ROLL OF THE GRADUATES
OF THE UNIVERSITY
OF ABERDEEN
1956–1970

PREVIOUS VOLUMES OF
ROLL OF THE GRADUATES OF THE
UNIVERSITY OF ABERDEEN

I

1860–1900
Compiled by Colonel William Johnston
Published by subscription as no 18 in Aberdeen University
Studies series. Aberdeen 1906

II

1901–1925
with Supplement 1860–1900
Compiled by Theodore Watt
Published by Aberdeen University Press 1935

III

1926–1955
with Supplement 1860–1925
Compiled by John Mackintosh
Published by University of Aberdeen 1960

ENQUIRIES ABOUT AVAILABILITY TO
ABERDEEN UNIVERSITY PRESS

ROLL OF THE GRADUATES OF THE UNIVERSITY OF ABERDEEN 1956–1970

WITH *SUPPLEMENT*
1860–1955

Compiled by
LOUISE DONALD MA LLB
W S MACDONALD MBE MA

PUBLISHED FOR THE UNIVERSITY OF ABERDEEN
BY ABERDEEN UNIVERSITY PRESS

First published 1982
Aberdeen University Press
A member of the Pergamon Group

© The Court of the University of Aberdeen 1982

The University of Aberdeen gratefully acknowledges
the assistance of the F. E. Bruce Bequest and the C. J. Weir Fund
in the production of this volume of the Roll of Graduates

British Library Cataloguing in Publication Data
University of Aberdeen
  Roll of the graduates of the University of
  Aberdeen 1956–1970: with supplement 1860–1955
  1. University of Aberdeen—Alumni
  I. Title   II. Donald, Louise   III. Macdonald, W. S.
  378.412′35   LF968

  ISBN 0-08-028469-8

PRINTED IN GREAT BRITAIN AT
ABERDEEN UNIVERSITY PRESS

PREFACE

In 1972 the University Court approved the proposal from the General Council that a fourth volume of the Roll of Graduates covering the period 1956–1970 should be compiled and that, as in the two previous volumes, a Supplement should be included bringing information up to date for graduates of the earlier periods. Mrs Louise Donald (née Turner) MA 1923 LLB 1972 was appointed editor and worked on the task from early 1973 until her death in December 1980. By that time all material for the 1956–1970 graduates had been edited and printer's galley proofs had partly been read and amendments made. The material for the Supplement had partly been edited and had begun to go into the printing stage.

The name Louise Donald had for many years been associated with Aberdeen University, notably as a member of the Business Committee of the General Council, as writer of a history of *Alma Mater* for the *Aberdeen University Review* and of a history of the General Council for the publication *The Fusion of 1860*. This volume of the Roll may well be seen to be her memorial as it is largely the result of her work during the last eight years of her life. Her successor as editor had worked closely with her from 1976 and was very willing to continue and bring her work to fruition.

Some information about the Roll as a whole may be appropriate. Volume I, published in 1906 the year of the University's Quatercentenary celebrations, dealt with graduates from 1860 to 1900, 1860 being the year of the 'fusion' of King's College and Marischal College to form the University of Aberdeen; volume II, published in 1935, dealt with graduates 1901–1925; volume III, published in 1960 the year of the celebrations marking the centenary of the 'fusion', dealt with graduates 1926–1955; and now volume IV covers the period 1956–1970. Each of volumes II, III and IV has a Supplement updating information about graduates in the previous volumes. As it has been the practice not to repeat in one volume material printed in an earlier volume, the information concerning the older graduate may start in volume I, continue in II and III and finish in volume IV. Where in the present volume *qv* is followed by (I), (II), (III) or (IV), or a combination of these, the numbers in parentheses refer to the respective volumes.

About 20,000 questionnaire forms were prepared for the initial mailing for this volume. Accompanying the forms for the pre-1956 graduates were copies of the information printed about them in volume III so helping them when updating the particulars of their careers. On the return of the completed forms the information supplied was condensed, typed and a copy sent to the graduate concerned for approval or amendment.

Section I (1956–1970)

It was decided to include in the main list the names of all graduates of the period. To achieve this Graduation Lists for the years 1956 to 1970 were checked against the 1971 General Council Register. There are close to 9,000 entries and about 35% of these show only names and degrees with dates, being all the information available. This is explained by the facts that many forms were never sent out as the Register showed no addresses; forms were returned marked 'gone away'; or the forms were never returned to the editor. In the case of many of the women graduates in this 35% category the Register showed a married surname and this has been printed. At a later stage addresses were found for some of these 'lost' graduates and a second issue of questionnaire forms was made up to as late as 1980. This proved relatively productive in replies.

Following precedent, married women graduates are recorded under their maiden names and identification of these, including any who graduated under their married names, may be aided by reference to the Section I list of Married Women Graduates on pp 374 to 392.

Information is presented in a standard pattern under five headings:

(1) Name and degree(s) with date(s) (Aberdeen University degrees only)
(2) Names and occupations of parents, and place and date of birth
(3) Further qualifications (other than those gained at Aberdeen University) and conferred honours
(4) Details of career
(5) Details of marriage with name and place of residence of father-in-law unless the spouse is an Aberdeen graduate when the degree and *qv* follows the name.

First degrees only have been given for parents, spouses of graduates and fathers-in-law. In connection with the death of graduates references are given to obituary notices in the *Aberdeen University Review (AUR)*.

Section I concludes with the Honorary Graduates 1956–1970 (pp 393 to 399). Their designations at the time of the conferring of the honorary degrees are as shown in the University Graduation Lists and a follow-up of the *AUR* references to the laureation addresses will give further information as to the sphere in which each gained distinction.

Section II (1860–1955)

Here are listed the names of those from volume I who graduated after 1890 and of all graduates from Sections I of volumes II and III—unless death has been intimated in one of these volumes. This Section contains approximately 11,600 names many with only basic information as they are in the Register without addresses or no replies have been received. Some are stated to be no longer on the General Council Register as contact has been completely lost for many years. While it is impossible to say if they are still alive, it is hazardous to assume they are dead.

A list of Married Women Graduates whose marriages have not been intimated in a previous volume of the Roll is included (pp 738 to 740) and the Section ends with a list of the Honorary Graduates for the volume III (1926–1955) period (pp 741 to 745).

The Appendix consists of a detailed analysis of the degrees and diplomas granted by the University during the period 1956–1970. The figures have been obtained from the Annual Statistics published by the University. One noticeable feature is the threefold increase in the annual number of degrees awarded over the period—from approximately 400 in 1956 to approximately 1,200 in 1970.

The structure of this volume of the Roll is similar to that of the earlier volumes but, to keep printing costs down, information has been condensed and words abbreviated without, it is hoped, leading to loss of intelligibility. The lists of Abbreviations and Degrees supplied should be material aids to the avoidance of ambiguity or misunderstanding. Punctuation has been reduced to a minimum as has the use of capital letters. An oblique line separates occupations which are thought to be contemporaneous, a comma if they follow on each other. A semicolon is used as the dividing device between posts held. The preposition 'from' has been used in front of the year when a graduate started in a post and so far as is known is still in that post unless a note to the contrary follows, e.g. 'retd'. In only a few cases have county names been added after place names.

In a book of this kind compiled over the long period of nine years errors of omission and commission and variations in style of recording and typographical presentation are almost inevitable and for this indulgence is claimed. From the very nature of the work the information given cannot be up-to-date. The main source of information has, of course, been the questionnaire forms, for the completion of which the editor expresses sincere thanks to the graduates concerned. Other information has been found in University records and the editor is indebted to the University Archives Department and the Registry for their willing cooperation and response to any enquiry. The personalia, obituary and marriage announcements in the *Aberdeen University Review* have been extensively drawn upon and for this there is further indebtedness.

A number of people have helped in the work. Miss Nora F. Glennie MA 1924, Lady Taylor (née Helen M. Jardine) MB ChB 1920, Dr Beatrix B. Law MA 1920, Miss Florence Mackenzie secretary to Principal Wright, and Miss Agnes M. Pittendrigh BSc 1926 helped in the preliminary years getting the volume under way. Mrs Flora M. Anderson (née Burley) MA 1923 acted as typist for some years. Mrs Roberta Morgan (née Gordon) MA 1932, Miss E. Ashley Scott MA 1930 and Mr Ian MacLean Smith MA 1931 were involved in the early stages and continued throughout. To all these the editors owe thanks. The office used by the editors was, conveniently, adjacent to that of the General Council and Mrs Ursula Price, assistant registrar, readily made records available and contributed to the work by typing and assisting in research. Guidance from Mr Harold M. R. Watt MA 1942 of Aberdeen University Press was a source of encouragement to both editors.

Aberdeen, January 1982   W. S. MacDonald

CONTENTS

ABBREVIATIONS
Explanations of some of the abbreviations and terms used

A period follows an abbreviation which in itself forms a word e.g. 'man.' for 'manager.'
An asterisk (*) indicates that the abbreviation is for the name of a university.
Note the difference between 'Aber' meaning Aberdeen city and 'Aberd' meaning Aberdeen University, 'Dun' Dundee city and 'Dund' Dundee University. In other cases the same abbreviation has been used in the text for city and university where it was thought no ambiguity would arise.

Aber	Aberdeen	auth	authority
*Aberd	Aberdeen	aux	auxiliary
*Acad	Acadia (Canada)	av med	aviation medicine
acad	academ-y-ic-ical-icus	AWRE	Atomic Weapons Research Establishment
acct	account-s-ing-ant-ancy	b	born
*Adel	Adelaide	BAC	British Aircraft Corporation
admin	administrat-ion-or	bact	bacteriol-ogy-ogist-ogical
adv	advanced	BAOR	British Army of the Rhine
advis	advis-er-ory	*BC, BrCol	British-Columbia
advoc	advocate-s	B of R	Book of Remembrance
advt	advertis-ing-ement	*Belf	Queens University Belfast
AEC	Army Educational Corps	BFES	British Forces Educational Service
AERE	Atomic Energy Research Establishment	BICC	British Insulated Callenders Cables
Af	African	BIM	British Institute of Management
ag	agen-t-cy	biochem	biochem-ist-istry-ical
agr	agricultur-e-al-alist	biol	biolog-y-ist-ical
AGS	Aberdeen Grammar School	*Birm	Birmingham
AHA	Area Health Authority	bld(g)(r)	build-ing-er
*Alex	Alexandria	BLMC	British Leyland Motor Corporation
*Alta	Alberta	BMA	British Medical Association
alum.	aluminium	bn	battalion
amb	ambulance	BOCM	British Oil and Cake Mills
anaest	anaesthe-tics-tist-sia	*Bom	Bombay
anat	anatomy	bor	borough
anim husb	animal husbandry	bot	botany
*ANU	Australian National University Canberra	BP	British Petroleum
app	apprentice	br	branch
arch	architect-ural	*Brad	Bradford
archae	archaeolog-y-ist	BR	British Rail
ARI	Aberdeen Royal Infirmary	brig.	brigad-e-ier
assoc	associat-e-ion	*Brist	Bristol
asst	assistant	Brit	Brit-ain-ish
assur	assurance	bs	building society
*Aston	Aston in Birmingham	BSBI	Botanical Society of the British Isles
ATS	Auxiliary Territorial Service	BSIP	British Solomon Island Principality
*Auck	Auckland	bus.	business
AUP	Aberdeen University Press	c	council-lor, county
AUR	Aberdeen University Review	CAA	Civil Aviation Authority
Aust	Australia-n	*Cai	Gonville and Caius College Cambridge

*Calc	Calcutta
*Calg	Calgary
*Calif	California
*Cantab	Cambridge
*Cape T	Cape Town
cardiol	cardiolog-y-ist
cas	casualty
cath	cathedral
cc	county council
CEGB	Central Electricity Generating Board
cent.	central
ch	church child-ren
chap.	chaplain
chem	chem-ist-istry-ical
chirop	chiropod-y-ist
chmn	chairman
civ	civil-ian
C of E	Church of England
C of S	Church of Scotland
cler	clerical
clin	clinic-al-ian
CMA	Canadian Medical Association
CNAA	Council for National Academic Awards
col	colon-el-ial
*Col	Columbia (NY)
coll	colleg-e-iate
comm	committee, command-er-ing, commer-ce-cial, commission-ed-ers
commun	commun-ity-ications
comp	company, comprehensive
compar	comparative
cong	congregation-al
conserv	conserv-ancy-ation-ative-ator
constit	constit-uency-utional
construct.	construction
consult.	consult-ant-ing-ancy
contr	contract-ing-or
*Corn	Cornell
corp	corporation
cott	cottage
CSIRO	Commonwealth Scientific and Industrial Research Organisation
cult.	cultural
curric	curriculum
d	daughter
d	died
DAFS	Department of Agriculture and Fisheries for Scotland
DDMS	Deputy Director of Medical Services
def	defence
dem	demonstrat-ion-or
dent	dent-al-ist-istry
dep	deput-e-y
dept	department-al
dermat	dermatolog-ist-y
des	design-er
dev	development-al
DHSS	Department of Health and Social Security
DIH	Department of Industrial Health
Dip.	diploma-tic
dir	director
diss	dissolved (marriage)
dist	district
distrib	distribution
div	division-al-divinity

D o E	Department of the Environment
doct	doctor-al
dom	domestic
DRI	Dundee Royal Infirmary
DSIR	Department of Scientific and Industrial Research (*see* SRC)
DTI	Department of Trade and Industry
DTp	Department of Transport
*Dub	Trinity College Dublin
Dun	Dundee
*Dund	Dundee
*Durh	Durham
dyn	dynamics
*E Ang	East Anglia
ecol	ecolog-y-ist
econ	econom-y-ist
*Edin	Edinburgh
edit.	edit-or-orial-ing
educ	educat-ion-ional-or
EIS	Educational Institute of Scotland
elect.	electric-al-ian
emb	embassy
EMS	Emergency Medical Service
eng	engineer-ing
Eng(1)	England (English)
ENT	Ear Nose and Throat
entomol	entomolog-y-ist
epis	episcopal
ERI	Edinburgh Royal Infirmary
esn	educationally sub-normal
estab	establishment
estim	estimat-ing-or
ESU	English Speaking Union
eval	evaluation
exam	examin-ation-er
*Exe	Exeter
exec	executive
exped	expedition
exper	experiment-al
ESTB	Employment Service Training Board
fac	faculty
fam	fam
FAO	Food and Agricultural Organisation
farm.	farm-er-ing
FCO	Foreign and Commonwealth Office
fd	field
f e	further education
fed.	federal
fell.	fellow-ship
fin.	financial
for.	forest-er-ry, foreign
FPA	Family Planning Association
Fr	French
GATT	General Agreement on Tariffs and Trade
GC reg	General Council Register
g d	general duties
gen	general
GEC	General Electric Company
geog	geograph-y-er
geol	geolog-y-ist-ical
geophys	geophysic-s-al-ist
Ger	German-y
geriat	geriatric-ian
*Glas	Glasgow
Glasg	Glasgow

gov(t)	govern-or-(ment)	*Leic	Leicester
g p	general pract-ice-itioner	lib	librar-y-ian-ianship
grad	graduat-e-ion	ling.	linguist-ic-ics
*Greg	Gregorian University Rome	lit	liter-ary-ature
g s	grammar school	*Liv	Liverpool
GTC	General Teaching Council(Scotland)	loc	local
guid	guidance	LMC	London Medical Council
gyn	gynaecolog-y-ical-ist	*Lond	London
haemat	haematology	LSE	London School of Economics
*Harv	Harvard	lt	lieutenant
HIB	Herring Industry Board	*Luck	Lucknow
HIDB	Highlands and Islands Development Board	m	married
hist	histor-y-ical	*Macq	Macquarie
h o	house officer	MAFF	Ministry of Agriculture, Fisheries and Food
hon	honorary	mag	magazine
h, hosp	hospital-s	man.	manag-er-eress-ement-ing
h p	house physician	*Manc	Manchester
h s	house surgeon, high school	*Manit	Manitoba
husb	husband-ry	manuf	manufactur-e-ing
hyg	hygiene	marr	marriage
HMFO	Her Majesty's Foreign Office	*Mass	Massachusetts
HM(C)IS	Her Majesty's (Chief) Inspector of Schools	mat.	maternity
HNC	Higher National Certificate	*McG	McGill
HSC	Hospital for Sick Children	*McM	McMaster
*H-W	Heriot Watt	MDC	Metropolitan District Council
I	infirmary	mech	mechan-ic(s)-ical-isation
IAEA	International Atomic Energy Agency	med	medic-al-ine
IBA	Independent Broadcasting Authority	*Melb	Melbourne
i/c	in charge	mem	memorial
ICI	Imperial Chemical Industries	merch	merchant
ICL	International Computers Ltd	met.	meteorolog-y-ist-ical
ICS	Indian Civil Service	metall	metallurg-y-ical
ILEA	Inner London Education Authority	meth	methodist
ILO	International Labour Organisation	metro	metropolitan
IMA	International Mineralogical Association	m h	mentally handicapped
indust	indust-ry-rial-rialist	MHSS	Ministry of Health and Social Security
inf	infirmary, infant	microbiol	microbiolog-y-ical
infect.	infectious	min	minist-er-ry, mineral-s-ogist
info	information	miss.	missionary
Inl Rev	Inland Revenue	MIT	Massachusetts Institute of Technology
insp	inspector	MN	Merchant Navy
inst	institut-e-ion	mod lang	modern languages
instr	instruct-or-ion	MoD	Ministry of Defence
insur	insurance	mo(h)	medical officer (of health)
Inv	Inverness	MoH	Ministry of Health
invest.	investment	*Montr	Montreal
Ital	Ital-y-ian	MoT	Ministry of Transport
ITA	Independent Television Authority	MoW	Ministry of Works
ITE	Institute of Terrestrial Ecology	MPNI	Ministry of Pensions and National Insurance
JMB	Joint Matriculation Board	MRC	Medical Research Council
JP	Justice of the Peace	munic	municipal
juris	jurisprudence	mus	music-al-ian, museum
*Kar	Karachi	NAB	National Assistance Board
*Kent	Kent at Canterbury (UK)	NAMH	National Association of Mental Health
kg	kindergarten	NASA	National Aeronautics and Space Administration(US)
*Khart	Khartoum		
Kt(d)	Knight(ed)	nat	natural, national
l a	local authority	NATO	North Atlantic Treaty Organisation
lab	labour (politics)-er, laboratory	NCB	National Coal Board
*Lake	Lakehead Canada	*N'cle	Newcastle
*Lanc	Lancaster	NCR	National Cash Registers
lang	language-s	NE	North East (Scotland)
Lat	Latin	NERC	Natural Environment Research Council
lect	lecturer	NESDA	North East of Scotland Development Association
leg.	legal	neurol	neurolog-y-ical-ist

*New Br	New Brunswick
*Nfld	Newfoundland
NFU	National Farmers' Union
NHS	National Health Service
NIAB	National Institute of Agricultural Botany
NOSCA	North of Scotland College of Agriculture
*Nott	Nottingham
NPL	National Physical Laboratory
NRC	National Research Council
NSHEB	North of Scotland Hydro Electric Board
*NUI	National University of Ireland
nurs	nurs-ery-ing
nutrit	nutrition-al-ist
NZ	New Zealand
obst	obstetric-s-al-ian
occup	occupation-al
ODA	Overseas Development Administration
ODM	Ministry of Overseas Development
OECD	Organisation for European Economic Development
off.	offic-e-er-ial
oper	operat-ing-ion-or
ophth	ophthalm-ic-ology-ologist
ordin	ordinance
org	organic
organis	organis-er-ation
orthop	orthopaedic
*Osm	Osmania
*Ott	Ottawa
*OU	Open University
OUP	Oxford University Press
O & M	Organisation and Method
*Oxon	Oxford
p a	personal assistant
paediat	paediatric-s-ian
*Panj	Panjab (Pakistan)
par	parish
path.	patholog-y-ist-ical
p e	physical education
*Penn	Pennsylvania
pers	person-al-nel
petr	petrol-ogy-eum
p h	public health, physically handicapped
pharm	pharmac-y-ist-eutical-ology
phc	pharmaceutical chemist
phil	philosoph-y-ical
*Phil	Philadelphia
phys	physic-s-ian-al-ist
physiol	physiolog-y-ical-ist
physioth	physiotherap-y-ist
plan.	plann-er-ing
PMG	Post Master General
PNEU	Parents' National Educational Union
pol	politic-s-al
poly	polytechnic-al
pop.	population
pract	pract-ice-itioner
prep	preparat-ion-ory
pres	president
presb	presbyter-y-ian
prevn	prevention
p or prim.	primary
prin	principal
pr(o)	public relations (officer)
prob	probation-er-ary

prod.	produc-tion-er-tivity-ts
prof	profess-or-ional
progr.	progr-amme(r)-ess
proj	project-ion-ionist
prop.	prop-erty-rietor-rietress
prot	protestant
prov	provinc-e-ial
p s	private secretary, primary school
psych	psycholog-y-ical-ist
psychiat	psychiat-ry-rist
ptnr	partner
publ	publi-c-city-cations-sher
QARANC	Queen Alexandra's Royal Army Nursing Corps
QEH	Queen Elizabeth Hospital
qv	which see
RA	Royal Academy
radiol	radiolog-y-ist
RAE	Royal Aircraft Establishment
RAEC	Royal Army Educational Corps
RA(E)HSC or	Royal Aberdeen (Edinburgh) Hospital for Sick Children
RACH	Royal Aberdeen Children's Hospital
RAI	Royal Alexandra Infirmary
RAM	Royal Academy of Music
RAMC	Royal Army Medical Corps
RANR	Royal Australian Naval Reserve
RASC	Royal Army Service Corps
RCAF	Royal Canadian Air Force
RCAMC	Royal Canadian Army Medical Corps
RCT	Royal Corps of Transport
*R'dg	Reading
RE	Religious Education
reg	regular, region-al
regist	regist-er-rar-ered-ration
regt	regiment-al
remed	remedial
rep	representative
reprod	reproduct-ion-ive
res	research
resid	resid-ent-ential-ing
retd	retired
RGC	Robert Gordon's College, Aberdeen
RGIT	Robert Gordon's Institute of Technology, Aberdeen (previously RGTC)
RGN	Registered General Nurse
RGS	Royal Geographical Society
RGTC	*see* RGIT
RHA	Regional Health Authority, Royal Horse Artillery
rheumat	rheumatology
*Rhodes	Grahamstown (SAf)
RHM	Rank, Hovis, McDougall
rly	railway
RMN	Registered Mental Nurse
RN	Royal Navy
RNI	Royal Northern Infirmary (Inv)
ROC	Royal Observer Corps
RRE	Royal Radar Establishment
RSPB	Royal Society for the Protection of Birds
RST	Rhodesian Selection Trust
s	son, school
S	South
SAf	South Africa
*St And	St Andrews
SAI	Scottish Agricultural Industries
*Salf	Salford

*Sask	Saskatchewan	tv	television
sc	science	temp	temporary
SCE	Scottish Certificate of Education	theol	theolog-y-ical
schol	scholar-ship	therap	therap-y-ist-eutics
scient	scient-ific-ist	*Tor	Toronto
SCM	Student Christian Movement	trans	transport
Scot.	Scot-land-tish	trav	traveller
sec	secondary	treas	treasurer
sect.	section-al	trg	training
secy	secretar-y-ial	*Trin	Trinidad
SED	Scottish Education Department	trop	tropical
sen	senior	trust.	trustee
serv	serv-ant-ice-ing	TSB	Trustee Savings Bank
*S Fraser	Simon Fraser Vancouver	tut.	tutor-ial
*Sheff	Sheffield	UAE	United Arab Emirates
SHHD	Scottish Home and Health Department	UCH	University College Hospital
*Sing	Singapore	*UCNW	University College of North Wales (Bangor)
soc	soci-ety-al	*UCW	University College of Wales (Aberystwyth)
sociol	sociolog-y-ist	UKAEA	United Kingdom Atomic Energy Authority
solic	solicitor	*UM(W)IST	University of Manchester (Wales) Institute of Science & Technology
spec	special-ist-isation		
SRC	Science Research Council (previously DSIR)	univ	university
s s	secondary school	URC	United Reformed Church
SSEB	South of Scotland Electricity Board	urol	urolog-y-ist
stat	station	util	utilisation
statist	statisti-cs-cian-cal	Vanc	Vancouver
*Stir	Stirling	vd	venereal disease
*S'ton	Southampton	vet.	veterinary
*Strath	Strathclyde	*Vic BC	Victoria British Columbia
struct	structur-es-al	virol	virolog-y-ist
stud.	stud-ent-ied-ies	vis	visual
subj	subject-s	VSO	Voluntary Service Overseas
subsid	subsidiary	WAIT	West Australian Institute of Technology
superv	supervisor	*Warw	Warwick
supt	superintendent	*Wash	Washington Seattle
*Sur	Surrey	WCC	World Council of Churches
surv	survey-or-ing	WEA	Workers' Educational Organisation
*Sus	Sussex	*Well	Victoria Wellington NZ
*Syd	Sydney	WHO	World Health Organisation
syst	system-s	*Wind	Windsor Ontario
TARO	Territorial Army Reserve of Officers	*Wis	Wisconsin
tech	techn-ical-ician-ology-ologist	*WOnt	Western Ontario
TEFL	Teaching (er) of English as a Foreign Language	WRNS	Women's Royal Naval Service
TESL	Teaching of English as a Second Language	WS	Writer to the Signet
tel	tele-phone-phonist-graph	YESTB	Youth Employment Service Training Board
telecom(m)	telecommunications	zool	zoolog-y-ist

DEGREES ETC
Degrees, Diplomas, Titles and Memberships of professional bodies

An asterisk (*) in front of an Aberdeen University degree indicates a degree with honours.
c or **d** indicates 'commendation' or 'distinction'. These indications are given *only* for the Aberdeen University degree(s) shown in bold type in line with the graduate's name. Throughout the text degrees not followed by a university name in brackets are usually Aberdeen degrees.

ABPsS	Associate Member of the British Psychological Society
ABSI	Associate Member of the Building Societies Institute
ACA	Articled Chartered Accountant
ACCA	Association of Certified and Corporate Accountants
ACGI	Associate of the City and Guilds of London Institute
ACII	Associate of the Chartered Insurance Institute
ADMS	Assistant Director of Medical Services
ADPA	Advanced Diploma in Public Administration
AFIMA	Associate Fellow of the Institute of Mathematics and its Applications
AFRAeS	Associate Fellow of the Royal Aeronautical Society
AHA	Associate of the Health Service Administration
AInstBM	Associate Member of the Institute of Builders' Merchants
AICMA	Associate of the Institute of Cost and Management Accountants
AICSA	Associate Member of the Institute of Chartered Secretaries and Administrators
AIInfS	Associate of the Institute of Information Scientists
AIL	Associate of the Institute of Linguists
AILA	Associate of the Institute of Landscape Architects
AInstP	Associate of the Institute of Physics
AIRI	Associate of the Institute of the Rubber Industry
AIWSc	Associate of the Institute of Wood Science
ALA	Associate of the Library Association
AMBIM	Associate Member of the British Institute of Management
AMInst F	Associate Member of the Institute of Fuel
AMICE	Associate Member of the Institution of Civil Engineers
AMIChemE	Associate Member of the Institute of Chemical Engineers
AMIEE	Associate Member of the Institute of Electrical Engineers
AMIHE	Associate Member of the Institute of Highway Engineers
AM(A)IMM	Associate Member of the (Australian) Institute of Mining and Metallurgy
AMIMSW	Associate Member of the Institute of Medical Social Workers
AMIStructE	Associate Member of the Institute of Structural Engineers
AMIWE	Associate Member of the Institute of Water Engineers
AMIWPC	Associate Member of the Institute of Water Pollution Control
ARAChem Soc	Associate of the Royal Australian Chemical Society
ARCM	Associate of the Royal College of Music
ARCO	Associate of the Royal College of Organists
ARCST	Associate of the Royal College of Science and Technology
ARIBA	Associate of the Royal Institute of British Architects
ARIC	Associate of the Royal Institute of Chemists
ARICS	Associate of the Royal Institute of Chartered Surveyors
ARMCM	Associate of the Royal Manchester College of Music
ATCL	Associate of the Trinity College of Music London

ATPL	Civil Pilot's Licence
BASc	Bachelor of Applied Science
BCL	Bachelor of Civil Law
BD	Bachelor of Divinity
BDS	Bachelor of Dental Surgery
BEd	Bachelor of Education
BL	Bachelor of Law
BMedBiol	Bachelor of Medical Biology
BPharm	Bachelor of Pharmacy
BSA	Bachelor of Agricultural Science
BSc	Bachelor of Science
BSocSc	Bachelor of Social Science
BTh	Bachelor of Theology
BVMS	Bachelor of Veterinary Medicine and Surgery
BVS	Bachelor of Veterinary Surgery (or Science)
CA ca	Chartered Accountant
Cand Med	Graduate in Medicine (Oslo)
CASS	Certificate in Applied Social Studies
CBE	Commander of the Order of the British Empire
CChem	Chartered Chemist
CCFP	Certificate of the College of Family Physicians, Canada
CD	Canadian Forces Decoration
C Dip AF	Certified Diploma in Accounting and Finance
CE	Civil Engineer
CEng	Chartered Engineer
ChB	Bachelor of Surgery
ChM	Master of Surgery
CIH	Certificate in Industrial Health
CMG	Companion of St. Michael and St. George
CRP(S)(C)	Certificate Royal College of Physicians (Surgeons) (Canada)
CRK	Certificate of Religious Knowledge
CS	Clerk to the Signet
CStJ	Commander of The Order of St John of Jerusalem
DA	Diploma in Art; Diploma in Anaesthesia
DABOS	Diplomate of the American Board of Orthopaedic Surgeons
Dip Ag Ex	Diploma in Agricultural Extension
DABPysch & Neurol	Diplomate of the American Board of Psychiatry and Neurology
DABS	Diplomate of the American Board of Surgery
DADMS	Deputy Assistant Director Medical Services
DBE	Dame of the Order of the British Empire
DBEA	Diploma of the British Esperanto Association
DC	District Commissioner
DCH	Diploma in Child Health
DCMT	Diploma in Clinical Medicine of the Tropics
DCP	Diploma in Clinical Pathology
DD	Doctor of Divinity
Dip Ed	Diploma in Education
DEP	Diploma in Educational Psychology
Dip FM	Diploma in Farm Management
Dip FMBO	Diploma in Farm Management & Business Organisation
DIC	Diploma of the Imperial College
DIH	Diploma in Industrial Health
Dip H&TEng	Diploma in Highway and Traffic Engineering
DL	Doctor of Laws; Deputy Lieutenant
Dip LA	Diploma in Landscape Architecture
Dip LD	Diploma in Landscape Design
Dip Lib	Diploma in Librarianship
DMJ	Diploma in Medical Jurisprudence
DMR	Diploma in Medical Radiology
DMRD	Diploma in Medical Radiological Diagnosis
DMRT	Diploma in Medical Radio Therapy
Dip Man St	Diploma in Management Studies
DO	Diploma in Ophthalmology
DOMS	Diploma in Ophthalmic Medicine & Surgery

Dip OR	Diploma in Operational Research
DObstRCOG	Diploma in Obstetrics of the Royal College of Obstetricians and Gynaecologists
DPath	Diploma in Pathology
DPA	Diploma in Public Administration
DPE	Diploma in Physical Education
DPH	Diploma in Public Health
DPM	Diploma in Psychological Medicine
Dip Pers Man	Diploma in Personnel Management
Dip R Ed	Diploma in Religious Education
DRSS	Diploma of the Royal Statistical Society
DSc	Doctor of Science
Dip Sec St	Diploma in Secretarial Studies
Dip Soc Ad	Diploma in Social Administration
DSCHE	Diploma of the Scottish Council for Health Education
Dip Soc Med	Diploma in Social Medicine
DSS	*see* DRSS
Dip Soc St	Diploma in Social (Sociological) Studies
Dip Stat	Diploma in Statistics
DTA(Trin)	Diploma in Tropical Agriculture
Dip TCP	Diploma in Town and Country Planning
DTM&H	Diploma in Tropical Medicine & Hygiene
Dip TP	Diploma in Town Planning
DUP	Docteur de l'Université de Paris
DVM	Doctor of Veterinary Medicine
DVSM	Diploma in Veterinary State Medicine
EdB	Bachelor of Education (later changed to MEd)
ERD	Emergency Reserve Decoration (Army)
FAAAS	Fellow of the American Association for the Advancement of Science
FAAP	Fellowship of the American Academy of Paediatrics
FACA	Fellow of the American College of Anaesthetists
FACCP	Fellow of the American College of Chest Physicians
FACMA	Fellow of the Australian College of Medical Administrators
FACOG	Fellow of the American College of Obstetricians and Gynaecologists
FACP(R)(S)	Fellow of the American College of Physicians(Radiologists)(Surgeons)
FAI	Fellow of the Chartered Auctioneers and Estate Agents Institute
FAMA	Fellow of the Aerospace Medical Association
FANZCP	Fellow of the Australian & New Zealand College of Psychiatrists
FAPA	Fellow of the American Psychological Association
FAPsS	Fellow of the Australian Psychological Society
FAS	Fellow of the Association of Surgeons of Great Britain and Ireland
FASA	Fellow of the American Statistical Association
FASCE	Fellow of the American Society of Civil Engineers
FASCP	Fellow of the American Society of Clinical Pathologists
FBA	Fellow of the British Academy
FBCS	Fellow of the British Computer Society
FBOA	Fellow of the British Optical Association
FBPsS	Fellow of the British Psychological Society
FCCP	Fellow of the College of Chest Physicians
FCFP	Fellow of the College of Family Physicians, Canada
FCIPA	Fellow of the Chartered Institute of Patent Agents
FCIT	Fellow of the Chartered Institute of Transport
FCMA	Fellow of the Institute of Cost and Management Accountants
FCS	Fellow of the Chemical Society
FCS(WAf)	Fellow of the West African College of Surgeons
FCSP	Fellow of the Chartered Society of Physiotherapy
FDSRCS	Fellow in Dental Surgery, Royal College of Surgeons of England
FEIS	Fellow of the Educational Institute of Scotland
FFA	Fellow of the Faculty of Actuaries
FFARACS	Fellow of the Faculty of Anaesthetists, Royal Australian College of Surgeons
FFARCS	Fellow of the Faculty of Anaesthetists, Royal College of Surgeons of England
FFARCSI	Fellow of the Faculty of Anaesthetists, Royal College of Surgeons in Ireland
FFB	Fellow of the Faculty of Building
FFCM	Fellow of the Faculty of Community Medicine
FFR	Fellow of the Faculty of Radiologists
FGAC	Fellow of the Geological Association of Canada

FGS	Fellow of the Geological Society
FHA	Fellow of the Institute of Hospital Administrators
FIA	Fellow of the Institute of Actuaries
FIB	Fellow of the Institute of Banking
FIBiol	Fellow of the Institute of Biology
FICeram	Fellow of the Institute of Ceramics
FICE	Fellow of the Institute of Civil Engineers
FICS	Fellow of the International College of Surgeons
FIDP	Fellow of the Institute of Data Processing
FIE (Aust)	Fellow of the Institute of Engineers (Australia)
FIEE	Fellow of the Institute of Electrical Engineers
FIEEE	Fellow of the Institute of Electrical and Electronic Engineers of America
FIEI	Fellow of the Institute of Engineering Inspection
FIFor	Fellow of the Institute of Foresters (GB)
FIFST	Fellow of the U.K. Institute of Food Science and Technology
FIHE	Fellow of the Institute of Highway Engineers
FIL	Fellow of the Institute of Linguists
FIMA	Fellow of the Institute of Mathematics and its Applications
FIME	Fellow of the Institute of Mechanical Engineers
FIMM	Fellow of the Institute of Mining and Metallurgy
FIMunE	Fellow of the Institute of Municipal Engineers
FIOB	Fellow of the Institute of Builders
FInstP	Fellow of the Institute of Physics
FInstPet	Fellow of the Institute of Petroleum
FIPHE	Fellow of the Institute of Public Health Engineers
FIRI	Fellow of the Institution of the Rubber Industry
FIStructE	Fellow of the Institution of Structural Engineers
FIWE	Fellow of the Institution of Water Engineers
FIWSc	Fellow of the Institute of Wood Science
FLA	Fellow of the Library Association
FLAS	Fellow of the Chartered Land Agents' Society
FLS	Fellow of the Linnaean Society
FMFCM	Foundation Member Faculty of Community Medicine
FMSA	Fellow of the Mineralogical Society of America
FPS	Fellow of the Pharmaceutical Society
FPhysS	Fellow of the Physical Society
FRACGP	Fellow of the Royal Australian College of General Practitioners
FRACI	Fellow of the Royal Australian Chemical Institute
FRACP(S)	Fellow of the Royal Australian College of Physicians (Surgeons)
FRAI	Fellow of the Royal Anthropological Institute
FRAS	Fellow of the Royal Astronomical Society or Royal Asiatic Society
FRAeS	Fellow of the Royal Aeronautical Society
FRCGP	Fellow of the Royal College of General Practitioners
FRCO	Fellow of the Royal College of Organists
FRCOG	Fellow of the Royal College of Obstetricians and Gynaecologists
FRCPath	Fellow of the Royal College of Pathologists
FRCP(C)	Fellow of the Royal College of Physicians, London (Canada)
FRCPE	Fellow of the Royal College of Physicians, Edinburgh
FRCPSGlas	Fellow of the Royal College of Physicians and Surgeons, Glasgow
FRCPysch	Fellow of the Royal College of Psychiatrists
FRCR	Fellow of the Royal College of Radiologists
FRCS(C)	Fellow of the Royal College of Surgeons, London (Canada)
FRCSE	Fellow of the Royal College of Surgeons, Edinburgh
FRCVS	Fellow of the Royal College of Veterinary Surgeons
FRES	Fellow of the Royal Entomological Society
FRGS	Fellow of the Royal Geographical Society
FRIAS	Fellow of the Royal Incorporation of Architects of Scotland
FRHistS	Fellow of the Royal Historical Society
FRIBA	Fellow of the Royal Institute of British Architects
FRIC	Fellow of the Royal Institute of Chemistry
FRICS	Fellow of the Royal Institute of Chartered Surveyors
FRIPHH	Fellow of the Royal Institute of Public Health and Hygiene
FRLS	Fellow of the Royal Literary Society
FRMS	Fellow of the Royal Microscopical Society
FRMetS	Fellow of the Royal Meteorological Society

FRS(C)	Fellow of the Royal Society (Canada)
FRSA	Fellow of the Royal Society of Arts
FRSE	Fellow of the Royal Society of Edinburgh
FRSGS	Fellow of the Royal Scottish Geographical Society
FRSH	Fellow of the Royal Society for the Promotion of Health
FRSM	Fellow of the Royal Society of Medicine
FRSS	Fellow of the Royal Statistical Society
FRSTM&H	Fellow of the Royal Society of Tropical Medicine and Hygiene
FSAScot	Fellow of the Society of Antiquaries, Scotland
FSAO	Fellow of the Scottish Association of Opticians
FSCA	Fellow of the Society of Company and Commercial Accountants
FSS	see FRSS
Grad BIM	Graduate British Institute of Management
Grad IEE	Graduate Institute of Electrical Engineers
Grad MechE	Graduate Institute of Mechanical Engineers
Grad Inst P	Graduate Institute of Physics
GMIPM	Graduate Member Institute of Personnel Management
Grad RIC	Graduate Royal Institute of Chemistry
idc	on staff Imperial Defence College
jssc	Joint Services Staff Course
LCP	Licentiate of the College of Preceptors
LDS	Licentiate in Dental Surgery
L-ès-L	Licencié-ès-lettres
LGSM	Licentiate Guildhall School of Music and Drama
LHA	Licentiate of the Institute of Health Service Administrators
LLA	Lady Literate in Arts
LL B	Bachelor of Laws
LLCM	Licentiate London College of Music
LLCO	Licentiate London College of Osteopathy
LL D	Doctor of Laws
LL M	Master of Laws
LM	Licentiate in Midwifery
LMCC	Licentiate of the Medical Council of Canada
LRAM	Licentiate Royal Academy of Music
LRCP	Licentiate of the Royal College of Physicians, England
LRCP(S)E	Licentiate of the Royal College of Physicians(Surgeons) Edinburgh
LTCL	Licentiate Trinity College of Music London
LTh	Licence in Theology
MA	Master of Arts
MAAPG	Member of the Association of American Petroleum Geologists
MANZCP	Member of the Australian & New Zealand College of Psychiatrists (Practitioners)
MAPLE	Member of the Association of Public Lighting Engineers
MASCE	Member of the American Society of Civil Engineers
MB	Bachelor of Medicine
MBA	Master of Business Administration
MBCS	Member of the British Computer Society
MBE	Member of the Order of the British Empire
MBIM	Member of the British Institute of Management
MBKS	Member of the British Kinematograph Sound & Television Society
MBNES	Member of the British Nuclear Energy Society
MBPS	Member of the British Psychoanalytical Society
MCEA	Member of the Canadian Electrical Association
MCFP	Member of the College of Family Physicians, Canada
MCIMM	Member of the Canadian Institute of Mining & Metallurgy
MCIT	Member of The Chartered Institute of Transport
MCPS	Member of the College of Physicians and Surgeons
MCRA	Member of the College of Radiologists, Australia
MCSP	Member of the Chartered Society of Physiotherapy
MD	Doctor of Medicine
MEd	Master of Education
MEIC	Member of the Engineering Institute of Canada
MF	Master of Forestry
MFCM	Member of the Faculty of Community Medicine
MFCP	Member of the Faculty of Community Physicians
MFHom	Member of the Faculty of Homoeopathy

MFO	Member of the Faculty of Ophthalmologists
MIA	Master of International Affairs (U.S.)
MIBiol	Member of the Institute of Biology
MICA	Member of the Institute of Chartered Accountants
MICE	Member of the Institution of Civil Engineers
MIEA	Member of the Institute of Engineering of Australia
MIEE	Member of the Institution of Electrical Engineers
MIERE	Member of the Institution of Electronic & Radio Engineers
MIFor (GB)	Member of the Institute of Foresters (GB)
MIH	Member of the Institute of Hygiene
MIHE	Member of the Institution of Highway Engineers
MIHVE	Member of the Institution of Heating and Ventilating Engineers
MILGA	Member of the Institute of Local Government Administrators
MILocoE	Member of the Institution of Locomotive Engineers
MIM	Member of Institute of Marketing
MInstMC	Member of the Institute of Measurement & Control
MIMechE	Member of the Institution of Mechanical Engineers
MIMH	Member of the Institute of Material Handling
MIMM	Member of the Institute of Mining & Metallurgy
MIMSW	Member of the Institution of Medical Social Workers
MIMunE	Member of the Institution of Municipal Engineers
MInstP	Member of the Institute of Physics
MIPHE	Member of the Institution of Public Health Engineers
MIPlantE	Member of the Institution of Plant Engineers
MIPM	Member of the Institute of Personnel Management
MIPR	Member of the Institute of Public Relations
MIQ	Member of the Institute of Quarrying
MInstR	Member of the Institute of Refrigeration
MIRSE	Member of the Institute of Railway Signal Engineers
MIStructE	Member of the Institute of Structural Engineers
MITAA	Member of the International Transactional Analysis Association
MIWES	Member of the Institution of Water Engineers and Scientists
MIWPC	Member of the Institute of Water Pollution Control
MIWSP	Member of the Institute of Works Study Practitioners
M Jur	Master of Jurisprudence
M Litt	Master of Letters
MMSA	Master of the Midwifery Society of Apothecaries
MNZIE	Member of the New Zealand Institute of Engineers
MPH	Master of Public Health (Yale)
MPS	Member of the Pharmaceutical Society
MRACGP	Member of the Royal Australian College of General Practitioners
MRCGP	Member of the Royal College of General Practitioners
MRCM	Member of the Royal College of Medicine
MRCOG	Member of the Royal College of Obstetricians & Gynaecologists
MRCP	Member of the Royal College of Physicians
MRCPE	Member of the Royal College of Physicians, Edinburgh
MRCPGlas	Member of the Royal College of Physicians & Surgeons, Glasgow
MRCPath	Member of the Royal College of Pathologists
MRCPsych	Member of the Royal College of Psychiatrists
MRCS	Member of the Royal College of Surgeons of England
MRCSE	Member of the Royal College of Surgeons, Edinburgh
MRCVS	Member of the Royal College of Veterinary Surgeons
MRI	Member of the Royal Institution
MRIC	Member of the Royal Institute of Chemistry
MRSForS	Member of the Royal Scottish Forestry Society
MRSH	Member of the Royal Society for the Promotion of Health
MRTPI	Member of the Royal Town Planning Institute
MRWEA	Member of the Royal West of England Academy
MS	Master of Surgery (of Science(USA))
MSA	Master of Science Agriculture
MSc	Master of Science
M Soc Pet Eng AIM & Mech Eng	Member of the Society of Petroleum Engineers of the American Institute of Mining and Mechanical Engineers
MSocW	Master of Social Work
MTAI	Member of the Institute of Travel Agents

MTh	Master of Theology
MVO	Member of the Victorian Order
MVSc	Master of Veterinary Science
MWD	Ministry of Works Department (NZ)
NDA(D)	National Diploma in Agriculture(Dairying)
NP	Notary Public
OBE	Officer of the Order of the British Empire
OStJ	Officer of the Order of St. John of Jerusalem
psc	Graduate of Staff College
PhD	Doctor of Philosophy
QHP(S)	Queen's Honorary Physician (Surgeon)
RD or VRD	Reserve Decoration Royal Navy
RGN	Registered General Nurse
RMN	Royal Mental Nurse
RSA	Royal Society of Arts
RSCN	Registered Sick Children's Nurse
SCM	State Certificated Midwife
SRN	State Registered Nurse
SSC	Solicitor before the Supreme Court(Scotland)
STB(M)	Bachelor (Master) of Sacred Theology
TD	Territorial Efficiency Decoration
ThM	Master of Theology

SECTION I

ROLL OF GRADUATES 1956–1970

ABBEY Heather Diane   MA 1966
m Bulmer

ABBOTT Ann Pringle   *MA 1967
d of Thomas P. A. CA and Christina Reid civ serv;
b Perth 2.5.45
Dip Lib (Lond) 1969
lib: arch. res unit Edin univ 1969–72, Roskilde univ
Denmark 1973–74; Danish min of environment from 1974
m Aber 9.6.72 Graham D. Caie MA 1968 *qv*

ABBOTT David Reid   *BSc(eng) 1965
s of Thomas P. A. CA and Christina Reid civ serv;
b Edin 26.11.42
MICE 1973
asst eng Scott Wilson Kirkpatrick & Ptnrs: Lond
1965–69, Brunei 1969–72, Lond 1972–74; res eng
Crouch & Hogg Inv from 1974

ABBOTT Derek Graham Cameron   *MA 1968

ABBOTT Elizabeth Margaret   *MA 1962
ward of Elizabeth R. A.; b Gloucester 29.5.41
teacher Stirling 1963–72
m Lossiemouth 12.4.69 Norman A. Black site eng s of
Albert Z. B. Stirling

ABBOTT John Granville   *BSc(agr) 1969
s of Kenneth G. A. civ serv MoH and Margery Brakell;
b Southport 9.8.45
sen res off. I, II Canberra 1969–73; Gaberone Botswana:
market. off. (agr)/res consult. dev 1973–78; educ plan.
Maseru Lesotho from 1978
marr diss

ABBOTT Susan   *MA 1969 Dip Ed 1970
d of Thomas P. A. CA and Christina Reid civ serv;
b Buckie 7.5.47
teacher: Cults acad 1970–73, Golspie h s from 1973
m Inv 27.7.73 Norman J. D. Wright MA 1969 *qv*

ABDELNOUR Hassan Osman   BSc(for) 1967
s of Osman Abdelnour Adam and Zeinab Mohamed
Ahmed; b Abu Usher Sudan 1.1.44
MSc(Khart) 1972
utilization off. for. dept Khartoum 1967–72; vice-prin
Forest Rangers' coll Soba Sudan from 1972
m Aber 3.2.65 Shane Moscati MA 1974 *qv*

ABDEL-TAWAB Gamal El Dín Mohamed   PhD 1957
BSc(Cairo)

ABDEL-WAHED Joseph   *MA 1959

ABDULAZIZ Abdullah   *MA 1963

ABDULAZIZ Mohammad Annuar Bin   BSc(for) 1960

ABDULMANAN Othman Bin   BSc(for) 1961

ABEL George   BSc 1965
s of George A. gas man. and Rose A. McRobb;
b Inverurie 13.8.42
jun tech off. inst of cancer res Lond from 1966

ABEL Joyce Audrey Katherine   MB ChB 1964

ABEL Patricia Margaret   MA 1969
d of John W. M. A. tel eng and Margaret B. Cooper;
b Aber 9.12.47
teacher Engl/hist Aber: Kaimhill s s 1970–71, Kincorth
acad 1971–73, Harlaw acad from 1974
m Aber 13.4.73 Arthur V. Duncan tech off. PO telephones
s of Lawrence D. Aber

ABEL Scott Adam   BSc(eng) 1964

ABELL Trevor Michael Barry   BSc(for) 1968
s of Kenneth W. A. HM insp taxes and Patricia E.
Turner; b Leicester 10.8.46
stud. ODM Oxon 1968–69; asst conserv for. Kitwe
Zambia 1969–75; scient off. land res div (for.) Tolworth
from 1976
m Wigtown 3.7.71 Helen F. B. McKay BSc 1970 *qv*

ABERDEIN James Douglas   BSc(agr) 1959
s of James A. radiographer and Christina Pope; b Aber
25.2.38
flying off. RAF 1959–63; helicopter pilot Bristow's
England, Pers Gulf 1963–65; farm. New Deer 1965–69;
teacher: Monquhitter 1966–68, Aboyne acad 1968–72;
head Lumphanan p s 1972–75
m Aber 17.10.64 Ethel Jamieson MA 1961 *qv*

ABERDEIN John Henry   *MA 1970
s of James M. A. lect in elect. installation and Marion
Smith shorthand typist; b Aber 23.3.46
teacher Fife from 1972
m Kirkcaldy 10.3.73 Penelope A. Shircore drama teacher
d of Winston S. Croydon

ABERNETHY Douglas Grieve   LLB 1970
s of Douglas G. A. mech and Agnes B. Grieve; b Aber
27.10.48
law app Edin 1970–72; Glasg: law asst 1972–75, ptnr in
law firm from 1975
m Aber 4.8.73 Pamela Green MB ChB 1974 med pract d of
Raymond G. Aber

ABOU AKKADA Abdelkadir Rashid   PhD 1961
BSc(agr) MSc(Alex)

ABOUL-KHAIR Sidky Abdallah   PhD 1964
MB ChB DCH(Alex)

ABUSAQ Muhammad Osman   *MA 1965
BA(Khart) PhD(Edin) 1971
s of Osman A. and Aishah; b Sudan 20.11.36
teacher Sudan 1961–62; lect teacher trg coll Khart 1965;
lect politics univ Khart 1965–74; secy for thought
Sudanese Socialist Union from 1974
m Khart 12.8.64 Safia M. Arabi BA(Khart) head community dev Khartoum d of Muhammad A.

ACQUAYE David Kpakpoe   PhD 1960
s of Samuel A. A. carpenter and Madam Kordey
Annan trader; b Accra 14.9.28
BSc(agr)(Mich)
res off. cocoa res inst Tafo Ghana 1960–66; univ of
Ghana: sen lect 1966, acting head dept of crop sc 1969,
dean fac of agr from 1972
m 23.12.62 Eugenia Quarty-Papifio sen tel superv d of
Samuel Q.-P. Kumasi Ghana

ACRES Bryan Douglas   MSc 1963
s of Ian S. A. MB BS(Lond) g p and Eileen O. L.
Bunday secy/missionary; b Bolobo Zaïre 9.5.37
BA(Lond) 1961
contr with Nigerian govt Ibadan 1964–66; sen scient off.
Sandakan Sabah 1967–72; with ODM Sana'a Yemen
1974–76
m Lond 28.9.63 Jannice M. Goode BSc(Lond) teacher d
of Alfred G. BSc(eng)(Birm) Sunbury-on-Thames

ADAM Alasdair Hugh Macqueen   LLB 1969
s of Robert J. A. MA(Oxon) univ prof and Frances

3

M. A. Macqueen; b Glasg 15.11.47
WS 1971
law app Edin 1969–71; solic: Kirkcaldy 1971–74, Alloa
and Alvah from 1975
m Edin 17.3.73 Judith A. Steele RGN d of John D. T. S.
MB ChB(Edin) Dumfries

ADAM Albert William *MA 1970
s of Keith C. R. A. BR signalman and Elizabeth
Hodgkinson GPO tel; b Alloa 19.11.48
trainee 'Ford Motor Co Warley and Richardson-
Merrell Lond 1970; trainee Conserv party ag 1972–73;
ag for Stirlingsh group from 1972
m Edin 16.7.71 Jennifer M. Saxby hotel man. trainee
d of George K. B. S. Hexham

ADAM Brian James *BSc 1970

ADAM Hazel May *MA 1966
d of Peter A. foreman and Violet Watt; b Aber 27.11.42
teacher Fr Ashford s Kent 1967–71; inf teacher
various schools Ashford 1971–72
m Aber 12.8.67 Stuart G. McRae BSc 1965 qv

ADAM Helen Margaret MB ChB 1967
m Cason

ADAM John MA 1966
s of John A. BR plant maintenance eng and Georgina
Keddie; b Perth 2.6.44
teacher Engl/mod stud. Hawick h s 1967–70; head Engl
dept Breckenbeds j h s Gateshead 1970–71; sen Engl
master Blaydon c s Co Durham 1971–73; dep head
Brumby c s Scunthorpe from 1973
m Aber 5.9.66 Lorna R. Cheyne MA 1966 qv

ADAM John Alexander *MA 1962

ADAM Kirsten *MA 1959
d of Archie D. A. MA 1929 qv(III) and Muriel M.
Cheyne MA(Edin) teacher; b Edin 22.7.37
Cert Ed(Leeds) 1960
teacher mus: Datchet 1960–63, Inverurie acad 1963–65;
prin mus Braehead s Buckhaven 1965–70; Fife: asst
organis mus 1970–74, organis arts from 1974

ADAM Malcolm MB ChB 1958

ADAM Margaret Eleanor *MA 1961 PhD 1967
d of Hyacinth A. G. A. chief p o RN and Eleanor M. E.
Fancourt secy; b Portsmouth 11.8.39
teacher mod lang Zurich 1961–64; temp asst lect: St
Michael's coll Toronto 1964–65, Magee univ coll
Londonderry 1967–68; lect tech coll Londonderry 1969–
74, head dept arts/soc stud. from 1974
m Aber 7.8.61 Walter Baumann DPhil(Zür) sen lect Ger s
of Jakob M. B. Switzerland

ADAM-SMITH Margaret Elphinston MA 1968
(conferred for long service of exceptional merit)
d of George A. S. MA(Edin) C of S min, prof Hebrew,
Principal & Vice-Chancellor Aberd 1909–35 and Alice L.
Buchanan; b Old Aber 3.9.10
advis to women stud. Aberd 1946–75
m Aber 7.8.34 Ian A. Clarke (d 1939) MA 1911 qv

ADAMS Angela Clare PhD 1970
d of William E. A. MB ChB prof anat and med dean
and Ena N. Mathewson typist; b Leeds 27.11.40

BSc(Otago) 1961
BECC res fell. Christchurch NZ 1961–63; res worker
Euratom Institut für Strahlensforschung Freiburg i Br.
Germany 1964–67
m Athens 28.3.71 Kosmas A. Kiossoglou MB ChB(Athens)
assoc prof paediat s of Anastasios K. Bourdourion Asia
Minor

ADAMS Christopher John *BSc(eng) 1968

ADAMS Frederick George MB ChB 1961
s of Lawrence A. and Catherine M. M. McPherson fish
curer; b Aber 24.9.38
DMRD 1968 (Lond) FRCR 1970
res hosp posts Aber 1961–63; g p Ilkeston 1964–66;
trainee radiol Sheffield 1966–70; consult. radiol Western
I Glasg from 1971
m Aber 4.10.63 Allison E. Richardson d of Joseph B. R.

ADAMS James Alexander *BSc 1960
s of William A. farm. and Jessie Chapman; b New
Aberdour 27.10.37
marine lab Torry Aber: scient off. 1960–66, sen 1966–72,
prin from 1972
m Aber 16.7.65 Elizabeth M. Elliot MA 1961 qv

ADAMS James Thomas Ward dLL B 1967 *1968
s of William S. A. MA(Glas) solic and Maisie T. Ward;
b Glasg 30.11.46
Hawker Siddeley Aviation: asst to leg. man. 1968–69,
sen contr off. 1969–71, asst contr man. from 1971
m Sanderstead 16.1.71 Rosemary C. Baker LL B 1968 qv

ADAMS John *BSc(agr) 1970
s of William A. BSc(agr) 1941 qv and Annie R. Pirie
MA 1941 qv; b Aber 16.7.47
auditor Ford Motor Co Brentwood from 1970
m Peterculter 30.10.71 Rosemary Henderson teacher
dom sc d of James H. St Cyrus

ADAMS John Mervyn *BSc(agr) 1969
s of George M. A. comp dir and Betty C. Davies loc
govt employee; b Walsall 14.4.46
MSc(Lond) 1970 DIC 1970 FRES(Lond) 1970
attached Oxfam grain storage proj as entomologist
Limbe 1971–72; sc off. grain storage Slough 1972–73;
proj leader ODA econ of storage proj Lusaka 1973–74;
FAO consult. Pakistan 1975; storage losses spec. ODM
from 1976

ADAMS Roy Douglas *BSc(for) 1966
s of Ronald S. W. A. and Edna W. Elton; b Wimbledon
7.3.44
MF(Vanc) 1969; PhD(Wash) 1974
univ instruct. Moscow Idaho 1969–71; stud. Washington
1971–76; wood scient Houghton Mich from 1975
m Aber 12.7.66 Fiona B. Clark MCSP physioth d of
Thomas M. C. BSc(Glas) Aber

ADAMS William Arthur *MA 1970

ADAMSON Helen Clark *MA 1960

ADAN George Edward MB ChB 1957
s of Edward A. carpenter and Isabella F. Lumsden;
b Aber 14.11.32
h o City hosp, Woodend hosp Aber 1957–58; army nat
serv Cyprus, Malta 1958–60; g p Cruden Bay 1960–62,
Spennymoor from 1962
m Blechingley 17.9.60 Patricia M. Murray SRN lieut
QARANC d of Thomas A. M. Blechingley

ADATIA Manharlal Harjivandas   MSc 1965
BSc(Bom)

ADDISON Barbara   *MA 1967
m Bancroft

ADDISON Eileen Patricia   MA 1964

ADDISON Jack Thomson   MA 1957
s of John T. A. comp owner and Violet Thomson;
b Cullen 22.5.32
Dip BA(Strath) 1968
Glasg: admin asst 1958–60; factory man. 1960–62; gen
man. 1962–66; man. dir from 1968

ADDISON James Lochore   *MA 1969
s of John A. man. and Elizabeth A. Lochore; b Aber
27.7.47
ergonomist Pilkington Bros St Helens 1969–70; temp posts
1971–72; teacher Glasg 1973–74; exec off. DHSS Glasg
from 1974
m Glasg 7.4.73 Judith M. Deacon lib d of David G. D.
Southampton

ADDISON John Douglas   *BSc(eng) 1970
s of Douglas J. A. boilermaker/welder and Gladys I.
Stuart; b Wartle 20.1.48
site eng Taylor Woodrow Construct. Lond 1970–73; des
eng: Kinnear & Gordon 1973–74, R. H. Cuthbertson &
Ptnrs Edin 1974–76, Steensen, Varming, Mulcahy &
Ptnrs from 1976
m Inverurie 6.11.71 Moira Ledingham staff nurse d of
Alfred F. L. Inverurie

ADDISON Marcus Leopold Gabriel   MB ChB 1960

ADDISON Margaret Ogilvie   MA 1964
d of John W. A. fisherman and Jeannie Hadden; b Inv
19.12.44
teacher: Fr/Ger Keith g s 1965–73, prin guid from 1973

ADDISON Violet Thomson   MB ChB 1957
m Coutts

ADDISON William George   BSc(agr) 1957
s of Alexander A. master baker and Mary Addison; b
Portknockie 12.9.35
Dip Agr(Cantab) 1958 DTA(Trinidad) 1959
Nyasaland: agr off. Rumpi 1959–62, soil conserv off.
Blantyre 1962–64; agr advis Elgin 1964–73; spec advis
crop husb NOSCA Aber from 1973
m Aber 12.6.59 Dorothy C. M. Stewart bus. asst d of
John H. S. Stonehaven

ADDO Stephen   BSc(for) 1959

ADEN Sandra   MA 1967
m Wilson

ADEOYE Isaac Adebayo   BSc(for) 1966
s of Emanuel A. A. ch worker and Julianah Adepate
trader; b Ibadan 11.9.37
CPA(Unife) 1974
sen asst conserv for. Ibadan, Oyo state, Nigeria from
1966
m Dun 11.4.63 Odunola O. Mipon nurse d of Adebola M.
Lagos

ADEY Gillian Dalton   MB ChB 1968
b Hull 27.8.44
FFARCS 1975
h o Aber 1968–69; sen h o Aber 1969–71; regist anaest

Aber 1971–75; res fell. biochem Aberd from 1975
m Kirkby Lonsdale 1973 Norman B. Bennett MB ChB
1963 *qv*

ADEYEMI Benjamin Omotunde   *BSc(eng) 1958

ADOMAKOH Christian Charles   MB ChB 1960
s of John Y. A. farm. and Rebecca Onemeng; b Ghana
14.1.31
DPM 1964 Dip Psych(Edin) 1965 MRCP(Edin) 1965
MRCPsych 1972
m o Accra 1961–71; sen lect med s Accra from 1971
m Accra 30.6.62 Victoria K. B. Davies nutrit/teacher d of
James B. D. Accra

ADU Samuel Victor   *BSc 1958 PhD 1968
b Abebifi Ghana 4.7.23
Ghana: scient off. min of agr 1959–63; inst soil res: res
off. 1963–69, sen res off. 1969–74, chief res off. from 1974
m Kumasi Ghana 1964 Victoria R. Larbi home sc tut.

AETHERIS Phoebus Sophroniou   MB ChB 1962

AFFLECK Georgina Stoddart   BEd 1969
d of George A. eng and Jean Blaikie; b Edin 15.1.42
teacher Engl Lasswade 1969–70, Glasg 1970–74, Fort
William from 1974
m Oban 14.6.74 Victor J. Scott elect eng s of Douglas S.
Glasg

AGBEKO Bertha Perpetua Bake   BSc 1966

AGBIM Charles Chuba   *BSc(eng) 1958
s of Felix O. A. civ serv and Grace A. Ilodigwe; b Nimo
Nigeria 6.10.34
DIC(Lond) 1959 PhD(Lond) 1961
site eng Tolworth Lond; Nigeria: exec eng min of works
Lagos 1963–64, lect univ of Lagos 1964–65, prin consult.
Agbim & Ptnrs (consult. eng) Lagos, Enugu, Kaduna,
Calabar from 1965
m Lond –.12.60 Ukamaka Okeke d of A. O. Arondizogu
Nigeria

AGBLE Theodore Komla   MB ChB 1959
s of Erastus L. A. storekeeper and Kate Ama Apo; b
Hohoe Ghana 21.7.31
BSc(Lond) 1954 MRCOG 1965 FCS(W. Af) 1974
m o Ghana 1960–62; sen h o obst/gyn: Southern gen hosp
Glasg 1963–64, St James hosp Leeds 1964–65; Kumasi
Ghana: sen m o 1965–70, spec gyn from 1970
m Leeds 1.10.65 Yolande Garraway nurse/midwife

AGERBAK Gullan Susanne   BSc 1966
d of Harry E. A. counsellor to Danish Embassy Lond
and Gudrun Rysgaard; b Stockholm 20.7.43
res asst (embryology) agr res council Edin 1966–67;
microbiol genetics (MRC) Lond 1967–68; Novo pharm
div, res inst Bagsvaerd Denmark 1968–73; scient prod.
man. from 1973

AGNEW John McMurray   MA 1969
s of James McG. A. ploughman and Mary C. McMurray;
b Stranraer 19.3.48
teacher maths: Stranraer acad 1970–72, St George's s
Vanc 1972–74, Stranraer acad 1974–75, Nanaimo B.C.
1975–76, Upper Canada Coll from 1976
m Vanc 6.7.74 Sharon Maclean

AH-SEE Antoine Kim-nen   MB ChB 1965 ChM 1975
s of Wong A. shopkeeper and Sin Y. Sew; b Mauritius
1.6.38
FRCS(Edin) 1970

h o Aber 1965–66; sen h o: Sidcup 1966–67, Bournemouth 1967–68; sen h o and regist Aber 1968–70; res fell. Uppsala Sweden 1970–71; regist Aber 1971–72; lect surg Aberd 1972–75; res fell. RN physiol lab Alverstoke 1975–77; sen lect surg Aberd/consult. ARI from 1977
m Aber 22.6.63 Catherine R. Matheson MA 1964 *qv*

AHMED Abul Hasan Moinuddin   MSc 1967 PhD 1969
BSc(Calc) MSc(agr)(West Bengal)

AHMED Fouad   BSc(for) 1959

AHMED Shammim Jehangir   PhD 1968
BSc MSc(Dacca)

AHMED Siddik Mohamed Shaheen   MSc 1970
BSc(Khart)

AHMED Tawfig Hashim   MSc 1964
s of Hashim A. acct and Zahra A. Rahman; b Omdurman 5.3.33
agr econ Khartoum 1964–67; agr econ advis Tripoli 1967–71; asst under-secy for plan., min of agr Khartoum 1971–74, dir dept of plan. from 1974
m Omdurman 28.3.60 Fathia el Baghir d of El Baghir Admed Ibrahim Omdurman

AHMED Yehia Youssef   PhD 1964
MB(Cairo) BSc(Lond)

AIDLEY Susan Mary   *BSc 1965

AIKEN Laura Jane   MA 1963 *1965
d of Agnes H. Aiken secy; b Bucksburn 10.3.43
Dip Ed(Lond)
teacher: Fort George Quebec 1966–68, Punnichy Sask 1968–71; peripatetic remed teacher Kincardine 1971–72; educ psych Aber and Kincardine 1972–73
m Burlington Vermont USA 17.12.73 David D. Blanchard BSc(Lehigh univ) headmaster s of Roger W. B. BA (Boston) NY USA

AIKEN Marigold Helen   BSc 1961
m Hall

AIKEN William Alexander   BSc(agr) 1967
s of Alexander F. A. farm. and Ella Scott; b Aber 14.3.45
Dip in Crop Protection (Edin) 1968
asst insp (GD) DAFS Oban from 1968
m Aber 23.8.68 Anne Davidson d of Hugh D. Lyne of Skene

AIKMAN David Powrie   *BSc 1961
s of Thomas S. A. BCom 1928 *qv*; b Aber 14.5.39
PhD (E Ang)
lect Univ of E Ang from 1965
m Aber 3.10.62 Margaret R. Morrice clerkess/typist d of Forbes M. M. M. Footdee

AIKMAN Peter Ramsay   BSc 1966
s of Thomson S. A. BCom 1928 *qv*; b Aber 18.4.43
prod. asst Erith 1966–68; Wrexham: prod. supt materials controller from 1969
m Huntly 14.7.66 Cathleen A. Munro MA 1964 *qv*

AIRD Iain Campbell   *MA 1968

AITKEN Alistair James   MA 1965
s of Walter J. A. and Isabella Black; b Fraserburgh 27.5.43
teacher Fr/Ger AGS 1966–69; prin teacher Powis acad from 1969

m Aber 4.7.70 Yvonne M. Mutch teacher d of Alexander F. M. Aber

AITKEN Gordon Brown   *BSc 1967 PhD 1970
s of Archibald B. A. man. and Dorothy A. Fraser; b Aber 15.3.45
ARIC 1970
res fellow: univ of Delaware 1970–71, Strath 1971–72; trained as teacher Aber 1972–73; lect chem univ Sains Malaysia from 1973

AITKEN Gordon Graham   MB ChB 1967
m Doreen L. Rettie MB ChB 1965 *qv*

AITKEN James Meff   MA 1967

AITKEN Joseph Caldwell   MA 1970
(conferred for long service of exceptional merit)
provisor univ union Aberd from 1950; retd 1970
d Aber 2.8.74

AITKEN Robin Elliot Guild   MB ChB 1963
s of Andrew A. civ eng and Isabella L. G. Guild teacher; b Edin 7.11.39
h o ARI, Inv RI 1963–64; regt m o 23rd Parachute Field Ambulance, Aldershot, Bahrain, Adelaide 1964–67; army health spec (major), York and Germany 1968–72; asst sen m o NE reg hosp board 1972–74; spec commun med Grampian health board from 1974
m Lond 26.7.69 Gillian A. Odell SRN d of Brig Benjamin A. O. Stanmore

AKALOO Nuvinchund   MA 1964
s of Ramnarain A. prop. and Sonia Beeharry; b Vacoas 3.10.37
educ off. Mauritius 1964–66; diplomatic off. freelance radio and tv broadcaster and interviewer in Engl with Mauritius Broadcasting Corporation from 1966; chief of protocol min of external affairs (Mauritius) from 1973
m Mauritius 11.2.66 Nalini D. Jhowry comp man. d of Ramroop J. Mauritius

AKHIDIME Samuel Olatunde   *BSc(eng) 1956

AKINKUGBE Ajibayo   Mb ChB 1957
s of E. A. A. trader and Victoria O. Akinnagbe; b Ondo 3.2.29
MRCOG 1965 FMCOG(Nigeria) 1971
m o W. Nigeria 1958–62; regist mat. hosp Aber 1962–66; consult. obst/gyn 1966–69; sen consult. & prin m o Ile-Ife hosp Nigeria 1969–74; assoc prof coll of med Lagos from 1974
m Lagos 15.12.60 Obafunke Femi-Pearse barrister d of J. T. F.-P. MB ChB(Edin) Lagos

AKPOM Cyril Amechi Odiakosah   MB ChB 1963

AL-AWADI Abdul Raman Abdulla   MB ChB 1963
s of Abdullah M. H. Al.-A. bus. man. and Mariam; b Kuwait 18.12.36
BSc(Beirut) 1958 DTM&H(Harv) 1965 FRCP(Dub) 1978 hon PhD(Si Chang Bon Korea) 1977
MoH Kuwait: h o, regist, member reporter of plan. comm 1963–69; asst dir, dir preventive serv 1969–75; min of health from 1975
m Kuwait 14.8.69 Sadika A. Al-wadi MD(Cairo) paediat d of Ali Al-A.

ALBERT Michael   *MA 1970

ALCOCK John Wright   BSc(for) 1956
s of Ralph T. A. comp dir and Edith D. Wright; b Morecambe 28.12.34

nat serv R.E.; trainee for. estates Lowther Castle Penrith;
Queensland for. comm 1960
m Brisbane 1.10.66 Carole Baldwin d of Alexander B.
Brisbane

ALCOCK Stephen Robert   MB ChB 1969
  s of Leonard G. A. eng and Marjorie I. Davis; b Sutton
Coldfield 24.6.45
h o ARI 1969–70; lect dept bact Aberd from 1970
m Tighnabruiach 30.6.72 Jean M. D. Paterson MA 1969 *qv*

ALDER Clive Philip   *BSc 1970
  s of Philip A. civ serv and Joan Murphy; b Romford
15.7.48
teacher chem Peebles h s from 1971
m Aber 31.7.71 Kathleen S. Paton BEd 1969 *qv*

ALEXANDER Anita June   BSc 1963
  d of Alfred A. farm. and Annie Rennie asst matron; b
Marykirk Laurencekirk 11.6.42
teacher biol Telford coll of f e Edin 1964–72, 1973–75
m Marykirk 26.8.73 William B. Hayton detective s of
James B. H. Wishaw

ALEXANDER Anne Elizabeth   BSc 1960
  m Normand

ALEXANDER Charlotte Mary Margaret   MA 1958

ALEXANDER Christine Moira   MA 1966
  d of John T. A. OBE MA(Edin) comp dir and Moira G.
Macdougall BSocSc(Edin); b Lanark 21.3.46
market res investigator Procter & Gamble Lond 1966–68;
res asst Procter & Gamble (Scandinavia) Lond 1968–69;
market res exec: L'Oreal Lond 1969–74, CPC (UK) Ltd
1974–76
m –.3.76 Ian A. Walker MA (St And)

ALEXANDER Dianne Marion   *LLB 1970
  d of Alfred H. A. butcher and Margaret L. Sproul secy;
b Aber 15.1.47
law app Edin 1970–72; sen conveyancing asst private WS
firm Edin 1972–75; solic, sen solic off. of Solic to Secy of
State for Scotland Edin from 1975
m Edin 18.10.76 Maurice M. Howieson man. dir eng comp
s of James S. H. Broxburn

ALEXANDER Donald Gerald   *MA 1962

ALEXANDER Duncan Kennedy   *BSc 1960
  s of John D. A. bank off. and Isabella D. Kennedy
shorthand typist; b Banchory 15.3.38
teacher sc Mackie acad Stonehaven 1961–66; prin sc
Lochaber h s Fort William 1966–69; prin chem Mackie
acad 1969–73; asst rector Elgin acad from 1973

ALEXANDER Elizabeth Margaret   MA 1963
  d of John D. A. bank acct and Isabella D. Kennedy
secy; b Banchory 5.9.42
teacher Fr/Ger Knox acad Haddington 1964–68; tut./
teacher Inv from 1969
m Aber 14.7.67 Neil A. Campbell MA 1967 *qv*

ALEXANDER Eric Richardson   MB ChB 1957 MD 1973
  s of James A. farm worker and Annie B. Smith reg
nurse; b Aber 31.3.33
DPM(Lond) 1969 MRCPsych 1972
h o Aber 1957–58; army Germany 1958–60; asst lect Dun
1960–63; army Germany 1963–67; regist Dumfries 1967–
70; sen regist Aber 1970–74, consult. Aber from 1974

m Orkney 15.1.60 Elizabeth I. S. Gray reg nurse d of
Robert G. Orkney

ALEXANDER George   BSc 1963
  s of George A. fisherman and Alexina C. Lamb; b
Peterhead 6.6.42
pilot RAF from 1964
m Old Deer 17.4.65 Dorothy M. Webster teacher d of
Henry W. Stuartfield

ALEXANDER Gwynyth Margaret   BSc 1970
  d of Alfred H. A. butcher and Margaret L. Sproul
secy; b Aber 26.6.49
teacher geog Johnstone from 1971, asst guid from 1973;
prin guid Renfrew h s 1975–78; teacher Furze Platt c s
Maidenhead 1978–79
m Aber 25.8.78 Kenneth R. Abernethy acct s of Thomas
A. Langbank

ALEXANDER Ian Kemp   BSc 1969
  s of Harry W. A. MA 1921 *qv* and Mabel Kemp MA
1929 *qv*; b Aber 15.5.47
comm asst ICI HOC div Lond 1969–70; rep ICI petrochem div Lond 1971–73; raw materials man. ICI petrochem div Billingham 1973–74; petrol prod. and bulk
sales man. ICI petrochem div Wilton from 1975
m Northwich 18.12.71 Susan A. Frith MA 1969 *qv*

ALEXANDER James Bremner   BSc(eng) 1957
  s of James A. farm serv and Anne B. Smith nurse;
b Cuminestown 27.9.35
grad trainee Scot. elect. trg scheme Glasg 1957–58; nat
serv REME sgt Cyprus 1958–60; teacher maths/sc
Hilton acad Aber 1961–62; computer customer eng IBM
Edin 1962–68; sen plan. rep Greenock IBM from 1968
m Aber 15.8.61 Marina A. Main typist d of John A. M.
Cuminestown

ALEXANDER James Irving   BSc(agr) 1956
  s of John A. MA(Glas) C of S min and Jane H. Irving;
b Kirkwall 8.12.31
DTA(Trin) 1958
dist agr off. Balovale N Rhod 1958–62; agr res off. Fort
Jameson N Rhod 1962–64; prin agr res off. Mount
Makulu Zambia 1964–68, asst chief agr res off. 1968–69;
farm. on own account Wigtown from 1969
m Balovale 3.11.59 Anne Lowrie SRN d of Wilfred L. L.
Halesworth

ALEXANDER John Ross   *MA 1968

ALEXANDER Margaret Jean   MA 1959
  d of Edward S. A. man. dir and Robina K. Ellis
cashier; b Aber 13.3.38
teacher Fr/Ger: Fraserburgh acad 1960–67; lect coll of
comm Aber from 1968

ALEXANDER Muriel Elizabeth   cLLB 1966
  d of Alastair I. L. A. acct and Muriel Gorman; b Aber
6.5.46
law app Arbroath 1966–68; leg. asst: Dun 1969–72,
Montrose 1972–75, ptnr 1975
m Montrose 21.10.72 Christopher R. C. Hardy journalist
s of Ronald H. Montrose

ALEXANDER Patricia Anne   PhD 1967
  b Glasg 12.11.42
BSc(Glas) 1963
biochem: Dun RI 1967–69, St Joseph's hosp Sarnia
Canada 1969–70; post doct res fell. Tor 1971–74, res
assoc since 1974
m Glasg –.12.66 Rae

ALI Faisal Mirghani   MSc 1966
s of Mirghani A. retd off. and Nagia Mohamed; b
Sudan 31.1.38
BSc(agr)(Alex) 1961; course maths Norwood tech coll
Lond 1963; pt I Dip Stat(Aberd) 1964
agr res corp Sudan: exper off. Sudan 1961-66; res worker
Wadmedani from 1966

ALI Zaffar   *MA 1962
s of Ameer A. and Nuroon Khan; b Trinidad 8.9.38
Dip Stat(Lond) 1964
statist Trinidad 1964; Univ of WI Jamaica: lect 1965-72;
educ statist from 1972
m Woking 27.7.63 Moira A. R. Fachie MA 1962 qv

ALLAM Hassan Nashaat Abdel Fattah   PhD 1967

ALLAN Alexander   *BSc 1966 PhD 1969
s of Alexander A. motor mech and Margaret I. Hay;
b Forres 26.2.44
scient Unilever res lab Port Sunlight from 1969
m Nairn 15.7.67 Margaret M. Baikie teacher d of John B.
Nairn

ALLAN Alexander Moir   *MA 1968

ALLAN Anne Mary   *MA 1963
d of John R. A. driver and Mary H. McRae; b Beauly
22.9.41
teacher geog: St Audrey's s mod s Hatfield 1963-64,
Loreto coll St Albans 1964-66, Harrytown h s Romiley
1966-72; prin St Bernard's g s for girls Slough from 1972
m Beauly 7.8.65 William A. Anderson BSc 1963 qv

ALLAN Barbara Gunn   BSc 1958
d of Donald A. farm. and Barbara G. Mathieson; b
Thurso 12.9.37
asst scient off. Wales 1958, Torry res stat 1959; teacher
p s Castletown 1960
m Castletown 1.6.61 Donald M. Sutherland civ eng/comp
dir s of Hugh D. S. Thurso

ALLAN Charles Maitland   *MA 1962
s of John R. A. MA 1928 qv and Jean A. Mackie MA
1929 qv; b Stirling 19.8.39
lect: Glas 1962-63, Dund 1963-65; lect, sen lect Strath
1965-74; farm. Methlick, writer, broadcaster from 1975
m Banchory-Devenick 23.2.61 Fiona Vine BSc(St And)
lect d of Reginald V. Dun

ALLAN Christine Susan   MA 1969
d of George D. A. CA and Blanche M. Eddie; b Aber
8.2.48
exec off. DHSS Dunfermline 1970-73
m Aber 13.4.71 Roger M. Needler civ serv s of William
H. N. Dun

ALLAN David Cameron   *MA 1969

ALLAN David Martin   *LLB 1968
s of Alexander J. A. comp dir and Margaret I. Caldwell
teacher; b Aber 25.10.46
law app, leg. asst Glasg 1968-73; ptnr Fergusson Robertson & Norrie Dun 1973-76; sen lect conveyancing/prof
pract of law Aberd from 1976
m Aber 16.6.69 Evelyn M. Black teacher d of Alan F. B.
BL(Edin) Elgin

ALLAN Dorothy May   MA 1968 DipEd 1969
d of John C. E. A. driving instr and Kathleen M.
Coutts; b Aber 29.4.47
teacher Engl/r e Lenzie acad 1969-72
m Aber 16.7.71 Sinclair B. Ferguson MA 1968 qv

ALLAN Douglas Kinmonth   BSc(agr) 1969 *1971
s of Charles P. A. printer and Jean K. Keay; b Perth
4.7.46
teacher W. Lothian from 1972

ALLAN Duncan Shearer   MB ChB 1966
s of Robert F. A. acct and Laura J. Fettes teacher;
b Insch 17.11.43
h o Aber: City hosp, cas dept ARI 1966-67, g p from 1967
m Aber 3.4.67 Valerie P. Allan MA 1966 qv

ALLAN Eric Robert   *BSc 1964
s of John C. E. A. driving instr and Kathleen M. Coutts;
b Aber 9.2.42
teacher sc West Calder h s 1965-66; Edin: teacher chem
George Heriot's 1966-71, prin chem from 1971
m Darlington 9.7.66 Valerie Cawthorn teacher d of
John C. Darlington

ALLAN Grant Alexander Thomas   *MA 1964
PhD(Alta)

ALLAN Helen Adcock   MA 1958
m (1) Imray
   (2) O'Neill

ALLAN Ian Malcolm Thomson   *MA 1957
s of John A. BSc(Glas) headmaster and Marjory
Thomson BSc(St And) teacher; b Fraserburgh 5.8.35
man. trainee Rugby 1957-61; works study eng Glasg
1961-63; man. bldrs and civ eng Aber from 1963
m Aber -.9.59 Mary Stewart radiogr d of Donald C. S.
Ellon

ALLAN Irene Pirrie   MA 1962

ALLAN Isobel Rose Campbell   MA 1964 Dip Ed 1965

ALLAN Keith Kellas Armstrong   *BSc 1962

ALLAN Lesley Marion   *MA 1965
d of Bertie A. theatre stage dir and Ellen M. Green civ
serv; b Aber 31.8.43
Charles McGregor mem prize for teaching 1966
teacher Engl Aber h s for girls 1966-72, year mistress
Northfield acad Aber from 1972

ALLAN Leslie Stewart   *MA 1965

ALLAN Mellis   *BSc 1962

ALLAN Patricia Margaret Isabella   MA 1967
d of Cecil E. A. A. bank teller and Annie C. Cunningham secy; b Glasg 3.2.46
teacher: Engl/hist 1968-70, Engl from 1970 Hermitage
acad Helensburgh
m Inveraray 30.10.71 Andrew W. Wiseman ACMA
internal audit. s of Andrew W. Pittenweem

ALLAN Roderick James   *BSc 1965
s of James A. mus teacher/piano tuner/mus and Mary
H. Mitchell; b Huntly 23.6.43
MSc(Wis) 1967 PhD(Dart) 1969
res geochem geol surv Ottawa 1969-74; chief nat water
res inst Western and Northern reg, Govt of Canada from
1974
m Quebec 28.12.72 Sandra E. Casey BA(Carleton) res asst
d of Joseph M. C. Ottawa

ALLAN Terrence William   *BSc(eng) 1970
s of William A. mason and Margaret L. M. McLeod
insur ag; b Forres 8.10.47

teacher coll of comm Aber from 1970
m Aber 5.8.72 Linda M. J. Low MA 1972 d of William
J. L. MA 1937 *qv*

ALLAN Thomas   *MA 1967
 s of Thomas A. clerk and Eileen Blain; b Glasg 29.7.45
asst teacher/dep head Worsley Canada 1968–71; prin
hist: Dumfries 1971–72, Fraserburgh from 1972
m Glasg 12.8.67 Anne Howatson teacher d of Robert H.
Glasg

ALLAN Valerie Pearl   MA 1966
 d of Duncan A. salesman/man. dir and Pearl Robinson;
b Aber 24.4.46
teacher private nurs s 1968–71
m Aber 3.4.67 Duncan S. Allan MB ChB 1966 *qv*

ALLAN William Craig   *BSc 1964
 s of William A. and Doris C. Bowman art teacher;
b Aber 8.11.42
PhD(Edin) 1971 AMA 1976
res stud. Edin 1965–68; res asst Hunterian Museum
Glasg 1968–72; dep curator and keeper of geol County
Museum Warwick
m Lighthorne 2.4.66 Ann M. Miller radiogr d of Robert
A. M. Gaydon

ALLAN William Sinclair   MB ChB 1957

ALLANACH Ian Gordon   *BSc 1969
 s of John A. and Jessie A. Cunningham; b Inv 1.11.47
teacher chem Dunf 1970–71; prin chem Glenrothes from
1972
m Inv 12.9.69 Patricia M. Loudon

ALLARDYCE Janette Harper   MA 1962
 m Taylor

ALLARDYCE Raymond Joseph Michie   *MA 1969
 s of Charles A. head porter Stir and Janet Michie; b
Crieff 3.1.46
teacher: Hanover Germany 1970–73, Stirling from 1973

ALLATHAN Alexander George   BSc(agr) 1960
 s of Alexander G. M. A. farm. and Roberta T. Rettie;
b Peterculter 8.9.37
asst agr advis Caithness 1960–62, acting agr advis Skye
1962–65, area agr advis Caithness from 1965
m Muir of Ord 25.10.68 Myra J. Johnstone secy d of
Archibald K. J. Invergarry

ALLATHAN Ronald Ewen   BSc(agr) 1964
 s of Alexander G. M. A. farm. and Roberta T. Rettie;
b Skene 26.6.43
agr advis Aber 1965–72; man. consult Aber from 1972
m Aber 22.3.66 Marilyn E. Simpson d of William S.
Rosehearty

ALLBROKE Raymond   *BSc(agr) 1968
 s of William A. farm. and Mary I. D. A. Mackie;
b Aber 25.4.45
agr advis W of Scotland agr coll: Campbeltown 1968–72,
Stirling from 1972

ALLEN Alistair Roy   *BSc 1969

ALLEN Hilary   *MA 1965
 d of Thomas W. A. C Eng and Florence E. Ironmonger; b Yorks 8.10.43
MA(Alta) 1967 PhD(Alta) 1972 Canada Council doct
fell. 1968–69

univ of Alta teaching asst 1965–68; Acadia univ: lect
1969–73, asst prof from 1973
m Halkirk 12.9.66 Raymond H. Thompson PhD(Alta)
asst prof head Engl dept Acadia univ s of Victor H. T.
Belf

ALLINSON Derek Wilfred   *BSc 1963

ALLISON James   BSc(agr) 1957

ALLISON Judith Elizabeth   MA 1970
 d of Thomas A. sales rep and Olive K. Matthew instr
spastic adolescents; b Newport-on-Tay 22.4.49
secy Lond 1971–73; teacher Engl Stuttgart W Ger 1973–
75; secy Lond 1975–77, Ingolstadt W Ger from 1977

ALLISON Margaret McGregor   *MA 1968 Dip Ed 1969
 d of Thomas M. A. dep secy board of man. Inv hosp
and Elizabeth L. Hunter; b Inv 2.11.45
teacher mod lang Greenock acad from 1969
m Elderslie 14.4.73 Ronald K. Thomson BSc(Strath)
teacher maths Johnstone h s s of Samuel J. T. MA(Glas)
Johnstone

ALLISON Stuart Norwood   MB ChB 1969 DMRD 1974
 s of Thomas B. A. shop man. and Ghislaine Turner
ladies' outfitter; b Annfield Plain 19.2.43
h o Woodend hosp, ARI 1969–70; trainee g p Aber 1970–
71; regist radiol/hon clin tut. ARI from 1974
m Aber 20.7.68 Marguereta M. F. Davie MA 1966 *qv*

ALLISTON John Charles   BSc(agr) 1969 *1970
 s of Gordon C. A. man. dir and Margaret T. Hay; b
Twyford 30.6.46
PhD(UCNW) 1974
lect anim prod. royal agr coll, Cirencester 1974–76; sen
scient off. animal breeding res organis Edin from 1976

AL-NAJAR Muthafar Haider   MLitt 1968
 BA(Cairo)
d 1976

ALPINE George   LLB 1968
 s of George D. L. A. MA(Cantab) marketing dir and
Josephine Azrak teacher; b Irvine 11.5.46
law app, leg. asst Paul & Williamsons advoc Aber from
1968
m Aber 17.9.71 Margaret A. Morrison secy d of Roderick
G. M. Huntly

ALSOP Gillian Eileen Margaret   BEd 1969
 d of William J. A. civ serv and Maud Arnold; b
Nuneaton 12.7.47
teacher: Summerhill acad Aber 1969–71, Heart of
England s Balsall Common from 1975
m Edin 28.6.69 Robin G. Peacock MA 1970 *qv*

ALSTON Alastair Summers   *BSc(for) 1961
 s of Thomas A. and Margaret R. Wilson art teacher;
b Glasg 27.9.39
dept of for. Fiji: div for. off. Lautoka 1962–64; util off.
Suva 1964–71; prin util off. Suva from 1971

ALVIS Patricia Ann   MA 1967
 m Robertson

AMAR Satya Swarup   MB ChB 1965 DMRD 1969
 s of G. S. A. MA(Punjab) dep dir educ; b Mathura
India 13.2.41
FRCR (1971)
ARI: m o 1965–66; regist 1967–69; sen regist 1969–72;
Nott gen hosp: consult. radiol from 1972
m Aber 1965 May E. Skinner MA 1967 *qv*

AMATRUDA Janina Maria Celeste   MA 1969
d of George A. shop owner and Celeste R. Vettraino
shop owner; b Dun 3.6.44
teacher Ital/Engl Lawside acad 1970–72; temp posts Scot.
and USA 1972–73; course shorthand/typing Dun 1974

AMOS Lilias Teresa   BEd 1969
d of William A. area man. E Scot. bus group and Jean
M. S. S. Lothian; b Edin 23.4.46
teacher Engl Galashiels acad 1969–70; res asst educ psych
univ of Virginia Charlottesville Va USA 1970–71; asst s
psych Exeter 1971–72
m Galashiels 25.7.70 James B. Reary BSc 1967 *qv*

AMOS Valerie Anne   MA 1967

AMSTELL Anthony David   LLB 1967
s of R. J. A. bus. man and Margaret Nathan numis-
matist; b Lond 6.1.45
AIL
barrister-at-law Lincoln's Inn from 1970
m Tonbridge 12.8.72 Ingrid J. Woodgate secy d of Harold
W. BDS(Lond) Tonbridge

AMUJO Stephen Jimo   BSc(for) 1964
s of Bale A. farm. and Dada Amujo Dada; b Odo-Ere
20.12.38
MSc(Oregon St Univ USA) 1970
posts in Nigeria: for. man. off. Bornu Prov 1964–65;
prov for. off. Bauchi 1965; res off. soil surv N Nigeria
1965–68; for. admin Kwara State 1970–71; acting chief
conserv for. Kwara State 1971–73; chief conserv for.
Kwara State from 1973
m Odo-Ere 23.12.65 Rachel I. Amujo d of Amujo Okejan
Odo-Ere

ANAKWENZE Francis Nwoye   BSc(for) 1958
s of Umeano O. A. farm. and Mgbeke Okafor;
b Nigeria 1926
conserv for. Calabar: asst 1958–60, sen asst 1961–63;
Enuga: dep chief 1963–69, chief from 1970; post grad
course at Commonwealth For. Inst Oxford 1964–65
m Akure, Nigeria 1951 Rebecca N. Ikeme d of Patrick I.
Awka Nigeria

ANDERSEN Ragnar Peter Axel   MB ChB 1962
s of Ragnar K. D. A. Cand Med (Oslo) surg and
Borghild Odegaard; b Harstad Norway 28.10.35
Cand Med (Oslo) 1962
asst dis g p/lt army med corps Oslo 1964–65; asst res dept
anaest various hosps Norway; asst anaest Sweden 1969,
Canada 1969–70, Oslo 1970–71; head dept anaest
Honefoss Norway 1971–73; asst chief dept anaest Aker
hosp Oslo from 1973
m Oslo 8.7.61 Merethe Mjelstad hosp pharm d of Hjalmar
A. M. Oslo

ANDERSON Aileen Anne   MA 1963
d of Alexander A. joiner and Annie S. Whitley; b
Aber 31.7.42
teacher: Fr Aber 1964–68, Fr/Lat Colchester from 1975
m Aber 5.4.66 Alexander D. Murray tech buyer s of
Archibald M. Aber

ANDERSON Alan Bain   *MA 1969

ANDERSON Alan John Bruce   *MA 1964 MSc 1966
s of John A. civ eng and Mary W. Moir; b Aber 14.1.41
FSS 1967
scient off. statist dept Rothamsted exper stat 1966–70;
chief statist MRC clin and pop. cytogenetics unit Edin
1970–74; lect statist Aberd from 1974

m Edin 26.6.74 Bridget I. Lowe BA(Hull) res off. SHHD
d of Patrick J. L. Carlow Eire

ANDERSON Alexander   BSc 1958
s of Alexander A. master mariner and Winifred D.
Riddell french polisher; b Aber 19.9.27
res asst Aberd 1958–66; res off. (grade I) from 1972
m Edin 25.3.61 Norma S. Hunter physioth d of John
N. W. H. MA(Edin) Edin

ANDERSON Alexander   BEd 1970
s of Alexander W. A. plumbing warehouse and trans
man. and Jessie T. B. Falconer secy; b Banchory 12.11.40
teacher sc Peterhead acad from 1970
m Longside 14.7.66 Moyra D. Henderson teacher home
econ d of William G. H. Inverurie

ANDERSON Alexander McRobert   MA 1958 cLLB1960
s of William M. A. farm. and Isabella Fyfe tailoress;
b Leochel Cushnie 11.7.36
leg. asst: Adam Thomson & Ross advoc Aber, ptnr
1967–71; secy supreme court leg. aid comm, Law Soc of
Scot. from 1972
m Aber 10.2.68 Brenda Main shorthand typist d of Charles
J. M. Dyce

ANDERSON Ann Ogilvie   MA 1963
b Elgin 24.2.42
secy Glas 1964–66; Apia W Samoa: teacher 1966–68,
admin asst 1968–70; careers off. Aber from 1970
m Aber 19.12.64 Alexander L. Walker BSc 1962 *qv*

**ANDERSON Anne Barbara Michie   MB ChB 1960
                                           cMD 1965**
d of James M. M. A. pharm and Jane A. Anderson
teacher; b Forres 10.2.37
D.ObstRCOG 1962 PhD (Univ of Wales) 1972
h o Inv, Aber, Glasg 1960–62; res fell. obst Aber and
Cardiff 1962–70; lect clin repro physiol Welsh Nat s of
med Cardiff from 1970

ANDERSON Arthur   BL 1958
d 1.3.68

ANDERSON Brian Alexander   MA 1963
s of John A. A. joiner and Isabella W. Davie bookkeeper; b Aber 8.1.42
DPE 1967
teacher geog/Engl/hist Northfield acad Aber 1965–66;
dip. in p e post grad course Scot. s of p e Jordanhill 1966–
67; teacher p e/geog Northfield acad; prin p e Powis acad
Aber from 1973
m (1) Aber Marianne E. H. Mackay MA 1964 *qv*
   (2) Aber 27.7.73 Mary R. Flockhart MA 1970 *qv*

ANDERSON Bryce Alexander   MA 1959 BD 1963
s of Alexander A. weighing machine mech and Maggie
Gaunt shop asst; b Aber 10.1.39
STM 1964
trainee urban training centre Chicago 1964–65; soc res
C of S Aber 1966–69; dir action res proj Youth dev trust
Manchester from 1969
m Aber –.10.69 Morag A. Booth cler asst d of Alexander
B. Aber

ANDERSON Catherine   MA 1964
d of Alexander H. A. teacher and Elizabeth M. D.
Smith teacher; b Airdrie 12.6.43
teacher hist Fort William 1965–69, spec asst 1969–72;
prin guid Lochaber h s 1972–75; prin hist Alness acad
from 1975

ANDERSON Catherine Mary *BSc 1969
  d of William A. BSc 1940 *qv* and Agnes W. Kerr BSc 1940 *qv*; b Aber 31.7.49
teacher VSO Shendam and Vom, Nigeria 1969–72; market. man. Unilever Lond 1972; proj acct J. R. McDermott Aber from 1977
m Aber 22.10.72 Thomas L. Mason BSc(eng)(Lond) civ eng/contr man., corporate plan., comm dir s of Harold P. M. Bishop's Stortford

ANDERSON Cecilia Patterson   MA 1970
  d of James P. A. fisherman and Cecilia C. Patterson; b Edin 23.1.49
teacher: p s Dalry 1971–74, New South Wales from 1974

ANDERSON Christopher David   BSc(eng) 1970
  s of Alexander G. A. BSc(eng) 1945 *qv*; b Aber 27.3.48
civ eng William Tawse Aber from 1970

ANDERSON Colin *MA 1966 Dip Ed 1967
  s of Simon P. A. factory worker, dustman and Amelia S. Steele factory worker; b Forfar 10.5.43
teacher Fr/Ger: Arbroath h s 1967–68, Grantown g s 1969–71, Elgin acad 1971–74; asst prin Fr/Ger Denny h s 1974–78; prin mod lang Deans Community h s Livingston from 1978
m Aber 1.8.69 Moyra M. Robertson teacher p e d of Alastair M. R. Bromley

ANDERSON Colin Henry   BSc 1970

ANDERSON David   BSc(eng) 1970
  s of David A. chief for. and Jessie W. Taylor; b Torphins 12.4.48
civ eng: Taylor Woodrow construct. Heysham 1970–73; James Williamson & Ptnrs Glasg from 1973

ANDERSON David George *MA 1968
  s of Adam G. A. and Winifred N. Haworth; b Orpington 31.5.45
res fell. geog univ of Newfoundland 1968–70; tut. asst Aberd 1970–71; lect geog Luton coll of tech from 1971
m Aber 3.8.70 Joy E. E. Ogston d of James A. O. Aber

ANDERSON David George   MA 1970

ANDERSON David John Boyd   MA 1970 BD 1973
  s of John B. A. author and Jessie M. Begg; b Glasg 23.6.49
asst C of S min Douglas & Angus ch Dun from 1973, min Bainsford ch Falkirk from 1974
m Edin 20.7.73 Eleanore St V. Dick MA 1970 *qv*

ANDERSON David Rae *MA 1958
  s of David A. marine eng and Alice M. Rae; b Stonehaven 27.1.36
LL B(Edin) 1960 LL M(ANU) 1966 WS 1961 NP 1969
Aust fed publ serv 1962–65; lect leg. and constit hist Canberra; asst solic Edin 1965–67; ptnr leg. firm Alloa and cent. Scot. from 1967
m Aber 6.1.62 Jean Strachan MA 1957 *qv*

ANDERSON David Sinclair *MA 1970
  s of Hope V. A. area controller Scot. (telephones) and Jean T. Sinclair cler off.; b Glasg 30.6.48
McGraw Hill Book Co Maidenhead: rep 1970; acad spec Dusseldorf from 1971

ANDERSON David William   MB ChB 1965
  s of John W. L. A. mining eng and Ivy E. H. Butler; b Nott 11.7.39

houseman ARI 1965–66; g p Aber from 1967
m Banchory 20.6.62 Janie W. F. Durward d of Lloyd G. D. Banchory

ANDERSON Dennis *BSc(eng) 1957
  s of James A. painter/decorator and Bella M. Middleton; b Aber 22.4.35
electronic des & dev eng Liverpool 1957–66; f e teacher elect./electronics Falkirk from 1966
m Aber 1960 Shirley Gray d of John S. G. Aber

ANDERSON Elizabeth Margaret Bain *BSc 1962
  d of Robert J. A. auctioneer/estate ag/factor/farm. and Laura M. Ligertwood MB ChB(Edin); b Aber 27.9.39
teacher Summerhill acad Aber 1964–65
m Aber 28.7.64 John Y. L. Hay BL 1962 *qv*

ANDERSON Eric *BSc 1957
  s of Robert H. A. eng and Eveline A. M. Kindness; b Aber 8.10.35
DPhil(Oxon) 1961
metallurgist group man. Geneva from 1961
m Geneva 21.12.63 Renate M. Kollrack metall tech d of Fritz K. Berlin

ANDERSON Frances Mary   MA 1970
  d of James M. A. farm. and Phyllis A. Taylor teacher dom sc; b Elgin 18.6.49
teacher Maisondieu s Brechin 1971–73
m Alves 30.12.72 Dennis Holland farm acct s of Charles C. H. Leeds

ANDERSON Gladys Margaret *BSc 1967
  m Watt

ANDERSON Gordon Ingram   MA 1967

ANDERSON Grant Mackenzie   MA 1966

ANDERSON Hamish Alexander *BSc 1962 PhD 1966
  s of Alexander J. A.; b Aber 8.5.40
Brit Council fell. faculté de sciences, Orsay France 1965–66; ICI fell. org chem Liverpool 1966–68; Macaulay inst for soil res Aber from 1968
m Aber 1964 Maureen L. Woollard MA 1959 *qv*

ANDERSON Hazel   MA 1969

ANDERSON Iain Howe *BSc 1958 PhD 1962
  s of John A. foreman (dyeing & cleaning) and Elizabeth March; b Glasg 8.2.37
FRIC 1971
lect chem H-W Edin 1961–71; asst secy Scottish assoc for nat certif and diplomas Glasg 1971–73; Scottish tech educ council Glasg: educ off. 1973–74, sen educ off. from 1974
m Stornoway 27.12.62 Anne I. Morrison BSc 1960 *qv*

Anderson Ian   MB ChB 1969
  s of William A. carpenter and Mary McDonald; b Aber 6.6.45
intern Vict Hosp, Lond, Ontario 1969–70; g p Pembroke, Ontario 1970–76; radiol Vict hosp London, Ont from 1976
m Turriff –.12.68 Lorna V. Elvin psychiat res worker d of William E. Turriff

ANDERSON Ian *LLB 1970
  s of Robert A. eng and Helen Marshall; b Paisley 4.7.43
LL M(Cape T) 1974
bar app Edin 1970–71, 72–73; advoc of sup courts of Scot.; member of coll of Justice 1973; lect in Roman Law, Witwatersrand 1973–74; advoc S. Af 1976

ANDERSON Ian Robert   *BSc(agr) 1968
s of Robert E. A. off. man./comp secy and Margaret
E. Baxter shop man.; b Elgin 6.11.45
MSc(Edin) 1970
pers trainee Shell Chem UK Carrington nr Manc 1970–72,
pers off. Shell R and M Stanlow 1972–74; remun advis:
Shell Venezuela Caracas 1975–78, Shell Internat Pet. Co
Lond from 1978
m Edin 13.8.71 Jane R. Langlands MA(Edin) Brit Council
off., BBC sen asst educ liaison d of Charles B. L. BSc(agr)
(Edin) Edin

ANDERSON Ian William White   MB ChB 1959
s of Alfred W. A. sales rep and Annabella M. Lyall;
b Aber 1.2.35
DObstRCOG 1965
h o ARI 1959–60; RAMC Brunei 1960–64; h o Raigmore
Hosp Inv 1964–65; g p: Saltcoats 1965–69, Kirkcaldy
from 1969
m Aber 13.12.60 Doris A. S. Leith physioth d of James L.
Aber

ANDERSON Isabel Barrie   BSc 1962

ANDERSON Isabella Ann   MA 1970
d of Herbert A. A. farm. and Isabel Walker; b Tough
14.5.49
teacher geog: Fife 1971–73, Ross-shire 1973–76
m Ballater 28.7.73 Ian D. Fraser mus instr s of Ernest F.
Crathie

ANDERSON James Allan   *MA 1964

ANDERSON James Andrew   *MA 1967
s of Gilbert A. crofter, fisherman and Robina S.
Williamson; b Whalsay 19.11.45
Dip Ed (Makerere Univ of E Africa) 1968
ed off. Kenya 1968–70; teacher Kaweran Coll NZ 1971;
sen town plan. asst Hamilton NZ from 1971

ANDERSON James Hugh   LLB 1966
s of David M. A. banker and Muriel E. Micklem MA
(Cape T) teacher; b Gwelo, Rhodesia 11.10.45
CA 1970
Johannesburg: comp acct subsid of Unilever SA 1970–72;
reg acct Western Bank (Anglo-Amer Group Co) 1972–75;
gen man. admin Ryan Niger corp (U.D.T. Group Co)
1975–76, dir from 1976
m Johannesburg 20.7.74 Anne V. Adcock p r consult.
(travel) d of R. A.

ANDERSON James Hunter   *BSc 1956 PhD 1959
s of Kenneth J. A. rly trans off. and Jessie R. S.
Hunter; b Romford 28.9.34
scient off. Long Ashton res stat Brist 1959–63; jun res
fell. univ of Brist 1963–66; sen res biochem, Fisons
Pharmaceuticals Loughborough 1966–69; sen scient off.
microbiol res estab Wilts 1969–71; teacher biol/chem
Lossiemouth h s from 1972

ANDERSON James Terry   MB ChB 1957
d Aden 14.5.67 *AUR* XLII 375

ANDERSON John   *MA 1960
s of George W. A. C of S min; b Oyne 20.11.37
teacher: RGC Aber 1961–65, prin geog Buckie h s 1965–
70; rector Speyside h s Aberlour from 1970
m Aber 17.7.63 Christina M. Murray MA 1958 *qv*

ANDERSON John   MB ChB 1964
s of Francis J. A. pharm and Elsie Falconer; b Lond
6.10.37

FRCSE 1968
hosp med pract Aber 1964–73; sen reg orthop surg from
1973
m Gatley 1966 Jennifer M. Brownhill nurse d of Albert B.
Gatley

ANDERSON John Leeds   *MA 1969
s of John L. A. foreman elect. welder and Alison Jolly;
b Aber 2.9.46
Lond: res asst inst for soc stud. in med care 1970–72,
Middx hosp med s 1972–75, lect in sociol 1975–78; lect
med sociol univ of Hong Kong from 1978
m Aber 25.7.69 Alison E. Grant MA 1969 *qv*; marr diss

ANDERSON John Peter George   MA 1968

ANDERSON Kathleen Guild   MA 1967

ANDERSON Margaret   *MA 1968
d 15.1.75

ANDERSON Margaret Louise Mary   *BSc 1966
d of George J. C. A. farm. and Margaret B. Barrie MA
1930 *qv*; b Aber 6.12.44
PhD(Lond) 1970
post doct. fell. Cold Spring Harbor lab Long Island USA
1970–73; scient staff Imp Cancer Res Fund Lond from
1973

ANDERSON Margaret Rosemary   MB ChB 1961
d of Thomas E. A. MB ChB 1926 *qv*; b Aber 17.11.37
m Aber 21.6.63 Murdoch W. MacLean MB ChB 1961 *qv*

ANDERSON Marvin Walter   PhD 1964
s of Walter R. A. BA(Pacific Lutheran univ) bapt min,
air force chap, coll pres and Faith E. Bennett; b Montevideo Minn 12.1.33
BA(Wash) 1955 BD(St Paul) 1959
asst to assoc prof ch hist Bethel Seminary St Paul Minn
1964–73, prof from 1973, visiting schol Cantab 1970–71
and 1977–78
m Spring Lake Park Minn 9.6.62 Ann M. Welin d of
Elmer C. W. Alvarado Minn

ANDERSON Myra Gordon   *MA 1964
d of James C. A. comm trav and Nellie G. Stables saleswoman; b Aber 10.5.41
teacher mod lang Aber 1965–69; participation in MA
course Russian at Aberd 1965–67; teacher Engl centre for
British teachers in Germany, Wipperfürth W. Ger
1969–71; dep dir of Centre for British Teachers in Europe
1971–74, admin from 1974

ANDERSON Nancy Lyons   *MEd 1966
d of David M. A. joiner/undertaker and Mary J. Kelly
nurse; b Kirkcaldy 23.10.11
BCom(Edin) 1932 DipEd(Edin) 1953 Dip RE(Edin) 1966
teacher: sen asst coll of comm Aber 1959–67; head comm
studies, Stranmillis coll of educ Belf from 1967

ANDERSON Peter George   *BSc(eng) 1969

ANDERSON Philip Edward   LLB 1969
s of Robert E. journalist and Catherine Martin;
b Glasg 9.6.49
Milne & Mackinnon Advoc Aber: app 1969–71, asst
solic 1971–73, ptnr from 1973
m Aber 28.6.68 Elizabeth M. Levie secy d of James M. L.
Aber

ANDERSON Raymond Kennedy   MA 1964 *1966
s of Francis W. A. police insp and Florence Kennedy
secy/bookkeeper; b Elgin 13.8.42
fin. exec: Ford Motor Co Essex 1966–72, BLMC Lond
from 1972

ANDERSON Robert   LLB 1966 MA 1969
s of James S. A. acct and Tony Levine nurse; b
Chelmsford 26.9.45
teacher: Adelaide 1969–71, coll of comm Aber from 1972

ANDERSON Robert   BSc 1970
s of Alexander A. agr worker and Maria J. Gordon;
b East Clyth 27.11.29
lect maths coll of comm Aber from 1971
m Exeter 14.2.63 Alison Black nurse d of Frederick B.
Devon

ANDERSON Robert John   *BSc 1966

ANDERSON Robert Moir Lechmere   MA 1962
                                               MB ChB 1967
s of David L. A. police off. and Mary Boyle head
teacher; b Doncaster 17.9.40
DPM 1974 MRCPsych 1975
major RAMC Germany, spec in psychiat
m Southport 1971 Mary T. Gavin MA 1970 qv

ANDERSON Roderick Stuart   *BSc 1969

ANDERSON Rosemary   *BSc 1966
m Smith

ANDERSON Sheila Buchan   MA 1964

ANDERSON Sheila Margaret   *BSc 1958
d of James C. A. coastguard and Alice M. A. Cocker;
b Aber 9.1.37
MSc(Manit) 1960
sc lib Manit 1960–61; dem bot: Sir George Williams
Univ Montreal 1961–62, Manit 1962–63; Manit: Lect bot
1965–66 and 1975, res asst bot 1975–76
m Winnipeg 7.7.62 Charles W. Anderson BSA(Manit)
farm./corporate secy grain exporting comp s of William
F. A. Manitoba

ANDERSON Violet   MB ChB 1962

ANDERSON William Alexander   *BSc 1963
s of William A. insur ag and Flora B. P. Christie;
b Forres 22.10.41
O R scient De Havillands Hatfield 1963–66; ICI paints
div: syst analyst Hyde 1966–69, bus. analyst Hyde 1969–
72, Slough from 1972
m Beauly 7.8.65 Anne M. Allan MA 1963 qv

ANDERSON William Craib   MA 1958 LLB 1961

ANDERSON William Peter   *BSc 1962
PhD(Edin)

ANDERSON-SMITH Gordon   MA 1966 *1969 BD 1971
s of Andrew M. F. S. master hairdresser and Nora N.
Forsyth; b Aber 29.12.40
ThM(Phil) 1972
asst min C of S Edin and Aber 1972–73; res stud. for
PhD Manc from 1973
m Aber 24.9.73 Myrtle I. Matthew MA 1964 qv
d Aber 4.3.80

ANDREW George Cassie   BSc MB ChB 1969

ANDREW Thomas Duncan   BSc 1962
s of William A. A. bus driver and Christina D. Ewen;
b Aber 7.10.35
teacher: maths/sc Robert Douglas mem s Scone 1963–72,
maths Perth g s from 1972
m Aber 4.4.64 Edith A. Wattie shorthand typist d of
Robert W. Aber

ANDREWS Peter John   BSc(for) 1961

ANGASTINIOTIS Michael Antoniou   MB ChB 1966
s of Anthony M. A. BEd(Athens) headmaster and
Helen Christaforou teacher; b Famagusta Cyprus 10.4.41
DCH(Glas) 1976
h o Aber 1966–67; regist neonatal paediat DRI 1968–69,
regist paediat Churchill hosp Oxford; paediat Famagusta
h from 1970
m Famagusta 27.8.61 Demetra McDonald d of James
McD. Glasg

ANGUS David   *MA 1969
s of George H. S. A. plumber and Jamesina Dalgarno
hosp cleaner; b Aber 7.12.46
clerk IPC bus. press London 1969–70; trainee journalist
IPC Mags 1970–71; asst edit. W. H. Smith & Son 1971–
72; sub edit. IPC Mags 1972–73; edit. Williams Mags
1973–74; free lance journalist from 1974
m Islington Sheila W. M. Fowlie secy d of James F. Aber

ANGUS David Nicol   MA 1958
s of James A. MA(Glas) teacher and Stella Nicol
MA(Glas) teacher; b Bettyhill 24.1.35
rly operating exec Lond from 1958

ANGUS Elizabeth Robb   MA 1970
d of John A. bus. man. and Agnes Shepherd; b Aber
23.10.18
teacher Engl Aber: coll of educ 1972–73, St Margaret's s
for girls 1973–74, Fr s of Total Marine 1974–78
stud. Aberd for M Litt from 1978
m Aber 8.4.41 J. Fergus Watt BL(Edin) town clerk Aber
s of James Watt CBE Aber

ANGUS George   BSc 1968
s of John A. sheet metal worker and Ethel Milne;
b Aber 6.2.47
teacher maths Huntly from 1969

ANGUS Jean   MA 1962

ANGUS Jeanette Alison   BEd 1970
d of Donald A. master butcher and Elizabeth M.
Hendry; b Wick 8.1.47
teacher Fr Wick h s 1970–72; man. staff Marks & Spencer
1972–74; teacher Fr/asst prin guid Wick h s from 1974
m Wick 23.12.77 Alan G. Mackenzie teacher, bus. man.
s of John G. M. Wick

ANGUS Jennifer Ann   MA 1967
d of Hector J. A. joiner and Ann M. Murphy shorthand typist; b Aber 3.4.44
teacher geog: Portobello s s 1968–69, Breadalbane acad
Aberfeldy 1969–74
m Aber 27.12.67 Michael Cooper MA 1968 qv

ANGUS Margaret Gardner   BSc 1960
d of Walter Angus police serg and Isabella Angus;
b Aber 2.10.38
Aberd: res asst med phys Foresterhill 1960–62; computing
asst Richard Thomas & Baldwins Newport Mon 1962–
64; teacher maths Glasg from 1973
m Aber 6.8.62 David Coutts BSc(eng) 1964 qv

ANGUS Michael George Noel *BSc 1962

ANGUS Zena June *MA 1964
 m Wight

ANNAND Gideon Scott MA 1962 *MEd 1967
 s of James S. A. banker and Wilhelmina E. A. Scott
MA 1932 qv; b Tullynessle 28.9.41
CA app 1962–64; educ off. Kenya 1967–72; teacher
Bannockburn h s Stirling from 1972
m Nairobi 7.2.72 Margaret R. Steer MA 1964 qv

ANNAND Patricia Ruth MA 1965
 m Somerville

ANNELLS Jane-Ann Ward *MA 1968
 d of Alfred G. M. A. and Dorothy J. Adsett; b
Brampton 6.3.45
m Aber 23.3.68 Ian K. M. Cameron MA 1966 qv

ANSTEY Clive BSc(for) 1968
 s of Frank F. Y. A. NZ rly publ and Nancy M.
Fairway; b Wellington 24.1.44
BSc(Well) 1965
dist for. Dunedin from 1968

ANTAO Anthony Juno Orlando MB ChB 1967
 s of Anthony J. P. A. MBE MBBS(Bom) 1937 and
Jesuina L. Carvalho; b Blantyre Malawi 4.6.43
DCMT(Lond) 1969 MRCP 1972
jun med off. Qn Eliz cent hosp Blantyre 1967–68; sen h o
infect. diseases E Birmingham hosp 1969–70; sen h o med
Knightswood hosp Glasg 1970; Milesmark hosp Dunfermline 1970–71; regist renal and gen med S Teesside
hosp group 1971–73; med regist and m o Westminster
hosp London 1973–75; sen asst consult. med min of publ.
health Doha Qatar from 1975

ANUMUDU David Ndubuisi MB ChB 1967
 s of Mathais O. A. merch and Janet Nwsahalu;
b Nigeria 25.11.37
h o: surg Ashington, med York, obst/gyn Leicester 1968–
69; sen h o obst/gyn Beverly 1968–69; sen h o genetic
med Sheffield 1969–70; regist obst/gyn Stockport 1970–
71; g p Warrington from 1971
m Aber 1.11.68 Alison J. Finnie DA d of David F. Cullen

ANWAR Ahmed PhD 1957
 MSc(Cairo)

APPERLEY Marion Barbara BSc 1970
 d of Eric R. A. estim eng and Dorothy A. Rowley;
b Birm 27.6.49
MSc(CNAA) 1974
metall chem Biometals Birm from 1970

APPIAH Robert Kwasi *BSc(eng) 1965

APPLIN Josephine Mary *BSc 1965
 m Corke

ARANDA Jose Martin PhD 1960

ARAP-SANG Francis Kiptorus BSc(for) 1968
 s of Barkoiyet Chepkeitany peasant and Kabon
Barkoiyet; b Kenya 27.3.42
MSc(for)(Tor) 1971
asst conserv of for. Kenya 1968–69; for. path. Kenya from
1971
m Kenya 16.8.69 Mary Jepkorir secy d of Jeremiah Kipyab,
Kenya

ARBUTHNOTT Gordon William *BSc 1964 PhD 1968
 s of Roy G. A. rly fitter and Maggie Lobban dom serv;
b Ellon 14.3.42
temp lect physiol Aberd 1968–69; Wellcome res fell.
Stockholm 1969–70; lect physiol Aberd 1970–73; MRC
staff scient Edin from 1973
m Aber 10.9.65 Joan E. Minto MA 1968 qv

ARCHEAMPONG Emmanuel BSc(for) 1963
 s of Robert Asiedu-Dentu min of relig and Madam
Adwoa Pokuaa farm.; b Larteh-Akwapim, Ghana
21.9.38
Ghana: asst conserv of for. 1964–67; for. supt Ashanti
Goldfields 1967–68; sen sc tut. Prempeh Coll 1968–73;
stocks supt State Gold Mines Corp, Tarkwa Goldfields
from 1973
m Bekwai-Ashanti –.12.65 Dorothy Kyei teacher d of
John D. K. Bekwai-Ashanti

ARCHER Rudolph MB ChB 1962

ARCHIBALD James Kennedy *BSc(eng) 1966
 resid Aber

ARDERN Richard John *BSc 1969
 MA(Sheff) 1971 ALA 1973
trainee univ lib St And 1969–70; lib HIDB Inv from 1971
m Inv 1970 Eileen M. Rhind BEd 1969 qv

ARGO Frances Elizabeth MA 1964
 d of John A. farm. and Annie I. Barron; b Ellon
22.2.44
teacher maths: Northfield s s Aber 1966–67, Duncanrig s
E Kilbride 1967–70, Ardersier s 1970–71, Victoria Drive s
Glasg 1971–74; asst prin maths Duncanrig s 1974–78
m (2) Glasg 20.7.73 Antony F. H. Henry CA comp secy
s of Samuel G. H. Cupar

ARGO Kenneth Barclay BSc(agr) 1970
 s of Douglas D. D. A. farm. and Edith Barclay MA
1944 qv; b Aber 19.8.48
MSc(N'cle) 1972
farm man. Cadbury/Typhoo/Schweppes Brechin 1972–76;
farm. Weldon Northants from 1976
m Aber 6.10.72 Helen M. Blyth teacher d of Robert B.
Laurencekirk

ARIDEGBE Michael Ojo BSc(for) 1961
 s of Josiah F. A. painter and Grace Ajayi dyer;
b Igbajo Oyo State Nigeria 4.11.22
Western and Oyo State Nigeria: asst conserv for. I and II
1961–67, sen asst 1968–72, conserv for. 1973–75, asst
chief conserv 1975–76, dep chief conserv from 1977
m Ibadan Nigeria 10.8.52 Grace Eyinade dressmaker d of
Daniel Adetona, Ogbomoshe Nigeria

ARKHURST Eustace MB ChB 1963
 BSc(McG)

ARKLEY Kenneth Ian *BSc(eng) 1966
 s of Alexander A. teacher and Victoria M. Grant;
b Laurencekirk 22.12.42
ICI Billingham: grad app 1966–67; plasterboard plant
man. 1967–69, plan. man. 1969–72, workshops man.
1972–76, comm man. waste water treatment from 1976
m Aber 10.4.64 Elizabeth S. Thomson secy d of James
I. F. T. MA 1936 qv

ARLIDGE Ernest Zane *PhD 1958
 BSc MSc(NZ)

ARMSTRONG Alison Margaret   MA 1970
 s of William A. A. paper mill worker and Alexandrina
Smith; b Aber 22.11.48
teacher: Fr/Ger Hazlehead acad Aber 1971–72, St
Joseph's s s Workington from 1972
m Aber 22.7.72 James K. Murdoch MA 1971 soc worker
s of James K. M. Aber

ARMSTRONG Colin Maxwell   *BSc 1970
 s of James M. A. MA 1936 qv; b Dun 19.10.47
MSc(N'cle) 1971
teacher chem St Andrews from 1972

ARMSTRONG Duncan   BSc(eng) 1958
 s of Allan A. MA 1925 qv; b Carrbridge 14.8.36
asst city eng dept Aber 1958–62; des eng pulp and paper
mills Vanc 1962–64; head of munic des dept corp for 1967
world exhib Montreal 1965–67; eng man. Warnock
Hersey Montego Bay 1967–69; proj eng Assoc Eng
Services Edmonton 1970–74; sen resid eng Cohos Evamy
& Ptnrs Fort McMurray from 1974
m Shetland 5.4.60 Jemima A. Peterson MA 1958 qv

ARMSTRONG Shona Inglis   MA 1970
 d of Matthew A. hotelier and Jessamy W. Hall;
b Burton-on-Trent 1949
secy posts S & E Africa 1971–72; secy: Amer consulate,
Edin 1972–73, Amer emb Lond from 1973

ARMSTRONG William George   *MA 1963
 s of William S. A. paper mill worker and Rena Smith;
b Aber 20.3.41
teacher: Whitehaven g s 1963–66, Longton h s 1967–70;
Stoke on Trent sixth form coll from 1970
m Aber –.7.64 Patricia Callum teacher d of Douglas C.
Aber

ARNOT Alexander Ian   LLB 1968
 s of Robert A. insur insp and Margaret E. O. Forbes
teacher; b Bridge of Allan 9.10.46
law app 1968–70; leg. asst 1970–72 Edin; solic Dunfermline from 1972

ARNOT Katharine Agnes Kinmond   BSc 1960
 d of Arthur W. A. BL(Edin) lawyer and Agnes M.
Watt MA(St And) teacher; b Forfar 8.6.40
asst biochem hosp lab Aber 1960–62; part time teacher
remed reading Stockton-on-Tees 1968–73; teacher biol/
chem Callander from 1975
m Strathpeffer 11.7.62 George H. Haddock RAF off./
sales eng s of Francis A. H. Coulsdon

ARRELL Margaret Olive   MA 1967

ARULANANTHAM David Cumaresan   *BSc(eng) 1969
 s of Daniel C. A. BSc(Calc) headmaster and Grace E. A.
Sathianadhan BA(Osm) teacher; b Jaffna Sri Lanka
2.6.44
plant eng Grangemouth from 1969
m Edin 1.6.74 Diana M. Knight BSc 1969 qv

ASARE Emmanuel Broni   BSc(for) 1957
 s of Isaac K. A. headmaster and Mary Afra Hemaa;
b Oda Ghana 7.3.33
Ghana: asst conserv for. Kumasi 1957–61; sen asst 1961–
63; conserv for. Koforidua 1963–71; dep chief conserv
for. Takoradi 1971–73; dir/dep chief exec Guksten (WA)
Sefwi Wiawso from 1973
m (1) Koforidua –.7.60; marr diss 1967
 (2) Koforidua –.8.70 Dora O. Kwane d of Emmanuel
O. Dapaa Agogo

ASHCROFT Thomas   MB ChB 1957

ASHCROFT William Alexander   *BSc 1958
 s of William G. A. BSc(Glas) schoolmaster and
Margaret S. Anderson; b Urquhart 16.6.36
MSc(Birm) 1963 PhD(Birm) 1967
geophys Seismograph Service, south Arabia, Nigeria
1959–62; res stud. Birm 1962–65; lect geol/mineral.
Aberd from 1966
m Lond 1961 Margaret J. Cotching BA(Liv) lect d of
Charles J. C. Carshalton

ASHER Lilian Stass   MA 1965
 d of William A. soldier/motor mech/commissionaire
and Maria E. H. Stass; b Inv 13.3.44
teacher Engl Inv h s from 1966

ASHFORD Anne Margaret   BSc 1965
 m Wolk

ASHFORD Judith   MA 1963

ASHLEY Michael John   MEd 1964
 s of John R. A. gold mine off. and Maud E. Darlow;
b Boksburg Transvaal 11.8.37
BA(Witwatersrand) 1958
lect educ: Johannesburg coll of educ 1964–66, Rhodes
univ Grahamstown 1967–71, sen lect 1972–78; prof educ
univ of Cape Town from 1978
m Aber 9.5.64 Angela M. D. Cort d of Frank C. MB ChB
(Manc) Brook I of W

ASHTON Robert William   *BSc(eng) 1970
 m Helen M. Barclay MA 1969 qv

ASHTON Shirley Elliott   MEd 1970
 d of Harry T. A. BSc(Adel) asst dir Aust bureau of met
and Melva G. V. Elliott Dip Com(Adel) teacher; b
Adelaide Aust 22.7.44
BA(Melb) 1965 AASD 1965 DipEd(Melb) 1966
teacher: Engl Bristol 1967–69; Engl/commun Aber from
1970
m Bristol 26.7.69 Charles R. A. Earl BSc 1971 scient off.
Rowett inst Aber

ASHUN Joseph Enimil   MB ChB 1958
 BSc(Lond)

ASIBEY Emmanuel Osei Agyeman   BSc(for) 1960
                                                            PhD 1974
 s of Kwaku O. A. farm./cocoa broker and Ama Omenaa
farm./ornamental beadworker; b Kwaso (Ashanti)
21.11.35
Ghana: Damongo- asst conserv for. 1961–62, asst, sen
asst game warden 1962–65, game warden 1965–67; chief
game and wild life off. from 1967; member: internat
comm park syst plan, 1963–65; Soc/agr/econ sub-comm
Volta Lake res proj from 1970; survival serv comm/nat
parks comm of internat union for conserv of nature and
nat resources (IUCN) from 1972; IUCN exec board from
1975
m Aburi 18.12.71 Joyce L. K. Kyei BA(R'dg) headmistress d of Thomas E. K. DipEd(Oxon) Kumasi

ASIEDU Emanuel Ransford   MB ChB 1959
 d Ghana 8.2.72

ASKEW James Alan   MSc 1963
 s of James E. and Gladys Askew; b Preston 10.7.39
BSc(eng)(Salf) 1962 CEng MIEE 1967
lect Harris Coll Preston 1964–68: sen lect 1968–73; sen
lect Preston poly from 1973
m Penwortham Preston 17.4.65 Joyce Ravenscroft

ATHANAS Christopher Nicholas   MA 1962 LLB 1964
 s of Nicholas A. BA(Columba NY) comp dir and
Elizabeth C. Tasker nurse; b Aden Arabia 26.8.41
WS 1969
law app Aber 1964–66; leg. asst: Aber 1966–68, Edin
1968–69; ptnr leg. firm Edin from 1969
m Aber 30.6.64 Sheena A. Stewart teacher p e d of
Peter M. S. Perth

ATKINSON Adrian Paul Charles   *MA 1960
 s of Edward P. F. A. naval off. and Christina C. M.
MacArthur; b Gourock 28.7.44
MSc(Aston) 1970 PhD(Aston) 1974
indust consult. Birm 1970–72; lect psych Aston from 1974
m Kingsley 1970 Christine L. Jones MA 1968 *qv*

ATKINSON Alison Mary   LLB 1969
 d of James E. M. A. safety off. and Heather A. Young;
b Edin 7.8.48
solic Edin from 1971
m Alloa 27.5.78 Douglas K. Tullis LLB 1971 solic s of
Ramsey T. BA(Oxon) Dollar

ATKINSON Douglas   BSc(eng) 1960
 s of John R. R. A. trans insp and Lizzie M. Will;
b Aber 1.9.39
MICE 1968
BR: Glasg—civ eng 1960–62, eng asst 1962–65, sen eng
asst 1965–67; Perth—asst (works & bridge) from 1968
m Clydebank 20.9.63 Elizabeth I. McKay d of John McK.
Clydebank

ATKINSON Geoffrey Eric   *MA 1969
 s of Eric A. A. loc govt off. Muriel E. Wicks; b Epsom
23.8.43
BA(econ)(Sheff) 1965 ARCO 1968
dir property comp Aber 1971–73; dir sports goods outlet
Aber from 1973; mus critic *Press and Journal* from 1968
m Aber 1967 Mary E. Macdonald BSc 1975 d of Thomas
K. M. BL 1937 *qv*

ATKINSON John Edmund   PhD 1967
 s of John G. A. eng and Eliza M. Burrell; b Barnard
Castle 19.8.40
BPharm(Lond) 1964 FCS 1965 MPS 1969 MIBiol 1970
ARIC 1972
post doct fell. chem dept Belf 1967–68; lect pharm RGIT
Aber from 1968
m Felling 7.4.66 Joan V. Nicholson teacher d of John
D. N. Gateshead

ATKINSON Kenneth   MSc 1963
 BA PhD(Durh)

ATKINSON Margaret May   BSc 1969
 d of Edmund A. MA(Cantab) income tax insp and
Kathleen Taylor teacher; b Renfrewsh 11.5.46
careers off. Teesside 1969–71; careers advis off. Darlington
1971–74; sen careers off. S Shields 1974–75; area careers
off. Crawley from 1975

ATMOWIDJOJO Sumadi   MSc 1966
 s of Tukardi A. police off. and Sajem Karsowidjojo;
b Yogyakarta Indonesia 21.1.36
PhD(Corn) 1978
jun res worker: Nat Biol Inst Bogor Indonesia 1966–72
and from 1978

ATTIN Kathleen Mary   MA 1967
 d of John A. tech and Cynthia Y. Young; b Trinidad
WI 25.3.44

secy Brit emb Helsinki Finland 1968; stud. soc work univ
of Alabama from 1976
m Helsinki 9.3.68 Mauri Valtonen MSc(Helsinki) res
astronomy s of Yrjo V. Kiljava Finland

AU NYUK CHENG Dorothy   MB ChB 1968
 d of William Au Ahwah LL B(Lond) and Mary Vu; b
Malaya 4.5.43
m o Malaysia from 1969
m Aber 25.7.66 Liew Meng Leong MBBS(Sing) consult.
obst/gyn s of Liew Him Yaw

AUCHINACHIE Isobel Margaret Taylor   MA 1960
 d of Henry W. A. bank man. and Edith R. Taylor
teacher; b Old Aber 8.7.39
teacher: Engl/hist Fochabers 1961–66, Castle Hill NSW
Aust 1966–68, Engl Tumut NSW Aust 1968–76
m Adelong NSW John L. Crain grazier s of William P. C.
Adelong

AUCHINACHIE Keith Taylor   MB ChB 1970
 s of Henry W. A. bank man. and Edith R. Taylor
teacher; b Kincardine 7.9.46
MRCGP 1974 D Obst RCOG 1973
h o ARI 1970–71; sen h o dept g p Aberd; fam phys
Brantford Ontario from 1977
m Aber 9.7.70 Gwen Porter teacher d of Peter P.

AULD Alan Graeme   *MA 1963
 s of Alan T. A. LLD 1970 *qv*; b Aber 14.8.41
BD(Edin) 1966 PhD(Edin) 1976 ordained Edin presb C of
S 1973
res in OT studies Edin, Jerusalem, W Germany 1966–69;
asst dir Brit s of archae Jerusalem 1969–72; lect Heb and
OT stud. Edin from 1972
m Sparkford 23.9.67 Sylvia J. Lamplugh secy d of
Stephen L. Sparkford

AULD Alison Mary   BSc 1969
 d of Alan T. A. LLD 1970 *qv*; b Aber 28.5.47
teacher: West Lothian 1970–73, Renfrewsh 1973–75
m Aber 2.7.73 Graham P. Angus arch. s of William A.
Aber

AUNG Maung Gyaw   MB ChB 1963
 s of Tha T. A. barrister and Daw Nee; b Akyab Burma
19.1.38
h s ARI 1964; h p Birkenhead 1964; h s Stracathro hosp
1964–65; regist path.: Mayfield 1966–69, Castleford from
1969
m Stracathro 1967 Margaret M. Ritchie SRN d of John R.

AUSTIN Euphemia Hall Hope (Fay)   MB ChB 1967
 d 20.12.70 *AUR* xliv 216

AVENT Yvonne Gladys   MA 1962 Dip Ed 1963
 d of Douglas J. A. pilot RAF and Muriel J. Murray;
b Perth 25.12.40
teacher: Pulteneytown acad Wick 1963–64, Halkirk j s
1964–67, Mt Pleasant s Thurso 1967–74; head: Bower p s
Wick 1974–76, Pulteneytown acad Wick from 1976
m Perth 3.8.63 Robert M. Gunn BSc(eng) 1961 *qv*

AVERY Moira-June Ingram   MA 1968

AWAD Mahmoud Mohamed Hassan   MSc 1963
 s of Mohamed H. A. and Sabah A. Nawar; b Kaha
Egypt 2.3.29
BSc(Ein Shams) Dip Soil Mech (France)
eng Monopia 1964; eng in min of irrig (barrages and
dams) Cairo 1964–68; chief eng from 1968
m Doki-Giza 5.7.52 Zinab A. E. R. Nawar d of Abd
El R. A. Elbaki N. Doki-Giza Egypt

AWON Ann Patricia   MA 1965

AWOUDA El Hag Makki   BSc(for) 1964

AWUNOR-RENNER Charles   MB ChB 1965

AYERST John Michael   BSc(for) 1961
s of William H. A. salesman and Muriel E. P. Stillwell
secy; b Perivale 10.12.38
asst for. comm Keith 1961–62; teacher sc: Kiltarlity
1963–64, Larkhall acad 1964–66; lect biol David Dale
coll f e Glasg 1966–69; sen lect environment stud.
Crewe & Alsager coll Cheshire from 1969
m Aber 31.8.63 Alice M. Cobb MA 1961 qv

AYERST Peter William   BSc(for) 1957 *1958
s of William H. A. comm trav and Elsie M. P. Stilwell
secy; b Perivale 10.12.38
asst conserv for. Tanganyika 1959–60; teacher: Hemel
Hempstead 1960–63, Nairobi 1963–73, Cape Town from
1973
m Aber –.8.60 Doreen E. Mitchell teacher d of Gordon
M. Aber

AYIVOR Gabriel Kodzovi   MB ChB 1964
s of Albert Y. A. tailor/storekeeper and Comfort
Amegashie; b Denu Ghana 29.9.31
BSc(McG) 1959 DPM 1971
h o Bridge of Earn 1965–66, sen h o, regist psychiat Ross
clin Aber 1966–71; Ghana: sen m o Ankaful psychiat
hosp 1971–77, psychiat spec from 1977
m Aber 8.10.71 Betty P. Thomson nurse d of William
F. T. Perth

AYLWARD Nigel Nunn   PhD 1967
BSc MSc(Birm)

AYRE John Fearnley   BSc(eng) 1970

BABALOLA Alexander Akinade Ajibola   *BSc(eng) 1969

BABBÉ Jean Evelyn Mary   BSc 1968
d of Peter M. F. B. horticulturalist and Vera E.
Guilbert; b Guernsey 26.7.46
Derby: computer progr 1968–70, sen progr 1970–72;
teacher maths: g s Burton-on-Trent 1972–74, Moreton
Wirral 1974–76; trg man. Transaction Data Syst Dawlish
from 1976
m (1) Derby 2.4.70 Rodney A. Firth dir Joshua Tetley
s of Norman F. Huddersfield; marr diss 1.1.76
    (2) Newton Abbot 26.7.76 John M. Watkins prod. rep
Marlow Ropes s of Leonard W. Dawlish

BACKETT Anne Louise   *BSc 1965 PhD 1969
d of Edward M. B. BSc(Lond) prof commun med Nott
and Shirley P. Thompson teacher; b Lond 17.10.43
res fell. pharm Aberd 1969–70; information scient in
pollution at MBA Plymouth from 1977
m Aber 21.6.66 James Cowie BSc 1964 qv

BADAWY Ahmed Mahmoud   PhD 1957
BSc(agr)(Alex) MSc(Alex)

BAGLEY Alexander John   *MA 1966 MLitt 1968
BA(Oxon)

BAHZAD Abdulla   MSc 1970
s of Abdulla Abdul-Kader lect mech and Sabiha Fawzi;
b Baghdad 12.3.36
BSc Comm(Baghdad) 1960
statist: Aber & dist milk marketing board 1971–72, USA
1972, self employed from 1973

m Aber 12.4.71 Christobel G. Terris MB ChB 1971 obst/
gyn d of David G. T. Grantown-on-Spey

BAILEY Colin David Howard   MB ChB 1968

BAILEY Mary Jane Greenlaw   BSc 1969
d of Gordon J. B. attendant nat phil dept Aberd and
Jane K. Hamilton beauty consult.; b Crowthorne 22.7.47
teacher sc Aber: Hazlehead acad 1970–73, Harlaw acad
1974–75, Hazlehead acad 1975–77
m Aber 9.8.69 David R. Franks MB ChB 1970 qv

BAILEY Warren Peter Neal   MSc 1969
MA(Oxon)

BAILEY-SMITH Robin   BMedBiol 1970 MB ChB 1973
b 11.4.48
resid Clackmannan

BAILLIE Alister Cameron   *BSc 1963 PhD 1966
s of Hugh B. mill worker and Margaret S. Macdonald
cook; b Brora 17.7.41
res fell. Atlanta, Georgia 1966–67; Chesterford Park res
stat: res chem 1968–72, sect. leader from 1972
m Dunphail 12.9.64 Elizabeth MacPherson MA 1963 qv

BAILLIE Ian James   BSc 1967

BAILLIE Kenneth Cameron   *MA 1963
s of Hugh B. mill worker and Margaret S. MacDonald
cook; b Brora 17.7.41
MSc(Lond) 1979
journalist: trainee Thurso 1963–65, sub edit. *The Scotsman*
Edin 1965–67; Lond: media res Gallup Poll 1967–71;
stud. Birkbeck coll 1971–73, trg advis printing/publ ITB
1973–75; self-employed pers and res consult. from 1975
m Wallington Marion Collins secy d of John R. C.
Wallington

BAILLIE Rita Marion   MB ChB 1959
d of Alexander M. B. MB ChB 1915 qv; b Eire 12.2.31
DCH 1962 (Lond) DPM 1964 (Lond) MRCPsych 1971
consult. psychiat Monyhull hosp Birm from 1972,
consult. from 1969

BAILLIE-HAMILTON Alexander Buchanan
                                        MB ChB 1956
s of John B.-H. tea planter and Bridgett E. Baker;
b Ceylon 2.11.32
DIH 1959
h o Aber and Stracathro 1956–57; chief m o tea estates
Peermade India 1957–58; sen h o Truro 1958–59; g p
Barbados 1959–64; indust m o Standard Telephones
1964–65; g p Maidenhead from 1965
m Caxton Hall 1964 Lilia M. J. Peters or Eaton boutique
owner d of Alan P. West Indies

BAIN Alexandrina Mary   MA 1963
d of Donald B. bldg contr and Johan C. Mackenzie
post mistress; b Tore 9.5.42
teacher maths: Bridge of Earn 1964–69, Penzotti s for
missionaries' children Lima Peru 1969–73, Invergordon
from 1974

BAIN Alison Anne   MA 1969

BAIN David Robertson   BSc 1960 *1964
b Thurso 8.4.39
PhD(Glas) 1968
res chem: UKAEA Dounreay 1960–63, 1964–65, univ of

Dayton Ohio 1968–70, Liv 1970–74; scient Unilever res lab Port Sunlight from 1974
m Aber 10.8.64 Elizabeth R. Baikie BSc(St And) teacher

BAIN Denis Warburton   MA 1961
s of James B. master slater and Jane Warburton; b Bolton 11.6.37
teacher: Engl/hist Grange s Alloa 1962–64, Engl Elgin acad 1964–67; instr lt RN Arbroath, Shotley Gate, Fareham 1967–72; teacher Aber: Hazlehead acad 1972–73, Craighill p s 1973–75, asst head Kittybrewster p s from 1976
m Aber 31.8.60 Jennifer B. Jack teacher d of James K. J. Aber

BAIN Derek Charles   *BSc 1966 PhD 1974
s of James B. blacksmith, insur ag and Jessie B. Taylor; b Buckie 30.4.44
mineralogist Macaulay inst for soil res Aber from 1966
m Fochabers 2.3.68 Grace M. Mackenzie BSc 1970 qv

BAIN Donald Straiton   *MA 1966
s of Donald B. MRCVS(Edin) vet surg and Isobel J. T. Finlay teacher dom sc; b Lanark 16.6.44
MSc(Strath) 1972
Dafoe fell. internat relations Manit 1966–67; res off. SNP Edin 1968–71; man. dir Res and Intelligence serv Stirling 1971–74; dir of res SNP Edin 1974–77; econ advis joint res centre of Europ communities Ispra Italy

BAIN Douglas John Geddes   MB ChB 1964 MD 1974
s of Douglas H. B. rly clerk and Margaret Geddes MA 1923 qv; b Aber 18.8.40
DObstRCOG 1966 DCH 1968 MRCGP 1970
res m o RACH, ARI, mat. hosp Aber 1964–66; g p Edin 1966–68; regist med, paediat Bangor and Kirkcaldy 1968–71; g p Livingston from 1971
m Sandra M. Souter p e teacher d of George M. S. LDS(Edin) Elgin

BAIN Edmund Donald Bruce   MA 1965
s of Robert B. BSc(Glas) lect agr and Christina M. Kirkman SRN; b Aber 7.6.40

BAIN Elizabeth Walker   MA 1969 Dip Ed 1970
d of John M. B. ship's steward and Isamay M. Logie; b Westray Orkney 27.7.48
teacher: Aber 1972–73, Engl Inv from 1975
m Orkney 12.6.68 Douglas A. Thomson MA 1973 teacher s of Douglas T. Kirkwall

BAIN George William   *MA 1963
s of George B. fishmerchant and Anne H. Gibb ptnr in fishmerchant's bus.; b Aber 4.11.40
articled CA app Aber 1963–64; asst res econ White Fish auth Hull 1965–67; econ Dunlop, Lond 1967–70; man. consult. Urwick Orr & Ptnrs Lond 1970–72; fish merchant Bain Bros Aber

BAIN John   MA 1970

BAIN Laurence Douglas   *MA 1962

BAIN Nigel Bruce   *MA 1967
BD(Glas)

BAIN Norman Brander   MB ChB 1968
s of Peter J. B. gamekeeper and Elizabeth Geddes; b Lossiemouth 2.1.41
DObstRCOG 1970
h o: King's Lynn, Norwich 1968–69, obst Gt Yarmouth,

anaest Worcester, York 1969–70, paediat Abergavenny 1971; g p/anaest Bromsgrove 1971; civ m o 1st regt RHA BAOR W Ger 1972–73; g p/anaest Wonthaggi Aust from 1973
m York 25.2.67 Anne M. Crichton MCSP Aber d of William S. C. Keswick

BAIN Priscilla Anne   MA 1969
d of Logie S. B. MB ChB 1937 qv; b Aber 30.11.48
Dip St Godric's secy coll Lond 1970
pa/secy to gen man. Ferranti Edin
m Aber 11.9.76 Robert J. M. Fraser prod. eng s of Robert F. Bathgate

BAIN Robert   *BSc 1956 PhD 1959
s of Robert Bain BSc(Glas) lect Aberd and Christina M. Kirkman; b Aber 17.2.34
paper indust in Scot. 1959–68; pulp and paper res Inst of Canada, Pointe Claire 1968–75; paper indust res assoc Leatherhead from 1975
m Aber 19.7.60 Helen C. Shirreffs MA 1955 qv

BAIN Sheila Margaret   *MEd 1965 PhD 1974
d of James M. B. wine and spirit merch and Isabella S. Robertson; b Dun 3.5.29
MA(Edin) 1952 Dip Ed(St And) 1954
lect Stockholm 1955–56; teacher Dun and Angus 1956–62; Aberd: asst, res fell. 1962–67, res asst, res off. from 1967

BAIN Stanley   *BSc 1960
s of Charles H. B. lab and Euphemia Curran; b Huntly 24.3.31
teacher biol: asst Dumfries 1960–62; prin Huntly from 1962
m Huntly 20.9.58 Irene M. Morrison health visitor d of Eric M. Huntly

BAINES William Robertson   BSc(eng) 1957
s of Sydney B. teacher of mus and organist; b Glasg 6.10.35

BAIRD Elizabeth   MA 1969
d of Alexander S. B. eng and Mary McWilliam teacher; b Buckie 12.3.46
m Aber 1969 Alexander W. L. Joss BSc 1967 qv

BAIRD Gabrielle Anne   MB ChB 1959
d of James A. B. BSc 1932 qv and Elizabeth M. Petrie MA 1936 qv; b Holyhead Anglesey 22.9.35
g p: Rhynie 1968–73, Aber from 1973
m Aber 22.9.59 George S. Sorrie MB ChB 1957 qv

BAIRD Jennifer Naomi
see Pinnock

BAIRD Margaret Davidson   MA 1962
d of David D. B. master plumber and Margaret M. Law; b Ellon 10.4.41
teacher Strichen 1963–67, Forres from 1967
m New Pitsligo 19.7.67 James A. Grant shopkeeper s of John G. Forres

BAKER Dennis Anthony   *BSc 1963 PhD 1966
MIBiol 1968
post doct fell. Nott 1966–67; sen lect biol Leic poly 1967–68; Sus: lect biol/sub dean biol sc 1968–72; reader biol from 1972

BAKER Penelope Anne   *MA 1969
d of Paul B. B. physioth and Alice M. M. Penney nurs. off.; b Walton-on-Thames 8.6.47
teacher: Christ's hosp girls' h s Lincoln 1970–72; Lubavitch House s London 1972–73; Lond: temp cler and

19   GRADUATES 1956–1970

bank work, Queen's secy coll 1973–74; edit. asst/secy
Wiedenfeld & Nicolson, Clapham from 1974
m –.9.75 O'Grady

BAKER Rosemary Clare   LLB 1968
  d of Norman H. B. tech illustrator GPO and Constance
E. Whiting bankruptcy clerk; b Croydon 31.1.47
asst solic Caterham 1971–72; lect law Ewell 1972–74;
private pract from 1974
m Sanderstead 16.1.71 James T. W. Adams LLB 1968 *qv*

BAKER Susan Jenifer   MA 1965 BSc 1969
  m Haddock

BAKIE Elspet Mitchell   MA 1960
  d of Joseph B. master joiner and Marie L. Gault;
b Lossiemouth 12.5.39
teacher: maths Forres 1961–63, Hopeman 1963–64; prim
and remed Kirkcaldy from 1972
m Aber 19.7.63 Donald C. Halliday BSc 1960 *qv*

BALAKRISHNAMURTI Thampu Saravanamuttu
                                    MSc 1966
  s of Thampu Saravanamuttu teacher/law stud. and
Mangayarkarasy Thamotharampillai; b Colombo, Sri
Lanka 19.10.21
BSc(Lond) 1947
teacher Colombo 1946–50; res off. Lunuwila, Sri Lanka
from 1950

BALD Lilian Urquhart   MA 1968
  d of David B. civ eng and Annie B. Urquhart; b
Dingwall 22.2.46
Lond: teacher Brixton 1969–72, audio-visual aids/head
remed dept Charlton from 1972
m Aber 3.7.69 David M. W. Martin BSc 1969 *qv*

BALDERSTON Mary Stewart   BSc 1966
  d of James B. eng and Mary Stewart; b Glasg 4.4.49
teacher geog: Johnstone h s 1967–70, Buenos-Aires
1970–72, Lond 1972–73, Hyndland s s Glasg 1973–76;
prin geog Kirkintilloch h s from 1976
m Paisley 4.4.77 Richard H. Thomas MA 1968 *qv*

BALDWIN David Kenneth John   *MA 1970 Dip Ed 1971
  s of Kenneth J. B. chlorination dept metrop water
auth and Lilias M. S. Cruickshank superv racecourse tot.
board; b Esher 3.11.47
MEd(Birm) 1976
asst teacher Aylesbury 1971–74; Cleveland educ auth:
trainee educ psych 1974–75, educ psych from 1976
m Aber –.9.70 Carol J. L. Martin MA 1970 *qv*

BALDWIN Jaroslav Raymond   *BSc(agr) 1963
  s of Anthony H. B. BMus(Durh) mus and Miluse
Policka; b Dun 9.8.39
teacher biol: Linlathen s Dun 1963–64, 1965–66; Kirklands s Methil from 1966
m Dun 1964 Daisy Sibbald lib, secy d of Archibald S. Dun

BALDWIN John Alexander   *MB ChB 1958 *MD 1969
  s of John A. B. LDS(Liv) dent surg and Margaret E.
Sewell SRN; b Lond 11.12.27
BA(Oxon) 1951 MA(Oxon) 1958 MRCPsych 1971 FFCM
1972
h o ARI 1958–59; clin & res fell. in psychiat Massa-
chusetts gen hosp and Harvard 1959–61; regist Kingseat
hosp 1961–62; dept ment health Aberd: sen res fellow
1962–64, Scot. hosp endow res trust fell. 1964–69; dir unit
clin epidemiology Oxon, med dir Oxon record linkage
study Oxford reg hosp board now RHA hon consult.
Oxon AHA(T) from 1969

m Aber 2.10.62 Joy H. Tremlett occup therap d of
Alfred J. T. Bristol

BALFOUR Anne Allan   MA 1964
  d of William Balfour eng BBC and Anne A. Ford;
b Sutton 20.7.42
f/lt WRAF educ branch UK and Ger 1965–71; p a to
dir educ Cumbria from 1972

BALFOUR Bernard Maitland   *MA 1966
  s of William C. B. trade union organis and Henrietta
Mitchell; b Aber 21.7.28
FSAScot 1976
teacher: spec asst lib stud. Summerhill acad Aber 1967–73,
prin hist Hazlehead acad Aber from 1973
m Aber 25.9.52 Isobel Davidson teacher d of Harry D.
Aber

BALFOUR Donald James Howland   *BSc 1970
  s of Walter B. insur ag and Margaret W. Howland secy;
b Fearn 29.4.48
post grad res Sheff 1970–73; teacher Isle of Harris from
1974

BALFOUR Walter Joseph   *BSc 1963
  s of Walter B. insur ag and Margaret W. Howland secy;
b Fearn 1.5.41
PhD(McM) 1967
post doct fell. Ottawa 1967–69; Vic BC: asst prof chem
1969–73, assoc prof from 1973
m Victoria BC 10.5.74 Rosemary Picozzi BA(Rdg) assoc
prof Ger lang and lit, Vic B.C. d of Nicholas P. MA(Glas)
Thorpe Bay

BALFOUR William John   BSc 1964
  s of Walter B. insur ag and Margaret W. Howland secy;
b Fearn 20.1.44
Surrey: insur clerk: actuarial 1964–67, pensions 1967–68,
work study off. 1968–70; computer progr from 1970
m Lond 16.9.74 Rosemary A. Philpot secy d of John W. P.
Lond

BALL Derrick Frank   PhD 1962
  s of Frank B. driver and Gladys Hanley; b Lond 7.5.30
BSc(Sheff) 1950 MBSc(Manc) 1975
lect chem Teesside poly 1962–66; sen lect chem Salf from
1966; visiting sen res fell. Manc bus. s 1973–74
m Stockton-on-Tees 25.2.56 Joyce Coffield d of John F. C.
Stockton-on-Tees

BALL John Christopher   PhD 1957

BALL Matthew Curry   PhD 1962
  ARIC

BALLANTYNE David Ferguson   LLB 1965

BALLANTYNE David John   *BSc 1970

BALLARD Peter   *BSc 1964
  s of Frederick B. rly eng dr and Ellen E. M. M. B.
Benton; b Crathie 15.9.41
post grad res Aberd 1964–65; teacher sc: Keith g s 1966–
68, RGC Aber 1968–73, prin phys/chem Turriff acad
1973–76, prin chem from 1976

BALLARD Sylvia Teresa   MB ChB 1959
  b Aber 14.7.35
h o RACH 1959–60; res asst lab City hosp Aber 1960–61;
res stud. Newham coll Cantab 1961–62
m Aber 10.8.60 Derek G. Land PhD(Liv) res biochem

BAMFORD John Michael   BSc(for) 1966
BSc(NZ)

BAMFORTH Malcolm   MB ChB 1957
s of Stanley B. woollen manuf and Lilian Pitchforth;
b Brighouse 20.10.31
FRSM 1966
g p Halifax 1958–66; med dir: Berk Pharm Godalming
1966–69, Winthrop Pharm Surbiton and USA 1969–72;
g p Halifax from 1972
m Halifax 13.7.57 June Hiller Dip Ed(Lond) teacher d of
Fred H. Halifax

BANCROFT David William   MA 1959
s of Sidney B. newsagent and Marion Schofield; b St
Helen's 29.3.38
nat service R.A. Hong Kong 1959–61; teacher Liv
1962–63; betting off. man. Liv 1963–73, ptnr Wigan
1973–74; civ serv HM customs & excise Liv from 1975
m Liv 10.10.70 Irene G. Wood off. superv d of Henry W.
Liv

BANG Ove   MB ChB 1961
s of Oscar B. Cand Med(Oslo) distriktslege and
Johanne C. Hammer; b Nore Norway 12.3.35
Cand Med(Oslo) 1961
distriktslege Norway: Gildeskal 1964–68, Bodo from 1968
m Trondheim 1962 Eva Andersen teacher d of Thorlief A.
Oslo

BANKS David Michael   *BSc(eng) 1967 MSc 1970

BANKS Diane   MB ChB 1962

BANKS Dorothy Anne   BSc 1962
d of David B. watchmaker/optician and Margaret
Mackenzie; b Forres 13.7.41
teacher maths: Inv 1963–68, London 1968–71, Cowdenbeath 1971–72; prin guid Cowdenbeath from 1972
m Dunfermline 10.4.71 David J. G. Scott BSc(S'ton)
teacher s of John T. S. Dunfermline

BANKS Ernest Alexander   LLB 1970
s of Ernest R. B. site clerk and Robina G. Tolan;
b Dun 5.1.49
law app Edin 1970–71; Dun: leg. asst 1971–74, self-
employed solic from 1974
m Dun 13.7.74 Ann V. Reilly teacher d of James R. Dun

BANKS Hazel Manson   *MA 1969
d of William J. B. master draper and Kathleen Coghill
shopkeeper & confectioner; b Thurso 9.10.46
housemother: Camphill village for handicapped adults
Yorks 1970–73; s for handic adolescents Napier NZ
1974–75; stud. Emerson coll, Sussex 1975–76

BANKS James Andrew   MA 1968
s of James A. B. prod. eng and Irene C. Stephen;
b Aber 13.1.45
DLC Loughborough coll 1969
teacher p e: Aber acad 1969–71, Queen's coll Nassau
1971–74, Kincorth acad Aber from 1975
m Aber 5.4.71 Jennifer S. Leslie teacher p e, d of Douglas
F. L. Stonehaven

BANNERMAN Emily   *MA 1966
d of Marcus B. crofter and Georgina Mackay; b
Bettyhill 27.6.44
teacher: prin hist Farr s Bettyhill from 1967, dep head
m Thurso 14.4.65 Marcus M. Campbell farm. s of
Donald C. Tongue by Lairg

BANNERMAN James Patrick Cochrane   *BSc 1969

BANNERMAN Roslyn   MA 1969
m Johnston

BANNISTER Peter   PhD 1963
s of John B. window cleaner and Gretchen A. S.
Taubald teacher; b Preston 2.5.39
BSc(Nott) 1960
Glasg: asst lect bot 1963–65, lect 1965–69; Stir: lect biol
1969–72, sen lect from 1972
m London 26.8.61 Margaret E. Hockley BSc(Nott)
teacher d of Reginald H. Lond

BARBER Elizabeth Anne   MA 1968
d of Henry C. B. agr seedsman and Winifred M.
Brocklehurst; b Grappenhall 30.6.45
teacher Fr and Ger: Huyton coll Liv 1969–71,
Tenbury s s Worcs 1971–73
m Stretton 11.8.71 Barnaby K. G. Miln man. dir seed
garden centre comp s of William W. G. M. Weaverham

BARBER Jennifer   MA 1967
d of John B. baker/confect and Gladys Milne shop asst;
b Aber 16.4.46
teacher Arbroath acad 1968–72, asst prin guid. from 1972

BARBER William   MA 1961 MEd 1972

BARBOUR Neil McLaurin   *BSc(eng) 1962

BARCLAY David John Chalmers   MB ChB 1969
s of John J. B. sales rep and Ruby B. Syme; b Aber
23.4.44
DObstRCOG 1974
h o, sen h o ARI 1969–71; S. Af: regist Durban 1971–
72, m o Ernest Oppenheimer hosp Welkom 1973–74;
g p Mudgee NSW Aust from 1974
m Edin 5.7.69 Jennifer A. Bryce MA 1967 qv

BARCLAY David Stewart   *BSc 1957
s of Hector G. B. foreman baker and Elizabeth
Summers; b Hatton of Cruden 20.11.32
teacher: gen subj Peterhead acad 1957–58, maths/sc Insch
1958–59; Perth h s: 1959–63, spec asst phys 1963–72, asst
prin phys from 1972
m Aber 28.3.72 Sheila C. Benzie MA 1966 qv

BARCLAY Gordon   MB ChB 1967
s of David B. MB ChB 1936 qv; b Pontardawe nr Neath
3.11.42
DRCOG 1969 MRCGP 1972/3
h o; casualty med, obst, paediat Aber 1967–69; g p
Braintree from 1969
m Aber 1.9.67 Meriel Gordon MA 1969 qv

BARCLAY Gordon Campbell   *BSc 1970
s of William R. B. stockbroker and Enid A. Strathern;
b London 25.1.49
Dip Stat(UCW)(Aberyst) 1974
Lond: asst statist/civ serv cadet Cabinet off. 1973–74,
asst Home off. from 1974

BARCLAY Hazel Doreen Emilie   BSc 1960
d of James B. farm worker and Emily Angus; b Turriff
25.9.38
teacher biol: Powis s s Aber 1961–63, Vincent Massey h s
Brandon Canada 1966–69; lab superv bot Brandon univ
from 1969
m Aber 5.7.61 James M. Skinner MA 1955 qv

BARCLAY Helen Margaret   *MA 1969 Dip Ed 1970
m Robert W. Ashton BSc(eng) 1970 *qv*

BARCLAY Ian Malcolm Taylor   BSc 1969

BARCLAY James Quarry   BSc 1958

BARCLAY John Edward   BMedBiol 1968 MB ChB 1971
s of John W. B. elect. eng and Margaret B. Begg;
b Aber 25.5.46
MRCP 1974
h o Woodend hosp Aber, ARI 1971–72; g p Aber,
Orkney 1972; lect chem path. Aberd 1972–73; regist
Wessex reg renal unit Portsmouth from 1973
m Aber 22.9.67 Alicia G. A. Cunningham speech therap
d of John C. Aber

BARCLAY Margaret   BSc 1958
d of Hector G. B. foreman baker and Elizabeth
Summers; b Hatton of Cruden 21.4.36
teacher sc: Goodlyburn j s s Perth 1959–63, Pitlochry h s
from 1963, prin guid
m Aber 12.10.63 John Brydone free-lance reporter s of
Archibald S. B. Pitlochry

BARCLAY Mitchell   BSc(Eng) 1958

BARCLAY Moira Todd   *BSc 1968

BARCLAY Peter Gordon   MA 1961

BARCLAY Rodney Gretton Esslemont   MA 1970
s of Alfred G. B. banker and Margaret K. Beedie;
b Aber 4.11.48
BAC Weybridge: computer progr 1970–71, organis and
methods off. 1971, jun syst analyst 1971–72; syst analyst
Nestlés Croydon 1972–74; bus. syst analyst BP Chemicals
Mayfair Lond from 1975
m Aber 2.8.71 Patricia E. Thomson teacher d of
Lesley J. T. Aber

BARCLAY Sheena Mary   *MA 1964
d of William A. B. MA 1939 *qv*(III) and Jean P. Buchan
MA 1941 *qv*; b Buckie 20.5.42
teacher Fr h s for girls Aber 1965–68
m Penang Malaysia 13.4.68 Karl D. Frankish elect. eng

BARCLAY William   BSc 1960 *1962
s of Adam S. H. B. elect. eng and Gudbjorg Jonsson;
b Aber 17.2.38
oil and gas exploration: geophys eng GSI Bromley 1963–
64; jr-sen geophys Mobil Oil Canada, Calgary 1964–73;
geophys Union Oil of GB Richmond 1973–74; sen geophys
Oil Exploration (Holdings) Edin from 1974
m Calgary 13.6.70 Leona D. Skibo BA(Calg) med res tech
d of Daniel N. S. Calgary

BARCLAY William Hector   *MA 1967
s of William P. B. lab and Ann C. McKenzie; b Aber
5.3.40
teacher: Engl Fraserburgh acad 1968–71, prin Engl
Larkhall acad 1971–73, Peterhead acad 1973–76; asst
rector Craigie h s Dun from 1976

BARCLAY William John   *BSc 1966
s of William B. pharm and Margaret C. Florence;
b Aber 15.9.43
FGS
geol Anglo-Amer corp Kabwe Zambia 1966–68; field geol
Inst of Geol Sciences Lond from 1968
m Aber 16.5.69 Rachel T. B. Taylor MA 1965 *qv*

BARCLAY William Wilkie   MA 1970
s of William G. B. policeman and Isabella H. Wilkie
nurse; b Stonehaven 23.1.49
dairy farm worker Tønsberg Norway 1970–71; teacher
Liberton s s Edin from 1972

BARCLAY Win Flora Margaret   MA 1962
d of James B. livestock auctioneer and Williamina M.
Duncan; b Insch 1.4.41
teacher Aber: Willowpark inf s 1963–69, St Margaret's
s for girls 1969–74
m Aber 9.10.74 Robert G. Strathdee s of Alfred G. S.
Milltimber

BARCLAY-ESTRUP Paul   PhD 1966
s of John B.-E. motel owner and Gudrun Kristensen
nurse/motel owner; b Calgary 13.2.31
BA(Br Col) 1957
Lake Thunder Bay Canada: asst prof 1966–72, assoc prof
from 1972
m Victoria B.C. Patricia M. Westwood BA(Br Col) 1958
book reviewer/radio drama critic d of Albert N. W.
Victoria B.C.

BARDEN Nicholas   *BSc 1967
s of Frank B. clerk and Mabel Nendick insur ag;
b Rotherham 8.7.46
D Phil(Sus) 1970
MRC stud. Sus 1967–70; Laval univ Canada: fell. 1970–
73, asst prof from 1973
m Rotherham 1968 Anne C. Chapman teacher d of Henry
C. Rotherham

BARKER Joyce   BSc 1970
d of Percy S. B. bricklayer and Janet M. Mackay
cashier; b Rotherham 16.10.47
teacher: Liberton s s Edin 1971–75, Windsor girls' s
Hamm W Ger from 1975

BARKER Veronica Frances   *MA 1968
d of James W. B. guard/motorman and Florence M.
West tailoress; b Worcester Park 3.4.37
ALA 1972 AIInfS 1974 MIInfS 1976 FLA 1977
asst lib Dund 1968–74; asst med lib Ninewells hosp/med s
Dund 1974–76; sen information off. centre for med educ
Dund from 1976

BARLATT Daphne Victoria Olakumbi   MA 1966

BARLOW Colin Hastings   PhD 1964
BSc(Lond) MS(Corn)

BARLOW William   BSc 1962

BARNES Keith Frederick   BSc 1968
s of Frank A. B. civ serv and Phyllis N. Vince; b East
Grinstead 27.5.43
MRIC 1973
lab tech: Inst of Cardiol Lond 1969–70, Kingston poly
1970–72; RIC course Medway and Maidstone coll of tech
Chatham 1972–73; res asst chem Thames poly Lond
1973–75; res stud. agr chem Wye coll(Lond) from 1976

BARNES Mavis   MA 1962 MLitt 1980
m Gray

BARNETT Bryanne Ethel Waldie   MB ChB 1961

BARNETT James   BSc 1966

BARNETT John *MA 1970
s of Joseph B. sheet metal worker and Rosina Wilson quality control superv electronics factory; b Glasg 2.10.48
teacher hist Fraserburgh acad 1971–74, prin hist from 1974
m Aber 13.12.69 Angela M. Bray teacher d of John A. B. Scrabster

BARNETT John Keith Ross *MA 1959

BARR Archibald John *MA 1964
s of Archibald J. B. publ and Grizel P. Alexander; b Glasg 25.11.42
CA 1968
man. dir McNaughton & Sinclair Glasg from 1968; dir and secy Munro-Marr publ Glasg from 1972, N Pitglassie Farm. Co Abdnsh from 1973, Scotgolf Serv Glasg from 1973
m Helensburgh 10.1.71 Helen R. Dundas physioth d of Ralph M. D. Helensburgh

BARR Kirsteen Holmes MA 1969
d of Archibald J. B. printer and publ and Grizel P. Alexander; b Kilmacolm 25.12.48
secy: Edin 1970–72, Glasg 1972–73; off. man. Aber from 1974
m Kilmacolm 9.9.72 Robert Davidson syst analyst s of Henry W. D. MA(Glas) Aber

BARR Margaret *MA 1967
d of Archibald J. B. man. dir/publ and Grizel P. Alexander; b Kilmacolm 26.2.45
teacher/lib Minden Germany 1968–69
m Kilmacolm 6.8.67 David H. White major s of Harry A. W. Upper Hatfield

BARR Peter BEd 1969
s of Thomas B. signalman RN, boot and shoe operative and Jean S. Dunlop off. worker, shop asst; b Northants 25.4.45
teacher geog Cumnock 1969–74; asst prin geog Ayr from 1974
m Lerwick 17.7.69 Maureen E. Hobbin BEd 1969 qv

BARR William *MA 1963

BARRACK Dianne Margaret MA 1961
d of Ian W. B. bank man. and Emily M. Anderson nurse; b Aber 11.3.40
pers asst: trg off. Nestlé Co Lond 1961–63, prof biochem and prof oceanography MIT USA 1963–69
m Aber 29.6.63 Jon A. McCleverty BSc 1960 qv

BARRACK Frances Mary MA 1966
d of William C. B. bank man. and Frances E. Wilson secy; b Ellon 21.5.45
teacher: Kirkhill p s Aber 1967–68, maths Kidderminster 1968–70, Bridge of Allan p s 1970–71
m Aber 27.7.68 Peter G. Morrison MA 1967 qv

BARRACK Iris Patricia MA 1966
d of Lewis B. farm. and Violet Moir; b Kinellar 1.11.43
teacher: Engl/Lat Inverurie acad 1968–70, Engl Glenrothes h s 1970–71 tut. Engl: Basil Paterson coll Edin from 1977
m Rayne 25.12.65 Frederick D. F. Shewan MA 1966 qv

BARRACK James White *BSc(eng) 1964
s of James R. B. farm. and Margaret S. White; b Ellon 6.10.41
MSc(eng)(Lond) 1972 DIC(Lond) 1972 MICE 1969 FRSA 1973

Sir R. McAlpine & Sons: civ eng on site—jun and sect. eng York 1964–65, Doncaster 1965–67; civ des eng Knutsford from 1967
m Aber 21.7.65 Betty T. Hardie MA 1963 qv

BARRASS Kenneth Neil BSc 1970

BARRETT William *MA 1963
s of Frederick B. operative cotton spinner, sheet metal worker and Bertha Bradley dressmaker; b Ashton-under-Lyne 1.11.29
psych: Belfast 1963–65, Sleaford 1965–66, Portsmouth 1966–67, Chichester 1967–73; clin psych St James hosp Portsmouth from 1973
m Lancaster 31.8.63 Kristin Maclennan MA 1962 qv

BARRETT-AYRES Ross BSc(eng) 1969
s of Reginald B.-A. Bac Mus(Edin) head mus dept Aberd and Elizabeth J. D. Ewing; b Edin 26.10.47
MICE
civ eng Aber c c 1970–74; asst lect (VSO) univ Benin, Nigeria 1974–75; civ eng Grampian reg from 1975
m Aber 21.12.70 Alexandra Berry MB ChB 1971 d of Alistair B. Stirling

BARRIE Gordon MB ChB 1968

BARRIT Derek Swaine MB ChB 1959
s of Jeffrey B. pharm and Gladys M. Swaine; b Hull 8.3.32
h o Aber, Perth, Middlesbrough 1960–61; g p Cold Lake Alberta 1961–62, Goodsoil Sask 1963–74; hosp m o Winnipeg from 1975
m Aber 6.7.56 Catherine W. G. Wood teacher d of George W. Aber

BARRON Aileen Ann MA 1968
d of James B. grocer and Mary B. B. Ferguson; b Edin 30.11.46
teacher Aber, Glasg from 1968
m Aber 4.7.69 James A. I. MacEwan MA 1969 qv

BARRON Anne Alexandra *BSc 1965 PhD 1978
d of Thomas B. gamekeeper and Lily Ross dom serv; b Dingwall 18.2.43
MSc(UCNW) 1971
res asst human cytogenetics Sheff 1966–69; jun tech off. MRC Harwell 1969–70; res asst immunology Aberd 1972–75
m St Albans 24.11.76 Malcolm Dye PhD 1976 res microbiol s of Jack E. D. Hunstanton

BARRON Charles Aitken *MA 1958
s of Charles F. B. storekeeper and Elizabeth M. Aitken; b Aber 11.1.36
teacher Engl Inverurie 1959–63; lect Glasgow 1963–70; head of drama coll of educ Aber from 1970
m Aber 1961 Margaret M. Shand MA 1961 qv

BARRON David James *MA 1965

BARRON Edward James MB ChB 1961
s of Edward B. stationmaster BR and Mary W. Dawson; b Keith 10.6.38
h o ARI, City hosp Aber 1961–62; Burnie Tasmania: sen h o 1962–63, g p 1963–70; g p Somerset Tasmania from 1970
m Aber 25.4.62 Elizabeth L. Lindsay nurs sister d of Charles D. L. Ballater

BARRON Hugh Wilson Taylor   *BSc 1964 PhD 1971
s of Edward B. stationmaster BR and Mary W. Dawson
b Portgordon 25.3.43
nat phil dept Aberd: asst lect 1968–70, lect from 1970
m Aber 11.12.71 Grace M. Scott secy, aux nurse d of
Ernest J. S. Aber

BARRON Joan Louise   MA 1970 CASS 1972
d of Douglas H. B. welfare off. for the blind and
Helen L. Ironside; b Aber 22.5.49
soc worker Aber assoc of soc serv from 1972
m Aber 5.7.72 Leslie Hutton teacher s of Alexander H.
Aber

BARRON Kathleen Elizabeth   *MA 1960
d of Charles F. B. storekeeper and Elizabeth M. Aitken
shop asst; b Aber 26.10.37
secy/translator STC Lond 1961–62; teacher: Fr/Ger
Woodford county h s 1962–64; Wombourne: teacher
Westfield jun s 1973–76, prin Fr Westfield middle s from
1976
m Aber 11.8.62 David A. Watkins BA(Birm) teacher s of
Frederick W. Luton

BARRON Margaret   MA 1969
d of John B. fisherman and Mary B. MacLean; b Nairn
8.3.48
teacher: Forres acad 1971–73; Ludenscheid W Ger
1973–74; Forres acad from 1974
m Senior

BARRON Norma Margaret   BSc 1957
d of Norman J. B. MA 1923 qv; b Aber 31.1.36
res asst zool: Nott 1958–61, Wye coll Ashford Kent
1962–63
m Aber 17.7.61 David J. Hannant BSc(Nott) lect civ eng
s of Eric L. H. New Barnet

BARRON Patricia   BSc 1959 *1960 PhD 1963
d of Norman J. B. MA 1923 qv; b Aber 1.1.39
res asst: anat Aberd 1963–64, biol Middx hosp med s Lond
1964–66; res fell. genetics Edin from 1967
m Aber 21.3.64 Iain B. R. Bowman BSc 1959 qv

BARRON Philip Thomson   MB ChB 1962
s of Robert T. B. civ serv and Ann Philip clerkess;
b Aber 18.5.38
FRCS(Can) 1971
h o ARI 1962–65; dem dept anat Manc 1965–66; res surg
Ottawa civic hosp 1967–72; lect dept surg Ott from 1973;
consult. surg Ottawa civic hosp
m Elgin 1963 M. Joan Mavor radiogr d of James M.
Elgin

BARRON Richard William   *MA 1970 Dip Ed 1972
s of James W. B. lect and Muriel T. Kennedy; b Aber
19.1.49
1st year div course Edin 1970–71; teacher classics
Dumbarton from 1972

BARRON Rosemary MacLean   MA 1970
d of John B. fisherman and Mary MacLean; b Nairn
30.8.49
teacher Fr Perth h s from 1971

BARRON Thomas James   *MA 1962
s of Thomas L. B. eng storeman and Mary A. Urquhart;
b Peterhead 20.1.40
PhD(Lond) 1969
post grad stud. Lond 1962–65; lect Edin from 1965

BARRON Veronica Moira   MA 1970
d of Stanley D. B. joiner and Moira M. Mann; b

Aber 10.3.49
cler asst DHSS Aber 1971–72
m Aber 15.1.72 James P. Robertson bldg mason s of
Alan R. Aber

BARRY John   BSc(eng) 1961
s of John B. B. mason/draughtsman and Alice E. L.
Wilson; b Aber 30.7.40
CEng MICE 1967
eng: asst Crouch & Hogg consult. Glasg, Angus 1961–63,
Williamson & Ptnrs consult. Glasg, Edin 1963–66; sen eng
Mitchell Construction Co Glasg, Peterborough 1966–67;
asst, sen, resid eng Lanark c c from 1967
m Aber 14.9.63 Marjory A. Stalker teacher d of William
S. Aber

BARTON Anne Margaret   BEd 1969
d of Roy B. carpet fitter/salesman and Margaret
H. Vass; b Inv 16.9.47
teacher Engl: Niagara Falls collegiate Ont 1969–71,
Dumfries h s 1971–73, Buckhaven h s 1973–76
m Inv 4.4.69 John G. Reid MA 1966 qv

BARTON Rae Colledge   MA 1958 cLLB 1960
s of George E. C. B. MA 1929 qv; b Aber 6.2.39
part time asst law Aberd 1960–68; ptnr Stronachs, advoc
Aber
m Glasg 10.7.63 Eileen E. D. Goodall teacher d of David
G. MA(Glas) Thornliebank

BASHAM Ian Reginald   BSc 1961 *1964 PhD 1968
s of Reginald J. B. (retired) and Flora Denoon;
b Quendon 8.12.39
FGS 1961
asst exper off. Macaulay inst Aber 1961–63; geol surv:
mineralogist Ghana 1964–65, mineralogist/tech aid
expert Sierra Leone 1969–70; prin scient off. in applied
mineralogy unit inst of geol sc Lond from 1970
m Aber 8.8.63 Sheena A. Macpherson teacher d of
William P. M. Huntly

BASIT Mohammed Abdul   MSc 1966 PhD 1969
MSc(Kar)

BATCHELOR Martyn Aubrey   *MA 1969
s of Aubrey R. B. OBE secy and Dorothy G. M. Ford;
b Sutton Coldfield 22.10.46
Dip LD(N'cle) 1971 AILA 1974
land arch. asst Derek Lovejoy & Ptnrs N'cle 1971; sen
city arch. dept N'cle 1971–74; prin landscape arch.
S Tyneside metro bor South Shields from 1974
m Sutton Coldfield 25.3.72 Lindsay J. Faulconbridge
BA(Durh) 1969 land. arch. d of Robert C. F. Glamorgan

BATES Russell   *MA 1969 Dip Ed 1970

BATESON John David   MSc 1968
BA(Durh)

BATSON Gerald Audley   cMB ChB 1960 MD 1969
s of Frederick E. B. gen man. Trinidad Sugar Estates and
Iris Pearce; b Trinidad 3.2.35
regist: cardiol N'cle gen hosp 1966–68, gen med Royal
Victoria I N'cle 1968–70; sen regist: cardiol N. gen hosp
Sheffield 1970–72, gen med Sheffield RI 1972–74; consult.
phys Scunthorpe health dist from 1974
m Gateshead 28.1.69 Pamela M. Scott SRN d of Archibald T. S. Gateshead

BAXTER Aldon Thompson   *MA 1966
d of Gordon A. B. MA(St And) teacher, headmaster
and Margaret S. A. Thompson MA(Edin) teacher; b
Fordyce 19.6.44

teacher Lond 1967–71 and from 1978
m Aber 16.7.66 James Williamson PhD 1965 *qv*

BAXTER Colin Henry   MB ChB 1966
s of Henry R. B. lect and Iris B. Young; b Jarrow 3.1.42
MCFP 1971 LMCC 1972
h o Stirling RI, ARI 1966–67; lect chem path. Aberd
1967–69; trainee g p Aber 1969–70; Toronto: g p York-
view med centre, m o Pilkington Glass Co from 1970;
active staff York Finch gen hosp
m Aber 23.12.65 Margaret E. Tough teacher art/artist d of
William T. Aber

BAXTER Kenneth   BSc 1961

BAXTER Margaret McLaren   MA 1961
d of John F. B. garrison works off. DoE and Margaret
M. Campbell; b Perth 28.11.39
teacher Perth 1962–66, Stirling 1966–72, Episkopi
Cyprus 1972–74, Gütersloh W Ger 1974–75; asst prin
Engl Kirkcaldy from 1975
m Dollar 29.7.66 Duncan M. Kennedy MA 1964 *qv*
marr diss 1972

BAXTER Margaret Sophia   MA 1961 Dip Ed 1962
m Alford 19.9.64 Geoffrey M. Telling MSc 1965 *qv*

BAYFIELD Neil Gillan   PhD 1967
BSc(Bangor)

BAYNE Rowan Stewart Ian Yelland *MA 1970 PhD 1977
s of James I. B. tv eng man. and Edna Wilder nurse;
b Reading 16.8.47
res stud. Aberd 1970–74; psych civ serv dept Lond 1974–
79; lect NE Lond poly from 1979
m Aber –.12.70 Elma Garden teacher d of Alister G. Aber

BEAR Keith Patrick *MA 1965
s of Robert T. B. hairdresser and Kathleen A. Mugan;
b Stafford 1.11.42
Dip Ed(Edin) 1966
teacher Engl: Trinity acad Edin 1966–69, spec asst
Kirkcaldy h s 1969–71; prin Engl St Patrick's h s Dumbarton 1971–74; asst rector St Saviour's h s Dun from
1974
m Aber 1.8.72 Jean E. Gray MA 1965 *qv*

BEATON Alasdair William Stewart   BSc(eng) 1966

BEATON George Alexander   LLB 1968
s of John G. B. and Nancy S. Milne; b Banff 22.7.47
law app, leg. asst Aber 1968–71; leg. asst Dun 1971–72;
leg. asst, ptnr Edin 1972–75; dep chief exec Sutherland
dist c Golspie from 1975
m Aber 18.7.70 Deirdre A. Smith LLB 1971 d of Richard
S. Kingussie

BEATON John McCall *BSc 1966 MSc 1969
s of Walter W. B. man. dir and Elizabeth H. S. McCall;
b Huntly 21.6.44
PhD(Alabama) 1973
sen res asst addiction res foundation Toronto 1969–71;
univ of Alabama Birm USA: instr 1971–73, asst prof
psychiat/psych 1973–76, assoc prof from 1976
m Aber 20.4.68 Eleanor Rose d of James R. Aber

BEATON Margaret Hamilton   MA 1970
d of Kenneth B. upholst/house furn and Catherine M.
Hamilton secy; b Dingwall 20.3.50
asst lib Aber from 1972
m Dingwall 17.7.70 Norman M. Macrae des eng s of
Farquhar M. Strathcarron

BEATON Mary   BEd 1968
d of David W. B. fishmonger and Mary A. Watt;
b Aber 22.12.17
Aber: teacher Engl/hist Summerhill acad 1968–72 and
careers mistress 1972–73; teacher Engl and year mistress
Torry acad from 1973
m Aber 15.10.41 John M. Loggie merch N off. s of George
R. L. Torphins; husb *d* 29.10.66

BEATTIE Alan Gordon   BMedBiol 1968 MB ChB 1971
s of Alexander G. B. MB ChB 1939 *qv*; b Aber 24.9.47
MRCP 1974
h o ARI 1971–72; res fell. dept med Aberd 1972–73; sen
h o gen med Aber city hosp 1973–74; regist gen med
Woodend hosp Aber 1974; res fell. therap Aberd 1974–
75; g p Aboyne 1975–76; regist gen med Aber from 1976
m Newton Mearns Christine A. Uytman nurs sister d of
Harold B. U. Newton Mearns

BEATTIE Alastair   MA 1958 LLB 1960
s of Archibald B. rly lengthman and Evelyn S. Bennett;
b Aber 11.10.37
leg. asst, sen, prin asst Dumfries c c 1961–67; dep clerk
Caithness c c Wick 1967–75; chief exec Caithness dist
council from 1975
m Dumfries 21.1.65 Rosaline Wright secy d of George
W. W. Dumfries

BEATTIE Eileen Margaret   MB ChB 1958

BEATTIE George *BSc 1959

**BEATTIE James Alexander Gordon   MB ChB 1967
                                        DMRD 1972**
s of Alexander G. B. MB ChB 1939 *qv*; b Aber 23.4.43
DObstRCOG 1970
ARI: h o 1967–69, sen h o, regist radio diagnosis 1970–72;
g p Edin 1972–74, Inverurie from 1974
m Aber 1.8.68 Jennifer B. Nichols teacher d of Walter
M. N. MB ChB(Glas) Glasg

BEATTIE Marilyn Watson *MA 1964
d of Bruce B. mill worker, masseur and Mary Watson;
b Forfar 13.10.41
MA(Manit) 1965
teacher: Turriff 1966–67, Monifieth 1967, teacher Fr:
Bottisham 1967–68, Exeter 1969–71
m Aber 12.8.67 William F. Hunter MA 1964 *qv*

BEATTIE Maureen Joan   MA 1970
d of David B. acct and Maud MacGillivray audit asst;
b Inv 14.6.49
teacher: Maisondieu s Brechin from 1971
m Inv 12.7.74 Iain A. Bain MA 1971 s of Alastair I. R. B.
Nairn

BEATTIE Robert Dennis   MA 1957

BEATTIE Sheena Margaret   MA 1963
d of Robert A. B. farm. and Margaret D. Skinner;
b Insch 10.9.42
teacher Gordon s Huntly 1964–67
m Kennethmont 23.7.66 George J. McConachie farm.
s of Robert McC. Wardhouse

BEAVINGTON Frank   MSc 1967
s of Edward N. B. farm. and Eva Shotbolt; b Hulcote
6.10.27
BA(Lond) 1954 PhD(Lond) 1961
visiting lect geog: univ of New Eng Aust 1967, univ of
Ibadan 1967–68; sen lect Wollongong univ coll Aust from
1969, prof geog Ahmadu Bello univ Kano 1974

m Sydney 20.6.70 Ruth B. Rainsford BA(Syd) teacher d
of Milton J. J. R. Turramurra NSW

BECERRA Luis Arcadio　MSc 1965
　BSc(agr)(Puerto Rico)

BECK Thelma Cecilia　PhD 1968
　d of Walter N. B. comm trav and Elsie F. Beresford;
b Lond 25.10.34
BSc(Lond) 1959 and 1961
Lond: tech King's coll hosp med s 1959, res asst univ coll
1959-63; Aber: res asst univ 1963-65, scient off. inst
marine biochem 1965-73, prin scient off. from 1973
m Lond 11.8.62 Hugo J. Fletcher BSc(Lond) lect s of
Walter J. F. Lond

BECKETT Edward George　MA 1967

BECKLEY Sandra Jane　MA 1966
　d of Vernon E. W. B. banker and Alma M. Houlgate;
b Sanderstead 25.4.44
m Sanderstead 6.8.66 John McQuillan MA 1965 qv

BECK-SLINN Iain　*MA 1970
　s of George A. B. S. banker and Hilda J. Gordon prob
off.; b Aber 1948
MSc(H-W) 1972 MRTPI 1974
plan. asst W Lothian c c 1972-73; sen plan. Banff c c
1973-75, Grampian reg from 1975
m Insch 1970 Elaine Cowie teacher d of William C. Insch

BEDDARD Susan Rydal　MA 1967
　d of Frederick D. B. MB BS(Lond) med admin and
Anne Porter teacher; b Windermere 13.2.45
secy: Ferranti Edin 1968-69, dept psych Edin 1969-70,
dept arch. Edin from 1973
m (1) Aber 3.8.68 Jeremy O'Regan MA 1967 qv
marr diss 1.9.74
　(2) Weymouth 22.10.76 Michael S. Spring MA(Cantab)
computer consult. s of Albert E. S. Warrington

BEDDOE Michael Richard　LLB 1968
　s of Jack E. B. BA(Cantab) chief exec Severn water
auth; b Aber 3.5.45
law app, solic Aber 1970-73; solic Edin from 1973

BEECH Maureen Theresa　MA 1964

BEGBIE Olivia Margaret Murdoch　BEd 1969
　b Edin 30.7.44
teacher geog Bellevue s Edin 1969-74, remed Drummond
h s Edin from 1974

BEGG Alan George　MA 1967

BEGG Alan John　MA 1969
　s of James B. paper-finishing man. and Gladys E.
Chilles lib; b Aber 19.11.48
Aber: app CA 1969-73, div acct from 1973
m Aber 24.1.72 Sheena E. Newby accounts clerkess d of
Albert W. N. Aber

BEGG Alistair Hendry Emslie　BSc 1956

BEGG Ian Stewart Darroch　MB ChB 1967 DMRD 1971
　s of Norman D. B. MB ChB 1929 qv; b Harrowby
21.7.44
DMRD(Lond) 1972
h o Inv and ARI 1967-69; trainee radiol Aber hosp
1969-71; regist radiol Aber 1971-72; g p Aber from 1972
m Aber 15.7.67 Carolyn I. Magee MA 1967 qv

BEGG Ingrid Edith　MA 1969
　d of William G. A. B. MB ChB(Glas) consult. psychiat
and Lucy M. R. Clarkson; b Ayr 22.10.45
teacher Engl: Kilmarnock 1970-71, Ayr from 1973;
Hodder & Stoughton publ Lond 1971-73

BEGG John Alexander Sutherland　MA 1959
　s of Daniel A. B. grocer and Elizabeth B. Sutherland;
b Castletown 2.7.38
BCom(Edin) 1961
man. posts Lewis's/Selfridge's dept store group Glasg
1961-73; dep chief exec Supa Centa (subsid of Lewis's)
Lond 1973-75; man. dir Supa Centa Northampton
1975-76; chief exec Lewis's Saverstore Ellesmere Port
1976-79; dir Lewis's Liv from 1979
m Irby 21.10.78 Lesley D. Nicol secy d of Donald N.
Thingwall

BEGG Lorna Marion　MA 1959
　d of Robert W. A. B. min of relig and Jessie H. Notman
nurse; b Unst 26.1.38
Dip R E 1960
teacher: Aber 1960-62, Stirling 1962-66; admin asst
Strath 1966-68; dep acad secy Stir from 1968
m Paterson

BEGG Norman Roderick Darroch　MA 1962 LLB 1964
　s of Norman D. B. MB ChB 1929 qv; b Islington
23.12.41
admin asst: E Ang 1964-66, Aberd 1966-68; asst secy
(acad) Aberd 1968-76; registry off. Aberd from 1976
m Aber -.7.65 Elizabeth J. Davidson teacher d of
Alexander M. D. Cults

BEGG Wilma Ann Cattanach　*MA 1962
　d of Alexander M. B. master butcher, hotelier and
Christina E. Bruce caterer, hotelier; b Montrose 7.5.40
teacher hist: Kinross 1963-66, Aber 1964-69
m 18.8.69 John K. L. MacLean BSc(St And) des and dev
eng s of Lindsay M. BSc(St And) Sandwick Shetland

BELL Agnes Davidson　BEd 1969

BELL Alfred Alan　*MA 1967

BELL David Scott　*MA 1970
　s of David B. MA(Edin) bus. man. and Irene S. Page;
b Edin 7.5.47
MSc(S'ton) 1971
post grad stud. Wolfson coll Oxon 1971-74; res fell.
centre for Europ stud. Sus from 1974

BELL Eileen Jessica　BEd 1969
　d of James A. B. shepherd and Margaret Nisbet;
b Kelso 4.4.48
teacher Engl Newbattle h s Dalkeith 1969-75
m Dalkeith 13.7.74 Charles B. S. Gibson MA(Edin)
teacher maths s of John E. G. Musselburgh

BELL Gavin Clement　*MA 1967
　s of Clement W. B. MA 1942 qv and Margaret I. R.
Angus MA 1942 qv; b Aber 14.4.44
res stud. Selwyn coll Cantab 1967-68; teacher George
Watson's coll Edin 1969-73; asst prin Ger Arbroath h s
1973-75; prin Ger Harlaw acad Aber from 1976
m Altrincham 29.12.70 Patricia M. Scott BA(Com)
(Manc) univ careers advis d of W. F. S. Cheshire

BELL Jennifer　MA 1970

BELL John Douglas Gordon　*MA 1969
　s of Douglas B. MB ChB(Edin) phys and Rose

Gordon nurs sister; b Aber 4.12.46
LRAM 1968
freelance arranger/composer Lond from 1969
m Aber 21.8.70 Angela M. James MA 1969 *qv*

BELL Kathleen Eleanor   *MA 1967

BELL Kathleen Taylor   MA 1969
d of Joseph B. aircraft fitter (Brit aerospace) and
A. J. Kathleen Taylor; b Elgin 5.6.48
teacher: Elgin 1970-75, BFPO Münster W Ger 1976,
Lossiemouth 1976-78, itinerant mus 1978, Lossiemouth
from 1978
m Elgin 25.3.78 Nigel S. Robinson flying off. RAF s of
Kenneth R. Whitby

BELL Margot   MA 1970
civ serv: Lond 1971-72, Elgin from 1973
m Edin 12.9.69 Graham Tuley BSc(for) 1970 *qv*

BELL Mary Rose   MB ChB 1967
d of Douglas B. MB ChB(Edin) chest phys and Rose
Gordon nurs sister; b Cairo 21.7.43
DA 1969
h o ARI 1967-68; regist anaest Falkirk 1969; occasional
locums from 1969; part time res work for NCB on
pneumoconiosis in miners inst occup med from 1974
m Aber 23.11.68 Peter H. Fettes MB ChB 1968 *qv*

BELL Thomas Matthew   PhD 1962
s of Thomas M. B. headmaster and Kate G. Lindsay;
b Greenock 22.8.36
BSc(Glas) 1959 MRCPath 1968 BA(OU) 1975
lect Aberd 1959-63; leader Afr proj imp cancer res fund
Entebbe 1963-69; sen virol MRC demyelinating dis unit
and hon lect N'cle 1969-72; lect virol N'cle 1973-74; sen
lect from 1974
m Glasg Fiona M. Downie civ serv d of Archibald D.
Dunoon

BELL Wendy Erskine Wetherly   MA 1963
d of Harold F. B. policeman, hotelier and Mary E.
Wetherly nurse; b Aber 19.5.43
secy: Lond 1964, Edin 1965-72, Houston Texas 1972-76,
Raleigh NC from 1976
m Aber 20.3.65 Gordon B. Burnett MB ChB 1964 *qv*

BELLIS Joanna Christine   MB ChB 1965
d of Herbert H. B. retailer and Marjorie D. Charlton
writer; b Woodford 31.10.39
DA 1968
h o RACH, City hosp Aber 1965-66; sen h o: med
Woodend hosp Aber 1967, sen h o, regist Guildford
1967-69; clin asst anaest Lancaster 1970-74; dept m o
commun health Barrow from 1974
m Ilford 3.9.67 David K. Lindley BSc(for) 1963 *qv*

BELLRINGER Alan Wayland   PhD 1968
s of Clarence W. B. carpet des and Edith G. M. Sayer
secy; b Croydon 26.8.32
MA(Glas)
lect Engl univ coll of N Wales Bangor 1968-74, sen lect
from 1974
m Bangor 5.7.65 Jean W. Taylor BA(Wales) tech coll lect
d of Thomas A. T. Belper

BELTON Sidney James   MA 1966

BEMBRIDGE Peter Christopher   LLB 1967

BENECKE Udo   BSc(for) 1961
s of Joachim A. B. PhD(Berlin) diplomat and Wilfriede

L. H. Brackemann; b Lemgo Germany 1.4.40
M Agr Sc(Canterbury NZ) 1968 Dr oec publ(Münich)
1972
NZ: scient Rangiora 1962-76, Christchurch from 1976
m Christchurch 1.5.65 Jennifer A. Jack nurse d of Gordon
D. J. Hokitika NZ

BENJAMIN Michael Ian   BSc 1969 MB ChB 1969
s of Cyril A. B. chem and Florence H. Warshowski;
b Leeds 15.7.44
Dip Psycho-therap(Tel-Aviv) 1978
Israel: h o Asof Marofe 1970-71; resid Beit Yam 1971-
72; army psychiat I.D.F. 1972-76; consult. psychiat: nat
insur/Israel milit industries/nat road safety council from
1976
m Tel-Aviv 10.11.78 Patricia R. Kelly admin (Hotel-
Sheraton T.A.), teacher of art

BENNET Anne Margaret   *MA 1961
m Chandler

BENNETT Colin   *MA 1963
d Glasg 5.8.73 *AUR* xlv 322

BENNETT David Stephen   BSc 1968

BENNETT James Roy   *BSc 1962 PhD 1967
s of Norman S. B. eng/man. dir and Mary Gowans;
b Perth 9.4.40
teacher: Falkirk h s 1967-69; head biol Graeme h s from
1969
m Brechin 5.8.66 Barbara M. Eunson BSc 1965 *qv*

BENNETT John David   MA 1970

BENNETT John Michael   PhD 1966

BENNETT Norman Bruce   MB ChB 1963 MD 1967
s of Norman S. B. eng and Mary Gowans; b Gorakphur
India 5.7.38
MRCP 1969 MRCPath 1973
Aberd: Ashley Mackintosh res fell. med 1964-65, MRC
jun res fell. med 1965-67, lect med 1967-70, Wellcome
res fell. and sen lect med from 1973; Eli Lilly internat
fell. Cleveland Ohio 1970-73
m Kirkby Lonsdale 1973 Gillian D. Adey MB ChB 1968 *qv*

BENNETT Peter James   *BSc(for) 1967

BENNETT Peter Norman   MB ChB 1963 *MD 1967
s of Norman B. tea planter and Jane E. Ogston teacher;
b Calcutta 25.11.39
MRCP(UK)
res fell., lect med Aberd 1964-71; Wellcome res fell. clin
pharm UCH med s Lond 1971-73; lect clin pharm Royal
post grad med s Hammersmith hosp Lond from 1973
m Kirkella 31.8.63 Jennifer M. Brocklehurst MB ChB
1963 *qv*

BENNETT Richard Dawson   *MA 1964 Dip Ed 1965

BENNETT Valerie   MA 1963

BENNISON George Mills   PhD 1959
BSc(Durh) 1943 MSc(Durh) 1951
lt REME 1943-45; asst geol Glas 1947-49; lect geol: Aberd
1949-60, Birm 1960-71, sen lect from 1971
m Lond 11.7.43 Gwendoline McQueen secy, teacher d of
William McQ. Lond

BENTINCK Susan Joyce   *BSc 1969
d of Gordon T. B. p o telecomm and Joyce Mearns
wages clerk; b Middlesbrough 15.5.47

teacher: Farnham Common 1970–71, Honiara Sol Is
1971–72
m Leeds 28.8.71 Christopher J. Lomas BSc(agr) 1970 *qv*

BENZIE Alexander Stewart   MB ChB 1970
s of Alexander B. farm. and Margaret S. Harcus MA
(Edin) teacher; b Glasg 24.11.46
DObstRCOG 1973 MRCGP 1976
h o Aber hosps 1970–71; sen h o Inv hosps 1971; m o
RAF 1971–77; g p Jeddah Saudi Arabia from 1977
m Aber 15.7.70 Dorothy C. Lunney MB ChB 1970 *qv*

BENZIE Carmen Hill Elmslie   MA 1957
d of Athol B. man. dir dept store and Carmen H. Allan
teacher, secy; b Aber 8.4.37
secy: export/import firm Lond 1958–59, to dir J. Lyons &
Co Lond 1959–63, to dir of prop. comp Glasg 1963–65
m Aber 1.5.65 George Ritchie man. dir dept store s of
William R. Glasg

BENZIE Heather Aileen   BSc 1956
d of James S. B. housing factor and Helen M. Rattray
loc govt off.; b Aber 12.5.35
teacher: sc Aber 1957–58, Wick 1958–62, Halkirk p s from
1970
m Aber 6.8.58 Hamish I. Gunn BSc 1955 *qv*

BENZIE Helen   MA 1962
m Welham

BENZIE Ronald John   MB ChB 1961

BENZIE Sheila Clark   MA 1966
d of James B. and Isabella Clark; b Perth 28.4.45
Dip Ed(Glas) 1967
teacher: Engl/Fr Perth 1968–73, asst prin guid from 1973
m Aber 1972 David S. Barclay BSc 1957 *qv*

BERG Peter Jack   BSc(for) 1969
s of Jack H. B. for. contr and Muriel E. Gray; b
Palmerston North NZ 23.9.45
BSc(Auck) 1966
NZ for. serv: for. Kaikohe, Thames 1969–70, dist for.
Waitemata 1970–75; chief for. off. Apia Samoa from 1978
m Waimate North 7.3.70 Glenda A. Hoult shorthand
typist d of Ralph W. H. Ohaeawai NZ

BERGER Jennifer   *BSc 1967
d of John B. MRCVS(Lond) vet surg and Leslie M.
Stewart; b UK 10.9.44
MA(Calif) 1969 (Zool) MPH(Calif) 1971
co-ordinator freedom commun clin Calif 1971; Nairobi:
Frederikson pop. fell./guest auxil FAO 1971–73, pop. educ
and eval spec in progr for better family living FAO from
1974

BERGER Vere   *MA 1969
d of John B. MRCVS(Lond) vet surg and Leslie M.
Stewart; b Wilmslow 8.1.46
MSocW(Sus) 1971
soc worker Berks c c from 1971

BERRIDGE Paul   MB ChB 1964
b Blackburn 23.9.39
DObstRCOG 1966

BERROW Michael Lloyd   PhD 1958
s of Leslie L. B. pharm and Winifred D. Brown;
b Norwood 20.7.32
BSc(Wales) 1955
soil chem agr dev and advis serv Bristol 1959–60; res staff
Macaulay inst for soil res Aber from 1960

m Aber 30.9.66 Sylvia M. Hartley asst scient off. d of
Harold B. H. Aber

BERRY Mary Alice Jane   *MA 1965

BERRYMAN Julia Clare   *BSc 1968
d of Eric R. B. solic and Jerameane R. Garnett;
b Luton 6.5.45
PhD(Leic) 1974
Leic: res asst dept psych 1969–74, res fell. dept psych
1974–75, lect psych dept adult educ from 1976

BERTRAM Barbara Costie   MB ChB 1956
d of William B. marine eng (insur) and Mabel Flett;
b S Shields 12.12.31
h o RI Inv 1956, S Shields 1957; sen h o: paediat Sunderland 1958, mat. N Shields 1958; g p trainee Inv 1959
m Inv 2.4.60 Duncan Livingstone LRCPGlas m o h
Kincardine s of George L. Inv

BERTRAM Julia Stanley   *BSc 1969
d of James S. B. eng and Evelyn Buchanan clerkess;
b Glasg 9.2.47
geol Zeehan Tasmania 1969–71, Perth W Aust from 1971
m Bearsden 7.8.69 Kenneth M. Ferguson BSc 1969 *qv*

BERY Jawaharlal   BSc(eng) 1957
s of Cate A. R. B. and Kaushalaya Handa; b Lahore
28.9.35
BSc(Calc) 1955 MIE(India) 1972
trainee Mitchell eng co Lond 1957–59; Bery Bros eng
workshop Calcutta: asst works man. 1959–67, purchase
off. 1969–76; commercial off. Bery Machin Manuf
Calcutta from 1976

BETTRIDGE Ann Elizabeth   BSc 1969
d of Robert C. B. man. sales eng and Audrey Weeder
playgroup organis; b Evesham 6.7.48
teacher: Elton county jun s Bury 1970–71, Hillside middle
s Skelmersdale 1971–72, games Oakdale middle s Poole
1972–75
m N'cle-u-Tyne 14.9.68 Neil W. Sharp MA 1970 *qv*

BEVERIDGE Thomas   MB ChB 1969
BSc(Glas)

BEVERLY Eric Angus   *MA 1967
s of Edwin A. B. bank off. and Alice Fleming teacher;
b Aber 18.11.43
res stud. Aber 1967–70; lect Fr: Warw 1970–71, poly
Plymouth from 1971

BEVERLY Gordon Maxwell   *BSc 1963 PhD 1966
s of John B. painter and Mary D. Bowie; b Huntly
18.3.41
post doct fell.: univ of Maine 1966–67, univ of N Carolina
1967–68; res chem ICI plastics div Welwyn Garden City
from 1969
m Huntly 17.9.66 Irene G. Brander dent nurse d of
Charles B. Huntly

BEWS Alan Alexander   MA 1966
s of James B. farm man. and Mary J. Robertson;
b Rhynie 6.9.45
Aber: CA app F. A. Ritson & Co 1966–72, acct JGB Oil
Serv Centres and assoc comps from 1972

BEWS Isobel Mary   MA 1962

BEWS Neil Davidson   BSc 1963
s of Donald B. tech advis and Adeline E. Davidson
clerkess; b Aber 9.4.43

Carshalton: shift man. chem firm 1963–70; asst prod.
man. from 1970
m Aber –.9.65 Joyce M. Reid secy d of Albert M. R.
Aber

BEY Norman Stewart   MA 1968

BEYTS Diana Mary   *MA 1968 Dip Ed 1973
   d of Clement E. B. asst lib Aberd and Edna M. Davidson; b Aber 13.2.47
field asst geog field centre Dale Fort 1968–70; teacher
Ashington 1971–72
m Bainbridge 5.9.72 Nigel Dower lect

BHATT Gunvant Shankerprasad   MB ChB 1966
   s of S. M. B. MBBs(Bom) and Vidya Dave; b Nairobi
8.9.38
LMCC 1970
h o Kilmarnock I and Ballochmyle hosp 1967–68; g p
Prescott Ont from 1968

BHATTI Perveen Akhtar   MB ChB 1965
   d of Abdul K. B. army off. and Feroza Janjua;
b Rawalpindi Pakistan 3.12.41
DObstRCOG 1967
h o Aber 1965–66, Cambridge 1967; g p Sudbury
Canada from 1968
m Manc 27.5.69 Iftikhar Hosain MSc(McG) geophys s of
Tassaduq H. MBBS(Punjab) Rawalpindi

BHATTY Muhammed Salabat Yar   PhD 1969
   MSc(Panj)
in USA

BICHAN Herbert Roy   *BSc 1964

BICHAN Robert Miller   MB ChB 1957

BICHAN Sydney John Eunson   BSc(agr) 1968
   s of Sydney B. farm. and Myrtle Tait; b Kirkwall
2.11.46
farm. ptnrship Drumoak and Swanbister, Orkney from
1968

BICKERTON Judith Carol   BSc 1967
   d of Richard S. B. MA(Cantab) eng and Ethel M.
Cheetham; b Farnborough 11.8.44
res asst Alta 1967–68; tech Calgary 1968–69; progr:
Lond 1969–71, (MRC) Lond and Edin 1971–74, Ferranti
Manc from 1974
m Siddington 21.9.74 James P. S. Bell BSc(Leic) s of
George T. B. BA(Cantab) Mobberley Nr Knutsford

BIDE Richard Willan   PhD 1964
   MSc(Alta)

BIGGAR Susan Mary   MA 1968
   d of Walter A. B. BSc(Edin) farm. and Patricia M. I.
Elliott; b Aber 18.2.47
Lond: BBC tv prod. asst 1968–72; Guinness Superlatives
publ res 1972–75; freelance sports res from 1975
m St Boswells 2.10.76 Michael R. Browne MA(Cantab)
oyster farm. s of Francis B. R. B. MA(Cantab) Pewsey

BIGGINS Peter   MB ChB 1969
   s of Sidney J. B. retailer and Doris Walters; b Mansfield 14.7.43
Jersey: h s gen hosp 1969–70; g p St Helier from 1970
m Guernsey 11.12.71 Mary E. Hamon SRN d of A. G. H.
Guernsey

BIGNELL Peter   *MA 1962 Dip Ed 1963
   s of Charles E. B. ship's eng and Isabella N. Hodgson

clerkess; b Lond 16.5.36
teacher: Tabora Tanzania 1963–65, Lond 1966–68,
Nairobi 1968–74; insp s Nairobi from 1974
m Aber 28.9.60 Patricia S. Morrison nurse d of George
J. M. Aber
marr diss 24.10.75

BIGWOOD Winifred Katherine   *MA 1957
   m Main

BILLAU Frances Joy   BEd 1969

BINNIE David Chalmers   *MA 1968

BINNIE, Lorna   MA 1966
   m Mitchell

BINNS Paul Edward   *BSc 1969
   s of Percy E. A. B. MA(Oxon) clerk in holy orders and
Edith Barker; b Greywell 27.7.42
PhD(Edin) 1975
geol Inst of geol sc Edin; scient off. 1969–71; sen scient
off. 1971–74, prin scient off. 1974–75; geol RD Shell
Explor and Prod. lab The Hague from 1975
m Richmond Surrey 13.8.66 Ceri L. Nelson airline clerkess
d of Brian N. Whitton

BINNS Richard Henry Fieldwick   BEd 1969

BIRCHALL Paul Malcolm Anthony   *BSc 1968

BIRD David Graham   LLB 1969
   s of Herbert B. process engraver and Muriel M. Adams;
b Aber 11.8.48
law app Henry J. Gray & Connochie Aber 1969–71; solic
Russell & Dunlop Edin 1971–73; solic and attorney-at-
law W. S. Walker & Co Grand Cayman BWI from 1973
m Dunblane 7.4.73 Catherine J. MacNaught d of David
C. MacN. Dunblane

BIRKBECK Helen Margaret Ann   MB ChB 1967
   d of John E. H. B. B. min of religion and Peggy
Simpson secy; b Aber 4.11.43
h o Woodend hosp Aber, RACH 1967–68; g p Aber
1969–76
m Aber 30.9.67 Gethyn Burgess univ lect

BIRKBECK Valerie Elizabeth Renner   MA 1956
   d of Philip L. B. ironmonger's man. and Elizabeth D.
Fraser; b Darlington 15.10.33
JP Denbighsh (now Clwyd) 1972
teacher: Quarryhill p s Aber 1957–60, Aber h s for girls
1960–61
m Aber 9.9.60 Michael A. Shields MB ChB 1954 qv

BIRNIE Alison Forbes Hunter   MB ChB 1959
   d of James A. B. MA 1927 qv; b Oldham 17.4.35
h o: RACH 1959–60; part-time g p Aber from 1970
m Aber 16.7.59 Frederick P. Lynch MB ChB 1955 qv

BIRNIE Donald James Forbes   MB ChB 1962
   s of James A. B. MA 1927 qv; b Farnworth 15.7.37
DA 1965 MRCGP 1972
h o ARI 1962–63; trainee asst Inverbervie 1964–65;
g p Aber from 1965
m Aber 1.12.62 Allison M. Tait d of James T. Aber

BIRNIE Gordon William Valentine   *BSc 1968
   s of William B. MB ChB 1936 qv; b Edin 15.10.43
teacher: Perthsh 1969–70; Abdnsh: asst 1970–71, spec
asst biol 1971–72, prin teacher from 1972
m Bridge of Earn 10.4.71 Margaret S. Paton health
visitor

BIRNIE Mae Lorimer   MA 1956
d of Allan B. baker and Elsie M. Buchan hotel worker;
b Glasg 13.12.34
teacher mod lang Fraserburgh 1957–64, Ellon 1964–71
m New Deer 29.12.71 William Mitchell farm. s of John
M. Ellon

BIRNIE Mary Jean   MA 1966
d of James B. farm./shop prop. and Christina J.
Robertson nurse; b Aber 15.9.45
teacher Engl Macduff h s 1967–69, New Deer j s s
1969–73; private tut: Engl Varberg Sweden 1973–74;
teacher Engl Brierton c s Hartlepool, Cleveland 1975–76,
New Deer s from 1977
m Aber 21.3.66 Gordon T. Whyte elect. eng s of Charles
G. W. Cuminestown

BIRNIE Myrtle Elise   BSc 1960
m McGregor

BIRRELL Brian William   *BSc 1968
s of Alexander B. actuary and Anne S. Deuchars;
b Kircaldy 26.10.46
teacher chem Armadale 1969–72; prin chem Kirkcaldy
from 1972
m Dun 28.12.74 Bronwyn M. Lauder BSc(Dund) teacher
d of George O. L. Dun

BIRRELL Elizabeth Fergusson   MA 1968
d of George D. B. motor mech and Christina F. S.
Ellis tel; b Edin 18.4.48
advt copywriter Edin 1968–69; teacher N'cle 1970–72
m Edin 27.6.70 Christopher J. Adams BSc 1968 qv

BIRSE Douglas James   MA 1960
s of Charles B. rly shunter and Elsie Wildgoose;
b Oyne 1.7.37
teacher Latin/Engl Creetown 1961–64; head: Lumphanan
1964–70, Dunecht 1970–74, Auchterellon 1974–76, Upper
Westfield s Bridge of Don from 1976
m Aber 25.7.61 Phyllis J. Third secy d of George T.
Premnay

BIRSE Muriel Jean   *MA 1960
d of George B. B. elect. eng and Agnes M. McLean;
b Dun 5.5.38
teacher geog Kirkton h s Dun 1961–62, Greycotes Oxon
1962–63, Headington 1963–64; part-time geog coll of
comm and mainly mus in p s Aber from 1970
m Dun 28.7.62 Ian J. Patterson BSc 1961 qv

BIRSE Sheila Margaret   MB ChB 1965
m Leslie

BIRSS James Gordon   MA 1961

BIRSS John Alexander Fullarton   MB ChB 1968
s of James F. B. CA and Dorothea H. Coutts MA
1932 qv; b Aber 28.7.45
h o: ARI, Woodend hosp Aber 1968–69; Tasmania:
resid m o NW gen hosp Burnie 1969–70, Mersey gen
hosp Latrobe 1970–71; g p Devonport Tasmania from
1971
m Devonport –.2.70 Heather D. Turner SRN d of John
G. R. T. Quoiba Tasmania

BIRSS Sheila Smith   MA 1964
d of William A. B. joiner and Isabel T. Smith; b Aber
1943
teacher: Currie 1965–70; prin guid Gorebridge from 1970

BISHOP Frances Margaret   *MA 1958
d of John B. bank teller and Margaret Dougherty MA
1928 qv; b Aber 19.11.36
teacher Engl: Morgan acad Dun 1958–59, Aber h s for
girls 1959–62, Peterhead acad from 1973
m Aber 13.7.60 Frederick Crawford MA 1958 qv

BISHOP Hugh William   MA 1968

BISHOP Iain Ritchie   *BSc 1959
s of John B. bank teller and Margaret Dougherty MA
1928 qv; b Aber 23.2.38
MSc(S'ton) 1962 OBE 1969
res asst S'ton 1959–63; lect: Guy's hosp med s Lond
1963–66, Leic 1966–72; on secondment to RGS exped
Mato Grosso Brazil 1967–69; dept zoology Brit Mus
(nat hist) from 1972

BISHOP Janet Margaret   BSc 1965
d of Frank B. nurse, eng and Frances S. Wallace
tailoress; b Whalley 26.10.41
res asst Aberd 1965–69
m Aber 22.6.68 Alan J. Hay BSc 1966 qv

BISHOP Margaret Elizabeth   MA 1968

BISHOP Marigold Rehan   MA 1968
m Cannings

BISHOP Prudence Margaret   *BSc 1968
m Vipond

BISSET Catherine Hutcheon   *BSc 1962
d of James B. B. sailmaker and Catherine H. Matthews;
b Aber 4.2.40
MSc(Exe) 1964
scient information off. Commonwealth mycological inst
1964–66
m Aber 16.9.66 Donald W. H. Stewart BSc 1960 qv

BISSET Derek   MA 1959

BISSET Gladys Margaret   MA 1958
m Hart

BISSET Iain Muir Fraser   MA 1961

BISSET James Martin   *MA 1956

BISSET Katrine McKenzie   MA 1959
m McLean

BISSET Morag Jane   *MA 1967
d of Robert D. N. B. MB ChB(Dunedin) surg and
Janet N. Sloan or Smillie radiographer; b Edin 1945
DipEd(Edin) 1968
teacher Engl Stirling h s 1968–72
m Auchterhouse Dun 25.8.67 Daniel S. Macleod MA
1967 qv

BISSET Raymond George   BSc 1963
s of William B. shop asst and Jean Thom clerkess;
b Ellon 16.8.42
teacher: Ellon 1963–64, sc Insch 1965–75; head Keithhall
p s from 1975
m Peterhead 10.4.47 Heather M. Smith teacher d of
James S. Peterhead

BISSET Reid Fyfe   MB ChB 1964
s of James B. PO eng and Mary L. Chasser shop asst;
b Aber 10.1.41
DObstRCOG 1967
h o: Woodend hosp Aber, ARI, Craigton mat. hosp St

Andrews 1964–65; Perth RI; sen h o 1966–68, regist anaest 1968–70; g p Perth from 1970
m Inv 26.5.66 Annette M. Mackenzie nurse d of David M. Foyers

BISSET Richard Alexander   *MA 1969
s of Thomas B. letterpress machineman and Dorothy M. Cardno; b Aber 26.3.47
teacher: Mackie acad Stonehaven 1970–72, prin geog Mackie acad 1972–79; asst rector Banchory acad from 1979
m Banff 23.3.78 Joyce A. Weir dental surg asst d of William W. Banff

BISSET Roderick Bruce   BSc 1968
s of George B. B. BSc(agr) 1924 *qv*; b Reading 31.8.47
electronic test eng Chelmsford 1968–70; electronic eng Inv from 1970

BISSETT George Norman   *MA 1963
s of George B. elect. and Johanna M. Shirsinger; b Burntisland 19.7.38
MPhil(Yale) 1969
lect Br Council Beirut 1964–66, head Engl dept pol sc fac Ankara Univ 1969–71; Anglo-Uruguayan cult. inst Montevideo: dir gen 1971–74 and cult. attaché Brit emb 1974–75; Br inst Barcelona: dir stud. from 1975
m Aber 9.8.65 Faith L. Svajian MA (Middlebury Vt) teacher Spanish d of George S.

BJØRNSON Leif Jan   MB ChB 1964
s of Olav B. grad pharm Oslo dir pharm comp and Liv Pallesen; b Oslo 6.11.39
spec intern. med 1974 MD(Oslo) 1978
Norway: h o Drammen, dist g p Senja 1965–66, milit m o 1966–67; Ulleval hosp Oslo univ clin: jun regist 1967–70, sen regist 1970–73, res fell. univ of Oslo 1973–77, sen regist from 1977
m Oslo 22.6.67 Elisabeth Bang teacher d of Hans B. Oslo

BLACK Adam Mackenzie   BSc(for) 1958
s of William J. L. B. teacher and Isabella Mackenzie secy; b Wick 7.11.34
nat serv BAOR 1956–58; teacher Wick 1958–59, prin biol Thurso h s from 1960
m Aber 1956 Anne S. Duthie shorthand typist d of Kenneth A. M. D. Aber

BLACK Alison Agnes Rankine   MA 1968 DipEd 1969
d of Archibald D. B. and Alice Rankine; b Loch Awe 12.9.47
teacher mod lang: Dunbarton 1969–70, spec asst Edin 1970–72; TEFL Unna W Ger from 1972

BLACK Allan William   *BSc 1965

BLACK David Alexander   BSc(for) 1958
s of Thomas A. B. preventive off. Customs & Excise and Mary T. Ferguson; b Edin 8.7.37
N Nigeria: asst conserv for. Maiduguri 1958–60, Bauchi 1960–64; NZ: for. Christchurch 1964–68, sen for. Auckland from 1968
m Darfield 3.9.60 Jeanette Barnes teacher d of Thomas S. B. Darfield nr Barnsley

BLACK Elizabeth Myrna Dowdy   MA 1957
d of James J. B. stat supt BEA Sumburgh and Mary A. Burgess; b Sumburgh 4.4.35
teacher: Lossiemouth 1958–61, Sandwick Shetland 1966–71, Dunrossness 1972–73, Sandwick from 1973

m Dunrossness 22.7.58 Andrew L. B. Flaws agr advis NOSCA s of Magnus F. Virkie Shetland

BLACK Francis Montgomery   *BSc 1970 PhD 1974

BLACK Gavin Thomas   BSc(eng) 1959

BLACK Gordon MacPherson   MB ChB 1956

BLACK Hugh Leggat   BSc(agr) 1957
s of Thomas B. LDS(Glasg) dent. surg and Agnes Leggat; b Huddersfield 31.5.35
Winston Churchill mem trust trav schol (Europ countries) 1971
man. Tarriebank estate Angus 1957–60; NOSCA: agr county and area advis from 1960 and farm man. from 1968
m Aber 21.7.61 Doreen M. Jeans teacher home econ d of Alexander J. Laurencekirk

BLACK Ian Macintosh   MA 1963
s of George S. B. civ serv, hotelier, prop. man. and Isabella R. Tait civ serv; b Inv 27.6.41
Aber: man. trainee 1964–65, sales man. 1965–66, dir 1966–68; Canada: teacher Winnipeg 1968–69, Port Alberni 1969–70, Victoria from 1970
m Aber 12.11.66 Alison M. Walker d of John W. Aber

BLACK James Howard Smith   MB ChB 1964

BLACK John Alexander Gordon   BSc(eng) 1968
s of J. Gordon B. MB ChB 1929 *qv*; b Camberley 7.1.44
BBC tv Lond from 1969
m Lond 3.6.72 Mary S. Kelly film/tv make-up artist d of James K. Telford

BLACK Margaret Catherine   BSc 1969
d of Charles D. B. farm./sub-contr and Mary H. Mathers; b Ellon 13.7.46
teacher sc Beauly 1970–74; prin guid Moray s Grangemouth 1974–78
m Aber 4.7.70 Allistair G. Matheson fin. acct s of Robert M. Tomintoul

BLACK Norval Marshall Burns   *MA 1966

BLACK Robert Leitch   LLB 1965

BLACK Robert William   *MA 1969

BLACK Ronald   MA 1970
s of Albert B. bus driver and Pearl J. D. Irvine off. worker; b Aber 3.7.49
housefather m h youths Pembury 1971–72; teacher: Dalmellington 1973–74, Lossiemouth from 1974
m E Kilbride 8.8.75 Kathleen M. Collier teacher dom sc d of Peter C. E Kilbride

BLACK Roy Peter   BSc 1968
s of Horace A. C. B. asst distillery man. and Isabella M. Bremner; b Knockando 3.12.46
Dip OR(Strath) 1969
Strath: res asst 1969–70, res fell. from 1970
m Johnstone 11.8.73 Eileen E. Townsend secy d of George A. T. Johnstone

BLACK William Broad   MA 1967
s of William J. B. joiner and Ella Broad; b Edin 7.4.46
BD(Edin) 1970
C of S min: asst Bathgate High ch 1970–72; min Durness linked Kinlochbervie from 1972

m Edin 18.7.70 Kathleen Clarkson MA(Edin) teacher d of William H. C. Huntly

BLACKBURN Alan Henry Hugh   BSc(agr) 1959

BLACKBURN Thomas Henry   PhD 1965
s of Thomas H. B. MA(Dub) headmaster and Mabel G. Shankey; b Sligo Ireland 8.8.33
BA MSc(Dub)
scient off. Rowett inst Aber 1957–67, assoc prof Br Col from 1967
m Aber –.4.63 Sheila E. Bell d of George B. Aber

BLACKHALL Margaret Isobel   MB ChB 1956 MD 1970
d of William G. B. master tailor and Jane S. Fowlie; b Tarland 17.12.32
DCH 1959 DObstRCOG 1960 MRCPE 1964
h o: RACH, Dumfries and Galloway RI, Cumberland I, Carlisle, Aber mat. hosp 1956–58; sen h o, regist paediat Duchess of York hosp Manc 1958–61; regist paediat RACH 1961–65; sen regist, res fell. Alderhey ch hosp Liv 1965–69; Aust: sen lect ch health Queensland univ 1970–73; visiting paediat Prince Charles hosp Brisbane/post-grad superv Royal ch hosp Brisbane from 1973
m Brisbane 23.10.72 Kenyon G. Fry MBBS(Queensland) s of Kenyon M. V. F. Brisbane

BLACKIE Ruth Violet   *MA 1967
d of Walter G. B. publ and F. Nancy S. Kerr; b Glasg 2.3.45
Dip Ed(Glas) 1968
teacher: Clydebank h s 1968–72; Dunbartonsh curric dev centre Clydebank from 1972
m Rhu 18.10.75 Andrew M. Currie MA (Edin) cartographic publ s of Robert E. C. Edin

BLACKIE Sheila Murray   MA 1970
d of Ian A. J. B. bus driver and Edith Murray; b Montrose 2.6.49
teacher Engl Arbroath h s 1971–72
m Hertford 11.10.73 John R. P. Abbott farm. s of Alexander I. A. Cape Town

BLACKLAW William   MA 1956

BLACKMORE Ian Raymond   *MA 1970
s of Donald I. B. solic clerk and Dorothea P. Corcoran; b Perth 26.10.46
pers off. Ford Motor Co Dagenham 1970–73; div pers and trg man. Lex Tillotson Manc from 1974
m Dunfermline 25.3.72 Moira F. McNeill teacher d of R. M. McN. Dunfermline

BLACKSTONE Anita Maureen   MB ChB 1963

BLADES Alexander William   MA 1959

BLAIR Alastair   BEd 1969
s of Duncan M. B. off. man. and Jessie L. Douglas; b Glasg 21.9.33
LGSM 1971
peripatetic teacher speech and drama Aber 1969–71; lect sp and drama Callendar Park coll of educ Falkirk from 1971

BLAIR David Antony James   *MA 1963
s of Alexander Y. B. master printer and Anne Smith; b Aber 27.7.40
teacher mod lang Arbroath h s 1964–68, Kirkcaldy tech coll from 1968
m Glasg 19.7.69 Laura M. A. Lees teacher p e, d of David L. MA(Glas) Glasg

BLAIR David Howie   LLB 1969
s of Alastair C. B. BA(Cantab) solic and Catriona H. Orr MA(St And); b Edin 10.4.48
trainee Swiss Bank Corp Lausanne 1969–70; Lond: invest. man. J. Henry Schroder Wagg 1970–74, invest. banker Dev West from 1974
m Arbroath 8.7.72 Carol L. Forbes MB ChB 1972 med pract d of Atholl G. F. MB ChB(St And) Arbroath

BLAIR Frances   *MA 1964
d of Francis B. dock lab and Alice Donaldson; b Aber 5.12.41
teacher: Dun 1965–67, Kirkcaldy 1973–74; educ off. Kano Nigeria 1967–70, Nairobi 1971–72, Maiduguri Nigeria from 1974

BLAIR Jennifer Ann   BSc 1970
d of Donald D. W. B. dir and Betty Cruickshank; b Lutterworth 14.1.49
Dip Exec & Secy Skills (Lond) 1971
clerk/tracer Brit Waterways Lond 1971–73; plan. asst: Hants c c Lyndhurst 1973–74, Winchester 1974–76; plan. off. Berks c c Reading from 1976

BLAIR Mary Stewart   *BSc 1970
d of William B. MB ChB(Glas) med pract and Alexina M. Paterson MB ChB(Glas) med pract; b Glasg 3.7.48
teacher: Glasg 1971–72, N'cle 1972–74, Louth from 1974
m Glasg 21.7.72 Ian R. Cubitt BSc(agr) 1971 plant breeder s of James C. Athens

BLAIR Robert   PhD 1960
b Beith 29.5.33
BSc(agr)(Glas) 1956
scient off. Rowett inst Aber 1957–60; Aberd: asst anim husb 1960–61, sen res fell. 1961–66; prin scient off. ARC poultry res centre Edin 1966–75; res assoc Corn. Ithaca NY USA 1969–70; dir nutrit Swift Canadian Co Toronto from 1976

BLAIRS Margaret Chalmers   MA 1967
m Chalmers

BLAKE Ian Kerr   *BSc(eng) 1970
s of James B. comp dir and Catherine Kerr comp dir; b Watford 7.4.48
civ eng from 1970

BLAKEMORE Marie   MSc 1970
d of Sydney R. B. blacksmith and Florence M. Morris; b Shrewsbury 13.7.31
BSc(Lond) 1953
res asst soil sc dept Aberd 1970–72
m Grinshill Shrewsbury 28.7.71 Christopher D. Bristow MSc 1969 qv

BLANCE George Gilbert   *BSc 1960
s of George W. B. MA 1927 qv; b Lerwick 21.7.36
teacher Fraserburgh 1961–64, spec asst 1964; Kirkwall: prin chem 1964–72, asst then dep rector from 1972
m Aber 1.4.63 Morag C. Smith teacher d of James S. Peterhead

BLANE William   *MA 1969
s of David B. miner and Helen Walker; b Cumnock 26 4.47
teacher: Ger/Russian Cumnock acad 1970–71, prin Ger from 1971

BLANKSON Henry Richard Sagoe   BSc(for) 1962

BLENCH Sheena Margaret   *BMedBiol 1969
MB ChB 1972
d of Ian B. MRCVS(Glas) vet surg and Jeanie
Mactaggart; b Aber 12.9.47
h o ARI, King's Cross hosp Dun 1972–73; sen h o
psychiat royal Dun Liff hosp 1973–74, regist psychiat
Aber from 1974
m Oldmeldrum 10.7.72 John E. Pollet BMedBiol 1969 *qv*

BLITZ Nicolas Martin   *BSc(agr) 1967 ᶜMB ChB 1978
s of Thomas J. Weihs MD(Basle) med consult. and
Marie Blitz teacher; b Aber 30.3.43
PhD(McG) 1970
res fell. McG univ 1970–71, Imp coll Lond 1971–73
m Peterculter 20.3.65 Karin G. Kunzer remed educ d of
Ernst K. Berlin

BLUM Alfred Ernest Gustav   BSc(eng) 1961

BLYTH Angus Campbell   MB ChB 1970
s of Joseph O. B. BR ticket coll. and Christina
Campbell; b Oban 6.5.45
h o: RACH, Woodend hosp Aber 1970–71; obst Royal
Free hosp Lond 1971–72; med off. Nsambya hosp
Kampala 1972–73; sen h o anaest Southend gen hosp
from 1973

BLYTH John Francis   *BSc(for) 1968 PhD 1974
s of Francis G. H. B. PhD(Lond) lect and Margaret G.
Crowley mus teacher; b Watford 18.1.46
area for. Fountain Forestry Cheddar 1968–70; res asst
soil sc Aberd 1970–73; land husb off. min of agr and nat
resources Karonga Malawi from 1974

BOA Donalda Forbes   MA 1957
d of Peter B. crofter and Elizabeth Forbes; b Kiltarlity
9.2.36
teacher: Engl Northfield acad 1958–59, Elm Tree House
s Cardiff 1971–74, supply S Glamorgan from 1977
m Aber 20.7.59 Alan R. Beattie BSc 1955 *qv*

BOA Hugh Forbes   MA 1962 LLB 1965
s of Peter B. crofter and Elizabeth Forbes; b Kiltarlity
20.2.40
law app, qualif asst Inv 1964–71; resid magist/dep regist
high court Kenya from 1971

BOA Mary Isobel   MA 1958
m Reinhardt

BOAG Ian Francis   BSc(eng) 1959
s of William J. B. rly clerk and Alexandrina Mackenzie
shop asst; b Inv 20.4.37
site eng (Wm Tawse) Skye, Harris 1959–62; Ross &
Cromarty c c: asst eng Ullapool 1962–67, Dingwall
1967–70, dist surv Black Isle 1970–73, asst county surv
maintenance Dingwall 1973–75; prin eng Highland reg
from 1975
m Inv 6.10.67 Anne M. Fraser teleph d of Donald F. Kyle

BOAL David   BSc 1959
b Edin 21.5.38
teacher sc: Northfield s Aber 1960–62, Auchterarder
1962–67, Oakbank approved s 1967–75, Northfield acad
from 1975
m Peterculter 21.1.61 Isla F. Douglas teacher d of
Crawford E. D. Peterculter

BOLLAND Allan   BSc 1963

BOLLINGTON David Ian   LLB 1967

BOLTON Alan   BSc(for) 1968 Dip Ed 1969
s of John B. dir and Muriel B. Galloway; b Manc
16.4.46
Bankhead acad Aber: teacher 1969–72, prin guid from
1972
m Aber 20.12.67 Isabella T. MacKay MA 1970 *qv*

BOND Margaret Jane   MA 1967
d of Robert B. farm. and Sophia Rimmer; b Southport
2.11.46
BA(St Albans) 1970
Ambassador coll of St Albans: secy to coll regist 1970–71,
secy to dir estate dept 1971–74

BONE Alan Barclay   BSc(agr) 1962
s of Robert B. B. marine eng and Betsy G. W. Nicoll;
b Calcutta 23.2.39
asst insp dept agr for Scot Aber from 1963
m Elgin 6.8.65 Frances Morrison teacher d of John M. M.
Fochabers

BONE Jessie Muir   *MA 1963
d of Alexander H. B. MA(Edin) min of relig and
Margaret L. Macpherson BSc(Edin) teacher mus; b Barr-
hill 5.3.42
LTCL(Lond) 1964
teacher mus: St Denis s Edin 1964–67, Tarbert s 1967–68
m Ruthwell Dumfries 2.6.67 John D. Sutherland MA
(Edin) min of relig s of John S. Edin

BONNICI Joseph John   MA 1960
s of S.B. and Catherine Barton; b Glasg 13.4.28
teacher Holy Cross p s Glasg 1961–66; housemaster:
St Mary's Hall Stonyhurst 1966–71, St Aloysius prep s
Glasg 1971–72; head St Joseph's p s Peebles 1972–74;
housemaster St Mary's Hall Stonyhurst from 1974

BONNYMAN Sheena Dutton   MB ChB 1965
d of James B. mason and Williamina J. Philip; b Keith
29.3.42
DPM(Lond) 1970
Aber: h o 1965–66; sen h o, regist psychiat 1966–70;
asst prof psychiat and neurol, Creighton univ Omaha
USA 1971–72; regist psychiat Aber 1972–73; asst prof
psychiat/behavioural sc Omaha from 1973

BONOMY Christine Margaret   *BSc 1969
d of William B. BD(Glas) C of S min and Margaret M.
Lindsay MA(Glas) teacher; b Chinsali, Zambia 9.6.47
scient edit. Oss Holland 1969–71; prod m o Beerse
Belgium 1971–72; prod. registration off. Ware Herts
1972–73; teacher Kano Nigeria 1975–78
m Perth 4.12.71 Rex A. H. Laycock BSc(Eng) 1969 *qv*

BOOTH Catherine Mary   BSc 1968
d of Ernest M. B. hydraulic eng and Mary A. Duncan;
b Cove Bay 20.6.47
teacher: maths/geog Stonehaven 1969–72
m Aber 25.7.70 Colin G. Berry joiner/carpenter s of John
B. Aber

BOOTH George Davidson   BSc(agr) 1967
s of George E. R. B. auctioneer/farm. and Annie J.
Davidson; b Aber 25.12.44
ptnr in fam farm. bus. Bucksburn from 1967
m Aber 19.6.70 Patricia Spence nurse d of John P. S. Aber

BOOTH James Connon Donald   MB ChB 1956
s of Alfred B. pharm and Agnes J. Connon shop asst;
b Aber 25.12.29
DPM(Lond) 1962 MRCPE 1969 MRCPsych 1971

h o Brechin, Bishop Auckland, Aber 1956–58; g p trainee Coatbridge 1958–59; jun psychiat posts Edin 1959–64; jun posts med psychiat Sedgefield, Bradford, Glasg 1964–69; consult. psychiat Glasg from 1969
m Edin 11.4.64 Rosemary H. Fraser MB ChB(Edin) med/psychiat posts d of Alexander F. Edin

BOOTH Kathleen Margaret Dawson   MA 1964
m Thomson

BOOTH Mary Ellen   MA 1961

BOOTH Michael John   *MA 1961

BOOTH Peter Frank   *MA 1964

BOOTH Rupert Guy Tempest   *MA 1968 Dip Ed 1969

BOOTH Thomas Calvin   BSc(for) 1970

BOOTHBY Patricia Mary   MA 1966
m Greig

BOOTHBY Robin John   *BSc 1969
s of Kenneth A. B. sales man. and Hilda M. Pardoe; b Lond 17.12.47
syst eng International Computers Lond from 1969

BORRIE John Peters   BSc 1964
s of Alexander P. B. arch. and surv and Vera E. Holdcroft; b Dumfries 5.1.40
teacher phys Perth acad 1965–74; prin phys Millburn acad Inv from 1974

BORTHWICK Leslie John   MB ChB 1969

BORTHWICK Sheila Ross   BSc 1970

BOSTOCK Fred Allan   PhD 1964
s of Horace B. painter/decorator and Adelaide Pegg; b Nott 27.9.30
BSc(Nott) MSc(Nott)
lect S'ton from 1965
m Nott 9.8.56 Margaret M. Thorpe d of William J. T.

BOTCHWAY Theophilus   *BSc(eng) 1965

BOULIND Peter Rodney   MB ChB 1969

BOURNER Sybil Audrey   MA 1968
d of Albert M. B. cler off. BR and Caroline B. Morgan; b Aber 27.2.47
TEFL Berlitz s of lang Paris 1969–76; translator/exec secy Beauté, Hygiène et Soins (Boots Co) Paris from 1976
m Aber 4.9.75 Jean-Luc J. Popineau (degree in econ (Paris)) res dept min of environment Paris s of Etienne P. Paris

BOUSFIELD Ivan John   PhD 1969
BTech(Brad)

BOWDEN Alexander Barclay   BSc 1970

BOWDEN Elizabeth Margaret Mitchell
                              *MA 1961 Dip Ed 1964
d of T. Mitchell B. LRAM mus organis Orkney, Moray and Nairn and Margaret W. Turner; b Ceres 27.4.39
teacher Aber from 1964

BOWDEN Thomas Neil   *BSc 1965
s of William L. B. admin man. and Ethel Howarth; b Blackpool 19.7.43

MSc(Manc) 1967 FRAS 1969
res stud. Manc 1965–69; analyst/progr Plessey Telcomms Liv 1970–73; sen syst progr Burroughs Machines Cumbernauld from 1973
m Aber 6.4.48 Margaret H. Horne BSc 1967 *qv*

BOWEN Gwladys Margaret   *BSc 1959

BOWEN Ian Hamilton   PhD 1967
s of Herbert L. Bowen p s v conductor and Sarah A. Hamilton; b N'cle-u-Tyne 3.11.42
BPharm(Lond) 1964 MPS 1970
res fell. chem Strath 1967–68; s of pharm Sunderland poly: lect pharmacognosy 1969–74, sen lect from 1974
m Sunderland 3.4.65 Margaret Hanson audio secy d of Reginald H. Sunderland

BOWEN Jennifer Ellen   *MA 1969
d of Edward L. B. bank man. and Alice M. Simpson; b Edin 5.3.46
Dip Ed(Edin) 1970
teacher Fr: Bathgate 1970–71, Edin 1971–72, coach Rudolph Steiner s Edin 1972–73; off. man. anim feed supplements York from 1974
m Edin 20.12.69 Keith S. Castell army off. s of Reginald T. C. C. Windlesham

BOWERS Anthony   BSc(for) 1960
s of Reuben O. B. banker and Esther I. Dando; b Stockton-on-Tees 29.6.33
Tokoroa NZ: investigation for. (silviculture) NZ Forest Products 1962–78, estab for. from 1978
m Findochty 19.7.55 Grace A. Campbell MA 1955 *qv*

BOWIE James Frederick Rognvald   MB ChB 1960
s of Frederick J. T. B. MB ChB 1924 *qv* and Victoria H. Reid BSc 1921 *qv*; b Aber 3.3.35
FRCP(C) 1972
h o ARI, Woodend hosp Aber 1960–61; sen h o Cromer/Aylsham 1961–65; regist phys med and rheumat Norfolk and Norwich area 1965–67; consult. Winnipeg 1967–72; prof and dir s med rehab Univ of Manit Winnipeg from 1972
m Aber 5.8.61 Lena C. Stephen d of John B.S. Aber

BOWIE Kenneth   *MA 1968
s of John B. eng and Jessie Duthie; b Fraserburgh 17.6.45
AICMA 1974
fin. analyst Lond 1968–71; Greenock: internal then materials audit. 1971–74; oper res analyst from 1974
m Aber 29.6.68 Yvonne Mathieson d of Nathaniel M. Aber

BOWIE Raymond Alexander   *BSc 1961 PhD 1964
s of Alexander B. civ serv and Catherine H. Watt; b Aber 23.12.38
post doc fell. (Fulbright schol) Wash USA 1964–65; res chem ICI pharm div Cheshire from 1965
m Aber 12.7.63 Sheila E. M. MacLeod BSc 1960 *qv*

BOWKER Christine   *BSc 1965

BOWLING Dudley James Francis   PhD 1961
s of Geoffrey B. eng and Ethel G. Smith; b Ganstead, Hull 20.5.37
BSc(Nott) 1958
asst bot Aberd 1961–63, lect from 1963
m Aber 9.4.62 Sheila M. Daun MA 1959 *qv*

BOWMAN Iain Bell Ramsay   *BSc 1956 PhD 1959
s of Alexander S. R. B. master baker and Agnes A. Bell; b Arbroath 8.10.34

NATO res fell. Wash USA 1959–61; sen res fell. Aberd 1961–62; scient staff MRC Mill Hill Lond 1962–65; Edin: lect biochem 1965–70, sen lect from 1970
m Aber 21.3.64 Patricia Barron BSc 1960 *qv*

BOWMAN Robert Miller *BSc(eng) 1956

BOWTHORPE Michael *BSc 1959
s of Leonard A. B. mus dir and Nancy Dickinson; b Belfast 26.11.37
FRMetS 1968
Aust: scient off. weapons res estab Adelaide 1959–63; phys Tasmania 1963–66 (Austral nat antarctic res exped Wilkes 1964–65) lect phys univ coll Townsville 1966–71; sen scient off. sc res council Lond from 1971
m Aber 12.9.59 June M. Ingram admin exec d of John I. Aber

BOWYER Elizabeth Alice MA 1956

BOWYER Leonard William BSc 1970

BOYACK Patricia Alison MA 1967 *1969
d of George W. B. tea planter and Agnes G. Johnston secy; b Dun 3.10.45
civ serv inl rev Edin and Blackpool from 1971
m Carnoustie 26.8.72 Christopher D. Smith MA 1966 *qv* marr diss

BOYCE Francis Angus BSc 1970
s of Anthony B. steamfitter and Margaret H. Angus saleslady; b Aber 11.4.45
teacher maths Aber from 1971

BOYD John Minto MA 1961
s of John M. B. comp dir and Margaret A. Gordon; b Huntly 20.1.40
trainee man. Glasg 1961–71; dir Boyds (Huntly) from 1971
m Edin 15.5.64 Jennifer A. G. Black d of John M. B. MB ChB(Edin), Edin

BOYD Joseph Ian PhD 1970
s of John A. B. LLB(Dalhousie) barrister and Thyrza J. McManus teacher; b Blaine Lake Sask Canada 23.1.35
BA(Sask) 1956 STB(Tor) 1964 MA(Tor) 1965
asst prof Engl Sask 1970–75, assoc prof from 1975; edit. *The Chesterton Review*

BOYD Peter David Armstrong *BSc 1970
s of James C. B. eng and Elaine C. Armstrong; b Woodford 4.5.46
Sheff: res geol 1970–74; cert educ 1975
m Aber 17.7.69 Evelyn Y. Fox MA 1969 *qv*

BOYD Rognvald *BSc 1969 PhD 1973
s of James H. T. B. MA(Glas) C of S min and Margaret Logie; b Glasg 22.7.46
geol Norway 1972–74; proj geol English Clays Lovering Pochin & Co St. Austell from 1974
m Petersham 3.4.71 Susan J. Reece agr d of Henry W. W. R. Basingstoke

BOYES Pamela Ann Margaret MA 1963
d of George B. MA(Edin) bus. man., admin asst in educ and Edith M. Abernethy MA(Edin) teacher; b Aber 22.3.43
teacher Fr: Perth h s 1966-67, Walthamstow Hall, Sevenoaks 1967–70
m Perth 3.8.68 Alan R. Crook BA(Cantab) teacher s of Reginald W. C. Bournemouth

BOYLE Douglas McKenzie BSc 1969

BOYLE John Garrett LLB 1969
s of James M. B. MA(Glas) solic/town clerk and Margaret Garrett; b Fraserburgh 27.5.48
law app Aber c c 1969–71; Lyall & Wood solic Turriff: qual asst 1971–73, ptnr from 1973
m Aber 2.6.72 Heather Green clerkess d of James N.G. Aber.

BRACEWELL Margaret Jeanette BSc 1968
d of George H. B. prod. worker and Margaret G. Morrice factory worker; b Aber 12.9.47
scient off. crop analysis Macaulay inst for soil res Aber 1969–72; tech dept pharm Aberd from 1976
m Aber 15.9.67 John D. Gray MA 1971 teacher s of George G. Aber

BRACK John Angus *MA 1964
s of John B. cashier and Agnes E. Dick shop asst; b Aber 14.10.42
MSc(Econ)(Lond) 1965
lect Warw from 1965

BRACK Margaret Holland BSc 1964
m Husband

BRADFORD Ann Patricia MB ChB 1960
d of Thomas B. army off. (killed WW II) and Annie Gossop clerk; b York 11.3.36
DPH(N'cle) 1966 MS(Prev Med)(Wash.) 1969 Prize soc epidemiologic res 1969
h o Derbysh RI 1960–61; g p trainee Leabrooks 1961–62; asst county m o Derbysh 1963–64; asst m o h S Shields 1964–66; Seattle: post doct fell. 1967–69, assoc dir Washington/Alaska reg med program 1969–74, asst prof epidemiology Wash. from 1969, dir mat. and inf care dept publ health from 1974
m York 11.10.58 Clive S. Carter BSc(Leeds) res metall s of Harry S. C. York

BRADFORD Helen Margaret BEd 1969
m Scott

BRADFORD Nial Charlton MB ChB 1969 *BSc 1972
s of Ernest F. B. BSc(Lond) geol and Phoebe Charlton MB ChB(Lond) med pract; b Lond 30.5.46
h o ARI 1972–73; MRC fell. res Aberd 1973–76; lect Dund from 1976

BRADFORD Richard Halsey Gordon *BSc 1970
s of Kenneth G. B. chartered surv and Helen G. Thompson; b Belfast 17.4.47
Mannlife Toronto: progr 1970–72, syst superv 1972–74, proj man. from 1974

BRADLEY Robert PhD 1965
s of Robert B. farm. and Frances A. Denny; b Blackburn Lancs 12.4.39
BSc(agr)(Leeds) 1962
field dev off.: white fish auth, fish farming Ardtoe 1965–68; farms man. fish farming Marine Harvest Lochailort from 1968
m Slaidburn Dorothy Wood SRN d of Wilfred W. Slaidburn

BRADSHAW Ian Robin MacDonald *MA 1967

BRADY Colin John PhD 1962
MSc(agr)(Syd)

BRAMLEY Paul Scotson PhD 1970
s of David S. B. farm./comp dir and Marjorie S.

Duckett; b Liverpool 21.5.40
BVSc(Liv) 1963
lect vet physiol Nairobi 1970–71; sen vet res off. ARC
inst Compton 1971–73; comp vet surg Glasg from 1973
m Cartmel 20.4.67 Fiona C. Townley nurse d of
Humphrey C. T. BSc(agr)(Edin)

BRAND John Arthur *MA 1956
s of John W. B. civ eng and Mary M. Anderson; b
Aber 4.8.34
PhD(Lond) 1962
asst politics Glas 1959–61, asst lect politics: R'dg 1961–63,
Lond 1963–64; sen lect politics Strath from 1964

BRAND Norrie Gordon   BSc 1967

BRAND Winifred Campbell Duncan   MA 1968
m Reid

BRANDER Colin   *MA 1970
s of Joseph M. B. riveter and Georgina S. Milne; b
Aber 7.9.32
teacher hist: Harlaw acad Aber from 1971

BRANDER Heather   MA 1963
d of William R. B. farm. and Isabel B. Innes; b Nairn
16.7.42
teacher: Liberton h s Edin 1964–65, E Calder 1965,
W Calder 1965–67; Aust: Coffs Harbour NSW 1968–69,
Albury NSW 1970–71, Shepparton Victoria 1973–74,
Wodonga Victoria 1974
m Aber 20.11.71 Frank D. Holden master mariner/
grazier s of Arthur C. H. Bright Victoria Aust

BRANDER John Gordon   MA 1969
s of John M. B. aircraft eng and Sheila Smith; b Aber
29.12.48
Dip Bus Stud(H-W) 1970
invest. analyst P & O shipping group Lond 1970–71;
airline pilot: Oxon CSE aviation 1970–71, BA Heathrow
Lond from 1971
m Aber 14.4.72 Elizabeth Naysmith BEd 1969 *qv*

BRANDIE WILLIAM   *BSc(eng) 1960
s of William B. naval off. and Nettie Bowie; b Aber
25.11.36
Edin: res eng electronics & computer syst 1960–64, group
leader computer syst 1964–69; sen electronics eng E
Lothian 1969–73; syst analyst-computer Edin from 1974
m Edin 21.7.62 Margot J. Wright teacher d of Frederick
W. Aber

BRANDS Sheila Johnston Campbell   MB ChB 1961
m Wiseman

BRANDT Halvor   MB ChB 1969
s of Olav B. min and Emma L. Midtbø; b Oslo 11.3.44
Norway: Mo i Rana h o 1970–71; g p 1971–72; army m o
Heistadmoen 1972–73; regist anaest Skien from 1973
m Mo i Rana 17.2.71 Eva Gronseth d of Torstein G.
MB ChB(Oslo) Mo i Rana

BRANSON Raymond Albert   * MA 1968
AFC

BRATT John Dudley   BSc(eng) 1962

BRAY Beverley Jane   MA 1970
m Hunter

BRAY John Terence   BSc 1958
s of George H. B. wholesale fish merch and Maggie
M. E. Crancher; b Grimsby 5.2.36

petr eng Kirkuk Iraq 1958–68; sen petr eng: Dukhan
Qatar 1969–74, Abu Dhabi UAE from 1974
m Glasg 5.8.63 Ann Johnson MA(Glas) teacher d of
Thomas R. J. Glasg

BRAZENDALE Anthony Henry   *MEd 1969
s of Henry B. sales rep and Bessie Connor; b UK
31.3.36
MA(Cantab) 1958
sen lect educ/psych Berks coll of educ Reading from 1969

BREBNER Alan   MA 1970

BREBNER Barbara Anne   MA 1957
d of John T. B. civ serv MoT traffic off. and Elsie A.
McKay; b Cruden Ba y 2.9.35
teacher: Seaton p s Aber 1958–61, Albyn s for girls Aber
from 1968
m Aber 5.8.61 Gordon H. Turner MA 1958 *qv*

BREBNER Eileen   MA 1966
d of William B. and Isabella A. Troup; b Turriff 15.3.45
Ibadan Nigeria: teacher/head dept arts Our Lady of
Apostles' g s 1968–75, vice-prin Isabatudeen girls' g s
from 1975
m Dun 9.11.67 Bandele A. Olusanya MB ChB(St And) g p
s of Allen O. O. Ijebu-Ode Nigeria

BREBNER George Grieve   BSc 1970
            (conferred for long service of exceptional merit)
s of William G. B. haulage contr and Johan McLennan;
b Aber 30.4.11
elected fell. inst of sc tech 1963
Aberd: member of staff from 1938, res asst dept geol &
mineral. 1965–70, sen res asst 1970–76; retd
m Aber 7.6.33 Christina Main d of John M. Portlethen

BREBNER John Main Thomson   *MA 1957
s of John M. T. B. trawl skipper and Lydia Buchan
shop asst; b Aber 17.5.35
PhD(Exe) 1965 PhD(Adel) 1970
res psych RAF Farnborough 1957–59; Nuffield res asst
Exe 1959–62; MoD res fell. Dund 1962–64; lect psych
Dund 1964–69; lect, sen lect psych Adel Aust from 1969
m Rolleston 29.7.59 Mary J. Fawkes BSc 1958 *qv*

BREBNER Ronald Martin   MA 1961 Dip Ed 1962

BRECHIN Derek Masson   *MA 1960

BRECHIN Neil Stuart   *MA 1957

BREED William Godfrey   *BSc 1965
s of Arthur W. B. MA(Cantab) schoolmaster and
Annie D. L. Marchant LRAM mus; b Redruth 27.6.41
DPhil(Oxon) 1968
fell: Calif 1968–69, Birm 1969–73; lect Adel Aust from
1973
m Hexham 7.8.72 Esther Richardson SRN d of Herbert
R. Hexham

BREMNER Alan   MB ChB 1960
s of David R. B. MA(Glas) HMIS and Alison L. Kent
MA(Glas) teacher; b Glasg 8.3.36
DObstRCOG 1962 MRCGP 1964
hosp jun posts Wales, Aber, Inv 1961–62; g p: trainee
Peebles 1962–63; asst Kemnay 1963–64; lect Edin 1964–
68; ptnr Market Drayton from 1968
m Aber 16.1.61 Shirley Jones MB ChB 1960 *qv*

BREMNER Catherine Margaret   MA 1965
d of Gerald F. B. MA 1968 *qv*; b Aber 29.11.44
teacher Ayr 1967–71
m Aber 12.8.67 John Brown BSc 1967 *qv*

BREMNER David Malcolm *BSc(eng) 1966
s of James S. B. works man. and Florence Leslie; b Aber 12.5.44
contr site eng Perth 1966–69, plan. site eng Anglesey 1969–71, plan. eng head off. Wallington 1971–76; UAE: asst man. Sharjah and Dubai 1976–77, br man. Dubai from 1978
m Aber 27.7.68 Alice S. Gibson BSc 1968 *qv*

BREMNER Douglas *BSc 1960
s of David R. B. MA(Glas) HMIS and Alison L. Kent MA(Glas) teacher; b Glasg 18.9.38
jun whaling insp/biol S Georgia sub-Antarctica 1960–61; res asst W Norwood tech coll Lond 1961–62; asst warden, warden Malham Tarnfield centre Yorks 1962–69; prin Culzean country park Maybole 1969–75; chief ranger Nat Trust for Scotland from 1975
m Kirkby Malham 11.6.66 Vivien Caton secy d of Frank C. Otterburn

BREMNER Gerald Falconer MA 1968
(conferred for long service of exceptional merit)
s of James B. pharm and Margaret Shearer; b Old-meldrum 27.6.10
Aberd: admin off. 1927–57, asst finance off. 1957–75; retd
m Stornoway 3.3.43 Catherine I. Macdonald d of John M. Stornoway

BREMNER Harold Alan MB ChB 1964
s of Harold A. B. pharm and Sarah Craib; b Lond 23.2.40
DRCOG 1969
h o Scotland 1964–68; g p Nairn from 1968
m Inv 27.3.65 Alison M. Maclean MA 1961 *qv*

BREMNER Ian *BSc 1960 PhD 1963
s of George P. B. joiner and Alexina M. Thomson; b Aber 19.2.39
res fell. Stockholm 1963–64; biochem: Fisons Holmes Chapel 1964–66, Rowett inst Aber from 1967
m Elgin 22.9.62 Kathleen Stewart teacher d of John S. Elgin

BREMNER Joan Ann MB ChB 1960
d of Harold A. B. pharm and Sarah Craib; b Lond 25.1.37
DObstRCOG 1962 DA 1964
h o Aber, Perth 1960–62; sen h o Aber 1963–64; govt m o: Nandi Hills Kenya 1967–70, Blantyre Malawi from 1971
m Aber –.9.64 Alexander C. McLean tea factories supt s of Daniel P. M. McL. Peterhead

BREMNER Maureen Anne MB ChB 1969

BREMNER Williamina MA 1957
m Ross

BRENNAN Donald Macrae MA 1968

BRENNAN Patricia Ann MA 1967
d of Kevin P. B. cler asst and Annie Stuart bookkeeper; b Forres 15.5.46
Dip Sec St(Strath) 1968
secy/pa: Fochabers 1968–72, N'cle 1973; admin asst Fochabers 1973–74; secy/pa: Lond 1974–76, Aber 1976; marketing asst Aber 1976–77
m Forres 24.10.70 William A. Dalgarno MA 1969 *qv*

BREW Eric James Collie *BSc 1967 PhD 1971
s of Frank B. shoemaker, hosp theatre orderly and

Agnes D. Collie clerkess; b Aber 19.3.44
res fell. Lond 1970–73; teacher: Marr coll, Troon 1973–75, prin chem Inverurie acad from 1975
m Aber 21.11.70 Marjory G. Mitchell MA 1966 *qv*

BREWSTER William David MA 1968

BRIDGE Christopher John LLB 1968
s of Joseph E. B. OBE TD Lt-col and Jeanne M. Pryor; b Cambridge 30.4.48
indust rel off. Rolls Royce Glasg 1968–71; pers off., sen pers off. BBC Lond from 1971

BRIERLEY John Clegg LLB 1964
s of John B. B. CA and Ruth Clegg; b Oldham 2.8.42
CA art. clerk Lond 1964–67, tax/audit man. 1967–70; CA self-employed Oldham from 1970
m Oxon 30.9.67 Susan J. Plummer MA 1965 *qv*

BRIGGS Peter Kemp PhD 1961
BSc(agr)(Syd)

BRIGGS Valerie Ann MB ChB 1961

BRIGGS William BSc(for) 1964

BRIGHT Peter Duncan *BSc 1970
s of Alec C. B. CA
MIBiol 1978
VSO teacher Vanua Levu Fiji 1972–73; teacher biol 6th form coll Ashford Middx from 1974

BRINKMAN David *BSc(eng) 1970

BRISTOW Christopher David MSc 1969
s of Arthur W. S. B. comm trav and Julie E. I. Cartwright teacher; b Worthing 1.8.39
BSc(S'ton) 1961 Dip Ed(S'ton) 1962
teacher Hounslow Lond 1962–63; geol: NCB opencast exec S Wales 1964–65, De Beers Consol Mines Cape Province S Africa 1965–67, Rio Tinto Zinc Abdnsh 1969–71; teacher: Aber 1971–73, Acton Reynold s Shropshire from 1973
m Shrewsbury 28.7.71 Marie Blakemore MSc 1970 *qv*

BRISTOW Peter Harold William *MA 1966
s of Harold E. W. B. comp dir and Marjorie N. Harper secy; b Bristol 21.10.43
admin asst univ E Ang 1966–67; asst lect Hunterian Mus Glas 1967–68; tech writer and computer syst progr and des Lond 1969–71; asst secy St Thomas's hosp med s univ Lond 1971–76; asst secy(acad) OU from 1976
m St And 28.6.69 Gillian Howey MA(St And) d of John H. Seaham

BRITTAIN John Michael *MA 1963
s of Harold B. banker and Dorothy Johnson; b Lincoln 14.8.38
res asst univ of Illinois USA 1963–64; res fell. S'ton 1964–68; sen res fell. Bath 1968–74; sen lect Loughborough from 1975
m Freshford 26.12.69 Hilary W. James marketing exec d of Harold J. MB ChB(Brist) Cardiff

BROCKIE Colin Glynn Frederick BSc(eng) 1963
BD 1967
s of Donald A. B. mech eng and Vera R. Thompson shop superv; b Westcliff-on-Sea 17.7.42
ordained prob Mastrick par ch Aber 1967–68; min St Martin's par ch Edin from 1968
m Richmond Surrey 28.9.68 Barbara K. Gordon BSc 1968 *qv*

BROCKLEHURST Jennifer Mary   MB ChB 1963
d of Eric A. B. pharm and Henrietta S. Taylor pharm;
b Hull 23.7.39
h o Woodend hosp Aber, ARI 1963–64; res Woodend
hosp 1964–66; g p Aber, Rickmansworth from 1970
m Kirkella 31.8.63 Peter N. Bennett MB ChB 1963 *qv*

BROCKS Ashley Margaret   MB ChB 1968
d of Basil E. B. MB ChB 1941 *qv*; b Aber 14.5.44
DCH 1971 FRCS 1974
h o Aber 1968–69; sen h o: paediat surg Carshalton
1970–71; cas and surg St George's hosp Lond 1971–72;
regist gen surg Orpington from 1972

BRODIE Andrew Francis   *BSc(eng) 1957

BRODIE Donald Ian Fordyce   BSc(eng) 1961
s of Ian F. B. plasterer and Kathleen Macleod; b Nairn
25.9.36
jun eng Switchgear des Manc 1961–63; transmission
plan. SSEB Glasg 1963–69; transmission plan. eng Belf
1969–76; power stat man. Kilroot Carrickfergus from
1976
m Huntly 19.8.61 Christine MacBain teacher d of
Alexander MacB. Huntly

BRODIE Iain Keith   *MA 1966 Dip Ed 1968
s of Stanley F. B. signalman in Royal Can Corps
Signals—killed in action Italy July 1944 and Agnes W. S.
Keith lib asst; b Edin 4.6.44
MSc(Edin) 1971
teacher: (VSO) Vidya Bhawan s Udaipur Rajasthan
India 1966–67; Bearsden acad 1970–72; prin maths
Cumbernauld h s from 1972
m Aber 26.7.68 Gillian I. MacLean MA 1968 *qv*

BRODIE Isobel Francis   BSc 1959
d of William B. sales supt Shell Oil and Agnes G.
Thomson teacher; b Brechin 2.2.39
lab tech GEC Coventry 1959–61; teacher: Coventry
1961–64, Brampton Ont 1964–66, Montreal 1966–67
m Forfar 27.7.63 Peter R. Fisher BSc(Warw) elect. eng
s of Frederick R. F. Southport

BROMFIELD Ian Derek   *BSc 1969
s of Leslie E. B. radio & tv eng and Dorothy T. Nicol
secy; b Aber 24.1.47
elect. eng: Loughton 1970–72, Leicester from 1972

BROOKS Alexander   *MA 1958

BROOKS David Wilson   BSc(eng) 1966

BROOKS Elizabeth Ada   BSc 1966 Dip Ed 1967
d of Alexander R. B. joiner, shipwright and Wilhelmina
I. Irvine; b Aber 1.11.44
teacher Munda Solomon Is 1968–69
m Aber 31.7.67 Michael B. Self BSc(for) 1966 *qv*

BROOKS Elizabeth Catherine   BSc 1970
m Petrie

BROOKS Marjorie   MA 1968 Dip Ed 1969
d of James B. and Sarah J. Wilson MA 1926 *qv*; b Edin
13.12.47
Nassau Bahamas: teacher Engl 1969–70 and year co-
ordinator 1973–75; lect Engl in coll of the Bahamas from
1975, lit co-ordinator, humanities div from 1978
m Aber 14.9.70 Winston G. Jones arch s of Geoffrey J.
Nassau

BROOKS Simon Alan Lawrence   MA 1969 MB ChB 1974

BROOMFIELD Sinclair George   *MA 1965

BROOMFIELD William McIntyre   BSc(eng) 1959
s of William P. B. comp dir and Eliza M. McIntyre;
b Aber 1.6.35
grad app Morris-Commercial cars Birm 1959–61; Aber:
asst serv man. Town & County motor garage 1961–63,
serv man. 1963–71, man. dir 1971–73; chmn Aber Motors
from 1973; dir Campbell & Sellar, T and C serv stat,
Grampian serv stat, County Garage (Fraserburgh) from
1976
m Aber 7.10.61 Mary C. Reid MA 1957 *qv*

BROUGH Alexander Hardie   BSc 1968

BROWN Aileen   MA 1969
d of Thomas A. B. bus driver, insur ag and Violet
McLeod shop asst, clerk; b Aber 17.8.48
Dip Pers Man.(RGIT) 1970
UKAEA: exec off. 1970–73, higher exec off. 1973–76
m Leigh 1973 Gordon C. B. Bull BSc(Brad) s of William
G. B. Sheffield

BROWN Alastair Nisbet   MB ChB 1961
s of Thomas R. B. airship des, teacher tech subj and
Marjorie S. D. Fowlie bank teller; b Aber 22.8.36
DObstRCOG(Lond) 1963
h o: ARI, city hosp Aber 1961–62, Motherwell mat. hosp
1962–63; g p: Crieff 1963, Aber/asst m o Craiginches
prison Aber from 1963
m Aber 28.1.63 Joan M. Garden med res asst d of Albert
E. G. Aber

BROWN Alastair William Scott
see Scott-Brown

BROWN Allan Guildford   PhD 1965

BROWN Anne Gordon   MA 1968
d of James B. overseer/custodian and Myra J. Stephen;
b Fyvie 6.5.47
teacher biol/geog Saltus g s Bermuda
m Aber 27.12.67 Leonard G. Cruickshank BSc 1968 *qv*

BROWN Anne McLean Gray   MA 1969

BROWN Anthony Leslie   LLB 1963
s of John W. B. police supt and Edith M. Goodwin;
b Banff 14.9.41
Dip Indust Ad(Strath) 1964
admin asst Glas 1964–65; res off. man. serv unit G. K. N.
Steel Co Cardiff, Scunthorpe 1966–68; lab relations off.
Yorks TV Leeds 1968–70; indust relations man. BL
Leeds 1970–74; div pers man. The Weir Group Leeds
1974–75; dir indust relations and pers: Weir Pumps Glasg
1976–80, Weir Foundries Leeds from 1980
m Glasg 10.9.66 Sandra K. Graham photogr d of James
G. Glasg

BROWN Audrey Beckett   *MA 1968

BROWN Barclay   MB ChB 1968
s of Alfred B. prod. eng and Helen B. Murray; b
Forfar 18.2.43
DObstRCOG(Lond) 1973
cas off. ARI 1968; h o geriat med Woodend hosp Aber
1969; med off. RAF Eng, Germ, Scot. 1969–74; fam pract
Simcoe Ontario 1974–76; g p Aber from 1976
m Aber 28.9.68 Patricia W. Angus d of Edward M. A.
Canada

BROWN Caroline Elizabeth   *MA 1967
m Davidson

BROWN Catherine Anderson   MA 1969
d of Adam B. mech eng and Catherine D. T. Anderson secy; b Aber 27.11.22
cler off. Edin from 1972

BROWN Charles   *BSc 1963 PhD 1966
s of Charles B. civ serv and Margaret A. Gunn; b Aber 13.5.42
FCS(Lond) FCS(USA)
res assoc Wis 1966–67; res fell. Kent; lect: Dund 1968–69, univ Kent from 1969
m Aber 30.7.64 Margaret R. Downie BSc 1963 *qv*

BROWN David Lawrence Keddie   *MA 1969
s of David K. B. water filtration plant oper and Frances McElroy accts clerkess; b Kennoway 17.5.47
teacher Ayr from 1970
m Aber 2.10.70 Margaret H. Burnett MA 1971 teacher d of Robert C. B. Fraserburgh

BROWN David Raymond   BSc 1970
s of Raymond T. B. printer and Mary H. E. Albans shop asst; b Nottingham 2.10.48
computer syst analyst Liverpool from 1970
m Bury 29.8.70 Rona G. Howarth BSc(Hull) teacher d of Charles H. Bury

BROWN David William   *BSc 1966

BROWN Dorothy May   MA 1968
d of Robert J. B. master draper and Jean A. Smith cashier/bookkeeper; b Aber 2.5.46
MIPM(RGIT Aber)
hosp soc worker Bilbohall hosp Elgin 1969–73

BROWN Duncan John Moir   BSc 1961

BROWN Edward Massie   *MA 1967

BROWN Eileen   MA 1965

BROWN Eric Macpherson   MA 1967

BROWN Evelyn Kaye   BSc 1964
d of Neil G. B. wine and spirit merch and Evelyn Simpson publican; b Aber 20.8.43
asst exper off. Nature Conserv Bangor Wales 1965–66; asst, later ptnr fam bus. from 1966

BROWN Frank Howell   MB ChB 1957
s of Frank L. B. secy and gen man. friendly soc and Emily B. Shaw; b Romiley 26.2.33
DTM&H(Liv) 1962 MRCGP 1966
med off. col serv Falkland Is 1958–62; g p: Stoke-on-Trent 1962–68, Isle of Mull 1968–70, Oban from 1970
m Aber 17.5.58 Margaret M. Stewart MA 1954 *qv*

BROWN Gordon Macdonald   *BSc 1970
s of Robert G. B. BSc(Edin) civ eng and Eleanor C. Macdonald; b Nigg Easter Ross 16.11.46
Dip TCP(H-W) 1975 MRTPI 1976
asst res off. Scot. dev dept Edin 1971–74; geog/plan. asst Inv c c 1974–76; plan./geographer Highland reg c from 1976

BROWN Graham Leslie   *MA 1968

BROWN Iain Alexander   BSc(for) 1961
s of John A. B. MA(Glas) schoolmaster and Elizabeth Killin teacher; b Glasg 10.2.40
asst plantation man. Guthrie Corp Malaysia 1961–65; Plant Protection (ICI) overseas tech serv Fernhurst Surrey, Canada, Israel, Aust, Asia 1965–67; ICI (Japan) agr advis 1968–70, Plant Protection (ICI) head tech serv Asia 1970–72; ICI (Malaysia) spec duties Kuala Lumpur 1972–73; Twiga Chem Indust (ICI assoc) agr coordinator E Africa Nairobi from 1974
m Midhurst 25.3.67 Diana Edwards d of Harold E. Midhurst

BROWN Ian Ross   BSc(for) 1957 *1958
s of William M. B. insur ag and Mary Ross; b Aber 16.2.36
MS(NY state coll of For. at Syracuse) 1960 PhD(Edin) 1964
Aberd for. dept: asst lect 1964–67, lect from 1967
m Aber 1.2.63 Madeline Morrison MB ChB 1962 *qv*

BROWN Irene   MA 1963
m Martin

BROWN James David Kingsley   MB ChB 1966

BROWN Janet Kathleen Thomson   MA 1969
d of Ian E. B. bank man. and Janet F. Spowart; b Ballater 6.1.49
teacher geog: Montrose acad 1970–73, St Andrew's h s Kirkcaldy from 1973

BROWN Jean   *BSc 1969 Dip Ed 1970
d of Henry B. gardener/chauffeur and Rebecca MacLennan; b Gourock 8.10.47
Renfrewsh: educ psych 1971–73, sen from 1973

BROWN John   *BSc 1967
s of Charles B. civ serv and Margaret A. Gunn; b Aber 11.3.44
res phys Stevenston 1967–71; coll lect Ayr from 1971
m Aber 12.8.67 Catherine M. Bremner MA 1965 *qv*

BROWN John Boyter   *BSc 1970
s of John B. aeroplane mech (RAF) civ serv and Margaret Boyter; b Cellardyke 13.2.48
teacher maths/geol: George Watson's coll Edin 1971–72, Mhlume cent s Swaziland 1972–73, St Augustine's s Edin 1973, Strathallan s from 1973
m Anstruther 4.8.73 Jennie E. Smith secy d of James W. S. Cellardyke

BROWN John Peter   BSc(agr) 1967
s of Peter J. G. B. civ serv and Mary Ross; b Inv 15.3.45
Dip FM(NOSCA) 1968
asst insp dept agr Scot. Aber from 1968
m Aber 15.8.69 Irene Taylor teacher dom sc d of Alexander T. Auchnagatt

BROWN John Robert   MA 1970

BROWN John Stuart   *BSc 1967 PhD 1972
MSc(Imp Coll)

BROWN Josie   BSc 1970
d of Leslie A. B. stoker and Olive Key; b Holbrook 5.2.49
Dip Ed(Leic)
teacher maths: Churchill Somerset 1971–72, Stockbridge 1972–73; computer progr Worthy Down 1973–74, Crossgates Leeds from 1974
m Shipham 22.7.72 Christopher D. Jackson BA(Durh) town plan. s of Ronald E. J. BSc(Nott)

BROWN Joyce Mary   *MA 1969

BROWN Karl Aubrey Leslie   *MA 1956
  b Georgetown Guyana 9.6.24
Dip Ed(Edin) 1957
Guyana: teacher geog Queen's coll 1957–60, head s s
Essequibo coast s 1960–65; teacher gen stud. tech coll
Aber from 1965
m Georgetown –.12.57 Moira H. McRobb MA 1954 *qv*

BROWN Kenneth   *MA 1964
  s of Stanley W. B. eng machine oper and Ann P. I.
Pirie; b Forfar 28.7.41
Aberd: tut. stud. psych 1964–65; asst lect psych 1965–67,
lect 1968; lect psych Queen's univ Belf 1968–75, sen lect
from 1975
m Brechin 3.8.64 Erica M. Johnston teacher d of John J.
Lerwick

BROWN Kenneth Joseph   *BSc 1968
  s of Charles H. B. farm grieve and Dorothy Duncan
shop asst; b Torphins 20.12.45
PhD(Dund) 1971
lect maths H-W Edin 1970–72; res fell. Sus Brighton
1972–73; lect maths H-W from 1973
m Aber 6.10.71 Elizabeth T. Lobban BSc 1967 *qv*

BROWN Linda Jane   MB ChB 1964
  d of William C. B. DA HMIS and Jane R. Lothian
teacher art; b Loanhead 10.6.40
FRCP(Aust) 1977
h o Aber 1964–66; lect path. Aberd/hon sen regist ARI
1968–70; NZ: regist path. Cook hosp Gisborne 1970–71,
part time g p Tapanui 1971–74, lect path. univ of Otago
from 1975
m Rangiora NZ 30.5.70 John S. Holloway BSc 1969 *qv*

BROWN Margaret   MB ChB 1956
  d of James H. B. butcher and Christina H. McCall linen
fact. worker/dom serv; b East Wemyss 7.2.31
DObstRCOG 1959
h o: Stracathro hosp, City hosp Aber 1956–57, obst &
gyn: Perth RI, Br of Earn 1957–58; sen h o Leic gen h
1958–59; g p: Leith 1959–60, Musselburgh 1961–63,
Peterhead from 1963

BROWN Margaret Jean Vernon   *MA 1962
  d of Alister B. pharm/optic. and Jean V. Halliday PO
clerk/tel; b Fraserburgh 29.6.40
teacher Engl/hist Inverurie acad 1963–65; sixth form
mistress county h s for girls Romford 1965–67; part-
time tut. Engl S Havering coll adult educ 1968; part time
teacher Engl Maylands s s for girls Hornchurch from
1976
m Aber 22.7.64 Alexander J. Kemp BSc 1961 *qv*

BROWN Mary   BEd 1970

BROWN Matthew Stephen Ross   *MA 1961 Dip Ed 1962
  s of Matthew B. and Isabella S. Ross; b Aber 1.1.33
Ruthrieston s s: teacher Engl/hist/geog 1962–66; spec asst
lib and careers master 1966–70; prin asst lib 1970–71;
prin teacher Engl 1971–73; prin teacher Engl Arbroath
acad from 1973

BROWN Michael   LLB 1967
  s of Rowland B. comp dir and Mona Furness; b
Blackpool 20.5.46
law app Glasg 1967–69; solic: Hamilton 1969–71,
Ayr 1971–75; asst dir of admin Kyle and Carrick dist
council Ayr from 1975
m Lenzie 20.1.72 Elaine R. Emmerson home serv advis/
dom supt d of John R. E. Bishopbriggs

BROWN Pamela Alison   MA 1968
  d of Robert P. M. B. MB ChB 1935 *qv*; b Aber 13.4.45
teacher: Fernielea s Aber from 1969

BROWN Pamela Margaret   BSc 1970
  d of Robert S.B. BSc(Glas) teacher, lect and Ada M.
Preece SRN; b Glasg 18.7.49
teacher biol: Tranent from 1971
m Aber 28.7.72 John R. Hart BSc 1971 teacher s of
Rupert A. H. Leeds

BROWN Patricia Helen   MA 1968
  m Shea

BROWN Peter Alan   *BSc 1970
  s of Norman M. B. BSc(Edin) for. and Sheila Cunningham teacher; b Hawick 22.5.45
MSc(Nfd) 1973
grad stud. St John's Nfd 1970–73
m Cullen 1971 Margaret G. Wilson MB ChB 1971 d of
John F. W. Cullen

BROWN Richard Alexander John   MA 1966
**   *MEd 1968**

BROWN Robert Edward   *LLB 1969
  s of Albert E. B. customs & excise off. and Joan B.
Powton tracer; b Newcastle-on-Tyne 25.12.47
law app, asst Aber 1969–72; part time lect Scots Law
Aberd 1970–72; proc fiscal depute Dumbarton 1972–74;
solic Rutherglen from 1974; prosp Liberal candidate
Rutherglen from 1974

BROWN Robert Morris   MB ChB 1969
  s of John H. B. headmaster and Rachel M. Clark secy,
nursery teacher; b Grantham 26.10.43
DCM 1976
QEH Barbados: h o med obst/gyn 1969–70, sen h o obst/
gyn, regist paediat 1970–72; m o Chivenor UK and Malta
1972–75; clin asst St George's hosp Lond 1975–76;
sen m o RAF N Ireland from 1976
m Aber 1.2.69 Patricia A. Swanson BSc 1969 *qv*

BROWN Ronald Scott
  see Scott-Brown

BROWN Rosalind Ann   *MA 1969
  d of Frederick C. B. BSc(Lond) schoolmaster and
Edith M. Goodhall teacher; b Middlesbrough 2.10.46
grad secy course Aber coll of comm 1969–70; various
secy posts from 1970
m Aber 30.5.70 Alan D. M. B. Samuel MA 1971 res
sociol s of John M. S. Edin

BROWN Ruby   MA 1968
  d of Christopher W. B. crofter/road foreman and
Barbara C. Gray; b Shetland 27.12.46
teacher maths: Whitburn acad 1969–72, Dunbar g s
1972–75, Kirkwall g s from 1975

BROWN Ruth Mary   MA 1956
  d of George W. B. paper mill worker and Margaret A.
McPherson SRN; b Aber 22.9.35
teacher Aber: St Clement St p s 1958–59, Springhill p s
1960–66, remed reading centre (ch guid serv) 1966–72;
head Carden House s for maladjusted pupils from 1972

BROWN Samuel Grieve   *BSc 1969
  s of Henry D. P. B. naval arch. and Mary G. M.
Currie; b Glasg 21.11.46
exploration geol Mount Morgan Queensland 1969–70;
mine geol Tennant Creek NT Aust 1970–71; exploration/

mine geol King Is Tasmania from 1972
m Mackay Queensland 4.1.74 Denise O. Tunnah teacher
d of John D. T. North Mackay Queensland

BROWN Sheila Anne   *MA 1962
 b Aber 23.6.41
resid Manc
m Aber 1963 Neil A. Simpson MA 1962 *qv*

BROWN Thomas Ian Spowart   MB ChB 1968
 s of Ian E. B. bank man. and Janet S. D. F. Spowart;
b Dunfermline 22.11.44
DObstRCOG(Lond) 1970 FRCSE 1973
h o, sen h o Bridgend, Glamorgan, Hexham, Newcastle,
Musselburgh 1968–71; Edin: regist surg 1971–74, orthop
surg from 1974

BROWN William   *BSc 1965 PhD 1969

BROWN William Alan   *BSc(agr) 1970
 s of Stanley B. agr worker and Jane Thornber; b
Fulwood Preston 24.11.45
consult. off. (MMB) Lancs from 1970
m Penwortham Preston 7.10.72 Juliet C. Taylor sales
superv Marks & Spencer d of Michael T. Penwortham
Preston

BROWN William Barton   BSc(eng) 1961
 s of William J. B. master bldr and Ethel M. Rutherford; b Aber 6.5.39
MICE 1968
Glasg: asst eng Crouch & Hogg consult. eng 1961–64,
site eng and des Reema (Scotland) contrs 1964–67;
sect eng: W. A. Fairhurst & Ptnrs consult. Glasg Inner
Ring Road, Kingston Bridge 1967–69, Charing Cross
1969–72; resid eng WAF on N Ayrshire District gen hosp
Kilmarnock 1972–73; dep resid eng WAF on Renfrew
Motorway Stage II Glasg 1974–76, resid eng from 1976
m Aber 21.3.62 Helen C. S. Hepburn shorthand typist
d of John S. H. Aber

BROWN William Campbell   MA 1969
 s of Joseph B. bldg contr and Flora Campbell; b Banff
25.5.48
stud. lang Frankfurt 1974

BROWN William Peddie   *MA 1956 PhD 1959
 s of William B. BL 1926 *qv*; b Aber 7.12.34
Dip Ed(Edin) 1960 FBPsS 1973 FPsSoc of Ireland 1973
Bedford coll Lond: asst lect psych 1960–62, lect 1962–64;
lect psych: Aberd 1964–68, Queen's Univ Belf 1969–70;
reader psych Queen's Univ from 1970

BROWNE Bernard James Forbes   *MA 1968
 s of Bernard L. B. teacher and Margaret Watson
teacher; b Aber 8.7.43
teacher Engl Dun from 1969
m Dunfermline 24.7.71 Frances E. Reid d of David R.
MA (St And) Dunfermline

BROWNE Felicia Ibironke   MB ChB 1963 MD 1972
 m Akinsete

BROWNE Michael   MB ChB 1970

BROWNING Matthew Peter   *MA 1966
 s of James B. grocer and Rowina S. Taylor; b Paisley
8.6.43
Dip Ed(Edin) 1967
teacher geog: South Eastham s s Newham Lond, Prince
Rupert s (BFES) Wilhelmshaven & Rinteln W Ger;

teacher geog/Engl Königin Mathilde Mädchen Gym-
nasium 49 Herford W Ger

BROWNLEE Norman Robert   *MA 1969
 s of James B. and Margaret N. Young MA(Edin);
b Markinch 16.2.47
teacher maths Cults acad Aber from 1970
m Aber 26.3.75 Elizabeth H. F. Hay d of A. D. F. H
Kintore

BROWNLIE Kathleen Anne   MA 1969
 d of Thomas A. C. B. BSc(Edin) civ eng and Marjorie
Bennetts; b Dumfries 16.6.48
post grad course statist LSE 1970–71; res asst prod.
assessment (food) Unilever Bedford 1969–70; asst statist
hosp board Cambridge 1971–74; statist sect. hosp auth
Croydon 1974–75; sen statist NW Thames reg health
auth from 1975
m Edin 28.8.72 Paul V. Griew BSc(Birm) computer syst
analyst, eng s of David G. Lond

BRUCE Alexander   MB ChB 1961

BRUCE Alexander Cobban   *BSc 1968

BRUCE Alexander Ritchie   BSc 1963

BRUCE Annie (Anne)   MA 1959
 d of Robert B. master baker and Charlotte N. Suttar;
b Peterhead 2.4.38
invest. asst Standard Life Assur comp Edin 1959–60;
secy Lindsay Jamieson & Haldane CA Edin 1960–62;
dir Thomas Murison Peterhead from 1969
m Aber 3.1.62 Thomas Murison MA(Edin) comp man.
dir s of Thomas M. Peterhead

BRUCE Audrey Bevin   *MA 1969
 d of Robert B. and Ethel Sim; b Ellon 4.10.47
plan. asst: Banff c c Buckie 1970–71, Coatbridge t c from
1972
m Aber 14.10.71 John R. T. Breckenridge off. customs
and excise s of John W. B. OBE Woking

BRUCE Carol Isabel   MA 1958
 d of David T. B. fish merch/comp dir and Isabella
Massie; b Aber 3.9.37
secy course Lond 1958–59
m Aber 27.6.59 William J. A. Innes MA 1956 *qv*

BRUCE Carole   MA 1966
 m Preshaw

BRUCE Charles John   *BSc 1959

BRUCE Charlotte   *MA 1961
 d of Robert B. master baker and Charlotte N. Suttar;
b Peterhead 10.12.39
m Singapore 11.11.61 Allan M. Thomson MB ChB
1957 *qv*

BRUCE Christine Flora Helen   *MA 1969
 m Thayer

BRUCE Clive   *MA 1967
 s of Robert B. master baker and Charlotte N. Suttar;
b Peterhead 10.7.43
teacher Grange acad Kilmarnock 1968–72; prin soc stud.
Queen Victoria s Dunblane from 1972
m Aber 14.9.66 Irene Guthrie teacher d of Alexander G.
Peterhead

BRUCE David Woodland   *MA 1956

BRUCE Donald McBeath   *BSc 1966

BRUCE Donald McCaskill   *MA 1969

BRUCE Dorothy Elinor   MA 1963
d of Alexander B. trawl owner and Helen M. Knowles;
b Aber 12.9.41
stewardess: BEA 1963–65; Caledonian 1965–71
m Aber 6.11.71 Charles J. Bell bus. man (eng) s of
Frederick B. North Walsham

BRUCE Elizabeth Jane Rose   MA 1960

BRUCE George Ian Copland   *BSc(eng) 1970 MSc 1972
s of George M. B. farm. and Christina M. Copland;
b Aber 22.11.48
des and dev eng (electronic) Ferranti Edin from 1972

BRUCE George Kerr   BSc(for) 1964
s of George O. B. merch/electronics expert and Amy
M. Kerr; b Aber 18.2.41
reg for. off: asst conserv, acting sen asst conserv for
Malawi 1964–70; branch man. Tilhill Forestry (Scot.)
Ripon 1970–72, Gifford E. Lothian 1972–74; for. consult.
Umtali Rhodesia from 1975

BRUCE George Leonard   BSc(eng) 1958
s of George R. B. cycle ag/shopkeeper and Kathleen S.
Murray cashier; b Aber 4.10.36
AMInstF 1966 MIME 1969
res eng Babcock & Wilcox Renfrew 1958–66; des eng
Clarke Chapman Wolverhampton from 1966
m Birm 20.7.68 Jean F. Knight BSc(Lond) computer
progr d of Leonard F. C. K. Birmingham

BRUCE Gordon McKay   MB ChB 1960
s of William B. MB ChB 1925 qv; b Aber 30.8.33
DObstRCOG 1962
h o: ARI, mat. unit Raigmore hosp Inv 1961–62; g p
Dingwall from Dec 1962
m Inv 12.8.66 Rosemary M. Souter nurse d of James P. S.
Fort William

BRUCE Graeme Maclean   *MA 1958 BD 1961

BRUCE Henry Thomson   MB ChB 1967
s of Henry T. B. hotelier and Elizabeth Selbie hotelier;
b Insch 25.10.43
h o: Maryfield hosp Dun, ARI 1967–68; regist path.
WI Glasg 1968–72; g p Glasg from 1972
m Glasg 27.9.68 Ellen J. Bishop MB ChB(Glas) d of
William B. Clydebank

BRUCE Iain Charles   *BSc 1969
s of John B. MB ChB 1941 qv; b Aber 17.1.46
PhD(Calg) 1975

BRUCE Iain Gordon   *BSc 1965
s of Robert B. farm. and Elizabeth Shand; b Methlick
6.5.43
BSc(Lond)) 1973
teacher: Perthsh 1966–71, Adelaide Aust from 1971
m Aber 19.2.66 Elizabeth A. Whyte nurse d of Robert W.
Aber

BRUCE Irene Margaret Jessie   MA 1958
d of Robert J. B. farm. and Jessie M. I. Collie; b
Nairn 2.1.37
teacher: Kinloss 1959–61, Lochside s Dumfries 1961–63;
comp secy Annan 1967–75; teacher Hecklegirth p s Annan
from 1975

m Findhorn 17.8.61 Raymond C. MacDonald civ eng/
comp dir s of Donald A. MacD. Elgin

BRUCE James Masson   MSc 1968 PhD 1971

BRUCE Jane Isabel   MB ChB 1960
d of Alexander G. B. MA(Edin) teacher and Ellen
Manson MA(Edin) teacher; b Wick 4.1.37
h o Inv, Perth, Inv 1960–61; g p Inv from 1970
m Aber 8.9.61 Ian Macpherson MB ChB(Glas) med asst
bact s of John M. Diabaig

BRUCE John   MA 1963

BRUCE John Clark   *BSc(eng) 1963
s of John M. B. blacksmith and Catherine J. Clark secy;
b Tarves 2.4.41
MICE 1969
eng: James Williamson & Ptnrs (power stat des) Glasg
1963–65, Tarmac Civ Eng (road and bridge construct.)
Hamilton and Cumbernauld 1965–67; Scott Wilson
Kirkpatrick & Ptnrs bridge des Glasg 1967–68, tunnel
des Lond 1968–69, sen eng in des of cross-harbour tunnel
and gen civ eng works Hong Kong from 1969

BRUCE Joseph Alexander George   BSc 1957

BRUCE Kate Margaret   *MA 1967
d of Douglass B. CA and Kate Hurrell BSc(Durh)
teacher; b Gravesend 23.12.43
secy Butterworths Lond 1968–70; prod. controller
Macmillan Lond 1970–72, prod. man. Maddox Editorial
1972–74; sales promotion exec The Radiochemical
Centre Amersham 1974–76
m Gravesend 25.3.72 Anthony A. Mortimer BSc(Lond)
marketing plan. s of Alexander M. Rickmansworth

BRUCE Lawrence   MA 1967

BRUCE Margaret Anne Mary   MA 1968
d of Allan M. B. haulage contr and Margaret B.
Moffatt; b Inverurie 16.3.47
teacher: Perth 1969–71, Rheindahlen W Ger 1971–73,
asst prin guid S Queensferry from 1973
m Aber 5.4.77 Peter R. Henderson CA s of Thomas W. H.
Edin

BRUCE Michael George   *MA 1966

BRUCE Michael Stewart Rae   MA 1959 cLLB 1961
s of Alexander E. B. MA 1921 qv; b Aber 26.7.38
law app: L. McKinnon & Son advoc Aber 1959–61,
Brodie Cuthbertson & Watson Edin 1961–62; member of
fac of advoc 1963
m Edin 27.12.63 Alison M. M. Stewart d of Alastair
M. S. Edin

BRUCE Patricia Helen   MA 1968
d of George R. B. motor/cycle ag and Kathleen
Murray secy; b Aber 13.1.47
teacher geog Kilmarnock acad 1969–72
m Aber 19.7.69 Robert G. Thomson tv film cameraman
s of William T. Edin

BRUCE Peter   BSc(eng) 1960 *1961
s of George B. fisherman and Jane Bruce; b Buckie
5.6.38
Edin: dev eng Ferranti 1960–68, tech writer ISI 1969–70,
dir Advanced Des Dev 1970–74, man. dir Bruce Anchor
from 1972

BRUCE Robert Gordon   *BSc(agr) 1963
s of Robert B. policeman and Isabella M. Gordon

hotelier; b Aber 19.1.41
PhD (Cantab) 1967
Glasg: asst lect 1966–70, lect zoology from 1970
m Camb 1963 Moira M. Christie MA 1960 *qv*

BRUCE Rosaleen Anne   BSc 1966
  m Norman D. Deans BSc 1966 *qv*

BRUCE Sheila   MA 1963

BRUCE William Craik   MA 1958 BD 1961
  s of William B. crofter and Elizabeth M. Craik; b
Dun 9.9.29
C of S min: asst St Giles Elgin 1961–62, min: St Andrews
ch Lochgelly 1962–68, Dalziel par ch Motherwell from
1968
m Forfar 20.9.58 Euphemia T. Sturrock secy d of William
S. Forfar

BRUNNEN Rosemary Ann   *MA 1968
  d of Peter L. B. MB ChB 1939 *qv* and Margaret C. T.
Brown MA 1942 *qv*; b Aber 1.11.46
MA(Nott) 1969
dem Nott 1969–71; Lond: soc worker 1972–76, sen clin
psych Charing Cross hosp/Gt Ormond St hosp 1976–78;
lect handicapped in commun OU Milton Keynes from
1978
m (1) Jones
  (2) Lond –.5.78 Derek M. Brechin MA 1960 *qv*

BRUNTON Jennifer Margaret   *MA 1970
  m Taylor

BRYANT Carl Leonard   BSc(for) 1957 MSc 1971
  s of Leonard B. steelworker and Marjorie A. Dixey;
b Coventry 12.10.35
Tanzania: asst conserv for. 1959–64, for. man. off.
hardwoods Dar-es-Salaam 1964–66, res off. hardwoods
Lushoto 1966–68; sen asst reg off. SWOAC Castle
Douglas from 1968
m Aber 23.7.62 Audrey M. Noble MA 1957 *qv*

BRYANT Jeremy Joseph   BSc(eng) 1964

BRYCE Andrew Bonner   BSc(eng) 1958 *1959
  s of Donald P. B. soldier, admin and Patricia I. Bonner
d of Thomas I. B. MA 1889; *qv*(I, II); b Yorks 6.6.36
MIEE CEng
grad app Rugby 1959–61; asst elect. eng HMTS *Alert*
1961–62; elect. eng RRS *Discovery* 1962–64; professional
eng Rolls Royce & Assoc at HMS *Vulcan* Thurso from
1964
m Lerwick 19.4.65 Elizabeth M. Inkster MA 1963 *qv*

BRYCE Graeme Findlay   *BSc 1960
  s of William C. B. master plumber and Veda M. H.
Findlay; b Aber 1.5.38
PhD(Lond) 1963
USA: res fell. univ of Indiana 1963–65, Yale 1965–69;
asst member Roche Inst of Molec Biol 1969–74; sen
scient Hoffmann–La Roche 1974–76, res fell. from 1976
m Connecticut 13.4.67 Mary A. Addelson BA(Hofstra)
secy d of Arthur E. A. New York

BRYCE Jennifer Anne   MA 1967
  d of George C. B. sports dealer and Annie M. Smith
civ serv, pharm; b Edin 23.6.45
Dip Soc Work(Glas) 1968
soc worker Aber 1968–71; almoner Durban hosp S Af,
dept ch welfare, Bantu children 1971–73; hosp
soc worker Mudgee NSW Aust from 1975
m Edin 5.7.69 David J. C. Barclay MB ChB 1969 *qv*

BRYCE Judith Helen   *MA 1970 PhD 1977

BRYDON Brenda Valerie   *BSc 1965 PhD 1969
  m Imlach

BRYER Kenneth Robert   *BSc 1967
  s of Robert G. B. BA(OU) res and des eng and Joan
Wallbank; b Hillingdon 18.10.43
CPA
tech asst chartered patent ag Lond 1967–70; chartered
patent ag Plymouth from 1970
m Aber 18.3.67 Patricia Nicholls d of Frank N. Aber

BUCHALA Antony Joseph   *BSc 1968 PhD 1971
  s of Stefan J. B. teacher, prof photogr and Anne Dick
nurse; b Aber 31.10.46
ARIC 1971
res fell. (Royal Society) Inst plant biol univ of Fribourg
Switzerland 1971–73; doctoral asst inst Cardiovascular
Res Fribourg from 1973

BUCHAN Alan Fraser   BSc(agr) 1968

BUCHAN Alexander   *BSc 1961 PhD 1965
  s of Robert B. bldr and Mary K. McDonald civ serv;
b Aber 4.9.39
res associate St Thomas hosp Lond 1964–67; lect Birm
from 1967
m Aber 12.8.65 Jennifer A. Cutt BSc 1962 *qv*

BUCHAN Alexander   MA 1970
  s of Alexander B. fisherman and Mary Crawford;
b Fraserburgh 1.4.35
BD(Edin) 1974
C of S min Stonefield and Burleigh with Anderson ch
Blantyre from 1974
m Paisley 1.5.67 Isabel C. Black BSc(Strath) d of David
C. B. Glasg

BUCHAN Alexander Greig   MA 1960 LLB 1962
  s of Charles B. fishselling man. and Mabel Greig;
b Fraserburgh 15.12.38
Aber: law app 1960–63, law asst 1963–65, ptnr J. & G.
Collie advoc from 1966
m Aber 11.7.62 Marie Marioni teacher d of Giulo A. M.
Fraserburgh

BUCHAN Alexander James   MB ChB 1959
  s of Alexander B. marine eng and Isabella Buchan;
b Fraserburgh 6.9.34
DObstRCOG 1964
ed off. RAMC Singapore, Maralinga Aust, Hong Kong
1960–63; h o mat. hosp Aber 1963; g p: Dagenham,
Airdrie 1963–64, Hobart Tasmania from 1964
m Aber 4.4.64 Aileen S. Dewar nurs sister d of Andrew D.
Aber

BUCHAN Alexander Reid   *BSc(eng) 1956
  s of Alexander R. B. fisherman and Davina C. Cruickshank; b Peterhead 6.9.33
MICE AMIHE CEng
asst BR Glasg 1956–58; nat serv (commissioned in Royal
Eng) RMCS Shrivenham 1958–60; chief asst eng capital
works Dumfries 1960–64; asst road eng Livingston dev
corp. 1964–65; lect: Napier coll of sc and tech Edin
1965–67, struct eng Strath from 1967
m Peterhead 22.12.56 Myra Booth secy d of George B.
Peterhead

BUCHAN Alexander Strachan   BSc(eng) 1969
  s of George W. B. shipwright and Mary T. Ironside;
b Fraserburgh 22.6.48
asst civ eng: Invergordon 1969–71, Lond from 1971

m Lochwinnoch 26.9.70 Sharon A. Smith secy d of Robert B. S. Lochwinnoch

BUCHAN Ann   MA 1962
 d of Arthur B. factory man. and Elsie R. Duncan; b Ellon 29.11.41
teacher: Engl/hist Peterhead acad 1963–66, p s Lagos 1967–69, p s Peterhead 1973–74, remed teacher
m Aber 3.4.64 Robert S. S. Summers asst buyer s of Gilbert S. Fraserburgh

BUCHAN Barbara Bruce   MA 1969
 m Thomas

BUCHAN Charles Cummin   BSc 1967
 s of Charles B. ship's capt, fisherman etc and Jeannie McGee; b Peterhead 13.10.45
G Inst P 1975
teacher Fraserburgh acad: maths/sc 1968–73, asst prin phys from 1973
m Fraserburgh 17.8.68 Georgina S. Buchan MA 1966 *qv*

BUCHAN Christina Sutherland   MA 1966

BUCHAN David Duncan   *MA 1960 PhD 1965
 s of Joseph D. B. civ serv/marine scient and Elsie A. Robb; b Aber 7.1.39
Gordon Bottomley fell. Aberd 1960–61, 1963–64; instr Engl univ Victoria Canada 1961–63, 1964–65; asst prof Engl Mass USA 1965–68; lect Engl stud. Stir 1968–71, sen lect from 1971
m Aber 2.9.65 Moyra J. Nisbet MA 1963 *qv*

BUCHAN Elizabeth Jean   BSc 1961
 d of James B. motor mech and Jessie A. A. Milne; b Huntly 19.12.35
res asst Lond 1961–64; teacher Aber from 1975
m Aber 21.12.61 John R. Sargent PhD 1961 *qv*

BUCHAN Georgina Stephen   MA 1966
 d of Gilbert M. B. fisherman and Christian Stephen; b Cairnbulg 10.4.44
teacher Fraserburgh acad: maths/sc 1967–69, r e 1971–72, prin guid from 1972
m Fraserburgh 17.8.68 Charles C. Buchan BSc 1967 *qv*

BUCHAN Jennifer Rosemary   MB ChB 1969
 d of Campbell B. MB ChB(Edin) surg and Marjorie Clark nurse; b Edin 27.9.45
DCH 1971
h o Aber, Inv 1969–70; sen h o Lond, Glasg 1970–72; g p Glasg 1972–73; Ayrsh: clin m o 1974–75, fam plan. off. from 1975
m Edin 28.4.73 John Cleland MB ChB(Glas) g p s of Gavin C. MB ChB(Edin) Mauchline

BUCHAN Joan Crawford   BSc 1970
 b Fraserburgh 12.11.48
clerkess NSHEB 1971–73
m Fraserburgh 14.8.71 Alan Rafferty bricklayer

BUCHAN John   MA 1968
 s of Alexander B. master butcher and Barbara S. Duthie teacher; b Fraserburgh 22.11.46
Dip Pers Man.(RGIT Aber) 1969
man. father's bus. Fraserburgh 1969–70; labour off. MoD Bishopton 1970–73; pers off. Ethicon Edin from 1973
m Aber 5.4.72 Ruth C. McInnes Dip Sp and Drama (Glas) drama teacher d of William D. McI. LLB(Glas) Aber

BUCHAN Kathleen Ina MacNicol   BSc 1964
                                                                    MB ChB 1967
 d of William A. E. B. teacher and Janet W. MacNicol teacher; b Ballater 21.2.43
DPM(Scot. conjoint) 1970 MRCPsych 1973
h o ARI/Woodend hosp Aber 1967–68; sen h o psychiat Ross Clinic Aber 1968–69; regist psychiat Cornhill and assoc hosps Aber 1969–73; locum regist RACH 1974–75; med asst psychiat Malvern Worcs from 1975
m (1) 1964
  (2) 1975 Richard E. Mackie BA(Cantab) psychotherap, writer s of Frederick P. M. MBBs(Brist) Mark Somerset

BUCHAN Leonard   BSc 1957

BUCHAN Mabel   MA 1969
 d of Charles B. fish salesman and Mabel Greig; b St Combs 11.1.48
teacher Peterhead 1970–74
m Rathen 6.7.71 Karl J. T. Revel BEd 1970 *qv*

BUCHAN Margaret Elizabeth   *BSc 1966
 d of William B. farm. and Margaret J. Shearer; b Turriff 12.11.44
teacher Queen Margaret acad Ayr 1967–71
m Aber 20.7.67 James A. Goodlad MA 1965 *qv*

BUCHAN Maynard Cowe   BSc 1968
 s of Samuel M. B. stat off. HM coastguard and Margaret J. Bowie; b Rattray Head 10.8.47
teacher maths Peterhead acad from 1969
m Peterhead 14.4.73 Lilian F. Melford MA 1969 *qv*

BUCHAN Muriel   MA 1958
 d of Charles M. B. installation insp and Alice W. Tocher; b Aber 4.5.38
teacher Aber 1959–66
m Aber 1.7.64 John W. Sim MB ChB 1964 *qv*

BUCHAN Neil   BSc(eng) 1961
 s of Alexander J. B. off. man. and Mabel Watson; b Aber 2.4.39
grad eng Crouch & Hogg consult. civ eng Glasg 1961–62; asst eng Glasg corp 1962–65; site eng/ag George Wimpey civ eng contr 1965–70; chief eng Scot. Myton civ eng/bldg contr 1971–72; sen eng, asst prin eng roads Strathclyde reg c from 1972
m Aber 26.7.62 Lesley H. Tough teacher d of Robert J. S. T. Knockando

BUCHAN Nigel Gordon   MB ChB 1966
 s of John B. trawl skipper and Jeannie Gray; b Aber 26.6.43
FRCSE 1972
h o Aber 1966–67; sen h o: Lincoln 1967–68, rotating surg Leeds 1968–70; regist surg Hull 1970–71; regist plastic surg Lond 1972–75
m Leeds 12.7.69 Verona Clemens nurse Thurscoe

BUCHAN Patricia Ann Bruce   MA 1960
 m Noble

BUCHAN Peter   MA 1967

BUCHAN Robert   *BSc 1959 PhD 1972

BUCHAN Robert   MB ChB 1960 MD 1965
 s of Robert A. B. b Peterculter 24.6.36
FRCSE 1968
h o ARI 1960–61; res fell. Aberd 1961–63; regist surg ARI 1966–69; sen regist Cardiff 1969–71; lect surg Edin 1971–74; consult. surg Kirkcaldy from 1974

BUCHAN Ronald MacDonald   MB ChB 1959
BDS

BUCHAN Sandra   MA 1966
d of Alexander B. journalist and Jane E. Ritchie; b
Peterhead 14.12.44
teacher Peterhead North s 1967–69; stud. Moray House
dip. in educ of the deaf 1969–70; nurs teacher Aber s for
deaf 1970–73; peripatetic teacher of deaf Aber county
from 1973

BUCHAN Sinclair   MA 1958 *BSc 1961
s of John M. B. B. JP man. fish-selling and ship
chandler's bus. and Robina Sinclair; b Fraserburgh
14.4.36
FRGS 1970
UCNW Menai Bridge: asst hydrographer 1961–64, res
asst 1964–68, temp lect 1968–69, lect phys oceanography
from 1969
m Garnfadryn nr Pwllheli 12.4.69 Sarah C. Hughes nurs
sister d of Griffiths J. H. Garnfadryn

BUCHAN William Arthur   *BSc(eng) 1961

BUCHANAN Jane Ann Macintosh   *MA 1969
d of Samuel M. B. insur insp and Margaret MacBean;
b Glasg 3.6.47
Dip Lib(Lond) 1971 ALA 1972
asst Sus lib Brighton 1969–70; audio visual aids lib
Newcastle-u-Tyne poly from 1971
m Newcastle-u-Tyne 28.7.73 Nigel M. G. W. Davey BSc
(Hull) res chem, materials tech s of Neville W. D. Maidstone

BUCHANAN Maria Theresa   MB ChB 1969
m Stoker

BUCHANAN William Andrew Petrie   MA 1970

BUCHANAN-SMITH Jock Gordon   BSc(agr) 1962
s of Rt Hon Lord Balerno MA 1922 qv; b Edin 9.3.40
BS(Iowa state univ USA) 1963 MS(Texas tech coll USA)
1965 PhD(Oklahoma state univ USA) 1969
USA: res asst: Lubbock Texas 1963–65, Stillwater Okla
1965–69; asst prof Guelph Ont Canada 1969–76, assoc
prof from 1976
m Dallas Texas 26.8.64 Virginia L. Maxson d of John
S. M. Dallas

BUCHMANN Karoly Francis Joseph   MB ChB 1969
s of Othar L. K. B. BSc(Budapest) indust pharm and
Erzsebet S. Varga secy; b Budapest 17.4.43
DA 1972 FFARCS 1975 DObstRCOG 1975
h o, trainee anaest ARI 1969–75; trainee anaest Stobhill
hosp Glasg 1975; consult anaest Tygerberg Cape Town
from 1975
m Glasg 14.9.73 Elizabeth R. Ewing SRN d of Walter E.
Glasg

BUCHMANN Othmar Laszlo Karoly Attila   *BSc 1967

BUCK Francis Norman   *BSc 1968
s of Alfred G. B. comp chmn textile trade and Cicely
Jackson; b Carlisle 16.4.45
prod. man. British Gypsum 1971–75, asst works man.
from 1976
m Carlisle 15.6.74 Janice Marshallsay d of James M.
Whitley Bay

BUCKLE Donald James   BSc(for) 1960
s of Hector D. B. comp secy and Doris M. Clark;
b Southampton 4.2.38

surv asst for. co New Forest 1960–61; for. man.:
Yattendon Estate Berks 1961–64, English Woodlands
Kent, Sussex, Surrey from 1964
m Aber 15.7.60 Verity M. Hutchison teacher d of Gordon
H. MB ChB 1930 qv

BUCKLE Ernest Roy   *PhD 1958
s of Ernest H. B. police constable, civ serv and Florence
M. Sinclair pianist; b Lond 23.9.26
ARIC 1955 FRIC 1961 CChem 1975 FIM 1976 CEng
1978
asst chem Aberd 1957–58; sen res asst Imp Coll Lond
1958–68; Sheff: lect metall 1968–75, sen lect 1975–77,
reader from 1977
m Sundridge 4.2.56 Shirley A. Brown bank clerk d of
John B. Sundridge

BUCKLEY Graham Peter   BSc(for) 1968
s of Frederick W. B. headmaster and Eileen Street
teacher; b Oswestry 11.4.47
MSc(Wales) 1970
res asst Leeds univ 1970–73; lect landscape/horticulture/
ecology Wye coll Lond from 1973

BUDDHOO Jayraz   BSc 1968

BUDGE Margaret   *BSc 1970
m Youngson

BUDGE Rosemary Kathleen   *MA 1964
d of James B. farm. and Ada M. Halcrow; b Bigton
Shetland 25.10.42
exec off. W. Pacific high commission Brit Solomon Is
1970–72; commissary superv Uniroyal Plantations
Liberia W. Af 1973–75; teacher Swaziland 1975–78
m Bigton 22.7.64 Ian W. Skea MSc(R'dg) anim prod. off.
ODM s of James S. Rendall Orkney

BUICK Ronald Nicoll   *BSc 1970 PhD 1974
s of Douglas S. B. consult. eng and Isobel J. Nicoll
teacher; b Dun 10.3.48
res biochem: Wis Madison USA 1973–76; inst of cancer
res Toronto from 1976
m Aber 3.7.70 Susan M. Wright BSc 1970

BUIE Christine Margaret   MA 1965
m Grant

BULLOUGH Frances Stewart   PhD 1967
d of Arthur S. B. MB ChB (Manc) consult. surg and
Margaret B. Stewart MA(Glas) foreign correspondent;
b Bellshill 10.12.41
BSc(Leeds) 1963 Dip Ed(Oxon) 1964
Brit Council Lond 1967–68; teacher Napier tech coll
Edin 1968–71
m Timperley 18.12.70 Peter J. Lindsay tech off. s of
David W. L. MB ChB(Glas) Edin

**BULMER Susan Rosalind   BMedBiol 1969
                                    MB ChB 1972**
d of Gerald B. BA(Cantab) rector Liv poly from 1970,
dir RGIT Aber 1965–70 and Greta L. Parkes BA(Cantab)
plant path.; b Herne Bay 23.12.47
h o RACH, Southampton gen hosp 1972–73; sen h o
clin path. United Sheffield hosp from 1973

BUNTING John Allen   *BSc 1969
s of Thomas A. B. RAF and Mary J. Massie teacher;
b Aber 12.11.46
geol with geol surv of W Aust from 1969
m Aber 1.9.69 Ann G. Sinclair MA 1968 qv

BUNTING Ronald Strachan   *BSc 1957
s of George B.; b Aber 18.10.34
jun geol, div explor supt several oil companies Calgary
Alberta from 1957
m Aber 29.6.57 Maureen A. W. Leslie

BURGESS Alexander Sharp   *MA 1970 Dip Ed 1971
s of John B. and Elizabeth J. Donaldson; b Elgin
29.4.48
teacher hist/mod stud: Elgin acad 1971–75, Arbroath
acad from 1975

BURGESS Anna Margaret   *MA 1956
d of Douglas B. BBC eng i/c and Evelyn Mackie; b
Aber 26.11.34
teacher Engl Perth acad 1957–63; prin Engl Dover g s
for girls 1963–65; lect Engl/commun New coll Durh
from 1970
m Aber 10.8.63 Brian A. S. Primmer BMus(Cantab) lect
mus Durh s of Harold P. Southsea

BURGESS Charles Smith   MB ChB 1964
s of Alexander G. B. farm. and Agnes Singer; b
Newmachar 28.1.41
MRCGP 1975
h o: ARI, city hosp, mat. hosp Aber 1964–65; g p Aber
1966–69, Ellon from 1969
m Aber 8.5.65 Doris M. Riddell teacher dom sc d of
James R. Whiterashes

BURGESS John Moncrieff   BSc(agr) 1958
s of George B. crofter and Catherine Moncrieff; b
Scousburgh 8.9.36
nat serv UK, Germany 1959–61; lect NOSCA Aber
1961–64; DAFS: asst lands off., lands off. Shetland,
Edin 1964–75; dir of res and dev Shetland Is Lerwick
from 1975
m Aber 31.7.65 Patricia M. Smith teacher d of Robert
W. S. Cults

BURGESS William Steven   *BSc 1962
s of William S. B. baker and Joey West; b Scalloway
Shetland 22.7.40
teacher chem: Perth h s 1963–66, spec asst 1966–72;
prin chem Galashiels acad from 1972
m Perth 29.9.63 Carmelita E. Brady secy, nurse d of
Joseph P. E. B. Aber

BURGHER George Stevenson   BSc(agr) 1960
b Ness, Westray 7.12.37
Orkney: teacher 1961–69, NFU area secy from 1969
m 10.7.63 Winifred S. Urquhart

BURN John Campbell   LLB 1966

BURN-MURDOCH Nigel Alexander Spencer
**   *BSc 1966**

BURN-MURDOCH Noel Gray   *BSc(for) 1965

BURNETT Alan Robertson   *BSc 1964 PhD 1968
s of Alexander B. bus prop. and Jeannie B. Cruden;
b Mintlaw 6.10.42
dem org chem Liv 1967–69; teacher chem/housemaster
Stirling h s 1970–73, prin chem Denny h s from 1973
m Larbert 27.2.72 Helen I. Mitchell BSc(Glas) teacher
d of George E. M. Larbert

BURNETT Alexander Walker   MA 1966
s of Alexander C. B. insp of works (col serv) and
Jessie F. Walker clerkess; b Aber 27.6.27
ALA 1970
trainee lib nat lending lib Boston Spa and Durham lib

1966–67; stud lib N'cle poly 1968–69; sc lib St And from
1969
m Aber 14.8.68 Marjory S. Middleton MA 1967 *qv*

BURNETT Alistair George Murray   LLB 1970
s of George M. B. BSc 1943 *qv* and Anne E. Bow MA
1946 *qv*; b Birmingham 18.5.50
NP 1972 WS 1974
Edin: law app Shepherd & Wedderburn 1970–72; asst
Baillie & Gifford WS from 1972
m Edin 10.6.72 Jennifer Edwards occup therap

BURNETT Frances Elizabeth   MA 1963

BURNETT Frances Helen   MA 1960
d of William J. B. mech eng and Helen J. Benzie; b Insch
1.10.39
teacher Engl girls' s s Chesterfield from 1973 after various
part-time posts
m Aber 4.7.61 Robert D. Porter BSc(eng) 1960 *qv*

BURNETT Gordon Bernard   MB ChB 1964 MD 1976
s of Joseph S. F. B. insur ag and Georgina C. Main
bookkeeper; b Aber 26.7.37
DPM(Edin) 1968 MRCPsych(Lond) 1972
h o Aber hosp 1964–65; regist royal Edin hosp 1965–68,
sen regist 1968–69; res fell. psychiat Edin 1969–72; asst
prof psychiat Baylor coll med Houston Texas; assoc
prof psychiat univ of N Carolina Chapel Hill from 1976
m Aber 20. 3.65 Wendy E. W. Bell MA 1963 *qv*

BURNETT Ian Anthony Julian   BSc(agr) 1969

BURNETT Irene Mary   BSc 1969
d of Robert B. joint prop. drapery store and Monica
M. Vincent cashier; b Nairn 3.3.46
Dip Comput Sc(Glas) 1970
analyst, progr Lucas Birm 1970–74
m Birm 6.4.74 Philip G. Grant maintenance plumber
Alberta govt tel s of Joseph G. Staffs

BURNETT James Brodie Crawford   MB ChB 1961
s of James W. M. B. wine & spirit merch and Elizabeth
S. McIntosh millinery/man. buyer; b Victoria BC Canada
3.3.31
DObstRCOG 1963 DA 1963
h o: Dumfries, Aber 1961–63; sen h o: Aber, Dumfries
1963–65; regist obst/gyn Aber 1965–67; g p Kirkwall
1967–68, med advis John Wyth & Son, Taplow 1968–70;
g p Caversham from 1970
m Aber 21.11.64 Josephine F. Stewart SRN nursing
sister d of William S. Ballater

BURNETT Janet Christine   MA 1967
d of Joseph B. BOAC radio oper, tv eng and Isabella B.
Arnott secy; b Aber 20.9.46
teacher: Lossiemouth h s 1968–69, Fr/Ger 1969–72
m Elgin 17.7.68 Charles M. Grant NDA farm. s of Ian
H. G. Lochhills Elgin

BURNETT Lorna Mary   MA 1964
d of David J. B. police sgt and Catherine Smith; b Aber
3.1.43
teacher: Inv 1965–69, Aber 1969–71, Brechin 1973–78,
Inv from 1978, acting asst head Holm s
m Aber 29.6.65 Nichol Thomson tech teacher

BURNETT Madeleine Anne   MA 1960
d of Joseph B. tv eng and Isabella B. Arnott secy;
b Lockerbie 26.8.40
teacher p s: h s for girls Aber 1961–64, Valley p s
Kirkcaldy 1964–66, Mauricewood p s Penicuik 1974–76,

asst head from 1976
m Aber 12.8.64 James R. Wight MA 1960 *qv*

BURNETT Panton Ironside   MA 1957

BURNETT Patricia Anne   BSc 1969
d of George M. B. BSc 1943 *qv* and Anne E. Bow MA 1946 *qv*; b Aber 30.8.47
edit. asst journal clin and exper immunol Edin 1970–71; secy asst vice-dean fac sc Edin 1971–73; med secy univ St John's Newfoundland 1973–75
m Aber 29.9.73 Richard G. Cawthorn BSc(Durh) sen lect geol univ Witwatersrand Johannesburg s of Thomas H. C. Bingley

BURNETT Sandra Mary Margaret   MA 1960

BURNETT William John   MA 1961
s of John W. B. farm. and Lizzie I. Panton; b Fraserburgh 13.3.40
teacher Aber from 1962
m Aber 7.8.67 Katharine J. M. West MA 1964 *qv*

BURNHAM Bruce   *MA 1965
s of Thomas C. B. headmaster and Margaret Ronald; b Hartlepool 27.3.43
BLitt(Oxon) 1971
teacher: Harrogate g s 1967–71; head hist Norwich h s from 1971
m Harrogate 19.12.70 Dorothy J. Hudson BA(Leeds) teacher d of Charles H. Leeds

BURNS Alasdair Michael   BSc 1969
s of Alexander S. B. art teacher and Kathleen McLean art teacher; b Aber 9.5.46
teacher: maths/phys/chem Peterhead acad 1969–70, phys/geol/sc Kincorth acad from 1971
m Milngavie 2.7.69 Sheila M. Garvie BSc 1970 *qv*

BURNS Alexander Julius   MA 1967
s of William A. B. MRCVS vet off. and Ilse Wohl; b Mpwapwa Tanganyika 8.7.45
Dip PE(Leeds) 1968 Cert Indust Man. (Hull coll of comm) 1975
teacher Span/Engl/Fr/PE Stockport s Cheshire 1968–70; Palma Mallorca: frogman ASA 1970–71; frogman/ptnr OSAN 1971–74; teacher Span Dartmouth h s, Birm from 1976
m Beverley 18.12.71 Ruth M. Whitfield BEd(Leeds) teacher d of Alfred H. W. Hull

BURNS James   MB ChB 1956

BURNS Marilyn Raynor   MA 1969
m Mackenzie

BURNS Philip   *BSc 1969
s of Denis B. boilermaker and Mary Stewart; b Glasg 24.1.31
Glasg: teacher biol 1970–72, prin biol from 1972

BURNS Robert Bruce   *MA 1962 *MEd 1965
s of Robert B. B. trans clerk and Mabel Cleminson; b Greenwich 17.6.39
PhD(Manc) 1973 ABPsS
teacher geog St Peter's s s Aber 1963–65; Manc: lect educ Didsbury coll of educ 1965–67, sen lect 1967–71, prin lect Mather coll 1972–74, lect educ Brad univ from 1974
m Manchester 17.12.66 Patricia M. Jackson d of Albert J. Levenshulme Manc

BURNS Robert John   *MA 1969

BURNS Rosalind Anne   *MA 1965
d of Arnold M. B. MA 1931 *qv* and Winifred Neilson MA 1930 *qv*; b Aber 20.7.43
teacher Kingston Surrey 1966–67
m Aber 3.9.65 David P. G. Williams MA(Cantab) sen prod. BBC(radio) s of David G. W. BSc(Bangor) Worcester Park

BURNS Sheila Anne Valentine   MA 1969
d of Norman B. chief supt police and Grace I. Valentine shorthand typist; b Aber 23.5.47
teacher maths: Aber 1970–72, Lossiemouth from 1972
m Elgin 8.7.72 Geoffrey Hanson RAF, insur broker s of John H. Rugby

BURNS William   BSc 1959
s of Adam B. gardener and Margaret D. Gibb teacher; b Insch 1.8.38
teacher maths: Knox acad Haddington 1960–64, Tillicoultry s s 1964–66; prin guid Alva acad from 1966
m Musselburgh 25.7.64 Elizabeth K. Thomson MA (Edin) teacher d of Thomas T. Musselburgh

BURR Robert John   MA 1956 *1958
s of Ebenezer B. shoemaker, estate employee and Helen A. Donald; b Tarves 10.4.34
teacher Engl: Leith acad 1959–63; prin Engl: Plockton h s 1963–66, Denny h s 1966–69, Peterhead acad 1969–72; head Plockton 1972–76; prin Engl Peterhead acad from 1976
m Aber 20.7.66 Eileen M. Strachan MA 1956 *qv*

BURROWES Esther Elizabeth Ann   *MA 1956
                                              *EdB 1961
d of Ernest E. B. bus. man and Olivia Nichols secy; b Georgetown, Guyana 31.5.32
Georgetown: teacher, sen mistress/dep head (ag) Bishop's h s 1957–71; asst chief educ off. (Min of Educ) 1971–74; dep chief educ off. (dev) (Min of Educ & Soc Dev) from 1974

BURT Cynthia Kinloch   MA 1956 *MEd 1958
m Dixon

BURT Michael William   *BSc 1970
s of Ernest H. W. B. MA(Glas) teacher and Margaret S. W. McCreath; b Glasg 2.8.48
various geol exploration posts Aust 1970–73; sen geol in field explor: Angola SW Af 1974–75, SW Af, S Af 1976–78; stud. chem univ of Natal in Durban from 1978

BURT Susan Helen Hay   MA 1967
d of Robert H. B. draughtsman and Eileen S. Singer; b Huntly 25.4.47
syst analyst, progr: Burmah Castrol Co Lond 1967–68, Aberd 1968–70, Philips Eindhoven Neths 1971–72, Lond 1972–73, Manc from 1973
m Lond 7.7.73 Christopher J. Davies BSc(eng) 1968 *qv*

BURT William Johnston   MA 1967
s of George A. T. B. police insp and Mabel G. Johnston secy; b Aber 14.11.45
Lond: exec off. min of publ bldg and works 1967–71, exec off. DOE 1971–72, higher exec off. oper res DOE 1972–78, sen exec off. from 1978

BURTON Richard Keith   BSc 1959 *1962

BUSBY Roger John Nicholas   BSc(for) 1960 *1961
s of Alfred E. G. B. teacher and Elsie E. Millward; b London 3.8.37
MSc(Sur) 1974

field asst Murphy chem co Wheathampstead 1961-62; dist off. for. comm Thetford & Princes Risboro' 1962-66; asst conserv for. (on secondment) Suva Fiji 1966-68; dist off. for. comm Cardiff, Malvern 1969-71; econ for. comm: Alice Holt 1971-75, Edin from 1975

BUSSEY Kenneth John   *MA 1969
s of John G. B. secy Brit Legion (Scot.) and Catherine Jamieson sales asst; b Inv 16.6.42
MPhil(Glas) 1971
res asst HIDB Inv 1971-1972; lect Paisley coll tech from 1972
m Hawick 4.12.71 Jennifer R. Johnstone teacher d of Gavin J. Hawick

BUTCHART Dorothy Anne Grace   MA 1967
m Yusuf

BUTLER Eileen Ann   *MA 1959
d of Sydney W. B. workshop superv and Annie I. Smith shorthand typist; b Aber 18.8.37
teacher: Engl Bell Baxter h s Cupar, Fife 1960-61, Leith acad 1961-64, part time remed subj Arbroath acad 1974-76
m Aber 28.7.60 John A. L. Cheyne MA 1957 qv

BUTLER Elizabeth Olive   *MA 1966

BUTLER James Sutherland   MA 1962

BUTLER Joyce Edith   MA 1969 Dip Ed 1970
d of Sydney W. B. PO superv and Anne I. Smith clerkess; b Aber 20.4.48
teacher Engl: Sidcup 1970-71, Harpenden 1971-74
m Aber 8.10.70 Ian A. Clegg MA 1970 qv

BUTLER Marilyn   MA 1961
m Watson

BUTLER Morgan   *BSc 1969
s of Alexander M. B. clerk and Anne C. Forman; b Ellon 29.10.46
GSM(Rhodesia)
software eng Marconi Space & Defence Hillend 1970-73; computer progr Lond 1973-74; comp dir Poole 1974-76; computer eng Johannesburg 1976-77; infantry off. Rhodesian army from 1977

BUTLER Noreen Isabel   *MA 1962
d of Sydney W. B. motor mech and Ella Smith shorthand typist; b Aber 6.8.40
teacher: Glasg 1963-67, remed Wigan 1969-71; ch guid Glasg from 1972
m Aber 3.4.63 William G. Thompson MA qv

BUTT Walter Dion   PhD 1959

BUTTERWORTH Ian Eric   *MA 1967
s of John B. and Vera M. Mellor; b Oldham 20.5.44
asst curate All Saints & Martyrs Church Middleton, diocese of Manc 1969-72; precentor St Andrew's episc cath Aber 1972-75; vicar St Matthew with St Barnabas Bolton diocese of Manc from 1975
m Manc 24.4.71 Valerie M. Storer

BUTTERWORTH Marilyn Holt   PhD 1960

BUTTLER Frank George   PhD 1958

BUXTON Ian William Derek   *MA 1958
s of William F. A. B. BA(Lond) HMIS and Janet A.

Mitchell teacher; b Alexandria Egypt 4.2.36
MBE 1972
Uganda govt: audit. Jinja, Kabale, Fort Portal 1958-62, sen audit. Gulu 1962-65, prin audit. Kampala 1965-68, dir of audit. Kampala 1968-71; loc govt off. Lond borough of Redbridge 1971-75; admin Commission for Local Admin in England from 1975
m Jinja 15.8.59 Elizabeth M. Gillies med lab res asst d of Neil G. Aber

BUXTON Neil Keith   *MA 1962
s of William F. A. B. BA(Lond) HMIS and Janet A. Mitchell teacher; b Alexandria Egypt 2.5.40
asst dept pol econ Aberd 1962-64; lect dept econ: Hull 1964-69, H-W Edin 1969-72, sen lect from 1972
m Aber 8.12.62 Margaret G. Miller d of William F. M. Aber

BUXTON Rosalind Carissa Clarence   MA 1968
d of Clarence E. V. B. BA(Cantab) col serv, farm. and Mavis J. B. Bromhead farm.; b Nairobi 21.7.46
Cert Ed TEFL(Lond) 1974
p r o Lond 1969-70; fam plan. asst Lond 1970-72; VSO teacher Engl Vientiane Laos 1972-73
m Limuru Kenya 7.9.74 Peter R. Nightingale BA(Cantab) indust man. s of Edward H. N. BA(Cantab) Lond

BUYERS William James Leslie   *BSc 1959 PhD 1963
s of William B. banker, rubber planter and Williamina B. McBey; b Aboyne 10.4.37
Aberd: asst lect 1962-64, lect 1964-65; AECL Chalk River Canada: NRC fell. 1965-66, assoc res off. 1966-74, sen res off from 1975; sen res fell. Oxon 1971-72, guest scient Oak Ridge 1972, AEC Denmark 1975, vice chmn Div Cond Matter Phys (Can Assoc Phys)
m Deep River Ontario 1.10.66 Marilyn J. Cliff BA(West. Ont) secy d of Walter C. S. Porcupine Ont

BYIERS Robert   *MA 1966
s of Robert B. porter univ hall of resid and Ellen W. Minty clerkess/typist; b Aber 26.12.42
MEd(Glas) 1972
teacher mod lang Glasg h s 1968-72; prin mod lang Kingsridge h s Glasg 1972-75; lect mod lang Notre Dame coll of educ Glasg from 1975
m Oban 6.7.68 Anne A. Irving MA(Glas) teacher d of Cunningham B. I. MA(Glas) Oban

BYRES Terence James   *MA 1958
s of James H. B. salesman and Annabelle Elder shop asst, shorthand typist; b Aber 6.10.36
BLitt(Glas) 1962
School oriental/Af stud. Lond: res fell. econ 1962-64, lect from 1964
m Aber 10.9.60 Anne C. MacKenzie lib d of Kenneth J. MacK. Crathie

BYRNE Pauline Jeannie   MA 1968

BYTH Robert William   LLB 1964

BYTH William   *MA 1962 PhD 1969
s of Alexander S. B. MA 1928 qv; b Edin 3.4.40
Aberd asst lect: psych 1965-66, lect 1966-71; lect psych Belf from 1971
m Aber 4.8.63 Irene B. Noble MA 1962 qv

BZDEGA Elizabeth Maria   *BSc 1969

CABLE William James Angus   MA 1966
s of James E. C. MB ChB 1915 qv; b Forfar 11.8.29
teacher: Hazlehead acad Aber 1967-70, spec asst 1970-

73; asst prin teacher 1973–74, prin teacher from 1974
m Perth 20.11.54 Elizabeth D. Smith asst warden school
of dom sc Aber d of John A. S. Lundin Links

CADENHEAD Alexander Thomson *MA 1970
Dip Ed 1971

CADGER John Mitchell Pirie *MA 1969

CAIE Christina *MA 1970
  d of John F. C. customs watcher and Katie B. Morrison; b Aber 6.12.48
Dip Lib(Strath) 1974
teacher Engl St Mungo's RC h s Falkirk 1971–72; stud.
asst Glas lib 1972–73; asst lib Andersonian lib Strath
from 1974
m Aber 18.9.70 John N. McSween chem s of Finlay MacS.
Is of Scalpay

CAIE Colin Fraser *MA 1969

CAIE Dorothy Elizabeth MB ChB 1966
  d of William C. group secy Aber gen hosps and
Adeline Donald shop asst; b Aber 9.12.42
MRCGP 1973
h o ARI, RACH 1966–67; MRC res worker The Gambia
W Af 1967–68; g p: Portlethen 1972–73, Skene 1974–77
m Aber 12.7.66 Alexander W. Logie MB ChB 1963 qv

CAIE Graham Douglas *MA 1968
  s of William C. secy/treas gen hosp Aber and Adeline
M. Donald; b Aber 3.2.45
MA(McM) 1969 PhD(McM) 1974
asst Engl dept McM univ Hamilton Canada 1968–72;
lect Engl univ Copenhagen from 1972
m Aber 9.6.72 Ann P. Abbott MA 1967 qv

CAIE Ronald Webster *MA 1960 Dip Ed 1963
  s of William W. C. supt marine eng and Elizabeth
Grant shorthand typist; b Aber 22.9.38
teacher Engl: London 1960–62, Aber 1963–68; spec asst
Kincardine 1968–70, prin teacher Aber from 1970
m Aber 19.8.61 Mary E. Stewart BSc 1960 qv

CAIRNCROSS Robert George MB ChB 1968
  s of George G. C. dir and Mary McInroy; b Dundee
6.7.44
MRCP 1974 MRCGP 1976
h o, sen h o ARI 1968–70; sen h o Birm, Dun 1970–72;
regist med Edin 1972–76; lect med educ Dund from 1976

CAIRNIE Alan Bruce PhD 1958
  s of John B. C. MA(Edin) teacher and Isabella Moodie;
b Ayr 18.11.32
BSc(Glas)
lect Aberd 1958–61; scient Inst of Cancer Res Lond
1961–67; assoc prof Queen's univ Kingston Canada
1967–76; head Radiation Biol defence res estab Ottawa
from 1976
m Troon 21.8.58 Agnes A. Blackwood

CAIRNS David Stitt MA 1968
  s of James G. C. bank man. and Margaret M. S.
Hunter teacher dom sc; b Aber 22.1.45
invest. analyst: JCI; Martin & Co Inc stockbrokers
Johannesburg 1968–71, asst to gen man. 1971–72; S Af
Cane Growers Assoc Durban from 1972
m Johannesburg 12.2.72 Susan J. Clews receptionist d of
Raymond A. C. Johannesburg

CALDER Alan *BSc 1965 PhD 1969
  s of John C. lorry driver and Margaret Goodbrand;
b. Wick 22.3.44

ICI organics: chem Stevenston 1968–72, sect leader from
1972
m Wick 8.7.66 Jean F. S. Sinclair tax off. d of Alexander
S. S. Wick

CALDER Alexander Charles *MA 1940
  s of Alexander C. master slater and Hilda Liddell;
b Aber 30.8.48
MA(Liv) 1974 BA(Lond) 1976
res Engl lang Liv 1970–72; civ serv DHSS Aber from 1977

CALDER Charlotte Newman BEd 1970
  b Aber 7.9.23
Biggar h s: teacher Engl from 1970, asst prin guid 1975–
77, prin guid from 1977
m Peterhead 1942 Skelsey

CALDER Hector John *MA 1959 *MEd 1968
  s of Charles C. man. and Helen Spalding; b Aber
8.6.37
teacher mod lang: Alloa acad 1961–65, AGS 1965–67;
Perth and Kinross: asst dir educ 1967–68, dep dir 1968–
75; div educ off and dep dir educ Tayside reg council
from 1975
m Falkirk 1.5.65 Diane M. Moore teacher d of Samuel
J. M. Falkirk

CALDER Iain Alexander Hamilton BSc 1969
  s of John H. C. surv customs and excise and Martha G.
Hamilton organis N of Scot FPA; b Asmara Eritrea
27.2.47
control chem i/c quality control lab/res and dev work
Edin from 1969
m Edin 12.5.72 Sheila N. Thomson lab asst d of William
T. Edin

CALDER Ian Mollison *BSc 1965 Dip Ed 1966
  s of Ronald M. C. hotelier and Athlene M. Henry hair
stylist, hotel prop; b Aber 12.7.43
teacher phys: RGC Aber 1966–69, spec asst 1969–70,
prin teacher from 1971

CALDER James Moir *BSc(agr) 1967
  s of John C. farm. and Annie Grant; b Dunphail 2.2.44
advis off. min of agr Armagh N. Ireland 1967–69;
NOSCA: asst econ Aber 1969–72, agr advis Keith from
1972
m Forres 6.8.66 Mary M. Ross teacher d of Archibald R.
Forres

CALDER James Rose MA 1958 *BSc 1961 PhD 1964

CALDER James Stewart Winton *MA 1962

CALDER Joan Christine MA 1965
  m Cumming

CALDER Stanley Shearer MA 1965

CALDER William James BSc 1961

CALLANDER James Dickson MA 1970
  s of John S. C. postmaster and Jessie M. M. Cross secy;
b Motherwell 9.6.48
Dip Bus Admin(Edin) 1973
postal h q (Scot): exec off. Edin 1970–72, asst postal
controller from 1973
m Aber 11.8.73 Jean Maxwell prod. secy d of Alexander
M. Edin

CAMERON Alan Graham MB ChB 1964

CAMERON Douglas Martin   BSc 1970
s of Thomas M. C. burgh chamberlain Kilmarnock and
Marion Anderson cler worker; b Kilmarnock 25.4.45
teacher maths Inverurie acad from 1971
m Aber 8.4.74 Moreen A. Simpson MA 1970 *qv*

CAMERON Elizabeth   MA 1968
d of William C. slater and Florence Sutherland; b Nairn
2.8.47
asst housemother children's home Rhynie 1968-69
m Forres 3.5.69 George A. M. Shaw porter-driver s of
Donald S. Forres

CAMERON Elizabeth Jane   MA 1968

CAMERON Graham John   *BSc(eng) 1969

CAMERON Hamish William   *BSc 1969
s of William D. C. farm. and Hannah Gillies; b
Cromarty 27.1.47
Glasg: proj leader 1970-78, syst man. from 1978
m St Cyrus 9.8.75 Edna Johnston BSc 1970 *qv*

CAMERON Henry Gordon   MA 1966
s of James H. C. cabinetmaker, univ tech and Florence
Dey; b Aber 27.5.43
teacher: hist/mod stud Oban h s 1967-69, econ/mod stud
Rosyth h s 1969; computer progr Nairn Williamson
Kirkcaldy 1969-70; NCR(Mfg) Dun: computer progr
1969-70, progr, head EDP Operations, syst des 1970-73,
computer proj controller 1973-76; sen syst des NSHEB
from 1976
m 12.8.67 Mary M. Stewart MA 1966 *qv*

CAMERON Henry Ogilvy   BL 1961
s of Henry O. C. police insp and Marion M. Burnett;
b Aber 9.12.39
app CA Aber 1961-64; dir agr and motor eng firm
Aberdeensh 1964-68; law app Aber 1968-70, ptnr C.
& P. H. Chalmers advoc Aber 1971-78; ptnr Cameron
& Thom advoc Aber from 1978
m Kent 25.7.64 Fiona C. Grant MA 1962 *qv*

CAMERON Hugh McKenzie   MA 1967
b Edin 3.4.46
teacher Engl Lockerbie 1969-71, asst prin Engl Craigshill
h s Livingston from 1971

CAMERON Ian Alexander   *d*LLB 1961
MA (Edin)

CAMERON Ian Kenneth Mackenzie   *MA 1966
s of Kenneth M. C. and Eileen Wright; b Fremington
15.8.40
Edin: journalist *Evening Post* 1966-68; labourer Scot.
Construct./supply teacher 1968; teacher Engl: Bankhead
acad 1969-72, Ingiliz Lisesi, Istanbul 1972-74; lang instr
univ petr and min Dhahran Saudi Arabia from 1974
m Aber 23.3.68 Jane-Ann W. Annells MA 1968 *qv*

CAMERON James   *BSc 1969 PhD 1973

CAMERON Jean Nicol   MA 1970 Dip Ed 1971
d of John G. C. letterpress foreman and Catherine M.
Nicol; b Kilmarnock 11.2.49
teacher Latin/Engl Dunfermline h s 1971-76
m Aber 3.7.73 Archibald Bennett BSc(Edin) teacher s of
John S. B. Kelty

CAMERON Joan   MA 1965 Dip Ed 1966
d of Alexander G. C. killed in action 1.7.44 and Evelyn
Fraser; b Aber 18.12.43

teacher Engl: Dunoon 1966-68, Aboyne 1968-74, asst
prin teacher from 1974

CAMERON John Francis   MA 1967 Dip Ed 1969
b Stanley 4.3.39
teacher Clydebank h s: Engl 1969-71, asst prin guid
1971-72, asst prin Engl 1972-74; prin Engl Dumbarton
acad from 1974
m Aber 6.8.69 Diana M. Douglas MA 1967 *qv*

CAMERON John Mowat   BSc 1956
s of Kenneth J. C. MA(Edin) C of S min and Barbara
J. S. Mowat teacher; b Aber 27.1.35
RAF: educ off. Cosford 1957-62, Halton 1962-64;
teacher sc Stranraer from 1964
m Coulsdon 31.12.60 Patricia M. Pink secy d of Joseph
E. P. Coulsdon

CAMERON Kathleen Isabel   MA 1964

CAMERON Kenneth John   *MA 1967
s of John C. Sudan govt off. and Kathleen M. Skinner
chirop; b Perth 27.4.45
PhD(Edin) 1971 Dip Lib(Strath) 1972
Dund: grad lib asst 1970-71, asst lib from 1973, res asst
dept mod hist Dund 1972-73

CAMERON Mairi Henrietta   MA 1965

CAMERON Margaret Elspeth Milne   *MA 1961
d of Norman A. C. MA 1929 *qv* and Elspeth M. Milne
MA 1969 *qv*; b Elgin 15.7.39
Dip Ed(Edin) 1964
Kansas univ USA: schol stud. 1961-62, lect Greek 1962-
63; St Andrews: teacher classics St Leonard's s 1964-66,
Madras s from 1970
m Stirling 15.8.64 Martin S. Smith MA(Glas) univ lect s
of Alexander D. S. Glasg

CAMERON Marie Sylvia   MA 1963

CAMERON Marion Brown   *MEd 1967
d of Thomas R. C. driver and Margaret T. Russell
waitress; b Edin 15.9.35
MA(Edin) 1957 Dip Ed(Edin) 1958
res assoc dept educ Manc 1967-68; lect educ psych coll
of educ Dun from 1968
m Edin 20.7.72 John E. C. de Quincey BA(Durh) s of
Arnold de Q. BA(Durh) Warwicksh

CAMERON Marjory Martin   MA 1961 Dip Ed 1962
d of John G. C. letterpress printer and Catherine M.
Nicol leg. secy; b Kilmarnock 2.4.40
teacher: Aber 1962-64, Manc 1964-66, Dun 1973-75,
Barrhead h s from 1975
m Aber 14.7.64 Alexander B. Wilson BSc 1962 *qv*

CAMERON Mary   MB ChB 1970

CAMERON Neil Duncan   *BSc 1970

CAMERON Rhona Cumming   LLB 1969

CAMERON Robert Ward   BSc 1970
s of Evan R. C. BSc(Glas) shipbuilding consult. and
Dorothy P. Ward; b Glasg 19.7.48
Lloyds broker Lond from 1970
m Exeter 4.9.71 Norma P. Edwards MA 1971 d of
Norman F. J. E. Exeter

CAMERON Roderick Francis   MA 1966
s of Stanley C. small tool worker and Gwendoline M. C.
Jackson; b Wolverhampton 26.4.44

teacher Craighill p s Aber 1967–73; asst head Tullos p s Aber 1973–77; head Inverurie Market Pl p s from 1977
m Aber 9.8.68 Catherine Ross MA 1966 *qv*

CAMERON Ruth Elizabeth LLB 1969
m Wilkie

CAMERON Seonaid Ealasaid MA 1970
d of John C. MA 1939 *qv* and Elizabeth W. Eddie BSc 1940 *qv*; b Inverness 15.9.49
Dip Soc Work(Edin) 1971
soc worker: Midlothian c c 1971–73, Roxburgh c c from 1973
m Aber 24.10.74 Richard D. Hollands BVMS(Edin) vet surg s of Frank G. H. LRCP(Lond) Derby

CAMERON Wilfred *MA 1965
m Dun 1969 Alison M. Low BSc 1965 *qv*

CAMERON-MACKINTOSH, Elizabeth BSc(agr) 1956

CAMPBELL Alan *MA 1965
b Thurso 6.12.42
teacher Thurso 1966–72; prin geog Montrose acad from 1972
m Wick 8.7.72 Maura C. Morrison teacher p e

CAMPBELL Alan Braidwood *MA 1970

CAMPBELL Alan Grant LLB 1968
s of Archibald G. C. master plumber and Catherine M. Morrison; b Aber 4.12.46
Aber c c: law app 1968–70, solic 1970–75; asst dir law/admin Grampian reg c from 1975
m Aber 29.6.74 Susan M. M. Black res worker d of John M. B. MB ChB(Edin) Aber

CAMPBELL Alan Tormaid MA 1967

CAMPBELL Alasdair *BSc 1968
s of William C. and Marion Morrison; b Struan 9.6.47
electronics eng Chelmsford 1968–73; des eng Nott 1973–74; computer syst analyst Somercotes from 1974
m Levenshulme Manc 12.6.71 Sylvia Wagstaff computer progr d of Francis T. W. Stockport

CAMPBELL Alasdair James *BSc 1963 MSc 1964
s of John R. C. joiner and Mary Grant; b Balmoral, Crathie 22.7.41
Assoc Fell. Inst Maths 1967
lect maths RGIT Aber from 1964
m Aber 23.8.68 Doris M. McLean MB ChB 1967 *qv*

CAMPBELL Alexander John MA 1968

CAMPBELL Alistair Robert MacBrair *BSc 1968
s of Bruce C. BSc(for)(Edin) author, broadcaster and Margaret Gibson-Hill MA(Edin) soc worker, writer; b Cardiff 9.5.46
Oxford: sub-edit. Blackwell scient publ 1968–69, edit. 1969–78; dir micromedia 1973–78, chmn Oxford microfilm publ 1975–78; dir Blackwell scient publ Oxford and vice-presid Blackwell scient publ N Amer/NY/Delaware from 1978; also writer
m Oxford 7.9.68 Frances R. Kirkwood teacher d of Kenneth K. BA(Wits) Oxford

CAMPBELL Angus BSc 1969
s of Angus C. gardener and Christine Tuach; b Plockton 6.4.48
MIBiol(Paisley tech) 1973
teacher biol Newton Stewart 1971–75; prin biol Eyemouth from 1975

m Stranraer 15.7.71 Elizabeth Purdie teacher home econ d of Stephen P. Stranraer

CAMPBELL Angus Iain Lionel *LLB 1969

CAMPBELL Calum Mackenzie *MA 1966
s of Tormaid C. MA 1933 *qv*; b Corgarff 14.10.43
PhD(Leeds) 1973
teacher: Malaskolinn Mimir Reykjavik 1966–73, Inverurie acad 1968; lect univ Iceland Reykjavik 1972–73; teacher Edin from 1974
m Strathdon 5.4.75 Sigridur Oladottir d of Oli K. Gudmundsson Cand. Med. (Laeknisprof Reykjavik) Reykjavik

CAMPBELL Cameron Robb Dixon MB ChB 1966
s of Peter C. Dip Ed(Durh) teacher, admin and Elizabeth H. Dixon; b S Shields 24.10.41
Dip Anaest RCS(E) 1969
h o Shotley Bridge 1966–67; sen h o, regist anaest Aber 1967–69; g p Norwich from 1969
m Aber 29.9.67 Patricia E. Morrice p e teacher d of Peter M. Aber

CAMPBELL Catherine Maciver *MA 1965
d of Norman M. C. joiner and Margaret J. Ross; b Avoch 22.1.43
teacher geog Aber h s for girls 1966–70
m Ullapool 2.4.68 Douglas P. Willis MA 1965 *qv*

CAMPBELL Clair MA 1969

CAMPBELL Colin Balnaves BSc 1964
s of Albert C. eng, works man. and Lizzie J. W. Balnaves saleswoman; b Aber 5.5.43
Dip Indust Man.(Strath) 1965
jun explor geol Sierra Leone 1966–67; Canada: staff geol INCO Sudbury 1969–70, proj geol Cerro mining comp Vancouver 1970–71; oper man. IRSCO Toronto 1971–78, VP marketing Crinan Toronto from 1979
m Toronto 30.6.69 Sandra L. Bromwich teacher d of H. Frederick B. Toronto

CAMPBELL Colin Grant BSc 1960
s of Wilson C. police janitor and Alice M. J. Grant; b Aber 17.6.38
teacher, spec asst Kaimhill s s Aber 1961–68; prin sc St Columba s s Kilmacolm 1968–73; prin chem Linlathen h s Dun from 1973
m Aber 3.7.65 Sandra V. T. Clements d of Frederick D. C. Aber

CAMPBELL Colin Kerr *MA 1964
s of Alan A. C.; b Edin 9.3.42
MA(Br Col) 1967 PhD(Brist) 1971
teaching asst Simon Fraser univ Vanc 1966–67; res fell. Strath 1967–68; asst prof geog Vict BC 1971–73; head res sect. BC parks branch Vict BC from 1973
m Victoria B.C. 1966 Linda Carol BSc(UBC) phys and occup therap

CAMPBELL Colin Murray LLB 1967
s of Isabel C. secy; b Aber 26.12.44
lect law: Dund 1967–69, Edin 1969–73; prof juris Belf from 1974

CAMPBELL Colinne BSc 1964
m Souter

CAMPBELL David Craig MA 1960

CAMPBELL David John BSc 1959
s of David R. M. C. civ serv and Dorothy M. Elgin clerkess; b Inv 29.8.38

teacher: AGS 1960–62, Hemel Hempstead g s 1962–66, Carleton Place h s Canada 1966–68, Niagara Falls adult educ centre 1968–70, Sundon Park j s Luton from 1970 m Aber 1.8.73 Gloria J. K. Whyte hosp cler off. d of Patrick W. Aber

CAMPBELL David Murdoch Armstrong *MA 1962
s of Murdoch C. MA(Edin) min of religion and Mary A. Fraser; b Glasg 11.8.39
asst lect, lect moral phil Glas from 1965

CAMPBELL David Stanley *BSc 1959 PhD 1962

CAMPBELL, Dorothy Mildred MA 1969
d of Donald C. gamekeeper and Mona Curr; b Aber 15.7.47
teacher: Inverallochy 1970–74, Aber 1974–75, Inv 1975–76
m Aber 15.7.75 Robert A. Masson BSc 1968 qv

CAMPBELL Duncan William BSc(agr) 1956
s of Duncan C. farm. and Helen R. Allan; b Elgin 28.5.33
farm man. Elgin 1956–60; teacher sc Forres acad 1961–66; farm. Elgin from 1966
m Perth 8.4.63 Glenda McDonald secy d of Gilroy B. M. Scone

CAMPBELL Frances Balnaves MA 1958
d of Albert C. eng, works man. and Lizzie J. W. Balnaves saleswoman; b Aber 22.5.36
Dip Pers Man.(Strath) 1966
teacher: Aber 1959–61, Glasg 1961–62; various posts Berlin, Paris 1962–63; teacher Glasg 1963–65; pers off., trg off. Lond 1966–69; tut., head of courses dept nat inst of indust psych Lond 1969–73
m Aber 30.12.71 Mohammed Y. Manjra BA(Rangoon) CA s of Yacoob M. M. Gujrat India

CAMPBELL Gillian Agnes *MA 1965
d of George A. C. shopkeeper and Jessie Macdonald nurs sister; b Dingwall 19.3.43
teacher geog/hist: Convent of Sacred Heart s s Aber 1966–71, Torry acad 1971–72
m Aber 23.3.67 John S. Smith MA 1963 qv

CAMPBELL Grace Stewart MA 1968 Dip Ed 1969
m Allanach

CAMPBELL Ian BSc(agr) 1959
s of William G. C. farm. and Isabel B. Steven; b Wick 31.12.36
dept agr: temp field off. Elgin 1960, asst insp Edin 1960–62, Kirkwall 1962–68, Dumfries 1968–74, insp Dumfries from 1974
m Kirkwall 25.3.65 Sonja M. O. Graham RGN d of Joseph O. G. Rimington Sheffield

CAMPBELL Ian James MA 1970

CAMPBELL Ian McDonald *MA 1964
s of Donald C. MA 1929 qv and Mary B. Cruickshank MA 1930 qv; b Lausanne 25.8.42
PhD(Edin) 1970 FSAScot 1970
Edin: res stud. 1964–67, univ lect from 1967; visiting lect Germany 1971; visiting lect, prof Canada, USA 1971, 1973, 1976

CAMPBELL James Buchan *BSc 1962
s of James B. C. eng and Janie T. Hugginson; b Fraserburgh 1939

PhD(Alta) 1965
post doct fell. Alta 1965–66; US publ health serv Wistar Inst Philadelphia: post doct trainee 1966–67, res asst 1967–68; univ of Toronto: asst prof virol 1968–70, assoc prof virol from 1970
m Aber 3.8.66 Sheena G. Hunter MA 1964 qv

CAMPBELL Jean Elizabeth MA 1968
b Aber 9.8.46
Edin: teacher 1968–71; civ serv from 1971

CAMPBELL Jean McEwen MA 1964
d of George C. master plasterer and Agnes Webster secy; b Fraserburgh 3.11.42
teacher hist: Inverurie acad 1965–68, St Mark's s s Mbabane Swaziland 1968–70
m Aber 16.7.68 George I. M. Martin BSc(Glas) agronomist/sen tut. coll of agr s of George M. Aber

CAMPBELL Jean Macrae MA 1964
d of Roderick M. C. MA 1929 qv; b Edin 20.3.43
teacher: Montreal, Weybridge, Fort William, Pereira (Colombia), Koratti, Kerala (India) 1965–75; head Glenelg p s from 1975

CAMPBELL Jessie MA 1964
d of James C. gardener/janitor and Isabella McArthur; b Perth 25.3.43
Cert Secy St (Strath) 1965
teacher secy stud. Moray & Nairn 1966–67; Perth: off. supervis 1969–73, asst acct from 1976
m Aber 15.5.65 John Hogg MA 1966 qv

CAMPBELL Joan Glen MA 1960
m Harding

CAMPBELL John Dugald *MA 1963
s of John C. C. MA(Edin) C of S min and Dorothy T. Torrance nurse; b Aber 19.2.41
teacher: Glenwood j h s Glenrothes 1964–66, Glenrothes h s 1966–69, prin hist Fortrose acad from 1969

CAMPBELL Joseph Mitchell MA 1969
s of Joseph M. C. fisherman and Margaret Main; b Lossiemouth 15.10.27
teacher geog Forres from 1971
m Lossiemouth 12.8.68 Isa Mackenzie d of Alexander B. M. Lossiemouth

CAMPBELL Kathleen Christine MA 1967

CAMPBELL Kenneth Murdoch MA 1967
s of Donald C. policeman and Ishbel Campbell; b Isle of Skye 26.8.40
BD(Penn USA) 1970 ThM(Penn USA) 1971 PhD(Manc) 1975
stud.res: Philadelphia 1967–71, Manc 1971–72, Tübingen, Germany 1972–73; Kampen, Holland 1973–74; Manc from 1974
m Aber 16.8.67 Christina MacLeod teacher d of Murdoch MacL. Stornoway

CAMPBELL Lachlan Alexander MA 1959 *1961

CAMPBELL Lawrence Curwen BSc 1960

CAMPBELL Lennox Hamilton *BSc 1970 PhD 1975

CAMPBELL Margaret Christine *MA 1967
d of James P. C. MB ChB(St And) orthop surg and Catherine A. Duncan MA(St And) teacher; b Nott 9.2.45

teacher: geog Bathgate acad 1968–69, soc stud./Engl Howe Sound s s Canada 1969–70; England: geog Rushcliffe s s 1970–71, Congleton girls' s s 1971–73, humanities Rothwell s s 1973–74
m Nott 28.8.71 Jeremy Nigel Sands prod. man. s of John W. S. Edin

CAMPBELL Mary Ann   MA 1959 Dip Ed 1960
d of Malcolm C. crofter; b Arnol Barvas Is of Lewis 13.3.35
teacher: Ruthrieston s Aber 1960–62; Longhope Orkney 1965–67; Brora h s 1969–73
m Perth 8.8.61 Charles Abel min of religion

CAMPBELL Mary Fraser   MA 1958 Dip Ed 1959
d of Murdoch C. MA(Edin) Free C of S min and Mary A. Fraser PO clerk/co-owner newsag bus.; b Glasg 21.9.37
teacher Cullicudden p s Black Is 1959–61; relief teacher Aber 1961–62
m Aber 13.9.61 James D. MacMillan MA 1963 qv

CAMPBELL Mary Slater   MA 1957
d of William C. fisherman/skipper and Margaret Liebnitz cook/dom worker; b Lossiemouth 4.4.37
teacher: Hopeman 1958–59, Elgin acad 1960–61; supply Elgin acad, Lossiemouth h s, Elgin h s from 1974
m Aber 17.7.59 Norman M. Stewart BL(Edin) solic s of George S. Lossiemouth

CAMPBELL Moira Ann   *MA 1957 Dip Ed 1958
d of George A. C. elect. contr and Margaret J. Niven; b Aber 29.8.35
CRK(Lond) 1965
teacher: hist/geog Fort William 1958–59, geog Inv r acad 1959–63; stud. Bible Training Inst Glasg 1963–65; Lond: teaching/ch work 1965–66, linguistics/missionary trg 1966–67; Taiwan: overseas missionary fell./lang study 1967–69, stud. work with Campus fell. 1969–70, work with tribal stud. from 1970

CAMPBELL Morag Clayton   MA 1969

CAMPBELL Myra Anne   MA 1965
m Jacobs

CAMPBELL Neil Andrew   *MA 1967
s of Frederick C. C. maintenance eng and Josephine M. Read BA(Leeds) teacher; b Durban 19.12.43
Dip Gen Ling(Edin) 1968
Inv royal acad: teacher Fr/Ital 1969–73, asst prin Fr/Ital from 1973
m Aber 14.7.67 Elizabeth M. Alexander MA 1963 qv

CAMPBELL Norma   MA 1970
d of Norman J. C. weaver and Christina Smith; b Brasar Is of Lewis 11.10.49
hotel man. Perth 1971–72, Aviemore from 1972
m 10.7.73 Kenneth P. MacKenzie hotelier s of W. H. MacK. Turriff

CAMPBELL Norman   *BSc 1966 MSc 1970

CAMPBELL Norman   MA 1966
s of Kenneth C. sub-postmaster and Rachel A. MacLeod; b Scalpay Harris 12.6.32
BA(Strath) 1972
teacher: Engl Kilmarnock tech coll 1967–74, asst prin Engl Ayr acad from 1974

CAMPBELL Norman   *BSc 1966

CAMPBELL Peter Ian   *MA 1959
d 6.10.63 AUR XL 304

CAMPBELL Richard Ewen   BSc(for) 1964

CAMPBELL Roy Hutcheson   PhD 1956

CAMPBELL Ruth Macdonald   MA 1956 Dip Ed 1957
d of John C. pharm and Hilda Manson LRAM mus; b Lerwick 29.3.34
teacher Richmond: h s 1957–59, convent s 1959–60; head dept sec mod s Uppingham; lect liberal stud. Beverley 1964–66; asst prin Engl Norwood comp s Lond; year mistress Croydon from 1974
m Cambridge 19.12.59 Peter G. Fletcher BA(Cantab) prof mus s of Eric F. Combe Martin

CAMPBELL Sheila Mary   MA 1959
d of Donald C. MA 1929 qv and Mary B. Cruickshank MA 1930 qv b. Lausanne 20.2.39
teacher: Mackie acad Stonehaven 1960–61, Culcabock p s Inv 1962–67, Inv h s from 1971, asst prin from 1976
m Inverbervie 27.12.61 Brian D. J. Denoon MA 1959 qv

CAMPBELL Sherry Elizabeth   *MA 1970 Dip Ed 1971
d of Keith B. C. judge and Betty J. Muffet; b Lond 18.7.47
m Lond 22.7.72 Thomas J. Wilkie civ serv

CAMPBELL Stewart James   *BSc 1966

CAMPBELL William James   *BSc 1959 MSc 1960

CAMPBELL William John   MA 1965
s of William C. MA(Glas) min of religion and Christina MacLean; b Garrabost Isle of Lewis 18.11.33
Grad Dip Theol(Free Ch Coll Edin) 1968
ordained Glasg 1968
min Detroit 1968–72, Park (Scot.) from 1972
m Glasg 24.8.64 Margaret M. Morrison RGN d of John A. M. Stornoway

CANNON Dorothy May Susan   MA 1970
d of John C. comp dir and Jane A. Keillor; b Galashiels 4.9.49
teacher Engl: Edin 1971–72, Perth W Aust from 1973
m Galashiels 14.7.71 Leo V. M. Forsyth struct eng tech s of Vincent H. F. Stow M'Lothian

CANT Derek George   MA 1966

CANT Helen Elaine   MA 1969
m Peterson

CANTLAY Evelyn Mary   *MA 1963

CANTLAY Jean Lesley   MA 1970
d of Leslie T. C. farm. and Mary B. Davie; b Ellon 23.2.49
teacher geog: Alford 1971–73, Vale of Leven acad Alexandria from 1973
m Cruden 30.7.73 Charles A. Murdoch LLB 1972 solic s of Robin M. MB ChB(Glas) Bearsden

CANTLAY John Simon   MB ChB 1969 DMRD 1973

CANTLAY Kenneth George   BSc(eng) 1969
s of William S. C. joiner and Elizabeth J. C. McRae clerkess; b Aber 29.1.48
CEng MICE 1974
asst eng Glasg: Babtie Shaw & Morton 1969–71, Scott

Wilson Kirkpatrick 1971–72; sect. eng Whatlings 1973–76; des eng Blyth & Blyth FFICE Inv from 1976
m Aber 4.4.72 Valerie A. Copland MA 1970 *qv*

CANTLAY Leslie Stuart   MB ChB 1969
s of William J. C. BSc 1943 *qv* and Sheila V. Innes MA 1966 *qv*; b Aber 14.7.45
Aber: h o 1969–70, sen h o psychiat 1970–71, psychiat regist 1971–72; milit serv r m o Belfast, Edin, Folkestone, S'ton (psychiat) and BAOR from 1972
m Aber 28.6.69 Sheila J. MacKenzie d of Hugh F. MacK. Inv

CANTLAY Valaine Innes   *MA 1967
m Middleton

CANTLAY William Shirras   MA 1966 LLB 1969
s of William R. C. teacher and Jane F. Shirras; b Aber 25.2.45
law app Elgin 1969–71; ptnr Cantley & Caithness solic St Andrews from 1971
m Aber 24.10.69 Rosemary J. Greig MA 1967 *qv*

CARBY-HALL Joseph Roger Rahbé   MA 1959
                                             LLB 1961
s of Daniel C-H army off., arch. and Nina A. Caruana; b Lydda Palestine 1.12.33
BA(Lond) RD 1974
asst leg. advis David Brown Indust Melham 1961–63; lect law Brist poly 1963–69; milit serv RA(TA) Sarawak and N Borneo 1965–66; RNR Intelligence from 1967; res stud. faculty of law Brist 1968–70; lect law univ Hull from 1970; author: *Principles of Industrial Law, Studies in Labour Law, Labour Relations and the Law, Cases in Managerial Law, Worker Participation in Europe;* edit. *Managerial Law*
m Southampton 3.3.62 Hilary V. Rudd stud. Aberd d of Thomas N. R. MB(Lond) Southampton

CARDEN Christopher Robert   BSc(for) 1970
s of Henry C. C. army off. and Jane StC. Daniell; b Lond 24.11.46
Papua, New Guinea: attached helicopter surv unit, for. dept 1970–71; asst dist for. off. Hoskins 1971; dist for. off. Nantambu 1972–73; sen lect utilization for. coll Bulolo 1973–74; Fiji: self-employed farm., relief estate worker NLDC 1975; car assembly worker NZMC Nelson NZ; man. off. Fiji pine commission from 1976
m Suva, Fiji 29.12.72 Sainimere Rokotuibau nurse, cosmetician, secy d of Isei R. Fiji

CARDNO David Donn   *MA 1962

CARDNO Edith Christina Jane   MA 1964
d of Andrew C. clerk and Lily Watt auxil nurse; b Fraserburgh 1.11.42
teacher Engl/Lat Fraserburgh acad 1965–76
m William T. Downie MA 1960 *qv*

CARDY James Charles   BSc 1970

CAREY Cynthia Laird   MA 1968 *1970
d of Bruce T. C. RN off. and Margaret Smith; b Aber 6.11.47
bilingual lexicographer Victoria, Canada 1971–74; Engl lang asst Paris 1974–75

CAREY Frances Elizabeth Gordon   *MA 1967
d of Gordon H. M. C. flt/sgt RAF (killed June 1944) and Barbara E. Thomson teacher; b Aber 24.8.44
secy/ling. course City of Westminster coll 1967–68; secy/pa London branch of Fr comp 1968–69; teacher Fr/Ger St Margaret's s Aber from 1970

CAREY Susan Veronica   MA 1963
d of B. John R. C. dir paper-making tech and Agnes B. Porteous secy; b Edin 11.3.43
sen secy course Wycombe coll 1963–64; pers secy to hosp admin Wycombe gen hosp from 1964

CARGILL Margaret Mary   MA 1961
d of George M. C. farm. and Margaret N. Forbes nurse; b Aber 30.4.40
Dip Soc St(Edin) 1962 Dip Child Care(Dund) 1968
disablement off. Stirling 1962–63; Edin: ch care off. 1963–67, 1968–70; soc worker 1970–73
m Aber 8.5.70 Myles M. Dryden BSc(Lond) univ prof Glas s of Robert P. D. Kirkcaldy

CARIDIS Dimitri Taki   PhD 1968
MD(Istan) FRCSE FRCAS

CARLE Alexander Robert   MA 1962 LLB 1964
s of Alexander R. C. clerk and Helen L. Rennie; b Aber 27.4.41
Aber: law app 1964–66, solic from 1966
m Aber 22.7.66 Judith M. Findlay MA 1965 *qv*

CARLISLE Eleanor McLaren   *MA 1964
d of Sydney S. C. CA and Elizabeth M. Webb; b Bombay 9.3.42
m Aber 15.9.65 James H. Stalker stationer/newsagent s of James M. S. Elgin

CARMICHAEL Barbara Morag   MA 1970
m Hamilton

CARMICHAEL David Alan   *MA 1968 Dip Ed 1969

CARMICHAEL Flora Christine Campbell   LLB 1963
d of William C. C. MA(Glas) chem and Elizabeth P. MacRae; b Glasg 19.8.41
Edin, Glasg: law app 1963–66; stud. Europ univs—Nancy, Düsseldorf, Hamburg 1966–68; lect compar law Glas 1968–71; jurist ling. Council of Min Brussels 1972–73; sen leg. asst, solic off. St Andrew's House Edin from 1973
m Edin 28.7.78 Leslie Hunt prod. man (aero. eng) s of Walter H. Alfreton

CARMICHAEL John Allan   BL 1965
s of John C. CA and Margaret R. F. Allan pharm; b Elgin 15.11.40
CA 1967
Aber: audit man. 1967–74; man. acct from 1974
m Aber 26.2.66 Kathleen Dutch staff nurse d of Norman D. Aber

CARMICHAEL Rosemary Catherine Dilys   MA 1962
                                                     LLB 1964
d of John H. C. MA 1929 *qv* and Alexandrina G. Dunlop MA 1932 *qv*; b Trawsfynydd Merioneth 2.11.40
law app: Aber 1964–66, Motherwell 1966; leg. asst: Carluke 1970–74, Glasg from 1975
m Aber 9.4.65 Ernest R. D. Smart MA 1958 *qv*

CARNEGIE Hazel May   *BSc 1969 PhD 1975
d of Alexander N. C. mech eng des and Betty Hampton; b Aber 16.3.47
res asst for. Aberd 1970; res stud. s of agr Aber 1970–73; scient off. natural envir res council Brathens res stat Banchory 1974; dem NOSCA from 1974

CARNEGIE Patrick Robert   PhD 1963
s of Robert Y. C. farm. and Catherine M. Leslie; b Kirkcaldy 16.12.34
BSc(St And) 1955

scient off. Ruakura NZ 1959; lect biochem univ Singapore 1960–64; sen res fell. Leeds 1964; sen lect biochem Melb Aust 1965–75, reader from 1975
m Hamilton NZ 1960 Mary E. Thompson p e teacher d of Robert M. T. Rutherglen Aust

CARNEGIE-SMITH Kaetrin   MB ChB 1966
 d of George C-S. BSc(eng) 1934 *qv*; b Shrewsbury 23.5.42
m John E. Black MB ChB(Belf) surg

CARNIE Ann   *BSc 1964
 MSc(Manit)
m Russell

CARNIE David Robertson   BSc 1958
 s of Thomas D. C. grocer and Edith Ross; b Laurence-kirk 13.11.37
BA(OU) 1974 G Inst P(IOP) 1975
teacher sc: Montrose acad 1959–66; Dingwall acad 1966–68, spec asst sc 1968–72; prin phys Dingwall acad from 1972
m Collieston 15.4.60 Isobel F. Cowie lab asst d of John C. Collieston

CARNIE Dorothy Frances   MA 1967
 d of Frank A. C. BSc 1935 *qv* and Anne J. S. Scroggie MA 1935 *qv*; b Stonehaven 29.4.47
m Aber 10.7.68 Alexander S. Craig BSc 1968 *qv*

CARNIE James Thomas   MA 1962

CARNIE John Allan   BSc 1958 PhD 1961
 b Aber 12.12.35
Manc: asst lect 1961–64, lect from 1964
m Aber 16.4.62 Marjorie I. Taylor

CARNIE Patricia Anne   MA 1965
 d of Frank A. C. BSc 1935 *qv* and Anne J. S. Scroggie MA 1935 *qv*; b Aber 15.5.44
m Aber 14.10.65 Jack R. Webb

CARNIE Thomas Ross   *BSc 1959
 s of Thomas D. C. grocer and Edith Ross; b Laurence-kirk 30.10.36
teacher math/sc Bell-Baxter h s Cupar 1960–62, spec asst phys 1962–65; prin phys: St Andrew RC h s Kirkcaldy 1965–67, Inverurie acad from 1967
m Aber 15.9.55 Elspeth J. G. McHardy d of Charles McH. Stonehaven

CARPENTER David William   BSc(eng) 1969
 s of K. N. C. schoolmaster and M. S. Sumner; b New-port, Mon 22.9.46
grad app Rolls-Royce aero div Glasg 1969–71; RAF coll Cranwell—pilot trg 1971–72; further flying trg Varsity and Hercules aircraft Oakington, Thorney Is 1972–73; Lyneham: Hercules co-pilot RAF 1973–76, Hercules capt RAF (flt-lt) from 1976

CARR Timothy Dominic Stephen   BSc(eng) 1964 *1965
 s of John M. C. BA(Cantab) solic and Edith M. Vincent; b Cambridge 27.5.43
Montreal: method eng Northern Elect. Co 1965–66, des eng United Aircraft of Canada 1966–69; Bristol: des eng Rolls Royce 1969–72, sales man. from 1972
m Hordle 30.8.75 Julia P. Child speech therap

CARRIE Brian James   *BMedBiol 1968 MB ChB 1971
 s of William W. C. BL 1940 *qv*; b Aber 16.4.47
MRCP 1975
h o ARI 1971–72; lect path. Aberd 1972–73; ARI: sen h o gen med 1973–74, regist gen med from 1974

CARROLL Helena Mary   MA 1964

CARRUTHERS David Robert   MA 1966 LL B 1968

CARRUTHERS James Philip   *MA 1967 Dip Ed 1968

CARSON Graham Margaret Gilston   *MA 1968
 d of William G. C. LRCPE g p and Margaret G. Munro nurs sister; b Edin 15.12.46
Dip Gen Ling(Manc) 1969
teacher Engl/Fr Montrose acad 1971–75
m Montrose 5.4.69 James P. Stevenson tel eng s of James P. S. Montrose

CARSON Joyce Marilyn   *MA 1960
 d of John M. C. estate gardener, school jan and Alice A. A. M. Thomson private serv/companion; b Aber 23.5.38
visiting lect relig kn/stud. Aber coll of educ 1960–61; part-time lect Engl/gen stud. Loughborough coll of f e 1962–64; lect Engl: coll of f e, tech coll Nott 1966–69, Burton-on-Trent tech coll 1969–74; sen teacher i/c career based courses Sixth Form coll Nott from 1974; TA: lieut WRAC 1958–62, 1965–66, capt 1967–76
m Aber 20.8.60 Arnold G. Fogg PhD 1961 *qv*

CARSS Alison Henderson   MB ChB 1958

CARTER Alyson Mary   MA 1968
 d of Andrew M. C. sheriff's off. and Mina M. Thomson; b Banff 1.10.46
teacher: Helensburgh 1969–70, Paisley 1970–71, Linwood 1972–75, Erskine from 1975
m Aber 6.12.69 Michael J. O'Leary MA 1969 *qv*

CARTER Caroline Katherine Horne   *BSc 1970
 d of William C. health phys monitor and Elizabeth Macdonald; b Wick 15.4.48
res asst Aberd 1970–71; teacher biol Edin from 1972
m Wick 29.3.75 Harold M. Gillespie BA(Cantab) s of John B. G. Currie

CARTER Jennifer Mary Talbot   *MA 1966

CARTER Peter Eric Graham   MB ChB 1968
 s of Eric T. G. C. army off. and Violet G. Penney; b Solihull 2.6.22
Croix de Guerre 1945 BA(Cantab) 1949 MBE 1960 MA(Cantab) 1968 DObstRCOG 1972
off. RE 1941–62, retd as major; h o ARI 1968–69; g p trainee Culter 1969–70; sen h o ARI: cas 1970–71, obst 1971–72; med off. stud. health serv 1972–74; phys i/c stud. health serv Aberd from 1974
m Accra 3.5.58 Alison C. Hare BBC secy d of Ivan L. O. H. Rottingdean

CARTER Robert Nattress   MB ChB 1958
 s of James V. C. acct and Gladys Nattress; b Trimdon Colliery Co Durham 9.8.34
DObstRCOG MRCGP
h o, sen h o Hartlepool 1958–60; trainee g p Edin 1960–61, lect g p Edin 1961–62; prin trainer in g p Easington, Peterlee (univ N'cle) from 1962
m Horden 13.8.59 Sheila Johnson teacher d of Frederick C. J. Horden

CARTNEY Michael William   BSc(eng) 1966
 s of William S. C. civ serv and Marjorie Rushton; b Maryport 18.9.43
MICE 1970
asst civ eng Cumberland c c highways dept Carlisle

1966–71; sen civ eng Stirling c c central reg highways from 1971
m Sulby I of M 12.8.67 Elaine B. Radcliffe MA 1967 *qv*

CARTWRIGHT Hugh MacLean   MA 1966
  s of Thomas C. soldier, miner, for. and Margaret Mac-Lean nurse; b Motherwell 22.10.43
Dip Free Ch coll(Edin) 1969
min Urquhart, Conon Bridge from 1969
m Daviot Inv, Mina M. Mackintosh farm. d of Alexander M. Dores

CASELEY Jane Rosamond   MB ChB 1956
  d of John R. C. BSc(eng)(Lond) civ eng and Katherine C. Spence MB ChB 1921 *qv*; b Singapore 15.4.31
h o: Aber, Brighton, Loughborough 1956–58; sen h o: Elizabeth J. Anderson hosp Lond 1958–59, Radcliffe I and Churchill hosp Oxford 1959–60; N Lond blood transfusion centre Edgware from 1960
m Lond –.7.61 Kurt Hellman DM(Oxon) cancer res

CASS David Roger Thoday   MA 1965

CASSELS Christine Thompson   MA 1968
  d of Kenneth J. C. retail man. and Jessie T. Lockhart; b Lanark 24.6.47
teacher geog/Engl/mod stud. Bearsden acad from 1969

CASSIDY John Edward   PhD 1968
  s of Edward C. and Elizabeth McDermott; b Manc 6.1.39
ARCST(Salf) 1962 ARIC 1962
res scient sect. leader ICI Runcorn 1966–77; tech man. ICI lime group Buxton from 1977
m Altrincham 6.6.64 Kathleen O'Connor

CASSIE Elizabeth Anne   *MA 1967
  d of William C. security advis and Isobel K. Reid; b Huntly 27.6.45
Dip Ed(Edin)
teacher Engl: Kirkcaldy h s 1968–71, Inv r acad 1971–74
m Aber 2.8.69 Peter N. Grainger BA(Durh) lect s of Francis L. G. BA(Lond) Upminster

CASSIE George   *BSc 1968
  s of Charles T. C. radio mech and Ella Ritchie; b Fraserburgh 31.1.46
army off. (capt) England, Germany 1968–78
m Grasmere 10.4.71 Marilyn A. Metcalfe teacher d of Joseph B. M. Whitburn

CASSIE Ralph   MB ChB 1964

CASTRO José López   MSc 1969
  s of Alejandrino C. vet surg and Nelida López teacher; b Tacuarembo 10.4.31
Ing Agrónomo(Uruguay) 1959
Uruguay: tech plan agropecuario Montevideo 1961–62, tech asst dept soil Sei Centro de Inv Agricolas La Estanzuela 1962–69, head dept soil sc agr res center 1969–74, head dept integrated res from 1974
m Tacuarembo 8.11.63 Violeta Albernaz d of Ursino A. Tacuarembo

CATER Alan John   LLB 1969

CATTANACH Helen Barlow   MB ChB 1962
  m Cooper

CATTO Christian May   MA 1966

CATTO Doreen Mary   BSc 1970
  d of William R. C. trackman and Maggie M. Thomson

nurse; b Maud 28.10.49
nurse auxil Maud 1970–73; stud. nurse Edin from 1973

CATTO Graeme Robertson Dawson   *MB ChB 1969
                                                    ***MD 1975**
  s of William D. C. MB ChB 1939 *qv*; b Aber 24.4.45
MRCP(UK) 1971
h o Aber 1969–70; dept med Aberd: res fell. 1970–73, lect from 1973
m Aber 14.7.67 Joan Sievewright LL B 1966 *qv*

CATTO Leslie Urquhart Macdonald   BSc 1969

CATTO Sheila Mary   MA 1964
  d of Patrick C. farm. and Mary Herd MA 1937 *qv*
b Fraserburgh 20.12.42
teacher Daviot Aberdeensh from 1965

CAWTHORN Nigel George   *BSc 1970
  s of James E. C. master tailor and Mary Monseair; b Pontefract 12.6.47
MSc(BC) 1973
mine geol Tungsten Canada from 1973
m Vancouver 7.5.71 Mary I. Florence BSc 1970 *qv*

CENTER Alexander Ross   *MA 1959

CEREXHE Ian   BSc 1970
  s of Ernest A. G. C. contr and Sophia M. M. McCracken nurse; b Portpatrick 9.9.46
UK, North Sea, Europe: operative, chargehand civ eng 1970–74, jun man., sen man. from 1974
m Shipley 1975 B. Lesley Anderson teacher d of James A. Shipley

CHADHA Rajendra Nath   PhD 1959
  s of Beant R. C. army off. and Krishna W. Suri; b Rawalpindi 1.8.30
BSc(Luck) 1951 MSc 1953 PhD(Luck) 1957
USA: post doct fell. Brooklyn poly New York 1959–60; sen chem W. R. Grace & Co 1960–63; dir res and dev Staufer Chem Co 1966–69; man. chem and polymers Marbon Chem Co 1966–69; chmn of board and chief exec off. Carroll Products Inc from 1969
m Washington D.C. Ajit Kaur Behl MD(Amritsar) phys d of S. Kundan S. B. Chandrigarh Punjab

CHADWICK Beryl   MA 1968
  d of Vincent C. eng and Ada Smith; b Accrington 28.12.45
careers off.: Prescot 1969–71, Middlesbrough 1971–73
m Aberfeldy 23.10.71 Robert T. Third MA 1966 *qv*

CHAINA Perviz   PhD 1968
  BSc MSc(Bom)
m Clifford

CHALLINOR Ronald   MA 1966
  s of Ronald C. and Mary Macleod; b Stornoway 25.5.45
teacher: Greenock 1967–73, Denny 1973–79; prin Engl Falkirk from 1979

CHALLIS-SOWERBY Loraine   *MA 1969 CASS 1975
  d of Derek C-S. teacher and Florence A. Bedworth shop asst; b Newton-le-Willows Lancs 2.8.47
commun worker Aber 1970–71; soc worker: Lancs 1971–74, Peterhead from 1974
m Aber 1.4.70 William Donaldson MA 1968 *qv*

CHALMERS Alastair   MA 1966 *MEd 1970

CHALMERS Anthony Alan   *BSc 1960 PhD 1964

CHALMERS David Johnstone   *BSc 1962 MSc 1964

CHALMERS George Lovie   MB ChB 1957
s of Roderick M. C. stonemason and Annabella
Strachan; b Aber 12.1.33
MRCPGlas 1965 MRCPE 1964
h o Inv R I, Victoria I Glas 1957–61; regist: gen med
Aber 1961–63, geriat med Dun 1963–65, sen regist 1965–
67; consult phys geriat med WI Glasg from 1967
m Inv 25.3.60 Jean Sutherland SRN d of William S.
Fearn

CHALMERS John Colin   *BSc 1960
s of Alan C. banker and Dorothy M. Polkinghorn; b
Tientsin 17.12.34
Belfast, Min of Agr, NI: asst prin 1960–64, dep prin
1964–68, prin 1968–74; asst secy dept agr from 1974
m Aber 11.7.61 Freda S. Rae teacher d of Harry R. Cults

CHALMERS Margaret Mitchell   MA 1969
d of Robert C. bus driver and Agnes H. M. Hepburn
shop asst; b Aber 11.7.48
teacher: Aber 1970–73, asst prin Engl Aber from 1973
m Aber 28.12.70 Ian T. Brodie teacher s of Daniel B.
Aber

CHALMERS Robert Alexander   DSc 1968
s of Alexander C. steelgrinder and Maud R. Nickolls;
b Birm 17.6.20
BSc(Manc) 1950 PhD(Edin) 1953 FRSE 1978
ICI res fell. Durh 1953–56; Aberd: from 1956 lect, sen
lect, reader
m Aber 4.8.62 Grace C. Turner MB ChB 1958 qv

CHALMERS William Skea   BSc(for) 1956
s of William S. C. BSc(agr) 1922 qv(II) and Violet E.
Richards; b Co. Durham 10.7.31
jun res fell. bot univ coll WI Jamaica 1956–58; Trinidad
and Tobago: res off. govt for. dept 1959–65, acting dep
conserv for. 1965–66 Port of Spain; UWI: res fell. cocoa
1966–73, asst regist 1973–76, sen asst regist from 1976
m 3.12.57 Alisha O. Westmaas d of Vivian O. W. Arima
Trinidad

CHAMBERLAIN Brian Richard   PhD 1965
s of Joseph H. S. C. aircraft eng and Ivy L. Bradshaw;
b Oxford 30.6.35
ARIC (1965)
res chem Pilkington Bros Ormskirk from 1964
m Aber 28.8.64 Helen S. Gilmour BSc 1962 qv

CHAMBERLAIN Janet Mary   PhD 1957
d of Clifford C. radio eng and Eva D. Curtis; b Desborough 14.5.31
BSc(Lond) 1952 MSc(Lond) 1953
res fell. dept of materia med Aberd 1963–68; res assoc
dept of internal med univ of Virginia USA 1965–66;
asst res dept biochem Cantab/fell. Lucy Cavendish coll
Cambridge
m Desborough 22.7.53 W. Peter G. Stein PhD 1955 qv

CHAMBERS Marcus Rex   *BSc 1965 MSc 1966
s of Laurence R. C. cotton manuf and Nellie C. Law;
b Rawtenstall 28.1.43
PhD(Liv) 1971
Edin: res asst nature conserv 1966–67; lect biol Napier
Coll 1967–68; res fell. zool Liv 1968–71; res fell. Aberd
1971–74; lect biol univ Sains Malaysia Penang from 1975
m Aber 18.1.75 Phyllis W. Booth SRN d of James B.
Aber

CHAMBERS Martin Alexander   LLB 1968 *1969
s of Alexander M. C. cabinetmaker and Robina H. T.

Sinclair; b Glasg 7.10.46
lang teacher Swaziland 1969–70; Glasg: law app 1970–72,
solic 1972–74; geol asst Namibia 1974–76; solic Melbourne from 1976
m Melbourne 18.3.78 Inez B. A. Prasad d of Andrew
G. P. Fiji

CHAN Edwin Wai   BSc 1970

CHAN Kwok Thye   *MA 1960
s of Chan Ah Hong AMN; b Malaysia 29.3.25
Kuala Lumpur: educ off. 1960–64, secy tariff advis board
Malaysia 1964–70, dir tariff div fed. indust dev auth from
1970
m Kuala Lumpur 18.8.62 Eleanor M. Berry teacher d of
P. P. B. Lundin Links

CHANDLER David Brendan   MA 1961

CHANDRASENAN Kochukunju   PhD 1966
BSc(Trav) MSc(Luck)

CHAPMAN Dianne Heald   BSc 1967

CHAPMAN Elizabeth Anne Mary   MA 1967

CHAPMAN Gwendoline Mary   MA 1969 CASS 1972
d of James P. C. garage prop. and Jessie A. de S.
Morison teacher; b Kirriemuir 22.8.48
soc worker Dun from 1972 (trainee 1969–70)

CHAPMAN John Sangster   *MA 1963
s of Harry C. and Lilias M. Sangster; b Aber 6.6.41
HM insp taxes Glasg 1964–65; Lond: salesman 1965–66,
town planning res off. 1966–70, computer progr from
1974

CHAPMAN Margaret Anne   MA 1965

CHAPMAN Martin John   *BSc 1967
s of Richard J. C. chem and Madeleine Rushforth
teacher piano; b Stanford-le-Hope 14.7.45
PhD(Lond) 1970
res asst Middx med s 1967–70, fell. Oklahoma city USA,
1970–72, publ health serv San Francisco 1972–74; res
investigator Paris from 1974

CHAPMAN Robert Sutherland   *MB ChB 1962
s of Robert C. bank man. and Edith G. Sutherland
teacher; b Cults 4.6.38
MRCPE 1965 (Lond) 1967
res fell. therap Aberd 1963–66, regist, sen regist dermat
ARI 1966–69; sen regist dermat Middx h Lond 1969–71;
consult dermat Glasg northern h and Stirlingsh/hon clin
lect Glas from 1971
m Meonstoke Rosalind S. Slater BSc(Leeds) scient res
worker (atherosclerosis) d of Ian G. S. BSc(Birm)
Meonstoke

CHAPMAN William   *MA 1963
s of George G. C. bank man. and Jane A. Cameron;
b Peterhead 26.1.40
teacher geog: Blairgowrie 1964–71, prin geog Perth g s
from 1971
m Perth 28.3.75 Kathryn L. Mackay MA(St And) teacher
d of G. L. M. Perth

CHARITONOWSKY Ariene   MA 1964
d of Nicolau C. LLB(Riga) barrister and Astrid von
der Pahlen secy, bus. prop.; b Riga Latvia 29.4.39
Dip Ed(Syd) 1972
shop asst to Fr consul, audit asst, clerk Blantyre Malawi

1961–62; teacher: Fr Kumasi Ghana 1964–65, mod
lang NSW Aust from 1968
m Aber 5.9.60 Alastair J. McLean BSc 1960 *qv*

CHARLES Benedict Augustine   MB ChB 1957
s of Richard C. farm. and Maude A. Batt; b St Andrews
Grenada WI 15.1.19
BSc(Wash) 1951
h o Stracathro h 1957–59; g p Grenada 1959–75; private
pract St Andrews Grenada from 1975

CHARLES Gaynor Barbara   MA 1969
d of Bryn C. teacher and Aileen F. Hutchison receptionist; b Rossett Wales 28.7.48
teacher: Aber 1970–71, Hastings NZ 1972–78
m Aber 28.12.71 Ian G. Cotching BSc 1971 teacher s of
John W. C. Aber

CHARLES Lauchlan Munro   BSc 1964
b Inv 8.10.39
sen biochem (NHS) Aber from 1964

CHARLESON Euphemia Barbara   BSc(agr) 1958
d of Charles W. C. crofter/postman and Jemima
Cheyne; b Shetland 11.8.36
asst exper off., exper off. Rowett inst Aber 1958–66
m Aber 27.6.62 Gordon M. Philip master butcher s of
Patrick C. C. P. Aber

CHARLTON Maureen   *BSc 1969
m Rose

CHAYTOR Daniel Emanuel Babatunji   *BSc 1958
s of Daniel A. H. C. civ serv and Adeline L. Lisk;
b Sierra Leone 13.4.31
PhD(Lond) 1961
Sierra Leone: lect zool Fourah Bay coll 1961–65; Njala
univ coll: sen lect 1965–66, dean sc 1966–67, vice-prin
1967–68; visiting prof biol Mass inst tech USA 1968–71;
prof zool Fourah Bay coll from 1971; dir inst marine biol
oceanog from 1973
m Lond 28.9.55 Trixie M. Thomas nurs sister d of
Emanuel H. T. MA(Durh) Freetown Sierra Leone

CHEADLE Yvonne Ada   MA 1961

CHEE Sek Por   PhD 1961
BCE(Melb)

CHEONG-LEEN Philip   MB ChB 1964
s of Edward C-L. merch and Elvira Low; b Hong Kong
8.3.38
FRCSE 1970
h o Aber 1964–65, sen h o Dun 1966–67; regist: Inv
1967–71, Lond 1971–74; sen orthop regist St George's
hosp Lond 1974–75; clin lect orthop univ of Hong Kong
from 1975; consult. orthop surg Queen Mary's hosp for
ch Carshalton/St James's hosp Lond from 1975
m Perth –.9.67 Dorothy J. Jackson nurse d of James J.
Newburgh Fife

CHERIYAN Joseph Kottukapally   MB ChB 1960

CHERMSIRIVATHANA Chirayupin   MSc 1964
BSc(Thaild)

CHESTER Michael Peter   *BSc(eng) 1968

CHEW Kenneth John   *BSc 1968 PhD 1978
s of John C. and Margaret M. MacEwan MA(St And)
statist; b Aber 24.8.45
sen asst geol Ontario dept mines Toronto 1968–69;
Aberd: res stud. geol 1968–69, 1971–73, SRC secy 1969–

70, pres 1970–71, rector's assessor univ court 1970–72;
geol BP Petr Dev 1974–76; lect geol univ coll Galway
from 1976
m Aber 6.4.71 Gillian G. Robertson MA 1966 *qv*

CHEW Moh-Koon   MB ChB 1961

CHEYNE Colin Fitzroy   MA 1970
s of George D. C. MA 1927 *qv*; b Edin 21.3.48
indust eng: Wiggins Teape S Wales 1970–71, MBO
advis St Neots 1971–72; Appleyard(Aber) p a to man.
dir 1972–73, marketing man. 1973–74; gen man, 1974–
76; quality control man. Simpson Wright & Lowe Notts
from 1976
m St Neots 9.9.72 Hilary K. Sheffield d of Ernest W. S.
St Neots

CHEYNE David George Mitchell   *MA 1969

CHEYNE Denis   BSc 1970

CHEYNE Gordon McLeod   MB ChB 1961
s of Robert G. C. banker and Margaret McLeod
teacher; b Insch 11.3.37
DObstRCOG 1963 MRACGP 1967
h o Aber, Nantwich 1961–63; g p Aber 1963–64; res m o
Burnie hosp Tasmania; Melbourne: g p 1965–69, anaest
from 1969
m Elgin 28.9.73 Sheila Telfer nurse d of James L. T. Elgin

CHEYNE John Alexander Leitch   *MA 1957
s of Charles D. C fish merch and Rosaline Leitch
typist; b Aber 5.10.34
BA(Oxon) 1959 MEd(Edin) 1970
secy Christian Council for overseas stud. Edin 1960–64,
min St Andrews cong ch St And 1964–65; chaplain Royal
h s Edin; lect educ dept coll of educ Dun from 1970
m Aber 28.7.60 Eileen A. Butler MA 1959 *qv*

CHEYNE Laurence Alexander   *MA 1970
s of James C. civ serv and Joyce L. Grant secy;
b Aber 5.12.47
teacher hist Glasg: Kingsbridge s s 1971–73, Bellahouston
acad 1973–74, prin hist Lochend s s from 1974
m Aber 6.2.71 Pamela A. Milne MA 1970 *qv*

CHEYNE Lorna Ruth   *MA 1966
d of William B. C. cost acct and Lila Mackenzie;
b Aber 22.8.44
teacher Engl: Hawick h s 1967–70, Riddings comp s
Scunthorpe from 1975
m Aber 5.9.66 John Adam MA 1966 *qv*

CHEYNE Muriel May   *MA 1959
m Nicol

CHEYNE William Mackenzie   *MA 1961 PhD 1965
s of William B. C. acct and Lila Mackenzie; b Aber
8.11.38
asst lect dept psych Strath 1964–66, lect from 1966
m Cumbernauld 10.5.74 Rona J. G. Lamont BA(Strath)
teacher d of John L. Glasg

CHIEDU Sylvester Okafor   BSc(eng) 1957

CHILD Mary Elizabeth   MA 1968
d of George C. BSc(Leeds) res chem ICI and Kathleen
Stevenson BSc(Leeds) magistrate; b Stockton-on-Tees
6.9.46
shorthand typist dept educ Stir 1969–70; secy Nott
1970–71, Aston 1971–72
m Stockton-on-Tees 17.7.68 Graham T. Maybank BSc
1966 *qv*

CHILMAN Paul Thomas   BSc(eng) 1964

CHILTON Kenneth John   *BSc 1968
s of John A. C. clerk and Joyce Borrill; b Aber 10.5.46
MSc(Essex) 1972
computer progr with ICL from 1968
m Lond 11.12.71 Linda M. Barnes BEd(Lond) teacher d
of Eric B. Downton

CHIN Leslie   *BSc 1962
PhD(Lond)

CHIN Sherlock Syn Lok   MB ChB 1966
s of Chin C. C. chief acct and Betty K. H. Tong
teacher; b Brunei 25.12.36
DTM&H(Liv) 1972
h o RNI Inv, RACH 1967–68; gen hosp Brunei: m o
1968–77, sen m o from 1977
m Aber 9.7.66 Vivienne M. Douglas MA 1955 *qv*

CHINNOCK John Henry   MB ChB 1959
s of William H. C. policeman and Eliza Whiston; b
Tamworth 26.10.33
DObstRCOG 1962
h o: N Staffs RI and ARI 1959–60, obst N Staffs mat.
hosp 1960–61; g p Stourbridge from 1961, clin asst obst/
gyn from 1966
m Tamworth –.8.63 Margaret L. Downing SRN d o
Arthur H. D. Stoke-on-Trent

CHIPHANGWI John David   MB ChB 1966
s of P. David C. farm. and Esther Z. Nsoma; b Malawi
17.12.36
DObs 1971 and MMed 1973(Makerere) MRCOG 1973
Malawi: h o Blantyre cent h 1966–67, dist m o Dedza
1967–69, acting med supt Zomba 1969–70; Uganda:
Mulago h Kampala 1970–73; Malawi: consult. Blantyre
cent h from 1973
m Blantyre 1974 Stella Thewe nurse

CHISHOLM Allan Donald   *MA 1967
s of Roderick C. MA(Edin) headmaster and Flora
Finlayson; b Grantown-on-Spey 16.6.45
econ: plan consult. Epsom 1967–68, Scot. dev ag Edin
1968–72; man. construct. comp Edin from 1973
m Inv 10.7.70 Anne L. Parkhill MA 1967 *qv*

CHISHOLM Duncan Douglas   MB ChB 1965
Dip Psychother 1970
s of Roderick C. MA(Edin) headmaster and Flora
Finlayson; b Grantown-on-Spey 8.10.41
DPM 1968 MRCPsych 1972
Aber: h o Glenburn Wing, ARI 1965–66; sen h o, regist,
Royal Cornhill h 1966–69; regist Ross Clinic 1969–70,
sen regist child psychiat RACH from 1970 (seconded
Clarke inst of psychiat Tor 1973–74)
m Aber 6.10.66 Rosemary G. Doyle MA 1964 *qv*

CHISHOLM James Alan   *BSc 1970
s of James C. tech UKAEA and Robina L. R. Brown;
b Edin 31.12.47
CEng MIEE 1977
PO exec eng telecom dev Lond from 1970
m Aber 22.12.70 Ruebena A. Duncan MA 1969 *qv*

CHISHOLM John Martin   BSc 1969

CHISHOLM Mairi   MA 1970
b Dingwall 20.5.48
teacher classics Millburn acad Inv 1971–75, asst prin
classics from 1975

CHISHOLM Neil William Thomas   BSc 1968

CHIZEA Leonard Governor   BSc(for) 1960
s of Obi C. Egumkonye farm. and Mary Elikwu; b
Asaba Nigeria 8.11.19
Nigeria: prov for. off. Ibadan 1960–63, for. off. Benin
1963–67, off. i/c regeneration Bendel State 1970–71, biol
master St Patrick's coll Asaba from 1976
m Benin city 9.1.45 Elizabeth Mokolo d of John O. M.
Asaba

CHONA Walter Dyson   MSc 1967
BSc(Rhodes)

CHOW Pak Shan   PhD 1970
b China 26.11.41
BSc(Chu Hai) MSc(R'dg)
lect Aberd from 1966
m Dun 25.9.71 Man C. Chiu MSc(Dund) computer progr

CHOY Stephen Tze Leung   MSc 1968 PhD 1969
BSc(Sun-Yat-Sen)

CHRISTIAN Glenda Angela   MA 1964
m Bastien

CHRISTIANSON Aileen Barbara   *MA 1966
d of Alan C. and Muriel Barker; b Colwyn Bay 8.8.44
res Engl dept Edin from 1966

CHRISTIE Alexander Ogilvie   *BSc 1956 PhD 1960

CHRISTIE Brenda Air   MA 1965
d of Robert E. C. off. man. and Agnes A. Young
clerkess; b Aber 17.10.44
teacher maths: Kaimhill s s Aber 1966–68, Queen Anne
s Dunfermline 1968–69, Douglas acad Milngavie 1970–
72, Summerhill acad Aber 1972, Mackie acad Stonehaven
1972–73
m Aber 18.10.68 Neil Robertson BSc(eng) 1967 *qv*

CHRISTIE Bryce   *BSc 1959
b Aber 27.6.37
prin teacher biol sc Peterhead acad from 1964; prin
examiner SCE exam board from 1976
m Aber 24.7.67 Priscilla Robb

CHRISTIE Colin   MA 1963

CHRISTIE Derek James   MA 1969

CHRISTIE Dorothy   MA 1968
m Riviere

CHRISTIE Dorothy Louise   MA 1968
m Kelso

CHRISTIE Evelyn Jane Campbell   MA 1968
d of William C. banker and Evelyn Dempster; b Edin
19.7.47
Dip Sec St(Strath) 1969
teacher ILEA from 1973

CHRISTIE Frances Mary   MA 1970

CHRISTIE Gayre   *MA 1970 MEd 1972
s of David C. eng and Isobel Gair; b Arbroath 16.3.45
teacher Arbroath acad 1972–73; educ psych Dun 1973–
75; lect psych Kelvingrove coll Brisbane Aust from 1975
m Aber 14.2.75 Carol A. Mullin d of Henry W. M.
Arbroath

CHRISTIE Gordon   *MA 1969
s of William G. C. chief supt E of Scot. Water Board

and Doris Thompson play s supt; b Aber 8.9.46
Dip Ed(Edin) 1970
teacher hist Ardrossan acad from 1970

CHRISTIE James McLean BSc 1963
s of Martin H. C. rly porter and Mary M. McLean
landscape artist; b Inverbervie 17.5.42
teacher maths/sc Laurencekirk 1964-66; RAF educ off.
SW Britain from 1966
m Laurencekirk Arlene E. H. Polson teacher, sales rep

CHRISTIE Janet Frances MA 1961
d of Richard N. C. army off. (G.H.) and Norah
Elsmie; b Gibraltar 30.1.36
secy: Collins publ London 1961-63, to Warden Rhodes
House Oxford 1963-70; secy/asst to prin Aberd 1971-73;
secy to prin Royal Holloway Coll univ Lond Egham
from 1974

CHRISTIE Jessie Mary MA 1958

CHRISTIE John Alexander MA 1956 LLB 1959
s of John C. lic grocer/gen merch and Mary W. B.
Sangster; b Tarland 2.6.35
solic Huntly from 1959, town clerk from 1970
m Huntly 17.3.63 Elizabeth M. Whitehouse d of Joseph
W. Huntly

CHRISTIE John Grant *BSc(eng) 1960
s of William C. MA 1929 qv and Isobel G. Bain MA
1923 qv; b Aber 12.4.38
MS(Harv) 1961
ICI: eng Billingham 1961-63, plastics Welwyn 1963-69;
Thetford: chief eng Vacuum Res 1969-73, dir Camvac
from 1973
m Aber 22.12.61 Patricia M. Shannon teacher d of
William P. S. MA(Glas) Aber

CHRISTIE John Lindley MB ChB 1961

CHRISTIE Kathleen Hardie MA 1962
d of Alexander C. insur man. and Catherine B. Hardie
secy; b Arbroath 9.7.41
teacher Engl Dalkeith h s 1963-68
m Aber 28.12.66 Forbes Marr BArch(Edin) arch./plan.
s of Archibald M. Aber

CHRISTIE Linda Sylvia Matthew MA 1966
m Hargrave

CHRISTIE Malcolm Andrew Bain *MA 1958
s of William C. MA 1929 qv and Isabel G. Bain MA
1923 qv; b Aber 9.7.36
dist off. N Rhodesia 1959-64; econ cent. plan. off.
Lusaka 1964-66; dev stud. Sus 1966-68; sen econ
M o Dev/Fin. Lusaka 1969-70, dir Walkover Estates
(irrigated farm. comp) Lusaka 1970-75; dir Landells
Mills Assoc (agr res and man. consult.) Lond, Bath from
1975
m Aber 3.11.62 Christian D. Fraser MA 1957 qv

CHRISTIE Margaret Barbara Anne MA 1965
Dip Ed 1966
d of Alexander C. farm. and Elizabeth M. Berry nursery
nurse; b Torphins 2.6.43
Dip. to teach deaf(Edin) 1978
teacher: Viewforth s s Kirkcaldy 1966-68, Elgin acad
1968-72, New Elgin p s 1972-73, Milltimber p s 1973-74,
Aber s for deaf from 1974

CHRISTIE Michael George Alexander MA 1966
cLLB 1968 *1969
m Margaret R. Sharp MA 1970 qv

CHRISTIE Michael James BSc 1970
s of James G. C. sheep man. and Rebecca M. M. Ross;
b Nigg Tain 15.6.49
Plessey telecomm Liv: tel syst des eng 1970-77, computer
facilities man. from 1977
m Liv 14.2.74 Sandra Y. Martin clerkess d of George S.
Liv

CHRISTIE Moira Macleod MA 1964
d of Alexander C. civ serv and Louise H. Johnston
cashier; b Aber 2.6.43
Dip Soc Ad(St And) 1965
soc welfare off. C of S Langlands Park s Port Glasgow
1965-66; Fraserburgh: asst to children's off. Aberdeensh 1966-69, soc worker counties of Aber & Kinc
1969-72; Aber: sen soc worker Aberdeensh/Kinc 1972-
75; soc work man. Grampian reg council (Aber city div)
from 1975

CHRISTIE Moira Margaret MA 1960
m Bruce

CHRISTIE Moyra Margaret MA 1958
m Burness

CHRISTIE Peter George Smith BSc(eng) 1965
s of Laurence S. postman/crofter and Magdalen
Christie knitter (cottage indust); b Skibhoull Cunningsburgh Shetland 28.6.41
trainee/jun eng Eng Elect. Co Burton-on-Trent and Edin
1965-69; steam turbine eng GEC Turbines Liddell Power
Station NSW Aust 1970-76; eng Construction Div GEC
(Aust) from 1976
m Lond 11.3.67 Lynette A. Wilson bank clerk d of
Reginald W. Southport

CHRISTIE Peter Laurie BSc(eng) 1959

CHRISTIE Reginald George LLB 1969
s of Reginald C. C. MA 1946 qv and Flora Barclay
MA 1942 qv; b Aber 1.7.48
Aber: law app, asst A. C. Morrison & Richards advoc
1969-72; ptnr Christie, Buthlay & Rutherford advoc
from 1972
m Aber 9.9.71 Yvonne M. H. Alden MA 1971 secy d of
Charles T. A. Dyce

CHRISTIE Robert Philip MA 1967
BSc(Lond)
res fell. occup guid proj sponsored by DES and DE
Hatfield poly 1974-76; prin off. psych/trg advis Hants
c c from 1976, consult. psych dyslexia remed organis from
1979

CHRISTIE Roy David BSc 1970
s of David A. C. publ works contr and Mabel F. Will;
b Aber 10.11.48
BVMS MRCVS(Glas) 1974
vet stud. Glas 1970-74; vet surg Grange, Adelaide S
Aust from 1974

CHRISTOPHER Moira Anne BEd 1969
d of David B. C. auto-elect. and Jean R. Bowie audio-
typist; b Elgin 8.5.48
teacher Mosstodloch 1969-72; relief teaching from 1978
m Aber 20.6.70 James L. Wilson farm worker/grieve,
self-employed contr s of William W. Keith

CHRYSTAL Kathleen May Robertson *MB ChB 1958
d of William A. C. law acct and Agnes M. Robertson
typist; b Aber 23.10.34
FRCSE 1964

h o ARI 1958–59; sen h o gen and orthop surg Inv hosps 1959–61; ARI: res fell. SHERT 1961–62, regist cas traumatic surg 1962–63, regist gen surg 1963–67; plastic surg: regist Westminster & Roehampton h Lond 1967–70, sen regist United Cardiff h 1970–71, SERHB Scot. Edin 1971–72; consult plastic surg N'cle RHB from 1972

CHU Cheong Wai   MA 1970

CHUA Dorothy Poh Luan   MB ChB 1958
d of Keh H. C. bank man. and Swee H. (Annie) Lee; b Singapore 9.7.30
Lond: h o 1960–61, cas off. 1961–62, sen h o paediat 1962–63; part-time m o Wandsworth 1964–73; clin asst Kingston hosp 1969–73, med asst from 1973
m Lond 31.1.59 Albert C. K. Looi comp dir s of Eng L. Penang; marr diss 1974

CHUNG Arthur Frederick   MB ChB 1967
s of Albert C. and Myrtle M. Minott; b Portland, Jamaica 12.10.42
h o Aber 1967–68; New York: resid obst/gyn 1968–72, fell. mem Sloan Kettering cancer centre 1972–74, asst prof coll phys and surg Columbia univ from 1974
d NY 16.12.78 AUR XLVIII 234

CHUNG PIN YONG Susan Sanne Hing   BSc 1968
m Lanhinglit

CHURCHARD Graeme Ogg   *BSc 1969
s of John C. C. head storekeeper and Jeannie E. Ogg; b Aber 19.9.47
geol: St And 1969–72; S Africa: geol surv Zululand 1973–74, Union Corp Orange Free State from 1974 (St Helena Gold Mines)

CIESLA Michael John   *MA 1969
s of Josef C. welder and Isabella Thomson; b Montrose 7.3.47
teacher, asst prin guid Arbroath 1970–72; prin geog Penicuik 1972–78; asst head S Queensferry from 1978
m Montrose 14.6.69 Patricia A. Beattie secy d of William F. B. Montrose

CLARK Adam Alexander   *BSc(eng) 1968
s of Adam A. C. farm. and Jessie I. Barclay; b Turriff 9.5.46
Dip Man Stud(Derby) 1969
Rolls-Royce: trainee aero-eng div Derby 1968–70; nuclear reactor course R.N. coll Greenwich 1970; operating eng RR & Associates Thurso 1970–76; asst resid eng RR & A Clyde submarine base Faslane from 1977

CLARK Alan Peter   *BSc 1970
s of Albert C. civ serv; b Cheshire 18.8.46
MSc(Stir) 1971 PhD(Stir) 1973
res fell. (SRC) theoret phys Stir 1973–77; prin res off. BSRA Wallsend N'cle-u-Tyne from 1977

CLARK Alastair James   *BSc 1962
s of James B. C. farm. and Barbara H. Rae; b Insch 29.5.40
chem tech BP Co Grangemouth 1962–68; res chem Arthur D. Little res inst Edin 1968–70; sen dev scient M.S.A.Co. Glasg 1970–72, res/dev man. from 1972

CLARK Alistair Verne   MA 1963 BD 1966
s of Alexander C. Christian missionary Bolivia, fin. secy to YMCA Aber and Mary O. Wood Christian missionary Bolivia; b Samaipata Bolivia 18.6.41
Baptist min: Oban 1967–71, Lossiemouth from 1971
m Aber 9.7.65 Audrey Smith teacher d of James S. Aber

CLARK Cecilia Marie   MB ChB 1962
d of William C. C. tech off. GPO tel and Cecilia Black; b Aber 2.1.38
h o ARI, RACH 1962–63; res fell. Brit heart foundation Aberd 1964–67
m Aber 19.7.63 Derek Ogston MB ChB 1957 qv

CLARK Christopher Geoffrey Hood   *MA 1966
s of Geoffrey B. H. C. barrister-at-law and Raymonde G. Gouache; b Fulmer 5.10.42
bank trainee, asst bank vice-pres New York 1966–71; bank man. Lond 1971–76, bank dir from 1977
m Lond 18.7.72 Fenella H. Bullen int decorator d of Paul G. B. Aboyne

CLARK David   *BSc 1969
s of John C. shipbuilder's yard man. and Helen S. Simpson; b Forfar 26.8.47
Aber: CA app Meston & Co 1969–73, asst acct W. G. Wilson & Co from 1973
m Aber 9.12.72 Mhairi D. Middleton bank clerkess d of William D. M. Aber

CLARK David Alexander   *BSc 1957
s of Alexander C. pharm and Sybil G. Paxton; b Aber 11.11.34
geol: Canada: Regina 1957–59, Calgary 1959–63 and from 1964; Tripoli 1963
m Aber 8.3.58 Jean M. Kirk lib d of Alexander K. MB ChB(Glas) Birmingham

CLARK David Arbuckle   MA 1969

CLARK David Mitchell   MA 1961 LLB 1964
s of Ronald M. C. comp dir and Clara Melville; b Aber 9.3.40
Aber: law app 1962–65, leg. asst 1965–67, ptnr Clark & Wallace advoc from 1967
m Aber 7.8.64 Lorna C. Ritchie receptionist d of Alexander R. Aber

CLARK David Robertson   *BSc 1965
s of William R. C. civ eng and Margaret E. Davies BSc(Aberystwyth) teacher: b Aber 7.10.43
MSc(Sus) 1967 FSAScot 1976
asst lect maths univ of sc and tech Kumasi, Ghana 1965–66; admin UKAEA Harwell 1968–73, Lond from 1973
m Dornoch 26.8.67 Genefer G. F. Wright MA 1966 qv

CLARK Denise Framar   MA 1961
d of Franck J. H. C. clerk and Marie T. MacDonald; b Aber 19.4.41
teacher Aber: Deeview p s 1962–67, Ferryhill p s 1974–78, nursery Walker Dam s from 1978
m Aber 12.7.63 Thomas A. Steele ARIBA arch. s of Douglas A. S. Coventry

CLARK Derek William   LLB 1967

CLARK Doris Helen   BSc 1964
d of James B. C. farm. and Barbara H. Rae farm.; b Chapel of Garioch 18.3.43
teacher maths Brechin h s 1965–73, asst prin maths from 1973

CLARK Dwight Bothwell   MSc 1968
s of Harold G. C. BS(Calif) chem and Lois H. Bothwell BA(Calif) teacher; b Long Beach Calif 1.2.38
BSc(Calif) 1961
progr man. (operational testing) Monterey Calif from 1968
m Minneapolis Minnesota 21.6.70 Margaret J. Kylander BS(Minn) teacher d of John B. K. Minneapolis

CLARK Eileen Mackenzie   BSc 1961
d of John A. S. C. bank teller, man. and Margaret H. Mackenzie; b Aber 1.10.41
teacher maths, spec asst Aber 1962–70; part time/temp teacher maths Methlick, Aboyne, Banchory from 1972
m Aber 8.8.69 Robert Paterson civ eng Aber c c s of Robert M. P. Aber

CLARK Frances Mary   MA 1958
d of Frank Reid insur ag and Ann M. Fraser; b Aboyne 19.7.30
teacher Aber: Engl/hist Powis s s 1958–68 Beechwood spec s 1968–71
m Aber 5.4.65 John F. Smith, Lord Kirkhill LLD 1974

CLARK Gerald Charles   BSc 1967

CLARK Gordon Milne   MA 1968
s of George A. C. golf club steward and Jessie Robertson golf club stewardess; b Glasg 30.4.47
foreign lang asst Munich 1969–70; teacher Bathgate 1970–71; foreign lang asst Lyon 1971–72; teacher: Stirling 1972–78, asst prin mod lang Wallace h s Stirling from 1978

CLARK Graham Sturrock   *MA 1965
s of John M. C. agr sales rep and Catherine M. Sturrock sub-postmistress; b Forfar 21.8.42
Dip Ed(Edin) 1966
Edin: teacher 1967–72, civ serv from 1972
m Haddington 24.7.71 Elizabeth A. M. Collins-Young MA(Edin) d of Joe R. Collins BA(Chicago) Philippines

CLARK Hamish   *MA 1970
s of David C. clerk/acct OS map agency man. and Mary D. Guthrie med secy; b Blantrye Malawi 27.12.47
post-grad stud. geog Belf 1970–72; res off. Scot dev dept, Scot. off. Edin from 1973
m Edin 15.9.73 Lynda J. Henderson BA(Belf) civ serv, lib d of Albert H. H. LLB(Belf) Belfast

CLARK Iain Mackinnon   MA 1961
s of Donald C. master mariner and Mary F. Mackinnon; b Glasg 24.11.33
teacher: Campbeltown 1962–66, Glasgow 1966–67, asst head Kirkconnel from 1967
m Helensburgh 1967 Anne V. C. Shuttleworth journalist d of Francis A. S. Broughty Ferry

CLARK Ian Anderson   MA 1965 BD 1971
s of John C. BR rep and Margaret Anderson; b Aber 19.7.38
teacher Lusaka s s Zambia; asst min N & E ch of St Nicholas Aber 1971–72; C of S min New Restalrig par ch Edin 1972–78; prin St Colm's coll Edin from 1978
m Aber 25.9.61 Elizabeth M. Cruden wages clerkess d of James C. Aber

CLARK Ian Cameron   BSc(eng) 1968
s of John Clark MA 1923 qv; b Aber 25.4.47
MS(eng) (Ohio) 1972
dev eng Goodyear Tyre & Rubber Co Glasg 1969–70; (stud. univ of Akron Ohio 1970–71) Goodyear International Tyre Tech Center Luxembourg: based Glasg 1972–74, based Wolverhampton from 1974, worked France, Germany, Luxembourg, Morocco, Philippines
m Aber 21.12.73 Teresita Lisano BBA (univ of E. Manila), exec secy d of Jose L. Philippines

CLARK Ian Douglas   *BSc 1956
s of James C. MA 1917 qv and Mary J. Rae MA 1921 qv(II); b Dingwall 7.2.34
teacher: Morgan acad Dun 1957–61; prin maths: Gran-

town g s 1961–63, Annan acad 1963–65, Aber (later Hazlehead) acad from 1965
m Dun 3.4.59 Christine Fitzwalter teacher d of Leslie C. W. F. Dun

CLARK Ian Illingworth   *MA 1966 Dip Ed 1967
s of John A. S. C. bank man. and Margaret H. McKenzie; b Aber 23.5.43
teacher: RGC Aber 1967–73, prin mod lang Kincorth acad Aber from 1973
m Aber 5.4.68 Joan G. Walker teacher d of Alexander W. Aber

CLARK John   *BSc 1966 MSc 1968 PhD 1970

CLARK John Kydd   MA 1969
s of William K. C. shopkeeper and Barbara B. Andrews bookkeeper; b Invergordon 24.3.48
teacher geog Loudon acad Ayrsh 1970; shopkeeper Invergordon from 1971
m E Kilbride 7.4.71 Elizabeth M. Murdoch MA 1969 qv

CLARK John Stuart Borthwick   BSc 1964
MSc(Edin)

CLARK Kathleen McKenzie   MB ChB 1968

CLARK Kenneth   *MA 1970
s of William C. butchery worker, prod. man. and Jessie A. F. Smith shop asst; b Aber 24.3.48
DPhil(Glas) 1972 Dip Commun Work(Aber) 1976
group worker in therap commun Lond 1972–74; voluntary commun work Aber 1974–75; commun worker Powis Aber 1976–77; dev off. with Langstane housing assoc Aber from 1978
m Aber 6.4.79 Helen J. C. Noble BSc 1975 lab tech d of Charles C. N. Longside

CLARK Margaret Elizabeth   *BSc 1964 PhD 1968
d of George C. machinist and Florence Robinson; b Sunderland 17.4.42
asst lect Belf 1967–69; dem univ coll Dub 1969–70
m N Ireland 24.5.69 William N. Osborough LLB(Belf) prof s of William T. O. Bangor Co Down

CLARK Margaret Jane   MA 1969
d of George S. C. comp dir and Elizabeth W. Brown; b London 22.4.48
ICL Lond 1969–72
m Lond 31.7.71 David J. Ewles haulage contr s of Douglas J. E. Lond

CLARK Margaret Smith   MA 1968 Dip Ed 1969
d of John S. C. publican, despatch clerk and Betsy G. de G. Garland restaurateur; b Broughty Ferry 7.6.47
invest analyst with advis serv to merch banks, insur co, stockbrokers etc. Lond 1969–71
m Dun 13.9.68 Kenneth M. Peebles lect civ eng Dund s of John A. P. Dun

CLARK Moira   MA 1966
d of James C. polit constit ag/agr show secy and Margaret S. Cruickshank MA 1936 qv; b Turriff 8.11.45
Dip Sec Sc(Strath) 1967
Lond: edit. secy *Architect and Building News* 1967–68; p a group insur man. De La Rue Co 1969–72; insur off. from 1973
m Aber 28.9.68 Robert W. George MA 1967 qv

CLARK Moira Grant   *MA 1960
d of Arthur C. oil drilling superv and Mary G. Fleming; b Aber 2.1.38
teacher mus Aber 1961–63, Aberdeensh from 1973

m Aber 5.7.63 Francis I. J. Fraser farm. s of Francis
W. V. F. Findhorn

CLARK Peter William   BSc(for) 1960

CLARK Ronald George   ᶜMB ChB 1956
 s of George C. rly traffic controller and Gladys Taylor;
b Aber 9.8.28
FRCSE 1960
h o ARI 1956–57; regist surg Western I Glasg 1958–60;
res fell. surg Harv 1960–62; lect surg Glas 1962–66;
Sheff: sen lect surg 1966–73, prof surg from 1973
m Dunbartonsh –.9.60 Tamar W. Harvie physioth d of
Walter H. Duntocher

CLARK Ronald Thomson   BSc(eng) 1967
 s of John C. comm trav and Elsie Thomson shopkeeper; b Elgin 17.1.46
computer: logic des/progr Chelmsford 1967–70, syst des
Stockholm 1970–72; computer consult.: Helsinki 1972–73,
Lond 1973–75; banking res Lond from 1975
m Kirkwall 1.4.70 Sandra R. Lloyd teacher d of Douglas
L. Kirkwall

CLARK Sally Ann   LLB 1970

CLARK Stanley Ross   MSc 1961
 s of Cecil C. C. elect. and Gertrude C. Beazer nurse;
b Berwyn Alta 8.3.37
BASc(Br Col) 1959 PhD(Manc) 1967
Athlone fell. 1959–61
def scient serv off. DRB Canada 1962–64; Commonwealth schol 1964–67; univ of Manit: res off. 1967–68,
asst prof 1968–69; univ of Victoria: asst prof 1969–73,
assoc prof c sc from 1973
m Nanaima BC 12.8.62 Mary Carney teacher d of Dennis
C. Bradford

CLARK Thomas Fetzer   PhD 1957
 AB BD(USA)

CLARK Vivien Mary Pamela   LLB 1970
 d of Charles C. MB ChB 1943 *qv*; b Woolwich 19.1.49
law app, solic Clark & Wallace advoc Aber 1970–77; lect
law Aberd from 1977
m Aber 26.2.72 Graeme L. Ogston LLB 1970 *qv*

CLARK William Gladstone Bartle   MB ChB 1960
 s of Evan C. civ serv and Lottie Johnston; b Invergordon 23.11.34
DA(Lond) 1963 FFARCS(Lond) 1967
h o ARI 1960–61; sen h o Leic RI 1961–62; resid anaest
Charing Cross hosp Lond 1962–63; lect anat Brist 1963–
65; anaest posts Brist, Manc, Salford, Stockport 1965–71;
consult. anaest N Birm health dist from 1971
m Aber –.6.62 Margaret Hepburn nurs sister d of
Alexander H. Aber

CLARK William James   BSc 1970
 s of William G. C. lorry driver and Jeannie A. Cheyne;
b Fraserburgh 22.11.47
sen assoc syst progr with IBM (UK) Greenock from 1970
m Greenock 12.5.79 Anne S. McNelis youth/commun
leader d of Roderick McN. Greenock

CLARK William Sneddon Reid   *MA 1965

CLARK Winifred Campbell   MA 1959
 d of Ronald M. C. comp dir/haulage contr and Clara
Melville; b Aber 29.6.38
teacher: Muirfield s Aber 1961–62, Middlefield s Aber
from 1969
m Aber 22.12.61 Charles S. A. W. Levitt MB ChB 1961 *qv*

CLARKE Alexander Gordon   MA 1965

CLARKE Audrey   MB ChB 1961

CLARKE Avril Robertson   MA 1965
 d of William R. C. eng and Janet Anderson; b Glasg
4.7.44
Bangkok: teacher Engl 1966–68, Mrs Clayton's s 1968–
74, Pattana s from 1974
m Aber 14.4.65 Prida Sananikorn BSc(agr) 1965 *qv*

CLARKE Mrs Margaret Elphinston
 see Adam-Smith

CLARKE Muriel   MB ChB 1957
 d of Charles R. C. shopkeeper and Maggie D. Stewart;
b Aber 15.9.33
h o, regist RACH 1957–60; trainee asst g p Aber 1960–61
m Aber 12.9.60 Donald A. Aitken MB ChB 1954 *qv*

CLARKE Peter Lawrence   *BSc 1969

CLARKSON Susan Trevor   MA 1964
 m Adam

CLEGG Ian Alston   *MA 1970
 s of Alan C. secy NFU and Eva Leaver; b Burnley
8.4.47
posts Nat West. Bank Lond from 1970
m Aber 8.10.70 Joyce E. Butler MA 1969 *qv*

CLEGG John Roger   BSc(eng) 1969
 s of William F. C. dir and Catherine I. Kane; b Rochdale 25.12.46
CEng 1972 MIMunE 1972 MIStructE 1974
eng: in loc govt Carlisle 1969–73, with consult. eng Liv
from 1973
m Rochdale 6.7.68 Judith H. Kirby d of Henry A. K.
Rochdale

CLEGG Kathleen Mary   PhD 1956
 b Lancs 12.12.27
BSc(Manc) 1948 MSc(Manc) 1952
sen lect food sc and nutrition Strath from 1960

CLEMENTS Cyril George   BSc 1970

CLERK Donald Edwin   *BSc(agr) 1970
 s of Archibald Clerk BSc(Glas) elect. eng and Cecilia
M. Hay; b Elgin 2.7.46
ARICS 1974
VSO Mazabuka Zambia 1970–71, asst Moray Estates dev
co Forres 1972–74; young farm. sponsored study tour
NZ and Aust 1974–75; farm/estate man. Hayes Hender-
son & Co Elgin from 1975

CLOUSTON Erlend David Roger   *MA 1970
 s of David S. C. vet surg and Sheila M. Roger teacher;
b Lerwick 3.5.46
sports journalist/arts correspondent *Liverpool Daily Post*
from 1970

CLOUSTON Robert William   BSc 1968
 s of Rognvald C. caterer and Catherine H. E. Sinclair
caterer; b Stromness 18.3.44
ALA 1970
Leeds: trainee lib 1967–70, lib inst geol sc 1970–73; Glos
tech information serv Cheltenham: tech serv lib 1973–74,
dep county tech information off. from 1974
m Aber 6.9.68 Vera F. Simpson MA 1966 *qv*

CLOWRY Brendan Patrick Michael   *MA 1969

CLUBB Dawson Robert   MB ChB 1964
s of William G. C. eng and Hannah M. Ironside; b
Ellon 5.12.39
h o Aber hosp 1964–66; sen h o 1966–67; g p Edin
1967–70, Shetland 1970–73, Mintlaw from 1973
m Aber 2.7.65 Roberta Ratter art teacher d of Gilbert R.
Lerwick

CLUNESS Anne Maureen   MB ChB 1958
d of Alexander J. C. excise off. and Ann H. Garriock;
b Lerwick 22.6.35
m Aber 5.7.58 Andrew P. Watt BSc 1955 *qv*

CLUNESS Sheila Margaret   MA 1957

CLURE Ann Elizabeth   LLB 1970
d of Denis J. C. civ serv and Elizabeth A. Brodie; b
Aber 22.1.49
law app Balfour & Manson SSC Edin 1970–72; leg.
asst James & George Collie advoc Aber 1972–73; solic
Scot. Health Serv central leg. off. Edin 1973–78
m East Saltoun 8.10.77 Nigel J. Pollock LLB 1970 *qv*

CLYNE Isobel Anne   MA 1956
d of William W. C. farm. and Isabella B. Forgie; b
Boddam 2.1.35
teacher: Markinch s Inv 1957–62, St Peter's RC s Aber
1962–69, Northfield acad 1969–72
m Aber 4.7.72 Roy Will farm. s of Robert W. W. Fordoun

COAD George Nicholas   MB ChB 1966
s of Evelyn Coad AMIEE chartered elect. eng and
Gladys Hodgson teacher; b Bowdon 2.10.33
h o ARI 1967–68; g p Newhaven from 1969; part-time
surg lt RNR 1969–73, dep police surg Seaford from 1969,
div surg Newhaven div St John's ambulance from 1971,
loc civ serv m o Newhaven from 1976
m Eastbourne 21.11.59 Barbara C. Welch d of Cuthbert
C. W. MD(Lond) Eastdean

COATES Eileen Susan   MA 1970

COBB Alice Margaret   MA 1961 LLB 1963
d of Thomas G. C. police off., security off. and Jane
Torrie; b Aber 25.4.41
leg. asst: c clerk Inv 1963–64, c clerk Lanarksh 1964–66;
self-employed solic E Kilbride 1966–69; lect publ law
N Staffordsh poly 1970–72, sen lect from 1972
m Aber 31.8.63 John M. Ayerst BSc(for) 1961 *qv*

COBB Ian   BSc 1967

COBB Judith Mary   BSc 1965
d of Martin Y. C. actuary and Mary Hay-Smith;
b Esher 15.4.43
pers asst-syst analysis Shell Internat Petr Lond 1965–67;
syst analyst Queen Eliz h Birm 1967
m Shere 15.4.67 John Cartmell BA(Cantab) chartered
mech eng s of Geoffrey S. C. BA(Cantab) Brampton

COBBAN Alan Balfour   *MA 1961
s of William C. fire off. and Annabella M. M. Balfour;
b Aber 25.9.39
MA PhD(Cantab) 1965 FRHistS
Trinity Coll Cantab: res hist 1961–63, fell. 1963–67; lect
med hist Liv 1966–75, sen lect from 1975

COBBAN Marion McArthur   *MA 1970
d of Robert J. A. C. baker and Marion M. McArthur
clerkess/typist; b Aber 24.2.49
Aber: cler off. HM Customs & Excise 1971–73; gen
admin asst hosp man. from 1973

m Aber 13.9.71 Alasdair G. Roberts off. MN, BSc 1975
s of George A. R. Aber

COCHRAN Francis Gordon   LLB 1960
s of David G. C. LLB 1925 *qv*; b Aber 7.4.34
BA(Oxon) 1957
advoc Aber from 1961
m Canford Cliffs 12.9.63 Ann J. S. Reynolds d of Leslie
R. Dorset

COCKBURN George Gordon   MB ChB 1956
s of George R. C. MA 1923 *qv*; b Aber 14.11.32
MRCGP 1962 DMJSoc Apoth(Lond) 1971
capt RAMC Dover, Edin 1957–60; h o mat. hosp Aber
1960–61; g p Aber from 1961; forensic med Aberd:
hon asst 1963, lect path. 1969, part time asst from 1974
d Aber 28.1.79 *AUR* XLVIII 234

COCKBURN John Alasdair Murray   LLB 1968
s of James R. M. C. MA(Cantab) indust man. and
Evelyn M. Mathieson BCom(Edin); b Glasg 10.7.46
CA 1972
Coopers & Lybrand: Glasg 1968–73, Montreal 1973–74,
Lond 1974–76, sen man. Glasg from 1976

COCKBURN John Shearer   MB ChB 1966 ChM 1973
s of James C. shoemaker and Olive J. Shearer nurs
sister; b Turriff 25.8.42
FRCSE 1970
h o, sen h o Aber 1966–68; sen h o Cardiff 1968–69; surg
regist Aber 1969–71; res fell. surg Uppsala Sweden
1971–72; regist cardiac surg Glasg 1973–74; sen regist
cardothoracic surg: Lond 1974–75, S'hampton from 1975
m Keith 30.4.69 Ethel M. M. Duncan shoe buyer d of
George A. D. Keith

COCKBURN Sarah Caudwell   *MA 1960

COCKER James Ian Burnett   BSc 1964
s of John W. C. joiner and Jeannie M. Allan shop
asst; b Banchory 6.3.42
teacher maths Banchory acad from 1965
m Stonehaven 1.7.67 Winifred C. C. Hopper teacher p e
d of Noel B. H. MB ChB 1950 *qv*

COCKERHAM Barry   *BSc(eng) 1969
s of George C. MA(Cantab) civ serv and Winnefred
Graver; b Edgeware 4.2.47
CEng MICE
asst eng(struct) with consult. eng Lond from 1969
m Ashtead 14.11.70 Mary M. Cooper bank clerkess d of
John C. Kirkwall

COCKSHOOT Ian   BSc 1968

COHEN Daniel   LLB 1966
s of Eli C. missionary and Olive M. Mackay nurse;
b Leeds 22.5.46
teacher: VSO Jaiama s s Sierra Leone 1966–67, grad
contract 1967–68; Aber: law app 1968–71; solic Fraser &
Mulligan advoc 1971–75, ptnr 1975–78; ptnr Cohen &
McCaw advoc from 1978
m Aber 10.4.72 Kathleen M. Buchan d of John W. B.
Aber

COHEN Grant Irving   MB ChB 1959
s of Sam N. C. MB ChB(Leeds) g p and Joyce Gillow;
b Sunderland 14.3.33
LRCSE LRCPE LRFPSGlas 1960
Sunderland: h o gyn gen hosp 1959–60; h o gen med RI
1960; g p from 1960; also clin asst diabetes in pregnancy
antenatal clin gen hosp 1973–76

m Newcastle 29.3.60 Laura Osterman lib asst d of Myer O. Newcastle

COLE Andrew John Latham   MB ChB 1969
s of John G. L. C. MB ChB(Birm) med pract and Peggy C. Bryant MB ChB(Birm) med pract; b Birm 30.12.43
h s Charles Johnson mem hosp Nqutu Zululand 1969; h p Gulson hosp Coventry 1970; E Birm hosp: sen h o 1970–71, sen h o infect. diseases 1971–72, sen h o path. 1972–73; regist radiol United Birm hosps 1973–75, sen regist radiol 1975–78; consult. radiol Dudley Rd hosp Birm from 1978

COLE James Kolawole   *BSc(eng) 1956

COLE John   MA 1967
s of John G. C. eng and Margaret I. H. Campbell nurse; b Buckie 2.12.45
teacher: spec asst Portessie 1968–72, asst prin guid Buckie h s from 1972

COLLERAN Ethel Mary   BSc 1958
d of James C. labourer/storeman and Mary J. Ingram; b Fochabers 20.12.35
lab tech biol Unilever Sharnbrook 1958–61; Bedford: lab asst agr Mander coll 1967–68; part-time teacher: Putnoe j s 1968–69, biol Mander coll 1969–70; full-time supply teacher from 1973
m(1) Bedford 18.2.61 Gordon W. Cruickshank nav off. s of Arthur L. C. BSc 1928 qv; husb d
(2) B cford 30.3.70 Terry Westgarth carpenter s of William A. W. Bedford

COLLERAN Nan Park Dunbar   BSc 1959
d of James C. labourer/storeman and Mary J. Ingram; b Ellon 20.11.37
exper off. geol surv of Gt Britain Edin 1959–66
m Edin 30.10.65 Robert Jackson BSc(eng)(H-W) civ eng, lect coll tech Dun s of Robert H. J. Edin

COLLEY Reginald James   PhD 1965
s of William H. C. BA(Cantab) headmaster and Martha-Jane O. Hayton; b Woodford Green 22.5.29
BSc(agr)(Leeds) 1951 Dip Agr(Leeds) 1952
internat civ serv OECD Paris from 1966

COLLIE George Scott   *MA 1961 Dip Ed 1962
s of George S. C. lab tech and Priscilla Hart teacher; b Liverpool 18.1.40
AFIMA 1971 MSc(Dund) 1974
teacher maths: St Andrew's h s Kirkcaldy 1962–65, spec asst Berwicksh h s Duns 1965–67; lect coll of tech Dun from 1967
m Aber 19.7.65 Barbara Gall MA 1960 qv

COLLIN Peter Paterson   MA 1968
s of George C. fisherman/security guard and Agnes Buchan; b Peterhead 24.1.46
teacher Clerkhill s Peterhead 1969–71, dep head 1971–75; head Hatton (Cruden) p s from 1975
m Peterhead 27.9.72 Anne M. Melville shop asst d of Ronald M. Peterhead

COLLINS Edwyn Patrick   MB ChB 1956
s of Edwin G. C. MB ChB(Edin) ENT surg and Elizabeth M. Baird art teacher; b Inv 31.10.31
h o ARI, Dr Gray's hosp Elgin 1956–57; RAF m o from 1957; wing comm from 1971
m Aber 9.2.60 Thelma K. McIntosh radiogr d of Robert P. McI. Aber

COLLINS Pamela Joy   BSc(agr) 1970

COLLINS Peter Munro   *BSc(eng) 1970
s of Herbert D. C. MB ChB 1941 qv; b Aber 1948
site eng Lond 1970–71; des eng Cardiff from 1971

COLMAR Kenneth Edwin   BSc(eng) 1957
s of Geoffrey C. C. lect and Agnes T. Forrester; b Aber 5.12.34
MIHE 1959 MICE 1961
grad asst eng Cumberland c c Carlisle 1957–60; asst eng Argyll c c Lochgilphead 1960–63; asst div surv W Perthsh Dunblane 1963–64; Ross & Cromarty c c: dist surv Black Isle Muir of Ord 1964–71, dep county surv Dingwall 1971–75; div eng (roads/trans) Ross & Cromarty div Highland reg Dingwall from 1975
m Lossiemouth 11.7.59 Morag C. Hardie teacher d of George A. H. Lossiemouth

COLQUHOUN Robert   *BSc(eng) 1965

COLVILLE Christine Peters   *MA 1970 CASS 1974
d of John C. nurseryman and Jessie Nichol; b Alloa 19.1.49
soc worker Aber 1974–75; lib asst Aberd 1976; res asst educ Aberd from 1977
m Aber 12.6.73 David W. Stewart MA 1973 journalist s of David L. S. MA 1930 qv

COLVILLE Penelope Mary   MA 1965
d of Duncan J. F. C. farm. and Catriona M. MacLean; b Campbeltown 9.2.45
educ edit Blackie & Sons Glasg 1966–69; teacher Mombasa Kenya 1971–72
m(1) Campbeltown 2.7.65 Ian G. Grossert BSc 1966 qv; husb d 10.11.73
(2) Johannesburg 12.12.75 Quentin D. Grearson BSc (Glas) prod. man. Ayliffe Cables, Edenvale S Af s of Lester D. G. Parkstone

COLVIN Michael Bruce   BSc(eng) 1969

COLWELL John Henry Murray   *BSc 1969 PhD 1977
s of Henry C.; b Buckie 22.4.47
ABPsS 1977
res stud. Aberd 1969–72; sen lect psych Middx poly from 1972
m Lond 4.9.71 Jennifer Fitzpatrick BSc 1972

COMLOQUOY Sheena   MA 1970
d of John H. C. MB ChB(Edin) g p and Christina H. Allan; b Edin 25.3.49
civ serv HIDB Inv 1970–71; teacher Dumfries 1972–77
m Edin 27.12.72 Alexander Wilson farm. s of Alexander W. Dumfries

CONDIE Adrian Peter   ᶜMB ChB 1956
s of Robert H. C. art teacher and Margaret G. Rennie art teacher; b Brechin 1.11.32
DObstRCOG 1959 MRCOG 1963
h o Aber hosps 1956–57; nat serv m o Singapore 1957–59; sen h o Durh, N'cle hosps: 1959–61, regist obst and gyn 1961–64; sen regist obst/gyn Birm hosps 1964–68; consult. obst/gyn NW Thames reg health auth—Edgeware gen hosp Middx from 1968
m Dun –.9.64 Marjorie R. Sword med secy d of Percy S. Dun

CONDIE Roy Gordon   MB ChB 1966 ᶜMD 1975
s of Robert H. C. DA artist/teacher and Margaret G. Rennie DA teacher art/dom sc; b Aber 6.3.42
DObstRCOG 1968 MRCOG 1971
h o, sen h o Aber 1966–70; regist obst Dun 1970–72; res fell. Aberd 1972–73; sen regist/lect Aber teaching hosps 1973–76; visiting sen lect univ of Brisbane 1975–76;

consult./sen lect obst/gyn Birm area health auth/Birm univ
m Aber 4.1.65 Wilma M. P. Cruickshank MA 1967 *qv*

CONN Brian Gordon *BSc 1968 MSc 1971

CONNOCHIE Henry John Gray BL 1957
s of William D. C. advoc in Aber and Muriel Milne; b Aber 17.2.29
NP 1962
Henry J. Gray & Connochie advoc in Aber: law asst 1957–59, ptnr 1961, sen ptnr from 1966; dir N of S board Eagle Star group from 1976
m Aber 29.8.57 Marguerita C. Cowie radiogr d of George C. Aber

CONNON Alexander MA 1964
s of George C. cooper and Mary A. M. Morrison weaver; b Peterhead 1.4.26
Aber coll of comm: teacher 1965–74, asst stud. advis from 1974
m Aber 26.9.52 Jessie C. Duthie secy, teacher shorthand typewriting d of Gilbert D. Aber

CONNON Gylymn John Douglas MA 1967

CONNON Rhoda Anne Elizabeth *MA 1961
d of John H. C. agr contr and Annie Barrack; b Daviot Aberdeensh 10.5.39
teacher: Fyvie 1962–65; part-time Wick h s 1969–74, Anna Ritchie s Peterhead from 1974
m Aber 21.4.62 Douglas M. Fraser BSc 1961 *qv*

CONNOR Richard Bridges *MA 1970
s of Richard C. bus conductor and Nellie Bridges; b Aber 4.5.38
teacher Engl: Summerhill acad Aber 1971–73, Studierrat-Gymnasium Nordhorn W Ger 1973–74, asst prin Engl Balwearie h s Kirkcaldy from 1974
m Aber 8.12.62 Audrey Porter

CONROY James William Hendry *BSc 1966 MSc 1971
s of William C. driver/timekeeper and Beatrice Munro receptionist; b Elgin 2.10.43
biol i/c ornithol res with Brit Antarctic Surv Aber, Lond, Huntingdon, Antarctica 1966–74; establishment div BAS 1974–77; inst terrestrial ecology Monks Wood exper stat from 1977

CONSTANTINIDES Costas Costa MB ChB 1956
s of Costas C. merch and Joanna Karletti; b Cyprus 10.2.28
DO(Lond) 1961 FRCS(Glas) 1965 FRCSE 1966
h o: Stracathro hosp 1957–58, ARI 1958–59; Glasg eye infirm: sen h o 1960–61, regist 1961–63, sen regist 1963–66; consult. ophth: Kuwait 1967–68, Abu Dhabi from 1968
m Aber 26.7.63 Dorothy M. Thorburn MA 1963 *qv*

COOK Aileen Barrie Swankie MA 1969 MEd 1971
d of John H. C. policeman, miner and Annie B. E. Swankie dispensing chem, teacher; b Dunfermline 20.4.47
teacher handicapped infants Aber 1970–76, asst head from 1976

COOK Archibald Noel *MA 1966

COOK David Ashley MB ChB 1967
s of Henry B. C. MB ChB 1921 *qv*; b Leeds 28.3.43
Aber: h o geriat, orthop, ophth 1967–68, ENT, dermat 1968–69; Hull sen h o: gen med 1969, neurol 1969–70, g p and neuro surg 1970; Dun: sen h o gen med renal

med 1971, regist gen med chest med 1971–73; Leeds: s h o obst and gyn 1973–74; g p: Beauly 1974–75, Thirsk from 1975
m York 2.4.71 Elaine P. Warren nurs sister d of Gerald W. York
d Thirsk 12.3.78 *AUR* XLVII 360

COOK Gordon James *MA 1970
s of Wilfred C. gen man. and Josephine Bartle; b Aber 1.4.48
DMS(Edin) 1973 AMBIM
salesman Edin from 1970
m Aber 1971 Maureen C. Thomson teacher d of James T. Aber

COOK Gordon Watt *MA 1961
s of Robert C. banker and Rose J. Wight; b New Deer 4.2.39
DRSS 1963
statist Cardiff 1962–65; lect statist: univ of Essex 1965–67, St And 1967–68, Aberd from 1968
m Aber 19.8.67 Frances O. Williamson MA 1962 *qv*

COOK Graham George BSc 1970

COOK Irene Brodie MA 1958
d of Andrew C. police off. and Isabella G. Brodie; b Lonmay 3.3.37
teacher Leeds 1959–63 and from 1973
m Aber 9.6.62 Alan Tiffany eng man. s of Frank T. Leeds

COOK Jennifer Valerie BEd 1970
d of Norman C. painter/decorator and Catherine Leslie shop asst; b Aber 30.7.49
teacher Engl Sir John Cass Redcoat s Lond 1970–73, head careers dept from 1973
m Aber 21.12.70 Roderick S. Anderson BSc 1969 *qv*

COOK Josephine Anne Harlow MA 1961
d of Harold H. C. RN, teacher and Mira S. Gyte teacher/authoress; b Settle 28.8.40
WRNS Reading and Petersfield 1961–62; radio oper Cornwall 1962–63, Gibraltar 1963–64
m Brazil 29.5.64 Michael J. Robinson telecomm eng (Cable & Wireless) s of Frank J. R. Tunbridge Wells

COOK Martin Robert MA 1968

COOK Ramsay *BSc(agr) 1964

COOK Richard Keith Daxon BSc(eng) 1969
s of Douglas R. J. C. mech eng/comp dir and Phyllis E. M. Smith; b Hillingdon 22.4.46
BAC Bristol: R & D test eng 1969–71, syst eng from 1971
m Amersham 3.8.68 Michelle M. Stoessl BSc(eng) 1969 *qv*

COOKMAN Gerald Philip *BSc(for) 1961
s of Giles C. CA and Laura E. Haines; b Devizes 9.10.39
MSc(Syracuse NY) 1964
agronomist Mexico, S America from 1964

COOKSON Henry John Angus BSc 1970
s of Robert P. C. LRCP med pract and Barbara A. Mair SRN; b Huntly 24.8.47
invest. analyst: stockbrokers Lond 1970–73, pension fund man. York from 1974

COOMBS Janet MA 1966
d of Ronald P. C. cutler and Jean H. Sanders nursing auxil; b Sheffield 4.3.45

Engl lang asst Arles 1967–68; teacher: Sheffield 1968–70, head mod lang 1970–73, Bassaleg Wales from 1973
m Sheffield 4.8.73 Peter B. Giles ship's off. MN s of Bernard G. Sheffield

COONEY Eileen   *MA 1970
 d of Robert H. C. political organis, bldr, crane slinger and Annie McPherson; b Aber 18.3.48
teacher Engl Cumbernauld 1971–72
m Aber 1971 Alan B. Grant MA 1968 *qv*

COONEY Neil   *MA 1965 Dip Ed 1966
 s of George T. C. watchmaker and Joan F. Howie comb-polisher; b Aber 17.8.43
teacher: hist Harlaw acad Aber 1966–70, prin hist Cults acad from 1970
m Aber 10.8.62 Aileen J. Thomson cashier d of David T. Aber

COOPER Alan Gordon   *MA 1968

COOPER Elaine Hilda   MA 1966
 m Stalker

COOPER Gillian Anne   MB ChB 1968
 m Robin F. Johnston MB ChB 1962 *qv*
killed in accident in Aust along with her two children

COOPER Ingrid Margaret Jane   MA 1969
 d of Harry J. C. C. physioth and Margaret J. Hay teacher; b Aber 8.12.47
teacher Fr/Ger: Stonehaven 1970–71, Stromness from 1971
m Orphir Orkney 2.4.74 Ronald E. Tait boatbuilder/chief steward, purser P & O ferries Orkney s of Edwin C. T. Toab Orkney

COOPER Kathleen Stuart   MA 1958
 d of James C. farm. and Georgina E. Wilson teacher; b Buckie 9.2.39
teacher: Aber 1959–63, W Lothian 1963–64, Moray 1964–66, Renfrewsh 1966–69
m Buckie 3.3.66 Robert J. Shiach aircraft eng s of Robert S. Kingston

COOPER Michael   *MA 1968
 s of Alexander S. C. clerk and Elsie Milne staff nurse; b Aber 13.10.43
teacher: asst prin Engl Breadalbane acad Aberfeldy from 1969
m Aber 27.12.67 Jennifer A. Angus MA 1967 *qv*

COOPER Robert Gary   MB ChB 1961

COOPER Simon John   BSc 1968

COOPER Stephanie   MA 1970
 m Wright

COOPER William David   *MA 1959 *MEd 1970
 s of William D. C. bookbinder and Florence M. Brown bookbinder's asst; b Aber 14.11.36
teacher: Engl Morgan acad Dun 1960–61, r e Waid acad Fife 1961–66, spec asst Engl RGC Aber 1966–71, prin Engl Bankhead acad 1972–74, asst head 1974–75; asst dir of educ Grampian reg council from 1975
m Edin 11.7.64 Gillian F. A. Porteous MA(Edin) teacher d of Norman W. P. MA(Edin), Edin

COOTE Audrey Elizabeth   BSc 1970
 d of William C. bus. man. and Janetta Agnew; b Omagh Co Tyrone 21.11.47

teacher maths Bearsden acad from 1971
m Omagh 5.8.71 Robert H. B. Gardiner BSc 1970 *qv*

COPEMAN Mary Evelyn   BSc 1963
 m Michie

COPLAND Alison Anne   *MA 1968 PhD 1971
 d of Gordon S. C. eng draughtsman and Agnes Fraser secy; b Aber 2.10.46
teacher mus: West Calder h s 1972–74, Mary Erskine s Edin from 1974; part-time tut. OU from 1974
m Aber 12.4.75 David H. Guest BSc(H-W) eng s of John H. G. Balerno

COPLAND Annabel Moira   *MA 1956

COPLAND Graeme McAllan   ᶜMB ChB 1956

COPLAND John Murray   *MA 1957
 MA(Oxon)

COPLAND Robert James   MA 1970

COPLAND Valerie Agnes   MA 1970
 d of Gordon S. C. draughtsman and Agnes Fraser secy; b Aber 20.7.49
teacher: Garrowhall 1971–73, Park s Glasg 1973–74, Crown s Inv 1975
m Aber 4.4.72 Kenneth G. Cantlay BSc(eng) 1969 *qv*

CORBETT Catherine Mary   BSc 1967 Dip Ed 1968
 d of Alexander R. C. bldg contr and Jessie A. Fraser nurse/asst matron; b Tain 6.3.46
teacher: maths/sc Inv 1968–71, maths Birm 1971–73, maths/sc Lond from 1973
m Tain 10.7.71 Alexander C. Skinner BSc 1968 *qv*

CORBETT Daniel Ferguson   BSc 1965

CORBETT Ian Leslie   BSc(eng) 1959

CORBETT James   BSc 1965

CORDINER Ian Callan   BSc 1965
 s of John H. C. MA 1935 *qv*; b Dalbeattie 11.10.42
teacher: Aboyne acad 1966–75, prin phys from 1975
m Huntly 29.7.67 Margaret R. MacDonald MA 1967

CORDINER Peter Stephen   *BSc 1970
 s of George L. C. and Janet C.; b Aber 5.10.42
Dip Ed(Belf) 1971
teacher: Kirkton h s Dun 1971–72, Kirkcaldy h s 1972–73; 2nd elect. off. MN 1973–74; teacher Summerhill acad Aber 1974–77; educ psych Elgin from 1977
m 6.8.77 Catherine Cameron hosp secy d of Hugh C.

CORDINER Sheila Elizabeth West   MA 1968
 d of Robert W. C. MA 1948 *qv*; b Aber 21.11.45
edit. asst D.C. Thomson Dun 1968–69; teacher Engl Joensun Finland 1969–71
m Peterhead 20.7.71 Thomas F. Taylor chief tech RAF

CORDINER Stella   BSc 1970
 m Sykes

CORFIELD John Richard   MSc 1970
 s of Ronald A. C. acct and Gladys E. Smith; b Stratford-upon-Avon 15.12.40
BSc(Brist) 1962
hosp physicist Lond 1963–65; med physicist: Copenhagen 1965–66, Aber 1966–69, Canterbury from 1969
m Copenhagen 1966 Agnes D. Seehuusen computer progr d of Sven T. R. S. Copenhagen

CORMACK Arthur Paterson   BEd 1969
s of Arthur P. C. and Jane E. Glass; b Aber 5.10.34
teacher Aber from 1969

CORMACK Elizabeth Anne   MA 1970
d of Robert J. C. shopkeeper and Ivy Sanders; b Dingwall 22.5.49
Aber: teacher trg 1970–71, shop asst 1971–72, clerkess computer changeover 1972–73
m Strathpeffer 6.8.71 Peter G. Savage MA 1972 s of George G. S. Edin

CORMACK Elspeth MacDiarmid   MA 1968
d of Alexander C. C. MA 1950 qv and Moira N. J. MacDiarmid MA 1941 qv; b Aber 7.5.47
RGN 1975
Engl lang asst Bonn 1968–69; Edin: teacher Engl Portobello s s 1970–72, Royal h s 1972–73; stud. nurse ERI 1973–75, staff nurse ERI 1975–76; Aber: dist nurse trg from 1977

CORMACK Geoffrey George   MA 1966

CORMACK Ian Richard   *BSc 1967 Dip Ed 1968
s of Alexander C. C. furniture store man. and Mary J. Farquharson; b Aber 24.3.45
teacher AGS 1968–75, prin geog Cults acad from 1975
m Aber 7.7.73 Moira Hunter teacher p e d of Sydney H. Cults Aber

CORMACK Ingrid Alexandra Jane   MA 1964
                                                    LLB 1966
d of Alexander K. C. insur off. and Elsie M. Dickson shorthand typist; b Dun 24.1.43
RGN 1973
law app Aber 1966–68; leg. asst: Edin 1968–71, Aber c c, Grampian reg c 1974–77
m Aber 2.12.77 John K. M. Dodds BSc(eng) 1967 qv

CORMACK James Gordon   MA 1961
s of James E. C. master carpenter/joiner and Jessie G. Smith MA 1930 qv; b Newmachar 15.3.40
Dip Bus St(Strath) 1965
syst rep Dun 1961–64; pers man. Linwood 1965–67; man. consult. UK and overseas; Lond: pers dir 1971–73, self-employed man. consult. from 1973
m Guisely 10.5.69 Carol A. Wood secy d of Alfred W. Guisely

CORMACK Jennifer Anne   MA 1970
d of John C. under-secy DAFS and Jessie M. Bain; b Edin 3.10.48
Dip Secy Ling(Westminster coll Lond) 1971
secy: Rank Xerox Lond 1971–73, conference asst *Financial Times* Lond 1973–74, pers asst joint res centre Ispra Italy from 1974

CORMACK John   *BSc 1967
s of George A. W. C. labourer and Ethel M. Youngson; b Aber 3.2.45
working in nuclear med in Aust
m Adelaide Aust 4.1.74 Jane Shearer d of James S.

CORMACK John Dickson   MB ChB 1962
s of Alexander K. C. insur off. man. and Elsie M. Dickson secy; b Aber 18.9.38
DObstRCOG 1965 DCH(Glas) 1971 LMCC 1972
h o: Aber hosps 1963–64, Bellshill mat. hosp 1964–65; g p Aber 1965–67; paediat regist Aber/clin tut. ch health Aberd 1967–71; g p Oakville Ont 1971–76; asst med dir Canada Life Ass. Co Toronto from 1976
m Laurencekirk 12.9.65 Katherine L. Spalding RGN d of David M. S. Laurencekirk

CORMACK Marjorie Forbes   MA 1961
d of Joseph C. castings controller and Janet S. Erskine pianist; b Fraserburgh 9.10.40
teacher: Aber 1962–64, Surrey 1964–65, Grangemouth part-time from 1973
m Aber 5.8.64 Allan J. Macarthur BSc 1961 qv

CORMACK Patricia   *MA 1957
d of James C. shopkeeper and Betty McKay; b Peterhead 19.7.35
teacher: Fr St Margaret's s Aber 1958–60, mod lang Aber acad 1960–63; housemistress Windsor girls' s BFES Hamm Germany 1963–66; dep head Downs s Compton Newbury 1966–69; lady advis Bellshill acad 1969–70; dep rector Hazlehead acad Aber from 1970

CORMACK Richard Melville   PhD 1961
s of William S. C. BSc(Glas) prin tech coll and Jean W. Niven teacher; b Glasg 12.3.35
BSc(Lond) 1954 BA(Cantab) 1955 MA 1962 Dip Math Stat(Cantab) 1956 FRSE 1974
Aberd: asst statist 1956–58, lect 1958–66; visiting asst prof univ of Wash. 1964–65; sen lect Edin 1966–72; prof statist St And from 1972
m Aber 1.9.60 Edith Whittaker BSc 1957 qv

CORMACK Robert John   *MA 1969

CORMIE David Ian   *MA 1962
s of David E. D. C. chartered surv and Jessie T. Brown; b Aber 18.8.38
trainee pers off. Lond 1962–66; pers off. Brentwood 1966–67; Lond: pers man. 1967–72, group indust relations advis from 1972

CORMIE Gordon David   *MA 1965
s of James C. C. painter and Nora M. Blandford lib; b Sleaford 15.4.43
Dip Town Plan(Leeds) 1970 MRTPI 1973
res off. min of housing and loc govt Leeds 1965–71; sen plan. asst Edin city plan. dept from 1971
m Worsbrough Bridge 2.12.67 June Mitchell town plan. d of Donald M. Worsbrough Bridge

CORMIE Stewart Dufton   BSc 1970

CORNER Alexander Wallace   *MA 1967 Dip Ed 1968
s of Alexander M. C. army off., ironmonger and Joan T. Paterson; b Bangalore India 19.9.44
teacher: Macduff 1968–69, Banff acad 1969–74, prin history Peterhead acad from 1974
m Aber 2.8.72 Sheila M. C. Bell teacher p e d of James B. Dumfries

CORNFORTH Hazel   MB ChB 1961

CORSE Douglas Alexander   *BSc 1963
s of David W. C. and Janet Tulloch; b Orkney 16.2.40
MS(Corn) 1966 PhD(Corn) 1968
grad asst Corn. 1963–68; England: res scient Nat Inst res in dairying 1968–73, nat cattle exec Cooper Nutrit Products Witham 1973–75; man. sales advis centre BP Nutrit (UK) Witham from 1975
m Kirkwall 5.8.65 Jennifer A. S. Harcus d of Edward S. H. H. Kirkwall

CORSE John Oliver   MB ChB 1968

CORSER Charles McKenzie   MB ChB 1959
s of James R. C. MA 1928 qv and Mona Meldrum MA 1928 qv; b Pluscarden 18.2.36
DObstRCOG 1960 MRCPsych 1975
h o: Woodend Hosp Aber 1959–60, Raigmore hosp Inv

1960–61; g p Bolton 1961–65, Elgin 1965–73, g p, psychiat Livingston 1973–76; consult. psychiat Bangour village hosp from 1977
m Aber 1.10.60 Sheila M. R. McKechnie nurse d of Duncan McK. Aber

CORSIE Edward Ogilvie   MA 1962
s of Robert G. C. bank man. and Jane A. O. Mattewson; b Hopeman 11.5.41
teacher: Engl/hist Newmill s s 1963–65, hist Lossiemouth h s 1965–69; head Boharm p s 1969–72; dep head Kinloss p s 1972–73; head Mosstodloch p s from 1973
m Buckie 5.8.67 Kathleen A. Hargreaves teacher d of John S. H. Elgin

CORSIE Mary   MA 1970
m Reid

COSTELLO Heather Pauline McKenzie   MA 1965
m Long

COTHLIFF Margaret Maud   *MA 1968

COULL Alexander Bruce   MB ChB 1957
s of David C. MRCVS(Edin) vet surg and Janetta Bruce MA 1921 qv; b Buckie 21.1.33
DObstRCOG(Lond) 1962
h o ARI 1957–58; short serv comm RAMC Ghana, Belgian Congo 1958–61; h o obst/gyn St Alfese's hosp Greenwich 1961; g p Thorpe Bay from 1961
m Aber Elizabeth J. L. Baxter civ serv d of William B. Turriff

COULL Dorothy Carnegie   MB ChB 1965 MD 1970
b Aber 27.3.42
MFCM 1974
Aberd: res fell. therap 1966–69, lect commun med 1970–79; commun med spec Grampian health board from 1979
m Aber 21.8.70 Moir

COULL Douglas   MA 1962

COULL Isobel Ronald   MA 1961
d of David B. C. mech and Isabella E. Ronald shop asst; b Aber 12.6.40
teacher: Glasg 1961–63, Leeds 1964–65, Hull 1965, Leeds 1967, W Wickham 1974–78; prin Lat/housemistress W Wickham from 1978
m Aber 9.3.63 Alexander W. Still BSc(eng) 1961 qv

COULL James Alistair Bruce   *MA 1966
s of James C. burgh surv and Isabella Bruce; b Aber 13.3.44
teacher classics: Brechin h s 1967–68, AGS 1968–71; prin classics Turriff acad from 1971

COULL James Reid   *MA 1957 PhD 1962
s of William C. fisherman and Jeannie Reid; b Peterhead 18.2.35
dept geog Aberd: asst 1959–61, lect 1961–71, sen lect from 1971

COULL James West   MA 1967

COULL John Taylor   MB ChB 1958
s of John S. C. fish merch and Ethel M. Taylor; b Aber 4.3.34
FRCS 1965
h o Aber 1958–60; sen regist: surg Edin 1963–65, traumolology Birm 1967–70; lect orthop Edin 1970–71; serv RAMC, later consult. orthop surg BAOR from 1971,

consult advis Br army orthop surg Lond from 1977
m Aber 27.12.58 Mildred Macfarlane MA 1956 qv

COULL Sandra Margaret   MA 1965
m Smart

COULL William   BSc 1961 MA 1962 MEd 1971
s of William C. fisherman and Jane R. Reid; b Peterhead 27.1.39
teacher Aber 1963–71; Elgin: educ psych 1971–74, teacher from 1974
m Buckie 17.7.68 Charlotte M. Thoresen teacher d of Otto T. Buckie

COUPER Alastair Dougal   *MA 1962 Dip Ed 1963
s of Daniel A. C. bldr and Devina Riley; b Aber 4.6.31
PhD(ANU) 1967 FCIT 1974
lect Durh 1966–69; prof UWIST Cardiff from 1969
m Aber 30.8.58 Norma Milton civ serv d of Clifford M. Aber

COUPER James Alexander   MA 1957
s of James W. C. butcher and Georgina Walker shop asst; b Aber 3.6.35
nat serv sergt instr RAEC, chief instr Engl app chef school Aldershot 1957–59; teacher Engl: Fernhill s mod s Farnborough 1959–60, Hilton s s Aber 1961–66; Aber: dep head Airyhall p s 1966–73, head Cloverfield p s from 1973
m Port Glasg 3.8.63 Jean R. Kane teacher d of George A. K. Port Glasg

COUPER Laureen Margaret   MA 1970
d of James C. clerk and Margaret A. Williamson; b Lerwick 18.12.49
teacher Engl/Fr: Webster h s Kirriemuir 1971–73, Aith j h s Shetland from 1973
m Voe Shetland 20.7.73 Allan Johnson bldr s of George J. Girlsta

COURT Roger James   *BSc 1963

COURT-BROWN Charles Michael   BSc 1970
s of William M. C-B. MB ChB(St And) prof genetics and Caroline G. S. Thom radiogr; b Edin 3.2.48
MB ChB(Edin) 1975
m Edin 6.7.74 Jacqueline Y. Q. Mok MB ChB(Edin) g p d of Mok To Leong BA(Nanking) Kuala Lumpur

COUSAR Charles Blanton   PhD 1960
s of Robert W. C. ThD(Virg USA) min and Irving Blanton; b Charlottesville Virg USA 7.2.33
AB(Dav Col NC) USA 1955 BD(Col Theol Sem) USA 1958
Col Theol Sem Georgia USA: asst prof NT 1960–64, assoc prof 1964–66, prof from 1966, dean of acad affairs from 1971
m Tallahassee Florida 10.9.55 Elizabeth C. Bowen AB (Oglethorpe) d of Reeves B. Tallahassee

COUSINS John Alexander   BSc(eng) 1958

COUSINS Roger Lee   *BSc(agr) 1969
s of Leonard H. C. sub-postmaster and Anne Eustace clerkess; b Coulsdon 11.6.46
MS(Corn) 1973
lect Corn. New York 1970–71; res assoc Edin 1973–74; sen res assoc E Ang 1974–75; sen res off. Dartington Amenity Res Trust (Dart) from 1975

COUTINHO Maria de Lourdes Pamela   MB ChB 1963
d of Basil M. T. C. auditor and Timothea D'Souza teacher; b Aden 11.2.38

BSc(Bom) 1956 DTM & H(Liv) 1965
h o: Ontario, Aber, Dun, Banstead, Lond, Nott 1962–69;
regist Lond: Whittington hosp, Royal Free hosp, St Ann's
1969–72, g p from 1972; FPA clin from 1970

COUTTS Alan Maxwell   MA 1967
s of William C. comm trav and Janet M. Barclay; b
Edin 28.7.45
CA 1971
Glasg: app 1967–71, audit asst 1971–73, taxation asst
1973–75, man. from 1975
m Bearsden 11.1.74 Dorothy Baird teacher d of William
N. B. Glasg

COUTTS David   *BSc(eng) 1962
s of George C. newsagent, hosp porter and Joan Gray;
b Aber 8.5.40
MIHE 1964 MICE 1965
asst site eng Newport Wales 1962–64; bridge eng: asst
Carlisle 1964–66; Glasg: chartered eng 1966–68, superv
from 1968
m Aber 6.8.62 Margaret G. Angus BSc 1960 qv

COUTTS Elizabeth Anne   *BSc 1962
d of Gordon C. farm. and Bella Taggart; b Durris
13.10.40
teacher biol High s for girls Aber 1963–66; lect biol
Cambridge coll of f e from 1966
m Aber 27.7.65 Alan J. Thomson BSc(agr) 1963 qv

COUTTS Evelyn Margaret   *MA 1959
d of Thomas C. pharm and Evelyn Gordon teacher;
b Aber 23.1.38
PhD(St And) 1972
teacher: Leeds 1960–61, Dublin 1961; asst lib Irish cent
lib and TCD Dublin 1962; teacher: Madras coll St And
1964–66, Bell Baxter h s Cupar 1966–68; univ lect
Columbia Mo USA 1969; prin geog Madras coll from
1970
m Aber 3.8.61 John A. Soulsby MA 1959 qv

COUTTS Findlay MacRury   MA 1964 LLB 1966
s of William L. C. barman and Kathleen Findlay secy;
b Aber 16.3.43
law app Hamilton t c 1966–69; town clerk Cupar 1969–
75; dir admin Dunferm dist c from 1975
m Aber 16.4.68 Christina G. Leathem MA 1966 qv

COUTTS Hamish Michael   BSc(agr) 1970

COUTTS Ian George Cormack   *BSc 1960 PhD 1964
m Aber 1968 Fiona Wood MB ChB 1968 qv

COUTTS John Gordon   MB ChB 1969

COUTTS John Isbister   MB ChB 1958
s of Thomas C. master mariner and Mary A. Peterson
nurse; b Aber 29.3.34
h o Woodend hosp Aber 1958–59; Tasmania: NW gen
hosp Burnie 1959–62, g p Somerset from 1963
m Wynyard Tasmania 7.3.69 Susan E. Harris nurse d of
Geoffrey P. H. Burnie

COUTTS Kathleen Margaret   BSc 1969
d of Frank Coutts PO worker and Jean A. T. Mackie;
b Stonehaven 29.8.48
Dip Ed(Edin) 1970
teacher Craigie h s Dun 1970–71; civ serv DHSS Dun
from 1971

COUTTS Penelope Ann   MA 1970
d of Alexander D. C.; b London 16.5.48
Cert for teachers of deaf(Manc) 1971

remed teacher s for deaf Aber from 1974
m Herts 9.1.71 Jeremy C. L. Saunders Stonehaven

COWAN George Sheppard Marshall   MB ChB 1964

COWAN Torquil Hamish   MA 1967
s of Robert J. C. civ eng/elect. consult./hotelier and
Agnes P. B. Borley secy; b Invergordon 10.9.46
Dip Ed(UCNW) Cert Curric Stud(Keele) 1974
Wales: teacher Holywell c s 1968–70; St David's h s
Saltney: head Engl 1970–74, head fac of commun and
lang from 1974
m Lloc 21.8.70 Enid W. Hughes loc govt clerk d of
Samuel H. H. Lloc

COWAP Sheila Mary Leslie   MA 1968
d of William L. C. film lib naval base and Mary
Strachan shop asst; b Ellon 3.6.46
Lond: Chelsea and Kensington hosp man. comm:
various admin posts 1968–72, New Charing Cross hosp
Fulham: admin off. equipping new hosp 1972–73; Civil
Aviation auth temp typing 1973; City and Guilds of Lond
Inst prod. of craft level exam papers and syllabus dev
from 1973

COWARD Helen Mary   MA 1967

COWE (Cowan) James McDonald   MA 1957
s of Andrew B. C. fisherman and Maggie McDonald;
b Fraserburgh 17.1.36
nat serv 1958–60; teacher Fraserburgh acad 1960–65;
dep head Fraserburgh centr s 1965–67; head: Kininmonth
p s 1967–71, Fraserburgh South Park p s 1971–75,
Fraserburgh Central from 1975
m Aber 4.8.59 Kathleen J. Dey teacher d of George A. D.
Fraserburgh

COWE Sybil Norma   MA 1957 Dip Ed 1958

COWELL Susan Elisabeth   MA 1965
d of John C. headmaster and Florence J. Atkinson
teacher; b Allerton Bywater 20.12.43
teacher Castleford 1966–68 and from 1975
m Leeds 5.8.67 Harry Cox headmaster s of Harry C.
Castleford

COWIE Alan   *MA 1959 Dip Ed 1960

COWIE Alexander Bertram   MA 1968

COWIE Alison Kilgour   MA 1965
d of John M. C. bank man. and Norah R. Kilgour;
b Aber 18.1.44
teacher Fr: Aber acad 1966–69, Perth acad 1970–72
m Aber 29.12.69 Hugh M. Smith asst man. insur s of
Hugh S. Aber

COWIE Alistair Gordon   *BSc(eng) 1970
s of Gordon C. nursery man. and Jessie Reid; b Portgordon 12.7.48
proj eng-struct Lowestoft 1971–72, Lond 1973–74; struct
des eng Sarawak Malaysia from 1975

COWIE Carol Ann Cummings   BSc 1966
d of James R. C. boardinghouse owner and Helen
McBeth shop man.; b Aber 27.6.45
exec off.: spectrochem Macaulay inst Aber 1966–67,
computer progr econ div NOSCA Aber from 1979
m Durris 7.1.67 Hugh M. Shepherd agr eng instr and
advis s of Kenneth J. S. Durris

COWIE Carol Mary   MA 1964
d of George A. C. master plumber and Caroline S.
Masson; b Glasg 9.5.43

teacher: Brandon 1965–67, Princes Risborough 1974–76, High Wycombe from 1976
m Stanley 24.7.65 Andrew Nall BSc(for) 1964 *qv*

COWIE Doris MA 1960

COWIE Ethel Margaret *MA 1957 Dip Ed 1958
d of Alexander E. C. upholsterer and Jessie A. Murray; b Aber 19.3.35
teacher: Montrose 1958–61, Lond 1962–66, Falkirk 1966–72, Lond from 1972

COWIE Frederick Cleveland Fulton MA 1962
s of Frederick M. C. eng and Evelyn M. Fulton; b Aber 7.4.41
teacher: RGC Aber 1963–67, Services p s Accra 1968–69, head humanities dept Gatow m s Berlin 1970–76, 4th yr co-ord Derby m s Osnabrück from 1976
m Aber 3.8.67 Jeanette I. Jack MA 1966 *qv*

COWIE Gordon Manson *BSc(for) 1966
s of Charles G. C. grocery man. and Flora M. Manson; b Insch 30.4.44
dist for. off. II Fort William 1966–68; asst educ off. Dean Foresters Training s; dist off. man. serv div For. Comm res stat 1971–74; dist off. I Fort Augustus from 1974
m Tidenham 6.3.71 Elizabeth M. O. Hewitt teacher ballet d of Arthur R. J. H. Chepstow

COWIE Isabell Catherine MA 1960
d of John M. C. bank man. and Norah R. Kilgour; b Aber 15.3.39
teacher Engl/Fr Perth 1961–62
m Aber 1.9.62 David Jack BSc(agr) 1954 *qv*

COWIE James BSc 1964 MB ChB 1969
s of James C. security off. and Annie Buchan; b Banbury 9.2.42
MRCP(UK) 1972
h o ARI 1969–70; sen h o, regist Lond 1970–73; sen regist Oxford 1973–77; consult. phys Plymouth from 1977
m Aber 21.6.66 Anne L. Backett BSc 1965 *qv*

COWIE James D. MA 1967
s of Patricia A. C. canteen asst; b Aber 6.8.45
MSc(Lond) 1974
res off. min of agr Leeds 1967–73, 1974–75, N'cle-u-Tyne from 1975
m Leeds 27.5.69 Mandy R. Ure teacher, civ serv

COWIE Jeannie Reid MA 1956
d of James C. farm. and Agnes Farquhar; b Cornhill 21.9.35
teacher maths: Keith 1957–58, Powis s s Aber 1958–61, remed maths Dun 1973–76
m Aber 2.8.58 Hance Fullerton BSc 1956 *qv*

COWIE John *BSc 1964 MEd 1978

COWIE Margaret Stephen *MA 1968

**COWIE Marion Patricia *MA 1957
Dip Medieval St 1968 MLitt 1970**
d of George S. C. men's outfitter and Edna M. Little-child bus. acct; b Aber 25.5.36
Dip Ed(Lond) 1958
teacher: Chatelard s Les Avants Switzerland 1958–59, Abbey s R'dg 1959–62, Engl lang Athens 1963, Kingsley s Leamington Spa 1964–67
m Aber 11.8.69 John H. Swogger BA(Kansas) Dip Medieval St Aberd 1969 s of Leo G. S. MA(Kansas) Topeka Kansas

COWIE Maureen Menzies MA 1970
d of Joseph C. journalist and Annie B. Menzies secy; b Aber 1.10.48
Dip Youth ESTB 1971
careers off. Stirlingsh 1971–72; soc worker Fraserburgh 1972–73; careers off. Aber from 1973
m Aber 15.8.72 James Murray BSc 1971 med res tech s of James M. Aber

COWIE Michael MA 1969
s of James C. credit ag and Vera T. Sutherland; b Aber 10.12.47
MEd(Glas) 1977
teacher St Thomas Aquinas s s Glasg 1971–73; house-master Bellshill acad 1973–75; asst prin mod stud. Camphill h s Paisley 1975–79; prin mod stud. Hawick h s from 1979
m Glasg 7.4.73 Jennifer A. Lake teacher d of Cecil C. F. L. Glasg

COWIE Nettie Isabella MA 1957

COWIE Stanley Windsor MA 1961
s of James C. trawl skipper and Agnes A. Smith; b Aber 25.7.37
teacher: Summerhill acad Aber 1962–64, Dailly p s Ayrsh 1965–68, Shortlees p s Kilmarnock 1969–75; trained as teacher of deaf 1975–76; teacher West Park s for partially hearing Crosshouse from 1976

COWIE William Pirie *BSc 1958

COWKING Thomas Leonard *MA 1968
s of Thomas C. bldr and Alice A. Harrison; b Settle 24.3.47
banker Lond from 1969
m Giggleswick 18.7.69 Philippa J. S. Jackson MA 1969 *qv*

COWLING Geoffrey John PhD 1968
BSc BD(Syd)

COWLING Terence Ian *BSc 1968
s of William C. motor mech and Edna M. Hook; b Aber 29.11.45
computer progr Winchester from 1968

COWN David John *BSc(for) 1967
s of William J. C. bldr and Isobel W. Diack MA 1933 *qv*; b Huntly 21.12.44
PhD(B Col) 1976
asst br man. Tilhill for. Elgin 1967–69; res scient for. res inst Rotorua NZ 1969–73 and from 1976
m Rotorua 19.12.70 Paula C. Hutton MA(Canterbury) teacher d of William M. H. BSc(Birm) Marapara

COWPER Hugh William MA 1968
s of John C. marine eng and Catherine M. P. Chisholm teacher; b Forres 10.9.46
teacher maths: Nairn acad 1969–73, Elgin acad 1973–74; asst prin maths Forres acad from 1974, asst prin guid from 1976
m Dallas Moray 16.7.76 Elizabeth Campbell MA 1977 museum asst d of Peter C. Kellas

COWPER Rosemary Hartell MA 1970
d of James A. C. cler off. Scot. gas and Joan S. Smith secy; b Penicuik 7.8.48
Dip Secy (coll of comm Aber) 1971
Edin: secy southern hosp board of man. 1971–72, to group eng 1973, to matron Elsie Inglis mat. hosp 1973–76, to gen admin Lothian health board s dist from 1976

COX Anthony Raymond Cole   BEd 1969

COX Cecil Joseph   MB ChB 1961
s of Henry C. prop. and Iris D. Hughes; b Trinidad 6.1.25
WHO fell. 1964 DPH(Tor) 1965 LMCC 1972
h o Aber hosps 1961–62; Trinidad: gen med, surg 1962–64, county m o h 1965–67; reg dir med serv Tobago 1967–69; m o h Port of Spain 1969–71; m o h Renfrew county Canada 1971–73; g p Cambridge Canada from 1973
m Aber 3.11.58 Franziska M. Nottelmann midwife d of Johann N. Gross-Reken Germany

COX Eric Frank   *BSc 1963
s of Albert C. grocer and Lillian L. Frost teacher; b Ely 3.2.41
PhD(Nott) 1966
res scient nat veg res stat Wellesbourne Warwick from 1966
m Nott 7.6.65 Avril H. Redfern nurs nurse d of Albert R. Nott

COXON Philip Stanley   MA 1970
s of Stanley C. ord surv and Ivy I. Rosher play s superv; b Derby 6.12.44
Aber: stud. teacher, stud. lib 1970–71; Inv: for. worker Dochfour estate, reindeer herder Aviemore 1971–72; asst warden Royal Soc Protection Birds Wales, England, Outer Hebrides from 1972

CRABB David Iain Charles   BSc(eng) 1961

CRAIB Margaret   *MA 1961
d of Andrew A. C. trawl skipper and Margaret R. Mair; b Aber 21.6.34
Aber: teacher Engl Aber acad, Hazlehead acad, St Margaret's s for girls, Rubislaw acad 1963–74; asst prin Engl Harlaw acad from 1975
m Aber 9.10.59 Anastasius Eleftheriou BSc 1964 qv

CRAIG Alexander Souter   *BSc 1968
s of Joseph C. fish merchant and Mary R. Souter; b Gourdon 20.12.46
phys: field trials Hawker Siddeley Dynamics Hatfield 1968–70, inst dev dept Barr & Stroud from 1970
m Aber 10.7.68 Dorothy F. Carnie MA 1967 qv

CRAIG Alison Margaret   *MA 1969
d of George A. C. acct and Dorothy Forbes telephonist; b Aber 10.4.47
Dip Ed(Edin) 1970
teacher: hist Dumbarton acad 1970–74, Jeddah prep s Saudi Arabia from 1975
m Aber 18.7.73 Robert H. Thomson BSc(Strath) civ eng s of James T. Dumbarton

CRAIG Alison Mary   MA 1958
d of Joseph C. and Mary R. Souter; b Gourdon 31.12.36
teacher: Mackie acad Stonehaven 1959–60, Killin s 1960–64, Prince Charles' s Kitwe Zambia 1964–66, Thurso h s 1968–74, Oban h s from 1974
m Aber 23.12.59 Ronald Mackay MA 1957 qv

CRAIG Amber Margaret   MA 1967
d of Andrew C. MA 1932 qv; b Aber 26.6.45
Dip Lib St(Belf) 1968; ALA 1970; Dip Hist of Art(Belf) 1972
sen lib asst Greenisland 1968–69; Down Co library 1969–70; asst lib Down Co 1970–71; sen asst lib Down Co Lib (later S-E Educ Lib Board) from 1971

m Peterhead 27.12.69 James R. R. Adams lib s of Alexander A. Ballybofey

CRAIG Andrew   MA 1966
s of Andrew C. MA 1932 qv; b Stonehaven 17.1.43
teacher-trg 1966–67; instr off. RN HMS *Ganges* 1967–69; transfer to gen list seaman spec HMS *Plymouth* Far East 1969–71, HMS *Lincoln* Far East 1971–73, HMS *Kent*, Medit 1973, HMS *Phoebe* 1973–74, RNC Greenwich 1974, HMS *Dryad* 1975, HMS *London* 1975–76, HMS *Excellent* 1976–77, HMS *Ark Royal* 1977–78
m Inv 13.4.68 Jennifer M. Hutchinson teacher d of Laurence H. BSc(Durh) Inv

CRAIG Cecilia   *MA 1966
d of Alexander M. C. fisherman and Elizabeth K. Gray; b Forfar 10.11.43
Lucy Fell(Aberd) 1966; MLitt(Cantab) 1972
univ teacher Waterloo Lutheran univ Ontario 1966–67 and 1972–73; teacher Wellshot s Glasg Jan–June 1972; lect Wilfrid Laurier univ Waterloo Ontario (formerly Waterloo Lutheran univ) 1973–74; teacher Mackie acad Stonehaven from 1975

CRAIG Evelyn Rose   MA 1962
m Scott

CRAIG Isobel Milne   MB ChB 1966
d of John C. civ serv and Gertrude M. Milne; b Aber 22.2.42
h o, sen h o gyn, dermat, gen med, psychiat Aber 1967–70; m o FPA: Teesside 1971–72, Birm 1973–75
m Aber 21.7.67 Peter A. Slater MB ChB 1966 qv

CRAIG James Alexander   MB ChB 1958

CRAIG James Boyle   PhD 1963
s of Albert C. machinist and Jessie Boyle; b Aber 12.7.32
CChem   MRIC
post-doct res asst Oxford univ 1963–64; scient off. Macaulay inst for soil res Aber 1964–66; post-doct res fell. Aberd 1966–67; lect chem Aberd from 1967
m Aber 11.11.70 Ann M. Bannerman telecomm traffic supt d of Charles L. B. Aber

CRAIG John Austin   BSc 1963

CRAIG Joseph   BSc(eng) 1960

CRAIG Lesley Catherine   *MA 1967 *MEd 1969
d of William G. W. C. comp man. and Catherine S. Ewen; b Aber 2.1.44
teacher Fr Hazlehead acad Aber 1969–75, asst prin mod lang Summerhill acad Aber from 1975

CRAIG Margaret Patricia   MA 1956

CRAIG Norma Rennie   *MA 1959
d of Daniel F. C. co-op soc man. and Jean A. Anthony secy; b Glasg 25.8.37
teacher hist: Keith 1960–62, Aber 1962–64; lib asst Glasg from 1974
m Aber 8.9.62 James G. Kellas MA 1958 qv

CRAIG Peter Michael   *BSc 1967
s of John P. Craig MA 1927 qv; b Ballater 13.8.45
govt geol: Honiara Br Solomon Is 1968–70, Edin from 1970
m Aber 22.11.47 Marjory A. Gall BSc 1966 qv

CRAIG Robert   MA 1960

CRAIG Robert Lawrence *BSc 1970
s of Robert E. C. BSc(Edin) marine phys and Dorothy
A. Lawrence MA 1967 *qv*; b Edin 16.8.48
phys Barr & Stroud Glasg from 1970
m Aber 17.7.71 Kathleen E. M. Robertson MA(Glas)
teacher d of Robert R. BSc 1965 *qv*

CRAIG Robin Alexander MB ChB 1969
s of James L. C. LLB(Glas) county clerk Aberdeensh
and Annie H. McCulloch; b Dumfries 18.12.44
Aber: h o ARI and city hosp 1969–70; sen h o Cornhill
hosp 1970–71, g p from 1971
m Aber 10.4.74 Lynda M. Sutherland teacher d of
William S. BL 1935 *qv*

CRAIG Roger Kingdon *BSc 1970 PhD 1974

CRAIGHEAD Peter Bruce BSc 1961 *1963
s of Peter C. journalist and Eliza B. L. Bruce typist;
b Aber 19.1.40
ARIC 1968
teacher Aber: chem RGC 1964–71, prin chem Kincorth
acad from 1971
m Aber 5.4.65 Margaret Hay teacher d of David H. Aber

CRAIGHEAD William Arthur MA 1957

CRAIGIE Alasdair Shaw BSc(eng) 1966
s of Hugh H. C. farm. and Margaret Shaw; b Inv
21.1.43
asst eng: Geo Wimpey & Co. Helensburgh 1965–66;
W. Tawse: asst eng Clacton-on-Sea 1966–68, site ag
Aber, Edin, Laurencekirk 1968–73, contr man. Aber
1973–76; dir CHAP Construct. (Abdn) from 1976
m Aber 4.4.74 Ada J. Newlands RGN d of William N.
Buckie

CRAIGIE James Alexander BSc(agr) 1961
s of James R. L. C. farm. and Tina S. Matheson
teacher; b Sandwick 15.1.39
poultry man. Inv 1961–64; farm. Cawdor 1964–67 and
from 1969; tech rep Isaac Spencer Aber 1967–69
m Nairn 6.10.62 Doreen Allan secy d of James A. Nairn

CRAIGIE Jean Roberta MA 1956
d of William I. C. master grocer and Jane S. Wilson;
b Fraserburgh 29.8.34
teacher: Middlefield s Aber 1957–62, Inverallochy 1962–
69, Fraserburgh inf s from 1969

CRAIGIE Peter Campbell MTh 1968
s of Hugh B. C. MB ChB(Manc) CBE chief m o mental
health Scot. and Lilia C. Murray SRN; b Lancaster
18.8.38
MA(Edin) 1965 Dip Th(Durh) 1967 PhD(McM) 1970
asst prof: Carleton univ Ottawa 1970–71, McM Hamilton
Ontario; assoc prof Calg Alberta from 1974, head of dept
from 1977; author *The Book of Deuteronomy* (Eerdmans)
1976
m Edin 5.9.64 Elizabeth Alexander MB ChB(Edin) phys
d of Charles A. Edin

CRAIGMILE Arthur Brown MA 1957

CRAIK Ian William *MA 1970

CRAMB Maurice Quentin *MA 1962 Dip Ed 1963
s of Maurice C. MA 1932 *qv*; b Aber 4.2.40
teacher Engl: Gordon s Huntly 1963–64, AGS 1964–69
(spec asst from 1967), prin Engl Madras coll St And
1969–72; HMIS: W of Scot 1972–75, national spec Engl,
convener Engl panel of HM Insp from 1975
m Aber 31.3.64 Diane P. Lawrie MB ChB 1967 *qv*

CRAMB Thomas James BSc(for) 1957

CRAN George Castle *MA 1969
s of William C. and Minnie Cran; b Inverurie 30.6.47
PhD(R'dg) 1973
operations analyst MoD Sevenoaks from 1973
m Prudhoe-on-Tyne 22.12.73 Catherine J. Harrand

CRAN Gordon William *BSc 1963
s of George W. C. cashier and Annie C. Scroggie; b
Aber 3.9.41
Dip Stat(Oxon) 1965 PhD(Belf) 1972 FRSS 1966
Queen's univ Belf: asst lect 1965–67, lect from 1967
m Belfast 4.8.73 Elizabeth A. Riddell staff nurse d of
William R. Belfast

CRAN James Douglas *MA 1969
s of James C. and Jane McDonald; b Kintore 28.1.44
Lond: res off. Conservative res dept 1970–71; secy nat
assoc of pension funds from 1971
m Lond 7.4.73 Penelope B. Wilson d of Richard T. P. W.
Lond

CRANE Nicola Hilary Francis *MA 1970
d of Bryant F. F. C. MA(Cantab) clerk in holy orders
and Gwendoline M. Hughes BA(Cantab) teacher; b
Brighton 6.4.47
Dip Secy St(Strath) 1971
secy to Inst fin. and invest. Stir 1971–72; admin asst
Midlothian c c Edin 1972–75; secy to acad board and
dir sixth form stud. Newton Abbot Devon group of s s
from 1976
m Congleton 15.7.72 Robin M. Orr BSc(agr) 1971 post
grad stud. s of Robert M. O. MA(Edin) Kirknewton

CRAVEN Janet Margaret MA 1970
d of Stanley N. A. C. BSc(eng)(Lond) C eng and
Margaret L. French, teacher; b Wakefield 29.3.49
ASO Dunstaffnage marine lab Oban 1971; ASO hill
farm. res organis: Edin 1971–73, Bush Estate, Penicuik
from 1974
m Oban 20.6.70 Robert M. Brown BSc(St And) elect. eng
s of Robert B. Tayport

CRAVEN Linda Joan Mary *MA 1969
d of Edward C. bank man. and Alice F. McWhor
comm artist; b Meols Wirral 6.9.46
Dip Soc Ad(Liv) 1970
Kirkby: asst playleader 1970–71; asst commun dev off.
1971–73; area commun dev off. Huyton Knowsley from
1974
m Huyton N Liverpool 18.12.71 Colin A. Brown instrument mech. s of George S. B. Maghull

CRAW William *MA 1967 Dip Medieval St 1968
s of Alexander M. C. turner and Jane H. Bain carpet
des, clerkess; b Paisley 10.3.38
post grad/part-time tut. Aberd 1968–69; res Paris 1969–
70; Rennes: lecteur d'Anglais univ de Haute-Bretagne
1970–72, lecteur in Institut universitaire de technologie,
univ of Rennes 1972–73; lect Fr Glas from 1973

CRAWFORD Derick Alexander BSc(agr) 1956
s of Theodore A. C. MB ChB(Edin) med pract and
Marjorie E. Leith; b London 5.12.31
Macheke Rhodesia: conserv and extension off. 1956–58,
tobacco farm asst 1958–63, man. 1963–65; Belfast: asst
man. cigarette dev 1965–71, prod. des man. 1971–73;
Montreal: gen man. res and dev 1973–74, dir res and dev
from 1974
m Aber 5.10.57 Elizabeth L. Donald MA 1957 *qv*

CRAWFORD Frederick *MA 1958
s of Frederick A. C. rly clerk and Alice C. Barron;
b Aber 13.8.36
teacher Engl Ellon from 1959; Ellon town councillor
1972–75
m Aber 13.7.60 Frances M. Bishop MA 1958 *qv*

CRAWFORD George Patrick Mitchell *MB ChB 1970
**   *MD 1975**
s of George C. insur comp man. and Nellie Mitchell
MA 1932 *qv*; b Aber 12.10.46
MRCP (UK) 1972
h o Aber 1970–71; res fell. dept med Aberd 1971–72;
MRC jun res fell. Aberd 1972–75; lect med Aberd 1975–
76; sen lect med haematol post grad med s univ Lond
1976–77; sen lect med univ W Aust from 1977
m Aber 27.7.67 Allison M. Irvine BSc 1967 *qv*

CRAWFORD John Richard   PhD 1958
BA(KCTenn) BD(Theol Sem Richmond Virg)

CRAWFORD Sarah Herdman   MA 1965
d of Ronald C. biscuit manuf and Isabel Herdman;
b Edin 23.11.43
secy course Lond 1965–66
m Kinloch Rannoch 21.5.66 Lionel G. D. Barclay farm.
s of Charles B. Dess

CRICHTON Rhoda   BSc 1961

CRICHTON Ronald   MA 1957 *1959

CRICHTON Roy Williamson   *BSc 1968
s of Alexander M. C. MA 1932 *qv*; b St And 8.4.46
Dip Ed(Makerere coll univ E Af) 1969
teacher: Kapsabet s Kenya 1969–71, housemaster Bishopbriggs h s Glasg 1971–74; prin guid Craigroyston h s
Edin from 1974
m Glasg 2.7.73 Hazel P. Barker MA(Glas) teacher d of
Benjamin B. Torrance

CRIGHTON Barbara Anne Moncrieff   MA 1964
d of David M. C. advoc Aber and Eileen A. Troughton;
b Portadown NI 31.5.43
teacher: Prestonpans p s 1965–70
m Aber 4.8.67 John H. McLaren arch./plan. consult. s of
John McL. Aber

CRIGHTON George Innes   BSc(eng) 1960

CRIGHTON Joan Beveridge   MA 1967 Dip Ed 1968
d of William C. C. postal and tel off. and Annie B. S.
Beveridge; b Glasg 7.12.46
teacher maths Mackie acad Stonehaven 1968–75
m Stonehaven 16.8.75 William M. Steele .MB ChB 1971
g p s of Edgar W.S. Loth

CRIGHTON John Watson   BSc(eng) 1960
s of Thomas T. C. county road surv/civ eng and Mary
D. Watson governess; b Elgin 15.5.39
MIMunE 1963 MICE 1966 MIHE 1978
asst eng Argyll c c 1960–64; asst eng, sen eng Perth &
Kinross joint c c 1964–75; team leader Tayside reg c from
1977
m Aber 17.7.64 Helen M. L. Kerr teacher dom sc d of
Joseph T. K. Aber

CRIGHTON Maureen Ross   MA 1965
m Smith

CRITCHLEY Carol Mary   MA 1966
d of Thomas A. C. civ serv/under secy and Margaret
C. Robinson; b Lond 24.12.43

teacher: Leyton Lond 1966–67, Basildon 1967–69, Kidderminster from 1969
m Hampstead 23.7.66 Alexander W. Mathieson MA
1966 *qv*

CROALL Margaret Matheson   *MA 1967
d of Peter S. C. man. dir and Peggy Matheson secy;
b Stornoway 5.1.45
gen admin asst NE reg hosp board Aber 1967–68; secy
Belford hosp Fort William 1968–69; sen admin asst NE
reg hosp board 1969–71
m Kelso 9.5.70 Alexander Halliday BSc(Glas) prod. man.
s of Alexander H. Wishaw

CROCKETT Edward John   *MA 1962

CROCKETT George Watt   MA 1964

CROCKETT Isobel Margaret   BSc 1967
d of Alexander S. C. BSc(eng) 1942 *qv*; b Aber 4.8.45
teacher Broughton s Edin 1968–72
m Edin 21.3.72 Michael S. Fisher MB ChB(Edin) g p
s of J. L. F. Huddersfield

CROCKETT Raymond Hughes   *MA 1965 *MEd 1969
s of George C. RNat Mission to Deep Sea Fishermen
Aber and Bessie Hughes ch sister; b Aber 10.5.43
teacher Engl West Calder from 1970

CROFTS Gillian Mary   *BSc 1965
d of Richard B. I. C. comp dir and Vera R. Bland;
b Shrewsbury 4.11.43
teacher: Liv 1965–66, Bebington 1966–69
m Aber 5.8.66 Alexander S. Philip BSc 1965 *qv*

CROFTS Harold Robert   MB ChB 1959

CROLL Hugh MacArthur   *MA 1965
s of John M. C. MB ChB 1929 *qv*; b Lincoln 3.7.42
ALA 1969
lib asst Aberd 1965–66; stud. s of librarianship Manc coll
of comm 1966–67; Edin univ lib: sen lib asst 1968–69,
asst lib from 1969

CROLL Neil Macarthur   *BSc 1960
s of John M. C. MB ChB 1929 *qv*; b Sheffield 6.7.37
health phys Manc 1960–66; Rolls Royce Derby: computer
progr 1966–69, information analyst from 1969
m Stretton-on-Dunsmore 18.3.61 Veronica M. Hill MA
1959 *qv*

CROMAR Neil   LLB 1966
s of Peter C. lab and Isabella Leys; b Aber 24.5.45
law app 1966–68; solic A. C. Morrison & Richards advoc
Aber from 1969
m Aber 4.4.70 Catherine F. H. Ross MA 1968 *qv*

CROMBIE Alan Shaw   BSc(eng) 1960
s of Theodore C. construct. eng and Jessie T. Shaw
MA 1931 *qv*; b Duns 19.10.38
Aber: asst eng city eng dept 1960–62, county eng dept
1962–64; Ross & Cromarty c c: asst eng 1964–70, sen
asst 1970–74; comp dir Dingwall from 1974
m Aber 2.4.62 Anne M. Wood bank clerkess d of John
J. W. Banff

CROMBIE Elspeth Mary   MA 1961
d of David L. C. BSc(eng)(Glas) man. dir and Barbara
C. Cumming; b Aber 14.4.40
shorthand typist: Ferranti Edin 1962–63, William Tawse
Aber 1964–65, secy soil sc dept Aberd from 1965

CROMBIE Margaret Harben   *MA 1961
m Ferguson

CROMPTON-NICHOLAS Eunice Lucinda *MA 1969
d of Carlton A. C. C-N. civ serv Jamaica and Margaret
L. Lidstone saleswoman; b England 18.1.46
interpreter/private secy Argentine emb Jamaica 1969–71;
exec asst/p r ag for private artist (painter) Jamaica, USA,
S Amer from 1971

CROOK Ian Clitherow BSc(agr) 1968
s of Sidney C. med rep and Ida C. Clitherow; b Liv
8.8.45
Dip FMBO(NOSCA) 1969
rural dev off. dept agr Papua New Guinea 1969–71;
W Aust: educ off. farm man. foundation of Aust Perth,
farm man. consult. Dowerin from 1974
m Prestatyn N Wales 22.8.69 Gillian M. Hughes teacher
d of Gwilym F. H. BA

CROOKSHANKS Noreen Meredith MB ChB 1958
d of George C. C. MA 1923 qv and Jean S. Gorrod
BCom 1923 qv; b Aber 18.3.35
h o Hairmyres hosp E Kilbride, RAHC, Yorkhill hosp
Glasg 1958–60; g p Stockport from 1971
m Aber 5.2.60 Hugh D. Baillie MB ChB(Glas) vascular
surg s of Hugh B. Glasg

CROSGROVE Torrance Pringle MB ChB 1960

CROSKERRY Patrick George *BSc 1968

CROSSLEY Peter John *BSc 1968

CROW Charles Gordon David MA 1965 MEd 1973

CROW Timothy John PhD 1970
s of Percy A. C. BSc(Lond) loc govt off. and Barbara
B. Davies; b Lond 7.6.38
MB BS(Lond) 1964 DPM 1971 MRCP 1972 MRCPsych
1972
lect mental health Aberd 1970–72; sen lect psychiat Manc
1973–74; head div of psychiat, clin res centre Northwick
Park hosp Harrow from 1974
m Lond 22.1.66 Julie C. Carter BSc(Lond) med pract
d of Eric G. H. C. PhD(Lond) Orpington

CROWE Walter Pressler MA 1969

CROXSON Jeremy Peter Gover BSc(eng) 1963
s of John A. G. C. oil comp exec, press and p/r and
Jessica J. I. White, secy to MP; b Sutton 25.9.41
MICE 1968 AMIHE 1969
Sir Frederick Snow & Ptnrs: asst eng Lond 1963–66,
resid eng 1968; site eng M62 Motorway Sir Alfred
MacAlpine & Sons Yorks 1967; civ eng Brit Petr Co
based in Lond from 1969
m Kenley Felicity Wilson-Brown airline receptionist d
of Malcolm W-B. Kenley

CRUDDAS John Wilfred *MA 1963
s of John W. C. and Mary A. T. Herron; b Shotton
Colliery 2.10.40
asst lect Engl and liberal stud. Darlington coll of f e
1963–64; liberal party organis for parl constit Roxburgh,
Selkirk, Peebles 1964; secy to fac of soc sc St And 1964–
67; secy to fac of soc sc and letters Dund 1967–68;
admin asst N'cle 1968–70; gen asst to secy/prin admin
asst univ coll Lond from 1970

CRUDEN John McNab BSc 1958 *1960

CRUDEN Norma Jeannette Margaret MA 1968
m Macdonald

CRUICKSHANK Alexander Esson BSc 1969
s of John C. hosiery mech and Agnes Esson; b Aber
3.4.48
Turriff: cost acct 1970–72, cost/wages man. 1972–74;
acct Aber from 1974
m Aber 30.6.72 Alison E. Merson MA 1971 teacher d of
John M. Aber

CRUICKSHANK Alfred Ian Duncan MA 1967

CRUICKSHANK Alistair Ronald *MA 1966
m Aber 29.3.67 Alexandra M. Noble MA 1965 qv

CRUICKSHANK Charles Ian *BSc(eng) 1961
s of Charles C. marine eng and Mabel Eddie; b
Singapore 30.8.39
CEng MICE 1966 MIEA 1972 MIE(Hong Kong) 1978
civ eng: site eng Lond, R'dg 1961–63, des eng Edin
1963–66, des eng Vancouver, Calgary 1966–69, assoc
Sydney 1969–77, ptnr John Connell & Assoc Hong Kong
from 1977
m Tomintoul 26.3.66 Jane A. Stuart SRN d of William S.
Glenlivet

CRUICKSHANK Colin James MA 1966

CRUICKSHANK David Keir Ross BSc(agr) 1957
s of Peter J. C. master butcher and Dorothy J. Ross
SRN; b Fochabers 11.6.34
Dip Agr(Cantab) 1958 DTA(Trin) 1959
Zambia: agr off. 1959–63, anim husb off. 1963–64, anim
husb res off. 1964–72, prin res off. from 1972

CRUICKSHANK Diana Christina *MA 1956
d of Ernest W. H. C. MB ChB 1910 qv; b Halifax Nova
Scotia 21.3.34
BA(Cantab) 1958
lect: Bergen univ Norway 1959–62, Engl City of Leeds
and Carnegie coll Leeds 1962–71, drama coll of educ
Aber from 1971

CRUICKSHANK Don William *MA 1965
s of William C. lab tech and Mary E. Duncan nurse;
b Fettercairn 16.8.42
PhD(Cantab) 1968
res fell. Emmanuel coll Cantab 1968–70; lect univ coll
Dub from 1970
m Aber 12.8.67 Margrit R. Ritchie MA 1965 qv

CRUICKSHANK Donald Gordon MA 1963
s of Donald C. C. MA 1933 qv; b Elgin 17.9.42
CA 1967 MBA(Manc) 1972
corporate plan. Alcan Alum Newport 1967–70; McKinsey
& Co Lond: man. consult. from 1972
m Aber 17.10.64 Elizabeth B. Taylor MA 1966 qv

CRUICKSHANK Edith Elsie *BSc 1964
m McBoyle

CRUICKSHANK Francis Robertson *BSc 1963
PhD 1966
s of Francis G. N. C. wood machinist and Margaret I.
Robertson secy; b Aber 30.1.41
res fell. Stanford res inst USA 1966–68; lect phys chem
Strath from 1968
m Aber 3.10.66 Joyce Muir cashier/telephonist d of James
W. M. Aber

CRUICKSHANK Gordon Dyce MA 1969
s of John C. factory stoker and Maggie A. H. Dyce
papermill worker, net braider; b Aber 29.9.26
teacher AGS from 1970
m Aber 23.3.51 Marion M. Stott MA 1946 qv

CRUICKSHANK Hugh Ogilvie Campbell *MA 1962
s of James C. rubber planter and Agnes Sherrif;
b Malaya 13.12.16
teacher geog Aberfeldy 1963–68; prin geog/mod stud.
from 1968
m Portsoy 2.8.58 Helen Wylie teacher home econ d of
William J. W. Port Glasg
d 10.12.75

CRUICKSHANK Ian MA 1962
d Ayr 20.2.67 *AUR* XLII 376

CRUICKSHANK Isobel MA 1961
d of Duncan J. C. pharm and Isobel Milne; b Insch
29.9.40
teacher: Dunf 1962–63; Ashton in Lancs, Makerfield
1963–64; Bowdon 1971–72
m Aber 12.8.63 George M. Bath dent surg s of George B.
Wigan

CRUICKSHANK James George *BSc 1957
s of Charles C. marine eng and Mabel Eddie receptionist; b Singapore 15.3.35
scient off. Macaulay inst for soil res Aber 1957–59;
lect geog Belf 1959–72, sen lect from 1972; visiting lect:
McM Ontario 1966–67, univ New England Armidale
NSW Aust 1973
m Rotherham 22.9.62 Margaret M. Bower BSc(Lond)
univ lect d of George B. Greasbrough

CRUICKSHANK John McRae cMB ChB 1966
s of William C. farm. and Mabel A. Cruickshank secy;
b Ellon 17.12.42
DObstRCOG 1971
h o ARI 1966–67; Perth RI: sen h o, regist med 1967–70,
sen h o obst and gyn 1970; g p Northallerton from 1970
m Beith 10.9.68 Ann L. Smith occup therap d of Robert
N. S. Beith

CRUICKSHANK Leonard George *BSc 1968
s of Donald C. C. MA 1933 *qv*; b Banff 15.8.46
teacher maths/geog Saltus g s Bermuda from 1969
m Aber 27.12.67 Anne G. Brown MA 1968 *qv*

CRUICKSHANK Marna MA 1959 Dip Ed 1961
d of James C. auctioneer and valuator and Grace M.
Boddie; b Cruden Bay 13.6.38
teacher: Engl/gen subj Kaimhill s s Aber 1961–66;
classics Peterhead acad 1966–77, asst prin classics (i/c
dept) from 1977

CRUICKSHANK Muriel Bremner MA 1962
d of George A. C. draper and Isabella Bremner;
b Cornhill 9.12.41
Norway: lab sister Tana 1967–69, Askim 1970–77; soc
worker Askim from 1977
m Aber 17.2.62 Per Spenning MB ChB 1965 *qv*

CRUICKSHANK Nancy Patricia MB ChB 1957
d of Robert C. MB ChB 1922 *qv*; b Milngavie 24.4.32
h o: Woodend hosp Aber, Farnham 1957–58; g p locum
work Edin from 1958; g p Dalkeith from 1977
m Edin 7.3.58 Kenneth McLean MB ChB 1956 *qv*

CRUICKSHANK Ruth Alexander MA 1966

CRUICKSHANK Sheila MA 1964
d of John C. timber contr and Helen F. Davidson;
b Aber 1.10.42
Dip Sec Sc(Strath) 1965
secy: to dir shipping comp Leith 1965–66, Edin univ
1966–73

m Aber 14.4.67 Robert H. C. Somerville shipbroker s of
Peter C. S. BCom(Edin) Edin

CRUICKSHANK Stanley MB ChB 1963
s of Robert C. foreman painter LNER and Mary A. G.
Aitken; b Insch 17.11.32
h o ARI, mat. hosp Aber 1963–64; g p Hull from 1965
m Aber 3.8.57 Mary E. Wallace MA 1954 *qv*

CRUICKSHANK William James BSc 1959 *1960

CRUICKSHANK Wilma Margaret Philip MA 1967
d of William C. farm. and Mabel A. Cruickshank;
b Aber 24.6.46
teacher: Mile-End p s Aber 1968–70, Fr Aber 1973–75,
Brisbane Aust 1975–76, Birm 1976–78; TEFL lang centre
Birm from 1978
m Aber 4.1.65 Roy G. Condie MB ChB 1966

CUDDEFORD Derek MSc 1968
s of Charles W. C. civ serv and Janet N. Williams;
b Hayes 10.5.45
BSc(Lond) MIBiol 1973
lect Edin from 1968
m Aber 17.2.68 Alison Lyall BSc 1966 *qv*

CULLEN Catherine Fraser *MA 1968 MLitt 1974
d of James C. teacher and Mary C. Fraser; b Hamilton
28.11.45
teacher Ger Harlaw acad from 1970
m Aber 12.7.74 Dirk Nikodem MA 1970 *qv*

CULROSS Brian Richard *BSc 1966
s of Kenneth A. C. printer's estimator and Marjorie
E. Savournin; b Lond 12.9.43
Dip Indust Chem Pract & Man 1966
market res exec: Berk, Lond and Harlow 1966–69, Baird
& Tatlock Chadwell Heath Essex 1969–70; E region Brit
Gas Corp, Potters Bar: sen marketing res asst 1970–75,
market res man. from 1975
m Lond 11.9.66 Lynn S. Davis secy d of Edgar H. D.
Lond

CUMINE Patrick Gerrie BSc(eng) 1963
s of Joseph G. C. bank man. and Elizabeth G. Peterkin:
b Dun 26.9.41
Aust: Sydney drawing off. 1965–67, Gladstone alum.
smelter 1967–70; alum. smelter Invercargill NZ 1970–71;
iron-ore conveyor belt Dampier W Aust 1971–73; cement
factory Jacarta Indonesia from 1973
m Brisbane 26.12.69 Heather Lawrie

CUMMINE Duncan Penny MB ChB 1957
s of John M. C. MRCVS(Edin) vet surg and Annie S.
Penny teacher; b Aber 17.3.34
DObstRCOG 1961 DCH(Lond) 1962 MRCGP 1976
h o ARI 1957–58; capt RAMC Nicosia Cyprus 1958–60;
sen h o royal hosp for sick ch Brist 1962–63; regist Aber
gen hosp 1963–65; g p Bo'ness 1965–69, Edin from 1970
m Edin 10.7.65 Sally J. Harris RGN nurse

CUMMINE John Anderson MA 1956

CUMMING Alastair McConnachie *BSc 1967
s of Alick C. fitter eng and Mary M. Innes; b Keithhall 19.8.45
res scient Whitehaven 1969–70; med genetics res asst
Aberd from 1971
m Aber 2.8.69 Kathryn A. Cole d of Harry C. Aber

CUMMING Alexander James *MA 1968
s of Alexander G. C. MA 1938 *qv*; b Aber 7.3.47
ACMA 1973

teacher VSO Calcutta 1968–69; trainee acct Fort William 1970–72; comp secy Aber 1972–76; acct Grampian health board from 1976
m Perth 21.7.73 Margaret A. Callan MA(Edin) teacher d of John A. C. Perth

CUMMING Ann Patricia   MA 1966
d of Patrick C. MA 1928 *qv*; b Broughty Ferry 6.11.43
Dip Sec St(Strath) 1967
m Aber 6.9.68 Malcolm S. Murray BSc(St And) brewer s of Randolph S. M. West Mersea

CUMMING Anne Davidson   BSc 1965
d of William G. D. C. CA and Jane G. Golightly; b Inv 22.6.44
teacher maths: Morrison's acad for girls Crieff 1966–72, Kincorth acad Aber 1972–73
m Inv 2.8.71 Brian A. Stalker BCom(Edin) CA s of Anthony S. Crieff

CUMMING Arthur   *MA 1960

CUMMING Elsie Jean   MA 1968
d of Leslie D. C. comm trav and Jeannie T. Morrison secy; b Aber 29.10.47
teacher Springburn p s Glasg 1969–70
m Aber 15.6.68 Russell D. J. Pollock-Smith granite merch s of David P-S. Lenzie

CUMMING Francis   BSc(agr) 1956 *1957

CUMMING Harold Greenfield   PhD 1966
s of Roy E. C. BScA(Guelph)agr and Alburtta A. Greenfield piano teacher; b Gore Bay Ontario 1928
BA(Tor) 1951 MWM(Mich) 1953
Ontario: superv big game man. 1967–71; moose/caribou biol 1971–73; assoc prof fish and wildlife man. Wakehead univ Thunder Bay from 1973
m Gore Bay 31.7.71 Wilma L. Nothrop BA(Melb) teacher d of Wilmot N. farm. Lake Rowan Victoria Aust

CUMMING Jean Elizabeth   MB ChB 1965
d of Alexander G. C. MA 1937 *qv*; b Lossiemouth 11.10.40
DObstRCOG 1967
h o: ARI, Woodend hosp 1965–66, paediat Inv RI 1966–67, obst Aber 1967; sen h o obst/gyn Taplow 1967–68; m o FPA clin Middx and Surrey from 1970
m Lond 27.12.67 Thomas G. Taylor MB ChB 1965 *qv*

CUMMINGS Leslie Peter Clement   *MA 1960
s of James D. C. taxi driver and Winifred C. Briggs; b Guyana 14.4.33
PhD(Iowa) 1967 FRGS 1956
various posts Guyana, Canada, USA 1960–67; sen lect, head geog univ Guyana 1967; commonwealth fell./ visiting asst prof univ Iowa USA 1968–70; visiting prof univ Papua N Guinea 1971; prof/dean fac Arts univ Guyana 1972–75; dir Mirev proj govt Guyana 1976; univ Guyana: dep vice chancellor 1976–79, vice chancellor 1979; Fulbright res fell. univ Puerto Rico from 1979
m(2) Guyana 22.12.78 Marva Scholl banker d of Cecil S. Guyana

CUNDILL Erica Dorothy   MB ChB 1960
d of Eric T. C. LLB(Rhodes) lawyer and Kate V. Lamsley teacher; b Komgha Cape S Af 15.11.16
BA(S Af)
h o Aber 1960–61; g p Bolsover and Claycross 1961–62; S Af: hosp m o Lovedale 1962–68; Frere hosp E Lond 1968–69, Lovedale 1969–74, Grey hosp King Williamstown 1974–75; prin m o/actg supt Victoria hosp Lovedale from 1975

CUNNINGHAM Alison Jane   *MA 1967
d of Alexander K. C. CA and Edith M. Dickson MB ChB(Glas); b Huddersfield 22.1.46
teacher Engl Ashington g s Northumberland 1968–70; caseworker Shelter Housing aid centre Edin 1970–71; asst reporter children's panel Lothian from 1972

CUNNINGHAM Donald Ian Alexander   MB ChB 1956
s of Donald E. S. C. MB ChB(Glas) g p and Barbara S. Hinds; b Wolverhampton 18.2.33
DObstRCOG 1963
Stourbridge: h o 1956–57, regist gen med 1957–58; SSC RAF med branch, mass radiography München Gladbach Germany 1958–61; sen h o obst/gyn Wolverhampton 1961–62; g p: Dudley 1962–71, Dufftown from 1971
m Dudley 14.1.57 Mary K. Malvena civ serv Rowett inst Aber d of Alexander M. Bucksburn

CUNNINGHAM Elizabeth Mary   MA 1968
resid Auchterarder
m Carmichael

CUNNINGHAM Gerald Andrew   MA 1956 LLB 1958
s of John C. sawmaker and tool dealer and Mary Degnan; b Aber 6.3.35
nat serv Bordon 1959–61; Aber: leg. asst: town council 1961–64, Burnett & Reid 1964–68; Hunter & Gordon from 1968—firm later amalgamated with others as Stronachs, ptnr from 1969
m Aber 30.9.61 Lyn Carragher tv announcer d of Norman G. C. Aber

CUNNINGHAM Heather   MA 1969
m Stern

CUNNINGHAM Margaret   MB ChB 1960

CURNOW Robert Nicholas   PhD 1959
s of Dr Reginald N. C. and Olive E. Curnow; b Derby 9.3.33
BA(Cantab) 1954 Dip Math Stat(Cantab) 1955
scient off. agr res council unit of statist Aberd 1955–61; Harkness fell. commonwealth fund USA 1959–60; R'dg: lect, reader, prof/head of dept applied statist 1961–74 and from 1977; dean faculty agr and food 1974–77
m Cornwall 1957 Vera J. Bull BA(Cantab) clin biochem

CURRIE Bruce McKenzie   *MA 1970

CURRIE Ian Fraser   *BSc 1961
s of John H. C. painter and Helen Murray; b Brechin 8.6.38
scient civ serv RRE Malvern 1961–72 and from 1973; Maitre de conference associé Grenoble univ 1972–73
m Brechin 1959 Evelyn F. Findlay art teacher d of Robert F. Glenlivet

CURRIE Kathleen Isobel   *MA 1969
m Harry

CURRIE Mairi Morrison   *MA 1969
d of George A. C. teacher and Ruth Bain; b Buckie 1.10.47
Dip YESTB(Napier coll) 1974
teacher Engl/Fr: Portree h s 1970–71, Grantown g s 1971–72; surv cler work Inv 1973; stud. careers off. Napier coll Edin 1974–75; careers off. Highland reg council Dingwall from 1975

CURRIE William Dawson   *BSc(eng) 1965

CURRY David John   *BSc(eng) 1965
s of Kenneth E. C. ARIBA arch. and Isabel L. Cox
secy; b Lond 18.4.42
eng AEI Leic 1965–68; SRC res stud. Loughborough
univ 1968–71; asst elect. eng RN eng serv 1971–76;
elect. eng RCNC from 1976
m Lond 23.7.66 Katharine G. Murray MA 1966 *qv*

CURTIS David John   MA 1966
s of P. Arthur C. man. dir indust plumbing contr and
E. Kathleen Lees prop. comp dir; b Wolverhampton
6.9.42
exec off. inland rev Birm 1966–70; Lond: higher exec off.
board of inl rev secys' off. 1970–73; sen exec off. organis
div inl rev from 1974
m Tettenhall Wolverhampton 3.5.69 Josephine G. Bate
loc govt off. d of Joseph J. B. Wolverhampton

CURTIS Kathleen Mary   MA 1964
d of Ronald F. C. and Marjorie S. Polson; b Lybster
26.6.44
Dip Sec Sc(Glas)
secy: Edin 1965–67, Cambridge 1967–68, Copenhagen
1968–73; translator: Brussels 1973–74, Luxembourg
from 1974

CURTIS Robert Bryan   BSc(for) 1960

CUSA Rosalind Jane   BSc 1967
d of Noel W. C. BSc(Lond) chem, patent off., artist and
Mary B. Oliver; b Cheadle Hulme 14.4.44
lab tech univ of Alberta Edmonton 1967–68; scient edit.
oceanographic inst DSIR Wellington NZ 1968–77
m Wellington 1976 Neil M. Robertson marine eng, farm.
s of Jock R. Nelson NZ

CUSHNIE Jennifer Anne Baird   *MA 1963
d of Albert P. D. C. comm trav/warehouseman and
Constance J. Stables hairdresser; b Aber 11.9.40
dir res and publ at an internat stud. house and conference
centre Geneva 1964–68; enrolled in MA programme
Span. dept Santa Barbara Calif 1969–71; teacher re-
evaluation counselling San Francisco from 1971
m Santa Barbara 10.10.70 Dennis W. Allen MA(Princeton) asst dean for. stud. and peace educ and organis s of
Lewis C. A. Arcadia Calif

CUTBUSH Elizabeth Ann   MA 1966
d of Richard C. BMus(Lond) prin teacher mus Aber
h s for girls and Doris Furlong radiographer; b Leeds
5.2.45
Huddersfield: part time lect Ger adult educ 1970–72;
head mod lang Almondbury s s from 1972
m Oxford 1965 Alan J. Foubister BSc 1966 *qv*

CUTHBERT John Alexander Mitchell   LLB 1968
s of Alan D. C. shipowner and Elspeth M. Mitchell;
b Glasg 19.5.46
Edin: law app 1968–70, asst solic 1970–71; Glasgow: leg.
asst 1971–73, ptnr from 1974
m Skene 28.8.71 Kirsty M. Frazer MA 1969 *qv*

CUTHBERT Mary McLaren Gordon   *MA 1956

CUTHBERTSON Alastair   BSc(agr) 1958
s of Sir David P. C. MB ChB(Glas) hon res fell. Glas
and Lady Jean P. Telfer; b Glasg 1.3.36
Dip Agr(Cantab) 1959
Cantab: res schol pig indust dev auth 1959–62, res fell.
1962–64; carcase evaluation off. pig indust dev auth
Hitchin 1964–68, head of carcase and meat quality, meat
and livestock comm Milton Keynes from 1968

m Reigate 24.8.63 Caroline L. Ferguson BSc(St And)
teacher d of Sir Gordon F. Reigate

CUTLER Timothy Robert   BSc(for) 1956
s of Frank R. C. bus. exec and Jeannie E. Badenoch
teacher dom sc; b Bihar India 24.7.34
nat serv 2nd lt RE Farnborough 1956–58; asst conserv
for. col for. serv Kenya 1958–64; NZ for. serv from 1964,
now dir prod. for. man. div head office Wellington
m Grangemouth 11.10.58 Ishbel W. M. Primrose teacher
d of James P. Grangemouth

CUTT Jennifer Allan   BSc 1962
d of James R. C. MA 1926 *qv*; b Aber 1.11.41
teacher maths: Montrose acad 1963–64, Lond 1965–67,
Birm 1967–68, home teacher Birm 1974–75; teacher ch
hosp s Birm from 1975
m Aber 12.8.65 Alexander Buchan BSc 1961 *qv*

DADI Samuel Olorun Femi   BSc(for) 1962
s of Elisha G. D. farm. and Racheal A. Oyo petty
trader; b Ikare W Nigeria 3.6.35
Nigeria: asst cons for. W State 1962–70; vice prin Bassa
Nge anglican g s Bibololeo Kware State 1971–76; sen
for. Skoup & Co assoc bus. consult. Enugu from 1976
m Aber 24.7.61 Josette Y. Lecafette teacher d of Leon L.
Tourcoing Nord France

DAFALLA Dafalla Ahmed   MSc 1965
s of Ahmed D. Abdelbagi merch and Aziza Hamadel-
niel; b Elodayia Sudan 1.1.36
BSc(agr)(Khart) 1960 PhD(N'cle) 1979
agr res corp Sudan: agronomist 1966–70, sen agronomist
1970–74, chief agronomist from 1974
m Sudan 7.11.68 Mahassin Suleiman d of Suleiman I.
Elbitain Sudan

D'AGOSTINO Laurence Cormack   BSc(eng) 1960
s of Louis D'A. shopkeeper and Gertrude S. Cormack;
b Torphins 9.1.39
grad app Ferranti Edin 1960–61; IBA: tech asst Durris
transmitting stat 1961–62, eng Durris 1962–68, sen eng
oper Lond 1968–72, sen eng methods/oper Winchester
from 1972
m Banchory 25.8.62 Maurelle L. Coutts soil analyst d of
Arthur D. C. Banchory

DAHL Peter Henry   *MA 1970
d of Peter C. D. hotelier and Edith M. K. Weierter;
b Edin 18.9.45
MSc(H-W) 1972
plan asst Notts c c 1972–74; sen plan. asst Bassetlaw
dist c Worksop 1974–75; sen plan. N'cle-u-Tyne metr d c
from 1975
m Aber 28.8.72 Dorothy M. Goldie BSc 1970 *qv*

DAILEY William Sebastian   PhD 1962
ARIC(Upminster)

DALE Brian Graeme   LLB 1968
s of Reginald C. D. chartered elect. eng/factory man.
and Marjorie A. Vousden; b Hanwell Lond 20.11.46
Edin: law app Shepherd & Wedderburn WS 1968–70;
solic Stuart & Stuart Cairns & Co WS from 1970, ptnr
1972–75; ptnr Brooke & Brown Dunbar from 1975;
treas diocese of Edin Epis Church 1971; chapter clerk
Cath Ch of St Mary 1972–75; dep regist of diocese
1973–75; regist/secy of diocese 1975
m Felton Common 23.5.70 Judith G. de B. Franklin SRN
d of Henry L. F. BA(Oxon) Felton

DALGARNO Frederick George Scott   LLB 1964
s of Frederick D. depot superv and Winifred H. Scott
clerkess; b Aber 17.6.43
Dip Indust Man(Strath) 1965 CA 1968
Aber: law app 1968–71; solic acting as invest. man. from
1971
m Aber 5.9.69 Moyra Ellis bank clerk d of William E.
Aber

DALGARNO Gordon   *BSc 1963
s of William W. D. clerk and Jean Gordon secy; b Aber
15.3.40
tech off. ICI Billingham 1963–64; York: phys Rowntree
1964–67, head phys Rowntree-Mackintosh from 1967

DALGARNO Laraine Massie   MA 1967
m Brown

DALGARNO Melvin Taylor   *MA 1966 PhD 1972
s of William W. D. clerk and Jane A. M. Gordon
shorthand typist; b Aber 4.12.43
asst moral phil dept Aberd 1969–70; lect phil inst of
extension stud. Liv 1970–71; lect moral phil Aberd from
1971

DALGARNO William Alexander   MA 1969
s of John A. D. fruit salesman and Mary Morrison;
b Elgin 26.9.46
entertainments ag Elgin 1969–72; trainee man. 1972–78;
retail store man. Harrogate from 1978
m Forres 24.10.70 Patricia A. Brennan MA 1967 qv

DALGETTY Yvonne Anne   MA 1958 Dip Ed 1959
d of Ian R. D. ARIBA arch. and Emma Sime secy;
b Alyth 22.8.37
teacher Blairgowrie 1959–62; resid Malaysia
m Blairgowrie 16.2.63 James G. Taylor rubber estate man.
s of Robert T. Buckie

DALRYMPLE John Allan   *MA 1961

DALZIEL Francis Robert   *MA 1956 PhD 1958
s of Francis D. capt MN and Agnes Shand; b Aber
30.7.34
lect: Indiana 1959–61, Adelaide univ Aust from 1961

DANBURY David John   BSc(for) 1958 *1959

DANIEL Anne Rosemary   MA 1967
d of William D. farm. and Louisa Smith; b Kirkcaldy
2.1.46
teacher mod lang Bo'ness acad from 1968

DANIEL James Donaldson   MA 1967

DANIELS Samuel Bannerman Martin   BSc(eng) 1962
s of Edwin P. D. gen merch and Faustina Coleman
dressmaker; b Cape Coast Ghana 22.3.35
DIC(Lond) 1964 MBA(Windsor univ Ont) 1976
M Gh IE 1976
asst eng: Oscar Faber & ptnrs Lond 1962–63, Tahal
consult. eng Tel Aviv 1964–65; Ghana: reg man. GWSC
1965–77, proj eng IISC Accra from 1977
m Ghana 18.8.68 Margaret R. Isliker secy d of Frederick
I. Accra

DARGIE Bryan Alfred   *MA 1963
s of Robert C. D. city chamberlain and Mary K. Bryan;
b Dun 24.9.41
stud. RAM Lond 1964–66; freelance violinist 1966–68;
teacher violin Aber from 1969
m Aber 17.7.70 Elizabeth M. Witte MA 1970 qv

DARLING Alan Jeffrey   BSc(eng) 1967 *1970
s of John N. Q. D. pers man. Hong Kong & Shanghai
Bank Lond and Elvira M. de Magistris teacher; b Sutton
13.11.48
MICE 1974
eng: civ des Lond 1970–72, resid construct. Aber 1972–
73; Rendel Palmer & Tritton consult. eng Lond: des
Thames Barrier 1973–74, resid construct. Thames Barrier
from 1974

DAUBE Jonathan Mahram   *MA 1957
s of David D. PhD(Cantab) univ prof and Herta B.
Aufseesser; b Cambridge 23.11.37
Acad Dip(Lond) 1960 EdD(Harvard) 1968
teacher: Engl/maths Watford g s 1958–60, Engl Manc g s
1960–63, Engl Newton h s Mass. USA 1963–65; teaching
fell. in educ Harvard univ 1965–67; asst to supt Newton
Mass. 1967–68; sen lect educ univ of Malawi Limbe
1968–70; supt schools Martha's Vineyard Mass. USA
1970–75; dir grad progr in educ Union Grad s Yellow
Springs Ohio from 1975
m Newton Mass. 29.8.64 Linda C. Lindquist BA(Minn)
d of Charles G. L. Minnesota

DAUN Sheila Mary   MA 1959 Dip Ed 1960
d of James C. D. bus driver and Mary R. Leven; b
Aber 11.6.38
teacher Torry acad Aber 1960–62
m Aber 9.4.62 Dudley J. F. Bowling PhD 1961 qv

DAVEY Brian Gregor   PhD 1957
BSc(agr)(Syd)

DAVIDSON Aileen Elizabeth   MA 1969
d of Thomas B. D. MB ChB 1940 qv; b Aber 12.7.48
teacher: Inchgarth p s Aber 1970–72, Tower coll Rainhill
1972–73
m Aber 8.7.72 Ian R. Gemmell elect. eng BICC s of
Stanley M. G. Aber

DAVIDSON Alan Ingram   MB ChB 1959 ChM 1973
s of Joseph D. shoemaker and Jean Dunbar; b Aber
25.3.35
DObstRCOG 1963 FRCSE 1968
h o ARI 1959–60; m o RAMC Jamaica/Brit Guiana
1960–62; sen h o ARI 1962–63; lect path. Aberd 1963–65;
ARI: regist surg 1965–70, sen 1970–74, consult. surg
from 1974
m Aber 14.10.67 Margaret E. Mackay nurs sister d of
Eric R. M. Inv

DAVIDSON Alexander   *BSc 1956

DAVIDSON Alexander Melvin   *BSc 1964 Dip Ed 1965
s of Alexander D. paperworker and Helen R. Duffus;
b Aber 15.3.42
Dip Stat(Strath) 1970 FRSS
teacher maths Langside coll Glasg 1965–67, lect maths/
statist Paisley tech coll from 1967

DAVIDSON Alicia Rose   MA 1969
d of George I. D. MB ChB 1935 qv; b Aber 9.12.47
teacher: kindergarten Edin acad 1970–74, nursery class
St Margaret's Aber from 1974
m Aber 11.3.78 Richard G. Brown comp dir s of Geoffrey
R. B. Westcott

DAVIDSON Angus William Black   *MA 1966

DAVIDSON Arthur Ian Greenwood   MB ChB 1960
**   *ChM 1965 PhD 1969**
s of Arthur D. civ eng/tea plantation man. and Sarah
F. Greenwood SRN; b Aber 29.1.37

FRCSE 1965
h o ARI 1960–61; lect anat Aberd 1961–62; lect/regist surg Aberd 1962–66; res fell. Western Reserve univ Cleveland USA 1963–64; sen regist surg Aber hosp 1966–71; consult. surg/sen lect surg Dund from 1971
m Montrose 27.4.67 Doreen R. Long SRN theatre sister d of Thomas L. MA(Glas) Ferryden

DAVIDSON Bennett Erskine   MA 1963
s of John B. D. cinema proj, film edit. and Raechel Erskine; b Aber 26.6.42
teacher phys: Aber acad 1964–68, prin phys: Albyn s for girls Aber 1968–73, Hilton acad from 1973
m Aber 26.12.67 Eileen Gordon CA civ serv d of Leslie W. G. Aber

DAVIDSON Brian John   *BSc 1966
MSc(Sheff)

DAVIDSON Catherine Mary   BSc 1962
d of James W. D. BR worker, caretaker Christ's coll Aber and Catherine E. Mutch; b Whitehouse 5.2.40
scient off. Torry res stat Aber 1962–63; teacher sc Forfar acad from 1970
m Aber 17.8.63 John F. Shepherd sales rep s of David S. Brechin

DAVIDSON Donald Allen   *BSc 1967

DAVIDSON Dorothy Hanna   MA 1956
d of Sydney G. D. MA 1920 *qv* and Gertrude C. McDonald MA 1922 *qv*; b Aber 29.10.35
teacher: Victoria Rd p s Aber 1960–62, Fernielea p s Aber 1962–64, part-time Oakfield s Lond 1966–67
m Aber 11.9.65 William P. Gill MA 1953 *qv*

DAVIDSON Elaine   BSc 1966
d of William L. D. g p o tel superv and Mabel Carr shop asst; b Aber 30.8.45
res asst: chem path. med s Aberd 1966–67, G. D. Searle res lab High Wycombe 1967–68
m Aber 23.9.66 James G. Knowles PhD 1967 *qv*

DAVIDSON Eleanor Fraser   MA 1956
b Aber 7.8.35
teacher: Kinneff p s 1957–59, Dumfries 1959–60
m Aber 27.6.59 Thomas G. Milne MA 1956 *qv*

DAVIDSON Elizabeth Joan   MA 1964
m Lingard

DAVIDSON Elizabeth Waiter   BSc 1960
m Hall

DAVIDSON Elsie Patricia Jane   *BSc 1969
d of William M. D. MB ChB 1934 *qv*; b Aber 2.3.45
post-grad stud. bot Aberd 1969–70; teacher biol Edin: Portobello s s 1971–72, Broughton h s 1972–77, prin biol from 1977
m Dirleton 8.7.72 Hugh M. Gordon BSc 1970 *qv*

DAVIDSON Eric George   *BSc(eng) 1966

DAVIDSON Fred Leith   MA 1960
s of Annie B. Davidson; b Oyne 2.8.39
BA(Lond) 1972
teacher: mod lang/Lat Dalbeattie h s 1961–73; Engl Bayonne France 1973–74; mod lang/Lat Dalbeattie from 1974
m Aber 19.8.61 Heather A. Duncan shorthand typist/cler off.

DAVIDSON Ian Alexander   MA 1970

DAVIDSON Ian Douglas   MA 1970

DAVIDSON Ian Gillespie   *MA 1967 *MEd 1969

DAVIDSON Irene Mary   *BSc 1962 MSc 1963
d of Alexander D. salmon fisherman and Eva E. Erskine; b Auchencairn 14.6.40
teacher sc: Nicolson inst Stornoway 1964–65, Bankhead acad Bucksburn 1965–66
m Aber 29.3.65 Alexander Matheson pharm/man. dir s of Alexander M. MB ChB 1931 *qv*

DAVIDSON Irene Urquhart   MA 1958

DAVIDSON James Alexander   BSc(agr) 1970
s of Thomas D. surv chainman and Catherine D. Lobban; b Aber 28.4.29
Fiji: sen agr off. Suva 1970–73, prin agr off. Lavtoka from 1973
m 2.6.56 Margaret H. Ross admin secy d of Douglas R. Lond; wife *d* Athens –.3.76

DAVIDSON James Russell   *BSc 1962

DAVIDSON Janice Mary   *MA 1970 Dip Ed 1971
d of John G. D. arch. and Frances M. Alexander teacher; b Aber 27.6.47
teacher Fr/Ger Mackie acad Stonehaven from 1971

DAVIDSON Jean Cooper   *MA 1968
d of James D. CA and Jean M. Cooper; b Aber 3.9.44
bilingual secy course City of Lond coll 1968; asst edit. dictionaries Collins & Sons publ Glasg 1969–70; teacher part-time coll of comm Aber 1972–73
m Aber 27.6.70 Christopher J. Gossip MA(Edin) univ lect s of Robin A. J. G. MA 1927 *qv*

DAVIDSON Jennifer   MA 1970
d of James H. D. comm cashier and Rosalie Menzies clerkess; b Aber 27.1.49
Dip Ed(Lanc)
teacher mod lang Carlisle from 1971
m Aber 10.8.73 Stewart Hudson plan. eng s of Kenneth H. Jarrow

DAVIDSON John Cunningham   MB ChB 1970
s of George I. D. MB ChB 1935 *qv*; b Aber 15.7.46
h o ARI 1970–71; sen h o, regist anaest Aber hosps 1971–73; g p in father's pract Aber from 1973
m Aber 10.7.73 Lorne M. McRoberts nurs sister d of James M. McR. MA 1962 *qv*

DAVIDSON John Forsyth   MB ChB 1957
s of John F. D. MA 1923 *qv*; b Lumphanan 11.1.34
MRCPE 1965 FRCPE 1974
h o ARI 1957–58; surg lieut RN UK and east of Suez 1958–61; med regist ARI 1961–65; Glasg RI: res regist 1965–66, sen regist haemat 1966–69, consult. haemat from 1969
m Paisley 30.7.59 Laura G. Middleton schoolmistress d of James E. M. Glasg

DAVIDSON John Gordon   *BSc(agr) 1967
s of John G. W. D. CA and Isabella Kemp art teacher; b Aber 17.4.44
agr advis Ayr/Wigtown 1967–72; gen man. farms, heavy plant hire and butchery Stranraer from 1972
m Aber 5.8.67 Margaret H. S. Robertson MA 1967 *qv*

DAVIDSON John Gregory Gordon   MB ChB 1968
s of Sydney G. D. MA 1920 *qv* and Gertrude C. McDonald MA 1922 *qv*; b Aber 21.11.43
h o ARI 1968–69; g p: Willesden 1969–71, Enfield 1972–78 Aber from 1978

DAVIDSON John Grieve   MA 1969
s of Samuel F. D. farm. and Mary Salter; b Torphins 14.3.46
teacher mus Walsingham s Kent 1970–71: actor as David Grieve: Argyle Theatre for youth 1971–72, Adeline Genée theatre E Grinstead 1972, Grand Theatre Swansea 1972–73, *At the End of the Day* Savoy Theatre Lond 1973–74; touring from 1974

DAVIDSON Joseph   BSc 1967
s of Joseph D. soldier and Ellen Harrison; b Birm 14.1.32
teacher: Rosemount s s Aber 1968–70, Kaimhill s s 1970–71, Castle Toward s 1971–73; asst prin maths Summerhill acad Aber from 1973
m Newhills Helen E. Raitt d of Walter R. Bucksburn

DAVIDSON June Rebecca Smith   MA 1969
m Mutch

DAVIDSON Kathleen   MA 1957
m Day

DAVIDSON Margaret Sharp   MA 1966

DAVIDSON Margarita Masson   MA 1962
d of John M. D. master mariner and Margaret E. Hynd MA 1933 *qv*; b Ellon 20.7.41
teacher: mod lang Elgin acad 1964–67, S Queensferry 1967–68, mod lang Morgan acad Dun 1968–69
m Huntly 5.10.68 Alexander G. Cooper comp rep s of Robert C.

DAVIDSON Marischal William   BSc 1963
s of Alexander M. D. civ serv and Jessie Brown civ serv; b Aber 18.9.37
teacher sc Aber from 1964

DAVIDSON Neil   *BSc 1963
s of Charles D. sen scient off. civ serv and Isobel Wood; b Aber 17.9.41
PhD (NY State) 1967
Downstate med center New York: teaching asst dep physiol 1963–64, res foundation fell. State univ NY 1964, asst instr 1966–67; grass foundation fell. marine biol labs Wood Hole Mass USA 1964; lect physiol Aberd from 1967
m NY 1965 Geraldine A. Fisher secy d of William J. F. The Wirral

DAVIDSON Peter Ian   LLB 1968
s of Peter D. C of S min and Elizabeth M. Winder; b Halifax 19.7.46
law app Aber 1968–70; asst solic Aber, Montrose 1970–74; ptnr T. Duncan & Co solic Montrose from 1974
m Kirkhill Invsh 3.11.73 Rosalind E. Munro RGN d of Alexander J. M. Kirkhill

DAVIDSON Rachel Chattan   *BSc 1969
d of William D. MB ChB(Leeds) consult. radiol and Jean M. Kerr; b Bradford 24.5.46
res chem ICI Billingham 1969–72; teacher sc Cleveland educ dept Middlesbrough 1972–76
m Hexham 6.9.69 Stuart L. Smith BSc(eng) 1967 *qv*

DAVIDSON Robert Hugh Clifford   MA 1968
s of Clifford A. D. rubber planter, farm. and Helen M. C. Buchanan nurse; b Malacca Malaya 27.1.47
RAF pilot from 1968
m Aber 24.12.68 Johan G. Whyte MA 1968 *qv*

DAVIDSON Roger George Leith   *MA 1963
s of George Davidson comp man. and Winifred Leith; b Glasg 2.10.41

fin. admin: Shell internat Lond 1963–66, Brunei, Sarawak 1966–68, Thailand, Laos 1968–70, Lond 1971–74, Lagos 1974–76, Lond from 1976
m Aber 27.7.64 Valerie E. Strang teacher d of Gavin S. Dinnet

DAVIDSON Ruth Isobel   BSc 1958 *1959
d of Sydney G. D. MA 1920 *qv* and Gertrude C. McDonald MA 1922 *qv*; b Aber 20.12.37
teacher Alberni Canada 1960–61; lib asst UBC Vancouver 1961–62; blood transfusion serv Edin 1963–64
m Aber 6.3.64 Malcolm Sutherland FSA Scot. merch s of Norman S. MBE Cults

DAVIDSON William   BSc(agr) 1958
s of F. W. D. farm. and Ada I. Norrie farm.; b New Deer 15.2.35
MSc(Durh) 1960
Glasg: lect agr eng 1960–68, sen mech advis from 1968
m Aber 15.12.60 Isobel McLean teacher d of John McL. Dinnet

DAVIDSON-LAMB Richard William   MB ChB 1968
s of William D.-L. MB ChB 1938 *qv*; b Bedford 26.11.42
DObstRCOG 1972 FFARCS 1975
h o Aber 1968–69; lect bact Aberd 1969–70; g p Aber 1970–71; h o obst 1971–72; s h o, regist anaest Aber 1972–75; sen regist anaest Edin RI 1975–78; consult. anaest ARI from 1978
m Aber 19.8.69 Nanette J. Flockhart MB ChB 1968

DAVIE Ann Margaret   MA 1967
d of James C. D. master mariner and Ellen M. E. Smith; b Montrose 22.4.44
Dip Sec St(Strath) 1968 ACII 1972
dealing with leg. documents Life assur co. Edin from 1968; later in Aust

DAVIE Anne   *MA 1968
m Paterson

DAVIE Fredric   *BSc 1967 PhD 1971
s of Percy D. asst pharm and Margaret S. Muir; b Aber 26.1.45
ICI: res chem Welwyn Garden City 1970–71, market dev off. 1971–76, proj man. 1976–79, gen man. RN plastics Leeds from 1979
m Aber 1.7.67 Carol C. Murray BA(Strath) teacher d of William M. Aber

DAVIE Isobel Marlene   MA 1964
d of George H. D. farm. and Christian Buchan; b Mufulira Zambia 27.8.42
teacher Engl/Lat: Inverurie acad 1965–66, Boroughmuir h s Edin 1966–68, Liberton h s Edin 1968–72
m Aber 26.7.69 Ian S. Mackay s of Donald M.

DAVIE Kathleen Fiona   *MA 1961
d of John W. D. barkeeper/chief steward Brit Leg. club and Bessie Donald; b Aber 1.7.37
Norway; part time teacher Fr/Ger Sandnessjøen 1966–71, teacher: Geir Borresen comp s Drammen 1971–72, Fr g s Sandnessjøen from 1973; also teacher Fr Norwegian corresp s (Engl dept) from 1972
m Münster Westfalen Germany 18.12.58 Tore Walen MB ChB (Münster) consult. surg s of Sigmund W. LLB(Oslo) Tromsø Norway

DAVIE Margaret Helen   BSc 1960
d of James D. ironmonger and Jeannie Morrison; b Nairn 10.11.38
teacher maths: Peterhead, Forres 1960–61, Chatham 1961–63; tech lib Camberley 1963–64; cardiol tech

Montreal 1965–67; ch welfare teacher Carshalton 1973–76; med rep from 1976
m Forres 28.12.61 Richard N. F. Dunbar BSc 1961 *qv*

DAVIE Marguereta Mary Ferguson   MA 1966
m Allison

DAVIE Ramsay Anderson Gove   BSc 1960

DAVIE Victoria Frances   BSc 1956 Dip Ed 1957
d of Alexander F. D. schoolmaster and Victoria E. Laing teacher dom sc; b Dun 27.5.35
teacher: sc Blairgowrie 1957–60, sc/maths Methven 1960–61, sc/maths Tain r h s 1961–62
m Perth 1960 Francis Young BSc 1956 *qv*

DAVIES Andrew Neil Brett   BSc(for) 1959

DAVIES Bronwen Veronica   MA 1969 Dip Ed 1970
d of George L. D. civ serv MoD and Irene M. Macie; b Wyke Regis 3.2.48
civ serv Inl Rev Manc 1970–71; teacher mod lang Perth from 1972

DAVIES Christopher John   BSc(eng) 1968
s of John A. D. civ serv and Phyllis Wiltshire secy; b Exeter 19.1.46
MICE 1973
Taylor Woodrow: site eng 1967–71, des eng (sect. leader) Southall 1971–73; des eng with consult. Sale from 1973
m(2) Lond 7.7.73 Susan H. Burt MA 1967 *qv*

DAVIES David Lewis   *BSc 1970

DAVIES Dorothy Valerie Ann   BSc 1969
d of Frank E. D. toolmaker and Doris A. Vickers; b Wolverhampton 16.9.47
teacher: Birm 1969–70, Wolverhampton 1970–71, head maths dept Bradford 1972–73, temp Fleet from 1973
m 26.12.71 Martin C. P. Burke BSc(Aston) phys, prod. man. s of Michael B. Birm

DAVIES Eileen Joan Alfreda   MA 1959
m Flavill

DAVIES Elisabeth Shona   MA 1969
m Raitt

DAVIES Ian Munro   *MA 1967
s of Joseph G. D. factory man. and Betty Munro; b Elgin 26.7.44
buyer Rootes Motors Coventry 1967–70; teacher Cheshire c c: Hyde 1970–72, 5th year tut. Bredbury 1972–77; dep head Macclesfield from 1977
m Hyde 8.5.71 Anne Shepley teacher/artist d of Peter K. S. Charlesworth

DAVIES James Andrew   MB ChB 1966

DAVIES Janet Elizabeth   BSc 1965
d of John H. D. BA(Sheff) area prin f e and Annetta Hough secy; b Stockton Brook 8.1.43
Cert Envir Sc(S'ton) 1974
teacher biol: Victoria Vancouver Is 1966–67, Poole 1967–68, Southampton from 1968

DAVIES Joan Margaret   MA 1968
m Macleod

DAVIES John Norman   MA 1966

DAVIES June Amelia   PhD 1967
d of John G. D. trans man. and Ethel A. Hutchings;

b Cardiff 26.5.43
BSc(Wales) 1964
lect univ coll S Wales 1967–70; edit. CEGB Leatherhead 1970–71
m Cardiff 25.7.69 David Byrom BSc (Cardiff) res Beechams res labs, ICI Teesside s of Tom B. Manc

DAVIES Lesley Ceridwen   MA 1970
m Golbourn

DAVIES Patrick Protheroe   LLB 1965
s of Kenneth D. D. MB ChB(Brist) med pract and Ethel G. Protheroe; b Cheltenham 5.10.44
Aber: law app 1965–67, solic, leg. asst 1967–70, solic, ptnr Milne & Mackinnon advoc from 1970
m Aber 19.9.80 Caroline Jane Gray LLB 1973 d of J. Hector Gray MA 1932 *qv*

DAVIS Betsy Maud Annies Ada   MB ChB 1959
d of Samuel D. teacher and Amy K. Speid teacher; b Priestman's River Jamaica 30.8.33
univ of Milan: Med Chir 1966 Dip Dent. 1969
h o Warrington 1959–60, Liv 1960–61, Kingston Jamaica 1961–70; g p Monza Italy from 1970
m Aber 1.10.58 Marcello Cavallo Med Chir(Milan) cardiol s of Alfredo C. Milan

DAVIS Elizabeth Ann   MA 1969
d of George W. E. D. tel sales rep and Isabella Beaton clerkess; b Aber 10.10.47
computer progr Manc reg hosp board 1969–70; computer progr (analyst) NW elect. board 1970–73
m Aber 26.12.69 Russell Milne MA 1970 *qv*

DAVIS Godfrey Peter   *MA 1969
s of Eustace B. D. BA(Brist) clerk in holy orders and Eva Henshall; b Liv 21.6.45
ARCO ARCM LRAM ATCL 1974
head mus St Andrew's s and organist/choirmaster Christchurch cath Nassau Bahamas 1970–73; stud. royal s of ch mus Croydon 1973–74; dir mus St George's s Clarens Montreux Switzerland 1974–76; dir mus Adams' g s Newport Salop from 1976 and organist/choirmaster collegiate ch of St Mary Stafford from 1977
m Aber 4.7.70 Stella R. Smith MA 1968 *qv*

DAVIS Lionel John   *MA 1966 Dip Ed 1967
s of Eustace B. D. BA(Brist) clerk in holy orders and Eva Henshall missionary in China; b Tachu Szechwan China 9.6.42
teacher: mod lang AGS 1967–70, prin mod lang Banchory from 1970
m Aber 14.7.67 Ingeborg I. Konig MA 1966 *qv*

DAVISON Elizabeth Armstrong   *BSc 1967 MSc 1970
d of Meredith H. A. D. MD(N'cle) consult. anaest and Ida F. Evans nurse; b Bicester 5.3.44
lect tech coll Aber 1970–72
m Chillingham 5.4.69 John P. Blakeman BSc(Wales) univ lect s of John C. B. Cranleigh
d N'cle 28.11.73

DAW Michael Richard   *BSc(for) 1962
s of William R. D. mental welfare off. and Florence L. C. Sampson; b Bath 23.5.40
for. man. Messrs. Clutton chartered surv Wells from 1963
m Inv 15.9.61 Anne P. L. Richards secy d of Robert L. R. MB ChB 1932 *qv*

DAWE Michael Charles Stewart   BSc(agr) 1965
s of Eric C. S. D. MRCVS(Edin) vet surg and Kathleen Barr hosp matron; b Johannesburg 9.11.40

Ukiriguru, Mwanza, Tanzania: pasture res ott. 1966–73; also acting sen res off. Western res centre 1971–73; agronomist lower Shire valley proj Ngabu Malawi from 1974
m Mwanza 8.7.66 Jennifer A. Beveridge d of Andrew W. B. Edin

DAWSON Alexander Richard   LLB 1968
s of Alexander D. comp chmn and Elisabeth G. W. Lakin MA(Glas) teacher; b Milngavie 23.1.47
law app Glasg 1968–70; solic, leg. asst Aber 1970–73; solic loc govt Aber from 1974
m Aber 7.9.70 Jennifer M. Maclean MA 1968 *qv*

DAWSON Audrey Anne   *MB ChB 1956 *MD 1966
d of Henry J. D. MA 1916 *qv*; b Aber 27.1.33
MRCPE 1959 FRCPE 1970 MRCPath 1971
h o: ARI 1956–57, Hammersmith hosp Lond 1957–58; Aberd: lect med 1958–67, sen lect haemat from 1967

DAWSON David George   *BSc 1963 PhD 1966
s of Robert G. D. BSc 1929 *qv* and Annie E. Adams MA 1928 *qv*; b Aber 28.7.41
res fell. chem: univ of W Ontario 1966–68, Aberd 1968–69; scient res dept ICI (paints div) Slough from 1969
m Aber 17.7.65 Caroline H. Munro MA 1963 *qv*

DAWSON Donald George   MB ChB 1959

DAWSON Elizabeth Helen   MA 1965
d of Robert G. D. BSc(eng) 1929 *qv* and Anne E. Adams MA 1928 *qv*; b Aber 31.7.44
Cert Sec Sc(Strath) 1966
asst lib inst chartered acct of Scot. Edin 1966–67; secy to advt man. Henry Birks & Sons, Montreal 1967–69; asst advt man. inst chartered acct of Scot. Edin 1969–70; secy Galashiels: to Bernat Klein des consult. 1970–72, J. & J. Hall & Co arch. 1972–73
m Aber 16.9.70 William T. M. Cleghorn CA s of William T. C. Galashiels

DAWSON Gavin Robert   MB ChB 1958

DAWSON Gordon Shepherd   *BSc 1963

DAWSON Margaret Caroline   MA 1956

DAWSON Margaret Jane   *MA 1961
d of Robert G. D. BSc(eng) 1929 *qv* and Anne E. Adams MA 1928 *qv*; b Berkhampstead 15.4.39
teacher Engl: Brechin acad 1962–67, Peterhead acad 1967–68
m Aber 5.4.66 Norman G. F. Russell MA(Edin) teacher s of George Y. R. Leven

DAWSON Moira   LLB 1965

DAWSON Robert Leslie   *MA 1958

DAWSON Ronald Peter Bond   *BSc(eng) 1970
s of Thomas F. D. lect tech coll and Elizabeth L. M. Brodie; b Aber 21.3.48
grad trainee tech eng Elgin 1970–72; Aber: gen eng NSHEB 1972–73, 4th eng 1973–74, 3rd eng 1974–76, 2nd eng from 1976

DAWSON William James   MA 1959

DAY Michael James John   *MA 1966
s of Hector J. D. wall and floor tiler and Winifred Myatt pottery decorator/clerk; b Manc 27.3.43
teacher Engl: Stamsund Lofoten Norway 1967–68, Peebles 1968–70; prin Engl Slidre Norway from 1970

DAY Nicholas Edward   PhD 1967
BA(Oxon)

DAYAL Radha Raman   PhD 1965
s of Amar S. Mathur lawyer and Jag R. Mathur; b Agra India 19.1.41
BSc(Agra) 1957 MSc(Agra) 1959
res assoc Penn state univ USA 1965–66; defence sc lab Delhi: pool off. 1966–69, sen scient off. 1969; NRC (Canada) fell. energy mines and resources Ottawa 1969–71; sen scient off. defence sc lab Delhi from 1972
m New Delhi 12.12.68 Rama Mathur MA(Luck) d of Govind N. M. Lucknow

DE JONCKHEERE Cyril Gustave   *BSc 1965
s of Cyril J. De J. civ serv/clerk of works and Mary B. Bremner; b Wick 20.11.41
FRMetS
scient off., sen scient met. off. Bracknell from 1968

DE SILVA Angela Rosemary   MA 1961
d of William de S. CA and Rhéa Parcon teacher; b Seychelles 17.2.38
MSc(Makerere) 1972
sen tut. zoology/bot univ of Makerere 1967–72; W Aust inst of tech dept of med tech Perth WA: lect: Engl/anat 1973–74, anat/physiol from 1974
m Aber 11.4.58 Gordon A. German MB ChB 1958 *qv*

DE SILVA Nihal Nemichandra   PhD 1960
BSc(Ceylon)

De SILVA William Raymond   *BSc(eng) 1968

DEADMAN Andrew James   MSc 1969 PhD 1973
BSc(Lond)

DEAN Alexander William   *MA 1968

DEAN Helen Millicent   MB ChB 1957
d of Charles A. Dean MB ChB 1925 *qv*; b Hull 13.7.32
DCH(Glas) 1960
h o St Luke's hosp Bradford 1957–58; Glasg: resid m o paediat royal mat. hosp 1958–59, royal hosp for sick ch 1959, jun h m o paediat Southern gen hosp 1959–62; school m o 1963–68; W Aust: m o intell handic serv Perth 1968–70 and from 1972; g p Kondinin 1970–72
m Renfrew 25.7.61 Henry Thornton Scott-Pillow s of Edward E. S-P; marr diss 1974

DEAN Peter Alexander   MA 1963 LLB 1966

DEANS Andrew   MA 1963
s of Andrew D. hotel prop. and Margaret R. Crozier; b Galashiels 3.5.40
superv with brewery 1963–67; teacher Galashiels acad from 1968
m Hawick 10.8.65 Evelyn Farish fashion des d of George F.

DEANS Isabella McDonell   MA 1962
m Pennington

DEANS Norman Dickson   *BSc(eng) 1966
m Rosaleen A. Bruce BSc 1966 *qv*

DEANS Thomas   MA 1962
s of Alexander S. C. D. head beekeeping dept NOSCA and Mary Young; b Edin 24.8.38
instr RA Nuneaton 1963–65; OCS S Arabian army Aden; instr Highland Bde depot Aber 1967–70; staff off. HQ 4 div Herford W Ger 1970–73; o c Sandhurst wing

Beaconsfield 1973–76; group educ off. Oxon Bucks & Berks Bicester 1976–79; staff off. SW dist Bulford from 1979, major RAEC
m Salisbury 23.5.79 Sybil M. Bromham d of Henry B. Acton

DEAR Alasdair George Wilbert   MA 1956 LLB 1959
s of Sidney W. D. BSc(St And) headmaster and Margaret E. Matheson teacher; b Crathie 14.9.35
Diplôme de Droites Comparées (univ of Luxembourg) 1959 WS 1972 TD 1976
parachute regt M East 1959–62; Edin: private leg. pract 1962–72, on own account from 1972
m Cockpen 30.7.67 Lesley A. Robertson d of Donald R. Edin

DEAR Elizabeth Margaret Anne   BSc 1962
d of Sydney W. D. BSc(St And) headmaster and Margaret E. Matheson teacher; b Crathie 15.1.42
res asst physiol Aberd 1962–66, sen tech physiol univ of Tor. Canada 1967–69
m Aber 23.12.64 Ian S. Hay MA 1963 qv

DEAS-DAWLISH Christopher Malcolm Keith
MA 1966

DEATON Mairi Rose   MA 1970
d of Leslie H. D. civ eng and Janet Wood; b Edin 11.6.49
teacher: Hawick 1971–76, Derby middle s Osnabruck W Ger from 1976

DEHDASHTY Akbar   BSc(agr) 1963

DELANEY Thomas   MA 1957

DEMIRALAY Ibrahim   PhD 1970
BSc(Ankara)

DEMPSEY Mary Henderson   MA 1959
m MacCallum

DEMPSTER Albert George   MA 1966

DEMPSTER Elaine Alexandria   MA 1970
d of Alexander J. D. bldg estimator/valuer and Irene C. Summers; b Caversham 20.10.48
visiting exec off. DHSS Manc 1970–72
m Huntly 1.8.70 Philip J. Coombes sheet metal worker/welder s of William C. Chester

DEMPSTER Walter   MA 1958
s of Walter D. acct Royal Bank of Scotland and Catherine Robertson clerkess; b Aviemore 4.3.37
teacher: Echt s 1959–69, head Arnage s from 1969
m Banchory 18.4.64 Annie Duncan nurse d of John D. Cullerlie

DENHAM Neil Leicester   MB ChB 1956

DENHOLM Alexander Carle   MB ChB 1957
s of Robert D. Scot. epis clergyman and Doris E. Dixon teacher dom sc; b Fraserburgh 23.3.31
h o Edin RI 1958–59; Royal Aust Air Force 1959–63; g p Perth W Aust from 1964 and clin tut. g p W Aust univ from 1976
m Edin 23.8.58 Myfanwy G. Owen occup therap d of John L. O. MB ChB(Edin)

DENNISTON Alexander Hastie   *MA 1966

DENOON Brian Donald James   MA 1959
s of Robert A. D. MA(Edin) teacher and Robina M.

MacPhee MA(Edin) teacher; b Inv 23.1.37
teacher Inv h s from 1960, asst prin from 1973
m Inverbervie 27.12.61 Sheila M. Campbell MA 1959 qv

DENOON Charles Alexander Royston   MA 1962

DENOON Deirdre Margaret Ann   MA 1962

DENT John Barry   PhD 1964
s of Cyril D. eng and Barbara R. Jackson; b Barrow-in-Furness 11.10.37
BSc(R'dg) 1960 MAgricSc(R'dg) 1962
lect R'dg 1964–70; reader Nott 1971–74; prof univ Canterbury NZ from 1974
m Sutton 1965 Sandra C. Webb BA(R'dg) teacher d of Edward W. W. Sutton

DENT Lesley Scott   PhD 1957   DSc 1972
d of Hugh A. D. civ serv and Marjorie Lord; b Grimsby 19.5.32
BA(Cantab) FInstP 1974
res fell.: Penn state univ USA 1957–59, Aberd 1959–66; Aberd: lect 1966–74, sen lect 1974–80, reader from 1980
m Pa USA 17.5.58 Fredrick P. Glasser DSc 1968 qv

DENTON Nigel George Martin   *MA 1966

DERIA Abdillahi   MB ChB 1966

DESOUGI Mohamed Abdo   BSc(for) 1970
BSc(Khart)

DEWAR Anne Armstrong   BSc 1970
d of Christopher A. D. dairyman and Elizabeth B. Wilson caterer; b St Andrews 24.3.50
teacher biol: Kirkland h s Methil 1971–73, Maltby g s Yorks 1973–74; analyst progr Sheff from 1974
m Denbeath 31.7.73 Andrew N. Brown BSc(St And) oper res scient s of George B. N. B. Methil

DEWAR Brenda Louise   *LLB 1969
d of Peter F. D. proof reader and Emily P. Dorian MA 1936 qv; b Aber 21.12.47
NP 1972
Edin: law app 1969–71, leg. asst Balfour & Manson 1971–76, ptnr from 1976
m Glasg 10.9.71 Donald G. Rennie MA 1968 qv

DEWAR David   BSc(eng) 1957

DEWAR Ian Alexander   *MA 1963
s of James A. D. civ serv and Mary Jessiman; b York 14.4.40
Ottawa: pers off. Canadian broadcasting corp 1964–66; pers off. dept fin. 1966–68; dept nat defence: dir labour relations 1968–70, dir biling programs 1970–72; dir biling programs Treasury 1972–74; dir exec staffing civ serv comm 1974–76; asst secy to Cabinet (pers) from 1976
m Aber 17.8.63 Julie Pack MA 1961 qv

DEWAR James Graham   BEd 1970
s of George D. butcher and Annie Graham; b Alloa 3.4.39
teacher geog RGC Aber from 1970

DEWAR James Wilson   *BSc 1956
s of John D. eng and Margaret H. Wilson teacher; b Maud 9.8.34
teacher geog: Montrose acad 1957–58, Forfar acad 1958–59, prin geog Kirkwall g s from 1959
m Kirkwall 15.7.66 Mary M. Hercus teacher of mus d of George H. Kirkwall

DEWAR John Willocks   MB ChB 1969
s of John M. D. insur ag and Mary F. Willocks; b Dun 31.1.39
BSc(St And) 1964 DA(Dub) 1975 FFARCSI 1977
resid m o: geriat Dun 1969–70, paediat Aber 1970–71, Burnie Tasmania 1971–72; g p locums NSW Aust 1972–73; regist anaest Perth, Ninewells hosp Dun from 1973
m Dun 1966 Alison J. R. Duncan lab asst d of Peter J. D. Dun

DEWAR Peter Saunders   *BSc 1968 PhD 1972
s of William D. poultry farm./market gardener/ museum attendant and Doris C. Stevenson milk off., lab steward; b Perth 15.12.45
FCS 1970
res fell. org chem S'ton 1971–73; org chem in chem process dev The Boots Co Nott 1973–75; chief chem Broomchemie: Almelo Neths 1975–77, Terneuzen Neths from 1977
m Aber 15.4.70 Anne H. Bowman insur clerkess, lib asst d of Albert H. B. Aber

DEWAR Robert   BSc(eng) 1959

DEY Elizabeth Milne   *MA 1967 Dip Ed 1968
m Moir

DEY Elizabeth Wilson   MA 1967
m Trevena

DEY Neil Alexander   *MA 1969

DHALL Dharan Pal   PhD 1968 cMD 1970
MB(Manc) FRCSE

DIACK Alistair Angus   BSc 1959

DIACK William George Hendry   MB ChB 1963
s of William D. MA 1930 qv(III); b Dunfermline 3.7.39
h o: City hosp Aber, ARI 1963–64; g p: Insch 1964–65, Inverbervie from 1965
m Aber 26.10.63 Patricia A. Bain lab tech d of William B. Aber

DIAMENT Morton Leonard   *MB ChB 1964 MD 1967
s of Robert D. bus. man. and Betty Gang; b New York 13.7.29
BA(Col) 1951
h o ARI 1964–65; Aberd: Garden res fell. med 1965–66, lect physiol 1966–69, h o obst, anaest 1969–70; g p: Stromness 1970–76, Dounby from 1976
m Edin 11.12.54 DeLille M. M. Porter MA(Edin) teacher d of James G. P. Aber

DIAMOND Anthony William   MSc 1968 PhD 1971
s of William H. D. BA(Cantab) civ eng and Dorothy G. Powell; b Calcutta 5.9.44
BA(Cantab) 1966
grad res asst to Dr Black FRS Oxford 1970–72; scient admin Cousin Is nature reserve Seychelles from 1973
m Canada 27.9.69 Elizabeth P. McIntyre MLitt 1968 qv

DIAZ Elgin   *MA 1969
s of Loyola E. D. teacher and Mavis Schumacher teacher, dressmaker; b Colombo 15.9.45
res assoc Leic 1969–73; stud. Derby coll of art 1973; potter Nott from 1973
m Leic 1971 Christina J. Schule BA(Leic) d of Freidrich S. Teneriffe and Hamburg

DICK Andrew Duthie   BSc 1959
s of Henry D. fishcurer and Elspeth Duthie; b Peterhead 27.9.36

teacher sc Peterhead acad 1960–68; head St Andrew's s Inverurie; advis prim educ Aber c c 1971–75; div educ off. Gordon div Grampian reg c from 1975
m Peterhead 1959 Olive McConachie d of Andrew McC. Peterhead

DICK Douglas McDonald   *BSc 1956 PhD 1959
s of Walter R. D. secy board of man. Moray hosps and Grace McDonald secy; b Elgin 22.1.35
chief analyst ICI Slough from 1959
m Aber 27.7.60 Irene E. Davidson secy d of Arthur G. D. Aber

DICK Eleanore St. Vernal   *MA 1970 Dip Ed 1971
d of William D. BSc(Glas) civ eng and Maisie M. Brown nurse; b Glasg 6.5.48
asst educ psych Angus c c 1971–74
m Edin 20.7.73 David J. B. Anderson MA 1970 qv

DICK Elizabeth Marjory   MA 1967
d of Thomas M. D. MA(Glas) headmaster and Petronella J. M. Roojackers; b Bellshill 8.3.47
teacher: Engl Eshwege Germany 1968, Ger/Fr asst Kaimhill s s Aber 1969–70, asst prin mod lang Holyrood s s Edin/oral examiner Ger for SED 1970–74; teacher Ger Melbourne from 1975
m Aber –.6.70 Robert Stevenson BSc(eng)(H-W) elect. s of Alfred S. Aber

DICK William Alexander   *MA 1958
s of James D. quarry worker and Isabella M. Barclay; b Elgin 11.3.35
man. trainee T. Wall & Sons Edin 1959–60; man. Simplicity Patterns Blantyre 1960–62; man. consult. F. B. Trethewey & Ptnrs Manc 1962–64; lect Strath from 1964
m Dun 3.4.65 Ruth Knight lect d of William L. K. Dun

DICK William Graham   *MA 1970

DICKIE Agnes   MA 1957   LLB 1959

DICKIE Arthur Coull   *BSc 1962 PhD 1965
s of Arthur J. D. marine eng and Elizabeth Coull; b Aber 2.2.40
res fell. St And 1965–67; sen biochem Aberd from 1967
m Aber 24.8.66 Barbara J. Thain tv prod. asst d of John T. Aber

DICKIE David Murray   *BSc 1968 Dip Ed 1969

DICKIE Douglas Sutherland   *BSc 1968
s of Douglas D. pharm and Sheila M. Wood; b Aber 6.1.47
BSc(City univ Lond) 1972
ophth optician Aber from 1973

DICKIE Gordon Lindsay   MB ChB 1968
s of James L. T. D. MB ChB 1942 qv and Alma C. Ritchie MB ChB 1942 qv; b Aber 25.2.45
DObstRCOG 1970 CCFP 1973
post grad g p training 1968–71; geog lect dept fam med univ of W Ontario Lond Ontario 1971–73, asst prof from 1973
m Aber 21.7.69 Margaret C. Leiper MA 1969 qv

DICKIE John Keay   *MA 1957
s of Alexander J. D. agr eng and Margaret I. Keay teacher; b Bankhead 17.5.35
nat serv RAF 1957–59; trainee acct man. chartered bank Lond 1959–60; teacher Renfrewsh 1961–64; prin teacher Turriff 1964–66; lect coll of educ Aber from 1966
m Aber 15.8.61 Anne H. W. Foley lib d of Augustine F. Dunfermline

DICKIE William Wood   *MA 1968
s of Douglas D. pharm and Sheila M. Wood; b Aber 12.5.41
Dip Ed(Edin) 1969
teacher hist St Mirins acad Paisley 1969–71; stud. phil pontifical Greg Rome 1972; lect lib stud. Peterborough 1973–75; head sixth form St Benedict's s Bury St Edmunds from 1975

DICKSON Alexander   MB ChB 1969
s of Alexander D. master tailor and Mary A. Thom tailoress; b Girvan 30.3.45
DObstRCOG 1971
h o Scot. and Eng 1969–73; g p New Cumnock from 1973
m Aber 30.4.71 Murdina V. MacInnes nurse d of Murdoch MacI. Gourock

DICKSON David Alexander   *BSc(for) 1958

DICKSON Fiona Jane   *BSc 1960
m Mellanby

DICKSON James Grant   MA 1959 LLB 1962
s of Lewis G. D. banker and Eleanor Ellis MA 1929 qv; b Glasg 17.6.38
leg. asst: Oban 1962–63, Edin 1963–66, Edin corp 1966–75; prin solic Lothian reg c from 1975
m Edin 14.10.66 Shirley Gray secy

DICKSON James Henderson   BSc 1964

DICKSON John   MA 1970

DICKSON Thomas   *BSc(eng) 1967

DICKSON William John   *MA 1968
s of George D. fruit merch and Magdalene Black; b Edin 5.6.45
res Paris 1968–70; lect Fr Glas from 1970
m Glasg 3.10.70 Michèle Bassi LèsL (Paris) teacher

DILLON Geoffrey   MB ChB 1958
s of John T. D. pers off. and Beatrice M. Smith; b York 17.9.28
MRCGP 1968
h o gen hosps Aber 1958–59; g p Cockermouth 1959–61; s h o gen hosps Aber 1961–63; g p Spalding from 1963
m 10.7.58 Helen F. B. Grieve MB ChB 1956 qv

DINNES James Annand   *MA 1956
s of Robert D. master butcher and Jane A. Keith; b Peterhead 25.8.27
FSAScot 1963 Dip TCP(H-W) 1964 Assoc M Royal Town Planning Inst 1965; Assoc M BIM 1975
farm man. spec Victoria BC 1957–59; plan. res off. Cupar 1960–64, county dev off. Buckie 1964–70; dep dev off. NESDA Aber from 1970
m Aber 22.9.52 Nancy R. C. Davidson MA 1949 qv

DINDA Paritosh Kumar   PhD 1960
BSc(agr)(Calc)

DINWIDDIE Robert   MB ChB 1969
s of Noel A. W. D. MA(Edin) master printer and May Kennedy MA(Edin); b Dumfries 23.2.45
DCH(Lond) 1971 MRCP(UK) 1974
h o Dumfries and Galloway RI 1969–70; paediat h p RACH 1970–71; res fell. ch health Aberd 1971–73; paediat regist RACH 1973–74; asst chief res phys ch hosp Philadelphia 1975–76; regist, sen regist hosp for sick ch Gr Ormond St Lond 1975–77; consult. paediat

Gr Ormond St, Queen Charlotte's hosp from 1977; hon sen lect inst of ch health, inst of obst/gyn univ of London from 1977
m Dumfries 23.10.71 Mary M. Saunderson RGN d of James S. Dumfries

DINWOODIE John Macmillan Walter   *BSc(for) 1957 PhD 1960
b Ayr 29.3.35
MTech(Brunel) 1976
Princes Risborough lab BRE: jun res fell. scient civ serv 1960–62, sen scient off. 1963–70, prin scient off. from 1970
m Aber 15.7.58 Margaret Johnson BSc 1957 qv

DIOMI Pierre   PhD 1969
MD(Paris)

DISBURY William Harold   BSc 1970
s of H. C. J. D. civ serv and Winifred E. Ryder; b Bootle 2.1.48
Thurso: barman 1970–71, UKAEA (SO) from 1971
m Thurso 4.2.71 Emily A. Barrons

DIX, Helen Main   BSc 1960
d of Harry W. D. civ serv and Nellie Lees civ serv; b Aber 5.2.39
teacher maths: Berwicksh h s 1961–64, Aber h s for girls 1964–65, Grove acad Dun 1965–66, Aber acad 1968–74
m Aber 2.10.65 Archibald B. Allan Anglican clergyman s of Archibald W. G. A. Glasg

DIXON Geoffrey Arthur   MB ChB 1965 Dip Psychother 1970
DPM(Scot. Conj)

DIXON George Andrew   *MA 1957
s of James W. D. and Beatrice R. Reid MA 1925 qv; b Grantown-on-Spey 12.5.36
BSc(Edin) 1967

DIXON John Michael Martin   *MA 1969
s of John M. D. journalist (killed on active service 1941) and Ena J. Harland; b Lossiemouth 25.3.42
Lond: O & M off. 1969–70; pers work from 1970
m Aber 30.1.71 Anne S. Murray MA 1968 qv

DIXON Margaret Doreen   *MA 1968

DIXON Roy George Ogilvie   *MA 1968

DOAK Noreen Mary Henderson   MA 1970
d of Matthew M. D. master butcher and Mary T. Sommerville; b Bellshill 3.8.49
RGN 1972 SCM 1975
staff nurse Aber and Edin 1973–74; stud. midwife Bellshill 1974–75
m Aber 14.6.75 John A. Young MB ChB 1973 s of Archibald G. Y. Longniddry

DOBSON Alan   PhD 1956
s of Albert P. D. clerk and Dorothy B. Hougham nurse; b Bethnal Green 20.12.28
BA(Cantab) 1952 MA 1970
Rowett inst Aber: scient off., sen scient off. 1952–61; sen scient off., prin scient off. 1962–64; Cornell univ Ithaca USA: visiting prof NYS coll vet med 1961–62, assoc prof 1964–71, prof vet physiol from 1971; Wellcome fell. Cantab 1971–72
m Aber 29.3.54 Marjorie J. Masson BSc 1948 qv

DOCHERTY Alistair George   *LLB 1969
s of James S. D. cashier and Jessie Burnett; b Dun

13.4.47
ACA 1974
Leeds: cashier/securities clerk Barclays Bank 1969–71, CA Guiseley from 1975
m Bradford 21.3.70 Wendy Howard secy d of Joseph E. H. Bradford

DOCHERTY Margaret Isabella   MA 1968
d of Robert H. D. head postmaster and Alexia M. Niven cler off.; b St And 9.5.47
teacher Banff acad 1969–71
m Banff 5.4.69 William R. McRobert insur insp s of Grant McR. Stonehaven

DODD Bernard Thomas   *MA 1962
s of Sydney T. D. caterer and Frances V. Stewart; b Lond 11.4.34
res DSIR, SSRC, Min of Lab Sheff univ 1962–71; Learning Syst (training des consult.) Richmond 1971–73; prin psych Admiralty res lab 1973–76; sen psych (Navy) div from 1976
m Lond 16.8.58 Hazel A. Moore bank clerk d of Edwin L. M. Lond

DODD Ingrid Helena   MA 1967
d of John A. A. D. comp dir/eng and Brenda C. Vale MB ChB(Edin) phys; b Kingsdown 25.6.47
MBBS(Lond) 1975 MRCS LRCP 1975
interpreter/teacher Rome 1967–68; med stud. Guy's hosp Lond 1968–75

DODD Sarah Margaret   *MA 1968
m Dukes

DODDS John James Anderson   *BSc 1965 PhD 1968
s of John Dodds coal miner and Lena Anderson; b N'cle-u-Tyne 9.6.41
teacher biol Dingwall acad 1968–73; prin biol Lochaber h s Fort William from 1973
m Aber 29.8.66 Anne Sinclair MA 1966 qv

DODDS John Keith Mathieson   BSc(eng) 1967
s of John M. D. MA 1928 qv and Anna L. McDonald MA 1934 qv; b Timperley 12.6.44
DMS (RGIT Aber) 1968 ACMA 1972
grad app Girling Cwmbran Wales 1968–70; trainee Connal & Co Glasg 1970–72; Lond: dir Imperial Cold Stores 1972–73, man. dir Bermondsey Cold Stores 1973–75; dir Charles Alexander & Ptnr (Transport) 1975–76; prop. Netherley bus. serv from 1977
m Aber 2.12.77 Ingrid A. J. Cormack MA 1964 qv

DOHERTY James   *MA 1962 *MEd 1965

DOHERTY Mary Margaret   MA 1967
m Murray

DOIG Dorothy Margaret   MA 1967

DOIG Jonathan David   *MA 1969
s of David T. D. journalist and Katherine W. Watters; b Dun 12.6.47
teacher Kirkintilloch from 1974
m Ullapool 9.4.74 Helen M. Hennessy BSc 1971 nurse d of Jeremiah D. H. MB ChB(Cork) Sweetly

DOIG Robert Jules   MB ChB 1956 MD 1973
s of Robert S. D. MB ChB(Glas) m o h Isle of Lewis and Lucienne Nizart teacher; b Lennoxtown 12.5.30
MRCPsych 1973
h o Aber 1956–57; resid phys Paris 1963–66; Lond: regist 1966–71, sen regist 1971–73, consult. psychiat from 1973

m Lond 9.8.73 Ruth Watson BSc(Lond) soc worker d of Robert W.

DONAGHEY Sean Francis O'Brien   *BSc 1969
s of Cyril F. O'B. D. BSc(eng)(Lond) eng, soc worker and Lois A. M. Daniels drama organis; b Sunderland 25.2.44
res stud. applied biol Cantab 1969–72; lect chem/biol Newark tech coll from 1972
m Nott 6.12.69 Margaret J. Ingram BSc 1969 qv

DONALD Alice Margaret   *MA 1958
d of David D. MA 1927 qv and Alice B. Morrison MA 1927 qv; b Aber 20.7.36
teacher maths: Bell-Baxter h s 1959–62; Edin: spec asst Trinity acad 1962–70, Ainslie Park s s 1970, spec asst Craigmount c s 1970–71
m Aber 30.7.70 Thomas B. S. Campbell MA(Edin) teacher s of William C. MA(Glas) Edin

DONALD Anne Fiona   LLB 1969
d of Douglas A. D. BA(Oxon) sheriff and Flora M. Macdonald; b Glasg 24.3.49
Edin: law app 1969–71, leg. asst from 1971

DONALD David   MB ChB 1965 PhD 1973
s of Maxwell A. W. D. garage prop. and Barbara A. Mearns; b Huntly 28.4.41
MRCPath
h o ARI 1965–66; lect path. Aberd 1966 and 1974–77; MRC travelling fell. res in USA and visiting asst prof path. Boston univ 1973–74; sen lect path. Aberd from 1977

DONALD David Alexander   BSc(agr) 1967
s of David A. D. MA(Cantab) teacher and Sheila C. M. Scott; b Dun 21.8.44
DFMBO(NOSCA) 1968
sales advis BOCM Aber 1968–69; farm man. Inverurie 1969–70; comp man. agri/hort co-op Fettercairn from 1970
m Inv 27.12.69 Lesley A. Ledingham MB ChB 1972 anaest d of Leslie A. L. MB ChB 1934 qv

DONALD David James Thomson   BSc(eng) 1961

DONALD Elizabeth Louise   MA 1957
d of Robert T. D. MA 1914 qv(II, III) and Louise Turner MA 1923 qv; b Aber 9.9.36
resid Montreal
m Aber 5.10.57 Derick A. Crawford BSc(agr) 1956 qv

DONALD Ethel Margaret   *MA 1963
d of William D. grocer/storeman and Maggie Ritchie; b Rhynie 23.7.40
res stud. for univ Lanc, Geneva, Paris 1963–65; lect Fr Glas 1965–71
m 27.7.76 Alistair H. Blyth MA(Glas) univ lect s of Henry M. B. Welwyn Garden City

DONALD George Francis John   *MA 1957
s of George C. D. lorry driver and Margaret J. U. Shand; b Huntly 16.6.34
teacher mod lang RGC Aber 1958–69; prin Ger Perth acad from 1969 and asst rector from 1973
m Aber 4.4.61 Isabella M. Roe MB ChB 1958 qv

DONALD Ian Benzies   *MA 1970
s of Forbes M. M. D. acct and Violet L. Benzies; b Aber 26.5.47
Dip Ger for foreigners(Hamburg) 1974
BP: supply asst Lond 1970–71, Hamburg 1971–74; oil trader Mabanaft Hamburg from 1974

DONALD John Gordon   MB ChB 1960

DONALD John Henry   *BSc(eng) 1963
s of Norman D. electro-plater and Isabella Short;
b Aber 6.12.41
Lond: electronic dev eng 1963–65, sen eng 1965–66,
proj eng 1966–68, man. proj eng 1968–71, tech dir from
1971
m Aber 28.5.66 Eileen McGrory MA 1964 *qv*

DONALD Leslie Forrest   *MA 1967 Dip Ed 1968
s of Robert R. D. shop asst and Helen F. Donald; b
Aber 7.4.44
teacher mod lang Mackie acad Stonehaven 1968–70, spec
asst 1970–72; prin mod lang Cults acad from 1972
m Aber 30.3.72 Mary K. Smith secy d of John S. Aber

DONALD Margaret Jessie   MA 1963
m Finnie

DONALD Maureen   BSc 1963
m Reid

DONALD Morag Russell   MA 1969
d of Charles R. D. and Hilda M. Russell; b Aber
19.3.49
ALA 1971
children's lib Bridge of Allan 1971–74; branch lib Stirling
from 1974
m Aber 16.3.73 Kenneth S. MacSween BSc(for) 1968 *qv*

DONALD Muriel Elizabeth   MA 1964

DONALD Robert   *LLB 1968
s of Robert S. D. van driver and Eleanor C. Findlay;
b Aber 26.2.46
law app Clark & Wallace advoc Aber 1968–70, leg. asst
Lefevre & Co advoc Aber 1970–74, ptnr from 1974
m Aber 25.6.69 Judith H. Stuart MA 1967 *qv*

DONALD Ruth Alicia   BSc 1966
d of Charles J. D. plumber and Alice Ewen teacher;
b Echt 25.10.45
teacher Muthill p s 1967–71
m Aber 13.7.68 Donald S. McLusky BSc 1966 *qv*

DONALD Sheila Elizabeth   *BSc 1968 Dip Ed 1969
m Welsby

DONALD Sylvia Margaret Bisset   MA 1961
d of George L. D. master mariner and Margaret B.
Gardiner; b Aber 27.11.40
teacher: Engl/Lat Possil s s Glasg 1962–63, Engl/commun
coll of comm Aber from 1963
m Aber 1.8.61 Norman A. Donald wholesaler/caterer
s of Alexander D. Aber

DONALDSON Alan Eunson   MB ChB 1967
s of Hector A. D. MA 1927 *qv*: b Aber 28.5.44
DObstRCOG 1969 MRCGP 1973
Aber: h o med City hosp, cas dept Woolmanhill, ENT
dermat and ophth Foresterhill and Woodend hosps,
obst mat. hosp 1967–69; g p Portlethen 1969, Ellon from
1970
m Aber 24.1.70 Christina J. Melhuish chiropodist d of
John W. M. Newtonhill

DONALDSON Anne Forbes   MA 1969
d of James I. D. hotelier and Elizabeth A. Robertson
teacher; b Kiel W Ger 8.5.48
teacher Edin 1970–71; secy Goethe inst Dublin 1971–73;
lect Engl univ of Jyväskylä Finland 1973–76
m Aber 29.12.71 Douglas C. Riach MA 1968 *qv*

DONALDSON John Dallas   *BSc 1956 PhD 1959
s of John D. chief welfare off. and Alexandrina M. R.
Dallas; b Hopeman 11.11.35
DSc(Lond) 1970 FRIC 1971
asst lect chem Aberd 1958–61; lect, sen lect inorg chem
Chelsea coll Lond 1961–72, reader 1972–80; prof indust
chem City univ Lond from 1980
m Aber 22.3.61 Elisabeth A. Forrest nurse d of George
E. F. Aber

DONALDSON Marjorie Ann   *MA 1970
d of Henry C. D. MA(Glas) min of relig and Kathleen
R. Anderson MA(Glas) SCM secy; b Glasg 7.4.48
careers advis in schools: Lytham 1970–71, Aber 1971–73;
secy course Edin 1973–74; secy Scottish Council of soc
serv 1974–76; volunteers organis Edin Council of soc
serv from 1976

DONALDSON Marjory Anne Russell   MB ChB 1970
d of James A. F. D. PO superv and Frances A. Russell
optician; b Aber 1.5.46
ARCM 1964
h o ARI and Woodend hosp Aber 1970–71; teacher
violin: Berks 1971–72, Downehouse s Berks 1974–75
m Aber 5.8.71 Douglas G. Fowlie MB ChB 1970 *qv*

DONALDSON William   *MA 1968 PhD 1974
s of William D. man. and Margaret G. Buchan nurse;
b Ellon 19.7.44
mobile lib Aberdeensh 1974–75; archivist Aber from 1976
m Aber 1.4.70 Loraine Challis-Sowerby MA 1969 *qv*

DONKIN Jean   BSc 1965

DONN George Cormack   *BSc 1966

DONNELLY Margaret Mary   BSc 1970
d of John P. D. soc worker and Mary Fox; b Barrhead
8.8.49
teacher: St Luke's h s Barrhead 1971, Nandom s s Ghana
1972–74, Holyrood s s Glasg from 1974

D'ORBAN Paul Theodore   MB ChB 1956
s of Charles D'O. landowner and Constance E. Hill;
b Lond 26.5.30
DPM 1961 MRCPsych 1972
m o publ hosp Georgetown Br Guyana 1956–59; psychiat
regist Friern hosp Lond 1959–62; psychiat Kingston
Jamaica 1962–65; Lond: m o HM prison Holloway
1966–74, consult. psychiat St. George's and Tooting Bec
hosps from 1974
m Aber 15.10.55 Laura S. F. Ho-A-Shu MA 1956 *qv*

DORCEY Anthony Hugh Joseph   *MA 1969

DORIS Coreen Wilma   BEd 1970

DORMAN David Kennedy   BSc(agr) 1968
b Cambridge 11.7.45
Dip Man St(Birm) 1972
Ely: man. trainee Dorman Sprayers 1968–69, marketing
asst, man. 1970–72; dir marketing and sales Dorman
Sprayers, A.C. Mouldings from 1973
m Birm 11.4.72 Pamela Small SRN

DORN Tola   *BSc 1969

DORWARD Gordon John   *BSc 1967 PhD 1978
s of John D. gen man. coachbuilding comp and
Elizabeth S. Easton; b Aber 28.3.45
ACMA 1973 MBA(New Jersey)
direct exchange schol Kansas USA 1967–68; res chem

Aberd 1968–71; trainee acct, marketing prod. group acct T. Wall & Sons (ice-cream) Gloucester from 1971
m Denver Colorado 22.12.74 Rebecca C. Ashley BA (Kansas) syst analyst d of Thomas E. A. BSc Aurora Colorado
d California 27.1.79 *AUR* XLVIII 234

DORWARD Lloyd Forbes   PhD 1962
  b Dublin 15.6.26
BSc(Lond) 1946 FIEE 1967
prin lect elect. eng Rutherford coll of tech N'cle-u-Tyne 1963–65; head eng dept Oxford poly from 1965
m Aber 14.8.50 Christina Munro secy d of John M. Aber

DOTT Harold Edwin Morton   BSc 1967 *1968
  s of Eric F. D. MB ChB(Edin) consult. phys (paediat) and Sarah D. Alexander artist; b Edin 5.3.45
res agr Brit overseas dev Cochabamba Bolivia 1969–71; teacher biol: Edin 1972, Lornshill acad Alloa 1972–73; collecting wild life specimens (self-employed) Cochabamba from 1974
m Cochabamba 3.10.74 Teresa Steinbach secy d of Franz S. Cochabamba

DOUDELL John Owen   *BSc 1970 Dip Ed 1971
  s of Herbert D. clerk and Mary J. Owen; b Liv 11.9.39
NDA 1960
teacher Huntly from 1971

DOUGHERTY Alan John   *MA 1961

DOUGHTY Flora Mary Scorgie   MA 1963
  d of William F. D. MA(Edin) headmaster and Flora Scorgie teacher; b Haddo 30.12.42
teacher: Mintlaw s 1964–70, Westfield s from 1970
m Tarves 6.8.65 Fergie Allan farm. s of William T. C. A. Mintlaw

DOUGLAS Alasdair Henry Mercer   *BSc 1970
  s of Alan D. MB ChB(St And) med pract and Alexandra D. Murray nurse; b Broughty Ferry 3.3.47
BR man. trainee 1970–71; lect Aberd from 1973
m Aber 23.7.74 Linda J. Forsyth MA 1971 d of Stanley F. MA 1939 *qv*

DOUGLAS Diana Margaret   MA 1967
  b Edin 27.2.46
secy mod lang dept Strath 1968–72
m Aber 6.8.69 John F. Cameron MA 1967 *qv*

DOUGLAS Ian   MA 1968

DOUGLAS John Forbes   *BSc 1965

DOUGLAS Lois Ernesta   MB ChB 1956
  d of Ernest G. D. LRCP(Edin) med pract and Mildred A. Case PO exec; b Jamaica 2.10.28
m o: Bridgetown Barbados 1958, Kingston publ hosp Jamaica 1959–62, Buea West Cameroon 1963, Jamaica 1963–67; asst m o h Bridgetown Barbados 1967–70, m o h from 1970
m Jamaica 8.2.58 Frederick G. Smith QC, SC, BA attorney-at-law Barbados s of Cecil S. Christchurch Barbados

DOUGLAS Louise Munro   MA 1970
  d of Percy R. D. eng and Muriel M. Sandison nurse; b Insch 24.9.49
teacher hist/mod stud.: Peterhead acad 1971–72, Dingwall acad 1972–73; relief teacher
m Inverurie 25.7.70 Neil F. Grant MA 1968 *qv*

DOUGLAS William Henderson   MA 1968
  s of Adam F. D. master bldr and Mary J. Cowie; b Elgin 1.12.36
teacher: Engl/hist Lossiemouth h s 1969–71; asst prin guid Buckie h s from 1971
m Buckie 12.10.60 Caroline Thomson d of William A. T. Buckie

DOUGLASS Lesley Helen   *MA 1969 *MEd 1973
  d of Edward E. D. bus. man. and Helen Brebner postmistress; b Sidcup 23.1.47
teacher: Livingston 1970–71, Aber 1972–73, educ psych Aberdeensh from 1973
m Aber 8.9.73 Harvey J. Aberdein LLB 1976 s of James A. Aber

DOULL Peter John Uilleam   *BSc 1962

DOUSE Michael John   *MEd 1964
  BSc(econ)(Belf) Dip Ed(Belf)

DOW Alexander Crawley   PhD 1957
  s of James M. D. c c arch. Renfrewsh and Elsie D. Crawley; b Paisley 12.10.05
MA(Glas) 1928 MC(Italy) 1945
C of S min Kelty 1932–48; chap. 8th Army Africa, Italy 1940–45; min East St Clements Aber 1948–50; chap. to forces Ger, Scot, Eng, Ireland 1950–58; min Stoneywood 1958–71, Westray and Papa Westray from 1971
m Paisley 20.7.32 Marion C. Anthony

DOW Gordon Edwards   MA 1965 Dip Ed 1966
  s of Alan B. D. joiner, store man., printer and Mary Edwards; b Glasg 19.4.44
teacher: Glenrothes p s 1966–68, Arbroath from 1968
m Aber 20.8.66 Linda J. Anderson d of Alister A. Aber

DOW Marion Baird Anthony   BSc 1960
  d of Alexander C. D. PhD 1957 *qv*; b Kelty 21.10.34
teacher: maths/sc Hilton s Aber 1961–64, sc Bankhead acad 1964–67, maths/sc Westray from 1967
m Bucksburn 8.7.63 Sydney M. Cooper lay missionary C of S s of William C. Bucksburn

DOW Michael Gillean Cameron McDonald   *BSc 1957

DOW Robin James   *MA 1970
  s of Alexander J. D. rly clerk, cost acct and Dorothy D. Muir s secy; b Glasg 10.5.39
teacher Balloch 1971–73; Rothesay s s from 1973
m Aber 1970 Wendy J. Gaffron MA 1969 *qv*

DOWDEN Hugh George Martin   BSc(for) 1956

DOWDS Stephen   LLB 1970

DOWER Michael James   BSc 1968
  s of James D. clerk civ serv and Doris M. Forsyth; b Aber 28.2.44
med copy-writer: Oss Holland 1968–71, Welwyn Garden City, Dagenham 1971–75; Lond: acct exec 1975–76, acct superv from 1976
m Aber 18.7.69 Moira Mackenzie MA 1968 *qv*

DOWEY Paul Wilson   MA 1967

DOWNIE Isobel Mary   *MA 1968
  d of Alexander J. D. post./tel off. and Eleanor H. Hay clerk; b Banff 13.8.46
Oxford: OUP gen catalogue 1969–70; copyright edit. and lib 1970–74; Sask Canada: sessional lect 1974–75, teaching fell. 1975–76
m Aber 26.7.68 Leonard M. Findlay MA 1967 *qv*

DOWNIE James Ritchie *BSc 1958
s of George D. fisherman and Sarah W. Ritchie; b
Rosehearty 23.9.36
Zambia: field geol Chartered Exploration Lusaka 1958–
68; asst chief geol NCCM Chingola div 1968–71; chief
geol NCCM: Broken Hill div Kabwe 1971–75, Konkola
div Chililabombwe from 1975
m Aber 5.1.62 Millicent M. Garrioch nurse d of David
B. G. MA(Edin) Milltimber

DOWNIE Margaret Rosaline *BSc 1963
d of William J. D. fisherman and Margaret M. West
teacher; b Rosehearty 22.7.41
teacher Aber acad 1964–66; res asst Wisconsin 1966–
67; various part-time teaching posts and at Simon
Langton g s Canterbury from 1968
m Aber 30.7.64 Charles Brown BSc 1963 qv

DOWNIE Mary Christine BSc 1970
d of Maxwell D. marine eng and Barbara A. Taylor
nurse; b Rosehearty 7.6.48
teacher biol: Lasswade 1971–75; Aber: Summerhill acad
1975–76, Hazlehead acad from 1976
m Rosehearty 10.8.74 Donald Maclean loc govt off. s of
Donald G. M. Dingwall

DOWNIE Norman William *MA 1966 Dip Ed 1967
s of William S. D. MA 1922 qv; b Aber 4.7.44
Lond: lect International Computers 1967–69; syst man.
Glaxo 1969–73; computer man. Oxford reg health auth
from 1973
m Aber 15.8.69 Cyndy A. Eastman dep computer man.
d of John F. Heasman Surbiton

DOWNIE Robert Taylor *MA 1964

DOWNIE Robert William Mackenzie MB ChB 1960
s of Robert D. auctioneer/valuator and Elizabeth R. C.
Mackenzie; b Aber 1.2.36
FRCSE 1966 Dip Laryngology & Otology(Lond) 1968
h o Woodend hosp Aber, ARI 1960–61; trainee g p
Ballater 1961–62; temp lect anat Aberd 1962–63; regist
ARI: surg 1963–65, ENT 1965–68; sen regist ENT
1968–72
m Durris 4.9.68 Aileen J. McHardy MB ChB 1966 qv
d Aber 9.5.72

DOWNIE Sheena Elizabeth MA 1965
d of Robert W. D. sales rep and Lillian E. Ferries;
b Aber 4.2.32
teacher Engl Aber: Northfield acad 1966–67, Kaimhill s s,
Kincorth acad 1967–73; asst prin Engl Kincorth acad
from 1973
m Aber 7.7.55 John L. C. Duthie sales rep s of John D.
Aber; husb d 1972

DOWNIE Susan Margaret MA 1964

DOWNIE William Alexander MA 1969
s of Alexander J. D. post./tel off. and Eleanor H. Hay
cashier/bookkeeper; b Banff 6.3.44
computer spec Lond from 1969
m Aber 11.10.68 Sandra G. Reid telex oper d of Alfred R.
Huntly

DOWNIE William Tytler MA 1960
s of William T. D. baker and Gertrude Leask; b Rosehearty 1.5.35
teacher Engl/hist: Possilpark s s Glasg 1963–66, Fraserburgh acad from 1966 and housemaster from 1972
m Fraserburgh 6.7.73 Edith C. J. Cardno MA 1964 qv

DOWNING Andrew John *BSc 1969

DOWNING Charles Stephen *BSc 1969

DOWNING Peter William BSc(eng) 1970

DOWNING Ronald Ernest *BSc 1969

DOWSETT Anthony Peter BSc(eng) 1965
s of Joseph D. loc govt off. and Irene D. Gould; b
Epsom 2.10.42
post grad app Bristol Siddeley Engines Watford 1964–66;
Carreras-Rothmans Belf: mech eng 1966–67, packing
dept man. 1967–71, prod. man. Unilever Croydon 1971–
73; fin. analyst Brit Leyland Birm from 1973
m Oxborough 8.10.66 Theresa M. Smith secy d of David
R. E. S. FRCS Norfolk

DOYLE Rosemary Galloway MA 1964
d of James M. D. hairdresser and Mary M. Sutherland
teacher; b Aber 16.6.41
teacher: Engl/Fr Fraserburgh acad 1966–67, Engl/hist
Mackie acad Stonehaven 1967–68; Aber: Engl/Fr Kaimhill s s 1968–69, Cornhill p s 1969–72
m Aber 6.10.66 Duncan D. Chisholm MB ChB 1965 qv

DRANE John William *MA 1969
PhD(Manc)

DRAPER Ivan Thomas MB ChB 1956
s of Thomas G. D. cost acct and Ethel A. Pearson;
b Derby 11.9.32
MRCPE 1959 FRCPE 1966
h o med, surg, neurosurg Aber 1956–58; sen h o gen med
Glasg 1958–59; regist and sen regist neurol Edin 1959–
65; Fulbright fell. Wellcome fell. and fell. clin physiol
Johns Hopkins univ Baltimore USA 1962–63; consult.
neurol inst of neurol sc S gen hosp Glasg from 1965
m Aber 4.7.56 Muriel M. Monro journalist d of John M.
Aber

DRAYSON Geraldine Munro BSc 1968
d of Eric G. D. loc govt off. and Marjory B. White;
b Ealing 20.9.46
teacher: sc Cults acad Aber 1968–69, Peterhead acad
1969; ptnr George C. McGowan (Contracts) civ eng contr
Banchory from 1969
m Aber 12.8.69 George C. McGowan BSc(eng)1966 qv

DREVER Michael James Flett MA 1963
s of Thomas A. D. clerk of works and Helen S. Flett;
b Harray 14.3.41
teacher Kirkwall g s from 1964
m Orkney –.7.68 Inga Tulloch bank clerk d of James T.
Kirkwall

DREW Elizabeth Helen MA 1969
d of Sidney F. D. radio and tv eng and Helen A.
Buchan shorthand typist; b Swindon 11.8.47
teacher Fr/Ger: Aberfeldy 1970–75, Fraserburgh 1975–
76; prin Fr/Ger Aberfeldy from 1976
d road accident 16.2.80 AUR XLVIII 443

DRINKWATER Barry William *MA 1966
s of Kenneth D. foreman joiner and Alice M. Broadley
distribution area man.; b Manc 6.9.42
grad pers off., man. recruitment of Standard Telephones
and Cables, part of ITT, Amer multinational corporation
based in NY mainly Lond 1966–77; pers man. LRC
International Lond 1977; recruitment dir Cambridge
recruitment consult. from 1977
m Epping 28.4.73 Christine Draine secy d of John F. A. D.

DRUMMOND Bruce Mackenzie   MA 1968
s of John A. D. ophth optician and Olive B. Parkinson;
b Aber 5.10.48
BSc(Ophth Optics)(Manc inst of sc and tech) 1971
ophth optician Aber from 1971

DRUMMOND Elizabeth Margaret   MA 1963
m Miller

DRUMMOND Iain Roderic   MA 1962
s of Henry T. H. D. MA(Cantab) lib Aberd and
Dorothea O. Mackintosh; b Stirling 22.5.41
acct/audit clerk Aber 1962-65; Inl Rev: exec off./
computer progr Aber, Perth, E Kilbride, Carlisle 1965-
72; insp of taxes/syst analyst Lond from 1973
m Aber 23.9.67 Ann E. Robertson d of William R.
Milltimber

DRUMMOND John Parkinson   MA 1961

DRUMMOND Neil   MA 1958
s of Robert H. D. supt eventide home and Christina
MacLeod matron eventide home; b Stornoway 21.11.36
MBCS 1973 FIDP 1973 MSc(N Lond poly) 1974
teacher Gordon s Huntly 1959-64; lect, sen lect coll of
comm Aber from 1964
m Dufftown 7.7.61 Winifred D. Shearer teacher d of
John S.

DRUMMOND Peter John   *MA 1970

DRUMMOND Sheelagh Margaret   BSc 1970
d of Charles W. D. bank man. and Kathleen A. Reid
teacher p e; b Galashiels 1.4.50
res asst microbiol MRC Edin 1970-71
m Cupar 7.8.70 George L. McQuitty LL B(Edin) solic s
of Gordon R. McQ. Cupar

DRY Frank Thomas   *BSc 1965
s of Jesse B. D. eng and Louisa Pilkington; b Manc
2.12.42
Macaulay inst Aber: soil surv off., scient off. 1965-72;
sen scient off. from 1972
m Aber 16.4.71 Helen M. Paterson MA 1966 *qv*

DRYDEN William Alexander Fraser   *MA 1970
s of William D. acct, bus. man. and Mary Mackay
tailoress; b Inv 24.3.48
Dip LA(Edin) 1972 Assoc Landscape Inst 1977
plan. asst (landscape) E Kilbride dev corp 1972-74;
landscape arch. Warrington dev corp from 1974
m Thurso 7.8.71 Sheila R. Chisholm teacher

DUCAT Thomas Nicholas   *MA 1965

DUDMESH Yvonne Margaret   MB ChB 1968
d of Stanley D. and Lilian M. Robins hotel prop.; b
Bournemouth 11.2.43
DRCOG 1970
h o Salisbury gen infirm. 1968-69; h o obst/gyn Odstock
hosp Salisbury 1969-70; trainee asst g p Teignmouth
1970-71; asst g p Hugglescote/cas off. Loughborough
gen hosp 1971-73; g p Hugglescote from 1973
m Teignmouth 12.6.71 Frederick A. Bladon spec eng s
of Frederick R. B. Teignmouth

DUFF Ernest Melvin   *MA 1964
s of Alexander D. tinsmith and Lily Kinsley; b Peterhead 21.4.39
teacher: Aber 1965-74; asst head p s from 1974
m Aber 21.5.66 Margaret M. Collier teacher/free-lance
writer d of John C. C. Aber

DUFF John   MA 1965

DUFF William Strath   *MA 1968
s of William D. elect. and Jeannie M. Cheyne; b Aber
9.2.45
teacher: Salford 1969-71, Corowa NSW Aust from 1972;
salesman NCR Manc 1971-72
m Alnwick 11.11.67 Lesley J. Meyer Dip Ed(Manc) art
teacher d of Wilfred H. M. Alnwick

DUFFTY Paul   MB ChB 1970
s of Stanley D. acct and Joan M. Pitman teacher;
b Leeds 1.9.46
MRCP 1976
h o: RACH, ARI 1970-71, Scarborough hosp 1971-72;
sen h o royal Manc ch hosp 1972; lect ch health Aberd
from 1972
m Aber 14.8.69 Lesley M. Macdonald MB ChB 1970 *qv*

DUFFUS Anne   MA 1959
m Clarke

DUFFUS Evelyn Elizabeth   MA 1959
d of Alexander C. D. clerk and Caroline M. S. Olley;
b Aber 19.7.39
teacher: Aber 1960-65 and from 1968
m Aber 2.8.63 Alistair Duncan BSc 1971 civ serv, teacher
s of Charles D. Aber

DUFFUS Gillian Marjorie   MB ChB 1964 MD 1969
d of George M. R. D. MB ChB 1931 *qv* and Marjorie
A. S. Third MA 1934 *qv*; b Aber 30.4.40
DObstRCOG 1966 PhD(Glas) 1975 MFCM 1977
h o Aber hosps 1964-66; res asst mat. hosp Aber 1966-
69; clin instr dept of obst/gyn Downstate med centre
State univ NY Brooklyn 1969-70; Wellcome res fell.
royal mat. hosp Glasg 1970-72; res fell. soc paediat unit
Glas 1972-75; fell. commun med from 1975
m Aber 30.10.70 Ronald J. McIlwaine MB ChB(Belf)
consult. psychiat s of Gilbert McI. Craigavon Co Armagh

DUFFUS John Logie Lyall   *MA 1969
s of George M. R. D. MB ChB 1931 *qv* and Marjorie
A. S. Third MA 1934 *qv*; b Aber 12.2.46
progr oper asst BBC radio Lond 1969-70; Scot. Opera
Glasg: pers asst to gen admin 1971-73, asst gen admin
1973-76, tech controller 1976-79; gen man. Hong Kong
Philharmonic Soc from 1979

DUFFUS Peter Ross Sinclair   MB ChB 1970
s of George M. R. D. MB ChB 1931 *qv* and Marjorie
A. S. Third MA 1934 *qv*; b Aber 18.8.47
DObstRCOG 1973 MRCGP 1974
h o ARI 1970-71; vocational trg scheme for g p Aberd
1971-74; g p from 1974; dep police surg from 1975
m Aber 25.9.70 Margaret M. Millar MA 1969 *qv*

DUFFY Gerard   MA 1961

DUGDALE Jeffrey   *MA 1970

DUGUID Eleanor Jean   MA 1969
d of Adam D. psychiat nurse and Helen F. Donald;
b Perth 22.3.48
teacher Dun 1970-72; civ serv Edin 1972-77
m Scone 14.10.72 Norman R. Weir civ serv

DUGUID Elizabeth Lillie   MA 1970
d of Alexander J. D. comp exec and Elizabeth Lillie;
b Aber 13.6.49
A Inst Pers Man 1975
teacher mod lang Surrey 1971-72; Lond: trg off. 1972-73,
pers off. from 1973; Qantas Airways, Chiswick 1976

DUGUID George Robertson   BSc 1966 Dip Ed 1967

DUGUID Hilda Margaret   MA 1969
    d of William H. D. papermaker and Elspet M. Hadden millworker; b Bucksburn 25.12.28
employment asst careers serv Aber town council, Grampian reg from 1970
m Aber 10.5.50 Swanson McKenzie MA 1969 *qv*

DUGUID Margaret Glegg   MB ChB 1957
    d of Alexander G. D. supplier off. equipment and Isabella C. Glegg; b Aber
DA(McG) 1966
h o, sen h o Aber 1957–59; rotating internship Plainfield New Jersey USA 1959–60; resid anest Hartford Connecticut 1960–63; fell. anaest: Montreal 1963–66; fell. anest univ of Vermont Burlington USA 1966–68; attending phys anest Plainfield New Jersey USA from 1968
m Aber Denis Gorvett s of Samuel G. Pontyridd; marr diss

DUGUID Martin Neil   MA 1969
    s of John D. baker, gardener and Elizabeth Christie; b Weymouth 28.9.45
teacher Aber from 1970
m Elgin 19.8.70 Sheila G. Henderson teacher d of James H. Elgin

DUGUID Robert Watson   BSc(eng) 1966
    s of Robert H. D. BCom 1926 *qv*; b Calcutta 9.2.45
MICE 1973
site eng UK 1966–71; Birm: des civ eng 1971–72; prod. eng (site) 1972–73; site ag from 1973
m St Albans 27.3.71 Elizabeth M. Rees occup therap d of William R. St Albans

DUNBAR Ian James Cameron   MB ChB 1961

DUNBAR John Manson   BSc(eng) 1959
    s of John M. D. civ serv dept agr(Scot.) and Jessie B. Manson; b Stirling 21.8.37
MICE 1965 PEng(Ont) 1966 AMIWPC 1968 MSc(Strath) 1968 MIPHE 1970
eng asst: Leeds 1959–62, Glasg 1962–66, London Ontario 1966; post grad stud. Glasg 1967; eng man. Paisley 1967; assoc ptnr consult. practice Glasg 1970–71, ptnr from 1971

DUNBAR Mary   MA 1959
    d of James D. omnibus driver and Mary Castle cook; b Aber 21.11.38
teacher maths: Northfield acad Aber 1960–62, Elgin acad 1963–66
m Aber 11.7.62 Andrew M. Philip civ serv s of Frank P. Aber

DUNBAR Patricia Mary   BSc 1956
    d of Alexander L. D. farm. and Margaret A. Watson; b Kemnay 19.8.34
AEO at AWRE Aldermaston 1956–57; res asst Milk Marketing Board Thames Ditton 1957–58; AEO at NIRD Reading 1958–61; part-time med phys tech Glasg S gen hosp from 1972
m Aber 21.7.59 Ronald H. Christie BSc(Glas) SSO at AWRE, lect Strath s of James C. Airdrie

DUNBAR Richard Neil Findlay   *BSc 1961
    s of James D. MA 1925 *qv*; b Margate 1.4.39
electronics eng: Chatham and Frimley 1961–65, Montreal 1965–67; Addlestone 1967–72; sales eng Dulwich 1972–74; sales man. Tolworth 1974–76, Slough from 1977
m Forres 28.12.61 Margaret H. Davie BSc 1960 *qv*

DUNCAN Alastair Barclay   *MA 1966 PhD 1976
    s of Eric M. D. MA 1929 *qv*; b Kirkpatrick Fleming 9.5.42
res stud. Aberd, Paris 1966–68; dem Fr Aberd 1968–69; temp lect Fr R'dg 1969–70; lect Fr Stir from 1970

DUNCAN Allan George   *BSc 1963
    s of Donald A. D. sales rep and Annabella Thom; b Aber 17.10.40
DPhil(Oxon) 1966
fell. univ of Calif Los Angeles 1966–67; res chem: US bureau of standards Colorado 1967–69; UKAEA AERE Harwell from 1969
m Aylesbury 5.5.73 Alison P. Reid occup therap d of Patrick R. Aylesbury

DUNCAN Allison Isabella   BSc 1962
    d of William D. paper millworker and Alice Lindsay; b Peterculter 24.11.41
prob. analyst Hawker Siddeley Hatfield 1962–64; teacher Dun 1964–65; free-lance progr NCR Dun 1965–66; part time progr Strath 1973–75; teacher: St Aldred's h s Paisley 1976–77, St Columba's s for girls Kilmalcolm from 1977
m Aber 30.3.64 Roy M. Johnson BSc(Brist) dynamics eng/lect s of Ernest A. J. Lond

DUNCAN Anne   *MA 1968
    m Noble

DUNCAN Anne Lawrence   *MA 1968
    m Cartshore

DUNCAN Brian Thomas Calder   MA 1967

DUNCAN Catherine Rose   MA 1962
    d of James S. D. banker, coal merchant and Catherine McPherson; b Grantown-on-Spey 21.7.41
pers secy Shell internat petr Co Lond 1962–65; teacher Haslemere 1965–67; resid Lagos 1973–77, The Hague from 1978
m Elgin 12.6.65 Richard R. Rayner oil co exec s of Ralph E. R. Twickenham

DUNCAN Cecil John   MA 1968

DUNCAN Charles George   MB ChB 1967
    s of Charles D. ship's carpenter and Margaret Smith; b Aber 6.7.43
CCFP 1974
Ont Canada: fam phys St Catharines 1970–72, Fonthill from 1972
m Aber 16.7.69 Patricia M. McAllister MA 1968 *qv*

DUNCAN Colin George   *MA 1969
    s of George M. D. gen merch and Nelly Forbes; b Torphins 28.8.47
Marks & Spencer: dept man. Aber 1969–70, Edin 1970–73; asst man. Stirling 1973–76, Preston from 1977

DUNCAN David Alexander   *BSc 1969
    s of William D. upholsterer and Elizabeth W. Anderson; b Elgin 12.4.47
FFA 1976
syst analyst Edin 1969–76, sen analyst from 1976

DUNCAN David Andrew McLaren   *MA 1967
    s of Andrew M. D. joiner and Ann H. Malcolm; b Auchtermuchty 13.2.43
L-es-L (Lettres Modernes) univ of Nancy France 1968
lect univ of Nancy 1967–68; teacher mod lang: Daniel Stewart's coll 1969–70, Schiller gym Hamelin 1970–71;

prin mod lang Alford acad from 1971
m Lindores 1967 Morag F. Rennie MA 1966 *qv*

DUNCAN David McPherson   *BSc 1962 MSc 1964

DUNCAN Douglas   *MA 1956
s of John D. garage prop. and Flora McBain; b Aber
13.11.32
Dip Russian Interpreter(Lond) 1958
teacher: George Watson's coll Edin 1959–68; prin Ger/
Russian Elgin acad from 1968
m Edin 1.4.61 Ayline C. Kerr nurse d of John Y. K.
Calcutta

DUNCAN Douglas James McKerrow   PhD 1961
b St And 14.6.31
MA(Oxon) 1953
lect Engl S'ton 1958–64; prof and head dept Engl univ of
Ghana 1964–67; visiting prof univ of Western Ontario
Lond Ontario 1967–68; prof Engl McM univ Hamilton
Ontario from 1968
m Stratford-on-Avon 18.9.65 Janet Hoskins

DUNCAN Douglas John Stewart   *LLB 1966

DUNCAN Elaine Margaret   MA 1968
d of Douglas D. bank admin and Clarice I. L. Fraser
civ serv; b Aber 29.3.47
teacher: Fr Liberton Edin 1970–71, Westbourne Glasg
1971–72, Engl/Fr Lenzie acad Kirkintilloch 1972–74
m Aber 5.8.71 James Ross BSc(eng) 1970 *qv*

DUNCAN Eleanor Margaret Cormack   MA 1970
d of Thomas S. D. MA 1938 *qv*; b Lossiemouth 5.12.48
teacher: East Barnet 1971–73, Ewell 1974–75, Peterhead
acad from 1975
m Aber 24.6.70 Harris J. Lacey; marr diss 1976

DUNCAN Elizabeth Ann   *MA 1966
m Mackie

DUNCAN Eric Thomson   MA 1956
s of Nathaniel J. D. D. farm. and Margaret D. Noble
teacher; b Newmachar 11.7.32
nat serv RAEC sgt/instr Harrogate 1957–59; teacher
Crieff p s 1959–62; head: Findo-Gask p s Perth 1962–68,
Errol p s from 1968
m Aber 29.6.57 Elaine M. C. Goodall bank clerkess d of
Joseph G. Wigtown

DUNCAN Erica Barbara Anne Weir   MB ChB 1962
d of Eric H. W. D. MB ChB 1931 *qv*; b Banff 7.9.38
DObstRCOG 1964 Dip Soc Med(Edin) 1969 MFCM 1973
h o: ARI, RACH 1962–63, Chase Farm hosp Enfield,
Edin RHSC, Simpson Mem Mat. Pav 1964–65; trainee
asst g p Edin 1965–66; res fell. Edin from 1966
m Aber 27.6.73 Hugh B. L. Russell MRCS(Lond) med
pract

DUNCAN Esmé Félicité   MA 1962
d of Harry F. D. tel and Elsie McKay off. man.; b
Aber 3.8.41
teacher Engl/r e Aber 1963–70; staff member Scripture
Union East Scot. from 1970

DUNCAN George   BSc(eng) 1969
s of George D. man. ship bldrs and Josephine Wyness
dist nurse; b Peterhead 26.1.49
civ eng county surv dept Lanarksh, Hamilton 1969–74;
sen eng Mears civ eng Peterhead from 1974
m Longside Doreen Hutchison MA 1972 teacher d of
Alexander M. H. Peterhead

DUNCAN George   *BSc 1965
s of Peter R. D. fish merch and Barbara L. Simpson;
b Peterhead 11.1.43
MSc(E Ang) 1966 PhD(E Ang) 1968
sen res asst Nijmegen Holland 1968–69; lect biol UEA
Norwich from 1969
m Saxmundham 3.6.67 Margaret A. Daniels secy d of
Bernard C. D. Saxmundham

DUNCAN Gordon Lindsay   *BSc 1956 PhD 1959

DUNCAN Hazel   MA 1958
d of William D. chief fisheries advis HIB and Isabella
McLean; b Peterhead 23.3.38
teacher: Peterhead 1959–60, Redruth 1960–62, Peterhead
1972–76, remed Buchan dist from 1976
m Peterhead 19.8.60 John L. Craze acct s of John L. C.
Redruth

DUNCAN Helen Pauline   *MA 1966
d of Harold D. bank man. and Phoebe P. Hulse; b
Kendal 16.6.44
res asst surv Engl dialects Leeds univ 1966–69; lect
Sedgley Park coll of educ Manc from 1969
m Duncan–Austwick

DUNCAN Isobel Margaret   *MA 1960
d of James D. bldg contr and Bessie I. Barclay MA
1924 *qv*; b Inverurie 26.6.38
BA(Cantab) 1962
res asst Nat lib of Scot. Edin 1962–64; part-time adult
educ tut. Leic 1964–66; dep regist births, marriages
deaths Ely from 1977
m Edin 3.4.64 George D. S. Galilee BA(Oxon) clerk in
holy orders C of E s of George A. G.

DUNCAN Jean Davidson   MA 1970
m Bryce

DUNCAN Jeanette Christina   MA 1969 Dip Ed 1970
d of Maxwell L. D. joiner and Jeannie A. Murray
teacher; b Torphins 22.10.48
teacher maths: Whitburn s s 1970–72, Boroughmuir s s
Edin from 1972, asst prin maths from 1973
m Aber 27.6.70 Derek M. Turpie MA 1969 *qv*

DUNCAN Jennifer Ethel   BSc 1964
m Steven

DUNCAN John   *MA 1970

DUNCAN John   *BSc 1960 MSc 1961
s of Albert G. D. joiner and Margaret B. Patterson
shop asst; b Aber 10.8.38
PhD(N'cle) 1964 FRSE 1974
lect maths Aberd 1963–70, sen lect 1970–71; prof maths
Stir from 1971
m Aber 8.8.63 Patricia Patterson BA(Mich) teacher d of
Adam G. P. Cleveland Ohio

DUNCAN John Alan   BSc 1970
s of John L. D. merch seaman and Joan E. Manson
machine-knitting instr; b Lerwick 14.4.48
teacher maths Brae j h s Shetland from 1971

DUNCAN Kenneth   MA 1960

DUNCAN Margaret Isobel   MA 1959

DUNCAN Margaret Josephine   MA 1966
d of Alfred J. D. bank man. and Margaret S. Willox;
b Ellon 15.10.45
teacher: Engl/hist Woodhill h s Dunfermline 1967–71,
Engl Ellon acad from 1971

DUNCAN Neil Alexander   MA 1961 BD 1964
s of William D. bank teller, acct, man. and Isobel J.
Moir bank clerk; b Aber 20.1.40
teacher: Glasg 1965–66, Banffsh 1966–68; field asst to
Exploration Ventures UK 1969–70; C of S min Keiss
from 1970

DUNCAN Nicolas Anne   MA 1967
d of Robert B. D. teacher and Nicolas Geddes teacher;
b Banff 5.5.45
teacher: Perth 1968–71, Dumbarton 1971–74, Alva from
1974
m Aber 28.12.71 John R. McIntosh BA(NSW) Aust
teacher s of Alvan D. McI. Waverton NSW

DUNCAN Raymond Grierson   *MA 1968
s of John C. D. man. and Margaret Coutts; b Aber
21.5.46
Dip Bus Admin(Edin) 1969
cadet dept of employment 1969–71; teacher Engl/hist
Perth h s from 1972

DUNCAN Robert   *MA 1969
s of George D. works man. and Josephine Wyness
nurse; b Peterhead 3.9.47
teacher hist Airdrie acad from 1970 and housemaster
from 1973

DUNCAN Robert Emslie   *MA 1970 MLitt 1977
b Forres 28.8.48
res assoc centre for study of soc hist Warw 1972–74;
joint author *Warwick Guide to British Labour Periodicals
1790–1970* 1977

DUNCAN Roderick   MA 1967

DUNCAN Ronald Wallace   MB ChB 1960
s of John D. master mariner and Jane Wallace; b Aber
21.3.35
MRCOG 1970
h o Aber hosps 1960–62; g p Aboyne 1962–65; HM
Forces consult. gyn Hanover W Ger from 1965
m Aber 12.7.60 Brenda M. Simpson teacher d of William
S. Cullen

DUNCAN Ruebena Ann   MA 1969
d of Walter D. boat-bldr/carpenter and Thomasina
Smith; b Lerwick 21.12.47
pers man. course RGIT Aber 1969–70; Lond: civ serv MHSS Blackheath 1970–72, Scot. off.,
Lord Advoc's off. Westminster 1972–75
m Aber 22.12.70 James A. Chisholm BSc 1970 *qv*

DUNCAN Sheila   MA 1967
m Harrison

DUNCAN Stuart Henry Weir   MB ChB 1965
s of Eric H. W. D. MB ChB 1931 *qv*; b Banff 7.9.41
DObstRCOG 1968 MRCGP 1976
h o ARI 1965–67; g p Peterculter from 1967 and clin asst
dept orthop ARI from 1969
m Marykirk 11.8.66 Irene A. Robertson MA 1965 *qv*

DUNCAN Walter   *BSc(eng) 1964
s of Walter D. boat-bldr/carpenter and Thomasina
Smith; b Lerwick 12.11.42
Coventry: post grad trg course 1965–67; des draughtsman
1967–70

DUNCAN William   MA 1957
s of Robert B. D. yard man. and Ethel Nicol; b Peterhead 4.2.36

teacher: Fraserburgh N s 1958–60; dep head Buchanhaven s Peterhead 1960–66; head: Ayton s 1966–70,
Chirnside s 1971–74; Culter s from 1974
m Peterhead 11.7.60 Mary C. Taggart teacher d of George
J. T. MA 1920 *qv*

DUNLOP James   PhD 1970
s of James A. D. and Lo-Ioma E. Palmer; b Palmerston
Nth NZ 4.6.42
BSc(Well) 1964 MSc(Well) 1966
scient DSIR Palmerston Nth NZ from 1970
m Palmerston Nth NZ 16.10.65 Frances M. Gerrand
nurse

DUNLOP Katherine Louise   MA 1966

DUNLOP Murray John   MA 1969

DUNLOP Sally Margaret Doris   *MA 1967
d of George G. D. lt col The Royal Scots, Scot. rep
Guide Dogs for the Blind Assoc and Aline T. Arthur
teacher; b Douglas I o M 16.4.45
edit asst Wm Collins Sons & Co publ Glasg 1967–69;
Lond: asst edit. George E. Harrap publ 1969–70; assoc
then dep edit. cookery books The Hamlyn publ group
1970–75; edit., publ man. Beaver books from 1975
m Edin 13.3.71 John N. Floyer MA(Cantab) oper res s
of Martyn du B. F. Milverton

DUNLOP Stewart Brice   *BSc(eng) 1964
s of John E. D. MB ChB(Edin) med pract and Ena P.
Simpson; b Steeple Bumpstead 11.5.42
tech asst serv dept (aero-engine) Rolls Royce Glasg
1964–65; army off. (capt) REME 1965–69; PA man.
consult.: man. consult. Edin 1969–73, Dublin from 1973
m Aber 23.4.69 Jennifer A. MacDonald MA 1964 *qv*

DUNN Elizabeth Ann   *MA 1966
d of Alexander D. MA(Glas) C of S min and Florence
M. S. Hourston nurse; b Portlethen 9.7.42
teacher geog: Bathgate 1965–67, St Serfs s Edin 1972–73;
lib asst Napier coll Edin 1967–68
m Portlethen 9.7.66 Allan G. Dodds MA(Edin) sen med
photogr s of Gilbert D. Edin

DUNN Euan Kennedy   *BSc 1967
s of Henry G. D. journalist and Phyllis Campbell; b
Aber 16.2.45
PhD(Durh) 1972
dept dem Edward Grey inst of field ornithology Oxon
1970–76; freelance writer Oxford from 1976

DUNN Marilyn Jennifer Lynette   MA 1965
d of Alexander D. MA(Glas) C of S min and Florence
M. S. Hourston nurse; b Portlethen 21.6.44
teacher Kaimhill s Aber 1966–70, Br of Don s from 1977
m Aber 20.7.68 Andrew F. Stronach BSc(eng) 1968 *qv*

DUNN William Dawson   *BSc(eng) 1970

DUNNETT Charles William   DSc 1960
s of William F. D. mech eng and Vera E. Holt; b
Windsor Ontario 24.8.21
MBE BA(McM) 1942 MA(Tor) 1946 FASA 1965
statist: dept nat health and welfare Ottawa 1949–53;
Lederle labs Pearl River NY 1953–74; prof biostatist
McM Hamilton Ontario from 1974
m Windsor Ontario 14.6.47 Constance W. MacDonald
nurse d of Roy S. MacD. Windsor Ontario

DUNSMUIR Martin Maxwell   *MA 1968 Dip Ed 1969

DURNIN Kenneth James McDonald   MA 1959
Dip Ed 1965
s of Joseph J. D. MA 1930 *qv*; b Aber 25.4.37
Cert Teacher of Deaf(Manc) 1969
teacher: p s Aber 1960–67, deaf Aber 1967–70, deaf
Perth W Aust 1970–75; dep head p cath s Morley Perth
W Aust from 1976
m Aber 26.12.62 Margaret A. Argo staff nurse d of
William A. Aber

DURNIN Monica Mary   *MA 1960
m Morales

DURNIN Patrick Joseph   MA 1957
s of Patrick J. R. D. master slater and Muriel T.
Keane; b Aber 13.3.29
teacher Aber 1958–64; head Selkirk p s 1964–65; dep
head Dumfries p s 1965–71; head: Annan p s 1971–77,
Brighouse from 1977
m Aber 3.1.55 Elizabeth A. Mutch MA 1952 *qv*

DURNO Denis   MB ChB 1960 MD 1972
s of Robert D. comm trav and Mabel Taylor milliner;
b Aber 19.5.36
MRCGP 1968
h o cas dept ARI, City hosp Aber 1960–61; g p Portlethen from 1961
m Aber 6.7.60 Audrey J. Angus cashier d of George A.
Aber

DURNO Joyce   MA 1964
d of Robert D. sales rep and Mabel D. Taylor milliner;
b Aber 1.5.43
Dip Soc St(Edin) 1965 MSocW(Br Col) 1973
soc worker: Aber 1965–67, Lond Ontario 1967–69,
Lions Gate hosp Vanc 1969–71 and from 1973
m Vanc 8.5.71 Edward G. Auld BASc(Br Col) prof phys
Br Col Vanc s of George W. A. Chilliwack BC

DURWARD Ian George   MA 1968
s of John Y. D. master confectioner and Nora Gordon
nurse; b Crieff 10.4.22
teacher: hist/mod stud. Peterhead acad 1969–71, geog/
mod stud. Cults acad Aber from 1971
m Fraserburgh 27.9.48 Margaret Donald catering superv
d of William J. D. Fraserburgh

DURWARD Wilma Anne Margaret   BSc 1963
d of Alexander F. D. master shoemaker/dir and Mary
R. Andrew asst father's bus.; b Torphins 7.2.42
teacher maths: Lasswade h s 1964–67, Inverurie acad
from 1977
m Aber 31.3.66 David S. Roberts BSc(H-W) teacher s
of Peter S. R. Dalkeith

DUTCH Eileen Watson   *MA 1957 Dip Ed 1958
m Gorie

DUTHIE Andrew   BSc 1957

DUTHIE Andrew Stewart   *MA 1968
s of Charles S. D. MA 1932 *qv*; b Edin 4.8.46
ACMA 1975
Vauxhall Motors Luton: grad induction course 1968–70,
statist fin. forecast sect. 1970–71, budget co-ordinator
1971–73; gen superv final budgets 1973–75, Europ
budget co-ordinator 1975–77, man. budgets/forecasts
from 1977
m Lond 9.9.72 Joy Musgrave florist d of Joseph M.
Gateshead

DUTHIE Anne Elisabeth   MA 1961
d of Alexander D. wholesale grocer and Jessie Robert-

son nurse; b Aber 30.6.40
Dip Soc Ad(Dund) 1963 CASS(N'cle) 1966
soc worker educ dept Dun 1963–65; N'cle: psychiat soc
worker RVI 1967–68, Nuffield ch psychiat unit 1968–69,
sen psychiat soc worker 1969–72; sen soc worker Morpeth
1972–73
m Aber 26.8.72 Eric H. Fisher BSc(N'cle) mech eng,
univ lect s of William H. F. Hartlepool

DUTHIE Ashley Mackintosh   MB ChB 1959 cMD 1976
s of Andrew M. D. MA 1920 *qv* and Christian M.
McDonald MA 1918 *qv*; b Chesterfield 31.1.32
DRCOG 1961 DA(Lond) 1962 FFARCS 1966
h o med and neuro-surg ARI 1959–60; sen h o obst and
gyn Scarsdale hosp Chesterfield 1960–61; ARI: sen h o
neuro-surg 1961–62, sen h o and regist anaest 1962–66;
sen regist anaest Westminster hosp Lond 1966–69; sen
lect anaest univ of Rhodesia from 1969, then prof anaest
Godfrey Huggins s of med, univ of Rhodesia
m Aber 19.9.60 Margaret S. Morrice radiogr d of
Alexander M. M. Aber

DUTHIE Elizabeth Jean Watson   MB ChB 1967

DUTHIE George   MA 1970

DUTHIE Iain Fraser   PhD 1961
BSc(Glas) BVMS

DUTHIE James Alexander   MB ChB 1959
b Peterhead 1.2.35
m Airdrie 9.9.66 Christine F. M. Chalmers BSc(Glas)
teacher

DUTHIE Jennifer Milne   MA 1968
d of James D. cooper and Jeannie Milne herring
worker; b Peterhead 29.3.47
m Peterhead 13.7.68 David E. Witts rly clerk s of Edgar
A. W. Portobello

DUTHIE John   MA 1965

DUTHIE John Scott   MB ChB 1962 ChM 1973

DUTHIE John Simpson   BSc 1969
s of Alexander D. D. butcher and Jane S. Simpson
nurse; b Rosehearty 13.9.32
teacher sc Fraserburgh 1971–78; share fisherman from
1979
m Peterhead 28.1.56 Vera Strachan d of Alexander S.
Peterhead

DUTHIE Joseph Graeme Munro   *BSc 1957
s of Frederick S. R. D. insur assessor and Maggie B.
Reid; b Aber 2.11.34
PhD(Brist) 1961
univ of Rochester NY: asst prof 1961–66, assoc prof
1966–74; visiting res assoc California inst of tech 1970–71;
Alfred P. Sloan res fell. 1970–72; dir C. E. K. Mees
observatory from 1974
m Hornell NY 11.8.62 Sue A. Roberts secy d of Clarence
S. R. Bath NY

DUTHIE Margaret Bruce   MA 1969
d of William C. D. joiner and Margaret B. Buchan;
b St Combs 2.1.48
teacher: Saline p s Dunfermline 1970–72, Fraserburgh
1972–74, Livingston from 1974
m Lonmay 17.10.75 Norman Raven MA 1969 *qv*

DUTHIE Pamela Ann   MB ChB 1962
d of Robert T. D. capt RFA, harbourmaster and Irene

King; b Fraserburgh 19.10.37
Co Durh: h o Shotley Bridge 1962–63; clin m o Bournemouth from 1972
m Aber 10.7.62 Kenneth Fleming MB ChB 1962 *qv*

DUTHIE Ruth   MA 1970 MEd 1972
  m(1) Trail
    (2) Thom

DWORZAK Antoinette Elsie   BSc 1970
  d of Anton H. D. bus. man. and May M. Jones
caterer; b Freetown Sierra Leone 31.12.40
MSc(Strath) 1972
forensic analyst Freetown from 1972
m Freetown 27.4.74 Kenneth A. B. Fergusson BSc(Lincoln USA) prin fisheries off. s of Adjai F. Freetown

DYAS John Charles   MA 1967

DYER Hamish McMillan   BSc 1964 MB ChB 1967
                                              PhD 1976
  s of Norman F. D. banker and Annie E. Rothnie
banker; b Aber 17.11.42
  h o Falkirk, Aber 1967–68; resid in g p Ottawa civic
hosp/Ottawa univ 1968–69; m o Zambia flying doct
serv Ndola 1969–70; Aberd: res fell. dept of embryology
1970–71; lect dept of dev biol from 1971

DYER Herbert Joseph   *MA 1959

DYER James Archibald Thomson   *MB ChB 1970
  s of Thomas J. D. MA(St And) C of S min and Mary
W. Thomson; b Arbroath 31.12.46
MRCPsych 1975
h o ARI, Woodend hosp Aber 1970–71; trainee g p Skene
1971–72; Royal Edin hosp: sen h o psychiat 1972–73,
regist psychiat 1973–75, sen regist 1975–77; res psychiat
MRC unit epidemiological stud. in psychiat Edin from
1977
m Aber 30.7.69 Lorna M. S. Townson MA 1969 *qv*

DYER Robin Maitland   MA 1960 MEd 1971
  s of Norman F. D. banker and Annie E. Rothnie
banker; b Aber 29.9.39
Aber: teacher Old Aber s s 1961–66; teacher, careers
master Hazlehead acad 1967–73; year master Northfield
acad 1973–75; asst div educ off. Aber div Grampian reg
from 1975
m Aber 20.7.63 Aileen M. Walker MA 1961 *qv*

DYKE Stanley Frederick   PhD 1958
  s of Albert E. D. BSc(Lond) metall and Kate E. Russell;
b Woolwich 15.9.31
BSc(Lond) 1955 DSc(Lond) 1969 FRIC
lect chem Aberd 1957–58; Bristol coll of tech: lect org
chem 1958–59, sen lect chem 1959–61, prin lect 1961–66;
univ of Bath: sen lect chem 1966–69, reader org chem
from 1969
m Aber 10.7.58 Alexandrina B. Sutherland MA 1954 *qv*

EADIE Jean Margaret   PhD 1956
  d of Robert G. W. E. BSc(Glas) indust chem and
Florence A. C. Paterson; b Glasg 17.5.31
BSc(St And) 1953
res protozoologist Rowett res inst Aber from 1953

EADIE Patricia Ann   BEd 1969
  d of David L. E. slater/plasterer and May Reid;
b Perth 24.10.44
teacher Fr Keith g s from 1969

EARL John Roderin   BSc 1968

EARLS John Crawford   PhD 1963
  s of Archibald E. eng and Jean Thompson; b Glasg
11.6.31
BSc(eng)(Lond) 1953 CEng 1959 FIEE 1973
RGIT Aber: sen lect 1963–65, prin lect 1965–70, head of
s of electronics and elect. eng 1970–76; asst prin
(resources) Sheff city poly from 1976
m Pitlochry 11.7.59 Constance A. Miller teacher p e
d of James A. M. Pitlochry

EASTLAKE John Jeffrey   MA 1968

EASTMAN Donald Sidney   MSc 1964
  BSc(Br Col)

EASTON David John Courtney   MA 1962 dBD 1965
  s of William C. E. missionary and Elizabeth Bennett
missionary; b Bogota Colombia 7.10.40
C of S min: asst St Andrew's ch Inverurie 1965–67,
Hamilton-Bardrainney ch Port Glasgow 1967–77, Burnside ch Glasg from 1977
m Port Glasgow 7.10.70 Edith Stevenson midwife d of
James S. Greenock

EASTON Eugene Gervais   *MA 1967 *MEd 1972

EASTON Thomas Bruce   BSc 1961
  d Aber 26.11.62 *AUR* xl 94

EATON Jane Patricia   *BSc 1970 Dip Ed 1971
  d of George E. dir environmental health/master of
works and Patricia J. Martin; b Banff 27.1.48
teacher biol/gen sc Firhill h s Edin, prin biol from 1972
m Banff 1.4.72 Ralph C. Wylie BSc 1970 *qv*

EBBON Gordon Patrick   *BSc 1965
  b 24.5.43
PhD(Lond) 1970
scient off. radiochem centre Amersham 1965–67; dem
St Thomas hosp med s Lond 1967–70; tech BP Grangemouth 1970–74; proj leader BP res centre Sunbury from
1974
m 31.8.68 Jean G. Shannon BSc 1966 *qv*

EBUADE-IYAMABO John Osoba   BSc(for) 1958

ECCLESTON Donald   MB ChB 1957
  b Preston 18.12.31
DPM(Lond) 1960 PhD(Edin) 1965 MRCPsych 1973
DSc(Edin) 1976
Edin: mental health res fund fell. 1962–64, consult.
psychiat royal hosp 1967–70; asst dir MRC brain metab
unit 1970–77; prof psych med N'cle from 1977

EDDIE Fiona Elspeth   *MA 1968 Dip Ed 1969
  m Burnett

EDDIE George   MB ChB 1962
  s of Joseph N. E. disablement re-settlement off. and
Euphemia C. Robertson; b Bradford 17.7.33
h o Aber: ARI, RACH 1962–64; h o Bellshill mat. hosp
1964; g p: Snaith 1964–69, Guernsey from 1969
m Aber 12.10.59 Mary I. Johnston MA 1959 *qv*

EDDIE Jean Lillian   *MA 1956
  m Wood

EDDIE Valerie Anne   MA 1969 Dip Ed 1970
  d of Robert M. E. tea planter and Elizabeth M. C.
Ross teacher; b Wick 4.8.44
teacher Dumfries from 1970
m(1) Alasdair R. R. Leonard; marr diss 1971

(2) 29.12.71 Ian Callander valuation surv s of Robert C. Dumfries

EDDON David Howard   *BSc 1969

EDEN Frederick John   BSc 1970

EDGAR Alison Mary   BSc 1960
 d of William M. G. E. MA(Glas) C of S min and Isobel M. Marr teacher p e; b Rhynie 28.7.39
teacher maths Nairn acad from 1961, also prin guid 1972–77

EDGAR Ian Alfred   BSc(agr)1970
 s of Alfred E. aircraft eng and Edna Holden; b Kilbarchan 19.8.47
A Inst BM
employed Miller, Morris & Brooker Slough from 1970, contr man
m Slough Carol Smith d of K. C. L. S. Slough

EDGE Rosemary Anne   *BSc 1968
 m Thompson

EDMOND Carol Mackenzie   MB ChB 1958
 g p Chiswick Lond from 1968
m(1) Cowie; marr diss
 (2) Lond 25.5.77 Ernest F. Roberts MA(Cantab) g p s of James B. R. MA(Oxon) East Grinstead

EDMOND David Michael   *MA 1969

EDMOND Margaret Grant   MA 1960
 m Aber 3.8.63 Stuart A. Middleton MA 1961 *qv*

EDWARD Alexander Thomas Hutson   BSc(Eng) 1964
 b Huntly 11.11.43
MICE 1969 MIWE 1973
resid eng Baptie Shaw & Morton consult. civ & struct eng Glasg, Loch Braden water treatment works Ayrsh from 1972

EDWARD Alison Jean Elphinstone   MA 1961
 d of Ian D. E. MA 1927 *qv*; b S India 19.3.40
Dip Soc St(Edin) 1962
res asst dept criminology Edin 1962–70; res assoc tourism and recreation res unit Edin from 1974
m Edin 5.8.63 Sidney J. Arnott MB ChB(Edin) lect, consult. s. of George A. Leeds; marr diss 1976

EDWARD Ian   MA 1956 LLB 1958
 s of Charles E. E. civ serv and Isobel T. Kynoch; b Aber 3.9.35
cadet col serv Cantab 1958–59; dist. off. col serv Mkushi N Rhod 1959–62; ptnr C & P H Chalmers advoc Aber from 1962
m Aber 20.8.58 Marguerite A. Leiper teacher p e d of George L. Aber

EDWARD Janice Elizabeth   MA 1967
 m Hepburn

Edward John   MB ChB 1965
 s of John E. grocer and Barbara J. Cormack; b Aber 14.2.40
h o Aber gen hosps 1965–67; sen h o obst/gyn Groote Schuur hosp Cape Town 1967–68; regist obst/gyn Grey's hosp Pietermaritzburg 1968–69; sen h o anaest Aber gen hosps 1969–71; g p Aber from 1971
m Aber 8.4.71 Elizabeth C. Duncan art teacher d of George D. D. Aber

EDWARD Kenneth George   *MA 1966 Dip Ed 1967

EDWARD Neil   MB ChB 1961
 s of Charles E. E. civ serv and Isobel T. Kynoch; b Aber 8.1.38
MRCPE 1965
Ashley MacIntosh res fell. med Aberd 1962–64; lect med Aberd 1964–73; sen regist Glasg RI 1971; tut. med Temple univ Philadelphia USA 1971–72; consult. phys Grampian area health board from 1973
m Aber 16.7.65 Vivien E. M. Smith MB ChB 1962 *qv*

EDWARD Patrick Duncan   *BSc(agr) 1968
 s of Duncan C. E. farm/grocer and Marjorie Duncan; b Methlick 19.5.45
res stud. Rothamsted 1968–70; field dev man. Yorksh 1970–73; lect NOSCA from 1973
m Udny 16.9.67 Mary A. Whyte civ serv d of Mormond W. Udny

EDWARDS David George Warrilow   BSc(for) 1959
 s of Richard H. E. paint tech and Gladys M. Lees; b Bloxwich 5.2.37
MF(Wash) 1963 PhD(Wash) 1969
res asst Wash 1959–60; lab tech for. comm Farnham 1961–62; teacher Walsall 1962–63; Wash: teaching asst 1963–65, res asst 1966–68; res scient Canadian for. serv Victoria BC from 1968
m Aber 14.8.61 Margaret H. Mitchell MA 1959 *qv*

EDWARDS John   *BSc 1970

EDWARDS John Charles Seaman   *MA 1957

EDWARDS Keith Ian Campbell   *MA 1956
 s of John G. E. grocer, security off. and Flora Jack; b Fort George 13.10.33
trg for C of S min Aber 1956–59; asst min Douglas and Angus ch Dun 1959–61; min Laurieston-Renwick ch Glasg 1961–68; warden Iona Abbey 1968–71; min the Michael ch Sheff from 1971

EDWARDS Meldrum Barclay   *BSc(eng) 1964
 s of Alfred J. M. E. MA 1924 *qv*; b Aber 2.12.42
MSc(Cantab) 1966 Dip H & T Eng(N'cle) 1967
res asst S'ton 1967–69; asst eng: Aber c c 1969–75, Grampian reg c from 1975
m Aber 28.10.72 Kareen A. M. Anderson soc worker d of Richard D. A. Aber

EDWARDS Michael Alexander   *MA 1969

EDWARDS Peter Stewart   MA 1969

EDWARDS Rex Richard Cyril   PhD 1968
 BSc(Hull)

EDWARDS Robert Norman   *BSc(eng) 1970
 s of Thomas C. E. BA(Wales) schoolmaster and Agnes H. M. Inglis; b Edin 14.8.47
MSc(Birm) 1973 MICE MIWE
asst civ eng R. H. Cuthertson & Ptnrs Edin 1970–72 and from 1974

EDWARDS Susan Mary   MA 1970
 d of Ronald D. E. prod. dev eng and Mary I. Smartt secy; b Woking 7.3.46
Dip Lib(UCW) 1978
Norway: teacher Lyngseidet 1971–72; Engl in s s/adult evening classes Tromsø 1972–74; lib asst univ lib Tromsø 1975–77

EDWARDS Timothy Drummond   BSc(for) 1967
 s of Colin C. E. MRCP consult. neurol and Lesley H.

Reynolds LRAM; b Lond 3.9.43
MA(Cantab) 1969
computer aided hist demographic res Cantab 1967–70;
syst dev with IBM Lond from 1970

EFFA Columbus Nsor   MB ChB 1965

EFOBI Onwuka Celestine   *MA 1959

EGBUONU Francis James Chukwodi   MB ChB 1963

EGLIN Stewart   *MA 1967

EHRHARDT Johanna Elisabeth Ursula Margarete
**   MB ChB 1960**
   d of Arnold A. T. E. LLB(Königsberg) lect law, clerk
in holy orders, sen lect ch hist Manc and Edit R. G. H.
Hahn   MA(Königsberg)   teacher;   b   Königsberg   Pr
Germany 6.9.34
h o: RACH 1960–61, Oldham 1961; m o Port of Spain
Trinidad 1961–62; Kenya: m o Kakamega, Kisii 1963–67,
g p Eldoret 1967–72, clin tut. med trg centre Nakuru from
1972
m Heywood 16.7.60 Roger W. Gray BSc(agr) 1960 qv

EL-ADEEMY Mahmoud Sadek Mahmoud   MSc 1966
   BSc(Ein Shams)

ELDER Elizabeth Fraser   MA 1959
   d of Ernest F. E. comp dir/hotel prop. and Isabella S.
Watson hotel man.; b Buckie 24.8.38
teacher: Glasg 1960, Hilton s s Aber 1961–63, Turriff
acad 1963–64, Macduff h s, Banff acad 1964–71, hist/Engl
Turriff acad from 1971
m Aber 28.12.67 Trevor L. Kenrick RAF pilot, garage
prop. s of Edward F. K. Llangollen

ELDER Keith Robert McMillan   *BSc 1956 PhD 1959

ELDER Lilian McIntyre   MA 1969 MEd 1977
   d of Alexander R. E. trawl skipper and Johnann M.
Cross fish worker; b Aber 8.7.42
part-time lect statist Aberd 1970–72, full-time from 1972
m Aber 14.11.59 James Gordon panel beater s of James
G. Aber

ELDER Michael Robert   MA 1969
   s of Alan R. E. insur off. and Ivy L. Morgan clerkess;
b Dun 16.4.47
Dip Lib(Wales) 1971 Ch Lib 1972
Luton: trainee lib 1969–70, sen asst lib Bedfordsh c lib
from 1971
m Belmont 14.9.74 Pauline A. Wiltshire chartered lib d
of Harold F. W. Sutton

ELDER Reynold Malcolm   MA 1965

ELDER Susan Winifred   *MA 1969
   d of Albert G. E. civ serv and Kathleen Yates civ serv;
b Aber 24.3.46
m Aber 29.8.69 Ronald C. Speirs MA 1969 qv

ELEFTHERIOU Anastasius   *BSc 1964
   s of Stephanos E. Eng Sc(Lausanne) chief telecomm
advis to Greek govt and Helen Rangou; b Athens 14.9.35
marine lab DAFS Aber: govt scient exper off., sen scient
off. 1964–74, prin scient off. from 1974
m Aber 9.10.59 Margaret Craib MA 1961 qv

ELERIAN Mohammed Kamal   PhD 1964

EL-GARHY Mohammed Talaat   PhD 1963
   MD(Ein Shams)

EL HAG Gaafar Abbas   MSc 1966 PhD 1969
   BSc(Khart)

EL HASSAN Babiker Ahmed   BSc(for) 1965

EL-HOSSADY Awad   MSc 1967 PhD 1971
   BSc(Libya)

ELKAROURI Mohamed Osman El Hassan   MSc 1965
   BSc(agr)(Khart)

ELLEN Judith Lesley   *MA 1970
   d of Eric M. E. Lloyds underwriter and Eunice Heath
MB ChB(St And) med pract; b Woking 1.7.48
au pair Moscow 1971–72; TEFL Lond, Milan from 1973
m 15.5.75 Archie Lambourne

ELLEN Signa Anna Main   MA 1968
   d of William M. E. trawl man. and Margaret F. F.
Baxter secy; b Aber 23.3.47
teacher Newtonhill p s 1969–76
m Aber 4.7.69 Ian V. Mackenzie hotelier s of Ian M. M.
MPS(Edin) Cults

ELLINGTON Henry Irvine   *BSc 1963 PhD 1969
   s of Henry K. T. E. eng and Alice B. Coutts; b Aber
17.6.41
scient off. AERE Harwell 1963–65; RGIT Aber: lect
phys 1966–73, lect i/c educ tech 1973–74, sen lect from
1974
m Aber 12.4.66 Lindsay M. Sheldon teacher d of James
A. S. Aber

ELLINGTON Kathleen Alice Tester   MA 1966
   d of Henry K. T. E. eng and Alice B. Coutts; b Aber
24.3.45
teacher: Tullos p s Aber 1967–69, Walker Rd p s, Tullos
p s 1974–78, Brit s Tripoli Libya from 1978
m Aber 30.6.67 John G. M. Sutherland BSc 1960 qv

ELLIOT Elizabeth Mary   MA 1961
   d of Richard E. teacher and Georgina C. McWilliam
nurse; b Lossiemouth 21.6.40
teacher: Engl/hist Nairn acad 1962–64, Summerhill acad
Aber 1964–66, part time remed dept Summerhill 1969–73;
part-time res asst inst med sociol Aberd from 1975
m Aber 16.7.65 James A. Adams BSc 1950 qv

ELLIOT James Rowland   MA 1970
   s of Rowland E. g p and May Pearson; b Edin 16.6.48
Dip Soc Work(Edin) 1972
trainee soc worker Bromsgrove 1970–71; Droitwich Spa:
soc worker 1972–74, asst team leader soc serv 1974–76;
asst trg off. Birm soc serv from 1976
m Birm 16.9.72 Linda A. Downey BSc(Swansea) soc
worker d of Thomas W. D. Birm

ELLIOTT James Montgomery   BSc(for) 1959
   s of James E. farm. and Katherine Maguire; b Tempo
NI 5.2.39
dist for. off. counties Londonderry/Tyrone 1960–64; farm.
Co Fermanagh from 1964

ELLIS Dennis George   *BSc 1967 PhD 1970
   s of George E. welder and Henrietta Simpson; b Aber
20.1.45
syst progr Bracknell from 1970
m Aber 15.7.72 Jennifer A. Irving staff nurse d of William
I. Kirkwall

ELLIS Dorothy Johanne Margaret   *MA 1968
   d of Arthur J. E. agr rep and Jane A. Stewart; b Aber
25.11.45

Dip Ed(Edin) 1969
teacher maths Hazlehead acad Aber 1969–72; asst prin
maths Hawick h s 1972–74; asst mistress Channing s
Highgate Lond 1974–76
m Aber 23.11.74 James W. Walton police off. s of James
W. W. Sunderland

ELLIS Ian Angus   *BSc 1959 PhD 1962
s of John E. marine eng and Helen Watt; b Liv 12.3.37
visiting post doct fell. res univ of Indiana Bloomington
USA 1962–64; Westfield coll Lond: asst lect 1964–66,
lect 1966–74; teacher sc Aboyne acad from 1974
m Aber 24.8.62 Sheila A. Marr typist d of John M. Aber

ELLIS Janet Elizabeth   *MA 1969
d of Richard T. E. MA 1939 qv and Jean B. M. Porter
BSc 1940 qv; b Aber 25.4.47
computer progr Esso Petr Lond 1969–72; sales forecaster
Scot. and Newc Breweries Edin 1972–73; computer syst
des Scot. Widows' Fund Edin from 1973
m Aber 24.6.72 Malcolm B. Baldwin MA(Edin) oper res
analyst govt statist s of John T. B. MB ChB(Edin)
Penicuik

ELLIS Susan Terry   PhD 1966
d of Humphry F. E. MA(Oxon) writer and Barbara P.
Hasseldine; b Lond 28.6.39
BA(Oxon) 1961 MA(Oxon)
res stud. St Bart's hosp Lond 1961–62; res asst: Aberd
1962–66, Oxford 1966–70, Sydney 1972, sen res asst 1978
m Somerset 1.11.69 Bruce J. Roser MB BS(Syd)

ELLISON Travers David   *MA 1967
s of Travers W. E. dir contr civ aviation auth and Enid
M. Atkinson; b Sutton Coldfield 11.8.43
DMS 1970
comm app Stevenage 1967–70; Lond: sen buyer 1970–74,
comm man. from 1974

ELLWAY Judith Margaret   MA 1969
d of Graham A. E. office man. and Phyllis D. Porter
cashier; b Lydney 31.3.48
post with task force Heanor 1970–71; soc worker Clay
Cross 1971–74, Cardiff from 1979
m Aber 5.6.70 Brian S. R. Harman MA 1970 qv

ELMAHI Abdu Rahman Gorashi   BSc(for) 1968
s of Gorashi E. farm. and Fatima Mahmoud; b Elrabwa
Sudan 1.1.45
MS(Utah) 1976
Sudan: instruct. for. rangers coll Khartoum 1968–69,
asst conserv for. 1969–75, conserv. for. Gezira from 1976
m Remaitab 25.7.74 Arafa Yousif d of Ahmed Y.
Remaitab

ELRICK John Davidson   BSc(agr) 1961

ELRICK Margaret Rose   MA 1967
m Marshall

ELSTON David Thomas   BSc(for) 1963

ELWELL-SUTTON Giles Paul   *BSc 1970

ELWICK Susan Ann   *MA 1970
d of Thomas H. E. plant eng and Constance A. Petty;
b Middlesbrough 26.7.47
Middlesbrough: teacher Engl St George's s s 1970–71,
St Peter's comp s 1972–73
m Middlesbrough 8.8.70 John A. Gardiner BA(OU)
teacher s of Thomas G. South Bank Teesside

ELWOOD Richard   *MEd 1963
MA(Edin)

ELY Elizabeth Mary Kidd   MA 1962
d of George E. mech and Rachel Wedderburn; b Glasg
22.1.41
teacher: Engl/hist Northfield s s Aber 1964–67, SW Ross
1967–71; head Achmore p s from 1971
m Aber 29.6.62 Christopher Mackenzie MA 1963 qv

EMSLIE Gordon Ritchie   *MA 1962
s of Charles R. E. arch. and Jessie K. Gordon; b Aber
30.6.40
Dip Psych(Lond) 1963 PhD(Queens univ Kingston
Canada) 1971 Regist Psych(Ont) 1966
Ontario: res asst dept psychiat Queen's univ Kingston
1963–65, clin psych gen hosp Kingston 1965–69, chief
psych commun psychiat hosp Guelph 1969–70; chief
psych Waterloo county board of educ Kitchener 1970–
72, Ryerson polytech inst Toronto: prof psych 1972–75,
chmn dept psych from 1975
m Kingston Ont 6.8.66 Judith R. Cafley

EMSLIE Helen Grant   MA 1959
m Wallace

EMSLIE Peter Forbes   LLB 1964
s of William E. MA 1926 qv and Elizabeth M. Dugan
MA 1926 qv; b Aber 11.12.41
law app Aber 1964–65; solic Edin 1965–72; solic Aber
from 1972
m Aber 18.1.68 Alexandra S. Mackintosh teacher d of
Alastair M. Insch

EMSLIE Ruth Anthea   MA 1966
d of William I. E. MB ChB 1936 qv; b Kirkwall 16.8.43
Denmark: p r asst ITT 1966–67, Engl secy advt ag
1967–68, asst liaison off. W A & Bates advt ag 1968–70;
Canada: secy JWT advt ag 1970–71, sales admin Knoll
internat 1971; England: market res asst Beecham 1971–
72; sen information off. Compton UK advt ag 1972–75;
market. off. Barclays bank internat from 1975

EMSLIE William James Ingram   MA 1962 LLB 1964
s of William I. E. MB ChB 1936 qv; b Aber 29.11.40
m Edin 9.9.67 Elizabeth K. Young tel d of John Y. Edin

ENDREDY Andrew Stephen   MA 1960
s of Andrew S. E. PhD(Budapest) pedologist and
Katalin Egressy; b Budapest 28.12.34
teacher maths: Alford s 1961–69, St Joseph's coll Dumfries 1969–70; sales rep CICA, SW Scot and N Eng 1970;
prop. Dumfries stamp shop from 1970; founder Palmerston philatelic auctions 1974
m Aber 28.12.61 Ruth Richardson MA(St And) lib d of
Alan R. BSc(Lond) Bridge of Weir

ENGESET Jetmund   MB ChB 1964 *ChM 1970
s of Arne K. E. MD(Oslo) med pract and Marta
Birkeland; b Vega Norway 22.7.38
FRCSE 1970
h o Aber hosps 1964–65; Aberd: res asst surg 1965–67,
sen h o gen surg and orthop surg 1967–68, lect surg
1969–74, sen lect from 1974; seconded to dept surg univ
of Gothenburg Sweden 1972–73
m Aber Anne G. Robertson SRN d of Allan G. R. Aber

ENGLAND Carol Susan   *MA 1966
m Bagnall

ENGLAND Esther Morrison Reid   MA 1970
                                             Dip Ed 1971
d of William R. E. eng machine man and Esther

Morrison shop asst; b Aber 24.1.49
Bowthorpe s Norwich: teacher Engl/hist 1971–74, dep
head Engl from 1974
m Aber 1971 Brian W. Henderson arch. s. of William J. H.
Aber

ENGLISH Peter Roderick   BSc(agr) 1959 *1961
PhD 1969
    s of William R. E. bldr, man. meat processing factory
and Lily MacDonald; b Glen Urquhart 9.3.37
NDA(Edin) 1960
farm man. Inverness-sh 1959–60; Aberd: asst lect 1961–
66, sen res fell. 1966–68, lect 1968–78, sen lect from 1978
m Inv 19.10.63 Anne D. Mackay BCom(Strath) college
regist/teacher d of James A. M. Balnain

ENNIS Elizabeth Jacqueline Ogilvy   MA 1970

ENTWISTLE Noel James   PhD 1967
    s of Joseph E. leather merch and Gladys Jackson
secy/man.; b Bolton 26.12.36
BSc(Sheff) 1960
lect, sen lect, prof dept educ res Lanc from 1968
m Hyde 8.8.64 Dorothy M. Bocking BA(Lanc) teacher
d of John W. B. Hyde

ENYI Patrick Ogbogu   MA 1963

ERRIDGE Robert   MA 1960 *1972
    s of Robert F. E. stone polisher and Emily Gauld;
b Aber 11.10.38
Lucy Fell., Senatus Prize in Engl Lit, Minto Mem Prize
in Engl 1971
teacher Engl: Peterhead acad 1961–62, Banchory acad
1962–63, Kaimhill s s Aber 1964–69; stud. Aberd 1969–
72; teacher Engl Rubislaw acad 1972–73, prin Engl
Linksfield acad from 1973
m Aber 15.7.60 Margaret C. H. Hossack asst scient off.,
teacher d of Robert H. Aber

ERSKINE-HILL Alexander Roger   LLB 1970
    s of Sir Robert E-H. BA(Cantab) CA and Christine A.
Johnstone mus teacher; b Biggar 15.8.49
app CA Edin 1971–72; shipbroker Lond from 1972

ESPLEY Sally Marion   *MA 1964
    d of Thomas H. E. BA(Oxon) civ serv, head teacher
and Marion M. J. Stott MA 1925 qv; b Chester 10.5.42
Dip Ed 1967 (Makerere coll univ of E Af)
VSO teacher Ibadan Nigeria 1964–66; teacher: Lond
1966, Korogwe and Machame Tanzania 1967–70, Swanley
1970–72
m Bromley 31.1.70 David C. Fletcher MSc(Lond) univ
lect s of Arthur L. F. Ipswich

ESSLEMONT Anne Russell   MA 1960
    d of Harold E. draper/comp dir and Roberta R.
Turnbull; b Aber 16.7.39
educ edit.: Lond 1961–64, Edin 1964–65; teacher p s
Buckhaven 1967
m Aber 5.9.64 James J. Stott MA 1960 qv

ESSLEMONT Ean William McLennan   *MA 1966

ESSLEMONT Elizabeth Mary   MA 1961
    d of J. Bryce E. BL 1929 qv; b Aber 17.10.40
teacher: Anderson S Carolina USA 1961–62, Dem s
Aber 1963–65
m Aber 13.7.65 Michael G. H. Gibb paper mill supt s
of Maxwell G. G. MB ChB 1928 qv

ESSLEMONT George Fowlie   *BSc 1969 MSc 1971
    s of Ernest J. E. man. dir and Marjory M. Duncan dir;

b Aber 12.12.46
res asst chem: Aberd 1969–70, R'dg from 1971

ESSLEMONT Iain   MB ChB 1956
    s of John C. E. BCom 1925 qv; b Aber 2.9.32
DObstRCOG 1960 MRCGP 1973
h o: Ayr c hosp 1956–57, gen hosp Dewsbury 1957;
Regt m o Gurkha Rifles Malaya, Hong Kong 1957–59;
h o obst Ayrsh cent. hosp Irvine 1960; Malaya: g p
Cha'ah 1960–62, Penang from 1962
m Penang 3.9.66 Mary G. Mars teacher d of James H. M.
Bishopbriggs

ESSLEMONT Marjory Elizabeth Helen   *MA 1959
    d of Ernest J. E. ironmonger, man. dir and Marjory
M. Duncan; b Aber 23.2.37
teacher hist: Aber h s for girls 1964–67, Powis acad
1970–71, prin guid Harlaw acad 1971–76; asst head
Linksfield acad from 1976
m(1) Fort Jameson Zambia 5.12.59 Alexander F. Florence
MA 1957 qv (d 31.3.63)
    (2) Aber 12.8.65 John I. Rose MA 1953 qv

ESSLEMONT Norman   MA 1964
    s of Harold E. comp dir and Roberta R. Turnbull;
b Aber 22.7.43
trainee store man. Bradford, Lond 1964–66; retail
clothing buyer 1966–70; comp dir Aber from 1971;
presid Jun Chamber Aber 1973
m Aber Rosalind M. MacAulay dom supt d of Robert G.
MacA. Glasg

ESSON George Michael   LLB 1969 *1970
    s of George E. tel eng and Christine W. Paterson;
b Aber 28.7.48
NP 1976
Aber: law app 1970–72, solic 1972, ptnr Esslemont &
Cameron advoc from 1974
m Aber 3.9.74 Lindsey A. Cameron MA 1971 cartographer d of James C. Aber

ETHERIDGE Nicholas Haggar Rowse   MLitt 1967
    BA(Vic Tor)

ETTLES James Anthony   BSc 1969
    s of William A. E. MA 1941 qv; b Aber 10.4.48
lieut RN reserve 1970; teacher sc: Cargilfield s Edin
1970–73, Haileybury coll Melbourne 1973–74, Kerang g s
Victoria Aust from 1974

EUNSON Barbara Miller   *BSc 1965
    d of George J. E. bank man. and Elizabeth G. Halbert;
b Stromness 5.8.44
teacher Falkirk 1966–69; asst educ psych Stirlingsh ch
guid centre 1969–72
m Brechin 5.8.66 James R. Bennett BSc 1962 qv

EUNSON John William   MA 1966
    s of Ellen Eunson; b Whalsay 31.5.20
teacher Engl Brumby comp s Scunthorpe from 1966
m Cleethorpes 26.8.41 Kathleen Webb d of Charles
W. W. Cleethorpes
d Banchory 15.9.78

EUNSON Ronald John   *MEd 1963
    s of James A. E. preventive off. Customs & Excise and
Madge Rodmell; b Kingston-u-Hull 28.1.38
BA(Durh) 1960
teacher mod lang Melville coll Edin 1963–66; lect educ
N'cle-u-Tyne from 1967
m Newcastle-u-Tyne Susan C. Tansley BA(N'cle) teacher
d of George E. T. BA(Birm) Newcastle-u-Tyne

EVANS Alexander Robert Matheson   MB ChB 1966
 s of Alexander C. E. civ serv and Gladys Hedley;
b Aber 6.11.42
DMRD(Lond) 1971
various trg posts in NHS hosps mainly in W Midlands;
consult. radiol NW Durham health dist from 1974
m Aber 2.8.76 Mary Linklater MB MS(Lond) med pract

EVANS David Victor   *BSc(eng) 1968
 s of Victor O. E. draughtsman, prod. man. and
Beatrice J. Shuck; b Birm 9.5.46
MICE 1973
Taylor Woodrow construct.: sect. eng Nott 1968–70,
des eng Southall 1970–72, chief site eng Derby 1972–76,
dep proj man. from 1977
m Newmill 15.9.74 Daphne E. Mark secy d of Stanley
B. M. Keith

EVANS Dita Marjorie Kaye   *MB ChB 1957

EVANS Ruth Eileen Margaret   BSc 1968
 d of Noel W. E. civ serv and Mary F. Cross; b
St Helens 15.2.42
BSc(Leeds) 1972
tech information off. Express Dairy Ruislip from 1978
m Guildford 14.10.78 David B. Clayton horticulturalist s
of Oswald J.C. Wisley

EVANS Thomas Russell   *MA 1970
 s of Thomas A. E. newspaper distrib man. and Marion
Russell; b Edin 20.11.47
HM insp taxes Dumfries, Leeds, York from 1970

EVERETT Richard John   *MA 1969
 s of John W. E. bldr and Hilda M. Hibling teacher; b
Hilgay Norfolk 13.12.33
Dip Ed(Lond) 1970
teacher/traveller Lond and Aust from 1969; prin geog
Woodlands g s Glenelg S Aust from 1979
m Lower Hutt NZ 25.7.64 Elaine M. Edridge teacher d of
Allan G. E. Lower Hutt

EVERITT Brian   MA 1960

EWBANK Corinna Valerie   MA 1964
 d of Henry V. E. BA(Cantab) army off. (col) and Joyce
M. Barrett teacher sp and drama; b Meopham 19.12.41
teacher: Engl St Winefride's s s Liv 1965–66, hist/r e
Stanley Park comp s Liv 1966–69, hist Sir William
Nottidge s s Whitstable from 1974
m Meopham 31.7.65 Christopher F. Cowie scient information off. s of Samuel R. C. Deal

**EWEN Alexander James   *MA 1966 MSc 1968
                                    PhD 1971 LLB 1979**
 s of Alexander S. E. house furnisher and Rosabell
Nicoll; b Glasg 1.10.43
Aberd: asst lect maths 1967–70, lect 1970–77; part-time
lect RAF Aber 1968–72; tut. OU Aber 1971–74
m Aber 8.7.75 Lindsay Watt B Ed 1975 teacher d of
Robert J. M. W. BL 1952 qv

EWEN Cameron Archibald   *BSc(eng) 1967
 s of William A. E. MA 1928 qv; b Aber 1.12.45
MICE 1973
civ eng Glasg 1967–75, Perth from 1975
m Elgin 11.9.70 Margaret A. Shirran BSc 1969 qv

EWEN George   BMedBiol 1970   MB ChB 1973

EWEN Graham   *MA 1962
 s of William A. E. MA 1928 qv; b Torphins 9.7.40
teacher Aber from 1963

m Tannadice 27.12.72 Jane A. Taylor midwifery sister d
of James D. T. MA(St And) Tannadice

EWEN Jane Helen Esslemont   MA 1968
 d of Herbert J. E. admin BR, shop owner and Laura
L. Geddie teacher sp and drama; b Aber 24.2.47
Dip Sec St(Strath) 1969
secy: educ trust careers res Lond 1969–70, univ admissions Lond 1971–72; p a to Brit judge at European Court
of Justice Luxembourg 1973–77
m 25.6.77 Andrew Durand barrister/lect univ coll
Buckingham

EWEN Norma Leslie   MA 1962
 d of Alexander L. E. member Shore Porters' Soc Aber
and Annabella B. Middleton; b Aber 15.3.41
teacher Kittybrewster p s Aber 1963–65; visiting teacher
mus Aber s 1967–68
m Aber 19.7.63 John Lockie BSc 1959 qv

EWEN Patricia Margaret   *MA 1967 MSc 1969
 d of George S. E. warehouseman and Elizabeth S.
Harkin; b Aber 1.7.45
PhD(Stir) 1973
teacher: Glasg h s for boys 1970–72, prin maths Bathgate
acad 1972–74, Mackie acad Stonehaven from 1974, asst
rector from 1976
m Aber 2.7.69 Iain E. Maclean MA 1967 qv

EWEN Richard   MA 1965

EWEN Robert   *MA 1961
 s of Robert E. insur ag and Helen L. McVie bank
clerk; b Clydebank 3.3.39
grad app Engl Elect. Co Bradford 1961–63; asst to dir
Glass Manuf Fed. Lond 1963–64; Aberd: admin asst
(acad) 1964–66, asst secy (acad) 1966–73, sen asst secy
(acad) and clerk to Senatus 1973–76, dep secy (acad)
from 1976
m Glasg 2.7.63 Eleanor I. Grayson teacher p e d of John
R. G. Glasg

EWEN Robert Robertson   MA 1961

EWEN Sheila Barbara   MA 1957
 d of Alexander L. E. member Shore Porters' Soc Aber
and Annabella B. Middleton; b Aber 17.9.35
teacher Kirkhill p s Aber 1958–60; teacher/lib Mitcham
tech s Melbourne Aust from 1974
m Aber 17.7.58 Francis A. Macnab MA 1958 qv

**EWEN Stanley William Barclay   MB ChB 1964
                                            PhD 1971**
 s of William B. E. pharm/optician and Jessie J.
McCallum pharm; b Aber 20.5.39
MRCPath 1972
Aberd: lect 1965–72, sen lect from 1973
m Aber 1965 Doreen J. R. Morrice nurs sister d of
Alexander M. Aber

EWIN Alison Margaret   *MA 1970
 d of Robert A. E. civ serv and Jean Burgess; b
Farnworth 4.10.48
admin asst Lancs c c Preston 1970–71; teacher: humanities Kirkcaldy 1972–73, outdoor educ Hexham 1973–77;
instr outdoor pursuits Crickhowell from 1977

EWING William Edward   *BSc 1965

EYIUCHE Godwin Chukunweike   MB ChB 1956
 s of Charles U. E. fitter Nigerian Rlys and Dinah E.
Odeluga; b Abacha Idemili ECS Nigeria 26.7.31

DTM & H(Liv) 1957 FRCSGlas 1963 FMCS(Nigeria) 1971 FICS 1974
Commonwealth schol in surg Glas 1961–63; h o; Elgin 1956, Windygates, Fife 1956–67; Nigeria: m o 1958–61, spec grade 1963–66, consult. surg 1967–72, sen consult. surg from 1972
m Arochukwu Nigeria 27.5.61 Rosaline Igomanta, stenog d of Kenrick N. I. Nigeria

FACHIE Moira Ann Ritchie   MA 1962

FADL Osman Ahmed Ali   PhD 1968
s of Ahmed Ali rly stationmaster and Zeinab A. Rahman; b Sudan 1.1.36
BSc(agr)(Khart) 1960 MSc(agr)(Khart) 1964
Wad Medani Sudan: scient, sen scient Gezira res stat 1968–78, asst res prof 1978, head soil sc sect. from 1978
m Sudan 30.5.66 Fatima d of Mohamed A. R. M. Kheir Jedda

FAIRBAIRN Ian Smith   BSc 1967

FAIRLIE Isobel Anne   MA 1969
d of Andrew K. F. MA(Glas) C of S min and Jane T. Buchanan; b Thurso 13.12.47
Dip Soc Ad(Manc) 1970 Dip Soc Work(Edin) 1975
trainee soc worker Dun 1970–71; Edin: clerical post 1972–74, trainee soc work 1974–75, soc worker from 1975
m Edin 20.10.75 John C. Lodge civ serv s of James O. L. Cape Town

FAIRWEATHER Keith John   LLB 1970
s of Stanley J. F. crew supt, civ serv and Jessie M. Smith civ serv; b Edin 24.3.47
Linlithgow: law app, leg. asst, sen leg. asst W Lothian c c 1970–74; Haddington: sen leg. asst, asst dir of admin E Lothian dist c 1974–77; leg. asst NCB Edin from 1977

FAJEMIYO Akinleye   *BSc(eng) 1965

FALCONER Alan David   MA 1967 *BD 1970
s of Alexander F. publ prod. man. and Jean B. Littlejohn secy; b Edin 12.12.45
Cert of Fac of Theol(Geneva) 1971
C of S min asst St Machar's cath Aber 1972–74; lect syst theol Irish s of ecumenics Dublin from 1974
m Edin 6.8.68 Marjorie E. Walters children's resid houseparent, secy d of Frederick J. W. Edin

FALCONER Atholl George   *BSc(eng) 1957
s of Robert F. and Eva Farquharson; b Aber 29.5.35
grad trainee Rolls Royce 1957–59; nat serv 1959–61; des eng Rolls Royce 1961–62; lect mech eng RGIT Aber from 1962
m Aber 9.8.67 Judith M. Weale

FALCONER Hugh Robert   MB ChB 1956
s of Hugh F. cler off. and Elizabeth Rhind; b Inv 21.9.32
h o ARI, Woodend hosp Aber 1956–57; surg lt RN 1957–60; sen h o Aber mat. hosp 1960–61; g p Aber from 1961
m(2) Aber 29.2.80 Annita Smith d of George A. S. Portlethen

FALCONER Ian Robert   PhD 1960
s of Robert H. F. elect. eng/dir and gen man. and Lilian W. Ball cashier; b Walton-on-Thames 12.5.35
BSc(Nott) 1957 DSc(Nott) 1971 FIBiol 1971 FRIC 1972
lect biochem Adelaide Aust 1960–64; reader animal biochem Nott 1965–71; univ of New England Aust: prof biochem from 1972, head s of biol sc from 1974

m Pavenham 20.9.58 Mary E. Roff BSc(Nott) res scient, teacher d of Joseph R. Pavenham

FALCONER James Parry   BSc 1966
s of John F. rly guard and Jessie A. M. Parry; b Wishaw 1.7.28
teacher: Kaimhill s s Aber 1967–68; maths tech coll Aber from 1968
m Wishaw 18.3.49 Gerda Gerst fashion buyer, lang lab steward d of Paul G. Bad Oeyhnhausen W Ger

FALCONER Robert   *MA 1963
s of David F. tel eng and Marjory M. U. Nixon; b Edin 28.12.40
market res exec: Cadbury Birm 1963–65, London Press Exchange 1965–67; dir market res subsid LPE Lond 1967–69; dir market res comp Commun Res Lond from 1969
m Aber 31.7.65 Eva M. Slessor BSc 1962 qv

FALK Alexander Jules   BSc(eng) 1967
s of Ernest F. Dip Ing(Hanover) mech and man. eng and Eva B. Halberstadt SRN; b Hampton 22.2.44
Cert Trans Stud(Lond) 1971 MICE 1973 MCIT 1975
sen tech off. chief civ eng off. BR (Eastern Reg) York and London 1967–73; sen eng asst London Midland Reg Lond 1973–75; Van Niekerk, Kleyn & Edwards consult. eng Johannesburg 1975–76; chief res off. nat inst for trans and road res Pretoria from 1976
m 20.2.76 Marion H. Rosenthal

FALK Robert Samuel   BSc(eng) 1968
s of Ernest F. Dip Ing(Hanover) mech and man. eng and Eva B. Halberstadt SRN; b Hampton 19.3.46
MIMechE
tech mech eng BP res centre 1968–73; trilingual tech eng Becorit (GB) Nott from 1973

FARQUHAR Dennis Alexander   LLB 1969

FARQUHAR Doreen Meldrum   MA 1969
m Mann

FARQUHAR Eric   MA 1959
s of John F. fisherman and Jean F. Sinclair; b Dunbeath 25.5.38
teacher maths: spec asst Fort William 1960–68 and f e off. 1968–70; head Tomintoul s s 1970–74; teacher maths Wick h s 1974–76, asst prin maths from 1976
m Inv 6.12.58 Audrey F. Fraser MA 1967 qv; marr diss 1977

FARQUHAR Fiona Margaret   MA 1966
d of H. Gordon F. BA(Oxon) consult. paediat phys and Jean Warden; b Oxford 31.3.45
Dip Soc St(Edin) 1967
secy Edin 1967–68; prob off./soc worker Cape Town 1968–72; med soc work Edin 1972–75; Oman: secy res dept Salalah 1975–76, secy palace dept of agr Seeb 1976, secy dairy proj Digdaga, Ras Al Khaimah 1976–79; resid N. Yemen
m Pittenweem 3.5.75 W. Alasdair S. Wyllie farm man. s of W.R.C.W. Bury St Edmunds

FARQUHAR Freda Jessie   MA 1964
d of Alexander D. F. trans man. and Jessie S. Gillan; b Ellon 18.10.42
m Aber 29.8.64 Stephen J. Carr RAF pilot s of James T. P. C. Aber

FARQUHAR George   *BSc 1970

FARQUHAR Ian Harry   MB ChB 1967
s of Harry F. master mariner and Catherine Bruce;
b Portgordon 22.12.41
DObstRCOG 1972 MRCOG 1972
h o Taunton, Aber 1967–68; m o med TTB Inv, obst
Kirkcaldy 1968–70; h o paediat Inv, gyn Kirkcaldy
1970–73; sen h o obst Glasg, obst/gyn Edin 1972–74;
regist obst/gyn: Lond 1974–75, Ninewells hosp Dun,
Perth RI 1975/77, Ninewells hosp from 1977

FARQUHAR Ian James   MA 1969
s of James M. F. bank man. and Irene M. Foot; b Banff
24.5.48
teacher VSO Mhlume Swaziland 1970–72; RAF off./pilot
trg Cranwell 1972–74; teacher: geog Linwood 1975–78,
asst prin outdoor educ Armadale from 1978

FARQUHAR Marian Donald   BSc 1957
d of Donald F. stonemason and Mary O. Dalgetty; b
Brechin 3.9.35
teacher: maths/sc Montrose 1958–62, maths St Austell
1962–65, head maths dept Fareham 1965–75, dep head
maths Bracknell from 1975
m Portsmouth 23.2.70 Francis G. Langton RN, civilian
instr off. MoD s of Francis G. L. Portsmouth

FARQUHAR Marjory Niven   MA 1958
m Innes

FARQUHAR Mary Easter   MA 1956
d of James F. farm. and Jane D. Scott; b Lhanbryde
21.4.35
teacher: p s Banchory acad 1957–60, Wellhouse p s Glasg
1960–65, Stepps p s Glasg 1971–76, asst head from 1976
m Aber 23.12.63 John L. Robertson journalist s of John
G. R. Glasg

FARQUHAR William John   *MA 1958
s of John C. F. gardener and Mary Whyte; b Maud
29.5.35
Dip Soc Ad(Manc) 1960 FHA 1963
NHS: nat trainee hosp admin Aber, Manc 1958–61;
Whitehaven: hosp secy 1961–64, dep group secy 1964–
66; reg staff off. Edin 1966–69; dep secy Eastern Reg
hosp board Dun 1969–74; dist admin S dist Lothian
health board Edin from 1974
m Aber 24.2.62 Isabel H. Rusk MA 1956 *qv*

FARQUHAR William Sinclair   *MA 1963
s of William F. trawl eng and Williamina Sinclair;
b Aber 4.10.40
teacher Engl Buckhaven h s 1964–67; prin teacher
Brockley c s Lond; lect Engl Jordanhill coll of educ
1971–74; asst rector Beath h s Cowdenbeath from 1974
m Aber 17.8.63 Eileen Hather d of Jack H. Aber

FARQUHARSON Alistair James Dawson
                                          MB ChB 1959

FARQUHARSON Graham Gibb   MA 1968

FARQUHARSON Malcolm James   MB ChB 1968

FARQUHARSON William Charles   BSc 1957
s of George F. carpenter and Lily Irvine; b Torphins
25.8.35
Dip Sc and Tech(Glasg) 1960 MICE 1964 CEng 1966
shop man. UKAEA 1960–65; process eng Demerara
bauxite comp Guyana 1966–67; metall Broken Hill dev
comp Zambia 1968–70; mill supt Sherbro Minerals
Sierra Leone 1970–71; prod. eng Chilanga Cement
Zambia 1972–73; sen chem eng Revere Jamaica Alumina

1974–75, sen process eng MMIC Surigao Nickel Project
Philippines 1976–78

FARR Valerie   MB ChB 1956   ^cMD 1966
b Darlington 2.10.30
DCH(Lond) 1959
h o: paediat Aber 1956–57, med Barnstaple 1957–58;
Aber: sen h o and regist paediat 1958–63, lect ch health
1963–66; asst obst from 1966

FARSI Ali Abdulla Suleh   MA 1962
d Texas USA –.12.73

FASEHUN Frederick Isiotan   MB ChB 1969
d car accident in 1977

FASHOLE-LUKE Edward William   PhD 1969
s of William F-L. acct GPO Sierra Leone and Cecilia
O. P. Macauley secy; b Freetown 6.12.34
BA(Durh)
visiting prof of relig Kalamazoo coll USA 1970; Fourah
Bay coll Sierra Leone: lect theol 1970–72; sen lect theol/
acting head and dean fac of arts from 1972
m Freetown 7.1.60 Henrietta A. P. Lynch-Shyllon teacher
d of H. L-S. Freetown

FAULKNER Clive   MA 1962

FAULKS James Neville Gardiner   *BSc 1962

FAULKS Judith Mary   MA 1967

FAULKS Norman Quinney   BSc 1965

FAWKES Mary Jill   BSc 1958
d of Harry I. F. schoolmaster and Lilian Broadhead
teacher; b Rolleston 27.5.37
asst res chem Ind Coope (Brewers) Burton-on-Trent
1958–59; lab tech MRC carcinogenic substances res unit
Exe 1959–61; teacher sc: Stover s Newton Abbot 1961–
62, Morgan acad Dun 1962–63
m Rolleston 29.7.59 John M. T. Brebner MA 1957 *qv*

FEARNLEY Arthur Herbert   *BSc 1967
s of Joseph E. F. BSc 1927 *qv*; b Banff 9.9.46
plan. asst Moray & Nairn joint c c Elgin 1967–74; sen
asst res plan. dept N Yorks c c Northallerton from 1974
m Grantown-on-Spey 5.4.69 Maureen M. Macaulay
teacher d of Alexander M. Grantown-on-Spey

FEATHER Elizabeth Ann   ^cMB ChB 1965
d of Herbert G. F. LLB(Lond) solic and Norah E.
Warman; b Fulmer 14.7.41
MRCP 1972
sen regist paediat Queen Elizabeth hosp for ch Lond
1974–75
m Frankley 17.8.74 John Seager MB ChB(Liv) paediat s
of Thomas S. MD(Liv) Heswall

FELL John Alexander   BSc(for) 1968
s of John W. F. (Cantab) and Evelyn A. Case; b Edin
9.6.43
BA(Cantab) 1965 MA(Cantab) 1969
for. invest. advis Edin 1968–71; gen fin. advis stockbrokers Glasg 1971–74; for. invest advis Econ For. Edin
from 1974
m Stenton 26.8.67 Mary A. H. Hunter MA(St And) d of
Hon Lord Hunter LLB(Oxon) Stenton Dunbar

FELL Margaret Eleanor   MA 1959
m Athawes

FELL Rosaleen Mabel   MA 1967
  m Bishop

FEMI-PEARSE Ayodeji   MB ChB 1959 MD 1970
  MRCPE DTM&H(Liv)

FENELON Anne Deirdre Sutherland   MA 1968

FENNELL John Allinson   BSc 1963

FENTON Winston   *BSc(eng) 1964 MSc 1966
                                                       PhD 1968

FERGUSON Charles Alexander   BSc(agr) 1970
  s of George F. farm. and Barbara Wilson; b Elgin
1.11.47
MSc(N'cle) 1972
farm. Forres 1972–73; working Aust, NZ 1973–74; farm.
Forres from 1974

FERGUSON David MacKay   *BSc 1963
  s of James M. M. F. loc govt off. and Margaret F.
Eggie; b Duns 26.12.40
PhD(Edin) 1969
dem physiol med s Edin 1965–66; ICI Alderley Park:
member physiol sect. indust hyg res lab 1966–70, head
physiol unit 1970–72, head acute toxicity unit, Central
Toxicology Lab 1972–75, toxicology advis Cent Med
Group from 1975
m Aber 28.4.67 Lois King d of Angus H. K. Winchelsea
Victoria Aust

FERGUSON Donald Ewen   *MA 1965

FERGUSON Donald Hugh Nicolson   BSc 1968
  s of Hamish N. F. hotel porter and Anne Fraser MA
(Edin) teacher; b Inv 4.7.47
ALA
salesman Farrington Data Processing Glasg 1968–69;
stud. N'cle-u-Tyne poly tech 1969–70; lib AWRE Aldermaston from 1971
m Lond 20.4.71 Patricia M. Simpson MA 1968 *qv*

FERGUSON Elizabeth Susan   MA 1970
  m Stuart

FERGUSON Fiona Margaret   MA 1970
  d of John W. F. PO tel eng and Christina M. Munro
nurs nurse; b Haslemere 25.9.49
teacher p s Lond 1971–76
m Invergordon 21.4.73 George D. Porter police sergeant
s of Alexander P. Alness

FERGUSON Gail Cooper   MA 1970

FERGUSON Iain Scoon   *BSc(eng) 1970
  s of Ian S. F. MB ChB(Edin) g p and Marjory H.
Walker; b Edin 7.4.48
Vickers defence syst div N'cle-u-Tyne: syst eng 1971–73,
tech asst to chief buyer 1973–76, purchasing off. from
1976
m Stocksfield 30.9.72 Mary E. Phillips d of Horace A. P.
Stocksfield

FERGUSON Ian Russell   *MEd 1956
  MA(Glas)

FERGUSON Irene Ramsay   MA 1960
  d of James M. M. F. loc govt off. and Margaret F.
Eggie civ serv; b Perth 25.6.39
teacher Fr: Stirling h s 1961–62, Aber acad 1962–64;

ptnr in farm. bus. from 1965
m Aber 2.8.62 William R. Strachan BSc 1959 *qv*

FERGUSON Joanne Audrey Lorne   BSc 1970
  d of John A. F. farm. and Lorna F. Conway dom
bursar; b Oban 30.4.48
teacher: Slough 1971–72, Brisbane Aust 1972–73,
Honiara BSIP 1973–78
m Aber 13.8.71 Steven E. Watson BSc 1971 pasture
agronomist s of George A. W. Strathtay

FERGUSON Kathryn Anne   *BSc 1969
  m Carmichael

FERGUSON Kenneth McIntosh   *BSc 1969
  s of David M. F. assur ag and Minnie T. MacDonald;
b Dingwall 25.7.47
geol Renison Bell Tasmania 1969–71; Perth W Aust:
univ stud. 1971–72, sen geol from 1973
m Bearsden 7.8.69 Julia S. Bertram BSc 1969 *qv*

FERGUSON Sinclair Buchanan   MA 1968 *BD 1971
  s of Robert B. F. manuf's ag and Emma H. S. S. S.
Munro bookkeeper; b Glasg 21.2.48
C of S min: asst St George's Tron ch Glasg 1971–74, par
of Unst 1974–76, asst edit Banner of Truth Trust Publ
from 1976
m Aber 16.7.71 Dorothy M. Allan MA 1968 *qv*

FERGUSSON Marjorie Hill   BSc 1964

FERNANDEZ-CARMONO Julio   MSc 1969
  Dr Ing Agr(Madrid)

FERRARI Leonella Lucia Anna Maria   *MA 1958
  d of Pietro F. restaurateur and Linda Acquistapace; b
Aber 6.4.35
private secy to Italian consul gen Toronto 1958–60; TEFL
European s Parma 1960–61; teacher Fr/Ital royal acad
Inv 1961–71, asst prin Fr/Ital 1971–72, prin from 1972
m Inv 29.9.58 Alexander B. G. Longmore MA 1956 *qv*

FERRARIS Mary   MA 1967
  d of Alfredo F. LL B(Torino) man. dir and Teresa
Santone; b Lond 27.1.47
MA (York univ Toronto) 1969
res asst Tor 1968–69; au pair, waitress Neuchatel, St
Cergue Switzerland 1970–71; secy Lond 1971–72; teacher
Ponteland Northumberland 1972–73; secy Tor 1974;
teacher Mississauga Ont from 1974
m Lond 1.8.73 William M. Kennedy BA (York Toronto)
teacher s of William M. K. Weston Ont

FERREIRA Robert Edwin Christopher   PhD 1958
  s of Edwin C. F. comp dir and Jessica G. Robinson
farm; b Windermere 30.8.31
BSc(Lond) 1954
bot: Nature Conserv Edin 1960–67, seconded from DOS
to govt of Uganda 1967–71, VSO Zambia 1972–74;
conserv biol and ecological advis Zambia Lusaka 1974–
76; plant ecol Nature Conserv Council Inv from 1977

FERRIES Isobel Jean   MA 1965

FETHNEY Hilary Ann   MA 1959
  d of John R. F. pharm and Janet F. McDonald; b
Bishopbriggs 16.4.39
m Aber 6.4.61 Robert I. Gloyer MA 1957 *qv*

FETHNEY Moira   *MA 1957
  d of John R. F. pharm and Janet F. MacDonald; b
Glasg 19.1.36

teacher mus: Gordon s Huntly 1958–60, Ripon 1960, Moray from 1972
m Aber 4.7.60 John A. Dickson RAF off. s of George F. D. BL 1928 *qv*

FETTES Douglas James   *BSc 1963
s of George F. F. fishmonger and Nellie Falconer; b Aber 24.12.40
PhD(Edin) 1968 FGS 1970
Edin: scient off. Inst of geol sc 1966–69, sen scient off. 1969–73, prin scient off. from 1973
m Dunfermline 8.11.68 Frances M. Hay secy d of William H. Dunfermline

FETTES Ian William   MB ChB 1969

FETTES Peter Hugh   MB ChB 1968
s of William Y. F. MB ChB 1938 *qv*; b Insch 1.5.42
h o ARI, City hosp Aber 1968–69; h o obst/gyn Falkirk and dist RI 1969–70; g p: Musselburgh 1970, Ardersier 1970–71, Gorebridge from 1971
m Aber 23.11.68 Mary R. Bell MB ChB 1967 *qv*

FIDDLER Alasdair Stuart   *BSc 1968
s of John R. F. and Margat J. Banks; b Kirkwall 23.10.46
Dip Chem Eng(Sur)
tech BP: Sunbury-on-Thames 1970–74, Lond from 1974
m Sunbury-on-Thames 15.9.73 Mollie A. Deacon copy-typist d of William E. D. Sunbury-on-Thames

FIELDING Jacqueline Anne   BSc 1970
d of William F. furn salesman and Gladys Greenwood lab tech; b Kendal 10.6.49
VSO teacher Kenya 1971–72; lect Exeter coll 1973; VS organis Exe Vale psychiat hosp from 1973
m Broadstone 13.9.69 Hamish Henderson MA 1971 insp taxes s of James L. H. Huntly

FIFE Alistair Angus   *BSc 1964
s of George F. MA 1930 *qv*; b Nairn 11.10.41
MSc(Alta) 1966 PhD(S Fraser) 1971
teaching asst: Edmonton 1964–66, S Fraser 1966–70; post doct fell.: S Fraser and Br Col 1971–72, univ Montr 1972–73; res phys CTF Syst Inc Port Coquitlam BC from 1973

FIFE William Alexander Anderson   BSc(agr) 1962

FILBY Alan George   *BSc 1969 PhD 1973

FINCH David William   MA 1965
s of William G. F. prod. eng and Annie E. Bollans; b Carshalton 6.2.41
MSc(Kansas) 1967
Lond: sub edit. The Assoc Press 1967–69; sen sub edit. BBC external serv 1969–74; edit. in resid Kansas univ 1974; foreign desk edit. The Assoc Press NY 1974–75; edit. Reuters NY from 1975
m Carshalton 30.8.69 Louise A. Riller BA(Kansas) lab tech d of Lowell E. R. BA(Kansas) Kansas City Miss.

FINCH Maureen Frances Heneage   *BSc 1970
d 19.8.70

FINDLAY Adam Herd   *MA 1970
s of Adam H. F. trawl eng and Isabella Sinclair; b Aber 16.10.44
teacher: Engl Fraserburgh acad 1971–72, Rubislaw acad Aber 1972–73; Engl/hist Kedron h s Brisbane Aust 1974–75; asst prin Engl Inverurie acad from 1976
m Aber 22.7.66 Patricia Ritchie MA 1966 *qv*

FINDLAY Alan Grant Reid   *MA 1964
s of William H. F. MB ChB(Glas) consult. phys, photographer and Marjorie J. Greenlees; b Stirling 10.8.42
BR: man. trainee Glasg 1965–67, asst to man. freight-liner terminal Glasg 1967–68; traffic asst Auchinleck 1969; teacher geog Inv royal acad from 1970

FINDLAY Alice Dawson   MA 1968 *MEd 1970
PhD 1974
b Aber 11.7.47
m Archbold

FINDLAY Angela Bisset   *MA 1964 *MEd 1966
m Duncan

FINDLAY David   *BSc 1957 PhD 1961
s of David F. cemetery supt and Frances Gordon; b New Pitsligo 30.5.35
FPhysS 1959
asst lect Aberd 1960–62; scient off. royal radar estab Malvern 1962–68; lect phys Queen's univ Belf 1968–72, sen lect from 1972
m Lerwick 14.7.60 Barbara E. Robertson teacher d of Thomas H. R. Mossbank

FINDLAY David Robert   MB ChB 1957

FINDLAY James Alexander May   MB ChB 1959
s of James W. F. water insp and Mary B. May; b Fraserburgh 1.1.35
FRCSE 1966
h o Aber hosps 1959–60; dem anat Aberd, Glas 1960–62; orthop: regist Glasg, chief resid Ottawa 1967–70, sen regist Leeds 1970–72; consult. orthop surg Paisley from 1972
m Hamilton 16.6.65 Mary E. W. Wright MB ChB(Glas) med pract d of William W. MA(Glas) Hamilton

FINDLAY James Slater   *MA 1963

FINDLAY John Bell Cuthbert   *BSc 1968
s of Robert F. dir sugar/rum prod. and Georgina Spence; b Georgetown Guyana 5.2.46
PhD(Leeds) 1972
univ Leeds: res assoc 1968–71, post doct fell. 1971–72; res fell./dept tut. Harvard univ USA 1972–74; lect Leeds from 1974

FINDLAY John William   *BSc(eng) 1969

FINDLAY John William Addison   *BSc 1966 PhD 1969
s of Alexander F. fisherman and Jessie R. Addison; b Buckie 27.3.45
USA: res assoc med chem Charlottesville Virginia 1969–72, clin res assoc Norfolk Virginia 1972–73; res scient Amersham 1973–75; USA: sen res scient (drug meta-bolism) Res Triangle Park N Carolina from 1975
m Aber 11.7.70 Jean M. Hey MB ChB 1970 *qv*

FINDLAY Judith Margaret   MA 1965
d of James A. F. insur surv and Mary Shewan; b Aber 29.3.44
teacher Fernielea p s Aber 1966–69
m Aber 22.7.66 Alexander R. Carle MA 1962 *qv*

FINDLAY June Mary   PhD 1959
d of Alexander F. master mariner and Miriam Stewart; b Hartlepool 8.6.31
BSc(Wales) 1952
teacher sc: Milford Haven g s 1953–54, James Gillespie's h s Edin 1954–56; res asst Rowett inst Aber 1956–60

m Aber 7.5.60 John S. Bevan-Baker FRCO(Lond) Sutton Coldfield

FINDLAY Leonard Murray *MA 1967
s of George F. ship's rigger and Irene Black; b Aber 14.12.44
DPhil(Oxon) 1973
Engl lit.: lect Birm 1972–74, asst prof Saskatoon Sask from 1974
m Aber 26.7.68 Isobel M. Downie MA 1968 *qv*

FINDLAY May Florence MA 1957
d of John F. county arch. Moray & Nairn and May S. Geddes; b Elgin 8.2.35
secy lit. side of *Journal* Glasg chamber of commerce 1958–60; prin teacher comm subj Brinnington s Stockport 1961–63; part-time nurs teacher Glasg from 1964
m Aber 17.8.60 Lewis A. Gunn MA 1957 *qv*

FINDLAY Neil Alexander *MA 1965
s of Thomas A. F. bank man. and Elspeth MacNeil; b Aber 1.7.42
Lond: teacher mus Beaufoy s 1968–69, head of mus Coopers' Company s 1969–73, head of mus Coopers' Company and Coborn s Upminster from 1973

FINDLAY Patricia Margaret MA 1966
d of James A. F. master butcher and Catherine Muldoon; b Selkirk 29.4.44
teacher: Engl Closeburn 1967–70, Engl/maths Melbourne, 1970, Toowoomba Aust 1970–72
m Dumfries 3.8.68 Christopher J. E. Newman BSc 1967 *qv*

FINDLAY Robert Campbell *MA 1962
s of Isaac M. F. taxi driver and Sarah J. Westland; b Aber 28.2.40
MA(Temple univ Philadelphia) 1967 PhD(Temple univ Phil) 1971
Philadelphia: staff psych ch hosp 1963–66, audiologist ch hosp 1966–68, audiol veteran's admin 1968–71; clin prof dept of speech univ of Pittsburgh from 1971
m Haddonfield NJ –.12.60 Judith G. Black MS(Drexel) lib d of Otis D. B. PhD(Ohio State univ) Haddon Hts NJ

FINDLAY Roderic Ian Garrioch *MA 1965
s of George I. G. F. MB ChB 1931 *qv*; b Ilford 21.12.41
Colston's s Bristol: teacher 1966–69, sen hist master from 1969

FINLAY Ian Chirnside BSc(eng) 1957 *1958

FINLAYSON Brenda Elizabeth BSc 1958
d of Eric C. F. MA 1926 *qv*; b Milltimber 27.7.37
teacher: Perth 1959–61, Reading 1961–64, Crediton from 1974
m Aber Wilson S. Mitchell livestock husb advis with ADAS s of A. Hunter M. Forfar

FINLAYSON Helen Rosemary BEd 1969 *MEd 1973
d of John F. fitter and Helen R. Findlay ch nurse; b Livingstonia Malawi 9.7.48
res asst educ surv and investig coll of educ Aber 1969–71; teacher Fr Rubislaw acad Aber 1972–75
m Aber 8.4.71 James H. Maycock BSc 1968 *qv*

FINLAYSON James *MA 1958
s of James F. master baker and Elsie Ogston embroiderer; b Stonehaven 28.3.36
educ off.: Sekondi Ghana 1959–61, Mbale Uganda 1961–71, Mackay Aust 1971–74; Toowoomba Aust from 1974
m(2) 14.8.67 Barbara Verest, Heeze Holland

FINLAYSON John *MA 1957
s of James F. master baker and Elsie Ogston embroiderer; b Aber 23.2.35
PhD(Cantab) 1962
res fell. Liv 1960–62; Canada: lect McG univ 1962–64; asst assoc prof Queen's univ Kingston from 1964
m Kingston Ont 4.8.67 Francien R. Mantin BA(Queen's univ) lib d of Joseph L. M.

FINLAYSON John Duncan MA 1969

FINNIE Helen Milne *MA 1968
b Banffsh 25.10.44
PhD(Edin) 1975
parliamentary res off. House of Commons Lond from 1974

FINNIE Ivor McIntosh MA 1969
s of William F. stationmaster BR and Betty S. Wilson; b Keith 23.1.45
Dip Man. St(RGIT Aber) 1970
marketing trainee Rowntree York 1970–72; Aber: C. E. Heath & Co insur brokers 1972–74, man. dir Crown Park estate agents and other companies from 1974
m Aber 15.4.68 Frances M. Buchanan secy d of Albert B. Aber

FINNIE Oswald Copland MA 1969
s of James S. F. agr eng and Clara W. Copland; b Fraserburgh 4.7.48
app CA Aber 1969–72; CA comp acct Edin from 1973
m Aber 21.7.72 Irene M. Ritchie MA 1969 *qv*

FINNIE William Wilson BEd 1970

FISH Melvin Raymond BSc(for) 1970 *MEd 1972
s of Joe F. fitter and Stella Caswell; b Bradford 26.12.47
teacher biol Prince Henry's g s Otley from 1972
m Bradford 19.8.72 Jean L. Wilson physioth d of Maurice W. Bradford

FISHER Peter McLaren MB ChB 1969 ᶜMD 1976
s of James F. laundry prop. and Elizabeth F. McDonald MA(Edin) teacher; b Aberfeldy 24.4.44
MRCOG 1976

FISHER Stanley Finlayson *MA 1965
s of Stanley P. F. lab and Frances B. Tosh fish worker; b Fraserburgh 6.12.42
indust trg off. Manc 1965–67; teacher: Stonehaven 1968–73, Aber 1973–76; blaster, oil-rig worker 1976–77; gen contr from 1977
m Stockport 13.7.68 Joan C. Wolstenholme MA 1973 soc worker d of Tom W. Stockport; marr diss 1976

FISHER Stuart Timothy BSc(eng) 1970
s of Leonard R. F. BSc(Lond) marine zool and Jean I. Elliott; b Chelmsford 2.8.48
Costain civ eng: jun eng Lond, Reading 1970–71, seconded to J. D. & D. M. Watson High Wycombe 1971–73, asst eng Birkenhead 1973–74; civ eng Transport and Road res lab des and site eng Crowthorne 1974–76; proj eng J. D. & D. M. Watson High Wycombe from 1976

FITCH Peter James BSc(for) 1965
s of James H. F. acct and Doris C. V. Langley; b Carshalton 22.12.43
Malawi: asst conserv for. Mzimba 1965–70, acting sen asst cons for. Limbe 1970–71; for. man. Accra Ghana 1971–75; man. Tilhill For. (Scotland) from 1976
m Aber 12.9.68 Helen M. Gibb d of James A. G. Aber

FITCHIE Logan Rodney George BSc 1969
s of George F. army off., eng and Jean H. A. Webster;
b Edin 25.8.46
S Af: trainee quality controller Vereeniging 1970–72,
sen work stud. off. Lever Bros Boksburg 1972–74, work
study off. Stewarts & Lloyds Vereeniging from 1974
m Vereeniging 6.2.71 Kathleen P. Mathers BSc 1969 *qv*

FITZROY Felix Rudolph MSc 1961
BSc(Lond)

FLANAGAN Elizabeth MB ChB 1959
b Aber
DPM(Dub) 1963 FRCPS(Can) 1968 LMCC 1969
MSc(Harvard) 1978
h o, regist, sen regist Aber 1960–68; spec psychiat
Vancouver 1968; dir mental health centre Vancouver
1969–77; consult. psychiat mental health serv Brit
Columbia from 1978
m Luke

FLEMING Christopher Alexander *BSc(eng) 1970
s of Brian A. F. insur comp dist man. and Marguerite
G. Allingham; b Lond 14.8.48
grad eng consult. eng Lond 1970–72; site eng consult.
eng Port Victoria Seychelles 1972; asst eng consult. eng
Lond 1972–73, PhD stud. Rd'g from 1973
m Aber 17.7.70 Christeen Maclean BEd 1969 *qv*

FLEMING Eleanor Shearer *MA 1963

FLEMING Fiona Margaret MA 1969
m Moir

FLEMING Hamish Kirkpatrick MA 1962
s of William S. F. CA and Jean H. Kirkpatrick; b Aber
17.3.37
div course New Coll Edin 1961–64; C of S min: Barrhead
South ch 1966–72, St Marnock's ch Kilmarnock 1972–75,
St Mark's ch Aber from 1975
m Barrhead 20.6.67 Agnes Duncan nurse d of Robert
M. D. Barrhead

FLEMING Jean BSc 1957
d of John F. farm. and Isabella Paterson; b Aber
24.12.35
biochem: Bangour hosp 1957–58, ch hosp Glasg 1958–60;
res asst ch hosp Toronto 1960–61; biochem East gen
hosp Toronto 1961–63; res asst univ of Pittsburgh USA
1963–64; biochem Homestead hosp USA 1964–66
m Aber 23.7.63 Ronald Gibson BSc(eng)(Belf) soils eng
s of Charles G. Belf

FLEMING Joan Mairi MA 1967
d of John F. BSc(Glas) teacher and Murdina Macleod
youth hostel warden; b Dunoon 12.6.46
teacher: Kirkhill p s Aber 1968–72, Banchory p s 1972–74,
remed from 1974
m Ullapool 30.3.68 Michael D. Lowndes BSc(eng) 1966 *qv*

FLEMING John Leslie MA 1968 *1970
s of John S. F. shop owner and Helen Leslie; b Dufftown 24.9.47
O and M off. Gen Accident Insur Perth from 1970

FLEMING Kathleen MA 1964

FLEMING Kenneth MB ChB 1962
b N'cle-u-Tyne 10.7.38
DObstRCOG 1964
h o Shotley Bridge gen hosp 1962–63; Aber: h o obst
mat. hosp 1963–64, sen h o, regist med ARI 1964–66;

g p Broadstone from 1966
m Aber 10.7.62 Pamela A. Duthie MB ChB 1962 *qv*

FLEMING Mark Roger Patrick MA 1968
s of Roger J. C. F. timber merch and Judith A. Q.
Jackson; b Aber 11.5.47
CA 1972
app CA Edin 1968–72, CA Paris 1972–73; timber merch
Glasg from 1973

FLEMING Rosslyn Muriel BSc 1970
d of Roland M. F. comp dir and Muriel A. S. Watt
nurse; b Redruth 4.10.49
progr Dublin 1970–72; syst progr Lond 1972–74; progr
Buffalo NY 1975–76; syst progr Boston USA from 1976
m Aber 1.9.72 Peter M. Bradley BSc 1971 res scient s of
Hunter W. B. MA 1946 *qv*

FLEMMING Christopher John MB ChB 1968
s of Clifford F. F. BSc(Manc) schoolmaster and Mary
W. Monaghan schoolmistress; b Buxton 1.5.43
Royal Alexandra hosp Rhyl: h o 1968–69, sen h o paediat
1969; sen h o obst/gyn Gt Yarmouth 1969–70; g p Capel
St Mary from 1970
m Rickmansworth 4.5.68 Lynda Ruff BSc 1968 *qv*

FLETCHER Alan McKay *BSc(for) 1960 PhD 1963
s of Sylvester T. F. comm trav and Annie M. Cook
clerkess; b Aber 25.2.37
geneticist with for. comm res div Edin from 1963
m Aber 28.8.64 Isobel J. Ritchie clerkess d of William R.
Dunecht

FLETCHER David James *MA 1960
s of Harry F. bank man. and Hilda Wood; b Burnley
20.12.37
res asst McG univ Montreal 1960–61; edit. asst D. C.
Thomson Dun 1961–62; cartographic edit. Clarendon
Press Oxford 1962–66; publ and edit. Wm Blackwood
Edin 1966–76; co-dir/edit. *Blackwood's Magazine* from
1976
m Aber 25.8.62 Margaret M. Stoney MA 1961 *qv*

FLETCHER Jane Margaret *MA 1965
d of Randall J. F. lathe oper and Jessie S. A. Waugh
midwife; b Birm 31.3.42
BA(Lond) 1968 MA(Toronto Ont) 1969
prof dept of Engl, Ryerson poly inst Toronto from 1970
m Tor Ont 22.6.74 Stanley T. J. Isherwood BTh(Tor)
clergyman/teacher s of Thomas W. I. MTh(Oxon)

FLETCHER Joan MA 1968

FLETCHER Terrence Albert Claude BSc(eng) 1962
s of James A. F. headmaster and Beryl C. Bourne
teacher; b Georgetown Guyana 15.2.39
MSc(Columbus Ohio) 1969
asst eng Lond 1962–63; Georgetown: eng 1963–68, spec
eng 1970–72, consult. eng from 1972
m Georgetown 26.3.64 Greta Perreira secy

FLETT Alexander Paul MA 1967

FLETT Alistair Murray *BSc 1959 PhD 1964
s of George F. BSc 1928 *qv*; b Inv 29.9.37
M Inst P 1965 FRAS 1972 TD 1972
Aberd: res stud. nat phil 1959–62, asst 1962–64, lect from
1964
m Aber 16.9.61 Aileen E. Mackie MB ChB 1962 *qv*

FLETT Allan Munro BSc 1962

FLETT Douglas Stewart *BSc 1957 PhD 1960
s of George F. BSc 1928 *qv*; b Inv 3.6.36
sen phys chem Permutit Co. Lond 1960–62; scient off.
DSIR Warren Spring lab Stevenage 1962–64; exch scient
Nat Inst of Metall Johannesburg 1964–65; sen scient off.
Warren Spring lab Stevenage 1965–66, 1968–71; guest res
nat res inst for metals Tokyo 1967–68; visiting prof univ
of Waterloo Ontario 1971; prin scient off. Warren Spring
lab Stevenage from 1972
m Aber 6.5.68 Mitsuko Hirano BA(Tokyo) clerkess d of
Torijiro H. BA(econ)(Tokyo) Fukioka City Japan

FLETT Hazel Margaret Gibb   MA 1956
d of George S. F. harbour master and Isabel G. Paul
insur ag; b Findochty 15.4.35
LTCL 1960
teacher: Aber 1957–60, Geilenkirchen Germany 1960–62,
Wyton 1970–72, Bracknell 1973–75, dep head 1974–76,
asst head Edin from 1976
m Finningley 22.12.62 Anthony G. Box BSc(Lond) RAF
off. (pilot), secy Scot. council for health educ from 1978
s of Ernest R. B. Market Drayton

FLETT James Crichton Smith   MA 1963

FLETT Joan   BSc 1970
d of John F. marine eng RN, seine fishing boat skipper
and Christina G. Edwards; b Lossiemouth 10.10.49
computer progr NCB computer centre Cannock 1970–73;
teacher biol/gen sc Lornshill acad Alloa from 1974
m Lossiemouth 21.4.73 Philip Dyer BSc(Liv) computer
progr, teacher s of Andrew D. Worsley

FLETT Joan Reid   *BSc 1969
d of George R. F. BSc(for) 1933 *qv*; b Bathgate 26.8.47
res asst Unilever Bedford 1969–70; teacher: sc Bannockburn j s s 1970–71, biol Broxbourne 1972–74; NZ: trade-
mark searcher at patent attorneys Wellington 1974,
teacher biol Erskine coll Wellington 1974, Naenae coll
Lower Hutt 1975–76
m Hertford 24.12.73 Neil W. Hindley BSc(Nott) civ eng s
of William C. H. Lowton

FLOCKHART Mary Rattray   MA 1970 Dip Ed 1971
d of Ian F. sales rep and Nan Allan; b Aber 13.11.49
teacher hist Northfield acad Aber 1971–76
m Aber 27.7.73 Brian A. Anderson MA 1963 *qv*

FLOCKHART Nanette Jamieson   MB ChB 1968
d of Ian F. and Nan Allan; b Aber 10.8.44
h o ARI 1968–69; trainee g p Aber 1969–70; sen h o
psychiat Aber 1970–71; clin m o Aber c c 1971–73; part-
time g p Aber 1973–75; clin asst: gen med Edin 1976–77,
part time paediat Aber from 1978
m Aber 19.8.69 Richard W. Davidson-Lamb MB ChB
1968 *qv*

FLORENCE Alexander Farquhar   *MA 1957
dist off. col serv Zambia
d Lusaka Zambia 31.3.63 *AUR* XL 207

FLORENCE Anne McKenzie   MB ChB 1962
d of Alexander A. F. police off., gen merch and Annie
G. A. Mitchell MA 1931 *qv*; b Aber 12.11.38
FFARCS 1966 (Nuffield Prize)
h o: Woodend hosp Aber, Victoria hosp Keighley,
paediat Edin 1962–63; sen h o anaest: Edin 1963–65,
Broadgreen hosp Liv 1965–66, regist 1966–67; res fell.
surg Liv 1967–68, sen regist paediat anaest 1968–69;
consult. anaest Liv reg cardio-thor unit from 1969, clin
lect Liv from 1969

FLORENCE Elizabeth May   MA 1959
d of George F. insur off. and Elizabeth T. Smith
teacher dom sc; b Aber 16.2.38
teacher maths/sc Mackie acad Stonehaven 1960–64
m Aber 1.10.64 Herbert D. Hay oil comp exec s of
William H. Pitcaple

FLORENCE Margaret Maitland   MA 1960
d of Kenneth S. F. law acct and Isabella L. Thomson; b
Aber 19.7.38
RGN(ARI) 1964 CMB(Aber)
staff nurse ARI 1964–67; Lond: private nursing 1968–70;
nurse Harley St clin 1970–71
m Lond 20.11.71 Salim H. Macki BSc(Moscow) petr eng,
min plenipotentiary Sultanate of Oman s of Hassan Y. M.
Muscat

FLORENCE Mary Isabel   BSc 1970
d of Alexander A. F. policeman, shopkeeper and Annie
G. A. Mitchell MA 1931 *qv*; b Braemar 1.12.47
geol Vancouver 1970–71 and 1973; part-time office work
Tungsten NWT Canada from 1974
m Vancouver 7.5.71 Nigel G. Cawthorn BSc 1970 *qv*

FLORY Flora Ann   MA 1966
d of Reid F. pharm and Sybil M. Lefleur tel; b Agra
India 16.5.45
teacher Summerhill s s Aber 1967–68
m Huntly 17.8.67 Alexander S. Milne BSc(eng) 1967 *qv*

FLUX John Etheridge Cormack   *BSc 1957 PhD 1962
s of Ronald C. F. BSc(eng)(Lond) civ eng and Charlotte
S. Cormack; b Maymyo Burma 20.12.34
scient with ecology div NZ DSIR Lower Hutt NZ from
1960, NZ nat res fell. Nairobi Kenya 1967–68
m Aber 30.7.58 Margaret M. West BSc 1956 *qv*

FOAD Roger John Michael   *MA 1969
s of John E. F. bank off. and Eileen M. Smeeton insur
ag; b Tendring 23.7.45
immigration off. Heathrow airport from 1971
m St Albans 17.2.73 Rosalind A. Carpenter nurse, civ
serv d of Alfred D. C. St Albans

FOGG Arnold George   PhD 1961
s of Richard F. cemetery regist/parks supt and Edith
Balmer; b Radcliffe 6.12.35
BSc(Lond) 1958 ARTCS(Salf) 1958
Loughborough coll of adv tech, Loughborough univ:
asst lect inorg chem/sub warden 1961–64, lect 1964–66,
lect analytical chem 1966–76, sen lect from 1976
m Aber 20.8.60 Joyce M. Carson MA 1960 *qv*

FOGG Lance Trevor   *BSc(eng) 1967

FOLEY Terence   *BSc 1968 PhD 1972
s of Michael F. RAF, antique dealer and Muriel
Yellowlees; b Selkirk 6.4.44
res fell. Imp Coll Lond from 1971

FONG Weng Cheong   MSc 1965
ARCFT

FOOT Janet Zoë   PhD 1969
d of Arthur S. F. MSc(R'dg) res scient and Dorothy
M. H. Irvine NDD; b Reading 7.7.46
BSc(R'dg) 1962 MAgrSc(Melb) 1965
scient with hill-farming res organis Edin from 1969;
visiting res fell. univ Melb s of agr Aust 1974–75

FOOTE Robert Lewis   MA 1970
s of Robert F. F. acct and Dorothy L. Forbes secy;

b Aber 5.3.42
teacher Engl Arbroath h s 1971–75; lect Engl Aber coll of commerce from 1975

FORBES Alan David   ***BSc 1956**

FORBES Alan George   **LLB 1965**

FORBES Alan Ritchie   ***MA 1956**
 s of James R. F. marine eng and Charlotte D. Kemp MA 1923 *qv*; b Edin 26.11.33
PhD(Otago) 1970
sen clin psych Crichton royal hosp Dumfries 1960–64; NZ: lect psych med Otago univ Dunedin 1964–67, lect, sen lect psych Otago univ 1967–75, prof psych Victoria univ Wellington from 1975, visiting prof Manc 1979
m Aber 7.8.58 Alison F. McCaskill teacher d of Francis W. McC. MA(Otago) Keith

FORBES Alexander   ***MA 1959**
 s of Alexander F. MA 1928 *qv*; b Lond 22.6.36
AInstLang(Madrid) 1957
teacher: Fr/Span Eastwood h s Glasg 1960–66, Harrison coll Bridgetown Barbados 1966–69; head Skinner comm coll Castries St Lucia 1969–71; teacher: guid Eastwood h s Glasg 1971–72, Internat s Singapore from 1972
m Aber 22.7.61 Moira Fraser teacher d of George F. Aber

FORBES Andrew King   **MA 1970**
 s of Frank M. F. MA 1947 *qv*; b Aber 7.5.49
police constable Lond from 1971

FORBES Anne   **MA 1960**
 d of John F. area off. Aber c c and Mary W. Duncan shop asst; b Keith 2.3.39
Dip Sec (Scot. coll of comm Glasg) 1961
p a to TU gen secy Lond 1961–65; admin asst MRC unit Edin 1965–67; pers secy to man. dir Lincs 1967–68; secy MRC med sociol unit Aberd 1968–74, admin asst from 1974

FORBES Atholl Roderick   **MB ChB 1966**
 s of Thomas F. bank teller and Annie H. A. Spain restaurateur b Aber 17.5.43
FRARCS 1970
h o Aber gen hosps 1966–67; sen h o, regist anaest united Sheff hosps 1967–71; sen regist anaest and tut. Hammersmith hosp Lond 1971–73; asst prof anaest univ Calif San Francisco from 1973
m Aber 2.8.67 Esmé Maxwell MA 1967 *qv*

FORBES Charles Leslie   **MB ChB 1957**
 s of Charles B. F. MA 1922 *qv*; b Aber 18.10.33
g p Aber from 1960
m Aber 10.3.58 Margaret M. Buthlay pharm d of Alexander B. Aber

FORBES David   ***MA 1965 Dip Ed 1969**
 s of Alexander F. MA 1928 *qv*; b Torphins 5.9.43
MA(Lond) 1968
exchange schol univ of Kansas USA 1965–66; trainee insp of taxes Aber 1966–67; teacher: Fraserburgh acad 1969–71, prin hist Golspie h s 1971–73; lect soc stud. Craigie coll of educ Ayr from 1973
m Aber 8.7.70 Marlene Chrystal tracer/draughtsman d of Robert C. Aber

FORBES Dorothy Kathleen   ***BSc 1966**
 m Richard W. Marriott BSc 1966 *qv*

FORBES Elspeth Ann   ***MA 1958**
 d of John S. F. (Bart) DSO R Eng farm. and Agnes J. Farquharson; b Bangalore S India 10.3.37

teacher mus: Aber 1959–60, Glasg 1960–61, Aber from 1969
m Glasg 1960 George M. Hardie comm artist/teacher art s of John H. Aber

FORBES Emily Coutts   **MB ChB 1969**
 d of William S. F. master draper and Rosanna Kelman dressmaker; b Insch 9.7.45
h o: med Greenock, gyn Aber 1969–70; sen h o Kingseat hosp 1970–71, regist 1971–72; regist Ross Clin Aber 1972–73, part time from 1973
m Aber 14.7.71 Peter G. Hamilton MB ChB 1972 g p s of Joseph S. H. MB ChB 1937 *qv*

FORBES Eric Alexander   **BSc(eng) 1966**
 s of John F. comp dir and Margaret J. Neish; b Forres 1.10.46
MICE 1974 CEng 1973
Aber: asst civ and struct eng (consult.) 1966–69, prin eng (consult.) 1969–72, dev eng (contr) from 1972
m Aber 22.9.66 Marguarite Urquhart d of Joseph U. Aber

FORBES Eric Simon   ***BSc 1956**

FORBES Gordon Gorrod   ***BSc 1961**

FORBES Hilda Mary   **MA 1969**
 d of Alexander F. agr worker and Isobella D. Simpson clerkess; b Insch 11.3.48
teacher geog/mod stud. Gordon s Huntly from 1970
m Aber 4.4.72 Brian T. Christie plant hire sales rep s of Thomas C. Banchory

FORBES Iain   **MB ChB 1968**
 s of John D. R. F. airline pilot and Elizabeth M. Macdonald; b Inv 23.10.42
LMCC 1976
h o Aber 1968–69; g p: Lond 1969–71, Lethbridge Canada 1971–76, Parksville Canada from 1976
m Lond 4.3.71 Anna D'Agostino DA teacher d of Louis D'A. Banchory

FORBES Iain Macdonald   **BD 1964**
 s of Alexander F. bank man. and Margaret F. Macdonald; b Johnstone 16.12.39
BSc(Edin) 1961
missionary/min Presb ch of E Africa Kiene settlement scheme Kenya 1966–69; home organis secy C of S overseas council Edin 1970–74; min Benbecula from 1975
m Aber 19.8.64 Margaret R. Macartney midwife d of William M. M. MA(Edin) Aber

FORBES Isabel Christina   **MA 1970**
 m Shearer

FORBES James Carnegie   ***BSc 1969 PhD 1973**

FORBES Margaret Iris Stuart   **MA 1964**
 d of Alexander A. F. shop man. and Margaret C. Miller; b Grantown-on-Spey 9.7.43
teacher: Pitcairn p s Almondbank 1965–67, Causewayend p s Aber 1967–69
m Grantown-on-Spey 12.4.69 Harry D. McIntosh pharm s of Donald S. McI. Turriff

FORBES Margaret Xanthe Patricia   **MB ChB 1964**
 d of John S. F. (Bart) DSO R Eng farm. and Agnes J. Farquharson; b Lond 25.3.40
h o RACH, Perth RI 1964–65; regist rheumatology ARI/ assoc hosps Aber from 1972
m Aber 16.7.64 James C. Petrie MB ChB 1964 *qv*

FORBES Michael Davidson   MA 1964
d of Harry C. F. fish merch and Jessie Massie; b Aber 14.4.43
Aber: CA 1969, man. acct Claben from 1970
m Limerick 21.6.72 Una M. Tobin nurse d of Michael T. Limerick

FORBES Patricia   MA 1963
m Ait-Hocine

FORBES Patrick Beaumont   MB ChB 1956
s of William F. MA 1922 *qv* and Margaret P. Beaumont MA 1922 *qv*; b Aber 20.1.33
DObstRCOG 1967 FRACGP(Adel) 1972
h o Woodend hosp Aber 1956–57; m o BMH RAMC Singapore 1959–61; h o mat. hosp Aber 1961–62; Terrace clin Naracoorte S Aust 1962–72; dep dir accident dept Box Hill hosp Melbourne 1973–75; g p Blackburn Melbourne from 1975
m Aber 10.4.58 Dorothy E. Mortimer MA 1953 *qv*

FORBES Ruairidh Alasdair   LLB 1970

FORBES Shona Macpherson   *BSc 1968 MSc 1970

FORBES Sinclair Thomson   *BSc 1960 MSc 1963

FORBES William Lithgow   BSc(agr) 1961

FORDYCE Andrew Patrick   LLB 1967
s of James P. F. lab/gen handyman and Minnie A. Thomson shop asst; b Unst 31.1.47
law app Aber 1967–69; Dumbarton: leg. asst 1969–71; ptnr firm of solic from 1971

FORDYCE Dennis Alexander   *BSc 1966
s of James A. F. foreman ganger with bldg contr and Patricia Chittenden; b Ashford Kent 7.5.44
MSc(CNAA)(Teesside poly) 1977
res phys Head, Wrightson & Co Thornaby 1966–69; elect. eng ICI petrochem div Billingham 1969–77; dev man. Electronic Serv (Manc) Middlesbrough from 1977
m Aber 24.6.67 Isobel Fife d of George F. MA 1930 *qv*

FORDYCE George   *BSc(eng) 1969
s of James F. farm worker and Violet Simpson; b Turriff 26.3.47
dynamicist Westland helicopters Yeovil 1969–70, des eng C. A. Parsons & Co N'cle-u-Tyne 1970–72; res eng CEGB Harrogate from 1972

FORDYCE James   *BSc(agr) 1969 MSc 1970
s of James F. farm worker and Violet Simpson; b Turriff 18.4.46
anim nutrit Dorset from 1974
m Turriff 28.11.70 Annie H. Pirie

FORDYCE Jane Elizabeth   MB ChB 1969
d of Gordon E. F. MB ChB 1932 *qv*; b Nunthorpe 5.2.45
DObstRCOG 1971 MRCOG 1974
h o ARI, Woodend hosp Aber 1969–70; h o and sen h o Elizabeth Garrett Anderson univ coll hosp Lond 1970–71; Glasg: sen h o Sick Ch hosp 1971–72, Vict Inf Samaritan hosp 1972–73, regist Queen Mother's hosp, Western I 1973–74; consult. genito-urinary med Glasg from 1974
m Middlesbrough 19.5.73 David T. Roberts MB ChB (Glas) dermat s of Trevor R. Llanelli

FORDYCE John   MA 1969 Dip Ed 1970
s of James F. farm worker and Violet Simpson; b Rathen 2.10.48
teacher Fr Woodmill h s Dunfermline from 1970

FORDYCE William Cairns   *BSc 1961 *MEd 1967
s of Lawrence S. F. indust chem and Euphemia D. Cairns; b Peterculter 27.8.39
res stud. Aberd 1961–63; teacher Aber: Northfield s, AGS 1964–66, prin teacher Albyn s for girls 1966–68; asst dir of educ: Dumfriessh 1968–69, Aberdeensh 1969–72, dep dir 1972–75; dep dir of educ (sec) Grampian reg Aber from 1975; member advis council on misuse of drugs from 1975
m Aber 13.7.61 Aileen M. Allan teacher d of Robert F. A. Aber

FORMAN Andrew   LLB 1966
s of William F. trawl skipper and Helen S. Bruce; b Peterhead 16.1.42
law app Edmonds & Ledingham advoc Aber 1966–68; asst Donaldson & Henderson solic Nairn 1968–70, ptnr from 1970
m Aber 13.9.68 Agnes M. Lindsay clerkess/typist d of James L. Aber

FORMAN Jennifer Constance   *MA 1968
m Kershaw

FORMAN Robert   BSc(eng) 1964
s of Robert F. driving instr and Margaret Duncan; b Peterhead 29.3.40
Aber: civ eng city eng's off. 1964–67, contr man. Lewis Middleton 1967–72, dir Hunter Construction (Abdn) from 1972
m Aber 2.8.63 Norma Robertson teacher d of George R. Cruden Bay

FORNA Mohamed Sorie   MB ChB 1962
d Freetown Sierra Leone 19.7.75 *AUR* XLVI 326

FORREST Alan Iain   *MA 1967
s of John F. MA(Edin) schoolmaster and Anne L. T. Miller; b Aber 19.12.45
DPhil(Oxon) 1971
res stud. hist Balliol coll Oxon 1967–70; lect hist Stir 1970–73; lect Fr hist Manc from 1974

FORREST Irene Joan   *MA 1969
m Oldman

FORREST James Tyson   BSc(for) 1958

FORREST Jean   PhD 1962
d of William F. eng and May E. M. Bennett; b Derby 29.8.26
BSc(Lond) 1951 MSc(Lond) 1957
tut. asst Queen's univ Belf 1963–66; tut./counsellor OU N Wales 1970–74; teacher John Bright's s Llandudno from 1974
m Aber 17.10.59 David W. M. Lindsay PhD 1962 *qv*

FORREST Robert Fowlie   *BSc 1965
s of Alexander C. F. butcher/bacon curer and Chrissiebell Fowlie tel; b Dyce 8.11.43
teacher: Onthank j s s Kilmarnock 1966–68, geog Cumnock acad 1968–70, prin geog Auchinleck acad from 1970
m Inv 1968 Sheena M. Macdonald teacher d of Donald J. M. Inv

FORREST Rosalind Elizabeth   *MA 1968

FORRESTER Alexander Robert   PhD 1963 DSc 1977
s of Robert J. F. eng and Mary Gavin; b Fife 14.11.35
BSc(H-W) 1959 MRIC 1963
Aberd: asst lect chem 1963–65, lect 1965–77, sen lect from 1977

m Stirling 4.4.61 Myrna R. Doull d of James D. BSc(Glas) Stirling

FORRESTER William MSc 1967

FORSYTH Audrey Thoirs MA 1968
  m Gibb

FORSYTH David James Cameron *MA 1962
  s of Joseph S. M. F. bank man. and Margaret J. Smith; b Elgin 4.6.40
Thomas Jefferson fell. univ of Virginia USA 1962–63; lect: econ Strath 1963–64, pol econ Aberd 1964–65, econ Strath 1965–71; visiting sen acad univ of Ghana Legon (Accra) 1971–72; sen lect Livingstone Inst Strath from 1973
m Stockport 7.9.69 Gillian A. Dunmore teacher d of H. Eric D. Poynton

FORSYTH David Rae *BSc 1968
  s of William A. F. sales rep and Gladys M. Rae secy; b Ellon 12.12.45
pilot plant man. St Helen's Lancs 1968–74; works man. Bolton from 1974
m Lancs 1968 Jane E. Anderson training advis d of Arthur A. Marple

FORSYTH Hope Glen Milne MB ChB 1967
  d of James P. F. MA(Glas) HMCIS and Joan W. McCulley; b Edin 10.2.44
DCH(Lond) 1969
h o: Aber hosps 1967–68, St Mary's hosp Lond 1969–70; m o Save the Children Fund Nigeria 1970–71; regist: paediat Reading 1971–73, Nuffield centre Lond 1974; m o commun health serv Edin from 1974
m Aber 24.6.74 John A. Sills MA(Cantab) med pract s of Oliver A. S. MRCS MRCP(Lond) Cambridge

FORSYTH Janet Marian Gibb *MA 1969
  d of James P. F. MA(Glas) HMCIS and Joan W. McCulley; b Edin 4.6.47
res asst sociol Aberd 1970–72
m Aber 28.12.70 David K. Yule MA 1969 qv

FORSYTH Kathleen Margaret MA 1969
  d of Charles F. lorry driver and Margaret C. M. Cumming; b Fyvie 24.3.48
teacher p dept Turriff acad from 1973
m Oldmeldrum 6.12.69 Albert M. Reid distill. worker/maltman s of Albert R. Oldmeldrum

FORSYTH Keith Wilson BSc(agr) 1959
  b Broughty Ferry 1.6.36
m Dumfries 20.12.69 Irene Hannay

FORSYTH Margaret Elizabeth MA 1965
  m Booth

FORTUNE James Duncan MSc 1967
  s of James A. F. livestock grader and Jessie G. F. Duncan; b Glasg 25.12.43
BSc(Glas) 1966 ARIC 1968 PhD(Glas) 1969
ICI polymer rheology(Glas) 1969–71; teacher chem Jordanhill s Glasg 1971–72, prin chem 1972–75; chem Strath reg council publ analyst's lab from 1975
m Glasg 15.6.74 Helen M. McLaverty BSc(Glas) teacher d of William McL. Glasg

FOSTER Charles Vincent *MA 1968

FOSTER David Deas MA 1970

FOSTER Jonathan Charles Brian *MA 1959
  s of John F. MA(Edin) schoolmaster, clergyman and Barbara Ludwig LRAM teacher mus; b Aber 2.5.38
BPhil(Oxon) 1964
Liv: asst lect Latin 1962–65, lect from 1965
external examiner Humanity Aberd 1973–76
m Aber 17.8.68 Joan A. Reid ARMCM teacher mus d of Graham R. Aber

FOSTER Joseph Redman MA 1959

FOSTER Thomas *BSc(eng) 1969

FOSTER William Warwick PhD 1957
  BSc(Lond)

FOTHERINGHAM Laurence James *MA 1958
  s of James F. traffic supt and Annie King; b Stonehaven 25.7.36
ICI: marketing exec fibres div Harrogate 1958–67, marketing exec Zürich from 1967

FOUBISTER Alan John *BSc 1966

FOUBISTER Glenn MC ChB 1959
  s of Thomas F. photographer and Elsie E. Glennie civ serv; b Peterhead 20.1.35
MRCPE 1967
h o Aber 1959–60; nat serv rmo Catterick garrison 1960–62; jun m o Lincoln, Oxford, Lond, Cambridge 1962–70; consult. geriat Reading from 1970
m Oviedo Spain 18.8.69 Adela A. Garcia stud. d of Antonio G. Rodriguez Oviedo

FOWDAR Youssouf MA 1966

FOWLE Heather Beatrice Antoinette White MA 1968

FOWLER Alexander Campbell *MA 1970

FOWLER Alexander Phillips MB ChB 1969
  s of Alexander P. F. and Helen M. Henderson; b Aber 25.9.44
h o ARI 1969–70; temp lect path. Aberd 1970–72; g p Aber 1972, Benbecula 1972–76, Fraserburgh from 1976
m New Pitsligo 20.7.70 Helen M. Watson MB ChB 1970 qv

FOWLER Frank Macpherson *MA 1957
  s of William A. F. bank man. and Jen C. Macpherson; b Inv 16.6.35
DPhil(Oxon) 1962
lect Ger: Aberd 1960–65, univ of Kent Canterbury 1965–66, King's Coll Lond 1967–70; Queen Mary coll Lond: reader Ger 1970–77, prof/head Ger dept from 1977

FOWLER Muriel Margaret BEd 1969
  d of David F. butchery man., off. clerk and Catherine M. T. Ross teacher; b Aber 26.3.47
teacher maths: Northfield acad Aber 1969–71, part time Kincorth acad 1976
m Aber 19.7.69 Raymond Inkster MA 1967 qv

FOWLER Ruth Kathleen MA 1967 Dip Ed 1968
  d of Neil H. C. F. foreman and Ruth A. Taylor; b Torphins 3.5.46
teacher hist/Engl/mod stud. Queen Anne h s Dunfermline 1968–72
m Torphins 1.8.70 Alan J. Campion prof and tech off. M o D s of John E. C. Rosyth

FOWLES Nathan Briggs *MA 1966
  s of Lloyd W. F. BA(Bowdion) teacher and Jane Briggs

BA(Wellesley); b Hartford Conn USA 13.6.43
reporter/feature writer *Evening Express* Aber 1967–69;
reporter *Evening Gazette* Middlesbrough 1969–74; Aber:
reporter *Scottish Daily News* from 1974; freelance labour/
indust reporter from 1975

FOWLIE Alan Smollett   MA 1963 LLB 1966
s of Harold F. driving instr and Helen Smollett nurse;
b Aber 8.3.42
syst analyst Sheepbridge Eng, Chesterfield 1967–68;
Sheff: admin asst, sen admin asst 1968–72; asst regist
Hull univ from 1972
m Coventry 17.4.71 Elizabeth A. Freeman BA(Sheff) soc
worker/univ admin d of Kenneth H. F. MB ChB(Birm)
Coventry

FOWLIE Douglas Gibb   MB ChB 1970
s of Herbert F. MB ChB 1930 *qv*(III); b Aber 16.1.46
MRCPsych 1976
h o ARI, City hosp Aber 1970–71; unit m o RAF
Marham, Benson 1971–72; trainee psychiat/spec in neuro-
psychiat Wroughton 1972–76, sen spec neuro-psychiat
Wegberg W Ger from 1976
m Aber 5.8.71 Marjory A. R. Donaldson MB ChB 1970 *qv*

FOWLIE Jean   MA 1961 Dip Ed 1962
m Fisher

FOWLIE John Leslie   BSc(agr) 1968

FOWLIE Peter   BSc(agr) 1970
s of John F. farm. and Elizabeth M. Leslie; b New
Deer 24.3.49
farm. New Deer from 1970
m Aber 31.8.72 Janet M. Mitchell teacher d of T. C. M.
Fordoun

FOWLIE Sylvia Mary   BEd 1969
d of Henry F. lorry driver and Mary B. Gow dom help;
b Aber 17.5.48
teacher Aber 1969–72 and from 1975
m Aber 11.7.69 Charles F. Western DA draughtsman/
off. man. s of Charles A. W. Aber

FOX Evelyn Yeats   *MA 1969
d of William F. F. bank man. and Eleanor MacLean;
b Buckie 7.4.47
ALA 1973
asst lib coll of educ Sheff 1970–71; Sheff univ: res worker
s of lib 1971–73, sen lib asst from 1973
m Aber 17.7.69 Peter D. A. Boyd BSc 1970 *qv*

FOX Richard Henry   *BSc(eng) 1970
s of Walter H. F. dep gen sales man. and Ethel A.
Ambrose; b Birm 20.7.48
MSc(Birm)
asst eng/hydrologist Robert H. Cuthbertson & Ptnrs
Edin from 1972

FRAME Ian Andrew   *MA 1966
s of John W. F. policeman, JP and Barbara M. Grant;
b Glasg 2.2.37
teacher geog Portobello 1967–70; prin geog: Tranent
1970–76, Lossiemouth from 1976
m Dunbar 18.10.75 Ann M. Ballantine DA art teacher d
of Stanley B. B. LRCPSE Dunbar

FRANCIS Heather Rosamund Dalton   MSc 1969
BSc(Rhodes)

FRANKLIN Andrew   *BSc 1966
s of Andrew F. carpenter and Elspeth I. Pirie; b Aber

19.5.44
marine biol: scient off., sen scient off. MÀFF fisheries
lab Burnham-on-Crouch from 1967
m Maldon 8.4.72 Frances L. Hyam marine biol d of
Laurence F. H. Burnham-on-Crouch

FRANKS David Robert   MB ChB 1970
                                            Dip Psychother 1977
s of Martin L. F. BSc(Brist) consult. civ eng and
Gwendolen M. B. Bailey BA(Cantab); b N'cle-u-Tyne
3.4.46
h o ARI 1970–71; sen h o, regist, sen regist Royal
Cornhill hosps Aber 1971–77; visiting prof psychiat
Creighton univ Omaha Nebraska USA from 1977
m Aber 9.8.69 Mary J. G. Bailey BSc 1969 *qv*

FRASER Alan William   *BSc 1969 PhD 1973
s of Alexander F. master butcher and Ann Ettles MA
1940 *qv*; b Forres 12.3.47
teacher chem: Buckhaven h s 1972–73, Kirkcaldy h s from
1973
m Forres 2.4.70 Edith H. Johnston MA 1969 *qv*

FRASER Alasdair James   BSc(agr) 1956
s of John F. farm. and Annabella M. Howar; b Inv
14.7.32
lect agr Melton Mowbray 1956–58; asst insp DAFS:
Inv 1959–66, Perth 1966–72; insp DAFS Stirling from
1972
m Groby 5.9.59 Averill Tweddle farm secy d of Joseph T.
Groby

FRASER Alastair Ian   BSc(for) 1957

FRASER Alexander   *MA 1968 Dip Ed 1969
d 15.3.71 *AUR* XLIV 216

FRASER Alexander Leslie   MA 1963
s of Alexander F. master draper and Maggie Chalmers
MA 1926 *qv*; b Ellon 6.10.41
pers off. Colvilles Bellshill 1963–65; youth employ. off.
Aber educ dept 1965–66; group trg off. Peterhead and
dist group trg assoc Peterhead 1966–68; trg consult.
indust trg serv Scot. 1968–71; trg man. Hiram Walker &
Sons Dumbarton 1971–74; manpower and trg off. Scot.
Eng Employers' Assoc from 1974
m Crail 26.9.64 Kathleen B. Riach teacher d of Ronald
A. C. R. Crail

FRASER Alison   *MA 1965
d of Alexander S. F. MA 1930 *qv*; b Aber 27.7.42
teacher: Lond 1966–67, Aber 1967–73
m Aber 25.11.73 John C. E. Allan driving instr s of
J. A. O. A. Aber

FRASER Angela   MA 1967
d of Orville L. P. F. comp secy and Williamina M.
Menzies; b Aber 6.2.46
teacher: Fr St Ive's St Ives 1968–71; i/c Fr St Colette's s
Cambridge 1971–75
m Aber 23.7.70 Roger W. Barlow MA(Cantab) lect s of
Vernon H. B. Rottingdean

FRASER Angus Charles   MA 1967

FRASER Archibald Kerr   *BSc 1968 PhD 1971
s of Alexander M. F. dist off. for. comm and Agnes
Kerr; b Stromeferry 27.8.46
teacher: sc Wishaw 1971–72, asst prin biol Peterhead
1972–74, prin biol Inv from 1974
m Inv 10.7.71 Kathleen M. Stewart MA 1970 *qv*

FRASER Arthur George   *BSc 1968
    s of Oliver G. L. F. bank cashier and Violet L. Persse
hosp sister; b Golspie 26.1.47
geophys computer Tripoli 1968–70; computer progr:
Lond 1970–75, IBM Portsmouth 1975, Teheran 1975–
77, IBM Portsmouth 1977, Singapore 1977–78, Amsterdam from 1978

FRASER Arthur Gilmour   *BSc 1959
    s of William G. F. trav, bookbinder and Mary B.
Wyllie; b Aber 1.8.37
PhD(Birm) 1964 FGS(Lond) 1965 Polar medal 1967
geol Brit antarctic surv: Antarctic penin Antarctica 1960–
62, Birm 1962–64; res fell. geol Brit antarctic surv Birm
1964–67; lect geol Hull from 1967
m Dyke 20.10.62 Marion E. Snedden MA 1957 qv

FRASER Audrey   MA 1967
    d of Francis R. F. journalist/shopkeeper and Christina
M. Fraser RAF (traffic control), hotelier; b Beauly 21.6.38
teacher: Lochaber h s Fort William 1968–70, Tomintoul
1970–76, Forres acad 1977
m Inv 6.12.58 Eric Farquhar MA 1959 qv; marr diss 1977

FRASER Callum   BSc 1968
    s of William A. F. bus driver and Mary M. Thain;
b Aber 14.7.47
syst progr: E Midlands gas board Leic 1969–73, Brit gas
corp Hinckley from 1973
m Banchory 3.6.72 Christina S. Sinclair MA 1969 qv

FRASER Callum George   *BSc 1966 PhD 1969
    s of Douglas C. F. eng and Bessie M. Johnstone secy;
b Dun 3.1.45
res fell. NRC Ottawa 1969–70; lect chem path. Aberd
from 1970
m Cults Aber 8.9.72 Stella Sim lib d of John S. Cults

FRASER Carole   MA 1970
    m Henderson

FRASER Christian Davidson   MA 1957
    d of Donald F. gamekeeper and Annie Davidson; b
Fordoun 3.11.36
Dip Soc St(Edin) 1958
child care off. Aber 1959–62
m Aber 3.11.62 Malcolm A. B. Christie MA 1958 qv

FRASER Christine Mary   *MA 1968
    d of Cuthbert W. F. policeman, soldier and Catherine
A. Crabb MA 1938 qv; b Fraserburgh 10.4.47
teacher Chapelpark s Forfar from 1973
m Forfar 8.6.68 Iain L. N. Dodds arch. draughtsman s of
John D.; marr diss 1977

FRASER Colin Hugh Thomson   *MA 1958
    s of Thomas F. gas worker/trade union off. and
Margaret R. Barron; b Aber 17.7.37
PhD(Brist) 1975
res stud. inst of psychiat Lond 1958–60; res assoc and
lect psych MIT Cambridge Mass 1960–63; res assoc
lab of soc relations Harvard 1962–63; lect: psych Exe
1963–64, soc psych Birm 1965–68, Brist 1968–74, Cantab
from 1975, fell. Churchill coll from 1976
m Birm 14.7.65 Carole M. Bell occup therap

FRASER Cristabel   MB ChB 1963
    d of Farquhar F. sales rep and Isabel R. Mackenzie
saleswoman; b Inv 13.9.38
DCH(Glas) 1969
h o RACH, City hosp Aber 1964–65; sen h o: clin path.
paediat ch hosp Birm 1965–67, Worcester 1967–68, regist

paediat Inv 1968–71; med asst mental subnormality Inv
1971–72 and from 1975
m Inv 11.7.70 William A. Macdonald bldg man. s of
Charles D. M. Inv

FRASER Derek James   *MA 1969

FRASER Doreen Catherine   MA 1965
    d of Angus F. master draper and Jean Y. S. Barclay;
b Aber 1.10.44
teacher Aber 1966–70
m Aber 7.8.68 John Hutcheson CA s of Herbert C. H.
MA 1929 qv

FRASER Douglas Morrison   *BSc 1961 Dip Ed 1962
    s of George F. BR foreman and Jane Balneaves; b Aber
17.1.39
teacher geog Turriff 1962–68, prin geog Wick 1968–74,
Peterhead from 1974
m Aber 21.7.62 Rhoda A. E. Connon MA 1961 qv

FRASER Elspeth Gray Mackenzie   MA 1963
    d of Arthur F. farm worker, crofter and Elizabeth G.
Gray farm worker; b Inv 2.9.41
teacher Engl/geog Banchory acad 1964–70, Tarradale
p s 1971
m Nairn 30.7.70 John G. C. Weir BSc(agr) 1966 qv
husb d 22.3.74

FRASER Evelyn Mairi   MA 1966
    d of William A. F. bank off. and Emma A. Matheson
stewardess MN; b Balmacara 28.5.44
teacher p s Aber 1967–74
m Aber William D. Topp offshore oper s of Alexander T.
Aber

FRASER Finlay Christopher   MA 1963

FRASER Frederick John Thomas   BSc(eng) 1956

FRASER George Balneaves   *BSc 1967 MSc 1971
    s of George F. BR workshop superv and Jane Balneaves;
b Inverurie 3.2.45
electronics eng: computers Borehamwood 1967–68, Dun
1968–69, commun Portsmouth 1970–73, servomechanisms
Winchester from 1973
m Carnoustie 26.6.68 Catherine M. Clerk civ serv exec
off. d of Archibald C. LDS(Glas) Carnoustie

FRASER George Leslie   *BSc 1956
    s of George F. MA 1917 qv; b Aber 21.6.31
prospecting geol Greenland, Fr Guinea 1956–58; educ
rep Scot., Ireland 1958–61; prin teacher geog: Ross h s
Tranent 1962–67, English s Nicosia Cyprus 1967–71,
Penicuik 1971–72; comp dir Broxburn from 1972
m Aber 11.3.59 Frances C. Gordon MA 1957 qv

FRASER George Lewis   BSc(eng) 1961
    s of George M. F. market gardener and Jean S. Mowat;
b Aber 10.9.40
grad app Mullard Radio Valve Co Mitcham 1961–63;
Foxboro-Yoxall Redhill: lect customer trg centre 1963–65,
digital support eng Foxboro USA 1965–67, digital syst eng
Redhill 1967–69, application spec (consult.) 1969–72, syst
spec 1972–76, man. market dev and sales support from
1976
m Aber 11.7.61 Rosemary P. Lowe secy

FRASER Gordon Alister   *BSc 1957

FRASER Gordon Davidson   MB ChB 1956
    s of Robert J. F. farm. and Anne M. Fyfe; b Strichen

6.11.32
MRCGP 1973
h o ARI 1956–57; surg lt RN 1957–60; jun h m o ARI
1960–61; g p Aber from 1961
m Aber 10.8.59 Doreen A. Henderson physioth d of
Alexander H. Aber

FRASER Graeme William   *MA 1966 Dip Ed 1967

FRASER Graham Campbell MB ChB 1956
 s of Eion R. F. bank man. and Dorothy S. Williams;
b Inv 20.6.32
Keith gold medal surg
FRCSE 1962 FRCS(Lond) 1962 LMCC 1967 FRCS(C)
1972 FACS 1973 Member Brit Pacif & Canadian Assoc
of Paediat Surgeons, American paediat surg assoc
h o ARI 1956–57: surg lt RN 1957–60, surg regist ARI
1960–63 resid asst surg HSC Lond 1963–67; consult.
paediat surg Vancouver from 1967
m Cupar 15.8.58 Rae S. McCallum museum lect d of
Thomas McC. Cupar

FRASER Helen Mary Alexander   MA 1970
 d of Robert S. F. MA 1925 *qv* and Kathleen M. B.
Smith teacher; b Aber 8.6.49
Dip St Godric's secy coll Lond 1971
p a Lond: Ibbs & Tillett concert ag 1971–74, Phonogram
1974–75; mus asst Scot. Arts Council Edin from 1975

FRASER Hugh Ross   MA 1966
 s of Ian S. F. BSc(eng)(Glas) eng and Elizabeth W.
Miller teacher; b Bath 2.9.43
journalist, staff reporter West Kirby 1967–68, Blackburn
1968, *Glasgow Herald* Edin 1968–69; San Francisco: asst,
man. edit. *Western Construction* 1969–72, edit. *California
Industry* 1972–73; *World Wood Magazine:* European edit.
Brussels 1973–74, edit. Brussels 1974–77, Harrow from
1977
m Edin 26.7.67 Victoria A. Greenamyer

FRASER Ian Charles   MA 1957
 s of John O. F. motor mech/driver bldg comp and
Edith I. Richardson; b Nairn 20.4.36
educ measurement univ of Melbourne 1963; Melbourne
s of printing and graphic arts 1965–67
teacher Bryans s Midlothian 1958–61; Aust: teacher
Taroona h s and Glenorchy state s Hobart Tasmania
1961–62; Aust council for educ res Melbourne: res off.
test dev div 1962–64, off. i/c publ div 1964–73; exec asst
to man. dir Thomas Nelson & Sons (spec proj) Sunbury
Mddx from 1973
m Newton-Grange 1.4.61 Elizabeth M. Sinclair secy d of
John B. S. Easthouses

FRASER Ian McGregor   *MA 1969

FRASER Ian Simon   MA 1957
 s of John F. foreman joiner and Joan B. Copeland;
b Aber 22.2.34
MTAI
Aber: clerk (bldg) 1957–59, trav salesman 1959–66; dept
man. trav Glasg 1966–72, branch man. Carlisle 1972–77,
Aber from 1977
m Aber 7.3.59 Ethel M. Reid d of Arthur R. Aber

FRASER, Irene   MA 1968
 m Rose

FRASER James Duncan Mackenzie   LLB 1963

FRASER James Kenny   *BSc(eng) 1967

FRASER Jean Elspet Elrick   *MA 1969
 m Smith

FRASER John   MA 1956 LLB 1958

FRASER John   *MA 1959
 s of John F. retail man. and Jessamine E. Mathieson;
b Inv 8.8.36
teacher Harris acad Dun 1960–66; prin teacher Buckie
1966–72; asst head Peterhead 1972–73, dep rector 1973–
75; rector Mackie acad Stonehaven from 1975
m Monifieth 29.7.63 Judith H. Procter bank clerk d of
Harold L. P. Dun

FRASER John   MA 1970
 s of John F. eng and Mary Bell; b Inv 30.7.47
Dip Soc Sc(S'ton) 1971 MSc(S'ton) 1972
lect govt: Fareham tech coll 1971–75, Isleworth poly
1975–76, sen lect Hounslow borough coll from 1976
m Aber 4.9.69 Pamela Brown teacher

FRASER John George Nevill   MA 1958 ^cLLB 1961
 s of James F. F. MA 1914 *qv*; b Aber 31.1.38
admin asst: St And 1962–64, Edin 1964–67; Aberd: asst
secy (acad) 1967–74, sen asst secy 1974–76, clerk to univ
court from 1976
m Aber 9.1.65 Helen F. Simpson teacher d of Vincent
J. A. S. Peterculter

FRASER John Watson   MA 1968 Dip Ed 1969
 s of John F. painter and Elsie Watson; b Forres 19.7.24
teacher: Allan Glen's s Glasg 1969–72; asst prin maths:
Banff acad 1972–73, Auchenharvie acad Stevenston from
1973
m Forres 19.5.51 Margaret E. Morrison

FRASER John William   PhD 1969
 s of John F. sen dep c clerk Ross and Cromarty and
Christina I. Jack; b Dingwall 9.10.18
BEM MA(Edin) 1947 BD(Edin) 1950 JP 1972
C of S min: Banchory Ternan 1950–59, Farnell and
Kinnell 1959–67, Farnell only from 1967
m Edin 12.7.50 Mary E. Purves bank clerk d of Robert
W. P. Edin

FRASER Julia Macphedran   MA 1970
 d of Alexander R. F. foreman steel erector and Margaret M. Breingan hotel man.; b Grantown-on-Spey
6.2.48
teacher Clydebank h s 1971–72; cler post hydro elect.
Aber 1972–73; teacher Millburn s s Inv 1973–77
m Nethybridge 26.8.72 James Macadie quantity surv s of
William B. M. Newtonmore

FRASER Julie   *MA 1963
 m Morris

FRASER Kathryn Joan   *MA 1969
 d of James W. F. army off. and Agnes Ford group VS
organis; b Edin 21.4.46
MSc(Strath) 1973 Dip Adult Educ(Glas) 1977 ABPsS
1976
VSO Akure Nigeria 1970; educ psych, sen educ psych
Fern Tower Glasg 1974–78; res fell. Stir from 1978

FRASER Leila Anne   BSc 1970
 d of William G. F. farm man. and Jean G. Milne hosp
records off., hosp interviewer; b Aber 17.7.49
teacher biol Aber from 1971
m Aber 18.9.70 Andrew G. Littlejohn banker s of
William L. Inverurie

FRASER Leslie William   *MA 1969

FRASER Lorna Kinkaid   MB ChB 1962
d of Andrew K. F. butcher and Elizabeth M. Munro; b Aber 20.8.39
h o Aber: City hosp, Woodend hosp, Ross clinic 1962–64, g p Aber 1964–68; part-time asst g p Colchester from 1968; m o FPA Wittam, Tiptree from 1971; clin asst venereology Colchester from 1973
m Aber 18.6.68 Gilbert Gray secy NE Essex commun health council s of Gilbert G. Ardersier

FRASER Margaret   MA 1966 Dip Ed 1967
d of Kenneth W. F. HM insp of taxes and Isabella Low; b Coventry 3.4.45
teacher Ferryhill p s Aber 1967–71
m Aber 29.7.67 Alexander G. Garrow BSc 1966 *qv*

FRASER Margaret Baird   *MA 1961
d of Alexander S. F. MA 1930 *qv*; b Aber 14.8.39
teacher geog Perth acad 1962–69, spec asst 1969; conserv off. Countryside Comm for Scot. Perth from 1969

FRASER Margaret Ethel   *BSc 1967 Dip Ed 1968
d of James D. F. ophth optician and Maureen A. Anderson dom sc teacher; b Aber 4.2.45
teacher sc Parkstone s Poole 1967–70
m Aber 27.7.68 Peter M. MacIntosh BSc 1966 *qv*

FRASER Margaret McBoyle   MA 1960
m Glass

FRASER Moira   MA 1961
d of John A. F. shoemaker, postman, filling stat owner and Helen J. Reid shop asst; b Ellon 8.10.40
teacher: Cowie Stirlingsh 1962–65, Peterhead 1965–66, East Plean 1966–67
m Inverurie 23.9.67 Frederick B. Brown, Dip Agr (WOSCA) distrib superv (lamps & elect. appliances) s of Frederick B. B. Giffnock

FRASER Norman   MA 1969 Dip Ed 1970

FRASER Norman Alexander   LLB 1970

FRASER Pamela Margaret   MA 1966
d of Henry F. MA 1927 *qv*; b Aber 8.2.45
Aber: teacher Hazlehead p s 1967–71, class singing in p s from 1971

FRASER Peter John   *BSc 1970 PhD 1973
s of William E. F. MA 1935 *qv* and Margaret R. G. Ferguson MA 1938 *qv*; b Aber 7.11.48
fell. res schol biol sc ANU Canberra 1973–75; lect zool Aberd from 1975
m Largo 31.10.72 Patricia C. G. Rodger BSc(Dund) teacher d of Hamish G. R. DA(Edin) Lundin Links

FRASER Peter Kerr   *MA 1969
s of Alexander S. F. MA 1930 *qv*; b Aber 20.5.47
syst analyst/progr Grampian Computer Facilities Aber 1970–73, syst and progr man. from 1974

FRASER Robert Alan   *MA 1968

FRASER Robert Dunbar   *MA 1967
s of Alexander W. F. FRIAS auctioneer and Christina Dunbar bus. woman; b Dingwall 30.11.45
teacher geog Dumfries 1968–71; prin geog: Thornhill 1971–73, Dumfries from 1974
m Aber 15.7.71 Annice P. Blackmore MA 1971 teacher d of Donald I. B. Tibbermore

FRASER Robin Charles   MB ChB 1963 MD 1974
s of Albert G. F. motor/agr ag and Jean Beaton; b Aber 15.2.40
MRCGP 1969 FRCGP 1974
h o ARI, RACH 1963–65; trainee g p Aber 1965; m o stud. health serv Aberd 1965–66; g p Leicester from 1966; part time lect g p, dept of commun health Leic from 1975
m Aber 20.7.64 Mary E. S. McAfee DA d of Andrew M. McA. BSc(Belf) Inv

FRASER Ronald   MB ChB 1970
s of Ronald F. farm. and Annie McCrae; b Inv 20.1.47
LMCC 1973
h o ARI, Woodend hosp Aber 1970–71; sen h o ARI 1971–72; asst m o Grand Bank Newfoundland 1972; private practice fam med Sault Ste Marie Ont from 1972
m Aber 14.1.71 Janette W. McCrone nurse d of James McC. Tighnabruaich

FRASER Rosemary Angela   MA 1970
m McAndrew

FRASER Sheila Maclennan   *MA 1966
d of Alexander F. master mariner and Muriel Harker; b Aber 9.5.44
teacher Engl Albyn s for girls Aber 1967–70
m Aber 24.7.68 Robin F. Scott MB ChB 1966 *qv*

FRASER Sheila Margaret   *BSc 1967
m Russell

FRASER Sheila Mary   *MA 1970
d of William R. D. F. LDS(St And) dent. surg and Mary Macdonald; b Aber 12.7.47
secy/p a to group trg off. Davidson Radcliffe group (paper indust) Bucksburn 1971–72; secy to head of Scott Sutherland School of Arch. Aber 1972–73; secy/p a to man. dir Borrell Sayward Burles Lond 1973–74; secy to dir and chief exec Bayer UK Richmond from 1974
m Aber 14.6.72 Colin G. E. Scotland LLB 1969 *qv*; separated 1978

FRASER Stephanie Ann   MA 1970
d of Campbell C. F. warehouseman and Florence M. Sayers factory man.; b Northampton 5.2.50
Aber: cler asst city police 1970–72, pers asst Impulse Publ 1973, teacher Sunnybank p s from 1974

FRASER Sylvia Rebecca   BEd 1970
d of Duncan F. livestock insp dept agr and Catherine Macdonald; b Drumnadrochit 7.12.48
teacher: Inv 1970–71, Drumnadrochit 1971–74
m Drumnadrochit 2.10.71 Kenneth J. Fraser mech s of Donald F. Glenurquhart

FRASER Wendy Paul   MA 1970
d of Orville L. P. F. comp dir and Wilhelmina Menzies; b Aber 3.3.49
teacher King James's s Knaresborough from 1971
m Aber 30.5.75 Thomas R. Evans MA 1970 *qv*

FRASER William Alistair   *BSc 1968
s of Roderick A. F. civ serv and Winifred G. F. Bristow teacher; b Dufftown 30.10.46
MPhil(Yale) 1972 PhD(Yale) 1972
res asst Imp Coll Lond 1972–73; radio pharm quality control Radiochem Centre Amersham from 1973
m New Haven Connecticut 27.12.69 Lynn C. Repsis BA(Colorado) reprod biol d of Anthony C. R. BA (Illinois) Denver

FRASER William Edward   MA 1957
s of William G. F. bookbinder and Mary B. Wyllie;

115

GRADUATES 1956-1970

b Aber 16.5.35
BD(Lond) 1959
Bapt ch min: St Andrews 1960–64, Crown Terrace ch
Aber 1964–76, Victoria Place, Paisley from 1976
m Aber 1.8.59 Lillian J. House midwife d of Charles
T. H. Aber

FRASER William Hamish   *MA 1963
s of Hugh R. R. F. loom turner and Charlotte Milne
shopkeeper; b Keith 30.6.41
DPhil(Sus) 1967
res stud. Sus 1963–66; lect Strath from 1966
m Aber 4.9.65 Helen Tuach MA 1965 *qv*

FRASER William Ross   BSc 1966 MB ChB 1972
s of William A. F. lorry driver and Beatrice J. Ross
nurse; b Aber 27.7.44
h o ARI 1972–73; sen h o g p vocational trg unit 1973–
76; g p Aber from 1977
m Aber 17.7.73 Alison F. A. Knox MA 1970 *qv*

FRATER Susan Elizabeth   MA 1967
m Sawyer

FRAZER George Bernard   MB ChB 1963
s of Theophilus E. F. elect. and Martha M. Peters;
b Freetown Sierra Leone 28.12.33
MRCOG 1968 FWACS
Aber mat. hosp: regist 1966–68, temp sen regist 1968–69;
sen spec obst/gyn Freetown from 1969
m Lond 1961 Frances A. Bowen-Wright teacher d of
Frank B-W. Freetown

FRAZER Kirsty Margaret   MA 1969
d of Frederick Y. F. BSc 1928 *qv*; b Manc 4.2.47
trainee surv Aber 1970–71; teacher Fintry 1973–78
m Skene 28.8.71 John A. M. Cuthbert LL B 1968 *qv*

FRAZER William Murdoch   BSc 1969
s of Robert F. eng and Agnes J. Murdoch; b Falkirk
28.12.46
RAF: trainee pilot 1969–72, pilot(Hercules) Cyprus
1972–75, careers off. N'cle-u-Tyne 1975–78, pilot
(Andover) flight checking from 1978
m Falkirk 15.2.69 Margaret E. Ivory teacher home econ
d of George I. Falkirk

FREELAND William John Walker   MB ChB 1958

FREEMAN Alan George   MSc 1960 PhD 1962
s of George R. F. bldr and Rose J. Bowater; b Birm
9.2.35
BSc(Birm) 1959
fell. Birkbeck coll Lond 1962–64; sen lect Victoria univ
Wellington NZ from 1964
m Wythall 4.4.63 Annie Drever SRN d of John D. Papa
Westray

FRENCH Catherine McLean   MA 1969
m Murray

FRENCH Chris (Christopher Norman)   *MA 1966
s of Frederick G. F. bldr and Kathleen R. D. Norman;
b Letchworth 8.11.42
PhD(Exe) 1975 ABPsS MBCS
res stud. Exe 1966–70; lect exper psych optics dept
UMIST from 1970
m Aber 18.2.65 Ann Watson BSc 1966 *qv*; marr diss
29.4.75

FRENCH Elspeth May   MA 1968
d of William G. F. MB ChB 1942 *qv*; b Aber 10.5.47
teacher: Glenbervie s Drumlithie 1969–71, Milltimber

p s Aber 1971–74, Croyland inf s Wellingborough 1974–
75
m Aber 14.7.71 Peter J. Gordon MB ChB 1971 s of Ian
G. BSc 1929 *qv*

FRENCH John Richard Joseph   BSc(for) 1963
b Wallasey 7.11.35
MSc(Syd) 1968 PhD(Oregon) 1972
for. off. Millicent S Aust 1963–64; res off. entomol
Sydney 1964–69, Corvallis USA 1969–72; res scient
entomol CSIRO Melbourne from 1972

FREW Euan Malcolm Shearer   MB ChB 1968
s of John F. M. F. MB ChB(Glas) consult. orthop surg
and Elizabeth M. Jack; b Aber 11.10.44
FRCSE 1973
h o City hosp Aber, ARI 1968–69; Garden fell. path.
Aberd 1969–70; sen h o surg rotation scheme Western
Inf Glasg 1970–72, regist from 1973; surg Royal Alexandra
Inf Paisley 1972–73
m Glasg 6.1.72 Anne I. Macdiarmid nurs sister d of
Malcolm M. Glasg

FRITH Susan Agnes   MA 1969
d of William F. acct clerk and Phyllis Rogerson; b
Northwich 17.9.47
teacher lang: Kentwood boys' s s Penge 1969–71, South
Norwood h s Lond 1971–73; head Ger dept Grange s
Stockton-on-Tees from 1973
m Northwich 18.12.71 Ian K. Alexander BSc 1969 *qv*

FRONDIGOUN Edward Miller   MA 1962

FROST Yvonne Marie   MA 1970
d of William H. F. master baker and Grace M. Gove
tel, typist; b Montrose 29.11.49
teacher: Engl Forfar acad 1971–74, asst prin Engl 1974–
76, Engl Oak Park h s Melbourne 1976–78; supply Engl
Wheathampstead h s from 1978
m Montrose 2.7.75 Vincent A. Arpino asst factory man
s of Vincent A. St Pauls Cray

FRYDMAN Anna   BSc 1967
d of Kaziemierz F. eng and Mattie H. Dowie comp
dir; b Nairn 9.12.45
MPhil(Lond) 1971 Dip Voc Guid(Kent coll for careers
serv) 1974
Lond: res asst MRC Hammersmith hosp and List inst
1967–72; asst secy royal inst of publ health and hyg
1972–73; careers off. ILEA 1973–74; careers advis PCL
from 1974
m Bolton 6.9.69 David M. Ewins acct s of William A. E.
Bolton

**FULLERTON Clare Elizabeth Oakes   *MA 1964
                                      PhD 1978**

FULLERTON Hance   BSc 1956
s of Robert F. fisherman and Jessie Smith; b Hamnavoe
6.12.34
Wiggins Teape: chem Stoneywood mill Aber 1959–63,
chem and asst paper prod. man. Fort William mill 1963–
67; prod. man. Caldwell paper mill Co Inverkeithing
1967–69; prod. man. Guardbridge Paper Co. 1969–72,
man. dir 1972–76; mill man. Wiggins Teape Stoneywood
mill Aber from 1976
m Aber 2.8.58 Jeannie R. Cowie MA 1956 *qv*

FULLERTON Michael John   *MA 1968

FULLERTON Robert Keith Ross   BSc(eng) 1967
s of Robert G. F. BSc 1924 *qv*; b Aber 12.1.46

CA 1971
sen acct Peat, Marwick, Mitchell & Co Paris/Lond
1971–73; man. Price, Waterhouse & Co Hong Kong
1974–75; group acct Swire Pacific Hong Kong from 1975

FULTON Anne Bradford Gray   MA 1969
d of James F. MA(Glas) teacher, headmaster and
Mary W. G. White; b Aber 31.3.48
Edin: computer progr 1969–73, sen progr 1973–77
m Aber 28.6.75 Ian G. Kirkpatrick BSc(Edin) syst des
(computers) s of John K. Edin

FURNELL James Rupert Gawayne   *MA 1968
s of Percy G. F. B Eng(Liv) elect eng and Margaret
K. A. Wray journalist; b Lond 20.2.46
Dip Clin Psych(Glas) 1970 ABPsS 1971 PhD(Stir) 1977
clin psych: Dumfries, Glasg 1968–70, RHSC Glasg 1970–
72; sen clin psych Stirling from 1972, hon lect Stir from
1978
m Glasg 14.9.74 Lesley A. Ross physioth d of John S. R.
Glasg

FURNESS Anthony John   *BSc 1969
s of Eric L. F. BSc(Lond) univ teacher and Enid B.
Bacon BA(Cantab); b Lond 31.10.46
teacher Lond 1970–72; Stockholm: TEFL univ 1972–73;
Engl St Erik's Folkhögskola from 1973
m Stockholm 15.6.73 Annika M. Erikson teacher d of
Karl E. Solna

FURNIVAL Colin Mitchell   MB ChB 1964
s of Ian M. F. acct and Martha R. Craik; b Edin
7.12.40
PhD(Leeds) 1971 FRCS 1972
h s ARI 1964–65; res asst physiol Leeds 1965–68; regist
surg univ hosp of Wales Cardiff 1968–72; lect surg Glas
1972–75; univ of Queensland Brisbane: sen lect surg
1975–79, reader in surg from 1979
m Aber 21.7.64 Isobel G. Souter MB ChB 1964 qv

FURRIE Brian Lawrie   MA 1963

FYDA Janina Cecilia Zofia   MA 1968
d of Charles J. F. eng/prop. garage and precision eng
comp and Jane D. King; b Ladybank 15.4.47
Aber coll of educ 1968–69
m Banff 22.3.69 John K. Walker bldg contr s of A. D. W.
Banff

FYFE Beryl   MA 1968
d of James F. clerk/stock controller and Rachel R.
Stephen; b Aber 12.12.46
teacher: geog Glenrothes 1969–73, Engl/geog Sultan
Omar Ali Saifuddin coll (sen), Bandar Seri Begawan,
Sultanate of Brunei from 1975
m Aber 16.8.69 Colin R. Mowat MA 1967 qv

FYFE Eric   *BSc(eng) 1970
s of Francis R. F. cashier/acct and Elizabeth R. Largue
clerkess; b Aber 17.2.48
electronic circuit des eng space div Hawker Siddeley
Dynamics Stevenage from 1970

FYFE Graham   *MA 1967
s of John B. F. test pilot/pilot RAF and Katherine G.
MacNab; b Frimley 14.6.37
teacher Kircudbright acad, Dalry s s, Castle Douglas h s
and assoc p s 1968–70; mus teacher Städtische Musik
und Singschule Heidelberg W Ger from 1971

FYFE Hans George Simpson   MA 1967
d 18.4.69 AUR XLIII 218

FYFE James Johnstone   MA 1957

FYFE John   *MA 1965
b Forfar 10.4.43
Dip Ed(univ of E Af) 1966
teacher: TEFL King's coll Budo Uganda 1966–71, Engl
St Joseph's coll Dumfries 1971–73, prin Engl Nairn acad
from 1973
m Sale 30.8.65 Susan M. Beckett

FYFE Lindsay Audrey   MA 1967
d of C. W. Kirkwood F. ophth optician and Audrey
H. Davidson tel oper; b Aber 14.5.46
teacher Airyhall p s Aber 1968–70
m Aber 16.6.67 Alexander I. Mitchell BSc 1972 res
biochem s of Alexander M. Kinellar

FYFE Ronald   MA 1960 MEd 1971
s of Francis R. F. acct/cashier and Elizabeth R. Largue
clerkess; b Aber 30.4.39
teacher: Northfield s s Aber 1960–62, Banchory acad
1963–66, Beechwood spec s Aber 1967–71; lect educ psych
Aber coll of educ 1971–76, sen lect from 1976
m Aber 20.3.63 Doris Kelman off. man. d of William K.
Aber

FYFFE Allen Frederick   *BSc 1968
s of Allen F. F. stereotyper and Charlotte Whyte;
b Dun 10.11.46
manual work 1968–69; teacher trg 1969–70; climbing
instr Glencoe 1970–71; outdoor pursuits instr Glenmore
Lodge Aviemore from 1971

FYSON Mary-Jean   MA 1966
d of Roger F. F. garage prop. and Winifred M. Heath
bookkeeper; b Dartford 15.8.42
secy Aber 1966–67; interviewer, man., pers off. employment ag Lond 1968–70; secy Guildford 1971; civ serv/
cler off. Eltham 1971–74; crown serv/exec off. Lond
1974–78; pers off. UBAF Bank Lond from 1978
m Eltham 24.9.66 Andrew M. Stewart MA 1965 qv; marr
diss 1.5.72

GACHARU Alex Micah   MSc 1970
BSc(agr)(E Af)

GACOKA Philip   MSc 1964
s of Ayub Githaiga farm. and Yunis Wambui farm.;
b Kenya 8.8.30
BSc(Lond) Makerere univ coll of E Africa 1957
Kenya: res off. Nairobi 1964–66; chief tech off., asst gen
man. Kenya tea dev auth 1967–74; gen man. nat irrigation board from 1974
m Kenya 1958 Damaris Njeri teacher d of James Kaberere,
Limuru

GADDIE John   MB ChB 1968 *MD 1975
s of John G. farm. and Elizabeth A. B. Wylie; b
Orkney Is 21.12.43
MRCP(UK) 1977
ARI: h o 1968–69, res fell. 1969–73, regist 1973–77,
sen regist respiratory med from 1977
m Aber 1.9.65 Patricia J. R. Kynoch d of James D. K.
MB ChB 1937 qv

GAFFNEY James Stewart Pettigrew   BEd 1969
s of Charles G. fisherman and Christina Pettigrew;
b Dunbar 26.2.47
teacher Engl Hawick 1969–73; asst prin Engl Elgin from
1973
m Aber 3.4.67 Elizabeth A. Cooney teacher d of George
M. C. MA(Edin) Invergordon

GAFFRON Wendy Jennifer *MA 1969
d of David J. G. MA 1948 *qv*; b Aber 26.12.46
teacher Engl: Vale of Leven acad Alexandria 1970–72,
Rothesay acad from 1972
m Aber –.8.70 Robin J. Dow MA 1970 *qv*

GAIT Peter William Dixon   MA 1966

GALBRAITH James Donald *MA 1967 MLitt 1970
s of James A. G. police off. and Ann G. Selbie; b Aber
26.4.43
res asst Scot Record Off. Edin from 1970

GALBRAITH Philip Andrew *BSc 1968 Dip Ed 1969
s of Andrew P. G. BSc(Edin) teacher and Dorothy
Hetherington; b Edin 8.7.46
teacher geog: The Marr Coll, Troon 1969–71, prin geog
from 1971; author *Geography in Action* I and II 1978
m Aber 1.8.69 Dorothy I. Liddle MA 1969 *qv*

GALL Barbara   MA 1960
d of John G. farm. and Mary I. E. Strath; b Ellon
17.11.38
teacher classics: Woodmill h s Dunfermline 1961–65;
Berwicksh h s Duns 1965–66; Dun: part time: Craigie
h s 1971–75, Dun h s from 1975
m Aber 19.7.65 George S. Collie MA 1961 *qv*

GALL Elsie Mary   MA 1962
d of Frank R. G. farm. and Elsie H. Booth; b Ellon
22.7.41
teacher Engl/hist/geog Crimond s Lonmay 1963–68;
relief p s teacher Monifieth area 1969–70
m Aber 29.8.68 Bruce T. Welch seed merch s of Robert
M. W. Monifieth

GALL Ian James   BSc 1959

GALL Kathleen Mary   MA 1966
d of Alexander N. G. insur ag and Agnes A. Smith; b
Aber 2.4.43
m Aber 28.12.64 Kenneth M. Hutcheon syst progr s of
Albert R. H.

GALL Marjory Anne   BSc 1966
d of Alexander N. G. insur ag and Agnes A. Smith
clerkess, shop asst; b Aber 21.7.45
teacher various short-term posts Edin 1967–74
m Aber 22.11.67 Peter M. Craig BSc 1967 *qv*

GALLACHER Jane Mitchell   MA 1969
m Ross

GALLICKER Patrick   MA 1961
s of Rose Gallicker textile worker; b Aber 3.11.39
Aber: teacher Engl Kaimhill j s s 1963–65, asst prin Engl
Northfield acad from 1965
marr diss 1979

GALLIE Nicholas Ian *MA 1969

GALLIE Roger Douglas *MA 1964
s of Douglas G. comp dir and Catherine Y. Stephen;
b Glasg 7.5.42
MLitt(Cantab) 1971
asst lect phil Leic 1966–69, lect from 1969
m Blandford Camp 12.8.72 Alison J. A. Lees asst dom
bursar d of Albert J. L. Blandford Forum

GALLOWAY Ann   MA 1960

GALLOWAY David Brian   MB ChB 1964
s of Harold W. G. bus man and Evelyn A. Johnston

teacher; b Aber 6.3.40
MRCP(Lond) 1971 DObstRCOG(Lond) 1966 FPA 1966
h o ARI 1964–65, Glasg Bellshill mat. hosp, Birm ch
hosp 1965–66; sen h o, regist Lond teaching hosps 1966–
70; regist, sen regist, lect Aber hosps/Aberd from 1970
m Lond 25.3.72 Diana E. Marshall MCSP(Lond)
physioth d of William M. Lond

GALLOWAY Richard Melvin *BSc(eng) 1967
m Aber 27.10.69 Patricia A. Howard MA 1968 *qv*

GAMBLIN Alfred Joseph   MB ChB 1969

GAMBLIN Sandra Anne   MB ChB 1968
d of Richard E. G. civ eng and Bessie I. Gray clerkess/
bookkeeper; b Aber 15.3.44
h o RACH, Woodend hosp Aber 1968–69; sen h o cas
dept RACH 1969–71; g p Aber from 1971
m Aber 28.12.68 William E. McIntosh MA 1965 *qv*

GAMMACK Evaline Anne Joan   MB ChB 1960

GAMMACK George Cooper   MA 1968

GAMMIE Agnes Davidson Ogg   MA 1956
d of Norman T. G. farm. and Elizabeth Davidson;
b Bieldside 20.2.36
teacher Kelowna BC Canada 1958–60; prin Fr Palmerston Ontario 1963–73; farm. Harriston Ont from 1973
m Ontario 1.2.58 George Strachan farm. s of John S.

GAMMIE Eileen Marie Cameron   MA 1968
m(1) Ledgard
(2) Tagart

GAMMIE Leslie *BSc 1968

GAMMIE Linda Rosemary *MA 1965

GAMMIE Michael John *MA 1968
MA(Glas)

GAMMIE Peter Alexander   MA 1969 *MEd 1972
s of James W. G. farm. and Flora M. McGibbon nurse;
b Aber 8.10.48
teacher Engl: Dumfries h s 1970–71, Arbroath acad
1971–72, Alloa acad 1972–75; asst prin Engl Alva acad
from 1975
m Rabastens, Tarn, France 1.8.73 Maryse C. M. Marty
BA(Stir) d of Jean R. B. M. Rabastens

GANSON Christine Jean *MA 1967

GANSON John Robert *BSc 1969

GARD John Alan   PhD 1956
s of John S. F. G. BSc(Durh) chem and Eliza Ainsley
teacher; b Washington, Co Durh 29.4.19
BSc(Durh) 1940 ARIC
res chem: Turners Asbestos Cement Co Manc 1940–45,
Washington Chem Co Durh 1945–49, Ferodo Chapel-en-
le-Frith 1949–52; Aberd: electron microscopist 1952–60,
res lect from 1960
m Washington Co Durh 3.9.45 Millicent Radford secy d
of Francis E. R. Heworth

GARDEN Brian   BSc 1965
s of Frank G. shipwright and Isabella B. Birnie;
b Aber 23.5.43
TD
Poole: progr 1966–69, syst analyst 1969–70; lect M o D
from 1970
m Cromarty 28.3.67 Catriona H. Thomson staff nurse
d of William T. Cromarty

GARDEN Eric Rae   BSc(eng) 1966

GARDEN Gordon Henderson   MA 1968
s of Alexander G. eng and Mary J. Towler; b Aber
3.7.23
teacher: tech coll Aber 1969-71, Beechwood s Aber from
1971
m Aber 1948 Ann Cardno nurse d of Alexander C. Aber

GARDEN Ian Allardyce   MB ChB 1958
s of Norman W. G. pattern maker, trans insp and Ruth
A. M. Allardyce tailoress; b Aber 6.2.33
h o Stracathro hosp Brechin 1959–60; m o RAMC
Singapore 1960–63; regist anaest Bridge of Earn, Perth
R.I. 1963–64; g p Kirkby-in-Ashfield from 1964
m Inv 7.5.60 Mary M. MacGruer SRN d of Thomas L.
MacG. Fort Augustus

GARDEN Isabel Stewart   MA 1962
m Gault

GARDEN Leonora   *BSc 1962
d of Charles P. G. decorator/signwriter and Williamina
M. Scroggie; b Aber 31.10.39
teacher: maths/geog Newtyle 1963–64, maths Ayr from
1972
m Aber 9.7.63 Hector R. Mackenzie MA 1956 *qv*

GARDEN Margaret Ann Flett   MA 1956
d of George G. capt MN and Mary A. Geddes;
b Portgordon 26.2.35
teacher: Fr/Engl Rhynie 1957–58, Fr Turriff 1958–59
m Aber 22.7.59 James W. Mackay master draper s of
James B. M. Buckie

GARDEN Thomas Buchan   MB ChB 1966
s of John A. M. G. capt MN and Martha Leadbetter;
b Stonehaven 11.3.42
h o Aber hosps 1966–68; g p: Elgin 1968–70, Rugeley
from 1970
m Aber 6.7.65 Alice T. Paterson teacher d of James H. P.
Fraserburgh

GARDINER Alexander Quentin   MB ChB 1962
PhD 1967
s of James M. G. OBE BCom 1926 *qv* and Nell W.
Sutherland SRN; b Aber 5.5.35
DPM(Edin) 1966 MRCPsych 1971
h o ARI, Ross Clin 1962–64; MRC jun res fell. psych
Aberd 1964–67; sen regist psych Royal Cornhill hosp
Aber 1967–70; fell. commun psych Yale univ s of med
New Haven, Conn 1970–71; consult. psychiat Grampian
area health board/clin sen lect mental health Aberd from
1971
m Aber 18.7.62 Rhoda M. Primrose teacher d of Norman
P. Aber

GARDINER Austen James Sutherland   MB ChB 1960
MD 1974
s of James M. G. OBE B Com 1926 *qv* and Nell W.
Sutherland SRN; b Great Bently 27.1.34
Anderson Medal 1960 MRCP(Lond) 1966 MRCPE 1977
FRCPE 1979
h o ARI 1960–61; res fell. surg, Garden res fell. med
Aberd 1962–64; regist ARI 1964–68; res fell. McG
Montreal 1968–70; sen regist, lect med Aberd 1970–76;
phys i/c Monklands hosp Lanarksh from 1976
m Edin 27.7.61 Ruth Duncan SRN d of Leslie D.
MA(Edin) Edin

GARDINER Celia Hamilton   MA 1963
d of George H. G., BSc(Leeds) teacher, farm. and

Diana M. Plummer; b Northallerton 25.5.42
ALA(Strath) 1964
sen lib asst Leeds univ med s 1964–66; dep lib Trinity and
All Saints coll of educ Leeds 1966–70; lib Friarage hosp
Northallerton from 1970

GARDINER James Kenneth   MEd 1956
s of John G. and Margaret Fothergill; b Dunfermline
5.8.27
MA(Edin) 1949 Dip Ed(Edin) 1952
dep dir educ Fife from 1967
m Edin 1.9.54 Ellenor Currie MA(Edin) teacher d of
James C. Edin

GARDINER Robert Hamilton Baxter   BSc 1970
s of Thomas B. G. MB ChB(Glas) surg and Elizabeth
H. Graham time and motion study observer; b Lennoxtown 8.10.48
chartering asst Glasg from 1970
m Omagh 5.8.71 Audrey E. Coote BSc 1970 *qv*

GARDINER William   *BSc 1960 MSc 1962

GARDNER Allan Buchanan   *MA 1958
s of Alexander B. G. arch.; b Aber 24.10.37
BA(Oxon) LL B(Cantab)
official Internat Labour Off. Geneva from 1964

GARDNER Elizabeth Charlotte Johnston   MA 1969
d of William G. G. G. master butcher and Louie E. J.
Reid MA(Glas) teacher; b Falkirk 29.11.48
staff man. Marks & Spencer S E England from 1969
m Falkirk 9.8.72 John D. Stevenson BA(Manc poly)
insur broker, stud. s of John C. S. Romford

GARDNER Hugh MacCallum   *BSc 1962

GARDNER Jean Stewart   BSc 1969

GARLAND Michael Stanley Ogilvie   MA 1959
Dip Ed 1960
s of Andrew W. G. comm trav and Barbara M. Moir
teacher; b Dun 7.9.38
teacher Andover s Brechin 1961–64; serv children's educ
auth: teacher Verden W Ger 1964–65, head p s Jever
W Ger 1965–70; head p sect. AFCENT internat s
Brunssum Holland 1970–72; head St Christopher's s
Rheindahlen W Ger 1972–76; head of Langlands s
Forfar from 1976
m Farnell 6.10.61 Margaret M. McNicol teacher d of
Duncan McN. Farnell

GARRIOCH David Brown   BMedBiol 1968
MB ChB 1971 MD 1978
s of David B. G. MA(Edin) headmaster and Millicent
Milne teacher; b New Aberdour 12.3.47
MRCOG 1977
h o ARI 1971–72; Lond: obst h o Hackney 1972–73;
regist obst/gyn St Thomas hosp and Pembury hosp Kent
1974–77, lect obst/gyn St Thomas med s from 1974

GARRIOCH Joanna Mackenzie   MB ChB 1966
d of James G. clerk of works and Margaret Mackenzie
nurse; b Kirkwall 13.5.42
h o Woodend hosp Aber 1966–67
m Aber 17.12.65 James A. Wattie MB ChB 1960 *qv*

GARRIOCK Kathleen Winifred Margaret   MA 1969
d of Francis G. man. dir and Barbara M. Jamieson;
b Lerwick 6.8.47
teacher Engl Landskrona Sweden 1970–71; teacher Fr:
Lerwick 1971, Nairn 1971–74; timber manager's asst

Lerwick from 1974
m Aber 2.4.73 William H. Stubbings asst man.

GARRISON Frederick Charles   *MEd 1970

GARROW Alexander George   *BSc 1966 Dip Ed 1967
 s of Alexander J. G. stone mason/blder and Elizabeth
M. Burnett; b Elgin 22.8.44
teacher phys AGS 1967–72; prin phys Kincorth acad
from 1972
m Aber 29.7.67 Margaret Fraser MA 1966 *qv*

GARROW Alice Anne   BSc 1959
 d of Frederick C. G. MA 1926 *qv* and Alice W. Stewart
BSc 1928 *qv*; b Aber 8.2.39
teacher sc: sen h s Dartmouth Nova Scotia 1960–61,
Sutton 1961–62, Shawlands acad Glasg 1963–64
m Aber 14.10.61 Alexander S. F. Mair BSc(eng) 1957 *qv*
d Worcester 29.12.75

GARROW Robert Stewart   *BSc(eng) 1963
 s of Frederick C. G. MA 1926 *qv* and Alice W. Stewart
BSc 1928 *qv*; b Aber 23.5.42
Dip Man. St(Strath) 1972
app/0 & M asst AEI Rugby, Leic 1963–66; Glasg: O &
M off. Rolls Royce 1966–67, man. serv off. SSEB 1968–69,
bus. consult. Arthur Andersen & Co 1969–72; man. advis
John Aird & Co Darvel 1972–73; bus. dev. exec Grampian
Oil Serv Glasg 1973–75; asst chief man. serv off. Glasg
dist c from 1975
m Milngavie 9.8.72 Christine W. McCracken inc tax insp
d of Dugald C. McC. Clarkston

GARTH Jeremy Robinson   *BSc 1970
 s of Geoffrey W. G. power stat supt and Freda M.
Robinson teacher; b Bradford 17.8.45
asst geol dept McM univ. Hamilton, Ont 1970–72;
press oper/machinist Burnley 1972–74; geol/well logger
based Aber from 1974

GARTMANN Jacqueline Hélène Elsbeth   MA 1963
 d of Anton G. confectioner and Alice R. L. Cugny
concert pianist; b Safien Switzerland 4.4.39
post grad stud.: Besançon 1963-64, Madrid 1964–65,
Berne 1965–66; Switzerland: teacher Engl Ftan 1966–69,
Engl translator in a major trust comp Zürich 1969–78,
free-lance translator Zürich from 1979

GARTSHORE Maurice John   MA 1969

GARVIE Christopher Ludwig   BSc 1962
 s of Denis S. G. BSc(eng) 1935 *qv*; b Aber 15.10.40
computer progr with Elliot Automation Lond, Den
Helder, Holland 1962–65; syst analyst: Seattle 1965–67,
Houston 1967–70, Munich, 1970–73, Houston 1973–77,
Friedrichshafen Germany from 1977
m Aber 2.4.65 Shirley R. J. Kidd d of Joseph I. K. Wick

GARVIE John Henry   *BSc 1970
 s of John G. butcher, factory sect. man. and Lydia M.
Black clerkess; b Aber 9.3.48
teacher: Stornoway 1971–75, prin phys Balfron from 1974
m Aber 20.8.71 Fiona M. Clark lib asst d of Alfred C.
Kingswells

GARVIE Sheila Margaret   BSc 1970
 m Milngavie 2.7.69 Alasdair M. Burns BSc 1969 *qv*

GARVIE William Hamilton Heslop   MB ChB 1956
 s of Hamilton A. G. bank man. and Elizabeth M.
Heslop p e teacher; b Kirkcaldy 15.6.30
FRCSE 1961 FRCS 1963

sen regist surg: Dun 1965–66, Aber 1966–67; Aberd:
lect surg 1967–68, sen lect 1968–69, consult. surg from
1969
m Aber 17.6.59 Katherine M. Matheson nurse d of
Alexander M. Aber

GASCOIGNE Michael Neil Clifton   LLB 1970
 s of C. A. Hector G. chartered land ag and Jean
Muller; b Inv 1.2.49
admitted WS; ptnr Messrs Brodies WS Edin from 1973

GASKIN Celeste Ellen   MA 1966
 d of Patrick G. dept store man. and Celesta M. Emslie;
b Aber 24.9.45
teacher: Engl/hist Fyvie s 1967–69; Engl lang British s
Milan 1969–72
m Aber 20.9.66 James H. Christie CA s of James C. Aber

GASTON Arthur Raymond Charles   MA 1958 BD 1961
 s of William J. G. min of relig(cong) and Mary M.
Chaplin; b Atherstone 25.5.36
Dip Scot. Cong Coll(Edin) 1961
prin theol coll/prof NT stud. Fianarantsoa Malagasy
Repub 1962–67; min Sauchie par ch Alloa 1969–75; min
Dollar West with Muckhart and Glendevon from 1975
m Glasg 12.6.62 Evelyn W. Mather civ serv d of James M.
Glasg

GAUKROGER Catherine Mary   MB ChB 1968
 d of Charles A. G. BA(Leeds) headmaster and Mary
Turner teacher; b Dunfermline 26.8.44
DObstRCOG 1971
h o Whitehaven, Aber 1968–69; sen h o; obst, paediat
Carlisle, Liv 1969–70, obst, med Wigan, Liv 1970–71;
g p: Aber 1971–72, Alva from 1972

GAULD Alexander George   *MA 1966
 s of William G. lorry driver, bus driver and Nellie
Manson; b Aber 11.2.43
teacher Fr/Span: Aber coll of comm 1967–69, AGS
1969–74, prin Span. Northfield acad Aber from 1974

GAULD George Alexander   MA 1959

GAULD James Alexander   BSc 1969

GAULD James Hendry   *BSc 1966 PhD 1969
 s of James G. insur man. and Dorothy I. Simpson;
b Aber 8.2.44
Royal Soc Leverhulme Schol 1966–67
soil surv staff Macaulay inst soil res Aber from 1969
m Aber 12.10.72 Lesley Baxter teacher d of William B.
Aber

GAULD Malcolm William Robertson   LLB 1964
 s of William R. G. MB ChB 1935 *qv*; b Cairo 10.10.43
CA 1967 AMBIM 1972
app Williamson & Dunn CA Aber 1964–67; audit sen
Price Waterhouse & Co. Glasg 1967–70; fin. controller
Hayward Tyler & Co eng E. Kilbride 1970–73; group
acct and comp secy Auchinleck Invest. Co Glasg from
1973
m Aber 2.8.68 Lesley M. H. Riddel med secy d of Johnston
R. Aber

GAULD Morton Alexander Edward   *MA 1959
 s of Charles G. G. naval off. and Gladys M. D. Eunson
teacher piano; b Edin 3.6.37
teacher classics Inverurie acad 1960–71; prin classics
Bankhead acad Aber from 1972

GAULD William   *MA 1963
s of William G. elect. welder and Rose Merchant; b Aber 5.4.41
exec off. BoT Lond 1963-68, civil aviation Highlands and Islands Edin 1968-69; higher exec off. Glasg 1969-73; far east rep civ aviation auth Hong Kong from 1973
m Aber 5.8.64 Yvonne Cormack d of George C. Aber

GAVIN, Irene Sise   MA 1963
m Cormack

GAVIN Kevin George   *MA 1970 Dip Ed 1971

GAVIN Mary Teresa   *MA 1970
m Southport 1971 Robert M. L. Anderson MA 1962 qv

GAVIN Neil Gow Sinclair   MB ChB 1970

GAVIN Pamela Ethel   *MA 1960
m Craig

GAVINE David Myles   *MA 1969
BSc(St And)

GEALS Michael Forbes   MB ChB 1968
s of James G. MA 1929 qv; b Aber 26.4.45
DObstRCOG 1972 MRCOG 1975
h o med, surg Woodend hosp Aber 1968-69; sen h o obst /gyn Dumfries 1969-71; regist: obst/gyn Inv 1971-73, surg St Leonard's hosp Lond 1973-74; obst/gyn Duke St hosp Glasg 1974-77; lect obst/gyn Aberd from 1977
m Aber 16.1.69 Jill Barker d of John B. Peterculter

GEAR Andrew David Davidson   BSc 1956
s of David M. C. crofter/boatman and Jemima A. Henry crofter; b Foula 3.6.33
nat serv 1957-59; teacher Mid Yell j h s Shetland from 1959
m Mid Yell 9.7.57 Wilma A. Hughson MA 1955 qv

GEAR Christine Anne   BSc 1960
d of John G. head postmaster and Margaret Dunbar teacher; b Lerwick 5.3.40
teacher: maths/sc Aberdeensh 1961-66, Kirkcudbrightsh 1966-67, maths Inverurie acad from 1977
m Aber 12.7.63 William F. Murdoch MA 1964 qv

GEDDES David Flett   *BSc 1966

GEDDES David Stewart   *BSc 1962 PhD 1967

GEDDES Elizabeth Marshall   MA 1967
d of George G. quarrymaster/farm. and Barbara M. Whitelaw BA(Lond) teacher; b Elgin 21.3.46
Dip Soc Ad(Edin) 1969 Dip Soc Work(Glas) 1974
soc worker: Falkirk 1969-75, Moray 1975-77 and from 1979; various posts (including vine-training) NZ 1977-79

GEDDES Ian Mackie   MA 1964

GEDDES James Clarke   MA 1958 *1960 Dip Ed 1961
s of James G. town chamberlain Inverbervie and Marjory A. B. Clarke; b Inverbervie 19.12.22
teacher hist/Engl RGC Aber 1961-64; head lib stud. Elmwood coll Cupar 1964-67; dir adult educ and extra-mural stud. St And from 1967
m Aber 28.12.55 Muriel L. McNab MA 1952 qv

GEDDES Jean Munro   MA 1966
d of William G. farm worker and Elizabeth W. Davidson; b Lintmill 22.5.46
teacher: Ayr 1967-68, Macduff 1968-71, Buckie from 1971

m Cullen 31.7.71 Alexander Watt acct s of Alexander W. Portknockie

GEDDES Margaret Elane   BSc 1963
d of George A. G. teacher and Isabella Kelman teacher; b Aber 20.10.42
teacher sc: Tynecastle s Edin 1964-66, Longbrook s Feltham 1966-67, Davies, Lains & Dick Lond 1967-68, Dalkeith s 1968-69
m Aber 31.3.67 Roger Gordon MRCVS(Edin) vet surg s of Robert G. Ballymena

GEDDES William Charles   *BSc 1959 PhD 1962
s of William R. G. farm. and Mary A. G. Anderson; b Buckie 2.9.38
Assoc Plastics & Rubber Ind 1975
asst lect chem Aberd 1962-63; sen scient off. rubber and plastics res assoc Shawbury 1963-67; sect. leader dev Nairn Floors Kirkcaldy 1967-70; lect polymer tech Napier coll of comm and tech Edin from 1970
m Fochabers 11.9.63 Barbara J. Morrison shorthand typist, hotel man. d of William M. Fochabers

GEE Isoline   PhD 1958
BSc(Wales)
res grant Rowett inst Aber 1958-59; part-time teacher sc Royal h s Edin 1959-60
m Aberystwyth 4.10.58 James F. D. Greenhalgh PhD 1959 qv

GELLATLY Ian Findlay   MA 1956 LLB 1958
s of John F. G. hairdresser, tobacconist, farm. and Janet Weir; b Stonehaven 18.4.35
teacher New Stevenston 1959-60; leg. asst Dunbarton c c 1960-65; leg. admin asst Stirling c c 1965-67; prin solic Motherwell & Wishaw t c 1967-69; prin dep town clerk, interim town clerk Coatbridge t c 1969-72, leg. advis 1972-75; solic (Scot.) British Airports Auth from 1975

GELLATLY Leonard James Weir   MA 1967

GELMAN Aubrey Louis   PhD 1967
s of Joseph G. rancher/mining comp dir and Ethel Smith; b Bulawayo Rhodesia 13.2.27
BSc(Cape Town) 1948 BSc(Rhodes univ S. Af.) 1949 Dip Agr Sc(Cantab) 1954
gen man. farming, ranching/mining Bulawayo 1949-53; jun exec Fisons Felixstowe 1954-57; consult. chem/gen man. farm./mining Bulawayo 1957-60; lect NOSCA Aber from 1961

GEMMELL Alastair Millar Duncanson   *BSc 1968
s of Alan R. G. PhD(Glas) univ prof and Janet A. B. Duncanson; b Ayr 9.2.46
PhD(Glas)1971
dem geog Keele univ 1971-73; lect geog Aberd from 1973
m Stair 27.2.71 June Hannah acct asst d of Andrew H. Drongan

GENTLE Terence Alexander   *BSc(eng) 1970
s of James A. G. taxi owner/driver and Lena I. Finlayson; b Aber 19.8.47
AMIEE
des eng Ferranti Edin 1970-72; eng/dir Pettamp Linlithgow 1972-74; sen eng Marconi space and defence syst Hillend 1974-76; instrument eng Kingsworth Marine Drilling Dun from 1976
m Aber 19.8.68 Ishbel M. Low MA(Edin) d of Robert A. L. Aber

GENTLES Myrna Grace   MB ChB 1961

GEORGALA Douglas Lindley   PhD 1957
BSc(agr)(Stellenbosch)

GEORGE Graham   BSc 1959

GEORGE Kathleen Margaret   MA 1970
d of Charles G. BSc 1939 qv; b Newcastle-u-Tyne
13.12.47
teacher Prestonpans 1971–74
m Newcastle-u-Tyne 6.4.74 Douglas I. Allan farm man.
s of William A. Symington

GEORGE Robert Wilson   *MA 1967
s of Robert W. G. loc govt off. and Elizabeth Newell
loc govt off.; b Ayr 6.4.44
econ res asst Lond 1967–68; p a to gen man. Varese, Italy
1968–69; Lond: econ 1969–70, man. consult. 1970–73, fin.
analyst 1973–74, corporate plan. 1974–77, invest. control
from 1977
m Aber 28.9.68 Moira Clark MA 1966 qv

GEORGE Sheila Catherine   MA 1967 Dip Ed 1968
d of Charles G. BSc 1939 qv; b Newcastle-u-Tyne
10.11.45
teacher Kirkhill p s Aber 1968–72
m Newcastle-u-Tyne 31.7.70 John N. Slater MB ChB 1971
med pract s of John S. MB ChB 1941 qv

GEORGESON James Arthur Hugh   MA 1969
s of Kathleen E. Hunter or Georgeson crofter; b
Shetland 18.11.47
teacher maths/geog Aith jun h s from 1970
m Aith 31.3.72 Evelyn H. Smith bank clerkess, comptometer oper d of George S. Aith

GEORGESON Vaila Mackenzie   *BSc 1970
d of James S. F. G. supt insur comp and Janet O.
Mackenzie; b Wick 10.12.48
vet regist off. (sect. head) pharm comp Dorking from 1973

GERMAN Gordon Allen   cMB ChB 1958
s of Gidley H. G. min of relig and Willeminia Gordon;
b Inverurie 12.5.35
DPM(Lond) 1962 MRCPE 1963 FRCPE 1971 MRCPsych
1972 FRCPsych 1973 MANZCP 1973 FANZCP 1975
sen h o, regist psychiat ARI 1958–63; regist, sen regist
psychiat The Maudsley hosp Lond; prof psychiat
Makerere univ Kampala, Uganda 1966–72; prof psychiat
univ of W Aust from 1972
m Aber 14.4.58 Angela R. de Silva MA 1961 qv

GERRARD Erica Margaret   MA 1966
m Downie

GERRARD Helen   *MA 1966
d of James G. and Jemima Kiloh; b Aber 5.9.43
lect geog Aber coll of comm 1967–74, sen lect gen stud.
from 1974

GERRARD Margaret Elizabeth   MB ChB 1968
m Herd

GERRARD Michael Alexander   MA 1968

GERRIE Anne   BSc 1959
d of John G. MB ChB 1929 qv(iii); b Aber 13.11.38
RSA(Lond)
secy to man. dir Lloyds Pharmaceuticals Lond 1961;
teacher Aber: RGC 1967, Albyn s 1967–70, Kincorth
acad 1971; own bus. 'The Windmill' Aber from 1972
m Aber 7.9.61 James F. Donald theatre man./comp dir
s of James R. D. Aber

GERRIE Roy Marnoch   *MA 1965
s of Alexander G. civ serv and Margaret Whyte; b
Edin 21.9.42
asst exam. Estate Duty Off. Edin 1965–66; admin asst
Strath 1966–74; asst regist univ of Kent Canterbury
1974–75; asst secy Dund from 1975

GERVAIS Lawrence Leonard   MA 1968

GHANEM Azza Muhammed Abdo   MA 1965

GHANEM Shihab Muhammad Abduh   BSc(eng) 1964

GHAURI Arif Ali Khan   MSc 1967
s of Hamid A. K. G. cloth merch and Fatima H. A.
Hussain; b Pilibhit (U.P.) India 22.9.38
BSc(Kar) 1961 MSc(Kar) 1962 Dip Fr(Peshawar) 1968
Peshawar univ Pakistan: lect 1967–72, asst prof geol
1972–77, assoc prof from 1977
m Karachi 12.10.67 Orooj B. M. Ullah BSc (Peshawar)
teacher d of Mohammad Ullah Khan, Karachi

GHAZALLI Baharuddin Bin Haji   BSc(for) 1963

GIBB Elizabeth Jean   MA 1959
d of John A. C. G. farm./hotel prop. and Jessie W.
Davidson; b Aber 24.5.38
teacher Aber 1960–61; floral art dem Scot. area from 1972
m Aber 27.6.60 Gerald Mortimer MA 1958 qv

GIBB George Gordon   BSc 1969

GIBB Jean   *MA 1970
d of Andrew R. G. estate factor and Jean R. Ritchie;
b Fraserburgh 19.3.48
teacher geog Perth acad 1971–75
m Fraserburgh 24.7.71 Duncan M. Pringle BSc 1970 qv

GIBB Jennifer Rosemary   BSc 1970
m Anderson

GIBB Judith Anne   MA 1967
d of Robert M. G. timber merch and Elspeth M. F.
Grant; b Aber 31.3.46
Dip Bus St(Strath)
secy to educ off. Grampian TV Aber 1967–72
m Aber 11.4.69 David G. Millar MB ChB 1967 qv

GIBB Margaret Carr   MA 1965
b Tarland 1.10.43
teacher mod lang: Inverurie acad 1966–67, Currie h s
1967–72
m Aber 5.8.66 Karl A. Linklater MRCVS(Edin) vet surg,
lect

GIBB Marilyn Rosemary   MA 1968
d of Robert M. G. timber merch and Elspeth M. F.
Grant; b Aber 22.9.41
teacher Fr: Norfolk 1969–73, RGC from 1974
m Aber 24.6.61 James G. Lowdon GD navigator RAF
s of James L. Elgin

GIBB Richard Alexander   *BSc 1958
MSc(Birm) 1959 PhD(Birm) 1961

GIBBONS June Evelyn Kathleen   MA 1970 *1972
d of Henry J. G. computer man. and Muriel Smith
shop man.; b Aber 21.2.50
asst soc work. Bellsdyke psychiat hosp Stirlingsh 1972–73
m Aber 14.3.71 Eoin M. Ross s lib s of John R. Bucksburn

GIBBONS Neil Mackintosh   BSc(eng) 1969

GIBSON Alastair *MA 1970 CASS 1975
s of Harold G. civ serv and Olive Hendry; b Aber
9.4.48
Aber: hosp admin 1970–72, soc worker 1973–77; sen soc
worker: Gateshead 1977–79, Aber from 1979
m Aber 8.4.72 Maureen Simpson d of Maurice A. S.
Muchalls

GIBSON Alice Sim BSc 1968
d of William G. clerk of works and Mary E. Ross; b
Aber 22.5.47
progr Perth 1968–69; exec off. (DPS) Lond 1971–73; syst
progr: Mitcham 1973–76, Dubai UAE from 1976
m Aber 27.7.68 David M. Bremner BSc(eng) 1966 qv

GIBSON Donald Mathieson *BSc 1964 PhD 1968
s of John M. G. warehouseman and Alice M. A. F.
Clark; b Aber 13.2.42
Torry res stat Aber: scient off. 1964–71, sen scient off.
1971–75, prin scient off. from 1975
seconded Laboratorium voor Microbiol univ of Ghent,
Belgium 1965–66
m Aber 12.12.66 Joan M. Cook secy d of Douglas C. Aber

GIBSON Hilary Marcia BSc 1963

GIBSON James George *BSc 1961
s of James S. G. delivery driver and May M. Nicol;
b Ellon 1.4.39
Anglo-Amer Corp of SA: field geol Mwadui diamond
mine Tanzania 1961–63, Lobatse, Botswana 1963–74;
mine resid geol Orapa diamond mine Botswana from 1974
m Serowe, Botswana 9.3.68 Cynthia M. Pretorius secy
d of Hendrik C. P. Serowe

GIBSON Joan Stephen Buchanan MA 1968
d of Donald S. G. asst eng PO tel and Phyllis Win-
stanley hairdresser; b Aber 28.4.47
TEFL: Berlitz s Rome 1971, Windsor centre ling.
Monza, Italy 1974, NIOGATE Teheran from 1977
m Aber 23.9.70 Enrico G. R. Nicoletti computer field
eng s of Leopoldo N. Forli Italy

GIBSON Peter James *BSc(eng) 1966

GIBSON Stewart Glen *BSc 1970

GIBSON Terence Michael MB ChB 1970
s of Patrick G. clerk and Edith J. Mason soc worker;
b Newcastle-u-Tyne 6.3.47
RAF from 1970
m Leicester 17.7.71 Alison F. Kibble cartographer

GIDNEY Alan Russell BSc 1965 *1966 PhD 1970
b S Shields 19.2.44
MIBiol 1969 scient fell. zool soc Lond 1970
lect NE Lond poly from 1969
m S Shields 6.8.66 Anna Rippon

GIFFORD Rosalind Mary *MA 1969
m Gilbert

GILBERT Philip Stanley MA 1970

GILES Louise Fleming *MA 1970
d of Alan M. G. MB ChB(Glas) consult. obst and
Winifred M. Hiddleston: b Glasg 19.9.48
Edin: asst res off. res and intell unit SHHD (now
information serv div common serv ag Scot. health serv)
1971–74, res off. 1974–76, sen res off. from 1976

GILL Angela Margaret *MA 1958
d of Alexander G. ARIBA arch. and Gladys M.
Bullock; b Oxford 8.4.36
teacher maths St Helen's girls' s Abingdon 1959–61;
computer progr: Boeing aircraft comp Seattle USA
1961–64, ICT Lond 1964–65, Boeing aircraft comp
Seattle 1965–66; sen applications analyst Control Data
Corp Lond from 1966
m Lambeth 9.7.77 Patrick H. Barnes comp dir s of Harold
A. B.

GILL Anna Berenice MA 1967
d of Thomas P. Gill MSc(Melb) lect and Kala R. Rudin
res asst; b Melbourne 18.10.45
Dip Ed(Melb) 1972 BEd(Melb) 1977
Melbourne: lect RMIT 1969–70, asst to acad regist tech
teachers' coll 1970–72, tech teacher Box Hill tech coll
1973–74, lect SCV Hawthorn from 1974
m Jean C. Pha MA 1967 qv; marr diss

GILL Brian MB ChB 1967
s of William G. blacksmith and Elsie Dickinson; b S
Shields 27.8.43
DMRD(Lond) 1971 FRCP(C) 1976
h o ARI 1967–68; sen h o path. Manc 1968–69; regist
radiol ARI 1969–72, sen regist 1972–74; consult. radiol
Calgary from 1974
m Bathgate 27.3.68 Mary N. Roberts teacher d of William
R. Bathgate

GILL Douglas Sutherland MB ChB 1960

GILL Elizabeth Ann MA 1963
d of Alexander G. G. shopkeeper, car salesman and
Barbara Cruden; b Aber 1.2.43
children's nurse NY 1963–64; teacher Peterhead 1964;
prob off. Aberdeensh/Kincardine 1964–68, soc worker
1968–72
m Aber 19.7.63 William Howie MA 1960 qv

GILL George Alastair Thomas MB ChB 1958
s of James W. G. MB ChB 1921 qv(II, III) and Margaret
E. Anderson MA 1919 qv; b Montrose 10.7.33
FRCS(C) 1969 CD 1974
Canada: m o RCAF 1959–74; private med pract (ENT)
Victoria BC from 1974
m St Hubert PQ 30.12.61 Marie A. Stewart secy d of
Gordon W. S. Matsqui BC

GILL George Barbour MA 1966

GILL John Joseph Bisset *BSc 1959
s of George G. grain merch and Agnes A. Barbour
clerkess; b Macduff 21.12.37
PhD(Liv) 1969
Liv: res asst 1960–61, asst lect, lect from 1961
m Aber 10.8.61 Sheila T. Urquhart teacher d of John U.
Banff

GILL Malcolm Alexander MA 1962
s of Alexander G. ARIBA arch. and Gladys M.
Bullock; b Oxford 22.3.40
TD 1972
exec The Thomson Organis Lond 1962–73; man. dir
Thomson Publ Johannesburg from 1974
m Newton St Loe 13.7.68 Jane Q. Roberts d of William
Q. R. CVO Newton St Loe

GILL Mark Andrew *MA 1964
s of Joseph G. aircraft eng and Rosemary Butcher
weight and stress tech; b Lytham St Annes 3.1.42
Dip PE(Loughborough)

trainee NFU Lond 1964–65; teacher: Kenya 1966–68, Turks and Caicos Is BWI 1968–71, royal g s High Wycombe 1971–73, Chalvedon s Basildon 1973–77, Fairham s Nott from 1977
m Hounslow 23.7.66 Maureen Smith nurse d of Hubert S. S. Hounslow

GILL Norman John   BSc(eng) 1959
s of James M. G. MB ChB 1927 qv; b Aber 14.4.36
ATPL(pilot civil licences) Qualified Pilot Instructor (Civil) RAF pilot Germany, UK, Malta 1959–75; civil pilot from 1975
m Inverurie 21.8.65 Lesley J. Stephen d of James A. S. Inverurie

GILL Rhoda Catherine   *MA 1966
m Peter J. Bennett BSc(for) 1967

GILL Robert Gerrard   *BSc 1970
s of Robert G. and Elsie R. Still; b Aber 15.12.47
man. trainee Reed Corrugated Cases 1970–71; prod. foreman 1971, work stud. eng 1972, prod. controller 1973–74, asst sales man. 1975–76; p a to chmn and chief exec Reed International from 1976

GILLAN Christopher John Archibald   LLB 1966
s of Archibald W. G. BL 1930 qv and Jane F. Mann teacher; b Stirling 4.9.45
Kinnear, Carlisle & Gillan solic Dun: app 1966–68, asst solic 1968–70, ptnr from 1970
m Dun 26.6.73 Carol A. Gordon teacher d of Arthur G. Dun

GILLAN Frances Leigh   MA 1970
d of Andrew G. rlyman and Maria Holmes s auxiliary; b Edin 28.9.48
Dip Sec St(Edin) 1972
Edin: secy indust des & consult. 1972–75; admin asst Lothian reg educ dept 1975–78, publ off. f e Lothian reg educ dept from 1978

GILLAN Robert Fairweather   MA 1958 LLB 1961
s of John F. G. advoc in Aber and Janet M. Thomson; b Aber 18.9.36
asst solic Alexander & Gillan advoc Aber 1961–66, ptnr from 1966
m Aber 29.6.67 Christian G. S. Gillan nursing sister d of Frederick R. G. Torphins

GILLANDERS Robert   MA 1963
s of Robert M. G. hairdresser and Isabella McKay; b Aber 9.10.41
teacher Aber: Muirfield s 1964–71, dep head Cummings Park s 1971–73, asst head Kittybrewster s 1974–75, head from 1975
m Aber 20.7.67 Wilma Buchan teacher d of Charles L. B. Aber

GILLESPIE Graham Alexander Mackay   *BSc 1968
s of Charles M. G. soldier, s attendance off. and Annie Mackay; b Lossiemouth 29.6.46
computer progr ICL Lond, Reading 1968–69; sen computer proj off. Brit Airways Lond 1970–76; real-time reservations syst controller Gulf Air Manama Bahrain from 1977
d 17.6.81

GILLESPIE Margaret Bella Dalgarno   MA 1957
d of William G. G. trans insp and Jane M. M. Porter; b Aber 13.3.34
teacher maths: Aber 1958–65, Croydon 1965, part time Aber from 1969, full time from 1977
m Aber 13.3.65 Norman W. Martin soldier, police off. s of William M. Edin

GILLIES Angus Reid   MA 1961 Dip Ed 1962

GILLIES Duncan Norman   MA 1963

GILMER Joan Margaret Morton   *MA 1969
d of James G. shop man., comp dir med serv and Elizabeth M. Morton teacher; b Glasg 26.6.47
scient asst anti-locust res estab Lond 1969–70; geol asst: site explor serv Aber 1970–72, R. C. Stewart 1972–73; exper off. geol country roads board Melb Aust from 1973

GILMORE George Malcolm   BSc 1967

GILMORE Linda Adams   PhD 1969
d of Allen A. G. BA(Amherst) univ prof and Althea Adams BA(Ohio State); b Boston USA 16.4.43
BS(Michigan State) 1965
Aberd: res fell. 1969–70, res asst 1970–72, res off. from 1972
m Aber 24.6.68 John E. Fothergill BSc(Brist) reader biochem Aberd s of Edward B. F. Bristol

GILMORE Stewart   MA 1963
s of Robert J. G. eng and Elizabeth Stewart; b Aber 8.5.35
teacher Perth 1964–67, sen teacher from 1967
m Beckenham 31.3.62 Jane H. Dixon staff nurse d of Arthur W. D. Beckenham

GILMOUR Helen Shirran   BSc 1962
d of Thomas G. master mariner and Margaret M. Bruce nurse; b Aber 20.1.41
analyst chem Aberd 1962–64; information scient Pilkington Bros Ormskirk 1965–71
m Aber 28.8.64 Brian R. Chamberlain PhD 1965 qv

GILMOUR Iain Fordyce   *MA 1969
s of Robert J. G. MA(St And) CA and Elnora M. Fordyce MA(Glas) teacher; b Colombo Sri Lanka 18.2.46
buyer Ford Motor Co Dagenham 1969–73; inventory man. Black & Decker Spennymoor 1973–77; head of manufacturing Berkey Colortran (UK) Thetford from 1977
m Ayr 21.8.70 Marjorie Y. Smith MA 1969 qv

GILMOUR Quentin William   LLB 1964
s of William G. solic and town clerk and Elizabeth B. Rennie; b Nairn 10.9.38
ptnr Gilmour & Co solic Lossiemouth from 1971

GILMOUR Tom Lister   *BSc(eng) 1966

GILMOUR William Mayne   MA 1965 BD 1968
s of George M. G. fitter BR and Ann R. Scott; b Glasg 18.10.42
C of S min: asst Cardonald par ch Glasg 1961–69, Coatbridge from 1969
m Glasg 22.8.69 Helen G. Dewar shorthand typist d of Ewan D. Glasg

GILROY Ian Shepherd   MA 1968
s of Alexander G. maintenance eng and Ella Hall shop asst; b Dun 17.11.45
teacher Dun 1968–69; stud. div St And 1970–71; teacher Engl St Mungo's acad Glasg 1971–76; asst prin Engl St Margaret's h s Airdrie 1976–78; prin Engl St Andrew's h s E Kilbride from 1978

GINZ Beryl   MB ChB 1964
d of Henry E. G. asst man. life insur and Winifred Welch; b Lond 12.1.39
MRCOG 1971 MSc(Leeds) 1974
h o Aber 1964–67; regist obst/gyn, paediat Auck NZ

1967–70; regist obst/gyn Cardiff 1970–73; MSc course steroid endocrinology Leeds 1973–74; lect obst/gyn Sheff from 1974

GIULIANI Maria Assunta *MA 1968
d of Edward G. shopkeeper and Maria Dalli; b Aber 10.11.46
TEFL Florence 1969–76
m Aber 14.2.70 Giustino Moni sales rep s of Giulio M. Gallicano Lucca Italy

GLADSTONE Patrick James *MA 1970
s of Archibald G. solic clerk and Mary J. Swanston; b Ayton 17.1.37
BSc(Edin) 1958
teacher: Engl Wick 1970–73, asst prin Engl from 1973
m Wick 29.10.71 Margaret M. Gunn BSc 1966 qv

GLASHAN Robin Wattie MB ChB 1958
s of Gordon M. G. bank man. and Alexandra Wattie art teacher; b Aber 8.9.33
FRCSE 1963 FRCSGlas 1964
h o Aber 1958–59; g p Dorset 1959–60; h o Angus 1960; dem anat Dund 1960–61; sen h o Bristol 1961–62; regist surg Glasg 1962–65; sen regist urol Glasg 1965–68; consult. urol Huddersfield from 1968
m Aber 21.7.59 Wilma M. R. Thomson nurse d of William J. T. Forgue

GLASS Duncan Alexander MA 1963
s of Duncan G. lab and Charlotte W. Jamieson; b Inv 9.8.30
teacher Engl Aber coll of comm from 1964
m Aber 14.7.58 Doreen Cumming hairdresser d of Robert W. C. Aber

GLASS Lesley Rose LLB 1966
m Davidson

GLASSER Fredrik Paul DSc 1968
s of David D. G. MSc(NY) teacher and Esther Glasser; b New Haven Conn USA 2.5.29
BA(Conn) 1952 PhD(Penn) 1958
res fell. Penn state univ USA 1957–59; Aberd: res fell. 1959–61, lect 1961–69, sen lect 1969–77, reader from 1977
m Pa USA 17.5.58 Lesley S. Dent PhD 1957 qv

GLASSMAN Robert Martin MB ChB 1969
s of Charles G. MB ChB 1934 qv; b Brooklyn NY 7.4.40
BSc(Penn) FACAnaest 1972 DA 1976
USA: intern med centre Nassau cty 1969–70, anaesthesiology resid 1970–72; attending and assoc prof anaesthesiology New Haven hosp Yale 1972–75; attending anaesthesiologist Waterbury hosp/St Mary's hosp Waterbury from 1975
m Aber 3.7.69 Kathleen J. Birnie MA(Edin) lib, proof reader d of George A. B. Aber

GLEN Eric Uprichard *MA 1966

GLEN Martyn Coulter BSc(agr) 1967
s of Robert S. B. G. estate factor and Williamina M. Combe; b Drymen 15.3.44
ARICS 1970
Inl Rev: valuation asst Aber 1967–70, main grade valuer to dist valuer's off. Aber from 1972
Rotary grad fell. Christchurch NZ 1970–72

GLENDINNING Catherine Milne MA 1957
d of Archibald D. G. acct and Mary M. Dewar; b Edin 19.4.36

teacher s for deaf Aber 1959–61; part time teacher: Kirkwall 1970–71, mus Aberdeensh s 1971–72, Logie Durno p s 1972–74; head Crathes p s from 1974
m Aber 23.7.60 George L. Parkinson MA 1957 qv

GLENDINNING Ian Archibald *BSc 1966 MSc 1968
s of Archibald D. G. acct and Mary M. Dewar; b Arbroath 24.9.44
field seismologist Sultanate of Oman and UK 1967–71; instrument eng Algeria 1972; geophys consult. Aber, Lond 1972–73; sen staff eng 1973–76 and operations man. from 1977 in geophys comp Swanley

GLENNIE Gwendoline Lorna *MA 1967
d of John A. S. G. MA 1928 qv; b Guildford 14.1.44
translator/interpreter Lond 1968–69
m Cruden Bay 5.10.68 Robin I. McConnachie MA 1961 qv

GLENNIE Hilda Isobel MA 1964
d of George G. shop asst and Hilda I. Mathieson teacher; b Aber 14.3.43
teacher: Ellon acad 1966–68, City of Lond s for girls 1968–70, Musselburgh g s 1970–71, Clydebank h s 1971–72, Northfield acad Aber 1972–75, asst prin Fr/Ger from 1975

GLENNIE James Harvey MA 1958

GLENNIE Janet Margaret *MA 1966
m Byth

GLENNIE John Alexander MB ChB 1962
s of James D. G. MA(Glas) teacher, headmaster and Alice Gammie secy; b Glasg 5.2.39
h o: Kilmarnock I, Ballochmyle hosp, Rotten Row hosp Glasg 1963–64; g p Wednesbury from 1964
m Kemnay 4.8.64 Frances M. Smart MA 1964 qv

GLENNIE John Moray McGregor BL 1961

GLENNIE William MA 1967
s of William R. G. farm. and Annabel Chalmers; b Dinnet 30.10.46
teacher: Chryston 1969–71, spec asst Rosehill h s Coatbridge 1971–73, asst prin hist Coatbridge h s 1973–77, prin hist Portree h s from 1977

GLENTWORTH Garth William *MA 1965
s of Robert Glentworth PhD 1941 qv; b Aber 27.11.43
MIA(Col) 1967 DPhil(Oxon) 1977
post-grad stud.: Columbia univ 1965–66, Edin 1966–67, Linacre coll Oxford 1967–68, 1972–73; lect/res fell. Makerere univ Kampala, Uganda 1969–72; lect univ of Botswana, Lesotho and Swaziland, Roma, Lesotho 1972; inst of loc govt stud. Birm from 1973

GLOVER David Robert MA 1970
s of George G. teacher and Frances M. J. Longhurst nurse; b Knolton 22.7.46
teacher Salop c c (Market Drayton, Wellington, Cleobury Mortimer) from 1971
m Shrewsbury 2.9.68 Eveline M. Hitzinger teacher

GLOVER Douglas Dwight BSc(eng) 1968

GLOYER Robert Irvine MA 1957 LLB 1959
s of Marshall H. G. photographer and Lizzie I. Whent; b Aber 7.1.36
short serv comm Royal Ulster Rifles 1960–63; asst Allan, Black and McCaskie solic Elgin 1963–65; ptnr Teague,

Leonard & Muirhead (later Leonards) Hamilton from 1965
m Aber 6.4.61 Hilary A. Fethney MA 1959 *qv*

GLUCK Martha   BSc 1960

GODDEN Michael John   MB ChB 1968

GODFREY Michael Eric Ray   BSc(for) 1967
s of Rex G. storeman and Olive M. Young stenographer; b Wellington NZ 26.5.42
BSc(Victoria NZ) 1964
NZ; dist for. King country 1967–70, scient, anim biol Rangiora 1970–73; MSc/PhD candidate ecology Davis, Calif (NZ govt burs/Jastro schol) from 1973
m Palmerston North NZ Anne C. Harris teacher d of Gordon S. H. BSc(Auck) Palmerston North

GOGOI Paramananda   PhD 1966
MBBS(Assam)

GOLBY Sean Anderton   *MA 1970

GOLDFARB Peter Samuel Gabriel   *BSc 1966

GOLDIE Dorothy Muirhead   *BSc 1970
d of Alexander G. BSc (Glas) headmaster and Janet M. Muirhead lect; b Edin 4.4.48
Dip Ed(Edin) 1972
field biol asst Field Stud. Council Malham 1970–71; teacher biol comp s Notts 1972–74, prin biol 1974–75
m Aber 28.8.72 Peter H. Dahl MA 1970 *qv*

GOLDIE Muriel Jean   *MA 1966 Dip Ed 1967
d of Alexander G. MA(Glas) headmaster and Janet M. Muirhead lect; b Doncaster 12.4.44
teacher mod lang Thurso h s 1967–72, prin mod lang 1972–75
m Aber 14.7.71 Donald A. K. Murray farm. s of George D. K. M. Castletown

GOLDING Harry Sutherland Walpole   MA 1966
Dip Ed 1972
s of Harry F. G. mech eng and Helen Sutherland bookkeeper/clerkess; b Glasg 15.1.21
lect Engl/gen stud. tech coll Aber from 1967
m Aber 10.7.54 Elaine T. Findlater teacher d of William A. M. F. Aber

GOLDSPINK Christopher Raymond   MSc 1967
s of Eric C. G. CA and Mary M. Smith; b Leicester 25.2.44
BSc(St And) 1966 PhD(Liv) 1971
res fell. limnological inst Neths 1967–70; lect: Didsbury coll of educ Manc 1971–76, Manc poly from 1976
m Maltby 19.9.70 Kathleen U. Hancox BA(York) med soc worker

GOLDSTRAW Brian Richard   *MA 1970
s of Richard H. G. sales rep, off. machine spec and Isobel M. Robertson typist; b Aber 20.12.46
asst postal controller Edin 1970–79, head of group from 1979
m Gladsmuir 22.5.76 Catherine W. Bruce BSc(Edin) postal serv d of Daniel C. B. Longniddry

GOMES Errol Henry   BSc 1967 MB ChB 1971
s of Frank G. and Lilian Nunes; b Singapore 4.8.41
MRCOG 1977
Aber: h o Woodend hosp, ARI, mat. hosp 1971–73; m o Kandang Kerban hosp Singapore 1974–76; g p

Linden Clinic Bundaberg Queensland Aust from 1976
m Wokingham 31.8.68 Margaret Read MA 1968 *qv*

GONNELLA Frances   BSc 1961
d of Joseph F. G. elect. eng and Eliza W. Yeaman; b Bendochy 26.12.40
teacher: Dun 1962–68, Dartmouth, Nova Scotia from 1968
m(1) Blairgowrie 11.9.61 Anthony S. Campbell art teacher s of Aldo N. C. Kirkmichael; marr diss
(2) –.4.76 Harry C. H. Wallace bank man.

GONZALEZ Carlos Adolfo   MSc 1967
s of Darwin G. bank man. and Maria C. Perez; b Montevideo Uruguay 17.11.29
FRSS 1977
lect universidad de la republica Uruguay 1968–73; statist INTA Castelar Argentina 1974–75; sen statist CNP-GL Embrapa Brasil from 1975
m Montevideo 5.4.62 Marta Diaz d of Wallace D. Montevideo

GOODALL Charles Morrison   MA 1956
s of William G. foreman finisher (textiles) and Margaret I. Morrison; b Keith 1.2.35
sgt/instr (RAEC) mod lang King Richard's s Cyprus 1957–59; Perth: teacher Craigie s 1959–68, dep head Letham p s from 1968

GOODALL James Alexander   BSc 1970
s of James G. farm worker and Grace Alexander shop asst; b Huntly 13.6.48
teacher sc Aberlour 1970–72, asst prin sc 1972–78, prin chem from 1978
m Rothiemay 22.7.72 Margaret A. Reid teacher d of Joseph R. Rothiemay

GOODALL John Charles   *BSc(eng) 1969
s of John G. police off., teacher and Ethel Goddard; b Garforth 3.3.47
CEng MICE 1975
site civ eng Wirral 1969–73; eng asst Chester 1973–76; sen asst eng Carlisle from 1976
m Wirral 6.11.71 Lynn B. Morgan BEd (Lanc) teacher d of Thomas J. M. Wirral

GOODALL Thomas   MA 1961
s of William G. shipyard worker, salesman and Jean King; b Glasg 7.1.29
teacher maths/sc Rhynie j s s 1963–65; head Eday South j s s 1965–72; teacher remed/ROSLA Kirkwall g s 1972–73, p s based Aberchirder from 1973
m Rothiemay 12.8.58 Phyllis J. Shearer MA 1957 *qv*

GOODBRAND Theodore Allan   MB ChB 1960
s of George D. G. hydraulics eng and Mabel B. N. Smith shop asst; b Aber 9.1.36
Aber: h o city hosp, Woodend hosp 1960–61; g p Longside 1961–62, Mintlaw from 1962
m Aber 1958 Isabella G. Mitchell man. d of William M. Aber

GOODFELLOW Carol Ann   MA 1969
d of John M. G. eng and Isabella Sutherland: b Inv 31.12.48
ALA(RGIT) 1970
sen asst lib Glenrothes 1970–72; asst lib Inv publ lib from 1972

GOODFELLOW Margaret Selbie   MB ChB 1965
d Glasg 31.7.67 *AUR* XLII 187

GOODLAD Charles Alexander   *MA 1965 PhD 1968
s of Henry G. fisherman and Williamina Guthrie;
b Yell 19.9.43
Newfoundland: asst prof/res fell. fisheries geog St John's
1968–70, fishing capt Stephenville 1970–71; fishing tech
FAO of UN Rome 1971–73, Casablanca 1973–74;
reg dir Arabco Bahrain from 1974
m Gibraltar 17.12.73 Myrtha Magloire d of Paul E. M. NY

GOODLAD James Adam   *MA 1965
s of Robert G. bank man. and Jemima B. Halcrow;
b Crayford 5.3.38
teacher: Ayr acad 1966–69, prin geog St Joseph's acad
Kilmarnock 1969–71, Cumnock acad from 1971
m Aber 20.7.67 Margaret E. Buchan BSc 1966 *qv*

GOODLAD Williamina Catherine   MA 1968
d of William G. fisherman and Robina Smith; b
Hamnavoe 21.5.47
teacher: Bathgate 1969–71, Edin 1971–73, exchange
teacher Aust 1973–74, Edin from 1974

GOPAUL Jaygobin   *MA 1970
s of Ramkwar G. chmn publ serv comm and Sonia
Billoo; b Mauritius 21.11.44
teacher Fr Qn Eliz coll and Royal coll Port Louis from
1970
m Mauritius –.4.77 Karini Bhunjun secy d of Tarkeshwar
B. Quatre-Bornes

GORDON Alexander   *BSc(eng) 1961
MEng(Glas)

GORDON Alexander Lobban   *MA 1958
s of George G. G. farm. and Elizabeth M. Lobban;
b Grantown-on-Spey 12.4.35
DUP 1965
univ of Manit: lect Fr 1961–65, asst prof 1965–70,
assoc prof from 1970

GORDON Allan Tawse   BSc(eng) 1964
s of Thomas T. G. rly eng(E Af) and Florence M.
Edward; b Methlick 15.8.43
RAF off.(navigator) UK, Singapore from 1965
m Dyce 12.7.66 Alison M. Milne teacher

GORDON Andrew George   *BSc(agr) 1963 PhD 1968

GORDON Anne   MA 1966

GORDON Anthony John   MSc 1970
s of Bruce C. H. G. farm. and Lorna M. Harris;
b Orange NSW Aust 7.10.46
B Rur Sc(New Eng) PhD(Guelph, Ont) 1974
sessional lect Guelph 1974; res fell. Wageningen, Nether-
lands 1974; then res scient Aust Wool Corp, Prospect
m Hobart Tasmania 29.12.70 Gwendolyn Bull BA(New
England) teacher d of Peter C. A. B. Midway Point
Tasmania

GORDON Barbara Katherine   *BSc 1968
d of G. A. Douglas G. MB ChB(Edin) ultrasonic radiol
and Hildegard M. Middleton SRN theatre sister; b
Ealing 15.8.46
biochem Western Gen Hosp Edin 1969–71
m Richmond 28.9.68 Colin G. F. Brockie BSc(eng) 1963 *qv*

GORDON Catherine Dillon   MA 1969
m Davidson

GORDON David Hendry   MA 1969
s of William H. G. LDS(Edin) dent. surg and Charlotte

Gauld; b Forres 28.5.46
timber yard lab Gothenburg Sweden 1970–72; teacher
Hazlehead acad Aber from 1972
m Gothenburg 10.6.72 Pia E. Ander midwife d of J.
Evert A. Gothenburg

GORDON Donald Ian   MA 1964
s of Forbes R. G. master signwriter, comm artist and
Eliza R. Robertson; b Becontree 12.12.30
SRN 1954 RMN 1957 BA(Strath) 1972
teacher Engl Airdrie 1965–69, spec asst Engl Larkhall
1969–70, asst prin Engl 1970–74, asst prin Engl Airdrie
from 1974
m Bankhead 26.3.55 Winifred Grier SRN d of Andrew G.
Ramelton Co Donegal

GORDON Eileen   BSc 1962
d of James S. G. farm. and Georgina Bruce; b Rothienorman 13.9.41
teacher: Perth acad 1963–65, Aber h s for girls 1965–66,
h s NY state USA 1966–70, Old Aber s 1970–71, part-time
Mackie acad Stonehaven 1976–77
m Aber 28.7.66 Donald MacLaren BSc(agr) 1966 *qv*

GORDON Elizabeth   MA 1969
m Johnstone

GORDON Frances Christina   MA 1957
d of Robert G. farm. and Frances C. Gauld; b Drumlithie 26.11.36
Dip Secy Pract(St Godric's coll Lond) 1958
secy classics dept Edin univ 1958–59; teacher Lasswade
p s 1962–67; teacher Engl/lib The Engl s Nicosia Cyprus
1967–71
m Aber 11.3.59 George L. Fraser BSc 1956 *qv*

GORDON George Park Douglas   *BSc 1960
s of George P. G. fish salesman and Chrissie A.
Douglas; b Peterhead 23.10.37
Grad RIC 1963 MRIC 1975 CChem 1975
teacher: sc Peterhead 1961–64, prin sc Dornoch 1964–67;
asst advis sc Glasg 1967–69; HMIS W Scot 1969–73;
HMIS Headquarters' staff Edin 1973–77; HMIS nat
spec sc from 1977
m Aber 16.7.63 Karein L. M. Fraser teacher d of Hector
M. F. Aber

GORDON George Philip   MA 1968
s of George G. G. hotel wine cellarman and Mary S.
Philip; b Aber 15.7.37
teacher Aber: Kirkhill p s 1969–72, Seaton p s 1972–76,
The Hillocks p s Bucksburn from 1976
m Aber 17.7.74 Joan M. S. MacLachlan MA 1963 *qv*

GORDON Hugh MacLeod   *BSc 1970
s of Ronald G. tweed mill man. and Ann MacLeod;
b Stornoway 28.8.47
teacher biol Craigmount h s Edin 1971–72, asst prin biol
1972–76; asst exam off. SCE exam board from 1976
m Dirleton 8.7.72 Elsie P. J. Davidson BSc 1969 *qv*

GORDON Ian   LLB 1963

GORDON Ian Livingstone   MA 1958
s of John D. G. MB ChB 1925 *qv*; b Bolsover 15.2.31
MA(Edin) 1968
teacher Dalkeith 1959–69, prin teacher from 1969 then
TEFL Lure, France
m Edin 18.3.61 Patricia C. A. Laidlaw MA(Edin) teacher
d of John W. L. MB ChB(Edin) Edin

GORDON Irving Philip   BL 1961
s of Albert G. footwear retailer and Rachael Green-
stein; b Aber 31.3.40
Cert Indust Ad(Glas) 1963
Geo Bassett & Co Sheff: grad trainee, prod. man. 1963–
65, pers/trg off. 1965–69; chmn/man. dir IPG group
selection and search consult. Lond from 1969
m Lond 15.11.70 Jacqueline Sinclair p a d of John T. S.
FRICS Surbiton

GORDON Jennifer Mirabelle   MA 1967
d of John A. S. G. grain merch and Margaret M. G.
Mitchell MA 1930 *qv*; b Inv 1.1.46
teacher: Inv 1968–70, Aber 1970–71, remed Aviemore
from 1977
m Inv 1.8.70 Angus MacNeill MB ChB g p s of Duncan
H. MacN. MA(Glas) Inv

GORDON Joan Elizabeth   MA 1969
d of James A. G. LDS(Sheff) dental surg and Dorothy
S. Sim market res; b Sheffield 26.9.47
teacher Edin 1971
m Aber 1968 Michael J. R. Stephen dentist s of William
R. S. MB ChB 1940 *qv*

GORDON John Fraser   MB ChB 1967
s of Robert A. G. foreman eng and Victoria W.
Cruickshank tailoress; b Aber 13.4.43
DObstRCOG 1968
h o ARI med, surg, obst/gyn 1967–69; g p: Aber 1969–70,
Peterborough from 1970
m Aber 1.9.65 Maureen C. Rae SRN d of Alexander R.
Aber

GORDON Kathleen Elisabeth   *MA 1969

GORDON Kenneth Ian   *BSc(eng) 1956

GORDON Malcolm Niall Duncan   *MA 1960

GORDON Margaret Anne   *MA 1970
d of Alexander G. gen merch and Christina B. M.
Duggie MA 1938 *qv*; b Nairn 28.1.48
Dip Soc Ad(Dund) 1971
soc worker Lisburn NI; med soc worker Newtonards
hosp NI 1973–75
m Huntly 3.4.72 James M. Maybin asst prin soc worker
s of Robert J. M. Belfast

GORDON Margaret Jean   MA 1956
d of James A. G. gen merch and Isabella Russell; b
Aber 19.3.35
teacher: Aber 1957–59, Toronto 1959–62, Sydney Aust
1963–64, Woking 1964–66, Sydney from 1966
m Rhynie 1.8.64 Errol S. Ward teacher s of Albert J. W.
Sydney

GORDON Martin   *BSc 1969
s of William M. G. car showroom attendant and
Jamesina H. Bruce; b Aber 17.3.47
CPA 1975
tech asst to chartered patent ag Lond 1969–72, Glasg
1973–75; chart. pat. ag Glasg 1975–77; chart. pat. ag/
European pat. attorney Worthing from 1977
m Lond 27.6.70 Jacqueline M. Simpson BSc 1969 *qv*

GORDON Meriel   *MA 1969
d of Ian Gordon MB ChB 1932 *qv*; b Aber 1.9.47
res asst econ univ of Essex 1969–70
m Aber 1.9.67 Gordon Barclay MB ChB 1967 *qv*

GORDON Nanette Lilian Margaret   cMB ChB 1965
d of Harold G. G. and Hannah L. C. Stephen; b Aber

27.4.42
FFARCS 1969
h o Woodend hosp Aber, ARI 1965–66; anaest Aber
hosps 1966–73
m Aber 16.7.65 Alan D. Milne MB ChB 1964 *qv*

GORDON Pamela Jane   MA 1962
d of Alexander M. G. timber merch and Violet Scorgie
comp dir; b Laurencekirk 29.1.42
teacher maths: Netherwood s for girls New Brunswick
Canada 1963–64, acad head 1964–65, Montrose acad
1965–68
m Laurencekirk 14.6.68 Ian D. Salmon farm. s of John
O. S. Montrose

GORDON Patricia Fairlie Leith   MA 1966
d of William G. tel eng and Williamina S. Leith; b
Wick 15.1.46
teacher: maths/phys city h s Chester 1967–69, maths/sc
Northmead s s Guildford 1970–71, maths Guildford
C of E s from 1971
m Aber 16.8.68 Derek Patch BSc(for) 1965 *qv*

GORDON Patricia Mary   MB ChB 1965
d of Alexander M. G. timber merch and Violet Scorgie;
b Laurencekirk 29.1.42
Memb Amer Psychiat Assoc
h o: Woodend hosp Aber, RAHC, RSC hosp Melbourne
1965–69; fell. haemat Melbourne 1969–70; resid, chief
resid ch psych Baylor coll of med Houston Texas 1975–79
m Adelaide S Aust 18.2.69 Ian J. Butler MB BS(Adel) ch
neurol univ of Texas s of John A. B. Adelaide

GORDON Robert Emslie   MSc 1970 PhD 1975
s of Samuel M. G. superv Scot. gas board, re-instate-
ment off. Greenock corp and Agnes M. McMaster
midwife; b Gourock 6.8.46
BSc(Glas) 1968
res asst med phys Aberd 1970–75; res fell. phys univ of
Kent from 1975

GORDON Robert Lennox   MB ChB 1960
s of Robert G. MA 1909 *qv*; b Aber 23.11.36
DObstRCOG 1963
h o ARI 1960–63; lect path. Aberd 1963–67; g p: Wednesbury 1967–72, Buchlyvie 1972, Wolverhampton from
1972
m Aber 1.4.65 Laura Wallace nurs sister d of Douglas W.
New Pitsligo

GORDON Rosemary Ellen   BSc 1968
m Michie

GORDON Ross Barclay   MB ChB 1967
s of Thomas B. G. MB ChB 1936 *qv*; b Cambridge
4.9.41
h o Peterborough 1967–68; g p Peterborough from 1968
m Downham Market 14.8.65 Helen M. Feetham d of
Frederick J. F. Downham Market

GORDON Sheila Edward   *MA 1964
d of Thomas T. G., PW insp E Af rlys, security off. and
Florence M. Edward; b Aber 17.8.41
teacher hist Whitburn j s 1965–67; spec asst Whitburn
acad 1967–72; prin hist Armadale acad 1972–78; prin
guid Penicuik h s from 1978
m(1) Dyce 4.8.65 John Ward designer/graphic artist s of
Arthur L. W. Ringwood
(2) Edin 9.7.77 Philip K. Templeton stud. Edin s of
John T. Kirkcaldy

GORDON Shelagh Ann Ormond   MA 1967 CASS 1969
d of Kenneth G. O. G. MB ChB(Edin) med pract and

Eileen P. Biggar; b Walton-on-Thames 1.10.46
soc worker Falkirk 1969–70, Aber 1970–71; sen soc
worker Falkirk from 1971
m Alloa 11.9.70 Ian M. Prentice LL B 1969 *qv*

GORDON Valerie   MA 1966
d of William S. G. bus driver, bus conductor and Jessie
Garden; b Aber 26.9.42
MA(N Carolina)
teaching asst univ of N Carolina USA from 1978
m Aber 22.9.61 Colin D. Hall MB ChB 1966 *qv*

GORDON William   *MA 1969

GORDON William Cleveland   MB ChB 1959
s of Sydney C. G. journalist and Georgina E. McKay;
b Tarbrax 3.10.35
DPM(Lond) 1969 MRANZCP 1971
surg/lt RN 1960–65; regist psychiat Sunnyside hosp,
Christchurch NZ 1966–69, consult. psychiat from 1971
m Aber 28.12.62 Adrien V. Fitch MA(Canterbury) clin
psych d of Lewis C. F. LL B(NZ) Christchurch NZ

GORIE James Sinclair   *MA 1959

GORMAN Hugh   MA 1966
s of Hugh G. bricklayer and Catharine McCallum;
b Milngavie 20.7.29
teacher Castle Douglas from 1967

GORMAN Martyn Lee   *BSc 1967 PhD 1970
s of John J. M. G. farm worker and Edna Fisher;
b Holmfirth 15.11.44
lect biol univ S. Pacific Fiji 1970–73; lect zool Aberd
from 1973
m Peterhead 27.7.68 Margaret Duthie teacher d of
Wilson D. Peterhead

GORMLEY George Donald   MB ChB 1960
s of George A. G. foreman baker and Marion F.
Ferguson nurse; b Elgin 13.6.36
h o Woodend hosp Aber 1960–61; g p Lossiemouth from
1961; part-time m o blood transfusion serv Aber from
1960; part-time cas off. Dr Gray's hosp Elgin 1962–67
m Aber 28.2.59 Grace E. McLeod teacher d of Thomas
McL. Dufftown

GORROD Kenneth Michael   BSc 1964
s of George G. comp dir and Jean Gibb; b Aber 18.7.43
CA 1968
Lond: fin. acct Glaxo Group 1968–72; man. consult.
Coopers & Lybrand 1972–75; fin. dir Airfix Prod. from
1975
m Aber 17.6.72 Fiona L. Galloway d of Harold W. G.
Aber

GOSS-CUSTARD John Douglas   PhD 1967
BSc(Brist)

GOTTFRIED Herbert   PhD 1963
ARIC

GOTTS Ian   *MA 1969 MLitt 1975

GOUDIE John Charles   BSc 1959

GOUGH Adrian Christopher   *BSc 1970

GOULD Grahame Warwick   PhD 1959
BSc(Brist)

GOULD Richard John   BSc(for) 1960
s of Walter H. G. tool maker, flt serg RAF, factory
man. and Eveline M. Philpott; b Lond 15.3.39
for. off. Queensland dept of for. Aust from 1961
m Brisbane 20.9.69 Charlene A. Reynolds-Thompson
BEd(Queensland) teacher d of Maurice R. J. R.-T.
Brisbane

GOULDING Christopher John   *BSc(for) 1968
s of Harry G. BEM W/O RAF and Phyllis Clare;
b Barnsley 13.10.46
PhD(Br Col) 1972
asst lect fac for. Br Col 1971–72; scient for. res inst
Rotorua NZ from 1972
m Inv 1967 Isobel P. Reid teacher d of John R. Avoch

GOVAN Eileen Tennant   BSc 1969
m Grant

GOVE Robert   BEd 1970
s of Robert G. fisherman and Marjory A. Lownie;
b Gourdon 19.7.35
FSA Scot 1973
teacher: Achnamara resid s Argyll 1970–73, hist/mod
stud. Peterhead acad from 1973

GOW David Drummond   MA 1964

GOW Elspeth Jean Ann   *MA 1970
d of Patrick H. G. bus. man. and Mary C. Shand
bus. ptnr; b Grantown-on-Spey 14.10.47
m Gt Yarmouth 27.6.70 Louis M. Smith MA 1969 *qv*

GOW Kenneth Shiach   *BSc(eng) 1969 MSc 1971
s of James G. insur salesman and Catherine R. Milton;
b Elgin 17.5.47
basic grade phys ERI 1971–74; dev eng Sonicaid, Livingston from 1974
m Elgin 1971 Christine M. Mathieson pers off.

GOW Sheena   MB ChB 1965 MD 1971
d of John G. agr eng and Margaret A. Stewart; b Aber
22.8.42
h o Aber hosps, Orkney 1965–68; res asst: Aberd 1968–
70, univ of Ottawa 1971–75
m Aber 29.12.70 Albert A. Tuttle MA 1969 *qv*

GOWAN Alastair Campbell   *BSc 1956 PhD 1959
s of Alexander E. G. BSc(Edin) headmaster and Agnes
C. Johnston; b Aber 30.3.35
res fell. univ of BC 1960; GEC NY: res and marketing
man. positions in chem businesses Mass., NY 1961–70;
gen man. polyester bus. 1971–72; pres GE Plastics BV,
Bergen op Zoom, Neths/chmn subsid comps in UK,
France, Germany, Italy from 1972
m Pittsfield Mass. 19.2.66 Silvia I. Kember

GOWANS David   MEd 1967
s of John G. comp dir and Elizabeth S. Stewart bank
clerkess; b St Monance 1.11.27
BSc(St And) 1949 Dip Ed(St And) 1950
educ off. RAF 1950–56; teacher maths/sc Buckhaven
1957–62; prin biol Aber acad 1962–67, dep head Ruthrieston s s Aber 1967–71; rector Menzieshill h s Dun from
1971
m St Monance 2.8.52 Margaret W. H. Fyall teacher d
of Thomas E. F. St Monance

GRACE Kenneth Frederick   BSc 1968
s of Howard F. G. distillery worker and Jessie Young;

b Montrose 19.12.45
teacher chem Montrose acad 1968–74; asst prin sc Balwearie h s Kirkcaldy from 1974

GRACIE Ian   *MA 1966

GRAHAM Alexander James   MA 1969
s of Alexander G. cooper and Helen Falconer; b Banff 9.6.48
Fraserburgh: teacher 1970–71, spec s (m h) teacher from 1971

GRAHAM Alexandrina Macdonald   MA 1956

GRAHAM Alexina   MA 1961
d of George G. tweed weaver and Margaret Campbell; b Back 26.10.39
teacher: Dingwall acad 1962, Nicholson inst Stornoway 1962–67, temp posts Back and Tolsta s 1969–73, Nicolson Inst from 1973
m Back 29.8.64 John Graham joiner s of John G. Portnaguran

GRAHAM, Ann Elizabeth   MA 1956
m Mackenzie

GRAHAM Carolyn Wendy   *MA 1970
d of Joseph L. G. bank off. and Sheila M. Blackburn; b Kendal 1.5.47
Dip Ed(Cantab) 1971
commun serv: volunt with spastics Lanarksh 1971, mentally handicapped Portsmouth 1972; teacher Friends' s Wigton from 1972

GRAHAM Christine   MA 1958
d of Robson G. met. off. and Margaret M. Mouat; b Carshalton 20.11.36
teacher: Fraserburgh 1959–62, Shetland 1962–69, Berlin 1969–71, Shetland 1972–73
m Lerwick 18.3.69 Sidney J. Carey commun eng s of John F. C. Thornton Heath

GRAHAM Donald Roderick   BSc(eng) 1963

GRAHAM Elizabeth Jane   MA 1969
m Edin 2.8.69 Christopher J. Ogilvie MA 1967 qv

GRAHAM Fiona Margaret   MA 1970

GRAHAM George Paterson   MA 1963
s of George G. chem worker and Dora L. Watt tailoress; b Aber 2.7.41
teacher: Insch 1964–68, Arbroath 1968–70; head: Gartly 1970–74, Aboyne p s from 1974
m Aber 4.8.65 Jennifer A. Pyper teacher p e d of Douglas P. Aber

GRAHAM Ian Wilson   *MA 1970
s of James W. G. colliery clerk and Sarah I. Mason civ serv; b Edin 17.11.47
Dip LA(Edin) 1972
asst landscape arch. Livingston dev corp 1972–74, landscape arch. E Sussex c c Lewes from 1974

GRAHAM James Gordon   *BSc 1970

GRAHAM Janet Sutherland   BEd 1968

GRAHAM Margaret   MA 1962
d of George G. tweed weaver and Margaret Campbell; b Back 6.11.41

teacher: Engl Glasg 1963–69, part time from 1973
m Glasg 6.8.65 John A. MacLean catering off. s of Murdo MacL. N Tolsta

GRAHAM Marjory Helen   MA 1956
m Mowat

GRAHAM Moray Keillour   *MA 1960
s of Reginald M. G. BA(Oxon) for. off. Kenya and Vera I. Ogle; b Nairobi 7.10.33
Dip Trop Ag(Trinidad) 1958
asst man.: Lobe estate Brit Cameroons 1956–60, Pamol estate N Borneo 1960–63; man. Sabah Palm estate Sabah 1963–77; consult. Agrotech Assoc Kota Kinabalu Malaysia from 1978
m Moniaive 12.6.75 Alison W. Gourlay d of James G. Thornhill

GRAHAM Thomas Carmichael   *MA 1956
s of John M. G. MA(Glas) prof of theol Aberd and Jessie H. Carmichael MA(Glas) teacher; b Clydebank 2.7.34
FI Pers Man. 1968
pilot RAF 1956–58; ICI pers man. posts Teesside, Grangemouth, Huddersfield, Manc, Ayrsh 1958–72, head of pers Hiram Walker (Scot.) Dumbarton 1972–74; pers man. Ciba-Cegy (UK) pigments div Paisley from 1974
m Aber 11.7.58 Jean J. Cran MA 1954 qv

GRAINGER Maureen Campbell   MA 1966
m Morrow

GRANT Adrian   *BSc 1970
s of Frederick A. G. off. serv and trans man. AA Manc and Winifred E. Pritchard; b Shawford 9.2.47
Manc: clerk dom contr dept NORWEB 1970–71, costing asst/stock controller HGV repair garage W. H. Cowburn & Cowpar chem mfrs Trafford Park from 1971
m Aber 20.8.71 Elizabeth D. Paterson teacher d of David P. Cumnock

GRANT Alan Bryce   MA 1968 LLB 1970
s of Peter B. G. linotype oper and Margaret M. C. Bell; b Falkirk 17.8.47
estate duty off. Edin 1971; law app, solic Cumbernauld dev corp 1972–74; solic Aber town c 1974–75; prin leg. asst Gordon dist c from 1975
m Aber 1971 Eileen Cooney MA 1970 qv

GRANT Alan James   BSc(eng) 1968 *1969
s of Kathleen M. Grant secy; b Cardiff 31.12.46
MSc(Cranfield inst of tech Bedford) 1971
Shell: res scient Thornton res centre Chester 1971–75, sen res scient The Hague from 1975
m Wilmslow 11.12.71 Elizabeth D. Saxon FSRTD teacher of radiography

GRANT Alasdair MacArthur   *MA 1969
s of Kenneth G. estate handy man and Margaret MacArthur; b Glasg 2.12.35
teacher: Engl/Gaelic Daliburgh S Uist 1970–72, Engl Glasg 1972–74, Lochgilphead from 1974

GRANT Alasdair Reid   BSc 1969

GRANT Alexander   *MA 1957
s of John C. G. postman and Margaret L. Grant clerkess; b Rothes 13.10.35
DIC 1959
scient off. UKAEA Dounreay 1958–60; lect: Thurso tech coll 1960–63, Nat coll of agr eng Silsoe 1963–75; sen lect s of agr eng Cranfield inst of tech from 1975

m Silsoe 1.1.72 Anne J. Tucker dom bursar d of John
R. T. Silsoe

GRANT Alexander   MA 1964

GRANT Alexander James   MA 1969
 s of James G. acct and Maria Morales; b Colombia
S Amer 28.6.48
distrib man.: Newcastle-u-Tyne 1969–70, Wakefield
1970–72; reg distrib man. Glasg 1972–75; Lond: plan.
man. 1975–78, comm man. from 1978
m Durham Marian Appleby teacher

GRANT Alison Elizabeth   MA 1969
 d of Alexander N. G. post./tel off. and Annie M. Pirie
typist; b Aber 12.1.48
asst edit.: *Hospital & Health Services Purchasing*, inst of
health serv admin Lond 1970–78; stud. Aber coll of
comm (post-grad biling secy course) 1979; admin asst
Peacock Printmakers Aber from 1980

GRANT Calum Roderick   *MA 1968 Dip Ed 1969
 s of Calum M. G. bldg consult. and Elaine C. Fraser;
b Edin 10.8.46
teacher: Stornoway p s 1969–72 and from 1974; remed
teacher Is of Lewis 1972–74

GRANT David Iain Montgomery   MA 1965 BD 1968
 s of Clifford M. G. wholesale confectioner and Edith
M. Taylor teacher; b Glasg 3.1.42
C of S min: asst Cathcart old parish Glasg 1968–69,
Trinity ch Dalry from 1969

GRANT David Renwick   MA 1963
 s of Leslie R. G. timber ag and Amy B. Macdonald;
b Edin 5.5.41
MSc(Edin) 1969
farm./sheep shearing Aust 1963–65; warden RSPB Loch
Garten 1966; asst reg off. nature conservancy Perthsh
1969–73; exped leader Quest 4 Algeria, Niger, Mali,
Upper Volta, Ivory Coast, Mauretania 1974–76; crofter/
fisherman Is of Skye from 1977
m Portree 28.4.78 Catherine E. S. Cochrane d of George
S. C. Southampton

GRANT Doris Margaret   MA 1969
 m Strachan

GRANT Elaine Margaret   MA 1965
 d of James C. G. edit. *Press & Journal* Aber and Hilda
L. Gordon; b Aber 15.5.44
Dip Soc Ad(Dund) 1966 Cert Med Soc Work(Edin) 1967
med soc worker: Hull RI, Cardiff RI, Southampton RI,
ARI, Lond, mat. hosp Aber 1968–72; generic soc worker
Hammersmith soc serv Lond 1972–74; trg and recruitment off. Fulham Lond 1974–76
m(2) Lond 14.6.75 John M. King soc worker, trg off.,
child care man., lect Aberd s of Leslie K. Lond

GRANT Elizabeth Helen   BSc 1967 Dip Ed 1968
 d of James G. security off. and Elizabeth C. MacBeth
quality controller; b Aber 12.1.46
teacher maths: Northfield s Aber 1968–69, Bellahouston
acad Glasg 1969–72; part time Penilee s Glasg from 1972
m Glasg 30.12.71 Roderick A. C. Murray merch seaman
s of Thomas G. M. Glasg

GRANT Elizabeth Jane   MA 1967

GRANT Elspeth Anne   *BSc 1967
 m Cooke

GRANT Eric George   *MA 1967

GRANT Fiona Christine   *MA 1962
 d of Ian W. G. navig off. merc marine and Emily W.
Salmon restaurant man.; b Farnborough 22.9.40
teacher phys/maths: Aber 1963–65, f e 1965–66, part-time
(mostly evening classes) 1968–74; part-time tut. phys
OU from 1971
m Kent 25.7.64 Henry O. Cameron BL 1961 *qv*

GRANT Gordon Duncan   BSc 1966
 s of Duncan G. loc govt off. and Williamina Blackley;
b Hamilton 12.10.43
MBA(W Aust) 1978
electronics eng Maidenhead 1966–68; computer syst eng
Lond 1968–72; Perth Aust: sen syst analyst 1972–76,
computer syst man. from 1976
m Perth W Aust 25.8.78 Lorraine J. Walker dep prin p s
d of Clifford W. Geraldton W Aust

GRANT Gregory Vincent   MA 1959 cLLB 1961
 s of Gregory V. G. and Mary H. Dawson; b Aber
26.12.37
solic Milne & Reid Aber from 1961

GRANT Helen Isobel   BSc 1956
 d of Benjamin G. tailor and Jane A. Forbes; b Forres
24.4.34
teacher maths Perth h s 1957–60
m Forres 24.9.60 George A. W. Ferguson farm. s of
William F. F. Forres

GRANT Ian   BSc 1959 *1963

GRANT Ian   MA 1960 LLB 1962
 s of Archibald S. G. butcher and Elspeth Johnston;
b Aber 11.11.38
law app Aber 1961–64; leg. asst Kincardine-on-Forth
1964–69; lands off. Blantyre Malawi from 1969
m Blantyre 5.5.73 Rahima Bhatti

GRANT Ian Alisdair Macgregor   *BSc 1964
 s of Ian G. lect Aber coll of educ and Gladys D. Tullo
typist; b Edin 31.12.42
Kodak, Harrow: res 1964–66, prod. technol from 1966
m Aber 6.3.67 June M. Lumsden MA 1966 *qv*

GRANT Ian Herbert Wynne Macdonald
**   *BSc 1964 Dip Ed 1965 MSc 1970**

GRANT Ishbel Sinclair   MA 1961
 d of Paul G. bar man. and Margaret J. Watson; b
Invergordon 15.9.40
teacher Torry acad Aber from 1962
m Aber 27.3.64 John Fraser letterpress machineman s of
John F. Aber

GRANT James Alexander   *BSc 1957

GRANT James Allister   *BSc(agr) 1957
 s of James A. G. slater and Margaret J. Walker;
b Aber 14.11.33
BLitt(Oxon) 1959
lect Cheshire coll of agr from 1960
m 2.1.60 Sheila M. Johnston lib

GRANT Kathleen Margaret   *BSc 1956
 d of David H. S. G. coach bldr and Margaret L.
Norrie clerk; b Aber 20.10.33
statist Coats res lab Paisley 1956–67; teacher maths/sc
Westwood s Reading 1957–58; asst exper off. AWRE
Aldermaston 1958–61; Basingstoke: teacher maths
Richard Aldworth s 1972–77, N Foreland Lodge from
1977
m Aber 24.7.57 Thomas O. Young BSc 1956 *qv*

GRANT Leslie Craib   *MA 1970 Dip Ed 1971
s of John G. master blacksmith and Annie Leslie; b
Lumphanan 14.4.29
teacher Engl/hist Torry acad Aber from 1971
m Fraserburgh 10.9.53 Sheila Doig waitress d of Robert
D. Fraserburgh
d Aber 19.2.76 *AUR* XLVI 418

GRANT Lilian Ann   MA 1964
d of William W. G. lab and Lily A. G. Kinnaird;
b Aber 19.3.43
teacher: Toronto 1966-70, Aber 1970-73
m Aber 6.8.65 John T. Brebner asst controller city police
Aber s of John T. B. Aber

GRANT Linda Mary   MA 1964
d of George R. G. MA(Glas) headmaster and Catherine
M. Morrison MA 1933 *qv*; b Aber 4.4.43
teacher: St Faith's prep s for boys Cambridge 1965-66,
Speedwell inf s Littlemore Oxon 1967, Albyn s for girls
Aber 1967-69
m Grantchester 8.8.66 Donald J. Morrison MA 1965 *qv*

GRANT Lionel   MB ChB 1956

GRANT Margaret Henrietta   *MA 1967 Dip Ed 1968
d of Alexander J. G. farm. and Marjory P. Watt;
b Dufftown 4.5.46
teacher: Bankhead acad 1968-71, part time Fleetwood
1974-75, Mytchett from 1975
m Aber 20.7.70 Charles W. Lyon Dean MB ChB 1971
army m o s of William J. L. D. MB ChB 1933 *qv*

GRANT Margaret Isabel   *MA 1961
d of Ian H. G. farm. and Isabella Milne MA 1930 *qv*;
b Elgin 28.2.39
Dip Sec St(Lond) 1962
prod./edit. asst OUP Lond 1962-64; teacher: Lond
1964-65, Bournemouth 1965-66
m Urquhart 22.12.64 Ralph J. Woodward BSc(City) syst
analyst s of William H. W. Doncaster

GRANT Margaret Mary   MA 1969
d of John G. gen merch and Mary J. Reid; b Tomnavoulin 19.12.25
med secy, translator, teacher Kinshasa univ Zaire
1970-73; teacher mod lang Lawside acad Dun 1974-76;
asst prin mod lang St John's s Dun 1976-78, prin mod
lang from 1978

GRANT Mavis   *MA 1960
m Elrick

GRANT McGregor Thom   BL 1958

GRANT Michael Murray   MA 1964
b Aber 8.11.41
FRSA 1968
sales man. Birm 1972-73; group dev exec Lond 1973-75;
teacher Staines 1975-77; bus. dev exec Colchester/Lond
1977-78; sen res exec Lond from 1978

GRANT Moira Booth   MA 1959
m Ewen

GRANT Moira Elizabeth   BSc 1968
d of James G. bank clerk, farm. and Patricia M.
Newbery nurse; b Keith 9.3.48
teacher: Banff 1969-71, Aberlour, Tomintoul 1971-73,
Tomintoul from 1974
m Tomintoul 14.8.71 Ian A. Mathieson farm. s of John
M. Tomnavoulin

GRANT Morag Henrietta Kerr   MA 1966
d of Robert G. van salesman and Maisie M. Martin
factory superv; b Fyvie 23.2.46
teacher Ayr: 1966-69, hist and asst prin guid from 1969
m Ayr 5.7.71 Robert R. Gibson apron operative s of
John G. Ayr

GRANT Neil Farquharson   MA 1968

GRANT Norman Marshall   MB ChB 1956
s of Robert F. G. man. dir/pharm and Doris M. Gable;
b Aber 20.7.26
h o sen h o Woodend hosp Aber, Lond, Essex 1956-58;
g p Grays 1958-59, Rochester from 1959
m Aber 5.12.53 Dorothy S. G. Banks DA med secy d of
Robert B. St Margaret's Hope

GRANT Raymond James Shepherd   *MA 1964
s of Bertie J. G. MA 1922 *qv* and Mabel S. Milne MA
1930 *qv*; b Aber 26.5.42
PhD(Cantab) 1971
Edmonton asst prof 1967-74, assoc prof dept Engl from
1974
m Vancouver 22.12.73 Pauline (Pieterke) Pearl Kits Dip
Chr Educ (Emmaus coll, Oak Park Illinois) girls' club rep
B.C. d of G. B. K. Red Deer Alta

GRANT Robert Morrison   MB ChB 1970
s of George R. G. MA(Glas) headmaster and Catherine
M. Morrison MA 1933 *qv*; b Aber 17.5.46
h o ARI 1970-71, res fell. surg Aberd 1971-72; regist
path. Wester I Glasg 1972-74; lect path. Glas from 1974
m Irvine 15.1.73 Joan C. Paton teacher d of Andrew P.
Irvine

GRANT Ronald Alexander   BSc 1958 *1959

GRANT Ronald Clark   *MA 1968
s of George A. G. insur off. and Margaret S. Clark;
b Elgin 19.5.44
post-grad res Glas 1968-71; tut. hist Glas 1968-71;
teacher AGS from 1972
m Aber 6.4.68 Audrey A. Menzies teacher d of John
A. M. Elgin

GRANT Ronald William   MB ChB 1967

GRANT Ruth Margaret   MB ChB 1970
m Collins

GRANT Sheila Margaret   MA 1965

GRANT Sheila Margaret   MA 1966
d of Archibald G. H. G. MA(Edin) min of relig and
Dorothy J. Paterson BSc(Glas) teacher; b Dunfermline
9.11.45
Dip Ed(Edin) 1967
teacher Peterculter p s 1967-74
m Aber 17.7.70 George E. Robertson MA 1970 *qv*

GRANT Victor Norman   MA 1963

GRANT Wilma Forrest   *MEd 1965
d of James W. G. bank off. and Mary B. Forrest;
b Keith 1.11.37
BA(NZ) 1961 BSc(Auck) 1971 MB ChB(Auck) 1973
NZ: teacher Engl/Fr Wellington E girls' coll 1966-67;
h o Cook hosp Gisborne 1974; m o NZ Red Cross S
Vietnam 1975; h o RACH 1975; med pract NZ from 1976

GRANT Wilma Taylor   MA 1970

GRASSICK Brian Douglas Miller   MB ChB 1961
s of Charles D. G. comp rep and Joan Miller; b Aber
13.5.34
DObstRCOG 1965
h o ARI 1962–63, Kuching/Miri gen hosps Sarawak,
Borneo 1963–64; sen h o obst Forth Park mat. hosp
Kirkcaldy 1964–65; regist obst/gyn Princess Margaret
hosp Nassau, Bahamas 1965–67; med advis Hoechst
pharm Lond 1967–70; g p Slough from 1970 and part
time indust m o with Slough indust health serv from 1970
m Aber 24.6.65 Annette Foo tel superv d of Francis F.
Kuching

GRASSICK Kenneth Alan   MB ChB 1966
s of Charles D. G. comp rep and Joan Miller; b Aber
7.6.35
h o Aber hosps 1967–68; m o, sen m o RAF Singapore,
England 1968–73; g p Newcastle-u-Tyne from 1973

GRASSIE Alexander Donald Campbell   *MA 1957
s of James C. G. DSc 1945 qv; b Aber 4.4.35
BA(Cantab) 1959 PhD(Cantab) 1962 FInstP 1979
lect phys Sus from 1962
m 1960

GRATTON Samuel Douglas Walls   MA 1961
s of Samuel G. bldg contr and Priscilla L. Walls; b
Glasg 5.3.37
tv prod.: Europe 1964–66, NYC, USA from 1966

GRAVES Peter Arthur   *MA 1966

GRAVES Rodney James   *MA 1970 Dip Ed 1971

GRAY Albert   BSc(eng) 1960

GRAY Alexander   *MA 1970

GRAY Alison Catherine   MA 1969
d of Edward G. comp dir and Muriel W. Fraser MA
1938 qv; b Aber 3.9.48
teacher Aber from 1970
m Aber 7.8.70 Eric E. Lachowski BSc 1970 qv

GRAY Catherine Jennifer   MA 1970
d of Robert A. A. G. stockbroker and Susannah I. H.
Thomson; b Glasg 6.4.49
Dip Sec St(Strath) 1971
secy: Ethicon Edin 1971–72, to man. dir Noble Grossart
from 1972
m Edin 22.6.74 Anthony D. D. MacIver LLB(Edin) solic
s of Donald D. MacI. Edin

GRAY Daniel   BL 1959
d Aber 11.6.61 AUR xxxix 205

GRAY Derek William George   MB ChB 1963
s of William G. house carpenter and Helen R. Sherriffs;
b Aber 28.4.38
h o ARI 1963–64; trainee g p Aber 1964–65; regist
paediat RACH 1965–69; g p Aber from 1969
m Aber 1.4.64 Allison Easton teacher d of Charles C. E.
Aber

GRAY Doreen Watson   *MA 1966
d of James A. G. slater and Barbara J. Lovie factory
worker; b Aber 18.11.43
HM insp taxes Aber, Lond 1966–72, higher grade from
1972

GRAY Elma   *MA 1956
m Howitt

GRAY Evelyn Mary Stewart   BSc 1967

GRAY Gordon   *MA 1967

GRAY Helen   BSc 1966
d of Alexander S. G. barman and Williamina Marr;
b Aber 27.3.45
res poultry res centre Edin 1967–68; teacher: Armadale
acad W Lothian 1968–69, Edin 1969–71
m Aber 19.7.69 Barry O. Hughes BA(Cantab) vet res off.
s of Leslie E. H. Cambridge

GRAY Ian   MA 1969 *1971
s of Charles G. P.O. tel and Elizabeth I. Kiloh; b Aber
20.6.48
teacher maths Rubislaw acad Aber 1972–75; asst prin
maths Kincorth acad Aber from 1975

GRAY Ian Alexander   MB ChB 1970
s of Alexander G. civ eng and Grace M. E. Jaffray;
b Aden Saudi Arabia 28.1.45
LMCC
h o: Gilbert Bain hosp Lerwick 1970–71, city hosp Aber
1971; g p: Thompson Manitoba 1971–73, Alliston Ontario
from 1973
m London –.10.65 Ellen M. McDonagh secy d of William
McD. Lond

GRAY Ian Gibson   MA 1965 LLB 1967

GRAY Ian Nicol   MA 1968

GRAY Ian Sharp   BSc 1956
s of John G. MA 1930 qv and Margaret C. Black MA
1929 qv; b Scalloway 27.4.36
soldier Munster Lager Germany 1956–58; teacher:
Lerwick 1959–62, Scalloway from 1972
m Lerwick 4.4.60 Marina J. Burgoyne hairdresser, secy
d of Robert C. M. B. Lerwick

GRAY Isabel Anne   MA 1969
d of Robert G. MA(Glas) C of S min and Johanna
I. M. Morison teacher dom sc; b Harthill 17.4.48
teacher Fr: Glenrothes 1969–71, Alloa 1972–73
m Stonehaven 29.12.71 David W. Hay BA(Stir) scient
civ serv s of Andrew A. H. St Fillans

GRAY Isobel Stewart   MA 1962
d of Alexander J. G. baker, NFU branch secy and
Christina S. Stewart shop asst, secy; b Aber 18.11.41
teacher Engl/Lat Fraserburgh acad 1963–64, Alford
s 1964–67; part-time remed teacher Alford acad 1972–77,
full time from 1977
m Alford 7.8.65 William J. Balfour painter/decorator
s of William J. B. Alford

GRAY James   *BSc 1963 MSc 1965
s of James F. G. master painter and Gladys Robertson
mus teacher; b Fort George 9.1.41
lect Aberd 1967–68; temp teacher Bervie 1968–69; div
man. Rockfall, Glasg 1969–71, comp dir site explor serv
Aber 1971–74; comp man. dir Grampian Soil Surv Aber
from 1974
m Tomintoul 29.7.67 Rhoda V. Murray BSc 1968 qv

GRAY James Anthony   MA 1959
s of James M. G. master draper and Monica M.
McKay teacher; b Dufftown 20.6.37
teacher maths Hilton acad Aber 1960–70, Cults acad from
1970
m Huntly 12.7.61 Margaret G. Grant teacher home econ
d of William M. G. Huntly

GRAY James Duncan   *MA 1970
MSc(Wales) 1971
statist civ serv from 1971; resid Newport Gwent

GRAY James Millar   *MA 1965
s of James M. G. chief eng MN and Jane W. Bate;
b Dun 8.11.43
RN instr lt 1966–71; teacher: asst prin Engl Harris acad
Dun from 1971

GRAY James Telfer   *MA 1964

GRAY Janet McNaught   *MA 1970
d of Colin M. G. civ serv and Murdina McArthur SRN:
b Glasg 22.5.49
Dip Bible Coll of Wales 1976
teacher Gaelic Stornoway 1971–74, lang Barra 1976–78,
Gaelic/r e Stornoway from 1978

GRAY Janice Margaret   BEd 1970

GRAY Jean Elizabeth   *MA 1965
d of John G. G. MA 1914 qv and Ida J. Cumming MA
1934 qv; b Aber 20.11.43
teacher Engl: West Calder h s 1966–70, Woodmill h s
Dunf 1970–72, Notre Dame h s Dumbarton from 1972
m Aber 1.8.72 Keith P. Bear MA 1965 qv

GRAY John Alexander   MA 1969
s of Robert G. prof and tech off. eng div M o D and
Annie J. Shand civ serv D o E dept; b Colombo Ceylon
20.3.48
teacher Engl subj: Queen Anne h s Dunfermline 1970–73,
St Andrew's Scots s Buenos Aires from 1973
m Kirkcaldy 3.4.72 Margaret A. Bogie BEd(Edin)
teacher d of John B. Kirkcaldy

GRAY John Peter Shaw   *MA 1970
s of John H. G. MA 1932; b Aber 11.3.47
LL B(Edin) 1972
law app Edin 1972–74, solic Gray & Kellas advoc Aber
from 1974
m Larbert 4.6.77 Lesley A. Reid LL B(Glas) solic d of
James B. R. Larbert

GRAY Joseph   BSc(eng) 1964
s of Joseph G. motor eng and Anne J. Smith; b Lerwick
6.8.42
MICE 1976
asst eng Zetland c c Lerwick 1964–75; dep dir construct.
Shetland Is c from 1975
m Hillswick 4.7.67 Agnes H. Williamson teacher d of
Robert J. W. Ollaberry

GRAY Laurence   MA 1966
s of John G. eng and Margaret S. Gibson; b Musselburgh 19.1.40
LTCL (speech) 1968 LGSM (drama) 1971 ADBEd
(drama) 1973
Aber: teacher Engl 1967–69, sp and drama 1969–71; asst
organis sp and drama 1971–76; advis drama Grampian
reg c from 1976
m Aber 7.7.69 Elizabeth S. Whiteford MB ChB 1967 qv

GRAY Laurina Gilberta Elizabeth   MA 1966
d of Robert G. quartermaster and Ann Christie;
b Vidlin Shetland 10.12.43
lib asst Aber publ lib 1966–67; tax off. Inl Rev Welwyn
Garden City from 1974
m Aber 4.3.67 Hennessey A. S. Thompson BA(Durh)
CA s of James T. Freetown Sierra Leone

GRAY Margaret Reid Russell   MA 1962
d of Andrew J. M. G. grocer, clerk and Margaret R.
Russell comptometer oper; b Aber 23.3.41
teacher: Engl Aber acad 1963–64, jun s RGC Aber
1964–69, remed Kirkhill p s Aber from 1974
m Aber 6.8.65 Derek J. Murison marine biol s of David
R. M. New Pitsligo

GRAY Marilyn   MA 1969

GRAY Marjory   MA 1968
d of Magnus H. G. fish merch and Elaine M. Martin;
b Aber 12.5.48
m Aber 29.12.67 Myles D. G. Hardie MA 1969 qv

GRAY Monica Mary   MA 1966
d of James M. G. draper and Monica McKay teacher;
b Dufftown 18.1.46
welfare off. Ayrsh 1967–68; soc worker Highland reg
from 1979
m Aber 6.8.69 Neil S. Campbell teacher s of Thomas
S. C. Ayr

GRAY Patricia   BSc 1963
d of John G. provender miller and Williamina S.
Banks printer's asst; b Aber 4.3.42
teacher maths: Barstable s Basildon 1965–66, Kaimhill s
Aber 1968, Portobello s 1969, Forester s Edin 1969–73,
Kincorth acad Aber 1973–79, Westhill acad Skene from
1979
m Aber 7.8.64 John W. Ritchie BSc 1964 qv; marr diss
1972

GRAY Peter Stuart   *BSc(eng) 1968

GRAY Roger Woodville   BSc(agr) 1960
s of Donald G. MA(Oxon) headmaster Bootham s York
and Janet K. Wright teacher: b York 30.8.34
Dip Agr(NOSCA) 1957 Nat Dip Agr 1957 DTA(Trin)
1962
Kenya: agr res off. min of agr Kakamega, Kisii 1962–67,
res off. E Af Tanning Extract comp Eldoret 1967–72,
man. seeds plant Kenya Seed comp Nakuru from 1972
m Heywood 16.7.60 Johanna E. U. M. Ehrhardt MB ChB
1960 qv

GRAY Russell   MA 1968
s of Andrew J. M. G. clerk and Margaret R. Russell;
b Aber 14.6.47
AGS: teacher, asst prin guid, prin guid, from 1969
m Aber 8.4.72 Sheila C. G. Baxter teacher d of Alexander
B. Aber

GRAY Sandra   BSc 1966 Dip Ed 1967
d of Alexander M. G. butcher shop man. and Agnes M.
Stephen; b Aber 10.4.45
teacher maths Summerhill s s Aber 1967–70; teacher
maths/asst house mistress Windsor g s Hamm Germany
1970–74, head maths dept from 1974

GRAY Sheenagh Mabel   *BSc 1956
d of Thomas G. farm. and Elizabeth M. G. Scott
tailoress; b Dyce 8.10.34
res biol: MRC AERE Harwell 1956–58, plant breeding
Pentlandfield 1958–60; teacher sc Inv h s 1960–62
m Aber 1.10.60 James Fitzpatrick indust photogr s of
Patrick F. Dun

GRAY Walter   BSc 1966

GRAY Walter Bignell   MA 1956

GRAY William Gavin   MA 1969   LLB 1971
 s of William G. eng and Gladys M. Taylor; b Aber
14.11.48
law app Aber 1972–73; ptnr Kinnear & Falconer solic
Stonehaven 1973–75; dir Royal Deeside Inns (Northern)
from 1975
m Aber 6.7.71 Pamela H. Jowett LLB 1970 *qv*

GRAY William Hugh   BSc 1964
 s of John Gray MA 1930 *qv* and Margaret C. Black
MA 1929 *qv*; b Scalloway 13.8.40
phys: Glasg 1964–68, Leic from 1968
m Leicester 9.7.66 Anne P. Sharp lib d of Leonard E. S.
Leicester

GRAY William Robert   MA 1967
 s of John H. G. carpenter/boat bldr and Mary S.
Anderson; b Baltasound Shetland 21.12.44
teacher: Perthsh 1968–75, central reg Scot. 1975–77;
head p s Cunningsburgh from 1977
m Killin 12.7.71 Margaret J. Lindsay teacher d of Michael
L. Edin

GREEN Andrew Braham   *MA 1968
 s of Henry G. clerk and Edith Pinkus; b Lond 29.4.45
Dip Pers Man (LSE) 1969
pers off. Masson Scott eng Lond, Brist 1969–73; pers
man.: J Blakeborough eng W Yorks 1974–78, Stone Platt
eng Crawley from 1978
m Helsinki Finland –.7.71 Riitta K. Salonen

GREEN Anne Mitchell   *MA 1970
 d of James G. MA 1929 *qv*; b Buckie 26.5.47
PhD(Cantab) 1975
grad stud. Girton coll Cantab 1970–73; lect LSE from
1973
m 21.6.75 J. B. Bullen MA(Cantab)

GREEN Christopher Stephen   BSc 1970
 s of Frederick R. G. sales consult. and Dorothy E. T.
Trobe; b Edgware, 29.8.48
Lond: articled clerk CA's off. 1970–73, exec off. in P.O.
(telecomms fin.) from 1973

GREEN Dorothy   LLB 1968
 d of Raymond G. gen man. and Louise G. Strachan;
b Aber 15.2.47
law app Aber 1968–70; leg. asst: Glasg 1970–74, part-
time Aber from 1975
m Aber 5.9.70 Ronald S. C. Shanks CA s of Robert I. S.
Dullatur

GREEN William Innes   BSc(eng) 1964
 s of Richard G. G. master joiner and Isabella Middleton, b Tarland 17.2.42
Birm: grad app 1964–65, prod. quality eng 1965–67;
Dun: indust eng 1967–68, asst head indust eng 1968–72;
man. MFG eng Waterloo, Canada 1972; head distribution Dun from 1973
m Ballater 25.9.65 Jennifer M. Bruce secy d of George
O. B. Ballater

GREENHALGH James Francis Derek   PhD 1959
 s of Cecil G. sales man. and Phyllis Woodmass buyer
in dept store; b Frodsham 4.10.32
BA(Cantab) 1953 MA 1957 MS(Illinois) 1954
lect agr chem Edin 1959–63; Rowett res inst Aber: head
pasture util sect. 1963–66, head cattle sect. 1966–70, dep
head of dept from 1970
m Aberystwyth 4.10.58 Isoline Gee PhD 1958 *qv*

GREENLEES Charles Victor   MA 1967

GREENSHIELDS Irene   MA 1969
 d of Frank G. gents' outfitter and Williamina Fraser;
b Cambuslang 3.5.48
Glasg: teacher 1969–70, 1971–73, asst prin mod lang from
1973
m Burnside 29.2.72 Alan S. Muir dir s of David M. Glasg

GREENSHIELDS Robert Archibald   *BSc 1958

GREENSMITH Isobel Moyra   *BSc 1968
 d of Leonard A. G. BSc 1928 *qv*; b Fowlis Easter
19.1.46
teacher maths Aber acad later Hazlehead acad 1969–74
m Aber 3.1.69 Christopher B. Howard BSc 1966 *qv*

GREENWELL George Rodney Lyndon   BSc(eng) 1965

GREENWOOD Duncan Joseph   PhD 1957 DSc 1973
 s of Herbert J. G. customs and excise and Alison
Fairgrieve MA(Liv); b New Barnet 16.10.32
BSc(Liv) 1954 Sir Gilbert Morgan medal of soc of chem
indust 1962
res fell. Aberd 1957–58; nat vegetable res stat Wellesbourne, Warwick: s o chem sect. 1959–62, s s o 1962–66,
head chem sect. 1966–74 (hon lect Birm from 1969 and
Leeds from 1974), s p s o and head soil sc from 1974

GREGORY Angela Christine   BSc 1965
 d of Andrew D. G. MA(Glas) acct, comptroller AEI
(Rugby) and Isabel M. Johnston; b Rugby 10.2.44
asst market res Ilford, Ilford 1965–66; econ/corporate
plan. Nairn Williamson (Holdings) Kirkcaldy 1966–68
m Kinross 28.9.68 John R. Crossland BA(Durh) market
res off, marketing man. s of Harold C. Barnsley

GREGORY Tudor John   *MA 1966
 s of Griffith J. G. bank man. and Phyllis M. Jennings
secy; b Bristol 20.9.42
pers man. ICI: Runcorn 1966–70, Brussels 1970–72,
Runcorn 1972–77, Kenya 1977–79, Widnes from 1979
m Widnes 6.6.70 Brigid M. Roach secy, receptionist d of
William R. Widnes

GREIG Allan   BSc 1962
 s of Thomas G. and Isabella McAllan; b Aber 1.12.40
teacher: S. Queensferry 1963–65, Chingola, Zambia
1965–68, Tripoli, Libya 1968–70, Corby from 1970
m Gorey 30.10.68 Breda O'Toole

GREIG Denis   PhD 1958
 s of Valentine G. bldg contr ag and Constance Cobban;
b Fettercairn 31.8.32
BSc(St And) 1953
phys: post-doc fell. nat res council of Canada Ottawa
1958–60, lect Leeds 1960–70, sen lect from 1970
visiting assoc prof Michigan State univ E Lansing, Mich,
USA 1969–70
m Brechin 4.9.57 Charlotte H. Webster MB ChB 1956 *qv*

GREIG Evelyn Margaret   BSc 1965
 d of Charles M. G. interior decorator and Evelyn A.
Flett; b Aber 21.12.43
teacher: Inverurie acad 1965, coll of comm Aber 1966–67;
air stewardess Lond 1967; teacher: Kampala Uganda
1968–71, Bauchi Nigeria 1972–73, Folkestone then
Beaconsfield from 1976
m Aber 27.12.69 William D. Wilkie BSc(Glas) teacher,
capt RAEC s of David G. W. Glasg

GREIG Irene Jean   *MA 1962

GREIG Isobel Elizabeth   MA 1961
 m Cook

GREIG James Robertson   MB ChB 1960
s of William H. G. police off. and Barbara M. Robertson civ serv; b Auchterless 14.5.36
MSc(Lond) 1973 DIH 1973
h o ARI and Aber city hosp 1960–61; lect Aberd 1961–62; m o RAF England, Aden, Scot., Guernsey, Lond from 1962
m Newton Mearns 1.8.63 Janet M. Morrison teacher p e d of Stanley M. Glasg

GREIG Linda Jean   *MA 1970
d of Alfred W. G. dept man. paper mill and Jean R. D. Innes secy; b Aber 8.9.48
teacher: Kincorth acad Aber 1973, Turriff acad from 1978
m Aber 4.12.70 Edward Shand MA 1970 qv

GREIG Marion Graham   BSc 1969
d of Alexander W. G. and Marion Graham; b Aber 25.4.48
teacher maths: Montrose acad 1970–72, Currie h s 1972–76
m Aber 31.7.72 David F. Goda MA(Oxon) statist (lect Aberd 1968–72) s of Lawrence G. Manc

GREIG Michael Andrew   *MA 1964

GREIG Norma Ann Mitchell   MA 1957
d of Charles G. bus driver and Mary M. McIntosh; b Fyvie 25.5.35
teacher: Ashley Rd p s Aber 1958–64, relief Crudie, Fyvie, Fintry, Ardmiddle p s 1972–73, Auchterless p s from 1973
m Fyvie 15.5.64 Harry P. Clark seeds exec s of Henry C. Turriff

GREIG Raymond   BSc 1963
s of Thomas G. house painter and Isabella M. McAllan; b Aber 31.8.42
teacher maths: Bo'ness acad 1964–68, Jarvis coll, Toronto from 1968
m(2) Toronto 24.6.77 Isobel Anderson d of William Hamilton Greenock

GREIG Robert   *MA 1958
s of Robert M. G. cattle dealer and Helen Y. Lumsden; b Aber 6.7.35
teacher mod lang Harris acad Dun 1959–64; prin mod lang Mortlach h s Dufftown 1964–66; Turriff acad: prin mod lang 1966–74, asst rector 1974–75, dep rector from 1975
m Aberlour 19.7.61 Isobel Miller MA 1958 qv

GREIG Rosemary Jeanette   MA 1967
d of Alexander W. G. chief insp police and Jessie M. Calder; b Arbroath 30.3.46
teacher p s: Aber 1968–69, Elgin 1969–71, St Andrews 1972–74
m Aber 24.10.69 William S. Cantlay MA 1966 qv

GREIG William Rattray   MB ChB 1959 *MD 1964
s of Hugh F. G. and Jessie Rattray; b Inv 28.9.35
MRCPGlas PhD(Glas)
sen lect Glas from 1969

GRENFELL James McNab   BSc 1968

GRIBBLE Colin Duncan   *BSc 1959
s of Joseph M. G. salesman and Elizabeth Duncan; b Lond 26.11.36
PhD(Edin) 1965 MIMM 1972
geol Williamson Diamonds Tanganyika 1959–62; lect

Glas from 1965; consult. geol Scot. quarry comp (AQS) from 1968

GRIBBLE Elizabeth Jean   MA 1960 cLLB 1962

GRIEVE Alasdair Aitken Hume   MB ChB 1965
s of William B. G. branch man. insur comp and Agnes Hume; b Glasg 31.12.39
h o RACH, city hosp Aber 1965–66; g p Aber from 1966
m Aber 1962 Irene H. Aitken hairdresser d of Alistair A. Aber

GRIEVE Alexander Millar   MB ChB 1970
s of James A. G. acct GPO Aber and Helen R. M. Miller p o clerk; b Aber 4.7.46
DObstRCOG 1972
h o Aber hosps 1970–72; army m o: Catterick 1972–74, Farnborough 1974–76, Hereford from 1976
m Kirkintilloch 20.12.69 Alexandra W. C. Taig midwife d of James T. Kirkintilloch

GRIEVE Andrew Alexander   MA 1970

GRIEVE David Rollo   MB ChB 1958
s of Charles B. G. MB ChB(Edin) med pract and Isabella H. Brown teacher; b Aber 25.2.35
MRCGP 1972
h o Aber hosps 1958–59; m o RCAF 1959–62; g p Aber from 1962
m Switzerland 3.1.59 Madeleine H. I. Schumacher PhD(Zurich) d of Eugen S. Wangs KtSt Gallen Switzerland

GRIEVE George Brown   *MA 1966
s of George G. painter and Mary Durham; b Glasg 20.2.35
teacher: geog Galashiels acad 1967–70, prin geog Campbeltown g s 1970–74; comp dir bldg comp Banffsh from 1974
m Aberlour 15.7.61 Patricia K. Munro comp secy d of Peter M. Carron Moray

GRIEVE Helen Ford Bayne   MB ChB 1956
d of Charles B. G. MB ChB(Edin) g p and Isabella H. Brown teacher; b Aber 27.6.32
h s RACH 1956; Woodend hosp Aber: sen h phys Glenburn wing (geriatric) 1957–58; s h o med 1961–64; clin med off. Lincolnshire AHA Sleaford from 1965
m 10.7.58 Geoffrey Dillon MB ChB 1958 qv

GRIEVE Ian Barr   MA 1963
s of William B. G. insur branch man. and Agnes Hume; b Glasg 22.2.42
teacher Engl: Hatton (Cruden) s 1964–69, Kaimhill s s Aber 1969–73, Kincorth acad Aber 1973–75, Bankhead acad from 1975

GRIEVE Kathleen Freda Seatter   MA 1958
d of William A. G. farm. and Clara Craigie; b Rousay 2.2.37
clerkess Moffat from 1972
m Rousay 17.7.58 William Murray MA 1959 qv

GRIEVE Richard Andrew Francis   *BSc 1965
MSc PhD(Tor)

GRIFFIN Anthony Roderick   *BSc(for) 1967
s of Anthony G. artist and Diana B. Long; b Watford 17.4.45
PhD(Oregon) 1974
Traralgon, Vict, Aust: for. res off. 1967–70, for. res off.

with Commonwealth govt (genetics and breeding of pinus radiata) from 1973
m Rosewell 13.2.65 Lindsay Jack MA 1967 *qv*

GRIFFITH Margaret Anne   *BSc 1967
m Davies

GRIFFITHS Arthur   BSc(eng) 1957

GRIFFITHS Freda Elizabeth   BSc 1962
d of Frederick N. G. machine oper and Elizabeth W. Nicol; b Lond 7.12.41
Govt actuary's dept Lond: cler off. 1964–70, exec off. 1970–76, higher exec off. from 1976

GRIFFITHS Peter Vernon   *MA 1970
s of T. Vernon G. acct and Nora Taylor; b Edin 6.12.47
MSc(Glas) 1972
clin psych RHSC Glasg from 1972

GRIGGS Daphne Ellen   MA 1967
m Vaughan

GRIGOR Norman   MA 1961

GRIMBLE Ian   PhD 1964
BA(Oxon)

GRIMES Katherine Mary Vincente   BSc 1965
d of Leslie E. G. off. customs and excise and Frances M. Rettie; b Turriff 29.3.44
Dip Ed(Edin) 1966
teacher maths: Knox acad Haddington 1966–67, Lossie-mouth 1967–70, Invernesssh 1971–72, Castle Douglas 1973, Nairn acad 1973–76
m Elgin 7.8.76 James M. Dixon flt lt RAF s of David F. D. Baldock

GRIMM Andrew Spalding   *BSc 1962
s of Robert J. W. G. farm. and Jean H. E. Spalding physioth; b Forfar 22.5.40
PhD(Glas) 1965
post-doc fell. nat res council of Canada Halifax Nova Scotia 1965–67, lect zool UCNW from 1967
m Aber 11.10.65 Marion Gordon BSc(Glas) reg plan., teacher d of Ernest J. G. Aber

GRINLY David   MA 1970
s of James G. civ serv and Anne W. M. Sharp textile worker; b Stirling 6.7.49
teacher geog Lornshill acad Alloa 1971–73 and from 1974; exec off. DTI Lond 1973–74
m Alloa 28.10.72 Eileen Mackison BSc(Edin) secy, civ serv d of Thomas M. Alloa

GRINSTED Carol Jean   MSc 1970
b Tunbridge Wells 30.10.47
BSc(S'ton) 1969 Dip Lib(Aberystwyth) 1973 ALA 1975
asst lib univ coll of Wales Swansea from 1973

GRISEDALE Alfred Catto   BSc(eng) 1957
s of Alfred G. shipyard worker and Stella D. Cardno; b Lancaster 8.8.36
MIEE 1970 CEng 1970
Bradford: grad app 1958–60; investigations eng Eng Elect. Co 1960–68; new prod. eng Lucas Aerospace from 1968

GRIVAS Jeffrey Peter   BSc 1970

GROSS Eric   *MA 1957 MLitt 1970 DMus 1975
s of Leo G. DL(Vienna) barrister and Ida Suchanek;

b Vienna 16.9.26
LTCL 1958 FTCL 1963
Sydney, Aust: teacher conservatorium mus 1959–60, univ lect mus 1960–71, sen lect 1971–73, assoc prof from 1974; pres fellowship of Aust composers 1970–73, 1976–77
m Plymouth 28.3.55 Pamela M. M. Davies d of John D. Mutley

GROSSERT Ian Gillies   BSc(eng) 1966
b 7.11.42
des eng Barclay Curle Glasg 1966–69; works man. John Grossert & Co Mombasa Kenya 1969–73
m Campbeltown 2.7.65 Penelope M. Colville MA 1965 *qv*
d Mombasa 10.11.73

GROSSET Arthur Early   *MA 1967

GROUNDWATER Gordon Thomas   MA 1967

GROUNDWATER James David   MA 1970

GROUNDWATER Myra Cumming   MA 1961
m Shearer

GROVE Eric John   *MA 1970
s of Gordon E. B. G. MB ChB(Manc) med pract and Irene Wilshaw; b Bolton 3.12.48
MA(Lond) 1971
lect dept of hist/Engl Britannia royal naval coll Dartmouth from 1971
m Lond 14.4.73 Elizabeth J. Stocks ALA asst lib Darting-ton coll of arts Totnes d of Thomas H. S. Bridlington

GROVES Arthur   *MA 1967

GRUBB Anthony Ainslie   *BSc 1966
s of Anthony J. G. MA 1933 *qv*; b Wroxham 27.7.44
MIEE and CE 1975 MIRSE 1975
rly signal eng BR Glasg from 1966

GRUBB John Alexander   *BSc 1964

GRUENLER Royce Gordon   PhD 1957
s of Walter P. G. machinist and Maude E. Gordon; b Laconia, New Hampshire, USA 10.1.30
AB(Williams coll) 1955 BD(Philadelphia) 1955
Hiram coll Ohio, USA: asst prof phil and relig 1957–64; chmn dept phil and relig 1962–66, assoc prof 1964–67; chmn dept of relig 1966–69, 1972–75, prof relig from 1967
m Laconia 6.9.52 Grace L. Sansom Dip Bible inst Penn. USA d of Frank S. Laconia

GUHA Madhabendra Mohan   PhD 1961
s of Surenda M. G. and Subarna Prava; b Barisal India 1.5.32
BSc(Calc) 1949 MSc(N Delhi) 1954
rubber res inst Malaysia: asst soils chem 1955–58 (study leave 1958–62) sen soil chem 1962–68; acting head of soils div 1968–70; dir agr res and advis bureau Malaysia from 1970
m Calcutta 1.5.64 Parul R. Paul BSc 1962 *qv*

GUNN Hugh James   *BSc(agr) 1963
d Bottisham 14.8.68 *AUR* XLIII 86

GUNN John Barnetson   LLB 1969

GUNN Lewis Arthur   *MA 1957
s of Lewis H. G. master butcher and Jane Arthur; b Aber 10.4.35
teaching asst Engl-speaking union Cornell univ USA 1957–59; asst lect, lect govt Manc 1959–66; lect, sen lect

politics Glas 1966–72; prof of admin Strath from 1972 and civ serv prof of admin civ serv coll London 1974–79 m Aber 17.8.60 May F. Findlay MA 1957 *qv*

GUNN Mairi Anne Macdonald   MA 1968

GUNN Margaret Mackay   BSc 1966
d of David G. process superv UKAEA and Jane B. Nicolson; b Wick 2.10.44
teacher maths Wick 1967–73
m Wick 29.10.71 Patrick J. Gladstone MA 1970 *qv*

GUNN Nancy Sim   MA 1959
d of Murdoch Y. G. asst area man. BR and Mary L. Boyes dent. recept; b Peterhead 9.1.38
teacher: maths Ellon acad 1960–65, spec asst from 1965
m Insch 28.7.62 Edward B. Wallace postman s of Edward B. W. New Pitsligo

GUNN Robert Morrison   BSc(eng) 1961
s of Donald B. G. acct and Williamina Miller; b Wick 2.4.40
eng Aber corp 1961–63; asst eng Caithness c c Wick 1963–69; area eng N of Scot. water board Wick 1969–75; div eng Highland reg c water and sewerage dept from 1975
m Perth 3.8.63 Yvonne G. Avent MA 1962 *qv*

GUNN William   MA 1959
s of William G. fish buyer and Isabella M. Webster; b Aber 18.6.36
FIL
teacher Westerton p s Aber 1960–62; lect Aber coll of comm 1962–70, sen lect Sp/Ital from 1970
m Aber 5.4.61 Moira I. Mitchell acct machine oper d of George A. M. Aber

GUNTON Tom William   BSc(eng) 1967
d 26.8.69

GURNEY Jill Diana   MB ChB 1967
d of John L. G. elect. eng and Molly B. Bracher; b Lond 8.3.42
FFARCS primary 1973
resid anaesthesiology NY USA 1969–71; regist anaest Charing Cross hosp Lond 1972–73; med advis Wellcome foundation from 1973

GUTHRIE Janet Margaret   *MA 1970
d of Duncan D. G. MA(Belf) charity dir and Prunella S. B. Holloway organis secy; b Newcastle-u-Tyne 2.2.48
cler off. DHSS Lond 1970–71
m Wandsworth 24.10.70 Alan R. Mearns fishmonger s of Allan E. M. Aber; husb *d* 15.12.73

GUTHRIE John Mowat   MA 1967
s of Henry F. G. farm. and Annie Mowat; b Pitsligo 17.2.41
teacher maths AGS 1968–74, asst prin maths from 1974
m Elgin 21.12.74 Kathleen E. Cantlie nurse, health visitor

GUY Alistair Ross   MA 1970
d Dingwall 29.12.70 *AUR* XLIV 216

GUYAN Alice McKnight   MA 1963
m Deans

GUYAN John McKnight   *BSc(eng) 1963

GYANG Emmanuel Afiakwa   MSc 1963 PhD 1965
s of Robert A. farm. and Emma Nyakoa farm.; b Ghana 21.10.23

BPharm(Lond) 1953
Ghana: lect univ of sc/tech Kumasi 1954–64, sen lect 1964–66, assoc prof from 1966
visiting prof pharm univ of Pittsburg USA 1972

HACKET Alastair   MA 1970
b Aber 16.6.49
resid Edin

HADDEN Norman Alexander   MA 1961
s of Alexander H. gardener and Ethel E. Ferguson; b Insch 18.10.38
teacher geog: Alford s s 1962–63, St John's j s s Dun 1963–65, also housemaster govt s s Yola, N Nigeria 1965–69, St Michael's s Dun; prin geog St Saviour's h s Dun from 1973
m Dun 10.7.63 Monica A. Feeney catering man. d of James F. Dun

HADDON Susan Mary   *BSc 1970

HADDOW John Foulds   BSc 1970

HAGGART David Ballantine   *MA 1956
s of William G. H. life assur man. and Isabella M. Patrick secy; b Dun 15.3.34
JP 1971
nat serv R Corps Sig 1956–58; teacher Perth 1958–59; youth employment off. Aber 1959–63; sen careers advis off. Aberd from 1963
m Aber 1.9.64 Gwendolen M. Hall MA 1964 *qv*

HAIGH John Beverley   *BSc 1970
s of William H. retailer and Nora Fern; b Huddersfield 22.7.46
syst analyst Lond 1970–73; teacher from 1974

HALCROW John Andrew   BSc 1967

HALDON Carol Anne   *BSc 1968

HALDON Robert Anthony   *BSc 1962 PhD 1965

HALEY David   BSc(for) 1961 *1962
b Goole 3.11.39
MF(Br Col) 1964 PhD(Br Col) 1966
Canada: lect for. econ Tor 1966–67, assoc prof for. Br Col Vancouver 1967–73; visiting reader for. econ univ of Ibadan, Nigeria 1973–74; assoc prof for. Br Col Vancouver from 1974

HALFHIDE Andrew George   BSc(for) 1963

HALL Alan Richard   *MA 1963
s of Francis C. H. comm trav and Winifred L. Low loc govt housing visitor; b Aber 28.8.40
admin off. govt N Nigeria, Gboko 1963–64; pers off. ICI agr div Stockton-on-Tees 1964–65; teacher econ Queen's Park s s, Glenwood s s Glasg 1966–68; Aber: lect econ coll of comm 1968–74; head of dept econ and acct AGS from 1974
m Glasg 16.2.68 Jean A. McIntyre art teacher d of Donald McI. Bathgate

HALL Alexander Urquhart   MA 1968

HALL Alison Margaret   *MA 1965
d of John K. H. bldg contr and Joyce Smith physioth; b Aber 15.12.42
UN Interpreters Dip(Holborn coll Lond)
m Paris 28.11.68 Patrick Giffin CA s of George W. G. BSc(eng) (Durh)

HALL Colin David   MB ChB 1966
s of David H. MB ChB 1955 *qv*; b Chester 11.5.41
DABPsych & Neurol 1976
h o, regist Aber gen hosp 1966–69; dept of neurol univ of
N Carolina USA; resid 1969–72, instr 1972–73, asst prof
1973–77, assoc prof from 1977, dir neuromuscular unit
from 1977
m Aber 22.9.61 Valerie Gordon MA 1966 *qv*

HALL David John   MSc 1967 PhD 1969
s of John W. H. loc govt off. and Gladys L. Briggs;
b Farnborough 25.9.43
BSc(S'ton) 1962 FIMA 1973 MBCS 1972
Aberd: res fell. dept mental health 1967–74, syst dir mental
health res unit 1970–74; sen lect Lond s of hyg and trop
med from 1974
m Sidcup 25.7.64 Janet Wells MB ChB 1968 *qv*

HALL David John   *BSc 1970
s of K. J. H. sales man. and S. M. Webb teacher;
b NZ 2.2.47
teacher: biol/gen sc Hazlehead acad 1973, biol/phys
Hulme g s Oldham from 1973
comm in RAF VR(T)
m Salford 25.9.70 Helen M. Murphy BSc 1970 *qv*

HALL Gwendolen Margaret   MA 1964
d of John N. H. C of S min and Roberta R. Clark
b Newport-on-Tay 12.5.43
teacher Ger Aber acad 1965–66
m Aber 1.9.64 David B. Haggart MA 1956 *qv*

HALL Hilda Rae   MA 1960
d of Norman J. A. H. farm. and Jeannie Rae; b Udny
1.1.39
teacher: Fraserburgh cent s 1961–63, Hayshead s
Arbroath 1963–68; Edin: Muirhouse s 1968–69, Gylemuir
s 1969–74 asst head from 1974
m Aber 23.3.79 Ian S. Robertson farm. s of David M. R.
Forfar

HALL Jean Valerie Aitken   *MA 1967
d of Gilbert B. H. textile dyer and Elizabeth C.
Andrew; b Dunbartonsh 15.2.45
teacher geog: Ainslie Park s s Edin 1968–69, Northfield
acad Aber 1969–70, part time coll of comm 1971–72
m Aber 15.7.69 Richard A. North BSc MB ChB 1969 *qv*

HALL Joan Mary Robertson   MA 1968
d of John K. H. comp chmn and Joyce R. Smith
physioth; b Aber 5.7.47
SRN 1974

HALL John Thackray   *MA 1968
s of John M. H. MA(Oxon) unitarian min and Hilda I.
Thackray MA(Oxon) teacher; b Wigan 14.5.44
Brit Council: admin asst Edin 1968–71, Lond from 1971

HALL Linda Frances   *MA 1970
d of Francis C. H. comm trav and Winifred L. Low
housing visitor; b Aber 5.10.47
teacher s s Burnham-on-Crouch 1970–72; exec off. DHSS
Chelmsford 1973–74
m Aber 13.9.69 Keith W. Wilson BSc 1967

HALL Maureen Yvonne   *BSc 1967 Dip Ed 1968
m Lorimer

HALL Mildred Lillington   MA 1970
b Newcastle-on-Tyne
MA(Oxon)
res fell. Aberd from 1970
m Kenneth L. Blaxter FRS Norfolk

HALL Pamela Mary   MB ChB 1969
d of Willie H. traffic man. BEA and Helen Duguid;
b Lisbon 26.4.45
DObstRCOG 1971 MRCOG 1977 FACOG 1978
h o Aber 1969–71; res fell. obst Aberd 1971–72; m o publ
health/regist path. Lond 1972–74; sen h o obst/gyn
Harrow 1974–75; regist obst/gyn Cape Town 1975–77;
asst prof obst/gyn Case Western Reserve univ Cleveland
Ohio from 1977
m Aber 12.7.69 Stewart M. Hamilton MB ChB 1968 *qv*

HALL Sandra   MA 1970
m Kelman

HALL Wendy Muriel Adanma   MB ChB 1968
m Amaechi

HALL William David   *MA 1959

HALL William Fergusson   MA 1968

HALLEY Jean   *MA 1970
d of David B. H. and Ethel J. Scott; b Lanark 10.12.47
higher exec off. D o I: Lond 1971–73, N reg off. Newcastle-u-Tyne from 1973
m Sudbury 18.9.71 Robin C. Moss BA(Sus) s of Charles
T. M. Sudbury

HALLEY Margaret Loosome   MA 1958

HALLEY Mary Rosalind   MA 1963
d of James R. H. insur supt and Mary M. Angus;
b Perth 3.8.43
teacher: Aber 1964–66, Wick 1971–75, Cumbernauld
1976–77
m Aber 29.12.65 Alan R. Reid MB ChB 1966 *qv*

HALLIDAY David   MSc 1967 PhD 1969

HALLIDAY Donald Catto   BSc 1960
s of Archibald S. H. millwright and Margaret M. Catto;
b Oldmeldrum 13.11.37
teacher maths Elgin 1961–72; prin maths Glenrothes
from 1972
m Aber 19.7.63 Elspeth M. Bakie MA 1960 *qv*

HALLIDAY George Sime   *MA 1966 MSc 1967
s of Archibald S. H. millwright and Margaret M. Catto;
b Oldmeldrum 10.11.44
PhD(Cantab) 1970
geophys: NCB Burton-on-Trent 1970–72, geophys serv
internat Croydon 1972–73; explor geophys Shell:
Lausanne 1973–74, The Hague, Kinshasa Zaire from 1974
m Aber 16.11.67 Patricia M. H. Neill MA 1967 *qv*

HALSTEAD Peter Howard   LLB 1968
s of Jack Halstead civ serv and Florence Howard;
b Flete 22.3.47
BA(OU) 1975 solic supreme court 1972
Telford: articled clerk 1969–72, asst solic 1972–75, chief
asst solic (loc govt) from 1975
m Cumbernauld 4.4.70 Margaret D. Leaker MA 1968 *qv*

HAMBANANDA Chumsri   MSc 1963

HAMBLIN Caroline Anne   *BSc 1967
m Taylor

HAMDARD Mohammad Siddique   MSc 1970
BSc(agr)(W. Pak)

HAMID Hamid Ibrahim   PhD 1964
MSc(N W Khart)

HAMILTON Angela Geraldine   *MB ChB 1968
d of Ronald K. H. bank man. and Mary K. A. Lloyd-Hall, SRN; b Lond 22.12.42
FFARCS 1973 fell. prize
h o RACH, ARI 1968–69; intern Montreal 1969–70; h o anaest Westminster hosp Lond 1970, sen h o Royal Berks hosp Reading 1971; Lond: sen h o Westminster hosp 1971–72, regist Royal Marsden hosp 1972–73, hosp for sick ch Great Ormond St 1973; sen regist anaest Wessex area health auth Southampton and Winchester from 1973

HAMILTON Brian Wallace   *MA 1970
s of David H. trans clerk and Mabel Todd; b Irvine 22.7.48
teacher mus: Aberdeensh 1971–73, Oldham from 1976

HAMILTON Elizabeth Ann   *MA 1962
d of David A. H. MB ChB 1936 qv; b Aber 9.10.39
teacher Engl: Aber h s for girls 1963–64, New Engl s Kuwait from 1975
m Aber 27.12.63 Ian A. Olson MB ChB 1962 qv

HAMILTON Elizabeth Muriel Jane   MB ChB 1957
d of Malcolm H. insur surv and Helen S. F. Henderson; b Aber 4.3.34
m Aber 26.7.57 James D. Rust granite merch s of James R. Aber

HAMILTON Frank Eric Graham   *MA 1966

HAMILTON Gilbert Brown   BSc(eng) 1969
s of Gilbert F. H. BSc 1933 qv and Margaret W. Monro MA 1934 qv; b Aber 21.12.45
grad eng BBC TV Lond 1969–74; man. (des/res) Aertech San Jose California from 1974

HAMILTON Ian Varcoe   MTh 1969
BEng BD(Melb)

HAMILTON Joan Isobel Sinclair   LLB 1967
d of David A. H. MB ChB 1936 qv; b Aber 23.10.46
solic Inv 1969–72; reporter to Inv burgh ch panel 1971–73
m Inv 20.1.68 Bruce A. Merchant LL B 1965 qv

HAMILTON Leslie William   *BSc 1967 PhD 1971
s of Norman M. H. civ serv and Eileen M. Inder; b Aber 6.10.45
asst prin teacher sc Powis acad Aber from 1971

HAMILTON Margaret Vera   MA 1969
d of Thomas H. chief off. MN and Margaret J. Marshall; b Aber 24.3.46
teacher Aber p s from 1970
m Aber 14.9.68 Thomas Wemyss MA 1969 qv

HAMILTON Stewart Maclean   MB ChB 1968
s of Joseph S. H. MB ChB 1939 qv; b Aber 22.1.45
MSc(Lond) 1974 MRCP 1972 Dip Amer board internal med 1978
h o Woodend hosp Aber 1968–69; lect path., med Aberd 1969–71; regist Aber 1971–73, Harrow 1973–75; spec regist endocrinology Cape Town 1975–77; med firm dir/dir metabolic unit/consult. endocrin Cleveland metrop gen hosp/asst prof med Case Western Reserve univ Cleveland USA from 1977
m Aber 12.7.69 Pamela M. Hall MB ChB 1969 qv

HAMILTON William Farquhar Douglas   MB ChB 1967
s of Douglas H. pharm/optic and Stella Farquhar MA 1931 qv; b Aber 24.7.43
DA 1970 FFARCS 1972
h o ARI 1967–68; res asst dept med Aberd 1968–69; sen h o (hon clin tut.) regist, sen regist (hon lect Aberd) 1969–75; consult. anaest (hon sen lect Dund) Tayside health board from 1975
m Aber 19.7.68 Frances T. Auchinachie teacher d of Henry W. A. Lonmay

HAMMERSTAD Bodil   MB ChB 1965
d of Erling H. MD(Oslo) chief m o Innherred Sykeheim Verdal and Else M. Borch; b Oslo 16.11.40
spec internal med(Norway) 1974 spec gastroenterology (Norway) 1974
jun regist surg Oslo 1965–66, h o surg and intern med 1966–67; asst publ health off. Andøy 1967; Oslo: regist geriat 1967–69, jun regist intern med 1969–70, regist int med 1970–75, res fell. from 1976
m Stiklestad, Norway 13.5.67 Reidar Selbekk Cand Psych (Oslo) clin psych s of Arne S. Selbekken

HAMPTON Alexander William Matthew   *MA 1964
s of Alexander J. C. H. marine eng and Isabella R. Matthew; b Aber 2.1.41
asst pers man. Peterhead 1965–67; Aber: welfare and accommodation off. 1967–73, stud. serv off. from 1973
m Aber 11.9.64 Kathleen Sangster d of William S. Aber

HAMSON Robin Barrington   BSc 1970
s of William S. B. H. teacher and Cynthia I. Parrish lib; b Cambridge 26.5.49
teacher: Liv 1971–72, Droitwich 1972–73, Leic from 1974

HANCE Raymond John   PhD 1961
BSc(R'dg)

HANKIN Ronald George   *MA 1956 Dip Ed 1958

HANNAY Margaret Kerr   MA 1968
m O'Hagan

HANSON Rosalind Irene   MA 1965
d of Sydney W. F. H. BSc(Liv) scient (food & nutrit) and Irene Tomlinson teacher; b Liv 15.10.43
m Aber 2.6.66 Charles J. E. McIver MA 1962 qv

HANTON Douglas Alexander   MB ChB 1964
s of Alexander P. H. bus. exec and Davinah A. Baxter; b Aber 25.4.38
DObstRCOG 1968
h o Woodend hosp Aber 1964–65; sen h o: DRI 1965–66, Bellshill mat. hosp Lanarksh 1966; g p: E Kilbride 1966–73, Strathpeffer from 1973
m Aber 22.10.66 Margaret I. McKendry banker d of William E. McK. Cults

HANTON William Baxter   *MA 1958

HARBINSON Heather   MA 1968

HARBOUR Anthony Bryan   *MA 1966
s of Harold E. M. MA(Cantab) tech dir and Mary P. McManus MA(Edin) teacher; b Edin 26.6.43
grad trainee Metal Box Lond, Manc 1966–68; Mars Slough: div sales man. 1974–77, pers man. from 1977
m St Albans 23.7.66 Jacqueline E. M. Wright MA 1965 qv

HARCUS Mary Elizabeth   MA 1960

HARDCASTLE Patrick David *BSc(for) 1968
s of Harold B. H. schoolmaster and Florence W.
Taylor clerk; b Nott 11.6.47
Malawi: asst conserv for. Limbe 1968–70, reg for. off.
Mzimba 1970–72, sen silviculturist Dedza 1972–75, sen
for. res off. Zomba from 1975
m·Blantyre Malawi 23.8.69 Moira A. G. Runcie MA
1969 qv

HARDIE Alexander Lewis BSc 1968

HARDIE Andrew David Kemp BSc(for) 1958 *1959
s of James M. H. estate factor and Isabella F. Kemp;
b Fochabers 10.4.36
FIWSc 1973
asst conserv for. W reg Nigeria 1959–63; dist off. for.
comm Ipswich, Hitchin, Princes Risborough 1964–66;
Kitwe Zambia: market. off., timber util res off. 1966–72,
chief for. prod. res off. 1972–73; temp lect for. and wood
sc univ coll N Wales (Bangor); branch man. Tilhill for.
(Scot.) Stirling 1974–76; indep for. consult. overseas
from 1976
m Dublin 31.8.73 Kathleen Cleary BComm(NUI)
teacher, indust trg off. d of John C. C. Ballylongford

HARDIE Audrey Fowler *MA 1956

HARDIE Betty Theresa MA 1963
d of George F. H. cc employee and Beatrice M.
McGillivray; b Ellon 20.11.41
teacher: Boddam 1964–65, Dunscroft 1965–66
m Aber 21.7.65 James W. Barrack BSc(eng) 1964 qv

HARDIE Elsie McPherson BSc 1964
d of Hans H. garage owner and Maria A. Murdoch;
b Aber 5.6.43
m Aberchirder 4.1.64 James H. W. Gray farm./wholesale
dairyman s of James G. Dufftown

HARDIE Hamish McGregor *BSc 1968
s of Hugh G. M. H. PhD 1948 qv; b Aber 5.7.46
syst eng (computer tech) Lond, Edin from 1968
m Aber 9.8.69 Joy S. Riddell tel/receptionist, tourist asst
d of Leslie R. Cults

HARDIE John David Morrison MSc 1968
BA(Cantab)

HARDIE Michael John MB ChB 1965
s of George M. H. col civ serv and Margaret G. F. Bell
nurse; b Aber 18.10.41
Dip Amer brd of paediat 1971 FRCP(C) 1972
h o Aber 1965–67; resid paediat New Haven USA;
Canada: fell. neo natal div hosp for sick ch Toronto
1969–72, asst prof paediat univ of W Ont 1972–77, asst
prof paediat and obst/gyn univ of Ottawa from 1977
m Aber 26.7.67 Betty F. McDonald nurs sister d of
Alexander McD. Inverurie

HARDIE Myles Douglas George MA 1969
s of George H. driver and Dorothy McIntosh; b Aber
19.6.45
teacher Engl Daniel Stewart's coll Edin 1970–73; prin
Engl: Auchterarder s 1973–76, Torry acad Aber from
1976
m Aber 29.12.67 Marjory Gray MA 1968 qv

HARDIE Raymond Alfred MA 1968
b Aber 30.9.46
publ man. Hallam group of Nottingham

HARDIE Richard Henry MB ChB 1963
s of Henry C. H. bldr and Elisabeth B. Buchan;

b Ellon 18.12.33
h o Aber 1963–64; capt RAMC r m o: 1st Tank regt
Hohne W Ger 1964–66, 1st para Aldershot 1966–68;
major RAMC: 21c 23rd Para Fd Amb Aldershot
1968–70, DADMS 4th div Herford, W Ger 1970–72;
lt col RAMC: c o 23 Para Fd Amb Aldershot 1972–77,
1st armd div Fd Amb Hohne from 1977
m Aber 10.7.62 Janet G. Warren MA 1961 qv

HARDIMAN Michael John MA 1964

HARDING Robert Blythe *BSc 1967

HARDMAN Lorna MSc 1968
d of Thomas Hardman civ serv and Hilda A. France;
b Edin 11.12.43
BSc(Edin) 1964
res asst chem dept Aberd 1964–69
m Dunfermline 25.7.67 Malcolm D. Ingram BSc(Liv) s of
Arthur I. BSc(Liv) Wallasey

HARGRAVE Stuart Anthony MB ChB 1968

HARGREAVES John Wilson BSc(for) 1967

HARHARA Feisal Bin Abdullah MB ChB 1967
s of Abdullah H. land-owner and Alyah Bajrai;
b Singapore 31.7.37
LMCC 1972 regd coll of phys and surg (Ont) 1972
h o med/surg Scot. 1967–68; Singapore: m o pass. ship
1968–69, publ health off. 1969–70; resid psychiat Kingston, Ontario 1970–71; fam pract Toronto from 1971

HARINCK Emmanuel MB ChB 1964

HARKINS Charles LLB 1970

HARLEY Roy MacGregor LLB 1970
s of John H. civ eng and Thelma D. MacGregor
teacher p e; b Glasg 29.10.48
law app Edin 1970–71; leg. asst E.D.C., Menzies,
Dougal & Milligan, Dan McKay & Norwell 1971–75;
Drummond & Co from 1975, ptnr from 1978

HARMAN Brian Sydney Robertson *MA 1970
s of Albert C. H. insur insp and Winifred I. Findlay;
b Aber 4.10.46
Cert Qual Soc Work (Keele) 1973
soc worker: Derbysh 1970–75, Northumberland 1975–78,
Cardiff from 1978
m Aber 5.6.70 Judith M. Ellway MA 1969 qv

HARMON William McIntosh BSc 1967
s of Roy J. H. clerk and Catherine McIntosh; b Nigg
Station by Tain 31.10.45
teacher: sc Glenrothes 1968–69, chem Dingwall from 1969

HARNDEN John Robert MA 1969
s of Noel J. H. Mus Bac(Edin) teacher and Agnes A.
Bee MA(Edin) teacher; b Edin 12.5.46
vandriver/storeman Hazlehead garden centre Aber 1970–
72; van driver gen store Lerwick 1973; exec off. Register
House (civ serv) Edin 1973–74; author from 1974 (resid
Alford, Orkney)

HARPER Douglas Ross BSc 1962 MB ChB 1967
cMD 1975
s of Louis R. H. eng and Margaret H. Cartwright secy;
b Aber 16.2.40
FRCSE 1971 FRCS 1972
h o ARI 1967–68; res fell. dept path. Aberd 1968–69;
ARI sen h o, regist gen surg 1969–73, vascular surg fell.
1972–73; sen regist gen surg ERI 1973–76; consult. surg

Forth Valley health board Falkirk RI from 1976
m Aber 19.7.68 Dorothy C. Wisely MA 1966 *qv*

HARPER Elizabeth Mackay   MA 1964
d of Donald H. soldier (*d* 1944) and Elizabeth J. Forbes
school meals attend.; b Thurso 4.11.42
teacher Engl/allied subjs Lochyside s Fort William
1965–66, Pulteneytown acad Wick 1966–67 and in 1977;
part-time tel Wick 1974–77; teacher remed/spec Engl
and maths Wick h s from 1977
m Aber 28.7.64 Fredrick G. McBoyle BSc(eng) 1958 *qv*

HARPER Elizabeth Shearer   MB ChB 1959

HARPER Hugh Alexander Barrie   MA 1960 LLB 1962
s of John H. MA(Glas) BBC educ off. and Agnes F. N.
Barrie teacher; b Glasg 29.3.39
MICA 1965 Dip Man. St BIM 1969 PhD(H-W) 1975
lect Aberd 1965; ptnr H. A. B. Harper & Co CA 1965–
73; man. dir. Kildonnan Invest. 1973–74; ptnr H. A. B.
Harper & Co solic from 1974
m Aber 26.8.67 Vivienne Eden secy d of Robert E. E.
Aber

HARPER John Louis   BSc(eng) 1958
s of Louis R. H. eng and Margaret H. Cartwright secy;
b Aber 30.5.36
MIMechE 1966 MIProdE 1970 MEng(Glas) 1978
Babcock & Wilcox: grad trainee Renfrew 1958–60, proj
eng Dalmuir 1960–64; contr eng John Brown Land
Boilers Clydebank 1964–65; mech eng Babcock &
Wilcox (operations) Renfrew from 1965 then prod. syst
man.
m Aber 5.7.61 Fiona M. Hunter MA 1959 *qv*

HARPER Lillian Helen   *MA 1964
d of Peter H. master butcher and Lily M. Murray
cook; b Aber 7.4.42
teacher Engl Mackie acad Stonehaven 1965–68
m Aber 30.3.65 Alexander R. Gallacher arch. s of Alexander R. G. Aber

HARPER Robin Charles Moreton   MA 1962

HARPER William   *MA 1966
s of Harry H. miller, road trans driver and Margaret
E. Clarke; b Norwich 15.4.44
asst plan. Norfolk c c 1966–68; head geog dept Langley
s Langley Park from 1968
m Woodbastwick 14.4.73 Mary E. Le Fevre nurse/riding
s prop. d of Donald Le F. Thorpe Hamlet Norwich

HARPER William Findlay   MA 1959 Dip Ed 1960
s of William M. H. BR insp and Isabella R. B. Findlay;
b Gartly 21.11.39
teacher: Aber 1960–61, Keith 1961–63, Banff 1963–71,
prin maths Inv 1971–76, asst rector Cults from 1976
m Aber 24.7.61 Cathleen J. Ogston teacher d of Charles
A. O. Botriphnie

HARRIES Harry Raymond   *MA 1969
s of Harry P. H. clothier and Gwendoline Hill comp
dir; b Cardiff 1.7.05
FIB
retd; resid Cheltenham
m Braintree 1.7.74 Mary F. Smithers lib Cheltenham
ladies' coll d of Kenneth O. S. BA(Oxon) Braintree

HARRIS Gillian Margaret   *MA 1968
d of Bernard F. D. H. BSc(Lond) teacher and Norah I.
Campbell; b Southborough 3.2.47

teacher: Gatehouse-of-Fleet 1969–70, f e tech coll Clydebank 1970–74, Queensland Aust 1974–75, Helensburgh
from 1976

HARRIS Iain Grant Nicolson   *MA 1968
s of Ian Nicolson (stepfather James F. G. H.) and
Christine Nicolson; b Edin 17.3.46
Lond: advt and p r man. 1968–74, dir, advt and p r
comp from 1974; mayor Royal borough of Windsor and
Maidenhead 1976–78
m Aber 8.8.69 Jane P. Robertson MA 1967 *qv*

HARRIS Paul Anthony   *MA 1970
s of John D. H. collector HM customs and excise and
Rita Harris; b Barnhurst 22.7.48
man. dir Impulse publ Aber from 1970

HARRIS Winifred Anne Charlotte   *MA 1969
d of Leslie F. H. comp dir and Winifred M. B. Wilson
MA(Glas) teacher; b Whyteleafe 1.1.47
Ford Motor Co (tractor oper) Essex: grad trainee
1969–70, admin asst 1970–71, trg off. 1971–72; pers asst
GATT UNO Geneva 1973; dept employment UK home
civ serv Lond: admin trainee 1973–75 H E O (A) 1975–77,
prin from 1977

HARRISON Christopher Peter Motte   *MA 1967

HARRISON Derek John   BSc(for) 1959
s of George H. H. RAF off. and Ethel M. Hutchins;
b Stoke Poges 11.6.26
FIFor 1969
Forres: woodlands man. Moray estates dev comp from
1959, man. Moray timber preserv (Forres) 1961–71,
man. dir from 1972; for. consult. in private practice
various estates in Scot. from 1964
m Edin 26.6.59 Janet L. M. Kennedy SRN d of A. E. K.
BSc(Edin) Portobello

HARRISON Ian Rodger   MA 1965

HARRISON Jacqueline Mary   MA 1961
m Wheeler

HARRISON Moira Ann   BEd 1969
b Aber 1.1.47
teacher Glenrothes from 1975
m Aber 11.11.67 James A. Wito BEd 1969 *qv*

HARRISSON John   *BSc 1969

HARROW Andrew Lewis   BSc 1960
b Aber 1.7.37
resid Milltimber

HARROW Iain Alastair Lewis   MA 1965 LLB 1968
s of William B. H. CBE trawlowner/comp dir and
Isobel W. Lewis; b Aber 3.3.32
app solic: Aber 1968–69, Stonehaven 1969–70
m Castle Eden 16.7.66 Diana Gordon-Russell MA(Edin)
teacher d of Rognvald G.-R. OBE MB ChB 1931 *qv*

HARROWER Margaret Elizabeth Mary   MA 1962
m Webster

HARRY Keith William   *MA 1968 PhD 1975

HART Roderick   *MA 1967

HART Stewart   PhD 1967
BSc(Edin)

HARTNOLL Gillian Pauline   MA 1967
m Tyrer

HARVAIS Gaëtan Hugues   BSc 1957 MSc 1963
PhD 1966
s of A. Roger H. acct gen, dep fin. secy and S. Lucette
Raffin; b Quatre-Bornes Mauritius 9.4.35
asst plant breeder sugar indust res inst Reduit Mauritius
1957–61; tut. dem Aberd 1963–65; res asst St And Dun
1965–66; Canada: asst prof biol: univ de Moncton NB
1966–67, Lakehead univ Thunder Bay Ont from 1967,
then assoc prof

HARVAIS Georges Roland   MB ChB 1957

HARVEY Lynette Patricia   MA 1966

HARVEY Michael Douglas   *MA 1968

HARVIE Thomas Gilchrist   BSc(eng) 1970
s of Thomas G. H. mech eng and Sarah Hutchison;
b Glasg 21.8.47
CEng MIMechE
stress eng Rolls Royce Hamilton 1970–71; mech des eng
Weir Pumps Alloa from 1971
m Dedham 24.7.71 Janet L. Turner MA 1968 *qv*

HARVIE Winifred Ann   MA 1966
m Thomson

HASAN Ghaziuddin   MA 1967

HASSAM Sadruddin Esmail   MLitt 1967
BA(Lond)

HASTIE Dennis   MA 1969
s of Peter T. H. colliery man. and Agnes L. Fisher;
b Edin 7.2.49
teacher Brechin from 1970
m Aber 24.7.71 Kathleen A. Owen MA 1970 *qv*

HASTIE Isobel Gerrard   MA 1968
d of Walter H. van driver and Mary A. Gerrard;
b Aber 4.4.47
teacher mod lang Banchory acad from 1969
m Aber 4.10.69 William S. Macdonald asst scient off.
marine res s of William F. S. M. Aber

HASTON Douglas Donaldson   MA 1958
s of Albert H. MA(Edin) teacher, headmaster and
Elizabeth S. C. Donaldson teacher; b Aber 8.7.31
LTCL 1969
teacher Westerton p s Aber 1959–71; mus instrument
(recorder) teacher Aber/Grampian from 1971
m Aber 6.8.55 Elspeth A. McMurtrie DA artist d of
John McM. MA(Edin) Skene

HATEM Ali Abdulla   MB ChB 1966

HATRICK Alan Arundel   *BSc 1969
s of Thomas F. H. chief collector taxes and Mary E.
Arundel; b Aber 13.2.47
Lic I Biol 1971
indust admin Glasg 1969–70; teacher biol Wolverhampton 1970–73; head s biol dept Walsall from 1973

HAUGLAND Anne   *BSc(eng) 1970

HAWCO George Thomas   BSc 1969

HAWKES Susan Gail   *BSc 1968

HAWKSWORTH Peter George   BSc(eng) 1968
s of Gerald G. H. aero eng fitter and Diana Davies;
b Burton-on-Trent 19.6.46

Clarke Chapman internat combustion div Derby: grad
app 1968–69, res and dev eng 1970–73 and fluid mech
group sect. leader from 1974
m Tutbury 3.1.70 Kay Harding man. hair stylist d of
Joseph B. H. Burton-on-Trent

HAWLEY John George   *MA 1969
s of George W. H. clerk in holy orders and Annie W.
Deans organist/accompan; b Insch 23.5.44
FRGS 1970
teacher: Queen Elizabeth's boys' s Barnet 1970–74, head
geog St Nicholas g s Northwood 1974–77, sen year tut.
Haydon s Northwood from 1977

HAWTHORN Lily Fleming   MA 1970

HAY Abigail Lyon   MA 1967
d of John L. H. eng fitter and Abigail F. S. Spence;
b Stromness 29.7.46
Aber: teacher sp and drama 1968–70, geog Powis acad
from 1970
m Aber 27.2.76 William G. Innes MA 1962 *qv*

HAY Alan James   *BSc 1966 PhD 1969
s of William H. BSc(agr) 1938 *qv* and Margaret H. G.
Crichton BSc(Glas); b Bexhill 16.10.43
post doct res fell. Duke univ USA 1969–71; res scient nat
inst for med res Lond from 1971
m Aber 22.6.68 Janet M. Bishop BSc 1965 *qv*

HAY Alexander John   *BSc(eng) 1969

HAY Alison Mary   MA 1968

HAY Audrey Mary Wilson   *MA 1970
d of Archibald H. LDS(Glas) chief dent off. Aber and
Mary W. Thomson MA(Glas) teacher; b Hamilton
23.5.48
teacher Westbury Park s Brist
m Aber 28.12.70 Peter A. Mitchell MA(Oxon) prod. man.
s of Eric R. M. MSc(Lond) Nott

HAY David Alexander   *MA 1968
s of George A. H. civ serv and Patricia M. McGregor;
b Aber 25.8.47
PhD(Birm) 1970
res fell. Birm 1970–72; lect La Trobe univ Victoria Aust
from 1972, then sen lect

HAY David Sinclair   BSc 1966
s of Alexander J. H. bus prop. and Catherine I.
Davidson teacher; b Elgin 21.2.44
teacher sc Summerhill acad Aber 1967, asst prin sc from
1973
m Elgin 7.8.70 Isobel L. Stuart teacher d of Robert P. S.
Elgin

HAY Douglas Middleton   MB ChB 1964
s of Charles M. W. H. foreman stevedore and Mary H.
Wyness; b Aber 21.4.41
DObstRCOG 1966 MRCOG 1973
h o RACH, Woodend hosp Aber 1965–66; Glasg: h o
obst/gyn South gen hosp, g p 1966; locum g p Kilsyth
1967; m o Tawau, Sabah E Malaysia 1967–70; regist obst/
gyn South gen hosp Glasg 1970–74; sen regist/hon lect
obst/gyn Ninewells hosp Dun 1974–78; consult. obst/gyn
Kingston-u-Hull from 1978
m Aber 23.7.64 Sheila R. Forsyth teacher d of John F. F.
Aber

HAY Elizabeth Mary   *BSc 1970
d of William E. H. MB BS(Durh) med pract and

Elizabeth Diericx BSc(Durh) teacher; b Newcastle-u-Tyne 22.3.48
lect biol coll f e Plymouth from 1971

HAY Gordon William   *MA 1970
d of William W. H. clerk and Agnes M. I. Dickie; b Aber 25.4.47
teacher: mod lang Kincorth acad Aber 1971–74, prin mod lang Turriff acad from 1974

HAY Ian Morgan   MA 1965

HAY Ian Stewart   *MA 1963
s of James C. H. clerk and Margaret F. Stewart secy; b Aber 9.10.40
teacher: RGC Aber 1964–67, Jarvis coll inst Tor Canada from 1967
m Aber 23.12.64 Elizabeth M. A. Dear BSc 1962 *qv*

HAY James Leslie   MB ChB 1959
s of Andrew L. H. MA 1925 *qv*; b Aber 13.4.35
g p: Kingston-u-Hull 1961–64, Aber from 1964
m Aber 10.12.75 Margaret Hurst health visitor d of Joseph H. London

HAY James Taylor Cantlay   *BSc 1957
s of James H. farm serv and Elsie M. Cantlay; b Huntly 13.6.35
FGS FInstPet Amer Assoc Pet. Geol
geol (IPC) Kirkuk Iraq; head geol dept Abu Dhabi petr comp 1967–71; lect geol Aberd 1971–74; chief dev geol BODL from 1975
m Aber 21.8.59 Mary G. Davidson MA 1955 *qv*

HAY Jean Margaret   *MA 1966
d of William H. garage owner and Hilda Martin teacher; b Birkenhead 11.4.44
Dip Ed(Lond) 1967
teacher: Lond 1967–69, Liv 1969–71, Cheshire 1971–73
m West Kirby 31.7.71 Ivor W. Phillips chauffeur

HAY John David Lumsden   *BSc 1958
s of John P. H. merch seaman and Isabella A. Lumsden; b Aber 23.6.35
MSc(Nott) 1962 DipEd(Nott) 1966
Nott: res digestive physiol 1958–61, teacher biol 1962–66, lect educ 1966–75; dir religious experience res proj Nott univ
Educ Information Book of the Year award by Times Educ Sup for book *Human Populations* publ Penguin Educ
m Sleaford 1964 Felicity J. Dilley teacher p e d of Percy J. D. Sleaford

HAY John Munro   *BSc 1959
s of William M. H. civ serv and Margaret I. M. B. Miller teacher; b Forres 7.10.38
PhD(Cantab) 1963 barrister at law of Gray's Inn
lect: Westfield coll Lond 1962–63, Aberd 1963–67, Imp coll Lond 1967–69; HM diplom serv: 1st secy Lond 1970–71, (AID) Vientiane Laos 1972–74, (chancery) Canberra from 1974
m Aber 16.8.60 Avril M. I. Menzies BSc 1960 *qv*

HAY John Yeaman Leslie   BL 1962
s of Andrew L. H. MA 1925 *qv*; b Aber 25.2.38
leg. asst Cooper & Hay advoc Aber 1963–64, ptnr from 1964
m Aber 28.7.64 Elizabeth M. B. Anderson BSc 1962 *qv*

HAY Kathleen Margaret   *MA 1968
d of Alexander J. H. bus prop. and Catherine I.

Davidson teacher; b Elgin 25.12.45
teacher inf s Lond 1969–77
m Elgin 4.8.72 Gregory P. Hayes computer consult. s of Edward P. H. Regina Sask

HAY Margaret Jean Wilson   *MA 1968
d of George H. master mariner, harbour master and Pearl G. Wilson; b Aber 24.6.45
ALA 1971
ref lib publ lib Aber 1968–69; rare books lib Glas 1971–75
m Aber 20.9.68 James A. Mellis MA 1968 *qv*

HAY Morag Cordiner   *BSc 1969
d of James C. H. NALGO off. and Margaret F. Stewart secy; b Aber 9.7.47
anim feedstuffs chem Aber 1969–78; consult. chem Ellon from 1978
m Aber 1.8.70 James Taylor MA 1971 teacher s of James F. T. Aber

HAY Norman   *MA 1956

HAY Robert King Miller   *BSc 1967
s of William M. H. civ serv DHSS and Margaret M. J. B. Miller teacher; b Edin 19.8.46
MSc(E Ang) 1968 PhD(E Ang) 1971
MRC post doct res fell. zool dept Edin 1971, s of agr Edin 1972–74; lect: crop prod. dept Bunda coll of agr univ of Malawi 1974–76, crop prod. s of agr Edin 1976–77, soil sc dept of environmental sc univ of Lanc from 1977
m Monifieth 31.5.69 Dorothea H. Vinycomb MA 1968 *qv*

HAY Rosalind Anne   MB ChB 1965
d of William M. H. civ serv DHSS and Margaret M. J. B. Miller teacher; b Edin 10.5.42
h o Bangour gen hosp, Leith hosp 1965–66; sen h o Bangour gen hosp 1966–68
m Aber 17.7.65 David G. Pyatt BSc(for) 1961 *qv*

HAY Sandra Yeaman   *MA 1959
d of Andrew L. H. MA 1925 *qv*; b Aber 26.7.36
assistante école normale d'institutrices Amiens France 1959–60; teacher Europ lang and educ centre Bournemouth 1961–63; Glasg: lect Langside coll of f e 1964–72, coll of tech 1972–73; asst chief off. Scot. bus. educ council Edin from 1974

HAY Stuart Scott   *MA 1969
s of Walter H. coll janitor and Annabella B. Scott shop man.; b Dun 6.4.47
Dip Ed(Dund) 1970
teacher hist/mod stud. Lawside acad Dun from 1970
m Dun 3.4.71 Eileen M. Ferguson machine oper d of Douglas M. F. Dun

HAY William Graham   *MA 1965

HAY William Thomas   MA 1970
s of William P. H. foreman slater and Lillian B. Hay; b Ellon 12.3.48
teacher: Peterhead acad 1971–74, Banksia Park h s Adelaide Aust from 1974
m Inverurie 7.8.71 Helen M. Minty d of George A. M. Inverurie

HAYES Norman Douglas   PhD 1957
BSc(R'dg)

HAYFRON-BENJAMIN Jonathan   MB ChB 1966
s of Charles F. H.-B. BA(Lond) barrister-at-law and
Grace Sackey; b Elmina Ghana 11.8.36
h o med/surg Glasg 1966–67; sen h o obst and gyn
Chatham 1967–68; m o min of health Tamale Accra
1968–73; resid paediat univ of Ott from 1973
m Leeds 1967 Ataa S. Koram nurse d of E. M. K.
BSc(Cantab) Accra

HAYMAN Jarvis Rigden   MB ChB 1966
s of Arthur G. R. H. w/off. RAF, civ serv, teacher
violin and Elizabeth J. Smith teacher; b Shrewsbury
18.2.42
FRCSE 1973 FRACS 1974
h o surg, med ARI 1966–67; sen resid m o surg, med
Ballarat Aust 1967–69; lect anat Aberd 1970–72; regist
surg: Inv gen hosps 1972–74, NSW teaching hosps
Sydney Aust 1974–76, private pract Goulburn NSW
from 1976
m Inv –.3.67 Kathleen R. Melville RGN d of William M.
Inv

HAYS Mark Stormont   BSc 1965

HAZEL Alan Walter   *BSc 1968
b Chelmsford 24.7.46
MBA(Harv) 1973
ESSO petr Co: marketing trainee 1968–69, salesman
Coleraine 1969–73; Lond: motoring analyst, invest.
analyst from 1973
m Cheadle Hulme 20.7.68 Jean M. Pepper MA 1968 qv

HEALEY Michael Charles   PhD 1969
s of Arthur G. H. ship's wireless oper M o T and
Elizabeth Clarke; b Prince Rupert BC Canada 31.3.42
BSc(BC) 1964 MSc(BC) 1966
Canada: leader fisheries man. res Winnipeg 1970–74,
Nanaimo from 1974
m Vancouver 2.7.66 Judy A. Takahashi BSc(BC) d of
Yosh T. Salmon Arm BC

HEAP Wilfrid   *MA 1962 Dip Ed 1963

HEARD Sheila Marilyn   MA 1970
m Macrae

HEATH Margaret Gowans   MA 1970
d of William G. J. H. marine eng and Ruby Gowans
shorthand typist; b Montrose 16.7.49
secy Montrose 1970–71; teacher Gourdon p s from 1972
m Aber 3.4.70 Graeme S. M. Calder asst mill man. s of
Albert I. C. Inverbervie

HECTOR Moira Eilona Margaret   MA 1970
m de Silva

HEDDLE Frederick William   BSc 1958

HEDLEY Anthony Johnson   MB ChB 1965 MD 1972
s of Thomas J. H. chem eng/man. dir and Winifred
Duncan secy; b Greenmount 8.4.41
MRCP(UK) 1973 Dip Soc Med(Edin) 1973 MFCM 1974
h o ARI 1965–66; Aberd: Garden & Phillips fell. materia
medica 1966–67, res fell. mat. med and therap 1967–69;
med regist Maryfield hosp and hon asst dept of pharm
Dund 1969–72; fell. dept commun med Edin 1972–74;
lect commun med Aberd 1974–76; sen lect commun
health Nott from 1976
m Aber 2.8.67 Elizabeth A. Walsh nurse/clin teacher
d of William H. W. Houston Renfrew

HEGEDUS Istva'n Imre Zsolt   MA 1966
s of I. I. H. DEcon(Budapest) lect maths and Klàra
G. A. Salamon lang secy; b Budapest 2.10.42
Cert Biol(Tor) 1973
teacher: biol Lond 1967–69, maths/sc Toronto from 1969

HEGGS Glenville William   *BSc(for) 1969
s of Thomas W. H. paintshop foreman and Mary J.
Philips packer; b Leicester 7.3.47
for. off. with logging comp responsible for logging and
for. progr Belize C America 1970–74; market. man. for.
co-op N Wales 1975–76; for. advis Windward Is/gen man.
Forest Indust Dev Corp Commonwealth of Dominica
from 1977
m Urquhart 17.1.69 Jeanette Henderson. MA 1968 qv

HEILPERN Jeffrey   MB ChB 1964

HEINZMAN Colin   *BSc 1968
s of George C. H. indust chem and Betty M. Auckland
cler off., civ serv; b Newcastle 5.7.46
Dip Ed(Sheff) 1969 Dip Admin(W Aust) 1976
teacher: chem Rutherford s Newcastle-u-Tyne 1969–71,
sc Perth W Aust from 1972
m Wilmslow 26.8.68 Lesley M. Short MA 1968 qv

HELGASON Bjarni   PhD 1959
BA (Iceland)

HELLSTRØM Per Arvid   MB ChB 1967

HENDERSON Aileen Jean Marshall   MA 1965
d of William D. H. teacher and Jean G. Marshall;
b Buckie 19.2.44
teacher Engl: Fraserburgh acad 1966–68, Aber acad
1968–71; remed Portlethen from 1978
m Aber 23.12.68 David N. Howie MA 1965 qv

HENDERSON Alasdair Ross   BSc 1969

HENDERSON Alastair Andrew Ross   *MA 1959

HENDERSON Alexander Scott   MB ChB 1959
                                                MD 1967
s of Alexander H. MB ChB(St And) phys and Mary E.
Charlton nurs. sister; b Aber 7.12.35
DPM(Lond) 1962 MRACP(Melb) 1964 MRCP(Lond)
1965 MRCPsych 1969 FRACP 1971
h o ARI 1959–60; h o, regist Ross clin Aber 1960–62;
regist psychiat Prince Henry hosp Sydney 1963–65;
member scient staff MRC unit epidemiological stud. in
psychiat Edin 1965–68; foundation chair of psychiat
univ of Tasmania 1968–74; dir NH and MRC soc
psychiat res unit ANU Canberra from 1975
m Sydney 1965 Priscilla H. Gill physioth d of William G.
Drummoyne NSW

HENDERSON Anne   MA 1968 Dip Ed 1969
d of James L. H. site ag and Alice M. Smith shop asst;
b Huntly 10.5.47
teacher Engl/hist: Kelso h s 1969–71, Perth h s from 1971

HENDERSON Antoinette Margaret   BSc 1957
d of Peter R. H. draper and Flora Cumming shop asst;
b Aber 19.5.36
chem Esso res Abingdon 1957–59; teacher sc Forres
acad 1960–63
m Aber 6.8.62 James Brown RAF/radio tech/telecommun
tech off (MOD) s of James B. Haswell

HENDERSON Brian Alexander   MA 1968

HENDERSON Charles Neil   *BSc 1961
s of Charles S. H. MA 1930 *qv*; b Peterculter 24.3.39
trainee paper tech Dartford 1961–62; dev chem Wiggins
Teape photogr paper mills 1962–66; tech man. Samuel
Jones & Co. Tillycoultry 1966–72; tech and comm man.
Guardbridge paper comp from 1972
m Birm 4.8.62 Susan M. Lambert BSc 1961 *qv*

HENDERSON Colin   *BSc 1964 PhD 1968

HENDERSON David John   MA 1968
s of David M. H. BSc(Glas) civ eng and Margaret G.
Inkster; b Perth 3.6.47
RAF pilot 1968–72; airline pilot BA Heathrow from
1972
m Perth 10.8.73 Patricia Z. Hall airline stewardess d of
Albert H. H. MB ChB(Lond) Stanley

HENDERSON David Munro   *MA 1965
s of Roderick B. H. sales man., C of S min and Isabella
C. Munro; b Inv 16.1.43
Dip Ed(Edin) 1968
post grad stud. univ of Virginia USA 1965–66; methods
analyst Vancouver 1966–67; econ master Daniel Stewart's
coll Edin 1968–69; lect bus. organis H-W 1969–72, lect
econ 1972–75; reg econ HIDB Inv from 1975
m Strathdon 7.9.68 Anna M. C. Webster teacher d of
Alexander W. Glenbuchat

HENDERSON David Scott   *MA 1958

HENDERSON Elisabeth Agnes Ross   MA 1967
m Gammie

HENDERSON Eric Alexander Macleod   *MA 1966

HENDERSON Eric Watt   BSc 1969
s of Charles B. H. foreman stonemason and Annabella
Soutar; b Forfar 25.4.46
scient off. in phys oceanography Marine lab Aber 1969–
73, higher scient off. from 1973
m Aber 27.7.79 Jennifer E. M. McLaren sales rep d of
Ian McL. Braemar

HENDERSON Ernest Allan   *BSc 1959

HENDERSON Fraser George   BSc(eng) 1966
s of George M. H. RN and Gertrude Calder bus.
woman; b Valetta Malta 27.4.39
MNZIE 1970 MICE 1971 Member Assoc Consult. Eng,
NZ 1974
asst eng city Aber 1966; Marks, Stiles & Sedcole consult.
eng and arch., Hamilton NZ: asst, sen des eng, assoc
1966–73, ptnr from 1973
m Hamilton NZ 1967 Elizabeth F. Grattan acct asst d of
Denis F. G. Toronto

HENDERSON George   *BSc 1967 MSc 1969

HENDERSON George William   MA 1959

HENDERSON George William   MA 1967

HENDERSON Hamish McNaughton   LLB 1957
s of James S. H. MA(St And) schoolmaster and Kate
M. McNaughton MA(St And) teacher; b Tannadice
19.9.26
BA(Cantab) 1949 MA(Cantab) 1957
lect Edin: constit law 1958–69, Scots law 1969–72; sen
lect from 1972

m Edin 1.9.60 Kathleen M. Guthrie MA(Edin) univ lect,
teacher d of Henry W. G. MA(Edin) West Linton

HENDERSON Ian Bruce   *BSc(eng) 1965
s of Jonathan H. haulage contr and Sarah Bruce;
b Oldmeldrum 30.7.43
MSc(Strath) 1971
ICI: plant eng agr div Billingham 1965–68, construct.
eng dyestuffs div Ayrsh 1968–70, proj eng petroleum div
Billingham 1970–75, sen staff from 1975
m Wick 5.6.70 Margaret G. Calder nurse d of John C.
Wick

HENDERSON Iona Mairi Clark   *MA 1967

HENDERSON James   *MA 1968

HENDERSON Jeanette   MA 1968
d of George H. H. master butcher and Elspeth M.
Cruickshank; b Rothes 29.6.48
Belize City: teacher Engl/hist 1970–71, lect Eng lit.
teachers' trg coll 1971; Wrexham: teacher Fr/Europ stud.
1975–76, Fr/Ger 1976, Engl/Fr 1976–79
m Urquhart 17.1.69 Glenville W. Heggs BSc(for) 1969 *qv*

HENDERSON Jennifer Jean   BEd 1969
d of William H. farm. and Dorothy Barton; b Fyvie
20.8.47
teacher Fraserburgh North p s 1969–70, Cowie p s
Stirlingsh 1970–73, stud. infant/nurs assoc and Froebel
Callander Park coll of educ Stirlingsh 1973–74
m Aber 7.7.70 Douglas L. Stewart teacher, advis outdoor
educ s of Douglas L. S. MA 1934 *qv*

HENDERSON Jonathan   *MA 1963

HENDERSON Mabel Christina   *MA 1967
s of David H. gamekeeper and Agnes A. W. Barr;
b W Hartlepool 3.4.45
teacher mod lang Harlaw acad Aber 1968–78
m Tongue 24.7.71 Leslie M. Baxter asst man. s of Alexander L. B. Aber

HENDERSON Margaret   MA 1957
d of George H. H. master butcher and Elspeth M.
Cruickshank; b Rothes 12.4.37
teacher: Engl Stanley j s s 1958–62, Logie Easter p s
1964–65, Tain p s from 1975
m Aber 18.4.62 Lawrence D. R. Allan CA s of David A.
Perth

HENDERSON Margaret Elizabeth   LLB 1967
d of Gordon H. H. MA 1937 *qv*; b Lurgan NI 9.12.46
law app Aber 1967–68; solic Burnett & Reid advoc Aber
from 1969
m Aber 3.7.71. John G. Sutherland estate fact. s of John
M. S.

HENDERSON Mary Fletcher   MA 1968
d of James H. customs and excise off. and Isabella H.
Leitch; b Edin 30.1.47
teacher mod lang Inverurie acad 1969–73
m Balerno 26.12.69 Neil D. Morrison res tech s of
Charles M. Aber

HENDERSON Michael George   MB ChB 1970

HENDERSON Peter   *MA 1960
s of Peter H. marine eng, TU off. and Mary Hepburn;
b Aber 28.5.37
res asst labour party Lond 1960–61; lect: St And 1961–66,

univ of Otago Dunedin NZ 1966–70, sen lect from 1970
m Aber 14.10.67 Doreen J. Davies BA lib Middx

HENDERSON Peter George   *BSc 1966

HENDERSON Reginald Laurence   MA 1956
                                      *MEd 1958
  s of Andrew H. dep chief constable, comp rep and
Johanna B. Gear secy; b Lerwick 8.8.34
2nd lt RAEC 1958–60; teacher Aber 1960–61; educ
psych Durh 1961–63, admin asst Northumberland 1963–
66; asst dir of educ Argyll 1966–72; dep dir of educ
Banffsh 1972–75 interim dir 1975, div educ off. Keith
from 1975
m Aber 12.7.61 Gladys Wilson MA 1958 *qv*

HENDERSON Robert Burnett Mackenzie   BSc 1968
  s of Robert G. B. H. man. and Elizabeth Burnett;
b Fraserburgh 23.1.40
teacher chem Inverurie acad from 1969

HENDERSON Robert Rait   *BSc(eng) 1962

HENDERSON Ronald Gordon   MA 1962

HENDERSON Rosalind Lyra   MA 1967 LLB 1970
  d of David H. MA(Glas) jeweller, ex-hon sheriff and
Lyra J. C. Gray; b Aber 26.5.46
law app Glasg 1970–72; leg. asst. Brander & Cruickshank
advoc Aber 1972–73
m Aber 15.11.72 John Flett fishery off. s of James T. F.
Buckie

HENDERSON Thomas William   MA 1968 Dip Ed 1969
  s of Thomas W. H. plumber and Eveline Evans; b Aber
28.5.27
teacher Aber: Rosemount s 1969–71, AGS 1971–73,
year master from 1973
m Aber 27.5.63 Margaret R. Walker pharm d of James W.
Aber

HENDERSON Vera Margaret   MA 1970
  d of John H. drainage insp and Vera M. McGovern;
b Aber 1.10.46
teacher Glasg from 1972

HENDERSON William Hillyard   *BSc 1969

HENDERSON William Lawrence   MSc 1961
  BSc(Edin)

HENDRIE Robert   *BSc 1969

HENDRY Alastair David Morrice   BSc(eng) 1962

HENDRY Albert Gordon   MA 1962
  s of Albert J. H. bakery vanman/man. and Helen H.
Robertson shop asst, clerkess; b Ellon 30.10.40
teacher: dem s Aber 1963–69, RGC j s from 1969
m Bearsden 24.7.71 Morag Mason teacher d of William
M. T. M. MA(Glas) Bearsden

HENDRY Alison Margaret   MA 1964
  d of John M. H. man. fishing comp and Amabel
Tawse typist; b Aber 30.7.43
Dip Soc St(Edin) 1965
ch care off. Midlothian c c 1965–67
m Aber 28.12.66 Charles J. Forbes arch. draughtsman
s of Charles F. Udny

HENDRY David Alexander Forbes   *BSc 1968
  s of Alexander F. H. MA(Glas) Scot. chmn conserv

party and Margaret Whitehead; b Falkirk 12.3.46
PhD(Cantab) 1972
univ lect Syd Aust from 1971
m 9.10.72 Mary Collard

HENDRY David Forbes   *MA 1966
  s of Robert E. H. hotel prop. and Catherine Mackenzie
hotel prop.; b Nott 6.3.44
MSc(Lond) 1967 PhD(Lond) 1970 fell. econometric soc
LSE: lect econ 1969–73, reader 1973–77; prof of eco-
metric from 1977; USA: visiting assoc prof Yale 1975,
UC Berkeley 1976
m Lond 7.10.66 Evelyn R. Vass MA 1966 *qv*

HENDRY Ian David   BEd 1969
  s of Norman D. H. MA(Edin) teacher and Annabella
M. Reid; b Kempston 1.6.41
teacher: Engl Arbroath acad 1969–71, Hayshead p s
Arbroath 1971–72; head: Carmyllie p s Arbroath 1972–
76, Torphins p s from 1976
m Aber 30.9.67 Elizabeth A. Hay teacher d of Adam H.
Newmachar

HENDRY Jacqueline Ann   BSc 1966
  m Simpson

HENDRY John Fraser   LLB 1968
  s of John M. H. asst progr controller and Amabel
Tawse typist; b Cottingham 28.2.47
Aber: app solic 1968–70, asst solic 1970–73, ptnr Campbell
Connon & Co advoc from 1974
m Aber 21.12.70 Margaret C. Robertson MA 1969 *qv*

HENDRY June Rennie   MA 1959
  d of George H. farm. and Maggie Rennie; b Banff
30.6.38
teacher: Fr/Engl/Lat Aberlour h s 1960–64, Linlithgow
acad and p s from 1970
m Grange 27.7.62 Alexander N. Adam teacher p e
s of Robert A. Aberlour

HENDRY Kathleen Anne   *MA 1968
  d of David H. mech eng merch N, oil comps and
Margaret Johnston secy; b Iran 19.3.46
teacher: Kelso 1969–71, Dun 1971–72, head hist Dormem
Wells h s Southall from 1972
m Dun 6.4.72 John A. Grocott landscape asst s of
Edmund S. G. Lond

HENDRY Robert Duthie   BSc 1959

HENDRY Sylvia Mattison   *MA 1964
  m Ramsay

HENEGHAN Kathleen Cecelia   MA 1969

HENRY Agnes Christina   *MA 1962

HENRY Michael Duff   MA 1958 ᶜLLB 1960
  s of Robert H. MA 1929 *qv*; b Harrow 29.8.37
leg./admin asst Renfrew c c Paisley 1962–65; leg. asst
Aber c c 1965–67; Renfrew c c Paisley: p a to county
clerk 1967–72, asst county clerk 1972–73, dep county
clerk from 1973 and chief exec off. to new Eastwood dist
council from 1974
m Aber 1962 Margaret C. Murray occup therap d of
J. M. M. Gardenstown

HEPBURN Alan Anderson   LLB 1965
  s of William R. H. sen exper off. and Jean C. Thomson;
b Kilmarnock 15.9.43
Dip Pers Man.(Strath) 1966 MIPM

Coventry: pers off. Bristol Siddeley Eng 1966–67; indust rel off. Rolls Royce 1967–68, Dunlop 1968–70; pers man. National Tyre Service Stockport; div pers man. Dunlop Semtex Brynmawr from 1974
m Aber 22.12.67 Olga F. Stephen catering man., teacher d of Robert J. S. BSc(Strath) Bieldside

HEPBURN Alexander Andrew   BSc 1967

HEPBURN Ian Ronald   *BSc 1969
  s of Stuart D. H. acct and Joyce E. Huggins; b Aber 27.5.47
syst progr nat eng lab E Kilbride 1969–71; Sperry Univac: sen syst progr, proj leader, group leader Zagreb Yugoslavia 1971–74, Europ h q data processing consult. Madrid, other Europ. capitals 1974–76; European syst spec Sperry Univac internat div Lond from 1976
m Elgin 30.6.69 Irene E. Slowey

HEPBURN Margaret Rennie   MA 1957

HEPBURN Robert   BSc 1970

HEPBURN Sheila Doreen   MA 1963
  d of James R. H. chief insp CID and Mary Noble shorthand typist; b Aber 2.7.29
teacher Aber: Sunnybank p s 1964–70, asst head Kittybrewster p s 1970–77, head Balnagask p s from 1977
m 12.4.55 Nicol P. Patterson; husb d Lond 6.3.62

HEPBURN Stanley   *BSc 1970

HEPBURN Stella   *MA 1970

HEPBURN Stuart Philip   *BSc 1967 PhD 1971
  s of Stuart D. H. farm cost acct and Joyce E. Huggins; b Norwich 15.4.45
ARIC 1969
ICI: res/market dev Runcorn 1970–74, USA market dev Wilmington Delaware from 1974

HEPPLESTON Paul Bernard   PhD 1968
  BSc(Wales)

HEPWORTH, Joan Susan   *MA 1970
  m Evison

HERBERT Alan Gordon   *BSc(eng) 1970

HERBERT David William   *BSc(eng) 1963

HERBERT Rodney Andrew   PhD 1970
  s of Harold H. loc govt off. and Dora Scarth; b York 27.6.44
BTech(Brad) 1967
res fell. Edin 1970–71; lect microbiol Dund from 1971
m Carlisle 4.9.71 Helen J. M. Millard MSc 1968 qv

HERD David James   *MA 1965

HERD Isabella Helen   BSc 1965

HERD Patricia Margaret   MA 1970
  d of James H. MB ChB 1944 qv; b Aber 18.4.49
post grad. secy ling course Aber coll of comm; Lond: secy/information asst 1971–73, edit. asst 1973–74, sub edit. BBC from 1974

HERD Peter Bruce   MA 1970
  s of Birrell H. trawler skipper/owner and Jeannie Bruce; b Buckie 2.7.48
CA 1977

Aber: asst acct, acct 1976–79, acct/comp secy from 1979
m Fraserburgh 2.6.73 Maureen P. McDonald beauty therap d of James McD. Fraserburgh

HERFORD Penelope Jean   PhD 1968
  d of Philip H. H. mech eng and Elizabeth J. Hawkins; b Reading 26.11.40
BSc(Glas)
asst lect agr biochem s of agr Aber 1968–69; scient off., higher scient off. poultry res centre Edin 1970–72
m Glasg 13.12.69 Dorian J. Pritchard BSc(Wales) biol, res fell. s of Oliver L. P. Caerphilly

HERRICK Peter William   BSc(for) 1966
  s of Neil C. H. clerk and Betty F. Findlay; b Auckland NZ 28.2.40
BSc(Canterbury NZ) 1964
for. NZ for. serv Rotorua 1966–69, prin for. trg centre 1970–74; prin for. Kaingaroa for. from 1975
m Christchurch 15.1.64 Kaye E. Webley artist d of Kasper G. W. Christchurch

HERRINGTON Reginald Nicholas   PhD 1966
  MB(Birm) DPM(Glas)

HESLOP Jane Stuart   MA 1964
  m Macnamara

HESLOP Rodney Eric Faber   *BSc(for) 1958
  s of Eric T. H. army off. and Kathleen E. Faber; b Hurworth-on-Tees 11.6.36
nat serv 5th royal tank regt Catterick, W Ger 1958–60; dist off. for. comm Farnham 1960–62; scient off., prin scient off. dept of soil surv Macaulay inst Aber from 1963

HETHERINGTON Alison Ann   MA 1967

HEWET Elizabeth Ann   MA 1967
  d of Alexander R. H. MA 1936 qv; b Aber 20.11.46
teacher: Aber 1968–69, Rosssh 1969–71
m Aber 1.8.69 Hugh G. J. Jamieson BSc(eng) 1967 qv

HEWINS Roger Herbert   *BSc 1962
  s of Herbert C. H. civ serv and Linda M. Marshall; b Farnham 29.11.40
PhD(Tor) 1971 NASA fell. 1972–75
geol: geol surv Georgetown Guyana 1963–65, Falconbridge Nickel Ontario 1965–67; grad stud., lect Tor 1967–72; USA: lunar sample co-investigator Lehigh univ Pa 1972–75, asst prof geol Rutgers univ NJ from 1975 (NASA grant to study meteorites)
m Georgetown 2.8.63 Catherine P. McDonald MA 1961 qv

HEWITT David Sword   PhD 1969
  MA(Edin)

**HEWITT Michael Ross   *BSc(eng) 1962 MSc 1964
                                        PhD 1968**
  s of Robert G. H. soldier, civ serv and Anna R. Priest MA 1924 qv; b Aldershot 14.5.40
T.D.
Aber: scient off. Torry res stat 1964–68, sen scient off. 1968–73, head of eng sect 1970, prin scient off. Torry res stat from 1973; AUOTC major 1970 21c 1974
m Aber 14.10.63 Catherine A. Watt MA 1963 qv

HEY Jean Marjorie   MB ChB 1970
  d of George B. H. BA(Cantab) insur actuary and Elizabeth H. Burns BA(Cantab) teacher; b N Shields 16.4.47
USA: clin assoc paediat Charlottesville Virginia 1970–72,

intern paediat Norfolk Virginia 1972–73; h o surg Amersham 1973–74; USA: resid, sen resid paediat Durham N Carolina 1975–77, private practice paediat Durham from 1977
m Aber 11.7.70 John W. A. Findlay BSc 1966 *qv*

HICKIE John Frederick   *MA 1968
   m Hessle 13.9.69 Rosemary Hings MA 1969 *qv*

HICKIE Sheila   *MA 1968 Dip Ed 1969
   d of Charles H. distillery employee and Margaret R. Anderson; b Montrose 14.8.45
teacher: mod lang Stirling 1969–72, Munster W Ger with BFES 1972–75, Engl Stadthagen W Ger 1975–77

HICKSON Bryan   MB ChB 1965
   s of Frank P. H. cabinetmaker and Winifred Grundy; b Reepham 9.1.40
MRCP(UK) 1970
h o, regist Aber hosps 1965–71; sen med regist St Bart's hosp Lond from 1971
m Aber 13.7.65 Kathleen Russell BSc 1962 *qv*

HIGGINS Helen Ritchie   *BSc 1967

HIGGINS Katharine   *BSc 1968
   m Jewitt

HIGSON John Michael   LLB 1966

HILL Avril Nicol   *MA 1956 Dip Ed 1957
   d of Harold G. H. MA(Glas) teacher and Elizabeth A. H. Nicol; b Nairn 5.4.34
teacher Perth 1957–64; spec asst geog: Perth 1963–64, Merritt Canada 1964–65; teacher Toronto 1965–67, head geog from 1967

HILL Guy Anthony   *MA 1966
   s of Arthur H. H. and Gladys Coleman; b Dartford 16.2.43
Cert TEFL(Lond) 1969
VSO teacher Engl Vientiane Laos 1966–68; lect Engl: univ of Belgrade 1969–70, Chulalongkorn univ Bangkok 1970–76; Edin lang foundation 1976–77; educ off. Brunei from 1977
m Edin 26.8.70 Dorothy A. Hare MA(Edin) TEFL d of James H. Edin

HILL Harry Joseph Charles   *MA 1963
   s of Henry B. H. SAI and May Curle; b Aber 17.10.40
Canada: grad asst Alta 1963–64, instr Engl univ of Victoria 1964–66; artistic dir RPA Productions Victoria acting/directing assignments 1968–69; lect Winona state coll Minn USA 1969–70; chmn CEGEP Engl dept Loyola coll Montreal 1970–75

HILL Veronica Marianne   *MA 1959
   d of Ronald H. MA(Oxon) civ serv and Elizabeth M. Rawson; b Lincoln 18.4.37
statist asst Macaulay inst Aber 1959–60; res asst dept geol Nott from 1974
m Stretton-on-Dunsmore 18.3.61 Neil M. Croll BSc 1960 *qv*

HILMI Haluk Ahmed   BSc(for) 1956

HILMY Yousef   PhD 1959
   BCom MSc(Cairo)

HILTON Anthony Victor   *MA 1968
   s of Raymond W. H. BSc(for) 1933 *qv*; b Ottringham 26.8.46

Lond: fin. journalist: *Guardian* 1968–69, *Observer* 1969–72, *Sunday Express* 1972–74; edit. *Accountancy Age* from 1974
m Bradford 29.3.69 Patricia Moore TV exec; marr diss 1974

HILTON John Geoffrey   *BSc 1970

HILTON Susan Nola   *MA 1964
   d of Raymond W. H. BSc(for) 1933 *qv*; b Ottringham 18.2.42
asst prin Scot. dev dept Edin 1964–66; man. eng services Boston, Mass from 1969
m Edin 15.3.68 James M. Carifio BA(Col) univ teacher, consult. s of Luigi J. C. Bradford Mass

HINCH Barry   *BSc(eng) 1969 MSc 1970

HIND Angela Joan   *MA 1969
   d of Francis P. H. physioth and Kate J. Page teacher; b Margate 25.6.47
teacher Engl girls' county h s Romford 1969–73
m Ramsgate 21.6.69 Richard S. Thomas MA(Oxon) prin home civ serv

HINDMARSH Paul Stewart   *BSc(agr) 1967
   s of Ralph H. hardware merch and Mabel P. Brigham; b Newcastle-u-Tyne 1.9.43
MSc(Lond) 1968 DIC 1968 MIBiol 1971
ODA stud. crop storage problems Yundum res stat The Gambia 1968–69; scient off. trop stored prod. centre 1970–72; sen scient off. from 1972 (seconded to Mt Makulu res stat Chilanga Zambia)
m Sunderland 16.8.67 Elizabeth A. Toyer MA 1965 *qv*

HINDOCHA Suresh Laljibhai   BSc(eng) 1966
   s of Laljibhai H. indust and Muktaben Lakhani; b Kakira Uganda 20.1.42
Pondicherry: dir New Horizon sugar mills from 1967; tech dir Auroville Electronics from 1968; man. dir Aummag Private from 1974

HINDS Enrique Roland   MA 1964

HINDS Eric Arthur   BSc(eng) 1969
   s of Wilfred H. bus driver and Lilian M. McCue shop prop., man.; b Houghton-le-Spring 10.2.47
MICE 1973 MIWE 1974
eng asst mid-Scot. water board Falkirk 1969–73; asst eng NE Scot. water board Aber 1973–75; group leader (operations) Gordon div dept of water serv Grampian reg c from 1975
m Buckie 4.4.70 Cathleen H. Geddes teacher d of Alexander G. Buckie

HINGA Godfrey   MSc 1964
   BSc(agr) Lond

HINGE Peter Leonard Graham   MA 1968

HINGS Rosemary   MA 1969
   d of Ronald H. tailor and Mavis Salmon; b Hessle 18.7.48
Southampton: acct asst Southern Gas 1969–70, p r asst 1970–71
m Hessle 13.9.69 John F. Hickie MA 1968 *qv*

HINTON Susan Jane   *MA 1969

HIRD Marilyn   BSc 1968
   m Murray

HITCHING Alan Victor   LLB 1968

HJORT Ove Johan   MB ChB 1963
s of Sven K. H. MB(Oslo) consult. surg and Harriet Backer-Groendahl; b Egersund Norway 25.6.36
Norway: resid surg/med Gjoevik 1964–65; asst g p V Slidre 1965; sen h m o/regist med Oslo 1965–72; consult. med Hammerfest 1970; regist cardiol Oslo from 1972; lt-col Norwegian army med corps and part-time consult. Red Cross clin Oslo from 1975
m Drammen Norway 1.10.66 Tove Vilstad d of Ivar V. Drammen

HO-A-SHU Laura Shirley Jocelyn   *MA 1956
d of David O. Ho-A-Shu acct and Dorothy A. Lee; b Guyana 29.4.32
teacher: Georgetown Guyana 1956–59, hist Kingston Jamaica 1962–65, hist Lond from 1965
m Aber 15.10.55 Paul T. d'Orban MB ChB 1956 qv

HOBBIN Maureen Elizabeth   BEd 1969
d of Norman G. E. H. sub postmaster and Agnes Goudie dist nurse; b Lerwick 2.12.47
teacher mod lang/Engl St Conval's R.C. h s Cumnock 1969–72
m Lerwick 17.7.69 Peter Barr BEd 1969 qv

HOBBS Alexander   *MA 1958
s of Alexander H. shopworker and Davidena Blacklaw hairdresser; b Aber 23.8.37
asst St And 1961–64; res fell. Strath 1965–67; lect: Edin coll of comm 1968–69, Jordanhill coll of educ Glasg 1969–75; sen lect Paisley coll of tech from 1975
m Aber 16.10.61 Mary L. Kemp BSc 1961 qv

HOBSON Christine Patricia   MB ChB 1961
b Ashton-u-Lyne 19.9.27
DObstRCOG 1963
g p Saddleworth Oldham

HODD Keith Tobias Burnett   MSc 1967
s of Frederick A. B. H. ophth optic. and Barbara J. Foster; b Hoddesdon 4.10.45
BSc(Lond) 1966
teacher sc Aberdeensh from 1973
m Hatfield 16.3.68 Patricia M. Berry BSc(Lond) res asst, teacher d of William B. Welwyn Garden City

HODGART Susan Wynne   *MA 1966
d of Charles G. H. MIMechE man. dir eng works and Dorothy M. H. Gillespie WAAF, BBC tech; b Aber 1.11.44
Lond: admin asst dept Engl Bedford coll 1967; edit. asst, asst edit., proj edit., gen edit. Macdonald & Jane's book publ from 1967
m Lond 6.7.73 Ian Fleming art dir and des consult. s of Ernest F. Worthing

HODGES Timothy   MA 1967
s of Thomas M. H. pers man. and Evelyn J. Foster; b Wolverhampton 18.5.44
lib Highfields s Wolverhampton 1970–73; teacher Engl Wood Green h s Wednesbury 1973–76; head Engl dept Pendeford h s Wolverhampton from 1976
m Aber 25.7.70 Angela J. G. Whyte BSc 1969 qv

HODGSON Ronald Arthur   BSc 1970

HOGAN James Philip   PhD 1957
BSc(agr)(Syd)

HOGG Cecil Archibald Grant   BEd 1970

HOGG Christine McColl   *MA 1970
d of James T. H. depot man., CA Inl Rev and Jessie M.

Garlick secy; b Edin 8.11.47
teacher Engl: Cumbernauld h s 1971–73, Banff acad 1973–75
m Aber 21.8.70 Bruce K. Gardner MA 1971 teacher s of Alexander M. G. scient instrum maker/res asst nat phil Aberd

HOGG John   *MA 1966
s of Alexander H. bldr and Margaret M. MacGillivray; b Nairn 8.5.42
teacher Engl Perth h s from 1967
m Aber 15.5.65 Jessie Campbell MA 1964 qv

HOGG Kathleen Louise   MA 1969
d of William W. H. baker and Christina Gillan; b Aber 11.1.48
teacher Engl: St Mary's acad Bathgate 1970–72, Morgan acad Dun from 1972

HOGG Nigel Robert Laurence   MA 1970
s of Peter L. H. chartered shipbroker and Elizabeth W. Humble; b W Hartlepool 6.1.49
F Inst Chartered Shipbrokers 1976
asst ag man. with loc shipbrokers Hull 1970–71; tanker chartering asst short sea chartering Göteborg Sweden 1971–72; Hartlepool: man. timber ag dept with loc shipbrokers 1972–74, comp secy, dir shipbrokers and fwdg ag from 1974
m Gifford 16.9.72 Elizabeth R. S. Taylor MA 1970 qv

HOGG William Murray   *MA 1966
s of Gavin M. H. draper and Rose Davie; b Brechin 20.1.18
teacher mod lang Brechin h s from 1967
m Liv 15.11.41 Grace W. Fairlie d of W. S. F. Brechin

HOLBOURN Frances Moira   *BSc 1966

HOLBOURN Sheila Catharine   *BSc 1964
d Athelstan H. M. H. MA(Edin) lect phys Aberd and Joyce H. Brown BSc(Oxon); b Oxford 9.3.42
crofter Foula from 1964
m Scalloway 9.9.64 James R. Gear fisherman/crofter s of David M. G. Foula

HOLDER Valerie Elinor   MA 1966 Dip Ed 1967

HOLDSWORTH Lily Florence Jane   MA 1960
d of Cyril H. ship's cook and Frances A. Woolverton factory worker; b Bo'ness 5.7.18
teacher: Peterhead 1961–67, spec s Orpington from 1967
m Bo'ness 11.4.44 Frederick Birks civ serv s of George F. B. Falkirk

HOLDSWORTH Patricia Dorothy   MA 1963
d of Douglas H. and Ethel F. Hunter; b Aber 18.12.42
teacher maths: High s for girls Aber 1964–65, Carolan g s Belfast 1965–68, Sir Wilfrid Laurier h s London, Ontario 1969–70, Bankhead acad 1970–74; asst prin maths Kincorth acad Aber 1974–75, prin guid Harlaw acad from 1975
m Aber 14.7.65 Niall A. Young BSc 1964 qv; marr diss 29.5.80

HOLLER Zeb North   PhD 1967
s of Zeb N. H. BA(Davidson coll NC USA) teacher, bus. man and Mary V. Harrison mus teacher; b Atlanta Georgia USA 2.8.28
AB(Davidson coll NC) BD(Richmond Va)
assoc pastor central presb ch Atlanta 1967–68; univ minister NC state univ Raleigh NC 1968–72; gen pastor Orange presb PCUS Durham NC 1972–75; pastor: Fort Hill presb ch Clemson SC 1975–79, presb ch of the

Covenant Greensboro NC from 1979
m Pensacola Fla USA 22.8.53 Charlene Levey BS(Richmond) teacher d of Charles H. L. Pensacola

HOLLIDAY Richard Durden   BSc(eng) 1962
s of Harry A. H. elect. eng comp dir and Kathleen Thomas teacher; b Watford 22.5.39
Lond: elect. eng 1962–67, reinsur broker 1967–73, insur underwriter Lloyds' from 1973
m Sevenoaks 10.6.67 Diana G. Reid secy, governess d of Nevile R. BA(Oxon) Kildary

HOLLOWAY Colin William   PhD 1967
BSc(Wales)

HOLLOWAY John Stevenson   BSc(for) 1969
s of John T. H. MSc(Otago) for. ecol, res admin and Una S. Stevenson Dip Home Sc(Otago); b Dunedin NZ 13.8.44
BSc(Otago) 1966
NZ for. serv: Gisborne 1969–71, dist for. Tampanui 1972–74, sen for. Dunedin from 1975
m Rangiora NZ 30.5.70 Linda J. Brown MB ChB 1964 qv

HOLLOWAY May Norma Duff   MA 1968
d of Norman W. H. civ serv and May D. Mallows; b Lond 20.10.46
Dip Ed(Dund) 1969
teacher Engl Harris acad Dun 1969–74; working in France 1974–75; teacher Engl/hist Newtyle s from 1975

HOLM Isabel   MA 1967
d of Evan M. H. farm. and Annie Ferguson farm.; b Resolis 13.6.46
teacher Avoch s 1968–72
m Dingwall 29.7.72 D. George Ross farm. s of John A. R. Fearn

HOLMES David   *BSc 1969

HOLMES Hazel Brown   MA 1969
d of Thomas B. H. farm. and Agnes A. Mitchell; b Edin 4.4.48
teacher Fr: Craigshill h s Livingston 1970–71, Douglas acad Milngavie 1971–72
m Currie 10.8.71 Robert Lamont farm. s of John L. Dumgoyne Glasg

HOLMES Paul Robin   *BSc 1970

HOLMES Sheila   MA 1970
m Aber 3.4.72 Stewart B. Telfer MSc 1969 qv

HOLMES William Alexander   MB ChB 1962

HONEYMAN Ian   MA 1962
s of John H. min of relig and Helen D. S. Aitchison; b Falkirk 12.1.42
div stud. licensed by C of S 1965; asst to regist univ Botswana, Lesotho and Swaziland 1965–66; asst min Aber 1966–67; admin asst Sus 1967–69; clerk to sc s Strath 1969–71; chief admin off. coll of tech Glasg 1971–73; plan. off. univ of S Pacific Fiji from 1973
m Lerwick 25.7.67 Eleanor J. Leask d of Laurence L. Lerwick

HONIGMANN Frederick John Reinhard   *MEd 1962
s of Hans D. H. PhD(Heidelberg) zool and Ursula M. Heilborn res tech zool; b Breslau Silesia 9.8.26
MA(St And) 1951 Dip Ed(St And) 1952 ABPsS 1965
teacher Aber acad 1962; educ psych ch guid serv Edin

1962–66; lect Craigie coll of educ Ayr from 1966
m Aber 9.7.55 Margaret M. L. Matheson BA(OU) d of John M. Aber

HOOD Charles Murray   MA 1970
s of William E. H. bank man. and Isobel M. Marr; b Edin 2.4.49
Assoc Chart. Inst Sec. 1974
admin asst W Lothian c c Linlithgow 1970–71; admin trainee Midlothian c c 1971–73, admin asst 1973–75; committee clerk Lothian reg c from 1975
m Edin 23.7.76 Catherine F. Wilkinson BSc(Edin)

HOOD Ellis   *BSc(eng) 1970

HOOD James Wilkie   *MA 1964

HOOD Margaret Elizabeth   BSc 1960
m Goudie

HOOD Virginia Agnes   MA 1970
d of Francis C. H. MA(Edin) univ prof and Muriel Dodds MA(Cantab) univ lect; b Newcastle-u-Tyne 29.3.48
secy: dept of Greek Edin 1971–73, part-time Strath 1974–75
m Durham 26.4.73 Gordon M. Thomson LL B 1969 qv

HOPKIN Duncan James   *BSc 1965 MSc 1970

HOPKIN Pamela Mary   BSc 1966
m Davidson

HORN Irene Elizabeth   MA 1969
d of Douglas J. L. H. civ eng and Agnes M. Tawse; b Kintore 6.11.47
teacher: Poole 1970–72, Glenrothes from 1972
m Aber 11.8.72 Alexander W. MacFarlane BSc 1970 qv

HORN Jennifer Rattray   MA 1965
d of Charles G. H. farm. and Barbara Simpson; b Fyvie 29.9.44
Dip Ed(Edin) 1966
teacher: Edin 1967–69, Sydney, Aust 1971–73, Gvarv, Norway from 1973; secy Oslo 1970–71
m Fyvie 29.9.69 Rein D. Follestad potter s of Einar F. Oslo

HORNBY Windham Brownrigg   *MA 1968 MEd 1979
stepson of John D. Brebner and s of Helen S. M. Lockhart; b Glas 7.4.46
teacher Malvern 1969–75; lect econ RGIT Aber from 1975
m Oxford 24.8.68 Allison J. Horncastle MA 1968 qv

HORNCASTLE Allison Jean   *MA 1968 Dip Ed 1969
d of Charles L. H. loc govt off. and Elizabeth D. Rae secy; b Grays 12.6.46
teacher Malvern 1969–71; Engl tut. 'A' level Worcester 1971–73; evening class tut. Higher Engl Aber 1977–79
m Oxford 24.8.68 Windham B. Hornby MA 1968 qv

HORNE Alexander Robert   *BSc(agr) 1966

HORNE Helen Edith   *BSc 1963
m John R. L. Howitt BSc 1962 qv

HORNE Jeanette Barbara   MA 1962
d of William A. H. garage man. and Jane H. Webster; b Edin 17.11.41
teacher maths: Annan acad 1963–64, Lossiemouth h s 1964–67; remed/adjustment teacher Elgin East End s

1967–68; staff man. Marks & Spencer 1968–71; teacher maths: Circencester Deer Park s 1971–72, Cliftonville s Northampton 1972, St Mary's s Northampton 1972–73, Annan acad from 1973
m Elgin 22.8.70 Nicholas J. Smith garage man., BL area superv s of William H. S. Bristol

HORNE Margaret Helen *BSc 1967
d of Alexander H. shopkeeper and Ruth Yule shopkeeper; b New Deer 22.10.44
teacher geog: Marist s Manc 1967–70, head dept 1969–70, evening classes Falkirk from 1975
m Aber 6.4.68 Thomas N. Bowden BSc 1965 *qv*

HORNE Norman John *MA 1960
s of James H. bus driver and Helen Riddoch; b Turriff 10.12.37
teacher classics Hamilton acad 1961–66; prin classics: Nicolson inst Stornoway 1966–71, Royal acad Inv 1971–72; asst head h s Inv 1972–77; rector Milne's h s Fochabers from 1977
m Aber 6.12.61 Ann Gavin shorthand typist d of Robert G. Aber

HORNE Ralph Ross *BSc 1962
s of Ralph A. H. MB ChB 1934 *qv*; b Aber 5.9.40
PhD(Birm) 1967 Polar medal 1971
geol: Brit antarctic surv Antarctica, Birm 1962–69, geol surv Ireland Dublin from 1969
m Leek 10.7.70 Margaret A. Horner nurse

HORROCKS Rodger BSc 1968
s of Sidney H. MB ChB(Liv) g p and Marjory C. Conners; b Derby 18.5.45
teacher biol Mackie acad Stonehaven 1969–73, prin biol from 1973
m Aber 11.5.66 Sandra J. Norrie BSc 1968 *qv*

HORSFALL George Lister MB ChB 1957
s of George A. C. H. master jeweller and Mabel Feavers tailoress; b Halifax 20.5.28
DA 1961
h o ARI 1957–58; sen h o anaest spec hosps Aber 1958–61; regist anaest S Teesside hosps Middlesbrough 1961–64; g p/anaest Thornaby-on-Tees from 1964
m Aber 22.5.61 Edna M. Fraser RGN d of James F. Bucksburn

HORSMAN Eileen Lesley MB ChB 1968
d of Squire R. H. teacher and Marjorie Plummer teacher; b Scarborough 2.3.44
FFARCS 1975
h o Aber 1968–69; sen h o: Jamaica 1969–70, Birm 1972–74; regist Birm 1974–75; sen regist Manc 1975–79; consult. Manc from 1979

HOSIE Linda Elizabeth Amy MA 1969
d of Manson B. H. elect. contr and Elizabeth Davidson; b Inverurie 12.9.48
teacher Aber from 1970
m Inverurie 16.8.69 Frank D. Davidson acct s of David D. Inverurie

HOSKISON Felicity Margaret *MA 1969

HOSSACK John James Grieve *MA 1969

HOUGHTON Thomas MB ChB 1964
s of Thomas H. insur man. and Kathleen Hargreaves; b Brighton 17.12.39
sen h o obst/gyn UCH Jamaica 1965–66; trainee g p Hatton and Cruden Bay 1966–67; sen h o anaest ARI 1967–68; g p Jersey from 1968

HOUSE Frank Raymond MSc 1968
Dip Tech(Lond)

HOUSE Judith Isa MA 1958
d of George H. A. H. superv Shell-Mex and Dorothy E. Ibbotson teacher; b Hedon 15.3.37
Dip Soc St(Leeds) 1959
Birm: soc case worker Council of Soc Serv 1959–60, youth leader The Settlement 1960–61; teacher county inf s Horncastle from 1966
m Hedon 19.4.60 Gerald B. Gorst div youth off. s of Gerald E. G. Preston

HOUSTON Neil Campbell MSc 1969
s of David H. red leader, welder and Nellie Campbell SRN; b Troon 1.12.40
BSc(Glas) 1963 FRMS 1974 MIBiol 1977
Torry res stat Aber: asst exper off., higher scient off. bact/electron microscopy from 1963
m Giffnock 3.6.66 Irene H. A. Dod data process. oper d of Credric N. D. BEng(Liv) Giffnock

HOUSTON Raymond MB ChB 1962

HOUSTON William Bernard MB ChB 1961

HOWARD Christopher Bernard *BSc 1966 MSc 1970
PhD 1976
s of Bernard H. H. BSc(Manc) prof biochem and Molly Rackett; b Stockport 9.3.44
Aberd: res asst 1966–73, res off. chem from 1973
m Aber 3.1.69 Isobel M. Greensmith BSc 1968 *qv*

HOWARD Geoffrey BSc 1964
s of Frank H. quantity surv and Margaret Baron; b Leeds 29.2.44
MSc(Lond) 1971
res asst Huntingdon res centre 1964–65; teacher: head biol dept Alleyns s Lond; lect: Trent coll Nott 1971–72, Park Lane coll Leeds 1972–77, sen lect from 1977
m Lond 20.10.69 Janet E. Franklin secy d of Harold F. Belvedere

HOWARD Patricia Anne *MA 1968
d of Harold G. H. head teacher and Violet E. Kelly; b Ayr 20.4.46
plan. off. town and county plan. dept Lancs c c 1968–73
m Aber 27.10.69 Richard M. Galloway BSc 1967 *qv*

HOWAT John Morrey BSc(for) 1958
b Edin 1.6.36
for. off, conserv for. E Nigeria 1958–67; teacher biol Perth 1968–71; conserv off. Countryside Comm for Scot. from 1971, media advis off. from 1975

HOWELL Joan Christine MA 1970
m Green

HOWELL John Bede Joseph BSc(for) 1962
s of Alfred J. H. wing comdr RAF and Mary A. Trinham; b Moasca Egypt 21.8.35
woodman France 1962–63; Worcs: jun consult. 1963–67; ptnr in firm of for. consult. from 1967
m Chelsea 11.9.65 Elizabeth M. Hungerford BSc(Belf) child nutrit d of Richard H. Dublin

HOWIE David Neville MA 1965 LLB 1967
s of Thomas W. H. MA(Glas) C of S min and Alexanderina McLennan; b Glenluce 28.1.43
Aber: law app 1967–69, leg. asst 1969–70, ptnr John Laurie & Co solic from 1970
m Aber 23.12.68 Aileen J. M. Henderson MA 1965 *qv*

HOWIE Ian Harrison　*BSc 1966 MSc 1967 PhD 1977

HOWIE John Mackintosh　*MA 1958 DSc 1970
s of David Y. H. MA(Glas) C of S min Ruthrieston S
ch Aber and Janet M. Mackintosh; b Chryston 23.5.36
DPhil(Oxon) 1961 FRSE 1971
asst dept maths Aberd 1958–59; asst, lect maths Glas
1961–67; visiting asst prof Tulane univ New Orleans
USA 1964–65; sen lect maths Stir 1967–70; regius prof
maths St And from 1970
m Aber 5.8.60 Dorothy J. M. Miller MA 1956 *qv*

HOWIE Kathleen Allison　MA 1964
m McCaig

HOWIE Margaret McLennan　MA 1964

HOWIE Robert　*MA 1958
s of Robert R. H. cloth finisher and Mary N. Allison;
b Aber 21.11.36
LRAM 1960
teacher mus: Torry acad 1959–60, Aber acad 1960–64;
lect mus Aber coll of educ from 1964
m Aber 3.8.62 Helen M. Smith secy d of William S.
Aber

HOWIE William　MA 1960 BD 1963 CASS 1972
s of Robert R. H. cloth finisher and Mary N. Allison;
b Aber 29.2.40
STM(NY) 1964
Aber: asst min Northfield par ch 1964–67; Aber assoc of
soc serv: dev off. 1967–70, asst secy 1972–73, secy from
1974
m Aber 19.7.63 Elizabeth A. Gill MA 1963 *qv*

HOWIESON James Stephen Paterson　BSc 1963

HOWIESON Margaret Paterson　MA 1963

HOWITT Angus Philip　*MA 1956

HOWITT David Scott　BEd 1969

HOWITT John Robert Lewis　BSc 1962
s of John H. bonus clerk and Annie S. McLellan;
b Aber 21.8.42
teacher Fraserburgh 1963–65; educ off.: N Nigeria
1965–69; RAEC Harrogate 1970–73, Herford W Ger
from 1973
m Aber 22.12.64 Helen E. Horne BSc 1963 *qv*

HÖYERALL Hans Martin　MB ChB 1963
b Oslo 13.5.36
Dr Med(Oslo) 1976
pre-reg posts Stavanger, Sortland Norway 1964–65;
m o h Skellefteå Sweden 1965–66; asst lege (g p) in clin
paediat: Umeå Sweden 1966–67, Bergen Norway 1967–70;
res worker in clin immunology and rheumat Oslo 1970–74;
asst lege in rheumat 1974–76, neurology 1976–77, internal
med from 1977
m Fredrikstad 27.7.63 Solveig E. Löken

HUCKVALE Eric Lindsay　*BSc(agr) 1970
s of Edward F. H. eng and Ella Urquhart; b Warwick
1.10.46
teacher: Sudbury g s 1970–71, Bransholme h s Hull from
1972
m York 12.7.72 Bertha F. Stirling BMedBiol 1969 *qv*

HUGGAN Robert Elliot　*MA 1964
no longer on GC reg

HUGHES Janice Butters　*MA 1970
d of James H. master baker/caterer and Elizabeth
Murray; b Aber 23.8.47
teacher: Fr Lond 1970–71, Fr/Ger Lewes 1971–73
m Aber 31.7.70 Ian M. Randall MA 1968 *qv*

HUGHSON Charles Bernard　*MA 1968

HUGHSON Robert Martin　*MA 1967

HULL Thomas Glenn　*BSc(agr) 1970
s of Robert H. steelworks foreman, linesman and
Dorothy Bradley; b Newcastle-u-Tyne 24.4.47
Newcastle: hosp porter 1970–72, insur ag 1972–73; exec
off. civ serv Lond, Newcastle 1973–76, higher exec off.
Newcastle from 1976
m Boldon Colliery Mary Coyme midwife d of William C.
Boldon Colliery

HUMES Walter Malcolm　*MA 1967 PhD 1972
s of David H. farm lab. and Agnes Graham; b Newton
Mearns 10.12.45
MEd(Glas) 1976
teacher Engl: Kingsdale s Lond 1968–69, Eastwood h s
Renfrewsh 1972–74; lect: Engl Notre Dame coll of educ
Glasg 1974–76, educ Glas from 1976

HUMPHREY Margaret　*MA 1964 Dip Ed 1965
d of Robert S. H. rly clerk and Margaret I. Cooper
governess; b Wick 4.5.42
teacher: geog Thurso 1965–66, asst, prin geog Hussey coll
Warri Nigeria 1966–67; temp asst head Hussey model s
1968; temp head CDC school Tiko Cameroons 1970;
secy Pentland geophys Wokingham from 1972
m Aber 6.4.66 Alistair M. Souter BSc 1964 *qv*

HUMPHREYS Douglas Eric Robin　BSc 1968

HUMPHRIES Wilfred Reynold　*MA 1969

HUMPHRIS Peter Maurice　BSc(eng) 1969

HUNG Wai Mun　MB ChB 1970

HUNT Andrew　LLB 1969
s of Frank H. H. H. civ serv and Nancy M. Smart;
b Edgeware 18.8.46
Perth: law app 1969–71, leg. asst 1971–73, ptnr solic
from 1973

HUNT Barbara Jean　MB ChB 1956

HUNT Jennifer　MA 1969 CASS 1971
m Wright

HUNT Stewart Marshall Sanderson　*MA 1970

HUNTER Alexander Freeland Cairns　MA 1960
　　　　　　　　　　　　　　　　　　LLB 1962

HUNTER Andrew Robb　*MA 1967
b Glasg 15.1.40
PhD(Stir) 1976
lect H-W from 1970

HUNTER Archibald Stewart　MB ChB 1960
s of Archibald M. H. MA(Glas) prof biblical crit
Aberd/Master Christ's coll Aber and Margaret W.
Swanson; b Comrie 7.3.36
DCH(Glas) 1962 MRCPGlas 1966 MRCPE 1966
h o, regist Aber hosps 1960–66; paediat cardiol: regist
Gr Ormond St London 1966–67, sen regist RHSC Edin

1967-69; sen res assoc dept ch health Newcastle 1969-72, res fell. Penn State univ USA 1972-73, consult. univ hosps Newcastle-u-Tyne/lect ch health N'cle from 1973
m Aber 9.12.60 Valerie M. Ewing bus. exec d of Andrew M. E. Aber

HUNTER Beatrice Josephine Nicholls   BSc 1962
d of Gordon W. H. farm. and Beatrice E. Taylor; b Banchory 4.11.39
computer progr Glas 1962-69
m Aber Frank F. D. Stott comp dir s of Frank W. S. Tayport

HUNTER Edward Bryce   BSc 1966
s of Edward H. butcher and Dorothy E. C. Davidson; b Aber 3.10.45
work study eng Lanarksh 1966-70; work study sect. leader/sen eng Dun 1970-73; sen man. consult. Nova Scotia from 1973
m Aber 17.9.66 Doreen H. Miller d of Norman M. Aber

HUNTER Elinor Isobel   MA 1970
m Forbes

HUNTER Elizabeth   *MA 1966
d of John H. farm./comp dir and Isabel J. Wallace; b Hitchin 23.4.44
teacher geog: Blyth s Norwich 1967-71, Dunstable s 1971-73; decorative arts course V & A museum Lond 1973-74; asst oriental art gallery 1974-75; lib/lect art hist polytech Stoke-on-Trent from 1975

HUNTER Fiona Mary   MA 1959
d of Archibald M. H. MA(Glas) prof biblical crit Aberd/Master Christ's coll Aber and Margaret W. Swanson; b Oxford 14.2.39
teacher Aber 1960-61; ch guid serv Glasg from 1969
m Aber 5.7.61 John L. Harper BSc(eng) 1958 *qv*

HUNTER Graham Cran   MA 1958 LLB 1960
s of John R. H. MA 1925 *qv*(II, III) and Janet D. Cran MA 1925 *qv*; b Huntly 4.10.36
law app Aber 1960-61; leg. asst Stornoway 1961-62, Inv 1962-63; leg. asst, ptnr Edmonds & Ledingham advoc Aber from 1963, joint clerk to Seven Incorporated Trades of Aber from 1976
m Aber 17.7.61 Janet C. Matheson MA 1959 *qv*

HUNTER Heather   MA 1959
d of John G. H. asst dir of educ and Jane B. Watt; b Lerwick 25.1.38
teacher: Aber 1960-62, Lerwick from 1974
m Aber 11.7.62 George A. Smith MB ChB 1962 *qv*

HUNTER Iain Hamilton   BSc 1969

HUNTER James Fraser   *MA 1966 Dip Ed 1967
s of William H. joiner and Jane S. Fraser secy; b Aber 25.2.43
Dip Soc Work (Stir) 1975
tut./house parent Murree Christian s W Pakistan 1967-71; soc worker Aberdeensh 1971-73: soc worker Grampian reg from 1975
m Aber 17.8. 67 Alison M. Craig nurse d of John C. Aber

HUNTER James Kirton   MA 1963
s of Andrew H. comp dir and Hilda Clark; b Peterhead 3.9.35
Edin: trainee 1963-67, stockbroker from 1967
m Aber 17.3.65 Vivien M. D. Alcock d of Thomas B. A. Keith

HUNTER James More   MB ChB 1961
s of James M. H. FRAS insur broker and Elsie A. Shirran; b Aber 10.8.30
g p Edin from 1965
m Aber 17.7.61 Margaret E. Ramsay d of Alexander C. R. Aber

HUNTER James Wood   MB ChB 1959

HUNTER Sheena Gordon   *MA 1964
d of Gordon H. salesman and Edith M. Law; b Aber 25.2.42
teaching asst univ of Alta, Canada 1964-66; ch psych Bancroft s New Jersey USA 1966-68; psych educ spec Sacred Heart Village Toronto 1968-71
m Aber 3.8.66 James B. Campbell BSc 1962 *qv*

HUNTER Thomas George   BSc(eng) 1958
s of James J. H. and Minnie F. Clark; b Victoria BC Canada 28.8.34
asst eng city eng's dept Aber 1958-61; Lerwick: eng Zetland county surv 1961-68, area eng N of S water board 1968-75, prin eng Shetland Is council from 1975
m Aber 22.7.60 Erica A. Laidlaw MA 1958 *qv*

HUNTER William Fiddes   *MA 1964
s of William H. joiner and Jeannie S. Fraser; b Aber 6.3.41
PhD(Cantab) 1972
lect Span.: Aberd 1964-65, Exe from 1968
m Aber 12.8.67 Marilyn W. Beattie MA 1964 *qv*

HURRY Anne Campbell   MA 1962
m Daniel

HURRY Patricia   *MA 1970

HUTCHEON Alexander Austin Clark Barnacle
BSc 1962 MSc 1967

HUTCHEON Andrew William   MB ChB 1968 MD 1977
s of George Hutcheon grocer and Elsie S. Murrison nurse; b Aber 21.5.43
MRCP 1971
h o ARI, Balfour hosp Kirkwall 1968-69; sen h o Woodend hosp Aber 1969-70; regist WI Glasg 1970-73; res fell. Glas 1973-75; lect med WI Glasg from 1975
m Kirkwall 14.7.66 Christine G. Cusiter teacher d of Francis G. C. Kirkwall

HUTCHEON Elizabeth Margaret   *MA 1970
Dip Ed 1971
d of George C. H. estate overseer and Matilda M. H. Fraser MA 1927 *qv*; b Inv 13.9.48
MEd(Glas) 1976
teacher Engl Bearsden acad 1971-73, Cathkin h s from 1973
m Aber 26.9.75 James G. Bell MB ChB(Glas) g p s of David G. B. Stepps

HUTCHEON Jean Gordon McKenzie   BSc 1958 *1959
d of James H. MB ChB 1924 *qv*; b Aber 26.5.37
teacher sc Aber h s for girls 1960-63
m Aber Hamish S. MacRae MA 1951 *qv*

HUTCHEON Muriel   MA 1960
m Wilson

HUTCHEON William Vincent   *BSc(agr) 1968
s of Andrew W. H. farm. and Lily Murison; b Aber 8.5.45
lect Aberd 1968-69; agr res Tafo Ghana 1969-78; lect NOSCA Aber from 1978

HUTCHESON Carole Jean   *BSc 1959
d of John M. H. farm. and Esther A. W. Munro; b Inv
25.12.37
MSc(Adel) 1962
univ dem Adel Aust 1959–62; asst warden Orielton field
centre Pembroke 1964–65; teacher biol Southend 1966;
tech off. in hosp lab Sunderland 1967–70
m Inv 7.4.69 John Bainbridge BSc(Leeds) teacher s of
John G. B. Ossett

HUTCHESON Christine Anne   MA 1964
d of John H. gen merch and Margaret A. Maclean
sub-postmistress; b N Kessock 17.2.43
teacher Engl: Dingwall acad 1965–66, Summerhill acad
Aber 1966–70; lect Engl/commun Aber coll of commerce from 1977
m Muir of Ord 1.4.66 William A. Milne med rep s of
William J. M. Aber

HUTCHESON Lilian Mary   BSc(agr) 1956
d of John M. H. farm. and Esther A. W. Munro; b Petty
Invsh 3.8.34
MSA(Tor) 1963 PhD(NSW Aust) 1968
res asst: Huntingdon res centre 1956–58, 1959–60,
Ontario agr coll 1958–59, 1960–64; res fell. univ of NSW
Aust 1964–68; clin biochem Canada: Vancouver gen
hosp 1968–72, royal Columbian hosp from 1973
m Guelph Ontario 27.6.64 Alistair Ewen

HUTCHESON Moira Mary   BSc 1969
d of James H. civ eng and Mary Marshall saleswoman;
b Stirling 21.5.48
teacher biol: Slough 1969–71, Newcastle-u-Tyne 1972–73,
Blackburn Lancs from 1973
m Tullibody 9.8.72 Peter C. Johnson sports complex man.
s of Robert J. Lond

HUTCHESON Rosemary Joan Fraser   MA 1970
d of John H. clerk and Margaret A. MacLean shop-
keeper/postmistress; b Inv 6.7.48
teacher Bonnyrigg from 1971
m Knockbain 1971 Andrew S. Barker BSc(Coventry) civ
serv, computer progr s of Kenneth S. B. Filey

HUTCHISON Alexander Howieson   *LLB 1966
s of Alexander S. H. min of relig and Grace M.
Ferguson; b Renton 12.4.44
AHA 1970
nat admin trainee NHSO SE Scotland 1966–69; hosp secy
Edin Royal Victoria hosp 1969–70, Simpson mem mat.
pavilion 1970–72; Lond: hosp secy Lewisham hosp
1972–74, gen admin Lewisham health dist from 1974

HUTCHISON Alexander Norman   *MA 1966
s of Gordon H. MB ChB 1930 qv; b Buckie 20.10.43
PhD(NW univ USA) 1975
lect Engl Vic BC Canada from 1966; Canada council
doct fell. 1968–70
m Victoria BC 28.12.71 Nora S. Seaborne BA(Vic BC)
univ lect d of Kenneth S. Victoria

HUTCHISON Charles   MA 1969

HUTCHISON Iain George Campbell   *MA 1967

HUTCHISON Kathleen Liston   PhD 1970
BSc(Glas)
m Cartwright

HUTCHISON William Watt   *BSc 1957
PhD(Tor) 1962

pres Geol Assoc of Canada 1973, secy gen Int Union of
Geol Sciences, dir gen Geol Survey of Canada from 1981

HUTH Herbert Erich   BEd 1969

HUTT Patricia Augusta   BSc 1963

HUTTON David George   BSc 1967
s of Kenneth B. H. MA(Oxon) and Barbara A. Britton
BA(Oxon); b Winchester 12.10.46
teacher: Uganda 1968, Basildon 1969–73, Gt Missenden
1973–75, Aylesbury 1975–76, Wigmore from 1977
m Harrogate 26.8.72 Janet M. Hambly BA(Exe) teacher

HUTTON Eleanor Jean   MA 1961 Dip Ed 1962
d of James G. H. rly investigating clerk and Ann
H. W. Keith clerkess; b Aber 21.5.40
teacher maths Aber from 1962
m Aboyne 22.10.76 Michael D. Watson BSc 1971 drilling
fluids eng s of Douglas C. W. Aber

HUTTON Elizabeth Mary   MA 1956
d of Alexander H. wholesale draper and Mary G.
Melvin secy; b Aber 18.1.36
information scient Mullard radio valve co Mitcham
junction 1956–59; teacher Engl Abbots Bromley 1970
information scient RARDE Halstead Sevenoaks from
1973
m Aber 31.7.59 Grahame V. J. Weston army off. s of
Victor J. W.

HUTTON Lisella Margaret   *BSc 1970
d of Hugh H. LRCPE g p and Mary D. Donald nurse;
b Carlisle 27.6.49
DipLA(Edin) 1972 AILA 1974
asst landscape arch.: Stonehouse and E. Kilbride dev
corp 1972–73, William Gillespie & Ptnrs Glasg from 1973

HUTTON Ray Forbes   MA 1969
m Hamilton

I'ANSON Annette Elizabeth   MA 1963 Dip Ed 1964
d of Leonard I'A. boiler attendant and Jeannie C.
Donaldson; b Aber 19.2.42
teacher Aber: Abbotswell p s 1964–68, King St p s
from 1968
m Aber 21.11.59 Kenneth C. R. Hepburn civ serv s of
George H. Aber; marr diss 1972

IBBOTSON Bernard Ross   *BSc(for) 1961

IBELL Robert Leslie   BSc(eng) 1967
s of William E. I. head teacher and Freda E. Hopwood
head teacher; b Woodford 11.1.46
MICE 1973
civ eng, site man. Taylor Woodrow construct. UK from
1967
m Middlesbrough 25.10.69 Patricia I. Wilkie MA 1967 qv

IBIAM Tolulope Idam Ngbo   MB ChB 1970

IBRAHIM Hassan Suliman   MSc 1968
BSc(agr)(Khart)

IKENWIWE Lawrence Ifeayin-Chukwu   BSc(eng) 1965

ILLINGWORTH William John   BSc(eng) 1961

ILLSLEY Raymond   PhD 1956
s of James I. potter's asst and Harriet Chamberlain

kitchenmaid; b Woodville 6.7.19
BA(Oxon) 1948
econ asst commonwealth econ comm Lond 1948–49;
soc & econ res off. Crawley New Town 1949–51; Aberd:
sociol MRC 1951–64, prof sociol 1964–75, prof med
sociol from 1975; hon dir MRC med sociol unit from
1965
m Oxford 15.6.48 Jean M. Harrison BA(Oxon) teacher
d of Arthur J. H. Oxford

ILOKA Lazarus Obidigeo   BSc(eng) 1965
 s of Ugonna O. I. and Nwalie Ezeodili; b Abatete
Nigeria 30.10.39
MSc(Loughborough) 1966 MBA(Loughborough) 1967
Dip Gen Man.(Turin) 1974 Dip Proj Appraisal(Milwau-
kee) 1976
dev eng BCC Wembley 1967–68; sen evaluation eng
Honeywell controls Glasg 1968–72; Nigeria: proj eng
Shell BP 1972–73, man. consult. centre for man. dev
1973–74, area man. dev bank from 1975
m Loughborough 1.10.66 Helen Okoye secy d of Francis
O. Abatete

IMAM Abubakar   MB ChB 1956
 s of Alkali Jafaru, chief Alkali of Kano and Hajiya H.
Yarshirayi; b Kano 13.7.31
MRCOG(Lond) 1963 FCS(W Af) 1964 FMCOG
(Nigeria) 1970 FRCOG 1977 OON (Off. of the Order of
the Niger) 1978
Kano Nigeria: m o 1957–64, consult. obst/gyn 1964–68,
sen consult. obst/gyn 1968, chief m o 1968–75, dir health
serv 1975–76, chief consult. 1974–76; voluntarily retd
govt serv 1977; med dir Mustapha mem hosp from 1977

IMAM Alkali Ja'Afaru Kalli Goni   BSc(for) 1957
 s of Goni Imam area court judge and Amina S. Imam
Hamsami; b Maiduguri 2.3.28
asst conserv for. N Nigeria 1957–59; Nigeria: prin for. s
Jos 1960–61, conserv, chief conserv for. Kaduna 1961–68;
perm secy: min of agr and nat resources Maiduguri NE
state 1968–75, min of health 1975–76, Brino state min of
finance/econ plan. from 1976
m Maiduguri 19.12.65 Hamra Mohammed BA (Ahmadu
Bello) asst regist univ of Maiduguri d of Mohammed
Shuwa Maiduguri

IMLACH Alexander Reid McLean   MA 1956
 s of James I. fisherman and Mary McLean; b Aber
27.1.36
Dip Soc Ad(Glas) 1969
teacher Engl Torry acad Aber 1959–60; teacher/house-
master Oakbank list D s Aber 1960–65; Rossie list D s
Montrose: third i/c 1965–69, dep head from 1969
m Montrose 28.3.64 Grace M. W. Amps teacher d of
William A. Fraserburgh

IMLACH James Alexander   BSc 1961 *1966 MSc 1967
PhD 1972

IMRAY Bryan Charles   BSc 1958
 s of Charles I. master grocer and Gladys Ingram;
b Aber 9.2.36
MEd(univ of Montana USA) 1974
geol govt surv Ghana 1958–62; educ off. Dar-es-Salaam
Tanzania 1963–68; teacher Grande Prairie Alberta
1968–72; prin Peace River h s Alberta from 1972
marr diss
m(2) Peace River 21.4.73 Jennifer E. Gray Dip Ed(N'cle)
d of James G. Ingleton

IMRAY James McGregor   MB ChB 1957
 s of William I. farm. and Barbara M. McGregor secy;

b Inv 24.9.33
DA 1962 FFARCS 1969
h o ARI 1957–58; regist: surg Hobart Tasmania 1958–61,
anaest ARI 1961–62; part-time farm. Abdnsh/anaest
ARI 1962–71; consult. anaest ARI from 1971
m Strathdon 20.8.65 Lucy C. Anderson SRN d of James
A. Strathdon

IMRAY John   MA 1958
 s of Robert C. I. docker and Elizabeth Stevenson;
b Edin 2.7.13
FEIS 1977
Aber: teacher Kirkhill p s 1958–66, dep head Victoria
Road p s from 1966
m Aber 22.7.36 Mildred Allathan teacher d of Alexander
A. Culter

IMRAY Mildred Marion   MA 1958
 m Davis

IMRIE Janet Yvonne   *BSc 1970
 m Henderson

INALSINGH Calvin Holmes Rajpat   MB ChB 1963
 s of Cyril H. I. chief clerk, crown solic's off. and
Charlotte S. Dookransingh prop.; b Trinidad 16.8.36
Trinidad: h o Port of Spain hosp 1964–65, dist m o
Sangre Grande 1965–72, dist m o, regist i/c Arima hosp
from 1972 and private pract from 1965
m Trinidad 8.2.68 Marina R. Persand d of Bharat P.
Trinidad

INALSINGH Carol Homer Amar   MB ChB 1961
 s of Cyril H. I. acct and Charlotte S. Dookransingh
prop; b Tunapuna Trinidad 26.10.34
DMRT(Lond) 1966
h o gen hosp Port of Spain Trinidad 1961–63; regist:
Hammersmith hosp Lond 1965–66, gen hosp Port of
Spain 1966–71; USA: asst prof radiol Johns Hopkins
univ Maryland 1971–75, dir of radiation oncology Blake
mem hosp Bradenton Florida 1975–79, Manatee mem
hosp Bradenton from 1979
m Trinidad 2.9.63 Mira Naipaul BA(Leeds) teacher

INALSINGH Vanessa Savriti   MA 1966
 d of Cyril H. I. chief clerk, crown solic's off. and
Charlotte S. Dookransingh prop.; b Trinidad 30.4.43
teacher Engl St Joseph's convent Trinidad from 1967

INGHAM Valerie   MA 1964

INGLIS David Simpson Blacklaw   BSc 1968

INGLIS Donald Bain Carrick   MA 1963 *MEd 1968
 s of William C. I. comm rep BR and Margaret A. C.
Bain; b Aber 17.12.41
BD(Glas) 1975
teacher: Engl/hist Northfield s s Aber 1964, Engl/hist
Eilon acad 1965–68; asst educ psych Lanarksh Hamilton
1968–71, sen educ psych 1971–72; asst min at Bathgate
high ch 1975–77; educ psych Fife reg c from 1977
m Glasg 24.9.74 Yvonne M. S. Cook secy d of James
D. C. San Paulo Brazil

INGLIS John Gladstone   BEd 1969

INGLIS John Proven   BSc 1970
 s of John P. I. contr off. NCB and Margaret H. Brand;
b Glasg 24.11.47
scient off. metrop police forensic labs Lond 1970–73;
teacher Dartford g s 1973–74; supt PO telecomm Lond
from 1975
m Aber 11.9.70 Elizabeth S. Moncrieff MA 1970 *qv*

INGLIS Julian Thomas   BSc 1967
s of Thomas I. BSc(St And) teacher and Patricia J.
Lake school lib; b Meikleour 29.7.46
MSc(Carleton univ Ottawa) 1975
teacher Peterhead, Toronto 1967–68; range biol Canada:
Inuvik N W terr 1968–70, Arctic Is 1970–73; land man.
biol and acting head land man. sect. govt of Canada
Ottawa from 1973
m Glasg 5.6.70 Aileen A. Urquhart BSc 1968 *qv*

INGLIS Leslie Glennie   MA 1963

INGLIS Mary Horne   *BSc 1970
m Smith

INGLIS Thomas   BSc(eng) 1968
s of Thomas M. I. security off. and Annie M. Patterson;
b Montrose 5.3.47
hydrologist to Forth River purif board Stirling 1968–72;
eng/hydrol Cheshunt: Lee conserv catchment board 1972–
74, Lea div Thames water auth from 1974
m Montrose 26.10.68 Frances P. Easton sales ledger clerk
d of George E. Montrose

INGLIS William Raymond   *MA 1970
s of William I. instrument tech and Mabel C. McEwan
receptionist; b Alloa 18.3.48
Alloa acad: teacher Engl 1971–73, asst prin guid 1973–74,
prin guid 1974–76; prin guid Lornshill acad from 1976
m Sauchie 22.8.70 Lorna I. Young MA(St And)teacher
d of Peter Y. Sauchie

INGOLFSSON Agnar   *BSc 1961
s of Ingolfur Davidsson Mag Sc(Copenhagen) botanist
and Agnes Christensen weaver; b Reykjavik 29.7.37
PhD(Mich) 1967
asst prof Mass USA 1967–71; dosent (lect) Reykjavik
1971–73, prof from 1973
m Reykjavik 25.12.72 Linda Wendel med tech d of
Andres W. Reykjavik

INGRAM Alexander Lindsay   BL 1957
s of Garson I. banker and Margaret N. Lindsay;
b Comrie 7.2.31
AIBankers(Scot) 1953
law asst WS firm Edin 1957–61; proc fiscal dep Cupar
1961–73, proc fisc Forfar from 1973
m Cupar 3.6.67 Margaret C. E. W. Meldrum adoption
off., play s supt d of Arthur G. M. Cupar

INGRAM Alex Simpson   *BSc 1968 PhD 1971
s of George I. woodcutter and Margaret J. Simpson;
b Huntly 5.6.45
tech off. St And univ 1971–73; res chem, plant man.,
team leader Fisons Loughborough 1973–77; sen chem
Lancaster synthesis from 1977
m Huntly 27.3.71 Marlene McIrvine MA 1971 d of
Robert I. McI. Forgue

INGRAM Anne Wilson   MA 1957

INGRAM Christopher Laidlaw   BSc(for) 1969
s of Lawrence I. MB BS(Durh) g p and Mary E.
Laidlaw teacher; b E Bolden 11.2.46
util off. Zambian for. dept Kitwe 1969–72; asst branch
man. Tilhill for.(Scot) Elgin 1973–74; reg man. Tilhill
for.(marketing) at Stirling 1974–76, Elgin from 1976
m Leith 31.7.69 Jean B. K. Mathie teacher d of Edward
J. M. Leith

INGRAM Greig Webster   MA 1969
s of William J. I. farm. and Margaret V. Booth teacher;
b Burnhervie 20.11.47
Glasg: teacher Holyrood s s 1970–72, Lourdes s s 1972–
74, prin mod stud. St Margaret Mary's s s from 1974
m Glasg 28.12.77 Patricia A. Miller bank off. d of
Duncan M. Glasg

INGRAM Margaret Jane   *BSc 1969
d of John L. I. man. flooring and Georgina L. Addison
nurs sister; b Nott 12.2.47
asst Molteno inst of biochem parasitology Cantab
1969–70
m Nott 6.12.69 Sean F. O'B. Donaghey BSc 1969 *qv*

INGRAM Roy   MA 1960

INKSON Dennis Wright   BSc(eng) 1969
s of James I. butcher and Violet Ledingham typist;
b Aber 25.2.48
grad eng Aber city eng 1969–74; site eng 1974–75; eng
Lothian reg c 1975–77; roads eng Dubai municipality
UAE from 1977
m(2) Aber 26.9.75 Lesley A. S. Allan LL B 1974 d of
Douglas A. Aber

INKSON James Henry Kerr   *MA 1963
s of John K. I. MA 1929 *qv* and Frances Wilson MA
1928 *qv*; b Aber 13.1.42
MPhil(Lond) 1968 PhD(Otago) 1980
post grad stud. Lond 1963–65; assoc res fell. Aston Birm
1965–68: lect psych Aston 1968–70; lect indust psych
univ of Otago Dunedin NZ, sen lect in indust psych
from 1973
m Muir of Ord 19.8.66 Nan Tuach BSc 1965 *qv*

INKSTER David White   MA 1961

INKSTER Elizabeth Mary   MA 1963
d of Walter W. I. fisherman and Barbara Inkster; b
Hamnavoe 21.7.42
teacher: maths/sc Wick 1964–65, sc Thurso 1965–66
m Lerwick 19.4.65 Andrew B. Bryce BSc(eng) 1958 *qv*

INKSTER Hugh   BSc(eng) 1970
s of Hugh C. I. comp secy and Dorothy Taylor;
b Kirkwall 2.5.47
man. trainee to prod. gen man. Keighley from 1971

INKSTER Raymond   *MA 1967 BD 1970
s of John I. and Kathleen I. Paterson; b Perth 20.6.45
Baptist ch min: Gilcomston Park ch Aber from 1971
m Aber 19.7.69 Muriel M. Fowler BEd 1969 *qv*

INNES Alan John   MA 1965 LLB 1967
s of John L. I. MA 1926 *qv*; b Aber 30.3.44
law app 1967–69; solic Peterkin & Duncans advoc Aber
from 1969

INNES Arthur James   MB ChB 1965
b Kemnay 5.6.42
DABS 1974
h o RI Perth 1965–66; USA: intern Norwalk hosp Conn
1966–67; lt, lt cdr US Navy 1967–69; surg resid Norfolk
gen hosp Virginia 1969–73; private pract gen surg
Springfield Oregon from 1973

INNES Brian Peter   BSc 1969

INNES Doreen Cormack   *MA 1962
d of John F. I. newsag and grocer and Thomasina
Cormack; b Aber 26.5.40

Ireland schol 1963 Classical hon moderations(Oxon) 1964
DPhil(Oxon) 1968 MA(Oxon) 1969
stud. Somerville coll Oxon 1962–65; res fell St Hugh's
coll Oxon 1963–67; lect classic stud. univ of Kent 1967–
69; fell. and tut. in Literae Humaniores St Hilda's coll
Oxon from 1969

INNES Eurwen Harries   MB ChB 1958
 d of John I. pharm and Sarah Harries; b Peterhead
12.6.34
DCH(Lond) 1960 DObstRCOG 1961 MRCP 1968
DPM 1971
h o Aber 1958–59; h o, sen h o, regist in various hosps
1959–72; consult. phys (rheumat and rehabilitation)
Hastings clin area from 1972

INNES Francis Albert Shaw   BSc(eng) 1968

INNES Graham Gilchrist   MA 1967

INNES Isabel Cunningham   *BSc 1969 MSc 1972
 d of Henry I. loc govt off. and Evelyn L. Cunningham
shop asst; b Aber 14.3.47
res chem Richards Aber 1969–73
m Aber 11.7.70 Ian Murray BSc 1971 agr chem s of
Cecil M. Aber

INNES Jean Alexandra   MA 1969
 d of William A. I. farm. and Sophie Anderson;
b Forres 29.2.48
ALA 1972
Aber city lib: lib asst 1969–70, asst lib 1971–72, lib i/c
central lending lib from 1972
m Aber 23.9.71 Fergus R. M. Dodds MA 1972 ptnr
Rainbow Enterprises (printer/publ) Aber s of John
M. D. MA 1926 *qv*

INNES John Michael   *MA 1963
 s of John S. I.; b Aber 13.11.41
PhD(Birm) 1969 ABPsS 1970
lect: dept of sociol Birm 1963–65, dept of psych Birm
1965–73, visiting lect dept of psych univ of Michigan
Ann Arbor USA 1972–73; lect dept of psych Edin from
1973
m Aber 1964

INNES Leslie Gordon   *MA 1958

INNES Lorraine Hilary   MA 1968
 d of Cameron R. I. MB ChB 1950 *qv*; b Glasg 26.6.46
Inst Pers Man.(Dun)
exec off. PO grad appointments centre Lond 1968–70;
stud. Dun coll of comm(IPM) 1978–79
m Corpach 25.4.70 Hugo Y. Shaw LL B(Dund) civ serv,
app solic s of Hugh S. Fort William

INNES Margaret Annie   MB ChB 1965
 m Cameron

INNES Norman Lindsay   *BSc(agr) 1957 PhD 1968

INNES Patricia Anne   *MA 1967
 m Falconer

INNES Patrick Gordon   BSc(eng) 1957
 s of John A. I. BSc 1913 *qv* and Elizabeth Stephen MA
1913 *qv*; b Aber 23.2.31
Guest Keen & Nettlefolds Midlands: grad app Birm
1957–58, pers asst to prod. dir 1958–60; The British
Screw Co Leeds: asst works man. 1960–64, dir and joint
gen man. 1964–66, man. dir 1966–72; Crompton Nettlefold Stenham Ashton-in-Makerfield: man. dir 1972–74;

GKN Fastener Tools div of GKN Screws & Fasteners
Birm: man dir from 1976
m Aber 15.9.56 Florence Hendry cook d of George H.
MA 1922 *qv*

INNES Sheila Valaine   MA 1966
 d of Cameron S. I. MBE col serv and Christian D.
Robb civ serv hosp admin; b Aber 9.5.23
teacher Luthermuir 1967–75
m Chapelhall 7.10.43 William J. Cantlay BSc(agr) 1943 *qv*

INNES William   MA 1960 Dip Ed 1961

INNES William   BSc 1961
 s of William G. I. fisherman and Mary A. Mair;
b Cullen 24.8.40
teacher: maths/sc Aberchirder 1962–65, maths Keith g s
1965–74, prin maths Fortrose from 1974
m Kirkwall 23.7.74 Moira L. Tait teacher d of Andrew T.
Kirkwall

INNES William George   MA 1962
 s of Gordon D. I. gamekeeper/for. worker and Maggie
Taylor; b Bucksburn 23.3.40
Powis acad Aber: teacher 1963–70, year master 1970–74,
asst head from 1974
m(2) Aber 27.2.76 Abigail L. Hay MA 1967 *qv*

INNES William George   MB ChB 1966

INNES William James Alexander   *MA 1956
 s of William J. I. insur ag and Helen M. M. Porter;
b Ballater 11.10.34
RAF off. gen duties branch 1956–72; prin Home Office
Lond 1972–76; asst secy N Ireland off. from 1977
m Aber 27.6.59 Carol I. Bruce MA 1958 *qv*

INNES-WILL Brian Norman   *MA 1967

INNOCENT Barbara Jean   *MA 1969
 m Jones

IORNS David Spencer   *BSc 1970
 s of Edward G. I. acct and Olive Chilton; b Aber
23.10.48
Grad RIC(Hatfield poly) 1972
process eng Welwyn 1970–75; prod. dev chem Leiden
Holland 1975–78; res dev man. Scarborough from 1978
m Aber 24.9.71 Alison Fraser MA 1971 d of William
C. F. Banchory

IRONSIDE Graham Johnston   MA 1958
 s of Basil I. MA 1926 *qv*; b Aber 14.6.37
CNAA Dip Educ Tech(Jordanhill) 1979
teacher: Aber 1959–63, Singapore 1963–65, Aber 1965–
66; lect: f e Aber 1966–79, sen lect educ resources Aber
coll of comm from 1979
m Aber 30.3.63 Joan T. Milne teacher p e d of George M.
Aber

IRUOHA Iruoha Oke   MB ChB 1965

IRVIN Carolyn Anne   *BSc 1959
 d of Richard I. trawl owner and Florence J. Ramsden;
b Peterculter 17.5.36
BA(Lond) 1968
Lond: edit. asst inst of phys 1960–62; teacher Sydenham
s 1962–64; stud. Bedford coll 1965–67
m Lond 18.3.67 Reginald G. Harlow BSc(Lond) lect s of
Alfred R. H. Lond

IRVIN Thomas Thoburn   MB ChB 1964 PhD 1968

IRVINE Alison McLean   BSc 1967 PhD 1972
d of Patrick F. B. I. stockbroker and Janette M. Johnson physioth; b Aber 28.5.47
path. dept Aberd: res asst 1967–69, Georgina McRobert fell. in cancer res 1969–72
m Aber 27.7.67 George P. M. Crawford MB ChB 1970 *qv*

IRVINE David Lawrence Morrison   MA 1967

IRVINE Edward Charles Fordyce   BSc(eng) 1956

IRVINE Elizabeth Marjorie   MB ChB 1965

IRVINE Gladys Christine   MA 1970
d of George I. farm. and Bella Dunn; b Aber 29.10.48
Dip Lib(Strath) 1972 ALA 1973
trainee lib Mitchell lib Glasg 1970–71; lib: Mitchell lib 1972–73, Paisley publ lib from 1974
m Aber 10.12.73 Alan D. Macmillan-Kelly bldg contr s of Donald M.-K. Wokingham

IRVINE James Robert Sinclair   MA 1970
s of Harry I. farm. and Hannah M. Henderson teacher; b Virkie Shetland 24.3.47
teacher: Lerwick p s 1971–73, asst head 1973–77, dep head from 1977

IRVINE Joseph Andrew   BSc 1966
s of Robert I. lorry driver and Jemima M. Hardy knitwear worker; b Mossbank Shetland 18.6.44
Lerwick: teacher sc 1967–68, maths from 1968
m Aber 3.4.68 Ishbel M. Cruickshank hairdresser d of John M. C. MA 1926 *qv*(III)

IRVINE Keith Robert   *BSc 1968

IRVINE Margaret Anderson   MA 1961

IRVINE Robert   *BSc 1956

IRVINE Ronald David   *MA 1967

IRVINE Veronica Mary   MA 1959
d of John A. I. streets/roads insp and Jean Scollay; b Aber 18.10.38
teacher: Marchburn inf s Aber 1960–62, Sholing inf s Southampton 1963–65, Guardbridge p s, Langlands p s St And from 1974
m Aber 4.7.61 George M. Phillips MA 1960 *qv*

IRVINE William Stuart   MA 1963
s of William S. I. man. fishcuring fact. and Agnes I. Paterson; b Aber 18.10.42
teacher: p s Lossiemouth 1964–65, p s Cumbernauld 1965–68; dep head p s St Ninians Stirling 1968–71; head: Shieldhill p s Falkirk 1971–75, Ellon p s from 1975
m Aber 18.12.65 Monica M. Davidson teacher d of Bertie M. D. Aber

IRVINE-FORTESCUE Margaret Ann   *MA 1966
d of William G. I.-F. army off. and Kathleen S. Bennett-Jones lect Dunfermline coll of p e; b Quetta Pakistan 20.7.44
Dip Soc Admin Stud(Oxon) 1967 Dip Ed(Edin) 1968
teacher Engl/soc stud. Middx 1968–70; asst apptments off. univ of E Ang Norwich from 1970

IRVING John Ramsay   *BSc(eng) 1969

ISAAC Philip Edward   *BSc(eng) 1969

IUTZ Josephine   MA 1962
d of Max C. F. I. man. wool export firm and Kathleen

E. Davey soc worker; b Bingley 10.8.41
part time teacher f e Ilkley from 1974; post-grad stud. hist and phil of sc Leeds univ
m Aber 20.10.60 Tokefat C. Pacsoo MB ChB 1962 *qv*

IZATT Jack Birrell   *BSc(eng) 1957 PhD 1959
s of William I. art lect and Winnifred Graham; b Buckhaven 13.7.35
FIEE 1974 CEng 1974
BBC res dept Kingswood Tadworth: eng aerial sect. 1960–62, sen eng receiver sect. 1962–65; Solartron Electronic Group Farnborough: team leader 1965–68, group leader 1969–71, chief eng dynamic analysis R & D 1972–75, res and dev man. syst div from 1976
m Aber 2.4.58 Katrine I. L. Macleod MA 1956 *qv*

IZATT Tom Graham   MA 1959
s of William I. art lect and Winnifred Graham; b Stonehaven 21.6.37
CEng MIEE 1973 MSc(Salf) 1977
res eng BBC Kingswood 1959–69; lect Preston polytech 1969–75, sen lect from 1975
m Sutton 12.4.66 Jacqueline Belchamber teacher

IZOD Jeffrey Edward   LLB 1966
s of Edward J. I. shop owner and Edith M. Esson; b Aber 17.11.43
oil marketing Lond: man. trainee 1967–68, area man. 1968–69, real estate negotiator 1969–71, sales man. 1971–74; agreements negotiator N Sea oil 1974–78; oil comp lawyer from 1978
m(2) Ashford 8.11.78 Cherry F. Hill secy d of Bertum W. H. Frimley

JACK Daniel MacPherson   *MA 1969
s of Daniel R. J. drift net fisherman and Jessie MacPherson; b Hopeman 15.11.30
teacher econ: Fraserburgh acad 1970–71, Moray coll of f e from 1971

JACK David Alexander   *MA 1967
s of George D. J. tel superv and Marjory Lee; b Inv 28.6.44
teacher: Portsmouth 1968–71, Lond from 1971
m Lond 10.8.74 Hilary M. Dove teacher d of Job D. Lond

JACK Edwin Alexander   BSc(eng) 1963 *1964
s of Wilfred J. J. mech supt and Mearl A. Younker; b Bartica Guyana 16.5.37
M.Phil(Lond) 1971
asst city eng city eng Georgetown Guyana 1964–72; sen eng Trinto Plan. Consult. Tacarigua Trinidad from 1972
m Port of Spain 31.10.64 Barbara P. Raymond MA 1962 *qv*

JACK George Clark   *BSc 1959

JACK George Wishart   *BSc 1967
s of George W. J. PO eng and Willexia Gardiner; b Wick 3.12.44
PhD(Brist) 1971
post doct fell. dept bact Brist 1970–71; sen scient off. microbiol res estab Porton Down from 1971
m Aber 16.7.68 Kathleen A. Robilliard MA 1965 *qv*

JACK Ian   MA 1970

JACK James Ironside   *BSc 1961
s of James I. J. farm., farm man. and Dorothy C. Gibb; b New Deer 23.4.39
MIMM
geol: Cape Province S Africa 1961–64, Aber 1965–66;

teacher Aber 1967–68; chief explor geol Nimba Liberia 1968–73; sen geol Elstree 1974; explor man. Tehran from 1974
m Aber 26.6.65 Lorna W. Brown d of William W. B. Aber

JACK James Wynd   *BSc 1966 PhD 1971
s of William A. J. civ serv and Margaret R. McKenzie nurse; b Portsmouth 21.7.44
MSc(Birm) 1967
Carnegie fell. Aberd 1971–72; syst eng Ferranti Edin from 1972

JACK Jeanette Isobella   MA 1966
d of James K. J. journalist and Annie Bruce man.; b Aber 4.3.45
teacher: Achimota prep s Accra 1968–69; Berlin: Spandau p s 1970–72, Gatow s 1973–76; Osnabrück: Wellington s from 1976
m Aber 3.8.67 Frederick C. F. Cowie MA 1962 *qv*

JACK Lindsay   MA 1967
d of Adam J. caretaker and Euphemia B. Laidlaw; b Thornton, 11.7.45
teacher Traralgon Vict Aust from 1970
m Rosewell 13.2.65 Anthony R. Griffin BSc(for) 1967 *qv*

JACK Shona Margaret   MA 1969
d of Alexander F. M. J. bank acct and Evelyn Harper nurse; b Aber 19.12.46
teacher: Crown p s Inv 1970–73, Gateside s Fife 1973–74, Levenvale p s Alexandria 1974–76, Haldane p s Balloch from 1976
m Aber 19.4.73 George H. Dickie hosp eng s of George G. D. MB ChB 1936 *qv*

JACK-HINTON Colin   *MA 1957
s of Harold H. indust, C of E clergyman and Elizabeth B. Jack; b Newchurch-in-Rossendale Lancs 1.1.33
PhD(ANU) 1963 MRInst Navig 1977
dist off./asst secy overseas civ serv BSIP 1957–59; res schol ANU Canberra 1960–62; lect univ of Singapore 1963–65; res fell. ANU 1965–66; sen curator W Aust museum Perth 1966–69; dir museums and art galleries of N Territory Darwin from 1970
m Aber –.4.56 Anne H. McDonald; marr diss

JACKARIA Abdool Carrim   MB ChB 1961
s of Abdool S. J. merch and Fatmah T. Salehmamode; b Mauritius 2.5.35
FFARCS 1968
h o Woodend hosp Aber, ARI 1961–62; Mauritius: r m o min of health 1962–66, asst spec anaest 1968–69, spec anaest 1969–77, consult. from 1977
m Mauritius 16.8.63 Salma Ebrahim d of Abdullah E. Mauritius

JACKSON Alistair   MA 1969

JACKSON Arthur David   BSc 1965 MB ChB 1968
s of Herbert G. J. min of relig and Jean Martin nurs sister; b Congo 13.7.42
DObstRCOG 1970 MRCGP 1974 FPA(Cert) 1977
h o Inv RI, ARI, Aber mat. hosp, paediat RACH 1968–70; med regist/clin tut. Aber spec hosp group 1971–73; g p: Stockton-on-Tees 1973–76, Holmes Chapel from 1976

JACKSON Peter Tulloch   *BSc 1962
s of Charles E. J. civ serv and Agnes H. R. Gair teacher; b Aber 3.4.40
PhD(Cantab) 1966

tech off. ICI Billingham 1966–69; tech serv eng with UOP Lond from 1969

JACKSON Philippa Judith Sagar   *MA 1969
d of Harold S. J. solic and Kathleen M. M. Heap BA(Manc) teacher; b Leeds 25.4.47
psych/civ serv Lond 1969–71; market man. Thames Ditton 1971–72; free-lance market res consult. Surrey 1972–73; prop. Philippa Cowking consult. Weybridge from 1973
m Giggleswick 18.7.69 Thomas L. Cowking MA 1968 *qv*

JACKSON Ruth Lesley   MSc 1967
BSc(Wales)

JACOBSON George Alexander   BSc(eng) 1967
s of Andrew L. D. J. lorry driver and Joan C. Eunson; b Dunrossness Shetland 30.9.45
asst eng Duncan Logan(Construct.) Ross-shire 1967–70; eng asst Herts c c 1970–73; asst resid eng Inv c c 1973–74, resid eng from 1974

JAFFRAY Alan   *BSc 1960
s of Arthur J. soldier and Ann Walker; b Aber 15.2.39
prod. dev & tech serv rep Delft Holland, Manc 1960–64; tech prod. man. PVC Grangemouth, Barry 1965–75; tech man. Manc from 1975
m Manc 25.7.64 Judith Osborne d of Leslie O. Manc

JAFFRAY Ian Alistair   BSc(agr) 1960
s of Charles J. farm. and Winifred M. Rennie; b Nakuru Kenya 4.4.38
man. wheat farm Njoro Kenya 1960–65; farm man. broiler chicken comp Cape Town 1965–68, farm. own bacon pig prod. farm Pietermaritzburg S Africa from 1968
m Nakuru Rosemary S. Foster teacher d of James C. F. Wye

JAFFRAY James Robertson   BSc 1963
s of James M. J. rep, bus comp owner, hotelkeeper etc and Isabella Robertson catering superv; b Aber 11.1.41
teacher: maths Forfar 1964–65, maths/sc Edzell 1965–69, maths/sc Brechin 1969–73, remed s s Brechin 1973–75; asst work stud. and methods man. Fraserburgh from 1976

JAFFREY Helen Elizabeth   MA 1964 Dip Ed 1965
d of William M. K. shoemaker, retailer and Alexerina Imray dressmaker; b Insch 19.12.42
teacher Engl: Denny 1965–68, Dunfermline 1968–70
m Insch 13.7.68 Charles S. Oram BSc(H-W) indust eng s of Douglas O. Dunfermline

JAGANI Himatlal Permanand   *BSc 1962
s of Permanand Sakerchand Depala clerk and Surajben P. Depala; b Aden 20.4.37
MSc(Alta) 1970
lect: tech inst Aden 1962–65, univ of Ife Nigeria 1965–77; sen lect univ of Ife from 1977
m Dhrangdra India 21.1.64 Kundanbala H. Depala d of Santilal B. D. BA(Bhavnagar) Gujrat State India

JAKOBSEN Arnt   cMB ChB 1963
s of Arnt J. prof of surg univ of Oslo and Solveig Solumsmoen nurse; b Oslo 2.7.38
MD(Oslo) 1973 spec gen surg from 1977
Norway: h o Fredrikstad 1964, g p Asköy 1965, lect army med corps Oslo 1965–66, surg h o Oslo 1966–67, res fell. surg inst Rikshospitalet Oslo 1967–71, jun regist surg Rikshospitalet, Oslo 1971–73, regist Oslo city hosp 1973–77, sen regist Rikshospitalet Oslo 1977–78, transplant surg Rikshospitalet Oslo from 1978

m Aber 18.8.64 Sheila M. Michie DA textile des/lect in art d of Arthur R. M. Peterhead

JAMES Alasdair Macleod   MA 1962

JAMES Alfred Timothy   BSc(eng) 1963

JAMES Angela Margaret   *MA 1969
    d of Robert E. J. CPO writer (RN), man. (health and safety) and Agnes Watt secy Aber fed. SWRI; b Aber 20.11.47
edit. asst (Engl, mod lang school books) Macmillan 1969–70; teacher Engl Southfields s Lond from 1972
m Aber 21.8.70 John D. G. Bell MA 1969 *qv*

JAMES William   PhD 1965
    s of William J. eng and Cornelia James; b Johannesburg 15.8.37
BSc(eng)(Natal) 1958 Dip Hyd Eng(Delft) 1961
lect, sen lect univ of Natal 1965–71; visiting prof Queen's univ Kingston Canada 1970; prof McM univ Hamilton Canada from 1971; guest prof Lund and Lukeå univs Sweden 1977–78
m Aber 19.3.65 Evelyn M. Stephen MA 1965 *qv*

JAMIESON Andrew William   *BSc 1970
    s of Basil A. J. TU secy and Grace Williamson; b Yell 18.7.48
elect eng Plessey Templecombe 1970–71; glaciologist Brit antarctic surv S Georgia, Fossil Bluff Brit antarctic territory 1971–75; eng Shell UK explor and prod. from 1977

JAMIESON Christine   MA 1965
    d of John J. BSc(agr) 1929 *qv*; b Shetland 23.7.43
teacher: Stanley p s 1966–67, Aber 1967–68
m Shetland 16.8.67 Alfred Langmead diesel mech s of Ernest L.

JAMIESON Colin   MB ChB 1968
    s of John G. J. civ serv and Minnie Stewart; b Aber 23.11.43
g p: Strathdon 1969–70, Dumfries from 1970
m Aber 13.7.68 June Anderson teacher d of John A. Torphins

JAMIESON Donald Gavin   cMB ChB 1958
    s of Thomas J. bank man. and Donella J. Sutherland teacher; b Aber 5.6.36
MRCPE 1963 MRCP(Lond) 1965 FRCPE 1974
h o Aber 1958–59; sen h o Edin 1959–60; med regist: Aber 1960–63, Smethwick 1963–65; sen med regist Dun 1965–67; consult. neurol Birm from 1967
m Aber 8.10.65 Grace K. R. MacRae MB ChB 1962 *qv*

JAMIESON Ernest   BSc 1969

JAMIESON Ernest Charles   MB ChB 1967
    s of John J. sen insp ACT and Esther P. Andrews; b Aber 19.4.43
Dip Av Med 1972
h o ARI, Woodend hosp Aber 1967–68; RAF: jun m o Valley Wales 1968–69; m o Seletar Singapore 1969–71; m o RAF inst of aviation med Farnborough 1971–72; lect aviation med RAF aviation med training centre N Luffenham 1972–74; g p Moulton nr Spalding from 1974
m Aber 15.7.67 Diane Bell teacher d of Albert D. B. Aber

JAMIESON Ethel   MA 1961
    d of William J. gen merch and Constance R. Gordon shopkeeper; b 12.12.40

Dip Soc Ad(LSE) 1962
family caseworker Aber 1962–65; soc worker Kinc/Deeside dist from 1975
m Aber 17.10.64 James D. Aberdein BSc(agr) 1959 *qv*

JAMIESON Gordon   MB ChB 1960

JAMIESON Hugh Gilbert John   BSc(eng) 1967
    s of Hugh T. J. foreman stevedore and Christina G. Robertson clerkess; b Lerwick 16.11.44
MICE MIMunE
jun eng (roads) Aber 1967–69; eng asst Ross-shire 1969–72; asst eng Stirlingsh from 1972
m Aber 1.8.69 Elizabeth A. Hewet MA 1967 *qv*

JAMIESON James Chilles   PhD 1967
    s of John M. J. youth organis and Margaret C. Chilles; b Aber 15.5.39
BSc(H-W) 1964 MRIC
asst lect biochem Aberd 1966–67; univ of Manit: post doct microbiol/sessional lect chem 1967–68, asst prof chem 1968–71, assoc prof chem from 1971
m Aber 19.8.67 Muriel M. Shaw MA 1966 *qv*

JAMIESON James Thomas   *MA 1968
    s of John J. BSc(agr) 1929 *qv* and Marjory J. Morrison MA 1931 *qv*(III); b Gluss Shetland 10.4.46
teacher Engl Elgin 1968–69; TEFL: Kaysere Turkey 1970–71, Emden Fed. Repub Ger 1971–73; teacher Engl Inv from 1973
m Inv 27.6.70 Jean S. Taylor MA(Edin) res asst d of Thomas G. T. Inv

JAMIESON, Jane Murray   *MA 1968
    m Darling

JAMIESON Lesley Mary   MA 1967
    m Peterculter 7.11.70 Malcolm D. Leiper Brechin

JAMIESON Norman   *MA 1968
    Dip TP

JAMIESON Peter Burnett   *BSc 1963 PhD 1966
    s of George J. cashier and Violet Burnett; b Aber 9.7.41
member tech staff Bell tel labs NJ USA 1966–68; res fell. chem Aberd 1968–69; res scient Ferrania-3M (Savona) Italy 1969–70; sen res scient Harlow 1970–75; res superv 3M St Paul MN USA 1975–77; res man. 3M Harlow from 1977

JAMIESON Susan Jane   MA 1970 CASS 1972

JAMIESON Thomas Dean   *BSc(eng) 1969
    s of William J. and Helen J. Fraser; b Peterhead 30.11.23
MSc(Essex) 1970
teacher: elect. eng Inv 1970–73, sc/maths Saudi Arabia for BAC from 1974

JAMIESON Walter Nicolson   *BSc(eng) 1956

JAMIESON William Stuart   MB ChB 1956
    s of John G. J. civ serv and Minnie Stuart; b Lerwick 23.4.32
MRCPGlas FRCP(Can)
nat serv RAMC Malaysia 1957–59; regist Gartcosh 1960–63; capt, lt-col RAMC England, Singapore 1964–70; consult. Westlock Canada from 1971
m Aber 1957 Ann Donald d of William D. Portsoy

JAMIESON Wilson   *MA 1969
    s of Andrew J. tailor and Emily C. Wilson; b Preston-

pans 21.12.31
Stirling : teacher St Modan's h s, spec asst, asst prin mod
stud., prin mod stud. 1970–73; lect Jordanhill coll of
educ Glasg from 1973
m Blantyre 8.8.59 Frances C. Milligan secy d of Hugh M.
Blantyre

JAN Li Men   MSc 1968
   BSc(Sun Yet Sen)

JANJUA Sadiq   MB ChB 1962
   BSc(Panj)

JAPPY James Reid   MB ChB 1961
   s of George J. fisherman and Jeannie Reid; b Buckie
9.8.17
DObstRCOG 1964
h o ARI, Woodend hosp Aber 1961–62; h o obst Lond
1962–63; locum, trainee g p Bathgate, Edin 1963–64;
g p Edin from 1964
m Motherwell 9.5.53 Mary E. Hamilton MB ChB(Glas)
g p d of James S. H. Bellshill

JARROLD Robert Murray   *BSc(for) 1967
   s of William S. J. min of relig, missionary and Martha
H. Cowan missionary; b Kachhwa UP India 20.10.44
PhD(Edin) 1971
asst conserv for. Kenya 1967–69; rural econ Songkhla
S Thailand from 1971
m Ealing 6.8.66 Valerie M. Bate teacher d of Alan B.
Ealing

JARVIS Anthony   MB ChB 1966
   s of Harold J. eng, tool maker and Marion Tyrer;
b Leic 17.7.37
DObstRCOG 1973 MRCGP 1974 FPA cert 1974
h o med, surg Leic 1966–67; m o RAF squad. ldr UK,
Sardinia, Germany 1967–73; g p Leic from 1973
m Syston 27.7.63 Josephine Shelton matron, nurs nurse
d of John S. Queniborough Leics

JARVIS Raymond Hugh   MA 1970
   s of Alfred J. solic and Violet L. Cox; b Woodford
22.2.43
teacher: housemaster Great Walstead s Sussex 1970–76,
prin geog Holmewood House s Kent 1976–78, St
Michael's s Devon from 1978
m Windsor 17.4.71 Daphne Holt audiologist d of Eric H.
Holbeach

JAYASINGHE Jinapriva Balachandra   PhD 1958
   BVSc(Ceylon)

JEEVARATNAM Jeevarajah   MSc 1960 PhD 1963
   BSc(Ceyl)

JEFCOATE Trevor Edward Stephen   BSc(agr) 1967
   s of Edward A. J. comp acct and Anne E. Page;
b Chesham 23.11.45
Scott Sutherland s of arch.—farm bldgs Aber 1967–68;
dev off. Stratford-u-Avon 1968–70; proj man. Selsey
1970–71; teacher biol comp s Havant 1972–74; head dept
environmental and rural sc Manc 1975–77; co-ordinator
of sciences Manc from 1977
m Glasg 2.8.69 Ann K. Thomson MA 1969 qv

JEFFERIES Frances Mary   MA 1965
   m(1) Dreisbach
    (2) Knight

JEFFREE Christopher Edward   *BSc 1969 PhD 1974
   s of Edward P. H. PhD 1957 qv; b Aber 19.8.46

JEFFREE Edward Percival   DSc 1957
   s of Frank H. J. civ eng and Maud M. Le Couteur;
b Woodford 23.4.08
BSc(Lond) 1930
head bee res dept NOSCA Aber 1946–60; sen lect sc
Hull coll of educ 1960–63; head sc dept Avery Hill coll of
educ Eltham 1963–73; assoc edit. *Annals of Applied
Biology* from 1973
m Lond 9.4.42 Daphne J. Arnold asst edit., headmistress
d of Arthur J. A. Leigh-on-Sea

JEFFREY James Martin   BSc 1960
   s of James P. J. BSc(Glas) CA and Belle E. Bain MA
1926 qv; b Aber 5.9.39
teacher Aber 1960–61; computer salesman: Dagenham
1961–66, IBM (UK) Edin from 1966
m Methil 21.4.73 Whilma A. Black secy d of John B. B.
Methil

JEFFREY Joan Patricia   *BSc 1956
   phys Rolls Royce Derby 1956–62
m Aber 19.9.59 Roland J. Hill MA(Cantab) phys

JEFFREY John Peter   MSc 1966
   s of James P. J. BSc(Glas) CA and Belle E. Bain MA
1926 qv; b Aber 1.7.41
ARGIT CEng MIEE 1971 PEng(Ont) 1971
res eng Ferranti Edin 1967–69; tech eng Grampian TV
Aber 1969–70; res and dev man. Littons: Toronto
1970–71, Los Angeles 1971–72; gen man. J. T. L.
Parkinson Aber from 1972
m Aber 1.9.72 Judith A. Carry secy d of Joseph R. C.
Aber

JEFFREY Sheena Isobel Burnett   *BSc 1958
   d of James P. J. BSc(Glas) CA and Belle E. Bain MA
1926 qv; b Aber 21.6.37
AEO with ARC unit of biometr genetics Birm 1958–60;
teacher Hilton j s s Aber 1960–61; part-time scient off.
govt fisheries dept Nkata Bay, Monkey Bay Malawi
1961–63; res asst Scot. dev dept river surv Pitlochry 1974;
soc worker Tayside reg c from 1975
m Aber 17.9.60 Robert B. Williamson BSc 1958 qv

JEFFRIES Colin Edwin   *BSc 1963 MSc 1964
   s of George E. J. RAF mech and Jean S. Brown;
b Forfar 26.11.40
teacher Hawick 1967–71; Eyemouth: prin teacher 1971–
74, asst head from 1974
m Aber 17.7.65 Rosemary Ogilvie MA 1964 qv

JELLEY Robert Michael   PhD 1961
   MA(Oxon)

JEMMETT Kathleen Elizabeth   MA 1970
   d of Eric J. farm. and Mary M. Forbes; b Newcastle
5.2.49
teacher Engl: Stranraer acad 1971–73, Forres acad
1973–74; bank clerkess Elgin 1974–75
m Dingwall 4.10.72 Brian H. Keenan BA(Strath) teacher
s of Hugh K. Glasg

JENKINS David Alwyn   BSc 1969

JENKINS Eileen Morven   *MA 1962
   m Archer

JENNER Robert Corfield   BSc 1967

JERMIESON John   *MA 1961
   s of Joseph F. J. baker and Norah Sutherland clerkess;
b Aber 9.7.39

teacher: Engl: Broughton sen s s Edin 1962–64, RGC
Aber 1964–72, prin Engl from 1972

JEROME Janet Morag Cameron   MB ChB 1965
  d of Brian S. J. army off. and Sara M. Cameron
BSc(Glas) microbiol; b York 22.8.38
DObstRCOG 1968 DA 1972
sen h o: surg/gyn Weston-Super-Mare 1966–67, obst
Cardiff 1967–68; res asst in breast cancer trial Cardiff
1968–69; g p trainee Somerset 1969–70; sen h o anaest
Weston-super-Mare 1970–72; regist anaest: Edin 1972–
73, Jersey 1973–75; g p Jersey from 1975

JESSOP Alexander Smethurst   MA 1964 LLB 1966
  s of Thomas A. J. draper and Ethel M. Robertson
teacher p e; b Montrose 17.5.43
ptnr leg. pract Montrose 1966–76; dep proc fiscal Perth
1976–78; prin asst Crown office Edin from 1978
m Montrose 16.9.67 Joyce I. J. Duncan physioth d of
David W. D. Montrose

JESSOP Chasser Robertson   *MA 1963
  s of Thomas A. J. draper and Ethel M. Robertson
teacher p e; b Montrose 12.12.39
L ès L (Rennes) 1964 MA(Leeds) 1973
France: lect d'Anglais: univ of Rennes 1963–64, univ of
Nancy 1964–66; lect: Fr univ of Brad 1966–70, Engl
univ of Oran Algeria 1970–72; dir of govt ling. centre
Abidjan Ivory Coast from 1973
m Guiseley 27.6.69 Susan M. Marshall secy d of Alwyn
M. Guiseley

JEZZARD Janet Elizabeth Isobel   MB ChB 1956
  d of Robert J. teacher and Isobel H. H. Anderson
teacher; b Lond 11.11.32
h o Aber 1956–57; cas off. Rotorua NZ 1961–66; g p
Bethesda Wales 1971–72; g p Rotorua NZ from 1974
m Aber 13.9.57 Stanley D. Richardson BSc(Oxon) prof
for./consult. s of George R. Culter

JOHN Malick Abdul Karim   BSc(eng) 1967
  s of Abdul K. J. bus. man and Mam Binta Jagne;
b Banjul Gambia 16.6.43
Eng. Degree(Grenoble)
asst eng Lond trans board 1967–68; exec eng Banjul
1968–70; co-man. Gambia river basin proj Banjul,
Dakar Senegal 1970–74; dir dept of hydrol and meteorol
Banjul from 1974
m Banjul –.10.72 Fatou Janneh secy d of Howsoon
O-S. J. Banjul

JOHN Reginald Samuel   PhD 1970
  BSc(agr)(Ceylon)

JOHNSON Agnes Harriet   MA 1965
  d of Thomas H. J. crofter and Elizabeth Ratter
crofter; b Voe 4.7.44
Dip Lib(Strath) 1968 ALA 1970
lib asst Aber 1966–67; asst lib Glasg 1968–79; resid
Shetland
m Lerwick 4.4.72 James M. Hannah BA(OU) teacher s of
William H. Alexandria

JOHNSON Brenda   BSc 1969
  d of John W. J. planer, baker and Doris Carr confectioner; b Gateshead, 16.12.47
lib course RGIT Aber 1969; res tech X-ray crystallo-
graphy soil sc dept Aberd 1970–73
m Aber 8.4.71 Donald M. Grant derrickman, wayleaves
off., mud eng (oil comp) s of Kenneth G. Blair Drummond

JOHNSON David Charles   *MA 1964
  s of Sir Ronald E. C. J. MA(Cantab) head SHHD and

Elizabeth G. Nuttall MA(Cantab) teacher/concert singer;
b Edin 27.10.42
BA(Cantab) 1966 PhD(Cantab) 1972
freelance composer and writer on mus Edin from 1970
m Edin 12.5.73 Maureen Bagnall BSc(Edin) d of Albert B
Ayr

JOHNSON Elizabeth Ann Dorothy   MA 1960
  d of Benjamin M. J. driver and Agnes Hay; b Voe
3.12.39
teacher: p s Firth 1961–65, Bells Brae p s Lerwick 1965–67
m Lerwick 18.7.62 Peter G. Williamson BSc 1958 *qv*

JOHNSON John Hector   BSc 1958

JOHNSON Lilian Ethel   MA 1968
  m Dixon

JOHNSON Margaret   *BSc 1957
  b Darwen 31.8.34
teacher sc: High s for girls Aber 1959–60, Princes
Risborough from 1966
m Aber 15.7.58 John M. Dinwoodie BSc(for) 1957 *qv*

JOHNSON Margaret Anne   *MA 1960
  d of Frederick A. J. RAF eng, civ eng and Alexanderina
McKerron bank clerk; b Aber 12.11.36
translator of Fr air ministry Lond 1961–62; teacher Fr
Brechin, Edin 1963–64
m Aber 28.8.65 William J. Ross elect. eng s of William R.
Aber

JOHNSON Matthew Francis   *BSc 1968
  s of Sir Ronald E. C. J. MA(Cantab) head SHHD and
Elizabeth G. Nuttall MA(Cantab) teacher/concert singer;
b Edin 20.9.46
Edin: res eng in nuclear med comm equipment, Nuclear
Enterprises 1968–71, chief exec scientology acad from
1971
m Edin 12.10.68 Ann H. MacGregor d of Archibald K.
MacG. BSc(Edin) Assam

JOHNSON Richard Patrick Craig   PhD 1967
  s of Cecil G. J. BSc(S'ton) entomologist and Margaret
U. Black; b Lond 3.3.36
BSc(Lond) 1960 MIBiol
res asst DSIR Bedford coll Lond 1960–62; bot dept
Aberd: res asst DSIR 1962–64, asst lect 1964–67, lect
1967–74, sen lect from 1974
visiting res worker biol dept Mount Allison univ Sackville New Brunswick 1970
m Georgeham 19.11.60 Philippa M. Boutwood SRN
d of Aubrey B.

JOHNSON Ronald George   *BSc 1957
  s of Thomas G. J. mech eng and Helen W. Cruickshank; b Elgin 28.10.34
grad app Manc 1957–60; flying off. RAF 1960–62;
eng Motherwell 1962–64, sect. leader Manc 1964–73, res
and dev man. Sidcup from 1973
m Aber 5.11.60 Sheila Y. McDonald MA 1957 *qv*

JOHNSON Roy Rowland   *MA 1961

JOHNSON Sylvia Mary   MA 1965 Dip Ed 1966
  d of Bernard J. foreman D o E and Alice M. Yewdall;
b Horsforth 20.10.43
Essex: teacher Eng/Fr Maldon g s 1966–70, Plume s
Maldon from 1970
m Maldon 10.4.71 John Carpenter P.O. tech off. s of
John C. Maldon

JOHNSTON Alexander McIntyre   *MA 1968
                                    MEd 1974

JOHNSTON Arthur George Leighton   *BSc(agr) 1966
    s of Arthur G. J. market gardener and Mary I. Henderson teacher; b Ellon 3.1.31
teacher: AGS 1968–70, prin biol Ellon acad from 1970
m Aber 16.8.69 Mary M. Hay secy d of John A. H. Aber

JOHNSTON Brenda Anne   *MA 1970
    m Conn

JOHNSTON Charles Stewart   MA 1964
    s of James J. confectioner and Carrie Davy; b Methven 29.10.27
teacher Beechwood s Aber from 1965
m Aber 21.8.53 Mildred R. Bisset clerkess d of Charles D. B.

JOHNSTON Derek William   *MA 1966
    s of John Johnston civ eng and Annie M. McInnes; b Langholm 1.12.43
PhD(Hull) 1970
sen res off. Oxon from 1970
m Aber 23.12.66 Mary B. Thom BSc 1966 *qv*

JOHNSTON Edith Helen   *MA 1969 Dip Ed 1970
    d of John H. J. asst barrack warden and Isabella J. Shipp off. worker; b Forres 23.4.47
teacher Aber 1970–73
m Aber 2.4.70 Alan W. Fraser BSc 1969 *qv*

JOHNSTON Edna   *BSc 1970 Dip Ed 1971
    d of Archie J. master baker and Annie M. Cruickshank; b St Cyrus 28.10.48
teacher geog Hutcheson's g s Glasg 1971–77
m St Cyrus 9.8.75 Hamish W. Cameron BSc 1969 *qv*

JOHNSTON Hugh Walker   MA 1962

JOHNSTON James Grant   *MA 1969

JOHNSTON James Laughton   BSc 1965
    s of James M. J. MB ChB(Edin) psychiat and Elizabeth Balneaves writer; b Aber 11.4.40
Shetland: teacher p s 1967–69; asst reg off. Nature Conserv Council 1969–75, teacher from 1978
m Brighton 10.9.66 Patricia M. Royces

JOHNSTON John Keith   MA 1970
    s of Sydney M. J. off. man. and Margaret M. McIntosh tel; b Keith 14.12.49
CA 1974

JOHNSTON Kathleen Ann   MA 1961
    d of George A. M. J. comp dir and Elizabeth A. Robb; b Aber 25.4.40
Dip Sec St(St Godric's coll Lond) 1961
Lond: secy leg. dept Brit fed. of master printers 1961–63, worked for exhibition organis 1963–64
m Aber 15.8.64 Charles A. Hicks indust rel exec s of George W. H. Fleet

JOHNSTON Margaret   BSc 1970
    d of Andrew G. J. marine arch. joiner and Williamina M. Laurenson hotel housekeeper; b Lerwick 11.2.48
teacher maths Currie h s 1971–73 and from 1978
m Aber 12.3.70 Frederick H. Tait marine elect. eng s of Laurence S. J. T. Aith

JOHNSTON Margaret Joan   *BSc 1956
    d of James W. J. BSc 1929 *qv*; b Aber 25.3.35

PhD(Edin) 1960
res chem ICI(fibres) Harrogate 1956–57; scient off. (agr chem) Hannah dairy res inst Ayr 1960–63
m Aber 3.6.63 David J. Green BSc(Edin) syst analyst s of Henry L. G. BA(Cantab) Salisbury

JOHNSTON Mary Isabella   MA 1959
    d of John H. J. soldier, civ serv and Isabella J. Shipp off. worker; b Edin 9.4.38
teacher Engl Hilton s s Aber 1961–62
m Aber 12.10.59 George Eddie MB ChB 1962 *qv*

JOHNSTON Neil Roderick   MB ChB 1960
    s of Herbert W. J. cable eng, exec and Elizabeth Leslie; b Rio de Janeiro 22.7.35
DObstRCOG 1962 MRCGP 1970
h o: Aber 1960–61, mat. hosp Hull 1961–62; g p: trainee Eastbourne 1962–63, Norwich 1963–64, Edin from 1964
m Aber 3.4.62 Moyra G. Coutts teacher d of Albert C. Aber

JOHNSTON Nigel McLauchlan   MB ChB 1970

JOHNSTON Norman Howard   *MA 1969

JOHNSTON Patricia Anne Margaret   *MA 1966
    m Boxall

JOHNSTON Robin Forsyth   MB ChB 1962

JOHNSTON Ronald Park   *MA 1970

JOHNSTON Shona Nan   MA 1970
    d of Ronald D. G. J. man. dir and Nancy F. Price; b Fenwick 17.3.48
hotel receptionist, secy etc: Cape Town, Johannesburg, Aust, NZ, Far East 1970–74; teacher inf 1975–77, TEFL Lond from 1978

JOHNSTON William Alan   *BSc(eng) 1965
    s of John J. farm. and Jessie P. M. Matthew; b Glenbuchat 2.2.43
trainee eng Jas Howden & Co Glasg 1965–66; Burroughs machines Dumbarton: prod. eng 1966–70, sen prod. eng 1970; des eng PED Babcock & Wilcox (OPS) Renfrew 1970–71; sen scient off. Torry res stat Aber DTI/MAFF from 1971
m Aber 4.4.67 Susanne L. Watson secy d of Alexander W. Gamrie

JOHNSTON William George   MB ChB 1958
    s of James S. J. blacksmith/agr eng and Magdalena R. Tocher; b Fintray 4.9.33
DTM & H(Lond) 1961 FRCSE 1967
h o ARI 1959–60; HM Forces RAMC trainee surg, consult. surg lt-col UK, Singapore, Nepal, Germany including Berlin, Oman, Belize from 1960
m Aber 25.7.60 Anne Ross MA 1955 *qv*

JOHNSTON William Ross   MA 1960 Dip Ed 1961

JOHNSTONE Dorothy Jane   MA 1966
    m Hughson

JOHNSTONE Frank Dennis   MB ChB 1967 cMD 1978
    MRCOG

JOHNSTONE Gavin Wildridge   PhD 1969
    s of Arthur S. J. off. RE and Mary Wildridge; b Broughton, Peblessh 15.5.41
BSc(Brist) 1963 Dip Conserv(Lond) 1964
Melbourne: biol Antarctic div Aust Nat antarctic res

exped at Macquarie Is 1969–71, Davis, Antarctica 1972;
head off. Melbourne from 1972
m Hobart 11.11.72 Kerry A. Nolan nurse d of Christopher
J. N. Tasmania

JOHNSTONE Lesley   *MA 1958
  PhD(Cantab)

JOHNSTONE Lesley Margaret Harriet   *MA 1969
  d of Frank C. J. BA(Glas) lect hist Aber coll of educ
and Margaret Foord teacher; b Ayr 26.2.47
Dip Soc St (Edin) 1974 Dip Ed(Edin) 1977
res fell. Aber 1969–72; soc worker Edin 1972–73, 74–76
m Aber 19.2.72 John R. Inglis BSc 1971 res stud. s of
John I. Aber

JOHNSTONE Margaret Jane   BEd 1970

JOHNSTONE Raymond George   MA 1969

JOHNSTONE Ronald Clark Beckett   MSc 1968
  BSc(for) Edin

JOINER Vera Margaret   MA 1958 Dip Ed 1959
  d of Edward J. baker and Margaret W. Gavin psychiat
nurse; b Banff 19.10.38
Dip Russian 1964
assistante anglaise Uzerche France 1959–60; teacher,
spec asst Galashiels acad 1960–72; teacher Elgin acad
1972–74
m Melrose 10.8.65 John S. Tweddle chartered surv s of
Alexander M. T. Melrose

JOLLY Caryl Ann Howard   BSc 1970

JOLLY Ian   *BSc(eng) 1959 MSc 1961

JONES Alexander Alfred Albert   *BSc(eng) 1962

JONES Ann Harriet   MA 1966

JONES Arthur Stanley   PhD 1960
  BSc(Durh)

JONES Christine Louise   *MA 1968

JONES Elinor Margaret   LLB 1968

JONES Elizabeth Helen   BEd 1970
  d of Arthur G. J. civ serv and Hilda J. Cumming
MA 1939 qv; b Ealing 7.8.48
teacher: Fr Blackpool 1970–71, Fr/Engl Selkirk 1971–72,
Congleton 1972–74
m Selkirk 1.8.72 Michael J. Godfree BSc(Sus) computer
progr s of Eric F. G. Bournemouth

JONES Gavin David   *MA 1962

JONES Glyn David   LLB 1966
  s of Clifford C. J. eng/works man. and Annie J.
Murphy; b Glenboig 15.3.46
asst Robinson Rentals Bedford 1967–68; lect in law
Aber coll of comm 1968–69; exec asst, man. chamber of
shipping of UK Lond 1969–75; asst dir nat assoc of Brit
and Irish millers Lond from 1975
m Glasg 1.4.70 Anne D. Muir teacher p e d of William
A. M. Glasg

JONES Helene Marie   MA 1956
  d of Joseph G. J. seaman MN and Jessie A. Robertson
nurse, shopkeeper; b Inverurie 15.6.34
teacher: Kinellar p s 1957–59, Insch p s 1959–64, Bucks-

burn p s 1964–65; temp relief teacher Aberdeensh s
from 1968
m Aber 13.7.63 Alexander Gray miller, mason's lab,
BR and NCL fitter s of John G. Newmachar

JONES Idwal Pryderi Vaughan   MA 1966

JONES Jeffrey   BSc 1967

JONES John Nicholas   BSc 1967
  s of John E. S. J. comp dir and Norah E. Daniel;
b Wells 6.1.45
stockbroker Lond 1967–70; comp dir (animal feed)
Wells from 1970
m Clayhidon 29.7.72 Pauline A. Tyrrell MB BS(Lond)
med pract d of Douglas A. T. Clayhidon

JONES Keith Greig   LLB 1969
  s of Stanley J. BSc(eng) Manc and Sybil V. Greig;
b Edin 10.9.48
law app Aber 1969–71; leg. asst Dun 1971–72; solic
Stonehaven from 1972; prin solic to Kincardine &
Deeside dist c

JONES Margaret Ann   MB ChB 1960
  d of Horace M. J. banker and Kathleen I. Burrell;
b Worcester 14.4.36
MRCPath 1977
h o ARI 1960–61; sen h s City hosp Aber 1961–62; lect
path. Aberd 1962–65; regist part time path. Glasg R.I.;
sen regist part time Chelsea and Kensington Lond
1970–72; locum consult. path. Eastbourne and Hastings
reg board 1973–75; sen regist path. Edin RI from 1976
m Aboyne 21.12.60 Angus K. McIntyre MA 1961 qv

JONES Marianne Elizabeth   BSc 1959 *1960
  d of William E. J. BA(Oxon) dean and hon canon of
Brecon cath and Rachel M. Powell BA(Lond) soc worker
Welsh nat gov of BBC; b Perth W Aust 15.12.36
med biochem univ coll hosp Lond 1960–62
m Brecon 1962 Bernard J. Aylett BSc(Cantab) univ
teacher chair of chem Lond univ s of Francis P. A.
Teddington

JONES Mary Cornelia   *MA 1959
  d of William I. J. BA(Cardiff) clergyman, missionary and
Swantina J. de Young BA(Mich) teacher, missionary;
b Chicago 13.9.37
teacher: classics Balfron 1960–61, Aber 1961–65; inf
mistress Lockerbie 1965–69; inf mist./superv jun classes
Linton Camp NZ 1970–71
m Palmerston N. NZ 2.1.71 Robert A. C. Stewart
PhD(Massey) univ lect, prof s of Robert A. S. MA(NZ)
Wellington

JONES Mary Ellis   MA 1969
  d of David J. J. BSc(Cardiff) m o h and Megan Jones
BA(Cardiff) teacher; b Northampton 28.2.48
Dip Pers Man.(Lond) 1972
pers off.: Canadian Pacific Co Lond 1970–72, insur comp
Sydney 1972–73; lect pers man. and psych Sydney poly
from 1973
m Rugby John Dickie BSc(Lond) master brewer s of
David D. Solihull

JONES Michael Hugh   *BSc 1967

JONES Michael John   PhD 1968
  BSc(St And)

JONES Olwen Margaret   *MA 1956
  d of William I. J. MA(Cardiff) clergyman/teacher and
Swantina J. de Young BA(Mich) teacher; b Aden

31.1.34
asst lib Aber publ lib 1957
m Aber 30.8.57 Paul M. Doe MA(Oxon) univ teacher
s of Maurice N. D. BA(Birm) Norwich

JONES Robert Bruce   *BSc 1967

JONES Shelagh Anne Lesley   MA 1967

JONES Shirley   MB ChB 1960
   m Bremner

JONES Susan Primrose   MA 1963
m (1) Pariente
   (2) Addison

JORDAN Neville Arthur Joseph   BSc(eng) 1964

JOSLIN Paul William Bamber   MSc 1967
   BSc(BCol) MA(Tor)

JOSS Alexander William Leslie   *BSc 1967 PhD 1972
   s of William J. and Rebecca Gilbert; b Rhynie 8.12.45
scient MRC Edin 1970–75; sen biochem Raigmore hosp
Inv from 1975
   m Aber 1969 Elizabeth Baird MA 1969 *qv*

JOSS Alison Margaret   BSc 1970
   d of Edward G. J. shipmaster and Patricia E. Carbery
secy; b Aber 2.11.49
admin off. GLC educ dept ILEA Lond 1970–76
   m Aber 24.10.70 Brian S. Smith MA 1970 *qv*

JOSS Gary Anthony   MA 1969

JOWETT Pamela Hardy   LLB 1970
   d of Christopher H. J. MA(Oxon) diplomat and
Mary D. Burnett-White teacher; b Falkirk 31.10.48
Aber: law app 1970–72; leg. asst Lefevre & Co advoc
1972–78
   m Aber 6.7.71 William G. Gray MA 1969 *qv*

JOWETT Richard Andrew   MA 1969

JUNGR Minoslav   BSc 1957

JUTAGIR Torrance   MB ChB 1964

KABAARA Adriel Mukatha   MSc 1960
   s of Reuben M. teacher/peasant and Miriam N.
Muceke; b Meru Kenya 1934
BSc(Lond) 1955 PhD(Brist) 1974
soil chem: Ukiriguru Tanzania 1960–63, Namulonge
Uganda 1963–65; Ruiru Kenya: soil chem 1966, dep dir
(R) 1966–71, dir of res from 1971
   m Meru Kenya 29.8.64 Ruth G. Mantu teacher d of
Josiah M. Meru

KADIO Kisaka Robert   MSc 1968
   BSc(agr)(W Pak)

KAGIA James   MB ChB 1965
   s of Joseph M. K. and Rakeli W. M. Wangeci; b
Kiambu Kenya 1931
MPH(Harv) 1977 Fell. Paediat and Statist(Harv) 1977
intern med Dumfries RI, surg Neath gen hosp, h o
Bradford gen hosp 1965–67; Kenya: m o Nakuru then
i/c Kapsabet hosp Nandi 1967, Karuri health centre
Kiambu 1968–70; lect dept commun health univ of
Nairobi 1970–79, prof from 1979
   m Nairobi 21.3.70 Ruth W. Munge BA(Nairobi) teacher
d of John M.

KAITIFF David Isaac   MB ChB 1961

KALE Vasant Dattatraya   MSc 1964 PhD 1968
   BSc(Poona)

KAMALUDDIN Abul Fazal Muhammed   PhD 1967
   MA(Dacca)

KANDIL Mohammed Fakhry Mahmoud   PhD 1966
   BSc(agr) MSc(Cairo)

KARIMU Sikiru Ajani   BSc(for) 1965

KARLSEN Steinar Johan   MB ChB 1969
   s of Oskar K. K. BSc(Trondheim) dir Voss elect board
and Gunnvor Holthe; b Trondheim 4.9.44
regist surg Oslo univ hosp Lørenskog
   m Voss 15.7.67 Olov G. Hallstensen radiographer d of
Ola H. Fitjar Norway

KARMODY Allastair Michael   MB ChB 1962 ChM 1969
   FRCSE FRCS(Lond) 1967 FACS 1973
sen regist surg ARI 1969–70; Albany NY: asst prof surg
1970–75, assoc prof surg from 1975
   m Aber Rhona S. Chisholm teacher home econ

KASENALLY Abu Twalib   MB ChB 1969
   s of Abdul R. K. headmaster and Bibi K. Beebeejaun;
b Mauritius 10.8.41
FRCSE 1974
h o ARI 1969–70; lect dept path. Aberd 1970–71; sen
h o gen/orthop surg Aber 1971–72; res fell. vasc surg
Aberd 1973–74; regist gen surg Aber teaching hosps from
1974
   m Mauritius 31.3.72 Najmabanu Abbasakoor d of
Ismael A. C. A. Port Louis

KASONDE Joseph Mwenya   MB ChB 1966 ᶜMD 1976
   s of Edmund K. teacher and Gertrude L. Sunkutu;
b Mazabuka Zambia 30.1.38
MRCOG 1972
h o Lusaka 1966–70; h o obst/gyn Oxford 1970–72; regist
obst/gyn Stirling 1972–73; res fell. Oxford from 1973
   m Lond 7.11.40 Mary C. Mukandi SRN d of Enock
S. M. Mbala Zambia

KAWA Mambu Alphan Barbington   MB ChB 1966

KAY Catherine Helen Maxwell   MA 1965
   d of James B. K. bank man. and Margaret P. M.
Meldrum; b Kirkcaldy 10.3.44
teacher Engl: Bridge of Don s 1966–70, Glenrothes h s
1970–71; asst prin Engl Glenrothes from 1971
   m Kirkcaldy 12.10.74 Ian R. Downie BSc(Edin) teacher
s of David D. Lundin Links

KAY Jennifer Ann Yule   MA 1958 LLB 1965
   d of Frederick R. K. LLB(Cantab) col serv and
Constance M. Yule; b Aber 17.12.37
lib McG univ Montreal 1958; lect Engl Makerere night
s Kampala Uganda 1961; lect Aber coll of comm 1969;
restaurateur Maryculter from 1970
m(1) 4.1.58 John Lothian MA 1958 *qv*; husb *d* 13.2.62
   (2) Aber 3.12.66 Iain R. Martin MA 1966 *qv*; marr diss
1975

KAY Jillian Gay Ashley   MA 1966
   d of Frederick R. K. MA(Cantab) col off. and
Constance M. Yule; b Aber 19.5.43
   m Montrose 12.9.64 Ivan C. F. Wisely MB ChB 1967 *qv*

KAY Michael   PhD 1963
   s of Herbert B. K. shoe retailer and Amy Griffiths; b

York 10.3.38
BSc(Leeds) 1960 ARIC 1964
prin scient off. Rowett res inst Aber from 1963
m Aber 6.4.68 Moira Murray d of William M. Bucksburn

KAYLL Albert James   PhD 1964
 s of Swinburne A. K. B Arch(Penn) arch. and Mary
Hardy; b Vancouver 21.1.35
BSF(BC) 1959 MF(Duke) 1960
Canada: res scient Chalk River 1960–68, asst prof for./
co-dir fire sc centre univ UNB Fredericton 1968–71,
assoc prof 1971–77, prof and chmn dept for resources
from 1977
m Chilliwack BC 12.6.62 Jennifer J. M. Wellington d of
John H. W. ScD(Cantab) Johannesburg

KEATING Christine   MB ChB 1970
 d of James M. K. BSc(Swansea) electronic eng and
Cecelia A. J. Rodda teacher; b Swansea 10.5.46
sen h o, regist, lect haemat Lond 1972–76; g p HM Forces
Münster W Ger from 1976
m Eastbourne 17.1.76 Andrew Borthwick-Clarke MB BS
(Lond) med pract s of Aubrey B.-C. Salisbury

KEAY David Malcolm   BSc(agr) 1959

KEAY Hugh John   *BSc(eng) 1962

KEAY Irene Hutchison   *MA 1967
 m Khan

KEAY Lorna Mary   MA 1957 Dip Ed 1958
 d of John K. MA 1919 *qv*; b Banchory 8.4.36
teacher: Aber 1958–59, Reading 1959–61, Welwyn
Garden City 1961–62, Norwich from 1975
m Reading 1.4.61 Robert W. McTear man. life assur
comp s of Ian McT. Reading

KEAY Marjorie Kilgour   MA 1961
 d of James T. K. shop man. and Margaret N. Anderson; b Aber 22.2.40
teacher inf Aber 1962–63, Leic 1963–64, Exeter 1964–66
m Aber 3.7.63 Robin N. Trezise bus. exec s of Nolan
T. T. Cullompton

KEAY Peter Neil   *MA 1970

KEDDIE Gordon James   *BSc 1966
 s of David G. A. K. draughtsman/sports reporter and
Norah S. Elder asst postmaster; b Edin 29.12.44
Dip Ed(Edin) MDiv(Pittsburgh PA) 1973 MIBiol 1979
teacher biol Trinity acad Edin 1967–70; min North Hills
reformed presb ch Pittsburgh USA from 1974
m Beaver Falls PA 18.5.74 Jane A. McMillan BA(Beaver
Falls) d of John M. McM. Marion Iowa

KEELAN John   *MA 1966
 s of Andrew K. fitter and Elizabeth Henry; b Glasg
15.3.26
DPA(Glas) 1954
teacher mod lang Cults 1967–70; prin mod lang: Clydebank 1970–72, Stirling from 1972
m Aber 14.7.69 Susan I. Somerville MA 1969 *qv*

KEENAN Colin Grant   *MA 1970

KEENLEYSIDE Clunie Bonner   MSc 1968
 d of Colin B. K. farm. and Isobel Routledge teacher;
b Haltwhistle 23.10.46
Agr Tripos(Cantab) 1967
asst res off. countryside comm Lond 1968–70; asst secy
N Pennines rural dev board Appleby 1970–71; sen

countryside asst Durham c c 1971–79; sen res off.
countryside comm Newcastle-u-Tyne from 1979

KEEPING Joseph Douglas   MB ChB 1970
 s of Joseph C. K. patent examiner and Dorothy K.
Hawkins; b Liverpool 18.2.44
MRCOG 1976 F Aust COG 1979
h o, regist Aber hosps 1970–76; sen regist Wellington NZ
1976–77; lect obst/gyn Brisbane Aust from 1978
m Aber 3.8.68 Roberta A. Nichol LL B 1968 *qv*

KEIL Cheryl Maureen   MA 1970
 m Wylie

KEILLAR Doreen Nan   MB ChB 1969
 d of John R. K. and Nan F. Mitchell; b Dun 6.1.46
h o royal Devon and Exeter hosp Exeter 1969–70; Aust:
r m o base hosp Maryborough, Queensland 1971–72;
g p: Alstonville NSW from 1972, Lismore psychiat
admission unit from 1975
m Alstonville 2.3.73 Richard A. Bacon grazier, real
estate ag s of Christopher H. B. BA(Cantab) Broughton
Chester

KEIR Hamish Alexander   MSc 1961
 A H-W C

KEIR Rhona Mary   MA 1970
 d of Duncan K. farm. and Betty H. Dunbar farm.;
b Aber 10.11.49
teacher maths Castle Douglas h s from 1974
m Alford 20.8.69 Marcel H. Rivard agriculturist s of
Marcel R. Canada

KEITH Gordon   BSc 1970

KEITH Ian Cameron   MB ChB 1967

KEITH John Macpherson   BSc 1970 *1973
 s of Alexander M. K. MA 1931 *qv*; b Glasg 20.9.47
res asst royal coll of surg dent. res unit teratology dept
Kent from 1973
m Aber 8.10.70 Alexandra A. Davidson computer oper
d of Alexander D. S. Queensferry

KEITH Kathleen   *MA 1965
 m Ewen

KELBIE David   *LL B 1967
 s of Robert K. elect. linesman and Monica E. Pearn;
b Inverurie 28.2.45
advoc Edin 1968–79; Sheriff of N Strathclyde at Dumbarton from 1979
m Aber 7.9.66 Helen M. Smith MA 1966 *qv*

KELLAS Alfred Gordon   *MA 1969
 s of Alexander K. racing motor cyclist/motor cyclist
salesman and Dorothy A. Brown hair stylist; b Aber
14.12.41
sales off. man. BSA Guns Birm 1969–70; sen organis and
methods analyst Scot. Widows' Fund & Life Assur Soc
Edin 1970–78, sen organis and methods off. Grampian
reg c from 1978
m Stonehaven 15.6.68 Joy A. Green secy d of Douglas
R. G. Stonehaven

KELLAS James Grant   *MA 1958
 s of James F. Kellas MA 1920 *qv*; b Aber 16.5.36
PhD(Lond) 1962
tut. fell. hist Bedford coll Lond 1961–62; asst hist Aberd
1962–64; lect politics Glas 1964–73, sen lect 1973–77,
reader from 1977
m Aber 8.9.62 Norma R. Craig MA 1959 *qv*

KELLAS Peter Duncan *BSc(eng) 1969
s of George D. K. MA 1930 *qv*; b Huntly 20.4.47
Grad IMechE 1970
Rolls Royce E Kilbride: grad trainee 1969-71, performance eng from 1971

KELLY Alastair Fraser MA 1966

KELLY Frances MB ChB 1967
MA(Edin)

KELLY George Watson *MA 1968

KELLY Irene MA 1968

KELLY Jane Avril MA 1966
d of Robert K. police off. and Mary A. Archibald;
b Stirling 5.4.45
Dip Sec Sc(Strath) 1967
Lond: exec secy 1967-68, asst brand man. 1968-71
m Alloa 22.3.69 John B. Chesworth BSc(eng) 1974 civ
eng construct. man. s of Joseph S. C. Kingsley

KELLY John *MA 1958

KELLY Winifred MA 1958
d of William C. K. tel exec and Winifred I. Toman;
b Aber 26.8.38
teacher, spec asst Aber 1959-73; teacher Inv from 1973

KELMAN Alice Jane BSc 1961
m Diack

KELMAN Celia MA 1967
d of Andrew L. K. BSc(St And) indust chem and
Catherine E. Robinson MA(Glas) teacher; b Newcastle-
u-Tyne 21.1.46
assistante lycée Coulommiers France 1967-68; teacher:
Fr Hull g s 1969-70, Engl Huelva Spain 1970-71, Engl
Zaragoza, Granada Spain 1971-72; Fr/Span Queen
Elizabeth g s Hexham from 1972

KELMAN Elizabeth Jane Cooper MA 1964
d of William J. K. bldg mason and Elizabeth J. Cooper
nurse; b Torphins 20.11.42
teacher: Engl/remed subjs Gordon s Huntly 1965-73
m Aber 1.8.70 William T. Duffton auctioneer s of Alexander D. Huntly

KELMAN James Smith MSc 1962
s of George S. K. BL 1950 *qv*; b Aber 29.5.39
CEng MIMechE 1972
grad app AEI Manc 1962-64, performance eng 1964-67;
lect RGIT Aber from 1967
m Manc 1.7.67 Dorothy M. Wilkinson SRN d of Reginald
W. Blackpool

KELMAN James Tarves MA 1965
          (conferred for long service of exceptional merit)
s of James K. tailor and Nellie Tarves dressmaker;
b Turriff 31.8.14
ARICS 1951 FRICS 1975
Aberd: asst secy (edilis & lands) 1957-63, dep secy (edilis
& lands) 1963-68, buildings off. and factor 1968-78; retd
m Aber 14.6.39 Helen Paterson jeweller's asst d of
William P. Aber

KELMAN John Matheson MA 1960

KELMAN Margaret Elizabeth MA 1964
d of George O. K. elect./mech eng and Alice J. Duncan
teacher; b New Deer 1.6.43
teacher: Lat/hist Brierley Hill 1965-67, hist Lasswade

1968-70, hist Dingwall 1970-76; secy at Aberd 1976-78,
teacher hist/mod stud. Inv from 1978

KELMAN Maureen McKenzie *BSc 1964
d of George S. K. BL 1950 *qv*; b Torphins 11.1.42
govt serv (patent examiner) Lond from 1964

KELMAN Patricia Elspeth MA 1960
m Lenehan

KELSALL John *MA 1970
s of Lawrence K. teacher and Catherine J. Fortune;
b East Retford 31.7.47
Fullerton Moir & Gray schol Aberd 1970; PhD(Glas)
1976 Member Composers' guild of G.B. 1973; Member
Royal Mus Assoc 1976
teacher mus Renfrew h s 1975-77; lect mus Kingston
poly from 1977; OU tut. from 1973; organist/choir-
master Christ Church, Sutton Lond from 1977
m Glasg 17.6.72 Heather J. Wilson MA(Glas) stud.
advis d of William R. W. Glasg

KELTY Roger Fyfe *MA 1960

KEMP Alexander George *MA 1962

KEMP Alexander John *BSc 1961 MSc 1962
s of Albert W. K. woollen manuf/wholesale draper and
Isabella D. McIntyre MA 1921 *qv*; b Aber 20.10.38
FRAS 1970 MSc(Lond) 1974
lect The City univ Lond from 1965; part time tut. astron
S Havering coll adult educ from 1973
m Aber 22.7.64 Margaret J. V. Brown MA 1962 *qv*

KEMP David Alexander MA 1957

KEMP John Cumming *MA 1966

KEMP Marjorie Isabelle MB ChB 1956

KEMP Mary Lois BSc 1961
d of William K. TU off. and Mary A. Baxter; b Glasg
17.12.39
res asst biochem DRI 1961-62; Glas: tech biochem
1966-67, res asst biochem 1967-70, part time tech elect.
eng dept from 1974
m Aber 16.10.61 Alexander Hobbs MA 1958 *qv*

KEMP William Charles *BSc(eng) 1964
s of William K. T U off. and Mary A. Baxter; b Glasg
11.3.41
MSc(Birm) 1966
eng Elliott Automation Rochester 1964-65; Ferranti
Bracknell: des eng 1966-69, sen syst eng from 1970

KENDLE Janet Margaret MSc 1969
d of Sidney F. K. eng, shopkeeper and May R.
Goldfinch; b Lond 12.6.47
BSc(Sus) 1968
res bot dept Aberd 1970-71; civ serv computer progr,
syst analyst Edin 1971-77; progr analyst Lond from 1977
m Edin 20.3.72 David C. Watterson MA(Edin) Dip Ed
(Aberd) 1969 teacher, admin s of Leslie C. W. Edin

KENNAWAY Nancy Gordon *BSc 1959
d of Charles G. K. MA 1922 *qv*(II, III); b Aber 20.3.37
DPhil(Oxon) 1967
exp asst Scot. nat blood transfusion assoc Edin 1960-62;
scient off. MRC Oxford 1962-67; Portland USA: res
assoc univ of Oregon med s 1968-69, fell. genetics univ
of Oregon med s 1969-73, instr med genetics 1974-77,
asst prof med genetics from 1977

KENNEDY Bryan Ross   MB ChB 1960
s of William D. K. MA 1921 *qv*; b Fraserburgh 19.6.35
FFARCS
lect anat Aber 1962–63; regist, sen regist united Cardiff
hosps 1964–67; lect anaest Welsh nat s of med 1967–68;
consult. anaest Aber from 1968

KENNEDY Craig Daniel   BSc(eng) 1959
s of Robert W. K. garage prop. and Constance A.
Daniel; b Aber 14.4.36
des eng Glasg 1959–63; resid eng Edin 1963–64; field eng
BC Canada 1964–66; resid eng Nova Scotia 1966–68;
sen eng/assoc ptnr Glasg from 1969
m Edin 8.8.64 Irene Galbraith examiner in estate duty off.
d of Alexander G. Edin

KENNEDY Duncan Meldrum   MA 1965
s of John K. banker and Cathie J. A. Macdonald health
visitor; b Tillycoultry 3.7.40
teacher Stirling 1965–71, asst prin teacher from 1971
m Stirling 2.8.72 Margaret A. Murdoch secy d of John
M. Stirling

KENNEDY Elizabeth Ann   MA 1970
d of Hamish K. gamekeeper/stalker and Elizabeth
MacPherson; b Urray 14.12.49
teacher Engl/hist Kinlochleven s 1971–75; asst prin Engl
Thurso h s 1975–78; asst rector Plockton h s from 1978

KENNEDY Eric   *MA 1961
d 1.10.68

KENNEDY James Douglas   *MA 1961
b Inv 18.3.39
m 6.7.67

KENNEDY Katherine Stuart   MA 1962
d of George G. K. grocer and Jessie A. McIntyre;
b Forres 9.10.41
teacher: Forres 1963–64, Peterhead 1964–65, Huntly
1967–73, Elgin 1974–76, Forres from 1976
m Forres 11.7.64 George D. Smith police sgt s of George
R. S. Nairn

KENNEDY Michael Thomas   MA 1967 Dip Ed 1968

KENNEDY Richard   *MA 1969

KENNERLEY Peter Charles   MB ChB 1969
s of Tordiff A. S. K. MB ChB(Birm) g p and Eleanor
J. Reynolds; b Birm 10.8.42
DCH 1971 DObstRCOG 1972 DA 1975
h o: paediat Middx hosp Lond 1971–72, Addenbrooke's
hosp Cambridge 1972–73, anaest Middx hosp 1973–76;
g p Brackley from 1976
m Exeter 21.9.74 Alethea M. S. Coleridge nurse d of
Anthony D. C. Newton Abbot

KENNEY John Richard   *BSc(eng) 1969
s of Gordon F. K. time study eng BR and Phyllis E.
Butcher; b Peterborough 29.6.47
grad asst eng Edin 1969–71; resid civ eng Dunoon,
Shetland from 1971
m Dunrossness 2.9.69 Mary E. Robertson MA 1969 *qv*

KENT Anthony William David Charles   BSc 1966
s of Charles A. K. RN and Isabella M. H. Fraser,
admin secy; b Inv 5.2.47
Dip Aquaculture & Fishing Man.(Stir) 1977
teacher biol: Perth 1967–68, Linlithgow 1968–71, prin
biol Campbeltown 1971–74; shipyard worker Campbeltown 1974–76; aquaculture stud. Israel, Scot. from 1976
m Fyfield 27.7.68 Susanna J. Leiper BSc 1968 *qv*

KENT Margaret Rena   MA 1960
m Thomson

KENT Michael   PhD 1967
BSc(Leic) MSc(Lond)

KERR Carolyn Margaret Landon   *BSc 1965 PhD 1970
d of Robert R. K. MA(Oxon) sheriff and Mona Kerr
ARCM; b Berkhamstead 8.5.43
res assoc/instr univ of Tennessee Knoxville USA 1970–72;
S'ton: SRC res fell. 1972–73, Royal Society res fell. from
1973

KERR Gordon Alexander   BSc(eng) 1969

KERR Janet Helen   MA 1970
m Gibbons

KERR Jean Johnston   MB ChB 1957
d of John N. K. seed and potato merch and Susanna
T. Johnston teacher dom sc; b Aber 21.4.34
DObstRCOG 1960
h o Aber 1957–58, Lond 1958–59, Bellshill 1959–60;
g p trainee Edin 1960–61; sen h o, regist dermat Glasg
1961–63, clin asst from 1970
m Aber 16.9.61 Alexander D. McNeill MB ChB (Glas)
consult. surg s of Lachlan McN. Glasg

KERR Margaret Mary Orr   *BSc 1970
d of William K. nurseryman and Janet B. Black;
b Kilmacolm 28.7.48
teacher: Port Glasgow 1971–73, remed Greenock 1973–74,
gen sc/biol Greenock 1974–77, Glasg from 1977
m Greenock 1.7.77 Martin Archibald MA(Glas) teacher
s of William A. Bearsden

KERR Olive Pandora de Maillard   MA 1967

KERRIGAN Herbert Aird   LLB 1967 *1968
s of Herbert K. BSc(Glas) chem and Mary A. W.
Hamilton; b Glasg 2.8.45
Dip Criminol(Keele) 1969 MA(Keele) 1970 Admitted to
fac of advoc Edin 1970
Edin: lect crim law and criminol 1969–72, Scots Law
1972–74, tut. constit law 1972–74, advoc from 1973 and
prof compar law univ of S California from 1976

KERRY Lionel Retna   BSc(eng) 1970
s of Leopold P. K. civ serv and Kathleen M. Gordon
b Berbice Guyana 18.11.41
AMIHE 1972
Aber dist council: grad asst eng 1970–72, asst eng 1972–
73, roads dept from 1973
m Lerwick –.8.65 Agnes C. Morrison teacher d of John
M. Bigton

KESHAVARZ Rahmati   BSc 1964

KEY Anthony Wallace   *MA 1960
s of John R. K. man. driving s and Mary M. Low;
b Edin 6.3.39
DPhil(Oxon) 1963
lect phys univ of Natal 1963–66; post doct fell. univ of
Toronto 1966–68, visiting scient Nat Accelerator Lab
Chicago 1968–70; asst prof univ of Toronto 1970–73,
assoc prof from 1973
m Oxford 10.1.63 Sandra M. D. Mills broadcaster d of
Algernon S. M. Salisbury Rhodesia

KHALIL Khalil El Sayed Ahmed   PhD 1965
s of Sayed A. K. LLB(Cairo) judge and Ihsan El
Yamani teacher; b Mahalla Egypt 14.10.38

BSc(Cairo) 1960
lect Cairo univ 1966–72; teacher phys Cults acad Aber
1973–75; lect phys Aber tech coll from 1975
m Aber 24.1.63 Irene M. Stuart MA 1966 *qv*

KHAN Indira Sphina-a-Naz   MA 1961
    m Pringle

KHAN Iqbal Hussain   MB ChB 1961
    BSc(Kar) FRCSE
h o ARI 1961–62; lect path. Aberd 1962–63; regist surg:
Ayr county hosp 1963–65, Kilmarnock I 1965–67, asst
surg from 1967
m Aber 30.3.64 June L. Banks teacher

KHAN Nagib Hamed   BSc(civ eng) 1966 *1968
                                   BSc(elect. eng) 1967

KHAWAJA Jahangir Ahmed   MSc 1968
    MSc(Panj)

KIDD Arthur Graeme   *BSc(agr) 1965
    s of Arthur L. K. plumber and Margaret M. Lobban
nurs sister; b Holm 23.8.42
farm man. dev off. ICI Cumberland 1965–68; res off.
W Kilimanjaro, Tanzania 1968–70; ICI: farm man. rep
W Yorks 1970–74, marketing off. Billingham from 1974
m Mwanza Tanzania 14.12.68 Shelagh Bland sales
trainer d of Bruce B. Windermere

KIDD James   *MA 1959
    s of Charles S. K. farm. and Elspeth Duncan; b
Drumoak 19.10.36
ALA(Glas) 1964
nat serv RHA Salop, Woolwich, Hants, Aden 1960–62;
St And univ: asst lib 1963–66, sub lib (chief cataloguer)
from 1966
m St And 25.7.72 Maureen S. Galbraith lib d of Maurice
S. G. St And

KIDD Sheena Ann Mary   MA 1968
    m Agnew

KILKENNY Terence Michael   *MA 1968
    s of John C. K. teacher/gp capt RAF/reg dir central
council for phys recreation and Gladys Booth teacher;
b Nott 15.4.45
Dip Psych(WAIT) 1974
Aust: teacher educ dept W A 1969–70, school psych educ
dept W A from 1971 (Albany s h s)
m Inv 31.8.68 Isabel M. Ross MA 1968 *qv*

KILLMAN John Cowling   *BSc 1963

KIMBER Victor Robert   MB ChB 1969
    s of Robert A. K. civ serv and Mary A. Gough secy;
b Manc 19.6.44
DObstRCOG 1973
h o Aber 1969–70; sen h o Aber mat. hosp 1970–71;
interne Nazareth hosp Israel 1971–72; g p: trainee Aber
1972–73, Clay Cross Chesterfield 1973–74, Marple 1975,
Stone from 1975
m Matlock 14.9.74 Wendy A. March secy d of William
A. M. Matlock

KINCAID James   MA 1957 BD 1960
    s of James S. I. K. eng, shop owner and Mary A. B.
Duncan; b Aber 21.2.34
C of S min: asst Aber 1960–63, Mossgreen and Cross-
gates 1963–70; missionary Transkei S Af 1970–76;
Fintray with Keithhall with Kinellar from 1977
m Aber 1963 Valerie R. Moir missionary d of Joseph
S. M. Aber

KINCAID Mary   BSc 1964
    d of Peter K. security off. and Isabella J. H. Hay;
b Ellon 18.9.43 teacher maths: Inverurie acad 1965–68
High s for girls Aber 1968–69
m Aber 29.12.65 John A. Webster BSc(eng) 1964 *qv*

KINDNESS Agnes Johnston   BSc 1958
    d of Robert K. examiner BR and Agnes L. Johnston;
b Aber 1.7.36
teacher maths: Aber h s for girls 1959–62, Albyn s for
girls Aber 1971–74; prin maths St Margaret's s for girls
Aber from 1974
m Aber 9.4.60 Alexander E. Urquhart BSc(Strath) lect
RGIT Aber s of Alexander R. U. Aber

KINDNESS Eileen Moir   *BSc 1966 Dip Ed 1967
    d of George M. K. LDS(Edin) dent. and Helen
Hutcheon; b Aber 1.4.44
teacher: Melbourne 1969–70, Vancouver from 1976
m Aber 27.12.67 John F. G. Mackay BSc 1965 *qv*

KINDNESS Lindsay Margaret   *MA 1970
    d of George M. K. LDS(Edin) dent. surg and Helen
Hutcheon secy; b Aber 7.8.48
trainee staff man. Marks & Spencer Glasg, Preston,
Blackpool 1970–73
m Aber 26.8.71 Anthony P. Haslam NDA(Lancs) agr
acct s of Edward M. H. Turton

KING Alexander   BSc(eng) 1965
    s of Thomas R. K. trawl master and Jessie T. Kay;
b Aber 26.9.43
M AssocProf Eng(Ont) 1969
struct des: Brit Reinforced Concrete co Glasg 1965–66,
Guest Keen & Nettlefold Glasg 1966–67, Gen Engineering
Toronto 1967–68; Albery, Pullerits, Dickson and assoc:
struct eng 1968–69, resid eng of construct. Welland
Tunnel Ont 1970–73, sen eng 1973–75, assoc from 1975
m Aber 23.10.64 Ellen C. Morrice secy d of Francis
H. M. Aber

KING Anthony Desmond   BSc 1965

KING Henry John Bell   *MA 1968
    s of Henry C. K. bank man. and Jane M. Dunn;
b Nairn 1.9.46
MBA(Strath)
BLMC Birm: trans proj asst 1969–72, progr analyst
1972–73; progr co-ordinator, progr analyst man. 1973–
74, sales progr man. from 1974
m Birm 4.3.72 Mary A. Dickson SRN d of Vincent D.
Rathfriland Co Down

KING Kathleen May   *MA 1962
    d of Frederick T. K. trans auth employee and Margaret
B. Sutherland; b Dornoch 15.10.39
teacher Paisley 1964–65 and from 1972
m Dornoch 4.9.63 John R. W. Maclaurin CA, textile
merch s of John D. M. Houston Renfrewsh

KING Linda Mary   MA 1966

KING Margaret Hay   MA 1963
    d of James K. comp dir and Elizabeth L. Robertson;
b Aber 29.4.42
teacher Fr/Ger Harlaw acad Aber from 1964

KING Margaret Rosalind   MA 1967

KING Melville Douglas   *MA 1967
    s of William M. K. MA(Edin) C of S min and Margaret
I. Black; b Ballater 29.7.44

GRADUATES 1956–1970

170

MEd(Edin) 1974
teacher Liberton s Edin 1969–72, prin geog 1973–76;
asst head Tynecastle h s from 1976
m Edin 26.7.69 Alison J. Reid MA(Edin) teacher d of
Donald D. R. MB ChB 1937 *qv*

KING Michael George *BSc 1965 PhD 1969*
s of George T. K. power loom tuner and Margaret A.
Smith clerkess; b Aber 31.7.42
FCS(Iowa) 1968 ACS 1975
post doct res fell. chem: USAEC Ames Iowa 1968–70,
Aberd 1971; lect chem Fourah Bay coll Sierra Leone
1971–73; USA: instr chem Iowa State univ 1973–74,
res chem ASARCO S Plainfield New Jersey from 1974
m Aber 18.9.71 Margaret A. Schaefer PhD(Iowa State)
res chem d of Frank S. BA(Concordia) Waltham
Minnesota

KING Roger Hatton *MSc 1965*
s of George H. K. sqn ldr RAF and Vera O. L. Coe;
b Barry Glam 16.12.41
BSc(UW) 1963 PhD(Sask) 1969
tut. univ coll Swansea 1969–70; univ of W Ontario: asst
prof 1970–76, assoc prof from 1976
m Swansea 28.8.65 Gillian M. Williams BA(Wales) d of
Emlyn W. Swansea

KINGDON Doris *MA 1960*
d of William J. K. insur ag, teacher and Jeannie A.
Stuart; b Kingston-u-Thames 24.2.40
secy to head almoner Guy's hosp Lond 1961–64; teacher
Engl comm s Oporto Portugal 1964–65; clerk mail order
dept Bourne & Hollingsworth Lond 1965; secy/trans-
lator/interpreter Oporto 1965–67; secy/pers man. Donside Paper comp Aber 1967–72
m Banchory-Devenick 23.12.71 Ernest Smith interior
decorator s of Harry S. Aber

KINGHORN Jean Ann *MA 1968*
d of Alexander G. K. farm worker and Margaret A.
Ewen; b Keig 23.11.47
teacher: Bathgate p s 1969–71, Inv 1971–73, Edin 1973–
74, Ringshall from 1974
m Oyne 28.9.74 Geoffrey D. Moore BSc(eng) (Imp Coll
Lond) civ eng s of Thomas C. M. Felixstowe

KINGHORN Peter David *LLB 1970*
s of James S. K. solic and Grace Nucho; b Brechin
30.3.49
law app Edin 1970–72 leg. asst, dep burgh prosec Thurso
1972–74; ptnr law firm Brechin from 1974
m Edin 17.12.71 Carol A. Sandeman BSc 1971 insur
clerk d of Arthur S. Brechin

KINGSLEY Reginald Graham *MSc 1970*
s of William K. and Olive Pilgrim; b St John's Newfoundland 13.9.44
Dip Eng(Nfld) 1964 BEng(NSTC) (Halifax Nova Scotia)
1966
lect coll fisheries, navig, marine eng and electronics
St John's Newfoundland from 1970
m St John's 15.5.68 Dianne Hoyles R.N. d of John V. H.
BA (Memorial univ) St John's

KINNAIRD Anne Barclay *BSc 1961*
d of Thomas K. farm. and Jessie B. Ross clerkess;
b Kinross 25.12.40
teacher: sc Kinross 1961–62, biol Ballingry 1963–65
m Scotlandwell 10.3.65 Charles A. MacGregor farm.
s of William M. Lauder

KINNAIRD Annice Macleod *MA 1962*
d of Alexander K. flesher and Catherine A. Macleod;

b Stornoway 9.4.40
teacher hist Sidney Nova Scotia 1963–65; prin hist
Fortrose 1965–69; teacher hist (BFES) Hamm Germany
1969–72; prin guid Gordon s Huntly from 1972
m Elgin 9.7.80 James Macleod retailer s of James M.
Stornoway

KINNAIRD June *BSc 1966*
m Irvine

KINNAIRD Moira Margaret *MA 1958*
d of William K. works man. and Annie W. Cobb;
b Aber 14.12.36
teacher Aber 1959–61, Uddingston 1961–63 and from
1975
m Aber 14.7.61 Alexander E. McIlwain MA 1954 *qv*

KINNELL Anne Hoare *MB ChB 1956*
d of G. J. K. BD(Lond) provost St Andrew's cath
Aber and Anne E. Dunford; b Aber 28.12.32
h o, sen h o, regist anaest England 1956–61; g p Danbury
from 1961

KINNELL Herbert Gladstone *MA 1968 MB ChB 1968*

KIRK Alexander Charles *MB ChB 1968*
s of Alexander K. MB ChB(Glas) g p and Margaret
M. C. Dickie nurs sister; b Birm 6.10.35
cas off. Aber 1968–69; Rhodesia: obst Mpilo hosp 1969–
70, g p Bulawayo from 1970; major Rhodesia AMC;
r m o Selous Scouts from 1976

KIRK Robert David *MA 1970*
s of Robert K. decorator and Grace Pearson; b Edin
20.1.47
MPhil(Glas) 1972
commun dev off. Motherwell burgh 1972–74; soc
facilities off. central Lancs dev corp 1974–75; sen policy
analyst Dun dist from 1975

KIRK William Logan *MTh 1969*
s of Henry B. K. MB ChB(Edin) g p and Catherine
S. P. Logan; b Gullane 6.6.31
MA(Edin) 1954 BD(Edin) 1957 Cert Agr(Edin) 1966
asst min St Giles Cath Edin 1957–59; farm work E
Lothian 1959–66, tractorman Duns from 1968

KIRKLEY James Colin *BSc 1960*

KIRKMAN John Henry *PhD 1965*
s of Thomas P. K. BR employee and Muriel M. Neale;
b Boston Lincs 29.9.38
BSc(agr)(Durh) 1960 BSc(Durh) 1961 MNZIC 1967
lect soil sc univ coll Dub 1964–66; sen lect soil sc Massey
univ Palmerston North NZ from 1966
m Broxburn Dorothy A. Jones theatre sister d of William
I. J. BA(Cardiff) Broxburn

KIRKPATRICK James Alexander *MA 1965*

KIRKWOOD Elizabeth Watson *MA 1964*
d of William K. butcher and Helen G. Ferguson;
b Kilmarnock 9.8.43
Dip Ed(Edin) 1965
teacher Fr/Ger: Penicuik 1965–67, Kidsgrove 1967–68,
Maidenhead 1968–70
m Boat of Garten 15.4.67 David R. Davidson BSc(Edin)
elect. eng s of David R. D. Grantown-on-Spey

KIRKWOOD Mary *MA 1959 *MEd 1962*
d of Peter K. elect. eng NSHEB and Jannetta Milne
teacher; b Brighton 3.8.38

teacher Fr/Lat Aber acad 1960–64; asst youth employment off. Buckie 1964–66; Peterhead acad: teacher
Fr/Ger, prin asst i/c careers 1966–71, prin guid from 1971

KIRTON Heywood Cameron   MSc 1966
s of Harry H. K. farm. and Jeannie C. MacLeod;
b Taree Aust 14.1.41
BSc(Syd) 1961
Sydney: biometrician NSW dept agr 1961–68, dep chief
biomet from 1968
m Taree 29.9.62 Lynne G. Kidd teacher d of Andrew
E. K. Taree

KITAKA Francis Xavier Saebampitako   BSc 1967

KITCHIN Alison Margaret   *BSc 1959 PhD 1967
d of Ian D. Kitchin MB ChB 1930 qv; b Lancaster
20.1.37
teacher biol coll of comm Aber 1967–72; lect agr bot
Aberd from 1972
m Lancaster 8.8.62 Robert Innes TD CEng MIMechE
prin lect tech educ Aber coll of educ s of George I. Nairn

KITSON Richard Frederick   MA 1968
s of Norman F. K. publican and Elizabeth M. Beaton;
b Aber 24.3.41
Ford Motor Co: buyer maintenance and contr Warley
1968–73, buyer truck manuf oper Romford 1973–75;
chief buyer Acme Signs & Displays Enfield from 1975

KLEIN Thomas   *BSc 1960

KLINE Paul   *MEd 1963
s of Maurice V. K. civ serv and Ivy Simmons; b Lond
8.3.37
BA(R'dg) 1958 Dip Ed(Swansea) 1959 PhD(Manc) 1968
ABPs S 1970
res assoc dept educ Manc 1963–66; lect Exe: educ 1966–
69, psych 1969–73, reader psychometrics from 1973
m Swansea 8.8.59 Frances S. Golding BA teacher d of
Reginald G. Bromley

KNAPMAN Mary Louise   MA 1960
d of George R. K. comp dir and Louise D. G. Brown
hotel prop.; b Brixham 27.11.38
teacher: Engl Northfield acad Aber 1961–64, Engl/Fr
High s Perth 1965–66
m Ballater 4.7.64 Duncan Mackenzie DA teacher art s of
Duncan M. Inv

KNIGHT Diana Maud   BSc 1970
d of Cecil K. comp man., comp dir and Ruby G.
Parris des, man.; b St Michael Barbados 28.6.46
BSc(Lond) 1971
travel admin Lond 1971–72; food scient nutrit centre
Bridgetown Barbados 1973; teacher: chem Airdrie
1976–78, chem/sc Edin from 1978
m Edin 1.6.74 David C. Arulanantham BSc(eng) 1969 qv

KNIGHT Donald William   MSc 1966 PhD 1969
BSc ACGI(Lond)

KNIGHT Jean Elizabeth   MA 1970
d of John A. K. police driver and Jean C. Smith
cashier; b Aber 4.12.48
teacher Engl/liberal stud. tech coll Aber 1971–74
m Aber 21.7.71 David T. Yacamini MA 1971 teacher
s of David T. Y. Perth

KNOWLES David Alexander   MA 1970
s of R. B. K. acct and Christine I. Rutherford; b Edin

11.1.49
CA
app Edin 1970–74, self employed CA from 1974

KNOWLES Iain Colin Campbell   *MA 1967
s of John K. teacher and Janet Campbell; b Banff
25.3.45
bus. econ Rolls Royce small eng div Watford 1967–71;
fin. analyst: long range plan. Chrysler International S.A.
Lond 1971–73, plan. Rank Xerox Welwyn eng dept
Welwyn Garden City 1973–74; bus. analyst: plan. Rank
Xerox res lab Milton Keynes 1975–76, syst Rank Xerox
manuf and supply oper Uxbridge from 1977

KNOWLES James Gordon   *BSc 1964 PhD 1969
s of James G. K. store man. and Margaret M. M.
Forbes; b Aber 26.6.41
sen scient off. Amersham from 1967
m Aber 23.9.66 Elaine Davidson BSc 1966 qv

KNOWLES Kathleen Melrose   *BSc 1967
m Watts

KNOWLES Maureen   MA 1968
m Innes-Will

KNOWLES Peter Mitchell   *MA 1969 Dip Ed 1970

KNOWLES Sheila Elizabeth   MA 1969
d of Robert B. K. acct and Christine I. Rutherford;
b Edin 3.9.47
teacher geog Boroughmuir s Edin 1970–75
m Edin 6.7.73 John A. L. Miller LLB 1970 qv

KNOX Alison Frances Ann   *MA 1970
d of Francis H. K. BL 1945 qv(III) and Frances M.
Strachan MA 1939 qv; b Edin 2.11.48
teacher Engl Cults Aber 1971–74
m Aber 17.7.73 William R. Fraser BSc 1966 qv

KNOX Ian Davidson   BSc 1963 Dip Ed 1964

KNOX Patricia Campbell   *BSc 1969
d of T. Marshall K. CA and Hazel Campbell; b Aber
29.6.47
MA(Sheff) 1972 MRTPI 1974
plan. asst: Aber c c 1969–70, Lancs c c Preston 1972–73;
asst then prin plan. off. S Ribble Boro' c Preston from
1973

KNUTZEN Hanna Berit   MB ChB 1965
d of Hans C. K. clerk/bus. man. and Kristine Larsen
bus. man.; b Oslo 9.10.40
spec in anaest from 1973; member Norwegian assoc of
anaest; sen h o anaest univ of Bergen 1967–68, resid
anaest univ of Oslo 1969–70, sen regist 1970–77; consult.
anaest Drammen from 1978

KOJECKÝ Roger Miroslav Francis   *MA 1966
s of Miroslav K. allied air force off. and Sheila B.
Watson; b Lond 29.1.43
DPhil(Oxon) 1969 George Adam Smith (D. M. Cowan)
prize Aberd 1973 for book *T. S. Eliot's Social Criticism*
(Faber) 1972
Brit Council lect Tokyo 1970–72; part time lect Harrow
coll of f e 1973–74; bus. multinat comp from 1974; part-
time lect Lond univ extra-mural dept from 1974
m Northwood 2.7.77 Marie-Christine Dieudonné d of
Gilbert H. D. Saint Paul de Vence France

KOLACZ Marie Leona MA 1968

KÖNIG Ingeborg Irma *MA 1966
d of John K. joiner and Eva König; b Jaworze Poland
9.8.42
teacher mod lang: St Margaret's s for girls Aber 1967–69;
Aboyne acad 1973–77
m Aber 14.7.67 Lionel J. Davis MA 1966 *qv*

KÖNIG John Charles BSc(eng) 1968

KONKAMKING Laval MB ChB 1965

KOSS Paul MA 1970
s of Pawel K. sales rep and Elsie Bruce; b Aber 27.7.47
teacher: Hawick 1971–72, Engl Chapelton Jamaica from
1972
m 24.2.68 Morag Russell teacher d of Hugh R. Shapinsay

KPEDEKPO Gottlieb Mawulor Kwasi Dip Stat 1963
PhD 1966
s of Winfried Kwami K. cocoa farm. and Aurelia
Semenu; b Adaklu Abuadi Ghana 25.12.35
BSc(Lond) 1961 FRSS 1965 FIS 1976
res fell., sen res fell. univ of Ghana 1966–71; UN tech
asst expert in statist with title of prof Makerere univ
Kampala 1971–77, personal prof. dept econ from 1977
m Aber 10.9.65 Margaret S. Burnett secy d of George
P. B. Aber

KRISS Anthony *BSc 1969

KUFAAS Torbjörn MB ChB 1962
s of Gunnar K. merch N capt, ships insp Norway and
Solveig Lie; b Trondheim 17.1.34
spec gen surg Norway Med Assoc 1969 spec paediat
surg Norw Med Assoc 1974
h o, m o h, g p Trondheim, Lofoten 1963–64; regist:
surg, orthop Trondheim 1964–67; regist surg Sahlgrenska
Sjukhuset, Gothenburg univ Göteborg Sweden 1967–68;
sen regist surg Trondheim 1968–72; regist paediat surg
Helsinki 1972–74, sen h o paediat surg Sheff 1975;
consult. paediat surg Trondheim from 1975
m Aber 12.7.62 Jill Walker MB ChB 1962 *qv*

KUMAR Indra PhD 1957
BSc(Agra) MSc(Alld)

KUMOLU Joseph Babalola Omoyele *BSc(eng) 1959
MSc 1962
s of Solomon K. farm. and Sarah Odumlami; b Imesi-
Ile Nigeria 14.10.34
GIMechE 1962 MNSE 1963
Port Harcourt Nigeria: jun eng Shell BP 1963, proj eng
1963–65, sen proj eng 1965–67; Warri: head eng serv
1967–72, chief eng 1972–75, exec dir and man. from 1975
m Manc 3.9.60 Gladys O. Olaiya nurse d of John O.
Lagos

KYD David Robertson *MA 1964
s of David R. K. greengrocer and Williamina Robertson; b Echt 13.4.41
member Internat Inst for Strategic Stud. Lond; member
Royal Inst of Internat Relations Brussels; news edit.
overseas serv Swiss BC Berne 1964–65; NATO: comm
secy Paris, Brussels, head Press Serv and spokesman
from 1974
m Wald Switzerland 3.8.66 Anna E. Schraner secy d of
Leo S. Wald

KYDD Douglas William Bruce *BSc 1967

KYDD Frances Ann MA 1970

KYNASTON Colin Moffat MA 1969
s of George M. K. fire safety off. and Isabella G.
Moffat hosp receptionist; b Dunfermline 18.3.48
met. Brit antarctic surv Antarctica 1970–73; teacher
1973–75; roughneck Amer drilling comp ODECO on
'Ocean Kokuei' North Sea 1975–76; directional surv of
bore holes with Eastman Whipstock North Sea, Gulf of
Suez from 1976

KYNOCH Douglas Robert MA 1959
s of Alfred B. K. man. fishing comp and Nan Morrison
chief cashier AUP; b Aber 23.8.38
teacher Engl in lang s Brunswick W Ger 1960–61;
announcer and progr presenter Grampian TV Aber
1961–67; Glasg: news presenter TV BBC Scot. 1967–73;
Christian work Gospel Radio 1973–74, free lance
Christian work, writing and broadcasting from 1974

LA HOVARY Nicholas John MB ChB 1965
s of Christopher La H. bus. man. and Ida Mercinier
painter of landscapes; b Cairo 19.8.30
BSc(agr)(Melb) 1953
h o Woodend hosp Aber 1965–66; sen h o Cornhill hosp,
RACH 1966–67; h o Bellshill mat. hosp Glasg 1967–68;
sen res paediat, anaest Ottawa civic hosp 1968–69; family
doctor Ottawa from 1969
m Bellshill 26.8.67 Françoise Perret nurse, sister tut.
d of Pierre-André P. Neuchatel Suisse

LACHOWSKI Eric Edward *BSc 1970 PhD 1977
s of Stanislaw L. sales rep and Elizabeth R. Main
clerkess; b Aber 1.2.48
res asst dept chem Aberd from 1970
m Aber 7.8.70 Alison C. Gray MA 1969 *qv*

LAD Mohanlal Bhulabhai MB ChB 1963

LAIDLAW Erica Ann MA 1958
d of Archibald S. D. L. and Erica A. Heller; b Aber
23.5.37
teacher: Springhill p s Aber 1958–60, Lerwick p s 1960–65
and 1970–78, asst head Sound p s Lerwick from 1978
m Aber 22.7.60 Thomas G. Hunter BSc(eng) 1958 *qv*

LAIDLAW James Foster *MA 1970

LAING Eric Thomas *BSc 1963
s of Eric C. C. L., bank man. and Jean Bathie; b Dun
7.6.41
MSc(Edin) 1973
teacher sc Leith acad Edin 1964–66; lect phys Napier
coll of sc and tech Edin 1966–71; asst dir of educ W
Lothian 1971–73; asst dir of educ Edin 1973–75; asst to
dir of educ Lothian reg from 1975
m Edin 28.8.67 Anne M. Napier teacher bus. stud. d of
William N. Edin

LAING (Frank) Keith Anderson MB ChB 1958
s of William F. L. off. customs and excise and Joan R.
Anderson; b Aber 8.4.30
DObstRCOG 1960 MRCOG 1965 FRCOG 1979
consult. gyn Caithness and Sutherland Thurso from 1966
m Aber 17.3.56 Barbara D. Nisbet MA 1957 *qv*
d Halkirk 27.6.79 *AUR* XLVIII 354

LAING Hamish *BSc 1968

LAING John Alistair BSc(eng) 1962
s of John S.L. comp dir and Isabella H. R. Blackwood;
b Edin 19.11.37
AMIHE 1962 AMICE 1969 MIHE 1972 FIHE 1974
MICE 1972

site eng Fife 1960–64; sen eng, site ag Dun 1964–70; estimator Dun 1970–71; Nigeria: contr dir Lagos 1971–74, man. dir Kaduna from 1974
m Aber 13.7.61 Fay A. Muir secy d of John M. Aber

LAING John Dennis   MA 1959

LAING Kenneth George   *BSc(eng) 1968

LAING Lewis Alexander   *MA 1968

LAING May Normana Agnes   MA 1964
m McCallum

LAING Susan Mary   *MA 1968
d of Andrew L. master plumber and Emily A. Adam; b Aber 4.5.46
computer progr Lond, Glasg 1970–72; syst analyst Edin 1973–75; computer advis NHS Edin from 1975

LAING Thomas George   *MA 1958
s of Thomas L. MA 1925 qv; b Kilmarnock 27.2.37
teacher: Dun 1959–65, Invergordon 1965–67; prin hist: Portree 1967–71, Kincorth acad Aber 1971–76; asst rector Forres acad from 1976
m Dun 9.7.65 Kathleen E. MacBain teacher d of Duncan MacB. Longforgan

LAING William   BSc 1960
                 (conferred for long service of exceptional merit)
s of William L. sawmill lab and Mary Dawson; b Aber 8.3.93
elected fell. Inst of Sc Tech 1955
Aberd: chief tech chem dept 1929–1961, trg off. (part-time) 1961–65; retd
m Aber 18.8.20 Margaret C. Mackie bookseller's shop asst d of George M. Aber
d Aber 7.9.65 AUR XLI III

LAIRD May Austen   MA 1966
d of Ian A. L. CA comp dir and Frances M. McKinlay; b Kilmalcolm 17.7.44
exec off.: min overseas dev Lond 1966–68, F O Lond 1968–69; pers asst to chmn Brit Printing Ink Co Lond 1969–70; part time work for prisoners' wives serv from 1977
m Kilmalcolm 13.6.70 Gilbert M. Woods MA(Oxon) banker, solic s of Ellison M. W. MA(Oxon) Lond

LAIRD Norman James   BSc 1970

LAKIN Francis Henry Grewar   MB ChB 1960

LAKIN Kathleen Elizabeth   MA 1964 Dip Ed 1965
d of Alexander M. L. marine eng and Elizabeth F. Beattie secy; b Aber 3.10.42
teacher, Lode 1965–66, Aber 1966–71
m Aber 12.8.66 David J. Northcroft MA 1964 qv

LAMB Charles Scott   *MA 1970
s of David B. L. watchmaker and jeweller and Dorothy H. Martin; b Stirling 2.12.47
teacher Croydon from 1972

LAMB Georgina   *MA 1970
d of George M. L. car park attendant and Helen A. W. Kirton; b Aber 1.10.48
teacher geog Glasg from 1972
m Aber 25.7.69 William J. G. Livingstone insur clerk s of William L. Aber

LAMB James Summers   *MA 1969

LAMB MacGregor Ashley Webster   MEd 1962
MA(Edin)

LAMB Norman Bruce Christieson   BSc(eng) 1957

LAMB Raymond Johnston   *MA 1965

LAMB Robert Esson   *MA 1965

LAMB Roy Scott   BSc(for) 1957
s of William G. L. eng and Winifred Scott; b Aber 21.7.31
dist for. off. Co Londonderry from 1957

LAMBERT Robert Alexander   BSc 1969
s of James R. L. clerk and Anne P. Matthew; b Salford 19.2.49
geophys data processing Lond 1969–71; geophys field data analyst: Muscat Oman 1971–73, Melbourne, Alice Springs 1973–74; geophys seismologist Brisbane, Perth Aust from 1974
m Aber Priscilla Walker cler off. d of William W. Aber

LAMBERT Susan Margaret   *BSc 1961
d of Norman L. BSc(Durh) HM insp factories and Doris L. Nolan b Middlesbrough 20.11.39
teacher: Birm 1961–62, High Wycombe 1962–63, Stirling 1969–72, Fife 1976–77
m Birm 4.8.62 Charles N. Henderson BSc 1961 qv

LAMBIE Elizabeth Anne   *MA 1968
d of John S. L. MA(Glas) teacher and Ada Garden clerkess; b Glasg 17.7.46
teacher: classics Mackie acad Stonehaven 1969–74, part time Lat Aboyne acad from 1978
m Stonehaven 28.3.70 Ian O. Ritchie BSc 1968 qv

LAMBRAKIS Demetrios Panayotis   PhD 1966
BSc(Athens) Dip Stat (Manc)

LAMOND Nelida Kathleen   M Litt 1970
d of S. Erroll L. BA(S. Af) schoolmaster and Kathleen S. Carlton; b Pietermaritzburg S Af 5.6.28
BSocSc(Natal) 1966 Dip Nurs Educ(Natal) 1956
prof and head of dept of nurs univ of Natal Durban 1971–77

LAMONT Alan McGregor   MA 1960
s of William A. L. MA(Glas) schoolmaster and Barbara H. McGregor; b Glasg 23.2.40
army off. RA UK, Ger 1961–64; teacher maths: Ellon acad 1965–67, Glasg acad 1967–74, Dunblane s 1974–75; prin maths Alness acad from 1975
m Aber 10.4.68 Alison F. Rae MA 1962 qv

LAMONT Alison Jean Katherine   MA 1960
d of Alexander L. rubber planter and Alexa L. Will MA 1922 qv; b Aber 26.5.39
teacher: Torry j s s Aber 1961, Fr Aber acad 1961–66
m Aber 9.5.64 Charles P. Skene photogr/comp dir s of Cecil R. S. Aber

LAMONT Anne Caroline   *MA 1966
d of Thomas L. printer and Jessie M. A. Hainey; b Dunfermline 29.12.43
teacher: John Neilson h s Paisley 1967–78, Renfrew h s 1969–70
m Dunfermline 12.7.67 Alan D. Carstairs DA(Dun) teacher of art(f e) s of David B. C. Cupar

LAMONT Ann Patricia   MA 1958 MEd 1961
d of William E. L. master baker MN and Helen M. F.

Campbell; b Aber 28.12.37
Dip Ed(Edin) 1959
teacher St Peter's p s Aber 1959–61; asst educ psych
Renfrewsh 1961–63; educ psych Dover ch guid clin from
1963
m Dover 9.11.63 Alexander S. Flint ship's capt, marine
supt, port master s of Keith F. Dalmuir

LAMONT Bruce Malcolm   MA 1956
s of John I. M. L. civ serv and Lillian Lynch bus.
woman; b Hong Kong 12.5.34
teacher: Engl/geog Turriff 1960–66, geog Nairn from 1966

LAMONT Colin Campbell   *MA 1966

LAMONT Daniel Richard   *MA 1966

LAMONT Donald Alexander   *MA 1970
s of Alexander L. rubber planter and Alexa L. Will
MA 1922 qv; b Aber 13.1.47
trainee syst analyst Brit Leyland motor corp Oxford
1970–72, p a to man. dir Austin-Morris group of Brit
Leyland motor corp Birm 1972–73; F & CO Lond
1974–77; first secy UK mission to IAEA and UNIDO
Vienna from 1977

LAMONT Margaret Bruce   BEd 1969
d of Alexander L. insur insp and Davina Bruce; b Aber
27.12.32
teacher Engl Brechin h s from 1969
m Aber 30.5.53 William F. Haining BSc 1952 qv

LAMONT Margaret Mary   MA 1967
d of William L. grocer and Flora I. Macdonald; b Edin
21.4.46
progr: Lond 1967–68, Glasg 1968–70; analyst/progr:
Aber 1971–73, Lond 1973–74, Glasg 1974–77: progr
data processing Aberd from 1977
m Aber 16.7.76 John M. R. Miller data processing man.
s of Robert M. Dun

LAMPERT Brigitte Anita   MA 1964

LAM SHANG LEEN Kee Kwee Chun Yun   BSc 1967
s of Look-Siong Ng Cheng Hin prop. shoe factory and
Chun Yun Lam Shang Leen; b Mauritius 27.4.42
MSc(Lond) 1969 CChem MRIC 1974
sen tech QMC Lond 1967–69; lect Imp coll Lond 1969–
72; biochem St Thomas hosp Lond 1973–74; analytical
chem Parke-Davis Ontario 1974–75; res and dev ag
CRIQ Quebec from 1975
m Aber 5.7.63 Man Lee Ng Wing Wye secy d of Ng Wing
Wye Mauritius

LAM SHANG LEEN Yong-Kwee Chun Yun   BSc 1969
s of Look-Siong Ng Cheng Hin prop. shoe factory and
Chun Yun Lam Shang Leen; b Mauritius 9.6.43
BSc(Pharm)(RGIT Aber) 1975
continental tel Lond 1969–70, various posts Montreal
1971–72; man. pharm Leyland, Leicester 1976–78; prop.
pharm Aber from 1978
m Aber 29.3.71 Sheila Seivewright MA 1969 qv

LANGLANDS Alison Agnes Graham   MA 1967

LANGLANDS James Patrick   PhD 1962
BSc(agr)(Lond)

LANGLANDS Marianne Margaret   MA 1968
d of George N. L. master plumber and Margaret W.
Hampton; b Forfar 12.7.47

Dip Secy(Dun) 1969
Nat brewery comp Lond: secy to marketing dir 1970–73,
fin. analyst 1973–75
m Forfar 18.6.70 William B. Plaskett BSc 1969 qv

LANGLEY Susan Elsie   MA 1970

LANGSTON David   *MA 1968

LAPPIN Henry Cameron   *MA 1963 Dip Ed 1964
s of George A. L. riveter and Bridget O'Neil; b Paisley
9.12.20
teacher: Engl Inverurie acad 1964–68, Engl/gen stud. Inv
tech coll 1968–69, Engl Inv royal acad 1969–72, Engl/gen
stud. Moray coll of f e Elgin from 1972
m Inverurie 4.4.56 Frances J. Donald nurse d of Robert
D. Inverurie

LARDER David Frederic   PhD 1968
s of Frederic R. A. L. pharm, hotelier and Lilian W.
Hadfield nurse; b Lowestoft 20.2.35
BSc(Edin) 1958 BSc(Strath) 1959 FRIC 1970
Nelson B.C. Canada: dean of acad stud. 1963–69, acting
pres and vice-chancellor 1969–70, prof 1970–72, vice-pres
(acad) from 1972
m Montreal 27.12.61 Corrine O'Donnell hotel bus. d of
Patrick O'D. Edin

LARNACH Alison Jean   MA 1960
d of William L. retailer and Alice Dunnett; b Wick
26.11.40
m Aber 14.8.63 John B. Stuart tea planter, retailer s of
Harry S. Aber

LARYEA Alexander William Daniel   MB ChB 1966
s of William D. L. sen insp of taxes and Sophia Amah;
b Accra Ghana 16.12.38
DObstRCOG 1968 MRCOG 1972
h o Hitchin, Banbury 1967–68; sen h o obst/gyn Kingston,
Hitchin 1968–70; regist obst/gyn: Ipswich gen hosp
1970–72, Farnham and Frimley Park hosp 1972–74;
spec obst/gyn Ghana: Mampong Ashanti mat. hosp
1974–77, Ridge hosp from 1977
m Golders Green 11.8.74 Harriet Dodoo nurs off. d of
Harry A. D. Accra

LATHAM Peter Edmunds   BSc 1968
s of Ronald G. L. acct and Annie C. White nurse;
b Manc 23.7.45
Sen For. Cert of RFS 1976
for. Ripon from 1968
m Aber 11.12.67 Rosalind S. Hayward d of John
C. U. H. Kilmacolm

LATIMER Sheila   MA 1970
m Holme

LAW David Gordon   BSc(eng) 1960
s of David D. L. comp dir/wholesale boot factors and
Caroline Lamb; b Aber 27.4.38
MIMechE C Eng 1971
construct. eng power stat sites 1960–65, comp secy Aber
1965–68, construct. eng Dungeness 1968–70, proj man.
Babcock & Wilcox, Renfrew from 1970
m Aber 12.3.66 Sandra Cromar nurse d of Alexander
A. C. Aber

LAW George Rae   MA 1957 *BSc 1961 MSc 1962
s of George L. grocer and Julia Rae nurse; b Aber
8.4.29
asst lect geol Aberd 1959–62; dir Site Exploration serv
Aber 1962–77; geol Zaire grit explor Kinshasa from 1977

m(1) Aber 5.4.60 Elizabeth A. Abernethy BSc 1945 *qv*;
marr diss 1974
 (2) 1976

LAW Robert David *BSc 1960

LAW Sidney James MA 1961

LAWRENCE Anne Cruickshank MA 1966

LAWRENCE Catherine MA 1969

LAWRENCE Dorothy MA 1967
 d of William L. shopkeeper and Alice M. Thorpe;
b Lond 9.1.21
m Newcastle –.4.44 Robert E. Craig BSc(Edin) civ serv
s of Robert M. C. BSc(St And) Edin

LAWRENCE Jean Stuart *MA 1966
 m Wilson

LAWRENCE Kathleen *MA 1969
 d of Alexander L. clerk and Eveline M. Menzies paper
mill worker; b Ellon 5.6.47
teacher hist Inverurie acad 1971–72
m Bucksburn 4.8.71 Angus T. Smith MA 1970 *qv*

LAWRENCE Richard Keith *BSc(eng) 1967
 s of Frederick E. L. salesman and Rita N. A. Harrington; b Oxon 11.2.45
AMIEE 1967 MIEE CEng 1979
BBC: grad trainee 1967–69, electronics des from 1970
m Crookham 23.6.73 Jennifer G. Mercer secy d of Henry
J. M. Fleet

LAWRENCE Roger MA 1963 LLB 1965
 s of Charles W. L. comm trav and Margaret Bruce;
b Aber 2.3.42
law app/leg. asst Aber 1965–71, ptnr Burnett & Reid
advoc Aber from 1971
m Golspie 1.7.70 E. Joan Percy teacher d of Harold S. P.
Golspie

LAWRENCE William Gordon MA 1957
 s of William G. L. joiner and Annie I. R. Imlah;
b Turriff 20.1.34
Dip Soc/Psych of Educ(Leic) 1967
RAEC 1957–61; rep Lloyds & Scot. Fin. Aber, Leic;
lect lib stud Charles Keene coll Leic 1962–64; sen lect
educ Bede coll Durh 1965–71; sen soc scient (consult.)
Tavistock inst of human relations Lond from 1971 and
hon consult. Rosehill inst of human relations Toronto
from 1975
m Leic 31.5.62 Eszter Nagy shoe manuf d of Gyula N.
Budapest

LAWRIE Diane Park MB ChB 1967
 d of William G. R. L. man. Patrick Thomson's Edin
then owner/man. Lawries of Barnton and Mary B.
Hardie; b Edin 2.6.42
m Aber 31.3.64 Maurice Q. Cramb MA 1962 *qv*

LAWRIE Eleanor Weir MA 1966
 m Simpson

LAWRIE Margaret Elizabeth BEd 1970
 d of Thomas L. gardener and Catherine H. Porteous;
b Aber 13.6.31
teacher: Skene Square p s Aber 1970–74, Drumgarth inf s
Aber 1974–76, Fintray p s 1976–78, Marchburn inf s Aber
from 1979
m Aber 11.7.53 William B. Milne joiner s of David M.
Aber

LAWRIE William Alistair Buchan *MA 1970

LAWRIE William George *MA 1966

LAWRIE William John Neilson BSc 1956

LAWS Dennis Walter *MA 1966

LAWS Iain McColvin MB ChB 1969
 b Banchory 23.2.38
BDS(St And) 1961 FDSRCS(Eng) 1964
consult. oral surg Royal Free/Whittington hosps Lond
from 1972

LAWSON Anne Elizabeth BSc 1964

LAWSON Charles Frank MA 1970
 s of Frank C. L. P O tel eng and Elsie M. Low; b Inv
2.7.37
teacher maths Millburn s s Inv from 1971
m Inv 2.9.59 Rosaleen M. Stewart

LAWSON Henry Florence MA 1956

LAWSON Terence Anthony *BSc 1963

LAWTON David Maxwell *BSc 1970 PhD 1974
 s of Stanley E. L. PhD(Manc) tech man. and Joyce
Airey man. asst; b Grappenhall 1.5.47
post-doct fell. in ultrastructural plant cytology, bot dept
univ coll Cardiff from 1974

LAYCOCK Rex Adrian Harding *BSc(eng) 1969
 s of Rex E. L. surv and Frances M. Wibberley teacher;
b Derby 9.7.47
MSc(agr eng)(R'dg) 1973
civ eng: contr Kitwe Zambia 1969–70, consult. Rhodesia
1970–71, Lond 1971, Kano Nigeria 1974–77; in private
pract own firm consult. eng Bedford from 1978
m Perth 4.12.71 Christine M. Bonomy BSc 1969 *qv*

LEACH Joseph Henry PhD 1969
 b Sturgeon Falls Ontario 20.2.31
BSA(Tor) 1954 MSc(Guelph) 1966
res scient Ontario min of nat resources Lake Erie res stat
from 1969
m Huttonville Ontario 8.10.55 Mary L. Fraser BHSc(Tor)
dietitian

LEAKER Margaret Dalton MA 1968
 d of Dudley R. L. arch. and Mary V. James secy;
b Bristol 12.1.47
teacher: VSO Fr/Engl Takoradi s s Ghana 1968–69,
Engl/mus The Charlton s Wellington 1970–75
m Cumbernauld 4.4.70 Peter H. Halstead LL B 1968 *qv*

LEASK Aileen Margaret MA 1970
 d of John L. MB ChB 1938 *qv*; b Inverurie 15.6.41
teacher: Edin 1971–73, Stirlingsh from 1973
m Aber 4.4.73 Alastair Masson bank clerk s of Alastair M.
Evanton

LEASK Audrey Kathryn MA 1968
 d of Laurence L. L. div road foreman and Kathleen J.
Manson; b Shetland 1.6.47
teacher Engl Crieff 1969–71; head South Nesting p s
Shetland 1971–77
m Bigton 4.4.73 Alistair W. Mulley BP AD depot superv
s of Andrew W. M. Bigton

LEASK Margaret MA 1958
 d of Magnus L. trans oper and Jessie Smith clerkess;
b Lerwick 19.4.37

teacher Lerwick: Engl/Lat Anderson inst 1960–63, p s 1963–65, part-time p s/relief Anderson h s 1966–73, Bell's Brae p s part-time from 1973
m Aber 20.12.58 Gordon R. Silver travel ag/trans oper s of Frederick W. S. Bucksburn

LEASK Margaret Emma *MA 1964
d of Henry A. L. motor eng, man. dir and Emma M. Scott secy; b Aber 13.9.42
BA(Cantab) 1966 barrister-at-law Lincoln's Inn 1972
teacher Engl Thessaloniki Greece 1966–67; lect in law Queen Mary coll univ of Lond from 1967
m Aber 30.3.68 Peter S. Noble BA(Cantab) lect s of Peter S. N. MA 1921 *qv*

LEASK Mary Janet *MA 1967

LEASK Susanna Jean Isbister MA 1962
b Stromness 1.11.40
m Orkney 22.9.67 Ronald K. Leonard

LEATHAR Douglas Sutherland *MA 1969 PhD 1975

LEATHEM Christina Gilray MA 1966
d of James L. shopkeeper and Robina Robertson shopkeeper; b Wishaw 15.6.44
teacher: Wishaw 1966–69, Auchmuty j h s Glenrothes 1969–72
m Aber 16.4.68 Findlay M. Coutts MA 1964 *qv*

LEDINGHAM Christine Jean MA 1968
d of Robert G. L. and Christina MacMillan; b Aber 27.6.47
Secy Dip. (Lond) 1969
pers asst Lond 1969–70; W Ger: teacher Bonn 1970–71, teacher Engl Bonn-Hardtberg g s from 1972
m Ballater 8.8.70 Klaus Eichner Staats Examen (1 & 2) (Bonn) civ serv s of Wolfgang E. PhD(Bonn) Bonn

LEDINGHAM Roderic Bentley *MA 1966
s of Leslie A. L. MB ChB 1934 *qv*; b Aston-on-Trent 29.12.42
Dip Cartography(Glas) 1970 JP(Adelaide)
met. Antarctica Brit. ant. surv 1966–69; geol Aust Selection Pty Kalgoorlie 1970–76 and from 1978; off. i/c Aust Antarctic res exped Macquarie Is 1976–77

LEDINGHAM Stewart Charles BSc 1965

LEE Chong Soon MSc 1969
s of Lee Eng Teng surv and Khoo Choo Lean; b Penang 10.7.42
BAgrSc(Malaya) 1966 PhD(NCSU) 1977
Kuala Lumpur: biometrician dept of agr 1966–71; statist Malaysian agr res and dev inst from 1971
m Malaysia 12.2.70 Chang Sue Lyn nurse d of Chang Hoey Chan MB BS(Sing) Malaysia

LEE June Rose MA 1968

LEE Richard Martyn *BSc 1957 PhD 1961
s of Frederick G. L. civ eng and Beatrice M. Butler acct; b Merton Lond 22.11.34
Dip Entomology(Lond)
res biochem Wellcome foundation Berkhamsted 1960–65; sen lect vet pharm Portsmouth 1965–67; dept head parasitology SK & F Labs Welwyn Garden City 1967–74; dept head biochem SK & F Labs from 1974
m Aber 29.3.61 Arthurina R. M. Black MA 1955 *qv*

LEE Rodney Alan MA 1968

LEEGAARD Jens Michael MB ChB 1961

LEES Gordon McArthur MB ChB 1961 PhD 1968
s of Neil M. L. MB ChB(Glas) g p and Emelyn N. Laing dom sc teacher; b Dun 6.9.38
ARI: h o neurosurg, med 1961–62; Aberd: res fell. physiol 1962–66; lect: physiol 1966–68, pharm from 1968; visiting prof dept of pharm Loyola univ med center Maywood, Illinois 1970 and 1974
m Aber 14.12.63 Doris I. Manson MB ChB 1948 *qv*

LEES Joan cMB ChB 1960
d of James L. monum sculptor and Jessie C. Main; b Stonehaven 10.4.36
DCH(Lond) 1962 DPH(Tor) 1977
h o: Stracathro hosp 1960–61, Dun RI 1961–62; Carnegie s Edin 1962–63; Canada: resid Kingston gen hosp 1963–64, hosp for sick ch Toronto 1964–65; assoc m o h Borough of N York Ontario
m Tor 9.7.65 Ian McCausland BSc(Belf) prof elect. eng Tor s of Joseph McC. MA(Londonderry) Belfast

LEES Louisa Nelson Sharman Waugh MA 1962
m Fiddes

LEES Martin McArthur MB ChB 1958 MD 1971

LEES Moyra Isobel *MA 1968
d of Alexander C. L. hotelier/shopkeeper and Robina M. Ironside hotelier; b Aber 26.12.31
teacher Engl Mackie acad Stonehaven from 1969
m Aber 10.9.71 Norman J. Elder jet fuel supt s of Norman M. E. Glenelg

LEES Peter *MA 1960 MSc 1962
s of Peter L. waiter and Ann Grant; b Aber 22.6.38
AFIMA 1967
lect maths RGIT 1962–66; lect eng Aberd from 1966
m Aber 26.12.66 Gail Moir d of James M. Newmachar

LEES Ronald Forbes Barton MB ChB 1956

LEFEVRE David BSc 1969
s of Norman L. motor trade rep and Lilian Cassie; b Aber 6.3.48
MIWSP 1971
Wiggins Teape Aber: work-study asst 1969–71, work study off. 1971–73, man. acct 1973–75; John Wood Group (Aber) man. exec 1975–76; Woodacon Oils sales man. 1976–77; John Wood Group Offshore admin and dev man. 1977, gen man. from 1977
m Aber 26.7.69 Margaret McLeod cashier d of Alexander McL. Aber

LEFEVRE Frank Hartley MA 1956 LLB 1958

LEGG William Clubb Robson *BSc(eng) 1964

LEGGATT Irene Joan MA 1964

LEGGE Gordon Fraser BSc(agr) 1961
s of John A. L. pharm and optician and Jean G. Fraser; b Glasg 16.1.37
resid bot Hill farm. res organis Glensaugh Laurencekirk 1962–64; teacher sc: Arbroath h s 1965–69, Montrose acad 1969–71, prin biol from 1971
m Aber 30.3.64 Rhoda I. Ross BSc 1960 *qv*

LEGGE Joseph Smith cMB ChB 1966 MD 1972
s of Robert C. L. fisherman and Lily J. Smith; b Portessie 12.11.43
MRCP(UK) 1973

h o ARI 1966–67; res fell. dept med Aberd 1967–72; regist gen med Aber hosps 1972–73; sen regist respir med Tayside health board 1973–77; consult. thoracic med Aber from 1977, hon sen lect thoracic med Aberd
m Kirkwall 25.7.69 Sandra E. Leith nurse d of Alex L. Kirkwall

LEGGETT Stuart Ernest   BSc(for) 1966 Dip Ed 1967

LEIGH Elizabeth Dowie   *MA 1959

LEIPER Alan   MA 1958 LLB 1960

LEIPER James George   BSc(eng) 1958

LEIPER Margaret Christie   *MA 1969
d of William L. fish merch and Gladys D. West; b Aber 25.6.46
MLS (univ of W Ontario Lond Canada) 1973
teacher Frederick St s s Aber 1970–71; acting lib coll of fam phys of Canada Lond Ontario 1974–75
m Aber 21.7.69 Gordon L. Dickie MB ChB 1968 qv

LEIPER Sandra May   MA 1964
d of Thomas L. insur ag and Mabel Craigmyle; b Aber 18.12.43
Powis acad Aber: teacher maths 1965–68, 1969–71 and from 1974
m Aber 30.7.66 Ian E. Donald insur ag s of John D. Aber

LEIPER Susanna Jean   BSc 1968
d of Robert C. L. BA(Oxon) solic and Janet M. Oakden; b Woodford Green Essex 27.4.46
med lab tech ERI 1968–71
m Fyfield 27.7.68 Anthony W. D. C. Kent BSc 1966 qv

LEIPER William   MA 1968
s of William L. fish merch and Catherine J. Boddie clerkess; b Aber 17.9.46
Dip Man. St(RGIT)(Aber)
fish merch Aber from 1968
m Aber 11.9.70 Audrey G. J. Walker MA 1971 teacher d of Andrew A. W. Aber

LEISHMAN Douglas Andrew   BSc(eng) 1963
s of Mathew R. L. L. bank man. and Nancy B. Watt; b Colombo Ceylon 6.8.38
MICE 1968
asst eng Glasg: sitework 1961–63, office and site 1963–67, publ health off. from 1967

LEITCH Robert Findlay   MA 1965

LEITH Duncan Meldrum Thomson   MA 1961

LEJEUNE Anne   MB ChB 1959
d of François L. (Roman, Liège) merch and Betty Careless; b Newcastle-u-Tyne 1.9.34
m Lond 25.8.59 John P. Llewellyn BSc 1954 qv

LENDRUM Elizabeth Ann   LLB 1966
d of John F. L. MA(Cantab) headmaster and Mary A. M. Campbell nurse; b Aden 14.5.44
market res off.: Standard Bank Lond 1966–67, Proprietary Perfumes Ashford Kent 1967–68, B A C Lancs 1968–69; teacher from 1976
m Great Chart 14.9.68 Robert M. Boddy journalist s of Robert A. B. Lytham St Annes

LENDRUM Robert Donald Currie   MA 1966
s of Alan C. L. BSc(Glas) prof path. and Elizabeth B. Currie MA(Glas) almoner; b Glasg 9.4.44

MB ChB BAO(univ coll Galway NUI) 1972 MRCGP 1977
h o: surg Perth RI 1972–73, med Stracathro hosp 1973; sen h o obst Perth RI 1973–74, med Bridge of Earn from 1974
m Dun 1.9.73 Sheila Whyte MB ChB(St And) med pract d of Thomas B. W. LLB(Lond) Bromley

LENEY Fiona Margaret   MSc 1970 PhD 1974
d of Alfred M. L. MA(Oxon) fruit grower and Patricia N. M. Liston physioth; b Edin 16.8.47
BSc(Brist) 1968
asst res off. Countryside Comm for Scot. Perth 1973–74; res off. Dartington amenity res Trust Devon from 1974

LENG John Edward   MB ChB 1958
s of John P. Leng MA(Edin) min of relig and Emma A. Fay; b Motherwell 21.6.35
DObstRCOG 1961 Dip Theol(Lond) 1962
hosp posts Aber area, Lanarksh 1958–60; supt mission hosp W New Guinea 1963–67; g p: Motherwell 1969–73, Lenzie from 1973
m Gourock 8.9.61 Fiona E. S. Forrest nurse d of Robert F. Gourock

LENMAN Bruce Philip   *MA 1960
s of Jacob P. L. fisherman, PO tel, dep dir of fin. for. comm and May Wishart PO tel; b Aber 9.4.38
MLitt(Cantab) 1964 FSAScot
lect: Commonwealth hist St And, Queen's coll Dund 1963–67, Commonwealth/Scot. hist Dund 1967–72, Scot. mod hist St And from 1972
m Perth 2.9.67 Sheila G. Wilson MB ChB(St And) g p d of William W. MB ChB(Edin) Perth

LENNON James   MA 1963
s of James L. and Isobel MacGillivray wages clerk; b Nairn 23.5.41
JP
teacher Seafield p s Elgin 1964–67; dep head Applegrove p s Forres 1967–73; head: Cawdor p s Nairn 1973–75, Muirtown p s Inv from 1975
m Lossiemouth 8.10.73 Elizabeth S. Campbell secy d of James S. C. Lossiemouth

LENNOX Donald Iain   *BSc 1965

LENNOX John Macdonald Williamson   MA 1963

LENNOX Leslie Grant   MA 1963

LEONARD Elizabeth Marjorie   LLB 1969
d of John L. L. tea planter and Elizabeth T. Robb; b Shillong, India 8.9.47
law app St And 1969–71, asst solic: Dun 1971–73, Leven from 1973

LEONTIADES Leontios Ioannou   BSc(for) 1958
s of Ioannis P. L. farm./secy Ashia co-op credit soc and Paraskevi Mattheou; b Ashia Cyprus 17.10.33
Member Brit Ornithologists' Union
Cyprus: asst conserv for. 1958–62, 63–66 (for. off. postgrad course Oxon 1962–63); conserv for. Class I 1966–73; seconded dir game and wildlife serv 1973–74; conserv for. Class I 1974–77; acting asst dir dept of for. from 1977
m Nicosia 21.10.61 Androula Nicolau d of Nicolaos Georghiou Nicosia

LESLIE Alan Gilbert   *BSc 1969
s of Gilbert L. compositor and Isabella McIntosh; b Aber 23.9.46
tech serv eng Monsanto Chemicals Ruabon Wales 1969–71; teacher maths Fairchildes h s Croydon 1971–73;

Orpington coll of f e: lect maths 1973–77, sen lect (sciences) from 1977
m Bromley 12 7.74 Norma R. Collins BA(Birm) teacher, lect d of Bernard M. C. Lond

LESLIE Alistair Winchester   BSc 1960 Dip Ed 1961
s of Charles L. upholsterer and Annie F. Winchester; b Stonehaven 11.4.27
teacher: Castle Douglas 1961–73, prin chem/biol Grangemouth from 1973
m Oldmeldrum 4.10.52 Isabel M. Cooper cook d of George C. Tarves

LESLIE Denis Falconer   BSc 1969 Dip Ed 1970
s of Charles L. upholsterer and Annie F. Winchester; b Stonehaven 7.1.48
teacher maths: Arbroath 1971, Kirkcudbright 1971–72; computer progr Aber from 1972
m Elgin 26.7.74 Joan E. McGowan MA 1972 teacher d of Robert McG. Elgin

LESLIE Elizabeth Margaret McKay   MB ChB 1957
d of George W. B. L. farm., factor, fisherman and Margaret M. Reid; b Shetland 31.7.33
h o Aber 1957–58; intern Stenford USA 1958–59; h o RACH 1959–60; resid anaest Chapel Hill USA 1960–61
m Aber 14.7.60 H. Thomas Frank PhD (Duke) USA prof of relig s of Dallas M. F. Newport News, Va

LESLIE George William Davidson   BSc(agr) 1960
d 1972

LESLIE Ian Stewart   BSc(eng) 1960

LESLIE James   *BSc(eng) 1959
s of William L. shepherd/sub-postmaster and Maggie A. Flaws; b Quendale 30.5.38
MBA(McG) 1967 Abex Indust schol. 1965 1st McGill winner of Seagram bus. fell. 1966
eng Blyth & Blyth Edin Inv 1959–62; Montreal eng comp: eng 1962–65, sen superv econ and valuation div 1967–69, asst man. econ and val div 1969–71, man.: man. sciences, man. consult. div 1971–74, dir of plan. 1974–75; vice-pres plan. from 1975 also pres/dir Monenco computing serv from 1975 and dir Monenco holdings from 1975
m Inv 3.11.62 Marjorie S. Ness secy d of William M. N. Inv

LESLIE James Charles   *BSc 1970
b 17.6.48
teacher Elgin from 1971

LESLIE Jean Hamilton   MA 1961
b Aber 12.8.40
teacher Engl/hist: Northfield s s Aber 1962–65, Larkhall acad 1965–66; prin guid Bankhead acad Aber 1970–75; asst head Northfield acad from 1975
m Aber 10.7.63 Eric Wilson contr rep

LESLIE Jennifer Stewart   *MA 1965
d of Theodore L. farm., miller and Jean R. L. Stewart; b Aber 2.11.42
teacher: mod lang Aber h s for girls 1966–69, Engl Düsseldorf W Ger 1969–70, mod lang St George's s Edin 1970–71, Engl Kiel W Ger 1971–73; prin mod lang Albyn s for girls Aber from 1974

LESLIE Joan Elizabeth Agnes   *MA 1968
m Speed

LESLIE John Alexander   MA 1963

LESLIE John Stewart   *MA 1970
s of John A. L. BSc 1938 qv; b Rugby 23.3.48
teacher Engl Larnaca, Cyprus 1970–71; HM insp taxes Fulham from 1971
m Woodhouse Eaves 2.11.74 Angela M. E. Porter MA 1970 qv

LESLIE Lydia   MA 1961
d of Ernest S. L. acct, lect and Williamina Smith shop asst, nursery s asst; b Aber 5.1.40
teacher Ferryhill p s Aber 1962–65
m Aber 5.4.63 Joseph C. Coutts tv eng s of Joseph C. India

LESLIE Norman Grant   *MA 1964

LESLIE Norman William   *MA 1967 Dip Ed 1968
s of William L. civ serv and Annie W. Petrie; b Aber 23.1.35
teacher Hillhead h s Glasg 1968–69; Canada: teacher Oakwood collegiate Toronto 1969–73; assoc chmn soc and phil stud. Cawthra Park s s Mississauga Ont from 1974
m Aber 13.7.68 Sheila A. Watt BSc 1968 qv

LESLIE Patricia Edith   MA 1968
m Logan

LESLIE Roy McIntosh   BSc 1970

LESLIE Stanley Macdonald   MA 1963
s of George M. L. conduct. BR dining car, hotel porter and Georgina W. Cox tailoress; b Aber 29.3.41
teacher Engl Peterhead acad 1964–73, asst prin Engl from 1973
m Aber 24.7.68 Charlotte J. MacWilliams shorthand typist MA 1977 d of John P. M. RAF killed in action 1945

LESSELLS Gordon Stewart   *MA 1970
s of James L. MA(Edin) teacher classics and Frances M. Taylor MA 1941 qv
MSc(Oxon) 1971
lect: Glas 1973–74, univ of Benin Nigeria from 1974

LETHAM Adam   MA 1967
s of Robert L. L. farm. and Margaret McNeil; b Lanark 2.8.44
Masaka Uganda: teacher Kako sen s s 1968–71, asst head from 1971

LETHAM John McNeil   MA 1964
s of Robert L. L. farm. and Margaret McNeil; b Carfin 5.3.43
teacher: Souillac France 1965–66, Lanark from 1966

LEVACK Hamish Hunter   BSc(for) 1969
s of William L. L. MA(Glas) clergyman and Deborah A. C. Mayer; b Mauritius 25.7.44
BSc(Auck) 1967
NZ: for. Rotorua 1969–75, Wellington from 1975

LeVANN Helen Patricia   MA 1967

LEVENE Lawrence Barry   BSc 1966

LEVERETT James William   *BSc 1962
s of Benjamin L. and Nell Lloyd; b Norfolk 11.10.22
teacher RGC Aber 1963–65, prin asst 1965–68; prin Cults acad Aber 1968–72, asst rector 1972–75, dep rector from 1975
m Dyce 27.6.47 Isobel Fearnside d of Alfred F. Dyce

LEVETT Barry Richard   *BSc(eng) 1970
s of Richard E. K. L. BSc(eng)(Cantab) mech eng and

Jessie Banks; b Bognor Regis 30.8.47
MICE 1973
asst eng Crouch & Hogg Glasg 1970–72; eng Ross &
Cromarty Dingwall 1972–74; resid eng Wallace, Stone
& Arcubos Peterhead 1974–77; asst proj eng Halcrow
Sharjah UAE from 1977
m Wick 15.8.70 Avril H. B. Banks radiogr d of Harold
B. Wick

LEVIE David Stuart Craigen   BL 1958
    s of William E. L. MA(by ordinance) 1945 advoc in
Aber/prof conveyancing and Catherine S. Craigen
teacher; b Aber 5.7.33
col serv dist off. Kadavu, Fiji 1958–61; advoc in Aber
ptnr Milne & Reid 1961–64, ptnr John Sergeant & Co
E Kilbride 1964–71, ptnr Burnett & Reid advoc Aber
from 1971
m Daviot 6.2.60 Mary M. R. Mackie MA 1958 *qv*

LEVISON Lionel Hana Lothar   MB ChB 1964
    BSc(econ) Lond

LEVITT Charles Samuel Alexander Wheatley
                                                            MB ChB 1961
    s of Charles W. L. MB ChB 1936 *qv*; b Aber 6.12.35
h o: City hosp Aber, ARI 1961–62; resid m o mat. hosp
Hull 1962–63; g p Alyth, Aber from 1963
m Aber 22.12.61 Winifred C. Clark MA 1959 *qv*

LEW HO CHEUN Lew Kum Yeung   MA 1966

LEWIS David Charles   MB ChB 1968
    s of Henry D. L. factory worker and Lilian M.
Wilkinson; b Hertford 23.5.43
FRCS(C) 1974
Canada: intern Kingston 1968–69, resid med Toronto
1969–70, resid ophth Montreal 1970–73; private pract
Barrie Ontario from 1973
m Owen Sound Ontario 4.10.69 Susan J. Scopis BA(Tor)
comp dir d of Nicholas W. S. Owen Sound

LEWIS Geoffrey Gordon   *BSc 1969 PhD 1972
    s of Eric W. L. comp rep and Joyce H. Davidson;
b Aber 4.12.46
res off. CEGB scient serv dept (NW reg) Manc from 1972
m Runcorn 1.4.74 Gwyneth H. Jarvis exper off. pharm
div ICI d of George H. J.

LEWIS Gerald Patrick Thomas   *MA 1970
    s of Thomas J. L. farm. and Theresa M. Jessett;
b Haverfordwest 17.3.26
Dip Soc St(Belf) 1971 Dip Soc Work(Belf) 1972 Dip
counselling in educ settings (univ of Aston, Birm) 1974
pres SRC(Queen's univ Belf)—sabbatical year 1972–73
m Adare, Ireland 31.8.74 Ann C. Barry lib d of Patrick
E. B. Limerick

LEWIS Karen Joan   MA 1968

LEWIS Robert Alexander   MA 1963

LEWIS Rosemary Ann   BSc 1958
    d of Robert M. L. timber merch, clerk in holy orders
and Dorothy M. L. Bisset; b Milford Haven 28.8.38
teacher: Sawston village coll Cambridge 1959–60, Nott
1966; tut. dem univ and tech inst Hamilton NZ from 1970
m Ripon 30.6.59 Kenneth M. Mackay BSc 1957 *qv*

LEWIS Sheila Maude   *MA 1961
    d of John A. L. shipbuilder/dir and Sheila Sandison
MA 1930 *qv*; b Aber 28.4.38
Dip Sec St(St Godric's coll Lond) 1962

secy: Mitchell & Muil Aber 1961–62, A. Walker fish
market Aber 1962–63; geog secy John Bartholomew
Edin 1963–66
m Aboyne 17.9.65 Ian A. G. Kinniburgh MA(Edin)
asst lect Glas, edit man. John Bartholomew & Son Edin
vice-pres Brit. Cartographic Soc s of John K.

LIDDELL Charles Richard Wilson   MB ChB 1969
    s of Charles M. L. MB ChB 1937 *qv* and Elsie J.
Thomson MB ChB 1937 *qv*; b Aber 17.10.44
trainee g p Aber 1970–71; g p Cults/Peterculter from
1971
m Bieldside 26.3.70 Jacquelyn K. R. Anderson teacher
d of William C. A. Bieldside Aber

LIDDERDALE Ian Gavin   *MA 1970
    s of Ian M. L. garage prop. and Grace B. Cooper;
b Stafford 27.1.48
MSc(Hull) 1971
sen psych MoD(RAF) HQ RAF SC, RAF Brampton,
Huntingdon from 1971
m Upper Largo 31.7.68 Pauline J. Lister MA 1969 *qv*

LIDDLE Dorothy Isabelle   MA 1969
    d of Robert L. BSc(Edin) customs off., teacher and
Janet A. Lambert BA(Edin) teacher; b Dunfermline
1.6.48
teacher mod lang Marr coll Troon 1970–72
m Aber 1.8.69 Philip A. Galbraith BSc 1968 *qv*

LIEBNITZ William Falconer   *BSc(eng) 1969
                                                            MSc 1973
    s of James S. L. fisherman and Elizabeth Falconer;
b Lossiemouth 2.10.47
S Queensferry: prod. eng 1971–73, prod. eng superv from
1973
m Alves 11.9.73 Judith J. Sim d of George S. Alves

LIGHT Jeremy James   *BSc 1968 PhD 1977

LIGHTBOWN Raymond George   *BSc 1970
    s of George L. indust contr maintenance painter and
Helen Hutton lect; b Blackburn Lancs 29.5.47
BPhil(Liv) 1972 ABPsS 1974
prob clin psych Liv 1970–72; basic grade clin psych
Brist 1972–74, sen clin psych from 1974

LILLIE John Gordon   MB ChB 1958
    d 1977

LI LUI SANG Roland Serge   BSc(agr) 1967

LILY Michael   *MA 1969

LIND John   BSc(agr) 1963
    s of John M. L. farm. and Jessie P. Fell masseuse;
b Methlick 24.6.41
farm. Methlick from 1963
m Fyvie 21.11.63 Doris M. Kinghorn d of James K.
Rothienorman

LINDLEY David Keith   *BSc(for) 1963
    s of George V. L. sales rep NCB and Annie G.
Griffiths nurse; b Birm 27.2.40
MSc(Mich) 1964
res stud. Aberd 1965–67; scient off. for. comm Surrey
1967–70; sen scient off. nature conserv Grange-over-
Sands 1970–74; prin scient off. ITE Grange from 1974
m Essex 3.9.67 Joanna C. Bellis MB ChB 1964 *qv*

LINDQUIST Roy Philip   MSc 1969
    s of Vincent C. L. elect. tech and Elizabeth J. Philip

nurse; b Aber 1.4.46
BSME(Mass) 1967 MBA(Mass) 1978 Member Amer Soc
of Mech Eng
1st lt/instr US army air defense s Texas 1970, tactical
duty off. 38th Air defense arty Osan, Korea AFEM,
NDSM (military decorations) Jan–Nov 1971; Foxboro Co
Mass: prod. eng 1971–72, dev eng 1972–74, res eng
1974–77; natl secy dynamic syst and control div of
ASME from 1977
m Aber 26.6.70 Wendy J. Bisset nurse d of Reginald
R. B. BSc(eng) 1937 qv

LINDSAY Allan Home   LLB 1966

LINDSAY Ann Hunter   MA 1968
d of Duncan E. L. bank acct and Margaret H. Thomson
BSc(Glas) teacher; b Dornoch 2.3.46
teacher Fr Cults acad 1969–73; teacher of deaf Aber s for
the deaf 1973–74
m Aber 24.9.75 Joseph P. Richards ACSM mining eng
s of Edward J. R. Truro

LINDSAY Anne Fettes   MA 1968
d of Charles L. insp GPO and Mary S. Singer; b Aber
14.6.47
teacher Engl Northfield acad Aber 1969–71
m Aber 18.12.69 Michael A. Forsyth ARICS chartered
quantity surv s of Albert F. Aber

LINDSAY David William MacDiarmid   PhD 1962
s of William L. L. MA(Edin) teacher and Elizabeth
MacDiarmid teacher; b Dunfermline 21.3.36
MA(Edin) 1957
asst Engl dept Aberd 1959–63; lect Engl: Queen's univ
Belf 1963–66, UCNW 1966–76, sen lect from 1976
m Aber 17.10.59 Jean Forrest PhD 1962 qv

LINDSAY Elizabeth Mary   MB ChB 1968
d of William T. L. comm RN, estate man. and Mary
Duncan; b Windsor 28.8.44
fell. Amer acad of paediat 1975
h o Stracathro hosp Brechin 1968–69; Baltimore USA
paediat intern 1970–71, paediat resid 1971–72, chief
resid paediat 1972–73, instr paediat univ of Maryland
hosp from 1973
m Aboyne 6.7.68 Peter G. Ruff BBA(Texas) importer
s of Paul G. R. Midland Texas

LINDSAY Hamish William Harrower   LLB 1970
s of Alexander R. L. bus. man and Isabel S. McLean;
b Harrow 31.3.49
Übersetzen-Munchen Dolmetscher Inst 1973
lumberjack Sweden 1970–71; translator Germany 1971–
74; Edin: law app 1974–76, solic 1976; solic Aber from
1976

LINDSAY Helen Martin   MA 1967
m Boyle

LINDSAY James Gordon   MA 1969

LINDSAY John Alexander   BSc(agr) 1969 *1970
                                                    MSc 1977
s of Alexander C. K. L. publ serv and Helen Blain
nurse; b Glasg 17.3.47
husb off. Queensland dept of primary industries from
1977

LINDSAY LeRoy Rader   PhD 1965
AB BD(Kentucky)

LINDSAY Nigel Bruce   *MA 1970 MLitt 1973
s of Duncan D. L. BA(Oxon) univ lect and Eunice A.

Harris teacher; b Scunthorpe 27.3.48
lib party organis W Aberdeensh 1973–74; reg organis
Shelter from 1975; member: Aber town council 1973–75,
Aber dist c from 1977, univ court Aberd 1976–80

LINDSAY Roger   *BSc(eng) 1961

LINDSAY Ronald McLean   BSc 1969

LINDSAY Stanley John Edwin   *MA 1965 PhD 1971
s of Stanley F. L. MB ChB 1937 qv; b Aber 12.9.42
res psych M o D Farnborough 1971–75; clin psych
Broadmoor hosp 1975–77; lect inst of psychiat from 1977

LINKLATER Maud   MA 1957 Dip Ed 1958

LINTS Alice Milne   MA 1967
m Collinson

LIPP Donald   MB ChB 1959
s of George R. L. MB ChB 1914 qv; b Sheffield 3.12.33
h o ARI, Woodend hosp Aber 1959–60; h o obst/gyn
Mansfield 1960–61; g p Killamarsh, Sheff from 1961
m Aber 17.10.59 Ida I. Haeseler nurse d of Caesar H.
Frankfurt-am-Main Germany

LIPSCOMB Pamela Grace   MB ChB 1968
d of Ernest J. L. chart. surv and Grace A. Hamilton
shop asst, clerk; b Upminster 27.2.43
m Romford 20.7.68 Victor C. Mason BSc(Glas) lect,
sen scient off., res leader Copenhagen s of Harold E. M.
DCM Marchwiel

LISLE Philip Neil Teasdale   *BSc(eng) 1970
s of John T. L. overseas civ serv/advis to Botswana
govt and Margaret I. Wilkinson; b Gosforth 16.9.47
consult. civ & struct eng Glasg: eng asst 1970–73, sect.
eng, resid eng on construct. site Straiton, Ayrsh 1973–77,
resid eng on construct. site Riding Mill, Northumberland
from 1977

LISTER David Hugh   *BSc 1965 MSc 1967
s of James T. L. BR perm. way insp and Janet W.
Drummond; b Forfar 6.2.44
res asst with GR-Stein Refractories Bonnybridge 1967–71;
dev chem Cape Insulation Stirling 1971–74; prod. dev
man. Flexible Ducting Milngavie from 1974
m Bonnybridge 9.8.69 Ann K. Macaulay lib/typist d of
James M. Cumbernauld

LISTER Doris Anne   MB ChB 1970
d of Douglas L. MA(Glas) C of S min and Marion W.
Read teacher mus; b Rothesay 9.9.46
h o ARI 1970–71, res fell. therap Aberd 1971–72; trainee
g p Lond 1972–73; sen h o: obst DRI 1974, paediat
Paddington Green ch hosp 1974–75; g p The Abbey med
centre Lond from 1975
m Upper Largo 1.10.77 James A. Mackonochie newspaper man. s of James S. M. Tonbridge

LISTER Pauline Janette   MA 1969
d of Douglas L. MA(Glas) C of S min and Marion W.
Read; b Hamburg 16.3.48
m Upper Largo 31.7.68 Ian G. Lidderdale MA 1970 qv

LISTON Elizabeth Margaret   MA 1970
d of William A. L. MBChB(Edin) obst and Elizabeth A.
Macaulay; b Edin 7.9.48
teacher Greendykes p s Edin 1970–74
m Edin 1974 Donald A. Bremner eng s of Donald D. B.
Edin

LISTON Margaret Petrie *MA 1970
 d of Thomas M. B. L. quantity surv and Marjorie F. Petrie; b Glasg 10.3.48
Engl lang asst école normale d'instituteurs Paris 1970–71; teacher Eastwood sen h s from 1972
m Glas 19.12.75 Evan Mawdsley BA(Haverford Coll USA) lect Glas s of Evan M. Dorset

LITTLE Joan *MA 1958
 m Dickson

LITTLE Joan Ross *BSc 1967
 d of Hugh W. L. dep chmn bldg firm and Eleanor J. Cumming; b Forres 11.8.45
teacher: Dumbarton acad 1968–70, Perth acad 1970–71, St Augustine's Edin 1971–73
m Aber 18.12.71 Adebayo Olusanya MB ChB(Edin) regist surg s of Josiah A. O. Ibadan, Nigeria

LITTLE Patricia Cumming MA 1967
 d of Hugh W. L. quantity surv and Eleanor J. Cumming; b Aber 7.9.46
teacher Skene St p s Aber 1968–73
m Aber 22.12.69 Robert A. Minett MA 1969 *qv*

LITTLE William MA 1966

LITTLEJOHN Alastair Lewis *BSc 1969

LITTLEJOHN Alistair George *BSc(eng) 1957
 s of James D. L. comm trav and Alice M. Henry MA 1925 *qv*; b Aber 17.2.35
civ des eng, hydraulics res site eng: Knutsford 1957–59, Trawsfynydd 1959–66; sen site eng, bldg proj man. Liv 1966–71; dir Lond from 1971
m Waenfawr 16.2.63 Mairwen L. Jones air stewardess d of Henry L. J. Waenfawr

LITTLEJOHN Elizabeth Jane Wilson MA 1968
LLB 1970
 d of Louis H. L. rubber planter and Anne Wilson; b Penang 1.5.47
law app, leg asst Milne & Mackinnon advoc Aber 1970–73; leg. asst Wilsone & Duffus advoc Aber 1973; hotel man. Aboyne 1973–77; leg. asst Lefevre & Co advoc Aber from 1977

LITTLEJOHN Margaret Isobel BSc 1964
 d of John A. L. head gamekeeper and Isobel Lamb clerk; b Aber 5.5.43
asst exper off. Edin 1964–67; teacher biol Aber 1968–72, in 1973, 1974–75 and from 1978
m Maryculter 10.4.71 Robert J. Robertson blacksmith s of James R. Archiestown

LITTLEJOHN Robert King MA 1968
 s of Robert H. L. comm clerk, shopkeeper and Doreen C. Barclay; b Aber 17.3.46
commissioned RAF educ br 1969; stat educ off. RAF Henlow 1970–74; stat educ off. and ground s educ off. No 4 flying training s RAF Valley, Wales 1974–76; stat educ off. RAF Luga Malta 1976–78; stud. Sus from 1978
m Crieff 9.11.68 Anna A. M. Devine DA(Edin) d of Daniel D. Crieff

LIVESEY Hilary Joyce *MA 1966 Dip Ed 1967
 d of Herbert L. exec off. civ serv and Doris Bamber clerk; b Accrington 12.10.44
teacher Engl Haslingden g s Lancs 1967–71

m Accrington 16.5.70 Brian P. Timson quantity surv s of Philip D. T. Blackburn

LIVINGSTON Roderick George BSc 1968
 s of Hugh L. MA 1927 *qv*; b Birm 10.12.44
ADPA(Exeter) 1969 ACIS 1972 FSAScot
univ admin: grad asst Aberystwyth 1969–70, admin asst 1970–72; Dund: sen admin asst 1972–75, asst secy from 1975
m Edin 23.9.74 Wilma Watt d of William W. Edin

LIVINGSTONE Andrew Hugh *BSc 1967
 s of David L. ironmonger and Anne W. McClements agr advis; b Campbeltown 7.12.44
Dip Ed(Glas) 1968
teacher: Glasg 1968–70, prin maths Paisley from 1970
m Airdrie 5.7.72 Christine M. Henderson teacher d of James H. MA(Glas) Dun

LLOYD David Ellrington Burton MSc 1968
 BA(Oxon)

LLOYD-LAWRENCE Adrian Hugh *BSc 1964
 s of Arthur J. L.-L. MA(Cantab) soil chem and Gladys M. Wilson BSc 1932 *qv*; b Harpenden 16.4.42
PhD(Lond) 1977
geol: min resources div govt of Tanzania Dodoma 1964–67, Hunting Geol & Geophysics Borehamwood 1967–69; dep chief prospector for CAST (Diamonds Ghana) Akwatia Ghana 1969–72; advis to Algerian govt from 1977
m Lond 21.8.69 Catherine E. Marshall teacher/graphic des d of Cyril F. M. Nice France

LOBBAN Dorothy Kidd BSc 1961
 d of James A. L. rep and Mary M. Kidd tailoress; b Aber 21.3.40
teacher Renfrewsh 1962–63, Lenzie 1963–64, Aber from 1964
m Aber 10.8.63 James G. Shand teacher s of William J. S. Aber

LOBBAN Elizabeth Taylor BSc 1967
 d of James A. L. comm trav and Mary M. Kidd tailoress; b Aber 26.8.46
systems progr: ICL: Lond 1967–70, Dalkeith 1970–72, Sus Brighton 1972–73, ICL Dalkeith 1973–74, contr progr from 1975
m Aber 6.10.71 Kenneth J. Brown BSc 1968 *qv*

LOBBAN Graeme Alexander BSc 1967

LOBBAN James George *MA 1964
 s of George A. L. maintenance eng and Christina T. Calder; b Aber 9.9.42
teacher mus Inverurie acad 1965–66, prin mus from 1967

LOCHHEAD James Robert David BSc(for) 1969

LOCK Roger John *BSc 1969
 s of Harold E. L. fishmonger and Enid M. Frost shop asst; b Thetford 22.9.47
teacher: Kilmarnock 1970–71, Birm 1971–73; prin biol/sc Trinity s Leamington Spa 1973–78; lect educ(biol) univ of Leeds from 1978
m Leamington Spa 22.4.74 Ann C. Lea typist/receptionist d of Christopher J. L. Birm

LOCKHART Brian Robert Watson *MA 1967
 s of George W. L. nurse and Helen Rattray nurs. s teacher; b Edin 19.7.44
Dip Ed(Edin) 1968

Edin: teacher hist 1968–71, spec asst 1971–72, head hist dept George Heriot's s from 1972
m Girvan 4.4.70 Fiona A. Sheddon MA(St And) teacher d of James B. S. Girvan

**LOCKHART Gordon Burgess   BSc(eng) 1964 *1965
MSc 1967**

LOCKIE David   BSc(eng) 1964
s of David L. shepherd and Helen U. Ross; b Wick 2.4.43
Glasg: grad trainee eng 1964–66, des eng-elect. motors 1966–67, des eng-temp controls 1967–70, sen des eng 1970–77, sen proj eng DIG clocks/timers from 1977
m Patna Ayrsh 31.10.69 Elizabeth M. M. Clark nurs, theatre supt d of William R. C. Patna

LOCKIE John   *BSc 1959
s of David L. shepherd and Helen U. Ross; b Bilbster 22.9.36
teacher sc AGS 1960–66, prin biol RGC Aber 1966–68; lect Craigie coll of educ Ayr from 1968
m Aber 19.7.63 Norma L. Ewen MA 1962 qv

LODGE Geoffrey Arthur   PhD 1958
s of Arthur L. master mariner and Winifred R. Whitfield; b Newcastle-u-Tyne 18.2.30
BSc(agr)(Durh) 1951 FIBiol 1978
royal tank regt 1951–53; scient off. Rowett res inst Aber 1954–59, sen scient off. 1959–61; lect anim prod. Nott univ 1961–66, reader 1966–68; sen res scient anim res inst Ottawa 1968–74, prin res scient 1974–78; Strathcona-Fordyce prof agr Aberd and prin NOSCA Aber from 1978
m Aber 7.4.56 Thelma Calder d of William F. C. Aber

LOFTHOUSE Adam Robert   BSc(eng) 1962

LOGAN Ian William   LLB 1963
s of Robert L. BSc(Glas) teacher, asst dir of educ, coll prin and Agnes Coutts MA(Glas) teacher; b Glasg 19.1.41
CA 1966
Aber: app CA, qual asst Meston & Co CA 1963–68; acct, comp secy J. & J. Crombie 1968–75; fin. controller/dir Aber min water co from 1975
m Drumnadrochit 22.10.77 Margaret F. Morrison MA 1969 qv

LOGAN Robert Malcolm   MB ChB 1960
s of Robert L. BSc(Glas) teacher, asst dir of educ, prin Aber tech coll and Agnes C. Coutts MA(Glas) teacher; b Glasg 22.2.36
h o ARI 1960–61; asst g p 1961–62, locums 1962–63; P & O ship's surg 1963–64; g p Fraserburgh from 1964
m Aber 8.8.64 Lena J. Watkins MA 1959 qv

LOGGIE Derek Leith   *MA 1966
s of William J. L. off. man. and Margaret J. Bain driving s prop.; b Aber 13.2.44
posts in prod. control man. Glasg from 1966
m Aber 13.7.66 Christine E. Oliver BSc(Nott) dairy advis, lect d of Thomas H. O. Burton-u-Trent

LOGGIE Evelyn Joan   MA 1961
m Hill

LOGGIE Ronald George Cran   *BSc 1956
s of William G. L. police insp and Joan G. Riddoch; b Aber 3.1.34
scient off. Harwell 1956–57, Dounreay 1957–65; lect phys Thurso tech coll 1965–69, sen lect from 1969

m Glasg 23.12.67 Alexandra M. S. Thomson chem d of Alexander M. T. Glasg

LOGIE Alexander Wylie   MB ChB 1963
s of David L. LDS(Edin) consult. orthodontist and Nancy L. Macmillan; b Aber 5.11.38
MRCP(UK) 1972 DA(Lond) 1965 DObstRCOG 1967
h o Aber hosps 1963–66; g p trainee Insch 1966–67; m o MRC The Gambia W Af 1967–69; regist med Aber hosps 1969–72; lect therap Aberd 1972–73; sen med regist Aber 1973–76; consult. phys Scot. borders from 1976
m Aber 12.7.66 Dorothy E. Caie MB ChB 1966 qv

LOGIE John Robert Cunningham   MB ChB 1970
s of Norman J. L. MB ChB 1927 qv and Kathleen M. C. Neill BSc 1940 qv; b Aber 9.9.46
FRCSE 1974 FRCS 1975
h o ARI 1970–71; res fell. surg Aberd 1971–73; lect surg Aberd from 1973
m Aber 16.7.70 Rosemary Bates radiographer d of Victor B. Banchory

LOGIE Patricia Margaret Cunningham   MA 1969
d of Norman J. L. MB ChB 1927 qv and Kathleen M. C. Neill BSc 1940 qv; b Aber 26.10.48
teacher: Causewayend p s Aber 1970–72, Grove acad Dun 1972–73, asst prin Engl Albert s s Glasg 1973–76, part time Engl Greenock h s 1978, John Neilson h s Paisley from 1978
m Aber 10.4.70 Stephen A. G. Taylor MA 1972 retail area man. (Dorothy Perkins) s of Robert T. Cowdenbeath

LOGIE Raymond Alexander   BSc 1970
s of Alexander L. steward and Barbara L. Fraser; b Forres 11.6.49
Brit Aluminium Invergordon: cell tech 1971–72, prod. superv 1973–74, prod. supt 1975–76; prod. supt Kinlochleven from 1976
m Elgin 17.9.69 Janine M. E. Forteath teacher d of Ronald B. F. Elgin

LOGIE Robert John Milne   BSc(agr) 1966

LOMAS Christopher James   *BSc(agr) 1970
s of Ernest L. farm. and Myra H. Broadhurst; b Cheshire 20.9.41
MSc(R'dg) 1971
agr stud. Honiara Solomon Is 1971–72; agr off. Jenoi The Gambia from 1973
m Leeds 28.8.71 Susan J. Bentinck BSc 1969 qv

LOMAX Donald Ernest   MEd 1962
s of Ernest H. L. steelworks foreman and Edith Howarth; b Bolton 21.8.34
BA(Belf) 1960 DipEd(Belf) 1961 PhD(Manc) 1969
teacher Engl Bolton g s 1962–64; prin lect educ Didsbury coll of educ Manc 1964–69; lect educ Manc from 1969
m Belfast 27.12.62 Anne F. Kirkpatrick BA(Belf) head mod lang dept g s d of William R. K. Belf

LOMAX Kathleen Susan   MB ChB 1968

LONG Muriel Wood   MA 1962

LONG William Frederick   MSc 1967 PhD 1970
BSc(Lond)

LONGBOTTOM Molly Elizabeth   MA 1966
d of William F. L. postman and Williamina Munro;

b Ullapool 5.1.46
teacher: Luanshya, Kabwe, Mongu Zambia 1967–69;
bank clerk Ullapool 1970–71
m Ullapool 25.10.66 Alasdair B. Maclennan BSc(agr)
1966 *qv*

LONGMOOR Peter Morrice   MA 1969
  s of Alexander P. L. tea planter/eng and Helena M.
Morrice MA(Edin) teacher; b Elgin 10.8.47
ARICS 1974
app, asst valuation surv Aber from 1969

**LONGMORE Alexander Bryan George   MA 1956
                                                                    LLB 1958**
  s of William A. L. BSc(agr) 1920 *qv*(II); b Evanton
30.4.35
trust off. Nat Trust Co Tor 1958–60; TEFL Europ s
Modena Italy 1960–61; solic Inv from 1961
m Inv 29.9.58 Leonella L. A. M. Ferrari MA 1958 *qv*

LONGMORE Isobel   BSc 1962
  d of George M. L. rly eng driver and Davina M. Slater;
b Aber 8.11.39
teacher: maths Aber 1963–64, p s Boddam 1969–73,
maths Banff from 1973
m Aber 1.4.63 George H. Gray art teacher s of James G.
Aber

LONIE, Alice   MA 1969
  m Stout

LONIE Valerie Margaret Young   MA 1969

LOPATOWSKA Danuta Eleanora   MA 1970

LOPES Anthony Damian   MB ChB 1964
  s of Caetano M. L. and Alexandra L. b 29.9.35
MRCOG 1969 FRCS(C) 1972
h o: ARI 1964–65; sen h o, regist mat. hosp Aber 1966–
71; Canada: chief resid obst/gyn Mt Sinai hosp Tor
1971–72, consult. obst/gyn Tor from 1972

LORENZONI Maria Vittoria   MLitt 1969
  d of Paolo L. Dottore (Padua) lawyer and Gigiola
Avancini Dip(Florence) civ serv; b Trento Italy 15.7.36
Dott Ling(Venice) 1966
fell. Bozsista Venice 1970–73; teacher Engl; inst for
tourism Venice 1973–74, univ of Venice from 1974
m Coredo 11.12.71 Bruno Palaja Dottore (Padua) teacher
phys s of Pasquale P. Treviso Italy

LORIMER Alan Gilmour Bruce   MA 1967
  s of Frederick G. L. MA (St And) teacher and Helen
B. Anderson MA(Edin) teacher; b Inv 8.1.45
BSc(H-W) 1975
teacher maths Loretto s Edin 1967–68; instr lt RN Portsmouth 1968–71; Edin: app CA 1971–72, teacher maths
Craigroyston s 1973–74, asst prin maths St Augustine's
h s 1975–77, lect maths/statist Stevenson coll from 1977

LORIMER James   MB ChB 1970

LORIMER James William   *MA 1964
  s of James W. L. dye house operative and Elizabeth
C. Clark; b Aber 4.10.41
teacher: mod lang Aber 1965–67, Engl/hist Fort Hall
Kenya 1968–70, Fr/guid Aber from 1970
m Aber –.3.67 Eileen M. Reid MA 1965 *qv*

LORIMER Patricia Rose   *MA 1960
  m Young

LORVIK Edgar   *BSc(eng) 1970
  s of Paul L. carpenter and Torny M. Valset; b Malvik
Norway 6.5.45
civ eng with Sir Robert McAlpine & Sons Edin from 1970
m Bearsden 25.10.71 Marjorie L. Heath MA(Glas)
teacher d of Daniel H. Bearsden

LÖSETH Harald   MB ChB 1968

LOTHIAN Alan Thomas   *MA 1970

LOTHIAN Annona Joan   MA 1969

LOTHIAN John Kermack Milne   *MA 1958
  s of John M. L. MA(Glas) prof Aberd and Barbara
Cattanach MA(Glas) teacher/lect; b Saskatoon Canada
1.5.35
lect McG Montreal 1958–59; Shell internat Kampala/
Nairobi 1959–62
m Aber 4.1.58 Jennifer A. Y. Kay MA 1958 *qv*
d in plane crash Corsica 13.2.62 *AUR* xxxix 387

LOTT Edna Mary   *MA 1969
  d of Joshua L. painter/decorator and Agnes P. Donald;
b Newcastle-u-Tyne 11.5.47
civ serv (syst analyst) DHSS N'cle-u-Tyne from 1969
m N'cle-u-Tyne 11.10.69 John Hinds publican s of
Martin H.

LOUGHRAN Verne Elizabeth   MA 1970
  d of John M. L. MB ChB(Edin) HM comm for mental
welfare in Scot. and Moyra E. Reid MA(Edin) teacher;
b Edin 27.3.49
asst p r off. Glasg Citizens Theatre 1971–72; exec off.
HMSO Norwich from 1972
m Edin 6.10.73 Peter A. Hardingham leg. exec s of
Harry H. Norwich

LOUW Hendrik Andries   PhD 1958
  s of William A. L. farm. and Wilhelmina A. Bruyns
teacher; b Paarl S Af 3.9.29
BSc(agr)(Stellenbosch) 1951 MSc(agr)(Stellenbosch) 1955
Stellenbosch S Af: sen lect microbiol 1959–61, prof
microbiol 1961–73, dean of fac of agr from 1973
m Tulbagh S Af 1.4.55 Carolina J. de Kock teacher d of
Frederick C. de K. Tulbagh

LOVE Edwin Dereck   *BSc 1970

LOVE John Alexander   *BSc 1970

LOVE Penelope Rose   MA 1969
  d of Hugh L. man. and Margaret Anderson art
teacher; b Stockport 12.5.45
m Maryculter 1969 Andrew D. Barbour MA(Cantab)
fell. of CAI s of David B. BA(Cantab) Amersham

LOVE Philip Noel   MA 1961 cLLB 1963
  s of Thomas I. L. gen merch and Ethel V. Philip;
b Aber 25.12.39
ptnr Campbell Connon & Co solic Aber 1963–74, consult
from 1975; Aberd: part time lect evidence and proced
1968–74, prof conveyancing and prof pract of law from
1974
m Aber 21.8.63 Isabel L. Mearns teacher d of Innes T. M.
Aber

LOVIE David Christian
  see Shepherd

LOVIE John Cormack   *BSc 1958 PhD 1962

LOW Aileen Jean   MA 1966
m Smith

LOW Alan James   *BSc(for) 1959 PhD 1963
s of Robert M. L. MA 1925 *qv* and Katherine L. Gow
MA 1926 *qv*; b Elgin 18.5.37
MScF(New Brunswick) 1960
asst dept for. Aberd 1960–63; dist for. off. for. comm:
Inv 1964–65, Lochgilphead 1965; dist for. off. res div for.
comm Edin from 1965

LOW Alison Mary   *BSc 1965
d of John N. L. lect and Annabella M. Grant; b Dun
31.12.43
Dip Cartography(Glas) 1966
tech asst dept town and reg plan. Glas 1966–69
m Dun 1969 Wilfred Cameron MA 1965 *qv*

LOW David Melvin   BEd 1969

LOW Elizabeth Grant   MA 1957
d of Andrew L. farm. and Elizabeth M. Grant; b Aber
15.12.36
teacher: Sunnybank s 1958–61
m Peterculter 1.11.61 Douglas M. Benton estate man.
s of Joseph B. Malaya

LOW George   *MA 1956
b Aber 7.11.20
McGregor prize Aber coll of educ. 1957
teacher gen stud. Ruthrieston s s Aber 1957–60; lect
Engl, sen asst Engl and lib stud., head dept Engl and
commun stud. Aber coll of comm from 1960
m Banff 14.12.39 Winnifred Gerrard

LOW Isobel   MA 1968
d of David L. BSc 1938 *qv*; b Aber 1.6.47
jun syst analyst with nat data processing syst PO Lond
1969–71
m Aber 1.1.71 Roger L. Jagger army capt REME s of
Walter L. J. Worcester Park

LOW James Alan Scott   MA 1965 *LLB 1967

LOW John Royston   *BSc 1967

LOW Katherine Jean   MA 1961
d of Robert M. L. MA 1925 *qv* and Katherine Gow
MA 1926 *qv*; b Fochabers 15.4.40
teacher Forres 1962–66
m Lossiemouth 7.10.66 Douglas J. Murray MB ChB
(Edin) g p s of Iain M. M. MA(Edin) Portree

LOW Lindsay Peter   *MA 1961

LOW Margaret   *BSc 1965
d of David L. farm. and Annie J. Pirie teacher; b
Ellon 18.3.43
PhD(Glas) 1970
res asst: Cantab 1965–67, Glas 1967–71; post doct fell.
Denver Colorado from 1971

LOW Margaret   *MA 1968
d of James L. joiner and Ruth McPherson typist;
b Aber 5.6.45
Dip Sec St(Strath) 1969
secy to man. of IEG prod. group Ferranti Edin 1969–71;
secy NATO h q Brussels from 1972

LOW Mary Fraser   BSc 1967 Dip Ed 1968
d of David L. BSc 1938 *qv*; b Fraserburgh 1.12.45
teacher maths Craigroyston h s Edin 1968–72

m Edin 5.4.71 Donald R. Murray BA(OU) teacher art
RGC Aber s of James M. Edin

LOW Ramsay Allan   *BSc 1966
s of William J. L. MA 1937 *qv*; b Rhynie 26.6.44
indust chem ICI Nobel div Stevenston 1966–71; teacher:
Kilmarnock 1972–75, asst prin chem Ayr acad from 1975
m Aber 15.8.70 Esther B. McTaggart secy d of Andrew
McT. Kilbirnie

LOW Rose Margaret   MA 1959
d of Peter F. L. nurse and Rose H. McDonald nurse;
b Portsoy 12.11.37
Dip R Ed 1960
teacher: Aberchirder p s 1960–62, Rothiemay s s 1962–64,
Milne's h s Fochabers 1964–68, Broughton p s Edin
1968–69, Grantown g s 1969–70, Milne's h s Fochabers
from 1970

LOW Sheila   MA 1957
d of Alexander G. L. gen merch and Annabella
Laurie; b Aber 15.6.36
Aber: teacher St Margaret's epis s 1958–60, Engl Northfield acad 1960–71, prin guid from 1971

LOW Sheila Murray   MA 1970
d of John M. L. shift foreman and Jane B. Johnston
shop worker; b Montrose 16.1.49
Dip Soc Ad(Dund) 1971 CASS(Dund) 1973
trainee soc worker Glenrothes 1971–72; soc worker
Clackmannan from 1973

LOW Thomas Alexander   MA 1969

LOWE Maurice Douglas   MB ChB 1960
s of William H. L. store man. and Janet B. Dick;
b Aber 29.10.35
h o Stracathro hosp Brechin 1960–61; sen h o, obst h o
Ayrsh hosps 1961–62; trainee g p Bruton 1963–64; g p
Clive from 1964
m Aber 25.7.60 Dorothy M. Silver BSc 1956 *qv*

LOWE Rudolf   BSc 1970

LOWNDES Michael Daniel   *BSc(eng) 1966 MSc 1968
s of Daniel E. L. comp dir and Dorothy S. Croft;
b Walsall 25.10.43
res asst Aberd 1968–72; lect RGIT Aber from 1972
m Ullapool 30.3.68 Joan M. Fleming MA 1967 *qv*

LOWNE Barbara Oliver   *BSc 1963
d of Ernest W. J. L. chem eng and Dorothy B. B.
Coutts bookkeeper; b Aber 1.11.40
MPhil(Lond) 1966
dem in mycology UCNW 1965–67; res asst in bot ANU
1968–72
m Rochdale 18.12.65 Michael P. Austin BSc(Lond) res
asst s of Philip V. A. Hornchurch

LOWRIE Agnes Elizabeth   MA 1964
d of John L. fisherman and Elizabeth B. Fairbairn; b
Dun 4.2.44
teacher Engl: Powis s s Aber 1965–67, Ruthrieston s s
Aber 1967–69, Inverallochy s 1969–71
m Eyemouth 6.8.66 Alexander G. R. McKay BSc 1962 *qv*

LUBICZ-NAWROCKI Andrzej Emil Piotr   *MA 1969

LUBICZ-NAWROCKI Christopher George   *BSc 1966

LUCAS Alison Mary   MA 1967
resid Sheffield

LUCK Beverly Arline   MA 1960

LUDGATE Langley Robert   *MA 1966 Dip Ed 1974

LULMAN Phillip David   *BSc 1969

LUMSDEN Alexander Thomson McIntosh
                                                BSc(eng) 1970
s of Alexander T. L. vehicle bldr and Edna H.
McIntosh insur ag; b Aber 26.8.35
proj eng elect. eng Ayr 1970–71; elect. supt shipping
comp Glasg from 1971
m Aber 31.7.72 Catherine A. Sutherland MA 1970 qv

LUMSDEN Duncan Stordy   *MA 1967

LUMSDEN Ian McAllister   MA 1967
s of Peter M. L. comp rep and Catherine M. McGilvray;
b Perth 20.10.46
asst O & M analyst Shepherd Building Group York
1967–70; man. serv off. New Town Dev Corp Irvine
1970–72; O & M man. with Halifax bldg soc Halifax
from 1972
m Huddersfield 29.6.68 Joan D. Parker MA 1969 qv

LUMSDEN June Margaret   MA 1966
d of James W. L. master elect./ch off. and Marion
Jamieson clerkess-typist; b Aber 21.4.45
teacher: head maths dept St Dominic's g s Harrow
1966–73; maths tut. RNO hosp s Stanmore 1970–74;
maths Adeyfield comp s Hemel Hempstead 1974
m Aber Ian A. M. Grant BSc 1964 qv

LUNDSGAARD Anne   cMB ChB 1959
d of Erik L. civ eng and Else A. Engelsen; b Copenhagen 26.7.25
h o Woodend hosp Aber, ARI 1959–60; h o Frederiksberg hosp Denmark 1960; h o Aber mat. hosp 1960–61;
Denmark: part-time clin asst blood bank state serum
inst 1961; jun surg Copenhagen county hosp Glostrup
1961–62; jun surg Frederiksberg hosp 1962; res and clin
asst bloodgrouping dept state serum inst 1962–67; assoc
med dir reg blood transfusion centre Aalborg from 1967

LUNNEY David Christopher   *BSc(agr) 1967
s of Alfred J. L. chief fire off. and Dorothy E. Proctor;
b Stoke-on-Trent 15.2.43
labourer bldg sites and fish factory Aber 1967–69; asst
farm man. NOSCA Craibstone farm Bucksburn Aber
from 1969
m Aber 15.7.67 Marguerite P. Pritchard teacher d of
Richard W. P. Alness

LUNNEY Dorothy Christine   MB ChB 1970
d of Alfred J. L. chief fire off. AERE and Dorothy E.
Proctor med secy; b Macclesfield 15.12.47
DObstRCOG 1973 MRCGP 1976
h o Aber hosps 1970–71; sen h o: Inv hosps 1971–72;
Swindon 1972–73; various posts for Wilts health auth
1973; g p: British Army Germany 1973–76; Jeddah
Saudi Arabia from 1977
m Aber 15.7.70 Alexander S. Benzie MB ChB 1970 qv

LUQMAN Hafedh Mohammed Ali   MB ChB 1966
s of Mohammed A. L. LL B(Bom) barrister-at-law and
Ruqaiya Nasser; b Aden 11.12.39
h o Brighton 1966–67; sen h o surg, orthop, gen med
Aden 1968–74; regist med Aden 1974–75
m Aden 20.12.69 Raga Shamach of Mombasa Kenya

LWANGA Stephen Kaggwa   MSc 1967
s of Benoni K. L. ch min and Victoria Manjeri;

b Mukono Uganda 21.11.40
BA(Lond) 1965 FRSS 1967 MS(Harv) 1970
Makerere univ Kampala: lect 1967–69, lect. sen lect, assoc
prof 1971–78; statist WHO TDRC Zambia from 1978
m Kampala 9.9.72 Peace Kivengere d of Festo K.
Uganda

LYALL Alison   BSc 1966
d of William L. MA 1932 qv; b Galashiels 7.12.44
teacher: Aber 1966–67, E Lothian from 1968
m Aber 27.2.68 Derek Cuddeford MSc 1968 qv

LYALL Ardyn Anne   MA 1959
d of Andrew L. MA 1927 qv and Elizabeth H. M.
Innes MA 1924 qv; b Newburgh Aberdeensh 3.9.38
teacher Waterlooville Hants from 1970
m Aber 15.12.59 Alastair W. S. Brown MB ChB 1958 qv

LYALL Francis   MA 1960 cLL B 1962 PhD 1973
s of Francis L. capt MN and Agnes A. Thomson MA
1930 qv; b Aber 24.1.40
LL M(McG) 1965
asst lect, lect law Aberd 1964–69; visiting lect law Auck
NZ 1968; Aberd: lect publ law 1969–72, sen lect publ
law 1972–73, prof publ law from 1974
m Aber 1.8.67 Heather F. Smith MA 1965 qv

LYALL George Auchmuty   *MA 1968
s of George A. L. town plan. and Katherine Auchmuty;
b Edin 31.7.46
MSc(Strath) 1970 MRTPI 1973
plan. asst, sen plan. asst Dun 1970–75; plan. off. Scot. dev
dept Edin from 1975
m Edin 17.4.71 Pamela J. Fox secy d of John F. F. Edin

LYDON Richard John   *BMedBiol 1968 MB ChB 1971
s of James A. L. printer and Ivy M. Pearshall; b Birm
23.11.46
h o Woodend hosp Aber 1971–72; res fell. pharm Aberd
1972–73; trainee g p Bucksburn Aber 1973–74; g p
Tutbury from 1974
m Aber 13.12.69 Yvette H. F. Johnstone MB ChB 1972
g p d of John A. J. Aber

LYLE Ronald Cameron   *MA 1970
s of John L. shipmaster and Marjory C. Wilson;
b Edin 26.5.48
MSc(Birm) 1972
lect clin psych dept psychiat Edin from 1972
m Edin 10.9.75 Marilyn C. Dunn secy at Edin univ d of
James D. Edin

LYLE Valerie Catherine   MA 1967
m Innes

LYNCH George William   PhD 1964
BSc(econ) MSc(econ)(Lond)

LYNCH Michael   *MA 1969
s of Francis J. L. eng insp and Kathleen Lynch;
b Aber 15.6.46
lect hist UCNW from 1971
m Lond 1971 Mary Moore MA 1970 qv

LYON David   *BSc 1964 PhD 1968
s of James L. fisherman and Evelyn L. Noble; b Banff
13.6.42
res scient Esso Abingdon from 1967
m Oxford 17.10.70 Ferraleth A. Standing chirop d of
Samuel S. Oxford

LYON John Alexander   MB ChB 1956
s of Douglas L. MB ChB 1916 qv; b Peterborough

27.12.32
h o City hosp Aber, ARI 1956–57; g p Lond from 1957
m Aber 28.2.59 Ada M. Christie nurse d of Peter C. Aber

LYON Joyce Hilda   MA 1959
   d of Duncan L. farm. and Hilda L. McAra; b Kemnay
20.4.38
teacher Engl Northfield acad Aber 1960–62 and 1964
m Aber 28.7.62 James G. Cormack MN capt s of John C.

LYON Marjorie Anne   *MA 1956
   d of Adam J. L. hotel prop. and Marjory Baird hotel
prop.; b Peterhead 7.12.33
translator commonwealth bureau of anim nutrit Bucksburn Aber 1956–58; lib asst McG univ Montreal 1958–61;
teacher Ger (part-time) convent of sacred heart Aber
1969–71; teacher Fr/Ger St Margaret's s for girls Aber
from 1972
m Aber 6.9.58 George D. Watt BSc(eng) 1955 qv

LYON Patricia Mary Harper   MA 1959
   m Sloan

LYON Phyllis Stewart   MA 1967
   d of Franklin L. fish merch and Maisie A. G. Ramsay
market res; b Aber 22.2.45
market res trainee, jun res 1968–70; cler off. milk marketing board Aber 1971–72; cler work from 1973, in Canada
from 1974
m Aber 17.7.72 Ian Hamilton journalist s of John M. H.
Stonehouse

McALLAN Francis   MA 1965

McALLAN Frank Thomson   MA 1968

McALLAN Murray   *MA 1962 Dip Ed 1963

McALLISTER James   *MA 1963

McALLISTER Patricia Mary   *MA 1968
   d of Frederick G. McA. maintenance eng and Mary B.
Jamieson; b Ellon 28.8.46
teacher geog Thorold sen s s Ontario 1970–75
m Aber 16.7.69 Charles G. Duncan MB ChB 1967 qv

MacALPINE Bridget Fiona   MA 1963
   d of James MacA. army capt and Deirdre P. M.
Doherty; b Jerusalem 20.3.41
teacher: Maldon 1964–65, Engl Philip Morant c s
Colchester 1966–72, prin Engl from 1972

McANDREW Carl Stewart Cowie   BSc(eng) 1956
   s of Charles S. N. McA. signwriter and Rosanna
Cowie sales man.; b Aber 12.3.34
site eng Sir R. McAlpine on oil refinery Is of Sheppey
1956–58; nat serv RE Gibraltar 1958–60; asst eng city eng
dept Aber 1960–61; W. A. Fairhurst & ptnrs Aber:
eng 1961–77, ptnr from 1977
m Gillingham Kent 11.5.57 Irene Erridge shorthand typist
d of Robert F. E. Nott

McANDREW Donald Colin   MA 1970

McANDREW Gordon Miller   MB ChB 1957
   s of John B. McA. cert acct and Violet Coutts; b Aber
20.5.33
MRCPE 1962 MRCP(Lond) 1966 FRCPE 1975
consult. phys geriat: York 1971–73, Edin from 1973
m Aber 20.7.62 Leonora J. H. Murray MB ChB 1959 qv

McARA Michael James Dinnie   *BSc(eng) 1969
   s of Francis J. McA. BCom(Edin) CA and Florence

E. Winter; b S Croydon 11.10.46
Johannesburg: jun eng des off. 1969–71, site eng 1971–72;
site eng Lilongwe Malawi from 1972
m Johannesburg 4.9.71 Margaret A. Whiting secy d of
Noel F. W. Johannesburg

McAREE Derek William   MA 1965
   s of William McA. grocery man. and Mary A. W.
Taylor; b Dun 1.12.43
teacher: Aber 1966–67, Stirling 1967–73, asst prin mus
Stirling from 1973
d in road accident Blairdrummond 11.6.79

McARTHUR Alison   MA 1964
   d of Douglas P. McA. acct and Jessie L. Beaumont
clerkess; b Aber 8.2.43
teacher Abbotswell p s Aber 1965–68; supply teacher
Hawkesbury Ontario 1968–69
m Aber 14.7.66 Ian M. Warrack MB ChB 1966 qv

MacARTHUR Allan John   *BSc 1961 PhD 1965
   s of Donald M. teacher and Catherine M. Martin
teacher; b Ness Is of Lewis 26.11.39
Dip Polymer Sc and Tech (Brunel) 1965
res chem: Epsom 1964–68, Grangemouth from 1968
m Aber 5.8.64 Marjorie F. Cormack MA 1961 qv

MACARTHUR Angus   MA 1962
   s of Donald M. headmaster and Catherine M. Martin
teacher; b Ness Is of Lewis 22.2.42
teacher Engl/geog: Kirkton h s Dun 1963–68, Perth h s
1968–70; asst prin guid Grove acad Dun 1970–75,
prin guid from 1975
m Urquhart 20.7.66 Edna Douglas catering man. d of
Edmund D. Urquhart

**MacARTHUR Deirdre Catriona Caoirtiona
                                                MB ChB 1957**
   d of Archibald MacA. MA 1930 qv; b Tientsin N
China 27.6.33
h o: Woodend hosp Aber, Bridge of Earn 1957–59;
m o blood transfusion serv Glasg 1960–61; sen h o ARI
1962–63; m o Stirling c c 1967–74; cytologist Falkirk RI
1968–78, now Stirling RI
m Aber 3.4.59 Thomas G. Sprunt MB ChB(St And)
consult. orthop surg s of Thomas S. MB ChB(Edin) Dun

MACARTHUR Donald   BSc 1966
   s of Norman M. weaver and Jessie B. MacLeod;
b Carloway Is of Lewis 12.5.44
teacher: spec asst maths Inv 1967–72, part-time maths and
warden of boys' hostel Inv 1972–78; prin guid Inv r acad
from 1977
m Broadford Skye 3.10.69 Elizabeth M. Robertson
matron of hostel d of John R. Broadford

MacARTHUR Donella Catherine   MA 1965

MACARTHUR Doreen MacLeod   MA 1967
   d of Donald M. joiner, trades foreman and Kate A.
MacLeod teacher; b Stornoway 24.10.43
Lanarksh: teacher Ridgepark spec s 1968–72, Knowetop
spec s (later Firpark s) 1972–73, prin tut. from 1973
m Aber 2.7.71 Murdoch M. Smith clerk, RAF welf off.,
soc worker s of Murdo S. Stornoway

MacARTHUR Grace Sutherland   MA 1969 *1974
   d of Norman MacA. MA 1929 qv; b Falkirk 16.10.47
teacher Engl: Bankhead acad 1971–72, 1974–75, St
Margaret's s for girls Aber 1975–76
m Aber 7.7.70 Alexander S. Mather BSc 1966 qv

MACARTHUR Hamish Ewart   BSc 1969

MACARTHUR James   BSc 1960
 s of Kenneth D. M. joiner/Harris tweed weaver and
Marion MacLeod; b Carloway Is of Lewis 29.11.39
Dingwall acad: teacher maths 1961–72, prin guid from
1972

McARTHUR Jean Hamilton   *MA 1962
 MA(Cantab)
m Oliver

MacARTHUR Mairi Catherine Ealasaid   MA 1956
 d of Archibald MacA. MA 1930 *qv*; b Aber 15.8.35
teacher: Errol 1957–59, Callander 1959–60, Winnipeg
1960–61, Flatbush and Fawcett Alberta from 1961
m Westlock Alberta 4.7.62 Edward M. Elgert farm. s of
Darius E. Fawcett

McARTHUR Malcolm   *BSc 1969

MACARTHUR Malcolm William   BSc 1961
 s of Malcolm M. crofter/weaver and Margaret
Morrison; b Barvas Is of Lewis 28.3.40
asst exper. off. UKAEA Dounreay 1963–66; chief
assayer Af Manganese Comp Nsuta-Wassaw W reg
Ghana from 1966

McARTHUR Margaret Beaumont   MA 1958
 d of Douglas P. McA. comm acct and Jessie L.
Beaumont; b Aber 28.6.37
teacher maths/relig instr: Aber 1959–60, Largs 1960–61,
Kilmarnock from 1972
m Aber 5.8.60 George L. Marr MA 1957 *qv*

MACARTHUR Murdo   BSc 1966
 s of Donald M. crofter/weaver and Jane Morrison
teacher; b Breasclete Is of Lewis 20.2.46
teacher maths/sc Tain r acad 1967–69; prin chem South-
peace sen s s Dawson Creek BC Canada 1969–70;
teacher: chem/phys Hazlehead acad Aber 1970–72,
maths/guid Dingwall acad from 1972
m Tain 2.8.73 Ishbel M. Robertson teacher d of William
R. Tain

MACARTNEY Elizabeth Morag   MB ChB 1970
 d of William M. MA(Edin) C of S min and Jessie
H. I. Low teacher; b Glasg 2.6.46
h o RNI Inv, City hosp Aber 1970–71; doctor i/c Maasai
dev centre Olooseos, Kenya 1972–74
m Hutton 28.8.71 Colin P. Crabbie farm. s of John P. C.
BA(Oxon) Edin

MACARTNEY Ian Millar   *BSc 1970

MACASKILL Chirsty   MA 1958

MACASKILL Kenneth Finlay   MA 1967

MACASKILL Margaret Ann   MA 1956

MACASKILL Norman Duncan   *BMedBiol 1979
                                          MB ChB 1973
 s of Donald M. MB ChB 1946 *qv*; b Stornoway 29.7.48
MRCPsych 1977
h o Woodend hosp Aber, ARI 1973–74; sen h o psychiat
Kingseat hosp Newmachar 1974–75; regist: royal Cornhill hosp Aber 1975–76, Ross clinic Aber 1976–77,
RACH 1977–78
m Aber 25.9.70 Ann Kelly MA 1974 d of Kenneth K.

MacASKILL Thomas   MA 1963
 s of Ewen MacA. crofter and Mary Campbell; b Is of
Skye 20.2.40

teacher Engl/gen subjs: Annan acad 1964–66, Dunvegan
s Skye 1966–69; civ serv Lond from 1969

MACAULAY Charles Garden   *BSc(eng) 1970
                                                  MSc 1972
 s of Charles M. M. postman and Elsie M. D. McAllan;
b Midmar 8.10.48

MacAULAY Donald John MacPhail   MA 1968
 s of Murdo MacA. MA(Edin) min of relig and Dolina
MacPhail; b Edin 21.3.47
Glasg: teacher Engl Possilpark s s 1969–70, Waverley s s
1970–73, lect Engl Anniesland coll from 1973

MACAULAY Ewen Duncan Macrae   BSc 1959

MACAULAY Ian Innes   MB ChB 1959
 s of John L. M. MB ChB(Glas) g p and Rose W.
Innes nurs sister tut.; b Lybster 19.9.32
DObstRCOG 1961
h o hosps Aber, Inv 1959–61; sen h o Maryfield hosp
Dun 1961–62; regist med Stracathro hosp 1962–63; g p:
Dunblane, Fortrose, Alloa 1963–68, Aber from 1968,
dep police surg Aber from 1972; diving doctor Dept
Energy from 1974; m o BP Dyce from 1977
m Alyth 24.3.62 Helen L. Graham nurse d of James G. G.
Alyth

MACAULAY Jennifer Ann   MA 1968 Dip Ed 1969
 d of Duncan M. factory foreman and Ann MacLarty;
b Dunoon 8.8.47
teacher Karlstad Sweden 1969–70, Summerhill acad
1970–75, prin guid 1973–75, Honiara Solomon Is
1975–78, Fraserburgh (spec unit for maladjusted) from
1979
m Taynuilt 17.7.71 John F. Kinnon MB ChB 1971 med
pract s of John H. K. Inv

MACAULAY Margaret Grant   MB ChB 1968
 m Macdonald

McAULAY Margaret Isobel   MA 1965

McAUSLANE Nancy Barr   MA 1970
 d of John S. McA. joiner and Elizabeth Aitken;
b Glasg 11.3.49
teacher mod lang St Ninian's s Kirkintilloch from 1971
m Kirkintilloch 7.7.72 John Broom BSc 1971 med stud.
Glas s of John T. B. Kirkintilloch

McAUSLIN Edith James   BEd 1970
 d of James McA. bank man. and Edith A. Forrester
off. worker/book-keeper; b Anstruther 15.6.40
MEd(Glas) 1975
Glasg: res asst on youth proj 1970–71, commun worker
1972–73
m Anstruther 21.8.65 Robert Hamilton MA 1973 youth
worker/lect poly Liv s of William C. H. Cardross

McBAIN Anne   MA 1959
 d of Alan McB. MA 1920 *qv*(II, III); b Aber 11.8.38
secy Conemsco Lond 1960–61; teacher: Fr Cults acad
1973–74, Fr/Ger Alford acad 1974–76, supply from 1976
m Aber 3.6.61 David K. Craik farm. s of James C. MA
(St And) Alford

McBAIN Ian William Arbuthnot   *MA 1962
 s of William McB. and Margaret Buchan; b Peterhead
16.9.37
RAF educ off. 1963–71; teacher Engl Lossiemouth h s
1972–79; SOAF educ off. Muscat Oman from 1979
m Stonehaven 13.12.74 Sieghild Naue

MACBEAN Ann Veronica   MA 1962 Dip Ed 1963
 d of David A. M. marine eng and Lillias L. Davidson;
b Aber 5.5.42
BLibSc(BrCol)
lib Canada till 1971; educ lib Goldsmiths coll univ Lond
1971; then asst lib i/c non-print material Brighton poly
m Brighton 24.3.79 David E. House dep lib Brighton poly

MACBETH Katharine Marion   MA 1964
 m Dawes

McBLANE Fiona Agnes   LLB 1970
 d of John McB. chief insp royal mint and Fiona M.
Laing nurs. nurse; b Dunfermline 7.2.49
law app: Cupar 1970–71, Kirkcaldy 1971–72; solic Edin
from 1972
m Aber 2.8.72 John D. Stephenson MA 1969 *qv*

McBOYLE Evelyn Marguerite   *MA 1963
 d of Joseph M. McB. bank man. and Alice E. Reid
nurse; b Huntly 5.11.40
teacher geog/hist: Perth 1964–66, (temp) Bridge of Earn
1967
m Aber 27.8.66 Alexander J. Taylor BSc(agr) 1962 *qv*

McBOYLE Fredrick George   BSc(eng) 1958
 s of John McB. farm. and Elizabeth Dempster; b
Turriff 19.1.38
MICE 1964 MIWE 1968
site eng (contractors) NE and highlands Scot. 1958–61;
des off eng Snowy Mountains Aust 1962–63; asst eng
water dept Aber 1964; site eng (contr) Inv, Fort William
1965–66; asst, dep, prin eng loc govt Caithness/Sutherland
from 1967
m Aber 28.7.64 Elizabeth M. Harper MA 1964 *qv*

McBOYLE Geoffrey Reid   *BSc 1964 PhD 1969
 lect geog univ of Waikato Hamilton NZ 1966–69;
univ of Waterloo Canada: asst prof geog 1969–72, assoc
prof geog from 1972, assoc dean fac of environmental
stud. 1974–75, chmn dept geog from 1975

McCAFFERTY John Kenneth   MA 1956

McCALLION Margaret Theresa   MB ChB 1960
 m Gair
d 27.3.68

McCALLUM Archibald   MA 1967
 s of Archibald McC. fisherman and Agnes Ritchie;
b Aber 6.2.45
BA(OU)
grad trainee syst analysis Birm 1967–68; teacher maths,
asst prin maths Aber 1969–79; prin maths Westhill
acad Skene from 1979
m Cornhill 28.12.68 Violet H. Thom teacher d of Robert
T. Cornhill

McCALLUM Cornelius George   MB ChB 1964

McCALLUM Forbes   MA 1968
 s of James McC. loc govt off. and Isabella F. Livingston; b Aber 10.6.47
Dip Pers Man.(RGIT) 1969 IPM 1969
pers off. Glaxo labs Montrose 1969–73; pers man.
Richards Aber 1973–75; lect s of bus. man. stud. RGIT
Aber from 1975; councillor city of Aber dist from 1977

McCALLUM Moyra   MA 1957
 d of Albert McC. eng and Ruby Kemp; b Fraserburgh
17.7.35
BD(St And) 1965

teacher Aber 1958–62; lect Aberd 1969–70; par. deaconess
Aber 1970–71; coll tut. Edin from 1971

McCALLUM Nancy Buchanan   MA 1963

MacCALLUM Patricia Mary   MA 1967
 d of William K. MacC. turbine driver/fitter NSHEB
and Constance M. Rawson; b Inv 2.6.46
teacher nr Turriff 1968–69, Grangemouth 1969–72
m Glenmoriston 14.8.70 Robert G. Scott process oper
BP refinery s of Adam G. M. S. Armadale

McCALMAN Ian Alister   *MA 1964

McCALMAN Stuart   *MA 1969

McCANCE Mary   *BSc 1962

McCARTHY Daniel Peter Justin   MB ChB 1967
 s of Thomas J. McC. G.M. supt police and Margaret
M. J. Bowden civ serv; b Bootle 4.7.39
T.D.
work in med Lond, member Inner Temple, Home
Counties from 1969; major RAMC(V)

McCARTHY James   BSc(for) 1959
 s of Jacob F. McC. antique dealer and Lilybell
McKenzie; b Dun 6.5.36
Churchill fell. USA 1976
Leverhulme res schol Makerere coll Univ E Af Kampala
1959–61; dist for. off. Tanzania 1961–63; Nature conserv:
dep reg off. Grange-over-Sands 1963–69, reg off. Edin
1970–75; dep dir (Scot.) Nature conserv council Edin
from 1975
m Kampala 30.7.60 Margaret J. Stebbings teacher d of
Fred S. Romford

McCASKIE Thomas Conrad   *MA 1967

McCASKILL Betty Dalziell Craig   MA 1956
 m Aber 23.8.58 William N. Gilchrist MA 1952 *qv*

McCAW Graeme   *LLB 1968
 s of Robert McC. motor factor and Dorothy Booth
bookkeeper; b Aber 17.12.46
solic Lefevre & Co Aber 1969; ptnr Cohen & McCaw
m Aber 22.12.72 Teresa McHardy secy d of James McH.
Aber

McCAW Patricia Joan   MA 1966
 b Kilmarnock 11.6.46
teacher Fr: Manc 1967–69, Derby 1969–70, E Lothian
1972–77, Cambridge from 1977
m Aber 10.8.68 John F. Smithson BSc(eng) 1967 *qv*

McCLELLAND George   BSc 1970

McCLEVERTY Jon Armistice   *BSc 1960
 s of John F. McC. treas Aberd and Agnes E. Melrose
approved s matron; b Aber 11.11.37
DIC(Imp coll Lond) 1963 PhD(ICL) 1963
res assoc MIT USA 1963–64; univ of Sheff: asst lect
1964–65, lect 1965–73, sen lect 1973–74, reader inorg
chem from 1974
m Aber 29.6.63 Dianne M. Barrack MA 1961 *qv*

McCLUCKIE Peter   MA 1967
 s of Andrew McC. MA(Glas) teacher, lect Aber coll
of educ and Marion Richmond; b Kilmarnock 6.4.41
MI Pers Man.(Liv coll of comm) 1969
pers man.: Plessey Chorley 1968–73, Yorks Imperial
Metals Dun 1973–76, Distillers Co Edin from 1976

m Aber 14.1.67 Jane Paterson MA(Edin) teacher d of
John P. Sauchie

McCLURG Kathleen Joyce   MA 1967
    m Harrison

MacCOLL Malcolm David   BSc(eng) 1965

McCOMBIE Brian   MB ChB 1967

McCOMBIE Charles   *BSc 1967
    s of George McC. and Christina Ross; b Aber 25.6.45
PhD(Brist) 1971
sen scient off. reactor phys dept UKAEA Winfrith
1970–74; Switzerland: reactor phys Swiss Fed Inst for
reactor res Würenlingen 1974–79; proj leader at nat
co-operative for disposal of radioactive wastes Baden
from 1979
m Aber 12.7.67 Elizabeth Rennie d of James R. Aber

McCOMBIE Eric Lumsden   *BSc(eng) 1967

McCOMBIE Hamish Murdoch   BSc 1960
    s of James G. McC. bank teller and Elizabeth J.
Murdoch teacher; b Aber 30.8.38
weather forecaster Entebbe Uganda 1961–62; met.
analyst Nairobi Kenya 1962–66; scient off. world met.
organis Geneva 1966–73; scient off. policy plan. off. UN
environment progr Nairobi 1974–76; chief Asia div
world met. organis Geneva from 1976
m Nairobi 6.10.62 Barbara J. McCulloch secy, airline
stewardess d of Leonard D. McC. Stanmore

McCONACHIE Elizabeth Margaret   *MA 1969
    d of John A. McC. MB ChB 1945 *qv* and Jean M.
Macpherson MB ChB 1946 *qv*; b Aber 16.4.47
asst prin Home Office 1969–70; teacher ILEA from 1970
m Aber 28.8.70 Robin D. Reid MA 1969 *qv*

McCONDICHIE Jean McGiven   MB ChB 1965
    m Turner

McCONNACH Michael James   BSc(agr) 1962

McCONNACHIE Gordon   *BSc 1970 PhD 1974

McCONNACHIE Robin Inglis   *MA 1961
    s of William McC. bank man. and Christine J. Macrae;
b Uig Skye 27.2.40
BA(Oxon) 1963
Lond: asst prin Inl Rev secy's off. 1963–68, prin IR
secy's off. 1968–71, assoc dir Orion banking group 1971–
73, prin p secy to head of civ serv from 1973
m Cruden Bay 5.10.68 Gwendoline L. Glennie MA
1967 *qv*

McCONNACHIE William Allan   *MA 1967

McCONNEL John Robert   BSc(agr) 1969

McCONNELL Rosalind Anne   MA 1970
    d of Martin J. McC. sales rep and Adele Marioni
shorthand-typist; b Ellon 8.11.47
teacher: hist/mod stud. Peterhead 1971–73, hist Aber
from 1973
m Aber 22.10.73 James M. Livingston BSc(Glas) civ eng
s of James L. Airdrie

McCORMACK Agnes   MA 1964 Dip Ed 1965

MacCORQUODALE Helen Mary Franklin   MA 1968

McCRACKEN James Spowart   MB ChB 1957
    s of James O. McC. wool spinner and Anne Spowart;
b Glasg 8.12.30
DObstRCOG 1960 MRCGP 1967 DCH RCPSGlas 1968
h o Stirling, City hosp Aber 1957–58, sen h o women's
hosp Nott 1958–59; g p Nott, lect g p univ of Nott, clin
asst geriatrics Sherwood hosp Nott, clin m o Notts
AHA(T) from 1965
m Nott 5.12.59 Annie Richmond radiogr d of David R.
Nott

McCRAE Elizabeth Murray   BSc(agr) 1956
    d of Robert H. B. McC. MB ChB (Glas) g p and
Rhoda M. Sinclair dom sc teacher; b Wick 16.10.34
agr bact NOSCA Aber 1956–57
m Aber 15.6.57 Charles A. McCombie farm. s of Charles
McC. Knock

McCRAW Ian Alexander   BSc(eng) 1961
    s of Alexander J. McC. insur man. and Isabelle J.
Armstrong; b Perth 17.5.38
MIEE 1971 C Eng 1971
BBC Lond: proj eng 1961–77, sen eng broadcast syst
from 1977
m Lacey Green 7.9.63 Margaret A. Pitcher SRN d of
Douglas P. Lacey Green

McCRINDLE Dorothy Jane   MA 1969
    m Clark

McCRONE Michael   *MA 1970
    s of Alexander McC. furn salesman and Mary Robert-
son; b Aber 20.10.48
teacher Lond 1972–74, head of dept from 1974

MacCUISH Christine Mary   MA 1968
    d of Angus M. MacC. C of S min and Dolina Mac-
arthur p o clerk, nurse; b Glasg 19.9.48
teacher Nicolson inst Stornoway from 1969

MacCUISH Dolina   MEd 1970
    d of Roderick MacC. lighthouse keeper and Elizabeth
Macdonald; b Kenmore Rosssh 18.5.29
MA(Glas) 1950 Dip Ed(Edin) 1951
teacher Ardersier 1970, asst head Lochardil s Inv from
1970

McCULLOCH Helen Cormack   *BSc 1964
                                                              Dip Ed 1965
    d of Andrew R. McC. motor eng and Helen Cormack
tailoress; b Aber 2.2.38
teacher: Perth 1965–70, Bathgate 1970–71, Blackburn
1972; lect Bathgate from 1973
m Aber 8.8.70 Anthony R. Dallison BD(Lond) min of
relig s of Kenneth J. D. MA(Cantab) Daventry

McDERMENT John   MA 1958
    s of John McD. roadman and Grace E. R. Dixon
teacher; b Aber 2.5.37
nurs asst as nat serv 1959–61; teacher Aber/shire 1962;
employed Campbell & Sellar Aber mainly taxi driving
1962–64; civ serv MPNI Lond 1964–66; on cler staff
PO tel Aber from 1967
m Paisley 8.4.72 Barbara Dickson nurse d of Robert D.
Barrhead

MacDERMID Gordon Edward   PhD 1967
    s of Edward K. MacD. boilermaker and Katherine M.
Morrison; b Sydney Nova Scotia 22.9.39
BA(Mt Allison univ New Brunswick) 1959 BD(Halifax
Nova Scotia) 1961
parish min West Bay Nova Scotia 1962–65; Halifax NS

prof ch hist Pinehill div hall 1967–71, prof ch hist Atlantic s of theol 1971–74, parish min St Andrew's united ch from 1974/prof ch hist (part time) Atlantic s of theol from 1974
m Kentville NS Marjorie P. McReynolds BSc(Mt Allison) dietitian d of Kenneth McR. Dorval Quebec

MacDONAGH Brian James   LLB 1970

MACDONALD Aileen Ann   *MA 1970 MLitt 1972
**   Dip Ed 1972**
   d of Allan M. joiner and Jessie I. Finnie ch nurse; b Turriff 12.5.47
part time res stud. Aberd from 1972; lect Fr RGIT Aber 1973–75, asst edit. OUP from 1975

MACDONALD Alan Gordon   MB ChB 1960

McDONALD Alexander Sutherland   *BSc 1967

MACDONALD Alison Margaret   MA 1970
   d of Alistair J. M. marketing man. and Agnes B. Garden; b Kirkcaldy 2.3.48
teacher: Hollywood s Perth W Aust 1971–75, Swanley Kent 1975–77
m Aber 26.6.70 Brian D. Outlaw BSc 1971 petr geol s of Arthur L. O. Cranbrook

MACDONALD Alistair Gerould   *MA 1968
   s of Thomas K. M. BL 1933 qv; b NY 30.1.46
res stud. Aberd 1968–72; teacher mus Peterhead acad from 1972

MacDONALD Allistair Morrison   BSc(agr) 1956
   s of Donald MacD. BSc 1922 qv; b Barberton S Af 24.8.33
agr off. Brit col serv Tanganyika 1959–62; agronomist S Af sugar cane res stat 1962–64; tech off. export Murphy chem co Wheathampsted 1964–72; area man. USSR Stauffer chem co USA from 1972

MACDONALD Alys Taylor   MA 1963
   b Inv 17.1.43
m Inv 8.7.67 Alan D. Weir CA

MACDONALD Angela Ishbel   MA 1961
   d of Angus M. police serg and Mary M. Mackinnon SRN nurse; b Inv 21.11.39
Dip Secy Sc(Scot. coll of comm) 1962
statist asst SAI Edin 1962–63; f e teacher: Esk Valley coll Newton Grange 1963–65, Engl in secy coll Stockholm 1965–67, central coll of comm Glasg 1967–70
m Glasg 10.4.70 Alasdair B. Gillies BDS(Glas) dent surg s of John M. G. Glasg

McDONALD Angus   *MA 1958
   s of Alexander McD. carpenter/joiner and Elizabeth Watson; b Aber 4.1.36
H.M. col serv and overseas civ serv admin off. N Rhod/Zambia Lusaka 1959–71; secy to govt: Gilbert Is Tarawa 1972–78, Tuvalu Funafuti from 1979

MACDONALD Angus   MA 1967
   s of John M. weaver and Katie A. Macleod; b Harris 31.10.45
nat trainee hosp admin Edin 1967–69; admin asst Ninewells hosp Dun 1969–70; hosp secy: Samaritan hosp for women, W ophth hosp Lond 1970–74, St Mary's hosp Lond from 1974
m Holcombe 12.9.70 Jean Price midwife d of William P. Holcombe nr Bury

MacDONALD Angus John Alexander   *MA 1969
   s of Alan MacD. crofter and Morag A. MacDonald; b N Uist 6.4.47
res in Gaelic folk tales of N Uist at Aberd and s of Scot. stud. Edin 1969–72; teacher: geog Lochen s s Glasg 1973–74, Gaelic Portree h s from 1974
m Kilmore Skye 24.3.70 Mary MacDonald MA 1969 qv

McDONALD Ann Louise   *MA 1970
   m Scott

MacDONALD Barry   MA 1957 Dip Ed 1962
**   *MEd 1963**
   s of John M. MacD. miner, soldier, clerk etc and Barbara Ross tailoress; b Aber 29.9.32
teacher: Coalsnaughton p s 1963–65; lect coll of educ Glasg; curriculum proj evaluator Lond 1968–70; sen lect in educ, centre for applied res in educ univ of E Anglia 1970–76, acting dir from 1976
m Aber 5.11.58 Sheila Buchan receptionist, secy d of Maxwell C. B. Aber

McDONALD Catherine Pirie   MA 1961
   d of James C. McD. farm. and Helen B. Pirie; b Aberchirder 6.6.39
teacher Fr: Helensburgh 1962–63, Toronto 1969–72, Northampton commun coll Pa USA 1974–77; Rutgers NJ USA: grad stud. from 1976, teaching asst from 1977
m Georgetown Guyana 2.8.63 Roger H. Hewins BSc 1962 qv

MACDONALD Catriona   MA 1968 Dip Ed 1969
   d of Allan M. MA(Glas) head teacher and Kathleen M. Harkness; b Epsom 20.11.45
Dip TEFL(R Soc Arts) 1971
TEFL Berlitz Paris 1969–70, King's s Bournemouth 1970–71; EFL teacher supervis educ centre Kuwait 1971–73, ESP teacher fac commerce Kuwait univ from 1973
m Kuwait 11.11.76 John M. S. Roberts audio vis aids off. s of Charles W. R. Shaldon nr Teignmouth

McDONALD Charles William Esson   MB ChB 1966
   s of William McD. master slater and Diana S. Harper draper; b Aber 27.5.43
FRCSE 1971
h o: ARI, city hosp Aber 1966–67; sen h o WI Glasg 1967–69; regist: Bridge of Earn hosp 1969–72, Greenock RI from 1972
m Glasg 1.3.69 Jennifer M. Brown nurse d of William B. Glasg

MACDONALD Christina   MA 1961
   d of Angus M. boarding-house prop. and Mary Macdonald; b Drinishadder Harris 9.1.40
teacher: Engl/geog Paible j s s N Uist 1962–66, Engl/hist/geog Dufferin j h s Toronto 1966–67, Engl Kingussie s s 1967–68, Eng/hist Iochdar j s s S Uist 1968–70, remed Engl Mallaig s s from 1977
m Glasg 10.7.68 Angus A. MacLean MA 1956 qv

MacDONALD Christina Annabella   MA 1964
   d of Angus MacD. sheep farm. and Annabella MacLeod; b Tierra del Fuego 1.5.44
Dip Pastoral/Soc Stud. (St And) 1974
teacher: Dunfermline 1965–67, Aber 1967–73

MacDONALD Donald   MA 1960
   s of Kenneth H. MacD. crofter and Malcolmina Finlayson; b Glasg 6.3.38
div stud. Free Ch coll Edin 1960–64; licensed Stornoway 1963; Free Ch min Carloway from 1964

m Inv 11.7.68 Mary E. Macleod teacher d of Duncan J. M. Carloway

MacDONALD Donald   *MA 1962

MacDONALD Donald John   MA 1966
 s of Donald MacD. seaman and Mary MacLeod; b Stornoway 26.3.44
teacher Mount s Greenock 1967–68; asst prin teacher h s Inv from 1968
m Aber 2.8.69 Heather C. Paynter radiog d of Lionel P. Aber

MacDONALD Donald Stewart   *BSc 1965

MacDONALD Donald William Buchanan   *BSc 1966
 s of D. W. MacD. min of relig and Isabella M. Mackenzie MA 1930 *qv*; b Torridon 1.10.44
PhD(E Ang) 1969 MA(Cantab) 1974
res stud univ of E Ang 1966–69; SRC res fell. Cambridge 1969–70; dept genetics Cambridge: univ dem 1970–75, lect from 1975
m Lower Kingswood 24.8.74 Mary V. Goddard BSc (S'ton) plant path. d of Wilfred H. G. Lower Kingswood

MACDONALD Donalda   MA 1969
 m Stewart

McDONALD Duncan Charles   MA 1958
 s of William A. M. McD. gamekeeper and Annie R. MacLeod; b Glenmoriston 5.7.37
nat serv RAF UK, Germany 1959–63; teacher Lanarksh from 1964

McDONALD Duncan Gladstone   *BSc 1961
DSc(Lond)

MACDONALD Duncan William   MB ChB 1966
 s of William D. M. tea planter and Margaret McLean head inf s; b Inv 4.8.41
MRCPsych 1974
m o Zambia flying doctor serv Ndola 1968–69; m o Mombasa Kenya 1969–71; regist psychiat Rochford 1971–74; sen regist Lond from 1975

MacDONALD Elaine Margaret   *BSc 1969 PhD 1973

McDONALD Elspeth Caldwell   MA 1965
 d of Alexander McD. bank man. and Sophie E. Young; b Kirkwall 20.11.43
teacher Aber 1966–71
m Aber 3.4.69 Peter W. Rockwell MA 1965 *qv*

McDONALD Eric James   *BSc(eng) 1969 MSc 1971
 s of James C. McD. agr eng and Mabel Smith; b Ellon 12.8.47
R & D electronics eng Ferranti Edin from 1971
m Aber 18.9.71 Hazel A. Beattie catering man. d of William B. Brechin

MACDONALD Farquhar Graham   MB ChB 1957
 s of John M. hotel prop. and Ann Graham; b Edinbane Skye 10.7.28
h o Inv, Aber 1957–59; sen h o Glasg 1959–60; g p Bearsden 1960–63; Glasg from 1963
m Birkenhead 24.3.62 June S. Grant MB ChB(Liv) g p d of Ross A. G. MB ChB(Glas) Birkenhead

MACDONALD Fiona Mary   MA 1968
 d of Colin D. J. M. MA 1929 *qv* and Elizabeth M. M. Nimmo BEd 1970 *qv*; b Peterhead 4.11.48
teacher: Inverdee inf s Aber 1969–74; Engl in Haupt-

schule, Aue-Wingeshausen W Ger 1974–75; post-grad secy/linguist course Aber coll of comm 1977–78

MACDONALD Flora Ann   MA 1960
 b Harris 17.11.40
teacher: Scalpay p s Harris 1961–68, asst prin Engl/hist Sir E. Scott s Tarbert Harris from 1971
m Inv 26.7.67 William Morrison

MACDONALD Fraser John Rigg   *MA 1964

MACDONALD Gavin Grant   *MA 1963
 s of Donald M. shopkeeper and Elsie D. McDonald shopkeeper; b Inv 23.10.41
trainee man. dept store Manc 1966–67; computer progr: Lond 1968–73, Glasg 1973–77; shopkeeper Elgin from 1977
m Manc 24.4.71 Maureen Todd shop superv d of Hugh T. Manc

MACDONALD Hazel Jean   MA 1968
 m Mackenzie

McDONALD Ian   *BSc 1970

McDONALD Ian Alexander   MB ChB 1969

MacDONALD Ian Bradley   BSc(agr) 1957
 s of Donald MacD. BSc(agr) 1922 *qv* and Bessie MacBean nurse; b Barberton Transvaal 4.11.34
Dip Agr(Cantab) Dip Trop Agr(Trin)
agr off. col serv Somaliland 1959–60; comm sales man. Richardson's Fertilisers (ICI NI) Belf from 1960
m Aber 29.7.61 Kathleen F. Smith BSc 1959 *qv*

MACDONALD Ian Robert   PhD 1970
 s of Robert H. M. acct diplom serv and Jannetje W. Marang secy; b The Hague 4.5.39
MA(St And) 1961
lect Span. Aberd from 1965
m Bolton 20.4.62 Frances M. Alexander MA(St And) secy d of James R. A. MA(St And) Bolton

McDONALD Ian Ross   *BSc 1970
 s of James R. McD. painter/decorator and Elizabeth R. Massie shop asst; b Aber 27.11.47
geol Aust: Kambalda 1970–75, Townsville 1975–79, Tasmania from 1979
m Dun 5.8.70 Margaret E. Waterston BSc 1970 *qv*

MACDONALD Iris Dickson   MA 1969
 m Warburton

MACDONALD James Alexander   BSc 1956
 s of William M. fencing contr and Helen Mackay; b Balintore 28.8.32
RAF from 1956
m Amesbury 1970

MacDONALD James Cameron   BSc(agr) 1969
 s of Davaid MacD. elect. eng and Jessie C. Mackenzie; b Inv 12.8.45
asst lands off. DAFS Aber 1969–70, Ayr from 1970
m Glenurquhart Jean M. Girvan SRN d of David L. G. Glenurquhart

MacDONALD James Grant   BSc(eng) 1958

MACDONALD James Murdo   BSc(eng) 1961

MACDONALD Jane   MA 1969

MACDONALD Janice   MA 1969
m Blackhall

MACDONALD Jean Ronald   MA 1969
d of Ronald M. M. postman/poultry keeper and
Margaret M. Watson clerk; b Aber 12.10.48
shorthand typist Leeds 1970–72; showroom asst Dewsbury 1972–79; secy Mirfield from 1979
m Strachan 9.8.69 Martin J. Webster bldg contr s of
Willie W. Mirfield

MACDONALD Jennifer Alison   *MA 1964
d of Archibald M. master baker/horse breeder and
Georgina Morrison man. dir; b Elgin 17.9.43
res asst univ coll Swansea 1964–65; teacher Engl Elgin
acad 1967–69
m Aber 23.4.69 Stewart B. Dunlop BSc 1964 *qv*

MacDONALD Jessie Norma   *MA 1969

MACDONALD John   *BSc 1964
s of Norman M. wool mill worker and Christina
Mackay; b Stornoway 9.6.43
chem Brit steel corp Motherwell from 1966
m Glasg 7.8.71 Catherine Campbell nurse d of Edward
C. West Kilbride S Uist

MACDONALD John Douglas   MB ChB 1956
s of Douglas R. M. MB ChB 1921 *qv*; b Nairn 11.1.33
MID 1958 DObstRCOG(Lond) 1960 MRCGP 1964
h o Aber hosps 1956–57; nat serv RAMC Cyprus 1957–
59; sen h o obst Inv 1959–60; g p Nairn from 1960
m Rochdale Joy M. King teacher p e d of Robert H. K.
Rochdale

MACDONALD John Gillies   BSc 1970
s of Alexander M. seaman, lt RNR, crofter, millworker and Christina Gillies crofter; b Shawbost Is of
Lewis 3.9.47
teacher maths Helensburgh 1971–73, asst prin maths
from 1973

MACDONALD John Stuart   MA 1964

McDONALD Joyce Margaret   MA 1970
d of Ewan McD. MA(Glas) headmaster and Mary
Rowntree MA(Glas) teacher; b Glasg 17.2.50
LLB(Edin)
Edin: examiner Estate Duty off. 1971–73, organis univ
settlement 1973–74, teacher maths 1974; teacher law f e
coll Kirkcaldy 1974–79; worker commun proj N'cle
from 1974

MACDONALD Katherine Campbell   MA 1967

MACDONALD Kathleen Montgomery   MA 1965
m Rose

MACDONALD Kenneth Ian   *MA 1966
s of Norman M. MA 1932 *qv* and Bella MacLeod MA
1931 *qv*; b Inv 13.8.44
BPhil(Oxon) 1968
sen res off. Nuffield coll Oxon 1968–70; lect univ of
Essex Colchester 1970–72; dir SSRC surv archive 1972–
74; sen lect Essex 1975–76; univ lect/fell Nuffield coll
from 1976

MACDONALD Lesley Marjory   MB ChB 1970
d of Walter J. M. MPS dispensing chem and Frances
C. Macdonald; b Nairn 18.3.47
h o ARI, Culduthel hosp Inv 1970–71; sen h o Hull,
Rochdale 1971–72; trainee g p Aber 1972–73
m Aber 14.8.69 Paul Duffty MB ChB 1970 *qv*

McDONALD Linda Gordon   MA 1969
d of Donald McD. painter/decorator and Mary A. S.
Gordon; b Elgin 6.4.48
teacher Engl: Elgin acad 1970–74, Whitehills s s Dennis-
toun Glasg 1974–75
m Aber 24.8.74 David J. Grieve tv camera man s of
Herbert J. M. G. Motherwell

MacDONALD Madeline Viola   MA 1966
d of William J. MacD. master mariner and Madeline
Watt secy; b Macduff 11.5.45
teacher: Engl/hist/geog St Mungo's h s Falkirk 1967–69,
geog Banff acad 1969–72
m Portsoy 22.7.71 Ian Flory art teacher s of Reid F.
Huntly

MacDONALD Margaret Anne   MA 1970
d of Alexander MacD. stalker/for. and Annabel
MacLennan; b Dingwall 11.2.48
teacher Muir of Ord p s 1971–73, head Kinlochewe p s
from 1973
m Inv 8.12.73 Donald J. MacLean bldg contr s of
William MacL. Dundonnell

McDONALD Margaret Annie   MA 1961
d of John McD. bus driver and Alice Gauld doctor's
receptionist; b Aber 8.11.37
teacher Fr/Ger: Peterhead 1962–67, Inverurie 1967–68,
Peterhead 1968–77, prin Ger from 1977

MACDONALD Margaret Macleod   MB ChB 1968
d of Finlay M. min of relig and Margaret Anderson;
b Strath Halladale 24.12.44
DPM(Lond) 1971
Liv: h o Whiston hosp Prescot, St Helen's hosp 1968–69,
sen h o psychiat Sefton gen hosp 1969–71, regist psychiat
1971, asst psychiat psych day hosp 1972
m Inv 20.7.68 Alistair D. MacKay teacher s of Hector M.
Lochinver

MACDONALD Margaret Rose   *MA 1967
d of George M. and Rose M. Taylor; b Huntly 25.6.45
teacher Aboyne acad from 1968
m Huntly 30.7.67 Ian C. Cordiner BSc 1965 *qv*

MacDONALD Marsaili Elizabeth   MA 1961 LLB 1963

MACDONALD Mary   MA 1969
d of John S. M. fisherman/crofter and Agnes Murchison; b Sleat Skye 21.6.49
teacher Engl: Dalkeith h s 1970–71, part time Lochend
s s 1974; dem model ag Edin 1973; teacher: Paible j s s
1977, hist Portree h s from 1977
m Kilmore Skye 24.3.70 Angus J. A. Macdonald MA
1969 *qv*

MACDONALD Mary Bell   MA 1968

MACDONALD Morag Ann   MA 1965
d of Allan M. crofter and Marion A. Macdonald cook;
b N Uist 17.12.43
teacher: maths Paible s 1966–77, guid 1975–77, maths
Hawick h s 1977–78, maths/guid Paible s from 1978
m Daliburgh S Uist 28.6.79 Allan MacIsaac bldr s of
Donald A. MacI. Locheport N Uist

MACDONALD Morag Holmes   *MA 1970
d of Ronald M. M. pattern maker/poultry farm./post-
man and Margaret G. Watson bank clerk; b Aber
12.10.48
caseworker in fam serv. unit Glasg from 1970

MACDONALD Murdina   MA 1968 CASS 1970
m Maciver

MACDONALD Murdo   *MA 1970

McDONALD Muriel   MA 1958 Dip Ed 1959
d of Edward McD. publican, insur man. and Betsy
Goodall clerkess; b Brechin 19.3.37
teacher: Errol 1959-60, Perth 1960-65, remed Kincardine
from 1973
m Brechin 22.7.61 John Adams roads eng/div road surv
s of Frederick A. Brechin

MACDONALD Neilalice   MA 1966

MACDONALD Norma Myra   *MA 1970

MACDONALD Paul   MA 1968
s of John M. charge eng (power stat) and Mary E.
Gardiner; b Dartford 4.7.46
Dip Career Guid (Strath) 1972
careers off. older leaver spec Glasg 1968-73; area trg
advis Furniture & Timber ITB Perth 1973-76; lect psych/
careers guid Hull from 1976
m Aber 4.9.70 Jennifer A. Cantlay d of William J. C.
BSc(agr) 1943 qv

MACDONALD Ranald Roderick   *BSc 1967
MSc(Stir)

McDONALD Raymond William George   MA 1966
CA

MacDONALD Rhoda   MA 1965
d of Norman MacD. crofter/weaver and Ina Mac-
Lennan; b Lurebost Is of Lewis 24.1.44
teacher Engl Dingwall acad 1966-72, asst prin Engl from
1972

McDONALD Ronald William   MA 1970 MEd 1974
s of Ronald McD. bulldozer driver and Annie M.
McIntosh; b Longside 31.5.35
FSAScot
prin teacher hist Torry acad Aber from 1971
m Aber 7.12.63 Sheena C. Jackson d of James J. Aber

MACDONALD Sandra Irene   MB ChB 1965
d of Walter J. M. pharm and Frances C. Macdonald;
b Nairn 13.3.41
h o: Dumfries, Aber, Inv 1965-67; sen h o Dunfermline
1967-68; regist gen med Inv 1968-70; regist geriat Oslo,
Norway 1971-72, bedriftslege Namdal sykehus from 1972
m Nairn 21.4.73 Arne J. Aursnes C.Ph.(Oslo) teacher
s of Ivar A. Namsos Norway

MACDONALD Sheila Mary   MA 1968

McDONALD Sheila Young   MA 1957
d of Alexander McD. bank man. and Sophia E.
Young; b Kirkwall 28.3.36
teacher: geog Aber 1958-60, Malmesbury 1961-62,
Aber 1962, high s Blantyre 1962-63
m Aber 5.11.60 Ronald G. Johnson BSc 1957 qv

MacDONALD Shina Ann   MB ChB 1967
d of Murdo MacD. joiner and Bessie B. MacKillop
teacher; b Inv 19.12.40
h o RACH, Woodend hosp Aber 1967-68; g p: Crieff
1968-69, Ontario 1970-71, Kinlochleven 1972-77; part-
time work later
m Kinlochleven 29.10.77 James M. Young contr s of
Archibald M. Y. Ballachulish

MacDONALD Theresa Elizabeth   *MA 1963
d of Donald MacD. for. and Margaret Henaghen cook;
b Glasg 18.2.42
teacher Haverhill 1963-64; part-time tut. extra-mural
dept Glas from 1969
m Fort Augustus 17.8.63 John F. Ross MA 1961 qv

MacDONALD Vernon   BSc 1966

MACDONALD William   MB ChB 1959

MACDONALD William James Douglas   *BSc 1967
                                              PhD 1970
s of A. W. M., MC TD JP free lance journalist and
Muriel F. Pirrie; b Aber 26.3.45
ARIC 1971 FCS 1972 ACCA 1974
lect: Makerere univ Kampala Uganda 1970-72, Cardonald coll of f e Glasg 1973-74, sen lect from 1975
m Aber 20.8.70 Patricia A. Craigen univ tech d of
William A. C. Aber

McDONALD William Reid   *MA 1956

McDONNELL Edwin Joseph Anthony   *BSc 1967

McDOUGAL Malcolm James   *MA 1968 Dip Ed 1969
s of James McD. cabinetmaker and Christina D.
Edmund shop asst; b Holyoke Mass USA 5.1.32
teacher: Engl AGS 1969-70, spec asst Banchory acad
1970-72, prin Engl Alford acad 1972-77
m Aber 6.4.57 Maureen Knowles mus teacher d of
George K. Aber
d Aber 1.11.77

McDOUGALL Alice Joan   MA 1969
d of Kenneth McD. lab/crofter and Catherine Mac-
Leod; b Barvas Is of Lewis 2.6.47
teacher hist/mod stud. Finnart h s Greenock 1970-74
m Crieff 5.8.72 Kenneth J. Allan BSc 1971 teacher s of
John R. A. Beauly

MacDOUGALL Carol Campbell   *MA 1969
d of Peter C. MacD. insur ag and Caroline D. Dallas;
b Stonehaven 26.9.46
teacher Fr/Ger Edin 1970-72; Germany: teacher Engl
Bottrop 1972-73, Freising 1973-75; asst prin mod lang
Edin from 1976

MACDOUGALL John Davidson   MB ChB 1968

McDOUGALL John Finlay   *MEd 1970
s of Thomas W. McD. MA(Glas) teacher and Emily F.
Marshall teacher; b Paisley 15.12.45
MA(Glas) 1967
admin asst Edin 1967-68; teacher: classics RGC Aber
1970-73, prin classics Dunoon g s from 1973

McDOUGALL Martin Andrew   LLB 1969
s of Andrew C. McD. bank man. and Mary A. Fry;
b Oban 24.7.48
solic Greenock from 1969
d 9.1.81

McDOWALL Judith Howie   *MA 1967
d of William C. McD. BA(Oxon) high court judge
(Anglo-Egypt, Sudan), chief exec Nobel explosives Co
and Margery H. Wilson BA(Oxon) member of commun
council, commun health council/JP; b Birm 16.2.45
VSO teacher econ Silliman univ Dumaguete City Philippines 1967-69; exec off.: P O Lond 1969-70, admin
postal man. coll Rugby 1970-73; post exec 'C' finance
div operations postal board h q in Scot. Edin from 1973

McDOWALL Robert John   *MA 1964

McDOWELL Lindsay Anne   *MA 1967
d of John C. McD., BCom(Lond) comp dir and Molly
Hirst lib/teacher; b Dun 19.6.44
m Broughty Ferry 25.8.67 Roger D. Watkins MB ChB
1968 *qv*

McEWAN Brian Grant   MA 1959

McEWAN Iain   *MA 1962
b Perth 26.10.39
teacher hist Lenzie acad 1963–67; prin hist Arbroath acad
1967–74, Morgan acad Dun from 1974
m Edin 14.7.66 Nancy Graham MA(Edin) teacher

McEWAN Irene Barbara   *BSc 1968
d of Andrew D. McE. CA and Irene M. Kinnear;
b Bradford 15.8.46
Manc: des progr for Internat Computers 1968–71; syst
progr reg computer centre from 1971
m Manc 9.3.73 Frederick Lawton draughtsman, computer
oper man s of Frederick L. Stretford

MacEWAN James Alex Iain   *MA 1969 BD 1972
s of James A. MacE. C of S min and Edith M. Culbert
teacher; b Glasg 27.7.47
C of S min: asst Lochwood par ch Easterhouse Glasg
1972–74; min Stockethill par ch Aber 1974–80, Abernethy, Cromdale and Advie from 1980
m Aber 4.7.69 Aileen A. Barron MA 1968 *qv*

McEWEN Andrew Durrad   BSc(for) 1968
s of Jock M. McE. LLB(NZ) and Ruth C. Durrad;
b Feilding NZ 12.6.44
BSc(Well NZ) 1966 PhD (Cant. NZ) 1976
NZ for. serv.: Invercargill 1968–71, scient. for. res inst
Rotorua from 1971
m Wellington NZ 17.12.66 Winifred M. Fleming BSc
(Vict NZ) teacher d of Charles A. F. BA(NZ) Wellington

MacEWEN David Martin   LLB 1967

McEWEN Gavin Thomas   *MA 1968
b Hawick 21.10.46
MA(Kansas) 1970 DPhil(Oxon) 1980
Aberd-Kansas univ grad exch scholarship, asst instruct
Lawrence Kansas 1968–70; res Bonn W Ger 1970–72;
stud. Queen's coll Oxon 1972–75; Inland Revenue from
1975
m Arbroath 10.7.71 Aileen M. Petrie teacher

McEWEN James Gordon Keith   MSc 1962
s of McEwen MD(West Ont) phys and Laura B. Errett;
b Ekfrid Township Ontario
BSc(for)(Tor)
Canada: res scient for. Ont 1962–70; lect Lakehead univ
Thunder Bay Ont from 1973
m Ottawa 16.6.45 Ruth E. Gill
d Ontario 10.1.75

McEWEN John Fraser   BSc(for) 1959

MacEWEN Lawrence Traquair   BSc(agr) 1964
s of William I. L. MacE. RN, farm. and Edith A. T.
Nicol BA(Cantab) marine biol; b Is of Muck 24.7.41
farm. Is of Muck

McFADDEN Eleanor Thomson   MA 1970
d of Jack R. McF. man. dir paint manuf and Agnes
H. D. Dunlop hairdresser; b Glasg 12.5.48
computer progr dept soc med Aberd 1970–74; comp
progr syst analyst Grampian health board Aber from
1974

McFADDEN Ian Andrew   BSc 1964
s of Jack R. McF. comp dir/secy and Agnes H.
Dunlop; b Ayr 15.11.42
Aber: trainee man. fish processing indust 1964–66, prod.
man. 1966–69, gen man. 1969–76, dir 1976–77, man. dir
from 1977
m Aber 3.10.66 Evelyn J. Churchard d of John C. Aber

McFADDEN John Alexander Crawford   MA 1959
LLB 1962
s of John A. McF. MA(Glas) C of S min and Johanna
L. D. Todd; b Dunoon 11.9.36
leg. asst, ptnr Edin 1962–68, Dumfries from 1968
m Surbiton 27.8.64 Patricia M. Thompson MB ChB
1963 *qv*

MACFARLANE Alexander   BSc(eng) 1959
s of Duncan J. M. farm. and Amelia B. P. Massie;
b Culsalmond 24.3.37
aircraft stress eng Warton 1959–61; aero eng repair eng
Glasg 1961–62; Hamilton: tech asst aero eng dev 1962–
64, sect. leader aero eng dev 1964–66, asst dev eng
1966–69; E Kilbride: dev eng aero eng 1969–73, proj
man. from 1974
m Glasg 25.9.68 Anne J. Sutherland MA(Glas) teacher
d of Donald S. Wishaw

MACFARLANE Alexander William   *BSc 1970
s of Frederick A. M. farm. and Mary Reid farm.;
b Insch 23.7.48
asst eng Plessey Co Poole 1970–72; des eng GIM Glenrothes from 1972
m Aber 11.8.72 Irene E. Horn MA 1969 *qv*

McFARLANE Barbara Lena   MA 1968 LLB 1971
d of Harry A. McF. area eng g p o tel and Lena R. C.
Still MA 1969 *qv*; b Aber 9.7.47
Aber: law app Paull & Williamsons advoc 1971–73,
leg. asst Burnett & Reid advoc from 1973

MACFARLANE Duncan John   *BSc 1963
s of Duncan J. M. farm. and Amelia B. P. Massie;
b Insch 23.12.40
DIC 1964 PhD(Lond) 1969
seismologist The Hague 1968–69, Lagos 1969–73, Lond
from 1974
m Lond 20.7.67 Margaret O. Conroy teacher

McFARLANE Gladys   MA 1968
m Taylor

McFARLANE Hugh   BSc(eng) 1965
s of William A. McF. MA(St And) C of S min and
Jeanie K. Roberts MA(Edin) teacher; b Edin 24.12.43
Aber: gen asst dist eng NSHEB 1967–69, 3rd asst dist
eng from 1969
m Glasg 21.7.73 Catherine S. Grant teacher d of Archibald G. Glasg

MACFARLANE Michael Watt   MA 1959

MACFARLANE Mildred   MA 1956
d of Francis T. M. policeman and Gladys Orr clerkess;
b Port Glasg 23.2.35
teacher: Tillydrone p s Aber 1957–60, Engl Prince
Rupert s Rinteln Germany from 1973
m Aber 27.12.58 John T. Coull MB ChB 1958 *qv*

MACFARLANE Murdoch   MA 1962
s of Murdo M. mill foreman and Henrietta M.
Mackenzie; b Is of Lewis 30.11.40
BEd(Sask)

teacher Hilton Ross-shire 1963–67; Saskatoon Sask:
teacher 1967–74, vice-prin 1974–77, prin from 1977
m Sturgis Sask Caroline D. Wilgosh d of Mike W.
Hazel Dell Sask

MACFARLANE Neil Archibald Arthur   *BSc 1967

McFARLANE Richard Hamilton   LLB 1970
 s of Ian D. McF. MA(St And) prof Fr Oxon and
Marjory N. Hamilton MD(St And) med pract; b Cambridge 5.5.47
law app, solic Cupar from 1971
m St And 14.4.73 Anne M. Steele nurs nurse d of
Andrew R. S. St And

McFARLANE Wilma   MA 1966
 d of William P. McF. linotype oper and Mary
Anderson; b Aber 11.7.46
exec off.: DHSS Lond 1967–69, soc sc res council Lond
from 1970
m Aber 30.7.66 Roderic G. McAra marketing exec
pharm s of Alistair R. McA. MA 1937 qv

MacFARQUHAR David MacGregor   *MA 1966

MACFARQUHAR Iain Alexander   MB ChB 1959
 s of John M. M. MB ChB 1923 qv; b Kintore 27.11.36
DObstRCOG 1961
g p Elgin from 1962
m Ilford 9.3.63 Margaret O. Bell asst purser d of William
T. B. Ilford

MACFARQUHAR Joan   MB ChB 1957
 d of John M. M. MB ChB 1924 qv; b Kintore 9.9.33
DA 1961
h o: Woodend hosp, mat. hosp Aber 1957–59; h o S C
hosp Glasg 1959–60; sen h o anaest Inv 1959–60; regist
anaest Aber 1960–62
m Aber 15.9.62 William J. Leishman MB ChB(Glas)
part-time anaest Stirling R I s of James L. Condorrat

MacFARQUHAR Roderick Campbell   *MA 1963

McGEOCH Gay Christine Kesteven   *MA 1966

McGHIE Duncan   MB ChB 1966

McGHIE Jean Grant   MA 1962
 d of John McG. MA(Glas) C of S min and Isabel R.
Allan; b Camelon 23.9.41
syst analyst Internat Computers Nairobi from 1963

McGHIE Rhona Robertson   *MA 1958
 d of John McG. MA(Glas) min of relig and Isabel R.
Allan; b Falkirk 5.11.36
teacher: Blairgowrie 1959–61, Aber 1961–66, Homa Bay
Kenya 1966–72
m Nairobi 19.6.71 Brian C. Hurst BA(Cantab) teacher
s of Robert J. H. BA(Cantab) Lond

McGIBBON Graeme   MSc 1964 PhD 1967

McGILL Gordon Ramsay   MA 1965

McGILL Janice Margaret   MA 1969
 m Burn

McGILL Robert Leiper Craig   MA 1969
 s of Patrick J. McG. univ hall porter, buyer elect. store
and Robertina Craig hosp superv; b Aber 8.3.45
teacher hist Peterhead acad 1970–73; asst prin hist from
1973; part-time teacher f e Peterhead from 1971

m Aber 4.4.67 Margaret Beattie teacher d of John B.
Cove

MacGILLIVRAY Alexander Jamieson   *BSc 1958
                                            PhD 1962
 s of Adam MacG. shoemaker and Isabella Jamieson;
b Insch 24.7.36
scient Imp Cancer res fund Lond 1961–67; sen scient asst
Beatson Inst cancer res Glasg 1967–76; reader in biochem
s of biol Sus from 1976

MacGILLIVRAY Alexander John   MA 1966
 s of Donald MacG. tweed merch and Effie Robertson
teacher; b Benbecula 31.10.43
teacher Castletown 1967–71; head: Knock p s Is of
Lewis 1971–75, Balivanich p s Is of Benbecula from 1975
m Inv 27.12.68 Annie MacLeod MA 1967 qv

McGILLIVRAY Rhonda Moray   MA 1968
 d of Donald R. McG. army major, hotel man. and
Henrietta MacLennan bookkeeper, hotel man.; b Aber
19.3.47
soc worker Aber c c 1968–72
m Aber 7.9.71 John A. G. Scott occupational therap
s of Alexander G. S. Aber

McGINLEY Michael Owen   MA 1969 LLB 1971

McGINN Barry Charles   MA 1966
 s of Ronald McG. turf comm ag and Susanna Lowdon;
b Inv 1.7.45
Dip Rose Bruford coll of sp and drama 1969
actor Provinces/Lond and for tv and films from 1969

McGLASSON John Christopher   *MA 1964

McGOOGAN James Alexander   LLB 1969
 s of James M. McG. BSc(Glas) teacher and Mary J.
Davies; b Coatbridge 22.6.48
Dip Criminology(Edin) 1970
soc work asst Glasg 1970–71; asst reporter to ch panel
Glasg 1971–72, dep reporter Paisley 1972–73; law app
Coatbridge 1973
m Aber 18.8.72 Euphemia Brand MB ChB 1973 path.
d of James B. Ford

McGOWAN George Cockburn   BSc(eng) 1966
 s of George McG. bank man. and Annabella Cockburn;
b Thurso 29.5.43
asst civ eng Marples Ridgway Aber, Port Talbot 1966–68;
site ag: F. J. C. Lilley (Marine) Aber, Shetland, Glasg
1968–71, W. H. Rankin Is of Mull 1971–72, F. J. C.
Lilley (Marine) Glasg, Montrose, Aber 1972–75; self-
employed civ eng contr George C. McGowan (contracts)
Banchory from 1975
m Aber 12.8.69 Geraldine M. Drayson BSc 1968 qv

McGOWAN Peter Anthony   *MA 1969

McGRATH Katharine Ann   *MA 1968

McGREGOR Alan Graham   *BSc(agr) 1970
 s of Ian G. McG. MB ChB(Edin) g p and Mary I.
Allan land army, ch welfare off.; b Edin 17.6.46
ICI agr div rep Shrewsbury area Staffs/Shropsh from
1970, later marketing rep Hereford/S E Wales

MacGREGOR Alan Mackenzie   *MA 1966
 s of Laurence MacG. acct and Henrietta A. Mackenzie;
b Inv 23.6.44
marketing exec York 1966–68; Lond: marketing man.
1968–71, man. internat fin. from 1972
m Lond –.7.77 Anne Roberts MA 1966 qv

MacGREGOR Alastair Scott Russell *MA 1966
s of Norman MacG. MBChB(Glas) and Mary D. R.
Roddick; b Glasg 30.6.43
sales exec: Xerox Ottawa 1967–74, Rank Xerox Glasg
1974–77; br man. Nashoa Ottawa from 1977
m Vancouver 21.2.69 Janet Myles d of Gwyn D. M.
Ottawa

MACGREGOR Andrew McPherson MA 1969

McGREGOR Ann Lewese *MA 1970
d of Lewis McG. PO exec eng and Maria M. Forbes
secy; b Aber 1.11.47
MA(McM) 1972, BEd (K'ston, Ont) 1974
m Aber 13.12.69 Marc O. M. Abrioux MA 1971 s of
Olivier M. A. PhD 1949 *qv*

MacGREGOR Campbell MB ChB 1968
s of Robert A. MacG. bank man. and Mary B.
Hamilton lib; b Edin 15.8.42
h o ARI, Woodend hosp Aber, RACH, mat. hosp Aber
1968–70; g p Aber from 1970
m Coatbridge 31.10.69 Jennifer W. Scott BA(Strath) soc
worker d of William T. S. Coatbridge

MACGREGOR Catherine Elizabeth MB ChB 1965
m Tucker

MacGREGOR Christina Una MA 1969

McGREGOR Colin Masson *BSc 1968 PhD 1971
b Aber 2.12.46
lect maths Glas from 1971
m Bearsden 29.6.79 C. Joyce Paterson

McGREGOR David *BSc 1967
s of Patrick D. McG. grocer and Alexandrina M.
McKay; b Aber 29.11.44
res asst Unilever res lab Aber 1968–70; tech Zool soc of
Lond 1970–73, res fell. 1973–76, higher scient off. MAFF
lab Weymouth from 1976
m Aber 5.7.69 Sheila M. McKenzie BSc 1966 *qv*

McGREGOR Douglas Robert *BSc 1961

McGREGOR Elizabeth Margaret MA 1965

McGREGOR Forbes Clement BSc(eng) 1965
s of David T. McG. army off. and Mary R. Forbes
tailoress; b Nairn 14.10.42
Canada: jun eng Northern Elect. Co Montreal 1965–67;
central off. equipment eng B C tel co Vancouver 1967–
68; asst master Cambrian coll Sudbury 1968–69; chief
numerical control instr Sperry-Rand Montreal 1969–71;
assoc master Sault coll Sault Ste Marie from 1971
m Montreal 2.9.67 Laura M. M. Demers secy d of
Louis T. D. Kiosk Ontario

MacGREGOR Gelda Margaret *MA 1968
d of Ian B-K. MacG. MB ChB(Edin) g p, reg m o and
Rosa F. McLaren MB ChB(Glas) g p; b Kilmarnock
5.9.46
MPhil(Edin) 1974
grad teaching asst univ of W Ont Canada 1968–69,
res asst dept educ stud. Edin 1970–72; home-school
relations off. 'Priority' educ proj Liv 1972–74; adult
literacy organis Dun 1974–75; adult literacy co-ordinator
Lothian reg. from 1975

McGREGOR Griselda Sarah MA 1969
d of Alexander D. MacG. army off. MBE MC TD and
Margaret S. M. Reid MB ChB 1926 *qv*; b Aber 25.5.47
medal for journalism from American Legion 1975

travel USSR, Poland, Czechoslovakia, W Europe 1969–
70; journalist D.C. Thomson's *Dundee Courier* from 1970
m Dun 18.7.75 Charles H. Main print man. s of William
M. Aber

MacGREGOR, Helen Elizabeth MA 1970
m Frew

McGREGOR Ian *BSc 1968
s of Robert L. McG. eng and Ruby Forman nurse;
b St Fergus 14.3.46
PhD (S Fraser) 1974
intramural superv dept recreation S Fraser univ B C
Canada 1974–77, dir of recreation from 1977

MacGREGOR Ian Duncan *BSc 1957

MacGREGOR John Donald *BSc(agr) 1970
s of James J. MacG. BSc(Glas) univ lect and Elizabeth
C. Millar MA(Edin); b Eynsham 12.8.46
MSc(Lond) 1971
farm man. consult. Lugg & Gould Burgess Hill 1971–74,
sen consult. and area man. from 1974
m Dumfries 24.9.71 Kathleen H. Wilson MA 1970 *qv*

McGREGOR Joseph Don MA 1970
s of Alistair J. McG. elect., motor mech and Catherine
J. Grant; b Braemar 6.6.49
app CA Aber 1971–75, CA with Whinney Murray & Co
from 1977

McGREGOR Keith Alexander LL B 1969

McGREGOR Peter Alexander *BSc 1964

McGREGOR Sheila Nicol *BSc 1968
m Joiner

McGREGOR William Stewart Petrie MB ChB 1958
s of Robert McG. elect. eng and Margaret H. Petrie;
b Fraserburgh 15.9.33
FRCSE 1967
h o Aber, Nott 1958–59; RAMC from 1959
m Aber 13.6.59 Doreen M. Macleod d of James A. M.
Aber

McGRORY Eileen MA 1964
d of John McG. publican and Catherine Bain;
b Fraserburgh 12.4.42
Lond: secy 1965–69, edit. asst 1969–71
m Aber 28.5.66 John H. Donald BSc 1963 *qv*

McGRORY Ian or John *MA 1963
s of John McG. publican and Catherine Bain; b
Fraserburgh 25.2.40
CA 1967
acct: Adelaide S Aust 1967–77, Salisbury S Aust from
1971
m Launceston Tasmania 13.1.68 Patricia A. Paterson
teacher d of Thomas M. P. Exeter Tasmania

McGRORY John Joseph *MA 1969
s of James McG. excavator driver and Mary A. Strain;
b Clydebank 31.5.43
teacher Dunbartonsh from 1970
m Clydebank 5.8.72 Anne Lennon teacher d of John L.
Clydebank

McHAFFIE Michael Ernest Ninian BSc 1964

McHARDY Aileen Jean MB ChB 1966
d of William J. McH. gardener and Helen J. Petrie;
b Torphins 29.8.42

h o Aber 1966–67; trainee asst g p Cults 1967–68; dept
m o Aberdeensh 1968–70; m o VD clin Aber from 1972
m Durris 4.9.68 Robert W. M. Downie MB ChB 1960 *qv*
husb *d* 9.5.72

McHARDY Ellen   MA 1964 Dip Ed 1965
   d of Archibald James McH. farm. and Margaret
Smith nurse; b Buckie 29.1.44
teacher Sunnybank p s Aber 1965–69
m Aber 16.8.66 Roderick Smith MA 1964 *qv*

McHARDY Marigold Margaret Anngela Helen
                                                        BEd 1969
   m Gray

McHARDY William James   *BSc 1958 PhD 1962
   s of William J. McH. gardener and Helen J. Petrie;
b Durris 28.3.36
scient off. Macaulay inst for soil res Aber from 1962
m Aber 29.5.65 Eileen E. Forbes secy d of John W. F.
Aber

MACHIN David Harry   *BSc(agr) 1969
   s of John M. man., dir and Edna Young; b Sheffield
24.6.46
MSc(UCNW) 1972
scient off. Spillers res centre Newmarket 1969–70;
lect univ of Botswana, Lesotho, Swaziland 1971–74; overseas tech exec Paulsard Whites International Ipswich
1974–76; nutrit-higher scient off. Trop prod inst Min of
Overseas Dev from 1976
m Romiley 10.7.71 Janet D. Bailey BSc 1971 chem,
quality controller d of Norman B. Romiley

MACHRAY Wilma Margaret   *MA 1961
   d of William M. and Nettie H. Youngson; b Inverurie
30.11.39
teacher: geog Aber 1962–66; prin geog: Bankhead acad
1966–70, Ellon acad 1970–72; lect Aber coll of educ
from 1972
m McDonald

McILVRIDE Sandra Mary   *MA 1961
   d of Donald G. McI. bulb farm man. and Gladys
Maxwell; b Spalding 11.11.39
teacher: Demonstration s Aber 1962–67, Inverurie acad:
p s 1967–72, dep head p s 1972–75; asst head Kellands p s
Inverurie 1975–76; head: Stoneywood p s 1976–79,
Hazlehead p s Aber from 1979

MacINNES Lindsay Jane   MA 1970 Dip Ed 1972
   d of Angus MacI. acct and Jean C. Anderson secy;
b Edin 4.4.50
asst in fin. off. H.-W. from 1976
marr diss

MACINNES Margaret Ella   MA 1965
   d of Niel G. M. insp taxes and Elizabeth L. Clunie;
b Halifax 23.12.35
teacher Hayshead p s Arbroath 1957–58
m Aber 31.10.58 Ian D. Herd publican s of Douglas H.
Aber

MacINNES Mary Flora   MA 1965
   d of John L. MacI. farm. and Euphemia MacDonald;
b Tiree 28.12.43
teacher: Engl/Gaelic/soc stud. Inv 1966–68, Engl
Edmonton 1968–69, prin Engl Vancouver 1969–72,
Engl Hong Kong 1972–73, govt trg off. (land div) Hong
Kong 1974–77
m Hong Kong 7.8.72 Alexander MacArthur police off.
s of Donald MacA. Tiree

MACINTOSH Alan Archibald   *MA 1965
   s of Daniel M. lect maths/navig and Anne T. Murphy;
b Glasg 11.8.43
teacher Engl: Wilkie h s Saskatchewan 1966–69, Stir h s
1968–69, head Engl dept Shiney Row s s Co Durh:
Engl Big River Sask 1969–71, Russell Manitoba 1971–75,
Yorkton Sask from 1975
m Morpeth 11.8.65 Susan P. Turner MA 1965 *qv*

MACINTOSH Alastair   BSc 1966

McINTOSH Alexander Selbie   MB ChB 1963

MACINTOSH Anne   MA 1965
   d of Donald M. model maker and Margaret Bruce;
b Peterhead 6.2.45
teacher Peterhead from 1966

McINTOSH Charles   MA 1963
   d 27.4.64

McINTOSH Charles Mearns   *MA 1956
   s of William McI. rly signalman and Jeannie F.
Mearns milliner; b Insch 23.12.33
FRGS
RNVR 1956–59; teacher geog Banff acad 1960–62 prin
geog from 1962
m Aber 4.7.59 Maureen M. Craighead teacher d of James
G. C. Aber

McINTOSH Colin Stephen   MB ChB 1964
   s of Alexander McI. eng and Ann Stephen; b Fraserburgh 13.12.40
MRCP 1970
h o ARI 1964–65; sen h o Woodend hosp Aber, ARI
1965–66; regist med ARI 1966–70; Lond: lect dept
nephrology St Bart's hosp 1970–72, sen med regist
Westminster hosp from 1972

MACINTOSH Fiona McLean   *MA 1966

McINTOSH Francis George   *BSc(eng) 1963 MSc 1965
   s of Alexander M. McI. hotel prop. and Jean Selbie;
b Inverurie 19.3.42
MIEE 1972 CEng 1972
grad app SETS Glasg 1963–64; lect electronics RGIT
Aber 1965–71, sen lect from 1971
m Kemnay 2.4.64 Frances M. Morgan teacher d of
Alexander M. Kemnay

McINTOSH Gordon   *BSc 1960

McINTOSH Graham Henderson   MB ChB 1967
   s of John D. M. McI. master butcher and Mary
Taylor; b Stonehaven 28.8.42
DObstRCOG 1971 MRCGP 1975
h o ARI 1967–69; sen h o anaest ARI 1969–70; g p:
trainee Aber 1970–71, Stonehaven from 1972
m Aber 3.4.68 Elizabeth M. Emslie teacher p e d of
William E. MA 1926 *qv*

McINTOSH Ian Alexander   *MA 1969
   s of Ernest McI. buyer chem indust and Mabel W.
Turner teacher; b Wanstead 18.11.44
TEFL(UCNW)
teacher (Brit Council) to Finnish Brit Soc Helsinki,
Turku 1969–71; lect Engl Turku/Åbo: Turku s of econ
1972–74, Åbo Akademi (Sudd univ) of Turku/Åbo from
1974

McINTOSH James   *BSc 1962

McINTOSH James Robert Barclay   *MA 1970
PhD 1976
    s of Robert T. McI. joiner and Isobel Barclay nurse;
b Banchory 5.12.46
Aber: MRC res stud. 1970–73, MRC res scient 1973–77;
res fell Glas from 1977
m Southport 24.6.72 Jean B. Creswell PhD 1976 d of
Barry E. C. Southport

McINTOSH James Stuart   MB ChB 1958
    s of James S. McI. comp dir and Bessie D. Nicol
teacher; b Turriff 10.11.34
DObstRCOG 1965
h o ARI 1958–59; m o Tasmanian govt Latrobe 1960–61,
m o royal women's hosp Melbourne 1961–62; g p:
Maffra Aust 1962–63, Coventry from 1963
m Aber 21.7.59 Norma Welsh MA 1958 qv

McINTOSH John Alistair Reid   *BSc 1958
    s of John D. M. McI. butcher and Mary H. Taylor
cashier; b Stonehaven 21.1.36
Aberd: res asst 1958–61, clin phys 1961–64, lect 1964–74;
chief phys Coventry area health auth from 1974
m Aber 3.7.63 Alison Grant nurse d of Ian G. Inverugie

McINTOSH John Leslie   MA 1959
    s of Wilfred D. McI. confectioner and Christina A.
Black confectioner; b Banff 4.1.37
FSA Scot. 1962 BA(Lond) 1975
teacher Engl Turriff acad 1960–62; Banff acad: 1962–67,
spec asst 1967–72, prin guid from 1972

MACINTOSH Kathleen Macdonald   MA 1962
    d of Donald M. stores clerk and Joan K. C. Ross
teacher; b Inv 1.1.40
Dip Pers Man.(Glasg tech) MIPM 1973
pers off.: Worthing 1963–68, Chichester, Cambridge
1971–75; tax off. higher grade Cambridge from 1976
m Cambridge 7.10.78 Peter S. Gates res chem ARIC
s of Eric S. G. Hunstanton

McINTOSH Kathleen Mary   MA 1965
    m Carle

MacINTOSH Peter MacCallum   *BSc 1966
    s of Peter MacI. fatstock off. and Andrina J. G.
Robertson; b Meikleour 5.5.44
computer electronics: sen eng Poole 1966–71, prin chief
eng Towcaster from 1971
m Aber 27.7.68 Margaret E. Fraser BSc 1967 qv

McINTOSH Stewart Mellis   MA 1968

McINTOSH Sylvia   *BSc 1961
    d of Keith N. McI. joiner and Isabel MacKenzie;
b Findhorn 28.3.39
teacher maths Madras coll St And 1962–69
m Findhorn 15.7.67 William M. Cockburn LRIC indust
chem s of Edwin J. C. Strathkinness
husb d 1.6.77

McINTOSH William Eric   MA 1965 *1967 Dip Ed 1968
    s of Wilfred R. D. McI. confectioner and Christina
Black; b Banff 20.8.44
teacher Bankhead acad 1968–72, prin Engl Ellon acad
from 1972
m Aber 28.12.68 Sandra A. Gamblin MB ChB 1968 qv

McINTOSH William McKenzie   BSc(eng) 1967

McINTYRE Alan   MA 1970
    s of Henry McI. shop asst and Nora McI. Bain;

b Aber 5.4.30
teacher Summerhill acad Aber 1971–74; asst prin Engl
from 1974
m Aber 26.1.52 Sarah Ogston audit clerkess d of William
O. Aber

McINTYRE Angus Kennedy   MA 1961
    s of Angus McI. marine eng and Jean H.; b Renfrew-
shire 30.8.36
journalist: Aber 1961–64, Glasg 1964–70, Lond 1970–75,
Edin from 1975
m Aboyne 21.12.60 Margaret A. Jones MB ChB 1960 qv

McINTYRE Charles Clouston   BSc(agr) 1958
    s of James C. F. McI. BSc(agr)(Edin) agr advis and
Florence M. Clouston agr advis (poultry/dairy); b Newport on Tay 10.9.36
NDA 1959
farm man. Lathrisk Fife 1959–62, farm. Lathrisk 1962–
68, E Lathrisk from 1968 and chief exec Fife Growers
(farm co-op) Cupar 1972–76; ptnr Kettle Produce, veg
pre-packing and wholesaling from 1976
m Freuchie 19.2.68 Elizabeth McLaren RSAM mus
teacher d of James McL. Cupar

MacINTYRE Donald Hutchison   *MA 1961
Dip Ed 1964

McINTYRE Elizabeth Pauline   MLitt 1968
    BA(BrCol)
m Diamond

MacINTYRE John   MB ChB 1965 PhD 1973
    s of George A. MacI. french pol and Ethel B. C.
Sutherland; b Inv 26.3.40
FRCSE 1971
h o Aber 1965–66; res fell. surg Aberd 1966–69; regist
surg ARI 1969–73; lect surg King's coll hosp med s Lond
1973–75, sen lect 1975–78; consult. surg Perth RI from
1978
m Inv 10.7.65 Anne MacFarquhar teacher

McINTYRE Patricia Joan   MA 1960
    d of Peter J. McI. CA and Caroline W. Lipp teacher
home econ; b Broughty Ferry 18.10.39
teacher maths St Andrews 1961–64; syst analyst Toronto
1964–65; computer progr Vancouver 1965–67
m Vancouver 1.4.67 Rudolph E. North B Com(Br Col)
invest. counsellor s of Albert E. N. Vancouver

McINTYRE Ruaraidh Wishart   MB ChB 1957

McINTYRE William John   *BSc 1969
    s of William McI. man. and Marion S. G. Whyte;
b Inv 22.6.45
Lic Inst Biol 1971
teacher: Gracemount s Edin 1970–74, Greenhall h s
Gorebridge from 1974
m Stirling 19.10.73 Margaret S. Hill MA 1972 d of
David H. Stirling

McIVER Charles John Esslemont   MA 1962 LLB 1964
    s of C Gordon E. McI. MA 1949 qv and Doris L.
Shiach MA 1951 qv; b Turriff 14.1.43
NP 1971
leg. asst Clark & Wallace advoc Aber 1965–67, ptnr
from 1967
m(1) Aber 2.6.66 Rosalind I. Hanson MA 1965 qv
    (2) Aber 5.7.75 Janise M. Barron

MACIVER Donald John Morrison   *MA 1967
    s of Norman M. teacher and Annie Morrison; b Is of

Lewis 12.11.42
teacher Gaelic Nicolson Inst Stornoway 1968–73, prin
Gaelic from 1973
m Stornoway 9.7.69 Alice MacLeod teacher d of
Alexander MacL. Stornoway

MACIVER Donald Norman   *MA 1963

MacIVER Iain Davidson   MA 1963
	s of Thomas MacI. MA(Glas) teacher, f e off. and
Ann C. Davidson cordon bleu; b Inv 18.8.42
organis Moray & Nairn liberal assoc 1963–64; stud s of
librarianship coll of comm Glasg 1964–65; trav lib
Herefordsh c lib 1965–67; mobile lib Lanarksh c lib
1967–74; dep br lib Lanark dist lib from 1974
m Hamilton 13.7.74 Jennifer Meers secy, soc work asst
d of Thomas P. M. Hamilton

MACIVER Iain Finlay   *MA 1965
	s of John A. M. MA(Glas) head teacher and Marion
M. Maclean MA(Glas) teacher; b Stornoway 12.11.43
MLitt(Edin) 1977
asst keeper dept mss nat lib of Scot. Edin from 1968
m Edin 17.7.71 Lesley M. Stewart lib asst d of Archibald
G. S. Edin

MACIVER Iain MacDonald   *MA 1969 *MEd 1973

MACIVER John   MA 1968
	s of Angus M. tech off. and Mary M. MacLeod;
b Stornoway 24.1.45
off. customs & excise 1968–70; teacher Stornoway from
1971
m Stornoway 29.9.73 Janet A. Burrough clerkess, typist
d of Hubert P. B. Mordialloc Victoria Aust

MACIVER Kenneth Maclean   LLB 1969

MACIVER Norma Euphemia   MA 1967 CASS 1969
	d of Norman M. headmaster and Annie Morrison
clerk; b Uig Is of Lewis 5.7.44
soc worker Aber 1969–72; prin soc worker Is of Lewis
1972–75; dep dir soc work W Isles 1975–78, dir soc work
from 1978
m Aber 8.7.65 Finlay MacLeod MA 1965 *qv*

MACIVER Norman   *MA 1967

McIVOR Colin McKenzie   BSc(eng) 1956

McKAY Alan Campbell   *BSc 1970
	s of George B. McK. shopkeeper and Jean M. Campbell
sub-postmistress; b Inv 29.10.48
barman Kingshouse hotel Argyll 1971–72; teacher:
geog/sc Lochaber h s Fort William 1972, geog Inv h s
from 1973

MACKAY Alasdair   MA 1966

McKAY Alexander Gordon Reid   *BSc 1962
	s of Alexander W. McK. trans driver and Elsie R.
Gordon; b Lossiemouth 10.2.40
quality control chem paint factory 1963–68; works
chem canning factory from 1968
m Eyemouth 6.8.66 Agnes E. Lowrie MA 1964 *qv*

MACKAY Alexander James Mackenzie   BSc(agr) 1965
	s of Andrew M. crofter and Janet Sutherland; b Bonar
Bridge 29.8.42
agr consult.: Fife 1965–68, Angus from 1968
m Aber 12.8.66 Elizabeth A. Cargill teacher d of Robert
C. Ruthvenfield Perth

MACKAY Alexander John Ramsay   LLB 1970

McKAY Alison   *MA 1970
	d of James McK. bank man. and Vera G. Frary;
b Fraserburgh 23.4.47
teacher: f e Aber 1971–72, asst prin classics Edin from
1972

McKAY Alison Bruce   MA 1968
	d of John F. McK. pharm and Hannah B. Walker; b
Aber 22.8.47
Dip Pers Man.(Strath) 1969
market. asst advt ag Lond 1969–73; market res exec in
res ag Lond 1973–76; sen res psych in res ag Lond 1977–
78; assoc dir in res ag from 1978
m Aber 19.9.73 Nicolas B. Palmer BSc(Lond) bank man.
s of Cyril P. Brighton

McKAY Alistair Paterson   MA 1956
	s of Alexander P. McK. and Elsie J. Gardiner; b
Cullen 6.3.35
teacher Buckie p s 1957–59; teacher, head Deskford p s
1959–62; teacher: Portgordon s s 1962–64, prin Ger
Buckie from 1965

McKAY Andrea   *MA 1967 Dip Ed 1968
	d of Andrew McK. painter and Annie G. McKenzie;
b Aber 12.2.45
teacher maths St Margaret's s for girls Aber 1968–70;
educ psych Aber c c 1971–73
m Aber 8.7.66 Edwin B. Grant fireman s of John G. Aber

McKAY Betty Jane   *BSc 1964
	d of John McK. for./estate man. and Betsy Duncan;
b Craigellachie 5.5.42
Edin: marine biol 1964–69, vet immunologist 1969–71
m Aber 12.2.68 Alistair E. Philip MA 1961 *qv*

MACKAY Cairine Duncan   MA 1961
	d of William D. M. law clerk and Elizabeth Robertson;
b Aber 9.10.40
journalist D.C. Thomson Dun 1961–62; teacher Engl
Dun from 1963
m Aber 3.4.65 Donald W. Smith comm artist/teacher s of
Peter S. Dun

MACKAY Calum   MB ChB 1960
	s of John M. headmaster, min of relig and Mary
Macdonald teacher; b N Uist 3.5.32
h o, sen h o ARI, Woodend hosp Aber 1960–62; g p:
West Riding Yorks 1962–64, Thurso from 1964
m Aber 18.12.57 Norna Pottinger MB ChB 1958 *qv*

MACKAY Catherine   MA 1970
	d of Peter M. crofter/driver and Flora Nicolson; b Uig
Is of Skye 19.1.49
teacher: Inv 1971–73, Garelochhead p s 1973; exec off.:
dept for nat savings Glasg 1974–75, customs and excise
Greenock from 1975

MACKAY Christina Orr   MA 1968
	d of George K. M. CA and Daisy D. Orr; b Dornoch
15.7.47
teacher Fr: Langholm 1969–70, Annan 1970–72
m Dornoch 23.12.69 James Black acct s of William B.
Annan

MACKAY Christine MacDonald   BSc 1967
	d of Neil M. fishing skipper and Mary B. Sutherland;
b Helmsdale 1.3.46
teacher maths: Golspie 1968–73, Helmsdale from 1974
m Helmsdale 10.7.70 David Cowie fishing skipper s of
David C. Helmsdale

MACKAY David John *BSc 1963

MACKAY David William *BSc(agr) 1969
s of William M. farm. and Harriet E. Moir; b Turriff
8.1.46
farm man. rep Durham 1969–75;-prod. man. Billingham
from 1975
m Aber 6.1.73 Mary R. Brown BA(Stir) d of Charles
W. B. MA 1942 *qv*

McKAY David Wood *BSc 1968

MacKAY Donald Iain *MA 1959
s of William MacK. banker and Rhona Couper
teacher; b Kobe Japan 27.2.37
Council R Econ Soc from 1976 Council Scot. Econ Soc
from 1977
syst analyst, cost controller Bradford 1959–62; asst lect,
lect pol econ Aberd 1962–66; lect, sen lect applied econ
Glas 1966–71; prof pol econ Aberd 1971–76; prof econ
H-W Edin from 1976; visiting prof Cornell univ Ithaca
USA 1974–75
m Aber 31.7.61 Diana M. Raffan MA 1961 *qv*

MacKAY Donald James MA 1967
s of James S. MacK. factory process worker and Agnes
K. D. Binnie MA(Glas) teacher; b Stirling 14.6.44
teacher Lat Allan Glen's s Glasg from 1968

MACKAY Donald John Norman MA 1965

MACKAY Duncan Roderick MA ChB 1959

MACKAY Eleanor Margery Sinclair MA 1968
d of William R. M. BSc 1934 *qv*; b Edin 10.8.47
ALA 1974
res bibliog univ of Guelph Canada 1969–70; asst Westminster city libs Lond 1971–73; sen asst Dund lib 1974–77;
asst lib med section N'cle univ from 1977
m Aber John D. C. Harte BA(Cantab) barrister/lect s of
John D. H. MB BS(Lond) Bedford

McKAY Evan Alexander *BSc 1970
s of Peter A. McK. foreman joiner and Helen A. Dick;
b Inv 26.11.48
Dip Ed(Edin) 1971
teacher chem Elgin acad 1971–74; preacher of gospel
from 1974

MACKAY Fiona Currie *MA 1969
d of Alexander M. motor mech and Christina Cumming; b Glasg 7.3.47
lib asst marine lab Oban 1970–71; teacher p s St Combs
from 1972
m Aber 28.12.68 John W. B. Stephen fisherman

MACKAY Fiona Susanne MA 1969
d of Gordon M. quantity surv and Margaret M.
Macpherson teacher; b Aber 5.1.49
Dip Grad Secy(Aber coll of comm) 1971
pers secy: Lond 1971–72, Glasg 1972–74, Brussels from
1974
m Hugh F. O'Toole

MACKAY Harry Allan *MA 1959
PhD(Kingston)

McKAY Helen Fiona Boyes BSc 1970
d of John R. McK. MRCVS(Glas) vet surg/farm. and
Agnes C. Hunter; b Manc 9.9.49
teacher: Kitwe Zambia 1971–75, Lond from 1976
m Wigtown 3.7.71 Trevor M. B. Abell BSc(for) 1968 *qv*

MACKAY Isabella Tulloch *MA 1970
m Bolton

McKAY James *MA 1968 *MEd 1971
s of Adam F. McK. grocer and Elsie E. Kemp; b Aber
21.10.46
teacher Aber: Engl Northfield acad 1969–76, asst prin
Engl Torry acad from 1976
m Aber 12.4.75 Linda J. Robb

MACKAY James Gordon *MA 1964
s of John K. M. bank clerk and Edith Bolton nurse;
b Aber 18.12.38
MEcon(Adel) 1974
tut. econ univ of Adelaide 1964–67; lect: Queen's univ
Belf 1967–69, RGIT Aber from 1967
m Aber 17.7.64 Hilda C. Davie SRN d of George H. D.
Newmachar

MACKAY James Murray *MA 1967
s of James M. M. C of S min and Elizabeth Stewart;
b Inv 14.5.45
teacher: Aber 1968–70, Nassau 1970–73, Lond from 1973
m Lond 10.8.74 Monica Sibson teacher, pers asst d of
Alan W. S. Banbury

MACKAY Jane Margaret Mackenzie MA 1969
d of John S. M. M. timekeeper and Waltrena M.
Mackenzie man./owner drapery bus.; b Cromarty 5.12.48
youth employ. off. Aber 1969–71; searcher (soc secur
off.) Inv 1971; teacher Inv tech coll 1971–72; educ dept
staffing clerk Dingwall 1972–73
m Cromarty 7.5.71 Lewis Patience skipper/share owner
MV s of George P. Avoch

MACKAY Joan Morrison MA 1969 Dip Ed 1970
d of John M. MA(Glas) min of relig and Jean L.
Morrison teacher; b Glasg 5.9.47
teacher Engl Perth h s 1970–72, Linlithgow acad 1972–73
m Munlochy 15.7.72 Andrew A. Cox MA 1972 teacher
s of Thomas L. C. Pershore

MacKAY John Angus MA 1969
s of Alexander MacK. weaver and Mary Macdonald;
b Stornoway 24.6.48
circulation rep D.C. Thomson Aber 1970–71; Glasg:
teacher Engl N Kelvinside s s 1972–75, asst prin Engl
Colston s s; commun co-operative field off. for HIDB
Lewis from 1977
m Skye 25.3.70 Joan Martin MA 1971 teacher d of
Malcolm M. Portree

MACKAY John Francis Graham *BSc 1965 PhD 1968
s of Alexander N. C. M. admin asst and Muriel J.
Smith; b Aber 9.4.43
res asst (for. products): Melbourne 1968–73, Vancouver
from 1973
m Aber 27.12.67 Eileen M. Kindness BSc 1966 *qv*

McKAY John William MA 1962
s of James S. McK. eng and Mary Noble MA 1969 *qv*;
b Burma 7.3.41
BA(Oxon) 1964 PhD(Cantab) 1969
teacher classics Ayr 1964–66; lect theol Hull 1969–74;
asst curate St Mary's Cottingham from 1970
m Aber 14.8.64 Elsie M. Sim MA 1964 *qv*

MACKAY Jonathan Angus MB ChB 1970

MACKAY Judith Ann MA 1968

MACKAY Kenneth MA 1958

MACKAY Kenneth Cameron   MA 1969
s of Donald M. MA 1922 *qv*; b Is of Lewis 26.7.33
teacher Engl Tain royal acad from 1970
m Aber 13.9.68 Christina Maclean nurse d of Murdo M.
MB ChB(Glas) Dunvegan

MACKAY Kenneth James   MA 1966 BD 1970
s of Kenneth A. M. lorry driver/storeman and Marion
C. Burgess; b Inv 14.9.41
C of S min Dun from 1970
m Birstall Leic 1972 Janet Rogers BA(Hull) soc worker
d of Arthur N. R. Birstall

MACKAY Kenneth Malcolm   *BSc 1957
s of John K. M. bank teller and Edith Bolton nurse;
b Aber 22.2.35
PhD(Cantab) 1960
asst lect Nott 1960–62, lect 1962–70; reader univ of
Waikato Hamilton NZ from 1970
m Thornton Watlass 30.6.59 Rosemary A. Lewis BSc
1958 *qv*

McKAY Leslie George   MA 1956
s of Alexander McK. fisherman and Maggie Hay;
b Sandend 17.8.35
Cert Pers Man.(Glasg) 1957
teacher Aberchirder s s 1957–67, dep head Inverurie acad
1967–72, head Kemnay s s from 1972
m Rothiemay 15.7.60 Helen Adam teacher d of Alexander
A. Huntly

MACKAY Margaret   MB ChB 1969
d of John D. M. army off., teacher and Winifred H.
Potterton SRN; b Norwich 25.3.45
h o: Bruntsfield hosp Edin 1969–70; g p: Edin 1970–71,
Leith from 1971
m Kincardine O'Neil 20.9.69 David M. Chambers
BPharm(Lond) lect pharm Edin s of Reginald H. D.
Brighton

MACKAY Margaret Collie   MA 1959
d of George K. M. CA and Daisy D. Orr; b Salford
7.2.39
teacher: Perth 1960–61, Dornoch 1961–62, Laurieston
from 1962
m Dornoch 20.7.62 John Macpherson chem eng, teacher,
life assur off. s of John M. Bonar Bridge

McKAY Margaret Helen   MA 1964
d of James D. McK. wireless oper and Ella Shirreffs
shopkeeper; b Aber 7.3.28
teacher Aber from 1965
d Aber 9.5.81 *AUR* XLIX 139

MACKAY Marianne Elizabeth Houston   MA 1964
d of George A. M. M. comp dir and Margaret
Houston; b Thurso 16.12.43
Dip St Godric's Secy Coll Lond 1965
Aber: private secy 1965–66, teacher from 1967
m(1) diss
(2) Aber 11.7.73 Iain J. Inkson BSc(eng) 1972 dev eng
s of James I. Aber

MACKAY Marlene Anne   MA 1968
d of Donald M. M. Harris tweed weaver and Annie M.
Morrison; b Stornoway 30.4.47
teacher: Innerleithen p s 1969–73, Dunkeld p s from 1973

McKAY Mary Beatrice   *MA 1967
m Maclennan

MACKAY Moira Eleanor   MA 1970
d of Hugh M. M. shepherd, crofter and Margaret

R. H. Ross; b Dingwall 29.9.49
teacher maths Dingwall acad 1971–73, Gledfield p s
Ardgay 1973–77
m Ardgay 21.7.73 William R. Cameron shepherd s of
Roderick C. Alness

MACKAY Norman Harold   MA 1958
s of Donald M. MA 1922 *qv*; b Barvas Is of Lewis
27.6.36
teacher: Peterhead acad 1959–62, Bankhead acad 1962–
68, Nicolson inst Stornoway from 1968
m Stornoway 20.7.67 Johanna Morrison teacher d of
Angus M. Laxdale Is of Lewis

McKAY Ralph Alexander   BSc 1965 Dip Ed 1966
s of Alexander McK. and Jessie R. Potter; b Elgin
30.7.44
EdB(Winnipeg) 1970
teacher maths: Aber 1966–69, Winnipeg from 1969
m Winnipeg 15.7.72 Claudette Berard teacher

MACKAY Roberta Duncan   *MA 1962
d of Stewart M. prison off. and Mary A. Alcorn
compositor; b Edin 25.1.40
teacher classics Aber 1964–70; prin classics: St Margaret's
s Aber 1970–73, Harlaw acad 1973–78; remed teacher
Aber from 1978
m Aber –.7.66 George J. Stephen MA 1960 *qv*

MACKAY Ronald   MA 1957
s of John M. headmaster, min of relig and Mary M.
Macdonald teacher; b Berneray Harris 13.7.36
teacher: Killin s 1960–64, girls' h s Kitwe Zambia 1964–
67, Thurso h s 1967–68; head: Lieurary s Caithness
1968–74, Park s Oban 1974–78, Banchory p s from 1978
m Aber 23.12.74 Alison M. Craig MA 1958 *qv*

MACKAY (Smith) Ronald George   *MA 1967

MacKAY Ronald Graham   *MA 1968

MACKAY Ronald Ross   *MA 1963
s of William M. banker and Rhona Couper teacher;
b Delhi 25.11.40
Dip Royal Econ Soc 1973
res asst Strath 1963–65; lect econ N'cle 1965–79; sen
lect econ/dir inst econ res Bangor from 1979
m Whitley Bay 17.12.66 Christine M. Wood secy d of
Edgar W. BSc(Imp Coll Lond) Whitley Bay

MacKAY Sheena Patricia   MA 1960
m Packham

MACKAY Sheila   MA 1967
d of Duncan M. stationmaster and Lily Reid; b Inv
17.2.45
teacher: Inv p s 1968–70, geog Inv from 1970

McKAY Shona Elizabeth   MA 1964
m Grant

MACKAY Thomasina   cLLB 1970
d of George C. M. farm man. and Isabella Henderson:
b Evanton 29.10.27
app, leg. asst Aber 1970–73; leg. asst Inv 1973–75, ptnr
from 1975

MACKAY William David   *MB ChB 1959

McKEAN Donald Campbell   DSc 1967
s of James McK. BSc(Lond) eng and Winifred M.

Gardner; b Sanderstead 6.5.28
MA(Oxon) 1953 D Phil(Oxon) 1953
Aberd: lect chem 1955–67, sen lect 1967–73, reader from 1973
m Guestwick 28.7.54 Lucy M. H. Thorpe BA(Lond) min of relig d of Archibald F. T. MA(Cantab) Guestwick

MACKEAN Elspeth Mary   *MA 1968
d of Andrew N. M. MA(Glas) C of S min and Janet E. Milne MA 1939 *qv*; b Port of Spain Trinidad 3.10.46
spec proof reader OUP 1968–70; teacher Dublin from 1974
m Wallasey 7.8.70 Michael J. Haren BA(NUI) civ serv s of James J. H. Fivemiletown Co Tyrone

McKEAND John Shorland   MA 1969

McKEANE Patricia Mary   *MA 1969
accidentally killed Baldock Herts 2.2.70 *AUR* XLIII 447

McKECHNIE Alasdair Alner   MB ChB 1960 MD 1978
s of Alexander J. McK. semi-skilled lab at factory for disabled and Margaret A. Parker teacher; b Inv 17.10.36
DPM 1966 MRCPsych 1971
h o Aber hosps 1960–66; sen res assoc dept psych med N'cle; consult. psychiat Bangor vill hosp W Lothian 1970–72, phys supt/consult. psychiat from 1973
m Aber 22.7.61 Sheila Smith teacher d of Arthur J. S. Aber

MacKEITH Neil James   *BSc 1968
s of Walter B. MacK. civ serv and Isobel Sutherland off. man.; b Aber 29.8.46
seismologist M East, Africa 1968–72; teacher sc Alford 1973–74; geophys Johannesburg from 1974
m Aber 16.4.74 June M. Moir MA 1965 *qv*

MACKELLAR Margaret Chesser   MA 1970
d of Archibald M. clerk and Mary Bruce postwoman; b Campbeltown 8.2.49
teacher Hounslow 1971–74, Bolton 1974–75, Chorley from 1975
m Tarbert Argyll 19.9.70 Graham Jackson BSc 1971 scient civ serv s of William J. Liv

McKENDRICK Archibald Stewart   *BSc 1970
s of William A. T. McK. MB ChB(Edin) med pract and Mary J. Stewart; b Bedford 18.6.48
teacher: biol Inverurie acad 1971–74, prin biol: Balfron h s 1974–77, Park Mains h s Erskine from 1977

McKENDRICK Barbara Vivian   MA 1969

McKENDRICK Sheila Ann Elizabeth   *BSc(agr) 1966
d of Robert E. McK. farm. and Mary G. Telfer; b Windygates 9.4.44
agr econ, sen agr econ Belfast from 1966
m Perth 9.5.70 Patrick J. Magee MSc(Edin) arch., town plan. s of Daniel M. Downpatrick NI

McKENNA John Alan   *BSc 1970

McKENZIE Alan   *BSc 1970

MACKENZIE Alan   *BSc 1970 MSc 1972
s of William A. M. gen lab and Christina Forbes; b Forres 4.10.48
teacher chem Peterhead from 1972
m Forres 26.8.72 Sandra L. Fraser shorthand typist d of Hugh M. F. Forres

MACKENZIE Alan   *MA 1963

McKENZIE Alastair John   *BSc 1963

MACKENZIE Alexander   *MA 1956

MACKENZIE Alexander Archibald   MA 1958
s of Alexander G. M. hotel man. and Christina M. Macdonald; b Ullapool 23.11.36
CA 1963
ptnr Macdowall & Co CA Dingwall 1964–74; practice on own account A. A. Mackenzie & Co Dingwall from 1974
m Inv 29.7.60 Isobel M. Macdonald secy d of John M. killed in action 1940

MACKENZIE Alexander Miller   BSc(eng) 1956
b Beauly 6.8.35

MACKENZIE Alexander Stewart   CMB ChB 1959
s of James S. M. master draper and Elizabeth M. Robertson; b Grantown-on-Spey 1.12.34
FRSM 1971
h o ARI 1959–60; g p Auchenblae, Rhynie 1960–62; h o Aber mat. hosp 1961–62; g p Banff from 1962
m Aber 16.7.59 Margaret J. D. Forbes teacher d of Alfred H. F. Forres

MacKENZIE Alisdair Grant   *MA 1969

MacKENZIE Alistair Donald   BSc(eng) 1959

McKENZIE Alastair George Stuart   *BSc 1966
s of Alexander McK. MA 1933 *qv*; b Lossiemouth 31.8.44
teacher N'cle 1967–68; res and dev phys Morganite Resistors N'cle 1968–71; teacher: N'cle 1968–71, Aber 1973–76; Bible coll 1976–78; teacher Cambridge 1978–79; lect Uxbridge from 1980
m Chelmsford 10.12.77 Jennifer White

McKENZIE Ann Jean   BEd 1970
d of James McK. relief foreman Dun corp trans and Eira C. Hood shorthand typist; b Dun 26.5.49
teacher Engl: Kirkton h s Dun 1970–73, Harris acad Dun 1973–74
m Dun 16.10.71 Robert R. Ballantine MA(Dund) tut. asst, soc worker s of Alexander P. B. Markinch

MACKENZIE Anna Vass   BSc 1970

MacKENZIE Annabelle   MA 1963
d of Angus MacK. tech teacher and Catherine M. MacPherson; b N Uist 27.6.43
teacher Engl: Hamilton 1964–69, part time Fochabers 1974–77 and from 1979
m Glasg 31.3.66 James Barnett BSc 1966 *qv*

MACKENZIE Anne   MA 1958

MACKENZIE Anne Margaret   MB ChB 1965
d of Colin M. MB ChB(Glas) g p and Margaret M. Robertson MB ChB 1937 *qv*; b Inv 12.3.41
FPA cert 1971
h o ARI, royal northern I Inv 1965–66; sen h o Ross clin Aber 1967–71; f p assoc m o Liv 1971–74; clin asst psychiat Leighton hosp Crewe from 1974
m Tain 19.9.66 George B. Rawsthorne MB ChB 1965 *qv*

MACKENZIE Catherine   MA 1966
d of John M. fisherman and Annie MacArthur; b Isle of Lewis 8.5.45
teacher Engl Woodside s s Glasg 1967–68; curric asst lib Ont inst for stud. in educ 1968–71; teacher Engl Stirling h s 1971–72

m Aber 15.7.68 Kenneth T. Kennedy BA(Strath) educ admin, res fell. s of Robert K. Glasg

MACKENZIE Catherine Joan   *MA 1963
d of Donald M. motor driver and Louise W. Campbell; b Ullapool 18.1.41
teacher: Hermitage acad Helensburgh 1964–67; Singapore: RAF g s Changi 1967–69, sen mistress RAF s s Seletar 1969–71; head of house/geog Denbigh s Bletchley 1971–73; sen mistress John Bunyan s Bedford 1973–75, dep head from 1975
m Bolton 16.7.71 Keith Cowcill des eng s of Stanley C. Bolton

MACKENZIE Catriona   BSc 1968
d of John D. M. MA(Glas) teacher and Chirstie Mackay nurse; b Stornoway 4.5.45
teacher biol Rosa Bassett s Inner Lond 1969–70; lect sc Queen Margaret coll Edin from 1970

MACKENZIE Christina   MA 1962

MACKENZIE Christine Craig   *MA 1968
d of Alexander A. M. furn des and Annie L. Craig leg. acct; b 28.1.47
Dip Lib(Lond) 1970 ALA 1979
lib Dartford from 1977
m St Leonards-on-Sea 1970 James D. Johnston BA(Durh) organist s of James H. J. BD(Edin) St Leonards-on-Sea

MacKENZIE Christopher   MA 1963 *1965
s of Angus MacK. crofter/joiner and Catherine Mac-Pherson cook; b N Uist 24.3.40
teacher: Engl Powis j s s Aber, prin Gaelic Plockton from 1967
m Aber 29.6.62 Elizabeth M. K. Ely MA 1962 qv

MACKENZIE Colin Campbell Bannerman   *MA 1970
s of Colin M. acct and Isabella W. Brown; b Aber 23.8.36
teacher Powis acad Aber 1971–73, prin hist from 1973
m Aber 26.7.69 Jean A. Birse d of John B. Aber

MACKENZIE Colin Ferguson   MB ChB 1968
s of Lewis M. LRCPE g p and Janet S. Ferguson physioth; b Sheffield 16.3.42
FFARCS 1973
h o ARI 1968–69; m o Zambia flying doctor serv Ndola 1969–70; sen h o anaest, paediat univ hosp WI Kingston Jamaica 1970–71; sen h o anaest Middx hosp Lond 1972–73; regist anaest Royal Free hosp Lond 1973–74; sen regist anaest St Thomas's hosp Lond 1974–75; asst prof anaest univ of Maryland hosp Baltimore USA from 1975

MACKENZIE Colin Norman Paterson   BSc(eng) 1961

MacKENZIE Colin Robert   MA 1967
s of Daniel L. MacK. cabinetmaker and Irene Davie; b Glasg 11.11.35
Dip Educ Tech(Lond) 1974
lect Glenrothes tech coll 1968–70; sen lect educ tech Stevenson coll of f e Edin 1970–77; prin lect i/c continuing educ Portsmouth coll of art, des and f e from 1977
m Aber 25.9.65 Yvonne G. Mennie MA 1964 qv

MACKENZIE David George   MA 1966

MACKENZIE David Shaw   MA 1969 Dip Ed 1970

MacKENZIE Deirdre Catherine Ruby   MA 1969
d of Alaister I. MacK. MA(Edin) C of S min and Deirdre Grenville (formerly Christine MacKenzie); b Kirkcaldy 29.8.47
teacher: Aber 1970–72, Airdrie 1973
m Aber 5.7.71 Charles McLaughlin MA 1972 insur broker/man. s of Charles McL. Glasg

MACKENZIE Derek   MA 1958 Dip Ed 1959

MACKENZIE Donald   BSc 1961 Dip Ed 1967
s of Alexander M. plumb. contr and Mary Macdonald teacher; b Plockton 12.11.40
teacher sc Portlethen s s 1962–69, Mackie acad Stonehaven 1969–76; prin sc Mearns acad from 1976; superv f e centre Mackie acad from 1973
m Aber 24.7.63 Sheila Walker teacher homecraft, lect Aber coll of educ d of John W. Turriff

MACKENZIE Donald   *MA 1970
s of Roderick M. MA(Glas) teacher and Mary A. Mackenzie teacher; b Stornoway 3.1.49
res stud. Cantab 1970–73; lect Engl lit. Glas from 1973

MacKENZIE Donald Bothwell   MA 1967 MEd 1970
s of Murdo J. MacK. MB ChB 1939 qv and Ethel Bothwell nurse; b Aber 14.7.46
ABPsS 1975
teacher Engl/psych N Lond h s 1968–70; educ psych Lindsey c c 1970–74, Lincs c c 1974–78; dir Toynton Hall f e centre for handicapped school leavers (Linkage commun trust) Toynton from 1979
m Aber 8.8.69 Eileen M. Thow catering superv d of William T. Aber

McKENZIE Donald Seaton   *BSc 1964
s of Donald A. McK. BSc(Glas) dir of stud. s of agr Aber and Sarah W. Seaton teacher home econ; b Tadcaster 2.8.42
PhD(Lond) 1967
post doct stud. univ Illinois Champagne-Urbana USA 1968–70; lect Queen Eliz coll Lond from 1971
m Urbana 13.2.70 Sati Parameswaran BSc(Delhi) res asst

McKENZIE Doris Irene   MA 1970
m Beedie

McKENZIE Dorothy Jane   MB ChB 1968
d of Alexander E. McK. iron driller, school jan and Lily W. Gavin cashier; b Aber 18.3.45
h o Hairmyres hosp Renfrewsh 1968–69, g p: Glasg 1969–71, part time Surbiton 1974–75, New Malden 1975–76, Long Ditton from 1976
m Aber 20.7.68 John A. MacKintosh BSc(agr) 1967 qv

McKENZIE Douglas   MA 1963
s of Peter McK. hairdresser and Annie B. Daniel bookkeeper; b Peterhead 5.7.39
teacher maths Northfield acad Aber 1964–73, asst prin maths from 1974
m Aber 1.8.68 Beryl Booth teacher d of Alexander B. Aber

McKENZIE Douglas Andrew John   *MA 1969

MACKENZIE Eona Flora   MA 1960
d of John M. bus driver and Florence E. Maclennan clerkess; b Inv 31.12.39
teacher: Engl/Lat/geog Inv 1961–63, Rothes 1963–66, Lossiemouth 1966–70, geog Huntingdon from 1971
m Forres –.12.68 Christopher J. Lawless RAF s of Christopher J. L. Dublin

McKENZIE Francis Neil   MB ChB 1968 ^CMD 1973
s of Donald A. McK. BSc(Glas) dir of stud. s of agr
Aber and Sarah W. Seaton teacher home econ; b
Wetherby 13.6.44
FRCSE 1973
h o AR1 1969, regist; lect Aberd
m Rattvik Sweden 26.6.71 Anette M. Wallenstål lab
tech d of Gôsta W. Uppsala

McKENZIE George Rodney   *BSc 1970
s of George McK. civ serv and Agnes Conlin; b Edin
7.9.46
genetics dept Aberd: res asst on ARC grant 1970–74,
res off. from 1974
m Edin 4.9.68 Marian E. Stewart dom bursar, cler off.

McKENZIE Gerald Wood   BSc 1964

MACKENZIE Gordon Ross   BSc(agr) 1969
s of Alexander M. gardener/estate worker and Freda
G. Johnston shop asst; b Nairn 8.1.48
BD(Glas) 1975
agr advis off. Benbecula 1969–72; C of S min Kirkmichael and Tomintoul par ch from 1977

MACKENZIE Grace Margaret   BSc 1970
d of John H. M. boatbuilder and Mary A. Bunyan;
b Buckie 6.5.44
m Fochabers 2.3.68 Derek C. Bain BSc 1966 qv

McKENZIE Hamish Stewart   BSc 1958

McKENZIE Hazel   BSc 1970

McKENZIE Heather Budge   MA 1969 Dip Ed 1970
d of Sinclair McK. deep sea diver, tobacconist and
Catherine W. Budge; b Thurso 22.3.48
Thurso h s: teacher Engl 1970–72, asst prin Engl 1972–76,
prin Engl from 1976

MacKENZIE Hector Ralph   *MA 1956
b Edin 8.8.34
FRGS 1962
lect geog Craigie coll of educ Ayr from 1965
m Aber 9.7.63 Leonora Garden BSc 1962 qv

MACKENZIE Helen Sey   MA 1962
m Grant

MACKENZIE Helen Steedsman   MA 1965
d of William M. shop owner and Helen Herd civ serv;
b Dun 1.7.44
teacher: Johnstone 1966–68, Glengarnock 1971–74, in
spec unit for ment handicapped Ballingry from 1974
m Aber 2.7.66 David Glover shop owner s of Douglas G.
BD(Aber) 1971

MACKENZIE Hugh Niven   MB ChB 1957
s of Herbert M. M. watchmaker and Leila M. Dunn
teacher; b St Margaret's Hope Orkney 9.6.33
DObstRCOG 1964
h o Aber hosps 1957–58; m o RN UK, overseas 1958–63;
h o obst Inv 1963–64; Canada: Nupawin Sask 1964–69;
resid anaest Vancouver 1969–70, g p/anaest Powell River
BC from 1970
m Croy –.10.64 Helen E. Glennie nurse d of William
C. G. Gollanfield

MACKENZIE Iain   MA 1964 BD 1967
s of Andrew H. M. carpenter, C of S min and Annie
B. Barbour; b Clydebank 30.5.38
asst min Northfield ch Aber 1967–68; C of S min

Blochairn ch Glasg 1968–73, St Martin's ch Port Glasg
from 1973
m Glasg 10.6.61 Anna D. Rennie d of George R. Glasg

MACKENZIE Iain(John) Douglas   BSc 1968

MacKENZIE Iain Grant   *BSc 1967
s of Alastair G. MacK. MA 1930 qv; b Aber 27.2.45
MSc(Lond) 1971
dyn eng H.S.D. Stevenage 1967–69; math/statist R.C.A.
Sunbury 1969–70; syst eng Elliott Bros Frimley 1970–71;
lect maths RGIT Aber from 1972

MacKENZIE Ian Campbell   MA 1966 BD 1969
s of John MacK. joiner and Jessie Dunsmore cashier;
b Inv 11.2.45
C of S min: asst then ordained asst St James' (Pollock)
ch Glasg 1969–70, min Gairbraid par ch Glasg from 1971
m Glasg 28.4.73 Mary J. Thomson secy d of James H. T.
Glasg

McKENZIE Ian McLennan   *MA 1964 MEd 1972

MACKENZIE James Alexander   *MA 1970
s of James M. gamekeeper and Nancy Baikie; b Lairg
13.4.48
progr, syst des Logica Lond 1970–73; market. rep for
computer syst Burroughs Wolverhampton 1973–77,
market. man. from 1977

MacKENZIE (Hannah) Joan   MA 1966
d of Angus Mack. carpenter/seaman and Mary M.
MacLennan; b Aultbea 24.1.45
teacher: Fauldhouse s s 1967–70, backward pupils Dingwall acad 1970–72
m Inv 31.7.69 Douglas J. W. Milne MA 1967 qv

MACKENZIE Joan Margaret   MA 1967 Dip Ed 1968
d of Murdo A. M. haulage contr and Margaret
Macaulay teacher; b Ullapool 10.9.46
teacher: Lornshill acad Alloa 1968–69, Nicolson inst
Stornoway 1969–71, Ullapool j s s 1971–74, Tain r acad
from 1974
m Ullapool 18.10.77 Roderick P. Smith BSc(Edin)
teacher s of Roderick S. Penicuik

MACKENZIE John   MA 1958

McKENZIE John Neil   MA 1970

MacKENZIE Kenneth   MA 1965

MACKENZIE Kenneth   *MA 1966
s of Daniel B. M. clerk and Emily S. Duthie; b Aber
27.6.44
Lond: econ Courtaulds 1966–68, dir's asst 1968–70;
comp dir Hunter Barr & Co. Glasg 1970–72; dir Wilkinson Riddell & Larkins Birm 1972–76, man. dir from 1976
and chmn I. R. Morley from 1977
m Aber 15.10.66 Marjorie C. Thomson d of Edwin J. T.
Aber

**MacKENZIE Kenneth Angus Duncan   *BSc 1969
                                                       PhD 1977**

MACKENZIE Kenneth Donald   BSc 1956 Dip Ed 1957
s of Kenneth J. M. civ serv and Louisa Mackenzie;
b Stornoway 20.5.30
FBCS 1969
teacher Aber 1957–60; exper off. AWRE 1960–63;
computer man. Atlas Computing Serv Lond 1963–68;
asst dir univ of Lond computing centre from 1968

m Aber 4.7.58 Margaret J. McDonald teacher dom sc
d of William M. McD. Cults

McKENZIE Kenneth John   BSc(eng) 1967, 1968

MACKENZIE Lilian   BSc 1970

MACKENZIE Malcolm Cumming   BSc 1964
s of John M. plumber and Mary B. Cumming; b Tain
28.2.37
teacher: maths/sc Aberfoyle 1965–69, sc Inv h s 1969–72,
prin biol from 1972
m Tain 23.4.57 Helen Macgregor hairdresser d of Alister
M. Tain

MacKENZIE Malcolm Kenneth   MA 1958
s of Kenneth M. MacK. and Emily Bryson; b Stornoway 9.7.37
BA(Lond) 1968 MA res (univ of E Af, Makerere Kampala) 1971 PhD(Lond) 1978
teacher Engl. hist, mod stud.: Fraserburgh acad 1959–61,
Kemnay s s 1961–64; head Engl/geog St Joseph's coll
Arua Uganda 1964–68; head geog Kololo sen s s Kampala 1968–71; teacher: Auchterderran j h s Glenrothes
h s in 1968 and 1971; lect geog Notre Dame coll of educ
Bearsden from 1971
m Aber 2.4.63 Mary S. Gardner nurse d of Hutton A. G.
Kirkcaldy

MACKENZIE Margaret Miller Marwick   MA 1970

McKENZIE Margaret Wood   BSc 1959
d of George D. McK. MM marine engineman and
Maggie A. D. Wood; b Aber 22.10.36
teacher maths: Aber acad 1960–65, part time Albyn s
for girls Aber from 1972
m Aber 20.7.62 George D. Matthew BSc(eng) 1952 qv

MacKENZIE Marsali   MA 1970

MACKENZIE Mary Isabel   *BSc 1964 PhD 1967
d of Donald J. M. gen merch and Janet M. Mac-
Culloch SRN; b Torridon 2.11.42
res asst potato market. board NOSCA Aber 1967–70
m Inv 21.9.68 William G. W. Paterson BSc(agr)(Glas)
s of Hugh D. P. Hamilton

MACKENZIE Mary Macfarlane   MA 1968 CASS 1970
b Applecross 3.5.47
soc worker Dunbartonsh from 1970

MACKENZIE Moira   *MA 1968
d of Roderick A. M. area man. BR and Margaret
Cowper; b Perth 8.5.46
freelance translator: Oss, Holland 1969–71, Lond from
1971
m Aber 18.7.69 Michael J. Dower BSc 1968 qv

MACKENZIE Mona Forbes   MA 1967
m Paterson

MACKENZIE Morag   MA 1961

McKENZIE Morag Anne   MA 1965
d of James McK. master bldr/slater and Annie
Stewart; b Aber 15.8.44
teacher: Engl/hist Aber 1966–68, Engl Elgin acad 1968–
69, Engl/woman advis Keith g s 1969–71, asst rector
from 1971
m Aber 2.8.68 Grant Munro acct s of Alexander B. M.
Cornhill

MACKENZIE Myra   MA 1962

MacKENZIE Nancy Baikie   BSc 1964
m Reid

McKENZIE Richard Holder   BSc(eng) 1968
s of John J. McK. fisherman and Doris E. Holder;
b Lossiemouth 3.12.46
MICE 1973
Edin: site eng 1968–71, asst des eng from 1971
m Brora Isobel A. Fraser teacher d of Edward W. F.
Brora

McKENZIE Robin Charles   MA 1966
s of Robert T. McK. gen man. and Edith R. Kidd
secy; b Castle Donnington 30.3.43
trg asst Stewarts & Lloyds (British Steel) Glasg 1966–67;
pers man. Thomson reg newspapers Edin, Lond, Hemel
Hempstead 1967–76; employee relations man. Weather-
ford/Lamb inc Aber from 1976
m Aber 26.8.67 Margaret Sinclair MA 1966 qv

MACKENZIE Robin Russell   *MA 1961
s of George R. M. master ironmonger and Margaret
K. P. Faulconbridge nurse; b Forres 8.10.39
MA(McM) 1966
Br. Council secondment Joensuu Finland 1962–63;
teacher Engl Glasg 1963–65; grad teaching fell. Hamilton
Canada 1965–66; Finland: dir EFL Helsinki 1966–67,
univ lect Tampere 1967–70; lect Engl coll of tech Dun
1970–74; sen Engl instr King Faisal dir acad Riyadh,
Saudi Arabia 1974–75; dir of stud. The Basil Paterson s
of EFL Edin from 1975
m Forres 12.7.67 Eva-Liisa H. Hukari lib d of Erkki
T. J. H. Viiala Finland

MACKENZIE Rosemary   *MA 1965
d of Muriel J. M. farm man.; b Glasg 9.2.43
teacher Engl/hist RGC Aber 1966–69
m Aber 15.7.66 John R. Souter BSc 1963 qv

MacKENZIE Sheila   BSc 1970
d of Simon M. prison off. and Nora A. Watt teacher,
headmistress; b Perth 30.3.49
Dip Pers Man. (RGIT) MIPM
Marks & Spencer: trainee staff man. 1971–72, asst staff
man. Lond (Kingston) 1972–73; teacher-training Perth
W Aust 1974

McKENZIE Sheila Margaret   BSc 1966 Dip Ed 1967
d of Allan McK. grocer and Margaret I. Watt; b Aber
22.10.45
teacher: Gordon Schools Huntly 1967–69, Powis s s
Aber 1969, Inverurie acad 1969–70, Holt s Wokingham
1971–75
m Aber 5.7.69 David McGregor BSc 1967 qv

MacKENZIE Stuart Gregor   *MA 1968

MACKENZIE Susan Patricia   MA 1967

McKENZIE Swanson   MA 1969
s of James McK. stone mason and Isabella Fowler;
b Aber 24.2.27
teacher Aber from 1970
m Aber 10.5.50 Hilda M. Duguid MA 1969 qv

MACKENZIE Terry Faulconbridge   *MA 1970
s of George R. M. master ironmonger and Margaret
K. P. Faulconbridge nurse; b Forres 20.2.48
youth leader key youth centre E Kilbride 1972–74;
museum educ off. Hamilton from 1974

m Aber 3.6.71 Patricia M. Hyslop MA 1972 d of James T. H. Huntly

McKENZIE Tessa   BSc 1959
m Cowie

MACKENZIE Theodora   MA 1959
d of William J. M. pre-cast cement bldr and Joanna W. Macdonald; b Alness 26.3.39
teacher: Engl/Lat Lenzie acad 1960–62, maths Netherhall, Cambridge 1962–64, head of dept 1964–66, maths/Latin Rumson country day s NJ USA 1967–68, chem Pike s Andover Mass USA from 1976
m Inv 26.7.62 John Logan BSc(Glas) dept head Bell tel labs USA s of Alexander J. L. Kildary

MacKENZIE Torquil   BSc 1965

MACKENZIE Torquil Bruce   MA 1961

MACKENZIE Vivianne Ross   LLB 1970
d of Hugh M. master outfitter and Williamina M. Ross shopkeeper; b Inv 1.11.49
law app Tain 1970–72; leg. asst 1972–74
m Tain 19.8.72 John M. Reid asst acct s of John G. R. Aber

MACKENZIE William Donald   *MA 1963
s of Matthew M. BSc(Glas) teacher and Jessie M. Campbell teacher; b Elgin 10.4.39
teacher Kirkcaldy 1964–67; sen fisheries dev off. Inv from 1967
m Aber 22.7.71 Eileen E. Bennett teacher d of John C. R. B. Aber

McKEOWN, John Robert   *MA 1969
s of Robert M. O. McK. MB ChB (Belf) g p and Isabel A. Owen SRN; b Islington 23.2.46
Dip Ed(Sur) 1972 MEd(Sus) 1974
teacher ILEA Lond 1970–72; area educ psych W Sussex c c from 1974

McKERCHER Robert Barrie   PhD 1966
s of James B. McK. farm. and Zelma E. Edgar; b Rosetown Sask Canada 3.1.31
BA(Sask) 1954 BSA(Sask) 1954 MSc(Sask) 1956
dept asst soil sc univ of Sask Saskatoon 1955–63; visiting res Macaulay inst for soil res Aber 1963–66; asst prof Sask 1966–71, assoc prof 1971–77, prof from 1977; visiting lect soil sc Aberd 1976–77
m Aber 26.3.65 Norma M. Mellis stenog d of Harry M. Aber

McKERLIE Marie Middleton   *MA 1962
d of James McK. mech eng and Edith Middleton secy; b Aber 21.3.40
Dip Ed(Edin) 1963
teacher Engl: Aber 1963–66, Greenock 1967–68, Kilmarnock 1968–69
m Aber 22.7.66 Robert Cormack BSc(c eng) (Edin) civ eng s of William C. MRCVS Wick

McKERRELL Euan Harvey   *BSc 1969
s of Robert McK. stat supt BEA Aber and Anna L. M. Harvey; b Kirkwall 25.3.45
scient Shell res Sittingbourne from 1969
m Aber 27.12.69 Sheena L. Forrest teacher d of James M. F. Aber

MacKERRON Donald Kinloch Lindsay   *BSc 1966   PhD 1972

McKESSACK Ian Cecil   MA 1964

MACKIE Aileen Elizabeth   MB ChB 1962
d of Thomas G. M. furniture sales man. and Theresa M. Mitchell; b Aber 2.9.38
Aber: h o 1962–64, sen h o 1971–72, cas off. 1972–73, res asst genetics 1973–75, res asst med from 1975
m Aber 16.9.61 Alistair M. Flett BSc 1959 qv

MACKIE Alan Graham   *MA 1970 MLitt 1972
s of Alan C. M. MA(Glas) teacher and Annie S. Graham MA(Glas) teacher; b Glasg 24.9.48
insp taxes Lond from 1971

MACKIE Alastair James   MB ChB 1969
s of Gordon M. M. BCom 1937 qv; b Aber 31.7.45
MRCPsych 1975
employed by Grampian health board from 1969, spec psychiat from 1972
m Aber 2.1.70 Jennifer N. Pinnock MA 1970 qv

MACKIE Alexander Milne   *BSc 1961 PhD 1965
s of Alexander M. joiner and Jemima Mathieson; b Aber 5.3.39
MIBiol 1972
res fell. dept chem Edin 1964–65, dept brewing and chem H-W 1965–66; res off. NERC inst of marine biochem from 1967

MACKIE Ann Elizabeth   *MA 1968
d of Alan C. M. MA(Glas) teacher and Anne S. Graham MA(Glas) teacher; b Glasg 18.9.46
teacher maths Br of Don s Aber 1969–70; asst exper off. statist 1970–71, Scot. 1970–71; statist asst and market res Leyland 1971–73
m Aber 31.7.69 Kenneth G. Murdoch acct

MACKIE Brian Melvin   BSc 1968
s of John A. M. civ serv and Catherine Hay secy; b Aber 24.4.47
Kingswood: actuarial stud. 1968–71; syst analyst from 1971

MACKIE Bruce George Wishart   MA 1962

MACKIE Charles Christopher   *BSc(eng) 1970
s of Alexander G. A. M. BSc 1932 qv; b Sandal 28.4.48
grad eng Freeman Fox & Ptnrs Lond 1970–76; eng Ninham Shand Cape Town from 1976
m Perth 3.3.73 Fiona J. Izatt d of Gordon W. I. Perth

MACKIE Charles Keith   *BSc(agr) 1967
s of Charles T. M. eng and Mary A. Slessor; b Aber 9.9.44
agr advis Aber/Orkney 1967–71; advis off. (grassland) Aber from 1971

MACKIE David Morson   *BSc 1967

MACKIE Dorothy Elizabeth   MA 1958
m Hopkins

MACKIE Elizabeth Ann   *MA 1969
d of Leask M. farm. and Annie Carnegie; b Ellon 4.9.46
Dip Cartog(Glas) 1970
asst cartog edit. map publ firm Lond 1971–72; asst translator and edit. Paris from 1972
m Dun 18.9.71 Ivan Sevo s of Jozo S. Trogir Yugoslavia

MACKIE Grahame John Sinclair   BSc 1968
s of James M. M. shipbroker and Esther E. Sinclair teacher dress and des; b Ellon 4.9.46
teacher phys Peterhead acad 1969–70; trainee CA Aber

1970 Davidson prize acct Aber
m Aber 7.8.70 Elizabeth A. Duncan MA 1966 *qv*

MACKIE Isobel Macleod   MA 1957
d of Adam G. M. bank man. and Mary A. Macaskill;
b Tarbert Harris 2.1.37
teacher: royal s of Dunkeld 1958–59, Rhynie j s s 1960–61
m Aber 14.7.59 James F. Scott min of relig s of Robert S.
Dalmally

MACKIE Isobel Margaret   BSc 1966
d of Irvine M. farm. and Isabella G. Innes; b Rathen
21.10.44
teacher maths: Goodlyburn s s Perth 1967–71, Elgin acad
1971–74, asst prin maths from 1974

MACKIE Kathleen Isobel   MA 1966
m McConkey

MACKIE Lesley Margaret Hall   BSc 1970
m(1) Jamieson
   (2) Anderson

MACKIE Maitland   BSc(agr) 1958 *MA 1971
s of Maitland M. BSc(agr) 1932 *qv*; b Aber 21.9.37
farm. Westertown Oldmeldrum from 1958
m Norway 30.7.62 Halldis A. Ramn MB ChB 1963 *qv*

MACKIE Margaret Clubb   BSc 1956
d of William A. J. M. shoemaker and Jane J. Clubb
shopkeeper; b Aber 23.3.35
teacher Aber: sc Ruthrieston s s 1957–60, biol coll of
comm 1967–73, sc/biol Kincorth acad from 1973
m Hatton 21.9.57 John F. Bruce arch. s of Fyvie B.
Cruden Bay

MACKIE Mary Elizabeth   *MA 1956
m Fraser

MACKIE Mary Mowat Ross   MA 1958
d of Maitland M. BSc(agr) 1932 *qv*; b Rothienorman
15.8.36
teacher: Bankhead acad Aber 1959–60, Kadavu prov
s Fiji 1960–61, Kintore 1961, Duncanrig s E Kilbride
1969–74, part-time Aboyne acad from 1974
m Daviot 6.2.60 David S. C. Levie BL 1958 *qv*

MACKIE Michael James   BMedBiol 1970
MB ChB 1973
s of James F. M. MB ChB 1947 *qv*; b Aber 17.11.48
h o ARI 1973–74; lect dept med Aberd from 1974
m Aber 22.5.70 Shiona E. R. Hambrook MB ChB 1972
trainee g p d of Frederick H. Malaya

MACKIE Neil Lorimer   BSc 1962

McKIE Penelope Jane   *MA 1968
Dip Mediaeval St 1969
d of James M. F. McK. quantity surv and Jane G.
Hendry; b Glasg 19.8.45
rare book cataloguer Lib Comp of Philadelphia USA
1970–72; asst archivist GLRO (Middx records) Lond
1973–75
m Aber 25.7.70 Colin S. Berry PhD(Lond) biochem s of
Joseph G. B. Hayes

MACKIE Robert Norrie   MB ChB 1960 *MD 1965
s of Robert C. M. man. dir N of S Orkney & Shetland
shipping comp, Lloyds underwriter and. Jessie A. Norrie;
b Aber 29.7.36
Strachan bursary 1959 Venn essay prize 1959 McQuibban
prize med 1960 Cash gold medal, Thursfield award 1965

h o Gilbert Bain hosp Lerwick, Woodend hosp Aber
1960–61; Aberd: Garden res fell./lect anat 1961–65, lect
med 1965–66; dep dir stud. health serv Aberd; sen resid
Balgownie Lodge Aber 1967–71; inaugural dir stud.
health serv univ of W Aust, Perth from 1971; many
locums g p and private pract UK, W Aust from 1961
and m o WA sec teachers' coll from 1976
m Aber 31.10.62 Beatrice W. Findlater teacher d of
John W. F. Aber

MACKIE Ruth Anne   MA 1967
m Hillen

MACKIE Sylvia Christina Winifred   MA 1956
m Lewis

MACKIE Thomas David   BSc 1966
s of Thomas M. elect. eng and Gladys N. Mathieson;
b Aber 24.12.42
Brit Petroleum Co: supply analyst Lond 1966–71, supply
asst New York 1972–73, proj analyst Lond from 1973

MACKIE William Alexander   BSc(eng) 1963

McKILLIGAN Margaret Jean   *BSc 1970
d of John McK. publican and Margaret Mathieson;
b Aber 24.1.49
Dip Lib(Strath) 1974
res Aberd 1970–73; abstractor/lib Edin 1974–76
m Aber 14.2.76 John R. Tillson BEng(UWIST) scient,
farm. s of Wilfred T. Boston Lincs

McKILLIGAN Neil Gordon   *BSc 1965 Dip Ed 1966

McKILLIGAN Sheila Ann   *BSc 1968 PhD 1971
d of Stanley M. McK. PO tel tech and Mary J. Gordon;
b Aber 27.6.46
Harkness fell. of commonwealth fund of NY univ of
Calif Berkeley 1971–73; lect maths Aberd from 1973

McKILLIGIN Gordon George   BSc(agr) 1962
s of Foster F. McK. bank man. and Lizzie I. Stewart;
b Ellon 20.5.37
civ serv: asst insp DAFS Thurso 1962–74, insp Ayr from
1974
m Turriff 21.3.64 Evelyn M. Stephen clerkess d of Walter
S. S. Turriff

McKILLIGIN Helen Rose   MB ChB 1958
d of Foster F. McK. bank man. and Lizzie I. Stewart;
b Ellon 29.8.34
DCH(Glasg) 1960 DObstRCOG 1960 FRCP(C)1965
MPH(Berkeley) 1974
resid regist sick ch hosp Yorkhill Glasg 1960–64; St
John's Newfoundland: paediat 1964–66, chief neonatology Grace gen hosp 1966–73, prof mat. and ch
health Memorial univ from 1974
m Tor 1966 Dexter Hawkins insur adjuster s of Harry H.
Mt Pearl Newfoundland

MACKILLOP, Morag Johnston   *BSc 1956
m Butler

MACKINNON Adèle Francis   MA 1968
(conferred for long service of exceptional merit)
d of Robert M. OBE civ serv and Georgette du Betier;
b Glasg 1917
Aberd: member of staff of dept of p e from 1943 and dir of
p e for women students from 1958; retd 1975

MACKINNON Catriona Jean   MA 1970

McKINNON Christina Margaret   MA 1962
d of Roderick McK. weaver and Mary A. Macdonald;
b Lochs Is of Lewis 12.11.39
teacher: AGS 1963–65, Reading 1966–69
m Aber 22.7.65 John Slater MA 1961 *qv*

MACKINNON John Angus   LLB 1968
s of Alexander M. postman and Margaret Macraild;
b Skye 22.1.47
law app Edin 1968–70; Fraserburgh: asst solic 1970–74,
ptnr in law firm from 1974
m Aber 2.7.71 Sandra M. Rankin MA 1969 *qv*

MACKINNON Kathleen Lamont   *MA 1962
d of John C. M. master mariner and Elizabeth L.
Macdonald teacher; b Inv 3.10.40
MA(Nova Scotia) 1964 Dip Psych(NUI) 1974
asst archivist St Francis Xavier univ Nova Scotia
1963–64; teacher Engl/Gaelic Bellahouston acad Glasg
1965–67; clin psych ch hosp Crumlin Dublin from 1974;
part time lect psych univ coll Dublin from 1974
m Glasg 30.8.67 John M. Kennedy PhD(Lond) lect UCD
s of David K. MSc(Belf) Belfast

MACKINNON Margaret Christine Macdonald
MA 1964
d of Hugh M. min of relig and Annie M. Mackinnon
MA(Glas) teacher; b Uig Is of Skye 4.11.41
teacher: St Andrew's p s Rothesay 1965–67, remed asst
Rothesay p s from 1967

MACKINNON Neil Bruce   MA 1964 *1966
s of Neil M. oil comp supt and Andrewina McKenzie;
b Aber 12.1.25
teacher: Aber 1967–75, Gaelic Argyll 1975–76; indep
Gaelic res Highlands and Islands/admin in oil and oil-
related indust from 1976
m Aber 9.11.55 Louise Reid bus. prop. d of Robert R.
Cults

MACKINNON Patricia Isabella   MB ChB 1968
d of John M. textile teacher and Isabella W. Hewat; b
Edin 12.1.44
LMCC 1971
h o: RNI Inv 1968–69, Whiston hosp Prescott 1969; g p
Brockville Ontario from 1969
m Aber 27.12.67 Alexander Slowey MB ChB 1968 *qv*

MACKINTOSH Elizabeth Cameron
see Cameron-Mackintosh

MACKINTOSH Frances Mary   *BSc 1965
d of Alexander W. P. M. textile machinery inventor and
Eunice M. Moulden; b Leic 17.3.43
m Toronto 31.12.65 Alan H. Výse BSc(for) 1964 *qv*

MACKINTOSH Helen Campbell   BSc 1963
d of Robert M. bank man. and Isobel M. J. C. Campbell; b Elgin 27.1.43
computer progr: BAC Weybridge 1963–66, Strath 1966–
69, CAP 1969–72
m Dornoch 16.12.72 Philip H. Baldwin comput oper
man., quality assur analyst

MACKINTOSH John Allan   *BSc(agr) 1967
s of Alexander M. crofter/agr merch and Catherine M.
Cameron; b Fort William 19.5.43
W of S agr coll: agr econ Glasg 1967–72, Ayr 1972–73;
man. prod. econ Milk Marketing Board Thames Ditton
1973–77, sen econ from 1977
m Aber 20.7.68 Dorothy J. McKenzie MB ChB 1968 *qv*

MACKINTOSH Marguerita Graham   MA 1964
d of Kenneth M. MA 1924 *qv* and Annie S. Brown MA
1927 *qv*; b Bombay 3.4.44
teacher Engl Prestonpans from 1965
m Edin —.3.75 Kenneth Mackenzie police off. s of
Kenneth M. Ardersier

MACKINTOSH Peter Jones   *MA 1970

McKIRDY Ian William   *MA 1970
s of William McK. salesman and Margaret Murphy
teacher; b Glasg 16.4.48
m Aber 25.6.70 Jennifer Wilson teacher d of William W.
Yetholm

MACKLAND Sheila   *BSc 1970
d of Alexander M. comm man. and Georgina K. Loveday; b Aber 1.8.48
children's lib Aber c lib 1970–75
m Aber 21.12.73 Ian Wildgoose BSc 1964 *qv*

MACKLIN Frederick Creswell   *MA 1958
s of Frederick C. M. comm trav and Elizabeth G. W.
Angus; b Aber 11.3.35
teacher Fr/Span: AGS 1960–66, Queen's s BAOR
Rheindahlen W Ger 1966–70; prin Fr Anderson h s
Lerwick 1970–72; lect mod lang Aber coll of educ from
1972
m Forres 20.7.62 Anne Paterson teacher d of William P.
Forres

MACKLON Alan Edward Stephen   PhD 1962
s of Charles S. M. civ serv and Olive A. Pinks GPO
tel; b Dover 2.10.36
BSc(Nott) 1959
scient off. Macaulay inst for soil res Aber from 1962; res
assoc Washington state univ 1966–67
m Cambridge 30.4.60 Bridget J. Carr SRN d of Oliver G.
C. Cambridge

MACKNESS Jennifer Mary   BSc 1968
d of Ronald A. M. BSc(Lond) dep dir gen meat & livestock comm and Mary E. Bird; b Northampton 10.8.46
res tech: vet coll Edin 1969–71, electron microscopic unit
vet coll Lond 1971–75
m Radlett 17.7.71 Alan W. Downie BSc(H-W) civ eng s
of David M. D. Edin

McKNIGHT Elizabeth Mary   MA 1959
m Duncan

MacLACHLAN David Connor   MB ChB 1966
BDS(Glas)

McLACHLAN Derek Neil   BSc 1967
s of Donald McL. surv. customs & excise and Eva
Blair; b Aber 21.10.46
computer progr: N'cle-under-Lyme 1967–69, Edin 1969–
74; sen computer progr Edin 1971–73; syst consult. Edin
1973–74; analyst/progr Vienna from 1974
m Edin 21,7.72 Catherine P. Brown SRN d of Andrew
B. B. Edin

MacLACHLAN Janet Low   MA 1969
d of John L. MacL. BSc. 1955 *qv*; b Inv 27.11.47
stud. interpreter/translator Aber from 1972; qualif as
interpreter/translator Aber coll of comm 1975

MacLACHLAN Joan Mairi Scott   MA 1963
d of John S. MacL. MA 1937 *qv* and Ena B. S. Duguid
MA 1937 *qv*; b Inv 27.5.42
teacher Aber: h s for girls 1964–69, Cornhill p s from 1969
m Aber 17.7.74 George P. Gordon MA 1968 *qv*

MacLACHLAN Robin Mathieson   MB ChB 1958
s of Albert MacL. prof footballer, hotelier, club steward
and Jean Mathieson; b Dumfries 8.1.34
DObst(NZ) 1961
Wanganui N Z: h s posts 1958-60, g p from 1961
m Wellington NZ Pamela A. Mirams d of L. Holden M.
N Z

McLANNAHAN James Maxwell   BSc(for) 1968
s of George G. McL. airline pilot, man. exec and
Marjorie Maxwell; b Cairo 19.1.44
conserv Lower Swansea valley proj 1968-69; asst dir of
for. Grosvenor Estates Chester 1969-71; area man.
Eastern Woodlands assoc Norwich 1971-75; lect for.
Cumbria coll of agr & for. Newton Rigg Penrith from
1976
m Plemstall 1.9.69 Heather M. C. Kneale D.Phil(Oxon)
res scient anim behaviour d of Thomas K. BSc(eng)(Liv)
Chester

McLAREN Alison Christine Muirhead   MA 1969
d of Hugh C. McL. MB ChB(Glas) prof obst/gyn Birm
and Lois E. J. Muirhead; b Birm 9.12.47
teacher: Fr Northfield comp s Birm 1972-73, Fr/Ger
Edgbaston h s for girls 1973-74
m Birm 28.12.73 Brendan M. Coughlan MB ChB(Dub)
consult. obst/gyn s of Rupert C. Dublin

MACLAREN (Archibald) Allan   *MA 1964 PhD 1971
s of William M. rly eng driver and Jane Ritchie; b
Brechin 3.11.33
lect: pol econ Aberd 1965-68, sociol Strath from 1968

McLAREN Brian Alfred   BSc 1969

MacLAREN Donald   *BSc(agr) 1966
s of Ian MacL. factor and Agnes W. Mitchell; b
Douglas Lanark 1.9.42
MS(Corn) 1968 PhD(Corn) 1970
lect agr econ Aberd from 1970; visiting assoc prof univ of
Gwelph Canada 1975
m Aber 28.7.66 Eileen Gordon BSc 1962 qv

McLAREN Elizabeth Drysdale   *MA 1968
d of Hugh M. McL. MB ChB(Glas) g p and Patricia
J. S. Drysdale nurse, dietitian; b Glasg 21.5.46
teacher geog: Helensburgh 1969-70, Allan Glen's s Glasg
1970-72, Cranhill s s Glasg 1972, prin geog Glasg h s for
girls (later Clevedon s) 1972-74
m Aber 21.9.73 James A. Wilson BSc(eng) 1968 qv

McLAREN James Fergus   *MA 1970 LLB 1972
s of Robert C. McL. MB ChB(Edin) g p and Elizabeth
M. Ross SRN; b Edin 29.2.48
law app Brodies W.S. Edin 1972-74, solic and leg. asst
1974-75, ptnr from 1975

McLAREN Jean   MA 1957
d of William McL. boilerman and Lizzie E. Gray; b
Keith 8.6.36
teacher Cairnie p s 1958-59, Aberlour s s from 1971
m Keith 15.4.59 William G. Stuart draper s of William S.
Keith

McLAREN Lorna Elizabeth   MA 1969
d of Archibald D. McL. squad ldr RAF and Eleanor
Macfarlane teacher; b Perth 27.7.48
teacher lang: Dun 1970-71, Maidstone 1971-72, Inv
from 1973
m Dun 10.7.71 Allan M. Robertson BSc(Dund) civ eng s
of Walter G. R. Dun

McLAREN Lyndon Edison   PhD 1956
s of Uriah A. McL. farm. and Eulah L. Mitchell

teacher; b St Thomas Jamaica 15.4.23
BSc(Edin) 1950 MRCVS 1950 MIBiol 1956
Min of Agr Jamaica: vet off. Montego Bay 1951-53,
anim nutrit off. Old Harbour 1956-65, dir live stock res
Old Harbour 1965-72, chief tech off. Kingston 1972-76,
permanent secy Kingston 1976-78; reg dir Antillean
Zone Inter American Inst of Agr Sciences Santo Domingo
Dominican Republic from 1978
m Kingston 30.6.62 Leonie G. Perkins BA(USA) jour-
nalist/broadcaster d of Kenneth G. P. St Ann Jamaica

McLAREN Maurice Paterson Ross   BSc(agr) 1967 *1968

McLAREN Morag   MA 1968
d of William McL. boilerman and Lizzie E. Gray; b
Keith 9.6.47
teacher: Fr/Engl Banff 1969-70, Keith from 1970
m. Keith 18.7.70 David A. Sadler elect. eng s of Jim S.
Northwich

McLAREN Peter   BSc(agr) 1961
s of James McL. farm. and Elizabeth W. S. Craig; b
St Andrews 17.7.39
farm. Fife from 1961
m Kettle 23.7.64 Margaret M. Sangster BSc(Edin) teacher
d of Harry S. BSc(agr) 1950 qv

McLARTY Donald Gillies   MB ChB 1965 cMD 1974
s of Donald McL. sea capt and Janet Duff civ serv; b
Ardrishaig 22.6.40
MRCP 1971
res asst, Hall fell., res regist med W I Glasg 1966-72; lect
materia medica Glas 1972-77; sen lect med univ of Dar
Es Salaam from 1977
m Edin 4.7.69 Dorothy C. T. Buchanan physioth d of
Thomas B. Gullane

McLAUGHLIN Robert Henry   *BSc 1961

MACLEAN Alasdair   *MA 1970

MACLEAN Alasdair Smith   MA 1965
s of Donald M. crofter/insur ag and Mary A. Smith; b
Stornoway 21.3.44
Dip. Bus. Man.(Strath) 1966
NAAFI: trainee dist man. Aden 1967-68, dist man.
Lincolnsh 1968-69, Persian Gulf 1969-70, Newcastle
1970-71, Glasg 1971-72, Londonderry 1973-74, Yorks
1974-75, Düsseldorf W. Ger from 1975
m Glasg 4.1.74 Dolina McInnes hosp caterer d of Donald
McI. Tong Is of Lewis

McLEAN Alastair John   *BSc 1960
s of Hugh McL. comm trav and Alice A. Elliot; b Aber
19.6.39
geol/geophys Nyasaland geol surv Blantyre 1960-64;
hydro geol/eng geol Ghana geol surv Kumasi 1964-65;
open cast exec nat coal board/site geol Westfield Fife
1965-66; NSW Aust: coal geol Broken Hill Proprietary Co
NSW and Queensland Newcastle NSW 1966-69; Clutha
Dev coalmining geol and exploration Aust and N Z: geol
Camden NSW 1969-71, sen geol 1971-74, chief geol from
1974
m Aber 5.9.60 Ariane Charitonowsky MA 1964 qv

McLEAN Albert   MA 1966
s of Albert F. McL. soldier and Jane D. Farquhar;
b Aber 17.5.42
teacher Aber: Holy Family p s 1967-70, Cornhill p s
1970-73, asst head Broomhill p s from 1973
m Aber 19.9.64 Christian B. McCallum secy d of George
McC. Aber

MACLEAN Alexander Fitzroy   MB ChB 1965
s of Donald M. master grocer and Mary M. Dickie
milliner; b Helensburgh 7.8.39
DObstRCOG 1968 MRCGP 1975
h o: ARI, City hosp Aber, Aber mat. hosp 1966–67; g p
Banchory from 1967
m Helensburgh 2.4.66 Margaret A. McKinlay teacher
mus d of James McK. Helensburgh

MACLEAN Alice Isobel   MA 1960
d of Duncan M. roadman and Margaret Maciver; b
Gairloch 17.9.39
teacher: inf Dingwall acad 1961–64, Poolewe 1964–69,
Gairloch from 1969
m Achnasheen 2.4.69 Roderick MacKenzie butcher s of
Kenneth MacK. Gairloch

MACLEAN Alison Mary   MA 1961
d of Ronald M. MB ChB 1930 qv; b Inv 14.3.40
teacher Engl/Fr Bridge of Don s Aber 1962–66
m Inv 27.3.65 Harold A. Bremner MB ChB 1964 qv

MacLEAN Alistair William   *MA 1965
s of Roderick C. MacL. MA 1940 qv and Gladys Calder
MA 1937 qv; b Aber 24.4.43
MA (Queen's univ Kingston Canada) 1967 PhD (Queen's
univ) 1969
commonwealth school Queen's univ Kingston Canada
1965–69; res assoc/post doct fell. Edin 1969–71; asst prof
psych Queen's univ Kingston 1971–75, assoc prof from
1975
m Edmonton 15.7.67 Helen E. Seth BA(Alta) ch psych/
univ instr d of William E. S. Castor Alta

MacLEAN Allaster Graham   *BSc(eng) 1967

MacLEAN Angus Alick   MA 1956
s of Allan McL. ferryman/storeman and Marion
MacDougall; b N. Uist 30.5.34
nat serv RAEC BAOR Germany 1957–59; teacher Paible
j s s N Uist 1959–62; housemaster Balmacara s 1962–65;
dep head Paible j s s 1965–68, head 1968–73; head
Mallaig j s s from 1973
m Glasg 10.7.68 Christina Macdonald MA 1961 qv

MACLEAN Christeen   BEd 1969
d of Jon L. MacL. driver and Hannah Macdonald book
keeper; b Isle of Lewis 4.4.48
teacher: drama Aber 1969–70, Engl/head of house Lond
from 1970
m Aber 17.7.70 Christopher A. Fleming BSc 1970 qv

MACLEAN Christina Anne   MA 1965
d of Lachlan J. M. seaman and Johanna Smith; b
Glasg 8.2.44
Dip. Soc Sc(Edin) 1966
ch care off. Dunbartonsh 1966–69; soc worker, area soc
worker Argyll from 1968

MACLEAN Christina Joan   MA 1961

McLEAN Doris Margaret   MB ChB 1967 MD 1973
d of James J. McL. MA 1931 qv; b Aber 24.1.42
DObstRCOG MRCOG 1974
h o Aber hosps 1967–69; res fell. dept obst Aberd 1969–73;
sen h o obst/gyn Aber hosps; temp lect dept obst/gyn and
physiol Aberd 1974–75; lect obst/gyn and physiol Aberd
from 1975
m Aber 3.8.68 Alasdair J. Campbell BSc 1963 qv

MacLEAN Douglas Gordon   BSc 1962

MACLEAN Effie   *MA 1957

McLEAN Elspeth Margaret   MA 1961
d of Robert K. McL. tea planter and Helen C. McLean
MA 1931 qv; b Assam 12.1.40
teacher Engl: Ijebu-Ode g s W Nigeria 1962–64, Duncanrig s s E Kilbride 1964–65, teacher trg coll Machakos
1969–70, Machakos boys' s Kenya 1970–71, Mumbuni s
Machakos 1971–72
m Aber 24.7.62 Alasdair G. MacLure MA 1957 qv

MacLEAN George Frederick   *MA 1970
s of Calum G. MacL. stevedore and Jessie C. MacBean
clerk/shorthand typist; b Middlesbrough 17.3.48
teacher Engl: Dingwall acad 1971–74, Millburn acad Inv
from 1974
m 20.7.76 Mary MacLeod MA 1969 qv

MacLEAN Gillian Isabel   *MA 1968
d of Roderick C. MacL. MA 1940 qv and Gladys
Calder MA 1937 qv; b Aber 25.7.47
Dip Lib(Strath) 1972
lib: mus dept publ lib Edin 1968–70, Wm Porteous Glasg
1970–71; contr res asst BBC Glas from 1972
m Aber 26.7.68 Iain K. Brodie MA 1966 qv

MACLEAN Graham Douglas   MB ChB 1962
s of Frank S. M. MB ChB 1925 qv; b Leicester 25.5.38
MRCGP 1973
h o: Gilbert Bain hosp Lerwick, Woodend hosp Aber
ARI 1962–64; resid m o Aber mat. hosp 1964; regist
dermat ARI 1964–68; g p Aber from 1969
m Aber 20.7.63 Margaret M. Hepburn teacher d of
Alexander J. H. MA 1930 qv(iii)

MACLEAN Hamish   *MA 1970
s of Alistair M. banker and Sandra M. Fraser; b Inv
4.10.48
teacher; Portobello h s Edin 1971–76, Bridge of Don acad
Aber from 1976

MACLEAN Hugh Alexander   *BSc 1970
s of Donald J. M. bldg contr and Margaret Sutherland;
b Dornoch 5.12.48
teacher geog Wallace h s Stirling from 1971

MACLEAN Iain Edgar   *MA 1967
s of John M. bank man. and Annie E. Hunter; b Aber
2.8.45
ABPsS
dem psych dept Strath 1967–69, lect 1969–71; lect educ
stud. Callander Park coll of educ Falkirk 1971–74; lect
educ psych Aber coll of educ from 1975
m Aber 2.7.69 Patricia M. Ewen MA 1967 qv

MACLEAN Iain Gilleasbuig   *MA 1967
s of Donald A. M. MA(Glas) head teacher and
Margaret J. C. Smith; b Waternish Is of Skye 1.1.45
BR: man. trainee Scot. h q Glasg 1967–69, asst area man.
Irvine 1969–71, relief superv Aber 1971–72, Scot. h q asst
greater Glasg trans stud. 1972–73, plan. asst Suburban
serv Glasg from 1973

MACLEAN Iain Lorne   *MA 1967

MACLEAN Iain Matheson   MB ChB 1962
s of Murdo M. MB ChB(Glas) g p and Catherine
Matheson SRN; b Dunvegan 12.2.36
DObstRCOG 1966
h o City hosp Aber, cas unit Aber 1963–64; govt m o
Darwin Falkland Is 1964–65; h o obst W Gen hosp Edin,
Barrow-in-Furness 1965–66; sen h o surg RI Glasg 1966–
67; regist obst Glasg 1967–69; g p: Edin 1969–74, Is of
Tiree from 1974

m Glasg 1968 Alexandra Macdonald SRN d of Doney
C. J. M. Inv

MacLEAN Ian George Armstrong   BSc(eng) 1970

MacLEAN Ian Teasdale   MA 1961 LL B 1963
s of Roderick MacL. master baker and Joan Teasdale;
b Stornoway 3.6.40
Aber: law app 1961–64, leg. asst J. D. Mackie & Dewar
advoc from 1965
m Aber 1.8.73 Lavinia M. Symonds d of Henry A. S.
Aber

MacLEAN Ian William   BSc 1964
s of William MacL. slater and Isabella Ross MA 1923
qv; b Inv 30.1.38
teacher phys Inv from 1965

MACLEAN Ishbel Macleod   MB ChB 1969
d of John M. bldg contr and Mary Macleod teacher; b
Skye 18.6.46
h o: City hosp, Woodend gen hosp Aber 1969–70; m o
Dun 1973–74; part-time med pract in leprosy/gen med
clin Taipei Taiwan from 1975
m Aber 27.12.68 Cameron Tallach MB ChB 1968 qv

MACLEAN Jeannie Bishop   MA 1967
d of Duncan M. M. farm. and Marion B. Learmonth;
b Carlisle 11.9.45
Dip Marketing(Strath) 1968
teacher Glasg 1968–69; pers asst Yorks 1969–71; Lond:
coordinator 1971–72, admin from 1972

MACLEAN Jennifer Munro   MA 1968 Dip Ed 1969
d of Donald B. M. gardener, engineer and Martha
Munro teacher; b Invergordon 12.6.47
teacher p s Glasg 1969–70
m Aber 7.9.70 Alexander R. Dawson LL B 1968 qv

McLEAN John   MA 1962
s of John McL. trawl skipper and Violet Harrison factory worker; b Aber 3.11.38
BD(Edin) 1965
C of S min: asst Edin 1966–67, mission. Nagpur India
1967–70, Bathgate from 1970
m Aber 18.3.63 Iris McDonald tax off. d of William McD.
Aber

MACLEAN John   BSc 1970
s of Neil M. crofter/weaver and Mary Macleod; b
Carloway Is of Lewis 17.12.48
MLitt(Edin) 1973
retail sales dept Procter & Gamble Glasg from 1973

McLEAN Kenneth   MB ChB 1956
s of Leslie G. McL. MB ChB 1924 qv(II, III) and Helen
I. Yuill MA 1924 qv; b Dun 28.4.32
Dip Soc Med(Edin) 1969 MRCGP 1972
h o ARI, Woodend hosp Aber; nat serv capt RAMC
1957–59; g p: Notts 1959–60, Dalkeith from 1960
m Edin 7.3.58 Nancy P. Cruickshank MB ChB 1957 qv

MACLEAN Margaret   MA 1965
d of Dugald M. butcher and Isabel M. Macrae nurse;
b Stornoway 26.9.42
civ serv: Lond 1965–70, Edin from 1970

McLEAN Margaret   *MA 1968

McLEAN Margaret Brodie   MA 1967
d of James McL. s admin asst and Mary B. McFarlane
cler asst; b Paisley 16.11.46

teacher Engl Paisley 1968–73, asst prin Engl from 1973
m Glasg 15.7.71 David Arthur MA(Glas) teacher s of
David A. Glasg

MACLEAN Margaret Park   MA 1962 Dip Ed 1963
d of Alexander J. M. MA 1929 qv; b Is of Lewis 26.6.41
teacher: p s Broxburn 1963–66, Prince Rupert s BFES
Wilhelmshaven, Germany 1966–67, Engl dept Fairchildes
h s Croydon 1967–69
m 12.8.67 John V. O'Brien BE(Dub) chem eng s of
John J. O'B. Lismore

MACLEAN Marion   MA 1965
d of Angus M. fisherman and Mary Macsween; b
Heswall 30.5.43
teacher Logan Ayrsh p s 1966–68, maths Hastings s s NZ
1968–71 and from 1975
m Hastings NZ 8.2.72 Winfried L. Heuser horticulturist
s of Andreas H. W Ger

McLEAN Marlyn Hamilton   MA 1969

MACLEAN Mary   *BSc 1968
m Panko

MACLEAN Murdina   *MA 1969
d of Neil M. crofter/weaver and Mary Macleod; b
Carloway Is of Lewis 25.1.47
teacher: Lochside RC j s s Fort William 1970–71, Kincorth acad Aber 1971–72
m Carloway 13.8.71 James A. Skinner MB ChB 1969 qv

MACLEAN Murdoch William   MB ChB 1961
s of Murdoch M. police off., hotelier and Lilian D.
Rolles hotelier; b Lond 9.11.35
DObstRCOG 1963 MRCOG 1967 ECFMG 1970 FRCOG
1980
h o Aber 1961–63; regist sen regist Aber hosps 1963–73;
consult. obst/gyn Highland health board/clin sen lect
Aberd from 1973
m Aber 21.6.63 Margaret R. Anderson MB ChB 1961 qv

MacLEAN Norman   *MA 1967
s of Dugald MacL. butcher and Isobel M. Macrae
nurse; b Stornoway 22.3.45
Dip Urb & Reg St(Birm) 1969
teacher 1968; GLC tree counter 1970; hosp porter, PO
clerk 1971; tv prod. 1972–74; elect. from 1975

MACLEAN Patricia MacDonald   *MA 1969

McLEAN Roderick   *MA 1962
s of McGregor McL. LDS dent surg and Margaret E.
Forbes nurse; b Aber 12.10.40
teacher Engl Fraserburgh 1963–72; prin Engl Banchory
from 1972
m Aber 29.6.63 Alice M. Stevenson pharm d of David S.
Aber

McLEAN Ronald Alexander   *BSc 1969

MacLEAN Ronald Deans   *MA 1964

McLEAN Sheila Stewart   MA 1968
d of Malcolm A. McL. publican and Lily M.
McGregor; b Torphins 4.7.46
teacher hist/mod stud. Dunfermline 1969–70
m Edin 27.6.70 Ian D. Miller LL B 1967 qv

McLEISH Alan Watson   MA 1970
s of James McL. baker and Agnes Smith; b Edin
14.2.47
teacher hist Penicuik 1971–76, asst prin guid from 1976

McLEISH David Nigel Kerr   *BSc 1969

McLEISH Robert   *MA 1968
s of Robert McL. clerk and Elizabeth H. Lang clerkess;
b Glasg 13.12.45
BMus(Liv) 1969
teacher mus: John Hampden s High Wycombe 1969–70,
RGC Aber 1971–75; prin mus Kirkcudbright acad from
1975

MacLELLAN Ailsae Mary   *BSc 1969
d of Angus J. MacL. MB ChB(Glas) g p and Anne B.
Martin nurs sister; b Dublin 27.3.45
Dip Plant Taxonomy(Edin) 1970
res stud. Aber 1971–74

McLELLAN Colin Currie   MA 1957
s of John S. McL. baker and Catherine Currie; b
Airdrie 7.8.30
teacher maths Lanarksh 1958–70; prin maths Strathclyde
reg from 1970
m Glasg 4.8.61 Margaret P. Munro d of John M. Glasg

McLELLAN John Currie McKellar   *MA 1956

McLEMAN Alexander Watt   BSc 1968 *1971
s of James McL. postman and Rosemary Watt; b
Fraserburgh 4.4.47
teacher chem: Peterhead acad 1969–70, Portobello h s
1971–73; asst prin sc Broughton h s 1973–80, prin chem
Lasswade h s from 1980
m Fraserburgh 24.7.71 Elizabeth C. Buchan teacher d of
James B.

McLEMAN Doreen   MA 1961

McLEMAN James   BSc 1970
s of James McL. lab, postman and Rosemary Watt; b
Fraserburgh 15.8.48
MInstAM 1976 MMS 1978
trainee organis and method Edin 1970–73; organis and
method analyst Stratford-on-Avon from 1973
m Aber 12.9.70 Dena Y. Robertson lab tech d of George
B. A. R. Aber

McLEMAN Margaret Fraser   MA 1967
d of George L. McL. dept foreman and Margaret F.
Johnstone; b Fraserburgh 18.6.46
teacher: Fr/Lat Fraserburgh acad 1968–72, prin guid
from 1972

MacLENNAN Alasdair Balfour   BSc(agr) 1966
s of William B. MacL. pilot and Jeannie Logan; b
Birkenhead 8.6.43
anim husb off. (seconded from ODM) Mongu Zambia
1966–69; scient off. nature conserv Edin 1969–71; res. off.
Lumle agr centre Nepal 1971–73; self-employed landscape
contr Ullapool from 1973; occasional consult. work for
Hunting tech serv Middle East from 1973
m Ullapool 1966 Molly E. Longbottom MA 1966 qv

MACLENNAN Annabel Ross   *BSc 1966
d of Andrew R. M. mason/crofter and Betsy Urquhart;
b Inv 20.8.44
teacher maths Dingwall 1967–74, asst prin maths from
1974
m Kirkhill Invernesssh 15.8.70 George Fraser farm. s of
Donald F. Kiltarlity

MACLENNAN Anne Margaret Welsh   MA 1956
m Farquharson

MACLENNAN Colin Breck   *BSc(eng) 1958

MacLENNAN Colin Hamilton   MA 1966
s of John D. D. MacL. farm. and Rosamund M. J.
Plowright artist; b Kingston-u-Thames 9.2.44
teacher Biggleswade j s from 1967/school lib from 1971/
1st yr group leader from 1972
m Bedford 26.5.69 Barbara A. Crawte teacher d of Jack C.
Bedford

MacLENNAN David Neall   *BSc 1962

McLENNAN David Orkney   *MA 1964
s of David E. McL. linotype oper and Mary J. S.
Orkney; b Edin 24.8.38
teacher Aber coll of comm 1965–70; adult educ tut.
organis Kirkcaldy tech coll from 1970
m Aber 15.7.67 Anne G. Gray secy d of James G. Aber

MACLENNAN Donald John   MA 1956

MACLENNAN Donald John   MA 1959
s of Donald J. M. crofter and Johanna Maclean; b
Stornoway 14.7.37
teacher: Engl subjs Aber 1960–63, prin Engl Lionel s s Is
of Lewis from 1963
m Aber 2.4.60 Rena C. Lawson teacher homecraft d of
Roy C. L. Colliston Arbroath

MacLENNAN Duncan   MA 1962
s of Colin MacL. carpenter/crofter/haulage contr and
Ann MacDonald; b Kiltarlity 14.4.37
teacher Engl Inv, asst prin Engl from 1963
m Inv 28.7.64 Deirdre M. A. Denoon MA 1962 qv

MacLENNAN Elspeth Ann   BSc 1965

McLENNAN George Alexander   *MA 1958

MACLENNAN Helen Margaret   MA 1969
m Mackie

MACLENNAN John   MA 1959
s of Alexander M. merch seaman and Jessie Mackay; b
Gress Is of Lewis 10.5.33
teacher Back s s Is of Lewis from 1960
m Johnshaven 12.7.61 Lily A. M. Ritchie MA 1959 qv

MacLENNAN Kenneth Alexander   *MA 1966
s of Kenneth J. MacL. postmaster and Christian
McLaren; b Dingwall 12.12.43
grad comm trainee G. Wimpey & Co Lond 1966–68;
Toronto: asst sales man. 1968–72, market. man. from
1972
m 14.7.73 Maré L. Rice nurse d of Robert D. R. San
Mateo Calif

MACLENNAN Kristin   MA 1962
d of Christopher M. MA 1927 qv and Mary E. Harvey
BSc MA 1933 qv; b Edin 27.4.42
Dip Ed(Edin) 1963
teacher: Larne and Lurgan 1963–65, mainly Hampshire
1965–68; civ serv Hants 1969–71 and from 1972–75;
internat civ serv Geneva 1971–72; volunteer Dar es
Salaam from 1975
m Lancaster –.8.63 William Barrett MA 1963 qv

MacLENNAN Lesley Davidson   MA 1969

MACLENNAN Marion Harvey   MB ChB 1963
MD 1971
d of Christopher M. MA 1927 qv and Mary E. Harvey
BSc MA 1933 qv; b Aber 5.5.39
MRCOG 1969

Aber: h o 1963–65, sen h o 1965–66, regist 1966–69;
Aberd: lect obst/gyn 1969–73, consult. from 1973
m Aber 17.2.59 Peter A. Hall BEd 1972 teacher s of
Thomas T. H. N'cle-u-Tyne

McLENNAN Marion Margaret   *MA 1970
 m Flett

MacLENNAN Randall Davidson   BSc 1968
 s of Alexander MacL. motor mech and Annabel
McIntosh; b Banchory 18.4.39
computer progr Lond 1968–71; teacher maths/computer
stud. Aber coll of comm from 1971

MACLEOD Alexandra   MA 1961
 d of Murdo M. dock lab and Mary Macleod; b
Stornoway 10.10.40
teacher: Nicolson p s Stornoway 1962–65, Stockbridge
p s Edin 1966–67, Whitdale p s Whitburn 1970–74,
Holmston p s Ayr from 1974
m Aber 3.8.65 Maurice J. Roberts BA(Durh) teacher,
min s of David R. Sale

MacLEOD Alison Ann   MA 1963
 d of Alexander MacL. MA(Edin) teacher and Rhona C.
Lawrie MA 1930 qv; b Stirling 7.10.41
teacher Fr/Ger: Guelph Ont 1968–71, Winnipeg 1971–
75, Ottawa 1975–78, Guelph from 1978
m Bridlington D. Peter Stonehouse BSc(agr)(Guelph)
agr econ s of Ronald G. S. Bridlington

MacLEOD Allan John   *MA 1970
 s of Kenneth MacL. crofter and Mary Smith; b Barvas
Is of Lewis 8.5.48
res. off. econ Belf 1970–77; proj off. Nairn Floors Kirkcaldy from 1977

MacLEOD Allan William   MA 1962
 s of Allan MacL. fishcurer and Ina Smith; b Cullen
30.6.25
teacher: Barrhead h s from 1963; spec asst from 1965,
housemaster from 1969, asst head from 1973
m Glasg 12.7.71 Elsa P. Brown MA(Glas) teacher d of
James P. B. Glasg

MACLEOD Angus Mackenzie   *MA 1965

MacLEOD Angus Norman   MA 1960
 s of John A. MacL. gardener and Christina MacSween;
b Ardvourlie Harris 18.8.38
teacher maths/warden s hostel: Lochaber h s Fort William
1961–68, Nicolson inst Stornoway 1968–74; prin maths
Plockton h s from 1974

MACLEOD Annie   MA 1967
 d of George M. fisherman/merch seaman and Annie
MacDonald; b Stornoway 13.6.46
teacher: Castletown p s 1968–71, Stornoway p s 1971–75
m Inv 27.12.68 Alexander J. MacGillivray MA 1966 qv

MACLEOD Catherine   MA 1960
 d of Alexander J. M. MA 1938 qv and Dolina MacPhail
BSc 1939 qv; b Is of Lewis 1.4.40
teacher: Kincardine 1961–66, Perth & Kinross 1967–71,
Lanarksh from 1971
m Aber 4.8.65 Hamish Anderson claims supt s of George
W. A. Kinellar

MacLEOD Catherine Isabel   MA 1961

MACLEOD Catherine Johanna   MA 1961
 d of John M. road surfaceman and Mary Macleod;

b Balallan Is of Lewis 1.6.38
teacher Bathgate j s s: asst Engl and gen subj 1962–64,
prin Engl 1964–67; lect Engl and lib stud. Esk Valley coll
Dalkeith 1967–73; prin guid Dunbar g s 1973–76, Preston
Lodge h s Prestonpans from 1976

MACLEOD Catherine Marion   MA 1970
 m Stornoway 3.4.73 Donald K. MacLeod MA 1970 qv

McLEOD Charles Conchie   *MA 1965
 s of Charles S. McL. MA 1924 qv and Janet B. M.
Conchie MA 1929 qv; b Glasg 30.5.44
MSc(Waterloo Ont) 1966 FSA 1969
actuarial asst Toronto 1966–68; Manuf Life Insur Comp:
actuary Johannesburg 1969–71, group actuary Toronto
1972–74, asst vice-pres from 1974
m Thunder Bay Ontario 9.8.69 Sharon F. Lee BSc
(Waterloo Ont) syst analyst d of Frederick L. Thunder
Bay

MacLEOD Charlotte   MA 1959
 d of John MacL. s janitor, f e teacher and Charlotte
McBain; b Peterhead 6.12.37
teacher Inverallochy 1960–65, Boddam p s 1965–70,
Buchanhaven p s Peterhead 1970–75, Stobhill p s Gorebridge from 1975

MACLEOD Christine Mairi   MA 1970
 m Leathar

MACLEOD Christopher James   BSc 1957
 s of Christopher J. M. coal merch and Elsie M.
Brimmel; b Lossiemouth 1.2.36
teacher: maths Nairn 1958–59, sc Rothes 1959–60, sc
Lossiemouth 1960–63; RAF educ off. UK, Germany
1963–68, squadron ldr from 1968
m Rothes 4.10.62 Alison G. Smith lab asst d of William
S. Rothes

MACLEOD Daniel Stevenson   *MA 1967
 s of Daniel M. MB ChB(Edin) med missionary, g p and
publ health doctor and Mary M. Stevenson MA(Glas)
teacher; b Kirkwall 23.10.44
MEd(Glas) 1975
teacher: Engl Dollar acad 1968–71, Stirling h s 1971–72;
res. off. reading res unit Edin from 1972
m Auchterhouse 25.8.67 Morag J. Bisset MA 1967 qv

McLEOD David Angus   MB ChB 1956

MACLEOD Dolina   MA 1969
 d of Roderick M. and Chirsty M. Morrison; b Isle of
Skye 31.12.47
Dip Sec St(Strath) 1970
private secy Glasg 1970–72; teacher Engl Glasg 1973–76,
prin remed educ Glasg 1976–79
m Inv 13.7.73 Kenneth S. Smith mech eng s of Kenneth S.
Kiltarlity

MacLEOD Dolleen Ross   MA 1965

MACLEOD Donald Alexander   MB ChB 1962

MacLEOD Donald Angus   *BSc 1958
 MA PhD(Cantab)

MACLEOD Donald John   MB ChB 1970
 s of Alexander J. M. MA 1938 qv and Dolina M.
MacPhail BSc 1938 qv; b Is of Lewis 10.10.47
DObstRCOG 1974 MRCGP 1974
h o Aber hosps 1970–71; sen h o g p vocational trg Aber
hosps, Peterculter health centre 1971–74; g p Portree from
1974

m Aber 28.12.70 Marjory T. Burnett dietitian d of Alastair S. M. B. Aber

MACLEOD Donald John   *BSc 1963
s of Donald M. crofter and Catherine Murray; b Ness Is of Lewis 20.7.41
teacher Fraserburgh 1964–69; prin chem: Kirriemuir 1969–72, Forfar from 1972
m Aber 19.9.66 Eileen M. Watts d of Sidney W. Aber

MacLEOD Donald John   *MA 1965
s of Donald MacL. and Morag MacDonald; b Ardhasaig Harris 1.1.43
PhD(Glas) 1969
lect Glas 1965–79; dir commun educ proj Western Isles from 1979

MacLEOD Donald Kenneth   MA 1970
s of Kenneth MacL. MA(Glas) headmaster and Mary A. Morrison nurse; b Ness Is of Lewis 19.11.48
lect f e Lews Castle coll Stornoway 1971–80; asst dir f e Western Isles from 1980
m Stornoway 3.4.73 Catherine M. Macleod MA 1970 qv

MacLEOD Donald Roderick Angus   MA 1962
s of John MacL. weaver/crofter and Christina Macleod; b Carloway Is of Lewis 26.9.40
teacher Engl: Crookston Castle Glasg 1963–66, Nicolson inst Stornoway 1966–73, prin Engl and allied subjs Shawbost s s Is of Lewis from 1973
m Inv 16.10.73 Jean C. Hamilton teacher d of William M. H. Irvine

MacLEOD Duncan Charles   *MA 1957

MACLEOD Effie MacPhail   MA 1966
d of Alexander J. M. MA 1938 qv and Dolina Macphail BSc 1939 qv; b Bragar Lewis 29.12.45
teacher: Ayr 1967–68, Lat Tarbert Harris from 1968
m Tarbert 16.7.69 John MacSween P O asst s of Donald A. MacS. Harris

MacLEOD Finlay   MA 1965 *1966 PhD 1969
s of John MacL. crofter and Catherine A. MacLeod; b Lewis 5.5.37
lect Aberd 1969–72; teacher Lewis 1972–73; p s advis W Isles 1973–78; asst dir of educ (primary) Western Isles from 1978
m Aber 8.7.65 Norma E. MacIver MA 1967 qv

MACLEOD Flora   MB ChB 1956
d of Angus M. BSc(agr) 1911 qv and Clara E. Graham MA 1919 qv; b Stornoway 19.9.32
h o: Lewis hosp Stornoway 1956–57; gyn ARI/midwifery mat. hosp Aber 1957–58; Long Beach Calif: rotating internship Seaside hosp 1958–59, rotating and mat. internship Mem hosp 1959–61; publ health phys ch health care from 1970
m Arcadia Calif 18.10.59 Robert W. Erickson MS(Eng) (univ of S Calif) s of Arthur W. E. Wollaston Mass

MACLEOD Hugh Sime Matheson   MB ChB 1964
s of Ian M. M. MB ChB(Edin) g p and Annie F. Sime; b Inv 30.7.40
h o ARI, city hosp Aber 1965–66; h o obst/gyn Irvine 1966; g p: Nairn 1966–67, Fearn from 1967
m Monimail 8.8.62 Isabel C. C. Laird teacher p e d of James M. L. Glasg

McLEOD Ian Ronald   LLB 1966
s of Ronald McL. MA 1939 qv; b Aber 23.9.45
Aber: law app 1966–68, law asst 1968–70, ptnr Allan

Buckley Allan & Co later amalgamated with Wilsone & Duffus advoc
m Banff 11.8.67 Jennifer Main teacher d of David M. Banff

MACLEOD Ian Torquil   *MA 1959
s of Ian T. M. lt col/pharm rep and Isabella M. McLaren MA 1916 qv; b Inv 6.5.36
lect d'Anglais univ of Rennes France 1959–60; teacher Fr Inv acad 1961–68; spec asst Fr 1968–70, prin asst 1970–72; prin guid from 1972

MACLEOD Innes Fraser   *MA 1959

MACLEOD Isabella Margaret   MA 1969
d of James S. M. postman/crofter and Elizabeth A. Dickson cook; b Westfield Thurso 28.2.48
teacher: Cranham p s Worc 1970–75, Woodside county junior s Telford 1975–76
m Thurso 1.6.72 Michael J. Hitchings BSc 1973 lab asst/sen scient off. s of Edwin T. H. Chipping Campden

MacLEOD Jessie Christina   MA 1968

MacLEOD Joan   MA 1959
d of John MacL. s janitor and f e teacher and Charlotte McBain; b Peterhead 6.12.37
teacher: Cockenzie p s 1960–61, Boddam p s 1961–71, Buchanhaven p s Peterhead 1971–75, Gorebridge p s 1975–76. Loanhead p s from 1976

MACLEOD John   MA 1960

MacLEOD John   MA 1967
s of Macleod MA(Glas) headmaster and Peggy Macleay; b Glasg 9.7.46
teacher Engl Glasg 1969–73, prin Engl from 1973
m Glasg 1969 Erica M. Maclean Laxdale Is of Lewis

MacLEOD John   MA 1969

MacLEOD John Ross   MA 1963
s of Alister MacL. policeman and Kathleen Macdonald; b Isle Ornsay Skye 20.8.42
teacher: Dunbarney j s s Perth 1964–66, Njumbi h s Kenya 1967–68; prin Engl Chadiza s s Zambia 1969–72, Kagumo h s Kenya 1973–78
m Chadiza Zambia –.10.71 Susan E. Ridley MB ChB 1968 qv

MACLEOD John William Bartholomew   MA 1970
s of Murdo D. M. prison gov/reg dir of prisons and Dolina Macleod; b Stornoway 2.5.49
teacher geog Dingwall acad from 1971
m Dingwall 25.7.74 Anne M. Maclean MA 1972 teacher d of William M. Glendale Is of Skye

MACLEOD Kathleen   MA 1968
d of John M. motor mech and Margaret Macrae; b Stornoway 1.1.47
RGN 1970 SCM 1972
post grad nursing course Aber 1968–70; midwifery trg Bellshill 1971–72; nurse missionary Central India 1973–78; temp matron eventide home Glasg 1978; part time stud. Bible coll Glasg 1978–79; stud. commun health Liv s of tropical med 1980; return to India 1980

MacLEOD Katrine Isabel Lewis   MA 1956 Dip Ed 1957
d of Angus MacL. MA 1927 qv and Helen E. Riddoch MA 1928 qv; b Aber 24.3.35
teacher Aber: Powis 1957, Quarryhill 1958–59; remed C of E s Cranleigh part-time 1970–75
m Aber 2.4.58 Jack B. Izatt BSc(eng) 1957 qv

McLEOD Kenneth   MB ChB 1966
s of Kenneth McL. grocer and Christina Simpson; b
Elgin 3.7.42
FFARCS(Lond) 1970
h o Aber 1966–67; regist anaest Aber 1968–71; sen res off.
N'cle 1971–75, consult. anaest from 1975
m Elgin 14.2.64 Sandra G. Grant nurse d of William G.
Elgin

MACLEOD Kenneth James   BSc 1960
s of Kenneth M. farm. and Anne Fraser MA(Glas);
b Conon Bridge 1.3.38
FRMetS 1974
met Nairobi 1961–75, UNEP Nairobi from 1975
m Nairobi 30.6.68 Anita D. Duncan d of Ivan D. H. D.
Nairobi

MacLEOD Lewis   *MA 1970
s of Kenneth MacL. bldg contr and Cathleen Harris; b
Stornoway 19.1.49
PhD res fell. St John's Canada 1970–73

MacLEOD Malcolm   MA 1963

MacLEOD Malcolm   BSc 1967

MACLEOD Malcolm   MA 1968

MacLEOD Margaret   MA 1964
d of Donald MacL. crofter/weaver and Christina
MacLeod; b Carloway Is of Lewis 2.3.43
teacher: Plean 1965–67, Montreal 1967–72, Lond 1972–
73, Denny 1973–74, Inv from 1974

**McLEOD Marguerite Fiona Logan   MA 1958
                                                    CASS 1971**
d of Peter McL. MA(Glas) teacher and Eva Munro law
stud.; b Inv. 14.5.38
Dip Secy Sc(Glasg) 1959
teacher: Croy 1960–64, Lossiemouth 1965–69; soc work
Elgin from 1971

MACLEOD Marjory Barron   MA 1960
m Macdonald

MACLEOD Mary   *BSc 1968
d of Murdo M. merch seaman, dock lab and Mary
Macleod; b Stornoway 3.12.46
MSc(Lond) 1969
planner: Rosssh 1970–75, Highland reg c from 1975
m Glasg 28.12.76 Donald H. MacDonald farm. s of
Alexander A. MacD. Duncanston

MACLEOD Mary   MA 1969
d of Donald J. M. weaver and Catherine A. Macarthur; b Carloway Is of Lewis 19.3.48
teacher: Nicolson inst Stornoway 1970–76, Inv r acad
from 1976
m Aber 20.7.76 George F. Maclean MA 1970 qv

MacLEOD Mary Anne Millar   MA 1966
m McCormack

MacLEOD Moragh Alison   *MA 1965
d of Alexander MacL. bank man. and Sheila M.
Caldwell; b Buenos Aires 21.4.43
VSO teacher Engl Amedzofe trg coll Ghana 1965–66;
teacher Engl: Stockland Green bilateral s Birm 1966–67;
Ghana: Kpandu s 1967–70, Tema s s 1971–75; Cameroon;
presb coll Bali 1976–78, Sacred Heart coll Bamenda from
1978
m Aber 2.9.67 David T. A. Gibson BA(Dub) teacher s of
Angus E. G. Lincoln

MACLEOD Murdo   *MA 1958
s of George M. gamekeeper and Dolina McKinnon; b
Ardhasaig Harris 24.2.31
teacher geog: Glasg 1959–65, Thornhill acad 1965–67;
lect Stevenson coll of f e Edin from 1967
m Aber 13.2.65 Evelyn J. E. Carle d of William C. C.
Cults

MACLEOD Murdo   MA 1958 Dip Ed 1959
s of Donald M. dock lab and Mary MacIver; b Stornoway 2.12.37
teacher: Leverburgh 1959–62, Glasg 1962–69, Stornoway
from 1969
m Stornoway 13.10.71 Katie M. Martin teacher d of
Alexander M. Stornoway

MacLEOD Murdo Alexander   MA 1963
s of Alexander MacL. min of relig and Catherine
MacLeod; b Ness Is of Lewis 15.10.35
Dip Free Ch Coll Edin 1966
min Drumchapel Free ch Glasg 1966–72, Free ch Dingwall from 1972
m Glasg 24.8.66 Annie B. Nicolson MA 1962 qv

MACLEOD Murdo Donald   MB ChB 1970
s of Murdo M. seaman/crofter/fisherman/wool carder
and Isabella Macaulay fish trade worker; b Knock Is of
Lewis 5.3.45
MRCGP 1977
h o royal N I Inv 1970–71; sen h o obst/gyn Raigmore
hosp Inv 1971–72; sen h o paediat Bridgend hosp Glam
1972, g p trainee N Middx hosp Lond 1972–74; g p
Aldershot from 1974
m Inv 5.3.71 Elizabeth G. Eunson RGN d of George J. E.
Brechin

MACLEOD Nan Shepherd   MA 1956
d of Mary M.; b Portnaguran Is of Lewis 7.1.35
teacher: Engl Selkirk 1957–59, Sandwick p s 1959–66,
Engl Bayble from 1974
m Inv 2.8.61 John M. Macleod insur ag s of Malcolm M.
Garrabost Is of Lewis

MACLEOD Neil Munro   *MA 1960

MacLEOD Robert Dewar Murray   MB ChB 1960
s of Robert B. M. MA(Glas) headmaster and Helen
T. S. Murray MA(Glas) teacher; b Aber 17.5.37
DObstRCOG 1962 MRCPE 1965
res asst Aberd 1962–63; regist Aber hosps 1963–66; sen
regist Edin hosps 1966–77; consult. phys/geriat Elgin
from 1971
m Aber 15.7.61 Gwendoline C. Mair lib d of John S. S. M.
Aber

MACLEOD Roderick   MB ChB 1970
s of Roderick M. bldr and Chirsty M. Morrison; b
Portnalong Is of Skye 14.11.45
h o Woodend hosp Aber, Bridge of Earn hosp 1970–71;
regt m o 1st Bn Gordon Highlanders Inv, Ireland, Singapore 1972–75; g p m o Paderborn Sennelager garr BAOR
Germany 1975–76; sen h o obst/gyn mil hosp Colchester
1976; g p Kilsyth 1976–77, Ballachulish/Duror/Glencoe
and m o to Glencoe hosp from 1977

MACLEOD Roderick Alexander   *MA 1970
s of Neil J. M. bldr's foreman and Alice Livingstone; b
Inv 23.5.47
syst analyst Aber 1970–72; syst sales man. Carlisle 1972–
75; reg sales man. 1975–77; manuf's ag UK and Middle
East based Brampton from 1977
m Inv 27.2.71 Elizabeth J. A. Urquhart d of George U.
Inv

MACLEOD Roderick John   MA 1960
s of John M. shipwright and Jessie Macleod; b Stornoway 11.10.39
teacher: maths Nicolson inst Stornoway 1961–72, prin guid from 1972, asst rector from 1974
m Stornoway 2.4.69 Anna M. Murray staff nurse d of Alexander M. Gress Is of Lewis

MACLEOD Roderick John   *MA 1960

McLEOD Ronald Erskine   BSc 1963

MACLEOD Seonaid   BSc 1957

MACLEOD Sheila Elizabeth Mairi   BSc 1960
d of Robert B. M. OBE MA(Glas) headmaster and Helen T. Murray MA(Glas) teacher; b Aber 19.6.39
teacher sc/maths Aber 1961–64; lab asst Wash USA 1964–65; Macclesfield: teacher p s 1965–66, part-time from 1972
m Aber 12.7.63 Raymond A. Bowie BSc 1961 qv

MACLEOD William   *BSc 1961
s of Donald M. farm. and Jessie T. Macdonald; b Strathnaver
MBA(Mass) 1976
geol: Nigerian geol surv Kaduna Nigeria 1961–67, Union Corp Springs Transvaal 1967–69; Mass: progr/syst analyst Norton Co Worcester 1969–74, Harvard bus. s Boston 1974–76
m Worcester Mass 9.11.58 Virginia L. Pierpont BA (Boston) d of Harlan T. P. Worcester

McLINTOCK Michael John   *MA 1968 Dip Ed 1969
s of Robert P. McL. BSc(Edin) analyt chem and Mary E. Sim civ serv, bookkeeper; b Edin 9.6.46
publ exec Aber Journals 1969–72, sen publ exec from 1972
m Burghead 12.7.68 Marion J. Ralph MA 1966 qv

MacLURE Alasdair Gow   MA 1957
s of John MacL. hotelier and Isabella D. Gow; b Buckie 12.6.35
teacher: Kaimhill s s Aber 1959–62, Ijebu-Ode boys' g s Nigeria 1962–64, Duncanrig sen s s East Kilbride 1965–67, Machakos boys' s Kenya 1968–72, Bankhead acad Aber from 1973
m Aber 24.7.62 Elspeth M. McLean MA 1961 qv

McLUSKY Donald Stewart   *BSc 1966
s of Robert F. McL. tel eng and Ethel C. Fellingham teacher; b Harrogate 27.6.45
PhD(Stir) 1969 FLS MIBiol
lect Stir from 1968
m Aber 13.7.68 Ruth A. Donald BSc 1966 qv

McMAHON James Donald Robertson   MB ChB 1966
s of James M. McM. surv customs & excise and Flora MacDonald bank clerk; b Huntly 24.9.42
h o ARI 1966–67; trainee g p Portlethen 1967–68; Ont Canada: g p Hawkesbury 1969–72, Ottawa from 1972
m Aber 12.7.68 Jessie S. Macrae MA 1966 qv

McMANUS Terence Charles   BSc(eng) 1964

MACMILLAN Andrew   MB ChB 1967
MA(Glas)
d Oxford 18.10.79 AUR XLVIII 354

MACMILLAN Colin Bonnar   LLB 1970

McMILLAN Helen   MA 1970
d of William G. McM. exec eng PO tel and Jessie M. B. McIntosh tel, teaching auxil; b Lerwick 5.11.48

teacher Crianlarich 1971–73
m Aber 6.10.72 John Sinclair foreman joiner s of Thomas S. Killin

MACMILLAN Ian Reid Anderson   MA 1960 LLB 1962
s of William G. M. BSc 1925 qv and Doris Farquhar MA 1928 qv; b Buckie 16.6.39
law app Aber 1960–63; solic Peterhead 1963–68; Canada: articled stud. Winnipeg 1968–69, barr and solic from 1969
m Aber 11.5.63 Joan E. C. Sinclair BSc 1961 qv

MacMILLAN James Bain   MA 1967

MacMILLAN James Douglas   MA 1963
s of James MacM. farm., bldg contr and Jessie MacLachlan dressmaker; b Achosnich Ardnamurchan 30.9.33
stud. theol Free Ch of Scot. coll Edin 1963–66; licensed by Free Ch presb of Lorn 1966; ordained and inducted St Columba's Free Ch Aber 1966, St Vincent st Free Ch Glasg 1974
m Aber 13.9.61 Mary F. Campbell MA 1958 qv

MACMILLAN Janette Mary   *MA 1968
d of Donald M. sea capt Burmah Oil Co and Jessie M. Groves secy; b Glasg 18.4.47
Dip Ed(Edin) 1969
teacher: Whitburn 1969–70, sec spec class Linlithgow 1970–71; Whitburn 1971–72; educ psych Aberdeensh from 1972
m Aber 21.9.72 David I. R. Fotheringham MRCVS(Glas) vet surg s of John F. Aber

McMILLAN Margaret Anne   MA 1969
m McKay

MacMILLAN Margaret Flora   MA 1962

McMILLAN Margaret King   MA 1963
d of Duncan McM. J.P. miner and Annie S. Wilson cotton winder; b Law Carluke 2.3.36
teacher mod lang. Aber h s for girls 1964–65, Lanark 1965–66, Gloucester 1966–67, Aber 1967, Uddingston 1967–68, Bellshill 1968–70, Wishaw from 1971
m Mtwara, Tanzania 13.8.65 Peter C. Henderson supervis pipe line maintenance with Arabian Gulf Explor s of Alexander R. H. Torphins

McMILLAN Mary   MB ChB 1965
d of Evan McM. BSc(Edin) teacher and Helen G. Hunter; b Elgin 29.11.41
h o: Woodend hosp Aber 1965–66, Dumfries 1966–67; regist path. Dumfries 1967–69
m Dumfries 25.11.68 Alistair B. Gavin BSc(eng)(Birm) eng, prod. man. s of Robert J. G. Royston

MACMILLAN Neil Norman   MA 1968
s of John M. army off. and Joan Kennedy; b Nairn 27.3.46
educ. off. Brit Steel Corp Motherwell 1967–69; pers off. Amp of Gt Brit Port Glasgow 1969–70: dir MCS group of comp, man. dir MCS Recruitment Serv/man. dir MCS Brockies Glasg/Lond from 1970
m Hamilton 18.4.70 Ishbel B. McLellan des d of William K. McL. Hamilton

McMILLAN Ronald Edwards   *MA 1969

McMILLAN Sadie Woods   MA 1964
d of Duncan McM. miner and Annie S. Wilson cotton winder; b Law 15.11.33
teacher Aber: Northfield acad 1965–70, Hilton acad

1970–73, year mistress Linksfield acad from 1973
m Khartoum 16.4.56 Mohamed E. Elsarrag DKSM
(Khart) med pract/consult. psychiat s of Hassan E.
Omdurman; marr. diss

McMULLEN Adrian James   *MA 1967
s of James McM. invest. man. and Joan E. Gilling;
b N'cle-u-Tyne 24.11.45
teacher: gen subjs St Wilfrid's s m s Gateshead 1967–68,
geog/maths/r e Hartlepool 1968–71; teacher reading to
backward ch St Andrew's p s Blyth from 1976

McMURTRIE John   MA 1959

MACNAB Francis Auchline   MA 1958 PhD 1960
s of James D. M. farm. and Mary A. L. Hughes; b
Aust 21.6.31
fell world acad scholars 1975 FAPsS 1975 FBPsS 1976
FACE 1977
Aust: dir Cairnmillar inst Melbourne from 1961 and min
presb ch Prahran Melbourne 1961–70, Collins Street
(indep) Uniting ch Melbourne from 1971
m Aber 17.7.58 Sheila B. Ewen MA 1957 qv

McNAB John Winton   BSc 1960 *1961 MB ChB 1967
DMRD 1975
s of J. Winton McN. bank man. and Elizabeth S.
Cooper; b Stranraer 17.5.36
FRCSE 1973 FFRRCSI 1977
works chem Grangemouth 1961–62; h o, sen h o ARI and
Shetland hosps 1967–70; regist surg Inv hosps 1971–73;
regist radio diagnosis ARI 1973–76; sen regist radio
diagnosis Dun from 1976
m Aber 30.4.77 Patricia Quigley nurs. off. d of Luke Q.
Clydebank

MACNAB Rachel   MA 1957
d of Gilbert M. estate surv and Elizabeth H. Aird; b
Bridgend Is of Islay 29.7.37
BLS(BC) 1967 ALA(RGIT) 1975
teacher Engl/hist/geog: Aber 1958–62, Montreal 1962–65;
lib asst univ of BC Vancouver 1965–66, lib New Westminster publ lib Vancouver 1967–69; tut/lib Thurso tech
coll from 1969
m 30.7.76 Clive E. Lovelace BSc(eng)(Lond) eng des s of
Garth E. L.

McNALLY Brian Peter   BEd 1969
s of Peter McN. MA(Glas) headmaster and Jeanette
Gallacher; b Glasg 7.7.41
teacher Ayr acad 1969–71, spec asst 1971–73, asst prin
guid from 1973
m Ayr 13.7.73 Constance A. McGuire teacher d of
William C. McG Mauchline

MacNAUGHTAN Elizabeth Mary   BMedBiol 1967
MB ChB 1970
d of Ian P. J. MacN. MB ChB(Edin) consult. surg and
Jean Wiseman BSc(St And) bact; b Edin 1946
h o Aber 1971; g p Leuchars from 1974
m Aber 1969 Roger W. Williams MB ChB 1969 qv

McNAUGHTON James Leslie   LL B 1965
s of William R. D. McN. advoc in Aber and Elizabeth
Duncan secy; b Aber 8.12.43
law app Aber 1965–68; leg. asst Banff 1968–70; ptnr
Stewart Watson solic Banff from 1970
m Aber 1.8.70 Pauline Booth teacher homecraft d of
Joseph C. B. Aber

McNAUGHTON John Davidson   BL 1956
s of William R. D. McN. advoc in Aber and Elizabeth

Duncan secy; b Aber 17.7.35
leg. asst: Ranken & Reid SSC Edin 1959–60, Furst &
Furst SSC Edin 1961–64; ptnr Patrick & James WS Edin
1964–68; dep proc fisc: Glasg 1968–69, Dunfermline
1970–75; proc fisc Dornoch from 1975
m Edin 3.10.64 Joan T. Lyall secy d of Joseph L. Kirkcaldy

McNAUGHTON William Robert Duncan   BL 1957

MacNAY Gordon Roberts   MA 1969
s of Gordon R. MacN. MA 1969 qv; b Aber 16.9.47
teacher Douglas acad Milngavie from 1970

MACNEIL Joseph   *MA 1970
s of Joseph M. master mariner and Elizabeth Currie; b
Blantyre 20.8.32
teacher St Patrick's h s Coatbridge 1971–73, asst prin mod
lang from 1973
m Glasg 4.8.71 Rose M. O'Boyle teacher d of Thomas
O'B. Glasg

McNEILL Anne Christina   MA 1960
d of William M. McN. MA(Oxon) asst conserv for.
Ceylon, sen lect for. Aberd and Dorothy N. Maw
BSc(Lond) hosp almoner; b Aber 22.12.39
Dip Soc St(Edin) 1961 M Inst Almoners(Lond) 1962
med soc worker: St Mary's hosp Lond 1962–64, dept g p
Edin 1964–66, city hosp Edin 1966–67 and occasional
work from 1969
m Aber 25.3.66 Edmund R. Seiler MB ChB(Edin) med
pract s of Henry E. S. MB ChB(Glas) Edin

McNEILL Bridget Margaret   MB ChB 1970
d of William M. McN. MA(Oxon) sen lect for. Aberd
and Dorothy N. Maw BSc(Lond) med soc worker; b
Aber 22.1.46
h o: city hosp, mat. hosp Aber 1970–71, Green Lane hosp
Auckland NZ 1971; m o Vaiola hosp Nuku'Alofa Tonga
1972–74; med/psychiat regist Timaru hosp NZ 1975–76;
m o i/c psychiat patients Vaiola hosp from 1977
m Otane, Hawkes Bay NZ 4.12.71 Filimoto M.
Taumgepeau DSM(Fiji s of med) m o govt of Tonga s of
Siosifa M. T. Ha'a pai Tonga

McNEILL Francis   *MA 1968

McNEILL Morag Deirdre   MA 1968
d of Daniel A. McN. BL(Glas) solic and Jean I. D.
Wilson; b Edin 23.1.47
secy course St Godric's coll Lond 1968–69
secy: chartered patent ag Glasg 1969–72, trade assoc
Edin 1973, dir publ comp Edin 1973
m Dunblane 1.5.71 James A. Brown CA s of Frank B.
Glasg

McNEILL Stuart   *BSc 1964
s of Donald S. McN. mining elect. eng, newsp man.,
market gardener and Dorothy L. Hodges; b Letchworth
9.3.42
PhD(Lond) 1969 DIC 1969
asst lect Imp coll Lond 1967–70, lect from 1970
m Aber 10.8.67 Jean M. Sinclair BSc 1965 qv

MacNICOL Essel Marie   MA 1967

MACNICOL Helen Joan   *BSc 1969
m Brough

McNICOL Maureen Ann   BL 1957
b Aber 29.7.37
employed Shell Lond
m 1958 R. Y. Birley

MacPHAIL Angus   LLB 1967 MA 1969
s of William D. MacP. MA(Glas) headmaster and Elizabeth Brown; b Bonhill 15.1.47
solic: Edin 1970–75, Saudi Arabia from 1975

McPHAIL Dennis McKinnon   MA 1968

MacPHAIL Douglas   *MA 1970
s of Mary MacP.; b Campbeltown 20.4.46
Dip Ed(Edin) 1971
teacher mod lang royal h s Edin from 1971

MacPHAIL Evelyn Ann   BSc 1960
d of Alexander MacP. hosp gov and Jessie D. Downie hosp matron; b Edin 6.6.39
teacher: maths/sc Kelso h s 1961–67, maths Mainholm Ayr 1967–68
m Tarbert 8.9.67 Robert A. Ross B Mus(Glas) lect mus s of Robert R. Kilmarnock

MacPHAIL James Brown   MA 1966 LL B 1968
s of William D. MacP. MA(Glas) headmaster and Elizabeth Brown; b Bonhill 5.12.45
self-employed econ Regina, Vancouver 1968–70; law app, leg. asst Edin 1970–73; court asst leg. pract Aber 1974–75; sen solic Lothian reg c 1975–78; comm and leg. advis petro-chem industry Reading from 1978
m Ayr 14.7.73 Vivienne S. Law secy d of David L. Ayr

MACPHAIL Joan   MA 1970
d of John M. haulage contr and Mary J. Scott; b Glasg 22.3.49
teacher: Engl/hist/remed Penicuik h s 1971–74, Engl Forrester h s Edin 1974–77, Engl lang Brit inst Thessaloniki Greece from 1977

MacPHAIL Kenneth Donald Weir   MA 1963
s of Murdoch MacP. MA(Glas) clergyman and Georgina M. McDougall; b Balvicar 2.7.34
teacher Invsh 1964–66, Oban 1967–69, Easdale 1970–72, Glasg from 1972

MacPHAIL Lachlan   BSc(eng) 1970

MacPHAIL Malcolm   LLB 1957
s of Malcolm M. MacP. civ eng and Jean F. P. Wyse; b Kuala Lumpur 26.6.28
BSc(econ) (Lond) 1954
leg. asst A. C. Morrison & Richards advoc Aber 1957–58; solic Scot. Midland Guarantee Trust Edin 1958–59; leg. asst corp of city of Aber 1959–62, proc fisc dep Dun 1962–73; proc fisc Kincardine Stonehaven from 1973
m Dun 15.9.66 Moira C. Bleackley teacher d of James B. Dun

MacPHAIL Murdoch   MA1960 LLB 1964
s of William D. MacP. MA(Glas) headmaster and Elizabeth Brown; b Renton 13.8.39
self-employed solic Dingwall from 1970
m Glenlyon 2.11.63 Brenda M. Martin nurse

McPHAIL Robert James Field   MA 1968 LLB 1970
s of Thomas F. McP. shipowner and Marjorie M. Gunn; b Edin 10.4.47
CA 1973
CA Graham, Smart & Annan Edin 1970–74, Gill & Johnson, Deloite & Co Nairobi from 1974
m Aber 21.10.72 Kathryn M. Murray MA 1971 Brit high commission Nairobi d of John N. M.

MacPHEE Anne   *MB ChB 1961
m Chew

McPHEE Christine Mary   *MA 1968 Dip Ed 1969

McPHEE Kathleen Isabella   MA 1970
d of William J. McP. gas fitter and Sadie McLean; b Inv 22.8.49
clerkess NSHEB 1971–78
m Inv 26.6.70 Finlay MacKintosh plumber s of Finlay MacK. Drumnadrochit

MacPHEE Kenneth John   BEd 1970

MACPHERSON Beatrice Gillian   MB ChB 1962
m Wood

MACPHERSON Charles Lachlan   *MA 1970

McPHERSON Christina Margaret   BSc 1966

McPHERSON David Ross   BSc 1969
s of George McP. clerk of works and Margaret McIntosh; b Peterhead 12.11.46
MIBiol 1971
teacher sc Peterhead acad 1971–73, asst prin sc from 1973

McPHERSON Duncan James   MA 1956
s of James McP. coffee exporter and Flora M. Macpherson; b Santos, Brazil 29.10.30
Dip Agr 1959
farm. Rosssh from 1959
m Aber 9.1.60 Vivian M. Wylie teacher p e d of William W. Carluke

McPHERSON Edith Joan   *MA 1968
d of George McP. MA 1939 qv and Isabel M. Ross MA 1937 qv; b Liskeard Cornwall 6.11.45
ALA 1972
asst lib civ serv from 1970

MACPHERSON Elizabeth   MA 1963 Dip Ed 1965
d of Ian M. 1928 qv(III) and Elizabeth Cameron MA 1928 qv; b Forres 12.5.42
teacher Engl Aber 1965–66; bank clerk Atlanta USA 1967–68
m Dunphail 12.9.64 Alister C. Baillie BSc 1963 qv

McPHERSON Frank Murdoch   *MA 1960
s of Frank McP. shop worker and Ethel Greenlaw shop worker, seamstress; b Aber 2.9.38
Dip Clin Psych (Edin) 1962 PhD(Edin) 1968 FBPsS 1977
asst lect Edin 1960–63, lect 1963–71; sen lect Dund from 1971
m Edin 14.9.62 Karin Maria Langenheim DPhil(Kiel) lect Edin d of Konrad L. DPhil(Kiel) Kiel W Ger

McPHERSON Harry   MB ChB 1959

McPHERSON Ian   *BSc 1961
s of John McP. GPO worker and Matilda Hemphill; b Lairg 18.9.38
PhD(Strath) 1972
scient off. admiralty Dunfermline 1961–65; lect phys Falkirk tech coll 1965–67; res asst Strath 1967–70; lect N'cle polytech 1970–73; sen lect Glasg coll of tech from 1973
m Inv –.7.72 Rachel L. Macrae MA(Glas) teacher, GPO tel d of Donald A. N. MA(Glas) Tarbert Is of Harris

McPHERSON Ian Alexander Douglas   *MA 1959
s of Alexander W. McP. solic and Kathleen N. F. Brown MA 1920 qv; b Macduff 12.2.36
teacher: Eastwood h s 1960–69, prin mod lang Barrhead h s 1969–73; asst head Peterhead acad from 1973

m Glasg 2.7.65 Maureen A. Fotheringham MA(Glas) teacher d of Ian S. S. F. Whitecraigs

McPHERSON Ian David   MB ChB 1967
s of John G. McP. mason and Jenny Henderson nurse; b Aber 21.12.42
CCFP(Can) 1971
g p Ottawa
m Aber 1968 Margaret Walker

MACPHERSON Ian Richard   *MA 1956
s of George M. clerk and Violet A. Warwick; b Aber 4.1.34
PhD(Manc) 1960
asst lect Manc 1959-60, lect univ of Wales 1960-64, lect Durh 1964-72, sen lect 1972-75, reader from 1975; visiting prof univ Wis USA 1970-71
m Cheshire 7.8.59 Sheila C. Turner BA(Manc) teacher

McPHERSON James King   MA 1970

MACPHERSON Jane Eileen   MA 1970

**MACPHERSON Jean Elizabeth   *BMedBiol 1970
                                         MB ChB 1973**
d of Ian M. MB ChB(Edin) g p and May Hails SRN; b Bradford 13.6.49
h o Bradford 1973-74, sen h o paediat 1974-75; sen h o path. Leeds 1975-76, regist from 1976
m Boddy

MacPHERSON John Fiddes   MA 1959

McPHERSON Joyce Anne   MA 1970   Dip Ed 1971
m Peckitt

McPHERSON Kathleen Elizabeth   MB ChB 1969

MACPHERSON Mary Elizabeth Fraser   MB ChB 1959
d of Donald F. M. MRCVS(Edin) vet surg and Mary Henderson MA(Edin) civ serv; b Nairobi 3.12.33
h o Victoria ch hosp Hull 1961-62
m Kingussie 26.3.60 Ian S. Robertson BSc 1955 qv
d Aber 6.1.78

MACPHERSON Mary Isabella   *MA 1956 Dip Ed 1957
teacher geog: Inv royal acad 1957-59, Torry j s s Aber 1959-60, part time St Margaret's s for girls Aber 1967-68
m Aber 15.7.59 Frederick C. H. Nisbet BSc 1955 qv

McPHERSON Stephen   MB ChB 1956

MacPHERSON Thomas Ian   *MA 1967
s of Thomas MacP. head stalker and Mary A. C. W. Stuart; b Invercauld 14.3.42
teacher: geog Madras coll St And 1968-71, prin geog Buckie h s from 1971
m Dun 7.10.71 Margaret E. Kay BSc(St And) teacher d of William D. K. Dun

McPHERSON William James   *BSc 1970
s of James McP. eng and Chrissie Cassie secy; b Fraserburgh 9.1.48
Courtaulds: res chem Coventry 1970-74, group leader (res and dev) Coventry 1974-76, sect. leader (implementation of res projects into prod.) Grimsby 1976-78, sect. leader res and dev acrylics Coventry from 1978
m Fraserburgh 6.9.69 Jean L. Watt teacher d of Owen J. W. Memsie

McPHERSON Winifred   MB ChB 1962
d of Robert M. McP. bldr/hotelier and Winifred

Buckner; b Inverurie 20.6.38
Aber: h o Woodend hosp 1962-63, sen h o, regist City hosp 1963-66; regist clin path. Bristol RI 1966-68; clin asst haemat Melbourne Aust 1969-71; clin asst radiol Leic/g p Leicsh 1972-76
m Aber 3.7.67 Alastair Bissett-Johnson LLB(Nott) barrister and assoc prof McG Montreal s of Edward O. B-J. Banstead

MACPHIE Anne Winning   *MA 1961
m Smith

McPHIE James Langley   MB ChB 1969
s of James McP. comp rep and Agnes Brown; b Denny 7.3.45
h o ARI 1969-70; terminable lect path. Aberd 1970-73, lect from 1973
m Aber 2.12.72 Margaret MacKenzie RGN nurs sister d of George MacK. Lhanbryde

McPHILLIMY William Noble   *MA 1968 *MEd 1972
s of Noble McP. foreman moulder and Mary Neil knitter; b Glasg 18.2.43
teacher Engl Inverurie acad 1969-71; educ psych (child guid) Aber 1972-73; lect educ psych coll of educ from 1973
m Aber 12.11.66 Dorothy C. B. McWee MA 1968 qv

McQUEEN Earl Ingram   *MA 1959
s of Earl I. McQ. piano tuner and Violet C. Reid; b Aber 12.4.37
BA(Cantab) 1961 MA(Cantab) 1964 MLitt(Cantab) 1966
lect classics Brist from 1964

MacQUEEN Shiona Catherine Joan   *MA 1969

McQUILLAN John   MA 1965
s of John McQ. foreman steel fixer and Christina Butler; b Glasg 3.7.39
teacher: Lat/Russian Dumbarton 1966-67, Lat Cheshire 1967-69, Engl Hereford 1969-73; asst head Hereford from 1973
m Sanderstead 6.8.66 Sandra J. Beckley MA 1966 qv

McQUISTAN Fiona Eugenie Winifred   MB ChB 1964
d of John K. McQ. asst works man. and Eugenie W. Kivlichan teacher; b Glasg 27.8.39
DObstRCOG 1966 DA 1970
h o: Dumfries and Galloway RI, Woodend hosp Aber 1964-65; sen h o gyn Leeds, h o obst mat. hosp Aber 1965; sen h o: Law hosp Carluke 1965-67, Nat Women's hosp Auckland NZ 1967; regist anaest Wellington hosp NZ 1968-70; regist anaest Dumfries and Galloway RI 1970-71, part-time from 1971
m Dumfries 16.12.70 John D. C. Smith MA(Glas) solic s of Andrew C. S. MA(Glas) Glasg

MacRAE Anabel Janet   MA 1969

MacRAE Catriona Flora Gillanders   MB ChB 1961
d of John A. MacR. bank man. and Mary R. Nicolson nurse; b Wick 3.3.38
h o Aber 1961-62; part-time g p Cirencester 1962-63; sessional clin work (publ health) Lincoln 1967-70; part-time publ health Glos from 1970
m Aber 1960 Gordon L. Smith MBChB 1961 qv
husb d 14.2.75

McRAE Derek James   *BSc(eng) 1968

MACRAE Donaldina Agnes   MA 1966
d of George M. carpenter and Catherine Morrison; b Stornoway 15.1.45

teacher: Engl/allied subj Edinbarnet s s Clydebank 1967–69, Engl Kingsridge s s Glasg 1969–72, asst prin Engl 1972–73; prin Engl: City Public s s now Allan Glen's Glasg 1973–75, Garthamlock s s Glasg from 1975
m Aber 1.3.75 Thomas M. Jess insur broker s of Joseph J. Glasg

McRAE Edith   MA 1968
m Stephen

MACRAE Grace Kathleen Roslyn   MB ChB 1962
d of Edward G. M. man. dir and Grace C. Ross secy/cashier: b Aber 31.3.39
DPM 1967 MRCPsych 1974
h o: Aber 1962–63, Lond, Birm 1963–64; sen h o, regist Birm 1964–65; regist Dun 1965–67; regist, sen regist Birm 1967–72; consult. psychiat Birm from 1972
m Aber 8.10.65 Donald G. Jamieson MB ChB 1958 *qv*

MACRAE Helen Shepherd Blake   MA 1966
b Inv. 30.6.45
teacher Engl Aber 1967–68, Stranraer 1968–71
m Inv 24.7.68 D. M. Rothwell

MacRAE Helen Sylvia   MB ChB 1961
m Wilkinson

MacRAE Hugh   MA 1958
s of Donald MacR. crofter and Margaret Mackinnon; b Applecross 19.11.36
teacher Aber: Frederick St s 1959–69, prin Engl 1969–72; prin guid Harlaw acad from 1972
m Aber 28.12.72 Shirley Hepburn cook d of Alexander H. Aber

MACRAE Jean Gillean Cameron   MB ChB 1966
m Turner

MACRAE Jessie Salmond   MA 1966
d of Farquhar M. bank teller and Jessie A. Cargill; b Inv 15.2.46
teacher Kittybrewster p s Aber 1967–68
m Aber 12.7.68 James D. R. McMahon MB ChB 1966 *qv*

MacRAE John Alexander   LLB 1969

MACRAE John Alexander Cargill   BSc(eng) 1965

MacRAE John Mackinnon   MA 1965

MacRAE Kenneth Duncan   *MA 1964 PhD 1970
s of John D. MacR. sailor and Henrietta Gunn; b Forres 27.10.42
FRSS 1970
asst lect psych Aberd 1965–67; lect: psych Belf 1967–69, med statist Belf 1969–76; sen lect statist Charing Cross hosp med s from 1976
m Belfast 5.9.69 Julie A. Thompson MSc(Belf) occup psych d of Malcolm G. T. Lond; marr diss 1976

MacRAE Madeline   MA 1963
m Millar

McRAE Mairi Margaret   BSc 1957
d of Hugh McR. MA(Glas) teacher, educ psych and Margaret Campbell BSc(Glas) teacher; b Bearsden 15.6.36
res asst: Macaulay inst of soil res Aber 1957–62, path. dept Swedish hosp Seattle USA 1962–64, asst, head chem Washington state lab Seattle 1964–69; various posts in NZ 1971–73
m Seattle 5.3.66 Ian M. Munro

MacRAE Mary Morrison   MA 1969
m Ferguson

McRAE Moira Ida Elder   BEd 1970
d of George J. McR. and Jean R. McIntosh lab tech; b Keith 29.1.47
teacher: Engl (employed by Brit centre for teachers in Germany) Augsburg 1970–73, Engl/Fr coll of f e Augsburg from 1973

McRAE Norma   MA 1968
m Thomson

McRAE Stuart Gordon   *BSc 1965
s of Donald McR. sales rep and Elizabeth H. Wood; b Aber 31.10.42
PhD(Lond) 1971
lect soil sc Wye coll, univ Lond from 1965
m Aber 12.8.67 Hazel M. Adam MA 1966 *qv*

MacRITCHIE Kenneth John   MB ChB 1960
s of John MacR. crofter and Margaret Macleod; b Barvas Is of Lewis 21.12.32
Dip Psych Med 1960 CRCP(C) 1967 MRCPsych 1972 FRCP(C) 1973
h o ARI 1960–61; regist psychiat: Aber 1961–62, Glasg 1962–64; fell. med/psychiat Rochester USA 1964–66; sen regist psychiat Aber 1966–67; psychiat Toronto 1967–71, asst prof fac of med univ of Toronto/chief in-patient serv dept psychiat Toronto gen hosp 1971–76; dep psychiat-in-chief Tor sen hosp from 1976
m Rochester USA Rhoda McDonald d of John McD. Stockinish Is of Harris

MacRITCHIE Murray   MA 1964
d Aber 8.4.74 *AUR* XLV 450

McROBBIE Margaret Ishbel   MA 1958
d of Alexander McR. Hong Kong police and Violet M. Cruickshank MA 1928 *qv*; b Hong Kong 10.12.36
teacher: central s Fraserburgh 1959–67, Hythehill p s Lossiemouth 1968–69, Torphichen W Lothian 1969–70
m Aber 22.7.69 Calum McCallum lect tech coll s of Malcolm G. McC. Campbeltown

McROBERTS James Montgomery   MA 1962
s of Hugh B. McR. master mariner and Annie Montgomery; b Carnlough Co Antrim 20.1.11
teacher AGS 1963–70; retd
m Kilmun 22.6.46 Ronalda D. B. Watson d of Mearns B. W. Aber
d Aber 8.9.78 *AUR* XLVIII 107

McROBERTS Milton Rudolph   PhD 1961
MSc(Purdue)

McSEVENEY Elizabeth Beattie   MA 1969

McSPORRAN Archibald McDonald   *MA 1958

MacSWEEN Kenneth Somerled   BSc(for) 1968
s of Kenneth J. MacS. bank acct and Flora J. Macdonald MA(Glas) teacher; b Lamlash 31.5.46
tech serv proj leader pulp & printing indust Fort William, Beaconsfield, Cardiff, Tillycoultry 1969–72; area for. Fountain Forestry Stirling 1972–75; sales man. Northern Nurseries 1975–77; self-employed salesman and broker consult. of nursery stock, landscape contr./for. contr from 1977
m Aber 16.3.73 Morag R. Ronald MA 1969 *qv*

McVEIGH Gerald   BSc(for) 1961

McVICAR Alasdair Harkness   *BSc 1967 PhD 1973
s of Donald McV. farm. and Frances Harkness nurse;
b Glasg 21.5.44
res asst zool Aberd 1967–70; sen scient off. DAFS marine
lab Aber from 1970
m Kirkwall 8.8.68 Elizabeth M. Thomson MA 1966 *qv*

McVIE Fiona Jean Richmond   MA 1969

McWATT Peter Joseph   MB ChB 1969

McWEE Dorothy Carol Bruce   MA 1968
d of Ernest McW. shop man. and Mary Graham
health visitor; b Glasg 19.3.46
teacher p s: Kemnay 1969–72, Rothienorman 1972–74,
Hillocks Bucksburn 1974–75; head Kingswells p s from
1975
m Aber 12.11.66 William N. McPhillimy MA 1968 *qv*

McWILLIAM Alan George   *BSc 1970
s of George P. McW. SPCA insp and Dorothy C. G.
Riddell MA 1935 *qv*; b Edin 8.7.47
Greenock: computer progr 1970–73, syst analyst IBM
(UK) 1973–75; syst analyst BMW München W. Ger
1975–78; syst eng IBM (UK) St Albans from 1978

McWILLIAM Alexander Davidson   *BSc 1961
MSc 1963 PhD 1968
s of Adam McW. eng, trg off. and Jessie Davidson
cashier; b Elgin 2.9.39
asst lect Aberd 1965–68; phys Hilger & Watts Lond
1968–70; Margate: dev man. 1970–74, prod. group man.
from 1974
m Aber 26.7.68 Valerie C. Waterston civ serv d of James
W. Aber

McWILLIAM Angus Anderson   *BSc 1968 PhD 1974

MacWILLIAM Anne Margaret   BSc 1956
d of John MacW. MA 1905 *qv*; b New Pitsligo 15.12.35
tech res asst Unilever Warrington 1956–57; teacher Hilton
s s Aber 1958–60, St Margaret's Aber 1960–63, internat s
Geneva 1964–68, St Margaret's Aber 1968–69, Lively h s
Ontario 1969–70, Hutcheson's boys' g s Glasg 1970–74,
dep prin phys Madras coll St And from 1974

McWILLIAM David Gordon   MA 1970

McWILLIAM Elizabeth   MA 1969 Dip Ed 1970
d of William J. McW. blacksmith and Helen M.
Taylor; b Huntly 25.10.48
teacher mod lang: Perth h s 1971–73, Holly Lodge h s for
girls Liv from 1973
m Huntly 4.8.73 Joseph E. Pardoe civ serv s of Joseph
E. P. Huntly

McWILLIAM Helen Ann Wood   MA 1961
d of William J. McW. sawmiller, warehouseman and
Euphemia Wood; b Lossiemouth 5.11.40
teacher mod lang Elgin acad 1962–66
m Elgin 13.7.63 Ian McKidd chief off. merch navy s of
James McK. Elgin

McWILLIAM Irene Wilson   MA 1956
d of James McW. civ serv and Alexandrina Wilson; b
Aber 24.8.35
teacher Westerton p s Aber 1957–60
m Aber 27.12.58 Albert Birnie sen scient off. s of
Alexander B. Aber

McWILLIAM Ralph Robertson   BSc(eng) 1959

McWILLIAMS Dennis   *MA 1965

MADDEN Craig Alexander   *MA 1969
s of Alexander L. M. insur off. and Mary S. McKenzie
secy; b Aber 16.12.46
PhD(Glas) 1976
Glasg: teacher Cathkin h s 1972–74, Hutcheson's g s
1974–75, asst prin hist Shawlands acad from 1975
m Aber 13.7.71 May Simpson MA 1969 *qv*

MADELEY Charles Richard   MB ChB 1961 cMD 1965
s of Charles L. A. M. furn consult. and Elsie J. Mann
MB ChB 1921 *qv*; b Birm 14.8.32
h o ARI 1961–62; polio fund res fell. dept of bact Liv
1962–65; lect med microbiol St Thomas's hosp med s Lond
1965–70; MRC res fell. inst of virology Glas 1970–72;
sen lect clin virol/hon consult. virol Glas 1972–79; prof
virol N'cle from 1980
m Burbage 25.7.63 Margaret A. Martin mus d of Gordon
O. M. Oare Marlborough

MAGEE Carolyn Isabel   *MA 1967
d of Frank M. LLD 1979 and Isobel M. Noble civ serv;
b Aber 21.12.44
teacher: Engl & Fr Inv 1967–68; Fr Aber 1971–72 and
from 1973
m Aber 15.7.67 Ian S. D. Begg MB ChB 1967 *qv*

MAGEE Margaret Frances   MA 1961 *1968
d of Frank M. LLD 1979 and Isobel M. Noble; b Aber
24.1.40
L-ès-L(Rennes) 1969 M-ès-L(Rennes) 1970 Dip App
Ling(Edin) 1971
teacher: Aber 1962–65, Hamburg 1965; lect H-W Edin
from 1971
m Edin 11.8.75 Andrew M. Lang M.Phil(Edin) arch. s of
Robert M. L. Spinningdale

MAGEE Penelope Jane   *MA 1969
d of Frank M. LLD 1979 and Isobel M. Noble; b Aber
7.10.46
teacher: Engl Rennes France 1971–73, Fr Aber from 1973

MAHMUD Mohammed Darus Bin   *BSc(for) 1962

MAIN Alan   MA 1957 BD 1960 PhD 1963
s of James E. W. M. gen fish merch and Mary A. R.
Black; b Aber 31.3.36
STM(NY union theol seminary) 1961
C of S min Chapel of Garioch 1963–70; presb moderator
1969–70; chap. Aberd from 1970–80; prof pract theol
Christ's Coll Aber/head dept pract theol Aberd from 1980
m Aber 30.7.60 Anne L. Swanson MA 1957 *qv*

MAIN Alexander Norman   *MA 1964
s of Alexander O. M. lab and Susan S. Cruickshank;
b Aber 14.11.41
post grad res Aberd 1964–66; lect psych Strath 1966–73;
co-ordinating off. comm of vice-chancellors and principals Lond 1973–76; advis educ methods to Strath from
1976
m Aber 17.12.66 Alison M. Walker d of Ronald P. W.
MA 1931 *qv*

MAIN David   *BSc 1969
s of David M. elect. and Ann H. Coull; b Buckie
28.12.45
Dip Ed(Makerere) 1970
teacher, prin chem: Njiris s s Kenya 1970–73, Sekolah
Menengah Sains Kuala Lumpur 1974–75; prin sc Kgari
Sechele s s Molepolole Botswana 1976–78, Naledi s s
Gaborone Botswana from 1978
m Ashford Surrey 27.10.73 Clare I. Walker secy d of
John C. W. Staines

MAIN Dorothy   MA 1966
m Francis

MAIN Douglas Edmund Thomson   *BSc 1961
s of Alexander R. M. garage attend. and Ann C. A.
Thomson; b Aber 2.12.38
teacher: Inverurie acad 1962–68, Machakos boys' board. s
Nairobi 1968–73, Banff acad 1973, John Forrest sen h s
Perth W Aust from 1974
m Aber 25.1.64 Rona A. McCarthy med photogr

MAIN James Jennings   BSc(eng) 1964

MAIN Margaret Mein   MA 1956
d of David M. M. fisherman and Christine Duggie;
b Nairn 12.2.34
ALA 1963
lib asst Aber publ lib 1957–63; lib Ottawa publ lib 1963–
64; res off. Scot. Nat Lib 1964–65; lib Ottawa publ lib
from 1965, head of adult serv from 1978

MAIN Rosemary Susan   MA 1970
d of George K. M. MA(Glas) customs and excise surv
and Edith M. Mole secy; b Lond 5.4.49
teacher Edin from 1972

MAIN Sandra   MA 1968
d of David M. banker and Jessa R. Dallas; b Aber
14.1.47
teacher geog Elgin acad 1969–71
m Nairn 1971 John G. McConnachie police constable
s of Joseph McC. Inv

MAIN William Eric   BSc(eng) 1965

MAIN William Mein   BSc(eng) 1956
s of Isaac M. M. fisherman and Christina Duggie;
b Nairn 6.12.35
MEng(McM) 1975
civ eng: Port Talbot, Glasg, Toronto, Lond(Ont),
Winnipeg 1956–59; civ eng instr tech coll Hamilton
Canada from 1969

MAINLAND Margaret Miller   MA 1959
d of Harold M. teacher and Margaret C. Jamieson
teacher; b Kirkcaldy 5.4.37
teacher prim subjs/Lat/Fr various schools, latterly
Arbroath acad from 1960
m Montrose 17.4.54 John Findlay MA 1954 qv

MAINLAND Thomas James   BSc(eng) 1957

MAIR Alexander Stirling Fraser *BSc(eng) 1957
s of Alexander W. R. M. farm./acct and Agnes W.
Stirling; b Drumblade 20.7.35
app Rolls-Royce Glasg 1957–71; tech off. RAF Lond
1960–62; man dir Caithness Glass Wick 1971–75; market
dir Worcester Royal Porcelain Co 1975–76; group man.
dir Caithness Glass Wick from 1977
m(1) 14.10.61 Alice A. Garrow BSc 1959 qv (d 29.12.75)
(2) Crieff 21.10.77 Mary C. Bolton d of Thomas B. Crieff

MAIR Brian Alexander   MA 1968
s of Alexander M. missionary and Helen E. Gaussen
missionary; b Lond 25.10.47
journalist: reporter Inv 1968–70, edit. Paris 1970–76,
edit. and translator Hong Kong from 1976

MAIR Frank Fentie   MB ChB 1969
s of Stuart G. M. farm. and Mary P. Bruce; b Turriff
19.5.45

h o ARI 1969–70; sen h o obst, dermat ARI 1970–71;
g p Banchory from 1971
m Aber 11.7.68 Morag R. Brown clerkess d of James
F. B. Turriff

MAIR George Wood   MA 1961

MAIR James   *MA 1958

MAIR John   BSc 1958

MAIR John Miller Mitchell   *MA 1959
s of Alexander W. R. M. acct and Agnes W. Stirling;
b Huntly 14.5.37
Dip Psych(Lond) 1960 PhD(Lond) 1964 ABPsS
lect psych Middx hosp med s Lond 1963–67, sen lect from
1967; fell. Neths inst adv study in humanities and soc sc
Wassenaar, Holland 1971–72
m Harpenden 20.1.62 Katharine J. Lindsay BA(R'dg)
clin psych/writer d of Robert L. BSc(Lond)

MAIR Joyce Willetta   MA 1958

MAIR Stuart Bruce   BSc 1959

MAITLAND Alison Isabel   *MA 1969 PhD 1972
d of James J. M. farm. and Isabella H. Monro; b Aber
17.7.47
asst to H. C. Robbins Landon, Haydn schol: Florence
1972–73, Vienna 1973–74, Aber from 1974
m Aber 31.8.74 Robert S. Shiel BSc(agr)(N'cle) horticultural advis s of Stanley H. S. Morpeth`

MAITLAND Dorothy Isobel   MA 1963
d of James M. insp of works and Margaret Wilson;
b Aber 30.9.40
teacher: Ballater p s 1964–65, Cloverfield p s Bucksburn
1965–73, asst head from 1973
m Aber 17.8.71 George D. M. Dow DA teacher of art s
of Marshall D. Aber

MAITLAND Ronald George   BSc 1967

MAKIN Michael John   MSc 1963
BA(Oxon)

MALCOLM Hugh MacGregor   *BSc 1966
s of MacGregor M. bank man. and Christina B. B.
MacFarlane; b Edin 28.5.44
STC E. Kilbride: tel exchange proj and dimensioning
eng 1966–69, circuit des lab 1970–72; circuit eng for
private and export Crossbar tel syst Plessey Beeston
Nott 1972–74; tel traffic and syst stud. eng STC E Kilbride
from 1974

MALCOLM Neil Law   BSc(agr) 1961

MALCOLM Ronald Innes   *MA 1960 Dip Ed 1961
                                         MEd 1963
s of Edward C. M. chartered mech eng and Evelyn
Frain secy; b Glasg 12.8.38
teacher: Laurencekirk 1961–64, Dun 1964–70, E. Kilbride
1970–72; asst dir of educ Moray & Nairn 1972–75; div
educ off. Highland reg c from 1975
m Aber 30.12.64 Christine J. Williamson teacher d of
Charles W. Dollar

MALCOLM Stella Margaret   *BSc 1960
d of Norman L. M. eng and Winifred M. Forrest SRN
nurs sister/midwife; b Lond 31.12.37
Unilever Isleworth: res chem 1960–65, sect. man. consumer stud. 1965–67

m Lond 18.1.64 Alfred J. W. Ludford gold marker s of Alfred W.L. Lond

MALINS Donald Clive   PhD 1967 DSc 1976
 s of Richard H. M. and Mabel M. Warner; b Lima, Peru 19.5.31
BA(Wash) 1953 BS(Wash) 1956
Seattle USA: univ prof/progr head NOAA 1967–74, also dir environmental conserv dir NOAA dept commerce from 1974
m Seattle 27.1.62 Mary L. Leiren univ stud. d of Linus L.

MALLEY Alexander Bruce   MA 1965
 s of Alexander M. sawmill foreman and Ann F. Bruce; b Ellon 25.8.42
teacher Kirkhill p s Aber 1966–69; head audio-vis aids dept Ardleigh Green j s Hornchurch 1969–72; head Daviot p s Inverurie from 1972
m Fraserburgh 15.8.69 Sandra J. Sim MA 1969 qv

MALLEY Ian   MA 1963 BSc 1968
 s of Alexander M. sawmill foreman and Ann F. Bruce; b Fraserburgh 6.7.40
ALA 1973
lib Maria Mercer phys lib univ of Brist 1970–77; information off. for user Educ Brit lib from 1977

MALLINSON Donald Leslie   BSc(for) 1959

MALLINSON Peter David   *BSc 1969 PhD 1972
 s of Harry M. div secy friendly soc and Phyllis Hargreaves; b Northampton 30.6.47
FCS 1972 CChem MRIC 1972
R'dg: asst edit. *Molecular Physics* 1972–73; SRC postdoct res asst 1973–75; applications progr univ of Lond computer centre 1975–77; computer progr user serv univ of Aston Birm from 1977
m Aber 16.12.69 Margaret C. M. Mair MA 1971 d of Arthur B. M. Aber

MALLOCH Susan Margaret Jennifer   *MA 1969
 d of George C. M. MB ChB(Edin) g p and Eileen M. Littlewood MA(Edin) SRN; b Edin 24.2.46
Lond: p a, secy to chmn opinion res centre 1969–70, secy to gen man. Brit wool market. board 1970–71; teacher: Fr Headington s s Oxford 1972–74; TEFL Oxf 1974

MALOIY Geoffrey Moriaso Ole   PhD 1968
 s of Rokoi O. M. farm. and Keis E. Korio; b Ngong Kenya 10.8.39
BSc(BC) 1964 MIBiol(Lond) 1968 Scient Fell. Lond Zool Soc 1968
Kenya: head anim physiol div E.Af vet res inst Muguga 1968–71; univ of Nairobi: head dept anim physiol from 1972, prof anim physiol from 1975, dean faculty of vet med from 1976: visiting scient inst of anim physiol Cambridge 1971; sen Fulbright Hays schol and res assoc biol labs Harvard USA 1975

MALONE Brian Francis   *BSc 1968 MSc 1970

MALONE Mary Elizabeth   *MA 1967

MALTHOUSE Ray Edward   *BSc(eng) 1969
 s of Edward M. civ eng and Joyce E. Podger; b Stockport 22.7.46
MICE 1973
asst eng: Taylor Woodrow Lond 1969–70; Poole burgh council 1970–71, Warks c c 1971–74; sen eng Oxfordsh c c Oxford from 1974
m Bournemouth 12.6.71 Janet L. Freegard draughtswoman d of Ronald A. F. Poole

MALYA Meenakshi Manjeshwar   MSc 1964
 MA(Madras)

MANGAL Subash   BSc 1965

MANGAT Sukhdev Singh   BSc(eng) 1968
 BA(Panj)

MANLEY Duncan John Russell   MSc 1961
 s of Ernest R. M. bank man. and Sarah Rees BA (Swansea) teacher; b Croydon 31.3.38
BSc(Exe) 1959
soil surv (of Eng and Wales) Devon 1961–64; scient liaison off. Rank Hovis McDougall Lond 1964–67; tech and dev man., tech and buying dir Chiltman Biscuits Lond 1967–77; food process tech Baker Perkins Peterborough from 1977
m Cheam 14.7.62 Jane M. Howell secy d of Arthur C. H. Cheam

MANN David Leask   *BSc 1970
 s of Stanley O. M. bact, prin scient off. and Anna M. Leask; b Aber 9.3.48
PhD(Strath) 1973
proj man. Unilever res Sharnbrook 1973–78; tech man. United Biscuits Glasg from 1978
m Aber 6.7.71 Brenda L. Green teacher d of Raymond G. Aber

MANN Maureen Elizabeth   MA 1969
 m Collin

MANN Thomas Leslie John   BSc 1962
 s of Thomas L. M. M. sales man. and Anne H. Purdy; b Norfolk 30.4.41
Dip Ed(Adel) 1975
exper off. Torry fisheries Aber 1963–64; Aust: res asst dept anim husb Sydney univ 1964–66, livestock res off. dept of agr Adelaide 1966–68, haemat off. IMVS Adelaide 1969, supt field stat CSIRO div of nutrit and biochem Adelaide 1970–72, farm man. nr Adelaide 1973–74, res off. agr Roseworthy coll S Aust from 1974
m Adelaide 28.10.67 Elizabeth A. Webb nurs sister d of Martin W. Marwell Victoria Aust

MANSI Morid Girgis   MSc 1965
 s of Girgis S. M. sen clerk Sudan railways Atbara and Afifa H. Toma; b Atbara 20.6.39
BSc(Alex)
Gezira res stat Sudan: agronomist 1965–67, statist 1967–69 PhD stud dept expt statist NCSU, USA 1969–72; sen statist/head of statist sect. 1973–78; prof biometrics agr res corp Wad Medani from 1978
m Alexandria Egypt 24.8.67 Nagat N. Bissada BSc(eng) (Alex) chief agr eng Sudan Gezira board d of N. B. Alexandria

MANSON David Leslie   *BSc 1958
 s of Frederick W. M. CA and Margaret R. McAdam; b Elgin 19.8.35
res stud. Aberd 1958–61; indust chem: Manc 1961–63, Middlesbrough 1963–70; computer analyst/progr Middlesbrough from 1970
m Aber 20.5.60 Margaret I. Robertson hostel housekeeper d of James A. R. Brechin

MANSON Donald McAllister   *MA 1962
 s of Donald M. M. fishmonger and Jean Wallace teacher needlework; b Aber 26.4.37
teacher: Caol 1964–65, Banff acad 1965–68; sen educ psych Cumnock ch guid centre from 1968
m Aber 6.7.63 Mary Mitchell MA 1960 qv

MANSON Doreen Mackenzie MA 1970 Dip Ed 1971
d of William C. M. police sergt and Margaret A.
Mackenzie clerkess; b Fearn 19.6.49
teacher p s Stirlingsh 1971–75, Invsh from 1975
m Aber 4.7.77 Bruce A. Matheson s of James M. Inv

MANSON Henry John MB ChB 1970
s of James M. farm. and Mary E. Peterson; b North-
mavine Shetland 9.2.46
ARI: h o 1970–71, sen h o anaest 1971–72, regist anaest
from 1972
m Errol 3.4.71 Edith M. McFarlane RGN d of William
P. McF. Glencarse

MANSON John George Mackay *BSc 1968
s of Francis M. insur ag and Johan Mackay; b Wick
26.1.46
teacher chem: Wick h s 1969–71; RGC Aber 1971–76;
prin chem Lochaber h s Fort William from 1976
m Wick 9.7.71 Anne M. Fraser nurse d of Victor F.
Wick

MANSON Marion Scott *MA 1962
d of Alexander M. and Christina Mair; b Peterhead
3.2.39
teacher
m David W. N. Stewart coll lect

MANSON Neil Bressay *BSc 1963 MSc 1966
PhD 1968
s of Frederick W. M. CA and Margaret R. MacAdam;
b Elgin 17.8.40
asst prof Los Angeles 1968–70; res assoc Queen Mary
coll Lond 1970–72; ANU Canberra: res fell. 1972–78,
sen res fell. from 1978
m Aber 13.9.68 Patricia A. Garland secy d of Victor H. G.
Aber

MANSON Roger John MB ChB 1956
d Coventry 2.3.61 *AUR* xxxix 205

MANSOUR Ali Hafez MLitt 1967
s of Hafez M. bus. man and Bahaya Mohamed; b Egypt
26.3.32
BCom(Ein Shams) 1956 PhD(St And) 1970
statist insur co Cairo 1956–59; Cairo univ: asst 1959–62,
lect literature, econ 1970–75, reader from 1975
m Egypt Wedad Tulup d of Marawan T. Egypt

MANTELL Helen Diana Mary *MA 1965
d of Henry P.M. dist supt ALC Zambia and Barbara
A. Lyall MA 1921 *qv*; b Zambia 4.1.44
teacher: Lond 1966–67, Lusaka 1967–69; curric dev off.
Lusaka 1969–73; teacher Banffsh 1974–76; lang teacher
Engl lang foundation Edin from 1976

MARCELLA Camille *MA 1969
d of Domenico M. insur salesman and Flora M.
Murray sales asst; b Aber 14.6.48
Lond: proof reader market res comp 1969–70, admin
asst publ 1970–72, teacher 1973–78; resid Hong Kong
from 1978
m Aber 2.7.71 George W. Simpson arch. s of Norman S.
Stoneywood

MARDON David Kenneth BSc 1966 MSc 1975
s of George F. F. RAF, insur ag and Edith G. Milligan
PO clerk; b Retford 13.5.43
res asst zool Aberd from 1969
m Aber 12.10.72 Glenda E. Tomlin hotel caterer

MARIONI Lina Della BSc 1964
d of Luigi A M. shopkeeper and Delina Barbieri;

b Ellon 13.5.43
teacher maths: Stirling 1965–69, Ellon 1970–73, prin
maths from 1973

MARIONI Norma Luigina MA 1969
d of Luigi A. M. shopkeeper and Delina L. Barbieri;
b Fraserburgh 18.5.48
teacher Engl: Bathgate 1970–72, Dun 1972–75, Aber
from 1975

MARK Colin Brown Downie MA 1959
s of Alexander M. lorry driver, blacksmith and Mary
Bruce; b Campbeltown 26.12.36
teacher p s: Turriff 1959–61, Peterhead 1961–68; head:
Burnmouth 1968–72, Gourdon from 1972
m 26.7.63 Jean C. Thom nursery worker d of James T.
Aber

MARKS Gillian Mary *MA 1969 Dip Ed 1970
d of Robert S. M. HMIS and Mary G. Pyne s secy;
b Stirling 10.12.47
teacher Engl: Bell–Baxter h s Cupar 1970–71, Tomlinscote
c s s Frimley from 1971
m Torphins 6.8.71 David I. Gould BSc(N polytech Lond)
lect/syst analyst s of Francis C. G. Stokenham

MARNOCH Jennifer Jean MA 1970
d of Daniel J. M. M. head for. and Margaret S.
Menzies hairdresser; b Glenalmond 15.12.49
teacher: geog Dunblane h s 1971–75, prin guid from 1975
m Perth 30.7.77 Michael S. McHale policeman s of
Patrick McH. Auchterarder

MARNOCH Patricia June BSc 1960
m Currie

MARQUISS Michael *BSc 1970 PhD 1977
s of Maurice M. elect. eng and Mary Simmons book-
keeper/typist; b N'cle-u-Tyne 2.2.47
PhD stud. Aberd mtn and moorland res stat Banchory
1970–73; h s o ITE (predator res) out-posted at Dumfries
from 1974
m Aber 4.8.72 Elizabeth A. Henderson physioth d of
William H. Aber

MARR Douglas *MA 1969 Dip Ed 1970

MARR George Laurie MA 1957 dBD 1960
s of George C. M. wood working machinist and
Margaret W. Stopper; b Aber 3.6.36
C of S min: St Adrian's ch Anstruther 1961–67, Grange
ch Kilmarnock from 1967
m Aber 5.8.60 Margaret B. McArthur MA 1958 *qv*

MARR Iain Lovat *BSc 1961 MSc 1963 PhD 1966
s of Donald H. M. life assur off. and Margaret Hooson;
b Aber 21.6.39
Fritz Feigl prize of Austrian microchem soc 1970
asst lect Aberd 1964–66; CIBA fell. technische hochschule
Vienna 1966–67; lect chem Aberd from 1967; visiting
lect univ Kuala Lumpur Malaysia 1970–71 and 1977
m Vienna 11.8.66 Eva Watzka teacher Engl d of Otto W.
Vienna

MARR Ian Scott BSc 1966

MARR Kathleen Ann *MA 1970
m Malone

MARR Sheena Margaret Smith MA 1965
m Furie

MARRIOTT Richard Welton *BSc 1966
 m Dorothy K. Forbes BSc 1966 *qv*

MARSH Elizabeth-Ann MB ChB 1967

MARSH Jennifer Frances *MEd 1966
 d of Andrew M. comp secy and Frances Chrystal translator; b Pinner 10.11.37
MA(Cantab) 1961
teacher geog Aboyne acad from 1966

MARSHALL Adrian Gerald *BSc(agr) 1963 PhD 1969
 s of C. F. M. BSc(eng)(Edin) eng and Marjorie M. K. Fry; b St And 10.10.40
MS(Calif) 1965
teaching asst UC Berkeley Calif 1963–65; lect zool Aberd from 1965; seconded lect univ of Malaya 1966–68

MARSHALL Alexandra Rose MA 1967
 d of William K. M. relief stat master and Elizabeth A. Lawson; b Kingussie 16.8.46
teacher Lossiemouth p s 1967–71, asst head 1971–77; head Portknockie p s from 1977

MARSHALL Hugh Gordon Walker BSc(for) 1962

MARSHALL Keir Cleland LLB 1970
 s of Thomas K. M. town clerk and Isabella Thomson; b Paisley 18.11.47
NP 1974
law app Elgin 1971; exec off. HIDB Inv 1972; law app Inv 1972–74; solic Inv from 1974
m Bishopbriggs 4.4.74 Heather E. Cousin MA(Glas) teacher d of William C. Bishopbriggs

MARSHALL Linda Joyce BSc 1968
 m Lamb

MARSHALL Margaret Williamson *MA 1967
 d of John M. MA(Glas) headmaster and Maria R. Williamson; b N. Berwick 5.7.44
post grad Certif Advanced Europ Stud.(econ)(Bruges) 1968
trainee Europ commun inst for univ stud. and EEC Brussels 1968–69; res asst centre for contemp Europ stud. Sus 1969–70; part-time TEFL Helsinki 1971; part-time teacher Ger f e/freelance writer and translator Cheshire 1972–74; res assoc dept soc admin and med s Manc 1974–77
m Aber 26.3.70 Richard J. Potton BSc(Sus) univ lect s of Sydney C. P. Epsom

MARSHALL Peter Michie MA 1969
 s of Alexander M. grocery man. and Mary A. McLeod nurse; b Banff 29.9.46
MICA 1974
CA Edin 1969–75, Lond from 1975
m Edin 5.5.73 Margaret W. Forbes secy d of James W. F. Edin

MARSHALL Robert *MA 1967
 s of Wilfred R. M. gas board employee and Margaret Duncan; b Aber 21.8.44
lect inst d'anglais univ de Strasbourg 1968–71; information off. Brit consul. gen Strasbourg from 1972
m Derby 24.7.71 Patricia Daly SRN, secy dip. serv d of William M. D. Winslow

MARSHALL Sheila Ross MA 1970
 d of Robert J. M. police insp and Jean M. Ross teacher; b St And 5.9.48
banker Paisley, Glasg 1970–74
m Cupar 10.7.70 Peter W. Mills BSc(eng) 1970 *qv*

MARTIN Anne Don *MA 1968 CASS 1970
 d of John M. clerk of works dept environment Aber and Alexandrina McIntyre teacher; b Glasg 24.3.46
Glasg: med soc worker Western I 1970–72, sen med soc worker Gartnavel gen hosp 1972–75, fieldwork teacher Western I 1975–77; soc worker Kingseat hosp Newmachar from 1977
m Aber 3.6.77 Alan K. Foulis BSc(Glas) med pract s of Keith F. MB ChB(Glas)

MARTIN Brian Anthony Bernard *BSc 1969
 s of Edward L. M. printer and Doris M. Allen; b Lond 22.11.45
PhD(Warw) 1973
SRC res stud. Warwick univ 1969–73; wissenschaftlicher asst Max-Planck inst für biochemie München from 1973

MARTIN Carol June Lofthus *MA 1970
 d of John M. M. foreman joiner and Ethel M. Lofthus; b Aber 24.1.49
asst teacher: Aylesbury 1971–74, Cleveland educ auth 1974–75; Cleveland educ auth: coll lect 1975–76 and from 1979
m Aber –.9.70 David K. J. Baldwin MA 1970 *qv*

MARTIN Christine MA 1964

MARTIN David Michael Weir BSc 1969
 s of Gavin L. M. teaplanter, farm. and Jean I. Gavin; b Aber 27.1.43
Lond: syst analyst ICL 1969–73, Dataskil (salesman) 1973–74; Sydney: salesman NCR 1975–77, comp dir Martin Henderson from 1977
m Aber 3.7.69 Lilian U. Bald MA 1968 *qv*

MARTIN Eleanor Marie MA 1968
 d of Alexander M. M. farm man. and Helen R. Thomson teacher; b Salisbury 3.7.47
trg off. installation of data prep syst and of comm computer packages for customers in computer bureau Lond 1968–77
m Lond 17.8.74 Roy K. Kunar BSc(Imp coll) consult. eng s of David P. K. AIEd(Lond) Guyana

MARTIN Elizabeth Margaret *BSc 1967
 d of David M. M. crofter and Margaret I. Morrice; b Kingswells 3.3.46
MSc(Dund) 1969
teacher maths Summerhill acad, Old Aber s s 1970–75
m Aber 6.6.75 Thomas C. Kirkpatrick tel eng s of Thomas K. Lockerbie

MARTIN George McKenzie *MA 1962
 s of David M. M. crofter and Margaret I. Morrice; b Aber 9.3.40
lect Ger Aberd from 1965
m Aber 22.12.73 Eleanor J. Henderson MA 1971 teacher d of Ross M. H. Aber

MARTIN Iain Robert MA 1967

MARTIN Ishbel McDonald *MA 1967
 d of John M. clerk of works and Alexandrina McIntyre teacher; b Glasg 4.12.44
Engl asst Rennes univ France 1967–68; res stud. Aberd/Paris 1968–71; lect Fr: Edin 1971–72, Nott 1972–73, Manc polytech from 1973
m Cheadle 24.5.75 John M. Coy MSc(Brad) lect accounting/author s of William H. L. C. Reevesby nr Boston

MARTIN James McBride MA 1961

MARTIN James Mulholland   MA 1970
BD(Dund)

MARTIN John Stuart   MA 1967
s of John L. M. dir fam bus. tea/coffee merch and Bessie Ewan secy; b Sale 7.9.45
CA(Eng and Wales) 1972
Thornton Baker & Co CA Manc: articled clerk 1967–70, audit sen 1970–72; audit man. Pannel Fitzpatrick & Co CA Manc
m Accrington 4.8.71 Nancy P. Lodge teacher d of Spencer L. Accrington

MARTIN Lesley Elizabeth McLeod   MA 1966
d of Stanley E. M. MA 1934 qv; b Aber 15.9.44
teacher: Peterhead 1967–69, 1971–72, Langholm acad from 1975, remed educ from 1976
m Peterhead 9.4.69 Alexander D. McBay ARCO mus teacher Galashiels, Langholm acad s of Alfred D. McB. Peterhead

MARTIN Mary Ann MacSween   MA 1966

MARTIN Pamela May   MA 1970 Dip Ed 1971
d of John M. M. joiner and Ethel M. Lofthus typist; b Aber 29.7.47
teacher Tullos p s Aber 1971–73; teacher/lib Overleigh Middle Chester 1973–75
m Aber 21.12.67 Alexander S. Robertson MA 1967 qv

MARTIN Ruaridh MacCuish   *MEd 1969
s of John M. radio oper/tech and Catherine A. MacCuish teacher; b Stranraer 6.9.42
MA(Edin) 1964 Dip Ed(Edin) 1965
teacher maths Golspie h s 1965–68; asst educ psych Sutherland 1969–72; educ psych Western Is reg Stornoway from 1973
m Dingwall 10.7.70 Marion A. MacLeod teacher d of William MacL. Dingwall

MARTIN Scott Russell   MB ChB 1964
s of James R. M. MB ChB 1932 qv; b Aber 11.2.38
LMCC(Can) 1973
h o ARI 1964–65; RAF med br 1965–70; g p Port Perry Canada from 1970
m(2) Port Perry 30.7.77 Susan Schwan nurse Whitby Ont
d Port Perry 9.79 car accident AUR xlviii 354

MARTIN Sheila Christina   MB ChB 1958
d of James N. M. papermill worker and Annabell Duncan papermill worker; b Peterculter 22.7.33
MRCOG 1963 MRCGP 1966
NHS hosp posts N Wales, Scot. 1958–67; private pract and hon work Christian hosp Quetta Pakistan from 1967
m Glasg 17.12.66 Jahansoz F. Patel BA(Punjab) elect. eng/bus. man. s of Framrose B. P. Quetta

MARTIN Sheila Smith   BSc 1957
d of John A. M. motor hirer and Mary M. Mann secy; b Inv 3.9.36
FCS 1972
teacher chem: Aber h s for girls 1958–65, spec asst 1965–69, royal acad Inv from 1969

MARTIN Valerie Claire   *MA 1969
d of Wilfred H. M. head attendant House of Lords and Annie E. Beddoes; b Coleraine NI 29.4.42
C Phil(Calif) 1975
exch schol univ of Kansas USA 1969–70; instr Swedish lang and lit. univ of Calif Los Angeles 1970–75; instr Swedish lang US army 1974; Calif: instr Swedish Pomona coll Claremont 1974–77, dir lang lab Pomona coll 1975–76, instr Swedish Reseda commun adult s from 1975, owner Nordic translation serv Claremont from 1977; instr Swedish lang: Chaffey coll Alta Loma from 1977, Calif state poly univ Pomona from 1978, Citrus coll Azusa from 1979, parent educ Claremont adult s from 1979, Swedish s Mar Vista from 1980
m Los Angeles 11.6.75 Robert L. Gustaveson BS(Utah) civ eng s of Robert T. G. Salt Lake City

MARWICK David Corrigall   *BSc 1964
s of William C. M. MA 1937 qv; b Stafford 16.5.42
teacher: VSO Lusaka Zambia 1965–66, Aber 1966–68, Lerwick 1968–70; nurs auxil 1970–72, stud. nurse Aber from 1972
m 11.7.68 Jean M. H. Sandison MA 1966 qv

MARWICK John Sinclair   *BSc 1970

MASING Jawie   MB ChB 1967
s of Masing Ak Jerenang farm. and Kumang Ak Emparan farm.; b Marau Sarawak 3.3.42
DPH(Singapore) 1972
h o Hairmyres hosp Glasg 1967–68; m o Simanggang Sibu Sarawak 1968–71, sen m o 1972–74; g p Sarikei, Sarawak from 1974
m Sibu, Sarawak 28.11.70 Mary Wong P. H. clerk d of Wong P. Kwong Sibu

MASON Lesley Marie   MA 1967
d of Thomas L. M. elect. and May A. McMillan cashier/bookkeeper; b Manc 15.1.45
Dip Ed(Belf) 1968
teacher Engl Belf 1968–70, prin Engl Dungannon NI 1970–72; lect Engl Portadown NI 1972–74; commun tut. for adult educ Peterborough from 1975
m Newtownards NI 4.7.70 William H. Stewart comp dir s of James S. Kircubbin

MASSEY Juliet Cathron   BSc 1968
d of Humphrey L. M. CA and Catheron J. R. Formoy; b Harlow 25.4.46
jun tech, med lab tech: Oxford 1969–71, Ibadan Nigeria from 1972
m Lochgilphead 27.11.71 Donald R. Clark MB BS(Lond) med pract s of Roger H. C. Battle

MASSIE Arthur   MA 1970

MASSIE Harry McKenzie   MA 1968
s of Harry M. police off. and Nellie I. McKenzie hairdresser; b Turriff 31.8.46
grad trainee acct Bradford city treas 1968–71; tech asst educ. fin. Leic city treas 1971–74; audit asst Leics c c from 1974
m Arbroath 6.6.70 Christine A. Robertson nurs sister d of Donald R. Arbroath

MASSIE Helen Watson   BSc 1969 MB ChB 1971
d of George M. stillman and Helen A. W. Watson; b Oldmeldrum 5.7.45
DObstRCOG 1973
h o Aber hosps 1971–72; sen h o obst/gyn Inv 1972–73; civ med pract Osnabrück Ger from 1973
m Aber 4.12.72 Roderick J. M. MacDonald MB ChB 1971 RAMC s of Duncan MacD. Conon Bridge

MASSIE Kathleen Forbes   BSc 1962

MASSIE Maureen   BSc 1956
d of Alexander M. bank teller and Isabella J. B. Masson; b Aber 7.5.35
teacher maths/sc: Northfield acad Aber 1957–60, part-time posts Aber 1962–70; sc Peterhead acad from 1971

m Aber 29.12.59 Alexander G. Armstrong pharm s of
Allan M. A. MA 1925 *qv*

MASSIE Maureen Elizabeth Symmers   MA 1969
d of James M. blacksmith and Mary M. F. Taylor
psychiat nurse; b Strathdon 14.6.46
m Bucksburn 25.11.69 George M. Dorward sales rep s of
Alexander G. M. D. Stirling

MASSON Aileen Justine   MA 1966
m Wilson

MASSON Andrew   *BSc 1970

MASSON Catherine Kelly   MB ChB 1958
m Skinner

MASSON Christina   *BSc 1962 MSc 1964
d of John M. fisherman and Annie Ritchie; b Inverallochy 12.3.40
lect: RGIT Aber 1963–64, H-W univ Edin 1964–65;
part-time asst Aberd 1966 and 1969; temp lect RGIT
1971–73; part-time dem H-W univ Edin from 1974
m Noble

MASSON George Fraser   BSc(eng) 1961
s of George M. scient instrum maker and Janet Dufton;
b Aber 5.6.40
MICE
grad eng Swindon 1961–63; Lond: site eng 1963–64,
asst eng 1964–67, eng 1967–69; tech rep Birm from 1969
m Swindon 5.9.64 Valerie S. Scott teacher d of Mervin
J. S. Swindon

MASSON Gordon Machray   MB ChB 1968 cMD 1973
s of Alexander M. firemaster and Dorothy M. Davie;
b Greenock 3.4.45
MRCOG 1974
h o ARI 1968–69; sen h o Gilbert Bain hosp Lerwick
1969–70; sen h o mat. hosp Aber 1970; MRC fell. obst
Aberd 1970–72; regist obst/gyn Aberd 1972–74; clin
instr obst/gyn med coll Wisconsin Milwaukee USA 1974–
75; lect obst/gyn Aberd 1975–77; sen lect human repro-
duction and obst S'ton/hon consult. obst/gyn Hants area
(teaching) from 1977

MASSON Margaret Dean   BSc 1957 *1958
d of Alexander C. F. M. eng(telecomm) and Margaret
I. Allan; b Elgin 4.5.35
teacher: Dalkeith h s 1959–62, prin geog Keith g s 1962–
65, Weymouth g s 1965–71, Helston comp s 1975–76,
Elgin acad 1978–81, Kincorth acad Aber from 1981
m(2) Elgin 3.7.65 Bruce E. Weightman electronics eng
s of William E. W. N'cle-u-Tyne

MASSON Mary Bella Ritchie   BSc 1961
m Steele

MASSON Peter Davie   MB ChB 1965
d 4.4.66

MASSON Robert Alan   *BSc 1968
s of Robert M. fish merch and Nellie G. T. Livingstone;
b Inverallochy 7.3.46
teacher sc Peterhead acad 1969–72; app CA Inv 1972–76;
CA Aber from 1976

MASSON Robert Edwin   *BSc 1969 PhD 1973
s of Robert M. painter and Isabella M. Masson;
b Stonehaven 20.5.47
teacher chem: Kirkcaldy h s 1973, Torry acad Aber from
1973
m Aber 27.12.72 Mary R. Taylor BSc 1970 *qv*

MASSON Sandra   BSc 1968
d of Alexander S. M. merch navy and Isabella M.
Morgan; b Aber 30.8.48
teacher: Alford acad 1969–70, St Mary's acad Bathgate
1970–72, Linksfield acad Aber 1972–75
m Aber 4.7.75 Andrew J. Bolsover BSc(St And) teacher
s of John F. B. Stockport

MASSON Sheila Ann   BEd 1970
d of Robert M. painter and Isabella M. Masson;
b Stonehaven 8.5.49
teacher: mod lang Perth h s 1970–74, Engl St Matthias
gym Gerolstein W. Ger 1974–76, mod lang/ housemistress
Hartcliffe comp s Bristol from 1976

MASTERMAN Michael   BSc(eng) 1970
s of Leonard M. mech eng foreman and Catherine
Burke; b Durh 25.1.47
asst eng: Perth 1968–69, Northallerton from 1969
m Spennymoor 3.6.72 Hazel Dixon bank clerk d of
William J. D. BSc(Lond) Spennymoor

MASTERMAN Veryan Loveday Serrell   BSc 1970
teacher Bucks 1971–73; recorder for *The Zoological
Record* Brit Museum (nat hist) from 1973

MATHER Alexander Smith   *BSc 1966 PhD 1972
s of Alexander S. M. farm. and Mary M. Smith MA
1924 *qv*; b Aber 17.9.43
lect geog Aberd from 1967
m Aber 7.7.70 Grace S. MacArthur MA 1969 *qv*

MATHER Arthur Cameron Mackay   *BSc 1963
s of Osmund K. M. army off. and Jean C. Allan shop
man.; b Thurso 18.9.41
MSc(City univ Lond) 1977
seismic computer Bromley 1963–65; scient information
off. Lond 1966–77; bookshop prop. Cowes from 1978
m Hampstead 21.3.70 Elizabeth Holdstock SRN d of
Raymond P. H. Lond

MATHERS Helen Tait   *MA 1966 Dip Ed 1967
d of David S. M. MA(St And) teacher and Jean K.
Rutherford BSc(St And) teacher; b Campbeltown 6.2.44
teacher Engl N Berwick h s 1967–69; head p s Fetlar
1969–71
m Aber 23.7.69 Anthony R. Mainwood BSc(Brist) asst
warden Fair Isle bird obs/RSPB warden Fetlar/lorry
driver/teacher s of Henry R. M. OBE Whitstable

MATHERS John Shirreffs   BSc(agr) 1956
s of James C. M. eng and Frances H. Findlater nurse;
b Edin 5.3.31
SDA NDA(Edin & E. Scot. coll of agr)
reg admin off. Scot. agr trg board Perth from 1970
m Aber 12.6.58 Jenny Johnston nurse d of James W. J.
Aberchirder

MATHERS John Walker   *BSc(eng) 1966

MATHERS Kathleen Paterson   BSc 1969
d of Alexander R. M. farm. and Jenny Paterson
teacher; b Kintore 16.2.48
Vereeniging S Af: bact Rand Water board 1970–71,
teacher from 1971
m Vereeniging 6.2.71 Logan R. G. Fitchie BSc 1969 *qv*

MATHESON Alasdair Burnett   MB ChB 1964

MATHESON Catherine Ross   MA 1964 Dip Ed 1966
d of James R. M. gamekeeper, crofter, s bagpipe instr
and Helen C. Tough; b Kinlochewe 16.6.43
teacher: Aber 1965–66, Sutherland 1968, Aber 1973–75,

Porchester from 1975
m Aber 22.6.63 Antoine K. Ah-See MB ChB 1965 *qv*

MATHESON Catherine Ross   *MA 1958

MATHESON Christina   *MA 1962
d of Alexander M. MB ChB 1931 *qv*; b Inv 12.9.39
Dip Clin Psych(Edin) 1964
clin psych Stratheden hosp Fife 1964–65; part-time lect
dev psych Euro section univ of Maryland Italy 1965–66;
part-time res asst Strath 1967–69; part-time clin psych
RHSC Glasg 1969–73; sen clin psych from 1973
m Aber 4.9.65 Bruno U. V. Del Priore arch. s of
Domenico Del P. Salerno Italy

MATHESON Donald William   MA 1956
s of Kenneth M. crofter and Catherine MacDonald;
b Brue Is of Lewis 10.6.33
MBE 1973
serv RAEC UK, Borneo, Malaya, Hong Kong from
1957; major, sen educ off. Guards depot Pirbright
m Aber 19.1.57 Alice I. Durno d of Ferguson D.
Oldmeldrum

MATHESON Iain James   MA 1963
s of Donald J. M. BSc 1933 *qv*; b Conon Bridge 1.8.42
higher exec off. HM Customs & Excise from 1963
m Glasg 1.7.70 Marilyn A. Boyd mus d of Arthur
T. H. B. Glasg

MATHESON Janet Catherine   MA 1959 Dip Ed 1960
d of Alexander M. MB ChB 1931 *qv*; b Edin 13.9.37
teacher: Engl Northfield s Aber 1960–61, Stornoway
1962, Inv h s 1962–63
m Aber 17.7.61 Graham C. Hunter MA 1958 *qv*

MATHESON Jennifer Ruth Victoria   MA 1966
m McGinn

MATHESON Margaret Norma   MA 1961
d of Malcolm M. MA(Glas) schoolmaster and Winifred
M. Spink teacher; b Aberfeldy 19.1.41
teacher: Engl Bridge of Earn 1962–63, Engl/hist
Breadalbane acad Aberfeldy 1963–68
m Strathtay 24.7.64 John Kidd joiner s of John I. K.
Strathtay

MATHESON Mhairi Lindsay   MB ChB 1957
d of David M. bank man. and Mary S. S. Lindsay
MA(Edin) teacher; b Kirkcaldy 9.4.33
h o: ARI 1957–58, Dumfries & Galloway RI 1958–59,
mat. hosp Aber 1959; g p: Crieff 1959–60, Kyle of
Lochalsh 1960–65, Falkirk also prin m o (indust) from
1965; factory doctor Falkirk 1966–72

MATHESON Norman Alistair   MB ChB 1956
*ChM 1965
s of Allan J. M. and Margaret A. Mutch; b Inv 26.3.32
FRCS 1961 FRCSE 1961
h o Aber 1956–57; lect Aberd: materia medica 1957–58,
anat 1958–59; surg regist Aber gen hosps 1959–61; lect
surg Aberd 1961–64, sen lect from 1964 and consult. gen
surg Aber gen hosps from 1967
m Aber 10.9.58 Helen I. Grant d of John G. Ballindalloch

MATHESON Stephen Charles Taylor   *MA 1961

MATHESON Susan Marie   MA 1968
d of Donald J. M. BSc 1933 *qv*; b Nairn 26.2.48
nurse Skye 1968–69; teacher Lossiemouth 1970–71
m Croydon 29.12.70 Roger A. Lockley pilot lt RN s of
Leslie H. L. Croydon

MATHEWSON Alastair George   *BSc 1962 MSc 1964
PhD 1967

MATHEWSON Iain   MB ChB 1959

MATHIESON Alastair Merchant   MA 1960 LLB 1962
s of Alexander M. master butcher and Constance E.
Coutts cashier; b Aber 12.6.39
exch schol bus. man. univ of Kansas USA 1963–64;
asst solic Aber: James & George Collie advoc 1964–65,
A. C. Morrison & Richards advoc 1965–66, Paull &
Williamsons advoc 1966–69, ptnr from 1969
m Aber 31.8.63 Sally A. Jack health visitor d of Frank
W. J. Inverugie

MATHIESON Alexander Willox   *MA 1966
s of Alexander M. plumber and Christina Bissett;
b Aber 3.4.44
MInstM FRGS
fin. analyst Ford motor co Brentwood 1966–69; British
Leyland (Austin Morris div) Birm: pricing supervis
1970–71, man. price and budget analysis 1971–74,
marketing man. 1974–75; marketing serv man. Leyland
cars from 1975
m Hampstead 23.7.66 Carol M. Critchley MA 1966 *qv*

MATHIESON George McKenzie   MA 1958 LLB 1960
s of William M. M. loc govt off. and Nell A. Main;
b Aber 20.3.38
MILGA 1972 AMBIM 1973
law app Aber 1958–61; leg. asst: Banff 1961–63, loc govt
Inv 1963–64; dep town clerk Elgin 1964–73, town clerk
1973–75; sen leg. asst Moray dist c from 1975
m Aber 18.6.60 Roseann Dunbar shorthand typist d of
Albert D. Aber

MATHIESON John Watt   *BSc 1965 PhD 1969
s of John R. M. stonecutter and Mary Watt; b Aber
31.12.42
res fell. Baylor univ USA 1969–71; teacher Aber from
1971
m Aber 30.7.65 Netta Skinner teacher

MATHIESON June   MA 1960
d of Harry R. M. crane driver/machineman and Alice
P. Fyfe; b Aber 10.6.39
teacher Northfield acad Aber 1961–73, asst prin remed
educ from 1973
m Aber 31.3.72 George A. Cruickshank teacher s of
George C. Aber

MATIER Kenneth Ogilvie   *MA 1963
s of William R. M. printing man. and Janet B. Pollock;
b Glasg 13.6.34
BA(Cape T)
univ lect classics: Salisbury Rhodesia 1963–64, Grahamstown S Af 1965–74, sen lect from 1974
m Wolmaransstad S Af 6.1.68 Rosemary Bach BMus
(Rhodes) teacher d of Marx B. Wolmaransstad

MATTHEW Andrew Murray   MA 1970

MATTHEW James Andrew Davidson   *BSc 1960
PhD 1964
s of James M. power stat eng and Georgina Milne
typist; b Aber 22.11.38
FInstP 1974
Aberd: res stud. 1960–62, asst 1962–64; res asst Cornell
univ USA 1964–65; lect York univ 1965–75, sen lect from
1975
m York 23.3.68 Kathryn A. McKenna BA(York) publ
relations off. d of Michael J. McK. Nott

MATTHEW Jean Greig   MA 1956
m Cheriyan

MATTHEW Myrtle Irene   *MA 1964
d of Robert S. M. papermaker/watchmaker/school
janitor and Myrtle I. Munro; b Aber 9.12.40
Dip Lib(Lond) 1970
lib: res asst Nat Lib of Scot. Edin 1964–65, asst Aberd
1965–73, coll of adult educ Manc 1973–75; lib asst Aberd
from 1975
m Aber 24.9.73 Gordon Anderson-Smith MA 1966 qv

MATTHEWS Angela Rosemary   *MA 1970
d of F. D. M. housing man. consult. and M. J. A.
Matthews; b Welwyn Garden City 11.5.48
PO exec off. Edin 1970–71; pers off. Invergordon 1971–
74; careers off. Fife from 1974

MATTHEWS Frances Smith   MA 1962

MAUGHAN Evelyn Mary   MA 1969
d of Francis M. eng and Elizabeth M. Smith bank
clerkess; b Rhynie 18.12.47
teacher Lockerbie 1970–74
m Lockerbie 20.12.73 Roy B. Carlyle farm. s of William
J. C. Moffat

MAXWELL Elsa Pricella Ann   MA 1970
d of James W. M. warehouse man. and Elma M. King
teacher dom sc; b Stronsay 11.11.49
teacher Dun from 1971
m Kirkwall 12.9.68 Stanley C. Nutt s of Stanley C. N.
Alloa

MAXWELL Esmé   MA 1967
d of Thomas B. M. farm. and Ella Johnstone; b Annan
3.4.45
lect Engl: coll of tech Rotherham 1967–71, coll of comm
Hammersmith Lond 1972–73
m Aber 2.8.67 Atholl R. Forbes MB ChB 1966 qv

MAXWELL Phyllis Kathleen   *MA 1958
d of Edwin A. M. MA 1928 qv and Greta L. Sykes MA
1929 qv; b Cambridge 24.2.35
teacher: Clitheroe g s 1959–61, Wycombe h s 1961–63;
head scripture: Northwich g s 1963–67, Pennywell comp
s Sunderland from 1967

MAY Andrew   BSc 1956

MAY Andrew   MA 1962
s of George M. M. fisherman and Helen Lawrence;
b Fraserburgh 4.9.40
teacher: Hilton s s Aber 1963–65, Inverallochy p s 1965–
68; dep head Fraserburgh cent s 1968–71; head: Inverallochy p s 1971–76, New Pitsligo and St John's s s from
1976
m Fraserburgh 15.9.62 Zena M. F. Gibb d of Thomas
M. G. Sandhaven

MAY Andrew Bruce   *MA 1968 Dip Ed 1969
s of John M. sea capt and Catherine R. Murray
dispensing asst; b Buckie 10.3.35
teacher Engl Brechin h s 1969–73, asst prin Engl from
1973
m 29.5.62 Marchia M. Clunie d of Andrew C. Brechin

MAY Jeanne Moir   BSc 1958
d of Roderick J. G. M. maintenance eng and Jane
R. M. Moir; b Aber 7.3.37
teacher biol Aber acad from 1959 and year mistress from
1970

MAY Joan Bruce   MA 1970
m Lawrie

MAY John   MA 1963
s of John M. fisherman and Catherine R. Murray
dispenser; b Buckie 2.1.42
teacher: St Peter's s Buckie 1964–65, hist/Lat Forfar
acad from 1965 and prin guid from 1972; supt Forfar f e
centre 1970–75
m Aber 4.10.67 Patricia M. Low teacher d of George L.
MA 1956 qv

MAY John Mathieson   BSc 1967
s of John M. restaurateur and Shiela Mathieson
teacher; b Aber 5.2.46
teacher maths AGS 1968–74, prin maths Bridge of Don
acad Aber from 1974
m Aber 23.5.69 Valerie A. Yeats shorthand typist d of
Alexander L. Y. Aber

MAY John Robertson   BSc 1969
s of George M. MB ChB 1947 qv and Margaret S.
Hamilton MB ChB 1947 qv; b Edin 5.4.49
LRCP MRCS 1976 MB BS(Lond) 1976
scient off. Lond 1970–71; h o Royal Free hosp Lond
1976–77; trainee g p Bridgend Wales 1977–79; sen h o,
regist anaest Sheff from 1979
m Pembrokesh 12.11.77 Janice E. Mathias physioth d of
Charles E. M. Fishguard

MAY Rhoda Kathleen   BSc 1969
d of Roderick J. G. M. maintainance eng and Jane R.
Moir; b Aber 4.8.48
teacher geog/sc Hilton acad Aber 1970–79
m Aber 20.10.75 Gary G. Wright BSc(N'cle) soil surv
s of George W. Solihull

MAY Robert Leslie   BL 1956
s of Robert C. M. BL 1927 qv; b Aber 12.11.32
solic: Edin 1956–57, ptnr Mackenzie & Wilson advoc
Aber from 1957

MAY William Stewart   *BSc 1961
s of William M. marine eng MN and Elizabeth M.
Stewart; b Lond 27.1.38
CChem MRIC 1976
AGS/Rubislaw acad Aber: teacher sc 1962–66, spec
asst 1966–73, asst prin sc 1973–74, prin chem from 1974

MAYBANK Graham Thomas   *BSc(agr) 1966
s of Thomas W. M. comp dir and Doris E. G.
Bartholomew; b Bath 29.10.41
PhD(Stir) 1971
forensic biol Home Office S O Nott 1971–72; lect/head
biol sect. Walsall and Staffs tech coll (now Walsall coll
of tech) 1972–76, sen lect from 1976
m Stockton-on-Tees 27.7.68 Mary E. Child MA 1968 qv

MAYCOCK James Hewitt   BSc 1968
s of Joseph M. MA(Liv) C of S min and Lilian Hewitt
nurse; b Kirkcaldy 7.7.43
G Inst P(RGIT) 1977
teacher phys Harlaw acad Aber from 1969
m Aber 8.4.71 Helen R. Finlayson BEd 1969 qv

MAYS Enid Margaret   MA 1970
d of William M. turner/eng and Eileen W. Nuttall
milliner; b Coatbridge 1.6.49
MA(Texas) 1973
teaching asst Engl/stud. W. Berlin 1970–71; teacher Fr/
stud. Austin Texas 1971–73; civ serv Lond from 1974

MEADOWS Martin Ivo   BSc(for) 1970

MEAGER Anthony   *BSc 1969
s of Donald J. M. house-bldr and Molly Birch off.
worker; b Bletchley 24.10.45
PhD(Warw) 1972 Beit Mem Fell. 1972–75
post-doct res MRC Mill Hill Lond 1972–75; MRC sen
res fell. Warwick univ from 1975

MEARES Patrick   DSc 1959
s of Thomas P. M. civ serv and Violet E. Warne;
b Croydon 1.7.23
MA(Cantab) 1947 PhD(Cantab) 1948 ScD(Cantab) 1975
FRSE
res stud. Cantab 1943–46; res fell. Lond 1946–49; Aberd:
lect chem 1949–60, sen lect 1960–65, reader 1965–69, prof
from 1969
m York 24.5.47 Rhoda M. Small MA(Cantab) teacher
d of Horace E. S. Mexborough

MEARNS Kathleen Mary   *MA 1967 Dip Ed 1968
d of John C. M. agr rep and Alice M. Taylor MA 1928
qv; b Aber 11.4.45
teacher Springburn p s Glasg 1968–69, Kelvinside acad
1969–74; asst educ psych Angus 1974–75; teacher
Southesk p s Montrose 1975–76
m Aber 22.3.75 Peter Strachan teacher

MEARNS Yvonne   *MA 1965

MEDFORD William Lisle   MA 1970 CASS 1974

MEGHU Beulah Barbara   MA 1960
d of Thomas M. grocer and Dolly A. Seepaul; b
Trinidad 19.12.26
Trinidad: teacher Naparima girls' h s from 1951, prin
from 1964

MEIKLEJOHN Dorothy   MA 1968 Dip Ed 1969
m von Weymarn

MEINERTZHAGEN Ian Anthony   *BSc 1966
PhD(St And) 1971
res stud. Gatty marine lab St And 1966–69; Aust nat
univ: res asst dept neurobiol 1969–71, post doct fell.
1971–73; sen post doct fell. Harvard univ USA from 1973

MELDRUM Ian Greig   *BSc 1961 PhD 1964
s of Robert U. M. foreman joiner and Isabella Greig;
b Aber 1.3.39
res fell. Glasg 1964–69; res chem: Sunbury 1969–73,
Epsom 1974–76, Sunbury from 1976
m Paisley 23.7.66 Ina F. Ritchie teacher d of William
F. R. Lochwinnoch

MELDRUM Maureen Wendy   MA 1967 Dip Ed 1968
d of Alexander M. baker and Ethel Dinnie; b Huntly
29.1.46
teacher: Ellon 1968–74, Inverurie from 1978
m Inverurie 27.12.68 Richard A. Cruickshank water insp
s of Richard C. Newmachar

MELDRUM Moira Sutherland   MB ChB 1958
d of Roy M. arch. and Gladys M. Sutherland; b Aber
16.4.34
DCH(Eng) 1961
h o Woodend hosp Aber 1958–59; sen h o: ch hosp Nott
1959–60, paediat Manc 1960–61; part-time asst m o
Lancs from 1964
m Aber 29.9.61 William H. Mellor MB ChB(Manc)
g p s of Hezekiah M. Manc

MELDRUM Patricia Mary   MA 1967
m Nile

MELDRUM Stuart James   *BSc 1966
b Forfar 8.2.44
M Inst P 1970 PhD(Lond) 1973
St Bart's hosp Lond: phys dept med electronics 1966–70,
sen phys 1970–74; lect med electronics St Bart's hosp
med coll 1974–76; prin phys St Bart's hosp from 1976
m Glasg 1.9.67 Claire K. Young MA 1967 qv

MELFORD Lilian Fleming   MA 1969
d of Michael J. M. factory dept man. and Jean A.
Fleming secy; b Ellon 14.6.49
teacher mod lang Peterhead acad from 1970
m Peterhead 14.4.73 Maynard C. Buchan BSc 1968 qv

MELLING John   *MA 1962

MELLIS James Alexander   *MA 1968 PhD 1977
s of Duncan M. M. employ. whisky indust and
Margaret G. Rennie; b Glasg 1.6.46
Aberd: res stud. 1968–70, asst Ger dept 1969; lect Ger:
Glas 1970–75, Aberd from 1976
m Aber 20.9.68 Margaret J. W. Hay MA 1968 qv

MELLIS Patricia Mary   MA 1961
d of John R. M. drapery man. and Mary Bond; b
Stonehaven 10.7.40
teacher: Eastwood s s Glasg 1962–63, Lossiemouth h s
1966–67, St Margaret's s for girls from 1973, asst head
from 1975
m Aber 12.7.64 Graham C. Stalker MN off. s of George
D. S. Aber

MELLOR Valerie Anne Clark   *MA 1970
d of Eric D. M. civ eng and Marion Young nurse;
b Middlesbrough 30.8.47
TEFL Kokkola Finland 1970–71; psychotherap with
disturbed adolescents Parkside hosp Macclesfield 1971–
72; teacher Fr Woodmill h s Dunfermline from 1973

MELOTTE Christopher John   *MA 1970

MELVIN James Stuart   *BSc 1966 PhD 1971
s of Archibald M. farm. and Annie Paul farm.;
b Glasg 4.4.40
lect nat phil Aberd from 1971
m Aber 2.10.63 Elizabeth M. Thomson MA 1963 qv

MELVIN Jennifer Margaret Ord   *BSc 1966
m Lawrie

MELVIN Marjory Catherine   MA 1962
m Paget

MELVIN Ray   MA 1968
d of Alexander W. M. farm. and Violet M. Cruickshank MA 1928 qv; b Huntly 12.3.47
res asst drug addiction stud. Toronto 1968–69; post grad
course Aber coll of comm 1969–70; Düsseldorf: asst
foreign advert. dept Ger newspaper 1970–71, asst to
publ of comm information serv 1971, asst to dir of admin
head of Ger off. of Brit manuf audio-visual teaching
aids 1971–76; advt admin co-ordinator for Culligan
(America) Brussels from 1976
m Kildrummy 8.9.79 Richard C. Marcus BSEE(City
Coll NY) dir internat marketing s of William J. M. New
York

MEMERY Kevin Stuart Rowden   *MA 1965

MENCHER June   *MA 1958
m McKimmie

MENDHAM Nicolette Claire *BSc 1967 MSc 1968
d of Norman V. M. BSc(Lond) teacher and Marie L. Robin BA(Lond) teacher; b Lancaster 8.5.45
rest asst to chief exec Flintsh c c Mold 1968–74, ecologist to county plan. dept Mold Clwyd 1974–75
m Ackworth 27.10.73 Michael T. Richardson BSA(Dub) tech serv man. ICI s of Thomas N. R. Sandyford Co Dublin

MENMUIR Patricia Margaret *MA 1960
d of Alexander M. BSc 1926 qv; b Aber 6.11.36
Dun: teacher mod lang 1961–71, woman advis 1971–72, asst rector (guid) from 1972

MENNIE Alexander Milne MA 1968

MENNIE Catherine Fraser MA 1957
d of Alexander M. insur salesman and Catherine F. Bandeen; b Aber 10.8.36
teacher: Byron Park p s Aber 1958–61, St John's RC s Perth 1961–63, Hunter's Tryst p s Edin from 1970
m Aber 29.7.61 William A. Steele chartered elect. eng NSHEB s of George S. Aber

MENNIE George Hardie MB ChB 1965
s of William P. M. police supt, farm. and Ethel A. Hardie; b Elgin 30.5.42
DObstRCOG 1967 MRCGP 1975
h o Falkirk 1966–67; g p Dumfries 1968; med and health off. S Pacific health serv Fiji 1969–71; g p Banchory from 1971
m Aber 5.4.68 Dianne R. Hepburn midwife d of Angus I. H. Stornoway

MENNIE Ian Low *BSc 1957 Dip Ed 1958
s of John H. M. insp SPCC Aber and Jean Low clerkess; b Aber 28.5.34
teacher: spec asst sc Inverurie acad 1958–65, prin phys St Margaret's s Aber 1965–68; Newfoundland: asst prof mem univ from 1968, conductor St John's symphony orch from 1969
m Aber 1962 Maureen E. Hay lib/teacher d of Alexander H. Aber

MENNIE Kathleen Sheila MA 1961

MENNIE Margaret Mary MA 1969
d of Alexander T. M. MB ChB 1949 qv; b Aber 26.4.48
teacher Victoria Road p s Aber 1970–72; Lanarkshire: rural schools 1972–78, head Auchengray p s from 1978
m(1) Desougi
(2) Carmichael 8.8.77 John L. Cooper farm. s of John C. Hyndford Bridge

MENNIE Yvonne Gillian MA 1964
d of James M. pharm RGIT and Rose Harris; b Aber 7.10.42
teacher: remed spec Tullos p s Aber, Carleton p s Glenrothes; lect in numeracy/literacy TOPS prep course Portsmouth coll of art des and f e from 1977
m Aber 25.9.65 Colin R. MacKenzie MA 1967 qv

MENZIES Anne Frances Mary MA 1962
m Cunningham

MENZIES Annie Elizabeth MA 1959

MENZIES Avril Margaret Isobel BSc 1960
d of Charles S. M. MA 1934 qv; b New Pitsligo 21.1.40
chem PYE Electronics 1960–62; translation edit. Pergamon Press 1965–71
m Aber 16.8.60 John M. Hay BSc 1959 qv

MERCER David *MA 1969 MEd 1973
s of William B. M. joiner and Ella Cooper; b Aber 4.10.46
teacher econ York 1973–76; admin off. MDC Sheffield from 1976
m Dunblane 18.8.73 Debbie A. Anderson cook d of Thomas H. A. Glasg

MERCER Roy MB ChB 1960
s of John M. credit trader and Mary M. Hector; b Lond 27.8.36
DA(Eng) 1964
h o RACH, city hosp Aber, Craigtown mat. hosp St And 1961–62; sen h o regist anaest Vict hosp Blackpool 1962–65; g p Gt Yarmouth from 1965
m Cleveleys 9.11.63 Susan M. Bond SRN d of Thomas B. Cleveleys

MERCHANT Bruce Alastair LLB 1965
s of Alastair D. M. solic and Marcia A. Bruce; b Edin 17.5.45
law app James & George Collie advoc Aber 1965–67, solic 1967–68; ptnr: Fredk A. Black & Imrie solic Inv 1968–71, South, Forrest, Mackintosh & Merchant solic Inv from 1971
m Inv 20.1.68 Joan I. S. Hamilton LLB 1967 qv

MERRICK John Brian *MA 1959
s of John M. iron moulder and Annie Unsworth; b Newton-le-Willows 12.1.36
Dip Man.(educ) 1976
teacher: Nantwich 1961, St Helen's 1961–64; prin lect (head of dept) coll of higher educ Manc from 1964
m Newton-le-Willows 23.7.63 Patricia F. Hankey secy d of Fred H. Newton-le-Willows

MICHAEL Ian MacRae *MA 1962
s of Robert M. bank man. and Harriet MacRae; b Lerwick 23.7.40
DPhil(Oxon) 1966
res stud.: Hertford coll Oxford 1962–64, Queen's coll Dund 1964–65, asst lect maths Queen's coll Dund 1965–67; post doct fell. McM univ Canada 1969–70; lect maths Dund 1967–77 and warden Chalmers hall 1973–77; theol stud. Westcott House Cambridge 1977–79; asst curate parish of All Saints Kings Heath Birm from 1979

MICHAEL-PHILLIPS Peter John Charles MA 1968
s of Albert H. M-P. MB BS(Lond) med pract and Edna M. Thompson nurse; b Kettering 7.11.45
teacher Fr/Ger: Wisbech 1964–73, Chipping Campden from 1973
m York 1971 Fiona M. Sinclair teacher d of Jack S. York

MICHAELIDES Euripides Damianou BSc(for) 1958
s of Damianos Hj Michael farm. and Anna Samara; b Arghaki Cyprus 1.11.26
Dip Sc Indust Man. 1970 AMBIM 1971
asst dir for. Nicosia Cyprus 1958–75 (stud. for. off. course Oxon 1961–62) dir dept for. Nicosia from 1976
m Kyrenia Cyprus 24.4.61 Rena Petrides

MICHIE Alexander John *MA 1964

MICHIE Alistair Davidson MB ChB 1956
s of William A. M. master mariner and Jean Kelly secy; b Aber 5.3.32
MRCGP 1968
h o Woodend hosp Aber 1956–57; capt RAMC Malaya, Singapore 1957–60; g p Portlethen 1960–61; sen h o obst ARI; g p/clin asst psychiat Lostwithiel/Bodmin from 1962

m Aber 24.10.57 Dorothy J. Gloyer lib d of Marshall G. Aber

MICHIE Helen Gordon   MB ChB 1968
d of Gordon A. M. bank man. and Jessie Currie MA 1940 *qv*; b Aber 16.11.45
MRCOG 1974
h o: City hosp, Woodend hosp Aber, EGA hosp Lond 1968–70; sen h o: Edin RI, Nott, N gen hosp, Jessop hosp Sheffield 1970–73; regist obst/gyn Dun hosps 1973–74; lect obst/gyn univ Edin 1974–75; locum regist obst/gyn Edin RI 1976; consult. obst/gyn republic of Seychelles from 1976

MICHIE Helen Kennedy   MA 1958
d of Alexander M. seed warehouseman and Annie O. Rennie typist; b Aber 30.3.37
teacher: Engl/hist Mortlach s s Dufftown 1959–62, St Andrew's p s Nassau Bahamas 1962–63, Engl/hist Williams Lake h s BC Canada 1963–64, Aber: Muirfield p s 1965–73, remed Walker Rd p s from 1973

MICHIE John Charles Alexander   BSc 1961

MICHIE Uisdean Macleod   *BSc 1968

MICHIE William Guthrie McGregor   LLB 1968
s of William M. MA 1930 *qv* and Vera C. A. Booth MB ChB 1945 *qv*; b Aber 20.12.47
CA(Edin) 1972
merch banker Lond from 1972
m West Camel Somerset 18.6.77 Susan J. Griffin d of Philip J. G. West Camel

MIDDLER Elizabeth Thomson   MA 1958

MIDDLER James Ian Findlay   MA 1960
s of James M. M. fireplace contr and Gladys Findlay store man.; b Aber 6.8.38
teacher: p dept RGC Aber 1961–67, Engl Kelowna s s BC Canada from 1967
m Aber 5.8.71 Caroline A. Murray teacher d of James M. (missing in action 1944)

MIDDLETON Alan James   *BSc 1967

MIDDLETON Alexander Bruce   BSc(eng) 1962
s of Charles G. M. bus driver and Alexandra Bruce; b Insch 4.2.41
grad trainee on SMETA course W of Scot. area 1962–64; prod. man. manuf of M/C tools Glasg from 1964
m Aber 10.10.64 Patricia A. Spalding clerkess d of Robert M. S. Inverurie

MIDDLETON Bryson Bannochie   BSc(for) 1956

MIDDLETON Elizabeth Fraser   MA 1960
d of Peter M. rly ganger and Mary M. Cassie; b Elgin 24.12.38
BEd(New Br) 1971
teacher Glas 1961–65; Canada: teacher Engl h s Shellbrook Sask 1965–66, Fredericton h s New Brunswick from 1967
m Strathroy Ontario 14.7.66 Walter Brereton res tech univ of New Br s of Thomas B. Liverpool

MIDDLETON Gordon George Alexander   MB ChB 1958
s of George P. M. MB ChB 1926 *qv*; b Aber 11.5.33
RAMC Major army fam med Singapore, Munster W Ger 1960–65; g p MoD Sungei Patani Malaya, Camb, Hong Kong, Tidworth 1966–72, g p Aylesbury from 1972

m Chichester 7.4.62 Janet M. Bradshaw nursery nurse, med secy d of James S. B. MB ChB(Liv) Chichester

MIDDLETON Irene Mitchell   MA 1958 Dip Ed 1959
d of Andrew M. M. baker and Ethel M. Rettie; b Aber 6.5.38
teacher Aber: Inchgarth p s 1959–67, RACH 1967–70, Cornhill p s 1970–74
m Aber 11.7.72 George M. Cordiner joiner s of James C. Aber

MIDDLETON Linda Mary   *BSc 1970
d of Arthur M. foreman bldr and Mary F. Kemp; b Torphins 6.4.48
Dip Ed(Edin) 1971
teacher biol: Penicuik 1971–74, AGS from 1975
m Aber 24.10.74 John Price BSc(Belf) res asst dept spectrochem Edin s of agr, field investig off. dept nutrit biochem Rowett res inst Aber s of John A. P. Newtonabbey Co Antrim

MIDDLETON Marjory Stevenson   *MA 1967
d of James W. M. PO overseer and Marjory C. B. Stevenson mus teacher; b Edin 10.12.44
teacher: N'castle-u-Tyne 1968–69, Fife 1969–71; asst educ psych Fife 1971–72; adult literary assessor from 1974
m Aber 14.8.68 Alexander W. Burnett MA 1966 *qv*

MIDDLETON Rose Elspet   MA 1957
m Hirsch

MIDDLETON Sheila Margaret Silver   MB ChB 1962
d of George P. M. MB ChB 1926 *qv*; b Aber 13.6.38
DObstRCOG 1965
h o Woodend hosp Aber, Whipps Cross hosp Lond 1962–63; trainee g p Ballater 1963–64; h s mat. hosp Aber 1964; res asst nat coronary drug proj Cleveland Ohio 1966–67; med off. FPA Cardiff 1971–72, Sheffield from 1973
m Ballater 15.5.65 Ian D. Cooke MB BS(Sydney) prof obst/gyn Sheff s of Douglas C. Sydney

MIDDLETON Stuart Auldjo   *MA 1961
s of Stuart A. M. CA and Irene M. Esson; b Aber 31.5.39
trainee advert copywriter Lond 1961–71; dir Ogilvy Benson & Mather Lond from 1971; man. dir Ogilvy & Mather Malaysia Kuala Lumpur from 1975; sen dir Ogilvy Benson & Mather Lond from 1978
m Aber 3.8.63 Margaret G. Edmond MA 1960 *qv*

MIDDLETON William Cordiner   BSc 1959

MIDDLETON William Craig Noble   MA 1965

MIDDLETON William John   MA 1960
s of John M. M. painter/decorator and Mary Henderson; b Lamlash 10.7.38
BD(Edin) 1963
C of S min: Rerrick and Auchencairn Kirkcudbright 1964–71, Carnwath Lanark from 1971
m Glasg 1963 Mary M. Kerr insur clerkess d of William K. Lochranza Is of Arran

MILBURN Christopher John   BSc 1967 MB ChB 1972
s of John F. M. insur comp man. and Kathleen Wilson; b York 15.12.43
DRCOG 1977 MRCGP 1978
h o City hosp Aber, ARI 1972–73; lect path. Aberd 1973–74; sqdn ldr RAF med branch 1974–79; g p Aber from 1979

m Aber 25.3.74 Catherine M. Pirie MB ChB 1972 med pract d of Alexander A. P. MA 1891 *qv*

MILBURN John Anthony   PhD 1964
   s of Tom M. headmaster and Agnes M. Johnson teacher; b Carlisle 7.8.36
BSc(N'cle) 1958
agronomist Bookers sugar estate Guyana 1958–61; lect bot Glas 1964–75; overseas visiting fell. (Brit Council) India 1972; Fulbright Hays schol/res fell. (Charles Bullard) Harvard univ 1973–74; sen lect bot Glas from 1975; visiting fell. Messina univ Sicily 1979

MILES Fiona Anne   MA 1970
   d of Robert M. joiner and Ellen P. MacIntyre; b Osterley 12.4.49
teacher geog: Glasg 1971–72, Thurso 1972–76
m Aber 1.8.72 Hugh G. Boyd lect in agr s of John M. B. Huntly

MILES Susan Henderson   MA 1967
   d of Leslie A. M. RAF and Ruth B. M. Torrington; b Tunbridge Wells 19.11.43
teacher Aber: maths Kaimhill s s 1969–70, Fr Summerhill acad 1971, Hilton acad 1971–72, maths American s 1973–75, prin maths 1975–79; supply maths Grampian reg from 1979

MILESON Jill Stroud   *BSc 1966

MILLAR David Gavin   MB ChB 1967
   s of William M. M. MB ChB(Edin) prof mental health Aberd and Catherine M. Rankin LDS(Glas) dentist; b Aber 23.4.47
MRCGP 1974
h o Aber, Inv 1967–68; sen h o: Kirkcaldy 1968–69, Aber 1969–70; lect path. Aberd 1970–71; g p Aber from 1971
m Aber 11.4.69 Judith A. Gibb MA 1967 *qv*

MILLAR Elizabeth Moyes   BSc 1964
   d of William M. M. MB ChB(Edin) prof psychiat Aberd and Catherine M. Rankin LDS(Glas) dentist; b Edin 14.6.43
VSO teacher Zaria Nigeria 1964–65; teacher: chem Firhill s s Edin 1966–68, maths/chem Fort Portal Uganda 1969–70, maths Powis acad Aber from 1970, prin guid from 1972
m Aber 23.6.79 Alexander J. Riddell MA 1965 *qv*

MILLAR Henry Rankin   *B Med Biol 1969 MB ChB 1972
   s of William M. M. MB ChB(Edin) prof psychiat Aberd and Catherine M. Rankin LDS(Glas) dentist; b Aber 23.4.47
MRCPsych 1976
h o ARI 1972–73; res fell./sen h o commun med/gen med Aber 1973–74; sen h o, regist psychiat Edin 1974–77, sen regist psychiat Dun from 1977
m Aber 30.3.70 Frances M. Lee catering man. d of Robert S.L.

MILLAR Jillian Joan   *MA 1968
   d of James T. G. M. men's outfitter and Irene H. Dorward teacher; b Dun 1.7.46
teacher Engl/hist Perth h s 1969–73
m Dun 3.8.71 Charles E. S. Cassie MA(Edin) teacher s of Charles E. S. C. Leith

MILLAR Margaret Malcolm   MA 1969
   d of William M. M. MB ChB(Edin) prof mental health Aberd and Catherine M. Rankin LDS(Glas) dentist; b Edin 19.2.49
Dip Soc Admin(Edin) 1970
soc worker soc work dept Aber 1970–74
m Aber 25.9.70 Peter R. S. Duffus MB ChB 1970 *qv*

MILLAR Peter William   MA 1965
   s of Gavin R. M. MA(Edin) hosp supt/g p and Mary R. Birrell; b Edin 24.5.43
BD(Edin) 1968 ThM(Princeton) 1969
teaching posts India, Aust 1969–70; asst min Crown Court ch Lond 1970–71; C of S min: Glasg 1971–77, Madras India from 1977
m Glasg 29.9.73 Dorothy A. Somerville BSc(Edin) univ lect/bact d of William C. S. BSc(Edin)

MILLAR Roslyn Jean   BEd 1970

MILLARD Helen Joyce Macpherson   MSc 1968
                                                       PhD 1974
   d of Arthur V. M. loc govt off. and Helen M. M. Docherty; b Barrow-in-Furness 3.12.45
BSc(N'cle) 1967
res asst Dund from 1971
m Carlisle 4.9.71 Rodney A. Herbert PhD 1970 *qv*

MILLER Alistair James Mitchell   MA 1958
   s of Alfred J. M. MA 1926 *qv*; b Aber 27.8.38
CA 1964
app, clerk Meston & Co CA Aber 1958–64; asst Cooper Brothers & Co CA Lond 1964–65; asst comp secy Newman Hender & Co Stroud 1965–69; group comp secy Pegler–Hattersley Doncaster from 1970
m Aber 18.8.65 Barbara S. Young MA 1960 *qv*

MILLER Bruce John Fleming   MSc 1970 PhD 1974
   s of Robert G. M. BSc(Edin) for. and Anne F. Fleming BA(Edin) mathematician; b Ndola Zambia 16.10.45
BSc(Guelph) 1969
grad clerk dept sc Canberra Aust 1974–77; asst to pro-rector polytech Huddersfield from 1978
m Honley 6.4.74 Aileen M. Slater BSc(UCNW) teacher d of James B. S. Huddersfield

MILLER Charles Bruce   BSc 1959
   s of Charles B. M. mus seller and Gladys R. Stuart; b Aber 29.5.37
teacher sc Aber acad 1960–62; joined C. Bruce Miller & Co mus sellers Aber 1962, comp dir from 1965
m Aber 26.7.63 Marjory L. Bain teacher p e d of Robin D. B. Stonehaven

MILLER Christine Elizabeth   MSc 1970
   d of Ian M. C of S min and Jean M. Watson MA(Glas) teacher; b Edin 27.2.63
BSc(St And) 1965
lect: univ of Loughborough 1967–68, St And 1969–75; stud. deaconess TEV course St Ninian's ch of Scot. Crieff 1975–76

MILLER Donald Wares   MA 1958
   s of Alexander M. fisherman and Mary A. Doull; b Wick 27.7.37
teacher maths Wick h s from 1959
m Wick 11.8.61 Georgina D. Coghill clerkess d of William C. Wick

MILLER Dorothy Joyce Mitchell   MA 1956
   d of Alfred J. M. MA 1926 *qv*; b Aber 6.10.35
teacher Sunnybank p s Aber 1957–60
m Aber 5.8.60 John M. Howie MA 1958 *qv*

MILLER Douglas   MA 1965
   CA

MILLER Frank Israel   *BSc 1968 MSc 1970 PhD 1973

MILLER Gordon Reginald   *BSc 1957
   s of Reginald E. M. cinema man. and Elizabeth A.

McIntyre secy; b Harrogate 28.9.33
PhD(N'cle) 1962
res asst agr MAFF grant to N'cle 1957–60; res scient
Nature Conserv: unit grouse and moorland ecology
Aber 1960–66, Banchory 1966–70; res scient ITE
Banchory from 1970
m Fyvie 16.10.58 Lesley M. Sleigh BSc 1955 *qv*

MILLER Heather Margo   MA 1961
m Liversedge

MILLER Hugh Graham   *BSc(for) 1963 PhD 1969
s of Robert G. M. BSc(for)(Edin) for. off. and Anne
Fleming MA(Edin) teacher; b Zambia 22.11.39
res scient Aberd from 1963
m Aber 4.7.66 Thelma Martin d of James M. Aber

MILLER Ian David   LLB 1967
s of John M. M. bldr/civ eng, dir and Dolores
McLaughlan; b Edin 13.7.48
ptnr A. & W. M. Urquhart solic Edin from 1974;
Austrian consul for Edin 1974
m Edin 27.6.70 Sheila S. McLean MA 1968 *qv*

MILLER Ian James   MA 1959
s of John B. M. house furn and Mary B. Herd;
b Fraserburgh 21.10.38
LLB(Edin) 1962
law app Edin 1959–62; solic Dun 1963–68; sen leg. asst
Inv c c 1968–70; dep county clerk, county clerk Ross &
Cromarty Dingwall 1970–75; chief exec Inv dist council
1975–77; dir of law and admin Grampian reg c from 1977
m Edin 19.9.64 Sheila M. Hourston secy d of William
A. M. H. Edin

MILLER Ina Margaret   *MA 1966
m Hughes

MILLER Isobel   *MA 1958
d of Alexander M. MA(Edin) teacher and Christina
Mackie; b Elgin 3.12.35
teacher Fr/Ger: Harris acad Dun 1959–62, Turriff from
1973
m Aberlour 19.7.61 Robert Greig MA 1958 *qv*

MILLER James   *BSc 1970
s of David G. M. fisherman and Janet W. Calder;
b Keiss 19.2.48
MSc(McG) 1977
VSO Cebu City Philippines 1970–73; grad stud. McG
univ Montreal 1973–74; awarded Max Binz burs McG
univ for continuation of grad stud. 1974–75; Brit Council
staff from 1975

MILLER James Gordon   MB ChB 1970
s of James R. M. bank man. and Lily H. Tait; b Perth
24.7.46
MRCGP 1975
h o Aber 1970–73; g p: Hull 1973–78, Mintlaw from
1978
m Aber 16.7.70 Judith M. A. Warden MA(Edin) teacher
d of William W. St Cyrus

MILLER John Ashley Laing   LLB 1970
s of George W. M. pharm and Elizabeth M. Laing
MB ChB 1929 *qv*; b Essex 4.8.48
Edin: law app 1970–73, solic from 1973
m Edin 7.7.73 Sheila E. Knowles MA 1969 *qv*

MILLER John Dow Booth   MB ChB 1968 ChM 1978
s of John B. M. wine and spirit merch and Hilda Dow;
b Aber 10.7.43
FRCSE 1974

regist surg Aber 1974–78; res fell. surg Harvard USA
1975–76; lect surg Aberd from 1978
m Aber 18.7.72 Isobel Murray teacher d of Robert M.
Aber

MILLER John Robertson   MB ChB 1957

MILLER Judith Gibson   MA 1970

MILLER Magnus Alexander   *BSc(agr) 1968
s of David B. M. farm. and Margaret G. Muir;
b Methlick 5.3.34
econ with meat and livestock comm Bletchley 1968–70;
tech advis Bayer UK agrochem div Kinross from 1970
m Aber 25.7.59 Doreen C. Urquhart teacher home econ
d of Sinclair M. U. Aber

MILLER Norman Melvin   MA 1965 Dip Ed 1966
s of George P. M. foreman shipbuilding and Isabella
C. Melvin laundress; b Aber 19.9.43
teacher Engl Arbroath acad 1966–67; rly clerk Lond
1967–71; warden model lodging house Aber from 1973

MILLER Peter Edmund   *MA 1963

MILLER Raymond   MB ChB 1958

MILLER Robert   MB ChB 1960
s of William F. M. insur off. and Ann H. Gunn;
b Dunfermline 11.7.37
h o Woodend hosp Aber, Edin RI 1960–62; Inv: sen h o
Raigmore hosp 1962, g p from 1962
m Edin 31.3.61 Mary C. Cowie teacher d of Joseph C.
Whithorn

MILLER Stanley Scott   MB ChB 1962 ChM 1976
s of Robert S. M. pharm and Mary Reid; b Whitley
Bay 24.12.38
FRCS 1970 FAS 1973
h o ARI 1962–64; lect physiol Aberd 1964–68; regist
surg ARI 1968–70, sen regist 1970–74; resid asst surg
hosp for sick ch Gt Ormond St Lond 1974–76; consult.
surg ARI from 1976
m Aber 24.7.64 Madeline E. McGown speech therap d
of Charles G. McG. MA(Glas) Forres

MILLER Stuart   BSc 1964

MILLER William John   BSc 1957

MILLERS John   BSc 1969
s of J. E. M. master mariner and E. Ozols; b N'cle
2.6.47
retail area rep Texaco oil comp 1969–72; UK wrought
sales responsib Alcan aluminium comp from 1973
m Lond 15.9.73 Gundega Jankavs physioth

MILLHAM Richard Henry George   MA 1960

MILLIGAN George Allan   BSc(agr) 1956

MILLS Jeremy Charles Risby   *BSc 1970

MILLS John Robert   *BSc 1970
s of Robert M. shopkeeper and Olwen Fitz-hugh
SRN; b Stockport 23.1.47
teacher Perth 1971–76; lect Dun 1976–77; asst prin
teacher chem Perth from 1977
m Perth 11.7.72 Helen L. Bonomy BSc 1971 teacher d of
William B. MA(Glas) Perth

MILLS Peter William   BSc(eng) 1970
s of Harry M. comp dir and Laura Shaw; b Marple

29.9.47
Babcock & Wilcox Renfrew: grad app 1970–72, tech eng 1972–73; sales eng T. A. Kennedy & Co Glasg from 1973
m Cupar 10.7.70 Sheila R. Marshall MA 1970 *qv*

MILLWOOD Arthur Edward **MA 1960*
s of William H. M. mech/elect. eng and Millicent R. MacKenzie; b Inv 25.1.38
sales Pilkington Bros: Glasg 1960–66, Johannesburg 1967–70; sales W. R. Grace (Africa) 1970–71; lect commun/bldg materials univ of Port Elizabeth S Africa from 1971
m Southport 1.5.72 Jean Timpany

MILNE Alan Ducat   MB ChB 1964
s of George P. M. MB ChB 1934 *qv*; b Carlisle 3.8.40
MRCGP 1971 DA(Lond) 1967
h o Woodend hosp Aber, ARI 1964–65; regist anaest Aber 1965–68; g p Aber from 1968
m Aber 16.7.65 Nanette L. M. Gordon MB ChB 1965 *qv*

MILNE Alan Henry   MB ChB 1967

MILNE Alexander Strachan   BSc(eng) 1967
s of William M. fisherman, lab and Christina S. Strachan; b Billingham-on-Tees 27.3.45
MIEE 1972
trainee Inveresk Paper Group Aber 1967–69; elect. eng Donside paper mills 1969–70; proj eng: Bowater Paper Group Northfleet 1970–75, R. H. Cuthbertson & Ptnrs Edin from 1975
m Huntly 17.8.67 Flora A. Flory MA 1966 *qv*

MILNE Alistair Angus   BSc(agr) 1961
s of William M. police off. and Margaret Angus nurse; b Aber 25.6.39
BVMS(Edin) 1965
vet res off. Stormont N Ireland 1965–69, vet pract Aber from 1969
m Aber 15.7.61 Margaret Reid d of Alexander R. Aber

MILNE Arthur Donald   *BSc 1969
s of Arthur M. banker and Alice M. Main; b Forres 5.10.46
Brit petrol. co: geol Yarmouth 1969–70, Djakarta 1970–71, Yarmouth, Aber 1971–75, NZ 1975–76, Singapore from 1976

MILNE Brian   MB ChB 1966
s of Joseph P. M. MB ChB 1934 *qv* and Margaret J. Strachan MA 1928 *qv*; b Elgin 9.1.42
DObstRCOG 1968 MRCOG 1972
h o Aber 1966–67; sen h o surg Orkney 1968; regist gyn/obst: Inv 1968–72, Glasg 1972–74; sen regist gyn/obst Leicester from 1974, spec from 1977
m Kildrummy 6.9.67 Mary I. B. Ellis SRN ultrasound tech d of James E. Alford

MILNE Catherine Morag   BEd 1969

MILNE David James   *BSc(eng) 1969
s of William C. M. eng and Flora Macdonald; b Aber 30.11.46
MICE 1974 MIHE 1976 CEng
asst eng Lond 1970–72; sect. eng Glasg 1972–74; asst resid eng Keswick northern by-pass 1974–76; proj eng Shell Expro Aber from 1976
m Aber 18.8.73 Wendy A. Wisely MA 1969 *qv*

MILNE David James   *BSc 1970
s of Alexander M. MA 1933 *qv*; b Wick 1.4.47
MSc(Warw) 1972

oper res BL Birm, Liverpool 1972–75; prod. control Smith's Industries Cheltenham 1975–77, with PE Consult. Group from 1977

MILNE Donald McLean   BSc(eng) 1961

MILNE Dorothy Christie   BSc 1958
m Sim

MILNE Douglas James Wood   *MA 1967 BD 1970
s of John A. M. MA(Edin) headmaster and Mary M. Wood; b Dun 1.1.44
ThM(Westminster theol seminary, Philadelphia) 1971
min Free Ch of Scot. Glenurquhart 1972–79, Aust from 1979
m Inv 31.7.69 (Hannah) Joan Mackenzie MA 1966 *qv*

MILNE Douglas Malcolm   *MA 1962 Dip Ed 1963
d Nairn 31.3.75 *AUR* XLVI 327

MILNE Eileen   MA 1963
d of Alexander M. banker and Luella Mackenzie, ch's nurse; b Forres 28.5.42
m Inv 22.8.64 William H. Burnett prod. man. s of William H. B. Inv

MILNE Elizabeth May   MA 1968
d of John N. M. eng and Margaret J. Thomson secy; b Guildford 1.7.47
Cert Soc St(Glas) 1969 Dip App Soc St(Glas) 1970
soc worker: Glasg 1970–72, Paisley 1972–74, Nairobi 1975; sen soc worker Crawley from 1975
m Nairobi 2.10.74 Robert C. K. Mbugua hosp admin s of Jotham M. Kenya

MILNE Euan Cameron   MA 1964

MILNE Florence   MA 1969
d of George S. M. clerk and Mary Williamson; b Aber 21.11.47
teacher Byron Park p s Aber 1970–72
m Aber 31.7.70 John H. Adam quantity surv s of John H. A. Aber

MILNE George Alexander   *BSc 1963 Dip Ed 1964
s of George S. M. clerk and Mary Williamson; b Aber 22.9.40
teacher biol: Gordon s Huntly 1964–65, Inverurie acad 1966–71; prin biol Arbroath h s from 1971
m Aber 7.10.72 Marjorie A. Watt or Downie BSc 1965 *qv*

MILNE Gladys Ledingham   MA 1959
d of John M. M. farm. and Anne B. Ledingham; b Echt 13.2.38
teacher: Alford s 1960–62; Perth: Goodlyburn s 1962–65, St John's s 1965–66, High s 1973–74; remed: Forrester h s Edin 1974–77, Aberdeensh from 1977
m Alford 28.7.62 Archibald M. Cobban civ serv s of Archibald C. Monymusk

MILNE Gordon Graeme   MB ChB 1968
s of George P. M. MB ChB 1934 *qv*; b Carlisle 4.7.43
DA 1971
h o ARI, Woodend hosp Aber 1968–69; trainee g p Peterculter 1969–70; sen h o, regist anaest ARI 1970–73; g p/part-time anaest Gray's hosp Elgin from 1973
m Aber 10.7.68 Margaret J. Milne MA 1965 *qv*

MILNE Hamish Kenneth   *BSc 1970

MILNE Helen Margaret   BEd 1970
d of John M. farm. and Helen D. Garden MA 1927

qv; b Aber 6.1.48
teacher infants St Stephen's RC s Blairgowrie 1970–75, Dun s Montrose 1975–76
m Fettercairn 25.7.75 David A. Ritchie master joiner s of John A. R. Fettercairn

MILNE Helen Mary   MB ChB 1968
d of Albert M. policeman, secur off., safety & fire prev off. and Alice Milton secy; b Keith 16.5.41
h o RACH, St Helen's hosp Lancs 1968–69; locum sen h o Chesterfield royal hosp 1969; sen h o anaest: Chesterfield hosp group 1969–70, united Sheffield hosps 1970–71, Chesterfield hosp group 1971–72; regist anaest: Chesterfield hosp group 1972–73, N Tyneside hosp group 1973–74; trainee g p Hemsworth 1974–75; locum regist anaest S Teesside hosp group 1975; clin off. ch health and fam plan. Cleveland area health auth 1975–76; clin off. ch health Staffordsh area health auth 1976–77; g p Tamworth from 1977
m Aber 21.6.76 Terry D. Kinnis MB BS(N'cle) g p Tamworth s of John F. K. Stockton-on-Tees

MILNE Henry   *BSc 1960 PhD 1964
s of William G. M. for. and Mary Robertson; b Huntly 16.9.35
Aberd: asst lect zool 1963–65, lect 1965–72, sen lect from 1972
m Aber 14.9.60 Margaret J. Machray display artist d of Alexander M.

MILNE Ian Alexander   BSc(eng) 1956
s of James S. M. elect. and Helen M. Dawson; b Rothiemay 9.6.35
asst site eng hydro-elect. Loch Shin 1956–59; div hydraul eng MoW Kisumu Kenya 1959–62; des eng hydro-elect. Lond 1962–65; proj eng indust hydro proj Niagara Falls 1965–70; exec eng hydro-elect. proj Buenos Aires 1970–73; exec eng power div Buffalo USA from 1973
m Perthsh 20.3.65 Hazel M. Ross pharm d of Donald J. R. Comrie

MILNE Ian McDonald   *MA 1957
s of John W. M. painter and Annie McDonald; b Aber 14.10.34
teacher: royal acad Inv 1959–61, Daniel Stewart's coll Edin 1961–66, prin mod lang Gordon s Huntly 1966–77, prin Fr AGS from 1977
m Aber 21.7.60 Katherine M. C. Allan teacher d of William D. A. Edin

MILNE Isabel Alice   MA 1963
m Hutcheon

MILNE Isabella Galbraith   MA 1958

MILNE Isobel Frances   *MA 1965
d of Robert L. M. auctioneer/valuator and Elsie I. Mackie teacher; b Aber 1.8.42
VSO teacher Sierra Leone 1965–66; res asst FO Lond 1966–69; Sudan: s s teacher Omdurman 1969–71, Amer s Khartoum 1971–73, lect Engl fac of econ univ of Khartoum from 1973
m Aber 25.5.71 Abdel G. I. Dafa'alla orthop/optician s of Ismail M. D.

MILNE James Campbell   *MA 1970

MILNE James Dawson   *BSc 1959

MILNE John Alexander Barclay   MA 1957
s of John A. M. MB ChB 1905 *qv*(II, III); b Aber 25.6.19
teacher: Powis acad Aber 1957–59, Banchory acad 1959–

79; retd
m Easingwold 22.7.41 Jessie L. W. Leonard bank clerk d of Samuel N. L. Paisley

MILNE John Gilbert   *BSc 1958

MILNE Lesley Mary   *BSc 1957 Dip Ed 1958
m McIntyre

MILNE Leslie   BSc 1969

MILNE Margaret Eveline   BSc 1964
d of John M. comm trav and Eveline M. Blair clerkess; b Aber 5.11.43
teacher maths: Aber 1965–69, Canterbury 1969–73
m Aber 30.7.70 Roger Price BSc(Birm) univ lect s of Stanley P. Swindon

MILNE Margaret Harris   MA 1958

MILNE Margaret Helen   *MA 1957
d of John C. M. MA 1922 *qv* and Jane W. Shewan MA 1917 *qv*; b Aber 8.4.34
teacher: Fraserburgh acad 1958–59, Springhill and Fernielea p s Aber 1959–62, Brockley jun mixed s Lond 1962–63, Engl/hist Tarves j s s from 1963

MILNE Margaret Jean   MA 1965
d of George M. farm. and Helen Mair catering superv; b Skene 6.9.44
teacher Ferryhill p s Aber 1966–69; part-time lect Moray coll of f e Elgin from 1975
m Aber 10.7.68 Gordon G. Milne MB ChB 1968 *qv*
d Aber 19.7.81

MILNE Margaret Joan   *BSc 1970
d of Ronald M. M. area superv Tennant Cal. Breweries and Margaret H. Reid teacher; b Forres 2.6.48
Dip Ed(Edin) 1971
teacher sc Armidale NSW Aust 1971; part-time dem bot James Cook univ N Queensland 1975–77; teacher sc Dunedin NZ 1978
m Armidale 17.7.71 Anthony P. Spenceley BSc 1970 *qv*

MILNE Margaret Joyce   MA 1959
d of Joseph P. M. MB ChB 1934 *qv* and Margaret J. Strachan MA 1928 *qv*; b Aber 22.5.38
teacher: Banffsh 1960–66, N Province Zambia 1967–69; proof reader Luanshya Zambia 1969–73; teacher Elizabeth Vale S Aust from 1974
m Aber 14.7.61 William R. Sutherland MA 1963 *qv*

MILNE Marjory   MA 1960
d of John I. W. M. MA 1931 *qv*; b Aber 2.9.39
teacher mod lang: Knox acad Haddington 1961–66, Stirling h s 1966–72, spec asst 1972–73, asst prin mod lang and asst prin guid from 1973

MILNE Melville Kermack   MB ChB 1965
s of Alexander K. M. bank acct and Agnes Austin shop asst; b Glasg 4.4.41
FFA 1971
h o Aber 1965–66; sen h o obst/gyn Perth 1966–67; regist anaest Perth 1968–70; sen regist anaest Dun 1970–73; consult. anaest Dun from 1974
m Aber 30.3.67 Wilma J. Mortimer BSc 1962 *qv*

MILNE Michael William   *BSc(eng) 1968
s of Cameron M. M. MA 1934 *qv*; b Turriff 26.12.46
Scot. elect. trg scheme 1969–70; dev eng Ferranti Edin from 1970
m Edin 22.6.74 Joan E. Muir MA 1969 *qv*

MILNE Morgan James BSc(agr) 1968
 s of Arthur J. M. farm. and Mary M. Garden; b Forfar 20.9.46
MSc(N'cle)
oper trainee-oil, oil terminal superv Lancs 1971–73; asst agr eng Grimsby 1973–74; agr eng man. Grimsby from 1975
m Aber 2.5.70 Nicola M. Gearing secy d of George D. G. Udny Station

MILNE Pamela Anderson MA 1970
 d of James R. M. garage prop. and Eunice R. Anderson; b Aber 5.7.49
Dip Soc Ad(Glas) 1973 Dip Soc Work(Glas) 1974
soc worker: Ruchill hosp Glasg 1971–72, Renfrew c c 1974–76
m Aber 6.2.71 Laurence A. Cheyne MA 1970 *qv*

MILNE Patrick Findlay Creighton MA 1962

MILNE Paul Stocks *MA 1964
 s of William M. lect and Ada L. Laing; b Aber 27.7.42
insp of taxes 1964–65; lect econ univ of Hull from 1965

MILNE Raymond Taylor *BSc 1970 PhD 1974
 s of Herbert M. fitter and Margaret S. Taylor; b Forfar 17.11.47
dev chem Billingham from 1973
m Aber 2.4.70 Irene M. Sandison teacher d of John P. S. Cullen

MILNE Rosemary Joyce MB ChB 1970
 d of George P. MB ChB 1934 *qv*; b Carlisle 11.6.46
DObstRCOG(Lond) 1973
h o: gyn ARI 1970, Aber City hosp 1971; sen h o gen surg Balfour hosp Kirkwall 1971–72; sen h o obst Aber mat. hosp 1972–73; g p Bray Eire from 1974
m Aber 28.4.72 James A. W. Lee restaurateur, med stud. s of William L. Belf

MILNE Russell MA 1970
 s of Albert E. M. maintenance man. and Edith A. W. Annand; b Aber 10.12.47
computer progr, analyst Manc 1969–74; sen syst analyst F. W. Woolworth Manc 1974–76; proj leader hydro-electric Aber from 1976
m Aber 26.12.69 Elizabeth A. Davis MA 1969 *qv*

MILNE Stella Dagmar MA 1959
 d of Andrew M. MN home trade master and Frances G. Connon shop asst; b Aber 19.9.38
teacher Aber 1960–62
m Aber 19.7.61 Alastair F. L. Esson MN chief off., maritime pilot Aber s of Herbert W. E. MA 1951 *qv*(III)

MILNE Stephen Halkerston *MA 1970 Dip Ed 1971
 s of John I. W. M. MA 1931 *qv*; b Aber 18.7.47
teacher: mod lang Alloa acad 1971–73, asst prin mod lang 1973–74, prin mod lang from 1974

MILNE Thomas Graham MA 1956 LLB 1958
 s of Archibald M. MA(Glas) teacher and Helen M. Brown teacher; b Finzean 22.3.35
leg. asst: Dumfries c c 1959–61, Aber c c 1961–65; leg. asst, dep town clerk Galashiels t c 1965–68; town clerk Forfar 1968–74; dep dir of admin Tayside reg from 1974
m Aber 27.6.59 Eleanor F. Davidson MA 1956 *qv*

MILNE Valerie MA 1967
 d of Alan M. despatch clerk and Nancy Smith; b Aber 11.11.44
teacher Engl/hist Torry acad Aber 1969–71

m Aber 21.8.65 Alan W. R. Brock eng, stock controller
s of Charles B. Aber

MILNE Victor Gordon *BSc 1957
 b Aber 1934
MA(Tor) 1958 PhD(Tor) 1962
Canada: geol geol branch Ontario dept mines Toronto 1962–72; chief geol/asst director Ontario geol surv div of mines Min of Natural Resources Toronto from 1972
m 1964 Florence M. Dore

MILNE William Burnett Proctor BSc 1960
 s of William P. M. MA 1903 *qv*; b Bristol 13.8.11
MC 1943 OBE 1947
teacher sc Northfield acad Aber 1961–72; retd; resid Aber
m Aber 29.1.52 Barbara F. Souper d of Hugh R. S. MA 1908 *qv*(II, III)
d Aber 8.5.81

MILNE William Hendry *MA 1966
 s of Gordon M. mason, insur ag and Jeanie Hendry dressmaker; b Aber 3.11.41
teacher hist Ellon acad 1967–71, prin hist from 1972

MILTON Aileen *MA 1964
 d of Robert D. M. farm worker and Margaret Innes; b Roseisle 23.9.42
teacher VSO Rawalpindi Pakistan 1964–65; asst lib Glas 1965–68
m Glasg 1.9.68 Richard Fletcher BSc(Manc) lect s of John R. F. BSc(Birm) Abergele

MILTON Alan John Simpson *BSc 1970 PhD 1975
 s of John S. M. insur ag and Mary M. Innes; b Aber 4.6.48
dev chem Wiggins Teape Stoneywood from 1973
m St And 29.6.74 Margaret E. Keracher teacher home econ d of Thomas M. K. St And

MILTON Colin *MA 1965 PhD 1974
 s of Harry L. M. carpenter and Anne B. Miller; b Aber 21.8.43
lect Engl Aberd from 1967
m Aber 9.5.64 Ailsa M. Sutherland MB ChB 1969 *qv*

MINETT Robert Anthony *MA 1969 Dip Ed 1970
 s of Albert M. lect automative stud. and Hilda Speed part-time s secy; b Wolverhampton 5.8.46
teacher mod lang Rubislaw acad 1970–73, asst prin mod lang 1973–74; sen lect Ger coll of comm Aber from 1975
m Aber 22.12.69 Patricia C. Little MA 1967 *qv*

MINIO-PALUELLO Maria-Luisa MLitt 1965
 D in L(Venice)
m Cochran

MINTO Joan Edith *MA 1968
 d of Robert W. M. eng, printer and Phoebe R. Gareh shorthand typist; b Inverurie 10.6.46
res asst Aberd 1968
m Aber 10.9.65 Gordon W. Arbuthnott BSc 1964 *qv*

MINTY Alistair Leslie MA 1968

MINTY Ian Stuart Harris MA 1970

MIRGHANI Tag El-Din MSc 1968
 BSc(Khart)

MIRRILEES Christine *MA 1968
 m Findlay

MISTRY Chandan   MB ChB 1966
m Ward

MITCHELL Alexander Brown   LLB 1970
s of George M. comp dir and Georgina Mitchell;
b Hamilton 20.3.49
law app Glasg 1970–72; leg. asst Glasg 1972–73; solic
John Stuart & Wilson Huntly/Keith 1973–76, ptnr from
1976
m Aber 29.7.71 Evelyn J. S. Wilson teacher home econ
d of Andrew S. Wilson MA 1934 *qv*

MITCHELL Alexander Grant   *MA 1962

MITCHELL Andrew Smith   BSc(for) 1968

MITCHELL Anita Mary Burgess   *MA 1968
d of Thomas B. M. insur sect. supt and Edith Nicol
secy; b Grantown-on-Spey 4.3.46
Edin: teacher Fr/Ger Firhill s s 1969–70, Trinity acad
1970–74
m Edin 29.12.72 James D. Nolan MA(Edin) teacher s of
John P. N. Dunfermline

MITCHELL Anne Clouston   *MA 1968
d of Alexander D. M.. insp fisheries civ serv and
Margaret B. Eddie teacher; b Aber 24.2.46
teacher: Engl Kirkcaldy 1969–71, asst prin Engl Lossiemouth 1971–74, Engl Lüdenscheid Ger 1974–75, Engl
St Leonards 1975–77, prin Engl N Berwick h s from 1977

MITCHELL Anne Stewart   MA 1960
d of George H. M. ship's eng and Anne S. Stewart;
b Lossiemouth 26.1.39
teacher Engl Elgin 1961–63 and from 1973
m Aber 26.7.62 William Coull cereals man. Scot. Malt
Distillers s of William J. S. C. Rothes

MITCHELL Barbara Anne Margaret   MA 1967
d of William M. MA(Glas) teacher, HMIS and
Patricia E. Duncan nurse; b Aber 22.9.46
teacher infants: Aber 1967–73, BFES Germany from
1973

MITCHELL Beryl   BSc 1969
d of D. Stephen M. quantity surv, man. dir bldg comp
and Isabella Shaw shorthand typist; b Aber 20.9.47
teacher maths: Aber 1970–71, Edin from 1979
m Aber 12.7.69 Stuart C. Poole MA 1971 trans plan. s of
Ronald B. P. Lond

MITCHELL Charles Hendry   BSc(eng) 1970
s of Henry M. grocer and Christina M. Watt; b Aber
28.12.48
eng, sect. eng, agent from 1970
m Fairlie 26.3.75 Elaine M. Archibald teacher d of
Gilbert M. A. Blantyre

MITCHELL Charles James   BSc(eng) 1964

MITCHELL Christopher John   *MA 1967

MITCHELL Colin Henry Whiteford   BSc(agr) 1965
s of Arthur N. M. farm. and Isabella M. Whiteford;
b Dun 31.5.43
DFMBO 1966
farm. Leuchars from 1966
m Crieff 11.7.68 Elizabeth M. Miller teacher p e d of
James R. M. BSc(Glas) Crieff

MITCHELL Colin Stephen   *BSc 1964
s of William A. M. bank man. and Christina M.
Stephen; b Aber 18.11.41

des eng Philips indust Croydon 1964–68; Philips elect.:
tech/comm asst Lond 1968–71, prod. man. VCR equipment Lond 1971–73; prod. man. TV Lond from 1973
m Lond 7.9.68 Joyce M. Watt civ serv d of George W. W.
Aber

MITCHELL Dorothy Mary   MA 1965
d of James G. M. eng and Dorothy M. Geddes tel
superv; b Aber 10.11.43
teacher Engl: Powis acad Aber 1966–68, Gracemount s s
Edin 1968–71, prin guid from 1971
m Aber 2.8.68 Ian R. Yule teacher tech subjs s of Thomas
D. Y. Mintlaw

MITCHELL Easton Anderson   *MA 1967
s of John W. T. M. traffic insp ACT and Annie
Christie; b Aber 22.11.43
teacher mod lang Aber h s for girls (Harlaw acad) 1968–
73; asst prin mod lang Kincorth acad Aber from 1973
m 5.4.76 Alison M. Gossip MA(St And) d of William
H. G. MB ChB 1931 *qv*

MITCHELL Eileen   MA 1965

MITCHELL Elizabeth Margaret   MA 1963
m Rattray

MITCHELL Evelyn   MA 1970
d of Alexander M. farm. and Evelyn G. Wildgoose;
b Aber 12.6.47
Aber: nurse 1970–72, unqual nurse tut. 1973–74, teacher
from 1975

MITCHELL Frances Elizabeth   *BSc 1965
m Baxter

MITCHELL George Robertson   *BSc 1969
s of George A. M. farm. and Elizabeth Robertson;
b Torphins 5.7.47
teacher sc: St Augustine's s Edin 1970–72, Hazlehead
acad Aber 1972–75, prin chem Banchory acad from 1975

MITCHELL Gordon David   *BSc(eng) 1968

MITCHELL Graham   *BSc(eng) 1966

MITCHELL Hamish Lewis Mackay   MA 1961
LLB 1963
s of Lewis M. M. acct and Gladys J. Martin MA 1923
qv; b Kuala Lumpur 2.6.40
Aber: law app Edmonds & Ledingham advoc 1963–64,
leg. asst Paull & Williamsons advoc 1964–67, ptnr from
1968
m Aber 31.7.65 May M. Fraser teacher d of George B. F.
Aber

MITCHELL Isabel Ross   MA 1968 Dip Ed 1969
d of John E. M. master cabinetmaker and Bella Fraser;
b Aber 28.9.32
teacher Aber: Kittybrewster p s 1969–70, Harlaw acad
1970–74, prin guid from 1974
m Aber 17.9.55 Joseph B. Coull marine eng s of Joseph
B. C. Aber

MITCHELL Janet Campbell   BEd 1970

MITCHELL Janet Elizabeth   MA 1968
m Riddler

MITCHELL Jessie Davidson Falconer   BSc 1958
d of Alexander M. baker and Jessie Falconer; b Aber
18.7.37
teacher Aber 1959–63

m Aber 12.8.61 James W. D. Smith MA 1973 teacher
s of William S. Aber

MITCHELL John   *MA 1958

MITCHELL John Ivor   *MA 1966
 s of Ivor M. man. serv dept Goodyear Tyre Co and
Myrtle E. M. Macdonald bank clerk; b Wolverhampton
18.11.43
teacher Engl St Austell g s Cornwall 1967–71; second
prin Engl royal g s High Wycombe from 1972
m St Austell 1970 Elizabeth M. Trudgian teacher d of
Percival J. T. St Austell

MITCHELL John Robertson   MA 1970

MITCHELL June   MA 1968
 d of Thomas B. M. bank man. and Margaret M.
Gordon; b Keith 4.6.47
Athens: teacher Hambakis lang s 1969–74, Ambelokipi
lang centre 1975–78; opened own lang s Glyfada 1978
m Athens 26.12.71 Dimitris Sachinides electronic eng s of
Maralambos S. Athens

MITCHELL June Margaret Ross   *MA 1959
 d of Alexander J. M. travel ag and Violet Ross; b Aber
21.10.35
secy to dir of res Molins Lond 1961–74, to man. dir
Concord Lighting Internat Lond 1974, to dir of eng
Rank Xerox Lond from 1974
m Skovshoved Denmark 20.10.64 Jørgen A. H. Orth
indust film prod. s of Frits O. LDS(Copenhagen)
Klampenborg

MITCHELL Kate Fowler Falconer White   MA 1966
 m Legg

MITCHELL Kathleen Mary Anderson   *MA 1965
 d of John M. MA 1928 qv; b Elgin 8.2.43
res asst M o D Lond 1965–69; attaché Brit High Commission Singapore 1969–71; edit. asst Graphmitre
Tavistock from 1979
m Aber 11.8.71 Robert W. Perkins lt-col Royal Marines
s of Robert S.P. Surrey

MITCHELL Lewis Stuart   MB ChB 1965
 s of John M. bookseller/newsag and Marjory C.
Stuart; b Keith 14.2.38
h o ARI, Raigmore hosp Inv 1965–67; g p: Bucksburn
1967–69, Hobart Tasmania from 1969
m Inv 29.7.64 Maragret L. J. Allison nurs sister d of
William D. A. Kirkhill Invsh

MITCHELL Lilian Maud   PhD 1960
 MA LL B EdB(Glas)

MITCHELL Margaret Anne   MA 1961
 d of Alexander M. fisherman and Edith Bainbridge
hairdresser; b Lossiemouth 18.9.40
teacher Lossiemouth from 1962
m Lossiemouth 7.10.67 Alexander Mackenzie shop
owner

MITCHELL Margaret Henderson   MA 1959
 d of Alexander M. eng insp and Margaret Allison;
b Crewe 10.2.39
M Libr(Wash) 1965
teacher: Bannockburn 1961–62, Ash Vale Surrey 1962;
univ of Wash: lib asst 1963–65, lib 1965–68; univ of Vict
BC: asst bibliographer soc sc res centre 1969–73, bibliographer from 1974
m Aber 14.8.61 David G. W. Edwards BSc 1959 qv

MITCHELL Marjory Gibbon   MA 1966
 d of Robert W. A. M. elect. and Helen D. Young shop
asst; b Edin 29.4.45
teacher: Clydebank h s 1967–69, Fraserburgh acad 1969–
70, Cardinal Wiseman s Greenford 1971–73
m Aber 21.11.70 Eric J. C. Brew BSc 1967 qv

MITCHELL Mary   *MA 1960
 d of Jean Edmondstone; b Aber 4.9.37
secy to edit. Lond 1961; teacher: Isle of Barra 1962–63,
Glasg 1963–64, Banff 1965–66, Cumnock from 1971
m Aber 6.7.63 Donald M. Manson MA 1962 qv

MITCHELL Michael James   *MA 1970
 b Stonehaven 22.2.48
MCIT 1977
rly man. Liverpool, Wolverhampton from 1970
m Edin 4.9.71 Jillian M. Tomory MA 1970 qv

MITCHELL Moira Taylor   MA 1964
 d of John C. S. M. baker and Jeannie D. P. Wight;
b Aber 30.9.42
teacher Northfield acad 1965–69, later teacher f e
m Aber 5.8.67 Joseph Leiper MA 1971 teacher s of
George L. Aber

MITCHELL Patricia   *MA 1969
 m Ashenford

MITCHELL Patrick John Stuart   *BSc 1959
 s of Patrick M. MA 1924 qv and Gertrude H. Stuart
MA 1930 qv; b Aber 8.1.36
post grad res Aber 1959–60; res chem: petro chem
Billingham 1960–62, tobacco Bristol 1962–70; works/dev
chem carbon paper Caribonum Turriff 1970–74 tech
eng petroleum explor/prod. industry Dowell Schlumberger
Aber from 1974
m Aber 16.2.60 Jorja M. Carnegie nurse d of George
F. C. Aber

MITCHELL Roger   MA 1967

MITCHELL Rose McNeill   MA 1956
 d of George M. saw doctor and Mary Downie;
b Fraserburgh 27.10.35
teacher: Pitlochry h s 1957–59, Sunnybank s Aber from
1970
m Aber 22.8.59 George S. Hall warehouse dept man. s of
Wilson H. Aber

MITCHELL Stuart John   *BSc 1965 PhD 1969
 s of Mark G. M. teacher and Jane H. Elder teacher;
b Brentwood 16.12.43
scient off. UKAEA Aldermaston 1968–71, sen scient off.
1972–73; sen scient off. MoD 1973–76; prin scient off.
MoD Lond from 1976
m Aber 7.4.66 Sheila B. Fulton radiographer d of James
G. F. BL 1952 qv

MITCHELL Trevor Anderson   *MA 1970
 s of William I. C. M. BSc(agr) 1924 qv; b Elgin 20.9.46
teacher Ger/Engl/Fr/geog Congleton c g s for girls 1971–
78; head Ger dept Wycombe h s High Wycombe from
1978
m Aber 5.7.69 Yuko Motomura MA(Waseda univ
Tokyo) interpreter, translator, teacher d of Takeo M.
Tokyo

MITCHELL William   BSc 1968

MITCHELL William Ingram   BSc(for) 1958

MITCHELL William Stuart   *MA 1970 PhD 1974

MITCHELL William Stuart Gabriel   *MA 1967

MITCHELL William Sutherland   *BSc 1969
s of Andrew A. S. M. MA 1930 *qv*; b Wick 25.9.43
MSc(Br Col) 1973
geol from 1973
m Tacoma Wash USA 28.7.73 Courtney E. Soule MSc
(Stanford)

MITTELSTEIN John Edward Cowie   *MA 1969
s of Edward S. A. M. seaman and Margaret Cowie;
b Skopun Faroe Is 9.8.47
trainee, shipping exec The Ben Line Steamers Edin from
1970
m Glasg 27.8.71 Kathleen Wotherspoon d of David W.
Glasg

MIZERA Franz   *BSc(agr) 1967
s of Franz M. machine tool indust, soldier and Wanda
Marciniak; b Wyrzysk Poland 11.9.43
M Econ(ANU) 1971
Canberra: res econ bureau of agr econ dept primary
indust 1967–70, sen fin. off. Commonwealth Treasury
1970–72; internat wool secretariat: res econ Lond 1972–
73, econ and market res man. Brussels from 1973
m Poznan Poland 29.6.74 Bożena Jożefowicz econ (publ
serv) d of Mieczylaw J. Poznan

MIZON Margaret Shaun   MA 1965

MMBANDO Charles Stanislaus   BSc(for) 1966

MOAR Ann Maxwell   MA 1963
d of William I. M. bldr and Eileen F. Horne; b 7.11.42
teacher (VSO) Freetown Sierra Leone 1963–65; Edin:
teacher Engl Ainslie Park s 1966–67, Niddrie Marischal s
1967–68
m Aber Peter A. Dean MA 1963 *qv*

MOAR Patricia Ann   MA 1970
d of John P. M. civ eng and Wilhelmina M. Pottinger;
b Lerwick 24.5.49
teacher Fr/Ger Lerwick from 1971
m Dunrossness Shetland 13.10.73 William B. Burgess
aich. tech s of William B. Dunrossness

MOAR Peter Windwick   MA 1968
s of John P. M. civ eng and Wilhelmina M. Pottinger;
b Lerwick 25.9.45
teacher: Kayseri Koleji, Kayseri Turkey 1970–71,
Kirkcudbrightsh 1971–74; lect: Dumfries and Galloway
coll of tech 1974–79, Eng lit Basrah univ Iraq from 1979
m Aber 24.9.69 Angela M. Robertson secy d of James
K. R. Aber

MOBBS Ian Gaynor   *BSc 1967
s of Eric E. G. M. marine supt and Sarah Tait; b Glasg
25.2.41
MSc(McM) 1969 PhD(UWO) 1975
univ of W. Ont: grad stud. 1969–74, sen instr 1972–73,
lect 1973–76; asst prof Dalhousie univ Nova Scotia from
1976

MOFFAT Alistair Gibson   MA 1961

MOFFAT Sheila Patricia   BSc 1963

MOFFETT Jonathan Wallace   BSc(for) 1959
s of Robert W. M. wholesale draper, soldier, driver
and Helen G. McCracken secy; b Belfast 30.4.37
dist for. off. Co Antrim 1959–63; itinerant 1963–67;
orchardist Hastings NZ from 1967

m Hastings NZ 17.12.64 Christine R. Walker nurse d of
Hector W. W. Hastings NZ

MOGGACH Gordon   MA 1965
s of William C. M. farm. and Olive Ingram; b Keith
21.7.43
Dip Bus Man(Strath) 1966 ACMA 1971
Lond: budget acct Air Products 1966–70, comp acct
Ingersoll Locks 1970–71; sen man. acct HIDB Inv from
1971
m Lairg 5.4.75 Elspeth D. Ross civ serv d of Andrew
J. A. R. Lairg

MOHAMED Babiker Fadlalla   PhD 1967
s of Fadlalla M. wholesale dealer and Nur E. El
Sheikh; b Khartoum 9.7.34
MSc(Khart)
Khart: dem 1958–63, lect 1967–79, assoc prof from 1979,
head bot dept from 1980
m Huntly 11.6.68 Elizabeth A. Russell staff nurse d of
Alexander R. Aber

MOIR Alan Clark   *MA 1970 Dip Ed 1971
s of Harry M. mill man. and Irene L. M. Clark;
b Elgin 18.4.47
teacher hist Belmont acad Ayr 1971–74, asst prin hist
1974–76; prin hist Auchinleck acad from 1976
m Prestwick 28.3.75 Margaret Aird teacher home econ
d of Alexander A. Prestwick

MOIR Alexander Ian   *BSc 1966
s of Alexander M. foreman links and parks dept Aber
and Robina Cruickshank; b Aber 3.3.44
teacher maths Inverurie acad 1968–71; prin maths Keith
g s from 1971
m Aber 2.8.74 Kathryn E. McKenzie teacher d of
Robert M. McK. Buckie

MOIR Annette Nicol   MA 1959
m Rogerson

MOIR Arthur John Goddard   *BSc 1969 PhD 1973
s of John H. M. woodworker and Ellen Scott; b Lond
25.11.46
post doct res fell. MRC Birm from 1973
m Aber 20.8.73 Anne McKenzie BSc 1971 post grad stud.
Birm d of John A. McK. Gartly

MOIR David Alexander   MA 1966
s of Alexander M. eng and Williamina C. Munro;
b Aber 11.12.45
Dip. Bus. Stud.(Strath) 1967 AMBIM 1974
Plessey & Co. Poole: progr/analyst 1967–69, proj
leader 1970–72, syst man. 1973–74; sen syst analyst
Farnborough from 1974
m Aber 14.1.66 Kathleen Robertson teacher d of John
B. R. Aber

MOIR Dorothy Watt   *MA 1961
m Caldwell

MOIR Elizabeth Drummond   MA 1968
d of David M. police sgt and Elizabeth Davidson secy;
b Keith 3.2.47
Dip Sec St(Strath) 1969
coll of estate man.: secy to secy Lond 1969–72, sen admin
asst to prin Lond/Reading 1972–73, controller of postal
course div Reading 1973–75, dir of courses Reading from
1975

MOIR Grace Gordon   MA 1956
m Morrison

MOIR Graeme Kelman   *BSc 1970 PhD 1974

MOIR Hamish David Alexander   BSc(eng) 1964

MOIR Ian Alexander   BSc 1960
s of William A. M. M. fireman and Wilhelmina Alexander nurse; b Dun 20.11.39
phys UKAEA Dounreay 1960-63; commissioning eng Trawsfynydd 1963-65; oper eng SSEB Hunterston 1965-67; fuelling eng CEGB Wylfa 1967-74; oper eng SSEB Hunterston from 1974
m W Kilbride 17.6.66 Helen L. Davidson computer progr d of Alexander McH. D. W Kilbride

MOIR Ian Andrew   MA 1956 BD 1959
s of Andrew F. M. banker and Mabelle M. Scott secy; b Aber 9.4.35
sub-warden St Ninian's trg centre Crieff 1959-61; supt Pholela inst Bulwer Natal S Af 1962-73; C of S overseas council Edin: staffing secy 1974-76, joint secy ptnrship from 1977
m Edin 25.8.61 Elizabeth M. M. Fraser teacher d of James F. Edin

MOIR James Chalmers   *MA 1970
s of James G. M. grocer and Mary M. Craig; b Aber 29.12.48
salesman Manc 1970-72, area man. Edin 1972-77, dist sales man. 1977-79, nat sales man. Manc from 1979
m Carnwath 6.4.74 Margaret M. Park MA(Edin) teacher d of T. M. P. MB ChB(Glas) Carnwath

MOIR James McGrath   MA 1965

MOIR Jessie Ann Hay   MA 1956
d of Alexander M. and Catherine W. Baird; b Aber 22.5.31
teacher: Aberdeensh 1957-65, Singapore 1965-66, Aber from 1968
m Assam 23.4.66 Andrew M. Tracey

MOIR John Donald   *MA 1962

MOIR June Milne   MA 1965
d of Alfred G. M. M. bank man. and Lily Smith; b Aber 22.6.44
Dip Soc Ad(St And) 1966
teacher Aber 1967-74, remed Johannesburg from 1974
m Aber 16.4.74 Neil J. MacKeith BSc 1968 qv

MOIR Kathleen Munro   MA 1962
d of Alexander M. eng and Williamina C. Munro; b Aber 29.6.41
teacher: maths/r e Grangemouth 1963-65, maths Ruthrieston s Aber 1965-66, maths/r e Aber h s for girls 1966-69
m Aber 11.8.65 Grahame M. Henderson BD 1972 C of S min s of David H. MA(Glas) Bieldside Aber

MOIR Maureen Catherine   *BSc 1969
d of Herbert B. M. joiner and Anne G. Allen; b Aber 5.12.47
teacher chem: Royal h s Edin 1970-74, Lower Hutt NZ 1974-76, AGS 1976-77, Cults acad Aber from 1977
m Aber 27.12.79 Nigel R. M. Scott tax acct s of Malcolm P. S. Montgarrie

MOIR Michael   *BSc 1969 PhD 1972
s of Benjamin M. butcher and Ina Hosie; b Huntly 21.6.47
FCS 1968 MInst Brewing 1978
res fell. Zürich 1972-73, Stirling 1973-77; sen res chem Scot. & Newcastle Breweries Edin from 1977

MOIR Michael   BSc 1967
s of William M. M. butcher and Jane Robertson; b Aber 31.10.33
teacher maths Hilton acad, Harlaw acad Aber 1968-73, asst prin maths from 1974
m Aber 9.3.57 Elizabeth M. Gordon bakery asst d of Jeremiah W. G. Aber

MOIR Michael Joseph   *MA 1962
s of Joseph S. M. elect. eng and Irene E. Barrett shop asst; b Aber 29.9.41
Black Prize for Latin Aberd 1962 BA(Cantab) 1964 MA(Cantab) 1968
teacher classics Peterhead acad 1965-66; lect Victoria univ of Wellington NZ: classics 1966-67, gen ling. 1968-70; prin translation div Neths min of foreign affairs The Hague 1970-73; lect ling. Engl inst univ of Amsterdam from 1973; translator The Hague dist court 1973

MOIR Patricia Margaret   MA 1967
m Copland

MOIR Philip Malcolm   MA 1969

MOIR William Leonard Neill   MA 1962
d 1972

MOJSIEWICZ Andrzej Bruno   *MA 1969

MONCRIEFF Elizabeth Sinclair   *MA 1970
d of James S. M. lab and Agnes C. Ewen; b Perth 7.4.48
lib asst Bexley 1971-72; Lond: market res asst 1972, res exec with Westward TV 1972-74, higher grade tax off. Inl Rev 1944-47
m Aber 11.9.70 John P. Inglis BSc 1970 qv

MONCRIEFF Mitchell William   *BSc 1967
s of Mitchell J. M. crofter and Eliza A. Scott; b Sandness Shetland 7.4.44
DIC 1968 PhD(Lond) 1970 FRMet Soc 1970
Imp coll Lond: post doct res fell. dept meteorology 1970-72, lect met. from 1972
m Shetland 6.9.67 Patricia M. M. Nicolson catering superv d of George M. N. Bixter

MONCUR Charles Cheyne   *MA 1969

MONRO Graeme Cooper   *BSc(eng) 1967

MONRO Stuart Kinnaird   *BSc 1970
s of William K. M. comp dir and Williamina M. Fothergill; b Aber 3.3.47
FGS(Lond) 1972 MIGeol 1978
geol S Lowlands unit of inst of geol sc Edin from 1970
m Aber 31.7.71 Shiela D. Wallace teacher p e d of Thomas A. L. W. Aber

MONTGOMERY Catherine   *MA 1960

MONTGOMERY Malcolm Nicolson   *MA 1959

MONTGOMERY Neil   *MA 1965
s of John M. millworker and Annie B. Macdonald; b Stornoway 6.2.43
teacher: Jordanhill coll s Glasg, Annan acad, Hillpark s s Glasg, Lourdes R C s Glasg, Nicolson inst Stornoway, Hillhead p s Glasg 1966-81 (prin geog at Annan acad and Hillpark p s)
m Glasg 11.10.69 Effie Smith nurse d of Donald S. Bragar Is of Lewis

MONTGOMERY Ronald   BSc 1960

MOON Gordon Michael   *BSc 1969

MOON Helen Janet   MB ChB 1969
d of John M. M. mental nurse and Helen Watt teacher, nurse; b Banff 14.7.45
DCH(Glas) 1972
Aber: h o 1969–70, trainee g p 1970–71, h o paediat 1970–72, m o publ health from 1972
m Aber 15.7.69 Innes R. Stephen journalist s of Leslie P. S. Turriff

MOON Helena Margaret   MA 1969
m Whitmore

MOONEY James   MA 1966
s of Charles M. chef and Annie Daly shopkeeper; b Port Glasg 27.5.25
MEd(Glas) 1970
teacher: Engl Greenock 1967–69, asst prin Engl 1969–71; prin Engl Port Glasg from 1971
m Greenock 6.5.52 Maureen Keogh dressmaker d of William K. Greenock

MOORE Adam Gillespie Nichol   MB ChB 1964
s of Merrill M. BA(Vanderbilt) phys/poet and Ann L. Nichol BSc(ed)(Tufts) pre-s educator; b Boston Mass 21.10.31
AB(Harvard) 1956 Struthers gold medal/prize Aberd 1959 Munday Prize Aberd 1962 Amer med assoc physician's recog award 1970–73, 1973–76, 1976–79 Dip Amer Board of fam pract 1975 Cert lib Comm of Mass dept of educ 1974
milit serv pvt to maj MSC 1951–67; Boolt mem home board & Gtr Boston adv board 1967–73; trustee rep Mass hosp assn 1970–72; L fell. Boston med lib (Tr 1975–80); prop. Boston Athenaeum from 1964; h o ARI 1964–65; Mass. USA: resid paediat Carney hosp 1965–66, asst phys UHS Harvard law s Cambridge 1968–72, private fam pract Squantum from 1968
m Aber 15.10.66 Rosamie Alexander med secy d of Robert A. LDS(St And) Aber

MOORE Brian Hendry   BSc 1969

MOORE Eileen Mary Campbell   MA 1961
m Rueckert

MOORE Mary   *MA 1970
m Lynch

MOORE Maurice John   *MA 1967

MOORE Michael Archibald   MA 1956

MOORE Roderick Francis Inglis   *BSc(eng) 1969

MOORHOUSE Mary Charlotte   MA 1959
d of Charles R. M. maintenance eng and Mary Reekie; b Aber 16.6.38
teacher: Aber 1960–65; prin relig educ Clacton 1965–71, St Osyth 1971–72, prin r e Colchester 1972–74; sen tut. Frinton from 1974

MORAN Peter Antony   *MEd 1968
s of Joseph M. MA(Glas) teacher, headmaster and Gertrude O'Callaghan MA(Glas) teacher, lect coll of educ; b Glasg 13.4.35
MA(Glas) 1963 LTCL 1974 Lic Phil(Greg) 1955 Lic S Theol(Greg) 1959
teacher classics, mus Blairs coll Aber from 1968

MOREY Colin Robert   *BSc 1967
s of Charles H. M. elect. eng/civ serv and Florence G. Langdon book-keeper loc govt; b Waterlooville 10.8.44
FGS 1968 MIBG 1972 Dip Man. Stud.(Plymouth poly) 1976 MPhil(CNAA) 1980
prod geol UK 1967–68; sen tut. Slapton Ley 1969–74; dep warden Orielton Pembroke 1974–75; lect geol Brooklands tech coll Weybridge from 1976
m Epsom 28.4.79 Maureen E. F. Symons BSc(Brist) teacher d of Stanley C. S. Stamford

MORGAN Alexander   MB ChB 1960
s of Andrew M. M. fisherman, naval off. RNR, tel eng and Jamesina O. Strachan fishworker, canteen server; b Peterhead 6.6.37
h o Woodend hosp Aber, ARI, Airthrey Castle Bridge of Allan 1960–62; g p Stuartfield from 1962
m Aber 15.10.60 Elizabeth M. G. Mackintosh nurse d of John G. M. MA(Edin) Cruden Bay

MORGAN Audrey Mackay   MB ChB 1959
d of Albert M. tech teacher and Jeannie Inverarity; b Aber 15.6.36
DA 1963 Educ Council for Foreign Med Grad(America) 1966
h o RACH, Woodend hosp Aber, Whittington hosp Lond 1959–61; sen h o, regist King George hosp Ilford 1961–64; part-time res fell. anaest (Harvard) Mass. gen hosp Boston USA 1966–67
m Aber 19.5.62 Harold S. Winsey MB BS(Lond) consult. gen surg s of Geoffrey C. W. Beaulieu

MORGAN Brian Robert   *MA 1969

MORGAN David Gordon   MA 1967 LLB 1969
s of Thomas N. M. MB ChB 1931 qv and Roberta Gordon MA 1932 qv; b Aber 3.5.46
law app, leg. asst James & George Collie advoc Aber 1969–72; leg. asst Fyfe Ireland & Co WS Edin 1972–74; ptnr James & George Collie from 1974

MORGAN David Ivor   *MA 1958 LLB 1961
s of Leslie P. M. off. customs & excise and Helen Fisher; b Giffnock 7.12.36
leg. asst G. H. Bower & Gibb advoc Aber 1961–62; solic Davidson & Garden advoc Aber 1962–64, ptnr from 1964
m Aber 28.4.62 Diane C. Scott MA 1958 qv

MORGAN Finlay McLeay   MA 1959 LLB 1962
s of Finlay M. pharm and Charlotte J. Jamieson pharm; b Farnham 11.11.38
law app Aber 1962–63; leg. asst Ayr 1963–64, Edin 1964–66, Glasg 1966–67; leg. asst Dove, Lockhart, Mackay & Young WS Edin 1967–72, ptnr from 1972
m Wisbech 24.8.68 Elizabeth M. S. Scrafton teacher dom sc d of Philip R. S. Wisbech

MORGAN George Eric   MA 1970
s of George M. M. wine and spirit rep and Violet Davidson; b Aber 23.1.43
FSA Scot.
teacher Engl Hilton acad Aber 1971–73; prin Engl/hist Langholm acad from 1973
m Aber 30.12.69 L. Susan Marr MA 1973 teacher d of Gordon P. M. chartered surv Aber

MORGAN John Adam   BSc(eng) 1959
s of John S. M. MA 1928 qv; b Aber 16.8.37
post grad trainee Marconi Chelmsford 1959–61; elect. eng Honeywell Motherwell 1961–65; IBM Greenock: assoc eng 1965–69, sen assoc eng 1969–73, staff eng from 1973
m Aber 2.4.64 Marjory G. Stuart MA 1960 qv

MORGAN John Alexander   BEd 1969

MORGAN John Francis   MA 1958

MORGAN Karen   BSc 1969
d of Thomas M. PO tech off. and Joan Adams
publican; b Glamorgan 5.3.47
teacher Buchlyvie p s from 1977
m Gilfach Goch 26.9.68 Angus A. McWilliam PhD 1974
teacher s of Stuart W. McW. MA(Edin) Glasg

MORGAN Lois Cecily   *MA 1967
d of George D. M. policeman and Eunice L. O'Neal;
b Bridgetown Barbados 29.8.40
teacher: Greatfield p s Hull 1968–70, Combermere
Barbados 1970–72
m Aber 22.7.64 Carl L. Ince BA(Hull) diplomat s of
Leon St. C. I. St Michael Barbados

MORGAN Margaret Anne   BSc 1957
d of James M. rubber planter and Kathleen L. Cormac;
b Batu Gajah Malaysia 16.4.36
Dip Bact(Strath) 1959
asst scient off. nat collection of indust bact Torry res
lab Aber 1959–61
m Aber 8.1.60 William M. Cooke BSc(Edin) soil chem
Macaulay inst s of William P.C. Edin

MORGAN Maureen Gladys   MA 1957

MORGAN Roslyn Elizabeth   BSc 1968
d of Arthur M. chartered surv/land ag and Margery R.
Jones; b Torquay 13.1.45
scient off. plant breeding dept of nat veg res stat Wellesbourne 1968–72
m Newton Abbot 11.4.70 David Gray BA(Oxon) sen
scient off. s of Hugh G. Ogbourne St George

MORGAN Sheila Elisabeth Gordon   MA 1961
d of Thomas N. M. MB ChB 1961 *qv* and Roberta
Gordon MA 1932 *qv*; b Aber 12.8.40
teacher
m Aber 5.7.63 Melville F. Watson MA 1959 *qv*

**MORGAN William Charles   *BSc 1961 MSc 1962
                                              PhD 1967**
s of Robert M. comm trav and Elizabeth J. Mann;
b Inv 30.9.39
dem geol N'cle 1964–67; temp asst geol Aberd 1967–68;
res scient geol surv of Canada Ottawa from 1968
m Aber 23.12.67 Rohays A. I. Morrison BA teacher d of
John A. M. Aber

MORICE George Pirie   *MA 1957
s of George P. M. barman and Mary Still; b·Aber 29.8.29
asst lect phil Edin 1959–62, lect 1962–77, sen lect from
1977
m Aber 28.7.55 Cecilia F. M. Innes teacher of art d of
Charles I. Aber

MORLEY Michael Charles David   BSc(eng) 1969
s of David M. farm man. and Margaret M. Winfield;
b Swaffham 28.4.46
civ eng contr and des; Sir R. McAlpine: site eng Bristol
1969–70, Glasg 1970–71; sect. eng Michelin factory Dun
1971–73; des eng Ove Arup Dun 1973, sen sect. eng
Ardyne Point (oil platforms) Argyll from 1974
m Aber 8.5.70 Marion G. McDonald millworker d of
Angus McD. Kintore

MORRELL Michael   *MA 1970 MEd 1974

MOREEN Alison Mary   MB ChB 1961
m Graham

MORREN David   BSc(eng) 1957

MORRICE Alan   *MA 1965

MORRICE Alan George   *BSc 1969
s of Harold M. M. insur ag and Catherine M. Cambell
off. supt; b Aber 20.5.47
M Chem Soc(Lond) 1970 PhD(Illinois) 1974
univ of Illinois Urbana USA: teaching asst 1969–70, res
asst 1970–72, teaching asst 1972–74; chem instr nat
acad of dance Urbana/teaching asst univ of Illinois from
1974
m Chicago 16.8.74 Elaine C. Mancini BA(Illinois) stud.
d of Edward A. M. Chicago

MORRICE Alexander Malcolm   *BSc 1963
s of Alexander M. ocean res vessel capt and Emily
McRuvie; b Aber 23.12.40
MSc(S'ton) 1974
joined RN 1963, lt-cdr 1969, commander from 1976
m Nursling 14.8.65 Sarah A. Taylor d of George T.
Romsey

MORRICE Alice Isabella   MA 1970
d of James M. farm. and Alice Lunan; b Mintlaw
23.7.49
teacher mod lang Fraserburgh from 1971
m Aber 24.7.73 Alexander G. Douglas farm. s of
Alexander G. D. Fraserburgh

MORRICE Andrew   BSc 1963

MORRICE Anne Marie   MA 1963

MORRICE Edward Dolan   MA 1965

MORRICE Gordon Wilson   MA 1965

MORRICE Graham Durward   MB ChB 1959
s of John M. eng and Gertrude Walker dressmaker;
b Aber 22.2.35
DRCOG 1967 DO(Lond) 1977
RAMC capt Far East 1960–62, m o Charteris hosp
Kalimpong India 1964–66, Quarriers Homes Bridge of
Weir 1966–76; sen h o ophth Woodend hosp Aber 1976–
77, regist ophth from 1977
m Aber 30.9.67 Sanchamaya Yonjan SRN d of Ranman
Y. Darjeeling

MORRICE Graham Taylor   MB ChB 1967

MORRICE Jennifer Elizabeth   MA 1970

**MORRICE Kenneth Ewan   MA 1965 Dip Ed 1969
                                                           MEd 1978**
s of Kenneth E. M. Gordon Highlanders (retd) and
Williamina M. Armstrong weaver; b Aber 31.3.39
teacher Peterhead cent s 1966–70; head Udny Green p s
1970–72; asst secy St And 1972–73; head: Foveran p s
1973–75, Buchanhaven p s from 1975
m Longside 24.12.60 Elspeth W. Birnie teacher d of
William B. Rora

MORRICE Margaret   MA 1964
m Reid

MORRIN Catherine Mary   MA 1966

MORRIS Graham   MB ChB 1965

MORRIS Megan Lumley BSc 1968
d of Robert L. M. bank man. and Anne M. James
LLB(Aberystwyth) solic; b Haverfordwest 6.3.47
Dip Ed(Aberystwyth) 1969
teacher: sc Bradford 1969–70, biol Rollestonon Dove,
Burton-on-Trent 1970–73, i/c biol from 1973
m Cemaes 9.8.69 Simon J. Cooper BSc 1968 *qv*

MORRIS Raymond John Fowlie BSc 1969

MORRIS Robert Irvine Simpson *BSc(eng) 1965
MSc 1967

MORRIS Rona Jane Steward MA 1970 Dip Ed 1971

MORRISH Ann Loxton MA 1960
m Wong

MORRISON Agnes Anne *MA 1970
d of John C. M. farm worker, tractorman, bakery
storeman and Helen Lorimer; b Fyvie 19.11.47
MA(Essex) 1971
lect pol econ Aberd 1971–74
d Aber 6.1.76 *AUR* XLVI 418

MORRISON Alastair MB ChB 1965
s of William M. seaman/crofter and Margaret
MacCuish; b Locheport N Uist 7.6.41
DObstRCOG 1967 MRCGP 1971
h o Inv 1965–67; sen h o Perth 1967–69; g p Crieff from
1969
m Edin 5.8.67 Eileen E. MacPherson MB ChB(Edin)
med pract d of Roderick MacP. Edin

MORRISON Alexander Ferguson BSc 1963

MORRISON Alexander George *BSc 1960

MORRISON Angus Norman MA 1967 Dip Ed 1968
s of Malcolm M. soldier, lab, min of relig and Mary A.
Nicholson ch's nurse; b Kinlochewe 31.7.36
RMN 1961 Dip R E
teacher: Engl Vale of Leven acad Dunbartonsh 1968–71,
prin guid: Paisley 1971–74, Greenock h s from 1974
m Glasg 12.6.67 Bella A. MacLeod teacher d of Roderick
MacL. Grimsay N Uist

MORRISON Anne Isabel *BSc 1960
d of Aulay M. wholesale comp dir and Christina M.
MacLeod nurse; b Stornoway 28.9.38
jun res fellow marine bact Torry res stat Aber 1960–61;
res asst biochem Edin 1961–64
m Stornoway 27.12.62 Iain H. Anderson BSc 1958 *qv*

MORRISON Carolyn Ann MA 1965
d of George J. M. clerk of works and Caroline Laird;
b Aber 1.8.44
teacher Engl/hist: Glasg 1966–67, Engl Inv 1967–73
m Aber 27.12.71 Pietro M. Bisset tel eng s of Alexander
B. Inv

MORRISON Charles *BSc 1970

MORRISON Chrissisabell MA 1966
d of Angus M. lab and Margaret Mackinnon; b Lochs
Is of Lewis 9.1.46
teacher: Engl/Gaelic Nicolson inst Stornoway 1967–74,
guid 1973–74
m Inv 22.12.72 Cameron M. MacLeay BSc(Strath)
teacher s of Duncan MacL. MA(Edin) Fearn

MORRISON Christina MA 1969
m Macdonald

MORRISON Christine Bews MA 1969

MORRISON David LLB 1969
s of Eric S. M. PO overseer and Ruth I. Andrews;
b Aber 8.11.47
law app Campbell Connon & Co. advoc Aber 1969–72,
leg. asst 1972–73, ptnr from 1974
m Aber 1.7 72 Sandra I. Barron teacher d of Alexander
M. B. Aber

MORRISON Donald John *MA 1965
s of John M. MB ChB 1939 *qv*; b Edin 12.12.42
res Brasenose Coll Oxford 1965–67; lect Aberd 1967–71;
teacher Aber, Fochabers from 1971
m Grantchester 8.8.66 Linda M. Grant MA 1964 *qv*

MORRISON Gordon James MA 1970

MORRISON Harvey Elmslie LLB 1969
s of Eric E. M. MA 1940 *qv*; b Aber 5.1.47
CA 1973
Williamson & Dunn CA, Aber: app 1969–73, chartered
acct from 1973, ptnr from 1976
m Aber 25.7.73 Lesley E. Adam d of James W. A. Aber

MORRISON Ian *MA 1970
b Is of Lewis 28.1.35
teacher Aber from 1971
m Windermere 13.4.63 Olive Nunns

MORRISON Ian Robin *MA 1968
s of Peter C. M. farm. and Maggie E. Taylor; b Edin
14.1.45
lect Fr stud. N'cle from 1970
m N'cle-u-Tyne 26.3.71 Janet S. Burnett MA(Tor) lect
politics d of James T. B. Sims N Carolina USA

MORRISON Isobel Chalmers MA 1965
d of William J. M. dairy farm. and Isobel S. Chalmers
dairy farm.; b Banff 26.3.44
teacher: Bracoden p s 1966–68, Toronto 1968–70,
nursery Aberchirder from 1977
m Macduff 27.12.67 Neil S. Duguid joiner s of James D.
Aberchirder

MORRISON James Arthur BSc 1970
s of George M. indust chem and Marjorie E. Ingram;
b Aber 16.2.49
man. trainee Norwich city c 1970–72; admin asst soc
serv dept Norwich 1972–74; sen admin off. mid Suffolk
dist council 1974–76, prin admin off. from 1976
m Aber 17.9.71 Margaret A. Stewart secy d of William
A. H. S. Aber

MORRISON James Edward MA 1968
s of Ronald C. C. M. draughtsman and Peggy E.
Maunder; b Glasg 3.8.46
teacher Engl: Summerhill j s s Aber 1969–70, The King's
s Macclesfield from 1970
m Poulton-le-Fylde 29.7.72 Susan M. Holt BSc(Manc)
syst analyst d of William O. H. Poulton-le-Fylde

MORRISON James Murray *BSc 1964
PhD(Glas)

MORRISON James Roger MA 1959
s of James R. M. chief marine eng and Lizzie Connon;
b Aber 16.5.31
teacher: Engl/hist/geog Northfield acad Aber 1960–71,
hist Cults acad 1971–76, hist/mod stud. Powis acad
Aber 1976–77, Engl/hist/mod stud. AGS from 1977
m Aber 11.4.58 Rona E. M. Mackay teacher p e d of
Donald M. BSc(agr) 1924 *qv* (II, III)

MORRISON James Wilson Rennie ***MA 1965**

MORRISON Jean Isobel **MB ChB 1962**

MORRISON Jessie **MA 1962**
d of Murdo M. crofter and Isabel Mackenzie; b High
Borve Is of Lewis 17.10.40
teacher: Engl Adelphi Terr s s Glasg 1963–65, gen subj
Kiltarlity 1965–70, Millburn Inv 1970–71, prin Engl
Bolobo-sur-Fleure Zaïre from 1971
m Inv 16.8.74 David L. Boydell BA(Durh) teacher s of
Ronald H. B. Leeds

MORRISON Jessie Mary **MA 1968**
d of Alexander M. warper and Duncanina Smith;
b Stornoway 22.4.47
lib: Aber 1970–72, Stornoway from 1972

MORRISON John Alexander **BSc 1969 *1970**

MORRISON John Archie ***MA 1965**
s of Peter M. lobster fisherman and Flora McLean;
b Lochmaddy 2.2.43
teacher: Engl Rubislaw acad Aber 1966–70, prin asst
Engl 1970–72, prin Engl h s Thurso 1972–76, prin Engl
Banff acad from 1976
m Aber 4.4.74 Patricia M. Cushnie BBC secy/producer's
asst d of Albert P. D. C. Aber

MORRISON John Bernard **MA 1969**

MORRISON Joyce Campbell **MA 1967**
d of James C. M. lorry driver and Anne F. Cameron;
b Ellon 9.8.46
market res investig Lond 1967–72; civ serv HM customs
and excise Lond 1972–75; soc worker Dun from 1975
m Bond

MORRISON Kathleen Isabel **BEd 1970**

MORRISON Leslie Valentine **MA 1960**
s of George L. S. M. baker and Margaret Simpson;
b Aber 14.2.39
FRAS(Lond) 1961 MSc(Sus) 1968
asst exper off., prin scient off. astronomy Royal Greenwich Observatory from 1960
m Eastbourne 2.6.65 Susan A. Bailey astronomer d of
Gerald P. B. Eastbourne

MORRISON Lewis Duncan **MB ChB 1960**
s of James M. police off. and Louisa R. Adams;
b Aber 1.12.35
h o Aber hosps 1960–61; sen h o Victoria I Glasg 1961–
63; regist Inv hosps 1963–66; g p/part-time hosp posts
Golspie from 1966
m Inv –.10.65 Jean M. Maxwell RGN d of Henry A. M
MA(Oxon) Inv

MORRISON Madeline **MB ChB 1962**
d of Alexander F. M. eng driver BR and Margaret
McKessock; b Aber 30.10.37
MRC Psych 1976
h o: Woodend hosp Aber 1962–63, city hosp Edin 1963;
sen h o (part-time) Cornhill hosp Aber 1970–73; regist
(part-time) RACH from 1973
m Aber 1.2.63 Ian R. Brown BSc(for) 1957 qv

MORRISON Marcelle Ritchie ***BSc 1967**
d of George C. M. MA 1930 qv; b Edin 8.8.45
PhD(Glas) 1971
post doct fell. biochem univ of Cincinnati 1971–75; asst
prof dept of neurol univ of Texas health sc center Dallas
from 1976

MORRISON Margaret Flora **MA 1969**
d of Neil M. farm./for. and Agnes Small hairdresser;
b Inv 28.10.48
Dip Pers Man. (RGIT Aber) 1970 MIPM
lect Inv tech coll 1970; pers off. J & J Crombie Grandholm Aber from 1970
m Drumnadrochit 22.10.77 Ian W. Logan LLB 1963 qv

MORRISON Margaret Isobel **MA 1967**

MORRISON Margaret June **MA 1968**
d of James M. farm. and Mary Robertson teacher;
b Pitcaple 27.6.47
Dip Pers Man.(Strath) 1970 MIPM 1975
pers asst Balfour Kilpatrick Paisley 1970–71; job evaluation off. NAAFI Lond 1972–73; asst pers off. Merton &
Sutton AHA Lond 1973–75, Camden & Islington AHA
Lond 1976–77
m Ilford 27.2.76 Roger Barber LLB(Lond) solic s of
Richard B. Sidcup

MORRISON Margaret Leslie **MA 1959**
d of George C. M. MA 1930 qv and Marjory L. Bruce
MA 1925 qv; b Aber 21.10.38
secy London, Auckland, Melbourne 1960–61; teacher:
Adelaide 1962–63, The Hague 1963–65, Melbourne
1965–67, adult educ Baden Switzerland from 1972
m Adelaide Aust 2.3.62 Dick La Hey eng s of Jacobus H.
Haarlem Holland

MORRISON Margaret Mary **MA 1967**

MORRISON Margaret Sheila **BSc 1966**
m Reid

MORRISON Marie Ewart **MA 1963**
d of Norman Morrison MA 1923 qv; b Aber 29.10.44
BDS(St And) 1967
h o Dun dent hosp 1967–68; regist Glasg dent hosp
1968–70; lect oral biology Glas from 1970
m Aber 24.7.67 Alexander Watt MA 1964

MORRISON Mary ***MEd 1961**
d of Murdo M. merch/sub postmaster and Annie M.
Montgomery dist nurse; b Laxdale Is of Lewis 16.5.35
MA(Glas) 1956 ABPsS 1966
asst educ psych Edin 1961–63, part-time 1964–70,
Midlothian part-time 1971–77, full-time sen educ psych
from 1977
m Glasg 26.3.62 Donald Macaulay MA(Glas) advoc s of
John M. Bragar Is of Lewis

MORRISON Mary MacLean **MA 1968 Dip Ed 1969**
d of Donald M. MA(Glas) teacher and Agnes MacLean
occup therap; b Glasg 28.12.47
teacher Engl: Govan h s 1970–71, Elliot Lake Ontario
1975–76
m Glasg 1.8.70 Stewart J. Christine mech eng s of
Stewart C. Oban

MORRISON Murdo Nicolson ***BSc 1956**
s of Donald M. joiner, piermaster and Mary Nicholson
teacher; b Tarbert Harris 22.6.33
ARIC (1960)
trainee BP Lond, Wales, Grangemouth 1957–59; BP
refinery Grangemouth: chem i/c gas analysis lab 1959–
63, dev chem tech dept 1963–67, sect. head distillation
area 1967–77, area controller from 1977
m Kilbarchan 2.4.60 Anne L. Dick nurse d of Robert
K. D. Kilbarchan

MORRISON Neil ***MA 1970 Dip Ed 1971**

MORRISON Peter   MA 1966

MORRISON Peter George   MA 1967
s of George M. indust chem and Marjorie E. Ingram seamstress; b Wellingborough 16.9.45
trainee progr, team leader Birm 1967–70; chief progr, progr man. Bonnybridge 1970–75; software eng Cumbernauld from 1975
m Aber 27.7.68 Frances M. Barrack MA 1966 *qv*

MORRISON Roderick Murray   MB ChB 1970

MORRISON Wendy Joan   *MA 1965

MORRISON William   MA 1964
s of William M. crofter and Catherine Gunn; b Thrumster 14.7.43
teacher: Glasg 1965–66, Wick from 1966
m Lybster 9.8.68 Diane Miller receptionist d of James M. Lybster

MORRISON William Alexander   *BSc(eng) 1968
d Glasg 11.12.76

MORRISON William James   MB ChB 1959
s of James C. M. milk roundsman and Caroline I. Bruce; b Turriff 22.4.36
DObstRCOG 1961
h o City hosp Aber, Gilbert Bain hosp Lerwick 1959–60; cas off. royal N infirm. Inv 1960–61; h o obst Robroyston hosp Glasg 1961; g p Insch 1961–62, Ellon from 1962
m Aber 31.3.65 Anna I. C. Robertson staff nurse d of James R. Cairnie

MORTIMER Gerald   *MA 1958
s of Adam M. rlyman and Isabella McIntosh; b Glassel 27.1.36
FSAScot 1969
educ off. 1st btn Gordon Highlanders Celle Ger 1958–60; teacher hist Harris acad Dun 1961–66; prin hist Invergordon acad 1966–68; lect soc stud. Hamilton coll of educ from 1968
m Aber 27.6.60 Elizabeth J. Gibb MA 1959 *qv*

MORTIMER Sheila Williamina   MA 1960
d of John M. insur br man. and Adeline S. Laing telegraphist; b Aber 15.12.39
Dip Soc St(Edin) 1961 Cert Inst of Med Soc Work(Lond) 1962
Aber: soc worker mat. hosp 1963–65, sen soc worker RACH 1965–68, mat. hosp 1968–69, Woodlands hosp from 1973
m Aber 5.4.66 Howard O. Smith BSc 1964 *qv*

MORTIMER Wilma Jean   BSc 1962
d of William C. G. M. car sales man. and Jane M. Simpson; b Aboyne 1.11.41
teacher: maths/sc Summerhill acad Aber 1963–67, Perth h s 1967–70, maths Summerbank s Broughty Ferry 1975–78, maths/sc Dun from 1978
m Aber 30.3.67 Melville K. Milne MB ChB 1965 *qv*

MORTON Alan David   *BSc 1968

MORTON Douglas George   BSc(eng) 1960

MORTON Neil   *BSc(agr) 1967
s of Norman M. B Com(Manc) passenger trans eng, trans plan. res and Florence Elliot; b Cheadle 12.8.42
MSc(Lond) 1968 DIC 1968 FRES(Lond)
Swaziland: govt res entomol 1968–71, entomol cotton res corp 1972–75; entomol ICI plant protection dir Bracknell from 1976

m Manc 5.10.68 Susan J. Thom physioth d of Alexander M. T. BSc(eng)(Glas) St Martin's Guernsey

MOSCATI Shane   MA 1964
d of Clifford G. M. smallholder/mussel farmer and Jean C. Vass; b Lond 28.2.43
teacher: Aber 1965–67, Invergordon 1968, Khart 1968–71; lect Engl Omdurman 1971–74; instr Khart from 1975
m Aber 3.2.65 Hassan O. Abdelnour BSc(for) 1967 *qv*

MOSS Christine Margaret   MA 1964

MOSS Robert   PhD 1967
s of Leonard M. clothing manuf/des and Lore Elkan; b Leeds 30.11.41
BSc(Lond) 1963
scient off., sen scient off., prin scient off. Nature Conservancy/ITE(NERC) Banchory from 1967

MOTT Brian Leonard   *MA 1969
s of Leonard M. printer and Beryl E. Cowland; b Lond 20.8.46
PhD(Barcelona) 1978
lect phonetics Engl dept: Zaragoza univ Spain 1969–72, Barcelona univ from 1972 and co-ordinator Engl dept univ lang s from 1976

MOUAT James Henry   LLB 1966

MOUAT Katherine Ann   MA 1960
d of John G. M. trans man. and Joan C. Smith; b Lerwick 26.2.39
teacher Engl/hist: McLaren h s Callander 1961–63, Scalloway j s s 1963–65, Dunblane s s 1965–67, Engl Mackie acad Stonehaven from 1976
m Lerwick 31.3.64 James A. G. Mathers marine eng s of James M. Port of Menteith

MOUAT Patricia   MB ChB 1966
b Shetland 7.9.41

MOUNCE Robert Hayden   PhD 1958
BA(Wash) BD ThM(Ful Theol Sem)

MOUNIB Mohamed Said   PhD 1956
BSc MSc(Alex)

MOUSSA Mohammed Ahmed Sayed Ahmed   PhD 1966
BSc(Ain-Shams)

MOWAT Alexander Parker   MB ChB 1958
s of William M. trawl fisherman and Isabella P. Mair; b Cullen 5.4.35
MRCP(Lond) 1963 FRCP(Lond) 1975
nat serv RAMC Hong Kong 1959–61; h o med, paediat Aber, Lond 1961–65; res fell., assoc prof paediat Yeshiva univ NY USA 1968–69; sen regist paediat Aberd 1965–70; consult. paediat King's coll hosp/Maudsley hosp Lond from 1970
m Cullen 23.9.61 Mary A. S. Hunter civ serv d of Samuel H. Cullen

MOWAT Anne Mary   MA 1965
d of Victor S. M. bank man. and Jemima B. T. McNicol lib; b Edin 7.12.44
comm asst BP Co Lond 1966–68; teacher BC Canada 1968–69
m Aber 25.3.68 George A. R. Stark BSc(Lond) econ BP Co s of Allan R.S. BSc(Glas) Sunbury-on-Thames
d Torphins 17.11.78

MOWAT Charles Donald   MB ChB 1957
s of Charles D. M. fish merch and May C. Middleton;
b Aber 7.1.32
h o Woodend hosp Aber 1957–58; m o RAF E Anglia
1958–61; g p: St Walburg Sask 1961–67, Barnard Castle
Co Durh 1967–69, Stony Plain Edmonton Alberta from
1969
m Aber 21.7.58 Joan B. Williamson secy d of P. de
L. H. W. BCom 1926 *qv*

MOWAT Colin Ralph   *MA 1967 Dip Ed 1968
s of William R. M. civ serv and Margaret M.
McClenaghen; b Aber 14.5.45
teacher geog: Bo'ness acad 1968–69, Kirkcaldy tech
coll 1969–74; educ off. (6th form) geog Bandar Seri
Begawan Sultanate of Brunei from 1975
m Aber 16.8.69 Beryl Fyfe MA 1968 *qv*

MOWAT Ian Robert Mackenzie   *MA 1968
s of Robert J. B. M. banker and J. Violet Mackenzie;
b Dingwall 20.4.46
MA(Sheff) 1970 BPhil(St And) 1975
asst lib: St And univ 1970–72, H-W 1972–75, asst keeper
Nat Lib Scot. 1975–78, head Reader Services Glas univ
lib from 1978
m Sunderland 24.8.68 Margaret L. Jackson teacher d of
Victor J. Sunderland

MOWAT John   *BSc(eng) 1961
b Douglas Lanark 20.5.39
trainee SETS 1961–63; eng: NSHEB Blairgowrie 1963–
66, SSEB Musselburgh 1966–67, UKAEA Dounreay
1967–78, Culham from 1978

MOWAT John Stuart Simpson   MB ChB 1958
s of Alexander G. M. MB ChB 1924 *qv*; b Stoke-on-
Trent 31.1.30
h o med, cas Bury St Edmunds 1959–60; RN from 1960
m N'cle-u-Lyme 3.6.61 Eva-Maria V. Borel SRN d of
Gustave A. B. Neuchâtel Switzerland

MOWAT Katherine Ann Mackenzie   BSc 1963
m Morrison

MOWAT Malcolm David Yuille   LLB 1966
s of John M. MA(Glas) min of relig and Margaret A.
Howie MA(Glas); b Aber 1.10.44
CA 1969
app Williamson & Dunn CA Aber 1966–69; auditor:
Price Waterhouse & Co Paris 1970–73, Lisbon 1973–75,
audit man. Whinney Murray & Co Aber from 1975
m Paris 26.8.72 Susan Tunningley d of Robert T. Lond

MOWAT Norman Ashley George   MB ChB 1966
s of William M. fisherman and Isabella P. Mair;
b Cullen 11.4.43
MRCP 1971
h o Woodend hosp Aber, ARI 1966–67; sen h o, regist
Aber hosps, clin tut. med Aberd 1968–72; lect med Aberd
1972–73; clin lect gastroenterology St Bart's hosp Lond
1973–74; consult. phys/clin sen lect Aberd from 1975
m Fordyce 23.7.66 Kathleen M. Cowie teacher d of
James D. C. Fordyce

MOWAT Stanley Ian   *BSc 1966 MSc 1968

MOWAT Thomas James Smith   BSc(eng) 1966

MOWAT William   MB ChB 1961

MOWATT Christina Cecilia   MA 1970
m Thomson

MOWATT John Edward Arthur   BSc 1957

MUIR Andrew   BSc(agr) 1968

MUIR George Watson   *MA 1968

MUIR Isabella   *MA 1956 Dip Ed 1957

MUIR Joan Elizabeth   MA 1969
d of James F. M. plan. eng and Katherine W.
Macgregor; b Inv 10.5.48
Dip Grad Secy(Edin coll of comm) 1971
Edin: secy Ferranti 1971–73; inst of CA of Scot. Edin:
secy to edit. *The Accountant's Magazine* 1973–75, edit.
asst 1975–76; edit. and prod. man. 1976–77, asst edit.
1977
m Edin 22.6.74 Michael W. Milne BSc(eng) 1968 *qv*

MUIR John Geates   BSc(agr) 1967
s of Stephen M. farm. and Bella L. A. Harcus;
b Sanday Orkney 31.1.45
Dip FMBO 1968
DAFS: asst insp Aber 1968–77, insp Thurso from 1977
m Aber 28.7.73 Morag Ross d of Ronald R. Aber

MUIR Lisbeth   *MA 1970
d of George M. M. driver (*d* 9.4.55) and Nellie Coull
shopkeeper; b Millport 19.4.48
Dip YESTB
careers off. Lanarksh 1970–75; area careers off. Strathclyde reg (Ayr div) from 1975
m Millport 23.6.73 Peter J. Lamb ACA s of John L. L.
Addington

MUIR Lynn   *MA 1970

MUIR Neil Marshall   LLB 1970

MUIR Richard Ernest   *MA 1967 PhD 1970

MUIR Sarah Jane   *MEd 1967
d of John I. M. BSc(Glas) headmaster and Jean C.
Howgate teacher dom sc; b Grahamstown S Africa
1.9.42
MA(Edin) 1964
educ psych: N'cle-u-Tyne 1967–72, Bexley Lond from
1972
m Dalmeny –.3.72 Charles F. Morley BSc(Manc) prod.
marketing man. s of Francis E. M. Manc

MUIRDEN Elaine   MA 1969
d of Alexander H. M. master grocer and Mary Bruce
master grocer; b Aber 7.10.48
teacher maths Crawley 1970–73
m Aber 28.8.71 William B. M. Rowlands BSc(Leeds)
process eng s of William R. R. Llandovery

MUIRHEAD Ronald Archibald   *BSc 1965
s of John S. M. master glazier and Martha Craig;
b Glasg 15.11.35
MSc(Liv) 1974
res asst immunochem Liv 1965–67; hosp biochem Sefton
gen hosp Liv from 1967
m Wolvey 10.9.66 Lorna E. Fox midwifery tut.
d of Donald R. F. Nuneaton

MUKHERJEE Debangshu Bhusan   PhD 1960
BSc(Agra) MSc(Alld)

MUKHI Lajpat Mangharam   BSc(eng) 1957
BSc(Bom)

MUKHTAR Nuri Osman MSc 1970
s of Osman Mukhtar Hussein and Miyasa Ahmed;
b Dongula Sudan 1.1.39
BSc(Khart)
m Cairo 20.11.69 Fatma I. D. Salih d of Izzel D. S.
Cairo

MUKTAR Omar Mohamed Ahmed BSc 1959
s of Mohamed Ahmed teacher and Zeinab Osman; b
Omdurman 21.9.31
Dip Agr(Khart) 1955 MSc(univ Wales) 1963 PhD(Texas)
1970
Sudan: agr advis serv W Sudan 1955–56; agr res div Wad
Medani 1959–60, co-man. soil surv div 1964–68, dir soils
dept min of agr Wad Medani from 1971
m Swansea Patricia M. Wright BA(UCW) teacher d of
Edward W. Loughborough

MULHOLLAND Alastair Brodie MB ChB 1956
s of Alexander B. M. sales rep and Isabella Hamilton;
b Aber 23.2.32
DA(Lond) 1960 FFARCS(Lond) 1965 Cert Anaest
RCS(C) 1965 Lic Med Council(Can) 1966
h o Aber 1956–57, m o RAMC Malaya 1957–59; sen h o
anaest. regist anaest Aber 1959–65; Canada: sen resid
anaest Vancouver 1965–66, staff anaest Vict gen hosp
1966–71, chief dept anaest Vict 1971–74
m Elgin 2.9.61 Isabella H. Turnidge nurse d of Stafford
T. Elgin

MULHOLLAND Freda Jane MB ChB 1969
m Brown

MULHOLLAND Mary Grant MA 1969
d of Joseph M. postal insp and Evelyn M. A. Jefferson;
b Elgin 20.9.48
teacher: Dun 1971–73, Brit high comm Dar-es-Salaam
Tanzania from 1973
m St And 27.10.72 Alexander R. Anderson customs &
excise off. s of Alexander A. Alford

MULKAY Michael Joseph PhD 1970
BA(Lond) MA(S Fraser)

MULLER Emil-Roy PhD 1962
BSc(agr)(Natal)

MULVEY Charles *MA 1963
s of Charles M. shopkeeper and Mary P. Bruce;
b Aber 13.2.41
Trinity coll Dublin; asst in econ 1963–64, lect econ
1964–72; econ advis to Sec of State for Scot. Edin 1972–
73; sen lect econ Glas from 1973
m Dublin 28.1.66 Gerarda E. Vermeulen d of Adrianus
V. Bray Co Wicklow

MUNIR Yasser Husein MSc 1970
BSc(Cairo)

MUNRO Alexander MB ChB 1967 ChM 1968
s of William G. agr contr and Jane A. McKay SRN;
b Jemimaville 5.6.43
FRCSE 1972
sen h o HSC Gt Ormond St Lond 1969–70; regist ARI
lect surg Aberd 1971–75; sen regist surg: Aber 1975–77,
St Mary's hosp Lond 1977–78; consult. gen surg Inv
hosps from 1978
m Edin 17.7.72 Maureen E. McCreath staff midwife d of
James McC. CA Glasg

MUNRO Alexander Falconer *MA 1967
s of William M. civ eng and Annie E. MacDonald
nurse; b Forfar 1.1.44

Glasg: man. trainee BR 1967–69, costing asst BR 1969–
70; p a to man. dir Caithness Glass Wick 1970; United
Glass: sales exec Bridge of Allan 1970–74, market. dev
man. Staines from 1974
m Wick 17.8.68 Julia A. M. Aitkenhead pharm d of
Robert C. A. Rhodesia

MUNRO Andrew *MA 1964 PhD 1971
s of Alexander M. dyer and bleacher and Janet
McCracken; b Port Glasgow 1.1.36
BD(Glas) 1967 Ordained C of S min 1972
prin teacher relig educ: Banff acad 1971–72; lect theol
Trinity coll Ghana 1972–76; prin teacher r e Elgin acad
from 1976
m Aber 27.7.63 Sheila Smith BSc 1962 qv

MUNRO Angus Archibald Donald *MA 1970

MUNRO Anne Macintosh BEd 1969
d of Duncan M. head for. for. comm and Mary C.
Galbraith MA(Glas) teacher; b Campbeltown 9.11.45
teacher: Engl Edin 1969–72, drama Aber from 1972

MUNRO Caroline Helen *MA 1963
d of Thomas A. M. cabinetmaker and Caroline
Gordon; b Wanlockhead 21.9.41
teacher geog coll of comm Aber 1965–66; asst lib sc lib
univ of W Ontario 1967–68
m Aber 17.7.65 David G. Dawson BSc 1963 qv

MUNRO Cathleen Anne MA 1964
d of Angus H. M. banker, farm. and Kathleen W. F.
Manson hotelier; b Nairn 27.4.43
teacher: Garrowhill 1965–66, Slade Green, Bexley 1966–
68, Malpas 1968–69, Ellesmere Port from 1975
m Huntly 14.7.66 Peter R. Aikman BSc 1966 qv

MUNRO Donald BSc 1956

MUNRO Donald *MA 1959

MUNRO Donald James *MA 1964
s of William M. civ eng and Annie E. Macdonald
nurse; b Forfar 22.2.42
asst dept mss John Rylands lib Manc 1964–66; inst of
hist res univ of Lond: bibliogr asst 1966–73, asst lib from
1973
m Ashton-u-Lyne 27.3.67 Beryl Swetnam teacher d of
James S. Ashton-u-Lyne

MUNRO Frances Helen MA 1957

MUNRO Gillespie Donald MA 1960
s of John B. M. comm trav and Emma McCallum
insur clerkess; b Aber 28.4.39
teacher: Lumphanan s s 1961–63, Ballater p s 1963–67;
head Monymusk p s from 1967
m Ballater 17.10.64 Mary H. Davidson teacher d of
Donald D. Ballater

MUNRO Hamish David *BSc 1964 PhD 1967
s of James S. M. pharm and Isabella Thomson;
b Kilwinning 24.4.42
Chartered Patent Ag 1975 Gill Prize 1975
res fell. univ of Mainz Germany 1967–68; chem Procter &
Gamble N'cle 1968–71; patent tech asst Carpmaels &
Ransford Lond 1972–75; Procter & Gamble: patent ag
Cincinnati Ohio 1975, man. of patents Europe Strombeek-
Bever Belgium from 1976
m Aber 6.1.68 Alison B. Walker BSc 1964 qv
d Lond 9.2.80 AUR XLVIII 443

MUNRO Ian Alexander MA 1966

MUNRO Jean Margaret   MA 1968
d of Frank A. M. motor mech, loc govt off. and Martha
M. Anderson seamstress, shop asst; b Inv 11.1.47
Dip Sec Sc(Strath) 1969
secy: Lond 1969–71, Edin 1971–73; res asst Edin from
1973
m Edin 14.4.73 Terence Foster BSc(Edin) teacher s of
George F. Birm

MUNRO John Gray   BSc(eng) 1961
s of John G. M. MA(Cantab) group capt RAF and
Rita M. Walkey nurs sister; b Bromley 8.4.39
GMIMechE
Bristol: grad app BAC 1961–62; organis and methods
asst etc United Builders Merchants 1962–72, dir UBM
Group from 1972
m Wraxall 26.6.65 Elizabeth R. Scantlebury d of Eric S.

MUNRO Margaret Catherine   MA 1967
d of William G. M. blacksmith and Margaret Mackay;
b Brora 13.8.46
teacher: mod lang Hillhead h s Glasg 1968–72, Engl
anglic mission s Nuku Alofa Tonga 1972–73, Millburn
acad Inv 1975–78
m Brora 17.10.70 John E. Rae MA 1965 *qv*

MUNRO Margaret Jean Waters   MA 1968
m Munro

MUNRO Margot Gunn   *MA 1963
d of Robert G. M. MB ChB 1923 *qv*; b Sheff 16.1.36
ARCM 1959 LRAM 1963 Dip Lib(Sheff) 1966
trainee lib Torry res stat Aber 1964–65; asst lib St And
univ from 1966

MUNRO Mary Dunbar   MA 1962
d of John M. butcher and Davina Sinclair; b Thurso
2.5.41
teacher Miller acad p s Thurso 1953–65 and from 1972
m Thurso 1963 David J. Lyall nuclear chem s of John L.
Duns

MUNRO Robert Alexander   *MA 1968

MUNRO Robert Charles   PhD 1966
s of Ralph M. manuf and Bertha L. von Melcher
BS(W Reserve univ) nurse, entrepreneur; b Mansfield
Ohio 25.11.38
B Foreign Serv(Calif)
proj superv B. F. Goodrich Co Akron Ohio 1966–67;
superv of accts internat B. F. Goodrich Frankfurt
Germany 1967–68; Jos. Schlitz Brewing Co: man. spec
assignments Milwaukee Wisconsin 1968–69, asst dir sales
Europe Ghlin Belgium 1969–70; man. market. plan. and
res ITT world directories Brussels 1970–72, man. market.
plan. dev and res Brussels 1972–76, res analyst ITT
world hq NY City 1976–77; man. market dev Fundacion
Chile Santiago 1977–78; ITT world hq NY City: asst
man.-corporate market. 1978–79, man. market and bus.
strategy 1979, man. corporate indust and employee
relations from 1979
m S Juan PR 10.2.75 Maria do R. de F. M. Ribeiro-
Fernandes BA(Lisbon) advis acct exec d of Joaquim
d'A R-F. Portugal

MUNRO Robert James   *BSc(eng) 1964

MUNRO Robert Kenneth   *MA 1968
s of Donald W. M. flt lt RAF and Ethel Stoten;
b Dunstable 7.4.46
teacher geog: AGS 1969–70, Whitburn acad 1970–71,
prin geog Douglas Ewart h s Wigtown 1971–74; lect geog

Hamilton coll of educ from 1974
m Blair Atholl 10.8.68 Janet S. Seaton teacher d of
Alexander S. Blair Atholl

MUNRO Robert Lawrence   *MA 1966
s of Hugh A. C. M. M. insp taxes and Elsie M.
Chapman; b Cromarty 12.6.44
insp taxes: Aber 1966–68, Glasg 1968–72, Ardrossan
1972–73, Lond from 1973

MUNRO Robin Murray   *MA 1969
s of Ian S. M. MA(Glas) lect and Mary M. Allan;
b Bute 10.5.46
Arts Council award 1973
writer Catterline and Shetland from 1971; teacher
Galloway from 1975; poetry collections: *Shetland, like the
World* 1975, *The Land of the Mind* 1975

MUNRO Roderic   MA 1968
s of Frederick A. M. and Annie Jessiman; b Forres
3.4.47
teacher: dep head maths dept Little Ilford comp s Lond
from 1970

MUNRO Sheila Margaret   MB ChB 1969
m Mathewson

MUNRO Wendy   MA 1969
m Chaligne

MUNRO William Alexander   BSc(eng) 1967
s of Thomas A. M. cabinetmaker and Caroline Gordon
shop asst; b Glasg 7.5.40
MInstHE 1968 CEng MICE 1971
measurement eng R. J. McLeod Drumnadrochit 1967–
68; Forfar: asst eng Angus c c roads dept, sen eng from
1972
m Aber Dorothy W. Neish hairdresser/man. d of
Archibald C. N. Brechin

MUNSADIA Ishwarlal Dahyabhai   MB ChB 1963

MURCHIE Anne   MA 1959
m Morton

MURCHIE Innes Fyfe   *MA 1966
s of Charles S. M. eng and Elizabeth L. Innes bookseller; b Aber 10.11.43
bank clerk Aber 1967–69; res asst Clydesdale bank Glasg
from 1970
m Aber 28.6.69 Heather Cobban secy d of Charles C.
Aber

MURCHIE Marjory Elizabeth   *MA 1968
d of James L. M. chief supt police and Marjory Dean;
b Glasg 27.3.46
teacher: Hillhead h s Glasg 1969–72, prin geog Knightswood s s Glasg from 1972
m Glasg 21.3.70 Hamish G. Reid BSc(eng) 1968 *qv*

MURCUTT Miriam Sinclair   MA 1969

MURDOCH Anne Grace   MA 1970
d of George M. garage serv man. and Annie G. M.
Robb nurse; b Dun 18.1.49
Dip Soc Ad 1971 Dip Soc Work 1972
soc worker: royal Edin hosp 1972–73, Lancs c c 1973–76
m Monifieth 23.3.74 Bernard Strawson BSc(Lond) pers
off. BL s of Bernard S. Liv

MURDOCH Elizabeth Margaret   MA 1969
d of George M. M. joiner and Janet C. Aitken comptometer oper; b Glasg 9.9.48

teacher: Lat Kilmarnock acad 1970–71, p s Evanton 1971–72, Lat Invergordon acad 1972–74
m E Kilbride 7.4.71 John K. Clark MA 1969 *qv*

MURDOCH James   BSc 1964

MURDOCH Keith Kinord Ian   MA 1966
s of Colin C. I. M. artist/art dealer and Rosalind A. J. D. Cruickshank; b Aber 4.2.44
teacher: direct method Engl Paris 1966–69, supply Engl Brighton 1969–70, Engl Cambuslang from 1970; other non-teaching temp posts

MURDOCH Robert Bell   MA 1956
s of Robert B. M. civ serv and Marguerita C. Bell newsagent; b Stonehaven 28.10.31
teacher: maths Arbroath h s 1957–58, Carnoustie p s 1958–60; dep head: p dept Carnoustie j s s 1960–67, p dept Laurencekirk s s 1967–71, Arduthie p s Stonehaven from 1971
m Stonehaven 19.9.53 Alice M. Ross pharm's asst d of William R. Aber

MURDOCH Ronald McLean   MA 1968

MURDOCH William Forman   MA 1964 *MEd 1966
s of William F. M. gardener and Jeannie Simpson; b Cruden 6.4.39
Kirkcudbrightsh: teacher 1966–68, educ psych 1968–70; Abdnsh: sen educ psych 1970–71, head spec s 1971–76, advis spec educ Grampian reg c from 1976
m Aber 12.7.63 Christine A. Gear BSc 1960 *qv*

MURISON Norma   MA 1967
m Smith

MURPHY Arthur John   *MA 1967

MURPHY Helen Margaret   *BSc 1970
m Salford 25.9.70 David J. Hall BSc 1970 *qv*

MURRAY Alexander   BSc(agr) 1957
s of James M. farm. and Margaret Mitchell teacher; b Cornhill 26.7.33
asst exper off. Scot. Soc for res in plant breeding Roslin 1958–60; asst agr advis NOSCA Stonehaven, Inv 1960–62; asst insp, insp DAFS Edin, Kirkwall, Dun from 1963

MURRAY Alexander Irvine   BSc 1969
s of Irvine M. M. accts man. and Margaret J. Mackenzie; b Nairn 25.9.46
trainee computer progr Barrow-in-Furness 1969–70; computer progr Inv 1970–72; computer syst analyst Norwich from 1972
m Edin 4.11.72 Alys G. M. Roberts teacher of art d of Arthur R. R. Edin

MURRAY Alistair William   *BSc 1958 PhD 1962

MURRAY Anne Scott   MA 1968
d of Malcolm S. M. p e instr and Noel J. Corrigall; b Lossiemouth 7.6.48
Dip Pers Man(RGIT) 1970
Lond: secy, admin asst various companies 1970–74, exec off. MoD 1974–79
m Aber 30.1.71 John M. M. Dixon MA 1969 *qv*

MURRAY Bernard Marshall   BSc(eng) 1969

MURRAY Bruce   BSc 1960
s of George J. G. M. agr rep and Bella G. Lamb;

b Aber 2.11.39
teacher maths/sc Ruthrieston s Aber 1961–65; various posts with IBM (UK) Greenock from 1965
m Aber 3.8.62 Sheila M. West RGN d of Malcolm W. Aber

MURRAY Catherine   MA 1960
d of Donald M. Harris tweed millworker and Murdina Morrison; b Stornoway 24.1.39
teacher: Laurencekirk s s 1961–63, Cloverfield p s Aber 1964–67, Tough p s Dunfermline from 1975
m Aber 29.3.65 Donald Smith BSc 1961 *qv*

MURRAY Charlotte   MA 1960 Dip Ed 1961
d of Charles M. cattleman and Lily R. Henderson; b Inv 12.6.39
teacher Engl/hist: Kirriemuir 1961–66, Stornoway from 1966
m Dun 1.8.69 Murdoch Macleod weaver s of George B. C. M. Tong, Is of Lewis

MURRAY Christina Margaret   MA 1958
d of Donald M. and Murdina Morrison; b Stornoway 20.3.37
teacher: Inverallochy p s 1959–62, Stoneywood p s 1962–65
m Aber 17.7.63 John Anderson MA 1960 *qv*

MURRAY Christopher Hugh   *MA 1969
s of William M. MBE MM for./head for. and Mary B. MacRae; b Inv 17.1.47
grad acct trainee Tannochside Viewpark 1969–72; cost acct Fochabers 1972–75; acct stud. Edin 1975–76; lect bus. stud. Elgin coll 1976–77; chief acct Fochabers from 1977
m Aber 12.9.69 Audrey F. A. Park BEd 1969 *qv*

MURRAY David Cairns   *MA 1964 Dip Ed 1966
s of Robert J. M. hortic advis NOSCA and Mary McGuckian secy, teacher; b Glasg 6.8.41
teacher geog AGS 1966–68; lt RN educ off. RNAS Culdrose 1968–73, lt comm RN met. off. HMS *Daedalus* Lee-on-Solent 1973–75; sen forecaster HMS *Ark Royal* 1975–77, staff met. off. to capt i/c Hong Kong from 1977
m Westbury 9.4.69 Monica J. Grenfell SRN d of Richard C. G. Westbury

MURRAY David Findlay   BSc 1969

MURRAY Donella   MA 1957

MURRAY Douglas   MA 1970 LLB 1972
s of John M. baker and Ida Leighton-Hall; b Perth 31.1.49
law app Edin 1972–74; leg. asst Paull & Williamsons advoc Aber 1974–80, ptnr from 1980

MURRAY Eleanor Margaret   MB ChB 1961 DPH 1966
m Steiner

MURRAY Elizabeth Cooper   MA 1959

MURRAY Ernest   MB ChB 1965
s of Alexander M. gardener and Charlotte Coutts; b Alford 15.3.41
h p Woodend hosp, City hosp, mat hosp Aber 1965–67; g p Poole from 1967
m Aber 30.9.65 Eva I. W. Law secy d of Robert L. Keig

MURRAY George   *BSc 1961 MSc 1962 PhD 1965
s of George M. trawl fisherman and Agnes Coull; b Aber 23.5.39

asst lect maths Queen's coll Dun 1964–66; lect nat phil
Aberd from 1966
m Aber 2.10.72 Margaret A. Scrimgeour MA 1964 *qv*

MURRAY Gordon   BSc(for) 1957
s of Alan D. M. teacher and Helen Bowick MA(St And)
teacher; b Forfar 2.4.36
MSc(Purdue univ Indiana) 1969 PhD 1972
2nd lt RE 1957–59; teacher sc Kirriemuir 1959–60;
exper off. Nature Conserv Monkswood 1960–66; grad
res inst Purdue univ 1966–72; Lakehead univ s of for.
Thunder Bay Ontario: asst 1972–77, assoc prof from 1977
m Lossiemouth 9.7.60 Laura Leask radiogr d of Robert
J. L. Lossiemouth

MURRAY Hazel   *MA 1958
d of John M. chef and Jean Ormiston; b N'cle-u-Tyne
22.12.36
teacher mod lang: Perth 1960–62, Elgin 1962–63; asst
prin mod lang Aberlour 1967–76, prin mod lang from
1976
m Aberlour 28.4.62 William Fraser postman

MURRAY Helen Kilpatrick   *MA 1970
m Matthews

MURRAY Hugh Bruce   *MA 1967
s of James M. bank man. and Anne Bruce health lect;
b Aber 11.5.45
Dip Ed(Glas) 1968
teacher: prin hist St Leonard's s Glasg, prin soc stud
Bermuda from 1970
m Bermuda 22.7.71 Mary M. Doherty MA 1967 *qv*

MURRAY Ian   BSc(eng) 1968

MURRAY Ian James   BSc(eng) 1970

MURRAY Isabella Reid   *MA 1970
m Macdonald

MURRAY James   *BSc 1964

MURRAY James Alexander   MB ChB 1957
s of James A. M. motor salesman and Robina Berry;
b Aber 24.3.34
RAF 1958–61; h o Forth Park mat. hosp Fife 1961;
g p Kirkcaldy from 1961
m Aber 10.4.57 Mabel M. Gavin d of William G. Aber

MURRAY James Charles   *MA 1970 Dip Ed 1973
s of James M. bank man. and Annie Bruce lect; b Ayr
7.8.47
L ès L(Clermont–Ferrand) 1971
lect Engl univ of Clermont–Ferrand France 1970–71;
res stud. Aberd 1971–72; lect econ Engl Paris 1973–74;
teacher Fr Hazlehead acad Aber 1974–75; asst prin mod
lang Cults acad Aber from 1975
m Sens France 15.7.74 Liliane C. L. Carreau L ès L
(Sorbonne) teacher d of Louis A. C. Sens

MURRAY James Frederick   *MA 1969
s of James G. M. pharm and Anne M. Taggart; b Aber
13.5.46
teacher St And 1970–74; lib asst Dun 1974–76; post
grad ALA stud. RGIT Aber 1976–77; lib asst Aber from
1977

MURRAY James Morrison   MA 1968

MURRAY Jennifer Anne   MA 1965 *MEd 1968
m Reid

MURRAY John Young   *MEd 1966
s of Charles M. MA(Edin) teacher, HMIS and
Margaret I. Young MA(Edin) teacher; b Kirkcaldy
5.2.43
BSc(Edin) 1964
teacher chem Annan 1966–72, prin chem from 1972
m Inv 4.7.66 Barbara A. Williams teacher d of Edwin
M. W. Inv

MURRAY Katharine Gale   *MA 1966
d of Andrew D. M. soc statist and Joan M. St Aubin
lect; b Lond 10.10.42
teacher Engl: Dunfermline 1972–74, Corsham s 1974–76
m Lond 23.7.66 David J. Curry BSc 1965 *qv*

MURRAY Laurence Oliphant Nairne   MA 1964

MURRAY Leonora Janet Hunter   MB ChB 1959
d of Robert H. M. bricklayer/mason and Jessie Sim
hotel prop.; b Cluny 20.2.34
h o Woodend hosp Aber, ARI 1959–60; sen h o: geriat
Woodend hosp, psychiat royal mental hosp Aber 1960–
65; regist psycho-geriat Royal Vict hosp Edin from 1975
m Aber 20.7.62 Gordon M. McAndrew MB ChB 1957 *qv*

MURRAY Margaret Jane Irvine   MA 1965
d of James D. M. mill worker and Eva M. Davidson
waitress; b Aber 19.9.30
teacher Aber from 1966
m Aber 3.10.51 William P. Booth painter/decorator s of
Alexander B. Aber; husb *d* 7.4.60

MURRAY Margaret Muir   MA 1970 Dip Ed 1971
d of Walter M. M. dist lib and Helen R. Brown school
lib; b Motherwell 26.12.49
teacher geog: Dumfries 1971–73, Lond 1973–76; educ
off. HM prison Perth 1977; teacher geog Perth from 1977
m Alloa 24.12.76 Robert J. C. Watt MA 1973 lect
Dund s of William S. W. MA (Glas) prof humanity
Aberd

MURRAY Marjory Henderson   MA 1970 Dip Ed 1971
d of William M. steelfixer/scaffolder and Loveday
M. D. Mackay off. man.; b Golspie 21.11.49
au pair France 1971–72; teacher Ger/Fr Golspie 1972–73,
Fr Manc 1973; exec off. civ serv Manc, Edin 1974–76
m Golspie 27.10.73 Stuart F. Carnegie BSc 1971 res
scient s of James R. C. Inverarity

MURRAY Matthew Archibald Gillespie   BEd 1970

MURRAY Muriel Gray Carnegie   MA 1958
d of George J. G. M. agr salesman and Bella G. Lamb;
b Aber 5.8.37
teacher: Crathes 1959–60, Fernielea s Aber 1961–69
m Aber 1.3.69 Ian D. Knight off. man. OPM s of James
K. Meikle Wartle

MURRAY Neil   MA 1959
s of James M. blacksmith/crofter and Marion MacIver;
b Back Lewis 3.3.36
teacher Laxdale j s 1960–65; sen lect Lews Castle coll
Lewis from 1965
m Aber 27.12.62 Catherine Graham shop asst d of Angus
G. Back

MURRAY Neil Macbeth   MA 1969
s of Stuart M. clerk and Christina I. McBeth; b Elgin
6.3.48
prof footballer: Edin 1969–73, Greenock 1973–74,
teacher s s Greenock from 1974

MURRAY Norman   MA 1967
   s of Donald M. crofter/weaver and Margaret Smith;
b Lewis 1.7.46
BA(Strath) 1973
Glasg: teacher hist 1968–72, asst prin guid 1972–73, prin
hist from 1973

MURRAY Rhoda Violet   BSc 1968
   d of George J. A. M. M. head for. and Rhoda Ralph
nurse; b Portskerra 9.4.45
asst scient off. Marine lab Aber 1969–72
m Tomintoul 29.7.67 James Gray BSc 1963 *qv*

MURRAY Rhona Mary   MA 1969
   m Mackenzie

**MURRAY Ronald Gordon Ireland Clark   MA 1958
                                        Dip Ed 1959**

MURRAY Rosemary Lilian   *MA 1964 Dip Ed 1978
   m Watson

MURRAY Roy   MB ChB 1967

MURRAY Sheila Margaret   *MA 1963
   d of Alexander M. bank man. and Elsie F. Nicol civ
serv, acct work; b Inv 4.4.42
teacher mus: Aber acad 1964–65, Thurso h s 1965–66;
prin teacher mus Lerwick c s 1966–70, asst Anderson h s
Lerwick from 1970
m Aber 29.7.66 James G. Bruce chief clerk banking s of
Alexander G. B. MA(Edin) Thurso

MURRAY Stewart   *BSc 1966
   s of Robert M. MN off. and Catherine N. Stewart;
b Aber 18.9.37
geol NCB: Wales 1966–69, Scot. 1969–74; lands off.
W Scot. from 1974
m Aber 26.7.71 Helen M. Kean MA 1952 *qv*

MURRAY Violet   MA 1968 BD 1972
   d of Allan M. Br Legion car park attend. and Nellie S.
Dodds; b Aber 10.8.26
teacher Peterhead from 1973

MURRAY William   MA 1959
   s of William K. M. joiner and Elsie Barber; b New
Byth 26.8.36
teacher Fr/prin guid Moffat acad from 1960
m Rousay 17.7.58 Kathleen F. S. Grieve MA 1958 *qv*

MURRAY William John   BSc(eng) 1964
   s of William M. farm. and Jeanne A. Milton; b Keith
27.7.42
Dip Man.(McG) 1971
N Telecom Canada: dev eng 1964–73, dept head digital
trans div from 1973
m Barbados 21.12.69 Sally J. Edghill physioth d of
J. H. C. E. Christchurch Barbados

**MURRAY-SMITH David James   *BSc(eng) 1963
                                          MSc 1964**
   s of William M-S. grain merch and Katherine B. Trail;
b Aber 20.10.41
PhD(Glas) 1970
res eng Ferranti Edin 1964–65, Glas: asst 1966–67, lect
1967–77, sen lect from 1977
m Aber 9.8.66 Effie M. Smith MA 1963 *qv*

MUSA Mohammed Musa   PhD 1963
   BSc(agr)(Khart)

MUST Christopher John   MB ChB 1957
   s of John S. M. BA(Cantab) clerk in holy orders and
Katrine Russell MA 1929 *qv*; b Lond 19.11.33
DO(Lond) 1961 FRCS(C) 1967
h o Aber hosps 1957–58; ophth RAF Eng, Aden 1958–63;
regist ophth Carlisle 1963–66; consult. ophth Peterborough Ontario from 1966
m Aber 26.7.58 Janella H. S. Baxter leg. secy d of John B.
Aber

MUST Michael James   BSc 1960
   s of John S. M. BA(Cantab) clerk in holy orders and
Katrine Russell MA 1929 *qv*; b Wembley 18.7.38
teacher phys co-ed g s Biggleswade 1960–62; oil comp:
clerk board statist Lond 1962–63, computer syst auditor
Hemel Hempstead 1963–65, superv auditor 1965–70,
costing unit man. Lond, computer syst audit man. PO
central audit dept 1972-76; computer audit superv oil
comp from 1976
m Roxton 18.4.64 Janet Bates nurs nurse, teacher d of
Charles J. R. B. Roxton

MUSTAFA Muktar Ahmed   MSc 1966
   BSc(Khart)

MUTCH Alexander James   BSc(eng) 1957
   s of William K. M. clerk and Violet French; b Insch
15.6.37
des eng: Scot. gas board Aber 1957–58, city eng's dept
Dunedin city council NZ 1958–62, Macdonald Wagner &
Priddle consult. eng Sydney 1962–73, assoc dir from 1973
m Dunedin 18.12.59 Melva R. Milne nurse d of Anthony
W. M. Aber

MUTCH Douglas Bruce   MA 1969
   s of Henry D. M. bus driver and Mary A. Bruce
superv; b Ellon 8.11.48
teacher mod lang: Bankhead 1970–71, Arbroath 1971–74,
Arran from 1974
m Aber 7.7.71 Hilary M. Rhodes MA 1969 *qv*

MUTCH George Porter   *MA 1970 MLitt 1974
   s of William M. cycle dealer and Elsie C. Milton law
clerkess; b Keith 28.9.49
stud. Oxon 1971–73; lect: école normale supérieure
Paris 1973–74, univ de Paris–III 1974–76, univ de Paris–
IV–Sorbonne from 1976

MUTCH Gwendoline   MA 1967
   m McCaskie

MUTCH John   *MA 1964 Dip Ed 1965

MUTCH John Robert Young   MA 1958   LLB 1961

MUTCH Lesley Margaret Mollison   MB ChB 1956
   d of Henry J. M. M. rubber planter and Myra M.
Watt MA 1910 *qv*; b Peterhead 17.1.34
h o RACH 1956–57; h o obst, sen h o med Antrim NI
1957–58; sen h o paediat Carshalton 1958–59; g p Bicester
1959–67; res MRC progr on foetal growth and dev
Oxford 1970–74; sen clin m o Avon area health auth
Bristol from 1975
m Bicester 3.7.65 David C. Smith FRS prof s of John
S. N. Harrow

MUTCH Margaret Forman   *BSc 1970 PhD 1980
   lect anat Aberd from 1970
m Inverurie 22.8.59 James J. Bruce LLB 1972 solic

MUTCH Richard Moir   *MA 1968
   s of Richard A. M. mason and Elma S. Moir; b Ellon

25.3.46
journalist: Aber 1968–72, Glasg 1972–73, Aber from 1973
m Aber 16.6.69 Pauline H. Hay staff nurse d of Joseph
M. H. Aber

MUTCH William Alexander Ritchie   MA 1961
LLB 1963
    s of William P. M. grocery storeman and Bella P.
Ritchie; b Aber 22.12.40
NP 1973
solic Edin 1968–71; Bank of Scot.: asst law secy 1971–73,
law secy from 1973
m Aber 29.7.66 Alison C. Rae MA 1964 *qv*

MUTURI David Symon   BSc(for) 1968
    s of Simeon M. farm. and Dorcas Wanjiru; b Othaya
Kenya 24.4.41
Kenya: for. Maji Mazuri 1968–69, div for. off. 1969–71,
for. man. plans off. h q 1971–78, conserv for. i/c insp hq
from 1978
m Nyeri 21.12.78 Rahab W. Kirathe BEd(Exe) teacher
d of Paul K. Othaya

NAIRN Audrey   *MA 1957
    d of James R. N. comm trav and Annie G. Spence;
b Aber 30.11.34
Dip Lib Archive Admin(Lond) 1959
asst lib: Glas 1958–60, Leeds univ 1960–63
m Aber 2.11.63 Adrian T. Hall MA(Leeds) lib s of
Arthur H. Hornsea

NAISH Peter Laurance   *BSc(eng) 1967
    s of Stanley J. N. insur ag and Grace E. K. Russell;
b Johnstone 14.12.44
MICE 1973
site civ eng Lond from 1967
m Peterlee 30.5.70 Lesley M. Coleman secy d of Leonard
E. L. C. BSc(Lond) Peterlee

NALL Andrew Redmarley   BSc(for) 1964
    s of Alfred K. N. comp secy and Marion Fletcher
teacher; b Rochdale 28.11.41
asst to for. consult. Berwicksh 1964–65; asst contr man.
Co Durh 1965–67; asst head for. Staffordsh 1967–69;
asst for. off. Bucks c c 1968–74; for. off. S Oxford dist
council from 1974
m Stanley 24.7.65 Carol M. Cowie MA 1964 *qv*

NALUSWA James Tucker   MSc 1970
    s of Stanley G. W. B. N. for. ranger and Eriosi M.
Tamunoza; b Iwemba Nabirere Uganda 26.5.38
BSc(for)(Sarajevo univ Yugoslavia) 1969
Uganda: dist for. off. Toro 1970–71, grad res asst
Makerere univ 1971–74, prov comm for. Gulu 1974–
76, Mbale from 1976
m Lond 22.7.67 Margaret Wampande nurs. sister d of
Zadoki W. Namungalwe Uganda

NAPIER James Frederick   *MA 1969
    s of William N. sales man. and Vera Gregory; b Perth
10.4.47
post grad trainee Rolls Royce Bristol; teacher: hist
Bristol 1970–72, sc/hist Leigh 1972–73; housemaster
boys' boarding s Oakham from 1974
m Stowe 29.7.72 Rosemarie J. Salway s matron d of
Austin H. S. Weston-super-Mare

NAPIER Thomas Macdonald   *BSc 1962 MSc 1963
    s of James K. N. MA(Glas) C of S min and Mary M.
Deans MA(Glas) teacher; b Forfar 20.1.41
res asst phys dept Leeds univ 1963–67, sen exper off.
1967–70; payload eng European space technol centre

Noordwijk Holland 1970–72; electronics eng health
phys Cern Geneva 1972–79, dev man. Nuclear Enterprises
Edin from 1979

NAPPER Adrian John   MB ChB 1970
    s of Percy T. R. N. off. HM customs and excise and
Catherine J. Carter RGN; b Northampton 4.2.46
h o Woodend hosp Aber, ARI 1970–71; res fell., sen h o
surg Aberd 1971–72; m o Nessie Knight hosp Qumbu
Transkei 1972–73; sen h o: paediat Darlington 1973–74,
psychiat Dun from 1974
m Aber 27.4.74 Rona M. Ferguson RGN d of Frederick
F. Aber

NARAYAN Lakshmi   PhD 1958
    BA(Patna) MA(Calc)

NARGUNDKAR Ashok Shankar   BSc(eng) 1968
    BSc(Bom)

NARGUNDKAR Mukund Shankar   BSc(eng) 1963
    MSc(Bom)

NASH Edward John   *MA 1959

NAYSMITH Elizabeth   BEd 1969
    d of Duncan N. master painter and Elizabeth Gammie
health centre receptionist; b Insch 25.4.48
teacher geog: St David's h s Dalkeith 1969–72, Ashford
c s from 1972
m Aber 14.4.72 John G. Brander MA 1969 *qv*

NDUKA Otonti Sunday Amadi   *MA 1957
    s of Isaiah Nduka Oludi farm. and Rosannah C. Amadi;
b Rumueme Nigeria 9.5.26
Dip Ed(Lond) 1962 MPhil(Lond) 1969 PhD(Ibadan) 1979
Nigeria: educ off. insp/admin Port Harcourt 1958–62,
lect phil univ Nsukka 1963–65; commonwealth schol
LSE 1965–67; Nigeria: sen educ off. Lagos 1967–68, lect,
sen lect educ Ibadan univ 1969–80; prof educ Port Harcourt univ from 1980
m Lond 20.1.58 Pamela E. M. Holderness educ asst d of
Frederick W. H. Harrow

NEAL Andrew Graham   BSc 1965

NEAVE David John Benjamin   MA 1956

NEEDHAM Adrian Douglas   *BSc(eng) 1969
    s of Charles D. N. MD(Lond) med consult. and
Margaret V. D. Roden; b Lincolnsh 2.6.47
MICE 1973 FGS 1976
Lond: asst civ eng Sir Alex Gibb & Ptnrs 1969–73, sen
eng Cementation Ground Eng 1973–74, assoc Dames &
Moore from 1974

NEEDHAM Michael Roy   MA 1964

NEILAN Henry Thomas   *MA 1958
    s of Henry N. staff superv and Mary McCallum;
b Hamilton 5.5.36
teacher Fr/Span: Motherwell 1959–61, Kingston Jamaica
1961–64, Aber 1964–69, Tarbes France 1969–70, Dumfries
from 1970
m Aber 30.6.59 Sheila Wood MA 1958 *qv*

NEILL Patricia Mary Helen   MA 1967
    d of Thomas F. N. min of relig and Jane Bruce;
b Lesmahagow 26.10.46
teacher: Godmanchester 1968–70, Burton-on-Trent from
1972
m Aber 16.11.67 George S. Halliday MA 1966 *qv*

NEILSON Robert Ewan *BSc(agr) 1967 PhD 1971
s of Robert B. N. tel eng and Ada Redford secy;
b Forfar 4.6.44
res off. bot dept Aberd from 1970
m Ellon 29.6.68 Helen A. Sangster secy d of John S.
Ellon

NEIZER Justice Amonoo BSc(eng) 1960
m Lond 2.9.75 Barbara A. Thompson MA 1952 *qv*

NELSON James Stanley PhD 1968
BA BD(Bethel Minn)

NELSON William James Adair MA 1960
(conferred for long service of exceptional merit)
b Aber 2.4.07
CA 1929
finance off. Aberd 1948–75; retd

NEOPHYTOU Joannis Polykarpou MA 1961
s of Polykarpos N. farm. and Victoria T. Rousou;
b Paphos Cyprus 8.12.29
MSc(W Ont) 1965
teacher phys Nicosia Cyprus 1961–63, stud. Lond Ont
1963–65, geophys: geol surv of Cyprus Nicosia from 1965
Br Council schol seismol Edin, Camb, Imp Coll 1973
m Nicosia 14.9.62 Elpiniki N. Papadopoulou d of
Nestor P. Nicosia

NERLAND Beate *MA 1970
d of Knut N. fisherman/farm. and Inger A. Kirkeslett;
b Sør-Aukra Norway 10.1.26
teacher Swedish/Norwegian Harlaw acad/coll of comm
Aber 1971–72, EFL/tech Engl Bergen coll of tech
Norway 1972–74; teacher/edit. own work course TEFL
(multi-racial classes) coll of comm/Harlaw acad Aber
1974–76, TEFL inst of foreign lang Baku USSR 1976–
77; teacher Engl/Free Ch mission s Tonga S Pacific
1978–80
m Meldal Norway 5.10.46 James C. Gibson master
mariner s of Robert G. St Abbs

NEVIN Brian McElroy PhD 1968
s of Samuel C. M. N. clerk and Iris L. Wheeler clerk;
b Durban 3.2.32
MA(Natal) 1954
sen lect maths univ of Natal Pietermaritzburg 1969–78,
prof maths from 1978
m Kloof S Af 20.7.57 Jennifer M. Robbins MSc(Natal)
lect d of Colin J. J. R. Kloof

NEWBIGGING Alice Ross MA 1969
d of John G. N. factory worker and Doreen Ross shop
asst; b Bucksburn 16.9.48
Dip Soc Admin(Edin) 1970 Dip Soc Work(Edin) 1973
trainee soc worker Aberdeensh 1970–72; soc worker
Livingston from 1973
m Aber 30.5.75 Thomas L. G. Leckie psychiat soc worker
s of James L. Falkirk

NEWLANDS Winnifred Jean MA 1967
d of John N. farm. and Jane Shand ch's nurse; b Forres
31.7.46
m Rothes 21.3.67 James Falconer Dyke

NEWMAN Briony Frances BSc 1970
d of Donald R. N. warrant off. RAF and Ella J.
Walker cler off.; b Lincoln 5.1.48
res asst genetics Glas 1970–73; teacher sc/maths Aberlour
from 1974

NEWMAN Christopher John Edwin BSc(eng) 1967
s of Harold E. M. N. army off. and Margaret H.

Smith; b Epsom 25.8.46
site eng: George Wimpey & Co Livingston 1967–68,
Shanks & McEwan (contr) Dumfries 1968–70; Aust:
eng Melbourne & Metrop board of works 1970, asst eng
state wheat board Toowoomba Queensland from 1970
m Dumfries 3.8.68 Patricia M. Findlay MA 1966 *qv*

NEWTON John *BSc 1968
s of William R. N. LLB(Lond) dist comm nat savings
and Joyce C. M. Ives; b Llandudno 13.3.46
biochem tech vet coll Lond 1968–73; field biol pest
control N Lond 1973–78; entomologist pest control from
1978

NEWTON Raymond Garbet *MEd 1967
s of Robert G. N. clerk and Alice L. Harding; b Southport 21.2.27
BSc(Lond) 1956
lect geog Aber coll of educ from 1962
m(2) Ellon 22.6.73 Gisèle Bessaguet

NEWTON Robert Ian *MA 1970
b Stranraer 21.1.49
sen clin psych Argyll & Clyde health board from 1977
m Stranraer 8.8.70 Christine Frew

NGANGA Francis BSc(for) 1968

NG CHENG HIN Raymond Louis Tsien Kwee
MB ChB 1963

NG CHENG HIN Thomas BSc 1967

NG WING WYE Ng Yiow Sem MA 1970

NICHOL Peter Howard *MA 1969

NICHOL Roberta Allan LLB 1968
d of Robert S. N. army off. and Gladys Allan; b Aber
30.10.47
law app, leg. asst Aber 1968–76
m Aber 3.8.68 Joseph D. Keeping MB ChB 1970 *qv*

NICHOLS Colston Edward BSc 1965
s of Colston E. N. warden Birch Lawn Home S'ton
and Helen G. Milne asst matron; b Aber 30.11.43
RAF from 1965
m Aber 25.2.67 Julie M. E. Duthie teacher d of Robert
P. D. Aber

NICHOLS Judith Ann *MA 1961
d of Walter M. N. MB ChB(Glas) neuro-surg and
Barbara L. Thompson SRN; b Manc 30.10.39
teacher Engl: Perth 1962–64, Glasg 1964–67
m Aber 21.12.63 Lachlan A. Cameron BA(Cantab) univ
lect s of Alexander R. C. BSc(St And) St Fillans

NICHOLSON Anthony Paul MB ChB 1958
s of Wilfrid N. loc govt off. and Jessie B. Sherwood;
b Tresco Is of Scilly 5.10.27
NHServ Aber from 1958
m Aber 25.9.59 Audrey Clark d of Herbert C. Aber

NICHOLSON Bertram Milton *BSc 1970

NICHOLSON Catherine Mary MA 1968
d of Andrew F. N. marine eng and Margaret D.
Clark; b Kirkcaldy 12.7.47
teacher: Ger Thurso h s 1970–74, asst prin mod lang
1974–75, prin mod lang 1975–78; W Ger from 1978

NICHOLSON George MA 1967

NICHOLSON John Wallace   MA 1967 Dip Ed 1968
s of Wallace B. N. MA(Edin) min of relig and Ann Macleod; b Bayhead N Uist 20.9.43
teacher maths Plockton from 1968
m Inv 18.8.67 Sarah Macmillan secy/machine oper (NCR) d of William M. Glenshiel

NICOL Alastair William   *BSc 1959 PhD 1962

NICOL Alexander John   BSc(agr) 1969 *1970
s of J. C. N. civ serv and Helen Hutcheon nurs sister; b Huntly 5.11.46
asst arable marketing man. R.H.M. agr Essex 1970–72; training advis Argyll 1972–74; agr advis NOSCA from 1974
m Aber 15.11.74 Catherine E. Munro nurs sister d of Murdo R. M. Conon Bridge

NICOL Andrew Dick   BSc 1961 *1963 PhD 1967
s of William G. D. N. shop asst, naval petty off., insur ag and Isabel Elder shop asst; b Aber 31.5.39
Aberd: biochem clin chem 1961–62, asst lect chem path. 1963–67; sen biochem REHSC 1967–72; prin biochem royal Alexandra hosp Rhyl from 1972
m Leeds 9.10.65 Julia M. Kingham MA(Edin) res asst, OU tut. d of Frank K. Leeds

NICOL Andrew Graeme   MB ChB 1958 PhD 1968
s of Andrew N. BCom 1922 qv (II, III); b Aber 28.1.35
MRCPE 1963 MRCPath 1967 FRCPath 1977
h o ARI, Woodend hosp Aber 1958–59; m o RAMC UK, Arabia 1959–61; lect, sen lect path. Aberd 1961–77; m o Abu Dhabi Pet. Co 1977–79; sen m o ADLO-ADMA Abu Dhabi UAE
m Aber 16.4.66 Christine F. Walker nurse, midwife d of Robert W. Motherwell

NICOL Ann Louise   MA 1966

NICOL Arthur McAllan   *MA 1960

NICOL Brian David   *BSc 1967 MSc 1970

NICOL Donald Rose   *BSc 1960

NICOL Eleanor Freda   BEd 1969
d of John N. rly signalman and Elizabeth A. N. Boyne waitress; b Nairn 27.4.48
teacher Engl Forfar 1969–73, asst prin Engl from 1973
m Udny 25.7.69 Ronald Fordyce policeman s of John F. Pitmedden

NICOL George Williamson   BSc 1965
s of Anderson Nicol MA(Glas) min of relig and Jane B. Williamson; b Edin 14.8.44
VSO Nigeria 1965–66; Sheffield: Unilever UCMDS trainee 1968–70, asst prod. man. 1970–73, prod. man. from 1973
m Paisley 17.8.68 Joy D. Crichton teacher d of George C. Paisley

NICOL Graeme Douglas   MA 1967
s of John N. asst chief constable Aber and Margaret S. Meakin; b Aber 2.7.46
trainee off. Goodyear Tyre Rubber Co Wolverhampton 1967–70; trg advis furn and timber indust trg board E Scot. 1970–74; man. dir Kilgour & Walker (sales) Aber from 1974
m Brora 17.8.68 Isobelle M. Sutherland teacher d of Andrew S. Brora

NICOL Helen   MA 1963
m Reid

NICOL Iona Agnes   BSc 1959
d of Anderson N. MA(Glas) C of S min and Jean B. Williamson; b Edin 7.2.38
Dip Ed(Edin) 1960
teacher sc Ainslie Park s s Edin 1960–63; USA: res asst Harvard med s Boston 1963–64, res asst Washington univ med s St Louis 1964–66, teacher sc W Ladue j h s St Louis 1966–68; program dir/instructor Spaulding racquet ball club St Louis from 1973
m Aber 13.6.66 John W. Long Bs(Ohio State) bonder Toledo Ohio

NICOL Isobel Helen   *BSc 1970
d of Alexander N. garage prop. and Mary Hay ptnr; b Aber 18.2.48
teacher: geog Thornes House s Wakefield 1971–72, geog/gen stud. Elgin tech coll from 1972
m Aber 1970 William A. Stark BSc 1969 qv

NICOL James   BSc 1958 *1966
s of James A. W. N. master baker and Florence Hutton; b Peterhead 3.3.33
teacher: sc Peterhead acad 1959–65, geog Fraserburgh acad 1966–68; Peterhead acad: prin geog 1968–73, asst head 1973–75, dep rector 1975–79; rector Crieff h s from 1979
m Peterhead 26.12.58 Ina Thores d of Edwin T. Peterhead

NICOL Leslie McKenzie   *BSc(eng) 1961

NICOL Margaret   MA 1961
d of James N. herring indust board off. and Margaret Buchan; b Peterhead 26.4.33
Dip R Ed 1962
teacher St Peter's epis s Peterhead from 1962
m Aber 30.7.54 Robert Buchan eng s of Andrew S. B. Peterhead

NICOL Mary Stuart   *MA 1957
m Barnes

NICOL-SMITH Colin Alexander   BSc(eng) 1959
s of Alistair N.-S. jeweller and Elizabeth M. Rankin teacher, occup therap; b Aber 16.3.38
Inst of C Eng 1966 Inst of Struct Eng 1967; Assoc of Prof Eng of BC 1965
civ/struct eng: Aber, Lond, Edin 1959–64, Montreal, Vancouver 1964–72; dev eng Council of For. Industries of BC Vancouver from 1972
m Montreal 12.1.65 Judy B. Shepherd teacher d of Alan W. S. Vancouver

NICOL-SMITH Ruth Mary   MA 1959
d of Alistair N.-S. comp dir and Elizabeth M. Rankin teacher art, occup therap; b Aber 14.10.39
BBC studio man. Lond 1961–65; youth employment off. Aber, Edin 1965–67; teacher Engl Woolston h s Warrington from 1975
m Lond 11.4.63 Robert A. Harrison BBC tv prod. s of Daniel H. Manc

NICOLL Edward Alexander   MA 1969

NICOLL William Duncan   BSc(agr) 1964
s of Andrew F. N. farm. and Sheila M. H. Hawkins nurs sister; b Nairobi 5.9.41
Rhodesia: conserv and extension off. min of agr Nyamandhlovu 1964–71, group off. Sinoia from 1971

m Bulawayo 10.12.66 Frances M. Ralph teacher d of Thomas D. M. R. Burghead

NICOLSON Annie Bella   MA 1962
d of Finlay C. N. millworker and Christina Campbell; b Stornoway 5.3.41
teacher Glasg, Rosssh 1963–66
m Glasg 24.8.66 Murdo A. MacLeod MA 1963 *qv*

NICOLSON James Peter   *MA 1968 Dip Ed 1969
s of Robert P. N. crofter, bldr's lab, seaman and Mary C. Ganson; b Shetland 28.7.46
teacher Aith j h s Shetland from 1969
m Sandwick 15.8.69 Lillian R. Sinclair bank clerkess d of Adam S. Levenwick

NICOLSON James Robert   MA 1956 BSc 1961
s of Frank H. N. crofter, seaman, coast preventive man customs and excise and Helen B. Tait; b Aith Shetland 10.7.34
FRGS 1961 FGS(Lond) 1961
geol Marampa Mines Sierra Leone 1961–67; Shetland: fisherman/author 1967–72, geol/author from 1972
m Lerwick 6.9.65 Violet H. Sinclair nurse d of Gideon S. Scalloway

NICOLSON Peter Balfour   BSc 1969
s of William H. N. man. dir and Eleanor M. Dunlop MA(Glas) teacher; b W Kilbride 26.11.41
instr p e Inverclyde nat recreation centre (Scot. sports council) Largs 1971–72; teacher geog/asst prin guid Glasg from 1972

NIDEROST Adrian Carl   MSc 1963
s of Carl N. Q.C. LLB(Sask) solic and Lillian I. Crum BA(Sask) teacher of mus; b Saskatoon 9.8.39
BSc(McG) 1961 B o T Athlone scholarship 1961–63
proj eng: Domtar Montreal 1963–65; Domtar Pulp Lebel-sur-Quevillon Quebec 1965–68; process eng 1965–68, pulp mill supt 1968–70, eng supt 1970–72; pulp prod. supt Domtar Fine Papers Windsor Quebec from 1972
m Montreal 30.8.61 Heather I. Attridge BA(McG) teacher d of Walter G. A. Montreal

NIKODEM Dirk   *MA 1970 MSc 1974
s of Wilhelm N. sales rep and Agnes Schilling secy; b Germany 13.9.45
progr/analyst Aber from 1972
m Aber 12.7.74 Catherine F. Cullen MA 1968 *qv*

NIMMO Elizabeth Macdonald Mackay   BEd 1970
d of Andrew N. steel erector and Alison G. Mackay; b Glasg 13.2.17
teacher Engl/remed Rosehearty s from 1970
m Paisley 25.12.45 Colin D. J. Macdonald MA 1929 *qv*
d 12.7.78

NISBET Barbara Darge   *MA 1957
d of James D. N. teacher, HMIS and Marjorie M. Macgregor lib asst; b Glasg 5.10.34
teacher Engl: Aber h s for girls 1958–61, Linlathen s Dun 1964–66; infants Lieurary s Caithness 1968–69, art Pennyland s Thurso 1969–73, Engl Thurso h s 1973–78; temp lect Engl univ of Maryland Thurso from 1979 and schools liaison off. Grampian TV from 1980
m Aber 17.3.56 Keith A. Laing MB ChB 1958 *qv*
husb d 27.6.79

NISBET James   BEd 1970
s of Henry A. N. mining/civ eng and Mary B. Wyllie SRN; b Glasg 14.12.37
teacher geog/mod. stud. Kirkland h s Methil 1970–73, prin mod. stud. from 1974

NISBET Jennifer Baillie   *MEd 1968
d of John N. grocer and Janet Ritchie; b Prestonpans 10.6.44
MA(Edin) 1966 PhD(Leic) 1979
res off. Joseph Rowntree higher educ res proj univ Lanc 1968–71, sen res off. 1971–73
m Lancaster 29.7.72 David H. Thompson BS(tech) (Cardiff) psych/counsellor univ of Keele appt and counselling serv s of James H. T. Bolton

NISBET Moyra Jean   *MA 1963
d of James D. N. teacher, HMIS and Marjorie M. Macgregor lib asst; b Insch 23.9.41
MA(Alta) 1966
Canada: post grad stud./teaching asst Alta 1963–64, instructor Engl univ of Victoria 1964–65; USA: part-time lect Smith coll Mass. 1965–67, edit. asst Corn. NY 1967–68; part-time extra mural tut. Glas 1973–75
m Aber 2.9.65 David D. Buchan MA 1960 *qv*

NIVEN Donald Ferries   *BSc 1970 PhD 1973
s of William N. and Margaret I. Donald; b Aber 5.3.47
res asst Aberd 1970–73; res fell. univ of Kent Canterbury 1973–76; res assoc Macdonald coll of McG Montreal from 1976
m Aber 22.5.65 Maureen Ferguson d of James F. Aber

NIVEN John Alexander   MA 1970
s of Alexander F. N. MB ChB 1940 *qv*; b Chatham 10.8.47
stud. pilot Oxford 1970–71; airline pilot BA (Europ div) Heathrow from 1971

NIVEN Sheila Mary   MA 1959

NIXON Alan John Chamberlain   *BSc 1969
s of Ian A. N. meteorologist and Margaret C. MacFadyen teacher; b Stirling 16.8.47
PhD(McM)
Canada: teacher Hamilton 1976–77, post doct fell. 1977–79, res assoc 1979–80
m 4.7.75 Martha J. Oliver BMus(McM) nurs stud. d of T. Leonard J.O. Brantford Canada

NIXON Julie Anne   MA 1967 Dip Ed 1968
s of Stanley N. solic and Phyllis Crowe; b Redcar 28.4.45
teacher Fr/Span Surrey, Kent 1968–70, Bucks 1970–74, prin mod lang s of St Mary and St Anne Abbots Bromley Staffs 1974–78

NIXON Karen Patricia   *MA 1961
d of Robert N. eng man. and Barbara Jordan; b Gillingham 30.11.38
teaching posts grammar/upper schools 1961–74; CSE examiner and private tut. from 1975
m Market Harborough 1973 Graham B. Jones bus. man s of John H. J. Peatling Magna

NJOKU Boniface Onogbo   MSc 1965
s of Njoku Anugwara farm. and Nwanyi Njoku Chikere; b Nigeria 5.2.36
BSc(Lond) 1963
res off. in agr res inst Ibadan Nigeria from 1966
m Umuabia Nigeria 2.5.70 Bernice A. Osuji BSc(Ibad) res off. d of Godson O. Owerri

NNODI Anukem Oparanozie   MSc 1964
BSc(agr)(Ibad)

NOBLE Alexandra Mary   MA 1965
b Edin 28.5.44

teacher: Summerhill s Aber 1966–67, Kingsdale s Lond 1967–70
m Aber 29.3.67 Alistair R. Cruickshank MA 1966 *qv*

NOBLE Andrea   MA 1961

NOBLE Andrew Alexander John   *MA 1963
s of Andrew M. N. insur ag and Catherine J. Duffy; b Stirling 24.2.39
DPhil(Sus) 1970
lect Engl Strath from 1966
m Drumnadrochit 22.3.68 Jennifer R. Mackay nurse d of James A. M. Drumnadrochit

NOBLE Audrey Mitchell   MA 1957
d of George N. town c employee and Jean D. Noble; b Fraserburgh 3.4.36
teacher: Dunkeld 1958–62, Dar Es Salaam Tanzania 1965–66, Lushoto 1967–68, Dalbeattie from 1973
m Aber 23.7.62 Carl L. Bryant BSc(for) 1957 *qv*

NOBLE Benjamin Wiseman   *MA 1958

NOBLE Charles   BSc 1966

NOBLE Christina Elizabeth   *MA 1969
d of Albert N. motor mech and Charlotte Paterson SRN; b St Combs 9.5.46
teacher: Fr/Ger Colston s s Glasg 1971–73, Engl with Centre for British Teachers Mädchen Gymn, Bünde Ger 1973–75, angestellte Lehrerin from 1975
m Glas 14.7.69 Gilbert Whitelaw eng s of John W. Glasg

NOBLE Elizabeth Mary   *MA 1967

NOBLE Fiona Winifred   MA 1970
d of John N. CA and Mae Bonnington; b Edin 28.1.49
teacher Fernielea p s Aber from 1972

NOBLE Gillian Mae   *MA 1969
d of John N. CA and Mae Bonnington; b Edin 18.11.47
MSc(Lond) 1974
econ DoE Lond 1969–76, HM Treasury from 1976

NOBLE Ian   *BSc 1965 Dip Ed 1966

NOBLE Irene   MA 1956
m Dyer

NOBLE Irene Buchan   *MA 1962 Dip Ed 1963
d of John N. insp sea fisheries and Christian T. N. Buchan; b Inverallochy 28.10.39
teacher: Aber 1963–65, Fleming Fulton s Belf from 1973
m Aber 14.8.63 William Byth MA 1962 *qv*

NOBLE Iris   MA 1965
m Main

NOBLE Isabella Bruce   BSc 1959
m Tandy

NOBLE John   *MA 1957 MEd 1968
s of John N. fisherman and Christina Duthie; b Fraserburgh 11.2.35
teacher Larbert h s 1958–61, Fraserburgh acad 1951–63, coll of comm Aber 1964–68; asst psych Aber 1969–72; sen asst psych Aberdeensh 1972–74; prin psych E Lothian from 1974

NOBLE John Crawford   BSc 1957
s of Alfred N. sailmaker and Kate McLean; b Rosehearty 7.10.33
Fraserburgh acad: teacher maths 1958–66, spec asst

maths 1966–73, asst prin maths from 1973
m Sandhaven 26.12.58 Helen R. S. B. Fraser d of George P. F. Sandhaven

NOBLE John Gardiner   MB ChB 1956

NOBLE Mary   MA 1969
d of William N. and Beatrice M. Porter; b Aber 10.5.13
m Strichen 23.4.34 James S. McKay eng Burmah Oil Co India s of John McK.

NOBLE Robert   BSc 1966

NOBLE Violet McClelland   MA 1960
(conferred for long service of exceptional merit)
b Udny Station 20.6.1900
member of admin staff Aberd 1918–60

NOBLE William   BSc 1961 *1962
s of Alexander N. baker, teacher p e, security guard and Dolina F. Mitchell secy; b St Combs 29.7.40
teacher biol Dun 1963–66; lect Kirkcaldy 1966–73; sen lect from 1973
m Lonmay 29.6.63 Mary I. Fyvie nurse d of Alexander C. F. Lonmay

NOKE Frederick James   BSc 1968
s of Leonard C. N. fisherman and Charlotte N. S. Criggie; b Gourdon 27.1.47
asst prod. chem Schweppes (foods) Montrose 1969–70, prod. supt 1971–73; cake man. Cadbury-Schweppes (foods) Moreton Liv from 1974
m St Cyrus 5.5.73 Sandra A. Ruxton off. worker d of Alexander F. R. St Cyrus

NORBROOK Hamish Thomas Ellis   *MA 1969
s of Donald H. E. N. BBC Aber, Nigeria, Singapore, Oxford and Eleanor I. M. Hutchison MA 1939 *qv*; b Lond 17.8.47
teacher: VSO Engl école secondaire de Matana Burundi 1969–71; Fr Faraday comp s E Acton Lond 1972; BBC Bush House Lond: studio man. external serv 1972–74, asst overseas dev auth scheme Engl by radio 1974–76, prod. Engl by radio from 1976
m Lond 24.7.76 Dominique J. Mandier L ès L(Lyon) teacher d of Pierre M. St Etienne France

NORFOLK Jeremy Paul   MA 1970

NORMAND Anne Margaret   MA 1969 Dip Ed 1970
d of George F. N. teacher and Margaret B. D. Paton; b Perth 12.9.48
teacher: Prestonpans p s 1970–72, Edin from 1972
m Perth 20.10.73 John Mowat MA(Edin) teacher s of Ian J. G. M. LDS(Edin) Dumfries

NORQUAY Margaret   MA 1970

NORRIE Jean Gibb   MA 1959
d of William P. N. master coach builder and Ella G. Mair typist; b Aber 27.2.38
teacher Engl/hist Aber 1960–65
m Aber 7.4.65 John McBain CA s of Alan McB. MA 1920 *qv* (II, III)

NORRIE Sandra Jane   BSc 1968
d of Alexander N. outfitter and Violet E. Anderson secy; b Aber 18.11.46
m Aber 11.5.66 Rodger Horrocks BSc 1968 *qv*

NORRIE William   BSc(for) 1960

NORRIS Derek John   BSc 1970
s of Douglas T. N. sales rep and Amelia T. Gilmour;
b Aber 6.4.49
ACA 1975
VSO Mauritius 1970–71; Thomson McLintock Lond
1972–76; Bank of America Eur M East Africa div from
1976

NORRIS John William   MB ChB 1957 MD 1971

NORRIS Linda Campbell   MA 1970

**NORTH Richard Alan   BSc 1969 MB ChB 1969
PhD 1973**
s of Douglas A. N. wool merch and Constance
Ramsden; b Halifax 20.5.44
h o Aber 1969–70; Marr Walker res fell. Aberd 1970–71;
MRC res fell. Aberd 1971–73; res assoc univ of Loyola
Chicago 1972–73; res fell. Aberd from 1974
m Aber 15.7.69 Jean V. A. Hall MA 1967 qv

NORTHCROFT David John   *MA 1964
s of Henry J. N. customs and excise off. and Jean M.
Murrell; b Cheadle 6.2.42
MLitt(Cantab) 1969
teacher Engl AGS 1967–71; lect Engl Aber coll of educ
from 1971
m Aber 12.8.66 Kathleen E. Lakin MA 1964 qv

NORTHCROFT Janet Heather   *MA 1968
d of Henry J. N. customs and excise off. and Joan M.
Murrell; b West Dulwich 2.9.46
Dip Soc Ad/Soc Work(Manc) 1970
probation off. Manc prob and after-care serv from 1970
m Altrincham 4.3.72 Michael Pickering computer progr/
prob off. s of James W. P. Oldham

**NORTON Katherine Judith Morren   MA 1966
Dip Ed 1967**
d of William H. hotelier and Jean D. Montgomerie;
b Ayr 16.4.44
teacher Engl Hilton acad Aber from 1967

NORTON Royan   *MA 1968

NORVELL Elizabeth Diana   BSc 1969

NOTTAGE Bernard Jonathan   MB ChB 1969

NOWLAND John Louis   MSc 1963
BA(Manc)

**NWACHUKU Nathan Iheanyichuku Chukudi
PhD 1970**
BSc(Lond) MS(Hawaii)
m Aber 25.1.64 Oludotun M. Odugbose MB ChB 1966 qv

NWANKWO Lawrence   BSc 1958 Dip Ed 1959
s of Anowi N. customary court judge and Angelina
Dijiure; b Umulogho Nigeria 1928
Nigeria: vice-prin Okigwi 1959–64; chmn dist council
Etiti 1964–66, member home defence Etiti 1966–69;
prin Arugo h s Oweri from 1970
m Umulogho 1961 Rosaleen Azuogu teacher

**NYLANDER Percy Palgrave Shaftesbury   MB ChB 1958
*MD 1976**
s of Africanus G. R. N. civ serv and Lucretia P.
Thomas; b Lagos 30.1.25
MRCOG 1962 MRCPE 1964 FRCOG 1974 FRCPE 1979
h o ARI, Aber mat. hosp, sen h o Withington hosp Manc,
regist Dudley Rd hosp Birm 1958–63; sen regist UCH

Ibadan; univ of Ibadan: lect, sen lect 1965–70, prof obst/
gyn from 1970
m Birm 1964 Carmen O. Hume nurse d of Sydney O. H.
Leic

OAKLAND Gail Barker   PhD 1956
s of Theodore J. O. hardware merch and Winnifred J.
Barker; b Lang Sask 11.2.14
BA(Sask) 1933 MA(Minn) 1939 FRSS 1958
Ottawa: sen biometrician 1956–59, sen math advis 1959–
62; prof statist univ of Mass. Amherst from 1962

OAKLEY John Stafford   BSc(for) 1959

OATES James   *MA 1963

OATES Leonard Francis   MSc 1970
s of James H. O. MSc(Loughborough) lect aeronaut
eng and Bessie Evans secy; b Loughborough 27.2.46
BSc(UCW) 1967 Dip Ed(UCW) 1968
lect chem Braintree 1970–72; Devon: bldr 1972–77,
dev chem 1977–79, teacher from 1979

OBODOECHINA Francis Okechukwu   *BSc(eng) 1961
s of Ojinnak O. farm. and Mary A. Azikiwe; b Onitsha
Nigeria 15.10.36
grad asst, asst civ eng Crouch & Hogg Glasg 1961–63;
Nigeria: exec eng MoW E Nigeria Enugu 1964–66,
water eng i/c water supply Old Port Harcourt prov
1967–69; sen exec eng i/c water supply Old Abakaliki
prov 1970–73; prin exec eng i/c plan. & des E.C.S. water
board Enugu 1973–75; chief proj eng Enplen Group
consult. eng Enugu from 1975
m Onitsha 2.1.65 Patricia N. Egbunike teacher d of
Simon Muonweoku

O'BRIEN Alison Burroughs   MA 1963
d of Thomas H. O'B. CA and Dora M. Burroughs;
b Brocket Hall 20.6.42
Lond: res asst Engl Elect. 1963–65, res analyst W. S.
Crawford 1965–66, market res exec market information
serv 1966–68; freelance market res consult. Croydon
1968–71; sen market res exec Richardson Merrell Lond
1971–72; res off. States of Jersey 1972–74; freelance
market res consult. from 1974
m(2) Jersey 3.3.73 Christopher S. Le Brun law clerk

O'BRIEN Eric Adam   *MA 1959
s of William O'B. church off. and Annie Murray;
b Alfrod 31.10.36
teacher Hawick h s 1960–62; prin geog: N Berwick h s
1962–65, Dumbarton acad 1965–67, Galashiels acad
1967–74; asst rector Galashiels acad from 1974
m Galashiels 3.10.69 Christina J. Anderson bookkeeper
d of Adam A. Melrose

O'BRIEN Kathleen Jean   MA 1966 Dip Ed 1967

O'CARROLL Brian William   BEd 1970

O'CONNELL John Richard   *MA 1961

O'CONNOR Peter John   PhD 1960
s of John E. O'C. wholesale/retail tobacconist and
Marjorie G. Griffin; b Ilkeston 16.5.32
BSc(Nott) 1956
teacher Oldham 1959–60; res asst Christie hosp and Holt
radium inst (Paterson labs) Manc from 1960; visiting fell.
dept pharm Yale univ New Haven Conn 1964–66; sen
scient Paterson labs from 1966
m Oldham 8.8.59 Barbara M. Nelson BSc(Nott) teacher
d of Leslie N. Oldham

O'DELL Duncan Shortreed   *BSc 1961
  s of Andrew C. O'D. BSc(Lond) prof geog Aberd and
Queenie L. Smith BA(Lond) teacher; b Lond 6.6.40
PhD(Cantab) 1965
res stud., res worker MRC Cambridge 1961–67; post-
doct fell. royal soc Europ progr Naples 1967–68; res
worker MRC Lond 1968–70; lect zool univ coll Lond
from 1970

O'DELL Felicity Ann   *MA 1969
  d of Andrew C. O'D. BSc(Lond) prof geog Aberd and
Queenie L. Smith BA(Lond) teacher; b Aber 4.7.47
PhD(Birm) 1975
post grad stud. centre for Russian/E Europ stud. Birm
1969–72; teacher mod lang St Philip's RC g s for boys
Birm 1972–73; part-time aux nurse Birm 1974; res asst
proj on Soviet vocational educ and soc stratification
Cantab 1974–76; TEFL Cambridge from 1976

O'DRISCOLL Dorothy   MA 1964

ODUGBOSE Batatunde Olusegun   BSc 1968

ODUGBOSE Oludotun Mofolusho   MB ChB 1966
  d of David O. O. headmaster and A. A. Majekoclunmi;
b Ibadan Nigeria 28.4.39
m o Ghana med serv 1967–71; prin m o Nigerian rly
corp Lagos from 1971
m Aber 25.1.64 Nathan I. C. Nwachuku PhD 1970 qv

OFFICER John Burness   *MA 1959

OGENDO Reuben Benjamin   *BSc 1960
  s of Zechariah Aloo farm. and Mariam Abo farm.:
b Nyahera Kisumu Kenya 29.7.28
PhD(Lond) 1967
prin teacher geog Maseno s s Kenya 1960–61; univ of
Nairobi: lect geog 1962–68, sen lect 1968–72, assoc prof
1972–78, prof from 1978, dean fac of arts from 1978
m Maseno 24.12.51 Truphosa Anyango teacher d of
Harun Adoche Yala Kenya

OGG Graeme McPherson   *MA 1965
  s of James O. ACT employee and Esther Paterson;
b Aber 26.9.42
teacher Fr/Span. Perth acad 1968–69; translator DTI
Lond from 1969

OGG Hilary Ruth   MA 1970

OGG John MacMillan   BSc 1964 Dip Ed 1965

OGG Lindsay Anne   *MA 1969
  d of Thomas O. civ serv and Amelia W. Veitch civ
serv; b Aber 11.11.46
teacher: geog/humanities and dep house head Wanstead
Lond 1970–73; W Ger: teacher Engl Wipperfürth 1974,
Engl centre for Brit teachers in Europe Cologne 1974–75
m Aber 21.7.70 Andrew J. D. Smith CA s of James D. S.
Aber

OGG Thomas Winchester   MB ChB 1964
  s of Thomas O. civ serv DHSS and Amelia W. Veitch
civ serv; b Aber 20.6.40
DA 1968 FFARCS(Lond) 1971
h o Woodend hosp Aber, Raigmore hosp Inv 1964–65;
major RAMC short serv comm; post grad course Lond
1965, cas off. Benghazi 1966–67, anaest Iserlohn, Hanover
Ger 1967–69, ARI, Hanover 1969–71; ARI: regist,
sen regist and clin lect anaest Aberd from 1971
m Aber 20.7.65 Monica M. Wilson MA 1963 qv

OGILVIE Anne Patricia   *MA 1967

OGILVIE Brian   BSc 1968

OGILVIE Christopher James   MA 1967
  s of George T. A. O. chartered land ag and Jean C.
Barrett; b Ravenglass 20.4.47
Dip Pers Man.(RGIT) 1968
man. trainee BR Glasg 1968–71; store man. trainee
Marks & Spencer Paisley 1971–72; Beecham pharm
Irvine: asst pers off. 1973–74, pers off. from 1974
m Edin 2.8.69 Elizabeth J. Graham MA 1969 qv

OGILVIE David Wilson   MA 1963

OGILVIE Eileen Millar   MA 1961
  d of George G. O. farm. and Nan Duthie secy; b Forfar
8.4.40
teacher Lond 1962–64; bus. prop./founded youth centre
Perthsh 1965–71; secy to hosp matron Angus 1971–73
m –.5.74 Gilbert Rimmer ship's capt/dredging consult.

OGILVIE Elizabeth Baxter McDonald   MA 1968
  d of Alexander M. O. comm man. and Leonora C.
Douglas; b Dun 8.1.47
teacher mod lang Kirkton h s Dun 1969–72, asst prin
mod lang 1972–73; teacher mod lang Elgin acad from
1973
m Dun 8.4.72 Robert M. G. O'Brien MA(St And)
organis outdoor educ Moray & Nairn s of William O'B.
Woolston

OGILVIE Isobel   MA 1956
  d of John W. O. meal miller and Isabella Mackay;
b Elgin 8.6.34
teacher Stanley 1957–61, Inv 1961–70; prim. staff tut.
Inv 1970–74, prim. advis Rosssh from 1974

OGILVIE Marjory   MA 1961
  d of Charles O. long dist driver (BRS) and Ann Smith;
b Aber 21.7.35
teacher: Smithfield p s Aber 1962–63, Coventry from
1963
m Aber 2.4.63 Brian Rattray tech rep West Midlands Gas
Board s of John R. Aber

OGILVIE Rosemary   *MA 1964 Dip Ed 1965
  d of George T. A. O. farm., land ag and Jean S.
Barrett; b Selkirksh 12.11.41
teacher Engl Aber 1965–67
m Aber 17.5.65 Colin E. Jeffries BSc 1963 qv

OGILVY Munro Michael   *BSc 1968 PhD 1972
  s of John O. fruit grower and Frances Monro; b Dun
25.11.46
res fell. univ of Warwick 1971–73, sen exper off. UMIST
Manc 1973–74; res chem The Wellcome Foundation
Dartford 1974–78, man. dev res from 1978

OGSTON David Dinnes   MA 1966 BD 1969
  s of James G. O. farm. and Mary C. Dinnes; b Ellon
25.3.45
C of S min: asst St Giles cath Edin 1969–73, parish min
Balerno from 1973
m Forres 6.8.70 Margaret C. Macleod teacher d of
William M. Forres

OGSTON Graeme Leslie   LLB 1970
  s of Harry O. MA 1936 qv and Iris C. Watt MA 1941
qv; b Aber 1.11.49
law app, solic A. C. Morrison & Richards advoc Aber
1970–73; solic Clark & Wallace advoc Aber from 1973
m Aber 26.2.72 Vivien M. P. Clark LLB 1970 qv

OGSTON Walter MacTavish   PhD 1966
   s of Walter H. O. E India merch and Josephine E. Carter; b Birkenhead 5.12.17
BA(Oxon) 1939 MA(Oxon) 1946 MS(Calif Tech) 1947 FIME 1973
Power Jets Lutterworth 1940–49; Commonwealth fell. Pasadena USA 1946–47; Eng Elect. Co Rugby 1949–56; Centrax Newton Abbot 1956–59; lect, sen lect eng Aberd from 1959
m Bilton Rugby 9.4.49 Freda Gibson soc worker d of Frederick J. G. Rugby

O'HAGAN Philip John   BSc 1969

O'HANLON Anne   *BSc 1964
   d of Andrew H. miner and Rosa Ward; b Blackhall 27.10.39
teacher: Co Durh 1964–67, Kingston Jamaica 1967–70, Coatbridge 1971–72, prin sc Peterlee from 1972
m Blackhall 23.10.76 Robert Potts BSc(Teesside poly) mech eng

OJO Gabriel Oluwole Ayodele   *BSc(for) 1965

OJO now OJO-ATERE Joseph Oluwatayo   MSc 1967
   BSc(Ibad)

OKAFOR Jonathan Chukwuemeka   BSc(for) 1962

OKARU Paul Newton   *BSc(eng) 1959
   s of David O. O. bldg contr and Nkwo Ossai; b Oguta Nigeria 27.7.28
BSc(Lond) 1953 CEng MIEE 1968 MNSE 1972
grad app AEI Manc 1959–60; Nigeria: eng elect. utility Lagos 1961–62; undertaking man. Abeokuta 1962–64, dist man. Jos 1964–65; transmission eng sen control eng HQ Lagos 1965–70; head transmission rehabilitation Enugu 1970–71; Lagos: sen oper plan. eng 1972–73, man. oper 1973–74; dir oper 1975–77, gen man. oper from 1977
m Aber 31.3.59 Valentina I. Olisa Dip. Dom Sc, asst chief educ off. Lagos d of His Highness R. R. O. Onitsha Nigeria

OKEKE Raphael Ekemezie Chukwubuike   BSc(for) 1961
   s of Alfred I. O. civ serv and Eunice Igwego; b Amawbia Nigeria 24.6.33
Nigeria: asst conserv for. Ikom SES 1961–66, sen asst conserv for. Umuahia, Amawbia ECS 1967–75, conserv for. Amawbia/Enugu 1975–77, chief conserv for. Enugu Anambra from 1978
m Enugu Bernice Ejindu teacher d of Moses E. Onitsha

OKIGBO Lawrence Chukwuemeka   BSc(for) 1960

OKOYE Humphrey Chigbo   *BSc 1961
   BSc(Lond)

OLAJIDE Samuel Omolayo   BSc(for) 1966
   s of Josiah O. farm. and Ibilola Ogundejie; b Isinbode-Ekiti Nigeria 1.12.36
Nigeria: asst conserv for. Ibadan 1967–72; asst conserv soils Oshogbo from 1973
m Isinbode-Ekiti –.12.59 Victoria I. Adeyemo

OLATUNJI Oladapo   MB ChB 1967
   s of Akanbi O.; b Nigeria
DTM & H(Lond) 1969 DCH(Lond) 1970 DPH(Liv) 1971 Fell. Nigerian Med Council in Public Health 1976
h p and h s Joyce Green hosp Dartford 1967–68; sen h o paediat Alder Hey ch hosp Liverpool 1969–70; sen h o infect. diseases Fazakerley hosp Liverpool 1970–71; dept m o Lancs c c 1971–72; sen m o, later acting chief m o

Ahmadu Bello univ Zaria Nigeria 1972–76; med dir Mobil Nigeria Lagos from 1976
m Lond –.8.69 Olabisi Akinlabi d of O. Akinlabi

O'LEARY Michael Joseph   *MA 1969
   s of Joseph O'L. civ serv and Winifred C. E. Ridgley secy; b Hammersmith Lond 2.4.46
Dip Man. Stud.(Strath) 1976
Chrysler Scot. Linwood; budget analyst 1969–70, sen budget analyst 1970–71, supervis acct methods/audit. 1971–75; United Biscuits: sen audit. North from 1975
m Aber 6.12.69 Alyson M. Carter MA 1968 qv

OLEJNIK Henry Hugh   MA 1969
   s of Edward O. distillery worker and Johanna C. H. Kemp; b Beauly 9.6.47
GMIPM(RGIT) 1970
pers off. Ruislip 1970–72; salary admin/indust rel off. Harrow 1972–75; pers man. Polaroid Milngavie from 1975
m Dingwall 23.11.74 Joan J. Fowlie Europ prop. invest. co-ordinator d of William S. F. Dingwall

OLEMBO Titus Wycliffe   PhD 1970
   s of Nahashon O. farm. and Damary Olembo; b Wanakhale-Bunyore Kenya 28.5.37
BA(NY State)
res for. (path.), head for. div EAAFRO, sen res off., prin res off. Muguga and throughout E Africa from 1970
m Bunyore 11.9.61 Priscah Achando nurse, secy d of Patrick Kweya Maseno Kenya

OLET Erisa Dickson   BSc(for) 1970
   BSc(Makerere)

OLIVER David Ruskin   *BSc 1968
   s of Arthur R. O. MB ChB(Edin) g p and Barbara H. Rhodes; b Edin 30.12.37
teacher biol Dunoon g s 1969–71; prin biol Wick h s from 1971
m Glasg 27.12.73 Angusina C. MacLeod MA(Glas) teacher d of George MacL. Edderton

OLIVER Thomas Dalgleish   BSc(agr) 1956 MSc 1973

OLIVER William Bruce   *BSc 1970
   s of William A. O. BSc(Lond) sqd ldr RAF and Florence I. Fitzpatrick MA(Glas) teacher; b Weston-super-Mare 3.9.46
PhD(H-W) 1975
res asst Birm 1970–71; res stud. H-W 1971–75; res scient Pauls and Sandars Ipswich from 1975
m Huddersfield 26.7.75 Heather A. Slater BSc 1973 civ serv d of James B. S. Huddersfield

OLSON Ian Alistair   MB ChB 1962 MD 1969
   s of Andrew G. O. BBC recording eng and Doreen Carlee midwife; b Aber 5.5.39
h o A RI 1962–63; lect anat Brist 1963–69; sen lect anat Nott 1969–75; vice-dean/prof anat Kuwait med s from 1975
m Aber 27.12.73 Elizabeth A. Hamilton MA 1962 qv

OMABEGHO Sonny   MB ChB 1962

OMAND Donald   *MA 1958
   s of Donald O. rly employee and Jean Ross; b Lybster 8.1.36
MSc(Strath) FSAScot. FRSGS
teacher geog Bingley 1959–60; admin UKAEA Dounreay 1960–63; teacher Halkirk 1963–66; lect f e Thurso 1966–70; univ tut./organis extra-mural dept Aberd Elgin/Halkirk from 1970
m Stronsay 15.7.59 Emma S. Peace MA 1959 qv

OMAND Jean Sandra *MA 1966
d of James O. BSc(Edin) vet surg and Nettie C. Jack
secy; b Ayr 16.11.42
teacher geog: Forfar acad 1967–73, Lossiemouth h s
1973–74; prin guid Lossiemouth h s from 1974

OMAR Ali MSc 1969
BSc(Makerere)

OMAR Medhat Omar Mohamed Hassan PhD 1970
MB(Cairo) MSc(Assuti)

OMER Banaga Mohamed Ahmed MSc 1967
BSc(eng)(Khart)

OMUFWOKO Henry Dickson BSc(agr) 1968
s of Jacton T. O. bus. man. and Grace Akhamuru bus.
woman; b W prov Kenya 15.1.40
Kenya: agr res off. Kisi 1968–70; teacher chem Kisumu
h s from 1971; later sen sc master St Mary's Yala
m Glasg 19.8.67 Alice B. Ochami teacher d of Daudi O.
Maseno Kenya

O'NEALE Eugene Charles Henry MA 1967
s of Henry O'N. wine merch and Violet E. Benfell;
b Lond 12.12.43
law app Haddington, Edin 1968–71; solic Edin 1971–73,
ptnr leg. practice spec in court work Edin from 1973, dir
comp owning hotels and mus publ
m Lond 22.4.71 Marjory Davidson hairdresser d of
Archibald D. Glasg

O'NEILL John Albert MSc 1966
BSc(Belf) 1963 MSc(Belf) 1964 PhD(Belf) 1974
sen scient off.: dept of agr, fac of agr Queen's univ Belf
1965–69; man. proj res and dev Gallaher (tobacco) Belf
1969–79, factory man. from 1979
m Belf 1965 Dama Green

O'NEILL Joseph Patrick *MA 1960

ONWELUZO Bennett Samuel Kanayochuku
                                        BSc(for) 1963
s of Phillip W. A. O. teacher and Elizabeth N. Okafor;
b Nnewi Nigeria 16.1.36
MSc(Ghent) 1966
Nigeria: for. res off. (soils) fed. dept of for. res Ibadan
1963–65, for. res off. Enugu (civ war in Nigeria) 1966–70,
for. res off. grade 1 fed. dept of for. res Ibadan 1970–72,
sen res off. 1972–76; prin res off. 1976; chief sc off. Nat
Sc and Tech Dev Agency (i/c for. div) from 1976
m Onitsha E.C.S. Nigeria 16.5.70 Keziah U. Ojukwu
teacher d of Daniel O. Nnewi

ONWUEGBUNA Okechukwu MA 1957
b Nibo Awka Nigeria 31.12.21
AIE(Lond) 1965
Nigeria: civ serv Enugu 1957–76, asst chief insp of educ
1976; chief and traditional ruler Nibo from 1977

OPENSHAW Keith *BSc(for) 1961 *MA 1967
s of Herbert J. M. O. teacher and Nellie Walter;
b Salford 20.12.36
res asst for. dept Aberd 1961–66; for. econ FAO(UN)
Tanzania, Thailand; for. consult. Aber from 1972

O'PRAY Michael *MA 1968
s of Hugh O'P. auto. eng and Elizabeth Stewart;
b Ellon 13.8.46
Ford Motor Co Liv: trg off. 1968–70, pers off. from 1970
m Liv 24.8.74 Linda Roberts typist d of Robert O. R. Liv

ORANGUN Cornelius Oluwasade *BSc(eng) 1960
s of Joseph O. farm. and Felicia Obisesan; b Erin-
Ijesha Nigeria 16.6.32
PhD(Leeds) 1963 MICE 1968 MASCE 1968
asst eng: William Halcrow & Ptnrs Lond 1960–61, W. V.
Zinn & Assoc Lond 1963–64; lect univ of Lagos 1964–72,
assoc prof 1972–74, prof from 1976; visiting prof univ
of Benin 1975–76
m Lond 1.8.64 Oluyemisi Sofekun BA(Keele) educ off.,
admin off. d of David O. E. S. Sagamu Nigeria

ORD Michael John MA 1966
s of John O. marine eng and Mary Howes; b Aber
20.10.45
DBM(Strath) 1967 CIPFA 1976
syst analyst Glasg 1967–73; fin. analyst Coatbridge 1973–
78; fin. acct Edin from 1978
m Glasg 11.7.70 Isabel M. G. Wood BSc(Strath) computer progr d of James W. Glasg

ORDOR Ihekachi Tamunonenginyeofori James
                                        BSc(eng) 1957
Nigeria: mech eng MoW Port Harcourt 1960–63; plant
eng Nigerian Petroleum Refining Co Port Harcourt
1964–68, eng consult. Fed Min of Indust Lagos 1970–71,
gen man. Aba textile mills 1971–72; gen man. Nigerian
Petroleum Refining Co Port Harcourt 1972–75; gen
man. Nigerian Nat Oil Corp Lagos 1975; man. dir/
chief consult. Unitech, consult. eng Port Harcourt from
1976
m Lond 9.11.57 Mabel Ekeke nurse d of Inglis E. Aba

O'REGAN Jeremy *MA 1967
s of Terence O'R. police off. and Jane Coffin; b Oxford
20.4.43
Dip Ed(Edin) 1968
teacher Edin 1968–69; lect psych Moray House coll of
educ Edin from 1969
m Aber 3.8.68 Susan Beddard MA 1967 qv; marr diss 1974

ORR Craig Smith MA 1957

ORR Robert John BSc 1970
s of Robert O. lect and Agnes R. Lannigan; b Bellshill
1.2.46
teacher Wishaw from 1971
m Eastwood 6.4.77 Gina J. Landles BSc(Glas) teacher
d of James R. L. Glasg

ORR William McLean BSc(eng) 1962
CA

O'SHEA Gerrard Joseph LLB 1968
s of John S. O'S. manuf ag and Frances E. Hamblet
teacher; b Cheadle 21.8.46
articled solic clerk Manc 1969–72; prosecuting solic
Middlesbrough from 1973

O'SHEA Martin John *MA 1965
s of John S. O'S. manuf ag and Frances E. Hamblet
teacher; b Cheadle 23.7.43
Engl lang asst Bédarieux France 1965–66; asst lect tech
coll Lurgan NI 1966–72; lect/students' union liaison off.
tech coll Darlington from 1972

OSHIKANLU John Adebayo MB ChB 1961
d Nigeria 1975

OSOBAMIRO Samuel Adewole *BSc(eng) 1957
s of James O. farm. and Odunaike Sigbeku; b Nigeria
22.8.32
MICE 1961

Lond: asst eng Sir William Halcrow & Ptnrs 1957–59; site eng Cleveland Bridge & Engr 1959–60, asst RE Mott Hay & Anderson 1960–61; Nigeria: eng, sen eng, prin eng M of W & Transport W state 1961–71, chief eng, tech dir LAO Banjoko & Co civ eng contr & bldrs Ibadan 1971–77, man. dir from 1977
m Lond 9.8.58 Omfunmilayo F. Kalejaiye BA(Dub) teacher d of E. O. K. Zaria Nigeria

OTIM Stephen Ildefonsi   BSc(for) 1965

OUSLEY William Rettie   MA 1967

OWEN Kathleen Ann   MA 1970
d of Thomas V. O. RAF and Lilias M. Morrice clerkess; b Aber 31.1.48
teacher Brechin from 1971
m Aber 24.7.71 Dennis Hastie MA 1969 *qv*

OWENS William Leo   PhD 1961
BSc(Wash) MSc(Calif)

OXFORD Karl Anthony   BSc(eng) 1967

OXLEY Edward Ralph Blackett   *BSc 1964

OYAPERO Samusi Aremu   BSc(for) 1966

OZGA Jennifer Teresa   *MA 1970 *MEd 1972

PACITTI John   *MA 1958

PACITTI Stephen Anton   MA 1959
s of Paolo A. P. ice cream vendor and cafe prop. and Jean M. Forrest; b Aber 14.7.38
min: Dundonell par ch 1963–72, Glencairn ch Pollokshields 1972–76; lect bib. stud. Yu Shan Theol coll Hualien Taiwan from 1977
m Aber 22.6.63 Sylvia A. Long bookkeeper/typist d of Stanley H. L. Aber

PACK Julie Macdonald   MA 1961
d of George B. P. comp dir and Janet M. Watson comp dir; b Fraserburgh 8.9.40
teacher Aber 1962–63; Ottawa: teacher oral Fr 1963–66; teacher via tv 1966–68; exper proj co-ordinator IRTV 1968–70; consult./admin educ tv and audio-visual progr 1970–72; teacher oral Fr adult educ div from 1973
m Aber 17.8.63 Ian A. Dewar MA 1963 *qv*

PACSOO Tokefat Christian   MB ChB 1962
s of Chia P. bus. man. and Fing K. Wong; b Mauritius 10.6.36
DMRD(Lond) 1968
h o Ayr, Leeds 1962–63; govt m o Georgetown Guyana 1963–66; training posts in radiology Glasg 1966–71; radiol Yorks from 1971
m Aber 20.10.60 Josephine Iutz MA 1962 *qv*

PADDISON Ronan   PhD 1969
BA(Durh)

PADMORE Lloyd Gregory   MB ChB 1963
b Trinidad WI 1.6.35
MRCOG 1969 FRCS(C) 1972
obst/gyn Toronto from 1972
m Aber 18.1.66 Johan MacSween midwife

PAGE John Graham   MB ChB 1968 ChM 1977
s of George R. P. BSc(Lond) lect pharm and Lilian A. Kay pharm; b Liv 16.2.43
FRCSE 1972

h o ARI 1968–69; lect path. Aberd 1969–70; sen h o surg ARI 1970–71; regist surg ARI 1971–77; res fell. surg Harvard univ Boston 1974–75
m Aber 30.8.69 Jessie S. Hossack nurs sister d of Ebenezer G. H. Menstrie

PAGE Kenneth Robert   *BSc 1966 PhD 1970
s of Robert W. P. dist man. Prudential Assur Co and Constance L. Fish; b Peterborough 17.5.37
ARIC 1972
Aberd: ICI res fell. 1969–71, lect biophys chem from 1971
m Varde Denmark 6.9.60 Ingrid von T. Sivertsen teacher d of Paul G. S. Med Lic(Copenhagen) Copenhagen

PAINTING Josephine   MA 1968
d of Harold G. C. P. man. NAAFI and Mabel H. Sotherton; b Kuala Lumpur 12.2.48
teacher Chatham from 1974
m Aber 30.12.66 Kevin Murphy salesman s of Gerald M. Birkenhead

PAKIANATHAN Samuel John Wright   MSc 1968
s of John M. P. acct and Emily R. David; b Kuala Lumpur 5.10.33
BSc(Adel) 1962 PhD(Lond) 1975 MIBiol
res biochem Adelaide 1962–63; rubber res inst of Malaysia: plant physiol res off. 1963–76, sect. leader, sen prin res off. from 1976
m Singapore 24.4.65 Sarojini D. Paul MB BS(Bom) med pract d of S. D. P. Singapore

PALIT Gordon Baladev   MA 1958 LTh 1967
s of Kanai L. P. LRCPE med pract and Marion R. Spence nurse; b Karachi Pakistan 4.10.29
LTCL(Lond) 1977
teacher: geog, Engl r e Turriff acad 1959–61, geog, Engl Dun 1961–64, geog Glasg 1967–69, prin r e Lond 1969–72; lect lib stud. Ayr tech coll 1972–74; teacher Engl as second lang Birm Educ Auth from 1979

PALIT Stephen   MA 1961
s of Kanai L. P. LRCPE med pract and Marion R. Spence; b Glasg 20.7.34
C of S min: asst St Nicholas ch Aber 1961–62; teacher Lanarksh 1962–64; min Dundonell par ch Rosssh from 1973

PALMER Christine Janet   MSc 1969
BA(Oxon)

PALMER John MacDougall   BSc 1968

PALMER Tessa Jane Helen Douglas   MA 1968
d of Kenneth N. V. P. MA(Cantab) consult. phys and Rosemary B. de M. Douglas radiogr; b Lond 17.9.47
Dip Soc Ad(Edin) 1969 Dip App Soc Stud.(Lond) 1972
Lond: child care off. 1969–72, psychiat soc worker 1972–73, asst dir nat assoc for ment health from 1974
m Lond –.3.79 David M. D. Mills BA(Oxon) lawyer

PARDOE Kathleen Frances   MA 1969 Dip Ed 1970
d of Joseph E. P. RAF P & TO and Helen M. Shand shop asst; b Huntly 7.4.48
teacher: Engl/hist Methlick j s s 1970–72, Engl Oban from 1972
m Huntly 6.8.71 David F. Whyte BSc 1971 teacher s of John W. Edin

PARIENTE David   MB ChB 1967
s of Samuel R. P. comp dir and Sara Benady disp chem; b Lisbon 9.12.39
DPM(Lond) 1973 MRCPsych 1974

h o ARI, Woodend hosp Aber 1967–68; Lond: sen h o Royal Free hosp 1968–69, g p 1969–71; regist psychiat Wembley hosp 1971–72, regist psychiat Napsbury hosp 1972–74, sen regist psychiat 1974–75, hon clin asst Univ Coll hosp 1974–75, consult. psychiat Napsbury hosp from 1975
m Lond 18.8.71 Judith Katzenberg med secy d of Moshé K. BEd(Wurtzburg) Lond

PARIS Walter Walker   MA 1962
   CA

PARK Anne   MA 1969

PARK Audrey Forbes Annand   BEd 1969
   d of Andrew P. ironmonger/salesman and Dorothea F. Taylor; b Newtonhill 26.5.47
teacher Tannochside p s Viewpark 1970–72
m Aber 12.9.69 Christopher H. Murray MA 1969 qv

PARK Frank George Stephen   MA 1969
   s of Frank S. P. postman and Janet A. Stephen sales asst; b Aber 15.9.48
computer progr Southampton 1969–72; computer consult. Lond from 1972
m Aber 26.12.69 Rita Eddie d of John T. E. Aber

PARK Helen Jean   *MA 1961

PARK Ian Michael Scott   MA 1958 LLB 1960
   s of Ian M. P. BSc 1924 qv (II, III); b Aber 7.4.38 leg. asst Paull & Williamsons advoc Aber 1961–63, ptnr from 1963; hon sheriff Aber
m Edin 20.6.64 Elizabeth M. L. Struthers BL(Edin) solic d of Alexander M. S. BSc(Glas) Edin

PARK John Charles   BSc 1969
   s of Alastair H. Park MB ChB 1954 qv and Annie B. Will MA 1936 qv; b Aber 27.2.47
teacher biol Hilton acad Aber from 1970

PARK Raymond   *MA 1963 ᶜLLB 1966
   b Aber 24.5.41
ptnr Park & McRae advoc Aber from 1969
m Aber 18.4.69 Marie Lines nurse

PARK Roy MacLean   MA 1956
   s of George P. draughtsman, shopkeeper etc and Jessie MacLean for.; b Insch 12.6.35
nat serv interpreter Cyprus 1957–59; teacher: Lat/Engl subjs New Deer s 1959–62, Engl/hist Galashiels acad 1962; sen asst Lindsey county lib h q Lincoln 1965–66; cataloguer MoT lib Lond 1966–69; dep lib MoAgr central vet lab Weybridge 1969–77; lib i/c Gt Westminster ho branch lib Lond from 1977
m N'cle-u-Tyne 1.6.66 Barbara B. Ewing BA(Melb) lib d of Allan R. E. Melbourne

PARK Sheila Nan Robb   MA 1956

PARK William McGillivray   MB ChB 1960
   s of William M.P. and Hannah N. McGillivray nurse; b Aber 6.4.36
DMRD 1964 ECFMG 1965 FFR 1969
h o Aber 1960–62; regist radiol WI Glasg 1962–64; instr radiol Yale s of med USA 1965–66; consult. radiol Oswestry from 1967
m Wellington Salop 1.7.61 Anne E. Staddon MB ChB 1959 qv

PARKER Brenda Mary   *BSc 1961 PhD 1964
   d of Ronald P. publ lighting eng and Alice M. Lovell

teacher; b Aber 4.12.39
SRC res asst UMIST 1964–67; scient civ serv RAE Farnborough from 1967

PARKER Elizabeth Susan   MA 1967
   d of Michael E. P. papermaker, publican and Florence M. C. Duffus; b Aber 23.1.47
Dip Sec St(Strath) 1968
Lond: secy to head of corporate plan. Cerebos 1968–69, secy/res asst head of market forecasting Consolidated Gold Fields 1969–71; Purnell Books: asst edit. 1971–73, asst foreign rights 1973–76, foreign rights man. from 1976

PARKER Ian Charles   *MA 1970
   s of Malcolm D. B. P. civ serv/crofter and Kathleen H. Sunderland civ serv; b Bradford 27.4.49
VSO Sennar and Shendi Sudan 1970–71; teacher Lerwick from 1973

PARKER Joan Dorothy   MA 1969
   d of Alan C. P. eng buyer and Mary A. Cameron typeroom man.; b Aber 11.6.47
clerk in pers with area health dept Huddersfield from 1974
m Slaithwaite 29.6.68 Ian M. Lumsden MA 1967 qv

PARKER Timothy Robert Walker   LLB 1967

PARKHILL Anne Lindsay   MA 1967
   d of John C. P. oil comp man. and Chryssie S. C. King secy; b Inv 8.4.46
teacher: Inv 1968–70, Edin 1970–71
m Inv 10.7.70 Allan D. Chisholm MA 1967 qv

PARKINSON Alexander Tough   MB ChB 1961

PARKINSON David Kelly   MA 1962
   s of John T. L. P. comp dir and Alice M. Tough; b Aber 25.2.41
CA 1966
fin. dir J. T. L. Parkinson Aber construct. group 1966–70; farms dir R. H. Leonard E. Yorks from 1970; man. dir Amatola Hotel Aber 1978
m Aber 18.6.66 Lilian G. Rannie d of William R. Cults

PARKINSON George Leslie   *MA 1957
   s of George W. L. P. C of S min and Helen Leslie waitress; b Aber 7.2.35
BD(Glas) 1960
C of S min: Kirkwall 1961–71, Chapel of Garioch 1971–73; visiting teacher of mus Aberdeensh 1974–75
m Aber 23.7.60 Catherine M. Glendinning MA 1957 qv
d Aber 2.3.81 AUR XLIX 139

PARKINSON John David   MB ChB 1962
   s of David P. elect. contr and Margaret T. Clubb; b Aber 15.9.33
h o Aber 1962–63; sen h o paediat Inv 1963–64; g p: Ballater 1964–65, Lond from 1965
m Boat of Garten 15.6.68 Margaret H. Gibson MB ChB (Edin) med pract d of George H. G. MB ChB(Glas) Boat of Garten

PARKS Valerie Sharon   MA 1967
   d of Harold P. eng and Marguerite I. Chivas tax off.; b Aber 24.4.46
teacher Aber from 1974
m Aber 28.10.67 Douglas A. Jamieson staff and fin. exec PO tel s of George J. Peterculter

PARLEY Sheila   MA 1960
   m Craig

PARRY David John *BSc 1965 PhD 1968

PARRY Stephen Byron Dove MA 1964
 b Portsmouth 15.12.43
Aber: teacher maths St Peter's RC s s 1965–68, Summerhill acad 1968–70, Rubislaw acad/AGS 1970–73, asst prin maths from 1973
m Aber 30.6.73 Barbara-Anne Munro food hyg off.

PARSLOW John Lewis LLB 1969

PARSONS Margaret MA 1968
 d of Harold P. man. printing and Frances M. Webster clerk; b Croydon 31.3.27
teacher maths Aber from 1969
m Manc 19.7.50 John J. Connell BSc(Manc) asst dir res s of John E. C. Manc

PARTINGTON Naomi Anne MA 1957
 d of James P. comp secy, fin. dir and Anne Williams; b Bolton 25.3.36
trainee buyer Harrod's Lond 1957–58; teacher Engl: Yew Tree comp s Manc 1958–60, Southland's girls' s Reading 1960–63, Heyward tech s Bolton 1963–64; teacher Engl/hist Umtali girls' h s Rhodesia, Gilbert Rennie s for boys Lusaka Zambia 1964–65; speed reading tut. Princeton USA reading lab 1965–66
m Bolton 7.8.65 Kenneth M. Young MA 1957 qv

PATCH Derek BSc(for) 1965
 s of Llewellyn P. pharm/optician and Alice Crabtree BSc(Manc) teacher; b Chadderton 5.3.44
Nat Dip Agr 1972 MIFor(GB)
for. off. Cheshire 1965–69; lect arboriculture Merrist Wood agr coll Worplesdon 1970–74, course tut. arboriculture from 1974
m Aber 16.8.68 Patricia F. L. Gordon MA 1966 qv

PATE Jean Lesley MB ChB 1968

PATEL Arvind Rai MB ChB 1963 MD 1973
 s of Dahyabhai C. P. bus. man. (automobiles) and Gangaben D. Patel; b Thika Kenya 27.2.36
MRCP 1970
h o Aber 1963–64; Glasg: regist med 1965–71, sen regist 1972–75, consult. phys from 1975

PATEL Minu Kaikhashru MSc 1960
 BSc(Bom) MSc(Agra)

PATERSON Alan Burness *BSc 1969
 s of Stanley B. P. insur off. and Irene M. Clayton; b Kirkcaldy 26.2.47
MSc(Aston) 1970
Bakelite Xylonite: scient off. polyethylene div Aycliffe, Grangemouth 1970–78, dev man. expanded rubber and plastics div Croydon from 1978

PATERSON Alan Keith Gordon *MA 1961
 s of Albert P. MA 1923 qv (II, III) and Helen T. Horne MA 1923 qv; b Aber 8.5.38
PhD(Cantab) 1965
asst lect/lect Queen Mary coll univ of Lond from 1965
m Lund Sweden 20.7.64 Anna T. Holm Med Kan(Lund) d of Tage H. Phil Mag(Lund) Malmö

PATERSON Alan Stuart BSc 1961

PATERSON Alistair Lawrence MA 1969
 s of Alexander J. P. fisherman and Frances J. Lawrence; b Banff 25.12.47
teacher Fr Banff 1970–72; prin Fr: St Columba's RC s s Perth 1972–78, St Andrew's s Nassau Bahamas from 1978

PATERSON Catherine Isabella MA 1968
 d of George E. P. salesman and Catherine Smith; b Kirkwall 30.8.47
m Aber 17.5.68 Douglas J. Stewart MB ChB 1969 qv

PATERSON Colin BSc 1968

PATERSON David Lawrence *MA 1968

PATERSON Doreen MA 1966
 m Cuthbert

PATERSON Eliza Martha MA 1968
 d of Andrew P. plumber and Martha M. Harrigan; b Inv 8.11.46
teacher: East Plean 1970–71, Edin 1971–72, Stonehaven from 1978; owner private nursery s Stonehaven 1973–75
m Fort Augustus 21.9.68 Ian N. Guthrie DA teacher, lect Aber coll of educ, asst keeper Aber Art Gallery s of John G. Sandwick

PATERSON Erna Jean MA 1968
 m Laing

PATERSON Geoffrey Forbes *BSc 1969

PATERSON Gordon Allan MA 1969
 d Cyprus 13.10.73 AUR XLV 450

PATERSON Helen Margaret MA 1966
 d of David P. dist man. Scot. gas board and Henrietta Blair; b Banff 25.2.45
teacher: Cumnock 1968–71, Kirkwall 1971–76.
m Aber 16.4.71 Frank T. Dry BSc 1965 qv

PATERSON Ian Arthur *BSc 1967

PATERSON Isobel MA 1965
 d of William J. P. farm worker, millwright and Lily Ironside; b Turriff 10.4.44
teacher: Smithfield p s Aber 1966–67, Crimond p s; exec off. Inl Rev Worthing 1970–72; teacher remed Campbeltown g s, Kinloch p s 1972–73
m Campbeltown 14.4.73 Peter S. Armour BA(Strath) clerk Hudson Bay Co, exec Ford Co, comp dir s of Peter S. A. Campbeltown

PATERSON Jean Margaret Diack *MA 1969
 d of Archibald P. civ eng and Margaret H. McRobert; b Glasg 13.5.48
ALA 1971
grad trainee lib Aberd 1969–70; dep lib marine lab Aber 1971–75; lib Macaulay inst for soil res Aber 1976–77
m Tighnabruaich 30.6.72 Stephen R. Alcock MB ChB 1969 qv

PATERSON Jeffrey Norman McCheyne *MA 1968 Dip Ed 1969

PATERSON Joan Stuart MA 1962
 d of Cyril D. P. loc govt off. and Margaret Stuart; b Forres 9.7.41
teacher Applegrove p s Forres from 1963

PATERSON John Simon *BSc 1969
 s of Thomas R. P. salmon fishing lessee and Mona F. Mackenzie MA 1967 qv; b St Andrews 21.12.47
analytical chem Enfield 1971–72; ptnr commercial sea salmon fishing bus. Strathy Thurso from 1972

PATERSON John Thomson MB ChB 1963

PATERSON Kenneth Norman BSc 1964
MEd(Glas)

PATERSON Laura Beedie MA 1964
m Levy

PATERSON Lily Jane MA 1963
d of William J. P. farm lab, painter and Lily Ironside;
b Turriff 17.1.42
teacher Engl Bankhead acad from 1974
m Turriff 14.9.62 Ian A. Scott ordnance surv/tech
Grampian roads dept s of Clifford S. Dewsbury

PATERSON Maureen Lilian MA 1969
m Akintewe

PATERSON Neil *BSc 1966 PhD 1970
b Forres 1944
lect chem path. Aberd from 1966

PATERSON Richard George *MA 1956

PATERSON Ronald McNeill LLB 1970

PATERSON Ronald Seaton BSc(agr) 1969
s of Colin S. P. farm. and Anna M. Smith typist;
b Alyth 11.5.48
Dip FMBO(NOSCA) 1970
asst lands off. Stirling 1970–75; lands off. Lerwick from
1975
m Stirling 26.12.70 Aileen Stephen teacher d of James
Stephen

PATIENCE Hugh James Mackintosh *BSc 1970
s of Hugh P. harbour pilot and Elma Maclauchlan;
b Inv 3.3.48
Dip Ed(Edin) 1973 MEd(Glas) 1978
teacher Beauly j s s 1970–71; actuarial stud. Legal & Gen
Assur Soc Lond 1971; teacher: Kirkton h s Dun 1971–72,
high s Inv 1973–75, Allan Glen's s s Glasg 1975–76,
Hillhead h s Glasg 1976–78, Harvey g s Folkestone from
1978
m Glasg 3.7.76 Edith M. Culbert teacher mus d of James
A. C. Glasg

PATON John Alexander MA 1966

PATON Kathleen Scott BEd 1969
d of John P. chiropodist and Grace I. Scott; b Ellon
19.7.48
teacher mod lang Peterhead acad 1969–71; Peebles h s
1971–74
m Aber 31.7.71 Clive P. Alder BSc 1970 qv

PATON Keith Alan *MA 1962

PATON Thomas John Grindley MB ChB 1966
s of Thomas D. P. meat livestock controller and
Isabella G. McLean; b Duns 23.8.42
h o Inv 1966–67; g p Perth 1968, Mahalapy Botswana
1969–71, Ottawa from 1971
m Aber 19.5.67 Kathleen Davidson d of Alexander D.
Fyvie

PATON Wilma Ann MA 1967 CASS 1969
d of William S. P. bricklayer, foreman, site superv and
Agnes J. Allan waitress; b Forres 20.9.46
soc worker/fieldwork teacher Aber 1969–76; lect in soc
work RGIT Aber from 1976

PATRICK Anthony Graham *BSc 1969 MSc 1971
s of Graham M. P. civ serv and Barbara A. Worboys;

b Royston 7.8.46
army maj from 1978

PATRICK Barbara Howie *MA 1969 Dip Ed 1970

PATRICK David Malcolm MA 1970
s of Thomas E. P. arch. and Dorothy B. Malcolm
chirop; b Edin 20.2.47
CA 1973
Edin: acct Deloitte & Co CA, Dalgliesh & Tullo CA
1970–79; group acct Eastern Motor Co from 1979
m Aber 20.7.73 Alyson T. Greig MA 1971 teacher

PATRICK Elizabeth Boyd MLitt 1967
MA(Glas)

PATRICK George *MA 1963

PATTERSON Donald BSc(for) 1956

PATTERSON Dorothy Elizabeth BSc 1965
d of James R. P. quantity surv and Marian E. McEwan
MA 1924 qv; b Aber 27.5.44
teacher Duddingston p s Edin from 1966
m Edin 21.10.72 John D. Rutherford motor eng s of
John R. Bonnyrigg

PATTERSON Ian James *BSc 1961
s of James A. P. rlyman and Mary C. N. Darling;
b Duns 30.3.39
D Phil(Oxon) 1964
res fell. zool Aberd 1964–66, lect zool 1966–77, sen lect
from 1977
m Dun 28.7.62 Muriel J. Birse MA 1960 qv

PATTERSON Kathleen Anne *MA 1970
d of Andrew P. civ serv and Daisy F. MacDonald;
b Aber 1.12.47
teacher geog/mod stud. Blairgowrie 1971–75, Aust 1975–
76, Malta 1976–78, Cyprus from 1978

PATTERSON Margaret Helen MA 1958
d of James R. P. quantity surv and Marian E. McEwan
MA 1924 qv; b Aber 2.8.37
teacher: Byron Park inf s Aber 1959–69, Royal High p s
Edin 1969–72
m Edin 31.3.71 David N. Smith bank man. s of Thomas
S. Edin

PATTERSON Michael Hugh *MA 1970
s of Henry B. W. P. BSc(Durh) chem eng and Constance
M. Wright; b Birkenhead 30.8.47
diagnostic and remed teacher Marshfield e s n s Peterborough 1971–76; sen clin psych paediat assessment centre
Chesterfield from 1976

PATTERSON Robin James Michael BSc(eng) 1964

PATTERSON Valerie Ann Newton MA 1963
m Wharton

PATTIE Ann More Williamson MA 1967
d of Robert S. P. prod./plan. eng and Margaret W.
Taylor nurse; b Glasg 27.9.45
teacher Riverside s s Glasg 1968–72, prin guid 1972–74
m Inverurie 5.4.69 George Brown driver s of Douglas B.
Rutherglen

PATTIE Robert BSc(eng) 1968
s of Robert S. P. engraver and Margaret Taylor;
b Glasg 14.7.47
CEng MIEE

grad eng Derby 1968–70; sen tech off. Glasg 1970–75; eng asst Lond from 1975

PAUL Anil Krishna   MSc 1968
s of Lal Mohan P. teacher and Kunja Kamini; b Dacca Bangla Desh 15.1.24
BSc(Dacca) 1944 MSc(Dacca) 1946 PhD(Calc) 1972
lect organ./biochem Calcutta nat med coll 1948–54; Haringhata farm W Bengal: res asst, asst res off., res off. anim nutrit directorate of anim husb 1954–67, res off. physiol chem 1969–73; physiol chem from 1973
m Calcutta 2.3.49 Bina Kundu d of S. S. K. MB(Calc)

PAUL Douglas Wyness Thomson   MB ChB 1968
s of Douglas A. P. gen man. Hall Russell & Co and Margaret M. Thomson lib; b Aber 4.9.44
MRCGP 1974
h o Aber, Wick 1968–69; sen h o Thurso 1969; g p Wick from 1969
m Aber 23.7.67 Alexandra M. Lee teacher d of Robert L.

PAUL Helen Margaret Wyness   MA 1970
d of Douglas A. P. naval arch./gen man. Hall Russell & Co Aber and Margaret M. Thomson lib Torry res stat; b Aber 22.2.49
teacher Aber from 1971
m Aber 24.7.70 George C. Stove BSc 1972 tut. geog dept Aberd s of George J. S. Sandwick Shetland

PAUL Parul Rani   BSc 1962
d of Radha K. P. Dip Eng(Dacca) tech asst and Promode K. Dutta; b Bangladesh 7.4.37
BA(Calc) 1958
teacher Convent s Malaya 1959 and 1965–67
m Calcutta 1.5.64 Madhabendra M. Guha PhD 1951 qv

PAYNE Dorothy Ruth   PhD 1969
d of Charles F. P. civ serv and Violet M. Denne civ serv; b Croydon 26.8.36
BSc(Lond) 1960 MIBiol(Lond)
lect physiol Aberd from 1964

PEACE Emma Smith   MA 1959
d of Donald P. farm. and Margaret Chalmers; b Stronsay 29.3.38
teacher: Lat Bradford 1959–60, remed Halkirk 1965–67, p s Thurso 1967–70, p s Elgin 1970–71, f e Elgin 1973–74, prin guid/Engl Thurso from 1975
m Stronsay 15.7.59 Donald Omand MA 1958 qv

PEACOCK Robin Geoffrey   MA 1970
s of Geoffrey P. civ serv and Irene D. Baker; b Ilford 8.7.47
Dip Man. St(RGIT Aber) 1971 Dip Marketing 1972
Kwikform Birm: export admin asst 1971–72, market res off. 1972–73; J. C. B. Rocester Uttoxeter market intell spec 1973–75; Massey Ferguson Coventry market and econ res spec 1975–77, marketing res man. Europe, Africa, Asia, Australasia—parts oper from 1977
m Edin 28.6.69 Gillian E. M. Alsop BEd 1969 qv

PEAD Beryl-Anne   BSc 1968

PEARCE Gordon James Martin   PhD 1959
s of Walter P. secy and Harriet Seager; b Lond 27.12.09
BA(Lond) 1937 MA(Birm) 1944
baptist min: Tamworth 1936–44, Bradford 1944–52, Crown Terrace Aber 1952–60; dean and tut. Oxon 1960–74
m Lond 25.1.36 Doris P. Hancock dressmaker d of Humphrey H. RN Brixton Lond
d 11.2.74

PEARCE Janet Elizabeth   BSc 1970
m Haworth

PEARSON Charles Arthur   *MA 1962
s of Douglas H. P. fl/lt RAF and Christina M. Campbell secy; b Tain 15.5.40
cler work Invergordon 1963–65; teacher hist Middlesbrough from 1965

PEARSON Ian Henderson   MA 1967
s of Magnus H. P. master bldr and Alice M. Scott MA 1925 qv; b Lerwick 29.10.45
Dip Man. St 1969
Scot. gas Edin: grad trainee 1969–70, organis and methods off. from 1970
m Aber 24.7.70 Kathleen J. Yeoman MA 1968 qv

PEARSON Isobel Gilfillan   MA 1958
d of William P. tobacconist and Isabella Mark nurse; b Keith 22.10.37
teacher Aber 1959–60
m Aber 22.7.59 Patrick A. Symon MA 1952 qv

PEARSON James Murray   *BSc 1959 PhD 1962
s of James S. P. tobacconist and Jeannie E. Hendry; b Aber 22.11.37
post doct res fell. NY state coll of for. Syracuse NY USA 1962–64; asst lect, lect chem Aberd 1964–66; assoc lect Polymer res inst NY state coll of for. Syracuse 1966–68; man. Polymer sc area xerographic tech dept Xerox corp Rochester NY from 1968
m Aber 30.5.62 Hilary L. Buckett d of Robert B.

PEARSON Jean Robertson   *BSc 1959
m Alison
d 26.3.67

PEARSON Nigel William   LLB 1965

PEAT Conrad Ian   BSc(for) 1961
s of Rex A. P. master butcher and Lily Barnes; b Sheff 16.5.40
Kenya: asst conserv for. Elburgon, Londiani, Thomson Falls, Nairobi 1961–66; sen work study off. papermaking indust Exeter, Lond, Fort William from 1966
m Inv 11.4.70 Margaret R. L. Richards catering man. d of Robert L. MB ChB 1932 qv

PEAT Elizabeth Booth   MA 1967
d of Reginald A. P. MB ChB 1943 qv; b Jamaica 26.3.46
Dip Pers Man.(Middlesex poly)(Hendon) 1970
Lond: admin attaché dip. serv 1967–69; exec off. civ serv 1971–73, admin asst Lond 1973–74; soc worker Lond from 1975

PECK Catherine Pryde   MB ChB 1968
d of George T. P. seaman/weaver and Janet R. Dickson nurse; b Strathaven 2.7.43
h o Stornoway, Stonehaven 1963–69; regist haemat Law hosp Carluke 1969–71; g p Hamilton from 1971
m Hamilton 9.4.71 John Braithwaite BA(Strath) organis and methods off./syst analyst s of William L. B. Hamilton

PEDEN Donald George   MSc 1968
s of Ernest E. P. man. agr and feed supply comp and Bernice L. Swanston; b Victoria Canada 23.1.46
BSc(Vict) 1967 PhD(Colorado State Univ) 1972 PDF (Calg) 1973
res scient (ecol) Canadian wildlife serv Saskatoon from 1973

PEDERSON   *BSc 1967
  s of C. P. P. eng worker and Georgina L. Wilson;
b Aber 9.4.34
teacher: Stonehaven 1967-73, asst prin maths Banff from
1973

PEDERSEN Roy Norman   MA 1966
  s of Hans N. P. supt Aber harbour board and Anne W.
Black; b Ardrossan 22.11.43
teacher Stevenston 1967; exec off. min of tech Lond,
DTI 1970-71; asst admin off. HIDB Inv 1971-73, freight
trans off. 1973, res off. from 1974
m Lond 21.11.70 Jennifer Walpole secy d of Herman
T. W. Lond

PEGG Christopher Arthur Sunley   ChM 1969
  s of Arthur T. P. MA(Sheff) headmaster, supt remand
home and Dorothy A. Sunley matron remand home;
b Norfolk 3.7.37
MB BS(Lond) 1962 FRCS 1966
h o/sen surg cas off. St Thomas's hosp Lond 1962-64;
h o Worthing gen hosp 1964; sen h o Gt Ormond St
HSC Lond 1964-65; regist, sen regist, hon clin lect surg
ARI/Aberd 1965-73; res fell. surg Harvard univ Boston
Mass 1968-69; consult. surg/hon clin teacher surg Nott
univ hosp from 1973
m Cheltenham 8.2.64 Ann J. Ault MB BS(Lond) med
pract d of Frederick H. A. Cheltenham

PENNIE David Alexander   *MA 1969
  s of Gibb N. P. MA 1930 qv; b Dalbeattie 19.7.46
Dip Lib Stud.(Belf) 1971 ALA 1973
trainee lib Durh 1969-70; sen lib asst S'ton 1971-76; asst
lib Hull from 1976

PENNIE Rona   MA 1970

PENNINGTON John Barry   BSc(eng) 1966

PENNY Helen   BSc 1970
  d of Charles P. MB ChB 1922 qv; b Derby 9.3.47
secy course Oxford 1970-71; res secy Bristol 1971-72;
radio secy Derby 1973; med rep Bristol from 1974
m Derby 17.6.76 Stephen B. Lyus BA(Warw) man.
consult. s of Brian G. L. Marlborough

PENNY Rebecca   *MA 1966
  d of Charles P. MB ChB 1922; b Derby 21.3.42
Dip Ed(Edin) 1967
teacher Fr/Ger Derby 1967-69; TEFL: Cologne Ger
1969-73, Madrid from 1973

PEPPER Jean Margaret   *MA 1968
  d of William A. P. and Lilian M. Weetman; b Lond
28.1.46
teacher Engl Ashford 1968-69; exec off. univ of Ulster
Coleraine 1969-71; temp posts Watertown Mass USA
1971-73
m Cheadle Hulme 20.7.68 Alan W. Hazel BSc 1968 qv

PEPPIETTE Geoffrey Charles Christopher
BSc(eng) 1962

PERCIVAL Alan   PhD 1960
  BSc(Manc)

PERCIVAL James Sidney   *MA 1963 Dip Ed 1964
  b Tandjong Kassau Indonesia 12.10.25
teacher mod lang: Aber acad 1964-65, Inverurie acad
1965-68, coll of comm Aber 1968-69; asst prin mod lang
Inverurie acad from 1969
m Inverurie 24.12.49 Elizabeth McRae

PERCY Graham Charles Booth   *MA 1968
  s of Ernest R. P. eng and Violet E. Booth lib; b Aber
2.3.46
BBC: progr oper Lond 1968-70, prod. radio Nott from
1970
m Ratcliffe-on-Trent Jennifer Meakin p a/des d of
William K. M.

PEREIRA Brian Anthony   *BSc(eng) 1968
  s of Anthony P. comp dir and Ursula Figueira;
b Guiana 7.12.45
computer eng Greenock from 1968
m Aber 14.9.68 Heather M. Petrie MB ChB 1967

PEREZALEMAN Salvador de Jesus   MSc 1970
  DVM(Venez)

PERFECT Martin John   MA 1968
  s of Ernest J. F. MA(Oxon) schoolmaster and Eleanor
P. D. Denton journalist; b Oxford 23.5.47
telephonist Lond from 1968
m Aber -.10.73 Brenda J. Thompson edit. d of Benjamin
C. T. Bridge of Don

PERKS Helen Marjorie   MA 1956
  d of Jackie P. CBE DSC capt RN and Isabel Burns;
b Portsmouth 22.4.66
teacher: Bracoden j s 1957-59, Macduff h s 1959-61,
drama Banffsh 1971-74, asst prin guid Banff acad from
1974
m Aber 4.8.60 James A. S. McPherson MA 1949 qv

PERMAN Anne   MA 1966
  b Kent 24.12.44
resid Buxton Derbysh
m Escritt

PEROMBELON Michel Marie Clement   *BSc 1962
MSc 1963

PERRIE James Fraser   *MA 1959 Dip Ed 1960
  d 5.3.70

PERRIE William Thomas   *BSc 1965

PERRINS Margaret Janet   MB ChB 1969

PETERS David James   *BSc(eng) 1967
  s of David F. M. P. exec eng PO tel and Daisy Grieve
hairdresser; b Aber 27.3.45
CEng 1971 MICE 1971 MSc(Strath) 1972 MIPHE 1972
Aff IWPC 1973
sect. eng Taylor Woodrow construct. Dounreay, Wylfa
Anglesey, Invergordon 1967-70; asst eng Babtie Shaw &
Morton consult. eng Glasg 1970-71; sen asst eng Dun
city eng dept 1972-75; sen group leader WPC Tayside
reg c water serv dept from 1975
m Elgin 1.8.69 Christine M. Guthrie nurs/inf teacher d
of William J. R. G. Elgin

PETERS Gordon   *MA 1958
  s of James R. P. farm. and Nellie Reid; b Cluny
26.12.35
teacher hist/Engl: Camphill h s Paisley 1959-60,
Inverurie acad 1960-64; prin hist Gordon s Huntly from
1964
m Aber 29.7.66 Edith I. Wilson MA 1956 qv

PETERS Gordon Grieve   *BSc 1970
  s of David F. M. P. exec eng PO tel and Daisy Grieve
hairdresser; b Ellon 8.9.48
PhD(Edin) 1974

res asst MRC Edin 1974; res fell.: univ of Wisc Madison USA 1974–77, Imperial Cancer res fund Lond from 1977

PETERS Mary Elizabeth   *MA 1963
   d of Bernard F. P. plan. eng (cars) and Nellie I. Faunch; b Luton 20.7.40
commonwealth schol univ of Sri Lanka 1963; teacher Walsall 1964–66; lect: Cornwall 1967–68, coll for deaf Walton from 1979
m Luton 26.8.67 William J. Warren solic s of William J. W. Camborne

PETERSON Anne Elizabeth   MA 1966

PETERSON Christina June   MA 1970
   d of Arthur P. lorry driver and Mary A. Robertson dom serv; b Lerwick 13.12.49
teacher Anderson h s Lerwick from 1971
m Lerwick 16.7.71 John A. E. Johnson joiner s of Sinclair J. Bixter

PETERSON Gordon Craig   *BSc 1965 PhD 1974
   s of William G. P. B Com 1927 qv; b Aber 1.2.43
scient Unilever res Port Sunlight from 1969
m Aber 1968 Helen E. Cant MA 1969 qv

PETERSON James Peter   MA 1960
   s of Alexander M. P. merch seaman and Jessie A. Pole; b Sandness Shetland 3.6.39
teacher Shetland: Hamnavoe 1961–68, Walls 1968–70, Aith 1970–75; dep dir leisure and recreation dept Shetland Is c from 1975

PETERSON Jemima Alice   MA 1958
   d of Alexander M. P. merch seaman and Jessie A. Pole; b Sandness Shetland 9.11.36
teacher: Aber 1959–62, Edmonton Alta 1970–72
m Shetland 4.4.60 Duncan Armstrong BSc 1958 qv

PETERSON John Magnus   MA 1970

PETERSON Louis Keith   *BSc 1957 PhD 1960
   s of James P. P.; b Shetland 12.8.35
res assoc USC California 1960–62; lect City univ Lond 1962–65; assoc prof Simon Fraser univ BC Canada from 1965
m Jill J. Macdonald

PETRIE Doreen Alexandra   MA 1969
   d of William A. P. bus driver and Marie W. L. Haldane; b Aber 17.2.48
advt canvasser: Aber 1971–72, Edin 1972–74; pers asst Edin 1974–75, admin asst in educ Stonehaven 1975–77
m Braemar 18.9.71 Brian J. Wood BSc 1971 teacher s of Frank W. Aber

PETRIE Hazel Christine   MA 1968
   d of Robert E. P. man. hardware shop and Mabel Allerton cler off.; b Stoke-on-Trent 29.1.46
Dip Soc Stud.(Edin) 1969
Edin: trainee welfare off. dept health and welfare 1969–70; loc auth soc worker 1970–72; soc worker for Shelter 1972–73
m Haddington 3.10.70 George M. V. Dier syst eng s of Hubert V. S. D. BA(Oxon) Dumfries

PETRIE Heather Margaret   MB ChB 1967
   d of James B. P. headmaster and Margaret McDonald; b Melksham 9.8.44
h o Raigmore hosp Inv, Woodend hosp Aber 1967–68
m Aber 14.9.68 Brian A. Pereira BSc(eng) 1968 qv

PETRIE Helen Cattanach   *BSc 1966
   d of James W. H. P. MA(Edin) teacher and Janet Cattanach MA 1935 qv; b Elgin 9.10.44
teacher geog/maths Kaimhill s Aber 1967–68, Bankhead acad Aber 1968–70; dir Ben Reid & Co Aber from 1970
m Aber 27.7.67 John Fraser nurseryman s of Robert F. MB ChB 1935 qv

PETRIE James Colquhoun   MB ChB 1964
   s of James B. P. MA 1932 qv and Cairine R. MacLean MA 1940 qv; b Aber 18.9.41
h o ARI 1964–65; sen h o/regist Aber hosps 1965–69; lect therap Aberd 1969–71; sen lect therap Aberd/hon consult. phys Aber hosps from 1971
m Aber 16.7.64 Margaret X. P. Forbes MB ChB 1964 qv

PETRIE Mhorag Jean   BSc 1961
   m Taylor

PFISTER Maria Regina   *MA 1966
   d of Charles P. asst man. American Express co inc Lucerne and Margaretha Buehler clerk; b Sirnach Switzerland 9.8.40
teacher Stadtische Töchterhandelsschule Luzern, Switzerland from 1966
m Lucerene 28.4.73 Hans B. Fricker chief eng Canton of Lucerne s of Hans F. Aarau Switzerland

PHA Jean Cyril   *MA 1967

PHEMISTER Elizabeth Reid   *MA 1957
   d of Thomas C. P. BSc(Glas) prof geol Aberd and Mary W. Reid MA(Glas) teacher; b Cambridge 8.7.34
secy to dir: Joseph Lucas (electrical) Birm 1958–62, world h q internat wool secretariat Lond 1962–65; teacher mod lang Leamington coll for girls Leamington Spa 1966–72; secy to man. dir L Maurer UK Warwick 1973–74; exec off. Midland road construct. unit DoE Leamington Spa 1974–75; dep admin off. Mid-Warwicksh coll of f e Leamington Spa from 1975
m Warwick 23.6.70 Dennis B. Matthews tooling investig eng s of Robert B. M. Lighthorne

PHILIP Alexander Schroder   *BSc 1965
   s of Andrew F. P. bank acct and Martha H. Schroder; b Aber 26.5.43
MIERE C Eng 1972
telecomm Liv: dev eng 1965–72, eng man. from 1972
m Aber 5.8.66 Gillian M. Crofts BSc 1965 qv

PHILIP Alistair Erskine   *MA 1961
   s of James P. dairyman and Gertrude M. Erskine; b Aber 10.7.38
PhD(Edin) 1968 Dip Clin Psych(Edin) 1963 ABPsS
prob clin psych SE(Scot.) reg hosp board Edin 1961–63; clin psych NE(Scot.) reg hosp board Aber 1963–65; scient staff MRC unit for epidemiological stud. in psychiat Edin 1964–71; prin clin psych Bangour village hosp W. Lothian from 1971
m Aber 12.2.68 Betty J. McKay BSc 1964 qv

PHILIP Alistair Fowlie   *BSc(eng) 1968
   s of John P. rubber planter and Helena M. Fowlie teacher; b Aber 9.3.46
MSc(Cranfield) 1970
helicopter pilot RAF: Odiham 1970–78, Aeroplane & Arm. Exper Est Boscombe Down from 1978

PHILIP Charles Ian   BSc(eng) 1959

PHILIP George   MA 1958

PHILIP Grace Cameron   MA 1960
d of Richard P. master grocer and Grace E. Cameron
piano teacher; b Aber 23.7.39
teacher p s RGC Aber 1961–64; part-time visiting mus
spec p s Aber from 1975
m Aber 17.7.62 Philip F. Simpson gen secy Aber YMCA
s of John A. M. S. Aber

PHILIP Ian   MA 1966 MEd 1968
s of James P. eng and Helen N. Mitchell; b Peterhead
31.12.43
Dip Applied Ling(Edin) 1972
TEFL Mumbwa Zambia 1968–71; lect inst of tech Kitwe
Zambia 1972–78; sen lect coll of tech Mumbane Swaziland 1975–78

PHILIP Margaret McKenzie   MB ChB 1957
d of Peter W. MB ChB 1924 qv (II, III); b Huntly
20.11.33
h o RACH 1957–58; m o (ch health) Aberdeensh 1972–
75; part-time regist (ment deficiency) Woodlands hosp
from 1975
m Aber 16.9.57 Geoffrey M. Gill MB ChB 1953 qv

PHILIP Maureen Anne   BSc 1963 Dip Ed 1964
d of Henry P. law acct and Janet M. Mitchell off.
worker; b Aber 29.1.42
teacher maths St Margaret's s for girls Aber 1964–68;
part time lect maths Aber coll of comm from 1979
m Aber 4.4.66 Thomas W. Simpson MB ChB 1964 qv

PHILIP Patrick Blake   BSc(eng) 1957

PHILIP Robert Finlay   *BSc(eng) 1960
s of Arthur P. PO eng and Christina Findlay printer's
asst; b Aber 26.4.38
MIEE CEng 1970
proj eng Ferranti Edin 1960–65; lect Dund from 1965
m Aber 3.4.64 Anne F. Simpson MA 1961 qv

PHILIP Robert Freeland   MA 1960
s of Robert P. foreman fish filleter and Christina R.
Sanders dressmaker; b Aber 5.12.39
stud. Scots cong coll Edin 1960–63; attendant Gogarburn
ment hosp Edin 1963–64; untrained teacher Crossgates s
Fife 1964; min: Forsyth mem cong ch Glasg 1964–70,
Mastrick cong ch Aber 1970–78, Avonbridge cong with
cong wing Grahamston United ch Falkirk from 1978
m Berwick-u-Tweed 1.8.64 Yvonne Ingles MA(Edin)
teacher of deaf d of John A. W. I. Berwick-u-Tweed

PHILIP Suzanne   *MA 1959
d of Peter W. P. MB ChB 1924 qv; b Huntly 18.3.36
teacher: Fr/Ger High s for girls Aber 1960–61, Bridge of
Don 1962–63; The Gordon s Huntly from 1963
m Aber 28.9.61 Gordon C. Shirreffs MB ChB 1957 qv

PHILIP Wilma   MA 1964

PHILLIP Sheena Mary   MA 1960 Dip Ed 1961
d of William C. P. MA(St And) teacher and Mary D.
Flight shorthand typist; b Dun 10.4.39
teacher Engl/hist: Mackie acad Stonehaven 1961–66, Old
Aber s 1966
m Aber 10.4.65 Clement A. Stewart MA 1962 qv

PHILLIPS Alexander   BSc 1969
s of John P. slater and Louisa Hendry; b Aber 7.11.47
various posts in computing Dunstable 1969–76; sen syst
analyst Edin from 1976
m Aber 1.7.69 Margaret P. Gibson d of Douglas G.

PHILLIPS Anne Clemency Sarah   cMB ChB 1961
d of Ernest B. P. MTh(Lond) min of relig/lect Biblical
lang and theol and Alice Gordon artist; b Rugby 26.5.36
h o ARI, RACH 1961–62; m o Empress Zauditu mem
hosp Addis Ababa 1962–63; sen h o Fulbourn hosp
Cambridge 1964; g p Binfield from 1972
m Binfield 30.12.63 Colin W. Mitchell PhD(Cantab) lect
geog s of Arthur C. M. Chelsea

PHILLIPS George McArtney   *MA 1960 MSc 1961
s of George P. dent mech and Elizabeth McArtney;
b Aber 30.7.38
PhD(St And) 1969
asst maths Aberd 1961–62; teacher Allhallows s Devon
1962–63; lect: maths S'ton 1963–67, St And 1967–73, sen
lect from 1973
m Aber 4.7.61 Veronica M. Irvine MA 1959 qv

PHILLIPS Ian George Knox   BEd 1969

PHILLIPS James Dawson   *MA 1959

PHILLIPS Michael William   BSc(eng) 1967

PHILLIPS Roger John   MA 1970

PHILLIPSON John Tobin   *BSc(eng) 1962

PHILLIPSON Nicholas Tindal   *MA 1958
s of Andrew T. P. BA(Cantab) prof Cantab and
Rachel M. Young; b Aber 15.8.37
BA(Cantab) 1962 PhD(Cantab) 1967
nat serv RAF Norfolk 1958–60; lect hist Edin from 1965;
visiting fell. Davis centre Princeton univ USA 1970–71,
visiting lect Yale univ USA 1977

PHILP Arthur Andrew Kinninmonth   *BSc 1970
s of Robert P. trans man. and Miriam L. F. Kinninmonth; b Dunfermline 7.5.48
trainee computer spec Lond 1970–73; Perth: computer
progr 1973–74, computer progr proj leader 1974–75,
syst analyst 1975–77, asst computer oper supt from 1977
m Aber 19.9.70 Joan Watson secy d of James W. Aber

PHILP Bruce   *BSc 1970
s of James T. P. hotelier and Dorothy King hotelier;
b Crieff 12.10.47
res asst Ibadan Nigeria 1970–71; teacher biol Portree
from 1972

PHILP Richard Paul   *BSc 1968

PICKARD James Roy   MLitt 1969
s of Reginald J. P. PhD(Sheff) headmaster and Eileen
M. Alexander; b Lindrick 20.8.42
BA(Lond) 1964
asst lib Aberd from 1965

PICKARD Joyce Isobel Helen   MA 1970
m Petrie

PICKEN Hilda Hamilton   MA 1966

PICKFORD Douglas Thomson   BSc 1961

PICKLES Ian Munro   *MA 1967
s of John W. P. MB ChB 1932 qv; b East London S Af
3.6.44
Master Town & Country Planning (Syd) 1977 Member
Royal Aust Plan. Inst
teacher Lond 1967–68; supermarket warehouse man.
Lond 1968–69; Aust: town plan. asst Sydney, Melbourne

1970–72, asst town plan. N Sydney munic council 1973–77, dep town plan. Waverley munic council Bondi Sydney from 1977
m Sydney 28.12.71 Kathleen A. Littler BA(Syd) teacher d of John E. L. BA(Syd) Sydney

PIERCY John David BSc(eng) 1970
s of Frederick J. P. LDS dent. surg and Rebecca F. Maugham; b Wimbledon 2.10.47
trg RAF Cranwell, Oakington, Thorney Is 1970–73; co-pilot *Hercules* Lyneham from 1973
m Aber 31.3.73 Mary L. Marshall LLB 1972 articled clerk d of Alexander M. Aber
d flying accident –.9.78 *AUR* XLVIII 107

PIGGINS James Milne *BSc 1969
s of James M. P. shipowner/shipbroker and Mary Milne; b Aber 2.12.47
PhD(Cantab) 1975
res stud. radio astron Cambridge 1969–72; hosp phys Inv 1972–74; non-destructive testing Babcock & Wilcox Renfrew 1975–78; res fell. med phys Edin from 1978

PIGOTT Colin Peter BSc(eng) 1967
s of Kenneth P. P. comp dir and Dora Goodman comp dir; b Maghull nr Liv 29.5.45
piling eng 1967–71; proj man. 1971–74; estimator Ormskirk from 1974
m Aber 23.11.68 Ray B. Watson LLB 1965 *qv*

PIKE James Adam BSc(eng) 1970
s of John T. P. fisherman and Catherine Clark; b Aber 19.6.47
Brinsley: grad app Plessey trg centre 1970–72, asst eng electro-mech syst Plessey Crossbar syst lab 1972–73, eng-electronic des 1973–75, sen eng 1975–77, prin eng advanced SWG div from 1978

PIKE Malcolm Cecil PhD 1963
BSc(Rand) Dip Math Stat(Cantab)

PILGRIM Roy Malcolm BSc 1970
s of Leslie P. steelworks foundry insp and Mary A. Simmerson stock control clerk; b Sheff 15.3.48
MICA 1974
Sheff: articled clerk CA 1970–74, man. acct Edgar Allen Tools 1974; group chief acct High Mead Eng Holdings

PINNOCK (Baird) Jennifer Naomi MA 1970
d of Malcolm R. P. MB ChB 1950 *qv* and Ethel Melville dispenser; b Aber 14.4.49
teacher: Aber 1971–75, Inverurie from 1976
m Aber 2.1.70 Alastair J. Mackie MB ChB 1969 *qv*

PINSENT Elizabeth Margaret *BSc 1967
d of Robert J. F. H. P. MB ChB(Cantab) med pract and Ruth M. Morrison MA(St And) civ serv; b St And 2.11.44
PhD(Edin) 1973
res assoc Edin 1967–71; lect biol sc Napier coll of sc & tech from 1971
m Birmingham 3.4.72 George M. Alder MA(Cantab) lect s of George V. A. BSc(Brist) Bristol

PINSENT Robert Hugh *BSc 1968
s of Robert J. F. H. P. MD(Cantab) med pract and Ruth M. Morrison MA(St And); b St And 10.3.46
MSc(Alta) 1971 PhD(Durh) 1974
explor geol Vancouver 1971–72; res stud. Durh 1972–76, econ geol Winnipeg 1976–79; explor geol Vancouver from 1979

PIRIE Alexander Flett *BSc 1957

PIRIE Edna Louise *MA 1956

PIRIE Gordon Douglas *BSc 1964 PhD 1968

PIRIE Harold Rothnie MA 1966
s of James P. master shoemaker and Mary S. C. Clyne shop asst; b Insch 28.11.44
teacher: Engl/geog/hist Cumnock 1967–68, Engl/geog/mod stud. New Deer j s s 1968–69, Engl Inverurie acad 1969–71, gen subj Entoto s Addis Ababa Ethiopia 1971–72, Engl Bankhead acad 1972–75; prin guid Tarbert s from 1976
m Hopeman 21.7.73 Evelyn A. Jack staff nurse d of John J. Hopeman

PIRIE Isobel MA 1960
d of James P. garage propr and Margaret I. Pittendreigh; b Kemnay 21.1.39
teacher: Aber 1961–63, Knopi Finland 1963–64, Aber 1964–65, Rio de Janeiro Brazil 1965–67, Aber 1972–73, Perth W Aust from 1977
m Aber 4.3.67 Ian M. Ramsay MA 1962 *qv*

PIRIE James *BSc 1966

PIRIE James Gordon BSc 1968

PIRIE John Alexander MA 1962

PIRIE John Douglas *BSc 1961 MSc 1963 PhD 1965
s of Alexander A. P. MA 1891 *qv*; b Oldmeldrum 1.9.39
lect nat phil Aberd from 1965

PIRIE Michael Douglas MA 1968

PIRIE Sandra Isabel MA 1969

PIRIE Sheila Margaret MB ChB 1965
d of Richard T. P. BSc(eng) 1949 *qv*; b Aber 29.3.40
LMCC(C) 1967
h o: ARI 1965–66, Perth RI 1966; g p and Queensway gen hosp Toronto from 1966
m(1) Lyon—marr diss
(2) Toronto 24.12.76 William Zatelny MD(Tor) phys/surg s of Casimirus Z. Portage la Prairie Canada

PITTENDREIGH David William MA 1969
s of David P. eng and Elizabeth M. Porter; b Aber 5.3.48
Aber coll of educ 1969–70; RAEC: educ off. Rhyl 1970–73, Belf 1973–74, Paderborn W Ger 1974–75, inst army educ Lond 1976–77; RAEC centre Beaconsfield from 1977

PLASKETT William Baskerville BSc 1969
s of Vincent C. P. min of relig and Margery Baskerville; b Nott 14.5.45
med rep Lond 1970–73, prod. man. Guildford 1973–78; publisher from 1978
m Forfar 18.6.70 Marianne M. Langlands MA 1968 *qv*

PLOWMAN Michael BSc 1964
s of William P. comm vehicle salesman/eng and Barbara A. Smith; b Aber 9.2.42
teacher maths Northfield acad Aber from 1965
m Aber 25.3.67 Carol A. M. Dale d of John F. D. Aber

PLUCINSKA Teresa *BSc 1969
m Dorcey

PLUMMER Rachel Mary   *MA 1968 Dip Ed 1969
 d of Mark M. P. MA(Oxon) fam bus. man. and
Margaret Rhodes MA(Oxon); b Guernsey 7.12.45
teacher Engl Hove g s Sussex 1969–73; external examiner
for Lond 1972–74; AEB, Middx & Metropolitan from
1974
m Guernsey 11.7.67 Malcolm K. Redford MEd 1969 *qv*

PLUMMER Richard Henry   BSc(eng) 1963

PLUMMER Susan Jane   MA 1965
 d of Alfred P. comp dir and Dilys M. Jenkins; b
Tredegar 29.5.44
syst analyst IBM Lond 1965–69
m Oxford 30.9.67 John C. Brierley LLB 1964 *qv*

POCKLINGTON Trevor   MSc 1967 PhD 1969
 s of Ernest F. P. fitter and Edna M. Senior; b Hull
8.7.44
BSc(N'cle) 1966
res asst med phys Aberd from 1971
m Aber 5.2.73 Priscilla E. Buchan lab tech d of David
G. B. Aber

POGUE Hilary Margaret   *MA 1969
 d of Victor C. P. BA(Dub) par min/Baird res fell. and
Emmeline Houston BA(Dub) teacher; b Kirkwall 26.10.47
MPhil(Warw) 1973
trainee lib Dub univ (SCONUL) 1969–70; teacher Engl:
Musselburgh 1973, Inverkeithing from 1973
m Cumnock 13.10.73 Michael D. Attfield BSc(Wales)
med statist s of Leonard P. A. Barnet

POLE Francis George   *BSc 1969
 s of Peter P. merch seaman and Margaret H. Frazer;
b Shetland 25.5.47
serving off. RAF from 1969
m Lorna C. Davidson MA 1971

POLLARD Janet Evelyn   *BSc 1967

POLLARD John Henry   PhD 1961
 BSc(Brist)

POLLET John Eugene   BMedBiol 1969 MB ChB 1972
 s of Maurice P. DLitt(Paris) prof min/Engl lit and Myrtle F.
Roberts BSc(R'dg) lect Engl stud.; b Woolwich 14.2.47
h o Aber 1972–73; lect path. Dund 1973–74; sen h o
surg Aber 1974–76; regist surg Aber from 1976
m Oldmeldrum Sheena M. Blench BMedBiol 1969 *qv*

POLLITT Alastair Buchan   *BSc 1970 MEd 1975
 s of Arthur G. P. comm man./polit ag and Lesley S.
Buchan MA 1935 *qv*; b Aber 20.10.48
VSO teacher chem Berbice h s Guyana 1970–72; teacher
chem Auchmuty h s 1974–75; res assoc Godfrey Thomson
unit for acad assessment Edin from 1975

POLLOCK John Gordon   MB ChB 1964

POLLOCK Nigel James   LLB 1970
 s of George A. P. MB ChB(Glas) consult. orthop and
Nora E. Ogilvie; b 12.2.48
Edin: law app 1970–72; qualif asst solic from 1972

POLSON Donald   MA 1970

POLSON Hugh Alistair Edwin   MA 1968
 s of Hugh P. customs & excise off. and Roma St C.
Wakelin; b Birm 27.6.46
dept man. Marks & Spencer Aber 1968–69; asst brand
man. Baxter's of Speyside Fochabers 1969–71; market.
serv exec Stats (MR) Birm 1971–72; prod man.: Mettoy

Northampton 1972–74, Cadbury Schweppes Birm from
1974
m Macduff 8.8.70 Brenda Wood hairdresser d of Charles
W. Macduff

POLSON Janet   BEd 1970

POLSON Walter Angus   BSc 1970

PONT Alice   *BSc 1959
 d of Henry B. P. eng and Alice Cowie; b Aber 7.5.37
teacher: Aber acad 1960–64, Marlborough girls' coll
Blenheim NZ 1965–67; prin phys Lockerbie acad 1968–
73; asst rector Arbroath h s from 1973

PONT Henry Barnett   *BSc 1960 *MEd 1963
 b 3.5.38
ABPsS
teacher sc Ellon acad 1961–63; educ psych Midlothian
1963–65; res assoc Edin/Manc 1965–69; lect educ Leeds
1969–72; lect psych Strath from 1972
m Aber 1964 Helen A. Hall

POOLE Freda Joan   MA 1967
 d of William F. P. prop. bus. equipment comp and
Winifred M. Gill; b Aber 13.2.46
teacher Engl: Whitburn 1969–71, N Kelvinside s Glasg
1971–75; West Park s for deaf Crosshouse from 1979
m Glasg 1978 George Gardner BA(OU) distrib serv man./
prod. man. s of George G.

PORTEOUS William Gunn   *BSc 1969 PhD 1974

PORTER Angela Margaret Elizabeth   *MA 1970
 d of Thomas P. dist man. SW gas (Bath) and Pearl I.
Allen BA(Brist) teacher; b Cinderford 13.3.48
TEFL Larnaca Cyprus 1970–71; trg off. with Caltex (UK)
Lond from 1971
m Woodhouse Eaves 2.11.74 John S. Leslie MA 1970 *qv*

PORTER Jessie Pirrie   *MA 1960

PORTER John Frederick   PhD 1969
 s of Frederick A. P. eng and Edith M. Rhodes;
b Dunstable 22.2.41
BSc(St And) 1964 MIBiol 1970
post doct res fell. Aberd 1969–71; biomed res secy internat
plan. parenthood fed. Lond from 1971

PORTER Robert Duguid   BSc(eng) 1960
 s of Robert P. grocer and Elizabeth Duguid; b Insch
14.9.39
asst civ eng publ works Argyll 1960–66; sen asst eng
(water supply): Cirencester 1966–69, Chesterfield 1969–
74; supply eng Chesterfield from 1974
m Aber 4.7.61 Frances H. Burnett MA 1960 *qv*

PORTER Ronald Wayne   PhD 1970
 BA(Mt All) BD MTH(Pine Hill)

PORTER William Henderson   MA 1970

PORTFORS Ernest Andrew   MSc 1963
 BSc(Alta)

POTRATZ Gisela Barbara   *MA 1968
 d of Erich P. bank man. and Elisabeth Hartung acct;
b Greifswald W Ger 18.12.43
teacher Aber 1969–71
m Düsseldorf 16.12.66 Robert M. Cumming BSc(Edin)
lect s of Ian C. Edin

POTTER Eva-Maria *MA 1970
d of David S. P. FCO and Maria Hadner; b Klagenfurt
Austria 23.9.46
teacher: Lond 1972–73, Colwyn Bay from 1974

POTTER Kenneth Evan Duke BSc(eng) 1958

POTTINGER Norma MB ChB 1958
d of Thomas B. P. farm. and Annie P. Tait teacher;
b Stronsay Orkney 22.5.32
h o Woodend hosp Aber, ARI 1959 and 1961–62;
j h m o ARI 1962; locums Yorks, Caithness 1963–66;
g p Thurso from 1966
m Aber 18.12.57 Calum Mackay MB ChB 1960 *qv*

POULET Roger John *BSc 1967
s of Maurice V. P. diplomat and Edith M. Stober
teacher; b Lond 18.7.42
PhD(Cantab) 1970
Lond: scient civ serv DoE 1970–72, man. consult. Peat
Marwick Mitchell 1972–74, man. consult./dir Reid &
Timpson Assoc from 1974
m Knightsbridge 18.9.71 Rebecca M. Grant barrister d
of John W. H. G. E Twickenham

POWELL Roderick Walter Morrison MA 1969

POWELL Wilfred *BSc 1970 PhD 1973
s of Wilfred V. P. machine oper glass indust and Jessie
Critchley; b St Helen's 25.8.47
res asst for. dept Aberd from 1973
m St Helen's 4.7.70 Anne Farnen MA 1972 psych d of
Kenneth J. F. Eccleston Park

PRAGNELL Frederick Anthony *MA 1970 MEd 1972
s of Laurence H. P. civ serv and Mary Bowens; b Lond
31.1.47
MA(Lond) 1975
teacher: Fr/Lat Lond 1972–76, Engl with BAC Saudi
Arabia from 1976

PRATHIPASEN Ratchani MA 1960
BA(Bangkok)

PRATT George Michael *MA 1968
s of George A. P. solic/clerk to magistr and Jessie
Booth teacher; b Oswaldtwistle 7.1.45
VSO teacher Bo Sierra Leone 1968–70; sales exec for
Africa Longmans Group (publ) Harlow 1970–71; teacher
Blackpool collegiate g s from 1972
m Bolton 22.6.68 Philippa S. Bellis radiogr d of Thomas
B. B. Bolton

PRATT Michael Alexander MB ChB 1967
s of Alexander P. BSc(St And) lect and Mary R. V.
Wilson; b Cupar 20.5.44
MRCP 1972
h o, sen h o ARI 1967–69; med regist ARI 1969–71; g p
Aber from 1971
m Aber 4.11.71 Norma E. Hodder SRN d of A. Norman
H. Aber

PREMPEH Thomas Bonsu MB ChB 1966

PRENTICE Ian Miller LLB 1969
s of John D. P. secy and Elizabeth Miller secy; b Stirling
15.1.44
Edin; CA app 1969–73, acct from 1973
m Alloa 11.9.70 Shelagh A. Gordon MA 1967 *qv*

PRESHAW Colin Taylor MB ChB 1967

PRESHAW Roy McFarlane MB ChB 1959 MD 1965

PRESLY Alexander Hadden *BSc 1970
s of Alexander C. P. master butcher and Jeanette K.
Hadden; b Aber 3.11.48
Dip(Imp coll Lond) 1971 MSc(Lond) 1971 PhD(Birm)
1978
scient off. plant path. nat veg res stat Wellesbourne from
1971
m Sedgefield 19.4.76 Lorna Gray BSc(Trent-poly) tech
microbiol Lanchester poly Coventry d of William G.
Stockton-on-Tees

PRESLY Allan Smith *MA 1963
PhD(Edin)

PRESLY Graham Charles BSc(eng) 1968

PRESLY James Gordon *BSc 1970 Dip Ed 1971

PRESTON Stanley David cMB ChB 1960

PRICE Wilfred John MA 1964 Dip Ed 1965
s of Jesse P. bldr and Alice M. Bevan; b Crickadarn
18.8.23
teacher maths Aber acad/Hazlehead acad Aber 1965–72,
yearmaster from 1972
m Aber 18.9.48 Hazel Mitchell clerkess d of John M.
Aber

PRIMROSE Mary Marr MB ChB 1970
d of William S. P. works man. Brit Steel Corp and
Marjory M. Marr; b Glasg 2.4.46
m o publ health dept Nassau Bahamas 1970–71; fam
practice Dartmouth NS Canada from 1973
m Biggar 23.8.71 Hugh A. J. Roddis BSc(Lond) proj
man. eng Hermes Electronics s of John W. R. BSc(Lond)
St John's Newfoundland

PRIMROSE Robert Chalmers *MA 1956

PRINGLE Alexander Ferguson MB ChB 1960
s of Alexander F. P. MB ChB 1924 *qv*; b Aber 21.5.35
g p: Aber 1961–68, Lower Largo from 1968
m Anstruther 21.2.70 Margaret Williamson secy d of
James W. Glasg

PRINGLE Duncan Macmillan *BSc 1970
s of Alexander J. P. clerk of works and Christina
Macmillan shopkeeper; b Tarbert 24.4.47
teacher geog Perth h s 1971–73, asst prin guid 1973–77;
prin guid Perth acad from 1977
m Fraserburgh 24.7.71 Jean Gibb MA 1970 *qv*

PRINGLE James Craighead BL 1957
s of William E. P. woollen manuf and Beatrice M.
Craighead secy; b Inv 29.5.35
CA 1960
Inv: acct James Pringle woollen manuf 1960–61; asst
John C. Frame & Co CA, ptnr from 1962 (firm now
Frame, Kennedy & Forrest CA); sole pract James C.
Pringle & Co CA from 1977
m Aber 22.7.60 Maureen M. Taylor MA 1958 *qv*

PRINGLE Katherine Gibson *MA 1969
d of Alexander K. P. BSc(Glas) field geol, univ lect,
prof and Janet R. Templeton MA(Glas) teacher; b Aber
20.3.48
Dip Educ Psych(Glas) 1971
educ psych Glasg corp ch guid serv from 1971
m Glasg 19.7.72 Alexander H. Adam MB ChB(Glas)
med pract s of Alexander Y. A. MB ChB(Edin) Galashiels

PRINGLE Robert Macaulay MB ChB 1964

PRIOR Colin James BSc(eng) 1965
s of Frederick J. P. prod. eng and Elizabeth C. Reeves;
b Watford 8.9.43
MICE C Eng 1969
grad eng Babtie Shaw & Morton Workington, Glasg
1965–68; resid eng Leonard & Ptnrs Huddersfield 1968–
69; sen des eng, estimator Taylor Woodrow internat:
posts in Romania, Aust, Oman, now Lond from 1969
m 1976

PROCTOR David Wilson ᶜMB ChB 1961
s of Sydney S. P. MB ChB 1922 *qv* and Margaret J.
Rennet MB ChB 1923 *qv*; b Chester 6.9.34
DRCOG 1969 FFARCS 1968
h o ARI, Raigmore hosp Inv, Perth RI, RHSC Glasg
1961–64; ARI: regist med 1964–66, regist anaest 1966–69;
sen regist anaest WI Glasg 1969–71; consult. anaest WI
Glasg from 1971
m Hexham 20.10.73 Jennifer Coulson MB BS(Lond)
anaest d of Joseph R. C. Whitley Bay

PROCTOR Patricia Lawson MA 1956
m Davidson
d 27.4.62

PROSSER Alan James BSc 1970
s of James W. P. civ serv and Barbara Mitchell; b Aber
8.1.49
teacher maths Hilton acad Aber 1971–77; asst prin
maths Kincorth acad Aber from 1977
m 28.7.73 Dorothy E. Foote receptionist d of Eric C. F.
Peterborough

PROUD Ian Philip Saxby *MA 1967

PROUDFOOT James MB ChB 1958
s of James L. P. rep and Margaret G. Lawson; b Dun
3.8.34
MRCGP 1974
h o ARI 1958–59; m o RAF UK/Germany 1959–64;
med advis Roche pharm Basle Switzerland 1964–65; g p
Kirby Maxloe from 1965
m Anstruther 21.1.59 Catherine A. Fowler d of Thomas
F. Anstruther

PROUDFOOT Winifred MB ChB 1959
d of Frederick J. P. comp dir and Winifred Crawford;
b Carlisle 22.6.34
m Carlisle 19.8.61 Peter J. T. Tait BSc 1956 *qv*

PROUT Lesley Jean Margaret Honor MB ChB 1970
m McMillan

PULLICINO Mark *BSc(eng) 1969
s of Philip P. MBE diplomat, ambassador and Laura
Cavarra; b Malta 23.3.46
Dip BA(Edin) 1971 AMBIM 1974 MICE 1975 MEd(Mich)
1975
grad asst civ eng Valetta Malta 1969–70; civ eng/arch.
Berlin 1971–72, prof eng/arch. from 1972
m 1977 Katherine Mackenzie, Tain

PUNI Michael Kwaku Tufuor MB ChB 1967
s of Nana K. Y. P. cocoa farm. and Margaret Adade;
b Ntronang Ghana 24.5.35
h o Queen Mary hosp Sidcup 1967–68; Ghana: m o
Effia Nkwanta hosp Sekondi 1969, m o i/c health centre,
central prisons, boys' remand home Essikado, Sekondi,
Esipon 1969–70; m o i/c govt hosp/dist m o Tarkwa
1970–72; trainee Hammersmith s of hyg & trop med
Lond 1973–76; phys spec Cape Coast hosp 1976–78;
med dir Kwame Tufuor mem hosp Oda Ghana from
1978

m Accra 20.12.69 Agnes V. Ntiful teacher d of Paul N.
Akrofuom Ghana

PUNK Jozsef BSc 1960

PURANG Iswurdut MA 1960
s of Ramdutti P. trader and Savitri Ramphul; b Port
Louis Mauritius 22.4.36
Dip Soc Ad(LSE)
Port Louis: admin asst 1961–63; asst secy 1963–70, prin
asst secy 1970–71, prin p secy to prime min 1971–75;
perm secy from 1975
m Curepipe Mauritius 5.2.64 Yassoda Ramtohul teacher
d of Jaymohunt R. Curepipe

PURCELL Giles Barclay MA 1965

PURITCH George Sydney PhD 1969
s of George W. P. auto mech and Isabella Lamond;
b Perth 5.9.43
BSc(Vic BC) MSc(Mass) 1966
res scient DoE Can. for. serv Victoria BC from 1969
m Victoria BC –.5.67 Elaine L. Downey teacher d of
Clair D. Sidney BC

PURSELL Patricia Ann MA 1957
d of Wilfred A. P. shopkeeper and Ann Macleod; b
Lond 1.4.36
Is of Lewis: teacher: p s Leurbost j s 1958–62, s s Laxdale
j s 1965–66; spec class: Aird 1968–71, Nicolson inst
Stornoway 1971–73; remed reading Leurbost and other
p s from 1973
m Stornoway 31.3.60 Donald Macleod joiner s of Colin
M. Leurbost

PYATT David Graham *BSc(for) 1961 PhD 1978
s of David S. P. teacher and Constance N. Basford
teacher; b Cheadle 30.3.39
dist off. for. comm (soil surv): Alice Holt Lodge Farnham
1961–65; Edin 1965–68; dist off. soils res for. comm
northern res stat Roslin 1968–74, head of site stud. res
1974–77, sen scient off. from 1977
m Aber 17.7.65 Rosalind A. Hay MB ChB 1965 *qv*

PYLE David MA 1968 Dip Ed 1969
s of Robert M. P. plumbers' warehouseman and
Kathleen McHattie; b Aber 18.8.47
educ off. Kigezi h s Uganda 1969–71; teacher dep head
Engl Hereford s Grimsby from 1972
m Aber 11.9.65 Irene H. Chester teleph/secy d of Edward
H. C. Aber

PYLE Ronald Leslie MB ChB 1958
s of Thomas D. P. MB ChB(Glas) med pract and
Mary A. Leslie poultry advis; b Hamilton 29.11.34
DObstRCOG 1960
h o: city hosp Aber, Bridge of Earn hosp, RI Perth 1958–
60; short serv comm RAMC 1960–65; g p Blairgowrie
from 1965
m Annan 25.11.66 Morna G. C. Vivers teacher dom sc
d of Robert C. V. Annan

PYLE William Dryden MB ChB 1958
s of Thomas D. P. MB ChB(Glas) g p and Mary A.
Leslie poultry advis; b Hamilton 29.11.34
DObstRCOG 1964 MRCGP 1968
h o Inv, City hosp Aber 1958–59; regt m o 13/18 R
Hussars Malaya, Germany 1959–61; h o: Aber mat.
hosp 1961–62, RHSC Glasg, Kirkwall 1963–66; g p:
Camborne 1966–74, Canisbay from 1974
m Kirkwall 31.3.66 Jacqueline I. T. Turfus SRN d of
John T.

PYPER Joy Patricia   MA 1970
m Aber 8.8.80 Norman J. Dunbar

PYPER Robert Ferguson   *BSc 1969

QAYUM Abdul   MLitt 1969
MA(Panj)

QUINN Kevin   BSc 1968

QURASHI Afzal Ahmad   MB ChB 1963
  s of Mohammed Rafique supt GIP rly Jhansi India
and Bano Begum; b Jhansi 10.4.37
BSc(Sind Kar)
h o Woodend hosp Aber, ARI, Bellshill mat. hosp 1964–
65; sen h o Kingseat hosp Aber 1965–66; m o City hosp
Kano Nigeria 1966–69; prin in g p Witham from 1969
m Inv 19.2.66 Maureen Smart

RADCLIFFE Elaine Barbara   *MA 1967
  d of Percy R. farm. member House of Keys (Manx
parl) and Barbara F. Crowe; b Ramsey I of M 2.4.43
part-time lect tech coll Carlisle 1968–69, stud. lib Napier
coll Edin from 1975
m Sulby I of M 12.8.67 Michael W. Cartney BSc(eng)
1966 qv

RADDON David John   *MA 1970

RAE Alison Christine   MA 1964
  d of Alan G. R. oil well eng and Aileen M. Henderson
MA 1925 qv; b Digboi Assam India 14.5.43
teacher Edin 1965–69
m Aber 29.7.66 William A. R. Mutch MA 1963 qv

RAE Alison Fay   MA 1962
  d of Bennett B. R. MA 1926 qv; b Aber 27.7.41
asste Lycée St Jean d'Angély, France 1962–63; teacher:
Montreal h s 1964–66, Ellon acad 1966–67, Cranhill s s
Glasg 1967–70
m Aber 10.4.68 Alan M. Lamont MA 1960 qv

RAE Angus Chisholm   BSc(agr) 1960 MSc 1962
  s of Donald J. R. grain merch and Annie Adam;
b Perth 10.7.38
grass breeder min of agr (NI) Loughgall 1962–63; plant
breeder with Sinclair McGill Ayr from 1963
m Perth 2.5.64 Alison M. Brooke MA(Edin) teacher d of
Peter T. B. Perth

RAE Annetta   MA 1966
  d of Charles S. R. elect. welder and Margaret
McGinley ch nurse; b Glasg 31.3.45
teacher: Summerhill acad 1967–69, Wainwright h s
Alberta Canada from 1969
m Aber 15.8.69 Donald M. Mackee BEd(Alta) teacher
s of John J. M. Dornoch

RAE Beverley Anne   BEd 1970
  d of Arthur C. R. BSc(BC) corp vice-pres and Joy V.
Robinson; b Paterson NJ USA 22.10.48
teacher Engl Kapuskasing h s Ont Canada from 1972
m Kapuskasing 22.6.73 Gérard Lalonde BEd(Montr)
teacher

RAE Doreen Anne   MA 1968 Dip Ed 1969
  d of George M. W. R. contr and Annie M. Laird;
b Insch 1.11.47
Aber: qual control asst 1969–70, teacher 1970, exec off.
civ serv (supp benefits) 1970–76
m Aber 14.4.72 David J. Cameron BSc 1973 lect RGIT
s of Thomas J. D. C. Aber

RAE Gordon   *MEd 1969
  s of John R. insur ag and Marion Dow nurse; b Rutherglen 21.7.45
BSc(Glas) 1967
teacher phys Aber 1969–71; lect educ psych Aber coll of
educ from 1971

RAE Gordon Hogarth   *BSc 1970
  s of Robert R. comp dir and Margaret N. Gordon;
b Huntly 10.4.47
fish farm. res: exper ecologist Unilever Lochailort from
1971

RAE Ian Livingstone   *BSc 1968
  s of William H. R. customs and excise off. and Irene B.
Bowler; b Birkenhead 30.11.46
MSc(Strath) 1971
res asst Strath 1969–70; geol Noranda Kerr Portmadoc
1971–72; stud. teacher Glasg 1972; teacher: geog Glasg
1972–75, head of soc stud. Morant Bay Jamaica 1975–77,
geog Stirling from 1977
m Blairlogie 9.12.78 Jane C. McLearie teacher d of James
McG. McL. Clydebank

RAE John Edward   MA 1965
  s of William M. R. MA(Glas) asst chief constable and
Grace B. Hutchison secy; b Glasg 24.5.44
CA 1970
CA Arthur Young McLelland Moores & Co Glasg 1970–
72; govt audit. of Tonga Nuko'Alofa 1972–74; man.
Thomson McLintock & Co CA Inv 1974–79; ptnr
Morris & Young CA Perth from 1980
m Brora 17.10.70 Margaret C. Munro MA 1967 qv

RAE Maureen   MA 1959
  d of Douglas H. S. R. master baker and Jessie Guyan;
b Aber 11.12.37
MEd(Exe) 1978
teacher: Engl/hist East Kilbride 1964–66, Glasg 1966–67;
lect Leic 1967–68; head Engl dept Slough 1968–70; lect
Engl Rolle coll Exmouth 1970–74, sen lect from 1974
m Largs 2.7.60 Sean Oliver (later called Lalor) liaison off.
Dartmoor nat park s of John Oliver

RAE Norman John   BSc 1967
  s of Francis J. R. foreman stonemason and Mary B. K.
Morrison shop asst; b Kintore 18.1.46
teacher maths/sc Kintore 1968–73; statist. Grampian
police Aber from 1973

RAE Patricia   MA 1970
  d of Alexander R. wholesale egg merch and Myra
Webster bookkeeper; b Aber 27.12.48
teacher geog Aber from 1971
m Aber 3.4.71 Alexander C. Wilson fish merch s of
Alexander W. Aber

RAE Richard Bennet   *BSc 1969
  s of Bennet B. R. MA 1926 qv; b Aber 12.11.46
scient off. MoD (PE) AWRE Aldermaston from 1969

RAE Richard Gordon   *MA 1964
  s of Richard S. R. grocer and Mary A. Jamieson
nurse; b Aber 23.11.32
LTCL 1960
teacher geog: Turriff acad 1965–67, Wallace Hall acad
Dumfriessh 1967–73, Lawside RC acad Dun 1973–77,
Menzieshill h s Dun from 1977
m Aber 10.9.68 Margaret M. Fraser civ serv d of William
M. F. Aber

RAE Spence   MA 1960

RAE William Philip   MA 1970
s of William N. M. R. foreman eng and Audrey Philip clerkess; b Aber 7.12.48
teacher geog/hist/mod stud. Torry acad Aber from 1971
m Aber 16.10.71 Eileen M. Andrews secy d of Frederick M. S. A. Aber

RAFFAN Diana Marjory   MA 1961
d of George A. R. men's outfitter and Betty K. Lamb; b Aber 20.12.40
teacher Bradford 1961–62, Aber 1962–64
m Aber 31.7.61 Donald I. MacKay MA 1959 *qv*

RAFFAN Jennifer Twort   MA 1967
d of Alfred W. R. MB ChB 1938 *qv* and Jean C. Twort MB ChB 1939 *qv*; b Aber 10.11.45
Dip Secy St(Strath) 1968
secy: FCO Lond 1968–70, Brit emb Vienna 1970–72, centre for indust consult. and liaison univ of Edin 1973–74
m Aber 22.9.72 Anthony G. D. Johnston BA(Oxon) CA s of Hon Lord Douglas H. J. MA(Oxon) Edin

RAFFAN Rosemary Frances   MA 1970
m Norfolk

RAHMAN Quazi Abu Taher Muhammad Habibur   PhD 1965
s of Quazi S. Ahmed marr regist and Saleha Khatun; b Jhalakati Bangladesh 16.7.36
BSc(Dacca) 1958 MSc(Dacca) 1959 F Zool Soc Bangladesh 1974
Bangladesh: asst prof zool govt coll Sylhet 1965–68, Titumir coll Dacca 1969, Jagannath coll Dacca 1970–74; assoc prof zool Jagannath univ coll from 1975
m Dacca 27.10.68 Sufia Rahman d of Muhammad A. W. MSc(agr)(Calc) India

RAITT David Gordon   MB ChB 1969
s of William J. R. MB ChB 1924 *qv*; b Aber 28.3.46
DA 1973
h o Aber 1969–70; m o RAF: Ballykelly NI 1970–71, Masirah Oman 1971–72; anaest RAF Ely Cambs from 1972
m Aber 1969 Elizabeth S. Davies MA 1969 *qv*

RAITT Douglas Ferrier Stewart   *BSc 1957 PhD 1967
d Rome 27.11.76 *AUR* XLVII 215

RAITT John Stewart   *BSc 1962
s of William J. R. MBChB 1925 *qv*; b Aber 13.6.39
Aust: geophys bureau of min resources Melbourne, Canberra 1962–65, Continental Oil Co Sydney 1965–68; Conoco: geophys Lond 1968–70, staff geophys Princeton USA 1970–72, area geophys Stamford USA 1972–74, man. geophys Cairo Egypt from 1974

RAKHA Ahmed Mohamed Hassan   PhD 1965
BVSc(Cairo) FRVCS(Stockholm)

RALPH Alan John   BSc 1970
s of Issac R. fisherman and Marion Snook; b Somerset 13.2.49
acct Edin from 1970
m Elgin 14.7.72 Susan M. Grant teacher d of Donald G. Elgin

RALPH Alison Joyce   MA 1966
d of Thomas D. M. R. fisherman and Jessie S. Main nurse; b Elgin 28.8.45
teacher Fr/Engl Grantown g s 1967–68
m Burghead 19.7.68 Harry M. Ross BVMS(Edin) vet surg s of Alexander M. R. MA(Edin) Bonnyrigg

RALPH Marion Jean   MA 1966
d of Isaac R. fisherman and Marion W. J. Snook retail asst/WRNS; b Butleigh 23.11.45
teacher Fr Peterhead acad from 1967
m Burghead 12.7.68 Michael J. McLintock MA 1968 *qv*

RAMADAN Isfendiar   BSc 1960

RAMANATHAN Manickavasagar   MB ChB 1961

RAMANATHAN Markandu   MB ChB 1963

RAMANATHAN Perumal Chetty   MSc 1964
BSc(agr)(Madras)

RAMCHARAN Conrad   MB ChB 1966

RAMM Halldis Aslaug   MB ChB 1963
d of Finn Kielland R. capt and Aslaug Ekeland; b Bergen Norway 1.10.37
DCH(Glas) 1969 DRCOG 1977
h o ARI, RACH 1963–64; g p: Fyvie 1965–66, Insch 1966–76; sen h o obst/gyn Raigmore hosp Inv 1976–77; g p Insch from 1977
m Fana Norway 25.7.61 Maitland Mackie BSc(agr) 1958 *qv*

RAMNAUTH Coomar Surendra   *BSc(eng) 1969
s of Jai R. priest and Bhanmatie Sungh; b Guyana 5.11.44
eng MoW and commun Georgetown, Guyana from 1969
m Guyana 17.12.72 Sattie Sankar d of Kayman S. Essequibo Guyana

RAMSAY Andrew Douglas Kirk   *MA 1970 Dip Ed 1973
s of William N. M. R. BSc(Edin) univ lect and Janet D. K. MacKendrick hosp sister; b Edin 5.7.47
MA(Manit) 1974 MEd(Tor) 1974
head warden Fetlar nature reserve Shetland 1972; teacher Edin, Lochaber h s Fort William, Kirkwall g s from 1975

RAMSAY Iain McRobert   MSc 1970
s of John C. R. foreman joiner and Katherine J. McRobert nurs. sister; b Aber 18.2.44
Dip Arch.(RGIT) 1968 RIBA 1974 ARIAS 1975
lect arch. RGIT Aber 1970–73; arch./plan. Baxter, Clark & Paul Aber 1973–74; lect arch. RGIT from 1974
m Aber 27.8.71 Sandra A. Reid school matron, hotel housekeeper, shop man. d of Alexander R. Aber

RAMSAY Ian McKay   MA 1962
s of William R. R. wine & spirit merch and Agnes S. Hill; b Dun 14.6.26
teacher hist AGS 1963–72, asst head 1972–74; sen master educ dept W Aust Perth; prin Carmel s Perth WA from 1976
m Aber 4.3.67 Isobel Pirie MA 1960 *qv*

RAMSAY Keith Michael Moynihan   *MA 1958
s of Andrew M. R. MA 1923 *qv*; b Molleno Cape Province S. Af 5.12.33
LRAM(Sp and Drama) 1973
teacher Engl Finchley 1959–62; Surrey: head Engl/drama Frenshaw Heights 1962–73, artistic dir W Surrey youth theatre 1957–73, drama dir Dolmetsch festival 1973–74; lect drama Bishop Grosseteste coll of educ Lincoln from 1973
m West Wittering 13.7.57 Isabella M. O. Richards MA 1958 *qv*

RAMSAY Roderick Alan Macgregor   *MA 1964

RAMSAY William Alexander   *MA 1956
d 29.6.69

RANDALL Ian Maurice   MA 1968 *1970
s of Leslie R. evangelist and Jeannie Ewen; b Wick
9.1.48
telecommun man. Lond 1970–72; admin elect. Brighton
from 1972
m Aber 31.7.70 Janice B. Hughes MA 1970 qv

RANDALL Richard Frank   *BSc(eng) 1967
s of Rex C. R. chartered surv/eng and Ethel Price;
b Luton 28.2.45
MICE 1973
asst eng Sidcup 1967–69; site eng Mombasa Kenya 1969–
71; des eng Lond 1971–73; sect. eng Potter's Bar Lond
from 1973
m Harpenden 15.7.72 Charmian L. Houslander-Green
BSc(S'ton) admin off. d of Derrick G. G. Kingswear

RANKIN Beryl Margaret Morton   MA 1963
m McKay

RANKIN Bryan John   MA 1966
s of Gerald M. R. pedigree cattle breeder/farm./comp
dir and Sheena M. Brown; b Dumfries 14.7.45
CA 1969
Robertson & Maxtone Graham CA Edin: app CA 1966–
69, qualif asst 1969–70, asst man. 1970–71, man. 1971–73,
ptnr from 1973
m Aber 10.7.65 Kathleen E. Savage MA 1965 qv

RANKIN James   MA 1965

RANKIN Sandra Mary   MA 1969
d of Alexander I. R. fish salesman and Mary J. Craig
shop asst; b Stonehaven 16.11.47
teacher maths: Peterhead acad 1970–72, Fraserburgh
acad 1972–75
m Aber 2.7.71 John A. MacKinnon LLB 1968 qv

RAO Hebbule Venkola Gundu   PhD 1963
MSc(Mysore)

RAPP Sandra Louise   MA 1968

RATTRAY George Cheyne   BSc(eng) 1960
s of George C. R. confectioner and Arthurina (Effie)
Strachan clerkess; b Fraserburgh 6.2.39
MICE 1966
asst eng: Sir M. MacDonald & Ptnrs Norfolk 1960–61,
Wm Tawse Banff/Aber 1961–62, Scot. dev dept Edin,
Fort William 1962–65; asst resid eng Notts c c Cromwell
1965; Reid, Carter & Wilson: eng i/c Perth, Edin,
Amersham from 1965, ptnr from 1969
m Denver 25.8.65 Ann Watson teacher d of Leslie R. W.
Denver Norfolk

RATTRAY Graham Alexander Lindsay   BSc(eng) 1968

RATTRAY Jennifer Elizabeth   MA 1962
d of John B. R. pharm and Jessie D. George; b Elgin
27.5.41
Cert Secy Sc(Strath) 1963
Edin: secy/edit. asst Accountants' Magazine 1963–65, secy
to sen ptnr Brodie, Cuthbertson & Watson WS 1965–68;
Lond: secy to mineral broker 1968–71, pers asst to
G. L. Bourne FRCS FRCOG Harley Street from 1971
m Russell

RAVEN John   *BSc 1959

RAVEN Norman   MA 1969 LLB 1971
s of Norman R. eng and Helen Buchan shop asst;
b Fraserburgh 8.8.48
law app Fraserburgh 1971–73; solic Blairgowrie 1973–74;
govt solic Edin from 1974
m Lonmay 17.10.75 Margaret B. Duthie MA 1969 qv

RAWSTHORNE George Brian   MB ChB 1965
s of Joseph L. R. bldg contr and Caroline D. Ball;
b Woolton Liv 5.5.37
FRCSE 1968 FRCS 1973
h o, sen h o Aber 1965–68; surg regist, sen surg regist Liv
1968–73; consult. surg Crewe from 1973
m Tain 10.9.66 Anne M. Mackenzie MB ChB 1965 qv

RAYMOND Barbara Pearl   MA 1962
d of Emmanuel C. R. plant supt and Violet E. R.
Gloudon; b Labrea Trinidad 27.5.37
teacher St Francois girls' s Port of Spain Trinidad 1962–
64, Georgetown Guyana: teacher St Rose's h s 1964–65,
St Joseph's h s 1965–67, Tutorial h s 1968–69; clerical
asst Trinidad Tobago high comm 1971–72; teacher
Providence girls' h s Port of Spain 1973–75, acting vice-
prin from 1975
m Port of Spain 31.10.64 Edwin A. Jack BSc 1963 qv

REA Alan Michael   *BSc 1970

READ Margaret   MA 1968 Dip Ed 1969
d of Jack R. publ man. and Doris E. Cooper; b
Richmond 1.12.43
teacher Aber: head mod lang dept Rosemount s s 1969–
72, year mistress Summerhill acad 1972–73; teacher Fr
Amer s Singapore 1974–76, Bundaberg Queensland
Aust 1976
m Wokingham 31.8.68 Errol H. Gomes BSc 1967 qv

REAMSBOTTOM Stanley Baily   *BSc 1968

REAPER Leslie James   BSc(eng) 1970

REARY James Brown   *BSc 1967 PhD 1970
s of James B. R. insur supt and Margaret R. Walker;
b Fraserburgh 2.5.44
res fell.: univ of Virginia USA 1970–71, univ of Exeter
1971–73; sen residue analyst Fisons, Chesterford Park
res stat from 1973
m Galashiels 25.7.70 Lilias T. Amos BEd 1969 qv

REASON Janet Mary   BSc 1964
d of Eric F. R. insur dir and Violet E. Walker;
b Worthing 19.11.42
asst clin path. ARI 1964–65; asst biochem Fisons Holmes
Chapel Cheshire, Loughborough 1966–71
m Lond 12.10.68 Peter G. Killingback MSc(Manc) MPS
res biol s of Ernest K. BSc(Lond) Enfield

REDFERN Derek Briddon   *BSc(for) 1963

REDFORD Malcolm Kenneth   *MEd 1970
s of Leonard K. R. BA(S'ton) dir educ and Mary
Gardner; b S'ton 29.12.44
BSc(econ)(Hull) 1967 M Psych Soc 1970
teacher econ Hove g s from 1969; external examiner
AEB from 1973, Oxford from 1976
m Guernsey 11.7.67 Rachel M. Plummer MA 1968 qv

REDSHAW Edward Stephen   *BSc 1958
s of George E. R. livestock off. Jamaica and Mary V.
Thomson; b Jamaica 24.9.35
M Agr(C Rica) 1965 PhD(Alta) 1968
agr off. govt Jamaica 1958–63; farms supt Reynold

Jamaica mines 1968–70; Canada: res assoc Alta 1970–73; head plant sect. soil and feed testing lab govt of Alberta from 1973
m Kingston 2.9.59 Marguerite A. Silvera hair stylist d of Chandos J. S. Jamaica

REECE Anne Pauline   *MA 1969

REED Alexander Cheyne   *MA 1957

REEKIE Gladys   *MA 1956
d of Richard M. R. travel courier, shipping clerk and Vera I. Faulkner shorthand typist; b Aber 25.3.34
Aber: lib asst 1956–57, spec tech reader to printer AUP from 1957
m Aber 29.3.63 George S. Menhinick civ serv

REES Wendy Anne   MSc 1966
BSc(Lond)

REEVES Thomas Joseph   PhD 1966
BA(S Carolina) BD(Columb)

REIACH Maureen Annand   MA 1961
m Johnston

REID Alan   MA 1967
s of William R. bank man. and Ellen S. Dunnett; b Edin 21.5.46
Dip Pers Man.(RGIT) 1968
pers off.: Manc 1968–73, Balloch 1973; reg pers off./training man. Glasg from 1973
m Manc 10.10.70 Linda Slater secy d of Harry K. S. Stretford Manc

REID Alan Robert   MB ChB 1966
s of Robert R. comm trav and Catherine M. Craigmile; b Aber 22.11.43
h o Aber hosps 1966–67; g p: Aber 1967–68, Wick 1968–75, Cumbernauld 1975–76; indust m o Middlesbrough from 1977
m Aber 29.12.65 Mary R. Halley MA 1963 *qv*

REID Alice Margaret Chree   MA 1957
d of Charles J. R. farm. and Mary Cockburn MA 1929 *qv*; b Stonehaven 8.10.36
teacher Kincardinesh 1958–62; secy SCSS Islay 1971–73; teacher Perth from 1978
m Aber 8.10.59 Alexander S. Collie MA 1954 *qv*

REID Alison Alexandra Margaret   *MA 1969
d of William R. civ serv and Margaret B. Smith nurse; b Irvine 26.8.47
LRAM 1970
teacher mus: Banff 1970–71, Elgin 1971–74; asst mus organis Moray and Nairn 1974–76; teacher mus Elgin 1976–77
m Elgin 26.7.75 William G. Knox marine eng s of William C. K. New Elgin

REID Alison Anne   MA 1970
d of Alexander R. gen merch and Christabel M. Stuart secy; b Aber 30.1.49
teacher Engl/relig educ Bankhead acad 1971–72
m Aber 31.8.70 William A. McWhirr MA 1971 teacher bus. stud. s of Peter F. McW. Banff

REID Atholl   *BSc(eng) 1964

REID Christina Legge   MA 1956
d of Thomas R. farm. and Eleanor A. McIntosh; b Rathven 22.5.36

teacher: Portessie j s s 1957–60, Lhanbryde j s s 1961–62, asst head Heathery Knowe p s from 1963
m Buckie 12.4.60 Donald S. Miller caterer s of William M. Wick

REID David Douglas   MB ChB 1957
s of Douglas R. rly clerk and Janet W. Stephen nurse; b Huntly 28.4.33
FRCGP 1968
h o: ARI, RACH 1957–58, Latrobe Tasmania 1959–61; g p Alford 1961–64; Tasmania: dist m o Maydena 1964–65, g p Wynyard from 1965
m Cooee Tasmania 3.4.61 Anne Turnidge teacher d of Leonard E. T. Burnie Tasmania

REID David Jackson   MA 1969
s of Eric W. R. BMus(Edin) teacher and Isobel S. Jackson BMus(Edin) teacher; b Edin 12.3.48
CA 1975
acct Edin from 1969
m Edin 7.10.72 Inez G. Henderson SRN d of James H. Runcorn

REID Dennis   MB ChB 1967

REID Derek Donald   MA 1967

REID Doreen Violet   *MA 1964
m Presly

REID Dorothea Lesley Thomson   MA 1969
d of John R. acct and Maria A. Smith teacher; b Peterhead 27.8.48
Dip Sec(City of Lond poly); MInst Health Serv Admin
Lond: secy: to chmn/man. dir Astor Petrochem 1970–71; to head of man. dev Brit inst of man. 1971–72; gen admin asst Hammersmith hosp 1972–75; dep sector admin St Mary's hosp from 1975

REID Dorothy Joan   *MA 1970 Dip Ed 1971
d of Albert G. R. asst distill man. and Harriet Simpson; b Rhynie 15.6.48
teacher maths Inverurie acad 1971–74
m Kennethmont 14.7.73 Ian D. Pirie farm. s of Ian D. P. Turriff

REID Duncan Harman   BSc(agr) 1957
s of Walter A. R. farm. and Christine N. Harman; b Brechin 4.9.35
nat serv UK, Christmas Is 1957–59; anim nutrit dept (farms) J. Bibby & Sons Liv 1960–65; poultry farm. Perth 1965–71, poultry and gen farm. Brechin from 1971
m Southport 17.8.62 Brenda M. Hughes BA(Liv) teacher d of Frederick H. Southport

REID Eileen Mary   *MA 1965
d of Joseph R. and Elsie M. McKenzie; b Ellon 6.5.44
teacher geog/Engl Bankhead acad 1966–67; head geog dept Murang'a s s Kenya 1968–69; acting prin teacher geog Northfield acad Aber 1971–72; teacher remed maths Summerhill acad from 1973
m Aber 23.3.67 James W. Lorimer MA 1964 *qv*

REID Eric James   MA 1957 PhD 1961
d 20.8.70 *AUR* XLIV 112

REID Euphemia Mitchell   MA 1968
d of William M. R. range oper MoD and Jessie B. McLean; b Rosehearty 3.4.47
teacher: Rosehearty p s 1969–70, Scotstown p s Aber from 1970
m Aber 5.9.68 James Taylor DA teacher sculpture/ceramics s of James T. Rosehearty

REID Gavin Clydesdale   *MA 1969

REID George Gordon   *MA 1968
   s of George R. burgh surv and Gertrude P. Scott;
b Forfar 20.11.46
Dip Pers Man.(RGIT) 1970
labourer Aber 1968–69; naval off. from 1970

REID George Greig Forbes   *MA 1961 MEd 1965

REID George Guilland   *BSc(eng) 1969
   s of George T. H. R. DD 1969 qv; b Edin 25.11.46
MSc(UCNW) 1970 MIEE C Eng 1975
des eng indust dev unit UCNW Bangor 1970–72; consult.
marine consults. YARD Glasg from 1972

REID George William   *MA 1967
   s of William R. papermaking machineman and Ethel
Young; b Aber 15.7.44
PhD stud. King's coll Lond 1967–69; lect phil univ of
IFE, Ile-Ife Nigeria 1969–72; asst rep Brit Council
Maseru, Lesotho from 1972
m Blackburn Aberdeensh 24.6.67 Sheila E. Sim MA 1967

REID Gordon Findlay   MB ChB 1968
   s of Alfred R. bank man. and Emil Catherine Findlay;
b Aber 6.8.45
FRCSE 1972
h o, sen h o ARI 1968–72; regist surg: N'cle hosps 1972–
73, ARI 1973–76; regist urology N'cle 1976–78; res
fell. Inst of Urology Lond from 1979

REID Hamish George   *BSc(eng) 1968
   s of James W. R. chief clerk of works Aber c and
Isabella C. Kennedy leg. secy; b Aber 3.2.46
asst civ eng: Scott Wilson Kirkpatrick & Ptnrs Lond
1968–69, Glasg corp 1969–76, sen civ eng Strath reg c
from 1976
m Glasg 21.3.70 Marjory E. Murchie MA 1968 qv

REID Hamish Peter   BSc(agr) 1959

REID Ian Maitland   BSc(agr) 1963
   s of Adam M. R. man. dir and Catherine C. Walker;
b Aber 5.11.41
Master Nutrit Sc(Corn) 1965 PhD(Corn) 1967
res asst Cornell univ 1963–67; post doct fell. Pittsburg s
of med 1967–70; exper path. ARC Newbury from 1970
m Aber 20.8.66 Sally M. Paterson nurse d of George
A. P. Aber

REID Ian Stewart   MA 1966 *1968

REID Ida Engel   MA 1970
        (conferred for long service of exceptional merit)
   d of Ernest V. Tetzner and Barbara Henderson; b Aber
11.7.05
member of admin staff Aberd 1929–70

REID Ivan William   *BSc 1969

REID James Bruce   BSc(eng) 1969

REID James Bryce   *MA 1967
   s of Gavin B. R. bank cashier and Emily E. Graham;
b Glasg 12.4.41
MSc(H-W) 1969
town plan. asst. asst Scot. dev off. Edin 1969–71; asst town
plan. Glasg 1971–74; developer Nairobi from 1974
m Edin 29.3.70 Mary Magrys secy

REID James Dures   *MA 1969
   s of James T. R. BL(Glas) solic and Ann Dures;

b Aber 9.4.47
NCB: admin asst 1969–71; Harrow: acct-opencast exec
1971–74, head contr sect.-opencast exec 1974–78; purchasing and contr man. Lond from 1978

REID James Milroy   BSc 1967 *MEd 1972
   s of David R. clerk and Mary Milroy; b Glasg 23.3.46
teacher Torry acad 1968–73; educ psych: Aber ch guid
centre 1973–74, Suffolk s psych serv Bury St Edmunds
from 1974
m Aber –.11.68 Moira K. Farquharson MA 1971 d of
John F. Aber; marr diss 1974

REID Joan Heather   *MA 1957

REID Joan McKenzie   MA 1963
   d of Joseph R. woollen mill worker and Elsie A. A.
McKenzie; b Ellon 16.1.42
teacher Aber: Engl Summerhill acad 1964–70, prin guid
Summerhill acad 1970–71, prin remed Northfield acad
from 1979
m Aber 15.7.64 Alexander J. Sadler MA 1961 qv

REID John   MB ChB 1959 MD 1967
   s of Stanley R. comp dir and Hilda Wood; b Leeds
15.3.33
h o Woodend hosp Aber, Nott city hosp 1959–60; lt,
capt RAMC Cyprus 1960–63; regist dermat Bradford RI
1963–65; Squibb res fell. skin hosp Manc 1965–67; g p/
dermat Jersey CI from 1967
m Cyprus 18.2.60 Alice P. A. Chua d of Kai Hai C.
Singapore

REID (Iain) John Cowie Dunlop   *BSc 1967 MSc 1970
   s of John D. R.; b Buckie 10.11.44
asst tech man. Harlow from 1974

REID John Geddes   *MA 1966
   s of John R. joiner and Mary Geddes; b Buckie 13.9.44
teacher geog: Powis s s Aber, Tertowie resid s 1967–68,
Aberlour s s, Mortlach s s 1968–69, A. N. Myer s s
Niagara Falls Can 1969–71, Maxwellton h s 1971–73,
Kirkcaldy h s, Balwearie h s from 1973
m Inv 4.4.69 Anne M. Barton BEd 1969 qv

REID John MacBean   *MA 1961
   s of John R. acct and Maria A. Smith teacher; b
Peterhead 3.11.38
Rowntree Mackintosh: market asst 1961–65, brand man.
1965–69, prod. group man. 1969–77, market dir from
1977
m York 17.10.64 Norma F. Kendall clerk d of Joseph K.
York

REID John Mackay   MSc 1964
   A H-W C

REID John Paul   *BSc 1968 MSc 1970

REID John Sinclair   *BSc 1964 PhD 1970
   s of Norman S. R. CA and Mildred E. Watkis;
b Rickmansworth 9.5.42
lect nat phil Aberd from 1968
m Aber 24.9.70 Aenea J. Nicol PhD 1974 progr advis d
of Anderson N. MA(Glas)

REID John Spence Grant   *BSc 1964 PhD 1967
   s of John G. R. painter/decorator and Helen Spence;
b Huntly 27.3.42
Royal Society European progr fell. univ of Fribourg
Switzerland 1967–69; asst lect biochem Nott 1967–69,
chef de travaux (lect) inst de Biologie Végétale univ of

Fribourg 1970–73; lect biochem Stir from 1974
m Aber 24.7.64 Maureen Donald BSc 1966 *qv*

REID Katharine Isabella   MA 1956
   m MacLennan

REID Kathleen Ann   *MA 1969
   d of John C. N. R. fish merch and Frances K. Horne
teacher; b Aber 12.10.46
Dip Soc Admin(Liv) 1970 Dip App Soc Stud.(Dund) 1971
med soc worker: Stracathro hosp Brechin, ARI 1971–72,
part-time ARI from 1974
m Aber 14.4.71 Colin D. Sinclair MB ChB 1971 g p s
of David C. S. MB ChB(St And) Perth W Aust

REID Kenneth Bannerman Milne   *BSc 1965 PhD 1968
   s of John R. acct and Maria A. Smith teacher; b
Peterhead 22.9.43
scient off. fisheries biochem res unit Aber 1968–69; ICI
res fell. biochem Oxon 1969–71; MRC immunochem
unit dept biochem Oxon: member MRC scient staff from
1971
m Aber 10.9.69 Margery R. Gilmour lab tech d of
Thomas G. Aber

REID Lorna Anne   MA 1965 Dip Ed 1966
   m Brown

REID Margaret Elspeth   *MA 1970
   d of Norman S. R. CA and Mildred E. Watkis secy;
b Watford 28.9.46
res asst Aberd 1970–71; post grad stud. Edin 1971–73;
lect med sociol Glas from 1973
m Glasg David F. Hamilton BSc(Edin) lect s of David
A. H. BA(Lond) Bury St Edmunds

REID Marjory Blair   *MA 1969
   m Dooley

REID Mary Catherine   *MA 1957
   d of Charles A. R. gardener and Elspeth R. Jaffray;
b Insch 19.12.35
teacher Walsall 1959–61
m Aber 7.10.61 William M. Broomfield BSc(eng) 1959 *qv*

REID Maureen   MA 1970
   d of Walter Reid sen insp and Dorothy W. Thomson;
b Aber 30.5.49
teacher Engl Karlshamn Sweden 1971–73; civ serv/
receptionist PER 1974; typist (Swedish and Spanish)
mod lang dept Aberd 1974–75, sen secy from 1975
m Aber 1.7.70 Stig Z. Fritzon chem eng s of Valter K. F.
Karlshamn

REID Norman Haydn   LLB 1969
   s of Harry R. civ serv and Marjory G. Christie;
b Aber 16.3.48
CA 1973
fin. acct Kleinerts of Europe Perth 1973–74; man. acct
Scotsman publ Edin 1974–76; asst acct St Cuthbert's
Co-op Assoc 1976–78; chief acct Northern Co-op Soc
Aber from 1979
m Aber 28.7.71 Patricia C. Robertson MA 1970 *qv*

REID Robert Leslie   PhD 1957
   BSc BAgr(Belf)

REID Robert Thomas Fraser   *MA 1969

REID Robin Davidson   *MA 1969
   s of Robert R. eng and Jessie E. Davidson MA 1928
qv; b Cairo 22.11.46

MA(Lond) 1973
teacher hist: Pollards Hill h s Mitcham 1970–74, Kingsdale s Dulwich Lond from 1974
m Aber 28.8.70 Elizabeth M. McConachie MA 1969 *qv*

REID Stella Frances   MA 1970
   d of Alexander W. R. tea planting advis and Mary E.
Simpson teacher; b S India 21.9.49
teacher: drama Edin 1971–73; Engl Örebro Sweden
1973–74; drama Edin from 1974
m Aber 5.8.74 Colin J. Youngson MA 1970 *qv*

REID Stewart   *MA 1966 Dip Ed 1967
   s of Stewart R. eng and Jeannie Skakle; b Aber 8.11.42
teacher AGS 1967–72; prin mod lang Linksfield acad
from 1972
m Elgin 1.8.69 Jennifer A. Masson teacher d of William
A. M. Spey Bay

REID Thomas Myles Sutherland   *BMedBiol 1969
                                                        MB ChB 1972
   s of George R. MA 1939 *qv*; b Aber 31.7.48
h o ARI 1972–73; lect bact Aberd 1973–78; consult.
bact City hosp Aber from 1978
m Perth 5.9.75 Marjory H. Robertson

REID Veronica   BEd 1969
   d of William R. farm. and Helen D. Morrison MA
(Edin) teacher; b Meikleour Perthsh 3.10.47
teacher Fr: Dun 1969, Essex 1970; lib asst Essex 1970–
73; admin asst: Oxford 1973, Hertford from 1973

REID William Gordon   BSc(agr) 1968
   s of William F. R. BSc(agr) 1935 *qv*; b Dun Montrose
25.12.46
BSc(Dund) 1979
farm. Montrose 1968–76; stud. Dund 1976–79; res
microbiol Brist from 1979
m Montrose 17.2.73 Alison H. Rae MA(Edin) market.
co-ordinator d of William R. Lond

REID William Macpherson   MA 1959 LLB 1962
   s of William A. R. master butcher and Mabel McLeod;
b New Elgin 6.4.38
admitted advoc 1963; sheriff: Lothian & Borders July
1978, Glasg & Strathkelvin Oct 1978
m Geneva 18.9.71 Vivien A. Eddy d of Thomas B. D. E.
FRICS Wisbech

REID William Mitchell   *BSc(eng) 1967

REID William Thomas   LLB 1965
   s of Thomas H. R. BSc(St And) teacher and Annabella
McIntosh MA 1930 *qv*; b Inv 5.12.44
law app Aber 1965–67; leg. asst: Aber 1967–69, Ellon
1969–70, Edin 1970–72; ptnr Edin from 1972
m Dun 24.7.71 Catriona M. Houston asst dom supt
Edin RI d of John G. H. Dun

REILLY John Francis   MA 1967

REILLY Patricia   *MA 1968
   d of John R. tile fixer and Catherine McKinlay;
b Glasg 14.6.47
Dip Ed(Glas) 1969
teacher Engl: Glasg 1969–74, Alva 1974–76; prin Engl
Alloa from 1976
m Glasg 28.6.74 James Rafferty BA(Stir) draughtsman,
teacher, man. s of George R. Glasg

REITH Edna Harrison   MA 1963
   d of Harrison R. baker and Jessie Stables; b Keith
6.9.42

teacher Prestonpans 1964–67; lib Montreal 1967; journalist Lond from 1967

REITH Margaret Elizabeth   *MA 1962
  d of Harrison R. baker and Jessie Stables; b Keith 11.9.40
teacher Newmarket 1962–66; part-time work in adult illiteracy progr Reading from 1975
m Cambridge 28.3.64 Colin H. Walker MSc 1961 *qv*

RENDALL Ian Alexander   *BSc(eng) 1970
  s of Alexander R. grocer and Elizabeth J. Macdonald; b Wick 9.7.48
eng Aber from 1970
m Aber 14.12.70 Johan Simpson teacher d of James S. Thurso

RENDALL Margaret   MA 1967
  s of David J. R. farm. and Mary C. Clyne; b Deerness Kirkwall 23.4.46
m Kirkwall 19.7.68 John C. Garden lorry driver s of James G. New Deer

RENDALL Ruth   MA 1969 Dip Ed 1970
  d of John R. farm. and Anne E. Harvey nurse; b Kirkwall 19.12.48
teacher Stromness 1970–75
m Finstown 19.12.73 Maxwell C. St C. Tait farm. s of Eric St C. T. Dounby

RENNEY Ian Telford   MB ChB 1965

RENNIE Alistair   MA 1968
  s of George R. shipyard worker and Edith R. Connon; b Aber 10.3.39
Rolls-Royce Derby: O & M off. 1968–69, expenditure plan. off. 1970–73, prod. support acct from 1973
m Aber 8.10.66 Sheila A. Ewen secy d of James E. Aber

RENNIE Clifford Alfred John   *MA 1969 *BD 1972
  s of Charles R. chief stoker and Margaret W. Rosser; b Aber 15.7.43
C of S min: asst Garthdee Aber 1972–74, Altnaharra and Farr Sutherland from 1974
m Aber 2.7.74 Fiona M. Sheach nurs sister d of James M. S. Dufftown

RENNIE Donald Gordon   MA 1968 LLB 1970
  s of Gordon R. bldr and Flora MacLeod; b Aber 25.4.47
Edin: law app 1970–72, leg. asst Bonar, Mackenzie & Kermack WS 1972–73, ptnr 1973–75; ptnr Connell & Connell WS from 1977
m Glasg 10.9.71 Brenda L. Dewar LLB 1969 *qv*

RENNIE Graeme William John   *MA 1970
  s of Francis J. R. area eng PO(tel) and Joan Davie nurse; b Aber 3.6.39
MA(Cantab) 1975
res asst hist Aberd 1970–72; admin off. Cantab from 1972
m Aber 30.3.63 Audrey M. E. Thomson secy d of James H. T. Dunphail

RENNIE Ian   *MA 1969

RENNIE James   BSc 1962

RENNIE Morag Flora   *MA 1966
  m Duncan

RENNIE Morna Mabel Wilson   BEd 1970
  d of William J. R. blacksmith/welder and Mabel B.

Wilson; b Aber 27.11.46
teacher p s Peterhead 1970–74
m Dyce 22.12.73 Alistair A. Clarke elect. eng s of Thomas C. Aber

RENNIE Pamela Margaret   MA 1965
  d of John H. M. R. shoe shop prop. and Frances D. Ingram; b Ellon 2.3.44
teacher Fr Aber acad 1966–68; peripatetic teacher prim. Fr Aber 1968–69
m Aber 15.8.67 Owen Rowlands MA 1967 *qv*

RENNIE Thomas George   LLB 1968

RENNIE William McKenzie   BSc 1965 Dip Ed 1966
  s of William H. R. shopkeeper and Alexandrina McKenzie shopkeeper; b Aber 8.7.27
teacher phys Bankhead acad 1966–68, spec asst phys RGC 1968–72, prin phys Keith g s from 1972
m Elgin 26.12.76 Mabel Coggs MA(Edin) teacher d of John M. C. Nairn

RENTON Ross Langlands   MB ChB 1958
  s of David R. R. pharm and Margaret C. Black; b Berwick-on-Tweed 28.11.33
DIH 1963
h o Woodend hosp Aber, N Ormesby hosp Middlesbrough 1959–60; govt m o Barakin Laki N. Nigeria 1960–62; asst indust m o Slough indust health serv 1963–65; Nicholas res lab Slough: med advis 1965–72, dir med serv UK 1972–74, dir group med serv 1974–76; g p from 1976
m(1) Aber 6.8.56 Kathleen Ironside
  (2) Beaconsfield 4.3.78 Jennifer Smith

RENUCCI Luigi Sileno   *MA 1968

REPPER Dorothy Aileen   MA 1956
  d of William R. shipbroker and Alice W. Alcock secy; b Aber 28.1.35
teacher Inchgarth p s Aber 1957–63
m Aber 25.7.62 Alasdair D. Campbell scient civ serv s of George I. D. C. Banchory

REPPER Margaret Alcock   MA 1959
  d of William R. shipbroker and Alice W. Alcock secy; b Aber 17.10.38
Dip Soc St(Edin) 1960 AMIMSW 1961
med soc worker Glasg RI 1961–69
m Aber 12.10.68 Richard C. Hill BSc(Glas) sen lect acct coll of tech Glasg s of Richard T. W. H. Bearsden

RETTIE Charles Young Stuart   MB ChB 1958

RETTIE Doreen Lilian   MB ChB 1965
  m Aitken

RETTIE Marlene Elspeth   MA 1959

RETTIE Sheila Mitchell   MA 1970
  b Aber 1949
admin asst Legal & Gen Insur Co Lond 1970–71; teacher: Lond 1971, Victoria educ dept Euroa Aust 1972–74

REVEL Karl Jarvey Thomson   BEd 1970
  s of William T. R. MA(Glas) C of S min and Lilian M. A. Cluness; b Lonmay 19.8.46
teacher Peterhead 1970–73; head: Maud p s 1973–77, Pitfour p s Mintlaw from 1977
m Rathen 6.7.71 Mabel Buchan MA 1969 *qv*

REVERON Ruido Angel Esteban   MSc 1968 PhD 1971
DMB(Venez)

RHEAD Celia Margaret   BSc 1968
d 13.7.68

RHIND Eileen Margaret   BEd 1969
d of John M. R. surv Customs & Excise and Beatrice Leigh; b Glasg 30.11.47
p s teacher: Methil 1969–70, Sheffie!d 1970–71, Inv 1971–72
m Inv 11.8.70 Richard J. Ardern BSc 1969 *qv*

RHIND Gordon Baird   MB ChB 1965
s of Gordon R. publican and Williamina M. Baird; b Huntly 30.8.38
h o ARI 1965–66; g p Cults, Aber from 1966
m Aber 12.8.66 Doreen A. Walker fashion buyer d of George A. C. W. Aber

RHODES Hilary Margaret   MA 1969
d of Albert S. R. comp secy/bursar and Helen M. Leach; b Shipley 6.6.48
teacher Fr/Span Brechin h s 1970–74
m Aber 7.7.71 Douglas B. Mutch MA 1969 *qv*

RIACH Alan Bryson   BSc(eng) 1968
s of William J. R. farm. and Isobel Tough; b Botriphnie 18.10.45
des internat harvester comp Doncaster 1968–70; des, sect. leader, des eng Scammell lorries Watford 1970–73; des eng Leyland motors Lancs 1973–77; eng man. Leyland vehicles Bathgate from 1977
m Watford 26.5.73 Cynthia I. Tingle teacher d of Trevor H. Walterstone

RIACH Alison-Mary   *BSc 1963
d of Joseph T. R. civ eng and Alison K. Christie clerkess/pa; b Aber 14.9.41
MIBiol 1975
teacher sc Currie h s Midlothian 1964–67; first asst biol Benwell s N'cle-u-Tyne 1967–69; prin biol Hylton Red House comp s Sunderland 1970–72, head sciences from 1972
m Aber 3.4.67 Hedworth F. Oliver eng, ski instructor, ski s and sports man. s of Hedworth O. Sunderland

RIACH Doreen Mary   MA 1966
d of George R. bank man. and Eveline M. S. Tulloch teacher; b St Andrews 20.10.45
Froebel Cert 1968 Madeline McIver schol 1968
Marchburn inf s Aber: teacher 1968–69, i/c nursery class 1969–70; teacher i/c nursery Milton House Edin 1970–71
m Aber 27.12.70 Robert W. Black MA 1969 *qv*

RIACH Douglas Cameron   *MA 1968
s of Ronald A. C. Riach grocer and Margaret Douglas; b Crail 8.8.46
MLitt(Edin) 1970 PhD(Edin) 1976
visiting sen schol Amer council of learned societies 1972; lect Jyväskylä Finland 1973–76; res fell. Charles Warren Center Harvard 1976–77
m Aber 29.12.71 Anne F. Donaldson MA 1969 *qv*

RICE Alison Findlay   *MA 1969
d of James I. R. MB ChB 1939 *qv* and Jane M. F. Scroggie MA 1936 *qv*; b Stafford 19.11.47
BPhil(Oxon) 1971
lib asst Oxford 1971–73; teacher Harris 1974–77
m Aber 24.8.73 Andrew J. D. Johnson BA(Cantab) teacher, now hotel prop.

RICE Charles Duncan   *MA 1964
s of James I. R. MB ChB 1939 *qv* and Jane M. F. Scroggie MA 1936 *qv*; b Aber 20.10.42
PhD(Edin) 1969
Henry fell. Harvard USA 1965–66; lect hist Aberd 1967–69; Yale USA: fell. Amer council of learned societies 1969–70, asst prof hist 1970–75, dean Saybrook coll 1972–74, 1975–77, Morse fell. 1974–75, assoc prof hist from 1975
m Providence Rhode Is USA 2.7.67 Susan I. Wunsch MLitt 1970 *qv*

RICE William Patrick   BSc(agr) 1960
s of William J. R. MRCVS(Glas) vet surg; b Montrose 20.10.42
sugar agronomist Booker's sugar comp Blairmont Guyana 1960–62; agr advis/reg cattle advis Scot. and N Eng J. Bibby & Sons 1962–68; agr off. Bahamas Govt Nassau 1968–73; gen man. Caledonian farms Grand Cayman, Cayman Is BWI from 1973
m Chester 3.4.65 Dorothy Sharp d of John S. Abergele N Wales

RICHARDS David William Lawson   MB ChB 1965
s of Robert L. R. MB ChB 1932 *qv* and Margaret B. Howieson MA 1933 *qv*; b Mount Vernon 18.5.41
DObstRCOG 1967 MRCGP 1975
h o Aber hosps 1965–67; sen h o City hosp Aber 1967–68; regist Aber hosps 1968; g p Cults 1968–9, Cults/Culter from 1969
m Aber 23.9.66 Margaret R. Esslemont nurs sister d of J. Bryce E. BL 1928 *qv*

RICHARDS Isabella Margaret Olivier   MA 1958
d of William A. R. MB ChB(Lond) surg regist/g p and Noel Olivier MB ChB consult. phys/paediat; b Lond 4.5.33
m West Wittering 13.7.57 Keith M. M. Ramsay MA 1958 *qv*

RICHARDS Maureen Elizabeth   MA 1970
d of Frederick J. R. police serg and Elizabeth H. Davidson hosp receptionist; b Fraserburgh 7.6.49
teacher Fr/Engl Milne's h s Fochabers 1971–74
m Keith 7.7.72 George C. Newlands stone mason DoE s of George N. Lumsden

RICHARDS Peter Robin   *BSc 1970
s of Ronald R. supt regist and Olive C. Slater; b Brist 10.1.47
PhD(CNAA) 1977 FZS 1976 FLS 1976

RICHARDS Susan Jane   *MA 1970

RICHARDSON Colin Geoffrey   BSc 1967

RICHARDSON Fraser   MB ChB 1968
s of Frank R. exec off. HM customs and excise and Isobel A. Fraser secy; b Lynchmere 9.6.44
ARI: h o, sen h o 1968–70, regist gen med 1970–74; g p Aber from 1974
m Aber 20.11.71 Cynthia Ford nurse d of Sydney W. J. F. Dunfermline

RICHARDSON Ian Milne   PhD 1956
s of William A. R. solic and Elizabeth C. Milne; b Edin 4.3.22
MB ChB(Edin) DPH(Glas) 1948 MD(Edin) 1953 FRCPE 1956 JP 1960 FRCGP 1973
Aberd: sen lect group med 1956–68, reader gen pract 1968–70, James MacKenzie prof gen pract from 1970
m Glasg 12.10.46 Mary S. C. Gibb teacher d of William W. G. Wishaw

RICHARDSON William Henry   *MA 1967 MEd 1973

RICHES Kenneth Maurice   PhD 1962
s of Maurice W. R. compositor and Ivy Livermore;
b Lond 29.10.36
CChem MRIC 1959
res chem: Shell plastics lab Manc 1961–65, Deutsche
Shell Bonn Ger 1965–66, Shell agr res centre Kent 1966–
71, Shell res Thornton Chester from 1971
m Manc 21.12.63 Jean Stewart d of James S. Manc

RICHMOND Eileen Elizabeth Hope   MA 1965
d of John H. R. publican and Helen M. J. Mitchell
shopkeeper; b Aber 13.12.42
teacher maths/sc Summerhill acad Aber 1966–71
m Aber 19.12.69 John Martin coxswain/mech s of John
G. M. Aber

RICHMOND Helen Morag Hope   MA 1969
Dip Ed 1970
m Cults 1.9.80 Charles J. Croydon s of John C. Ipswich

RICHMOND William   *BSc 1965
s of James W. R. MRCS LRCP(Lond) g p and Joan
Brander BA(Lond) teacher, lect tech coll, magistrate;
b Peterborough 6.12.41
Dip Indust Man. 1966
agr zool, tech market. asst Lond 1966–71; teacher
Croydon 1971–75; fin. admin Lond from 1975

RICHMOND-WATSON Marilyn Olivia   MA 1967

RICKETTS John Anthony   LLB 1966

RIDDELL Alexander Gall   MA 1956
d 18.6.71

RIDDELL Alexander John   MA 1965 Dip Ed 1966
s of John M. R. blacksmith and Elizabeth S. L. Gray;
b Aber 4.1.44
teacher: Engl/hist Middle s s Aber 1966–68, hist Powis
acad from 1968, prin guid from 1973
m Aber 23.6.79 Elizabeth M. Millar BSc 1964 qv

RIDDELL Andrew Alexander   MA 1967
s of George A. R. BCom 1929 qv; b Lond 15.3.44
MA(E Ang) 1975
trainee lib Birkbeck coll Lond 1967–68; bookseller
Cologne, tech translator Paris 1968–69; teacher:
Hillingdon educ auth 1970–72, Engl g s centre for Brit
teachers in Europe Braunschweig W Ger 1972–74, Engl
g s centre for Brit teachers in Europe Rheinberg W Ger
1975–76; trainee interpreter, asst interpreter EEC Comm
Brussels from 1976
m Lond 20.7.74 Carol A. Ross BA(Tor) teacher d of
Clancy A. R. Toronto

RIDDELL George Steedman   *BMedBiol 1970
MB ChB 1973
s of George S. R. MD 1949 qv; b Aber 27.2.48
h o: Dumfries 1973–74, Aber 1974; Aber: sen h o anaest
1974–75, regist anaest 1975–78; sen regist anaest Cardiff
from 1978

RIDDELL Joan Harriet   MA 1966 Dip Ed 1967
d of Robert R. bank man. BA(OU) and Janet G.
Sutherland; b Inv 30.6.45
teacher: Helmsdale p s 1967–71; relief Fr/Engl/prim. and
remed subj Sutherland from 1971
m Kirkmichael 26.7.69 George T. H. Murray joiner/
woodwork instr f e centre

RIDDELL Linda Elizabeth   MA 1968
d of John M. R. blacksmith and Elizabeth S. L. Gray

tailoress/shop asst; b Aber 19.4.47
teacher: Menstrie 1969–74, Grangemouth from 1974

RIDDELL Margaret Isobel   *MA 1965 Dip Ed 1966

RIDDELL Patricia Ann   BSc 1962
m Daniels

RIDDELL Robert Gordon   *BSc 1968
s of Albert R. poultry farm. and Anne Drummond
poultry farm.; b Glasg 9.5.46
paper-coating tech: Cardiff 1968–72, Blackburn from
1972
m Weston-s-Mare 13.3.71 Kay Reeks nurse d of Eric
W. R. Calcutta

RIDDELL Ronald   MA 1957
s of Frederick G. R. monumental mason/blacksmith's
hammerman and Violet Urquhart sales asst; b Aber
24.3.35
2/lt RAEC garrison educ off. SAAA Manorbier Wales
1958–60; teacher: Middlefield p s Aber 1960–62, spec in
relig educ Bell–Baxter h s Cupar 1962–64, prin asst relig
educ Aber acad 1964–68; lect relig educ Jordanhill coll
of educ Glasg 1968–74; advis in relig educ Aber educ
comm 1974–75; Gramp reg councillor from 1975
m Aber 26.7.63 Agnes Webster MA 1978 lab asst d of
Alexander W. Aber

RIDDLE Michael   MA 1968
s of William R. dairyman and Jean M. Campbell;
b Nairn 8.4.47
BA(OU) 1978
teacher hist/mod stud. St Columba's h s Dunfermline
1969–78, prin guid 1970–78; asst head (guid) Speyside h s
from 1978
m Nairn 21.9.68 Elizabeth I. Campbell teacher d of
Peter C. Nairn

RIDDLER Alexander Marryatt Hay   BSc 1959
s of Marryatt G. R. tech off. DAFS and Helen D. Hay;
b Aber 25.4.36
Dip Integrated Surveying ITC–Unesco centre Enschede
The Neths 1973
teacher maths Inverurie acad 1959–60; soil surv NSW
DA Sydney from 1960
m Sydney NSW 31.8.63 Laurel J. Thompson paymistress
d of William R. T. Port Stephens NSW

RIDDLER Gordon Peterkin   *BSc 1967

RIDDOCH Ella Falconer   MA 1966
d of Henry J. R. farm. and Agnes Jamieson; b Huntly
30.5.45
teacher: Engl Glasg 1967–69, maths 1969–71, prin maths
1971–72, maths Aber 1972–73, asst prin maths Glasg
from 1973
m Drumblade 10.8.73 Francis W. Lawrence bank clerk s
of John L. Fraserburgh

RIDDOCH Hilda Ellen   MA 1970
m Armour

RIDDOCH James Skene   BSc(eng) 1970
s of Walter S. R. driving instruct. and Isabella H.
Skene; b Dufftown 1.10.39
bus. man
m Dufftown 11.7.65 Anne E. W. Niven d of John N. Aber

RIDDOLLS Anthea   MSc 1969
BSc(St And)

RIDLEY Susan Elizabeth   MB ChB 1968
d of Ernest F. R. MB ChB(St And) g p and Catherine

M. Malcolm MB ChB(St And) g p; b Glasg 20.6.44
DObstRCOG 1972
h o Aber 1968–69; rotating intern Edmonton Alberta
1969–71; consult. m o Nyeri hosp Kenya 1972–78
m Zambia 2.10.71 John R. Macleod MA 1963 *qv*

RILEY Alasdair James   MA 1968
s of James F. R. MB ChB(Edin) g p and Marina E.
Fraser; b Perth 31.1.46
journalist: *Kent Messenger* 1968–71, *Evening Standard*
Lond 1971–76, Scottish TV Glasg 1976–78, *The Sun* Lond
from 1978

RILLEY Charles   MA 1963

RILLEY Elizabeth Jean   MA 1956
d of Norman S. R. insur acct and Sophie M. Work;
b Aber 9.3.35
LTCL(Lond) 1969
teacher Portlethen p s from 1957

RINGE James Peter   PhD 1956
BSc(Lond) ARIC

RINGSLEBEN Mary Ruth Elizabeth   PhD 1956
d of William C. R. MSc(Queen's Ont) mining eng and
R. Dorothy Sharp BA(Queen's Ont); b Timmins Ontario
30.7.28
BA(Tor) 1950 Dip Archives Admin(Liv) 1957
admin asst Leeds from 1957

RITCHIE Alan Alexander   BSc(eng) 1970

RITCHIE Alison Mary   MA 1967
m Monro

RITCHIE David Alexander   *BSc(eng) 1970
s of David S. R. nurs off. and Margaret F. Wood nurs
sister; b Banff 30.6.49
MIEE 1978
eng ICI Ardeer 1970–73; gen man. Motherwell Bridge
Electrical Motherwell 1973–79; elect. eng Roche Prod.
Dalry from 1979
m Banff 12.4.68 Margaret I. Falconer MA 1971 teacher
d of George F. Banff

RITCHIE David Andrew   *BSc 1970
s of David R. eng and Henrietta R. Mair; b Philippine
Is 21.10.47
Lond: tech rep 1970–73, sen sales exec from 1973
m St Albans 23.9.72 Kathleen W. McDonagh SRN d of
John T. McD. St Albans

RITCHIE Doris Jean   MB ChB 1957
d of Gordon R. millwright and Jeanie Law; b Huntly
23.9.33
h o RACH 1957–58; g p: asst Stonehaven, Hayes 1958–
63, ptnr Aber from 1974
m Aber 17.10.59 George D. Dalgarno higher exec off.
Customs & Excise s of George H. D. Aber

RITCHIE Ethel Margaret   MA 1959
d of Kenneth R. motor mech, shopkeeper and Annie
C. Allardyce shop asst; b Peterculter 27.6.39
teacher: maths/geog Aboyne acad 1960–62, sc Peterhead
acad 1963; Blackhills p s 1966–74, acting head 1974–75,
Anna Ritchie spec s Peterhead from 1975
m Peterculter 30.6.62 James R. Cruickshanks plumber,
prison off. s of James C. Banchory

RITCHIE Ian Ogilvie   *BSc 1968
s of Charles O. R. baker and Isabel M. Simpson;
b Johnshaven 13.5.46
res stud. Aberd 1968–70; teacher: AGS 1971–72, Stonehaven 1973–77, Aboyne from 1977
m Stonehaven 28.3.70 Elizabeth A. Lambie MA 1968 *qv*

RITCHIE Irene Allardyce   MA 1964
d of Kenneth R. shopkeeper and Annie C. Allardyce;
b Peterculter 7.4.42
teacher: maths Banchory acad 1967–70, p s Banchory
acad 1970–72, maths St Columba's RC s Perth 1973–75,
maths Perth acad from 1975
m Banchory 12.10.60 Robert W. Singer gen man. s of
George S. Banchory

RITCHIE Irene Mary   MA 1969
d of James A. R. machine oper and Georgina H. M.
Raeper; b Aber 5.12.47
teacher: Aber 1970–72, Linlithgow 1972–76
m Aber 21.7.72 Oswald C. Finnie MA 1969 *qv*

RITCHIE Jean McCurrach   MB ChB 1958
d of George F. T. R. rly guard and Mary McCurrach
nurs sister; b Aber 13.6.34
DA(Eng) 1960
Glasg: h o sick ch hosp Yorkhill, Stobhill hosp 1958–59,
sen h o anaest Stobhill hosp, RI 1959–63; g p Brighton
m Aber 27.2.63 John M. Howat MB ChB(Glas) paediat
surg s of Robert H. Irvine

RITCHIE John   BSc(eng) 1970

RITCHIE John Miller   MA 1968

RITCHIE John Russell   BSc(eng) 1964
b Fraserburgh 29.3.42
MIEE 1972 AMBIM 1974
elect. eng NSHEB from 1964
m Aber 26.7.67 Mary M. Davidson

RITCHIE John Winter   *BSc(eng) 1964

RITCHIE Kenneth Brian   MB ChB 1967
s of Kenneth R. newsagent and Annie C. Allardyce;
b Stonehaven 31.12.43
h o Dumfries 1967–68; obst Falkirk 1969; paediat Ayr
1969; g p: Dalry 1970–72, Inverkeithing from 1972
m Aber 17.12.66 Maureen Kelly civ serv d John K. Aber

RITCHIE Lily Ann McBay   MA 1959 Dip Ed 1960
d of Charles O. R. master baker and Isabel M.
Simpson; b Gourdon 2.1.39
teacher: Mackie acad Stonehaven 1960–61, mod lang
Nicolson inst Stornoway 1968–73, Fr Back s/Leurbost s
Is of Lewis from 1973
m Johnshaven 12.7.61 John Maclennan MA 1959 *qv*

RITCHIE Margaret Janet   MA 1967
b Aber 11.6.46
teacher Aber from 1968
m Aber 25.7.74 John M. Elsom MSc(E Ang) res asst

RITCHIE Margaret Murray   MA 1969
d of David R. haulage contr/farm worker and Jean R.
Macleman SRN; b Inv 4.1.48
teacher Crown p s Inv 1970–72
m Cromarty 24.7.71 James M. Scott ptnr fam garage/
motor mech s of Hugh S. Conon Bridge

RITCHIE Margrit Rose   *MA 1965
d of Alfred A. R. banker and Anna-Margarethe Kull
nurse; b Aber 26.7.42
teacher: Fr/Ger Aber 1966–67, Cambridge 1967–69
m Aber 12.8.67 Don W. Cruickshank MA 1965 *qv*

RITCHIE Patricia   MA 1966 Dip Ed 1967
d of Joseph R. postman and Robina S. Galbraith clerk; b Aber 11.12.44
teacher: Aber 1967–72, Brisbane Aust 1974–75
m Aber 27.7.66 Adam H. Findlay MA 1970 *qv*

RIVIERE Marc Serge   *MA 1970

RIXON Frank Gerald   *LLB 1967

ROAF Jane Isobel   *MA 1966
m Stubbes

ROBB Catherine Roberta Steele   MA 1969
m Haggart

ROBB Christian Mackenzie Thomson   MB ChB 1959 DPH 1963
d of James A. T. R. marine eng and Christian R. Norrie pers secy; b Ilford 11.6.36
MFCM 1972
h o, sen h o Woodend hosp Aber 1959–61; rotating internship Vancouver gen hosp 1961–62; m o, sen m o health dept Aber 1963–74; commun med spec Grampian health board Aber from 1974

ROBB Colin Collie   MA 1963 LLB 1965
s of Stanley L. R. soldier, checkweighman and Ena Collie; b Aber 9.3.42
Aber: law app 1965–67, solic 1967–75; Grampian reg c: asst dir law & admin 1975–79, dep dir from 1979

ROBB David Strachan   *MA 1969
s of Erland S. B. R. civ serv and Margaret M. Strachan; b Aber 6.1.47
asst instr in lit State univ NY New Paltz NY USA 1969–70; lect Engl Dund from 1973

ROBB Eileen May   *MA 1969
m Halborg

ROBB George Alan   *MA 1964
s of George R. solic and Phyllis M. Allan; b Aber 20.5.42
LLB(Edin) 1966 WS 1968
law app Davidson & Syme WS Edin 1966–68; leg. asst Edmonds & Ledingham advoc Aber 1969–71; lect publ law Aberd 1970–73; leg. asst Brander & Cruickshank WS Aber 1971–72, ptnr from 1973
m Aber 3.8.73 Moira A. Clark teacher d of Sydney M. C. Aber

ROBB John Bertram Leslie Macdonald   MB ChB 1960
s of Bertram G. R. rep and Anne M. Peters MA 1930 *qv*; b Edin 23.2.36
regist psychiat Bangour Midlothian 1964–69; g p Fauldhouse from 1970
m Morebattle 12.10.63 Pauline E. Yearnshire midwife d of William Y. Alnmouth

ROBB Margaret Niven Davidson   *MA 1968
m Buchan

ROBB Norah Mary Steele   MA 1969

ROBB Ronald Reith   *MA 1961

ROBBIE Alice Mary   MA 1962
m Curley

ROBBIE Angus Abercrombie   MA 1958
s of James R. horticulturist and Margaret J. Abercrombie; b Aber 28.5.37

Dip Voc Guid 1966 gen serv medal 1960
educ off. RAEC/1st batt RHF Aden 1958–60; youth employ. off. Edin 1960–63; careers off. Birm 1963–67; careers off. Aberd from 1967
m Cambridge 7.7.62 Patricia G. Pollock med secy

ROBBIE John Forsyth   BSc(eng) 1958 *1965
s of John D. R. for. and Jane M. Souter MA 1917 *qv*; b Alves 25.3.35
eng: Freeman Fox & ptnrs N Wales 1958–60, James Williamson & ptnrs Glasg 1960–64; lect Aberd 1965–72, sen lect from 1972
m Aber 2.5.59 Sheila M. Inkster radiogr d of Andrew R. I. Banchory

ROBBIE Sheila Catherine   MA 1960
d of John G. R. gen man. dept store and Catherine Craigmyle; b Aber 25.8.39
interpreter/translator Fr/Engl Noumea New Caledonia 1970–71; teacher Engl at Fr s Bucharest Rumania from 1973
m Noumea 21.2.61 Marcel L. Ropert L-ès-L(Rennes) univ lect Melb, diplomat Tokyo, Bucharest s of Marcel M. R. Saint Brieuc France

ROBBINS Alan Marcus James   *BSc(for) 1970
s of Eric R. J. R. farm. and Margery Bryant; b Osterley 7.3.47
MSc(Oxon) 1971
for. res asst Commonwealth for. inst Oxford 1971–72; for. res ODM tech aid Matagalpa Nicaragua from 1972

ROBERTS Anne   *MA 1966 Dip Ed 1967
d of Llewelyn L. R. univ admin and Marjorie Wear; b Aberystwyth 26.10.42
cler off. civ serv Leic 1967–68; trainee careers off. Leic 1968–69, Kent 1969–70, careers off. Leic 1970–71, sen careers off. 1971–77
m(2) Lond 20.7.77 Alan M. MacGregor MA 1966 *qv*

ROBERTS Celia Frances   MA 1967
m Reid

ROBERTS Joyce Cameron   MB ChB 1970
d of Robert C. R. off. fire brigade and Eleanor D. Cameron; b Aber 24.1.47
FFARACS
h o Aber 1970–71; Brisbane Aust: sen resid 1971–72, regist anaest 1972–74; regist anaest Middx Lond from 1975
m Brisbane –.10.72 Ralph G. Cobcroft MB BS(Queensland) phys s of Athol J. C. Redcliffe Queensland

ROBERTSON Aileen   BEd 1969
d of Hugh R. MA 1950 *qv*; b Aber 28.9.47
teacher: Fochabers 1969–71, Kinloss 1971–73, Glasg East 1973–76, Glasg West 1976–77
m Forres 13.10.73 Donald M. Davidson BA(Strath) CA s of Thomas S. D. Inv

ROBERTSON Alan Mackenzie   BSc(agr) 1961
s of Ian R. joiner and Elsie R. Pope; b Banchory 29.1.37
exper off. ARC farm bldg unit Silsoe 1961–64; farm bldg advis PIDA and MLC Bush estate Edin 1964–69; investigator SFB IU NOSCA Craibstone, Bucksburn from 1969
m Tarland 2.6.62 Margaret Walker civ serv d of Allan W. Tarland

ROBERTSON Alastair Ogston   LLB 1967
s of Ian R. clerk of works and Edith V. Silver teacher;

b Aber 13.7.46
Aber: law app Clark & Wallace advoc 1967–69, solic, ptnr Burnett & Reid advoc from 1969
m Cullen 3.8.68 Catherine E. Robertson MA 1967 *qv*

ROBERTSON Alastair Thomson   LLB 1969

ROBERTSON Alexander   MA 1960
 s of Alexander R. fish merch and Helen R. Robb; b Aber 13.8.39
Dip Soc St(Edin) 1961 PhD(Edin) 1974
trainee psychiat soc worker N'cle-u-Tyne 1961–62; res asst Leic 1962–64; res off. Essex 1964–66; lect Ipswich civ coll 1966–68; res off. MRC unit for epidemiological soc stud. Edin 1968–72; lect soc admin Edin from 1972
m Leic 26.9.64 Elaine Walden soc worker d of Henry G. F. W. Sanderstead

ROBERTSON Alexander Stewart   *MA 1967
                                                        ***MEd 1972**
 s of Alexander J. R. MA 1925 *qv*; b Forfar 17.10.45
teacher RGC Aber 1967–73; head Engl/communications/related stud. fac Castell Alun h s Hope Wales 1973–78; dep head Yogol Bryn Elian, Colwyn Bay from 1978
m Aber 21.12.67 Pamela M. Martin MA 1970 *qv*

ROBERTSON Alison Kinloch   MA 1966
 m Smith

ROBERTSON Alistair Charles   MB ChB 1968
 s of George P. R. R. R. soldier, woodman and Annie S. Smith shop asst; b Huntly 18.4.44
h o Aber, Dumfries 1968–69; asst g p Annan 1969–70; sen h o Lancaster 1970–72; g p: Arbroath 1972–73, Hessle N Humberside from 1973
m Aber 20.7.70 Susan M. Gallantry teacher d of Tom G. Aber

ROBERTSON Andrew   *MA 1958 *MEd 1960
 s of John R. trawlmate/fish market porter and Williamina D. M. Barnie; b Aber 28.8.36
teacher: Culter 1959–60, New Deer 1960–61; lecteur Rennes univ France 1961–62; teacher/spec asst Banchory acad 1962–68, prin Fr Kaimhill s s Aber 1968–71, prin Fr/asst head/dep head Kincorth acad from 1971
m Aber 14.7.60 Edna M. Sangster lab tech/dispensing asst d of Norman F. S. Aber

ROBERTSON Anne Christine   MB ChB 1968
 m Napier

ROBERTSON Anne Wilson   MA 1966 Dip Ed 1967
 d of Charles W. R. MA 1934 *qv*; b Dumfries 11.2.46
teacher Thornhill p s Dumfries 1967–76
m Belhelvie 7.7.72 James Boyle master painter/decorator s of Robert H. B. Thornhill

ROBERTSON Annette Walker   BSc 1957
 d of Robert W. R. gen merchant, clerk and Emma S. Stevenson tailoress; b Aber 19.11.34
electron microscopist: Surrey 1957–59, Hampshire 1959–61; sub-postmistress from 1974
m Aber 1958 Michael B. Bagley brewery sales man. s of Walter E. W. B. Portsmouth

ROBERTSON Barbara Reid   MA 1960
 d of Thomas F. R. grocery br man. and Barbara C. Reid; b Aber 6.6.39
teacher inf Aber 1961–67
m Aber 31.7.65 Ian G. Morrice CA s of Alexander T. M. Aber

ROBERTSON Brian Kellock   *BSc 1970 Dip Ed 1971

ROBERTSON Catherine Edith   MA 1967
 d of George A. R. retail outfitter and Catherine E. Clark nurse; b Aber 17.8.46
teacher Engl/Fr Bankhead acad 1968–70
m Cullen 3.8.68 Alastair O. Robertson LLB 1967 *qv*

ROBERTSON Christian Scott   MA 1967
 m Tait

ROBERTSON David   MA 1966
 s of Edwin J. R. wireless mech/radio tv shop prop. and Fanny T. Moir prop. hi-fi tv radio bus.; b Aber 23.2.38
prop. hi-fi tv radio bus. Aber/Fraserburgh from 1966
m Aber 27.3.68 Norma C. Simpson MA 1969 *qv*

ROBERTSON David Alasdair   MB ChB 1959

ROBERTSON David Lewis   *BSc 1958
 s of David R. BSc 1924 *qv* and Margaret W. Lewis MA 1929 *qv*; b Bieldside 2.2.37
grad app Ericsson Telephones Beeston 1958–60; electronics dev eng: Ferranti Bracknell 1960–64, Elliott Automation Camberley 1964–72; man.: Quality Assurance, Marconi Space and Defence Systems Camberley from 1972
m Oxford 19.12.59 Winifred G. Macgillivray d of Alexander M. Oxford

ROBERTSON David Stewart Malcolm   MA 1958
 s of William H. R. civ serv and Isabella B. Malcolm; b Glasg 1.6.28
teacher: Engl/allied subj Rothiemay s s 1959–61, Engl Nairn acad 1961–74, prin Engl Glenurquhart s s from 1974
m Streatham 29.4.50 Eileen M. Adams d of William F. A. Streatham

ROBERTSON Edwin   BSc(eng) 1958

ROBERTSON Eleanor Margaret   BSc 1968
 d of Ogston R. farm. and Rosaline B. Adams secy; b Stonehaven 9.8.47
teacher: maths/geog Montrose acad 1969–71, maths/sc Tarves s 1971–73
m Aber 4.8.71 John S. Law farm. s of William S. L. Fyvie

ROBERTSON Elizabeth Ann   MA 1959
 d of John R. CEng F I Mun E county road surv and Margaret G. Wright; b Inv 26.6.38
teacher Engl Hilton j s s Aber 1960–63
m Kirkwall 21.5.63 Robert G. Bain farm. s of Robert G. B. Tankerness Orkney

ROBERTSON George Ewen   *MA 1970 *MEd 1972
 s of Donald E. R. asst gen man. dept store and Heather G. Sutherland; b Aber 21.4.47
teacher Fr/Ger Mackie acad Stonehaven 1972–75; asst prin Fr/Ger Bankhead acad 1975–78; prin Ger Inverurie acad from 1978
m Aber 17.7.70 Sheila M. Grant MA 1966 *qv*

ROBERTSON George Lindsay   MB ChB 1967

ROBERTSON George Malcolm MacNeill   BSc 1968
 s of George A. R. man. dir and Morag D. Wark; b Aber 21.7.47
med rep: Wellcome Foundation central Scot. 1969–73, ICI Aber from 1973
m Aber 19.12.70 Irene P. Henderson teacher d of Alexander S. H. Aber

ROBERTSON George Ross   MA 1961

ROBERTSON George Slessor   MB ChB 1958 MD 1973
s of John B. R. garage prop. and Alice J. S. Clyne
teacher; b Peterhead 31.12.33
Struthers gold medal 1963 FFARCS 1964
h o Aber, Lond 1958–61; lect anat Aberd 1961–63; sen
h o anaest, regist, sen regist anaest Aber 1963–67; asst
anaest Winnipeg Canada 1967–68, consult. anaest/hon
sen lect anaest Aberd from 1969
m Aber 21.9.60 Audrey E. McDonald med res asst d of
Hector McD. Aber

ROBERTSON Gillian Gibbs   MA 1966
d of Thomas G. R. MA 1926 *qv*; b Elgin 17.12.43
teacher mod lang: Whitburn acad 1967–70, Edin 1970–71,
Ellon 1971, Harlaw acad Aber 1971–73 latterly asst prin
mod lang
m Aber 6.4.71 Kenneth J. Chew BSc 1968 *qv*

ROBERTSON Gordon Watson   *BSc(agr) 1969

ROBERTSON Graeme William   BSc 1969
s of William R. bank man. and Marjory J. Thain PO
civ serv; b Aber 30.1.47
higher scient off. Macaulay inst for soil res Aber from
1971

ROBERTSON Hamish Thomson   MA 1970

ROBERTSON Helen Lawrence   MA 1956
BEd(Manit)
m Caswell

ROBERTSON or Johnston, Helen Mary   MB ChB 1962
b Aber 21.3.38
m Sumner

ROBERTSON Ian   *BSc(eng) 1966
s of Robert C. R. grocer and Daisy A. M. B. Masson
nurse; b Cardenden 12.12.44
MICE 1971 MEng(Glas) 1972
eng: Aber 1966–67, Longannet 1967–68, Stirling 1968–71;
sub-ag Erskine 1971–73; ag Coulport from 1973
m Aber 28.10.67 Muriel E. R. Leiper computer oper d of
Alexander W. L. Aber

ROBERTSON Ian   *MA 1967
s of John R. bank man. and Alice R. Walton; b Lond
17.1.45
Dip Ed(Cantab) 1968
teacher Engl Fettes coll Edin 1968–72; BBC sports
broadcaster/rugby commentator Lond from 1972

ROBERTSON Ian Graeme   *BSc 1964

ROBERTSON Irene Adams   MA 1965
d of William R. farm. and Katherine P. Adams
teacher; b Aber 23.12.43
Dip Soc St(Edin) 1966
fam case worker Aber assoc soc serv 1966–68
m Marykirk 11.8.66 Stuart H. W. Duncan MB ChB 1965 *qv*

ROBERTSON Isobel Margaret   MA 1961
d of James G. R. farm. and Jane S. Cruickshank;
b Insch 1.1.38
teacher of blind Dorton House s for the blind Seal
Sevenoaks from 1963
m Aber 23.12.63 Charles B. Yule tv tech s of Charles
N. D. Y. Huntly

ROBERTSON James Albert   *BSc 1961
s of James S. R. farm. and Anne Gillanders; b Boyndlie

Fraserburgh 17.12.38
teacher: Galston 1962–63, chem Dumfries acad 1963–71,
prin chem Wallace Hall acad from 1971
m Aber 10.8.66 Sheana McGregor teacher

ROBERTSON James Alexander   *BSc 1956
s of Robert R. R. MA(Edin) C of S min and Jessie
G. S. McCready MA(Edin) teacher; b Edin 3.3.35
Kilgour sen schol(Aberd) 1956–58 R S McLaughlin resid
fell. Queen's univ (Kingston Ont) 1956–57 MSc(Ont) 1960
Ont Canada: summer geol asst 1954–56, field party
leader 1956–60, geol Ont dept mines 1960–72, chief
mineral deposits geol Ont div of mines Min of nat
resources Toronto from 1972
m Toronto 20.1.68 Reima M. Bogle secy d of Leslie P. B.
Toronto

ROBERTSON James Edwin   *BSc 1967

ROBERTSON James Forsyth   BSc(eng) 1961

ROBERTSON James Youngson   MA 1961
s of James R. grocer and Eileen G. Nicol cashier;
b Aber 21.9.40
teacher: Inverkeithing p s 1962–64, Townhill, Dunfermline
p s 1964–65, Bridge of Don, Scotstown p s Aber 1965–
70; head O'Neil Corse p s from 1970

ROBERTSON Jane Petrie   MA 1967
d of John C. R. RN police and Joan W. Petrie dressmaker; b Perth 8.6.45
teacher geog: Lond 1968–69, Windsor 1969–73, head
geog 1973–75
m Aber 8.8.69 Iain G. N. Harris MA 1968 *qv*

ROBERTSON Janet Gibson   MA 1962
m Maclaren

ROBERTSON John Gordon   MB ChB 1959

ROBERTSON John Grant   *BSc(eng) 1967
s of John M. R. sales man. and Betty C. Edmonstone;
b Edin 3.1.44
MEng(Glas) 1971 MICE 1973
des eng/site RE Edin 1967–72; des eng Lagos Nigeria
1972–75; sen des eng Edin 1975–76; sen designer/loc off.
man. Kuwait from 1976
m Arbroath 5.4.68 Elma C. Bishop teacher d of Richard
S. B. BD(Edin) Arbroath

ROBERTSON John Hamish   *MA 1969
s of Eric D. R. BSc(for) 1934 *qv*; b Delhi 18.3.45
edit. coins, medals and currency weekly Indep Mags
Lond 1969–72; radio journalist Aust broadcasting
commission publ affairs sect. Sydney/Brisbane from 1972

ROBERTSON John Macdonald   *BSc 1969
s of Wilfred R. mill worker and Jane L. Rothnie;
b Ellon 29.1.47
Dip Genetics(Edin) PhD(Edin) 1973
m Portobello 28.11.70 Moira S. M. McKenzie BSc(Edin)
1967 tech off. d of John R. McK. Edin

ROBERTSON John Watt   MB ChB 1959
s of William R. fishing skipper and Maggie J. Watt
dressmaker; b Gardenstown 3.10.23
DRCOG 1962 MRCGP 1965
h o Aber 1959–60; trainee g p Aber 1960–61; h o Inv
1961–62; g p: Aber 1962–70, Tarbert Harris from 1970
m Kirkintilloch 27.7.57 Alexandrina Gillies SRN d of
Donald G. Kirkintilloch

ROBERTSON Kathleen Jean   MA 1968
m Edmiston

ROBERTSON Kathleen Mary   *MA 1959
resid Glasg

ROBERTSON Kenneth George *MA 1963 Dip Ed 1964

ROBERTSON Kenneth Gordon   *MA 1970
s of Norman M. R. off. man. and Jane H. Gordon;
b Aber 14.3.47
PhD(R'dg) 1980
lect sociol R'dg from 1972
m New York 9.4.78 Ellen F. Greenberg BA(NY) market
res Metal Box corp d of William G. Rockaway Beach

ROBERTSON Laurna Mary Scott   MA 1965

ROBERTSON Leonora Wood   MA 1957 Dip Ed 1958

ROBERTSON Lindsay   BSc 1963

ROBERTSON Lorraine Irvine   MA 1970
d of George R. bookbinder and Helen L. Wilson ptnr
in fam bus. (Geo Jolly); b Aber 29.3.48
teacher Engl: Summerhill acad Aber 1972–74, Kincorth
acad Aber 1974–76; signwriter (own bus.) Orkney from
1976
m Aber 22.4.77 David H. Bichan BSc 1976 shipping ag
s of Howard B. Deerness

ROBERTSON Margaret Cormack   MA 1969
                                                    Dip Ed 1970
d of Henry S. R. fish merch and Isabella M. Baxter;
b Aber 27.7.48
teacher St Margaret's s for girls Aber 1970–73
m Aber 21.12.70 John F. Hendry LLB 1968 qv

ROBERTSON Margaret Hamilton Stewart   MA 1967
d of Stanley G. R. BSc(Glas) sen scient papermaking
and Margaret B. Stewart; b Hamilton 19.1.46
teacher: Catrine 1968–69, Stranraer 1969–71
m Aber 5.8.67 John G. Davidson BSc 1967 qv

ROBERTSON Marion Isabel   BSc 1956
d of Mark R. master joiner/cabinetmaker and Marie
C. C. Reilley secy; b Aber 23.11.34
BA(OU) 1979
aircraft des Brist 1956–57; teacher maths Aber: High s
for girls 1958–63, Kincorth acad 1970–74, Torry acad
from 1974, prin guid from 1975
m Aber 4.4.60 Edward D. Turner teacher s of Harry T.

ROBERTSON Marjorie Anne   MA 1969
m Mitchell

ROBERTSON Marjory Elizabeth   *MA 1970
                                                    Dip Ed 1971
d of William R. bank man. and Marjory J. Thain;
b Aber 30.1.47
teacher Fr/Ger Perth h s from 1971
m Aber 27.7.76 John Lewis BSc(Sheff) teacher s of
Sydney L. Cardiff

ROBERTSON Mary Elizabeth   MA 1969
d of Adam A. R. merch seaman/weaver and Tina M.
Mouat; b Lerwick 14.7.48
asst soc worker Edin 1970–72; soc worker Argyll 1972–
73; p o tel Lerwick from 1973
m Dunrossness 2.9.69 John R. Kenney BSc 1969 qv

ROBERTSON Michael Lawrance   MA 1967
s of William V. R. eng man. and Christina F. Smith

hairdresser; b Aber 22.2.44
trg off. Bolton 1968.–69; man. consult. Bolton 1969–72;
prod. dir Londonderry 1972–75; man. consult Belf from
1975
m Aber 28.10.67 Marjorie J. Gilbert tel d of George G.
Aber

ROBERTSON Michael Mundie   *BSc 1958 PhD 1962

ROBERTSON Myrtle Emslie   BSc 1965
m Watson

ROBERTSON Neil   MA 1966 LLB 1968
s of George R. bank man. and Margaret R. Stephen
teacher; b Dufftown 24.12.45
law app Aber 1969–71; admin asst: loc auth Inv 1972–73,
secy's off. Aberd from 1973
m Aber 22.12.71 Sylvia J. Yeats secy d of Alexander
C. Y. Aber

ROBERTSON Neil   BSc(eng) 1967
s of William F. R. insur area man. and Daisy Sutherland ch's nurse; b Aber 4.12.42
MICE 1974 MIMunE 1975
asst eng Rosyth 1967–69; asst eng then sect. leader Glasg
1970–72; asst eng Aber 1972–75; sen eng Stonehaven
from 1975
m Aber 18.10.68 Brenda A. Christie MA 1965 qv

ROBERTSON Ouaine Mitchell   MA 1962
m Bain

ROBERTSON Patricia Clare   MA 1970
d of William J. R. granite merch and Clare Hodge
teacher; b Aber 21.7.49
post grad stud. nurse Aber 1971–72
m Aber 28.7.71 Norman H. Reid LLB 1969 qv

ROBERTSON Patricia Mary   *MA 1957
d of Peter D. R. bookseller and newsagent and Mary
H. R. Rhind; b Insch 30.9.35
Lond: export/import bi-ling secy 1958–59, embassy
translator/secy 1960–62, bi-ling confidential secy (statist)
1962; bi-ling p a: invest comp 1963, eng 1963–65,
comm radio 1965–66; teacher mod lang 1971–75; secy
(architects) 1975–76; secy (univ) from 1977
m Chelsea 18.5.63 Christopher P. Downey elect. distrib
eng s of Michael J. D. Lond

ROBERTSON Robert   BSc 1965

ROBERTSON Robert Elrick   MB ChB 1962

ROBERTSON Robert John   MB ChB 1958
s of Lindsay R. tourist information off. and Joan C.
Johnson; b Aber 4.3.32
trainee g p Lerwick 1959–60; g p: Unst 1960–78, Voe
from 1978
m Lerwick 1.3.59 Marion E. Gamble midwife d of
James G. Cardonagh Co Donegal

ROBERTSON Ronald Charles Ramsay   *BSc 1970
s of James B. R. marine eng and Elizabeth L. Ramsay
ch's nurse; b Glasg 20.3.44
grad stud. McM univ Hamilton Ont 1970–71; explor
geol Eire 1971; grad stud. Queen's univ Kingston Ont
1972–79; explor geol: Peru and Bolivia 1977 and 1978,
Alaska from 1979
m Kingston Ontario 18.1.75 Maria del Pilar Rosario Belon
BEd(Catolica Santa Maria) teacher d of Miguel B.
Arequipa Peru

ROBERTSON Sandra Mary Stewart   *MA 1965
m Morrison

ROBERTSON Sheena   MB ChB 1963
d of John W. R. fisherman and Christina McLeman;
b Fraserburgh 4.12.38
h o ARI, Addenbrookes hosp Camb 1963–65; asst m o
Caernarvon 1965–73; g p Stirling 1973–75; regist virol
W I G Glasg 1975–78; temp lect Middx med s Lond
from 1978
m Aber 1.8.64 Stewart R. Sutherland MA 1963 *qv*

ROBERTSON Sheila   MA 1966
d of George R. farm serv and Agnes Duncan; b Longside 30.1.45
teacher Seaton p s Aber 1967–69
m Aber 21.7.67 Gordon J. Fraser police serg s of James F.
Ellon

ROBERTSON Sheila Margaret   MA 1969 Dip Ed 1970
d of James A. R. farm. and Mabel Cameron nurse;
b Huntly 12.8.48
Lond: trainee computer progr 1970–71, progr 1971–72,
sen progr 1972–73, analyst/progr from 1973
m Huntly 10.6.72 Steven R. Johnson ACA s of Kenneth
C. J. BSc(eng)(Leeds) Sheffield

ROBERTSON Shonaid Elizabeth   MA 1960
m Barr

ROBERTSON Stuart Forrest   MB ChB 1964
s of James A. R. sales man. and Alice S. Forrest nurse;
b Aber 24.7.40
h o: Woodend hosp Aber 1964–65, Bridge of Earn hosp
1965–66; sen h o Manc royal eye hosp 1966–68; lect
anat Aberd 1968–71; asst m o h Kincardine c c 1971–74;
clin m o commun health div Grampian health board(south
dist) Aber from 1974
m Aber 7.2.72 Morag Macleod RGN d of Kenneth M.
Melbost Borve Is of Lewis

ROBERTSON Susan Florence   MA 1969
d of John S. R. fish merch and Dorothy L. Bittiner
secy; b Aber 9.3.48
Düsseldorf Ger: bi-ling secy 1970–73, acct exec in
advertising ag 1973–77
m Düsseldorf 22.6.76 Gerhard H. Hermenau prod. (tech
serv dept) in advertising agency s of Bruno H. H.
Ahrensburg W Ger

ROBERTSON Thomas Wilson   BSc(agr) 1969
s of John R. farm. and Mary F. Wilson; b Keith 23.2.47
MSc(N'cle) 1971
farm worker nr N'cle-u-Tyne 1971–72; jun res assoc
N'cle 1972–74; mechanisation advis NOSCA Aber from
1974
m Aber 18.8.70 Linda G. Coletta journalist d of Guido C.
Aber

ROBERTSON Vincent Charles   *BSc 1961
s of Alexander S. R. janitor and Helen F. Buckle;
b Elgin 31.8.39
De Havilland aerobatics trophy winner 1972
RAF: trainee pilot South Cerney, Weeming, Valley 1961–
63, Vulcan pilot Scampton 1963–66, Canberra pilot/flt
comm Laarbruch Ger 1966–69, qualified flying instr
Bristol 1969–72; central flying s instr Little Rissington
1972–73; comm off./sqdn ldr Queen's univ air squadron
Belf 1973–76; Brit Commanders in Chief Mission to
Soviet forces in Ger (Berlin) from 1976
m Aber 10.12.60 Christine F. Owen civ serv d of Robert
S. O. Aber

ROBERTSON Violet   *MA 1961

ROBERTSON William   *BSc(eng) 1967 MSc 1969

ROBERTSON Winifred Helen Joyce   *MA 1963
d of Alexander S. R. janitor and Helen F. Buckle;
b Elgin 22.8.41
teacher: Kirkton h s Dun 1964–67, Elgin acad 1967–68,
Aber acad (Hazlehead) 1968–73, Cardinal Manning
Boys' s Lond 1973–74, Hazlehead acad from 1974
m Elgin 23.7.68 Donald T. Graham tut/prin s of radiography s of John G. Is of Raasay

ROBILLIARD Kathleen Anne   MA 1965 Dip Ed 1966
d of Henry S. R. bldr and decorator and Lilian le
Gallez; b Hyde 12.10.43
teacher Fr/Engl: Northfield acad Aber 1966–68, Kingswood boys' s Bristol 1968–70; employ. off. (civ serv)
Salisbury 1971–74
m Aber 16.7.68 George W. Jack BSc 1967 *qv*

ROBIN Sara Veronica   BSc 1970 *1971
d of Angus H. R. BA(Cantab) admin and Katharine V.
Harvey; b Edin 21.9.49
Dip Ed(Syd) 1977
teacher VSO Kamuli Uganda 1971–72; Brit Council
admin Lond 1973–74; Oxfam/youth organis Glasg
1974–76
m Balfron 29.8.75 Hugh MacPherson BSc(eng) 1971 civ
eng s of Duncan H. MacP. BSc(eng)(Edin) Edin

ROBINSON Iain Robert   MA 1970
s of Douglas R. R. farm./agr merch and Isabel M. W.
Nicol; b Hutton 10.5.49
app acct Glasg 1970–73; farm man. trainee Whauphill
Newton Stewart from 1973

ROBINSON Keith   PhD 1966
BSc(Leeds)

ROBINSON Patricia Joan Martin   MA 1966
d of Wilfred M. R. MB ChB(Glas) g p and Joan B. S.
Davie MA(St And); b Glasg 19.10.45
passenger ag Air Canada Vancouver 1966–67; staff man.
Marks & Spencer Oxford 1968–69; secy Glasg 1970–71
m Kilmacolm 4.6.71 George M. Morton MA(Glas) solic
s of John M. Paisley

ROBISON Douglas   *BSc 1964
s of George D. R. plumber/gas meter collector and
Madeline P. Harris dressmaker; b Aber 28.9.41
Dip Ed(Makerere coll univ of E Af) 1965
teacher: head maths KNCU s s Moshi Tanzania 1965–
67, head maths Robinson Rd h s Nassau Bahamas 1967–
70, maths Ainslie Park comp s Edin 1970–73, maths
Ingiliz Linesi Istanbul 1973–74, head maths from 1974

ROBSON Donald Selby   BSc 1963

ROBSON Edith   MA 1962

ROBSON Fraser McPherson   *BSc(eng) 1970 MSc 1972
s of William L. M. R. comp dir and Muriel M. A.
Fraser; b Elgin 22.1.48
civ eng Binnie & ptnrs Lond from 1972

ROBSON Primrose Christine   *BSc 1969
m Brown

ROCKWELL Peter   MA 1967
s of Lloyd W. R. BSc(Harvard) oil broker and Grace
M. Sutton; b Tunbridge Wells 30.7.18
teacher mod lang Powis acad Aber from 1968
m Aber 12.8.42 Wilma G. Philip d of William P. OBE
MC TD Aber

ROCKWELL Peter William   MA 1965 LLB 1967
s of Peter R. MA 1967 *qv*; b Aber 16.11.43
solic Aber from 1967; ptnr Adam Thomson & Ross (now
Adam Cochran & Co) advoc Aber; secy Law Soc of Scot.
Aber and NE leg. aid committee
m Aber 3.4.69 Elspeth C. McDonald MA 1965 *qv*

RODDIS Linda Judith Ann   MB ChB 1970
s of John W. R. BSc(Lond) lect elect. eng and Muriel
E. R. Chard teacher comm subjs; b Plymouth 21.11.45
h o Aber, Dumfries 1970–71; Newfoundland Canada:
resid St John's 1971–72, St Anthony 1972–73; g p
Wimbledon 1973–76; part-time g p Halifax Nova Scotia
from 1977
m Aber 26.4.71 Alan D. Thomson MB ChB 1971 phys s
of Angus M. T. MB ChB(Glas) N'cle-u-Tyne

RODGER George David   *BSc 1962
s of George A. R. farm. and Annie I. Kidd; b Bridge
of Cally 5.8.40
teacher sc: Kintore 1963–67, Alford from 1967

RODGERS Patricia Elaine Joan   *MA 1970
d of Kenneth V. A. R. MB ChB(Edin) phys/surg and
Anatol C. Reeves MA(Atlanta) headmistress; b Nassau
Bahamas 13.7.48
Dip Internat Relations(Grad Inst Internat Rel Univ of
W Indies) 1972 PhD(Geneva) 1977
Min External Affairs Nassau: admin cadet 1970–71, asst
secy 1972–73, member of Bahamas delegation to 3rd UN
conference on the law of the sea in Caracas 1974 and
1975, 1st asst secy 1977–78; counsellor Bahamas emb
Washington from 1978 and chargé d'affaires ad interim
Aug 1979 to March 1980

RODGERS William Alan   MSc 1966
BSc(Lond)

ROE Isabelle Marie   MB ChB 1958
d of Frederick C. R. MA(Birm) prof French Hull,
Aberd and Claire A. Frebault L es L(Lyons) teacher/
writer Fr text books; b Aber 25.11.33
Aber: trainee asst g p 1959–60, sen h o paediat City hosp
1960–61, med asst radio therap ARI 1962–69; sen h o,
regist psycho-geriat Murray royal hosp Perth from 1970
m Aber 4.4.61 George F. J. Donald MA 1957 *qv*

ROGER Anne Young   BSc 1966

ROGER Brian Mitchell   MA 1967

ROGERS Howard Clive   MA 1969
s of David R. consult. comp pension scheme and
Gladys I. Goddard; b Ealing 22.7.48
Croydon: export man. sales trainee 1969–71, computer
input clerk 1971–72; teacher Fr: Tividale comp s Warley
1972–74, St Michael's h s Sandwell from 1974

ROGERS John Simon Blackford   MA 1970

ROGERS Teresa Anne   MA 1965
d of William B. L. R. teacher, army capt, trainee RC
priest and Dora M. Carnelly soc worker; b Folkestone
5.11.35
BA(Lond) 1972 Dip Lib(Aberystwyth) 1969
asst lib Lond: Tower Hamlets 1965–67, Wandsworth
1969–71; edit. asst OUP Lond 1972–73; Orion insur
clerk Folkestone 1976–77; recept/tel Inter-city Tours
Folkestone 1977–78; lib asst Lond 1978–79

ROLAND Philip Godfrey   BSc 1969
s of Egbert R. headmaster and Joan R. Severs valu-

ation off. loc govt; b Exeter 9.11.47
AMICE 1970 AMIStructE 1970
civ eng Lond 1969–72; gen man. Seven Seas Dredging
Weybridge from 1976
m Eltham 5.8.72 Lindsey J. Perkins teacher d of Leslie
G. F. P. Eltham

ROLBIN Cecil   MB ChB 1956

ROLLAND Fiona Mary   BSc 1970
d of Charles F. R. MB(Cantab) g p Edin and Venetia
G. Payne nurse; b Edin 22.11.48
air stewardess BEA 1970–72; Lond; sub-edit. *Brit Journal
of hosp med* 1972–73, sub-edit. *Over 21* mag. from 1973
m Cox

ROLLASON John David   LLB 1969
s of William N. R. MB ChB(Birm) consult. anaest
and Margaret Rowbotham dietitian; b Scunthorpe
27.9.48
Lond: consult. fin. serv 1969–74, insur broker from 1975
m Lond 6.10.73 Sarah P. Lunn SRN d of Eric J. A. L.
France

ROLLO Elizabeth Anne   MA 1969
d of George R. mason and Lizzie McKnight; b
Fraserburgh 7.8.47
for. lang secy Freiburg W Ger 1970–72
m New Pitsligo 7.8.69 Klaus Jordan (staatsexamen
Freiburg 1969) teacher s of Günter J. Bohringen W Ger

ROLLO Sheila Noble   BSc 1966
d of Robert N. R. farm. and Evelyn R. Bisset; b
Crimond 31.1.45
teacher maths: Peterhead acad 1967–71, Fraserburgh
acad 1971–73
m Crimond 31.7.65 Alexander J. Miller baker s of
Alexander M. Blackford

ROLTON Hilary Ann   *BSc 1968 PhD 1972
d of Grahame W. R. des eng and Ann Riley; b Melton
12.6.46
res fell.: Max Planck inst Berlin 1972–73, Beatson inst for
cancer res Glasg 1973–76; biochem Monklands dist
council hosp Airdrie from 1976
m Edin 28.12.74 Robert K. S. Gray BSc(Edin) teacher
s of Robert K. S. G. Edin

RONALD Alison   LLB 1970
m Carruthers

RONALD Guinevere   *MA 1968
b Aber 28.10.44
teacher Aber 1969–77; prin Ger AGS from 1977
m Aber 3.8.64 Jürgen K. A. Thomaneck MEd 1970 *qv*

RONALDSON John Blues   *MA 1957 Dip Ed 1958
s of Traill S. R. contr and Christina L. Blues; b Brough
Caithness 5.8.35
MEd(St And) 1968
asst école normale d'instituteurs Arras France 1958–59;
teacher mod lang Anstruther 1959–67; educ psych ch
guid clin Kirkcaldy 1967–69; staff tut. psych of ado-
lescence N'cle 1969–73; lect applied psych N'cle from
1973
m St And 6.7.63 Juliet E. Corden d of William C.
Cambridge

**ROOK David Anderson   BSc(for) 1957 *1958
                                          PhD 1963**
s of John I. R.; b Bukoba Tanzania 27.6.36
MSc(NY state coll of for.) 1960

asst lect for. Aberd 1960–64; scient in for. res inst Rotorua NZ from 1964
m Aber 19.7.61 Dorothy M. Pirie

ROPER Philip John   BSc(for) 1968

RORIE Neil Iain George   *MA 1967 *MEd 1969
s of James H. K. R. acct and Gertrude Yeaman; b Dun 29.5.44
teacher Dun h s 1969–71; head hist/sen housemaster Wombwell h s Yorks 1971–75; dep head Frogmore s from 1975
m Dun 4.4.70 Susan H. Gibson MA(St And) teacher d of Alexander G. Dun

ROSE Alwyn Lionel Edgar   MB ChB 1968
BSc(How Wash)

ROSE Christopher John   BSc(for) 1969
s of Charles R. painter/decorator and Ruby M. E. Frost asst matron; b Scunthorpe 9.11.47
for. Lincs 1969–70; trainee man. Civic Trees Nationwide 1970–71; for. Lincs; asst for. off. Milton Keynes dist council 1973–74, for. off. from 1974
m Folkestone 12.8.72 Judith B. Winspear teacher d of Terence W. Folkestone

ROSE George Charles Robert   *BSc(eng) 1967

ROSE Isla Margaret   BSc 1959
d of John R. BSc(agr) 1911 qv(II, III); b Port Charlotte Islay 1.9.37
eng White Waltham 1959–60; computer progr: Chelmsford 1960–64, Dounreay 1964–69; teacher maths Thurso from 1970
m Inv 24.9.66 David Thom asst man. fast reactor fuel reprocessing s of David T. Dun

ROSE James Hendry   BSc 1959
s of James R. works eng and Barbara Hendry; b Aber 22.5.38
nat serv (RE) Germany 1959–61; teacher: maths/sc Oldmeldrum 1963–68, maths Bankhead acad from 1968
m Aber 2.6.62 Sheila C. Anderson secy d of Alfred J. S. A. Aber

ROSE John   MA 1964
s of William R. clerk and Margaret Stronach; b Keith 20.1.44
teacher: Fr Bankhead acad Aber 1965–72, prin Fr Ellon acad from 1972

ROSE John Laurence   *BSc(eng) 1966
s of John R. BSc(agr) 1911 qv(II, III); b Rodel Is of Harris 17.1.40
MICE 1970
Glasg: grad eng Sir Wm Halcrow & ptnrs 1966–67, asst eng Cowan & Linn 1967–70, sen eng 1970–74, sen proj eng 1974–76; head of struct dept James Williamson & ptnrs from 1976
m Dunbeath 30.8.63 Elizabeth M. Sutherland BSc(Glas) teacher d of James E. P. S. Thurso

ROSE Norman   *MA 1970

ROSS Aileen Mary   MA 1962
d of George H. R. mason and Mary Davidson off. worker; b Inverurie 10.6.41
teacher: Foxbar p s Paisley 1962–63, Inverurie acad 1965–68; housemistress/dep head Limuru girls' s Kenya 1969–73; teacher/housemistress Harrogate coll 1973–74; teacher/year mistress Powis acad Aber from 1974

ROSS Alexander Hugh   MA 1956
d Caputh 24.1.74 AUR XLV 450

ROSS Alison Clark   MA 1962
d of John A. R. banker and Elspet M. Clark; b Aber 22.1.41
Dip Soc St(Edin) 1967
Engl asst Schleswig Ger 1963–64; teacher mod lang: Turriff 1964–66, Kelvinside acad Glasg 1967–71
m Aber 6.8.70 Ian B. McKellar MA(Glas) lect hist Jordanhill coll of educ s of Donald McK. Dalmuir

ROSS Andrew Alexander   *MA 1963
s of George R. BCom(Edin) acct clerk Unilever and Elspet I. Milne nurse, hosp matron; b N Cheam 27.9.41
man. trainee, jun man. steelworks Consett Iron Co Durh 1964–66; teacher: prin geog/sen housemaster Old Moshi African boys' resid s s Moshi Tanzania 1966–69, geog Boroughmuir s s Edin 1969–71, John Street s s Glasg 1971–73, asst prin geog Duncanrig s s E Kilbride 1973–75, prin geog Doon h s Dalmellington from 1975
m Glasg 10.7.71 Patricia A. Tait MA(Glas) teacher d of Alexander W. T. Glasg

ROSS Angus Roderick   BSc 1969

ROSS Avril Elizabeth   MA 1965
d of Donald C. R. pharm and Elizabeth Macleod; b Lairg 26.4.44
teacher Fr Inv royal acad 1966–69
m Cromarty 21.12.68 Robert G. Ritchie CPO RN s of Archibald G. R. Chessington

ROSS Barbara Adams Fenton   *BSc 1966
m McKenzie

ROSS Barbara Bruce   MA 1959

ROSS Catherine   MA 1966
d of James R. fireman NEFB and Johana N. Livingstone shopkeeper; b Lochgilphead 21.5.45
teacher: Willowpark inf s Aber 1967–72, 1974–77; nursery Drumgarth inf s from 1977
m Aber 9.8.68 Roderick F. Cameron MA 1966 qv

ROSS Catherine Anne   BEd 1969

ROSS Catherine Frances Hay   MA 1968
d of John H. R. off. man. and Kathleen M. R. Hay comptometer oper; b Aber 29.8.47
teacher Engl Aber 1969–73
m Aber 4.4.70 Neil Cromar LLB 1966 qv

ROSS Catherine Lindsay   MA 1961
d of James R. R. gen merch and Jessie S. MacPherson teacher; b Helmsdale 18.4.40
teacher dem p s Aber 1962–63; Norway: lib Molde 1974–75, Tromsø from 1975
m Aber 3.10.60 Sigurd B. Wisløff MB ChB 1963 qv

ROSS Charles Melville Brown   *MA 1958
s of Charles R. haulage contr and Christy M. MacAskill teacher; b Inv 12.12.36
teacher Stirling h s 1959–66 (spec asst 1965–66); prin classics: Turriff acad 1967–71, Banff acad from 1971
m Falkirk 26.12.59 Elizabeth C. Henderson clerkess/typist d of John W. H. Falkirk

ROSS Christine Donaldson   BSc 1967
d of Murdo A. R. salesman and Janet G. Donaldson typist; b Inv 7.4.47
computer syst eng Edin 1967–72

m Nairn 25.9.71 Howard W. Corfield BSc(Strath) computer eng s of Howard L. C. Clydebank

ROSS Claude Marie Louise MA 1960
d of R. H. R. man. dir and Germaine Lery L ès L(Paris); b Paris 24.6.23
m Edin 31.10.44 Norman S. Whitehead man. dir s of Frank W. Aber

ROSS David MA 1969
s of Robert R. lab. and Hughina McPherson; b Nairn 27.3.48
Dip Youth Commun Work(Edin) 1974
teacher Aber: Bankhead acad 1970–73, Harlaw acad 1974–77, Summerhill acad 1977–78, Bankhead acad from 1978

ROSS David Alexander *MA 1962
s of David R. bldr and Lena N. Davidson nurse; b Forres 23.4.40
PhD(Lond) 1967
lect Fourah Bay coll univ of Sierra Leone Freetown 1965–68; assoc prof hist Simon Fraser univ Burnaby BC Canada from 1968

ROSS David Sinclair *BSc 1967 MSc 1969 *BD 1977
s of William F. S. R. plasterer and Elspeth Black; b Aber 24.7.45
PhD(Glas) 1971
res chem with Philips Aachen W Ger 1971–74; min C of S Peterhead from 1978
m Aber 6.7.68 Heather G. Watt BSc 1970 qv

ROSS Donald Forrester MA 1963
s of Edward S. R. MA 1923 qv; b Aber 14.6.42
CA 1967
CA app G & J McBain Aber 1963–67; audit asst Thomson McLintock & Co Glasg 1967–69; C of S asst treas Edin 1969–75, dep treas from 1975
m Glasg 25.6.70 Dorothy R. Nelson teacher d of Jack N. Glasg

ROSS Donald George MB ChB 1967
s of John R. civ serv customs & excise and Barbara Cruickshank teacher; b Lonmay 6.6.44
FFARCS 1973
h o, sen h o Queen Mary's hosp Sidcup 1967–69; ARI: sen h o, regist, sen regist anaest 1969–77; consult. anaest from 1977
m Aber 12.12.69 Doreen A. Garvin radiogr d of Thomas G. Coleraine NI

ROSS Donald Hugh *MA 1964
s of John R. MA 1930 qv and Elizabeth Fraser MA 1930 qv; b Balintore 8.3.42
sub-edit. *Scotsman* Edin 1964–69; Lond: polit edit. gallup poll 1969–71, edit. *Labour Weekly* from 1971
m Glasg 28.9.70 Anne Macleod BA(OU) 1977 teacher d of Angus M. Shawbost Is of Lewis

ROSS Dorothy Susan Aitken MA 1967 CASS 1969

ROSS Douglas Fraser MA 1961
s of Simon D. R. BSc 1930 qv and Lilias M. Garland MA 1932 qv; b Pretoria S Af 25.11.40
CA
acct/comp secy: J. T. L. Parkinson–Twaddle Glasg 1969–70, J. T. L. Parkinson Aber 1970–71; acct inter-city transport Cumbernauld 1971–74; gen man. John Russell (Grangemouth) Grangemouth from 1974
m Glasg 6.7.68 Marjorie A. McNaught exec off. BoT d of Arthur B. McN. MA(Glas) Glasg

ROSS Edward Forrester *MA 1960
s of Edward S. R. MA 1923 qv; b Aber 13.6.37
teacher: coll de Geneva Geneva 1961–62, St Albans 1962–63, Bremen Ger 1963–66; head upper s Gilberd s Colchester from 1966
m Bremen 1966 Rosemarie Balzereit

ROSS Flora Munro *MA 1961
d of Angus W. R. farm. and Emily J. Hill clerkess; b Invergordon 1.12.39
BLitt(Oxon) 1968
post-grad stud. Oxon 1961; lect in Engl Liv 1963; Aber 1965
m Aber 8.9.70 John H. Alexander DPhil(Oxon) univ lect s of John A. Bath

ROSS Frank Leslie *BSc 1962 PhD 1965

ROSS Freda Mary MA 1964
m Binns

ROSS Gemmell Bowman MA 1970
s of Charles W. R. printer and Winifred C. Rennie secy; b Aber 6.6.49
RAF pilot flying Harriers No 3(F) sqdr Wildenrath W Ger (rank flt lt) from 1970
m Aber 20.12.73 Maureen L. Mathison MA 1973 pers secy d of George D. M. Aber

ROSS George MA 1960 dLLB 1962
s of George R. master baker and Ruby Nicol shop-keeper; b Aber 6.3.37
leg. asst Stephen & Smith advoc Aber 1962–65, ptnr from 1965; Aberd: part-time asst Scots Law 1962–70, part-time lect Scots Law/Private Law from 1970
m Aber 5.9.62 Anne Bruce hosp secy d of Alexander B. Aber

ROSS Glen Stewart Adam BSc 1964
s of Archibald R. master elect./plumber and Patricia Stewart (d 1943); b Aber 31.1.43
Cert Radiation Safety(Manc) 1975
teacher maths Bervie s s 1965–67; prin phys/area exams secy Lango coll Lira Uganda 1968–72; teacher phys/sc Lossiemouth h s 1972–76; prin sc/phys Speyside h s from 1976
m Aber 20.6.70 Isabella A. Russell teacher (d 1975) d of John D. R. MA(Glas) Rosemarkie

ROSS Graham Garland *BSc 1966

ROSS Gwyneth MA 1962
d of George W. R. MA 1928 qv; b Aber 7.8.41
Dip Sec Sc(Strath) 1963
m Edin 8.7.67 Raymond A. McCabe MA(Glas) fin. dir s of James O. McC. BA(Edmonton) Glasg

ROSS Hamish Fordyce *BSc 1959

ROSS Helen MA 1956
d of Stanley A. N. R. telecomm mech and Elizabeth B. Cocker tailoress; b Aber 23.7.36
teacher Renfrewsh 1957–61, Kent 1961–62
m Inv 29.12.62 Leslie P. Best

ROSS Helen Margaret MA 1969
m Antcliffe

ROSS Hilary Anne *MA 1967
d of John R. assur dist man. and Annabella C. Milne; b Ellon 9.12.44
DEP(Glas) 1969

asst educ psych Notre Dame child guid clin Glasg 1969–70; teacher Long Eaton p s Derbysh 1970–71; biometrician med dept Ciba–Geigy Basel from 1971
m Manc 31.5.69 M. Jamil Chaudri BSc(Salf) mathematician s of M. Khalil C. Toronto

ROSS Iain Paul   BSc 1965 PhD 1970
s of John R. customs off. and Barbara Cruickshank teacher; b Lonmay 28.1.43
res stud. med s Aber 1965–70; clin biochem W gen hosp Edin 1970–73; lab scient univ hosp Edmonton Alberta 1974; truck driver Edmonton 1974–75; civ serv Alberta prov govt from 1975

ROSS Iain Sutherland   MB ChB 1964 PhD 1970
s of William S. R. man. dir farm comp and Ruby Clark; b Enfield 18.9.38
sen lect chem path. Aberd from 1973
m Aber 12.2.66 Joan A. Bell d of James M. B. Bearsden

ROSS Isabel MacDonald   *MA 1968
d of John Ross MA 1930 *qv* and Elizabeth Fraser MA 1930 *qv*; b Dingwall 4.10.46
Dip Psych(WAIT) 1974
W Aust: teacher soc stud. Armadale h s 1969–70; res asst Melbourne 1970; teacher Engl Balcatta h s 1971–72; guid off. Loreto convent Claremont 1974; tut. psych to external WAIT stud. Albany 1975; school psych Albany 1976–77
m Inv 31.8.68 Terence M. Kilkenny MA 1968 *qv*

ROSS James   MA 1964 BD 1967
s of David R. fisherman and Elizabeth Johnston; b Port Seton 26.4.33
C of S min: Kilsyth from 1968
m Tranent 1.9.55 Mary C. Somerville typist d of Robert S. Port Seton

ROSS James   BSc(eng) 1970
s of John R. maintenance worker process ind and Andrewina M. Crawford; b Fraserburgh 13.4.43
instrumentation eng dev Glasg 1970–72; Cambuslang: process dev eng 1972–73, asst works eng from 1973
m Aber 5.8.71 Elaine M. Duncan MA 1968 *qv*

ROSS James MacLean   MA 1963

ROSS John   *BSc 1964

ROSS John   BSc 1961 PhD 1964

ROSS John Alexander   *MA 1970
s of Samuel T. R. comm clerk and Helen M. Christie hotel receptionist; b Aber 1.2.38
Dip Lib(Strath) 1973
Esso petr comp: market. trainee Lond 1970–71; oper superv N Shields 1971–72; lib Lanark c c E Kilbride 1973–74, dep lib Bishopbriggs dist lib from 1974

ROSS John Fraser   *MA 1961
s of John R. MA 1930 *qv* and Elizabeth Fraser MA 1930 *qv*; b Inv 27.6.40
MA(Alta) 1962
lect Glas from 1964
m Fort Augustus 17.8.63 Theresa E. MacDonald MA 1963 *qv*

ROSS Kathleen Anne   MA 1969
d of Frederick G. R. pharm and Lily H. Munro; b Ellon 11.7.48
stud. YESTB Manc poly 1970–71; careers off. Bolton corp 1970–72

m Stonehaven William A. Wright sub edit. *Daily Mail* Manc s of William W. Didsbury

ROSS Lorna Alison Ishbel   MA 1968

ROSS Margaret Isobelle Fraser   MA 1968 Dip Ed 1969
d of John A. R. mech, traffic warden and Margaret C. Fraser; b Maryburgh 8.6.47
Edin: teacher mod lang Tynecastle h s 1969–73, asst housemistress 1972–73, prin Fr from 1973

ROSS Marion Catherine   MA 1965
m Robb

ROSS Marjory Millikin   MA 1962
b Peterhead 18.12.40
Perth h s: teacher Engl 1963–70, spec asst 1970–72, asst prin Engl from 1972

ROSS Mary Jane Storey   MA 1958

ROSS Maureen Vallely   MA 1966
m Watts

ROSS Patricia Frances Bernadette   MA 1968
d of John R. MB ChB 1937; b Fraserburgh 22.3.47
Lond: marketing asst 1969–70, proj admin 1970–71, pers asst 1971–76
m Aber 30.8.71 Richard G. L. Stileman BSc 1968 *qv*

ROSS Philip Wesley   MB ChB 1960 cMD 1970
s of George W. R. MA 1928 *qv*; b Aber 6.6.36
MIBiol 1970 FLS 1973 TD 1974
lect bact: Aberd 1961–64, Edin 1964–73; sen lect bact/hon consult. bact Edin RI from 1973; sen warden outward halls and student houses Edin from 1972
m Aber 12.8.60 Stella J. Shand MA 1958 *qv*

ROSS Rhoda Isabella   *BSc 1960
d of David R. clerk and Christina S. Allan photog asst; b Aber 26.3.38
res stud. dept bot Aberd 1960–61; teacher Montrose 1962–68
m Aber 30.3.64 Gordon F. Legge BSc(agr) 1961 *qv*

ROSS Sheila Margaret Craig   MA 1970
d of William G. R. market gardener and Isabella H. C. McHarg; b Laurencekirk 3.3.49
teacher Fr/Ger Arbroath acad from 1971

ROSS Simon Fraser Robertson   *MA 1965
s of Finlay R. R. welding eng and Mary V. Fraser secy; b Inv 24.6.40
jun, middle, sen man. posts Indust & Comm Fin. corp Lond, Leic, Lond 1965–70; Edin: Scot. rep Williams Glyn & Co 1970–73, man. dir Royal Bank Dev 1973–76, man. dir Monross Investments from 1976
m Dingwall 26.9.70 Patricia M. Longmoor MA(Edin) soc worker d of Alexander P. L. Kincraig

ROSS Susan Christine   *MA 1968
m Tinch

ROSS Susan Janet Ferguson   MB ChB 1970
m Morrison

ROSS Valerie Anne   MA 1962
m Begg

ROSS William Alexander   MA 1968
s of William R. ironmonger and Annie M. Knox nurse; b Forfar 7.4.46

teacher: Arbroath 1969–70, Aber from 1970
m Arbroath 1.8.70 Marjory E. H. Drever teacher d of
Samuel D. MA(St And) Arbroath

ROSS William James   *BSc 1964

ROSS Wilson   MA 1968

ROTHIN David John   *MA 1969
s of Arthur R. carpet fitter and Ethel Moore; b
Wolverhampton 17.4.47
computer progr: GPO Lond 1969–71, Morrison's assoc
comps Glasg 1971–74; computer analyst/progr Lanarksh
c c Hamilton from 1974
m Motherwell 20.4.73 Aileen M. Sinclair MA 1972
teacher d of John S. Inv

ROTHNIE Douglas William   MB ChB 1957
s of Alexander R. farm worker and Barbara Duguid;
b Fyvie 6.11.30
h o royal ment hosp, City hosp Aber, ARI 1957–58;
m o RAF UK, Aden, Persian Gulf 1959–62; sen h o:
cas Woolmanhill Aber 1962–63, Risedale mat. hosp
Barrow-in-Furness 1963–64; g p Barrow-in-Furness from
1964
m Denmark 8.5.60 Edel H. Henriksen nurse d of Peder H.
Staellands Odde

ROWELL Michael John   MSc 1969
s of Basil W. R. marine eng and Claire D. Heather;
b Lond 6.1.46
BSc(Hull) 1967 PhD(Sask) 1974
Canada: sessional lect soil microbiol Saskatoon 1972–73,
post doct fell. Edmonton 1974, sess lect 1974–75

ROWLANDS Brian MacLean   *MA 1968
s of Arthur W. R. banker and Helen C. S. MacLean
MB ChB 1936 qv; b Aber 3.7.46
Dip Ed Psych(Lond) 1969
teacher Greenwich (ILEA) 1969–71; educ psych Bradford from 1971
m Greenwich 2.10.70 Valerie Burton teacher d of Samuel
H. B. MA(Cantab) Dulverton

ROWLANDS Owen   *MA 1967
s of William M. R. teacher and Gladys Hunt teacher;
b Wolverhampton 19.1.44
teacher Fr/Ger RGC Aber 1968–70; prin mod lang:
Earlston 1970–72, Galashiels acad from 1972
m Aber 15.8.67 Pamela M. Rennie MA 1965 qv

ROWLING Christopher Lewis   *BSc(eng) 1968
s of Gerald A. R. bank off. and Edna Pearman;
b Croydon 17.12.45
Lond: tv elect. circuit des eng IBA 1969–72, oper
broadcast eng 1972–73, broadcast eng Capital Radio from
1973
m Bitteswell 29.6.74 Janis L. Moignard loc govt off. d of
C. George M. Bitteswell

ROWORTH Colin Campbell   *BSc 1970
s of William L. R. ARIBA arch. and Mary O. S.
Campbell nurse; b Edin 17.1.49
proj leader (res and dev) papermakers Wiggins Teape
Beaconsfield 1970–72; res and dev tech Tullis Russell &
Co Glenrothes 1972–76; group leader (chem tech serv)
Tullis Russell from 1976
m Beaconsfield 14.10.72 Susan Lockhart teacher d of
Clement L. Beaconsfield

ROY Bharatendu Narayan   PhD 1957
MSc(Calc)

ROYLE Trevor Bridge   *MA 1967
s of Kenneth B. R. army off. and Kathleen B. Page;
b Mysore India 26.1.45
Edin: edit. William Blackwood 1968–70, lit. dir Scot. arts
council from 1971
m(1) Shrivenham 26.8.67 Jane B. Sibbald MA 1968 qv;
marr diss 1.2.73
(2) Edin 27.4.73 Hannah M. Rathbone MB ChB(Edin)

RUBBI Saiyid Fazl-I   PhD 1964
MSc(Dacca)

RUBIN Freda   *MA 1967

RUDDIMAN Kenneth Wilson   *MA 1962
m Helene A. Stewart MA 1962 qv

RUFF Lynda   *BSc 1965 PhD 1968
d of Wilfred S. R. dir eng firm and Laurel W. Dexter
secy; b Radlett 27.9.41
asst res path. Denbigh 1968–69
m Rickmansworth 4.5.68 Christopher J. Flemming MB
ChB 1968 qv

RUKUBA Martin   BSc(for) 1959

RULE Frank   *BSc 1962
s of George W. R. rly guard and Winifred Gray;
b Cambridge 29.7.24
teacher biol Blairgowrie 1963–65, prin biol 1965–69;
lect coll of educ Aber from 1969
m Lusaka Zambia 5.11.49 Margaret Keith nurs sister d
of William K. Mintlaw stat

RUNCIE Moira Anne Gardiner   *MA 1969
d of William R. pharm/optic and Margaret Tait
teacher; b Aber 6.6.47
lect Engl univ of Malawi Blantyre 1969–70, Zomba from
1976
m Blantyre Malawi 23.8.69 Patrick D. Hardcastle BSc(for)
1968 qv

RUNOLFSSON Sveinn   BSc(agr) 1970
s of Runolfur Sveinsson BSc(Copenhagen) dir soil
conserv serv and Valgerður Halldrösdóttir; b Hvanneyri
Iceland 28.4.46
MSc(Corn) 1972
Gunnarsholt Iceland: asst soil conserv 1970–72, dir soil
conserv serv from 1972
m Iceland 27.12.73 Oddný Saemundsdóttir nurse d of
Saemundur Jónsson

RUSH Christopher   *MA 1968

RUSHTON Sarah Ruth   *MA 1970
d of Edwin P. K. R. MB ChB(Birm) med pract and
Joyce W. Newman nurse; b Bristol 14.2.49
asst solic Northampton 1974–79
m Leeds 10.7.70 Anthony P. Sturdee BSc 1968 qv

RUSHWORTH Alison Louise   MA 1970
d of William R. R. BA(Lond) teacher and Dorothea A.
Gladstone headmistress; b Wimbledon 24.4.49
BA(Lond) 1973
teacher Engl to adults in Volkhochschule: Stuttgart
Ger 1973–74, Heidelberg from 1975

RUSK Isabel Henderson   *MA 1956
d of William M. R. R. MA(Glas) lect r e and Constance
A. Henderson; b Glasg 3.4.35
Cert Soc St(Edin) 1957
ch care off. Aber 1958–62
m Aber 24.2.62 William J. Farquhar MA 1958 qv

RUSSELL Agnes Jean   MLitt 1968
   BA(Lond)
m Short

RUSSELL Alan Gordon   MA 1963

RUSSELL Alison Margaret Joan   BSc 1969 *MEd 1973
   d of James K. R. hotel man. and Ivy J. Hill; b Aber
9.7.48
teacher maths: Kingussie 1970–72, internat s Geneva
1973–75
m Aber 15.4.74 David J. Ryan teacher s of John J. R.
Weymouth

RUSSELL Andrew   BSc 1970
   s of James R. telecomm supt and Joan A. Finch BBC
receptionist; b Huddersfield 20.8.49

RUSSELL Brian Montgomery   *BSc(eng) 1970
   s of Andrew M. R. MA(Glas) C of S min and
E. Pauline Allan nurse; b Arbroath 19.10.48
des progr 1970–73; team leader progr 1973–77; sen eng
LSI Exploitation ICL Manc from 1977
m Pudsey 19.8.72 J. Margaret Kingman BSc(Leeds)
progr d of Reginald K. Pudsey

RUSSELL Dorothy May   *MA 1962
   m Ellis

RUSSELL George   MB ChB 1959
   s of George R. merch/farm. and Elizabeth M. Law
teacher; b Insch 2.7.36
MRCP(Lond) 1964 FRCP 1977
h o, sen h o, regist Aber 1959–65; res fell. univ Colorado
med center Denver USA 1965–67; lect ch health Aberd
1967–68; consult. paediat Grampian health board Aber
from 1969; prof paediat univ of Riyadh, Saudi Arabia
1977–78 (leave of absence)
m Aber 20.8.62 Gillian D. Simpson radiogr d of Douglas
B. S. Kirriemuir

RUSSELL Helen May   *BSc 1965
   d of George S. R. baker and Catherine Buchan teacher;
b Inv 9.12.43
town plan. asst Aber 1965–67
m Aber 17.9.66 Ian P. Souter MA 1964 qv

RUSSELL Ian Farquhar   *BMedBiol 1970
                                    MB ChB 1973
   s of Alexander R. gamekeeper and Kathleen M.
Baxter nurse, bookkeeper; b Insch 11.11.48
FFARCS 1977
resid m o Latrobe Tasmania 1973–74; sen resid m o Sir
Charles Gairdner hosp Perth Aust 1975–76; regist anaest
ARI 1976–77; spec paediat anaest Janeway hosp Newfoundland 1978; sen regist anaest ARI from 1977
m Aber 15.7.72 Helen S. Campbell BSc 1973 tut.
histology d of Thomas G. M. C. Aber

RUSSELL James   *BSc 1958 PhD 1963
   s of James R. foreman shoe repairer and Jane W.
Youngson; b Aber 24.11.35
FCIPA 1970 European Patent Attorney
patent off. min of aviation Lond 1961–64; patent off.
liaison with US govt Brit emb Washington DC 1964–67;
sen patent off. RAE Farnborough 1967–78; prin pat.
off. MoD Lond from 1978
m Aber 19.12.60 Elspeth R. Geggie teacher p e d of
Thomas W. G. Glasg

RUSSELL James Gordon   MB ChB 1966
   s of Alexander R. butcher and Eileen J. Emslie;
b Fyvie 11.4.42

DObstRCOG 1968 MRCGP 1972 DPharm Med 1977
h o ARI 1966–67; sen h o: obst Northampton gen hosp
1967, med Killearn hosp 1968, paediat Alder Hey ch's
hosp Liv 1968–69; ship's surg royal fleet auxil MoD 1969;
g p Bucksburn 1969–75; med advis Ciba–Geigy (UK)
from 1975
m Aber 6.5.72 Jennifer M. Renton occup therap d of
David R. R. Aber

RUSSELL Jennifer Mary   MA 1968
   d of Archibald R. R. man./comp dir and Irene
Rowlings; b Falkirk 14.9.47
Dip Ed(Glas) 1969
teacher: geog Dalry h s 1969–70, geog/mod stud.
Garnock acad Kilbirnie 1970–72, asst prin guid 1972–74;
prin guid Auchenharvie acad Stevenston 1974–76
m Largs 11.7.75 Crawford W. Logan BSc(Paisley tech
coll) gen man. s of James W. L. MB ChB(Glas) Largs

RUSSELL John Grant   BSc(eng) 1969

RUSSELL Kathleen   BSc 1962
   d of George S. R. baker and Catherine Buchan
teacher; b Inv 17.3.41
teacher maths: Inv 1963–65, Aber 1965–66, Lond from
1973
m Aber 13.7.65 Bryan Hickson MB ChB 1965 qv

RUSSELL Leslie   MA 1962
   s of William R. baker and Mary Leslie shop asst;
b Aber 1.6.41
Higher Dip R Ed(Aber) 1963
teacher relig educ: Falkirk h s 1963–68, Aber acad/
Hazlehead acad 1969–73, asst prin r e 1973–75, prin r e
from 1975
m Aber 10.4.65 Anne W. S. Douglas shorthand typist d of
Alexander D. Aber

RUSSELL Mhairi Ballantyne   MB ChB 1966
   d of Robert S. B. R. LDS(Glasg) dent. and Mabel E.
Duthie; b Torphins 28.4.43
Aber: h o City hosp, RACH, mat. hosp 1966–68;
trainee g p Elgin 1968–69, part-time g p Cullen/Portsoy
from 1969
m Aber 25.8.69 Iain D. Legge agr insp Dept Agr(Scot.)
s of John A. L. Invergordon

RUSSELL William   *BSc 1964
   s of James R. foreman shoe repairer and Jane W.
Youngson; b Aber 4.2.41
Cert Computer Sc(Brunel) 1972
VSO lect Guyana s of agr corp 1964–65; Lond: scient off.
police scient dev branch Home Office 1965–68, sen
scient off. 1968–71, prin scient off. civ serv dept 1971–77,
sen prin scient off. 1977–79; dep town clerk/chief exec
Aber from 1979
m Aber 1.7.67 Sandra Ross civ serv d of Alexander I. R.
Aber

RUST Mary Wilson   MA 1957 Dip Ed 1965
   d of James H. R. MA(Edin) C of S min and Mary
Wilson mission.; b Moukden China 26.11.36
teacher Dumfries 1959–64 and from 1970; head Dunsyre
p s 1965–70

RUTHERFORD Andrew Adams   PhD 1963
   s of James S. R. MA(Royal Univ Ireland) presb min
and Bertha C. Robb; b Warrenpoint Co Down 3.1.25
B Agr(Belf) 1951 M Agr(Belf) 1957 FRSS 1959
off. i/c field exper Loughry agr coll Cookstown Co
Tyrone; post grad stud. statist Aberd 1954–56; off. i/c
field exper Macaulay inst for soil res Aber 1956–57;
scient off., prin scient off., consult. statist ARC unit of

statist Aberd; dept agr NI/head agr biometrics Belf 1964–76; head statist dept East Malling res inst from 1976 m Rostrevor Co Down Harriet M. Clarke receptionist stud. health centre d of William C. Newry

RUTHERFORD Barbara Anne   MA 1962
d of John R. flt lt RAF eng fitter/farm. and Mary C. I. Collingwood shop asst; b Aber 9.12.40
teacher Engl: to for. stud. Kent 1964–65, Brit council scheme Halden Bodø Norway 1965–67, Willington Co Durh from 1968

RYAN Pamela   *MA 1970 MLitt 1972
d of Angus C. R. HGV driving instr and Euphemia Mundie; b Glasg 31.3.49
teacher: Brittons s Essex 1972–74, Walthamstow girls' h s Waltham Forest from 1974
m Helensburgh 12.8.72 Graham H. Munn MA(Glas) civ serv s of Thomas M. Cardross

RYDER Carol Ann   *BSc 1969

SAAD Zakaria Abdalla Mohamed   BSc(for) 1969
BSc(Khart) MSc(Khart)

SAAKWA-MANTE Kwaafo   MSc 1964
s of Saakwa-Mante merch and Korkoi Mensan; b Accra Ghana 17.2.24
MB ChB(Leeds) 1952 DTM&H(Lond) 1954 DPH 1956 MFCM 1974
sen m o Accra 1964–68; chief med statist centre for health statist Ghana from 1968
m Crewe 8.6.54 Nora Clegg d of Thomas C. Rochdale

SABRI AL-OZAIRI Sudad   PhD 1968 *ChM 1972
MB ChB(Bagh)

SACHS Monica Trevor   MA 1966

SADLER Alexander James   MA 1961
s of George S. area man. petr comp and Mary Cruickshank; b Lairg 7.12.40
BA(OU) 1977
teacher maths Aber: Hilton s s 1962–70, coll of comm 1970–73, prin maths Torry acad from 1973
m Aber 15.7.64 Joan M. Reid MA 1963 qv

SADLER Glenn Edward   PhD 1967
AB(Ill) MA(Calif)

SADLER Michael George   LLB 1967 *MA 1970
s of William R. S. LRCPGlas med pract and Margaret T. Marshall MA(Glas) teacher; b Stranraer 25.2.47
ACCA 1972
acct manuf indust N'cle-u-Tyne 1970–73; plant acct man. Manc 1973–75; Melton Mowbray: fin. acct man. manuf indust 1975–77, fin. controller from 1977
m Edin 10.8.70 Susan W. Stewart MA 1969 qv

SADLER Robin Mischa   *BSc(for) 1964
s of John S. teacher and Eveline M. Sanders artist; b Macclesfield 8.10.41
Brit Council schol inst for Skogskjøtsel Vollebekk Norway Bergen, Vollebekk 1964; teacher: Congleton s mod s Congleton 1965, biol King's s Macclesfield 1965–79; sheep farmer Laxey I o M from 1979
m Laxey 30.7.66 Margaret H. Clague textile des d of Robert Q. C. Laxey

SADLER Rodney Grayston   BSc(eng) 1958
s of Frederick W. S. sales rep and Ellen M. Annison; b Aber 11.7.36

CEng MICE 1964
engineer: asst Wimpey 1958–61, exec with water supplies div of Govt West Nigeria 1961–63, section Taylor Woodrow 1964, section to proj man. Costain Civil 1964–74, reg man. Wales Shellabear Price contr 1975–76, div man. SE England Bovis Civil 1977–80, comm dir Protern des bldg Wales from 1980
m Aber 11.9.59 Elizabeth A. S. Metcalfe comptometer oper, cler asst d of George M. Aber

SAID Abdullah Babiker Mohamed   MSc 1967
s of Babiker Mohamed S. and Elhassan El Sania Fatima; b 1.1.39
BSc(agr)(Beirut)
Sudan: land use off. Elfasher Darfur prov 1967–68, Elobeid Kordofan prov 1968–69; co-man. Savanna dev proj Khartoum 1969–73; asst dir proj: rural dev dept 1973–75, soil conserv and land use dept from 1975
m Omdurman Sudan Abdel Halim Ahmed Fathia secy d of Abdel Halim Ahmed Omdurman

SAINT Christine   MA 1969
m McLaren

SAINT Lorna Sinclair   MA 1956
d of Ernest S. police off. and Anne G. Sinclair; b Aber 21.12.35
admin secy Internat Airadio Lond 1957–58; teacher Engl govt s for boys Bo Sierra Leone 1958–59
m Bo Sierra Leone 23.6.58 William D. Carslake BSc(for) 1955 qv

SALARDINI Ali Akbar   MSc 1962 PhD 1965
BSc(agr)(Teheran)

SALIH Fathi Mohamed   BSc(for) 1967

SALIH Hussein   BSc(for) 1964

SALVIN Janice Lillian   MA 1968
m Reid

SAMA Daniel Sundima   MB ChB 1963
s of Thomas S. farm. and Marie S. Ndomahina; b Njala Sierra Leone 24.12.30
DTM & H 1965 FRSocTM & H
Sierra Leone: m o 1965–68, m o Njala Un Coll 1968–70; regist psychiat Haddington 1970–73; s m o Njala Un Coll from 1973
m Aber 30.11.60 Olivia T. Caulker d of Alphoso C. Shenge Sierra Leone

SAMPSON Alan John   BSc(for) 1961
s of Ronald D. S. heating eng and Dorothy M. Jarman; b Milton Regis 7.4.37
physiol asst, sen agronomist Shell biosciences lab Kent from 1961
m Sittingbourne 5.9.59 Geraldine Gutsole

SAMPSON Enid Elizabeth   MSc 1970
d of John H. S. marine eng and Eleanor M. Douglass teacher; b Middsx 1918
BSc Sp(Ext) (Lond) 1942
asst to rural plan. consult 1970–72
m Cambridge 1943 John S. D. Bacon ScD(Cantab) res scient and univ teacher s of Charles H. B. BSc(Lond) Lond

SAMUELS Digby John   LLB 1970

SANANIKONE Prasong   BSc(agr) 1969

SANANIKORN Prida *BSc(agr) 1965
  s of Thao Peng Sananikorn banker/politician and Boonthan bus. woman; b Vientiane Laos 4.8.40
Thailand: sen man. (marketing) Bangkok 1965–68, sen exec (advt) 1968–71, chief sales div Construct. Material Marketing Comp Bangkok from 1971
m Aber 14.4.65 Avril R. Clarke MA 1965 *qv*

SANDERS Penelope Jane *MA 1969
  d of Brian G. S. ophth optician and Edith M. Holt; b Walsall 7.4.47
Dip Clin Psych(Br Psych Soc) 1976
secy: FCO Lond 1970, Royal Free hosp Lond 1970–71, Price Waterhouse Assoc Lond 1971–72, Brit dom appliances Peterborough 1972–73; prob clin psych: Peterborough dist hosp 1972–73, Norfolk area health auth Norwich 1974–76; clin psych Broadmoor hosp 1976–77
m Coleshill 15.7.72 John E. Spinks LLB(Lond) retail exec s of Ronald L. S. King's Lynn

SANDERSON John Graham *BSc(eng) 1968

SANDISON Alan George *MA 1958
  s of William A. S. farm. and Bella J. Meston; b Ballater 13.11.32
PhD(Cantab) 1963
asst Engl Aberd 1960–62; lect Engl: Exe 1963–71, Durh 1971–74; prof Engl Strath from 1974

SANDISON Derek James BSc 1966
  s of James S. S. clerk (retd) and Margaret H. Burnett; b Ellon 17.9.45
aerodynamics eng BAC Brist 1966–68; sen scient computer analyst de Havilland aircraft Toronto 1968–78; syst man. HG Engineering Toronto from 1978

SANDISON Jean Mary Harrison MA 1966
  d of Arthur M. S. crofter/road lab. and Peterina Brown clerkess; b Heylor Shetland 15.1.45
teacher Anderson inst Lerwick 1967–71
m 11.7.68 David C. Marwick BSc 1964 *qv*

SANDRINGHAM Peter Rankin LLB 1966

SANDS David Clifford MB ChB 1969

SANDS Jeremy Nicol *MA 1958
  s of Harvey T. N. and Alice R. E. Benzie; b Glasg 18.1.37
resid California USA

SANDSTRAND Ivar Peter Kaare MB ChB 1963

SANGSTER Alan John *BSc(eng) 1963 MSc 1964 PhD 1967
  s of William J. S. postal worker and Edna M. Walker teacher; b Aber 21.11.40
CEng MIEE 1971
res eng Ferranti Edin 1964–69; sen eng, prin eng, group leader Plessey Radar Is of Wight 1969–72; lect H-W Edin from 1972
m Aber 12.4.69 Barbara M. Wilkie staff nurse d of James W. Aber

SANGSTER Alistair Scott MA 1970

SANGSTER Barrie MB ChB 1968
  s of Joseph S. bank man. and Mary A. McPherson; b Elgin 16.9.45
h o: ARI, Law hosp Carluke 1968–70, Stirling hosp, RACH 1970–72; g p Leeton NSW Aust from 1972

m Fyvie 14.8.70 Mary A. K. Hosie d of Alexander H. Fyvie

SANGSTER Christopher Leslie Gordon BEd 1969
  s of James H. S. MA 1930 *qv* and Mary A. Stewart MA 1929 *qv*; b Elgin 20.5.47
teacher Perthsh 1969–73; lect educ tech S Thames Coll Lond 1973–74; advis educ tech SCET Glasg 1974–75; organis i/c teachers' resource centre Portsmouth 1975–78; trg consult. Guardian BS Lond from 1978
m Broughty Ferry 18.7.70 Gillean H. B. Thomson

SANGSTER Gillian Mary MB ChB 1962
  d of James H. S. MA 1930 *qv* and Mary A. Stewart MA 1929 *qv*; b Elgin 10.8.39
h o RAHC, ARI, Woodend hosp Aber 1962–64; trainee g p Mells Frome 1964–65
m Aber 14.4.65 Alastair M. Suttie MB ChB 1961 *qv*

SANGSTER Harry Maxwell *BSc(agr) 1964
  s of Harry S. BSc(agr) 1950 *qv*; b Perth 6.2.42
agr dev off. Edin, Lanarksh from 1964
m Methven 4.8.66 Sheena M. Wann chirop d of John W. Methven

SANGSTER Lorna Mary BSc 1966
  d of Edwin H. S. sales rep and Daisy H. Youngson; b Aber 3.1.45
teacher maths: St Peter's s Aber 1967–68, Powis acad Aber 1968–70, Fleetwood s Chessington 1970, Darroch s Edin 1970–71, Kincorth acad Aber 1972
m Aber 20.7.69 Willson D. Taylor MB ChB 1969 *qv*

SANGSTER Michael James Lyon *BSc 1964
  s of James H. S. MA 1930 *qv* and Mary A. Stewart MA 1929 *qv*; b Elgin 14.9.42
PhD(R'dg) 1968
lect R'dg from 1968; res fell. Frankfurt/Munich 1968–69
m Bootle 4.8.73 Mary C. McTegart BSc(Liv) teacher d of Charles W. McT. J.P. Bootle

SANGSTER Moira Helen MA 1967
  d of George T. S. joiner and Helen Moir; b Aber 2.9.46
teacher Cults, Dyce p s from 1968

SANGSTER Rosemary MA 1962
  m Logan

SANGSTER Valerie Joan *BSc 1970 PhD 1974
  d of William M. S. and Joan M. M. Davis; b Aber 2.4.48
post doct res asst s of agr Nott 1974–76, res fell. from 1976
m Aber 15.12.73 Colin R. Black BSc 1971 lect

SANN Alan BSc 1967 Dip Ed 1975

SANTOS Francis Olayimika BSc(eng) 1957 *1958
  s of Stephen O. S. pharm and Christiana A. Onasanya bus. woman; b Nigeria 22.4.33
MICE 1963 F Nigerian Soc Eng 1979
eng: jun C. S. Allots & ptnrs Manc 1957, asst Aber city c 1958, asst F. A. Macdonald & ptnrs Kirkcaldy 1958, Ove Arup & ptnrs Edin 1960–61, exec Western Nigeria dev corp Ibadan 1961–63, chief Obi Obembe & assoc Lagos 1963–71, ptnr Olaniyan Omotoso Santos & assoc Lagos from 1971
m Manc 5.10.57 Grace A. Johnson nurse, journalist d of Iubueabeokun J. Benin City Nigeria

SAPRA Parkash Chander BSc(eng) 1959

SARELIUS Sonja Marie   MSc 1969
    MA(Well)
m McKinlay

SARGENT Alice Anne   *BSc 1968
    m Smith

SARGENT John Reid   *BSc 1958 PhD 1961
    s of Alexander C. S. fisherman and Annie Reid;
b Buckie 12.10.56
Bond gold medal of Amer oil chemists soc 1977
res fell. Courtauld inst Lond 1961–64; lect biochem
Aberd 1964–70; prin scient off. NERC inst marine
biochem Aber 1970–77, merit sen prin scient off. from
1977
m Aber 21.12.61 Elizabeth J. Buchan BSc 1961 *qv*

SARSON David Michael   MA 1966 Dip Ed 1969
    s of Ronald H. S. man. dye works and Marjory E.
Whalley; b Leic 17.10.43
teacher Powis acad Aber 1967–69; dep prin maths
Ashfield s Kirby-in-Ashfield 1967–71, dep prin maths,
prin maths Kirkley h s Lowestoft from 1971, later also
sen master
m Aber 10.9.66 Patricia Morrison staff nurse d of William
S. M. Keith

SAUNDERS Jennifer Jane   BSc 1966

SAVAGE Kathleen Elaine   MA 1965
    d of William S. BA(Lond) teacher, civ serv and
Florence M. Barclay civ serv; b Aber 21.11.42
teacher p s St George's s for girls Edin 1969–71
m Aber 10.7.65 Bryan J. Rankin MA 1966 *qv*

SAVAGE Robert Henry   MSc 1962
    BSc(eng)(Alta)

SAVEGE Jill Margaret   MB ChB 1967
    d of David S. CA and Colinda Geddes; b Arbroath
28.3.44
DPM 1970 MRCPsych 1972 LGSM(Lond) 1970 LTCL
(Lond) 1971 FTCL(Lond) 1972 Cert Adult Psych 1976
Child Psych 1977 (Amer Board Psychiat & Neurol)
h o Woodend gen hosp Aber 1967–68; sen h o Ross
Clinic Aber 1968–69; regist Dingleton hosp Melrose
1969–70; regist, sen regist commun psychiat royal Edin
hosp 1970–72, sen regist gen psychiat 1972–73; sen regist
adolescent psychiat Tavistock clin Lond, Hillend hosp
St Albans 1973–74; fell. adolescent/fam psychiat George
Washington univ DC USA 1974–75; fell. ch psychiat
ch's hosp DC USA 1975–76, part-time private pract from
1976
m Bethesda 12.10.75 David E. Scharff MD(Harv) psycho-
analyst and child psychiat s of Nicholas S. St Louis USA

SAVIDGE Malcolm Kemp   *MA 1970

SAVIN Anne   *MA 1966
    m Knowles

SAVORY Christopher John   *BSc 1967 PhD 1974

SAW Choo Ban   MSc 1967 PhD 1974
    s of Seng H. S. shop keeper and Geck K. Tan; b Penang
27.1.40
BSc(Peking) 1963
struct eng: Penang 1963–64, Lond 1964–66; res stud.
Aber 1966–69; asst lect eng Aber 1969–70, lect from
1970
m Lond 3.6.67 Koon Tee Lim midwife d of Lan K. L.
Penang

SAWYER Madlene Marina   BSc 1967 MB ChB 1972
    d of John N. S. and Doris H. Brooks; b Nassau
Bahamas 25.9.44
h o: St James' hosp Leeds 1972–73, Law hosp Lanarksh
1973; m o paediat Princess Margaret hosp Bahamas
1973–74, regist obst/gyn from 1974

SAYLE Timothy George   BSc(eng) 1966

SAYLES Elisabeth Anne   BSc 1965
    d of Henry S. S. BA(Cantab) chem mech eng and
Betty A. Allen secy; b Middleton St George 2.12.43
teacher: sc Goodlyburn j s Perth 1966–67, biol Morgan
acad Dun 1967–69, part-time biol Kirkton h s Dun from
1972
m Largs 8.7.67 John W. Vigrow MA 1965 *qv*

SAYLES Hilary Margaret Jean   MA 1961
    d of George O. S. MA(Glas) historian and Agnes J.
Sutherland; b Glasg 30.6.40
cataloguing rare continentals Folger lib Wash DC USA
1961–63; teacher Bedales, Petersfield 1965–66; indexing
emblem books Art Hist inst Utrecht from 1966

SAYLES Michael George Alexander   BSc 1959
    s of George O. S. MA(Glas) prof hist Aberd and
Agnes J. Sutherland; b Glasg 30.5.37
Member Inst Trg Dev 1979
RAF off. (sqn ldr) Cyprus 1960, UK 1963–71, Arabian
Gulf 1971–72, UK and RAF staff coll Bracknell from
1972
m Church Fenton 20.6.64 Jacqueline V. S. Beaumont d of
Lesley S. B. Yorks

SCACE Robert Chaston   *MA 1964
    s of Norman C. S. actor and Isobel Robertson dental
nurse; b Aber 20.10.42
MA(Calg) 1968 PhD(Calg) 1972
Canada: grad asst, instr univ of Calg 1964–72; lect Red
Deer coll 1968, Mt Royal coll 1971–74; pres Scace &
Assoc environmental consult. Calgary 1971–78; geogr
Reid Crowther & Ptnrs consult. eng and plan. Calgary
from 1978
m Sylvan Lake Alberta 9.6.73 Margaret E. Wright
biochem res tech d of Kenneth A. W. Three Hills
Alberta

SCARGALL Isabel Anne   *MA 1966

SCARGILL Sally Penelope   *MA 1969

SCARLETT Stewart McLaren   MA 1961
    s of Stewart L. S. bricklayer, mason, bldg contr, BR
employee and Margaret Wisely; b Aber 3.4.38
teacher: asst Ayr 1962–65, prin Engl Singapore 1965–71,
dep head Ayr 1971–74, dir guid United World coll SE
Asia Singapore from 1974
m Maybole 16.10.64 Hazel Rodgers teacher d of James R.
Maybole

SCHARF Eric Manfred   BSc(eng) 1970
    s of Erich F. A. S. indust des and Ida M. G. Scheffel;
b Brist 5.10.47
MSc(Wales) 1971 PhD(Sur) 1977
res Sur Guildford from 1971

SCHIRMER Lise   MB ChB 1967
    d of Helge S. bank off. and Gunvor Drangsholt;
b Aber 22.10.38
Norway: h o Narvik 1968–69, g p Finnmark 1969, jun
regist Vadsø 1969–71; g p Gøtene Sweden 1971; regist:
Porsgrunn Norway 1971–76, Uyo Nigeria 1972, univ
clin Bergen from 1976

SCHOOREL Pauline Marie   BSc 1960
m Shand

SCHWARZ Pamela Margaret   MA 1968
d of Edward S. BSc(Lond) head teacher and Kathleen
R. Ratcliffe secy, teacher, lib; b Burgess Hill 17.4.47
Dip Housing Man. Member Inst Housing 1975
teacher maths: Sussex 1968–69, Internat Vol Serv
Mbabane Swaziland 1970–71, temp work Sussex 1972;
Mosscare Housing Manchester: trainee housing man.
1973–74, asst housing man. 1975–76, housing man. 1977–
78, sen housing man. from 1979

SCLATER John Bingham   BSc(for) 1957
b Dun 3.2.31
for. off. Perth Aust 1957–69 and from 1972; sen for.
Lau-Aust Reforestation Proj Vientiane Laos 1969–72;
for. off. W Aust 1972–74

SCOALES Robert Alexander   MA 1959

SCOBBIE Valerie Ann   MA 1970
d of William R. S. security consult. and Vivien M.
Pirie; b Aber 7.6.49
cler asst educ dept Aber 1970–73
m Aber 25.7.70 Samuel D. Sinclair police serg LLB 1975
s of John G. S. Dornoch

SCORGIE Anne Moyra   *MA 1959
d of William S. nurse and Sarah A. McFarquhar;
b Daviot Aberdeensh 23.2.36
admin asst Manc 1959–61; teacher Engl Graeme h s
Falkirk from 1972
m Aber 23.8.61 Graeme M. Bruce MA 1958 qv

SCOTLAND Colin George Emmerson   LLB 1969
s of James S. MA(Glas) prin Aber Coll Educ and Jean
Cowan MA(Glas); b Glasg 27.7.48
CA 1973
app CA Aber 1969–73; merch banker Lond: invest. exec
1973–75, man. 1975–78, assoc 1978–79, dir from 1979
m Aber 14.6.72 Sheila M. Fraser MA 1970 qv; separated
1978

SCOTT Alexander John   BSc 1970 CASS 1976
s of Charles A. N. S. MA 1933 qv and Isabella G.
McDonald MB ChB 1944 qv; b Elgin 6.8.48
teacher Edin 1972–73; trainee soc worker Aber 1973–74;
commun worker Aber 1976–79; fieldwork teacher
(commun work) Aber from 1979
m Aber 25.3.75 Alison M. M. Smith MA 1972 teacher
d of Malcolm S. Dingwall

SCOTT Alison Hunter   MLitt 1968
d of Harold S. MB ChB(St And) g p and Phyllis M. P.
Baird; b Glasg 23.2.45
MA(St And) 1966
m Brackley 23.7.73 Duncan S. James

SCOTT Alison Mary   MA 1965
m Clark

SCOTT Allan David   BSc(eng) 1966

SCOTT David Baillie Crichton   *BSc 1957
s of John S. comp dir and Helen M. A. Crichton nurse;
b Calcutta 4.8.34
PhD(Glas) 1963
res asst, asst lect Glas 1958–63; seconded: tropical fish
culture res inst Malacca Malaya 1960, E Af freshwater
fisheries res organis Jinja Uganda 1962–63; lect zool St

And from 1963
m Glasg 1961 Sybil G. Ward BSc(Leic) d of Peter A. W.

SCOTT Dennis   PhD 1964
BSc(Durh)

SCOTT Derek Alexander   *BSc 1958

SCOTT Diana Hendry   BEd 1970
d of Charles S. BSc 1934 qv; b Aber 25.1.48
teacher mus: Pitmedden area Aberdeensh 1970–71,
Turriff acad from 1972
m Montgomery

SCOTT Diane Cowperthwaite   *MA 1958
d of James S. shoemaker instr and Hannah Laing
milliner; b Aber 12.2.36
BA(Cantab) 1961
lect Engl Dalhousie univ Halifax Canada 1958–59, part-
time lect RGIT Aber; journalism from 1968 founder/
edit. *Leopard* mag. Aber
m Aber 28.4.62 David I. Morgan MA 1958 qv

SCOTT Eleanor Mary   *BSc 1961
d of Charles W. S. BSc(Glas) for. off. and Isobel G. M.
Stewart; b Aber 27.3.38
tech asst haemat dept med s Cantab 1961–65
m Aber 16.8.61 Roger H. Fairclough MA(Cantab) map
lib s of James F. Carnforth

SCOTT Elizabeth Mora Joan   MB ChB 1968
d of Gordon I. S. MB ChB(Edin) surg and Mora J.
Craig MB ChB 1940 qv; b Aber 21.5.44
h o Bridge of Earn hosp, East Ham mem hosp Lond
1968–69; h o, sen h o City of Lond mat. hosp, royal
northern hosp Lond 1969–71; g p Woking from 1972
m Elgin 8.1.72 David K. Wilson CA s of Peter R. W.
Inverkeilor

SCOTT Elspeth Susan   MA 1969
d of Arthur S. bank off. and Agnes I. M. Hutcheson
teacher dom sc; b Edin 11.12.48
CA 1975
hotel waitress S Queensferry 1969–70; trainee computer
oper NCB Edin 1970; app CA 1970–75; CA T. Hunter
Thomson & Co Edin
m Queensferry 15.10.77 Alexander W. W. Munro CA
app, salesman, driver s of Alexander F. M. Dalkeith

SCOTT Frederick   MA 1969
s of Robert S. papermaker and Elizabeth K. Adams;
b Aber 10.6.25
teacher Fyvie from 1970
m Aber 20.6.64 Barbara J. Lewis BSc N(Lond Ont) nurse,
superv of nurs d of Frederick C. L. Sudbury Canada

SCOTT Helen Massie   *MA 1969
m Edwards

SCOTT Hugh Lawrence   *BSc(eng) 1963 MSc 1965
s of John S. master baker and Ethel Urquhart master
baker; b Aber 3.7.41
res eng Eng Elect. Whetstone 1965–68, sect. leader 1968–
70; tech eng Simon–Carver Stockport 1970–72; self
employed gen merch 1972–78; constr insp man. Hunt
Co Int Iran from 1978
m Aber 15.12.64 Margaret S. Whitton nurse d of David
M. W. Arbroath

SCOTT Ian Malcolm   *MA 1958 PhD 1980

SCOTT James Norman Gallie   BSc(eng) 1970
s of Charles W. S. BSc(Glas) for. and Isobel G. M.

Stewart; b Oxford 30.12.46
dev eng Ferranti Edin 1970–78, Littet W Ger from 1978
m Banbury 6.4.74 Joy L. Barratt MA 1971 careers off.
d of Albert G. B. Adderbury

SCOTT Joan Frances MA 1968
d of Frank A. S. draper and Robertha J. Ollason;
b Lerwick 8.2.47
teacher Scalloway j h s Shetland 1969–72
m Lerwick 9.7.69 David W. Pottinger draper s of David
S. P. Burra Isle Shetland

SCOTT Kathleen Charleston MA 1970
d of George A. S. MA 1930 qv; b Banff 14.6.49
asst staff man. Marks & Spencer Glasg 1971–73; pers
dept HIB Inv 1973–74; teacher from 1976
m Aber 12.7.73 Roderick M. Manson MA 1971 teacher
s of Anderson M. BSc(agr) 1933 qv

SCOTT Kathleen Mary Winifred MA 1967
d of Albert S. T. S. crofter and Catherine B. Tulloch;
b N Ronaldsay 11.9.45
teacher: Mintlaw 1968–71, Linlathen h s Dun; seconded
from Dun educ auth for cert in youth/commun work
1974–75; prin guid Linlathen h s Dun from 1976

SCOTT Linda Kathryn MA 1969
d 15.10.71

SCOTT Margaret MA 1964
d of Alexander R. S. chief display advt clerk Aber
Journals and Alexis Smith; b Aber 3.2.43
Cert Soc St(Glas) 1965
ch care off. Lanark c c 1965–67
m Aber 6.3.67 Kenneth R. Young asst hotel man./
teacher catering s of Lachlan B. Y. MA(Glas) Perth

SCOTT Michael Lennox BSc(eng) 1960
s of John S. S. tea planter and Irene Bird-Wilson lect,
man.; b Calcutta 11.11.38
M Eng Sc(NSW) 1965 CEng(Aust) MIHE(Lond)
civ eng dept main roads NSW Aust 1960–66; sen asst eng
traffic Kingston-u-Thames 1966–68; civ eng dept main
roads NSW 1968–70; hwy eng Vallentine Laurie & Davies
Bangkok, Kuala Lumpur 1970–71; resid eng N. D. Lea &
Assoc Bangkok 1971–73; proj eng Ibadan Nigeria 1973;
resid eng, sen hwy eng Ibadan, Kano 1973–74
m Cairns Queensland Aust Penelope J. Watsford teacher
d of Stephen D. W. MD, BS(Melb) Yorkey's Knob
Queensland

SCOTT Michael McGillivray MB ChB 1967
s of George A. S. MA 1930 qv; b Banff 4.10.43
DObstRCOG 1971 FRCSE 1975
h o, sen h o Aber gen hosps 1967–69; m o flying doctor
serv Ndola Zambia 1969–70; sen h o Aber gen hosps
1970–71; surg sen h o Derbysh RI 1972–73; regist surg
univ of W Manc Salford 1973–75; sen regist orthop and
clin lect United Birm hosps from 1975

SCOTT Norman Marshall PhD 1967
s of Charles S. farm. and Williamina C. Marshall;
b Aber 2.7.24
FRIC 1976
prin scient off. Macaulay inst Aber from 1967
m Aber 18.12.55 Margaret McFarlane d of Robert McF.
Aber

SCOTT Owen Rae *MA 1969
s of James R. S. cler worker insur comp and Euphemia
B. Jones wages clerk insur comp; b Dunoon 24.7.46
Ford Motor Co. Essex: job eval off., organis analyst

1969–72, pers policies analyst 1972–73; staff advis Brit
Leyland Preston from 1973

SCOTT Patrick William BSc 1959
s of William S. civ serv and Mary L. Gray; b Huntly
10.10.37
teacher maths AGS from 1961, prin guid from 1972

SCOTT Peter Allardyce *MA 1970

SCOTT Robert James *MA 1970

SCOTT Robin Douglas Murray MB ChB 1964
s of Ian M. S. MB ChB(Edin) med pract and Liebe B.
Rankine; b Carlisle 2.2.41
MRCPE 1968 MRCP(Lond) 1968
h o, sen h o Aber 1964–66; regist med Aber 1966–71; res
fell. Washington univ s med St Louis USA 1969–70; lect
med Edin 1971–75; consult. phys Windsor from 1975
m Aber 14.7.64 Alexandria Shearer secy d of Alexander S.
Aber

SCOTT Robin Ford cMB ChB 1966
s of Laurence F. S. master mariner and Barbara H.
Wilson loc govt off.; b S Shields 8.9.42
MRCGP
h o RACH, ARI 1966–67; terminable lect path. Aberd
1967; trainee g p 1970; g p Grays, Dun from 1970 and
asst tut. dept g p Dund from 1972
m Aber 24.7.68 Sheila M. Fraser MA 1966 qv

SCOTT Ronald LLB 1970
s of William S. and Christina M. Finnie; b Turriff
19.10.48
law app John Laurie & Co Aber 1970–72; law app, leg.
asst corp of City of Aber from 1972
m New Byth 24.7.71 Edna Imray teacher d of Gordon
J. I. New Byth

SCOTT Rosemary MA 1969
d of James S. for. and Helen Turner; b Kelso 26.6.48
teacher maths Galashiels acad 1970–78
m Duns 8.7.77 Roger H. Wardman B Tech(Brad) lect
s of Ernest W. Otley

SCOTT Sinclair Tulloch BSc(eng) 1960
s of Albert S. T. S. crofter and Catherine B. Tulloch;
b Kirkwall 19.1.37
nat serv 1960–62; Ranco Motors: grad app Tantallon
1962–64, res dev Uddingston Glasg 1964–66; des eng
Montreal 1966–68; crofter N Ronaldsay from 1968
m Glasg 29.3.65 Catherine Marquis d of Alexander M.
Glasg

SCOTT William Forbes *MA 1968
s of William S. MA 1936 qv; b Aber 12.11.46
PhD(Dund) 1971 FFA 1974
temp lect maths Glas 1970–71; lect actuarial maths/
statist H-W from 1971
m Aber 5.8.70 June Leys teacher d of Alexander M. L.
Portsoy

SCOTT William John *BSc 1961
s of William S. plumber and Hannah M. Rutherford;
b Perth 19.11.39
asst exper off. Macaulay inst Aber 1961–63; teacher:
Govan h s Glasg 1964–66, Douglas Ewart h s Newton
Stewart asst prin guid, prin guid from 1966
m Glasg 27.3.67 Wendy E. Pearson nurse d of Kenneth
B. P. Glasg

SCOTT William Oliver BSc(agr) 1957

SCOTT-BROWN Alastair William   MB ChB 1958
                                 Dip Psychother 1972
s of Sir William Scott-Brown MA 1912 *qv*; b Madura
S India 12.11.34
DPM(Lond) 1965 MRCPsych 1971
h o Woodend hosp Aber 1958–59; RN UK and Far East
surg lieut 1959–63, training in psychiat and spec posts
1963–74; surg comm RN consult psychiat and clin tut.
Royal Victoria hosp Netley Southampton from 1974
m Aber 15.12.59 Ardyn A. Lyall MA 1959 *qv*

SCOTT-BROWN Ronald   MA 1958 LLB 1960
s of Sir William Scott-Brown MA 1912 *qv*; b Madras
14.2.37
solic and invest. man. 1961–66; ptnr Brander &
Cruickshank advoc Aber from 1966; dir East of Scot.
Invest. Man. from 1973
m Aber 8.9.66 Jean L. Booth lect Aber s of dom sc d of
Albert B. Aber

SCRIMGEOUR Margaret Aitken   *MA 1964
b Forfar 5.7.41
teacher Fr: Perth 1965–68, Banchory from 1968
m Aber 2.10.72 George Murray BSc 1961 *qv*

SCROGGIE Brian Charles   *MA 1968

SEATON John Gow   BSc(eng) 1969
s of Alexander S. gen merch and Janet Gow MA(Edin)
teacher; b Aberfeldy 16.6.47
asst eng; D. Logan Invsh 1969–70, Tarmac constr
Forres 1970–71; des eng Fairhurst & Ptnrs Aber 1971–72;
sect. eng Tarmac constr Forres 1972–73, ag from 1973
m Kintore 13.9.69 Patricia E. Davidson d of Alexander
D. Kintore

SEATTER Kathleen   *MA 1965
d of William Y. S. blacksmith, male nurse and Margaret
Sim laundry worker; b Aber 28.5.42
teacher: High s for girls Aber 1967–70, Cults acad Aber
from 1970
m Aber 20.12.68 Arun K. Naha BSc(Calc) syst dev eng
govt serv s of Jogendra C. N. Calcutta

SEDDON Thomas Michael   MB ChB 1962
s of Thomas S. cotton manuf and Edith Houghton;
b Rochdale 30.10.33
h o Blackpool 1962–63; sen h o Kendal, Blackpool 1963–
64; lect anat Aberd 1964–65; g p Slyne-with-Hest from
1965
m Rawtenstall 3.1.59 June Coleman d of Frederick C.
Rawtenstall

SEED Carol Irene   MA 1965
m Lockhart

SEIVEWRIGHT Sheila   MA 1969
d of Charles E. S. shoemaker and Martha Lowe;
b Lancs 1.8.47
continental tel Lond 1970–71; various posts Montreal
1971–72
m Aber 29.3.71 Yong-Kwee Lam Shang Leen BSc 1969 *qv*

SELAND Johan Harald   cMB ChB 1965
s of Harald S. S. BSc(pharm)(Oslo) pharm and Rachel
Sunde; b Stavanger 7.6.41
Cand Med(Oslo) 1965
Norway: h o county hosp Kristiansund 1966–67, asst
dist doct Meløy 1967, indust doct Glomfjord 1967–68,
m o Norw air force Sola air base 1968–69, h o ophth
univ hosp Bergen 1969–71, res fell. ophth univ of Bergen
from 1971

m Stavanger 18.12.65 Kari M. Galta nurse d of Daniel G.
Sørbø Norway

SELF Michael Barnard   BSc(for) 1966
s of Peter B. S. BSc(Lond) teacher and Beryl Y. Wood;
b Brist 25.2.45
for. off. Munda Solomon Is 1967–72; timber contr Brist
1972–73; for. off. Honiara Solomon Is 1973–77;
harvesting and marketing man. Tilhill For. Farnham
from 1977
m Aber 31.7.67 Elizabeth A. Brooks BSc 1966 *qv*

SEMEONOFF Irina   *MA 1964
d of Boris S. MA(Edin) univ lect and Catherine I.
Davie MA(Edin) teacher; b Edin 9.2.43
stud. occup psych Birkbeck coll Lond 1964–67; part-
time quality control eng Rochester 1968
m Lond 4.12.65 Alfred J. Alexander eng s of Alfred A.
Laurencekirk

SERWANGA Edward Kiddugavu   BSc(for) 1962

SESHADRI Holavanhalli Srinivasaiyengar   PhD 1963
s of Srinivasaiyengar S. MA(Madras) supt of police and
Laxamma Laxamma; b KGF India 30.1.27
BSc(Bangalore) 1948 MSc(Bangalore) 1959
India: lect chem Mysore 1948–59, lect biochem univ of
Mysore 1959–71, reader biochem from 1971
m 29.5.49 Narayanachar Anandam d of Narayanachar,
Hindupur

SHACKLES Charles John Dalglish   *BSc(agr) 1964
s of Derek H. S. CBE solic. and Lella D. Kirkland;
b Edin 20.10.39
MIBiol(Nott) 1968
asst reg off. nature conserv council E Anglia from 1970

SHAH Rajnikant Prabhulal   MB ChB 1962

SHAHID Khalil Akhtar   MSc 1969 PhD 1971
MSc(Panj)

SHAKSPEARE Anthony Evan   MA 1967

SHAND Aeneas John   *BSc 1959 PhD 1962
s of John S. S. cashier Elgin burgh council and
Elspeth T. Robertson; b Elgin 6.9.37
FCS 1957 FRIC 1976 CChem 1976
group ldr Miles lab Stoke Poges 1962–65; lect organ.
chem Middx polytech: Enfield 1965–66, Hendon 1966–
70; sen lect organ. chem Napier coll of comm and tech
Edin from 1970
m Bridgend 6.4.63 Margaret W. Dickson shop asst d of
Henry D. Tweedmouth

SHAND Eden Lennox Arthur   *BSc(for) 1963

SHAND Edward   MA 1970
s of Edward S. painter/decorator and Mary
Mackintosh; b Aber 10.9.49
teacher: Hilton acad Aber 1971–73, Banff acad from 1973
m Aber 4.12.70 Linda J. Greig MA 1970 *qv*

SHAND James Sim   MB ChB 1964
s of Herbert D. S. fire off. and Marjory G. Wilson;
b Aber 27.10.39
h o Woodend hosp, City hosp Aber 1964–65; g p Aber
from 1965
m Aber 17.7.64 Valerie H. Stewart insur clerkess d of
Hugh S. Aber

SHAND John Fordyce   *BSc 1967
b Ellon 12.2.45

SHAND John Herbert   *BSc 1970 PhD 1977

SHAND Margaret Moncrieff   *MA 1961
 d of Hector S. man. dir and Isabella Leishman; b Perth
27.9.36
teacher: Turriff 1962–63, Glasg 1963–65, 1969–70, Aber
1970–72; Aber: prin teacher guid 1972–74; asst head
teacher from 1974
m Aber 1961 Charles A. Barron MA 1958 *qv*

SHAND Michael Robertson   BSc 1966
 s of John S. S. cashier and Jean Stevens; b Elgin
13.2.45
syst progr Plessey Co Liv 1966–69; diagnostic progr/
analyst NCR Dun 1970–74; syst progr ICL Dalkeith
1974–76; teacher maths/computer stud. Elgin from 1977
m Dun –.7.73 Mary Lynch teacher d of James L. Errol

SHAND Rory Alexander   BSc 1970

SHAND Roy Cooper   BSc(eng) 1960

SHAND Stella Joyce   MA 1958
 d of Joseph S. head for. and Marie Sargent secy;
b Methlick 17.9.36
teacher: Culter s 1959–62, Peffermill from 1976
m Aber 12.8.60 Philip W. Ross MB ChB 1960 *qv*

SHAND William Alexander   *BSc 1961 MSc 1962
**   PhD 1965**
 s of James A. S. MA 1936 *qv*; b 30.4.40
lect nat phil Aberd 1965–68; govt serv Christchurch
1969–79, Malvern from 1979
m Keith 28.8.65 Moyra E. King d of Alfred J. F. K.
Keith

SHAND William Fraser   *BSc 1963

SHANKS Gordon William   MA 1967
 s of William A. S. banker and Muriel H. Boyd tracer;
b Arbroath 10.12.45
teacher maths Stranraer h s 1968–70; asst prin maths
Shoeburyness comp s 1970; prin maths/sc Pilton s and
comm coll Barnstaple 1971–74; asst head Logie s s Dun
from 1974
m Stonehaven 23.9.67 Margaret E. Carr d of James C.
Stonehaven

SHANKS Michael Fraser   BMedBiol 1968

SHANNON Jean Greig   *BSc 1966
 d of William G. S. waterguard supt HM customs and
excise and Maud D. Hamilton; b Glasg 20.10.44
PhD(Lond) 1969
Lond: res asst St Mary's hosp 1966–69; lect 1969–70;
dem/lect Edin 1970–72; OU tut. Camberley from 1975
m Aber 31.8.68 Gordon P. Ebbon BSc 1965 *qv*

SHARP David Williamson   *BSc 1969 PhD 1972

SHARP Evelyn Mary   MA 1959
 d of George M. S. farm. and Mary C. F. Wood
cashier; b Cookney 10.10.38
teacher: Mackie acad Stonehaven 1960–62, New Byth
1962–64, Angus, Kincardine 1972–75, Fettercairn from
1976
m Cookney 1.8.62 Stuart Riddell farm worker s of
Joseph R. Alford

SHARP Margaret Rothnie   *MA 1970 MLitt 1975
 m Michael G. A. Christie MA 1966 *qv*

SHARP Neil Wood   *MA 1970
 s of James H. W. S. PO tel eng, head of plan. N of
Scot. PO telecom board and Finlayson W. M. Neil lib,
cler off. Inl Rev; b Glasg 14.8.47
MA(Lanc) 1972
lect in sociol: Bournemouth and Poole coll of f e Poole
1972–79, i/c soc sciences coll of arts and tech N'cle-u-
Tyne from 1979
m N'cle-u-Tyne 14.9.68 Ann E. Bettridge BSc 1969 *qv*

SHARP Ronald James   *MA 1970

SHARP Rosemary Elaine Christine   *BSc 1968

SHAW Alexander Martin   *MA 1963 LLB 1965

SHAW Cecilia Helen   MB ChB 1961
 d of John C. Shaw teacher and Agnes C. Page; b Alyth
20.9.36
h o RACH, Ipswich and E Suffolk hosp 1961–62; sen h o
anaest Ipswich and E Suffolk hosp 1962–63; regist
anaest Law hosp Carluke 1963–64; resid anaest Ottawa
1975–77
m Pitlochry 20.9.63 Colin T. Downie BSc(H-W) phys s
of Alistair D. Blairgowrie

SHAW Christopher Patrick James   BSc 1968

SHAW Edwin Louis   *BSc 1970
 s of Noel S. eng and Elizabeth Sievewright; b Perivale
15.11.47
FCS 1972 CEng MIProd.E 1979
res stud. Aberd 1970–73; sect. man. Internat Sports Co
Horbury 1973–74, dept man. 1974–75; sect. leader work
study Tower Housewares Wombourne 1975–77; chief
work study eng T.I. Sunhouse Walsall 1977–78, indust
eng man. from 1978

SHAW Josephine May   MA 1968 Dip Ed 1970

SHAW Milton William   PhD 1965
 s of William S. clerk to urban dist council and Margaret
Brown; b Colne 21.9.24
BSc(agr)(Leeds) 1944 MSc(Leeds) 1953   FR Ent Soc
(Lond) 1959
asst entomol: Harper Adams agr coll Newport Shropsh
1945–46, MAFF Tettenhall 1946–50; asst advis entomol
NOSCA Aber 1950–63, advis entomol from 1963
m Edgmond Newport 3.5.49 Iris Bolas secy d of Samuel
G. B. Edgmond

SHAW Muriel Margaret   MA 1966 Dip Ed 1967
 d of John G. S. reader Aber journals and Muriel
Norrie clerkess; b Aber 18.12.44
teacher Engl h s Winnipeg from 1967
m Aber 19.8.67 James C. Jamieson PhD 1967 *qv*

SHAW Robert   *MA 1958
 s of Robert S. grocery asst and Violet H. Scorgie;
b Aber 2.5.36
BPhil(Oxon) 1960
asst lect econ Keele 1960–62; lect pol econ Aberd 1962–
70, sen lect from 1970
m Aber 24.9.60 Valerie Hunter occup therap d of
Frederick A. H. LDS(Edin) Stonehaven

SHAW William Peterkin Gordon   *BSc 1963

SHEACH Gordon Chisholm   BSc(eng) 1969
 s of Alexander S. master bldr and Emily H. Watt;
b Dufftown 7.4.48
site eng Lond 1970–73, site eng and sub ag Tayside

1973–77, estimator Lond from 1978
m Ilford 26.8.72 Barbara J. Gorman teacher d of John
H. G. Cardiff

SHEARER Blanche Anne   MA 1967
 d of Raymond P. S. joiner and Blanche S. Wilson s
canteen attendant; b Cornhill 21.9.46
teacher maths Banff acad 1968–74
m Cornhill 17.7.70 Ronald G. L. Sim BDS(Glas) dent
surg s of George S. S. Cornhill

SHEARER Charles Anthony   BSc 1970

SHEARER Elsa Margaret   LLB 1968
 d of Ernest J. M. S. BSc(Edin) path./bact and Helen M.
Lenman MB ChB(Edin); b Edin 4.6.47
Edin: law app 1968–70; teacher Tollcross p s 1971–72
m Laurencekirk 20.12.69 David Christie BA(Strath) lect
econ/author s of William C. Menstrie

SHEARER John Robertson   cMB ChB 1966 PhD 1975
 s of John A. S. MB ChB 1934 qv; b Aber 29.8.42
FRCSE/1971
h o ARI 1966–67; res fell. Aberd 1967–69; MRC jun
res fell. Aberd 1969–70; regist surg Aber 1970–72; sen
orthop regist 1972–74; lect orthop surg Oxon 1975–76;
prof orthop S'ton from 1976
m Leven 18.10.68 Gloria A. Lemon physioth d of
William L. MA(Strath) Leven

SHEARER John William   *MA 1966

SHEARER Kathryn Isobel   MA 1968
 d of William S. butcher and Catherine D. A. Findlay;
b Saskatoon 11.5.47
teacher Engl: Elgin acad 1969–75, Buckie h s from 1975
m Aber 3.8.66 Charles Boyle swimming pool man. s of
Charles B. Glasg

SHEARER Margaret-Ann Milne   MA 1966
 m Kaloo

SHEARER Peter John   *MA 1967

SHEARER Phyllis Jean   MA 1957 Dip Ed 1958
 d of Mary S.; b Glasg 28.1.37
teacher: Slains p s 1958–60, Eday p s Orkney 1965–72,
remed Grampian ch guid Huntly area from 1975
m Rothiemay 12.8.58 Thomas Goodall MA 1961 qv

SHEARMAN Duncan Ward   BSc 1970
 s of John R. S. clerk and Vera M. Knowles; b Preston
20.9.48
Cannock: progr (computer) 1970–72, computer syst
analyst from 1972
m Deerness Orkney Jennifer M. Bichan MA 1971 d of
James H. B. Deerness

SHEDDEN Alfred Charles   MA 1966 LLB 1967
 s of Alfred H. W. S. bookkeeper and Jane M. Kay; b
Edin 30.6.44
law app Arbroath 1967–68, Glasg 1968–69; leg. asst
Glasg 1969–70; ptnr McGrigor, Donald & Co Glasg
from 1971
m(1) E Kilbride 3.8.68 Rosalyn E. M. Terris MA 1967 qv;
marr diss 19.7.79
 (2) Glasg 6.12.79 Irene Munro

SHEDDON Dorothy Joanna   BSc 1968
 d of Alexander C. S. town clerk/burgh chamberlain
and Josephine M. Johnston; b Dunfermline 6.7.45
Dip Ed(univ of E Af) 1969

teacher maths, head dept Tororo girls' s Uganda 1969–74;
teacher maths Westfield s Watford from 1974

SHEEHAN William   MSc 1968
 s of William S. blacksmith and Margaret R. Mahoney;
b Farranfoxe Co Kerry 27.7.32
BSc(Cork) 1961 PhD(Dub) 1976
prin res off. agr inst Creagh Ballinrobe

SHENNAN Andrew Theodore   MB ChB 1967
 s of Edward T. S. MB ChB 1939 qv; b Aber 22.3.43
MRCP 1972 LMCC 1974
h o RACH 1967–68; sen h o paediat Musgrove park
hosp Taunton 1968–69; lect ch health Aberd 1969–71;
regist paediat RACH 1971–73; Coutts clin fell. in
neonatology sick ch hosp Toronto from 1974
m Aber 20.1.68 Anne Stewart MA 1965 qv

SHENNAN Jean Lindsay   *BSc 1959
 d of Theodore S. MB ChB(Edin) med pract and Ann L.
Thomson MB ChB 1930 qv; b Aber 5.4.36
PhD(Glas) 1973
schol (May & Baker) post-grad res W of Scot. agr coll
1959–63; microbiol BP Proteins Grangemouth 1964–78;
microbiol BP Co res centre Sunbury-on-Thames from
1978

SHEPHERD Allan Nicol   BSc(eng) 1970
 s of George S. farm. and Jessie I. Wilson clerkess;
b Stonehaven 27.7.48
site eng (contr) Loch Duich 1970–71; grad eng Dumbarton
1971–73; sen asst eng (consult.) Glasg from 1973

SHEPHERD Brian   *BSc 1970

SHEPHERD Charles Henderson   *BSc 1969
 s of Charles A. S. dev insp and Agnes M. Henderson;
b Aber 30.12.46
MSc(Sheff) 1970 PhD(Salf) 1976
res fell. Salf 1974–79; nuclear phys Nuclear Power Comp
Whetstone from 1979
m Leeds 25.8.79 Jill E. Thirsk BSc(Salf) d of Harold
E. T. Knottingley

SHEPHERD David Christian   MB ChB 1965
 s of James G. L. caretaker and Christina D. Main;
b Birse 29.12.37
DObstRCOG 1968
h o ARI, city hosp Aber, RACH, mat. hosp Aber 1965–
67; sen h o Ross clin Cornhill Aber 1967–68; g p
Chatham from 1968
m Ballater 4.8.62 Kathleen M. Shepherd d of William
J. S. Ballater

**SHEPHERD David Ian   MB ChB 1968
 *MD 1976 (Thursfield Award)**
 s of James I. R. S. comp secy and Mary M. Baird MA
1933 qv; b Aber 4.10.44
MRCP(UK) 1973
h o ARI, Dumfries RI 1968–69; sen h o ARI 1969–70;
Sir Ashley Mackintosh res fell. dept med Aberd 1970–71;
regist gen med Aber 1972–74; sen regist neurol: Aber
1976, S'ton from 1976
m Aber 15.5.70 Hilary J. Sharp RGN d of Thomas V. S.

SHEPHERD George Wilson   *BSc(agr) 1965
 s of George S. farm. and Jessie I. Wilson secy; b
Cookney 5.4.42
agr dev off. Cambridge 1965–69; agr consult. Cleveland
1970–73; asst fertiliser marketing man. Edin 1974–75,
area sales man. Guildford from 1977
m Cambridge 12.7.69 Diane M. Maskell secy d of
Claude C. M. Cambridge

SHEPHERD Ian *MA 1968
s of John S. MA(St And) teacher; b Dun 12.3.44
res stud. Belf 1968–70; lect geog ABU Nigeria 1970–73;
teacher Dun coll of comm from 1973

SHEPHERD James BSc(eng) 1956

SHEPHERD Malcolm Gaul MA 1958 LLB 1960
s of Frederick M. S. police supt and Maggie B. M.
Simpson; b Banchory 14.1.37
leg. asst A. C. Morrison & Richards advoc Aber 1960–
62, ptnr from 1962
m Aber 9.2.63 Edna M. McKenzie tel oper d of George
D. McK. Aber

SHEPHERD Margaret MA 1958
d of Andrew C. S. master plasterer and Jessie J.
Mackintosh; b Nairn 20.5.37
teacher: p s Hawick 1959–60, Fr/Ger Brora 1962–70,
Fr/Ger Inv from 1970
m Edin 12.12.59 John M. McFeat MA(St And) teacher
s of James McF. Auchterarder

SHEPHERD Marion PhD 1968
d of Hector S. insur man. and Mary Pope; b Dun
25.11.29
BSc(St And) 1950
hon fell. Aberd 1968–70
m St Andrews 18.3.52 Samuel C. Frazer MB ChB(Glas)
prof chem path. Aberd s of John K. F. Airdrie

SHEPHERD Patricia Joanna MA 1959

SHEPHERD Roger Edward *BSc 1968

SHEPHERD Ronald *BSc(agr) 1956
s of John J. S. farm. and Catherine C. Cruickshank;
b Rafford Moray 4.4.34
Malaysia: res off. Prang Besar estate Kajang 1957–65,
dir of res Prang Besar res stat Kajang 1966–75; dir res
Harrisons & Crosfield Malaysia from 1975
m Aber 4.4.68 Elsie M. Main MA 1954 *qv*

SHEPHERD Ronald Shearer Gordon MB ChB 1961

SHEPPARD David Dawbarn MA 1970

SHERAN John Duncan *MA 1968
d 26.6.72 *AUR* xlv 128

SHERET Brian Sydney *MA 1966 *BD 1969
s of Sydney G. S. chief clerk and Ruth Park; b Aber
9.6.44
DPhil(Oxon) 1972
C of S min: asst Corstorphine Old ch Edin 1972–73;
locum Northfield Aber 1973–74, St Columba's Kilbirnie
1974–75, Aber 1975–77, John Knox Ch Gerrard St
Aber from 1977

SHERWOOD Robert Tom BSc(for) 1956
s of Gerald B. S. civ serv and Margaret E. Harper
teacher; b Epsom 2.11.30
dist for. off. Co Down from 1956
m Newcastle Co Down 9.8.58 Shirley C. Wheeler
teacher dom sc d of Charles C. W. Newcastle Co Down

SHEVELS Terence *BSc 1970

SHEWAN Doreen Baxter MB ChB 1970

**SHEWAN Frederick David Fitzgerald MA 1966
BD 1969**
s of Albert S. farm./sheep dealer and Mary J. Fitz-

gerald nurse; b Whiterashes 24.3.42
C of S min: asst Glenrothes 1969–70, Northesk par ch
Musselburgh from 1970
m Rayne 25.12.65 Iris P. Barrack MA 1966 *qv*

SHIACH Donald McGregor *MA 1960

SHIACH Gordon McGregor MA 1965 *MEd 1968
head Donaldson's School for the Deaf Edin
d Edin 24.4.77 *AUR* xlvii 215

SHIELS David Anthony MA 1962
MEd(Glas)

SHIELS Murray Brett *MA 1963 Dip Ed 1966

SHIMMINS James George *BSc 1960

SHIPMAN Nigel Christopher Leslie *MA 1967
s of Leslie H. S. bank man. and Violet Dawson fashion
buyer; b Louth 1.9.44
asst prin civ serv Edin 1967–72, prin from 1972

SHIPP John McKenzie BSc 1957

SHIRAZI Rahmati Keshavarz BSc 1964

SHIRRAN Margaret Anne *BSc 1969
d of Andrew G. S. banker and Winifred M. Falconer
secy; b Elgin 26.10.47
Dip Cartog(Glas) 1970
cartographic edit. Glasg 1970–75
m Elgin 11.9.70 Cameron A. Ewen BSc(eng) 1967 *qv*

SHIRRAN William Alexander Andrew *BSc(eng) 1967
s of Andrew G. S. banker and Winifred M. Falconer
secy; b Elgin 15.4.45
MICE 1972
asst eng Glasg, Evanton, Peterhead 1967–75, eng with
Highland reg (Evanton) from 1975
m Aber 1.8.68 Lorna M. Campbell teacher d of Ephraim
C. MA 1933 *qv*

SHIRREFFS Gordon Chisholm MB ChB 1957
s of William S. banker and Tomina F. Gordon; b
Cochin S India 26.3.34
DA(Lond) 1962
h o ARI 1957–58; surg lt royal Aust navy 1958–60; sen
h o anaest ARI 1961–62; g p Huntly from 1962
m Aber 28.9.61 Suzanne Philip MA 1959 *qv*

SHIRREFFS Marjorie Anne MA 1970
d of Andrew G. S. CA and Georgiana (Nan) C. Kelman
MA 1940 *qv*; b Aber 15.2.50
teacher classics Inverurie acad 1971–72
m Aber 5.4.72 John W. Graham comp dir s of Charles
F. G. Aber

SHIRREFFS Murdoch John MB ChB 1970
s of John S. bank acct and Isobel Campbell; b Aber
25.5.47
DObstRCOG 1973 MRCGP 1974
h o ARI 1970–71; trainee g p Aber 1971–74; g p prin
Bucksburn from 1974
m Aber 17.7.71 Jennifer A. McLeod BSc 1976 d of James
A. McL. Aber

SHIRREFFS Richard Cameron MA 1968 ᵈLLB 1970
s of Andrew G. S. CA and Nan C. Kelman MA 1940
qv; b Aber 25.2.47
law app 1970–72; solic/ptnr Mackie & Dewar advoc Aber
from 1973; secy AU Alumnus Assoc from 1973

m Aber 18.4.73 Gillian M. Fisher MA 1972 med soc worker d of John W. F. MA(Cantab) Oxford

SHIRREFFS Wallace BSc(eng) 1960
s of William W. R. S. ship's rigger and Margaret E. Warrender; b Aber 21.5.38
MIHE 1962 MICE 1967
dept main roads NSW Aust Sydney 1960–61; grad eng: city eng's dept Aber 1961–63, chief eng's dept Cumbernauld 1963–64; highway des eng Scott Wilson Kirkpatrick & Ptnrs Glasg 1964–66; des eng Cowan & Linn consult. eng Glasg 1966–67; superv eng Lanarksh c c Hamilton 1967–72; group leader Inv c c 1972–74; dep county road surv Kincardine c c Stonehaven 1974, asst div road surv Kincardine–Deeside div Grampian reg c from 1975
m Rutherglen Glasg 9.9.67 Rose G. Murphy teacher d of John M. MA(Glas) Rutherglen

SHIRRIFFS George Geddes cMB ChB 1963
s of William S. S. master painter and Mary A. Geddes MA 1926 qv; b Aber 10.2.40
h o ARI 1963–64; Aberd: Garden res fell. 1964–66, dept res fell. therap 1966–68; g p Aber from 1969
m Aber 12.3.65 June V. Sinclair nurs sister d of John S. Aber

SHODERU Rasheed Omokayode BSc(eng) 1967

SHORT John Robert Thomas DSc 1957
s of Victor A. S. army off. and Marion D. von Langen; b Perth W Aust 26.6.24
BSc(Univ W Aust) 1946 DPhil(Oxon) 1950
lect, sen lect agr zool Aberd 1952–65; ANU Canberra: sen lect zool and warden Garran Hall 1966–73, later reader zool from 1973
m Cambridge 6.8.52 Elizabeth Y. Campbell MA(Edin) lib, res asst d of John Y. C. DD(Edin) Cambridge

SHORT Lesley Margaret MA 1968
d of Frank S. acct and Margaret Hill secy/typist; b Manc 1.8.46
Dip Ed(N'cle) 1970
teacher Fr/Ger Perth W Aust 1972–73, part-time Fr 1975–77, part-time remed Engl from 1977
m Wilmslow 26.8.68 Colin Heinzman BSc 1968 qv

SHRUBSOLE Martin Richard *MA 1970
s of Stanley A. H. S. loc govt off. and Margery Hutt lib; b Maidstone 29.7.47
BR Scot. reg: traffic man. trainee 1970–72, asst stat man. Waverley stat Edin 1972–73, freight comm intelligence asst Glasg 1973–75, asst area man. Partickhill 1975–77; area man. BR Grantham from 1977
m Maidstone 14.8.71 Wendy E. Lawson BA(Bangor) teacher d of Walter G.A.L. Maidstone

SHUTTLEWORTH Graham Rex *BSc 1963
s of Norman H. S. eng (aeronautical) and Mabel L. French; b Wolverhampton 16.5.41
MSc(Birm) 1966
hosp biochem: Birm 1963–73, Bournemouth from 1974
m Wolverhampton 21.3.64 Susan M. Jenkins teacher d of Trevor I. J. BSc(Swansea) Claverley nr Wolverhampton

SIAFA Salu Franklin MB ChB 1963

SIBBALD Jane Bonnie *MA 1968
d of John S. soldier, teacher and Rita M. Hall; b Farnborough 31.12.44
Edin: asst antique shop 1968–69, MoT cler asst 1970–71; exec off. SED 1971–73; admin trainee MoD Lond 1974–76, higher exec off. (admin) 1977, prin 1978

m Shrivenham 26.8.67 Trevor B. Royle MA 1967 qv; marr diss 1973

SIBLEY Graham Hugh Milne BSc(agr) 1967

SIEVEWRIGHT David Campbell BL 1957
s of James A. D. S. loc govt off. and Ann G. Campbell; b Aber 16.8.37
leg. asst: Aber c c 1960–64. Lanark c c Hamilton 1964–65; private pract Hamilton from 1965
m Aber 18.9.61 Hazel M. Wilson pharm d of James W. Aber

SIEVEWRIGHT Joan LLB 1966
d of James A. D. S. treas Aber c c and Ann G. Campbell; b Aber 30.4.46
Aber: law app 1966–68; solic 1968–70, part-time from 1970
m Aber 14.7.67 Graeme R. D. Catto MB ChB 1969 qv

SILVER Dorothy Mary BSc 1956
d of James S. insp taxes and Isabel R. McLaren; b Selby 19.4.35
teacher Aber 1957–60
m Aber 25.7.60 Maurice D. Lowe MB ChB 1960 qv

SILVER Patricia Cameron BSc 1957 *1958
m Reid

SILVER Sheila Allison MB ChB 1961

SILVER William Allan MSc 1970
s of Harold A. M. S. farm. and Mary B. Watson teacher; b Oxbow Sask Canada 3.10.32
BA(Sask) 1953 BSc(Sask) 1954 MD CM(McG) 1956 FRCS(C) 1967
med res fell. Sask 1968–69; McLaughlin trav fell. Aberd 1969–70; asst prof surg (orthop) Sask from 1970
m Hudson Bay Sask 6.8.54 Eunice S. Black BA(Sask) asst lib d of John A. B. Sask

SILVERSTONE Peter Isaac MB ChB 1968
s of Michael S. locksmith and Ada Oland secy; b Hampton Court 27.5.41
DObstRCOG 1970 MRCOG 1974
h o geriat/gyn Aber 1968–69; sen h o: Carlisle 1969–71, N'cle-u-Tyne 1971–73; regist obst/gyn N'cle-u-Tyne 1971–73; res fell. obst N'cle-u-Tyne 1973–75, sen regist 1975–77; consult. obst/gyn Gateshead hosps from 1977
m Lond 14.2.71 Beryl Lux BA(Lond) teacher

SIM Alan James *BSc(eng) 1970
s of James H. S. shopkeeper and Anne McWilliam; b Aber 13.12.47
MICE 1973
eng city eng's dept Aber 1970–73; Aber: des eng W. A. Fairhurst & Ptnrs from 1973
m Aber 3.10.70 Nancy Ramsay secy d of George H. R. Aber

SIM Alan William Paterson MA 1966

SIM Betty May *MA 1961
d of Robert L. S. mason and Christina R. Hay MA 1928 qv; b Ellon 21.8.39
teacher Thurso: geog 1962–63, geog/Engl from 1973
m Aber 2.8.63 Derek Bradstreet physicist s of James B. Norfolk

SIM Catherine Mary MB ChB 1970
m Legg

SIM David Morrice MB ChB 1963

SIM Denis O'Brien MA 1967
s of John S. police off. and Ruth O'Brien MA 1930 *qv*;
b Huntly 27.8.46
teacher: Dumbarton 1968–69, New Pitsligo 1969–71;
exec off.: Metrop Police Civil Comm Lond 1971–73,
Scot. Home and Health Dept Edin 1973–78, higher exec
off. SED Edin from 1978
m Edin 27.10.73 Anne P. Broderick dept man. John
Lewis d of Joseph B. Dublin

SIM Dorothy BSc 1960
d of William R. S. joiner and Mary Low; b Aber
25.3.39
teacher: Perth 1961–64, Montreal 1964–67, Edin from
1967
m Low

SIM Elsie Marguerite MA 1962
d of Alexander A. S. quarry man. and Marguerite B.
Low; b Old Deer 15.11.40
teacher: Fr/Engl/hist Hopeman s s 1963–64, Fr/Engl
Auchinleck 1964–65, Lat/Fr/Engl Drumley House, Ayr
1965–66, Ely h s Cambridge 1966–67
m Aber 14.8.64 John W. McKay MA 1962 *qv*

SIM George Hugh Bremner *BSc 1960
b Aber 28.5.37
comp dir
m Aber Dorothy C. Milne BSc 1959 *qv*

SIM Johann Christine MA 1960
m Bowen

SIM John McBain BSc(eng) 1963

SIM John Robert MA 1968
s of William S. sales rep and Margaret M. Harcus
clerkess, nurse; b Kirkwall 9.12.46
merch seaman 1969–70; teacher: Engl Dunfermline
1970–72, Engl/hist Kirkwall from 1972
m Westray Orkney 12.7.72 Thora H. Drever hosp dom
d of Stewart B. D. Westray

SIM John Wilson MB ChB 1964
s of John J. W. S. elect. and Isabella K. Beattie; b Aber
16.1.37
h o ARI, Perth, Irvine 1965–66; g p Yorks from 1966
m Aber 15.7.64 Muriel Buchan MA 1958 *qv*

SIM Lesley Beatrix MA 1959
m Milligan

SIM Marta (Martha) Gorrod *MA 1957
d of George G. S. plasterer and Nelly W. Sim; b Aber
10.1.35
teacher mod lang: Morrison's acad Crieff 1958–60, Aber
acad 1960–63, spec asst 1963–69; prin mod lang Rose-
mead s Littlehampton 1969–73; acad tut. from 1973
m Aber 9.4.69 Alexander G. Watt mushroom grower s of
George W. Littlehampton

SIM Morag Kathleen O'Brien MA 1961
d of John S. police serg and Ruth S. O'Brien MA 1930
qv; b Ellon 15.11.40
teacher maths: Bankhead acad 1962; part-time Aber
coll of comm 1968–71, Inverurie acad 1971–75, asst prin
maths Bankhead acad 1975–76
m(1) Fraserburgh 4.8.62 William G. Innes MA 1962 *qv*;
marr diss
  (2) Fraserburgh 13.8.76 Andrew J. Cooper master
printer s of Dennis R. C. Fraserburgh

SIM Sandra Jean *MA 1969
d of Alexander S. security off. and Helen W. Ritchie
kitchen asst; b Aber 10.5.47
clin psych: Warley hosp Brentwood 1969–72, Royal
Cornhill hosp Aber 1972–75
m Fraserburgh 15.8.69 Alexander B. Malley MA 1965 *qv*

SIM Sheila Elizabeth *MA 1967
d of John S. electric pylon erector and Elizabeth Harvey;
b Aber 31.3.46
teacher: Engl/hist Lond 1967–69, Engl Ife Nigeria 1970–
72; curric dev, Engl and edit. Distance Teaching Maseru
Lesotho 1973–76; teacher Engl Lond 1977–79; PGCE
in Engl as foreign lang at Inst of Educ Univ London
from 1979
m Kinellar 24.6.67 George W. Reid MA 1967 *qv*

SIMISON Aileen Margaret MA 1963

SIMMERS Gillian Jean MA 1968
d of William S. farm. and Jeannie R. Morrison MA
1937 *qv*; b Fraserburgh 22.5.47
teacher: geog Bannockburn 1969–70, geog/remed Nairn
acad 1970–74, remed Forfar acad 1974–77
m Aber 16.7.75 Robert A. Gall BSc(St And) teacher s of
Robert G.

SIMMONDS John Stewart MA 1969
s of Wilfrid T. S. clerk and Margaret Campbell; b Elgin
17.1.47
teacher hist/mod stud. Forres acad 1970–73; capt RAEC
Pirbright 1973–74; comm Sandhurst 1974
m Lossiemouth 1.4.72 Anne Campbell civ serv d of
John C. Lossiemouth

SIMMONS Thomas Caithness BSc(for) 1960

SIMMS Ian Howard MA 1968
s of Louis S. BSc(Lond) headmaster and Edna J.
Joseph vice-prin coll of adult educ; b Lond 15.7.46
salesman Lond 1968–69; area man. (sales/admin) Brist
1969–73; man. dir of own comp Brist from 1973

SIMPSON Alan BSc 1970
s of Kenneth S. and Edith M. Cruickshank; b Aber
19.11.49
Sterling Winthrop Group Surbiton: computer progr, syst
analyst 1970–74, unit man. from 1974
m Ashford Middx 21.9.74 Marion Walker export clerk
d of Edward W. E Molesey

SIMPSON Alexander *MA 1965 *MEd 1978
s of William B. S. cinema man. and Jane E. S.
Goldsmith; b Aber 22.7.35
Dip Ed(Lond) 1971
Aber: lect geog coll of comm 1966–72, prin teacher geog
Northfield acad 1972–78, lect psych coll of comm from
1978
m Aber 22.3.58 Hilda D. Brown teacher d of Alexander
B. Aber

SIMPSON Alexander BSc 1969
s of James S. farm., tech off. dept of agr and Colina
MacLellan shopkeeper; b Campbeltown 27.5.48
scient off. (field geol) inst of geol sc Lond 1969–73;
teacher geog Falkirk from 1974

SIMPSON Alexander *MA 1968
s of Alexander S. fisherman and Mary M. Sutherland;
b Lossiemouth 10.8.43
MSc(Strath) 1975
teacher Lond 1969–71; computer progr civ serv Lond
1971–72; teacher Airdrie 1972–73

m Nairn 22.3.67 Jean H. Munro civ serv d of James A. M. Nairn

SIMPSON Alexander Milne   BSc 1957
s of Alexander M. S. process oper and Maggie A. Easton; b Lonmay 28.3.36
UK AEA Dounreay 1958–62; asst exper off. Winfrith Heath Dorset 1962–65; tech off. ICI organics div Stevenston from 1965
m Aber 12.8.57 Margaret I. Adie med lab tech d of Norman J. A. Aber

SIMPSON Ann   *MA 1961
d of W. Douglas S. MA 1919 univ lib Aberd and E. Dorothy Mason bank employee; b Aber 25.4.38
secy stud. Lond 1961–62; translator Paris 1962–66; Lond: cler off. Central Bureau for educ visits and exchanges 1966–67, admin asst Council for Brit Archaeology 1967–68, various posts MRC 1968–78, sen admin asst (internat relations) NALGO from 1978

SIMPSON Anne Frazer   MA 1961 Dip Ed 1962
d of George S. detect. insp/regist man. for trawl fishermen and Margaret Frazer lab tech/chem; b Aber 9.3.40
teacher: Engl/hist/geog Torry s s Aber 1962–64, Engl Firrhill s s Edin 1964–65; part-time lect Engl f e College of Art Dun
m Aber 3.4.64 Robert F. Philip BSc(eng) 1960 *qv*

SIMPSON Bernard Alan   MA 1965 Dip Ed 1966

SIMPSON Brian Dalgleish   BSc 1966
s of James M. S. tweed indust man. and Kate Little; b Aber 12.10.44
teacher phys: Cults acad 1967–72, RGC Aber 1972–74; asst prin phys RGC from 1974

SIMPSON Catherine Mary   MA 1957
d of Douglas J. S. elect. eng and Catherine R. Reid; b Aber 17.3.37
Dip Ed(Hong Kong) 1969
teacher Engl Diocesan girls' s Kowloon Hong Kong 1969–72, sen Engl mistress from 1972
m Brit Solomon Is Protectorate 28.9.57 Robin R. Mason BSc(Lond) agr scient s of Alfred H. M. Ashby-de-la-Zouche

SIMPSON David Clark   *MA 1966
b Johnshaven 20.11.35
teacher Engl/hist Bervie 1967–69; Mackie acad Stonehaven: teacher hist/year master 1970–72, teacher hist/ prin guid 1972–73, prin hist from 1973

SIMPSON Dorothy Anna   BSc 1959 *1960
m Williams

SIMPSON Douglas John   *BSc(eng) 1956

SIMPSON Duncan Simmie   BSc(eng) 1962

SIMPSON Eileen Mary   MA 1967
d of James D. G. S. blacksmith and Mary A. Cowie milliner; b Aber 20.11.46
teacher: Engl/hist Whitburn 1968–73, prin Engl/hist Tranent from 1973

SIMPSON Elizabeth Ann Brand   *MA 1959
m Dare
d 27.4.66

SIMPSON Elma Watt   MA 1967
d of James W. S. farm. and Mabel J. Watt; b Fraser-

burgh 22.6.46
teacher mod lang: Camphill h s Paisley 1968–71, Woodfarm h s Renfrewsh 1971–73; asst prin mod lang Castlehead h s Paisley from 1973
m Rosehearty 29.7.72 Ian L. H. Cummings MA(Glas) teacher s of Robert M. C. Paisley

SIMPSON Frank   BSc 1965

SIMPSON George   MA 1961

SIMPSON George Henry   *MA 1956
s of Joseph H. S. master cabinetmaker and Janet M. Henderson; b Leeds 6.12.14
Higher Dip RE (Aber coll of educ) 1957
teacher: Engl Viewforth s s Kirkcaldy 1957–59, Aber Tech coll: teacher lib stud. 1959–63, head gen stud./man. dept from 1963
m Aber 11.6.48 Frances T. Wilson d of Robert M. W. Aber

SIMPSON Hamish Milne   BSc 1969
s of Thomas S. distill man. and Margaret A. Milne; b Rothes 6.6.48
jun geol Geosurv of Aust Adelaide 1969–70; geol: Rockfall Co Barrhead 1970–73, Foundation Eng Lond from 1973
m Ilford 26.7.75 Christine M. Tomlinson teacher d of James T. Ilford

SIMPSON Helen Joyce   MA 1965

SIMPSON Ian Grahame   MB ChB 1966
s of John W. S. licensed grocer and Hilda Milne; b Aber 2.7.42
Dip Soc Med(Edin) 1970
h o Aber 1966–67; trainee g p Aber 1967–68; regist med Aber 1968–69; fell. in med admin Aber, Edin 1969–72; asst sen m o NERHB Aber 1972–74; spec commun med Aber 1974–75; dist m o Aber 1975–78; asst secy med def union Lond from 1978
m Aber 20.7.68 Heather W. McLaughlin BA lib d of William R. D. McL. Portlethen

SIMPSON Jacqueline Margaret   *BSc 1969
d of Alexander S. BSc(Lond) prin navig coll and Yvonne M. White typist; b Glasg 1.11.46
PhD(Lond) 1973
m Lond 27.6.70 Martin Gordon BSc 1969 *qv*

SIMPSON Janis Mary   MA 1970
d of Charles D. S. elect. eng and Mary S. Forsyth; b Aber 9.4.49
teacher: Engl/hist Lossiemouth h s 1971–73, remed Northfield acad Aber from 1973

SIMPSON John Cruer   *MB ChB 1965 PhD 1975
s of Alexander N. S. acct and Isabella Noble; b Toronto 15.5.41
MRCPath 1973
h o ARI 1965–66; Aberd: Garden res fell. dept med 1966–67, MRC fell. dep med 1967–68, lect path. 1968–75; visiting prof Mich univ 1975–77; sen lect path. Aberd from 1978

SIMPSON Leonard McPherson   BSc(for) 1959

SIMPSON Lilian Janet Weir   MA 1961
d of George S. grocery vanman and Lily M. Menzies cook; b Rothes 7.12.39
teacher Struy p s 1962–64, Beauly j s 1964–67; head Struy p s 1967–71; part-time remed Inv 1974–78; teacher

Knockbain p s from 1978
m Strathpeffer 20.7.63 John Gordon carpenter, contr s
of Hugh G. Struy

SIMPSON Margaret Elizabeth   *MA 1963
   d of Robert S. cashier and Elizabeth C. Rennie bookkeeper; b Aber 19.4.41
teacher Aber acad 1964–66
m Aber 3.8.63 William D. Hardie MA 1953 *qv*

SIMPSON Marnel   MA 1961
   d of Johnston O. S. and Dorothy Bremner; b Peterhead
20.6.40
asst lib univ of Edin from 1963
m Peterhead 6.8.66 Valnor Powell BA(Bangor) univ lib

SIMPSON May   *MA 1969
   d of Philip S. joiner and Elsie Beattie nurse; b Tarves
15.5.47
teacher classics Hutcheson's girls' g s Glasg 1970–74
m Aber 13.7.71 Craig A. Madden MA 1969 *qv*

SIMPSON Moreen Anne   *MA 1970
   d of Alexander D. S. audit asst and Kathleen Beedie
uphol sewer; b Aber 22.2.48
journalist Aber from 1970
m Aber 8.4.74 Douglas M. Cameron BSc 1970 *qv*

SIMPSON Neil Alasdair   *BSc 1966

SIMPSON Neil Alexander   *MA 1962
   b Blairgowrie 20.2.40
ALA 1966
lib asst Fulwood 1962–63; asst lib Guildhall lib Lond
1964–68, various posts Manc publ lib 1968–74; prin asst
(pers) cultural serv dept Manc 1974; asst chief lib (oper
serv) Tameside 1974–77; asst dir (culture) Stockport from
1978
m Aber 18.9.63 Sheila A. Brown MA 1962 *qv*

SIMPSON Neil Norman   *MA 1968
   s of Neil M. S. motor mech, gardener and Ann
W. G. W. Webster; b Aber 24.3.37
teacher hist Aber acad (later Hazlehead acad) 1969–73;
prin hist/mod stud. Bridge of Don acad Aber from 1974
m Aber 6.6.61 Sheila Main teacher d of William M.
Aber

SIMPSON Norma Craigmile   *MA 1967 PhD 1971
   d of Alexander C. S. flower/fruit shop prop. and
Isabella H. Allan shorthand typist; b Aber 12.6.45
Aberd: res asst mental health dept 1967–69, res fell. from
1969
m Robertson

SIMPSON Norman Stanley Riach   *MA 1962

SIMPSON Patricia Marion   *MA 1968
   d of Robert G. E. S. dental tech, licensed victualler and
Mary W. Edgar MA(Glas) teacher, physioth; b Glasg
4.7.47
Dip Lib(Strath) 1970 ALA 1972
trainee lib Milngavie 1968–69, asst bibliographer J.
Whitaker & Sons Lond 1970–71; sen asst lib Basingstoke
from 1971
m Lond 20.4.71 Donald H. N. Ferguson BSc 1968 *qv*

SIMPSON Robert   MA 1966

SIMPSON Robert William   *MA 1963
   s of William T. S. sheet metal worker and Annie C.
Mearns; b Aber 30.7.41

B Phil(Oxon) 1965
lect moral phil Aberd from 1965
m Aber 27.9.63 Gladys D. Murison teacher d of Robert
M. Aber

SIMPSON Sandra Mary   MA 1969

SIMPSON Sheena Grant   *MA 1958
   d of Walter S. S. and Harriet H. Wills; b Peterhead
22.1.38
Engl lang asst Beauvais France 1958–59; teacher Fr/
Ger Aber 1960–64, Fortrose from 1972
m Aber 30.3.63 Graham Munro MA(Edin) teacher s of
William D. M. Dingwall

SIMPSON Sheila Margaret   MA 1965
   d of George S. and Nan Hay; b Huntly 23.9.44
teacher geog/hist Keith g s 1966–68, spec asst 1968–73;
prin geog Abbott's coll Cape Town S Af from 1974
m Elgin 19.7.72 Edward S. R. McAllister navig off. MN
s of Alexander S. McA. Tomintoul

SIMPSON Sybil Elizabeth Gray   MB ChB 1959
   d of Thomas S. stationmaster BR and Thomasina D.
Redpath ch's nurse; b Edin 12.4.34
DObstRCOG 1963
h o, sen h o Woodend hosp Aber, Perth, Bridge of Earn
1960–62; Perth: trainee g p 1962–63, sen h o regist anaest
1963–67, med asst anaest from 1967

SIMPSON Thomas William   MB ChB 1964
   s of Thomas F. S. civ serv and Sarah V. McDade
secy; b Aber 23.2.39
DA 1968
h o: Dumfries RI 1964–65, Woodend hosp Aber 1965–66;
regist anaest ARI 1966–68; g p Aber from 1968
m Aber 4.4.66 Maureen A. Philip BSc 1963 *qv*

SIMPSON Vera Fraser   *MA 1966
   d of William S. police serg, gen merch and Margaret
J. A. Milne gen merch; b Aber 16.5.44
Dip Engl as second lang(Leeds) 1968
VSO teaching fell. Njala univ coll Sierra Leone 1966–67;
Bradford: teacher Engl to immigrant children 1968–70
and 1972–74; res asst computer based learning proj
Leeds univ 1970–72; teacher Engl Chosen Hill s Church-
down from 1974
m Aber 6.9.68 Robert W. Clouston BSc 1968 *qv*

SIMPSON Vincent Leslie   BSc(eng) 1960
   s of Vincent J. A. S. paper mill worker and Florence
Leslie; b Peterculter 1938
asst eng Argyll c c Strachur 1960–63; asst eng/sub ag
Wm Tawse Aber: Strachur, Mull, Clacton 1963–66;
Argyll: ag/civ eng man. W. H. Rankin Sandbank 1966–
73, ptnr/dir Bonnar construct. co civ eng contr Kilmun
from 1973

SIMPSON William Barber   *BSc 1959 PhD 1962
   s of William S. baker and Margaret Barber; b Aber
31.5.36
res fell. Nott 1962–64; lect: Trinity coll Dublin 1964–68,
RGIT Aber from 1968
m Aber 7.6.61 Hazel M. Grant civ serv d of Robert G.
Aber

SINCLAIR Alan George   *BSc 1957 PhD 1960
   s of Samuel S. weaver/crofter/grocer's asst and Anne S.
Johnston; b Sandwick Shetland 7.7.35
Lincs: indust chem 1960–65, lect coll of tech 1965–69;
scient agr res Mosgiel NZ from 1969
m Aber 8.8.58 Isabella M. Bruce indust radiogr, saleswoman d of John B. Aber

SINCLAIR Ann Gordon   MA 1968
d of Duncan T. R. S. bank insp and Charlotte G. Hay
postal worker; b Aber 1.3.47
teacher lang Perth W Aust 1970–72
m Aber 1.9.69 John A. Bunting BSc 1969 *qv*

SINCLAIR Anne   MA 1966
d of George S. S. man. herring trade and Johan R.
Strachan; b Peterhead 12.1.44
teacher: St Peter's R C s Aber 1967–68, Dingwall acad
1968–70, Invernesssh from 1972
m Aber 29.8.66 John J. A. Dodds BSc 1965 *qv*

SINCLAIR Catherine Croy   *MA 1957

SINCLAIR Christina Sandra   MA 1969
d of John S. farm man. and Elizabeth L. W. Tait;
b Peebles 31.7.49
computer syst progr throughout UK from 1969
m Banchory 3.6.72 Callum Fraser BSc 1968 *qv*

SINCLAIR Douglas Walker   BSc 1964

SINCLAIR Duncan Alexander   MA 1961

SINCLAIR Duncan John   *MA 1958

SINCLAIR Elizabeth Burness   MA 1967
d of David B. S. estate worker and Lizzie K. Rutherford; b Perth 26.4.41
teacher: Kaimhill s s Aber 1968–69, Milnes h s Fochabers
1969–71, Porchester s s 1973–75
m Elgin 1.8.70 Raymond V. Bennett off. RN s of Arthur
B. Dawlish

SINCLAIR Elizabeth Katherine   MA 1960
m Dawson

SINCLAIR Ernelyn Jean   MA 1968

SINCLAIR Janet Anne   MA 1965 Dip Ed 1966
d of Robert S. crofter and Mary M. MacRae teacher;
b Inv 17.1.44
teacher: Croy 1966–70, Inv 1970–73; staff tut. Inv educ
auth from 1973
m Fraser

SINCLAIR Jean Milne   BSc 1965
d of Farquhar C. S. joiner and Jessie Paterson; b Aber
7.1.44
teacher girls' g s Newbury 1966–69
m Aber 10.8.67 Stuart McNeill BSc 1963 *qv*

SINCLAIR Joan Elisabeth Cumming   BSc 1961
d of Ian J. S. indust consult. and Janet F. Ross teacher
dom sc; b Lossiemouth 26.10.40
res asst biol Aberd 1961–64; relief teacher Peterhead
acad 1965
m Aber 11.5.63 Ian R. A. Macmillan MA 1960 *qv*

SINCLAIR John   *BSc 1956
s of Arthur J. S. farm. and Frances A. Anderson;
b Lhanbryde 17.11.31
AMBIM 1972
process supt SAI: Leith 1956–57, Aber 1957–61; Ilford
photogr materials manuf Cheshire: dept man. 1961–71,
dep works man. 1971–76; pers man. Inveresk Paper Co
(coated papers) Macclesfield from 1976
m Macclesfield 20.10.70 E. Doreen Lytton soc worker and
estate ag sales d of Robert J. L. Timperley

SINCLAIR John   *BSc(eng) 1967
s of Alexander H. S. eng and Elizabeth McPherson;

b Findochty 29.5.46
MICE MIWES
grad eng Sunbury 1967–68; asst eng Lond 1968–71; eng:
Bristol 1971–74, Piuca Peru 1974–76, Ankara Turkey
1976–78, Najran Saudi Arabia 1978–79
m Elgin 20.6.70 Frances S. Taylor d of James M. T. Elgin

SINCLAIR Joyce Elaine   MA 1964
m Mawson

SINCLAIR Margaret   MA 1966
d of Alister J. S. tech teacher and Isobel Rilley dem;
b Aber 5.4.45
computer syst progr Edin 1966–70
m Aber 26.8.67 Robin C. McKenzie MA 1966 *qv*

SINCLAIR Margaret Florence   MA 1968
d of Harold S. draper and Blanche Rossetter; b Golspie
18.12.46
teacher Fr Creighton s Lond 1969–75
m Lond 28.8.73 Bernard Whiting civ serv s of William
G. W. Robertsbridge

SINCLAIR Morag Anne Stuart   MA 1963
d of Ernest J. S. farm. and Ivy J. L. Hourston sub-
postmistress; b Orkney 18.6.42
Orkney: teacher Finstown p s 1964–66, remed Birsay p s
1973–74, remed Rendall 1977–78
m Orkney 22.7.66 James M. Rendall farm. s of Alexander
S. R. Stromness

SINCLAIR Morag Margaret   MA 1968
d of William P. S. photogr man. and Margaret White;
b Aber 24.2.46
teacher Fr/Ger Newbattle h s Dalkeith 1969–73, Craigroyston s s Edin from 1973
m Aber 13.7.73 James H. Robertson MA(Edin) C of S
min s of James R. Stirling

SINCLAIR Neil Thomson   *MA 1967
s of Duncan S. bank man. and Doris M. Thomson
LDS(Glas) dentist; b York 20.6.44
Assoc Museum Ass. 1973
trainee museum asst Cheltenham 1967–72; sen asst
museum curator Sunderland 1972–75; curator: Monkwearmouth Station Museum 1975–77, Sunderland
Museums from 1977

SINCLAIR Norma Murray   *MA 1968 Dip Ed 1969
d of Benjamin M. S. auctioneer and Ann B. Mackenzie
teacher; b Wick 28.5.46
teacher phys Wick from 1969

SINCLAIR Peter Rayment   *MA 1969
PhD(Edin)

SINCLAIR Robert Andrew   *BSc 1960 MSc 1962
PhD 1965
s of Robert S. merch seaman and Jemima A. Peterson;
b Trondavoe Shetland 18.3.38
FCS 1960 Fulbright schol(S Calif) 1965–67
asst lect Lond 1963–64; post doct fell.: S Calif Los
Angeles 1965–67, Lond 1967–68; sen scient: 3M Co
Harlow 1968–73, 3M St Paul USA from 1973
m Lossiemouth 18.7.63 Jean R. Smith BSc 1961 *qv*

SINCLAIR Robert Forbes   BSc(eng) 1963
s of Alfred M. S. turner and Christina C. Ritchie;
b Aber 10.10.41
AMIEE 1963
trainee eng Glasg 1963–65, 4th asst eng Bathgate 1965–66;
3rd asst eng: Ardrossan 1966–67, Kilmarnock 1967–74,
2nd eng Glasg from 1974

SINCLAIR Wilma   MA 1960
d of William J. H. S. RNVR and trawl skipper and
Christina Slater; b Aber 25.5.39
teacher Errol 1961–63, Toronto 1965–67
m Aber 24.8.63 Carl W. Groskorth RCAF fighter pilot,
capt Air Canada s of Carl L. G. Parry Sound Ontario

SINGER Derek Alexander   LLB 1964
s of Alexander S. sqdn leader RAF and Marjory W.
Pullar; b Forfar 2.7.43
BA(Cantab) 1968
law app Edin 1964–66; solic, called to bar 1966–69;
Lond: trainee merch bank. 1969, leg. asst F. A. R.
Bennion barrister 1969–71; leg. draftsman min of fin.
Jamaica, Kingston 1971–74; gen counsel to merch bank
Kingston from 1974
m St Andrew Jamaica 25.12.72 Sandra A. G. Abrahams
BMus(Kentucky) off. man. d of William V. A. St Andrew

SINGER Linda Mary Coutts   MA 1970
d of James C. S. CA and Helen S. Niven; b Fyvie
12.4.49
teacher: Fife 1972–73, Musselburgh 1973–75, Prudhoe
1976–78
m Kintore 8.8.75 Roland W. J. McKinney BSc(St And)
biochem s of Robert McK. Galashiels

SINGER Wilma Wallace   *MA 1970
d of William S. tyre serv rep and Dora Ewen accts
clerkess; b Aber 28.8.49
teacher hist Lanarksh 1971–72; Lond: actuarial dept life
assur comp 1972–73, trainee fin. planner 1973–74, life
and pensions plan. consult. from 1974
m Aber 20.12.75 Duncan D. Simpson-Fraser BSc(Glas)
elect eng, comp dir s of S. S-F. Lochwinnoch

SINGH Kesar   MB ChB 1964

SINGH Kulbir Kartar   *BSc(eng) 1963 MSc 1965

SINGH Kulrajmohinder   MB ChB 1968
s of Kartar S.; b Tanga Tanzania 13.4.42
h o: Lond 1968–69, paediat Aber 1970–71, Nuneaton
1971–72, anaest Burnley 1972–73; g p Fillmore Sask
Canada from 1973
m Nairobi 23.8.70 Tejinder K. Jabbal

SINGH Madan Mohan   MB ChB 1965

SINGH Manik   PhD 1960
s of Shri P. S. farm. and Shrimati Pasinda Kuer;
b Patna India 1.10.21
BSc(B.H.U. India) 1940 MB BS(Patna) 1946
lect anat Aberd 1960–61; prof/head dept anat P.W. med
coll Patna from 1962
m Bihar India 11.5.46 Shakuntala Singh PhD 1962 qv

SINGH Neville Bharat   BSc(eng) 1966
s of Udho S. farm./bus. man. and Meghbati Singh bus.
woman; b Georgetown Guyana 14.9.38
MICE 1972 MSc(Ohio) 1973
Guyana: resid eng Mackenzie highway Demerara 1966–
68; proj eng Corentyne Highway E Berbice 1968–69;
spec eng: structures roads div MoW/hydraulics 1969–70,
maintenance, hydraulics & supply 1970–72, plan. Central
Transport plan. unit Min of econ dev from 1973
m Aber 26.2.66 Aileen S. Forbes teacher d of H. M. C. F.
Aber

SINGH Shakuntala   PhD 1962
d of Sarju P. S. LLB(Patna) judge and Moti Singh;
b Brahampur Bihar India 10.6.31

BA(Patna) 1947 MA(Patna) 1949 MEd(Patna) 1954
lect Hindi MM coll Patna univ from 1957
m Bihar 11.5.46 Manik Singh PhD 1960 qv

SIOU Leon Ange Pierre Mee   *BSc(eng) 1969
s of Leon L. M. A. S. land surv and Lucia C. K. Hong
hairdresser; b Port Louis Mauritius 31.5.44
asst eng LCC 1969–70; Toronto: field eng for contr
1970–71, proj eng/estimator/proj man. for contr 1971–
74, VP/gen man. from 1974
m Toronto 3.12.71 Brenda V. Cannon med secy d of
Alfred C. Enfield

SIYO Wells Jones   *MEd 1966
BA Dip Ed(SA) BEd(Natal)

SKARDHAMAR Torfinn   *BSc 1958
s of Odmar S. comm attaché for Faroese trade affairs
and Ingeborg Poulsen; b Tórshavn Faroe Is 25.8.35
MSc(Birm) 1960
phys: inst for atomenergi Kjeller Norway 1959–61, AB
atomenergi Stockholm 1962–68; phys/proj leader Kjeller
1968–75, sen phys/group leader Kjeller from 1976; also
sen consult. Scandpower A/S Norway
m Horten Norway 17.10.70 Anne-Karí Raaen Cand.
Philol.(Oslo) teacher

SKEETE Maureen Valeria Harford   MB ChB 1969
d of Lee H. S. MA(Durh) teacher, headmaster and
Myra M. A. Nicholls teacher; b Barbados 18.1.44
Dip Dermat(Lond) 1974
h o Queen Elizabeth hosp Barbados 1969–70; sen h o
univ hosp of WI Jamaica 1970–71; chief med asst, regist
univ of WI 1971–72; m o Wandsworth Lond 1973; sen
h o dermat, res fell. St John's hosp Lond 1974–77; sen
regist dermat univ hosp of WI 1977; asst consult. (Queen
Eliz hosp Barbados)/assoc lect dermat univ of WI from
1978
m Barbados 9.5.70 Henry S. Fraser MB BS(univ of WI)
s of Robert S. F. Barbados

SKENE Alfred   MA 1969

SKENE Donald Scott   *BSc 1959
s of Kenneth C. S. S. MD(Lond) g p and Margaret P.
Paterson; b Lond 16.7.36
PhD(Lond)
Blackman stud. E Malling res stat 1959–63; res off.
CSIRO Melbourne Aust 1963–68; Cabot found. fell.
Harvard univ USA 1968–70; res sc E Malling res stat
from 1970
m Grantham 12.3.63 Ella J. Basker BSc(Nott) horti-
culturist

SKENE Elizabeth Ann   *MA 1969
d of William R. R. S. insp BR and Jessie B. Taylor
teacher home econ; b Insch 19.3.47
teacher Bankhead acad 1970–71
m Peterculter 25.7.70 Stephen R. Duthie wholesale
grocer s of Walter S. D. Cults Aber

SKENE John Robert   MB ChB 1962
s of Kenneth C. S. S. med pract and Margaret P.
Paterson secy; b Willesden 8.3.33
DObstRCOG
h o surg/med/obst Aber 1962–64; sen h o gyn Aber 1964–
65; g p Taunton from 1966
m Bournemouth 3.7.65 Wendy H. Taylor RGN d of
Ian H. T. MB ChB(Glas) Bournemouth

SKENE Richard Mackie   LLB 1969

SKENE William George   cMB ChB 1962

SKINNER Alexander Cumming   *BSc 1968
s of Alexander S. bldr and Jessie Cumming; b Dingwall 24.11.47
FGS(Lond) 1972
geol: Brit antarctic surv Stonington Base E Antarctica, Birm 1968–72, overseas div inst of geol sc Lond, Shan States Burma, Lond, Lobatse Botswana from 1972
m Tain 10.7.71 Catherine M. Corbett BSc 1967 qv

SKINNER Alexander Morrison   MA 1963
s of James B. S. MA 1934 qv; b Aber 23.9.42
FFA 1969 F Pensions Man. Inst 1977
trainee actuary, actuary Edin 1963–70; asst group actuary Montreal 1970–71; actuarial/pensions advis Kingston Jamaica 1971–72; pensions (sales) man. Edin from 1972
m Aber 16.7.66 Gay H. Brown teacher home econ d of William B. Aber

SKINNER Annie Mackenzie   MA 1959
d of David A. S. merch seaman and Christian E. Harkus; b S Shields 12.6.38
teacher: Inv 1960–65, Helmsdale 1965–66, Golspie from 1969
m Balintore 3.4.65 Allan C. Barclay BSc(Glas) teacher/asst rector s of John B. B. Inv

SKINNER Craig   *MB ChB 1965
s of James S. acct and Jane A. Craig; b Stonehaven 1.10.40
MRCP(Lond) 1970
h o ARI 1965–66; lect path. Aberd 1966–67; sen h o, regist, sen regist med Aber gen hosps 1967–74; sen regist respir med Sheffield from 1974
m Lond 15.11.61 Beryl Findlater teacher d of James F. Aber

SKINNER George   BSc(eng) 1961
s of George S. fisherman and Barbara Allan; b Balintore 28.9.40
MICE
Montreal eng co Calgary Alberta in 1974
m Tain Margaret Vass teacher d of Kenneth V. Tain

SKINNER Ian Ross   MA 1968

SKINNER James Allan   MB ChB 1969
s of George S. fisherman and Barbara Allen; b Balintore 12.9.46
h o RACH, Woodend hosp Aber, Inv 1969–70; sen h o obst Bellshill 1971; g p Aber 1971–72, Fearn from 1972
m Carloway Is of Lewis 13.8.71 Murdina Maclean MA 1969 qv

SKINNER Martha Helen   MA 1969
m Lennox

SKINNER May Elizabeth   MA 1967
d of George C. S. farm. and Marguerite C. Reid teacher; b Aber 15.5.42
m Aber 1.9.65 Satya S. Amar MB ChB 1966 qv

SKINNER Michael John   *BSc 1970

SKINNER Morna Logan   LLB 1967
m Hinch

SKINNER Peter Jackson   MA 1967

SKINNER Tom Anthony   *BSc(eng) 1965
s of David A. S. seaman and Christian Harkus; b Balintore 20.11.42

MEng(Carleton) 1972
eng: Ferranti Edin 1965–66, Canadian gen elect. 1966–67; res eng (scient staff) Bell Northern res Ottawa 1967–73; sen eng Telesat Canada, Ottawa 1973–74; prin Miller commun Ottawa 1974–76; pres Kantel Ottawa from 1976
m Balintore 22.7.66 Angela R. Thompson teacher d of Alexander T. Tain

SKOYLES Douglas   *BSc 1968 PhD 1971

SLACK Margaret Mary   MB ChB 1963

SLATER Francis William   *BSc 1970

SLATER John   PhD 1956
ARIC

SLATER John   *MA 1961 MSc 1962 PhD 1969
s of David J. S. fish salesman and Martha Summers clerkess; b Fraserburgh 23.9.39
asst lect, lect R'dg 1964–68; syst eng IBM Lond 1968–69; ass prof computer sc Calgary univ Alberta 1969–72, assoc prof from 1972
m Aber 22.7.65 Christine M. McKinnon MA 1962 qv

SLATER Peter Anderson   cMB ChB 1966
s of William S. MB ChB 1941 qv; b Aber 6.9.41
FRCSE 1972
h o ARI 1966–67; lect path. Aberd 1967–68; sen h o ARI: surg 1968–69, orthop 1969–70; regist: surg Middlesbrough gen hosp Teesside 1970–72, orthop Selly Oak Birm accident hosps 1973–75; sen regist orthop surg ARI 1975–78; consult. orthop surg Stracathro hosp from 1978
m Aber 21.7.67 Isobel M. Craig MB ChB 1966 qv

SLATER Rosalyn Jane   *MA 1970
s of William S. MB ChB 1940 qv; b Nairobi 2.9.46
res asst med sociol Aberd 1971–72
m Aber 20.8.70 David Stephen civ serv (Scot. off. audit unit) s of John S. J. S. Aber

SLEIGH or Kennedy, Allison Margaret   MB ChB 1960
d of F. R. S. MB ChB 1923 qv; b Hampton Hill 28.4.36
h o Aber: RACH, Woodend hosp 1960–62; FPA/MRC Cardiff 1966–68; BTS Aber 1968–70
m(2) Aber 1.12.73 Iain Fraser BL(Glas) advoc in Aber s of Donald F. Glasg

SLEIGH Elizabeth Anne   MA 1969

SLESSOR Eva Margaret   BSc 1962
d of William M. K. S. teacher and Eva J. K. Ross teacher; b Aber 23.10.39
teacher: Torry acad 1963–65, Sheerwater s s Woking 1965–68, Holme j s Headley from 1975
m Aber 31.7.65 Robert Falconer MA 1963 qv

SLESSOR Ian Munro   MB ChB 1956
s of John S. costing clerk and Helen B. Milne cashier; b Aber 19.5.32
MRCGP 1967 MSc 1978
h o Aber gen hosps 1956–58; dem anat dept Queen's coll Dund 1958–60; regist surg Aber gen hosps 1960–62; g p Aber 1962–69; med advis Astra Chemicals Watford from 1969

SLESSOR William Ross   BSc 1964 Dip Ed 1965
s of William M. K. S. teacher and Eva Ross teacher; b Aber 12.3.41
teacher sc Torry s s Aber 1965–68; injured in climbing accident 1968

SLETTEN Jorgen   MB ChB 1964
s of Andreas S. man. elect. works and Helga Kviteng;
b Mo Norway 18.4.37
FRCGP 1972
h o Stornoway 1964–65; Norway: g p Ardal 1965–66,
g p/loc m o h Laerdal 1966–70; g p trainee Bangour
(Scot.) gen hosp 1970–72; g p/distriktslege (m o h) Løten
Norway from 1972
m Aber 3.4.64 Annabel J. Bain teacher, med secy d of
James B. St Fergus

SLORACH Ronald George   BSc 1960

SLOWEY Alexander   MB ChB 1968
s of Frank S. publ works contr and Margaret More;
b Burghead 2.2.42
LMCC 1970
h o Inv, Liv 1968–69; g p Brockville Ontario from 1969
m Aber 27.12.67 Patricia J. Mackinnon MB ChB 1968 *qv*

SMALL Alan   *MA 1959
s of Frank S. eng and Alice M. Carnie; b Westminster
Lond 25.8.37
FSAScot. FSA(Lond)
asst lect, lect geog Aberd 1961–68; sen lect, reader geog
Dund from 1969
m Oslo 30.8.68 Sigrun Holdhus Cand Real(Oslo) res
worker/teacher d of Sigurd H. Oslo

SMALL Basil Oscar Samuel   MSc 1962
BSc(New Br)

SMALL Olwen Margaret Henderson   MA 1970

SMALLWOOD Michael John   BSc 1969 *1975
                                                        MSc 1976
s of John S. and Kathleen Dixon; b Bradford 3.11.44
teacher Aber 1969–70; asst trans man. Lond 1970–72

SMART Allan Gordon   *MA 1956 MEd 1973

SMART Ernest Ross Duncan   MA 1958 LLB 1961
s of Percy C. S. buying man. and Abigail Tawse;
b Aber 19.3.37
BD(Glas) 1978
law app Aber 1958–61; admin asst Lond 1961–63; stud.
Christ's coll Aber 1963–66; C of S min: asst Motherwell
1966–67, Carluke 1967–74, Merrylea Glasg from 1974
m Aber 9.4.65 Rosemary C. D. Carmichael MA 1962 *qv*

SMART Frances Mary   MA 1964
d of George S. maintenance eng and Isabella A.
Robertson; b Aber 22.2.44
m Kemnay 4.8.64 John A. Glennie MB ChB 1962 *qv*

SMART Hazel   MA 1962
d of Charles R. S. foreman textile waterproofer and
Mabel C. D. Kemp; b Aber 24.10.41
teacher: Middle s, Powis s Aber 1963–65; part-time Aber
coll of comm 1968–70
m Aber 27.7.63 James F. Reaper scient off. s of Robert
W. R. Aber

SMART James Alexander   MA 1966

SMART Jane Frances   BSc 1969
d of George G. J. S. MA(Cantab) dir salmon fishings
and Frances B. McFadyean; b Montrose 20.1.48
secy Lond zool gardens 1969–70; temp secy etc Aust
1971–73; curator biol sc museum of NT Darwin Aust
1973–74; secy 1974–77
m Melbourne Aust 26.4.74 David C. Tucker BSc(James

Cook univ) geol s of Horace F. T. MB BS(Melbourne)
Sandringham Vic Aust

SMART John Kirkton   BSc(for) 1958
s of John K. S. manuf's ag and Margaret C. Cathro;
b Aber 20.6.34
prof off. W Aust govt for. serv Perth W Aust from 1958
m Aber 27.4.57 Margaret I. Smith potter d of Andrew S.
Aber

SMART Judith Mary   *MA 1970
d of Gordon A. S. arch. and Mary Anderson MB
ChB 1938 *qv*; b Lond 4.6.48
teacher, secy for Finnish, Brit soc Jyväskylä Finland
1970–71; Lond: sub edit. med dept Butterworths, house
edit. Bailliére Tindall, med publ 1972–75; sub edit. John
Wright med publ Bristol
m Aber 28.4.73 Alan Watt jun man. life assur off. s of
Charles N. W. Edin

SMART Lynne Watkins   MA 1965 LLB 1967
d of James S. soc worker and Beryl M. Watkins;
b Hertford 9.3.44
law app town clerk's dept Aber 1967–69; leg. asst
Burnett & Reid advoc Aber 1970–71
m Aber 22.12.69 Dennis J. Williams comp chmn s of
Percival J. W. BSc(eng) Lond

SMART Marjory Ann   *MA 1968
d of Alexander W. S. rly clerk and Christina Taylor
shop asst; b Aber 15.9.45
Lond: stud. secy duties City of Westminster coll 1968–69,
private secy to dir of import/export comp 1969–72
m Aber 12.9.70 Roy R. Dover cler off. BR s of Thomas
R. D. Lond

SMART Norman Alexander   MA 1964

SMART Peter Alexander Fordyce   BSc 1964
s of Douglas G. S. rubber estate man. and Annie W.
Porter; b Malang Indonesia 10.7.42
Dip App Ling.(Edin) 1973
various posts Scot. 1964–67; TEFL: Sweden, Saudi
Arabia, W Ger 1967–72, Poland, Saudi Arabia, W Ger
1973–78; teacher Colchester from 1978
m Kirkcaldy 6.9.74 Jean Ford MA(St And) d of James F.
Kirkcaldy

SMELLIE Isabel Ann   MA 1961
m Johnston

SMITH Aileen Andrea   MA 1970

SMITH Aileen Campbell   MA 1970

SMITH Alan Howard   *BSc 1969

SMITH Alan Wilson   BSc(for) 1956
b Middlesbrough 1.9.35
reg man. Flintshire Woodlands; resid Shrewsbury

SMITH Alastair Davidson   MA 1966

SMITH Alexander Adams   MA 1970

SMITH Alexander Gordon   *BSc 1956
s of James W. S. BSc(agr) 1929 *qv*; b Inv 18.8.34
PhD(Lond) 1961
geol, geol surv dept Lusaka Zambia 1959–65; site geol
Consol. Gold Fields Strontian 1965; patent examiner
DTI Lond from 1966
m Bushey 5.5.73 Mary V. Glanville SRN d of Arthur
V. G. Bushey

SMITH Alexander John *MA 1966 Dip Ed 1967
s of Alexander G. S. bank acct and Jessie R. Kistler;
b Edin 25.8.43
Edin: teacher Engl Boroughmuir s s 1967–70, Craigmount s s 1970–73 and asst housemaster 1972–73, prin
guid Trinity acad from 1973
m Berwick-u-Tweed 29.12.67 Shona F. Geggie teacher
d of Peter G. G. Berwick-u-Tweed

SMITH Alexander Low *MA 1969 Dip Ed 1970
s of Alexander L. S. baker and Jeannie Lindsay;
b Forfar 7.3.47
teacher: geog Forfar acad 1970–73, prin geog Forres
acad from 1973

SMITH Alistair Joseph Watt *MA 1962

SMITH Angus Thomson *MA 1970
s of Leslie S. S. BR rly clerk and Nellie Thomson;
b Aber 30.5.27
teacher hist Keith g s from 1971
m Bucksburn 4.8.71 Kathleen Lawrence MA 1969 qv

SMITH Ann MA 1960 Dip Ed 1961

SMITH Anne Josephine MA 1968

SMITH Basil Forbes Lowden BSc 1956
s of James S. bank man. and Eva McIntosh; b Insch
4.5.34
radar fitter RAF UK, Malaya 1957–59; analytical chem
SSO Macaulay Inst Aber from 1959
m Ansley Nuneaton 10.9.66 Mary E. Woodward BSc
(Birm) statist d of Aubrey F. W. Atherstone

SMITH Ben *MA 1966
s of Benjamin S. and Mildred W. Stephen MA 1935 qv;
b Woking 17.1.44
ANU Canberra: res schol 1966–68, sen tut. 1968–71;
lect Strath from 1972
m Stonehaven 21.9.66 Elizabeth Synge BSc 1966 qv

SMITH Brian Stuart *MA 1970
s of Reginald J. S. wireworks gen man. and Irene
Bowles attend. blood transfusion serv; b Aber 13.1.48
Ford Motor Co 1970–76; sales progr and distribut man.
Leyland Vehicles Leyland 1976–80; man. dir Leyland
Vehicles (Ireland) from 1980
m Aber 24.10.70 Alison M. Joss BSc 1970 qv

SMITH Brian William Wright *BSc 1969

SMITH Callum Ian MA 1968
s of Malcolm S. shopkeeper/crofter and Allanina
Martin; b Leurbost Is of Lewis 18.7.46
teacher maths Oban h s from 1969

SMITH Campbell David MA 1970
s of David S. headmaster and E. Sylvia East; b Ellon
14.4.49
RAF off. UK, Cyprus from 1970
m Tankerness Orkney 10.4.71 Isobel Robertson BEd 1971
teacher d of George R. Kirkwall

SMITH Charles Crombie BSc(eng) 1961
b Huntly 19.1.40
MI Mun E 1963 M Inst HE 1964
city eng dept Aber: grad asst 1961–63, asst eng 1963–69,
prin eng from 1969

SMITH Charles Graham *BSc 1965

SMITH Christopher David MA 1966 *1968 PhD 1978
s of Richard E. S. schoolmaster and Doris Lowry;
b Wolverhampton 3.3.46
lect, sen lect psych Harris coll Preston, Preston polytech
from 1971
m(1) Dun 26.8.72 Patricia A. Boyack MA 1967 qv; marr
diss
(2) Hereford 29.12.78 Rhiannon Phillips Powell BA
(Durh) res fell. Strath d of Charles P. P. MA(Oxon)

SMITH Colin James Webb MA 1969
s of Auckland R. S. baker and Elspeth M. Carnie;
b Aberchirder 26.5.47
teacher hist Earlston from 1970
m Earlston 20.7.74 Shirley H. Paterson stud. d of William
D. P. Earlston

SMITH Colin Peter BSc 1969

SMITH Conal Robertson Cumming *MA 1969

SMITH Craigie Alexander Donald BL 1959

SMITH David Allan Addison MA 1965

SMITH David Balfour *BSc(eng) 1967 MSc 1969
                                                    PhD 1978
MIEE 1974 CEng

SMITH David Christopher MSc 1968 PhD 1976
s of Bertram T. H. S. warden hall of resid Leic poly
and Florence M. Drage asst warden; b Leic 29.5.46
BA(Cantab) 1967 MA(Cantab) 1971
lect geol N Lond poly 1972–74; geochemist geol surv
Trondheim Norway 1974–77; res fell. Edin 1977–80; dep
dir mineralogy dept nat hist museum Paris from 1980
m Bois-Guillaume France 7.7.77 Elisabeth Delaunay
documentation eng d of Henri D. Bois-Guillaume

SMITH Dennis *MA 1967
s of Winifred M. J. Smith clerkess; b Aber 7.3.45
post-grad stud. Queen's coll Oxon 1967–70; res asst Nat
Lib of Scot. Edin from 1970

SMITH Derek Stewart Hunter *BSc 1969 PhD 1973

SMITH Diana Margaret BSc 1970
d of Dennis N. R. S. res scient and Hilda H. Williams
nurse; b High Wycombe 3.11.48
sen tech in plant path. lab RHM res centre from 1970
m High Wycombe 1.9.74 Douglas W. Taylor MA(Glas)
records off., information off. s of Ian G. T. Prestwick

SMITH Donald BSc 1961 *MEd 1968
s of Roderick S. weaver and Normina Macphail;
b Bragar Is of Lewis 28.7.39
teacher Aberdeensh 1962–68; lect Aber coll of comm
1968–70; prin teacher maths Woodmill h s Dunfermline
1970–77; asst rector Inverkeithing h s from 1977
m Aber 29.3.65 Catherine Murray MA 1960 qv

SMITH Donald Robert MA 1962
CA

SMITH Doreen MA 1964
m Gilmour

SMITH Douglas McKinnon *MA 1968
s of Alexander D. S. insur ag and Annie McKinnon;
b Aber 27.9.46
MBA(Strath) 1969
Lond: marketg exec Rank Hovis McDougall 1969–74,
marketg man. RHM Foods from 1974

SMITH Edward Alistair   *MA 1961 PhD 1967
  s of Archibald S. bank man. and Jean M. Johnston;
b Aber 16.1.39
asst lect geog Aberd 1963–67, lect from 1967

SMITH Edward Gordon   *BSc 1962
  s of Frank G. S. textile worker and Isabel Anderson;
b Fochabers 10.11.39
Dip Ed(Glas) FCS
teacher: Lira Uganda 1963–65, Kisumu Kenya 1967–69,
Glasg from 1970
m Isel Cumberland 6.7.66 Annie Sutton BA(Nott) soc
worker d of Sydney S. Blindcrake

SMITH Effie Macphail   MA 1963
  d of Roderick S. crofter/weaver and Normina
Macphail; b Stornoway 9.4.43
teacher: Fife 1964–66, Dunbartonsh 1966–68 and 1975–
76; trainee computer progr. from 1976
m Aber 9.8.66 David J. Murray-Smith BSc 1963 *qv*

SMITH Elaine Grace   MA 1967
  m Niven

SMITH Elizabeth Ann   *MA 1968

SMITH Elizabeth Ann Scott   MA 1962
  d of Wilson H. S. MA 1926 *qv*; b Aber 24.1.42
Dip Secy Pract(Glasg)
secy to dir Mugiemoss Mill Bucksburn 1963–64
m Aber 4.10.63 Keith W. Ferguson MA 1953 *qv*

SMITH Elizabeth Mary   BSc 1966

SMITH Eric Leslie   MB ChB 1959
  s of William R. S. licensed grocer and Martha D. Lees;
b Aber 3.2.35
MRCPE 1964 FRCP 1978
regist dermat venereology ARI 1959–63; sen regist and
tut. Middx hosp and St John's hosp for diseases of the
skin Lond 1964–66; head dermat and vd dept Mowasat
hosp Kuwait 1967–68; prin in pract consult. dermat
Camberley dist gen hosp 1969–74; head dermat and vd
dept cent hosp United Arab Emirates from 1975
m Aber 6.8.64 Ethne I. Cook d of Andrew C.

SMITH Esmé Agnes   MA 1957
  m Reid

SMITH Esther Margaret   BEd 1970
  d of William W. S. farm. and Esther M. Lowe;
b Cardenden Fife 7.1.49
teacher geog/mod stud. Lesmahagow 1970–73
m Dun 28.7.70 John C. Bicket farm. man. asst s of
David B. Kirriemuir

SMITH Eva Roberta   *MA 1957
  m Foote

SMITH Fay Whyte   MA 1965
  m Simpson
d 9.10.71 *AUR* XLIV 322

SMITH Francis William   MB ChB 1970 DMRD 1975
  s of William S. BSc 1934 *qv*; b Colchester 8.1.43
ARI: h o, sen h o 1970–72, regist nephrol 1972–73, regist
radiodiagnosis from 1973
m Newcastle-u-Tyne 5.12.70 Pamela A. Cox SRN nurs
sister d of James C. Whitley Bay

SMITH Geddes   MA 1957 *MEd 1977

SMITH George   MB ChB 1970
  s of Benjamin S. ship's eng and Edith M. S. Bond;
b Banff 13.6.47
DA(Lond) 1973 DObstRCOG 1973 FFARCS 1977
med off. RAF med br 1970–78; sen regist anaest Derbyshire RI, Groby Road hosp Leic and Nott City hosp from
1978
m St And 17.7.70 Fay R. Marshall dom sc teacher d of
John R. M. St And

SMITH George   MA 1969
  s of George A. S. elect. eng and Mary C. D. Murray;
b Portlethen 15.3.48
pilot RAF Leuchars from 1969
d air crash Canary Islands 26.5.78

SMITH George Alexander   MB ChB 1962
  Lerwick: g p from 1965, anaest from 1970
m Aber 11.7.62 Heather Hunter MA 1959 *qv*

SMITH George Bruce Pirie   °LLB 1967
  s of William S. master coach painter and Anna Pirie;
b Aber 15.6.47
law app, leg. asst James & George Collie advoc Aber
1967–70; leg. asst Paull & Williamsons advoc Aber 1970–
72, ptnr from 1972

SMITH George Cowie   MA 1969

SMITH George Nicholson   *MA 1969
  s of George N. S. turbine driver and Isabella D. Begg;
b Aber 15.6.47
MSc(Oxon) 1974
res asst dept psych Dund 1969–70; dept man. Marks &
Spencer Kirkcaldy 1970–72; dep supt boys' remand home
Grimsby 1972; soc worker Oxon soc serv Abingdon from
1974

SMITH Gerald Sutherland   MA 1967

SMITH Gladys Jane Hogarth   MA 1965
  d of Robert S. farm./driver and Gladys G. Bisset civ
serv; b Buckie 15.3.44
teacher Broomhill p s Aber from 1966
m Aber 30.7.71 Richard Little civ serv (ordnance surv) s
of John J. E. S. L. Leith

SMITH Gordon   *BSc 1963 PhD 1968
  s of Allan S. and Margaret S. Willocks; b Aberfeldy
6.11.41
lect bot univ of Malaya Kuala Lumpur from 1968

SMITH Gordon Anderson
  see Anderson-Smith

SMITH Gordon Ansell Morrison   MA 1957
  s of James M. S. MB ChB 1924 *qv*; b York 27.11.35
teacher Engl Northfield acad Aber from 1960
m Antrim NI 27.7.61 Ethel E. Marquess teacher home
econ d of Harold F. M. Muckamore Co Antrim

SMITH Gordon Laird   *MA 1968 MSc 1973
  s of William E. S. g p and Elsie G. Chisholm; b Glasg
20.4.47
FRSS 1969
res fell. dept statist Aberd 1968–71; Torry res stat Aber:
scient off. DTI 1971–72, MAFF 1972–73, higher scient
off. MAFF 1974–77, sen scient off. MAFF from 1978

SMITH Gordon Lamont   MB ChB 1961
  s of Howard L. S. civ eng and Doris Sharples; b Aber
12.4.34
D Av Med 1974

m Aber 1960 Catriona F. G. MacRae MB ChB 1961 *qv*
d Farnborough 14.2.75 *AUR* XLVI 240

SMITH Grace Neilson MA 1956
d of John R. S. insur ag and Mary R. Neilson; b Aber 24.6.36
teacher Tillydrone p s, Braeside p s Aber from 1957
m Aber 5.8.60 Michael E. Welsh admin off. Aberd s of Eric St C. W. Aber

SMITH Graham Francis *MA 1960
b Lond 30.5.33
PhD(Cantab) 1963
asst prof Calif Los Angeles 1963–65; lect univ of Wales Swansea 1965–70; sen lect Stir from 1970
m 18.7.64 Angela M. BA(Birm) univ lect

SMITH Hamish George *BSc(eng) 1970

SMITH Hance Duncan *BSc 1968 PhD 1973
s of Hance S. ferry boat owner/oper and Emmie J. Duncan; b Lerwick 12.11.45
post-grad res, tut. stud. geog Aberd 1968–72; lect geog: Aber coll of educ 1972–74, N'cle-u-Tyne poly 1974–76, univ of Wales inst sc and tech from 1977

SMITH Hazel *MA 1967

SMITH Heather Fiona Cameron *MA 1965
d of James L. S. comm trav and Mary W. Robertson shop asst; b Glasg 12.5.43
Dip Cartog(Glas) 1966
grad cartog Aberd 1966–70; Brit council exchange fell. univ of Budapest Hungary 1967; visiting lect geog Auck univ NZ 1968
m Aber 1.8.67 Francis Lyall MA 1960 *qv*

SMITH Helen Ann MA 1961
d of John N. S. Harris tweed mill worker and Christina MacMillan; b Stornoway 2.7.40
teacher: Bathgate j s s 1962–64, Uphall W Lothian 1964–66, Dun 1966, Edin 1966–67
m Dun 1.10.66 Ian Ferguson electronics eng s of Donald F. Lochmaddy N Uist

SMITH Helen Isobel MA 1960
m Reid

SMITH Helen Mary MA 1966
d of William R. S. farm. and Helen M. Paterson teacher; b Aber 15.12.45
teacher: Engl Whitburn s s 1967–68, Linlithgow p s 1968–72
m Aber 7.9.66 David Kelbie LLB 1967 *qv*

SMITH Howard Ogilvie *BSc 1964
s of George O. S. elect. eng and Dora Dickson; b Aber 7.7.42
RGC Aber: teacher 1965–69, housemaster Sillerton house 1969–73, prin geog from 1973
m Aber 5.4.66 Sheila W. Mortimer MA 1960 *qv*

SMITH Humphrey Graham MSc 1968
b Farnworth 6.6.45
BSc(Edin) 1967 PhD(Edin) 1973
biol Brit antarctic surv: Signy Antarctica 1968–71, Edin 1971–74; lect ecology Lanchester poly Coventry 1974–77, sen lect from 1977

SMITH Iain Graham LLB 1970
s of Donald S. civ serv and Margaret Urquhart; b Glasg 14.4.49

man. trainee Hayes 1970–71; law app Aber 1971–73, solic from 1973
m Glasg 26.6.71 Anna D. Wilson MA 1973 ground hostess Air Anglia d of Hugh T. W. Dallas Moray

SMITH Ian MB ChB 1961
b Chapel of Garioch 29.6.37
DObstRCOG 1963 FFARCS 1969
h o Aber, Dun, Inv 1961–63; sen h o, regist, sen regist anaest Aber 1964–72; staff anaest Toronto 1972–73; consult. anaest Aber from 1974
m Aber 6.8.66 Mary Donald

SMITH Ian *MA 1969

SMITH Ian Barclay *BSc 1962 PhD 1965
s of James B. S. process engraver overseer and Margaret A. Drunsfield; b Aber 3.10.39
CChem MRIC 1970
post doct fell. Atlantic reg lab NRC(Can) Halifax Nova Scotia 1965–67; assoc res off. NRC(Can) 1967–72; sect. leader cement phys sect. res lab Blue Circle Industries 1972–76, dep man. basic res dept from 1976
m Aber 5.9.64 Elizabeth M. E. Hay d of William Hay MB ChB 1933 *qv*

SMITH Ian Beveridge BSc(eng) 1960

SMITH Ian James BSc 1970 *1971
s of John S. plumber and Jeannie Cowling; b Aber 1.7.46
teacher sc Northfield acad Aber 1972–74 asst prin sc from 1974
m Aber 24.9.66 Elizabeth Benzies teacher d of Charles F. B. Aber

SMITH Ian Slessor BSc 1956 BL 1959
s of George F. S. wholesale fruiterer and Anne Shaw; b Inv 4.2.35
solic Munro & Noble Inv from 1961
m Edin 9.7.60 Jennifer A. Casson MA(Edin) law app

SMITH Jacqueline East MA 1965 Dip Ed 1967
d of David S. schoolmaster and Evelyn S. East; b Grimsby 6.5.45
VSO El Obeid Sudan 1965–66; teacher Engl Finnish/Brit soc Imatra Finland 1967–68; lect Engl at Finnish lang inst trg translators and interpreters Turku Finland from 1972
m Imatra 3.7.68 Ismo J. Lento syst analyst s of Kaarlo L. Salo Finland

SMITH James *BSc 1956 PhD 1959
s of Andrew S. fisherman and Jeannie Murray; b Buckie 12.11.35
ARIC 1963 FRIC 1973
asst lect Aberd 1958–63; DSIR sen res fell. NATO univ of Zürich 1960–61; lect, sen lect, prin lect chem Slough coll of higher educ from 1963
m Huntly 20.8.60 Mary A. Featch teacher d of Alexander F. Huntly

SMITH James BSc 1966
s of Alexander S. fisherman and Katie Smith; b Edin 26.4.44
teacher maths Whitburn 1967–69, Lossiemouth 1969–72; prin maths Lendrickmuir from 1972
m Lossiemouth 5.4.68 Margaret E. Riddell teleph, nurse d of Douglas B. R. Lossiemouth

SMITH James David Blackhall *BSc 1962 PhD 1965
s of James S. master butcher and Marion MacQueen; b Peterhead 25.4.40

FCS 1963 ARIC 1965 ACS 1968 MIEEE 1976
Fulbright res fell. Syracuse univ NY USA 1965–66; sen
scient Laporte Indust Luton 1967–68; fell. scient
Westinghouse elect. corp res center Pittsburgh Pa USA
from 1968

SMITH Jean Reid   BSc 1961
d of John S. shopowner and Grace Souter; b Edin
23.8.39
teacher maths: Hopeman 1962–63, Lond 1963–64, Los
Angeles USA 1965–66
m Lossiemouth 18.7.63 Robert A. Sinclair BSc 1960 *qv*

SMITH Jennifer Margaret   MA 1968
d of William L. S. market gardener and Margaret A.
Bell shorthand typist; b Torphins 2.2.48
teacher Aber 1969–71
m Skene 11.7.69 Alexander D. Leys chef s of Alexander L.
Sauchen

SMITH Jennifer May   MA 1962
b Aber 13.2.42
teacher Quarryhill p s Aber 1962–64; res off. educ dept
Aberd from 1964
m Welsh

SMITH Jenny Ford   MA 1969

SMITH Joan Doreen   *MA 1959 PhD 1964
m Taylor

SMITH John   BSc 1963
s of John D. S. baker and Helen Gordon; b Aber
27.11.19
teacher: phys AGS 1964–66, maths Aber coll of comm
1966–70; sen teacher computer stud. Aber coll of comm
from 1970
m Aber 4.8.71 Constance Paterson bakery man. d of
Alexander P. Aber

SMITH John   MB ChB 1968
s of Finlay S. haulage contr and Catherine MacIver;
b Breasclete Is of Lewis 28.1.45
MRCGP 1975
h o Belford hosp Fort William, city hosp Aber 1968–69;
sen h o mat. hosp Middlesbrough 1969–70; g p Portree
1970, Stornoway from 1970
m Inv 10.4.70 Muriel K. MacDonald nurse d of Roderick
MacD. Lochs Is of Lewis

SMITH John Angus   MB ChB 1962 MD 1966
s of John S. blacksmith and Henrietta MacKay;
b Shader Is of Lewis 6.8.36
FRCP(C) 1971
h o Aber 1962–63; asst lect bact Aberd 1963–64; lect
microbiol Monash univ Melbourne 1964–67; lect infect.
diseases Glas 1967–69; assoc prof med/med microbiol
Tor. Canada 1969–77; assoc prof path./assoc in med
univ of Br Col from 1977
m Aber 2.10.63 Elizabeth Thomson nurse d of George
F. T. Aboyne

SMITH John Hay   *BSc 1966 PhD 1969
s of John S. fisherman and Mary Hay; b Sandend
23.1.46
res and dev chem ICI Grangemouth from 1969
m Grangemouth 30.10.71 Dorothy Mentiply secy d of
James A. C. M. Grangemouth

SMITH John Lane   MA 1968

SMITH John Smart   *MA 1963 PhD 1969
s of John A. R. S. civ eng and Vera M. H. Campbell;

b Aber 14.2.41
FSAScot.
asst lect geog Aberd 1965–68, lect 1968–74, sen lect from
1974
m Aber 23.3.67 Gillian A. Campbell MA 1965 *qv*

SMITH June Ellison   MA 1967 Dip Ed 1968
d of Charles C. S. merch N and Frances E. Skene;
b Aber 12.6.40
teacher Engl/r e: Bankhead acad 1968–69; journalist
Hemel Hempstead from 1971
m Nairn 8.8.70 John Z. Chisholm supermarket man. s
of James C. Nairn

SMITH Karl Alworth   MB ChB 1960 ᶜMD 1977
b St Ann Jamaica 3.3.29
WHO fell. 1964–65; Milbank fac fell. 1966–71; Ford
found. grant Yale 1967–68
MPH(Yale) 1965 DrPH(Yale) 1971 MFCM 1973
h o ARI 1960–61, h o/jun regist univ hosp WI Jamaica
1961–62; spec m o/MRC epidemiol res unit UWI MoH
Jamaica Lawrence Tavern 1962–66; dept soc and
preventive med UWI Jamaica: lect, sen lect 1968–77;
dir fam plan./epidemiol unit 1972–74; visiting assoc prof
dept h care & epidemiol UBC Canada 1975–76; h
sciences rep Internat Dev Res Centre reg off. E & Cent
Africa from 1978

SMITH Kathleen Forbes   BSc 1959
d of Campbell G. S. civ serv and Catherine H. Pointer;
b Aber 16.7.38
teacher Aber and NI 1960–76; head sc dept Forthill
girls' s Lisburn NI from 1976
m Aber 29.7.61 Ian B. MacDonald BSc(agr) 1957 *qv*

SMITH Kathleen Jessie   BSc 1957
d of James W. S. BSc(agr) 1929 *qv*; b Inv 18.9.36
chem Esso petr co Southampton 1956–57; Canada: lab
tech NB hosp Frederickton 1957–58; res tech NRC
Ottawa 1958–61; chem Calopet Foods Oakland Ca USA
1961–72
m Frederickton 15.2.58 William L. M. McKillop BSc(for)
1954 *qv*

SMITH Linda   MA 1969
b Scone 20.1.48
teacher Engl Livingston 1970–74
m Aber 1.8.67 Denis Cheyne BSc 1970 *qv*

SMITH Lindsay Scott   *BSc 1964
s of Daniel S. S. motor mech and Margaret A. Irvine;
b Lerwick 17.9.39
asst seismologist Sultanate of Muscat of Oman 1964–66;
seismol Onitsha Biafra 1967–68; sen seismol: Donala
Cameroons 1968–70, Asaba Nigeria 1970–72; dep dev
off. Lerwick 1972–74; asst man. (Ocean Inchcape)
Lerwick 1974–76; oper man. (Norscot Serv) Lerwick
from 1976
m Lerwick 3.10.63 Agnes G. Williamson d of William
T. W. Yell Shetland

SMITH Lorna Anne   *MA 1970 MLitt 1972 PhD 1980
m Stewart

SMITH Lorraine Josephine Jeannie   MA 1970
m Donnelly

SMITH Louis Mark   *MA 1969
s of George W. S. eng and Genevieve Kenny; b
Sheffield 7.8.44
oil rig catering N Sea in 1974
m Gt Yarmouth 27.6.70 Elspeth J. A. Gow MA 1970 *qv*

SMITH Lynda Kaye Storm   BSc 1963
m McDowall

SMITH Malcolm Murdo   MA 1965
d 3.2.68

SMITH Margaret Scott   MA 1969
d of Edward S. lab and Mary Scott; b Buckie 31.12.47
lect maths/statist Aber coll of comm 1969-70; computer
progr UKAEA Thurso 1970-71; part-time lect Thurso
tech coll 1972-77
m Buckie 27.9.69 Alexander Bruce elect. eng s of
Alexander B. Findochty

SMITH Marjorie Young   MA 1969
d of James Y. S. comp dir, agr seedsman and Margaret
A. S. Russell; b Ayr 17.11.48
teacher: Havering 1970-72, Hatfield Peverel 1972-74,
Darlington 1974-75
m Ayr 21.8.70 Iain F. Gilmour MA 1969 qv

SMITH Mary Frances   BSc 1967 Dip Ed 1968
d of Edward S. crane driver, lab, storekeeper and
Mary Scott; b Buckie 15.5.46
teacher maths: Ellon acad 1968-69, Buckie h s 1969-74,
asst prin maths from 1972
m Buckie 7.8.71 Langley C. Forbes photogr s of John
C. F. Buckie

SMITH Mary Reid   MB ChB 1970
d of Maurice W. S. farm. and Ann R. Mutch clerkess;
b Huntly 6.12.46
DObstRCOG 1972 FPA certif 1974
h o: Woodend hosp, City hosp Aber, Yorkhill hosp
Glasg, mat. hosp Aber; sen h o Gray's hosp Elgin; res
regist mat. hosp Aber; clin m o (fam plan.) GGHB
m Aber 3.5.74 Thomas M. Scott MB ChB(Glas) s of
Thomas S. MB ChB(Glas) Inv

SMITH Maureen Rose   MA 1961
m Paterson

SMITH Michael   *MA 1966

SMITH Muriel Glenda   MA 1959

SMITH Neil Gordon   BSc(agr) 1958

SMITH Patricia Anne   MA 1968
d of James B. S. process engraver overseer and
Margaret A. Drunsfield; b Aber 29.4.47
Canada: soc worker Halifax 1969-70, caseworker
Ottawa 1971-74; Engl tut. Würzburg W Ger 1974-76;
clerk Ottawa 1976-77
m Ottawa 22.10.70 Gregory S. Bezanson PhD(Carleton)
microbiol s of Gerald E. B. Nova Scotia

SMITH Patrick Fleming   *MA 1965 MSc 1967

SMITH Peter   MA 1969

SMITH Peter McGregor   *BSc 1966 PhD 1974

SMITH Reginald George   PhD 1962
BSc(Edin)

SMITH Robert Allan   MA 1970 BSc 1973

SMITH Robin Bailey
see Bailey-Smith

SMITH Roderick   MA 1964 Dip Ed 1968
s of William S. gen merch and Alexina Macleod

postmistress; b Keose Is of Lewis 9.2.40
lect RAEC Scot. infantry depot Br of Don Aber from
1965
m Aber 16.8.66 Ellen McHardy MA 1964 qv

SMITH Roderick John   MA 1969
s of Malcolm S. crofter and Allanina Martin; b
Leurbost Is of Lewis 16.11.47
teacher maths Western Is from 1970
m Stornoway 31.3.72 Annie Campbell d of Norman C.
Sandwick

SMITH Ronald George
see Mackay (Smith) Ronald George

SMITH Ronald Ian Lewis   *BSc 1964 PhD 1968
s of Ian L. S. BSc(eng) 1935 qv; b Aber 29.1.42
bot Brit antarctic surv S Orkney Is Antarctica 1964-67,
Aber 1967-69, South Georgia Subantarctica 1969-71;
head B.A.S. bot sect. Birm from 1971
m Stronsay Orkney 1.7.70 Elinor M. M. Groat staff
nurse d of John G. Stronsay

SMITH Rosalind Ailsa Hamilton   *BSc 1968

SMITH Rosemary   MA 1965

SMITH Rosemary Anne   *MA 1963 Dip Ed 1964
d of Reginald D. W. S. quality control insp and Megan
Whitely; b Welwyn 1940
lect coll of educ Hitchin 1964-66; head Engl dept The
Bishop Perowne s Worcester 1966-71
m Hitchin 1965 John A. Cattanach area/branch sales
man. computers s of Alexander B. C. BSc 1931 qv

SMITH Sandra   *MA 1968
m Campbell

SMITH Sandra Whyte   MA 1965
d of Robert W. B. S. BOAC navig, oper off. BAA
and Margaret H. Whyte home help organis; b Airth
30.12.42
Penguin books: i/c sale of foreign rights contr dept
Harmondsworth 1965-67; asst book edit. univ of Lond
Press 1967-71; freelance book edit. royal coll of nurs/
ULP from 1971
m Burnham 4.1.69 Hugh M. R. Dawson journalist/chief
sub edit. *Daily Mail* s of William D.

SMITH Sheila Murdoch   *BSc 1962
d of Charles H. I. S. acct and Janet R. Ross lab asst;
b Edin 11.11.40
teacher Ruthrieston j s s Aber 1963-64
m Aber 27.7.63 Andrew Munro MA 1964 qv

SMITH Sheila Taylor   MA 1968

SMITH Sheila Thomson   MA 1967
d of George T. S. serv eng and Annie G. McKnight;
b Banff 4.10.46
teacher: Perth 1968-71, Glenrothes 1971-72, Aber from
1972
m Aberchirder -.7.71 Edward F. McLerie draughtsman
s of John F. McL. Newburgh Fife

SMITH Simon Fleming   *BSc 1958 Dip Ed 1960
s of William R. S. marine eng and Winifred M.
Fleming; b Singapore 18.3.37
teacher maths AGS 1959-65; prin maths: Banchory
acad 1965-66, Cults acad Aber from 1966
m Aber 21.7.61 Irene M. Rannie teacher d of William
S. R. Milltimber Aber

SMITH Stanley Leith   *MA 1960 Dip Ed 1962
s of Stanley L. S. comp dir and Alice Johnston;
b Aber 17.12.35
ACCA 1976
trainee man. Peterhead 1960–61; teacher geog Arbroath
acad 1962–65, prin geog N Berwick 1966–70; comp secy/
dir New Pitsligo Aber 1970–76, comp acct from 1976
m Aber 15.7.66 Jessie Bremner nurs sister

SMITH Stella Rankine   MA 1968
d of David S. farm. and Muriel C. Smith secy; b
Stonehaven 1.6.47
Dip Secy 1969
secy Leeds 1969–70; teacher: Engl govt h s Nassau
Bahamas 1970–73, Fr/Engl Monks Hill h s Croydon
1973–74; TEFL St George's s Montreux Switzerland
1974–75; part-time tut. Fr Walker tech coll Wellington,
Telford from 1976
m Aber 4.7.70 Godfrey P. Davis MA 1969 qv

SMITH Stewart Mitchell   MA 1966
s of Gordon S. S. policeman and Barbara A. Mitchell;
b Aber 23.12.31
teacher Fr/guid Linksfield acad Aber from 1967
m Aber 1.8.59 Heather G. Douglas

**SMITH Stuart Lauchlan   MA 1964 *BSc(eng) 1967
MSc 1970**
s of James C. S. elect. eng and Jean Stuart; b Kilmarnock 24.4.44
plant eng chem indust ICI Wilton 1969–75, proj eng
chem indust from 1975
m Hexham 6.9.69 Rachel C. Davidson BSc 1969 qv

SMITH Trefor Leslie   *MA 1970
s of Leslie J. S. MA 1931 qv; b Aber 4.7.48
BMus(Liv) 1971 Assoc R Manc Coll Mus 1973
Diplomprüfung (piano) Hamburg 1977
pianist Hamburg from 1973

SMITH Vivien Evelyn Mark   MB ChB 1962
d of Louis A. S. bank man. and Evelyn K. Mark;
b Aber 19.2.36
DCH(Lond) 1964
h o: RACH 1962–63; Whipps Cross hosp, Qu Eliz hosp
for ch Lond 1963–65; regist psychiat Aber 1965–71;
instr psychiat Temple univ Philadelphia 1971–72; regist
psychiat royal Cornhill hosp Aber from 1972
m Aber 16.7.65 Neil Edward MB ChB 1961 qv

SMITH Walter John Scott   BSc 1963
s of William B. S. cabinetmaker/stone polisher and
Mary A. Beattie; b Aber 31.1.26
Aber acad: teacher 1964–65, i/c careers 1966–70, year
teacher (later Hazlehead acad) from 1970
m Aber 24.3.51 Hannah Webster d of John A. W. Aber

SMITH Wendy Anne   *BSc 1966
m Ratcliffe

SMITH William   *MA 1970
s of Alexander S. S. elect. eng and Margaret E. L.
Aitken; b Glasg 22.2.46
MSc(McG) 1972
univ lect geog: Christchurch NZ 1972–76, McG Montreal
from 1976

SMITH William   BSc 1968

SMITH William Gordon   BSc 1966 *1972

SMITH William Holmes Macfarlane   *BSc 1967
s of Alexander M. S. OBE gen man./eng Dun harbour

trust and Catherine P. Macfarlane; b N'cle-u-Tyne
23.4.42
MIBiol 1970 PhD(R'dg) 1976
res dem genetics dept agr bot R'dg 1967–71; res fell.
genetics dept biol sc Dund 1971–72; barley breeder/
tech man. Rothwell plant breeders Lincs 1972–78; admin
head brassica dept Scot. Plant Breeding Stat from 1978
m Sandford St Martin 18.4.70 Daphne Henderson BSc
(R'dg) res asst d of Frank H. Enstone

SMITH William Merson   MB ChB 1969
s of William S. farm./bus. man. and Daisy Merson;
b Rathven 18.2.44
h o Aber 1969–70; m o RAF 1970–72; lect aviation med/
physiol RAF from 1972
m Belf 5.5.71 Roberta A. Stevenson RGN d of Howard
M. S. MB ChB(Belf) Ballylesson

SMITHSON John Franklin   BSc(eng) 1967
b Adlington 30.4.45
CEng MICE MIWES
asst eng Manc 1966–69; asst resid eng Derby 1969–70;
resid eng Haddington 1970–74; civ eng Edin 1974–77;
sen eng Cambridge from 1977
m Aber 10.8.68 Patricia J. McCaw MA 1966 qv

SMYTH Elizabeth Anne   *MA 1968
d of Sidney G. C. S. bus. man. and Vivian A. Donn
BA(Lond) teacher; b E London S Af 28.11.44
member of authors' soc 1979 MA(Essex) 1980
studio man. BBC Lond 1968–71; VSO teacher univ of
Indonesia 1971–73; univ lect Saudi Arabia 1974–77;
ELT advis Brit Council Lond 1977–79

SNAITH Sybil Mary   PhD 1968
BSc(Lond) 1965
res biochem Rowett inst Aber 1968–76
m Birm 29.3.74 W. R. McAleese dir teaching centre Aberd

SNEDDEN James Leishman   BSc 1960
s of George F. S. teacher and Elizabeth S. Ruthven;
b Glasg 30.11.38
teacher sc Kirriemuir s s 1961–63; spec asst, prin asst,
prin teacher Brechin h s from 1963
m Aber 12.7.62 Jean McLeod teacher d of James McL.
Lerwick

SNEDDEN Marion Elspeth   MA 1957 *EdB 1960
d of Andrew S. gamekeeper and Christina Morrison
teacher; b Forres 4.8.36
teacher Torry s s Aber 1958–60; asst educ psych Perth
1961–62, educ psych St Francis esn s Birm 1962–64
m Dyke Forres 20.10.62 Arthur G. Fraser BSc 1959 qv

SNOW Thomas D'Oyley   *MA 1969
s of George D. S. BA(Oxon) headmaster, bishop and
Joan M. Way piano teacher; b Godalming 8.2.45
area off. nat union of public employees Kent from 1969

SNOWIE Anne Fowlie   MA 1967
d of George B. S. farmer and Anne W. Fowlie; b Echt
9.4.45
teacher: Echt s 1968–69, Kinellar s 1969–71
m Echt 6.8.68 Douglas J. Burnett farm./haulage contr s
of James B. Echt

SOBACZEWSKA Marysia Bernadine   MA 1967

SOBEY Douglas George   MSc 1970 PhD 1976
s of George A. S. mech and Rowena A. Lockhart
secy/stenog; b Summerside Prince Edward Is Canada
10.6.47

BSc(Mt All) 1969
teaching asst bot Belf 1973–74; lect Stranmillis coll Belf from 1974

SOHAIL Mahmood Ali   MSc 1970
BSc(AH)(Panj) Dip TVM(Edin)

SOKOLOWSKI James   *BSc(eng) 1967
s of Antoni S. maintenance eng and Elizabeth Lowson; b Glasg 2.1.45
MICE 1972
asst site eng Balfour Beatty & Co Brist 1967–69; asst des eng EPDC Sidcup 1969–70; asst resid eng Sir M. MacDonald & Ptnrs Baghdad Iraq 1970–72; sect. eng, asst construct. man. Reed & Mallik Brist from 1972
m Brist 4.10.69 Lesley L. Bailey tracer/draughtswoman d of H. W. F. B. Brist

SOLIMAN Mohamed Hassan Mohamed   PhD 1967
s of Hassan M. S. merch and Saida Hegazy; b Alexandria 16.4.33
BSc(Alex) 1958 MSc(Cairo) 1962 MA Clin Bioch 1965 Alexandria: lect 1958–74, asst prof 1974–80, prof biochem med res inst from 1980
m Alexandria 1965 Nahed E. El-din BA(Alex) teacher Engl d of Joseph E. E. Alexandria

SOLSTAD Karl Jan   MLitt 1970
Cand Mag(Berg) Mag Art(Oslo)

SOMERVILLE David Henry Norman   *MA 1963
                                   *MEd 1965**
s of David H. P. S. mining eng and Christian T. Flannery; b Edin 11.6.40
teacher Fr/Lat Kelvinside acad Glasg 1965–68; lect psych: coll of educ Hamilton 1968–70, Liv univ 1971–72, Craigie coll of educ Ayr from 1972

SOMERVILLE Susan Isabel   *MA 1969
d of James L. S. ARIBA(Edin) arch. and Marjory S. Prophet; b Aber 22.12.46
teacher mod lang Clydebank 1970–72
m Aber 14.7.69 John Keelan MA 1966 qv

SOPER Frederick Robert Charles   MB ChB 1957
s of Frederick C. S. comm man. and Evelyn Fiddes; b Aber 31.10.32
h o ARI 1957–59; g p: Porth S Wales 1959–69, New Deer from 1969
m Merthyr Maur Glam 4.1.58 Maureen Lewis BSc (Cardiff) d of Robin L. Nantmoel

SOPPITT Alastair Ian   MA 1963
s of John A. W. S. clerk and Eliza J. McWilliam; b Aber 16.6.42
LHA 1971
admin asst NERHB 1963–65; sen admin asst board of man. Aber gen hosps 1965–69; prin admin asst NERHB 1969–71, asst secy 1971–74; dist admin southern dist Highlands health board Inv from 1974
m Aber 27.6.64 Elizabeth A. Sim statist asst d of Henry M. S. Aber

SORLEY Alison Mary   MA 1957
m Morrice

SORRIE George Strath   MB ChB 1957
s of Alexander S. baker and Florence Strath secy; b Lynn Mass USA 19.5.33
DPH(Lond) 1963
asst m o h Reading 1962–65; lect statist Lond s of hyg/trop med 1965–67; g p: Rhynie 1967–73, Aber

1973–75; employment med advis for NE Scot. Aber from 1975
m Aber 22.9.59 Gabrielle A. Baird MB ChB 1959 qv

SORRIE James Maclean   BSc 1960

SOUDEN Carol Elizabeth   MA 1970
d of Robert S. trans insp and Mary H. Paul auxil nurse; b Aber 1948
m Aber 29.12.70 Lesley Wiseman MA 1971 fin. consult. s of Bertram W. Aber

SOULSBY John Allan   *MA 1959
s of Sydney H. S. BSc(N'cle) marine eng and Alice M. Allan; b Grosmont Whitby 18.1.35
MA(Dub) 1964 PhD(Dub) 1970
res asst Leeds 1959–61; lect geog: Trinity coll Dub 1961–64, St And from 1964; visiting prof univ of Missouri Columbia USA 1968–69; visiting lect W Washington state coll Bellingham USA 1969; prof Earth Sc univ Malawi Zomba 1976–79 on secondment
m Aber 3.8.61 Evelyn M. Coutts MA 1959 qv

SOUTAR Lynda Margaret Hay   MA 1967
d of William H. S. bank. man. and Joan M. Biltcliffe; b Ellon 22.6.46
teacher Galashiels acad: Engl/r e 1968–70, esn class 1970–72; maladjusted class Kingsway h s Chester 1972–73, esn class Dee Point Middle s Chester 1973–74; Careers/Engl Stanney c s Ellesmere Port from 1974

SOUTAR Marjorie Elizabeth   *MA 1969 PhD 1972
d of Alexander A. S. advis mus Dun and Lisbeth A. B. Anderson; b Arbroath 19.11.46
MA(St And) 1967 LRAM ARCM 1967
teacher mus Dollar acad 1973–75; lect mus Glas from 1975
m Glasg 17.8.76 David S. Rycroft BSc(Lond) res fell. chem Glas s of Kenneth R. Clitheroe

SOUTER Alan Cunningham   *BSc 1965

SOUTER Alistair McMillan   *BSc 1964
s of George S. lighthouse keeper/handyman and Maude S. McMillan ch nurse; b Montrose 7.8.42
asst seismologist Seismograph Serv UK, Denmark 1964–66; seismol UK, Nigeria 1966–67; party chief various seismic crews Nigeria, Cameroons 1968–72; consult. geophys own comp Pentland Geophysical Lond from 1972
m Aber 6.4.66 Margaret Humphrey MA 1964 qv

SOUTER Christina Imlach   MA 1961 Dip Ed 1963
d of Alexander S. fisherman and Christina A. Murray; b Buckie 9.5.41
teacher: Fr Kaimhill s s Aber 1962–64, Fr/Lat Aber acad 1964–66, Fr/Ger Elgin acad 1966–71
m Aber 31.7.70 Ian S. Suttie BSc 1964 qv

SOUTER Elizabeth Margaret   MA 1970
d of Roy S. skipper/owner/inshore fisherman and Lizzie M. H. Ritchie; b Stonehaven 14.3.50
teacher: geog Kirkcaldy h s 1971–73, Engl Wick h s 1973–76
m Aber 11.7.73 Iain Johnston MB ChB 1973 g p s of Douglas J. Lochore Lochgelly

SOUTER George Robert Fraser   MA 1968

SOUTER Graham William   BSc 1969

SOUTER Ian Alexander   BSc(eng) 1970

SOUTER Ian Patrick   MA 1964
 s of Maitland E. S. clerk and Annie M. Burr nurse/
teacher parentcraft; b Aber 15.3.43
CA 1967
app CA Aber 1964–67; audit sen, man. Lond 1967–75;
ptnr Whinney Murray & Co Aber from 1975
m Aber 17.9.66 Helen M. Russell BSc 1965 *qv*

SOUTER Isobel Gove   MB ChB 1964
 d of John G. S. self-employed and Elisabeth Stephen;
b Gourdon 4.5.39
DMRD 1972 MR Aust Coll Radiol 1978
h s: ARI 1964, St James' hosp Leeds 1965; res asst surg
univ of Wales 1968–70; regist radiol: univ hosp of Wales
Cardiff 1970–72, Western I Glasg 1972–73; sen regist
radiol RI Glasg; radiol and dir of radiol Mater hosp
Brisbane Aust 1976–78; radiol in private practice
Brisbane from 1978
m Aber 21.7.64 Colin M. Furnival MB ChB 1964 *qv*

SOUTER John Randell   *MA 1966
 s of Andrew W. S. MA(McG) and Florence M.
Randell; b Johnshaven 5.2.44
edit. asst Collins & Co Glasg 1966–67; teacher Almonte
h s Ontario from 1968
m Smith's Falls Ontario 26.5.73 Mary L. Murphy BA
(Carleton Ottawa) lit critic d of W. Ormond M. MD
CM(Queen's univ Kingston Ont) Smith's Falls

SOUTER John Reginald   *BSc(eng) 1963 MSc 1967

SOUTHWICK Christopher Alexander Patrick
                                                         *BSc 1970**

SPATE Gordon Robert   MA 1966
 s of Leslie E. S. dept store man. and Isabel M. Craig
stenogr; b W Kilbride 18.10.41
RAF off. (helicopter pilot) from 1967

SPEAKMAN Kenneth   PhD 1965
 s of Frank S. eng and Irene Graham; b Middlesbrough
3.2.38
FRIC 1972
Watford: res scient bldg res stat 1965–73; scient UK
DoE from 1973
m Teesside 19.3.60 Pauline Reed d of Aaron R.

SPEED Robert Malcolm   MSc 1970
 BSc(Wales)

SPEIRS Margaret Gray   BSc 1967

SPEIRS Ronald Cowan   *MA 1969
 s of Andrew C. S. civ serv and Joyce Aird nurse;
b Inv 15.8.43
PhD(Stir) 1974
lect Ger Birm from 1971
m Aber 29.8.69 Susan W. Elder MA 1969 *qv*

SPELLS Angela Kathleen   *MA 1969
 b Watford 7.1.45

SPENCE Andrew   BSc 1970
 s of John C. S. lab and Williamina M. Sutherland;
b Unst Shetland 27.2.49
teacher: maths Anderson h s Lerwick 1971–78, asst prin
guid from 1973
m Unst 11.8.71 Williamina Laurenson typist d of James
W. L. Unst

SPENCE Charles   BSc 1965
 s of John C. S. lab/crofter and Williamina M.

Sutherland; b Unst Shetland 21.11.42
teacher: Lerwick 1966–67, Alloa 1967–71, Stromness
1971–72, Unst from 1972
m Unst 3.4.68 Mary J. Laurenson clerkess d of James
W. L. Haroldswick Unst

SPENCE Edith Lochrie   MA 1970
 s of William D. S. civ serv and Isabella Percy nurse;
b Lennoxtown 2.4.49
teacher Port Glasg 1971–74; prin mod lang Greenock
1974–75; prin Ger Largs from 1975
m Gourock 1.8.73 James M. Leckie BSc(Strath) teacher
s of William L. Greenock

SPENCE Elizabeth Ann   MA 1961

SPENCE Elizabeth Catherine   *MA 1965
 m Young

SPENCE Graham Cruickshank   *MA 1969
 s of James C. C. S. GPO overseer and Elsie M.
Wilson; b Inv 27.6.47
teacher hist Inv 1970–73; prin hist Portree 1973–77; asst
head Alness from 1977
m Inv 29.8.69 Helen M. McIntyre d of Duncan McI.
Inv

SPENCE Ian William   *BSc 1968

SPENCELEY Anthony Philip   *BSc 1970
 s of Kenneth du G. S. teacher and Dulcie V. Cowan
teacher; b Ilford 21.8.47
grad res stud. univ New England Aust 1971–73; tut.
geog James Cook univ of N Queensland Aust 1973–77;
asst lect geog univ Otago NZ 1977–78; lect geog univ
Papua N Guinea from 1978
m Armidale NSW Aust 17.7.71 Margaret J. Milne BSc
1970 *qv*

SPENCER Joan Margaret   MA 1965

SPENCER Peter Frederick   BSc(for) 1962 *1963

SPENCER Ruth Elizabeth   BMedBiol 1969
 d of Harold S. PhD(Edin) prof oriental stud. and
Hilda Nunn BA(Durban) secy, lib; b Hyderabad India
27.3.48
MB ChB(Birm) 1972
h o: Worc RI 1972–73, Mpilo hosp Bulawayo Rhodesia
1973, Ronkswood hosp Worc 1973–74; g p Halesowen
1974–75; clin asst: Nott ch's hosp 1975–79, haemat
Royal Liv hosp from 1980
m Edin 12.1.74 Roger Ferguson MB ChB(Birm) consult.
phys s of Alan H. F. BA(Oxon) Lincoln

SPENNING Per   MB ChB 1965
 s of Knut L. S. MA(Oslo) rector and Signe Eilifsen
MA(Oslo) teacher; b Bergen 6.1.40
ECFMG 1965
Norway: Vadsø/Tana 1965–66, m o h Tana 1966–69,
private practice Askim 1969–77, soc med Fredrikstad
from 1977
m Aber 17.2.62 Muriel B. Cruickshank MA 1962 *qv*

SPERRING Peter   *BSc(eng) 1970
 s of Frank S. headmaster and Margaret Reynolds
teacher; b Ruislip 10.8.48
civ eng Kitwe Zambia from 1970

SPICER Hugh Joseph Michael   MB ChB 1958
 s of Elvon L. S. prop. and Irene P. Woodroffe;
b Trinidad 3.5.33

h o Port of Spain gen hosp Trinidad 1959–60; private pract Port of Spain from 1960
m Barbados WI 16.10.71 Ann G. Kerr man. reservations Air Canada d of William K. MB ChB(Edin) Bridgetown Barbados

SPILSBURY Sarah Vivienne   MLitt 1969 PhD 1973
d of Charles A. S. outfitter and Gladys Britton; b Bristol 19.5.41
BA(Brist) 1965
lect French Aberd from 1970

SPITTAL Robin Mackay   *MA 1967

SPRAGINS Conway Fitzhugh   PhD 1965
s of John D. S. MA(Davidson univ) presb min and Mary M. Fitzhugh BA(Arkansas) teacher; b Little Rock Arkansas 4.9.35
BA(Arkansas) 1957 BD(Union Theol Seminary Richmond Va) 1963 MDiv 1971
prof of religion Arkansas coll Batesville from 1965
m Batesville 25.8.60 Ann Westmoreland BA(Arkansas) teacher d of Weldon O. W. Batesville

SPROUL Edna Winifred   MA 1964
d of Munro D. S. carpenter and Barrie M. Crichton; b Kintore 26.1.43
teacher: Gordon s Huntly 1965–66, Irlam s s Lancs 1966–68, Murrayburn p s Edin 1968–69
m Aber 2.7.66 David M. Wildgoose MA 1964 qv

SQUIRES James Finlay Robertson   MA 1957
s of Alfred G. S. comm trav and Isabella Cairncross; b Glasg 21.2.32
BD(Glas) 1960
post-grad s Huntly Peter Marshall bursar Princeton USA 1960–61; Brown-Downie fell. Marburg 1961–62; teacher Riverside s s Glasg 1961–62; lect: syst theol Glas 1962–65, r e Aber coll of educ 1965–66, prin lect from 1966
m Glasg 9.9.60 Catherine Hamilton nurse d of Alexander D. H. Glasg

STABLES Ronald Alexander   BSc 1969
s of Alexander S. joiner and Freda Hopkins; b Aber 29.5.47
teacher Nassau Bahamas 1970–73; stud. UCNW 1973–74; teacher Grampian reg from 1974

STADDON Anne Elizabeth   MB ChB 1959
d of Frederick W. S. horticulturist and Edith Clegg teacher; b Wellington Salop 25.6.34
DObstRCOG 1961
h o Woodend hosp Aber, ARI 1959–60; h o obst Aber mat. hosp 1960–61; trainee g p Church Stretton Salop 1961–62; sen h o med Barrow-in-Furness 1962; s m o Salop c c 1968–72; g p Oswestry from 1972
m Wellington 1.7.61 William M. Park MB ChB 1960 qv

STAFFORD David Kenneth Bryce   *MEd 1970
MA(Edin)

STALKER Anne Elizabeth Richards   MA 1968
Dip Ed 1969
d of Alexander L. S. MB ChB 1943 qv and Mary E. C. McLean MB ChB 1943 qv; b Aber 7.9.47
teacher: prin geog Slough 1969–73, Engl lang Helsinki Finland 1973–74, prin geog Lond from 1974

STALKER Heather Leith   MA 1970
m Begg

STALKER William   MA 1967

STAMPER Christopher Paul   *BSc 1969
s of Frank S. superv plastics div ICI and Eva Griffiths; b Blackpool 29.4.47
scient off. soil surv Engl and Wales Wolverhampton 1969–70; teacher: goeg Ash Green h s, joint prin adult educ centre Coventry 1970–73, Sixth Form coll Darlington from 1973, head geog dept from 1978
m Aber 28.11.69 Shiona R. Cantlay teacher d of William J. Cantlay BSc(agr) 1943 qv

STANBRIDGE Catherine Clark   *MA 1969
d of Elias S. factory worker and Gladys W. Singer; b Aber 28.6.47
secy/typist Aberd 1970–73; teacher Banchory p s from 1974
m Aber 7.7.78 George M. McA. Slater herring curer s of William G. S. Aber

STANGER Ian Leslie   MA 1962

STANLEY Terence Eric   *BSc 1965
s of Eric W. S. civ serv and Winifred M. Longman; b Watford 11.1.43
MSc(N'cle) 1966 PhD(Lond) 1970
lect maths The City univ Lond 1968–78; sen lect from 1978
m Burton-u-Stather 5.8.72 Margaret R. Armstrong secy d of Rev Wilfred T. A. OBE MA(Oxon) Scunthorpe

STARK Ronald David   cMB ChB 1965 PhD 1969
s of John S. comm trav and Williamina Chalmers secy; b Edin 12.6.41
MD(Birm) 1973 MRCP 1973
h o Aber gen hosps 1965–66; Garden res fell. physiol Aberd 1966–68; Canadian MRC fell./lect pharm Manit 1968–70; clin res fell. med Birm 1970–74; clin physiol ICI pharm Macclesfield from 1974
m Aber 22.7.66 Alexandra M. Gray nurse d of Alexander G. Kirriemuir

STARK William Alexander   BSc 1969
s of William B. S. mill man. and Margaret Kidd; b Perth 15.1.47
Assoc Member Textile Inst 1973
trainee man. Darlington 1969–72; asst mill man. Keith from 1972
m Aber 1.9.70 Isobel H. Nicol BSc 1970 qv

STARKS Richard Gordon   *BSc 1968 MSc 1970
s of John F. S. naval arch. and Violet L. Veazey authoress; b Portsmouth 30.3.47
tech edit. *Canadian Pulp and Paper Industry Magazine* Toronto 1970–72; asst edit. *The Financial Post* Toronto from 1973

STAUNTON Irene Anne   MA 1969

STAVE Rolv Elias   MB ChB 1965

STEELE Donald Hamish   *MA 1966
s of James S. headmaster and Elsie J. Gordon teacher; b Inv 28.7.44
Dip Ed(Edin) 1967
teacher geog George Heriot's Edin 1967–70, prin geog Bathgate acad 1971–76; asst rector Royal h s Edin 1976–78, seconded as asst to Dir of Educ Lothian reg
m Aber 27.12.68 Moira J. L. Welsh MA 1966 qv

STEELE Dorothy Robertson   MA 1963
m Mein

STEELE Grace Mitchell Fairley   MA 1969
d of Robert B. D. S. BSc(St And) schoolmaster and

Helen D. Jamieson MA(St And); b Perth 6.1.49
teacher r e Galashiels acad 1970–78; asst prin guid
Breadalbane acad Aberfeldy from 1978

STEELE John Douglas   LLB 1969
s of Andrew R. S. teacher and Janet O. Y. Dalgleish;
b St And 21.2.48
law app Dun 1969–71; solic Glasg from 1971

STEELE Joyce Mary   MA 1956
d of Archibald S. wholesale confectioner/grocer and
Georgina A. Yule; b Aber 16.11.35
teacher Engl/geog Angus 1957–59
m Aber 11.9.59 Brian K. Crookshanks MA 1949 *qv*

STEELE Patricia Marr   *MA 1970
m Bedford

STEER Margaret Rose   MA 1964
d of John M. S. power loom tuner, lab, inventor and
Violet J. Ross millworker; b Aber 5.5.42
teacher: Nairobi, Johannesburg 1964–66, Bishopbriggs,
Knightswood Glasg 1967–70; artist/printmaker Chewoyet
Kenya 1970–72; teacher Stirling, Glasg 1972–75
m(2) Nairobi 7.2.72 Gideon S. Annand MA 1962 *qv*

STEEVES Martin Paul Taylor   *MA 1964

STEIGERWALT Mary Susan   PhD 1967
AB(Calif)

STEINER Mark Rudie   LLB 1968

STENHOUSE Donald   cMB ChB 1961

STENHOUSE Robert James   BSc(agr) 1964
s of Robert J. S. farm. and Rebecca Pyper; b Stonehaven 2.8.40
DAFS: tech asst Edin 1964–66, asst insp Perth 1966–74,
insp Perth from 1974
m Kinneff 4.8.64 Glenda L. Duncan d of Alexander D.
Catterline

STEPHEN Alison Margaret   MA 1958
m Sibbald

STEPHEN Allan Grant   MA 1968
s of Mary Findlater; b Turriff 14.12.45
teacher Engl: Auchterarder s s 1969–70, Turriff acad
from 1970
m Aber 10.4.73 Joan M. Gorman teacher d of John
N. G. Balmedie

STEPHEN Anne   MA 1969
d of James S. BR train guard and Mary R. Garvock;
b Aber 3.5.48
Dip Soc St(Glas) 1970 CASS(Dund) 1973
soc worker Dun from 1970
m Miller

STEPHEN Charles Gordon   BSc(eng) 1963
s of Charles S. fisherman/clerk and Gordon Noble;
b Cairnbulg 23.4.28
prod. eng Burrough Machines Cumbernauld 1963–67;
dev eng: Rolls Royce Hamilton, E Kilbride 1967–71,
manuf of counting devices Veeder Root Dun 1971–75;
teacher tech educ from 1976
m Stirling 5.4.68 Christian C. Taylor boarding s matron
d of Hugh T. Auchnagatt

STEPHEN David James   LLB 1969

STEPHEN David Sheriff   *MEd 1967
BSc(St And)

STEPHEN Dennis Duncan   *BSc(eng) 1966
s of Samuel S. agr worker and Anne McKandie;
b Banff 27.1.44
electronic eng Chelmsford 1966–70; prod. man. (computers) Kidsgrove from 1970
m Nantwich 26.6.71 Bridget M. Smith midwifery sister
d of Thomas E. S. Kells Co Meath Eire

STEPHEN Dorothy   *BSc 1961

STEPHEN Evelyn Mary   MA 1965
d of Robert S. banker and Vera S. Smith; b Aber 23.1.44
Dip Ed(Natal) 1967 PhD(Natal) 1971
m Aber 19.3.65 William James PhD 1965 *qv*

STEPHEN Frank Graham   BEd 1970
s of Frank S. master farrier/blacksmith and Helen E.
Paterson; b Brechin 6.6.42
teacher Southesk p s Montrose from 1971

STEPHEN George   MB ChB 1970
s of George S. depot man. and Eileen E. Garrett;
b Fraserburgh 11.5.46
h o, sen h o ARI, RACH 1970–73; g p Portlethen from
1973
m Rothiemay 28.8.71 Norma G. Birnie nurse d of
William B. Rothiemay

STEPHEN George John   *MA 1960

STEPHEN George Willson   MB ChB 1961
s of Alexander S. MA 1918 *qv*; b Aber 12.2.37
DObstRCOG(Lond) 1963 DA(Lond) 1972
h o ARI 1961–62; sen h o: obst, anaest Middlesbrough
1963–64; ship's surg Royal Fleet auxil serv Far East
1964–66; g p Thornaby from 1966; clin asst anaest
S Teesside from 1970
m Hong Kong 6.8.65 Patricia McAlpine teacher d of
Douglas McA. Whitley Bay

STEPHEN George Wilson   MB ChB 1956
s of George S. fish salesman and Margaret Duthie;
b Mallaig 9.10.31
FFARCSI 1962 FFARCS 1963
h o Stockton, Aber 1956–57; sen h o anaest Dun, Liv
1958–60; regist anaest Derby 1961–64; res asst anaest
Philadelphia USA 1964–66; lect anaest Edin 1967–70;
consult. anaest Lond from 1970

STEPHEN Ian Berneaud   *MA 1962 Dip Ed 1963

STEPHEN Isobel Marion   *BSc 1966

STEPHEN James Flockhart   MA 1965
s of James F. S. eng and Sophie E. Mutch midwife;
b Aber 31.3.26
teacher: maths Cults acad 1966–71, spec asst maths/
careers 1971–72; maths/prin guid Cults acad Aber from
1972
m Aber 7.3.53 Frances M. Allan oper theatre sister d of
Francis A. Aber

STEPHEN James Gordon   BSc(agr) 1958

STEPHEN John   *BSc 1956 PhD 1960
s of Thomas S. fisherman and Jeannie M. Smith;
b St Monance 15.11.34
scient off. Rowett res inst Aber 1956–62; sen res fell.
microbiol res estab Porton 1962–65; lect Birm 1965–74,

sen lect from 1974
m Peterhead 21.6.58 Elizabeth F. Buchan teacher d of George B. Peterhead

STEPHEN John Matthew   *MA 1965
s of George M. S. comm trav and Christina F. Matthew; b Aber 25.3.43
radio journalist Swiss shortwave serv Bern 1965–68, asst edit. news dept 1968–69; chief sub-edit. BBC external serv news dept Lond from 1969
m Aber –.8.66 Diane K. McAra d of Alastair R. McA. MA 1937 *qv*

STEPHEN Kenneth James   *MA 1964
s of William S. S. clerk and Annie M. Sim; b Fraserburgh 13.3.42
teacher Engl: Inverurie acad 1965–68, Blairgowrie h s 1968–72, asst prin Engl 1972–74; prin Engl Lossiemouth h s from 1974
m Fyvie 16.7.69 Margaret C. Cowie DA teacher of art d of Peter C. Oldmeldrum

STEPHEN Lorna Margaret   MA 1962
d of Andrew D. S. clerk/f-lt RAF and Helen M. Byers nurse; b Glasg 2.8.42
secy mod lang sect. school broadc dept BBC Lond 1963–71
m Grantown-on-Spey 30.8.69 Adrian Banks ophth optic s of Reginald F. B. Orpington

STEPHEN Margaret Elizabeth   MB ChB 1967
s of William D. S. pharm asst and Jessie Bell pharm; b Aber 11.7.43
h o Woodend hosp Aber, Bangour gen hosp Broxburn 1967–68; trainee g p Edin 1968–69; g p Armadale from 1969
m Edin 23.9.72 Smith Tennant comm clerk s of Smith T. Bathgate

STEPHEN Mary Lindsey   MA 1965

STEPHEN Maureen Youngson   *MA 1962
m Morrison

STEPHEN Richard Leslie   MA 1969

STEPHEN Robert Brown Sangster   *MA 1962
s of Robert A. S. fisherman and Sophia Cordiner self-employed shopkeeper; b Boddam 6.11.38
Glasg: teacher geog Crookston Castle s s 1963–67; prin geog Grange s s 1967–71, Queen's Park s s 1971–74; asst head Cathkin h s Cambuslang from 1974
m Motherwell 11.7.64 Emily J. Campbell nurse d of John C. Motherwell

STEPHEN Thomas George   BSc(agr) 1956 MSc 1976
s of Leslie S. teacher and Christina E. A. Soutar teacher; b Nuneaton 14.5.33
agr off. HM overseas civ serv Kumasi Ghana 1956–60; agr advis: BOCM Inv 1960–64, PIDA Aber 1964–68; dev off. meat and livestock comm Aber 1968–76; lect Clinterty agr coll 1976–77, NOSCA from 1977
m Aber 9.1.58 Margaret H. B. Gray teacher d of James G. C. Bucksburn

STEPHEN William   *MA 1956
s of James S. fisherman and Harriet Noble dressmaker; b Fraserburgh 29.10.33
nat serv 1956–58; teacher Musselburgh g s 1959; Aber coll of comm: teacher 1959–61, sen econ 1961–63, head of prof stud. 1963–70, second dep prin from 1970
m Aber 15.9.56 Eleanor Goodrum typist d of James G. Aber

STEPHEN William Strachan   *MA 1958
s of James S. eng and Andretta W. Noble; b Fraserburgh 21.11.34
teacher Engl: Arbroath h s 1959–61, Buckhaven h s 1961–65, Aber acad 1965–70, prin guid 1970–73, asst head Hazlehead acad from 1973
m Aber 27.12.60 Anita M. Young teacher d of George Y. Aber

STEPHENSON Christopher Stanley   BSc 1967
s of Stanley R. S. newsagent/stationer and Kathleen M. Irwin bookkeeper; b N'cle-u-Tyne 28.5.44
fisherman 1967–68; man. retail newsagency Morpeth 1968–70; self-employed fisherman Oban from 1970
m Derby 7.9.68 Marion M. Martin teacher dressmaking/millinery d of Gideon M. M. Derby

STEPHENSON Gillian   MB ChB 1957
m Craig

STEPHENSON Joan MB ChB 1959

STEPHENSON John David   *MA 1969 Dip Ed 1970
s of Ernest S. clerk and Ada Clunie teacher; b N'cle-u-Tyne 4.2.45
teacher Daniel Stewart's and Melville coll Edin 1970–73, housemaster from 1973
m Aber 2.8.72 Fiona A. McBlane LLB 1970 *qv*

STEVEN Robert Lewis Tocher   *BSc 1961 MSc 1963

STEVENSON David William Stewart   MA 1969

STEVENSON Ian McLeod   BEd 1970

STEVENSON James Alexander Stewart   MA 1969

STEVENSON John Campbell   MA 1966
s of Alexander N. S. lab and Jean M. Campbell; b Johannesburg 27.1.45
bank clerk Clydesdale Bank 1967–68; teacher Engl/hist Aboyne acad 1968–71; head Towie p s from 1971
m Dinnet 18.12.71 Seonaid E. Grant stud. d of James I. S. G. Dinnet

STEVENSON John Thomas MacSween   *BSc 1967 MSc 1969
s of William A. S. farm. and Mary S. Firth postmistress; b Stromness 21.11.46
dev eng Ferranti Dalkeith 1968–74, res fell. Edin from 1974
m Glenesk 9.10.68 Winifred M. Sanderson milk and food hyg off. d of Allan A. S. Arbroath

STEVENSON Margaret Paplay   MA 1969
d of Henry S. joiner and Maggie Paplay MA 1932 *qv*; b Kirkwall 12.12.48
Cardiff: teacher kindergarten Elm Tree House s 1972–73, Engl Bryn Hafren comp s 1973–74; secy to firm John Jolly Kirkwall 1975–76
m Stromness 31.7.71 James W. Spence BSc(Wales) naval off. s of James W.S. Stromness

STEVENSON William   BSc(eng) 1960

STEVENSON William   *MA 1963
s of Raymond W. H. S. BA(Oxon) prof phys and Stephanie B. Roberts MA(Rhodes); b Charlottetown PEI Canada 27.5.41
FRCO 1963
teacher Edin 1964–69; prin mus Morgan acad Dun from 1969
m 16.7.66 Lorna Murray teacher d of David M. Aber

STEWART Alan Duff *BSc 1961 MSc 1962 PhD 1965
s of John D. S. MA 1924 *qv*; b Aber 29.11.38
lect phys Dund from 1965
m Aber 18.3.66 Frances G. Pirie teacher d of Thomas P.
Aber

STEWART Alexander *BSc 1967
b Elgin 22.11.45
MIEE C Eng
dev eng: Marconi Radar Syst Chelmsford 1969–72,
Ferranti Edin from 1972

STEWART Alison BSc 1965
d of John S. MA 1926 *qv*(III); b Aber 6.6.45
m Aber 21.10.66 John A. Simpson fisherman s of
William S. Whalsay

STEWART Andrew MA 1966
s of George S. crofter and Catherine Graham; b Back
Is of Lewis 3.7.43
RAF off. from 1966
m Lond 13.12.69 Patricia A. Malloy MA(St And) med
soc worker d of Joseph H. M. MB ChB(Dund/St And)
Abbotts Bromley

STEWART Andrew Macmillan *MA 1965
s of Howard M. S. BSc(Lond) consult. civ eng and
Sybil D. Thornton ballet dancer/teacher; b Esher 9.8.42
MBPsS Foreign Affiliate Amer Psych Assoc   Assoc RC
Psych FSS
res stud. Aberd 1965–67; asst lect Surrey univ 1967–69;
pers man. IBM(UK) 1969–74; sen fell. (seconded 1972–
74) inst of manpower stud. Sus 1972–77; ptnr Macmillan
Stewart & Ptnrs, dir Macmillan Stewart from 1978
m(2) Guildford 8.5.72 Valerie G. Haycock PhD(Sheff)
indust psych d of Alec T. H. Coalville

STEWART Anne MA 1965
d of Harvey S. bank man. and Annie Gray teacher;
b Ellon 25.7.42
teacher Engl Gordon s Huntly 1966–68
m Aber 20.1.68 Andrew T. Shennan MB ChB 1967 *qv*

STEWART Audrey Fraser MB ChB 1960
m Gunn

STEWART Brian Richard *BSc(eng) 1969
s of Richard S. elect. eng and Edith M. Wallaker;
b Aber 7.4.47
CEng MICE 1973
site eng Birm 1969–70; asst eng Edin from 1970
m Aber 10.10.69 Margaret W. Speirs clerkess/typist d of
Joseph S. S. Aber

STEWART Catherine Anne MA 1970 CASS 1972
d of James S. MRCVS(Edin) vet surg and Ella Dunse;
b Kendal 1.9.49
soc worker Perth 1972–74; Harpenden: part-time youth
worker 1977–79, soc worker sessional from 1979
m Aber 4.7.72 Edward Pattison

STEWART Charlotte Forbes MA 1967
m Duncan

STEWART Clement Allan MA 1962 *MEd 1970
s of Henry T. S. MA(St And) teacher and Evelyn
Ogilvie teacher; b Strichen 9.1.41
teacher: maths AGS 1963–69, spec asst maths 1969–70;
prin maths Dunoon g s 1970–72, asst rector 1972–74,
dep rector 1974–77; head Lochgilphead h s from 1977
m Aber 10.4.65 Sheena M. Phillip MA 1960 *qv*

STEWART Donald Herbert MA 1968 MEd 1970

STEWART Donald Robert *MA 1963
s of Alexander B. S. MA 1925 *qv* and Alice F. Bowman
MA 1921 *qv*; b Aber 21.9.40
res stud. Aberd 1963–66; lect Ger UCNW 1966–72; asst
secy St And univ from 1972

STEWART Donald William Hugh BSc 1960 MA 1962
s of Alexander M. S. farm. and Elizabeth I. Macleod;
b Inv 17.11.32
teacher Invsh 1963–64; scient information off. Aber from
1964
m Aber 16.9.66 Catherine H. Bisset BSc 1962 *qv*

STEWART Donella Kinmond MA 1970
m Cooper

STEWART Douglas James MB ChB 1969
s of Douglas G. S. CA and Anne Dunbar; b Aber
30.6.46
FRCSE 1973
h o ARI 1969–70; Anderson and Thomson fell. path.
Aberd 1970–71; sen h o surg ARI 1971–72; regist surg
Aber teaching hosps 1972–76; sen regist surg ERI from
1976
m Aber 17.5.68 Catherine I. Paterson MA 1968 *qv*

STEWART Douglas Lunan BSc(eng) 1959
s of James D. S. MA 1931 *qv*; b Aber 19.2.38
Dip H&TEng 1972
asst eng: Sir William Halcrow & Ptnrs Inv 1959–60,
W. A. Fairhurst & Ptnrs Aber, Dun 1960–66; asst eng
to traffic eng Aber c c 1966–75; prin eng Grampian reg c
1975–79; self-employed Aber from 1979
m Aber 1.4.66 Lesley J. Watt MB ChB 1968 *qv*

STEWART Evelyn MB ChB 1961

STEWART Evelyn Ogilvie BSc 1962 cMB ChB 1964
d of Henry T. S. MA(St And) headmaster and Evelyn
Ogilvie teacher; b Fraserburgh 26.10.39
h o ARI, RACH 1964–65; Garden ress fell. Aberd 1965–
66; res asst anaest Glasg RI from 1973
m Aber 25.7.64 Geoffrey D. Parbrook MB ChB(Birm)
anaest s of George H. P. Torquay

STEWART Frances Lindsay *MA 1969
d of James D. S. MA 1931 *qv*; b Aber 17.4.46
MSc(N'cle) 1974
teacher: Brentwood p s 1969–70, ESN(M) Sheff 1970–71,
ESN(S) Sheff 1971–72; educ psych N'cle-u-Tyne 1974–76;
advis pre-s handicapped ch N'cle from 1976
m Aber 9.4.79 Keith A. Humphreys BEd(Lond) teacher,
lect s of Joseph H. Barrow-in-Furness

STEWART George James Lionel BSc(eng) 1967

STEWART George Macleod MB ChB 1959 DPH 1969
s of James G. S. marine eng and Mary D. Stephen
nurs sister; b Singapore 1935
DTM&H(Lond) 1964 DIH(Lond) 1970 MFCM 1972
h o ARI, Woodend hosp Aber 1959–60; gen duty m o
RAMC Singapore, Malaya, N Borneo 1960–63; r m o 1st
Bn Grenadier Guards BAOR & UNFICYP Ger, Cyprus
1964–65; dem army health RAM coll Lond 1966; instr s
of army health Ashvale Aldershot 1966–68; dep asst dir
army health Brisbane Aust 1970–72; dep asst dir army
health and res MoD Lond 1972–74, asst dir from 1974
m Aber 4.8.60 Audrey W. Young MB ChB 1959 *qv*

STEWART Gordon Grant *MA 1957
resid Perth

STEWART Hélène Annette   MA 1962
m Kenneth W. Ruddiman MA 1962 *qv*

STEWART Hugh McKenzie   MA 1957

STEWART Ian Malcolm Alexander   *MA 1962

STEWART Ian Murdoch   *BSc 1956
s of William S. MA 1913 *qv* and Jessie K. Davie MA
1913 *qv*; b Aber 17.4.33
Stafford: res tech Nelson res lab Eng Elect. Co. 1956–64,
head phys metall sect. 1964–70; man. Electron Optics
Group Walter C. McCrone Assoc Inc Chicago USA from
1970
m Aber 14.6.56 Shirley M. Kelman BSc 1955 *qv*

STEWART Ilene Robertson   MA 1969 Dip Ed 1970
d of Ian D. S. hairdresser and Sarah D. Bradley;
b Meikleour 1.2.48
teacher maths: f e Aber 1970–74, Driffield from 1974
m Auchterarder 18.7.70 Michael A. Hall MB ChB 1974
h o Hull RI s of Antony H. Rushden

STEWART Iris   MA 1956
b Nairn 28.2.36
resid Edin

STEWART Isabella Davidson   MA 1956

STEWART James Harvey   *MA 1962
s of Harvey S. banker and Anne Gray teacher; b Ellon
15.8.39
Dip Adv St (Soc Admin)(Manc) 1964
hosp admin Edin 1965–67; prin admin asst hosp man.
York 1967–68, dep group secy York 1968–73; area admin
Northumberland area health auth Morpeth from 1973
m Aber 24.4.65 Fiona M. M. Reid teacher d of John R.
Peterhead

STEWART James John   BSc 1958
s of William S. fisherman and Agnes H. Murray;
b Lossiemouth 23.1.37
HM forces intellig corps 1958–61; Wiggins Teape: prod.
trainee Stoneywood 1961–65, paper mill foreman Scot.
pulp and paper mills Corpach 1965–68; chief papermaker
Empire Paper Mills Kent 1968–71; paper mill supt
Bowater Scott Corp Barrow-in-Furness 1971–74; tissue
mill supt Harir Pars Co Haft Tappen Khuzestan Iran
1975–77; comm supt Sulzer Bros Basrah Iraq 1977–78;
consult. paper tech from 1978
m Aber 18.11.61 Christina A. Stephen asst pharm d of
William J. S. Aber

STEWART James Keith   MA 1969

STEWART Jamesina Sinclair   MA 1963
m Milne

STEWART Joan Helen   MA 1963

STEWART John   MA 1966 LTh 1969
s of Alexander S. gen merch and Annabella Cameron;
b Glasg 6.11.31
MTh(Lond) 1971
C of S min Bowmore Islay 1970; min United Reform ch
(St Andrews) Canterbury from 1971; dist chmn 1972–73;
on univ court of univ of Kent at Canterbury from 1974
m Glasg 11.12.57 Joyce B. Woods d of Alfred G. W.

STEWART John Macfarlane   *BSc 1960 PhD 1966
s of James M. S. master grocer and Mary Keillor;
b Dun 29.4.39

MRC schol zool Aberd 1960–63; Georgina McRobert
res fell. cancer dept path. Aberd 1964–67; lect biol Stir
from 1967; biol inst (Carlsberg foundation) Copenhagen
1974–75
m Dun 4.4.62 Kamala M. Saggar MA(St And) teacher
d of Jainti D. S. MB ChB(St And) Dun

STEWART John Marsh   *MA 1970
s of John M. S. dir/gen man. Ulster Steamship Co
and Anne Thompson; b Belf 20.7.47
econ Courtaulds Lond from 1970

STEWART John McLeod   BSc 1959 Dip Ed 1961

STEWART Joseph   *BSc 1969 PhD 1973
b Elgin 16.2.47
teacher Perth acad 1972–76, Whitfield h s Dun from 1976
m Fochabers 12.9.70 Lorna A. Smith MA 1970 *qv*

STEWART Kathleen Anne   MA 1957

STEWART Kathleen Mairi   MA 1970
d of Allan S. farm. and Ella M. L. Harman; b Cromarty
11.4.49
teacher: Carfin p s 1971–72, South Park p s 1972–73
m Inv 10.7.71 Archibald K. Fraser BSc 1968 *qv*

STEWART Kathleen Ross   *MA 1963
m Macpherson

STEWART Kenneth George   *BSc(eng) 1970

STEWART Laspic Gilchrist   LLB 1966

STEWART Magnus   *BSc 1962
s of John S. MA 1926 *qv*; b Aber 2.11.40
teacher: maths/sc Banchory acad 1963–64, chem AGS
1964–73, prin chem Northfield acad Aber from 1973
m Aber 12.6.64 Norah Hogg nurse d of Charles H. Aber

STEWART Margaret Ollason   MA 1962 Dip Ed 1963
d of Douglas L. S. MA 1934 *qv* and Christina M.
Laurenson MA 1936 *qv*; b Lerwick 20.10.41
teacher: p s Bonnyrigg 1963–66, partially deaf Sydney
Aust 1966–69, remed Bedford 1971–73, p s Macduff from
1974
m Aber 3.3.66 Henry J. L. Mantell arch. s of Henry
P. M. Macduff

STEWART Mary Edmar   *BSc 1960
d of Edwin S. storeman and Elizabeth A. B. Macdonald
civ serv; b Aber 16.2.38
steroid biochem: St Mary's hosp Lond 1960–62, res
unit Aber 1962–65
m Aber 19.8.62 Ronald W. Caie MA 1960 *qv*

STEWART Mary McBeth   MA 1966
d of James S. rly worker and Mary McBeth; b Oban
16.1.45
teacher: Oban h s 1967–69, hist Kirkton h s Dun 1971–74,
prin hist from 1974
m Dun 12.8.67 Henry G. Cameron MA 1966 *qv*

STEWART Mary Smith   MA 1958

STEWART Morna Grace   MA 1968
d of William R. S. BSc(St And) man. dir and Irene
E. G. Henderson MA(St And) teacher; b Dun 11.8.46
teacher Engl/hist Belf 1970–72; TEFL: Aber 1972–73,
Cambridge from 1973

STEWART Murdina   MA 1968
d of John S. crofter and Peggy Campbell; b Skye

17.4.46
teacher Gaelic: Badenoch 1969–73, Nova Scotia 1973–78,
bilingual educ proj Skye from 1978

STEWART Murray Lessels   *MA 1959

STEWART Neil   BSc(eng) 1962

STEWART Neil   MA 1964
s of Archibald S. farm. and Catherine Buchanan;
b Isle of Skye 1.12.34
stud. divinity at Free ch coll Edin 1964–67; min of Free
C of S Conon Bridge

STEWART Patricia Louise   MA 1957
d of John H. S. bank man. and Ada C. L. Paterson
BCom(Edin) secy Amer consular serv; b Aber 5.2.36
Cert for Teachers of Deaf(Manc) 1958
teacher of deaf: Woodford Green 1959, Edin 1959–60,
Herts 1967–68, Edin from 1969
m Aber 10.10.59 James E. Fraser MA 1953 qv

STEWART Peter James Neilson   *MA 1967
s of William N. S. granite merch and Dorothy Chalmers
BSc 1926 qv; b Aber 11.1.45
reporter *Highland News* Inv 1967–68; edit. *Caithness
Courier* Thurso 1968–69; sub-edit. *Evening Echo* Hemel
Hempstead 1969–71; Hong Kong: dep chief sub-edit./
features edit. *China Mail* 1971–73, asst to edit. *Sunday
Standard* 1973–74, news edit. and fin. edit. *Hong Kong
Standard* 1974–76, chief edit. Rediffusion (Hong Kong)
TV 1976–78
d Hong Kong 26.5.78

STEWART Ralph Robertson Ferguson   *MA 1964
   MA(Sask)

STEWART Ronald Ramsay   MA 1960 *1962
s of William S. salesman and Lavinia Macdonald jute
weaver; b Dun 5.5.39
teacher Engl Hozier s s Lanarksh 1962–63; prob clin
psych Lancs 1963–65; res assoc N'cle 1965–67, res fell.
Liv 1967–72; lect educ psych Liv from 1972

STEWART Susan Winifred   MA 1969
d of James G. S. acct and Winifred E. Hooker; b Glasg
7.7.48
teacher Fr: Harpurhey h s Manc 1970–71, Shiremoor
mid s Northumberland, Balliol mid s Longbenton N'cle,
Seaton Sluice mid s Northumberland, N Manc h s for
girls 1971–74
m Edin 10.8.70 Michael G. Sadler LLB 1967 qv

STEWART William Brodie   MA 1965 Dip Ed 1966

STEWART Winifred Margaret   MA 1964

STEWART Winthrop Rodney   PhD 1965
s of Winthrop F. S. industrialist and Martha Rediger;
b Hollywood Ca USA 31.12.33
BA BD(Calif)
Arizona USA: pastor Hope Baptist ch Phoenix 1965–72;
exec dir Esperança Inc from 1972
m Norwalk CA 4.2.56 Regina Bullinger nurse

STEYN John Hofmeyr   PhD 1967
s of Johannes S. S. MD(Groningham) ophth surg and
Blanka Hablutzel; b Johannesburg 3.10.29
MB ChB(Cape Town) 1952 FRCS(Eng) 1957 FRCSE
1973
consult. urologist ARI/Aberd 1967–69; consult. in admin
charge dept urology Aber from 1969

m Johannesburg 6.4.53 Daphne M. Nelson BA(Witwatersrand) d of Bernard N. LLB(Witwatersrand)
Johannesburg

STILEMAN Richard Graham Learmonth   *BSc 1968
s of Peter L. S. insur exec and Rhoda E. C. Garrick;
b Reigate 20.12.44
Chapman & Hall book publ Lond: edit. 1969–75, man.
dir from 1975
m Aber 30.8.71 Patricia F. B. Ross MA 1968 qv

STILL Alexander William   BSc(eng) 1961
s of Alexander I. S. gardener and Helen A. Jamieson;
b Redhill 2.4.39
consult. eng Glasg 1961–63; site eng Yorks 1964–67;
sen civ eng Aber 1967–70; chief estimator/comm. man.
Lond from 1970
m Aber 9.3.63 Isobel R. Coull MA 1961 qv

STILL Elaine Lily   MA 1967
d of Albert E. S. cashier and Lily Frain; b Aber
25.6.46
teacher: Walker Dam inf s Aber 1968–70, Oxford p s
Münster Germany 1970–73, Catcott County p s nr
Bridgwater from 1974
m Morpeth 29.7.72 Philip Gosling army off. s of
Christopher F. J. G. Gateshead

STILL Joan   MA 1961
d of Johnstone S. master butcher and Jean Milne shop
asst; b Aber 27.6.41
teacher Engl/hist Powis s s Aber 1962–68
m Aber 28.3.67 Ronald G. Walker auctioneer and
valuator s of Alfred W. Rothienorman

STILL John Mackenzie   MA 1963
   CA

STILL Lena Robson Cooper   MA 1969
b Aber 3.2.21
Aber: teacher maths coll of comm 1970–73, St
Margaret's s for girls from 1973
m Aber 3.8.44 Harry A. McFarlane area eng GPO tel

STILL Ronald David   *BSc(eng) 1969

STIRLING Bertha Fiona   BMedBiol 1969 MB ChB 1972
d of Charles S. res eng and Bertha M. Wescott nurse;
b Darlington 12.8.47
Hull: h o med/surg 1972–73, surg clin asst 1973–74
m Haxby 12.7.72 Eric L. Huckvale BSc(agr) 1970 qv

STIRLING Hamish   MA 1959 LLB 1961
s of James S. BSc(St And) univ lect and Ann W. Black
teacher; b Liv 9.7.38
law app Jameson, McGhie & Munro solic Elgin 1961–62;
proc fisc dep: Dun 1963–70, Duns/Hawick/Jedburgh/
Selkirk 1970–74, Glasg 1974–75; admitted fac of advoc
1976
m Aber 15.8.63 Margaret D. Bottomley nurse d of
Harry B. MA(Oxon) Milltimber

STIRRAT Helen Margaret Rosemary   MB ChB 1967
d of Hugh S. BSc(Lond) lect econ RGIT and Helen M.
Oakes civ serv; b Enfield 6.1.43
DPM(Lond) 1973
h o Lond, Tor 1967–68; g p trainee Lond 1969–70; sen
h o, regist psych Ilford, Epsom 1970–73; m o fam plan.
assoc Woking 1970–73; res fell. inst of psych Tor from
1973
m Aber 15.7.67 Peter F. Meier solic s of Frederick J. M.
Diessenhofen Switzerland

ST LOUIS Patrick Joseph *BSc 1967 PhD 1971

STOCKAN Kathleen Irida Harcus MA 1967
d of James D. S. farm. and Agnes W. Harcus; b
Orkney 25.3.46
ALA 1972
Aber publ lib: lib asst 1968–69, asst lib from 1970
m Aber 18.7.69 John M. Corall teacher s of Thomas
M. C. Aber

STOCKDALE Christopher Leo *BSc 1969 MSc 1971

STODDART David Michael *BSc 1965 PhD 1968
s of James H. S. BSc(Glas) prin examiner HM patent
off. and Elizabeth M. McCutcheon; b Lanark 19.4.43
post doct fell. natural environm res Council Oxford 1968–
69; lect zool King's coll Lond from 1969
m Aston Clinton 27.12.69 Lydia B. Treutler teacher d of
Hermann H. W. T. Aylesbury

STOESSEL Horace Edward PhD 1962
AB(K Coll, Tenn) BD ThM(UTS NY)

STOESSL Michelle Madeline BSc(eng) 1969
d of Edmund S. acct/comp dir and Alice H. Schweitzer;
b Lond 26.11.48
m Amersham 3.8.68 Richard K. D. Cook BSc(eng) 1969
qv

STOKER Roger *BSc 1965 PhD 1968

STONE Beryl Margaret MB ChB 1959
d of Archibald C. S. ironmonger and Ruth L.
Dodsworth SRN; b High Wycombe 15.6.23
BSc(Lond) 1953 Affiliate RCPsych 1962
h o Royal Halifax I, Crumpsall hosp Manc 1959–60; sen
h o Barony hosp Nantwich 1960–61; regist: Herrison
hosp Dorchester 1961–62, St George's hosp Morpeth
1962–65; asst psychiat Lawn hosp Lincoln 1965–73
m Aber 14.4.61 John McN. White MB BS(Lond) asst
psychiat Lawn hosp s of William L. A. W. Hornchurch
d Charleville-Mézieres Ardennes France 26.4.73 *AUR*
xlv 321

STONE Gordon Victor MB ChB 1969
s of Victor J. S. bookkeeper/cashier and Madeleine O.
Imlach secy dept chem Aberd; b Lond 4.10.45
DCM(Edin) 1976 MFCM 1977
h o Aber 1969–70; unit m o RAF: Anglesey 1970–71,
Laarbruch Ger 1971–74; sen m o RAF Gloucester 1974–
75; Scot. Health Serv Fell. in commun med 1975; spec in
commun med Grampian health board from 1978
m Aber 16.7.69 Aileen S. Wilson BSc 1969 *qv*

STONE Michael Terence MA 1967

STONES William Clark BSc(for) 1956
s of John G. S. farm. and Ada J. Tiplady teacher;
b Richmond Yorks 6.7.34
nat serv 1956–58; for. comm surv Argyll 1959–60; farm.
N Yorks from 1960
m Crook Greta Nicholson bank clerk d of Joseph S. N.
Crook

STONEY David Thomas William BSc 1968

STONEY Margaret Marshall MA 1961
d of John A. S. banker and Margaret M. Fullerton
secy; b Glasg 5.4.41
teacher: Aberdeensh 1961–62, Oxfordsh 1962–63, part-
time Midlothian 1972–76, full-time 1976, prin remed
dept Penicuik h s from 1977
m Aber 25.8.62 David J. Fletcher MA 1960 *qv*

STOPPER Irene May MA 1968
m Sinclair

STORM Isabella MA 1958
d of George S. fisherman and Christina Campbell;
b Nairn 11.1.37
teacher: Kinloss p s 1958–62, Dalneigh p s Inv 1962–68,
Fort William p s from 1978
m Nairn 1.8.62 Alexander McIntosh policeman s of
Robert McI. Nairn

STORRY John Edgar PhD 1960
s of Ernest R. S. textile ag and Norah M. Burchell
teacher; b Nott 14.5.35
BSc(Nott) 1957
post grad schol physiol min of agr Rowett res inst Aber
1957–60; scient off., sen scient off., prin scient off. chem
dept Nat Inst Res Dairying Reading from 1960
m Edin 9.7.60 Catherine I. Dickson chem d of William D.
Portobello

STOTT Eileen May MA 1965
d of John W. S. farm. and Georgina G. Cumming;
b Aber 25.7.44
teacher: Bankfoot p s Perthsh 1966–69, Albyn s for girls
Aber from 1969

STOTT James Joseph MA 1960
s of James S. eng, hotelier, farm. and Oslena E.
Prosser secy; b Aber 7.6.37
BD(Edin) 1963
C of S min: asst Broughton Pl par ch Edin 1963–65,
Denbeath par ch Buckhaven 1965–70; independent
evangelist Aberdeensh from 1973
m Aber 5.9.64 Anne R. Esslemont MA 1960 *qv*

STOTT John LLB 1970
s of John S. elect. board off. and Doreen Davidson;
b Aber 6.5.49
tourist (6 mths) India 1970; law app, leg. asst Paull &
Williamsons advoc Aber 1971–75; leg. asst Wilsone &
Duffus Aber from 1975
m Sutton-cum-Lound 19.8.72 Elizabeth M. Morton BSc
1972 teacher d of Alexander F. M. BA(Oxon) Retford

STOTT Mary Louise MA 1966
m Tait

STOTT Peter LLB 1967
s of F. Floyd S. stockbroker and B. Marjorie Henderson; b Aber 13.9.45
law app Aber 1967–69; solic: Glasg 1970–71, Aber 1972;
ptnr Paull & Williamsons advoc Aber 1973; corporate
lawyer Westburne Internat Indust Calgary Alberta from
1974
m St And 25.5.74 Priscilla M. Cook secy d of David C.
Cook MA(Edin) Elie

STOTT Roderic Michael *BSc(eng) 1964

STOUT William MA 1965

STOW Philip Roger *BSc(eng) 1970
s of Cedric A. S. man. timber merch and Doris
Leeming; b Keighley 21.5.48
MICE 1978
Sir Alfred McAlpine: temp works des eng Wirral 1970–
71, site eng: Runcorn 1971–72, Ince 1972–74; plan. eng
Dowsett Engineering Harrogate 1975–78; temp works &
plan. eng Robert McGregor Manc from 1978
m Keighley 27.9.69 Susan E. Cook nurse d of Willie C.
Keighley

STRACHAN Alexander   BSc 1970

STRACHAN Arnold   BSc 1970
   s of Norman W. farm. and Annie Brodie; b Aber
12.1.49
teacher geog Eastwood h s Newton Mearns from 1972
m Aber 26.12.73 Mary Jarvie hair stylist d of John J.
Aber

STRACHAN Benjamin   BSc 1959
   s of Benjamin S. fisherman and Jane S. Ritchie; b
Inverallochy 30.5.38
teacher sc Northfield acad Aber 1960–69, prin asst
teacher 1969–73, prin phys from 1973
m Aber 5.4.61 Catherine Third d of Andrew T.
Inverallochy

STRACHAN Bruce Cordiner   BSc 1968

STRACHAN Christina Helen   MA 1970
   d of John R. S. farm. and Helen B. Anderson; b
Huntly 12.2.49
teacher Paisley from 1971
m Aber 18.8.71 Peter H. Cowie BSc(eng)(Strath) mech
eng s of Alfred H.C. Inverurie

STRACHAN Daphne Mary Andrea   MA 1956
   d of Andrew A. S. BSc(St And) dir telecomm Fed.
Malay States and Mary L. McIntosh; b Malaysia 4.3.35
asst to Lond rep univ of Ife Ibadan Nigeria 1965–72;
Lond rep univ of Ife 1972–78; prin asst secy nat univ
comm (Nigeria) Lond from 1978

STRACHAN David Gillan   BSc 1970
   s of George S. foreman joiner and Annie Maitland;
b Aber 2.12.48
work stud. off.: Philips Hamilton 1970–71, Pye Airdrie
1971–73, Aber c c from 1974
m Aber 19.9.70 Moira Jamieson MA(Glas) teacher d of
George J. Aber

STRACHAN Diana   MA 1970
   d of Roy S. news ag and Gladys Dinnie; b Insch 1.8.49
lib asst King's coll lib Aberd 1971–73
m Aber 21.7.71 Keith Nicol sales rep s of William N.
Kintore

STRACHAN Dugald James John   *MA 1965
   s of William J. S. bank man. and Mary S. McDonald;
b Elgin 15.4.43
NERC grant dept geog Aberd 1965–66; teacher geog:
Aber acad 1967–68, Elgin acad 1968–70, prin geog from
1970
m Elgin 24.7.68 Jennifer A. Barclay teacher d of Herbert
A. B. Elgin

STRACHAN Eileen Mary   MA 1956
   d of William S. and Isabella M. MacIntosh; b Peterhead 20.2.35
Dip Secy St(Glasg) 1957
secy officers' assoc Glasg 1957–58; Bankhead acad:
teacher classics 1959–64, spec asst 1964–66; prin teacher
classics Denny h s 1966–67, asst prin teacher classics
Ellon acad 1976
m Aber 20.7.66 Robert J. Burr MA 1956 qv

STRACHAN Euan Simpson   *BSc(eng) 1960
   s of George M. S. bank man. and Mary A. Mutch;
b Aber 9.2.38
MIEE
elect. eng: Ferranti Edin 1961–65, Rolls Royce & Assoc
Derby from 1965

m Kincardine O'Neil 5.5.62 Helen A. Smith teacher d of
James S. Glassel

STRACHAN Fiona Katherine   MA 1965
   m Peacock

STRACHAN Graham   MA 1958 LLB 1961
   s of John S. law acct and Annie I. Sutherland; b
Fraserburgh 14.4.36
law app Davidson & Garden advoc Aber 1961–62, ptnr
from 1962
m Breda Neths 8.1.66 Elizabeth M. G. B. de Koning soc
worker d of Jacobus de K. Breda

STRACHAN Helen Scott   MA 1963
   m Bell

STRACHAN Ian Munro   MA 1965
   s of Joseph M. S. elect. eng and Sophia Munro; b Keith
20.11.42
teacher Glenwood j h s Glenrothes 1966–67; TEFL
Benghazi Libya 1967–69; head O'Neil Corse p s 1969–71;
lect Engl Gulf tech coll Bahrain from 1971
m Aber 12.8.65 Isobel M. Bisset teacher d of James A. B.
Keithhall

STRACHAN James Wood   LLB 1966
   s of James D. S. PO eng and Edith Wood; b Aber
26.10.45
law app Aber 1966–68; solic Montrose from 1968
m Aber 7.5.71 Christine M. Ayrton clerkess d of Tom A.
Aber

STRACHAN Jeannie   MA 1957
   d of William D. S. fisherman and Jeannie Mair; b
Peterhead 6.5.37
Dip Sec Sc(Strath) 1958
educ off. Stewart & Lloyds Glasg 1958–59; secy to asst
man. dir Reed Paper Group Lond 1959–60; teacher
Engl/hist Lond 1960–61; admin asst Aust nat univ
Canberra 1962–65; personnel off. (leg. off.) Edin 1966–67;
teacher Alloa 1968–73
m Aber 6.1.62 David R. Anderson MA 1958 qv

STRACHAN Marlene   MA 1965
   d of Robert S. butcher and Christian B. W. Murison
armature winder; b Fraserburgh 30.9.44
teacher: Cultercullen s Aberdeensh 1966–67, Bucksburn s
1967–69, Scalloway s 1969–71
m Aber 9.8.67 William Y. Doverty customs off. s of
John D. D. Aber

STRACHAN Mary Catherine   *MA 1967
   m Hardie

STRACHAN Peter   *MA 1968 Dip Ed 1969

STRACHAN Robert   MA 1959
   s of John W. S. harbour pilot and Elizabeth J.
Strachan fishworker; b Fraserburgh 25.12.38
nat serv Hildesheim Ger 1960–62; teacher: Govan 1963–
65, Jedburgh from 1965
m Old Deer 10.7.68 Maureen Ritchie secy d of Henry R.
Mintlaw

STRACHAN Robert Alexander   MB ChB 1966

STRACHAN Robert George   MB ChB 1957
   s of Robert G. S. fisherman and Agnes Buchan;
b Peterhead 13.8.33
DObstRCOG 1959 DCH(Lond) 1972 MRCGP 1974
Dip Ven 1977

h o Aber, Glasg, Aber 1957–59; ship's surg **Canada** 1959–60; g p Pudsey from 1960
m Leeds 28.5.60 Muriel Hopkins nurse/midwife d of Reginald H. Leeds

STRACHAN William **BSc 1957**

STRACHAN William Reith ***BSc 1959**
s of Ian W. S. farm. and Isobel S. Reith; b Aber 18.5.37
soil surv Macaulay inst Aber 1959–62; agr sales rep Aberdeensh 1962–64; farm. West Balquhain from 1964
m Aber 2.8.62 Irene R. Ferguson MA 1960 *qv*

STRACHAN William Watson ***BSc 1969 MSc 1971**
s of William S. fatstock off. DAFS and Georgina Esslemont; b Aber 22.11.46
MRTPI 1976
plan. asst Salop c c 1971–73; sen plan. asst Inv c c 1973–74; prin plan. off. Tewkesbury borough council 1974–77, asst borough plan. off. from 1978
m Peterculter 3.8.68 Christine F. Bambrick teacher home econ d of Martin F. B. Peterculter

STRANG Ian William **MB ChB 1967**
s of Gavin S. farm. and Katherine I. Lawson; b Dinnet 12.5.41
FCM 1972 Dip Soc Med 1973 MFCM 1977
virologist Burroughs Wellcome Lond 1969; lect bio eng Strath 1970; dep med supt Glasg northern hosps 1972; sen regist commun med 1973; consult. epidemiologist to Scot. Head Injury Study 1977; CMS Argyll and Clyde Health Board 1977

STRATFOLD Anthony Leslie John **BSc(eng) 1967**

STRATTON Thomas Mackie **BSc(eng) 1958**

STRAW Jennifer Ann **MA 1965**
d of Leonard S. sales rep and Edna M. Aldred clerk; b Nott 6.10.44
teacher: Birm 1967–71, Mitcham 1971–73; exec off. MAFF Lond from 1973

STRONACH Andrew Fraser ***BSc(eng) 1968**
s of Andrew S. brewer and Elizabeth I. Webster; b Elgin 18.8.46
res stud. Aberd 1968–69; lect Aberd from 1969
m Aber 20.7.68 Marilyn J. L. Dunn MA 1965 *qv*

STRONACH Charles George ***MA 1965 Dip Ed 1966**

STRONACH Ian Macdonald ***MA 1967**
s of Peter D. S. bank acct and Louie Moir teacher; b Aber 16.3.45
MEd(Brist) 1978
teacher: Huntly 1968–69, Zambia 1969–72, Peterhead 1972–74, Zambia 1974–77; educ res Glasg from 1978
m Banff 21.6.69 Kathleen M. Falconer nurse d of Stanley F. Banff

STRONACH Patrick Moir ***BSc(eng) 1966**
s of Peter D. S. bank acct and Louie E. Moir teacher; b Aber 7.10.43
CEng MICE 1973
Aber: civ eng 1966–77, resid eng 1977–78, sen eng from 1978
m Aber 4.3.67 Margaret J. Forbes nurse d of Alexander F. Fordoun

STRONG Paul James Henry **BSc(agr) 1970**
s of Kenneth S. BSc(R'dg) farm. and Phyllis Drane; b Norfolk 16.1.47

Dip Milk Prod./Processing (Seale Hayne agr coll) 1971
farm man. consult. (consultancy comp mainly in undev countries) from 1971
m Winchester 8.7.72 Helena R. Franks farm secy d of Colin B. F. Basingstoke

STROUD Marjory **BSc 1968**
d Edin 6.8.75

STRUDWICK Christine Mary **MA 1968**
d of Leon A. S. civ serv and Ethel M. Stephenson teacher; b Richmond Yorks 3.4.48
teacher: Crawley 1969–73, Barrhead from 1973

STRUDWICK Michael John ***BSc 1969**
s of Leon A. S. civ serv and Ethel M. Stephenson teacher; b Richmond Yorks 3.4.48
teacher chem Harlaw acad Aber from 1970
m Aber 4.8.73 Alison J. Troup occup therap d of George T. Perth

STRUTHERS Eileen ***MA 1966**
m Ferguson

STRZALKOWSKA Wanda Christina **MB ChB 1969**

STUART Alison **MA 1966**
d of William S. farm. and Agnes F. Oliphant secy; b Ellon 20.7.45
secy to dir *Encounter* mag Lond 1967–68; information off., sen information off. with consumers' assoc publ of *Which?* Lond 1968–72; teacher Lond from 1973
m Lond 17.9.71 Colin P. Loxley comp dir/wine importer s of John L. L. Ashtead

STUART Ann Grant **MA 1970**
d of John S. mech eng REME and Marion N. G. Paterson MA(Edin) teacher; b Grantown-on-Spey 6.3.50
Dip Soc Ad(Edin) 1973
VSO teacher mod lang/dep head Sagamu Nigeria 1970–72; Orangeville Canada: ch care worker 1973–74, teacher arts/crafts from 1974

STUART Brian Sansom **MB ChB 1969**

STUART Charles Alexander ***BSc 1967**

STUART Charles James **MA 1969**
s of Charles S. prod. man. woollen mill and Barbara E. Angus; b Keith 17.1.49
teacher asst prin guid Speyside h s Aberlour from 1970
m Aberchirder 13.10.73 Lorna A. Stephen d of George S. Aberchirder

STUART Christina Carol **MA 1970**

STUART Irene Margaret **MA 1966 Dip Ed 1968**
d of John M. S. tel eng and Gladys W. Johnston; b Insch 13.9.43
MA(TEFL)(Cairo) 1971
teacher Engl Amer univ Cairo 1969–72; prin guid Inverurie acad from 1972
m Aber 21.1.63 Khalil E. A. Khalil PhD 1965 *qv*

STUART James Campbell **BSc(agr) 1969**
s of James D. S. MRCVS(Edin) vet surg and Marjorie E. Campbell; b Inv 14.9.46
MSc(N'cle) 1971
farm. Conon Bridge from 1971
m Leeds 12.1.74 Mary M. Travers MRCVS(Edin) d of Thomas T. Leeds

STUART John Thomson   MA 1965
s of John T. S. soldier, civ serv, clerk and Elen H. Petrie; b Aber 4.12.28
chaplain: Highland Brig depot Aber 1965–66; 1st batt Scots Guards Malaya 1966–67, Scots Guards Edin, Pirbright 1967–69, Scot. Infantry depot Aber 1969–71, St Andrew's ch Aldershot 1971–74, St Andrew's ch Tidworth 1974–76, Scot. Infantry depot Glencorse 1976–78; minister Bedrule, Denholm and Minto from 1978
m(1) 1.5.57 Audrey Thomson nurse d of James E. D. T. Aber; wife d 17.6.73
(2) 23.3.78 Elsie M. Ogilvie catering off. d of John W. O. Pluscarden

STUART Judith Helen   MA 1967
d of Alexander G. S. pharm and Dolly C. Scott; b Aber 21.11.46
Aber: computer oper 1968–69, cler asst 1970–71
m Aber 25.6.69 Robert Donald LLB 1968 qv

STUART Margaret Mary   MA 1968
d of John S. and Marion Paterson MA(Edin) teacher; b Grantown-on-Spey 3.5.47
Dip Sec St(Strath)
secy WCC Geneva 1969–70; secy translator: Battelle inst Geneva 1971, UNESCO Paris from 1971

STUART Marjory Grace   MA 1960
d of George S. mech eng and Marjory A. D. Grant; b Aber 8.4.38
teacher Muirfield p s Aber 1962–64
m Aber 2.4.64 John A. Morgan BSc 1959 qv

STUART Michael John   *BSc 1969
s of John A. S. master painter and Gladys M. Penny PO clerk; b Fraserburgh 24.11.46
teacher: geog Fraserburgh 1970–71, Glasg 1971–72; prin geog Irvine from 1972
m Aber 5.7.71 Danièle M. Bathier teacher d of Marcel U. B. Clermont-Ferrand France

STUART Norman   BSc 1970 Dip Ed 1971
s of Hugh H. C. S. process worker and Jessie A. Copland; b Banff 10.12.46
teacher maths Queen Anne h s Dunfermline 1971–73, asst prin maths from 1974
m Renfrew 30.6.73 Rosaleen M. Miller soc worker d of William M. MA(Glas) Renfrew

STUART Roderick   *MA 1970

STUART Sheila Mary Amelia   MA 1967

STUART Thelma Lorraine   MA 1969
m Dickie

STUART Valerie Madeleine Garrick   MA 1966
d of Thomas S. master joiner and Eliza Stuart teacher; b Tomintoul 2.4.46
teacher Fr: Alford acad 1967–70, Invergordon acad 1970–72
m Tombae Glenlivet 9.10.71 John A. Hill elect. s of Joseph H. Cullen

STURDEE Anthony Peter   *BSc 1968
s of E. P. L. S. farm., acct and Pilar C. Fuller arch. asst; b Gerrards Cross 3.3.45
PhD(Leeds) 1972
res asst anat Leeds 1969–72; lect developmental biol Wolverhampton poly 1972–75; sen lect cell biol Coventry poly from 1975
m Leeds 10.7.70 Sarah R. Rushton MA 1970 qv

STURDY Robin Geoffrey   MSc 1966
BA(Cantab)

STURM Maxwell Graeme de L'Isle   BSc 1961
s of Maxwell G. de L. S. MB ChB 1927 qv; b Darlington 6.12.35
MSc(Lond) 1969 PhD(Univ of West Indies) 1975
teacher LCC 1962–64; res off. fisheries dept of game and fisheries min of nat resources Zambia 1965–68; res dem univ of WI Trinidad 1970–75; lect zool Bayevo univ Kano Nigeria from 1977

STURROCK Isabel Anne   MA 1962
m Oxley

STURROCK Jane Traquair   *MA 1968
d of Alexander P. S. MA(St And) journalist and Chrissie M. Traquair MA(St And) secy; b Glasg 13.4.46
staff man. Marks & Spencer Doncaster, Huddersfield 1968–69; secy univ of Edin 1969–74; secy ICFC Edin from 1974
m Edin 1.4.72 Michael Williamson marketing man. s of Henry R. W. ARIBA(Edin) Musselburgh

SUBIOTTO Arrigo Victor   PhD 1969
MA(Lond)

SUDWEEKS Anthony William   *MA 1961

SUE-A-QUAN Cerise Delphinium   *BSc 1970
d of Kelvin S-A-Q and Edna E. Lee; b 8.12.47
m Aber 30.6.70 Jerry Sue-Chue-Lam MB ChB 1971 postgrad stud. surg s of Frank S-C-L. Toronto

SUMMERS Andrew   MA 1957
s of Andrew S. fisherman and Elsie Bruce; b Peterhead 13.6.35
teacher Sauchie 1961–64; dep head Tullibody 1964–65; head Maryculter 1965–68; lect Dun from 1968
m Peterhead 1961 Helen M. Stephen des tweed mill d of William M. S. Peterhead

SUMMERS Patricia   *BSc 1960 MSc 1961
d of Peter R. S. fishing skipper and Maggie Goodbrand; b Fraserburgh 8.8.38
biochem: Rowett inst Aber 1961–62, city hosp Aber 1962–64; teacher chem Fraserburgh acad from 1973
m Aber 22.12.61 Oddstein Uri MB ChB 1964 qv; marr diss 1975

SUMMERS Ronald Watson   *BSc 1970 PhD 1974
s of Ronald S. MB ChB(St And) med pract and Doris Bulloch; b Dun 26.6.47
post doct res asst univ of Cape Town S Af 1974–77; employed by ODM to work for Grasslands Trial Unit Falkland Islands
m Aber 16.5.74 Judith A. Dunnet secy d of George M. D. BSc 1949 qv

SURAPHIBUL Kannica   PhD 1968
BSc(B'kok)

SURGEONER James Hamilton   LLB 1967

SUTHERLAND Aileen Mackenzie   *MA 1963
d of Alexander W. S. gen merch and Elizabeth M. McKenzie nurse; b Mulben 10.3.42
careers off. educ auth Edin 1964–66; town plan. asst: Stirling 1966–67, N'cle 1967–70; careers off. Aberd from 1970

SUTHERLAND Ailsa Margaret   MB ChB 1969
d of James H. S. elect. eng/farm. and Eleanor E.

Walton; b Frimley 9.5.43
Aber: h o 1969–70, g p trainee 1970–71, psychiat regist
1971–73, part-time from 1974
m Aber 9.5.64 Colin Milton MA 1965 *qv*

SUTHERLAND Alexander Dermot   MA 1967

**SUTHERLAND Anne Elizabeth   *MA 1959
                                          *MEd 1963**

SUTHERLAND Astrid Elizabeth   MA 1969

SUTHERLAND Barbara Elizabeth   MA 1960 *1962
    d of William S. farm. and Barbara M. Taylor; b
Lancaster 12.11.38
teacher geog: Grove acad Dun 1963–66, Liberton s s
Edin 1966–68
m Aber –.7.66 Norman G. Robb BSc(H-W) electronics
eng/sen computer progr s of William C. R. MA(Glas)
Hawick

SUTHERLAND Catherine Ann   *MA 1970
    d of George S. MA(Edin) miss., C of S min and Margot
Davidson MA(St And) teacher; b Edin 22.12.47
teacher Engl: Smithycroft s s Glasg 1971–73, Stirling
1973–75, Hermitage acad Helensburgh from 1976
m Alexander T. M. Lumsden BSc(eng) 1970 *qv*

SUTHERLAND Colin Robert   BSc(eng) 1963
    s of Robert S. MA 1922 *qv*; b Aber 1.4.42
CEng MICE 1969
eng Sir Robert McAlpine & Sons UK, Bahamas from
1963
m Scunthorpe 12.8.67 Margery Foster lect in art, teacher
d of Lawrence F. Scunthorpe

SUTHERLAND David George   *MA 1962
    s of David A. P. S. eng, s janitor and Flora George shop
asst; b Aber 28.9.40
DPhil(Oxon) 1966
Cern fell. Geneva 1966–67; lect phys Glas from 1967

**SUTHERLAND David Ivor Macpherson   *MA 1960
                                          *MEd 1962**
    s of David S. MA 1932 *qv*; b Wick 22.1.38
teacher mod lang AGS 1962–66; lect: educ Stranmillis
coll Belf 1966–69, psych Craigie coll Ayr 1969–72; asst
dir of educ Sutherland c c 1972–75; div educ off. Inv
1975–79; dep dir of educ Highland reg c from 1979
m Aber 16.7.64 Janet H. Webster teacher d of Alexander
S. W. Aber

SUTHERLAND Denis Ian   MA 1961 BD 1963
    s of James S. master grocer and Jessie K. Balfour;
b Aber 5.1.39
C of S min: asst Aber 1963–64, evangelist to Scotland's
travelling families Perth 1964–70; co-ordinator of socio-
educ proj to travelling families Perth 1970–73; parish
min Glasg from 1973
m Aber 1.9.62 Norma M. Carroll nurse, health visitor
d of Charles C. Aber

SUTHERLAND Donald Fraser   *MA 1965

SUTHERLAND Gerald Murray   BSc(eng) 1968
    s of William G. M. S. road haulage contr and Eleanor
M. Milne secy; b Forres 2.8.47
MICE 1978
eng asst, asst eng Banff c c 1968–75; eng Grampian reg c
Elgin 1975–79; sub ag Morrison constr Elgin from 1979
m Banff 14.8.70 Catherine H. Smith clerkess d of James
A. M. S. Banff

SUTHERLAND Iain Alexander   MB ChB 1967

SUTHERLAND Ian Raffan   BSc 1968
    s of James R. S. banker, gen merch and Mary
Mitchell leg. secy, gen merch; b Fraserburgh 18.9.45
applications eng in refrig (indust) Dartford 1968–72;
acct Aber from 1972
m Fraserburgh 12.8.67 Sylvia C. Park teacher d of John
S. P. Fraserburgh

SUTHERLAND Inga Maxine   MA 1961
    d of Andrew S. postman and Ivy E. E. Sutherland
sub-postmistress; b Orkney 28.9.40
teacher: Kirkwall g s 1962–63, Bell-Baxter h s Cupar
1963–65, supply Orkney from 1965
m Orkney 10.3.66 George S. G. Rosie coxswain/marine
oper s of James R. S. Ronaldsay

SUTHERLAND Jane Mitchell   MA 1958
    d of William J. S. banker and Jane H. Mitchell;
b Colombo Ceylon 15.12.37
edit. asst AEI Lond 1959–61
m Lond 5.3.61 Alexander Hamilton BA(Cantab) civ eng
s of John H. Bolton

SUTHERLAND Joan More   *BSc(agr) 1967
    d of John S. farm. and Alice A. Bremner; b Latheron
MSc(Carleton univ Ottawa) 1976
plant path. agr res stat Tanzania 1967–69; res asst:
Carleton univ 1971–76, biol sc Dund 1976–79, fell. from
1979; PhD stud. from 1976

SUTHERLAND John Graham Martin   BSc(eng) 1960
    s of John G. G. M. S. man. iron foundry and Elizabeth
S. S. Forbes cashier; b Aber 1938
CEng 1966 MICE 1966 MIMunE 1969 MIHE 1970
eng Sir Robert McAlpine & Sons Port Talbot, Gloucester,
Lond 1960–62; civ eng consult. Flint & Neill Lond,
Cambridge 1962–64; asst eng Aber c c 1964–66; prin
asst eng, group leader (roads) Aber 1966–76; sen civ eng
Sir Frederick Snow & Ptnrs Scot. 1977; asst proj dir
Arab Union Contr Co Libya, Syria, Egypt 1978
m Aber 30.6.67 Kathleen A. T. Ellington MA 1966 *qv*

SUTHERLAND John Matheson   MA 1961
    s of Robert S. boat bldr/hirer and Mary A. Matheson
teacher; b Portree 23.9.30
teacher sc Old Aber s s 1962–66; dep head Cornhill p s
Aber 1966–75; head Hanover St p s Aber from 1975
m Aber 15.9.61 Jean MacDonald cler asst d of James
MacD. Aber

SUTHERLAND John William   MA 1970

SUTHERLAND Kathleen Mitchell   MA 1960
    d of James R. S. banker, gen merch and Mary
Mitchell leg. secy; b Fraserburgh 13.9.39
man. gen merch bus./sub p o Rathen from 1961

SUTHERLAND Keith Farquhar   *MA 1970 *MEd 1976

**SUTHERLAND Laurence Anderson   *BSc(eng) 1962
                                          MSc 1963**
    s of John D. S. farm. and Eliza I. Williamson MA
1925 *qv*; b Orkney 8.1.41
res asst Aberd 1963–66; scient off. nat eng lab E Kilbride
1966–69; lect Napier coll of sc/tech Edin from 1969
m Aber 1965 Angela M. Tinsley teacher d of Joseph T.
BSc(R'dg) Aber

SUTHERLAND Mackenzie Stewart   MB ChB 1962
                                                    Dip Psychother 1971
    b Carluke 31.3.33
MRCPsych 1972

SUTHERLAND Margaret Shepherd   MA 1968
                                                    Dip Ed 1969
    d of William J. S. elect. and Mary A. Macleod;
b Brora 7.5.47
teacher: Bathgate 1969-71, Bournemouth from 1971
m Glasg 22.7.71 Hugh F. Walding PhD 1968 qv

SUTHERLAND Marian Will   MA 1965
    d of James R. S. banker, gen merch and Mary
Mitchell leg. secy; b Fraserburgh 1.3.43
teacher Fr/Ger Glasg 1966-67; lib asst Aber from 1967
m Aber 23.3.73 Alastair C. Beaton journalist s of Robert
A. B. Stonehaven

SUTHERLAND Mary Margaret   MB ChB 1960
    d of John S. audit acct and Annie F. Mackay RGN;
b Aber 30.9.36
DPM(Lond) 1972 MRCPsych(Lond) 1973
h o Lerwick, Aber 1961-62; regist med Peel hosp
Galashiels 1962-64, Northallerton hosp 1964-66; regist
geriat N'cle gen hosp 1966-70; regist royal Cornhill hosp
Aber 1970-75; consult psychiat Dingleton hosp 1975-76,
Bilbohall hosp Elgin from 1976
m Aber 22.8.64 Alexander I. Simpson MB BS(Durh) s of
Alexander J. S. Durh

SUTHERLAND Michael Alexander Owen   MA 1966
    s of Donald A. S. bus. man., hotelier, confectioner and
M. Jean Hackett; b Wick 31.8.42
Dip Bus. Man.(Manc) 1967
Metal Box Co: trainee, comm asst, comm man. from
1971; resid Wrexham
m Lond 27.11.67 Sally Kirkwood secy/pa d of John H. K.
Vict Aust

SUTHERLAND Nan Elizabeth   MA 1959
    m Martin

SUTHERLAND Ray Duncan   *MA 1969
    d of William G. S. master baker and Margaret E. Rae;
b Aber 17.9.46
Dip Ed(Dund) 1971 LLB(Dund) 1974
law app Dun 1974-76; solic Dun 1976-77, Glasg from
1977
m Aber 28.12.70 Stanley L. Mann MB ChB(St And)
radiol s of Allan S. M. Arbroath

SUTHERLAND Robert   *BSc 1969
    s of Robert S. factory supt and Hilda Whyte; b
Peterhead 15.11.46
teacher Ayr acad 1970-73; prin teacher Prestwick acad
from 1973

SUTHERLAND Sandra Mackenzie   MB ChB 1962
    m Dymock

SUTHERLAND Stanley   BSc 1961
    s of James Esson shipyard painter and Selina
Sutherland glove stitcher; b Aber 7.5.22
Master Mariner (foreign going) certif(Aber) 1956
lect navigation Aber 1962-64; teacher phys/maths/sc
Aber from 1964
m Aber 9.2.43 Mary B. Styles d of Herbert S. Aber

SUTHERLAND Stewart Ross   *MA 1963
    s of George A. C. S. comm trav and Ethel Masson;
b Aber 25.2.41

BA(Cantab) 1965 MA(Cantab) 1969
asst lect phil UCNW 1965-68; lect phil Stir 1968-72,
sen lect 1972-76, reader 1976-77; visiting fell. humanities
res centre ANU Canberra 1974; Gillespie visiting prof
relig coll of Wooster Ohio USA 1975; prof hist and phil
of religion King's coll univ of Lond from 1977
m Aber 1.8.64 Sheena Robertson MB ChB 1963 qv

SUTHERLAND Susan Mary   BSc 1960
    d of George S. excise off. and Catherine Rainbird;
b Edin 2.5.39
teacher: maths Edin 1961-63, jun s Derby 1963-64,
Beverley 1964-66
m Forres 7.9.63 Anthony C. Stewart BVM&S(Edin) vet
surg s of Henry G. S. MRCVS(Glas) Binfield

SUTHERLAND Thelma Ann   MA 1967

SUTHERLAND William John   MA 1970

SUTHERLAND William Ross   MA 1963
    teacher: Banffsh 1964-67, N Province Zambia 1967-
69; lect correspondence educ Zambia 1969-73; teacher
S Aust from 1974
m Aber 14.7.61 Margaret J. Milne MA 1959 qv

SUTHERS Susan   *MA 1969 Dip Ed 1970
    d of George A. S. bank clerk and Doris Hargreaves;
b Bury 10.5.47
teacher Engl: Bo'ness 1970-72, Edin 1972-74, Lond from
1974
m Lond 10.4.76 Vivian W. Willson BSc(Bolton) PO tel
eng s of William H. J. W. Woking

SUTTIE Alastair Mackintosh   MB ChB 1961
    s of John S. MRCVS(Edin) vet surg and Annie S.
Miller MA(Edin) teacher; b Enniskillen NI 5.4.38
DObstRCOG 1963 MRCGP 1975
h o: Woodend hosp, Ross clin Aber, Raigmore hosp
Inv 1961-63; g p: locums Scot., Canada 1963-64, Hawick
from 1964
m Aber 14.4.65 Gillian M. Sangster MB ChB 1962 qv

SUTTIE Ian Simpson   *BSc 1964 Dip Ed 1965
    s of John S. MRCVS(Edin) vet surg and Annie S.
Miller MA(Edin) teacher; b Forres 13.2.42
teacher biol Elgin acad 1965-68, prin biol from 1968
m Aber 31.7.70 Christina I. Souter MA 1961 qv

SUTTIE James McDonald   BSc(agr) 1956 MSc 1970
    s of James M. S. gardener and Jane L. Nicoll; b
Kirkmichael Perthsh 13.6.34
Dip Agr(Cantab) 1957 DTA(Trinidad) 1958
agr off. Kenya 1958-69; pasture spec FAO of UN India
1970-71, Madagascar 1971-77, Pakiston Punjab from
1977
m Nyeri Kenya 10.2.61 Elizabeth R. Andrews MA 1955
qv

SUTTLE Neville Frank   PhD 1964
    BSc(R'dg)

SUTTON Alastair Morris   LLB 1966
    s of Ernest E. M. S. trans man. and Nancy Venn;
b Bristol 6.1.45
LLM(Lond) 1967 Dip Air and Space Law(Lond) 1967
barrister-at-law(Middle Temple) 1971
lect in laws Lond/tut. Lond inst of world affairs 1967-73;
prin admin/dir gen for external relations comm of
Europ communities Brussels from 1973
m Aber 2.9.68 Eileen Taylor BSc 1966 qv

SUTTON Anthony Hubert   PhD 1964
ARIC

SVEINBJORNSSON Sveinn   *BSc 1970
s of Sviensson S. capt/shipowner and Laufey Gud-
laugsdottir; b Neskaupstadur Iceland 5.3.45
sen scient off. fisheries biol pelagic species Reykjavik
from 1970
m Reykjavik 29.12.74 Margret Samuelsdottir clerk
criminal court Reykjavik d of Samuel Kristjansson
Reykjavik

SVENDSEN Johan Harald
see Seland

SVOBODA Andrew Pavel   MA 1966

SWAN Thomas Clarke   *MA 1969

SWANSON Anne Louise   MA 1957
d of Alexander J. S. head postmaster and Georgina W.
Sutherland civ serv; b Annan 30.5.37
teacher Engl Thurso h s 1958–60; NY: teacher Brick
presb ch s 1960–61, St Hilda's/St Hugh's s 1961; Aber:
teacher Engl Northfield s s 1961–63, remed educ
Linksfield acad from 1972
m Aber 30.7.60 Alan Main MA 1957 *qv*

SWANSON James Macaulay   BSc(agr) 1963

SWANSON Patricia Anne   BSc 1969
d of Thomas G. S. accounts man. and Edith M. Gray
secy; b Aber 11.2.47
teacher sc Harrison coll Barbados WI 1969–71; tech i/c
blood transfusion dept N Devon RI from 1972
m Aber 1.2.69 Robert M. Brown MB ChB 1969 *qv*

SWANSON Ruth Agnes   MA 1966
m Walker

SWIFT Margaret Jeanne   BEd 1970
d of Maurice S. eng and Margaret Jaques artist; b
Chorlton-cum-Hardy Manc 7.1.24
teacher Harlaw acad from 1971
m Aber 8.6.46 Ronald M. Dick plumber/insp house
drainage s of Alexander D. Aber

SYME David Couper   MA 1963
s of Colin R. S. civ serv and Lucy H. Richmond secy,
bank clerkess; b Perthsh 22.6.42
Dip Russian Lang(Strath) 1968
teacher: mod lang Bankhead acad, Inverurie acad 1966–
69, TEFL Schwerte W Ger 1969–71, mod lang Summerhill
acad 1971–73; instr/off. RAEC Guards depot Pirbright
from 1973
m Halstead 7.7.69 Patricia M. Wood nurse d of Nowell
W. W. Halstead

SYMON Doreen   MA 1956
m Grieve

SYMON Jennifer   *MA 1968
d of Lindsay J. S. MB ChB 1944 *qv*; b Aber 31.5.46
teacher: inf Gt Dunmow 1969–71, spec class juniors
Montrose 1971–72
m Lossiemouth 16.8.69 Robert W. Y. Martin MB BChir
(Cantab) g p s of Thomas Y. M. Tottington

SYMON John Charles   *MA 1957
s of Charles S. traffic supt Aber corp and May Devlin
typist; b Aber 19.1.30
LTh(Greg) 1953

teacher hist Blairs coll Aber 1957–61; lect phil/theol
St Andrew's coll Melrose 1961–72; parish priest Aber
1972–74; teacher r e Edin 1974–77; parish priest Thurso
from 1977

SYMON Robert John Charles   MA 1960 LLB 1965

SYMON Sheena Margaret   *MA 1958
m Crozier

SYMONS Gordon Leonard   *MA 1966

SYNGE Elizabeth   *BSc 1966
d of Richard L. M. S. BA(Cantab) res biochem and
Ann Stephen MB B Chir(Cantab) doctor, teacher; b St
Albans 3.5.44
PhD(ANU Canberra) 1970
Aust nat univ Canberra: res schol 1966–70, res asst
1970–71; Glas part-time: dem 1972–74, res asst from
1974
m Stonehaven 21.9.66 Ben Smith MA 1966 *qv*

SYNGE Jane   *MA 1964
d of Richard L. M. S. MA(Cantab) res biochem and
Ann Stephen BA(Cantab) doctor, teacher; b Leeds 11.4.43
PhD(LSE) 1971
asst prof sociol: univ of Illinois Urbana USA 1970–72,
McM univ Hamilton Ontario from 1972
m Philadelphia 1.1.70 Bunli Yang BA(Harv) trans analyst
s of T. Yang MA(Harv) Villanova Penn

SYPULA Pauline Zofia   MA 1969
m Lane

TAGGART William John   BSc(agr) 1956
s of John A. T. granite merch and Annie W. Ross;
b Aber 9.9.34
PhD(Edin) 1972
farm. Kincardine 1956–61; agr advis NOSCA Aber 1961–
65; res fell. agr dept Edin 1965–67; lect agr Edin 1967–69;
agr bus. consult. Cumberland 1969–74; agr advis to
Clydesdale Bank Glasg from 1974
m Aber 2.7.58 Ann C. Falconer teacher d of James D. F.
Aber

TAILOR Thakorbhai Jinabha   *BSc 1963

TAIT Andrew   MA 1963
s of Andrew D. T. fisherman and Maria L. McKenzie;
b Fraserburgh 3.4.41
teacher AGS 1964–69; dep head Culter p s 1969–71;
head: Crimond p s 1971–73, Hillocks p s Bucksburn
1973–76, Mill O' Forest p s Stonehaven from 1976
m Fraserburgh 10.8.63 Rosemary Green teacher d of
Joseph G. Fraserburgh

TAIT Brian Copeland   MA 1967

TAIT Catherine Joyce   MA 1967
d of John O. T. wholesale fruit/potato merch and
Muriel Chubb; b Perth 7.9.46
teacher: Uddingston 1968–70, Whitburn 1970–72, asst
prin Fr from 1972

TAIT Douglas John   BSc(eng) 1962

TAIT Elspeth Muriel   MA 1958

TAIT George Henry   *BSc 1958
s of Henry J. T. shipmaster and Margaret J. Barron;
b Aber 27.12.36
PhD(Lond) 1961

St Mary's hosp med s Lond: res fell. 1961–64, asst lect 1964–65, lect 1965–70, sen lect from 1970
m Edin 6.9.62 Deirdre E. Ross med lab tech

TAIT Helen Stewart   MA 1964
d of Walter S. C. T. loco eng and Harriet Mackie; b Aber 3.4.42
teacher: p s AGS 1967–68, Engl Hazlehead acad Aber 1974, Summerhill acad Aber from 1975
m Aber 28.10.61 Henry Barber eng/chief tech nat phil dept Aberd s of John B. Aber

TAIT Ian Sim   MA 1965
s of Alexander D. T. store man. and Jean N. Sim; b Fraserburgh 15.10.42
BA 1979
teacher: asst prin maths Fraserburgh acad 1966–74; lect computer educ Aber coll of educ from 1974

TAIT John   *BSc 1960
s of Andrew T. farm. and Jemima A. J. Dalziel nurse; b Aith Shetland 20.12.38
teacher: prin maths Lerwick s s 1961–66; comp dir Whalsay Shetland from 1966
m Whalsay 20.12.63 Charlotte H. Sutherland dom worker d of Hugh S. Whalsay

TAIT John Mervyn   *BSc 1969 PhD 1973
s of John T. bus driver and Enid Annal hotelier; b Kirkwall 30.3.47
electron microscopist Macaulay inst for soil res Aber from 1972
m Kirkwall 3.4.70 Heather A. Tullock midwifery sister d of Robert T. T. Kirkwall

TAIT Katherine McAdie   BEd 1968
d of John T.; b Wick 13.5.44
teacher Wick h s 1968–71; grad asst Stir 1971–77, asst dir p e Stir from 1977

TAIT Peter John Thomas   *BSc 1956 PhD 1959
s of John T. fisherman and Elizabeth Tulloch; b Lerwick 22.10.34
Ramsey mem fell. Aberd 1959–61; sen lect chem UMIST Manc from 1961
m Carlisle 19.8.61 Winifred Proudfoot MB ChB 1959 qv

TALLACH Cameron   MB ChB 1968
s of James A. T. min of relig and Elizabeth D. Fraser shopkeeper; b Kames 5.12.43
h o Aber gen hosps 1968–69; temp lect physiol Aberd 1969–70; sen h o surg Aber gen hosps 1970–72; m o Dun publ health serv 1972–74; med missionary Taipei Taiwan 1974–77, Taichung Taiwan from 1977
m Aber 27.12.68 Ishbel M. Maclean MB ChB 1969 qv

TALLACH James Ross   MB ChB 1967

TAMBER Einar Rolf   MB ChB 1970
s of Ragnvald A. T. DSC admiral royal Norwegian navy and Nini M. Aas; b Edin 16.11.43
Norway: resid path. Norwegian radium hosp Oslo 1970; h o Lillehammer 1971; asst m o Skjervøy Troms 1972; lt (med br) royal Norwegian navy (ship's surg on frigate) Bergen 1972–73; cas off. Bergen 1973; m o Namdalseid from 1974
m Sandvika Norway 31.7.71 Daisy S. H. Wong MB ChB 1970 qv

TAMLYN Lynda Kay   MA 1969
d of Charles W. C. T. chain store man. and Olive E. Meecham; b Cardiff 8.7.48

Bristol: soc worker 1969–70, prin nurs s 1970–74, stud. Redland teacher trg coll 1974

TARBAT Lorna Mary   MA 1963
d of Henry T. civ serv and Violet Scrimgeour clerkess; b Aber 1942
teacher
m Aber –.7.65 Ian F. Hall lithographic artist s of John H. Edin
d Edin 7.2.74

TASIE Godwin Ohyemaechi Mgbechi   PhD 1969
BA(Nig)

TASKER Helen Anne   MA 1969
d of Norman H. T. elect. welder and Elizabeth H. Thomson shop asst; b Aber 24.11.47
teacher Engl: Powis acad Aber 1970–71, Dumbarton acad from 1971
m Aber 6.8.71 Bruno R. Dimambro civ serv s of Rossato D. Aber

TAUSJØ Johan Elling   MB ChB 1970
s of Johan T. M. T. MD(Oslo) surg and Aasta Mjaaland mus teacher; b Haugesund Norway 24.5.44
Spec in Oncology & Radiotherapy(Norway) 1980
h o Stavanger 1970–71; milit serv (lt, capt) Oslo 1971–72; regist radium hosp Oslo 1972–74; fell. oncology univ hosp Madison Wisc USA 1974–76; sen regist radium hosp Oslo from 1976
m Madison 10.8.69 Janet L. Ficken MA(Wisc) teacher d of Robert F. BA(Wisc) Wisconsin

TAVADIA Hosie Byram   MB ChB 1964
s of Byram C. T. stock exch broker and Gool S. Patel; b Canton China 24.2.37
DObstRCOG 1966 MRCPath 1971
grant from leukaemia res fund 1974–75
h o Raigmore hosp (RI Inv) 1964–65; sen h o Perth RI, Ayrsh gen hosp Irvine 1965–66; regist lab med southern gen hosp Glasg 1966–70; lect path. Glas hon sen regist path. Glasg RI from 1970; consult. histopathologist Forth Valley health board from 1975
m Aber 19.7.65 Catherine W. M. Ross teacher d of Menzies M. R. Invergordon

TAVADIA Phiroza   MB ChB 1961
d of Byram C. T. stock exch broker and Gool S. Patel; b Hong Kong 5.2.34
h o RACH, ARI 1961–62; Lond: sen h o Prince of Wales hosp 1962, h o Elizabeth Garrett Anderson hosp 1963–64; g p 1964–69; clin asst gyn Elizabeth Garrett Anderson hosp 1972–75; g p Hong Kong from 1975

TAVENDALE Bruce   *BSc 1960

TAWSE Euan William   *MA 1969

TAWSE Peter Alexander Lagrange   *BSc 1968
s of Peter C. T. council lab and Edith M. H. Walker MA 1929 qv; b Insch 14.1.46
res stud. Aberd 1968–71; Banff acad: teacher geog 1972–73, asst prin guid 1973–74; lect geog Trinity & All Saints' colleges Leeds from 1974
m Peel IOM 2.8.73 Bernadette M. McHugh MB ChB 1972 g p d of Hubert McH. Peel

TAYLOR Alan Murray   *BSc 1969
s of Henry G. T. MA(Edin) priv secy (lit) and Mary W. Hughson MA(Edin) teacher; b Lerwick 29.3.47
man. trainee Brit Ropes Doncaster 1969–71; pilot RAF flt/lt from 1972

m Conisbrough 30.9.72 Sheila Ross secy d of Samuel R. Southend

TAYLOR Alec Stuart BSc 1967

TAYLOR Alexander John BSc(agr) 1962
s of Alexander T. farm. and Elsie McKinnon; b Longside 13.7.40
agr advis NOSCA Perth from 1962
m Aber 27.8.66 Evelyn M. McBoyle MA 1963 *qv*

TAYLOR Alexander Kinnear BSc 1970

TAYLOR Alison Cursiter BSc 1958

TAYLOR Andrew Thomas *BSc 1965
s of Thomas M. T. MA 1920 *qv* and Helen M. Jardine MB ChB 1920 *qv*; b Aber 20.11.43
M Inst P 1969
instrum man. ICI Teesside from 1965
m Redcar Margaret S. Coyle secy d of Joseph H. C. Redcar

TAYLOR Anne Vaughan MA 1969

TAYLOR Annette Mollison MA 1964
d of George S. T. foreman maintenance eng and Annie M. Proctor tailor's cutter; b Forfar 8.1.43
teacher mod lang Montrose acad 1965–69; part-time lect Engl lang Angus tech coll Arbroath from 1976
m Montrose 23.7.66 James A. Thomson plan. eng, app instr, trg man., comp man. s of James A. T. Montrose

TAYLOR Arthur MA 1968

TAYLOR Catherine Margaret *MA 1970
adopted d of Henry W. T. millwright and his sister Margaret Taylor; b Aber 6.2.49
Aber: lib asst 1971–73, stud. lib RGIT 1973–74, trainee publ lib 1974–75; asst ref lib Aber city dist lib from 1975

TAYLOR Charles Cormack Greig *MA 1970
Dip Ed 1971

TAYLOR Christina Chirrey Smith MA 1957
m Macdonald

TAYLOR Christopher Martin *BSc 1968

TAYLOR Colin Ross MB ChB 1964
s of Colin F. T. MA 1932 *qv* and Edith I. Dargie MA 1930 *qv*; b Inv 7.12.40
DCH(Glas) 1966 ECFMG(USA) 1974 MD(Connecticut) 1977
h o Stracathro hosp, RACH 1964–65; sen h o paediat Stobhill hosp Glasg 1965–67; sen h o, regist Stobhill hosp Glasg 1967–70; assoc, sen assoc dir clin res Pfizer Inc Connecticut USA from 1970, also on med staff of Lawrence hosp New Lond Conn; holder of USA patents in electocardiography and drug treatment; co-chmn American coll of cardiology annual meeting 1978
m Buckie 11.7.64 Helen M. Calder artist d of James C. Buckie

TAYLOR David *MA 1965

TAYLOR David McKinlay *MA 1967 Dip Ed 1968
s of Colin F. T. MA 1932 *qv* and Edith I. Dargie MA 1930 *qv*; b Madderty 27.7.45
MEd(Glas) 1975
teacher hist Dunfermline h s 1968–71; prin hist Garnock acad Kilbirnie 1971–77, asst rector from 1977
m Glasg 1.8.68 Jacqueline M. Thomson MA 1967 *qv*

TAYLOR Denys Anthony Walton BSc(agr) 1970
s of Denys R. W. T. comp dir and Margaret M. Forster; b Durh 16.6.44
trainee man. Lond 1971–72; teacher: sc Lond 1972–73, biol Surrey from 1974

TAYLOR Dianna Louise MA 1965

TAYLOR Duncan McKay *BSc 1963

TAYLOR Edward Thomson *MA 1970
s of Edward E. T. civ serv and Jemima Yule; b Dun 22.5.35
export man. Peterhead 1970–71; lect coll of comm Aber from 1971
m Trier Ger 17.4.66 Ursula D. Spring teacher d of Arthur S. Eng(Bingen W Ger) Trier

TAYLOR Eileen BSc 1966
d of Nelson T. teacher and Vaunda E. Murray clerk; b Dunfermline 16.10.45
computer progr NCB Cannock 1966–68; software progr internat bus. machines Lond 1968–70
m Aber 7.9.68 Alastair M. Sutton LLB 1966 *qv*

TAYLOR Elizabeth Buchan *MA 1966
d of Alexander W. T. toolmaker and Elizabeth M. Buchan; b Fraserburgh 13.2.44
res asst educ tech Sur 1974–75; teacher Godalming coll Surrey from 1975
m Aber 17.10.64 Donald G. Cruickshank MA 1963 *qv*

TAYLOR Elizabeth Royda Sinclair MA 1970
d of William T. textile des and Elizabeth R. Hargreaves; b Edin 14.12.49
Secy/Ling Dip(City of Westminster coll) 1971
p a to publ Lond 1971–72; secy to arch. Edin 1972–73; secy to man. chem comp Hartlepool 1973–74; p a gen man. Mineral Grinding Co Hartlepool 1974–76
m Gifford 16.9.72 Nigel R. L. Hogg MA 1970 *qv*

TAYLOR Elizabeth Wilson BSc 1967 Dip Ed 1968
d of Alexander T. farm. and Agnes E. L. Maxwell farm.; b Elgin 18.12.46
teacher: sc Lossiemouth acad 1969–72, p e Laurencekirk 1972–74, p e and guid Laurencekirk 1975; purser/watchkeeper on STS *Robert Gordon* RGIT Aber from 1975

TAYLOR Ethel Ann MA 1966 Dip Ed 1967
d of Alexander T. supermarket owner and Ethel Garden off. man.; b Aber 30.12.45
teacher Bexley Heath 1967–72; home teacher Hillingdon 1974–75
m Aber 17.8.68 James A. M. Gilmour man. bldg soc s of James G. Helmsdale

TAYLOR George Abel MB ChB 1958
s of Alexander T. farm. and Margaret J. Abel receptionist; b Home Hill Queensland Aust 11.8.33
MRCGP 1972
h o Woodend gen hosp Aber, ARI 1958–59; sen h o Woodend hosp 1959; nat serv m o (army) Edin, Glasg, W Isles 1960–62; g p Aber from 1962
m Aber 3.10.64 Margaret E. Willox BSc 1959 *qv*

TAYLOR Graeme Charles Stuart LLB 1970

TAYLOR Iain James Gray *MA 1970
s of Charles G. S. T. MA 1921 *qv*; b Stornoway 8.3.48
Dip Town Reg Plan.(Glas) 1972
teacher: Victoria Dr s s Glasg 1973–74, Oban h s 1974–

75, Nicolson inst Stornoway 1975-76; lib asst Dingwall from 1976

TAYLOR James Mann   *BSc 1958

TAYLOR John   MB ChB 1958
s of John T. credit draper/salesman and Margaret S. Hamilton factory process worker; b Saltcoats 29.9.34
MRCGP 1972
h o Woodend hosp Aber, Kilmarnock I 1958-59; m o Colchester milit hosp 1959-61; h o Forth Park mat. hosp Kirkcaldy 1961-62; g p: Kilwinning 1962-64, Greenock from 1964
m Stevenston 15.7.59 Alison G. Cameron teacher d of William O. C. Stevenston

TAYLOR John   *MA 1967

TAYLOR John Murray   *MA 1964 Dip Ed 1965
s of John M. T. MA 1931 qv; b Aber 18.7.42
teacher classics: Dunfermline h s 1965-68, spec asst classics 1968-70; prin classics: Kirkcudbright acad 1970-74, Liberton h s Edin 1974-76, McLaren h s Callander 1976-78; asst dir of educ Central reg from 1978

TAYLOR John Randolph   PhD 1956
s of H. Kerr T. BD(Richmond Va USA) clergyman and Fanny B. Graham missionary; b Taichow Kiangsu Province China 12.1.29
AB(Davidson coll NC) 1951 BD(Richmond) 1954 DD(Oglethorpe Atlanta Ga) 1974
pastor: ch of the pilgrims Washington DC 1956-67, central presb ch Atlanta 1967-76, Myers Park presb ch Charlotte NC from 1976
m Shreveport La 1.6.51 Arline Johnson BA(Centenary coll) d of William M. J. Shreveport

TAYLOR Judith   MA 1969
m Salkeld

TAYLOR Kathleen Anne   BSc 1963

TAYLOR Keith   *MA 1961
s of James T. warehouseman and Leslie Clubb; b Aber 3.11.38
teacher Engl Mackie acad Stonehaven from 1962, year master from 1972

TAYLOR Lesley Jane   *BSc 1965
m Dickson

TAYLOR Linden Estelle   MA 1970

TAYLOR Margaret Watt   BSc(agr) 1956
d of Alexander W. T. farm. and Helen M. Crichton teacher; b Aber 4.4.35
asst exper off. Torry res stat Aber 1956-57; area organis Scot. Assoc of Young Farmers' Clubs 1957-60
m Aber 1.7.60 William Anderson farm. s of Ronald A. MB ChB 1923 qv

TAYLOR Mary Ross   *BSc 1970 PhD 1975
d of William S. T. pharm and Winifred M. Ross MB ChB(St And) med pract; b Aber 25.2.48
res asst dept chem Aberd 1970-72, res off. from 1972
m Aber 27.12.72 Robert E. Masson BSc 1969 qv

TAYLOR Maureen McGrotty   MA 1958
d of George G. T. civ serv and Frances H. S. McGrotty teacher; b Aber 29.1.38
teacher: Kirkhill p s Aber 1959-60, Hilton p s Inv 1961-63; pers secy Inv from 1973
m Aber 22.7.60 James C. Pringle BL 1957 qv

TAYLOR Michael James   LLB 1969

TAYLOR Michael William   BSc 1970 MB ChB 1975
s of James A. T. comp dir and Doris M. R. Webster; b Aber 19.7.48
MRCP 1977
Aber hosps, Grampian health board: h o, sen h o 1975-77, med regist from 1977
m Aber 28.4.75 Anne M. Skinner SRN d of Henry G. S. MB ChB 1938 qv

TAYLOR Patricia Mary   MA 1964
d of John G. T. head janitor Ellon acad and Mary C. Taylor; b Ellon 29.7.43
Marks & Spencer: head pers dept Leeds, Oxford, Liverpool 1964-68, selector/merchandiser head off. Lond 1969-71
m Ellon 1.5.71 Michael J. Turner man. dir internat merch bank in Hong Kong s of Alfred T. Taunton

TAYLOR Pauline   MA 1967
d of George M. T. munic off. and Amy Jackson; b Sheffield 5.2.46
Somerset: teacher Churchill 1968-71, Huish epis s 1971-73, dir first yr stud. 1973-74, head lower s from 1974
m Bridgwater 30.5.73 John A. S. Clarke schoolmaster s of Frank E. S. C. Fordingbridge

TAYLOR Peter Bruce   MB ChB 1967
s of George H. C. T. MB ChB 1940 qv; b N'cle-u-Tyne 30.6.44
FFARCS 1972
h o Raigmore hosp Inv 1967-68; stat m o RAF Leeming, Sharjah, Muharraq (Trucial Oman States), N Luffenham 1968-72; sen h o, clin asst anaest St Thomas hosp Lond 1972; spec anaest RAF hosp Halton 1972-74; regist anaest ARI from 1974
m Scalloway Shetland 8.8.69 Jamesina M. Robertson midwife d of Thomas J. R. Scalloway

TAYLOR Rachel Thomson Brown   MA 1965
d of Albert G. T. farm man. and Janet R. Morrison; b Carnwath 21.5.44
teacher Edin 1966-69
m Aber 16.5.69 William J. Barclay BSc 1966 qv

TAYLOR Robert Smart   *MA 1963

TAYLOR Robin Dempster   *BSc 1970 PhD 1974

TAYLOR Ross Jenkins   MB ChB 1966
s of Neil T. clergyman and Mary E. Livingstone MA (Edin) teacher; b Bearsden 16.4.43
DCH 1970 MRCGP 1972
m o/spec phys RAF sqn ldr 1966-73; lect g p Aberd 1973-78, sen lect from 1978
m Thurso 7.9.65 Armida M. Craig nurse d of Donald A. C. Thurso

TAYLOR Stewart McConachie   BSc 1958

TAYLOR Thomas Gilchrist   MB ChB 1965
s of Thomas G. T. supt works Inv c c and Catherine S. Cross; b Hamilton 18.2.40
MRCPath 1974
h o Woodend hosp Aber, RNI Inv 1966-67; sen h o: Inv, St George's hosp Lond 1967-68; regist: path. W Middx hosp 1968-70, haemat St Mary's hosp Lond 1970-71; sen regist haemat Kingston hosp Surrey, St Thomas' hosp Lond 1971-75; consult. blood transfus/ haemat Highland health board Inv from 1976
m Lond 27.12.67 Jean E. Cumming MB ChB 1965 qv

TAYLOR Timothy John   *BSc 1967

TAYLOR William Alexander   MA 1961
s of Colin F. T. MA 1932 *qv* and Edith I. Dargie MA
1930 *qv*; b Aber 22.5.39
BA(Lond) 1970 FSA Scot. 1973
teacher Summerhill acad Aber 1962–67, spec asst 1967–
73, asst prin 1973–76; prin hist Linksfield acad from 1976
m Aber 30.6.62 Margaret J. Allan teacher d of Robert
F. A. Aber

TAYLOR William Hay   *MA 1957 *MEd 1959
s of Walter F. T. cooper and Jessie R. Maclennan
nurse; b Findochty 30.8.35
MSc(Kansas) 1960
teacher Engl/hist Hyndland acad Glasg 1960–62; lect:
Falkirk tech coll Stirling 1962–64, St Luke's coll of educ
Exeter 1964–78, Exe from 1978
m Buckie 9.7.61 Odile G. M-L. Saunier L ès L(Caen)
teacher d of Bernard S. Etretat, Seine Maritime France

TAYLOR William James   *MA 1966 LLB 1969
s of Cecil T. clerk and Ellen Daubney clerkess; b Nairn
13.9.44
law app Aber, Edin 1969–71; Scot. bar Edin from 1971;
councillor Edin corp, Lothian reg council from 1973
m Aberlemno 31.7.71 Margaret U. Russell MA(St And)
admin d of A. Colin R. CMG MA(Oxon) Aberlemno

TAYLOR Willson Davidson   MB ChB 1969
s of Williamson A. T. newsag and Margaret M. J. T.
Davidson shop asst; b Aber 25.11.45
MRCP 1974
h o Woodend hosp Aber 1969–70; m o Queen's Own
Highlanders Edin, BAOR 1970–72; phys milit hosp
Catterick 1972–74; regist dermat N'cle-u-Tyne 1974–75;
sen spec dermat Brit milit hosp Hong Kong 1975–78; sen
regist dermat RVI N'cle-u-Tyne from 1978
m Aber 18.7.69 Lorna M. Sangster BSc 1966 *qv*

TELFER Alison Shaw   MA 1969
d of John H. T. man. dir spinning mill and Alice Shaw;
b Hawick 20.10.48
Dip Soc Work(Glas) 1975
asst ch's home Edzell Lodge Edin 1969–70; nurs asst
royal Edin hosp 1970–71; trainee soc worker Crichton
royal hosp Dumfries 1971–73; stud. Glas 1973–75

TELFER Stewart Bryson   MSc 1969
s of Thomas B. T. MBE chartered quantity surv and
Isabella M. Young; b Edin 15.11.45
BSc(Glas)
lect anim physiol & nutrit univ of Leeds from 1971
m Aber 3.4.72 Sheila Holmes MA 1970 *qv*

TELLING Geoffrey Morgan   MSc 1965
s of Robert E. T. master carpenter and Elsie G. Morgan;
b Newport 10.2.32
Grad RIC 1960 MChemA 1969 CChem FRIC 1970
res chem Unilever res Sharnbrook from 1964
m Alford 19.9.64 Margaret S. Baxter MA 1961 *qv*

TEMPLETON Alexander Allan   MB ChB 1969
s of Richard T. and Minnie Whitfield; b Glasg 28.6.46
MRCOG 1974
Aber: h o 1969–73, res fell. dept obst 1973–74, regist
obst/gyn from 1974

TEMPLETON Helen Margaret   MA 1969 Dip Ed 1970
d of George M. T. LDS(Glas) dent. surg and Margaret
J. Coutts; b Turriff 28.8.48
teacher Plaistow Lond 1970–71, Harringey Lond 1971–72,
Cheshunt 1972
m Turriff 12.8.72 Malcolm McMillan MA(St And) syst
analyst s of Donald McM. Northwood

TEMPLETON Margaret Barbour   MA 1958

TEMPLETON Richard   *BSc 1959 PhD 1963

TENGEY James Gbeze Kofi   MLitt 1969 PhD 1973
BA(Ghana)

TENNANT Charles   MA 1958 Dip Ed 1959
b Aber 23.11.36
teacher: Engl Northfield s s Aber 1959–64, Engl/commun
Aber coll of comm from 1964
m Aber 4.8.61 Loretta A. M. Pole

TENNANT John Milton   MA 1965
s of John T. MA 1937 *qv*; b Gartly 22.11.29
C of S min St Andrew's ch Lochgelly from 1968
m Dun 31.3.56 Jean McMillan teacher d of Martin P. E.
McM. Dun

TENNANT Maurice Henderson   MA 1968

TENNENT Justine Rose   MA 1969
d of William T. comp dir and Justine Clark mus; b
Glasg 18.10.48
Dip Pers Man. (RGIT) 1970
pers man.: Fine Fare superstore Aber 1970–72, Skean
Dhu hotel Dyce Airport 1973–76; lect Aber coll of
comm from 1976
m Aber 1.6.70 Donald K. McIntosh prod. group man.
s of Milton McI. Burton-u-Trent

TENNENT Ruth Margaret Goodwin   MA 1962
m Ndakala

TERRIS Rosalyn Elizabeth Marlin   MA 1967
d of John M. T. MBChB(Edin) med pract and Edith
H. D. Robertson secy, teacher; b Newtongrange 2.3.47
teacher Glasg: asst Woodside nurs s 1969–71, head Mile
End nurs s 1971–72, head Ayr St nurs s 1972–73, asst
Anderson St nurs s 1976–77, asst Kelso nurs s 1977–79
m(1) E Kilbride 3.8.68 Alfred C. Shedden MA 1966 *qv*;
marr diss
(2) Glasg 17.8.79 Douglas D. Faulds quantity surv

TETHER John Gordon Gurney   *BSc 1965
s of Cyril H. G. T. fin. journalist and Marjorie L.
Gurney; b Hatfield 28.7.42
geol surv off.: Moroto Soroti Uganda 1967–73, Lusaka
Zambia from 1974
m Aber 6.4.66 June E. Ballantyne teacher d of Samuel B.
MA(Glas) Aber

TEWNION Alexander   *BSc 1961 Dip Ed 1962
s of John T. master bldr and Alice G. Cran; b
Auchnagatt 8.9.20
teacher sc Dollar acad 1962–65, prin biol from 1965
m Aber 21.9.51 Agnes D. Richards BSc 1944 *qv*

THAIN Alexander Buchan   MB ChB 1959
s of James T. fisherman and Margaret Buchan; b
Peterhead 25.2.35
DObstRCOG 1966 CIH(Dund) 1974
h o, sen h o psychiat Montrose 1959–61; trainee g p/
hosp Inv 1961–63; regist dermat Inv 1963–64; sen h o
obst Stirling 1964; g p Invergordon 1964–65; regist med
Inv 1965–66; g p: Fort William 1966–71, Ardersier/Nairn
from 1971
m Aber 28.2.64 Helen K. Simpson RGN d of John S.
Inv

THAIN John Forrest   *BSc 1961 PhD 1964
s of John F. T. metal turner and Margaret A. M. Moir
envelope maker; b Aber 20.10.39
univ of E Ang Norwich: sen res assoc biophys 1964–67,
lect biol from 1967
m Hemel Hempstead 22.10.66 Vivien M. Pratt BSc(Brist)
teacher d of Charles E. P. Hemel Hempstead

THAIN Linda Mary   *MA 1969
d of Harold B. T. civ serv and Alice McKimmie secy,
admin asst; b Aber 5.7.47
teacher Aber: Engl Summerhill acad 1970–71, Powis acad
1971–72; part-time r e St Margaret's s for girls from 1973
m Wolviston 18.7.69 David Henderson police constable s
of Dawson H. Methlick

THAIN Rita Frances   MA 1970
d of Henry F. T. Aber c c worker (amenities dept) and
Rosetta L. Black; b Alford 8.3.49
teacher Engl Dumfries h s 1971–72; exec off. Customs &
Excise Aber 1972–74, Dun 1974–79
m Aber 9.8.73 Graham R. I. Milton MA 1974 careers
off. s of John S. M. Aber

THAIN William   MSc 1964 PhD 1967
ARGTC

THAKUR Vikram Chandra   MSc 1967
BSc MSc(Panj I)

THINN Anne Buyers   MA 1963
m Sinclair

THIRD David   *BSc 1963
s of Hugh B. T. eng and Annie A. Whyte; b Peterhead
23.6.41
MSc(S'ton) 1972 C Eng MIEE 1976
teacher chem Ellon acad 1964–66; lect phys RAF
Cosford Wolverhampton 1966–70; teacher Engl RAF
Upwood Huntingdon 1970–71; lect electronic eng RAF
coll Cranwell 1971–77; trg consult. M o D(TSS) from
1977
m Aber 7.8.64 Sandra E. T. Young teacher d of Adam
H. Y. Aber

THIRD George Thomas   BEd 1970 MEd 1972
s of Taylor M. T. hotelier/farm. and Annie Matthew;
b St Fergus 30.4.45
teacher Scotstown s Aber 1972–73, Balgownie s 1973–74;
educ psych: Aber 1974–76, city div Grampian reg from
1976
m Aber 2.8.68 Eileen M. Macleman teacher d of
Alexander MacL.

THIRD Marion Jessica   MA 1966

THIRD Robert Taylor   *MA 1966
s of Taylor M. T. farm./publican and Annie Matthew;
b St Fergus 27.7.43
publ man. Aberdeen Journals 1967–69; creative serv
superv *North Eastern Evening Gazette* Middlesbrough
1969–73, man. Keyhead hotel St Fergus 1973–78
m Aberfeldy 23.10.71 Beryl Chadwick MA 1968 qv

THOM Alan Mackay   *MA 1969 Dip Ed 1970

THOM Anne Shirley   *BSc 1964
d of Robert J. T. MA 1934 qv; b W Cults Aber 2.3.41
VSO Malawi 1964–65; ICL Lond 1965–70 and from 1973

THOM Florence Margaret   MA 1958

THOM Ian Alexander James   MA 1965

THOM James Alistair   MB ChB 1960
s of Neil T. bus. consult. and Susan H. Johnston;
b Cargill 21.2.36
DTM & H 1965 MSc(Lond) 1973 DIH 1973
h o Aber, Glasg 1960–62; m o RN med serv 1962–78;
sen lect environ mental health univ Sydney from 1978
m Aber 23.3.61 Agnes M. Smith polit ag d of Ogilvie
M. S. Whitestripes Bridge of Don

THOM Mary Beatrice (Marie)   *BSc 1966
d of George J. T. lorry driver and Mary Morrison;
b Aber 6.7.44
PhD(Hull) 1970 Dip Clin Psych(Brit Psych Soc) 1977
res off. Kingswood approved s 1968–71, Oxon 1971–77;
lect clin psych Royal Free hosp s of med Lond univ from
1977
m Aber 23.12.66 Derek W. Johnston MA 1966 qv

THOM Peter McGregor   MB ChB 1970
s of Alexander M. T. BSc(eng)(Glas) and Jane S.
Robertson; b India 30.6.43
h o Woodend hosp Aber, RACH 1970–71; vocational trg
scheme g p Wessex reg hosp board Bournemouth, Poole
1971–74
m Aber 17.7.71 Margaret E. Peebles teacher d of David
S. P. Aber

THOMANECK Jürgen Karl Albert   *MEd 1970
b Stettin 12.6.41
DPhil(Kiel) 1969
lect Ger dept Aberd from 1969
m Aber 3.8.64 Guinevere Ronald MA 1968 qv

THOMAS David Hugh   MSc 1967
BSc(Sheff)

THOMAS David Kashope   BSc 1967
s of David A. T. govt printer Sierra Leone and Kezia A.
Sawyerr; b Freetown Sierra Leone 5.2.36
M Assoc Clin Biochem 1968 Dip Clin Biochem(Sur) 1971
MSc(Sur) 1971 PhD(Ibad) 1978 MIBiol 1979
clin biochem govt of Sierra Leone, Connaught hosp
Freetown 1967–78; lect clin biochem univ Ife Nigeria
from 1978

THOMAS Elizabeth Mair Trefor   *MA 1967
m Hope

THOMAS Oswald Augustus   PhD 1966
BSc(agr)(Corn) MNS(Corn)

THOMAS Richard Howard   *MA 1968
s of Alan T. publ/bookseller/off. man. and Linda
Barnes secy; b Preston 24.9.44
asst man. mail order publ/retail gift store Preston 1968–
70; asst edit. dictionaires Collins publ Glasg 1970–74,
sen edit. 1974–78, publ man. from 1978
m Paisley 4.4.77 Mary S. Balderston BSc 1966 qv

THOMIS Helen Rosemary   *MA 1966
m Macdonald

THOMPSON David Squire   *BSc(eng) 1970
s of Squire T. garage prop. and Elsie Eden; b Sunderland 20.2.48
self-employed motor trader Sunderland from 1970
m New Silksworth 19.6.71 Karen M. Sanderson nurse d
of William G. S. Vancouver

THOMPSON Derek   MA 1959
s of Henry E. T. fruiterer/confectioner and Vida I.
Garthwaite; b Hartlepool 17.6.37
Dip PE(Leeds)

teacher p e Middlesbrough 1960–62; Hartlepool: head of p e 1962–73, head of year from 1973
m Hartlepool 1960 Sylvia M. Robson d of Frederick R. Hartlepool

THOMPSON Diana Mary   BSc 1970
d of George D. T. teacher and Sylvia F. Franklin teacher; b Sleaford 7.3.49
univ tech lung function ARI 1971–73; tech respir dept royal post grad med s Hammersmith Lond from 1974
m Dun 31.7.71 Ian R. Hunter MA 1972 supplies off. NHS Northwick Park hosp Harrow s of Jim H. Dun

THOMPSON Diana Ruth Brodie   *MA 1960

THOMPSON Ethel Dorothy Barbara   PhD 1965
d of Fred T. civ eng and Helen Bolton teacher; b Stretford 15.8.21
BA(Manc) 1946 Dip Soc St(Manc) 1947 AIMSW 1948 fell. Eugenic Soc 1967
sociologist: MRC obst med unit Aber 1951–65, MRC med soc unit from 1965; seconded MRC labs Gambia W Af 1961–64

THOMPSON Francis   BEd 1969

THOMPSON Joseph Kell   PhD 1968
s of William K. T. farm. and Elizabeth Milliken teacher; b Mallusk Co Antrim 2.7.29
BSc(Belf) 1950 BAgr(Belf) 1951 MS(Purdue univ Indiana) USA 1955
asst lect NOSCA Aber 1951–67; nutrit advis NOSCA/ recognised teacher Aberd from 1967
m Aber 22.7.60 Margaret R. Summers teacher d of John B. S. Cairnbulg

THOMPSON Margaret Mary   *MA 1958
d of Alexander G. T. tea planter, sub-postmaster and Lizzie E. J. Davidson sub-postmistress; b Fordyce 13.4.37
teacher maths: Banff 1959–61, part-time St Peter's s Buckie 1965–66, Buckie h s from 1966
m Fordyce 12.7.61 Alexander Wilson farm. s of John W. Buckie

THOMPSON Mary Belle Elizabeth   MA 1969
d of Gilbert T. T. tel eng and Elizabeth F. Bain; b Lerwick 21.1.47
teacher Engl Lasswade 1970–71; relief teacher Engl Grampian reg from 1972
m Lerwick 10.7.70 John E. Inglis civ eng s of George L. I. Aber

THOMPSON Patricia Mary   MB ChB 1963
d of Charles H. T. PhD(Manc) archivist and Norah M. Cann headmistress; b Plymouth 3.10.38
h o: paediat, gen med Aber, rheumat Edin 1963–65; g p: Edin 1966–67, part-time Dumfries 1969–75, ptnrship g p from 1975
m Surbiton 27.8.64 John A. C. McFadden MA 1959 qv

THOMPSON William Gilbert   *MA 1962
s of Gilbert S. T. merch seaman, PO linesman and Robertha A. Thomason nurse; b Edin 10.4.39
PhD(Strath) 1970
teacher Glasg 1963–66; asst lect econ hist Wigan tech coll 1969–70; lect hist Glasg coll of tech from 1971
m Aber 3.4.63 Noreen I. Butler MA 1962 qv

THOMPSON William John   *MA 1965

THOMSEN John Kenneth   *BSc(eng) 1968

THOMSON Alan James   *BSc(agr) 1963 PhD 1966
s of Alexander T. dent. tech and Jane N. Adams; b Aber 3.3.40
scient off. plant breeding inst Cambridge from 1966
m Aber 27.7.65 Elizabeth A. Coutts BSc 1962 qv

THOMSON Allan McLean   MB ChB 1957

THOMSON Angus William   *BSc 1970 PhD 1975
s of Angus T. housing insp and Jessie Macdonald; b Inv 13.2.48
MSc(Birm) 1971
MRC res stud. Birm 1970–71; Aberd: SRC res stud. 1971–74, Marr Walker res fell. 1974–75, lect immunology from 1975; sub-warden Johnston Hall 1977

THOMSON Ann Kilpatrick   MA 1969
d of John T. taxi driver and Ann D. Troup; b Glasg 27.10.47
tut. McLenan proj Kirklands Selsey 1971–73; teacher: St Luke's s Portsmouth 1972, Havant g s Hants 1972–74; head econ dept Havant Sixth form coll 1974
m Glasg 2.8.69 Trevor E. S. Jefcoate BSc(agr) 1968 qv

THOMSON Anne Macdonald Collie   *BSc 1969
d of William T. sales rep and Georgina Collie cloth examiner; b Aber 7.2.47
teacher: Ruthrieston s Aber 1970–73, Ellon acad from 1973
m Aber 10.8.72 Clifford Brown med lab tech s of James B. Aber

THOMSON Austin Mathers   LLB 1966
s of Matthew O. T. dent. surg and Ann S. Mathers; b Ellon 20.9.45
Edin: law app Shepherd & Wedderburn WS 1966–68, leg. asst Brodies WS 1968–71; ptnr A. C. White, Silver, Young & Cosh solic Ayr from 1971
m Edin 6.10.69 Felicity A. Vaughan d of Mansel C. M. V. RAF Ger

THOMSON Barbara Ann   MA 1969
d of John T. and Veronica Ironside admin asst Aberd; b Haslemere 26.6.48
teacher: Sunnybank p s Aber 1970–72, Beechwood s Aber 1972–75, Inverurie acad 1975–77
m Aber 29.7.72 Colin D. Adamson MA 1973 teacher, roustabout s of David L. A. Aber

THOMSON Christina Philip Gillanders   MA 1968
d of James T. RN and Elizabeth S. Gillanders tailoress; b Aber 22.4.29
BEM
teacher Torry acad Aber 1969–72, asst prin geog from 1972

THOMSON Colin Barron   BSc(eng) 1964

THOMSON David Bryan   BSc(agr) 1962

THOMSON David Sinclair   *MA 1965
s of David S. T. merch seaman and Wilhelmina Cooper; b Aber 13.3.43
Dip Ed(Makerere) 1966
teacher: Manjasi h s Tororo Uganda 1966–68, Engl Birm 1968–74, St George's j s Birm from 1974

THOMSON Dereck   *MA 1962 Dip Ed 1963

THOMSON Diane Nicolson   MA 1964
d of John T. fisherman and Margaret I. Ritchie; b Whitehills 9.6.43
Dip Soc St(Edin) 1965

fam casework Sheffield 1965–67; Edin: ch care off. 1967–68, play group superv 1968–70
m Whitehills 30.3.68 Paul W. Williams MA(Edin) lect s of Peter D. W. Salt River, Cape, S Af

THOMSON Donald Maclean   MB ChB 1968
s of Donald T. MA 1929 *qv*; b Oban 1.6.43
g p: Aber 1968–70, Ontario from 1970
m Aber 8.6.66 Mary M. Shepherd secy d of John S. Alford

THOMSON Dorothy Anne   MA 1969
d of Robert P. T. eng and Millicent F. Mayers; b Aber 5.11.48
teacher Musselburgh g s 1970–71
m Aber 19.9.69 Ivor J. A. Moir CA s of Joseph M. Aber

THOMSON Douglas   MA 1963
s of George C. T. lab and Helen Baxter fishworker; b Aber 6.4.29
teacher: Powis acad Aber 1964–67, prin hist Old Aber s s 1967–74, also dep head 1970–74; dep head Summerhill acad Aber from 1974
m Aber 2.4.54 Mary A. Dempster d of George D. Aber

THOMSON Douglas Gavin   MB ChB 1964

THOMSON Douglas King   BSc 1967
s of William J. T. crofter, postman, lorry driver and Henrietta M. McBeath soc work care asst; b 12.10.45
teacher maths: Peterhead acad 1968–74, also housemaster Banff acad from 1975

THOMSON Elizabeth   MA 1970
d of James T. master butcher and Catherine B. Henderson teacher; b Longside 28.2.36
m Aber 8.8.60 George R. Duguid BSc 1966 *qv*

THOMSON Elizabeth May   MA 1963
d of Douglas T. shop man./ch off. and Isabella C. Grant; b Insch 24.5.42
teacher: maths Aber h s for girls 1964–66, part-time maths/sc Aber tech coll from 1966
m Aber 2.10.63 James S. Melvin BSc 1966 *qv*

THOMSON Elizabeth Mowat   MA 1966 Dip Ed 1967
d of William R. G. T. grocer and Robina S. Mowat nurse auxil; b Kirkwall 22.6.45
teacher Skene 1967–71
m Kirkwall 8.8.68 Alasdair H. McVicar BSc 1967 *qv*

THOMSON Geoffrey Riddell   MA 1969
s of Edward R. T. MA 1938 *qv*; b Kintore 21.7.48
Dip Cartog(Glas) 1970
cartogr geog dept univ of Winnipeg from 1970
m Winnipeg 26.10.74 Erlinda A. Elefante BSc(Manila) d of Miguel E. Manila

THOMSON Gordon Matthew   LLB 1969
s of Matthew O. T. LDS(Glas) dent. surg and Ann S. Mathers; b Girvan 22.1.48
law app Edin 1969–71; Glasg: leg. asst, solic 1972–78, ptnr MacRobert Son & Hutchison from 1978
m Durh 26.4.73 Virginia A. Hood MA 1970 *qv*

THOMSON Helen Laing   MB ChB 1956
b Uddingston 21.5.32
DA(Lond) 1958 FFARCS 1964
sen h o anaest Aber 1957–59; regist anaest Liv 1959–66; clin asst anaest Carlisle from 1968
m Aber 5.12.64 Brian J. Spencer BA(Dub) med pract

THOMSON Iain Urquhart   MA 1967 BD 1970
s of Charles M. T. ironmonger, bus. rep and Ann L. Urquhart; b Dun 13.12.45
C of S min: Ayr 1970–72, par ch Skene from 1972
m(1) Inv 11.8.72 Shona G. Kinnon MB ChB 1973 d of John K. Inv; wife *d* 15.10.73
(2) Aber 30.7.75 Christine S. Freeland secy d of Patrick F. Aber

THOMSON Ian   *BSc 1964

THOMSON Ian Sim   MA 1969
s of John M. T. postman and Annie Sim; b Aber 20.7.44
teacher Aber from 1970
m Aber 5.7.73 Jennifer A. Yule teacher p e d of Davie Y. Aber

THOMSON Irene Edna   *MA 1965
d of Michael T. fish merch and Edna M. Kinloch; b Aber 7.11.41
asst edit. Thos Nelson publ Lond 1965–66; edit. William Collins publ Glasg 1966; teacher geog Keith g s 1968–70; lect geog Aber coll of comm 1970–79
m Lond 9.8.75 Peter J. Bates tech s of John H. B. Lond

**THOMSON Jacqueline Margaret   MA 1967
Dip Ed 1968**
d of James H. T. lt RSF, insp Glasg city police and Jane I. Scott MA(Glas) soc worker, bookshop asst; b Glasg 9.5.46
teacher Engl/geog: Queen Anne h s Dunfermline 1968–71, Garnock acad Kilbirnie 1971–72; temp Kilbirnie from 1973
m Glasg 1.8.68 David M. Taylor MA 1967 *qv*

THOMSON James Alan   *MA 1967

THOMSON Janette Davis   MA 1967
d of Robert D. T. baker, stillman and Phyllis E. C. Watt canteen asst, newsp reporter; b Grantown-on-Spey 4.6.46
RSA Dip TEFL 1979
teacher Engl: Glasg 1968–74, asst prin Engl Glasg 1974–75; peripatetic teacher immigrant pupils Dunbartonsh from 1978
m Grantown-on-Spey 16.8.69 Peter J. Robertson packag tech, postman s of Peter R. Clydebank

THOMSON Jean Ann   BSc 1970
d of Allan S. T. watchmaker/instrum repairer and Jane Simpson; b Torphins 15.7.49
civ serv Lond from 1971

THOMSON John   *MA 1968
s of John T. fisherman and Isobel M. Ritchie lib; b Whitehills 28.1.46
area salesman Procter & Gamble E Anglia from 1974
m Belfast 25.10.71 Mary B. Hopkirk teacher d of Frederick J. H. Belfast

THOMSON John Campbell   BSc 1958 *1959
s of John C. T. fisherman and Elsie Farquhar; b Lossiemouth 15.9.37
MSc(Wales) 1974
teacher Elgin acad 1960–62; RN instr/meteorol and oceanographic duties Portsmouth, Arbroath, Singapore, Northwood, Plymouth, Lossiemouth, Oslo, Antarctica, Helston 1962–77; gen man. Ocean Routes (UK) Aber from 1977
m Arbroath 13.4.63 Anne H. Farmer teacher d of George W. F. Southampton

THOMSON John Edward Fraser   LLB 1965
s of John E. T. wholesale stationer, hotel prop. and Helen S. Johnston prop.; b Aber 5.4.44
Aber: law app 1966–68, leg. asst 1969–70, ptnr Stronachs advoc Aber from 1970
m Aber 16.8.67 Patricia I. Johnston secy d of George J. Aber

THOMSON John McEwan   *MA 1967

THOMSON Kenneth James   *MA 1967
s of Angus M. T. MB ChB(Glas) med res scient and Alice A. C. Lyon MA 1936 qv; b Aber 30.9.45
MSc(Lond) DIC(Lond) 1968 MS(Iowa) 1972
stud.: Imp coll Lond 1967–68, Edin 1968–69; res assoc dept agr econ N'cle 1970–71; res Iowa state univ 1971–72; lect agr econ N'cle from 1972

THOMSON Lorna Kathleen   MA 1962
m Paterson

THOMSON Mary Helen   MA 1967
d of John T. farm. and Lizzie H. Robbie MA 1931 qv; b Torphins 24.5.43
teacher: Kirkhill p s Aber 1968–69, Middlefield p s Aber 1969–70, supply Kincardine/Deeside 1977–79, Mill o' Forest p s Stonehaven from 1979
m Aber 8.2.68 Kenneth G. Stuart sales exec s of John S. Inverurie

THOMSON Michael John Duthie   *MA 1968
s of Henry T. civ serv and Jean Duthie; b Fraserburgh 29.10.46
MSc(Dund) 1973
oper res: British Steel Corp Corby 1970–73, United Biscuits Liv 1973–78; stock man. United Biscuits Lond from 1978
m Liv 18.8.75 Joanna C. Deane clerk d of Antony D. Liv

THOMSON Nichol Gilbert   *MA 1969

THOMSON Robert Nairn   *BSc(eng) 1958

THOMSON Rosemary Doreen   *MA 1969
d of David T. MA(Glas) schoolmaster and Doreen S. Rose secy; b Johnstone 11.4.47
PhD(Cantab) 1975
res stud. Newham coll Cambridge 1969–73; lect Engl: Birm 1973–74, univ coll Lond from 1974
m Cambridge 7.8.71 Gerard Ashton BA(Cantab) univ lect s of Gerard A. Hindley Green Wigan

THOMSON Sarah   MA 1967

THOMSON Stella Helen Campbell   *MA 1961
m Donaldson

THOMSON William Farquhar   *BSc 1957 Dip Ed 1958
s of John C. T. and Elsie Farquhar; b Lossiemouth 17.10.35
teacher: Nairn acad 1958–62, Elgin acad from 1962
m Aber 4.4.61 Elizabeth H. Donald d of William D. Aber

THORAT Padmakar Laxman   MSc 1967 PhD 1969
MSc(Agra)

THORBURN Ailsa Catriona   *MA 1967
d of Adam T. MA(Edin) univ lect and Mary M. Christie sculptress; b Haddington 8.5.43
lang asst Lycee d'Anthony Paris 1967–68; teacher: Fr St Frideswides s Didcot 1969–70, Fr/Ger Falkirk h s

1970–71, Fr/Ger St Modan's h s Stirling 1971–75
m Aber 22.8.67 Alastair B. Duncan MA 1966 qv

THORBURN Dorothy Margaret   MA 1963
d of William T. banker and Isabella K. Forsyth; b Turriff 21.3.40
teacher: Glasg 1965–68; teacher Engl Arabic s Abu Dhabi
m Aber 26.7.63 Costas C. Constantinides MB ChB 1956 qv

THORBURN Richard Thomas   MA 1967 LLB 1969
s of David R. T. MA(Glas) teacher and Mary G. Sutherland; b Aber 12.8.47
law app Edin 1969–72; stud. D.A.A.D. course—Ger law Düsseldorf and Freiburg W Ger 1972–73; barrister at Middle Temple Lond 1973–76; solic: Edin 1976–77; ptnr McGoogan Thorburn & Co solic Coatbridge

THORES Orison Alistair   MB ChB 1960

THORNTON David Conrad   *BSc 1970 MSc 1972
s of Frank W. A. T. ladies'/gentlemen's outfitter and Jane R. Webster ladies' outfitter; b Arbroath 1.1.48
Aberd: res stud. nat phil 1970–73, res asst from 1973

THORNTON Douglas   *MA 1970
s of Douglas S. T. and Mary L. McWilliam; b Fraserburgh 11.9.47
Dip LD(N'cle) 1972
landscape arch. Tyne and Wear c c plan. dept N'cle-u-Tyne from 1974
m Lily N. Watt

THORNTON Patricia Anne   *MA 1970 PhD 1980
d of Edwin P. G. T. man. dir BICC (cables div) and Joyce I. Partridge; b Manc 15.1.48
res fell. inst of soc/econ res St John's Newfoundland Canada 1970–73; res Aberd from 1973

THORNTON Roger Vincent   BSc(for) 1965
s of James W. T. master butcher and Ethel Clarkson; b Leeds 26.4.44
prod. man. Aber 1965–69; timber buyer Bowaters Cheshire 1969–72; purchasing dir STP Cowie 1972–77; man. Scotland Taylor Maxwell Timber from 1977
m Aber 27.7.67 Norma Reid teacher d of George R. Macduff

THORP Carole Jean Strathdee   MA 1968
d of Leonard M. T. comp dir and Gertrude K. M. Strathdee; b Aber 10.2.47
Lond: secy: to dir Weidenfeld & Nicholson publ 1969–70, Gordon Harbord theatr and lit. ag 1970–71; Ottershaw s Chertsey from 1971
m Aber 12.6.71 Philip G. Hogarth-Gaute insur loss adjuster s of Joseph H. H. G. Woking

THORPE Hugh Rankin   PhD 1963
s of Fred T. market gardener and Isobel J. McCaw deaconess; b Otaki NZ 30.9.36
ME BSc(Canterubry NZ) 1960
NZ: asst eng MWD Wellington 1964–65, eng i/c MWD central labs. Lower Hutt 1965–69; Colombo plan. advis univ of Khon Kaen Thailand 1970–72; sen eng MWD water/soil div Wellington 1973–77; scient MWD water/soil div Christchurch from 1978
m Lauriston Canterbury NZ 19.12.59 Rhona M. Scarth BA(Canterbury NZ) teacher d of George W. S. Lauriston and Mary A. Anderson MA 1926 qv

THORPE William   BSc(agr) 1968 *1969
s of Sidney W. T. farm. and Joan M. Feary; b Wisbech

4.3.46
VSO with Oxfam, rural dev team Chizera Zambia 1969–70; res stud. anim breeding res organis Edin from 1970

THORSTEINSSON Vilhjálmur   BSc 1970
s of Thorsteinn Loftsson and Vilhelmina Tymstra BSc(Amster); b Iceland 9.9.43
teacher Reykjavik Iceland 1970–74; scient off. Icelandic marine lab. Húsavik N Iceland from 1974
m Reykjavik 8.3.74 Stefania Juliusdottir BA(Iceland) teacher d of Július Júliusson Kópavogi Iceland

THOW John   BSc(eng) 1957

TIETJEN Rodney Stephen   MA 1968
s of Albert T. draughtsman and Brenda Schofield; b St Helens 6.5.46
tech selection off. Lond 1968–69; teacher Whiston 1969–70, prin Engl from 1970
m Lond 31.3.69 Stella M. Thompson teacher d of Walter T. St Helens

TIKU Moti Lal   PhD 1964
s of Mahishwar N. T. eng and Tarawati Pandit; b Kashmir India 10.1.36
BA(Kashmir) 1955 MA(Panj) 1957 MA(Patna) 1960
lect applied statist R'dg 1964–68; Canada: assoc prof maths Guelph univ 1968–69, assoc prof statist McM univ 1969–74, prof statist McM from 1974
m Kashmir 17.1.57 Govri Dhar BA(Kashmir)

TIMMIS Roger   *BSc(for) 1966
s of William T. maintenance mech and Barbara Davies shorthand typist; b Altrincham 21.7.44
PhD(Br Col) 1973
VSO asst conserv for. N Nigeria Lokoja 1967–68; grad stud. B.C. Vancouver 1968–72; post doct fell. B.C. for. serv res div Victoria Canada 1973–74; for. regeneration physiol Weyerhaeuser Comp Centralia Washington state USA from 1974

TIMMONS James   BSc 1968
s of Andrew T. coal miner and Helen O'Hear; b Chapelhall 14.8.26
MIBiol 1971
teacher: Lanarksh 1969–71, prin biol Coatbridge from 1971
m Glasg 27.8.55 Janet Shields teacher d of Henry S. Glasg

TIMOTHY Robin Reginald Warren   *BSc 1969
s of George A. T. RAF off., schoolmaster and Daisy K. Frary; b Hunstanton 5.3.47
computer syst eng IBM: Lond 1969–70, Birm 1970–73; computer salesman IBM Birm from 1974

TIMPERLEY David John   MA 1964
s of Robert T. and Edith E. H. Dickinson; b Burnley 19.1.42
articled clerk Blackburn 1964–67; acct Oswaldtwistle from 1967
m Whalley 9.5.71 Patricia M. Nutter secy d of Kenneth N. Whalley

TINCH Robert Templeton   *BSc 1968 MSc 1970

TINCH William Robson   BSc(eng) 1965 MSc 1968
                                                    PhD 1973
s of William T. comp chmn, chartered surv and Martha Templeton; b Barrhead 4.10.42
Aberd: asst lect 1968–69, lect eng 1969–72; contr man. A. Hall & Sons (Bldrs) Edin 1972–77; prod. man. J. Fyfe

Aber 1977–78; man. dir Autospeed Cars Aber from 1979
m Dalkeith 10.5.80 Carol J. Reid d of James R. Dalkeith

TINKLIN Richard   PhD 1966
s of Ernest S. G. T. clerk and Phyllis S. Parry; b Bristol 19.9.40
BSc(Brist) 1963
asst lect agr botany Wye coll univ Lond 1966–68; lect biol Norwich city coll 1969–71; sen lect microbiol Hull coll of tech 1972–76, sen lect biol Hull coll of higher ed from 1976
m Wye 31.8.67 Irene G. Cozens BSc(Lond) d of William J. C. BSc(Edin) Watford

TINSTON David James   *BSc 1969
s of Sydney J. T. progress chaser and Margaret H. Jardine; b Stockport 14.4.44
respiratory physiol central toxicology labs (ICI) Macclesfield from 1970

TINTO James Ferguson   *MA 1962
s of James F. T. MA(Glas) univ lect and Isabella Calder; b Carluke 4.12.15
teacher Engl: Aber acad 1963–68, Rubislaw acad (AGS) 1968–73, asst prin Engl from 1973
m Aber 21.5.53 Ethel J. J. Gerrie soc worker d of George D. G. Aber

TISDALL Jeremy Peter   *BSc(eng) 1963

TITTENSOR Andrew Malcolm   *BSc 1966
b Wolverhampton 31.4.44
PhD(Edin) 1970
sen scient off. min of agr Worplesdon from 1970
m Edin 4.9.68 Ruth M. White MA(Oxon) free-lance ecologist

TOCHER Alison Margaret   MA 1961

TOCHER Frances Mary   *MA 1969
m Bell

TOCHER Kathleen Anne   MB ChB 1967
d of Wilfred I. M. T. MA 1945 qv; b Aber 24.4.43
LMCC 1969
Canada: rotating intern Saskatoon 1967–68; private pract Port Coquitlam 1968–75; asst m o Vancouver health dept from 1976
m New Westminster 4.10.69 David G. W. Carter commun tech s of Francis B. C. Surrey Canada

TOD Anne Stuart   MA 1969
d of Alexander A. T. pharm and Mary-Jane Stuart nurse; b Fyvie 3.6.48
AIL(Lond)
teacher Fr: Craigroyston s Edin 1970–72, Whitney inst Smith's Bermuda 1972–75
m Roberts

TODD James Martin   PhD 1968
s of James T. LDS(Leeds) dent. surg and Elsie Hey teacher; b Kingston-u-Hull 24.6.33
LRCP(Lond) 1958 MRCS 1958 DPM(Leeds) 1963 MRCPsych
h o, sen h o: Leeds, Lancaster 1958–61; regist psychiat Hull 1961–63; sen regist psychiat Ross clin Aber/clin tut. ment health Aberd 1963–66; dep phys, supt, consult. psychiat Dingleton hosp Melrose 1966–67, dir day center Soundview/Throgs Neck ment health center/clin asst prof Albert Einstein coll of med, consult. psychiat Bronx State hosp NY USA 1968–69; staff psychiat/med dir Rutland ment health serv Rutland Vermont USA 1969–71;

private pract psychiat Rutland 1972–74; staff psychiat Brattleboro Retreat Vermont from 1974/clin asst prof psychiat univ of Vermont Burlington USA 1969–75; asst prof psychiat Dartmouth med s Hanover NH USA from 1975
m Leeds 30.11.56 June A. Kirkcaldy nurse d of Donald K. Bradford

TODD Ronald   MA 1965

TOMASSON Thorsteinn   *BSc(agr) 1970
s of Thomas Tryggvason Phil lic(Uppsala) geol and Kerstin Jancke cashier; b Uppsala Sweden 17.7.45
res off. agr inst Iceland 1970; plant-breeding stud. Uppsala univ from 1974
m Reykjavik 6.7.68 Sophie I. L. Kofoed-Hansen BSc (Boston) teacher of deaf d of Agnar K-H. Reykjavik

TOMKINS Richard George William   BSc(agr) 1968
s of Charles R. T. farm./seed merch and Constance A. Dewis; b Northampton 28.11.46
Dip Farm Bus. Ad(Wye) 1972
farm man. Rutland 1969–71; farm man., farm. Northants from 1972
m Kettering 11.7.75 Penelope J. Bilson BSc(Leic) prob off., teacher d of W. Antony R. B. Kettering

TOMLINSON Christopher Malcolm   BSc(eng) 1968
s of Norman T. machine tool merch and Joan E. Taylor; b Manc 4.1.47
site eng civ eng contr: Birm, Warrington 1968–72, Lond 1972–73; machine tool merch Manc from 1973
m Ollerton Knutsford 26.10.74 Janet A. Stirling teacher d of Alexander F. S. Ollerton

TOMLINSON Sheila Mary   BSc(agr) 1966
d of Henry T. bank man. and Wyn Milne ptnr/asst stock and share broker; b Rochdale 29.5.44
sen res asst Unilever Bedford from 1962
m Chadderton 11.5.68 Tom Irvine, Udny

TOMORY Jillian Mary   *MA 1970
d of Kenneth A. M. T. MB ChB(Edin) RAMC and Evelyn F. McGuinness teacher; b Dublin 6.2.48
Dip Lib(UCW) 1971 ALA 1974
Liverpool: secy/p a 1972, asst lib 1972–75; branch lib Wirral 1975–77
m Edin 4.9.71 Michael J. R. Mitchell MA 1970 qv

TOOLAN Paul   MA 1965

TORRIE Stephen Milne   *BSc 1961 Dip Ed 1962

TOSH Agnes   MA 1961
d of John T. civ serv and Constance Stevenson; b Aber 11.3.40
teacher Kaimhill s s Aber 1962; lektor Engl Folk-universitet Maricstad, Ludköping Sweden 1962–64; TEFL Bexhill 1964–70; teacher: hist Blackfen s for girls Sidcup 1970–73, Engl/hist Lyndon s Solihull from 1974
m Aber –.12.64 Cornelis M. Groeneveld tech eng s of Cornelis M. G. Amsterdam

TOSH Victor Lamont   MB ChB 1958
s of William A. T. salesman and Jessie Lamont; b Bankhead 1.12.32
DObstRCOG 1961
h o, sen h o: Woodend hosp, Ballochmyle hosp, Forth Park mat. hosp Kirkcaldy 1959–60; RAMC: sen h o Princess Louise Margaret hosp Aldershot 1960–61, gen duties m o Brit milit hosp Kingston Jamaica 1961–62, BAOR Hohue W Ger 1962–63; g p Fraserburgh from 1963

m Aber 19.7.58 Eva M. Smith teacher d of Alfred F. S. Aber

TOUCH Peter Gerald   *BSc 1967
s of Arthur G. T. CMG MA(Oxon) phys/civ serv, chief scient min of supply, M o D, FO and Phyllis Wallbank MA(Oxon) teacher; b Washington DC, USA 21.2.44
Beecham labs Brockham Park: dev chem 1967–68, pharm regist off. 1968–70, head of regulatory affairs unit from 1970
m Dorking 2.8.69 Frances A. Weatherhead teacher d of Christopher S. W. BA(Cantab) Dorking

TOUGH Alexander Henry Furneaux   *MA 1962

TOUGH Elizabeth Agnes   MA 1970 Dip Ed 1971
d of Alexander T. works foreman and Elsie M. Furneaux; b Aber 9.7.49
teacher Engl Kincorth acad from 1971
m Aber 24.7.70 Colin R. Russell policeman s of Andrew M. R. MA(Glas) Aber

TOUGH Harry Gordon   MB ChB 1956

TOUGH John Richard   BSc 1968
s of Robert J. S. T. distillery man. and May G. Munro; b Knockando 22.11.47
SSEB Glasg: trainee computer progr, progr, sen progr, sen analyst progr from 1968
m Turriff 24.4.70 Marian J. Connon MPS hosp pharm d of Alexander W. C. Turriff

TOUGH Laurence Michael   *LLB 1970
s of Alfred T. teacher and Margaret Milne; b Aber 10.7.47
law app Stewart & Murray advoc Aber 1970–72, solic from 1972
m Edin 30.3.74 Sandra E. C. Shaw d of Norman M. S. Edin

TOUGH Michael Cameron   *BSc(eng) 1970
s of George T. distillery worker and Edith M. Cameron; b Dufftown 31.7.48
asst civ eng: Glasg 1970–72, Helensburgh 1972–73; resid eng: Craignure Mull 1973, Stromness 1973–75, Peterhead power stat site from 1975

TOUGH Ronald Brebner   MA 1957

TOUGH Sheila Violet   *MA 1961 Dip Ed 1962
b Clatt 26.6.38
teacher Greenhall h s Midlothian from 1969

TOWELL Richard John   *MA 1969

TOWERS George Alexander   MA 1969
s of William J. T. instrum mech and Violet Ward; b Dunfermline 11.3.46
budget accts man. Glasg 1970–71; prin teacher geog Kelvinside acad Glasg from 1972
m Bearsden 21.8.71 Moira E. Connell med secy d of Stewart J. C. Dunoon

TOWNS Alan Thomas   LLB 1969
s of Thomas C. T. off. man. and Helen McPherson; b Aber 8.3.49
law app John & W. G. Craigen advoc in Aber 1969–71; leg. asst: John & W. G. Craigen 1971–73, corp of city of Aber 1973–75, prin leg. asst city of Aber dist council from 1975

TOWNSEND Alan Brian   *MA 1968

TOWNSEND Helen McGregor   MA 1967

TOWNSON John Michael   PhD 1967
s of Allan T. cashier and Edith M. Hird teacher;
b Silsden 19.7.36
BSc(eng)(Lond) 1957 Assoc City & Guilds Inst 1957
MICE 1961
lect Aberd 1962–68; prin lect Teesside polytech 1968–70;
sen lect Strath from 1970
m Helensburgh 28.7.62 Judith M. Peel teacher home econ
d of Robert A. P. Helensburgh

TOWNSON Lorna Mary Stephen   *MA 1969
d of Edward B. T. army off., insur ag and Amelia J.
McLean secy; b Crieff 21.1.47
teacher Old Aber s s 1970–71; freelance work with
Times Ed Supp, BBC and ante-natal teacher trg with
National Childbirth Trust 1971–73; asst head Engl dept
Musselburgh g s from 1973
m Aber 30.7.69 James A. T. Dyer MB ChB 1970 qv

TOWSE John Beckwith   MSc 1970
s of David B. T. comp dir and Margaret B. Watson
teacher; b Leighton Buzzard 20.5.44
BSc(Lond) 1969 GRIC 1969
post grad res: Aberd 1970–72, Brittany 1972–73; marketing radio chem centre 1973–74; marketing (export) High
Wycombe from 1974

TOYE Michael Ian Andrew   BSc(eng) 1963

TOYER Elizabeth Anne   MA 1965 Dip Ed 1966
d of Harvey C. A. T. papermaker and Doreen
Skinner; b Worksop 27.12.43
teacher: prin hist/Engl Mintlaw j s s 1966–67, hist
Bagshot s mod s 1967–68, Engl the Convent Banjul The
Gambia 1968–69, Engl Chilanga s Zambia 1971–73,
Amer s Dacca Bangladesh from 1977
m Sunderland 16.8.67 Paul S. Hindmarsh BSc(agr) 1967 qv

TOZER Ralph Arthur   MB ChB 1958
BA(Brist)

TRAIL Marjorie Webster   *MA 1970

TRAILL Alister Barron   *BSc 1970

TRAILL Carol Irene   MA 1970
d of Francis P. M. T. shopkeeper and Edith E. M.
Daws civ serv; b Helmsdale 29.9.49
teacher: Fr/Ger Invergordon 1972–73, Fr Golspie 1973–
76; TEFL St Gym Wermelskirchen Ger 1976–78; teacher
Fr/Ger Galashiels 1978–79, Lossiemouth from 1979

TRANTOR Moira Rosalind   MB ChB 1970
m Milne

TREDINNICK Beatrice Anne   *MA 1966
m Pollard

TREVELYAN John Francis   BSc(for) 1958
s of Charles W. T. MA(Oxon) teacher and Maud D.
Dixey; b Wokingham 5.2.34
NZ: for. Tokoroa 1959–64, teacher Te Puke 1964–76,
orchardist Te Puke from 1976
m Weston-super-Mare 1.11.58 Elizabeth M. Brockenshaw
BSc(Brist) microbiol d of Harvey B. Weston-super-Mare

TREVENA Iain Christopher   *BSc 1966 PhD 1970

TRICKER Edward Forbes   MA 1967 MEd 1972
s of Edgar H. T. naval off. RN, hotel prop. and Helen
Forbes waitress, hotel prop.; b Gillingham 4.10.37
HNC(naval arch.) 1959
ship's draughtsman 1953–59, 1961–64; des draughtsman
Ford Motor Co 1959–61; teacher maths AGS 1968–72;
prin guid Powis acad Aber 1972–79; asst head Ellon
acad from 1979
m Aber 19.3.60 Robina Annand tracer d of Robert A.
Aber

TRIGGS Peter Ronald   *MA 1969

TROUP Annette   *BSc 1962
d of Ronald C. T. market gardener and Mary
Farquhar cook; b Ellon 26.9.39
teacher Summerhill s s Aber 1963–66; headmistress
Kampala Uganda 1967
m Belhelvie 6.4.63 Colin P. Neave CA s of David J. N.
Aber

TROUP Norma   MA 1964
d 19.4.68

TROUP Richard Forbes   LLB 1968
s of Arthur D. T. MA 1925 qv; b Peterhead 16.9.47
Edin: law app 1968–70, solic from 1970
m Edin 10.2.73 Sandra E. Sinclair secy d of Alastair S.
Edin
d Edin 3.7.75

TRUSLER Gillian Anne   *MA 1970
d of Donald C. T. solic's clerk and Ann L. Argo sewing
machinist; b Lond 31.7.48
teacher mus: Ruthrieston s s Aber 1971–73, Harlaw acad
Aber 1973–76, AGS from 1976

TUACH Ann Ishbel   MA 1967 Dip Ed 1968
d of Kenneth D. T. farm worker/bldg lab and Jessie
Finlayson; b Fearn 13.7.46
teacher: Falkirk 1968–70, Lond 1970–71, Leeds 1971–72,
Wetherby from 1972
m Aber 28.8.71 Roger J. K. Tibbett sales ag s of James
D. K. T.

TUACH Helen   *MA 1965
d of Kenneth D. T. farm worker/bldg lab and Jessie
Finlayson; b Fearn 20.6.43
teacher W-central Scot. 1966–71; lect infant work
Callendar Park coll of educ Falkirk 1971–72
m Aber 4.9.65 William H. Fraser MA 1963 qv

TUACH Nan   BSc 1965
d of James A. T. fencer and Hannah Mackenzie;
b Muir of Ord 21.3.44
teacher sc: Duddeston Manor bilat. s Birm 1966–69,
Kaikorai Valley h s Dunedin NZ 1971–72
m Muir of Ord 19.8.66 James H. K. Inkson MA 1963 qv

TUCKLEY Catharine Mary   MB ChB 1962
d of Laurence T. clerk in holy orders and Mary A.
Hill; b Stafford 19.6.33
h o: ARI, Woodend hosp Aber, city hosp Derby 1962–
64; g p Derby from 1964

TULEY Graham   *BSc(for) 1970
m 1969 Margot Bell MA 1970 qv

TULLETT Adam   MB ChB 1956

TULLO Alan William   *BSc 1970
s of William S. T. shopkeeper and Janet E. Milne

SRN; b Elgin 7.2.48
PhD(Stir) 1974
lect maths Edin 1973-74; oper res scient Brit Steel (Teesside) from 1974

TULLOCH Andrew Thomas Hawick   BSc(eng) 1956
s of John T. bus. man and Elizabeth M. Hawick teacher; b Shetland 11.1.36
jun eng Sir Robert McAlpine & Sons Kent 1956-58; county surv dept Zetland c c Shetland 1958-63; dir knitwear manuf comp Shetland from 1963
m Bedford -.9.60 Wilhelmina V. Scott d of John S. Lerwick

TULLOCH Ian   BSc(eng) 1964

TULLOCH John William   *MA 1958

TULLOCH Marian Isabella   BSc 1961 PhD 1966
d of Margaret I. T. hosp cook; b North Ronaldsay 8.5.40
Aberd med s: res asst med phys 1961-67, res fell. therap 1967-74
m Aber 17.5.68 John K. Chesters BA(Cantab) biochem s of John H. C. BSc(Sheff) Sheffield

TULLOCH Ragna   MA 1970
d of Robert G. T. BSc 1941 qv; b Elgin 8.5.49
teacher maths/sc: Stornoway 1971-72, Fochabers 1973, Stornoway 1973-74, Elgin 1974-75, São Paulo Brazil 1975-77, Bexley 1977-78; woman police constable Lond from 1978

TUNNARD Christopher Timothy   LLB 1970
s of Thomas N. T. MA(Oxon) teacher/organist, HMIS and Noreen M. Petherick; b Kidlington 3.8.48
solic's articled clerk/law stud. Birm 1971-74; asst solic: Birm 1975-76, Tadcaster from 1976

TÜRKER Hilmi   MSc 1969 PhD 1971
BSc(Ankara)

TURNBULL Andrew Robert   *MA 1967 PhD 1973

TURNBULL David Alexander   LLB 1959
BA(Oxon)

TURNBULL Ian William   BSc 1969
s of William S. T. man. dir and Nora S. Henderson; b Glasg 5.8.48
CA 1974
app CA Glasg 1969-74; CA Arthur Young McClelland Moores 1974-77; dir/comp secy Grays of Fetterangus (1972) from 1977

TURNER Charles Cason   PhD 1956
AB(Davidson Coll) BD(Union Theol Sem Va)

TURNER George Alexander   MA 1963

TURNER Gordon Hepburn   MA 1958
d of Percy J. T. rly off. and Evelyn Hepburn; b Lincoln 13.9.36
MEd(Manc) 1976
teacher Fr/Ger: Gordon s Huntly 1959-61, Aber coll of comm 1962-67; prin Fr Aber coll of comm from 1967
m Aber 5.8.61 Barbara A. Brebner MA 1957 qv

TURNER Grace Constance   MB ChB 1958 cMD 1963
d of Edward T. civ serv and Christina A. Paterson; b Aber 22.8.34
h o RACH 1958-59; g p trainee Auchinblae 1959-60;

lect bact Aberd 1960-63; regist bact city hosp Aber 1963-64; part-time lect bact Aberd 1971-72; part-time g p Bucksburn from 1978
m Aber 4.8.62 Robert A. Chalmers DSc 1968 qv

TURNER Janet Lesley   MA 1968 Dip Ed 1969
d of Cyril G. T. publ consult. and Katharine S. Elder MA 1930 qv; b Colchester 14.9.46
teacher Fr/Ger: Edin 1969-71, Alva 1971-74
m Dedham 24.7.71 Thomas G. Harvie BSc(eng) 1970 qv

TURNER Juliet Wilson   MA 1962
d of Harry E. T. BSc(Manc) teacher, C of S min and Jean Wilson; b Dumfries 5.7.40
Dip Theol(Lond) 1967 Dip Bible-training Inst Glasg 1967
teacher Engl/hist: Cumnock acad 1963-67, Hampton Park s S'ton 1967-68; part-time teacher needlework St Judes s Islington Lond 1974-76
m Peebles 10.8.68 Brian K. Mann teacher s of Vernal K. M. Loughborough

TURNER Paul Barrie   BSc(for) 1968
s of Harold F. T. gardener and Doris Irvin bookkeeper; b Birkenhead 28.2.44
man. trainee Thames Board Mills (Unilever) Warrington 1969-72; tech sales rep Milchem inc Houston Texas from 1973

TURNER Susan Patricia   MA 1965
d of James F. T. RAF, gen merch and Jean Lackie; b Cheltenham 21.1.45
Canada: teacher Russell Manitoba 1971-74, freelance journalist/columnist for weekly newspaper Yorkton Sask from 1975
m Morpeth 11.8.65 Alan A. Macintosh MA 1965 qv

TURNER William Robert Clyne   MB ChB 1960
s of Edward Turner civ serv and Christina A. Paterson secy; b Peterhead 1.11.37
DObstRCOG 1963
h o: Stracathro hosp Brechin, Falkirk RI, ARI 1960-62; lect anat Aberd 1962; g p: Aber, Purley, Lincoln 1965-67 and clin asst Linc 1967; private pract Banff Alta Canada 1967-77; pres med staff Mineral Springs hosp Banff Canada 1973-74 (active staff 1967-77); g p Tunbridge Wells Kent 1977-78; private pract Calgary/courtesy staff Rockyview and Holy Cross hosps from 1978
m Aber 22.6.63 Patricia E. Kelly RGN d of Christopher K. Falkirk

TURPIE Derek McDonald   MA 1969
s of Alexander M. T. wagon repairer, park ranger and Mary J. Mackie midwife; b Aber 19.7.48
teacher geog Whitburn from 1970
m Aber 27.6.70 Jeanette C. Duncan MA 1969 qv

TURRIFF William   *MA 1968 *MEd 1972
s of William T. postman and Mary S. McDonald; b Peterhead 6.9.45
DEP(Glas) 1970
teacher Causewayend p s Aber 1970-72; educ psych Exeter 1972-74; sen educ psych Stonehaven from 1974
m Aber 2.8.68 Geraldine O. Smith teacher d of John S. USA

TURTON John Neville   *MA 1969 *MEd 1975

TURTON John Samuel   PhD 1966
s of Colin T. civ serv and Annie G. Brown; b Sale 28.12.29
BSc(eng)(Lond) 1955 MSc(eng)(Lond) 1959 C Eng MIMechE(Lond) 1961

lect mech eng Sus univ from 1966
m Battersea 1957 Margaret D. Stockley teacher d of
Ernest W. S. London

TUTTLE Albert Austin   MA 1969
s of Albert T. eng and Margaret H. Ballingall; b Forfar
27.9.47
MEd(Ottawa) 1975
teacher: Motherwell 1970-71, Ottawa from 1971
m Aber 29.12.70 Sheena Gow MB ChB 1965 *qv*

TUTTLE Angus Swanson   MB ChB 1968

TUTTLE Irene Margaret   MB ChB 1970
d of Albert A. T. eng and Margaret H. Ballingall;
b Dun 9.10.45
DObstRCOG 1972
h o Aber 1970-71; g p Pembroke Ont Canada 1970-72
and from 1973; sen h o obst Stirling 1972-73
m Pembroke Ont 13.1.78 Floyd D. Skuce pres Dalmar
Paving s of Lloyd S.

TWATT John William   BSc(agr) 1970
s of Stephen M. T. farm. and Brenda Tait; b Kirkwall
24.11.47
temp posts Canada 1970-73; asst insp DAFS Aber, Oban
1973-78; insp DAFS Orkney from 1978

TWEEDIE Quentin William   BSc(eng) 1967

TWIGGS Arthur Ronald   *BSc 1969
s of Sydney T. RAF off. and Frances G. Cumming;
b Lincs 18.3.48
field geol/mine geol NT Aust 1969-71; field geol W Aust
1971-72; sen geol (eng) Lond based from 1973

TYRRELL Marcus Alexander   BSc(for) 1959

TYSON Robert Donald Grigor   MA 1966

TYTLER Peter   *BSc 1964 PhD 1968
s of Peter T. MB ChB 1940 *qv*; b Stirling 11.9.42
Stir: NERC res fell. 1967-69, res lect attached to SMBA
Oban 1969-72, lect biol 1972-78; asst prof univ of
Kuwait 1978-80
m Stirling 9.4.70 Stephanie Flaherty prin's secy Stir d of
Stephen F. Stirling

U'REN William Graham   *BSc 1970
s of Henry G. U. MA 1976 (by ordin) and Catherine C.
Graham; b Glasg 28.12.46
Dip TP(Strath) 1974 MRTPI 1974
town plan. asst: Clacks c c 1970-72 Lanark c c 1972-75;
prin plan., chief plan. off. Lanark dist c from 1975
m Glasg 15.10.70 Wendy M. Hogarth

UDDOH John Adewa   *BSc(eng) 1960
s of Samuel M. U. and Ugioro Ogiefa; b Agbani
Nigeria 22.4.32
Dip Civ Eng(Yaba tech inst) 1953 AF Inst Pet 1964
Regd Eng(Coren, Nig) 1973
exec eng (roads) M o W Umuahia Nigeria 1960-61; BP
Nig: oper eng Lagos 1961-63, dist oper eng Kano, Jos,
div eng Port Harcourt Benin 1964-70, gen man. Gwato
Nig Benin (road constr comp) 1970-73, man. dir Progress
Eng comp Benin from 1973
m Lond 15.8.59 Patricia M. Mudahy nurse d of J. M.
Kingston Jamaica

ULLMANN Liselotte Ludovicka   PhD 1957
MA(Oxon)
m De Kock

UMAR Mohammad   PhD 1968
s of Haji C. Din bus. man and Wazir Begum; b Lahore
Pakistan 6.9.36
BSc(Punj) 1958 MSc(Punj) 1964
sen res off. PCSIR Lahore 1968-70; lect analyt chem
Punjab univ Lahore 1970-74, asst prof from 1974
m Lahore 7.1.62 Hamida Shafi d of Haji M. S. Lahore

UNDERWOOD Ian Richard   MB ChB 1968

URE James Murray   BSc(for) 1957

URI Oddstein   MB ChB 1964
s of Jonas U. farm. and Halldis Brekke; b Valldal
Norway 30.12.34
Spec Pediat(Bergen) 1971
Norway: intern Flekkefjord 1965; jun regist Tromsø
1966-68, Voss 1969-70, Bergen 1970-72; private pract
Tønsberg 1973-77; chief m o Ibb, Yemen 1977-78;
private pract Tønsberg from 1978
m(1) Aber 22.12.61 Patricia Summers BSc 1960 *qv*; marr
diss 14.2.75
(2) Tønsberg 24.2.75 Turid Lutnes physioth d of Magne
L. Rena Norway

URQUHART Aileen Alexander   *BSc 1968
d of George F. U. BSc(Strath) civ eng/comp dir and
Elizabeth E. Stiller secy; b Glasg 20.9.45
res asst plant biol Bangor univ coll N. Wales; Canada:
tech med biochem Ottawa univ 1971-74, grad stud. PhD
plant physiol Carleton univ Ottawa from 1974
m Glasg 5.6.70 Julian T. Inglis BSc 1967 *qv*

URQUHART Alastair Alfred   MA 1961
s of Alfred U. comm trav and Violet Duncan; b Turriff
13.1.40
teacher: Turriff acad 1962-73, Toronto from 1974

URQUHART Alison Anne Mairi   MA 1964
d of Alexander U. MA(Glas) teacher and Annie B.
Scott MA 1925 *qv*; b Inv 11.5.43
teacher: Mosspark p s Renfrew 1965-69, Portessie p s
1969-74, Stornoway p s from 1974

URQUHART Barrie Stephen   LLB 1966
s of Stephen U. dent. tech and Gladys Barrie; b Aber
12.5.45
law app 1967-69 Greenock; solic Greenock, Hamilton
1969; solic Aber from 1969
m Glasg 25.4.70 Irene F. Harvey bank clerkess d of
David L. H. Glasg

URQUHART Gillian Rose   MA 1967 Dip Ed 1968
d of George S. U. gen grocer and Mavis O. Davis: b
Lucknow India 1.11.45
teacher Engl/Amer hist Philadelphia dance acad USA
1968-69; teacher: Engl/hist Kinning Park Glasg 1969-71,
asst prin Engl Barrhead h s 1971-72, Engl Verdin comp s
stud. induction course for spec educ Hartford 1974;
teacher p h s Winsford from 1975
m Hatfield Alan E. Howes loc govt off. s of Eric H. H.
Hatfield; marr diss

URQUHART Gordon Alexander   *MA 1959 MSc 1964

URQUHART Gordon Greig   BSc(eng) 1963

URQUHART Helma Muriel   MA 1957
d of James L. U. civ serv and Wilhelmina Forsyth;
b Stornoway 18.4.36
tech lib Aber/Beaconsfield Cambs 1961-67; lib tapes for
blind stud. Lond from 1967

URQUHART Jean McDonald BSc 1967

URQUHART Robert George Inglefield BSc(eng) 1963
s of Colin U. grocer and Agnes I. Mitchell; b Portsoy
18.9.42
MICE 1968 MIHE 1967
grad asst eng Aber c c 1963–65; asst eng Banff c c 1965–68;
sen eng: SE roads conserv unit Maidstone 1968–72, Perth
c c 1972–74; supt eng defence dept Muscat Sultanate of
Oman from 1974
m Grangemouth 22.7.67 Rosalind W. Jeffreys computer
oper d of William J. Grangemouth

URQUHART Ronald John *MA 1959

**UYANWAH Philomena Obiageliuwah MB ChB 1964
MD 1978**
m Akpom

VADLAMUDI Babu Pitchi PhD 1968
BSc(Andhra) MSc(Saugar)

VALENTINE John Murray BSc(for) 1967
s of J. Stuart V. BA(Vict Well NZ) teacher and Nancy
P. Rutherford; b Wellington NZ 8.4.43
BSc(Well) 1965 PhD(Wash) 1975
NZ for. serv: for. Tuatapere 1967–69, scient Rotorua
1969–78, prin for. Wellington from 1978

VALENTINE Maurice Keith BSc 1970
s of William W. V. regist of births, deaths, marriages
and Elsie Rowe; b Dun 10.11.49
syst analyst: Babcock & Wilcox (Ops) Renfrew 1970–74,
Renfrew c c Paisley 1974–75, Strathclyde reg c Glasg from
1975, proj leader
m Aber 4.8.72 Kathleen Bruce MA 1972 teacher d of
Colin S. B. Aber

VALENTINE Ranald John Harben *BSc 1959

VALENTINE Wyn Patricia *BSc 1966
d of Henry W. V. MA 1931 qv and Winifred Stoddart
MA 1931 qv; b Aber 1.8.44
computer progr Lond 1966–67; teacher Longniddry p s
from 1977
m Aber 28.1.67 Andrew J. Williamson MA 1966 qv

van der KAMP Bart John PhD 1967
s of Walter van der K. headmaster and Derkje van Dyk;
b Kampen Neths 30.12.41
BSF(Br Col) 1964
univ of Br Col Vancouver Canada: asst p a 1967–74,
assoc p a from 1974
m Capelle a. d. Yssel Holland 22.12.64 Adriana Schippers
d of Hendrik S. a. d. Yssel

van der TOORREN Vivien Lois MA 1967 Dip Ed 1968
d of Jan van der T. airline pilot and Lorna R. Murray;
b Londonderry NI 9.6.45
teacher: VSO Freetown Sierra Leone 1966–67, Brent
Lond 1968–69; publ Longmans Harwell 1968–69;
teacher Reading 1969–73
m Aber 29.11.69 William J. Attenborough BSc(R'dg)
farms man. s of William A. East Carlton

VANN Janet Petronella *BSc 1966
d of C. Roland V. schoolmaster and Eileen M. Norris
head teacher; b Mansfield 25.7.43
teacher geog Royal Masonic s Herts 1966–68; Procter &
Gamble: sales prom dept 1968–72, brand man. 1972–76;
Braun AG, W Ger: group prod. superv 1976–78, internat
marketing man. *Hair Care* 1978–79, prod. line dir *Oral
Care* from 1980

VARGAS CUBIDES Esperanza MSc 1968
Chem(Nat Univ Coll)

VARRIE Melvyn Keith *MA 1969
s of George A. W. V. painter/decorator and Elsie
Jacques; b Dumfries 26.1.47
Dip Ed(Edin) 1971
teacher Dumfries 1969–70, post-grad stud.: UCW 1970–
71, Edin 1971–72; teacher: Dun 1972–75, Irvine from
1975

VASS Evelyn Rosemary *MA 1966
d of John V. MA 1937 qv; b Aberfeldy 5.12.44
MSC(Lond) 1967 PhD(Lond) 1973
Lond: clin psych 1967–70; sen psych Guy's hosp 1970–74,
prin psych from 1974
m Lond 7.10.66 David F. Hendry MA 1966 qv

VASS Mary McIntosh Forbes MA 1958
d of Alexander V. works man. and Isabella Forbes; b
Fraserburgh 30.8.36
admin asst Strath 1965–69; asst secy Jordanhill coll of
educ Glas 1969–72
m Glasg 17.12.71 Campbell B. Burns MA(Glas) prof of
bus. law s of James B. Glasg

VAUGHAN Gordon Henry MB ChB 1957
s of Henry E. V. caterer and Nellie B. Yoxall; b Aber
19.3.33
FRACGP 1973
h o Woodend hosp Aber 1957–58; capt RAMC(NS)
Tidworth 1958–60; phys Stanvac Sumatra Indonesia
1960–62; med supt KI. gen hosp S Aust; med pract
Turramurra NSW Aust from 1965
m Glasg 14.7.55 Anne L. Gibson BSc(Glas) teacher d of
William G.

VAUGHAN Ian MA 1965

VAUGHAN Ludlow Murcot MA 1963
s of Aaron T. V. clerk and Albertha Robinson; b
Montego Bay Jamaica WI 20.5.25
Dip Ed(Glas) 1966
teacher Edinbarnet s s Faifley Clydebank 1964–69; dep
head Dalreoch p s Dumbarton 1969–72; head Edinbarnet
p s Faifley from 1972
m Glasg 15.5.48 Archibaldina M. Rough d of Archibald
R. Glasg

**VAZ PORTUGAL Apolinário José Barbosa da Cruz
PhD 1964**
s of Apolinario P. Ms Chem(Coimbra) chem and
Celeste da C Vaz prof; b Murtosa Portugal 9.11.30
Dip Nutrit Physiol(Sorbonne) 1959 D Vet Sc(Lisbon) 1967
res fell min of agr Lisbon 1967; head of biochem/anim
nutrit dept of inst of anim prod. Vale de Santarem,
Portugal 1967–69, dir of inst prod. res from 1973; prof
anim prod. fac of vet sc Lisbon from 1969; secy of state
for agrarian dev from 1978
m Portugal 3.10.69 Ana M. G. Correia d of Manuel da
Silva C.

VEITCH Angela Georgette *BSc 1967
d of George B. W. V. teacher of art and Margaret M.
Gordon; b Inv 9.4.44
biochem Raigmore hosp Inv from 1967

VELAYUTHAM Mariappan PhD 1968
MSc(Madras)

**VELLACOTT Terence Charles Frederick Bishop
*MA 1967**
s of Jack F. B. V. elect. eng and Elsie M. Pedder; b

Romford 27.11.42
teacher: Engl Eton coll 1968–69, Engl/Lat St Paul's cath choir s 1969–76; prin classics Montpelier prep s Paignton from 1976

VERMOUTH Paul Clinton   *MA 1969
s of Paul C. V. bus. man and Shirley L. Johannis; b Keene NH USA 6.10.46
MA(Lond) 1970
grad stud. Af stud. Lond 1969–70; fell. Af stud. center Boston univ Mass 1971–73, also sen teaching fell. from 1973

VICCA Mario Luigi   MA 1959 LLB 1961
s of Peter V. restaurateur and Elvira Zumpani; b Aber 22.10.37
NP 1978
ptnr Storie, Cruden & Simpson advoc Aber from 1963
m Glasg 21.5.63 Joan M. Carroll teacher p e d of William C. Glasg

VICKERS Ivan George   BSc(agr) 1966 *1967
s of George D. V. and Violet G. Maplestone; b Lincoln 23.8.43
BA(Cantab) 1974 Vet MB MRCVS 1977
livestock husb advis min of agr ADAS Chelmsford 1967–72; stud. vet med Churchill coll univ of Cambridge 1972–77; min of agr vet off. Bury St Edmunds from 1977

VIGROW John Will   *MA 1965
s of John W. V. engraver and Florence Clarkson; b Aber 24.8.32
Morgan acad Dun: teacher geog 1966–68, spec asst 1968–70, prin asst 1970–72, prin guid from 1972
m Largs 8.7.67 Elisabeth A. Sayles BSc 1965 *qv*

VIGROW Mary Louisa Mitchell   *MA 1963
d of George W. V. factory worker and Jessie Lakin photographer; b Newhills 12.2.24
teacher Engl Bankhead acad from 1964
m Bucksburn 12.8.46 Frederick Crade master upholsterer and coach trimmer s of Samuel C. London

VINCENT Clifford   BSc 1970
b Aber 4.5.49
teacher maths Powis acad Aber 1971–73, asst prin maths 1973–75; prin guid Bankhead acad from 1975

VINYCOMB Dorothea Harden   MA 1968
d of Godfrey B. V. BA(Cantab) eng and Christina J. Glendinning; b Belfast 29.8.47
ch care off. Norwich 1968–69; med soc worker Liv 1969–70; teacher Engl Mitundu s s Malawi 1974–76
m Monifieth 31.5.69 Robert K. M. Hay BSc 1967 *qv*

VIPOND Peter Wilfred   *BSc 1966 PhD 1969

VIRGO Keith James   MSc 1965
s of Alfred J. V. wholesale grocery/comp dir and Doris M. Portwine; b Woking 9.4.41
BSc(agr)(Lond) 1962 Dip Agr Eng(NCAE) 1976)
soil surv/pedologist: Hunting tech serv Sudan, Middle East 1964–67, dept agr Canada 1967–68; sen soil surv/land classifier Hunting tech serv Thailand, Niger, Côte d'Ivoire, Ethiopia, Swaziland, Somalia, Bahrain from 1968
m Sandown I of W 6.4.68 Sandra G. Martin cartogr d of Stanley A. M. Sandown

VIVEKANANDAN Kandavanam   PhD 1970
s of Kanapathipillai K. and Sinnathamby Sinnammah; b Ceylon 6.9.36

BSc(Ceylon) 1961 MIBiol 1970
res off. for. dept Colombo Ceylon from 1970
m Ceylon 26.1.72 Arulmanidevi Thambirajan d of Ponniah T. Batticaloa, Ceylon (Sri Lanka)

Von KUENSSBERG Verity Constance Evelyn   MA 1968
m Duncan

VORHAUS David Glyn   BSc 1966

VYSE Alan Horsley   *BSc(for) 1964
s of Adam V. fish merch and Joan H. Horsley teacher; b Tynemouth 31.8.42
MScF(Tor) 1971
for. econ Canadian for. serv Victoria BC 1966–73; res for. BC for. serv Williams Lake from 1974
m Toronto 31.12.65 Frances M. Mackintosh BSc 1965 *qv*

WADDELL Sheila Buchanan   MA 1969
d of Roy W. bus. man. and Maureen C. Buchanan teacher dom sc, nurse; b Glasg 24.4.48
Assoc I P R 1975
leader writer *Glasgow Herald* 1969–70; teacher Engl Douglas acad Milngavie 1972; information asst (p r off.) Babtie Shaw & Morton consult. civ & struct eng Glasg 1972–74, teacher: Engl/hist Barrenjoey h s NSW Aust 1975, Engl Bishopbriggs h s Glasg from 1976

WADDS Geoffrey Alan   *BSc 1966 PhD 1970
s of Edward A. W. aircraft insp and Joan Dilley civ serv; b Oxford 20.6.43
res analyst Lankro chem Eccles 1969–72; analyst/biochem Beecham pharm Harlow 1972–78; head analytical dept Anstead Billericay from 1978
m Cheadle 28.12.68 Linda P. Will nurse d of Thomas W.

WADSWORTH Ronald Stuart   ᵈLLB 1968
s of Arnold W. woollen textile spinner and Margaret S. Chree; b Huntly 3.11.47
law app, qualif asst, ptnr Mackie & Dewar advoc Aber 1968–73; ptnr Philip & Wadsworth advoc Aber from 1973; part time asst private law Aberd from 1968
m Luton 29.3.69 Margaret Clarke SRN d of Thomas S. C. Luton

WADSWORTH Sheila   LLB 1967
d of Stanley W. CA and Eva Whitworth; b Middleton 17.8.46
qualif solic Aston, Manc 1968; articled clerk Epsom c 1968–71; lect in law tech coll Ewell from 1971
m Rochdale 12.6.71 James H. Surgeoner LLB 1967 *qv*

WAITE James Howard Raymond   LLB 1969
s of Ralph R. W. and Margaret E. H. Pearson BSc(Lond); b Gloucester 7.4.48
solic Guildford from 1973

WAITER Sheila   MA 1956
d of Hugh G. W. fish merch and Julia M. Imrie clerkess; b Inverbervie 1.4.35
m Inverbervie 6.7.57 Alexander D. Mathieson farm., conservative ag s of Andrew M. Laurencekirk

WAKELIN Derek Raymond   *BSc 1970 PhD 1974
s of Bernard W. fitter and Lillian Holdsworth; b Rugby 20.10.46
lect: Aberd 1973–74, N'cle poly 1974–79, sen lect from 1979

WAKEMAN Norman Henry   *MA 1959
s of Henry E. W. soldier/painter and Elizabeth Cooper; b Hartlepool 30.10.36
sergeant instr RAEC 1959–61; Hartlepool: teacher 1961–

63, careers and exam. master 1963–73, head careers dept from 1973
m Hartlepool 9.9.60 Jean C. Fraser SRN/midwife d of Alexander E. F. Hartlepool

WALDING Hugh Frederick   PhD 1968
 s of Frederick E. W. off. at Law Soc and Lilian E. Bridge secy; b Norbury 24.7.43
MA(Oxon) 1965
res asst agr Glas 1968–71; lect Bournemouth coll of tech from 1971
m Glasg 22.7.71 Margaret S. Sutherland MA 1968 *qv*

WALDON Geoffrey   MB ChB 1961

WALKER Aileen Isobel Anne   MA 1968 Dip Ed 1969

WALKER Aileen Margaret   MA 1961
 d of William B. W. fisherman and Annie Parley waitress; b Aber 28.3.41
Aber: teacher Mile End s 1962–66; visiting teacher of mus prim. schools 1969–74; teacher Kintore s from 1974
m Aber 20.7.63 Robin M. Dyer MA 1961 *qv*

WALKER Alastair Alexander Wallace   *MA 1965

WALKER Alexander Davidson Ross   BSc 1961 *1963

WALKER Alexander Lyell   BSc 1962
 s of Alexander W. teacher and Jean R. Cook teacher; b Hamilton 30.7.41
Dip Ed(Glas) 1963
teacher: Glasg 1963–66, Western Samoa 1966–68; prin teacher RGC Aber 1969–72, Kincorth acad Aber from 1972
m Aber 19.12.64 Ann O. Anderson MA 1963 *qv*

WALKER Alison Barclay   BSc 1964
 d of Edward W. insur off. and Christina Barclay shorthand typist; b Aber 16.5.43
teacher maths Arbroath h s 1965–67
m Aber 6.1.68 Hamish D. Munro BSc 1964 *qv*

WALKER Andrew   BL 1957
 s of Thomas W. trawl owner and Margaret L. Mitchell; b Aber 29.2.36
Aber: trawl owner 1957–60, fish merch 1960–78, fish broker from 1978
m Aber 17.8.60 Christina M. Clark d of James G. C Aber

WALKER Anne   MA 1970 *MEd 1977
 d of Alfred W. W. cabinetmaker and Marion Esslemont secy; b Aber 28.11.48
teacher: Engl Torry acad Aber 1971–75, asst prin Engl Powis acad Aber from 1975
m Aber 8.8.70 Russell R. Orchard data control clerk s of Anthony R. O. Lond

WALKER Arthur Wellesley   *BSc 1962 Ph D 1966

WALKER Brian James   *BSc 1968

WALKER Christopher Howard   *MA 1966
 s of Harold W. min of relig and Kathleen Ushaw; b Birm 1.4.44
Dip Soc Admin(Manc) 1968
nat trg scheme for hosp admin Aber, Manc 1966–68; dept of soc admin univ of Hull: res asst 1968–69, asst lect 1969–71, lect from 1971
m Shere 10.4.71 Sarah J. Thompson BA(Hull) teacher d of Graham B. T. Dorking

WALKER Christopher Royston   BSc 1969
 s of Stanley W. clerk and Muriel N. Brown; b Norton Malton 30.7.48
computer progr: Nat West. bank Lond 1969–78, team leader corp of Lloyds insurers Chatham from 1978
m Cullen 29.5.71 Jane A. N. Woollam MA 1969 *qv*

WALKER Colin Harold   MSc 1961
 s of Harold H. W. prop. mus shop and Eleanor M. Bashford; b Thornton Heath 28.4.36
BSc(R'dg) 1959
scient. off., sen scient off. The Nature Conservancy, Abbots Ripton 1962–67; lect physiol/biochem R'dg from 1967
m Cambridge 28.3.64 Margaret E. Reith MA 1962 *qv*

WALKER Colin Nairn   *BSc 1968

WALKER Daniel Graham   *BSc 1961
 s of Daniel G. W. insur ag and Thomasina Mahaffey; b Aber 22.6.38
teacher NZ: maths/sc New Plymouth 1961–64, Bay of Islands coll from 1965
m New Plymouth 19.4.62 Carol E. Evans d of Idris L. E. Brit army Singapore

WALKER Doreen Isobel   MB ChB 1966
 d of Ian W. man. and Doris I. Stewart hairdresser; b Aber 6.5.42
h o gyn, med ARI 1966–68; sen h o psychiat Ross clin Aber 1968; part-time m o publ health Dun 1970–73; commun m o (sessional) Glenrothes and Leslie from 1973
m Aber 1.9.64 Thomas P. Reid sen process eng in electronics s of Thomas P. R. Aber

WALKER Edith Harriet   MA 1963
 m Beanan

WALKER George Stuart   BSc(eng) 1962

WALKER Ian Cossar   BSc 1967

WALKER Ivy Ada   MA 1967 Dip Ed 1968
 d of Alfred W. gen merch/grocer and Christina Duguid; b Rothienorman 30.10.46
teacher: Engl/hist Northfield acad Aber 1968–74, Turriff acad 1974–76
m Aber 12.4.73 William Cruickshank farm. s of William M. C. Rothienorman

WALKER James Findlay   MB ChB 1967
 s of John W. fish merch and Annie Findlay; b Aber 3.9.43
DObstRCOG 1971
h o: Perth RI, Victoria I Kirkcaldy 1967–69; g p Edin 1970–73; dir of res: Merrell nat labs Cincinnati Ohio 1973–76, Merek, Sharp & Dohme Philadelphia from 1976
m Aber 22.7.67 Yvonne E. Souter secy d of Robert S. Aber

WALKER James Stewart   *BSc 1959

WALKER Jean Middleton   *MA 1965
 m Riach

WALKER Jill   MB ChB 1962
 d of Thomas W. trawl owner and Margaret L. Mitchell teacher; b Aber 19.7.38
m Aber 12.7.62 Torbjørn Kufaas MB ChB 1962 *qv*

WALKER John Anderson   BSc 1970 Dip Ed 1971
 s of Robert W. tech instr. and Muriel W. Webster; b Aber 11.12.47

teacher sc Haddington 1971–74, prin chem Eyemouth from 1974
m Aber 19.7.72 Patricia A. Kelman nurs nurse d of John C. K. Aber

WALKER John Marshall   MB ChB 1966
s of Alexander C. W., BSc(H-W) eng consult. and Jane Ross; b Aber 27.2.43
FFARCS 1972
h o: ARI, Tasmania 1966–68; g p/anaest Perth Aust 1968–70; anaest/regist: Inv 1970–72, Edin 1973–74; anaest Diaconessenhuis Heemstede Neths from 1974
m Nairn 11.7.66 Elisabeth Ker d of John K. Nairn

WALKER John Murray   MA 1969
s of John A. W. grocer and Jane Y. Murray grocer; b Keith 1.7.48
teacher p s Lossiemouth h s 1970–73; dep head Speyside h s Aberlour 1973–76; head Cullen p s from 1977

WALKER Katharine Alice   MA 1962
(conferred for long service of exceptional merit)
d of George W. MA(Edin) clergyman DD 1922 qv(II) and Isabella Strong; b Aber 21.4.1900
asst lib Aberd 1922–65

WALKER Margaret Ann   MEd 1967
d of John C. W. BA(Cantab) civ serv and Mollie Wallwork civ serv, teacher; b Bamford 18.3.43
MA(St And) 1964
VSO teacher Magburaka Sierra Leone 1964–65; lect Engl lang Ahmadu Bello univ Zaria Nigeria from 1973
m Hertford Heath –.4.63 Michael J. Jones PhD 1968 qv

WALKER Marget Blackwood   MA 1960

WALKER Margaret Helen   MA 1961 Dip Ed 1962

WALKER Michael George Russell   *BSc 1969

WALKER Michael Grant   MB ChB 1964 ChM 1976

WALKER Norma Ann   BSc 1960
d of Alfred W. gen merch and Christina Duguid; b Rothienorman 12.2.39
teacher biol: Blairgowrie 1961–63, Inverurie 1963–64, Huntly 1965–67
m Aber 25.11.64 James J. F. Fawns farm. s. of James F. Huntly

WALKER Patricia Eveline   *MA 1968
d of William G. W. mech eng and Grace Cobban; b Aber 8.3.46
teacher Fr: Marple Hall g s Cheshire from 1969
m Aber 16.8.68 Gordon M. Coull quantity surv s of William C. Aber

WALKER Patrick John   MA 1962
s of John W. carpenter and Isabella Barron; b Aber 20.12.39
teacher: Powis s 1963–65, New Deer p s 1965–68; head: Tough p s 1968–71, Hatton (Cruden) p s 1971–75, Kellands p s Inverurie from 1975
m Aber 20.8.65 Phyllis Wyness d of Philip W. Kintore

WALKER Peter Anthony   MB ChB 1965
s of Richard J. W. MB ChB 1937 qv; b Aber 19.10.41
FRCSE 1970 MRCPath 1977
h o: ARI, Woodend hosp Aber 1965–66; terminable lect path. 1966–67 and 1969–70; sen h o: ARI, Glasg Western hosp 1967–69; lect path. Aberd 1972–81; Fife health board: consult. histopathologist Victoria hosp Kirkcaldy from 1981

m Aber 27.7.72 Gillian U. Price nurs sister d of John A. P. MA(Glas) Kintore

WALKER Thomas   PhD 1966
BSc(Dunelm)

WALKER William   *BSc 1966
s of William W. farm. and Isabella Legge; b Banff 11.12.43
teacher AGS 1967–73; prin phys Inv royal acad from 1972

WALKER William Brimlow   BSc(for) 1965
s of John M. T. W. furniture manuf and Mary K. Brimlow; b Glas 9.4.43
MIFor(GB) 1968
conserv lower Swansea valley proj (univ res proj) 1965–67; sen for. off. Norfolk c c Norwich 1967–69; for. man. Midlands private for. comp Shrewsbury 1969–72; reg man. S Scot. private for. comp Moffat from 1972
m Devizes 2.9.67 Diane R. Hiscox d of Stanley G. H. Devizes

WALKER William Thomson   MA 1965

WALLACE Bruce   MA 1966 BD 1969

WALLACE Elizabeth Ann Hay   MB ChB 1965
d of George E. E. surv of customs and excise and Margaret E. Hay teacher; b Elgin 6.8.32
MA(Edin) 1955 DPH(Glas) 1970
h o: Raigmore hosp Inv, Bridge of Earn, Craig Dunain Inv 1966–67; sen h o geriat Ashludie Dun 1967–68; asst m o Banffsh 1968–74, Grampian health board from 1974

WALLACE George Noble   *MA 1966
s of George H. W. eng and Mary S. Trail; b Fraserburgh 11.4.44
teacher Engl: Peebles 1967–68, Turin 1968–75, Dun 1975–76, and interpreter/translator Alba Italy from 1976

WALLACE Glenis Winifred   MA 1963
m Humphreys

WALLACE Ian Grant   MA 1957
s of Alexander R. B. W. hosp porter and Jane T. Innes; b Aber 1.12.34
BPhil(Oxon) 1959 Dip Ed(Edin) 1960 MEd(Glas) 1966 PhD(Glas) 1971
lect Glas: logic 1960–66, psych from 1966
m Banchory 9.7.59 Elva J. F. Durward teacher d of Alexander F. D. Banchory

WALLACE Irene Isobel   *MA 1966
m Hughson

WALLACE Janice Clare   MA 1968
d of Alexander F. W. arch. and Jeannette MacDougall; b Strathblane 22.6.47
secy: admin Wolsey Hall Oxford 1969–70, cognition proj psych Edin 1970–71; teacher: Easthall p s Easterhouse Glasg 1972–73, Harestones p s Kirkintilloch from 1973

WALLACE Judith Carol   *MA 1968

WALLACE Margaret Alison   *MA 1966
d of Alexander B. W. MB ChB(Edin) surg and Marguerite I. Burke nurse; b Edin 24.2.44
Edin: secy/edit. asst cartographic bus. 1967–68, edit. publ firm 1968–69
m Ceres 17.1.70 Alan J. Masson BSc(Edin) lect(Kodak) s of Hamish M. MA(Edin) Edin

WALLACE Martha Walker   MA 1967

WALLACE Michael Kennedy   BSc 1969
s of Ian H. W. plumber and Irene Kennedy clerkess; b
Aber 17.11.47
teacher sc Kaimhill j s s Aber 1970–71; exec off. M o D
Lond from 1971

WALLACE William   BSc(eng) 1970

WALLIS Richard Godfrey   *MA 1958
s of Richard H. W. customs & excise off. and Grace
Godfrey; b Aber 15.2.35
teacher mod lang Dunfermline h s 1959–63, spec asst
1963–65; prin mod lang Peterhead acad 1965–67; prin Fr
Dunfermline h s 1967–72; rector Bridge of Don acad
Aber from 1972
m Kirkpatrick-Fleming 30.3.64 Mary Beattie BSc(Edin)
teacher d of Thomas L. B. Kirkpatrick-Fleming

WALMSLEY Rosanne Mary   MA 1967

WALSH Alan Robertson   BSc 1970

WALSH Kieran James   *BSc 1969
s of James W. headmaster and Winefride M. Little
teacher; b Wrexham 21.9.43
teacher Summerhill acad Aber 1970–73; asst prin guid
1973–74, prin guid from 1974

WALTERS Jacqueline Mary   MB ChB 1963
m Bressan

WALTERSON Laurence Imlach   MB ChB 1957
s of Peter W. policeman and Jessie M. Imlach nurse; b
Lossiemouth 7.6.33
h o Woodend hosp Aber 1957–58, ARI 1958–59,
Woolmanhill Aber 1959; ship's surg 1959–60; sen h o
Woolmanhill 1960–62; g p Aber from 1962
m Aber 19.6.64 Jean Anderson MA 1955 *qv*

WALTON Michael John Stewart   MA 1967
s of John K. W. oil merch and Ruth G. Stewart; b Alyth
22.10.44
NCR: spec assignments Dun 1967–68; oil merch J.
Walton & Son Newtyle from 1968
m Perth 13.6.66 Penelope J. Rogers MA(St And) d of
John R. MB ChB(Glas) Dun

WALUDA Jerzy Marian   BSc(eng) 1969
s of John W. quarry chargehand and Maria Zon; b
Lancaster 2.8.47
asst eng highways/bridges Carlisle 1969–74; resid eng
Greta Bridge Co Durham from 1974
m Hawes 13.9.69 Marjorie Whitehead stud. nurse d of
Jason W. Gayle

WANG Stanley Way Shien   MB ChB 1969

WANN Kenneth Taylor   *BSc 1970 PhD 1975

WARBURTON David Hart   BSc(for) 1969

WARD John   PhD 1969
MAgrSc(R'dg)

WARD John Neve   MA 1968
s of Albert E. W. shop man. and Marget D. Finlayson
shop asst; b Nairn 24.1.48
indust dev off. HIDB Inv from 1968
m Fort William 26.10.74 Georgina R. Walker dent. nurse
d of Alexander I.M.W. Inverlochy

WARD John William   BSc 1966

WARD Nuala Clare   MA 1965
d of James J. W. MA(Glas) teacher/headmaster and
Catherine J. Goulding hairdresser, for. worker; b Lond
26.1.43
MA(St And) MRTPI 1973
plan. asst: Lanarksh 1965–67, Perth 1967–68; res asst, res
off. Perth 1968–74, plan. off. from 1974

WARD Stephen David   PhD 1968
BSc(Wales)

WARDELL Heather Lucy   MA 1968

WARDLAW Don Mark   PhD 1959
BA(Columbia univ NY) BD(Union Theol Seminary,
Richmond Va)

WARDLE Clement Shreen   *BSc 1962 PhD 1973
s of Arthur C. W. eng, teacher and Frances T.
Schensinger MA(Oxon) lect; b Mere 1.10.39
dev comm fisheries stud. Lowestoft 1962–64; Aber: jun res
fell. Torry res 1964–66, sen res fell. marine lab 1966–70,
sen scient off. marine lab 1970–72, prin scient off. from
1972
m Birm 17.7.62 Penelope A. Stripp teacher d of H.A.S.
Dar-es-Salaam Tanganyika

WARDLE Penelope Margaret   MA 1964

WARES Roy   *BSc 1964 MSc 1979
s of James W. and Mary D. Taylor; b Aber 16.8.42
MSc(Kingston Ont) 1971
Canada: field geol Ont 1964–68, proj evaluation geol
Vancouver 1968–74, sen geol Vancouver 1974–77; plan.
Grampian reg c Aber 1979–80; res geol Squamish Canada
from 1980

WARNOCK John Fraser   BSc 1969
s of John C. W., BSc(Glas) civ serv and Flora M.
Fraser teacher; b Glas 18.2.47
CA 1974
app acct Turner, Hutton & Lawson Glasg 1969–74

WARNOCK Shaw William   *MA 1967
s of Samuel S. W. freight man. and Marion I. Burns; b
Stirling 24.3.45
M Litt(Cantab) 1973
stockbroker's clerk (res dept) London from 1970

WARRACK Ian McArthur   MB ChB 1966
s of John W. MB ChB 1932 *qv*; b Doncaster 26.12.41
CCFP 1973
h o Woodend hosp Aber, ARI 1966–67; trainee g p
Culter 1967–68; Canada: fam phys Hawkesbury Ontario
1968–74, Ottawa 1974–77, lect family med univ of
Ottawa from 1977
m Aber 14.7.66 Alison McArthur MA 1964 *qv*

WARREN Andrew   *BSc 1959
s of Thomas W. MA(St And) teacher and Janet S.
McPhail teacher; b Kalimpong N Bengal 27.10.37
PhD(Cantab) 1967
soil surv Hunting tech serv UK, W Pakistan 1960–61;
lect univ coll Lond from 1964; fell. ACLS Lincoln
Nebraska USA 1967–68
m Aldringham 19.8.67 Inga M. Kerridge occup therap d
of Peter K. Ongar

WARREN Geoffrey Austin Richard   BSc 1966

WARREN Janet Gwyneth   *MA 1961
d of Thomas W. MA(St And) teacher and Janet S.
Macphail teacher; b St And 25.11.39

part time lect Farnborough tech coll 1967–70; TEFL Engl lang coll Bielefeld, W Ger 1970–72; Farnborough: teacher comp s 1973–75, part time lect tech coll from 1975
m Aber 10.7.62 Richard H. Hardie MB ChB 1963 *qv*

WARREN Susan Elizabeth   BSc 1968
d of Harold J. M. W. elect. eng and Phyllis Todd; b Grays 26.9.47
teacher sc Hilton s Aber 1969–71
m Aber 8.10.70 Douglas J. Grimes drilling fluid eng s of Harold C . G. Aber

WARRENDER, Jean   MA 1964
m Morris

WARRINGTON Brenda Elizabeth   MA 1969
d of Clifford W. head warehouseman and Margaret C. Johnston saleswoman; b Inv 13.1.48
exec off.: SED Edin 1969–72, dept for nat savings Glasg from 1972
m Inv 17.6.72 Norman Fawcett asst landscape off. s of John F. Workington

WARRINGTON Sandra   BSc 1966
d of Clement E. W. vicar and Euphemia M. Mackenzie; b Glasg 20.8.44
Dip Dietetics(Glasg) 1976
scient information off. Commonwealth Bureau of Nutrition Rowett res inst Aber 1966–73; dietitian Manc area health auth Manc RI 1976; sen dietitian Rochdale area health auth Birch Hill hosp 1976–78, area dietitian from 1978

WARWOOD Alasdair Iain   MA 1968
s of Kenneth A. I. W. hotelier and Helen I. N. Turnbull; b Newbury 17.7.48
syst analyst Burroughs Machines Birm 1968–72; dep computer serv man. BSG Birm 1972–74; syst analyst delegacy of loc exams. Oxford 1975–76; asst secy Finance Houses Assoc Lond from 1977

WASHINGTON Angela Mary   *BSc 1967
d of Noel W. MA(Cantab) teacher and Pauline M. Jarvis; b Rotherham 7.10.45
teacher geog Gloucester h s for girls 1968–72; lect geog/geol Gloucester City coll of tech from 1972

WATERFIELD Angela Alice   *BSc 1969 PhD 1973
d of Thomas W. prod. man. and Margaret Murphy; b Leigh 25.7.45
Aberd: res asst 1969–73, res fell. from 1973

WATERHOUSE Sheena Mary Alexandra   *MA 1965

WATERS Robert Pearse   BSc(for) 1960
insp of taxes from 1961

WATERSTON Margaret Elizabeth   *BSc 1970
d of William H. W. MA(Dund) assay clerk and Margaret Bore clerkess; b Dun 14.2.48
geol Kambalda Aust 1970–75
m Dun 5.8.70 Ian R. McDonald BSc 1970 *qv*

WATERSTON William George   LLB 1970
s of George W. LLD(Dund) ornithol and Nancy G. Ritchie; b Edin 2.2.49
Edin: WS ptnr Pearson, Robertson & Maconochie WS from 1974
m St Andrews Andrea L. Bennett SRN d of Peter H. B. BA(Oxon) Ottawa

WATKINS Lena Joan   *MA 1959
d of George A. W. man. dir light eng comp and

Elizabeth M. Smith teacher; b Bexley 1.4.37
teacher Aber h s for girls 1960–64
m Aber 8.8.64 Robert M. Logan MB ChB 1960 *qv*

WATKINS Roger Dexter   MB ChB 1968
s of Dudley D. W. cartoonist/illustrator and Doris E. Taylor; b Dun 21.7.43
MRCGP 1977
h o Inv 1968–70; g p Helensburgh from 1970
m Broughty Ferry 25.8.67 Lindsay A. McDowell MA 1967 *qv*

WATSON Alan Edward   *BSc(eng) 1970
s of Edward B. W. papermaking foreman and Muriel Forrester; b Fyvie 3.9.48
grad asst civ eng: Bucks c c Aylesbury 1970–72, Aber city eng dept 1972–74, Grampian reg water serv from 1974

WATSON Ann   *BSc 1966
d of James W. BSc 1932 *qv*; b Aber 25.5.45
res asst Exe 1967–70; computer progr: Bristol univ 1970–72, Birkbeck coll Lond 1972–75, Bristol univ from 1975
m Aber 18.2.65 Christopher N. French BSc 1966 *qv*; marr diss 1975

WATSON Anna Galbraith   MA 1961
d of Melville E. W. livestock auctioneer and Kate A. Forsyth; b Aber 29.11.40
market res investig Lond 1961–62; N'cle-u-Tyne: market res plan. 1962–65, asst pers superv for women 1965–69
m Aber 23.3.68 Peter R. Pearks BSc(chem eng)(Swansea) process dev eng s of Eric J. P. Torquay

WATSON Arthur   *BSc(eng) 1964 MSc 1965

WATSON Arthur Vincent Reid   MB ChB 1958
s of Vincent M. M. W. MB ChB 1921 *qv*; b Aber 18.2.30
DObstRCOG 1961 MRCGP 1971
g p Birmingham 1960–67, Torphins from 1967
m Arbroath 10.6.61 Linda M. G. McMaster d of Thomas McM. Arbroath

WATSON Brian MacDonald   *MA 1970

WATSON David Beresford   BSc 1961

WATSON Derek   *MA 1965
s of James W. man. dir and Elizabeth Wilson; b Aber 14.12.42
Lond: computer progr 1966–68; syst analyst 1968–74; lect computer stud. coll of tech Dun from 1974
m Wimbledon Lond 7.9.68 Beryl Johnson computer consult. d of Albert J. Wimbledon

WATSON Edith   *MA 1966
d of George W. farm. and Edith M. Morison MA 1939 *qv*; b Aber 5.1.44
Dip Ed(Edin) 1967
teacher geog Edin 1968–71; lect geog Craiglockhart coll of educ Edin 1971–76
m Aber 19.4.73 Robert A. Sykes BSc(eng)(Strath) civ eng s of Hubert S. Kirkmahoe Dumfries

WATSON Eleanor McLeod Munro   *MA 1963
d of William H. W. clerk and Helen M. M. Boyd piano teacher; b Aberlady 4.4.42
teacher geog E. Kilbride 1964–65
m E. Kilbride 10.7.64 David Butters min of relig s of Joseph B. Lochgelly

WATSON Gillian Mary   MA 1963
d of Philip E. W. comp dir and Mary E. Burton; b Aber
2.4.43
Dip Soc Sc(Edin) 1964, MIMSW(Lond) 1965
med soc worker ERI 1965–66
m Aber 9.10.65 Dennis A. Carswell BSc lect geol s of
Dennis L. C. Howwood

WATSON Graham   MA 1962

WATSON Helen Margaret   MB ChB 1970
d of George W. farm. and Edith M. Morison MA 1939 *qv*;
b Aber 27.2.46
h o Aber 1970–71
m New Pitsligo 20.7.70 Alexander P. Fowler MB ChB
1969 *qv*

WATSON Iain Scott Michie   *MA 1967
s of John S. W. MB ChB 1936 *qv* and Elizabeth
Michie MA 1936 *qv*; b Aber 21.6.45
joint man. dir Northern Jewellers (Scot.) Aber from 1968
m Aber 4.5.70 Marilyn Smith comp dir

WATSON Ian Rees   BSc(agr) 1970
s of John F. W. carpenter/joiner and Mary M. Rees; b
Croesgoch Haverfordwest 16.7.46
MSc (UCW) 1974
res asst UCW Aberystwyth till 1973; commercial diver
from 1974

WATSON Irene Abercromby   MB ChB 1959
d of William H. W. MA 1929 *qv* and Dorothy J. M.
Smith MA 1929 *qv*; b Loudon Malawi 9.8.34
m o city hosp Aber, RACH Aber 1959–61; part-time
govt m o: Mwenzo/Isoka Zambia 1961–74; private pract
Lusaka 1974–76
m Aber 15.7.59 James L. Wilkie MA 1956 *qv*

WATSON James Sinclair   MA 1967
s of James G. W. san insp and Mary M. Sinclair
clerkess; b Glasg 12.5.45
BA(OU) 1976
teacher maths Kelso h s 1968–74, asst prin maths from
1974
m Gordon 5.4.74 Muriel H. Ford d of James R. F.
Gordon

WATSON John Richard   PhD 1970
b Otley Yorks 2.5.46
BSc(Durh) Grad Dip Rec(WA) ARIC
res fell. soil sc univ of Western Australia 1970–76;
environmental off. dept conserv and environment Perth
1976–78

WATSON Kathleen   MA 1970
d of James W. warehouse foreman and Kathleen
Wallace; b Aber 18.12.48
cler asst city assessors Aber 1971–72 cler off. customs &
excise Edin from 1972
m Aber 12.1.74 Robin G. M. Mutch quantity surv s of
Eric G. M. Hayes

WATSON Ken Murray   BSc(agr) 1965
s of Robert P. W. farm. and Valerie L. Wood teacher
p e; b St And 25.6.43
Dip FM(NOSCA) 1966
agr advis: Inverurie 1967–68, Orkney 1969, farm man.
Fife from 1969
m St And 19.6.70 Pamela B. Millar nurse d of Tom B. M.
St And

WATSON Melville Forsyth   MA 1959 LLB 1961
s of Melville E. W. livestock off. and Kate A. Forsyth;

b Edin 30.8.38
law app, leg. asst Aber 1959–64; ptnr Storie, Cruden &
Simpson advoc Aber from 1964; chmn nat insur appeal
tribunal Aber from 1972
m Aber 5.7.63 Sheila E. G. Morgan MA 1961 *qv*

WATSON Michael John   BSc(eng) 1968
s of Daniel S. W. BSc(eng) 1932 *qv*; b Portsmouth 9.8.45
eng Rolls Royce Derby 1968–71; instr RN 1971–77;
teacher Woodbridge s 1977–80; RAF from 1980
m Aber Josee A. Lentz d of Emile E. L. Lond

WATSON Nancy Hunter   MA 1966

WATSON Nigel John Fairley   *MA 1970

WATSON Ray Buchanan   LLB 1965
d of William W. oil comp exec and Elizabeth J. Rae;
b Aber 11.7.44
leg. app Aber 1965–67, solic Aber from 1967
m Aber 23.11.68 Colin P. Pigott BSc(eng) 1967 *qv*

WATSON Robert Haldane   BSc(for) 1956

WATSON Roderick Bruce   *MA 1965
s of Mearns B. W. BSc 1933 *qv*; b Aber 12.5.43
PhD(Cantab) 1971
lect Engl lit univ of Vict BC Canada 1965–66; res stud.
Cambridge, Edin 1966–70; Arts Council grant for own
poetry 1970–71; lect Engl lit Stir from 1971
m Aber 14.7.66 Celia H. Mackie d of Stanley M. Aber

WATSON Rosemary Anne   MA 1959
d of Philip E. W. man. dir and Mary E. Burton secy; b
Aber 20.6.38
secy to prod. overseas talks and features BBC 1960; pers
secy to dir Rowett res inst Aber 1960–65
m Aber 29.12.65 James N. Hay BSc(Glas) univ lect s of
John H. Alloa

WATSON Stanley James   *MA 1969 Dip Ed 1970
s of William H. W. MA 1929 *qv* and Dorothy J. M.
Smith MA 1929 *qv*; b Aber 25.11.38
teacher Engl AGS 1970–72, prin guid Ellon acad from
1972
m Aber 4.7.66 Elizabeth M. Jones teacher d of Frederick
J. J. Colwyn Bay

WATSON Valerie   MA 1969
d of Henry M. W. bus. man. elect./radio/tv and
Gertrude A. Milne; b Banff 8.12.37
teacher: Quarryhill p s Aber 1960–64, St Christopher's
ch s Manama Bahrain, RAF s Muharraq Bahrain 1965–66
m Aber 1963 Frederick D. Routledge pilot/mooring
master s of Frederick S. R. Elgin

WATT Aileen Elizabeth Clare   BEd 1969
d of Archibald W. MA 1936 *qv*; b Machyllneth N
Wales 20.11.46
teacher Fr Portobello h s 1969–73; asst prin mod lang
Craigmount h s Edin from 1974
m Aber 20.1.73 Matthew M. Little BSc(Edin) teacher,
insur clerk s of Arthur L. Langholm

WATT Alan Charles   MB ChB 1958
s of Charles W. asst postmaster and Charlotte
McGregor nurs sister; b Keith 5.1.34
LMCC 1976
h o Woodend gen hosp Aber, Perth RI 1958–59; m o
colony of N Borneo Beaufort and Keningaw now Sabah
Malaysia 1959–62; h o mat. hosp Aber 1963; termin lect
anat Aberd 1963–64; med pract Westlock Alta Canada
from 1965

m Aber 29.7.59 Margaret O. Willox RGN d of Alexander W. Cuminestown

WATT Alan Stewart Mitchell   *BSc 1970

WATT Alastair   BSc(eng) 1970

WATT Alastair Douglas   BSc(eng) 1966
s of James W. eng and Isabella S. Ferguson; b Aber 25.7.44
jun, intermed eng Racal Bracknell 1966–68; sen eng, proj man. RDL (EMI) Camberley 1968–71; sole prop. Hillhouse Systems Camberley from 1971
m Weybridge 28.9.65 Veronica S. Handy d of Dennis J. H. Walton on Thames

WATT Alexander   *MA 1964 PhD 1967
s of Alexander M. W. farm. and Elma Taylor; b Ellon 24.11.41
asst lect nat phil Aberd 1967–68, lect Glas from 1969
m Aber 24.7.67 Marie E. Morrison MA 1963 qv

WATT Alexander   *BSc 1967
s of James C. W. fisherman and Helen A. Watt; b Crovie 2.9.37
teacher: sc Bankhead acad 1968–74, chem Aber tech coll from 1974
m Fraserburgh 2.1.62 Christine Murray d of John M. Gardenstown

WATT Alexander John   MB ChB 1956
s of Adam N. S. W. MB ChB 1925 qv and Margaret A. Mackay MB ChB 1926 qv(III); b Dagenham 3.7.33
h o ARI, Raigmore hosp Inv 1957–58; g p: Grimsby 1958–67, Perth from 1967; CAA authorised examinr Perth/part time m o Perth aerodrome from 1968
m Whitekirk 24.3.62 Elizabeth A. Brash BSc(Edin) teacher d of George M. B. BSc(Edin) Edin

WATT Alexandra Adam   *MA 1964
m West

WATT Andrew John   *BSc 1963 PhD 1966

WATT Andrew Robin   LLB 1970
s of Andrew W. CBE BA(for)(Oxon) comm of for. and Helen M. McGuffog; b Edin 31.3.49
law app Edin 1970–72, solic from 1972

WATT Ann Elizabeth   MA 1963
m(1) Hendry
   (2) Seymour

WATT Ann Marie   MA 1957
d of Charles W. W. man. draper's shop, clerk and Ellie H. Hutcheon; b Aber 9.11.35
teacher Aber: Muirfield s 1958–64, RGC 1964–68
m Aber 27.12.68 William I. Campbell eng draughtsman, tech coll lect s of Hugh C. North Shields

WATT Avril Martin   *MA 1966

WATT Catherine Allardyce   MA 1963
d of William A. W. long dist driver, trans foreman and Elisabeth B. Cross waitress, superv; b Aber 4.8.42
part time teacher mod lang coll of comm Aber from 1964
m Aber 14.10.63 Michael R. Hewitt BSc(eng) 1962 qv

WATT Charles Cameron   *BSc(agr) 1969
s of Walter W. police/ch's panel and Jean R. Wood; b Haddington 20.11.46
lands off. DAFS Oban 1970–73; reg tech advis Atcost Scot./N Eng 1973–74; lands off. DAFS Glasg, Orkney,

Stirling from 1974
m Tranent 26.8.70 Margaret Hart teacher dom sc d of William H. Elphinstone

WATT Chrissy   MA 1956
d of Charles W. acct and Williamina Fraser; b Aber 9.7.36
teacher Pitmedden p s 1957–68; teacher/housemistress Albyn s for girls Aber 1968–74; teacher Balgownie p s 1974–77; asst head Cults p s Aber from 1977

WATT David Alexander   *BSc(for) 1969
s of Alexander S. W. oil refinery superv and Doris G. Paine; b Lond 26.6.48
landscape asst (for.): Kent c c estates ·dept Maidstone 1970–74, Islington (Lond) plan. dept 1974–78, arboricultural off. parks dept from 1978

WATT David Alexander Fraser   *MA 1964

WATT Donald Alexander   ᵉLLB 1966
s of James W. civ serv and Jamesina McLennan; b Spey Bay 27.2.45
law app Dun 1966–68; solic: Clydebank 1968–69; Kirkcaldy 1969–73; solic/town clerk Burntisland 1973–75; dep dir of admin Kirkcaldy from 1975
m Hamilton 6.12.69 Yvonne R. Jennings nurse d of Patrick J. Middlesbrough

WATT Donald William Clement   MB ChB 1962
s of James C. W. fisherman and Mary Macdonald nurse; b Macduff 21.1.37
DMRD(Lond) 1965 CRCP(C) 1969
h o, sen h o ARI 1963–65; regist RI Glasg 1965–67, sen regist Victoria I Glasg; consult. radiol, dir radiol Holy Cross hosp Calgary Canada from 1968
m Glasg 10.9.60 Elizabeth Lambert secy d of James L. Glasg

WATT Elspeth Murray Richards   BSc 1970
d of Harold M. R. W. MA 1942 qv and Elizabeth F. C. Richards MA 1941 qv; b Aber 26.4.49
teacher: Elphinstone p s Tranent 1971–72, Speke, Liv 1972–73; insur clerk Guardian Royal Exchange Insur Co Preston 1973–76
m Aber 22.9.72 Alastair S. Leaver BSc 1971 brewer s of Harry L. Largs

WATT Eric   *MA 1961
s of James W. W. fisherman and Charlotte Johnston; b Banff 25.3.39
brand man. York 1961–66; asst marketing man. Peterborough 1966–68; marketing man. Birm 1968–72; Lond: European man. 1972–76, marketing controller 1976–78, comp dir from 1978
m Camberley 14.9.63 Diana M. White BA(R'dg) psych, teacher d of Richard H. W. Camberley

WATT Forbes   *MA 1967
s of Joseph W. tailor, fisherman and Rose Forbes gen merch; b Pennan 13.9.35
Cert Master Mariner 1960
teacher: geog Fraserburgh acad 1968–70; Buchan tech coll Fraserburgh: teacher soc/gen stud. 1970–71, lect navigation 1971–72, head dept naut stud. from 1972
m Gardenstown 17.3.56 Mary W. Robertson nurse/sister d of William R. Gardenstown

WATT Francis   *BSc(eng) 1967
s of George A. W. fisherman and Jamesina Smith; b Aber 1.1.44
Canada: lubrication eng Saskatoon 1967–68, petr eng Edmonton 1968–70; pilot RAF UK, Cyprus from 1970

m Aber 30.7.66 Sylvia E. Reeve teacher d of Terence C. R. RN

WATT Francis Austen   MA 1966
s of Francis W. BSc 1933 *qv*; b Kelso 26.2.44
Chrysler UK (purchasing): fin. analyst, office man. Coventry 1966–70; Internat Computers (ICL) sales exec Harrow, Glasg, Manc 1971–75; acct Finnie, Ross, Allfields CA Lond 1976–79; fin. controller P & O Consultancy & Computer serv Watford from 1980
m Stoke-on-Trent 3.4.71 Ursula M. Regan teacher; wife *d* 1.10.72

WATT Francis James   MB ChB 1965
s of James W. eng and Isabella Ferguson; b Aber 5.4.40
DA 1967 DObstRCOG 1968 FRCP(C)Anaes 1977 FACA 1978
h o Aber 1965–66, sen h o Sheffield, Irvine 1966–68; g p Cinderford, Keswick 1968–72; resid anaest Toronto 1972–75; consult. anaest Newmarket Ontario from 1975
m Perth 29.4.66 Adena Thomson nurse/midwife d of George T. Perth

WATT Gavin William   BSc 1970
s of William N. W. toolmaker and Violet Cockburn teacher; b Aber 13.5.46
teacher Paignton 1970–71; res chem Nott 1971–77; PGCE Nott univ 1977–78; teacher Hawick from 1978
m Aber 29.8.70 Christine A. Davidson clerkess d of Alexander D. Fraserburgh

WATT Gordon Alastair James   *MA 1965

WATT Graham Gordon   *BSc 1967

WATT Guy Ridley   *BSc(for) 1969
s of Alexander J. W. and Audrey Z. D. Ridley; b Surrey 3.10.45
BLitt(Oxon) 1971
Min Overseas Dev Lond 1971–72; consult. FAO Rome 1972; asst conserv for. Honiara Solomon Is 1972–74; consult. Min Overseas Dev Lond 1974–75; for. res inst Rotorua NZ from 1975
m Newick 26.2.72 Rosemarie J. Jenkins d of Neville C. J. Farnborough

WATT Heather Güldmar   BSc 1970
d of William G. W. teacher, min of relig and Thelma G. Taylor secy, teacher; b Aber 4.5.47
res asst pharm Strath 1968–69; teacher sc in NATO s Brunssum Holland 1972–73; trainee acct: Aber 1977–78, Peterhead from 1978
m Aber 6.7.68 David S. Ross BSc 1967 *qv*

WATT Ian Joseph   MA 1967 MEd 1972
s of Joseph W. fisherman and Christina W. Duncan; b Lerwick 25.8.40
teacher Lerwick 1968–71
m Lerwick 25.9.67 Eleanor J. Paton d of James J. P. Lerwick

WATT James Currie   MB ChB 1969

WATT James Dennis MacPherson   *MA 1967
d Bristol 8.3.69 *AUR* XLIII 218

WATT James Norman Mackenzie
***MA 1968 Dip Ed 1971**

WATT Janet Farquhar   *BSc 1956
m Stollery

WATT Jill Emerson   *MA 1969
m Crofts

WATT John Alexander   MB ChB 1962
s of William J. W. farm. and Marjory McRobb farm.; b Rothes 19.8.38
DPM 1966 CRCP(C) 1968 MRCPsych 1972 FRCP(C) 1972
h o, sen h o ARI 1962–63; Garden res fell. bact Aberd 1963–64; lect Aberd 1964; regist psychiat Ross clin Aber 1965–66; regist Kingseat hosp Newmachar 1966–67; visiting clin instr psychiat Strong mem hosp univ of Rochester NYS, USA 1967–68; staff psychiat: Clarke inst Toronto 1968–71, Homewood sanatorium Guelph Ont 1971–72, med dir from 1972
m Whithorn 2.7.62 Olga Petrucci teacher d of Italo P. Whithorn

WATT John Alexander Menmuir   BSc(agr) 1956
s of William B. S. W. farm. and Margaret E. Menmuir teacher; b Stonehaven 1.3.35
farm. NSW Aust 1956–57; nat serv 1957–59; reg advis R. Silcock & Sons Midlands 1959–68; W & J Pye NW England: tech advis 1968–78, tech & market. man. from 1978, also dir Nutrition Control Services Lancaster
m Southport 16.12.61 Elizabeth A. Wollaston nurse d of Geoffrey G. W. Southport

WATT John Ritchie   MA 1969

WATT John Simpson   MB ChB 1956
d Edmonton 14.11.68 *AUR* XLIII 86

WATT Joyce Stephen   MA 1957 *MEd 1965 PhD 1980
d of William M. W. circuit man. oil comp and Josephine M. Stephen; b Aber 28.5.37
teacher St Margaret's s for girls Aber 1958–65; lect Dun coll of educ 1966–72, Aberd from 1972

WATT Lesley Jane   MB ChB 1968
m Stewart

WATT Linda May   MA 1970
d of William W. surv and Doris E. McLeod teacher; b Aber 9.5.49
governess Algeria 1971–72; teacher Royal h s Edin 1972
m Edin 29.8.72 Michael Naismith-Beeley naval off. s of Bruce N-B. Irvine

WATT Margaret   MA 1958
m Lyall

WATT Margaret   MA 1969

WATT Margaret Ann   BSc 1967
m Chalmers

WATT Marjorie Anne   BSc 1965
d of John W. man. and Annie S. Henderson secy; b Aber 2.5.44
teacher maths: Inverurie acad 1966–68, Grove acad Dun 1968–69, Bridge of Don s Aber 1970–72
m(1) Downie
(2) Aber 7.10.72 George A. Milne BSc 1963 *qv*

WATT Mirren Adams   MA 1958
d of Walter A. W. acct and Margaret C. I. Coulter teacher; b Aber 12.3.37
teacher Engl Northfield acad 1959–70, prin asst Engl/guid/careers 1965–70
m Aber 21.12.68 Joseph Watson branch man. s of Joseph W. Aust

WATT Morag Elizabeth   MA 1962
m Tamisari

WATT Nicol Lumsden   BSc 1956 *1958
s of George W. san insp and Mary W. S. Lumsden; b
Turriff 6.8.35
MInstP 1967 CEng MIEE 1968
phys: Assoc Elect. Indust Manc 1958–63, Hammersmith
hosp Lond 1963–67, Patent off. Lond 1968–69, univ of
Manitoba Winnipeg 1969–71, poultry res centre Edin
from 1972
m Bonn 12.6.70 Sigrid M. G. Stegert nurse Marburg

WATT Pearl Wiseman   BSc 1970
m Noble

WATT Sheila Anne   BSc 1968
d of Douglas A. W. cashier and Anne B. Stewart; b
Aber 25.2.47
BEd(Tor) 1970
res proj Glasg RI 1968–69; Tor: teacher maths Winston
Churchill coll inst 1970–73, L'Amoreaux coll inst 1973–
75, asst head maths from 1975
m Aber 13.7.68 Norman W. Leslie MA 1967 *qv*

WATTIE James Alistair   MB ChB 1960
m Aber 17.12.65 Joanna M. Garrioch MB ChB 1966 *qv*

WATTS-RUSSELL Grayling Jessica Pepita   MA 1968
d of David R. W. R. W-R. landowner and Gina S.
Baker BA(Rome); b Hamburg 5.10.47
Dip Vocat Guid(R'dg) 1973
TEFL: Vientiane Laos 1968–70, Cambridge 1970–71;
careers off. Surrey c c 1972–74
m Reading 10.2.73 Andrew M. Wright BA(Cantab) med
pract s of John W. W. BSc(Cantab) Effingham

WEATHERLEY Jill Margaret   *MA 1967 Dip Ed 1980
d of Paul E. W. BA(Oxon) univ prof Aberd and
Margaret L. Pirie poultry man.; b Kampala Uganda
13.9.45
m Irvine

WEAVER Ian Robert Sidney   *BSc(eng) 1960
s of Sidney W. dir of amenities Aber c c and Grace T.
MacGregor; b Winchester 14.7.39
MICE 1966
asst eng: Angus c c 1960–61, Midlothian c c Edin 1961–
64; eng asst R. H. Cuthbertson & Assoc Edin 1965–66;
teacher sc: Bearsden 1968–71, Montrose 1971–72; sen
asst eng, resid eng Forfar, Brechin from 1972
m Forfar 9.10.71 Sheila E. Blair MA(St And) teacher d of
William B. Forfar

WEAVER Rhoda Jean   MA 1964
m Murdoch

WEBB Alastair Richard John   MA 1970
s of Richard J. W. environmental health off. and
Margaret M. Johnston; b Glasg 29.5.48
teacher: geog/Engl Glasg 1971–73, geog Perth 1973–75,
geog/guid from 1975
m Glasg 5.4.72 Helen W. Moffat art teacher d of David M.

WEBB Ian Scott   *BSc 1969 PhD 1976
s of Kenneth R. W. solic and Gwen L. Scott artist; b
Berkhamsted 13.10.46
soil scient with land resource surv team Honiara Solomon
Is 1969–70; post grad stud. soil sc dept Aberd 1971–73;
sen scient off. min of agr Auki, Honiara 1973–77; res
scient (ODM) Rothmansted exper stat 1977–78; soil
scient/plan. Electrowatt Eng Serv (Lond) Lond, worldwide from 1978

m Aber 4.4.72 Linda A. McKay MA 1971 teacher d of
William D. McK Winchester

WEBB John MacLeod   BSc 1966
s of Arthur B. W. eng and Margaret MacLeod nurse;
b Barnet 11.1.45
Lond: computer progr, syst des 1966–71, syst/progr man.
1971–73, syst exec 1973–74; data base man. Tehran Iran
1975–77; proj man. Bath, Reading from 1977
m Aber 19.3.66 Pamela N. Pollock LL B 1971 computer
syst analyst d of Capt K. P. Poole

WEBB Michael John   MSc 1966
s of Harry F. W. optical eng and Dorothy A. M.
Butler; b Birm 8.5.44
BSc(N'cle) 1964
res stud. Lanc 1966–69; scient, sen scient Shell Res(agr
chem) Sittingbourne from 1969
m N'cle-u-Tyne 25.5.68 Judith Greenwood BSc(N'cle) d
of Maurice G. N'cle-u-Tyne

WEBB Moraig Anne MacLeod   MA 1961
d of Arthur B. W. eng and Margaret MacLeod nurse;
b Barnet 8.7.40
teacher: Engl/hist Macduff 1962–67, Engl/Latin Elgin
1967–68
m Nairn 11.7.64 George M. Gray farm. s of Robert G.
Banff

WEBER Ursula Hilde   MB ChB 1965

WEBSTER Alexander David
                                BSc 1956 *1957 Dip Ed 1958
s of David A. W. licensed grocer and Jemima
Hutchison; b Brechin 30.1.35
teacher chem Perth acad 1958–64; prin chem Nairn acad
from 1964
m Brechin 5.8.64 Donna J. Robertson d of George S. R.
Brechin

WEBSTER Alistair Kellas   MB ChB 1964
d Hereford 31.7.70 *AUR* XLIV 112

WEBSTER Brydon   MB ChB 1961
d 26.1.63 *AUR* XL 208

WEBSTER Charlotte Hutchison   MB ChB 1956
d of David A. W. lic grocer and Jemima Hutchison; b
Brechin 24.5.32
h o Strachathro hosp Brechin 1956–57; sen h o ARI
1957–58; chest phys royal Ottawa sanatorium 1958–60;
Leeds: lect path. 1961–64, m o FPA from 1969
m Brechin 4.9.57 Denis Greig PhD 1958 *qv*

WEBSTER Colin James   *BSc 1964 PhD 1967
s of James W. lorry driver and Coleena McIntosh; b
Aber 29.7.42
post doct res Tor Canada 1967–68; scient ICI organics
div Stevenston 1968–77, asst oper man. Manc from 1977
m Aber 3.9.65 Margaret Harper med secy d of Hugh
M. H Aber

WEBSTER Elizabeth Ann   MB ChB 1970
d of Harold V. W. postman and Vera B. Reed; b Lond
28.8.47
h o: ARI 1970–71, Lond 1971–72; sen h o Ilford 1972–74;
g p Ilford from 1974
m Ilford 14.8.71 John B. Houston bank clerk s of Joseph
H. MA(Dub) Glengarnock

WEBSTER Elizabeth Joan   MA 1964
d of John W. farm. and Elizabeth Thomson; b Turriff
30.3.43

remed teacher sec dept; Rosehearty and Turriff 1965–74; prin guid and remed teacher Turriff acad from 1974
m Turriff 16.7.66 David R. Christie farm. s of James C. Fordoun

WEBSTER Ewan Burgess   *BSc 1969
s of William W. bank man. and Mary H. Burgess SRN; b Keith 12.9.47
scient off., sen scient off. AEA Dounreay from 1969

WEBSTER Gordon Johnstone   MA 1959 Dip Ed 1960

WEBSTER James   MB ChB 1969
s of James G. W. soldier and Kathleen M. Cowie; b Aber 16.9.30
h o Woodend hosp Aber 1969–70; g p: Aber 1970–71, Oldmeldrum/Fyvie, Aber from 1971
m Fyvie 24.7.71 Caroline J. Mair physioth d of Scott M. M. Aber

WEBSTER John   BMedBiol 1970 MB ChB 1973
s of William J. W. fisherman and Emma Watt; b Aber 17.3.48
MRCP 1975
h o ARI 1973–74; temp lect therapeutics/clin pharm Aberd 1974–75; sen h o med Woodend gen hosp Aber 1975; lect therap/clin pharm Aberd from 1975
m Fraserburgh 20.5.76 Mary G. Simpson midwife d of William J. C. S. Maud

WEBSTER John Alexander
            *BSc(eng) 1964 MSc 1965 PhD 1968
s of John A. W. man. dir bldg/civ eng contr and Lilias W. Wilson; b Aber 12.2.43
Aberd: asst lect eng 1965–66; lect eng maths 1966–69; res scient CSIRO Canberra Aust 1969–72; res eng MWD Wellington NZ 1972–75; sen lect arch. Well from 1975
m Aber 29.12.65 Mary Kincaid BSc 1964 qv

WEBSTER Michael Joseph   BSc 1968
s of Francis W. dir textile comp and Nancy K. Elsmie; b 25.4.46
Dip Acct(Strath) 1974 CA 1978
man. trainee Arbroath 1968–73, app CA Aber 1974–77, acct Arbroath from 1977

WEBSTER Nicol Ewen   *MA 1968

WEBSTER William Gordon   MSc 1964
s of Gordon W. W. BSc(Alta) chem eng and Ena Youngblood nurse; b Calgary Alta 24.5.39
BSc(elect.eng)(Alta) 1961
Athlone fell. BoT UK 1962–64; Canada: res eng trans eng CN Rail from 1964
m Edmonton Alta 9.7.62 Phyllis G. Roos BSc(Alta) nurse d of Val K. Roos BEd(Alta) Edmonton

WEDDELL Ann   *BSc 1968

WEDDLE Richard Braid   *BSc 1969
s of Hugh E. W. BSc(Durh) solic's clerk and Margaret A. Braid solic's clerk; b 13.2.47
res asst (food tech/biochem) Unilever res Aber from 1969

WEIGHTON David Michael   *BSc(agr) 1966
s of David W. storekeeper and Betsy W. Hardie; b Forfar 24.12.42
MSc(UCNW) 1967
Boots Co: tech off. insecticide dev Nott 1967–69, tech off. Sydney Aust 1969–71, sen tech off. insecticides/fungicides res Nott 1971–76, sen dev off. from 1976

WEIR Elizabeth McDonald   MA 1970
d of John D. M. W. teacher tech subjs and Agnes D. Irvine piano accompan dance in schools; b Aber 19.2.49
Dip Grad Sec(Edin coll of comm) 1971
secy; Alex Hall & Son (bldrs) Aber 1971–72, Aber Construction Group 1972; secy/pa Colin Wood Antiques Aber 1972–74; secy/typist fac of Arts Aberd 1975–78, sen secy/typist mod lang from 1978

WEIR Iain Thomson   MA 1968

WEIR James Alexander   BSc 1961
s of James W. farm. and Louisa Farquhar; b Portnockie 13.3.39
teacher sc Powis acad Aber 1962–71; prin sc Old Aberdeen j s s 1971–73; prin phys Powis acad from 1973
m Aber 8.8.67 Mary M. Tod teacher d of David J. T. Kirkcaldy

WEIR James William Henderson Cameron
                        BSc(agr) 1961
s of John N. C. W. BSc(agr)(Glas) agriculturalist and Jessie F. Henderson nurs sister; b Aber 24.1.39
BVMS(Glas) 1966
asst vet surg Aber 1966–69; ptnr vet surg Aber 1969–75, prin from 1975
m Aber 29.3.68 Yvonne D. C. Carle teacher dom sc d of Robert C. Aber

WEIR Jane Gibb   *MA 1969
d of John S. W. RAF, postman and Evelyn Moir shop asst; b Abingdon 24.4.47
m Aber 20.12.68 Roderick H. Cameron eng draughtsman s of Roderick C. Greenock

WEIR John Grant Colin   BSc(agr) 1966
s of John N. C. W. BSc(agr)(Glas) agriculturalist and Jessie F. Henderson nurs sister; b Aber 31.1.42
Dip FM(Aber) 1970
agr advis NOSCA: Benbecula 1966–69, Dingwall 1970–72; farm man. NOSCA farm Aldroughty Elgin 1972–74
m Nairn 30.7.70 Elspeth G. M. Fraser MA 1963 qv
d Elgin 22.3.74 AUR xlv 450

WEIR Marion Preston   BSc 1959
d 23.10.66

WEIR Robert James   BSc 1962
s of Robert W. textile des and Jessie A. Tough mill worker; b Keith 3.6.41
teacher: maths/sc Edzell j s s 1963–65, chem Mackie acad Stonehaven 1965–73; prin chem Bankhead acad from 1973
m Aber 14.8.65 Sheila M. Adam sen lab tech d of Walter A. Aber

WELCH Linda May   MA 1969

WELFORD John George   BSc(for) 1958
d 19.1.64

WELFORD Peter Alexander Rex   BSc 1970
s of Peter G. W. MA(Oxon) teacher and Enid D. Blackmore teacher; b Weymouth 22.6.48
lab Is of Skye 1971–72; teacher: Edin 1972–77, New York 1977–78, Edin 1978–79; Is of Skye: bldg contr 1979–80, mus from 1980

WELLS Janet   MB ChB 1968
d of John A. N. W. eng and Joan Broadman secy; b Clacton 13.6.45
Aber: h o ARI 1968–69; Aberd res fell. dept path. 1969–

71; trainee g p Torphins 1972–73; med co-ordinater NE
Scot. reg hosp board 1973–74; m o Bexley and Greenwich
area health auth 1974–75; m o Kent area health auth
1975–79; regist commun med SE Thames area health
auth from 1977
m Sidcup 25.7.64 David J. Hall MSc 1967 *qv*

WELLS Judith Angela   MA 1959
  d of Joseph N. W. fish merch and Thirza Robertson; b
Grimsby 3.11.37
Secy-Dip Bi-lingual(Ealing tech coll) 1960
bi-ling secy Dow-Unquinesa SA Bilbao Spain 1960–61
m Aber 9.9.61 Jose L. Gervas BEcon(Bilbao) capt SpMN
s of Victor G. Sestao-Vizcaya Spain

WELLS Michael   *BSc 1957 PhD 1968
  s of Stanley R. W. clerk and Jessie P. Featherstone
cashier; b Norwich 25.4.34
teacher sc Ellon acad 1958–60; asst exper off. DAFS
Perth 1960–62; res asst dep mat. med-therapeutics Aberd
1962–68; lect biol sc H-W Edin from 1968
m Aber 28.12.59 Elizabeth M. Gloyer shorthand typist d
of Marshall H. G. Aber

WELLS Russell Emerson   PhD 1970
  s of Emerson H. W. farm. and Vera E. Wheatland; b
Unity Sask Canada 2.6.33
BSc(agr)(Sask) 1956 MSc(Alta) 1961
Can. dept agr soil surv Edmonton 1956–62; organis of
Amer states soil surv Chile 1962–63; Can. land inventory
(soil surv and land classif) Newfoundland 1963–67; Can.
for. serv (environmental surv): Newfoundland 1967–73,
Quebec from 1973
m St John's Newfoundland 28.12.67 Elizabeth R. Carter
d of John C. St. John's

WELSH Elizabeth Katherine Cochrane   MA 1965
  d of Graham C. W. MA 1937 *qv*(III) and Bessie King;
b Edin 4.1.45
Dip Secy Sc(Strath) 1966
secy ag work Edin 1965–66; staff secy Kennet comp s
Thatcham from 1977
m Edin 23.7.66 Gareth J. Rowlands MA(Cantab) statist
s of Vernon W. R. BA(Bangor) Liv

WELSH Jane Alexandra Cochrane   MA 1968

WELSH Jean Saddler   BSc 1970
  d of William P. W. joiner, teacher and Esther Saddler;
b Fraserburgh 2.12.48
computer progr Aber c c 1971–72
m Aber 18.2.72 John G. Smith BSc 1972 scient off. s of
James S. Fraserburgh

WELSH Margaret Cramond   MB ChB 1968
  m Underwood

WELSH Moira Jean Lennox   *MA 1966
  d of Martin W. mech eng and Helen R. Hislop clerkess;
b Edin 26.6.44
Dip Ed(Edin) 1967
teacher Silverknowes p s Edin 1967–70; educ psych Edin
1970–73
m Aber 27.12.68 Donald H. Steele MA 1966 *qv*

WELSH Norma   MA 1956
  d of Norman G. M. W. vanman/gen store owner and
Mary W. Watson; b Inverurie 31.3.35
teacher: Johnstone 1957–58, Aber 1958–59
m Aber 21.7.59 James S. McIntosh MB ChB 1958 *qv*

WEMYSS Robert Duncan   *MA 1970
  s of Duncan W. male nurse and Duncanina McKinnon;

b Inv 28.3.48
MSc(H-W) 1972 MRTPI 1974
town plan. asst Ayr burgh 1972–75; asst dir (plan.)
Cumnock and Doon valley dist c from 1975
m Inv 12.9.70 Marilyn H. Lobban clerkess d of George
I. L. Inv

WEMYSS Thomas   MA 1969
  s of James A. W. factory foreman and Margaret G.
McKay filleter; b Fraserburgh 2.6.46
teacher sp/drama: Aber corp 1970–72, Aber coll of comm
from 1972
m Aber 14.9.68 Margaret V. Hamilton MA 1969 *qv*

WENHAM Martin William   PhD 1966
  BSc(Wales)

WERNHAM Archibald Garden   LLB 1967

WESSEL Ivar   MB ChB 1968

WEST Alexander William   MA 1963
  s of Alexander W. W. and Rose N. Davidson; b Stonehaven 14.11.39
teacher Aber 1964–76; prin geog Linksfield acad Aber
from 1976; leader Sandy West's Jazzmen band
m Aber 23.5.72 Edith S. Crabb

WEST Carole Margaret   MA 1965
  d of Stephen W. MA 1930 *qv* and Mary C. Scroggie MA
1933 *qv*; b Huntly 16.12.44
assistante d'Anglais Riom France 1966–67; teacher
Cuminestown 1967–68; civ serv Winchester 1968–74;
free-lance computer progr from 1975
m 4.8.71 Anthony W. Cox tech asst s of Sidney C.
Winchester

WEST Edna   MA 1962
  d of Francis W. fisherman, comp dir and Emily West;
b Gardenstown 15.6.41
teacher maths Rosyth 1963–68; Malawi: teacher maths
Blantyre 1969–70, maths and gen subj Limbe 1970–71;
computer progr Limbe 1971–72, secy-wages clerk
Lilongwe 1972–73
m(1) Grant
  (2) Lilongwe 26.8.72 Roger Kennington owner steel
work comp s of Jack H. K. BSc Embangweni S Africa

WEST James Scott   MA 1959
  s of Forbes W. fisherman and Barbara J. Watt; b
Macduff 1.12.36
teacher Portsoy, Banff from 1960
m Macduff 17.7.63 Elizabeth M. Thain teacher d of
Robert T. Macduff

WEST Katharine Jane Mitchell   *MA 1964
  d of George W. bank clerk and Jane Mitchell; b Inv
8.1.42
asst lib Aberd 1965–68
m Aber 7.8.67 William J. Burnett MA 1961 *qv*

WEST Margaret Munro   BSc 1956
  d of Gordon R. W. banker and Mary A. Aird nurse; b
Rangoon Burma 8.11.33
teacher sc Aber 1957–60, Lower Hutt NZ 1970–71; sc
tech Lower Hutt from 1973
m Aber 30.7.58 John E. C. Flux BSc 1957 *qv*

WESTWATER Gary David   MA 1970

WESTWOOD Carole   MA 1967
  d of Clifford J. W. scrap metal dealer and Ethel M.
Crosby; b Middlesbrough 8.10.44

teacher Fr Bertram Ramsey comp s Middlesbrough 1967;
cler off. DHSS Middlesbrough 1968–69; clerk Brit pass-
port off. Kampala Uganda 1969–71
m Middlesbrough 5.8.67 David Watkins PO telecom eng
s of Walter W. Middlesbrough

WESTWOOD William Dickson   *BSc 1959 PhD 1962

WETHERLY Vivien Joyce Erskine   MA 1964
d of William R. W. elect./mech eng, insur underwriter
and Isabella MacKintosh; b Aber 25.11.46
Dip Sec St(Strath) 1965
res asst, secy to Prof Charles Wilson, Jesus coll Camb,
writing hist of Unilever, Lond and Camb 1965–66; res
asst/secy external serv BBC African serv Lond 1966–67;
teacher Addison p s Lond 1968–70 and from 1972
m Lond 4.11.67 Mihalaki Fotiadis BSc(eng)(Istanbul) civ
eng dir civ eng comp s of Yani F. Istanbul

WHALLEY Margaret Joyce   BSc 1965
d of Geoffrey W. man. and Edith M. Brueton; b Aber
14.3.44
computer progr Internatl Computers Kidsgrove 1965–70
m Aber 24.2.68 Samuel A. Alcock BA(OU) prod. control
man. s of Samuel A. Stoke-on-Trent

WHEATLEY James Alexander McIntosh
                                        *BSc(eng) 1962

WHELCHEL Michael Anthony   PhD 1966
BA(Belhaven) BD(Columbia Theol Sem Georgia)

WHIGHT Evelyn Ann   PhD 1970
d of Thomas B. W. BA(Queensland) teacher, headmaster, sen tut. maths Macq univ and Nellie E. L.
Williams secy; b Chatswood NSW Aust 10.9.38
BSc(Syd) 1959 MSc(Syd) 1961
Aust: lect maths/statist univ of Syd 1968–72, Macq from
1973
m Blockley Glos 2.1.65 Roger W. Eyland PhD(Cantab)
univ lect s of Thomas W. E. Sylvania Waters NSW

WHINN Marjorie   *BSc 1967

WHITAKER Ian Michael   BMedBiol 1969

WHITAKER Margaret Anne   MA 1968

WHITCOMBE Kenneth Barry   *MA 1968
s of Douglas H. W. trans man. and Gwendoline I.
French; b Nantwich 17.7.46
teacher geog Cults acad 1969–71; prin geog Cowdenbeath
from 1971

WHITE Alexander Robert   MB ChB 1960

WHITE Anthony   MB ChB 1966
s of Cyril W. miner and Florence M. Dicks; b Warsop
nr Mansfield 11.11.39
h o 1966–68; g p: trainee Aber 1968–69, Glasg from 1970
m Glasg 30.9.72 Margaret A. Christison SRN d of David
C. MB ChB(Glas) Glasg

WHITE David Alexander   *MA 1969
s of Peter M. W. shop prop. and Catherine P. Peters;
b Kilwinning 12.12.46
teacher Kings Rise s s Birm 1969–72, prim. supply East
End Lond 1972–73; lect psych & commun Falkirk coll of
tech from 1973; examiner in child educ for Scot. nursery
nurse exam. board from 1978
m Largs 20.4.76 Janette Williamson teacher p e d of
James W. Largs

WHITE Edward James Milner   *BSc 1967
s of Leslie M. W. landscape arch. and Mary N. Muir;
b Woking 28.4.45
PhD(Lond) 1971
res asst as Leverhulme fell. muscular dystrophy Guy's
hosp Lond 1967–71; lect biochem Glas from 1971

WHITE Frances Geraldine   LLB 1967
d of Harold G. W. civ serv and Margaret McInally civ
serv; b Perth 30.3.45
Lond: solic's articled clerk 1967–70; solic: N Thames gas
board 1970–72, CEGB from 1972
m Cookham 20.5.78 Noël C. O. Mizen eng s of Dennis
G. M. Cookham

WHITE George Baird   MB ChB 1968
s of George D. W. joiner and Dorothy M. Triptree; b
Aboyne 9.10.42
h o ARI, Maryfield hosp Dun 1968–69; trainee g p Aber
1969–70; sen h o Aber mat. hosp, ARI 1970–71; g p
Congleton 1971–72, Mold Clwyd N Wales 1972, Chester
from 1972
m Banchory 5.8.67 Carole W. H. Tincker secy d of
Maurice A. H. T. MA(Cantab) Banchory

WHITE Graham Robert   BEd 1969
s of Robert W. welf off. loc auth and Isobel L. C.
Veitch lib; b Aber 23.3.46
teacher: Hazlehead p s Aber 1969–71, Scotstown p s
Aber 1971–73; dep head Cults p s 1973–75; lect Jordanhill coll Glasg from 1975
m Aber 10.7.71 Alison C. McKenzie teacher d of
Alexander McK. Aber

WHITE Ian Hendry   *BSc 1970 PhD 1977
s of John G. W. baker, fisherman and Bessie Joiner; b
Banff 29.6.48
res asst: dept of chem path. Aberd 1970–74, dept of biochem Liv 1974–76; lect dept of chem path. Aberd from
1976
m Portsoy 9.10.71 Isobel M. Cooper HCO Scot. telecom
d of James C. Portsoy

WHITE Isobel Anne   MA 1967 Dip Ed 1968
d of William W. blacksmith and Maria Lindsay; b
Aber 14.6.44
teacher Fr-Ger Aber h s for girls 1968–73, asst prin mod
lang Summerhill acad 1973–75
m Aber 23.12.69 John W. Malcolm MA(Glas) journalist,
teacher, lect s of Andrew R. M. Glasg

WHITE Janet Elizabeth   MA 1967
d of Reginald W. works man., pers man. and Annie L.
Mercer secy; b Wakefield 11.6.47
teacher: Ossett g s 1968–70, Summerhill acad Aber 1970–
71, Hilton acad Aber 1971, Douglas acad 1971–76, part-
time Clevedon s from 1979
m Wakefield 30.3.70 Frederick D. Yule MA 1968 qv

WHITE Michael George   MA 1967
s of Frederick G. W. grocer and Dora J. Smith; b
Wolverhampton 21.11.46
AMBIM 1976 AIPM 1978
exec off. PO Birm 1967–69; Lond: asst postal controller
1969–71, higher exec off. PO 1971–77, head of group PO
from 1977

WHITEFIELD Elizabeth McCombe   BEd 1970
d of James P. W. comp dir and Mary F. Thom; b Glasg
28.8.47
teacher mus/Engl Airdrie 1970–76
m Glasg 6.8.71 James Noble BSc(Glas) surg s of John
R. N. Glasg

WHITEFORD Elizabeth Sim   *MB ChB 1967
d of John W. BSc(Glas) and Elizabeth Strachan MA
1927 *qv*; b Forres 12.4.44
MRCPath 1976
h o ARI 1967–68; lect path. Aberd from 1968
m Aber 7.7.69 Laurence Gray MA 1966 *qv*

WHITEFORD Michael Hugh McLeod   *BSc(eng) 1966
d 11.2.67

WHITEHEAD Paul Bryant   *BSc(eng) 1967
s of Jack W. sales man. and Peggy Calligan; b Huddersfield 2.5.44
MICE 1974
sect. eng Edmund Nuttal civ eng contr 1967–69; civ
constr eng ICI 1969–73; sen eng Edmund Nuttal 1973–75;
proj man. Christiani & Nielsen civ eng contr from 1975
m Aber 22.7.66 Wilma E. Barrack d of William J. B.
Aber

WHITEHEAD Peter John   BSc 1968
s of John W. loc govt off. and Alice Richardson; b Liv
25.3.46
dev off. Birds Eye foods Liv 1968–71, asst prod. man.
1972–73; teacher sc Kincorth acad Aber 1974–78, Cults
acad from 1978; also part-time farm. from 1974
m Fetternear 22.8.69 Frances A. Wilson teacher d of
Robert W. Kemnay

WHITEHOUSE Alan John   MA 1961 LLB 1965

WHITELAW Francis George   PhD 1962
s of Francis G. W. and Hannah M. Taig; b Ardrossan
29.5.35
BSc(agr)(Glas) 1958
res scient Rowett inst Aber from 1958
m Aber 26.3.63 Anthea W. W. Bickford BSc(UCW) res
scient, teacher d of Humphrey A. B. Malaya

WHITELEY David   *BSc(for) 1965
s of Sidney W. BSc(Manc) res chem and Margaret E.
Simon; b Hatch End 16.2.43
MSc(ANU) 1974
various posts/schol. Sweden 1965–66; Canberra Aust:
for. off. logging res for./timber bureau 1966–73; clerk for.
policy sect. Aust dept of agr 1973–75; asst div for. off.
WA dept of for. Manjimup Aust from 1975

WHITELEY Fleur St Clair   *MA 1965
d of Archibald W. M. W. MA 1929 *qv*; b Aber 22.2.43
Dip D'Etudes Francaises(Sorbonne)1963 B Litt(Oxon)
1971
res stud. Oxon 1965–68; teacher Fr Manc g s 1968–69;
asst lect Belf 1969–70; lect Manc 1970–71
m Oxford 11.7.70 Walter J. Houston MA(Cantab) min of
relig s of Henry H. MA(Penn) Stockport

WHITELOCK Cecil Elizabeth   MB ChB 1968
m Macdougall

WHITLEY Michael William   MB ChB 1970

WHITTAKER Edith   *BSc 1957 PhD 1960
d of James E. W. BSc(eng)(Lond) elect. eng area man.
NSHEB and Edith Hopkinson; b Bradford 28.7.35
res fell. dept bot Aberd 1960–63
m Aber 1.9.60 Richard M. Cormack PhD 1961 *qv*

WHITTINGHAM Thomas Anthony   MSc 1967
BSc(Lond)

WHYTE Alastair Graham Donald
                                   *BSc(for) 1960 PhD 1964**
s of Alistair G. D. W. MA 1927 *qv* and Eveline S.

Mackie MA 1927 *qv*; b Aber 8.2.39
Dip For.(Oxon) 1964 MIFor(NZ) 1970
NZ: res scient Rotorua 1964–69; lect Christchurch univ
from 1969
m Rotorua 14.12.69 Rosemary E. Harris teacher d of
John M. H. MSc(Well) Rotorua

WHYTE Alistair John   *MA 1962

WHYTE Angela Jean Graham   BSc 1969
d of James S. W. MA 1933 *qv* and Janet R. Graham MA
1934 *qv*; b Kirkcaldy 17.6.48
Wolverhampton: teacher maths girls' h s 1970–73, The
Regis s Tettenhall from 1973
m Aber 25.7.70 Timothy Hodges MA 1967 *qv*

WHYTE Brenda Agnes   *BSc 1959
m Lenssen

WHYTE Colin Graham   BSc(eng) 1965
s of James S. W. MA 1933 *qv* and Janet R. Graham
MA 1934 *qv*; b Aber 2.7.44
post-grad trainee Brechin 1965–67; market res eng
Brechin 1967–68; market. eng Coventry 1968–69;
Brechin: sales market. eng 1969–70, commercial sales
man. 1970–76, sales dir 1976–79, sales & market. dir
from 1979
m Tannadice 12.12.70 Margaret S. Bell secy, hotel
receptionist d of George B. MA(Edin) Montrose

WHYTE George Garden   MB ChB 1960

WHYTE Johan Geddes   *MA 1968
d of Gilbert W. painter and Johan Geddes bonus clerk;
b Peterhead 2.3.46
teacher Stow-on-the-Wold from 1972
m Aber 24.12.68 Robert H. C. Davidson MA 1968 *qv*

WHYTE Kathleen Anderson   MA 1965
m Winter

WHYTE Roderick James   *BSc 1960
s of Roderick W. tradesman and Helen Taggart; b Inv
8.11.38
MSc(RS of Mines) 1973 DIC 1973 MIMM 1974
explor geol: Malawi 1960–63, Ghana 1963–65, UK 1965–
66; Zambia: chief mining geol Chibuluma 1966–72, asst
geol supt 1974–75; geotech eng Maidenhead 1975–77,
proj eng Johannesburg from 1977
m Inv 29.2.64 Diana I. A. Sutherland nurs sister d of
John S. Kilmarnock

WHYTE Roger William   *MA 1970

WIEBE Paul Arthur   MSc 1963
b Winnipeg Manitoba 11.2.38
BASc(Br Col) 1960 Athlone fell. 1962–64 DIC(Lond) 1964
jun civ eng Vancouver BC 1960–62, sen hydraulic eng
Niagara Falls Ont 1964–69; spec advis to Epwapda on
hydraulics & hydrology Dacca E Pakistan (now Bangladesh) 1969–71; head water resources div Montreal from
1971
m Vancouver 1962 Joanne W. Rosene BA(Br Col) teacher

WIGHT James Reid   *MA 1960 *MEd 1964
s of James M. W. bakery van salesman and Alice Reid;
b Inverurie 6.9.36
teacher Aber 1961–64; asst dir of educ Fife 1965–69; lect
educ man./admin Moray House coll of educ Edin from
1969
m Aber 12.8.64 Madeleine A. Burnett MA 1960 *qv*

WIGHT Wendy Jean   *MA 1960

WILD Valerie Frances   *MEd 1969
d of Barton R. W. man. English Elect. subsid and Flora
F. C. Lewis BSc(Lond) teacher; b Preston 20.8.46
MA(Oxon) 1967 Dip Ed 1968
Aber: res asst psych Aberd 1969–70; lect coll of comm
1970–71, lect coll of educ 1971–75; teacher Barthol Chapel
1975–79; head Cairnorrie p s from 1979
m Oxford 26.8.67 David A. Smart MA(Oxon) forensic
biol s of George A. K. S. Glossop

WILDGOOSE David Middleton   MA 1964
s of Alexander M. W. civ serv and Alice H. R. Milne;
b Aber 5.10.43
Dip Pers Man.(Strath) 1965 MSc(Strath) 1976
trg off. AEI Manc 1965–68; pers off. Thomson Organis
Edin 1968–70; pers man. Collins publ Glasg 1970–76;
lect Dun coll of tech from 1976
m Aber 2.7.66 Edna W. Sproul MA 1964 qv

WILDGOOSE Ian   BSc 1964
s of Robert W. W. farm. and Mary H. Stewart; b
Urquhart 22.9.43
teacher chem: Lossiemouth h s 1965–73, Bankhead acad
from 1973
m Aber 21.12.73 Sheila Mackland BSc 1970 qv

WILKEN Ronald   *MA 1959

WILKENS Thomas Gene   PhD 1968
BA BD(Luther USA)

WILKIE Brenda   MA 1968
d of William J. W. eng and Jessie A. Milne teacher; b
Batu Gajah Malaysia 24.2.49
teacher Engl: Forrester s s Edin 1969–71, Eastbank acad
Glasg 1971–74, Perth acad 1974–76
m Glasg 18.7.74 Melvin C. Cooper adv plumber s of
Charles W. C. Bridge of Alford

WILKIE Charles Alexander Spark   MA 1970
d Aber 13.1.74

WILKIE David Sharp   *BSc 1970

WILKIE Iain James   MA 1967
s of John W. salmon fisher, factory worker and Annie
D. Robertson secy; b Perth 17.11.46
police constable Aber 1967–73, sgt from 1973
m Aber 4.6.71 Esmé E. McDerment health visitor d of
John McD. Aber

WILKIE James   *MA 1963 M Litt 1974
s of George R. W. blacksmith and Jane M. Poustie; b
Dun 1.2.38
teacher hist Perth 1964–67; prin hist Golspie 1967–71;
lect coll of educ Aber from 1971
m Aber 8.6.63 Agnes McLennan nurse d of William A.
McL. Findochty

WILKIE James Lindsay   *MA 1956 BD 1959
s of James L. W. comm trav/news ag and tobacconist
and Annie Hamilton teacher; b Dunfermline 30.1.34
C of S min: asst St Machar's cath Aber 1959–60; Zambia:
missionary min of ch of Central Africa in Rhodesia,
Mwenzo 1961–65, miss. min of united ch of Zambia Isoka
1965–69, synod treas of UCZ Lusaka 1970–71, Christian
Council chaplain to stud. in univ of Zambia 1971–76;
exec secy (Africa) Brit Council of Churches from 1976
m Aber 15.7.59 Irene A. Watson MB ChB 1959 qv

WILKIE Patricia Isabel   MA 1967
d of Peter W. P O eng and Isabella M. Craig french
polisher; b Aber 8.7.46

off. Nat West Bank Lond, Middlesbrough, Shepperton
1969–73
m Middlesbrough 25.10.69 Robert L. Ibell BSc(eng) 1967 qv

WILKIE Victor Macfarlane   BSc 1966 Dip Ed 1967
s of William W. joiner, clerk of works and Margaret
Pirie; b Elgin 1945
MI Gas E 1973 C Eng 1973
eng (Scot. gas) Edin, Aber, Uddingston from 1967
m Crook of Devon Kinross 19.3.74 Barbara Whitson
nurse d of Donald W.

WILKIN Jennifer   MA 1967
d of John A. W. mech eng and Williamina Tait; b Aber
20.1.46
teacher: Skene Sq p s Aber 1968–69, Cornhill p s Aber
from 1969

WILKINS Brian   *BSc 1969
s of William S. W. headmaster and Elizabeth A.
Cordiner; b Cruden Bay 12.12.46
MSc(Sus) 1970 DPhil(Sus) 1973
teacher chem Crawley from 1973
m High Wycombe 12.8.72 Hazel J. Shapter BSc(Sus)
teacher d of Ronald F. S. High Wycombe

WILKINS Roberta   *MA 1970

WILKINSON David   MB ChB 1956
s of Ernest W. MA(Cantab) HM insp taxes and Muriel
M. Wyatt; b Derby 13.2.32
h o Stracathro hosp Brechin 1957–58; m o RAF fl lt
Wilmslow, Upavon 1958–61; g p Potton 1961–62; h o
obst Farnham 1962; g p S Elmshall from 1962
m Aber 10.6.57 Katharine P. Carter RGN d of Charles
C. OBE BSc(Leeds) Aber

WILKINSON Martin Arthur   BSc(for) 1970
s of Arthur W. teacher and Agnes G. Harrison; b
Leigh 9.10.48
private for. man. comp: for. asst, asst br man. Lhanbryde
1970–72, asst br man. Jedburgh 1972–73, br man. Ludlow
from 1973
m Jedburgh –.7.74 Alison A. Ritch teacher d of Leslie
S. S. R. Jedburgh

WILKINSON Norma Jean Ross   MA 1964

WILKS Jocelyn   PhD 1963
BA(Brist)

WILKS Robin John   PhD 1967
BSc(Brist)

WILL Alexander James   BSc(eng) 1959

WILL Alexander Ogilvie   MA 1962
s of Alexander O. W. butcher and Annie B. Milne; b
Peterhead 17.8.41
teacher Peterhead cent s 1963–68; head: Rothienorman
p s 1968–75, South Park p s Fraserburgh from 1975
m Peterhead 25.7.64 Eileen F. Milne teacher d of Joseph
M. Peterhead

WILL Diana Beatrice Robertson   *MA 1959
d of Hunter M. Will MA 1928 qv; b Aber 27.5.37
teacher: geog Edin 1960–65, Lugton s Dalkeith from 1975
m Aber 7.4.62 John M. Legge arch. s of Andrew L. Aber

WILL Duncan   BSc 1956
s of Sydney W. master stevedore and Helen Watt; b
Fraserburgh 23.4.35
Grad Inst Phys(Paisley coll of sc and tech) 1969

teacher: maths/sc Fraserburgh acad 1957–63, phys Berwicksh h s 1963–65; prin sc Forebraes s Alloa 1965–69; prin phys Lornshill acad Alloa from 1969
m Inverallochy 30.3.63 Grace B. Crawford clerkess d of John W. C. Inverallochy

WILL Frank   BSc(eng) 1970
s of Elizabeth M. Will; b Ellon 2.11.49
grad asst eng Perth and Kinross c c Perth 1970–75; prof grade asst Tayside reg c from 1975
m Aber 15.7.72 Diane H. Mackie MA 1972 computer progr d of George M. Aber

WILL Hunter Alexander Bonnar   *BSc(eng) 1966
s of Hunter M. W. MA 1928 qv; b Aber 12.12.44
CE MICE 1971
des eng: Aber 1966–67, Glasg 1967–68; eng asst Aber 1968–77, prin eng from 1977

WILL Patricia   MA 1959

WILL Peter Milne   *BSc(eng) 1958 PhD 1960
s of James W. cooper and Margaret Milne; b Peterhead 2.11.35
res scient: AEI Manc 1960–61, AMF Sonning Common Reading 1961–64, AMF Springdale Conn USA 1964–65; res staff member IBM T. J. Watson res centre Yorktown Hts NY from 1965; also lect univ of Conn Stamford Branch grad s in elect. eng 1966–71
m Aber 21.3.59 Angela H. Giulianotti

WILL Sylvia Jennifer   *MA 1965
m Fulton

WILLCOX Graham   *MA 1962

WILLETS Lynn Denise   *BSc(agr) 1970
d of Harold W. gen man. textile firm and Bertha Ramsden; b Farnworth 13.8.47
res stud. Tillycorthie farm Udny 1970–72
m Aber 23.6.72 John Gilbert HGV driving instr s of John G. Kintore

WILLETTS Patricia Mary   MA 1970

WILLIAMS Angela Catherine   *MA 1965
m David S. Hewitt PhD 1969 qv

WILLIAMS Frances Ann   MA 1967
d of John A. W. and Charlotte K. Morrison; b Huntly 1.8.46
Dip Pers Man.(Strath) 1968
tech sales corresp Edin 1968–70
m Aber –.2.70 David G. M. Carpenter mar. eng s of Albert G. C. Tarbet

WILLIAMS Gaynor Myfanwy   MA 1965 Dip Ed 1966
m(1) Sinclair-Gieben
(2) Hamilton

WILLIAMS Geraldine Mary   BSc 1970
d of Arthur W. aircraft eng and Dorothy M. J. Lee secy; b Gainsborough 26.3.49
teacher: p s Sydney Aust 1971–72, Sheppey Kent from 1972

WILLIAMS Jacqueline Ann   *MA 1969

WILLIAMS Paul   MA 1968

WILLIAMS Richard Peter   BSc 1967
s of William R. W. supt marine eng and May Deakin; b Bristol 17.6.46

quality controller food indust Grimsby 1967–68, entomologist Arusha Tanganyika 1968–70; quantity controller food Cleethorpes 1971–72; teacher: Gt Coates 1974–77, Jamaica, El Salvador (cent Amer) from 1977

WILLIAMS Roger Walford   MB ChB 1969
s of John E. W. comp rep and Elsie J. S. Evans teacher; b Shrewsbury 12.5.45
h o Aber hosps, Airdrie and Coatbridge hosps 1969–71; g p Fife 1971–72; sen h o Dunfermline hosps 1972–73; g p Fife from 1973
m Aber 1969 Elizabeth M. Macnaughtan B Med Biol 1967 qv

WILLIAMSON Alastair Mitchell   BSc 1964 *MA 1966

WILLIAMSON Andrew John   *MA 1966 Dip Ed 1967
s of Arthur S. W. fisherman/cooper and Mary Anderson; b Whalsay 31.5.44
teacher Alloa acad 1967–70, prin geog: N Berwick h s 1970–71, Musselburgh g s 1972–74; asst head Dalkeith h s from 1974
m Aber 28.1.67 Wyn P. Valentine BSc 1966 qv

WILLIAMSON Anne Margaret   *MA 1958
d of George J. W. farm. and Janet Walker; b Inverurie 17.9.36
teacher: Perth h s 1959–62, exchange Indianopolis USA 1962–63
m Indianopolis 3.8.63 Gale M. Helft AB(Indiana) teacher s of Nathan H. Indianopolis

WILLIAMSON Brian   PhD 1969
s of Ronald W. T. W. BA(Lond) teacher and Jean Walsh; b Rossendale 6.4.44
BSc(UCW) 1965 MSc(Nott) 1966
NATO post doct res fell. biol Woolwich polytech, med fac Mem univ of Newfoundland St John's Canada 1970–72; post doct res asst for. NERC Aberd 1972–73; plant path. Scot. hortic res inst Invergowrie from 1973
m Ringwood 1971 Janet M. Saunders radiogr d of Alan S. St Leonards nr Ringwood

WILLIAMSON Elliot Allen   MB ChB 1961
s of Alexander A. W. bldg contr and Jane J. Martin; b Aber 10.8.38
DObstRCOG 1965
h o: paediat Inv 1962, obst/gyn Irvine 1963; g p Balloch; h o anaest Perth 1965–66; g p Oakville Ont Canada from 1966; pres med staff Oakville hosp from 1975
m Dunbar 1963 Helen E. Bruce teacher p e d of Archibald B. Dunbar

WILLIAMSON Frances Olwen   MA 1962
d of Alexander A. W. bldg contr and Jane J. Martin; b Aber 18.3.42
teacher: Aber 1962–67, Dun 1967–68, Aber 1968–71
m Aber 19.8.67 Gordon W. Cook MA 1961 qv

WILLIAMSON Grace Agnes   MA 1963 Dip Ed 1964

WILLIAMSON James   MSc 1963 PhD 1965
s of Thomas W. supt marine eng and Kathleen Simpson; b Liv 5.4.39
BSc(Nott) 1967
Imp Coll Lond: res fell. metall 1965–70, lect metall/materials sc from 1970
m Aber 16.7.66 Aldon T. Baxter MA 1966 qv

WILLIAMSON John   MA 1970 Dip Ed 1971
s of Robert J. W. chef and Edith M. Crofts; b Aber 11.3.39
teacher geog Glenrothes 1971–74, asst prin mod. stud.

from 1974
m Aber 3.8.63 Maureen Yeoman acct machine oper d of Douglas E. Y. Aber

WILLIAMSON Kenneth Harry   *BSc 1970
s of Thomas L. W. c'erk of works (loc govt) and Harriet E. Anderson; b Lerwick 8.2.48
PhD(Lond) 1975
sen scient off. hydrogeology unit inst geol sc Lond (work concerns geothermal explor proj overseas) from 1975

WILLIAMSON Laurence Angus Leslie   BSc(eng) 1956
s of William T. H. W. BSc 1910 qv; b Cairo 17.10.34
De Havilland Eng Co Edgware: app 1956–58, tech asst rocket tech office 1958–60; tech sales, power plant dept George Cohen Machinery Lond; assoc edit. *Machine Design Engineering* Rowse Muir publ./Mercury Ho publ Lond 1965–68; p r o Rolls Royce Derby 1968–71; press off. eng div Tube Investments Lond 1971–77; publicity man. machine div Tube Investments Coventry from 1977
m Aber 29.3.61 Diana J. Findlay occup therap d of Frank A. F. Kingswells

WILLIAMSON Marjory Johan Duncan   MA 1960

WILLIAMSON Mary McIntosh McConnell   MA 1970
d of Archibald W. comm trav and Jean H. McIntosh shop asst; b Glasg 27.9.40
ALA 1973
loc hist lib NE Scot. lib serv Aber from 1972

WILLIAMSON Peter Garrick   *BSc 1958
s of Robert W. seaman/crofter and Ursula M. Garrick sub postmistress; b Ollaberry Shetland 30.1.36
teacher sc Anderson h s Lerwick from 1960
m Lerwick 18.7.62 Elizabeth A. D. Johnson MA 1960 qv

WILLIAMSON Robert Buchanan   *BSc 1958
s of Archibald M. M. W. MA 1920 qv(II, III); b Edin 12.4.35
fishery res trg grant fisheries lab Pitlochry 1958–60; Malawi: govt fisheries res off. Nkhata Bay, Monkey Bay 1960–65, govt chief fisheries off. Zomba 1966–70; Freshwater Fisheries lab Pitlochry: sen scient off. 1970–76, prin scient off. from 1976
m Aber 17.9.60 Sheena I. B. Jeffrey BSc 1968 qv

WILLIAMSON Sheila Mary   MA 1970
m Russell

WILLIS Douglas Peter   *MA 1965 MLitt 1967
b Methlick 19.7.43
tut./stud. geog Aberd 1965–67; prin teacher geog: Cults acad 1968–75, Fortrose acad from 1975
m Ullapool 2.4.68 Catherine M. Campbell MA 1965 qv

WILLOX Alexander   *BSc(eng) 1962

WILLOX John Brand   MA 1963
s of Sydney M. W. pharm and Elizabeth M. Brand; b Aber 14.4.40
ITA teacher fell. Glas 1969 Churchill fell. Scandinavia 1970
teacher: Ellon 1964–65, Peterhead 1965–66; head: Laggan p s 1966–67, Knockando p s 1967–70, Dufftown p s 1970–72; p s advis Caithness 1972–76; asst dir BFES from 1976
m Peterhead 22.7.64 Sheena F. Grant teacher d of Charles G. Peterhead

WILLOX Margaret Elizabeth   BSc 1959
d of James W. man. dir Aber hide skin & tallow comp and Elizabeth Mitchell secy; b Aber 19.9.38

AEO biochem/microbiol Torry res stat. Aber 1959–66
m Aber 3.10.64 George A. Taylor MB ChB 1958 qv

WILLS Leslie Charles   MB ChB 1966
s of Charles L. W. draper and Anne E. Wright; b Aber 21.2.40
FRCSE 1972
h o Aber hosps 1966–67; sen h o ARI 1967–68; lect anat Aberd 1969–71; regist ENT ARI/tut. Aberd 1971–72; sen regist ENT ARI/lect Aberd 1972–75; sen regist/lect prof unit royal nat nose throat ear hosp Lond 1975; consult ENT surg ARI/sen lect surg Aberd from 1975
m Aber 19.6.67 Frances C. Gove teacher d of David G. Cults

WILSON Aileen Susanna   *BSc 1969 MSc 1971
d of James M. W. wholesale grocer and Christina F. Livingstone; b Aber 20.10.47
res asst computer dept Aberd 1970–71; oper res. analyst Düsseldorf W. Ger 1971–72; res fell. computing centre Aberd 1978
m Aber 16.7.69 Gordon V. Stone MB ChB 1969 qv

WILSON Alan Chaney   *BSc 1968 PhD 1972
s of William A. W. MD(Lond) med statist and Mary L. Harvey; b Kampala Uganda 30.7.45
trav fell. Boehringer Mannheim corp 1971 held in univ of Bari Italy; res assoc biochem Baylor coll of med Houston Texas USA 1971–76; res fell. biochem univ of Ottawa 1976–77; NRC visiting fell. Ottawa res stat agr Canada from 1977

WILSON Alexander   BSc(for) 1964

WILSON Alexander Bruce   *BSc(eng) 1962 MSc 1964
s of Alexander W. MA 1925 qv and Jessie C. Bruce MA 1922 qv; b Kirkcaldy 8.8.40
turbine des Manc 1964–67; refrig des Dun 1967–75; res eng Renfrew from 1975
m Aber 14.7.64 Marjory M. Cameron MA 1961 qv

WILSON Alexander Dey   *BSc(eng) 1963
s of Alexander D. W. MA 1936 qv and Mary C. Anderson BSc 1938 qv; b Stromness 7.4.41
grad trainee Scot. elect. trg scheme 1963–65; asst eng NSHEB: Keith 1965–67, Huntly 1967–68, Peterhead 1968–69; ICI: elect. eng (plastics div) Wilton works Cleveland 1970–76, sen elect. des eng (paints div NW) Hyde 1976–78, works elect. instrument eng (paints div) Newton Works Hyde from 1978
m Aber 27.7.66 Eleanor M. Coutts teacher d of William C. MA 1925 qv

WILSON Alexander George   *MA 1969
s of Joseph S. W. lab attendant and Adeline H. Crockett; b Aber 25.2.47
LTCL 1965 LRAM 1970
res stud. St John's Cambridge 1969–73; violinist Bergen S O Norway from 1973
d Norway –.6.75 *AUR* XLVI 328

WILSON Alexander John   MA 1969
s of Alexander J. W. master stove enameller and Anne Milne; b Aber 15.10.46
trainee admin man. Aber 1969–70; Glasg: asst admin man. 1970–71, admin controller 1971–77, admin man. Poole branch Marley Tile Co from 1977
m Kirkintilloch 7.7.73 Sheena E. Turnbull teacher d of James T. Lenzie

WILSON Alexander Shand   BSc(agr) 1964
s of James O. W. farm. and Mary S. Shand nurse; b Banff 15.8.41

farm. Banff from 1964
m Banff 24.5.69 Mary G. Duff bank clerk d of George D.
Banff

WILSON Anthony James   *MA 1970
s of James T. W. admin and Elsie A. Merrick; b Aber
1947
res stud. Oxford univ 1970-72; lect Paisley from 1972

WILSON Barbara Helen   *MA 1966
d of Henry J. S. W. BA(Cantab) headmaster and
Marjorie L. Cruden horticulturalist; b Market Harborough 11.3.43
Dip Ed(Edin) 1967 ALA 1969
asst lib: Street 1967-68, Liv 1970; tut. lib Kirkby coll of
f e Liv 1970-72, chief lib N Warks coll of tech and art
Nuneaton from 1972
m Sheffield 14.7.68 Stuart L. Heaton BA (Warw)
draughtsman/lect s of Jack H. Bridgwater

WILSON Brian   LL B 1969
s of George C. W. BL(Glas) solic and Margaret I.
Lavers nurs sister; b Perth 20.2.46
law app Banff c c 1969-71, leg. asst 1971-72; sen leg. asst
Inv c c 1972-73; dep county clerk Banff c c 1973-75; dir
of admin and leg. serv Banff and Buchan dist council
Banff 1974-78; chief exec Inv dist c from 1978
m Buckie 9.4.69 Isobel Esson teacher d of John E. Buckie

WILSON Catherine Martin   MA 1964
d of Hubert M. W. MA(Cantab) dir of educ Shropsh
and Ida M. Samuel BA(Cantab) county organis Shrops
WRNS, member Telford dev corp; b Shrewsbury 11.11.42
trainee, buyer D. H. Evans 1964-67; boutique buyer Swan
& Edgar 1967-72; opened own shop for young fashion in
Pinner 1972
m Lond 15.2.69 David A. Aubrey buyer BHS s of
Geoffrey E. A. Lond

WILSON Cynthia Dolores   BSc 1956
d of Archibald W. fisherman and Mabel Gault nurse;
b Aber 27.11.33
analytical chem Peterhead 1957-65; teacher: Peterhead
acad 1966-67, Summerhill acad 1967-70, prin guid 1970-
73; prin guid Linksfield acad from 1973
m Aber 10.10.59 Archibald McRaw MA(Glas) lect bus.
man. RGIT s of James McR. MA 1908 qv(II, III)

WILSON Denis Maclean   *MA 1960 MSc 1961
s of George S. W. silver engraver and Jean S. Maclean
lib; b Elgin 6.8.37
asst lect maths Aberd 1961-63; syst progr IBM UK labs
Hursley 1963-64; lect computing sc Aberd from 1964

WILSON Donald Fraser   *MA 1964

WILSON Dorothy Lawrence   *MA 1965
d of James W. W. bank man. and Anne L. Stewart nurs
sister; b Aber 10.3.43
teacher mod lang: Albyn s for girls Aber 1966-68, King's
s Gütersloh Germany 1968-74
m Aber 19.8.71 Philip G. Snell BSc(Brist) teacher s of
Gerald T. S. Umberleigh

WILSON Edith Isabel   MA 1956
d of Alexander W. MA 1925 qv and Jessie C. Bruce MA
1922 qv; b Kirkcaldy 6.4.35
teacher maths: Brechin h s 1957-59, Inverurie acad 1959-
63; spec asst maths Inverurie acad 1963-66, Gordon s
Huntly 1966-72, prin guid Gordon s Huntly from 1972
m Aber 29.7.66 Gordon Peters MA 1958 qv

WILSON Elizabeth Whyte   MA 1965
m Thom

WILSON Erlend Ramsay   *MA 1957

WILSON Gavin Bruce   MA 1962 ᵉLL B 1964
d 3.10.69

WILSON Gladys   MA 1958
d of George G. W. carpenter and Maggie A. Paterson;
b Macduff 10.10.36
teacher: Aber 1959-61, part time Banffsh and Grampian
reg from 1974
m Aber 12.7.61 Reginald L. Henderson MA 1956 qv

WILSON Gladys Helen   MA 1960
d of George P. W. bldr and Elspeth J. Law; b 3.12.39
m Aber 30.7.65 Charles E. Simpson arch.

WILSON Gladys Maclean Watt   MA 1956
m Srivastava

WILSON Hamish Robert McHattie   *MA 1967
s of James W. teacher and Margaret A. P. McHattie; b
Aber 19.1.46
BA(Cantab) 1969 MA(Cantab) 1973 PLD(Cantab) 1976
Croom Robertson res fell. Emmanuel coll Cambridge
1969-72; health serv admin Aber from 1972
m Aber 18.6.70 Ann M. V. Shewan RGN d of James M. S.
BSc 1931 qv

WILSON Harold   MEd 1966
s of Albert W. trade union off. and Ann Reay; b
Stanley Co Durh 11.9.42
BSc(Manc) 1964 ABPsS 1972
teacher maths: Peterhead 1966-67, Stonehaven 1967-68;
educ psych Lanarksh 1968-71; prin psych: Clackmannan
1971-75, Central reg from 1975
m Stonehaven 23.12.68 Dorothy T. Campbell teacher d of
John C. C. MA(Edin) Glenrothes

WILSON Helen Irene   *MA 1966
d of John W. trawl skipper and Elizabeth Gardiner; b
Aber 5.10.44
teacher Fr: Aber h s for girls 1967-70, private tuition
Frodsham 1970-73, part-time Helsby county g s for girls
from 1973
m Cullen 12.9.70 Humphrey C. Bowen MA(Oxon) res
man. ICI s of Edward A. B. MA(Oxon) Oxford

WILSON Ian Alexander   BSc(eng) 1966

WILSON Isabel Ann   MA 1956
m Middleton

WILSON James Anthony   *BSc(eng) 1968 MSc 1970
s of Alexander D. W. MA 1936 qv and Mary C.
Anderson BSc 1938 qv; b Aber 25.7.46
asst consult. eng: Glasg 1970-72, Helensburgh 1972-73;
sen consult. eng Glasg 1973-75; proj eng from 1975
m Aber 21.9.73 Elizabeth D. McLaren MA 1968 qv

WILSON James George
                    ***BSc(eng) 1961 MSc 1963 MA 1966**
s of James W. marine eng and J. Farquhar; b Buckie
29.11.30
BA(OU) 1974
teacher maths AGS 1967; lect maths Aber tech coll from
1967
m 1960 Moira Wood BA(OU) d of Angus M. W.

WILSON James Moir   *BSc 1960 MLitt 1975
s of William G. W. fisherman and Alexanderina McKay;
b Whitehills 20.4.38
M Inst P
teacher: phys AGS 1961-64, prin phys Nairn acad 1964-

70, Inv royal acad 1970–71; Aber coll of educ: lect phys sc 1972–77, sen lect i/c phys sc dept from 1977
m Aber 21.7.66 Jean G. Duncan secy d of George L. D. Aber

WILSON Jean   MA 1965
d of George W. seaman and Alice Wilson; b Turriff 6.1.44
teacher: Engl Friern Barnet g s 1966–68, nat soc for ment handicapped ch Lond 1968–70, Edin 1970–72, asst prin Engl Craigroyston s Edin from 1972

WILSON John Allan   *BSc 1969
s of George P. D. W. elect. and Isobella W. Allan; b Forfar 24.1.48
res stud. Imp coll 1969–73; res assoc Birm from 1973

WILSON John Dewar   PhD 1969
s of Stuart W. exec eng GPO telecom and Jenny R. Jamieson shop asst; b Edin 27.5.39
MA(Edin) 1960 Dip Fd(Edin) 1961 MEd(Glas) 1964
lect educ Aberd 1969–70; prin lect educ Moray House coll of educ from 1971
m Glasg 27.7.65 Margaret A. Miller teacher d of Robert M. M. Glasg

WILSON John Haldane   BSc(eng) 1963

WILSON John Smith   *MA 1970
s of John W. bldg contr and Mary H. Smith; b Lossiemouth 30.3.25
teacher Engl AGS 1971–75; asst prin Engl Kincorth acad Aber from 1976
m Lossiemouth 17.11.50 Irene Smith teacher d of James A. S. Lossiemouth

WILSON Kathleen Helen   MA 1970
d of Alexander W. farm. and Kathleen M. Ling nurse; b Dumfries 13.1.49
soc worker: Kent c c Canterbury 1970–71, Brighton soc serv 1972–73
m Dumfries 24.9.71 John D. Macgregor BSc 1970 qv

WILSON Keith William   *BSc 1967 PhD 1974
s of James G. H. W. farm lab and Isobel E. Cound; b Shrewsbury 29.9.44
scient civ serv sen scient off: MAFF Burnham-on-Crouch 1970–77, NW water auth Warrington from 1977
m Aber 13.9.69 Linda F. Hall MA 1970 qv

WILSON Lorna Murray   MA 1957 Dip Ed 1958
d of Gordon D. W. papermaker and Annie T. Murray; b Bucksburn 11.3.36
teacher: maths Tarbert Is of Harris 1958–62, high s for girls Glasg 1962; mathematician UKAEA Windscale 1962–64
m Aber 17.10.63 Philip R. Stanwix BSc(Glas) res chem s of William P. S. Darlington

WILSON Margaret Anderson   MA 1968
m Mikulsiti

WILSON Margaret Elizabeth   BSc 1962
d of Frank J. W. foreman maltman and Isabella Younie; b Rafford 9.3.41
teacher: sc Goodlyburn s s Perth 1963–65, spec asst 1965–66, maths St Stephen's h s Port Glasgow 1974–76, High Tunstall comp s Hartlepool from 1976
m Rafford 10.7.65 Hamish A. Copland radar tech RAF, electronic test eng IBM s of Robert S. C. Abernethy

WILSON Margaret Hill   MA 1970
s of David D. W. painter/decorator and Helen Hill; b

Stirling 25.5.48
journalist *Weekly News* Glasg from 1970

WILSON Moira   MA 1969
d of Alexander W. orthop tech and Mary H. Sangster lib, stock superv; b Perth 6.8.47
Inv: temp sales asst, temp clerkess Inv t c 1969; asst collector of taxes Inl Rev from 1970

WILSON Monica Mary   MA 1963
d of James O. W. farm. and Mary Shand nurs sister; b Banff 11.10.42
teacher: p s Stonehaven 1964–65, Amer s s Benghazi Libya 1966
m Aber 20.7.65 Thomas W. Ogg MB ChB 1964 qv

WILSON Muriel   MA 1967
m Greig

WILSON Neil   *BSc 1957

WILSON Peter Richard   BSc(for) 1962

WILSON Philip Melvin   MB ChB 1969

WILSON Robert Charles Duncan   MB ChB 1956
s of Charles D. W. MB ChB 1924 qv(II, III) and Margaret T. Munro MA 1925 qv; b Darlington 19.7.32
ECFMG(USA) 1962 LMCC 1962 CCFP(C) 1970
h o Aber 1956–58; internship Calgary Alta 1958–59; h o Westminster hosp Lond Ont 1959–60; clin lect fam med univ of W Ont Canada from 1967; g p Lond Ont from 1962
m Lond Ont 1.2.74 Maureen A. Gregory d of George E. G. Gravesend

WILSON Robert Keith   BSc 1967
s of Robert W. farm. and Frances Gray teacher; b Aber 4.5.44
advt exec J. Walter Thompson Co Lond 1967–70; asst advt man. Scottish & N'cle Breweries Edin 1970–72; advt exec Roche Prod. Lond 1972; sen acct superv McCann Erickson Lond from 1973

WILSON Robert Murray   BSc(eng) 1966
s of Peter M. W. chmn/man. dir and Agnes B. Calder teacher elocution; b Bearsden 30.3.43
Montreal: boiler des eng 1966–67, sales eng 1967–68; Clydebank: sales eng 1969–75, sales and marketing dir from 1975

WILSON Robin George   MA 1969

WILSON Roger Victor   *MA 1966
s of Robert W. W. tech auth, pers off. and Ada S. Rickwood; b Lond 30.6.44
ABPsS 1969 MPhil(Lond) 1972
psych, sen psych MoD Farnborough 1966–72; univ careers advis Leeds from 1973

WILSON Ronald George   MB ChB 1961
FRCSE 1970
lect surg Nott

WILSON Stewart Roger Devine   *MA 1966

WILSON Susan Margaret   MA 1965

WILSON Wendy Scott   MLitt 1970
d of John D. W. comp pres and Shirley J. Mansfield; b Litchfield Illinois 21.1.46
BA(Wells) 1968
USA: teaching fell. Northeastern univ Mass. 1970–71, teacher Lexington s Mass. from 1971, lect Northeastern

univ from 1972, writer Prentice-Hall publ from 1980
m Weston Mass. 24.11.71 Lloyd M. Thompson BA(North-eastern) teacher s of Lloyd M. T. Scituate Mass.

WILSON William Alan   MB ChB 1968
  s of William C. W. MB ChB(Edin) emeritus prof surg Aberd and Ivy M. Allan; b Aber 13.1.42
MRCGP 1974
h o ARI, RACH 1968–69; g p Aber from 1969, med asst ARI from 1975
m Aber 26.12.63 Eileen M. Machray teacher d of John W. M. Lyne of Skene

WILSON William Stewart   *BSc 1960
  s of Robert S. W. civ serv and Elizabeth K. K. Hamilton; b Aber 15.5.37
teacher AGS 1961–66; prin maths Banchory acad 1966–72, dep rector 1972–78, rector from 1978
m Aber 3.8.66 Elizabeth A. Gorrod bank teller d of George G. Aber

WILSON Wilma Elizabeth Bruce   MA 1963
  m Hunter

WINCHESTER Alexander   MA 1957

WINCKWORTH William Haydn   LLB 1968 *1969
  s of Wilfrid H. W. highways eng and Joan F. Thurlow; b S'ton 8.6.47
admitted solic Eng 1972
articled clerk, asst solic Lancs c c Preston 1970–73; sen solic Telford dev corp Salop 1973–78; solic Lond & Manc Assur Co Exeter from 1978
m Aber 3.4.71 Jean Middleton teacher d of William M. Aber

WINGFIELD Nigel Richard Haydon   MA 1970

WINNING Timothy John   MB ChB 1970

WINPENNY Alexander Rae   *MA 1963

WINTON Douglas   BSc 1957

WINTON Peter Garden   BSc 1966

WIRK Harwant Kaur   MB ChB 1968

WISELY Dorothy Constance   MA 1966
  d of Norman F. W. haulage contr/farm. and G. Constance Robertson; b Aber 18.12.45
teacher p s Cults acad Aber 1967–69
m Aber 19.7.68 Douglas R. Harper BSc 1962 *qv*

WISELY Ivan Charles Fraser   MB ChB 1967
  s of John A. K. W. teacher and Elizabeth A. M. Fraser MA 1927 *qv*; b Aber 28.1.43
DA 1971
h o, sen h o, regist anaest ARI 1967–73; g p: Aber 1973–74, Dyce/Bucksburn from 1974
m Montrose 12.9.64 Jillian G. A. Kay MA 1966 *qv*

WISELY Kathleen   MA 1965 *MEd 1970
  teacher: Engl/hist Northfield acad Aber 1966–74, prin guid Kincorth acad Aber from 1974

WISELY May   *MA 1969

WISELY Norman Robertson   *BSc(eng) 1969
  s of Norman F. W. haulage contr/farm. and G. Constance Robertson; b Aber 4.1.48
Dip Man. St(Strath) 1974
prod. dev eng Gen Motors Scot. Newhouse 1969–73;

sales dev eng Baker Perkins Jaxons Glasg from 1973
m Aber 5.8.72 Margaret A. Sinclair MA 1972 teacher d of Iain A. M. S. Aber

WISELY Wendy Adie   *MA 1969 Dip Ed 1970
  d of Albert J. W. salesman and Jane Aitken; b Aber 23.3.47
MSc(Strath) 1973
teacher p s Lond 1970–72; educ psych Dunbartonsh 1974; teacher: i/c tut. centre Workington 1974–75; p s Arlecdon 1975–76
m Aber 18.8.73 David J. Milne BSc(eng) 1969 *qv*

WISEMAN Alasdair   BSc(agr) 1963
  s of Alexander W. gen merch and Elizabeth A. Shaw teacher; b St Fergus 29.12.40
BVMS(Glas) 1967 PhD(Glas) 1978 MRCVS
dept vet med Glas vet s: asst lect 1967–70, lect 1970–77, sen lect from 1977
m Culsalmond 24.12.69 Patricia A. Duncan hairdresser d of William D. Insch

WISEMAN Alexander Sutherland   MB ChB 1958

WISEMAN Carl McQueen   MB ChB 1961
  s of Alfred R. M. W. hairdresser and Isobel McQueen nurse; b Banff 16.4.37
CRCP(C) 1971 FRCP(C) 1972
h o Norwich 1961–62; g p Essex 1962–63; sen h o, regist psychiat Norwich 1963–65; Canada: staff phys Brandon Manit 1965–68, resid psychiat St Boniface 1968–69, staff phys/clin dir Brandon, private pract (psychiat) Brandon from 1972
m Dovercourt 1961 Patricia A. McCurry teacher d of Patrick McC. Dovercourt

WISEMAN David   MB ChB 1959
  s of Joseph G. W. fisherman and Barbara Wiseman; b Gardenstown 28.2.35
DObstRCOG 1968
h o Woodend hosp Aber, Stracathro hosp Brechin 1959–60; sen h o Royal Vict hosp Blackpool 1960–61; regist anaest royal Salop hosp Shrewsbury 1961–62; g p: Kirkwall 1962–67; Withernsea 1967, Auchenblae from 1967
m Aber 16.1.60 Hazel Anderson nurse d of James D. B. A. Kirkwall

WISEMAN Graham Richmond   *MA 1956
  b Aber 30.10.32
teacher mus AGS 1957–58, Aber acad 1957–61; prin mus Inverurie acad 1961–67; county mus organis Moray and Nairn 1967–75; advis in mus Grampian reg from 1975
m Aber 11.7.62 Winifred R. Emslie shorthand-typist

WISEMAN Margaret Macdonald   MA 1967
  d of Henri R. W. plumber and Jessie S. Birss; b Inv 28.7.47
part-time teacher Engl, mod lang, r e Wick h s 1970–77; asst regist Wick from 1978
m Dufftown 5.8.67 Kenneth G. Wood MA 1966 *qv*

WISEMAN Raymond   MB ChB 1964
  s of Joseph G. W. fisherman and Barbara Wiseman; b Gardenstown 4.1.41
MRCPath 1970 Dip Bact(Lond) 1970
h o Woodend, City hosp Aber 1964–65; terminable lect bact Aberd 1965–69; asst, sen bact Luton 1969–72; consult. bact Bangour from 1972
m Aber 3.4.65 Esther H. Wood teacher d of Alexander W. Aber

WISEMAN Robert Lindsay   *BSc 1963 PhD 1967
s of James C. W. MA 1930 *qv* and Winifred A. I.
Melvin MA 1930 *qv*; b Elgin 18.12.40
USA: post doct fell./res staff Yale 1968–72, res assoc publ
health res inst NY from 1973
m NY 15.9.73 Anca M. Vasiliu MA(Bucharest) teacher d
of Constantin V. MSc(Bucharest) Tuckahoe NY

WISLEY Ada May   MA 1968
m Bain

WISLØFF Sigurd Brun   MB ChB 1963
s of Carl F. W. DD(Oslo) prof ch hist and Ingrid Brun;
b Oslo Norway 13.3.36
Norway: h o Stavanger 1964–65, m o h/g p Bratvaag/
Haram 1965–69; regist: soc med Molde 1969–70, psychiat
Molde 1970–73, consult. psychiat Molde 1974, chief
consult Åsgård sykehus univ psychiat hosp Tromsø
m Aber 3.10.60 Catherine L. Ross MA 1961 *qv*

WITO James Alexander   BEd 1969
b Arbroath 19.1.42
teacher Arbroath 1969–70; prin Fr Kinross 1970–73; asst
prin mod lang Dunfermline 1973–75; prin mod lang
Ballingry from 1976
m Aber 11.11.67 Moira A. Harrison BEd 1969 *qv*

WITTE Elizabeth Mary   *MA 1970 PhD 1980
d of William W. PhD 1935 *qv* and Edith M. S. Melvin
MA 1932 *qv*; b Aber 13.12.47
teacher mod lang Harlaw acad Aber 1971–74; stud. PhD
Aberd from 1974
m Aber 17.7.70 Bryan A. Dargie MA 1963 *qv*

WONG Cheong Ngan   BSc 1970

WONG Daisy Sai Hui   MB ChB 1970
d of Ngiong H. W. bus. man and Chung I. Chong; b
Sarikei Sarawak 30.5.42
h o: Aber, Kirkwall 1970–71; asst radiol Bergen Norway
1972–73
m Sandvika Norway 31.7.71 Einar R. Tamber MB ChB
1970 *qv*

WONG David Kwok Hung   MB ChB 1968

WONG Shing Lai Alexis   BSc(eng) 1969
s of Wong Kam merch and Sui Ping Leung; b Hong
Kong 3.7.45
Hong Kong: jun site eng 1969–70, grad eng 1970–71, asst
resid eng 1971–73, asst eng 1972–73, des eng 1973–77,
proj man. from 1978
m Hong Kong 12.10.74 Florence Foon Hang Chan secy d
of Chan Chik Yuen, Hong Kong

WOOD Alastair James   *MA 1956

WOOD Alexander Stewart   *BSc 1968

WOOD Alfred Wallace   *MA 1959

WOOD Ann Veronica   *MA 1963
d of William W. MA 1930 *qv* and Margaret S. Geddes
MA 1932 *qv*; b Dufftown 4.8.40
Cert Soc Work(Exe) 1964
ch care off. Hertford c c Hemel Hempstead 1965–67; soc
worker Edin 1967–71; lect soc work Goldsmiths Lond
univ from 1971

WOOD Anne Elizabeth Harthill   BSc 1965 Dip Ed 1966
m McDonald

WOOD Annie Mary   MA 1962

WOOD Catherine Margaret   MA 1964
m Craig

WOOD Douglas Simpson   *MA 1958
s of George T. N. W. master plumber and Dorothy M.
Simpson; b Aber 25.12.36
nat serv UK, Germany 1958–60; market res exec: Lond
1960–64, Hull 1964–65; market res man. Lagos 1965–67,
Kuala Lumpur 1967–68, Singapore 1968–71; Lond:
market res ag dir 1971–73, proj dir Soc Res inst from 1973
m Borehamwood 11.7.64 Elizabeth P. J. Hooton secy d of
Gordon H. Borehamwood

WOOD Ella   BSc 1970
m Smith

WOOD Fiona   MB ChB 1968
DObstRCOG 1970
m Aber 1968 Ian G. C. Coutts BSc 1960 *qv*

WOOD Frank   BSc 1960

WOOD Geoffrey Edward   *MA 1967
s of Edward W. coach painter and Ellen Ross; b Aber
19.8.47
lect univ of Warwick 1968–71 and from 1973; res econ
Bank of England (on leave from Warwick univ) 1971–73
m Aber 8.4.69 Lesley A. Henry BA(Lond) teacher d of
George H. Mansfield

WOOD Ian Clark   *BSc 1964
s of John W. comp dir and Margaret Clark; b Aber
21.7.42
man. dir John Wood Group (Abdn) Aber from 1964
m Aber 25.9.70 Helen MacRae d of Murdo MacR. Inv

WOOD James Falconer   MB ChB 1960

WOOD Jane Anne McLeod   MA 1968
d of William W. plasterer and Lilian Walters; b Mansfield 26.11.46
BA(Strath) 1978
teacher Engl Glasg from 1971

WOOD John   *BSc 1965
s of John W. sea capt and Isabella Slater; b Portknockie
28.3.43
MSc(W Ont) 1970
Canada: field geol Toronto 1965–68, exploration geol
NW Territories 1969–70, Alberta 1970–71; Precambrian
surveys geol Ontario from 1971
m Norwich Ontario 1969 Janet J. Pollard BA(W Ont)
teacher d of James I. P. Norwich Ont

WOOD John Bruce Murray   LLB 1970
s of Arthur E. S. W. MB ChB(Edin) g p and Robina
Bruce; b Edin 30.6.49
Edin: asst examiner 1970–73, executry asst 1973–74, cler
off. Lothian reg c 1977–78, cler off. Lothian reg trans 1978

WOOD John Keith   MA 1968 Dip Ed 1969
s of Alfred J. W. farm. and Mary C. Keith dist nurse; b
Kirkwall 10.10.47
teacher Engl: Forfar 1970–71, Stromness 1971–77; asst
head Stromness from 1977
m Kirkwall 14.8.69 Fiona C. Groundwater bank clerkess
d of Alexander G. Kirkwall

WOOD Kenneth George   MA 1966
s of Albert G. W. indust civ serv MoD and Amy B.
Sandoe; b Queenborough 10.7.44
teacher mod lang Eastwood h s 1967–70; Wick h s: asst

prin mod lang 1970–78, asst prin guid from 1978
m Dufftown 5.8.67 Margaret W. Wiseman MA 1967 *qv*

WOOD Kenneth McDonald   LLB 1968
   s of Gordon W. slater, night superv and Edna M.
Falcon; b Aber 21.1.48
invest analyst: Philips & Drew stockbrokers Lond 1968–
69, Gilbert Eliott & Co stockbrokers Lond from 1969
m Lond 19.12.70 Diane B. Freedman stockbroker's clerk
d of Philip F. Leyton Lond

WOOD Margaret Ann   MA 1963 Dip Ed 1964

WOOD Margaret Ann   MA 1969
   d of Robert S. R. W. eng and Anna Reid florist; b
Fraserburgh 2.2.48
Dip Biling Secy (Aber coll of comm) 1973
teacher Fr Grimshaw Alberta 1970–72; Peace River
Alberta: stenog dept indust, trade & comm 1973–74,
teacher p s 1974–76, Fr 1977–78, p s from 1979
m Fraserburgh 29.6.73 Michael A. S Arnold BEd(Alta)
vice-prin elem s s of Stanley A.S.A. Lond

WOOD Margaret Buchanan   MA 1970
   d of James S. L. W. MA 1929 *qv*; b Newtonmore 5.1.49
tut./translator Ger/stud. medieval Ger Munich 1972–73
m Torphins 18.8.73 Gerhard Weber Dip Biochem(Munich)
s of Gerhard W. Niederbayern

WOOD Margaret Mair   MA 1960
   d of William M. W. lt-comm RNR, fishing skipper-
owner and Williamina Campbell; b Rothesay 21.10.40
teacher Engl/hist Macduff h s 1961–62, Portknockie j s s
1962–69
m Findochty 22.12.62 James G. King lect p e s of
Archibald W. W. K. Keith

WOOD Maureen Jessie   *BSc 1968
   d of Joseph W. manuf's ag and Jessie Burton; b
Cartmel 8.2.46
PhD(Belf) 1975
Belf: post grad stud. 1968–71, teaching asst 1971–72;
post doct res asst King's coll Lond 1972–74; teacher biol
Sunbury-on-Thames 1975; cryobiol MRC lab ans centre
Carshalton from 1975

WOOD Michael   *BSc 1963
   s of James S. L. W. MA 1929 *qv*; b Insch 25.6.41
Dip Cartog(Glas) 1964
Glas: res asst 1964–66, asst lect 1966–69; lect geog Aberd
from 1969
m Aber 6.8.66 Margaret R. L. Barr MA(Glas) teacher d
of James C. B. Stevenston

WOOD Moira Jean Campbell   MA 1965
   d of William M. W. fisherman and Williamina
Campbell; b Findochty 30.10.45
teacher: geog Kintore 1966–68, Engl Cambridge 1968–69,
Engl Welwyn Garden City 1969–72
m Findochty 4.4.70 John M. Knapman MA(Cantab)
computer syst eng s of Gordon A. K. Lond

WOOD Sheila   MA 1958
   d of Edwin W. marine eng and Josephina Smith; b Aber
25.7.37
teacher: Carfin 1959–61, Fr The Priory s Kingston
Jamaica 1963–64; lect mod lang Galloway coll of tech
Dumfries from 1978
m Aber 30.6.59 Henry Neilan MA 1958 *qv*

WOOD Stanley   *BSc 1957

WOOD Susan Elizabeth   MB ChB 1967
   d of Gordon W. MA(Edin) solic and Agnes E. Stephens
physioth; b Walton-on-Thames 16.5.43
DCH(Lond) 1970
h o Inv, Aber, Maidstone 1967–68; sen h o paediat Luton,
Kingston 1969–70; regist paediat Chelmsford 1971–72;
clin m o commun med Kingston from 1972
m Aber 14.4.72 Gordon P. R. Antonio electronics eng s
of Oscar R. A. Bangalore India

WOOD Sydney Arthur Rankin   BSc 1967

WOOD Thelma   MA 1966 *MEd 1970
   d of John W. master mariner and Fanny C. McKenzie;
b Stonehaven 14.3.45
teacher mod lang Linlithgow 1967–69; asst educ psych
Edin 1970–72; sen educ psych Forfar 1972–74
m Stonehaven 19.9.70 George F. Ritchie BSc(H-W)
electronics eng s of George F. R. Stonehaven

WOOD William Rae   *MA 1959
   s of Alexander C. W. taxi driver and Ethel Rae bakery
worker; b Aber 30.11.36
Dip Ed(Lond) 1960
educ off. N Nigeria 1960–71; teacher hist Bellahouston
acad Glasg 1971–73, prin hist Whitehill s s Glasg from
1973
marr diss

WOOD Willina Ross   MA 1957
   d of William W. trawlmaster and Williamina R. Wood;
b Aber 13.11.36
Lond: trainee life dept Royal Insur Co 1958–60, off.
superv Paterson Eng Co 1960–62, priv secy Peter Lind &
Co 1962–63
m Aber 17.6.61 Iain H. Muir bank trust off. s of John
C. M. Glasg

WOODBURN Winifred Margaret   MA 1969

WOODFORD Helen   MA 1969
   d of Leonard A. W. postman, farm., ambul driver and
Eileen M. Baker dist nurse, midwife; b Crawley 7.6.47
Dip Ed-TEFL(Manc) 1972
Brit council teacher Engl Kokkola Finland 1969–70;
TEFL Padworth coll Reading 1970–77; Brit council
teacher Engl Vientiane Laos 1972–75

WOODHEAD William David   BSc(for) 1958 *1959

WOODHOUSE Sylvia   BEd 1969
   d of Denis K. W. arch. and Rosa M. S. Barclay
governess; b Toronto 9.9.17
teacher: Blackburn Lancs 1969–70, Rishton 1970–76
m Aber 22.9.51 William T. Main linotype oper, prod.
man. s of William M. Aber

WOODROW James Dow   MA 1963

WOODS Ian Cecil Cordner   *MA 1970

WOODS William John Francis   LLB 1970

WOOE-CHUNG Rudolph Theodore   MA 1959

WOOLFENDEN David   BSc(for) 1956
   s of Edward W. hat manuf and Muriel Gill teacher; b
Denton 12.4.32
for. off.: NI 1956–66, Kasama Zambia 1966–69, NI 1969–
74, Roseau Dominica WI from 1974
m Enniskillen NI 9.7.66 Gillian M. West teacher d of
James W. Ballycassidy Co Fermanagh

WOOLLAM Jane Anne Nelson   MA 1969
d of Frederick W. master grocer and Phyllis Nelson hairdresser; b Banff 7.10.48
teacher hist/Engl Lond 1970–71, accts asst *Daily Express* Lond 1971–72; supply teacher (home tuition dept) Gillingham Kent from 1978
m Cullen 29.5.71 Christopher R. Walker BSc 1969 *qv*

WOOLLARD Maureen Lydia   MA 1959
b Aber 5.1.37
secy in Aberd 1960; teacher: Aber 1962–65, Wallasey 1966–68
m Aber 15.7.64 Hamish A. Anderson BSc 1962 *qv*

WOOLVERTON Peter Roy   *MA 1970
s of Michael W. estate surv and Isabella Smith; b Edin 17.10.47
Liberton h s Edin: teacher geog from 1971, later asst prin outdoor educ

WORLING Michael James   BSc 1966

WORRELL Joy Irma Cecil   MA 1968

WRAY Aileen Isabel Mackie   MA 1958
d of Vincent L. W. man. nat carriers Aber and Edith Walker MA 1925 *qv*; b York 6.6.37
teacher mod lang: W Midlands 1958–65, Notts from 1972
m Aber 18.8.60 Peter B Knott teacher s of Harold A. K. Reading

WRIGHT Alan Beattie   BL 1960
s of John M. W. MA 1929 *qv* and Jane H. Beattie MA 1930 *qv*; b Aber 2.5.39
CA 1962
acct Lond 1962–66; chief acct/comp secy Kampala Uganda 1966–69; proj auditor Teheran Iran 1969–72; divisional acct Sale 1972–75; gen man. Dun 1975–79; acct in profession Dun from 1979
m Banff 28.5.66 Isabel G. Wood teacher d of John J. W. Banff

WRIGHT Alexander Neill   PhD 1958
BA(Oxon)
resid Faversham

WRIGHT Constance Clarice Mathieson   *MA 1963
d of Thomas M. W. basketmaker and Clarice Brett french polisher; b Aber 24.5.41
BD(Lond) 1978
teacher Engl: Hermitage acad, Helensburgh 1964–68, Aber acad 1968–74; stud. Birm Bible Inst 1974–78; teacher r e/Engl/hist Lea Mason C of E s Birm from 1978

WRIGHT David Gerard   *MA 1966

WRIGHT David Glover   *BSc(eng) 1969

WRIGHT Dorothy Gillian   *MA 1967

WRIGHT Genefer Gail Finlayson   MA 1966
d of William C. W. BL 1939 *qv*; b Inv 28.5.45
FSA Scot 1974
teacher Leeds 1967–68; interviewer for govt soc serv 1968–69
m Dornoch 26.8.67 David R. Clark BSc 1965 *qv*

WRIGHT Grace Elberta   *MA 1961

WRIGHT Ian James   *BSc 1968 PhD 1971

WRIGHT Jacqueline Elizabeth Margaret   MA 1965
d of John W. elect. and Agnes A. Watt; b Aber 19.12.44
m St Albans 23.7.66 Anthony B. Harbour MA 1966 *qv*

WRIGHT Jean Anne   MB ChB 1958
m Cameron
d Watford 8.2.66 *AUR* XLII 91

WRIGHT John David Maitland   *MA 1964
s of Edward M. W. BSc(Lond) princ Aberd 1962–76 and Elizabeth P. Harris; b Aber 20.5.42
Simpson Prize, De Gurbs Schol
DPhil(Oxon) 1967 FRSE 1978
lect Christ Church Oxford 1965–68; fell./tut. St Catherine's coll Oxford 1968–70; prof pure maths R'dg from 1971
m Aber 17.9.65 Helen Butler

WRIGHT John Richard   BSc(eng) 1970
s of Herbert W. police off., civ def off., law off. and Kathleen Rogers; b Wallasey 18.12.48
Brit Aerospace: flight test instrumentation dev eng Warton Lancs 1970–73, sen FTI calibration eng from 1973
m Aber 18.3.72 Sandra M. Marr bank clerk, secy d of Walter A. M. Aber

WRIGHT Norman John Duncan   MA 1969
s of William C. W. BL 1939 *qv*; b Inv 4.4.48
LL B(Edin) 1971
post grad res sociol of law Edin 1971–73; law app Dornoch 1973–75; leg. asst Arthur & Carmichael, Dornoch 1975–77, ptnr from 1977
m Inv 27.7.73 Susan Abbott MA 1969 *qv*

WRIGHT Susan Margaret   BSc 1970
d of John N. W. MA 1951 *qv*; b Lond 12.7.48
lab asst; psych dept Aberd 1970–74, med lab Wis Madison USA from 1974
m Aber 3.7.70 Ronald N. Buick BSc 1970 *qv*

WRIGHT William George   *BSc 1956
s of Frank W. textile worker and Margaret I. Ellis shopkeeper; b Garmouth 27.12.33
jun tech RAF UK, Germany 1956–58; res chem Birm 1959–62; sen scient off. (textiles) Dun 1962–71, post-grad res work Dund 1971–73; tech man. (textiles) Dun 1973–76; chem (distilling indust) Tormore from 1977
m Urquhart 31.10.59 Isabella B. Farquhar shorthand typist d of Alexander F. Garmouth

WU San San   MB ChB 1965
d of Shu H. W. BA(China) bus. man and Siok H. Ng; b Sarawak 11.8.35
DPH(Singapore) 1972 MFCM 1974
Singapore: m o Kerdang Kerbau mat. hosp and paediat unit gen hosp 1967–68; health off. mat. and ch serv 1968–70, trg and health educ unit min of health 1970–72, sen regist mat. and ch health serv from 1973

WUNSCH Susan Ilene   M Litt 1970
d of Samuel W. bus. owner and Etta H. Waldman; b Providence Rhode Is USA 7.3.46
BA(Wellesley coll USA) 1967
Yale USA: electron microscopist 1969–73, asst dir undergrad admissions 1973–74, dean Saybrook coll 1974–75, 1978–79; asst dean Yale coll 1977–78
m Providence 2.7.67 Charles D. Rice MA 1964 *qv*

WYCHERLEY Gwyneth   MA 1957
m Henderson

WYLIE Alastair Graham   PhD 1965
s of Hance G. W. police off. and Isabella P. Neilson; b Glasg 26.4.36
BSc(Strath) 1961
ICI Cheshire: res chem 1965–66, res and dev chem 1966–72, res and dev group man. from 1972

m Cheadle-Hulme 12.9.68 Norma Atkinson med lab tech
d of Joseph A. Cheadle-Hulme

WYLIE Brian Gilfillan   MA 1969

WYLIE Ralph Clark   *BSc 1970
   m Banff 1.4.72 Jane P. Eaton BSc 1970 *qv*

WYLIE Roslyn   MA 1968
   d of Drummond W. bank man. and Doris Lancashire;
   b Dunfermline 2.10.47
   Dip Soc Ad(Edin) 1969 CASS(Brist) 1971
   trainee soc worker Edin 1969–70; asst psychiat soc
   worker Murray royal hosp Perth 1971; soc worker/
   commun worker Roxburghsh Hawick 1972–73
   m Scone 30.10.71 Alan Anderson LL B(Edin) solic s of
   Andrew A. Coldstream

WYLIE-RITCHIE John Young   MA 1969

WYLLIE Andrew David Hamilton
               BSc 1964 *MB ChB 1967 PhD 1975
   s of Andrew M. W. MB ChB(Glas) phys supt Royal
   Cornhill hosp Aber and Marjorie H. Maxwell BSc 1930
   qv; b Aber 24.1.44
   MRCP 1970 MRC Path 1975
   h o ARI 1968–69; termin lect path. Aberd 1969–70; MRC
   jun res fell. Lond 1970–72; lect path. Edin 1972–75; res
   fell. cancer res campaign Cambridge 1976–77; sen lect
   path. Edin from 1977
   m Leic 18.9.71 Hilary Walder

WYLLIE Anne Margaret   *MB ChB 1960
   d of Andrew M. W. MB ChB(Glas) phys supt Royal
   Cornhill hosp Aber and Marjorie H. Maxwell BSc 1930
   qv; b Dumfries 8.7.38
   Dip Ophth(Lond) 1963 Fell. Ophth(Edin) 1966
   h o Perth, Aber 1960–62; sen h o Glasg 1962–63; regist
   Aber 1963–65; sen regist 1965–70; consult. Portsmouth
   1970–77, Lanarksh from 1977

WYLLIE Marjorie Rose   *BSc 1957
   d of Andrew M. W. MB ChB(Glas) phys supt Royal
   Cornhill hosp Aber and Marjorie H. Maxwell BSc 1930
   qv; b Dumfries 17.6.35
   PhD(Glas) 1961
   grad dem zool Glas 1957–60; Glas: asst lect 1960–61,
   part-time res asst/dem 1961–64; temp lect zool Jordanhill
   coll of educ 1964–65
   m Aber 17.9.60 John B. Wilson MA(Glas) electronics eng,
   forecasting man., man. consult. s of Frank B. W. Glasg

WYNESS Helen Pirie   MB ChB 1965
   d of Gordon W. and Betty M. Pirie teacher homecraft;
   b Aber 11.10.43
   Dip Av Med 1967 Dip Hyperbaric Physiol(Calif) 1975
   m o RAF Halton, Wroughton, Kinloss, Farnborough
   1966–69; g p Cardiff 1971; cas off. St Davids Cardiff
   1972–73; m o publ health Aber 1973–75; m o oceaneering
   internat diving comp from 1975; med advis royal Omani
   army Muscat
   m(1) Lee-Mason
      (2) Aber 11.2.76 Austin Tobin

WYNESS Phyllis Jane   MB ChB 1969

WYNN Michael   MB ChB 1964
   s of Michael J. W. comp dir and Mary A. McDonald;
   b Elgin 20.11.38
   h o: ARI, Bridge of Earn 1965–66; sen h o: Bellshill mat.
   hosp, anaest Preston RI 1966; g p Glasg 1966–67, Buckie
   from 1967
   m Falkirk 16.6.69 Jennifer D. Bruce nurs sister d of
   Andrew D. B. Falkirk

WYNNE Rosalind Clare   *MA 1964
   m Gow

WYNTER Roderick Anthony   MB ChB 1958
   s of Hugh H. W. and Clare Oritinaire; b Jamaica
   12.6.30
   DCH(Lond) 1964
   h o: Woodend hosp Aber, Kingston publ hosp Jamaica
   1958–59; g p Antigua WI/dist m o 1959–62; rotating
   regist univ of WI 1963; SC hosp Toronto: sen asst resid/
   fell. cardiol/assoc resid 1964–66; Sunnybrook hosp
   Toronto jun asst resid med 1966; SC hosp Toronto
   teaching fell./post grad med course/fell. nephrol 1967–68:
   g p Toronto 1968–72; clin teaching fam pract Wellesley
   hosp univ of Toronto/courtesy staff Toronto W hosp/
   staff fam phys Wellesley hosp from 1972, lect fam/commun
   med/courtesy staff Women's coll hosp

XENOPHONTOS Constantinos   BSc 1966 *1967
   s of Xenophon Polycarpou farm. and Styliani
   Constantinou; b Nicosia 24.3.40
   MSc(eng)(Queen's univ) Kingston Ont 1972 F Geol Soc
   Greece Fulbright schol PhD(Calif)
   geol grade II with geol surv Cyprus 1968–70; commonwealth s Queen's univ Canada 1970–72; geol grade I
   Cyprus 1972–75
   m Nicosia 22.7.68 Rosalind M. Mitchell MA(St And)
   teacher d of Andrew F. M. Dun

YACKIMINIE Ann Bona   *MA 1961 Dip Ed 1962
   d of Alexander Y. eng and Barbara Shivas; b Aber
   26.8.39
   teacher: Hong Kong 1963–66, Sutherland 1966–70,
   Cyprus 1970–73
   m Aber 10.8.62 Stewart Simpson civ serv s of George S.
   Aber

YASSIN Tag Elsir   MSc 1968
   BSc(agr)(Khart)

YEATS Ian Martin   *MA 1963
   s of Alfred Y. MA 1929 *qv*; b Aber 14.2.41
   BA(Oxon) 1965 BCL(Oxon) 1966 MA(Oxon) 1970
   barrister (Inner Temple) 1972
   lect law Q Mary coll Lond from 1966; visiting lect univ
   of Adelaide Aust 1974

YEATS Katherine Hilda   MA 1969
   d of James C. R. Y. lib and Mary Barclay; b Bristol
   10.6.48
   au pair Paris, Berlin 1969–70; temp clerkess Lond, Aber
   1970–71; lib asst Aber publ lib 1972–73; lib trainee RGIT
   Aber 1973–74; lib asst Aberd 1974–77; temp clerkess
   from 1978
   m Aber 21.7.75 Peter S. C. Smith ARICS quantity surv s
   of William C. B. S. Lochgoilhead

YEE Chee Pong   BSc(eng) 1963

YEOMAN Hilda McLean   BSc 1962
   d of Charles Y. painter/decorator and Mabel D.
   Edwards; b Stonehaven 25.4.41
   teacher maths/sc Laurencekirk s s (Mearns acad from
   1977) 1963–72, asst prin guid 1972–75, prin guid from
   1975

YEOMAN Joyce Elizabeth   *MA 1970
   d of William S. Y. proj eng and Jessie McKenzie; b
   Aber 27.7.48
   computer progr Baric Glasg 1970–73
   m Aber 13.5.72 Joseph T. McAdie lorry driver s of
   Alexander J. McA. Ardgarten by Arrochar

YEOMAN Kathleen Janice   MA 1968
d of James Y. hosp audiology tech and Daisy M. Cook;
b Aber 8.7.47
teacher: Aber 1969–70 Midlothian 1970–72
m Aber 24.7.70 Ian H. Pearson MA 1967 *qv*

YING David Andrew   *MA 1969

YORKE Douglas McKenzie   *LLB 1968
s of Guy U. Y. MB ChB 1964 *qv*; b Aber 6.1.46
LLM(Penn) 1969
lect law Glas 1969–73; sen lect Glasg coll of tech from
1973
m Old Kilpatrick 17.3.73 Izella C. Dunbar secy d of
James D. Old Kilpatrick

YORKE Guy Ultan   MB ChB 1964
s of Harold L. Y. shipping comp clerk and Onra L.
Powell; b Christchurch NZ 5.11.24
BSc(Canterbury NZ) 1953
h o, sen h o royal northern hosp, W Fife hosp Dunferm-
line, Balfour hosp Orkney 1965–66; g p Aber, Inv,
Tokanui and Mataura, Runanga NZ 1966–69; cas off.
Southland hosp NZ 1970; supt Riverton hosp/g p NZ
1971–74; port health off./indust m o Ocean Beach/g p
Bluff NZ from 1974
m Aber Margaret T. Mackenzie shop man. d of William
McK. Aber

YOUNG Alan John Ward   MA 1966
   CA

YOUNG Alastair Cushnie   MB ChB 1964
s of Robert Y. rly signalman and Helen R. T. Gillespie
secy; b Comrie 28.2.41
MRCP 1970
h o Aber hosps 1964–65; h o, sen h o neurol/neurosurg
Killearn hosp 1965–66; regist Aber hosps 1966–71; regist
neurol inst of neurol sc Glasg 1971–73; sen regist neurol
Oxford from 1973
m Kilbirnie 5.7.69 Myra R. Rabey teacher d of Robert
R. R. Kilbirnie

YOUNG Alexander Douglas   BSc(agr) 1957

YOUNG Ann Lesley   *MA 1966
d of Alexander Y. insur exec and Annie Muir; b Edin
8.6.44
teacher geog: Perth h s 1967–68, Powis s s Aber 1968–70
m Aber 12.7.68 Neil G. Meldrum teacher of mus s of
William J. S. M. Aber

YOUNG Anne Elizabeth   MA 1965
d of John Y. and Marjory F. James admin asst corp of
Aber; b Aber 11.3.44
Dip Soc St.(Edin) 1966 Dip App Soc St.(Harris coll Preston) 1971
soc worker Angus from 1966
m Aber 11.4.74 Gerald L. Crighton DA arch. s of Leslie
C. Aber

YOUNG Antony Richard   *BSc 1970
MSc(Lond) 1972 PhD(Lond) 1980
Lond: teacher 1972–76, res asst 1976–79, res assoc from
1979

YOUNG Audrey Winifred   MB ChB 1959
m Aber 4.8.60 George M. Stewart MB ChB 1959 *qv*

YOUNG Barbara Shand   MA 1960 *BSc 1963
d of John Y. MA 1929 *qv*; b Singapore 2.12.39
teacher: Ladies' Coll Cheltenham 1964–68, York Coll for
girls from 1977
m Aber 18.8.65 Alistair J. M. Miller MA 1958 *qv*

YOUNG Christina Jean Taylor   MA 1969
d of Alexander F. T. Y. MA(Glas) C of S min and
Phyllis M. R. Chisholm MA(St And) teacher; b Dumfries
3.10.47
teacher geog Shoreditch comp s Lond 1970–73, prin geog
from 1973
m Edin 15.8.75 James A. Fadden BSc(Lond) teacher s of
Thomas J. F. Liverpool

YOUNG Claire Keir   *MA 1967
b Glasg 14.6.45
teach Engl: cent foundation girls' s Lond 1968–71,
Queensbury s Dunstable 1971–75; res asst Hatfield poly
1976–78
m Glasg 1.9.67 Stuart J. Meldrum BSc 1966 *qv*

YOUNG Colin McIntyre   PhD 1964
s of Archibald Y. Y. farm., soldier, civ serv and
Florence Stirling; b Kelvington Sask Canada 27.7.36
BSA(Tor) 1961
Canada: post doct fell. univ of Guelph 1964–65, sessional
lect 1965–66, asst prof Laurentian univ 1966–68, assoc
prof from 1968

YOUNG David Paterson   *MA 1960
s of James P. Y. steel worker, shopkeeper and Elizabeth
J. Rugg shopkeeper; b Rutherglen 30.11.37
FRGS 1961
teacher: Cumnock acad 1961–64, prin geog 1964–70; dep
rector Grange acad Kilmarnock 1970–77; rector Kilwinning acad from 1977
m Edin 30.11.68 Jean M. Brown lect d of John B. Edin

YOUNG Donald Stirling   MB ChB 1957
s of John S. Y. BSc(Glas) prof path. Aberd and Ruth M.
Whipple BA(Cantab) econ; b Belfast 17.12.33
PhD(Lond) 1962
lect materia medica Aberd 1958–59; regist post grad med s
Lond 1962–64; USA: visiting scient nat inst of health
Bethesda 1965–66, chief clin chem sect. nat inst of health
1966–67, head sect. clin chem Mayo clin Rochester from
1977
m Rockville MD USA 1972 Silja Meret BS(Vassar)

YOUNG Douglas   *MA 1961 PhD 1969
s of James Y. gasfitter and Isabella Brand; b Aber
15.6.40
instruct. univ of Victoria Canada 1962–64; teacher Engl
Aber acad 1964–67; lect Engl Aber coll of educ from 1969
m Auldearn 18.7.64 Margaret Forbes teacher d of
Kenneth F. Auldearn

YOUNG Eileen Margaret   *MA 1958
d of Alexander L. Y. CBE MA(Glas) teacher and then
dir educ Aberdeensh and Ellen O. Duffy MA(Glas)
teacher; b Glasg 23.7.37
LRAM 1954 MA(Oxon) 1964 LLM(Harvard) 1961
barrister-at-law (Lincoln's Inn 1963); asst lect law Brist
1961–63; asst leg. advis, leg. counsellor FCO from 1963
m Lond 8.10.66 John Denza MA 1956(Cantab) FCA s of
Luigi C. F. D. Lond

YOUNG Francis   BSc 1956 Dip Ed 1957
s of Fanny B. Young; b Logie Pert 19.12.34
teacher sc Perth acad 1957–61; prin sc Tain royal acad
1961–63; prin phys: Vale of Leven acad 1963–65, RGC
Aber 1965–71; sen lect phys Kingsway tech coll Dun from
1971
m Perth 16.4.60 Victoria F. Davie BSc 1956 *qv*

YOUNG George   BEd 1970

YOUNG Gordon   *MA 1964

YOUNG Gordon Anthony   BSc 1967
s of Albert T. Y. sales rep and Eileen E. Eden shop-keeper; b Nantwich 8.11.45
BVMS MRCVS(Edin) 1972
tech asst (MRC grant) psych Aberd 1967-68; vet g p Sevenoaks 1972-73, Etwall from 1973
m Edin 14.7.72 Dorothy A. Hogg d of James E. H. Edin

YOUNG Hazel Mitson   MA 1968
d of Norman W. Y. MA(Glas) and Margaret Mitson cler off.; b Torphins 21.8.47
m Aboyne 17.8.68 Robert D. Knorr arch. tech, plan. tech s of Lawrence E. K. Aboyne

YOUNG James Alexander Taylor   *BSc 1962
s of Alexander F. T. Y. MA(Glas) clergyman and Phyllis M. R. Chisholm MA(St And) teacher; b Peebles 4.4.40
PhD(Edin) 1966
univ dem Edin 1962-66; lect Edin from 1966; visiting lect Nairobi 1975
m Sheff 16.7.66 Gillian M. Randall MA(Edin) teacher d of John A. R. Sheff

YOUNG John   BEd 1970 MEd 1973
s of James Y. joiner and Janette R. Y. Halkerston; b Perth 15.2.43
teacher Engl/hist Stonehaven 1970-73: educ psych Edin 1973-76; sen educ psych from 1976
m Jedburgh 14.7.71 Valerie A. J. Bennett teacher of art d of John B. FRCO Jedburgh

YOUNG John Charles   MA 1965 LLB 1975
s of John Y. lorry driver and Marjory F. James secy; b Aber 11.3.44
MITransport 1969
various post road trans indust Aber, Newport (Mon), Livingston, Dun 1965-72; law app, leg. asst Glasg; solic Stornoway

YOUNG Johnstone Oliphant   *BSc 1960
s of Johnstone O. Y. and Winifred C. Morrison; b Huntly 15.3.38
PhD(UCNW) 1963
asst lect zool Leic 1963-64; lect zool Liv 1964-77; sen lect from 1977; visiting lect zool univ of Nairobi 1971-72
m Bangor 31.8.63 Beryl M. Randall BA d of Ernest F. R. Bangor

YOUNG Kenneth Moir   *MA 1957
s of John S. Y., BSc(Glas) prof path. Aberd and Ruth M. Whipple BA(Cantab) econ; b Belf 13.12.35
PhD(Princeton) 1969
stud. app AEI Manc 1957-59; res scient AEI Aldermaston 1959-63; grad stud. res staff member plasma phys lab Princeton univ NJ 1963-70; lect phys UMIST 1970-74; res phys plasma phys lab Princeton univ from 1974
m Bolton 7.8.65 Naomi A. Partington MA 1957 qv

YOUNG Marilyn Elizabeth   MA 1968
m Douglas

YOUNG Niall Andrew   *BSc 1964 MSc 1966
s of Andrew Young loc govt off. and Marion M. Watt; b Glasg 16.6.43
PhD(Belf) 1968
res fell. Lond Canada 1968-70; lect computing sc Aberd from 1970
m Aber 14.7.65 Patricia D. Holdsworth MA 1963 qv

YOUNG Oswald Courtenay   BSc 1963
s of Urias M. Y. bookkeeper and Mabel E. Kong; b

Trinidad WI 5.4.29
med/clin biochem gen hosp Port of Spain Trinidad from 1963
m Port of Spain 19.3.50 Rita C. Affonso d of Silvano A. Port of Spain

YOUNG Pamela Anne   *MA 1968
m Morris

YOUNG Prudence Ann   *MA 1960
d of Archibald G. B. Y. MB ChB 1937 qv and Annie S. Bain MB ChB 1931 qv; b Aber 6.5.38
m Aber 23.7.60 John A. King BSc(eng) 1952 qv

YOUNG Robert Macfie Douglas   LLB 1970
s of Robert M. Y. MA(Edin) solic and Margaret A. MacCaig; b Inv 23.10.48
NP 1973
law app Edin 1970-73; solic: Edin 1973, Inv from 1973

YOUNG Ronald Noble   *BSc 1960 PhD 1963
s of Charles E. Y. shop man. and Mary S. Noble; b Aber 15.5.38
res fell.: Akron univ Ohio USA 1963-64, Hull univ 1964-65; lect chem Sheff from 1963; visiting prof: Syracuse univ NY USA 1973, Akron univ 1972 1976 1978
m Aber 2.6.62 Mally Tompkins

YOUNG Susan Margaret   MA 1967
d of John D. Y. ship broker and Isabel Macdonald physioth; b Cardiff 11.10.45
civ serv Lond 1967-71; E Sussex c c Lewes: traffic eng 1971-79, pers off. indust relations from 1979
m Bromley 11.4.70 Arthur J. M. Hammond BA(Birm) civ serv s of Arthur H. Bisley

YOUNG Sylvia Jean   *MA 1962
d of R. H. Y. and Jane H. Webster; b Forfar 7.8.40
m Aber 1963 Alistair J. W. Smith MA 1962 qv; marr diss 1971

YOUNG Thomas Ogilvie   *BSc 1956
s of James D. Y. piano tuner and Elizabeth S. Carr; b Aber 11.6.34
scient off., sen scient off. MoD AWRE Aldermaston 1956-76; prin insp health & safety exec Lond from 1976
m Aber 24.7.57 Kathleen M. Grant BSc 1956 qv

YOUNG Valerie May   MA 1958 Dip Ed 1959
d of James A. Y. pharm and Rachel Cowling private secy; b Aber 13.1.38
teacher maths Aber 1959-69 and from 1974
m Aber 22.7.64 Dennis Kelly comp dir s of Bruce K. Cults

YOUNG William Fisher
                    MA 1969 *BSc 1972 MSc 1973
s of Charles G. Y. civ serv Inl Rev and Frances O. Fisher teacher; b Inv 24.4.47
scient off. sub div of soil sc, ITE, natural environment res c, based at Banchory res stat

YOUNG William James   MA 1958
s of Alexander C. Y. quarry man. and Annie Shand; b Garmouth 25.12.37
teacher: Kaimhill s s Aber 1960-62, prin geog Gambia h s Bathurst The Gambia W Af 1962-66; asst head Elgin East End p s 1967-71; head: Logie p s 1971-75, Burghead p s from 1975
m Aber 15.3.62 Joyce H. A. Murray d of Stewart M. Aber

YOUNG William McDonald
*BSc 1960 MSc 1961 PhD 1964
s of Robert Y. salmon fisher and Jessie A. McDonald;
b Inverbervie 23.4.39
res stud. nat phil Aberd 1960–63, asst 1963–64, lect phys
Dund from 1964

YOUNGSON Alan Falconer   *BSc 1970

YOUNGSON Alexander Hovell   MA 1961

YOUNGSON Colin James   *MA 1970 Dip Ed 1971
s of James A. Y. man. multiple tailors and Flora J.
MacOwan head Causewayend p s Aber; b Aber 27.10.47
teacher Engl Kelvinside acad Glasg 1971–73; TEFL
Örebro Sweden 1973–74; teacher Engl Craigmount h s
Edin from 1974
m Aber 5.8.74 Stella F. Reid MA 1970 *qv*

YOUNGSON James Andrews Robert   MA 1957

YOUNGSON Linda Clare   *MA 1968
d of William C. Y. arch. and Muriel Windsor; b
Milngavie 1.4.46
Dip Lib(Strath) 1970
grad trainee Stir univ lib 1968–69; asst lib Stirling c lib
1970–72; sen lib asst Stir univ from 1972

YOUNGSON Marika Elizabeth   MA 1969
d of John A. Y. MSHAA consult. audiologist and Rita
E. Milonopoulou; b Aber 17.6.48
computer progr Lond 1969–70; asst to sen progr Perth
1970–73
m Aber 31.8.68 Denis I. Squire ARICS bldg surv s of
Ronald A. S. Aber

YOUNGSON Richard Windsor   *BSc(for) 1964
s of William C. Y. arch. and Muriel Windsor; b
Milngavie 19.5.42
exper off. Nature Conserv red deer res Scot. 1964–69; res
off. Unilever salmonid cultivation Lochailort 1969–75;
field off. Red Deer Comm red deer man. from 1975
m Nairn 17.7.75 Margaret F. Macnaughton d of Charles
C. M. Lochailort

YOUNIE Peter George Hugh   BL 1956
s of John Y. MA(Edin) judge ICS and Dorothy
Mitchell MB ChB 1921 *qv*; b Aber 12.8.31
WS 1959 TD 1967
law app Watt & Cumine Aber 1953–56, Edin 1956–58;
solic Hunter Harvey Webster & Will WS Edin 1958–60,
ptnr from 1960
m Edin 3.3.61 Morag A. Tod MA(Edin) 1959 admin secy
d of John L. T. Lasswade

YOUNIE Richard David   BSc(eng) 1964

YOUSOF Abdul Mohsin   MB ChB 1961
s of Alabdul R. Y. bus. man and Noon Yousof; b
Singapore 27.10.34
MRCPGlas 1966 PhD(Prague) 1973 FRCPGlas 1976
h o Aber 1961–62; h o, regist Kuwait 1962–64; visiting
regist Aber 1964–65; Kuwait: regist 1965–67, sen regist
1967–68, consult. cardiol 1968–74, prof med & founding
Dean of s of med from 1974
m Kuwait 8.5.64 Shuaa Al Sumait d of Jassem H. A. S.
Kuwait

YSART Adèle Louise   MA 1970
d of Paul M. Y. glassmaker and Margaret Irvine; b
Perth 30.9.47
man. Mackays hotel Wick 1970–76; exec secy Dubai

colour tv Dubai UAE from 1976
m Dubai 28.2.80 Lewis M. Robertson BSc(Belf) electronics eng s of Duncan McR. R. Aber

YSEBAERT Marie-Josée Margherita   MA 1962
d of Sylvain Y. factory owner and Elodie Loeys bus.
ptnr; b Moldegem Belgium 17.4.25
teacher: Fr Aber 1962–68, Fr/Engl Manitoba 1968–69,
Fr/Engl Kettwig Germany from 1969
m Belgium 27.3.47 Fraser

YUILL Robert Alexander   ^eMB ChB 1959
s of William Y. master baker and Jeannie Raffan; b
Aber 2.11.34
DObstRCOG 1962 MRCGP 1976
h o Woodend hosp Aber, ARI, Perth RI, Bridge of Earn
hosp 1959–62; g p: Auchterarder, Perth 1962–65, Aber
from 1966
m Aber 25.7.59 Mary M. Hunter secy d of James W. H.
Aber

YULE David Kenneth   *MA 1969
s of Kenneth R. J. Y. sales man. SAI/farms man. and
Jane Johnston; b Aber 14.5.47
post grad stud.: computing centre Aberd 1969–70, pers
man. RGIT Aber 1970–71; Aberd: admin asst tech trg
1971–74, clerk to faculty of med from 1974
m Aber 28.12.70 Janet M. G. Forsyth MA 1969 *qv*

YULE Denis Noble   LLB 1970
s of James F. Y. des eng and Phyllis M. Noble secy; b
Aber 7.6.48
law app Aber 1970–72; leg. asst Aber 1972–73; ptnr L.
Mackinnon & Son advoc Aber from 1973
m Aber 30.7.70 Yvonne I. Smith teacher d of John W. S.
Aber

YULE Frederick Duncan   *MA 1968
s of Alasdair B. Y. baker, shopkeeper and Margaret
McNeil hairdresser, shopkeeper; b Peterhead 8.3.46
res stud. Aberd 1968–71; lect Glasg coll of tech from 1971
m Wakefield 30.3.70 Janet E. White MA 1967 *qv*

YULE Roy   *MA 1966

YULE Sheila Kathleen   MA 1957
m Lenthall

YULE William   *MA 1962
s of Peter C. Y. fam grocer and Mary A. Moir mental
nurse; b Aber 20.6.40
Dip Psych(Lond) 1963
res off. MRC soc psych res unit Lond 1963–64; res off.,
lect ch dev inst of educ Lond 1964–69; lect psych inst of
psychiat Lond 1969–73, sen lect from 1973
m Sudbury 6.3.72 Bridget A. Osborn BSc(econ)(Lond)
res worker ch psychiat d of Mark G. O. Hartest

YULL Leonard Louis   BSc(for) 1957
s of Louis A. Y. tree felling/land clearing contr and
Fanny H. M. Holloway secy; b Lond 21.10.35
nat serv RE UK, Cyprus 1957–59; Tanganyika: dist for.
off. Rondo, for. man. off. Dar es Salaam 1960–69;
promotions off. Edon For. Kendal Cumbria 1969–73;
dir Econ For.(Northern) Kendal from 1973
m Glasg 26.9.69 Elizabeth C. Martin teacher p e, secy d of
David P. M. Glasg

ZAFAR Mukhtar Muhammad   PhD 1968
BSc MSc(Punj)

ZANRE Michael Luigi Peter   LLB 1969
s of Joseph D. Z. publican and Linda M. Ostacchini; b

Lond 2.10.47
CA 1975
Aber: app CA 1969–73, asst to group acct Davidson
Radcliffe 1973–74, chief acct PSF offshore (Scot.) 1974–
76, fin. controller Wm Hay & Sons from 1976
m Aber 15.1.72 Annabella B. Ritchie asst scient off.
Rowett inst Aber d of George S. R. Fraserburgh

ZELUFF James Daniel   PhD 1964
  s of Ulrich C. Z. BS(Mich) off. US treasury dept and
Ruth I. Yeats; b Tampa Florida 28.4.30
BS(Florida) 1953 M Div(Union Theol Seminary Richmond Va) 1956
USA: assoc prof Queen's coll Charlotte NC 1964–68,
assoc dir of Interpreter's House Lake Junnluska NC and
clin psych Asheville Psychiat Assoc 1968–77, pres Zeluff

& Assoc Asheville NC (stress and time man. consult.)
from 1978; author *There's Algae in the Baptismal Font*
1978
m Staunton Va 28.5.55 Elizabeth Sheffer pres Snelling &
Snelling Asheville

ZIEDAN Ibrahim Elsayed Mohammed
                              MSc 1964 PhD 1967
  BSc(eng)(Cairo)

ZORAB Richard Arthur   *BSc 1970
  s of Edward C. Z. MBBS(Lond) ophth surg and Janet K.
Baillie nurs sister; b Tomsey Hants 28.2.46
outdoor activities instruct. Aviemore 1970–71, Europe
1971–72; edit: Wm Collins publ Glasg 1972–73, Churchill
Livingstone Edin from 1973

MARRIED WOMEN GRADUATES 1956–1970 WITH HUSBANDS' NAMES IN ALPHABETICAL ORDER

An asterisk (*) indicates an Aberdeen University graduate.
The year of graduation follows the name if there is another graduate of the same name or if, in the case of a husband, he graduated outwith the 1956–1970 period.

ABBOTT John R P
*ABDELNOUR Hassan O
ABEL Charles
*ABELL Trevor M B
ABERDEIN Harvey J
*ABERDEIN James D
ABERNETHY Kenneth R
*ABRIOUX Marc O M (1971)
ADAM
ADAM Alexander H
ADAM Alexander N
*ADAM John
ADAM John H
*ADAMS Christopher J
*ADAMS James A
ADAMS James R R
*ADAMS James T W
ADAMS John
*ADAMSON Colin D (1973)
ADDISON
AGNEW
*AH-SEE Antoine K
*AIKMAN Peter R
AIT-HOCINE
*AITKEN Donald A
*AITKEN Gordon G
AKINSETE
AKINTEWE
AKPOM
ALCOCK Samuel A
*ALCOCK Stephen R
*ALDER Clive P
ALDER George M
ALEXANDER Alfred J
*ALEXANDER Ian K
ALEXANDER John H
*ALI Zaffar
ALISON
ALLAN Archibald B
ALLAN Douglas I
*ALLAN Duncan S
ALLAN Fergie
ALLAN John C E
*ALLAN Kenneth J (1971)

BLACKIE Sheila M
MOSCATI Shane
CAMPBELL Mary A
MCKAY Helen F B
DOUGLASS Lesley H
JAMIESON Ethel
ALEXANDER Gwynyth M
MCGREGOR Ann L
CLARKSON Susan T
PRINGLE Katherine G
HENDRY June R
CHEYNE Lorna R
MILNE Florence
BIRRELL Elizabeth F
ELLIOT Elizabeth M
CRAIG Amber M
BAKER Rosemary C
MCDONALD Muriel
THOMSON Barbara A
JONES Susan P
KIDD Sheena A M
MATHESON Catherine R
MUNRO Cathleen A
FORBES Patricia
CLARKE Muriel
RETTIE Doreen L
BROWNE Felicia I
PATERSON Maureen L
UYANWAH Philomena O
WHALLEY Margaret J
PATERSON Jean M D
PATON Kathleen S
PINSENT Elizabeth M
SEMEONOFF Irina
FRITH Susan A
ROSS Flora M
FACHIE Moira A R
PEARSON Jean R
DIX Helen M
GEORGE Kathleen M
ALLAN Valerie P
DOUGHTY Flora M S
FRASER Alison
MCDOUGALL Alice J

ALLAN Lawrence D R
ALLANACH
*ALLISON Stuart N
AMAECHI
*AMAR Satya S
ANDERSON
ANDERSON
ANDERSON Alan
ANDERSON Alexander R
*ANDERSON Brian A
*ANDERSON Brian A
ANDERSON Charles W
*ANDERSON David J B
*ANDERSON David R
ANDERSON Hamish
*ANDERSON Hamish A
*ANDERSON Iain H
*ANDERSON John
*ANDERSON Robert M L (1962)
*ANDERSON Roderick S
ANDERSON William
*ANDERSON William A
*ANDERSON-SMITH Gordon
ANGUS Graham P
*ANNAND Gideon S
ANTCLIFFE
ANTONIO Gordon P R
*ARBUTHNOTT Gordon W
ARCHBOLD
ARCHER
ARCHIBALD Martin
*ARDERN Richard J
ARMOUR
ARMOUR Peter S
ARMSTRONG Alexander G
ARMSTRONG Duncan
ARNOLD Michael A S
ARNOTT Sidney J
ARPINO Vincent A
ARTHUR David
*ARULANANTHAM David C
ASHENFORD
ASHTON Gerard
*ASHTON Robert W

HENDERSON Margaret
CAMPBELL Grace S
DAVIE Marguareta M F
HALL Wendy M A
SKINNER May E
GIBB Jennifer R
MACKIE Lesley M H
WYLIE Roslyn
MULHOLLAND Mary G
FLOCKHART Mary R
MACKAY Marianne E H
ANDERSON Sheila M
DICK Eleanore St V
STRACHAN Jean
MACLEOD Catherine
WOOLLARD Maureen L
MORRISON Anne I
MURRAY Christina M
GAVIN Mary T
COOK Jennifer V
TAYLOR Margaret W
ALLAN Anne M
MATTHEW Myrtle I
AULD Alison M
STEER Margaret R
ROSS Helen M
WOOD Susan E
MINTO Joan E
FINDLAY Alice D
JENKINS Eileen M
KERR Margaret M O
RHIND Eileen M
RIDDOCH Hilda E
PATERSON Isobel
MASSIE Maureen
PETERSON Jemima A
WOOD Margaret A
EDWARD Alison J E
FROST Yvonne M
MCLEAN Margaret B
KNIGHT Diana M
MITCHELL Patricia
THOMSON Rosemary D
BARCLAY Helen M

CARTSHORE
CARTWRIGHT
CASON
CASSIE Charles E S
CASTELL Keith S
CASWELL
CATTANACH John A
*CATTO Graeme R D
CAVALLO Marcello
*CAWTHORN Nigel G
CAWTHORN Richard G
CHALIGNE
CHALMERS
CHALMERS
*CHALMERS Robert A
*CHAMBERLAIN Brian R
CHAMBERS David M
CHANDLER
CHAUDRI Mohammed J
CHERIYAN
CHESTERS John Knight
*CHESWORTH John B (1974)
CHEW
*CHEW Kenneth J
*CHEYNE Denis
*CHEYNE John A L
*CHEYNE Laurence A
*CHISHOLM Allan D
*CHISHOLM Duncan D
*CHISHOLM James A
CHISHOLM John Z
CHRISTIE Brian T
CHRISTIE David
CHRISTIE David R
CHRISTIE James H
*CHRISTIE Malcolm A B
*CHRISTIE Michael G A
CHRISTIE Ronald H
CHRISTINE Stewart J
CLARK
CLARK
*CLARK David R
CLARK Donald R
CLARK Harry P
*CLARK John K
CLARKE
CLARKE Alistair A
*CLARKE Ian A (1911)
CLARKE John A S
CLAYTON David B
*CLEGG Ian A
CLEGHORN William T M
CLELAND John
*CLOUSTON Robert W
COBBAN Archibald M
COBCROFT Ralph C
COCHRAN
COCKBURN William M
*COLLIE Alexander S (1954)
*COLLIE George S
COLLIN
COLLINS
COLLINSON
*CONDIE Roy G
CONN

DUNCAN Anne L
HUTCHISON Kathleen L
ADAM Helen M
MILLAR Jillian J
BOWEN Jennifer E
ROBERTSON Helen L
SMITH Rosemary A
SIEVEWRIGHT Joan
DAVIS Betsy M A A
FLORENCE Mary I
BURNETT Patricia A
MUNRO Wendy
BLAIRS Margaret C
WATT Margaret A
TURNER Grace C
GILMOUR Helen S
MACKAY Margaret
BENNET Anne M
ROSS Hilary A
MATTHEW Jean G
TULLOCH Marian I
KELLY Jane A
MACPHEE Anne
ROBERTSON Gillian G
SMITH Linda
BUTLER Eileen A
MILNE Pamela A
PARKHILL Anne L
DOYLE Rosemary G
DUNCAN Ruebena A
SMITH June E
FORBES Hilda M
SHEARER Elsa M
WEBSTER Elizabeth J
GASKIN Celeste E
FRASER Christian D
SHARP Margaret R
DUNBAR Patricia M
MORRISON Mary M
MCCRINDLE Dorothy J
SCOTT Alison M
WRIGHT Genefer G F
MASSEY Juliet C
GREIG Norma A M
MURDOCH Elizabeth M
DUFFUS Anne
RENNIE Morna M W
ADAM SMITH Margaret E
TAYLOR Pauline
EVANS Ruth E M
BUTLER Joyce E
DAWSON Elizabeth H
BUCHAN Jennifer R
SIMPSON Vera F
MILNE Gladys L
ROBERTS Joyce C
MINIO-PALUELLO Maria-Luisa
MCINTOSH Sylvia
REID Alice M C
GALL Barbara
MANN Maureen E
GRANT Ruth M
LINTS Alice M
CRUICKSHANK Wilma M P
JOHNSTON Brenda A

CONNELL John J
*CONSTANTINIDES Costas C
COOK
*COOK Gordon W
*COOK Richard K D
COOKE
COOKE Ian D
COOMBES Philip J
COOPER
COOPER
COOPER Alexander G
COOPER Andrew J
COOPER John L
COOPER Melvin C
*COOPER Michael
*COOPER Simon J
COOPER Sydney M
COPLAND
COPLAND Hamish A
CORALL John M
CORDINER George M
*CORDINER Ian C
CORFIELD Howard W
CORKE
CORMACK
CORMACK James G
*CORMACK Richard M
CORMACK Robert
*COTCHING Ian G (1971)
COUGHLAN Brendan M
COULL Gordon M
*COULL John T
COULL Joseph B
COULL William
*COUTTS David
*COUTTS Findlay M
*COUTTS Ian G C
COUTTS Joseph C
COWCILL Keith
COWIE
COWIE
COWIE Christopher F
COWIE David
*COWIE Frederick C F
*COWIE James
COWIE Peter H
*COWKING Thomas L
COX
*COX Andrew A (1972)
COX Anthony W
COX Harry
COY John M
CRABBIE Colin P
CRADE Frederick
CRAIG
CRAIG
CRAIG
*CRAIG Alexander S
*CRAIG David M (1954)
*Craig Peter M
CRAIG Robert E
CRAIK David K
CRAIN John L
*CRAMB Maurice Q
*CRAWFORD Derick A

PARSONS Margaret
THORBURN Dorothy M
GREIG Isobel E
WILLIAMSON Frances O
STOESSL Michelle M
GRANT Elspeth A
MIDDLETON Sheila M S
DEMPSTER Elaine A
CATTANACH Helen B
STEWART Donella K
DAVIDSON Margarita M
SIM Morag K O'B
MENNIE Margaret M
WILKIE Brenda
ANGUS Jennifer A
MORRIS Megan L
DOW Marion B A
MOIR Patricia M
WILSON Margaret E
STOCKAN Kathleen I H
MIDDLETON Irene M
MACDONALD Margaret R
ROSS Christina D
APPLIN Josephine M
GAVIN Irene S
LYON Joyce H
WHITTAKER Edith
MCKERLIE Marie M
CHARLES Gaynor B
MCLAREN Alison C M
WALKER Patricia E
MACFARLANE Mildred
MITCHELL Isabel R
MITCHELL Anne S
ANGUS Margaret G
LEATHEM Christina G
WOOD Fiona
LESLIE Lydia
MACKENZIE Catherine J
EDMOND Carol M
MACKENZIE Tessa
EWBANK Corinna V
MACKAY Christine M
JACK Jeanette I
BACKETT Anne L
STRACHAN Christina H
JACKSON Philippa J S
ROLLAND Fiona M
MACKAY Joan M
WEST Carole M
COWELL Susan E
MARTIN Ishbel M
MACARTNEY Elizabeth M
VIGROW Mary L M
GAVIN Pamela E
PARLEY Sheila
WOOD Catherine M
CARNIE Dorothy F
STEPHENSON Gillian
GALL Marjory A
LAWRENCE Dorothy
MCBAIN Anne
AUCHINACHIE Isobel M T
LAWRIE Diane P
DONALD Elizabeth L

*CRAWFORD Frederick
*CRAWFORD George P M
CRAZE John L
CRIGHTON Gerald L
CROFTS
*CROLL Neil M
*CROMAR Neil
CROOK Alan R
CROOKE William M
*CROOKSHANKS Brian K (1949)
CROSSLAND John R
CROYDON Charles E J
CROZIER
*CRUICKSHANK Alistair R
*CRUICKSHANK Don W
*CRUICKSHANK Donald G
CRUICKSHANK George A
CRUICKSHANK Gordon W
CRUICKSHANK James R
*CRUICKSHANK Leonard G
CRUICKSHANK Richard A
CRUICKSHANK William
*CUBITT Ian R (1971)
*CUDDEFORD Derek
CUMMING
CUMMING Robert M
CUMMINGS Ian L H
CUNNINGHAM
CURLEY
CURRIE
CURRIE Andrew M
*CURRY David J
CUTHBERT
*CUTHBERT John A M

DAFA'ALLA Abdel G I
*DAHL Peter H
DALGARNO George D
*DALGARNO William A
DALLISON Anthony R
DANIEL
DANIELS
*DARGIE Bryan A
DARLING
DAVEY Nigel M G W
DAVIDSON
DAVIDSON
DAVIDSON
DAVIDSON
DAVIDSON
DAVIDSON David R
DAVIDSON Donald M
DAVIDSON Frank D
*DAVIDSON John Gordon
DAVIDSON Robert
*DAVIDSON Robert H C
*DAVIDSON-LAMB Richard W
DAVIES
*DAVIES Christopher J
DAVIS
*DAVIS Godfrey P
*DAVIS Lionel J
DAWES
DAWSON
*DAWSON Alexander R

BISHOP Frances M
IRVINE Allison M
DUNCAN Hazel
YOUNG Anne E
WATT Jill E
HILL Veronica M
ROSS Catherine F H
BOYES Pamela A M
MORGAN Margaret A
STEELE Joyce M
GREGORY Angela C
RICHMOND Helen M H
SYMON Sheena M
NOBLE Alexandra M
RITCHIE Margrit R
TAYLOR Elizabeth B
MATHIESON June
COLLERAN Ethel M
RITCHIE Ethel M
BROWN Anne G
MELDRUM Maureen W
WALKER Ivy A
BLAIR Mary S
LYALL Alison
CALDER Joan C
POTRATZ Gisela B
SIMPSON Elma W
MENZIES Anne F M
ROBBIE Alice M
MARNOCH Patricia J
BLACKIE Ruth V
MURRAY Katharine G
PATERSON Doreen
FRAZER Kirsty M

MILNE Isobel F
GOLDIE Dorothy M
RITCHIE Doris J
BRENNAN Patricia A
McCULLOCH Helen C
HURRY Anne C
RIDDELL Patricia A
WITTE Elizabeth M
JAMIESON Jane M
BUCHANAN Jane A M
BROWN Caroline E
GLASS Lesley R
GORDON Catherine D
HOPKIN Pamela M
PROCTOR Patricia L
KIRKWOOD Elizabeth W
ROBERTSON Aileen
HOSIE Linda E A
ROBERTSON Margaret H S
BARR Kirsten H
WHYTE Johan G
FLOCKHART Nanette J
GRIFFITH Margaret A
BURT Susan H H
IMRAY Mildred M
SMITH Stella R
KÖNIG Ingeborg I
MACBETH Katherine M
SINCLAIR Elizabeth K
MACLEAN Jennifer M

*DAWSON David G
DAWSON Hugh M R
DAY
*DEAN Peter A
DEANS
DEANS
DEKOCK
DELPRIORE Bruno U V
*DENOON Brian D J
DENZA John
DESOUGI
de QUINCEY John E C
de SILVA
*DEWAR Ian A
DIACK
*DIAMOND Antony W
DICK Ronald M
DICKIE
DICKIE George H
*DICKIE Gordon L
DICKIE John
DICKSON
DICKSON
DICKSON John A
DIER George M V
*DILLON Geoffrey
DIMAMBRO Bruno R
*DINWOODIE John M W
DIXON
DIXON
DIXON James M
*DIXON John M M
DODDS Allan G
*DODDS Fergus R M
DODDS Iain L N
*DODDS John J A
*DODDS John K M
DOE Paul M
*DONAGHEY Sean F O'B
*DONALD George F J
DONALD Ian E
DONALD James F
*DONALD John H
DONALD Norman A
*DONALD Robert
DONALDSON
*DONALDSON William
DONNELLY
DOOLEY
*d'ORBAN Paul T
DORCEY
DORWARD George M
DOUGLAS
DOUGLAS Alexander G
DOVER Roy R
DOVERTY William Y
DOW George D M
*DOW Robin J
*DOWER Michael J
DOWER Nigel
DOWNEY Christopher P
DOWNIE
DOWNIE Alan W
DOWNIE Colin T
DOWNIE Ian R

MUNRO Caroline H
SMITH Sandra W
DAVIDSON Kathleen
MOAR Ann M
BRUCE Rosaleen A
GUYAN Alice M
ULLMAN Liselotte L
MATHESON Christina
CAMPBELL Sheila M
YOUNG Eileen M
MENNIE Margaret M
CAMERON Marion B
HECTOR Moira E M
PACK Julie M
KELMAN Alice J
McINTYRE Elizabeth P
SWIFT Margaret J
STUART Thelma L
JACK Shona M
LEIPER Margaret C
JONES Mary E
LITTLE Joan
TAYLOR Lesley J
FETHNEY Moira
PETRIE Hazel C
GRIEVE Helen F B
TASKER Helen A
JOHNSON Margaret
BURT Cynthia K
JOHNSON Lilian E
GRIMES Katherine M V
MURRAY Anne S
DUNN Elizabeth A
INNES Jean A
FRASER Christine M
SINCLAIR Anne
CORMACK Ingrid A J
JONES Olwen M
INGRAM Margaret J
ROE Isabelle M
LEIPER Sandra M
GERRIE Anne
McGRORY Eileen
DONALD Sylvia M B
STUART Judith H
THOMSON Stella H C
CHALLIS-SOWERBY Loraine
SMITH Lorraine J J
REID Marjory B
HO-A-SHU Laura S J
PLUCINSKA TERESA
MASSIE Maureen E S
YOUNG Marilyn E
MORRICE Alice I
SMART Marjory A
STRACHAN Marlene
MAITLAND Dorothy I
GAFFRON Wendy J
MACKENZIE Moira
BEYTS Diane M
ROBERTSON Patricia M
GERRARD Erica M
MACKNESS Jennifer M
SHAW Cecilia H
KAY Catherine H M

FOTHERGILL John E
FOTHERINGHAM David I R
FOTIADIS Mihalaki
*FOUBISTER Alan J
FOULIS Alan K
*FOWLER Alexander P
*FOWLIE Douglas G
FRANCIS
FRANK H Thomas
FRANKISH Karl D
FRANKS David R
FRASER
FRASER
FRASER
*FRASER Alan W
*FRASER Archibald K
*FRASER Arthur G
*FRASER Callum
*FRASER Douglas M
FRASER Francis I J
FRASER George
*FRASER George L
FRASER Gordon J
FRASER Henry S
FRASER Iain
FRASER Iain D
*FRASER James E (1953)
FRASER John
FRASER John
FRASER Kenneth J
FRASER Robert J M
FRASER William
*FRASER William H
*FRASER William R
FRAZER Samuel C
FRENCH Christopher N
FREW
FRICKER Hans B
FRITZON Stig Z
FRY Kenyon G
*FULLERTON Hance
FULTON
FURIE
*FURNIVAL Colin M

*GALBRAITH Philip A
GALILEE George D S
GALL Robert A
GALLACHER Alexander R
*GALLOWAY Richard M
GAMMIE
GARDEN John C
GARDINER John A
*GARDINER Robert H B
*GARDNER Bruce K (1971)
GARDNER George
*GARROW Alexander G
GATES Peter S
GAULT
GAVIN Alistair B
GEAR James R
GEMMELL Ian R
*GEORGE Robert W
*GERMAN Gordon A
GERVAS Jose L

GILMORE Linda A
MacMILLAN Janette M
WETHERLEY Vivien J E
CUTBUSH Elizabeth A
MARTIN Anne D
WATSON Helen M
DONALDSON Marjory A R
MAIN Dorothy
LESLIE Elizabeth M McK
BARCLAY Sheena M
BAILEY Mary J G
MACKIE Mary E
SINCLAIR Janet A
YSEBAERT Marie-Josée M
JOHNSTON Edith H
STEWART Kathleen M
SNEDDEN Marion E
SINCLAIR Christina S
CONNON Rhoda A E
CLARK Moira G
MACLENNAN Annabel R
GORDON Frances C
ROBERTSON Sheila
SKEETE Maureen V H
SLEIGH Allison M
ANDERSON Isabella A
STEWART Patricia L
GRANT Ishbel S
PETRIE Helen C
FRASER Sylvia R
BAIN Priscilla A
MURRAY Hazel
TUACH Helen
KNOX Alison F A
SHEPHERD Marion
WATSON Ann
MacGREGOR Helen E
PFISTER Maria R
REID Maureen
BLACKHALL Margaret I
COWIE Jeannie R
WILL Sylvia J
MARR Sheena M S
SOUTER Isobel G

LIDDLE Dorothy I
DUNCAN Isobel M
SIMMERS Gillian J
HARPER Lillian H
HOWARD Patricia A
HENDERSON Elisabeth A R
RENDALL Margaret
ELWICK Susan A
COOTE Audrey E
HOGG Christine M
POOLE Freda J
FRASER Margaret
MACINTOSH Kathleen M
GARDEN Isabel S
McMILLAN Mary
HOLBOURN Sheila C
DAVIDSON Aileen E
CLARK Moira
DE SILVA Angela R
WELLS Judith A

GIBB
GIBB Michael G H
GIBBONS
GIBSON Charles B S
GIBSON David T A
GIBSON James C
GIBSON Robert R
GIFFIN Patrick
GILBERT
GILBERT John
*GILCHRIST William N (1952)
GILES Peter B
*GILL Geoffrey M (1953)
*GILL William P (1953)
GILLIES Alasdair B
GILMOUR
*GILMOUR Iain F
GILMOUR James A M
*GLADSTONE Patrick J
GLASS
*GLASSER Fredric P
*GLENNIE John A
GLOVER David
*GLOYER Robert I
GODA David F
GODFREE Michael J
GOLBOURN
*GOMES Errol H
*GOODALL Thomas
*GOODLAD James A
*GORDON George P
*GORDON Hugh M
GORDON James
GORDON John
*GORDON Martin
*GORDON Peter J (1971)
GORDON Roger
*GORIE
GORST Gerald B
GORVETT Denis
GOSLING Philip
GOSSIP Christopher J
GOUDIE
GOULD David I
GOW
GRAHAM
GRAHAM Donald T
GRAHAM John
GRAHAM John W
GRAINGER Peter N
GRANT
GRANT
GRANT
GRANT
*GRANT Alan B
GRANT Charles M
GRANT Donald McA
GRANT Edwin B
*GRANT Ian A M
GRANT James A
*GRANT Neil F
GRAY
GRAY
GRAY Alexander
GRAY David

FORSYTH Audrey T
ESSLEMONT Elizabeth M
KERR Janet H
BELL Eileen J
MACLEOD Moragh A
NERLAND Beate
GRANT Morag H K
HALL Alison M
GIFFORD Rosalind M
WILLETS Lynn D
McCASKILL Betty D C
COOMBS Janet
PHILIP Margaret M
DAVIDSON Dorothy H
MACDONALD Angela I
SMITH Doreen
SMITH Marjorie Y
TAYLOR Ethel A
GUNN Margaret M
FRASER Margaret M
DENT Lesley S
SMART Frances M
MACKENZIE Helen S
FETHNEY Hilary A
GREIG Marion G
JONES Elizabeth H
DAVIES Lesley C
READ Margaret
SHEARER Phyllis J
BUCHAN Margaret E
MACLACHLAN Joan M S
DAVIDSON Elsie P J
ELDER Lilian M
SIMPSON Lilian J W
SIMPSON Jacqueline M
FRENCH Elspeth M
GEDDES Margaret E
DUTCH Eileen W
HOUSE Judith I
DUGUID Margaret G
STILL Elaine L
DAVIDSON Jean C
HOOD Margaret E
MARKS Gillian M
WYNNE Rosalind C
MORREN Alison M
ROBERTSON Winifred H J
GRAHAM Alexina
SHIRREFFS Marjorie A
CASSIE Elizabeth A
BUIE Christine M
GOVAN Eileen T
MACKAY Shona E
MACKENZIE Helen S
COONEY Eileen
BURNETT Janet C
JOHNSON Brenda
McKAY Andrea
LUMSDEN June M
BAIRD Margaret D
DOUGLAS Louise M
BARNES Mavis
McHARDY Marigold M A H
JONES Helene M
MORGAN Roslyn E

GRAY George H
GRAY George M
GRAY Gilbert
*GRAY James
GRAY James H W
*GRAY John D (1971)
*GRAY Laurence
GRAY Robert K S
*GRAY Roger W
*GRAY William G
GREARSON Quentin D
GREEN
GREEN David J
*GREENHALGH James F D
GREIG
GREIG
*GREIG Denis
*GREIG Robert
GRIEVE
GRIEVE David G
GRIEW Paul V
*GRIFFIN Anthony R
GRIMES Douglas J
GROCOTT John A
GROENEVELD Cornelis M
GROSKORTH Carl W
*GROSSERT Ian G
GUEST David H
*GUHA Madhabendra M (1951)
GUNN
*GUNN Hamish I (1955)
*GUNN Lewis A
*GUNN Robert M
GUSTAVESON Robert L
GUTHRIE Ian N

HADDOCK
HADDOCK George H
HAGGART
*HAGGART David B
*HAINING William F (1952)
HALBORG
HALL
HALL
HALL
HALL Adrian T
*HALL Colin D
*HALL David J (1967)
*HALL David J (1970)
HALL George S
HALL Ian F
*HALL Michael A (1974)
*HALL Peter A (1972)
HALLIDAY Alexander
*HALLIDAY Donald C
*HALLIDAY George S
*HALSTEAD Peter H
HAMILTON
HAMILTON
HAMILTON
HAMILTON Alexander
HAMILTON David F
HAMILTON Ian
*HAMILTON Peter G (1972)
*HAMILTON Robert (1973)

LONGMORE Isobel
WEBB Moraig A M
FRASER Lorna K
MURRAY Rhoda V
GRAY Elsie M
BRACEWELL Margaret J
WHITEFORD Elizabeth S
ROLTON Hilary A
EHRHARDT Johanna E U W
JOWETT Pamela H
COLVILLE Penelope M
HOWELL Joan C
JOHNSTON Margaret J
GEE Isoline
BOOTHBY Patricia M
WILSON Muriel
WEBSTER Charlotte H
MILLER Isobel
SYMON Doreen
MCDONALD Linda G
BROWNLIE Kathleen A
JACK Lindsay
WARREN Susan E
HENDRY Kathleen A
TOSH Agnes
SINCLAIR Wilma
COLVILLE Penelope M
COPLAND Alison A
PAUL Parul R
STEWART Audrey F
BENZIE Heather A
FINDLAY May F
AVENT Yvonne G
MARTIN Valerie C
PATERSON Eliza M

BAKER Susan J
ARNOT Katharine A K
ROBB Catherine R S
HALL Gwendolen M
LAMONT Margaret B
ROBB Eileen M
AIKEN Marigold H
DAVIDSON Elizabeth W
MACLENNAN Marion H
NAIRN Audrey
GORDON Valerie
WELLS Janet
MURPHY Helen M
MITCHELL Rose McN
TARBAT Lorna M
STEWART Ilene R
MACLENNAN Marion H
CROALL Margaret M
BAKIE Elspet M
NEILL Patricia M H
LEAKER Margaret D
CARMICHAEL Barbara M
HUTTON Ray F
WILLIAMS Gaynor M
SUTHERLAND Jane M
REID Margaret E
LYON Phyllis S
FORBES Emily C
MCAUSLIN Edith J

*HAMILTON Stewart M
HAMMOND Arthur J M
HANNAH James M
HANNANT David J
HANSON Geoffrey
*HARBOUR Anthony B
*HARDCASTLE Patrick D
HARDIE
HARDIE George M
*HARDIE Myles D G
*HARDIE Richard H
*HARDIE William D (1953)
HARDING
HARDINGHAM Peter A
HARDY Christopher R C
HAREN Michael J
HARGRAVE
HARLOW Reginald G
*HARMAN Brian S R
*HARPER Douglas R
*HARPER John L
*HARRIS Iain G N
HARRISON
HARRISON
HARRISON Robert A
HARRY
HART
*HART John R (1971)
HARTE John D C
*HARVIE Thomas G
HASLAM Anthony P
*HASTIE Dennis
HAWKINS Dexter
HAWORTH
*HAY Alan J
HAY David W
HAY Herbert D
*HAY Ian S
HAY James N
*HAY John M
*HAY John Y L
*HAY Robert K M
HAYES Gregory P
HAYTON William B
*HAZEL Alan W
HEATON Stuart L
*HEGGS Glenville W
*HEINZMAN Colin
HELFT Gale M
HELLMAN Knut
HENDERSON
HENDERSON
HENDERSON Brian W
*HENDERSON Charles N
HENDERSON David
*HENDERSON Grahame M (1972)
*HENDERSON Hamish (1971)
HENDERSON Peter C
HENDERSON Peter R
*HENDERSON Reginald L
*HENDRY David F
*HENDRY John F
HENRY Antony F H
HEPBURN
HEPBURN Kenneth C R

HALL Pamela M
YOUNG Susan M
JOHNSON Agnes H
BARRON Norma M
BURNS Sheila A V
WRIGHT Jacqueline E M
RUNCIE Moira A G
STRACHAN Mary C
FORBES Elspeth A
GRAY Marjory
WARREN Janet G
SIMPSON Margaret E
CAMPBELL Joan G
LOUGHRAN Verne E
ALEXANDER Muriel E
MACKEAN Elspeth M
CHRISTIE Linda S M
IRVIN Carolyn A
ELLWAY Judith M
WISELY Dorothy C
HUNTER Fiona M
ROBERTSON Jane P
DUNCAN Sheila
MCCLURG Kathleen J
NICOL-SMITH Ruth M
CURRIE Kathleen I
BISSET Gladys M
BROWN Pamela M
MACKAY Eleanor M S
TURNER Janet L
KINDNESS Lindsay M
OWEN Kathleen A
MCKILLIGIN Helen R
PEARCE Janet E
BISHOP Janet M
GRAY Isabel A
FLORENCE Elizabeth M
DEAR Elizabeth M A
WATSON Rosemary A
MENZIES Avril M I
ANDERSON Elizabeth M B
VINYCOMB Dorothea H
HAY Kathleen M
ALEXANDER Anita J
PEPPER Jean M
WILSON Barbara H
HENDERSON Jeanette
SHORT Lesley M
WILLIAMSON Anne M
CASELEY Jane R
FRASER Carole
IMRIE Janet Y
ENGLAND Esther M R
LAMBERT Susan M
THAIN Linda M
MOIR Kathleen M
FIELDING Jacqueline A
MCMILLAN Margaret K
BRUCE Margaret A M
WILSON Gladys
VASS Evelyn R
ROBERTSON Margaret C
ARGO Frances E
EDWARD Janice E
I'ANSON Annette E

*HERBERT Rodney A	MILLARD Helen J M	HUSBAND	BRACK Margaret H
HERD	GERRARD Margaret E	HUTCHEON	MILNE Isabel A
HERD Ian D	MACINNES Margaret E	HUTCHEON Kenneth M	GALL Kathleen M
HERMENAU Gerhard H	ROBERTSON Susan F	HUTCHESON John	FRASER Doreen C
HEUSER Winfried L	MACLEAN Marion	HUTTON Leslie	BARRON Joan L
*HEWINS Roger H	MCDONALD Catherine P		
*HEWITT David S	WILLIAMS Angela C	*IBELL Robert L	WILKIE Patricia I
*HEWITT Michael R	WATT Catherine A	IMLACH	BRYDON Brenda V
*HICKIE John F	HINGS Rosemary	IMRAY	ALLAN Helen A
HICKS Charles A	JOHNSTON Kathleen A	INCE Carl L	MORGAN Lois C
*HICKSON Bryan	RUSSELL Kathleen	INGLIS John E	THOMPSON Mary B E
HILL	LOGGIE Evelyn J	*INGLIS John P	MONCRIEFF Elizabeth S
HILL John A	STUART Valerie M G	*INGLIS John R (1971)	JOHNSTONE Lesley M H
HILL Richard C	REPPER Margaret A	*INGLIS Julian T	URQUHART Aileen A
HILL Roland J	JEFFREY Joan P	INGRAM Malcolm D	HARDMAN Lorna
HILLEN	MACKIE Ruth A	*INKSON Iain J (1972)	MACKAY Marianne E H
HINCH	SKINNER Morna L	*INKSON James H K	TUACH Nan
HINDLEY Neil W	FLETT Joan R	*INKSTER Raymond	FOWLER Muriel M
*HINDMARSH Paul S	TOYER Elizabeth A	INNES	FARQUHAR Marjory N
HINDS John	LOTT Edna M	INNES	LYLE Valerie C
HIRSCH	MIDDLETON Rose E	INNES Robert	KITCHIN Alison M
*HITCHINGS Michael J (1973)	MACLEOD Isabella M	*INNES William G	HAY Abigail L
*HOBBS Alexander	KEMP Mary L	*INNES William G	SIM Morag K O'B
*HODGES Timothy	WHYTE Angela J G	*INNES William J A	BRUCE Carol I
HOGARTH-GAUTE Philip G	THORP Carole J S	INNES-WILL	KNOWLES Maureen
*HOGG John	CAMPBELL Jessie	IRVINE	KINNAIRD June
*HOGG Nigel R L	TAYLOR Elizabeth R S	IRVINE	WEATHERLEY Jill M
HOLDEN Frank D	BRANDER Heather	IRVINE Tom	TOMLINSON Sheila
HOLLAND Dennis	ANDERSON Frances M	ISHERWOOD Stanley T J	FLETCHER Jane M
HOLLANDS Richard D	CAMERON Seonaid E	*IZATT Jack B	MACLEOD Katrine I L
*HOLLOWAY John S	BROWN Linda J		
HOLME	LATIMER Sheila	*JACK David (1954)	COWIE Isabell C
HOPE	THOMAS Elizabeth M T	*JACK Edwin A	RAYMOND Barbara P
HOPKINS	MACKIE Dorothy E	*JACK George W	ROBILLIARD Kathleen A
*HORNBY Windham B	HORNCASTLE Allison J	JACKSON Christopher D	BROWN Josie
*HORROCKS Rodger	NORRIE Sandra J	*JACKSON Graham (1971)	MACKELLAR Margaret C
HOSAIN Iftikhar	BHATTI Perveen A	JACKSON Robert	COLLERAN Nan P D
HOUSE David E	MACBEAN Ann V	JACOBS	CAMPBELL Myra A
HOUSTON John B	WEBSTER Elizabeth A	JAGGER Roger L	LOW Isobel
HOUSTON Walter J	WHITELEY Fleur St C	JAMES Duncan S	SCOTT Alison H
*HOWARD Christopher B	GREENSMITH Isobel M	*JAMES William	STEPHEN Evelyn M
HOWAT John M	RITCHIE Jean M	JAMIESON	MACKIE Lesley M H
HOWES Alal E	URQUHART Gillian R	*JAMIESON Donald G	MACRAE Grace K R
*HOWIE David N	HENDERSON Aileen J M	JAMIESON Douglas A	PARKS Valerie S
*HOWIE John M	MILLER Dorothy J M	*JAMIESON Hugh G J	HEWET Elizabeth A
*HOWIE William	GILL Elizabeth A	*JAMIESON James C	SHAW Muriel M
HOWIESON Maurice M	ALEXANDER Dianne M	*JEFCOATE Trevor E S	THOMSON Ann K
HOWITT	GRAY Elma	*JEFFRIES Colin E	OGILVIE Rosemary
*HOWITT John R L	HORNE Helen E	JESS Thomas M	MACRAE Donaldina A
*HUCKVALE Eric L	STIRLING Bertha F	JEWITT	HIGGINS Katharine
HUDSON Stewart	DAVIDSON Jennifer	JOHNSON Allan	COUPER Laureen M
HUGHES	MILLER Ina M	JOHNSON Andrew J D	RICE Alison F
HUGHES Barry O	GRAY Helen	JOHNSON John A E	PETERSON Christina J
HUGHSON	JOHNSTONE Dorothy J	JOHNSON Peter C	HUTCHESON Moira M
HUGHSON	WALLACE Irene I	*JOHNSON Ronald G	MCDONALD Sheila Y
HUMPHREYS	WALLACE Glenis W	JOHNSON Roy M	DUNCAN Allison I
HUMPHREYS Keith A	STEWART Frances L	JOHNSON Steven R	ROBERTSON Sheila M
HUNT Leslie	CARMICHAEL Flora C C	JOHNSTON	BANNERMAN Roslyn
HUNTER	BRAY Beverley J	JOHNSTON	REIACH Maureen A
HUNTER	WILSON Wilma E B	JOHNSTON	SMELLIE Isabel A
*HUNTER Graham H	MATHESON Janet C	JOHNSTON Anthony G D	RAFFAN Jennifer T
*HUNTER Ian R (1972)	THOMPSON Diana M	*JOHNSTON Derek W	THOM Mary B
HUNTER Thomas G	LAIDLAW Erica A	*JOHNSTON Iain (1973)	SOUTER Elizabeth M
*HUNTER William F	BEATTIE Marilyn W	JOHNSTON James D	MACKENZIE Christine C
HURST Brian C	MCGHIE Rhona R	JOHNSTONE	GORDON Elizabeth

JOINER	McGREGOR Sheila N	LAND Derek G	BALLARD Sylvia T
JONES	INNOCENT Barbara J	LANE	SYPULA Pauline Z
JONES Graham B	NIXON Karen P	LANG Andrew M	MAGEE Margaret F
*JONES Michael J	WALKER Margaret A	LANGMEAD Alfred	JAMIESON Christine
JONES Winston G	BROOKS Marjorie	LANGTON Francis G	FARQUHAR Marian D
JORDAN Klaus	ROLLO Elizabeth A	LANHINGLIT	CHUNG Pin Yong
*JOSS Alexander W L	BAIRD Elizabeth	LAW John S	ROBERTSON Eleanor M
		LAWLESS Christopher J	MACKENZIE Eona F
KALOO	SHEARER Margaret-Ann M	LAWRENCE Francis W	RIDDOCH Ella F
*KEELAN John	SOMERVILLE Susan I	LAWRIE	MAY Joan B
KEENAN Brian H	JEMMETT Kathleen E	LAWRIE	MELVIN Jennifer M O
*KEEPING Joseph D	NICHOL Roberta A	LAWTON Frederick	McEWAN Irene B
*KELBIE David	SMITH Helen M	*LAYCOCK Rex A H	BONOMY Christine M
*KELLAS James G	CRAIG Norma R	LEATHAR	MACLEOD Christine M
KELLY Dennis	YOUNG Valerie M	*LEAVER Alastair S (1971)	WATT Elspeth M R
KELMAN	HALL Sandra	LeBRUN Christopher S	O'BRIEN Alison B
KELSO	CHRISTIE Dorothy L	LECKIE James M	SPENCE Edith L
*KEMP Alexander J	BROWN Margaret J V	LECKIE Thomas L G	NEWBIGGING Alice R
*KENNEDY Duncan M	BAXTER Margaret M	LEDGARD	GAMMIE Eileen M C
KENNEDY John M	MACKINNON Kathleen L	LEE James A W	MILNE Rosemary J
KENNEDY Kenneth T	MACKENZIE Catherine	LEGG	MITCHELL Kate F F W
KENNEDY William M	FERRARIS Mary	LEGG	SIM Catherine M
*KENNEY John R	ROBERTSON Mary E	*LEGGE Gordon F	ROSS Rhoda I
KENNINGTON Roger	WEST Edna	LEGGE Iain D	RUSSELL Mhairi B
KENRICK Trevor L	ELDER Elizabeth F	LEGGE John D	WILL Diana B R
*KENT Anthony W D C	LEIPER Susanna J	*LEIPER Joseph (1971)	MITCHELL Moira T
KERSHAW	FORMAN Jennifer C	LEIPER Malcolm D	JAMIESON Lesley M
*KHALIL Khalil E S	STUART Irene M	LEISHMAN William J	MACFARQUHAR Joan
KHAN	KEAY Irene H	LENEHAN	KELMAN Patricia E
KIDD John	MATHESON Margaret N	LENNOX	SKINNER Martha H
*KILKENNY Terence M	ROSS Isabel M	LENSSEN	WHYTE Brenda A
KILLINGBACK Peter G	REASON Janet M	LENTHALL	YULE Sheila K
KING James G	WOOD Margaret M	LENTO Ismo J	SMITH Jacqueline E
*KING John A (1952)	YOUNG Prudence A	LEONARD Ronald K	LEASK Susanna J I
KING John M	GRANT Elaine M	LESLIE	BIRSE Sheila M
KINNIBURGH Ian A G	LEWIS Sheila M	*LESLIE John S	PORTER Angela M E
KINNIS Terry D	MILNE Helen M	*LESLIE Norman W	WATT Sheila A
*KINNON John F (1971)	MACAULAY Jennifer A	*LEVIE David S C	MACKIE Mary M R
KIOSSOGLOU Kosmas A	ADAMS Angela C	*LEVITT Charles S A W	CLARK Winifred C
KIRKPATRICK Ian G	FULTON Anne B G	LEVY	PATERSON Laura B
KIRKPATRICK Thomas C	MARTIN Elizabeth M	LEWIS	MACKIE Sylvia C W
KNAPMAN John M	WOOD Moira J C	LEWIS John	ROBERTSON Marjory E
KNIGHT	JEFFERIES Frances M	LEYS Alexander D	SMITH Jennifer M
KNIGHT Ian D	MURRAY Muriel G C	*LIDDERDALE Ian G	LISTER Pauline J
KNORR Robert D	YOUNG Hazel M	LIEW Meng Leong	AU NYUK CHENG Dorothy
KNOTT Peter B	WRAY Aileen I M	*LINDLEY David K	BELLIS Joanna C
*KNOWLES James G	DAVIDSON Elaine	LINDSAY David W M	FORREST Jean
KNOX William G	REID Alison A M	LINDSAY Peter J	BULLOUGH Frances S
*KUFAAS Torbjörn	WALKER Jill	LINGARD	DAVIDSON Elizabeth J
KUNAR Roy R	MARTIN Eleanor M	LINKLATER Karl A	GIBB Margaret C
		LITTLE Matthew M	WATT Aileen E C
LACEY Harris J	DUNCAN Eleanor M C	LITTLE Richard	SMITH Gladys J H
*LACHOWSKI Eric E	GRAY Alison C	LITTLEJOHN Andrew G	FRASER Leila A
LA HEY Dick	MORRISON Margaret L	LIVERSEDGE	MILLER Heather M
LAING	PATERSON Erna J	LIVINGSTON James M	McCONNELL Rosalind A
*LAING Frank K A	NISBET Barbara D	LIVINGSTONE Duncan	BERTRAM Barbara C
LALONDE Gérard	RAE Beverley A	LIVINGSTONE William J G	LAMB Georgina
LALOR Sean O	RAE Maureen	*LLEWELLYN John P (1954)	LEJEUNE Anne
LAMB	MARSHALL Linda J	*LOCKIE John	EWEN Norma L
LAMB Peter J	MUIR Lisbeth	LOCKLEY Roger A	MATHESON Susan M
LAMBOURNE Archie	ELLEN Judith L	LODGE John C	FAIRLIE Isobel A
*LAMONT Alan M	RAE Alison F	LOGAN	LESLIE Patricia E
LAMONT Robert	HOLMES Hazel B	LOGAN	SANGSTER Rosemary
*LAM SHANG LEEN Yong-Kwee		LOGAN Crawford W	RUSSELL Jennifer M
C Y	SEIVEWRIGHT Sheila	*LOGAN Ian W	MORRISON Margaret F

LOGAN John
*LOGAN Robert M
LOGGIE John M
*LOGIE Alexander W
*LOMAS Christopher J
LONG
LONG John W
*LONGMORE Alexander B G
LOOI Albert C K
LORIMER
*LORIMER James W
*LOTHIAN John
LOVELACE Clive E
LOW
LOWDON James G
*LOWE Maurice D
*LOWNDES Michael D
LOXLEY Colin P
LUDFORD Alfred W L
LUKE
*LUMSDEN Alexander T M
*LUMSDEN Ian M
LYALL
LYALL David J
*LYALL Francis
*LYNCH Frederick P (1955)
*LYNCH Michael
*LYON DEAN Charles W (1971)
LYUS Stephen B

MACADIE James
MCADIE Joseph T
MCALEESE W R
MCALLISTER Edward S R
MCANDREW
*MCANDREW Gordon M
MCARA Roderic G
MACARTHUR Alexander
*MACARTHUR Allan J
MACAULAY Donald
MCBAIN John
MCBOYLE
*MCBOYLE Frederick G
MCCABE Raymond A
MCCAIG
MACCALLUM
MCCALLUM Archibald M
MCCALLUM Calum
MCCASKIE
MCCAUSLAND Ian
*MCCLEVERTY Jon A
MCCOMBIE Charles A
MCCONACHIE George J
MCCONKEY
MCCONNACHIE John G
*MCCONNACHIE Robin I
MCCORMACK
MACDONALD
MACDONALD
MACDONALD
MACDONALD
MACDONALD
MACDONALD
MCDONALD

MACKENZIE Theodora
WATKINS Lena J
BEATON Mary
CAIE Dorothy E
BENTINCK Susan J
COSTELLO Heather P M
NICOL Iona A
FERRARI Leonella L A M
CHUA Dorothy P L
HALL Maureen Y
REID Eileen M
KAY Jennifer A Y
MACNAB Rachel
SIM Dorothy
GIBB Marilyn R
SILVER Dorothy M
FLEMING Joan M
STUART Alison
MALCOLM Stella M
FLANAGAN Elizabeth
SUTHERLAND Catherine A
PARKER Joan D
WATT Margaret
MUNRO Mary D
SMITH Heather F C
BIRNIE Alison F H
MOORE Mary
GRANT Margaret H
PENNY Helen

FRASER Julia M
YEOMAN Joyce E
SNAITH Sybil M
SIMPSON Sheila M
FRASER Rosemary A
MURRAY Leonora J H
MCFARLANE Wilma
MACINNES Mary F
CORMACK Marjorie F
MORRISON Mary
NORRIE Jean G
CRUICKSHANK Edith E
HARPER Elizabeth M
ROSS Gwyneth
HOWIE Kathleen A
DEMPSEY Mary H
LAING May N A
MCROBBIE Margaret I
MUTCH Gwendoline
LEES Joan
BARRACK Dianne M
MCCRAE Elizabeth M
BEATTIE Sheena M
MACKIE Kathleen I
MAIN Sandra
GLENNIE Gwendoline L
MACLEOD Mary A M
CRUDEN Norma J M
MACAULAY Margaret G
MACLEOD Marjory B
MORRISON Christina
MURRAY Isabella R
TAYLOR Christina C S
THOMIS Helen R
WOOD Anne E H

*MACDONALD Angus J A
*MACDONALD Colin D J (1929)
MACDONALD Donald H
*MACDONALD Ian B
*MCDONALD Ian R
MACDONALD Raymond C
*MACDONALD Roderick J M
  (1971)
MACDONALD William A
MACDONALD William S
MACDOUGALL
MCDOWALL
*MACEWAN James A I
*MCFADDEN John A C
*MACFARLANE Alexander W
MCFARLANE Harry A
MCFEAT James
*MACGILLIVRAY Alexander J
MCGINN
*MCGOWAN George C
MCGREGOR
*MACGREGOR Alan M
MACGREGOR Charles A
*MCGREGOR David
*MACGREGOR John D
MCHALE Michael S
*MCILWAIN Alexander E (1954)
MCILWAINE Ronald J
*MACINTOSH Alan A
MCINTOSH Alexander
MCINTOSH Donald K
MCINTOSH Harry D
*MCINTOSH James S
MCINTOSH John R
*MACINTOSH Peter M
*MCINTOSH William E
MCINTYRE
*MCINTYRE Angus K
MACISAAC Allan
MACIVER
MACIVER Anthony D D
*MCIVER Charles J E
MCKAY
MCKAY
*MCKAY Alexander G R
MACKAY Alistair D
*MACKAY Calum
*MACKAY Donald I
MACKAY Ian S
MCKAY James S
MACKAY James W
*MACKAY John F G
*MCKAY John W
*MACKAY Kenneth M
*MACKAY Ronald
MACKEE Donald M
*MACKEITH Neil J
MCKELLAR Ian B
MACKENZIE
MACKENZIE
MACKENZIE
MACKENZIE
MCKENZIE
MACKENZIE Alan G
MACKENZIE Alexander

MACDONALD Mary
NIMMO Elizabeth M M
MACLEOD Mary
SMITH Kathleen F
WATERSTON Margaret E
BRUCE Irene M J

MASSIE Helen W
FRASER Cristabel
HASTIE Isobel G
WHITELOCK Cecil E
SMITH Lynda K S
BARRON Aileen A
THOMPSON Patricia M
HORN Irene W
STILL Lena R C
SHEPHERD Margaret
MACLEOD Annie
MATHESON Jennifer R V
DRAYSON Geraldine M
BIRNIE Myrtle E
ROBERTS Anne
KINNAIRD Anne B
MCKENZIE Sheila M
WILSON Kathleen H
MARNOCH Jennifer J
KINNAIRD Moira M
DUFFUS Gillian M
TURNER Susan P
STORM Isabella
TENNENT Justine R
FORBES Margaret I S
WELSH Norma
DUNCAN Nicolas A
FRASER Margaret E
GAMBLIN Sandra A
MILNE Lesley M
JONES Margaret A
MACDONALD Morag A
MACDONALD Murdina
GRAY Catherine J
HANSON Rosalind I
MCMILLAN Margaret A
RANKIN Beryl M M
LOWRIE Agnes E
MACDONALD Margaret M
POTTINGER Norna
RAFFAN Diana M
DAVIE Isobel M
NOBLE Mary
GARDEN Margaret A F
KINDNESS Eileen M
SIM Elsie M
LEWIS Rosemary A
CRAIG Alison M
RAE Annetta
MOIR June M
ROSS Alison C
BURNS Marilyn R
GRAHAM Ann E
MACDONALD Hazel J
MURRAY Rhona M
ROSS Barbara A F
ANGUS Jeanette A
MITCHELL Margaret A

*MacKenzie Christopher
*MacKenzie Colin R
MacKenzie Duncan
*MacKenzie Hector R
MacKenzie Ian V
MacKenzie Kenneth
MacKenzie Kenneth P
*McKenzie Robin C
MacKenzie Roderick
*McKenzie Swanson
McKidd Ian
Mackie
*Mackie Alastair J
*Mackie Grahame J S
*Mackie Maitland
Mackie Richard E
*McKillop William L M (1954)
McKinney Roland W J
*Mackinnon John A
MacKintosh Finlay
*Mackintosh John A
Mackonochie James A
Maclaren
McLaren
*MacLaren Donald
McLaren John H
*McLaughlin Charles (1972)
Maclaurin John R W
McLean
McLean Alastair J
McLean Alexander C
*MacLean Angus A
MacLean Donald
MacLean Donald J
*MacLean George F
*MacLean Iain E
MacLean John A
MacLean John K L
*McLean Kenneth
*MacLean Murdoch W
MacLeay Cameron M
Maclennan
Maclennan
*MacLennan Alasdair B
*MacLennan Duncan
*MacLennan John
Macleod
*MacLeod Daniel S
MacLeod Donald
*MacLeod Donald K
*MacLeod Finlay
MacLeod John M
*MacLeod John R
*MacLeod Murdo A
MacLeod Murdoch
McLerie Edward F
*McLintock Michael J
*MacLure Alasdair G
*McLusky Donald S
*McMahon James D R
McMillan
*Macmillan Ian R A
*MacMillan James D
McMillan Malcolm
Macmillan-Kelly Alan D

Ely Elizabeth M K
Mennie Yvonne G
Knapman Mary L
Garden Leonora
Ellen Sigma A M
Mackintosh Marguerita G
Campbell Norma
Sinclair Margaret
Maclean Alice I
Duguid Hilda M
McWilliam Helen A W
Maclennan Helen M
Pinnock Jennifer N
Duncan Elizabeth A
Ramn Halldis A
Buchan Kathleen I M
Smith Kathleen J
Singer Linda M C
Rankin Sandra M
McPhee Kathleen I
McKenzie Dorothy J
Lister Doris A
Robertson Janet G
Saint Christine
Gordon Eileen
Crighton Barbara A M
Mackenzie Deirdre C R
King Kathleen M
Bisset Katrine M
Charitonowsky Ariane
Bremner Joan A
MacDonald Christina
Downie Mary C
MacDonald Margaret A
MacLeod Mary
Ewen Patricia M
Graham Margaret
Begg Wilma A C
Cruickshank Nancy P
Anderson Margaret R
Morrison Chrissisabell
McKay Mary B
Reid Katharine I
Longbottom Molly E
Denoon Deirdre M A
Ritchie Lily A M
Davies Joan M
Bisset Morag J
Pursell Patricia A
MacLeod Catherine M
McIver Norma E
MacLeod Nan S
Ridley Susan E
Nicolson Annie B
Murray Charlotte
Smith Sheila T
Ralph Marion J
McLean Elspeth M
Donald Ruth A
Macrae Jessie S
Prout Lesley J M H
Sinclair Joan E C
Campbell Mary F
Templeton Helen M
Irvine Gladys C

*Macnab Francis A
Macnamara
McNeill Alexander D
*MacNeill Angus
*McNeill Stuart
Macpherson
*MacPherson Hugh (1971)
Macpherson Ian
*McPherson James A S (1949)
McPherson John
*McPhillimy William N
*McQuillan John
McQuitty George L
Macrae
*MacRae Hamish S (1951)
Macrae Norman M
*McRae Stuart G
McRaw Archibald
McRobert William R
MacSween John
McSween John N
*MacSween Kenneth S
McTear Robert W
*McVicar Alasdair H
*McWhirr William A (1971)
*McWilliam Angus A (1974)
Macki Salim H
*Madden Craig A
Magee Patrick J
Main
Main
*Main Alan
Main Charles H
Main William T
Mainwood Anthony R
*Mair Alexander S F
Malcolm John W
*Malley Alexander B
Malone
Manjra Mohammed Y
Mann
Mann Brian K
Mann Stanley L
*Manson Donald M
*Manson Roderick M (1971)
Mantell Henry J L
Marr Forbes
*Marr George L
*Marriott Richard W
Marshall
Martin
Martin
*Martin David M W
Martin George I M
*Martin Iain R
Martin John
Martin Norman W
Martin Robert W Y
*Marwick David C
Mason Robin R
Mason Thomas L
Mason Victor C
Masson Alan J
Masson Alastair
*Masson Robert A

Ewen Sheila B
Heslop Jane S
Kerr Jean J
Gordon Jennifer M
Sinclair Jean M
Stewart Kathleen R
Robin Sara V
Bruce Jane I
Perks Helen M
Mackay Margaret C
McWee Dorothy C B
Beckley Sandra J
Drummond Sheelagh M
Heard Sheila M
Hutcheon Jean G M
Beaton Margaret H
Adam Hazel M
Wilson Cynthia M
Docherty Margaret I
Macleod Effie M
Caie Christina
Donald Morag R
Keay Lorna M
Thomson Elizabeth M
Reid Alison A
Morgan Karen
Florence Margaret M
Simpson May
McKendrick Sheila A E
Bigwood Winifred K
Noble Iris
Swanson Anne L
McGregor Griselda S
Woodhouse Sylvia
Mathers Helen T
Garrow Alice A
White Isobel A
Sim Sandra J
Marr Kathleen A
Campbell Frances B
Farquhar Doreen M
Turner Juliet W
Sutherland Ray D
Mitchell Mary
Scott Kathleen C
Stewart Margaret O
Christie Kathleen H
McArthur Margaret B
Forbes Dorothy K
Elrick Margaret R
Sutherland Nan E
Brown Irene
Bald Lilian V
Campbell Jean M
Kay Jennifer A Y
Richmond Eileen E H
Gillespie Margaret B D
Symon Jennifer
Sandison Jean M H
Simpson Catherine M (1957)
Anderson Catherine M (1969)
Lipscomb Pamela G
Wallace Margaret A
Leask Aileen M
Campbell Dorothy M

*MASSON Robert E
*MATHER Alexander S
MATHERS James A G
MATHESON Alexander
MATHESON Allistair G
MATHESON Bruce A
MATHEWSON
MATHIESON Alexander D
*MATHIESON Alexander W
MATHIESON Ian A
*MATTHEW George D (1952)
MATTHEWS
MATTHEWS Dennis B
MAWDSLEY Evan
MAWSON
*MAYBANK Graham T
MAYBIN James M
*MAYCOCK James H
MBUGUA Robert C K
MEARNS Alan R
MEIER Peter F
MEIN
MELDRUM Neil G
*MELDRUM Stuart J
MELLANBY
*MELLIS James A
MELLOR William H
*MELVIN James S
MENHINICK George S
*MERCHANT Bruce A
MICHIE
MICHIE
MIDDLETON
MIDDLETON
*MIDDLETON Stuart A
MIKULSITI
MILLAR
*MILLAR David G
MILLER
MILLER
MILLER Alexander J
*MILLER Alistair J M
MILLER Donald S
*MILLER Ian D
*MILLER John A L
MILLER John M R
MILLER Thomas H
MILLIGAN
MILLS David M D
*MILLS Peter W
MILN Barnaby K G
MILNE
MILNE
*MILNE Alan D
*MILNE Alexander S
*MILNE David J
*MILNE Douglas J W
*MILNE George A
*MILNE Gordon G
*MILNE Melville K
*MILNE Michael W
MILNE Russell
*MILNE Thomas G
MILNE William A
MILNE William B

TAYLOR Mary R
MACARTHUR Grace S
MOUAT Katherine A
DAVIDSON Irene M
BLACK Margaret C
MANSON Doreen M
MUNRO Sheila M
WAITER Sheila
CRITCHLEY Carol M
GRANT Moira E
McKENZIE Margaret W
MURRAY Hellen K
PHEMISTER Elizabeth R
LISTON Margaret P
SINCLAIR Joyce E
CHILD Mary E
GORDON Margaret A
FINLAYSON Helen R
MILNE Elizabeth M
GUTHRIE Janet M
STIRRAT Helen M R
STEELE Dorothy R
YOUNG Ann L
YOUNG Claire K
DICKSON Fiona J
HAY Margaret J W
MELDRUM Moira S
THOMSON Elizabeth M
REEKIE Gladys
HAMILTON Joan I S
COPEMAN Mary E
GORDON Rosemary E
CANTLAY Valaine I
WILSON Isabel A
EDMOND Margaret G
WILSON Margaret A
MACRAE Madeline
GIBB Judith A
DRUMMOND Elizabeth M
STEPHEN Anne
ROLLO Sheila N
YOUNG Barbara S
REID Christina L
McLEAN Sheila S
KNOWLES Sheila E
LAMONT Margaret M
STEPHEN Anne
SIM Lesley B
PALMER Tessa J H D
MARSHALL Sheila R
BARBER Elizabeth A
STEWART Jamesina S
TRANTOR Moira R
GORDON Nanette L M
FLORY Flora A
WISELY Wendy A
MacKENZIE Joan
WATT Marjorie A
MILNE Margaret J
MORTIMER Wilma J
MUIR Joan E
DAVIS Elizabeth A
DAVIDSON Eleanor F
HUTCHESON Christine A
LAWRIE Margaret E

*MILTON Colin
*MILTON Graham R I (1974)
*MINETT Robert A
MITCHELL
MITCHELL
*MITCHELL Alexander I (1972)
MITCHELL Colin W
*MITCHELL Michael J R
MITCHELL Peter A
MITCHELL William
MITCHELL Wilson S
MIZEN Noël C O
MOIR
MOIR
MOIR
MOIR Ivor J A
MONI Giustino
MONRO
MONTGOMERY Kenneth M
MOORE Geoffrey D
MORALES
*MORGAN David I
*MORGAN John A
MORLEY Charles F
MORRICE
MORRICE Ian G
MORRIS
MORRIS
MORRIS
MORRISON
MORRISON
MORRISON
MORRISON
MORRISON
MORRISON
*MORRISON Donald J
MORRISON Neil D
*MORRISON Peter G
MORRISON William
MORROW
MORTIMER Anthony A
*MORTIMER Gerald
MORTON
MORTON George M
Moss Robin C
MOWAT
*MOWAT Colin R
MOWAT John
MUIR Alan S
MUIR Iain H
MULLAY Alistair W
MUNN Graham H
MUNRO
MUNRO Alexander W W
*MUNRO Andrew
MUNRO Graham
MUNRO Grant
*MUNRO Hamish D
MUNRO Ian M
MURDOCH
*MURDOCH Charles A (1972)
*MURDOCH James K (1971)
MURDOCH Kenneth G
*MURDOCH William F
MURISON Derek J
MURISON Thomas

SUTHERLAND Ailsa M
THAIN Rita F
LITTLE Patricia C
BINNIE Lorna
ROBERTSON Marjorie A
FYFE Lindsay A
PHILLIPS Anne C S
TOMORY Jillian M
HAY Audrey M W
BIRNIE Mae L
FINLAYSON Brenda E
WHITE Frances G
COULL Dorothy C
DEY Elizabeth M
FLEMING Fiona M
THOMSON Dorothy A
GIULIANA Maria A
RITCHIE Alison M
SCOTT Diana H
KINGHORN Jean A
DURNIN Monica M
SCOTT Diane C
STUART Marjory G
MUIR Sarah J
SORLEY Alison M
ROBERTSON Barbara R
FRASER Julie
WARRENDER Jean
YOUNG Pamela A
MOIR Grace G
MOWAT Katherine A M
ROBERTSON Sandra M S
ROSS Susan J F
STEPHEN Maureen Y
GRANT Linda M
HENDERSON Mary F
BARRACK Frances M
MACDONALD Flora A
GRAINGER Maureen C
BRUCE Kate M
GIBB Elizabeth J
MURCHIE Anne
ROBINSON Patricia J M
HALLEY Jean
GRAHAM Marjory H
FYFE Beryl
NORMAND Anne M
GREENSHIELDS Irene
WOOD Willina R
LEASK Audrey K
RYAN Pamela
MUNRO Margaret J W
SCOTT Elspeth S
SMITH Sheila Murdoch
SIMPSON Sheena G
McKENZIE Morag A
WALKER Alison B
McRAE Mairi M
WEAVER Rhoda J
CANTLAY Jean L
ARMSTRONG Alison M
MACKIE Ann E
GEAR Christine A
GRAY Margaret R R
BRUCE Annie

MURPHY Kevin
MURRAY
MURRAY
MURRAY Alexander D
*MURRAY Christopher H
MURRAY Donald A K
MURRAY Donald R
MURRAY Douglas J
*MURRAY George
MURRAY George T H
*MURRAY Hugh B
*MURRAY Ian (1971)
*MURRAY James (1971)
MURRAY Malcolm S
MURRAY Roderick A C
*MURRAY William
*MURRAY-SMITH David J
MUTCH
*MUTCH Douglas B
MUTCH Robin G M
*MUTCH William A R

NAHA Arun K
NAISMITH-BEELEY Michael
*NALL Andrew R
NAPIER
NDAKALA
NEAVE Colin P
NEEDLER Roger M
*NEILAN Henry T
NEWLANDS George C
*NEWMAN Christopher J E
NICOL
NICOL Keith
NICOLETTI Enrico G R
NIGHTINGALE Peter R
*NIKODEM Dirk
NILE
*NISBET Frederick C H (1955)
NIVEN
NOBLE
NOBLE
NOBLE
NOBLE
NOBLE James
NOBLE Peter S
NOLAN James D
NORFOLK
NORMAND
*NORTH Richard A
NORTH Rudolph E
*NORTHCROFT David J
NUTT Stanley C
*NWACHUKU Nathan I C

O'BRIEN John V
O'BRIEN Robert M G
O'GRADY
O'HAGAN
*O'LEARY Michael J
O'NEILL
*O'REGAN Jeremy
O'TOOLE Hugh F
*OGG Thomas W
*OGILVIE Christopher J

PAINTING Josephine
FRENCH Catherine M
HIRD Marilyn
ANDERSON Aileen A
PARK Audrey F A
GOLDIE Muriel J
Low Mary F
Low Katherine J
SCRIMGEOUR Margaret A
RIDDELL Joan H
DOHERTY Mary M
INNES Isabel C
COWIE Maureen M
CUMMING Ann P
GRANT Elizabeth H
GRIEVE Kathleen F S
SMITH Effie M
DAVIDSON June R S
RHODES Hilary M
WATSON Kathleen
RAE Alison C

SEATTER Kathleen
WATT Linda M
COWIE Carol Mary
ROBERTSON Anne C
TENNENT Ruth M G
TROUP Annette
ALLAN Christine S
WOOD Sheila
RICHARDS Maureen E
FINDLAY Patricia M
CHEYNE Muriel M
STRACHAN Diana
GIBSON Joan S B
BUXTON Rosalind C C
CULLEN Catherine F
MELDRUM Patricia M
MACPHERSON Mary I
SMITH Elaine G
BUCHAN Patricia A B
DUNCAN Anne
MASSON Christina
WATT Pearl W
WHITEFIELD Elizabeth M
LEASK Margaret E
MITCHELL Anita M B
RAFFAN Rosemary F
ALEXANDER Anne E
HALL Jean V A
MCINTYRE Patricia J
LAKIN Kathleen E
MAXWELL Elsa P A
ODUGBOSE Oludotun M

MACLEAN Margaret P
OGILVIE Elizabeth B M
BAKER Penelope A
HANNAY Margaret K
CARTER Alyson M
ALLAN Helen A
BEDDARD Susan R
MACKAY Fiona S
WILSON Monica M
GRAHAM Elizabeth J

*OGSTON Derek (1952)
*OGSTON Graeme L
OLDMAN
OLIVER
OLIVER Hedworth F
*OLSON Ian A
OLUSANYA Adebayo
OLUSANYA Bandele A
*OMAND Donald
ORAM Charles S
ORCHARD Russell R
*ORR Robin M (1971)
ORTH Jørgen A H
OSBOROUGH William N
*OUTLAW Brian D (1971)
OXLEY

PACKHAM
*PACSOO Tokefat C
PAGET
PALAJA Bruno
PALMER Nicolas B
PANKO
PARBROOK Geoffrey D
PARDOE Joseph E
PARIENTE
*PARK William M
*PARKINSON George L
*PATCH Derek
PATEL Jahansoz F
PATERSON
PATERSON
PATERSON
PATERSON
PATERSON
PATERSON Robert
PATERSON William G W
PATIENCE Lewis
*PATTERSON Ian J
PATTERSON Nicol P
PATTISON Edward
PEACOCK
*PEACOCK Robin G
PEARKS Peter R
*PEARSON Ian H
PEEBLES Kenneth M
PECKITT
PENNINGTON
*PEREIRA Brian A
PERKINS Robert W
*PETERS Gordon
*PETERSON Gordon C
PETRIE
PETRIE
*PETRIE James C
*PHA Jean C
*PHILIP Alexander S
*PHILIP Alistair E
PHILIP Andrew M
PHILIP George G
PHILIP Gordon M
*PHILIP Robert F
*PHILLIPS George M
PHILLIPS Ivor W
PICKERING Michael

CLARK Cecilia M
CLARK Vivien M P
FORREST Irene J
MCARTHUR Jean H
RIACH Alison M
HAMILTON Elizabeth A
LITTLE Joan R
BREBNER Eileen
PEACE Emma S
JAFFREY Helen E
WALKER Anne
CRANE Nicola H F
MITCHELL June M R
CLARK Margaret E
MACDONALD Alison M
STURROCK Isabel A

MACKAY Sheena P
IUTZ Josephine
MELVIN Marjory C
LORENZONI Maria V
MCKAY Alison B
MACLEAN Mary
STEWART Evelyn O
MCWILLIAM Elizabeth
JONES Susan P
STADDON Anne E
GLENDENNING Catherine M
GORDON Patricia F L
MARTIN Sheila C
BEGG Lorna M
DAVIE Anne
MACKENZIE Mona F
SMITH Maureen R
THOMSON Lorna K
CLARK Eileen M
MACKENZIE Mary I
MACKAY Jane M M
BIRSE Muriel J
HEPBURN Sheila D
STEWART Catherine A
STRACHAN Fiona K
ALSOP Gillian E M
WATSON Anna G
YEOMAN Kathleen J
CLARK Margaret S
MCPHERSON Joyce A
DEANS Isabella M
PETRIE Heather M
MITCHELL Kathleen M A
WILSON Edith I
CANT Helen E
BROOKS Elizabeth C
PICKARD Joyce I H
FORBES Margaret X P
GILL Anna B
CROFTS Gillian M
MCKAY Betty J
DUNBAR Mary
BURNETT Irene M
CHARLESON Euphemia B
SIMPSON Anne F
IRVINE Veronica M
HAY Jean M
NORTHCROFT Janet H

*PIGOTT Colin P
PIRIE Ian D
*PLASKETT William B
POLLARD
*POLLET John E
*POLLOCK Nigel J
POLLOCK-SMITH Russell D J
*POOLE Stuart C (1971)
POPINEAU Jean-Luc J
PORTER George D
*PORTER Robert D
POTTINGER David W
POTTON Richard J
POTTS Robert
POWELL Valnor
*PRENTICE Ian M
*PRESHAW Colin T
PRESLY
PRICE John
PRICE Roger
PRIMMER Brian A S
PRINGLE
*PRINGLE Duncan M
*PRINGLE James C
PRITCHARD Dorian J
*PYATT David G

RAE
*RAE John E
RAFFERTY Alan
RAFFERTY James
*RAITT David G
RAMSAY
*RAMSAY Ian M
*RAMSAY Keith M M
*RANDALL Ian M
*RANKIN Bryan J
RATCLIFFE
RATTRAY
RATTRAY Brian
*RAVEN Norman
*RAWSTHORNE George B
RAYNER Richard R
REAPER James F
*REARY James B
*REDFORD Malcolm K
REID
REID
REID
REID
REID
REID
REID
REID
REID
*REID Alan R
REID Albert McK
*REID George W
*REID Hamish G
*REID John G
REID John M
*REID John S G
*REID Norman H

WATSON Ray B
REID Dorothy J
LANGLANDS Marianne M
TREDINNICK Beatrice A
BLENCH Sheena M
CLURE Anne E
CUMMING Elsie J
MITCHELL Beryl
BOURNER Sybil A
FERGUSON Fiona M
BURNETT Frances H
SCOTT Joan F
MARSHALL Margaret W
O'HANLON Anne
SIMPSON Marnel
GORDON Shelagh A O
BRUCE Carole
REID Doreen V
MIDDLETON Linda M
MILNE Margaret E
BURGESS Anna M
KHAN Indira S
GIBB Jean
TAYLOR Maureen M
HERFORD Penelope J
HAY Rosalind A

ALEXANDER Patricia A
MUNRO Margaret C
BUCHAN Joan C
REILLY Patricia
DAVIES Elisabeth S
HENDRY Sylvia M
PIRRIE Isobel
RICHARDS Isabella M O
HUGHES Janice B
SAVAGE Kathleen E
SMITH Wendy A
MITCHELL Elizabeth M
OGILVIE Marjory
DUTHIE Margaret
MACKENZIE Anne M
DUNCAN Catherine R
SMART Hazel
AMOS Lilias T
PLUMMER Rachel M
BRAND Winifred C D
CORSIE Mary
MACKENZIE Nancy B
MORRICE Margaret
MORRISON Margaret S
NICOL Helen
ROBERTS Celia F
SALVIN Janice L
SILVER Patricia C
SMITH Esme A
SMITH Helen I
HALLEY Mary R
FORSYTH Kathleen M
SIM Sheila E
MURCHIE Marjory E
BARTON Anne M
MACKENZIE Vivianne R
DONALD Maureen
ROBERTSON Patricia C

*REID Robin D
REID Thomas P
REINHARDT
RENDALL James M
*RENNIE Donald G
*REVEL Karl J T
RIACH
*RIACH Douglas C
*RICE Charles D
RICHARDS
RICHARDS Joseph P
RICHARDSON Michael T
RICHARDSON Stanley D
*RIDDELL Alexander J
RIDDELL Stuart
RIDDLER
RIMMER Gilbert
RITCHIE David A
RITCHIE George
RITCHIE George F
*RITCHIE Ian O
*RITCHIE John W
RITCHIE Robert G
RIVARD Marcel H
RIVIERE
ROBB
ROBB Norman G
ROBERTS
*ROBERTS Alasdair G (1975)
ROBERTS David S
ROBERTS David T
ROBERTS Ernest F
ROBERTS John M S
ROBERTS Maurice J
ROBERTSON
*ROBERTSON Alastair O
*ROBERTSON Alexander S
ROBERTSON Allan M
*ROBERTSON George E
*ROBERTSON Ian S (1955)
ROBERTSON Ian S
ROBERTSON James H
ROBERTSON James P
ROBERTSON John L
*ROBERTSON Neil (1967)
ROBERTSON Neil M
ROBERTSON Peter J
ROBERTSON Robert J
ROBINSON Michael J
ROBINSON Nigel S
*ROCKWELL Peter W
RODDIS Hugh A J
ROGERSON
ROPERT Marcel L
ROSE
ROSE
ROSE
*ROSE John I (1952)
ROSER Bruce J
ROSIE George S G
ROSS
ROSS
*ROSS David S
ROSS Donald G
ROSS Eoin M

McCONACHIE Elizabeth M
WALKER Doreen I
BOA Mary I
SINCLAIR Morag A S
DEWAR Brenda L
BUCHAN Mabel
WALKER Jean M
DONALDSON Anne F
WUNSCH Susan I
STRZALOWSKA Wanda C
LINDSAY Ann H
MENDHAM Nicolette C
JEZZARD Janet E I
MILLAR Elizabeth M
SHARP Evelyn M
MITCHELL Janet E
OGILVIE Eileen M
MILNE Helen M
BENZIE Carmen H E
WOOD Thelma
LAMBIE Elizabeth A
GRAY Patricia
ROSS Avril E
KEIR Rhona M
CHRISTIE Dorothy
ROSS Marion C
SUTHERLAND Barbara E
TOD Anne S
COBBAN Marion M
DURWARD Wilma A M
FORDYCE Jane E
EDMOND Carol M
MACDONALD Catriona
MACLEOD Alexandra
ALVIS Patricia A
ROBERTSON Catherine E
MARTIN Pamela M
McLAREN Lorna E
GRANT Sheila M
MACPHERSON Mary E F
HALL Hilda R
SINCLAIR Morag M
BARRON Veronica M
FARQUHAR Mary E
CHRISTIE Brenda A
CUSA Rosalind J
THOMSON Janette D
LITTLEJOHN Margaret I
COOK Josephine A H
BELL Kathleen T
McDONALD Elspeth C
PRIMROSE Mary M
MOIR Annette N
ROBBIE Sheila C
CHARLTON Maureen
FRASER Irene
MACDONALD Kathleen M
ESSLEMONT Marjory E H
ELLIS Susan T
SUTHERLAND Inga M
BREMNER Williamina
GALLACHER Jane M
WATT Heather G
HOLM Isabel
GIBBONS June E K

Ross Harry M
*Ross James
*Ross John F
*Ross Philip W
Ross Robert A
Ross William J
Ross-Browne Michael
Rothwell D M
Routledge Frederick D
Rowlands Gareth J
*Rowlands Owen
Rowlands William B M
*Royle Trevor B
*Ruddiman Kenneth W
Rueckert
Ruff Peter G
Russell
Russell
Russell
Russell Colin R
Russell Hugh B L
Russell Norman G F
Rust James D
Rutherford John D
Ryan David J
Rycroft David S

Sachinides Dimitris
*Sadler Alexander J
Sadler David A
*Sadler Michael G
Salkeld
Salmon Ian D
*Samuel Alan D M B (1971)
*Sananikorn Prida
Sands Jeremy Nigel
*Sargent John R
Saunders Jeremy C L
*Savage Peter G (1972)
Sawyer
Scharff David E
*Scotland Colin G E
Scott
Scott
Scott
Scott David J G
Scott Ian A
Scott James M
Scott John A G
Scott John F
Scott Nigel R M
Scott Robert G
*Scott Robin F
Scott Thomas M
Scott Victor J
*Scott-Brown Alastair W
Scott-Pillow Henry T
Seager John
Seiler Edmund R
Selbekk Reidar
*Self Michael B
Senior
Sevo Ivan
Seymour
*Shand Edward

Ralph Alison J
Duncan Elaine M
MacDonald Theresa E
Shand Stella J
MacPhail Evelyn A
Johnson Margaret A
Biggar Susan M
Macrae Helen S B
Watson Valerie
Welsh Elizabeth K C
Rennie Pamela M
Muirden Elaine
Sibbald Jane B
Stewart Helene A
Moore Eileen M C
Lindsay Elizabeth M
Carnie Ann
Fraser Sheila M
Williamson Sheila M
Tough Elizabeth A
Duncan Erica B A W
Dawson Margaret J
Hamilton Elizabeth M J
Patterson Dorothy E
Russell Alison M J
Soutar Marjorie E

Mitchell June
Reid Joan M
McLaren Morag
Stewart Susan W
Taylor Judith
Gordon Pamela J
Brown Rosalind A
Clarke Avril R
Campbell Margaret C
Buchan Elizabeth J
Coutts Penelope A
Cormack Elizabeth A
Frater Susan E
Savege Jill M
Fraser Sheila M (1970)
Bradford Helen M
Craig Evelyn R
McDonald Ann L
Banks Dorothy A
Paterson Lily J
Ritchie Margaret M
McGillivray Rhonda M
Mackie Isobel M
Moir Maureen C
MacCallum Patricia M
Fraser Sheila M (1966)
Smith Mary R
Affleck Georgina S
Lyall Ardyn A
Dean Helen M
Feather Elizabeth A
McNeill Anne C
Hammerstad Bodil
Brooks Elizabeth A
Barron Margaret
Mackie Elizabeth A
Watt Ann E
Greig Linda J

Shand James G
Shanks Ronald S C
*Sharp Neil W
Shaw George A M
Shaw Hugh Y
Shea
Shearer
Shearer
*Shedden Alfred C
*Shennan Andrew T
Shepherd Hugh M
Shepherd John F
*Shewan Frederick D F
Shiach Robert J
Shiel Robert S
*Shields Michael A (1954)
Shirreffs Gordon C
Sibbald
Sills John A
Silver Gordon R
*Sim George H B
*Sim John W
Sim Ronald G L
Simpson
Simpson
Simpson Alexander I
Simpson Charles E
Simpson John A
*Simpson Neil A
Simpson Norman
Simpson Philip F
Simpson Stewart
*Simpson Thomas W
Simpson-Fraser
Sinclair
Sinclair
*Sinclair Colin D (1971)
Sinclair John
*Sinclair Robert A
*Sinclair Samuel D (1975)
Sinclair-Gieben
Singer Robert W
*Singh Manik
Skea Ian W
Skelsey
Skene Charles P
Skinner
*Skinner Alexander C
*Skinner James A
*Skinner James M
Skuce
Slater George M McA
*Slater John
*Slater John N (1971)
*Slater Peter A
Sloan
*Slowey Alexander
Smart
Smart David A
*Smart Ernest R D
Smith
Smith
Smith
Smith

Lobban Dorothy K
Green Dorothy
Bettridge Ann E
Cameron Elizabeth
Innes Lorraine H
Brown Patricia H
Forbes Isabel C
Groundwater Myra C
Terris Rosalyn E M
Stewart Anne
Cowie Carol A C
Davidson Catherine M
Barrack Iris P
Cooper Kathleen S
Maitland Alison I
Birkbeck Valerie E R
Philip Suzanne
Stephen Alison M
Forsyth Hope G M
Leask Margaret
Milne Dorothy C
Buchan Muriel
Shearer Blanche A
Hendry Jacqueline A
Lawrie Eleanor W
Sutherland Mary M
Wilson Gladys H
Stewart Alison
Brown Sheila A
Marcella Camille
Philip Grace C
Yackiminie Ann B
Philip Maureen A
Singer Wilma W
Stopper Irene M
Thinn Anne B
Reid Kathleen A
McMillan Helen
Smith Jean R
Scobbie Valerie A
Williams Gaynor M
Ritchie Irene A
Singh Shakuntala
Budge Rosemary K
Calder Charlotte N
Lamont Alison J K
Masson Catherine K
Corbett Catherine M
Maclean Murdina
Barclay Hazel D E
Tuttle Irene M
Stanbridge Catherine C
McKinnon Christina M
George Sheila C
Craig Isobel M
Lyon Patricia M H
Mackinnnon Patricia I
Coull Sandra M
Wild Valerie F
Carmichael Rosemary C D
Anderson Rosemary
Crighton Maureen R
Fraser Jean E E
Inglis Mary H
Low Aileen J

SMITH	MACPHIE Anne W	STEELE Thomas A	CLARK Denise F
SMITH	MACRAE Catriona F G	STEELE William A	MENNIE Catherine F
SMITH	MURISON Norma	*STEELE William M (1971)	CRIGHTON Joan B
SMITH	ROBERTSON Alison K	*STEIN (Walter) Peter G (1955)	CHAMBERLAIN Janet M
SMITH	WOOD Ella	STEINER	MURRAY Eleanor M
*SMITH Alistair J W	YOUNG Sylvia J	STEPHEN	MCRAE Edith
SMITH Andrew J D	OGG Lindsay A	STEPHEN David	SLATER Rosalyn J
*SMITH Angus T	LAWRENCE Kathleen	*STEPHEN George J	MACKAY Roberta D
*SMITH Ben	SYNGE Elizabeth	STEPHEN Innes R	MOON Helen J
*SMITH Brian S	JOSS Alison M	STEPHEN John W B	MACKAY Fiona C
*SMITH Christopher D	BOYACK Patricia A	STEPHEN Michael J R	GORDON Joan E
SMITH David C	MUTCH Lesley M M	*STEPHENSON John D	MCBLANE Fiona A
SMITH David N	PATTERSON Margaret H	STEVEN	DUNCAN Jennifer E
*SMITH Donald	MURRAY Catherine	STEVENSON James P	CARSON Graham M G
SMITH Donald W	MACKAY Cairine D	STEVENSON John D	GARDNER Elizabeth C J
SMITH Ernest	KINGDON Doris	STEVENSON Robert	DICK Elizabeth M
SMITH Frederick G	DOUGLAS Lois E	STEWART	MACDONALD Donalda
*SMITH George A	HUNTER Heather	STEWART	SMITH Lorna A
SMITH George D	KENNEDY Katherine S	*STEWART Andrew M	FYSON Mary J
*SMITH Howard O	MORTIMER Sheila W	*STEWART Clement A	PHILLIP Sheena M
SMITH Hugh M	COWIE Alison K	*STEWART David W (1973)	COLVILLE Christine P
*SMITH James W D (1973)	MITCHELL Jessie D F	STEWART David W N	MANSON Marion S
SMITH John D C	MCQUISTAN Fiona E W	*STEWART Donald W H	BISSET Catherine H
*SMITH John F (Lord Kirkhill) 1974	CLARK Frances Mary	*STEWART Douglas J	PATERSON Catherine I
*SMITH John G (1972)	WELSH Jean S	STEWART Douglas L	HENDERSON Jennifer J
*SMITH John S	CAMPBELL Gillian A	*STEWART Douglas L	WATT Lesley J
SMITH Kenneth S	MACLEOD Dolina	*STEWART George M	YOUNG Audrey W
*SMITH Louis M	GOW Elspeth J A	*STEWART Joseph	SMITH Lorna A
SMITH Martin S	CAMERON Margaret E M	STEWART Norman M	CAMPBELL Mary S
SMITH Murdoch M	MACARTHUR Doreen M	STEWART Robert A C	JONES Mary C
SMITH Nicholas J	HORNE Jeanette B	STEWART William H	MASON Lesley M
SMITH Peter S C	YEATS Katherine H	*STILEMAN Richard G L	ROSS Patricia F B
*SMITH Roderick	MCHARDY Ellen	*STILL Alexander W	COULL Isobel R
SMITH Roderick P	MACKENZIE Joan M	STOKER	BUCHANAN Maria T
*SMITH Stuart L	DAVIDSON Rachel C	STOLLERY	WATT Janet F
*SMITHSON John F	MCCAW Patricia J	*STONE Gordon V	WILSON Aileen S
SNELL Philip G	WILSON Dorothy L	STONEHOUSE D Peter	MACLEOD Alison A
SOMERVILLE	ANNAND Patricia R	STOTT Frank F D	HUNTER Beatrice J N
SOMERVILLE Robert H C	CRUICKSHANK Sheila	*STOTT James J	ESSLEMONT Anne R
*SORRIE George S	BAIRD Gabrielle A	STOUT	LONIE Alice
*SOULSBY John A	COUTTS Evelyn M	*STOVE George C (1972)	PAUL Helen M W
SOUTER	CAMPBELL Colinne	STRACHAN	GRANT Doris M
*SOUTER Alistair M	HUMPHREY Margaret	STRACHAN George	GAMMIE Agnes D D
*SOUTER Ian P	RUSSELL Helen M	STRACHAN Peter	MEARNS Kathleen M
*SOUTER John R	MACKENZIE Rosemary	*STRACHAN William R	FERGUSON Irene R
SPEED	LESLIE Joan E A	STRATHDEE Robert G	BARCLAY Win F M
*SPEIRS Ronald C	ELDER Susan W	STRAWSON Bernard	MURDOCH Anne G
SPENCE James W	STEVENSON Margaret P	*STRONACH Andrew F	DUNN Marilyn J L
*SPENCELEY Anthony P	MILNE Margaret J	STUART	FERGUSON Elizabeth S
SPENCER Brian J	THOMSON Helen L	STUART James F	MACQUEEN Shiona C J
*SPENNING Per	CRUICKSHANK Muriel B	STUART John B	LARNACH Alison J
SPINKS John E	SANDERS Penelope J	STUART Kenneth G	THOMSON Mary H
SPRING Michael S	BEDDARD Susan R	STUART William G	MCLAREN Jean
SPRUNT Thomas G	MACARTHUR Deirdre C C	STUBBES	ROAF Jane I
SQUIRE Denis I	YOUNGSON Marika E	STUBBINS William H	GARRIOCK Kathleen W M
SRIVASTAVA	WILSON Gladys M W	*STURDEE Anthony P	RUSHTON Sarah R
STALKER	COOPER Elaine H	*SUE-CHUE-LAM Jerry	SUE-A-QUAN Cerise D
STALKER Brian A	CUMMING Anne D	SUMMERS Robert S S	BUCHAN Ann
STALKER Graham C	MELLIS Patricia M	SUMNER	ROBERTSON Helen M
STALKER James H	CARLISLE Eleanor M	*SURGEONER James H	WADSWORTH Sheila
STANWIX Philip R	WILSON Lorna M	SUTHERLAND Donald M	ALLAN Barbara G
STARK George A R	MOWAT Anne M	SUTHERLAND John D	BONE Jessie M
*STARK William A	NICOL Isobel H	SUTHERLAND John G	HENDERSON Margaret E
STEELE	MASSON Mary B R	*SUTHERLAND John G M	ELLINGTON Kathleen A T
*STEELE Donald H	WELSH Moira J L	SUTHERLAND Malcolm	DAVIDSON Ruth I

*SUTHERLAND Stewart R
*SUTHERLAND William R
*SUTTIE Alastair M
*SUTTIE Ian S
*SUTTON Alastair M
SWOGGER John H
SYKES
*SYMON Patrick A (1952)

TAGART
TAIT
TAIT
TAIT Frederick H
TAIT Maxwell C St C
*TAIT Peter J T
TAIT Ronald E
*TALLACH Cameron
TAMBER Einar R
TAMISARI
TANDY
TAUMGEPEAU Filimoto M
TAYLOR
TAYLOR
TAYLOR
TAYLOR
TAYLOR
TAYLOR
*TAYLOR Alexander J
*TAYLOR David M
TAYLOR Douglas W
*TAYLOR George A
*TAYLOR James (1971)
TAYLOR James
TAYLOR James G
*TAYLOR Stephen A G (1972)
TAYLOR Thomas F
*TAYLOR Thomas G
*TAYLOR Willson D
*TELFER Stewart B
*TELLING Geoffrey M
TEMPLETON Phillip K
TENNANT Smith
THAYER
*THIRD Robert T
THOM
THOM
THOM David
*THOMANECK Jürgen K A
THOMAS
*THOMAS Richard H
THOMAS Richard S
THOMPSON
THOMPSON David H
THOMPSON Hennessey A S
THOMPSON Lloyd M
THOMPSON Raymond H
*THOMPSON William G
THOMSON
THOMSON
THOMSON
THOMSON
THOMSON
*THOMSON Alan D (1971)
*THOMSON Alan J
*THOMSON Allan M

ROBERTSON Sheena
MILNE Margaret J
SANGSTER Gillian M
SOUTER Christina I
TAYLOR Eileen
COWIE Marion P
CORDINER Stella
PEARSON Isobel G

GAMMIE Eileen M C
ROBERTSON Christian S
STOTT Mary L
JOHNSTON Margaret
RENDALL Ruth
PROUDFOOT Winifred
COOPER Ingrid M J
MACLEAN Ishbel M
WONG Daisy S H
WATT Morag E
NOBLE Isabella B
McNEILL Bridget M
ALLARDYCE Janette H
BRUNTON Jennifer M
HAMBLIN Caroline A
McFARLANE Gladys
PETRIE Mhorag J
SMITH Joan D
McBOYLE Evelyn M
THOMSON Jacqueline M
SMITH Diana M
WILLOX Margaret E
HAY Morag C
REID Euphemia M
DALGETTY Yvonne A
LOGIE Patricia M C
CORDINER Sheila E W
CUMMING Jean E
SANGSTER Lorna M
HOLMES Sheila
BAXTER Margaret S
GORDON Sheila E
STEPHEN Margaret E
BRUCE Christine F H
CHADWICK Beryl
DUTHIE Ruth
WILSON Elizabeth W
ROSE Isla M
RONALD Guinevere
BUCHAN Barbara B
BALDERSTON Mary S
HIND Angela J
EDGE Rosemary A
NISBET Jennifer B
GRAY Laurina G E
WILSON Wendy S
ALLEN Hilary
BUTLER Noreen I
BOOTH Kathleen M D
HARVIE Winifred A
KENT Margaret R
McRAE Norma
MOWATT Christina C
RODDIS Linda J A
COUTTS Elizabeth A
BRUCE Charlotte

*THOMSON Douglas A (1973)
*THOMSON Gordon M
THOMSON James A
THOMSON Nichol
THOMSON Robert G
THOMSON Ronald K
TIBBETT Roger J K
TIFFANY Alan
TILLSON John R
TIMSON Brian P
*TINCH Robert T
TOBIN Austin
TOPP William D
TRACEY Andrew M
TREVENA
TREZISE Robin N
TUCKER
TUCKER David C
*TULEY Graham
*TULLIS Douglas K
TURNER
TURNER
TURNER Edward D
*TURNER Gordon H
TURNER Michael J
*TURPIE Derek M
*TUTTLE Albert A
TWEDDLE John S
TYRER

UNDERWOOD
*URI Oddstein
URQUHART Alexander E

VALTONEN Mauri
VAUGHAN
*VIGRON John W
VIPOND
VON WEYMARN
*VYSE Alan H

*WALDING Hugh F
WALEN Tore
WALKER
*WALKER Alexander L
WALKER Christopher R
*WALKER Colin H
WALKER John K
WALKER Ronald G
WALLACE
WALLACE Edward B
WALLACE Harry C H
WALTON James W
WARBURTON
WARD
WARD Errol S
WARD John
WARDMAN Roger H
*WARRACK Ian M
WARREN William J
WATKINS David
WATKINS David A
WATKINS John M
*WATKINS Roger D

BAIN Elizabeth W
HOOD Virginia A
TAYLOR Annette M
BURNETT Lorna M
BRUCE Patricia H
ALLISON Margaret M
TUACH Ann I
COOK Irene B
McKILLIGAN Margaret J
LIVESEY Hilary J
ROSS Susan C
WYNESS Helen P
FRASER Evelyn M
MOIR Jessie A H
DEY Elizabeth W
KEAY Marjorie K
MACGREGOR Catherine E
SMART Jane F
BELL Margot
ATKINSON Alison M
McCONDICHIE Jean M
MACRAE Jean G C
ROBERTSON Marion I
BREBNER Barbara A
TAYLOR Patricia M
DUNCAN Jeanette C
GOW Sheena
JOINER Vera M
HARTNOLL Gillian P

WELSH Margaret C
SUMMERS Patricia
KINDNESS Agnes J

ATTIN Kathleen M
GRIGGS Daphne E
SAYLES Elisabeth A
BISHOP Prudence M
MEIKLEJOHN Dorothy
MACKINTOSH Frances M

SUTHERLAND Margaret S
DAVIE Kathleen F
SWANSON Ruth A
ANDERSON Ann O
WOOLLAM Jane A N
REITH Margaret E
FYDA Janina C Z
STILL Joan
EMSLIE Helen G
GUNN Nancy S
GONNELLA Frances
ELLIS Dorothy J M
MACDONALD Iris D
MISTRY Chandan
GORDON Margaret J
GORDON Sheila E
SCOTT Rosemary
McARTHUR Alison
PETERS Mary E
WESTWOOD Carole
BARRON Kathleen E
BABBÉ Jean E M
McDOWELL Lindsay A

WATSON	BUTLER Marilyn	*WILLIAMSON James	BAXTER Aldon T
WATSON	MURRAY Rosemary L	WILLIAMSON Michael	STURROCK Jane T
WATSON	ROBERTSON Myrtle E	*WILLIAMSON Peter G	JOHNSON Elizabeth A D
WATSON Joseph	WATT Mirren A	*WILLIAMSON Robert B	JEFFREY Sheena I B
*WATSON Melville F	MORGAN Sheila E G	*WILLIS Douglas P	CAMPBELL Catherine M
*WATSON Michael D (1971)	HUTTON Eleanor J	WILLSON Vivian W	SUTHERS Susan
*WATSON Steven E	FERGUSON Joanne A L	WILSON	ADEN Sandra
WATT	ANDERSON Gladys M	WILSON	HUTCHEON Muriel
WATT Alan	SMART Judith M	WILSON	LAWRENCE Jean S
WATT Alexander	GEDDES Jean Munro	WILSON Alexander	COMLOQUOY Sheena
*WATT Alexander	MORRISON Marie E	WILSON Alexander	THOMPSON Margaret M
WATT Alexander G	SIM Mart(h)a G	*WILSON Alexander B	CAMERON Marjory M
*WATT Andrew P (1955)	CLUNESS Anne M	WILSON Alexander C	RAE Patricia
*WATT George D (1955)	LYON Marjorie A	WILSON David K	SCOTT Elizabeth M J
WATT James F	ANGUS Elizabeth R	WILSON Eric	LESLIE Jean H
*WATT Robert J C (1973)	MURRAY Margaret M	*WILSON James A	MCLAREN Elizabeth D
WATTERSON David C	KENDLE Janet M	WILSON James L	CHRISTOPHER Moira A
*WATTIE James A	GARRIOCH Joanna M	WILSON John B	WYLLIE Marjorie R
WATTS	KNOWLES Kathleen M	*WILSON Keith W	HALL Linda F
WATTS	Ross Maureen V	WINSEY Harold S	MORGAN Audrey M
WEBB Jack R	CARNIE Patricia A	WINTER	WHYTE Kathleen A
WEBER Gerhard	WOOD Margaret B	*WISELY Ivan C F	KAY Jillian G A
WEBSTER	HARROWER Margaret E M	WISEMAN	BRANDS Sheila J C
*WEBSTER John A	KINCAID Mary	WISEMAN Andrew W	ALLAN Patricia M I
WEBSTER Martin J	MACDONALD Jean R	*WISEMAN Lesley (1971)	SOUDEN Carol E
WEIGHTMAN Bruce E	MASSON Margaret D	*WISLOFF Sigurd B	Ross Catherine L
WEIR Alan D	MACDONALD Alys T	*WITO James Alexander	HARRISON Moira A
*WEIR John G C	FRASER Elspeth G M	WITTS David E	DUTHIE Jennifer M
WEIR Norman R	DUGUID Eleanor J	WOLK	ASHFORD Anne M
WELCH Bruce T	GALL Elsie M	WONG	MORRISH Ann L
WELHAM	BENZIE Helen	WOOD	EDDIE Jean L
WELSBY	DONALD Sheila E	WOOD	MACPHERSON Beatrice G
WELSH	SMITH Jennifer M	*WOOD Brian J (1971)	PETRIE Doreen A
WELSH Michael E	SMITH Grace N	*WOOD Kenneth G	WISEMAN Margaret W
*WEMYSS Thomas	HAMILTON Margaret V	WOODS Gilbert M	LAIRD May A
WEST	WATT Alexandra A	WOODWARD Ralph J	GRANT Margaret I
WESTERN Charles F	FOWLIE Sylvia M	WRIGHT	COOPER Stephanie
WESTGARTH Terry	COLLERAN Ethel M	WRIGHT	HUNT Jennifer
WESTON Grahame V J	HUTTON Elizabeth M	WRIGHT Andrew M	WATTS-RUSSELL Grayling J P
WHARTON	PATTERSON Valerie A N	WRIGHT Gary G	MAY Rhoda K
WHEELER	HARRISON Jacqueline M	*WRIGHT Norman J D	ABBOTT Susan
WHITE David H	BARR Margaret	WRIGHT William A	Ross Kathleen A
WHITE John H M	STONE Beryl M	WYLIE	KEIL Cheryl M
WHITEHEAD Norman S	Ross Claude M L	*WYLIE Ralph C	EATON Jane P
WHITELAW Gilbert	NOBLE Christina E	WYLLIE William A S	FARQUHAR Fiona M
WHITING Bernard	SINCLAIR Margaret F		
WHITMORE	MOON Helena M	YACAMINI David T (1971)	KNIGHT Jean E
*WHYTE David F (1971)	PARDOE Kathleen F	YANG Bunli	SYNGE Jane
WHYTE Gordon T	BIRNIE Mary J	YOUNG	LORIMER Patricia R
WIGHT	ANGUS Zena J	YOUNG	SPENCE Elizabeth C
*WIGHT James R	BURNETT Madeleine A	*YOUNG Francis	DAVIE Victoria F
*WILDGOOSE David M	SPROUL Edna W	*YOUNG John A (1973)	DOAK Noreen M H
*WILDGOOSE Ian	MACKLAND Sheila	*YOUNG Kenneth M	PARTINGTON Naomi A
WILKIE	CAMERON Ruth E	YOUNG Kenneth R	SCOTT Margaret
*WILKIE James L	WATSON Irene A	*YOUNG Niall A	HOLDSWORTH Patricia D
WILKIE Thomas J	CAMPBELL Sherry E	*YOUNG Thomas D	GRANT Kathleen M
WILKIE William D	GREIG Evelyn M	YOUNGSON	BUDGE Margaret
WILKINSON	MACRAE Helen S	*YOUNGSON Colin J	REID Stella F
WILL Roy	CLYNE Isobel A	YULE Charles B	ROBERTSON Isobel M
WILLIAMS	SIMPSON Dorothy A	*YULE David K	FORSYTH Janet M G
WILLIAMS David P G	BURNS Rosalind A	*YULE Frederick D	WHITE Janet E
WILLIAMS Dennis J	SMART Lynne W	YULE Ian R	MITCHELL Dorothy M
WILLIAMS Paul W	THOMSON Diane N	YUSUF	BUTCHART Dorothy A G
*WILLIAMS Roger W	MACNAUGHTAN Elizabeth M		
*WILLIAMSON Andrew J	VALENTINE Wyn P	ZATELNY William	PIRIE Sheila M

HONORARY GRADUATES 1956–1970

The designations are as at the time of laureation.

The first *AUR* reference is to the laureation address. Where available some later information has been added.

An asterisk (*) is prefixed to the names of those who hold, or have held, degrees of Aberdeen University other than honorary degrees and further information about these may be found in the appropriate Section(s) of this volume and earlier volumes of the Roll of Graduates.

ADAM SMITH or Carleton, Janet Buchanan LL D 1962
author and journalist; literary edit. *New Statesman and Nation* 1952–60; *AUR* xxxix 346

AITKEN Robert Stevenson (Sir) LL D 1960
MD (NZ) DPhil(Oxon) LL D (Dalh, Melb, Panj, McG, Penn) DSc(Syd) FRCP (Lond, Edin) FRACP
vice chancellor Birm univ; chmn comm of vice chancellors and principals; *AUR* xxxix 40

ALEXANDER Charles LL D 1968
businessman and farmer; *AUR* xlii 308

ALEXANDER Peter LL D 1966
CBE FBA
regius prof Engl lit. Glas univ 1935–63; *AUR* xli 307
d 18.6.69

ALLEN George Vance (Sir) LL D 1963
d 2.10.70

ANDERSON Colin Skelton (Sir) LL D 1963
Hon ARIBA Hon Des RCA Officer of the Order of Orange-Nassau
chmn Trustees of the Tate Gallery; chmn joint deptmental comm on grants for students 1958–60; *AUR* xl 174
d –.10.80

ANDREWES Christopher Howard (Sir) LL D 1963
MD(Lond) FRS
dep dir National Institute for Medical Research 1952–61; *AUR* xl 171

ANGUS William Stephenson LL D 1969
MA LL B
secy and factor Aberd 1952–67; *AUR* xliii 186

ASHBY Eric (Sir) LL D 1958
DSc(Lond) ScD(Dub) LL D(St And)
pres and vice chancellor Queen's univ Belfast from 1950; *AUR* xxxvii 393

ASHMOLE Bernard LL D 1968
CBE MC MA BLitt(Oxon) Hon ARIBA FBA
Lincoln prof classical archaeology Oxford univ 1956–61;

Geddes Harrower prof Greek Art and archaeology Aberd 1961–63; visiting prof archaeology Yale univ 1964; *AUR* xlii 313

ATHOLL His Grace the Duke of
nominated for the award of LL D degree but *d* 8.5.57 before the day of graduation

ATTLEE Clement Richard, The Rt Hon Earl LL D 1956
AUR xxxvi 414
d 8.10.67

AULD Alan Talbert LL D 1970
secy of the Aberdeen Association of Social Service from 1945; member of the Scottish Council of Social Service; *AUR* xliv 91

BAIRD Dugald (Sir) LL D 1966
MD(Glas) FRCOG LL D(Glas) DSc(Manc)
regius prof obst/gyn Aberd 1937–65; *AUR* xli 313

BAIRD May Deans (Lady) LL D 1960
BSc MBChB(Glas)
chmn N E Reg. Hosp Board, Scot.; *AUR* xxxviii 553; nat governor BBC in Scot. 1965–70

BANNERMAN John Macdonald LL D 1958
OBE MA BSc(Glas)
rector Aberd 1957–60 *AUR* xxxviii 175; Life Peerage 1967 Lord Bannerman
d 10.5.69 *AUR* xliii 332

*BARTLETT Henry Matthew DD 1963
MA(Aberd) 1923 BD(Aberd) 1926
min par of Logie from 1928 and clerk to Dundee presb; *AUR* xl 168
d 21.12.80 *AUR* xlix 136

BERKHOF Hendrik DD 1965
ThD
prof systematic theol Leiden univ; *AUR* xli 123

BETJEMAN John LL D 1965
CBE Hon DLitt(R'dg, Birm) Hon ARIBA
poet and author; *AUR* xli 116; Kt 1969; Poet Laureate from 1972

BILSLAND The Rt Hon Alexander Steven (Lord)
LL D 1956
AUR xxxvi 414
d 10.12.70

***BODONHELYI Jozsef DD 1960 (in absentia)**
PhD(Aberd) 1926 DD(Debrecen)
vice dean of Theol seminary of the Hungarian Reformed
Church, Budapest; *AUR* xxxviii 552
d Budapest 1966 *AUR* xli 341

BOEGNER Marc DD 1960
DTheol(Paris)
pres French Academy of Moral and Political Sciences;
AUR xxxix 39
d 1972

***BROWN William Scott (Sir) LL D 1956**
KCIE CSI MA(Aberd) 1912
rector's assessor on univ court Aberd from 1951; *AUR*
xxxvii 82
d Aber 17.5.68 *AUR* xlii 350

***BRUCE Frederick Fyvie DD 1957**
MA(Aberd 1932, Cantab)
prof biblical hist and literature Sheff univ from 1955;
AUR xxxvii 176

BRUFORD Walter Horace LL D 1958
MA(Cantab)
Schroder prof Ger in Cambridge univ from 1951; fell. St
John's Coll, Cambridge; corresponding member of The
Deutsche Akademie, Munich; *AUR* xxxvii 395

***BURNS Hendry Stuart Mackenzie LL D 1956**
BA(Cantab) MA(Aberd) 1921 BSc(Aberd) 1922
pres Shell Oil Company Inc USA; *AUR* xxxvii 82
d 28.10.71 *AUR* xliv 319

CADMAN William Healey DD 1956
MA BLitt(Oxon) BD(Lond) DTheol(Stras)
prof biblical stud. Mansfield Coll Oxon from 1944; *AUR*
xxxvii 82
d. 12.9.65

CAIRD George Bradford DD 1966
DPhil DD(Oxon)
prof O T lang and lit Alta univ 1946–50; prof N T lang
and lit McG univ 1950–59; sen tut. Mansfield Coll Oxford
from 1959 and Grinfield lect in The Septuagint at Oxford
from 1961; *AUR* xli 315; prin Mansfield Coll from 1970

***CALDER John DD 1957**
MA(Aberd) 1900
min emeritus of St Peter's Church North Sydney Aust;
AUR xxxvii 177
d Sydney Aust 19.10.62 *AUR* xl 74

***CAMERON George Gordon DD 1962**
MA(Aberd) 1925 STM (NY)
min Glenburn Paisley; *AUR* xxxix 344

CAMPBELL Archibald Hunter LL D 1963
regius prof public law Edin univ from 1945; dean of fac
of law from 1958; *AUR* xl 175

CAMPBELL David (Sir) LL D 1960
MC MA BSc MD(Glas) LL D(Glas, Dub, Liv) DCL
(Durh) FRFPSGlas FRCP(Lond) FRSE
regius prof materia medica Aberd 1930–58; *AUR* xxxviii
554
d Aber 30.5.78

CLAPHAM Arthur Roy LL D 1970
CBE PhD(Cantab) FRS FLS
prof bot Sheff univ 1944–69; member successively of the
Nature Conservancy and the Natural Environment Re-
search Council from 1956; chmn Brit nat comm for the
International Biological Programme; *AUR* xliv 93

CLYDE The Rt Hon Lord (James Latham McDiarmid
Clyde) LL D 1960
PC BA(Oxon) LL B(Edin) LL D(Edin, St And)
Lord Justice-General of Scotland; *AUR* xxxix 41
d –.6.75

COATS The Rt Hon Thomas, The Lord Glentanar
LL D 1966
member of the governing bodies of the Rowett Research
Inst and of NOSCA; chmn Advisory Council for Scotland
of the Air Training Corps; chief of the Boy Scout Association in Scotland; *AUR* xli 262
d 28.6.71

COGGAN Frederick Donald DD 1963
DD
the Most Reverend and Rt Honourable Archbishop of
York; *AUR* xl 169; Archbishop of Canterbury 1975–80;
created Baron of Canterbury and Sissinghurst in the
county of Kent 1980

COING Helmut LL D 1968
Dr Juris(Gott) Dr(hc) (Lyons, Montpellier, Vienna)
prof law and former rector of Frankfurt-am-Main univ;
dir the Max Planck Inst of European Legal History; *AUR*
xlii 310

COURVOISIER Jaques DD 1956
prof church hist Geneva univ; some time dir ecumenical
commission for P o W's set up by the World Council of
Churches; *AUR* xxxvii 82

***CRAIG Albert DD 1967**
MA(Aberd) 1932 MB ChB(Aberd) 1936 DTM(Calc)
C of S med missionary Charteris hosp Kalimpong from
1937; *AUR* xlii 160

***CRAIG John LL D 1964**
MB ChB(Aberd) 1921 FRCPE
prof ch health Aberd 1948–63; *AUR* xl 378
d Aber 19.4.77 *AUR* xlvii 211

***CRAMB Maurice LL D 1966**
MA(Aberd) 1932 LL B(Aberd) 1934
member of the bus. comm of the General Council Aberd
from 1949 and vice convener from 1963; member univ
court Aberd from 1960; *AUR* xli 308

***CROMBIE James Ian Cormack (Sir) LL D 1957**
KCB KBE CMG MA(Aberd) 1925
chmn Board of Customs and Excise from 1955; *AUR*
xxxvii 178, 205
d Lond 22.5.69 *AUR* xliii 214

CROSS Frank Leslie DD 1959
BSc(Lond) MA DPhil DD(Oxon)
Lady Margaret prof divinity and Canon of Christ Church
Oxford from 1944; *AUR* xxxviii 173
d 30.12.68

***CRUICKSHANK Ernest William Henderson LL D 1959**
MD(Aberd) DSc(Lond) PhD(Cantab) MRCP FRSE
regius prof physiol Aberd 1936–58; *AUR* xxxviii 176
d 29.12.64 *AUR* xli 109

*CRUICKSHANK Robert   LL D 1968
CBE MD(Aberd) 1925 FRCP(Lond, Edin) FRSE
prof bact Edin univ 1958–66; prof soc and preventive
med univ of the West Indies from 1966; *AUR* XLII 311
d Edin 16.8.74 *AUR* XLV 108

CURSITER Stanley   LL D 1959
CBE RSW RSA FRSE
Her Majesty's painter and limner in Scotland from 1948;
AUR XXXVIII 176
d 22.4.76

de VALOIS Ninette (Dame)   LL D 1958
DBE Mus Doc(Lond) DLitt(R'dg) DMus(Sheff) Chev.
Leg. d'H
dir Sadler's Wells Ballet, the Sadler's Wells Theatre
Ballet and Sadler's Wells Theatre; founder of the Sadler's
Wells School of Ballet and of the National School of
Ballet Turkey; *AUR* XXXVII 395

de VAUX Pere Roland   LL D 1964
Dr Theol
superior of l'Ecole Biblique de St Etienne, Jerusalem and
dir of the French School of Archaeology in Jerusalem
from 1945; dir of the Palestine Archaeological Museum;
AUR XL 377
d –.9.71

de VISSCHER Fernand   LL D 1961
Dr-en-Droit(Ghent) Dr h.c. (Grenoble, Strasbourg,
Paris, Rennes, Lille)
member of the Belgium Royal Academy; member of the
Italian National Academy; prof law Louvain univ 1936–
59; pres International Society for the History of the Laws
of Antiquity; *AUR* XXXIX 175
deceased

*DIACK Peter   DD 1957
MA(Aberd) 1912
min of the Park Church Glasgow; *AUR* XXXVII 177
d Edin 4.5.67 *AUR* XLII 181

*DICKSON John Abernethy   LL D 1969
MA(Aberd) 1936 BSc(for)(Aberd) 1938
successively dist off., divisional off. and conserv and from
1968 dir-general of the Forestry Commission; *AUR* XLIII
192

*DIKE Kenneth Onwuka   LL D 1961
BA(Durh) MA(Aberd) 1947 PhD(Lond)
prin and prof of hist in univ coll Ibadan Nigeria; *AUR*
XXXIX 176

DINWIDDIE Melville   DD 1959
CBE DSO MC
controller in Scot. of BBC 1933–57; *AUR* XXXVIII 174
d Edin 12.6.75

**DOUGLAS-HOME The Rt Hon Sir Alexander Frederick
LL D 1966**
Prime Minister and First Lord of the Treasury 1963–64;
AUR XLI 261

*DOWNIE Allan Watt   LL D 1957
MB ChB(Aberd) 1923 MD(Aberd) 1929 DSc(Aberd)
1938
prof bact Liverpool univ from 1943; *AUR* XXXVII 179

DURNO James   LL D 1960
CBE
farmer and stockbreeder; *AUR* XXXVIII 555
d Aber 7.1.71 *AUR* XLIV 216

ELDJÁRN Kristján   LL D 1969
MA PhD
curator and head of the National Museum of Iceland
1947–68; pres of the Republic of Iceland from 1968; *AUR*
XLIII 187

*FALCONER Ronald Hugh Wilson   DD 1960
MA(Aberd) 1934 BD(Aberd) 1937
organiser of religious broadcasting for Scotland; *AUR*
XXXIX 40
d Glasg 20.5.77 *AUR* XLVII 213

FISON Joseph Edward   DD 1958
MA BD(Oxon)
Canon of Truro, Cornwall; *AUR* XXXVII 392
d. 2.7.72

FOHRER Georg   DD 1969
DTheol
prof O T studies Erlangen univ from 1962; *AUR* XLIII 194

FORBES-LEITH Robert Ian Algernon Bt (Sir)
MBE JP   **LL D 1967**
Lord Lieut of the county of Aberdeen from 1959; *AUR*
XLII 154
d 17.3.73

GARDNER Helen Louise (Dame)   LL D 1967
DBE DLitt FBA FRSL
fell. of Lady Margaret Hall and Merton prof Engl Oxford
univ from 1966; *AUR* XLII 155

*GEDDES Alexander Ebenezer McLean   LL D 1956
OBE MA(Aberd) 1906 DSc(Aberd) 1915 FRSE
FRMetS
member of the staff of dept nat phil Aberd from 1909 and
reader until retirement in 1955; *AUR* XXXVII 82
d 26.12.70 *AUR* XLIV 145

GIBB Andrew Dewar   LL D 1957
MBE QC MA LL B(Glas)
advoc and barrister at law, regius prof of law Glas univ
from 1934; *AUR* XXXVII 179
d 24.1.74

GIBSON Alexander   LL D 1968
CBE FRCM
mus dir of Sadler's Wells Opera 1957–59; prin conductor
and mus dir of Scottish National Orchestra from 1959;
artistic dir of the Scottish Opera Company from 1962;
AUR XLII 312; Kt 1977

GOLLWITZER Helmut   DD 1966
DTheol DD
ordinarious prof theol univ of Bonn 1950–57; ordinarious
prof theol Free univ of Berlin from 1957; *AUR* XLI 316

**GORDON (née Boissier) Beatrice Mary June (Countess
of Haddo)   LL D 1968**
FRCM
conductor of the Haddo House Choral Society; *AUR*
XLII 308; Marchioness of Aberdeen

GRAHAM John Macdonald   LL D 1964
CBE DL JP DD
Lord Provost of the city of Aberdeen 1952–55 and 1961–
64; prof systematic theol Aberd from 1937; *AUR* XL 380;
retd; resid Comrie

*GRANT Joseph   DD 1958
MC MA(Aberd) 1925
C of S min Cromdale Grantown-on-Spey; *AUR* XXXVII
392

GUTHRIE (William) Tyrone (Sir)   LL D 1965
administrator of the Od Vic and Sadler's Wells Theatres 1939–45; chancellor of Queen's univ Belfast
d 15.5.71

HALL John Fiddes   LL D 1965
CBE
convener Aberdeen Education Committee 1950–52; chmn governors of Robert Gordon's Colleges 1952–63; *AUR* XLI 117
d 17.12.68

HARDY Alister Clavering (Sir)   LL D 1962
MA DSc(Oxon) FRS FLS FZS
regius prof natural history Aberd 1942–45; fell. Merton Coll and Linacre prof zoology and comparative anatomy Oxford univ 1945–61; *AUR* XXXIX 347

HARROD Roy Forbes   LL D 1956
MA(Oxon) FBA
Nuffield reader in internat economics in Oxford univ and joint edit. of the *Economic Journal*; *AUR* XXXVII 82; Kt 1959
d –.3.78

HEPBURNE-SCOTT The Rt Hon Henry Alexander the Lord Polwarth   LL D 1966
chancellor Aberd 1966; *AUR* XLI 258; governor Bank of Scotland 1966–72; chmn then pres Scottish Council (Development and Industry) 1955–72

HETHERINGTON Hector James Wright (Sir)   LL D 1961
KBE DL MA(Glas) LL D(Glas, Liv, St And, Sheff, Wales, Prin, Cantab, London, Edin, Belf, Tufts(USA), Br Col) DLitt(McG) D-es-L(Laval) LHD (Wooster, Ohio) Hon ARIBA Hon FRFPSGlas FKC Hon FEIS
vice chancellor and prin Glas univ from 1936; *AUR* XXXIX 177
d 15.1.65

HEUGHAN William   LL D 1964
agent and chief trustee of the MacRobert Estates, Tarland; *AUR* XL 381
d 15.8.65 *AUR* XLI 155

HIRST Edmund Langley   LL D 1960
CBE MA BSc PhD LL D(St And) DSc(Birm) MSc (Manc) FRIC FRS FRSE
Forbes prof of organic chem Edin univ and pres of the Royal Society of Edinburgh; *AUR* XXXIX 42
d 29.10.75

HOGG Norman   LL D 1967
JP
Lord Provost of the City of Aberdeen and ex-officio member of univ court Aberd 1964–67; *AUR* XLII 152
d 25.6.75

*HOWIE James William (Sir)   LL D 1969
MB ChB(Aberd) 1930 MD(Aberd) 1937 FRCP FCPath
head of dept of path. and bact in The Rowett Research Inst Aber 1946–51; prof bact Glas univ 1951–63; dir of Public Health Laboratory Service from 1963; pres of Coll of Pathologists from 1966; pres BMA 1969–70; *AUR* XLIII 236

HUDDLESTON Ernest Urban Trevor   DD 1956
MA(Oxon)
member of the Community of the Resurrection from 1941 and lately Provincial of that Order in S Af; *AUR* XXXVII 82; Suffragan Bishop of Stepney 1968–78; Bishop of Mauritius from 1978

HUGGINS Charles   LL D 1966
MD DSc MS FRCS FRCSE FACS
dir Ben May Lab for cancer res in univ of Chicago from 1951; *AUR* XLI 310; dir Ben May Lab 1951–69; chancellor Acadia univ 1972

*IRVINE Archibald Clive   DD 1958
MA(Aberd) 1913 MD(Aberd) 1925
head of Chogoria hosp and sen missionary of the C of S mission in Kenya; *AUR* XXXVII 392
d Nairobi 7.6.74 *AUR* XLVI 107 & 235

JACKSON Willis (Sir)   LL D 1960
DSc(Manc, Brist) DPhil(Oxon) Dr Sc Tech(Zur) FRS MIEE MIMechE FInstP
pres of Institution of Electrical Engineers; *AUR* XXXVIII 555
d 17.2.70

*JARDINE or Taylor, Helen Margaret (Lady)   LL D 1966
MB ChB(Aberd) 1920 MD(Aberd) 1937
member of Board of Directors of ARI 1944–48; member NE Scotland Regional Hospital Board 1948–58; chmn NE Scotland Regional Nurse Training Committee from 1952; member of the Academic Advisory Committee of St And univ; *AUR* XLI 309

*KEITH Alexander   LL D 1967
MA(Aberd) 1916
farmer and writer; *AUR* XLII 155
d Stonehaven 5.10.78 *AUR* XLVIII 103 & 61

KENNEDY Archibald Cowan   LL D 1963
DD
regius prof Hebrew and semitic lang Aberd 1932–62; *AUR* XL 170
d 1.3.66

KLOSTER Robert   LL D 1962
Kt of Order of St Olav MA PhD(Oslo)
dir of the Vestlandske Kunstindustrimuseum Bergen from 1949; *AUR* XXXIX 348
d 7.2.79

KNEALE William Calvert   LL D 1960
MA(Oxon) FBA
fell. and tut. in philosophy at Exeter Coll Oxford; *AUR* XXXVIII 556

LARSEN Carl Syrach   LL D 1966
MF Dr Agr PhD
dir of the Arboretum of the Royal Veterinary and Agricultural College at Horshølm Denmark from 1937; *AUR* XLI 311
deceased

LASCELLES The Rt Hon George Henry Hubert the Earl of Harewood   LL D 1966
artistic dir of the Edinburgh International Festival of music and drama 1961–65; *AUR* XLI 263

LAUTERPACHT Hersch (Sir)   LL D 1959
QC MA LL D(Cantab) Dr Jur Dr Sc Pol(Vienna) FBA
judge of the International Court of Justice at the Hague; *AUR* XXXVIII 177
d 8.5.60

*LAWRENCE Philip Douglas   DD 1966
MA(Aberd) 1919
minister of Rubislaw church Aber from 1940; *AUR* XLI 314
d Aber 1.6.67 *AUR* XLII 184

LEAVIS Frank Raymond   LL D 1970
 PhD Hon Litt D(Leeds, York)
reader in Engl Cambridge univ 1959–62; fell. Downing
coll 1936–62; edit. *Scrutiny* 1932–53; *AUR* XLIV 95
d –.4.78 *AUR* XLVII 361

LEDERER Edgar   LL D 1968
 DrPhil(Vienna) Dr-ès-Sc Phys(Paris)
prof biol chem univ of Paris at Orsay 1959; dir of the Institute for the Chemistry of Natural Substances at Gif-
sur-Yvette (Central National de la Recherche Scientifique)
from 1960; *AUR* XLII 317

*LEITCH Isabella   LL D 1965
 OBE MA(Aberd) 1911 DSc(Aberd) 1919
dir of the Commonwealth Bureau of Animal Nutrition
1946–60; *AUR* XLI 118
d Aust 21.7.80 *AUR* XLIX 66

LENNOX Robert Smith   LL D 1970
 JP
Lord Provost of the City of Aberdeen and ex-officio mem-
ber univ court Aberd 1967–70; *AUR* XLIV 92

*LILLIE John Adam   LL D 1967
 QC MA(Aberd) 1906 LL B(Edin)
sheriff of the counties of Fife and Kinross from 1941 and
Convener of the Sheriffs 1960–65; *AUR* XLII 153

*LOCKHART Robert Douglas   LL D 1965
 MB ChB(Aberd) 1918 ChM(Aberd) MD(Birm)
prof anat Birm univ 1931–38; regius prof anat Aberd
1938–64; *AUR* XLI 119

*MacDONALD Donald   DD 1961
 MA(Aberd) 1913 BD(Aberd) 1920
chap. on the Indian Ecclesiastical Establishment 1924–46;
min of Well Road ch Moffat 1946–58; *AUR* XXXIX 173

*MACDONALD Donald John   LL D 1957
 MA(Aberd) 1923
rector Inverness r acad from 1944; *AUR* XXXVII 182

*McHARDY William Duff   DD 1958
 MA(Aberd) 1932 BD(Aberd) 1935 MA(Edin) DPhil
(Oxon)
Samuel Davidson prof O T stud. London univ from 1948;
AUR XXXVII 393

*McINTOSH Ian Donald   LL D 1962
 MA(Aberd) 1930 MA(Cantab)
head George Watson's coll Edin 1953–58; head Fettes
coll Edin from 1958; *AUR* XXXIX 349
d Edin 18.1.75 *AUR* XLVI 238

MACIVER Robert Morrison   LL D 1969 (in absentia)
 MA DPhil Hon Litt D Hon DSc Hon LHD Hon LLD
lect political sc Aberd 1907–15; prof political sc univ
Toronto 1915–27; prof at Barnard coll USA 1927–29;
prof sociology Columbia univ 1929–50; *AUR* XLIII 189
d 16.6.70 *AUR* XI III 189 & XLIV 112

MACKIE James Alexander   LL D 1958
 CBE JP FCIS
magistrate and member Aberdeen town council from
1940; governor of Robert Gordon's Colleges Aber from
1938; *AUR* XXXVII 397
d Aber 9.11.63

MACKIE Maitland   LL D 1957
 OBE
chmn Board of Governors of NOSCA 1947–56; *AUR*

XXXVII 180
d Tarves 30.7.75

MacKINNON Donald MacKenzie   DD 1961
 MA(Oxon)
regius prof moral phil Aberd 1947–60; Norris-Hulse prof
of divinity Cambridge univ from 1960; *AUR* XXXIX 174

McMILLAN William   LL D 1957
 CVO RA RBS
Sculptor; *AUR* XXXVII 183

MARWICK Hugh   LL D 1956
 OBE MA DLitt(Edin) Chevalier of the Royal Norwegian Order of St Olaf
hon sheriff substitute of Orkney from 1936; dir of educ
for Orkney 1929–46; *AUR* XXXVII 82
d Orkney 21.5.65 *AUR* XLI 155

MATTHEWS James Robert   LL D 1960
 CBE MA(Edin) FLS FRSE
regius prof bot Aberd 1934–59; *AUR* XXXVIII 557
d Banchory 12.4.78

MAYNEORD William Valentine   LL D 1969
 CBE DSc FRS FInstP
prof of physics as applied to med Lond univ 1940–64;
trustee of the National Gallery from 1966; *AUR* XLIII 193

MELVILLE Harry Work   LL D 1957
 PhD(Edin, Cantab) DSc(Edin) MSc(Birm) FRS
prof chem Aberd 1943–48; secy DSIR from 1956; *AUR*
XXXVII 181

*MILNE John Nelson   LL D 1960
 BCom(Aberd) 1922 MA(Aberd) 1946 LL B(Aberd)
1947
convener of the bus. comm of the General Council Aberd;
AUR XXXIX 43

MITTON Charles Leslie   DD 1964
 MTh PhD
prin Handsworth (Methodist) coll Birmingham from
1955; *AUR* XL 382

*NEILL Robert Macfarlane   LL D 1965
 MC MA(Glas) DSc(Aberd) 1941 FRSE
successively asst lect and reader in dept of natural hist
Aberd 1920–64; *AUR* XLI 120
d 30.7.69

NEUBERGER Albert   LL D 1967
 CBE MD PhD FRS FRIC
prof chem path. St Mary's hosp Lond univ from 1955;
AUR XLII 156

NICHOLSON Edward Max   LL D 1964
 CB
dir general of The Nature Conservancy from 1952; *AUR*
XL 378

*NICOL Thomas James Trail   DD 1968
 MBE MC MA(Aberd) 1938
asst chap. general to the Forces; *AUR* XLII 314

NISSIOTIS Nikos   DD 1967
 DD
prof theol Athens univ; prof theol and, from August 1966,
dean of the Graduate School and dir at the Ecumenical
Inst at Bossey; *AUR* XLII 161

*NOBLE Thomas Alexander Fraser   LL D 1968
 MBE MA(Aberd) 1938
vice chancellor Leic univ from 1962; *AUR* XLIII 70

PERY Edmund Colquhoun 5th Earl of Limerick
LL D 1961

GBE KCB DSO TD
Lieutenant of the City of London; chmn of the Medical
Research Council 1952–60; *AUR* xxxix 178
d 4.8.67

PITT Harry Raymond   LL D 1970
PhD FRS
lect maths Aberd 1939–42; prof maths Queen's univ Belfast 1945–50; prof pure maths Nott univ 1950–64; vice
chancellor R'dg univ from 1964; *AUR* xliv 94

PLEYDELL-BOUVERIE William, Seventh Earl of
Radnor   LL D 1959
KCVO
chmn Forestry Commission from 1952; *AUR* xxxviii 177
d 23.11.68 *AUR* xliii 86

POLANYI Michael   LL D 1959
DSc(Princ, Leeds) MD PhD (Budapest) MSc(Manc)
FRS
prof soc stud. Victoria univ Manc 1948–58; *AUR* xxxviii
178

*RAE Francis William   DD 1965
MA(Aberd) 1931 BD(Aberd) 1924 STM
min par of Cardonald in Glasg presb from 1948; *AUR* xli
124

*RAE James   DD 1956
MA(Aberd) 1910 BD(Aberd) 1914
lately moderator of the General Assembly of the Presby-
terian Church of England; *AUR* xxxvii 82
d Lond 4.5.60 *AUR* xxxviii 589

RAILTON Ruth   LL D 1960
OBE FRAM FRMCM
founder of the National Youth Orchestra of Great
Britain; *AUR* xxxviii 557

REID George Thomson Henderson   DD 1969
MC MA BD(Edin)
min W Church of St Andrew Aber from 1955; *AUR* xliii
195

RENGSTORF Karl Heinrich   DD 1962
ordinary prof N T theology and exegesis in the West-
fälische Wilhelms Universität Münster from 1948; *AUR*
xxxix 345

RIEGER Clarence Oscar Ferroro (Sir)   LL D 1969
CBE MB BS FRCSE
hon consult. surg at Adelaide Children's hosp; past pres
of the Blue Cross Association of Australia; pres of the
Australian Medical Association from 1967 and immediate
past pres of the BMC; *AUR* xliii 238

*ROBERTSON Alexander   LL D 1958
MA(Aberd) 1919 BSc PhD(Glas) FRS
Heath Harrison prof chem Liv univ 1933–57; member of
the University Grants Committee; *AUR* xxxvii 397
d Grantham 9.2.70 *AUR* xliii 444

ROBERTSON James Jackson   LL D 1956
OBE MA(Glas) BD(Lond) FRSE FEIS JP
rector Aberdeen Grammar School from 1942; *AUR*
xxxvii 82
d 9.6.70 *AUR* xliv 112

ROE Frederick Charles   LL D 1958
MA(Birm) L-es-L(Lyons) D de l'univ (Paris, Rennes,

Cler Ferr) Chev Leg d'H Laur Fr acad
prof French Aberd 1932–57; *AUR* xxxvii 398
d 6.12.58 *AUR* xxxviii 12

ROSS Frank Mackenzie (The Honourable)   LL D 1961
CMG MC KStJ LL D(Br Col)
Lieut Governor of the province of British Columbia
1955–60; *AUR* xxxix 178
d 11.12.71

RUPP Ernest Gordon   DD 1962
MA DD(Cantab)
prof ecclesiastical hist Manc univ from 1956; *AUR* xxxix
346

SCOTT Peter Markham   LL D 1963
CBE DSC
rector Aberd 1960–63; *AUR* xl 176

SCOTT Robert Balgarnie Young   DD 1968
MA BD PhD DD(Tor)
prof religion Princeton univ from 1955; *AUR* xlii 314

SHAW Charles James Dalrymple, The Honourable Lord
Kilbrandon   LL D 1965
QC BA LL B
senator of the College of Justice in Scotland and Lord of
Session from 1959; chmn Scottish Law Commission;
AUR xli 117

*SHEPHERD Anna (Nan)   LL D 1964
MA(Aberd) 1915
lect Engl at Aberdeen Training Centre for Teachers 1915–
56; *AUR* xl 382
d Aber 27.2.81 *AUR* xlix 136

*SIMPSON William Douglas   LL D 1960
OBE MA(Aberd) 1919 DLitt(Aberd) 1924 FSA
FSAScot
lib Aberd and regist of the General Council; *AUR* xxxix
44
d Aber 9.10.68 *AUR* xliii 24, 27

SKYDSGAARD Kristen Ejner   DD 1968
DTheol
prof dogmatics and N T exegesis in Copenhagen univ and
dir of the Ecumenical Institute, Copenhagen; *AUR* xliii
71

*SMITH John   LL D 1965
MBChB(Aberd) 1915 MD DSc(Aberd)
chief bacteriologist in the City Hospital Aber 1920–58;
AUR xli 121
d Aber 19.6.76

SMITH Thomas Broun   LL D 1969
QC MA DCL LL D FBA
prof Scots law Aberd 1949–58; prof civil law Edin univ
1958–68 then prof Scots law there; *AUR* xliii 188

SOUCEK Josef Bobuslav   DD 1969
Hon D Theol
prof of N T in Prague univ and dean of the Comenius
Faculty of Protestant Theol in the univ from 1966; member of the Ecumenical Council of Churches in Czechoslovakia; *AUR* xliii 197
d –.9.72

*STEEL David   DD 1964
MA(Aberd) 1932 BD(Aberd) 1935
min par of St Michael's Linlithgow from 1959; *AUR* xl
383

STEPHEN George   LL D 1959
  Lord Provost of the City of Aberdeen and ex-officio member of the univ court Aberd from 1955; *AUR* xxxviii 178
d Aber 18.1.72

STEVEN Henry Marshall   LL D 1964
  CBE PhD FRSE
prof for. Aberd 1938–63; *AUR* xl 379
d 15.2.69

STEVEN William   DD 1960
  min Queen's Park West Church Glasg; *AUR* xxxviii 553
d 31.8.64 *AUR* xli 61

STRÖMBACK Dag Alvar   LL D 1958
  Fil Dr(Uppsala)
prof Scandinavian and Comparative Folklore Uppsala univ from 1948; *AUR* xxxvii 399
d 1.12.78

SUNDKLER Bengt Gustaf Malcolm   DD 1967
  D Th
prof church history Uppsala univ from 1949; dir of the Swedish Institute for Missionary Research from 1951; bishop of Bukoba Tanzania 1962–65; *AUR* xlii 162

SUTHERLAND Joan (Mrs Richard Bonynge)
                                                    LL D 1968
  CBE
prima donna of the Royal Opera House Covent Garden from 1952; *AUR* xlii 309

SWANN Michael Meredith   LL D 1967
  MA PhD FRS FRSE
prof natural hist Edin univ 1952–65; prin and vice chancellor from 1965; *AUR* xlii 157; Kt 1972; chmn BBC from 1973

*SWAPP George   LL D 1961
  DCM MM JP C St J MB ChB(Aberd) 1924
g p in the city of Aberdeen; *AUR* xxxix 179
d Aber 24.5.69 *AUR* xliii 213

*TAYLOR William   LL D 1962
  CB MA(Aberd) 1913
under secretary at Min of Labour 1946–52; chancellor's assessor to the univ court Aberd from 1955; *AUR* xxxix 349

*THOMSON Arthur Landsborough (Sir)   LL D 1956
  CB OBE MA(Aberd) 1911 DSc(Aberd) 1920
second secy to the MRC from 1949; *AUR* xxxvii 82
d 9.6.77 *AUR* xlvii 286

THURIAN Pere Max   DD 1964
  dep prior to the community of Taize; *AUR* xl 384

TOOTHILL John Norman (Sir)   LL D 1966
  published the *Toothill Report on the Scottish Economy* 1961; *AUR* xli 264

VON ALLMEN Jean-Jacques   DD 1970
  Dr Theol
prof practical theology in Neuchatel univ; *AUR* xliv 96

WADDINGTON Conrad Hal   LL D 1966
  CBE ScD DSc FRS
Buchanan prof anim genetics Edin univ from 1947; *AUR* xli 312
d Edin 29.9.75

*WALKER Horace   DD 1967
  MA(Aberd) 1932 BD(Aberd) 1935
secy depute of the Home Board of the Ch of Scot. 1948–57; secy from 1957; *AUR* xliii 158

WALKER Norman Thomson   LL D 1966
  OBE PhD
successively lect and reader in education and head of the dept of educ Aberd 1925–60; dir of extra mural stud. Aberd 1955–65; *AUR* xli 310
d 20.4.75 *AUR* xlvi 327

*WATSON William Hay   DD 1964
  MA(Aberd) 1929
missionary of the C of S in Livingstonia and Blantyre from 1933; *AUR* xl 385

*WATT Archibald   DD 1959
  MA(Aberd) 1923 STM
min of Edzell par ch and convener of the social service comm of the General Assembly of C of S; *AUR* xxxviii 175
d Aber 1.1.81 *AUR* xlix 137

WATT William Montgomery   DD 1966
  MA BLitt PhD
lect, then reader and from 1964 prof of Arabic in Edin univ; *AUR* xli 316

WILSON William Combe   LL D 1963
  FRCSE
regius prof surg Aberd 1939–62; *AUR* xl 172
d 12.3.74 *AUR* xlv 451

WOOTON Barbara Frances (Baroness Wooton of
                                       Abinger)   LL D 1969
  MA Hon LHD Hon LL D Hon DSc
prin Morley coll for Working Men and Women 1926–27; dir of stud. in adult educ Lond univ 1927–44; reader, later prof in soc stud. London univ 1944–52; *AUR* xliii 190

YOUNG Frank George   LL D 1965
  FRS FRIC DSc PhD MA
prof biochem Cambridge univ from 1949 and master of Darwin coll; *AUR* xli 122

YOUNG John Stirling   LL D 1963
  MC MD FRSE
regius prof path Aberd 1937–62; *AUR* xl 173
d Aber –.10.71

SECTION II

SUPPLEMENT
TO ROLL OF GRADUATES 1860–1955

ABD-EL-ALL Mostafa Shukri Abd-el-Halim
PhD 1955

ABEL or Falconer, Catherine Florence   MA 1935
d 29.12.71

ABERCROMBY Ann McLean Riddell   MA 1917
d Aber 21.3.70 *AUR* XLIII 442

ABERCROMBY Edward George   BSc(eng) 1931
FICE MIWE
dep new works eng from 1959: King Geo VI reservoir
Staines, Qu Eliz II reservoir Walton-on-Thames, filtrat
works Ashford Common, Thames–Lee Tunnel main;
retd 1.4.68

ABERCROMBY Norman Jackson   *MA 1923
officier de l'ordre des Palmes Académiques 1970;
head of Fr dept George Heriot's s Edin 1940–63; retd

ABERDEEN Jennie Watson   *MA 1919 PhD 1934
lect Engl and dep prin Avery Hill coll Lond 1934–
58; retd; resid Aber

ABERNETHY Barclay Chivas   MB ChB 1949
b Aber 18.1.28
FRCSE 1958 FRCS 1959
sen surg regist E Fife hosp 1960–66; consult surg
E Fife hosp based at Vict Hosp Kirkcaldy from 1966

ABERNETHY David Forbes   BSc(agr) 1955
farmer Rosehearty from 1958
m Rosehearty 16.7.66 Mary Duncan teacher d of
George S. D. Rosehearty

ABERNETHY Elizabeth Anna
BSc 1945 *1947 MB ChB 1958
sen h o dermat and vd Aber 1960–61; asst clin chem
dept Aber 1961–62; res asst dept mental health Aber
1968–72; regist mental deficiency Woodlands hosp
Aber 1972–75; consult mental deficiency Ladysbridge
hosp Banff from 1975
m Aber 5.4.60 George R. Law MA 1957 *qv*; marr. diss
1974

ABERNETHY or Anderson, Hilda Mary   MA 1949

ABERNETHY James   BSc(eng) 1951
d Cupar 17.9.68 *AUR* XLIII 86

ABERNETHY James Smart   MA 1929 LLB 1931
d Kingston Moray 25.5.76

ABRIOUX Olivier Marie   PhD 1949

ADAM Alexander   MB ChB 1942
clin lect surg Aberd 1962–70, clin sen lect from 1970

ADAM Ann Ida   MA 1931
LRAM 1933
teacher: Badenscoth 1949, Inverurie 1953; retd 1971
m 1934 George D. Rowe
d Inverurie 17.5.75

ADAM Anne Grigor   MA 1935

ADAM Catherine Kennedy   MB ChB 1951
FFARCS 1960
regist anaest: Southampton 1957–59, Mt Vernon hosp
Northwood 1959–60, sen regist anaest Sheffield 1960–
61, consult. anaest Kirkcaldy from 1961

ADAM David Thain   BSc(agr) 1923
member of tc Royal Burgh Forfar from May 1961
wife d 1.9.55

ADAM or Cameron, Eliza Smith   MA 1942
d 2.5.75

ADAM George   BSc 1910
no longer on GC reg

ADAM Gertrude Bryce   MA 1935
teacher Mile End s from 1937

ADAM Hugh Grant   MA 1912

ADAM James Horatius George   MA 1929

ADAM Jane   MA 1935

ADAM or Falconer, Janet Scott   MA 1922
no longer on GC reg

ADAM John   MB ChB 1926
no longer on GC reg

ADAM John Law   MB ChB 1890

ADAM or Lawson, Olive Bessie
***BSc 1946 PhD 1960**
univ of Melbourne: sen dem bot 1960–73, prin
tut. from 1973

ADAM Peter   *MA 1936
d 9.9.65 *AUR* XLI 250

ADAM William   MA 1902 *BD 1908
d Milnathort 13.7.61 *AUR* XXXIX 270

ADAM William   MA 1947 BSc(agr) 1949
farm. Banchory

ADAM William James   MB ChB 1922
d Eastbourne 24.7.67 *AUR* XLII 359

ADAMS or Dawson, Anne Elizabeth   MA 1928
resid Fingask Fraserburgh

ADAMS Arthur Richard   MB ChB 1949
FRCPE 1972 RD
Western Aust: phys in charge chest unit repatriation
gen hosp Hollywood 1964–68, Sir Charles Gairdner
hosp Shenton Park, clin lect Univ of W Aust from
1968
surg comm RANR

ADAMS or Sim, Christina Margaret   MA 1948

ADAMS Eleanor Mary   MB ChB 1954 ᶜMD 1960
g p Derby: asst 1961–62, prin from 1962
d Derby 14.7.79 *AUR* XLVIII 354

ADAMS George   MB ChB 1951
g p: Seahouses 1961–69, Spennymoor from 1972

ADAMS James Henderson   BSc 1947
MIPlantE 1961 CEng 1972 FInstF 1974
NCB East Midlands: fuel tech 1959–64, area fuel tech 1964–68; Midlands Sales reg area fuel tech from 1968

ADAMS John Charles   MA 1927
d Natal S Af 31.7.76

ADAMS John Jackson   *MA 1954 MEd 1956
asst dir of educ Dun 1961–62, Lanarksh 1962–66; dep dir of educ Glasg 1966–71, sen dep dir of educ from 1972
d Plymouth 1.6.74 *AUR* xlvi 111

ADAMS or Anderson, Lily Christine Gray   *MA 1920
d Forres 21.10.72

ADAMS or Alexander, Margaret Ross   *BSc 1931
resid Banchory

ADAMS or Ritchie, Marjory Mabel   MA 1954

ADAMS William   MB ChB 1924
g p Leeds; retd 1970

ADAMS William   BSc(agr) 1941
farm. Anguston Peterculter

ADAMS William Main   BSc 1949 BSc(eng) 1953

ADAMSON or Petrie, Elma   MA 1949

ADAN Harold George Wickham   *BSc 1897
d Aber 20.12.65 *AUR* xli 236

ADDIE Annie Frances   MA 1933
teacher Oakbank s Aber; retd 1964

ADDIE or Pickard, Margaret Sybil   MA 1925
resid Lond

ADDISON Alexander   MB ChB 1954
DObstRCOG 1960 MRCGP 1966
h o Woodend hosp Aber 1954–55; capt RAMC jun med spec 1955–58; h o Bellshill mat. hosp Lanarksh 1958–59; g p Douglas, Lanarksh from 1959
m Aber 24.8.55 Joan Wood RGN d of John W. Bucksburn

ADDISON George Munro   MA 1931
d Botriphnie 24.9.69 *AUR* xliii 331

ADDISON John   BSc(eng) 1945
d 1981

ADDISON Rodney Murison   BL 1949
ABSI 1963 FIA 1967 OBE 1976
staff solic and loans man. Malaya Borneo Bldg Soc Kuala Lumpur 1957–63; ptnr Wilsone & Duffus advoc Aber from 1964; tech asst expert ODM 1963, 1967, 1969; chmn Scot. group bldg soc inst 1969–71; secy City of Aber savings comm 1963–70, chmn from

1970; chmn Grampian reg sav comm and vice chmn Nat sav comm for Scot. from 1975; hon secy Aber branch RNLI 1965–74, chmn from 1974; member exec comm Scot. Life Boat council from 1965; secy treas Victoria model lodging house Aber 1966–75

ADDISON William   MA 1908 BSc 1909
d Banff 9.4.62 *AUR* xxxiv 376

ADDISON William Eric   PhD 1953
BSc(Glas) 1948
sen lect inorg chem Nott from 1964; dep regist UMIST from 1967

ADEL Emanuel Paul   MB ChB 1934

ADIE Albert Reith   MA 1936
headmaster Braemar s

ADIE Margaret   *MA 1933
teacher Engl Aber until 1975; retd

AGASSIZ Cuthbert Delaval Shafto
                MB ChB 1908 DPH 1910 *MD 1912
d 16.11.72

AHMED Mohammed Abdel Maged   MA 1955

AIKEN or Brebner, Doris Margaret
                MA 1944 Dip Ed 1953
Kingston Canada: fac admin off. Queen's univ 1967–75; asst regist from 1976
m(2) Kingston 1.8.73 Bruce K. Laughton MA(Oxon) univ prof s of Norman B. L. MB(Edin) Fordingbridge

AIKEN Edith Elizabeth Smith   MA 1938
teacher Aber until 1944

AIKEN or Reid, Gladys   MA 1952

AIKMAN Thomson Smith   BCom 1928
retd 1973
d Aber 8.4.74 *AUR* xlv 448 and xlvi 109

AIRD Robert   MA 1897 MB ChB 1901
d 1.3.64

AIRLIE William Higgins   MA 1948
b Glasg 26.10.20
prin teacher Engl/maths Kintore s from 1960

AITKEN or Clunie, Agnes Smith   BSc 1924
d 4.12.68

AITKEN Albert Stuart   MA 1953 LLB 1955
TD
ptnr A. C. Morrison & Richards advoc Aber from 1959 major RASC/RCT(TA) 2 1/C 153 Regt RCT Dunf from 1967

AITKEN Angus   *BSc 1950 PhD 1954
sen scient off. MAFF exper factory Aber 1959–61; sen scient off./prin scient off. Torry res stat Aber from 1961
m Aber 30.9.61 Wilma W. Smith BSc 1954 *qv*

AITKEN Arthur Jeffrey Hood   MB ChB 1944
 d Clacton 9.2.63

AITKEN Donald Andrew   ^cMB ChB 1954

AITKEN Dorothy Ritchie   MA 1954
 teacher: Beauly 1960–61, Inzievar s Oakley 1961–
62, Blacklaw s Dunfermline 1962, St Leonards,
Dunfermline 1968–70, Lat Dunfermline h s from
1970
m Dunf 24.10.60 Allan Hempseed surv s of Henry H.
Rosyth
d 15.2.74

AITKEN or Bradley, Elizabeth Handley   MA 1945
 teacher: Magwa Asian j s s Jinja Uganda 1960–62,
Victoria Nile s Jinja 1963–64, Arusha s Tanzania
1964–71, Victoria Nile s 1971–72, Jinja sen s s 1972;
ptnr/prop. with husb gen store/sub PO Skegness from
1973

AITKEN or Hancock, Elizabeth Mary   BSc 1954

AITKEN or Reid, Ella Taylor   MA 1916
 d 1972

AITKEN Elsie Mary   MA 1925

AITKEN Henry   MB ChB 1928
 FRCSE 1938
consult. surg oto-rhino laryngology Royal Victoria
hosp, Ulster hosp Belfast; retd 1972

AITKEN Hilda   MB ChB 1947 DPH 1965
dept m o health dept city of Aber now dept commun
med Grampian health board from 1965

AITKEN or Gilmore, Isobel   MA 1951
 teacher: Victoria Rd p s Aber until 1960, temp
teaching Scone and Perth 1975–77, Robert Douglass
mem s Perth from 1977

AITKEN John   BSc(for) 1922
 retd 1964

**AITKEN or Griffith, Leslie Mercy Veronica
　　　　　　　　　　　　　　MB ChB 1948**
 clin asst Hurstwood Park hosp Haywards Heath
1968–70; g p (ptnr) Worcester from 1971

AITKEN Margaret Ferrier   BSc 1920
 d 1962

AITKEN or Chalmers, Margaret Stuart   MA 1945
 teacher Camberley from 1970

AITKEN Robin Christopher   BSc(eng) 1945

AITKEN Thomas   *MA 1949

ÅKERBERG Blenda Clarice   MA 1949
 teacher: Walker Rd p s Aber from 1972
d Aber 30.10.75

ALEXANDER Alexandra Duncan   MA 1916
 d Nairn 15.6.74 *AUR* xlvi 107

ALEXANDER or Dale, Audrey Jean   MA 1944
 Aber: teacher Kaimhill s 1955–60, part-time pre-
nursing coll, coll of comm 1960–77

ALEXANDER Doreen Wood   *MA 1950

**ALEXANDER or Taggart, Doris Elizabeth
　　　　　　　　　　　　　　MA 1948**

**ALEXANDER or Storm, Elizabeth Ann Murison
　　　　　　　　　　　　　　*MA 1915**

ALEXANDER Eric Archie   BSc(eng) 1945
 tech Derby from 1949
m Derby 2.6.62 Jean M. Toms d of Arthur T. Derby

ALEXANDER George Sim   MA 1930
 d Kemnay 4.9.62 *AUR* xl 93

ALEXANDER Harry William   MA 1921
 teacher: dep head Victoria Rd s Aber; retd 1966
d 14.1.81

**ALEXANDER or Caird, Helen Catherine Elizabeth
　　　　　　　　　　　　　　MA 1953**

ALEXANDER Henry Gavin   MA 1944
 MA(Oxon) 1954
commonwealth fell. Univ of Minnesota 1956–57;
teacher: Maidstone g s 1960–65; head Guisborough
g s 1966–69, Hampton s Mddx from 1970
m Kew 31.3.64 Barbara A. Richards BA(Oxon) 1961
teacher d of Sydney R. Manchester

ALEXANDER Herbert Alexander Darg   MA 1915
 d 2.1.81 *AUR* xlix 135

ALEXANDER Isobel Bisset   MB ChB 1949
 DPH(Leeds) 1965 MFCM 1972
sen dep m o West Riding c c Harrogate and dep
m o h Knaresborough 1965–74; sen m o h Harrogate
N Yorks AHA from 1944

ALEXANDER James   BSc(eng) 1931
 Hong Kong: asst dir of publ works 1961–64, govt
civ eng 1964–68, retd from col serv 1968

ALEXANDER John   *MA 1898 BSc 1906
 d Aber 23.2.68 *AUR* xlii 345

ALEXANDER Joseph   MB ChB 1918
 no longer on GC reg

ALEXANDER Mary   MA 1935
 sen exper off. DSIR Lond 1938–53; tech asst to sc
attaché Br embassy Washington DC 1953–58; exec
vice-pres Herner & Co from 1958
m Washington 7.8.54 Saul Herner BS(Wisc) pres
Herner & Co

**ALEXANDER or Miller, Mary Ramsay
　　　　　　　　　　　　　　MB ChB 1942**
 N'cle: sen res assoc gyn dept 1961–63, Nuffield res
assoc midwif dept 1966–67, fam plan. from 1964 and
from 1971, loc auth Newcastle and Northumb 1971–
75; sen m o (child health) N Tyneside from 1975

ALEXANDER or Macaree, Mary Watson
MA 1943

ALEXANDER or Moffat, Maud Kilgan MA 1933

ALEXANDER Stella Margaret BSc 1936
Aber: prin teacher sc Rosemount s until 1972,
Kincorth acad 1972–73; retd

ALEXANDER William MA 1912
d Aber 14.4.66 *AUR* XLII 83

ALEXANDER William MA 1951 LLB 1954

ALEXANDER William Johnstone BSc(eng) 1945
MSc(Leeds) 1973
chief eng ITT Bell & Gossett Letchworth 1961–66;
grad certif in educ Leeds 1967; lect eng Bradford tech
coll 1967–75, sen lect from 1975

ALISON Crichton MB ChB 1915
no longer on GC reg

ALLAN Alexander MA 1931
d Aber 31.12.73

ALLAN Alice Mary MA 1928

ALLAN Alice Williamina MA 1929
retd 1971

ALLAN Charles Baird MA 1948 LLB 1950

ALLAN Charles Davidson
MB ChB 1921 DPH 1941
d Edin 4.12.74 *AUR* XLVI 236

ALLAN Cuthbert Alastair *MB ChB 1921
g p Dun
d Dun –.6.67

ALLAN Donald McKay MA 1939
d Midhurst 1973

ALLAN Douglas John Innes MA 1936
FEIS 1972 JP 1975
head Prestonpans p s from 1957

ALLAN Eva Mary MA 1928
SCM 1933
Nurs trg ARI, ERI 1929–33; midwifery trg Mother's
hosp Hackney 1933–34; Queen's nurse E Barnet
1935–40; asst supt Queen's trg home Hackney 1940–
43; supt midwives/health visitors Aber 1943–45; asst
supt nurses E Suffolk 1945–48; Queen's nurse/asst
supt Aber 1948–66; retd

ALLAN Frances MB ChB 1953
DPM(Lond) 1970 MRCPsych(Lond) 1973
asst m o h Inverness-sh 1962–66; psychiat regist
Rainhall hosp Liverpool 1966–69; sen m o (mental
health) Stirling cc; sen regist Lea Castle hosp
Kidderminster 1970–72; consult. psychiat Royal Scot.
Nat hosp Larbert from 1972

ALLAN George James MA 1923 MB ChB 1927
d 29.6.65

ALLAN George William[s] MB ChB 1901
no longer on GC reg

ALLAN Gertrude Alice Bisset MA 1932
teacher Ashley Rd s Aber from 1947; retd 1975

ALLAN or Adie, Hazel Elizabeth MA 1950
teacher until 1955

ALLAN or Palmer, Helen Margaret BSc 1942
teacher sc Bo, govt s Sierra Leone 1946–47
resid Bexhill-on-Sea

ALLAN Hellen Anderson *MA 1929
teacher mod lang; retd 1970; resid Dufftown

ALLAN Isabella May Ogg
MA 1924 MB ChB 1928 DPH 1938
d Aber 3.7.72 *AUR* XLV 127

ALLAN James Gray MA 1954
teacher: first asst Sanday s 1958–62, prin Engl
Jedburgh g s 1962–68 also dep rector 1968–76; head
Moray middle s Grangemouth from 1976

ALLAN James Sunley MB ChB 1954
DPH(Lond) 1960 DIH(Lond) 1973 FRSM
post grad stud. Lond s of hyg & trop med 1959–60;
m o Unilever Lond 1960–74; sen m o UML (Unilever)
Port Sunlight from 1974
m Glasg 1959 Mary M. Tannahill MB ChB(Glas)
1957 consult. psychiat d of Andrew R. T. Glasg
d 14.6.79 *AUR* XLVIII 354

ALLAN or Robinson, Jessie Roberta Forgan
*MA 1928

ALLAN John MA 1889

ALLAN John Birnie MA 1931 BD 1934
MBE 1963
retd 1974; resid Rochester

ALLAN John Black MA 1926 BD 1928
m Myra T. Duncan MA 1926 *qv*
resid Edin

ALLAN John Mearns MA 1904
d –.1.62

ALLAN John Murray MA 1922

ALLAN John Robertson *MA 1928
writer; resid Methlick, then Lincoln

ALLAN Leslie Christie MB ChB 1938
m o h Calgary 1960–73; dep m o h Edmonton from
1973

ALLAN Lindsay Hay MB ChB 1939
g p Barrow-in-Furness from 1946

ALLAN or Stewart, Maggie   MA 1923

ALLAN or Donaldson, Margaret   MA 1952

ALLAN or Henderson, Margaret Manson Oman
                                   MA 1943

ALLAN or Kernoff, Margaret Pirie   MB ChB 1938
   part time m o fam plan clin LCC 1948–73

ALLAN or Ritchie, Margaret Stephen   MA 1917
   Lady Ritchie 1941
d Banchory 2.6.76 *AUR* XLVII 102

ALLAN Marjorie Jane Gordon   MB ChB 1945
   res asst Royal Marsden hosp Lond from 1963

ALLAN Marjory Fyfe   MA 1927
d Montrose 4.2.73

ALLAN or MacLeod, Mary Anderson   MA 1943
   teacher: Mortlach 1961–71, Keith p s from 1971
husb *d* 27.5.72

ALLAN Mary Davidson   MA 1927 *MEd 1946
   Zambian Distinguished Service Medal 1979
prin psych M o D (air) Lond 1946–65; dir of tech aid
in occup psych Zambia 1965–67; dir of occup assessment for govt of Zambia from 1967–73
d –.9.81

ALLAN Moira Margaret   MA 1942
   teacher Rothes s from 1949

ALLAN Norman Duncan   MB ChB 1930
   retd from g p and St John ambul brig 1973
d 7.9.80 *AUR* XLIX 68

ALLAN Richard George Gordon   MB ChB 1951
   g p Scunthorpe

ALLAN Robert   MA 1948
   Dip Deaf (Chaplain) 1973
min St Andrew's North Church Kilmarnock 1961–73;
chap. to the deaf Ayrsh from 1972

ALLAN Robert Milne   MB ChB 1942
d Kilmarnock 8.1.78

ALLAN Robin Thomas Phillips   BSc(agr) 1949
   ICI: agr dev off. Yorks & Co Durham 1954–65;
tech rep agr Isle of Man from 1965

ALLAN Theodore Martin   MB ChB 1941
   asst dir N E Scot. blood transfusion serv from 1956
m Conon Bridge 1953 Isabel M. Sellar LLB(Edin) d
of Rev. John S. MA(Edin)

ALLAN William   MB ChB 1909 DPH 1912
d 30.12.66

ALLAN William Garland Leith
                        MB ChB 1946 MD 1980

ALLARDYCE Alexander   MA 1904 *BL 1907
   no longer on GC reg

ALLARDYCE or Cameron, Jean Garden   MA 1945
   soc work for handicapped and deprived ch
Portugal, Turkey, Philippines, Uruguay, Austria from
1952

ALLARDYCE Marian Jane   *MA 1912
   d Pagnell 8.1.65 *AUR* XLI 55

ALLARDYCE William Frank Gray   BSc(eng) 1953
   MICE 1959 MIWE 1964
Angus c c eng dept: asst 1956–58, sen asst 1958–64,
chief asst 1964–74, dep county eng 1974–75; asst dir
(new works-des) water serv dept Tayside reg c from
1975

ALLAWAY Ernest Edward   MB ChB 1907
   no longer on GC reg

ALLCROFT William Miller Ord
                        BSc(agr) 1930 PhD 1934
   retd from min of agr 1965; settled in NZ 1968

ALLENBY or Hughson, Myrra Hutcheon Sewell
                        ered *MA 1939 BD 1951
   teacher Aber 1972–76; retd

ALLISON Brian Johnstone   BSc(for) 1951

ALLISON Ernest Russell   BSc 1921 MB ChB 1928
   d Aber 10.7.66 *AUR* XLI 338

ALLISON Robert Whitelaw   MA 1922
   no longer on GC reg

ALLISON Thomas Philip Gray   MB ChB 1950
   g p Aber

AMONOO Kofi Alfred   *BSc 1952
   d Accra –.8.58 *AUR* XLIII 86

ANDERSON Adam Connan   BSc(agr) 1955
   asst advis NOSCA Keith, Inverurie 1957–62; tech
advis N E Farmers Aber 1962–67; farms man. Strutt
& Parker Elgin 1967–71; g p farm man. (own bus.)
Forres from 1971
m Boat of Garten 24.7.58 Shona G. MacDougall
teacher d of James M. Grantown-on-Spey

ANDERSON or Hepburn, Agnes Forbes   *MA 1953
   ARCM(violin teaching) 1968
mus critic *Press & Journal* Aber 1956–58; free lance
violinist (from 1964) e.g. for Scot. Opera; Edin: private
teacher violin from 1969, teacher violin George
Watson's coll 1968–72

ANDERSON Alan Gauld   *MA 1955
   BOCM Co: market res man. Scot. 1958–62,
asst chief cattle advis Lond 1962–66, Tomkinsons
GMBH: gen man. Hanover 1966–68, export man.
Kidderminster 1968–74; man. dir Anderson Exports
from 1974

ANDERSON Alexander   MB ChB 1932 MD 1946
   FRSM 1960
chief m o BP 1963–69; retd
d Glasg 16.9.75 *AUR* XLV 417

ANDERSON Alexander Donald Stewart   MA 1927
d Lond 5.6.62 *A UR* xxxix 383

ANDERSON Alexander George   BSc(eng) 1945
dir Aberdeen Construction Group 1969–72; chmn/
joint man. dir William Tawse Aber from 1972

ANDERSON Alexander Greig
    MA 1905 *MB ChB 1909 *MD 1914 LLD 1949
d Aber 21.5.61 *A UR* xxxix 200

ANDERSON Alexander Wilson   BSc 1913

ANDERSON Alred Lyall Smith   MB ChB 1941
g p Holmfirth from 1950

ANDERSON or Lawrence, Amanda Margaret
    MA 1949

ANDERSON Andrew Black   *MA 1923
d 22.1.63

ANDERSON or Watson, Angelica
    ***MA 1914 *BSc 1914**
d 9.3.62 *A UR* xxxix 380

ANDERSON or Esslemont, Annabel Margaret
    MA 1947
head teacher: Aldbar by Brechin 1964–73, Careston
by Brechin from 1973

ANDERSON or Ferguson, Annie   MB ChB 1919

ANDERSON Annie   MB ChB 1920
MBE 1970
g p Oldmeldrum from 1947

ANDERSON or Hill, Annie Cecilia Stewart
    MA 1935

ANDERSON or Christie, Annie Isabella   MA 1927
teacher Sunderland 1929–32

ANDERSON Annie Jane   MA 1919 BSc 1922

ANDERSON Archibald Stirling Kennedy
    MA 1909 *MB ChB 1914 DPH 1921
d –.3.72

ANDERSON Audrey Lucy   MA 1949

ANDERSON or Bourne, Barbara Eileen
    MB ChB 1945
part time clin m o Barnet AHA from 1974

ANDERSON Beatrice Margaret   MA 1946

ANDERSON Betty Ann Forbes   MA 1949
teacher: BFES s Sennelager Germany 1958–61,
Highgate h s Kuala Lumpur 1961–64, Buckie h s
(p dept) 1965–67, head Inveravon p s Ballindalloch
from 1967

ANDERSON Caroline Mary   MA 1929
teacher Methlick; retd 1970

ANDERSON or Macdonald, Catherine   MA 1944

ANDERSON Catherine Gifford Isbister   MA 1927

ANDERSON Charles   MB ChB 1926
g p Burnley 1937–62; retd
deceased

ANDERSON Charles Ernest   BSc(eng) 1952
contr eng (elect.) Bowater Paper Corp North Fleet
1952–70; retd

ANDERSON Charles James Barton   MB ChB 1940
surg Arbroath from 1957

ANDERSON David   *BSc 1952 MEd 1954
d 16.10.77

ANDERSON David Bruce   *BSc 1955 PhD 1959

ANDERSON Davidson Wallace   BSc 1948
asst head/prin maths Moray s s Grangemouth
1961–68; rector: Camelon h s Falkirk 1968–74,
Woodlands h s Falkirk from 1974

ANDERSON or Taylor, Dora   *MA 1922
head teacher Engl Mortlach s s Dufftown 1923–25;
tut. asst Engl univ of Cape Town 1927; lect in
children's lit Buxton Nursery School Training Centre
Claremont Cape 1938–40; secy to jun lit soc Cape
Town 1942–62; writer of articles on S Af lit for '*Trek*'
Cape Town 1942–48
d Hemel Hempstead 12.10.76

ANDERSON Edith Kathrine   MA 1934
teacher until 1950

ANDERSON Edward   MB ChB 1946
MRCGP 1968 JP
g p Glenlivet from 1965

ANDERSON Edward James   BSc 1946
NCB: reg opencast man. (dev) W. Midlands 1964–
68; reg opencast man. (dev) Central 1968–74; reg
opencast geol Central E from 1974
m 15.3.52

ANDERSON Edwin   MB ChB 1942
b 20.8.1918
g p Gillingham from 1947
m Gillingham 7.5.60 Rosalind M. L. Darby LRCP g p
d of Frederic M. D. Warrington

ANDERSON Elizabeth Margaret   MA 1954

ANDERSON Elizabeth Margaret Davidson
    MA 1926

ANDERSON Elizabeth Mary Stewart   MA 1951
teacher Engl: Ballater s 1956–67, Cults acad from
1967

ANDERSON or Twatt, Elizabeth Norman
    MA 1933

ANDERSON or Nesbitt, Ella   MA 1931
   teacher kindergarten Albyn s for girls Aber 1960–71; retd; resid Oldmeldrum

ANDERSON or Pirie, Ella Edith   MA 1904

ANDERSON Eric Alexander
                     MA 1949 Dip Ed 1956

ANDERSON Ernest Arthur   BSc(for) 1942

ANDERSON Ethel Margaret   MA 1930
   teacher geog Ellon acad 1947–70
d Aber 17.9.74

ANDERSON Francis   MB ChB 1904
   no longer on GC reg

ANDERSON George Menzies   MB ChB 1923
   g p Manchester from 1926

ANDERSON George Stevenson   MB ChB 1938
   consult. surg Inv from 1964

ANDERSON George Walter   MA 1955 MEd 1957
   DEP(Glasg) 1965
psych Glasg 1963–68; head Nerston resid s E Kilbride 1968–70; dep prin psych Fife from 1970
m Aber 14.4.62 Lilian M. Brockie

ANDERSON George Walter Fraser
                     MA 1928 MB ChB 1933
   Tangier from 1934

ANDERSON George William
                     MA 1953 *MEd 1968

ANDERSON Gordon Rae   *MA 1949
   MA(Cantab) 1966
asst secy Aberd 1963–65; Cambridge: asst registrary 1965–70, sen asst registrary from 1970

ANDERSON Hazel Leith   *MA 1944
   prin teacher classics Aber h s for girls 1964–73; asst head Harlaw acad Aber from 1973

ANDERSON or Geddes, Helen Isobel   MA 1914
   d Aber 20.8.71 *AUR* XLIV 316

ANDERSON Henry Francis   BSc(eng) 1939

ANDERSON Ian Alfred
            BSc 1929 *1930 *MB ChB 1933 *MD 1950
   FRCPath
retd 1970
m Aber 31.10.36 Kathleen I. W. Duthie d of David H. D. MA 1893 *qv*(I, II)

ANDERSON Ian Hall   MB ChB 1952
   MIH (Harv) 1960 Certificate Military Medicine (Air) (Canadian Forces Med Council) 1968 FAMA 1970
RCAF: 1 Air Div Zweibrucken Germany 1960–65; inst of aviat med Toronto 1965–71; sen consult. civ aviation med–fed govt Ottawa from 1971

ANDERSON Ian Vernon   MB ChB 1955

ANDERSON Irene Rosalind   *MA 1950
   teacher Engl Vigo, Spain 1960; free-lance translating of books etc., abstracting scient papers, edit., mss, original writing from 1963
m(2) Pitlochry 12.6.79 Garth Logan

ANDERSON or Child, Isabel Cruden   MA 1938

ANDERSON or Ritchie, Isabel Innes   MA 1938
   teacher Engl Old Aber s from 1959; retd

ANDERSON or Manley, Isabella Lamont   MA 1935
   d Aber 18.1.62

ANDERSON or Mackworth, Isabella Largie
                     MA 1903
   d 13.7.67 *AUR* XLIV 178

ANDERSON or Way, Isobel Margaret   MA 1938

ANDERSON James   MA 1890

ANDERSON James   MA 1912
   no longer on GC reg

ANDERSON James   BSc(agr) 1938

ANDERSON James Adams   MB ChB 1951
   g p Skegness from 1957

ANDERSON James Bruce   MA 1910 MB ChB 1910

ANDERSON James Reid   *BSc 1921
   d Montrose 12.8.71 *AUR* XLIV 319

ANDERSON James Stirling
            MA 1914 *1919 *MB ChB 1921 *MD 1923
   retd 1956; resid Barrington

ANDERSON Jane Barbara Carrie
                     MA 1925 BSc 1925 *1926
   retd 1962

ANDERSON Janet Watson   MB ChB 1945
   m o (mat. & ch health) Nairobi 1965–71
m Nairobi 1966 James O'Gorman agr eng

ANDERSON Jean   MA 1955
   resid Aber
m Aber 19.6.64 Laurence I. Walterson MB ChB 1957 *qv*

ANDERSON or Ferguson, Jean Stuart   MA 1948
   resid Glenrothes

ANDERSON or Geddes, Joan Grant   MA 1954
   teacher: asst prin biol Banff acad from 1969

ANDERSON John   MB ChB 1916

ANDERSON John   MB ChB 1938
   g p Shaftesbury, Stockton and Seaham Harbour from 1947

ANDERSON John Christie   MB ChB 1904
deceased

ANDERSON John James Hall   MB ChB 1921
d Jersey –.9.64 *AUR* XL 399

ANDERSON John Leonard   BSc(agr) 1954

ANDERSON John Rognvald   MB ChB 1943
g p: Scourie 1963–65, Gloucester from 1965

ANDERSON or Hall, Katherine Evelyn   MA 1933

ANDERSON or Gare, Margaret Ann Taylor
MA 1941

ANDERSON Margaret Brown   MA 1935
teacher Hanover St s Aber 1936–73; retd

ANDERSON or Angus, Margaret Collie   *MA 1941
admin asst St. Andrew's House Edin 1941–42; war
service in ATS 1942–43; various teaching posts
Roxburgh from 1964; cler asst SSEB Galashiels from
1975

ANDERSON or James, Margaret Constance
MA 1952
teacher Melbourne from 1973

ANDERSON or Gill, Margaret Elsie   MA 1919
teacher Aber 1941–65; retd
d Aber 28.11.78

ANDERSON Margaret Jane   MB ChB 1923
asst bact S Af inst of med res Johannesburg
seconded to publ health dept municipality of
Johannesburg to initiate immunisation serv
m Cape Town 9.11.35 George Park eng s of George P.
Strichen

ANDERSON or Stephen, Margaret Jane   MA 1929
farm. 1960–79; resid Nairn
husb d 26.9.60

ANDERSON or Pardy, Marie Hogg
BSc 1924 *1925
resid Aber from 1957
d Aber 1.10.79

ANDERSON or Duguid, Marie Louise
MB ChB 1941
h o RACH 1941–42; g p: Elgin 1942–44, Coventry
1944–47

ANDERSON Mary (May)   *MA 1915
d Edin 27.4.61 *AUR* XXXIX 202

ANDERSON or Smart, Mary
MB ChB 1938 DPH 1942
resid Aber

ANDERSON Mary Ann   MA 1925
teacher NSW Aust: maths Bowral h s 1929–30,
Hay h s 1930–34, Katoomba 1934, Sydney girls' h s
1935, Hay h s 1936

m Christchurch NZ 12.9.36 George W. Scarth farm. s
of James S.

ANDERSON or Wilson, Mary Craigie   BSc 1938
teacher maths Elgin acad 1967–74; retd

ANDERSON or Dewar, Mary Sinclair   MA 1926
resid Edin

ANDERSON or Wilson, Mary Still   MA 1905

ANDERSON Patrick Hector Roberts
BSc(agr) 1922 MB ChB 1934 MD 1954
div m o h Surrey c c Epsom 1946–65; m o h
borough of Epsom and E. Ewell 1965–67; retd

ANDERSON Robert   BSc(eng) 1949
sen asst eng Edin from 1960

ANDERSON Robert   *MA 1951
sen lect Fr univ of Durh from 1967

ANDERSON Robert John   MB ChB 1943
JP parish of Rosemarkie 1972
g p Fortrose from 1947
d Fortrose 14.2.80 *AUR* XLVIII 443

ANDERSON Robert Leslie   BSc 1952
teacher maths Dalkeith from 1958

ANDERSON Robert Moir Lechmere   MB ChB 1910
d 1969

ANDERSON Robert Moir Lechmere   MB ChB 1942
g p Stainforth and Hatfield, Doncaster from 1946

ANDERSON Ronald   MB ChB 1923
d Chelmsford 26.1.68 *AUR* XLII 360

ANDERSON Ronald Elrick   BSc 1953

ANDERSON Sarah Tulloch   MA 1929
d Inv 31.3.74

ANDERSON or Liston, Shona Isobel   MA 1950

ANDERSON or Sheldon, Sophie   MA 1930

ANDERSON Sylvester Campbell   MB ChB 1938

ANDERSON Thomas Edge
*MB ChB 1926 *MD 1930
FRCPE 1962 Member Brit Assoc of Dermatology
from 1938 (President 1967–68); retd 1968
d Aber 21.9.73 *AUR* XLV, 319

ANDERSON Thomas Gordon Greig
BSc 1955 Dip Ed 1958
teacher sc Oban h s from 1962

ANDERSON Thomas Kennedy
BSc(agr) 1925 *1927 *BSc 1926
d Aber 19.1.65 *AUR* XLI 58

ANDERSON Una   MA 1954

ANDERSON or Robson, Valerie Elizabeth
                              MA 1949 MB ChB 1954
  resid Potton

ANDERSON or Hossack, Vera Isobel   BSc 1945
  part-time teacher chem and archae Vancouver from 1968

ANDERSON Wardlaw   MB ChB 1940

ANDERSON William   MB ChB 1915
  no longer on GC reg

ANDERSON William   MB ChB 1919
  d 19.3.73

ANDERSON William Ainslie   MB ChB 1947
  consult. gen surg Derbysh RI from 1961

ANDERSON William Alexander   BSc 1940
  SAI 1945–75; retd

ANDERSON William Archibald   MA 1951
  MC TD

ANDERSON William George   MA 1938
  head Peterhead c s from 1970

ANDERSON William John   *MA 1940
  lib and teacher Engl sixth form coll Brockenhurst from 1962

ANDERSON William John Moir   MA 1931
  retd 1972; resid Boddam

ANDERSON William John Ronald   MB ChB 1946
  consult. obst/gyn Coventry from 1961

ANDREW or Buchan, Ella Mary   MA 1945
  teacher Aber until 1953

ANDREW Herbert Francis   *BSc 1952

ANDREW Robert Alexander   MB ChB 1951
  g p: Mansefield 1955–63, Leven Yorks from 1967

ANDREW or Fraser, Shirley Margaret   MA 1955

ANDREWS Elizabeth Ross   MA 1955
  teacher: BFES Malacca, Malaya 1959–60, Hospital Hill s Nairobi 1968–70
  m Nyeri Kenya 10.2.61 James M. Suttie BSc(agr) 1956 *qv*

ANDREWS or Anderson, Margaret Walker
                              MA 1952
  resid Dun

ANGELO or McKellar, Paula Marjorie
                              MB ChB 1954

ANGUS Douglas John   *BSc(eng) 1950
  Trent poly Nott sen lect 1966–73; prin lect from 1973

ANGUS Hamish Thomas Ingram   MA 1930
  teacher Peeblesh; retd
  d 5.4.80

ANGUS Ian Alexander   MB ChB 1939
  MRCPsych 1972
  HM Prisons: sen m o Winchester 1960–63, Birmingham 1963–67; prin m o Home Office prison dept Manchester 1967–75
  d 11.12.77 *AUR* XLVII 360

ANGUS or Craig, Jeannie Gertrude   MB ChB 1923
  retd from g p 1967
  d Aber 9.4.77 *AUR* XLVII 212

ANGUS Magnus Miller   *MA 1951
  teacher Newmachar p s from 1969

ANGUS or Bell, Margaret Isabella Rennie
                              *MA 1942
  civ serv until marriage; resid Edin

ANGUS Margaret Jean   MA 1941

ANGUS or Sibley, Margaret Mitchell   MA 1930

ANGUS Ronald George   *MA 1947 Dip Ed 1948
  lect RGIT Aber from 1949

ANGUS William   BSc(agr) 1900
  no longer on GC reg

ANGUS William George Stewart   BSc(agr) 1931
  d Sandiacre 4.1.72

ANGUS William Rogie
                  MA 1924 BSc 1926 *1927 DSc 1940
  sen lect in phys chem UCNW Bangor; retd 1970

ANGUS William Stephen   MB ChB 1908
  d Aber 18.5.64 *AUR* XL 395

ANNAND Dudley Nicolson   MA 1954 LLB 1957
  ptnr Esslemont & Cameron advoc Aber from 1961

ANNAND Duncan Matheson   MA 1936
  d Aber 24.6.71 *AUR* XLIV 321

ANNAND James Mitchell   MA 1952 BD 1955
  min Dryfesdale church Lockerbie from 1966

ANNAND John Carmichael
                              MA 1932 MB ChB 1937
  g p Broughty Ferry from 1945
  m Aber 27.7.40 Elizabeth D. McEwan d of David McE. Aber

ANNAND Pearl Jane   MA 1941

ANNANDALE James Scott   MB ChB 1910
  d Stonehaven 19.5.64 *AUR* XL 397

ANTON Alexander Elder   MA 1946 LLB 1949
  CBE FBA 1972
  member of Scot. Law Comm: part time 1966–73, full time from 1973; resigned chair of juris Glasg 1973

ANTON Charles Edward   MA 1955 LLB 1957
ptnr Adam Thomson & Ross advoc Aber from 1961

ANTON Henry Craigen   MB ChB 1946
DMRD(Edin) 1957 FFR 1961
consult. radiol Stobhill hosp Glasg from 1963

ANTON Ian Robert   MA 1949
no longer on GC reg

ANTON John Bernard   MA 1953
solic Lond and W. Aust 1962–68; stipendiary magistrate: Kalgoorlie W Aust 1968–72, Midland W Aust from 1972

ANTON or Donald, Lucy Margaret   *MA 1948
JP 1966
resid Aboyne
m Blairs 20.2.56 James R. Donald, Aber

ARCHDALE Arthur Joseph   MA 1950
head York House s Rickmansworth from 1963

ARCHIBALD Alexander   *MA 1890 MB CM 1894
deceased

ARCHIBALD Alexander Spring   MA 1926
retd from Crawford Church 1972
wife *d* 27.3.66

ARCHIBALD Charles   MA 1902
no longer on GC reg

ARCHIBALD John Ingram   BSc 1948

ARGO or Price, Isobel Mary   MA 1944
comp secy with T. Norman Price (Dudley), Dudley from 1966

ARGO or Collins, Jean   MA 1947
teacher Exeter from 1970

ARGO John Duncan   MA 1933
teacher Aboyne and Torphins 1935–45 (not 1941); head Canberra p s East Kilbride 1963–74; retd

ARKHURST Frederick Siegfried   *MA 1952

ARKLAY James Taylor   BSc 1934
d Forfar 6.1.80 *AUR* xlviii 442

ARKLIE Eileen Agnes Stuart   MA 1948
head Balgay s Dun 1960–61; teacher Aber 1961–63, lect soc stud. RGIT Aber from 1963

ARMSTRONG Alexander William   *BSc 1925
no longer on GC reg

ARMSTRONG Allan MacLeod   MA 1925
retd from teaching 1968; resid Dyke

ARMSTRONG or Gray, Dorothy   MB ChB 1950
g p New Cross Lond from 1952

ARMSTRONG James Muir   *MA 1936
Arbroath h s: prin asst 1968–71; asst prin Engl 1971–77; retd

ARMSTRONG John Bruce Ormiston   MB ChB 1953
g p Croydon from 1956

ARMSTRONG Peter Charles   BSc 1948
s of Philip G. A. sales rep and Doris A. Matthews; b Glasg 23.12.26
tobacco chem Bristol, Glasg 1950–57, tech & prod. man. Salisbury Rhodesia 1957–65; tech & dev man. Belf 1965–70; prod. dir Lurgan, Andover 1970–75; dev man. Lond, Jos Nigeria from 1976
m Bristol 19.9.53 Betty P. Merchant d of Stanley V. M. Bristol

ARNAUD Frederick Cooper   BSc(eng) 1939

ARNAUD John Charles Stanley   *MA 1948 Dip Ed 1949
JP for Banffshire 1972
prin teacher Engl Keith g s from 1960

ARNAUD Stanley William   BSc(eng) 1950

ARTHUR George Gordon   *MA 1950
teacher mod lang: Aberlour h s 1960–65, Aber coll of comm 1965–68; asst prin mod lang RGC Aber from 1968

ARTHUR Helen Elizabeth   MA 1936

ARTHUR John Hay   MB ChB 1924
MBE
d Eccleston 4.4.78 *AUR* xlvii 356

ARTHUR William Hay   MB ChB 1929
g p Bridlington and member of staff of Lloyd hosp Bridlington from 1930; retd 1963
d 9.5.80

ASHBY Arthur Sinckler   MB ChB 1937
visiting surg gen hosp Barbados from 1948

ASHER William Alexander   MA 1919
no longer on GC reg

ASHWORTH Michael Raymond Frederick   PhD 1941

ATKINSON James Leslie   *MA 1952
staff man. Ford Motor Co 1959–67; personnel man. Celanese Corp 1967–69; manpower man. Plessey Co 1969–71; organis and pers planning man. British Leyland from 1971

ATKINSON Thomas Henry   *BSc 1953
tech off. (chem) Billingham from 1953

ATTISHA Paul Elias   MB ChB 1930
g p Basrah Iraq 1946–71; retd

ATTYGALLÉ John Wilhelmus Samuel
                                    MB ChB 1897
deceased

AUCHINACHIE Douglas William
            MA 1924 BSc 1926 *1927 PhD 1931
d Wakefield 1.2.61 *AUR* xxxix 203

AUCHINACHIE or Nugent, Elizabeth Eleanor
                                    MA 1915
d 25.2.64

AULD Mary Innes Ruxton
                    MB ChB 1951 DPH 1956
asst m o h Kincardine 1958−74; clin m o Grampian
health board from 1974

AULD or Hardie, Phyllis Amy Isobel   MA 1934
teacher: relief work St Margaret's s for girls Aber
1955−63, part time Bristol 1966−68; resid Cromarty

AULD William Harry Ruxton
                    MB ChB 1944 *MD 1954
FRCPath 1968 FRCPGlas 1975
consult. chem path. group lab St Mary Abbot's hosp
London 1956−61; consult. med biochem Ballochmyle
hosp from 1961

AUTY or Duncan-Brown, Eunice Mary
                                    MB ChB 1941
g p Greenock from 1947

AYMER Alexander Lindsay   MB ChB 1913
no longer on GC reg

AYMER Charles Alastair   MB ChB 1921
g p Lond 1931−76; retd

AYMER or Gordon, Frances   MA 1909
no longer on GC reg

AYRTON or Jones, Elsie Elizabeth   MA 1926
retd 1966; resid Lond

BADDON or Wardlaw, Catherine Ann   MA 1926

BADENOCH Agnes Margarete   MA 1923
d 20.9.73 *AUR* xlv 318

BADENOCH Alexander Guthrie
            MA 1919 *MB ChB 1923 *MD DPH 1934
d Edin 5.12.63

BADENOCH Alexander William
            MA 1923 MB ChB 1927 MD 1929 ChM 1944
Lond: visiting urol Royal Masonic hosp till 1970,
civ consult. urol RAF, consult. surg St. Peter's hosp
for Stone and St. Bart's hosp; consult. urol Samaritan
hosp for women till 1959; pres: Hunterian Soc 1959,
urol sect. Royal society of Med 1958, British Assoc
urol surg 1968−69; awarded St. Peter's medal 1974;
joint-edit. *European Urology*

BADENOCH David Sutherland   MB ChB 1912
d Lichfield 1.8.69 *AUR* xliii 328

BADENOCH Emily Mary
                    MB ChB 1920 DPH 1921
d Aber 1.3.72 *AUR* xliv 429

BADENOCH George   MA 1897
no longer on GC reg

BADENOCH or Third, Hilda Jean   MB ChB 1923
g p Nelson 1923−66
resid Skipton

BADENOCH Jessie   MA 1904
d 15.2.64

BADENOCH Mary   MA 1926
retd 1965; resid Buckie

BADENOCH or Davidson, Nancy   MB ChB 1955
LMCC (Ott) 1973
part time m o publ health serv Glasg 1958−64;
Toronto: school health serv 1966−68, m o rehab
centre 1970−74; g p Dundas Ontario from 1974

BADENOCH Sarah Graham   MA 1922
no longer on GC reg

BAGGLEY Charles Arthur   MB ChB 1944

BAGGLEY or Sidery, Margaret Evelyn   MA 1935
resid Burgess Hill

BAIKIE or Lennie, Lucy May   MA 1907
resid Beauly
d 23.9.80 *AUR* xlix 66

BAILEY Gordon Raymond   BSc 1952
PhD (Br Col)

BAILEY Henry Patrick   *BSc(eng) 1936
Vickers (ship-bldg group) Barrow-in-Furness: elect
eng i/c nuclear proj des team 1957−67, man. spec serv
dept 1967−72; man. spec proj elect. dept from 1972

BAILEY-THOMSON or Dillon, Joyce Doreen
                                    MB ChB 1938
g p Nott from 1938

BAILLIE Alexander Main   MB ChB 1915
d Torquay 10.1.74

BAILLIE Angus William   BSc(agr) 1954
agr advis in E Perthsh and East of Scot. coll of agr
from 1954

BAILLIE David Main   MB ChB 1909 MD 1912
d 6.2.71

BAILLIE Donald John   MA BSc 1937 MEd 1949
dir educ Kirkcudbrightsh
d Dumfries 28.2.75 *AUR* xlvi 239

BAILLIE Elizabeth Crosse   BSc 1926
retd 1966; resid Nairn

BAILLIE George Roderick Bannerman
                                    MA 1930 BSc 1932
 d New Pitsligo 24.2.70 *A UR* XLIII 446

BAILLIE James   MA 1903
 no longer on GC reg

BAILLIE James Francis   MA 1929
 DBEA
 v-pres Edin Esperanto Soc; resid Auldearn

BAILLIE or Laird, Margaret Bell   BSc 1941
 teacher sc/biol Sittingbourne 1957–70; resid Elgin

BAIN Alexander Adam Ness   MB ChB 1936
 d Inv 26.8.66 *A UR* XLI 341

BAIN or Young, Annie Simpson   MB ChB 1931
 g p Aber from 1939

BAIN or Brown, Annie Wilson   MA 1930
 teacher: Bradfield 1931–38, Ipswich 1952–63, prin
 maths Leicester 1963–68; retd; resid Woodbridge

BAIN or Gibson, Barbara Cheyne   MA 1932
 teacher Edin 1960–68; resid Edin

BAIN or Jeffrey, Belle Emslie   MA 1926
 teacher: Tillydrone s Aber 1958–71; retd; resid
 Bieldside Aber

BAIN Catherine Brown Wilson   MA 1930

BAIN Charles Stewart   MA 1927

BAIN Ewen Grant   MA 1935
 head Logie Durno s 1958–75

BAIN Flora Elizabeth   MA 1946

BAIN George Munro   MA 1908
 d 4.1.63

BAIN Ian McPherson   *MA 1910
 BA(Oxon)
 resid Broughty Ferry
 d Dun 9.8.81

BAIN or Christie, Isabel Grant   *MA 1923
 d Aber 8.9.72

BAIN James Andrew   BSc 1954 *BSc 1956
 Lond: mineralogist min resources div overseas geol
 surveys 1960–67, prin scient off. mineralogy unit Inst
 Geol Sc from 1967

BAIN John Alexander   *MA 1938
 asst edit. *The Iraq Times* Baghdad 1946–50; edit:
 The Singapore Free Press 1960–63, *The Malay Mail*
 Kuala Lumpur 1963–67; sen sub edit. *The West
 Australian* Perth W Aust from 1967
 m Leeds 20.9.63 D'Orise Timmins teacher d of
 William T. Cape Town

BAIN John William Laing   MB ChB 1936
 d Aber 24.10.78 *A UR* XLVIII 106 and 232

BAIN Lawrence Weir   MB ChB 1913
 no longer on GC reg

BAIN Logie Samuel   MB ChB 1937
 D Phys Med (Lond) 1953 DL MRCPGlas 1975
 resid Aber

BAIN Margaret Amelia   MA 1908
 d 4.1.67

BAIN Margaret Isobel   *MA 1923
 Dip Univ Paris 1931
 Prin Edge Hill trg coll Ormskirk 1947–64
 resid Edin

BAIN or Horne, Marjorie   MA 1927
 teacher Abdnsh: Lyne of Skene s 1956–59, Cluny s
 1959–70

BAIN or Craig, Marjorie Simmonds   MB ChB 1942
 resid Glenbuchat

BAIN or Wrigglesworth, May Murray   MA 1931

BAIN Robert   MA 1902
 d 12.6.64

BAIN Robert   *BSc(eng) 1948

BAIN Roderic   MB ChB 1944
 g p Stainland Yorks from 1946
 d Stainland –.10.80 *A UR* XLIX 135

BAIN Roderick McLean   MB ChB 1947 DPH 1951
 MFCM 1972
 sen clin m o Wigan from 1961

BAIN William   BSc(agr) 1949
 teacher sc Bridge of Don s from 1952

BAIN William Alexander   *MA 1904
 d Dunlop Ayrsh 28.7.68 *A UR* XLIII 77

BAIN William Cranna   MA 1942 *BSc 1948 PhD 1951
 sen prin scient off. Appleton Lab Slough from 1964

BAINES Doreen   *MA 1949
 m Dawson

BAIRD Agnes Alexandra   MA 1931

BAIRD Anna Frances   MA 1928

BAIRD or Graham, Annie Frances   MA 1925

BAIRD Eba Crichton   MB ChB 1943 DPH 1948
 MFCM 1972
 m o h Burgh of Hamilton from 1970

BAIRD Edward George   *MA 1925 MB ChB 1932
 d 25.1.67

BAIRD or Gimingham, Elizabeth Caroline
                                    MA 1945 Dip Ed 1946
 Aber: lib Harlaw acad 1967–72, asst lib Bankhead
 acad from 1973

BAIRD James Alexander *BSc 1932 MA 1934
DipEd (Lond) 1962 JP 1969
head New Pitsligo and St. John's s Aberdeensh from
1965

BAIRD Jessie Elizabeth Crichton MB ChB 1939
FRCOG 1976
consult. gyn/obst Royal Samaritan hosp for women
and Rutherglen mat. hosp Glasg

BAIRD John Wilson *MA 1950

BAIRD or Penman Splitt, Joyce Deans
MA 1949 MB ChB 1954
MRCPE 1973
Edin: res fell. and clin asst dept therap univ and R.I.
1957–64; MRC res fell. and clin asst dept med univ
and W Gen hosp 1965–68; m o Scot. Home and
Health dept St. Andrews House 1969–70; lect med
univ and W Gen hosp from 1971; sen lect med univ
and consult. phys W Gen hosp from 1976

BAIRD or Shepherd, Mary Margaret MA 1934
resid Milltimber Aber

BAIRD William Scott *MA 1937
head Elgin West End s 1954–76; retd

BAKER Joseph John BCom 1931
retd J. W. Baker Aber 1971

BAKER Sheila Marian MB ChB 1943
consult. diag radiol East Dorset dist Wessex RHA
from 1959

BAKHSHI Rewati Raman MB ChB 1926

BALCH or Taylor, Dorothy Janet MA 1946
resid Dunedin NZ

BALCH Douglas Freeman BSc 1933
retd teaching 1971; resid Aber

BALCH Hubert William MB ChB 1937
consult phys med and rheumat Grampian reg hosp
board from 1963 sen clin lect rheumat Aberd from
1966

BALFOUR or Dufton, Eleanor Youl *MA 1921
resid Huntly

BALFOUR Jean MA 1945

BALL Hayward Percy MA 1901
no longer on GC reg

BALLANTYNE Thomas Arnott
MA 1950 LL B 1953
solic: Mayer & Fraser Keith 1956–58, Brown &
McRae Fraserburgh 1958–61, Wight & Aitken Aber
1964–70; man. dir Marcliffe hotel Aber 1961–70;
retd; resid Edin

BAND Robert William Ingram MA 1929

BANISTER or Sutherland, Anne Elizabeth BSc 1951
Hobart Tasmania: teacher biol Friends' s 1966–71,
sen Fahan Presb girls' coll from 1971

BANKS Charlotte MA 1910 *1912
no longer on GC reg

BANKS Francis Sinclair *MA 1932 BD 1935
min Strachur and Strathlachlan par ch Argyll from
1965
d 29.1.79

BANKS Janet *MA 1935
resid Forres

BANKS Mary Margaret Mitchell MA 1948
teacher Inchgarth s Aber from 1949

BANNERMAN Agnes Winifred *MA 1928
retd teaching 1968; resid Sherborne

BANNERMAN or Fleming, Lizzie (Elizabeth)
MA 1915
no longer on GC reg

BANNERMAN Mary Macleod MA 1951
teacher George Watson's Ladies' coll Edin from
1962

BANNERMAN Norman George BSc(eng) 1954

BANNERMAN Robert Chalmers *MA 1928
retd 1967
d Coldwaltham Pulborough 15.8.75

BANNOCHIE or Godward, Dorothy Mary
MA 1920
resid Milltimber Aber

BAPTY Leonard MB ChB 1936
FRCS(C) 1972
Victoria BC Canada: on active staff Victoria gen
hosp, on visiting staff Royal Jubilee hosp from 1972

BARBER Allan *MA 1953

BARCLAY Alexina McConnachie MA 1926
no longer on GC reg

BARCLAY Ann Freeman Stewart MA 1954

BARCLAY or Rowe, Annie McConnachie MA 1927
d Banff 17.8.76

BARCLAY Annie Taylor MA 1933
teacher: Dem s Aber 1935–38, Woodside s 1938–50,
Rhenish g h s Stellenbosch Cape Province SA 1950–
51, Davidson's Mains p s Edin 1951–68, mistress i/c
p dept James Gillespie's h s for g Edin 1968–73, head
James Gillespie's p s 1973–76

BARCLAY or Duncan, Bessie Isabella *MA 1924
resid Bieldside Aber

BARCLAY David   MB ChB 1936 DPH 1939
JP
Provost Stonehaven 1972–75

BARCLAY or Argo, Edith   MA 1944
resid Laurencekirk

BARCLAY or Paterson, Elizabeth   MA 1921
d 15.2.72

BARCLAY or Main, Emily Margaret   MA 1947
Dip Spec Educ(Glasg) 1976
teacher Merkland spec s Kirkintilloch 1970–75 and from 1976

BARCLAY or Fraser, Ethel   MA 1914
no longer on GC reg

BARCLAY or Christie, Flora   MA 1942
resid Banchory

BARCLAY George Copland   *MA 1950
teacher: sp asst Engl Hawick 1951–64, prin Engl Scunthorpe 1964–66, asst prin Engl Hawick from 1966

BARCLAY Gordon Powell   MB ChB 1936
d Glensford 21.1.62 *AUR* xxxix 385

BARCLAY Hector Summers   MA 1949
Hamnavoe Shetland: teacher maths/sc 1958–65, head from 1965

BARCLAY Ian Campbell   BCom 1926
resid Aboyne

BARCLAY James Alexander
                    MA 1930 BSc 1933 MB ChB 1937
physiol dept med s Birm: retd

BARCLAY Jane Scott   MA 1930
secy Brander & Cruickshank advoc Aber 1954–68; retd 1968

BARCLAY Jeanie Gordon   *MA 1938
asst Hilton nurs s Aber from 1968; retd 1974

BARCLAY or Stephen, Jeannie Margaret
                                ***MA *BSc 1914**
d Aber 18.6.71 *AUR* xliv 317

BARCLAY John Wood   MA 1954
d Aber 6.1.75

BARCLAY Louise   MA 1927

BARCLAY Mary Dorothy   MA 1949
teacher maths: Govan s s 1955–58, 1959–66; Gladstone h s Vancouver BC (on exchange) 1958–59
m Aber 18.9.65 Norman Maclean radio off. M N s of Alexander M. Glasg

BARCLAY or Kemp, Nora Burgess   MA 1951
teacher Aber: Middlefield s 1952–58, Deeview s 1969–74, Greenfern s 1974–75; asst head (early stages) Hanover St s from 1975

BARCLAY or Mavor, Sheena Watson   MA 1932
resid N'cle-u-Tyne

BARDSLEY Raymond Alan Peter   BSc(agr) 1951
served RA (field branch) U.K., Burma, India 1943–47, final rank capt; Lancashire: field off. pig indust dev auth 1963–68, dev off. meat and livestock comm 1968–73; spec at h q Bletchley from 1973

BARKER Horace Armstrong   MB ChB 1925
d 12.4.77

BARKER Noël Camilla Berners   MA 1948
m Peel

BARKER or Peel, Rosalind Cordelia   MA 1944

BARKLEY or Landsberg, Sylvia Yuille   PhD 1955
resid Southampton

BARLOW or Girvan, Florence   MA 1926
resid Kirkcaldy

BARLOW or Gray, Juliet   MA 1923
d Airdrie 13.11.77

BARNET John Brebner   MB ChB 1941
g p Dun from 1948
d 27.4.76 *AUR* xlvi 418 and xlvii 106

BARNETT or Glasson, Adeline Elizabeth   MA 1924
no longer on GC reg

BARNETT Christopher Charles   MA 1925 BD 1927
d 18.9.63

BARNETT Eleanora Mary   MA 1910
retd 1954; resid Wishaw

BARNETT Elizabeth   MA 1917 ^dLLB 1921
sen ptnr A. C. Morrison & Richards advoc Aber until retd 1966; only woman member Soc of Advoc Aber until 1973

BARNETT Euphemia Cowan   BSc 1918 DSc 1940
d Aber 12.3.79 *AUR* xliii 442

BARNETT George   BSc 1950
flying off. RAF 1950–52; Canada BC Hydro Vancouver: distrib des 1954–56, indust rep 1956–62, rates analyst 1963–65, cost of serv superv 1965–68, man. rates/cost dept from 1968
m Abbotsford BC 2.5.59 Patricia J. O'Neill home econ d of Peter O'N. Co Cork

BARNETT James Grubb   MB ChB 1953
resid Iver Bucks
d Iver 24.10.80 *AUR* xlix 70

BARNETT James William   MB ChB 1907
d Farnham 31.5.65 *AUR* xli 145

BARR James   MB ChB 1945
d 19.3.80

BARR John Edwin   BSc(eng) 1936

BARR John Hamilton   BSc(agr) 1953

BARR or Kidd, Margaret Miller   MA 1938
res Christchurch NZ

BARR-SIM Albert Edward   MB ChB 1916
d Inverurie 31.1.68 *AUR* XLII 354

BARRACK or Andrew, Mary Frances   MA 1953
resid Kingswells Aber

BARRACK or Rutherford, Robina Robertson
MA 1941
teacher Kincardine O'Neil p s from 1968

BARRACLOUGH Ronald   MB ChB 1935
col late RAMC, late hon surg HM The Queen;
resid Gyfelia Wrexham 1976

BARRETT William   *MA 1909
d Guisborough 6.12.60 *AUR* XXXIX 101

BARRIE James Alexander   *BSc 1949 PhD 1952
Brit rayon sen res fell: Aber 1952–54, Lond 1954–
55; lect Imp Coll Lond 1955–67; visiting prof MIT
Boston USA 1961–62, sen lect Imp Coll Lond from
1967
m Lond 3.4.61 Maureen M. Wantstall secy d of
Robert W. Lond

BARRIE or Anderson, Margaret Bowman   MA 1930
resid Fordoun

BARRON Alfred Saunders   MA 1912 BD 1915
d Crieff 20.11.73 *AUR* XLV 317 and 446

BARRON Annie   *MA 1926
teacher classics: Madras coll St And 1927–43,
Morgan acad Dun 1943–64
m St And 14.7.45 William Ramsay security off. s of
James R. Armadale

BARRON or Mackay, Annie Knight   MA 1910
d Turriff 2.12.60 *AUR* XXXIX 201

BARRON Arthur Morison
**   *MB ChB 1924 MD 1932**
d Poole 10.10.79 *AUR* XLVIII 353

BARRON Bruce Morison   MB ChB 1951
g p Poole from 1959

BARRON Catherine Ann   MA 1948
teacher Aberdeensh: Rosehearty 1961–62, Inverurie
1963–70, Oldmeldrum 1973–76
m Oldmeldrum 21.7.76 Alfred J. Burns, Billingham

BARRON Charles Leith   MB ChB 1931
d Dunblane 1.12.72 *AUR* XLV 128

BARRON or Robertson, Dorothy Elizabeth
MB ChB 1947
g p Aber from 1955

BARRON Eliza Christina Margaret   MA 1900
d 13.5.70 *AUR* XLIII 440

BARRON Elizabeth Walker   MA 1928
teacher Aber 1954–60, Drumgarth inf s Aber
1960–72; retd 1972
resid Aber

BARRON or Routledge, Elsie   MA 1939
teacher Derbysh: Cromford 1960–63, Bakewell
1969–73

BARRON or Dickson, Enid May   MA 1952
resid Prestwick

BARRON James Smith   MA 1914
no longer on GC reg

BARRON Jane Gray   *MA 1917
d Stracathro 23.3.74

BARRON or Anderson, Jane McGee   BSc 1950

BARRON Jeannie Helen Mary   MA 1926
teacher: St Clement St s Aber 1927–37, Linksfield s
Aber 1944–47, Oxgangs s Edin 1948–66
m Aber 4.3.38 Herbert Rae master mariner

BARRON or Marshall, Jessie Eliza Coutts   MA 1928
d 29.5.75

BARRON John   MB ChB 1949
MRCPsych 1971
consult. psychiat E Surrey and W Sussex from 1971

BARRON John McKay   BSc 1949
head: Rayne N s Aberdeensh 1962–65, Melrose g s
from 1965

BARRON or Mackay, Lucy Maud   MA 1907
d 24.8.77

BARRON Marjory Henderson   MA 1936
teacher Aber: Middlefield p s from 1943; retd 1976

BARRON Robert Mackay   MB ChB 1930
Police surg retd 1960; chmn Dudley Worcs exec
council from 1961, med off. Dudley coll of educ from
1944

BARRON or Duggie, Seonaid Margaret   MA 1953

BARRON William Douglas   MA 1909
d Edin 1.5.70 *AUR* XLIII 440

BARRON William James   MA 1924
d Aberlour 9.2.73 *AUR* XLV 225

BARRON Williamina Agnes   *MA 1918 BSc 1920
no longer on GC reg

BARTLET James Eric Alexander
MB ChB 1939 MD 1947

BARTLET Leslie Bow   MB ChB 1951
DCH 1959 MRCPsych 1972
sen psychiat regist Herts C G Clin 1957–60; consult
child psychiat Hampshire ch guid serv 1960–65;
consult ch psychiat S'ton hosps/clin teacher med
faculty S'ton
m Lond 23.4.60 Suzanne M. Brilliant BSc(LSE) stud.
counsellor S'ton d of Charles B. Wembley Park

BARTLET Margaret Taylor   MA 1919
MBE 1966
head Tynepark approved s for girls Haddington till
retd 1966; resid Edin

BARTLETT Henry Matthew
                         MA 1923 BD 1926 DD 1963
part time chaplain DRI 1955–69; awarded City of
Orleans medal 1963; clerk Synod of Angus and
Mearns 1967; dir City of Dundee educ trust; retd as
min of Logie 1969; retd as clerk to presb Dun 1972
d 21.12.80 *A UR* LXIX 136

BARTON George Edward Colledge   MA 1929
head jun s Robert Gordon's coll Aber from 1933;
housemaster 1937–64; retd

BATE Phillip Argall Turner   *BSc 1931

BATTEN Ronald Mortimer   MA 1947

BATTISBY Christina   MA 1921
teacher: retd from Frederick St s Aber 1962

BATTISBY or Barber, Keturah Mary Connon
                                        *MA 1930
teacher Edin: Norton Park s s 1957–61, Boroughmuir s s 1961–64; lady advis David Kilpatrick s s
1964–72; retd
d West Calder 1.4.80

BAUER David   BSc 1948
deceased

BAXTER or McAllister, Alexandra   MA 1927
inf teacher Paisley: Carsbrook St s 1956–62,
Williamsburgh 1962–69
d Paisley 30.5.76

BAXTER Archibald Green   *MA 1932

BAXTER or Coutts Milne, Catherine Hannah
                         MB ChB 1925 DPH 1927
resid Farnham

BAXTER Flora Leslie   MB ChB 1927
m (2) Amersham Bucks 14.2.70 Hugh W. Broatch
AIB banker s of Richard B. J.P. Lochmaben

BAXTER Helen Robertson   *MA 1902
no longer on GC reg

BAXTER Ian Francis George   MA 1936 LLB 1938
prof law Tor from 1966; dir Fam Law Study for
Ont Law Reform Comm 1965–68; co-dir Vanier
res proj on fam support 1967–70; dir Leg. Res

Proj for Canadian Pharm Assoc 1970; co-ordinator
Connaught Progr on Fam Law and Soc Welfare
1976–78; NATO prof univ of Louvain Belgium 1967;
visiting prof Brist 1975–76

BAXTER or Eccles, Isabella Anne   MB ChB 1922

BAXTER James Houston   BD 1920
d St And 1.4.73 *A UR* XLV 224

BAXTER William   MB ChB 1913
no longer on GC reg

BAXTER William Gordon   *BSc 1941
OBE 1970
W. A. Baxter & Sons Fochabers: prod dir 1946–49,
man. dir 1949–69, chmn from 1969; chmn Best of
Scotland Fochabers from 1970; loc dir Bank of
Scotland Aber from 1972

BAYER Jacob Max   MB ChB 1923
no longer on GC reg

BAYER Philip   MB ChB 1925

BAYNHAM John William   *BSc 1952 PhD 1955

BEAN or Chileen, Elizabeth Helen   MA 1910
no longer on GC reg

BEANGE Margaret Helen   *MA 1931
teacher mod lang Turriff acad Abdnsh 1967–73
m Boddam 14.11.63 James Cummine farmer s of
James C. Turriff

BEARSLEY Eleanor Emma   *MA 1916
resid Edin

BEATON Arnold   BSc(for) 1952

BEATON James   MA 1929
d 1965

BEATON Lily   MA 1936
teacher Edin; retd

BEATON Mabel Margaret   MA 1931
no longer on GC reg

BEATON or Wyness, Millicent   MA 1927
resid Bramhall

BEATTIE Alan Gordon   MB ChB 1951
g p Poole from 1954
m Aber 2.4.53 Isabel Coutts teacher d of Andrew C.
Aber

BEATTIE Alan Rae   *BSc 1955 PhD 1959
res staff Texas Instruments Inc Dallas USA 1959–
63; univ coll Cardiff: lect applied maths 1963–68, sen
lect from 1968; visiting lect Nairobi univ 1974–75

BEATTIE Alexander Gordon
                         MB ChB 1939 DPH 1958
FRCGP 1972
g p Aber from 1945

BEATTIE Alexander William   MA 1936

BEATTIE Arthur James   *MA 1935
prof Greek Edin from 1951

BEATTIE George Fisher   *BSc 1940
res chem Manchester from 1943; retd

BEATTIE or Wright, Jane Hastings   MA 1930
resid Aber

BEATTIE John   MA 1941
head dept Sheerness tech s 1966–70; div tut. Sheppey s from 1970

BEATTIE Katrina   *BSc 1954
m Kolizeras

BEATTIE Margaret Carroll   *MA 1924
teacher maths head dept Oakdene Beaconsfield 1953–71
d Banchory 22.8.76

BEATTIE or Wisely, Margaret Watson   MA 1927
resid New Pitsligo

BEATTIE Nellie (Helen)   MA 1901
no longer on GC reg

BEATTIE Peter Henry   MB ChB 1936 MD 1949
Ophth regist Addenbrooke's hosp Cambridge 1946; consult ophth Norfolk and Norwich hosp from 1947; retd 1974

BEATTIE or Gruer, Rosamund   *MB ChB 1950
Dip Soc Med(Edin) 1968
g p Kemnay 1964–67; dept soc med Edin: res fell. 1968–73, sen res fell. from 1973

BEATTIE or Hay, Violet   MA 1928
d Auchterless

BEATTIE Walter Gordon   MA 1953 BD 1956
min W Parish ch Fraserburgh from 1962

BEATTIE William Forbes   MB ChB 1912
deceased

BEAUMONT or Forbes, Maggie Porter   *MA 1922
d Aber 18.6.70 *AUR* XLIV 110

BECK-SLINN Kathleen   MA 1931
MBE 1972
retd Torry Res Stat 1972

BEDDIE Alastair James   MB ChB 1934
retd 1974; resid Kelowna BC Canada

BEDDIE Lewis Beaton   MA 1888
d Aber 23.1.65 *AUR* XLI 34

BEEDIE or Hogg, Hazel Gill   MA 1948
resid Tawa NZ

BEEDIE James   MA 1942
prin teacher Engl: Arbroath acad 1962–68, Powis acad Aber 1968; asst head Powis acad from 1973

BEEDIE William   MB ChB 1904 MD 1914
no longer on GC reg

BEER Keith Edward   *BSc 1949
CEng FIMM 1975
prin geol SW Eng unit Inst of Geol Sc Exeter from 1963; part time lect Exe 1969–74

BEGG Alan Duncan   *MA 1954

BEGG Albert Tulloch   *MA 1923
d Aber 8.3.65 *AUR* XLI 57

BEGG Andrew Macdonald   MA 1952
ptnr with father and wife in Andrew Begg & Son Elgin and Buckie; also ptnr with wife in Andrew Begg, Forres from 1973; town councillor Elgin from 1960, Dean of Guild then Bailie/JP from 1967

BEGG Charles Michael Macintyre
                                    MA 1939 *BSc 1942
FRS(Edin)
reader zool Aberd
m(1) wife died
(2) 1966 Lavender Miller d of Donald M. Aber

BEGG Donald Leslie Bartlett   *MA 1938
teacher: Hilton acad Aber from 1947, prin hist from 1965
d Aber 2.1.80 *AUR* XLVIII 443

BEGG Francis William   MB ChB 1903
d 12.6.61 *AUR* XXXIX 271

BEGG Ian Forbes   MA 1931 DD 1971
Aber: priest i/c St. Ninian's Seaton till 1973; canon St. Andrew's Cath 1965; dean diocese Aber and Orkney 1969; bishop Aber and Orkney from 1973

BEGG John Hudson   MB ChB 1939
LAIHA (New South Wales) 1958 FACMA 1968
med supt: Queen Victoria hosp Adelaide S Aust 1950–60, Ballarat base hosp Victoria Aust 1961–71; S Aust dept publ health Adelaide from 1971

BEGG or Ross, Muriel Jean   MA 1925
d 6.5.73

BEGG Thomas Leslie   MB ChB 1947 DPH 1950
prin m o (mental health) lect (admin mental health serv) Liv from 1952; retd 1974

BEGG William   MB ChB 1906 DPH 1908

BELL Aluinn Neil   *MA 1955
teacher geog
m Cults, Fife 21.7.60 David S. Petrie MA(Glas) teacher classics/dep head

BELL Andrew Farm Hamilton
                                    MA 1930 ᵈLLB(c) 1932
Assoc Aust Soc Acct 1964

asst solic: Aber, Glasg 1932–39, 1945–51; Sydney Aust: asst acct 1952–72, internal auditor 1972–79; retd

BELL Archibald Brown Ross   BSc(agr) 1954
farm. Ardormie from 1963

BELL Clement Wood   *MA 1942
BA(Lond)
dep prin Daniel Stewart's & Melville coll Edin from 1966

BELL Elizabeth Andrew   MA 1949
Glasg: teacher classics: Albert s s till 1963, Allan Glen's 1964–68; prin teacher guid: Riverside s s 1968–72, Albert s s 1972–74; asst head Grange s s from 1974

**BELL or Turnbull, Elizabeth Paterson Nicol
MB ChB 1950 MD 1954**
resid Oxford

BELL Harry McAra   *MA 1924
MA(Cantab) 1927 M.Ed(Glas) 1932
rector Dollar acad till 1960; hon res fell. St. And from 1972
m Glasg 9.10.33 Sophia M. Fulton d of Alexander B. F. Glasg

BELL James Clark   MB ChB 1929
g p East Ham from 1934

BELL John Hamilton   MB ChB 1924
d Lond 4.1.69 *A UR* XLIII 213

BELL Kenneth Hamilton   LLB 1935
admitted solic of Supreme Court NSW Aust 1960 held 4 positions in law off. Sydney 1959–69, Queensland 1969–71; retd; resid Manly NSW

BELL Kenneth Mackenzie   MB ChB 1939
MRCGP 1954
g p Harrow; chmn Harrow and Hillington BMA 1969

BELL Michael William   BSc(Eng) 1951

BELL or Strath, Rhoda Duncan   *MA 1951
Aber: teacher lang part-time High s for girls 1960–62, Albyn s for girls 1968–74, Cults acad from 1974

BENNET James Anderson   PhD 1953
sen lect elect. eng Dund from 1964
wife *d* 1963
m(2) Edin 1964 Anne T. B. Fraser civ serv d of James F. Edin

BENNET Robert Alasdair   MB ChB 1955 MD 1967
b Glasg 27.10.30
h o ARI and Manor hosp Nuneaton 1956–57; m o RAMC 1957–61; res fell. orthop dept Edin 1961–64; lect path. dept Dund from 1964

BENNETT Harold Stanley   MB ChB 1945
consult. radiol Royal Cornwall hosps Truro from 1954

BENNETT Margaret Edith   *MA 1936
head Lansdowne House s Edin till 1974; retd

BENNETT or Blank, Miriam   MB ChB 1950
Fell. Amer Board Fam Practice 1976
g p Bridgeport Conn USA from 1951

BENNETT or Smith, Violet Jane   MA 1910
d Aber 8.5.73 *A UR* XLV 316

BENSON or Fraser, Kathleen Elizabeth   MA 1944
resid Edin

**BENSON or Lachman, Mary Isobel Falconer
MA 1940**
JP 1969
teacher Colne: head lang Park County s s 1958–68, sen lang Grammar s 1968–78

**BENTON or Duthie, Alexandra Hay
MB ChB 1924 DPH 1934**
resid Chichester

BENTON James Lipp Brown   BSc 1941 *1947

**BENZIE or Duguid, Agnes Mildred Emslie
MB ChB 1922 DPH 1925**
d near Aber 13.1.73 *A UR* XLV 225

BENZIE Alexander Swan   MB ChB 1923
g p retd; resid Pamber Heath nr Basingstoke 1976

BENZIE Annie Ronald   MA 1926
resid Fraserburgh

BENZIE or Gordon, Helen Watt   MA 1930
teacher: temp relief Kennethmont, Gartly 1957–61, Rhynie 1962–69, Gordon Schools Huntly 1969–74

BENZIE Jeannie   MB ChB 1924
resid Fraserburgh

BENZIE Robert James   *MA 1940
d 2.1.72

BENZIE Sheila Allan   MA 1952
m Aber 1.6.63 John Tanner
resid Buckhurst Hill

**BENZIE William
MA 1953 *1955 MEd 1957 PhD 1967**
lect Engl Vic BC Canada from 1958

BERGER Michael Jona   *MA 1950
M Jur (Hier) 1965 admitted Israel Bar 1968
sen dir of control State comptroller's off. Jerusalem 1962–73; dep leg. counsel Securities Authority of Israel from 1973

**BERKLEY Arnold Ber (BERKOWITZ Abraham Ber)
MB ChB 1923**
no longer on GC reg

BERLINGUET Lorne Francis Caven   MB ChB 1935
gen surg St Joseph Hosp Three Rivers Canada

from 1939 geriat spec Cooke hosp Three Rivers
Canada from 1960
m(2) –.11.74 Frances Keating

BERNARD George Reid   MB ChB 1939
RAF 1941–46; g p Ipswich from 1946

BERNARD Robert McFarlane   MB ChB 1940

BERRY Alexander Ian   MA 1940

BERRY Douglas Austen Oldfield   *MA 1951

BERRY Douglas Wales
                MB ChB 1915 DPH 1922 *MD 1923
d East Fortune 13.6.73 *AUR* xlv 317

BERRY or Duncan, Elsie Janet Isobel   MA 1916
d Aboyne 27.7.80 *AUR* xlix 66

BERRY Harriet Ann Ford   MA 1908
d Basle Switzerland 5.1.70 *AUR* xliii 440

BERRY Janet Clerihew   MA 1926
d Aber 27.7.62 *AUR* xl 92

BETENSON William Francis Whitaker
                MB ChB 1917

BETHUNE or Kerr, Anna Macleod   MA 1926
d Rosskeen, Invergordon 15.4.62 *AUR* xxxix 383

BETHUNE or Sangster, Barbara Una Doull
                MA 1932
resid Edin

BETTSON Denis John   BSc(agr) 1949

BEVERIDGE or Notholt, Agnes Arnot   MA 1949
teacher Breakspear s Ickenham Lond boro Hillingdon 1957–59 and from 1969

BEVERIDGE Evelyn Eleanor   MA 1950
teacher Kingswells p s Abdnsh from 1952
m Aber 8.8.67 Douglas Shirran printer

BEVERIDGE John Walker   MB ChB 1954
g p Great Harwood 1962–63; Tasmania Aust d m o
Flinders Island 1963–65, g p Launceston 1965 and
from 1969, d m o Evandale 1965–69; capt RAAMC
army reserve from 1969

BEVERIDGE Margaret Edith   MB ChB 1955
FFARCS 1967
regist anaest hosp for sick children Gt. Ormond St
Lond 1966–67; consult. anaest Aber gen hosps from
1969

BEVERIDGE Robert Noel   *BSc(eng) 1950
ICI: plant eng metals div Liv 1955–57, sen des eng
Nobel div Glasg 1957–60, proj eng plastics div
Welwyn Garden City 1960–63, sect. man. plastics div
Darwen 1963–65, head off. Millbank Lond 1965–68;
plastics div Welwyn Garden City: tech co-ordinator
1968–70, head admin from 1970

BEVERLEY or Clarke, Gladys Margaret Watt
                MA 1938

BEWGLASS Mary Melven Law   BSc 1937

BEWS or Orr, Barbara Jessie   *MA 1941

BEWS or Cheyne, Jean Fyfe   MA 1952
resid Br of Don

BEWS John William Simpson   MA 1926
d Aber 2.6.68 *AUR* xliii 84

BHANDARI Kodlamogati Lakkana   BSc(agr) 1924
coffee planter: man. coffee estates Coorg India
1928–61
m Mangalore India 29.5.28 Sarsa Saraswathi land
owner d of B. Mahabaleshwara Shetty, Brahmavar,
S Kanara, India

BICHAN Isabella Hepburn   MA 1905
no longer on GC reg

BICHAN Patrick Isbister   BSc(agr) 1951
b 22.11.25
BOCM: farms man. Yorks 1953–59, farms dir Yorks
and Leicester 1959–65; cattle husb advis Eng/Scot.
1965–72; man. dir Farm Ptnrs Lincs from 1972

BICKERSTETH Jean Elfride   *MA 1945
Cert Ed (Lond) 1971
Hull: tut. Kingston-u-Hull coll of educ 1967–71, univ
lect theol and warden Lambert Hall from 1972

BICKERSTETH Ursula Mary   *MA 1950
teacher: head classics Wimbledon h s 1976

BIEDA Kazimierz   *MA 1948
asst lect econ Singapore 1949–51; lect econ
Auckland NZ 1951–57; sen lect econ: Kumasi Ghana
1957–59, Armidale Aust 1959–66; reader econ
Brisbane from 1966

BILLE Ian Robertson   MA 1955
b 1.8.21
teacher Aber from 1956

BINNS William Osborne   *BSc(for) 1955

BIRD Dorothy Mary   MA 1944

BIRKETT Nichol Thomson   MA 1948 *MEd 1950
visiting prof educ nat inst educ univ of Delhi/
consult spec educ to Nat Council Educ Res and Trg,
Govt of India 1963–65; sen lect dept spec and remed
educ Jordanhill coll of educ Glasg 1965–75, prin lect
from 1975; hon lect psych Glas 1976

BIRKS Colin Alastair   MB ChB 1940
g p Sleaford from 1949

BIRNIE or Ross, Ada Mary   MA 1952
teacher Mile End s Aber from 1973

BIRNIE Alexander   BSc(agr) 1926

BIRNIE Alexander Brodie   *MA 1933
chmn traffic comm Scot. traffic area Edin from 1965

BIRNIE Alexander John Milne   MB ChB 1954
FRCSE 1968
orthop: m o Stracathro hosp 1960–61, regist Ipswich and E Suffolk hosp 1961–64, Royal South Hants hosp S'ton 1964–65, Queen Mary's hosp for children 1965–66; regist gen surg Newcastle gen hosp 1966–68; sen regist orthop Middlesbro gen hosp 1968–71; consult. orthop surg Dryburn hosp Durh, orthop and accident hosp Sunderland, from 1971
m(1) diss –.2.67
(2) Newcastle-u-Tyne 18.3.67 Audrey J. Fairservice SRN d of B. W. F. Mitcham

BIRNIE Bella Garden   MA 1931
teacher Engl/hist Banff acad 1947–69; retd

BIRNIE Charles John   MA 1949
teacher Engl/allied subj orphanage Aberlour 1961–63; relief teacher Banffsh 1963–67; div course Aber 1967–69; C of S min Annbank from 1969

BIRNIE Edith Bennett   BSc 1946
Banffsh: teacher maths/sc Portessie 1969–72; maths Buckie h s from 1972

BIRNIE Ian Malcolm   BSc(eng) 1942
turbine eng CEGB NW reg from 1975

BIRNIE James Arthur   MA 1927 MB ChB 1931
MBE 1972 FRCGP 1973
g p Aber from 1948

BIRNIE or Clarke, Jeannie Morrison   MB ChB 1921
d Malmesbury 8.6.79

BIRNIE Mary Morrison   MA 1929

BIRNIE Norman   MA 1932
min Bannockburn 1936–42, Guyana 1943–50, Monquhitter 1951–54, Stockton-on-Tees 1955–60, Cardiff 1960–71; mod. gen assembly Presb C of E 1969–70; min St. George's ch Bexhill-on-Sea from 1971

BIRNIE William   MB ChB 1936
g p Garelochhead till 1964; Kingseat hosp Newmachar: locum regist Apr–Aug 1965; med asst psychiat August 1965–75; retd 1975

BIRSE or Cameron, Emma Leslie
                              MB ChB 1951 MD 1956
DPM(Lond) 1970 MRCPsych 1975
asst m o h Fife c c 1963–67; sen asst m o h Dun 1967–68; med asst: Strathmartine hosp Dun 1968–70, Stratheden hosp Cupar 1970–72; psychiat Weston Day hosp Cupar from 1972

BIRSE Eric Leslie   *BSc 1950
soil scient Macaulay inst for soil res Aber from 1953

BIRSE or Dunlop, Margaret Williams   MA 1927
no longer on GC reg

BIRSE William Milne   *MA 1910 *BSc 1911
d Ontario 3.9.67 A UR XLII 180

BIRSS or Munro, Ann Grace Fulton   BSc 1954
resid Edin

BIRSS John Gordon Michie   MA 1946

BIRSS Ronald   MA 1937

BISHOP David McLean   *MA 1942
sect. man. control eng ICI petro chem div Teesside from 1963: vice pres Inst Measurement and Control 1971–74, pres 1974–75

BISSET Alexander   MB ChB 1900
d 1968

BISSET Alexander Andrew   MB ChB 1908 MD 1910
no longer on GC reg

BISSET or Hall, Alice Joyce   *MA 1940
resid Guildford

BISSET Anna Black   *MA 1941
CRK(Lond) 1966
teacher mod lang Selhurst g s for girls Croydon 1954–60; head Fr dept later dep head Farrington s s for girls Chislehurst 1961–70; teacher Engl Karnataka theol coll Mangalore S India 1971–76; pers secy *Christians Abroad* Lond from 1976

BISSET or Fyvie, Anne McRae   MA 1952
LLB(Edin) 1955 Dip Ed(Edin) 1955
teacher Sutton from 1964

BISSET Arthur James   MA 1938 LLB 1946
ptnr Connon, McRobert & Bisset solic Stonehaven from 1947

BISSET or Dawson, Catharine   *MA 1909
d Haddington 29.8.62 A UR XL 78

BISSET Charles Barron   MA BSc 1923
d Edin 16.6.66 A UR XLI 339

BISSET Charles Bruce   MA 1940
Aber: last head Rosemount s s 1969–72; dep head Harlaw acad from 1973

BISSET David Gove   MB ChB 1941

BISSET David Robert   BSc(agr) 1943
sen agr advis Kincardinesh from 1968

BISSET or Rogers, Doris Isobel   MB ChB 1948
resid Moffat

BISSET Eleanor   *MA 1914
d Torphins 18.4.71 A UR XLIV 209

BISSET or Ritchie, Frances Margaret   MA 1944
teacher Haddington p s from 1965

BISSET George Bruce   BSc(agr) 1924
MS(Corn) 1924
sen lect R'dg univ until 1965; retd

BISSET or Spackman, Georgina   *MA 1919
resid Blackburn

BISSET or Lyall, Iva Isabella   MA 1913
d Ashton-under-Lyne 20.8.69 *AUR* XLIII 329

BISSET John Davidson   MA 1919
rector St Modoc's Doune and St Mary's Aberfoyle
till 1966; retd; canon St Ninian's Cath Perth 1965–66;
hon canon from 1967

BISSET May Simpson   MB ChB 1946
sen regist anaest Middlesex hosp 1954–57; part
time anaest Boston Mass USA 1957–58; consult.
anaest: Queen Mary's hosp Carshalton 1960–62, Mt
Vernon hosp and Harefield hosp Northwood Lond
1962–72; private anaest practice nursing homes in loc
area and Lond from 1972
m Aber 3.4.56 Gerald P. Blanshard BA(Cantab)
consult. phys s of William B. Doncaster

BISSET Rita   MA 1924
teacher Buckie h s till 1963; retd

BISSET Reginald Rust
                    BSc(civ eng) 1937 BSc(elect eng) 1938
Elgin: man. dir David Forsyth & Co civ eng contr
1972–78, consult. civ eng i/c northern off. Cowan &
Linn consult. civ/struct eng Glasg from 1978

BISSET Ruth Johnstone   MA 1941
teacher Aber: Central s s, Aber acad, Hazlehead
acad 1950–78
d Aber 24.5.78

BISSET or Findlay, Sheila Stodart   BSc 1924
resid Fochabers

BISSET Walter Davidson   MA 1921
resid Herne Bay
d Herne Bay 3.10.80 *AUR* XLIX 67

BISSET William John George   BL 1929

BITTINER John Bruce   MB ChB 1943
TD 1965
consult. Nott from 1963; clin teacher Nott from 1973

BLACK Agnes   *MA 1912 *BSc 1913
no longer on GC reg

BLACK Alfred Alexander   MA 1895
d Aber 11.8.65 *AUR* XLI 236

BLACK Arthurina Rosemary Margaret   MA 1955
teacher: Lyne of Skene 1960–61, Berkhamsted
1961–66; part time: Waterlooville 1966–68, Hitchin
from 1968
m Aber 29.3.61 Richard M. Lee BSc 1957 *qv*

BLACK or Bain, Catherine Helen   MA 1933
teacher Abdnsh: Logie Durno 1961–67, Chapel of
Garioch 1968–72

BLACK Flora Weir   *BSc 1940
scient civ serv Building Res Stat D o E from 1951

BLACK Gertrude May   MA 1924 BSc 1926 *1927
woman advis Nicolson Inst Stornoway till 1968;
retd

BLACK Isabella   MA 1910
head Ardmiddle s Turriff 1945–54; retd

BLACK or Christie, Isabella   MA 1917
no longer on GC reg

BLACK or Henderson, Isabella Ferguson   MA 1902
no longer on GC reg

BLACK Jane   MA 1912
teacher various posts Scot. 1913–17; spec qualif
Ger 1918; teacher mod lang Huddersfield Greenhead
h s for girls 1925–45; various posts Caithness 1947–51
d 5.12.81

BLACK or Atkins, J. Marguerite   *MA 1932
BA(Oxon) 1937
prin and prof Engl Maharani univ coll for women
Mysore India 1937–40; member HM diplom serv
1966–72; tut. in tut. coll from 1972

BLACK John Gordon   MB ChB 1929
DDMS: (BR) corps NW Europe 1958–60, h q TPS
Malta 1960–61; retd as brig. 1961; civ m o RNAS
Lossiemouth 1962–72; retd

BLACK or Petrie, Kathleen Jean   MA 1933
teacher classics/Fr St John Rigby g s later 6th form
coll Wigan from 1965

BLACK or Neville, Margaret   BSc 1954
part time lab asst nat rubber prod. res assoc Welwyn
Garden City 1970–73; part time teacher maths
Verulam s St Albans from 1974

BLACK or Gray, Margaret Carmichael   MA 1929
teacher Scalloway j s Shetland till 1966; retd

BLACK Marjorie Macadie
                            MB ChB 1944 DPH 1949
MFCM 1972
sen clin m o Dun from 1970

BLACK Morrice Alexander   MA 1886
no longer on GC reg

BLACK or Siviter, Nancy Mary Briscoe   *MA 1930
resid Kingswood Surrey

BLACK or MacVicar, Nellie Maria   MA 1919
resid Dunbar
d 16.2.81

BLACK Robert Alexander Ross   *BSc 1948

BLACK Russell   *BSc 1950 PhD 1958

BLACK Stanley Alfred Briscoe
MB ChB 1931 DPH 1933 MD 1944
wife *d* 1963
dep sen admin m o NE reg hosp board Aber from 1963; retd 1974

BLACK Thomas Muir   BSc(for) 1953 *1954 PhD 1957
d 2.11.72

BLACK William George   *MA 1928
retd Beverley 1972
d Lond –.11.78

BLACK Winifred Constance Robertson   *MA 1922
teacher: spec asst mod lang High s for girls Aber till 1965; retd

BLACKADDER or Evans, Isabelle Rosemary
*MA 1941

BLACKBURN Raymond Forrester
MB ChB 1951 DPH 1958
DObstRCOG 1957 MFCM 1972 MBIM 1975
2 i/c 23 para fd amb 1963–66; c o 23 para fd amb/s
m o AB forces 1967–70; c o BMH Hong Kong
1970–72; ADMS Eastern dist Colchester 1973–74;
dep cmdt RAMC TC 1974–75, ADG MoD 1975–76;
ADMS SE dist Aldershot from 1976
m(2) Farnborough 4.6.66 Ann D. Hubbard d of
William G. H. Richmond Surrey

BLACKHALL or Carlyle, Agnes Ethel Sharp
MA 1941
teacher Barassie p s Troon 1970–73; asst head
Bank St s Irvine from 1973

BLACKHALL Alexander   BSc 1949 *1950 PhD 1953
res chem ICI: dyestuffs div 1956–62, petro chem
and polymer lab Rincorn 1962–65, dyestuffs div
Blackley Manc 1965–71, sen res scient fibres div
Harrogate 1971–76; lab admin ICI Fibres Harrogate
from 1976

BLACKHALL or Robertson, Isabella Ewan   MA 1913
no longer on GC reg

BLACKHALL John Anderson   *BSc 1951
indust chem ICI Manc from 1955
m Manc 12.7.58 Sheelagh M. M. McKay secy d of
Charles S. McK. Middleton

BLACKIE Mary Jane Garden   MA 1915

BLACKLAWS Hector Ross   MA 1924 BCom 1926
S Africa from 1933: dir wool marketing comp Adolf
Mossenthal Port Elizabeth, secy civ serv club Cape
Town
d Cape Town 21.3.79

BLACKLAWS or Steele, Joan Mathieson   MA 1951
teacher Aber: part time pre nurs coll 1960–62 and
1964–74, Northfield acad 1974–75, prin guid Powis
acad from 1975

BLACKLAWS Peter Campbell   *MA 1951
Dip Ed(ESN)(Lond) 1966
Lond: teacher spec s 1962–66, head remed dept
1966–69; remed advis borough of Waltham Forest
1969–73; Wales: sen tut. Caerleon coll of educ Mon
1973–75, dir of stud. Gwent coll of higher educ from
1975
m Lond 20.8.65 Ann M. Evans Glam

BLACKWELL Alistair Macleod   MB ChB 1950
Derby: clin asst psychiat Pastures hosp Mickleover
from 1964, ptnr in group pract from 1971

BLAIR Edith   MA 1908
no longer on GC reg

BLAIR or MacNeill, Gwendolyn Ann   *BSc 1955

BLAIR or Leyland, Margaret Johnstone Grieve
MA 1952

BLAKE or Donald, Adelaide Victoria   BSc 1925
no longer on GC reg

BLAKE Isabella Downie   *MA 1924
resid Aber

BLANCE George William   MA 1927
JP 1966
head Central p s Lerwick till 1966; retd
d Lerwick 11.3.77

BLANCE or Barclay, Laura Margaret   MA 1951
teacher Hamnavoe Shetland from 1965

BLANCE Thelma   *MA 1953 PhD 1956
Glasg corp plan. dept 1957–73; Aber NESJPAC
sen plan. 1973–75; Grampian reg c: dep dir phys plan.
from 1975
TA: Aberd OTC 1952–57; signals regiments Glasg
(capt, sqdn cmdr) 1957–69

BLUES Ernest Thompson   *BSc 1953
PhD(R'dg)

BLUES Roy Gibb   MB ChB 19848
g p Lochgelly from 1959

BLYTH John   MA 1910

BLYTH Norman Macgregor Downie   MB ChB 1948
FRCOG 1973
regist obst/gyn St Mary Abbots hosp Lond 1960–62;
locum consult. obst/gyn Welsh hosp board 1962–64;
consult. obst/gyn E Glamorgan gen hosp Wales from
1964

BOCHEL Alexander Main   BSc(eng) 1949
sen asst W. A. Fairhurst & Ptnrs (formerly F. A.
Macdonald & Ptnrs) consult. eng Glasg from 1954

BODDIE or Laing, Margaret Sim   MA 1943
teacher Springhill p s 1962–72; Powis acad: remed
teacher from 1972, also year mistress from 1973

BODENSTEIN Nicholas Combrink   *MB ChB 1921
d S Africa 29.9.74

BODIE Samuel Murphy Walford   MB ChB 1940
d Aber 1.1.74 *A UR* XLV 449

BODONHELYI Joseph   PhD 1936 DD 1960
d Budapest 1966 *A UR* XLI 341

BOGGIE Robert   *BSc 1953 PhD 1956
Macaulay Inst for soil research Aber from 1956

BOND or Connon, Margaret Donaldson   MA 1946
teacher Weymouth: div educ comm 1963–70, sen mistress Engl dept Convent of the Sacred Heart from 1970

BONNAR Beatrice Dunnett   MA 1926 BD 1937
min EU Congr church Langholm 1941–66; retd Langholm

BONNER or Garden, Davidina Barclay   *MA 1931
teacher Engl High s for girls Aber; retd

BONNEY Henry Claude   MB ChB 1925

BOOKER Patrick Kilgour   *MA 1949
OBE 1968
Aden: asst chief secy 1961–63, sen then prin advis Br High Comm 1963–67; seconded as dev secy Fed of S Arabia 1965–66 then perm secy Min of Finance Fed of S Arabia 1966–67; retd from HM overseas civ serv 1968; contr admin Rolls Royce 1968–69; Aberd: sen admin asst 1969–70, asst secy from 1970

BOOKER Robert Kilgour   MA 1950 ᵈLLB 1950
sen ptnr Allen & Gledhill advoc and solic Singapore from 1960; advoc and solic of the High Court of Singapore and Malaysia; solic Scot. and Eng, n p, comm of oaths; dir of numerous publ and private comps Far East from 1960; chmn Brit Assoc of Singapore; gov of United World Coll of SE Asia; member Internat Council of United World colleges; chmn or pres of several charitable organis Singapore m Singapore 8.10.58 Hazel E. Nathan d of J. S. N. BA(Cantab) Singapore

BOON-LONG Twee Swasdi   BCom 1926

BOOTH Alan James   MB ChB 1948
FFARCS 1958
sen anaest regist Liv 1958–60; consult. anaest: Liv 1960–62, Inv from 1962

BOOTH Alexander   MA 1900
d Kingston, Jamaica 15.8.61 *A UR* XXXIX 268

BOOTH Alexander Graham   MB ChB 1929
d Bedford 28.3.74 *A UR* XLVI 109

BOOTH Herbert Watt   MB ChB 1941
d Aber 31.10.64 *A UR* XLI 60

BOOTH Ian Farquhar   *MA 1932
rector Maxwelltown h s Dumfries 1970–74; retd

BOOTH James
                BSc 1924 *1925 PhD 1929 MB ChB 1938
d Aber 4.9.75 *A UR* XLVI 322

BOOTH James Graham Mackenzie
                                MA BL 1919 LLB 1922
d Stonehaven 4.12.69 *A UR* XLIII 444

BOOTH or Gauld, Kathleen   MB ChB 1924
d Dumfries 28.9.77 *A UR* XLVII 286

BOOTH or Horne, Lorna Leslie   MA 1946

BOOTH or Simpson-Craib, Moyra Louise   MA 1939
resid Fochabers

BOOTH Robert George   MA 1933
head Fraserburgh central s 1954 to 1974

BOOTH or Michie, Vera Constance Anne
                                        MB ChB 1945
part-time m o casualty dept ARI from 1970
husb d 23.3.78

BOOTH William   MB ChB 1925
d Derby 12.7.65 *A UR* XLI 150

BORTHWICK Edward Kerr   *MA 1946
Edin: sen lect Greek 1967–70, reader from 1970

BORTHWICK or Yuill, Mary Murdoch   *MA 1944
city/county councillor Nott 1972–77; member South Nott commun health c from 1978
marr diss 1973

BOSE Probodh Kumar   PhD 1955

BOTHWELL Alexander Fairweather
                                MA 1915 MB ChB 1922
d Aber 13.3.78 *A UR* XLVII 356

BOTHWELL Beatrix Bennet   MA 1929
retd 1968; resid Aber

BOTHWELL James   BSc 1935
Peterhead acad: prin teacher phys from 1960; retd 1975

BOTHWELL James Edward   MA 1927 LLB 1929
sole ptnr Macqueen & Findlater advoc Aber from 1936; Soc of Advoc Aber: lib from 1966, secy 1967–79
d Aber 14.11.80 *A UR* XLIX 68

BOTHWELL or Herbert, Jessie Anderson   MA 1936

BOTHWELL Peter William
                MB ChB 1946 DPH 1950 ᵈMD 1961
lect epidemiology and publ health Brist till 1967; head motor cycle res unit Birm 1967–69; head bio-eng BSA/Triumph res estab Warwicksh 1969–71; consult. bio-eng to Denver res inst USA 1971–72; man. dir Caliber Design Stratford-on-Avon from 1972

BOW or Burnett, Anne Edith   MA 1946
resid Edin
husb d 4.9.80

BOWEN Neville Arthur   PhD 1949
sen lect maths: Aberd 1959–61, Leic 1961–65; prof maths Royal univ Msida Malta from 1965; dean eng, arch. and sc from 1972
m Rome 21.7.58 Jacqueli1e Arrighi, Licence es Lettres (Grenoble) teacher Engl Casablanca d of Jacques F. A. Rome

BOWER Haddon Graham   *MA 1933 LLB 1935

BOWER or Barron, Mary   MA 1933
teacher Strichen till 1972; retd

BOWICK John   BSc 1955
LIBiol (Wolverhampton Poly) 1972
teacher biol Bankhead acad: asst 1967–72, prin from 1973; post-grad study plant path. s of agr Aber

BOWIE Frederick John Thomas
**   MB ChB 1924 DPH 1927**
d Aber 14.11.73 *AUR* xlv 447

BOWIE Harold Ian Cameron   MB ChB 1942

BOWIE Helena Mary   *MA 1920
d 21.7.75

BOWIE James Cameron   MB ChB 1940
Birm: asst m o till 1970; dep m o 1970–73; phys health serv 1973–75

BOWIE Mary Taylor   MA 1933
d Fochabers 17.7.68 *AUR* xliii 85

BOWIE Sheila Mary Lumsden   *MA 1951
asst prin teacher Engl Edin: Liberton s s 1961–74, Cranley from 1974

BOWIE Stanley Hay Umphray   *BSc 1941 DSc 1969
silver medal RSA 1959 FMSA 1963 FRS(Edin) 1970 FIMM 1973
Lond: chief consult. geol UKAEA 1955, asst dir chief geochem Inst of Geol Sc 1968; visiting prof applied geol Strath 1968; chmn Internat comm on ore microscopy (IMA) from 1970

BOWMAN or Stewart, Alice Fisher   *MA 1921
resid Aber

BOWMAN Frank James Sandison   MB ChB 1933
retd g p 1973
resid Milltimber Aber

BOWMAN John Wilson   MB ChB 1917
resid Southampton

BOWMAN Margaret Philip
**   MA 1919 MB ChB 1922**
g p till 1965; retd; resid Newcastle-u-Tyne

BOWMAN Robert   MA 1918 LLB 1920

BOWMAN William   MA BSc 1933 MB ChB 1940
lect clin chem Aberd from 1952; retd 1974
d Aber 18.3.77

BOWRING Michael John   BSc(for) 1952
m Aber 1956 Margaret N. Stewart DA d of William N. S.

BOWYER Alexander Albert   MA 1932 BD 1936
min of C of S North ch Aber from 1958; retd 1976; resid Stonehaven
d Aber 19.6.78 *AUR* xlviii 104

BOXHALL John Alfred   *MA 1951
overseas course B Oxon 1958–59; Tanganyika: d c Kilbondo 1959–60; treas off. Dar es Salaam 1960–62; asst master Crosfields s Reading 1962–66; asst secy s Oriental and African stud. Lond 1966–71; secy inst adv leg. stud. from 1971

BOYD Alexander Millar   MA 1902
no longer on GC reg

BOYD Angus Archibald William   MB ChB 1949
g p Bolton from 1970

BOYD, Annabella Constance Eva   BSc 1925
d Aber 16.5.67 *AUR* xlii 365

BOYD Annie Evelyn   BSc 1913
d 13.9.73 *AUR* xlv 317

BOYD Catherine Thomson   MA 1935

BOYD Elizabeth Johnstone   MA 1909 BSc 1910
d 6.1.68

BOYD James Rodgers   MB ChB 1940
visiting phys Bannockburn I D hosp Stirling from 1958
m 16.2.42 Kathleen M. T. Black, Fyvie

BOYD Jeannie Strathdee   MA 1928
d Northallerton 15.9.67 *AUR* xlii 186

BOYD Leslie George   MB ChB 1936
g p Northallerton from 1946; retd 1976
d Northallerton 27.8.80 *AUR* xlix 69

BOYD or Davidson, Mary Falconer   MA 1903
no longer on GC reg

BOYD or Buchan, Olwyn   *MA 1925
teacher mod lang Peterhead acad 1956–59

BOYD Percy Stuart   *MA 1948 PhD 1952

BOYD Roderick MacSwan   MA 1945
min C of S Amulree and Strathbrann ch Dunkeld 1961–71; retd; resid Edin
d Edin 31.8.76 *AUR* xlvii 106

BOYD William Hugh Falconer   MB ChB 1941
sen anaest Bangour hosp W Lothian from 1950; retd

BOYNE Alexander William   BSc 1944 *1948
FRS(Edin) 1973
head statist dept Rowett inst Aber from 1948

BOYNE James Anderson   MA 1923
d Aber 4.4.71 *AUR* xliv 211

BOYNE or Witheridge, Jean McDonald   MA 1944
resid Stony Stratford
husb *d* 29.12.73

BRADLEY Hunter Witley   MA 1946
teacher: head geog/geol dept John Marley s
N'cle-u-Tyne from 1959

BRADY Harold Samuel   MB ChB 1934
no longer on GC reg

BRAID Kenneth William   BSc(agr) 1913 BSc 1914
retd; resid Skene

BRAND Hamish Douglas Ferguson   MB ChB 1913
no longer on GC reg

BRAND Jane   *MA 1928
teacher mod lang Perth acad till 1966; retd

BRAND Margaret Hilda   MA 1924

BRAND Margaret Mary   MA 1947
teacher Aber: Ferryhill s 1961–62, High s for girls
1962; secy/translator to man. dir USM (France) Paris
from 1962
m Aber 19.10.62 Paul E. Darmon; marr diss 1971

BRANDER James Melvin   *BSc 1953

BRANDER or Paterson, Lillian Mary   BSc(agr) 1940

BRANDS Alexander Campbell   MA 1930 LLB 1931
d Aber 21.1.67 *AUR* xlii 369

BRANDS John   BSc 1948
FRSS 1956
plan. man. Ciba Labs Horsham from 1969

BRANNEN Ian Cameron   MB ChB 1947
MFCP(Lond) 1972
dep county m o Norfolk 1963–73; dist commun phys
Norwich from 1974

BRASH Robert Alexander   BSc 1944

BREBNER Allan   MB ChB 1929
reg m o Min of Health Lond till 1968; retd; resid
Aber

BREBNER Arthur   *BSc(eng) 1947 PhD 1952
prof eng Queen's univ Kingston Ont from 1957

BREBNER George Gill   *MA 1948
def res staff British Emb Wash DC 1959–62; RAE
Farnborough from 1962

BREBNER Hugh   *MA 1905 BSc 1906
retd
d Bearsden 4.12.73 *AUR* xlv 444

BREBNER Hugh   MB ChB 1943 MD 1954
FRCPGlas 1968 FRCP(Lond) 1972

consult. phys West I Glasg and hon clin lect Glas
from 1955

BREBNER or Speirs, Inez Mary   MB ChB 1942
part time g p 1942–63; asst m o h Stirlingsh
1963–73; m o DHSS from 1966

BREBNER James Joseph   *MA 1953

BREBNER John Low   *BSc 1955 PhD 1959
asst lect nat phil Aberd 1958–60; NRC post doct
fell. Ottawa 1960–62; res scient CERI Geneva 1962–
68; assoc prof Montr 1968–74, prof from 1974
m Geneva 24.7.69 Eva M. Pobitschka, Dip Biol
(Geneva) res asst immunology d of Ernst A. P. Dip
Ing(Dresden) Dormagen Germany

BREBNER Lilias White   *MA 1951
Univ Leeds: warden Lupton Hall till 1960, lect Ger
till 1968
m Leeds 18.4.68 Richard F. M. Byrn, BA(Dub) lect
Ger univ Leeds s of Francis M. B. MB ChB(Dub)
Kilmacanogue Co Wicklow

BREBNER Margaret Evelyn   MA 1954 Dip Ed 1955
teacher mod lang Turriff acad 1956–65; spec asst
from 1965

BRECKENRIDGE Mary Morrison   MA 1949

BREEZE John   MB ChB 1950
MRCOG 1958 FRSM 1968 FRCOG 1974
consult. obst/gyn Gt Yarmouth and Waveney dist
from 1968

BREMNER Charles   *MA 1925
d 1.2.64

BREMNER James George   MB ChB 1926
no longer on GC reg

BREMNER Mary Aileen Anne   MA 1944

BREMNER or Allan, Mary Christina
resid Crookston Glasg   **BSc 1923 MA 1924**

BREMNER or Christie, Mary Flett   MA 1928
husb *d* 1969
teacher Smithfield s Aber 1965–67
d Fochabers 31.8.80

BREMNER Robert Yool   *MA 1904 BSc 1907
no longer on GC reg

BREMNER William   MA 1907
no longer on GC reg

BREMNER William Andrew Alexander   *BSc 1953

BREMNER William James   MB ChB 1927
g p Hale till 1964; consult. anaest Wythenshowe &
N Cheshire hosps 1964–70; retd; resid Ramsey IOM
d Sutton Coldfield 4.12.79

BREMNER William John   *BSc 1952

BRÉTONIÈRE or Bamford, Marianne de la
MA BCom 1936
secy trg Lond 1936–37, secy posts Lond/ARP h q Aber 1939–41; secy to dir Fraserburgh/Lond 1941–45; organis secy Scot. marr guid council Edin 1952–64; teacher: bus. stud. Edin 1965–69, prin bus. stud. from 1969

BREWSTER Gordon Watt   MA 1952
head teacher Aberdeensh: Finzean 1962–66, Tarland 1966–69, Clerkhill Peterhead 1969–74, Dyce from 1974

BRIDE John William   BSc(for) 1951

BRIDGES or Rae, Mary Davidson   *MA 1939
resid Glasg

BRIEN Thomas Ralph   *BSc 1951
head sc dept St Gregory's comp s Kirkby 1960–64; lect Jordanhill coll of educ Glasg from 1964

BRIGHT Edgar Bulmer   MB ChB 1937
hon phys to H.M. the Queen 1971–72; dir of health and res (RAF) Lond 1970–71; off. comm Princess Alexandra's hosp Wroughton 1971–72

BRISTER Graham Harrold   BSc(for) 1953
PhD(Wash) 1970
col for. serv till 1964; post grad course Oxon 1959–60; Wash. USA: timber eng 1964–65, teaching asst 1965–70; asst prof Georgia from 1970

BRITTAIN David Antony   MA 1952 LLB 1954

BROCKIE Arthur Alexander   MB ChB 1941
d Northland NZ 1.3.71

BROCKIE Edward Henry   MA 1952

BROCKIE Margaret Millicent   MA 1912
d Aber 29.7.77

BROCKIE or McCrea, Mary Davidson   MA 1915
teacher Kirkcaldy 1916–28
resid Newark-on-Trent
d 1977 *AUR* XLVII 284

BROCKS Arthur William   MA 1948
(conferred for long service of exceptional merit)
d Aber 7.4.75 *AUR* XLVI 325

BROCKS Basil Ernest   MB ChB 1941
d Brentwood 14.1.79 *AUR* XLVIII 232

BRODIE or Read, Alison Garland   MB ChB 1944
resid Blebo Craigs

BRODIE Douglas MacBean   MB ChB 1941
d Altrincham –.11.78

BRODIE Edward Adam   MA 1930 LLB 1932
sole ptnr A. and E. A. Brodie solic Banff 1933–76; then consult.
wife d 20.1.70

BRODIE James Hurrie   MB ChB 1937
m o DHSS Blackpool from 1971
m Singapore 28.10.59 Winifred M. Hiscock DPH(Lond) med pract d of Walter G. H. PhD(Lond)

BRODIE or MacGillivray, Margaret Ann   MA 1912
d Newtonmore –.1.74

BROMBERG or Jay, Helena June   *MA 1949
Lond: freelance broadcaster 1955–65; market res p r asst 1965–72; organis secy/admin dir from 1972

BROMBERG Priscilla Betty   MA 1952
Toronto: secy Shell Oil Co 1959–61; off. man. lib board of educ 1962–63; lib asst univ of W Ont Lond Ontario from 1963; private scholar working in field of 16th cent. Engl printing from 1970
m Tor 1.10.60 Robert W. Tracy BA(Tor) city plan.

BROOK David Whiteley   PhD 1952
sen tech off. Br Titan Products Billingham 1962–66; tech serv man. Titanium Intermediates 1967–75; teacher chem Cleveland educ auth from 1976

BROOKER Ian Mackintosh   MB ChB 1950
g p Shetland: Yell till 1965, Levenwick from 1965

BROOKER William Dixon   BSc 1953 *1958
prin teacher geog Aberlour h s 1959, Keith g s 1960–62, 65–66; seconded King Richard s Dhekelia Cyprus 1962–65; tut. organis extra-mural stud. Aberd: Elgin 1966–69, Aber from 1969

BROOKS Alexander   MB ChB 1925
major RAMC; on staff Blaina hosp Nantyglo Mon from 1955

BROOKS Helen Porter   MA 1948
teacher Inverurie acad 1964–75, Kellands s Inverurie from 1975

BROUGH Esther Jones   MA 1911
no longer on GC reg

BROWN Alexander   MB ChB 1936
consult. anaest Hull and E Riding from 1950

BROWN Alexander Aitken Lawson   *MA 1952
prin teacher classics Ellon acad 1950–76

BROWN Alexander Phimister   LLB 1949
d Aber 18.6.78 *AUR* XLVIII 107

BROWN or Stewart, Alice Ann   MA 1918
resid Aber
husb d Aber 14.7.66 *AUR* XLI 338
d Aber 25.3.80

BROWN Andrew Hunter
MA 1912 BSc 1912 MB ChB 1915
d 14.9.73

BROWN or Robertson, Anna Maria Margaret
MA 1937
d 6.4.67

BROWN or House, Annie   MA 1942

BROWN or Mackintosh, Annie Stewart   MA 1927
d Cullen 14.2.72 *AUR* XLIV 431

BROWN Augusta Elizabeth Rudmose   *MA 1904
d Westbury on Trym, Bristol 13.12.66 *AUR* XLII 80

BROWN or McLachlan, Barbara Annie   MA 1917
resid Aber

BROWN Beatrice Rose   MA 1922
retd 1962; resid Aber
d Aber 7.1.79 *AUR* XLVIII 228

BROWN or Steen, Catherine Elizabeth
                                    MA 1950 *1951
teacher Westholme indep s Billinge End Blackburn
till 1960; emig Australia 1963

BROWN or MacLaren, Catherine McKay   MA 1923
teacher Aber till 1957; resid Aber
d Aber 23.10.79

BROWN Charles Alexander
                    MA 1935 MB ChB 1939 MD 1946
consult. ophth surg Bristol Eye hosp and SW reg
health auth from 1951

BROWN Charles Grant   MA 1927 LLB 1929
   JP
sen ptnr Burnett & Reid advoc Aber from 1943; dir
publ and private comps
d Aberlour 11.8.81

BROWN Charles Wilson   MA 1942
   BA(OU) 1973
teacher phys: Aber tech coll 1959–77 (seconded to
Ifunda tech coll Tanzania 1966), Inverurie acad from
1977

BROWN or John, Christine Beatrice Anderson
                                    MB ChB 1947
d 1.12.66 *AUR* XLII 374

BROWN Donald Duncan   MB ChB 1942 MD 1946
no longer on GC reg

BROWN or Murray, Dorothea Catherine Wallace
                                    BSc 1948
relief teacher Kensaleyre s Skye 1957–73; vice-
county-recorder Skye for BSBI from 1966

BROWN Douglas Alexander   BSc(eng) 1950

BROWN Douglas Watson   BSc(eng) 1933

BROWN Eelin Mary   MA 1953

BROWN Ellen Mary   MA 1931
youth and commun serv organis Aber educ comm
till 1972; retd

BROWN or Gould, Florence Elisabeth McCaw
                                    *MA 1951
   ABPsS 1954

Southampton: part-time teacher 1962–65; member
res team surv of disturbed adolescents Wessex 1965;
publ as *Stress in Youth* 1971; part-time educ psych
from 1966

BROWN Frances Mary   *MA 1919
no longer on GC reg

BROWN Francis Frederick   MB ChB 1913
no longer on GC reg

BROWN Frederick William Campbell
             MB ChB 1915 DPH 1921 *MD 1922
d 22.2.71

BROWN George Taylor   MA 1919
d Aber 1.5.66 *AUR* XLII 85

BROWN Georgia Ella   MA 1919
d Aber 21.12.77 *AUR* XLVII 356

BROWN Helen Clow   MB ChB 1954

BROWN Hilda   MA 1919
no longer on GC reg

BROWN Ian Macdiarmid   MB ChB 1942
consult geriat Eastbourne hosp group from 1965;
BMA: member council 1968–69, and chmn group
med admin 1972–76

BROWN Ian Mitchell   LLB 1949

BROWN or Singer, Isabel Mary   MA 1947
radon asst Aberd 1947–49; teacher: ISS Centre
Awali Bahrain 1962–64, Mackie acad Stonehaven
1965–70, Lochaber h s Fort William from 1970

BROWN Isobel Campbell   MB ChB 1920

BROWN Isobel Janie   MA 1929
teacher Aber till 1968; retd

BROWN James   BSc 1923
no longer on GC reg

BROWN James   MB ChB 1944 MD 1956
   FRCR
consult. radiol: Manc and Lanc from 1954

BROWN James Donald   BSc(agr) 1924
   CBE 1976
Orkney: DL from 1968, convener c c from 1970
d Stromness 1.5.78

BROWN James Mortimer   *MA 1950
Essex: head Engl dept Torells c s Grays, head sen s
Hassenbrook c s Stanford-le-Hope; head Beacon Hill
s Aspatria Cumberland

BROWN or Clark, Jenny Brewster   *MA 1922
retd 1958; resid Stonehaven
husb *d* 3.9.64

BROWN John   MA 1953
teacher Aber: Ruthrieston s s 1961–64, 1st asst jun

s RGC 1964–73/housemaster RGC boarding house 1964–69, Kittybrewster p s 1973; asst head: Cummings Park p s 1974, Walker Rd p s from 1974

BROWN John Gatherer   MB ChB 1914
  d 10.12.62

**BROWN or McPherson, Kathleen Nora Frances
                                                                MA 1920**
  resid Aber
  husb *d* –.6.49

**BROWN or Glogan, Lesley Elizabeth Melville
                                                                MA 1948**
  resid Hastings

BROWN or Hudson, Louise   MA 1914
  resid Aber

BROWN Mabel Kathleen   MA 1955
  teacher: Mufulira h s Zambia 1960–62, Aber coll of comm 1965–67, Oldhall s Hethersett 1967–70, Dereham h s Norfolk from 1971
  m Mufulira 9.12.61 Raymond H. Rawlins sales dir s of Henry R. Newbury

BROWN Maggie   MA 1948
        (conferred for long service of exceptional merit)
  d Aber 28.10.64 *AUR* XLI 60

BROWN Margaret   MA 1929

BROWN Margaret   MA 1932
  d Peterhead 28.2.68 *AUR* XLII 370

**BROWN or Brunnen, Margaret Christian Thomson
                                                                MA 1942**
  Aber: part-time soc worker child guid centre 1953–55, part-time interviewer soc surv soc dept Foresterhill 1962–64, part-time case worker Assoc Soc Serv from 1964

BROWN Margaret Eliza   *MA 1915
  resid Aber
  d Aber 10.7.76

BROWN or Macleod, Margaret Florence   MA 1919
  retd; resid Darlington

**BROWN or Parker or Saxby, Mary Murray
                                                                MA 1943**
  MSc(Louisville)
  d 19.8.75

BROWN Patricia Margaret   *BSc 1953
  Aberd: res asst dept chem 1964–72, res off. from 1972

BROWN or Steventon, Rachel Mitchell   MA 1913
  no longer on GC reg

BROWN Richard Petrie   *MA 1949

BROWN Robert   *MB ChB 1905 *MD 1907
  no longer on GC reg

BROWN Robert   MB ChB 1951
  MRCP(C) 1965 FRCP(C) 1969
Canadian Decoration and clasp
sen m o Metz France 1958–63; asst head dept psychiat nat def med centre Ottawa 1963–68 promoted lt col; chief psychiat Can. Forces hosp Kingston, Ont from 1968; now med dir reg psychiat centre (Ont) for Canadian penitentiary serv

BROWN Robert Pearson Masson   MB ChB 1935
  h o Hereford gen hosp 1935–36; g p: Inv 1936–37, Edzell 1937–45, W Bromwich 1945–48, Aber from 1948

BROWN Robert Walker   MB ChB 1913
  d Peterhead 19.3.62 *AUR* XXXIX 380

BROWN Roy Dudley   MA 1935 LLB 1937
  Lond: dep dir Shipbuilders & Repairers Nat Assoc and secy Shipbuilding Corp from 1938

BROWN William   BL 1926
  ptnr Esslemont & Cameron advoc Aber from 1944; secy Aber and N E legal aid comm 1952–70; member Council Law Soc of Scot. 1961–75; member Scot. solic discip comm from 1971; hon sheriff from 1974

BROWN William Baxter Brodie   MB ChB 1925
  d Aboyne 6.4.63 *AUR* XL 205

BROWN William Cairns   *MA 1945

BROWN William Imray   *MA 1950

BROWN William Peddie   MA 1956

BROWN William Scott (Sir)   *MA 1912 LLD 1956
  d Aber 17.5.68 *AUR* XLII 350

BROWNE Francis James   MB ChB 1906 *MD 1919
  d Sydney Australia 17.8.63 *AUR* XL 300

BROWNE Magdalene Gordon   MA 1928
  d Aber 19.12.69 *AUR* XLIII 446

BROWNE Ronald Austin   MB ChB 1953

BROWNE William   BD 1911
  d 19.5.69

**BROWNIE William Campbell
                                            *BSc(eng) 1947 MA 1953**
  MIMechE 1958 CEng 1962
AEI(M/c):grp ldr 1958–68; Thurso Tech coll: lect 1968–74, sen lect from 1974

BROWNLEE Robert Wyness   *MA 1925
  FEIS 1950
prin teacher maths St. Modan's h s Stirling till 1969; retd
wife *d* 1966
m(2) Bridge of Allan 27.12.67 Jane M. Anderson or Dean milliner d of Charles A. Hamilton

BROWNLEE William   BSc(eng) 1953

BRUCE or Lamb, Agnes   MA 1926
b Peterhead 20.11.26
resid Christchurch NZ

BRUCE or Dobie, Agnes Gladys   MB ChB 1922
d 3.11.63

BRUCE Alexander   BCom 1924
no longer on GC reg

BRUCE Alexander   *BSc 1931 MA 1932
prin teacher chem Aber g s 1962–74; retd
m Aber 29.3.69 Agnes F. Gray Aber

BRUCE Alice Margaret   MA 1948

BRUCE or Pearson, Alice Mary   *MA 1947

BRUCE Andrew Buchan   MA 1922
d Wick 9.11.64 *AUR* xli 57

BRUCE Andrew Watt   MB ChB 1947

BRUCE Charlotte Diverall   MA 1928
teacher: Pegswood 1930–33, Carlisle 1933–35,
Ashington 1935–38, Windsor 1938–43, Newport
(Salop) 1943–46, Chichester from 1946; retd 1965

BRUCE David   MA 1951
teacher Nairn acad: 1964–73, asst prin classics from
1973
m Inverurie 24.7.64 Rosella Gall d of William G.
Inverurie

BRUCE David Breckinridge   *BSc 1949 PhD 1953
head chem lab Courtauld's chem eng Coventry
1958–67; tech man. Internat Paint Co Birm 1967–70;
dev dir Goodlass Wall & Co Liv from 1970

BRUCE or Milne, Doris Margaret   MA 1923
resid Reading

BRUCE Douglas James   BSc(eng) 1945
MIMechE 1957 SA Govt Certif Mech Eng 1958,
Elect Eng 1959 MIEE 1966 CEng 1966
chief eng Nat Chem Products Durban 1960–62;
Atomic Power Constructions Lond: sen eng 1962–68,
group eng 1969–75; Eptisa-Ghesa-TRSA Madrid:
chief eng mech equip sect. from 1975

BRUCE Douglas Walter   MB ChB 1909
deceased

BRUCE Duncan McKenzie   MA 1949
C of S min N Parish Ch Stirling from 1963

BRUCE Edward George   MA 1914 BSc(agr) 1919
resid Aber

BRUCE Elizabeth Alexandra   MA 1926
teacher sc pre-nursing coll Aber till 1969; retd

BRUCE Ethel Mary   *MA 1916

BRUCE or McGlashan, Frances Elizabeth
                                MB ChB 1927
no longer on GC reg

BRUCE Frederick Fyvie   MA 1932 DD 1957
MA(Manc) 1963 FBA 1973
prof bibl crit and exegesis Manc from 1959

BRUCE George   MA 1908
retd 1952; resid Edzell
d Edzell 24.6.79

BRUCE George   MB ChB 1948
g p: Dornoch 1952–53, Woking from 1953

BRUCE George Gordon   MB ChB 1915
retd; resid Aber
wife *d* 5.11.73
d Inverurie 6.6.76 *AUR* xlvii 102

BRUCE George Macpherson   MA 1936
dep rector Br of Don acad Aber from 1972

BRUCE George Robert   *MA 1932
retd BBC 1970; first fell. creative writing Glas
1971–73; extra mural lect Glas 1973; USA: visiting
prof Union theol seminary Richmond Virginia Jan
1974; poet in resid Orescott coll Prescott Arizona
from Feb 1974; visiting prof Coll of Wooster 1976–77

BRUCE George Smith   BSc(agr) 1922
d Edin 24.2.67 *AUR* xlii 360

BRUCE or Holmes, Isobel Annie   MA 1927
no longer on GC reg

BRUCE James   MB ChB 1954
h s mat hosp Dumfriessh 1958–62; g p Edin from
1962
m Edin 27.7.64 Patricia A. McAinsh MA(Edin) d of
James McA. Edin

BRUCE or Coull, Jannetta   MA 1921
resid Brentwood

BRUCE or Noble, Jean Malcolm   MA 1937
resid Hamilton Ontario

BRUCE or Pirie, Jeannie Reid   MA 1926
head Dunecht s till 1961; teacher maths Cults acad
1964–68
husb *d* –.9.60

BRUCE or Macpherson, Jeannie Robertson
                                MA 1949
teacher Aber: Kittybrewster s till 1960, St Peter's
RC s 1966–67; Fernielea s from 1967, sen remed
teacher from 1972

BRUCE or Wilson, Jessie (Janet) Coull   MA 1922
retd (teaching) 1962
d Aber 30.11.73

BRUCE John   MB ChB 1941
g p Crowle from 1970

BRUCE John   BSc 1944

BRUCE John Brantingham   BSc(for) 1947
for. serv BC Canada from 1947

BRUCE Kenneth   *MA 1916
no longer on GC reg

BRUCE or Dick, Margaret   MB ChB 1946
g p: Rotherham and clin asst Sheffield and
Rotherham hosp till 1965, Wakefield 1965–71; locum
sen h o ERI from 1973

BRUCE or Bowman, Margaret Jamieson Hill
                                    ***MA 1949**
teacher Fr/Lat Aboyne acad from 1950

BRUCE Margaret Morrice   MA 1924
no longer on GC reg

BRUCE Marjorie Graham   *MA 1951

BRUCE or Morrison, Marjory Leslie   MA 1925
teacher Ferryhill s Aber; retd 1964; resid Aber
d Aber 7.8.79 *AUR* xlviii 441

BRUCE Mary Brown   MA 1948
prop. pharm Balfron from 1969

BRUCE Mary Helen   MA 1947
Lond: asst prin mental health soc worker City of
Westminster 1965–70; soc work sen off DHSS
Alexander Fleming House from 1970

BRUCE or Lindsay, Mary Wilson   MB ChB 1944
resid Aboyne

BRUCE or Burnett, Muriel Georgina   MA 1941

BRUCE Nan Helen   MB ChB 1947
DA 1966
anaest: Leeds area, Hull 1957–59, Aber 1959–61,
Teesside, N'castle reg from 1961

BRUCE or Davidson, Priscilla Constance   BSc 1954
resid Mintlaw

BRUCE Robert   *MA 1933
OBE 1962
cultural attaché Brit emb Budapest 1963–65; rep Brit
council Hong Kong 1966–68; assoc prof polit sc
Eastern Kentucky univ USA 1968–69; prof polit sc
Prescott coll Arizona from 1969

BRUCE Robert Anderson   *MA 1933
head dept gen educ Singapore polytech 1957 to
retd; resid Aber

BRUCE Robert Douglas   MB ChB 1928
OStJ 1963
RAF med br 1939–63; m o M o D Lond from 1963

BRUCE Robert Gauld   MB ChB 1955
MRCGP 1965
sen h o: Gorleston hosp Gt Yarmouth 1958–59,

West Norwich hosp 1959; g p Oulton Broad Lowestoft
from 1959

BRUCE Ronald John   MB ChB 1945

BRUCE Ronald Marshall   *MA 1950
teacher Dun: Harris acad 1952–61, coll of comm
1961–67; prin hist Forfar acad from 1967

BRUCE Ronald Reith   BSc(eng) 1947

BRUCE or Birch, Sheila   MA 1950
resid Romford

BRUCE or Brown, Stella   MA 1950
teacher Abdnsh: Hatton 1960–69, Boddam from
1969–74, Auchterellon from 1974

BRUCE Wilhelmina   MA 1910

BRUCE William   MB ChB 1925
d Inv 18.4.62 *AUR* xxxix 383

BRUCE William Anderson   MA 1951

BRUCE William Riddoch   MB ChB 1950

BRUCE Winifred Mary   MA 1952
teacher maths Norfolk: Westcliff h s 1964–70, head
of dept King's Lynn 1970–78; head maths dept Alice
Harpur s Bedford from 1978

BRUNNEN Peter Lance   MB ChB 1939
FACCP 1958
consult. thoracic surg Grampian Health Board from
1952; clin sen lect thoracic surg Aberd from 1970

BRYANT Ronald William Gower   *MA 1937
Canada: dev plan off. Halifax Nova Scotia 1961–62;
asst prof Univ de Montréal 1962–66, assoc prof
Concordia univ Montreal from 1966; consult. to
Quebec prov govt and govt Canada from time to
time; author of *Land, Private Property, Public Control*
(Montreal 1972) and numerous papers

BUCHAN Agnes King   *MA 1938
teacher Fr High s for girls Aber 1963–66; lect coll
of educ Aber from 1966

BUCHAN Alexander   MB ChB 1936
consult. obst/gyn E Reg hosp board from 1946

BUCHAN Alexander McIntosh   *MA 1919
d St Louis USA 16.7.69 *AUR* xliii 329

BUCHAN Alexander Presley
                        MB ChB 1942 DPH 1947
med supt and consult. psychiat St. Margaret's hosp
Birm from 1957
d Tamworth 18.5.81

BUCHAN Alexander Reid   BCom 1926

BUCHAN Alexander Reid   BSc(eng) 1956

BUCHAN Alfred John   MB ChB 1922
d Ilford 15.12.68 *AUR* xliii 212

BUCHAN Andrew   *MA 1934
teacher Peterhead: jun instr centre 1938–40, acad 1940–41, Central s 1946–57; RA intellig corps Europe 1941–45; spec ag Prudential insur co of America Montclair 1957–79; retd
m Montclair NJ 20.7.57 Jean C. Cowe

BUCHAN Andrew Robertson   MA 1946 LLB 1949
d Nassau, Bahamas 1.10.79

BUCHAN or Suckling, Anna
                              BSc 1930 *1931 PhD 1935
d 19.7.64 *AUR* xl 400

BUCHAN Christian   *MA 1946

BUCHAN or Nieuwenhuyzen, Dorothy May
                              MA 1951

BUCHAN Edith   MA 1928
d Rhyl 28.7.77

BUCHAN or Merchant, Elizabeth   MA 1916
resid Torphins

BUCHAN Elsie Isabel   MA 1925
teacher maths/sc Kaimhill s Aber till 1964; retd

BUCHAN Forbes   MB ChB 1924

BUCHAN Ian James   MB ChB 1942
g p Poole from 1947

BUCHAN Isobel Bruce   *MA 1935
teacher mod lang: Gordon s Huntly 1941–48, Perth acad 1948–73; retd

BUCHAN or MacInnes, Jean Park   MA 1941
remed teacher Engl Stromness acad Orkney from 1972

BUCHAN or Black, Jeanetta   MA 1946

BUCHAN Jim   *MA 1949 *MEd 1954
prin teacher Engl subj and dep head Culter s 1960–66; prin teacher hist and dep rector Cults acad 1966–71; dep rector 1971–75; rector Peterhead acad from 1975

BUCHAN John   BSc(eng) 1953

BUCHAN John Andrew Noble   MA BCom 1929

BUCHAN Joseph   MA 1950

BUCHAN Joseph Forrest   MA 1924
d Elgin 3.3.79 *AUR* xlviii 228

BUCHAN Lavina Evelyn   MA 1938
Northfield s Aber: woman advis 1963–72, dep head from 1972

BUCHAN or Pollitt, Lesley Smith   *MA 1935
prin teacher guid Inv h s from 1972

BUCHAN or Merchant, Lizzie   MA 1916
no longer on GC reg

BUCHAN or Duchovny, Margaret   MA 1951

BUCHAN Margaret Mary Cordiner   MA 1946
Peterhead: teacher Buchanhaven p s 1963–66, dep head 1966–76; head Meethill p s from 1976

BUCHAN or Collin, Margaret Noble   MA 1928

BUCHAN or Wilkie, Martha Third   MA 1926
teacher Engl/Fr/geog/hist Skene s s 1960–67; retd; resid Aber

BUCHAN or Adams, Mary   MA 1919
resid Grangemouth
d Grangemouth 12.5.79

BUCHAN or Martin, Mary Simpson   MB ChB 1942
school m o Birm from 1957; sen clin h o Birm

BUCHAN Ogilvie Milne Clarke   *MA 1951
lect hist of polit thought univ of W.I. Jamaica 1960–63; staff tut. phil Durh from 1964
m(2) London 22.8.58 Wendy I. M. Oldridge; marr diss 1964
(3) Durham 14.10.67 Janet M. Rennie

BUCHAN Robert   BSc 1954
Member Assoc Prof Eng of Ontario 1965
Ontario: field geol Sudbury 1954–61, geol/mineralogist Falconbridge Nickel Mines Thornhill from 1961
m Copper Cliff Ontario 15.12.56 Mema Nicoli secy
d of Joseph N. Copper Cliff

BUCHAN Robina Smart   MA 1928
Walthamstow: teacher St Mary's C of E s 1930–38, Beaconsfield s s 1938–52, dep head 1952–67; retd; resid Rosehearty

BUCHAN Samuel   MA 1925 BSc 1927 *1928
works dir Wright Dental Co Dundee 1959–70; retd

BUCHAN Stevenson   BSc 1929 *1930 PhD 1934
CBE 1971 FRSE 1962
dep chief scient off./asst dir spec serv geol surv 1960–67; chief geol Inst Geol Sc 1967–68; chief scient off./dep dir Inst Geol Sc 1968–71; retd 1971

BUCHAN William   BSc 1931
d Aber 2.1.68 *AUR* xlii 370

BUCHAN William
                    MA 1916 MB ChB 1918 *MD 1926
second asst to prof path. Aberd 1921–22
Aber: g p till 1958, member med board MPNI 1940–66; part-time asst reg m o N E reg board 1958–75; m o i/c limb clin ARI 1969–73

BUCHAN William Robertson   MB ChB 1950
CCFP 1970
Canada: g p Whitehorse Yukon till 1972; asst prof univ BC dept fam pract Vancouver from 1975

BUCHANAN Donald   MB ChB 1908 MD 1911
no longer on GC reg

BUCHANAN or Crichton, Isabel Alison
*MA 1935 *MEd 1937
resid Bieldside Aber

BUCHANAN John Brownlie   *BSc 1951

BUCHANAN John Robert Mungo
MA 1947 Dip Ed 1949
Aber: dep head Muirfield p s 1958–66; dep head Middlefield p s 1966–70, head Springhill p s from 1970

BUCHANAN Malcolm   MA 1925
retd 1972; resid Conon Bridge

BUCHANAN or Davison, Mary Alston   BSc 1951
part-time teacher Dunfermline from 1965

BUCHANAN Michael Stuart   *BSc 1951
geol surv Nigeria: geol 1951–61, sen geol Jos 1961–64, prin geol Ibadan 1964–65, asst dir 1965–66; lect geol Aberd from 1966

BUCHANAN Percival William
*MA 1951 LLB 1954
town clerk Alloa from 1963; dir admin and leg. serv reg c from 1974
m Aber 6.6.64 Anna D. Barron shorthand typist d of John B. Aber

BUCHANAN Robert Thomson   *MA 1951
PhD(Edin) 1958
lect econ Brist 1961–68; lect indust relations Strath from 1968
m Edin 7.9.69 Eunice M. Allan MA(Edin) teacher d of Ebenezer A. Arbroath

BUCHANAN-SMITH Alick Drummond
MA 1922 BSc(agr) 1923
Hon DSc (H-W) 1972
vice chmn pigs indust dev auth till 1966; created Baron Balerno of Currie in the County of Midlothian; life peer 1963; chmn Court of H-W 1966–72; disting alumnus Iowa State univ 1967; pres Royal Scot. Geog Soc 1968–74; hon assoc Royal Coll of Vet Surg 1970; hon member Royal Vet Assoc 1976; treasurer Royal Soc Edin 1966–77
wife d 1947

BUDGE Catherine Christina   MB ChB 1948
DPH(Glas) 1966
Glasg: asst m o corp health dept 1966–73, g p from 1973

BUDGE Neil   MB ChB 1942

BUIE or Maclennan, Catherine Mary   MA 1955
d S Africa 6.6.71

BULLEN Jennie   MA 1947
teacher Dounby Orkney 1952–61

m Stromness Orkney 4.4.61 David R. Corse master mariner s of Robert W. C. Falkirk

BULLEN John Herbert   BSc(eng) 1943

BULMER George Gordon   MA 1921
sen master Cedarhurst prep s Solihull 1963–73; retd

BULTITUDE Frederick William   *BSc 1953
PhD(Lond) 1957
prin scient off. AWRE Aldermaston from 1964
wife d 17.7.71

BUNDY Colin Thomas   BSc(for) 1954
Nyasaland: asst conserv for. 1957–64; Zomba, Malawi: sen asst conserv for. 1964–67, man. for. indust div 1967–71; Rhodesia: asst man. prod./sales Umtali 1971–76, man. timber promotion council Salisbury from 1976
m Glasg 31.7.63 May F. McLaughlin d of David McL. Glasg

BUNTING Julia   MA 1923
d Aber 26.5.61 *AUR* xxxix 203

BURGER Roelof du Toit   PhD 1955
prof soil sc univ of O.F.S. Bloemfontein S Africa from 1960

BURGESS Annabella   MA 1921
d 30.11.65

BURGESS Margaret   MA 1923
no longer on GC reg

BURGESS Stanley Everatt   MA 1930 *EdB 1956
d Grantham –.9.62 *AUR* xl 94

BURGESS Wilson Merchant   MB ChB 1937
JP 1957
g p Middlesbrough 1937–38; h s Sunderland RI 1938–39; g p Longside 1939–42 and from 1945; hon med supt Peterhead cott hosp 1962–73
d Longside 2.4.77 *AUR* xlvii 214

BURLEY Flora Macdonald   *MA 1923
resid Aber
m Aber 10.10.72 Alexander C. Anderson BA(Cantab) MRCS LRCP lt col IMS (retd) s of Sir John A. MA 1877 *qv*(I, II)

BURN John Kenneth Arthur   MB ChB 1941
MRCGP 1959
sen h m o anaest Grimsby, g p of hosps from 1955

BURNESS Alexander   MB ChB 1936
d Sunderland 29.11.70 *AUR* xliv 215

BURNETT Agnes Howe   MA 1921
teacher Aber till 1960; retd

BURNETT Alexander Ramsay   MB ChB 1948
MRCGP 1960
Thurso: g p from 1962; anaest Dunbar hosp from 1966

BURNETT Alice Mary   MA 1925
teacher lang Oldmeldrum s till 1963; retd
d Aber 15.3.79 *AUR* XLVIII 228

BURNETT or Ross, Catherine Redpath   MA 1926

BURNETT Charles   *MB ChB 1924
d Edin 17.12.67 *AUR* XLII 361

BURNETT David   *MA 1921 *BSc 1922
prof maths Rhodes univ Grahamstown S Af till
1960; high altit observatory Boulder USA 1961–64;
lect Aberd 1965–69; retd

BURNETT Donald James   *BSc 1951
indust chem Kodak Harrow from 1954

BURNETT or Thomas, Elspeth Helen   MA 1942
resid Kingussie

BURNETT Ernest Wood   MA 1931
C of S min Rothiemay from 1966; retd 1975

BURNETT or Birse, Evelyn Mary   *BSc 1951
resid Aber

BURNETT George Murray   *BSc 1943 PhD 1947
FRSE 1957 JP Aber 1968
Aberd: prof chem 1955–74, vice prin 1966–69; vice-
chancellor and prin H-W from 1974
d Edin 4.9.80 *AUR* XLIX 70 & 139

BURNETT Gerrard   *MB ChB 1921
Pontefract Yorks: g p retd 1959, m o Remploy
Factory from 1948 (except 1972); retd 1976

BURNETT Hugh   MB ChB 1934

BURNETT James Donald   *BSc 1946 PhD 1949

BURNETT Janet Findlay Martin
                              MA 1907 MB ChB 1923
d Swindon 11.8.62 *AUR* XL 77

BURNETT Muriel   BSc 1950
Dip Ed(Sheff) 1969
indust chem Manc 1949–63; teacher Rotherham
1969–71
m Sale 5.1.57 Harold G. Glover BSc(Lond) scient s of
Thomas G. Timperley

BURNETT Robert Alexander   *MA 1919 *BSc 1920
d Stockport 23.1.75

BURNETT Ruby Alice   MA 1945
Dip Teacher of Physioth 1962
teacher Aber hosp s of physioth from 1962

BURNETT Walter Sinclair   BSc(for) 1954
for. consult. and land agent Munlochy from 1965

BURNETT William   MA 1931
headmaster Boddam till 1973; retd

BURNETT William   *MB ChB 1943 *ChM 1957
FRCPSGlas 1961 FRACS 1964
Brisbane: prof/head dept surg univ of Queensland
and hon sen surg royal Brisbane hosp from 1963; on
royal Brisbane hosp board 1973–76; sen commonwealth res fell. UK 1967
d 30.8.81

BURNETT William Ronald Barrington   MA 1938
second dep city chamberlain Aber from 1967; retd
1975; later on part time basis

BURNETT or Scott, Winifred Elizabeth   MA 1920
teacher Albyn s for girls: 1945–62, head jun s
1962–65; retd

BURNS Andrew Sheridan   MB ChB 1924
no longer on GC reg

BURNS Arnold Marischal   MA 1931
Aber: JP from 1955, member town council till 1975

BURNS Charles   BSc 1938

BURNS or Macdonald, Elsie Jessie   MA 1920
resid Rothes
d Aber 1.8.80

BURNS or Smith, Ethel Annie   MA 1924
resid Sutton

BURNS Hendry Stuart Mackenzie
                        *MA 1921 *BSc 1922 LLD 1956
d 28.10.71 *AUR* XLIV 319

BURNS or Munro, Hilda Elizabeth   MA 1931
teacher Kirkcaldy till 1969; retd

BURNS James   BSc 1923 *1924 PhD 1927
CBE 1967
North Thames Gas Lond: chief eng 1949–59, dep
chmn 1959–62; chmn: Northern Gas N'cle 1962–67,
Southern Gas Southampton 1967–69; retd; fell. and
hon life member Inst of Gas Engineers, Pres 1958–59,
fell. Inst of Fuel, pres 1960, fell. Inst Chem Eng

BURNS James Henderson   PhD 1952

BURNS Malcolm McRae   PhD 1936
KBE 1972 FNZIC 1943 FNZIAS 1968 FRSNZ
1963 FAAAS 1966 hon DSc(Canterbury) 1974
prin Lincoln agr coll NZ 1952–74; chmn phys
environment comm 1968–70, fact-finding g p on
nuclear power 1976–77; member: nat dev council
1969–74, nat museum council from 1974, beech for.
council 1972–78; trustee Norman Kirk mem etc.
chmn DSIR res council 1959–62; NZ rep Harkness
fell. 1961–76

BURNS or Sharp, Mary Stuart   *MA 1943
teacher Fr/Ger Morrison's acad Crieff from 1960

BURNS William   BSc 1932 MB ChB 1935 DSc 1944
CBE 1966 FRCP 1973
prof physiol Lond (Charing Cross hosp med s) from
1947

BURNS William George   MA 1915
no longer on GC reg

BURR George Paterson   MB ChB 1911
d Aber 24.3.62 *A UR* xxxix 378

BURR Graham Erskine   BSc(eng) 1950

BURR Mary Gladys   MA 1933
teacher Kittybrewster s Aber 1961–72; retd

BURR Patrick Dickie   BSc(eng) 1935

BURRELL Joan Mary   MB ChB 1945 ᵈMD 1953
DCH 1955
g p Aber from 1953

BURRY Harris Sheffield   BSc 1945

BURRY John Neilson   MB ChB 1950
MRCPE 1964
private pract Alice Springs NT Aust 1957–60; dermat
St. John's hosp Lond and Wilkinson 1961–64; dermat
in private and hosp practice Adelaide S Aust from
1964; lect i/c dermat teaching univ Adel; member edit.
comm of journal *Contact Dermatitis*

BUSHELL Peter John   *BSc 1955
MA DPhil(Oxon) 1962
Oxon: res lect Christ Church 1959–62, lect Magdalen
1962–63, Dartmouth coll USA 1963–64, Sus 1964–75,
reader Sus 75; Nairobi 1967; assoc prof Dartmouth
coll USA from 1972–73; sen visiting fell. Wis Madison
USA from 1973
m Oxford 1963 June Walton MA(Oxon)

BUTCHART or Bull, Catherine McKenzie   MA 1935
resid Cambridge

BUTCHART Henry Jackson   BL 1905 LLD 1952
OBE DSO TD
d Aber 30.8.71 *A UR* xliv 231

BUTHLAY Alan Donald   *MA 1953
teacher: spec asst Inverurie acad 1959–64, prin
Engl Banchory acad 1964–68, lect Engl Aber coll of
educ from 1968
d 9.10.81

BUTHLAY Eric   BL 1949
ptnr Christie, Buthlay & Rutherford advoc Aber
1962–75, Raeburn Christie Buthlay & Rutherford
from 1975

BUTHLAY Kenneth George   *MA 1949
Dip App Linguistics (Edin) 1966
lect Scot. lit Glas from 1966, sen lect from 1975

BUTT Raymond Alexander   BSc(for) 1944
HM Overseas Civ Serv (for. serv) 1944–64; for.
consult. Scot. Woodland Owners Assoc Co Edin from
1964

BUXTON Robert Edward   BSc(eng) 1945

BUYERS Jessie   MA 1903
d Banchory 4.10.64 *A UR* xli 53

BUYERS or Gilchrist, Winifred   MA 1913
d 29.2.64

BYARS John Robbie   MB ChB 1934 DPH 1938
dep county m o h Leicestersh 1949–74; retd

BYRNE Charles   BCom 1937
head of war pensions DHSS (sen prin) Blackpool
from 1961

BYTH Alexander Skinner   MA 1928
JP 1963
wife *d* 5.5.72
headmaster Cluny s 1944–72; retd
d Aber 15.11.78 *A UR* xlviii 104

BYTH George Lawrence   MB ChB 1936
g p Liverpool from 1947

BYTH John Gordon   MB ChB 1936
Ernest and Minnie Dawson Cancer Trust Prize
1959
g p: Blackpool 1947–66, Jersey 1966–72; retd
d Jersey 20.12.76

CABLE James   MB ChB 1915
d Forfar 3.3.71 *A UR* xliv 210

CADENHEAD Robert McNeil   MB ChB 1937
g p Lerwick from 1950

CADGER Alexandrina   MA 1946
teacher Tore s Rosssh from 1950

CAHILL Dennis Neville   BSc(agr) 1951
Dip Agr Ext (Melb) 1970
asst prov conserv and extension off. Bulawayo,
Rhodesia 1962–65; Victoria, Aust: soil conserv off.
Heathcote 1965–67, dist soil conserv off. Heathcote
1967–68, sen conserv off. Horsham 1968–72, reg
conserv off. Horsham from 1972

CAHILL John Alfred   BSc(eng) 1945
AMIMechE 1953 CEng 1971
grad app GEC Witton, Erith 1947–48; jun des eng
turbine des off. Fraser & Chalmers Erith 1948–49;
contr eng Sturtevant Eng co Lond 1949–53; asst
mech eng(dev) Steetley Magnesite Co W Hartlepool
1953–57; dev eng Chem Insulating Co Darlington
1957–61; Laporte Industries Grimsby: proj eng 1961–
63, des/proj man. 1963–76, site eng man. from 1976

CAIE or Phillips, Frances Stewart   MA 1929

CAIE Jane Ann   *MA 1925
d Aber 30.8.62 *A UR* xl 91

CAIE John   *MA 1932 MB ChB 1938
g p Warwick and Leamington Spa from 1943

CAIE Rachel   MA 1927 BSc 1930
d Aber 26.4.76

CAIN Alexander Mathieson   *MA 1950 PhD 1954
asst keeper Br Museum 1954–66; lib syst analyst

and assoc prof Upstate med center Syracuse NY 1966–69; rare book lib state univ of New York Buffalo 1969–71; spec collections lib and assoc prof univ of Illinois med center Chicago 1971–73; asst keeper Nat Lib of Scot. from 1973

CAIRD or Searle, Catherine Annie   MA 1933
teacher Engl/hist/commerce St Margaret's s Exeter till 1974; retd; teacher Crediton prep s 1974–78; retd

CAIRD or Bailey, Margaret MacCallum   MA 1935

CAIRNS or Stuart, Elizabeth Richardson
MB ChB 1929

CAIRNS Robert Hill   *MA 1950

CALDER Alexander   BSc(agr) 1925
FRSE 1929 OBE 1953
chief marketing off. Pigs Marketing Board Lond 1935–53 and dir of pig supplies Min of Food Lond 1945–53; dir pig indust board Rhodesia 1953–63; retd; resid Denbigh
m Pwllheli N Wales 1948 Iona Williams civ serv d of John T. W. Pwllheli

CALDER Alexander Chalmers   MA 1946 LLB 1949
Edin: leg. asst 1961–62, ptnr in leg. firm 1962–69, leg. asst 1969–77

CALDER Alexander John Williams
MA 1906 MB ChB 1910
d Hornsea 11.6.62 AUR xxxix 375

CALDER Alistair Davidson   MB ChB 1952

CALDER Andrew   BSc(agr) 1921
no longer on GC reg

CALDER or Logan, Annie Mary   MA 1921
no longer on GC reg

CALDER Charles Cumming   BSc 1908 BSc(agr) 1908
d Aber 18.4.62 AUR xxxix 376

CALDER Charles Cumming   MA 1936 LLB 1940
sole ptnr W. J. C. Reed & Sons solic Laurencekirk
m Aber 30.7.45 Isobel E. R. Pirie d of John W. P. Aber
d Laurencekirk 6.12.77

CALDER Edith Ellen   MA 1915

CALDER Enid   MB ChB 1920
d Lowestoft 4.1.63 AUR xl 202

CALDER or MacLean, Gladys   MA 1937
Milngavie: teacher 1955–69, asst head from 1970; retd 1976

CALDER or Goodwin, Gladys   MA 1955

CALDER Hew Maclaren Neville   MB ChB 1925
d 16.5.75 AUR xlvi 322

CALDER James   BSc(agr) 1934

CALDER James Black   MA 1910
d 18.4.72 AUR xliv 427

CALDER or Breedon, Jessie Catherine   MA 1941

CALDER John   MA 1900 DD 1957
d Sydney Aust 19.10.62 AUR xl 74

CALDER or Watson, Margaret Winifred
MA 1912 *1913 MB ChB 1920
d Distington 20.1.66 AUR xli 242

CALDER Mary Lawrence   *MA 1944

CALDER William John   MA 1906 MB ChB 1909
d Aboyne 1.6.69 AUR xliii 208

CALDER William Norman   MB ChB 1939
g p Aber from 1947

CALDER William Victor   BSc(for) 1936

CALDWELL Ian Wingate   MB ChB 1939 MD 1954
FRCP 1970
S'ton med s hosps: consult. dermat from 1962, hon lect from 1971

CALDWELL James McAuley   BSc(eng) 1946
C.Eng 1967 FIEE 1967
NSHEB Edin: sen eng transmission construct. 1963–71, chief transmission and distrib eng from 1971

CALDWELL John   *MA 1951
MSc (Cranfield Inst Tech)
d Macclesfield 18.3.75 AUR xlvi 240

CALDWELL John Stewart   MB ChB 1945
MRCGP 1964
g p Aberlour from 1949

CALDWELL or Mair, Marie Isobel   MB ChB 1940

CALDWELL Thomas Douglas   BSc 1952
Lond: sen master Risinghill comp s 1960–65, head South Hackney comp s from 1965

CALDWELL William Mitchell Hunter   MA 1945

CALLAN or Davidson, Sheila Margaret Jane
MA 1932

CALLANDER David   BSc(agr) 1951

CALVERT Norman Hillbrook   BSc(eng) 1953
CEng MIMechE 1964
Baker Perkins Peterborough: asst proj eng 1960–64, proj eng 1964–68, sen proj eng from 1968
m Peterborough 27.2.60 Isabella M. Donn teacher d of Robert C. D. Glasg

CALVERT Rhoda Margaret   MA 1942 *MEd 1944
prin educ psych Dunbartonsh from 1949

CAMPBELL or Hobsley, Jane Fairlie
MB ChB 1945
clin m o Enfield Lond from 1967

CAMERON Albert James *BSc 1931 *1932
d Kingston Surrey 20.7.69 *AUR* XLIII 331

CAMERON Alistair Simpson MB ChB 1937
g p Brighton S Aust from 1958

CAMERON Allan *MA 1908
d 2.5.64 *AUR* XL 395

CAMERON Allan Ross *BSc(eng) 1948
MInstMC 1957 FIEE 1962 FIMechE 1969 MBNES
Lond: res eng and dep chief eng nuclear div
Elliott Brothers (Lond) 1948–57; chief control and
instrumentation eng/chief elect. eng Atomic Power
Construct. 1957–70; chief elect. eng (Sutton) then
chief eng KoRi proj Brit. Nuclear Des and Construct.
1970–76; chief eng Roject dept Assoc Nuclear Serv
from 1976
m Edin 22.6.51 Sheila M. C. Dovey d of Rev Archibald
C. D. MA(Edin)

CAMERON or Campbell, Anna Magdalen MA 1949
teacher Kemnay from 1968

CAMERON or McCaskie, Annie Maria Grace
MA 1911
d Elgin 31.10.75 *AUR* XLVI 320

CAMERON or McKay, Annie May MA 1925
no longer on GC reg

CAMERON Charles William Morrison
MB ChB 1923
d 25.8.71

CAMERON Colin *MA 1952

CAMERON or Macpherson or Bremner, Elizabeth
*MA 1928
freelance journalist from 1929
resid Nethybridge

CAMERON Eva Margaret *MA 1927
since retirement in 1960 relieving posts in Engl
depts Elgin acad and Lossiemouth

CAMERON Frances MA 1932 BCom 1934
MBE 1963
trg coll and s s teacher SE Nigeria with Presb Ch
1938–68; teacher Banchory acad 1968–71; retd

CAMERON Francis MA 1922
head teacher: Skene Street s Aber 1948–57,
Sunnybank s Aber 1957–62; retd
d 17.11.81

CAMERON George Gordon MA 1925 DD 1962
C of S min: Glenburn ch Paisley 1958–69, assoc
min St Columba's, Pont St Lond 1970–75
d Edin 20.11.80 *AUR* XLIX 67

CAMERON Hugh Fraser MB CM 1890
no longer on GC reg

CAMERON Iain Angus BSc(agr) 1951
chief agr off. Lusaka, Zambia 1966–69; proj co-
ordinator HIDB Inv from 1969

CAMERON Ian *MA 1952
asst c clerk Selkirk 1968–70, town clerk Linlithgow
1970–75; dep dir admin Stirling dist c from 1975
m Edin 3.4.65 Kathleen A. Beevers insur clerkess d of
John C. B. Edin

CAMERON Iona McDonald *MA 1955

CAMERON or Milton, Isabel Jean BSc(agr) 1953
resid Deskford

CAMERON or Grant, Isabella Mary *MA 1944
teacher Fr Inv acad from 1969

CAMERON James BSc(eng) 1945
Dip Internat Man. (NW Univ USA) 1968
Rugby: commercial man. Power Generation group
Eng Elect. Co 1966–68, contr dir GEC Turbine
Generators 1968–77; reg dir GEC Turbine Generators
Seoul S Korea from 1977

CAMERON James *BSc 1939 DSc 1957
FIMM 1972
tech advis uranium resources (field expert) of IAE
Agency of UN, Turkey, Philippines, Uruguay, Egypt,
Ecuador, Somalia 1962–68; tech advis uranium resources HQ for IAEA Vienna from 1968
d Vienna 2.4.80

CAMERON James McKilligan
MA 1949 Dip Ed 1950
head Fraserburgh N p s from 1969

CAMERON or Mitchell, Jane Thomasina MA 1927
resid Banff

CAMERON or Hobbes, Janet Seaton MB ChB 1922
retd; resid Birm

CAMERON Jean Bremner *MA 1930

CAMERON or Stokes, Jeannie Rose-Innes
MA 1915
d Sutton 19.1.77

CAMERON Jessie Mortimer MA 1933 BSc 1934
teacher maths/sc h s for girls Aber till 1972; retd;
resid Peterculter

CAMERON or Ross, Joan Duncan BSc(agr) 1950
teacher: sc Auchmuty 1959–61, biol Invergordon
1973–74, asst prin guid 1974–75, prin guid from 1975

CAMERON John MA 1939
teacher Dingwall acad from 1971
d Inv 22.7.73

CAMERON John Andrew MB ChB 1933
g p New Pitsligo till 1966
resid Grantown-on-Spey

CAMERON John Brunton *MA 1932 BD 1935
C of S min Flowerhill ch Airdrie 1956–76; resid
Aber
d Aber 23.6.78 *AUR* XLVIII 105

CAMERON John Macphail　MA 1909
d 29.7.68

CAMERON John Mowat　BSc 1956

CAMERON John William Gillanders　MA 1909
d Aber 9.11.65 *AUR* XLII 82

CAMERON Kenneth　MA 1900
no longer on GC reg

CAMERON Kenneth Sutherland　MB ChB 1951
FFARCSI 1964
consult. anaest NW Durh group hosps from 1964

CAMERON Lewis Legertwood Legg
　　　　　　　　　BSc(agr) 1920 DD 1953
d Edin 19.3.73 *AUR* XLV 225

CAMERON or Harvey, Lilias Margaret　MA 1938
retd ill health 1958; resid Aber

CAMERON or MacLeod, Lily McKenzie　MA 1912
d 1963

CAMERON Margaret Dickson　MB ChB 1937

CAMERON or Baker, Margaret Robertson
　　　　　　　　　　　　　MA 1947
d Boston Lincs 9.4.72

CAMERON Norman Austin　*MA 1929

CAMERON Patrick Stephen Gerrard　MB ChB 1918
d N Shields 13.4.70 *AUR* XLIII 443

CAMERON Scott　MB ChB 1941
g p Manc till 1964; Lond: m o Treasury med serv
1964–68, dept m o borough of Waltham Forest from
1968; retd

CAMERON Sheila Smith　BSc 1951

CAMERON Thomas William Ferguson
　　　　　　　　　　　　　MB ChB 1929
g p Chatham till 1967; retd; resid Iver Heath
d 28.3.77 *AUR* XLVII 212

CAMERON or McCracken, Una Margaret Isabel
　　　　　　　　　　　　　MA 1925
resid Barnes, London
d 30.7.78

CAMERON William　MB ChB 1901
d Bromley 7.4.66 *AUR* XLI 236

CAMERON William James　MB ChB 1935
g p: Luddendenfoot till 1966, New Mills, Fife
1966–68, Halifax from 1969

CAMERON William John　MA 1907
d Dunfermline 31.8.67 *AUR* XLII 179

CAMERON or Hoyte, Wilma Emelda Mary
　　　　　　　　　　　　　MB ChB 1953

CAMPBELL Alan Newton　DSc 1929
Manit, Winnipeg: retd head chem dept 1966, retd
teaching staff 1969, emeritus prof 1969

CAMPBELL Alexander Elmslie
　　　　　　　MA 1911 *BSc 1912 *MB ChB 1914
no longer on GC reg

CAMPBELL Alexander George　MA 1910
d Saskatoon Canada 22.6.73

CAMPBELL Alexander Gibson　*MA 1939
ABPsS 1964 MEd(Edin) 1966 FSA Scot 1968
Edin: educ psych/careers counsellor George Heriot's s
1956–64; lect Scots law corp f e serv 1964–67; sen lect
leg. stud. Napier coll of sc and tech 1967–74; head
dept law Napier coll of comm and tech from 1974

CAMPBELL Alistair Matheson　*MA 1927
Montreal: pres Sun Life Assce Co of Canada
1962–70, chmn from 1970

CAMPBELL Angus Murdo　MA 1950
head Fidigary s Lewis from 1969

CAMPBELL or MacLean, Anne Thomson　MA 1929
teacher: Portsoy 1959–60, Milne's h s Fochabers
1960–69; resid Stromness
husb *d* 5.7.77

CAMPBELL or Greig, Christina Mitchell　MA 1930

CAMPBELL Colin William　*MA 1954

CAMPBELL Constance Gill　MA 1947
BEd(Sask) 1970 MS(Syracuse NY) 1971
educ consult. publ s board of educ Saskatoon Canada
from 1972

CAMPBELL or Mackay, Constance Maud
　　　　　　　　　　　　　***MA 1942**
resid Aber
husb *d* 28.2.77

CAMPBELL David　BSc 1921
d Aber 15.3.62 *AUR* XXXIX 382

CAMPBELL David Davidson
　　　　　　BSc(mech eng) 1955 BSc(civ eng) 1956
eng asst Kincardine c c 1961–67; eng McAdam
contr Aber from 1967

CAMPBELL Donald　MB ChB 1922
g p Poole 1935–63; retd

CAMPBELL Donald　MA 1929
C of S min Bervie from 1958
wife *d* 29.3.47

CAMPBELL Donella　MA 1950
d Hamilton NZ 13.3.71 *AUR* XLIV 216

CAMPBELL or Duthie, Dorothy Frances　MA 1941
resid Purley

CAMPBELL Duncan Ian *MA 1938
prin Brummana h s Lebanon till 1962; teacher gen subj comp s Lond 1962–64; lect dept educ stud. Edin 1964–73, sen lect from 1973

CAMPBELL Edward Arthur Dudley MB ChB 1937
no longer on GC reg

CAMPBELL or Macmurray, Elizabeth Hyde
MA 1915
husb deceased
stud. painting Lond, writer of fiction from 1930

CAMPBELL or Marsh, Elizabeth McCutcheon
BSc 1938

CAMPBELL or Fitzwilliam, Elizabeth Mary
MA 1947
resid Esher

CAMPBELL Ephraim MA 1933 *BSc 1936
Elgin acad: spec asst sc 1962–72; asst prin teacher guid from 1972; retd 1975

CAMPBELL or Garry, Flora MacDonald
MA 1922
Arts Council Award (*Bennygoak and Other Poems* publ 1974); resid Comrie

CAMPBELL George William Douglas
MB ChB 1943
d Kingston Jamaica 30.11.78

CAMPBELL or Bowers, Grace Alexandra MA 1955
resid Tokoroa NZ

CAMPBELL Gregor Mackenzie BSc 1931 *1933
head Drumsmittal p s 1958–67
d North Kessock 25.3.67 *A UR* XLII 186

CAMPBELL or Thomson, Helen Donaldson
MA 1940
teacher maths Glasg from 1956

CAMPBELL or Chalmers, Helen Morris MA 1929
resid Aber

CAMPBELL or Tonge, Helenora Seymour MA 1910
d Thurso 28.6.66 *A UR* XLI 336

CAMPBELL or Peuschel, Ishbel Patricia MA 1951

CAMPBELL James MA 1910
d 15.4.66

CAMPBELL James Duthie BSc 1947

CAMPBELL or Burgess, Jane Wilhelma Burgess
MA 1912
temp work civ serv Edin 1956–60; retd

CAMPBELL or Smith, Jean Johnstone MA 1907
d Lerwick 9.5.68 *A UR* XLII 345

CAMPBELL Jean Menzies MA 1951
teacher Engl Dunbar g s from 1956
m Edin 12.7.63 John S. McKie MA(St And) teacher

CAMPBELL or Falconer, Jessie Catherine
MA 1947
resid Auldearn

CAMPBELL or Hall, Jessie Mackintosh MA 1946
teacher: Kinloss 1965–69, Forres from 1969

CAMPBELL John MA 1902 BL 1905
no longer on GC reg

CAMPBELL John Duthie MB ChB 1951
cas off. St Tydfil's hosp Glamorgan 1958–64; g p Luton from 1964

CAMPBELL Kenneth MA 1948

CAMPBELL Lilias Ann Turnbull MA 1909
no longer on GC reg

CAMPBELL or MacGregor, Margaret Christina
MA 1913
no longer on GC reg

CAMPBELL or Maguire, Margaret Frances
MA 1939

CAMPBELL or Ross, Margaret Gault *MA 1943

CAMPBELL or Watt, Margaret Jemima MA 1954
teacher Barnehurst s Kent from 1969

CAMPBELL Margaret McKay MA 1919
no longer on GC reg

CAMPBELL Marie Dorothy MA 1942
lect soc stud. RGIT Aber 1968–74; lect soc work Monash univ Melbourne Aust from 1974

CAMPBELL or Morrison, Marion Pitt *MA 1932
teacher Lat Wallace Hall acad 1941–42; teacher Fr: Benedictine convent 1942–44, Dumfries acad 1958–70

CAMPBELL or Glen, Mary Grant MA 1943
teacher: Bretby House New Malden from 1971

CAMPBELL or Crotty, Mary Sinclair MA 1942
MA(Dub) 1961
dir practical trg dept soc stud. Dub from 1959
m(2) Patrick Lynch MA(NUI) prof econ univ coll Dub(NUI) s of Daniel L. Dublin

CAMPBELL Murdo MA 1951
JP Invernesssh 1966
head: Croy s Inv 1965, Merkinch s Inv from 1975

CAMPBELL Nancy Allan MA 1952

CAMPBELL Neil MA 1952
Inv: head: Inchmore p s Kirkhill 1968–71, Tomnacross p s Kiltarlity from 1971

m Glasg 4.7.62 Janet Macleod teacher d of Norman M. Leverburgh Harris

CAMPBELL Peter   MA 1910
d Forres 8.6.67 *AUR* XLII 180

CAMPBELL Robert Clark   MB ChB 1955
FRCSE 1963 FRCS 1963
regist: surg ARI 1960–64, plastic surg Norwich 1964–66; sen regist plastic surg Leeds 1966–68; Robert W. Johnson fell. plastic surg univ of Miami USA 1968; consult. plastic surg Cantab from 1971

CAMPBELL Robert Mackenzie   BSc 1952
dep head Helmsdale s from 1966

CAMPBELL Roderick George   MA 1933
d Dingwall 20.5.80 *AUR* XLIX 68

CAMPBELL Roderick Macrae
                    MA 1929 *MB ChB 1933
OBE 1972 FFCM 1972
Inv: dep sen admin m o 1950–62, sen admin m o North reg hosp board 1962–73

CAMPBELL Rosa Margaret   BSc 1934
sen exper off. Rowett Inst Aber from 1951; resid Bieldside Aber

CAMPBELL Rosemary Elizabeth   MA 1955
teacher army s Hong Kong from 1958
m Aber 10.9.60 John E. Flowers army off. s of Charles E. F. Lond

CAMPBELL Tormaid   MA 1930
d –.6.66

CAMPBELL or Winter, Violet Mary   BSc(agr) 1949

CAMPBELL William Beaton   MA 1905
d Inverurie 30.9.71 *AUR* XLIV 316

CAMPBELL William Henry McKay   BSc(agr) 1950
area agr advis NOSCA

CAMPBELL William Robert Hugh   *MA 1933
prin teacher classics Fortrose acad from 1964; retd 1965

CANT or Young, Mary McPherson   MA 1944
MA(Alta) 1968 PhD(Alta) 1974
asst prof depts anthrop and relig stud. Alta Edmonton

CANT Ronald Fraser   MB ChB 1948
consult. radiol Isle of Thanet group of hosps from 1958

CANTLAY Alexander   MA 1931

CANTLAY or Mutch, Isabella Christian   MA 1947

CANTLAY or Bartlet, Isabella Margaret   MA 1917

CANTLAY Violet May   MA 1922
retd 1961; resid Blackpool

CANTLAY William John   BSc(agr) 1943
teacher: Northfield s Aber 1960–67, Laurencekirk s 1967
d 29.11.77

CANTLIE James   MB ChB 1942
g p Christchurch Dorset from 1954
m Bournemouth 22.6.71 Eva von Hofmann secy d of Rolf von H. BSc(Berlin) Esslingen-Nechar W Ger

CANTLIE Keith   *MA 1908
Kt
d Lond 29.4.77

CANTLIE Neil   *MB ChB 1914
d Lond 16.5.75 *AUR* XLVI 321

CARCARY Mary McLeod   *MA 1945

CARDNO George Watt   MB ChB 1951
g p Howe of Fife from 1956
m Kilmacolm 14.9.63 Kathleen Calder MB ChB(Glas) d of Rev Alastair S. C. TD MA(Edin) Kilmacolm

CARDNO Harry Spark   BSc 1942
d Aber 13.10.80

CARDNO Ian Robertson   MA 1931
head Culter s Peterculter from 1966; retd 1974

CARDNO James Alexander   *MA 1938
MA(Cantab) 1946 FBPsS 1962 FAPsS 1966 FAPA 1972
assoc prof psych univ Tasmania 1961–65, prof from 1965

CARDNO James Halliday   MA 1912 BSc 1915
d Peterhead 3.6.67 *AUR* XLII 181

CARDNO James Stuart   MA 1930
asst dir educ Kincardinesh 1963–70, dep dir from 1970

CARDNO John Alexander   MB ChB 1931 ᶜMD 1938
retd 1973; resid Kinross

CARDNO Rachel   MA 1943
teacher: Winnipeg and New Westminster, Canada 1959–60, Knox acad Haddington 1960–67, Dunnikier s Kirkcaldy from 1967

CARGILL William McHardy   MA 1930
teacher maths: Fyvie 1958–66, Turriff acad 1966–72; retd

CARLE Annie Cook   MA 1930
teacher: spec asst Fr Harlaw acad Aber from 1962

CARLE or Weir, Jeanie Strath   MA 1918

CARLE John Leslie   MB ChB 1932
d Southend-on-Sea 5.7.63 *AUR* XL 303

CARLISLE Alan   PhD 1954
sen res off. Imper Forest Inst Oxford 1956–58;

prin scient off. Nature Conserv Merlewood res stat Grange-over-Sands 1958–68; progr man. Canadian For. Serv Petawawa for. exper stat Chalk River Ontario from 1968

CARMICHAEL Dennis Dickinson   MB ChB 1950
univ of NC Chapel Hill NC USA: resid in psychiat 1958–61, fell. in child psychiat 1961–63, asst clin prof psychiat from 1966; Charlotte NC: child psychiat mental health center 1963–66, private pract child psychiat from 1964

CARMICHAEL John Harald   *MA 1929 BSc 1931
retd 1973; resid Badenscoth

CARMICHAEL Norman Bayne
MA 1930 MB ChB 1941
g p Derby from 1947
d Derby 22.2.78 *AUR* xlvii 358

CARMICHAEL William   BSc(for) 1948
FLS 1965
Tanzania: reg for. off. Mwanza 1960–62, Tabora 1963–64, Mwanza 1964–65, conserv for. Arusha 1965–69; Edin: stud. New coll 1962–63, 1967 and 1970, C of S asst min Holy Trin ch 1970–71, min Restalrig ch from 1971

CARNEGIE Agnes Crighton   *MA 1934
High s for girls Aber (Harlaw acad from 1971): prin teacher Engl 1957–64, dep head 1964–72; lect univ of Sacred Heart Tokyo 1973–75; retd

CARNEGIE Austen Ogston   *MA 1951
teacher: Northfield s Aber 1956–60; Auchterderran j h s Cardenden: prin Engl 1960–70, dep head from 1970

CARNEGIE Charles   BSc 1914
d Perth 13.7.73 *AUR* xlv 317

CARNEGIE Isabel Margaret   MA 1937

CARNEGIE James   MA 1935

CARNEGIE Leslie Thompson   BL 1941
county clerk and other posts Dumfries from 1954; clerk: SW Scotland Water Board from 1960, SW Scotland dev auth from 1972; chief exec Dumfries and Galloway reg c from 1974

CARNEGIE-SMITH George   BSc(eng) 1933
Bedford: sen eng MOT 1964–70; dept environment: sen eng 1970–72, prin prof and tech off. from 1972; retd 1974
d Bedford 10.9.77

CARNIE Frank Alexander   *BSc 1935
rector Banchory acad 1967–77; retd

CARNIE or Dawson, Margaret Isabel   MA 1929

CARNIE Mary Helen   MA 1920
Dun: teacher 1921–37, sc 1940–59, retd; resid Kintore

m Dun 1.7.37 George Campbell MA(Edin) teacher s of Hugh C. Melvich

CARNIE or Fullerton, Maud Mary Adams   BSc 1937
resid Trail BC Canada

CARR or Elder, Agnes Lawson Stewart   MA 1943
resid Aber

CARR Thomas Lauder   MB ChB 1942 ChM 1956
consult. orthop surg ARI from 1954

CARRIE Alistair Ramsay   BSc(eng) 1951

CARRIE James   MB ChB 1924
d 25.5.64 *AUR* xl 399

CARRIE William Wilson   BL 1940
d Aber 23.9.80 *AUR* xlix 70

CARSLAKE William Dodd   BSc(for) 1955
FBCS 1972
asst conserv for. Bo Sierra Leone 1957–61; IBM Lond from 1961

CARSWELL Robert Finlayson   BSc(eng) 1945

CARTER Andrew McKenzie   MA 1951

CARVER Evelyn Beckett Faber   MA 1924
no longer on GC reg

CARVER John George Campbell   MA 1926
head Sandhead s Wigtown till 1970; retd; wife *d* 1966
m(2) Glasg 12.7.69 Jessie B. M. Stevenson or Buchanan BSc(Glas) teacher d of Archibald M. S. Paisley

CASEBY Joy Murray Rodger   *MA 1948

CASSIE Alexander   MA 1937

CASSIE Alexander Whyte   MA 1897 MB ChB 1901
d 29.6.63 *AUR* xl 198

CASSIE or Walker, Barbara Bathea   MA 1927
resid Bexhill

CASSIE or Routledge, Elizabeth Mary   MA 1951

CASSIE Francis George Monro   BSc(eng) 1947
d Aber 6.3.76

CASSIE George   MB ChB 1952 DPH 1957
MFCM 1973
Lanarksh: asst sen m o 1960–66, sen m o from 1966; commun med spec Greater Glasgow health board 1974

CASSIE Gordon Fordyce   MB ChB 1944 ChM 1958
Gorham-Peters res fell. Harvard med s USA 1957–58; consult. surg Queen Eliz II hosp Welwyn Garden City from 1962

CASSIE or Henderson, Joyce   MA 1947
teacher: Kent till 1957, Bexley from 1969

CASSIE Margaret   MA 1934
teacher Walker Road p s Aber 1936–76; retd

CASSIE or Johnston, Margaret Duff   BSc 1943
resid Richmond Surrey

CASTLE or Hay, Margaret Anne   MA 1948
Dip. in Reading Dev (OU) 1977
teacher: Turriff p s, Bredalbane p s 1962–65, Banff acad 1965–72, remed Banff p s from 1972

CASTLE or Kilgour, Frances Christina   MA 1931
resid Banchory

CATO George Christopher   *MA 1931 BD 1938
sen lect phys univ of Natal, Durban from 1963; retd 1975

CATTANACH Alexander Belmont Leslie   BSc 1930

CATTANACH or Tough, Edith Julienne   *MA 1954
teacher Fr Oakhill s Stoke on Trent 1971–75

CATTANACH or Petrie, Janet   *MA 1935
teacher Gordonstoun till 1969; resid Elgin

CATTANACH Ronald Gibson   BL 1951
advoc in Aber

**CATTANACH or Milne, Sandra Isobel Don
MA 1955**
teacher Burnside s Aber 1956–62
m Aber 4.4.61 Thornton G. Milne chartered surv s of George S. M. New York

CATTERALL Sydney   MB ChB 1940 MD 1954
Assoc MBPS 1960 FRCPsych 1973
psychiat Edmonton 1963–67, consult. psychiat Liff hosp Dun from 1968

CATTO Alexander Godsman   MA 1905 BD 1908
d Edin 21.5.67 *AUR* XLII 345

CATTO Anne   *MA 1921
retd teaching Maxwellton s Dumfries 1966; resid Aber
d 4.6.77

CATTO David   *MA 1926
teacher Engl, prin Engl, dep head Frederick Street s s Aber 1927–64; retd
m Aber 29.6.40 Annie J. Connon d of James C. Dufftown

CATTO Forbes Shepherd   MB ChB 1923
d 15.2.76 *AUR* XLVI 416

CATTO Gavin Anderson   BSc(agr) 1939
JP(Perthsh) 1967 OBE 1968 FRAgrS 1969 (found. fell.)
prov dir E of Scot. coll of agr Edin from 1967
d Bridge of Earn 19.4.75 *AUR* XLVI 240

CATTO Gordon Duffus   BSc(eng) 1951
CEng MIMechE 1966
proj eng Scottish & Newcastle Breweries Edin 1961–67; sen mech eng Andrews-Weatherfoil (Scot.) Paisley from 1968
m Edin 10.9.60 Agnes J. W. Marshall secy d of James M. Hamilton

CATTO Henry Gray   BL 1938
Aber c c: solic 1960–72, dep c clerk 1972–75; clerk NE Scot River Purif Bd from 1975

CATTO or Cormack, Isabella Ogg   MA 1932
d Aber 11.1.68 *AUR* XLII 371

CATTO James Alexander   BCom 1923
d 20.3.71

CATTO James Rankine Wilson   MB ChB 1942
g p Coventry from 1947

CATTO John   BL 1947
d Edin 22.2.67 *AUR* XLII 373

CATTO Laura Deas   MB ChB 1924

CATTO William Dawson   MB ChB 1939
MRCGP—founder member
g p Aber from 1946
wife d –.7.78

CAY David Robert Bellamy   MA 1949 LLB 1952
advoc Scot. from 1954

CAY Edward   MB ChB 1934
d Edin 8.12.74

**CESSFORD Edward Allan Macpherson
MA 1940 *MEd 1944**
AMBPsS 1960
dep prin psych Ayrsh from 1973

CHADWICK John Peter   MB ChB 1950
m o Brit Alum. Comp Awaso, Ghana from 1952

CHALMERS Adeline Knox   BSc 1933
d Sittingbourne 7.4.78

CHALMERS Alan Ferguson   *BSc(eng) 1953
AFRAeS 1960
b Dunblane 12.10.31
aerodynamicist to asst chief stressman Hayes 1953–62; sen progr to div man. Boreham Wood 1962–73, marketing exec from 1973

CHALMERS Alexander   *MA 1930
teacher Loughborough coll 1946–68; retd

CHALMERS Alexander   MB ChB 1931
MRCGP 1952 C St J 1968
g p Sittingbourne

CHALMERS Alice Lesley   *MA 1931
retd 1970; resid Stevenage

CHALMERS Audrey Miller   BSc(agr) 1949
agr econ NOSCA till 1969
m Broughty Ferry 12.8.69 Lachlan G. Low-Mitchell

CHALMERS Davena Annie   *MA 1947
prin teacher mod lang: Bridgwater girls' g s
Somerset 1962–68, Hamilton acad 1968–76; prin
teacher French Peterhead acad from 1976

CHALMERS Derek   MB ChB 1954
regist ARI 1958–59; Edin RI: regist 1960, sen regist
1961–63; dir med affairs E. R. Squibb & Sons
Twickenham from 1964; dermat Gt Ormond St hosp
from 1969

CHALMERS or Stewart, Dorothy   BSc 1925 *1926
resid Cults

CHALMERS Edmund   MA 1912

CHALMERS Frederick Grant Duncan   MA 1916
no longer on GC reg

CHALMERS George Quinton   MA 1919
no longer on GC reg

CHALMERS or Reid, Isobel Mary Smart
                       MB ChB 1942
d nr Thirsk 31.7.67 *A UR* XLII 186

CHALMERS James Alastair   MB ChB 1945
g p Westcliff-on-Sea from 1951

CHALMERS James Durno   MB ChB 1945
MRCGP 1963
g p Insch from 1952

CHALMERS or Stewart, Jeannie Ann Gordon Fenton
                       MA 1924
no longer on GC reg

CHALMERS John Taylor   MA 1930
head Hatton Fintray s from 1951; retd

CHALMERS or Fraser, Maggie   MA 1926
resid Oldmeldrum

CHALMERS or Spira, Margaret   MA 1922

CHALMERS or MacKay, Margaret   MA 1944

CHALMERS Margaret Irvin   PhD 1951
biochem Rowett res inst Aber from 1946

CHALMERS or Nairn, Margaret Johnstone
                       MA 1938
resid East Sheen, Lond

CHALMERS or Ainscow, Mary Ann
                 MA 1912 MB ChB 1916
d Cumberland 9.5.69 *A UR* XLII 328

CHALMERS or Fraser, Mary Ewen   MB ChB 1943
med asst dept obst and gyn Aberd from 1964, clin
lect cervical cytology

CHALMERS or Gray, Norah Ellis   MA 1944
resid Cape Town

CHALMERS or Inglis, Norma   MA 1928
resid Portsoy

CHALMERS Robert Westland   MB ChB 1909
no longer on GC reg

CHALMERS Theodore   MB ChB 1906
d Inv 1.2.73 *A UR* XLV 223

CHALMERS William Gordon   BL 1948
Edin: sen proc-fiscal dep 1959–63; sen leg. asst in
Crown Office 1963–67; dep Crown Ag 1967–74,
Crown Ag from 1974

CHAMBERLAIN Charles Deryck   BSc 1944
DipEd(Oxon) 1965
teacher maths the Priory s for boys Shrewsbury from
1965

CHAMBERS Graham Peter   *MA 1950

CHAMBERS Henry Daniel
                 MB ChB 1932 ᶜMD 1938

CHANCE Robert Maxwell   MB ChB (1910 *MD 1912
no longer on GC reg

CHANNON Anthony Guy   *BSc 1952

CHANOCK Leon   MB ChB 1925
lect surg anat univ of Cape Town from 1940

CHAPMAN or Esslemont, Isobel Barbara   MA 1946
teacher Fyvie from 1963

CHAPMAN or Gibbs, Mabel Scott   MA 1919
no longer on GC reg

CHAPMAN Wallace Milne   MB ChB 1936
g p Shaftesbury 1938–73; retd
d 1981

CHAPMAN William   MB ChB 1909
d S Af 16.7.62 *A UR* XL 78

CHAPMAN William Gordon   *MA 1950
d Oxford 9.2.68 *A UR* XLII 374

CHARLES Audrey Elsie   MA 1950
head teacher Aber: Cairncry inf s 1967–69, Braeside
inf s from 1969

CHATTERJI or Ghosh or Sutherland, Leila (Savoja)
                       MB ChB 1922

CHEN Foong Kong   MA 1917 MB ChB 1921

CHEN Chung   PhD 1944

CHESSAR Lilias Robina   MA 1910
retd headmistress; resid Turriff

CHESSOR George Clinton   MB ChB 1943
g p Alloa from 1955

CHEYNE Agnes Christina   MA 1923
teacher Engl Ellon acad 1959–61; retd; resid Inverurie

CHEYNE Alexander   *MA 1912
d 23.3.76 *A UR* XLVII 286

CHEYNE Alexander Ian   MB ChB 1954
DPM 1966 MRCPsych 1972
g p: Littleport 1958–64, Dalkeith 1964–65; regist Crichton royal hosp Dumfries 1965–67; psychiat Hillcrest hosp Adelaide S Aust 1967–68; Gartnavel royal hosp Glas: sen regist 1968–70, consult. psychiat from 1971

CHEYNE Alexander Ingram
                    MB ChB 1923 MD 1940
d Leamington Spa 23.4.72 *A UR* XLV 126

CHEYNE Alfred William Harper
                    MB ChB 1914 DPH 1920

CHEYNE Douglas Gordon
        MB ChB 1910 MD 1914 DPH 1914
d Lond 26.6.66 *A UR* XLI 336

CHEYNE Eleanor Rose Lornie   MA 1926
no longer on GC reg

CHEYNE George Collie   MA 1907 BSc(agr) 1909
d Maud 6.1.65 *A UR* XLI 54

CHEYNE George Duguid   MA 1927
SSC
ptnr W H Mill, McLeod & Rose WS Edin from 1931

CHEYNE Janet Forbes   MA 1911
no longer on GC reg

CHEYNE or Leslie, Lorna Birnie   MA 1941

CHEYNE Margaret Annetta Boon   *MA 1921
no longer on GC reg

CHEYNE William George   MB ChB 1921
d Cosham Portsmouth 24.12.73 *A UR* XLV 447

CHINN Gertrude Annie   MA 1912
d Aber 21.3.65 *A UR* XLI 148

CHINNIAH Samuel Ernest Nalla-nayagam
                    MB ChB 1928

CHISHOLM Alexander Gordon   MB ChB 1952
DPM(Leeds) 1962 MRCPsych 1971
sen h m o De La Pole hosp 1963–71; consult. ch psychiat dept ch and fam psychiat N Tees gen hosp Stockton-on-Tees from 1971
m Hull 1962 Margaret W. Jenkins MA 1955 *qv*

CHISHOLM or McDermott, Christina Isobel
                    MA 1946
teacher geog St David's h s Dalkeith from 1970

CHISHOLM Donald   MA 1949

CHISHOLM Fanny Bisset   BSc 1926
d 7.2.78

CHISHOLM Georgina   MA 1920
no longer on GC reg

CHISHOLM or Innes, Margaret Ann Jamieson
                    MA 1933

CHISHOLM Ronald Harry Eddie   *MA 1949
Edin: head mod langs Melville coll 1960–72, head Ger/Russian dept Daniel Stewart's and Melville coll from 1972

CHITTY Edward Charles   *MB ChB 1924
FBOA(Emeritus) 1966
consult. surg St Stephen's hosp Lond 1948–60; retd

CHRISTIE Albert   MA 1932 MB ChB 1936
consult. anaest Glasg from 1939; retd 1977
m Glasg 9.12.39 Eva E. Walker d of Robert W. Aber

CHRISTIE or Conacher, Alexa Margaret Davidson
                    MA 1952
teacher Aber 1958–62 and from 1971
husb *d* 8.10.76

CHRISTIE Alexander   BSc 1953

CHRISTIE Alexander Wesley   *MA 1920
d Huntly 4.3.75

CHRISTIE Alexander William   *MA 1948
prin scient off. trans and road res lab D Tp Crowthorne from 1955

CHRISTIE Alexandrina Margaret   *MA 1932
head Engl dept Nairn acad 1943–71; retd

CHRISTIE Andrew   MA LLB 1951
solic Aber
m Aber 16.10.59 Hazel L. Souter chirop d of Charles M. S. Aber

CHRISTIE Andrew Barnett
            MA 1930 MB ChB 1935 ᶜMD 1939
DCH 1948 FRCP 1972 FFCM 1972
head dept infect diseases Liv 1946–74; prof infect diseases Benghazi from 1975

CHRISTIE or McDonald, Betty Margaret
                    MA 1953
Nairn: teacher Millbank s 1967–73, remed 1973–77, remed Rosebank s from 1977

CHRISTIE Charles Mowat   *BSc(eng) 1954
MInstMC 1975
Wiggins Teape Stoneywood paper mill: head spec investig sect. tech dept 1960–62, head paper dev tech dept 1962–65; instrument man. ICI paints div Hyde group Cheshire from 1965

CHRISTIE or Ure, Dorothy Margaret Jane
MA 1944 *1964
res asst Aberd 1964–66; educ psych: Aberdeensh educ dept 1967–71, Aber city educ dept from 1972

CHRISTIE Elizabeth   MA 1923
teacher: Alves s s 1944–54, Lhanbryde j s s 1954–56, East End p s Elgin 1956–66; retd

CHRISTIE Elizabeth   MA 1926
JP 1970
teacher: Dunnottar s Stonehaven 1940–67; retd

CHRISTIE Forbes Grant   BCom 1926
no longer on GC reg

CHRISTIE Frances Rumgay
MB ChB 1945 DPH 1963
FMFCM 1972
dept m o: Banff c c 1963–66, Aber c c 1966–69, sen m o child health Grampian health board from 1969

CHRISTIE George Alexander Geddes
BSc(agr) 1952
farm. Fordyce from 1952

CHRISTIE George Davidson   BCom 1924
no longer on GC reg

CHRISTIE Gwendoline   MA 1955

CHRISTIE Harcourt Lawrence   MA 1925
d Aber 16.2.69 *AUR* xliii 214

CHRISTIE Harry Donald   MB ChB 1926
g p Lond retd; resid Stonehaven

CHRISTIE or Thomson, Isabella Mary   MA 1935
teacher part-time Kirkhill s Aber 1969–71

CHRISTIE James Gray   MB ChB 1908
no longer on GC reg

CHRISTIE James McDonald   MB ChB 1936
g p Leeds from 1941

CHRISTIE James Walker Melvin   MB ChB 1931
retd 1971; resid Betwys-y-Coed N Wales

CHRISTIE John Duncan   *MA 1932
teacher maths Wallace Hall acad Dumfriessh 1967–71; retd

CHRISTIE Joseph Dryden   MA 1938
BA(Lond) 1972
RN 1948–64, teacher Dun: Grove acad 1964–65, Kingsway tech coll from 1965
d Dun 1975 *AUR* xliv 417

CHRISTIE Lyall Lees   BCom 1923
MCIT
retd 1962; resid Herne Bay

CHRISTIE or Dalgleish, Mabel Alexandra   MA 1929

CHRISTIE or Cooke, Margaret Anderson   MA 1948
resid Lossiemouth

CHRISTIE or Duncan, Mary   MA 1924
d 23.11.66

CHRISTIE or Brown, Mary Burnett   MA 1939
teacher Findochty 1940–42, Loreburn St John's Dumfries 1942–46, Cogrieburn Dumfriessh 1946–50; NZ: clerk soc security dept Auckland 1952, teacher Gisborne 1953, part time Te Anau and Manapouri from 1953
m Otorohanga North Is NZ 21.8.54 John A. B. Brown bushman, carpenter and hotel man. (now deceased) s of John A. B. B. Riverton Southland NZ

CHRISTIE or MacKellaig, Mary Jane   MA 1924
teacher Nethybridge 1930–31; resid Fort William

CHRISTIE Reginald Cecil   MA 1946 LLB 1949
advoc Aber from 1949
d Aber 13.4.80

CHRISTIE Robert Alexander   MB ChB 1951
d Manitoba 11.2.62 *AUR* xxxix 386

CHRISTIE or Henderson, Sheila Isobel   *MA 1928
resid Oxford

CHRISTIE Thomas John   MA 1947
shoe retail bus. from 1947; resid Petworth

CHRISTIE William   MA 1921
d Aber 26.1.66 *AUR* xlii 85

CHRISTIE William   *MA 1925
PhD(St And) 1968
HMIS: western div 1946–54, north eastern div 1954–63; retd; resid Dun
d 27.9.79

CHRISTIE William   *MA 1929 LLB 1976
JP
head Summerhill s s Aber 1961–67; retd; law app Aber from 1976

CHRISTIE William   BSc 1952
chief works chem Whakatane board mills, NZ 1966–73; prod. supt from 1973

CHRISTIE William Sam George   MB ChB 1924
retd 1963; resid Aber

CHRYSTALL Dorothy Mitchell   MB ChB 1935
g p Ladywell med centre Edin from 1971

CHRYSTALL or McGregor, Margaret McGregor
MB ChB 1949
MRCGP 1960
g p Turriff from 1966

CLAMP or McHardy, Gertrude   PhD 1932
resid Pulborough

CLAPPERTON or Lock, Marian Nichol   *MA 1930
teacher: QASM Moascar garrison Egypt 1951,

Aber 1952, Nairobi 1957–59, Surrey 1963–67; resid
Wimbledon

CLAPPERTON Mary Frederica   MA 1904
no longer on GC reg

CLAPPERTON Thomas   MB ChB 1907
d 10.12.69

CLARK or Reid, Agnes Mary   MA 1925
d in Australia

CLARK Alexander John   MA 1954

CLARK Alexander John Ogilvie   MA 1946

CLARK Alexander Mackenzie   BSc 1945
res eng (electronics) Ferranti Edin from 1948

CLARK Alexander William   *MA 1924
head Darvel h g s Ayrsh 1947–68; retd; part time
tut. double bass Ayr c c 1968

CLARK Andrew   MA 1906
no longer on GC reg

CLARK Ann   MA 1906
no longer on GC reg

CLARK or McDonald, Anna Bella   MA 1933
teacher Dun from 1959; retd; resid Dun

CLARK Anne Elizabeth   MA 1937

CLARK or Cooper, Anne Paterson   MA 1948
teacher Broomhill p s Aber from 1968
husb *d* 6.10.69

CLARK Annie   MA 1933
teacher Aber h s for girls 1944–71; retd
d Aber 7.10.77

CLARK Annie Simpson   MB ChB 1924
g p Leyton Lond from 1935; retd; resid Aber

**CLARK or Brennan, Catherine Johana
                    MB ChB 1923 DPH 1924**
g p Dowlais Glam; clin asst Merthyr and Cynon
Valley Mid Glam; retd 1961

CLARK Charles   MB ChB 1943
barrister-at-law Middle Temple 1957: HM coroner
county of Essex from 1960

CLARK Charles Alexander   *MA 1941
prin teacher hist Kirkwall 1956–62; lect econ RGIT
Aber 1962–67; head econ dept Dun coll of commerce
from 1967
m Aber 24.7.56 Norah C. Milne teacher

**CLARK Charles Grant
                    ᶜMB ChB 1953 MD 1960 *ChM 1966**
sen lect surg Aberd 1961–64; reader surg Leeds
1964–67; prof surg univ coll hosp Lond from 1967

CLARK or Crabb, Christianna Amy   MA 1911
d Aber 7.5.73 *A UR* xlv 224

CLARK David Findlay   *MA 1951 PhD 1975
FBPsS 1969
prin clin psych Leicester area psych serv 1960–66;
consult. clin psych Grampian HB for mentally handicapped Ladysbridge hosp Banff and clin sen lect dept
ment health Aberd from 1966

CLARK or Watt, Dorothy Cameron   MA 1946
resid Alford

CLARK or Stawart, Elma Hay   *MA 1941
resid Berwick-on-Tweed

CLARK or Dean, Elspet Forrest   MA 1929
resid Aber

CLARK Francis   MB ChB 1949

CLARK George Norman   *MB ChB 1927
Alberta: g p Coal Valley 1954–58, Morinville from
1958; retd 1970
coroner Province Alberta from 1970

CLARK George Ogilvie   *MA 1915 *BSc 1920
d Aber 24.10.66 *A UR* xlii 84

CLARK George Ogilvie   MB ChB 1946
consult. surg Wolverhampton & Dudley group of
hosps from 1957

CLARK Hannah Hendry   MA 1936
teacher inf: Sandhaven p s 1937–40, Aber: King St
p s 1941–68, Ashley Rd p s 1968–79; retd

CLARK Helen Smith   MA 1954

CLARK Ian Jardine   .*MA 1937
prin teacher mod lang Hilton acad Aber 1968–79;
retd 1979
wife *d* 1963
m(2) Aber 5.8.75 Katherine M. Keith or Nicol nurs
nurse d of James K. Clola

CLARK Isabella   MA 1933
dep head p dept Banchory acad from 1965

CLARK Isabella Ewen   MA 1927
no longer on GC reg

CLARK James   MB ChB 1904 *MD 1907
d 13.12.71 *A UR* xliv 426

CLARK James   MA 1917 BSc 1920
rector Invergordon acad 1939–59; retd; resid Aber

CLARK James   BL 1925
proc-fiscal Dun 1946–64; retd; resid Jedburgh
d 19.10.80

CLARK James   *MA 1950
Ontario civ serv comm: sen staff dev off. 1963–72,
policy dev off. 1972–76, chief exec dev from 1977

CLARK James Alexander Macdonald
                    MB ChB 1907 MD 1913
  resid Holsworthy
d 19.2.74 *A UR* xlv 446

CLARK James George   ***MA 1930**
  d 27.4.67

CLARK James McKillican   **MB ChB 1906**
  no longer on GC reg

CLARK James Reid   ***MEd 1947**
  CBE 1966 FEIS 1967
dir educ city of Aber 1957–75; retd

CLARK Jean Marion Findlay   **MA 1927**

CLARK or MacIntyre, Jenette Annabelle Graham
                                    MA 1924

CLARK or Bisset, Jessie Ann   **MA 1922**

CLARK John   ***MA 1923 *BSc 1924**

CLARK John   **BSc(agr) 1925**
  d Aber 31.7.75 *A UR* xlvi 322

CLARK John Gordon   **BSc 1949**

CLARK Leah   **MA 1917**
  no longer on GC reg

CLARK or Stewart, Lillias Jean Fowlie   **MA 1923**
  resid Aber

CLARK Lillie Dunbar   **MA 1945**
  teacher Aber: High s for girls till 1966; inf mistress:
Seaton p s 1966–70, asst head Mile End p s from 1970

CLARK or Dey, Magdalene   **MA 1945 Dip Ed 1958**
  teacher St. Margaret's s for girls Aber 1964–69; lect
Engl Speech and Drama coll of educ Aber from 1969

CLARK or Abel, Margaret Rutherford
                                    MB ChB 1937
  retd; resid Norwich

CLARK or Aitken, Mary Ann   **MA 1928**
  teacher Dun coll of comm 1968–70; retd 1970

CLARK Mary Anton   **MA 1912**
  resid Blairgowrie

CLARK or Hutcheon, Moira   **MA 1954**
  Inv: lect Engl/soc stud. tech coll 1963–66, asst head
Cent s from 1970, head teacher Cent p s from 1976

CLARK Muriel Mary   **MA 1948**
  teacher maths Turriff acad from 1949

CLARK Norman Stuart
                    BSc 1933 MB ChB 1936 *MD 1955
  FRCP 1964
reader ch health Aberd from 1964

CLARK Norman Walker McNicol   **MA 1933**
  d Edin –.8.73 *A UR* xlv 449

CLARK Robert James   **MB ChB 1916 DPH 1929**
  d Grappenhall –.12.70 *A UR* xliv 210

CLARK Robert Towers   **MA 1922 BCom 1924**
  Fell. Inst Admin/Comm of S Af 1935
retd prin tech coll E London S Af 1964; lect: Natal
tech coll 1965–74, univ of Durban-Westville from
1975
d Durban S Af 5.3.80

CLARK or Gibson, Rona Williamina McLennan
                                    MA 1936
  teacher: p dept Turriff acad 1962–69, dep head
from 1969; retd 1975

CLARK Victoria Elizabeth   ***MA 1915**

CLARK William Duncan   **BCom 1924**
  no longer on GC reg

CLARKE Agnes Dorothea Barr   **MA 1940**
  secy in Aberd from 1948, admin asst Aberd from
1974

CLARKE Alison   **MB ChB 1941**
  MRCGP 1953 FRCGP 1970
m o (part time) stud. health serv Glas till 1971; m o
(part time) reg m o SHHD Glasg; clin tut. undergrad
med educ Glas from 1972

CLARKE or Niven, Barbara Dorothy Theresa
                                    MA 1951

CLARKE Christine Lyon   **MA 1917**
  d Aber 15.9.69 *A UR* xliii 329

CLARKE Edward Colin   **BSc(for) 1950**

CLARKE Ian Anderson   **MA 1911 BSc(agr) 1912**
  d 1939

CLARKE John   **MB ChB 1923**
  hon surg Porth & dist hosp from 1928

CLARKE John Innes   ***MA 1950 PhD 1956**
  FRGS
prof geog univ coll Sierra Leone 1963–65; reader geog
Durh 1965–68; visiting prof univ of Wisconsin USA
1967; prof geog Durh from 1968

CLARKE William Alexander   **MB ChB 1931**

CLARKSON Alexander   **MA 1928 BCom 1929**
  d Aber 13.9.70 *A UR* xliv 110

CLARKSON or Hynes, Marion Mackay Petrie
                                    MB ChB 1937
  d 9.1.69

CLAY Arthur John Mackenzie   **BSc(for) 1953**
  for. off. London Yorksh motorway 1957–60; land-

scape consult. 1960–65; Canberra: arboriculturist with parks and gardens 1966–73, landscape des and consult. horticulturist from 1973

CLAY Austin Cuthbert   MB ChB 1940 MD 1942
g p Aber from 1945; retd
d 22.12.81

CLEGHORN Robert Allen   DSc 1932
FRCP(Can) 1965 FRCPsych 1972
dem dept med Toronto 1933–46; major RCAMC No. 1 res lab Italy, NW Europe 1943–45; dir lab exper therap and asst to prof psychiat Allan mem inst Montreal 1946–64; dir Allan mem inst, chmn dept psychiat McG univ Montreal 1964–70; hon consult. McG univ from 1971; emeritus prof
m Aber 2.4.32 Sheena M. Marnoch BA(Oxon) d of Sir John M. MA 1888 *qv*(I, II, III)

CLIFFORD Margaret   MA 1951
d 30.5.73

CLIFFORD Sydney Charles   MB ChB 1950
g p Royston Barnsley from 1956

CLOUSTON John Herbert Thomas   MA 1936
d Orkney 29.11.75

CLOUSTON or Jones, Sheila   MB ChB 1955
part time locum health and welfare dept Aber 1959–73; retd
m Aber 4.7.53 Rodney Jones BSc(Liv) marine biol s of Henry J. Cheltenham

CLOW Archibald
**   MA BSc 1929 *1931 PhD 1934 DSc 1940**
scient and tech historian sen consult. BBC/OU from 1970

CLOW or Tulloch, Enid Matilda Murray
**   MB ChB 1937 DPH 1942**
Bristol: asst s m o 1965–70, sen dept m o from 1970
husb *d* 4.1.65

CLUBB Alexander William   MB ChB 1955
MRCOG 1964 FRCOG 1977
capt RAMC 1958–61; regist obst and gyn City gen hosp Sheffield 1961–64; sen regist united Birm and reg hosps 1964–66; consult. obst and gyn N Staffordsh hosp centre from 1966

CLUBB or Leatherby, Ethel Forbes   MA 1950
secy pers asst. High Wycombe from 1957

CLUNAS or Fraser, Dorothy Isobel   MA 1945

CLUNIE James Gourlay   PhD 1952
no longer on GC reg

CLUNIE Thomas   MB ChB 1924

CLYNE Andrew Christopher   MB ChB 1944
no longer on GC reg

CLYNE Henry   MA 1920 MB ChB 1924

COBBAN Andrew Christopher   MB ChB 1944
g p Aber 1952–54; Alberta: Barrhead 1954–56, Westlock from 1956

COBBY John England   BSc(for) 1944
conserv for. Nairobi 1960–64; dist for. off. Cape Town 1964–74; reg dir for. King Williams Town S Áf.
wife *d* Cape Town 22.11.70
m(2) Cape Town 15.9.73 June E. Morecroft or Chisholm travel consult. d of Herbert T. M. Hoylake

COBURN Alexander Milne Wilson   MB ChB 1941
g p Seaton Devon from 1946 and div surg St John ambul brig.

COCCALIS Nicholas   *MA 1952
MEd(Alta) 1968 PhD(Alta) 1970
Canada: teacher Calgary publ sen h schools 1959–66, Alta 1966–70; McG univ: asst prof 1970–76, assoc prof from 1976

COCHAR William Smith   MB ChB 1921
retd 1959; resid Ashton-u-Lyne
m Manc 6.4.33 Eleanor J. Wallace teacher d of Alexander W. MRCS Ashton-u-Lyne

COCHRAN David Gordon   LLB 1925
d Aber 3.1.72 *AUR* XLIV 430

COCHRAN Duncan Scott   MB ChB 1931
o c: milit hosp Catterick 1960–64, royal Herbert hosp Woolwich 1964–66; retd col late RAMC; m o army careers information off. Birmingham from 1966
d Dun 8.8.81

COCHRAN Ian McIntosh   MB ChB 1949
d Glasg 12.3.69 *AUR* XLIII 218

COCHRAN William   MB ChB 1949
consult. paediat surg Ulster hosp and royal Belfast hosp for sick ch from 1962

COCHRANE Helen Bain Tainsh   MA 1952
asst head Gracemount p s Edin from 1968
m Edin 29.10.70 John E. King MA(Cantab) schoolmaster s of Herbert A. K. MA(Cantab) Holt Norfolk

COCHRANE or Dishington, Mary Margaret Campbell
**   BSc 1950**

COCK Gilbert Henry   BSc(agr) 1923

COCKBURN Arthur George   BSc(eng) 1943
TD 1964 C Eng 1951 FIWE 1969 FICE 1972 FRSH 1972 MBIM 1973
chief eng (water) Perth c c 1965–68; dep eng (oper) east of Scot. water board Invergowrie by Dun 1968–75; sen dep dir water services Tayside reg c Invergowrie from 1975

COCKBURN Charles   MA 1929 MB ChB 1933
consult i/c ophth depts Aber hosps from 1960: pres Scot. ophth club 1972; retd

COCKBURN George Rae   *MA 1923
head Hilton s s Aber 1955–65; retd

COCKBURN Lucy   MA 1912
d Market Drayton 24.11.69 *A UR* xLII 328

COCKBURN Mary   MA 1929
m Aber 30.11.34 Charles J. Reid farm. s of Alexander
R. Slains; resid Johnshaven

COCKBURN William   MB ChB 1938
d 14.8.71 *A UR* xLIV 321

COCKBURN William Charles
MB ChB 1936 MD 1963
FRCP 1971
dir central publ health lab Colindale 1958–60; m o
virus diseases WHO Geneva 1961–74; dir div com-
municable diseases from 1974

COCKER Francis   MA 1939

COCKER Phyllis Margaret   MB ChB 1955
h o obst and gyn Dunfermline mat. hosp 1958–59;
sen h o cas and orthop Raigmore hosp Inv 1959–60
m Inv 29.4.61 Kenneth J. Macdonald MB ChB 1954 *qv*

COCKIE Bruce Mavor   MA 1951
teacher: spec asst Engl/geog Bervie j s s 1965–69;
Mackie acad Stonehaven: spec asst Engl/geog 1969–
70, prin asst coordinator Brunton stud. 1970–72, asst
prin guid from 1972

COGHILL John George Jamieson   MB ChB 1922
d 14.3.71

COLDWELL or Williams, Joan Margaret
*MA 1938

COLE Emmanuel Latundi   *MA 1952

COLE Enid   MA 1955 Dip Ed 1956 MLitt 1973

COLEMAN Andrew Leslie Edmund Filmer
MB ChB 1907 MD 1912
d 25.1.64

COLLIE Alexander Shepherd   MA 1954
head: Johnshaven p s Kincardinesh 1964–69, Port
Ellen p s Islay 1969–72, Stanley p s Perthsh from 1973

COLLIE Benjamin   *BSc 1931
ICI prod. plan. man. (leathercloth div) 1962–71;
retd; resid Wilmslow

COLLIE Donald Cumming   *BSc(agr) 1951

COLLIE George Francis   BL 1933
CBE (civil) 1964
ptnr James & George Collie Aber from 1934; vice-
chmn board of man. for Aber spec hosps 1952–60,
chmn 1960–68; hon col 51st (H) div RASC(TA) then
hon col 153 highland regt RCT(V) 1964–71; dir then
chmn Aber univ press from 1953; pres soc of advoc
Aber 1974–76

COLLIE or Stephen, Hester Margaret   MA BSc 1928
teacher: human biol with BFES Hamm W Ger

1961–63, anat and physiol pre-nursing stud. Littlehampton from 1963

COLLIE Ian   *MA 1955 Dip Ed 1956
MEd(Glasg) 1966 MBIM 1971 FSA(Scot) 1975
teacher: Eastwood s Clarkston 1958–64, Langside
coll Glasg 1964–66; asst dir of educ Stirlingsh 1966–
69; dep dir educ: Dunbarton 1969–72, Stirlingsh
1972–74; dir educ Central reg from 1974; hon lect
dept Educ Stir 1977
m Clarkston 3.7.64 Helen S. Meikle MA(Glas) teacher
d of Robert M. Clarkston

COLLIE John   BSc(eng) 1935

COLLIE Joyce Philip   *MA 1951 PhD 1954

COLLIER or Durbin, Joyce   *MA 1915
d 10.9.78 *A UR* xLVIII 227

COLLIER Mary   MA 1923
teacher Banff acad till 1961; retd

COLLINGWOOD Margaret Walker Hill   MA 1926
retd 1975; resid Montreal

COLLINGWOOD or Thomson, Marian Stancliffe
BSc 1924
resid Montreal
husb *d* Quebec 20.10.64 *A UR* xLI 56

COLLINS Henry Duckworth   MB ChB 1933

COLLINS Herbert Davidson   MB ChB 1941
d Aber 17.3.74 *A UR* xLV 449

COLLINS Kenneth Thomas
***BSc 1952 Dip Ed 1955 *MEd 1957**
Exeter: head educ dept and dean of stud. St Luke's
coll 1973–77, dep prin from 1977

COLLINS or Finlayson, Margaret Mackie   MA 1927
teacher maths Leith acad 1940–66; retd; resid Edin

COLLINS Mitchell   MA 1950

COLLINS Thomas   MA 1950
prin teacher relig knowledge RGC Aber from 1955

COLT Joan Margaret Roper
***MA 1953 MB ChB 1959**
h o Lond 1959–60; sen h o: Ashford Middx
1960–61, S'ton 1961–62; asst ship's surg Brit India
SN Co Lond 1963–64; part-time asst m o BBC Lond
1964–65; part-time m o Bromley A H A from
1976
m Lond 3.10.64 John M. Campbell BA(Cantab) pers
man. s of Arthur J. C. Lyme Regis

COLVIN Robert Cowan   MA 1914 BSc(agr) 1914

COLWELL Jeffrey David   PhD 1955
BA(ANU) 1966
Aust: analyst NSW dep agr Sydney 1950–52; res fell
Macaulay inst Aber 1952–55; Aust: res off. dept agr

Wagga Wagga NSW 1955–60, res scient Commonwealth scient and indust res organis Canberra from 1960

CONACHER Gilbert Stewart   MA 1955
   teacher Aber: 1956–60, maths Kincorth acad 1960–76
d Aber 8.10.76 *AUR* xlvii 106

CONCHIE or McLeod, Janet Borrowman   MA 1929
   resid Claygate Surrey

CONCHIE or Dorrell, Julia Grant Wilson
**   MA 1938 BSc 1940**
   Dip Soc Sc (Glas) 1941
pers man. Newcastle, Lond 1941–44, scient admin (gas indust) Lond 1944–47; salesman, waitress etc USA 1947–50; scient admin (coal indust) Lond from 1950
m Lond 14.10.55 Peter G. Dorrell BSc(Lond) lect archaeology

CONN George Keith Thurburn   *MA 1933
   OBE FInstP FRAS
   dir Norman Lockyer Observatory Sidmouth from 1961
d 4.6.75 *AUR* xlvi 325

CONNOCHIE Charles Cumming   MB ChB 1926
d Lochaber 18.4.75 *AUR* xlvi 323

CONNON Campbell   MA 1941 LLB 1949
d Cairngorms 18.12.63 *AUR* xl 303

CONNON Edwin William   BSc(eng) 1929

CONNON Frank Clark   MA LLB 1951
   Aber: leg. asst Burnett & Reid till 1961; own practice 1961–63; sen ptnr Campbell Connon & Co solic from 1963

CONNON George Leslie   BSc(eng) 1947
   scient MoD Portland: exper off. till 1959, sen scient off. 1959–66, prin scient off. from 1966

CONNON William Catto   BL 1949
   town clerk and chamberlain Dufftown 1955–71; part time town clerk and chamberlain Aberlour 1960–73; town clerk Grantown-on-Spey 1971–73; disposed of solic bus. Dufftown 1973; sen solic East Kilbride and Stonehouse dev corp 1973–77; prin solic Dumbarton dist c 1977

CONNON William Lewis   BL 1949
   ptnr Mackenzie & Wilson solic Aber from 1954

CONOCHIE Douglas Alexander Ferguson
**   BSc 1949 MA 1951 MEd 1958**
   FBPsS
educ psych Cambridge 1961–65; prin educ psych counties of Aberdeen and Kincardine 1965–75; dep reg educ psych Grampian from 1975
wife deceased
m(2) Aber 11.10.80 Cairine R. McLean or Petrie MA 1940 *qv*

CONOCHIE Jean Barbara   *MA 1955 Dip Ed 1956
   b Lerwick 14.4.33
sen clin psych child psychiat serv Cambridge 1961–63; part-time sen clin psych royal hosp for sick children Edin from 1971 and part-time res psych dept ch life and health Edin from 1972
m Cambridge 3.12.60 Frank Bechhofer MA(Cantab) reader in sociol Edin s of Ernest B. Nottingham

COOK Allan Montague   MB ChB 1950
   MRCPsych 1971
Ladysbridge hosp Banff: consult. and psychiat 1962–64

COOK Bertram John   MA 1905
   no longer on GC reg

COOK David Kay   MA 1910
d Ballater 2.7.62 *AUR* xl 79

COOK David Lamb   *BSc 1950
   Canadian Pratt & Whitney Aircraft Montreal: chief of perf & control 1963–70, chief proj eng turbofans 1970–79, proj man. PTT turboprop from 1979

COOK Ethel   MA 1915
   teacher Fife: Kelty s 1915–20, West Wemyss s 1920–45, West j s s Kirkcaldy 1945–56; retd; resid Strichen
d Fraserburgh 2.3.79

COOK Henry Burness   MB ChB 1921 MD 1929
d Cults 25.3.74 *AUR* xlv 447

COOK Iain Anderson   MB ChB 1949 *MD 1959
   b Glasg 26.9.26
FRCPath 1972
consult. haemat and reg dir N of S blood transfusion serv Inv from 1960

COOK John   *MA 1912
   part-time teacher Herefordsh/Yorks 1953–65 publ *The Strad and Other Poems* (Lond) 1967
d Inv 21.2.74 *AUR* xlv 447

COOK or Duncan, Linda Ritch   *BSc 1955
   asst lect biochem dept Aberd 1956–58
resid Elgin

COOK or Laidlaw, Margaret Morgan   *MA 1937
   teacher mod lang Keith g s 1939–40, prin mod lang Mortlach s s 1940

COOK or Harris, Mary Jane Smith   *MA 1908
   resid Minehead
d Minehead 17.2.79

COOK Michael   *MA 1954

COOK Nicholas   *MA 1923
   retd 1970; resid Buenos Aires

COOMBE Robert Gorton   BSc(agr) 1923
   no longer on GC reg

COOPER Alexander   MA 1917 MB ChB 1921
d Dundee 27.6.73

COOPER Alfred   *MA 1948
man. family bus. millwrights and joiners Strichen from 1954

COOPER Alfred William Howden   MA 1919

COOPER or Christie, Anna Jessie Durno   MA 1939
resid Grange

COOPER Constance Stewart   MA 1931
Dun: transferred to St Mary's 1967, released from community of St Peter to work in Dun 1972, Rev Mother Superior St Mary's sisterhood from 1973

COOPER Douglas Alexander   BSc(agr) 1954
Edmonton Alberta: man. mill oper N Alberta 1958–71, gen man. seed oper for prov of Alta and Brit Col from 1971

COOPER Geoffrey   MA 1955
prin teacher Engl/hist Alford s 1961–62; head Tullynessle p s 1962–65, Rayne North p s 1965–69, Newtonhill p s from 1969

COOPER George   MB ChB 1906
g p Lond 1907–61; retd; farm. Insch from 1925

COOPER George   BSc 1952
prin teacher: maths/sc Culter s s 1960–66, sc Cults acad 1966–68, sc Bridge of Don acad from 1968–76, phys from 1977
d 23.8.80

COOPER Hamish Rae   *BSc 1946 PhD 1950
prin res off. Shirley Inst from 1961

COOPER or Carle, Harriet Thomson   MA 1928
resid Aber

COOPER Herbert George   MA 1908
no longer on GC reg

COOPER Isabel   BSc(agr) 1950
resid Bourtie Inverurie

COOPER James   MB ChB 1924
g p Birm 1928–62; retd; resid Aber
d Worcestersh 6.6.77 *AUR* XLVII 286

COOPER James Young   *BSc 1950 PhD 1954

COOPER Jessie   MA 1936
d Aber –.4.68 *AUR* XLII 371

COOPER John   BSc(agr) 1915
no longer on GC reg

COOPER John George   BSc(eng) 1949
sect eng GEC–Elliott Process Automation Leicester from 1966

COOPER or Sanderson, Margaret   BSc 1953
resid Inverurie

COOPER Margaret Jessie Corrigall   MA 1935

COOPER Patrick Ashley (Sir)   LLB 1912
d at sea 24.3.61 *AUR* XXXIX 202

COOPER William Davidson   *MA 1925 *BD 1927
hon canon St Andrew's cath Aber from 1962; retd 1977
d Peebles 27.2.78 *AUR* XLVII 356

COPELAND or MacLean, Lily Rennie   MA 1922
resid Aber
husb d Aber 26.3.77

COPEMAN Graeme James Frank   BSc(agr) 1948
head dept of grassland husb NOSCA Aber from 1956; pres Brit Grass Soc 1976–77

COPLAND George Alistair   BSc 1954
scient Inveresk res labs Weybridge 1960–61; Jointine Prod. comp (paper converters) N Hykeham: chief chem 1961–74, man. tech serv from 1974
m Aber 24.6.61 Aileen Melvin clerk d of Alexander M. Stoneywood

COPLAND Helen Ellis   MA 1906
d Aber 16.1.69 *AUR* XLIII 208

COPLAND or Stephens, Helen Margaret   MA 1935
teacher: Crookedholme Ayrsh 1946–49; teacher Engl: Frederick St s Aber 1949–52, Glasg 1957–60, Aboyne 1962–68; resid Ballater
m Aber 28.12.45 Alexander Stephens, Kilmarnock

COPLAND or Barry, Janet Ellis Webster
                                        MB ChB 1944
resid Cork, Eire 1976

COPLAND Myra Frances   BSc 1941
FBCS 1968
computer progr DH Propellers/Hawker Siddely Dynamics Hatfield 1952–64; computing man. CI Data Centre Aldershot from 1964

COPLAND William Alexander   MB ChB 1946
FFR 1956 FRCSE 1975 FRCR 1976 VRD
member clin teaching staff Edin univ from 1962 consult. radiol Lothian health board; QHP 1972–73; retd (surg capt) RNR 1973

CORALL John Mitchell   MB ChB 1936
DMR(Lond) 1947
consult. radiol Medway and Gravesend and mid-Kent group of hosps from 1950

CORBETT Donald Cameron MacRae   *BSc 1953

CORBETT or Davies, Evelina Isabella
                                MB ChB 1922 DPH 1923
resid Bosbury

CORBETT or Hansford, Lizzie Marjory   MA 1914
d 1978

CORDICE Gideon John   MB ChB 1950

CORDINER Adelaide Russell Balfour　MA 1916
   d 24.2.62 *AUR* xxxix 380

CORDINER or Ritchie, Jean Mowat　MA 1940
   resid Peterhead

CORDINER John Hutchison　MA 1935
   JP 1975
teacher Ellon acad 1935–72; retd; RAF 1940–45;
provost Ellon 1958–65

CORDINER John Noble　MA 1924
   d Stirling 16.8.78

CORDINER Robert William　MA 1948
   teacher Peterhead N s 1949–55, dep head 1955–77;
retd

CORMACK Alexander　BSc(eng) 1951
   CEng MIMechE 1959 OBE 1980
works man. AEI turbine generator works Glasg
1964–65; N Ireland: gen man. GEC turbine generator
works Larne 1965–73, man. dir Everton engineering
Newton Abbey from 1973, pres N Ireland engineering
employers assoc Belfast from 1973

CORMACK Alexander Allan　*MA 1913
   author of various publications and of numerous
articles to *AUR* etc; orig member/chmn of Aber
county rent appeal committee 1955–73
d Aber 9.6.76 *AUR* xlvii 101

CORMACK Alexander Cumming
           *MA 1950 Dip Ed 1959 MEd 1962
   head dept remed and spec educ coll of educ Aber
from 1975
marr. diss 1973
m (2) Aber 22.6.73 Margaret Ritchie or Waite lect coll
of educ Aber d of Alfred R. BSc 1926 *qv*

CORMACK or Bond, Barbara Stevenson　MA 1955
   resid Gidea Park

CORMACK Edwin James　BL 1954
   leg. asst firm of patent ag Salisbury Rhodesia 1955–
58; ptnr Fisher Cormack and Botha patent and trade
mark ag Salisbury, Lusaka, Blantyre 1959–79; man.
patent ag dept Spoor and Fisher patent attorneys
Pretoria from 1979
m Salisbury Rhodesia –.4.66 Kathleen M. A. Gale
teacher d of William D. G. Salisbury

CORMACK or Berrie, Ella　MA 1904
   no longer on GC reg

CORMACK or Simpson, Elsie Stott Pickering
                   MA 1941
   teacher: Orpington 1957–67, Upper Poppleton
York from 1968

CORMACK George　MB ChB 1939
   g p Cambo from 1944
marr. diss 1968

CORMACK Gertrude Elizabeth　MB ChB 1920
   retd

CORMACK James Maxwell Ross　*MA 1932
   regius prof Greek Aberd from 1965
wife *d* 1968
m(2) Reading 14.8.68 Sybil P. Dadley BA(R'dg)
teacher d of Harry G. D. Reading
d Aber 4.6.75 *AUR* xlvi 324

CORMACK or Murray, Janet Isabella　MA 1941
   resid Aber

CORMACK John William　*MA 1912
   d Glasg 16.11.69 *AUR* xliii 328 and 441

CORMACK Robert　MA 1912
   no longer on GC reg

CORMIE James Ernest Dingwall　BL 1951
   dep town clerk Perth from 1966

CORMIE or Tough, Robina Andrew　BSc 1948
   scient ICI dyestuffs div 1948–71; organics div from
1971; resid Rochdale

CORNER Harold Hartmann　BSc(agr) 1919
   agr advis Roxburgh till 1961; retd
wife *d* 1968
d 16.2.79

CORNER Malcolm Manford　MA 1922 BD 1925
   C of S min West Church Grangemouth 1960–69;
retd; resid Edin

CORNER William　*MB ChB 1916 *MD 1924
   DTM & H (Lond) 1925
g p Hove from 1930
wife *d* 1971
d Hove 15.8.81

COROON John　MA 1949
   d Lond 3.4.75

CORRIGAL Donald　MA 1904
   d Rothiemay 24.5.66 *AUR* xli 335

CORSER James Ronald　MA 1928
   head Findhorn p s 1963–66; dep head Kinloss p s
1966–70; retd; resid Elgin

COSTIE Isaac　MA 1933 *MEd 1936

COTTERILL Leonard　MB ChB 1899
   no longer on GC reg

COULL Alexander　*BSc(eng) 1953 PhD 1961
   FRSE 1971 FICE 1973 FIStructE 1973
lect: eng Aberd 1957–62, civ eng univ of S'ton 1962–
66; prof struct eng Strath from 1966–76; regius prof
civil eng Glas from 1977
m Aber 22.12.62 Frances B. Moir teacher d of Francis
T. C. M. Aber

COULL or Atkins, Catherine Mary　MB ChB 1943
   MFCM 1972
sen m o county borough Southampton 1967, prin m o
1971–74; spec commun med Dorset A H A 1974

COULL David Carnegie   MB ChB 1940
ophth surg Aber from 1947

COULL George Morrison   BCom 1923
prin Weybridge tech coll 1958–63; retd; resid Bognor Regis

COULL James   BSc 1924

COULL James Riddell   *MA 1933
no longer on GC reg

COULL John   BSc 1955

COULSON Thomas William Gibson   BSc(for) 1950
dist off. For. Comm from 1952; resid Campbeltown

COULSON William James   BSc 1947 *1948
MRIC 1963 C Chem 1976
teacher sc Galashiels acad 1957–60, Kelso h s 1960–62, Graeme h s Falkirk 1962–69; teacher chem Paisley: Oakshaw p s 1969–74, St Mirin's and St Margaret's comp h s from 1974

COULTHARD James William   *MEd 1952
lect educ/psych Moray House Edin 1953–65; visiting Fulbright prof univ of Toledo Ohio USA 1965–66; Moray House: sen lect psych 1966–72, prin lect/head dept psych from 1972

COUPER John Mill   *MA 1935 PhD 1948
Sydney: lect Engl univ of NSW 1959–72; assoc prof Engl Macquarie univ from 1972

COUPER Robert Scott   *MA 1942
rector Forres acad from 1968

COURT Helen Elizabeth   *MA 1927
no longer on GC reg

COUTTS or Donald, Bertha Mary   MA 1955
resid Milltimber Aber

COUTTS Catherine Elizabeth   BSc 1949

COUTTS David   *MA 1910
no longer on GC reg

COUTTS or Birss, Dorothea Harper   MA 1932
teacher Aber: King St s 1956–62, Summerhill s 1962–69, Middle/Frederick St s 1969–72; retd

COUTTS Elizabeth Milne   MA 1906 BSc 1917
d 4.3.79 *A UR* XLVIII 226

COUTTS George   MA 1949
JP Aber 1971
Aber: dep head King St s 1962–66; head: Tillydrone p s 1966–73, Mile-End p s from 1973

COUTTS or Patterson, Helen   MA 1941
resid Montrose

COUTTS or Sexton, Helena Martha Lumsden
MA 1925

COUTTS Isabella Leys   MA 1908
d Aber 8.2.61 *A UR* XXXIX 201

COUTTS James   MB ChB 1926
dep med supt S Wales sanat Talgarth 1947–69; retd; resid Cardigan
d 28.6.78

COUTTS or Butt, Janet Grant   MA 1947
resid Edin

COUTTS or Macdonald, Jessie Milne   MA 1927
d 30.8.76

COUTTS or Harris, Margaret Constance   MA 1913
no longer on GC reg

COUTTS or Murray, Margaret Janet   MB ChB 1922
d Aber 30.6.75 *A UR* XLVI 322

COUTTS or Monkhouse, Marion Charlotte
MA 1914
retd 1949; resid Harrogate

COUTTS or Anderson, Mary   MB ChB 1924
resid Banstead

COUTTS or McKerrigan, Mary Jane   MA 1907
d Leeds 22.7.70 *A UR* XLIV 107

COUTTS or Price, Patricia Jane MacLeod
MA 1925
d W Kilbride 4.4.74 *A UR* XLV 448

COUTTS Thomas Gordon   *MA 1955 ᶜLLB 1957
QC 1973

COUTTS Vera Cecile   MB ChB 1953
b Glenfarg 27.6.28
DPM(St And) 1959 MFCM 1972
asst m o h: Perth & Kinross c c 1959–62, Fife c c 1962–65; sen asst m o h Fife c c from 1965; sen clin m o Fife health board

COUTTS William   MA 1925
d Portgordon 27.6.63 *A UR* XL 205

COUTTS William Ernest   MA MB ChB 1937
g p Cardiff from 1946

COUTTS William Shivas   MB ChB 1924
d Leeds 15.9.68 *A UR* XLIII 84

COW Alexander Strachan Miller   *MA 1927
teacher maths Kelso h s 1928–67; retd; resid Matlock

COW Catherine Mair   MA 1947
teacher Peterhead acad from 1948; resigned 1969
m 30.7.80 Hurry

COWAN Ian Campbell
BSc 1936 MB ChB 1943 MD 1952
dir phys med (consult. status) Sunderland area from 1952

COWAN James   *MA 1918
no longer on GC reg

COWAN Nigel Smart   BSc(eng) 1933
retd army brig 1960; admin Nat Trust Waddesdon Manor Aylesbury 1960–70; ag Waddesdon estate from 1969
d 2.4.80

COWE Alexander May   *BSc 1953 MB ChB 1958
h s mat. hosp Aber 1961–63; g p Ilkeston from 1963

COWIE Alexander Carnegie   BSc 1955
BVMS(Glas) 1961 MRCVS(Glas) 1961 DVSM(Edin) 1967
vet surg Stonehaven 1961–64 and from 1964; vet off. min of Agr Cornwall 1964–76; div vet off. anim health div Min of Agr Tolworth from 1974
m Aber 27.9.61 Muriel M. Black teacher d of Alexander L. B. Aber

COWIE Alexander Smith   MA 1907

COWIE Alfred   MB ChB 1933
g p Leeds 1951–73: retd; resid Cults

COWIE Catherine Mary   MA 1920

COWIE or Murison, Christian Ewen   MA 1915
d 7.6.72 AUR xlv 125

COWIE Clement Alexander   MB ChB 1923
g p Warwicksh till 1958; retd to Dalkeith W Aust
d Felixstowe 14.12.79

COWIE Douglas George   BSc(eng) 1953
eng Traction proj dept Metro Vickers Elect. Co Manc later AEI 1955–65; elect. des eng ICI Fibres Harrogate 1965–67; elect. maintenance eng Wilton 1967–70; mech plant eng petro chem div ICI 1970–77; eng supervis Chevron Petroleum (UK) Aber from 1977
m Barton Lancs 16.7.60 Patricia R. Taylor teacher d of William E. T. Glazebrook Warrington

COWIE or Kinghorn, Elizabeth Jane   MA 1947

COWIE Frank Philip   MA 1952
DipEd(Dund) 1970 *MEd(Dund) 1971
prin teacher maths: Goodlyburn s s Perth 1964–69; Perth g s 1971–73; asst rector Perth g s from 1973
m Clunie 2.4.60 Lorna C. Allardice RGN nurse d of James M. A. Blairgowrie

COWIE George   *MA 1931
rector Alva s 1958–70; retd; resid Elgin

COWIE George   MB ChB 1955
DObstRCOG 1960
h o gyn and obst gen hosp Northampton 1958; g p Ashington 1958–59, Great Barr Birmingham 1959–61, Grimethorpe Barnsley 1961–66, Stockport from 1966
m Birmingham –.7.65 Joyce P. Wright secy d of Arthur W. Birm

COWIE George Alexander   *MA 1927
d Montrose 14.12.73 AUR xlv 448

COWIE George Robert   *MA 1933 ᵈLLB 1935
OBE 1977 LLD(Belf) 1980
secy Queen's univ Belf 1948–77; retd
wife d 28.5.72

COWIE or Johnston, Gladys May   MA 1917
d Norway 11.12.70 AUR xliv 210

COWIE Gordon Strachan   *MA 1955 LLB 1958
nat serv 2nd lieut RPC 1958–60; lect internat and compar law Queen's Coll Dundee, St And 1960–67; sen lect publ law Glas 1967; prof publ law Glas from 1973; dean fac law Glas from 1977; admitted to fac of advoc 1962
m Dusseldorf 11.8.61 Angela M. Whelband d of Rowland G. W. BAOR

COWIE or Hutchison, Helen Alice Creswell
                 MA 1944

COWIE Howard Elphinstone   BSc(agr) 1923

COWIE Isabel Proctor   *MA 1933
teacher Fr/Ger: Keith g s 1944–62, spec asst Gordon Schools Huntly 1962–72; retd

COWIE Isabella Sutherland   MA 1952
teacher: Strichen 1953–60, Perth acad 1960–61, San Fernando Trinidad 1961–63; resid Mbabane, Swaziland
m Port of Spain Trinidad 13.8.60 John C. Philip bank man. s of William P. Strichen

COWIE James Hay   *MA 1948
prin teacher mod lang Morgan acad Dun from 1963
m Newcastle Staffs 29.6.68 Vera Porter secy d of George P. Madeley nr Crewe

COWIE James Macrae
         MB ChB 1898 DPH 1900 *MD 1903
d Burton on Trent 9.3.61 AUR xxxix 198

COWIE James Strachan   *MA 1952
dist off. N Rhodesia 1953–66; asst regist univ of Kent at Canterbury from 1966
m Aber 13.9.52 Sheila Mackay

COWIE Jane   MA 1923
d Portsoy 10.10.69 AUR xliii 330

COWIE Jessie Geddes   MA 1955
teacher: Findochty 1956–60, Middlefield s Aber 1960–62; Inverallochy 1962–65 and from 1974; resid Fraserburgh
m Buckie 24.12.60 Gordon Clark eng s of Peter C. Aber

COWIE John   MB ChB 1946
d Lond 24.6.70 AUR xliv 111

COWIE John Lawless   MA 1947
C of S min Rosyth parish Dunfermline 1960–70; exper team min Richmond Craigmillar Edin 1970–77; Christian Fellowship of Healing Edin from 1977

COWIE Lillis Marion   MA 1924
  teacher Engl: Arbroath till 1960, Brechin h s 1960–63; retd

COWIE or Clark, Mabel Margaret   MA 1920
  d 19.10.75 *AUR* XLVI 322

COWIE Nellie Durno   MA 1914
  no longer on GC reg

COWIE William   *MA 1951

COWIE William Archibald Douglas   MA 1923
  retd 1968; resid Cummertrees Annan
d Cummertrees 8.3.76

COWIE William Bagrie
                    MA 1930 BCom 1932 LLB 1934
  d 1.11.71 *AUR* XLIV 432

COWIE William George   *MA 1934
  Jordanhill coll of educ Glasg: lect econ/mod. stud. 1973–77; retd; lect adult educ (WEA) Strathclyde from 1977

COWIE William John Gavin   *MA 1951
  lect fac of agr N'cle from 1963

COX George Frederick   *MA 1910
  d N Berwick 7.12.64 *AUR* XLI 55

COX or Glascodine, Margaret Elizabeth   MA 1953
  temp teacher Lennoxtown p s 1962–68; teacher Engl Townhead j s s 1968–71; asst prin Engl Kirkintilloch h s from 1972

COX Reginald Tom   MB ChB 1915
  d 15.7.80

COX Richard   *MA 1946
  prin teacher maths Forrester s Edin 1959–65; head Sutherland tech s Golspie 1965–68; head W Calder h s from 1968

CRABB or Fraser, Catherine Amy   *MA 1938
  teacher Colliston Angus from 1956
marr diss 1961
m(2) Guthrie 18.9.63 John Strachan MBE eng s of George M. S. Guthrie

CRAGGS Joyce   MA 1950
  Graz Austria: exchange teacher 1966–68; Lehrbeauftragte univ Graz 1967–68; teacher g s from 1968
m Graz 10.7.69 Franz Scherz gymnasiat prof Mag Phil(Graz) s of Franz S. Graz

CRAIB David Andrew   MB ChB 1939
  g p Eastbourne from 1947

CRAIB Kathleen   MA 1953 MEd 1958
  educ psych Glasg ch guid serv 1962–65; sen clin pysch Douglas Inch clin for psychiat Glasg 1965–70; tut. organis ch panel trg, dept extra-mural and adult educ Glas
m Aber 14.9.62 Robert I. Murray farm. s of Sir Robert A. M. Glasg

CRAIB William   BSc(agr) 1929
  CBE
d Edin 30.10.72

CRAICK William   BSc(eng) 1942

CRAIG or Thomson, Agnes McCulloch   *MA 1955
  sen psych clin NERHB 1961–69; lect psych Aberd from 1970

CRAIG or Cooper, Ailsa   BSc 1953
  teacher sc Hilton acad Aber from 1967

CRAIG Alan Gordon   MB ChB 1951
  St Louis Missouri: res psychiat Wash univ 1963–66, chief resid psychiat 1966–67, instr psychiat 1967–68, asst prof from 1968; pres med staff St Vincent's hosp from 1975

CRAIG Albert   MA 1932 MB ChB 1936 DD 1967
  ordained presb Glasg 1947; C of S min St Andrew's ch Peebles from 1967

CRAIG Alexander Henderson   MB ChB 1916
  d Lichfield 26.5.61 *AUR* XXXIX 203

CRAIG Andrew   MA 1932 LLB 1934
  b Aber 16.6.11
town clerk Peterhead 1946–75, harbour clerk Peterhead 1946–76; retd

CRAIG Andrew Hugh   *MA 1952
  teacher mod lang Alloa acad 1956–67; prin teacher Lornshill acad Alloa from 1967
m Aber 7.8.63 Grace R. M. Henderson florist d of William H. Udny

CRAIG or Barron, Ann   MA 1926
  teacher Mile-end p s Aber 1942–46
husb *d* 4.5.65

CRAIG Annie   MA 1935
  retd 1973; resid Aber

CRAIG David Main   *MA 1954
  lect Engl univ Ceylon 1959–61; organis tut. WEA North Yorks 1961–64; univ Lanc: lect and sen lect Engl 1964–72, sen lect without dept duties from 1972

CRAIG David Ogilvie   MB ChB 1946

CRAIG Doris Agnes   MA 1925
  no longer on GC reg

CRAIG Elma Cruickshank   MA 1953 Dip Ed 1966
  Dip Ed of Deaf (Manc) 1958
teacher of deaf: Ohio s USA 1962–64, Aber s 1964–66; lect educ of deaf univ Lond inst of educ 1966–70; res fell. R'dg 1970–73, hon lect N'cle schol educ 1973–76; lect City Lit Inst London from 1976
m McMillan

CRAIG Eric   MA 1955
  BD(Edin) 1960
C of S min Chalmers-Lauriston ch Edin from 1966

CRAIG Eric John Dickson   MB ChB 1946
clin asst radio therap Essex county hosp Colchester
from 1957

CRAIG Ernest Duncan   MA 1911
no longer on GC reg

CRAIG Esther Mary   *MA 1955
mus mistress King's Norton g s for girls Birm
1958–62; sen mus mistress North Kesteven g s
Lincolnsh 1962–64
m Aber 12.12.64 Reginald Barrett-Ayres BMus(Edin)
reader in music Aberd s of Frederick G. B-A.
Aviemore

CRAIG George Alexander Barclay   MA 1942
HMIS Edin from 1964

CRAIG Ian George Logan   MB ChB 1942
g p Stanford-le-Hope from 1953

CRAIG Isla   MB ChB 1955 MD 1963
MRCPath 1965 FRCPath 1977
regist clin path. Sunderland RI 1960–63; sen regist
path. Manchester teaching hosps 1963–65; consult.
path. Selly Oak hosp Birm from 1965

CRAIG James   MA LLB 1937
OBE 1970
sole ptnr R. Addison-Smith & Co WS Edin; now in
ptnrship with son James L. J. C.

CRAIG James Alexander   MA 1932 BD 1939

CRAIG James Wood   MB ChB 1924
d Stirling 8.6.68 *AUR* XLIII 84

CRAIG or Still, Jane Douglas   MA 1915
resid Aber
d 1.2.79

CRAIG or Melville, Jean Forrest   MA 1934
d of James C. MA 1902 qv(II, III)
teacher Aber: Porthill p s, Seaton, King St, Hanover
St 1936–42; Rugby: New Bilton c s 1942–43, Hill-
morton Paddox j s 1943–47
m Rugby 25.7.42 William S. Melville BSc(eng) 1938 qv

CRAIG John   *MA 1906
declined CBE 1939, elected member Athenaeum
1943; resid Hazlemere
d Wimbledon 9.6.81

CRAIG John   *MB ChB 1921 LLD 1964
Hon FAAP 1958
prof ch health Aberd 1947–63; retd
d Aber 19.4.77 *AUR* XLVII 211

CRAIG John McLennan   MB ChB 1950
FACOG(Lond) FRCS(C) FRCOG
Calgary: consult. gyn and obst Holy Cross hosp,
Calgary gen hosp 1962–73; consult i/c foetal monitor-
ing chief dep obst and gyn Holy Cross Hospital
Calgary Alberta
m Farnham 9.3.57 Elisabeth Schuler

CRAIG John Peter   *MA 1927
head Ballater s 1943–67; retd
d Aber 22.7.77 *AUR* XLVII 286

CRAIG Joseph   *BSc(eng) 1942
b Aber 29.9.21
dir Craig Stores Aber from 1951

CRAIG Mackenzie Melville   MB ChB 1943

CRAIG or Daniel, Margaret Forrest   BSc 1955
teacher: Beath h s Cowdenbeath 1960–62, Northfield acad Aber 1970–75, Sunnybank p s Aber from
1975

CRAIG or Gibson, Mary   MA 1935

CRAIG Mary Ann   MA 1919

CRAIG Mary Ann   MA 1931
teacher: Fordoun s 1938–70; retd; resid Auchenblae

CRAIG or Macdonald, Mary Jessie   *MA 1917
d 1.3.65 *AUR* XLI 56

CRAIG or Scott, Mora Joan   MB ChB 1940
g p Elgin from 1941
husb d –.12.71

CRAIG Norah Alison   MA 1925
d Aber 25.4.71 *AUR* XLIV 211

CRAIG Norman James   *MA 1930 MB ChB 1935
d 9.6.65

CRAIG Ronald Anderson   BL 1936
consult. MacDiarmid & Craig solic Aber from 1976

CRAIG Sheila Phillips   MA 1953
teacher Inverurie acad from 1954

CRAIG or Blackburn, Sheila Wood   MB ChB 1951

CRAIG Theodore Watson   BSc(agr) 1921
d Kirkhill Invernesssh 4.8.54

CRAIG Victor   MA LLB 1952
solic Glasg 1952–57 and from 1960; pers off. Paisley
1957–60
m Glasg 24.6.54 Catherine M. McEwen comptometer
oper/typist d of William McE. Glasg

CRAIG William   *MA 1907 *BD 1913
d Nairn 15.1.67 *AUR* XLII 346

CRAIG William   MA 1931
CA

CRAIG William Elliot   BSc(agr) 1938
area man. SW Scot Chem Bldg Prod. Lond from
1950, man. Scot. off from 1976; ROC 1947–77; bar
to long serv medal 1970

CRAIG or David, Winifred Anne   MA 1950
resid Aber

CRAIGEN or Beedie, Patricia Young   MA 1944

CRAIGEN William Gordon Cameron   MB ChB 1945
d 14.2.69 *A UR* XLIII 217

CRAIGHEAD Edward Alexander   *MA 1948
prin Quinte s s Belleville Ontario from 1969

CRAIGHEAD Robert   BSc 1930

CRAIGHEAD William   MA 1922
d Grangemouth 5.6.67 *A UR* XLII 185

CRAIGIE Betty   MA 1952
teacher: Inverallochy 1962–69, Fraserburgh inf s from 1969

CRAIGIE John Dustan   *BSc 1933
sc master/dep rector Sanquhar acad; retd 1971

CRAIGMYLE Alexander Donald   *MA 1907
retd; resid Newburgh Aberdeensh
d Newburgh 7.1.78 *A UR* XLVII 355

CRAIK David   MA 1907

CRAMB Finlay Ross   *MA 1912
d Aber 4.2.62 *A UR* XXXIX 378

CRAMB Maurice   MA 1932 LLB 1934 LLD 1966
head dept Rom Law 1947–51; convener bus. comm of General Council Aberd 1971–79; General Council assessor 1960–63 then (to 1979) Chancellor's assessor univ court Aberd; executive trustee Carnegie Trust

CRAMOND David Stephen   MB ChB 1945

CRAMOND James   MB ChB 1941 DPH 1947
Lond: g p Knightsbridge 1945–59, advis occup health to various organis from 1955–69; Northern reg hosp board (Scot.) Inv 1969–71; g p Kent 1971–73, Lond Kensington and Farnham Surrey from 1973; consult. aviation med

CRAMOND Tom   BSc(agr) 1951
MBE 1973
prin teacher agr and rural subj Stranraer acad from 1965

CRAMOND William Alexander
                                MB ChB 1947 ᶜMD 1954
FANZCP 1969 FRCPsych 1971 FRACP 1973
S Aust: dir mental health 1961–65, prof mental health Adel 1963–71; prin m o mental health Scot. home and health dept Edin 1971–72; dean of fac of med and prof mental health Leic 1972–75; prin and vice-chancellor univ Stir 1975–79

CRAN Brennan Scott   *MB ChB 1928 *MD 1931
consult. surg and urologist Tees-side hosps from 1945; retd

CRAN Doris Kellas   MA 1929
head Craigellachie p s 1948–73; retd; resid Lower Cabrach

CRAN Douglas   MB ChB 1915
retd army col; resid Kilmacolm

CRAN or Jamieson, Edith   MB ChB 1924

CRAN Edward Gray   BSc(eng) 1950
eng insp Scot dev dept Edin from 1971
m Aber 18.8.61 Wendy I. M. Diack

CRAN Eva Margaret   MA 1931 MB ChB 1936
acting div m o Division I LCC 1964–65; dep m o Lond bor of Hammersmith 1965–69; retd full time, working on sessional basis Hammersmith from 1969

CRAN or Bruce, Helen Jean Geddes   MA 1934
resid Keith

CRAN or Blair, Helen Johnston   BSc 1927
resid Milltimber, Aber

CRAN Ian Mitchell   MB ChB 1947
consult. surg Queen Alexandra milit hosp Lond 1966–69; joint prof milit surg RCS England and royal army med coll Lond 1969–70; retd army 1970; g p Taree NSW Aust 1970–72; consult. surg Manning River dist hosp Taree from 1973

CRAN James   MB ChB 1941
g p Wellingborough from 1953

CRAN James Hunter   *MA 1947
rector Falkirk h s from 1962
d Carronshore 27.1.71 *A UR* XLIV 215

CRAN or Hunter, Janet Davidson   *MA 1925
teacher Gordon s Huntly: inf dept 1938–50, asst then spec asst mod lang 1950–68; retd
husb *d* 1.2.38

CRAN or Graham, Jean Jamieson   MA 1954
resid Troon

CRAN John   BCom 1927
no longer on GC reg

CRAN Victor Alexander   MB ChB 1938
g p Tilbury from 1949

CRANNA or Robbie, Ella   MA 1930
teacher Tarves from 1963

CRANNA or Farquhar, Helen Jane Christian Park
                                                        MA 1915
no longer on GC reg

CRANSTON or Mann, Chrissie Coutts   MA 1923
d Forres 3.12.73 *A UR* XLV 447

CRANSTON Margaret Isabella   MA 1908
resid Forres
d 26.12.77

CRANSTON Thomas   MA 1912
d Edin 30.8.66 *A UR* XLI 337, XLII 83

CRANSTON William Ian   *MB ChB 1949 MD 1957
MA(Oxon) 1962 FRCP 1965
first asst RPM dept Oxon 1960–64; prof med St
Thomas' hosp med s Lond from 1964

CRAWFORD or Holland, Anna Margaret   MA 1935

CRAWFORD David Chalmers
                          MA 1901 BSc(agr) 1906 BSc 1909
no longer on GC reg

CRAWFORD Douglas Murray   BSc(agr) 1952

CRAWFORD or Macdonald, Elizabeth   MA 1934

CRAWFORD Ian Milne Cay   MA 1948

CRAWFORD John Henry Forbes   MB ChB 1951
LM(Dub) 1955 MRCGP 1961
ship's surg: M.S. *Meteor* 1969–71, Royal Fleet
Auxiliary from 1974

CRAWFORD Kenneth Stewart   MB ChB 1938
consult. anaest Nottingham groups of hosps from
1946

CRAZE Margaret Catherine   MA 1939
vice-prin h s Montreal 1964–69; co-ordinator of
curric Prot school board of Greater Montreal 1969–
70; asst supt PSBGM 1970–76; reg dir PSBGM from
1976

CRAZE Mary Betty   MA 1943
teacher Montreal 1958–63; head maths dept
Lachine h s from 1963

CREIGHTON Barbara Helen   *MA 1915
no longer on GC reg

CREIGHTON Mary Anne Findlay   MA 1912
d Aber 15.4.73 *AUR* XLV 224

CRERAR Archibald   MB ChB 1935
JP 1949
g p Millport from 1953

CRICHTON Alexander   MB ChB 1940
d Wellington 30.7.75 *AUR* XLVI 325

CRICHTON Alexander McKerrow   *MA 1932
McLaren h s Callander: prin teacher classics 1947–
59, also dep rector 1959–72; dep rector from 1972;
retd 1975
wife *d* 2.9.72

CRICHTON Arthur   MA 1914 BSc(agr) 1920
TD
d Brechin 12.1.72 *AUR* XLIV 428

CRICHTON or Kellas, Isobel Margaret   MA 1939
resid Ballater
husb *d* 17.2.68

CRICHTON John Andrew   MA BSc(agr) 1922
dep dir Rowett Inst Aber 1963–64; agr res consult.
Havana Cuba 1964–66; retd; resid Aber

CRICHTON William McKerrow   *MA 1934
OBE 1968
head Ntare sen s s Mbarara, Uganda 1955–72; retd;
resid Bieldside Aber

CRICHTON William Paterson   BSc(eng) 1953

CRICHTON or Bremner, Jemima Findlay   MA 1925
teacher E. Lothian 1964–70; retd; resid Prestonpans

CRICHTON or Petrie, Jessie Allan   MA 1926
teacher Peterhead cent s 1953–64; retd

CRICHTON Margaret Murray
                          MA 1953 Dip Ed 1956
teacher: Aber 1956–64, W Lothian 1964, Edin
1964–65, Glasg 1965–73, asst prin teacher from 1973

CRICHTON William George   BSc(agr) 1942
vet pract New Deer 1950–70; vet off. Lawson's
Dyce from 1970 and vet dir Aber and dist MMB cattle
breeding div from 1973

CROCKART or Jolly, Margaret Clementina
                                          MA 1910
d 11.9.74

CROCKETT Alexander Stewart   BSc(eng) 1942
FIStructE 1958 FIMunE 1958 FICE 1970
borough eng and surv Chesterfield 1960–65, sen dep
city eng Edin 1965–74; city eng Edin 1974–75; dir of
highways Lothian reg c from 1975

CROCKETT Charles Stephen   MB ChB 1955
MRCGP 1968
g p: New Pitsligo from 1956, Oakville Ontario 1969
m(2) Glasg 13.4.78 Carol I. Cross BEd(Glasg) secy
BBC d of John C. Glasg

CROCKETT Joseph   MA 1950 LLB 1953
LLM(Lond) 1968
sen admin asst nat superan scheme Lond 1957–60;
asst secy Cocoa Choc & Confect Alliance Lond 1960–
62; lect/sen lect Hatfield polytech 1962–69; prin lect
law polytech Newcastle-u-Tyne 1969–71; head of
dept leg. stud. polytech Wolverhampton from 1971

CROLL or Paterson, Eirene Victoria   MB ChB 1924
d 14.1.61

CROLL Jean Flett   MB ChB 1935
asst county m o h Northants from 1953; retd 1975
m Cheltenham 26.8.64 Thomas Woolfenden clerk in
holy orders s of Thomas W. Kettering

CROLL John MacArthur   MB ChB 1929 DPH 1931
FRCPath 1963
retd 1971; resid Lincoln
d Derby –.6.81

CROMAR Alexander   MA 1953 *MEd 1965
prin teacher maths Torry s s Aber from 1964; asst
head Torry acad 1973, dep head from 1974

CROMAR Arthur Clement   MA 1935 LLB 1937
law app Cochran & Macpherson advoc Aber

1934–37; leg. asst Hogart & Burn Murdoch WS Edin 1938–39, Cochran & Macpherson advoc Aber 1939–40; RAF wireless oper/intell off./flt lt 1940–46; leg. asst Merchant Co Edin/secy & solic Scottish YH assoc Edin/Stirling 1946–68; dep town clerk Stirling 1968–75; asst dir admin & leg. serv Cent reg c 1957–78; retd
m Edin 22.9.64 Elizabeth C. F. Smith MA(Edin) teacher d of William S. MA(Edin) JP Edin
d Comrie –.8.81

CROMAR Colin Douglas Leslie   MB ChB 1932
FRCS(USA) 1973 Assoc Fell. Amer Proctological Soc 1959
resid North Jackson Mississippi 1961–62; surg pract Pasadena and Houston Texas from 1962
marr diss

CROMAR Peter Law   MA 1952 MEd 1962
ABPsS 1965
asst educ psych child guid serv Edin 1962–66; Moray & Nairn joint c c: educ psych Elgin 1966–71, prin educ psych from 1971

CROMBIE Alan Alexander Cran   BSc(eng) 1945

CROMBIE George Edmond   *MA 1930
counsellor H M Emb Dublin 1961–65; Brit High Comm Bathurst, The Gambia 1965–67; retd 1968
d Aber 9.12.73 AUR XLV 226

CROMBIE Hugh Mackenzie   MB ChB 1925
d Aber 23.4.61 AUR XXXIX 204

CROMBIE Irene Helen   MA 1932
JP 1964
secy to Lord Provost Aber 1951–72; retd; resid Aber
d Middlesbrough 22.11.76

CROMBIE James Ian Cormack (Sir)
                                  ***MA 1925 LLD 1957**
d Lond 22.5.69 AUR XLIII 214

CROMBIE or Brown, Katherine Isabel MA 1928
m Aber 26.8.43 James Brown
resid Aust 1944–77
d Ashford Middx 3.11.77

CROMBIE or Parker, Kathleen Mary   *MA 1935
resid Middlesbrough

CROMBIE or Croll or Finlayson, Margaret Mary
                                               MA 1926
d 16.4.71

CROMBIE Peter   *MA 1933
d Aber 1.11.75

CRONE or Bruce, Anna Hunter   *BSc 1945
resid Liverpool

CROOKE Myles   PhD 1950
for. entomol (for. comm) Farnham 1951–60; lect Aberd from 1960

CROOKSHANKS Allan Stephen   MA 1927
d Dumfries 19.3.71 AUR XLIV 211

CROOKSHANKS Brian Kerrington
                              MA 1949 dLLB 1952
TD 1967
Aber: asst solic Cormack, Cramb & Gibb 1966–75, dep proc fiscal from 1975; comm serv 51(H) signal regt TA 1955–67

CROOKSHANKS George Coutts   MA 1923
d Aber 8.3.70 AUR XLIII 445

CROSBIE Alexander John   *MA 1952
FRGS 1956 PhD(Edin) 1965
lect univ Edin 1964–72, sen lect from 1972
wife d 19.12.62
m(2) Logie 2.6.65 Nicola J. Watson MA(Edin) d of A. J. S. W. Bridge of Allan

CROSBIE or Donald, Jane   MA 1915
resid Aber

CROSSLING Frank Turner   MB ChB 1949
FRCSGlas 1970
consult. surg Stobhill hosp Glasg 1964–67 and from 1968; sen lect surg Nairobi Kenya 1967–68

CROUCHER Barbara Margaret   MA 1942
head PNEU s Harlow 1961–64; Lond: sen mistress Jewish s Manor House 1964–67, sen mistress Garden House s Sloane Square 1967–71; teacher in ILEA schools from 1971, in Falconbrook j m s Wandsworth from 1973

CROW Henry James   MA MB ChB 1949 cMD 1964
MRCPsych 1971 FRCPsych 1977
clin dir Burden neurol hosp and inst Bristol from 1956

CROW Robert Stewart   MB ChB 1945 cMD 1958
FRCP 1971
consult. phys Torquay from 1962

CROW William Conacher   MA 1934

CROWLEY Eamon   BSc(eng) 1940
RAF 1940–46; des eng Ont hydro Toronto 1947–57; Canada: dir of eng BC power comm Victoria BC 1957–61, gen. man. internat power eng consult. (IPEC) Vancouver/pres Canadian eng consult. Ottawa 1961–73, vice-pres IPEC/man. syst des & construct. BC hydro and power auth Vancouver from 1973
m London Ont 11.12.48 Marion W. Neil nurse

CROWLEY Gerald Patrick   BSc 1935
d Bury 13.2.78 AUR XLVII 359

CROWLEY Thomas Michael   MA 1940

CROWLEY Timothy John   MB ChB 1952
g p Woodchurch and part time anaest Wirral group hosps 1960–66; then surg Royal Fleet Aux. Serv MoD Lond from 1966
d 6.6.75

CROZIER Theodore James   MA 1950

CRUDEN or Hacket, Christina Melville   MA 1949

CRUDEN James McNab   BSc(eng) 1950
  resid Canada

CRUICKSHANK Alan Hamilton
                        ***MB ChB 1936 *MD 1942**
  MRCPath 1963
reader path. Liv from 1966

CRUICKSHANK Alexander
                        MB ChB 1922 *MD 1934
  m o min of health Lond 1951–65; med advis
Tenovus Cancer information centre Cardiff 1965–70;
retd; resid Crail

CRUICKSHANK Alexander
                        MA 1922 MB ChB 1925
  d Walton-on-Thames 6.8.80 *AUR* XLIX 67

CRUICKSHANK or Davidson, Alice Lawrie
                                      MA 1947
  resid Forres

CRUICKSHANK or Semple, Alison Ballenden
                                      ***MB ChB 1939**
  med asst (part-time) E of Scot. blood transfusion
serv from 1955; resid Dun

CRUICKSHANK Alistair   BSc(agr) 1953
  conserv and extension off. Filabusi S Rhod 1953–61;
farm. Fyvie 1961–77

CRUICKSHANK Andrew   MA 1899
  d Bearsden Glas 10.10.64 *AUR* XLI 52

CRUICKSHANK Andrew Whyte   MA 1949
  head: Holytown p s Lanarksh 1967–71, Petersburn
p s Airdrie from 1971

CRUICKSHANK or McGillivray, Anne Calder
                                      MA 1925
  resid Helmsdale
husb *d* 24.2.72

CRUICKSHANK Annie   MA 1928
  teacher maths NSW Aust 1929–37; head Rogart p s
1941–68; retd
m Grantown-on-Spey 3.12.37 Mackay Mackay MA *qv*
husb *d* 5.3.67

CRUICKSHANK or Davidson, Annie Wilson Corrie
                                      MA 1933
  resid Nairn

CRUICKSHANK Arthur Lewis   *BSc 1928
  chief telecomm supt Bedford 1953–69: retd; resid
Ringwood

CRUICKSHANK or Watt, Caroline Margaret
                                      MA 1918
  d Inv 31.3.78

CRUICKSHANK Charles Burr   MA 1893
  no longer on GC reg

CRUICKSHANK Charles Greig   *MA 1936
  FRHistS 1971
exec secy Commonwealth econ comm 1964–66; dir

commodities div Commonwealth secretariat 1967–68;
BoT (reg export div London and SE) 1969–71;
Channel Is occupation official historian 1970–71;
insp FCO 1971–72; asst secy civ aviation auth Lond
1971–72; asst secy DTI Lond 1972–73; retd; resid
Lond

CRUICKSHANK Charles Ian Thomas
                                      MB ChB 1953
  MRCGP 1961
g p: Gairloch W Ross 1960–64, Kintore 1964–67 and
in group practice Inverurie from 1967

CRUICKSHANK Cyril Edgar   BSc(eng) 1932 *1933
  AMICE 1939 AMIWE 1945 FIWE 1969
eng asst Westminster 1935; chief asst Aber c c 1959–
68; area eng cent area NE of Scot water board from
1968; retd 1973

CRUICKSHANK Daniel   MA 1942 LLB 1949
  ptnr leg. firm Dun from 1955

CRUICKSHANK Donald Campbell   *MA 1933
  dep rector Banff acad on closure of Fordyce acad
1964; retd 1971; resid Fochabers

CRUICKSHANK or Macdonald, Dorothy Mary
                                      ***MA 1925**
  resid Aber

CRUICKSHANK Douglas Scott   BCom 1926
  CA
no longer on GC reg

CRUICKSHANK Douglas William   MA 1927
  sen met. off. and lect climatology RAF Thorney Is;
retd 1970; resid Aber
d Aber 1.7.81

CRUICKSHANK or Doig, Elizabeth   MA 1949

CRUICKSHANK Elizabeth Scott   MA 1921
  d Aber 5.8.71 *AUR* XLIV 319

CRUICKSHANK or Jolly, Elizabeth Walker
                                      MA 1946
  Glasg: teacher handicapped (m h and p h) children
1960–69; dep head Kennyhill s for m h children
1969–73; head Rottenrow (later Abercorn) s for m h
children from 1973

CRUICKSHANK Elsie Margaret   MA 1940
  teacher Smithfield s Aber 1965–66; clerkess Aber
from 1967

CRUICKSHANK or McGee, Elsie Margaret
                                      MA 1950
  resid Aber

CRUICKSHANK Eric Hugh   *BSc 1953 PhD 1956

CRUICKSHANK Eric Kennedy
                        ***MB ChB 1937 *MD 1948**
  OBE 1960 FACP 1970 FRCPGlas 1972
dean post grad med and prof post grad med educ Glas
from 1972
marr. diss

m (2) Kingston Jamaica 6.11.69 Josephine W. Williams nurse d of Theodore R. W. CMG MA(Oxon) Jamaica

CRUICKSHANK Ernest William Henderson
MB ChB 1910 *MD 1920 LLD 1959
 d 29.12.64 *AUR* XLI 109

CRUICKSHANK Ethel Margaret
BSc 1923 PhD 1926
 MA(Cantab) 1965
res under MRC Dunn nutrit lab Cambridge 1940–73; retd; resid Cambridge

CRUICKSHANK or Sayce, Ethel Margaret Lindsay
*MA 1930
 resid East Kilbride

CRUICKSHANK George   *MA 1913 *BSc 1920
 OBE BA(Cantab)
d Weybridge 11.9.72 *AUR* XLV 124

CRUICKSHANK George Alexander
MA 1931 BSc(agr) 1933
 SAI Edin from 1945

CRUICKSHANK George Grant   MA 1953
 teacher Dyce s from 1969

CRUICKSHANK George Watt   MB ChB 1951
 g p Lond from 1959

CRUICKSHANK Gordon   BSc(eng) 1944

CRUICKSHANK Hector   MA 1932 BSc(for) 1934
 d Aber 11.3.63 *AUR* XL 206

CRUICKSHANK Helen Margaret   BSc 1944
 teacher sc Keith g s from 1949; resid Lhanbryde

CRUICKSHANK or Smith, Helen Taylor   *MA 1952
 on edit. staff Canadian Med Assoc Journal 1956–62; resid Oakville, Ontario

CRUICKSHANK Isobel Watt   MA 1912
 no longer on GC reg

CRUICKSHANK Jack Naughton   *BSc 1941
 prin scient off. MoD from 1959
m Birm 11.5.51 Joan Corbett

CRUICKSHANK James   BSc 1922
 no longer on GC reg

CRUICKSHANK James Henry
*BSc 1933 PhD 1936
 asst gen man. ICI Europa Brussels 1968–72; retd; resid Stockport

CRUICKSHANK James Robert Leslie
MA 1925 LLB 1928
 WS 1937
Edin: leg. asst 1927–36; ptnr Menzies & White, WS later Menzies, Dougal & Milligan, WS from 1936
m Edin 5.9.35 Norah Burke d of Matthew J. B. Middletown Armagh N Ireland

CRUICKSHANK James Stephen   MB ChB 1936
 d Sheffield 20.12.72 *AUR* XLV 227

CRUICKSHANK James William   *BSc 1951

CRUICKSHANK Jeannie Ann   *MA 1920
 retd 1960; resid Inv

CRUICKSHANK John Alexander   MA 1937
 teacher Engl/hist/geog Aber/Aberdeensh 1939–40; war serv RAF N. Af/Italy 1940–45; various teaching posts 1945–47; teacher Aber: Engl/hist/geog Frederick St s, prin hist/geog/mod stud. Linksfield acad 1947–76; retd

CRUICKSHANK John Benton   MB ChB 1937
 d Glasg 1.4.69 *AUR* XLIII 216

CRUICKSHANK or Downie, Katherine   MA 1932
 resid Salcombe

CRUICKSHANK Katie Isabella   MA 1911
 no longer on GC reg

CRUICKSHANK Leslie Duffus   MB ChB 1955
 Aber: h s (obst) mat. hosp 1959, trainee asst 1960; g p Forfar from 1960; (locum tenens Parry Sound Ontario July Aug 1972)

CRUICKSHANK Leslie Valentine   *MA 1931
 OBE
sqn ldr RAF; retd
d Shaftesbury 26.3.81 *AUR* XLIX 138

CRUICKSHANK Lorna Collie   *MA 1950
 Edin: teacher mod lang St. Denis s 1963–70, head of dept from 1970; Goetheschule Hanover (centre for Brit teachers) 1975–77

CRUICKSHANK Maggie Bell   MA 1924
 spec asst teacher maths Airdrie acad; retd 1966

CRUICKSHANK or Clark, Margaret Stewart
MA 1935
 teacher Turriff acad from 1967

CRUICKSHANK Martin Melvin
BSc 1911 MB ChB 1912 *MD 1925 ChM 1927
 d 19.10.64 *AUR* XLI 32

CRUICKSHANK Mary   MA 1922
 teacher Hilton s s Aber 1932–61; retd

CRUICKSHANK or Campbell, Mary Barbara
*MA 1930
 d Lausanne Switzerland 29.3.47

CRUICKSHANK or Lawson, Mary Elizabeth
MA 1923
 resid Inv

CRUICKSHANK Peter   BSc(eng) 1955

CRUICKSHANK Peter Bruce   BSc(for) 1950
 NE reg man. Bowaters Forest Products Fordoun from 1968

CRUICKSHANK Robert
                              *MB ChB 1922 *MD 1925 LLD 1968
FRSE 1957 FRCPE 1962 CBE 1966
prof soc and preventive med univ of WI, Kingston
Jamaica 1966–68
d Edin 16.8.74 *A UR* xlv 108

CRUICKSHANK or Houston, Thelma Cromarty
                              MB ChB 1943
clin med off. Camden and Islington A H A from
1972

CRUICKSHANK or McRobbie or Melvin, Violet Mary
                              MA 1928
resid Huntly
husb (A. W. Melvin) *d* 1965

CRUICKSHANK William Durward   MB ChB 1915
d Rustington 10.10.61 *A UR* xxxix 278

CRUICKSHANK William Leslie   BSc(eng) 1940

CRUICKSHANK William Walker
                              *MA 1901 *BD 1915
d 6.4.69 *A UR* xliii 208

CRUICKSHANK or MacKay, Williamina
                              MB ChB 1925
g p; retd 1939; resid Bexhill-on-Sea

CRUICKSHANK or Milne, Williamina Hay
                              MB ChB 1938
Royal Cornhill hosp Aber 1968–72; part time g p
from 1972

CRUICKSHANKS John   MA 1937
dep dir educ Moray and Nairn 1967–75; div educ
off. Moray div Grampian reg c from 1975

CRUSE Clara   *MA 1921 BSc 1922
teacher maths Lemington g s Northumberland
1926–59; retd; resid N'cle-u-Tyne

CULLEN or Isles, Alice May   MA 1946

CUMMING Alexander Farquharson   BSc(agr) 1906
no longer on GC reg

CUMMING Alexander George   MA 1938
FEIS 1963
head Portknockie s s from 1961; retd 1977
d 10.10.80

CUMMING Alexander (R.)   *MA 1901
no longer on GC reg

CUMMING Alexander Robertson Ritchie
                              MB ChB 1935 MD 1940
d Cottingham 31.5.66 *A UR* xli 341

CUMMING or Graham, Alexandrina Wilson
                              MA 1922
no longer on GC reg

CUMMING Annie Ogilvie   MA 1931

CUMMING or Bisset, Catherine Munro
                              BSc 1925 *1926
d Lond 9.11.61 *A UR* xxxix 282

CUMMING Douglas   BSc(agr) 1954
DAFS: asst insp Aber 1958–71, insp Ayr 1971–78,
insp Aber from 1978

CUMMING or Schofield, Ella   *MA 1909

CUMMING George   MA 1904
no longer on GC reg

CUMMING George Ingram   MA 1929

CUMMING or Jones, Hilda Jamieson   *MA 1939
teacher: Engl Galashiels acad 1963, Selkirk h s
1963–77; retd 1977

CUMMING or Gray, Ida Jean   MA 1934
resid Aber

CUMMING or Young, Isobel McRae   MA 1927
resid Insch

CUMMING James Collie   *MA 1929

CUMMING James Munro   *MA 1930
d Tain 30.11.67 *A UR* xlii 369

CUMMING John   *MA 1936
HMIS 1950; HM(dist)IS from 1962
d 5.4.78 *A UR* xlviii 106

CUMMING Joyce Edith   MA 1953
resid Menorca Balearic Is Spain
m Mahon Menorca 4.4.73 Juan Cardona maker of
costume jewellery s of Antonio C.

CUMMING Mary   BSc(agr) 1948
farm. Newburgh Aberdeensh

CUMMING Mary   *MA 1952
teacher Fr: Insch 1958–60, Bankhead acad from
1960

CUMMING Patricia May   MB ChB 1955
DPH 1961
Banff c c: asst m o h 1961–64, dep m o h 1964–65, clin
m o h Glasg from 1973
m Craigellachie 23.7.65 Neil M. Jack DA(Edin) arch.
s of Donald D. J. FRIBA

CUMMING Patrick   MA 1928 LLB 1930
joint clerk univ court St And and secy Council
Queen's Coll Dundee 1954–63; ptnr Gray, Robertson
& Wilkie solic Dun 1963–67; town clerk Banff
1967–70; retd 1970

CUMMING Robert Alexander   MB ChB 1933
FRCPath 1964 (founder fell.) FRCPE 1970
FRCSE 1971
reg dir SE Scot. blood transfusion serv from 1947;
retd 1974
hon con phys (Blood Transf) ERI

CUMMING Ronald Anderson   MB ChB 1925
retd 1961; resid Banchory
d Aber 12.2.79 *AUR* XLVIII 229

CUMMING Ronald Patrick   MB ChB 1945
consult. surg to Shetland hosps from 1957

CUMMING or Cunningham, Rosa Mary Gordon
MA 1914
d 12.8.65

CUMMING William James   MB ChB 1928

CUMMINS Gordon Theodore Martineau
MB ChB 1948

CUNNINGHAM Donald Cameron
*MA 1955 MEd 1957
Aber: teacher Engl Hilton s 1960–61, Aber acad
1961–63, RGC 1963–66; lect coll of educ from 1966

CUNNINGHAM Henry Campbell   MA 1915
no longer on GC reg

CUNNINGHAM Ira James   PhD 1931
d NZ 29.8.71

CUNNINGHAM Shirley Margaret
*MA 1952 *MEd 1967
journalist 1952–65; Aber: teacher hist/Engl 1967–
69; lect educ coll of educ from 1969

CURR Alexander Ian   MB ChB 1921
d Poole 7.11.69 *AUR* XLIII 329

CURRID John Gilbert   *MA 1919 MB ChB 1924
d Chadwell Heath 31.5.70 *AUR* XLIV 109

CURRID Patrick Grant   MA 1920 MB ChB 1923
d Lond 22.5.68 *AUR* XLII 358

CURRIE Alan   BSc(eng) 1945

CURRIE Andrew   MB ChB 1941
MFCM 1971
N Nigeria: sen m o hosps admin M of H Kaduna
1959–61; sen m o admin Kano med div 1961–62;
Scot.: dept med supt Inv hosps 1963–65, med supt Inv
hosps 1965–73, dep sen admin m o Northern reg hosp
board 1973–74; c m s Highland health board 1974–75;
c m s Argyll and Clyde health board from 1975

CURRIE Annie Watson   MA 1915
d Keith 9.8.72

CURRIE George Alexander
*BSc(agr) 1923 DSc 1936 LLD 1948
LLD (Dalhousie Can) 1958 LLD (NZ) 1961
LLD (univ of Papua and New Guinea) 1976
vice-chanc univ of NZ 1952–61; chmn comm on educ
in NZ 1960–62; chmn comm on higher educ Papua
and New Guinea; resid Canberra

CURRIE Helen Littlejohn   MA 1950
Ellon acad: prin teacher mus 1959–72, prin teacher

guid 1972–73; Aber: year mistress Harlaw acad from
1973; organist and choir mistress Ferryhill N church
Aber from 1971

CURRIE James   BSc 1951
Aber: prin teacher maths Powis acad 1963–73; asst
head Harlaw acad from 1973

CURRIE James Glen   BSc(agr) 1955

CURRIE or Michie, Jessie   MA 1940
teacher Engl Ijebu-ode g s W Nigeria 1949–56;
Zaria N Nigeria: lect Engl coll of arts sc and tech
1958–61; head Ahmadu Bello staff s 1963–66; View-
lands p s Perth: teacher 1970–74, asst head from 1974

CURRIE Norman Lamont   MA 1928 BCom 1930
head Bonhill p s Dunbartonsh 1965–72; retd; resid
Dumbarton
d Dumbarton 2.8.76

CURRIE Robert   MA 1949
C of S min Dowanhill ch Glasg from 1969

CURSITER William Nisbet   *BSc(eng) 1951
FIStructE MICE
chief eng Dorman Long & Amalgamated Eng Lagos
1961–62; asst to export dir Dorman Long & Co Lond
1962–67; contr man. (export) Redpath Dorman Long
Glasg 1967–75; contr man. Redpath Dorman Long
Glasg from 1975

CUSHNIE or Robertson, Agnes Jean Carswell
MA 1941
teacher Rosebank s Nairn from 1966

CUSITER Douglass James   MB ChB 1937
m o h and div m o West Riding c c: Mexborough,
Conisbrough and Dearne 1961–72, Rotherham,
Kiveton Park and Maltby from 1972
d Scarborough 27.5.74 *AUR* XLVI 110

CUSITER Hilda   *MA 1932
Fairfield h s Manc: sen classics mistress 1950–58,
dep head from 1958; retd 1975

CUTHBERT or Young, Jean Spiers   *BSc 1955

CUTHBERT Mary McLaren Gordon   MA 1956

CUTHBERTSON Iain   *MA 1952 LLD 1978
gen dir of prod. Citizens' Theatre Glasg 1961–64;
asst dir Royal Court Theatre Lond 1965–67; dir
Perth Theatre from 1967: Rector Aberd 1975–78
m Glas 6.1.64 Anne C. K. Biles actress d of Reginald
N. B. Glasg

CUTHBERTSON Lilias Margaret   MA 1953
m Aber 15.10.60 William E. Strachan MB ChB
1954 *qv*
resid Plymouth

CUTHILL James Caithness   BSc 1941

CUTLER James Raymond   *BSc 1954
civ serv Fed Govt of Nigeria, Kano 1955–59; stored prod. entomologist/pesticides DAFS Edin from 1959

CUTT James Ritch   MA 1925
Aber: head Cornhill s 1951–63, Sunnybank s 1963–65, Mile End s 1965–69; retd

CUTTS John Raymond   *MA 1953

DAKERS John   BSc 1923 *1924
prin teacher chem Portobello s s 1962–68; retd

DALE Alexander Robb   MA 1949
FEIS 1972 RNVR lt (A) (O) 1942–46
Aber coll of comm: teacher 1959–63, sen teacher 1963–73, acting head of dept 1973, later head of dept

DALE Brian Bozier   MB ChB 1953
MLCO 1969 MFHom 1976
dir stud. Lond coll of osteopathy and at Harley House Marylebone Rd from 1967

DALGARNO Charles William   BSc(eng) 1950
civ eng Wm Tawse Aber from 1954
d Aber 10.5.78

DALGARNO Christian Edith   MA 1939

DALGARNO or Reid, Ethel Margaret   MA 1907
d S Af

DALGARNO Helen Ruth   MA 1927
retd 1955; resid Edin

DALGARNO John   BSc(eng) 1955

DALGARNO Myra Theresa   *MA 1948
teacher mod lang Tunbridge Wells 1960–71; head of dept from 1971

DALGARNO Wilfred Tait   MA 1928 BSc(agr) 1930
teacher: Old Rayne 1960–61, Bucksburn 1961–72; retd; resid Princes Risborough

DALGLEISH George Robert White   BSc(eng) 1948
Peterhead: asst civ eng Admiralty 1948–50, resid eng harbour improvement work 1950–53; civ eng Sir Alex Gibb Ptnrs Edin 1953–54; plan. ag contr man. Holland & Honnen & Cubitts (Scot.) Edin and N'cle 1954–61; contr man. Richard Costain Construct. N'cle and Leeds 1961–66; Higgins Hill Northern Leeds: contr man. 1966–68, reg. man. 1968–72, dir from 1970

DALGLEISH James White   MA 1937 LLB 1939
Cardiff: dir C H Bailey 1962; dir Allseas Shipping Services and subsids 1965; dep chmn C H Bailey from 1970

DALGLEISH or Leyton, Sheila Robertson
MB ChB 1943
Eng: g h m o Powick hosp 1960–62, clin asst path. Bromsgrove gen hosp 1962–63; Horsham Aust: private psychiat 1968–71, school m o from 1973

DALLAS Marjorie Gordon   MA 1908
no longer on GC reg

DALLAS Robert Duncan   MA 1933
teacher Banchory acad from 1947

DALTON Alfred Hyam   *MA 1948
CB 1976
Inland rev: dep chmn from 1973

DALY Robert   MA 1948
JP Perth 1967
C of S min: Inchture and Kinnaird ch linked with Longforgan ch from 1963; mod Dun presb from 1973

DALZIEL or Wetherly, Agnes Johnston   MA 1946
teacher: Commercial Rd p s Sunderland 1964–66, Hillview p s Sunderland 1966–68, asst head St Margaret's s for girls Aber 1968–75, asst head Cults p s 1975–77; head Greenbrae p s Bridge of Don Aber from 1977
husb d 1963

DANIEL Leslie Morren   BSc(agr) 1952

DANIEL Renwick St. Clair Calder   *MA 1951
ACMA 1962 FCMA 1966
area cost dev off. NCB Fife area, Dysart 1961–66; lect man. acct RGIT Aber from 1966

DANSON James Gordon   MB ChB 1908 MD 1922
d Bath 18.6.69 AUR XLIII 327

D'ARCY Rosina Cannon   MA 1952

DARGIE or Taylor, Edith Isabella   MA 1930
remed teacher Ferryhill s Aber 1966–72; retd
husb d 12.1.66
d Aber 13.2.80

DARK Victor Marshall   BSc(eng) 1951
CEng MICE 1957 MIWES 1959
eng with various consult. on water supply, harbour and bldg proj in UK, Libya, Saudi Arabia, Brunei 1965–78; Moxley Jenner & Ptnrs Swindon from 1979

DARLING James Grahame   BSc 1908
no longer on GC reg

DARNLEY Ernest Marshall   MB ChB 1934

DARNLEY William Russell   MB ChB 1935
no longer on GC reg

DAS Nadella Vinkata   BSc(agr) 1924
no longer on GC reg

DASTOOR Jamshed Khorsted   MB ChB 1915
no longer on GC reg

DASTUR Ratan Edulji   MB ChB 1912
no longer on GC reg

DAVID Ian Ainsley Fearon   BSc(eng) 1943 MA 1949
FSA Scot 1970
retd; resid Aber

DAVIDSON Adrian Cyril BSc(eng) 1945
  supt Central Thermal Serv Ontario hydro Toronto
from 1972

DAVIDSON Alastair Grant MB ChB 1948
  g p Helmsdale from 1957

DAVIDSON Alexander Dyce
MA 1929 MB ChB 1933
  g p Steyning from 1945
d W Chiltington 20.2.77 *A UR* XLVII 212

DAVIDSON Alexander Masson MB ChB 1937
  Lond: consult. ch welfare Borough of St Pancras
1946–48; clin asst St Mary's hosp for women and
children Plaistow 1950–62; patron soc of portrait
sculptors from 1962; retd from med pract 1971; resid
Oxford
d Oxford 2.11.80

DAVIDSON Alexander Munro BL 1951
  ptnr C & P H Chalmers advoc Aber from 1952
m Hampstead Lond 23.5.59 Anne P. Hayes
d Cults Aber 23.4.78 *A UR* XLVII 360

DAVIDSON Alexander Robert *MA 1922
  d Kilmarnock 15.9.69 *A UR* XLIII 330

DAVIDSON Alfred MA 1949
  teacher: Townhill Dunfermline 1952–54. Gordon
Schools Huntly 1954–60; Huntly: head Largue s
1960–66; Gordon Schools Huntly: dep head (prim)
1966–72, head from 1972
m Huntly 15.8.56 Elizabeth M. McIrvine teacher d of
John McI. Glass

DAVIDSON Alfred Harry BSc 1923
  FEIS 1962
retd
d Leicester 10.9.76 *A UR* XLVII 105

DAVIDSON or Innes, Amelia Shaw Ethel MA 1949
  resid Huntly

DAVIDSON or Lobban, Annabella Lobban
MA 1903

DAVIDSON or Bruce, Annie Bertha MA 1932
  resid Buxton

DAVIDSON or Jones, Annie Dawson MA 1941
  teacher St Luke's Brighton 1964–66, post of spec
responsibility for mus from 1966

DAVIDSON or Hutchinson, Annie Margaret
McKessar MA 1936 *BSc 1938
  resid Poole

DAVIDSON Annie Milne MA 1920
  no longer on GC reg

DAVIDSON or McNab, Bessie MA 1915
  teacher: maths/Fr Anderson inst Lerwick 1916–17,
maths Fraserburgh acad 1917–56, spec asst 1956–62;
retd
d Fraserburgh 12.12.76

DAVIDSON Charles Ingram BSc(eng) 1951
  d Aber 14.2.60 *A UR* XXXVIII 600

DAVIDSON Constance Annie MA 1924
  teacher: Inverurie acad 1925–28
d Aber 24.11.74

DAVIDSON Donald MA 1926
  d Edin 26.8.65 *A UR* XLI 246

DAVIDSON Donald Arbuthnot BL 1923
  ptnr Wilsone & Duffus advoc Aber 1936–73; retd

DAVIDSON Donald Falconer BSc(for) 1938

DAVIDSON Douglas Steel BL 1951
  d Edin 15.3.72 *A UR* XLIV 433

DAVIDSON or Skene, Edith Anne MA 1907
  d Aber 18.4.66 *A UR* XLII 82

DAVIDSON Edith Margaret *MA 1945
  teacher: second master Engl Dundee h s 1965–73;
prin guid Grove acad Broughty Ferry from 1973

DAVIDSON Edwin Maxwell Murray BD 1913
  C of S min: retd from Markinch 1960; resid Perth
d 29.3.77

DAVIDSON or Fyvie, Eleanor M. MA 1941
  teacher Fyvie from 1969

DAVIDSON or Harper, Elizabeth Cruickshank
MA 1924
  teacher Fyvie s till 1967; retd
d 22.9.76

DAVIDSON or Gray, Elizabeth Mary BSc 1945
  teacher maths: Airdrie acad 1971–73, Woodmill h s
Dunfermline from 1973; in spec class unit Ballingry
jun h s from 1976

DAVIDSON or Abbas, Elma Rutherford
MB ChB 1946
  doctor i/c trg Internat Planned Parenthood Fed reg
off. Nairobi from 1971

DAVIDSON Ethel Margaret May MA 1929
  d Brechin 28.8.61 *A UR* XXXIX 282

DAVIDSON or Mathie, Ethel Mary Falconer
MA 1930

DAVIDSON Flora Mary *BSc 1954 PhD 1957
  biochem: Lond chest hosp 1959–73, Willesden gen
hosp from 1973

DAVIDSON Frank George Shepherd
MA 1932 BL 1934
  advoc in Aber

DAVIDSON Frank Norrie BSc(eng) 1942
  MICE 1951 ERD 1965
dep dir roads Tayside reg c from 1975

DAVIDSON George   MB ChB 1908 DPH 1909
retd 1965; resid Bedford 1965–70, Aber from 1970
d Aber 6.11.76 *AUR* xlvii 211

DAVIDSON George Chessor   BSc(eng) 1945
FIEE
NSHEB: area eng Elgin from 1966

DAVIDSON George Ian   MB ChB 1935
d Aber 9.3.74 *AUR* xlv 449

DAVIDSON or Dickie, Georgina Christian   MA 1925
matron Tertowie resid s Kinellar 1945–60; teacher
Aber 1960–73; retd
husb *d* 27.3.60

DAVIDSON Gilbert   MA 1934
FEIS 1972
head St. Ronan's s s Inverleithen from 1945

DAVIDSON Graham MacGregor   MB ChB 1949
g p Bradford from 1954

DAVIDSON Hector   BSc(agr) 1952

DAVIDSON or Sleigh, Helena Margaret
　　　　　　　　　MA 1920 MB ChB 1923 DPH 1924
Lond: organis of courses Women's Corona soc
1958–63; overseas med advis Save the Children Fund
1963–73; resid Tunbridge Wells
d 13.7.81

DAVIDSON Henry William   MA 1899
no longer on GC reg

DAVIDSON Iain Francis William Knowles
　　　　　　　　　*MA 1954 EdB 1956
teacher St. Peter's RC s Gloucester 1960–63; educ
psych Bexley 1964–67; Ontario inst for stud in educ
Toronto: res assoc 1967–69, PhD stud. 1969–71; lect
dept of spec educ from 1972
m Aber 19.8.67 Barbara A. Marshall teacher d of
Joseph M. East Sheen Lond

DAVIDSON Ian   *BSc(eng) 1952
lect eng Queen's coll univ St. And/Dund univ from
1967

DAVIDSON Ian Mackenzie   BSc 1951
teacher maths/sc Alford 1956–61; relief teacher
maths/sc/prim. subjs various schools Aber/Aberdeensh
1961–73

DAVIDSON Ian Winsted   BSc 1929

DAVIDSON or Chalmers, Ida Helen   MA 1916
no longer on GC reg

DAVIDSON Irene Girdlestone   MA 1940
teacher: Colegio Internacional Arequipa Peru till
1961; Aber: teacher prim. relief staff 1962, geog/mod
stud/scripture Aber h s for girls—Harlaw acad—
1961–75, geog from 1975

DAVIDSON James   MB ChB 1902
no longer on GC reg

DAVIDSON James Johnston   *MA 1924
d Hythe Kent 5.6.71 *AUR* xliv 320 & 430

DAVIDSON James Meldrum   MA 1942
C of S min: Dalziel h ch Motherwell 1960–67, St.
Andrew's ch Inverurie from 1967; town councillor
1969–75

DAVIDSON James Smart   *MA 1926
FEIS
d 3.10.75

DAVIDSON James Watt   MB ChB 1944
g p Clevedon Avon from 1960

DAVIDSON James Watt   ᶜMB ChB 1953 MD 1969
MRCP & SGlas 1963 FRCP(C) 1972
regist med N'cle reg hosp board 1960–61; sen regist
radiol: DRI 1962–63, Western Inf Glasg 1963–65;
Canada: staff radiol Toronto gen hosp 1965–71, assoc
prof radiol univ of Toronto 1971–74; dir radiol
Chedoke hosps Hamilton and assoc clin prof radiol
McM univ Hamilton 1974, dir radiol Henderson gen
hosp Hamilton Ont 1977

DAVIDSON or Gibson, Jane Isabella
　　　　　　　　　　　　*MB ChB 1940
FRCPath 1965
lect path. Aberd from 1970

DAVIDSON or Thomson, Janet Anderson   MA 1947
resid Towthorpe York

DAVIDSON or Milne, Janet Dorothy
　　　　　　　　　　　　MB ChB 1954
med asst dept of venereology Bristol RI; sen m o
fam plan. clin from 1977

DAVIDSON or Jackson, Jean Lawrie
　　　　　　　　　　　　MB ChB 1949
m Edin 11.1.52
resid North Bay Ontario

DAVIDSON or Taylor, Jean Margaret   MA 1947
resid Dyke Forres

DAVIDSON or Reid, Jessie Elizabeth   MA 1928
resid Aber

DAVIDSON John   BSc 1948
d 4.10.64

DAVIDSON John   BSc 1951 *1952

DAVIDSON John   PhD 1953
CChem FRIC 1962
head dept chem and phys analysis Rowett res inst
Aber from 1970

DAVIDSON John Bruce   BSc(eng) 1949

DAVIDSON John Farquhar
　　　　　　　　　　MB ChB 1922 DPH 1926
d 20.7.79 *AUR* xlviii 351

DAVIDSON John Fergus Chalmers   MA 1955
　MBKS 1971
teacher: Mile-End p s Aber 1956–62, Aber g s 1962–
63; lect audio-visual media Aber coll of educ 1963–66;
asst dir Scot Film Council Glasg 1966–70; head educ
film div Encyclopaedia Brit Lond from 1970–73;
elected vice-pres internat council for educ media
Stockholm 1969; man dir educ and trg div Trans-
media (W H Smith group) 1974; formed own co
Fergus Davidson Associates to distribute film television audio and video materials 1975, chmn and man
dir

DAVIDSON John Forsyth   MA 1923
　JP FRES
d Banchory 25.2.76

DAVIDSON John Maxwell   MB ChB 1925
　no longer on GC reg

DAVIDSON or Davidson, Julia Forgie
　　　　　　　　　　　　　　MB ChB 1946
　Aberd: res asst dept soc med 1968–73; part time res
asst dept commun med from 1973

DAVIDSON Lawson Douglas   MB ChB 1945
　O St J 1971
consult. anaest NE reg board (Scot.) from 1963; hon
med supt St. John nursing home Aber

DAVIDSON Lily Robertson   MA 1923

DAVIDSON or Walker, Margaret Elizabeth
　　　　　　　　McKenzie   MA 1943 Dip Ed 1957
　m(2) Surrey 6.8.60 Francis E. Benwell army off. s of
Frederick B. Johannesburg
resid Bushey

DAVIDSON or Massie, Margaret Elizabeth Meta
　　　　　　　　　　　　　　MA 1925
　no longer on GC reg

DAVIDSON Margaret Isobel   MB ChB 1955
　g p Aber from 1957

DAVIDSON or Hunter, Marion   MA 1916
　no longer on GC reg

DAVIDSON Marjory Stuart   MA 1920 BSc 1923
　d Bournemouth –.9.72

DAVIDSON or Hay, Mary Gordon   MA 1955
　resid Aber

DAVIDSON or Murray, Mary Maxwell   MA 1946
　resid The Hague, Holland

DAVIDSON or Dinnes, Nancy Rosemary Chalmers
　　　　　　　　　　　　　　MA 1949
　asst town clerk Cupar 1959–64; secy: Scot. Boat-
owners Mutual Insur Assoc Buckie 1965–70, Peterkin
& Duncans advoc Aber 1970–73, Brander & Cruickshanks advoc Aber from 1974

DAVIDSON Norman James Hunter   MB ChB 1938
　FRCPath 1963
path. All Saints hosp Chatham from 1956

DAVIDSON Patricia McKenzie   MA 1951

DAVIDSON Peter McLaren   BSc 1924
　retd from Pilkington Bros 1967; resid Eccleston
St. Helens

DAVIDSON or Slessor, Phyllis Eileen
　　　　　　　　　　　　　　MB ChB 1939
　resid Edin

DAVIDSON Rachel Mary   MA 1926
　retd; resid Aber

DAVIDSON Rena Mayor Simpson   MA 1923
　teacher: Culloden s 1942–45, Canonmills s Edin
1945–55, Carrick Knowe s Edin 1955–64; retd

DAVIDSON Richard Charles   BSc(eng) 1950

DAVIDSON Robert   MB ChB 1923

DAVIDSON Robert   BSc(agr) 1947

DAVIDSON Robert   MA 1949 *MEd 1952
　teacher Aber and Banffsh 1950–54; asst dir of educ
Kincardinesh 1954–63; dep head Ferryhill p s Aber
from 1963

DAVIDSON Robert   MB ChB 1951
　MRCPsych 1971
Glasg: sen m o Woodilee hosp 1957–65; consult.
psychiat: Hartwood hosp 1965–67, Woodilee hosp
from 1967

DAVIDSON Robert Andrew Welsford   BCom 1923
　no longer on GC reg

DAVIDSON Robert Murray   MB ChB 1955
　g p Atherstone Warks from 1966

DAVIDSON Stephen   *BSc 1951 PhD 1954
　lect nat phil Aberd from 1958

DAVIDSON Sydney Gordon
　　　　　　MA 1920 MB ChB 1924 LLD 1975
　surg ARI; retd 1965
d Aber 22.3.80 *AUR* XLVIII 440

DAVIDSON or Preece, Sylvia Hendry Miller
　　　　　　　　　　　　　　MA 1955

DAVIDSON Thomas Bendelow   MB ChB 1940
　g p Aber from 1947

DAVIDSON Thomas John
　　　　　　　　　MB ChB 1922 DPH 1923
　DTM & H 1929
IMS 1923–48; retd col; resid Bridport
m Loughborough 1951 Ethel I. Harvey

DAVIDSON or Shewan, Vera Eileen Jeannie
                                        MA 1931
resid Aber

DAVIDSON William   BSc(eng) 1952

DAVIDSON William Campbell
            ***MB ChB 1928 MD 1934 DPH 1938**
retd 1966; resid Matua Tauranga NZ

DAVIDSON William Gordon   MB ChB 1931
d Grimsby 31.8.64 *AUR* XL 400

DAVIDSON William Mackay
                    MB ChB 1934 *MD 1957
FRCPath 1963 FRSE 1964
prof haemat King's coll hosp med s Lond from 1959:
emeritus prof Lond univ from 1974

DAVIDSON William Sharp   MB ChB 1931
DPH 1948 FACMA 1968 CBE 1980
RN surg lt 1932–35; IMS 1938–48 retd with hon rank
of lt col; dep commissioner of publ health and dep
prin m o of West Aust 1949–62, comm publ health
and prin m o WA 1963–74

DAVIDSON-LAMB William   MB ChB 1938

DAVIE Alexander   MA 1910
d Insch 1961 *AUR* XXXIX 273

DAVIE Alexander Brodie   MB ChB 1936
g p fam doctor unit health centre Hounslow from
1970
d 7.2.78 *AUR* XLVIII 232

DAVIE or Oughtred, Armorel Margaret   *MA 1950
resid Ottawa

DAVIE Christian Stephen   MA 1929
retd 1969; resid Hatton

DAVIE Doris Helen Gordon   MA 1933

DAVIE or Robertson, Elaine Agnes   MA 1944

DAVIE Frederick   *BSc 1948

DAVIE George Forbes   BSc 1927
d 9.4.64

DAVIE Hilda Stephen   MA 1939
teacher: year mistress Hazlehead acad Aber from
1970

DAVIE James Ferguson   BCom 1932
teacher Ruthrieston s s 1940–73, Harlaw acad from
1973; retd

DAVIE Jean Keith   MA 1949
teacher Aber: various schools 1949–50, maths/sc
Kaimhill s s 1950–71, maths Kincorth s s 1971–74,
asst prin (admin) Kincorth s s from 1974

DAVIE or Butterworth, Jessie Henderson   MA 1927
retd 1967; resid Aber
d Aber 5.7.80

DAVIE or Stewart, Jessie Keith   MA 1913
d 25.7.66 *AUR* XLI 338

DAVIE Louis Helen Gordon   MA 1933
no longer on GC reg

DAVIE or Fyfe, Margaret Ann Birnie   BSc 1949
teacher sc Torry acad and Cults acad Aber from
1970
husb d 1.2.68

DAVIE Violet Cameron   *MA 1914
retd; resid Banff

DAVIE or Barbour, Wendy Jean Alison
                                        MB ChB 1948

DAVIE William Alexander James   *BSc 1953
FBCS 1959 MInstP 1971 MSc(eng) (Cranfield Inst
Tech) 1955
tech man. Elliott Bros Birchamwood 1966; Welwyn
Garden City: man. dir Direct Data 1966–74, man. dir
Automated Lib Syst from 1974
marr diss 1978

DAVIE William George   *MA 1924
teacher maths Boroughmuir s s Edin 1956–68; retd

DAVIES Edwin Braithwaite   PhD 1937

DAVIES Rupert Meredith   BSc 1924

DAVIS Arthur Joseph   MA 1940 Dip Ed 1947
awarded papal Benemerenti medal for serv to
church and commun 1979 retd head Corpus Christi s
Wilford Nott when amalgamated with indep g s to
form Becket comp s 1975; counsellor Becket comp s
1975–79; retd

DAVIS Brian Noel Kittredge   BSc 1955
PhD(Nott)

DAVIS or Anderson, Eileen   MB ChB 1950
dental anaest Derby from 1961

DAVIS or MacTaggart, June Mary   MB ChB 1948
MFCM 1973
sen m o Torbay county borough 1968–74; spec
commun med Devon A H A from 1974

DAVISON John Landfear   *MA 1952
prin teacher Engl Wallace Hall acad Dumfriessh
from 1969
m Dumfries 17.7.59 Barbara A. Douglas teacher d of
George D. Dumfries

DAWSON Alexander   MB ChB 1905
resid Aber
d Aber 21.6.80 *AUR* XLIX 66

DAWSON Allan Alexander
                            BSc(agr) 1927 PhD 1930

DAWSON Andrew Erskine   BSc(agr) 1952

DAWSON or Duncan, Annie Alexandra   MA 1924
resid Aberlour

DAWSON Daniel Sutherland   BSc 1909
no longer on GC reg

DAWSON or Steven, Dorothy   MA 1927
no longer on GC reg

DAWSON or McWilliam, Eileen Vanora   MA 1909
no longer on GC reg

DAWSON Emma   MA 1912
no longer on GC reg

DAWSON Ernest Vincent Coutts   MB ChB 1944
MRCGP 1959 FRCPE 1971
g p Elgin from 1952

DAWSON George Forbes   MA 1903 MB ChB 1906
d Musselburgh 20.6.66 *AUR* XLI 335

DAWSON George Gardiner   MA 1910
d Elgin 12.2.71 *AUR* XLIV 209

DAWSON Gladys   MA 1935
d Aber 7.4.71 *AUR* XLIV 212

DAWSON or Gibson, Helen Mary   MA 1925
d Falkirk 20.1.73

DAWSON Henry James
                MA 1916 MB ChB 1921 DPH 1931
d Aber 10.3.69 *AUR* XLIII 211

DAWSON James Gordon
        *BSc(mech eng) 1937 *BSc(elect eng) 1938
Zenith Carburetter Co Lond: man. dir 1970–76,
chmn from 1976

DAWSON James Norman   BSc 1955

DAWSON or Sobecki, Jean   MA 1949 Dip Ed 1950
teacher Edin: Liberton p s 1959–62, Bruntsfield p s
from 1967

DAWSON or Stewart, Jenny Naomi   MA 1920
resid Alloway

DAWSON John Alexander
                MA 1915 *MB ChB 1918 MD 1933
d Aber 24.1.72 *AUR* XLIV 428

DAWSON or Dunbar, Kathleen Mary
                        MB ChB 1949
school m o Forth Valley from 1970

DAWSON Leslie Knight   MB ChB 1945
MRCGP 1965
g p Skene from 1966

DAWSON Margaret Elizabeth   MA 1939
d 1950

DAWSON or Trubshaw, Margaret Isobel   MA 1926
no longer on GC reg

DAWSON or Coburn, Mary Lindsay   MA 1942

DAWSON Philip   MA 1940 LLB 1949
ptnr James & George Collie advoc in Aber from
1952

DAWSON Reginald David   BSc 1914

DAWSON Robert   MA 1914 MB ChB 1921 MD 1932
g p Middleton-in-Teesdale from 1921; retd 1963

DAWSON Robert Ernest   BSc(eng) 1939

DAWSON Robert George   BSc(eng) 1929
MIEE 1962
farm. Phingask Fraserburgh from 1945

DAWSON or Purchase, Sheila Marshall
                        MB ChB 1951
JP(Hove)
g p Brighton from 1954

DAY Stephen Lunan   MA 1938
dep head Middlefield p s Aber from 1970
d 29.11.81

DEAN Agnes Mary   MA 1930

DEAN Alan Charles Barclay   MB ChB 1954 ChM 1970
res asst, lect surg King's coll hosp med s Lond
1959–65; sen lect surg Edin from 1965; hon secy
Royal coll of surg Edin from 1978
m Lond 14.9.60 Fidelity J. Montagu-Pollock d of Sir
William M-P. BA(Cantab) Copenhagen

DEAN or Mackenzie Stuart, Amy Margaret
                        *MA 1918
chmn John Reid and Robert Nicol Trusts, Aber
d Aber 13.10.78

DEAN Charles Alfred   MB ChB 1925
d Brechin 22.2.72 *AUR* XLIV 430

DEAN or Bryce, Constance Elsie   MA 1929
retd 1970; resid Sunderland

DEAN Douglas   MB ChB 1923
d Crosby Liverpool –.2.68 *AUR* XLII 360

DEAN or Manson, Elma Fraser   MA 1929

DEAN or Borowiak, Helen   MA 1922
no longer on GC reg

DEAN Ian   MA 1953 LLB 1956

DEAN Isabella   MA 1917
teacher: inf mistress Ferryhill p s Aber till 1961;
retd

DEAN or Grant, Isabella Lyon   *MA 1917
d 26.6.1977 *AUR* XLV 120

DEAN Jessie Clara   MA 1924
d Aber 24.4.76

**DEAN or Macfadyen, Laura Margaret Isobel
                          BSc 1924 *1925**
no longer on GC reg

DEAN Myra   BSc 1948

DEAN William John Lyon   MB ChB 1933
g p Lossiemouth 1945–66; chmn joint c c Moray
and Nairn 1962–71; member white fish auth from
1953; chmn herring industry board from 1971; resid
Edin

DEANS or Milligan, Ethel   *MA 1931
resid Aber

DEANS Hilda Agnes   MB ChB 1944 DPH 1954
MFCM 1972
sen asst commun med Dun from 1968

DEANS Maxwell Duncan   MA 1928 LLB 1931
retd; resid Edin

DEANS Winifred Margaret   *MA 1922 *BSc 1923
retd; resid Aber

**DEMPSTER Douglas George
                          BSc 1938 BSc(agr) 1939**
sen lect agr Aberd superv univ farms from 1954

DEMPSTER Mary Rae   *MA 1952
Dip Man St(RGIT) 1975
teacher Harlaw acad Aber 1960–74; admin/pers asst
Comex Diving Aber 1976–77
m 30.3.77 George G. Niven CA

**DENHAM Robert Henry George Hector
                          MB ChB 1923 DPH 1928 MD 1933**
FRSH 1964 MFCM 1974
member NE Somerset hosp man. comm 1948–68;
secy W of Eng branch soc of m o h 1947–63; member
council soc of m o h 1947–63; publ health rep Bath
div BMA 1950–64; retd; resid Bath

DENNEHY Moira Whitley   PhD 1935

DENOON David   MA 1925
d 19.3.64

DENOON Marjory   MA 1937
teacher Newmachar p s 1964–76; retd

DENOON or Thomson, Mary McKenzie   MA 1930
resid Aber

DENTON Eric James   PhD 1952
ScD(Cantab) 1964 FRS 1964 FIBiol 1964 Fell. univ
coll Lond 1965
physiol Plymouth 1956–64; res prof Royal Society
Bristol from 1964

DERIDDER Johannes   MB ChB 1923

DESAI Anand Devarao   PhD 1939
Hyderabad India: agr dem 1931–33, chem asst
1933–40, agr chem 1940–46; retd; resid Karnatak
state

DESSON Robert Gregor   *BSc 1941

DEVENISH Walter John   MA 1947

**DE VILLIERS Isaac Bernhardi
                          MB ChB 1905 *ChM 1906**
no longer on GC reg

DEVLIN or Downham, Elizabeth Stirling   MA 1935
Sunderland: lect maths Monkwearmouth coll f e
1963–64; teacher maths St Anthony's g s 1965–75

DEVLIN or Hay, Winifred Marguerite   MA 1946

DEWAR Eric   BSc(eng) 1955

DEWAR James   MA 1887
d 31.1.62 *AUR* xxxix 369

DEWAR Ranald Somerled   MB ChB 1939
g p Queensland Aust
m(2) Brisbane 15.1.76 Ursula E. Prestwood nurse d of
William P. W Aust

DEWARS Jane Laing   *MA 1923
retd 1966; resid Brechin

DEY Annie   MA 1907
no longer on GC reg

DEY Dorothy Margaret   MA 1933
teacher Skene Square s Aber 1939–74

DEY George Alexander   BSc(for) 1950
dist off. for. comm: Kincardine/Angus 1950–54,
Argyll 1954–64, Glamorgan 1964–70, Aberdeensh/
Banff 1970–73; acquisitions/plan. off. Aber 1973–76,
Wester Ross dist from 1976
m Auchenblae 27.3.54 Mary B. G. Watson clerkess
d of Barclay W. Auchenblae

DEY James Alexander   MA 1949
teacher Knox acad Haddington 1950–74; prin
Preston Lodge h s from 1974

DEY James Riddoch   MA 1926
d Aber 20.9.70 *AUR* xliv 110

DEY Jenny Louise Riddoch   MA 1953
teacher mod lang: Aber h s for girls 1961–63,
Banchory acad 1963–68, Hazlehead acad Aber from
1968

DEY Walter Lewis   MA 1940
teacher: prin phys Torry acad Aber from 1962

DEY William Harley   BSc(eng) 1947
civ eng Sir Robert McAlpine & Sons Lincolnshire
from 1949

DEZSO Ladislas PhD 1930
pastor Debrechen 'Great Church' Reformed Church from 1953; member gen synod of Hungarian Reformed Church

DIACK Alan George BSc(eng) 1955
RAF sqdn ldr from 1974

DIACK Hugh MA 1951
teacher: Glasg acad 1967–68, A G S/Rubislaw acad from 1968

DIACK Hunter *MA 1930
sen lect educ Nott from 1964
d Nottingham 12.12.74 *AUR* XLVI 237

DIACK or Cown, Isobel Wyness MA 1933
d 16.9.72

DIACK James Ian Donald MB ChB 1951
j h m o orthop ARI 1959–60; trainee g p Southborough 1960–61; g p Littlehampton from 1961, clin asst orthop Bognor Regis war mem hosp from 1963

DIACK or Morrison, Lillias Mary Helen MA 1952
teacher Oxgangs p s Edin from 1966

DIACK Mary Margaret MA 1948
teacher geog and remed Peterhead acad from 1968
m Aber 31.3.65 Alexander H. Aird depot eng

DIACK or Brown, Nellie Shaw MB ChB 1921

DIACK Peter MA 1912 DD 1957
d Edin 4.5.67 *AUR* XLII 181

DIACK Peter MA 1948
C of S min Elgin S par ch from 1956

DICK Andrew James Mennie *MA 1928

DICK George Robert Farney *BSc 1939
asst head The Gordon Schools Huntly from 1974

DICK Janet Young *MA 1932
retd 1972; resid Aber

DICKIE Alexander Ironside *MA 1934
OBE 1969
retd 1972; resid Muckhart Dollar
d Stirling 25.4.80 *AUR* XLVIII 442

DICKIE David Bannerman Wood MA 1930
head Broomhill p s Aber 1960–69; retd

DICKIE George Green MB ChB 1936 DPH 1938
d Aber 19.7.73 *AUR* XLV 321

DICKIE James Lindsay Tocher
MB ChB 1942 DPH 1947
g p Crimond from 1952
d Crimond 6.1.79 *AUR* XLVIII 233

DICKIE or Armstrong, Jessie Ann *MA 1920
d S Af 22.9.77

DICKIE John Mackinlay *MA 1915
edit. Chambers's *Twentieth Century Dictionary* 1957–58; retd: publications: *Great Angling Stories* (anthology 1941; reprints 1941, 1947, 1955); *How to Catch Trout* (1963); resid Edin

DICKIE Marie Louise MA 1925
retd 1962; resid Aber

DICKIE or Collie, Myra Catherine *MA 1931
resid Wilmslow

DICKIE or Whitmarsh, Phyllis Margaret MA 1939
resid Aber

DICKIE William Macfarlane *MA 1918 PhD 1926
FLA 1930
Aberd: asst logic and metaphysics 1918–22
retd 1961; resid Dun

DICKIE William Wood *MA 1927
retd 1966; member 1st GTC for Scot 1970–71, 2nd GTC from 1971: resid Aber

DICKIE-CLARK William Findlay MB ChB 1939
ENT surg Cape Town and Groote Schuur hosp Cape Town from 1947

DICKINSON Ada MA 1924
no longer on GC reg

DICKSON Alexander BSc(for) 1953

DICKSON Alice *MA 1942
Lond: admin asst Uganda dev corp 1954–62; asst secy inst of health sen admin from 1962

DICKSON Andrew MB ChB 1928
g p Old Deer 1936–62; asst dermat ARI 1962–68; asst photobiol unit Dund from 1968; retd
d 16.8.79

DICKSON or Simmons, Barbara Macdonald
MA 1943
resid Lethbridge Alberta

DICKSON Dugald Macdonald MB ChB 1946
g p Bristol from 1951

DICKSON or Currie, Elizabeth Helen MA 1941
resid Deskford

DICKSON George Fortune BL 1928
Huntly: solic from 1929, man. British Linen Bank from 1940, burgh prosecutor from 1929

DICKSON Iain Alexander BSc(agr) 1951
MAgric (Purdue univ Indiana USA) 1959
spec anim husb W of S agr coll from 1963; seconded to Min Overseas Dev member of team reporting agr indust in Falkland Is 1969–70

DICKSON Jessie Isabella MA 1925
retd 1967; resid Aber

DICKSON John Abernethy
MA 1936 BSc(for) 1938 LLD 1969
CB 1970 FBIM 1975
dir Scot. for. comm Edin 1963–65; Lond: comm
(harvesting and marketing) 1965–68; dep chmn and
dir gen 1968–76; chmn standing comm on Commonwealth Forestry 1968–76; chmn Commonwealth
Forestry Assoc 1972–75, vice-pres 1975–76: retd 1976

DICKSON John Chisholm　MA 1950
C of S min St Fittick's ch Aber from 1957; chap:
Craiginches prison Aber 1959–69, army cadet force
from 1951; moderator presb of Aber from 1976

DICKSON Kathleen　MA 1946
teacher: remed work infants/juniors Smannell
Hants 1970, Vernham Dean 1971–73, Weyhill 1974–
76
m Andover 28.10.61 Andrew K. Briant BA(Cantab)
late dir agr Zanzibar s of Alfred B. Newbury
husb d 1966

DICKSON Margaret Laing　MA 1930
resid Fraserburgh
m Aber 20.9.41 William A. P. Reid master baker s of
William A. R. Dinnet
husb d 1969

DIKE Kenneth Onwuka　*MA 1947 LLD 1961
Hon DLitt: (Boston Mass) 1962, (Birm) 1964,
(Ahmadu Bello) 1965, (Ibadan) 1979;
Hon DSc (Moscow) 1963
vice chancellor Ibadan univ 1960–67; chmn Assoc of
Commonwealth univs 1965–66; Andrew W. Mellon
prof Afr Hist Harvard from 1973

DINGLEY or Brown, Vera Mary　BSc 1944
teacher phys Badminton s Brist from 1967

DINGWALL Hilda Anderson　*MA 1922 BSc 1923
teacher Aber acad 1944–64; retd; resid Fetterangus

DINGWALL Ian Macdonald　MB ChB 1951
med supt Texaco Trinidad Inc W Indies from 1955

DINGWALL or Sorley, Jessie Ross Grant
MB ChB 1925 DPH 1927
d Aber 15.11.76 *A UR* XLVII 287

DINGWALL Robert Crichton Macdonald
MB ChB 1943

DINNES or McKenzie, Agnes Ferguson　MA 1905
d 18.2.71 *A UR* XLIV 208

DINNIE Doreen Audrey　MA 1954
kindergarten teacher Newark Delaware USA from
1975 (completed pre-s curric & child dev courses univ
of Delaware 1976, 1977)
m Aber 19.7.68 Robert Rayne mech des eng s of
Andrew R. Philadelphia

DOBBIE or Thom, Hazel　*BSc 1950 PhD 1953
lect dept ch health Aberd from 1958; resid Aber

DOBSON James Samuel　MA 1950
d 29.3.64

DOCKAR Alexander Watt　MB ChB 1924
Birm: g p 1924–62, dep m o HM prison 1937–61;
retd; resid Droitwich

DODDS Edwin Mathieson　*MA 1923 DSc 1937
d Minehead 30.7.74 *A UR* XLVI 108

DODDS James George　*BSc 1950 PhD 1956
lect bot Edin from 1954

DODDS John Mathieson
***MA 1926 BSc 1926 *BSc(eng) 1928**
res dir AEI Manc 1961–70; retd; resid Strathdon

DODS or Laing, Julian Ursula　MB ChB 1945
resid Oxted

DODSWORTH Thomas Little　PhD 1951
JP Aberdeenshire 1961 FRAgrS 1973
Head anim husb dept NOSCA and lect dept of agr
Aberd from 1947

DOIG Barbara Mary　MA 1952
teacher: Aber 1953–55, Reading 1962–64; Somerset:
dep head Backwell 1964–72; Surrey: head Compton
1973–75, Shere from 1975
m Aber 26.6.54 Michael J. Hannagan BSc(agr) 1953 *qv*

DON Alexander Victor Reid
MB ChB 1920 ChM 1922
retd 1971
d Ashford 5.11.76 *A UR* XLVII 103

DON Charles Sydney Douglas
***MB ChB 1925 ᶜMD 1928**
d 7.9.73 *A UR* XLV 319

DON Eric George　*MB ChB 1922 ᶜMD 1929

DONALD Agnes　MA 1938
teacher Portlethen p s 1946–76; retd

DONALD Alexander　MA 1924
d 31.12.63

DONALD Alexander　MA 1942
no longer on GC reg

DONALD Alexander Bothwell
MB ChB 1933 MD 1937
retd 1970; resid Edin

DONALD or Radcliffe, Alexandra Margaret
MA 1936

DONALD Amy　MA 1905
no longer on GC reg

DONALD Annie Isabella　MA 1921 BSc 1924
resid Fleet
d Fleet 9.5.80 *A UR* XLVIII 440

DONALD Charles *BSc 1932 PhD 1936
ICI (organics) man. tech dev dept Grangemouth 1965–72; retd

DONALD or McKay, Christobel MB ChB 1953
g p Whitehaven from 1958

DONALD Daniel Barker BCom 1923
d Paris 11.2.33

DONALD David *MA 1927
retd 1971; resid Aber

DONALD David Mitchell Cooke BL 1935
Lond: man. dir Robert Fleming & Co merch bankers from 1960; chmn: Invest Trust Corp and London and Holyrood Trust from 1972

DONALD Derek George Mansell BSc(for) 1952
MSc(for) (Stellenbosch) 1964
DSc (Stellenbosch) 1968
S Af: sen lect silviculture Stellenbosch univ 1960–75; prof Merensky Chair of Silviculture from 1975

DONALD or Rayne, Elizabeth *MA 1921
no longer on GC reg

DONALD or Barrie, Elizabeth Florence MA 1937
deceased

DONALD or McIntyre, Elizabeth Walker MA 1925
no longer on GC reg

DONALD Ella MA 1950
head woman asst Peterhead cent s 1970
m Peterhead 28.6.69 John H. Sheran trans man. Crosse & Blackwell s of William S. Peterhead

DONALD Francis Cantlie MA 1905
resid Nairn
d Inv 18.1.74 A UR xLv 446

DONALD Frederick John BSc(for) 1950

DONALD George BSc(agr) 1919
d Oxford 18.1.62 A UR xxxix 280

DONALD George McIntyre BSc(agr) 1922
no longer on GC reg

DONALD Heather Margaret *MA 1949
retd joint intell bureau 1961; publ The Life of Lord Mount Stephen Vol I 1965, Vol II 1977; occasional hist articles for learned journals; wrote quarterly econ reviews for Economist intell unit 1963–66, articles on Maghreb for Annual Register
m Lond 2.7.60 Ian G. Gilbert MA(Edin) civ serv, asst secy DHSS s of Alexander G. G. DCM Kenya

DONALD Ian MB ChB 1954
g p Aber and attachment ARI from 1959

DONALD or Shepherd, Isabel MA 1939
teacher: sen mistress Greenhead Sixth Form coll Huddersfield from 1973

DONALD James *MA 1930
d Arisaig 30.7.75

DONALD James Alexander *MA 1938
CBE 1962
man. dir: Borneo Co Lond from 1962, Inchcape (WA) Pty Perth West Aust 1968, Jaxon Construction Pty Perth WA from 1975
m Singapore 24.1.48 Joan L. McLean d of Frank A. McL. West Perth WA

DONALD James Booth *MA 1938

DONALD James Crosbie MB ChB 1954
Cert Competence in Pediat Surg RCS(C) 1976
surg resid Seattle 1963–68; consult. surg Royal Jubilee hosp Victoria BC Canada from 1968
m Victoria BC 26.5.62 Ann M. Clarke nurse d of Hugh E. C. Victoria BC

DONALD James Knight MB ChB 1924
d Fleet 31.12.71 A UR xLiv 430

DONALD Jessie MA 1925
retd 1966; resid Fleet

DONALD or Smith, Joan Grant MA 1948

DONALD John George MB ChB 1951
OBE 1971 DTM & H(Edin) 1964 (Greig medal in trop med) MRCGP 1971 MFCM 1972 FRCGP 1977
sen m o RAF Waddington 1960–64; stud. RAF staff coll Bracknell 1965; sen m o HQ AFCENT Fountainbleau France 1956–68; dep dir med pers MoD Lond 1968–72; comm off. RAF hosp Akrotiri Cyprus 1972–76, RAF hosp Ely 1976–78, prin m o HQ Germany from 1978

DONALD Laurence BSc(eng) 1953

DONALD or Sargison, Mabel MA 1926
retd 1960; resid Majorca

DONALD MacKenzie Munro MA 1903
no longer on GC reg

DONALD Margaret MA 1931
retd 1969; resid Aber

DONALD or Thomson, Margaret Patricia *MA 1942
lect Sus 1964–66; visiting prof State univ of NY at Buffalo USA 1966–67; reader Sus from 1967
m(2) Brighton 20.5.66 Maurice Evans PhD(Cantab) univ prof Exe

DONALD Margaret Smith Mowat MA 1950 Dip Ed 1958 *MEd 1960
asst educ psych ch guid serv Aberdeensh and Kincardine 1966–75, Grampian reg c from 1975

DONALD or Merrifield, Margaret Wason MA 1909
resid Acme, Alberta
husb d 20.1.73

DONALD or Robson, Marion Gordon   MA 1910
resid Edin

DONALD or Jobson, Mary   MA 1917
no longer on GC reg

DONALD or Rodger, Mary Ann   MA 1951

DONALD Norman   BSc 1947
dep head Insch s from 1966; elected member Gordon dist council 1974–80

DONALD Norman Frederick   *MA 1927
retd 1970; resid St And
wife d 29.6.76

DONALD Priscilla Thomson   MA 1922

DONALD Robert Turner   MB ChB 1951
MRCGP 1961 DPM 1979
g p Lenham Kent 1956–76; clin asst psychiat Oakwood hosp Maidstone 1970–76; g p Montrose from 1976/hosp pract psychiat from 1980

DONALD Thomas Hunter   MA 1902
no longer on GC reg

DONALD Walter   *MA 1933
d Blairgowrie 24.3.68 *AUR* XLII 371

DONALD William John   BSc(agr) 1953

DONALD Winifred Wilson   *MA 1939
prin teacher Engl Lansdowne House s Edin from 1959; educ publ Collins 1963–65

DONALDSON Alan Malcolm   MB ChB 1948
MRCGP 1968 DIH (soc of apothecaries) 1972
g p Lincoln 1959–74; reg m o DHSS Lincoln from 1974

DONALDSON Alistair   BSc(eng) 1955
FIHE 1957 DipTE 1963 MAPLE 1966 FIMunE 1969 MBIM 1972 FIPHE 1974 MILGA 1974 FICE 1975
sen asst (roads) Peebles c c 1959–62; Cumberland c c: sen eng 1962–65, asst surv 1965–71; county surv Fife c c 1971–75; county surv Clwyd c c from 1975

DONALDSON or Shaw, Catherine   MA 1918
d 10.7.65

DONALDSON or Runcie, Christina   MA 1942
Grantham: teacher Engl/drama girls' central s 1963–65; head Engl dept Walton girls' s from 1965

DONALDSON Elizabeth   *MA 1914
resid Stirling

DONALDSON Elsie   MA 1928
teacher maths Portknockie 1969–70; retd; resid Portknockie

DONALDSON George Gregor   MB ChB 1940
consult. anaest Gateshead hosp group 1949–74; retd

DONALDSON Hector Alexander
MA 1927 BSc 1929 *1930
d Aber 30.4.68 *AUR* XLII 367

DONALDSON Helen   MA 1916
retd 1968; resid Peterhead

DONALDSON John Edward   *MA 1928
d Wick 23.2.67 *AUR* XLII 368

DONALDSON Robert Fyfe   BCom 1923
no longer on GC reg

DONALDSON Sheina Margaret   MA 1954
teacher: Linlithgow 1959–62, Darlington 1962–64; resid Keyworth
m Edin 27.7.62 Roy Francis Weston BSc(eng)(Lond) civ eng

DONALDSON William John   *MEd 1948
FRIC 1950
sen lect Aber coll of educ 1963–75; retd

DORIAN or Dewar, Emily Prout   MA 1936
teacher Glasg 1970–75

DORIAN or Douglas, Sheila   MA 1949
resid Leatherhead

DORIAN Thomas Charles   *MA 1924
head Albert sen s s Glasg 1960–67; retd

DORNHORST Hubert Karl Wilhelm Haartsz
MB ChB 1906
no longer on GC reg

DORNLEY Ernest Marshall   MB ChB 1934

DOSS Paul Thangasami Jesu   MB ChB 1927
no longer on GC reg

DOUGALL or Walsh, Jean Barr Marshall   MA 1945
resid Pointe Claire Quebec

DOUGHERTY Charles   *MA 1933
no longer on GC reg

DOUGHERTY or Bishop, Margaret   *MA 1928
teacher i/c Craigielea reception and assessment centre Aber 1957–67
d Aber 4.11.75

DOUGLAS Andrew Morrison   MA 1954
C of S min: Bon-Accord St Paul's ch Aber 1963–72, Gardner Mem with West and St Columba's ch Brechin from 1972

DOUGLAS Arthur Wallace Murison   MB ChB 1924
resid Braishfield
d 28.1.78

DOUGLAS Edward Annand   MA 1906
no longer on GC reg

DOUGLAS Hugh Brown   MA 1950
Lond: p r staff Brit hotels & restaurants assoc 1960–74, BR from 1974
m Belf 4.4.62 Sheelagh S. Knox BA(Belf) teacher d of Albert E. K. Limavady

DOUGLAS Ida Constance   MA 1927
resid Banchory

DOUGLAS or Halton, Isobel Jean   *MA 1938

DOUGLAS James Murray   MA 1945
Lond: Treasury 1960–63, asst secy min of housing and loc govt 1964–66, secy royal comm on loc govt in England and Wales 1966–69, secy gen county land-owners assoc from 1970

DOUGLAS or Kamsley, Janet Evelyn   MA 1939

**DOUGLAS or Wilkinson, Margaret Helen Keith
MA 1942**

DOUGLAS or Murphie, Margaret Isabel   *MA 1920
Fort William: provost till 1959, made freeman of burgh 1967

**DOUGLAS or Deans, Marjory Cumming Sutherland
*MA 1944**

DOUGLAS Muriel Mary Ogilvie   *MA 1923
d 2.5.71

DOUGLAS Vivienne Mary   *MA 1955
teacher Engl and relig educ Albyn s for g Aber 1956–67; resid Brunei 1976
m Aber 9.7.66 Sherlock S L Chin MB ChB 1965 qv

DOVE Ian Mayor   MB ChB 1923
d 12.4.72

DOVERTY or Laird, Lilian Helen   MA 1951
teacher Edin 1956–65

DOW Alexander Rattray   MB ChB 1952
Sunderland: g p 1954–73, consult. A/E unit RI from 1973

DOW or MacLennan, Alison Agnes Smith   MA 1934
husb d 14.4.75
d Aber 22.6.77

**DOW or Cooper, Dorothy Janet
MA 1919 MB ChB 1922**
no longer on GC reg

**DOW or Cox, Elizabeth May
MA 1918 MB ChB 1919**
asst anat dept Aberd 1919–20; h o Nottingham: ch hosp 1920–22, gen hosp 1922–25
resid Nott

DOW Herbert   MA 1955

DOW James   MB ChB 1937 DPH 1957
MFCM 1972

retd surg cdr RN 1964; asst m o h/sen m o West Lothian 1964–68; Midlothian and Peebles: sen m o 1968–71, dep m o h 1971–72; resid Edin
d Edin 27.12.79 AUR XLIX 69

**DOW or Fraser, Margaret Mary Maclaren
MA 1928 BSc 1929**
teacher Harris acad Dun 1962–72; retd
husb d 15.7.62

**DOW or Cooper, Marjorie Johanna Macpherson
MB ChB 1925 DPH 1929**
resid Dun
husb d 27.6.73

DOW Ronald   *MA 1952
Preston: head organis and methods Engl Elect. Co 1959–62, BAC 1962–65; Ashridge man. coll Berkhamsted: lect 1965–69, progr dir from 1969

DOW Thomas McLaren   BSc(for) 1948

DOWNIE Allan Watson   MB ChB 1946
FRCP 1972
asst/assoc prof neurol univ of N Carolina 1958–65; sen lect med and hon consult. neurol Aberd and NE reg hosp board from 1965

**DOWNIE Allan Watt
*MB ChB 1923 *MD 1929 DSc 1938 LLD 1957**
FRCPath
retd prof bact Liv 1966; visiting prof paediat univ of Denver Colorado 1966–69; res work on MRC grant 1969–72, part-time consult. path. Sefton gen hosp from 1973

DOWNIE Balfour   *MA 1909
d Aber 25.2.68 AUR XLII 348

DOWNIE Dorothy McIver   MA 1928
d Aber 30.1.79

DOWNIE George   *BSc 1954
lect geol Aberd from 1960

DOWNIE John George   MA 1926
retd 1970; resid Culsalmond

DOWNIE or McIntosh, June   MA 1954

DOWNIE Richard Duthie   *MB ChB 1923
OBE 1966 MRCGP (founder member)
g p Sheffield 1923–66; locum work since retirement; resid Salcombe
d Southport 27.8.78 AUR XLVIII 104

DOWNIE William Spence   MA 1922 BSc 1924
Aber: head Ruthrieston f e centre 1956–58, dep head Sunnybank p s 1939–62; retd

DOYLE George Mitchel   BSc 1948 *1949

DOYLE Thomas   *MEd 1955
d Bridgend Wales 3.11.75

DRAPER William   MA 1952

DREVER or Rutter, Daisy Don   MA 1916
no longer on GC reg

DREWERY James   *MA 1952

DRON Kenneth Walker   *MA 1951 Dip Ed 1954
dep rector Falkirk h s 1966–69; rector Brechin h s
from 1969

DRON William Douglas Duff   BSc(agr) 1949

DRUMMOND Edith Margaret   MA 1938
DBE 1966
dir WRNS Lond 1964–67; retd; resid Holt Norfolk

DRUMMOND James Gilmour
                                    ***MA 1907 DD 1951**
d Glasg 20.2.63 *AUR* xl 199

DRUMMOND John Alexander   BSc(for) 1947

DUCAT Eric Francis   MB ChB 1945
g p Bath from 1948

DUCAT or Webster, Helena Mary Lawson
                                    ***MA 1934**
resid N Berwick

DUCKWORTH Ronald Barrett   PhD 1952
FIFST 1968
sen scient off. MAFF Aber 1955–56; lect food sc
Strath 1956–66, sen lect 1966–70, reader from 1970
m Aber 22.2.55 Margaret C. Johnston teacher d of
James W. J. Aberchirder

DUFF Agnes Helen   MA 1908
d Edin 16.3.78 *AUR* xlvii 355

DUFF Alexander Dewar   MB ChB 1927
d 10.6.77 *AUR* xlvii 287

DUFF Alistair Duncan Stewart   *BSc(agr) 1950

DUFF Caroline Stevenson   MB ChB 1951
g p Dover from 1954

DUFF or Fish, Dora Grant   MA 1931
d Camberley –.8.67

DUFF or Ritchie, Elizabeth Helen   *MA 1913
chief escort to 500 evacuee ch by sea to Canada
1940; resid Edin

DUFF Harold Bissett   BSc(eng) 1932
civ eng Ford Motor Co Dagenham 1947–65
d Streatham 19.11.77

DUFF Rachel Tolmie   *MA 1911
d Paisley 15.5.68 *AUR* xlii 350

DUFF Stewart   MB ChB 1939
g p Grimsby from 1949

DUFFTON Robert Alexander Lawson   BL 1937
retd 1978; resid Cheltenham

DUFFUS Adrian Michael Campbell   MB ChB 1948
MRACP 1961 FRACP 1972
clin res dir Roche Products Welwyn Garden City
from 1962

DUFFUS Alan Alexander   MB ChB 1920 DPH 1922
Watford: m o and surg/med supt Shrodells hosp
1931–45, g p till 1961; resid Fernhurst Haslemere

DUFFUS Alexander James   BL 1950
ptnr Wilsone & Duffus advoc Aber from 1953

DUFFUS Beatrice   MA 1940
resid Fraserburgh

DUFFUS George Macnaughton Rae   MB ChB 1931
g p Aber 1936–39 and from 1952
d Aber 27.1.81 *AUR* xlix 138

DUFFUS Helen Mary Isabella   MA 1942
d 1971

DUFFUS James Catto   MA 1912 ᵈLLB 1914
d 17.8.62 *AUR* xl 80

DUFFUS Janet Rennie   MA 1925
resid Aber
d Aber 16.8.81

DUFFUS or Penman, Jeannie McKenzie   MA 1936
teacher N'cle-u-Tyne from 1960; retd

DUFFUS Stanley Herbert   MA 1949
teacher Galashiels acad from 1950

DUFTON Alexina Margaret   MA 1955

DUFTON or Smith, Margaret Johnston
                                    MB ChB 1918

DUGAN Alexander Mathieson
                                    MB ChB 1918 DPH 1921
Manchester educ comm 1926–59; retd
d Aber 29.8.75 *AUR* xlvi 322

DUGAN or Sommerville, Alice Henrietta
                                    MA 1931 BSc 1934
keeper of herbarium dept of bot Aberd 1954–77;
retd

DUGAN or Burnett, Dorothy Jane Elizabeth
                                    BSc 1922
resid Aber

DUGAN or Emslie, Elizabeth Madeline
                                    MA 1926 BSc 1929
resid Banchory
husb *d* 14.5.72

DUGGIE or Gordon, Christina Baillie Main
                                    MA 1940
resid Huntly

DUGGIE David Main   BSc(for) 1948

DUGUID Alexander George *MA 1949
Wing Cmdr

DUGUID Annabelle Murdina
MA 1948 MB ChB 1953
regist anaest UCH Kingston Jamaica 1956–57; sen
h o anaest Edin 1959–61; anaest Medicine Hat Alberta
1963–64; med asst anaest Wrexham Wales
m Kingston, Jamaica 16.6.56 Jan F. Bras MB
(Amsterdam) ophth surg s of Johannes B. Indonesia

DUGUID David Shepherd *MA 1914
d Aber 1.3.68 *AUR* XLII 352

DUGUID or Pirrie, Ellie Forbes **MA 1908**
husb d 1956
resid Keith
d 11.7.78

DUGUID or MacLachlan, Ena Bauchope Sutherland
MA 1937
teacher: h s for girls Aber 1966–68, speech and
drama dept Aber 1968–74, Smithfield p s 1974
husb d 7.9.71

DUGUID or Oldershaw, Frances Marjory
MB ChB 1921
no longer on GC reg

DUGUID Francis Massie **BSc 1947 *1948**
prin teacher sc Ellon acad from 1957

DUGUID Helen Leslie Duff
MB ChB 1944 MD 1951
FRCPath 1971
consult. path. i/c cytology and assoc histopath RI
Dun from 1963
m Helensburgh 23.9.63 Alistair S. L. Rae
MB ChB(Edin) consult. psychiat s of Alexander R.
Edin

DUGUID Ian McIver **MB ChB 1948 MD 1959**
FRCS 1961 PhD(Lond) 1962
Lond: consult. ophth surg Lond hosp 1962–63, ophth
surg Moorfield eye hosp from 1963, ophth surg
Westminster hosp from 1964

DUGUID John **MB ChB 1939**
d 2.1.73

DUGUID John Bright **MB ChB 1920 *MD 1925**
d 21.12.80 *AUR* XLIX 136

DUGUID or Lamont, Margaret Sinclair
MB ChB 1942
m o Sunnyside psychiat hosp Christchurch NZ
from 1972

DUGUID Raymond Maurice **MB ChB 1942**
g p Coventry from 1946
d 7.10.76

DUGUID Robert Hutton **BCom 1926**
retd bus. admin Prot s board of Greater Montreal
1962; Aber: acct Middletons (Aber) 1965–72; asst
acct James Blake 1974–77; retd

DUGUID William **MB ChB 1909**
d 21.8.76

DUNBAR Alexina **MA 1929**
d 23.4.72

DUNBAR David Milne **MB ChB 1942**

DUNBAR or Gray, Elizabeth Alexina
MB ChB 1923
resid Portsoy
husb d 1.2.72

DUNBAR Elsie Williamina **MA 1914**
no longer on GC reg

DUNBAR Helen **MA 1905**
d Cullen 19.4.77

DUNBAR or Ponting, Helen Milne Cooper **MA 1942**
head teacher Bexley Lond from 1967

DUNBAR James **MA 1925 MB ChB 1929**
MRCGP 1967
g p Gillingham Kent from 1933

DUNBAR Jane *MA 1913
d Cullen 8.6.71 *AUR* XLIV 316

DUNBAR Jessie Isabella *MA 1930
retd 1969; resid Bearsden

DUNBAR Joan Gordon Thain **MB ChB 1927**
d of Duncan D. shepherd; b Fordyce 20.12.1900
resid Cullen

DUNBAR Joseph **MA 1955**
dep head Meldrum s 1966–72; asst prin teacher
Bankhead acad responsible for school/industry liaison
career work from 1972

DUNBAR Leslie **MB ChB 1948**
g p Dunblane from 1951

DUNBAR or Simpson, Lorna Margaret
*MA 1950 Dip Ed 1951
lect educ psych coll of educ Aber from 1966

DUNBAR Margaret Stewart **MA 1907**
d Buckie 11.9.72 *AUR* XLV 123

DUNBAR or Innes, Mary Jessie **MA 1911**
d Hull 2.11.75 *AUR* XLVI 320

DUNBAR or Foster, Norah May Esson
MB ChB 1929
retd; resid Cullen

DUNCAN or Philip, Adeline Myron *MA 1925
resid Elgin

DUNCAN Albert Tait **MB ChB 1925**
g p Banff 1925–30; Falkirk 1930–31, Portsoy 1931–
35; Dun 1935–67; retd; resid Banff
d Banff 14.9.77 *AUR* XLVII 287

DUNCAN Alexander   BL 1950

DUNCAN Alexander Stuart   BSc(for) 1932
estate man.: Argyll 1959–62, E Anglian estates 1962–73; retd; resid Elgin

DUNCAN Alfred George Brown
                    MB ChB 1915 ^cMD 1919 DPH 1920
retd 1960; resid Aboyne

DUNCAN Alfred Henry   MB ChB 1948
g p Blackburn Lancs from 1951
m Manc 6.1.68 Ruth Thompson nurs sister d of George R. T. Manc

DUNCAN or MacLeod, Alice Lindsay   MA 1953
teacher hist Arbroath h s from 1967

DUNCAN or Pullar, Amy Rose   MA 1929
b Lhanbryde 24.12.06
teacher maths/hist Forres acad 1964–68; retd; resid Lossiemouth

DUNCAN Angus   MA 1923 BD 1926
d Edin 19.9.71 *A UR* xliv 429

DUNCAN Anne   MA 1943
Aber: teacher Rosemount s 1948–72, woman advis from 1959; Harlaw acad teacher and careers mistress from 1972

DUNCAN or Esslemont, Anne Elizabeth
                    MA 1923 ^dLLB 1925
d Wick 20.9.72 *A UR* xlv 126

DUNCAN or Fleming, Betty Fraser   MA 1930
resid Keith

DUNCAN Charles   MA 1944 LLB 1949

DUNCAN or Munro, Christian Brown Smart
                    MA 1932 LLB 1935
d 31.1.66

DUNCAN Cyril Gordon McKenzie
                    BSc(agr) 1955 *1966
asst insp DAFS Edin 1960–64; farm. Elgin from 1964

DUNCAN David   MB ChB 1924 DPH 1929 MD 1934

DUNCAN Donald   *MA 1950
computer progr Crosse & Blackwell Lond 1961–64; trg off. Distillers Co Epsom 1964–66; Unilever Merseyside Port Sunlight: head man. trg centre 1966–70, company pers man. from 1970

DUNCAN Douglas Mackenzie   BCom 1930

DUNCAN Douglas Stanley   *MA 1937 BSc 1938
FEIS 1965
dep head Northfield acad Aber from 1967

DUNCAN or Purdie, Edith   *MA 1935
resid Gatehouse of Fleet

DUNCAN Edith Mackenzie   MA 1928

DUNCAN or Ogston, Edith Margaret   MA 1944
resid Elgin

DUNCAN or Shewan, Elizabeth Christina   MA 1924
resid Lochearnhead

DUNCAN or Bruce, Elizabeth Craven   MA 1929
resid Edin

DUNCAN Elizabeth Deans   MA 1930
m Smith

DUNCAN Elizabeth Eleanor   MA 1953
private secy J & J Crombie Grandholm works Aber 1955–61
m Aber 18.12.61 George F. Howie CA s of William H. Aber

DUNCAN or Carlisle, Elsie Mary   BL 1936
resid West Huntingtower Perth

DUNCAN Eric Henry Weir
                    MB ChB 1931 DPH 1949
g p Culter from 1953

DUNCAN Eric Marr   *MA 1929 BD 1934
retd 1972; resid Stirling

DUNCAN Ethel Helen Laing   *MA 1931 BSc 1933

DUNCAN Ethel Mary Maudaline   MA 1936
retd 1975; resid Peterhead

DUNCAN Forbes   MA 1930
head Camdean s Rosyth 1953–72; retd; resid Dunfermline

DUNCAN or Wood, Freda Campbell   MA 1945

DUNCAN George   BCom 1928
d 1980

DUNCAN George Douglas
                    MB ChB 1948 DPH 1952
FFCM 1972
sen admin m o E Anglia reg hosp board 1968–73; reg m o E Anglia reg health auth from 1973

DUNCAN George Gordon   MB ChB 1950 DPH 1955
g p Rothes from 1959
m Wilmslow 2.3.57 Hilary J. Piggin nurs sister d of Edward P. Weston Crewe

DUNCAN Helen Margaret Eveline   *MA 1930
volunt soc worker Red Cross from 1945; resid Aber

DUNCAN Henry Charles   BSc(agr) 1946
NOSCA: hort advis Aberdeensh/Banffsh 1962–73, head hort div from 1973
d 8.10.77

DUNCAN James   MB ChB 1923
d Frinton-on-Sea 4.12.72 *A UR* xlv 127

DUNCAN James   BSc(eng) 1947
comp dir Methlick from 1957
wife *d* 11.8.71

DUNCAN James George   MB ChB 1945
FRCSE 1967 MRCPGlas 1971 FRCPGlas 1975
FRCR 1975
visiting prof univ of Rochester USA 1969; consult.
radiol in admin charge Glasg RI and assoc hosps from
1969

DUNCAN James Hugh   *BSc 1954
FICeram 1972
geologist fed of Malaya 1954–60; min/ceramist
English Elect. Co Stafford 1960–69; sen prin scient
off. BR board r & d div Derby from 1969

DUNCAN James Robertson   MA 1932
head Strathdon s 1947–61; Melbourne Aust:
teacher Princess Hill h s 1962–63, Camberwell s
1963–64; sen asst (post of responsib) Box Hill h s
from 1965; retd 1975

DUNCAN Janet Campbell   MA 1947 MB ChB 1951
C of S missionary Charteris and leprosy hosp
Kalimpong India 1955–69; Wick: part-time g p 1969,
part-time h s Bignold hosp 1973; C of S missionary
rural health progr Kalimpong from 1973
d Wick 10.9.78 *AUR* XLVIII 107

DUNCAN or Smith, Jessie Edgell   MA 1907

DUNCAN John   MA 1927
head Udny Green s Aberdeensh 1960–70; retd;
resid Aber

DUNCAN John McWilliam   MB ChB 1936
g p Worcester from 1947

DUNCAN or Sproat, Kathleen Watson   MA 1955
resid Kirkcudbright

DUNCAN or Torrance, Lorna Lawrence
                                    MB ChB 1942
JP (Leicestersh) 1962
g p Leicester from 1946

DUNCAN Maggie Ann (Madge)   MA 1917
d Lond 30.1.64 *AUR* XL 398

DUNCAN Margaret Garden   MA 1945
DipEd(Oxon) 1946
resid Kirkcaldy
m Buckie 16.9.59 David J. L. Innes BA(Oxon) textile
manuf s of John L. I. LLB(Edin) Kirkcaldy

DUNCAN Margaret Simpson   MA 1909
d Aber 29.6.70 *AUR* XLIV 107

DUNCAN or Talbert, Marjorie Ada   *MA 1952

DUNCAN or Hunter, Mary   MA 1915
d 17.11.72 *AUR* XLV 224

DUNCAN Mary Ann   MA 1909

DUNCAN or Butterworth, Mary Elizabeth
                                    MA 1916 *1917

DUNCAN Mary Elizabeth   MB ChB 1953

DUNCAN or Atkinson, Mary Hattle   *MA 1944

DUNCAN Mary Lawson Philip   *MA 1926
d Aber 1.3.56 *AUR* XXXVI 436

DUNCAN Mary Patricia   *MA 1946

DUNCAN or Davis, Moira Manton   *BSc 1948
resid Harrogate

DUNCAN or Allan, Myra Thomson   *MA 1926
resid Edin

DUNCAN Norman Alistair   MB ChB 1912
no longer on GC reg

DUNCAN Norman James   BSc(eng) 1955

DUNCAN Peter   MB ChB 1940
d 10.1.79

DUNCAN Robert Alexander Low   BSc(agr) 1933
d Fraserburgh 15.11.71 *AUR* XLIV 321

DUNCAN Robert Erskine Burt
                                    *BSc 1951 PhD 1954
FRIC 1964
man. Glenochil res stat Distillers Co Menstrie from
1974

DUNCAN Robert Hendry   MB ChB 1951
USA: clin dir High Point hosp Portchester NY
1960–63; dir mental health serv NE New Mexico
1963–65; dir Courts' clinic Rochester NY 1965–69;
consult Rochester City school dist NY from 1965; dir
mental health serv Livingston and Wyoming countries
NY from 1969

DUNCAN Robert Morris Turner
                                    MA 1950 Dip Ed 1954

DUNCAN Robert Reid   MB ChB 1905 DPH 1910
no longer on GC reg

DUNCAN or Watson, Sheila Margaret   MA 1945
husb *d* 1968
Cert Soc Work (RGIT) 1974
soc worker Aber from 1973

DUNCAN or Wood-Smith, Sybil Mary Anderson
                                    MA 1929

DUNCAN Thomas   MB ChB 1938
psychiat i/c Essex Hall, royal E Counties hosp
Colchester 1966–68; clin dir King's County hosp
Waterville Nova Scotia 1968–73; consult. in Bury St
Edmund's health dist from 1974

DUNCAN Thomas McPetrie   MA 1924 BD 1928
d Bishopbriggs 9.8.71 *AUR* XLIV 320

DUNCAN Thomas Strachan   *MA 1938
prin maths teacher Peterhead acad from 1961

DUNCAN Walter   *MA 1929
d Aber 23.5.68 *AUR* XLII 368

DUNCAN William   MB ChB 1954
FFR(Lond) 1962 FRCPE 1972 FRCSE 1977
consult radiotherap Christie hosp and Holt radium
inst Manc 1964–71; prof radiotherapy Edin from
1971

DUNCAN William Alexander James   MA 1954

DUNCAN William Gavin   BCom 1928
d Newport 5.11.68 *AUR* XLIII 84

DUNLOP or Carmichael, Alexandrina Gladys
MA 1932
teacher: spec asst Fyvie 1966–74; retd; resid
Badenscoth

DUNLOP Charles Moir   MB ChB 1946
MRCGP 1968
g p Eastbourne from 1950

DUNLOP Harry Young   BSc(agr) 1954
agr advis NOSCA from 1966; resid Dinnet
d Dinnet 4.7.81

DUNN Alexander Simpson   *BSc 1949

DUNN Edward   BSc 1934 *1935

DUNN George Alexander Farquhar   MA 1951
asst prin teacher maths Peterhead acad from 1973
m Aber 29.7.61 Jean A. Harris teacher bus. stud. d of
Andrew H. Aber

DUNN Helen Ann   MA 1924
no longer on GC reg

DUNN or Coull, Irene Jean   MA 1945
prin teacher: Engl Rosemount s s Aber 1969–72,
guid Harlaw acad from 1972

DUNN or George, Jessie Addison   MA 1930
d Hillside 5.3.66 *AUR* XLII 88

DUNN or Clements, Margaret Jane Heron MA 1919

DUNNE Eileen Carmel Kober   MA 1944 *1948
asst head Sacred Heart h s Paisley from 1971
m Old Kilpatrick 2.7.60 Lawrence Peacock mech
eng/teacher s of William P. Dumbarton

DUNNE Jane Ann   MA 1926
dep head St Mary's RC s Aber 1959, St Joseph's
1960–64

DUNNE Joseph Peter   MB ChB 1940
supt m o 1942–50; regist to med psychiat units
1950–60; j h m o psychiat Pastures hosp Meikleover
Derby 1960–66; med asst psychiat Moorhaven hosp
Ivybridge from 1966

DUNNET Charles William   MA 1920
d 14.10.71

DUNNET George Mackenzie   *BSc 1949 PhD 1952
FRSE 1970 FIBiol 1974
Aberd: sen lect nat hist 1966–71; prof zoology 1971–74
regius prof nat hist from 1974

DUNNET William Nicholson
MB ChB 1944 MD 1961
MFCM 1974 FFCM 1978
DHSS HQ Lond: m o epidemiological sect. 1963–65,
sen m o 1965–77, prin m o head of div of communi-
cable diseases from 1977

DUNNETT Arthur Hugh   MB ChB 1941
DPH(St And) 1961 FACMA 1967
m o Norfolk Is 1961–63; commonwealth dept of
health Canberra Aust from 1963

DUNNETT May   MA 1930
no longer on GC reg

du PREEZ James John   MB ChB 1910
no longer on GC reg

DURIE Frederick Lewis   *BSc(eng) 1933

DURIE or Dugan, Isobel Forbes   MA 1926
resid Aber

DURNIN John Valentine George Andrew
MA 1942 MB ChB 1946
DSc(Glas) 1961 MRCPGlas 1963 FRCPGlas 1969
FRSE 1976
prof physiol Glas 1973

DURNIN Joseph John   *MA 1930
head Holy Family RC s Aber 1959–72; retd; resid
Aber

DURNO Charles   *MA 1903
d Aber 9.1.67 *AUR* XLII 345

DURNO John Fyvie   MB ChB 1924
g p Lond 1956–63; blood transf Sutton 1963–66;
retd
d Glasg 29.8.75 *AUR* XLVI 322

DURNO or Leyden, Mary Bannerman   BSc 1953
resid Pitlochry

DURNO Mary Margaret Grant Mearns   MA 1909
d Aber 7.8.61 *AUR* XXXIX 273

DURNO Robert   BSc(eng) 1944 BSc(civ eng) 1948
d Dun 8.5.72

DURNO Sydney Elmslie   BSc 1949 PhD 1967
MIBiol 1951
Macaulay inst for soil res Aber from 1949

DURWARD James   *MA 1919
d 2.12.71

DURWARD James Mortimer   *BSc(eng) 1940
MBE 1957
Lagos Nigeria: sen eng in fed min of works 1957–70, chief eng from 1970

DUTCH John Henry   MA 1947 BD 1949
d Helensburgh 10.11.68 *AUR* XLIII 86

DUTCH Ralph Douglas   *MA 1951 *MEd 1953
prin lect educ psych Aber coll of educ from 1963

DUTHIE or Finniecome, Alice Mary   MA 1910
no longer on GC reg

DUTHIE Andrew May
                    MA 1920 *MB ChB 1924 MD 1929
retd: resid Newtonhill
d 14.10.81

DUTHIE Andrew Ritchie   MB ChB 1954
trainee asst Inverurie 1957–58; g p Turriff from 1958

DUTHIE Austin Leslie Smith   MB ChB 1950
d Leeds 15.4.76 *AUR* XLVI 418

DUTHIE Birnie Winchester   MB ChB 1949
MRCGP 1973
g p Aber from 1954

DUTHIE Charles Sim   *MA 1932 BD 1935 DD 1952
prin New College Lond 1964–77; pres: Cong Union of Scot. 1952–53, Cong Ch in England and Wales 1971–72
d Edin 11.1.81

DUTHIE Clifford Raymond   BSc(eng) 1948
FInstPet. 1962 CE 1958 MIMechE 1958
refinery supt eng Mina-al-Ahmadi Kuwait 1961–67; construct. supt Stone & Webster Eng 1967–73; mech eng consult. London Bridge Eng from 1973

DUTHIE Douglas Watt
                    MA 1925 *BSc 1927 PhD 1935
d Keynsham nr Bristol 20.6.69 *AUR* XLIII 330

DUTHIE Edwin   MA 1932
retd 1965; resid Aber

DUTHIE Edwin William   MB ChB 1931
d 2.1.70

DUTHIE Effie Mitchell   MB ChB 1924
g p and m o Hulme s s for girls Chadderton Oldham 1931–69; g p and dental anaest (schools) 1969–72; retd nat health practice 1969; contd private practice till 1973 and s m o Hulme g s for girls Oldham till 1972; retd

DUTHIE or Cameron, Eileen Marischal MB ChB 1942
m o in dept Waltham Forest, Lond from 1966; m o Salop AHA from 1976

DUTHIE or Miller, Elsie Cowie   BSc 1926
resid Aber

DUTHIE Eric Edmonston   *MA 1926
d Thorndon Cross Devon 22.10.74 *AUR* XLVI 109 & 236

DUTHIE or Gill, Eveline Elizabeth   MA 1935
resid Edin

DUTHIE Frank   BCom 1922
d 10.3.65

DUTHIE Frederick Mitchell   MB ChB 1931
retd surg cdr RN from 1953; med exam. off. RN/RM Manc from 1958; resid Oldham
d 10.4.78

DUTHIE George Stewart   BSc 1949
Aber: prin teacher maths/sc Old Aber s s 1961–66; dep head Torry acad 1966–74, head Torry acad from 1974

DUTHIE or Ross, Gladys Belle   MA 1931
rural head teacher Aberdeensh

DUTHIE Ian Wilson   *BSc(eng) 1930
3 awards for inventions
res scient with RN Admir HQ Lond till 1966; QAD insp and res plastics Haslemere from 1966

DUTHIE James Leask   *BSc 1952
W. J. Emmons award 1972 (AAPT)
geophys Brit petr co: UK, Senegal, Iran 1955–63; bituminous materials eng BP res centre 1963–74; BP southern Africa 1974–76

DUTHIE Joan Noble   MA 1929

DUTHIE John   MB ChB 1948

DUTHIE John   BSc(eng) 1954
MICE 1962
site eng Mitchell construct co Invernesssh 1959–60; des eng James Williamson & Ptnrs Glasg 1960–61; superv eng Montreal eng co 1962–69, sen superv eng from 1969

DUTHIE John James Reid   MB ChB 1935
Edin: reader dept of med 1964–68, prof med (rheumat) from 1968
m Edin 4.4.73 Kathleen W. Beaton area off. soc work dept Edin d of John M. B. Edin

DUTHIE John Milne   MA 1929 BSc 1931
JP
head Skene j s s 1947–69; retd
d Aber 4.3.72 *AUR* XLIV 432

DUTHIE John Stephen   MA 1939
NCB London 1959–63; Blue Circle Group: chmn Malayan Cement 1963–68, man dir Assoc Pan Malaysia Cement group Kuala Lumpur and Singapore 1967–68, dir Assoc International Cement Lond 1970, dir Blue Circle Group 1975, chief exec Blue Circle Cement UK 1977

DUTHIE Louis Herbert   MB ChB 1937
surg capt RN 1964–72; retd; civilian m o RN coll Greenwich from 1972

DUTHIE Louisa   MA 1915
no longer on GC reg

DUTHIE Margaret Alexander   BSc 1924
retd 1958
no longer on GC reg

DUTHIE or Traill, Margaret Stephen   BSc 1927
no longer on GC reg

DUTHIE Maureen Benton   BSc 1949 MB ChB 1954
Christie hosp and Holt radium inst Manc: sen regist 1963, asst radiotherap (s h m o) 1963–66, consult. radiotherap from 1966

DUTHIE Phyllis   MA 1919
no longer on GC reg

DUTHIE Robert   *MA 1949

DUTHIE Robert James   MB ChB 1922 *MD 1924
d Chichester 4.1.71 AUR XLIV 210

DUTHIE Stephen   *MA 1931 BSc 1932
prin teacher sc h s Inv 1951–72; retd

DUTHIE or Bruce, Winifred Margaret   *MA 1928
teacher Fr/Ger Aber h s for g 1938–45; Fr Hamilton Park s Glasg 1956–59; head Fr dept Broomlea s Whitecraigs Glasg 1959–62; asst Fr/Ger Hutchesons' girls' g s Glasg 1964–68; resid Callander

DUTHIE or Skinner, Winifred Rose Margaret
                                        MA 1925
resid Cambridge

DYKER or Gauld, Janet McCallum   *MA 1947
resid Vancouver

EADY George Edward   *MA 1953
sen dep prin Aber coll of comm from 1962

EAGER Richard   MB ChB 1905
no longer on GC reg

EAGGER Arthur Austin   MB ChB 1922
med dir Slough indust health serv 1947–63, retd, consult. from 1963; resid Exeter

EAGGER Mary Thomson   MA 1914
d Aber 22.12.62 AUR XL 82

EASSON William McAlpine
                    ***MB ChB 1954 ᶜMD 1967**
Dip Gen Psychiat 1963 Dip Ch Psychiat 1966 MRCPsych 1972
inst psychiat univ of Sask 1959–61; USA: fell. ch psychiat Menninger Clin Topeka 1961–63, consult. 1963–67; prof and chmn dept of psychiat Med Coll of Ohio, Toledo 1967–72, prof univ of Minnesota Minneapolis 1972–74, prof and head of dept of psychiat Louisiana State Univ med s New Orleans from 1974

EASTON James David   MA 1911
d Daviot Abersh 6.3.65 AUR XLI 55

EASTON Robert Morrison   MA 1907 MB ChB 1911
d Erith Kent 23.10.69 AUR XLIII 327

EASTWOOD Wilfred   PhD 1949
FIStructE 1959 FICE 1963
pres inst of struct eng 1976–77; Univ of Sheffield: prof civ eng 1964–70, consult. eng from 1970

EATON David   BSc 1906
d Stonehaven 6.11.70 AUR XLIV 208

EDDEY Leslie George   MB ChB 1938
d Salisbury Rhodesia 22.10.67 AUR XLII 372

EDDIE Alfred Alexander Pratt   MA 1913
d Aber 2.1.71 AUR XLIV 209

EDDIE or Badenoch, Christina Snowie   *MA 1923
resid Clifford Yorks

EDDIE or Cameron, Elizabeth Watt   BSc 1940
Dip Spec Educ (Jordanhill coll Glasg) 1963
teacher: St Andrews s Inverurie 1963–71, Dingwall acad 1971–73, Brimmond assessment centre Aber 1973–75, Woodlands hosp s Aber from 1975
husb d 22.7.73

EDDIE or Mitchell, Irene   MA 1950
resid Aber

EDDIE or Saunders, Mabel   MA 1953

EDDIE Robert William   MB ChB 1909
d Aber 22.10.62 AUR XL 79

EDDIE Vernon James   MA 1927 BCom 1929
d Lond 15.3.69 AUR XLIII 215

EDDISON John Michael   *BSc(eng) 1952
MIStruct E 1961 MEIC 1966 FICE 1974 FASCE 1975
Scott Wilson Kirkpatrick and Ptnrs Lond: Lond off. 1963–66; res eng dept of trans Vancouver 1966–67; res eng Belize Br Honduras 1967–68; res eng Brunei 1969–73; off. Hong Kong 1973–74; res eng Sabah 1974–77; proj eng (airports) Asian Dev Bank Manila from 1977

EDIE Charles Benjamin   *MA 1937
C of S min ch of the Holy Rude Stirling from 1955

EDIE or Mackie, Katharine Mary   MA 1939
resid Edin

EDMOND James Taylor   *MA 1940
FInstP 1967
RN scient serv Baldock 1948–59; res off. CEGB Leatherhead 1959–67; sen lect Dund from 1967
m Sutton 5.10.63 Judith M. E. Vincent secy d of Albert V. Sutton Surrey

EDMOND John Stephen   MA 1955
b 28.5.33
teacher: Bankhead acad 1959–66, prin geog Northfield acad Aber 1966–71, Hillpark s s Glasg 1972–73,
prin geog John St s s Glasg from 1973
m Aber 2.4.62 Dorothy A. Thomson BSc 1953 *qv*

EDMOND Neil Lennox   MB ChB 1953 DA 1957
g p Rochdale from 1960

EDMONDS Donald Thomas   *BSc 1955
res fell. Oxon 1957–61; on staff univ of California
1960–61; fell. Wadham coll Oxon from 1962, lect
Oxon 1965–67; Yale univ USA 1967–73; sen tut.
Wadham Coll Oxon 1973–76

EDWARD or Buchan, Evelyn May   MA 1933

EDWARD Henry   BSc(for) 1931
civ serv min of trans from 1958; retd 1975

EDWARD Ian David   MA 1927
d 6.2.66

EDWARD James Falconer   BSc 1932

EDWARD Margaret Duguid   *MA 1947
Aber acad: spec asst maths 1956–65, prin asst
maths 1965–70, year mistress Hazlehead acad Aber
from 1970

EDWARD Mary   *MA 1928
retd 1968; resid Stonehaven

EDWARDS Alan Tawse   MB ChB 1950
FRCPath 1972
consult. path. Halifax area hosps from 1959

EDWARDS Albert Gray   BSc(eng) 1945

EDWARDS Alexander Fraser   *MA 1948
prin teacher mod lang Douglas-Ewart h s Newton
Stewart from 1956

EDWARDS Alfred   *MA 1923
retd 1962; resid Aber
d Glasg 23.11.80 *AUR* xlix 67

EDWARDS Alfred John Meldrum
MA 1924 BCom 1927
head Skene Square p s Aber 1958–63; part-time
teacher Robert Gordon's coll Aber 1963–77; retd

EDWARDS Daniel   BSc 1949 *1950
head pharm s RGIT Aber from 1959

EDWARDS David (Sir)   MA 1912 ᵈLLB 1914
d Lond 28.2.66 *AUR* xli 242

EDWARDS or Jamieson, Elizabeth Mary
MB ChB 1912
venereologist Arcoats hosp Manc 1941–48; retd
d Hemel Hempstead 7.2.77 *AUR* xlvii 211

EDWARDS or Wood, Ezel Anna Bella   MA 1936

EDWARDS Farquhar Duncan   MB ChB 1947
g p Brechin from 1951

EDWARDS Harold George   *BSc 1951
housemaster Tonbridge s from 1965

EDWARDS Henry William McGregor
MB ChB 1948
med off. NCB S Midlands from 1972
d Nuneaton 11.7.79

EDWARDS Herbert John   BL 1922 MA LLB 1923
retd 1973; resid Aber

EDWARDS James Gordon Hastings   LLB 1948
d Cults Aber 9.3.72 *AUR* xliv 433

EDWARDS Jane Lucy   MA 1952
dep head approved s Warrington 1959–61; area off.
ch's dept Lancs c c 1961–66; lodging & welfare off.
Birm 1966–69; insp ch's dept Home Office Birm
1969–71; soc work serv off. DHSS Birm from 1971
m Birm 22.9.73 Farhang Bakhtar BSc(Birm) univ lect
s of Mostafa B. Iran

EDWARDS Jean McGregor
MA 1940 MB ChB 1950 DPH 1956
sen m o (clin) Wigan AHA from 1956
m Bolton 9.2.63 Edward J. Desmond MB ChB(Cork)
sen m o (occup health) Greater Manc council s of
Jeremiah F. D. Cork

EDWARDS Lindsay Duncan   BSc 1955
teacher: Glasg 1958–59; maths/sc Douglas Ewart
h s Newton Stewart 1959–70; comm educ branch
RAF from 1970
m Edin 19.7.58 Margaret A. C. C. Teese teacher d of
Thomas K. T. Glasg

EDWARDS Phyllis Allan   MA 1948
teacher Engl Elgin acad 1960–61; ch guid serv Aber
from 1971
m Lossiemouth 30.7.60 William A. Taylor ACII insur
insp s of Hector M. T. New Elgin

EDWARDS or Simmons, Phyllis Mary   MA 1939
teacher: head Engl dept Sholing g s S'ton from 1959

ELDER Charles Gordon   *MA 1910 MB ChB 1940
d Aber 23.10.69 *AUR* xliii 328

ELDER George William   MB ChB 1915
no longer on GC reg

ELDER Ian   *MA 1949 Dip Ed 1950 MEd 1965
Aber: asst dir educ 1967–72, dep dir from 1972

ELDER James Bremner   MB ChB 1902
no longer on GC reg

ELDER James Evan   MA 1904
d 1.1.67

ELDER John George   MB ChB 1912
no longer on GC reg

ELDER John Rawson
                    ***MA 1902 DLitt 1914 LLD 1943**
d Dunedin NZ 12.4.62 *AUR* xxxix 373

ELDER or Turner, Katharine Silver   MA 1930
resid Colchester

ELDER Norma McDonald   MA 1920
no longer on GC reg

EL HADIDI Moustafa Saleh   PhD 1953
dean higher inst of agr Kafi El Sheikh Egypt
1958–68; visiting prof Baghdad univ Iraq 1969–73;
head/prof bot fac of agr: Kafi El Sheikh 1973–74,
Mansoura Egypt from 1974

ELLIN or Booker, Catherine Scott   *MA 1952
resid Banchory

ELLINGER Gabrielle Marianne   PhD 1951
res biochem Rowett res inst Aber from 1946

ELLIOT Elizabeth Patterson   *MA 1949
prin teacher mod lang Mackie acad Stonehaven
from 1968

ELLIOT Isabella Craig   MA 1923
retd 1961; resid Aber

ELLIS Alexander Gordon Glennie   BSc(agr) 1911
d Elgin 21.9.62 *AUR* xl 80

ELLIS Clarence Isidore   MB CM 1896 MD 1901
d 19.11.61

ELLIS or Dickson, Eleanor   MA 1929
resid Aber
d Hayle 7.7.81

ELLIS Elizabeth Helen   MA 1947

ELLIS or Sutcliffe, Ethel   MA 1916
d Nairobi 21.1.77

ELLIS Frederic Stuart   BSc(eng) 1949
FBCS 1968
educ serv man. Systems Reliability Luton from 1975

ELLIS John   BSc(agr) 1922
farm. from 1947; resid Alford; retd

ELLIS John Alexander Gordon   BSc(for) 1949
acting conserv of for. Kumasi Ghana 1959–60; retd
from HM overseas for. serv 1960; teacher: sc Elgin
acad 1961–64; biol Kirkcaldy tech coll 1964–65; prin
teacher biol Glenrothes 1965–74; dep rect Milne's h s
Fochabers from 1974

ELLIS Richard Tunstall   MA 1939 LLB 1948
OBE 1970 DL
ptnr Paull & Williamsons advoc Aber from 1949;
chmn board of gov Dunfermline coll of phys educ
1964–67; chmn Scottish area TSB assoc 1967–76;
memb TSB cent board from 1976

ELMSLIE or Garden, Eleanora Johnston
                    MA 1948 MB ChB 1953
g p Timaru NZ from 1965

ELMSLIE Elizabeth Esther   MA 1910
d Balmedie 8.7.66 *AUR* xli 337

ELMSLIE Gordon Sinclair   BSc(eng) 1951
FInstHE 1956 MICE 1958 MAmer Soc CE 1963
constr supt/asst chief eng Reynolds Jamaica Mines
Jamaica 1959–65; contr man. (overseas) Middle
East/reg man. Sydney Green & Sons (Contractors)
Henley-on-Thames 1965–71, resid eng Sandford
Fawcett Wilton & Bell consult. eng Lond 1971–72;
group ldr Inv c c Isle of Skye 1972–73; sen eng Blyth
& Blyth consult. eng Inv from 1973

ELMSLIE John Alexander Grant   MB ChB 1951
g p Halifax from 1957

ELMSLIE John Grant   MB ChB 1920
d Aber 3.1.67 *AUR* xlii 358

ELPHINSTONE John Joseph
                    MB ChB 1932 MD 1946
Perth W Aust: dept publ health 1958–68; g p from
1968

ELRICK or Hatvany, Doris Margaret   *MA 1946

ELRICK Joan Davidson   MA 1915
no longer on GC reg

El Shazly Khaled   PhD 1951
nat res award agr sc 1961, 1969
univ of Alexandria: lect dept anim prod. 1951–58, asst
prof 1958–65; prof 1965–70, head of anim prod. dept
1970–74; nutrit off FAO Rome 1974–76; Dep Min of
Agr 1976; prof anim nutrit 1977

ELWELL Harry Willmott   MB ChB 1902
no longer on GC reg

EMMANUEL Antoine Fathallah   MB ChB 1927
m o various govt hosps and clins from 1927 to
1958; private practice in afternoons; retd 1968
d Baghdad 16.10.75

EMSLIE Alfred George   *MA 1928
PhD(Corn)

EMSLIE Alfred George
                    ***MB ChB 1929 ʿMD & DPH 1933**
FRCP(Lond) 1969
hon consult. phys Eastbourne group of hosp from
1972

EMSLIE Alfred William   *MA 1950

EMSLIE Alice   MA 1937
teacher Engl and remed Harlaw acad Aber from
1971

EMSLIE Arthur Raymond Gordon   DSc 1934
d Ontario 27.9.65 *AUR* xlii 89

EMSLIE Calthorpe MA 1950
teacher Penicuik from 1965

EMSLIE or Angus, Charlotte Sylvia Smith MA 1949
resid Radcliffe-on-Trent

EMSLIE Dorothy Margaret Jane MB ChB 1919
retd 1964; resid Lond

EMSLIE Ethel Richmond
⠀⠀⠀⠀⠀⠀⠀⠀⠀**MB ChB 1922 DPH 1927 MD 1932**
retd 1960; resid Ballater

EMSLIE Harold George MA 1950
⠀Aber: dep head Craighill s 1964–70, Fernielea s
1970–75, Mile End s from 1975
m Peterculter 5.8.64 Olive A. Jamieson teacher d of
William J. Peterculter

EMSLIE John BSc(agr) 1923
⠀head Slains s 1937–65
d Ellon 4.4.76

EMSLIE John Alexander Simpson MB ChB 1922
⠀MRCGP 1964
g p Eastbourne from 1946

EMSLIE John William BSc(agr) 1922
⠀*d* Troon 1.6.73 *AUR* xlv 318

EMSLIE Michael John ᶜMB ChB 1954
⠀MRCGP 1972
g p Eastbourne from 1957
m Lond 14.11.59 Jill Smyth d of Stanley C. S.
Kensington

EMSLIE or Attisha, Victoria Clare
⠀⠀⠀⠀⠀⠀⠀⠀⠀**MB ChB 1926 DPH 1929**
⠀g p Basrah Iraq 1934–71; retd
d Calgary 13.12.79 *AUR* xlviii 441

EMSLIE William MA 1926 LLB 1928
⠀*d* Banchory 14.5.72 *AUR* xlv 127

EMSLIE William Harold Lees MB ChB 1927
⠀phys homoeopathic hosp out patients Glasg from
1945

EMSLIE William Ingram MB ChB 1936
⠀g p Kirkwall 1939–63; ARI: sen h o anaest 1963–65;
regist anaest 1965–68; med asst anaest from 1968
wife *d* 1973
m(2) Stromness 31.8.74 Edith S. Horrie med secy/
matron eventide home d of Thomas R. H. Firth
Orkney

EMSLIE-SMITH Alan Hugh
⠀⠀⠀⠀⠀⠀⠀⠀⠀**MB ChB 1937 ᶜMD 1958**

EMSLIE-SMITH Donald MB ChB 1945 *MD 1957
⠀FRCPE 1965 FRCP(Lond) 1968
sen regist and tut. royal post grad med s of Lond and
Hammersmith hosp 1958–61; sen lect med St And
and hon consult. phys DRI 1961–67; Dund: sen lect
med and hon consult. phys DRI 1967–71; reader med

and hon consult. phys DRI and Ninewells hosp from
1971
m Lond 19.9.59 Ann E. Milne d of Col Thomas M. CB
DSO Milford-on-Sea

ENDEAN Frank BSc(for) 1954 *1955
⠀asst conserv for. Kitwe, Zambia 1956–67; res scient
Canadian for. serv Edmonton 1967–73; consult. for.
Forestal Internat Vancouver from 1973

ENGLISH or Bain, Elizabeth Barbara MA 1953
⠀resid Aber

ENGSTROM Victor Ralph Whitcomb BCom 1930

ENTWISTLE Jessie MA 1920
⠀*d* 18.2.71

ERSKINE or Stronach, Janet MA 1948
⠀vol serv organis board of man. for Moray hosps
from 1973; resid Elgin

ERSKINE or Innes, Marguerite Norah Laidlaw
⠀⠀⠀⠀⠀⠀⠀⠀⠀**MB ChB 1941**
⠀locum tenens Aber 1948–54

ESCOFFERY William Henry MB ChB 1941

ESCOFFERY William Ignatius MB ChB 1913

ESPLIN or Lord, Elizabeth Grant MA 1944

ESSLEMONT Alexander Gordon BCom 1923
⠀retd 1967; resid Harrow
m(2) Harrow 12.5.79 Winifred D. G. Wheeler d of
James T. Leach Sheerness

ESSLEMONT Donald Alexander Logie *MA 1951
⠀prin teacher classics Inverurie acad from 1958

ESSLEMONT Elizabeth MA 1914

ESSLEMONT George Beedie
⠀⠀⠀⠀⠀⠀⠀⠀⠀**MA 1925 BCom 1927 LLB 1930**
⠀city chamberlain Glasgow 1943–70
d Glasgow 21.11.75 *AUR* xlvi 416

ESSLEMONT James Bryce BL 1928
⠀ptnr Wilsone & Duffus advoc Aber 1936–75; retd;
consult. Wilsone and Duffus

ESSLEMONT John Connon BCom 1925
⠀man. dir John E. Esslemont Aber 1961–74; retd

ESSLEMONT Margaret Christina Taylor MA 1942

ESSLEMONT or Williamson, Marianne Rollo
⠀⠀⠀⠀⠀⠀⠀⠀⠀**MA 1936**

ESSLEMONT Mary
⠀⠀⠀⠀⠀**BSc 1914 MA 1915 MB ChB 1923 LLD 1954**
⠀founder member RCGP FRCGP FBMA Vice-pres
BMA
member univ court Aberd 1946–74; retd 1962; resid
Aber

ESSLEMONT or Scott or Clay, Mary Gerrie
                                        MB ChB 1940
    resid Aber

ESSON Alexander George Duncan   MA 1915

ESSON George Alexander Cockburn   MB ChB 1936
    retd; resid Elgin

ESSON or Walker or Warren, Mary Bella   MA 1910
    d Portsoy 18.12.70 *AUR* XLIV 209

ESSON Norman Watson   MA 1952
    teacher sc Bawating s Sault Ste Marie Ontario from 1967

ESSON Walter Louis   MA 1920 MB ChB 1924
    O St J 1970
member, chmn war pensions and indust boards Manc 1952–70
m Aber 9.12.27 Elizabeth Reid d of William R. Johannesburg
d Manchester 29.2.80 *AUR* XLVIII 440

ETOE Owen Mansell   *MA 1951

ETTLES or Fraser, Ann   MA 1940
    resid Forres

ETTLES William Alexander   *MA 1941
    clasp to VRD 1967 JP
lt cdr RNR retd
teacher Engl Keith g s Banffsh 1962–69; prin teacher Engl Buckie h s from 1969

ETTMAN Irving Kelsey   MB ChB 1934
    FACR 1964
clin prof radiol univ of Tennessee Memphis from 1970

EUNSON Leonard Harvey   MB ChB 1924

EVANS Gwynfryn Pugh   *MEd 1947

EWAN or MacLean, Alice May   MA 1906
    retd; resid Inv

EWAN James   MA 1951

EWAN John Muir   *MA 1955

EWAN Mary Strachan   *MA 1930
    prin lect maths Crewe coll of educ 1959–73; retd; resid Aber
d Aber 30.9.79 *AUR* XLVIII 353

EWAN Matilda Annie (Ramsay)   *MA 1912
    resid Aber
d Aber 18.9.78 *AUR* XLVIII 102

EWAN William Alexander   BSc(eng) 1950

EWAN William John Strachan   MB ChB 1936
    FRCP(Lond)
consult. phys Haroldwood hosp and Rush Green hosp Essex

EWART Hugh James   PhD 1936

EWEN Alan Burness   MA 1941

EWEN Alastair Hamilton   MA 1923
    retd; resid Ellon

EWEN Douglas Richard   *MA 1949
    assoc prof Laurentian univ Canada 1965–66; sen lect univ of WI Trinidad 1968–70; chmn Engl dept York univ Toronto from 1973

EWEN or Murray, Elsie May   MA 1918
    d 21.12.70

EWEN James Barclay
                    MB ChB 1927 ᶜMD 1933 DPH 1934
    d Royston 20.3.71 *AUR* XLIV 211

EWEN or Inkson, Jane   MA 1914
    d Aber 31.1.61 *AUR* XXXIX 202

EWEN or Farquhar, Jeannie May   MA 1919
    d 19.5.71

EWEN Robert   MA 1902
    no longer on GC reg

EWEN William   MA 1910 BD 1914
    d Banff 16.2.71 *AUR* XLIV 209

EWEN William Alexander   MA 1928
    head Demonstration s Aber 1964–70; retd

EWING or White, Isabella Helen   *MA 1907
    d 18.5.74

EWING James   MA 1910 BSc 1911 DSc 1916
    no longer on GC reg

EWING Maggie Anderson   MA 1916

EWING or Macdonald, Mary Angus   MA 1921
    no longer on GC reg

FAIRBAIRN Nellie   MA 1916

FAIRLEY or Macpherson, Aileen Margaret Crichton
                                        MA 1949
    resid Trumpington

FAIRLIE Andrew Lindsay   BSc(agr) 1945

FAIRWEATHER or Cruickshank, Joan Isobel
                                        MA 1953
    resid Fyvie

FAIRWEATHER or Watt, Kathleen Adela   MA 1910
    d 25.7.71 *AUR* XLIV 427

FALCONER Alfred   *MA 1925
    retd 1968
d Aber 23.2.78 *AUR* XLVII 356

FALCONER Bernard Paul Anthony   *MA 1954

FALCONER Catherine Jean   BSc(agr) 1955
m McCorkindale

FALCONER or Dawson, Dolina Barbara   *MA 1926
no longer on GC reg

FALCONER or Barbour, Eva Farquharson
                                        MA 1950
teacher: Middlefield s Aber from 1968

FALCONER Ian McLeod   BSc(eng) 1953
MICE 1961
des eng Sir Wm Halcrow & ptnrs consult. eng Lond 1959–60; sen eng, at A. A. Stuart Aigas of Kilmorack hydro schemes Invsh 1960–64; Crudens bldg and civ eng contr: proj eng Ninewells hosp Dun 1964–71, proj man. phase III Dun coll of art 1971–73, Dun coll of tech 1973–76; contr man. Taylor Woodrow Glasg 1976–79; bldgs off. Dund from 1979

FALCONER James   *MA 1906
d Perth 3.11.70 *AUR* XLIV 167

FALCONER James Duncan   *BSc 1952 PhD 1955
tech marketing superv Ruabon Wrexham from 1972

FALCONER John   *MA 1920
no longer on GC reg

FALCONER or Cowan, Kathleen   MA 1915
no longer on GC reg

FALCONER Margaret Sim   MA 1911
no longer on GC reg

FALCONER Neil Douglas   *MA 1954
comm asst ICI till 1962; Scot Adhesives Co Glasg from 1963, latterly dir
m Glasg 7.1.63 Roseanne S. M. Anderson BA(Dub) d of Samuel A. BSc(Glas) Glasg

FALCONER or Smith, Rachel   MA 1948
teacher: Crieff 1965–73, maths Crieff s s from 1973

FALCONER or Macdonald, Rona Morven   MA 1945

FALCONER Ronald Hugh Wilson
                        MA 1934 BD 1937 DD 1960
William Thyne schol of ESU for first visit of Scotsman to Aust and NZ branches of ESU 1970
OBE 1971
retd BBC 1971; advis on relig TV: to NZ broadcasting corp 1971–72, to S. Afr. churches from 1972; consult. radio and TV World Assoc for Christian Commun from 1971; convener C of S dept of publ and publication from 1971; retd; resid Glasg
d Glasg 20.5.77 *AUR* XLVII 213

FALLOWFIELD or Mackay, Patricia Mackay
                                        *MA 1947
m(2) Wilson

FALLOWFIELD Thomas Leslie   MB ChB 1955
MSc(Birm) 1960
RN(perm serv) from 1956

FARKAS Paul Lapislas   PhD 1931

FARMAN or Crozier, Gertrude Elizabeth   MA 1933

FARMER Victor Colin   PhD 1947
FRIC 1964
sen prin sc off. Macaulay Inst for soil res Aber from 1968

FARQUHAR Alexander Proven   MA 1950
teacher Aber: 1951–63, first asst RGC 1963–66; dep head Cults s 1966–73, head Milltimber s from 1973

FARQUHAR Alice Margaret Mary   *MA 1946
woman advis St Peters RC s Aber from 1965

FARQUHAR or Collie, Barbara   MA 1924
retd; resid Crimond

FARQUHAR or Rankin, Barbara Drummond
                                        MA 1915
resid Invercargill NZ

FARQUHAR or MacMillan, Doris   MA 1928
d 4.3.71 *AUR* XLIV 212

FARQUHAR George Greig   MB ChB 1900
d Darlington 12.8.63 *AUR* XL 299

FARQUHAR Ian Ewen   *BSc 1954 PhD 1957
lect maths Queen Mary coll Lond 1961–68; res fell. theoret phys Norges Tekniske Høgskole Trondheim, Norway 1966–67; lect/sen lect theoret phys St And from 1968

FARQUHAR or Temple, Irene Elizabeth   MA 1952
teacher Engl: Aber h s for girls 1965–70, Beath sen h s Cowdenbeath from 1970

FARQUHAR or Baxter, Isobel Reid   MA 1949

FARQUHAR or Grant, Isobel Rust   MA 1924
retd 1965; resid Aber
husb d 7.5.81

FARQUHAR James Alexander   MA 1900
d 22.5.64 *AUR* XL 394

FARQUHAR or Stobbs, Jean Floyd   MB ChB 1923
resid Hartlepool
husb d 1965

FARQUHAR or Simpson, Jessie Margaret   MA 1941

FARQUHAR John   BSc(for) 1947

FARQUHAR John David   BSc(for) 1944

FARQUHAR or Sellar, Mary Morison
                        MB ChB 1925 DPH 1951
resid Aber

FARQUHAR Moira   BSc 1953
analytical chem ICI Ardeer, Stevenston 1953–61

m Aber 6.5.61 Norman S. Wallace BSc(Glas) res chem
s of Norman G. W. Falkirk

FARQUHAR Oswald Cornell   PhD 1951

FARQUHAR Robert Forbes   BSc(eng) 1950

FARQUHAR Robert Warrender
                BSc(agr) 1925 MB ChB 1937 DPH 1947
d Lancaster 15.2.68 *AUR* XLII 365

FARQUHAR or Hamilton, Stella   MA 1931
resid Fraserburgh

FARQUHARSON Charlotte Simpson   BSc 1932

FARQUHARSON Edward   MB ChB 1930 MD 1934
d Bournemouth 26.1.61 *AUR* XXXIX 283

FARQUHARSON or Locke, Eva Grant   MA 1928
d 15.2.74

FARQUHARSON Gordon Booth   MB ChB 1950
MRCGP 1970
g p Inv from 1963

FARQUHARSON or Gardiner, Grace Helen Gordon
                                MA 1945
teacher Aboyne p s from 1965

FARQUHARSON Henry   MA 1936 LLB 1937
life insur indust, spec in estate plan. Toronto from
1954

FARQUHARSON Horace   BSc 1954
med rep G. D. Searle & Co., Aber 1960–64; Scot
div man. Searle lab pharm div Scot. 1964–74; reg sales
man. from 1974

FARQUHARSON Ian Glennie   *MA 1950
prin teacher classics Kirkcaldy h s 1966–75; dep
rector Blairgowrie h s from 1975

FARQUHARSON or Harper, Isobel   MA 1908
d Aber 19.4.73

FARQUHARSON James Kennedy
                BSc(for) 1932 MB ChB 1937
retd 1973; resid Ellon
d 14.11.81

FARQUHARSON John
                BSc 1926 *1927 PhD 1930 DSc 1939
d Surrey 22.8.64 *AUR* XL 399, XLI 247

FARQUHARSON John Ogilvie
                MA 1940 ᵈLLB 1949
ptnr Brander & Cruickshank advoc Aber from
1952

FARQUHARSON or Elphinstone, Kathleen Rhoda
                                BSc 1949

FARQUHARSON or Corlette, Margaret
                        MB ChB 1948
resid Sydney Aust

FARQUHARSON or Irvine, Margaret Elizabeth Ann
                                MA 1954
teacher mod lang Arundel s Salisbury Rhod 1960–
63

FARQUHARSON Myrtle   MB ChB 1954
DA(Lond) 1957 D Obst RCOG(Lond) 1963
DPH(Glas) 1964
jun h m o chest diseases Ruchill hosp Glasg 1959–60;
sen h o obst Kirkcaldy 1963; s m o Glasg 1963–66;
m h o Peace River Area BC Canada 1966–68, g p
White Rock BC from 1968

FARQUHARSON William Cowie   MA 1923
secy Scot. Bible Soc Edin from 1966
retd 1968; resid Edin

FARRANT John Frederick Ames
                MA 1951 BD 1958 MTh 1980
rector: Holy Trinity epis ch Motherwell 1965–70,
All Souls' Anglican ch Lae, Papua New Guinea
1970–74, St Bride's epis ch Glasg 1974–77, canon St
Mary's cath Glasg from 1977

FARRELL Edna Bessie   MA 1955
teacher Aber: Cummings Park p s 1956–70,
Broomhill p s from 1970

FARRELL James Malcolm   MB ChB 1951
g p Fochabers from 1966

FASKIN Annie   MA 1920
no longer on GC reg

FAULKNER Roy   BSc(for) 1948
for. comm res div: asst geneticist Edin 1959–62,
prin geneticist Roslin from 1962

FEARNLEY Doris Ethel   MA 1931
teacher Engl Harrogate 1938–71; retd; resid
Harrogate

FEARNLEY or Clark, Gladys   *MA 1935
resid Harrogate
husb *d* 1966

FEARNLEY Joseph Eric   *BSc 1928
retd 1966; resid Harrogate

FEINSTEIN Samuel   MB ChB 1922
no longer on GC reg

FELL William Ian Andrew   MB ChB 1930
d Thurso 29.3.62 *AUR* XXXIX 384

FENTON Alexander   *MA 1951
dep keeper Nat Museum of Antiquities of Scot. i/c
Scot. country life sect. Edin from 1959; hon fell. s of
Scot. stud. Edin from 1969

FENTON Edward Wyllie
                MA 1912 BSc 1913 DSc 1936
d 16.9.62 *AUR* XL 81

FERGUSON Allan William George   BSc(eng) 1955

FERGUSON or Cowie, Beatrice Doreen   MA 1944
resid Aber

FERGUSON or Rahman, Doreen   MB ChB 1954
m o: packages factory Lahore 1961–63, outpatients' dept Holy Family hosp Rawalpindi 1966–67; resid Benghazi Libya

FERGUSON Elizabeth Margaret Graham
                                    MA 1950
Weston Park s Southampton: head geog dept 1958–66, dep head 1966–74; dep head Harlaw acad Aber from 1974

FERGUSON Elizabeth Mowat   MA 1925
retd; resid Edin

FERGUSON or Smith, Evelyn   MA 1915
no longer on GC reg

FERGUSON Fergus Graeme   *BSc(eng) 1940
MIWE 1973
eng Sir Alexander Gibb & Ptners Reading from 1949

FERGUSON or Drummond, Hilda   MA 1947

FERGUSON or Jack, Jean Alexandra
                                    MB ChB 1939
resid Carlops Penicuik
husb *d* 16.5.64

FERGUSON John   BSc(agr) 1947
FRICS 1969 BA(OU) 1973
sen lands off. dept agr for Scot: Thurso 1968–71, Inv 1971–75; tech dev off. DAFS Edin from 1975

FERGUSON Keith   MA 1948 ᵈLLB 1952
DPA(Lond) 1973
town clerk Buckhaven and Methil 1959–62; secy and leg. advis Glenrothes dev corp from 1962

FERGUSON Keith Webster   MA 1953 LLB 1955
leg. asst L. Mackinnon & Son advoc Aber 1958–62, ptnr from 1962
m Aber 4.10.63 Elizabeth A. S. Smith MA 1962 *qv*

FERGUSON Malcolm   MA 1953
prod.: schools dept BBC Edin 1962–71, audio-visual unit Strath 1971–76; dir television 1976–77; dir audio-visual serv Glas univ from 1977

FERGUSON or Cattell-Jones, Margaret Kidd
                                    ***MA 1922**
d 1972

FERGUSON or Fraser, Margaret Redman Gibson
                                    ***MA 1938**
resid Kingswells, Aber

FERGUSON Mary Ann Hay   *MA 1924
d Edin 19.2.66 *AUR* xli 340

FERGUSON Vivian Leslie   MB ChB 1920
d 17.11.69

FERGUSSON or Macfarlane, Marian Melville
                                    MB ChB 1939
resid Montrose

FERRES Gordon Kemp   ᵈMB ChB 1928
retd 1963; resid Banchory
m(2) Chichester 6.10.58 Sheila E. Bennett physioth d of Stephen B. Guildford

FERRIER or Gammie, Anne Taylor   MA 1950

FERRIER William Roderick   BL 1948
Clydesdale Bank: trust. off. Aber 1960–65, asst man. trust. dept 1965–69; man. trust. dept Lond 1969–71; dep trust. man. head off. Glasg 1971–72, trust. man. 1972–76; asst gen man. from 1976

FERRIES Catherine Anderson   MA 1951
teacher: Fr/Lat Aboyne j s s 1953–62, maths/ remed subj Gordon s Huntly from 1968
m Aber 15.8.62 George Stephen farm. s of George S. Rothienorman
husb *d* 8.10.76

FERRIES or Donald, Elizabeth Williamina   MA 1941

FERRIES or Stewart, Evelyn Mary   MA 1949
resid Chilliwack BC Canada

FERRIES George William   *MA 1951
lect applied psych univ of Aston Birm from 1963

FERRIES Harvey   BL 1950
sole ptnr Carle Duthie & Ferries advoc Aber from 1961

FERRIES John Morrison   MB ChB 1948
consult. North Vancouver gen hosp from 1957

FERRIES Magdalene   MA 1946 Dip Ed 1969
Dip Educ Deaf (Edin) 1970
teacher: Aber s for deaf 1968–71, Gateside centre for educ of deaf Paisley 1972–74; Aber s for deaf from 1976

FETTES Frances   MA 1910
d Aber 1.10.74

FETTES William   MB ChB 1928 DPH 1931
retd 1970; resid Lytham St Annes

FETTES William Youngson   MB ChB 1938
retd 1971
d Ardersier 10.11.73 *AUR* xlv 449

FIDDES Christopher   MA 1932
retd 1971; resid Edin

FIDDES Douglas Alexander   BSc 1947
d Salisbury Rhodesia 29.4.75 *AUR* xlvi 325

FIDDES John   MB ChB 1919 *MD 1926

FIDDES John Douglas
                      MA 1905 *BSc 1907 MB ChB 1909
d Billericay Essex 24.6.66 *AUR* xli 335

FIDDES Mary Elizabeth   *MA 1930
teacher: prin Fr/Ger Aberlour h s 1944–59, asst
Fr/Ger Elgin acad 1960–61, spec asst Keith g s
1962–69; retd; resid Keith

FIDDES William Ogilvie   BCom 1923
d 8.5.78

FIDLER Mysie (Jemima)   MA 1911
d Berwick 26.2.65 *AUR* XLI 147

FIELD or Cowie, Valerie Aileen
                              ᶜ**MB ChB 1948** ᶜ**MD 1951**
PhD(Lond) 1967 FRCPsych 1971
asst dir MRC psychiat genetics res unit London
1959–69; consult. psychiat Fountain and Carshalton
group hosps Surrey 1961–67; USA visiting scient nat
inst of health Bethesda and res assoc in neurol ch hosp
dist of Columbia Washington 1968–69; hon consult.
psychiat: Maudsley and Bethlem royal hosps Lond
1967–68, Mayday hosp Croydon 1968–75; hon
consult. St George's hosp from 1975; chmn ment defic
sect Royal Coll Psychiat from 1975
husb *d* 1970

FINDLATER Alexander George Craig
                                              MB ChB 1945
DA(Lond) 1967
g p Launceston, Tasmania from 1969
d 6.11.78

FINDLATER or Cairns, Helen   *MA 1944
dep head: Wood Green s Lond 1964–67, Haringey
s 1967–69; head High Cross s Haringey from 1969

FINDLATER William Thompson   BSc(agr) 1953
vis aids off. s of agr Aberd from 1971

FINDLAY Adam Fyfe
                          ***MA 1889 DD 1923 LLD 1948**
d Aber 19.1.62 *AUR* XXXIX 268

FINDLAY Alexander
              ***MA 1895 *BSc 1897 DSc 1902 LLD 1944**
d 14.9.66 *AUR* XLI 286

FINDLAY Alexander   MB ChB 1923
retd; resid Chigwell

FINDLATER Alexander John
                              MA 1907 BSc(agr) 1909
chief agr advis col serv S Nigeria; retd 1954
d Aboyne 26.12.76

FINDLAY or Kitz, Alice Duff   MB ChB 1939
d Halifax Nova Scotia 20.5.69 *AUR* XLIII 216

FINDLAY Annie   MA 1912
no longer on GC reg

FINDLAY or Strang, Bella   MA 1934

FINDLAY Charles Bruce   MB ChB 1936
insp of aliens port of Folkestone 1956–64; med
advis Carter Wallace pharm Folkestone from 1964

FINDLAY or Cox, Diana Avril   *MA 1953

FINDLAY Francis   *BSc 1941
no longer on GC reg

FINDLAY Garden Whyte   MA 1951
DTI from 1961

FINDLAY George Alexander   MB ChB 1943
g p Chryston, Glasg from 1950

FINDLAY George Daniel   BSc(agr) 1951

FINDLAY George Ian Garrioch   MB ChB 1931
d Askerwells 23.12.76 *AUR* XLVII 213

FINDLAY Graham   MB ChB 1953
g p Ilford from 1954

FINDLAY Harry David   MA 1924 MB ChB 1928
g p Marlow-on-Thames from 1969

FINDLAY Henry Ritchie   MB ChB 1939
g p Huddersfield from 1949

FINDLAY Ian Douglas   MB ChB 1946
DPH(Tor) 1960 Cert Publ Health(Can) 1961
BC Canada: m o h S central health unit Kamloops
1959–69; g p Irving clin Kamloops from 1969

FINDLAY Ian James   MA 1931 BSc 1935
d 23.7.75

FINDLAY James   MA 1954
teacher Portsoy s s 1960–64; Buckie: dep head h s
1964–69; head p s from 1969
m Dingwall 16.7.60 Jessica M. Young teacher d of
John Y. Dingwall

FINDLAY James   BL 1954
town clerk dep Aber 1972–75; dep dir law and
admin Grampian reg c from 1975
m Aber 2.3.63 Wilma A. Anderson secy/police off. d of
William A. A. Aber

FINDLAY James George   MA 1952
head teacher: Fintry, Turriff 1965–67, Monquhitter
1971–75, Turriff p s from 1975

FINDLAY or Robertson, Jean   *MA 1939

FINDLAY or Duthie, Jeannie   MA 1951
teacher Wester Langlee p s Galashiels 1964–68, asst
head from 1968

FINDLAY John   MA 1954 Dip Ed 1955
teacher mod lang: Laurencekirk j s 1958–62, dep
head Sanday j s s Orkney 1962–67, Stranraer h s
1967–68; dep head Park p s Stranraer 1968–71; head:
transition s Macduff 1971–76, Ladyloan p s Arbroath
from 1976

FINDLAY John Angus   MB ChB 1955 MD 1973
h o ARI 1958–60; lect anat Aberd 1960–61; univ
coll S Wales and Mon, Cardiff: lect anat 1961–72,

serv lect from 1972
m Grantown-on-Spey 1.5.59 Elisabeth Allan Durh

FINDLAY John Gray   BSc 1924
no longer on GC reg

FINDLAY Leslie   MA 1915
no longer on GC reg

FINDLAY or Ennals, Margaret Buyers   MA 1930
d Camberley 1.1.73 *AUR* xlv 226

FINDLAY or Cumming, Mary   MA 1909
no longer on GC reg

FINDLAY or Stuart, Mary Isabella   MA 1942

FINDLAY or Gall, Rhoda Gertrude
MB ChB 1924 DPH 1926
retd 1963; resid Aber

FINE Samuel Harry   MB ChB 1925
no longer on GC reg

FINLAYSON Bruce   MA 1954 MEd 1956
teacher Engl AGS 1960–67, prin asst Engl 1967–71; prin Engl Kincorth acad Aber from 1971

FINLAYSON Eric Cameron   MA 1926
CA Aber from 1932; retd 1976

FINLAYSON Horace Courtenay Forbes   *MA 1907
d St Leonards-on-Sea 3.12.69 *AUR* xliii 440

FINLAYSON Isobel Eleanor Mary   MA 1911
no longer on GC reg

FINLAYSON James Kerr
** *BSc(eng) 1943 *MB ChB 1954**
FRCP(Lond) 1973
instr and fell. in med Rochester NY 1958–60; ARI: sen regist med 1960–64, consult. phys from 1964

FINLAYSON John Dugald   MA 1904
no longer on GC reg

FINLAYSON Kenneth Macdonald   MB ChB 1928
no longer on GC reg

FINLAYSON or Shupe, Lily Helen   MA 1939
teacher BC Canada: Mission City 1958–60, Fort St John 1961–63, Salmon Arm 1966–74; retd

FINLAYSON Margaret Scotland   MA 1931
teacher Edzell 1948–73; retd

FINLAYSON Margaret Watt   MA 1941
teacher Walker Rd p s Aber from 1949

FINLAYSON Roderick Alexander   MA 1919
retd 1966; resid Edin

FINLAYSON Sidney Knight   MA 1913
d Orpington –.7.69 *AUR* xliii 329

FINLAYSON William   MA 1910
d 1.2.71

FINNIE Alison Murray   MA 1915
no longer on GC reg

FINNIE Andrew Scott   MA 1938
MICA(Scot)
Aberd: part-time lect acct 1960–66, head of dept from inception in 1966 to 1973; ptnr Whinney Murray & Co m(2) Peterculter 5.6.64 Johne S. Balmain CA d of Kenneth F. B. Edin

FINNIE or Gray, Davina Milne   MA 1955
teacher: Portknockie p s 1965–66, Portsoy p s 1966–68, remed Banff acad 1968–71; head Botriphnie p s from 1971

FINNIE Isabella   MA 1925
retd 1968; resid Edin

FINNIE James Sadler   MB ChB 1946 MD 1959
g p Aber from 1951

FINNIE Margaret Maud Keith   MA 1927
teacher Cults s 1935–68; retd; resid Aber
d 22.10.81

FINNIE or Kant, Rosemary Stewart   MA 1951
secy phys dept Portland state univ Oregon USA 1968–70; teacher Dumfriessh 1970–72; pers secy to man. dir Century Aluminium Co Sanquhar 1972–75; Jordanhill coll of educ 1975–76; sec cert Lat/Engl teacher Glasg from 1976

FINNIE Williamson Jackson
BSc 1935 MB ChB 1938
consult. anaest Bradford hosp group from 1947; retd

FIRTH Ian George Macdonald   MB ChB 1915
no longer on GC reg

FIRTH James Stevenson   MB ChB 1928
retd 1969; resid Rousay

FIRTH Norman John   MA 1929
head Tankerness s Orkney
m 1931 Helen Hendry teacher
d Tankerness 21.10.52

FITZPATRICK Ewart Adsil   PhD 1951
sen lect dept of soil sc Aberd from 1969

FLAWS Muriel   MA 1925
no longer on GC reg

FLEMING or Robinson, Anne Elsie   MA 1929
resid Belfast

FLEMING Eric James   MA 1949

FLEMING Stanley David   BSc(agr) 1955

FLEMING Thomas Aitchison   BSc(for) 1949

FLETCHER David Livingstone   MB ChB 1938
g p Pickering from 1945

FLETCHER Edith Eleanor   MA 1934
teacher Woodside s Aber from 1943; retd 1975

FLETCHER Grace   MA 1955

FLETCHER Harold Roy   PhD 1933
hon DSc(Edin) 1971 hon DSc(St And) 1972
regius keeper Roy Bot Gdn Edin 1958–70; pres Bot
Soc of Edin 1959–60; vice-pres Royal Soc Edin 1961–
65; pres internat assoc of bot gardens 1964–69; HM
botanist in Scot. from 1966; hon prof bot Edin from
1968
d 27.8.78

FLETCHER John Robert   BSc(for) 1950
for. comm: for. off. Chester 1953–58, Bakewell
1958–67, Kendal 1967–72, Thetford 1972–76, Edin
from 1976
m Adel Leeds 2.11.57 Maureen Hobson

FLETT Alexander Campbell   BSc 1955 PhD 1958

FLETT Alexander Smith   MA 1948
d Aber 1.2.75 *AUR* XLVI 240

FLETT or Howie, Constance Florence   MA 1923
resid Aber
husb *d* 2.12.76
d Aber 13.2.81

FLETT George   BSc 1928 MA 1930
head Inverallochy 1962–71; retd; resid Torphins

FLETT George   BSc 1949
teacher Dunbartonsh: guid post Bradfield s from
1972

FLETT George Reid   BSc(for) 1933 BSc 1935
teacher: Blackburn p s W Lothian 1936–37, Lindsay
h s Bathgate 1937–40; educ off. RAF 1940–45; head
Longridge p s 1945–46; head of sc: Russel s E
Croydon 1946–54, John Newnham s E Croydon
1954–56; asst head internat s Geneva 1956–64;
exchange teacher Chadwick s Los Angeles 1964–66;
Lossiemouth h s 1966–75; retd; resid San Diego Calif

FLETT Helen Jane   MA 1905
no longer on GC reg

FLETT Ian Stark   *MA 1943 *MEd 1948
dep educ off. Kingston-u-Hull 1963–66; dir educ
Fife 1966–75; dir educ Fife reg c from 1975

FLETT or Hughes, Isabella   MA 1924
d Aber 16.4.71 *AUR* XLIV 211

FLETT John Alexander   *MA 1946
teacher maths AGS from 1950
m Macduff 2.7.55 Jean P. Thomson health visitor d of
George T. Macduff

FLETT John Alexander   MA 1949

FLETT or Reid, Margaret   MA 1946

FLETT or Tarlton, Nelly   MA 1920 MB ChB 1924
d Bristol 22.11.65 *AUR* XLII 85

FLETT or Stone-Wigg, Sheelagh Mairi   BSc 1954
Kericho p s Kenya: teacher 1967–70, head from
1970

FLETT or Elder, Sheila Margaret   MA 1949
Malaya: head Engl dept Bentong h s Pahang
1964–65, Uplands s Penang 1965–66; teacher
Causewayend p s Aber 1968–75, asst head from 1975

FLETT William   MA 1911
no longer on GC reg

FLETT or Kilpatrick, Williamina Smith
                        BSc 1944 *1946
MEd(Tor) 1976
Toronto: teacher St Clement's s for girls 1960–63,
Don Mills C I 1963–69, asst head maths G. S. Henry
s s from 1969

FLOCKHART David   BSc 1936

FLOCKHART Helen Rattray   BCom 1929
d 17.12.65

FLORENCE Alexander Leslie   MB ChB 1950
g p Tawa, Wellington NZ from 1966

FLORENCE Elsie Mary   MA 1932
teacher Aberdeensh from 1933: Buchanhaven s,
Chapel of Garioch s

FLORENCE Janet Leslie   MA 1911 *1912
retd 1954
d Stirling 4.2.77

FLORENCE or Chalmers, Patricia Barbara   MA 1951

FLORY Janet   MA 1952
retd; resid Ellon
d Ellon 31.1.79 *AUR* XLVIII 233

FLOWERDEW Richard Edward   MB ChB 1908
d Nairobi 9.12.71 *AUR* XLIV 427

FORBES or Robb, Agnes Kate   MB ChB 1932
part time school m o Leicester from 1965

FORBES Alexander   MA 1928
head Ferryhill p s Aber 1964–67; retd; resid Tarland
d 8.8.81

FORBES Alexander   *MA 1948
dep rector Fraserburgh acad from 1969

FORBES Alexander Riach   MB ChB 1919
retd: resid Tadworth

FORBES Allan Massie   BSc(agr) 1951
nutrit advis Farm Feed Formulators Northallerton
from 1970

FORBES Andrew   MB ChB 1932
  d 3.12.73 *AUR* XLV 448

FORBES or McDonald, Annabella Allan   *MA 1942
  prin teacher maths Hamilton g s Lanarksh from 1970

FORBES or Robertson, Annie   MA 1907

FORBES or Paul, Barbara Anderson   *MA 1947
  Cambridge electron accelerator Harvard univ 1956−62; teacher Fr Lexington publ s Mass USA 1964−66, 68−71

FORBES Charles Brown   MA 1922
  retd 1964; dir Aber FC from 1936
  d Aber 15.4.80 *AUR* XLVIII 441

FORBES Charlotte Clark   *MA 1913
  retd 1952
  d Daviot Abdnsh 11.1.80

FORBES or Fraser, Christina   MA 1924
  resid Beauly

FORBES or Angus, Christina Findlay   MA 1951
  d 2.8.77

FORBES David Albert   MB ChB 1943
  d Chesterfield 18.10.70 *AUR* XLIV 111

FORBES Donald Fraser Christopher   BSc(for) 1952
  m Innerleithen 11.7.64 Agnes H. Dodds civ serv d of James W. D. Peebles

FORBES Eleanor Margaret   MA 1924
  secy posts mainly with ICI Lond 1924−36
  m Aber 23.7.36 James P. Norrie BSc(eng)(Glas) consult. mining eng RST Rhodesia s of William N. Cape Town
  husb *d* Cape Town 1978

FORBES or Rendle, Elizabeth Ann   MA 1928
  resid Okehampton

FORBES Elsie McKenzie   MA 1916
  no longer on GC reg

FORBES Etta Broughton   MA 1914
  resid Tunbridge Wells
  d 31.3.78

FORBES The Hon Sir Ewan   MB ChB 1944
  Bart JP
  resid Brux Alford

FORBES Ewen Maitland   MA 1955

FORBES Francis Dawson   MB ChB 1938
  d Hartford Huntingdon 29.6.62 *AUR* XXXIX 386

FORBES Frank Mathieson   MA 1947 LLB 1949
  solicr; retd 1975

FORBES Frederick Alastair   MB ChB 1939
  g p Aber from 1946; retd

FORBES Frederick Stanley Arnot   MB ChB 1941 DPH 1947
  JP 1971 O St J(Wales) 1973
  g p Chepstow from 1949

FORBES George   MA 1905
  d Peterhead 15.8.68 *AUR* XLIII 77

FORBES George Barnet   MB ChB 1937 MD 1951
  FRCPath 1963
  consult. path. Kent & Canterbury hosp Canterbury from 1948

FORBES George Wilson   MB ChB 1942
  g p Watton-at-Stone from 1952

FORBES Gordon   BCom 1923
  resid Tunbridge Wells
  d 28.3.76

FORBES or Pratt, Grace Christina   MA 1948
  Aber: teacher maths Hilton acad 1970−73, year mistress Northfield acad from 1973

FORBES Ian   MA 1951
  Aber: teacher 1952−73, asst head guid from 1973

FORBES Ian Mackenzie   MA 1948
  PhD(Glas) 1977
  C of S min Dalziel par ch Motherwell 1966−77, Kemnay par ch from 1977

FORBES Isabelle Mary   *MA 1946
  Glasg: sen teacher mod lang Langside coll 1964−70, head lang dept Cardonald coll from 1970

FORBES Isobel Munro   MA 1947
  asst head/guid The Gordon Schools Huntly from 1971

FORBES or Adamson, Jane   *MA 1923
  resid Cullen

FORBES Jane Mearns Mackie   MA 1935
  Birm: teacher 1954−58, dep head 1958−60; Stonehaven: mus asst Mackie acad 1961−62, teacher Fetteresso and Arduthie p s till 1973; retd
  m Stonehaven 30.3.46 Douglas C. W. Stewart pol constable s of Agnes S. Shrewsbury; marr diss

FORBES or Campbell, Janet Jane   MA 1935
  teacher: head maths dept Bulstrode g s Hounslow 1955−68, head Green House Hounslow Manor s GLC 1968−74

FORBES or Kay, Janet Syme   MA 1949
  teacher North s Kirkcaldy from 1964

FORBES Jessie Margaret   MA 1925
  teacher James Clark s s Edin 1943−69; retd
  d 7.6.77

FORBES John   MB ChB 1900
  no longer on GC reg

FORBES John   MB ChB 1954
DA 1960
asst anaest Teesside from 1965
m Stockton-on-Tees 5.10.63 Winifred Peacock SRN
d of Alfred M. P. Stockton-on-Tees

FORBES John Alexander
                    MA 1947 MB ChB 1951 MD 1963
MRCGP 1962 FRCGP 1971
Southampton med s: sen lect commun med 1969–72,
prof primary med care from 1972

FORBES John Clark   MB ChB 1924
retd 1958; resid Aber
d Aber 29.6.79 *AUR* xlviii 351

FORBES John Edward   MA LLB 1952
solic John Wilson and Turnbull Falkirk from 1961

FORBES Lesley Lumsden Wilson   MA 1939
teacher Aber from 1941

FORBES Lyla Catherine   MB ChB 1922
d 19.1.71

FORBES or Innes, Margaret   MB ChB 1936

FORBES or Burnett, Margaret Elizabeth Alexandria
                                        BSc 1920
d Stockport 31.3.73

FORBES or Orr, Margaret Jane   MA 1921
d Rothesay 9.8.75 *AUR* xlvi 322

FORBES or Graham, Margaret Jean   MA 1949
resid Glasg

FORBES or Gray, Margaret Shepherd   MA 1928
retd 1969; resid Aber

FORBES or Millar, Margaret Thomson   *MA 1949
teacher: Aber acad 1955–57, Elgin acad 1957–58,
Nairn acad 1960–62, Perth acad 1963–65, Rothesay
acad 1966–68, asst prin mod lang Dunfermline h s
from 1969

FORBES Margaret Valentine   MA 1936
Aber: teacher Woodside p s from 1941

FORBES Mary Isabella   MA 1913
no longer on GC reg

FORBES or Middleton, Mary Isobel   MB ChB 1937
resid Broughty Ferry

FORBES or Shiach, Mildred   MA 1935
d Dumfries 16.2.63

FORBES Patricia Rose   MA 1951
teacher Inv r acad from 1954

FORBES Robert Fraser   MA 1913
no longer on GC reg

FORBES or Brittain, Rosa Jean   MA 1931
resid Calne

FORBES Stanley   *MA 1950
Oakbank s Aber: asst head 1961–66, dep head from
1966

FORBES William   *MA 1922
d Aber 21.12.69 *AUR* xliii 444

FORBES William Henry Brough   BSc(for) 1951

FORBES William Skene   MA 1952
no longer on GC reg

FORBES or Sim, Willma Coutts   MA 1953
Inf Mist. endorsement 1969 Inst of Ling Exam Ger
Grade II 1973 Intermed Grade Pts I and II 1974
Aber: teacher Mile-End s 1967–73, Fr and Ger in
prim. schools from 1973

FORD William   MA 1946
d Elba –.7.73 *AUR* xlv 321

FORDYCE or Donovon, Elizabeth Jane   *MA 1933
OBE 1968
retd 1972; resid Verwood
husb d 1976

FORDYCE Gordon Esslemont   MB ChB 1932
consult. surg N'cle-u-Tyne reg hosp board from
1952; retd 1975

FORGAN or Findlay, Margaret Rose
                        MA 1909 MB ChB 1912
retd 1957; resid Leven

FORGAN Robert
                    MA 1911 MB ChB 1915 *MD 1924
retd 1971
d Brentwood 8.1.76 *AUR* xlvi 414

FORGIE Alexander Davidson
                        MB ChB 1927 MD 1945
d Lond 11.6.64 *AUR* xl 400

FORGIE or Walker, Jane Ross   MB ChB 1934
resid Edin

FORMAN Bruce   *BSc 1949 PhD 1956
FRSA 1971
The Nature Conservancy: reg off. E. Anglia Norwich
1961–66, spec scient advis Lond 1966–67, conserv off.
(England) Lond 1967–74, dep dir England from 1974

FORMAN Frank   *MB ChB 1922 *MD 1932
d Israel 9.3.80 *AUR* xlix 67

FORRAI Gabriel Louis   MB ChB 1955
g p: Crook, Durh 1960–63, Ilford, Barking,
Dagenham from 1963

FORREST or Austin, Aileen   *BSc 1949
resid Sheffield

FORREST Alastair William Fordyce   MA 1950
Aber: dep head Cummings Park p s 1965–67,
Abbotswell p s 1967–69; head Causewayend p s
1969–71, Abbotswell p s from 1971

FORREST Alistair William *MB ChB 1927
FRCGP 1972
g p Aber 1954–74; retd
m(2) Aber 8.9.60 Agnes E. Whitter MB ChB 1951 *qv*

FORREST Elsie Marjorie MA 1940
teacher Fernielea p s Aber from 1961
m Aber 18.3.72 John M. Telfer MA(Edin) army/MN
s of Thomas M. T. Edin

FORREST James *MA 1899
no longer on GC reg

FORREST James Sim MA LLB 1950
employed Union Castle Mail Steamship Co Lond
and Capetown 1950–72; off. man. housing dept Edin
1972–75, chief asst admin from 1975

FORREST or Cowie, Jean Ailsa MA 1948
resid Edin

FORREST John *MA 1948
deceased

FORREST John Berry MA LLB 1950
ptnr Adam Thomson & Ross advoc Aber from
1954

FORREST Robert Andrew Dermod *MA 1914
d –.1.77 *AUR* xlvii 211

FORREST Stanley MA 1920 MB ChB 1924
coronation medal 1937 KPR medal 1963
hon m o Kenya police reserve 1949–63; retd; resid
Kenya
d Nairobi 17.5.81

FORRESTER Robert Smith MB ChB 1947
DCP(Lond) 1956 MRCPath 1963
DMJ(Path)(Lond) 1967 FRCPath 1974
surg cmdr RN retd; late consult. path. RN; c m o
HMS *Raleigh* Cornwall
m Stanwell 27.10.48 Elizabeth C. Wright nurse d of
Francis W. W. Aber

FORRESTER Thomas Martin
*BSc 1949 ᶜMB ChB 1957
d Aber 17.3.71 *AUR* xliv 216

FORSTER Dorothy BSc 1925 EdB 1945

FORSTER Frank Northman MB ChB 1944
g p Kemnay from 1970; retd 1977

FORSTER George Robert *BSc 1949
Plymouth marine lab: on scient staff dept sc and
indust res from 1951
m Plymouth 8.8.61 Alison M. Livingstone d of
Duncan L. Plymouth

FORSTER Margaret Gena
MA 1927 BSc 1929 *1930
retd 1972; resid Aber

FORSTER Reginald Arthur MB ChB 1905

FORSYTH Alexander BSc 1935
BA(OU) 1979
man. dir group of chem firms formed by T. & H.
Smith (latterly joined to Glaxo group) 1957–70; full
time member HIDB Inv 1970–75; OU stud. 1975–80;
retd

FORSYTH Archibald Goodall BSc(agr) 1949
d Edin 15.3.63 *AUR* xl 207

FORSYTH Barbara *MA 1922
retd 1962; resid Fortrose

FORSYTH Douglas Charles Tetley *BSc 1954
sen scient off. inst for marine environmental res
Edin from 1954; retd 1977

FORSYTH Gordon *MA 1948
war serv Scots Guards, 6th Gurkha Rifles India,
Middle East, Italy 1940–46; teacher Aberdeensh
1949–57; overseas civ serv educ off. Port of Spain
Trinidad 1958–69; lect coll of comm Aber from 1969
m(2) 14.2.58 Mairi W. Stewart d of James S. S.
MB ChB 1913 *qv*

FORSYTH Gordon *BSc 1949
ICI tech serv dept plastics div from 1965

FORSYTH John BSc 1951 *1952
lect agr entomology univ of Ghana 1959–62;
entomologist royal horticultural soc Wisley, Surrey
1963–66; lect nat hist dept of extra-mural stud.
Queen's univ Belf 1966–76, sen lect from 1976

FORSYTH John Alexander MA 1946
teacher: Engl/Lat Bracoden j s 1947–51, Lat/geog
Fordyce acad 1951–64; county drama advis from
1964

FORSYTH Robert McCallum BSc 1953
teacher: sc Portsoy j s s 1962–68, phys Banff acad
from 1968
m Aber 11.7.61 Velta Piksis MA 1953 *qv*

FORSYTH Stanley *MA 1939

FORSYTH Theodore *MA 1933
d Dumfries 21.8.74 *AUR* xlvi 109

FORSYTH William George Cameron PhD 1946
United Brands Co hq New York: i/c corporate res
and dev

FORTH Dorothy Mary Margaret MB ChB 1942
MRCGP
g p Cromarty 1962–76; m o Kingseat hosp Aber from
1976

FORTUNE Ronald Denis *BSc 1951
DSc(Gen)

FORTUNE William James MA 1908 *1910
Dip(Caen) 1907 Dip Phonetics(Marburg) 1908
retd 1951; resid Crieff
m(2) Crieff 21.11.68 Sybil J. E. Mackintosh MA(St

And) d of William F. M. Dun
d Crieff 15.1.81

FOSTER Margaret Stoddart   MA 1934
teacher: Cullen s s 1962–69, Whitehills 1969, Engl
Banff acad from 1969

FOSTER or Watson, Winifred Mary
                              MB ChB 1922 DPH 1927
d Willington 21.8.68 *AUR* XLIII 80

FOTHERINGHAM or Thomson, Euphemia Mary
                              MA 1929
resid Comrie

FOTHERINGHAM Ian King   *BSc(eng) 1948

FOTHERINGHAM Ian Murray   *BSc 1952

FOTHERINGHAM Thomas   BCom 1923
no longer on GC reg

FOTHERINGHAM William Milne   MB ChB 1931
part time indust m o BTR from 1942

FOUBISTER Donald MacDonald   BSc 1924
no longer on GC reg

FOUBISTER John Bichan
                    MA 1901 BSc 1904 MB ChB 1914
d Aber 15.12.68 *AUR* XLIII 208

FOUBISTER Thomas Benjamin
                    MA 1936 MB ChB 1941
g p Echt from 1955

FOUBISTER William James   BSc(eng) 1949
MICE 1951 MIWE 1955 FIMunE 1973
civ eng: Paisley corp 1949–51, Aber c c 1951–62; div
road surv Aber c c 1962–75; area road surv Grampian
reg c from 1975

FOUIN Francois Louis Pierre   MB ChB 1954
MRCGP 1966
g p Cults/Culter dist from 1959

FOWLER Alexander Burn   BSc(agr) 1928

FOWLER or Lewes, Alice Lyon   MA 1908
d 28.6.61 *AUR* XXXIX 273

FOWLER Andrew   MB ChB 1916
d Aber 18.11.71 *AUR* XLIV 317

FOWLER or Hardie, Catherine Jane   MA 1925
resid Aber

FOWLER Edna Violet Moir   *MA 1949
teacher Inverurie acad from 1959

FOWLER Elijah   MB ChB 1939
g p Stockport from 1946

FOWLER Elizabeth Fordyce   MA 1921
d Aber 25.11.71 *AUR* XLIV 319

FOWLER James Archibald   MB ChB 1953
g p Victoria BC Canada from 1959

FOWLER James John   *MA 1923
d 11.10.65 *AUR* XLII 86

FOWLER Joanna Aitken   MA 1915
no longer on GC reg

FOWLER or Smith, Mary Jean
                              MA 1933 *MEd 1948
sen educ psych Dun 1960–72; retd
m Aber 8.7.50 Stewart F. Smith civ serv

FOWLER Thomas Mair   MB ChB 1936
promoted col RAMC 1964; retd 1971; resid Ellon

FOWLIE or Finlayson, Anna Beatrice   MA 1935
resid Hawick

FOWLIE George Gordon   BSc 1941 *1947
MInst P
Nobel's Explosives Co Stevenston Ayrsh: sen plant
man. 1970–73, comp safety dept man. from 1973

FOWLIE Hugh   MA 1920 BSc(agr) 1921
d 1941

FOWLIE or Sparke, Gertrude Elizabeth   MA 1930
resid Aber

FOWLIE or Watmough, Jessie Robertson   MA 1933
teacher: Cleethorpes 1951–70; retd; resid Humber-
ston Grimsby

FOWLIE John   MA 1926
d Aber 6.3.70 *AUR* XLIII 445

FOWLIE Mary Susan   MA 1910
d Aber 24.11.77

FOWLIE Spencer Stephen   MA 1912
retd 1956; resid Buckie
d Elgin 17.2.79 *AUR* XLVIII 226

FOX Andrew Fraser   MA 1939
Broughton, Peeblessh: head cent p s from 1952

FOX Edgar Alexander   MB ChB 1949
g p Bishop Auckland from 1951

FRAIN or Grant, Elizabeth Rae   *MA 1922
resid Aber

FRAIN Ian Miller   MA 1951
head Laurencekirk s s from 1965; provost burgh
Laurencekirk from 1960; chmn Kincardine Deeside
dist c from 1974

FRANCE Ronald Spalding   MA 1946
chmn and man. dir J. Haighton & Sons Nantwich;
gen comm of Inland Revenue Crewe from 1961

FRANCIS Jacqueline Olive Priscilla McKay
                                          MA 1947

FRANÇOIS Charles Arthur　MB ChB 1928

FRANKLIN Montague　MB ChB 1938
g p Glasg from 1948

FRASER Alan John　MA 1928

FRASER Alan Norman　BSc(eng) 1932

FRASER Alastair Hugh　BSc(agr) 1955

FRASER Albert Grant　MB ChB 1943
DObstRCOG 1961 FRCGP 1973
g p Aber from 1948

FRASER Alexander　MA 1951

FRASER Alexander Birnie　MB ChB 1949
no longer on GC reg

FRASER Alexander Mackenzie
　　　　　　　　　　MB ChB 1924 DPH MD 1929
d Inv 27.7.61 *AUR* xxxix 281

FRASER Alexander Skinner　MA 1930
d Aber 18.2.67 *AUR* xlii 369

FRASER Alfred　BSc(agr) 1921
d 7.9.69

FRASER Alistair Mearns　*BSc 1950

FRASER Allan　BSc(for) 1950

FRASER Allan Henry Hector
　　　BSc 1925 MB ChB 1928 *MD 1929 DSc 1953
d Aber 12.7.79 *AUR* xlviii 351

FRASER or Murray, Anita Garden　BSc 1947
resid Currie

FRASER Annie　MA 1936
d Aber 1.11.76

FRASER or Jamieson, Annie　*MA 1939

FRASER Archibald Stewart　*BSc 1955
lect geog: univ of Auckland NZ 1961–65, later univ
of W Aust, Perth; sen lect Flinders univ of S Aust
Bedford Park from 1967
m Beverley W Aust 20.5.63 Sarah M. Barrett-Lennard
farm./banker d of Geoffrey B.-L. Beverley

FRASER Arthur　MA 1906
no longer on GC reg

FRASER or Walker, Bessie　MA 1934
resid Haddington

FRASER Campbell Victor　MB ChB 1953
g p Bedford from 1954

FRASER Catherine Margaret　MA 1944
teacher Quarryhill p s Aber from 1954

FRASER Charles George　BSc(eng) 1953

FRASER or Goodbody, Charlotte Mary　*BSc 1951
part-time dem zool dept univ of W.I. Kingston
Jamaica from 1956

FRASER Christine Grace　MA 1954 LLB 1956
solic Inv: ptnr MacArthur & Co from 1967
m Killearnan 30.10.76 Daniel MacWilliam

FRASER or Sutherland, Constance Elizabeth Anderson
　　　　　　　　　　MA 1947 LLB 1950
lect in law s of bus. man. stud RGIT Aber from 1967
marr diss

FRASER David Edward　MB ChB 1949
FRCGP 1973
g p Bucksburn from 1955

FRASER Donald　BSc(agr) 1922
no longer on GC reg

FRASER Donald　MB ChB 1929
retd 1971; resid Winchester

FRASER Donald Edward Kerr　BSc(eng) 1955
MICE 1968
D. Logan: asst civ eng Gartcosh Strip mill 1959–62,
sub ag Dunbar cement works 1962–63, sub ag Tay
road bridge 1963–66; W A Fairhurst & Ptnrs Dun:
asst civ eng 1966–68, sen civ eng from 1968
m Invergordon 5.9.62 Marguerite C. G. Mackenzie
Queen's nurse d of Thomas A. M. Invergordon

FRASER Donald Robertson　*MA 1937 BD 1942
C of S min Balquhidder par ch from 1973

FRASER Donald William　MA 1955

FRASER or Simpson, Dorothy Mary
　　　　　　　　　　BSc 1952 PhD 1955
MRC fell. Birm 1956–58
resid Hartlepool

FRASER Douglas James　MB ChB 1934

FRASER Douglas McLaren　MB ChB 1949
g p Swallowfield from 1959

FRASER Douglas Morrison Milne
　　　　　　　　　　MA 1913 MB ChB 1916
d 17.3.63

FRASER Duncan　*BSc 1933 PhD 1951
secy for Asia and Aust overseas council Edin
1965–71; retd; resid Kiltarlity

FRASER or Ross, Elizabeth　MA 1930
resid Fearn

FRASER or Wisely, Elizabeth Ann Mutch　MA 1927
teacher: spec asst maths Albyn s for girls Aber from
1948; retd
d Aber 15.11.77

FRASER or Macdonald, Elizabeth Clark
                               MB ChB 1936
part-time g p/PH and Treasury med serv 1942–68;
resid Brisbane

FRASER Elizabeth Donaldina
            MA 1941 *EdB 1943 PhD 1955
Aberd: sen lect psych 1963–64, Anderson prof
psych from 1964; dean fac Arts and Soc sciences
1976–79

FRASER or Quarman, Emily   MA 1931
resid Balham Lond

FRASER or Lyall, Fiona Jane
            MB ChB 1954 DPH 1958
Grampian reg councillor Mearns 1974; g p
Laurencekirk and the Mearns

FRASER Forbes John   MA 1949
teacher Longside s 1950–69; farm. Longside from
1969

FRASER Francis Stewart Gordon   *MA 1925
d Monifieth 15.7.62 *AUR* XL 91

FRASER George   MA 1917
retd 1953; resid Aber

FRASER George Angus Paterson   MB ChB 1927
retd 1965; resid Bourne
d Lond 5.2.79

FRASER George Knowles
            MA 1911 BSc 1912 BSc(for) 1919
no longer on GC reg

FRASER George Paterson   *BSc 1949 PhD 1952

FRASER Georgina Fowler   MA 1911
no longer on GC reg

FRASER Hector Alexander   *MA 1932
Edin: group man. Standard Life Assur co 1961–69,
asst gen man. 1969–72; retd 1972
hon secy Faculty of Actuaries 1968–70
wife *d* 21.8.66
m(2) 7.4.67 Christine E. Walker

FRASER or Wilson, Helen   MA 1910
no longer on GC reg

FRASER or Wilkie, Helen   MA 1924
no longer on GC reg

FRASER or McLean or Macdonald, Helen Cumming
                               MA 1931
teacher: Bridge of Don 1945–68, Scotstown 1968–69
resid Fintray Aberdeensh

FRASER or Sutherland, Helen Elizabeth   BSc 1952
resid Cults

FRASER Helen Mackenzie   MA 1944
teacher: Milne's h s Fochabers 1950–60, Mortlach

s s Dufftown 1960–67, Hopeman s s 1967–70; resid
Dufftown
m Aber 12.12.70 Alan D. Bennett civ serv

FRASER or Clarke, Helen Susanna   MB ChB 1942
resid Lond

FRASER Henry   MA 1927
head Inchgarth p s Aber 1965–70; retd; resid Aber

FRASER Hugh Simon   MB ChB 1936 MD 1938
chest phys Wessex reg hosp board 1948–73; retd;
resid Llandrindod Wells Wales

FRASER Iain Alexander   MB ChB 1943

FRASER Ian Charles   MB ChB 1954
DTM & H(Lond) 1963 DPH(Lond) 1964
DIH(Lond) 1965 MFCM 1972
m o 2nd Bn Royal Tank regt Libya, Germany, UK
1959–60; RAMC: army health spec 1961–68, sen spec
in army health; lt-col from 1968; retd 1973; univ m o
Leeds from 1973
m Montrose 31.5.58 Lancetta D. Archibald secy d of
Lancelot A. Montrose

FRASER Ian Ross   *MA 1953 MEd 1955
prin teacher geog Elgin acad 1960–66; rector Waid
acad Anstruther 1966–71, Inv r acad from 1971

FRASER or Gill, Isabel Mary   MA 1947
teacher: Boddam 1963–64, Peterhead cent s 1964–
65, Kinnoul s Perth 1966–69, Quarryhill p s Aber
from 1974; resid Milltimber Aber

FRASER or Wood, Isabella Macdonald   MA 1948
resid Brora

FRASER or Hvistendahl, Isabella Milne   MA 1917
resid Tonsberg Norway
husb *d* 1972

FRASER Isabella Murray   MA 1927
no longer on GC reg

FRASER James   MB ChB 1914
d France 5.4.63 *AUR* XL 201

FRASER James   MA 1919
d Alness 18.9.62 *AUR* XL 85

FRASER James   MA 1928
teacher: Dingwall acad 1951–69; retd; resid Inv

FRASER James   MA 1929
Petrol Indust serv; retd 1974; resid S Croydon

FRASER James Cobban   MA 1929 MB ChB 1939
g p Aber 1948–67; retd; resid Inverurie

FRASER James Edward   *MA 1953
Scot. office: p secy to perm. under-secy of state
1960–62, p secy to parl under secy of state 1962; prin
Home and Health dept 1962–64, Cabinet office 1964–
66, HM Treasury 1966–68, SHHD 1968–69; asst secy

SHHD 1970–76; under secy Scottish off. (Fin. Div) from 1976

FRASER James Fowler   MA 1914 *MB ChB 1922
retd; resid Aber
d Aber 23.2.79 *AUR* xlviii 226

FRASER James George Davidson   BSc(eng) 1937

FRASER James Henry   *MA 1899

FRASER Jamesina Rose   MA 1911
d 4.8.72 *AUR* xlv 124

FRASER Jane Ellen   *MA 1910
d Aber 9.1.76 *AUR* xlvi 414

**FRASER or Kestner, Jean Grace Sutherland
                                        *MA 1941**
scient information off. Commonwealth Bureau of agr econ Oxford from 1965

FRASER or Hunt, Jeannie Drummond   MA 1911
no longer on GC reg

FRASER or Maclean, Jemima   MA 1922
teacher: Kinross j s s 1946–65: town councillor 1956–59; retd; resid Aber

FRASER Jessie Elspet   MA 1937
teacher Grantown g s from 1948; retd 1977

FRASER or Florence, Joan Mary   MA 1936
teacher: Ross-shire 1938–40, Aber 1941–47 and from 1958; retd 1975

FRASER John   MA 1914 BD 1919
d Aber 9.8.63 *AUR* xl 302

FRASER John   MB ChB 1937 MD 1954
med supt Astlie hosp Edin 1949–76

FRASER John Annand   MA 1919 DD 1951
Chaplain to HM The Queen 1952–64, extra Chaplain from 1964
C of S min Aberdalgie & Dupplin 1960–70; conv bus. comm of Gen Ass. 1962–67; conv gen admin comm of Gen Ass. 1962–67; chmn judicial comm of Gen Ass. 1962–66; chmn C of S Trust 1962–66; member Broadcasting Council for Scot. 1963–67; retd 1970; resid Perth

FRASER John Milner Ross   MA 1949
teacher: Mile End p s Aber 1950–69, Tulliallan p s Fife from 1973

FRASER John Stuart   MB ChB 1953
g p East Bridgford from 1959

FRASER Kenneth   MA 1921
no longer on GC reg

**FRASER Kenneth Boyd
                    MB ChB 1940 *MD 1950 DSc 1961**
FRSE 1961

res fell. (Nuffield award) Walter and Eliza Hall inst Aust 1951–52; res fell. (NIHA award) dept genetics Glas 1959–61; sen lect inst virol Glas 1961–66; prof microbiol Queen's univ Belf from 1966

FRASER or Fraser, Leslie Winifred   MB ChB 1942
part-time dem bact dept Melb univ Aust 1951–52; resid Belfast

FRASER Malcolm   BSc(agr) 1955
estate man. Lovat Estates from 1973
m Inv 12.8.62 Juliana S. Ferguson d of Hugh F. Muir of Ord

FRASER Margaret Ann   MA 1920
d Inv 30.5.66 *AUR* xli 338

FRASER or Ramsay, Margaret Elizabeth   MA 1946
teacher Aber 1947–53; resid Bieldside Aber

**FRASER Margaret Fowlie
                    MA 1917 MB ChB 1921 DPH 1930**
resid Milltimber Aber

FRASER Margaret Helen   MA 1939
teacher Grantown g s from 1961; retd 1977

FRASER Margaret Lilias Ross   BSc 1923
retd 1963
d 14.2.75

FRASER Margaret Rose   *MA 1916
no longer on GC reg

FRASER Mary   MA 1911
d Forres 24.1.74 *AUR* xlvi 446

FRASER or Grigor, Mary Ann   MA 1941

FRASER or Brown, Mary Bella   MA 1933
teacher: Cults p s 1959–66, Cults acad 1966–74, Cults new p s from 1974; retd 1975

FRASER or Chivas, Mary Gault   MA 1942

FRASER or Hutcheon, Matilda Margaret   MA 1927
no longer on GC reg

FRASER or Jones, Murdina Isabella   MA 1911
retd 1952; resid Tain
d Tain 26.2.75 *AUR* xlvi 320

FRASER or Mathieson, Muriel Alice   MA 1943
teacher Aber: King St p s 1958–60, high s for girls 1960–70, Muirfield p s from 1970

FRASER Muriel Gordon   MA 1940

FRASER or Gray, Muriel Winifred   MA 1938
d Banchory 20.7.78
husb *d* 24.1.69

FRASER Norman Grant   MB ChB 1950
MRCPsych 1973
res fell. psychiat univ of Pittsburgh USA 1959–60;

consult. psychiat and dep phys supt Woodilee hosp Lenzie, Glasg from 1961
m Aber 30.12.61 Daphne Inglis d of William H. I. Aber

FRASER Ogilvie Murray   MB ChB 1927
RAF: civ m o Felixstowe 1959–62, dep pres med board off. and aircrew selection centre Biggin Hill 1962–76; resid Bath

FRASER Olive   *MA 1931
Chancellor's Medal for Poetry (Cantab) 1935
d Aber 9.12.77 *AUR* xlvii 359

FRASER Ranald Lamont   MA 1917
d 1965

FRASER Robert
　　　　　MB ChB 1935 DPH 1937 MD 1946
chest phys NE reg hosp board from 1948; retd 1977

FRASER Robert James Alexander   MB ChB 1939
clin sen lect neuro-surg Aberd from 1958

FRASER Robert Sherriffs   MA 1925
teacher: maths/sc Girvan h s 1926–43, maths Central s s Aber 1943–49; prin maths: Old Aber s s 1949–51, Hilton s s Aber 1951–66; retd; resid Cults Aber
m Stonehaven 21.8.48 Kathleen M. B. Smith teacher d of William F. S. Stonehaven
d Cults 5.5.78 *AUR* xlvii 356

FRASER Ronald George Juta   *BSc 1924 PhD 1926
exec secy internat council of scient unions 1949–63; retd; resid Lower Hutt NZ

FRASER Ronald McWilliam   MB ChB 1954
LMCC 1970 CCFP(Can) 1973
g p Clarkston 1958–62, Fochabers 1962–66, Hinton, Alberta from 1966

FRASER or Stellman, Rose Margaret   MB ChB 1939
MFCM 1972
sen m o London boro' of Bexley health dept 1970–74; prin m o child health Bexley health dist from 1974

FRASER or Gray, Sheila   MA 1929
resid Inverurie

FRASER or Campbell, Sheila   MA 1944
resid Ardrossan

FRASER or Spensley, Sheila Ross   MA 1953 EdB 1955

FRASER Simon John Coulter
　　　　　MB ChB 1893 MD 1903
d 30.5.67

FRASER Thomas   BSc 1923 *1924
retd 1966; resid Inv

FRASER Thomas Alexander
　　　　　MB ChB 1929 MD 1934
d 7.12.65 *AUR* xli 249

FRASER Thomas Donald Noble   MA 1926
no longer on GC reg

FRASER or Scott, Violet Muriel   BSc 1923
no longer on GC reg

FRASER Walter Allan   MA 1906
d Findhorn 18.7.61 *AUR* xxxix 273

FRASER William   BSc(eng) 1936

FRASER William Augustus Carr   DSc 1931

FRASER William Donald   BSc(agr) 1942

FRASER William Elrick
　　　　　MA 1935 BSc 1936 *1938 PhD 1957
Aberd: sen lect geol and mineralogy 1963–70, reader from 1970

FRASER William Gordon   *MA 1914
d 5.1.66

FRASER William Jack   *BSc 1955

FRASER William Thompson   MA LLB 1952
various leg. posts 1952–70; founder/ptnr Fraser & Mulligan advoc Aber from 1970; part-time member Rent Assessment panel for Scot. from 1975; part-time lect agr law Aberd from 1976

FRASER or Masson, Winifred Margaret   MA 1946
teacher Lusaka Girls' s Zambia from 1964

FRATER Clifford Sydney Horler   BSc(eng) 1947
reg army off. col home and overseas from 1948; resid Farnham
m Andover 21.4.51 Grace P. M. Curtis

FRAZER Allan Cameron   *MA 1934 LLB 1937
Chevalier in the Order of Orange Nassau 1972
sen ptnr Hagart & Burn-Murdoch WS Edin from 1948; hon consul for Neths in Edin from 1965; rector's assessor Edin 1967–68; dean consular corps Edin–Leith 1976–77; pres Edin Sir Walter Scott Club 1975

FRAZER Fred Young   BSc(eng) 1928
d Aber 20.12.63 *AUR* xl 302

FREELAND Alexena Walker   MA 1948
teacher Aber from 1963

FREELAND or Morrice, Helen   MA 1950

FRENCH or Ferguson, Christina Moir   MA 1925
no longer on GC reg

FRENCH Isobel   *MA 1942
prin teacher hist Elgin acad from 1969

FRENCH William George   MB ChB 1942
g p Stonehaven from 1951

FREW or Robertson, Christina Rose   MA 1902
no longer on GC reg

FRIEDLAND Garson   MB ChB 1926

FRIEDLÄNDER or Young, Ernestine Hannah
                                    MA 1950

FRITH Anthony Charles Gauvain   BSc(for) 1945

FUGLESTVED Per Bengt   MA 1951

FULLERTON or Caldwell, Enid   MB ChB 1951
    Founder Member R C Psych 1971: Member Brit
Psycho-Analytical Soc 1976
consult. psychiat Lansdowne clin Glasg 1963–66;
assoc psychiat McLean hosp Belmont Mass from
1966

FULLERTON Harold Williams
                    MA 1925 *MB ChB 1931 MD 1937
    d 14.7.70 *AUR* XLIV 28

FULLERTON or Bothwell, Isobel   MA 1946
    resid Stratford-on-Avon

FULLERTON John   MA 1938
    min United ch of Canada Trail BC from 1972

FULLERTON Robert Gerrard
            BSc 1924 *MA 1925 PhD 1932 MB ChB 1938
    g p Aber 1939–66; boarding m o min of soc security
Aber from 1966
d Aber 12.4.79 *AUR* XLVIII 228

FULLERTON Thomas Anderson   MA 1901
    no longer on GC reg

FULTON Graeme Lascelles   *BSc 1946

FULTON James Graham   BL 1952
    OBE FCIS
ptnr Brander & Cruickshank advoc Aber from 1952;
dir: Aber Univ Press from 1959, East of Scot. Trust
from 1963, Scot. Fishermen's Organis from 1973, East
of Scot. Investments Managers from 1975; chmn Scot.
Herring Producers' Assoc from 1957

FYFE Albert   BSc 1948
    lect Enfield coll of tech 1961–74, sen lect Middx
polytech Enfield from 1974
m Barnet 5.8.61 Georgina R. Smith secy d of Arthur S.
Lond

FYFE Edwin Reginald   MB ChB 1951
    g p Culross from 1962
d Dunfermline 1.2.68 *AUR* XLII 375

FYFE Forest William   MA 1933 MB ChB 1937
    prof anat Dalhousie univ Nova Scotia 1964–78;
retd

FYFE George   MA 1930

FYFE Grace Cameron   MA 1938
    teacher: Castleton and Catterline p s Kincardine
1939–47, Pitlochry h s 1959–64, maths Breadalbane

acad Aberfeldy 1964–72, Perth g s from 1972
m Dunnottar 27.9.47 William J. Duguid (*d* 1972)

FYFE or Boyle, Isabella Stuart Chalmers   MA 1910
    no longer on GC reg

FYFE Malcolm Hewer Durke Findlay
                        BSc(agr) 1953 MSc 1965
    dir agr S Cameroons 1960–63; MMB res fell. Aberd
1963–65; agr econ NOSCA 1965–69, sen agr econ
1969–75; dir studies from 1975
m Buea, S Cameroons 12.5.61 Avril A. Pitcher d of
Raymond P. P. Cape Town

FYFE or McAusland, Sheila Glennie
                                MA 1941 LLB 1947
    d 13.11.81

FYFE William Stuart Fraser   BSc(agr) 1954

FYFFE or McCutcheon, Joan   MA 1948

FYVIE or Campbell, Agnes   MA 1933
    teacher: Newhall p s Ross & Cromarty 1958–63,
Drumsmittal p s from 1963
husb *d* 1967

FYVIE Elizabeth Mary   *MA 1937

FYVIE or Raven, Elizabeth Milne   *MA 1938
    resid Aber

FYVIE Norman Gammie   MB ChB 1954
    d 17.7.75

GADSBY James Burnet   MB ChB 1944
    g p Burnley from 1952

GADSBY Norman Burnet   MB ChB 1919
    d Aber 8.6.69 *AUR* XLIII 211

GADSBY or Main, Sheila Mary   *MA 1950
    teacher Engl Penicuik 1952–53, Eskisehir coll
Turkey 1956–58, Portobello h s from 1966

GAFFRON David John   MA 1948
    teacher Ashley Road p s Aber 1949–74; retd

GAFFRON Sonia Anne   MA 1955
    Assoc Memb Market Res Soc 1965
A C Nielsen Co. Oxford 1960–64, Lond: market res
Monsanto 1964–66, United Biscs 1966–70; teacher
maths ILEA from 1970

GAGE Albert   MB ChB 1951
    MRCPsych 1971 MA(Cantab) 1977
consult. ch psychiat: Manc 1961–63, Cambridge from
1963

GAIR Charles Ian Mackenzie   BSc(agr) 1945
    dir Royal Highland and Agr Soc of Scot. Edin
1966–73; chmn nat dairy exam board Lond 1969–71;
member north of Scot. milk marketing board Inv
from 1967; chmn Scot. Milk Records Assoc Paisley
1977–79

GAIR or Doig, Janette Jane Elizabeth Henrietta
MA 1913

GAIR or Roberts, Margaret Milne   MB ChB 1925
resid Craigellachie

GAIT James   MA 1929
rector St Palladius' ch Drumtochty, St Andrew's ch Fasque and St Laurence's ch Laurencekirk from 1954

GAITER John Alexander   MB ChB 1924
d 12.12.70

GALBRAITH or Brameld, Edith Minnie Staveley
MA 1903
no longer on GC reg

GALBRAITH Frederic Winbolt Staveley   MA 1904
no longer on GC reg

GALBRAITH or Wilson, Jean   MA 1954
teacher: Woodside p s 1957–59, Goodlyburn j s s Perth 1960–64; resid Crieff

GALL Annie Catto   MA 1934
d Aber 12.1.68 *AUR* XLII 371

GALL Christian Jane Wedderburn   BSc(agr) 1933
d 12.8.77

GALL or Rintoul, Eliza   MA 1923
teacher Kennoway Fife 1924–27
resid Abergavenny

GALL or Brown, Elizabeth   MA 1928
resid Edin

GALL Frederick   BSc(eng) 1945

GALL or Mackay, Harrietta   MA 1950

GALL Henderson Alexander   *MA 1952
with Reuters in S Af and the Congo 1960–63; foreign correspondent ITN worldwide incl Vietnam 1965–75; newscaster/for. corr ITN from 1970; publ *Gold Scoop* 1976; rector Aberd from 1978

GALL John Reid   MA 1912
d Aber 22.8.66 *AUR* XLI 337

GALL or Elmslie, Lilian Fyfe   MB ChB 1921
d Aber 15.1.76 *AUR* XLVI 415

GALL or Harvey, Margaret Joan   MA 1925
no longer on GC reg

GALLIE John MacLean   MA 1932
rector of St Machar's ch Bucksburn 1950–67; canon St Andrew's cath Aber from 1967
d Aber 12.12.77 *AUR* XLVII 359

GALLOWAY Alexander   MA 1921 MB ChB 1925
d Alresford 24.9.66 *AUR* XLI 244

GALLOWAY Alexander Ogilvy   MA 1907
d Tasmania 10.6.65 *AUR* XLI 239

GALLOWAY Ethel Lawrence Rutherford
MB ChB 1924
d Mansfield 30.6.62 *AUR* XL 90

GALLOWAY Ian Charles Robert
*MA 1952 Dip Ed 1955

GALLOWAY or Thompson, Jane Henderson
MA 1919 MB ChB 1922 MD 1959
MRCPsych 1973
consult. psychiat and dep med supt Northgate and dist mental deficiency hosp Morpeth 1952–67; hon med dir and consult. psychiat to Newcastle and dist counselling centre from 1965

GALLOWAY Margaret de Villeneuve   *MA 1930
d Aber 1975

GALLOWAY Maurice Edgar Emslie   BSc(agr) 1924
retd; resid Banff

GALLOWAY Rudolph William   MB ChB 1914
d 22.3.76 *AUR* XLVI 415

GALT George Gordon   *MA 1925
retd 1967; resid Banchory

GAMMIE Alastair James   *MA 1951 MEd 1956
Aberd: asst lect educ 1960–62, lect 1962–72, sen lect from 1972

GAMMIE Alexander Edward   *MB ChB 1919
d 27.12.70

GAMMIE Douglas Strachan   *MA 1930

GAMMIE James   *BSc(eng) 1944
supervis Bell tel labs N Andover Mass USA from 1956
m Providence Rhode Is Emily P. Stickney BFA (Rhode Is s of Design) advt man. d of Charles A. S. BA(Dartmouth) Lancaster Mass

GAMMIE John Wilson   MB ChB 1941
DA 1958
g p Elgin from 1946; spec anaest Elgin from 1967

GAMMIE Robert Petrie   MB ChB 1923 MD 1930
OBE 1967 MRCGP
retd 1966; resid Cambridge
wife d 24.6.71

GAPPER William Frederick
MB ChB 1930 DPH 1935
d 11.12.60

GARCIA-PINEDA Maria Dolores   PhD 1954
USA: biochem dept NYU 1961–62; investigator junta de energia nuclear Madrid from 1962

GARDEN Alexander   *BSc 1934
HMIS: Ayrsh 1948–59, Edin 1959–64, Orkney, Caithness, Sutherland from 1964
resid Lossiemouth

GARDEN Alexander Davidson   MB ChB 1924
   private med pract and res Lond 1925–28; private study econ Battle 1929–34; private aeronaut res (patients) Lond 1935–39; war serv major RAMC Gloucester 1940–43; g p and med/aeronaut res (patients) 1943–63; retd; resid Westcliff-on-Sea
d Westcliffe-on-Sea –.6.75

GARDEN Alexander Murray   MA 1909
   d Toronto 11.7.66

GARDEN Allan   *BSc 1952

GARDEN David William   MA 1922 BSc 1924
   prin teacher maths/sc Macduff h s till 1960; retd; resid Macduff

GARDEN Edwin   MB ChB 1924
   d Leytonstone 18.12.70 *AUR* XLIV 211

GARDEN Edwin Laurie   MA 1940
   d Aber 16.5.66 *AUR* XLI 342

GARDEN George   BSc 1945

GARDEN or Milne, Helen Davidson   MA 1927
   resid Fettercairn

GARDEN James   BL 1939
   ptnr Alexander George & Co solic (formerly George, Riddell & McPherson) Macduff from 1950

GARDEN James David   MB ChB 1953
   g p Timaru NZ from 1965

GARDEN James Taylor   BSc(agr) 1922
   retd 1959; resid Inverugie Peterhead

GARDEN James Waddell   MB ChB 1944
   anaest Stracathro hosp from 1953

GARDEN John Flett   *BSc 1953 PhD 1956
   FRIC 1964
sen lect Slough coll of tech 1962–63; dep head chem dept Portsmouth poly from 1963

GARDEN Lewis Beattie   *MA 1936
   C of S Edin: secy dep comm on soc serv 1961–66; dir soc serv from 1966
d Edin 6.10.80 *AUR* XLIX 69

GARDEN or Bruce, Linda Agnes
                              *BSc 1951 PhD 1954

GARDEN Margaret Helen   MA 1931
   teacher Auchmuty h s Glenrothes 1961–69; resid Edin
m Edin 10.12.60 William G. R. Bodie arch. and plan. s of John M. B. Aber

GARDEN Margaret Isabella   MA 1937
   resid Lossiemouth

GARDEN Ralph   BSc(eng) 1947
   prin teacher phys Perth acad from 1972

GARDEN Richard Ramsay
                    MA 1914 *MB ChB 1917 DPH 1920
   d Bristol 11.4.66 *AUR* XLI 243

GARDEN Robert Symon   MB ChB 1934
   FRCS 1969
hon consult. orthop surg Preston R I from 1975

GARDEN Ronald Jamieson Beattie
                              *MA 1930 M Litt 1977
   Aber: head Rosemount s s 1965–66, head Ruthrieston s s 1966–72; retd

GARDEN Ruth Jane Morgan   MA 1930 *MEd 1949
   d 5.1.67 *AUR* XLII 370

GARDEN or Shaw, Vera Margaret   MA 1938
   no longer on GC reg

GARDEN William John   MA 1922
   no longer on GC reg

GARDEN William Sim   MB ChB 1902 MD 1908
   no longer on GC reg

GARDINER Alexander   MA 1954 Dip Ed 1955
   prin teacher navigation Buckie h s from 1967
m Cullen 4.4.63 Isabella J. Mair bank clerkess d of John W. M. Cullen

GARDINER Alexander James   MB ChB 1927
   g p Coventry 1931–64; retd; resid Brixham

GARDINER Audrey Isabel   MA 1949

GARDINER James Aitken   *MA 1949

GARDINER James Martin   BCom 1926
   OBE 1967
retd; resid Bieldside Aber
m Buckie 3.3.34 Nell Sutherland

GARDINER James Stewart
                              MB ChB 1946 MD 1972
   MRCGP 1959 DIH 1973
g p Falkirk 1952–66; Grangemouth: part time works m o ICI 1959–66, full time 1966–74; div m o pharm div Alderley Park 1974–76, organics div Blackley from 1976; hon lect dep soc and occup med Dund from 1973

GARDINER Joseph   MB ChB 1943

GARDINER or Wells, Margaret Findlay
                              MB ChB 1929
   resid Totnes

GARDINER Margaret Hay   MA 1950

GARDINER or Rae, Mary Wilson   MA 1943
   teacher Engl Styles s s Gt Yarmouth 1967–73; soc worker Gt Yarmouth from 1974

GARDINER Robert   MB ChB 1951
   MFCM(RCP) 1972

sen asst m o Fife County health dept 1966–67, sen m o 1967–74; spec commun med Fife health board from 1974

GARDNER Alastair   *BSc 1951

GARDNER Alfred Gordon   MA 1937
asst clerk Middx c c 1964–65; GLC: prin solic 1965–69; dep solic and parliamentary off. 1970–74; dir leg. serv 1974–76; retd

GARLAND or Mitchell, Irene Stevenson   *MA 1936
part time teacher Fr/Lat Rosebery g s Epsom 1962–78; retd

GARLAND or Ross, Lilias May   *MA 1932
resid Aber
husb *d* 16.5.65

GARNER Mildred Maxine   PhD 1952
fell. Amer Inst of Indian stud. Poona India 1962–63; Wallace Eugene Rollins prof of relig Sweet Briar coll, Virginia USA from 1969

GARRIOCH or Begg, Isabel Mary Taylor   MA 1953
ptnr A. Begg & Son Elgin and Buckie from 1957; man. ptnr A. Begg Forres from 1973

GARROW Duncan Smith   MA 1910
d Inverurie 8.12.74

GARROW Frederick Campbell
        MA 1926 BSc 1928 *1930 MB ChB 1940
d Canso Nova Scotia 27.5.63 *AUR* XL 205

GARROW George   BSc 1950
head Thornhill p s Stirling from 1963

GARROW or Macleod, Isabel Mary   *MA 1935
head Raigbeg s Tomatin Invshire from 1968
husb *d* –.6.68

GARROW or Hart, Jane   *MA 1909
resid Edin

GARROW Robert Philip   MB ChB 1907 *MD 1911
d Strathkinness 1.3.71 *AUR* XLIV 208

GARSON Magnus Sinclair   *BSc 1949
PhD(Leeds) 1961 FIMM 1973
sen geol Zomba, Malawi govt 1962–64, prin geol 1964–66 (independence medal); prin scient off. inst geol sciences 1967–77 (gold medal of consolidated goldfields); seconded as proj man. UNDP Cairo 1972–74

GARSON Mary (Sister)   MA 1942
charitable foundations for destitute India, Sri Lanka; resid Worth Abbey Crawley

GARSON Ronald David   MB ChB 1953
Dip Board of Life Insur Med 1973
Canada: g p Port Arthur 1962–69; assoc med dir Metropolitan Life insur comp Ottawa from 1969; addiction res foundation Ottawa from 1969

GARVIE Denis Scott   BSc(eng) 1935
OBE

GARVIE Donald William   BSc(eng) 1933

GATHERER Alexander   MB ChB 1951 ᶜMD 1960
FFCM 1973
dep county m o h Northamptonsh 1962–65; m o h Reading from 1965

GATHERER or Coutts, Margery   MA 1948
resid Aber

GATHERER William Alexander   *MA 1948
HMIS Glasg 1961–73; head educ advis serv Edin from 1973

GATT or Bonsell, Williamina Forbes   MA 1946

GAUL or Norrie, Jean Margaret   MA 1951
resid Turriff

GAULD or Elder, Alice Mary   *MA 1946
asst teacher W. Kirby g s for girls Lea, Wirral from 1976

GAULD Charles Edward   BSc(agr) 1925
d Glen Tanar 17.8.62 *AUR* XL 92

GAULD Charlotte Mary   MA 1944
lect tech coll Aber 1972–78, sen lect from 1978

GAULD Edgar Norman   MB ChB 1937
FRCP(Can) 1972
chief dept of med Chedoke gen hosp Hamilton, Ontario 1960–70; consult. phys Hamilton Civic hosps from 1972

GAULD Edgar Reuben   MB ChB 1928
m o BR (S region) from 1954

GAULD Elspeth Jean   MA 1947
Aber: teacher Seaton p s 1964–70, Hazlehead p s 1970–71; dep head Walker Road p s 1972–74, asst head Springhill p s from 1974

GAULD Forbes Fraser
        BSc(mech eng) 1947 *BSc(civ eng) 1948
Canada: struct eng BLM Regina 1960–64; div eng Wright Engineers Vancouver 1964–67; sen eng Acres consult. serv Vancouver from 1967

GAULD or Struthers, Frances Charlotte   MA 1936
teacher: Engl/Fr/RI Paignton girls' s s Torbay 1965–69, Fr Hatton s s Sevenoaks 1969–71
widowed 1964
m(2) Torquay 5.4.69 John J. G. H. Harbord army off. (capt) (PSC)/educ off. s of John J. H. Gillingham

GAULD or Thompson, Isobel Margaret   MA 1943
teacher St Denis s for girls Edin from 1969

GAULD James   MB ChB 1939
FRCGP 1971
g p Aber from 1947

GAULD Jessie Ann   MA 1928

GAULD or Wallace, Katharine Winifred   MA 1926
Dip univ Poitiers 1926
teacher Watford 1962–67
m(2) Harrow 29.3.67 John Wagner JP retd bank man.
s of William F. W. Harrow

GAULD Lawson   MA 1950
RAF air crew WO 1941–46 India/Burma; head
King Edward p s from 1961

GAULD Mary Begg   *MA 1950 Dip Ed 1951
lect hist Aber coll of educ 1966–67, prin lect from
1967

GAULD Patricia Mary   BSc 1952

GAULD William Gordon James   BSc 1950
prin teacher maths/sc Kemnay s s from 1959

GAULD William Robertson
                    MB ChB 1935 MD 1938
FRCP 1962
reader clin med Aberd from 1975; retd

GAULD William Wallace   *MA 1943
under-secy DAFS Edin from 1972

GAULD or Greenaway, Winifred Ogston   MA 1942
Devon: teacher Mount Radford s Exeter 1957–67;
dir Dartmouth Potteries from 1969

GAVIN Alexander Cram   MB ChB 1901
no longer on GC reg

GAVIN or Ashcraft, Catherine Irvine
                    ***MA 1928 PhD 1931**
awarded Medal of Honour Helsinki univ Finland
1970
chief publications: non fict *Liberated France* 1955; fict
Madeleine 1957, *The Cactus and the Crown* 1961, *The
Fortress* 1964, *The Moon into Blood* 1966, *The Devil in
Harbour* 1968, *The House of War* 1970, *Give Me the
Daggers* 1972, *The Snow Mountain* 1973, *Traitors'
Gate* 1976
resid San Francisco

GAVIN or Calder, Doreen Mary Alexander
                    MA 1939
teacher Crumpsall Lanc inf s Manc from 1946; retd

GAVIN Evelyn Edith   *MA 1953
PhD(Strath) 1969
lect in law Strath 1964–70, sen lect from 1970
m Glasg 16.4.63 Christopher Iain MacDonald

GAVIN Hamish Crilley Reid   BSc(for) 1952
DPA(Vic BC)
for. BC for. serv Canada 1953–64; insp BC Lands serv
1964–66; govt of Canada: Manitoba: plan. nat parks
serv 1966–71, dev off. dept of reg econ expansion
1971–72, man. environmental protection serv from
1972

GAVIN John Abernethy   MB ChB 1945
reg m o DHSS Lond from 1975

GAVIN Lewis   *MA 1912
d Strichen 26.4.65 *AUR* xli 149

GAVIN Lewis Den Munro   MB ChB 1939 MD 1947
FRSTrop Med & Hyg 1943 MRCGP 1968 Memb
Soc Occup Med
exam med off. DHSS 1955–74; chief med off. Southern
Elect. Board from 1974

GAVIN Robert   MA 1926 LLB 1928
chief ILO mission to Congo 1960–61; chief off.
relations and conference serv and secy governing
body 1961–66; retd 1966; indust relations consult.
Ford Foundation India 1967–68; resid St Etienne du
Grès, France

GAVIN William   MB ChB 1925
h o mat. hosp Aber, RACH RAHSC 1925–26; g p
Yorks 1927–28; h o Park hosp Davyhulme, Manc
1929–30; locum g p Lancs 1930–32; g p Horwich,
Bolton 1932–66 (RAMC Europe and M. East 1939–
45); retd; resid Muchalls
m Penistone 7.7.39 Phyllis A. Lawrence SRN d of
George A. L. Dunford Bridge

GAWN Ernest King   MB CM 1895 MD 1904
no longer on GC reg

GEALS James   *MA 1929
teacher classics RGC Aber 1933–70; retd; resid
Cults Aber

GEARY Malcolm Walker   MA 1937
teacher Rosemount s s Aber till 1969

GEDDES Alexa Margaret Brownie   MA 1936
asst lib Lancs county lib Preston 1938–45; lib
Macaulay inst soil res Aber from 1945

GEDDES Alexander   MB ChB 1955
g p firm of Geddes, Gray and Davies Clacton-on-
Sea from 1957

GEDDES Alexander Ebenezer McLean
            ***MA 1906 *BSc 1907 DSc 1915 LLD 1956**
d 26.12.70 *AUR* xliv 145

GEDDES Alexander Marr   MB ChB 1909 MD 1928
d Aber 10.1.73 *AUR* xlv 223

GEDDES Alexander Slater   MA 1938 BD 1941
C of S min: Huntly par ch 1961–67, St Mary's par
ch Banff from 1967

GEDDES Charles John McWilliam   MB ChB 1930
MRCGP 1953
g p New Eltham and clin asst Eltham hosp from 1948

GEDDES or MacTaggart, Christina Carnegie
                    BSc(eng) 1947
resid Maidenhead

GEDDES Edith Elsa   *MA 1947
d Aber 14.1.72 *AUR* XLIV 433

GEDDES or Dawson, Elizabeth Taylor
                                       MA 1921 *BSc 1924
resid Grantown-on-Spey

GEDDES or Milton, Emma Margaret   MA 1926
resid Aber

GEDDES George   MB ChB 1932
g p Lancaster from 1935

GEDDES George Barclay   *MA 1946
teacher: Inverurie acad 1957–67, prin mod lang
Bankhead acad Aber from 1968

GEDDES Godfrey Power   *MA 1915
d Aber 27.6.64 *AUR* XL 398

GEDDES or Davidson, Helen Alisoun   MB ChB 1954
part time work in publ health clin from 1956; resid
Broughty Ferry

GEDDES or Feggetter, Helen Winchester
                                       MB ChB 1939
resid Keswick

GEDDES James   MA *BSc 1927
d Stirling 13.12.74 *AUR* XLVI 236

GEDDES or Law or Watson, Jean   MA 1938

GEDDES Jeannie   MA 1908
no longer on GC reg

GEDDES Jeannie   *MA 1920
resid Aber

GEDDES or Bradley, Jessie Watson   MA 1913
no longer on GC reg

GEDDES John   *BSc 1933
FRIC 1954
rector Peterhead acad 1964–75; retd

GEDDES John   BSc(agr) 1940
agr insp: Aber 1946–56, Edin from 1956
m Nott 28.10.50 Doris S. Daft

GEDDES John Fowlie   MA 1925
d Drumoak 24.1.70 *AUR* XLIII 445

GEDDES or Bain, Margaret   MA 1923
woman advis Inverurie acad 1950–66; retd

GEDDES Margaret Calder   MA 1948
Mackie acad Stonehaven: teacher 1958–69, asst
prin guid 1969–72, prin guid from 1972

GEDDES or Wood, Margaret Simpson   *MA 1932
resid Aberlour
d Elgin 29.4.80

GEDDES Marjory Inglis   *MA 1910
d Murtle Aber 24.12.60 *AUR* XXXIX 102

GEDDES Mary   MA 1936
d Fordyce 3.11.74

GEDDES or Shirriffs, Mary Allan   MA 1926
d 2.5.64

GEDDES Mary Thomson   MA 1925
retd; resid Drumoak

GEDDES Walter   BL 1949
Civ Def long serv medal 1966 Dip Scot. Council
Health Educ 1972
county clerk Peeblesh 1955–75; chmn Scot. council of
health from 1973; chmn Borders loc health council
from 1975

GEDDES Walter   MB ChB 1953
DPH(St And) 1966 MFCM 1974
g p Thurso 1958–67; publ health Aber from 1967
d 13.11.81

GEDDES William   MA 1909
no longer on GC reg

GEDDIE Colin More   MB ChB 1914
no longer on GC reg

GEDDIE John Moncrieff   MB ChB 1938
g p Aber from 1945

GEDDIE Marie Murdoch Cameron   MA 1924
retd 1963; resid Dufftown

GEERSHON or Chanock, Dorothy Florence
                                       MB ChB 1928
resid Cape Town

GEILS James   *MA 1938 ᶜLLB 1940
solic Davidson & Garden Aber 1946–48; lawyer
Shell leg. dept Lond 1948–63, dep head 1963–73; secy
The Shell Transport & Trading Co Lond from 1966
m Pentir Caerns, N. Wales 19.7.47 Heather N.
MacLeod 3rd off. WRNS d of Donald MacL. Pentir
Caerns

GEILS Mary Milne   MA 1942

GELLATLY or Duncan, Joyce Mary   MB ChB 1954
resid Edin

GEORGE Charles   BSc 1939 *1940
teacher r g s N'cle-u-Tyne from 1950
d Gosforth N'cle-u-Tyne 25.1.78 *AUR* XLVII 359

GEORGE Charles Mathieson
                                       MA 1930 BSc 1930 *1932

GEORGE Ernest Alan   BSc(agr) 1955

GEORGE Gordon Young   MA 1951
prin teacher Engl Sanquhar acad Dumfriessh 1966–
69; asst head Kinross h s from 1969

GEORGE or Tavener, Katharine Jameson   MA 1919
resid Aber

GEORGE Rosemary Violet   MA 1923
teacher: jun s RGC Aber 1928–64; retd; resid Aber
d Aber 18.8.80

GEORGE Walter Henry   BSc 1936

GEORGESON Alice Margaret   *MA 1933
teacher classics Holmwood prep s for boys Formby
1940–61; retd; resid Aber

GEORGESON or Shaw, Charlotte Gordon
*MA 1929
resid St Lucia Queensland Aust

GEORGESON William Wares   *MA 1927
retd; resid Thames Ditton

GERARD William Wilson   *BSc 1955
man. dir Eli Lilly & Co, 1963–71; man. dir and
chief exec Berk pharmaceuticals from 1972

GERRAND Waistel Gordon   BSc 1951
BVMS(Glas) 1959 MRCVS 1959 DVSM(Edin)
1965
vet pract Montrose 1959–61; vet off. Beverley 1961–
71; div vet off. min of agr Lond from 1971
m Rutherglen Elizabeth E. Hamilton med lab tech/
teacher d of William M. H. Rutherglen

GERRARD or Emslie, Evelyn Winifred   MA 1950
teacher Applegrove s Forres from 1965

GERRARD James Dennis   MA 1953
teacher: prin Engl Stranraer acad 1963–70, asst
prin Engl Stranraer acad (comp) 1970–73; prin Engl
Drummond s s Edin from 1973
m Stranraer 15.7.67 Dorothy C. Graham med secy
d of Alexander J. G. Stranraer

GERRIE or Menzies, Grace Stewart   MA 1947

GERRIE Mary Hannah   MA 1904
no longer on GC reg

GERRIE Norman   *MA 1951 Dip Ed 1958

GERRY Harold Joseph Cruickshank   *MA 1949
FIL 1969
tech translator Lond 1952–71; freelance tech translator St. Albans from 1971

GIBB Alan George   MB ChB 1941
sen ENT consult. Tayside area Dun 1960–69; hon
sen lect otolaryngology Dund from 1969
m Invergowrie 6.9.66 Elisabeth A. Addison nurse d of
George A. Invergowrie

GIBB Alexander   MA 1945 LLB 1950
ptnr Stewart & Watson solic Turriff from 1953

GIBB Alexander John Brown   MB ChB 1948

GIBB Dorothy Constance   BSc 1931 PhD 1935
employed by H. Tempest Nott from 1953

GIBB or MacFarlane, Isobel Margaret   MA 1934
teacher inf: Walker Rd s Aber 1936, AGS 1936–39,
St Martin's, Lincoln 1941–44; part-time AGS 1957–
66, Kingswood s Aber from 1966; retd 1974

GIBB Jean Ford   MA 1954

GIBB John   MA 1943 BD 1947
d Selkirk 19.9.74 *AUR* XLVI 236

GIBB or Leslie, Margaret   MA 1954
resid Alford

GIBB Margaret Winifred   *BSc 1936 MB ChB 1945
g p Aber from 1950

GIBB or Malcolm, Mary Robertson   MA 1936

GIBB Maxwell Grant   *MB ChB 1928
MRCGP 1958
retd; resid Aber

GIBB Muriel Elizabeth   MA 1932
sen hosp m o ENT: Lanarksh 1960–61, Ayrsh
1962–63; consult. ENT Ayrsh from 1965

GIBB Robert   MB ChB 1942
hon memb sociedade Brasileira de Radiologia 1966
FRCR 1975
dep dir radiotherapy Christie hosp Manc 1964–66;
lect radiotherapy Manc from 1966; hon treas RCR
1973

GIBB Robert Alexander Stephen   MB ChB 1941
g p Salford from 1947

GIBB Thomas   BL 1937
retd 1975; appted hon sheriff Aber 10.10.72
d Aber 2.11.80 *AUR* XLIX 69

GIBB William Scott   MA 1943
FSCA 1974
joint controlling interest as dir in G. L. Gibb & Co
timber merch Aber 1958–76

GIBB or Macdonald, Winifred Inglis Buchanan
MB ChB 1931
resid Budleigh Salterton

GIBBON or Coulter, Dorothy Isobel McKay
MA 1913
no longer on GC reg

GIBSON Charles Anderson   *MA 1931
d Australia 1973

GIBSON David Hall   *BSc(eng) 1955 PhD 1958
MICE 1963 FIOB 1971
eng J. Mowlem, Hunterston 1958–61; des eng C. S.
Allot Manc 1961–63; man./man. dir F. J. Gibson (bld)
Wilmslow from 1963; member council Keele univ
from 1969
m Wilmslow –.9.64 Angela C. Heslop BSc(Manc)
pharm d of John P. H. Wilmslow

GIBSON or Stuart, Eileen   MA 1933
   teacher: Ellon acad 1935–41, 1944–60, maths Hilton acad 1960–71, prin guid 1971–77; retd

GIBSON George   MA 1924
   d Aber 19.2.74 *AUR* XLV 448

GIBSON Harrison Raymond   MB ChB 1955
   BSc(Otago) 1949
g p Silverdale NZ 1966–75; Ruakaka Northland NZ from 1975

GIBSON Ivor   *MA 1954
   C of S min Kelty 1959–65; tut. organis adult educ Fife 1965–69; res St And 1967–69; teacher re Glenrothes 1970–74, Edin from 1974
m Kelty 6.8.60 Margaret T. B. Gillespie teacher d of William G. Kelty

GIBSON Jane   *MA 1921
   retd 1958; resid Edin
m Robert W. Urquhart MA 1920 *qv*

GIBSON John Stalker   BSc(eng) 1952
   CEng MIMechE
lt-col REME
War Office equipment sponsorship 1963–66; min of tech proj off. with Canadair in Montreal 1966–69; Quality Assur and equipment support plan. appts with REME tech group Lond 1969–79

GIBSON or Dutch, Mary Kerr
                              ***MA 1952 Dip Ed 1953**
   teacher Engl Aber coll of comm 1969–71; lect Aber coll of educ 1971–73; teacher Engl Banchory acad 1973–74; year mistress Rubislaw acad Aber from 1974

GIBSON William Cameron   *MA 1934
   capt (signals intelligence) Burma 1940–45; prin teacher/dep rector Galashiels acad 1965–72; dep rector 1972–75; retd; resid Aber
d Aber 29.4.79 *AUR* XLVIII 232

GIBSON William Naldrett   BSc(for) 1932
   FIF(GB)
dist for: Inv/Edin/Dumfries 1935–51; asst conserv for. Dumfries 1951–66; branch man. Filhill Forestry Stirling 1966–69; reg man. Econ Forestry from 1969
m Inv 11.6.52 Janet M. Stewart secy d of Angus S. Fort William

GILBERT or Allen, Elspet Frances   MA 1944

GILCHRIST Robert Niven   *MA 1909 *1910
   d Aber 21.1.72 *AUR* XLIV 427

GILCHRIST William Niven   MB ChB 1934
   g p Barnes, Lond till 1971; sessional work DHSS Lond 1971–75; retd

GILCHRIST William Normandale   *MA 1952

GILCHRIST William Scott   BL 1950
   teacher Aber 1964–73; retd

GILES Alexander Rennie   BSc(agr) 1933
   farm. Tarves from 1945, also Moss-side of Gight, Fyvie from 1965
d St Katherines 25.5.79

GILES Andrew Milne Mitchell   MA 1927
   retd 1967; resid Carnoustie
d 12.9.81

GILES Archibald William   MA 1926
   MBE 1946
CA Aber 1930; Lond: acct (ca) 1930–39; RAF sq/ldr accts dept 1939–46, banker/man. dir Baring Bros & Co 1947–68, comp dir from 1968
m Lond Alison F. Z. Judd MB BS MD(Lond) med pract d of Harold G. J. CA Hampstead

GILES or Duncan, Catherine Margaret   MA 1943

GILES Florence May   MA 1944
   teacher Aber: Muirfield p s 1957–62 and from 1966, Sunnybank p s 1963–66

GILES George Marr   MA 1903
   no longer on GC reg

GILFILLAN or McLachlan, Helen Urquhart
                                              MA 1939

GILL Alexander John   BSc(agr) 1949
   lect Ont agr coll Guelph till 1959; farm. Macduff from 1959

GILL Alexander McIntosh   BSc(eng) 1952
   MICE 1960
Aber: civ eng Wm Tawse contr 1960–71; man. dir Bon-Accord Construction struct eng from 1972

GILL Bella   *MA 1912
   resid Aber

GILL David James   MB ChB 1947
   FRCP(C) 1974
man. dir James Gill & Sons Aber 1962–68; Canada: resid psychiat univ of Alta 1968–72, phys (psychiat) Alberta hosp Edmonton from 1972

GILL or Buchan, Doreen Clark   MA 1946

GILL Geoffrey Munro   MB ChB 1953
   MRCGP 1963
g p Inverurie from 1957

GILL or Ebsworth, Gladys Mary Badenoch
                                            MB ChB 1945
   g p Farnborough from 1957

GILL Helen Mitchell   MA 1927
   teacher: Cults p s till 1968; retd; resid Aber

GILL or Bruce, (Isobel) Dorothea   *MA 1951
   resid Bourne End

GILL James Cruickshank   BSc(agr) 1948
   asst farm man. Rowett res inst Aber 1963–72, sen scient off. from 1972

GILL James Munro Christie   MB ChB 1927
 FBMA 1966 founder member RCGP, elected FRCGP 1970
 g p Inverurie till 1967; retd

GILL John Frederic   *MB ChB 1906
 no longer on GC reg

GILL John Murray Dunlop   MB ChB 1955
 regist obst/gyn: Creigton hosp Fife, Irvine cent hosp 1957–61; private pract Kingston Jamaica 1961–63; resid radiol Princess Margaret hosp Toronto 1964–65; fam plan. admin univ of Michigan 1966; med advis fam plan. progr govt of Kenya 1966–69; private pract Toronto 1970; WHO consult. Philippines 1970; assoc dir health sc internat dev res centre Ottawa 1971–75, dir from 1975

GILL John Paterson Beveridge
 MA 1929 MB ChB 1935
 m o dist of Canisbay (incl Is of Stroma) Caithness till 1968; retd; resid Peterculter

GILL or Payne, Margaret   *MA 1949
 resid Lytham St Anne's

GILL Margaret Macgillivray   MA 1931

GILL Norman   MB ChB 1935
 d Preston 18.12.76

GILL Norman   MB ChB 1936
 g p Wakefield from 1946

GILL Robert Douglas   *MA 1949
 prin teacher: mod lang Peterhead acad 1962–65, Ger Perth acad 1965–68; prin examiner mod lang for SCE exam board 1966–69; rector Beath sen h s Cowdenbeath 1969–72; head Rubislaw acad (AGS) from 1973

GILL Wallace John   MB ChB 1923
 d Sonning-on-Thames 15.2.72 AUR XLIV 429

GILL William MacGregor   *MA 1946
 head hist dept: Stranraer h s 1962–70, Stranraer acad from 1970

GILL William Proctor   MA 1953 BL 1955
 acct Spicers paper makers and merch Lond 1960–62 and Sawston Cambridge 1962–64; Lond: asst secy Reed Paper Group Lond 1964–69, fin. controller Charterhouse Indust later Charterhouse Group Lond 1969–76; fin. dir Alenco (internat) fittings manuf Henley-on-Thames from 1976
 m Aber 11.9.65 Dorothy H. Davidson MA 1956 qv

GILLAN Alexander Stuart   *MA 1930
 d Kirkcaldy 30.3.70 AUR XLIII 446

GILLAN Archibald Wedderburn   BL 1930
 d Dun 19.11.76

GILLAN Ian Thomson   *MA 1937 BD 1940
 curate Musselburgh 1970–72, par priest Jedburgh 1972–73; received into Anglican Communion by Bishop of Moray Inv 1973, licensed to serve as priest in Epis ch (Scot.); asst priest St Andrew's cath, Aber 1973; precentor St Andrew's cath Inv 1974; priest in charge St Clement's ch Mastrick Aber from 1976

GILLAN John Thomson Clifford
 *MA 1950 LLB 1953
 ptnr: Alexander & Gillan advoc Aber 1963–75, Wilsone & Duffus advoc Aber from 1975
 m Aber 15.3.65 Isobel M. Wood MA 1948 qv

GILLAN Percival Milne   *MA 1926
 d 15.9.78 AUR XLVIII 104

GILLAN Robert Urquhart   MA 1920 MB ChB 1924
 DOMS(Lond) 1934
 hosp ophth serv Lond 1948–63, gen ophth serv Lond from 1963

GILLAN William George   *MA 1935
 prin teacher classics Elgin acad 1961–77; retd; resid Elgin

GILLANDERS Anne Cruickshank   BSc 1932
 sen haemat tech Sorrento mat. hosp Birm till 1970; retd; resid Aber

GILLANDERS or Scott, Helen Georgia   MA 1954
 teacher Middlefield p s Aber from 1970

GILLESPIE or Swapp, Anne Margaret   MA 1952
 LTCL 1963
 teacher Aber 1960–64; resid Aber

GILLESPIE or Smart, Hilda Annie Mary   MA 1933
 resid Dunecht

GILLESPIE James Ross   MB ChB 1954
 g p Hull from 1956

GILLIES Angus John   MA 1942
 MA(Windsor) 1964
 Canada: head Engl dept W. D. Lowe tech s Windsor, Ont 1960–64; head Engl dept A. B. Lucas s s London, Ont 1964–67; Windsor board of educ: asst supt of schools 1967–73, supt of progr from 1973
 m Windsor Ont 21.12.63 Merle L. Worthy secy

GILLIES Daisy   MA 1910
 no longer on GC reg

GILLIES Hugh Donald Mackay   MB ChB 1944
 g p Stornoway from 1947
 d Inv 29.3.77 AUR XLVII 214

GILLIES John MacDonald   MA 1918
 C of S min S. Knapsdale till 1964; retd; resid Lochgilphead

GILLIES Kenneth   MA 1922
 C of S min Gardner St ch Glasg from 1924
 d Glasg 26.7.76

GILLIES Neil Radasi   MB ChB 1954
 g p Stornoway from 1957

GILLILAND Susan Mary   MA 1950
publ relations exec Lond 1958–60; teacher Engl Tormead s Guildford from 1972
m Lond 6.12.58 Michael Milliken MA(Oxon) man. consult. s of E. Kenneth M. MA(Oxon) Tunbridge Wells

GILLIS Allan Webster   BSc 1949

GILMORE Elizabeth Duthie   MA 1910
no longer on GC reg

GILMOUR John   BSc 1948
spec asst maths Aber acad 1966–73, asst prin maths (now Hazlehead acad) from 1973

GIMINGHAM Charles Henry   PhD 1948
FRSE 1961 FI Biol 1967
Aberd: sen lect bot 1961–64, reader 1964–69; pers chair 1969–72, second chair 1972

GIULIANI Raffaello Giuseppe
                              ***MA 1948 Dip Ed 1949**
teacher Engl Natick Mass USA (chmn Engl) 1964–65
m Castelfiorentino, Florence 20.7.68 Maria Innocenti secy d of Nino I. Castelfiorentino

GLASCODINE John Kenneth   BSc(eng) 1952
C Eng MIMech Eng FInstF MCIBS
man. nat indust fuel efficiency serv Glasg from 1971

GLASHAN Alexander James   BSc 1944 *1948
rector Turriff acad 1961–64, Elgin acad from 1964

GLASHAN Sheila Esslemont   MA 1948 Dip Ed 1969
teacher Aber: Walker Rd p s till 1959, Rosemount s s 1960–71, year mistress Kincorth acad 1971–73, dep head from 1973

GLASS Alexander Gibb   MA 1899
no longer on GC reg

GLASS Cecil Bentley-Innes   PhD 1952
civ serv: prin scient off. 1961–72, sen prin scient off. (head of oper res group govt comm hq Cheltenham) 1972; dep chief scient off. 1977 (head of electronics res and dev div govt comm hq Cheltenham)

GLASS Charles Alexander   MB ChB 1930
g p Manchester till 1968; retd

GLASS Charles Stanley   MB ChB 1911
d 21.4.66

GLASS Isabella Adeline   MA 1923
spec asst Engl/lib Brandon h s Motherwell 1960–65; retd; resid Aber

GLASS James Gerald   MA 1926 BSc 1927
head New Byth s till 1968; retd; resid Fochabers wife d 29.12.72

GLASSMAN Charles   MB ChB 1934
b 29.8.1903

g p Brooklyn NY USA 1934–73; retd; resid Jamaica NY

GLASSMAN Max Samuel   BSc 1934 MB ChB 1937
d New York 9.1.78

GLEGG or McRae, Agnes Alice   BSc 1947 *1949

GLEN Archibald   BSc 1950
Isaac Spencer Aber: tech serv man. 1960–64, man. paints div 1964–70, dir paints div 1970–75, man. dir from 1975

GLEN Marjory Ann Duncan   MA 1908
no longer on GC reg

GLEN-CAMPBELL Edward Arthur Dudley
                              MB ChB 1937

GLEN-CAMPBELL Maynard Joscelyne
                              MB ChB 1940

GLENNIE Agnes Elisabeth   BSc 1926
DSIR Cambridge/Lond till 1963; retd; resid Lond

GLENNIE or Clarke, Cicily Margaret
                              ***MB ChB 1936**
MFCM 1972 (founder member)
asst res med psych Cambridge till 1963; sessional m o Merton/Richmond-u-Thames 1967–68; sen m o commun care Richmond 1969–74; area spec commun med (soc serv) Kingston/Richmond AHA from 1974

GLENNIE or Cameron, Ethel Wilma Whyte
                              MA 1948
teacher Arnage p s 1958–61; resid Fraserburgh

GLENNIE or Tanner, Evelyn Winifred   MB ChB 1935
locum anaest apptments under S W reg hosp board at various hosps; asst F P clin univ coll hosp Lond from 1967

GLENNIE Harry Philip   MA 1928
man. dir J. A. Prestwich Indust from 1958

GLENNIE Henry Hay Ian   MB ChB 1936
surg P & O steam navig comp/NZ shipping co 1959–62; g p Hamilton NZ from 1962

GLENNIE Herbert Charles   *MA 1925
rector Linlithgow acad till 1967; retd; resid Edin

GLENNIE James Cruickshank   *MA 1931
C of S min Mauchline old ch from 1948
d 13.1.80

GLENNIE James Stephen   MB ChB 1940

GLENNIE John Acton Sinclair   MA 1928 LLB 1930

GLENNIE Nora Frances   *MA 1924
prin maths Albyn s for girls Aber from 1953; retd 1967
d Aber 6.12.75 *AUR* XLVII 212

GLENNIE or Grant, Norma Grant Hay
                              MA 1931 ^dLLB 1933
    resid Lossiemouth

GLENNIE Ronald Edward   MB ChB 1933 MD 1951
    d Cambridge 18.7.70 *AUR* XLIV 111

GLENTWORTH Robert   PhD 1941
    head soil surv of Scot. Macaulay inst of soil res
Aber from 1946; retd 1976

GLEW Denis Richard   BSc(for) 1949

GLOVER Ian   BSc(eng) 1930
    no longer on GC reg

GLOVER William Edward   MB ChB 1911
    no longer on GC reg

GODDEN Wilfred John   MB ChB 1936

GODFREY Elizabeth Robertson   MA 1906 *1907
    d Aber 20.9.62 *AUR* XL 77

GODSMAN or Watt, Lilian   BSc 1928
    teacher Stoneywood p s 1929–32; resid Bieldside
husb *d* Bieldside Aber 7.1.77

GOLDIE or Brown, Evelyn   MB ChB 1926
    g p Lond from 1930

GOLDIE William   MA 1927 MB ChB 1932
    d Leeds 13.2.70 *AUR* XLIII 445

GOODALL or Scott, Catherine Jane   MA 1941
    resid Glasg

GOODALL or Troup, Ethel Dolly Allan   MA 1949
    temp teacher Winchester Virginia USA from 1970

GOODALL Isabella Cooper   MA 1932
    teacher: spec asst maths Keith g s 1943–73; retd

GOODALL John   *MA 1929
    prin teacher sc: Fortrose acad till 1965, Tain royal
acad 1965–66; retd; resid Fortrose

GOODALL or Wilson, Murial Olive   MA 1944
    resid Bucksburn

GOODALL or McGregor, Shirley Cameron
                                             MA 1954
GOODBODY Ivan Miles   PhD 1954
    Jamaica: sen lect zool univ of W.I. 1962–64, prof
from 1964

GOODBRAND Alan Reid   BSc(eng) 1942

GOODBRAND Stephen   MB ChB 1908
    d Banchory 16.1.68 *AUR* XLII 348

GOODBRAND Stephen   MA 1949
    moderator: synod of Merse and Teviotdale 1961–
62, presb of Jedburgh 1972–73; min Southdown par
ch linked with Hobkirk from 1973

GOODLAD John Fordyce Robertson
                              MA 1930 MB ChB 1934
    d Lincoln 18.3.76 *AUR* XLVI 417

GOODSPEED Morley James   *BSc 1949
    CSIRO div of land res Canberra, Aust from 1962
wife *d* 1963
m(2) Melbourne 7.7.65 Marie P. F. Murphy d of
John M. Mt Martha Vict Aust

GOODWIN John Francis   BSc(for) 1945
    chief educ trg off. for. comm from 1970; resid
Basingstoke
m Cinderford 31.12.52 Edith Usherwood

GORDON Agnes   MA 1925

GORDON Agnes May   MA 1928
    d Aber 31.1.69 *AUR* XLIII 215

GORDON Alice   MA 1910
    no longer on GC reg

GORDON Alistair James   BSc(eng) 1950

GORDON Andrew   MA 1913
    d Dun 30.7.75 *AUR* XLVI 321

GORDON or Macpherson, Annie   MA 1927
    no longer on GC reg

GORDON Annie Isabella
                              BSc 1933 MA 1934 BD 1945
    min presb C of E Rankin mem ch Liv 1961–66; tut.
St Andrew's Hall Selly Oak Birm 1966–68; retd; resid
Edin

GORDON Charles Eddie Talbot   MB ChB 1946
    g p Fraserburgh from 1949

GORDON Charles Harold   *MA 1929
    FEIS 1963
rector Dunfermline h s till 1968; retd; dir. time-tabling
advis serv Scot. Moray House coll of educ from 1968
and for dept of educ in Eire from 1972

GORDON or Georgeson, Charlotte Helen   MA 1901
    d Aber 25.9.65 *AUR* XLII 80

GORDON Christie Wilson   MB ChB 1938
    FRCP 1971 FFCM 1972
reg m o W. Midlands reg health auth Birm 1976
d Birmingham 9.8.79 *AUR* XLVIII 353

GORDON Christina Scott   MA 1928
    retd 1967; resid Macduff

GORDON or Hamilton, Christine Jean
                                             BSc(agr) 1940
    resid West Calder

GORDON or Dixon, Clara   MA 1912
    no longer on GC reg

GORDON Coral Ogilvie   MB ChB 1919
    no longer on GC reg

GORDON Daniel George John
                          MA 1921 MB ChB 1924
FBMA 1958 FRCGP 1971
g p Ellon till 1961; retd; resid Inverurie

GORDON Diana Mary   MA 1954 MB ChB 1965
SRN(Lond) 1958
h o Longmore hosp Edin 1965–66, ARI 1968; part-time m o Lindsey c c Lincs 1968–72; part-time g p Lincoln 1971–72; resid Swaziland; m o i/c St Teresa's clin Manzini
m Shirebrook 15.4.63 William J. Reeves BS(Lond) s of Ernest R. Clapton-on-the-Hill

GORDON Donald Hugh McKay   *MA 1945
gen man. Tootal Licensing Manc from 1947

GORDON Donald McDonald   *MA 1944
CMG 1970
HMFO: first secy Rangoon 1960–62, counsellor S Af 1962–66, Imperial def coll Lond 1966–67, counsellor and consul-gen Saigon 1967–70; FO 1970–72, dep high comm Kuala Lumpur 1972–75; Brit High Commissioner Cyprus from 1975

GORDON Donald Roderick   BSc(agr) 1954
field off. min of agr Lincoln 1958–60; lands off. DAFS Thurso from 1960
m Inv 5.6.65 Helen W. Shepherd cler off. civ serv d of Alexander R. S. Inv

GORDON Dorothy Belle   MA 1937
Aber: prin asst teacher Engl High s for girls 1965–73 (now Harlaw acad); asst prin teacher 1973–75; retd
d Aber 13.5.80

GORDON Douglas McKenzie   MA 1937
min cong ch Montrose from 1947; chmn Cong union of Scot. 1965–68

GORDON Douglas Thomson
                    MB ChB 1950 DPH 1954 ᶜMD 1962
res asst phys Ham Green hosp Bristol till 1960; Plymouth: sen h m o Scott hosp 1960–67; g p from 1967

GORDON Duncan   MA 1954
teacher Engl: Inv h s 1955–60, Lachine h s Montreal 1960–65, Inv h s 1965–66; spec asst Engl Fortrose acad Rosssh 1966–72; prin Engl Millburn s s Inv 1972–75; Fortrose acad from 75
m Inv 2.4.60 Margaret E. Sinclair teacher p e d of James M. S. Inv

GORDON or Beveridge, Elizabeth Anderson
                                        MA 1947
resid Glasg

GORDON or Jones, Elizabeth Annie Watts
                                        MA 1933

GORDON Elizabeth Helen   MA 1941

GORDON or Simpson, Elizabeth McVicar   MA 1914
d Edin 18.3.74 *AUR* XLV 447

GORDON Eric Christie   MB ChB 1923
d Cornwall 12.5.73

GORDON or Morrison, Ethel Mary   BSc 1923
no longer on GC reg

GORDON Evelyn Mary   *MA 1945
spec asst mod lang Fraserburgh acad 1951–62; Aust: teacher mod lang Bendigo h s 1962–70, sen mistress from 1970

GORDON Frederick William
                    ***MA 1919 MB ChB 1922 ᶜMD 1935**
d 16.3.71

GORDON George Alexander Connell
                          MB ChB 1914 DPH 1920
d 18.10.75 *AUR* XLVI 415

GORDON George Hector Miller   MB ChB 1951

GORDON George Norrie   BSc 1925 BL 1931

GORDON or Black, Georgina Berry   MA 1937

GORDON Grace Forbes   MA 1928
retd 1964; resid Aber

GORDON or Harrison, Grace Thomson   MA 1947
teacher biol Bartholomew s Eynsham Oxford from 1967

GORDON Harold Cowie   MA 1948 *BSc 1951
teacher: AGS 1952–56, London area 1956–58, Aske's Hatcham boys' s Lond 1958–67; lect Britannia RN coll Dartmouth from 1967

GORDON or Robson, Hazel   MA 1952
teacher Rothes 1958–65, Aberlour 1966–73, prin guid 1973–76, prin guid Speyside high commun s from 1976

GORDON or Abercrombie, Helen   MA 1920
no longer on GC reg

GORDON Helen Elizabeth   MB ChB 1943
DA 1947 FFARCS 1954 FFARCSI 1955
consult. anaest N W Durh hosp group 1955–74; retd
m Shotley Bridge Co Durh 6.3.71 Kenneth G. F. Mackenzie MB BChir(Cantab) consult. surg s of John M. MA 1896 *qv*(I, II, III, IV)

GORDON Henry Gray McKerron
                                        MA 1948 PhD 1952
d St And 7.6.63 *AUR* XL 207

GORDON Ian   BSc 1929 MB ChB 1932
hon clin reader med Aberd from 1948

GORDON Ian Alastair   BSc(agr) 1951
tech off. SAI till 1969; reg sales man. (Scot.) Rumenco from 1969

GORDON Ian Stuart   BSc(for) 1935

GORDON Ian James   MB ChB 1946
 FRACS 1961
Aust: hon surg Bendigo N dist base hosp from 1961, hon urologist from 1969

GORDON Ian Lionel Victor Lumsden   MB ChB 1923

GORDON Isabella   *BSc 1922 DSc 1928
 Commonwealth Fund Fellowship 1926–28
OBE 1963 FLS 1931 FZS 1932 FInstBiol 1964
member edit. board of *Crustaceana* from inception, publd in Holland 1959–66; retd; resid Lond

GORDON James   MB ChB 1924
 g p Hull 1929–75; retd; resid Cottingham E Yorks
m(2) Hull 18.7.41 Elsie Hatfield d of Walter H. Hull
d Cottingham Yorks 24.9.79 *AUR* XLVIII 351

GORDON James Alexander   MA 1922 MB ChB 1925
 d Aber 27.4.76 *AUR* XLVI 416

GORDON James Alexander   *BSc 1928
 d 14.9.63

GORDON James Bremner   MB ChB 1942
 d Peterhead 29.10.74 *AUR* XLVI 240

GORDON James Burgess   BSc(eng) 1947

GORDON James Gray   BSc 1925
 no longer on GC reg

GORDON James Lawrie   *BSc(eng) 1952
 MASCE MEIC MCEA MCSCE regist prof eng in Quebec & Alta
Montreal Eng Co: asst man. hydro div 1964–72, chief hydraulic eng from 1971

GORDON James William   BSc 1955

GORDON or Felgate, Jamesina   MB ChB 1937
 d Leeds 28.10.75

GORDON (Jane) Margaret Cockburn   MA 1930
 retd from teaching 1967; resid Aber
d Aber 12.7.81

GORDON or Hay, Jean Innes
                                MB ChB 1940 DPH 1965
 h o RACH 1940–41; sen h o Maidenhead hosp 1941; flt lt med res RAF 1941–46; j h m o Bellsdyke mental hosp Larbert 1956–58; m o ch health Aber health dept/Grampian N area health board from 1962
m Aber –.6.46 Spottiswood R. Hay farm. s of Thomas R. H. Edin

GORDON or Mackay, Jean Morrison   MA 1950
 teacher: Lat Alexandra g s Singapore 1960–62; remed reading Bannockburn from 1969

GORDON Jeannie Wallace   MA 1929
 d Stornoway 30.10.66 *AUR* XLII 86

GORDON or Smith, Jessie   MA 1950
 teacher Canada: Lester Pearson sen s s New

Westminster 1961–62, Alberni dist s s Port Alberni BC 1962–66, Gold River s s BC from 1967

GORDON Jessie Ann   MA 1926
 d Stornoway 30.10.66 *AUR* XLVI 86

GORDON or Stewart, Joan Cameron   MA 1938
 teacher: temp Alford area 1960–62, Engl Alford acad from 1963

GORDON or Reid, Johan Aiken
                                MA 1953 Dip Ed 1954
 teacher Aber High s for girls till 1962; resid Bieldside Aber

GORDON John   BSc(for) 1940

GORDON John Alexander   *MB ChB 1928
 d Lond 14.7.73 *AUR* XLV 320

GORDON John Duncan   MB ChB 1925
 d Aber 30.1.69 *AUR* XLIII 215

GORDON John Grant   BSc(agr) 1948 PhD 1955
 JP 1969
prin scient off. Rowett inst Aber from 1965

GORDON John Robert   *MA 1954
 Canada: plan. res dir metro Tor plan. board 1957–68; h s teacher geog Borough North York, Tor from 1968

GORDON John Younie   BSc 1954
 Aber: prin teacher chem RGC 1966–71, asst head from 1972
m Aber 30.3.61 Anna R. Bremner teacher homecraft d of William T. B. Aber

GORDON Joseph Evans   BSc(agr) BSc(for) 1920
 dep prin E of S coll of agr/sen lect agr Edin till 1961; retd; resid Longniddry
d Haddington 14.9.77

GORDON or Middleton, Margaret Augusta
                                ***MA 1936**

GORDON or Gordon, Margaret Grant   MA 1919
 no longer on GC reg

GORDON Margaret Sinclair   MA 1945
 prin speech therap Caithness c c from 1973

GORDON Mary   MA 1914
 resid Aber
d Aber 23.2.79

GORDON Mary Paton   MA 1912
 d 10.6.66

GORDON or Greenshields, Muriel Glenesk
                                MA 1951

GORDON or Snartt, Netta Terras   *MA 1905
 Charing vicarage Kent 1955–59; retd Gander Newfoundland 1959–63; resid London 1963–79, resid

Victoria BC from 1979
husb *d* London 1976

GORDON Peter Mitchell   *MA 1952 BD 1957
C of S min Brechin cath from 1965
m Edin 21.10.61 Fiona S. McDonald MA(St And)
deaconess/teacher d of Thomas P. McD. MA
LLB(Edin) Edin

GORDON Robert   MA 1909
d Aber 2.4.65 *AUR* xli 146

GORDON Robert Fraser   BSc 1930 DSc 1947
CBE 1972 FRCVS 1970 hon DVSc(Liv) 1970
dir poultry res stat Houghton, Huntingdon; chmn
and non-scientific dir The Animal Health Trust Lond;
edit. *The World's Poultry Science Journal*
d –.2.81 *AUR* xlix 137

GORDON or Morgan, Roberta   *MA 1932
resid Aber
husb *d* 4.5.69

GORDON Ronald Macgregor   BSc(eng) 1954
civ eng corp of Trinity House Lond 1961–64; man.
construct. dept MB Dredging Co Erith 1964–66;
Lond: sect leader Rendel Pelmex & Tritton 1966–68,
HM civ eng insp of factories from 1968

GORDON Ronald Murray
                              MB ChB 1937 DPH 1939
MFCM 1974
sen m o SHHD Edin 1955–75; retd
wife *d* –.4.68
m(2) Edin 31.12.69 Doris M. Imrie BA(Oxon) d of
William C. I. Dun
d 21.8.81

GORDON or Cowan, Rosemary   MA 1951

GORDON Thomas Barclay   MB ChB 1936
g p Littleport from 1941; retd 1974
d Peterborough 29.9.79 *AUR* xlviii 353

GORDON Thomas Robert   MB ChB 1925
retd; resid Canada 1977–79, Bexhill from 1979
wife *d* Vancouver 15.11.78

GORDON Walter Mitchell   *MA 1954
market res exec and man. posts Lond 1954–66;
asst secy univ apptments board Liv 1966–70; sen
counsellor OU NW reg England from 1970
m Lond 29.6.60 Anne P. Woods secy d of John W.
Beckenham

GORDON William   MA 1898
no longer on GC reg

GORDON William James   MA 1933
s of William J. G. hosp gov; b Kirkcudbright 24.4.12
dep head King St p s Aber 1958–62, head from 1962;
retd

GORDON William Johnston   MA 1905
d Ratcliffe-on-Trent 15.12.64 *AUR* xli 53

GORDON William Law   *MA 1919
retd; resid Sunningdale

GORDON William Leslie   MB ChB 1938
d –.9.66

GORDON William Lindsay Drummond
                                 BSc(agr) 1935

GORDON William Morrison
                      MA 1953 LLB 1955 PhD 1963
Glas: sen lect private law 1965–69, Douglas prof civ
law from 1969

GORDON William Thomson   MB ChB 1935

GORDON-RUSSELL James Bertrand
                                 MB ChB 1943
MRCP(Lond) 1948 DPM 1950 FRCPsych 1971
FRCP(Lond) 1973
sen reg psychiat SW metro reg hosp board 1950–52;
consult. psychiat S Somerset clin area 1953–57;
consult. psychiat and phys supt Roundway hosp
Wiltshire/consult. psychiat Swindon hosp group
1957–64; dep chmn Melbourne mental health auth
State of Victoria, Aust 1964–66; consult. psychiat
Bristol clin area/clin tut. and reg tut. post grad
psychiat Brist/reg advis Royal Coll of psychiat/chmn
vocat trg sub-comm SW reg/visiting consult. psychiat
BRHSC/consult. psychiat Bristol ch and fam guid
serv from 1967
m 28.6.50 Margaret M. O'Byrne

GORDON-RUSSELL William Colin   MB ChB 1937

GORROD Charles Elgar   MB ChB 1936 DPH 1939
m Aber 25.12.45 Margery Aspinall

GORROD or Crookshanks, Jean Soutar   BCom 1925
resid Aber
d 18.12.81

GORROD William Cowie   MB ChB 1924
g p Sheffield 1927–73; retd

GORTON or Ford, Isabel Mary Simpson   MA 1946

GOSSIP Margaret Elizabeth   *MA 1925
MA(Oxon)
dep head N. Lond Collegiate s till 1962; retd; resid
Edgware

GOSSIP Robin Arthur John   *MA 1927
d Edin 21.2.62 *AUR* xxxix 384

GOSSIP William Henderson   MB ChB 1931
MRCGP 1961
g p Dun till 1973; retd
d Dun 5.6.80 *AUR* xlix 68

GOURLAY Alice Edith   MA 1948
teacher maths Kirkton h s Dun 1963–74
resid St Cyrus

GOVE Daisy Dugid   *MA 1951
teacher Luanshya h s N Rhodesia 1962–74,

Randfontein h s Transvaal from 1974
m Luanshya 12.12.59 Lawrence J. Greeff eng s of
Johan C. G. Springs Transvaal

GOVE or Anderson, Doreen May Mowatt
MB ChB 1949
  JP 1971
dept m o Wakefield AHA from 1966; staff surg to
W Yorks police from 1965

GOVE James George   MA 1945
  HM for. serv: FCO 1946–73; Berlin, Paris, Lond
1958–73; retd; now with Gallaher group

GOVE or Ironside, Mary Jack   MB ChB 1947

GOVE Reginald Bisset   MB ChB 1949 MD 1967
  MRCP(Lond) 1955
phys MoH Cent. Af Fed. 1960–63; sen spec phys
dept health Zambia 1964–76; phys Wenela spec hosp
Johannesburg from 1976
resid Johannesburg S Af republic

GOVE Robert Morrison   *BSc(eng) 1947

GOW Alistair Ian Stuart   BSc(eng) 1953

GOW Edward   MA 1935

GOW Edward James   MB ChB 1947
  med asst psychiat Craig Dunain hosp Inv from
1963

GOW Florence Helena   MA 1902
  no longer on GC reg

GOW James John   BL 1947 PhD 1952 LLD 1964
  member Fac of Advoc from 1952

GOW Jenny   MA 1924
  no longer on GC reg

GOW John   *MA 1913
  no longer on GC reg

GOW or Low, Katherine   MA 1926
  resid Lossiemouth

GOW Katherine Mary   MA 1947
  teacher Aber: Springhill p s 1961–68, Woodside p s
from 1968

GOW or MacDonald, Mary   MA 1916
  no longer on GC reg

GRAFTON Mabel   BCom 1930
  Lond: bookkeeper Stonehouse & Ptnrs insur
brokers 1932–33; secy work Charles Packer & Co
1933–34; resid Twickenham
m Aber 7.4.34 Thomas C. Young CA s of Archibald Y.
MA(Glas) Aber

GRAHAM Alexander John   MB ChB 1951
  MRCPE 1961 FRCPGlas 1974
sen hosp m o Woodilee hosp Lenzie 1959–62; consult.

psychiat Hartwood hosp Lanarksh 1962–69, phys
supt from 1969

GRAHAM Amelia Lillie   MA 1932
  teacher Aber from 1936

GRAHAM or Macleod, Clara Eliza   MA 1919
  d Stornoway 1.8.68 *AUR* XLIII 80

GRAHAM David Alan   *MA 1954

GRAHAM David Spence   *MA 1950 Dip Ed 1953
  lect Moray House coll of educ Edin 1961–65;
HMIS Glasg 1965–72; HM dist insp Aber 1972–75,
HMCIS West of Scot. from 1975

GRAHAM Duncan John Macfarlane   BSc(for) 1953
  teacher geog Stanstead coll Quebec from 1958;
consult. Inst for World Order NY from 1971; pres
Global Citizens Assoc from 1975

GRAHAM or Thomson, Elizabeth Ann Frances
MA 1951
  teacher: Rayne N 1960–62, Brackens s Dun 1967–
74, Dyce nursery s 1974–76, Beechwood s Aber from
1976

GRAHAM Frederick Duncan   BSc 1926
  FEIS 1955
retd 1969; resid Dun

GRAHAM or Whyte, Janet Russell   *MA 1934
  teacher maths St Margaret's s for girls Aber 1961–72

GRAHAM Marion   *MA 1924
  retd 1967; resid Aber

GRAHAM Robert Henry   BSc(for) 1952

GRAHAM Walter   MB ChB 1925 MD 1928
  g p St John's Wood Lond from 1928

GRAINGER or Gordon, Emily   MA 1925
  d Lond 14.7.65 *AUR* XLI 150

GRANT or Poole, Agnes Strachan   MA 1929
  resid Winchmore Hill Lond

GRANT Alan   MA 1929 MB ChB 1933 *MD 1938
  MRCP(Lond) 1949 FRCPath
sen lect forensic serology Guy's hosp med s Lond/hon
consult. forensic serologist Guy's hosp

GRANT Alan John   *MA 1926
  awarded Coll of Educ gold medal for distinguished
serv to educ
head Jeppe h s for boys Johannesburg 1943–62; retd;
lect maths Johannesburg coll of educ 1962–76
m Johannesburg 28.6.32 Catherine R. Barclay d of
John B. Aber

GRANT Alastair Burness   MA 1948
  d in Nigeria 27.3.77

GRANT Alastair Neish   BSc(eng) 1947

GRANT Alastair Patrick   BSc(agr) 1937

GRANT Alastair Robertson
                        MB ChB 1913 MD 1924
retd; resid Goosnargh, Preston

GRANT Alexander   BCom 1922
d Dun 29.2.72 *AUR* XLIV 429

GRANT Alexander   BSc(agr) 1948
  Dip Agr Econ(Oxon) 1949 ACMA 1953 BSc(econ)
(Lond) 1965
agr econ NOSCA Aber 1949–66; lect: Galashiels coll
of f e 1967–69, Scot. coll of textiles Galashiels 1969–73;
sen lect Falkirk tech coll from 1973

GRANT Alexander Christie   BSc 1949 *1950
  ICI dyestuffs sales man. Scot. Glasg from 1969

GRANT Alexander Dow   BSc(for) 1934

GRANT Alexander Flett   MA 1955
  teacher maths Aber: St Peter's RC s 1956–67,
Kaimhill s s 1967–71; spec asst maths Kincorth acad
1971–73; prin teacher maths Hilton acad from 1973
m Aber 7.7.69 Patricia A. Milne teacher d of James
D. M. Aber

GRANT Alexander Rae   *MA 1920 BD 1922
retd; resid Aber

GRANT Alexandra Mariel   MA BSc 1926
  teacher maths/biol and woman advis Grantown g s
1957–67; retd

GRANT Alison Marion   MA 1914
d Milltimber Aber 15.4.77

GRANT or Innes, Anna Helen   MA 1930

GRANT Anna Thomson   *MA 1922
retd 1962; resid Aber

GRANT Anne   MA 1927 BCom 1928
  pers off. in industry till 1939; squad off. WAAF
1939–45
m Lond 8.1.44 Arthur B. W. Greenhough (capt) MBE
MC FRSA arch. s of Edward G. MA(Cantab)
Eardisland
husb *d* 22.9.74

GRANT or Miller, Annie Mary Jane   MA 1926
  teacher mod lang: Hyndland s s Glasg 1961–62,
Fortrose acad 1962–68; retd

GRANT or Speight, Annie Mabel   MA 1908
  d Hanover New Hampshire USA 4.10.66 *AUR* XLII
82

GRANT Bertie James   *MA 1922
d Aber 23.7.71 *AUR* XLIV 320

GRANT Charles   MB ChB 1943
  MRCGP 1968
asst g p Insch 1944–45; g p Crail from 1950

GRANT Charles Murdoch   MA 1937

GRANT Charles Murdoch Stronach   BSc(agr) 1931

GRANT Christina Bruce   MA 1915
  d Golspie 20.6.70 *AUR* XLIV 109

GRANT or Youngson, Daphne Margaret   MA 1949
  lect Engl Nanyang univ Singapore 1967–69; resid
Hong Kong

GRANT Donald Austin   MB ChB 1940
  g p Brechin from 1946

GRANT Donald Cumming   *MA 1951 Dip Ed 1952
  prin teacher geog: Aberlour h s 1960–67, Dunbar g
s 1967–72; asst head Dunbar from 1972
m Aber 22.12.62 Margaret M. Campbell MA(St And)
teacher d of Alexander D. C. Montrose

GRANT Donald Stewart   *MA 1952

GRANT Donella   MA 1953
  teacher/stud. Canterbury NZ 1953–55; teacher
Glasg 1957–59, Invsh 1959–62, Fort Augustus from
1974
m Edin 22.12.62 Patrick D. C. L. MacDonald garage
owner

GRANT Edith   MA 1918
  no longer on GC reg

GRANT or Craig, Edna Jane Fordyce   MA 1951

GRANT Edward   BSc(eng) 1953
  MICE 1959 MIMunE 1962 MSc(N'cle) 1968
FIHE 1969
city eng dept latterly prin eng(traffic) Aber 1957–75;
chief asst eng Aber div dept of roads Grampian reg c
from 1975
m Aber Patricia R. Glennie tech d of George G.
Bicester

GRANT or Baird, Elizabeth Innes   *MA 1911
  d Wishaw 23.1.68 *AUR* XLII 350

GRANT Eric Donaldson   *MA 1951

GRANT Ethel Stewart   MA 1917
  d Buckie 25.11.70 *AUR* XLIV 210

GRANT or Noble, Ethel Stewart   MA 1938
  teacher Aberdeensh: Birkenhills s 1957–64, Ardallie
s 1965–67, Ellon p s 1967–70; resid Aber

GRANT or Kellock, Evelyn Marjory Forbes   MA 1944
  teacher Caol s from 1967

GRANT Florence Liddell   MA 1930
  LCP 1935
retd 1966; resid Bath

GRANT George Lockhart   MB ChB 1946 DPH 1961
  DIH(Dun) 1968 MFCM 1972
commun med spec Dun from 1974

GRANT Gordon Couper   BSc(for) 1922
retd 1969; resid Peterculter

GRANT Hamish Brown   MA 1933 LLB 1935
CBE 1975
Scot. secy Federation of Brit Indust 1953–65

GRANT Henry Frederick Lyall   MA 1898
no longer on GC reg

GRANT or Mackie, Isabella   MA 1906
d Banff 23.3.54

GRANT Isabella   MA 1923
d Fochabers 23.5.65 *AUR* XLI 50

GRANT James   BSc(agr) 1931
d Pitlochry –.12.75

GRANT James   BSc(eng) 1951
prin dev eng GEC Commun Coventry 1962–70, superv eng from 1970

GRANT James Forgan   MB ChB 1906
d Bexhill 24.12.66 *AUR* XLII 82 & 346

GRANT Janet Macpherson   MA 1912
resid Lossiemouth
d Elgin 5.9.78

GRANT or Anderson, Jessie   MA 1924
resid Aber

GRANT Jessie   MA 1925
teacher and chief prim. asst Hopeman s 1935–69; retd; resid Fochabers

GRANT or Hepburn, Jessie Margaret   *MA 1940
resid Dunkeld

GRANT John   MA 1915
d 25.11.65

GRANT John   MB ChB 1921
d Orpington 30.3.61 *AUR* XXXIX 203

GRANT John George   MB ChB 1929
d –.4.67

GRANT John King   MB ChB 1924
d Brechin 22.3.76

GRANT John Philip   BL 1953
prof acct Arthur Young McClelland Moores & Co Aber from 1970

GRANT John William   MA 1919 BSc(agr) 1921

GRANT John William   BSc(agr) 1937
NDD(Glasg) 1937
reg dir NOSCA Aber from 1947
m(2) Caddonfoot 30.8.63 Meave M. MacLeod cler asst d of Alasdair MacL. Beauly

GRANT Joseph   MA 1925 DD 1958
C of S min Cromdale and Advie 1959–71; retd;

resid Grantown-on-Spey; chmn Moray and Nairn educ comm 1958–60

GRANT Lawrence Barron   MA 1924 *BSc 1925
retd 1976; resid Glasg

GRANT Lesley Dunbar   MA 1954
teacher Crossroads s Durris 1963–73, head from 1973
member Banchory t c from 1971, Dean of Guild from 1971; hon treasurer until 1975; member selection comm for Scot. women's golf 1976

GRANT Lewis Neish   *MA 1950

GRANT or Speight, Mabel   MA 1908
no longer on GC reg

GRANT or McArthur, Maggie Irvine   MA 1908
no longer on GC reg

GRANT or Burton, Margaret Isabella   MA 1910
d Victoria BC 6.3.80

GRANT Margaret Janet   MA 1910
resid Forres

GRANT or Melvin, Margaret Macpherson   MA 1918
farm. Brechin; resid Brechin

GRANT or Craig, Margaret Paterson   MA 1928
no longer on GC reg

GRANT or Bremner, Margaret Shand   MA 1931
resid Forres

GRANT Marjory Jean   MA 1954
teacher: Alford s 1960–66, Insch s 1967–69, Keith g s from 1969

GRANT or Wilson, Mary Philip   BSc 1944
teacher maths Ruthrieston s s (later Harlaw acad) Aber 1964–77; retd

GRANT or Thomson, Moira   MA 1955 Dip Ed 1956
head Fetternear p s 1963–68; asst prin teacher Inverurie acad 1968–71, Stoneywood p s Aber from 1971
husb *d* 5.10.64

GRANT or Whittaker, Moyreen   MA 1955
resid Aber

GRANT Murdo Macdonald
                MA 1952 *1954 Dip Ed 1955
prin teacher Engl Golspie h s 1964–68, head Kingussie h s from 1968

GRANT Muriel Catherine   MA 1941
High School Asst Cert(Tor) 1959 Dip Lib Sc 1968
teacher Moray and Nairn 1942–44; teacher/lib Port Elgin, Ont from 1959
m Lossiemouth 1944 W. James Meikle stained glass artist s of William M. Toronto

GRANT or Hedges, Nora Christina   MA 1936

GRANT Norma Cissy   MA 1948

GRANT Patrick Thomas   *BSc 1951
FRSE 1969 FIBiol 1970 OBE 1980
reader biochem Aberd and dir fisheries biochem res
unit 1963–70; dir inst of marine biochem and hon lect
marine biochem Aberd from 1970

GRANT Quentin Alexander Frain Rae
                                    ***MB ChB 1951**
Foundation FRCPsych 1972
USA; asst dir ch psychiat Johns Hopkins univ,
Baltimore 1960–61, dir ment health St Louis
county Missouri 1962–64, chief soc psychiat NIMH
Washington DC 1966–68; Canada: psychiat-in-chief
hosp for sick ch Tor and prof child psychiat Tor from
1968

GRANT Robert   MA 1946 *BSc 1949
sen prin scient off. and head of soil surv of Scot.
Macaulay inst for soil res Aber from 1950

GRANT Robert Charles   MA 1893
no longer on GC reg

GRANT Ronald Kirkham   MB ChB 1921

GRANT or Farquhar, Sheila Leonard
                            MA 1950 ᵈLLB 1953
resid Radlett

GRANT Stuart Cowie   BSc(eng) 1944
d –.1.62

GRANT William   MA 1915
d Monifieth 28.6.70

GRANT William Gordon   MB CM 1895 MD 1898
d Dunbar –.11.60 *AUR* xxxix 95

GRANT William Ligertwood Main   MA 1905
no longer on GC reg

GRANT William Morton
                        MA 1919 BD 1922 PhD 1928
C of S min Falkirk W ch 1927–67; retd

GRANT William Sutherland   *MA 1926
d 9.8.65 *AUR* xli 246

GRASSICK Donald McCombie   BSc(eng) 1944
d 2.10.71

GRASSICK John Robertson   MA 1949
teacher Engl Selkirk h s
d Galashiels 17.10.78

GRASSICK William James   MA 1919
d 1.10.63

GRASSIE Dorothy Isobel   BL 1952

GRASSIE or Hibbard, Elizabeth Donald
                            MB ChB 1951 MD 1963
lect dept of obst and gyn Liv 1963–73; stud
counsellor Welsh nat s med from 1974

GRASSIE James Campbell   DSc 1948
Aberd: reader dept of eng till 1963
d Glasg 14.5.76 *AUR* xlvii 106

GRASSIE John Taylor   MB ChB 1934
g p Cheltenham from 1935; anaest Cheltenham gen
hosp 1937–62

GRASSIE Norman   *BSc 1945 PhD 1948
DSc(Glas)

GRATE Robert Alexander   MA 1932
d 6.3.66

GRATTIDGE Alan Edwin Thomas   BSc(eng) 1950
FIMechE 1969
Aber: tech dir John M. Henderson & Co from 1965;
dir C. F. Wilson (1932) & Co from 1973

GRATTIDGE Isobel Riddell   MB ChB 1942
g p Nott from 1949

GRAY Adam   MB ChB 1909 MD 1912
d 13.2.70 *AUR* xliii 440

GRAY or Graham, Aileen Jean   MA 1952
resid Bieldside, Aber

GRAY Alan Taylor   MA 1953
head maths dept Castle s Taunton 1966–71; dep
head Barnoldswick s West Riding, 1971–74; head La
Mare de Carteret s Guernsey from 1974

GRAY Albert Henry   *MA 1928
asst actuary Sun Life Assur Co of Canada from
1954

GRAY Alexander   MA 1909
d Stonehaven 17.6.68 *AUR* xliii 78

GRAY Alexander   MA 1911
d Portsoy 1.2.72 *AUR* xliv 427

GRAY Alexander   MA 1925 LLB 1927
ptnr Gray & Kellas advoc Aber from 1930
d 10.10.81

GRAY Alexander   BSc(eng) 1947
Banff c c: chief asst eng 1965–67, dep county surv
from 1967

GRAY Alexander James   MB ChB 1953
Tasmania: dist m o Cygnet 1967–69, Evandale
from 1969; also m o to tuberculosis div Launceston
from 1969

GRAY Alexander Pirie   MB ChB 1924
retd 1964; resid Durh
m Wheatley Hill, Durh 1962 Ann Gribbens

GRAY Alexander Robertson   MA 1921 LLB 1922
d 6.11.76 *AUR* xlvii 105

GRAY Alexander Thomson   *BSc(eng) 1948

GRAY Andrew Latto Craig   MA 1951
min Pinelands presb ch Cape Town from 1959

GRAY Andrew Paton   MB ChB 1912
d 19.11.63

GRAY Barbara Mary Young   *MA 1933
d –.10.71

GRAY or Ross, Bella Rainy   MA 1909
d 4.11.76

GRAY Brian Scott   *BSc 1953 PhD 1970
MIBiol 1968
dir of res Harrison & Crosfield Malaysia 1960–70;
on staff World Bank Jakarta, Indonesia 1970–75,
Washington DC from 1975
m Kuala Lumpur 24.8.68 Adèle M. Surin bus. woman
d of Herbert P. S. Ipoh Malaysia

GRAY Charles Duncan Stewart   *MA 1940
asst man. periodicals advt dept *The Times* Lond
1961–65; man. *The Times* Edin off. and advt man. *The
Times Educational Supplement Scotland*
m Aber 11.11.66 Barbara B. Smith
d Edin 15.6.74 *AUR* xlvi 110

GRAY Charles Hugh   MA 1900
no longer on GC reg

GRAY Daniel   BL 1959
d Aber 11.6.61 *AUR* xxxix 205

GRAY David George   MB ChB 1955
FRCP(C) 1966
Canada: phys royal Ottawa sanatorium 1957–62,
resid Ottawa gen hosp 1962–66, radiol Ottawa gen
hosp/assoc prof univ of Ottawa med s 1966–76, chief
dept of radiol Queensway-Carleton hosp Ottawa
from 1976

GRAY or Spence, Diana Norma   MA 1949

GRAY or Hartgerink, Dorothy   *MA 1944
ALA(Aust) 1972
part time lib in arch. and univ lib Sydney Aust from
1967

GRAY Douglas   MA 1944 *1949
man. dir and founder Park Film Studios Glasg
from 1959; man. dir Campbell Harper Films Edin
from 1972

GRAY Douglas Alexander Gordon   BSc(eng) 1953
d Sutton Coldfield 4.11.70 *AUR* xliv 216

GRAY or Stuart, Elizabeth   MB ChB 1915
d 11.1.71

GRAY Eric   *MA 1951
prin teacher mod lang: Lasswade h s 1960–65,
Mary Erskine s Edin 1965–70; Airdrie acad: head
upper s 1970–71, dep rector 1971–73; rector Beath
sen h s Cowdenbeath from 1973

GRAY Eric Duff   MA 1919 MB ChB 1922 MD 1933
retd 1965; resid Manchester
wife *d* 2.7.53

m(2) Manc 26.9.59 Helen P. Hampson almoner d of
Francis C. H. Bramhall

GRAY Ethel Elizabeth Maitland
                              MB ChB 1921 DPH 1923
d Aber 19.11.68 *AUR* xliii 80

GRAY or Shirreffs, Eva Cecile Gordon
                              MB ChB 1945
clin asst Leic RI from 1957

GRAY or Smylie, Evelyn Allan   MA 1949
part-time remed teacher RACH 1968–72, full-time
from 1972

GRAY Francis Gillespie   MA 1922
d Edin 11.2.73

GRAY George   *MA 1946
asst lib univ St And from 1946

GRAY George Milne   MA 1916 MB ChB 1920
d Lamarsh 6.8.62 *AUR* xl 84

GRAY Hamish William   *MA 1949
schoolmaster Lond from 1954

GRAY Harry   MB ChB 1951

GRAY Hector Mulholland   MB ChB 1928
med pract Johannesburg from 1930; retd
m(2) Johannesburg Grace Pease d of John P. Illinois
USA

GRAY Helen Mackay
                    MA 1909 BSc 1911 MB ChB 1915
d Lond 1.9.70 *AUR* xliv 107

GRAY Isobel Margaret   MA 1942

GRAY James   MA 1946

GRAY James Garden   MA 1892
no longer on GC reg

GRAY James Smith   MA 1901 MB ChB 1904
d 21.1.61 *AUR* xxxix 98

GRAY or Watt, Jane Henderson   MA 1925
d 19.5.65

GRAY or Ironside, Jeannie Moir   MA 1913
d 15.2.70

GRAY John   MA 1930
Shetland: head Scalloway j s s till 1966; retd

GRAY John   MB ChB 1942
g p Thornley from 1948

GRAY John Alexander   *BSc 1942
chem res and dev dept Bakelite Birm from 1959

GRAY John Gordon   MA 1914
retd; resid Aber

GRAY John Hector　　MA 1932 ʿLLB 1939
　ptnr Gray & Kellas advoc Aber from 1946

GRAY John William Reid　　*MA 1949 LLB 1952
　resid magistrate Uganda till 1962; temp proc-fiscal
dep Glasg 1962–63; Dund: lect private law from
1964; warden Airlie Hall 1966–75

GRAY or Gray, Lilian Elizabeth　　MA 1926
　resid Kenilworth Cape Town
husb *d* 14.1.62

GRAY Malcolm　　*MA 1939
　Aberd: sen lect econ hist dept of pol econ 1962–66,
reader econ hist 1966–69; reader econ hist dept of
econ hist from 1969

GRAY or Comfort, Margaret Ann　　MA 1942
　teacher Lat/Engl Alford acad from 1943

GRAY or Hector, Mary Forrest　　MB ChB 1945
　g p Maseru Lesotho 1960–66; part time lect dept of
path. Aberd 1967–75, res asst dept genetics 1977–80

GRAY or Allan, Priscilla Elizabeth　　MA 1948
　resid Scunthorpe

GRAY Robert　　*BSc 1951
　asst rector Mackie acad Stonehaven from 1972
m Aber 27.3.59 Edith Smith

GRAY Robert Alexander Harper　　MA 1901
　no longer on GC reg

GRAY Ronald　　MB ChB 1955
　h o St James hosp Tredegar 1959–61; g p:
Cwmbran 1961–72, Birm from 1972
m(2) Merthyr Tydfil 25.10.69 Nina Davis midwife d of
Sidney D. Merthyr Tydfil

GRAY Stuart Thomas Gordon
　　　　　　　　　　　　MB ChB 1935 DPH 1937
　O St J 1963 C St J 1971 FFCM 1972
C MoH and prin school m o E. Suffolk 1952–74; retd
wife *d* 11.11.75
m(2) Eye 29.12.77 Lucille B. Stables or Swinney d of
William S. Aber

GRAY Theodore Grant　　MB ChB 1906
　d Wellington NZ 8.9.64 *AUR* XL 394

GRAY Trevor
　　　　　BSc(mech eng) 1936 BSc(elect eng) 1937

GRAY or Gordon, Vera　　MA 1937
　resid Edin

GRAY William Cowan　　MB ChB 1901
　d Jersey 2.6.67 *AUR* XLII 345

GRAY William Hedley　　*MA 1949

GRAY Williamina　　MA 1910
　retd; resid Aber
d Aber 1977

GRAY Winniefred Margaret
　　　　　　　　MA 1910 MB ChB 1913 DPH 1914
　d Perth 9.11.72 *AUR* XLV 124

GREEN or Brown, Annie Bella　　MA 1912
　d 25.4.66 *AUR* XLII 84

GREEN or Fyfe, Annie Fraser　　MA 1911
　d Aber 29.9.73

GREEN Elizabeth Aimée　　MB ChB 1951
　DPM MRCPsych
Cell Barnes hosp St Albans: sen regist 1962–67,
consult. psychiat from 1967

GREEN George Dunbar　　BSc 1933 MA 1938
　lect maths Thurso tech coll 1967–77; retd

GREEN James　　*MA 1929
　d Aber 11.9.73

GREEN Mabel　　MA 1953
　Dip Phonetics (Edin) 1963
sen lect speech unit Engl dept Moray House coll of
educ Edin from 1971

GREEN Marion Winifred　　*MA 1936
　retd 1970; resid Aber

GREEN or Crook, Nancie Hilda　　*MA 1936

GREEN Patrick John　　MA 1901
　d Aber 24.2.66 *AUR* XLII 80

GREEN Peter　　BL 1938

GREENE or Biezanek, Anne Campbell
　　　　　　　　　　　　BSc 1947 MB ChB 1951
　g p Wallasey Cheshire from 1963
marr diss July 1972
m(2) Wallasey 9.11.72 Frank Le R. Perrée retd soc
worker High Wycombe

GREENHORNE Marcus Fernando Hillarion
　　　　　　　　　　　　　　BSc(eng) 1931
　d Aber 27.3.71 *AUR* XLIV 212

GREENLAW Karl Stewart Guthrie　　MA 1937
　d Edin 15.1.75 *AUR* XLVI 239

GREENSMITH Leonard Alexander　　*MA 1928
　teacher maths Stirling h s 1960–68; retd; resid Aber
d Aber 12.8.79

GREESON Clarence Edward
　　　　　　　　　　　MB ChB 1910 MD 1913
　d 10.6.79 *AUR* XLVIII 350

GREGOR or Berry, Emily Isabella　　MA 1931

GREGOR Ewen William　　BSc(for) 1955

GREGOR Robert　　MA 1912
　retd 1949; resid Edin

GREGOR Walter   MB ChB 1922
d Bridge of Earn 21.9.71 *AUR* XLIV 320

**GREGOR or Murdoch, Winifred Montgomery
                                        MA 1950**

GREIG or Irvine, Alice Mary Geddes   MA 1910
d 12.8.62 *AUR* XL 80

GREIG or Cheetham, Clara   MA 1944
  teacher: King's House Calcutta 1955–60, Bishop-briggs Glasg 1961–62, Engl Lenzie acad Glasg 1962–65; form mistress/teacher Engl Foundation of King Edward VI Macclesfield 1965–67; head: Maryton s Montrose 1967–70, Sandford s Strathaven from 1970

GREIG or Gardiner, Georgina Imray   MA 1929
  resid Brixham

GREIG Hazel Williamina   MA 1941
  lect in craft Aber coll of educ 1962–65
m Aber 17.12.65 Leslie Wilson comp dir s of Thomas W. Cleckheaton

GREIG John   *MA 1949
  FSAScot 1971
col off. Devonshire Ho Lond 1950–51; col admin serv Nyasaland 1951–55; asst prin col off. Lond 1955–57; sen lab off. Blantyre, Nyasaland 1957–60; asst comm of lab Aden 1960–64; teacher hist Bell-Baxter h s Cupar from 1969

GREIG John Lyall   BSc(agr) 1924 BSc 1926
  OBE 1956
schol: Oxon/Imp coll of trop agr Trinidad 1926–28; dept agr Malaya 1928–50; dir agr N. Borneo 1950–56; advis (World Bank) govt of Iran 1957–61; chief of mission FAO of UN to Ethiopia 1962–67; resid Guildford

GREIG or Crabb, Kathleen Ogilvy Lindsay   MA 1949

**GREIG or Maclagan, Laura Mary Hutcheon
                                        *MA 1930**

**GREIG or Macaulay or Dodd, Margaret Helen Ingram
                                        BSc 1942 *1943**
  St And: Nuffield res fell. 1951–57; res fell. 1957–60; MRC res fell. Leeds 1963–68; SRC res fell. Bangor Wales from 1970

GREIG Thomas Paton   BSc(eng) 1949

GREIG William James   BSc(eng) 1948
  civ eng Cementation Co UK, Iraq, India, Israel, Spain, USA 1949–71; man. dir Carbeth construct. co Airdrie 1972–76; construct. man. Mass transit rly corp Hong Kong from 1976
m Bearsden 22.6.74 Catherine Morrison MA 1955 *qv*

GREY Robert   MB ChB 1914
  no longer on GC reg

GRIBBLE James George   MA 1954

GRIEVE Donald McLeod   BSc(agr) 1941
  farm. Dumfriessh 1941–50; col agr serv Nigeria 1950–60; chartered land ag Dumfries 1960–65; ptnr Bell–Ingram chartered survs Perth from 1965
m Eckford, Roxburgh 23.7.58 Ann E. Scott d of George S. Kelso

GRIEVE Edwin   MA 1953 LLB 1955
  ptnr: Donaldson & Henderson solic Nairn 1958–68, Rollo, Steven & Bond solic Dun 1968–70, A. C. Morrison & Richards advoc Aber from 1970

GRIEVE Elizabeth Anderson   MA 1908
d –.4.61

**GRIEVE or Mitchell, Elizabeth Napier
                                        MB ChB 1953**
  resid Aber

**GRIEVE George McKenzie Denny
                                        *MA 1941 BD 1944**

GRIEVE James   MA 1918 MB ChB 1922
  retd 1961; resid Ferring

GRIFFIN Mona   MB ChB 1943 DPH 1948
  g p Aber from 1954

GRIFFITH Frank   MB ChB 1913
  no longer on GC reg

GRIFFITH or Wardell, Sheila Munro   *BSc 1954
  Chelmsford: school lab tech 1969–73; res eng Marconi wireless tel comp from 1973

GRIFFITHS David Ronald   BSc(eng) 1946

GRIFFITHS George Ian   MA 1939 BD 1942
  C of S min Chalmers ch Wishaw 1950–76, High Cross ch Melrose from 1976

GRIFFITHS or McLeod, Margaret Evans   MA 1928
  teacher maths/Engl RGC Aber 1966–73
husb *d* Port Harcourt Nigeria 8.3.66

GRIGOR James   BSc 1931 *1933
d Forres 30.1.74 *AUR* XLV 448

GROENEWALD Pieter Fourie   MB ChB 1933

GROUNDWATER Randolph Cumming   MA 1949
d Ontario Canada 15.3.72

GRUBB Anthony James   MA 1933
  C of S min Deer from 1954

GRUBB Craig McIrvine   *BSc(eng) 1953

GRUER Edith Mary   *MA 1910
d Edin 30.12.66 *AUR* XLII 82

GRUER Kenneth Terence   MB ChB 1950
  g p Kemnay 1953–67; Scot home & health dept Edin: reg m o 1967–70, sen m o from 1970

GUILD Alexander Eddie   BSc(eng) 1930
FIWE 1951 FICE 1968 OBE 1973
President IWE 1969−70
eng and man. Newport: Newport & S Mon water
board 1960−70, Gwent water board 1970−74, Welsh
water auth to retirement 1974

GULLETT or MacDonald, Adeline Isabel   MA 1936
head Walker Dam inf s Aber from 1967

GUNN Alasdair James Manson   BSc(agr) 1955

GUNN Alastair James   MA 1924
insp of schools Europ educ dept N Rhodesia
1953−55; retd; part-time teaching posts: NZ 1955−57,
boys' g s Eng 1957−66; resid Downderry nr Torpoint

GUNN Alexander   MA 1925
head Castletown j s s Caithness from 1938
deceased

GUNN Alexanderina   MA 1950

GUNN Benjamin Williamson   MA 1928 ᶜLLB 1931
retd 1968; resid Fochabers
d Buckie 12.6.81

GUNN Christina Alexandra   MB ChB 1936
retd 1972; resid Bognor Regis

GUNN Colin Fraser   MA 1907
no longer on GC reg

GUNN Flora McKenzie   MA 1955
d 31.7.65 AUR XLI 252

GUNN Hamish Iain   BSc 1955
asst head Halkirk 1962−67; Thurso h s: teacher sc
1967−72, prin guid 1972−74 and asst head from 1974

GUNN John Alexander   MA 1915
C of S min: St Fittick's ch Aber till 1956; chaplain
H.M. Prison Craiginches, Aber 1943−58; resid Bridge
of Weir
d Bridge of Weir 18.1.80 AUR XLVIII 440

GUNN or McVay, Marie McKenzie   MA 1924
no longer on GC reg

GUNN or Beardmore, Marion Ellen Maggie
                                        MA 1906
d 18.7.69 AUR XLIII 327

GUNN Murdo MacKenzie   MB ChB 1923
no longer on GC reg

GUNN or Tait, Norma Mary   MA 1953

GUNN William   MA 1919 *MB ChB 1924
d Wick 18.1.68 AUR XLII 357

GWYNN Arthur Montague   MB ChB 1942
MA(Dub) 1967
dep edit. Medical Journal of Australia Sydney 1960−77,
edit. from 1977

GYLE John McGregor   BSc(agr) 1950
farm. Esslemont, Ellon from 1950
m Dun 25.10.52 Doreen G. Paterson d of Donald
F. P. Dun

HAASE or Rosowsky, Erika Ernestine   MA 1944
resid North Hill Lond

HACKET or Johnstone, Dorothy Christian Liddle
                                *MA 1935 *1937
Gwilym Gibbon res fell. Nuffield coll Oxon 1973−74
comm of customs and excise 1964−76; excise advis
BAT Lond 1976−77
d 24.2.81 AUR XLIX 138

HADDEN Charles Strachan   MA 1912
no longer on GC reg

HADDEN George Campbell   MB ChB 1944
g p Blackheath Birm from 1950
m Sedgley 25.6.60 Patricia Baker MB ChB(Birm) med
pract d of Henry B. B. Sedgley

HADDEN Helen Elizabeth   MA 1915
no longer on GC reg

HADDEN Jeannie   MA 1936
teacher King St s Aber from 1950

HADDEN Jeannie Chalmers   MA 1931
retd 1970; resid Aber

HADDEN Jessie Harper   *MA 1919
retd 1959; resid Inverurie

HADDEN or Gould, Winifred Reith   MA 1925
resid Bo'ness

HADDOCK William   *MA 1954
MInstP 1963 MRInst Navig 1964
prin eng Marconi Space and Defence Syst (Combined
GEC, Engl Elec Co, AEI) Stanmore from 1968

HAINING Kenneth Anderson   BSc 1949
RAF serv in Korea, Cyprus, Philippines, Brunei,
Aden, UK; retd 1965; teacher Nott: Eastwood s mod
s 1965−72, head sc Eastwood comp l s from 1972
m Kegworth 14.2.68 Rosalie I. Swann comp dir d of
Henry S. Liv

HAINING William Fulton   BSc 1952
teacher maths/sc Hatton 1961−63; head Kinneff p s
from 1963

HALCROW Marjory Elizabeth Agnes   MA 1943
resid Aber

HALDANE William Duncan   BSc(for) 1933
retd 1970; resid Crockey Hill York

HALKETT or Brebner, Evelyn   *MA 1928
resid Turriff

HALL or Saxby, Agnes Milne   MA 1929
resid Leighton Buzzard

HALL Agnes Taylor Cameron MA 1930
head Kirkhill p s Aber 1957–61; retd
m Aber 8.4.61 Alexander Keir MA 1905 *qv*
husb *d* 3.1.71

HALL Alan Stirling *MA 1954
FSA(Lond) 1973
lect classics Keele 1961–72; sen lect from 1972;
visiting lect dept classical stud. univ Pennsylvania
Philadelphia 1968–69; hon secy Brit inst of archae
Ankara 1973
m Cambridge 7.7.63 Gillian M. Carver BA(Keele) ch
care off. d of Ralph C. Sawston

HALL Alfred Petrie MB ChB 1906
d Aberfeldy 31.3.63 *A UR* XL 198

HALL David MB ChB 1955
g p Milton Keynes

HALL Eric George
　　　　　　　　BSc(elect eng) 1944 BSc(civ eng) 1948
FICE 1973
Edin: dep res eng James Williamson & Ptnrs 1953–66;
dir Mitchell construct comp (Scot.) 1966–73, gen
man. Farrans 1973–74; associate James Williamson
& Ptnrs from 1974

HALL Frederick *MA 1952
col educ serv: prin coll in Kenya 1953–66; univ of
Malawi 1966–68; dep head educ Doncaster coll of
educ from 1968
marr diss

HALL George William Hutchison BCom 1926
no longer on GC reg

HALL James Christian MB ChB 1920
d Stowmarket 17.10.66 *A UR* XLII 85

HALL John Alexander BSc 1950
retd 1973; resid Alness
d 5.3.77

HALL Leonard Duncan BSc(eng) 1951
SAI: prod. controller Edin 1961–69, works eng
Aber 1969–73, eng sen man. from 1973

HALL or Gates, Mary Jane Cruickshank MA 1940

HALL or Rugg, Vera Winifred Duguid
　　　　　　　　　　MB ChB 1941 DPH 1948
dep m o h Caithness from 1963

HALLIDAY Alastair George Brand *MA 1937
trained for Presb min Westminster coll Cambridge
1969–71; asst Trinity presb C of E Harrow 1971–72;
ordained and inducted Trinity presb C of E Streatham
Lond 1972

HALLIDAY George BSc(for) 1922
no longer on GC reg

HALLIDAY or Jope, Henrietta Margaret *BSc 1937
hon res fell. geobiochem Belf from 1965

HALLIDAY John Alexander *MA 1927
retd 1970; resid Perth

HAMILTON Daniel Currie BSc(agr) 1949
Edin: man. dir SAI (horticulture) 1964–70, consult.
from 1970

HAMILTON David Anderson MB ChB 1936
d Montrose 2.3.62 *A UR* XXXIX 386

HAMILTON Elizabeth Findlay MB ChB 1954
ophth inst Glasg: sen regist 1960–62; sen h m o
(part time) 1962–71, med asst from 1971

HAMILTON Gilbert Frewin
　　　　　　　　　　BSc 1933 MB ChB 1938
visiting prof Marquette univ Milwaukee USA 1961
d Aber 10.6.74 *A UR* XLVI 110

HAMILTON John BSc(eng) 1945

HAMILTON Joseph Stewart
　　　　　　　　　　MB ChB 1939 DPH 1947
founder FFCM 1971 FRSH 1961
area m o Staffs from 1964

HAMILTON Malcolm Thomas Henderson
　　　　　　　　　　　　　　　MA 1952
asst rector Blairgowrie h s from 1972

HAMILTON or Newton, Margaret Macfarlane
　　　　　　　　　　　　　　MA 1949
resid Wells

HAMILTON or May, Margaret Steedman
　　　　　　　　　　　　　　MB ChB 1947
BA 1978
g p Bolsover from 1961

HAMILTON Ronald Thomas BSc(eng) 1953
CEng MICE 1959
dir Mitchell Construction Co: Stockton-on-Tees
1961–73, Stamford from 1973

HAMILTON Thomas Graham MB ChB 1954

HAMILTON William Aitken Brown *MA 1931
dir pers/under secy-gen of UN NY 1959–62; asst
under secy of state F C O Lond 1962–68; retd; resid
Tunbridge Wells

HAMILTON-BELL Patrick MB ChB 1937
g p Richmond Surrey from 1950

HAMILTON-PEARSON Edgar Alan
　　　　　　　　　　　　　　MB ChB 1912
d Alderney 23.5.61 *A UR* XXXIX 274

HAMLEY Kenneth Norman MA 1952

HAMPTON Myron Grant *BSc 1953
tech off. SAI Edin 1958–67; head eng R & D div
Brooke Bond Liebig Reading from 1967
m South Weald 9.9.61 Virginia M. Davis SRN d of
Edward D. South Weald

HANNAGAN Michael John   BSc(agr) 1953
Dip Agr (Cantab) 1954 DTA(Trin) 1955
agr off. col serv Tanganyika 1955–61; agr advis
Spillers S Eng and S Wales 1961–71; formulations
man. Spillers farm feeds Lond from 1971
m Aber 26.6.54 Barbara M. Doig MA 1952 *qv*

HARBRON Patrick   *MA 1953
Uttoxeter: sixth form master Alleyne's g s 1964–74,
head sixth form/sen teacher from 1974
m Pontesbury 17.4.63 Blanche Malcolm BA(Nott)
teacher d of Lewelyn-Bar M. Pontesbury

HARDCASTLE Edward John Brierly   BSc(for) 1950
TD
man. dir Engl for. assoc Reading 1958–67; major: 4th
KOSB(TA) till 1960, 4/6th Royal Berks regt (TA)
1960–66; dir Engl Woodlands Uckfield from 1968

HARDIE Alexander Merrie
                    MA 1931 *BSc(elect eng) 1933
                    ***BSc(mech eng) 1934 PhD 1959**
MRWEA 1970
vice-prin Bristol coll adv tech 1963–66; prof phys univ
of Bath from 1966 and pro-vice-chancellor 1966–71

HARDIE Alexander Waldie   MB ChB 1937
consult. anaest royal Surrey county hosp Guildford
from 1947

HARDIE or Johnston, Annie   MA 1910
no longer on GC reg

HARDIE or Sussex, Elizabeth   *MA 1953
Lond: contrib to Brit film inst publ from 1962,
edit. asst *Sight and Sound*, asst edit. *Monthly Film
Bulletin* 1964–66, freelance writer and res from 1966;
publ works: *Lindsay Anderson* (Studio Vista) 1969;
autobiog novel under pseudonym 1971; prod. and
directed docum film *Can Horses Sing?* 1971; *The Rise
and Fall of British Documentary* (Univ of Calif Press)
1975
m Aber 15.6.59 Alan Sussex BA(Oxon); husb *d* 1965

HARDIE Ethel Louisa   MA 1921

HARDIE Frances Irene   MA 1952
teacher Glasg from 1961

HARDIE Frederick William   MA 1909
d 8.4.68 *AUR* XLII 348

HARDIE or Bruce, Helen Glennie Yule   MA 1954
dept econ dev Victoria BC Canada from 1965

HARDIE Hugh Grant Macpherson   PhD 1948
retd 1972; resid Cults Aber

HARDIE James Leslie   MB ChB 1950
g p: Southland NZ 1967–70, York from 1970

HARDIE Peter   MA 1926 BCom 1929
retd; resid Aber

HARDIE Raymond Ledingham   *BSc 1954 PhD 1957

HARDIE William Dunbar   *MA 1953
FHA 1970
asst secy: NE reg hosp board Aber 1963–76, Grampian
health board from 1976
m Aber 3.8.63 Margaret E. Simpson MA 1963 *qv*

HARDING Albert William   *MA 1952
MEd(St And) 1962 PhD(Dund) 1976
lect hist Dun coll of educ from 1962

HARDY Eric Gordon   *MB ChB 1940 MD 1954
first asst dept surg Durh from 1954; consult. surg
Chester R. I. from 1959

HARE Christopher Leighton   PhD 1941

HARGREAVES Claude Christian   MB ChB 1915
retd; resid Brighouse

HARGREAVES Herbert   MB ChB 1909
no longer on GC reg

HARKER Alan Brook   BSc(agr) 1951
farm man. N Walsham 1951–56; BOCM: advis
Suffolk 1956–60, prod. man. Erith 1960–62, advis
Glasg 1962–68, p r and training man. Basingstoke
1968–73; sales man. Boe & Silcock Shrewsbury
1973–75; agr advis Glasg from 1975
m Leic 10.5.52 Sheila M. V. Boddy BSc(agr)(Lond)
res asst d of James A. V. B. Leic

HARKINS or Simpson, Anne   MA 1948
farm. Karoi, Rhodesia
m(2) Salisbury Rhodesia 26.2.64 John P. Adams farm.
s of John W. A. MB ChB(Lond) E Lond S. Afr

HARKINS Denis   MB ChB 1937
d Derby 20.5.75 *AUR* XLVI 325

HARKINS or Gammie, Helen Davidson
                    MB ChB 1941
g p Elgin from 1961

HARKINS William   *MA 1926 MB ChB 1931
retd 1972; resid Strichen

HARLEY Robert Chalmers   BSc(agr) 1952
insp DAFS from 1953; resid Keith

HARPER Alfred Alexander
                    MA 1929 MB ChB 1932 *MD 1947
N'cle: prof physiol 1963–72, emeritus from 1972

HARPER Alister Donald   *MA 1942
Brit Council: asst rep Buenos Aires 1961–65, overseas "A" div 1965–73, home div from 1973; retd 1981

HARPER or Rhind, Charlotte Cockburn   MA 1950
teacher: Huntly 1960–70, Scotstown 1970–73, Cults
Aber from 1973

HARPER or Wallace, Daisy Isabel Margaret
                    MA 1931
d Inverurie 27.11.79

HARPER Douglas   MA 1902 *BL 1905
no longer on GC reg

HARPER Elizabeth   MA 1911 BSc 1915
d Manchester 20.6.67 *AUR* XLII 181

HARPER Eric Imlay   MA 1933 MB ChB 1938
g p Swindon from 1946; retd 1978

HARPER Francis Gordon   BSc(for) 1931
owner and man. Glebe farm and nursery Aboyne
from 1958

HARPER James Hall McPherson   BSc 1941

HARPER John Stuart   MB ChB 1924
d Trowbridge 9.9.77 *AUR* XLVII 286

HARPER or McKay, Mary Scott   MA 1928
resid Banff

HARPER Peter Charles   BSc 1948 *1949

HARPER William Francis   MA 1904
no longer on GC reg

HARRINGTON Albert Blair
                        MB ChB 1938 MD 1944
FMFCM 1972
chief med advis civ serv dept from 1976

HARRIS or Allan, Barbara Munro   MA 1950

HARRIS or Gordon, Dorothy Morton
                        MB ChB 1925
g p Goodmayes 1926–63
d Vancouver 15.11.78

HARRIS Herbert Reginald   MB ChB 1927
d Ipswich 12.10.69 *AUR* XLIII 330

HARRIS Matthew Hughs   MB ChB 1903
no longer on GC reg

HARRISON John Clive   BSc(for) 1949
dist off. for. comm: E England 1950–54, New Forest
1954–62; Kent 1962–73, Malvern from 1973
m Southampton –.9.56 Marie J. Murray d of William
M. Southampton

HARROW John Alexander   MB ChB 1941
g p Keswick from 1947

HARROW Mary Elizabeth
            MA 1930 MB ChB 1934 DPH 1938

HART Alis   MA 1932
retd 1966; resid Stonehaven

HARVEY Charles Alexander
                        MB ChB 1917 DPH 1921
d Bedfordsh 12.9.76 *AUR* XLVII 102

HARVEY Derek John   *MA 1954

HARVEY Douglas   MA 1923 BSc 1924 PhD 1927
commonwealth bureau of anim nutrit Rowett inst
Aber: scient asst 1952–56, asst dir 1956–60, dir 1960–
66; retd

HARVEY Helen Margaret   MA 1920
no longer on GC reg

HARVEY Ina Berry   MA 1926
d –.12.62

HARVEY Jeanie   MA 1928
teacher: Logie Durno 1942–47, Old Rayne 1947–66
m Insch 28.1.30 Charles W. Ross farm. s of Alexander
R. Insch

HARVEY or Sutherland, Margaret Mary   MA 1932
d Kirkcaldy 16.12.78

HARVEY Mary Elizabeth   MA 1928
retd 1971; resid Aber

HARVEY or Maclennan, Mary Elizabeth
                        BSc MA 1933
teacher maths/sc Perthsh 1955–70; resid Blairgowrie

HARVEY Peter   MB ChB 1952
d Leeds 27.12.69 *AUR* XLIII 447

HARVEY William Alexander   BCom 1935
retd 1969; resid Market Harborough
d 4.10.76

HASSAN Ali   MB ChB 1929

HASSAN Hassan Mohamed   MA 1955

HASSAN Kamal   PhD 1947

HASTINGS Alexander Gordon   MB ChB 1926
no longer on GC reg

HASTINGS or Page, Ann Wilson   MA 1915 *1916
d London 23.3.75 *AUR* XLVI 236

HASTINGS Edward   *MA 1913 DD 1950
joint-edit. *The Expository Times* 1922–64; edit.
and published *The Speaker's Bible* in 36 vol; other
publications
d Aber 31.7.80 *AUR* XLIX 66

HATT or Forbes, Mabel   MA 1923
resid Auckland NZ

HAUGHS Margaret Agnes   BSc(agr) 1949
NOSCA: agr econ 1955–71, sen agr econ from
1971

HAWES Arthur Joseph   MB ChB 1916
d 27.11.74 *AUR* XLVI 236

HAY or Begg, Alice   MA 1938
head Glenlyon s Aberfeldy from 1968

HAY or Auchnie, Alice   MA 1947
resid Keithhall Inverurie

HAY Andrew Bertram   MB ChB 1936

HAY Andrew Leslie   MA 1925 ᵈLLB 1927
sen ptnr Cooper & Hay advoc Aber; part-time lect
Aberd: evid and proced 1945–64, tax. law 1961–77

HAY Arthur Colson   MA 1937
MB ChB(St And) 1943
g p Wallasey from 1949

**HAY or Mitchell or Dunn, Barbara Helen Douglas
MA 1952**

HAY or Gillies, Camilla Hill   *MA 1934
asst lect Fr/Lat univ of Leeds from 1945; asst
examiner JMB Lond, Oxon, Cantab from 1940
d Harrogate 20.6.78 *A UR* xLvIII 105

HAY Charles Albert   MB ChB 1920
d Aber 7.11.76

HAY or Sim, Christina Riddell   MA 1928
m Aberdeensh Robert Lumsden Sim
d –.5.58

HAY David   MA 1951
head Rainford h s St Helen's from 1961

HAY David Sinclair   BL 1932

HAY David Stuart   BSc(agr) 1952
ICI agr div: dep chmn 1977
m Hitchin 20.8.60 Patricia K. Jespersen BA(Lond)
teacher/pers off. d of Svend A. J.

HAY Francis Walker Christie   MA 1947 *1949
teacher: prin hist/mod stud. Aberfeldy h s 1962–65,
prin hist Banff acad 1965–70, asst rector from 1970
national convener R. Brit Legion (Scot.) from 1967

HAY George   BSc(eng) 1945
control construct. eng: 1958–70, proj. man. Lond
and Renfrew from 1970

HAY George Gordon Wallace   MB ChB 1921
d 23.10.69

HAY Gladys Ann Campbell   MA 1941
teacher: Whitehills 1942–44, Dufftown 1944–46,
Charleston USA 1946–47, Dufftown 1947–52,
Chilliwack BC Canada 1952–53, Elgin 1954–78; retd

HAY Gladys Rose   MA 1948
Aber: year mistress Summerhill acad 1970–72, dep
head Hilton acad from 1972

HAY Hamish Gordon   *BSc 1948
teacher-missionary meth coll Uzuakoli E Nigeria
1958–62; head phys Matthew Murray s Leeds 1962–
70; head sc Tong comp s Bradford from 1970

HAY Harold Mills   BSc(eng) 1947

HAY or McDougall, Helen Jane   MA 1916
d Tribune Sask 4.8.75

HAY or Fairley, Helen Mary   MA 1910
d Lanark 9.7.77

HAY Ian Kennedy   MB ChB 1941
FACMA 1968
Aust: m o h NSW 1960–67, metrop m o h Sydney
1967–72, prin m o h health comm NSW Sydney from
1972
d Sydney 13.5.77

**HAY James Robert William
MB ChB 1926 DPH 1928 *MD 1930**
m o h Kirkcaldy 1937–64; retd; resid Kinnoull
Perth

HAY Jane Laing   MA 1931
retd 1970; resid Fortrose

HAY or Webster, Janet (Jessie)   MA 1913
husb *d* 1957
d Aber 21.2.80

HAY Janet Guthrie   MA 1943
teacher Engl/hist Rothes s s 1963–68
m Elgin 14.9.68 Norman Burns chief supt police s of
James D. B. Kincardine o' Neil

HAY or Brown, Jean Cameron   MB ChB 1951
dept m o Herts c c 1968–75; m o Rudolph Steiner
curative schools from 1975

HAY Jessie Helen   MA 1925 BSc 1925 *1926
retd 1967; resid Elgin

HAY John McKay   BSc(eng) 1952

HAY John Rae   BSc(agr) 1927
no longer on GC reg

HAY John Sutherland   *MA 1945
prin teacher classics James Gillespie's h s Edin from
1966

HAY or Birch, Lorna May   *MA 1936
d Lond 23.8.69 *A UR* xLIII 331

HAY Margaret Ann   MB ChB 1936
retd 1974; resid Lond

HAY or Cowan, Margaret Geddes   MB ChB 1948
asst m o Edinburgh corp from 1969; clin m o
Lothian health board
husb *d* 1967

HAY Mildred Barnett   MA 1944
higher exec off. govt commun hq from 1965

HAY Robert Gall   *MA 1939
rector Arbroath h s from 1962

HAY Ronald John   *BSc 1945 PhD 1948
ICI Fibres: chem eng Harrogate 1959–64, tech asst
indust market res from 1964

HAY or Summers, Ruth Watson   *MA 1941
resid Portknockie
d 14.11.79

HAY William   MB ChB 1933
g p Aber from 1947

HAY William   BSc(agr) 1938

HAYES Norman Frank   *BSc 1952 PhD 1955
res chem Allen & Hanbury's Ware from 1958

HAYMAN Ann Elizabeth   MA 1950
teacher: sc Fort William 1967–68, maths Laurencekirk from 1977
m Fort William 20.6.60 Robert S. Hunter

HAYMAN Edward William   BL 1954
sen leg. asst Ayr c c 1961–69, chief leg. asst 1969–75;
asst dir admin Strathclyde reg c from 1975

HAYWOOD Laurence   MA 1951 Dip Ed 1952
Aber: dep head: Tillydrone p s 1965–67, Muirfield
p s 1967–70; head Quarryhill p s from 1970

HAZELWOOD James Scott   MA 1925
no longer on GC reg

HEAD Malcolm John   PhD 1950
visiting reader anim nutrit Sur, Guildford; consult.
anim nutrit

HEALD Peter Joseph   PhD 1952
DSc(Manc) 1962 FRSE 1967
head dept anim biochem Twyford Lab 1961–66; prof
biochem Strath from 1966

HEARD or Peet, Helen Asher   MA 1929
no longer on GC reg

HEARNE Arthur Ambrose   MB ChB 1916 MD 1925
d –.5.67

HECTOR George Pittendrigh
                    *MA 1901 BSc 1906 DSc 1922**
d Aber 12.11.62 *AUR* XL 74

HECTOR or Fowler, Irene   BSc 1951
teacher: Scotland, England, Canada till 1957
m 16.7.53 James A. Fowler MB ChB 1953 *qv*
d Victoria BC 12.7.80

HECTOR or Bradfield, Joyce Marguerite   BSc 1951
resid Aber

HECTOR Ralph Melville   MB ChB 1937
CBE 1963
consult. radiol military hosp: Catterick 1957–60,
Accra 1961–63 and sen m o Brit joint serv trg team;
consult. radiol Cambridge milit hosp Aldershot 1963–
74; retd

HECTOR William Litster   *MB ChB 1922
d Brighton 2.9.72 *AUR* XLV 125

HEDDLE Christine Louise   MA 1953

HEDDLE Harald Scott   MB ChB 1945
g p Benbecula and S Uist from 1955

HEDDLE Inga Pirie   MA 1949
teacher: Arusha Tanganyika 1958–61, St Andrew's
private s Maraval, Trinidad 1962–76; resid Burnley
m Port of Spain 31.1.74 John E. Pritchard textile tech

HEGGIE David John Gordon   BSc(agr) 1947
dairy farm. Wigtownsh from 1953

HEGGS Thomas Barrett   MB ChB 1902 MD 1904
no longer on GC reg

HELMRICH or Clow, Nan Louise
                    *BSc 1931 MA 1934**
scient historian
d Welwyn Garden City 10.2.73

HEMS John Macqueen   PhD 1954
tut. Engl/soc stud. Langside coll Glasg 1959–66;
Canada: prof phil Carleton univ 1966–67 (Canada
council grant 1968), assoc prof phil univ of Guelph
1967–69, prof phil from 1969 (Fr govt grant 1970)

HENDERSON or Rae, Aileen Margaret   MA 1925
resid Dollar

HENDERSON Alastair Gordon   BSc 1951 *1952
teacher: sc Stonehaven 1953–64, prin sc Alford
1964–65, sen teacher Aber from 1965

HENDERSON Alastair Wingate
                    MB ChB 1927 MD 1934
retd g p 1969; part time m o Bicester Ordnance
Oxon and part time assessor MHSS from 1969

HENDERSON Alexander Davidson
                    *MA 1950 MSc 1969**
statist NE reg hosp board Scot. Aber from 1967,
Grampian health board from 1974

HENDERSON Alexandra   MA 1909
retd; resid Heswall
d 1977

HENDERSON Alistair Mitchell   BSc(agr) 1925
no longer on GC reg

HENDERSON or Millington, Arabella Victoria
                    MA 1909
resid Seaview Is of Wight
d Is of Wight 28.1.80

HENDERSON Arthur Graeme   BSc(eng) 1950
FInstPet MSPERIM & Mech eng Professional eng
Trinidad
Trinidad: dist petr eng for. reserve 1960–63, dist supt
Barrackpore 1963–66, consult. petr eng 1966–68;
man. Singapore 1968–69: SE Asia man. Jakarta
1969–73; spec proj man. Santa Flora Trinidad from
1973

HENDERSON Caroline Lamond   MA 1910
d 23.10.71

HENDERSON Charles Shaw   *MA 1930
retd 1969; resid Scone

HENDERSON Christina Dickson
                              MA 1927 BSc 1930
retd 1967; resid Aber
d Newmachar 10.5.81 AUR XLIX 137

HENDERSON David   BSc(for) 1950

HENDERSON David   MA 1951 Dip Ed 1952
Dunfermline: teacher Engl/gen stud. Lauder tech coll 1960–64, sen asst i/c dept Engl/gen stud. from 1964

HENDERSON David   *BSc 1952

HENDERSON Denys Hartley   MA 1953 LLB 1955
ICI: various posts/dir i/c fertilisers agr div Billingham from 1957
m Aber Doreen M. Glashan d of Robert C. G. Aber

HENDERSON or MacKenzie, Dorothy Catherine
                              ***MA 1926**
d Falkirk 27.8.62 AUR XL 92

HENDERSON or Esson, Dorothy Johanna Margaret
                              MA 1932
teacher Ellon 1940: resid Huntly

HENDERSON or Thomson, Dorothy May
                              MA 1931
d Lond –.8.42

HENDERSON or Turner, Edith Mary   *MA 1935
resid Forfar

HENDERSON Elizabeth Harriet Mitchell   MA 1944
teacher Burnside inf s Aber from 1954

HENDERSON or Forrest, Elizabeth Mary
                              MA 1918
resid Bromley

HENDERSON Ellen Mary   *MA 1924
acting prin hist Central s s Aber 1943–49; prin Engl/hist Banchory acad 1949–64; retd; resid Banchory

HENDERSON Eric Douglas   BSc 1950

HENDERSON Esther Williamina   MA 1929

HENDERSON Forbes Wilson   MB ChB 1943
g p Sheffield from 1948

HENDERSON George David Smith   *MA 1953
MA PhD (Cantab) 1961 FSA
Graham Robertson res fell. Downing coll Cantab 1960–63; lect dept hist of art Manc 1962–65; lect dept fine art Edin 1966–71, reader 1971–73; lect and head of dept hist of art Cantab from 1974

HENDERSON George Richard   BSc(agr) 1946

HENDERSON Gordon Harvey   MA 1937 LLB 1939
d Aber 20.3.70 AUR XLIII 446

HENDERSON Gordon Nicol   BSc(eng) 1949
FICE 1972
sen ptnr A. Henderson & Ptnrs Aber from 1972

HENDERSON Hector McBain   MB ChB 1934
d 25.5.81

HENDERSON or Leslie, Helen McIntosh   MA 1942
resid Cleadon village Nr Sunderland

HENDERSON Henry   *MA 1931
resid Inv

HENDERSON Henry Laurence   MA BCom 1925
retd 1965; resid Musselburgh

HENDERSON Isabella Barclay   MA 1926
resid Edin

HENDERSON James   MB ChB 1924
d Scarborough 14.7.73 AUR XLV 319

HENDERSON James   BSc(for) 1951
Aberd: lect for. 1964–72, sen lect from 1972; lieut cdr RNR Aberd RN unit from 1968

HENDERSON James Gordon
                              cMB ChB 1949 MD 1970
FRCPsych 1971
consult. psychiat Grampian area health board from 1959 and clin sen lect mental health dept Aberd

HENDERSON or Lund, Jane Dalrymple   MA 1913

HENDERSON or Haddock, Jane Reid   *MA 1920
resid Inverurie

HENDERSON Jean   *MA 1926
prin teacher Ger Aber acad 1960–69; retd; resid Garlogie Skene

HENDERSON Jeannie Elizabeth   MA 1912
no longer on GC reg

HENDERSON Jessie Jane   MA 1934
teacher Gordon s Huntly from 1954

HENDERSON John   MA 1910
d 9.3.61

HENDERSON John Dunlop   MB ChB 1904
no longer on GC reg

HENDERSON John Hope   MB ChB 1954
DPM 1960 FRCPsych 1971 MFCM 1972 FACP 1973
sen m o Woodend hosp Aber 1960–61; consult. psychiat/phys supt Dr Gray's and Bilbohall hosps Elgin 1962–69; Edin: consult. psychiat/phys supt Bangour village hosp and Western gen hosp 1969–72,

prin m o/consult. psychiat SHHD 1972–76; advis on mental health WHO from 1977

HENDERSON John Murdoch   MA 1926
  d Aber 10.11.72 *AUR* xlv 127

HENDERSON John Peter   BSc(eng) 1947

HENDERSON John Wishart   MA 1904 BL 1906
  no longer on GC reg

HENDERSON Kenneth Douglas
                              ***MA 1952 Dip Ed 1953**
  spec asst Engl AGS 1957–65; lect Engl Aber coll of educ from 1966; co-edit. *Education in the North*; recog teacher for BEd degree Aberd 1972

HENDERSON Laurence Peter   MA BSc(agr) 1923
  d 16.12.69

HENDERSON or Fraczek, Louise Buchanan
                                                MA 1942
  d Barnes 5.7.79

HENDERSON or Murtock, Mabel Adams
                                          MB ChB 1938
  resid Sunderland

HENDERSON or Millar, Margaret Elizabeth
                                                MA 1955

HENDERSON or McCreadie, Marjorie Muriel
                                                MA 1940
  resid Mequon Wisconsin USA

HENDERSON or Williams, Mary Margaret
                                                MA 1944

HENDERSON or Macrae, Mary Simpson   MA 1952
  Dip Nursery Educ(Aber) 1972
inf teacher Cloverfield s Bucksburn 1960–72, nursery teacher i/c Oldmeldrum 1973–76, asst head March-burn inf s Aber from 1976

HENDERSON Moira Elizabeth Keill
                              ***BSc 1952 PhD 1955**
  scient off. microbiol dept Macaulay inst for soil research Aber 1952–64
m Aber 26.10.63 Alexander R. Wilcox man. s of Thomas H. W. Aber

HENDERSON or Lemerle, Muriel Osbourne
                                          MB ChB 1942
  g p Southborough Tunbridge Wells from 1944
husb *d* 1969

HENDERSON or Stephen, Nancy Falconer
                                                MA 1930
  resid E. Grinstead

HENDERSON Peter   MB ChB 1929 MD 1931
  CB 1965
sen prin m o dept educ and sc 1964–69; retd; hon phys HM Queen 1964–67; short term consult. WHO SE Asia and Middle East 1969–74; resid Guildford

HENDERSON or McCallum, Rica   BSc 1924
  resid Edin

HENDERSON Richard Bruce   *MB ChB 1924
  DTM & H 1929 LM (Dub) 1935
RAMC hon rank capt 1945
resid Bexley Heath

HENDERSON Robert Dalrymple
                              MA 1927 MB ChB 1931
  FRSM 1946
retd 1972; resid Epping
d 29.5.79

HENDERSON Robert Gregory
                    MB ChB 1929 DPH 1931 MD 1933
  consult. phys and med supt Southern hosp Dartford 1939–59; resid Brenchley Tonbridge
m Brenchley 18.11.60 Josephine E. Merricks or Beeney d of Walter M. Icklesham

HENDERSON Robert Thomas Smith
                                          MB ChB 1950

HENDERSON Thomas George   *MA 1927
  dir educ Argyll 1946–71; retd; resid Dunoon

HENDERSON or Conn, Violet Lindsay   MA 1937

HENDERSON William   MB ChB 1912
  d 16.11.67

HENDERSON William Gordon   MB ChB 1944

HENDERSON William Lewis   BSc(agr) 1939
  d Aber 8.8.66 *AUR* xli 342

HENDRIE or Duffus, Elizabeth Catherine
                                          MB ChB 1947
  resid Aber

HENDRY Alexander William
                              MB ChB 1914 MD 1918
  d Aber 22.7.72 *AUR* xlv 124

HENDRY Amy   *MA 1916
  no longer on GC reg

HENDRY or Hay, Annie Mary Hay   MA 1913
  d 17.9.69

HENDRY Anthony Morrice   *MB ChB 1924
  d Birmingham 10.9.67 *AUR* xlii 185 & 362

HENDRY Arnold William
                    ***BSc(eng) 1941 PhD 1946 DSc 1954**
  prof bldg sc Liv 1957–63; prof civ eng Edin from 1964
wife *d* 1966
m(2) Edin 1968 Elizabeth L. A. Inglis admin asst d of Harry R. G. I. Edin

HENDRY or Addison, Charlotte Patricia   MA 1914
  no longer on GC reg

HENDRY or Jones, Charlotte Souttar
                 *MB ChB 1923 DPH 1924

HENDRY Elizabeth   *MA 1925
no longer on GC reg

HENDRY Eric Grassick   MB ChB 1940
g p Buckie from 1946

HENDRY or Welbourn, Esther
                MB ChB 1936 ᶜMD 1939
MA(Cantab) 1964
Cambridge: clin asst dermat Addenbrooke's hosp
from 1963; dir stud. in med sc New Hall from 1964;
fell./lect anat New Hall from 1966

HENDRY Frederick William Firman   BSc 1923
no longer on GC reg

HENDRY George   MA 1903
no longer on GC reg

HENDRY George   MA 1922
d Stratheden Fife 22.3.66 *AUR* XLII 85

HENDRY George Alexander
                BSc 1935 MB ChB 1938
d N'cle-upon-Tyne 13.7.71 *AUR* XLIV 321

HENDRY George Alexander
                MB ChB 1948 MD 1971
d Leigh-on-Sea 2.5.76

HENDRY George Stuart   *MA 1924 DD 1949
pres Amer theol soc 1971; prof emeritus Princeton
theol soc NJ 1973

HENDRY Gordon Frederick   *MA 1942
Scot. office Edin: econ advis 1965–67; asst secy
from 1967

HENDRY or Fyfe, Gwendoline McKenzie   MA 1940

HENDRY Harold Gordon   BSc(eng) 1953
MIHE 1955 AMBIM 1976 FICE 1976
eng prov roads dept Pietermaritzburg 1953–60;
Burmah Oil Co: supt eng Calcutta 1960–63, proj
man. Lahore 1963–73, consult. Adelaide 1973–74;
BP (North Sea oil dev) 1974–76; consult. Nairobi
from 1976
marr diss

HENDRY Helen   MA 1909
no longer on GC reg

HENDRY Ian Murdo   *MA 1948
rector: Dunoon g s 1969–75, Dollar acad from 1975

HENDRY Innes Craig   *BSc 1951
MInstP 1969 FInstPet 1975
lect/res fell. Stir 1968–72; lect RGIT Aber from 1972

HENDRY James   MB ChB 1947 DPH 1953
Cert Path(Can) 1960 FRCPath(Can) 1972
path. Brandon gen hosp Manitoba from 1957

HENDRY or Cumming, Jessie Elizabeth   MA 1930
resid Inverurie

HENDRY Jessie Tait   MA 1927
retd 1966; resid Aber

HENDRY John   *MA 1929

HENDRY John Smith   BSc 1953
Dornoch acad: teacher maths 1962–67, prin maths
1967–72; prin guid Cults acad from 1972

HENDRY Joseph   MA 1952
prin teacher geog Grantown g s Grantown-on-Spey
from 1956

HENDRY or Gardiner, Mabel Blaikie   MA 1914
d Edin 27.11.71

HENDRY or Gerard, Margaret Edith   MA 1955
resid Kingsworthy

HENDRY or Black, Margaret Garden   MA 1950
teacher Hightae Dumfriessh from 1974
husb d 1972

HENDRY Neil Geddes Clarkson   MB ChB 1939
CBE 1976
clin sen lect orthop Aberd from 1968

HENDRY Robert William   MB ChB 1926
retd 1970; resid Halifax

HENDRY or Paterson, Ruth Davidson   MA 1928
resid Edin

HENDRY Thomas Begg Tawse
                MA 1922 BCom 1924
no longer on GC reg

HENDRY William Ewart   BSc 1935 *1936
head Inverarity s Angus from 1952
wife d 1963
m(2) Inverarity 1.7.67 Catherine L. B. Mills SRN
theatre sister d of Charles M. Tealing

HENDRY William Garden   MB ChB 1936
consult. surg Highlands gen hosp Lond from 1946

HENDRY William Gordon   MA 1940 LLB 1947

HENDRY William Thomson   MB ChB 1944
g p Aber from 1951; lect forensic med Aberd from
1957; police surg Aber from 1956

HENEKE Paul Michael   MB ChB 1942
g p Cape Town from 1946

HENFIELD Marie Adelaide Gordon   MA 1933

HENRIQUES Stella Grace Alice   MB ChB 1923
retd 1964; resid Stamford

HENRY Alexander Falconer   MB ChB 1950
CCFP 1977

g p Ottawa Ont 1956–72; chief emerg dept Ottawa civic hosp from 1972
m 1.7.54 Christina H. Mitchell d of John M. Stornoway

HENRY or Littlejohn, Alice Mary   MA 1925
    resid Aber

HENRY Annie   MA 1925
    dept head prim. dept Laurencekirk s s 1965–67; retd

HENRY or Gillis, Daisy   MA 1942
    teacher Fr Northwich girls' g s Cheshire from 1965

HENRY John Alexander   BSc(agr) 1949

HENRY or Hall, Kathleen Margaret Ross   MA 1946
    d 31.7.68

HENRY Kathleen Mary   PhD 1933
    retd 1965; resid Glenageary Co Dublin

HENRY or Norrie, Margaret Ogston   MA 1923
    Aber: teacher Engl Albyn s for girls 1942–46; temp post asst teacher s for deaf 1954–63; retd

HENRY Norman Fordyce McKerron
                                    *MA 1931 *BSc 1934
    Cantab: lect mineral.-petrology from 1947; fell. St. John's coll 1960

HENRY or Hunter, Phyllis Roberta   MA 1928
    retd 1967; resid Scalloway
d Shetland 4.2.78

HENRY Robert   *MA 1929
    retd 1969; resid Macduff

HENRY Sheena Landsborough   MA 1950

HENRY or Spark, Sophia Ogston   *MA 1924
    resid Ringwood
husb d 8.4.69

HENRY William Millar   MA 1903
    d Lond 20.12.61 AUR xxxix 271

HENSON Ronald   *MA 1930
    d Aber 11.10.68 AUR xliii 84

HEPBURN Alfred   *BSc 1954

HEPBURN Athol Noble   MB ChB 1954
    DPH(Lond) 1961 surg cdr RNR(Lond) RD 1971
m o BOAC Lond 1961–69; sen m o RAF Farnborough 1969–72; dir civ med serv procurement exec MoD Lond from 1972
m Lond 26.10.63 Julia E. B. Smith SRN d of Leonard B. S. Llangoedmor Cardigan

HEPBURN or Sants, Elsie Ann Watt
                                    MA 1943 *MEd 1948
    Bangor N Wales: educ psych ch guid clin 1961–63, part-time sen lect St Mary's coll 1963–66: miscellaneous lect/res Sus from 1966

HEPBURN or Stokoe, Helen Rose   MA 1925
    d Lond 6.2.61 AUR xxxix 105

HEPBURN John   MB ChB 1954
    MRCGP
g p: Barnhill 1962–63, Skelmorlie from 1963

HEPBURN Mark Ireland   MB ChB 1941

HEPBURN Ronald William   *MA 1951 PhD 1955
    prof phil Edin from 1964

HERBERT Ellenor   *MA 1916
    d Aber 14.4.76

HERBERT George Leslie   MB ChB 1942
    g p Kexborough nr Barnsley from 1948

HERBERT Norman   MEd 1950
    d Banchory 18.1.71 AUR xliv 216

HERBERT William   MB ChB 1937

HERD or Galt, Bethia Cooper Rodger   MA 1928
    resid Aber

HERD George McLeman   MA 1954
    teacher: Kaimhill s Aber 1964–65, Cent s Fraserburgh 1965–69; head New Byth s from 1969

HERD or Ferguson, Isabella Flett   MA 1925
    resid Aber

HERD James   MB ChB 1944 DPH 1948
    g p Banchory from 1948

HERD or Catto, Mary   MA 1937

HERON Ernest Mercer   *MA 1927
    d Edin 23.7.69 AUR xliii 330

HERRIOT Alexander   MB ChB 1951
    FRCOG 1972
sen regist obst and gyn: Leeds RHB 1961–63, Southern gen hosp Glasg 1964–66; consult. obst and gyn E Fife hosps from 1967

HERVEI Geyza Joseph   *MA 1928
    d 25.1.71 AUR xliv 431

HEUCHAN or Thomson, Mary Jane   MA 1902
    no longer on GC reg

HEWET Alexander Ross   *MA 1936
    lect maths Aber coll of educ 1962–68, sen lect from 1968

HEWETT or Edwards, Alison Hayward
                                    MB ChB 1952
    m 1.7.50
resid Tonbridge

HILL Alexander Campbell   MA 1916 MB ChB 1918
    d Hove 15.11.67 AUR xlii 352

HILL Alfred   BSc 1909 BSc(agr) 1911
d Auckland NZ 3.1.61 *AUR* xxxix 101

HILL Amelia   MA 1952
teacher: Iraq petr comp Dukhan Qatar 1959–62;
Brechin from 1972
m Brechin 9.6.62 Dudley Waller garage prop. s of
Edwin H. W. Streatham

HILL Ethel Massie   MA 1932
teacher AGS from 1950; retd 1974

HILL John Kingsley   BSc(eng) 1945

HILL Robert Dougan   MB ChB 1951 MD 1976
g p Isle of Barra from 1963

HILL Ronald Johnstone   *MA 1949
Chevalier des Palmes Academiques 1970
prin teacher mod lang Liberton Edin 1960–62; advis
mod lang Edin corp from 1970

HILLS or Thorpe, Frances Elizabeth   BL 1940
resid Lond

HILSON Norman James Macfarlane   MA 1919
resid Aber

**HILTON Raymond Walwork
                    BSc(for) 1933 MB ChB 1950**
d Oswestry 24.8.75 *AUR* xlvi 325

HINDS Lesley   PhD 1952
ICI plastics div Welwyn Garden City from 1952

HINGSTON Alfred Alwyne   MB ChB 1900
no longer on GC reg

HIRD Alexander   MB ChB 1949
asst g p Ashington 1951–56, g p Aber 1957–77;
resid Aber

HIRD Gordon   MB ChB 1947

HIRST Herbert Alexander   BSc(eng) 1938
d 1.10.63

**HOARE or de Navarro, Agnes Dorothea Mackenzie
                    *MA 1923**
PhD(Cantab) 1929
pres assoc of Newnham coll 1958–63; memb par
council Broadway from 1967; founder memb
Broadway Trust (regd with Civic Trust), secy 1963–72,
chmn 1972–76, vice pres from 1976

HOARE Florence Margaret   MA 1909
no longer on GC reg

HOARE Janette Mary   *MA 1913
d 1967

HOARE or MacTavish, Margaret Wilma   MA 1925

HOARE Samuel   *MA 1919
d Cheltenham 31.3.76 *AUR* xlvi 415

HOBART Nettie   MA 1906

**HOBBIN Gordon Marnoch
                    BCom 1931 MB ChB 1936**
d Burnham Bucks 15.8.69 *AUR* xliii 331

HOBBIN Ruby Gordon   MA 1929
no longer on GC reg

HOBSON Bruce Morris   *BSc 1948
Edin: sen lect obst & gyn 1959–66; reader from
1966

HODGE or Shea, Isabella   *MA 1906
d –.6.70

HODGE John Brian Symons   BSc(for) 1948
timber trade from 1952; resid Surbiton

HOGAN Elsie   MA 1910
no longer on GC reg

HOGG Alexander Adam McDougall   *MA 1952
Aber coll of educ: lect geog 1964–69, sen lect from
1969
m Arbroath 30.9.61 Moira MacKenzie hotel man. d of
Duncan MacK. Aviemore

HOGG Cecil Berisford   MB ChB 1914
no longer on GC reg

HOGG Charles Gordon   MA 1932 LLB 1933
proc-fiscal: Cupar 1961–68, Dun from 1968

HOGG or Champion, Margaret Mary   MA 1939

HOGGARTH Frank Evans   MA 1928
d Lond 12.4.74

HOGGARTH Marion Duncan   *MA 1927
retd; resid Aber

HOLDEN George Walker   BSc(agr) 1955

HOLIDAY John Edward   MB ChB 1955
DA(Lond) 1969
g p Rowlands Gill Tyne & Wear 1960–65; clin asst
anaest Gateshead hosp group from 1965

HOLLANDS Edwin James   MA 1931
rector: St George w St Barnabas Manc 1958–60, St
Congan Turriff 1960–74; elected canon of St Andrew's
cath Aber 1969; retd; resid Poulton-le-Fylde

HOLLOWAY Christopher John   DLitt 1955
LittD(Cantab) 1970
Cantab: reader Mod Engl 1966–72, prof from 1972

HOLM Davina *MA 1938
teacher: asst prin mod lang Invergordon acad
1961–71; prin Ger Dingwall acad from 1971

HOLM or McLeod, Isabella Deas   MA 1930
d Tain –.6.55

HOLM or Campbell, Isabella Fraser Mackenzie
MA 1939
head Killen s Rosssh from 1961

HOLM or Riddell, Peploe Campbell   MA 1934
Edin: teacher inf mistress Prestonfield s 1960–64;
James Gillespie's h s 1964–69; asst head inf
S Morningside s from 1969
marr diss 1954

HOLMAN Howard Henry   PhD 1937

HOLMES or Carpenter, Daphne Elizabeth
*MA 1953

HOLMES Dorothy Mildred   MB ChB 1920
no longer on GC reg

HOOD or McAllan, Alison   MA 1955
secy Victoria League in Scot. from 1956; resid Wick

HOOD or Macpherson, Ena   *MA 1927
resid Dunfermline

HOPKIN Vincent David   *MA 1954
prin psych and head psych sect RAF inst of aviation
med Farnborough from 1965

HOPKINS Herbert Desmond   BSc(eng) 1935
dir Lyds & Scot. fin. Nott 1963–68; man. dir
Internat Factors Brighton 1968–71; dir pers and
admin Lyds & Scot. fin. Edin from 1971

HOPKINS Herbert Owen   *MA 1924
d 1974

HOPKINS Ronald Isaac   BSc(eng) 1951

HOPKINSON Andrew Douglas   BSc(agr) 1911
d 8.10.69

HOPPER Albert St Clair   BSc(eng) 1942

HOPPER Noel Brian   MB ChB 1950
MRCGP 1954
g p Stonehaven from 1951
wife d 13.3.63
m(2) Stonehaven 30.12.75 Carolyn S. M. French staff
nurse d of David M. F. Newburgh Fife

HORÁNSZKY DE HORA Ladislaus   PhD 1927
no longer on GC reg

HORN Alexander   MB ChB 1907

HORN Annie Keir   *MA 1919
retd 1964; resid Buckie
d Aber 13.3.80

HORN David   MB ChB 1934

HORN Eleanor Jean   *MA 1949 Dip Ed 1950

HORN Ian Ross   MB ChB 1934
no longer on GC reg

HORNE Dorothy Louisa May   MA 1947
teacher Northfield acad Aber from 1963

HORNE Elizabeth   MA 1944

HORNE or Paterson, Helen Taylor   *MA 1923
no longer on GC reg

HORNE Henry James   MB ChB 1922
d Blackpool 22.9.65

HORNE Henry Murray   MB ChB 1951
Tasmania: g p Latrobe 1966–76, Devonport from
1976

HORNE Ralph Alexander   MB ChB 1934
g p Portlethen 1937–73; retd; resid Portmahomack

HORNE William Donald   *MA 1919
no longer on GC reg

HORNE William Ian   MB ChB 1950 ᶜMD 1963
FRCPath 1972 FRCP(Can) 1972
path. Hotel-Dieu hosp Windsor Ontario from 1963

HORROX Fred   MA 1911
d 1.2.77

HOSIE Stewart MacGregor   BSc 1953
ptnr site explor serv 1956–72; geol with C. H.
Dobbie & Ptnrs consult. eng Lond 1972–76
m (2) 3.9.66 Janet Hodgkinson teacher
d Aber 2.3.78

HOSSACK Christina Ross Forbes   MA 1914
resid Coupar-Angus

HOSSACK William Strachan   MB ChB 1953
g p Banff from 1958
m Aber 27.8.60 Catherine R. Sellar cashier d of James
S. S. MacDuff

HOUGHTON William Nusum   MB ChB 1900
no longer on GC reg

HOUSTON Bradford George   *BSc(agr) 1952
sen res off. Tengeru Tanzania 1964–68; Aber:
teacher biol AGS 1968–72, prin biol Northfield acad
from 1972

HOUSTON John Anderson   MB ChB 1939

HOUSTOUN George Provan   *MA 1952
prin teacher Queen Anne h s Dunfermline 1962–65:
Dun: dep head Rockwell s s 1965–72, rector Rockwell
h s from 1971
d 31.10.81

HOWARD Stewart Carlisle
MB ChB 1906 *MD 1908
no longer on GC reg

HOWELL Frances Helen Kemp
*MA 1954 Dip Ed 1955
prin teacher hist Craigholme s Glasg from 1960

HOWIE or Hopkins, Cecil Don   BSc 1927

HOWIE David Porter   MA 1909
d Kilmarnock 5.7.73 *AUR* xlv 316

HOWIE George   *MA 1937 *MEd 1939
PhD(Leeds) 1961
assoc prof educ univ of Sydney Aust from 1965
d Sydney 16.5.80 *AUR* xlix 69

HOWIE or Ross, Helen Doris   BL 1948

HOWIE James William
                   *MB ChB 1930 *MD 1937 LLD 1969
HM hon phys 1965–68 Kt 1969 FRCPGlas 1958
FRCP 1963 hon fell. Path. Soc (GB and Ireland) 1977
hon fell. Assoc Clin Path. 1977 hon assoc RCVS 1977
Pres: BMA 1969, RCPath 1966–69, assoc clin path.
1972–73; prof bact Glas 1951–63, dir publ health lab
serv Eng and Wales 1963–73; retd resid Newtonmore

HOWIE or Peterson, Jean Nicol
               MB ChB 1926 DPH 1928 MD 1933
med asst venereology dept RI Edin from 1967

HOWIE Robert George Porter   MA 1914
d 19.9.64 *AUR* xl 398

HOWIE Thomas Wilson   BD 1941

HOWIESON or Richards, Margaret Beattie
                                    MA 1933
d Inv 24.8.69 *AUR* xliii 331

HOWISON James William   *BSc 1954 PhD 1957
member Aust pulp & paper Indust tech assoc 1968
Wiggins Teape (Stoneywood): chief chem Aber/
Nowra NSW Aust 1962–67, chem Shoalhaven Mill
Nowra NSW 1968–77; paper tech Allied Colloids
(Aust) Pty Sydney from 1977
m Sydney 25.3.72 Robyn L. Pattrick d of Eric P.
Shellharbour NSW

HOWITT Kelvin Stewart   *MA 1946
d 20.9.62

HOWITT Lewis Finnigan   MB ChB 1951 DPH 1955
MFCM 1972
Edin: asst m o h 1960–61, sen asst m o h 1962–63;
dep m o h Midlothian and Peebles 1963–68, s m o
SHHD Edin from 1968
m Dalkeith 23.7.55 Sheila H. E. Burns MA(Edin)
teacher d of William B. Linlithgow

HOYLE Nancy Jean Campbell   *MA 1948
teacher: Engl Findochty 1952–54, rural Greysteele,
NI, Engl/hist Bridlington 1960–61
m Buckie 1.9.54 Jack Austin air signaller FAR s of
Albert E. A. Leeds

HUGHES Albert Lewis   MB ChB 1939
g p Wellington NZ 1965–67, Forestburg Alberta
1968, Torryburn Fife 1968–69, Pudsey 1969–76
m NZ 16.9.65 Maureen E. Chapman d of James G. C.
d 23.11.76

HUGHES John Stanley   BL 1934

HUGHSON or Rennie, Christina Peterson   MA 1929
d Aber 17.1.67 *AUR* xlii 368

HUGHSON or Gear, Wilma Anne   MA 1955
teacher Mid Yell j h s Shetland from 1956

HULSE Norman Laing   MB ChB 1938
FMRCGP
g p Blackley Northants from 1948

HUMBLE Henry   MA BSc 1922
OBE 1970
rector Elgin acad 1950–64; retd
d Elgin 23.12.81

HUMBLE or Rae, Katherine Izobel
                              *MA 1913 BSc 1914
d 1.7.77

HUMBLE or Phimister, Margaret
                          MA 1942 MB ChB 1948
d Aber 20.7.78

HUMBLE or Taylor, Renée Myles   BSc 1949 *1950
Inverurie acad: teacher chem 1962–66, woman advis
1966–72, asst head guid from 1972

HUME or Cope, Isobel Dorothy   MA 1915
d Lond 16.12.62 *AUR* xl 83

HUME or Harper, Joan Winifred   MA 1924
resid Glasg

HUME William John   MA 1927
no longer on GC reg

HUMPHREY John   MB ChB 1913
no longer on GC reg

HUMPHREY or Niven, Kathleen Jane   BCom 1928

HUMPHREY Reginald Alexander Milne
                                    MB ChB 1926
d Geelong NSW –.6.73 *AUR* xlv 318

HUMPHREY Stanley Frank Walker   MA 1925
semi-retired; resid Rivonia Transvaal
m Kalk Bay Cape Province S Af 17.7.43 Una K.
Fowler d of Hugh C. E. St James Cape Province

HUMPHRIES James Ernest   DSc 1926
d Aber 25.2.79 *AUR* xlviii 229

HUMPHRIES Walter Robson   *MA 1928
d Aber 11.3.80 *AUR* xlviii 442

HUNT David Laurence
               BSc(elect eng) 1951 BSc(mech eng) 1952
MIEE
GEC Rugby: chief eng mining and spec drives elect.
proj 1969–71, div chief eng Elliott indust controls
1971–76, div man. mining elect. proj from 1976

HUNTER Alexander   MB ChB 1939
    FRCOG(Lond) 1966
obst & gyn Smith clin Hawkesbury Ont from 1952

HUNTER Alexander   MB ChB 1947
    g p Middlesbrough from 1952

HUNTER Allan   BSc 1947 *1948

HUNTER Allan Thomson   *MA 1926
    prin teacher Engl and dep head Old Aber s s
1948–70; head f e centre Aber 1949–70
d Aber 15.10.76 *A UR* xlvii 105

HUNTER David Ian   MB ChB 1954
    g p: Aber from 1963

HUNTER Douglas Alexander
                                ***MB ChB 1921 MD 1941**
    d Lond 10.12.69 *A UR* xliii 444

HUNTER or Cowley, Eilean Annand   MB ChB 1942
    resid Hartfield

HUNTER or McCoss, Ellen Jane Martin   MA 1912
    d Aber 10.12.72 *A UR* xlv 224

HUNTER or Trendell, Ethel Clementina Margaret
                                ***MA 1917**
    d 10.10.77

HUNTER Florence Muriel   MA 1925
    resid Aber

HUNTER Gillies Connan   BSc 1947 *1948
    agr res council grantee Edin 1948–50; biol res
worker Rowett res inst Aber from 1950

HUNTER Grace Beverley   *MA 1948
    secy/lib centre of African stud. Edin from 1962

HUNTER Graham William Galloway
                                MB ChB 1955
    DPH(Edin) 1961 DTM & H(Lond) 1963
m o fed. health serv Aden 1959–67; g p Cumnock
from 1968
m Wallington 31.8.63 Fiona M. S. McNairn art teacher
d of Edward S. McN. MA(Glas) Wallington

HUNTER or Bruce, Helen Elizabeth   MA 1935
    resid Kildrummy

HUNTER or Barrack, Isobel Mary   MA 1947
    resid Amersham

HUNTER James Douglas   MB ChB 1949
    FFARCS 1964
regist anaest county hosp Lincoln 1955–59; gen hosp
Newcastle-u-Tyne: sen regist anaest 1960–64, consult.
anaest from 1964

HUNTER James Greig   MB ChB 1942

HUNTER or McBoyle, Madaleine Jean   MA 1951
    cler asst Linden centre Huntly from 1971

HUNTER Robert Ferguson   BSc(agr) 1949

HUNTER Stanley Beveridge   *MA 1942

HUNTER Thomas   MB ChB 1941
    consult. orthop surg Barking and Havering from
1957

HUNTER William Drummond   MA 1912
    C of S min: Middle ch Perth 1926–63; clerk to
presb of Perth 1948–70
d 12.7.79

HURST Roger Trevellian   BSc(for) 1955
    for. comm: asst dist off. Mansfield 1958–59,
Helmsley 1959–61; dist off. Wakefield 1961–64,
Kendal 1964–68, Aberfoyle 1968–72; conserv and
recreation off. W Scot. from 1972
m Windermere 20.1.73 Denise M. Panton SRN nurs
sister d of D. P. Windermere

HUSBAND Valentine Margaret   MB ChB 1943
    FRCOG 1971
Lond: sen regist W Middx hosp 1958–62; consult.
gyn Italian hosp 1963–69; consult. obst/gyn NE
Thames AHA from 1966
m Craig

HUTCHEON Archibald   MA 1900
    BL(Edin)
no longer on GC reg

HUTCHEON Gladys Gladstone   MA 1925
    no longer on GC reg

HUTCHEON Harry   MB ChB 1936
    d Kingswells 21.11.67 *A UR* xlii 371

HUTCHEON Isabel   *MA 1921
    resid Dun

HUTCHEON James   MB ChB 1924
    d Aber 19.6.68 *A UR* xliii 84

HUTCHEON James Eddie Harper   *MA 1955
    teacher: Inv 1958, prin Engl Inv acad from 1968

HUTCHEON Mary   MA 1924
    no longer on GC reg

HUTCHEON Mary Hosie   MB ChB 1944
    FRCOG 1976
sen regist obst & gyn univ coll hosp Jamaica 1959–60;
Hammersmith hosp: sen regist obst & gyn 1963–65;
Harrogate & dist hosp: consult. obst & gyn from 1965

HUTCHESON Herbert Cecil   MA 1929
    head: Westerton p s Aber 1966–69, Mile End p s
Aber 1969–73; retd

HUTCHINSON Ralph Thomas   MA 1948

HUTCHISON Alexander Cantlay
                                MA 1936 *BSc 1938 PhD 1945
    tech man. ICI HQ Lond 1960–62; Ardeer: gen

man. silicones dept 1962–69, plan. man. Nobel div 1969–71; man. dir BOH Chemicals Poole from 1971

HUTCHISON Charles Alexander   *MA 1922
no longer on GC reg

HUTCHISON Charles Strachan   *BSc 1955
PhD(Malaya) 1966 FGS FIMM
oilfield geol Fyzabad Trinidad 1955–57; univ of Malaya: asst lect Singapore 1957–58, lect Kuala Lumpur 1958–67, asst prof Kuala Lumpur 1967–77; prof univ of Kansas USA 1970–71; prof applied geol univ of Malaya Kuala Lumpur from 1977
m Kuala Lumpur 5.7.60 Ann Chan d of Chan Poh, Negri Sembilan Malaysia

HUTCHISON or Ogilvie, Edith Mary   MA 1935
teacher: Liv 1959–63, Aber 1963–70; retd; resid Weymouth

HUTCHISON or Norbrook, Eleanor Isobel Margaret *MA 1939
teacher Nigeria 1957–59
resid Bletchingdon

HUTCHISON Gordon   MB ChB 1930
d Kintyre 13.5.71

HUTCHISON Laura Ann   MA 1939
teacher Ashley Rd s Aber from 1952

HUTCHISON or Chater, Margaret   BSc 1928 *1929
resid Aberystwyth

HUTCHISON Robert Nicholson   MA 1954 Dip Ed 1955
d Scalloway 2.2.62 *AUR* xxxix 386

HUTCHISON Thomas Mundie   BSc(eng) 1936
CEng FIMechEng 1939 FIAgrEng 1948 MBIM 1950 FIMC 1960
Urwick, Orr & Ptnrs: India, NZ, Malawi, Turkey, Nigeria, Ceylon, Kenya 1967–76; private practice from 1976

HUTTON Agnes Forbes   *MA 1934
teacher Notre Dame h s Battersea 1961–75; retd; resid Abergavenny

HUTTON Marjorie Smith   MA 1928

HUTTON Stewart William Reid   MB ChB 1944
DA 1966
g p: Walsall 1949–66, Ramsgate from 1967

HYND or Davidson, Margaret Elizabeth   MA 1933
resid Huntly

HYND or Baird, Nora   MA 1940
head Kinnoir s Huntly from 1953

HYTTEN Frank Eyvind   PhD 1954
MD(Sydney) 1962 FRCOG 1970
pers prof human reprod physiol N'cle from 1971

IGGO Ainsley   PhD 1954
FRSE 1962 DSc(Edin) 1963
Locke res fell. Royal Society 1960–62
prof vet physiol Edin from 1962; visiting prof Kyoto univ Japan 1970, guest prof Heidelberg 1972; dean vet fac Edin 1974–77

IHSANULLAH Mohammed   BSc(agr) 1923

ILLINGWORTH Keith   BSc(for) 1953 *1954

IMLACH Alexander Robert   BSc(eng) 1944
FIEE 1965 CEng 1965
sub lieut RN 1944–46; various eng posts elect. generating boards SW England 1946–56; reactor eng man. AEA Thurso from 1956
m Dartmouth 1.9.46 Audrey E. Le Blanc

IMLACH or Reid, Jeannie Murray   MA 1947
teacher Bervie s Inverbervie from 1960

IMLAH Gertrude   MA 1930

IMLAH Keith Cameron   BL 1949
Lond: leg. asst 1955–67, asst leg. advis 1967–73, sen asst leg. advis 1973–77, comp secy/leg. advis from 1977
m Lond 21.12.63 Marjorie Harrington 2nd off. WRNS d of William C. H.

IMLAY or Agrell, Jean Elspeth   *BSc 1933
mineralogist Tube Investments res inst Hinxton, near Cambridge 1955–60, res asst dept min petr Cantab 1969–76; Russian translator

IMLAY or Muirhead, Joan Betty   *BSc 1933 PhD 1938
resid Grahamstown S. Af

IMLAY Joice Margaret   MB ChB 1944
g p Manc

IMPER Albert David   BSc(agr) 1924 PhD 1928
d Edin 18.5.71 *AUR* xliv 320

IMPER or Gordon, Lilian Clara   MA 1949
prin teacher Renfrew; resid Milngavie

IMPEY Cecil Vernon   MB ChB 1906

IMRAY Herbert Alexander   MB ChB 1954
g p Portree/Callander 1958–62; m o Fiji and Gilbert and Ellice Is 1962–71; regist psych Craig Dunain hosp Inv 1972–75, med asst psych from 1975

INGERSENT Kenneth Arthur   BSc(agr) 1949
lect econ Nott from 1970
m Allestree Derby 31.8.60 Elizabeth M. Sadler BA(Oxon) d of Wilfred J. S. Derby

INGLIS Alexander   MA 1926
d Banff 12.9.73 *AUR* xlv 319

INGLIS Douglas Johnstone   BSc(eng) 1949 *1950
man. AST div Nat Welding comp Montreal 1957–

61; man. pollution control div Stenberg-Flygt AB Montreal/Stamford USA 1961–71; lect eng Aberd from 1971

INGLIS or Muller, Jean Elizabeth Winton
　　　　　　　　　　　　　MB ChB 1938
　FFACS 1954
m o i/c nurs staff Groote Schur hosp Capetown 1958–70, part time m o from 1970

INGLIS or Muir, Jean Milne　MA 1955
　teacher: maths Banff acad 1956–58, maths Jedburgh g s from 1970 and asst prin guid from 1977

INGLIS Margaret Rose　MB ChB 1948
　MRCPsych 1972
consult. psychiat Ailsa hosp Ayr from 1964

INGLIS William Grant　*BSc 1953 DSc 1965
　Adelaide, Aust: dir S Aust museum 1968–70, dir environ & conserv 1972–76, permanent head D o E 1976

INGRAM Agnes Matheson　MA 1926

INGRAM Anne　MA 1952 Dip Ed 1953
　teacher Colegio San Silvestre Lima, Peru 1958–62 and from 1969
m Lima 22.12.61 Alfons Buck photogr bus. s of Ludwig B. Stuttgart Ger

INGRAM Bruce Millar　MA 1953

INGRAM Charles Greig　MB ChB 1951

INGRAM Edward Alexander　MB ChB 1942
　sen regist surg ARI 1959–63; g p Lerwick from 1963

INGRAM or Gilchrist, Elizabeth Evelyne　*MA 1933
　resid Barnes Lond

INGRAM George Alexander　*BSc 1950
　prin scient off. sc civ serv from 1964
m Aber 8.10.63 Margaret H. Youngson catering man. d of James Youngson MA 1921 *qv*

INGRAM George Bremner　BSc(agr) 1948
　teacher rural sc Llandrindod h s from 1972

INGRAM or Constable, Harriet Gordon　MA 1900
　no longer on GC reg

INGRAM Helen Smith　*MA 1926
　retd 1966; resid Aber

INGRAM Ian William　MA 1946
　teacher indep s till 1971; rep NFU Nott 1971–73; sales exec Lonsdale & Bartholomew printers Nott from 1973
d 1.2.81

INGRAM James Brown　MA 1950 BD 1953
　teachers' coll Bulawayo, Rhodesia: head div dept 1962–65, acting then asst vice-prin 1964–65; lect inst of educ UC Rhodesia, Salisbury 1965–70; lect City of

Leeds & Carnegie coll of educ Leeds 1970–72; prin lect curric stud. Margaret McMillan coll of educ Bradford from 1972

INGRAM Katherine　BSc 1940
　resid Keith

INGRAM Lilias Jean　*MA 1932
　scient work MoD from 1939
d 13.1.76

INGRAM or Patterson, Margaret Angus
　　　　　　　　　　　　　MB ChB 1944
　MBE 1962
med supt: Dooars & Darjeeling tea assoc hosp & surg to hosp 1957–61; surg i/c surg unit Tung Wah hosp Hong Kong 1964–73; consult. in neuro-electric therap Lond from 1972

INGRAM Peter Willoughby　MB ChB 1934
　FRCS 1960
retd 1969; resid Maidenhead

INGRAM William Fasken　MB ChB 1925
　d 28.2.64

INGRAM William Wilson　MB ChB 1912 *MD 1919
　FRACP 1938
retd; resid Sydney

INKSON or Slater, Elsie Lilian Blackhall　BSc 1944
　resid Manc

INKSON John Kerr　*MA 1929
　prin teacher mod lang Dingwall acad 1946–68; retd
d Inv 16.4.79

INKSON Robert Henry Ewen　*BSc 1948
　FRSS 1949 FIStat 1969
Macaulay inst for soil res Aber: prin scient off. 1963–68, head dept statist from 1968

INKSTER Davina　MA 1916
　own s at Peterculter 1940–61; interim work in small schools in Perthsh 1962–68; retd; resid Peterculter

INKSTER John　MB ChB 1909 *MD 1913

INKSTER John Scott　MB ChB 1946
　Lond: member council assoc of anaest 1971–73, examiner final FFARCS examination from 1973; resid Gosforth N'cle-u-Tyne

INKSTER Mary　MA 1909
　d Poole 20.2.78

INKSTER or McMenemey, Robina
　　　　　　　　　　　　　MB ChB 1920 MD 1928

INNES Alexander Henry　MB ChB 1952
　Royal Cornhill hosp Aber: med asst 1964–74, consult. forensic psychiat from 1974

INNES or Jenkinson, Alice Mabel Lee　MB ChB 1920
　resid Towcester

INNES Annie   MA 1922
retd 1967; resid Fraserburgh

INNES Cameron Roy   MB ChB 1950
JP 1965
g p: Foyers 1963–67, Fort William from 1967
d Fort William 1.6.77 *A UR* xlviii 107

INNES or Fischer, Catherine Donaldson   MA 1951
resid Luseland Saskatchewan

INNES Charles John Alexander   MA 1949
Cong ch min: Saughtonhall ch Edin 1960–69,
Coatdyke ch Airdrie from 1969

INNES or Cockburn, Christine Rose   MA 1934
lect LSE (Lond) 1943–66; soc affairs off. UN Geneva
1966–68; res off. internat soc security assoc ILO
Geneva 1968–74, dir res and documentation sect.
from 1975

INNES David   BSc(agr) 1959
mech advis NAAS Silsoe 1965–68; farm. Fordoun
from 1968

INNES or Farquharson, Elizabeth Ann Forbes
MA 1945
resid Fyvie

INNES or Lyall, Elizabeth Hughina McDonald
MA 1924
teacher Newburgh Aberdeensh 1943–64; retd

INNES or Mitchell, Elizabeth Jane   MB ChB 1908
d Aber 19.8.74 *A UR* xlvi 107

INNES Eric Milner   BSc 1935 MB ChB 1940
d Edin 7.11.78 *A UR* xlviii 106

INNES Francis Lumsden Farquharson
MB ChB 1941
consult. plastic surg Norwich from 1959

INNES George   MB ChB 1950 DPH 1957 MD 1959
MRCPsych 1971 MFCM 1972
sen res fell. dept mental health Aberd 1959–64, lect
1964–68; sen lect dept commun med Aberd 1968–76,
reader from 1976

INNES George Smith   BSc 1930 *1931
OBE 1971
retd 1970; resid Esher

INNES Gordon   *MA 1950
PhD(Lond) 1961
lect s of Oriental & African stud. Lond 1953–74,
reader from 1974; visiting prof of ling Indiana univ
Bloomington USA 1966–67

INNES Helen   MA 1908
no longer on GC reg

INNES or Will, Helen Reid   BSc 1913
resid Coventry

INNES Helen Watt   MA 1933
no longer on GC reg

INNES Ian Adam
BSc(mech eng) 1945 BSc(civ eng) 1948
proj man. UN surv geotherm resources in N Chile
Santiago from 1967

INNES Ian Dunbar   MB ChB 1943
VRD 1959 FRCGP 1970
g p Hull/part-time clin asst in dermat Hull RI from
1948; RNVR and RNR 1949–64; final rank surg lt cdr
d Hull 8.2.78 *A UR* xlvii 360

INNES Ian George   MA 1911 BSc 1912
BSc(agr) 1913 MB ChB 1918 ᶜMD 1928
d 18.2.65 *A UR* xli 147

INNES Ian Rome   MB ChB 1937 *MD 1955
Manit: assoc prof dept pharm & therap 1960–64,
prof from 1964/head of dept from 1967

INNES James   MA 1898
no longer on GC reg

INNES James   MA 1920 MB ChB 1924
g p: Hull 1928–39, Bournemouth 1939–60 (war
serv RAF 1942–45); retd 1960; resid Farnham
Common

INNES James Gilchrist   MA LLB 1949
ptnr Wilsone & Duffus advoc in Aber from 1952

INNES James Thomson   BSc(eng) 1945

INNES or MacDonald, Jane Helen   MA 1932
teacher cent. s Peterhead 1948–59; resid Deskford
husb *d* Inverboyndie Banff 21.5.73

INNES or Bruce, Jane Lunan   MA 1940

INNES or Law, Joanna Kean   MA 1911
d Toronto 8.11.64 *A UR* xli 55

INNES John   *MB ChB 1924 DPH 1927 ᶜMD 1930
d 8.9.72 *A UR* xlv 127

INNES John   BSc(eng) 1928 MB ChB 1937
d 23.12.72 *A UR* xlv 226

INNES John Lyall   MA 1926 LLB 1933
d Lond 2.8.69 *A UR* xliii 330

INNES John Robert Stephen   MB ChB 1940
g p Aber from 1946 and m o Aber prison from 1949

INNES John William
MA 1910 MB ChB 1915 *DPH 1919
FRSH 1951
retd; resid Thornhill
wife *d* 1972

INNES or Ross, Lizzie Paul   MA 1911
d 10.3.65

INNES or Macpherson, Maggie Robertson   MA 1909
d 22.8.64

INNES Margaret Eleanor   MA 1931
retd 1974; resid Aber

INNES of Macpherson, Margaret Howat Pagan
MA 1923
d Edin 2.5.79

INNES Margaret Jane   MA 1928
retd 1968; resid Peterculter

INNES or Steel, Mary Margaret Shaw   MA 1918
no longer on GC reg

INNES Maxwell   BSc(eng) 1951

INNES Maxwell Alexander Allan   MA 1952

INNES Norman Duncan   MB ChB 1952
g p Aber from 1952

INNES or Chitty, Penuel Mary   MB ChB 1924
resid Beckenham

INNES Robert   *BSc 1953 PhD 1957

INNES Robert Alexander   BSc(for) 1947
MRSFS 1950 MIFor(GB) 1951
for. comm Inv: div for. off. 1956–65, asst conserv
1965–70, conserv of for. from 1970

INNES Stephen George Begg
MA 1946 *MB ChB 1951

INNES Thomas Christie   MB ChB 1904
d N'cle-u-Tyne 15.8.64 *A UR* xl 394

INNES Thomas Christie   MA 1931

INNES William   MA 1940
JP 1972
dep rector Dunblane h s from 1962

INNES William   BSc(agr) 1949
farm Kincardinesh from 1949

INSCH Audrey Gordon   *MA 1955
PhD(Durh) 1958
teacher: Aber acad 1959–61, head Engl Grey Coat
hosp Lond 1961–68; sen lect Stockwell coll Bromley
from 1968

INSCH Herbert Saunders   BCom 1926
gen man. (Scot.) Bowmaker Stirling 1962–68; retd;
resid Gatehouse of Fleet

IRELAND Alfred James   MB ChB 1914
no longer on GC reg

IRONS William   MA 1919 BSc(agr) 1919
no longer on GC reg

IRONSIDE Alastair Grant   MB ChB 1953
FRCPE 1976

sen regist thoracic med united Oxford hosps 1963–64;
sen lect clin epidemiology Glas 1964–66; consult.
phys infect. diseases Monsall hosp Manc/part time
lect commun med Manc; smallpox consult. DHSS
from 1966
d Marple 24.8.80 *A UR* xlix 70

IRONSIDE Basil   MA 1926
d Aber 8.9.69 *A UR* xliii 330

IRONSIDE Charles Edward   MA 1919
D Phil
d Florida –.4.80

IRONSIDE David George   BSc(agr) 1922
d 16.10.62 *A UR* xl 86

IRONSIDE Eva Constance   MA 1913 MB ChB 1916
d Torbay 8.3.72 *A UR* xliv 428

IRONSIDE or Shepherd, Jane Ann Sherrin
MA 1913
d Forfar 12.11.76

IRONSIDE or Rixon, Margaret   MA 1950
Grays Essex: teacher Little Thurrock p s 1961–64;
head mus Deneholm p s 1966–73; remed teacher
E Tilbury from 1974

IRONSIDE Marjory   MA 1925
retd 1967; resid Glasg

IRONSIDE or Cox, Nellie Burns   MA 1906
no longer on GC reg

IRONSIDE Redvers Nowell   *MB ChB 1922
d Eastbourne 18.7.68 *A UR* xliii 81

IRONSIDE or Merkley, Rosemary Elizabeth
MA 1944

IRONSIDE Wallace   MB ChB 1940 MD 1954
FRANZCP 1964 FRCPsych 1971 FRACP 1971
univ of Rochester NY: Fulbright res schol 1959, sen
Buswell fell. 1959, fell. found. fund for res in psychiat
1960; Leverhulme res fell. All India inst of med sc
India 1971 asst prof psychiat univ of Rochester NY
1959–61, found. prof psych med: univ of Otago NZ
1962–69, Monash univ Aust from 1969

IRONSIDE William Bickerstaff   BSc(agr) 1953
farm. near Wick from 1954
m(2) Inv 5.10.63 M. A. Moir NDD

IRONSIDE William McIntosh Sinclair
MB ChB 1945
consult. ENT Huddersfield from 1959

IRVINE Alastair Munro   BSc(eng) 1952
MIEE 1960 AMBIM 1965
sen eng (constr) NSHEB Aber area from 1962

IRVINE Archibald Clive
MA 1913 MB ChB 1917 MD 1925 DD 1958
d Nairobi 7.6.74 *A UR* xlvi 107 & 235

IRVINE Charles Ross   *BSc 1930 MA 1931
retd 1971; resid Basingstoke
d 21.1.79 *AUR* XLVIII 231

IRVINE Elizabeth Fergusson   MA 1916
study and writing 1946–63; author of *A pioneer of the New Psychology* publ 1963; resid Suffolk

IRVINE George Bruce   BSc(eng) 1945
dep head Sandwick jun h s Shetland from 1974
m Bigton Shetland 29.12.59 Catherine M. S. Manson teacher d of Thomas M. Maywick

IRVINE James Geddes Greig   *MA 1946

IRVINE Jane Elizabeth   MA 1947
teacher: Prince Rupert s BFES Wilhelmshaven W Ger 1960–63, asst prin Engl Northfield acad Aber from 1963

IRVINE John Locke   MA 1915
d 8.6.69

IRVINE or Newman, Lilian Lloyd   *MA 1924
d Cambridge 13.5.73 *AUR* XLV 225 & 322

IRVINE or Barrie, Margaret Elizabeth Mary
MA 1948

IRVINE Mary Edith   MA 1930
retd; resid Portknockie

IRVINE Sidney Herbert   *MA 1954 MEd 1956
PhD(Lond) 1964 Fell. Eugenics Soc 1968
FBPsS 1974
lect educ: univ coll Rhodesia 1959–64, Brist 1964–67; visiting schol. educ testing serv Princeton NJ USA 1967–68; assoc prof educ/psych univ W Ont 1968–71; Brock univ Ont 1971: prof/dean coll of educ 1971–76, prof educ res from 1976

IRVINE William Alexander   MB ChB 1955
d Inv 22.4.77 *AUR* XLVII 360

IRVINE-FORTESCUE James William   *MA 1937
CA 1948 JP 1957 DL (Kincardine) 1975
Kt Order of St Lazarus of Jerusalem 1975
councillor Kincardine c c/chmn Lower Deeside dist council 1964–73

IRWIN William Knox   MB ChB 1908 MD 1913
d 18.7.73

ISBISTER Samuel   BSc(agr) 1934
dep chief insp DAFS 1960–71; retd; resid Culbokie
wife *d* 1960
m(2) Edin 21.4.62 Mary M. M. Anderson teacher
d Culbokie 9.12.79 *AUR* XLVIII 442

IZATT or Miller, Annie Milne   MA 1925
resid Carluke

IZATT or Troup, Ella Shand   MA 1922
teacher Greenock 1949–67
husb *d* 1.8.48

JACK or McBain, Annie May   MB ChB 1922
husb *d* 1964
resid Inv
d –.2.79

JACK David   BSc(agr) 1954
farm. Jackstown,Rothienorman from 1963; also joint man. dir Jacks drapers/outfitters Peterhead
m Aber 1.9.62 Isabell C. Cowie MA 1960 *qv*

JACK Dorothy Elizabeth   *MA 1930
retd 1968; resid Stonehaven

JACK or Christie, Elizabeth Turner   MA 1926
d Glasg 12.9.80

JACK Ernest Munro   MB ChB 1945
MRCGP 1962
g p Bolton from 1948; serving brother St John from 1967

JACK George   MA 1890
no longer on GC reg

JACK George Polson   MA 1936
d Edin 16.5.64 *AUR* XL 401

JACK or Falconer, Georgina Sutherland   MA 1941
teacher Elgin acad: Fr 1960–72, prin guid from 1972

JACK Helen Margaret   MA 1923
no longer on GC reg

JACK or Fraser, Jean Elizabeth   MA 1935

JACK or Griffith, Jessie Munro   *MA 1921
teacher part-time St Margaret's s Aber 1944–49; resid Aber

JACK John Argo   *MA 1926
no longer on GC reg

JACK Margaret Helen Bruce   MA 1936
retd 1979; resid Grantown-on-Spey

JACK Marjorie   MA 1955
m Cairns

JACK or Miller, Millicent Isobel   MA 1923
resid Mosstodloch Fochabers

JACK William Begg   MA 1923
d 27.11.71 *AUR* XLIV 320

JACKSON James   BSc(agr) 1951
farm. Brechin from 1951
m Colliston Angus 26.10.66 Maureen Geddes

JACKSON James Archie Donaldson   BSc(for) 1947
MBE 1964
conserv of for. N Nigeria 1959–70, for. advis (Brit tech aid) Ethiopia from 1971

JACKSON Jessie Elizabeth Catherine   MA 1944
secy loc govt Inv from 1952

JACKSON John Harrison   MA 1928 BSc 1930

JACKSON or Norrie, Mary Baird   MA 1926

JACKSON Philip Mott   MB ChB 1940
JP St Andrew Jamaica 1972
m o and police surg Kingston Jamaica 1962–64; retd
col med serv 1964; private pract St Andrew Jamaica
from 1965

JACKSON Robert Hay   BSc(eng) 1953
d Sabah Borneo 28.12.73 *AUR* xlv 450

JACKSON Tom Forbes   *MA 1915
d 27.3.70

JACKSON William Welsby   PhD 1933

JACZYNSKA Alexandra   *MA 1953

JAFFRAY or Morrison, Agnes Baxter   MA 1929
resid Aber

JAFFRAY Alastair Blackburn   MB ChB 1932
d Rayton 21.6.60 *AUR* xxxviii 598

JAFFRAY Annie Ada   MA 1908
no longer on GC reg

JAFFRAY David Mitchell   *MA 1939
d Lond 1976 *AUR* xlvi 417

**JAFFRAY or Eyre-Smith, Fanny Ewerdine
MA 1918**
no longer on GC reg

JAFFRAY Isabella   MA 1911
d Glasg 26.10.71 *AUR* xliv 316

JAFFRAY or Pollock, Jessie Isobella   MA 1916
no longer on GC reg

JAFFRAY Kathleen Mary   MA 1924
d 20.2.72

JAFFRAY Reginald Andrew Baxter   MB ChB 1926
retd; resid Bromley

JAFFRAY Victor Wallace   MA 1940
LLB(Edin)
d 8.7.77

JAFFREY Leslie James   BSc 1949 *1950
MICE 1963
prin scient off. Hydraulics res stat Wallingford from
1961

JAMES Alexander Souter   *BSc(eng) 1954
consult. Lond 1958–60; man. UK branch site
investig comp Aust 1960–63; prin A. S. James Pty
geotech eng Melbourne from 1963

JAMES Catherine Masson   MA 1938
teacher Forres acad 1956–77; retd

JAMES or Shivas, Catherine Philip   MA 1930
resid Peterculter

JAMES Edward   MB ChB 1923 ᶜMD 1928
consult. phys to Romford and Chelmsford hosps
till 1970; p/t consult. in infect. diseases Chelmsford
1954–70; retd; resid West Mersea

JAMES John Courtenay   BD 1907
no longer on GC reg

JAMESON Alexander Pringle   *BSc 1911 DSc 1920

**JAMESON William Wilson
MA 1905 *MB ChB 1909 *MD 1912 LLD 1940**
d Lond 18.10 62 *AUR* xl 75

JAMIE Elizabeth Davidson   MB ChB 1955
DMJ(Lond) 1965 Member Inner Temple 1971
LLB(Lond) 1972
Lond: ophth Clerkenwell med mission Haxton group
of hosps and clin, clin asst eye dept Westminster,
Great Ormond St. and Royal eye hosps from 1959

JAMIESON Alan   *BSc 1952
prin res fell. MAFF fisheries lab Lowestoft 1965–69,
prin scient off. 1969–74, individual merit award graded
sen prin scient off. from 1974

JAMIESON Alexander   MB ChB 1937
DPH(Edin) 1962 MFCM 1972
Edin corp: asst m o p h dept 1962–66, sen m o
1966–74, sen m o and designated m o Lothian health
board commun health dept from 1974

JAMIESON Alexander Slessor   *MA 1926
retd 1970; resid Edin
m –.7.31

JAMIESON or Thompson, Elizabeth   BSc 1934
teacher phys Ardrossan acad 1968–72; resid
W Kilbride

JAMIESON Frederick   *BSc 1950

JAMIESON George Grant   *MA 1920
d Nairn 9.9.73

JAMIESON George Stuart   MA 1920

JAMIESON or Warrander, Irene Patricia   MA 1953
teacher maths Aber: Middle s 1963–66, Powis acad
from 1966

JAMIESON John   MA 1923
d Edin 2.3.67 *AUR* xlii 185

JAMIESON John   BSc(agr) 1929
retd 1972; resid Ollaberry Shetland

JAMIESON John Robert   MA 1901 BSc 1907
no longer on GC reg

JAMIESON Julia Ann   BSc 1924
retd 1962; resid Stonehaven
d Stonehaven 18.7.80

JAMIESON or Stephen, May Keith   *MA 1941
form mistress Blairmore prep s for boys Glass from 1959

JAMIESON Michael Sutherland   *MA 1953
lect Engl: Keele 1960–62, Sus from 1962; warden Falmer House Sus 1962–72; fell. Salzburg Seminar in Amer stud. 1965; visiting prof Facolta di Magistero univ of Rome 1969; res Berg collection NY 1973

JAMIESON Ruth Campbell   *MA 1917
retd 1960; resid Banchory

JAMIESON Samuel   PhD 1949

JAMIESON or Brylowskie, Violet   *MA 1942

JAMIESON William George   MA 1921
no longer on GC reg

JAMIESON-CRAIG Catherine Isabella Anderson   MA 1915 MB ChB 1927 MD 1934
d 27.3.60

JAPPY or Mitchell, Jeannie   MA 1941

JAPPY John Flett   BSc(eng) 1943

JARDINE or Taylor, Helen Margaret (Lady)   MB ChB 1920 MD 1937 LLD 1966
JP Aber
chmn NE Scot. reg nurse trg comm 1952–72; resid Edin
husb, Sir Thomas M. Taylor, Principal Aberd, *d* 1962

JARVIE Elizabeth Ellis   MA 1941

JEANS Henry Williams   MB ChB 1904
no longer on GC reg

JEFFREY David Sinclair   BSc(for) 1953

JEFFREY Florence Winifred   MA 1922
no longer on GC reg

JEFFREY John Colin Somerville   MB ChB 1949
MBE 1945
g p Lochgilphead from 1959

JENKINS Annie   *MA 1922

JENKINS Margaret Wilson   MA 1955
m Chisholm

JENKINS May Chalmers   MA 1940
journalist Aber Journals from 1968

JENKINS William Leyshon   *BSc 1952

JERMEY Kevin Gerard   *MEd 1952
MIM 1962
asst to gen man. Tracy petr comp Kirkuk Iraq 1958–59; comm man. of subsid Darlington Chem 1959–64; Lond: MSL consult. 1965–67, Rank Organis exec apptments advis 1967–70, assoc dir Canny Bowen &

Associates 1971–73, dir Berndtson Internat from 1973

JESSAMINE Alexander Gordon   MB ChB 1948
Ottawa: sen phys royal Ottawa san 1959, head dept med 1961–68; phys i/c Ottawa reg tuberculosis prevn serv Ontario M o H from 1968

JESSAMINE Austin Steele   MB ChB 1939
MRCGP
g p Aber from 1939
d Aber 15.3.81

JESSIMAN James Brown   MB ChB 1922 MD 1933
retd; resid Bromley
d Bromley 27.2.79 *AUR* XLVIII 228

JESSIMAN or Ward, Janetta Mary Gray   MA 1915
no longer on GC reg

JEWERS John Milne Everett   MB ChB 1941
consult. surg W Dorset group of hosps from 1965

JOCKEL Charles Marshall   MB ChB 1946
g p Bolton 1949–65, Tawa NZ from 1965

JOHNSON Allan   BD 1952
no longer on GC reg

JOHNSON or Semple, Dorothy   MA 1951

JOHNSON Edward   MB ChB 1908
d 3.6.63

JOHNSON Francis Hernaman-   MB ChB 1904
no longer on GC reg

JOHNSON James Charles Manson   *MA 1929
no longer on GC reg

JOHNSON Joan Mortimer   MA 1949
m Chopin

JOHNSON Laurence Leask   BSc 1922
resid Lerwick

JOHNSON Louis   MA 1955
Shetland: relief teacher Lerwick, Fetlar, Yell 1956–57; teacher j s s Urafirth 1957–62; head North Roe p s from 1962
m Lerwick 6.4.59 Lilias M. Hawkins teacher d of Reginald C. H. Sandness Shetland

JOHNSON or Ensor, Mary Kinross   MB ChB 1945
FPA Bishop's Stortford from 1952; clin asst venereol Lond from 1974

JOHNSON Maurice Buchan   MB ChB 1903
no longer on GC reg

JOHNSON Rosemary Agnes   *MA 1955
teacher Engl Torry s s Aber 1957–61
m Aber 27.12.60 William P. Baxter DA(Edin) artist/teacher s of George B. Aber

JOHNSTON Adam   MB ChB 1906
  d Aber 5.3.66 *A UR* XLII 82

JOHNSTON or Reid, Adiell Durward   *MA 1923
  resid Strathdon

JOHNSTON Alexander   MA 1925
  pres Retd Teachers' Assoc (Scot.) 1977–79
retd 1965; resid Dumfries

JOHNSTON or Mowat, Aline Cameron   MA 1949
  teacher Wick: p s 1966–70, mus s s 1970–78; full
time mus spec for four prim. s in Wick from 1978

JOHNSTON Anthony   BSc 1942 *1943
  FIBiol 1970
Kew: asst dir commonwealth mycological inst 1965–
68, dir from 1968

JOHNSTON David William Douglas   MA 1948
  Co S min Auldearn and Ardclach 1963–76;
moderator Inv presb 1973–74; county c Nairnsh from
1969
d Auldearn 28.11.76

JOHNSTON or Rice, Dorothy Margaret   MA 1926
  d Doncaster 28.9.69 *A UR* XLIII 330

JOHNSTON Edward Alexander
                MA 1923 MB ChB 1927 DPH 1931
  retd 1967; resid Inv

JOHNSTON Edwin   *MA 1923
  d Lond 28.1.69 *A UR* XLIII 212

JOHNSTON or Höy, Elizabeth Marguerite Angela
                                MA 1944
  Norway: translator Kristiansand from 1955, lect
tech Engl Air Force tech coll from 1965

JOHNSTON Elizabeth Russell   BSc 1940

JOHNSTON Elizabeth Whyte   MA 1948

JOHNSTON or Michie, Ellenina Catherine
                                MA 1952
  teacher Kirkcaldy 1959–60; resid Aber from 1967

JOHNSTON George Andrew   MA 1912
  d 13.8.66 *A UR* XLI 337

JOHNSTON or Manson, Helen   MA 1940
  resid Peterhead

JOHNSTON Henry Watt   MA 1911
  d Bishop Auckland 15.1.74 *A UR* XLVI 107

JOHNSTON or Thompson, Isabella   MA 1935
  teacher Aber 1940–46, 1957–74; retd
husb *d* 1969

JOHNSTON Isabella Ivy   *MA 1928
  prin teacher Fr/Ger and woman advis Banchory
acad; retd 1966; resid Insch

JOHNSTON James Bruce   MB ChB 1947
  d Eastbourne 24.4.79 *A UR* XLVIII 233, XLIX 70

JOHNSTON James Cooper   MA 1911
  no longer on GC reg

JOHNSTON James Douglas   MB ChB 1953
  d –.11.66

JOHNSTON James Weston   BSc 1950

JOHNSTON James William   BSc(agr) 1929
  farm. Fintray Dyce from 1948

JOHNSTON or Marr, Janet   MB ChB 1925
  d Lond 13.5.73 *A UR* XLV 319

JOHNSTON Janetta Maria   MA 1933
  teacher Keith g s 1957–68; retd

JOHNSTON or Hedges, Janey Alison Donald
                                ***MA 1948 *EdB 1951**
  resid Didcot

JOHNSTON John   MB ChB 1909
  d Aber 31.12.62 *A UR* XL 79

JOHNSTON John Edward   MA 1922 *1923
  no longer on GC reg

JOHNSTON or Grieve, Kathleen Zia   BSc 1941
  BBC tech staff Aber 1941–44; nat pres C of S
Woman's Guild 1966–69; organis BBC's Scot. tele-
phone referral centre for adult literacy from 1975

JOHNSTON Margaret Cadger   MA 1933
  retd 1971; resid Fraserburgh

JOHNSTON Margaret Helen   MA 1955
  m Stuart

JOHNSTON or Potts, Margaret Taylor   BSc 1955
  resid Caton

JOHNSTON or Reid, Mary   *MA 1939
  resid Inv

JOHNSTON or Murray, Mary Elizabeth   MA 1924
  resid Aber

JOHNSTON or Esslemont, Mary Gray   MA 1952
  teacher; Aber 1953–56; Keithhall from 1956

JOHNSTON or Grover, Mary Ross   MA 1936
  teacher Hanover St p s Aber 1938–74; retd
husb *d* 1966
m(2) Aber 30.3.66 Harold J. Boorer headmaster s of
Walter J. B. Wolverhampton

JOHNSTON or Birss, May   MA 1941

JOHNSTON Neil Campbell   MA 1944 *MEd 1948
  prin teacher mod lang Bankhead acad Aber 1961–
67; advis mod lang Aber educ comm 1967–75; asst dir
educ Grampian reg from 1975

JOHNSTON Robert Neilson
           *MB ChB 1943 MD 1953
FRCPE 1963 FRCP 1972
hon sen lect respir diseases Dund from 1965
m(2) Aber 14.5.64 Elizabeth M. Semple capt WRAC
d of Robert Semple MB ChB 1910 *qv*

JOHNSTON Thomas   BSc(agr) 1954

JOHNSTON Violet Elspet Lawson   MA 1933
   retd 1970; resid Fraserburgh

JOHNSTON William Forsyth   MA 1930
   head Portgordon j s s 1963–71; retd; resid Buckie

JOHNSTONE Albert James   *MA 1936
   Inverurie acad: prin teacher maths from 1962, asst
head from 1972; retd 1977

JOHNSTONE Alexander
           MA 1914 MB ChB 1916 DPH 1920
   no longer on GC reg

JOHNSTONE Alexander Fordyce   MB ChB 1947
   FRCPsych 1974
consult. psychiat Craig Dunain hosp Inv from 1957

JOHNSTONE Charles George   MA 1934
   head Buchanhaven p s Aberdeensh from 1958; retd
1975

JOHNSTONE George Erskine   MB ChB 1939

JOHNSTONE or Ogilvie, Helen Macleod   MA 1916
   d Liverpool 31.8.74 *AUR* XLVI 107

JOHNSTONE or Williams, Irene Constance
           MA 1934

JOHNSTONE James George   MB ChB 1913
   no longer on GC reg

JOHNSTONE James Hugh   *MA 1950
   Inv royal acad: prin teacher geog 1960–71, dep
rector from 1971

JOINER Henry   MA 1904
   d Meigle 17.4.66 *AUR* XLII 82

JOINER John Herschel   MA BSc 1925
   CA firm Glasg 1925–34; Lond: statist 1934–41, CA
asst 1941–46, ptnr 1946–73, sole ptnr from 1973

JOLLY or McKinnon, Elsie McKenzie   MA 1933

JOLLY Eric James   MB ChB 1923
   d Huntingdon 12.1.68 *AUR* XLII 360

JOLLY Flora Jessie   MA 1931
   retd 1967; resid Aber

JOLLY George Mann   BSc 1942 *1947
   market gardening Skye 1958–61; statist (prin scient
off. grade) ARC unit of statist: Aberd 1961–66, Edin
from 1966

JOLLY Robert Alexander   *MA 1931
   d Bampton 21.3.74

JOLLY William Crockart   *MA 1946
   teacher maths Mackie acad Stonehaven from 1955
m Aber 11.8.66 Elizabeth J. Goddard secy d of James
S. G. Aber

JONES Benjamin Wignall   MB ChB 1917
   no longer on GC reg

JONES Bronwen Jean   *MA 1935
   teacher Craig-y-nos prep s Swansea 1936–38;
Cardiff: pers man. Gripoly Mills 1939–41, caseworker
fam welfare assoc 1961–66, soc worker educ dept
1966–73; retd
m Cardiff 18.10.40 Herbert S. W. Jones chartered
marine and mech eng s of William M. J. Resolven

JONES David Arthen   PhD 1951
   d Aber 11.11.75

JONES Joan Mary Glyn   *MA 1955

JONES John Gareth Watkin   PhD 1955
   prin scient off. Grassland Res Inst Hurley
Maidenhead 1965–70; sen res fell. dept agr R'dg
1970–75; sen lect dept agr R'dg from 1975
m Dolgellau Merioneth 30.6.73 Hilary A. Evans
MA(Edin) lib d of William G. E., MBBS(Lond),
Dolgellau

JONES Mair Lewys   MB ChB 1951
   g p Aberdulais 1957–59; resid Hamilton Mass USA
m 24.9.59 Gwyn Walters BA BD PhD(Edin) prof
theol Mass USA

JONES or Humphrys, Margaret Irvine   MA 1946

JONES Marion Gwyneth Cornwall   MA 1920
   retd 1957; resid Ilkley
d Ilkley 10.5.77

JONES or Hatch, Megan Owen Ceiron   MA 1942

JONES or Watkins or Le Moine, Menna Owen Ceiron
           MB ChB 1940
   FACCP
phys Oxford reg centre Woodstock Ontario 1960–77;
retd

JONES or Buchanan, Nina Roberta Ceiron
           MA 1951

JONES Thomas   BSc 1950
   d Aber 25.8.65 *AUR* XLI 251

JONES William Park   MA 1926
   d Aber 26.1.63 *AUR* XL 205

JORDAAN William Petrus   MB ChB 1921

JORDAN David Alma   BSc(for) 1953
   MIFor 1956 MA(Cantab) 1961 AIWSc 1963
Hull: dir Riplington Estates from 1951; dir Anlaby

Estates from 1963; dir Ferriby Construction Co from 1964; bldg surv for Alma Jordan 1959–73; dir South Hunsley Marketing Combine from 1973; man. dir Alma Jordan (Builders) from 1976 and (Farms) from 1975; dir Shawland Vegetable Growers from 1976
m Kirkella 2.6.36 Sheila J. Clark bank cashier d of Donald C. Hull

JOSLIN Anthony   BSc(for) 1955
Dean Glos: asst educ off. 1963–68, dist off. from 1968
m Weston-under-Penyard 3.9.70 Barbara M. Bevan d of Francis J. B. Ross-on-Wye

JOSS or Brister, Alison Patricia   MA 1953

JOSS or Cunningham, Dorothy Mackintosh
MA 1950

JOSS George Smith   MB ChB 1950
FRCSE 1960 FRSM member: Brit Assoc of Plastic Surg, Fr Soc Plastic et Reconstn Surg, Europ Assoc of Maxillo-Facial surg
sen regist plastic surg Middx hosp/Mt Vernon centre 1960–64 plastic surg: consult. United Norwich hosps Ipswich and E. Suffolk gen hosp from 1964, hon consult. Addenbroke's hosp Cambridge 1964–69, hon consult. US Air Force in Britain from 1965

JOSS or Lawrence, Margaret Robertson   MA 1933
no longer on GC reg

JOSS William Taylor Barron   MB ChB 1923
retd 1960; resid Edwalton
d –.2.73

JOYNER Charles   MA 1915
no longer on GC reg

JOYNT Geoffrey Henry   MEd 1951

JUNOR or Mackenzie, Mary Paterson   MA 1930

JUPP or Wilson, Alice Marion   MA 1923
no longer on GC reg

KABATA Zbigniew   BSc 1955 PhD 1959 DSc 1966
parasitology: marine lab DAFS Aber 1955–67, dept environ fisheries and marine serv Nanaimo BC Canada from 1967

KAINAN (Ibrahim) Sasson Yacov   BSc(eng) 1949
sen prod. eng on A/C hydraulic components Israel A/C Indust from 1969
m Israel 5.2.59 Evette Ben-Shlomo teacher d of Obadia B-S Kiriat Ono Israel

KANE or Collier, Mary Anne   MA 1933

KANGA Burjorji Sorabji   MB ChB 1916 MD 1919
FRIPHH(Lond) 1929
resid Bombay

KAY Margaret Horne   MA 1909
d Elgin 24.1.72 *AUR* xliv 427

KAY or Williams, Valerie Margaret Mary
MA 1950 ᶜMB ChB 1955
m o cytology unit path. dept Aber

KAY William Hunter   MB ChB 1915

KEAN Helen Margaret   MA 1952
teacher: Muirfield p s Aber 1959–62, Sunnybank p s Aber 1963–66, maths Llywn-y-Bryn girls' g s Swansea 1967–69, phys Lanark g s from 1969
m Aber 26.7.61 Stewart Murray BSc 1966 *qv*

KEAY John   *MA 1919
d 4.4.76

KEAY Margaret Elizabeth   MA 1949 MB ChB 1955
g p: Birm 1961–72, Gloucester from 1972
m Sutton Coldfield 23.10.60 Chris P. Van Zyl BSc (O F State) lect Birm s of Christian V. Z. Bloemfontein

KEIR Alexander   MA 1905
m(2) Aber 8.4.61 Agnes T. C. Hall MA 1930 *qv*
d Aber 3.1.71 *AUR* xliv 208

KEIR or Phelan, Isabella Bruce   MA 1925
no longer on GC reg

KEIR James   MA 1904
no longer on GC reg

KEIR Robert Macdougal Stewart   MB ChB 1940
sen consult. anaest Dumfries and Galloway R. I. from 1951

KEIR Walter Alexander Stewart   *MA 1947
sen lect Engl Aberd from 1971

KEITH Alexander   *MA 1916 LLD 1967
farm. 1944–71; author *A Thousand Years of Aberdeen* 1972; resid Stonehaven
d Stonehaven 5.10.78 *AUR* xlviii 103 & 61

KEITH Alexander McPherson
MA 1931 MB ChB 1935
d Paisley 30.7.75 *AUR* xlv 324

KEITH David Tully   *MA 1951
teacher Boddam p s 1964–67; head: Logie Coldstone p s 1967–71, Whitehills from 1971
m Lond 15.4.62 Winifred H. Hopgood shop man. d of Albert H. Muswell Hill

KEITH Donald Ritchie   *MA 1938 *MEd 1945
teacher Powis acad, Torry acad 1966–79; retd

KEITH Elizabeth Margaret Jeannie   MA 1928
retd 1968; resid Peterculter

KEITH Elizabeth Meston   MA 1949
teacher Mearns acad Laurencekirk 1953–61 and from 1971
m Stonehaven 11.10.58 Alexander J. D. Nicoll consult. eng

KEITH Frederick Leonard   MB ChB 1904 MD 1918
d Aboyne 23.3.70

KEITH or Cameron, Grace   MA 1955

KEITH Ian Fyvie   BSc(agr) 1948

KEITH James Duncan Lindsay
          ***BSc(mech eng) 1935 BSc(elect eng) 1936**
sen mech eng Merz & McLellan consult. eng from
1945
m Northwich 11.5.44 Edith M. P. Tharme army, lab
asst d of Alfred C. T. Stourton

KEITH Marshall William   MB ChB 1930 DPH 1932

KEITH or Hood, Mary Jane   MA 1918
teacher sc/maths Glenrothes 1954–65; retd; resid
Leslie

KEITH Nelson   *MA 1926
d Abernethy 14.4.66 *A UR* XLII 88

KEITH William Brooks   MB ChB 1906 MD 1914
d 13.5.63

KELBIE Emmanuel Buckland   BSc(eng) 1955

KELLAS Arthur Roy Handasyde   *MA 1936
counsellor HM Emb Tehran 1958–62; Imperial
Defence Coll Lond 1963; counsellor HM Emb: Tel
Aviv 1964–66, Kathmandu 1966–70, Aden 1970–72;
High Commissioner Dar-es-Salaam 1973–75

KELLAS Derek Mario Mitchell   BSc(for) 1938
d 17.2.68 *A UR* XLII 373

KELLAS George Duncan   MA 1930 LLB 1932
solic and notary: war serv RAF 1941–45; commissioned Malta 1942; town clerk Inverurie/clerk to
Garioch dist council 1946–75

KELLAS Henry Ronald   MB ChB 1936
g p Swindon from 1948

KELLAS or Legge, Isabella Dey McDonald
                                            MA 1930

KELLAS James Forrest   *MA 1920 *BD 1923
C o S min Durris 1958–66; moderator Synod of
Aber 1964–65; retd
d Aber 9.1.77

KELLAS or Brand, Janetta Margaret   MA 1929
retd 1972; resid Benwick

KELLAS John   MA 1920 *1921 DD 1950
d Edin 12.11.67 *A UR* XLII 358

KELLAS Lorna Mary   BSc 1943 *1947
resid Cambus o' May

KELLAS Robert   MB ChB 1910
d Lismore NSW 1.1.66 *A UR* XLII 83

KELLAS Robert Lloyd   MA 1947
head Arrochar p s Dunbartonsh from 1968

KELLOCK Alexander Moir   MB ChB 1932
d 27.11.73

KELLY Francis Charles   *BSc 1923 PhD 1926
FRSM 1937
commander of the Chilean Order of Merit 1969
retd 1971; resid Lond

KELLY George Carmichael
          ***BSc 1923 MB ChB 1926 *MD 1930**
CBE 1959 hon MA(Brist) 1964
sen admin m o SW reg hosp board 1947–65
resid Clevedon
d Clevedon 25.7.77

KELLY Mary Carmichael   MA 1916
d Edin 15.2.76

KELLY Terence O'Neil Fraser   MB ChB 1942

KELLY William   MB ChB 1925
d Bexhill-on-Sea 23.5.75 *A UR* XLVI 323

KELMAN Emily Thom   *MA 1933

KELMAN George Smith   BL 1950
joint man. dir mech supplies Aber from 1969
d 3.10.81

KELMAN or Ray, Jane Thain   MA 1936
teacher: Kittybrewster p s Aber 1937–45, Horley
Surrey 1955–78

KELMAN John   MA 1909 BSc 1911
no longer on GC reg

KELMAN or Macleod, Muriel Hay   MA 1947
resid Oban

KELMAN or Shirreffs, Nan Cameron   MA 1940
resid Aber

KELMAN Richard Cameron   MA 1930
MIQ 1975
chmn and man. dir of companies in extractive indust
including Shirman enterprises (Aber), Craigenlow
Quarries, Road Seal associated with Tarmac
Roadstone

KELMAN or Stewart, Shirley May   BSc 1955
resid Downers Grove Illinois USA

KELSEY Vernon   BSc 1953
res chem Coalite & Chem Prod. Chesterfield from
1956

KELSO Arthur Allardyce   BSc(eng) 1948

KELSO Olga   MA 1934
retd 1971; resid Stonehaven

KELTY Arthur   BSc 1910
no longer on GC reg

KEMP or Macleod, Agnes Helen   *MA 1943
Herts: head mod lang St Francis coll Letchworth 1964–72, dep head St Angelo's s Stevenage from 1973; dept chmn N Herts bench from 1973

KEMP Alastair   BSc(eng) 1954

KEMP Alastair Taylor   MA 1951
d Aber 26.2.76 *AUR* XLVII 215

KEMP or Huffam, Alice Rae   BSc 1932 *1933
resid Cottingham

KEMP or McLaren, Alison McIntyre   MA 1954

KEMP Annie   MA 1905
no longer on GC reg

KEMP or Forbes, Charlotte Davidson   MA 1923
teacher Engl Peterhead North j s s 1945–67
d Dunedin NZ 30.5.76

KEMP or Buckland, Ethel Elizabeth Mary   MA 1942
resid Winchester

KEMP or Howell, Ethel Hope   *MA 1913
d Aber 19.6.62 *AUR* XLI 55

KEMP or Alexander, Mabel   MA 1929
resid Shrewsbury

KEMP or Rutherford, Margaret Cooper
MB ChB 1942
part-time asst m o with Aber burgh publ health dept from 1964; retd

KEMP Margaret Ellen   MA 1908
d Letchworth –.11.73

KEMP Marion Davina Sutherland   *MA 1917
d Dufftown 24.9.72 *AUR* XLV 125

KEMP or Brodie-Browne, Marjorie Paterson
**   *MA 1937**
Leamington Spa: teacher Fr/Ger Leamington coll for girls, head mod lang dept from 1966–76; retd

KEMP or Stark, Mary Ann   MA 1920
resid Whitburn

KEMP Moyra Strachan Mortimer   MB ChB 1947
lect anat Aberd from 1966
m Aber 14.8.62 George W. Anderson

KEMP Nellie   MA 1929

KEMP Robert   *MA 1929
d Edin 25.11.67 *AUR* XLII 368

KEMP or Smith, Rose   MA 1913
d Aber 19.3.69 *AUR* XLIII 210

KEMP Thomas Ian   MB ChB 1952
g p Enfield from 1959

KENDALL Richard Haddon   BSc(for) 1949

KENNEDY Agnes   MA 1935
d Aber 23.9.65 *AUR* XLI 250

KENNEDY Alan Campbell   BL 1954
Aber: prin leg. asst Town clerk's dept 1962–69, burgh proc fisc 1969–75; chief exec Gordon dist c from 1975

KENNEDY Margaret Chalmers   MA 1938

KENNEDY or Grant, Margaret Jane
**   *MA 1903 *1904**
teacher Mortlach s s 1904–08
d Dufftown 9.10.75

KENNEDY or Kemp, Mary Elizabeth   *MA 1911
d Aber 24.2.77

KENNEDY William Birnie   MB ChB 1948
DPH(Edin) 1964
RAF dep s m o 18 group Pitreavie 1961–63; s m o: Persian Gulf Bahrein 1964–66, Manby 1966–69, Hockering 1969–73; member med board OASC Biggin Hill from 1975

KENNEDY William Duff   *MA 1921
retd 1962; resid Fraserburgh

KENNEDY William John   BSc(eng) 1952

KENNER Lionel   *MA 1953

KENWORTHY Brian John   PhD 1952
sen lect Ger Aberd from 1968

KEPPIE Joseph Lockhart   *BSc(agr) 1953

KER or Gray, Audrey Isabella   MA 1933 LLB 1934
d Ipswich 11.11.75

KERMACK William Ogilvie
**   *MA *BSc 1918 DSc 1925**
d 20.7.70 *AUR* XLIV 25

KERR or Anderson, Agnes Wishart   *BSc 1940
teacher Aber h s for girls from 1965

KERR or Campbell, Alexandra Jean Robson
**   *BSc 1930 PhD 1936**
resid Winnipeg

KERR Cecilia Elizabeth Sommerville   *MA 1940
teacher girls' g s Tunbridge from 1952

KERR or Deall, Christina Ferguson   MB ChB 1923
d Nott 11.8.73 *AUR* XLV 318

KERR Colin Mackay   MA 1903
no longer on GC reg

KERR Elizabeth   MA 1922
retd 1962; resid Retford

KERR Fergus Gordon Thomson   *MA 1953
ordained priest 1962; prior of Blackfriars Oxford from 1969

KERR George Robert England   MB ChB 1933
d Inv 7.5.72 *AUR* XLV 128

KERR Ian McDougall   MB ChB 1938
FRCP(C) 1975
NY, USA: dir St Lawrence county mental health serv Potsdam 1959–72; dep dir clin St Lawrence state hosp Ogdensburg 1972–76; retd
d New York 29.11.78

KERR or Nicol, Margaret Isobel Goldie   MA 1940
resid Aber

KERR or Rae, Mary High   MA 1942

KERRIN Albert Eric   MA 1951
Stranraer: part time priest i/c St John's Stranraer with St Ninian's Portpatrick from 1970; asst teacher Lochan's p s 1970–71, dep head Park p s from 1971

KERRIN Daniel   *MA 1921
teacher Engl Newton acad Ayr 1957–61; retd; resid Johannesburg

KERRIN John Charles
                 MB ChB 1922 DPH 1925 *MD 1930
d Cheadle 29.6.68 *AUR* XLIII 83

KERRIN Richard Elual   MA 1920
retd 1969; resid Kemnay

KESTNER Friedrich Julius Theodor   *BSc(eng) 1939
FRGS 1970
prin scient off. hydraulics res stat DSIR Wallingford from 1958

KEYS or Harkins, Annie Elizabeth Martin   MA 1925
resid Aber

KEYT Frederic Dudley Ross
                 MB ChB 1920 DPH 1921
d 5.10.67

KIDD Andrew   *MA 1925
retd BBC Lond 1964; lit edit. *Evening Argus* Brighton from 1964

KIDD Dorothy Rose   MA BSc 1939
retd 1976; resid Milltimber Aber
member univ court Aberd from 1978

KIDD Douglas Alexander   *MA 1934
prof classics univ of Canterbury Christchurch NZ from 1957; retd 1979

KIDD Francis Tosh   MA 1928

KIDD James   MA 1922
d Glasg 2.11.71 *AUR* XLIV 320

KIDD Neil Malcolm Lee   BSc(agr) 1954
farm man.: Lincs 1957–58, Kincardinesh 1959–63, Fife 1963–70; farm. Angus from 1970
m Careston 14.7.61 Mary H. Falconer MA(Edin) teacher d of John M. F. Finavon

KIDD or Brown, Sheila Joan   MA 1948
teacher: Steward st inf s Birm 1959–60, Ferryhill p s Aber from 1965

KIDD William Gordon   *MA 1951

KILGOUR James Gray   MA 1923
woollen manuf Aber from 1926

KILGOUR John Lowell   MB ChB 1947
psc(Camberley) 1959 jssc(Latimer) 1964
MRCGP 1961 MFCM 1973
gen staff coll Camberley 1959–60 ADMS GHQ Farilf Singapore 1960–63; joint serv staff coll Latimer 1964–68; sen m o DHSS London; head internat health div DHSS from 1971/chief med advis FCO overseas dev admin from 1973

KILGOUR or Gill, Lilian Elsie   MA 1924
teacher Engl/hist Methlick j s 1960–70; retd; resid Ellon
husb *d* 13.11.68
d Aber 30.6.78 *AUR* XLVIII 104

KILLAH James   BSc 1949
AInstP 1969
Gordon s Huntly: spec asst 1959–73, prin teacher phys/chem from 1973

KILLOH Ronald Bruce   MB ChB 1940 DPH 1947
smo Croydon 1958–64, Bournemouth 1964–67; NSW Aust: d m o h 1967–77; retd

KILOH James Robertson   *MA 1951
prin teacher mod lang: Graeme h s Falkirk 1961–64, Trinity acad Edin 1964–73, asst head from 1973

KINDNESS or MacLean-Bryant, Elizabeth Brodie
                 MacLean   MA 1929

KINDNESS or Hutchison, Gladys   MA 1926
resid Kirkcaldy

KINDNESS Jane   *MA 1925
educ off. Sierra Leone 1944–45; head mod lang dept St Leonard's s St And 1959–66
m Lond 12.9.45 Geoffrey L. Jobling barrister/law off. col leg. serv/judge col judic serv s of Robert J. Celebes

KINDNESS Mary Allan   MA 1930
teacher Ashley Rd s Aber 1956–68; retd

KINDNESS or Steel, Winifred Mary Allan
                 MA 1914 MB ChB 1918 DPH 1921
retd 1972; resid Lond

KINEL Zofia Krystyna Wanda   MB ChB 1950
m Laszewski

KING Andrew Palfrey   BSc 1945

KING or Johns, Jessie Forrester   BCom 1929

KING John Abercromby   BSc(eng) 1952
m Aber 23.7.60 Prudence A. Young MA 1960 *qv*

KING John Alexander Hay   BCom 1929
no longer on GC reg

KING or Lory, Mary Merrily   MA 1948
resid Charlwood Horley Surrey

KING Norman William   *MA 1949 Dip Ed 1953

KING Oswin James Albert   BSc(eng) 1940
MICE 1948
vice-pres Eng Alcan Jamaica Mandeville 1956–75;
proj dir Construction Alumina Plant Madrid 1975–
78; ptnr/rep Alumina Co of Canada/Royal Dutch
Shell Anaconda USA/Construction Alumina Plant
Limerick from 1979
m Leicester 23.9.48 Margaret E. Skene

KINGHORN Alexander Manson
                         MA 1947 *1950 PhD 1953
Kingston Jamaica: lect Engl univ coll of W I 1960–
63, sen lect 1963–67, reader from 1967

KINGHORN Doris Elizabeth Catherine   MA 1948
Peterhead acad: teacher 1951–66, spec asst 1966–
72, prin guid/spec asst mod lang from 1972

KINGHORN John Mackie   MA 1921
d 10.1.64

KINGSTON Brian   BSc(for) 1955
Uganda: asst conserv. for. 1958–66, working plans
off. Entebbe 1966–69, sen working plans off. 1969–74;
FAO proj Turkey 1975–77, consult. in Thailand for
FAO 1978

KINMOND David   MA 1951 Dip Ed 1952
teacher: prin Engl Powis s s Aber 1966–68, dep
head 1968, latterly head Summerhill acad Aber
d Aber 11.8.76 *AUR* XLVII 106

KINNAIRD Frank Ferguson   MB ChB 1949
DObstRCOG 1953 DIH(Eng) 1970
DHSS: m o Yorks and Humberside reg 1968–73, sen
m o Norcross Blackpool 1973–74, sen m o/secy (med
attendance allowance board) HQ Lond from 1974

KINNELL John Dunford   MB ChB 1954
regist anaest Southend gen hosp 1958–60; sen
regist Leeds gen I 1961–65; Burroughs Wellcome fell.
Calif L A 1963–64; consult. anaest York hosp from
1965
m Wetherby 18.8.65 Christine Demain physioth d of
John C. D. Wetherby

KINSELLA William Peter   MA 1952

KIRBY Oswald   *MA 1896 BSc 1901
no longer on GC reg

KIRBY Percival Robson   MA 1910
d Grahamstown SA 7.2.70 *AUR* XLIII 441

KIRK Dudley Walter   MB ChB 1924
no longer on GC reg

KIRK or Barron, Gertrude Mary   MA 1947
d Inverurie 29.3.65 *AUR* XLI 60

KIRK John Fraser   MA 1951 BD 1955 PhD 1979
C of S min: St James' par ch Forfar 1962–70, publ
St James' Forfar 1965, Morningside par ch Edin from
1970; sen county chaplain ACF Fife 1959–77, awarded
Cadet Forces Medal and clasp

KIRKBY Norman Stephen   BSc(eng) 1954

KIRKNESS Marion Hamilton   MA 1911
d 21.4.64

KIRKWOOD John   BSc(agr) 1926
retd; resid Lanark

KIRSNER Morris Harold   MB ChB 1934
MD(NY)
d New York –.1.73

KIRTON Harry Morrison   *BSc 1938

KIRTON Ian Wilkison   BSc(for) 1951
teacher biol: Berwicksh h s Duns 1960–71, St
Mungo's acad Alloa from 1971

KIRTON John   MA 1911 MB ChB 1914 *MD 1921
d 12.5.64 *AUR* XL 397

KIRTON Ronald Alexander   MB ChB 1951
g p Saundersfoot from 1968

KITCHIN Ian Douglas   MB ChB 1930
d Westmorland 3.9.76 *AUR* XLVII 105

KLOKOW or Jamieson, Edna   MA 1947

KNIGHT Colin Robert   *MA 1931
sen Engl master The Latymer School Lond 1966–
75; gentleman H.M. Chapels royal St James's Palace
Lond 1946–68; retd

KNIGHT Kenneth William   *MA 1952

KNOWLES or MacPhail, Elizabeta   BSc 1947
teacher maths/sc Forrester s s Edin 1968–72

KNOWLES or Lawrie, Ella May   MA 1954

KNOWLES James   MB ChB 1949
LMCC(Can) 1958
g p Aurora Ontario from 1959; member nucleus
comm on ethics CMA 1967–70; past pres: York
County hosp Newmarket Ont, York County med soc

KNOWLES Mary   BSc 1914
retd 1945; resid Edin

KNOWLES William Henderson   BSc 1923
no longer on GC reg

KNOX Alexander Campbell White   MB ChB 1913
d Lond 13.11.61 *AUR* xxx 275

KNOX Alexander Cruden   *MA 1907
d Lond 20.6.64 *AUR* XL 345

KNOX Alexander Mavor   MB ChB 1945
g p Kelso from 1953

KNOX Edward Wilson   MA 1925
d Innellan 12.3.62 *AUR* xxxix 383

KNOX George Boddie   MB ChB 1954
g p: Glasg 1958–62, Beauly 1962–65, Isle of Lewis
1965–66, Braemar 1966–67, Vale of Leven from 1967
m Glasg 18.6.66 Catriona Mackay d of Charles M.
Isle of Barra

KNOX or Shepherd, Harriet Doreen   MA 1938

KNOX Joseph   *BSc 1900 DSc 1907
d Glasg 14.9.66 *AUR* XLII 80

KNOX or Hill, Kathleen Mary   MB ChB 1943
resid Lond

KNOX Robert Strachan   *MA 1910
d Toronto 12.2.75

KOPERSKA or O'Dwyer, Janina Elizabeta Maria
MB ChB 1950
regist cas off. Ballinasloe Galway 1962–65; g p Edin
1965–67; asst psychiat Gogarburn hosp from 1967
m(2) Edin 2.4.66 Kazimierz P. Durkacz MD (Edin)
dentist s of Jan D. Przemysl Poland

KOSTERLITZ Hans Walter
PhD 1936 DSc 1944 LLD 1979
FRSE 1951
Aberd: prof pharm from 1968; emeritus prof and dir
of unit for res on addictive drugs from 1973

KRAMER Alexander Eric
BSc(civ eng) 1950 BSc(elect eng) 1952
SM(MIT) 1962 PhD(Aston) 1972
sect eng Hydro Quebec, Montreal 1959–61; res asst
MIT Cambridge USA 1961–62; res eng Hydro
Quebec, Montreal 1963–64; lect fluids Aston Birm
from 1965
m Birm 21.3.68 Pauline A. Taylor d of Sidney T. Birm

KRAMER or Medhurst, Mary Rose   MB ChB 1951
g p Bracknell from 1960

KROGH Grace   MB ChB 1929

KWO Chia-wei   MA 1921

KYNOCH James Davidson   MB ChB 1937
MRCGP 1958
g p Aber

KYNOCH Joseph Bonniman   BCom 1927
CA
d 20.4.77

KYNOCH or Paterson, Mary Thomson   MA 1924
teacher Rosehearty 1955–65; retd; resid Cults

LAIDLAW Andrew Alec   BSc(for) 1933

LAIDLAW Hilda Lucy   MA 1915 *MB ChB 1919
resid Forfar

LAIDLAW Jean Johnstone   MA 1936

LAIDLAW William Brittain Rutherford   DSc 1932

LAIDLAW William Young   MB ChB 1942

LAING Alexander   *MA 1936 *MEd 1938
life fell. univ of Leeds 1979
univ of Leeds: part time advis to overseas stud. 1956–
72, sen lect in educ/educ psych 1961–79; retd

LAING Alexander Walker   MB ChB 1905
d 1970

LAING Alexander Wood   MB ChB 1950
d Lerwick 13.6.71 *AUR* XLIV 322

LAING Alice Fyvie   MEd 1954
PhD(Wales) 1972
lect in educ univ coll of Swansea 1968–73, sen lect
from 1973

LAING or Phease, Amelia Henderson   *MA 1914
resid Worthing Sussex
husb d 1958

LAING Annabella Petrie   MA 1925
retd 1969; resid Aber

LAING Annie   *MA 1930
retd 1968; resid Scone

LAING Arthur Gordon   MB ChB 1948
MRCGP 1962 JP 1970
g p Tarves from 1956

LAING Christina Ross
MA 1919 MB ChB 1923 DPH 1925
retd 1958; resid Cults Aber

LAING or Irvine, Christine Doig   MA 1950
remed teacher Broomhill p s Aber from 1964

LAING David Burnett   MB ChB 1925
d Sheffield 10.1.79 *AUR* XLVIII 229

LAING Donald   BSc 1947 *1948
sen scient off. dept soil surv Macaulay inst Aber
from 1954

LAING Elizabeth   MA 1948
teacher in Angus from 1949

LAING Elizabeth Campbell
                    MB ChB 1946 DPH 1951 MD 1952
asst m o h Aber from 1955

LAING or Miller, Elizabeth Margaret
                                        MB ChB 1929
doctor in out-patient hosp Harari, Salisbury, Rhodesia 1962; resid Saffron Walden

LAING Ellen Macgregor Ross   MA 1930
Aber: head Inverdee inf s 1966–72, mus in infant s 1972–77; retd

LAING Frederick   MA 1912 *BSc 1913
d Putney 10.12.65 *AUR* XLI 242

LAING George   BL 1940
d 5.9.72

LAING George Duncan   MB ChB 1953
g p Eston 1956–66, New Deer 1966–69; reg m o DHSS Newcastle-u-Tyne from 1969

LAING George Innes   *MA 1924
teacher Banffsh: classics Banff acad 1925–27, prin classics Fordyce acad 1927–30, prin classics Keith g s 1930–68/dep rector 1950–68; head f e centre Keith 1944–56
m Enzie 23.6.56 Mary T. Gray MA(Glas) teacher

LAING or Robertson, Gertrude Moir   MA 1945

LAING Gordon Smith   BSc(eng) 1936

LAING Harry Gordon   MB ChB 1941

LAING Iain Morrison Ross   MB ChB 1951

LAING Ian Watson   *MB ChB 1923
d 8.4.66 *AUR* XLI 245 & 399

LAING or Hall, Isabel Margaret MacDonald
                                              BSc 1944
resid Alness
husb *d* 5.3.77

LAING or Baird, Isabella   *MA 1946
teacher Engl Invergordon acad 1963–70; asst lib Gordon s Huntly 1970–72; teacher Engl Keith g s from 1972

LAING James Allan   MA 1939
C of S min: Duddingston par ch Edin 1947–62, St Andrew's Lhanbryde par ch Elgin 1962–75; moderator: Elgin presb 1972–73, Synod of Moray 1973–74; retd; resid Elgin

LAING or Walls, Jean   MA 1951
teacher Buckie area p s from 1971

LAING or Thomson, Jean Ramsay Henry   MA 1941
resid Victoria BC Canada

LAING John Gordon   *MA 1898
no longer on GC reg

LAING Kenneth Macrae   *MA 1928
retd 1972, resid Inv

LAING Leslie Gordon   MB ChB 1955
h o mat. hosp Aber 1959; g p Aber 1959–60, Peterborough 1960–62, Loughborough 1962–69, Brampton Ontario/active staff Peel mem hosp from 1969

LAING or Sabiston, Margaret   MA 1942
sen teacher maths Blurton h s Stoke-on-Trent from 1967
husb *d* Stoke-on-Trent 11.8.79

LAING Margaretta Lilias   MA 1943 MB ChB 1954
g p Saltaire med centre Shipley from 1965

LAING Marshall George   MA 1946 LLB 1949
leg. asst J. L. Anderson & Co solic Cupar 1960–62, ptnr Craig & Geddes solic Dumfries 1962–75, ptnr Symons & Macdonald solic Dumfries from 1975
m Hong Kong 25.4.56 Hikmat Talhouk d of Amin T. Beirut

LAING Nancy   MB ChB 1943
g p Inverurie 1944–77; retd

LAING Peter Duncan   *BSc(eng) 1951
CEng MIMechE 1959 Dip Man. St.(Glasg) 1962 AMInst Refrig 1964
Howden Compressors Glasg: dev eng 1955–60, head dev sect 1960–65, eng man. 1965–69, gen factory man. 1969–74 and dir from 1971

LAING or Harper, Rhoda   MA 1944
d 8.1.66

LAING Thomas   *MA 1925
prin teacher classics and dep rector Kilmarnock acad 1960–68; retd
d Nairn 13.8.77

LAING Thomas James   *MA 1928
retd 1972, resid Dinnet

LAING William   *BSc 1951 PhD 1954
s of William L. BSc(by ordinance) 1960 *qv*
ICI Stevenston: Nobel div res chem 1954–60; prod. man. Indian Explosives Bihar India 1960–63; ICI Stevenston: prod. man. 1963–66, petr-chem div prod. pers man. from 1966

LAIRD Alistair Noble   MB ChB 1955
milit serv Cowglen hosp Glasg 1958–60; g p Penkridge 1960–61, Coventry from 1961

LAIRD Bowman Stiven   BSc(eng) 1947
MICE M(A)ICE
eng min of works Benmore and Wellington NZ 1968–73
d Wellington NZ 3.8.73

LAIRD or Laird, Clara   MA 1933
Kirkwall g s: teacher maths/lady advis 1965–73, prin guid 1973; retd

LAIRD George Stephen   MB ChB 1950
RD 1972 JP 1975
g p Ashton-under-Lyne 1957–73; serv in RN reserve
from 1954

LAIRD John Alexander Grant   BSc(eng) 1949
contr man. Marples Ridgway (constructors) Edin
1965–68; chief eng Nairn Floors Kirkcaldy from 1968
m Aber 23.12.50 Morag S. Smith dom sc supt hosps d
of Murdo S. Benbecula

LAIRD William   MA 1950 LLB 1953
ptnr Allan McDougall & Co SSC Edin from 1961

LAKIE John Annand   MA 1949
prin teacher Engl Linlathen h s Dun from 1959

LAMB Annie Elizabeth   MA 1926
d 5.2.72

LAMB George Fairbairn   MA 1908
d 4.2.69

LAMB or Law, Isabella Rebecca   MA 1919
resid Edin

LAMB or McKenzie, Isabella Thom   MA 1947

LAMB John Garden   MA 1913 BSc(agr) 1914
FRMetS 1916
resid Prestwick
d Ayr 14.12.78 AUR xlviii 226

LAMB Kenneth Beldon   *BSc 1952

LAMB Kenneth Malcolm   BSc(for) 1950
b Turriff 27.11.24
conserv of for. Buea S Cameroons 1960–61; teacher sc
Aber 1963–66; for. NZFS Christchurch NZ 1966–72,
sen for. from 1972

LAMB Theodore Mitchell George   MA 1922
d Tor-na-dee Aber 30.1.66 AUR xlii 85

LAMB William Andrew   *MA 1951
Aber coll of comm: teacher gen stud. 1961–65, sen
teacher hist 1965–75, sen lect publ admin and soc
stud. from 1975

LAMBERT John Lewis Mackenzie   *BSc 1951

LAMBIE Hugh Rodger   MB ChB 1922

LAMONT Angela   MA 1933
d Perth 26.1.79

LAMONT Dugald Lennox Daniel   MB ChB 1929
g p St Albans 1939–73; retd; resid Holt Norfolk

LANCASTER Margaret Stephen   *MA 1951
teacher geog Aber acad 1959–69
m Birse 1.7.68 Francis M. Synge BA(Dub) geol s of
Victor M. S. MB(Dub) Dublin

LANDELS John Gray   *MA 1951
MA(Cantab) 1953 PhD(Hull) 1961
lect classics R'dg 1960–77, sen lect from 1977

LANDGREBE Frank Walter   DSc 1941
prof materia medica univ of Wales 1952–77; now
emeritus prof

LANE Peter Hamilton   *MA 1952
flt-lt RAF educ branch 1964–72, sqr ldr admin
(educ) from 1972
m Valerie M. Butts BA(Lond)

LARG Ann Henderson   *MA 1915
Dip de Langue et Litterature Francaises (Rennes)
1922
resid Rothesay

LARG David Glass   MA 1915
no longer on GC reg

LASCELLES Clarence Felix   MB ChB 1944
MRCPsych 1971 FRCPsych 1974
consult. psychiat Cherry Knowle hosp Sunderland
1956–68; clin tut. univ N'cle from 1968

LASCELLES or Beaux, Gladys Mary   *MA 1947
husb d 1961
m(2) Lyon France 13.6.63 Jacques Reynaud DL(Lyon)
bus. dir s of Pierre R. DL(Lyon)

LASCELLES Raymond George
                                    ***MB ChB 1955 MD 1964**
FRSocMed 1960 DipPsychMed(Lond) 1961
FRCP(Lond) 1974
Lond: regist neurol St Thomas' hosp; sen regist
neurol nat hosp Queen Sq 1962–65, sen regist neurol
Guy's hosp 1965–70; consult. neurol and lect neurol
MRI and univ Manc from 1970
m Lyon France 1966 Martine Reynaud d of Paul R.
St Didier au Mont d'or Rhône France

LASDON Albert Harold   MB ChB 1934

LAUDER Helen Mary   MA 1933
asst head Banff p s 1965–72; retd

LAURENSON Angus Scollay   BSc 1948 *1949
prin teacher sc Anderson h s Lerwick 1960–69, prin
chem 1969–73, teacher sc Aboyne acad from 1973
d 23.11.75

LAURENSON or Stewart, Christina Margaret
                                                    MA 1936
teacher Insch 1965–78; retd

LAURENSON Rae Duncan
                                    MB ChB 1953 MD 1963
in Edmonton Canada

LAURIE Gavin   BSc(agr) 1938
d 22.5.64

LAW Anthony Charles   *MA 1925
no longer on GC reg

LAW Beatrix Bennett
MA 1920 MB ChB 1923 *MD 1928
 sen ophth surg NE reg hosp board 1946–61; part time lect ophth Aberd 1946–61; retd

LAW or Jenkins, Edith Ann McPherson   MA 1911
 no longer on GC reg

LAW Eleanora Margaret Patricia
MA 1918 *MB ChB 1921
 retd 1958; resid Dinnet and Aber
d Aber 11.12.79 *AUR* XLVIII 440, XLIX 67

LAW Elizabeth Alexandra   *MA 1925
 no longer on GC reg

LAW or Stewart, Frances Mary   MA 1928
 woman advis Carnoustie h s 1966–72; retd

LAW Frederick William   MA BSc(agr) 1912
d Stoke-on-Trent 29.6.70 *AUR* XLIV 109

LAW George   *MA 1912
d Girvan 25.5.61 *AUR* XXXIX 202

LAW Ian McConachie   *BSc 1924
 retd 1962; resid Huntly
d –.7.81

LAW or Henderson, Isabel Alice   *MA 1926
 resid Oldmeldrum

LAW James Gordon   BSc(eng) 1947
 eng ag firm of quarry masters Glasg from 1960

LAW or McDonald, Jean Innes   *MA 1924
 resid Oldmeldrum

LAW John Dickson   BSc(eng) 1954
 MICE 1961 FICE 1972 MASCE 1972
resid eng Sir M. MacDonald & Ptners Lower Diyala irrig proj Iraq 1961–64; area eng Balfour Beatty & Co Kainji hydro elect. proj Nigeria 1964–68; claims eng ECI Denver Colorado USA Athens 1968–69; area eng Balfour Beatty & Co Lynemouth smelter proj Northumberland 1969–70; asst resid eng TAMS Int Corp NY Tarbela H-E proj Pakistan 1971–73; resid man. Agrar- und Hydrotechnik Emb H Essen W Ger, Semper Dam & Irrigation Proj Central Java 1974–76; eng rep Bahrain (John Taylor & Sons) 1976–77; dep constr man. Shiroro HE proj Nigeria Chas. T. Main Int Inc Boston Mass USA 1978
m New Brighton Cheshire 8.10.60 Barbara England SRN nurs sister d of Clem E. MB ChB(Sheff) Wallasey

LAW or Fraser, Margaret Nellie Stuart   MA 1931
 resid Aboyne

LAW Noel Pottinger   MA 1951

LAW Sheila   MA 1951
 head Finzean s from 1970
m Aber 27.12.61 Alexander R. Harper teacher s of Alexander H. Inverurie

LAW William George   MA 1952
 Aber: prin teacher geog Ruthrieston s s 1965–73; co-prin teacher geog Harlaw acad from 1973
m Aber 3.8.62 Norah M. MacLeod cler off. d of Donald MacL. Lochganich Isle of Lewis

LAW William Proctor   *MA 1912 BSc 1915
d Aber 27.2.73 *AUR* XLV 224

LAWIE Alexander   MA 1952

LAWIE William   MB ChB 1922
d Colchester 9.6.67 *AUR* XLII 185

LAWRANCE or McLeod, Ida Walker   MA 1939
 resid Collieston

LAWRENCE or Richards, Agnes McKillop
MA 1908
d 17.2.64

LAWRENCE Albert Alexander   MB ChB 1953
 g p Buckie from 1957
m Aber 2.3.61 Edith M. Adam d of Herbert D. A. Inverurie

LAWRENCE or Forbes, Annie   MA 1910

LAWRENCE Doreen Ross   MA 1929
 retd 1967; resid Aber
d Aber 7.2.80

LAWRENCE or Anton, Doris May   MA 1942
 lib catalog asst Edin city lib; resid Edin

LAWRENCE Emily Ann Spence   MA 1926
 teacher Fr Summerhill s s Aber 1962–65; retd

LAWRENCE George Morton   *MA 1936 LLB 1939
 ptnr James & George Collie advoc Aber from 1949

LAWRENCE George Smith
MA 1910 MB ChB 1916
d 14.8.71 *AUR* XLIV 316

LAWRENCE or Jaffray, Isobel Mary   *MA 1940

LAWRENCE James   MB ChB 1953
 g p Aberlour from 1958

LAWRENCE Margaret Helen   MA 1913
 resid Cullen
d Buckie 26.10.78

LAWRENCE or Black, Marjory Irene
MB ChB 1934
d Aber 2.6.63 *AUR* XL 206

LAWRENCE Philip Douglas   MA 1919 DD 1966
d Aber 1.6.67 *AUR* XLII 184

LAWRENCE Robert Daniel
MA 1912 *MB ChB 1916 MD 1922
d Lond 29.8.68 *AUR* XLIII 78

LAWRENCE William Calder Macphail
                          MB ChB 1953 DPH 1969
MFCM 1973
dep m o Banff c c 1966–74; spec commun med Forth
Valley health board from 1974

LAWRENCE-SMITH, Alexander Maxwell
                          MB ChB 1929
m o Port of Lond auth 1947–50, prin m o from 1950

LAWRIE Charles James Reid   BSc(eng) 1950

LAWRIE George Walker   MA 1937

LAWRIE Helen Margaret   BSc 1950

LAWRIE John Samuel   MB ChB 1928
no longer on GC reg

LAWRIE or MacLeod, Rhona Cameron   MA 1930
d 27.3.63

LAWRIE Thomas Ruthven   MB ChB 1951
Cert Diag Radiology(Can) 1962 FRCP(C) 1972
Canada: serv in RCN 1956–67; radiol ch hosp/Grace
mat. hosp Halifax; asst prof radiol Dalhousie univ
Halifax from 1967
marr diss

LAWRIE Thomas Scott   MA 1948
prin teacher geog Hilton acad Aber from 1965
m Aber 3.4.58 Janet E. Cunningham teacher d of
David C. Aber

LAWRIE Una   MB ChB 1947 DPH 1952
sen asst m o h Notts 1957–60
m Aber 1960 John T. Cockburn BSc(Glas) teacher s of
John T. C. Lanark

LAWSON or Cowie, Ann Chapman   *MA 1941
Herefordsh: teacher Engl/hist and asst lib Bluecoat
s s 1960–66, head hist dept Cannon Frome s s
1966–69, hist tut. The Grange Bredenbury 1969–72

LAWSON or Geddes, Annie Mary   MA 1924
no longer on GC reg

LAWSON Donald Boyd Cameron   MB ChB 1925
d Sheringham 26.11.69 *AUR* XLIII 445

LAWSON Gordon Cecil
                          MA 1907 *BSc 1909 DSc 1920
d Hereford 8.3.76

LAWSON or Kennedy, Helen Cecilia   MB ChB 1950
med missionary: Senegal 1954–68, Abidjan Ivory
Coast 1968–75; part time clin m o Hillingdon AHA
from 1975

LAWSON Ian Richard   MB ChB 1954 MD 1958
MRCPE 1960 FACP 1970 FRCPE 1971
consult. phys Aber gen hosps 1961–66, dept med
Christian med coll Ludhuana India 1967–68; USA:
med dir Hebrew home for aged 1970–76; assoc clin
prof univ of Connecticut med s from 1972; vice pres

for med affairs Danbury hosp Connecticut from
1976

LAWSON Janet McFiggans   MA 1948
m Hatch

LAWSON John Dempster   PhD 1951
Mast. Eng(Melb) 1963 MASCE 1963
FIE(Aust) 1973
prof civ eng univ of Melbourne Aust from 1970

LAWSON John Simpson   MA 1935 BCom 1937
prin teacher bus. stud. Aber acad/Hazlehead acad
1960–73; advis in bus. stud. Aber educ dept 1973–
75; advis bus. stud. Grampian reg 1975–76; retd

LAWSON Mabel Gordon   MA 1916 MB ChB 1918
d Folkestone 8.8.72 *AUR* XLV 125

LAWSON or West, Margaret Officer   MA 1949
teacher maths: Middle s Aber 1950–52; Birm:
King's Norton g s 1952–54, Selly Park s mod s
1960–61, Harrison Borrows g s 1961–63; Croydon:
Ashburton s s 1970–73, Coloma g s 1973–75; resid
Aber

LAWSON William Graham   BCom 1924
no longer on GC reg

LAWSON William Wilfred James   MB ChB 1904
d 23.12.63

LEACH Gweneth Rose   *MA 1953
m Parker

LEAHY or Mulcahy, Patricia   MA 1951
B Soc Work(W Aust) 1976
W Aust: soc worker mental health serv Perth 1977–78,
sen soc worker commun ch health serv from 1978

LEARMONTH or Fleming, Barbara Drever
                                        BSc 1953
resid Greenlaw

LEASK Caroline Martha Mackenzie   *MA 1928

LEASK James Christopher   MB ChB 1941
Zambia: m o Zambian govt Livingstone 1970–73,
sen m o Anglo-Amer Corp Lusaka 1973–77; m o
Livingstone hosp Port Elizabeth SA from 1977

LEASK John   MB ChB 1938
g p Inverurie 1948–74; retd; resid Ballindalloch

LEASK or Cameron, Margaret   MA 1952

LEASK Mary Isabel Milne   MA 1926
teacher: Insch, Woodside Aber, Kintore, Kent,
Inverurie 1958–65
m Aber 7.8.48 Robert Jezzard teacher s of Edward J.
Sandwich

LEASK Millicent Florence   MA 1940

LEASK Peter   MA 1903
no longer on GC reg

LEATHAM or Smiles, May Morris   MA 1910
d Aber 31.10.64 *AUR* XLI 55

LEDINGHAM Alexander   MA 1952
ptnr Edmonds & Ledingham advoc Aber from 1958
m Aber 26.1.63 S. Rosemary Mackintosh teacher p e d of Harvey G. M. LDS(Edin) Durris

LEDINGHAM Isabella Culbert Chessar   BSc 1919
resid Gillingham Kent

LEDINGHAM James   MB ChB 1933
g p N Hykeham from 1947

LEDINGHAM James George   MB ChB 1953
g p Edin from 1956

LEDINGHAM John   *MB ChB 1922
d Lond 23.6.70 *AUR* XLIV 110

LEDINGHAM Leslie Andrews   MB ChB 1934
d Inv 25.7.73 *AUR* XLV 321

LEDINGHAM or Cox, Louisa Lemmon   BCom 1939
exec clerk J Lyons & Co Lond 1940–45; Victoria BC Canada: secy to asst judge advoc Canadian armed forces 1958–59; secy to admin asst min of highways 1959–65

LEDINGHAM Robert Mackay   MA 1913 LLB 1920
d Aber 27.2.69 *AUR* XLIII 210

LEDINGHAM William Lemmon Stewart
                                        MB ChB 1937
g p Tunbridge Wells from 1946

LEDINGHAM William Marshall   MB ChB 1923
d 1.7.73

LEDINGHAM William Wilson   MA 1950
BA(Lond) 1964
dep rector Alford acad from 1966

LEDINGHAM or Stopper, Winifred Ewen   *MA 1948
Aber: teacher Engl AGS/Ruthrieston s s 1949–50, Rosemount s s 1950–57, St Margaret's s for girls 1959–72; prin Engl St Margaret's s from 1972

LEE or Stevenson, Beryl Agnes   *MA 1943
teacher Dumfriessh from 1954

LEE John   MA 1941 BD 1944
d 17.4.80

LEE Margaret Helen   MB ChB 1946
g p Chesterfield from 1950

LEEFE John Dixon   BSc(for) 1951
for. comm: dist off. Brecon Wales 1962–63, Grantham 1963–67; proj off. Linsey (Lincs) proj for. improvement of environment Lincoln 1967–70; HQ man. trg off. with for. comm Basingstoke 1970–73; prin for. coll (Brit tech assistance) Prodromos Cyprus from 1973

LEES Frank Jamieson   MB ChB 1928
g p Banff from 1930

LEES John   *MA 1950 PhD 1953
FInstP 1968
res phys/sen scient off. National Eng Lab E Kilbride 1958–61; phys/res man. Standard Telecomm Labs Harlow from 1961
m 6.12.58 Sheila M. Reilly

LEES John Drennan   MB ChB 1933
d 21.10.65 *AUR* XLI 250

LEES William   MA 1932 BD 1943
d Aber 4.7.75 *AUR* XLVI 325

LE FANU George Ernest Hugh   MB CM 1901
no longer on GC reg

LEFEVRE Isabel Margaret Murray   *MA 1934
prin teacher Engl St Margaret's s for girls 1959–72; retd

LEGG George Alexander Hendry   BSc(eng) 1949

LEGGAT George MB ChB 1911 DPH 1913
d Grange-over-Sands 24.1.72 *AUR* XLIV 427

LEGGAT Peter Ogilvie   MB ChB 1941 MD 1951
FRCP 1968
clin lect dept of med N'cle from 1965

LEGGE James Roger   *MA 1922
d 24.9.64

LEIGHTON John Crichton   BSc(eng) 1950
Frederick Snare Corp NY: field eng Miragoave, Haiti 1956–57, constr eng NY 1958–59, constr man. Vallenar Chile 1960–64; Kaiser Eng Calif proj man.: Renukoot India 1965–67, Melbourne 1968–72; exec vice pres Milder-Kaiser Sao Paulo 1973–75, vice pres Latin Amer oper from 1975
m Vallenar Chile 26.5.62 Anita Del C Miranda teacher d of Gregorio M. Atacama Chile

LEIGHTON Kenneth Macrae   MB ChB 1947
FRCP(C) (Br Col) 1967
Vancouver: resid dept anaest Vancouver gen hosp 1963–67; asst prof dept anaest 1968–75, assoc prof from 1975; recipient BC heart foundation grant from 1968; examiner Royal Coll Physicians and Surgeons of Canada from 1972

LEIGHTON or Forbes, Mary   MA 1947
pers man. J & P Coats Anchor Mills Paisley 1948–51; youth employment off. Aber educ auth 1951–53; part time med soc worker: Queen Mother's hosp Glasg 1965–67, Law hosp Carluke 1967–76, tut. soc work Motherwell tech coll; med soc worker ARI 1977

LEIPER Doreen Florence   BSc 1952
teacher maths/sc/chem Aber acad 1961–70, year mistress from 1970 (later Hazlehead acad)

LEIPER or Keith, Dorothy   *MA 1950

LEIPER Edwin James Reid
                    MA 1925 *MB ChB 1930 *MD 1937
FRCP(Lond) 1969
retd 1972; resid Bishops Stortford

LEIPER John   MB ChB 1927 MD 1937 DPH 1938
  MBE 1964 JP 1961
retd 1968; resid Aber
m(1) Aber 10.7.31 Robina Wood Aber
  (2) Aber 14.10.59 Mabel Robertson Aber

LEIPER or Ashforth, Margaret Vera   *MA 1952
  Edin: part-time teacher maths Princess Margaret
Rose hosp s from 1976

LEITCH Isabella
            MA 1911 BSc 1914 DSc 1919 LLD 1965
  OBE 1949
dir (Imperial) Commonwealth Bureau of anim nutrit
Rowett res inst Aber 1946–60, contd in service of
Bureau preparing syst for coding and retrieval of
information on nutrit and part time appointment to
staff of Agr Res Council 1960–74 to prepare (with
A. W. Boyne) report on composition of Brit feeding
stuffs published 1976
d Aust 21.7.80 *AUR* xlix 66

LEITCH Madelina Alison   MA 1908
  d 15.2.76

LEITH Elizabeth Jean   MA 1944
  teacher Middlefield p s Aber from 1945

LEITH or Grant, Helen Simmil   MA 1948
  head Armiddle s Aberdeensh 1962–76; head
Monquhitter s from 1976
husb *d* 1962
m(2) Aber 3.4.69 James Pennie radio and elect. off.
Merch N

LEITH James Alexander   MA 1954 LLB 1956

LENCZ Sandor (Alexander) Geza   PhD 1933

LENDRUM or Hale, Dorothy Mary   MA 1922
  resid Lond

LENDRUM or Rennie, Gertrude Helen
                              MB ChB 1920
  retd 1958; resid Aber

LENG or Shewan, Audrey Ashill   MA 1952
  teacher: Tulloch p s Perth 1972–78, Perth h s from
1978

LENNON or Sorrie, Evelyn Mary   MA 1952
  resid Middlesbrough

LENNON George Gordon
                    MB ChB 1934 *ChM 1945
  Hon Fell. Gyn Soc 1956
prof obst and gyn Brist 1951–67; visiting prof:
Istanbul/Ankara 1956, Durban, Johannesburg,

Pretoria, Kampala 1958, Teheran 1965; dean fac of
med univ of W Aust from 1967

LEONARD or Russell, Christina   MA 1923
  d 1974

LEONARD-SMITH or Garten, Anne Leslie
                    Armstrong   *MA 1945
  lect Maria Grey coll of educ Twickenham 1967–70,
sen lect from 1970

LE PIVERT John Alfred   *BSc(eng) 1947
  FICE FIArbitrators FPWI CEng
ptnr Livesey & Henderson Lond 1962–71; proj dir
GEC Elliott Automation Borehamwood Herts from
1972
freeman of City of Lond

LERCHS Armin   BSc(eng) 1954
  Bureau Ingeco Gombert: man. consult. tech dir
Cairo, Alexandria 1957–59, dir Lisbon 1959–66;
Ingeco Gombert Portuguesa: chmn board of dir
Lisbon, Luanda, Lourenco Marques, Rio de Janeiro
from 1966
m Alexandria Egypt 20.3.59 Alice B. Djanian d of
Sarkis D.

LE ROUX or Brodie, Katherine McEwen
                              MB ChB 1949
  g p trainee Lochwinnoch 1963–64, locums in Beith,
Lochwinnoch and Johnstone 1964–68; g p Beith from
1969

LESLIE or Riley, Agnes Kidd   MB ChB 1942
  anaest Radcliffe I Oxford, Stoke Mandeville hosp
Aylesbury; h s Warneford hosp Leamington Spa

LESLIE Annie   MA 1935
  work study Scot. & N'cle Breweries Newcastle
1968–75; retd; resid Huntly

LESLIE Charles McKay   BSc(eng) 1949 *1952
  MIEE 1966 Dip Man. St(Strath) 1970
MIProdE 1969 AMBIM 1970
temp controls group Honeywell Newhouse Lanark:
chief eng 1964–66, chief prod. eng 1966–71, prod. eng
man. Bellshill 1971–74, des eng man. from 1974

LESLIE David Alexander   MA 1955

LESLIE Donald Alexander   MB ChB 1944
  FRCPath 1963
consult path. Sunderland from 1952

LESLIE Douglas   MB ChB 1953
  g p Oakville Ont Canada from 1959

LESLIE Douglas Macbeth   BSc(eng) 1945

LESLIE George Christie   BL 1954
  ptnr McVey & Murricane solic Glasg from 1963

LESLIE George Erskine   *BSc 1951

LESLIE or McLaughlin, Gladys Irvine   MA 1937

LESLIE Gordon James Booth   MB ChB 1955
Dip Ophth RCS 1961
sen h o eye dept ARI 1959–60; regist ophth Glasg
eye I 1960–63, ophth spec Sarawak Malaysia 1963–68;
clin asst ophth inst Glasg from 1968; regt m o 71st
Roy Eng regt Yorkhill Glasg from 1973
m(2) Bearsden 22.8.75 Kirsten L. Plehn d of Villy
S. P. Odense Denmark

LESLIE Ian   BSc 1942
d Lond 8.6.67 *AUR* XLII 186

LESLIE James Campbell   MA 1921 BSc(agr) 1922
d –.7.74

LESLIE Jane   MA 1910
no longer on GC reg

LESLIE John Angus   BSc(eng) 1938
d Loughborough 12.11.80

LESLIE John Erskine   BSc(for) 1950

LESLIE or McCallum, Lizzie   MA 1910
d Richmond Yorks 7.1.71 *AUR* XLIV 209

LESLIE Mansfield Alastair   *MA 1948
prin teacher Engl Waid acad Anstruther from 1958

LESLIE Margaret Ethel   MA 1953
teacher Aber: Mile End p s 1971–73, asst head
Sunnybank p s from 1973
m Aber 27.7.62 William M. Currie s of James C. Aber

LESLIE or Rose, Mary Horn   *MA 1903
d 4.6.67

LESLIE Muriel Roy   MA 1932
no longer on GC reg

LESLIE Norman Hector   MB ChB 1922
dep anaest Royal Victoria Inf N'cle-u-Tyne 1943–45
d N'cle-u-Tyne 9.7.74 *AUR* XLVI 108

LESLIE Phyllis Davidson   MB ChB 1937
retd; resid Aboyne

LESLIE William   MA 1910 MB ChB 1915
no longer on GC reg

LESLIE William   ᵈLLB 1953
WS/ptnr J C Brodie Cuthbertson & Watson WS
(now Brodies) Edin 1955–76; a chmn industrial
tribunals (Scot.) from 1976
m(2) Dalton 29.11.69 Elizabeth J. Bowden-Smith d of
Ralph P. B-S. Ecclefechan

LESLIE William Allan   ᵈBL 1926
ptnr Frame & Macdonald solic Glasg from 1936;
prov grand secy A F & A Masons Glasg from 1954

LESLIE William Norman   MA 1898
no longer on GC reg

LESLIE Wilson Summers   MA 1915 BD 1918
d Aber 25.12.70 *AUR* XLIV 210

LESSEL Elizabeth Isabella   *MA 1917
retd 1955; resid Aber
d 15.12.81

LETHBRIDGE William   MB ChB 1895
no longer on GC reg

LEVACK David Proudfoot   *MB ChB 1924
retd; resid Drumoak
d Aber 26.2.79 *AUR* XLVIII 228

LEVACK John William   MB ChB 1931
d Aber 1.9.73 *AUR* XLV 320

LEVACK or Aitken, Mary Robertson
                         MA 1920 MB ChB 1924
retd 1957
d Maidstone 30.4.74

LEVITT Charles Wheatley   MB ChB 1936
d 16.6.78

LEWIS or Knight, Annie Walker   MA 1929

LEWIS Anthony Vincent   MA 1954

LEWIS Cecil Arthur   *MA 1915
no longer on GC reg

LEWIS George Alfred   MB ChB 1946
FRCOG 1973
regist/sen regist obst & gyn Westminster hosp Lond
1961–69; consult. obst & gyn Gloucester from 1969

LEWIS Ivor Howells   MB ChB 1949
MFCM 1974
m o, asst sen m o Manc reg hosp board 1962–64; asst
sen m o, prin asst sen m o Leeds reg hosp board
1964–74; spec commun med Yorks reg health auth
from 1974

LEWIS James Howells   MB ChB 1952
m o commonwealth dept of health Melbourne
1959–62; g p: various UK locums 1962–77, Falkirk
from 1978
m(2) Middlesbrough 29.11.68 Winifred A. Small
teacher d of John W. S. Skelton

LEWIS or Robertson, Margaret Walker   MA 1929
resid Bieldside Aber

LEWIS or Graham, Mary Patricia Havard
                                MB ChB 1949
DPH(Manc) 1962 MFCM 1975
m o LHA Warrington 1955–68; sen m o Warrington
dist Cheshire AHA from 1968

LEWIS Mercedes Louisa   MA 1949

LEY Francis James   *BSc 1953

LEYS George Murray   MA 1919 *MEd 1921
d 4.5.67 *AUR* XLII 358

LEYS Thomas   *BSc 1954

LIANG Lone   MA 1917 LLB 1918 LLD 1945
d Yonkers NY State 12.6.67 *AUR* XLII 355

LIANG Shih-Chen   PhD 1948

LIDDELL Charles Mitchell   MB ChB 1937
d Milltimber Aber 15.6.74 *AUR* XLVI 110

LIDDELL Leslie Carse   MB ChB 1938
g p Pennycraig Glam from 1947

LIGERTWOOD John Catto   *MA 1925
retd 1968; resid Bridge of Allan

LIGHTBODY Alexander
               ***BSc(mech eng) 1938 *BSc(elect eng) 1939**
OBE 1967
tech exec naval weapons div Hawker Siddeley
Dynamics Hatfield from 1963
d Herts 9.2.74

LIGHTBODY John Cumming   MB ChB 1942
d 25.6.77 *AUR* XLVIII 287

LILLIE or Garrett, Helen
               MA 1910 MB ChB 1914 MD 1920
C of S Missionary in Punjab 1920–46; lib asst Glas
univ 1948–63
d 22.1.77

LILLIE Isobel Milne   MA BSc 1913
d Caithness 31.3.73 *AUR* XLV 224

LILLIE James Pickford   MB ChB 1923
d 1966

LILLIE John Adam   MA 1906 LLD 1967
KC 1931; sheriff of Fife and Kinross 1941–71; dep
chmn and leg. comm of gen board of control for Scot.
1944–60; retd; resid Edin

LILLIE Mary Purves   *MA 1915
resid Lybster

LILLIE William   *MA 1921 DD 1948
lect Bibl stud. Aberd 1953–69; retd

LIND William Charles Morrison   MA 1936
d Kildary 23.9.70 *AUR* XLIV 111

LINDSAY Albert George   MA 1932
retd; resid Aber

LINDSAY Angus William   BSc(eng) 1949
Gulf Oil Corp: chief eng E & W dist Venezuela
1959–66, proj man. Bantry Bay Ireland 1966–69,
consult. Kuwait, Okinawa, Canada 1969–70, exec
Venezuela 1970–73; Gulf Oil/Texaco: supt Ecuador,
Quito 1973–74, feasibility stud. Paraguay and N Sea
Scot. 1974–75; co-ord of transport Gull Is. hydro
elect. proj Labrador from 1975

LINDSAY David Grant   MB ChB 1944
NSW Aust: m o dept of publ health Sydney
1961–65, med supt Peat Is. hosp Brooklyn from 1965

LINDSAY Gordon Forbes   MB ChB 1944
g p Aboyne from 1948

LINDSAY James Martin   *MA 1945 PhD 1950
prof Ger univ W Aust Perth from 1969

LINDSAY or Wood, Jean Elizabeth   MA 1947

LINDSAY or Thompson, Johan Dunlop   BSc 1918
d Sydney Aust 1959

LINDSAY John Grant   MB ChB 1930

LINDSAY or Strachan, Marjorie Gertrude Helen
                                    ***MA 1933**
resid Ealing Lond

LINDSAY or Pounder, Mary Grant   MA 1929
no longer on GC reg

LINDSAY Sheila Taylor   BSc 1927
d Edin 13.12.68 *AUR* XLIII 215

LINDSAY Stanley Frederick   MB ChB 1937
d Banchory 11.8.71 *AUR* XLIV 321

LINKLATER Eric Robert Russell
                        ***MA 1925 LLD 1946**
d Aber 7.11.74 *AUR* XLVI 10

LINKLATER James Reith   BCom 1922

LINKLATER John Roy   MA 1938 *MEd 1940
admin off. Edin div Lothian reg c 1975–79; retd

LINTS William Alexander   BL 1940
sen ptnr Cornillon Craig & Co WS Edin

LIPP or Flett, Dorothy   BSc 1925
resid Edin

LIPP George Robertson   *MB ChB 1914
d 24.6.62

LIPP or Spence, Isobel   *MA 1925
no longer on GC reg

LIPP Kenneth Lewis   MB ChB 1952
asst g p: Thurso 1953–54, Willington Co Durham
1954–56; sen h o orthop ARI 1956–57; g p: Aber
1957–66, Oban and police surg/anaest Oban hosps
from 1966

LIPP or Castle, Margaret   MA 1917 MB ChB 1921
S Af med corps 1939–45; resid Dartington

LIPP Robert James Grant   MA 1910 BSc(agr) 1911
d 21.8.65

LIPP Samuel   *MA 1912 BSc 1913 BSc(agr) 1914
d Newport-on-Tay 11.9.69 *AUR* XLIII 328

LISTER George   MA 1903
no longer on GC reg

LISTON John   PhD 1955

LITTLE Edwin   *BSc 1952

LITTLE Frank Bamford   BSc(agr) 1947

LITTLE James Robertson   *MA 1926
 acting rector Leith acad 1969–70; retd; resid Edin

LITTLE Jean Webster   MA 1938
 Edin: edit. Thomas Nelson & Sons 1952–64, publ Oliver & Boyd 1964–76

LITTLE or Copland, Margaret McNeill
                                   MA 1931 MB ChB 1935
 DPH(N'cle) 1960 MFCM 1970
Sunderland: sen m o 1967–70, dep m o h from 1970

LITTLE Robert   *MA 1926
 d –.3.65

LITTLE Robert Davidson   MB ChB 1953
 FRCS(Can) 1973
Canada: g p/surg spec Edmonton 1960–73, surg spec Immaculata hosp Westlock Alta from 1973
wife *d* 1967
m(2) Edmonton 9.10.68 Margaret H. McKay nurse d of William McK. MD(McG) Edmonton

LITTLEJOHN Alastair Ironside   MB ChB 1955

LITTLEJOHN David   *MA 1951

LITTLEJOHN George Sandison   BSc 1952
 FRSH 1961 FIFST 1964
res man. Metal Box Co of India Calcutta 1960–72; head overseas res serv div Metal Box Co Overseas Lond from 1972

LITTLEJOHN James George   MA 1923
 retd 1965; resid Ayr
d Ayr 7.5.80

LITTLEJOHN or Hopes, Margaret Primrose
                                   MA 1920
 resid Torphins

LITTLEJOHN or Flavel, Mary Victoria
                                   MB ChB 1919

LITTLEJOHN Michael Peter   BSc(eng) 1951

LITTLEJOHN Robert Cruickshank   *MA 1925
 retd 1966; resid Torphins
wife *d* Glasg –.4.60
d Torphins 21.4.79 *A UR* XLVIII 229

LIVINGSTON David Fettes   MB ChB 1944
 g p Sheffield from 1953
d Glasg 5.2.80

LIVINGSTON David Munro Sheldon
                     BSc(agr) 1954 *1955 PhD 1959
 FIFST 1971
Aber: sen scient off. dept applied nutrit Rowett res inst 1961–66, head dept of nutrit sc RGIT 1966–71, head s of nutrit sc RGIT from 1971

LIVINGSTON Hugh
                     MA 1927 MB ChB 1931 ᶜMD 1935
 retd 1974; resid Sutton Coldfield
d 25.10.81

LIVINGSTON Hugh Gibson   BSc(agr) 1950
 res off. Rift Valley prov Nakuru Kenya 1957–60; EAAFRO (East Af high command) SSO anim husb dept Kikuyu Kenya, Uganda, Tanganyika 1960–62; dir advis serv Colborn Vita Feeds Canterbury Kent 1962–67; sales dir/nutrit Burgess Feeds Thornton-le-Dale 1967–71; marketing man. Trouw & Co (G.B.) Cambridge; group tech dir Farm Feed Formulators Northallerton from 1972

LIVINGSTON or Ross, Nancy   MA 1942
 ACTL 1941
teacher Aber from 1942

LIVINGSTONE Cyril Joseph   MB ChB 1938

LIVINGSTONE Mary   MA 1918
 d Aber 16.7.71 *A UR* XLIV 317

LLEWELLYN John Patrick   *BSc 1954 PhD 1958
 s of John M. W. L. stockbroker and Mary K. Horsey; b Bishop's Stortford 14.1.33
asst lect nat phil Aberd 1957–58; łect phys univ coll of N. Wales Bangor from 1958
m London 1959 Anne Lejeune MB ChB 1959 *qv*

LOBBAN Agnes   MA 1914
 d Aber 24.8.76

LOBBAN Alfred William Clark   MB ChB 1940
 DPH 1967 RCP & S 1967 MFCM 1972
g p Gamlingay Beds 1946–65; asst c m o Beds 1965–67; m o h N Beds dist 1967–69; sen m o Kingston-on-Thames 1969–70; 2nd dep c m o h and p s m o Beds c c 1971–72; m o h and p s m o Luton 1972–74; dist commun phys Beds AHA from 1974
wife *d* 1968
m(2) Lond 4.1.69 Ivy M. Sandover SRN d of William S. MA(Oxon) Richmond Surrey

LOBBAN or Blackmore, Catherine Margaret
                                   MA 1927
 d Exeter 27.3.68 *A UR* XLII 367

LOBBAN Hilda Cook   MA 1927
 retd; resid Glasg

LOBBAN James Wilson
         MA 1924 MB ChB 1927 DPH 1929 ᶜMD 1930
 retd 1969; resid Birkenhead

LOBBAN Lina Ross   *MA 1931
 retd 1959; resid Huntly

LOBBAN or Dott, Sybil Margaret Gray   MA 1924

LOBBAN William George   BSc(eng) 1949

LOCKE Alton William   BCom 1926

LOCKE Donald Erskine   MA 1936 ᵈLLB 1938
Lond: prin dept of econ affairs 1965–67, prin nat board for prices and incomes 1967–70, prin DTI 1970–74; retd

LOCKHART Robert Douglas
                    MB ChB 1918 ChM 1924 LLD 1965
FSA Scot 1951 FRSE 1954
retd 1965; hon curator Aberd anthrop museum from 1939

LOCKHART William   BSc(for) 1922
no longer on GC reg

LODGE John Blakestone   *MA 1950
chief press off. O U 1970–72; reporter *Evening Express* Aber from 1972

LOGAN or Simpson, Annie Welsh   *MA 1930
BD(Edin) 1975
teacher: Engl Esdail s Ayton 1946–47, Edin acad 1947, Engl La Martinière for girls Calcutta 1947–50; relief teacher Lanarksh 1953–70

LOGAN Charles   *BSc 1953

LOGAN Donald Macpherson   BSc(agr) 1948
teacher chem/bot/zool Fortrose acad from 1966

LOGAN John Black   MA 1927 BD 1930
Order of St Mark 1970 (conferred by patriarch of Alexandria); retd 1970; resid Crieff; Lee lect 1977

LOGAN or MacIntyre, Katherine Jean   MB ChB 1947
resid Kuwait

LOGAN or Raffan, Marie Margaret   MA 1937
resid Bridgend Glam

LOGG Matthew Hannah   MB ChB 1921
no longer on GC reg

LOGGIE George Alexander   MA 1951
prin teacher: Engl Kaimhill s s Aber 1966–73, guid Hazlehead acad from 1973

LOGGIE William John   MA 1955
Aber: teacher maths Northfield s s 1961–66, prin maths Old Aberdeen s s 1966–71, year master Kincorth acad 1971–73, asst head from 1973

LOGIE Norman John   ᵈMB ChB 1927
retd 1969
d Aber 15.3.72 *AUR* xliv 431

LOHR Alexander George   MA 1921 BCom 1924

LOMAX-SIMPSON Josephine Mary   MB ChB 1948
MRCPsych 1973
med asst Wimbledon hosp 1962–77; consult. E Grinstead fam consult. clin 1963–77; founder Messenger House Trust 1970 for unsupported young mothers, Hutchinson settlement 1977 for students

LONG John Dennis   BSc(for) 1945

LONG Michael   BSc(for) 1936

LONG Richard Arthur Kingslow
                    BSc(eng) 1950 *1951 PhD 1954

LONGBOTTOM Keith Illingworth   BSc(for) 1953
no longer on GC reg

LONGMORE Herbert John Alexander
                    MB ChB 1954
MRCGP 1966
Surg regist ARI 1959–61; g p Lochmaben from 1961

LONGMORE William Andrew
                    Dip Agr 1915 BSc(agr) 1920
no longer on GC reg

LORIMER Alan   MB ChB 1949
LMCC 1961 FASCP 1967 Canadian Centennial Medal 1967 MASC 1972 FRCPath 1973 FRCP(C) 1973
lect path. Aberd 1957–59; path.: Salford royal hosp 1959–61; dept of health New Brunswick Canada from 1961
m Bolton 1956 Helen M. Greenhalgh teacher d of Frank G. Manc

LORIMER Archibald Harkness   MB ChB 1948

LORIMER Garth   MB ChB 1950
g p Singapore 1952–76; Aust from 1976

LORIMER John Alexander   BSc 1941
no longer on GC reg

LORIMER Peter   MA 1916
retd; resid Peterculter

LORIMER William Robert Wells   BSc(eng) 1945
eng N E reg hosp board Aber from 1967

LOTHIAN or Watt, Marion Isabel   MA BSc 1911
d Tunbridge Wells 12.2.72 *AUR* xliv 427

LOTHIAN (William) Arthur Cunningham (Sir)
                    MA 1908 BSc 1909 LLD 1950
d Lond 16.11.62 *AUR* xl 77

LOUDON John Russell   *BSc 1953
PhD(Tor) 1960 MIMM(Can) FGeolAssoc(Canada) MGeolSoc(S Af)
Vancouver: geol Amer Metal Climax 1960–65, dist geol Texas Gulf Sulphur Inc 1965–69; reg man. Southern Africa Texas Gulf Inc Johannesburg 1970–75; man. dir Pandora Mining (Johannesburg) from 1976

LOUTTIT or Ross, Mary Sandison   MA 1944
resid Alness

LOVIBOND Catherine Betty Jerrard
                    BSc 1933 *1934

LOVIE Margaret Isabella   MA 1933
no longer on GC reg

LOVIE Peter   MA 1926
d Kilsyth 5.2.66 *A UR* XLII 88

LOVIE Susan Milne   MA 1932
retd 1970; resid Banff

LOW or Thom, Adamina Middleton   MA 1921
no longer on GC reg

LOW or King, Agnes Mary   MA 1946

LOW Alistair   *BSc 1952
plant breeder Etton res corp Serere Uganda 1961–65; CSIRO 1965–77; prin res scient plant breeding in oil seeds sunflower and safflower CSIRO Griffith Aust from 1976

LOW or Fraser, Betty Gordon
BSc 1948 *1949 PhD 1953
lect phys Dun coll of tech 1965–67; vice-prin Trevelyan coll Durh 1967–70; asst secy Ox & Camb s exam board Cambridge from 1970

LOW Charles   MB ChB 1939
MBE 1973
g p Tomintoul 1956–75; retd; resid Kessock

LOW Charles Alexander   MA 1929
no longer on GC reg

LOW David   *BSc 1938
Ellon acad: prin teacher of maths from 1947 and dep rector from 1956

LOW Edward Oliphant   MB ChB 1931
d Tynemouth 4.10.68 *A UR* XLIII 85

LOW Ethel Isobel   BSc 1952

LOW James Alexander   MA 1936 LLB 1938
d Aber 2.11.76

LOW or Vannet, Jean Farquhar   MA 1938
teacher Engl: Kirton h s Dun 1963–68, Grove acad Broughty Ferry 1968–76

LOW or Robertson, Jeannie Anne   MA 1915
d Maud 22.2.81

LOW John
*BSc(mech eng) 1933 BSc(elect eng) 1934

LOW John Alexander   *BSc 1941
prin teacher phys: Golspie 1958–65, Perth from 1965

LOW John Robertson   *MA BSc 1924
d 21.12.70

LOW Margaret Ross   MA 1945
teacher Hilton acad Aber from 1948

LOW or Mackintosh, Muriel Agnes   *MA 1933
resid Nairn

LOW Norma   MA 1953
secy/translator: Glasg 1954–56; Internal Air Trans Assoc Geneva from 1975
m Aber 10.2.56 Robert C. McIntosh CA Europ controller s of Alexander McI. Aber

LOW Robert Milne   *MA 1925
retd 1963; resid Lossiemouth

LOW or Bremner, Ruby Cameron   MA 1949

LOW William James   MA 1937
head: Hatton (Cruden) s 1961–70, Kintore s 1970–76; retd; resid Banchory

LOW William Robin Milne   *MA 1954
Honiara Br Solomon Is: admin off. class 'A' from 1972, secy for soc serv 1972–73

LOW William Smith   MA 1926
retd 1967; resid St And

LOW William Stewart   BSc 1948
teacher: spec asst sc Mearns acad Laurencekirk from 1949

LOWE Anne Margaret   MA 1951
teacher: Banff p s 1962–67, Engl/hist Banff acad from 1967

LOWE Donald Neil   MA 1912
d 10.7.70

LOWE Florence Lyall   MA 1914
d 30.3.65

LOWIT Ian Michael   MB ChB 1953
MRCPE 1959 MRCPsych 1973
sen regist Kingseat hosp and Ross Clin Aber 1959–61; consult. dept ch and fam psychiat RACH from 1961

LOWSON David Sturrock   BSc(for) 1950

LOWSON or Ross, Marion Catherine   MA 1922
resid Leabrook S Aust

LUCKHOO Maurice Stanley   MB ChB 1955
regist N Cambs hosp Wisbech 1957–58; clin off. RAMC (nat serv) BMH Singapore 1958–60; N Cambs hosp Wisbech: regist 1960–67, asst phys from 1967

LUDWIG Brian   *MA 1950
d Aber 11.1.73 *A UR* XLV 228

LUKE or Strachan, Iris Winifred   MA 1949
resid Montrose

LUMSDEN Alexander Gow   *MB ChB 1917
d Lond 23.4.75 *A UR* XLVI 236

LUMSDEN Andrew Anderson   BL 1922
d Aber 8.2.66 *A UR* XLII 86

LUMSDEN Charles Edward
MB ChB 1936 *MD 1948
d 23.6.74 *A UR* XLVI 110

LUMSDEN Charles Gordon   MA 1915 LLB 1922

LUMSDEN Charles Ian   BSc(agr) 1950

LUMSDEN or McLean, Edith Ross   *MA 1916
d Haddington 21.6.64 *A UR* xl 398

LUMSDEN George Henry Charles   *MB ChB 1907
d 15.2.61 *A UR* xxxix 273

LUMSDEN George Innes   MB ChB 1946
g p Peterhead
d 25.10.81

LUMSDEN George Innes   *BSc 1949
FRSE 1967
dist geol inst of geol sc Edin from 1970

LUMSDEN William   BCom 1928 MB ChB 1938
g p Aber from 1947

LUNAN or McLaren, Ivy Scott   BSc 1927
resid Wilmslow
d Wilmslow 4.4.79 *A UR* xlviii 229

LUNAN Netty Margaret   *MA 1918
d Aber 22.3.68 *A UR* xlii 356

LUNAN or Catto, Ruth Anderson   MA 1947
lib MRC 1969–71

LUNDIE John Ernest   MA 1921
d Aber 18.6.73 *A UR* xlv 318

LUNN James Glover Thomson   MB ChB 1937
d Blackpool 8.11.65 *A UR* xli 250

LUTTRELL Arthur Brocklehurst
see Munro-Ferguson

LYALL or Sleigh, Ada Shirley   MA 1954
Stirling: teacher St Ninian's p s 1962–73, asst head
Braehead p s from 1973

LYALL Alan Richards   MB ChB 1951
DObstRCOG(Lond) 1957 MRCGP 1963
g p Laurencekirk from 1956

LYALL Alexander
    MA 1920 *MB ChB 1923 *MD 1926 LLD 1971
d Aber 11.5.74 *A UR* xlv 341

LYALL Alexander David   MB ChB 1950
accidentally drowned Shetland 22.7.65

LYALL André   BSc 1943

LYALL Andrew   MA 1927
head Newburgh Mathers s 1935–64; retd; resid
Newburgh Aberdeensh

LYALL Anne-Marie   MA 1945

LYALL or Mantell, Barbara Ann   MA 1921
retd 1965; resid Macduff

LYALL Barbara Clarke   *MA 1952
b 19.7.30
teacher maths Perth acad 1961–73, asst prin maths
from 1973

LYALL Constance Edina   *MA 1915
d Crieff 21.11.74 *A UR* xlvi 236

LYALL Douglas Jolly   MB ChB 1945
d Edin 5.6.63 *A UR* xl 207

LYALL or Lowe, Florence   MA 1914
d 30.3.65

LYALL Gordon   MA 1907
d Lond 16.3.68 *A UR* xlii 347

LYALL Ian Hodge   BSc 1955
d 30.5.64 *A UR* xl 401

LYALL Joseph Watt   MB ChB 1927

LYALL Maggie   *MA 1922 BSc 1923
retd 1962; resid Scone Perth

LYALL Malcolm George   MA 1951 MB ChB 1956
FRCS 1970
sen h m o Aber hosps 1961–72; consult. ophth surg
Essex from 1972

LYALL Ronald Alexander   MA 1949 LLB 1952
ptnr: Kinnear & Falconer solic Stonehaven 1960–
64, Walter Gerrard & Co. Solic MacDuff from 1964

LYALL Thomas   MB ChB 1936 MD 1954
consult. venereologist Stockport, Macclesfield,
Crewe from 1961

LYALL William   *MA 1932
teacher phys: Edin 1933–39, Dunfermline 1939–40:
RAF(S/L) Cranwell 1940–46; teacher phys Edin
1946–73; retd; resid Gifford
m Edin 25.11.39 Jane Mann teacher d of Donald M.
Fortrose

LYNCH Frederick Passmore   MB ChB 1955
DObstRCOG 1962 MRCGP 1966
Aber: h o mat. hosp 1958–59; g p from 1959

LYNCH Robert   MB ChB 1953
g p Kilwinning from 1958

LYNN Harry Belford   MA 1948
prof Engl San Antonio coll Texas from 1973

LYON Alexander   MB ChB 1951
h o City hosp Aber 1951; m o RAF 1951–56; g p
Inv 1956–58, Golspie 1958–60, Doncaster from 1960;
clin asst anaest Doncaster RI from 1968
m Aber 6.2.54 Joan I. Paterson nurse d of William P.
Aber

LYON or Thomson, Alice Anne Cowan   MA 1936

LYON Christina Helen   MA 1927
retd 1968; resid Alford

LYON Dorothea Mary Anton   MA 1921
retd 1938; resid Aber
d 4.2.78 *AUR* XLVIII 227

LYON Douglas   MB ChB 1916 DPH 1921
d –.3.67

LYON Katherine Elizabeth   MA 1946

LYON Louis Carlyle   MB ChB 1927
d 30.1.70 *AUR* XLIII 446

LYON Mabel Margaret Annand   MA 1927
resid Aber

LYON Mary   MA 1910
d Aber 11.6.65

LYONS James Michael   *BSc 1949 PhD 1952*
MChemInst(Can) MCIC
dir continuing educ Lachute Quebec 1967–69;
Montreal: chmn chem dept Dawson coll 1969–71;
chmn sc and tech John Abbott coll from 1971

MACALDOWIE John   BL 1947
trustee man. Clydesdale Bank 1950–72; retd; resid
Glasg

McALLAN or Emslie, Betty   MB ChB 1951
asst m o h Midlothian 1961–68; g p Oldham from
1968

MacALLAN James Brown   MB ChB 1908
no longer on GC reg

McALLAN James Lewis   MA 1937 LLB 1939
dep county clerk Aberdeensh 1954–75; dir law and
admin Grampian reg c 1975–77; retd

McALLAN James Watt   MB ChB 1944

McALLAN James William Mackie   MA 1895
d Aber 13.1.66 *AUR* XLII 79

McALLAN John Gilbert   BSc 1944
dev eng Standard Telephones & Cables from 1944
m Golders Green 27.1.51 Margaret Bickford-Smith
d of Alan B-S. Liss

McANDREW Albert Grassick Cumming
                        BSc(eng) 1951
sen prof tech ML Aviation Co. White Waltham
1967–75; proj man. from 1975

McANDREW or Munro, Isabella Margaret
                        MA 1943
head Ae p s Dumfries from 1958

MACANDREW Margaret Cameron   *MA 1942*
resid Bramhall

MACANDREW or Anscombe, Maureen Maxwell
                        MB ChB 1944
clin asst St Mary's hosp Manc from 1965

MACANDREW Ronald Maxwell   DLitt 1929
d 20.4.62 *AUR* XXXIX 384

MACANDREW Ronald William   MB ChB 1954
g p Aber from 1956

McARA Alastair Ross   MA 1937
d Aber 1.4.73 *AUR* XLV 227

MACARA or Barnett-Smith, Margaret Elizabeth
                        MA 1948

McARTHUR Alexander Allan   PhD 1952
C of S min: Peterhead old par ch 1952–56,
Pollokshields-Titwood par ch Glasg 1956–65, St
Mary's par ch Edin from 1965
publ *The Evolution of the Christian Year* 1953, *The
Christian Year and Lectionary Reform* 1958

MacARTHUR Allan Alexander   MA 1912
no longer on GC reg

MacARTHUR Archibald   MA 1930
retd 1968; resid Milltimber Aber
d Stirling 18.6.78 *AUR* XLVIII 104 & 353

McARTHUR Effie Kate   MA 1925
teacher Laxdale j s s 1958–64
m Edin 1.5.65 Angus Macleod retd headmaster s of
Malcolm M. Carloway Is of Lewis

McARTHUR Gordon   *MA 1952*
PGCE(Lond) 1961
bank off.: Chartered Bank Singapore 1953–55,
Indonesia 1956–57; educ off.: Sabah, Malaysia 1961–
67, Hong Kong 1968–72; sen govt trg off. Hong Kong
1972–73; prin lect polytech Hong Kong from 1973
m Sabah 21.11.69 Glynis Wong Chew Ngoh teacher
d of Wong Wai Chek Singapore

McARTHUR Ian   BSc(for) 1937
no longer on GC reg

MACARTHUR John   MB ChB 1925
d Worthing 28.10.74

MACARTHUR John   MA 1939
dep head Stornoway p s 1964–74, head from 1974

MACARTHUR John Gordon   *MB ChB 1937*
FRCPGlas 1964 FRCPE 1969
sen lect materia medica Glas and consult. phys
Stobhill gen hosp Glasg and 1950
wife *d* 13.1.74

McARTHUR Julia   MA 1929
retd; resid Edin

MACARTHUR or Clarkson, Kathleen Daisy
                        MA 1947
teacher: h s Dun 1967–71, Gillburn s Dun from
1971

MACARTHUR or Mackenzie, Mary Alexandra
MB ChB 1944
part time asst m o h Kidderminster from 1970

MacARTHUR Norman   MA 1929
JP Ross and Cromarty 1960
retd 1971; resid Inv

MacARTHUR William Gordon   MB ChB 1908
d Yorksh –.1.71

MacASKILL Alexander John   *MA 1948
prin teacher Gaelic Nicolson inst Stornoway 1960–
66; head Portree h s 1966–71; rector McLaren h s
Callander from 1971

MACASKILL Angus   MA 1923
C of S min London Road ch Edin 1947–64;
officiating chaplain RAF Turnhouse Edin 1947–64;
C of S min Cults and Kettle, presb of Cupar Fife
1964–69; retd; resid Bridge of Earn
m Arbroath 23.11.32 Maureen R. Anderson d of
Norman B. A. Arbroath

MACASKILL Donald   MB ChB 1946
JP Ross and Cromarty
h o St Luke's hosp Bradford 1947; locum tenens
Borve 1947–49; g p: Wolverhampton 1949–51,
Galson Is of Lewis from 1952

MACASKILL or Vince, Margaret   MA 1928

MACAULAY Alexander   MA 1922
d –.9.63

MACAULAY Allan John   MA 1947
head Crathie s from 1961
d Crathie 18.4.77 *AUR* XLVII 214

MACAULAY Callum Alexander   *MA 1952
pers man.: Burmah–Shell refinery Bombay 1958–
63, Brunei Shell Co Seria, Borneo 1963–69; pers
asst Shell Internat Lond 1969–70; pers man. Shell
Malaysia Kuala Lumpur 1970–72; pers sen man.
Saudi Arabian airlines Jeddah 1973–74; pers admin
Southeastern Drilling Serv Aber 1974–75; head of
personnel Total Oil Marine from 1976
m(2) Bombay 11.10.58 Jillian R. Anderson d of
Kenneth H. A. Johannesburg

MACAULAY Donald   *MA 1953
lect: dept of Engl lang Edin 1957–60; dept of Irish
Trinity coll Dublin 1960–63; dept of applied ling Edin
1963–67; head dept of Celtic Aberd from 1967

MACAULAY Donald Campbell   *MA 1951
prin teacher mod lang Summerhill acad Aber 1967–
74, prin teacher Fr Hazlehead acad Aber from 1974

MACAULAY Donald Roderick   MB ChB 1938
sen dept m o Ross and Cromarty from 1970, sen
m o Western Isles health board

MACAULAY Joyce Alexander   BSc 1951 *1952

MACAULAY Malcolm   MA 1921 BSc 1923
no longer on GC reg

MACAULAY or Pringle, May Isabella   MA 1925
resid Perth
d Perth 17.9.79

MACAULAY Murdina   MA 1947
Aber: teacher Rosehill inf s 1948–62, Cornhill p s
1962–65, asst head Cornhill s from 1965
m Aber 1961 David K. Cowie
d Aber 17.8.78 *AUR* XLVIII 107

MACAULAY William   BSc(agr) 1936

McAUSLANE Stella Maxwell   MA 1955
teacher Gordon s Huntly from 1961

McBAIN Alexander Cruden   MA 1929
Lond: dir team man. consult. 1964–73, dir inter-
scope man. serv from 1973
no longer on GC reg

McBAIN Alexander Walker
MB ChB 1940 DPH 1947
d Aber 30.11.70 *AUR* XLIV 215

McBAIN Archibald Patrick   MB ChB 1953

McBAIN Charles Stewart   BSc 1950
AMIGasE 1955
chem eng Menstrie 1960–63; asst distillery man.
Girvan 1963–69; oper man. Keith from 1969
marr diss
m(2) Fraserburgh 1.7.72 Kathleen M. Innes teacher

McBAIN Douglas   MB ChB 1939
DMJ 1962
g p Aber from 1948; sen police surg Aber from 1957
m(2) Strathdon 16.10.76 Mildred M. Fraser

McBAIN or Sim, Elizabeth Stephen   MA 1927
teacher comm subjs Hilton acad Aber 1953–68;
retd but contd part-time till 1972

McBAIN or Sadler, Flora Munro   *MA 1934

McBAIN William   BSc 1949
BA(OU) 1973
dep head Laurencekirk s s from 1961

MacBEAN Alexander Fraser   BSc 1934 MB ChB 1938
reg m o h from 1957; resid Exeter

MacBEAN Coila Christina   MA 1933
d 30.12.63

McBEAN Donald Henderson   BSc(agr) 1950
farm. Balblair from 1951
m Inv 4.4.61 Charlotte G. Holm secy d of Thomas H.
Balblair

MacBEAN or Coles, Dorothea Fraser
BSc 1935 MB ChB 1938
off./sister order of St John from 1960; commander/

sister order of St John from 1964; med advis joint commission St John and Red Cross Cyprus in 1964

MACBEAN Innes Black **MA 1938*
teacher Fr Ampleforth coll York from 1956

MACBEAN John **BSc(agr) 1937**
prin: Kersewell agr coll Carnwath 1953–60, Balmacara agr s Kyle Rosssh 1961–65, Lawmuir agr coll E. Kilbride 1965–74; retd

MacBEAN Robert John Laing **MB ChB 1937**
d Dunbeath 11.1.69 *A UR* XLIII 216

MacBEATH John **BCom 1922 *BL 1923**
d 15.4.66

McBEATH or Wilson, Margaret Allan **MA 1931**
head partially-sighted dept Claremont OAS Salford 1960–68; teacher Leuchars p s 1968–74; retd; resid Mintlaw

MacBEATH Ronald Angus **BSc 1950**
housemaster Wingate coll Addis Ababa 1953–56; Sudan govt off. (educ) Khartoum, Port Sudan 1956–60; (Brit council) sen housemaster cadet coll Chittagong Bangladesh 1960–64; teaching posts in Scot. 1964–69; head Temple p s M'Lothian 1969–74; head Whitecraig p s Musselburgh from 1974
m Inv 21.8.52 Ann-Mairie Macleod secy d of John M. Nairobi

McBEY William George **BSc 1949 *1950**

McBOYLE or Gordon, Helen Maggie **MA 1910**
resid Hamilton NZ
d NZ 17.9.77

McBOYLE John Rae **MB ChB 1938**
TD 1960 MRCGP 1971
g p Sheffield 1946–62; reg m o from 1962

McBOYLE Patrick George **MB ChB 1943**
JP 1958
g p Huntly from 1947

McCALL Andrew **MA BSc 1950**
teacher maths Tain acad 1958–61; head Lochinver s s from 1961
m 4.8.62 Sheena L. Conway civ serv; wife *d* 2.4.77

McCALLUM Aenea Janet **MA 1940*
duties in War Office (MI6) Richmond Surrey 1940–45; Lond: in advt 1946–49; edit. asst Royal Inst of Internat Affairs 1949–51; edit. secy of Oriental & Af stud. univ of Lond 1951–55
m Cambridge 11.8.55 W. Sidney Allen MA(Cantab) prof compar philol univ of Cambridge s of William P. A.

McCALLUM or Duff, Bethea Janet **MA 1950**
teacher: geog/Engl 1963–65, commerce 1965–71 West Calder h s Midlothian; lect commerce Steventon coll of f e Edin from 1971
marr diss 1961

McCALLUM Eoin Leslie Richardson **MB ChB 1944**
d Richmond Yorks 28.11.71 *A UR* XLIV 433

McCALLUM Isabella **MA 1925**
teacher Johannesburg 1950–66; resid Cape, S Af
m Grange Banffsh 8.4.39 Daniel S. Crichton CA s of Robert C. Errol Perthsh

McCALLUM Jennie Whitelaw **PhD 1929**
retd 1961; resid Edin

McCALLUM or MacLaren, Margaret Jane **MA 1920**
resid Edin

MacCALLUM or Henderson, Margaret Paxton **MA 1924*
resid Aber

McCALLUM Mary Kennedy **MA 1904**
d Edin 2.6.71 *A UR* XLIV 316

McCALLUM Norman Hugh Ross **MB ChB 1933**
d 10.2.69

McCALLUM Robert Francis Gordon **MA 1923*
head Queen's Park s Glasg; retd
d Edin 24.4.76

McCALLUM Thomas Watson **MA 1904**
no longer on GC reg

McCANN or Mitchell, Marjory Grace **MA 1952**
USA: volunteer teacher reading Schenectady 1968–70; grad stud. in s of soc work 1972
marr diss 1974

McCANN or Cahill, Mary Walker **BSc 1954**

McCASKIE or Macaulay, Gertrude Rhodes **MA 1922**
no longer on GC reg

McCLELLAN or Rybka, Hester Nicholas **MA 1951*
MA(Oxon) 1966 Outstanding educators of America award 1974
Palmer jun coll Davenport Iowa: instr 1966–71, head dept Engl/phil from 1971; Nat Endowment for The Humanities fell. in resid univ of Calif at Santa Cruz 1977–78

McCLELLAN John Forrest **MA 1954*
civ serv: p s to perm under-secy of state for Scot. Edin/Lond 1959–60, asst secy S.E.D. Edin 1969–77; asst under-Secy of State Scot. off. Lond/Edin from 1977

McCLURG Hamish Greig **MA 1954 LLB 1957**
solic Carrington & Sealy, Bridgetown Barbados from 1958

McCOMBIE Arthur Leiper **MA 1950*
prin teacher hist AGS/Rubislaw acad 1961–73; dep head Rubislaw acad 1973–77, dep rector AGS from 1977

m Aber 25.7.61 Vaila M. J. MacLeod teacher p e
d of Donald MacL. Nairn

McCOMBIE Charles William   *MA 1948 PhD 1951
   FRSE 1970
sen lect Aberd 1963–64; prof phys R'dg from 1964;
visiting prof univ of Illinois USA 1972

McCOMBIE Donald Johnson   MB ChB 1943

McCOMBIE or Gleeson, Effie   MA 1902
   no longer on GC reg

McCOMBIE Elizabeth Winton   MA 1955
   Aber: infant mistress Smithfield s 1969–74, head
Rosewood inf s from 1974

McCOMBIE George Henry   MA 1932 LLB 1936
   Huntly: ptnr John Dickson & Son solic 1965–70;
solic on own account from 1970

McCOMBIE Hamilton   MA 1900
   d 31.5.62 A UR xxxix 372

McCOMBIE Harry Duncan   MA 1948
   teacher accounting/computer progr/law/Fr h s
Listowel Ontario from 1968

McCOMBIE or Shepherd, Hazel   MA 1950
   d –.10.72

McCOMBIE Isabella   MA 1909
   d Glasg 11.2.66 A UR xli 241

McCOMBIE James Daniel   BL 1927
   d Aber 10.11.74 A UR xlvi 237

McCOMBIE John   MA 1888 BD 1891
   d Dumfries 10.10.47

McCOMBIE Kathleen   MB ChB 1947
   g p; retd 1964
m Aber 5.12.64 Edward G. C. Rhind MB ChB 1935 qv

McCOMBIE Meta   *MA 1902
   no longer on GC reg

McCONACHIE Allan Milne   MB ChB 1953
   g p Luton from 1955

McCONACHIE Bert Stewart   BSc 1944
   Ontario: electronics eng Canadian Westinghouse
Hamilton 1952–57; man. radar eng Raytheon Canada
Waterloo 1957–74; man. Tactical Data Syst Litton
Syst Rexdale from 1974
m Hamilton Ont 1957 Hannah P. L. Robinson path.
secy/newsp proof reader d of John L. R. Burlington
Ont

McCONACHIE or Sprunt, Elizabeth Mary
**   MB ChB 1955**
   vocational trg 1974–78; locum work Dun from
1978
husb d 1971

McCONACHIE George William   MA 1924
   head Dunnottar p s Stonehaven 1954–67; retd;
resid Stonehaven
d Stonehaven 6.5.81

McCONACHIE or McGregor, Helen Isabel
**   *MA 1943**
   resid Banavie, by Fort William

McCONACHIE Isabella   MA 1935
   teacher Kinloss p s 1959–76; retd

McCONACHIE John Alexander   MB ChB 1944
   g p Lossiemouth from 1951

McCONACHIE or Englefield, Margaret Lipp
**   MA 1913**
   no longer on GC reg

McCONNACH Bruce   *MA 1955
   Lond: acct exec Young & Rubicam 1960–64; advt
man. *L'Oreal of Paris* 1964–65, head of sales and
subscriptions consumers' assoc *Which?* 1965–70; mag
sales man. *Reader's Digest* 1970–72, head of marketing
consumers' assoc *Which?* from 1972

McCONNACH or Haywood, Jean Morag   BSc 1951
   resid Aber

McCONNACHIE or Forbes, Anne Gray   MA 1926
   resid Pitmedden

McCONNACHIE Catherine Elizabeth
**   MA 1926 BD 1959**

McCONNACHIE Duncan Campbell
**   MA 1934 LLB 1936**

McCONNACHIE George William Ritchie
**   BSc(agr) 1920**
   no longer on GC reg

McCONNACHIE Helen   MA 1934

McCONNACHIE Helen Isobel   MA 1941

McCONNACHIE or Stevenson, Isabella Kemp
**   *MA 1908**
   d Aber 9.6.68 A UR xliii 78

McCONNACHIE James Lock   BSc(eng) 1950
   M Inst Eng(Aust) 1954
plant and supply eng Melb metro Board of Works
Melbourne from 1968

McCONNACHIE James Stewart
**   BSc 1935 *MB ChB 1938**
   consult. surg Welsh reg hosp board from 1949

McCONNACHIE or Hughes, Jeanie Simpson
**   *MA 1913**
   resid Bearsden

McCONNACHIE or Donaldson, Jeannie Anne
**   MA 1922**
   resid Grantown-on-Spey

McCONNACHIE or Johnson, Mary Walker
MA 1924
resid Te Aroha NZ

McCONNACHIE Ronald William   MB ChB 1946

McCOSS or Scott, Evelyn   MA 1925
retd 1968; resid Galashiels

McCOWAN Daniel   BSc(agr) 1953
sen scient off.: Nature Conservancy Edin 1964–72,
ITE Banchory from 1974
m(2) Glasg 15.6.73 Catriona F. Finlayson MA(Edin)
teacher d of Kenneth F. MA(Glas) Glasg

McCRAE Marion (Mona)   MA 1941

McCRAE Stuart Rice   BSc(eng) 1950

McCREADIE Samuel Robert McNay
ᶜMB ChB 1951
Dip Amer Board of Path. 1958 Fell Amer Acad
Paediat 1961
dir path. ch hosp Milwaukee Wisconsin USA/assoc
prof path. med coll of Wisconsin (formerly Marquette
univ) from 1960

McCREADY Margaret Scott   PhD 1947
dean Macdonald inst univ of Guelph Ontario
1964–69; head home sc dept fac of agr univ of Ghana,
Legon near Accra 1969–71; retd; resid Toronto

McCREATH Helen Margaret Ross   MA 1942
secy Shipbuilding Conference (called Shipbuilders
and Repairers National Association from 1967) 1946–
77; gen secy Nat Council of Women (GB) 1977

MacCRIMMON Padruig René   BSc(agr) 1953
ICI plant protection div HMOCS Nigeria 1954–63;
dev off. Europe from 1963

MacCUISH Alexander John   BSc 1932
d Fortrose 29.8.78 *AUR* XLVIII 105

MacCUISH Catherine   MA 1924
d 28.6.66

MacCUISH Donald   MA 1926

MacCUISH Donald John   MA 1931
member crofters' comm Inv from 1975

MacCUISH or McDonald, Hannah Margaret
MA 1942
resid Mapperley

MacCUISH Roderick Kenneth   MB ChB 1942
FRCP
consult. phys Bradford hosps from 1958

McCULLOCH David James   MB ChB 1950
d Bulawayo Rhodesia 3.2.70 *AUR* XLIII 446

McCULLOCH Gordon Louis   MB ChB 1922
FRCGP 1968

provost, E Anglia fac royal coll g p's 1963; author
Man Alive Aldus books 1967

McCULLOCH or Hutchinson, Margaret Wedderburn
MA 1913
no longer on GC reg

McCULLOCH William Edward
MB ChB 1923 ᶜMD 1929
no longer on GC reg

McCULLOCH Winifred Sophia   MA 1912
retd 1950; resid Glasg
d Glasg 8.4.80

McCURRACH Margaret Davidson   MA 1933
teacher: Frederick St s s Aber 1948–69, Bridge of
Don acad from 1969

McCURRACH or Watt, Mary Smith   MA 1936
resid Croydon

McCURRACH William George   MA 1938
d Aber 4.7.78 *AUR* XLVIII 106

McCURRIE Janet Grierson   MA 1955 LLB 1958

McCUTCHEON George Buchanan   MB ChB 1952
Aust: m o spec hosp Toowoomba 1958–68, med
supt Ipswich from 1968
marr diss
m(2) Toowoomba 13.2.68 Helga Waschier nurse
educator d of Hans W. Karnten Austria

MacDIARMID or Hatrick, Christine Bannerman
BL 1939
d Aber 31.8.75

MacDIARMID James Breadalbane   MB ChB 1905
practised in NZ: Auckland, Tauranga
d NZ

MacDIARMID or Cormack, Moira Noel Jean
MA 1941
teacher Engl Aber 1956–72; off. i/c Richmondhill
House (Aber mother and baby home) from 1972
marr diss 1973

MACDONALD Agnes   MA 1954 LLB 1956
leg. asst J & F Anderson WS Edin 1957–60; asst
solic: Scot. spec housing assoc Edin 1968–73, Cuthbert
Marchbank Paterson & Salmon SSC Edin from 1973
m Edin 25.7.58 Finlay Mackenzie res and dev eng/
prod. market. man. (electronics)

MACDONALD Alastair Alexander   *MA 1948
mem univ of Newfoundland: assoc prof Engl 1961–
69; prof from 1969; contributor to magazines, reviews
etc in UK Canada and USA; poetry publ *Between
Something and Something* (1970), *Shape Enduring Mind*
(1974), *A Different Lens* (1981)

MACDONALD Alexander   *MA 1925
DD(St And)
vicar: St Augustine's Tonge Moor Bolton 1933–40,

All Souls Leeds 1940–46; sen chaplain Leeds I 1940–45; rector All Saints St Andrews from 1946; retd 1976
d –.6.80 A UR XLIX 67

MACDONALD Alexander   MA 1929

MACDONALD Alexander
                    ***MA 1931 *MB ChB 1937 *MD 1943**
retd 1978; emeritus prof; resid Aber

McDONALD Alexander   *MA 1931
joiner Portsoy from 1931
d Portsoy 7.9.79 *A UR* XLVIII 354

MACDONALD Alexander Henry   MA 1932
teacher Fraserburgh from 1940

MACDONALD Alexander Hugh   BSc(agr) 1923
Argentine: ranch asst Las Petocas 1925–28, ranch under-man. 1929–34, frigorifico buyer Buenos Aires 1934–36, ranch under-man. Las Petocas 1937–42, 1946–57, ranch admin San Luis 1958–65
m Santa Fé 31.1.48 Gwendoline S. Smith d of Walter B. S. prov of Cordoba, Argentine

MACDONALD Alexandrina   MA 1910
d Conon Bridge 13.3.68 *A UR* XLII 348

MACDONALD Alfred Emerson
                         MA 1929 *MB ChB 1932

MACDONALD Alison Margaret Graham   BSc 1951
lect chem Birm 1962–72, sen lect from 1972

MACDONALD Alistair   *BSc 1949

MacDONALD Alistair Cameron
                         MA 1913 *MB ChB 1916
d Elgin 12.1.71 *A UR* XLIV 209

MacDONALD Alistair Cameron   MB ChB 1948
MRCGP 1974
g p Norton, Stockton-on-Tees from 1963

MACDONALD Alistair David
                         MB ChB 1930 MD 1934
asst m o h King's Lynn, Norfolk c c 1960–66; asst m o h Inv c c 1966–69; retd
m(3) Kendal –.4.68 Margery M. Bridges d of Donald B. King's Lynn

MACDONALD Alistair Philip   MB ChB 1934
g p Newark 1935–40 and from 1945; retd 1974

McDONALD Alistair Phinn   BSc 1949
mill chem C. Davidson & Sons Bucksburn 1950–51; prod. man.: Umtali Board and Paper Mills S. Rhodesia 1951–55, C. Davidson & Sons/group tech off. Davidson Redcliffe from 1955
m Glasg 4.2.47 Mary W. Stewart

MACDONALD Allan   *MEd 1953
asst psych Edin 1953–57; educ psych Berksh 1957–62, sen educ psych Glos from 1962

MACDONALD Allan Duncan   MB ChB 1947
DPH(Edin) DIH(Lond) 1961
Unilever fell. indust med Lond/Gloucester/Warrington 1961–62; reg m o T. Wall & Son Gloucester 1962–64; area m o BR southern reg E Croydon from 1964
m Cirencester 20.3.65 Ann D. M. Bullock BBC secy/ antique dealer d of Humphry B. CIE OBE FRHS FRGenS Cirencester

MACDONALD Andrew   MA 1929
no longer on GC reg

MACDONALD Angus Lewis   MA 1903
no longer on GC reg

MACDONALD Angus William Bertram
                    BSc 1935 MB ChB 1938 MD 1951
consult. chest phys Dudley and Stourbridge group of hosps from 1952
m Helen R. Chignell

McDONALD or Dodds, Anna Low   MA 1934
resid Strathdon

MacDONALD Annie   **MA 1915 and 1916
d 3.9.78 *A UR* XLVIII 102

MACDONALD or Campbell, Annie   MA 1932
d 1.4.61

MACDONALD Anson   BSc(agr) 1950
sen lands off. Thurso from 1971

MacDONALD Archibald James   BSc(agr) 1925
no longer on GC reg

MacDONALD Betsy   MA 1954
m Howieson

MACDONALD Catherine   MA 1912
resid Hamilton Ont Canada 1961–71; retd 1971; resid Glasg
m Stirling 24.8.60 James McKenzie hydro employee Ont s of James McK. Keiss

MACDONALD Catherine   MA 1955
teacher: Hilton p s Inv 1957–65, Engl Mimir s of lang Reykjavik Iceland 1965–71, Cowdenbeath p s from 1979
m Stornoway 12.9.67 Sven Bjarnason, Cand Theol (Reykjavik) C of S min s of Bjarni B. Reykjavik

MACDONALD Catherine Isobel   MA 1930
teacher: Lond 1931–51, Inv 1951–69, Drumnadrochit 1967–69; retd; resid Drumnadrochit

MacDONALD or Heriot, Catherine Jane   *MA 1914
no longer on GC reg

MACDONALD Charles John   MA 1930

McDONALD or Duthie, Christian Milne   MA 1918
d Daviot 1.3.73

MACDONALD Christina Fraser MA 1921
teacher Glenurquhart s s s 1930–62; retd; resid Drumnadrochit

MacDONALD Christopher MB ChB 1935

**MACDONALD Colin David John
                          MA 1929 BSc(for) 1932**
head Maud s 1965–73; retd; resid New Aberdour

McDONALD David *MA 1950
MBE 1974
sen classics master Opoku Ware s Kumasi, Ghana 1958–63; commissioned educ branch RAF (sqn/ldr 1966) 1963; Durh univ and Mecas, Lebanon (Arabic interpreter) 1968–70; GC HQ 1970–73; Engl lang instr Kuwait milit acad from 1974
m Coatbridge 29.7.58 Margaret M. Gillespie teacher d of Charles E. G. Coatbridge

McDONALD David Sandeman MB ChB 1951
DGM(Melb) 1977
m o Dr Gray's hosp Elgin 1952; g p Kirkoswald Cambs 1952–53, New Pitsligo 1953–56; Aust: sen m o base hosp Mildura, Victoria, Aust 1957–58, g p Red Cliffs 1958–71, Merimbula 1971–73; geriat m o Beechworth Aust from 1973
m Aber 22.8.52 Elizabeth M. Thomson secy d of John S. B. T. Inv

MACDONALD Donald MA 1913
d Kilmun 17.10.75

MacDONALD Donald MA 1913 BD 1920 DD 1961
retd; resid Montrose

MACDONALD Donald MA 1914
d Stornoway 29.10.61 *AUR* xxxix 275

MACDONALD Donald BSc(agr) 1922
d 6.5.60

MACDONALD Donald MA 1928 BCom 1930

MACDONALD Donald *MA 1937
prin teacher Fr/Ger Fort William s s s later Lochaber h s from 1947
d 12.5.76

MACDONALD Donald MB ChB 1942
deceased

MacDONALD Donald MA 1948
JP 1969
head Aberdour s New Aberdour Aberdeensh from 1969

MacDONALD Donald Alexander MB ChB 1931
d 18.7.67

MacDONALD Donald Douglas MA 1928

MACDONALD Donald Farquhar *MA 1930
FRHistS 1967
emeritus prof mod soc and econ hist Dund 1976

MACDONALD Donald John *MA 1923 LLD 1957
retd 1962; chmn N reg hosp board 1965–71
wife *d* 1961

MacDONALD Donald John *MA 1955

McDONALD or Sim, Doreen Ellen MA 1942

MACDONALD Douglas Reginald *MB ChB 1921
d Nairn 12.1.77

**MACDONALD Douglas Stephen
                          *MA 1922 MB ChB 1931**
d Budleigh Salterton 2.2.78 *AUR* xlviii 103

MacDONALD Duncan BCom 1924
retd 1968; resid Drumnadrochit
m Chicago 25.4.28 Marion MacDonald d of Murdo MacD.

**McDONALD or Edwards, Edith Mary Hutcheon
                          MA 1942**
head Fryern j s Chandler's Ford from 1963

MACDONALD or Humphreys, Eleanor MA 1914
no longer on GC reg

MacDONALD or Snowden, Elizabeth Ann MA 1940
resid Abingdon

**MacDONALD or Godden, Elizabeth Frances
                          BSc 1932**
resid Guildford

**MACDONALD or Somerville, Elizabeth Mary
                          MB ChB 1948**
resid Edin

MACDONALD or Taylor, Ella MB ChB 1946
g p Bradford from 1967

**MACDONALD or Robertson, Elsa Milne
                          *MA 1954**
teacher: mod lang Aber h s for girls 1958–69, prin Ger 1969–75, Engl/Ger at French s Aber from 1975

MACDONALD or Elliott, Elsie Souter MA 1942
supply teacher Kent c c 1960–61; sen clin psych: (part-time) St Augustine's hosp Canterbury 1961–69, Little High Wood, Brentwood 1970–78, m h Medway commun health serv from 1978

MACDONALD Eric Alexander Mackay MA 1905
no longer on GC reg

MACDONALD Flora Helen Grant MB ChB 1924
g p Bradford-on-Avon 1940–66; retd; resid Aber

McDONALD Frank Edward *MA 1948

MACDONALD George Alexander *MA 1949
FIL 1966
Colvilles Glasg: export sales admin 1955–64, staff translator 1964–67; staff translator Br steel corp, gen steels div Motherwell from 1967

McDONALD George Alexander
MB ChB 1954 ᶜMD 1960
MRCPath 1963 MRCPGlas 1968 FRCPGlas 1972
FRCPath 1976
sen regist haemat Glas RI and assoc hosps 1962–64,
consult. haemat in admin charge from 1964; hon lect
haemat Glas, hon consult. W Scot. blood transfusion
serv

MACDONALD George Grant   BSc(agr) 1909
d Cambridge 18.7.60 *AUR* xxxix 102

McDONALD or Davidson, Gertrude Chessor
MA 1922
resid Aber

McDONALD Gladys Elsie   MA 1939
teacher Frederick St s s Aber, later Linksfield acad
from 1947

MCDONALD or Duthie, Gladys Margaret
MA 1946
teacher Rosehearty 1947–50, Stoneywood 1950–51,
Aber 1964–66, Beechwood s Aber from 1966

MACDONALD Hannah Margaret   MA 1922
teacher Engl/hist Ruthrieston j s s Aber 1943–62;
retd

McDONALD or Bohdanowicz, Harriet   *MA 1933

MACDONALD Hector   MA 1951
teacher: Fyvie s 1958–63, Culter s 1963–66, Cults
acad 1966–68, prin geog Summerhill acad Aber from
1968

MACDONALD or Exton, Helen Cantlie   MA 1926
resid Port Erin, Is of Man
husb *d* 1969

McDONALD Herman Ewart Theodore
MB ChB 1931
retd 1970; resid Mexico
wife *d* 1977

MacDONALD Hester May   MA 1935
d Aber 12.4.71 *AUR* xliv 212

MACDONALD Hugh   MA 1944

MacDONALD Iain Alasdair   *MA 1931
HMIS 1951–69; retd

MACDONALD Ian   *MA 1926
no longer on GC reg

McDONALD Ian Arthur   BSc 1951
JP
Aber: prin teacher sc Summerhill s s 1961–67, dep
head Summerhill acad 1967–71, head Old Aber and
Middle and Frederick St s 1971–73, head Linksfield
acad from 1973

MACDONALD Ian David   *MA 1954
DSc(Manc) 1970 LGSM 1977

res fell. Aust nat univ Canberra 1961–64; prof maths:
univ coll Newcastle NSW 1964–67; reader in maths
univ of Queensland 1967–68; visiting lect in maths
Dund 1969; sen lect maths univ of E. Anglia 1969–70;
sen lect maths Stir from 1970
m(1) Tintagel 20.12.65 Sheila Oates BA(Oxon)
mathematician; marr diss 1972
(2) Alloa 24.2.73 Ann B. C. Fleming d of James F.
Alloa

MacDONALD Ian Robert   *BSc 1952 PhD 1955
sen Fulbright travel award 1960
res plant physiol univ Calif Los Angeles 1960–61; prin
scient off. dept soil org chem Macaulay inst Aber from
1974

MacDONALD Ian Robert   *BSc(agr) 1954
insp DAFS from 1959

MacDONALD Isabella   MA 1917
resid Inv
d 7.6.77

MACDONALD Isabella Craig   MA 1933
dep head The Park s for Girls Glasg 1972–76; retd

McDONALD or Scott, Isabella Gardner
MB ChB 1944
asst m o h Moray and Nairn 1963–74; sen clin m o
W Grampian dist from 1974

MacDONALD or MacDougall, Isabella MacGillivray
MA 1914
ptnr guest house Kensington 1954–63; retd; resid
Elgin

McDONALD or Paul, Isobel Mary   MA 1923
d –.11.38

MACDONALD Isobel Mary   MA 1928

McDONALD James   MA 1901
d Aber 1.11.60 *AUR* xxxix 99

MACDONALD James David
BSc(for) 1930 BSc 1932
FRSE 1962
retd 1968; resid Brisbane

McDONALD James Hector   MB ChB 1925
Argyll: g p Is of Colonsay 1951–59, Appin 1959–62;
retd; resid Port Appin

MACDONALD James Mearns   MB ChB 1906
no longer on GC reg

MACDONALD Jamesina   MA 1946
teacher Engl/Lat Barrhead h s Renfrewsh from
1962

McDONALD Jane   MA 1928

MACDONALD or Crombie, Janet   MA 1925

MACDONALD or Mackenzie, Janet Bisset
Wotherspoon   MA 1925

MACDONALD or Howie, Janet McPherson
                                    MA 1937
 resid Edin

McDONALD Janet Mary   MA 1924
 no longer on GC reg

McDONALD Janetta Mary   *BSc 1938
 sen res fell. dept agr biochem Aberd 1960–63; biol
testing pharm prod. Liv from 1963; retd

McDONALD or Taylor, Jessie Ann Anderson
                                    MA 1933
 resid Torphins
d 10.9.74

MACDONALD John   MA 1902
 d Cults 7.6.61 *AUR* xxxix 199

MACDONALD John   MA 1907
 d Callander 9.5.72

MACDONALD John   *MA 1909
 d Nairn 17.12.70 *AUR* xliv 208

MACDONALD John   MA 1915
 no longer on GC reg

MACDONALD John   MA 1919
 d 30.3.67

MACDONALD John   MA 1920
 d Aber 6.9.66 *AUR* xli 338

MACDONALD John   MA 1922
 C of S min: Kilmuir-Easter Rosssh 1948–60,
Lochcarron 1960–66; retd; resid Torridon

MACDONALD John   MB ChB 1924

MACDONALD John   *MA 1926
 no longer on GC reg

MacDONALD John   MB ChB 1938
 hon phys to H.M. the Queen 1963
NZ: surg capt RNZN 1963, dir naval med serv
RNZN 1963–70; dir med serv armed forces northern
reg from 1970

MACDONALD John   MA 1948
 Air Efficiency Award
C of S min Lochee old par ch (formerly St Ninian's)
Dun from 1949

McDONALD John   *MA 1954
 teacher geog: Elgin acad 1958–60, spec asst Nairn
acad 1960–63, prin 1963; Inverness h s: prin teacher
1963–70, dep head from 1970

MacDONALD John Bruce   MB ChB 1955

MACDONALD John Charles Mackie
                                    MB ChB 1942
 g p and anaest Elgin
author *The Wolf* 1977; *Blood of the Wolf* 1978

MacDONALD John Donald Graham   MB ChB 1940
 d Inv 10.5.73 *AUR* xlv 321

MACDONALD John Grant   *MA 1935
 no longer on GC reg

MacDONALD John Norman   MA 1937
 d 15.6.62

MACDONALD John Stewart   MA 1897
 no longer on GC reg

MacDONALD or Mackinnon, Kathleen Jean Povo
                                    MA 1949

MACDONALD Kenneth James   MB ChB 1954
 g p: Invergordon 1959–60, Forres 1960–62, Bonar
Bridge from 1962; m o Migdale geriat hosp and loc.
Treasury m o
m Inv 29.4.61 Phyllis M. Cocker MB ChB 1955 *qv*

McDONALD Lizzie   MA 1934
 teacher Aber from 1936
d Aber 21.9.76

MACDONALD Malcolm   *MA 1926
 deceased

McDONALD Malcolm Edward   MB ChB 1951
 CCFP 1970 FRSTM & H
Newfoundland, Canada: m o i/c Brookfield hosp
1962–67, chief dept of g p Sa Grace Gen hosp St
John's 1969–75, clin instr dept of fam med Memorial
univ of Nfld St John's 1970–74, clin asst prof fac of
med from 1974

MACDONALD Margaret   MA 1912
 resid Inv
d 26.8.77

MACDONALD Margaret   MA 1919
 resid Inv
d Inv 10.6.81

MACDONALD or Hogarth, Margaret Cameron
                                    MB ChB 1907
 resid Lond

MacDONALD or Fowler, Margaret Jane
                                    BSc(agr) 1937
 teacher: rural sc Colne Valley h s Huddersfield
1959–61, biol Ongar s s Essex 1961–66, p s Stapleford
Abbotts 1966–75, dep head from 1975
husb *d* –.12.69

McDONALD Marie Wyness   MA 1953
 scient information off. Commonwealth Bureau of
Nutrition Bucksburn Aber from 1960
m Aber 26.3.73 Alexander Walker asst man.

McDONALD Marjory Elizabeth   MA 1925
 no longer on GC reg

McDONALD or Woodcraft, Mary   MA 1945
 resid Loughton

MACDONALD or Reid, Mary   MA 1922
resid Inv

McDONALD Mary Graham
                    MB ChB 1943 DPH 1954
MFCM 1972
asst m o Inv c c 1961–70, sen m o from 1970
m Longniddry 18.9.71 James Campbell civ eng s of
George C. Glasg

McDONALD or Catto, Mary Isabella Philip
                    MA 1932

MACDONALD Mary Isobel   MA 1945
teacher Conon p s Ross and Cromarty from 1951

MACDONALD Mary Jane Watt   MA 1927
retd 1969; resid Nairn

McDONALD Mona Margaret Cruickshank
                    MA 1950
member diplom serv 1951–70; teacher Engl in
home for emotionally disturbed ch Biesfeld W Ger

McDONALD Moraig Mary   MA 1952

MACDONALD or Scott, Morna Catherine
                    MB ChB 1941
g p Alyth from 1947

MACDONALD Murdo   BSc 1951
B Ed/M Ed(Winnipeg) 1961/1972
teacher Winnipeg from 1958

MACDONALD Neil   MA 1931
dep head Mallaig j s 1963–70; teacher Engl/hist Inv
h s 1970–73; retd
d Inv 6.4.79

MACDONALD Norma   *MA 1955
M Litt(Edin) 1971
teacher: Brit inst s Madrid 1957–60, Oban h s 1960–
65, f e Edin 1966–69, Jordanhill coll Glasg 1969–70;
res work ch lang dev Jordanhill coll 1972–73
m Edin 28.12.68 Leslie Dickinson BA(Keele) lect
univ/coll of educ

MacDONALD Norman   MA 1929
retd 1970; resid Inv

MACDONALD Norman   MA 1932 *BD 1938
retd 1970; resid Conon Bridge

MACDONALD Patrick David Alexander
                    MB ChB 1925
d Lond 6.2.68 *AUR* XLII 366

MACDONALD Patrick Thomson Tulloch
                    ***MA 1903**
d 1972

MACDONALD Peter Chalmers   *MA 1936

MACDONALD Ranald   BSc(agr) 1919
d 1962

MACDONALD Ranald Roderick
                    ***MA 1921 BSc 1922**
d 10.7.63

McDONALD Robert   MB ChB 1937 DPH 1947
FRCPsych 1973
retd 1979; resid Ilkley

MACDONALD Robert Fraser
                    ***MB ChB 1937 *MD 1940 DPH 1941**
m o W reg hosp board 1948, later commun med
spec Greater Glasg health board

MACDONALD Robert Gordon   MA 1907 DD 1954
d 17.12.70

MACDONALD Roderick   BSc(for) 1947
no longer on GC reg

MACDONALD Roderick   BSc(agr) 1952
lands off. DAFS Thurso 1964–67; head land dev
div HIDB Inv 1967–72; sen lands off. DAFS Edin
1972–75; div agr off. Edin from 1975
m Inv 27.4.62 Elizabeth Macleod SRN d of Norman
J. M. MA 1926 *qv*

MACDONALD Roderick Scott   *BSc 1954
teacher sc Elgin acad 1957–60, spec asst chem
Nairn acad 1960–63, prin sc Tain royal acad 1963–66,
head sc/prin chem Wishaw h s 1966–70, prin chem
Fraserburgh acad 1970–73, asst head Fraserburgh
acad from 1973

MACDONALD or Archdale, Sheena Margaret
                    MA 1947
admin and teaching in husband's prep s Rickmansworth from 1963

McDONALD or Buchan, Sheila   MA 1949
resid Peterhead

MACDONALD or McLennan, Sheila Mary
                    MA 1943
resid Fraserburgh

MACDONALD Simon   BSc(eng) 1952

McDONALD Stella Leslie   *MA 1948
woman advis Milne's h s Fochabers 1956–72; asst
rector from 1972

MacDONALD Thomas James Chalmers
                    MB ChB 1924 ᶜMD 1928
d 12.10.66 *AUR* XLII 86

MACDONALD Thomas Kyd   BL 1937
ptnr J. D. Mackie & Dewar advoc Aber from 1948

MACDONALD William Bass   MA 1922
teacher: first asst Newmilns j s s Ayrsh and supt f e
centre 1931–61; retd; resid Kilmarnock
m Kilmarnock 25.12.31 Janet W. Highet

MacDONALD William David Elder   MA 1929

MACDONALD William George   MB ChB 1908
no longer on GC reg

MACDONALD William George   MB ChB 1950
g p Elgin from 1957

MACDONALD William Nevins   MA 1901
d Aber 30.1.61 *A UR* xxxix 199

MacDONALD William Smith   MA 1923
MBE 1968
head Inchgarth s Aber 1949–65; retd; group commandant No 29 group ROC Aber 1963–68; edit. vol IV *Roll of Graduates* from Jan 1981

**MACDONALD or Hides, Williamina Fletcher
MA 1923 BSc 1925**
teacher Musselburgh g s 1946–69; retd; resid Edin husb *d* –.3.37

**MacDONALD or Overton, Wilma McKimmie
BSc 1951**

**McDONALD or Lumsden, Winifred Wright
MB ChB 1950**
m o publ health Fife 1961–68; sen m o commun med Angus dist from 1969

**MacDONELL or MacPhail, Christina Rose
MA 1949 DipEd 1950**

MacDONELL Eileen Emma Mary   MA 1942

McDOUGALL Christina Henry   MA 1941
prod. progr organis radio and tv, talks and publ affairs CBC Toronto 1957–68; spec proj off. (communications) UN inst for trg and res (Unitair) NY from 1968

McDOUGALL Edith Jean   PhD 1934

MACDOUGALL Hugh   BCom 1938
MICA(Scot) 1946
ptnr Lond firm c a 1946–65, fin. consult. from 1965 marr diss 1960
m(2) Dunning 4.4.62 Christina H. MacNab priv secy d of William MacN. Inverkeithing

MacDOUGALL or Gale, Janet Isabel   MA 1950
resid Lond

MacDOUGALL or Carter, Martha Park   MA 1949
resid Windsor

McDOUGALL May Currie   MA 1941

McDOWALL Alan Robert   *MA 1952
FRSSoc 1954
Shell Internat: Lond 1960–65, and from 1971; Shell Eastern Singapore 1965–71

MacECHERN Christian Victor Aeneas   MA 1907
C of S min Kirkmabreck ch Kirkcudbrightsh 1938–65; retd moderator presb of Wigtown
d 20.10.77 *A UR* xlvii 355

McEWAN George Lamb   MB ChB 1940
g p Coventry from 1953; retd 1977

MacEWAN Ian   *MA 1932
d Inv 29.12.67 *A UR* xlii 371

McEWAN or Patterson, Marian Elizabeth   MA 1924

McEWEN Margaret Melrose   *MA 1932
clerkess Aber c c NE counties valuation comm from 1957; retd

McFARLAND Henry Stewart Noel   *MA 1946
d Durh 4.11.73 *A UR* xlv 450

McFARLANE Angus Alexander   MA 1952
MInstP 1980
UK AEA (indust group): asst exper off., exper off. reactor materials lab Culcheth, higher scient off. nat centre for tribology Cheshire 1971–78, sen scient off. from 1978 RNL Risley
m(1) Dun 28.3.59 Jessie M. C. Cuthbert; marr diss –.2.77
(2) Leeds 26.8.77 Sandra A. Ingham BSc(Nott)

MacFARLANE Donald Alexander   MA 1910
min of relig F P ch Dingwall and Beauly 1930–73; retd; resid Inv
m Dingwall 8.5.57 Isabella Finlayson teacher homecraft d of Angus F. Dingwall
d 25.10.79

McFARLANE Isabel Jean   MA 1935
soc worker LCC 1938–65; prin soc worker health dept Westminster city council Lond 1965–75; retd

MACFARLANE James Matthew   *MA 1948
sen admin off. Edin univ from 1957
d 10.9.80 *A UR* xlix 139

MACFARLANE John Brownlie   MB ChB 1931
army rank in 1961 Brigadier
d Edin 6.12.72

MACFARLANE John Clarkson   MB ChB 1925
Derby: g p 1931–70; retd
obst Nightingale mat. hosp 1937–61; retd; locum g p surgeries 1971–74; m o occup health clin cent and S Derbysh hosp 1973–78

McFARLANE Robert Forbes   BCom 1929

**MacFARQUHAR Alexander (Sir)
*MA 1925 LLD 1980**
Internat Co-operation medal 1965
USA: spec advis to UN secy-gen for civ affairs in Congo NY 1960–61; under-secy (dir of pers) UN NY 1962–67; retd; resid Kingston-on-Thames

MACFARQUHAR John Mackenzie   MB ChB 1924
d Fochabers 1.7.74 *A UR* xlvi 108

McGEACHIE or Saunders, Janie Gardiner   MA 1951

McGEE James Ivor   *MA 1951 DipEd 1955
teacher Engl: AGS 1958–63; sen teacher coll of comm Aber from 1963

McGEE William   MA 1955

McGHEE Thomas Wilson   *MA 1953

McGILL Alexander David   MA 1934 MB ChB 1939
 d Penarth 14.1.75 *AUR* XLVI 239

McGILL or Smith, Edith Kathleen Finlayson
                                              BSc(agr) 1950

McGILL Jane Craig   MA 1948

McGILLIVARY Peter Walker   MA 1925
 d Stonehaven 20.11.77

McGILLIVRAY Alexander Shaw   MA 1933

McGILLIVRAY Elaine   *MA 1950
 teacher mod lang Havergal coll Toronto 1960–67, head mod lang from 1967

McGILLIVRAY Eric Laing   *MA 1931 BCom 1933
 Lanarksh: prin teacher maths Gateside j s s 1961–70, Stonelaw h s from 1970

McGILLIVRAY George Mortimer   MB ChB 1912
 d Aboyne 19.4.67 *AUR* XLII 350

MacGILLIVRAY Ian   BSc 1950

MacGILLIVRAY Ian Brodie   BSc(agr) 1954
 man. Cluny estate Newtonmore from 1958
 m Kingussie 20.6.58 Joan M. Mackay teacher d of Kenneth A. M. MB ChB(Glas) Laggan

McGILLIVRAY William Harrison Jamieson
                                              MB ChB 1924

McGILLIVRAY William Harthill   MB ChB 1942
 consult. ENT surg Lanark county area from 1954

McGLASHAN Agnes Margaret
                         MA 1949 MB ChB 1954
 consult. psychiat and med dir: Watford ch and fam psychiat clin 1964–77; dir outpatient serv Thistletown reg cent for ch and adolescents Toronto Canada from 1977; asst prof ch psychiat Tor univ from 1977
 m Lond 26.8.60 Ronald M. Gabriel LRCPE psychiat s of William G. G. Hove

McGLASHAN or Mason, Dorothy   MA 1905
 d 28.10.70

McGLASHAN or Napier, Frances
                                      MA 1954 DipEd 1955
 resid Tain

McGLASHAN George   MA 1932
 d Aber 27.12.64 *AUR* XL 59

McGLASHAN or Runciman, Helen   MB ChB 1904
 no longer on GC reg

McGOWAN Christina Jessie   MA 1936
 teacher Aber 1938–45, Forfar from 1960

m Elgin 22.7.42 Andrew MacKay dir eng firm s of Charles MacK. Glasg

McGOWAN or Catto, Rowla   MB ChB 1938
 resid Wolfhill by Perth
 husb *d* 1975

McGOWAN William Barber   MB ChB 1942
 Rhodesia: govt m o Filabusi 1956–66; med supt Gatooma 1966–67, med supt Umtali from 1967

McGRATH Margaret Mary   MA 1927
 no longer on GC reg

McGREGOR Alexander   MA 1904
 d Maud 24.3.72 *AUR* XLIV 426

MACGREGOR Alickina   MA 1920
 d Rosemarkie 25.11.73

McGREGOR Archibald   MB ChB 1949
 MRCGP 1960
 g p Turriff from 1966

MACGREGOR or Laird, Christina   MA 1945

MACGREGOR Duncan Ronald   *MA 1948

MACGREGOR or Spark, Elizabeth   MA 1923

MacGREGOR Elizabeth Bennett   *MA 1921 BSc 1922
 no longer on GC reg

MacGREGOR George William Gordon   BSc 1955
 Alyth h s: prin maths 1964–71, rector from 1971

McGREGOR Helen   *MA 1927
 d of Alexander M. quarryman; b Newhills 10.2.05
 retd 1963; resid Aber

McGREGOR Henrietta Hay   MA 1925
 d Elgin 10.1.76

MacGREGOR Ian Wyness   MB ChB 1923
 retd; resid Hereford
 m Brompton, Lond 17.12.42 Violet M. Rose-Richards d of Thomas P. R-R. Laugharne

McGREGOR James   MA 1901
 no longer on GC reg

McGREGOR James Anderson   MB ChB 1949
 MRCGP 1963
 g p: Auchenblae 1962–67, Edin from 1967

McGREGOR James Morrison   MA 1930
 JP 1958–74
 teacher: Louth 1931–37, teacher/dep head Walker Rd p s Aber 1937–52, dep head Woodside p s Aber 1952–56, head Muirfield p s Aber 1956–68; retd

MACGREGOR James Murdoch   *MA 1947
 free-lance writer short stories, novels, film scripts, radio scripts, books on photog., wine making etc from 1952

m Aber –.7.60 Margaret Murray d of RQMS Alexander M.

McGREGOR Jean Anderson   MA 1952
teacher: Gwelo, Rhodesia 1957–59, Middlesex 1960–63, Torphins 1964–68, Fr/Ger Inverurie acad 1968–74, prin guid Cults acad Aber from 1974

McGREGOR or Macdonald, Jean Campbell
MA 1943
teacher: Fr Ellis Guilford s Nott 1964–68, Fr/Italian Rushcliffe s Notts 1968–72, Fr/Lat Rawlins upper s Quorn from 1972

MacGREGOR or Aitken, Joan   MA 1927
head Blarich p s Sutherland 1937–68; retd; resid Rogart

McGREGOR John Clark   MB ChB 1934
MRCGP 1957 JP(Caithness) 1965 DL(Caithness) 1977
g p Thurso from 1946; member Scot. med practices comm Edin from 1968; retd 1976

McGREGOR John George   *MA 1934

McGREGOR John Grant   MB ChB 1906
no longer on GC reg

MacGREGOR Kenneth Stuart Hall   MB ChB 1948
g p Sutton-in-Ashfield from 1954

MacGREGOR Malcolm   *MA 1924
no longer on GC reg

MacGREGOR or Fry, Margaret Una Cameron
*MA 1923
resid Weymouth

MacGREGOR or Hogg, Mary Emily Watt   MA 1917
resid Edin
d Edin 25.3.80

McGREGOR Norah   MA 1934
teacher Mile End p s Aber 1948–75; retd

MACGREGOR Rosabel Elizabeth   *MA 1929
teacher: prin Lat/Ital Beacon s for girls Bridge of Allan 1957–73; retd; resid Alloa

McGREGOR or Hamilton, Yvonne Margaret Hogg
MB ChB 1949
m o Dunfermline from 1972

MacGRUER or Noble, Christina Anne   MA 1912
no longer on GC reg

McHAFFIE Alexander Taylor   MA 1951

McHAFFIE Margaret Allan   *MA 1947 PhD 1954
sen lect Ger Glas from 1967

McHARDY Alexander Smith   *MA 1923
retd; resid Banff
d Banff 9.12.77 *AUR* xlvii 356

McHARDY or Slesser, Alice Mary   MA BSc 1909
no longer on GC reg

McHARDY Barbara Jean   MA 1933

McHARDY Elizabeth   MA 1906
d 30.10.65 *AUR* xli 239

McHARDY or Finegan, Elizabeth   MB ChB 1909
resid Hayward's Heath Sussex

McHARDY Francis   MA 1925
no longer on GC reg

MacHARDY Hamish Chisholm   *MA 1950
teacher: head of mod stud. Viewforth h s Kirkcaldy 1960–65, head hist Tain royal acad from 1965

McHARDY or Anderson, Isabella Murray   MA 1930
missionary: W and NW China 1936–51, Bihar NW India 1953–54, Saiburi S Thailand 1954–68; resid Denny

McHARDY James Brown   MA 1954

McHARDY John   MA 1903
d –.12.69 *AUR* xliii 440

McHARDY or Hendry, Margaret Jean
MB ChB 1943
resid Aber

McHARDY or Milne, Margaret Munro   MA 1951
d Glasg 18.5.77

McHARDY or Muir, Marjory Ann   MA 1933
lib Blenheim Ontario from 1959

McHARDY or Markham, Mary Elizabeth Garden
MA 1925
retd 1966; resid Clarkston Glasg

McHARDY or Dawson, Mary Robertson   MA 1927
teacher maths Kemnay 1967–69; retd

McHARDY William Duff
MA 1932 BD 1935 DD 1958
prof OT stud. Lond 1948–60; regius prof Hebrew and student of Christ Church Oxon from 1960

McHARDY or Reid, Winifred Clara   MA 1926
resid Nairn
d Nairn 23.7.77

McHATTIE or Williams, Annie Jane   *MA 1935
resid Exeter

McHATTIE Robert   MA 1938
Aber: teacher Engl Torry s s 1949–62, Old Aber s s 1962–70, prin Engl 1970–75; asst prin Engl Linksfield acad from 1975

McILWAIN Alexander Edward   MA 1954 LLB 1956
pres SRC Aberd 1956–57
leg asst: Gray & Kellas Aber 1960–61, John Y.

Robertson solic Hamilton 1961–63; ptnr Teague, Leonard & Muirhead (later Leonards) Hamilton from 1963; notary publ SSC 1966, county secy Scout Assoc Lanarksh from 1967; burgh prosec Hamilton 1967–75; dist prosec Hamilton dist c 1975–76; member council of Law Soc of Scot. from 1972
m Aber 14.7.61 Moira M. Kinnaird MA 1958 *qv*

McILWRAITH or Worrell, Joyce Duddingston
                                                  BSc 1950

MacINNES Angus   MB ChB 1951

MacINNES Donald   MA 1930

McINNES Hector John   BSc(agr) 1954

MACINNES or Smith, Jean Armour   MA 1946
    teacher Dingwall p s from 1968

McINNES Kenneth Guthrie   BSc 1949

MacINNES Marion Margaret   MA 1939
    teacher Engl Millburn s s Inv 1961–72, also prin guid from 1972; retd 1977

MACINNES Niel Iain   *MA 1953
    Lloyds Bank Lond: sect. man. overseas dept 1969–73, dep man. city, overseas br 1973–77, asst man. docum div overseas dept from 1977

McINTOSH Alastair Donald   BCom 1934
    teacher bus. stud. Peterhead acad 1966–69, prin bus. stud. from 1969

McINTOSH Alexander   *BSc 1950

McINTOSH Alexander Wilson
                  MB ChB 1950 DPH 1956 MD 1962
    MFCM 1972
sen asst m o h Aber 1963–64; dep county m o and dep prin school m o N Riding Yorks c c Northallerton 1965–74; dist commun phys York health dist from 1974

MacINTOSH Alistair Eoin   MB ChB 1943
    FRCP(Can) 1972
g p Georgetown Ont from 1967

McINTOSH Annie Bell   MA 1930
    teacher: Helmsdale 1932–40, Airdrie 1950–52; head Ballindalloch s 1953–60; teacher Aberlour 1960–61, Grantown g s 1961–70
m Lairg 3.4.40 Thomas H. Reid BSc(St And) teacher s of Andrew D. R. Dun

McINTOSH Annie Greig   *MA 1901
    d Aber 7.10.63 *AUR* XL 300

McINTOSH Donald   MB ChB 1947
    consult. phys i/c Hounslow chest clin, Ealing Hammersmith and Hounslow AHA and W Middx hosps from 1972

MACINTOSH Donald   MB ChB 1953

McINTOSH Edward   *MA 1915
    d Exmouth 23.3.70 *AUR* XLIII 442

McINTOSH or Burness, Frances Rae
                                    MA 1931 MB ChB 1936

McINTOSH or Scrimgeour, Helen Dalziel   MA 1930
    resid Frittenden
husb *d* 1974

McINTOSH or Cowie, Helen Geddes   MA 1943
    resid Insch

McINTOSH Iain Alexander   MB ChB 1948
    DPH(Lond) 1959 DIH 1960 MFCM 1972
RAF med branch from 1949
d Halton 5.2.78 *AUR* XLVIII 107

McINTOSH Ian Donald   *MA 1930 LLD 1962
    d Edin 18.1.75 *AUR* XLVI 238

McINTOSH Irene Margaret   MA 1946
    teacher Engl: Kincardine 1947–51, Aber 1952–61; supply teaching 1962–73; teacher Engl Cults acad from 1973
m(1) Aber 29.9.51 Alfred J. Marr shop man. s of Alfred J. M. Aber; husb *d* 1974
(2) 3.7.78 Ian G. M. Petrie BSc(St And) teacher

McINTOSH or Macinnes, Isobel Margaret
                                                  ***MA 1948**

MacINTOSH James Archibald   BD 1904
    no longer on GC reg

McINTOSH James McInroy Dalziel   MB ChB 1935
    retd g p 1972; part-time ACMO health dept Hertfordsh c c from 1972

McINTOSH or Ross, Jessie (Janet)   MA 1932
    resid Bo'ness

McINTOSH John   MB ChB 1938
    m o DHSS Edin from 1966
d 19.11.81

MacINTOSH John Leitch   MA 1949
    no longer on GC reg

McINTOSH John Taylor   *MA 1950
    head: Towie s 1962–69, New Deer s from 1969

McINTOSH or Harte, Lilian   MA 1937
    resid W Bridgford

McINTOSH or Ferris, Margaret   MA 1942

McINTOSH Murdoch   BL 1939
    d –.1.72

McINTOSH or Campbell, Nancy Rebecca   MA 1949
    d Glasg 25.1.74

MacINTOSH or Forbes, Rena Crum   BSc 1950
    teacher maths/sc Aber from 1951

McINTOSH Robert Fyfe   BSc(eng) 1953

McINTOSH William   MA 1951 *MEd 1953
d Leamington Spa 4.7.76

McINTOSH William Craib   MA 1923 MB ChB 1927
retd; resid Northam, Bideford
wife *d* 1968
m(2) Bideford 22.11.69 Jeannetta P. Way or Mortimer
d of Stanley W. Bideford

McINTOSH or Sutherland, Williamina   MA 1912
no longer on GC reg

MACINTYRE Donald Gordon   MA 1955 MEd 1957

McINTYRE Ian Sinclair   MA 1950
teacher Lumphanan 1950–59; head: Berefold s
1959–65, Slains s from 1965

McINTYRE or Kemp, Isabella Downie   MA 1921
teacher Fr/Engl Westlands h s Rugby 1961–67;
retd

McINTYRE Peter Farnworth   BSc(for) 1949
d Banchory 24.9.70 *A UR* XLIV 111

MACINTYRE or Palmer, Ruby Crombie   MA 1929

McINTYRE William   MB ChB 1950

MACINTYRE William Campbell
                                MA 1950 *MEd 1954

MACIVER Alexander   MA 1955
teacher City Publ s s Glasg 1962–64; head: Poolewe
p s Wester Ross 1964–70, Carloway p s Is of Lewis
1970–75, Knock p s Is of Lewis from 1975
m Glasg 30.12.64 Mary A. Campbell d of Kenneth C.
Point Is of Lewis

MacIVER Angus Stuart   MA 1931
retd 1970; resid Westerdale Halkirk

McIVER or MacBean, Barbara Campbell   MA 1911
no longer on GC reg

McIVER Charles Gordon Esslemont   MA 1949
dir Lawson Turnbull & Co Aber from 1954

McIVER Colin John   *MA 1907
d Aber 31.10.69 *A UR* XLIII 327

McIVER or Murray, Dorothy Coutts   *MA 1923
resid Knaresborough
husb *d* 1967

MacIVER Ian Frederick   BSc(for) 1949
dist off. for. comm: Malvern 1950–64, N Devon
1964–68, S Cowal 1968–72, Stirling from 1972

McIVER Ian Ronald   *MA 1931
teacher: asst prin mod lang Banff acad 1964–72;
retd

MacIVER John   MA 1919
retd; resid Braco

MacIVER John Angus   MA 1950
head Hopeman p s from 1970

McIVER Kenneth Esslemont   MB ChB 1945
g p Staveley from 1949

MacIVER Kenneth Ian   BSc(agr) 1954
area superv potato market. board for Fife, Kinross,
Clackmannan at Cupar from 1957
d Cupar 26.5.80 *A UR* XLIX 70

MacIVER Kennethina Macpherson   MA 1946
teacher Kelvindale p s Glasg from 1976

MacIVER Madeline   MA 1940 *MEd 1966
d Stornoway 29.10.66 *A UR* XLII 89

MACIVER Malcolm   MA 1929
headmaster Knock 1952–64; retd; resid Breasclete
Is of Lewis
m(2) Glasg 2.2.74 Annie S. Macleod P O clerk d of
Roderick J. M. Balallan Is of Lewis

MACIVER Malcolm Morrison   MA 1922
d 1973

MacIVER or Crawford, Margaret Barbara
                                        ***MA 1936**
d Inv 24.7.78 *A UR* XLVIII 106

MacIVER Mary   MB ChB 1951

MacIVER Murdo   BSc(eng) 1948
MBE
dist man. NSHEB Western Isles Stornoway from
1968
d Stornoway 8.4.75 *A UR* XLVI 326

MacIVER Ranald Murdo   BSc(agr) 1949
Dip Animal Genetics(Edin) 1950
scient off. poultry res centre Edin 1950–53; lect dept
of agr Edin 1953–60; geneticist Dale Turkeys Ludlow
1960–64; lect UCNW Bangor from 1964

McIVOR William Benjamin   MA 1955
head: Thrumster p s 1960–70, Miller acad Thurso
from 1970
m Wick 28.3.59 Margaret E. Sutherland med receptionist d of James S. Wick

McKAIN William Thomas   BSc(eng) 1952

McKAY or Kelly, Agnes Jessie   MA 1923
retd 1962; resid Aber
d Aber 30.4.80

MACKAY Alexander   MB ChB 1921
g p Thornaby-on-Tees 1922–58; retd; resid
Northallerton

McKAY Alexander Duncan Den   *MA 1919
d Dun 10.4.70 *A UR* XLVI 444

MACKAY Alexander Henderson   MB ChB 1924
no longer on GC reg

MACKAY Alexander Murray   MB ChB 1947
g p Edin from 1969

MACKAY Alexander Taylor   *MA 1950
teacher: mod lang Ellon acad 1955–66, Schiller coll
Germany 1966–71, acad dean 1970–71; prin mod
lang Torry acad from 1971
m Edin 16.7.71 Dorothy L. A. Craig teacher d of
William C. Edin

MACKAY Alexandrina   MA 1903
d Golspie 22.11.63 *AUR* XL 300

MACKAY Angus Sim   *BSc(eng) 1934

MACKAY or Morrison, Ann   MA 1945
part-time teacher Laxdale p s from 1972

MACKAY Anne   MA 1944
no longer on GC reg

MACKAY Annie   MA 1902
no longer on GC reg

MACKAY or Smillie, Catherine Elizabeth   MA 1949

MACKAY or Darby, Catherine Yvonne   MA 1938
teacher maths/sc Goodall Rd s mod s Leyton 1948–
55; prin maths Leyton Manor Co sec girls 1958–60;
teacher: human biol/maths Ruckholt Manor Co s s
Waltham Forest 1961–72, maths Woodford Co h s
girls Essex 1972–73, Caterham h s Ilford 1973–77;
retd

MACKAY Charles   BSc(agr) 1947
MSc(Kentucky) 1960 W. K. Kellogg found. fell.
1959–60
insp DAFS Aber 1954–64, sen insp Ayr 1964–70;
Edin: tech dev off. DAFS 1970–73, dept chief agr off.
1973–75, chief agr off. from 1975

MACKAY Charles Kenneth
                              BSc 1954 MEd 1960 PhD 1978
teacher Aber 1958–60; county educ psych Bedford
1961–64; lect Aberd 1964–72, sen lect from 1972

MACKAY Christina   MA 1904
d Aber 15.3.63 *AUR* XL 198

MACKAY or Macleod, Christina   MA 1933

MACKAY Christina Mary   MA 1953
teacher: remed Nicolson inst Stornoway from 1969
m Aber 4.4.60 Allan D. Whiteford MA 1954 *qv*

MacKAY Christine Ann   MA 1953
woman advis Inv h s from 1964, asst head from
1972

MACKAY Coinneach Ian   BSc(eng) 1951

MACKAY David Nicol   *MA 1951

MACKAY Dennis   *BSc 1954 PhD 1958
SKF res fell. Queen's coll Dund 1958–61; lect
pharm Leeds univ 1961–65; US publ health fell.
pharm Los Angeles 1965–66; sen lect pharm Leeds
univ from 1973
m Forres 23.3.68 Moira McLennan clerkess d of John
A. McL. Forres

MacKAY Donald   MA 1915
d Dunfermline 15.5.1973 *AUR* XLV 318

MACKAY Donald   MA 1922
asst teacher Nicolson Inst Stornoway 1922–25;
head Tarradale j s s Muir of Ord till 1961; retd

MACKAY Donald   *BSc 1954 PhD 1957
asst prof univ of Waterloo Canada 1960–62; Oxon:
NATO res fell. 1962–63; DSIR res fell. 1963–64; assoc
prof univ of Waterloo from 1964

MACKAY Donald George   MA 1938 MB ChB 1943
med statist gen reg off. Somerset House 1951–56;
dep med supt Inv hosp group 1956–58; med statist off.
N reg hosp board (Scot.) 1958–66; sen med off.
(commun med) SE Thames reg health auth from 1966

MACKAY Donald John   MA 1953
highlands off. Scot. Agr Organis Serv Edin 1958–61;
man. trg off. UK AEA Dounreay 1961–64; training/
pers off. Brit Alum. Co Kinlochleven/Fort William
1964–65; dir An Comunn Gaidhealach Inv 1965–70;
pers man. Brit alum. Co Invergordon from 1971

MACKAY Donald Ross   BSc(agr) 1954
overseas col serv agr dept Lusaka Zambia 1964–69;
gen man.: Tobacco Board of Zambia Lusaka 1969–72,
General Farming Co Lilongwe Malawi 1972–73; tech
advis Overseas Dev Admin Windward Is from 1974
m Lundazi Zambia 1962 Maureen J. Whitaker nurse
Derby

MACKAY Doris Badenoch   MA 1947
teacher Milne's h s Fochabers from 1948

MACKAY or Leeson, Dorothy Jean   MB ChB 1942

McKAY Douglas Charles   *MA 1951
head Tillycoultry s 1963–67; rector: Alva acad
1967–71, Leith acad from 1971; chmn Port of Leith
housing assoc

MacKAY Duncan   MA 1901
no longer on GC reg

MacKAY Duncan William   MB ChB 1917
no longer on GC reg

MACKAY or Clarkson, Elizabeth   MA 1907
no longer on GC reg

McKAY or Rendall, Elsie Sutherland   MA 1938
teacher Pierowall j s s Westray Orkney from 1950;
retd 1977

McKAY Eric   *MB ChB 1948 ᶜMD 1965
FRCPE 1971 MRCPsych 1971

res fell. paediat Tor 1960–61; Aberd: lect ch health 1961–69, consult. dev paediat from 1975

MACKAY Eric Beattie   MA 1948
edit. *The Scotsman* Edin from 1972

MACKAY Ethel Elizabeth Lauder   *MA 1919
retd 1960; resid Edin
d Edin 22.11.79

McKAY or Fraser, Ethel Mary   MA 1923
retd 1963; resid Shaftesbury

McKAY or Birnie, Félicité Rolland   *MA 1934
teacher: Grangefield gr s for girls Stockton-on-Tees 1956–60, Howell's s Llandaff Cardiff 1963–71, Charters Towers s Bexhill-on-Sea from 1973

McKAY or Begg, Fiona Hunter   MA 1955
teacher: maths King's Rd s Rosyth 1959–61, McLean p s Dunfermline 1965–66, remed Pathhead s Kirkcaldy 1966–69, relig educ Kirkcaldy h s from 1969

MacKAY Flora Mary   MA 1939
teacher: Galloway House s Garlieston 1966–67, Ferryhill p s Aber from 1967; retd 1977

MACKAY George Patrick Gordon   *MA 1937
CBE 1962 Kt 1966
gen man. E. Af Rlys & Harbours 1961–64; World Bank: 1965–78 (dep dir 1974–75, dir Saudi Arabia 1975–77); retd; resid Haslemere

McKAY George Shiach   MA 1898 MB ChB 1902
no longer on GC reg

**MACKAY George William MacBeath
                              MA 1920 MB ChB 1924**
retd 1964; resid Farnham
d Hampton 29.9.77 *A UR* XLVIII 103

McKAY Gilbert Watt   *MA 1950
D Litt (Schiller coll Germany) 1965
sen dean St Peter's coll Oxon from 1970
m 7.12.60 Elizabeth M. Norman D Phil(Oxon) mus. and musicologist d of Sir Edward J. N. Dorking

MACKAY Hugh   MA 1913
retd 1954; resid Connel

MacKAY Hugh   BSc(eng) 1931

MACKAY Ian   MB ChB 1950
d 13.7.73

MACKAY Ian   BSc(eng) 1952
Stornoway: div road surv 1956–71; asst county surv 1972–75, dir engineering from 1975

MACKAY Ian Anderson   *BSc 1936
d Birkenhead 27.4.63 *A UR* XL 206

MACKAY Ian James Hendry   BSc 1951
JP 1971

area off. White Fish auth from 1953
councillor: city of Aber 1966–74, reg seat Hazlehead in Grampian reg from 1974
d Aber 28.2.77 *A UR* XLVII 215

McKAY or Ironside, Iona Margaret   BSc(agr) 1952

**MACKAY or McIntyre, Iris Fowler
                              *MA 1953 DipEd 1954**
Canada: pres sec assoc teachers of Engl BC 1970–71, pres BC Engl teachers' assoc 1971, pres elect Canadian council of teachers of Engl 1973–74

MACKAY or Williams, Isabel   MA 1946

MACKAY Isabel Scott   *MA 1927
d Elgin 30.4.75 *A UR* XLVI 323

MACKAY or Fenelon, Isabella Gray   MA 1953

MACKAY Ivor Macdonald   BSc(eng) 1952
CEng MIEE 1961
head elect. eng and sc coll of f e Barrow-in-Furness from 1962
d 7.10.77

McKAY James   MB ChB 1950
g p Richmond Va USA from 1959

MACKAY James Finlayson   MB ChB 1937
consult. venereol N Lancs/S Westmorland from 1950

McKAY James MacGregor   MB ChB 1942
consult. radiol Morriston hosp Swansea/Swansea gen hosp/Llanelly hosp from 1956

MACKAY James Ross   *BSc 1955
head biol dept Inverurie acad from 1963
m Alford 21.10.61 Mary B. Brown clerkess/typist d of Frederick W. B. Alford

MACKAY James Slater   MA 1938
d Lossiemouth 31.3.73 *A UR* XLV 227

MACKAY or Brown, Jane Laughton   MA 1901
no longer on GC reg

MacKAY or Sharp, Jean Grant   MA 1949
resid Aber

**MacKAY or Cruickshank, Jean Murrion Finlayson
                              *MA 1924**
retail staff man. Scotch wool shops h q London/Greenock 1959–61; consult. retail trades educ council h q Lond 1961–63; resid Yarm-on-Tees
marr diss 1966

MACKAY or Husband, Jean Reay   *MA 1951

McKAY or Cross, Jean Weir   MA 1927

McKAY Jeannie Anderson   MA 1927
teacher Peterhead cent s 1929–37, Inverallochy s 1937–48, North s Fraserburgh 1948–69; retd

MACKAY Jessie Margaret   MA 1932

MACKAY John   MA 1893
d Yarm-on-Tees 14.2.66 *AUR* XLII 79

MACKAY John Alexander   *MA 1912 DD 1939
retd 1959; resid Washington DC 1959–69, Hightstown NJ USA from 1969

MacKAY John Bruce   MB ChB 1925
g p Bromley-by-Bow, Lond 1925–64; retd; resid Bexhill-on-Sea

MACKAY John Henry   BSc(for) 1924

McKAY John Hutchison   BSc(eng) 1944
MIEE 1966
sect head Kent c c supplies dept Maidstone from 1971

MACKAY John Kinnear   MB ChB 1939
g p Middlesbrough from 1946

McKAY John Mair   MA 1942

MACKAY John Simpson Bain
                    MA 1926 MB ChB 1931 DPH 1933
retd 1968; resid Bury

MACKAY John Swinton   MB ChB 1935
surg spec RAMC 1942–46; consult. surg Victoria I Glasg 1948–72; retd; resid Blairgowrie
m(2) Newton Abbot 17.11.46 Margaret H. Selby-Smith nurse d of Ronald S-S. Newton Abbot

MACKAY Kenneth   BSc(eng) 1948
rep Procter & Gamble (formerly Thomas Hedley & Co) Redcar from 1957

MACKAY Kenneth James   MB ChB 1954

MACKAY Kenneth William Peter   BSc(agr) 1940
d Mauchline 2.1.77

MACKAY Lena   *MA 1953
teacher: hist/Engl Dunbar 1968–77, prin guid and leisure from 1977
m Inv 30.7.60 James R. Glass loc govt. off. s of Alexander G. Dunbar

MACKAY Mackay   MA 1928
d Rogart 5.3.67 *AUR* XLII 186

MACKAY Margaret Marr Esslemont   MA 1928
no longer on GC reg

MACKAY Marion Elizabeth   MB ChB 1953
MRCP 1965 Dip Psych Med(Manc) 1968
MRCPsych 1971
consult. psychiat Bolton from 1971

McKAY or Barron, Marjorie Kate Mabel   MA 1931
resid Skene

MACKAY or Fraser, Mary Anna   MA 1920

MACKAY Mary Elizabeth   MA 1943

MACKAY or Button, Mary Ross   *MA 1917

MacKAY Mary Ross   MA 1917
retd 1961; teacher sc Invergowrie Perthsh 1963–64

MACKAY Matthew   BSc(eng) 1952

MACKAY Moira Gunn   MA 1953
teacher classics Nicolson Inst Stornoway from 1966

MACKAY Mona Elspeth   *MA 1930
teacher Fr/Engl Grantown g s 1961–70; retd; resid Advie

McKAY Mona Isobel   MA 1950
lib/tut. Loughborough coll of educ 1965–77; sub lib Loughborough univ of tech from 1977

MacKAY Murdo John   BSc 1936

MACKAY Murdoch   MB ChB 1950
d Staffordsh 11.5.73 *AUR* XLV 321

MACKAY Murdoch Macbeth   MA 1937
chaplain royal Cornhill hosp Aber from 1961; hon lect mental health Aberd from 1973

MACKAY Muriel Helen   *BSc 1944 PhD 1948
resid Didsbury

MACKAY Neil Melvin   BSc(eng) 1951
FICE 1966 MIWE 1972
prov eng min of works Kenya, Nyeri 1962–63; resid civ eng Ratcliffe Power stat Nott 1964–67; resid eng M6 motorway Killington/Tebay 1967–70; proj eng Kenya coast water supply augmentation Nairobi 1971–74; proj eng Renfrew motorway from 1974

MACKAY Robert John   *MA 1911 LLB 1918
d 24.11.67

MACKAY Robert Watt   *BSc 1950
retd 1977; resid Middlesbrough

MacKAY Roderick   MA 1901 MB ChB 1904
no longer on GC reg

MACKAY Roderick
                    MB ChB 1924 DPH 1931 ᶜMD 1934
d 7.9.66

MACKAY Roderick Duncan   BSc(eng) 1951

MACKAY Ronald   MA 1950
JP Midlothian 1972
Midlothian: head Pumpherston p s 1965–73, Harrysmuir p s from 1973

MACKAY Roy Stuart   MA 1950 DipEd 1951
teacher Lat: Queen's s Rheindalen Germany 1962–65, St Modan's s Stirling 1965–67; careers off. Stirling from 1967

MACKAY William Bremner **BSc 1952*

McKAY William Graham MB ChB 1951
g p Whitehaven Cumbria from 1958

McKAY William Macgilvary PhD 1939
Academician (Bologna univ) Italy 1969 FIBiol Lond 1971
agr scient co-ordinator for Europe, Lederle labs 1957–65; consult. from 1965

MACKAY William Roderick BSc 1934
JP County of Inv 1962
chaplain Inv hosps from 1961

McKEE Catherine Dora MA 1949
civ serv; resid Lond

McKEE John Low MA 1949 DipEd 1950

MACKEGGIO George Alexander
                              MA 1911 BD 1914
retd; resid Prestwick

McKELLAR Kenneth BSc(for) 1947
FRSA 1969
dir Radio Clyde Glasg from 1973

McKENDRICK Anderson Gray DSc 1927
no longer on GC reg

MACKENZIE Alan Theodore Louis BSc(eng) 1935
asst gen man. Keymer Bagshawe & Co Calcutta 1948–52; dir Barrow Hepburn & Gale (machinery) Leeds 1953–70; man. dir Mackenzie eng Keighley from 1970
m Lerwick 4.5.55 Thelma K. Lennie

MACKENZIE Alasdair Urquhart MA 1942
head: Munlochy j s 1956–68, Bridgend Alness from 1968

MACKENZIE Alastair Chisholm *MA 1924
d Falkirk 27.8.62 *A UR* XL 90

McKENZIE Alastair Grant MA 1930
d Aber 16.5.78 *A UR* XLVII 359

McKENZIE Alastair Still *MA 1950
prin teacher classics James Gillespie's p s Edin 1961–66; exam. off. SCE exam. board Edin; dep rector Stirling h s from 1971, rector Tain r acad from 1975

MACKENZIE Alexander *MA 1914 *BD 1919
d Glasg 16.3.70 *A UR* XLIII 441

McKENZIE Alexander *MA 1933
prin teacher mod lang Elgin acad 1957–75; retd

MACKENZIE Alexander William Riddoch
                              MB ChB 1928

MACKENZIE or Paterson, Alexandrina Morag
                              MA 1944

MACKENZIE Alice MB ChB 1940
g p Aber from 1962

McKENZIE Andrew Stuart *MA 1951 *MEd 1953
Fife: prin teacher Engl Balwearie s s 1962–65, dep head 1965–67; head King's Rd s s 1967–72; rector Inverkeithing h s from 1972

MACKENZIE Angus BSc(agr) 1926
no longer on GC reg

MACKENZIE or Bowie, Anne *MA 1937
teacher Sellypark s Birm 1956–75

MACKENZIE Annie BSc 1928 *1929
retd Keith 1966; resid Elgin

MacKENZIE or Slater, Annie Johanna MA 1940
d Aber 18.12.71 *A UR* XLIV 433

MACKENZIE or Murray, Annie Macleod
                              *MA 1945 PhD 1955

McKENZIE Archibald BSc(for) 1934
tea planter N Bengal 1934–40 and 1946–48; war serv 8th Gurkha Rifles 1941–46; Windsor Ontario: self-employed 1948–56, budget analyst Chrysler Canada 1956–72; retd 1973
m Ealing 21.6.45 Ivy F. Alliband d of William A. Lond

MACKENZIE Barbara BSc 1954
biochem Stirlingsh from 1959
m Glasg 7.4.61 Stuart O. Kermack BA(Oxon) advoc/ sheriff Forfar s of Stuart G. K. MA(Edin) Connell

McKENZIE Betty MA 1954
teacher: army s Famagusta Cyprus 1960–63, Mile End s Aber 1963–64, Farley j s Luton 1964–69, Engl s Addis Ababa Ethiopia 1969–74, Fraserburgh inf s from 1974

MACKENZIE or Gordon, Catherine Cowan
                              MA 1946
teacher: Victoria Rd s Aber 1947–49, Madras coll St And 1955–72, asst head Canongate s St And from 1972
husb d 7.6.63

McKENZIE or Cameron, Catherine Hay MA 1933
d Perthsh 16.10.74

MacKENZIE or Stratford, Cecilia Mary *MA 1932

McKENZIE Charles BSc(eng) 1954
sen eng AEI Automation Knutsford 1960–64; sect. eng GEC-Elliott Process Automation Leic 1964–69; chief eng GEC elect. proj Rugby from 1969
m Oldham 20.2.59 Margaret N. Oates SRN

MacKENZIE Charles Duncan PhD 1935
no longer on GC reg

McKENZIE Christina Frances MA 1920
no longer on GC reg

MACKENZIE Colin   MB ChB 1954
g p Stockton-on-Tees from 1959

MACKENZIE David Hart   MB ChB 1923
d 7.9.67 *AUR* XLII 185

MACKENZIE Donald   MB ChB 1928

McKENZIE Donald   BSc(agr) 1922
no longer on GC reg

MACKENZIE Donald   MA 1930
d 23.4.70

MacKENZIE Donald Kenneth Munro   MA 1954

MACKENZIE Donaldina   MA 1928
teacher Gravir p s Isle of Lewis 1929–42, Fr/Maths
Nicolson inst Stornoway 1942–67, spec asst 1967–69;
retd; resid Laxdale

McKENZIE Douglas Christie   MA 1924 BCom 1925

MACKENZIE Duncan Murdo   MA 1939
C of S min West par ch Kinross from 1962

McKENZIE Edith Middleton   *MA 1944

McKENZIE or Maclean, Eileen Mary   MA 1944

MACKENZIE or Cowell, Elizabeth Graham
                                           MA 1925
resid Findochty

MACKENZIE Elizabeth Margaret Fraser   MA 1946
sen exec off. MRC Lond till 1970
m Buckie 17.10.70 George C. Wilson BL(Glas) solic
s of George C. W. Coatbridge

McKENZIE or Cocker, Ethel Middleton   MA 1944

MACKENZIE Evan Alexander
                        MB ChB 1914 DPH 1920
d 24.8.68

MacKENZIE or MacLeod, Flora Elizabeth
                                           MA 1909
d Edin 18.9.76

MACKENZIE Forbes Alexander   MB ChB 1954
g p Eccles Lancs from 1955

MACKENZIE or Fraser, Frances Mary Clara
                        *MA 1949 *MEd 1951

MacKENZIE Francis Fiddes   MA 1901
no longer on GC reg

McKENZIE George Clark   *BSc 1949
prin teacher maths Elgin acad 1961–66; rector
Buckie h s from 1966

MACKENZIE George Doughty   MB ChB 1924
d Inv 30.1.61 *AUR* XXXIX 204

MacKENZIE George Anderson   *MA 1950
prin teacher mod lang: Bishopbriggs p s 1965–70,
Cathkin h s Cambuslang 1970–71; head upper s
Cathkin h s 1971–73, dep rector from 1973   – *cillin* 30/7/95

McKENZIE George Duncan
                        MB ChB 1930 DPH 1933
d Heaton, Bolton 13.12.74 *AUR* XLVI 238

MacKENZIE George Grant   BSc(agr) 1926
d Inv 30.8.73

McKENZIE George Horatius   *MA 1917 *BSc 1918
retd 1957; resid Saltcoats

MACKENZIE George Ironside   BSc(for) 1932
conserv for.: Cardiff 1960–64, Aber 1964–69; retd;
resid Lochcarron

MacKENZIE George Stephen   MA 1910
no longer on GC reg

MACKENZIE Grace   *BSc 1926
no longer on GC reg

MacKENZIE Hector Lyle   *MA 1929

McKENZIE or Newman, Helen Mackay
                        MA BSc 1930
res chem Brit indust sand Redhill 1950–72; retd;
resid Purley

MacKENZIE or Garden, Henrietta   MA 1921

MacKENZIE Hugh   BSc(agr) 1938
nat agr advis serv 1946–72; retd; tech rep Weston
pharm Spalding from 1972

McKENZIE Hugh Pearce   *MA 1951

MACKENZIE Hugh Skinner   *MA 1899 BD 1904
d Edin 28.2.60 *AUR* XXXVIII 584

MACKENZIE Ian   BSc(eng) 1953
group leader eng Inv c c from 1974

MACKENZIE Ian Alexander Ross   MB ChB 1939
g p Tutbury Burton-on-Trent from 1947; pres
Derby med soc 1974–75; retd 1976; resid Norfolk

McKENZIE Ian Kindness   *MA 1951

MACKENZIE Ian Lorimer   BSc(agr) 1939
DAFS: sen insp (GD) N area Thurso 1959–66,
NE area Aber 1966–71; div agr off. St Andrew's Ho
Edin from 1971

MacKENZIE or Mills, Iris Susan   MA 1935
resid Inv

MacKENZIE Isabel   *MA 1911
no longer on GC reg

MACKENZIE or James, Isabel Elizabeth
                        MB ChB 1940 DPH 1957
resid Bieldside Aber

MacKENZIE or Milne, Isabella Flora
               MB ChB 1922
   retd; resid Sutton Coldfield
husb *d* 9.9.71

MACKENZIE or Macdonald, Isabella MacIntosh
               MA 1930
   d Skye 29.1.80 road accident

McKENZIE James   MB ChB 1924
   d Lumsden 5.10.67 *AUR* XLII 363

McKENZIE James   MB ChB 1944
   FRCS(Eng) 1961 FRSM 1962
ENT regist Manc R I 1957–61; sen ENT regist royal
hosp Wolverhampton 1961–62; consult. ENT surg
Wolverhampton and Dudley/Stourbridge group of
hosps from 1962

McKENZIE James Alexander   MB ChB 1937
   retd 1971; resid Bibury Cirencester

MacKENZIE James Ross   MB ChB 1906 *MD 1912
   d Aber 24.9.63 *AUR* XL 301

MACKENZIE James Ross   MB ChB 1946

MacKENZIE James Strath   MA 1939
   ptnr Brander & Cruickshank advoc Aber from
1954

MACKENZIE Jane   *MA 1925
   retd; resid Stornoway

MACKENZIE or Holt, Jane   MA 1936
   d 20.4.71

McKENZIE Janie   MA 1909
   d 22.10.69

MACKENZIE or Dunlop, Jean Gordon   MA 1945
   resid Eastbourne

MACKENZIE or Smeeton, Jeanette Campbell
               MA 1949

McKENZIE or Reid, Jessie   MA 1929
   teacher Engl: Blackwell s mod s Headstone Harrow
1949–56; Heath Park girls' s Romford 1956–68; retd;
resid Peterculter

McKENZIE or Harvey-Williams, Jessie Agnes
               MA 1932
   teacher Brecon Wales from 1964
husb *d* –.10.64

McKENZIE or Hudson, Jessie Marian
               MB ChB 1937
   d Lond 3.1.68 *AUR* XLII 371

MACKENZIE Jessie Marie Ursula   *MA 1931
   d Aber 1.1.80

MACKENZIE John   MA 1896 MB ChB 1900
   d 2.11.70 *AUR* XLIV 107

McKENZIE John   BSc 1931
   head Crimond s from 1956; retd 1971; resid
Stonehaven

MACKENZIE John   MA 1939
   no longer on GC reg

McKENZIE John   MB ChB 1944 MD 1957
   Aberd: sen lect embryol 1955–63, reader 1963–69,
reader and head of dept of dev biol from 1969

McKENZIE John   *BSc(agr) 1951
   no longer on GC reg

MacKENZIE John Angus   MA 1912
   no longer on GC reg

McKENZIE John Grant   MA 1910 BD 1912 DD 1939
   d Edin 17.5.63 *AUR* XL 199

MacKENZIE John Mearns   MA 1949

MacKENZIE John Moir   MA 1911 MB ChB 1915
   d Aber 25.12.71 *AUR* XLIV 428

McKENZIE John Robbie   MA 1909
   d Aber 24.3.69 *AUR* XLIII 209

McKENZIE John Ross   MA 1918
   no longer on GC reg

McKENZIE Joseph Morrison   MB ChB 1923
   g p Dewsbury 1923–26, Newport E Yorks from
1926

MacKENZIE Kenneth   MA 1922
   d Inv 1.1.65 *AUR* XLI 57

MACKENZIE Kenneth   PhD 1931

MacKENZIE Kenneth   MA 1940
   d Edin 18.2.71 *AUR* XLIV 215

MACKENZIE Kenneth Campbell   MB ChB 1925
   g p Kent; retd; emigrated to NZ 1976

MacKENZIE Kenneth Pirie   MA 1910 MB ChB 1914
   d Inv 7.3.68 *AUR* XLII 348

MACKENZIE or Wishart, Lilian   *MA 1929
   resid Bromley

MacKENZIE or Clark, Lilias Stuart Fraser
               *MA 1932
   resid Juniper Green, Midlothian

MACKENZIE Maimie Margaret   *MA 1952
   asst youth employ. off. Maidenhead 1964–65, lect
Engl E Berks coll of f e 1965–68; resid Reading
m Maidenhead 28.10.67 Arthur E. Tucker acct/bursar
Birkbeck coll Lond s of Frederick T. Muddiford nr
Barnstaple

MACKENZIE or Gow, Mairi   MB ChB 1951
   assist psychiat Craig Dunain hosp Inv from 1967

MACKENZIE Margaret Elizabeth Fraser
MB ChB 1946
hosp apptments Scot., Canada, England to 1955; g
p: Beauly 1955–60, Inv from 1960

MACKENZIE or Craig, Margaret Findlay Brown
MA 1942
teacher: Engl/maths W Byfleet c s s Surrey 1957–64,
Engl Robert May's s Odiham 1964–69, maths St
Nicholas indep s Fleet from 1969

MACKENZIE Margaret Jean   MA 1941
head Lochcarron p s from 1966

MACKENZIE Margaret Rankin   *MA 1913
resid Beauly
d Inv 9.3.78

McKENZIE or Laws, Margaret Ross
MA 1934 MB ChB 1939
g p Hetton le Hole Co Durham (Tyne & Wear)
1954–70, ptnr in Hetton group pract from 1970

MACKENZIE Margaret Troup
MA 1913 ᵈBL 1921 ᵈLLB 1922
d Golspie 11.2.71 *A UR* XLIV 209

MacKENZIE Mary   MA 1937

MacKENZIE or Murchison, Mary Flora   MA 1943
teacher classics Plockton sen s s from 1947
husb *d* 20.7.69

McKENZIE or Cook, Mary Gillieson   MA 1941
b 6.2.21
pers man. Brit Indust Plastics Oldbury, Warley, W
Midlands from 1942
husb *d* 20.8.74

MacKENZIE or Walker, Mary Mollison   MA 1915
d 30.3.81

MACKENZIE May Orme   MA 1904
no longer on GC reg

MacKENZIE or Rundle, Moira Elizabeth Grace
MA 1951
resid Crieff

MacKENZIE Murdo   MA 1915
no longer on GC reg

MACKENZIE Murdoch Roderick   *MA 1951
asst prin teacher Engl Kirkcaldy h s 1959–68; prin
Engl Broxburn acad W Lothian 1968–70, Perth acad
from 1970

MACKENZIE Myra Aileen   MA 1954
m Gill

McKENZIE Nellie Baring   MA 1945
teacher: Markinch 1945–48, Muir of Ord 1948–51,
Blantyre Malawi 1951–52, Tokoroa NZ 1952–60,
Ullapool from 1964
m Blantyre Malawi 9.6.51 Louis O. Vernon bus. man.
s of René L. V. Beja, Tunisia

MACKENZIE Niven St Clair   *MA 1932
retd 1974; resid Aber

MACKENZIE Norman   BSc 1949 *1950 PhD 1953
indust liaison off. RGIT Aber from 1963

MACKENZIE Rhoda Jane   MA 1931
teacher Rosssh: Munlochy 1939–48, Fodderty from
1948

MACKENZIE Robert Fraser   *MA 1931
prin teacher Engl Templehall j s Kirkcaldy 1952–57;
head: Braehead j s Buckhaven 1957–68, Summerhill
acad Aber 1968–74; retd
m Kingston-on-Thames 5.2.45 Diana C. Lister d of
Harold S. L.
publ: *A Question of Living, Escape from the Classroom,
The Sins of the Children, State School, The Unloved
Head*

McKENZIE Roderick Eddison   MB ChB 1938

MacKENZIE or Paterson, Rosabelle   MA 1935
resid Crieff

MACKENZIE Roy John   MB ChB 1928

MacKENZIE or Hunter, Sandra Ishbel   MA 1951
teacher Fr/Ger Nairn acad 1961–70, prin Fr/Ger
1970–73; prin teacher mod lang Millburn acad Inv
from 1974
m(2) Nairn 5.10.73 Daniel B. Grant MA(Edin) prin
teacher geog s of Daniel A. S. G. Inv

MACKENZIE or Lawn, Sheila Isabelle   MA 1946

McKENZIE or Sinclair, Sheila Kennedy   MA 1951
resid Aber

MACKENZIE Somerled Macdonald   MB ChB 1954
d Aber 9.6.76 *A UR* XLVII 106

MACKENZIE Thomas   MA 1926
min health & local govt Lond: chief exec off.
1958–65; retd; higher exec off. 1965–70; temp serv:
with Road trans and gen insur comp Putney 1970–71,
with Leach Bright & Co CA Richmond 1971–72;
retd; resid E Sheen

MacKENZIE William Alexander
BSc 1949 *1950 MEd 1976
ARIC 1962
prin teacher sc Peterhead acad 1962–68; lect chem
coll of educ from 1968
m Aber 4.7.60 Dorothea M. Still bank clerk d of
James S. Aber

MacKENZIE William Henry   MA 1948

McKENZIE William Thomas Daniel   MB ChB 1948
MRCGP 1952
g p Thornhill Dumfriessh and clin asst Thornhill hosp
from 1961; assoc advis g p

MACKENZIE or Camps, Winifred Mary Ross
MB ChB 1936
d Lond 15.4.75

McKERLIE Alan   MB ChB 1937

McKERRON Robert Gordon   *MA 1922
d Cape Town 14.4.72 *AUR* XLV 225

McKERRON Charles   MB ChB 1910
no longer on GC reg

McKERROW William Alexander Hogg
***MB ChB 1906**
d 9.3.72

McKESSACK Peter   BSc 1892 MB ChB 1896
no longer on GC reg

MACKESSACK Robert John   MA 1899
d 9.3.70 *AUR* XLIII 440

McKIDDIE John Macdonald   MB ChB 1937
FRCOG 1965
consult. obst/gyn Wakefield from 1950

MACKIE Adam Argo   MB ChB 1942
d Maryfield, Sask 14.9.69 *AUR* XLIII 331

MACKIE Alastair Webster   *MA 1950
teacher Engl: spec asst Ward acad Anstruther from 1974

MACKIE Alexander George Angus   *BSc(eng) 1932
MInstCE 1939
RE (supp reserve) 1935–41; final rank capt; civ eng Holloway Bros (Lond) 1941–59; man. dir Beechdale Eng from 1959
m Sandal 10.10.42 Joan Froggart d of Frank F. Sandal

MACKIE or Sim, Annie   MA 1931
head Cookney p s Stonehaven till closed 1969; teacher Newtonhill p s from 1969

MACKIE or Aitken, Catherine Hay   MB ChB 1945
part-time clin m o Enfield & Harringey AHA 1970–72; part-time g p Hornsey 1972–77; clin asst dermat Whittington hosp from 1977

MACKIE or Shepherd, Elizabeth Reid   MA 1940
resid Newburgh Aberdeensh

MACKIE or Horne, Elsie   MB ChB 1921
no longer on GC reg

MACKIE or Whyte, Eveline   MA 1927
resid Peterhead

MACKIE Evelyn Mary   MA 1950

MACKIE or Birkett, Gertrude Joan   MA 1948

MACKIE Gordon Moggach   BCom 1937
prin teacher comm subj Peterhead acad 1939–70; retd

m Aber 19.7.41 Winifred G. McGibbon d of Robert McG. Edin

MACKIE or MacDonald, Helen   MA 1913
d Lond 18.5.60 *AUR* XXXVIII 590

MACKIE Ian Alexander   MB ChB 1954

MACKIE Isabella Farquhar   MA 1917
teacher: Monymusk p s 1939–40, maths St Margaret's s for girls Aber 1944; retd; resid Monymusk
d 4.9.81

MACKIE James Farquharson   MB ChB 1947
MRCGP 1958
g p Walthamstow from 1950
wife *d* 1967
m(2) Lond 10.10.68 Marjorie Eaves d of George E. Worksop

MACKIE James Robertson Monro
MB ChB 1932 *MD 1934
FRCP(Lond) 1970 FRCPsych 1972
consult. psychiat Leeds & Bradford area 1950–71; retd; resid Lumphanan

MACKIE James Sinclair   *BSc 1951 PhD 1956
Canada: post grad fell. NRC Ottawa 1954–56; res chem Can. indust lab McMasterville and Kingston Ont 1957–69; tech man. Chancell Montreal from 1969
m Montreal 6.5.60 Jeanine Enos

MACKIE or Allan, Jean   *MA 1929
dir St Nicholas s Aber/Aberdeensh 1949–72
resid Methlick and Lincoln

MACKIE Jean Grant   MA 1915
d 19.7.64 *AUR* XL 398

MACKIE Jessie Christina   MA 1929
teacher Broomhill p s Aber 1961–70; retd

MACKIE Lewis   MB ChB 1944
MRCGP 1965
g p Oldmeldrum from 1959

MACKIE Maitland   BSc(agr) 1932 LLD 1976
JP 1964 CBE 1965 FEIS 1971 FR(Ag)S 1973 KtOStJ 1977
Lord lieut Aberdeensh from 1975; convener Aber county council 1970–75; chmn Aber and dist milk market. board from 1960; vice chmn NOSCA 1975
wife *d* Rothienorman 1960
m(2) Texas 19.10.63 Pauline M. McCalip BSc(Baylor Texas) d of Edwin L. McC. MD(Vanderbilt) Weslaco Texas

MACKIE Margaret   MA 1920
no longer on GC reg

MACKIE Margaret Isobel   *MA 1936
MVO 4th class 1958; Officer of the Order of Orange Nassau 1958; 1st secy dip serv
d Auchencairn 13.6.71

MACKIE or Large, Mary   BCom 1935 MA 1936
farmer: memb BBC agr advis comm; chmn Kesteven coll of educ
husb *d* 19.9.73

MACKIE or Johnston, Mary   MA 1955

MACKIE or Mucha, Muriel Jean   MB ChB 1950
d Dumfries 18.1.67 *AUR* XLII 374

MACKIE Ninian   *MA 1945
solic Arthur Hunt & Hunt Lond
d Lond 20.11.69 *AUR* XLIII 446

MACKIE William   MB ChB 1931 DPH 1948
dep sen admin m o SE reg hosp board Edin 1963–69; retd from NHS 1969; consult. to Johnson & Johnson Slough and to Smith & Nephew Welwyn 1970–71; retd; resid Chudleigh

MACKIE William Souter   *MA 1906
MA(Oxon) 1970
resid Cape Town
wife *d* 1965
d Cape Town 17.6.80 *AUR* XLIX 66

MACKIE Williamina Stephen   MA 1924

McKILLIGAN Robert Falconer   MA 1910

MacKILLIGAN Winifred   MA 1915
no longer on GC reg

McKILLIGIN or Banyard, Eileen Mary   *MA 1929
resid Dorchester

McKILLOP Annie Buchanan Erskine   MA 1950
teacher: Craighill p s Aber 1966–71, remed Tullos p s Aber from 1971

MACKILLOP or Donald, Elizabeth Mary   MA 1951
resid Stellenbosch S Af

**McKILLOP William Lawie Mitchell
                           BSc(for) 1954 *1957**
MSc(for) (univ of New Brunswick Can) 1959
PhD/MA (Berkeley Calif USA) 1965
for. off. Can dept for. Ottawa 1958–61; USA: asst prof univ of Calif Berkeley 1964–69, assoc prof from 1969

McKIM Mary Agnes Gardner   MA 1908
d Glasg 9.12.72

McKIM Roberta Jane   MA 1912
d Paisley 2.11.67 *AUR* XLII 350

McKIMMIE Michael McKerrow   *MA 1952

**McKINLAY or Sheale, Margaret
                           MA 1941 *MEd 1943**
educ psych Ealing from 1966

MACKINNON or Cummins, Agnes Evelyn   MA 1949
supply teacher: Currie 1966–68, Edin 1968–70; teacher Blackhall Edin from 1970

MACKINNON Alan   *BSc 1911 *MA 1924
d Belfast 28.3.71 *AUR* XLIV 209

**MACKINNON or Beedie, Christina Margaret
                                            MA 1942**
year mistress Hilton acad Aber from 1971

MacKINNON Donald Norman   MB ChB 1925
d Wigan –.8.71

**MACKINNON Douglas Nelson
                           MA 1937 MB ChB 1943**
OBStJ 1968 MRCGP 1969
g p Bolton from 1947

MACKINNON Edgar Charles   MA 1949

**MACKINNON or Cochran, Elizabeth Agnes
                                            MA 1934**
various posts since leaving Kenya 1968; resid Ballitoville, Natal

MacKINNON Fiona Rose   *MA 1955
teacher Falkirk h s 1956, later actg prin Woodlands h s Falkirk

MACKINNON George Duff Gordon   MA LLB 1949
Chevalier De L'Ordre National Du Mérite France 1974
ptnr L Mackinnon & Son advoc Aber from 1949; relinquished comm 51(H) div signal regt TA 1960; chief signal off. Highland dist with rank of col 1960–64

MACKINNON or Greig, Helen   MA 1947
d Sedgefield 22.4.72 *AUR* XLV 128

MACKINNON or Spicer, Jane Gordon   *MA 1950
on staff of *Queen* mag from 1954; resid Putney Lond

MacKINNON Kenneth   MB ChB 1905

**MACKINNON Lachlan
                           MA 1906 ᵈBL 1908 LLB 1910**
d Aber 10.8.73 *AUR* XLV 316

MACKINNON Neil Ormiston   MB ChB 1924
d Lond 22.10.65 *AUR* XLII 86

McKINNON Norman   BSc(for) 1923

MACKINNON Roderick   MA 1928
jubilee medal 1935
C of S min: Contin 1960–70, Is of Barra from 1970
m Nigg Rosssh 22.8.42 Eileen G. Mackay d of Norman D. M. Nigg

MACKINNON Ronald Lee   BL 1951
ptnr Milne & Mackinnon advoc Aber from 1969

**MACKINNON Walter Grieve
                           BSc 1923 *MB ChB 1935**
g p Derby from 1936
d Derby 17.4.78 *AUR* XLVII 356

MACKINNON William Calthorpe
                    MA 1913 MB ChB 1917
 d Aber 22.5.73 *AUR* XLV 317

MACKINNON William Lunan   *MA 1911 *1912
 no longer on GC reg

MACKINTOSH Alexanderina   **MA 1919**
 teacher maths Inv h s 1922–63; retd
d Inv 15.1.81

MACKINTOSH Angus   **MB ChB 1911**
 no longer on GC reg

MACKINTOSH or Cramond, Bertine Janet Cameron
                    MB ChB 1947
 psychiat m o Adelaide S Aust 1962–71; regist dept
psych med RHSC Edin 1971–72; asst ch psychiat
Leics ch guid clin and adolescent unit 1972–75; part
time regist, sen regist dept ch and adolescent psychiat
RI Stirling from 1976 and at RHSC Glasg

MACKINTOSH Christina Mary   **MA 1917**

MACKINTOSH or Garrett, Elizabeth   *MA 1953

MACKINTOSH or Raithby, Elizabeth Ashen
                    MA 1914

MACKINTOSH or Chisholm, Fanny Bissett
                    *BSc 1926
 retd 1969; resid Strathpeffer
d 7.2.78 *AUR* XLVIII 104

MACKINTOSH Finlay George   **MB ChB 1937**

MACKINTOSH Herbert   **MA 1921**
 no longer on GC reg

MACKINTOSH Hugh Stewart   **PhD 1941**
 FEIS 1958 LLD(Glas) 1969
dir of educ Glasg 1944–68; retd

MACKINTOSH Ian   **MB ChB 1927**
 part time indust m o Kodak 1954–64; chief m o
Shell-Mex and BP Lond from 1964

MACKINTOSH or Park, Isabella Jean Robertson
                    BSc MA 1935
 resid Aber
husb *d* Aber 3.12.76

MACKINTOSH James   **MA 1929**
 d Inv 22.12.61 *AUR* XXXIX 282

MACKINTOSH James Maclean   **BSc(agr) 1950**

MACKINTOSH John   **MA 1916 *1919**
 edit. vol III *Roll of Graduates* published 1960
d Aber 11.12.67 *AUR* XLII 354

MACKINTOSH Kenneth   **MA 1924**
 clergyman/teacher Milne's h s Fochabers 1951–68;
retd; resid Cullen
wife *d* 14.2.72

MacKINTOSH Lily Fraser   **MA 1931**
 no longer on GC reg

MACKINTOSH or Brooker, Mabel Wilson   **MA 1920**
 resid Aber
d Ballater 25.2.81

MACKINTOSH or Stewart, Nini Isabel   **MA 1928**
 teacher Seremban convent s Malaya 1952–65; retd;
resid Nairn

MACKINTOSH Robert   **MA 1910 DD 1950**
 d Edin 1.1.62 *AUR* XXXIX 273

MACKINTOSH Thomas   **BSc(agr) 1921**
 no longer on GC reg

McKINTY Henry Bernard   **BL 1922 BCom 1922**
 d Aber 13.10.68 *AUR* XLIII 83

MACKNIGHT James Russell Chalmers   **BSc 1952**
 farms man. Aberdeensh 1952–57; crop husb advis
Dept Agr Malta 1958–60; agr advis Fisons NI/Scot.
1962–73; dep secy Royal Highland & Agr Soc
Ingliston Edin from 1973
d 2.8.81

MACKWORTH Norman Humphrey   **MB ChB 1939**

McLACHLAN Douglas Gordon   **BSc(agr) 1950**
 RD 1969
asst lands off. DAFS: Thurso 1964–68; lands off. Inv
1968–75; sen lands off. Oban from 1975
RNR from 1956 lt comm
marr diss 1964
m(2) Oban 7.4.64 Mary F. Hunter teacher

MacLACHLAN John Low   **BSc 1955 DipEd 1956**

MACLACHLAN John Scott   **MA 1935 LLB 1937**
 d Aber 7.9.71 *AUR* XLIV 321

McLAGGAN John Douglas
                    MA 1914 *MB ChB 1920
 d 1.1.67 *AUR* XLII 182

McLAREN Alexander   *BSc 1941 PhD 1948

MACLAREN Atholl Hutchison   **MB ChB 1942**
 MRCGP 1960
Nott: g p from 1948, clin asst phys med city hosp from
1961; chmn Notts loc med comm; vice chmn Notts
fam pract comm; pres elect Nott Medico Chirurgical
Soc

MACLAREN David Martin   *MA 1950
 MRCPE 1963 MD(Lond) 1967 FRCPath 1977
David Bruce labs Wiltshire 1960–61; lect bact Guy's
hosp Lond 1961–64; consult. group path. Stockport
Cheshire 1964–74; prof clin bact Amsterdam from
1974

McLAREN George Neil   **MB ChB 1925**
 g p Darlington 1935–61; retd; resid Dalbeattie
d Kippford 16.5.77

MACLAREN Hugh McCallum *MA 1954
prin teacher sc West Calder h s 1960–63; prin phys Stirling h s 1963–69; HMIS North div from 1969; resid Bieldside, Aber

McLAREN or Macleod, Isabella Morrison MA 1916
d Inv 9.10.66 *A UR* XLII 85

McLAREN John MA 1897
no longer on GC reg

MacLAREN Mary Jane Mowat MB ChB 1918
d 21.5.76

McLAREN Robert Gordon Alexander
                    MB ChB 1927 MD 1938
retd 1968; resid Maidstone

McLAREN or Hutchings, Shelagh Isobel MA 1947
appliance off. ARI from 1959

McLAREN Agnes MA 1916
d Fraserburgh 4.3.70 *A UR* XLIII 442

MacLEAN or Wedderspoon, Agnes King Johnston
                    MA 1953

McLEAN Alexander *MA 1919
d Alloa 16.5.64 *A UR* XL 399

MACLEAN Alexander MA 1939
bldg contr Sydney/Bathurst Aust from 1949

MACLEAN Alexander John MA 1929
retd 1971; resid Isle of Lewis

MACLEAN or Macaulay, Alexandra Campbell
                    MA 1930
d 6.7.73

MACLEAN Allan James *MA 1931
prin teacher phys Dunfermline h s from 1944; retd 1974

MACLEAN Andrew Iain MB ChB 1943
g p Hull from 1947

McLEAN Andrew Lewis BSc(agr) 1951

MACLEAN Angus MA 1922
d Kingussie 27.2.69 *A UR* XLIII 212

MACLEAN Angus MA 1929

MACLEAN Anne Matheson MA 1928
teacher Nicolson inst Stornoway/Stornoway p s 1959–72; retd; resid Tong Isle of Lewis

MACLEAN or Brakebill, Annie (Nan) MA 1941

MACLEAN or Petrie, Cairine Ross
                    *MA 1940 *MEd 1954
ABPsS
teacher Ruthrieston s Aber 1958–68; sen educ psych Aber c c 1968–75; prin psych NE List 'D' schools Scotland from 1975

publ: Backward or Maladjusted Children in Secondary School (Ward Lock) 1970; *Child Guidance* with D. A. F. Conochie (Macmillan) 1975
husb *d* 1966
m(2) Aber 11.10.80 Douglas A. F. Conochie BSc 1949 *qv*

MacLEAN Colin George *MA 1950
sub edit. *Daily Telegraph* Lond 1960–61; asst edit. letters to edit. *The Times* Lond 1961–65; edit. *Times Educational Supp* Scot. Edin 1965–77; gen and educ edit. W. & R. Chambers Edin 1977–79; publ dir AUP from 1979

MACLEAN Donald *MA 1902
d Edin 4.1.62 *A UR* XXXIX 270

McLEAN Donald Patrick *MA 1940
dir admin Fife reg; retd

McLEAN or Henderson, Dorothy Elizabeth
                    MA 1930
teacher Rosehill s amalgamated with Cornhill s Aber 1962–70; retd
marr diss 1947

McLEAN Douglas Gordon MA 1920
retd 1963; resid Longniddry

MACLEAN Duncan MA 1949
head Barvas s Is of Lewis from 1961

McLEAN or Clark, Eileen Mary MA 1946
resid Wolverhampton

MACLEAN Ewen MA 1906
no longer on GC reg

McLEAN Frank Summers MB ChB 1925

McLEAN or Smith, Helen MA 1910
d Aber 13.4.66 *A UR* XLII 83

MACLEAN or Rowlands, Helen Campbell Smith
                    MB ChB 1935
d Aber 3.1.71 *A UR* XLIV 212

MACLEAN Henry Ross Colquhoun MB ChB 1944
g p Brentford from 1954

McLEAN Ian Cook MB ChB 1953
g p: Corinda Brisbane Aust from 1963

MACLEAN Isabel Grant Morrice
                    MA 1943 LLB 1949
resid Aber

McLEAN James Alexander Forbes
                    *MB ChB 1937 DPH 1941
MRCPath 1964 FRCPath 1965
consult. bact Mile End hosp Lond from 1964

McLEAN James Johnston MA 1931
d Aber 24.4.67 *A UR* XLII 370

McLEAN Janetta Christian   MA 1926
retd 1964; resid Glasg

McLEAN or Murray, Jessie Fraser   MA 1919
d Aber 20.1.75

MACLEAN John   *MA 1909 BSc 1910
d 5.10.64

MacLEAN John   BSc(agr) 1923
retd 1966
d Aber 26.3.77

MACLEAN John Alexander
                    MA 1925 LLB 1930 PhD 1939
    CBE 1968
dir educ Invernesssh 1943–68; retd 1968; chmn N reg
hosp board from 1971; resid Inv

MACLEAN John Stewart   *MA 1940
    FEIS 1967
prin teacher Engl Buckie h s 1960–69; rector
Stromness acad from 1969
d 5.7.77 *AUR* xlviii 106

MACLEAN Kenneth John   MB ChB 1950
    DPH(Lond) 1965
surg cmdr RN 1959–68
d N'cle-u-Tyne 17.8.69

McLEAN Maitland Naisby   BSc 1944 *1949
    res/dev tech Kodak Harrow 1950–62; dev man./dir
Salford 1962–66; man. staff Kodak Harrow from
1966

McLEAN Margaret Elizabeth Bennet   MA 1938
    part time teacher mus Banffsh s from 1972

MACLEAN or Stalker, Mary Elizabeth Carmichael
                                MB ChB 1942
    g p Aber 1967–77; resid Banchory

McLEAN Muriel Margaret MB ChB 1942 ᶜMD 1955
    consult. paediat Clwyd AHA from 1957

MACLEAN Neil   MA 1949

McLEAN Nigel Hugh   BSc(eng) 1950

MACLEAN Nigel Ross   MA 1937 BD 1940
    C of S min St Paul's ch Perth from 1954

MACLEAN Roderick Charles
                    ***MA 1940 *MEd 1948**
    dir tv Glas univ 1965–69; dir audio-visual serv
Glas and Strath 1969–76; head centre for educ pract
Strath from 1976

MACLEAN Ronald   MB ChB 1930
    d Inv 28.10.68 *AUR* xliii 85

MACLEAN William Gordon   BD 1912
    min emeritus First Presb ch Winnipeg; moderator
Presb ch in Canada 1946–47
d 29.2.80

McLEAY Ella   MA 1935
    retd 1972; resid Auchenblae

McLELLAN Duncan Morison
                    ᶜMB ChB 1950 DPH 1958
    MFCM 1971
asst sen admin m o N reg hosp board 1961–65; dep
s a m o E reg hosp board 1965–68; group med supt
Ninewells and assoc hosps Dun 1968–71; m o/acting
dir Scot. hosp centre Edin from 1971

McLELLAN John Hugh Crawford   MA 1906
    d Crieff 10.1.75 *AUR* xlvi 234

McLEMAN Daniel   MB ChB 1955

McLEMAN Malcolm   *BSc 1951

McLEMAN William John Murdoch   BSc(eng) 1954
    MICE 1960
des off. Sir William Halcrow & ptnrs Lond 1959–60;
dir Smokeless Heating Bromley 1960–67; dir J.
McLeman Heating Chislehurst Kent from 1967
m Aber 2.3.61 Mary B. Mann d of Robert M. Aber

MacLENNAN Alastair   MB ChB 1934
    col staff appts Germany/Egypt/UK 1952–64; insp
trg army med serv M o D Lond 1964–66; DDMS h q
1st (Br) Corps Germany 1966–67; promoted to brig
DDMS h q southern command Hounslow/DD gen
army med serv Lond 1967–69; curator RAMC hist
museum Aldershot from 1969; rank of maj-gen as
retd off.
m Lond 4.7.40 Constance A. M. Cook d of Ambrose
C. Rowlands Castle

MACLENNAN Alexander Bain   BSc(eng) 1950

MACLENNAN or Mackenzie, Ann   MA 1913
    no longer on GC reg

MACLENNAN or Gallagher, Anne Gordon Innes
                                MB ChB 1925
worked for Nat Blood Transfusion Serv and Pension
Boards for Min of Pensions and locums Weymouth
1958–73
husb *d* 1956

MacLENNAN or Morrison, Catherine Mary
                                    MA 1923
    resid Croy

MacLENNAN Christopher   *MA 1927
    retd 1967; resid Blairgowrie

MacLENNAN Donald   MB ChB 1924
    Wales: consult. surg Llanelli hosp/Glamorgan
hosp/Carmarthen Inf 1934–68; retd
m Lond 18.7.38 Margaret Evans

MacLENNAN Donald Alexander   MA 1955

MacLENNAN Donald McKay   MA 1953

McLENNAN Douglas George   BSc(eng) 1945
    Assoc Brit Inst Radio Eng 1947

GEC Glasg branch: various appts from 1951
resid Crieff

MacLENNAN Duncan Anderson Macgregor
                                    MB ChB 1934
  d Dufftown 14.4.75 *AUR* XLVI 325

MACLENNAN or Young, Flora   MA 1906
  d Yorkshire 7.11.75

MACLENNAN George William Grant
                        MA 1926 BSc 1928 *1929
  no longer on GC reg

MacLENNAN Harrie   MA 1924
  retd 1969; resid Inv

MacLENNAN or Mackenzie, Janet   BSc 1920

MacLENNAN or Mackenzie, Joanna   MA 1924
  teacher Sanquhar acad Dumfriessh 1926–71; retd

MacLENNAN John   MB CM 1895 MD 1925
  d Nairn 8.5.61 *AUR* XXXIX 198

McLENNAN John Duncan   MB ChB 1934 *MD 1939
  d Washington DC 4.6.62 *AUR* XXXIX 385

MacLENNAN J. Munro   MA 1923 BSc 1925
  scient edit. Canberra Aust 1958–61; freelance
Russian–Engl translator Britain, Eire, Spain, Portugal,
Canada from 1961
  d Ottawa 4.12.75 *AUR* XLVI 416

MacLENNAN Kenneth   BSc(agr) 1912
  no longer on GC reg

McLENNAN Kenneth   MA 1896 BD 1903
  no longer on GC reg

McLENNAN or King, Lydia Mary   MA 1951
  teacher Hythehill p s Lossiemouth 1965–74, head
from 1974

MACLENNAN Norman Macpherson
                  MB ChB 1921 DPH 1923 MD 1924
  d 8.3.67

MacLENNAN Robert Cran   MB ChB 1920
  d –.12.65

MacLENNAN Robert William   MA 1902
  no longer on GC reg

MacLENNAN Roderick George Squair   *BSc 1955
  field and mining geol S Africa 1955–63; mining
geol: Nchanga Zambia 1963–66, Welkom OFS S Afr
1966–67; chief geol Vaal Reefs E & M Co S Af from
1967
  wife *d* 6.6.71
  m(2) Queenstown S Af 8.12.72 Gillian A. May d of
Harry W. M. Queenstown

MacLENNAN William George Duncan   *MA 1922
  retd 1966; resid Edin
  d –.2.81

MACLEOD Agnes Percy   *MA 1933

MACLEOD Alasdair Macgillivray   MA 1910
  no longer on GC reg

MACLEOD Alexander   MA 1920
  no longer on GC reg

McLEOD Alexander   MA 1951
  head Caol p s Fort William from 1963

MACLEOD Alexander Crichton
                            BSc 1954 PhD 1958
  DIC 1958
  scient off. AWRE 1958–60; sen scient Morganite res
and dev Lond 1960–67; sen lect metallurgy Strath
from 1967
  m Lond 11.3.61 Muriel O. Smith BSc(Swansea) res
phys chem/admin Stir d of James S. Bridgend Glam

McLEOD Alexander Grant   MA 1909
  no longer on GC reg

MACLEOD Alexander John   MA 1938
  teacher Gaelic Sir E. Scott s s Tarbert Harris
1955–74, dep head from 1974

McLEOD Alexander Luias   MB ChB 1924
  no longer on GC reg

MACLEOD Alice MacLennan   MA 1954

MACLEOD Alick John   MA 1949
  teacher Oban h s from 1953

MACLEOD Alister Ian   MB ChB 1945
  reg m o DHSS Manc from 1966

MACLEOD Allan John   MB ChB 1910
  no longer on GC reg

MACLEOD Angus   BSc(agr) 1911
  tech off. DAOS Stornoway 1958–62; retd; resid
Stornoway
  wife *d* 1.8.68

MacLEOD Angus   MA 1927
  d Fordoun 22.7.64 *AUR* XL 400

MACLEOD Angus   MA 1929
  d 17.6.67

MACLEOD Angus Maclennan   MB ChB 1952
  g p: Arisaig 1958–65, Mallaig 1965–68, Fort
William 1968–69, Strachur Argyll 1969–75, Dunoon
from 1975

MACLEOD Anne Stewart   MA 1954
  DipEd(Edin) 1963
  teacher Bathgate: j s s 1963–65, tech coll 1965–67;
Canada: teacher Merritt h s B C 1967–68, L V Rogers
h s Nelson B C 1968–70; teacher Clackmannan coll of
f e Alloa from 1970
  m Muckhart Perthsh 28.12.73 William G. Sanderson
BSc(H-W) mining eng

McLEOD or Clarke, Barbara Louie   MA 1952

MACLEOD or Macdonald, Bella   MA 1931
resid Conon Bridge

MACLEOD Calum Alexander   MA 1955 LLB 1957
comm RAEC Belfast/Manc 1958–60; ptnr
Paull & Williamsons advoc Aber from 1964; chancellor's assessor Aberd from 1979
m Inv 21.7.62 Elizabeth M. Davidson teacher d of
David D. Inv

MacLEOD Calum Murray   MA 1952 LLB 1964
teacher Bervie j s Inverbervie 1961–63; leg app and
solic 1964–70; solic: Dun 1970–73, on own account
Broughty Ferry 1973–77; acquired law firm T. & J. W
Laverock Dun 1977

MacLEOD or MacLure, Catherine   MA 1950

McLEOD Charles   MB ChB 1946
short serv comm RN 1957–61; g p: Ripley 1961–67,
Elgin from 1967
m Lond 1959 Margaret E. Redman SRN d of
Christopher E. R. Southwold

McLEOD Charles Stewart   *MA 1924
OBE 1961 FCIT C St J
BR from 1948: chief indust relations off. 1962–68;
retd. Author *All Change* Rly indust relations in the
Sixties publ Gower Press 1970

MACLEOD Christina   MA 1911
d Inv 25.9.71 *A UR* XLIV 316

MacLEOD or Mackay, Christina Margaret
                                              *MA 1941

MACLEOD or Reid, Christine Soldan   *MA 1938
head mod lang dept Lady Eleanor Holles s
Hampton from 1966; retd 1975
husb d 26.3.77

MACLEOD David Macgregor
                          BSc 1949 *1950 PhD 1953

MACLEOD Donald   MA 1932
d Bettyhill 14.5.77

MACLEOD Donald   MA 1936
JP
d 10.12.71

MACLEOD Donald   MA 1950
teacher W. Calder h s Midlothian 1960–63; prin
maths Tarbert s s from 1963
m Dennyloanhead 7.4.66 Janet C. W. Thomson
teacher dom subj d of William T. Banknock by
Bonnybridge

MACLEOD Donald John   MA 1947
dep head Shawbost j s s 1949–65; head Valtos s Uig
1965–74; asst head Stornoway p s from 1974
m Glasg 15.7.65 Alexina Macdonald teacher d of
Donald M. Shawbost

MACLEOD Donald John   MA 1954
d 1972

MACLEOD Donald Norman   MA 1947

MacLEOD Donovan Hutcheson   MB ChB 1953
d Essex 23.2.72 *A UR* XLIV 434

MacLEOD Douglas Haig   *BSc(agr) 1941

MACLEOD Duncan   MB ChB 1924
d Stornoway 17.10.60 *A UR* XXXIX 204

MacLEOD Duncan   MA 1927
d Aber 11.3.65 *A UR* XLI 151

MacLEOD Duncan   MA 1934
head Gairloch j s s Ross from 1949; retd

MACLEOD Elizabeth Jane   MA 1952
teacher Engl Fortrose acad 1973–74; asst prin Engl
from 1974

MACLEOD or Catto, Elizabeth Kate   MA 1917
d Stracathro 15.2.79 *A UR* XLVIII 227

MACLEOD Eric Campbell   MB ChB 1954
DPM 1960 LMCC 1965 MRCPsych 1973
FRCP(Can) 1973
sen regist dept psych med Glas 1961–64; Canada: dir
psychiat unit Sudbury gen hosp Ont/consult. psychiat
Sudbury mem hosp and Sudbury Algoma sanatorium
from 1964

MACLEOD George   MA 1948
JP
d 10.5.69 *A UR* XLIII 217

McLEOD George Johnston   *MA 1932
prin teacher classics Montrose acad 1952–71; retd

MACLEOD Hughina Aird   MA 1912
no longer on GC reg

MACLEOD Ian   MB ChB 1948
g p Kilwinning from 1968

MacLEOD Ian Ingram Scott   ᵈBD 1952
C of S min St Andrew's ch Arbroath from 1959

MACLEOD Isabella   MA 1910
no longer on GC reg

MACLEOD James   MA 1939
dep head Aber 1957–64; head Skene Square s Aber
from 1964

MacLEOD James William   BSc(eng) 1935

MACLEOD or Cumming, Jean   MA 1954
teacher Contin from 1968

MACLEOD or Lawrie, Johanna Annabella   MA 1950
teacher Inv h s 1963–70; head Aldourie p s Inv from
1971

MACLEOD John   MA 1908
  no longer on GC reg

MACLEOD John   MA 1936

McLEOD John Alexander   BSc(agr) 1951

MACLEOD John Angus   MA 1910
  retd 1950; resid Sunderland

McLEOD John Bryce   *MA 1950
  DPhil(Oxon) 1958 Whittaker Prize Edin math soc
  1965 FRSE 1974
  fell./lect Wadham coll Oxon from 1960; jun proctor
  1963–64; visiting prof univ of Wisconsin Madison
  USA 1964–65, 1970–71; visiting prof univ of
  Minnesota Minneapolis 1977–78

MACLEOD John Morrison   MA 1948
  JP
  head Dalneigh p s Inv 1961–68; Invernesssh: county
  advis for prim. educ 1968–73; asst dir of educ 1973–75;
  dep dir educ Highland reg c from 1975

MacLEOD John Murdo   MA 1923

MACLEOD John William   *BSc 1949

MACLEOD Kenneth   MA 1929
  d Lochaber –.5.63

MacLEOD Kenneth   MA 1951

MACLEOD Lachlan   MA 1921
  d Inv 30.3.66 *AUR* XLII 85

McLEOD Laura Stewart   *MA 1914
  no longer on GC reg

McLEOD or MacDonald, Lilian Mary   MA 1945
  retd 1971; resid New Elgin; resumed teaching Elgin
  acad 1976
  husb deceased

MACLEOD Mairi Elizabeth   MB ChB 1949
  g p Somercotes from 1964
  m Derbysh 9.5.64 George R. M. Sterland farm. s of
  George M. S. Pentrich

MACLEOD Mairi Matheson   MA 1954

MACLEOD Malcolm   MB ChB 1939 MD 1960

MACLEOD Malcolm   *MA 1950
  teacher classics/hostel warden Nicolson Inst
  Stornoway 1970–74; asst prin relig educ from 1974;
  prin classics from 1975

MACLEOD Malcolm Donald   *BSc(eng) 1950
  prof eng Shell-Mex & BP Lond 1962–63; reg eng
  Shell & BP Scot. Glasg 1963–75; Shell UK Oil:
  aviations oper man. Lond 1975–76, reg oper man.
  Glasg 1976–79, man. plant & admin dept Lond from
  1979
  m Glasg 26.4.62 Anne MacDonald secy d of Angus
  MacD. Glasg

MACLEOD Malcolm Murdo   MA 1950

MACLEOD Malcolmina   MA 1935

MACLEOD Margaret Jean   MA 1931

MacLEOD Margaret MacLennan   MA 1950
  teacher: Crimond s 1951–67, Strichen s from 1967
  m Inv 28.12.60 Stanley J. Buchan farm. s of Patrick
  B. B. Philorth Fraserburgh

McLEOD or Beveridge, Margaret Patricia   MA 1925
  resid St And

MacLEOD or O'Gorman, Marie Eaton   *BSc 1941

MACLEOD Marion   MB ChB 1938
  no longer on GC reg

MACLEOD or MacAskill, Marion Macaulay
                                            MA 1930
  d 22.11.68

MACLEOD or Caie, Mary   MA 1901
  d 22.2.69

McLEOD or Burton, Morag Grace   *BSc 1955
  resid Warrington

MacLEOD Murdo   MA 1922
  d 25.4.64 *AUR* XL 399

MACLEOD Murdo   MA 1928
  JP 1953
  teacher Shawbost s Ross & Cromarty 1936–43, head
  1943–53; head Bayble j s s 1953–71; retd; resid Brue,
  Barvas Is of Lewis
  m Aber 2.8.44 Isabella Morrison nurse d of Alexander
  M. Upper Barvas

MACLEOD Murdo   *MA 1950
  HMIS from 1969
  m Inv 4.4.63 Catherine Fraser RGN d of Alexander F.
  MA(Edin) Inv

MACLEOD or Clark, Muriel Rhoda   MA 1947
  resid Botswana
  m Drumnadrochit 16.12.52 Alexander J. F. Clark

MacLEOD Neil   MA 1927

MACLEOD Norman   MA 1933
  retd 1968; resid Aber

MACLEOD Norman   ᶜMB ChB 1951

MacLEOD Norman John   MA 1926
  d 24.3.66

McLEOD Patricia Ann Moir   MA 1923
  retd 1966; resid Aber

MACLEOD Roderick   MA 1927
  head Rothiemurchus s 1952–68
  d Inv 1.6.68

MACLEOD Roderick Forbes **MA 1953*
prin teacher Engl Grove acad Dun 1967–73; dep rector Webster's h s Kirriemuir from 1973

MACLEOD Roderick Macrae MA 1925
no longer on GC reg

MacLEOD Roderick Torquil BSc(for) 1955
assoc B C reg for.
Canada: asst for. Kamloops for. dist Br Col for. serv—silviculturist and gen management—1960–66; dist silviculturist and gen timber admin Prince Rupert for. dist 1966–72; dist appraisal off. and for. i/c East Kootenay zone Nelson for. dist from 1972

McLEOD Ronald **MA 1939*
prin teacher classics AGS from 1964; sqn ldr RAFVR 1961–77

MACLEOD or Lawrence, Sheila MA 1951
teacher Buckie p s from 1966

McLEOD Susie Milne MA 1922
head kindergarten dept RGC Aber 1947–54; retd; resid Aber

MacLEOD Thomas Finlay Bidgood MA 1949
JP
d Dufftown 27.5.72 *AUR* xlv 128

MACLEOD William **MA 1932*
d 24.1.66

MACLEOD William Ferrans MB ChB 1943
g p Cowdenbeath from 1947

McLUSKEY or Davidson, Margaret Beedie MA 1929

MACMAHON Antoinette Margaret Helen
MB ChB 1943
MRCPE 1962
med regist paediat Northern group of hosps Edin 1961–63; sen regist paediat S Warks hosps 1964–66; asst paediat Dumfries & Galloway Inf 1966–68; med missionary Serabu hosp via Bo Sierra Leone from 1969

MacMAHON Charles Grant MB ChB 1904
no longer on GC reg

MacMAHON or Burnett, Joan Elizabeth MA 1942

McMAHON John Robertson MA 1954

McMAHON Sheila MA 1947

MacMAHON or Christie, Teresa Mary MA 1949
resid Aber
d 4.3.81

MACMILLAN Alexander MA 1898
d Liverpool 2.1.61 *AUR* xxxix 98

MACMILLAN Alexander **MA 1910*
d 11.6.65

McMILLAN or MacDougall, Alice Malcolm
*MA 1933 BSc 1935 *1936
teacher Cornaigmore j s s Is of Tiree 1939–70; retd

McMILLAN or Dawson, Bethia Ross MA 1947
teacher: maths/sc Inverurie acad 1955–58, maths Milne's h s Fochabers 1963–72; maths and asst prin guid Milne's h s from 1972

MACMILLAN Duncan MA 1955
teacher Uddingston g s 1958–61; spec asst Whitehill s s Glasg/teacher Russian 1961–71; teacher Fr/asst prin guid Bishopbriggs h s 1971–73, prin guid from 1973
m Glasg 10.7.63 Margaret M. Shaw market res interviewer d of John J. S. Kildonan Is of Arran

McMILLAN Duncan Stewart **MA 1930*
d Lond 19.7.69 *AUR* xliii 331

MACMILLAN Elizabeth MA 1952

MACMILLAN James MA 1932
CA 1936
fin. dir John Summers & Sons Shotton Chester 1963–68, Holst & Co Watford 1968–72 chmn from 1969, Norwest Holst Bootle 1972–75

MACMILLAN John Murdo MA 1938
OBE 1972
head Back s s Is of Lewis from 1969

MacMILLAN or Watt, Lilias MacGregor MA 1915

MACMILLAN or Shepherd, Margaret Wallace
MA 1930
resid Grimsby

McMILLAN or Winchester, Mary **MA 1945*

MACMILLAN Matthew **MA 1950*
OBE 1976
assoc prof Engl univ coll of Cape Coast Ghana 1962–64; prof Engl univ of Khartoum 1965–70; Engl teaching div Brit Council Lond 1970–74; 1st secy educ Brit high comm New Delhi from 1974

McMILLAN Neil BSc 1952 **1953*

MACMILLAN William Boyd Robertson
MA 1951 *d*BD 1954
C of S min: Fyvie par ch 1960–67, Bearsden S ch 1967–78; St Mary's par ch Dun from 1978
m Aber 22.8.62 Mary A. B. Murray MB Chb 1955 *qv*

MACMILLAN William George
BSc 1925 **1926* PhD 1930
d Andreas Isle of Man 16.5.77

McMURTRIE or Tessier, Beatrice Somerville Brodie
*MA 1948
France: Bronze medal, Salon d'Erquy 1972, lauréate Salon des Femmes Peintres de l'Ouest 1976, Prix de la Peinture à l'Eau Salon de Baugé 1978
one-man shows Nantes, Angers, St Brieuc, group

exhibitions Aber, Paris, La Baule, St Nazaire, Breton painters' group, Musée de Nantes etc 1968–79

McMURTRIE or Gardner, Isobel Jean   BSc 1951
resid Curepipe, Mauritius

**McNAB or Macalister, Annabella Johnstone
MA 1937**
teacher: Nethybridge p s 1953–54, Westerton p s Aber from 1965

McNAB Ian Stephen   BSc 1950 *1951
MICE 1958
asst chief estimator Crudens Musselburgh 1964–71; sen contr man. Wm London & Son Bothwell 1971–74; contr man. Murdoch Mackenzie from 1974

McNAB James   MB ChB 1953
resid Halifax Nova Scotia
m 1954 Hazel G. MacLean man. dir

McNAB Mary Davidson   MA 1948
d Fraserburgh 24.9.69 *A UR* XLIII 331

McNAB or Geddes, Muriel Lesley   MA 1952
teacher Fr: Auchmuty s Glenrothes 1965–66; Madras coll St And from 1968

McNAIR Gordon Peter   ᶜMB ChB 1948
consult. surg RAF UK/Germany/Bahrain/Aden, retd 1969; coll m o RAF Cranwell 1969–70; g p Rhayader Wales from 1972

McNAIR James Jamieson   MB ChB 1941
DTM & H(Liv) 1960 FFCM 1973 C St J
Ceylon: sen m o AHQ and CO RAF hosp 1957–59; o c RAF inst of hyg Freckleton 1959–62; DGMS staff RAF Lond 1962–65; o c RAF hosp Changi Singapore 1965–67; p m o fighter comm RAF Bentley Priory; o c joint serv med rehabit unit Chessington 1968–71; M o D Lond: dir health and res RAF 1971–73, dep dir gen med serv RAF 1974–77; retd
m Valetta Malta 5.9.45 Zobell Pyper nurse; wife *d* 20.1.77

**McNAUGHT Duncan Arthur Hutchison
MB ChB 1940**
sen h m o Bangour hosp W Lothian 1962–69; consult. anaest Peel hosp Galashiels from 1969

MACNAUGHTON or Watt, Agnes   *MA 1922
resid Comrie

McNAUGHTON Alastair Ronald   MB ChB 1951

**McNAUGHTON or Thomson, Jean Herron Love
*MA 1925**
resid Banchory

McNAUGHTON John Love   MA 191.
d Buckie 2.11.64 *A UR* XLI 55

MacNEILL Donald   MB ChB 1951
g p: Crieff 1959–60, Montrose from 1960; Stracathro hosp: clin asst (orthop) 1960–77, g p hosp pract (orthop) from 1977

McNICOL Alexander Stuart   BL 1928
proc fiscal Aber 1960–69; retd; resid Arbroath

McNICOL Duncan   MB ChB 1950
MRCGP 1969
g p Glasg from 1954; part time tut. in g p Glas from 1973

MACNIVEN Catherine Jane   MA 1921

McNUTT Margaret Rosemary   MA 1942 Dip Ed 1957
Aber: teacher Powis s s 1958–63, lect coll of comm 1963–67; leg. asst A C Morrison & Richards advoc Aber 1967–69; lect coll of comm Aber 1969–70, sen lect from 1970

MACONACHIE Gordon William   MB ChB 1903

McOUAT Alexander   MA 1907
no longer on GC reg

MacOWAN Kenneth Duncan Simpson   BSc 1932
CBE 1960
anim health advis Min of overseas dev 1963–68; retd; resid Ramsey I of Man

**MacOWAN or Cunningham, Marion Margaret
MA 1928 BSc 1929 PhD 1932**
NZ: teacher sc Chilton St James s Lower Hutt 1950–55, head sc girls' h s Palmerston North 1961–71 husb *d* 29.8.71

McPETRIE James Duncan   MA 1895
no longer on GC reg

**McPETRIE James Stuart
*BSc 1924 PhD 1934 DSc 1939**
CB
dir gen electronics res and dev min of aviation Lond 1958–62; dir Racal Electronics Bracknell 1962–66; dir Mac Farms Slapton Devon 1966–68

MacPHAIL Angus   MB ChB 1924
no longer on GC reg

MacPHAIL or Macleod, Dolina   BSc 1939
resid Tarbert, Is of Harris

MACPHAIL Hugh Norman   MB ChB 1950
g p Edin from 1952

MACPHAIL Ian   *MA 1949

MACPHAIL Jessie Ann   MA 1909
no longer on GC reg

MacPHAIL John Critchfield   MA 1930
d Portpatrick 3.5.68 *A UR* XLII 370

MACPHAIL or Macleod, Mary   MA 1940
inf mistress Contin s 1962–68; relief teacher Easter Ross from 1974

MacPHAIL Norman   MB ChB 1912
d Carloway Lewis 31.1.61 *A UR* XXXIX 202

McPHERSON Barbara   MA 1952
teacher Millbank p s Nairn from 1956

MacPHERSON or McLean, Catherine Mary
BSc 1944
asst dev and des (electronics) Hayes 1945–46;
publisher's tech sub-edit. Lond 1946–57; bldg soc br
man. Chorkywood from 1975

McPHERSON Charles Ronaldson   MA 1924
head Tarves s 1943–65; retd; resid Milltimber

McPHERSON Charlotte Anderson   MA 1926

McPHERSON Christine Catherine Mary   MA 1955
teacher Forres from 1964

MACPHERSON Colin Campbell Reith
*MA 1952 ᵈBD 1955
C of S min St Margaret par ch Dunfermline from
1966

McPHERSON David   BSc 1940 MA 1943

MACPHERSON Ewen Donald   *MA 1950
prin teacher hist Aber acad 1959–66; lect hist Aber
coll of comm from 1966

McPHERSON George   MA 1939 *BSc 1947
sen exper off. marine lab Aber from 1957

MacPHERSON George Milne   MA 1955
retd 1972
d Aber 24.1.78 *AUR* xlvii 360

MacPHERSON George Robert   MB ChB 1944
g p Inv from 1955

McPHERSON Hamish Grant   MB ChB 1927
retd 1970; resid Hastings NZ

MACPHERSON Harry Gordon   *BSc 1952

MACPHERSON Ian William   MA 1943 *1948
member HM diplom serv: Ankara 1958–59, Geneva
1959–60, Budapest 1963–66, Athens 1972–75

MACPHERSON Ishbel Eliza   MA 1930
d Huntly 14.12.75

MACPHERSON or Reid, Isobel Margaret   MA 1946
teacher Broomhill p s Aber from 1969

McPHERSON James   *MA 1904
no longer on GC reg

McPHERSON James Alexander Strachan
MA 1949 ᵈBL 1952 LLB 1952
ptnr Alexander George & Co solic Macduff from
1955; member Macduff t c and Banff c c 1958–75;
provost Macduff 1972–75; chmn Banffsh educ comm
1967–70; convener Banff c c 1970–75; member
Grampian reg c and chmn Public Protection Comm
from 1974; hon Sheriff Grampian, Highlands and Is

from 1972; member Grampian health board from
1974; member of the Post Office Users' Council for
Scotland; DL Banffsh
m Aber 1960 Helen M. Perks MA 1956 *qv*

MACPHERSON James Cluny   BSc 1952

McPHERSON James Ritchie   MB ChB 1945

MacPHERSON James Stewart   *MA 1937

MACPHERSON or McConachie, Jean Margaret
MB ChB 1946
g p Lossiemouth; m o Gordonstoun school

MACPHERSON John   MA 1905 BSc(agr) 1906
no longer on GC reg

McPHERSON John   MB ChB 1909

MACPHERSON John   MB ChB 1940
FRGOG 1964
sen consult. obst/gen Torbay dist hosps from 1954

MACPHERSON Kenneth Manchip   *MA 1955

MACPHERSON Malcolm   BSc(for) 1949
for. comm: dist off. Fochabers 1966–71, Craven
Arms Salop from 1971

McPHERSON Margaret Ann   *MA 1942
Edin: chief exec off. Scot. dev dept 1965–70; Scot.
off. superann div: chief exec off. 1970–71, prin 1971–
74; asst secy from 1974

McPHERSON or Russell, Margaret Murray
MA 1928
DipDomSc(Birm) 1959
trainee dom sc Radbrook coll Shrewsbury 1958–59;
teacher dom sc Glanford s s Brigg 1959–63

MACPHERSON Mary Jean Grant
MA 1952 BSc 1954

McPHERSON Mary Margaret Mackenzie
*MA 1938

MACPHERSON or Taylor, Mary Tait   MA 1931
resid Laurencekirk

MACPHERSON Norman Letham
MA 1924 BSc 1927 *1928 PhD 1931
d Quebec 7.2.72 *AUR* xliv 430

MACPHERSON Robert William
MB ChB 1906 DPH 1911 MD 1913
no longer on GC reg

MACPHERSON Ronald Taylor   MB ChB 1950
FRCPath 1971
path. McKellor hosp Thunder Bay Ont from 1971

MACPHERSON or Burnett, Rosina Margaret Mill
MA 1946

MACPHERSON William John *MA 1950
tut. Cai Cantab 1960–70, sen tut. 1964–65, coll lect from 1964

MACPHERSON William Noel John MA 1952

McQUEEN Andrew Milroy BSc(eng) 1953

McQUEEN David James BD 1907
d Edin 8.4.62 *AUR* xxix 375

McQUEEN Elizabeth Milroy *MA 1901
d Aber 5.3.63 *AUR* xl 198

McQUEEN James Milroy
                              MA 1903 *BSc 1906 *MB ChB 1907
d Aber 1963

MACQUEEN John MA 1914
d Inv 14.3.60 *AUR* xxxviii 591

McQUISTAN Robert Ian BSc(agr) 1954
farm. Montrose from 1963

MacQUOID Margaret Kathleen MA 1920
retd 1962; resid Newport Fife
d 7.6.79

MacQUOID Peter Craik MA 1919
C of S min Turriff St Ninian's par ch 1927–66; retd

McRAE or Mackie, Agnes Irvine MA 1916
no longer on GC reg

MACRAE Alastair Douglas
                              MB ChB 1940 *MD 1950
MRCPath 1964 FRCPath 1969
dir virus reference lab Colindale Lond 1961–70; consult. virologist reg virus lab city hosp Edin 1970–74; consult. virol/sen lect dept microbiol and publ health lab univ hosp Nott from 1974

MACRAE Alexander Duncan MA 1939

MacRAE Alick John MA 1949
teacher Engl Methlick s s 1950–53 head Badcall Inchard s Sutherland 1953–58, Bualnaluib s Ross and Cromarty 1958–67, Drumsmittal s from 1967
m Aber 26.12.53 Margaret J. Shand d of Alexander S. Methlick

McRAE Alister Murray *MA 1928
d 7.10.65

MACRAE or Smith, Ann MA 1913
d 6.5.78

MACRAE or Macfarlane, Anne Ishbel MA 1945
teacher: Engl/hist Whitehills j s s 1963–69, Engl Banff acad from 1969

MACRAE Anne Margaret Smith MB ChB 1939
Bradford: h o ch's hosp 1940–41, g p 1941–46; med asst (geriat) Southport Lancs from 1963
m Bradford 20.6.40 George M. C. Smith MB ChB 1939 *qv*

MACRAE Archibald Campbell MB ChB 1912
d 19.9.61

MACRAE Calum Og MB ChB 1953
nat serv RAF 1955–57; g p Uig Skye 1957–75; group pract Portree from 1975
m Inv 28.1.61 Sarah MacRae teacher dom sc d of Archibald MacR. Inv

MACRAE Christina Catherine MA 1906
d Inv 22.7.74 *AUR* xlvi 106

MACRAE or MacDougall, Christine MB ChB 1924
private pract Ruislip from 1948
husb *d* 1959

MACRAE Christopher BSc(for) 1954

MACRAE Christopher Donald MB ChB 1923
g p Huddersfield; retd
d 29.10.80 *AUR* xlix 136

MACRAE Donald Kenneth *MA 1909 BSc 1910
d 19.6.64 *AUR* xl 396

MACRAE Donald Robert BSc(agr) 1924
vet surg Banff 1935–68; retd

MacRAE Donald Roderick BSc 1951

MACRAE Duncan MA 1895
no longer on GC reg

MACRAE Duncan James MB ChB 1903
d Kyle 27.5.62 *AUR* xxxix 373

MacRAE Duncan Keith MA 1950 LLB 1953
ptnr Jenkins & Jardine solic Stirling from 1963

MACRAE or Montgomery, Duncina MA 1927
resid Kyle of Lochalsh

MACRAE or Macrae, Edith Mary
                              MA 1919 MB ChB 1922 BSc 1925
resid Portsoy
husb *d* Portsoy 22.7.63

MACRAE Elizabeth Robertson Smathers MA 1931

MACRAE Finlay Milne BSc(for) 1951
for. off.: Inv 1951–53, Fort William 1953–63, Dingwall from 1963

MacRAE Hamish Simpson *MA 1951

MACRAE Herbert Alexander MA 1909
d Aber 12.12.67 *AUR* xlii 348

MACRAE Hugh Ross BSc(agr) 1924
no longer on GC reg

MACRAE or Taylor, Isabella *MA 1925
resid Alvesford
d 16.6.77

McRAE Ishbel MA 1926
teacher Kinloss p s 1966–71; retd; resid Findhorn

MACRAE Ishbel Margaret   MB ChB 1943
spec accreditation RCOG 1974
clin asst Univ Coll hosp, Queen Charlotte's and
Chelsea hosps Lond 1966–77; sen spec obst/gyn
Benghazi Libya 1968–69; clin advis in fam plan. York
from 1977
m Kingston-u-Thames 29.11.62 Edward J. Monks
MBE lt col

MACRAE or Soutter, Johann   MA 1923
d Dunfermline 15.6.72 *AUR* xlv 127

MACRAE John   MA 1906
d Stornoway 7.5.54

MACRAE John Duncan   MA 1913
no longer on GC reg

MACRAE John Smith   MA 1929 MB ChB 1934
g p Bradford
d 2.1.80 *AUR* xlix 68

MACRAE John William   MB ChB 1921
d Portsoy 22.7.63

MACRAE or Shields, Julia Macdougall   MA 1903
no longer on GC reg

MacRAE or Duval, Katreen Ismay Ferguson
                                                    *MA 1953
resid Paris

MacRAE Lachlan   *MA 1909
d 11.5.62 *AUR* xl 79

MACRAE Margaret   MA 1917
no longer on GC reg

McRAE Mary Rose   MA 1919
no longer on GC reg

MACRAE Robina Ann   MA 1926
no longer on GC reg

MACRAE Roderick   MA 1907
retd 1947
d Cheltenham 3.4.77

MACRAE Roderick   MA 1911
no longer on GC reg

MacRAE Roderick Alexander   *MA 1937
no longer on GC reg

MACRAE Ronald Duncan
                            MB ChB 1929 DPH 1931
m o BAOR Rheindahlen Germany and München
Gladbach 1964–69; cas off. Catterick milit hosp
1969–72; retd; resid Portsoy

MACRAE or Yorston, Sheila   MA 1949
teacher Balmedie s from 1972

MACRAE William John   MB ChB 1954
asst g p Ullapool 1957–58; sen h o med Belvidere

hosp Glasg 1959–60; g p: Glasg 1960–62, Dalmally
from 1962
m Inv 3.12.58 Isabel B. Macdonald

MACRAE or Graham, Williamina   MA 1927
no longer on GC reg

McRITCHIE or Harrison, Bella Jane   MA 1904
no longer on GC reg

McRITCHIE Douglas   *MA 1908 *1909 BD 1913
no longer on GC reg

MacRITCHIE Farquhar   MA 1925 LLB 1929
LLD(Edin) 1965 CBE 1968
prof conveyancing Aberd 1946–74; retd

MACRITCHIE John Donald   BSc(agr) 1954

McROBB or Farquharson, Annie Masson   MA 1925
d Sutton 15.9.73 *AUR* xlv 319

McROBB Keith McLeod   *MA 1937
TD 1965
C of S min Balshagray par ch Glasg 1960–74, Dalserf
par ch Lanarksh from 1974; chaplain TA forces
1948–67

McROBB Moira Helen   MA 1954 *1956
d of Farquharson McR. indust packing case manuf
and Sarah J. Hughson; b Aber 25.12.32
teacher: Fisherie 1956–57, Georgetown Guyana
1962–65, Aber tech coll 1967–68; piano teacher
Harlaw acad/Broomhill s Aber from 1972
m 23.12.57 Karl A. L. Brown MA 1956 *qv*

McROBB Neil Farquharson
                    BSc(elect eng) 1955 BSc(mech eng) 1956
Ferranti Edin: dev eng 1956–62, prod. support eng
1963–66, sen prod. supp eng 1967–71, syst eng group
leader prod. supp dept from 1972
m Penicuik 16.6.61 Jean H. Keiller SRN d of William
T. L. K. Penicuik

McROBBIE Alexander   MB ChB 1904 DPH 1905
no longer on GC reg

McROBERT George Reid
                            *MB ChB 1917 *MD 1923
hon FRCPE 1970
med advis to Secy of State for commonwealth relations
Whitehall Lond 1958–62; pres RSTM & H Lond
1961–63 nominated governor of publ bodies by Secy
of State for CR including board of man. royal post
grad med s 1958–71
d Nayland 6.6.76 *AUR* xlvii 102

McROBIE or Wagstaff, Dorothy Margaret
                                                        MA 1916
part-time dem phys Durh 1942–46; resid Leeds
d Leeds 17.3.80

McROBIE or Swapp, Frances Elizabeth   MA 1926
d Stonehaven 29.8.75 *AUR* xlvi 323

McRONALD Angus Duncan *BSc 1950
ME(Calif) 1969 PhD(Calif) 1974
sen res off. AAEC Sydney Aust 1962–64; prin scient off. NPL Teddington UK 1964–65; member tech staff JPL Pasadena USA from 1965

MACSWEEN John   MA 1922
no longer on GC reg

MACSWEEN John   MA 1928
head Broadford j s s Skye 1944–69; retd; resid Breakish
d 7.12.78

MACSWEEN Murdo   MA 1929

MacSWEEN Murdo   MA 1949 DipEd 1950
teacher Engl/soc stud Aber trades coll 1950–59; head gen stud. dept Aber coll of comm 1959–64; third i/c Oakbank approved s Aber 1964–70; dep head Kerelaw approved s from 1970

MacTAGGART Douglas Keith
                         *MA 1944 MB ChB 1949
MFCM 1973
m o h and dir soc serv Torbay county borough 1967–74; dist commun phys Torbay health dist from 1974

MACTAGGART William Keith   BSc(eng) 1948
CEng 1966 FIMechE 1973 FRAeS 1974
RAF: C O eng squadron Tengah Singapore 1960–63; Lond: M o D intell off. 1963–65, syst analyst def oper analysis/estab 1965–67, wg/cdr des and introduction of Air Force maintenance computer syst M o D 1967–71; gp capt/C O RAF stat Newton 1971–73; dep mech eng RAF strike command 1973: air cdre/dir of air armament M o D(PE) Lond from 1973

McTAVISH or Davidson, Katrina   MA 1949
Inv: teacher Merkinch s 1958–66, remed work Bishop Eden's s 1971–72, Dalneigh p s from 1972

McVEAN or Wood, Isobel Christie   MA 1926
resid Bournemouth

McVICAR or MacBean, Barbara Campbell
                                    MA 1911
no longer on GC reg

MacVICAR Donald   MA 1916 BSc 1922
teacher sc/geog and dep head g s 1931–60; retd

McVICKER John Louis Armitage   MB ChB 1943
MRCGP 1952 DIH 1969 FRSM 1972
g p Coventry 1948–66; W Bromwich: indust med practice 1966–69, med dir W Midlands indust health serv from 1969

McWILLIAM Charles Keith   MA 1919 BD 1920
clerk: synod Clydesdale 1952–66, presb Hamilton 1938–67; retd
wife *d* 14.12.72
d Cleland 11.5.76

MacWILLIAM Elizabeth Bethune   MA 1942
teacher Forres acad from 1943

McWILLIAM or Hendry, Elizabeth Jean   MA 1946
resid Bearsden

McWILLIAM or Berry, Elizabeth Mae   MA 1953

McWILLIAM Euphemia Jemima   BSc 1923
teacher maths/sc Banchory acad 1941–55; Bankhead acad Aber: teacher sc 1955–61, prin sc 1961–65; retd; resid Aber

MacWILLIAM George   *MA 1906 *BD 1909
d Edin 3.4.61 *AUR* xxxix 200

McWILLIAM George Porteous   MA 1915

McWILLIAM or Donald, Helen Margaret   MA 1949
resid Stonehaven
husb *d* 1.4.68

MacWILLIAM Jean Hepburn   MA 1936

MacWILLIAM John   *MA 1905 *BD 1908
d Aber 10.2.61 *AUR* xxxix 200

McWILLIAM or Fraser, Margaret   MA 1910
d 20.8.72

McWILLIAM or Chalmers, Margaret   MA 1949

McWILLIAM or Hunter, Margaret Shewan
                                    MA 1932

MAGEE Hugh Edward   DSc 1924
d 4.3.63 *AUR* xl 204

MAGUIRE Michael Finnbarr   PhD 1953

MAIN Arthur William Alexander
                         *MA 1949 BD 1953
C of S min: Douglas and Angus par. ch Dun 1955–64, St David's mem par ch Kirkintilloch 1964–70; stud. Jordanhill coll of educ Glasg 1970–71; teacher classics/relig educ Douglas acad Milngavie 1971–75, prin r e from 1975

MAIN David George Ewen   MA 1920
d Aber 29.1.62 *AUR* xxxix 382

MAIN David McDowall Gordon   MA 1904
d 1.5.64

MAIN or Shiach, Doreen Elizabeth   MA 1949
head Balgownie p s Aber from 1975

MAIN or Rees, Elizabeth Margaret   BSc 1952
teacher chem Farrington girls' s Chislehurst Kent from 1968

MAIN Elsie Margaret   MA 1954 BSc 1956
teacher sc Bankhead acad 1962–68
m Aber 4.4.68 Ronald Shepherd BSc 1956 *qv*

MAIN Ernest   *MA 1912
d North Berwick 25.2.66 *AUR* XLII 84

MAIN George Walker   *MA 1950
  teacher: Engl Niddrie Marischal s s 1959–63, Fr, asst prin Fr Portobello h s from 1963 prod./actor Fr plays Fr inst from 1953

MAIN James Mein   *BSc(eng) 1950

MAIN James Mein   BSc(eng) 1955

MAIN or Inglis, Jane   MA 1936
  teacher Aber: King St p s 1937–38, Skene St p s 1964–77

MAIN Joseph   MB ChB 1953

MAIN Kenneth Ritchie   BSc(eng) 1950

MAIN or Hendry, Margaret Wallace   BSc 1950
  teacher infants: Dunbar 1964–70, Banff from 1971

MAIN Peter Tester   MB ChB 1948 MD 1963
  ERD 1957 FRSocMed 1957
lt col RAMC reserve (Suez) Egypt 1956–57; Boots Co Nott: asst dir of res 1964–68, dir of res 1968–73, dir main board 1973–77, chief exec indust div from 1977

MAIN Roland Gemmell   MB ChB 1939
m o Roan Consolidated Copper Mines Mufulira Zambia from 1964

MAINLAND Malcolm Smythe   BSc 1922
d 28.1.70

MAIR Alexander   *BSc 1930
d 9.10.72

MAIR Alexander   BSc(eng) 1931

MAIR Alexander
                    MB ChB 1942 DPH 1947 MD 1950
  FRCP 1967 FFCM 1974
prof/head of dept publ health and soc med St And, later Dund, from 1955

MAIR Catherine Elizabeth   *MA 1936

MAIR or Davidson, Charlotte Geddes   *MA 1935
  resid Dun

MAIR or Imlah, Elizabeth   MA 1945
  teacher Peterhead acad from 1966

MAIR Elizabeth Georgina   MA 1932
d N'cle-u-Tyne 1.11.73 *AUR* XLV 321

MAIR Elsie Reid   MA 1929
  no longer on GC reg

MAIR or Laing, Ethel   MA 1939
  teacher: St Peter's s s Buckie 1960–69; Aboyne acad 1973–75; retd; resid Dinnet

MAIR Georgina   MA 1925
d 31.5.76

MAIR or Kerr, Grace   MA 1928
  resid Aber
d Inv 2.1.79

MAIR Greta   MA 1937
  teacher Fraserburgh cent s 1959–77; retd

MAIR Ian Geddes   *BSc 1952
  prin teacher sc Keith g s from 1960

MAIR James Campbell   BSc(eng) 1951

MAIR or Hutcheson, Jane Eliza   MA 1925
  resid Aber

MAIR John Alexander Paterson   *MA 1926
  retd 1964; resid Aber

MAIR John Magnus   MB ChB 1937
  MFCM
Edin: part time lect soc med 1959–75; sen dep m o h 1964–69; dir soc work from 1969

MAIR Joseph   *BSc(eng) 1951
  MIEE 1969
head elect. group assoc eng group res and dev Rugby 1965–69; head phys and elect. eng Clayton Dewandre Co Lincoln from 1969

MAIR or Boyd, Lily Gardiner   MA 1945

MAIR or Scott, Margaret   BSc 1951

MAIR Margaret Helen   MA 1923
  retd 1962; resid Kirk Ella, Yorks

MAIR Mary Elizabeth   *MA 1928
  retd 1967; resid Banff

MAIR Mary Hay   MA 1941
  asst prin teacher Fr Torry acad Aber from 1972

MAIR or Thom, Mary Jane   MA 1942

MAIR Robert   MB ChB 1954
  Dip Psych(Edin) 1963 LMCC 1977 ECFMG 1977
consult. psychiat Bellevue hosp Kingston, Jamaica 1965–68; govt psychiat Zomba, Malawi 1969–73; psychiat Sudbury Algoma sanatorium Ont 1974–76

MAIR Robert George   MB ChB 1947

MAIR Stanley David   MA 1935
d Glasg 1.8.76

MAIR Thomas James Anderson
                    ***MA 1938 *MEd 1940**
  RAF educ br Cranwell/Far East 1949–71; group capt RAF (retd) 1971; resid Aboyne

MAIR Victoria Helen Anne   MA 1916
  no longer on GC reg

MAIR Vida   MA 1934
    teacher: spec asst Portsoy j s s 1965–69, Engl
Buckie h s 1969–72, asst prin guid Buckie h s from
1972

MAIR William George   MA 1905
    d Peterhead 16.6.61 *A UR* xxxix 200

MAIR William George Parker
                              MB ChB 1936 MD 1956
MRCPath 1963 FRCPath 1968
consult. neuropathologist Nat Hosp for nervous diseases Lond 1958–78, hon consult. from 1979/hon
consult. neuropath Northwick Park Harrow from
1979

MAITLAND or Brzostowski, Dorothy   *MA 1949
    asst dir Internat Hosp Federation Lond from 1969

MAITLAND Gladys Lucy   *MA 1935
    teacher: Edin 1940–44, Dyce 1950–53, Coatbridge
1954–59, Dun 1961–74
m Peterhead 12.8.41 Thomas I. Mackay min of relig

MAITLAND Helen Donaldson   MA 1917
    retd 1959
d Aber 20.1.77 *A UR* xlvii 211

MAITLAND Helen Mary   MB ChB 1953
    MRCGP 1968
g p: Peebles 1961–62, Aber from 1962

MAITLAND or Selbie, Margaret Helen   *MA 1934
    resid Huddersfield

MALCOLM or Harper, Eliza Morris   MA 1918
    no longer on GC reg

MALCOLM Ernest William   MB ChB 1927
    no longer on GC reg

MALCOLM Florence Johnston
                              MB ChB 1923 DPH 1926
    d Invercargill NZ 7.6.64 *A UR* xl 399

MALCOLM Ian   *MA 1948 PhD 1952
    teacher RGC Aber: spec asst 1963–67, prin asst
1967–71, prin maths from 1971

MALCOLM Robert Mackinnon   BSc(for) 1947
    Canada: timber appraiser BC govt Victoria 1960–
72, consult. for. in private pract from 1973

MALCOLM William   *MA 1950
    Aber coll of comm: teacher 1959–63, sen hist 1963–
64; head gen stud. 1964–73; retd
d Aber 13.10.78

MALLOCH Christina Muir   MA 1922
    no longer on GC reg

MANN Charles   MA 1911 ᵈLLB 1914
    d 6.11.72 *A UR* xlv 124

MANN or Smith, Elizabeth Helen   MA 1919
    resid Richmond Surrey

MANN or Madeley, Elsie Jane   *MB ChB 1921
    FRSocMed 1925–65
retd 1966; resid Lond
d Lond 7.1.79 *A UR* xlviii 227

MANN George Donald   MA 1922
    d Lond 10.1.80 *A UR* xlviii 441

MANN James Alexander   BSc(agr) 1923
    no longer on GC reg

MANN James Angus   MA 1913
    d Inv 28.4.72 *A UR* xlv 124

MANN James Wallace   MA 1916 MB ChB 1918
    no longer on GC reg

MANN William Thomson   MA 1930
    no longer on GC reg

MANSON Anderson   BSc(agr) 1933
    retd 1968; resid N. Kessock

MANSON Ann Elizabeth   MA 1913
    d Aber 1.12.69 *A UR* xliii 441

MANSON Cecil George Russell   MA 1951

MANSON Charles Stewart   BSc(eng) 1947

MANSON Doris Irene   MB ChB 1948
    lect dept med Aberd 1949–63
m Aber 14.12.63 Gordon M. Lees MB ChB 1961 *qv*

MANSON or Elder, Edna Burness Inglis   BSc 1944
    resid Kirriemuir

MANSON George Inglis   MB ChB 1944
    OBE 1974
Peterhead: g p from 1948, m o HM prison from 1955

MANSON or Cameron, Jean Margaret   MA 1948
    temp relief teaching Lusaka, Zambia 1958–69; resid
Inv

MANSON or Leland, Katherine Mabel   BSc 1946

MANSON Margaret Frances   MA 1945
    teacher Woodside p s Aber 1946–49; Portree h s inf
1949–52, Engl 1963–72, prin guid from 1972
m Portree Is of Skye 23.11.51 Norman N. Mackinnon
postman

MANSON or Jones, Margaret Mimie   *BSc 1943
    resid Scarborough

MANSON William George Campbell   MB ChB 1949
    JP Gordon dist Grampian reg 1963
g p Alford from 1956

MANSON William Isbister   BSc(eng) 1947
    res eng BBC from 1947; resid Tadworth

MANT Forbes Allan   MA 1952

MANTELL Ruth Margaret   MA 1942
  head Ramsay/Boyndie spec s Banff from 1969

MARDON Austin   MA 1948

MARGACH Alastair James   BSc(agr) 1927
  d Uganda 4.5.62

MARIONI Giovanni Emilio Lorenzo   BSc 1942
  d Aber 28.10.68 *A UR* XLIII 85

MARIONI Peter   MB ChB 1947
  FRCSE 1963 FRCS 1964 Cert gen surg Canada
  1964 FRCS(Aust) 1967
  h o thoracic surg gen hosp Vancouver 1959–60; regist
  thoracic surg Broadgreen Liv 1960–61; lect physiol
  Liv univ 1961–62; regist gen surg Warrington gen
  hosp 1962–63; chief resid gen surg Edmonton Royal
  Alexandra hosp 1964–65; consult. gen surg Ashburton
  gen hosp NZ; private pract Windsor Ont from 1967

MARK or Davidson-Innes, Alexandrina Margaret
MA 1927
  no longer on GC reg

MARKS George Maurice   MA 1948
  d 15.3.67

MARMION John   BSc(eng) 1948

MARNIE Ronald James Rattray   BSc(for) 1954

MARNOCH Derek George   BSc(eng) 1955
  ACMA 1975
  Claben Aber: prod. man. 1970–75, gen man. from
  1976
  m Aber 23.8.63 Kathleen Howard

MARNOCH or Burnley, Mary Fowler Ritchie
MA 1927
  resid Kirkcaldy
  d –.2.80

MARNOCH Sheila Middleton   MA 1940
  teacher inf Aber from 1942

MARR Alexander John   MA 1913
  d Datchworth 28.12.62 *A UR* XL 81

MARR David Murdoch   MB ChB 1914 MD 1919
  d Inv 9.11.70 *A UR* XLIV 109

MARR Douglas John   MB ChB 1906
  d 27.3.64

MARR Douglas Stuart Sandeman
MA 1936 LLB 1939
  d 28.3.61 *A UR* XXXIX 283

MARR Elizabeth Stewart   MA 1913
  d Inv 17.10.66 *A UR* XLII 84

MARR or Clowes, Isobel Margaret   *MA 1946
  lib asst from 1948
  resid Horton-cum-Studley, Oxford

MARR James William Slesser
MA BSc 1925 DSc 1963
  d Surrey 29.4.65 *A UR* XLI 150

MARR or Esson, Mabel Agnes   MA 1942
  resid Slains Ellon

MARR Neil George   MB ChB 1927
  d 15.10.72 *A UR* XLV 226

MARR Thomas Deans   *MB ChB 1924
  g p retd 1959; retd reg med c 1969; resid Lond
  d 5.5.78 *A UR* XLVIII 104

MARRIOTT Francis Henry Charles   PhD 1951
  lect biomaths Oxon from 1965; fell. Wolfson coll
  Oxon from 1969
  m Edin 19.12.64 Catherine F. Broadfoot SRN/tut.
  Glasg

MARRIOTT John Draper Middleton   MA 1950
  Aber: dep head Seaton p s 1962–65, dep head
  Middlefield p s 1965–66, head Tullos p s from 1966

MARSDEN or Marsden, Elizabeth Abernethy
MB ChB 1931
  asst m o and asst s m o Merthyr Tydfil from 1948;
  resid Aberdare

MARSH Charles Arnold   PhD 1953
  sen lect univ of NSW Aust 1965–72, assoc prof from
  1972

MARSH Dane Ernest Marshall   BSc(for) 1949
  JP gazetted Nigeria 1961
  dist for. off. and prin for. s Ho Togoland Tarkwa and
  Sunyuni Gold Coast 1950–55; asst lect Mander coll of
  f e Bedford 1956–58; Nigeria: prov for. off. Ikom
  1959–61, reg res off. E reg Enugu 1961–63, for. advis
  Niger delta dev board Port Harcourt 1963–66; dir
  Launderettes (Bedford) from 1968 and also antique
  dealer Sharnbrook Beds from 1970
  m Chippenham 15.10.61 Dorothy Campbell d of
  Archibald C. NZ

MARSHALL Doreen Gilchrist   MA 1953
  teacher Culter j s s till 1961; resid Aber
  m Aber 4.4.60 Antony D. Cameron eng consult. s of
  James D. C. Carshalton

MARSHALL or Smith, Evelyn Duncan   MA 1952

MARSHALL or MacDonagh, Gillian Rosemary
Struan   MB ChB 1948
  consult. accident and emergency dept royal Portsmouth hosp from 1965
  husb d 1965

MARSHALL or Milne, Helen Mary   MA 1913

MARSHALL Ian Alexander Robert Burns
                                    BSc(for) 1945
Brit for. comm in Eng from 1946; resid York

MARSHALL Ian Howard
                    *MA 1955 BD 1959 PhD 1963
asst tut. Didsbury coll Bristol 1960–62; methodist
min Darlington 1962–64; lect NT exegesis Aberd
from 1964; pers sen lect Aberd 1970–77, reader 1977–
79, prof from 1979
m Carlisle 25.3.61 Joyce E. Proudfoot MA(Edin) ch
care off. d of Frederick J. P. Carlisle

MARSHALL Norman   MB ChB 1950 DPH 1958
g p Manly NSW Aust from 1965

MARSHALL Wilfred
            MA 1922 *MB ChB 1927 *MD BSc 1928

MARTIN Agnes Clark   BL 1930
retd 1976; resid Peterhead

MARTIN Alasdair Peter   MA 1955
head Fort William RC s from 1964

MARTIN Andrew   BSc(agr) 1947
NOSCA: county agr advis Moray and Nairn 1960–
67, supervis and sen lect Craibstone 1960–71; dep
prin s of agr Aber from 1971

MARTIN Basil William   MB ChB 1908
no longer on GC reg

MARTIN Derek Walker   MA 1955 LLB 1957
leg. and admin posts c clerk's dept Inv 1960–62; leg.
asst W. & J. S. Gordon solic Forfar 1962–64, ptnr
1964–67; asst c clerk Sutherland c c Golspie 1967–69,
dep c clerk from 1969
m Aber 11.2.61 Lydia A. W. Howard asst city
chamberlain's dept Aber d of John A. H. Aber

MARTIN Douglas   *MA 1935
retd 1973; resid Kirn, Dunoon

MARTIN or Collie, Elizabeth   MB ChB 1935
retd 1971; resid Brechin

MARTIN Elizabeth Ferguson   MA 1925
d 18.3.66 *AUR* xlii 86

MARTIN Ellen Margaret   MA 1926
no longer on GC reg

MARTIN or Mitchell, Gladys Jeannie   MA 1923
retd 1965; resid Aber

MARTIN or Cameron, Gladys Mary Elizabeth
                                    MB ChB 1926
d Chatham 21.6.66 *AUR* xli 340

MARTIN Hamish William Thomson   MB ChB 1932

MARTIN or Stevenson, Helen Catherine Halley
                                    *MA 1943
teacher mod lang: The Westbourne s for girls Glasg
1964–71, spec asst from 1971

MARTIN Hugh Thomson   BL 1947
solic Montrose from 1947

MARTIN James Ramsay   MB ChB 1933
retd 1969; resid Ellon
d 1.11.81

MARTIN John   MA 1920 BD 1922
retd 1958; resid Cardonald Glasg
d 29.8.76

MARTIN Kenneth Gavin   BSc(agr) 1952
farm. 1952–73; lect agr Oatridge agr coll from 1974
m Aber 20.10.73 Moira G. Monteath secy d of William
A. M. Glasg

MARTIN or Hunter, Mary Margaret
                            MB ChB 1936 DPH 1947
dept m o h Aber corp. 1947–71; retd; resid Aber

MARTIN or Davis, Maureen Joan   MA 1949

MARTIN or Steel, Sheila Eunice Nanette   *MA 1935
resid Edin

MARTIN Stanley Ephraim   *MA 1934
head St Peter's s Peterhead from 1939

MARTIN Victor David Randall   MB ChB 1942
    MFCM 1972
m o h Doncaster from 1960

MARTYN Robert Godfrey   MB ChB 1912
no longer on GC reg

MARWICK David Gibson   *BSc(agr) 1936
d 30.10.73

MARWICK Robert Craigie   MA 1949

MARWICK William Corrigal   MA 1937
d Nairn 8.1.76 *AUR* xlvi 417

MASON Ethelwyn Margaret   DSc 1938

MASOR Philip Leon   MB ChB 1935
USA: assoc attending surg (ophth) NY Eye and
Ear inf from 1946

MASSEY Allan   MB ChB 1908
no longer on GC reg

MASSEY John Edwyn   BSc(for) 1950

MASSIE Francis Edward   MB ChB 1928
g p Thornton Heath from 1933

MASSIE George Campbell   MA 1942
head Bucksburn s from 1969

MASSIE or Allen, Gladys   *MA 1954 Dip Ed 1955
teacher maths Boroughmuir s Edin from 1971

MASSIE Leslie Alexander   MA 1935 LLB 1936
solic-gen (hon QC) Malaya 1959–60; advoc Scot.
Bar from 1961
resid Edin

MASSIE or Watson, Letitia   MA 1925
resid Whitehills Banff

MASSIE or Wallace, Louise Christian   MA 1911
d Bradford 17.1.78 *AUR* XLVII 356

MASSIE or Sutherland, Margaret Elizabeth
MA 1923
resid Christchurch NZ

MASSIE or Hendry, Margaret Mary Strachan
MA 1947
resid Aber

MASSIE or Hogg, Mary   MA 1917
resid Aber; freelance writer of verse
husb *d* 1967

MASSON or Jackson, Anne Madeline   MA 1936

MASSON Charles Robb   BSc 1943 PhD 1948
nat res council of Can: assoc res off. 1955–59, sen
res off. 1959–65, prin res off. from 1965; resid Halifax
Nova Scotia

MASSON Charles Will   BSc 1950
head: Inchture p s Perthsh 1961–66, Doune p s
Perthsh from 1966

MASSON David Norman   MA 1912 BD 1917
d Aber 13.4.66 *AUR* XLII 84

MASSON or Todd, Frances Anne   *MA 1939
resid Crieff

MASSON Gordon Baxter   MA 1955 LLB 1957
advoc in Aber; ptnr W. Kirkwood & Smith Aber
from 1960

MASSON or Milne, Isabella Margaret   BSc 1949
teacher biol Elgin acad from 1961, also asst prin
guid 1973–77, prin guid from 1977

MASSON James Leiper   BSc(for) 1949
conserv of for. Kano Nigeria 1959–62; for. expert
FAO: Sudan 1962–63, Thailand 1964–67, Malaysia
1967–69, Rome 1969–70, Cuba 1970–74, Peru from
1974

MASSON John Richard   *MA 1951
MBE 1962 OBE 1970
asst fin. secy UK high comm off. S Africa 1961–63;
Swaziland: acting secy fin. 1964–68, secy for fin. 1968–
72; retd from publ serv 1972, dir of companies from
1972

MASSON or White, Katharine Isobel Mary
** *MA 1943**
resid Edin

MASSON or Rogers, Marion Gibbins   MA 1946

MASSON or Dobson, Marjorie Jean   BSc 1948
resid Etna NY USA

MASSON William David   MB ChB 1955
DTM & H(Lond) 1963 DCH(Glas) 1964 MRCPE
1969
lt col RAMC; g p Acharacle Argyll from 1977

MASSON William Peterkin   MA 1914
resid Nethy Bridge

MATHER George Strathdee   MB ChB 1916
Durham: m o h Stockton RDC 1923–58; chmn
hosp man. comm Hartlepool 1955–59; retd; resid
Penrith

MATHER Stuart Smith   BSc 1952
LRAM (pianoforte) 1967
head Strathmartin s by Dun from 1963

MATHERS Cecil George   BSc 1941 *1947
sen exper off. AEA Chem II UKAEA, DERE
Dounreay from 1958

MATHERS Eleanor Anderson   MA 1948

MATHESON Alexander   MB ChB 1931
MRCGP
g p Stornoway/visiting phys Lewis hosp 1933–48
d Stornoway 19.12.78 *AUR* XLVIII 232

MATHESON Alexander John   MA 1934

MATHESON or Beattie, Catherine Fiona   MA 1954
teacher Fraserburgh inf s 1966–77; remed Warddykes s Arbroath from 1978

MATHESON Colin   MA 1918 BSc 1921
d 1980

MATHESON Donald
MA 1924 *BSc 1927 PhD 1932
OBE 1965
Lond: HM chem insp of factories 1938–57, HM dep
sen chem insp 1957–60, HM sen chem insp/head of
chem branch 1960–68; retd; internat lab off. Geneva
1969
m Luddendenfoot 12.7.39 Hilda Spencer nurse d of
William S. Luddendenfoot

MATHESON Donald   *MB ChB 1937
col RAMC 1961–70; retd; civ med pract milit
corrective training centre Colchester from 1970

MATHESON Donald   MB ChB 1938
anaest Vancouver gen hosp from 1955

MATHESON Donald   MA 1948

MATHESON Donald John   BSc(agr) 1933
retd 1964
d Inv 29.1.76

MATHESON Donald William   BSc(eng) 1945

MATHESON Ellen   MA 1928
teacher: Mackie acad Stonehaven 1958–61,
Summerhill acad Aber 1961–67, retd; resid Aber

MATHESON George Philip   BSc(agr) 1932
   farm. Marykirk/potato merch Montrose 1955–80;
retd; resid Montrose
d Aber 1.7.80

MATHESON Harry Ririe   *BSc 1950

MATHESON or Waudby, Hectorina   MB ChB 1951
   Hong Kong relief doctor in Leprosarium Hay
Ling Chau 1960–75; g p: Peace clin Kowloon 1965–
66, locum for tuberculosis m o Haven of Hope
Sanatorium 1966; part-time asst gyn and inf welfare
clin Nethersole hosp 1968; part-time asst res Leprosy
Study Centre Lond from 1976; m o Leprosy Mission
Lond from 1978

MATHESON James Alexander   *MA 1909
   d Inv 6.6.61 *AUR* xxxix 201

MATHESON James Roderick   BSc 1919
   resid Ullapool
d Inv 17.5.81

MATHESON or MacPhail, Jemima Muriel   MA 1914
   resid Carloway Is of Lewis
husb *d* 31.1.61

MATHESON John Gunn   MB ChB 1941
   consult. anaest Shotley Bridge gen hosp Co Durh
and N'cle gen hosp from 1952

MATHESON Katherine Dunlop   *MA 1934
   d Ayr 24.12.48

MATHESON Knut Cecil Cyril   *MA 1925
   no longer on GC reg

MATHESON or Sweeney, Margaret   MA 1931

MATHESON or Bowdler, Margaret Mary   MA 1948

MATHESON Mary Grace   MA 1920
   no longer on GC reg

MATHESON Mary Helen   MA 1931

MATHESON Murdo   MA 1930
   head Kiltearn p s Ross and Cromarty 1963–72;
retd; resid Evanton

MATHESON Norman Allan   *BSc 1950 PhD 1954
   sen scient off. Rowett res inst Aber 1961–65, prin
scient off. from 1965

MATHESON Peter   MB ChB 1937
   JP Ross and Cromarty 1968
m o West Uig Lewis from 1945

MATHEWSON or Wilson, Annie Allardyce
                                        MA 1921
   resid Kintore
d Jedburgh 12.7.78 *AUR* xlviii 103

MATHEWSON Annie Clugston   MA 1915
   d 26.1.73

MATHEWSON or MacLean, Elizabeth Swanson
                                        MA 1928
   resid Edin

MATHEWSON or Ratcliff, Ishbel Margaret
                                        MA 1932
   d Lond 25.7.71 *AUR* xliv 321

MATHEWSON James   MA 1939
   farm. Tarves from 1945

MATHEWSON John George   BL 1932
   d Aber 9.1.75 *AUR* xlvi 239

MATHEWSON or Wilson, Mary Elizabeth
                                        MA 1919
   teacher Greenness p s, Cuminestown p s 1941–42;
head: Largie p s 1942–51, Craigdam 1951–63
d Aber 21.6.79

MATHEWSON William Gray
                          BSc(agr) 1949 MSc 1974
   sen agr off. Mbeya Tanzania 1951–65; asst secy
NFU of Scot. Edin 1965–68; assoc prof Nova Scotia
agr coll Truro Nova Scotia from 1968
m Calgary Alberta 15.3.58 Greta M. L. Ekstrand reg
nurse d of Daniel E. Calgary

MATHIESON or Thomson, Ada Isobel   MA 1925

MATHIESON Agnes Duguid Ferrier   MA 1935
   d 5.12.64

MATHIESON or Lawson, Agnes Margaret
                                        MA 1931
   teacher Kittybrewster p s Aber 1951–56; head Birse
p s 1956–60; teacher: Tarland s s 1960–63, maths
Aboyne acad 1963–75; retd
husb *d* 9.2.69

MATHIESON Alexander McLeod   BSc 1941 *1942
   Fell. Aust Acad of Sc 1967
chief res scient chem phys div CSIRO Melbourne
from 1965

MATHIESON or Smith, Catherine   MA 1915
   d Ballater 12.3.73 *AUR* xlv 318

MATHIESON Charles Edward   MB ChB 1925
   retd 1972; resid Leeds
wife *d* 28.11.58
d Leeds 1.7.80 *AUR* xlix 67

MATHIESON Constance Mina
                          MA 1947 *MEd 1949
   sen clin then prin psych NE reg hosp board now
Grampian area health board from 1960; also Aberd:
clin lect mental health dept 1966–73, hon sen clin lect
from 1973
m 18.11.63 Alexander M. Cordiner tea planter, fish
merch

MATHIESON David Wyllie   MB ChB 1943
   med pract N Vancouver from 1960

MATHIESON or Mackay, Elsie Craig Durward
                                    MA 1927
  resid Bury, Lancs (metrop county of Manc)

MATHIESON or Macdonald, Evelyn Margaret Helen
                                    MA 1940
  resid Wellington NZ

MATHIESON Gordon   MB ChB 1949
  MSc(McG) 1960 FRCP(C) 1968
Montreal: asst prof McG univ 1957–63, assoc prof
from 1963; also neuropath Montreal Neurol Inst
from 1957; hon res fell. dept path. Aberd 1973–74
m Montreal 22.8.70 Julia C. Parker reg nurse Quebec
province d of Herbert H. P. Montreal

MATHIESON or Walmsley, Isabel Mary
                                    MB ChB 1937
  resid St And

MATHIESON James Moir   MB ChB 1907
  no longer on GC reg

MATHIESON or Goldie, Marie Agnes   *MA 1933
  resid Leeds
husb d Leeds 13.2.70

MATHIESON Marjory Winifred   *MA 1945
  resid Aber

MATHIESON Sheila   MA 1950
  teacher Stoneywood j s from 1954

MATTHEW George Douglas
                          ***BSc(eng) 1952 PhD 1961**
  MICE 1959
Aberd: sen lect eng 1967–70, reader from 1970
m Aber 20.7.62 Margaret W. McKenzie BSc 1959 qv

MATTHEW Hilda Cruickshank   MA 1934
  teacher; retd 1975

MATTHEW Ian   *MA 1952
  teacher: geog Aber acad 1958–67, prin geog
Douglas acad Milngavie 1967–71; asst rector Douglas
acad from 1971
m Aber 7.4.65 Miriam E. Buchan teacher Peterhead

MATTHEW or Williams, Jessie Donald
                                    MA 1944 *1947
  Salisbury: teacher maths/geog St Edmunds s for
girls 1965; maths La Retraite Convent s (formerly
Leehurst) from 1965
husb d 17.10.64

MATTHEW John Low   MB ChB 1954
  g p Kirkby-in-Ashfield from 1961

MATTHEW Keith Ronald Thomson   MB ChB 1929
  g p Glasg from 1929

MATTHEWS Annie Peill   *MA 1902
  d Aber 19.8.67 AUR XLII 178

MATTHEWS or Matthews, Elizabeth Agnes
                                    MA 1927
  teacher Fr/Ger Bankhead acad 1963–68; retd; resid
Aber
husb d 15.11.62

MATTHEWS George Irvine   MA 1945 LLB 1948

MATTHEWS Ian McPherson   *BSc 1953

MATTHEWS John Drake   BSc(for) 1948
  FRSE 1964 FIFor 1966 FIBiol 1968
prof for. Aberd from 1963

MATTHEWS Keith Morton Lille   BSc(agr) 1953

MATTHEWS Robert Begbie   BSc(eng) 1952
  sen dev eng GEC Coventry 1959–60; Enfield coll of
tech: asst lect 1960–61, lect 1961–66, sen lect 1966–72;
sen lect Middx polytech from 1973

MAVOR George Edward
                    MA 1939 *MB ChB 1944 ChM 1953
  d Aber 4.12.73 AUR XLV 449

MAVOR or Knox, Janet   *MA 1908
  d Stonehaven 5.1.73 AUR XLV 223

MAVOR William Ferrier   *MA 1934
  FRSA 1968
admin asst s of phys N'cle 1968 and counsellor
(Humanities) O U northern reg from 1972

MAXWELL Edwin Arthur   *MA 1928
  FIMA
fell. Queens' coll Cantab till retd 1974; thereafter life
fell.; keeper of records 1946–72; sen bursar 1958–65;
hon secy internat comm math instr 1970–74

MAXWELL or Wyllie, Marjorie Hamilton
                                    BSc 1929 MA 1930
  resid Glasg
husb d Oyne 8.1.76

MAXWELL-JOYNER Charles
                                    MA 1915 MB ChB 1921
  MCPS(Alta) 1932 St John's medal
private pract Nassau Bahamas 1958–70; life member:
British red cross; Amer med soc Vienna; co-founder
Bahamas cancer soc

MAY Alexander   MA 1929 BD 1935
  C of S min Innerleven E ch Methil from 1949
d Leven 23.8.81

MAY George   MB ChB 1947
  g p Bolsover from 1950

MAY James   MA 1887
  no longer on GC reg

MAY James Robertson   BSc(eng) 1952
  MICE FIStructE
bridge eng Invsh 1959–60; Scot. dev dept Edin:
bridge eng 1960–66, sen bridge eng from 1966

MAY or Good, Phyllis   MA 1931
resid Southport Merseyside

MAY Robert Crouch   BL 1927
ptnr Mackenzie & Wilson advoc Aber from 1937

MAY William   *MA 1933
dep rector Dornoch acad 1965–68, rector from 1968

MEADOWS or Todd, Elza Harris   MB ChB 1942
MFCM 1972
Surrey: asst m o h Mitcham 1961–63, dep m o h
Richmond and Barnes 1963–65, sen m o Sutton;
Merton (Lond borough): dep m o h 1968–72, m o h
1972–74; dist commun phys Roehampton dist 1974–
78; dir occup health Charing Cross hosp from 1978
husb d 25.4.61

MEARNS Henry Balfour   MA 1919
no longer on GC reg

MEARNS Ian Andrew   MA 1954 LLB 1957
leg. asst Moray & Nairn joint c c Elgin 1968–70,
chief leg. asst 1970–73; town clerk Girvan 1973–75;
dep dir admin Kyle and Carrick dist c Ayr from 1975
m Elgin 28.4.62 Elizabeth A. M. Sutherland med secy
d of Allan S. Elgin

MEARNS or Towers, Isobel Margaret   *MA 1934
teacher: remed classes Fraserburgh North s 1958–
61, Engl Fraserburgh acad 1961–72; retd

MEARNS James Godsman   BSc(agr) 1923
rubber planter man. Selangor Malaysia 1923–41,
1947–48 interned Singapore 1941–45/6; retd; resid
Banchory
m Aber 5.12.46 Marguerite M. Dean indust nurse d of
George M. D. Ellon
d 13.2.80

MEARNS James Michie   *MA 1952

MEARNS William Anderson
**   MA 1899 MB ChB 1903 DPH 1913**

MEARNS William Ramsay   MA 1954 LLB 1956
post grad stud. bus. admin Harvard bus. s 1956–57;
pers/indust relations positions Massey-Ferguson: Tor
(Can) Detroit, Des Moines, Racine (USA), Coventry,
Vereeniging (S. Af) 1957–72; dir pers/indust relations
Perkins eng co (subsid of Massey-Ferguson) Peterborough from 1972

MEE or Stephen, Annie Margaret   MB ChB 1940
g p Fochabers from 1961

MELDRUM Andrew McGregor   MA 1892
no longer on GC reg

MELDRUM or Moir, Annie   MA 1915
no longer on GC reg

MELDRUM or McGillivray, Doreen
**   MB ChB 1948 DPH 1951**
g p Aber 1950; later resid Cambuslang

MELDRUM or Kynoch, Elsie Jane Gillanders
**   MA 1928**

MELDRUM Frederick James   MA 1947
Aber: asst man. Barton Abrasives 1947–55; man.
dir John Lawrie & Co from 1961; dir Barton & Sons
Dudley from 1977

MELDRUM Helen   MA 1923
retd 1963; resid Ballindalloch

MELDRUM Margaret Ann   MA 1922
d Aberlour 12.3.66 *AUR* XLII 86

MELDRUM or Irvine, Margaret Catherine
**   MA 1942**
Aber: visiting teacher p s languages from 1969

MELDRUM or Wade, Mary Elizabeth Helen
**   MA 1951**

MELDRUM or Corser, Mona   MA 1928
resid Elgin

MELDRUM Neil Ian Wilson   MA 1940 LLB 1947

MELDRUM Walter James   MB ChB 1921
d Norwich 31.10.71 *AUR* XLIV 429

MELDRUM William James Gillan   MB ChB 1941

MELROSE John Kidd Ramsay   BSc(agr) 1950
sen insp DAFS S.W. area Ayr from 1970

MELVILLE or Rae, Gladys Evelyn   *MA 1945
resid Aber

MELVILLE John Douglas Scott   MB ChB 1944
d Inv 12.1.79 *AUR* XLVIII 233

MELVILLE Mattie Fraser   MA 1929
retd 1971; resid Bearsden

MELVILLE or Flett, Vivien Mary   MA 1947
resid Bearsden

MELVILLE William Gordon   MA 1950
BA(Lond) 1967
Aber: teacher Cummings Park p s 1951–64; dep head
Hanover St p s 1964–66, dep head Sunnybank p s
from 1966

MELVILLE William Simm   BSc(eng) 1938
FIEE 1951 OBE 1963
BTH Co Rugby: grad app 1938–40, res eng 1940–50,
eng man. (radar); gen man. (radar & defence) AEI,
Leicester; proj man. GEC-Marconi, Chelmsford from
1968
m Rugby 25.7.42 Jean F. Craig MA 1934 *qv*

MELVIN Alfred   MA 1902 *BL 1904
no longer on GC reg

MELVIN Andrew George   *MA 1929
dep rector Tain acad 1968–70; retd

MELVIN Anne   MA 1951 MB ChB 1956
DA 1959
regist anaest S Manc hosp group 1960–63; asst anaest Preston RI from 1964; anaest Lancs c c from 1968
m Leeds 22.9.61 James P. Lythgoe MB B Chir(Cantab) consult. surg s of Sir James L. MA(Manc) Wilmslow

MELVIN or Cruickshank, Annie   *MA 1929
retd 1967; resid Kemnay
d Kemnay 31.7.75

MELVIN or MacKay, Annie Elizabeth
MB ChB 1920
g p Northampton and Thornaby-on-Tees 1920–23 and 1939–46; retd; resid Northallerton

MELVIN or Witte, Edith Mary Stenhouse *MA 1932
asst Ger dept Aberd 1944–47; teacher Ger part time Aber h s for girls 1963–70
d Daviot Aberdeensh 19.1.79 A UR xlviii 232

MELVIN James   MB ChB 1915
d East London S Afr 29.4.72 A UR xliv 429

MELVIN John Middleton   MA 1950 LLB 1952
ptnr A. C. Morrison & Richards advoc Aber from 1957; clerk of the peace county of Aber 1970–75

MELVIN or Durcan, Katherine Jessie Walker
**   *MA 1942**
resid Baldrine Is of Man

MELVIN Kenneth Stewart   MB ChB 1903
no longer on GC reg

MELVIN Kenneth Thomson   *MA 1955 Dip Ed 1956

MELVIN or Morrison, Marion Gertrude   *MA 1936
teacher Ger: various schools 1954–75, Clifton h s for girls from 1975

MELVIN Redvers George   MA 1920 MB ChB 1924
d 14.3.64 A UR xl 399

MELVIN Robert William McIntosh   BSc(eng) 1928
FICE
pres Brit waterworks assoc 1972–73; dir Brit waterworks comp; dir Bristol & West bldg soc

MELVIN or Wiseman, Winifred Anne Isobel
**   MA 1930**
resid Aber

MENMUIR Alexander   MA 1926
d Aber 16.2.73 A UR xlv 226

MENNIE Alexander Thomson   MB ChB 1949

MENNIE or Thompson, Annie Isabella Beaton
**   *MA 1917**
d Brechin 15.11.70 A UR xliv 208

MENNIE Douglas   MA 1942 MEd 1957
resources dev off. Grampian reg from 1975
wife d 5.9.77

MENNIE Duncan Mackenzie   *MA 1929
prof Ger/Scandavian stud. N'cle 1959–74; emeritus prof from 1974

MENNIE Elma Rae   *MA 1938
head Laurel Bank s Glasg 1963–68; headmistress' fell. Ger dept univ coll S Wales Cardiff 1968; dep head Walbottle g s N'cle-u-Tyne from 1968 (Walbottle h s from 1972); retd 1977

MENNIE or Henderson, Gertrude Mary
**   MB ChB 1945**
clin asst chest clin and mass radiography RI Sheffield from 1964

MENNIE Gordon   MA 1939

MENNIE or Shire, Helena Mary   *MA 1933
Cantab: assoc lect Engl King's coll/asst dir of stud. in Engl Fitzwilliam coll from 1964; member acad council and lect to Brit and Europ stud. group Lond from 1972; foundation fell. Robinson coll Cantab from 1974

MENNIE John   MA 1948 *MEd 1953
d Aber 20.9.66 A UR xli 342

MENNIE Robert Alexander Esslemont   *MA 1942
F Inst Pet
BP: Lond 1943–48, oper man. Zürich 1948–55, asst to man. dir Hamburg 1955–57, various assignments Lond 1957–63, shareholders' rep Hamburg 1964–67, asst gen man. supply Lond 1968–76; dir publ affairs (Scot.) from 1977
m Belfast 8.12.41 Dorothy S. A. Moat B Com Sc(Belf)

MENZIES Angus   MB ChB 1937

MENZIES Charles Sparke   MA 1934
JP Aberdeensh 1961
retd 1974; resid Aber
d 1.9.81

MENZIES Elizabeth Ross   MA 1931

MENZIES Graeme Mitchell Mill   MB ChB 1925
d Aber 5.6.72 A UR xlv 127

MENZIES Joan Isobel   MA 1947
teacher Engl Edin/Aber 1948–68; lady advis Niddrie Marischal s s Edin 1968–72, asst head 1972–74, dep head Castlebrae h s from 1974
m Currie 31.7.68 Thomas A. Miller DFC teacher p e s of Robert P. M. Hamilton

MENZIES Kenneth John   MA 1947
head Stoneywood p s 1965–76; retd; resid Dyce

MENZIES Mathilda Fisher
**   MB ChB 1920 DPH 1921 *MD 1928**
retd 1958; resid Lond

MENZIES Norman   MB ChB 1940
g p Acton and Chiswick Lond from 1948

MENZIES Robert Forbes   MB ChB 1941
lect bact Aberd from 1946
wife *d* 13.10.66

MENZIES Thomas   MB ChB 1915
d Dun 17.10.69 *A UR* xliii 329

MENZIES Thomas   MB ChB 1945
FRCS(Eng) 1962 FRCS RCPSGlas 1973
consult. surg Glasg RI and hon clin lect surg Glas
from 1966

MENZIES Walter Neil   *MA 1936
asst lib: Edin univ 1959–62, Aberd 1962–65; sub lib
Aberd 1965–76, sen lib asst Aberd from 1976

MENZIES William   MB ChB 1925
d 13.1.73 *A UR* xlv 226

MERCHANT Ethel   MA 1928

MERCHANT James Murray   BSc 1947 *1948

MERCHANT Janet Mitchell   MA 1946
teacher: Stockethill S p s Aber 1947–61, Northfield
acad Aber 1961–74, Cloverfield p s Bucksburn from
1974

MERCHANT Margaret Elizabeth Strachan
                                              ***MA 1945**
Alford acad: prin teacher Engl/hist from 1965,
woman advis from 1966, asst head from 1973
m Lumphanan 25.7.64 John A. Cooper s of James C.
Alford

MERCHANT William John Shaw   BSc(agr) 1941
county advis Caithness 1948–49; Dingwall: agr
advis Rosssh 1949–72, sen agr advis Ross/Sutherland
from 1972

MERRIMAN Jemima Mary Phillips   MA 1932
retd; resid Stromness

MERSON Alan Edmond   BSc(agr) 1951
dir S. T. Law Aber from 1968

MERSON or Bonner, Dorothy Mary   MA 1915
d Aber 31.3.61 *A UR* xxxix 202

MERSON George Polson   MB ChB 1933
DPH(Lond) 1953 MFCM 1974
m o Zanzibar 1940–50, sen m o Tanganyika 1950–62;
m o h Gravesend 1962–76; port m o Denton
Gravesend 1976–79; retd; resid Dartford

MERSON William   *MA 1932

MESTON Alexander Marshall   *BSc 1949 PhD 1952
ICI Stevenston: sen scient Nobel div 1969–71, dep
man. NSM dept organics div from 1971
d Bury 25.12.78 *A UR* xlviii 233

MESTON Gertrude   MA 1913
d Aber 21.6.73

MESTON Michael Charles   *MA 1954 LLB 1957
JD(Chicago) 1959 hon sheriff City of Aber 1972
Aberd: sen lect compar law 1964–68, prof juris 1968–
71, prof Scots law from 1971

MESTON William   *MA 1910 BSc 1912
d Aber 26.9.65 *A UR* xli 241

METCALFE or Whyte, Joan Anne   *MA 1937
resid Kenilworth

MICHAEL James   MA 1903
no longer on GC reg

MICHELSEN or Larg, Isabella Beaton   *MA 1915
no longer on GC reg

MICHELSON Everett Gladstone   MB ChB 1921

MICHIE Alexander McGregor
                                    MB ChB 1933 DPH 1935
FFCM 1972
med supt Aber gen hosps 1948–71; PASMO NE reg
hosp board from 1971

MICHIE Arthur Cumming   *BSc 1900 DSc 1906
d Corbridge 17.5.74 *A UR* xlvi 234

MICHIE Charles   MB ChB 1940
m o pneumoconiosis med panel DHSS Sheffield
1963–74; retd; now part time appt: m o pneumoconiosis med panel DHSS Glasg, indust injuries and
war pensions med records DHSS Glasg and clin asst
cytology dept Glasg RI

MICHIE Charles Watt   *MA 1929
OBE 1943 Defence Medal 1945 Coronation Medal
1953 GMG 1960
m Edin 1933 Janet L. G. Kinloch MA(Edin) teacher d
of David K. Kirkcaldy

MICHIE or Rose, Dorothy May
                                              ***MA 1952 Dip Ed 1953**
d Aber 3.4.63

MICHIE or Watson, Elizabeth   MA 1936

MICHIE Elizabeth Woodrow   MB ChB 1955

MICHIE Eric Raymond   MA 1951

MICHIE Ernest James Stewart   BSc(for) 1955
dist off. for. comm: Carlisle 1958–63, Fort Augustus
1963–67, Inv 1967–75, Dornoch from 1975

MICHIE Ethel Lilian   MA 1941
teacher Scotstown p s Aber 1969–72
m Aber 9.7.71 Daniel J. Stephen artist

MICHIE Francis William   *MA 1894
d Aber 18.3.62 *A UR* xxxix 370

MICHIE Hellenor Ramsay Watson Thomson
                                                        ***MA 1907**
d Ballater 4.10.69 *A UR* xliii 327

MICHIE James Alexander *MA 1947 D Litt 1961
sen lect Engl univ of Hull from 1966

MICHIE James Alexander Davidson
*MA 1951 MEd 1958
sen dep dir of educ Dun 1965–67; sen dep dir of educ Aberdeensh 1967–68, dir of educ 1968–74; dir educ Grampian reg from 1974

MICHIE James Ernest BSc(agr) 1945
prin teacher sc Kaimhill s s Aber 1961–69, dep head from 1969

MICHIE or Smith, Jean Christian MA 1952
resid Brighton

MICHIE John BSc 1933
head Longside p s 1966–73; retd
d Longside 23.5.81

MICHIE Robert Cook BSc(eng) 1941
hon Sheriff Fort William from 1972
man. dir Highland Lime Co Fort William 1952–77, man. from 1977

MICHIE Victor Gordon BSc(eng) 1948
MCIT
man. dir Charles W. Michie haulage contr Aber from 1970 and man. dir Boyne Bay Lime Co Aber from 1977

MICHIE William MA 1930 MB ChB 1935
b 27.1.11
consult. surg ARI from 1947; councillor Royal coll of surg Edin from 1971; pres assoc of surg of GB & Ireland 1972; elected member of James IV assoc of surg (internat) 1972; member of UK specialist advis comm in gen surg from 1973
d Aber 23.3.78 *A UR* xlvii 359

MICHIE William David *MA 1952
Dip Ed(Lond) 1968
insp of s Salisbury Rhodesia from 1971

MICHIE Winifred Margaret Ross MA 1944
teacher Meldrum s from 1946

MICKLEBURGH Walter Edward
BSc 1949 MB ChB 1953
DPM(Melbourne) 1964 MANZCP 1965
MRCPsych 1973
Aust: psychiat mental health serv Adelaide 1964–73, dir of mental health Aust Capital Territory Canberra from 1973

MIDDLER Dorothy Findlay MA 1954
m West Vancouver 7.9.68 David E. W. Thomas comp dir s of William J. T. Hove

MIDDLETON or Brebner, Agnes Ann MA 1915
resid Bearsden
husb *d* 4.12.73
d Stirling 27.2.79

MIDDLETON or Durno, Alfreda Gordon MA 1938

MIDDLETON or Kinnes, Alice MA 1901
no longer on GC reg

MIDDLETON or Johnston, Cecilia Douglas
BSc 1934 MB ChB 1940
Aber: locum tenens g p until 1974, co-ordination SAFUR from 1974; resid Longside

MIDDLETON David MB ChB 1932
g p Sunderland from 1935; chmn Sunderland div BMA 1955; member Sunderland hosp man. comm from 1967; member Sunderland AHA (N reg health auth) from 1973; retd 1977

MIDDLETON David Austin MB ChB 1954
FRSM 1965
g p: Bucksburn 1959–61, Aber 1961–65; med advis in pharm indust: Isleworth 1965–69, Ingelheim, Germany from 1969
m Frankfurt/Main Germany –.4.61 Angelika Ankele teacher d of Heinrich A. MD(Giessen) Frankfurt

MIDDLETON or Florence, Dorothea Watson
MA 1950
resid Tawa, Wellington NZ 1976

MIDDLETON Douglas George Lawson
BSc(eng) 1944

MIDDLETON or Cunningham, Emma *MA 1955
teacher Engl New Deer s 1957–59; resid Aber

MIDDLETON George Proctor MB ChB 1926
KCVO 1962
retd from g p Ballater and from surg apothecary HM household at Balmoral 1973
wife *d* 24.11.64

MIDDLETON Isabella Annie *MA 1944
teacher mod lang Aber h s for girls (later Harlaw acad) from 1951, prin Fr from 1966

MIDDLETON or Reid, Isabella Annie Alexandra
MA 1946
resid Grantown-on-Spey

MIDDLETON or Gow, Janie Emslie MA 1923
resid Newbury

MIDDLETON John MA 1929
retd 1971; resid Lond

MIDDLETON Lewis BSc(eng) 1936
dir: Aber Construct. Group 1967–72, Hunter Construct. (Aber) from 1972

MIDDLETON or Hill, Muriel Agnes *MA 1947
teacher mod lang: Buckhaven h s 1950–58, St Thomas of Aquinas s s Edin 1971–76, Broughton h s Edin from 1976

MIDDLETON Richard Stevenson Will
MB ChB 1949
MRCPGlas 1966 fell. Council of Europe 1973
assoc consult. phys Oxford 1967; consult. phys geriat

med Swindon/Cirencester 1967–70; sen consult. phys/
sen clin lect dept geriat med St James's univ hosp
Leeds from 1970

MILLAR Andrew Gerrie   *MA 1948
   prin teacher Fr Perth acad 1962–65; rector
Rothesay acad Bute 1965–68; rector Dunfermline h s
from 1968

MILLAR or Boyne, Janet Cuthbertson   *MA 1947
   teacher Engl/hist h s for girls (Harlaw acad) Aber
from 1964

MILLAR or Yorston, Jessie Campbell
                         MB ChB 1953 ^cMD 1956
   sen clin m o commun health Southampton and
Winchester from 1967

MILLAR Josephine Beatrice   MA 1929

MILLAR Joyce Margaret   MB ChB 1951
   MFHom 1960 LLCO 1962
h o: gyn royal Lond hom hosp 1954–55, S'ton 1955–
56; g p Addlestone 1956–58; clin asst Lond royal
Lond hom hosp; osteopath phys 1960–62; private
pract from 1962; clin asst royal Lond hom hosp from
1967

MILLAR or Rudram, Mary Davies   *BSc 1940
   analyst with Wessex water auth Somerset rivers div
Bridgwater Somerset from 1970

MILLAR William Davidson   BSc(eng) 1949 *1950
   lect civ eng RGIT Aber from 1960

MILLER Alexander Loudon   *MA 1955 Dip Ed 1958
   d 23.5.77

MILLER Alfred James
                         MA 1926 LLB 1937 LLD 1975
   MBE 1961 OBE 1969 Hon FSBI 1965
retd 1972; resid Aber
d Aber 7.5.80 *AUR* XLVIII 441

MILLER Allan Douglas Stewart   BSc(for) 1949

MILLER or Mackenzie, Annie Alexina   MA 1918
   resid Inverurie
d 8.5.77

MILLER Charles   MB ChB 1949

MILLER Charles Wilmar   MA 1949
   C of S min: Munro ch Rutherglen Glasg 1959–65,
Cruden par ch 1965–73, Anstruther ch from 1973;
Scot. council member inst of adv motorists, pres Scot.
groups assoc

MILLER or Richardson, Daveen Elizabeth   MA 1949
   teacher: Ware 1964–69, Broxbourne 1973–76

MILLER Donald John   *BSc(eng) 1947
   app eng/eng: metro Vickers Manc 1947–53, Brit
elect. auth Kingston-on-Thames 1953–55, Preece
Cardew & Rider consult. eng Lond 1955–66; chief eng

NSHEB Edin 1966–74; dir eng SSEB 1974–78, gen
man. from 1978
m Edin 19.4.73 Fay Herriot MA(St And) teacher d of
James H. LLB(Edin) Duns

MILLER Duncan   MB ChB 1911
   no longer on GC reg

MILLER Ernest   *MA 1952 LLB 1955
   NP 1964
exec asst Glasg 1956–57; court asst Hamilton 1957–
60; proc fisc dep Glasg 1963; part time burgh prosec
Rutherglen 1965–75; part time chmn DHSS tribunal
Motherwell from 1966; sen ptnr John Y. Robertson &
Co Hamilton and Giffnock Glasg 1963
m Glasg 30.3.59 Renee Kay leg. secy

MILLER Florence Mary   MA 1922
   no longer on GC reg

MILLER George   MA 1950
   head: Fetterangus p s 1960–65, Rhynie p s 1965–75;
Insch from 1975

MILLER George Norman   MB ChB 1937
   g p Leigh-on-Sea from 1939

MILLER Ian   BSc(agr) 1950

MILLER James   BSc(agr) 1936

MILLER James Webster   MB ChB 1903
   no longer on GC reg

MILLER or Kennedy, Jessie Nicol   MA 1906
   no longer on GC reg

MILLER or Mills or Paul, Joan Mary   *MA 1946

MILLER John   BSc(agr) 1916
   no longer on GC reg

MILLER John Lawrence   *BSc(eng) 1945

MILLER John Whyte   MB ChB 1942
   s m o Longbenton and Killingworth, Northumberland from 1973

MILLER Mackenzie   MA 1951

MILLER or Buchan, Margaret   MA 1951
   m(2) Duchovny

MILLER Nancy Hamilton   *MA 1942
   lect Engl Padgate coll of educ Lancs 1960–61; prin
teacher Engl Mary Erskine s Edin from 1961

MILLER or Stewart, Patricia Scott   MA 1955

MILLER Peter   MA 1923
   no longer on GC reg

MILLER Robert Candlish   BSc 1951
   CEng MIERE AMBIM MIMC
staff apptment war off. Lond 1958–63; cmdr REME

wing s of artillery Larkhill (lt col) 1963–66; dept commandant s of elect. eng REME Arborfield (lt col) 1966–69; man. consult. Harold Whitehead & Ptners Lond 1969–72; man. dir Avonmouth Eng Bristol 1972–74; man. consult. Whitehead Consult. from 1974

MILLER Stephen James Hamilton
                    MB ChB 1937 MD 1953
surg-oculist HM household 1965–69; dep hospitaller St John's hosp Jerusalem from 1968; edit. *British Journal of Ophthalmology* from 1973; surg-oculist to HM The Queen from 1974

MILLER Thomas Balfour   *BSc 1949 PhD 1952
d Aber 10.12.76 *AUR* xlvii 214

MILLER Walter Taylor   MB ChB 1946

MILLIGAN Frederick Patterson   MA 1890
d Edin 17.5.61 *AUR* xxxix 198

MILLIGAN James Cameron   *MEd 1950
retd; resid Aber

MILLIGAN or Mackenzie, Margaret Cranston
                    MA 1951

MILLS or Mills, Margaret Mary   MB ChB 1922
DA RCSI 1949 FFARCSI 1962
consult. anaest St Michael's hosp Dunlaore, Ireland from 1948
m 29.5.39 Joseph E. Mills BE(UCD) Co Dublin; husb *d* –.7.64

MILNE Adam   BSc 1934 MB ChB 1937
d Hailsham 19.3.75 *AUR* xlvi 239

MILNE Alastair   MA 1951 *MEd 1953
lect, prin lect psych Dun coll of educ 1961–69; HMIS SED from 1970
wife *d* Glasg 18.5.77

MILNE Alexander
                    MA 1932 *BSc 1934 PhD 1938 DSc 1950
FIBiol 1963
hon member staff King's coll Durh (later univ of N'cle) and off. agr res council N'cle 1943–67; sen prin scient off. agr res council N'cle 1963–67; prof/head of dept agr zool N'cle 1967–75; emeritus prof from 1975
wife *d* 27.10.70

MILNE Alexander   *MA 1933
dep rector Wick h s 1964–73; retd

MILNE Alexander   MA 1936 LLB 1939
d Aber 31.1.75 *AUR* xlvi 239

MILNE Alexander   BL 1937
d Aber 27.10.79 *AUR* xlviii 354

MILNE Alexander Andrew Philip   *MA 1935

MILNE Alexander Berkeley   *MA 1946
OBE 1968
first secy Brit emb Brussels 1961–64; Brit residual

mission Salisbury Rhodesia 1966–67; Brit emb Jedda 1968–71; counsellor Brit FMB Tehran 1974–77; FCO Lond from 1977

MILNE Alexander George   MB ChB 1948
g p Portland from 1951

MILNE Alexander John Buchan   MA 1922
retd 1960; resid Aber
d 18.12.78

MILNE Alexander Minty   *MA 1924
no longer on GC reg

MILNE Alexander Robert   MA 1926
d 2.12.65 *AUR* xli 246

MILNE Alfred Pyper
                    MA 1924 BCom 1926 BSc(agr) 1932
no longer on GC reg

MILNE or Caie, Alice Jane   *MA 1932
resid Warwick
d Leamington 13.8.81

MILNE Andrew   *MA 1913
d S Af 11.7.72 *AUR* xlv 124

MILNE Andrew Maitland   MB ChB 1955
FDSRCS(Edin) 1966
RADC became major, sen spec dent. surg UK/Germany 1959–69; lect oral path. Welsh Nat s 1970–72; reg dent. off. Yorks DHSS Leeds from 1972

MILNE Andrew Noble   BSc 1946 MB ChB 1953
sen accident and emergency off. Grimsby gen hosp from 1964

MILNE Angela Alica   *BSc 1948 PhD 1952
MSc(Melb) 1967
prin univ women's coll Melbourne 1960–67; teacher Henley g s 1970–71; sen exper off. univ R'dg from 1971
m Melbourne 24.5.62 Lloyd H. P. Jones BAgrSc(Melb) sen prin res scient CSIRO Aust

MILNE or Duthie, Anne   MB ChB 1946
h o RACH 1946–47; Birm accident hosp 1947–48; Lond: dem anatomy Charing Cross 1948–49, regist obst/gyn St Mary's hosp 1949–51; g p Leeds from 1951
husb *d* 15.4.76

MILNE Annie Watt   MA 1912
d Aber 15.4.72 *AUR* xliv 428

MILNE Archibald Cousland   MB ChB 1946
Edin: sen anaest city hosp/consult. anaest RI from 1965

MILNE Arthur Hay   MA 1934
war serv capt RA 1940–46; head Hobkirk p s Roxburghsh 1946–55; lect Aber tech coll from 1955
m Sunbury-on-Thames Elma A. Brown pers secy d of William E. B. Wanstead Lond

MILNE Arthur John   MB ChB 1901 DPH 1903
no longer on GC reg

MILNE Arthur Young   MB ChB 1917
d Willesborough Ashford Kent 11.4.62
AUR xxxix 381

MILNE or Dickson, Barbara   MA 1916
d 20.2.63 *AUR* xl 201

MILNE Bryan Coutts   MA 1953 LLB 1955

MILNE Cameron McPherson   MA 1934
head Kennethmont p s from 1955

MILNE or Smith, Catherine Mathers   MA 1930
teacher Kintore p s 1958–70

MILNE Charles   BSc(agr) 1916
d Aber 20.12.67 *AUR* xlii 355

MILNE Charles Buchan   *MA 1949
Aber: dep head Frederick St s s 1966–73, Hilton
acad from 1973

MILNE Charles Gordon Shaw
                MA 1914 MB ChB 1917 MD 1929
retd lt col RAMC(India) 1935 ED(Efficiency Decor.
India) 1934
Fell. Brit Orthop Assoc 1975
sen orthop surg; retd 1967

MILNE Christian Park Newlands   MA 1914
teacher; retd 1954
d Aber 21.5.78

MILNE or Ingram, Christina Jane   MA 1917
d 2.11.60 *AUR* xxxix 280

MILNE Comyn   BL 1954
FRSA 1962
ptnr Wink & Mackenzie solic Elgin from 1961; TA
(Seaforth, 3 Queen's own Highlanders, 51 Highland
volunteers) attaining rank of major 1962–72; dir Sun
Alliance Assur (local); clerk to county Income Tax for
Moray

MILNE David Coutts   *MA 1931
supt Carnoustie f e centre 1945–59; spec asst
Arbroath h s 1969–73; retd; resid Carnoustie
d 25.11.77

MILNE David Dean   MB ChB 1955
FRCSE 1963
regist surg: Aber 1957–59, Falkirk 1959–66; surg
spec: Sandakan Borneo 1966–69, Tripoli Libya 1969–
72; consult. surg N'cle-u-Tyne from 1972
m Banff 30.7.60 Elizabeth A. Kerr nurs sister d of
George G. K. Banff

MILNE Derek Allardyce   MB ChB 1941
resid Woking

MILNE Dorothy Reid   *MA 1934
lect relig educ Neville's Cross coll Durh 1960–63;

sen lect r e W. Midlands coll of educ Walsall 1963–74;
lect r e City of Birmingham coll of educ and City of
Birmingham poly 1974–77

MILNE Douglas Graeme   MB ChB 1942 DPH 1952
FFCM 1973 QHS 1974
dep dir gen army med serv, rank major gen from 1975

MILNE Douglas Mearns   MB ChB 1940
sen consult. thoracic surg SW reg hosp board from
1951; resid Bristol

MILNE Duncan   MB ChB 1951
DPH(Dund) 1969
m o in dept Dun 1968–73, Angus from 1973
m Montrose 27.10.72 Davena Reid RGN SCM HV;
wife *d* 1973

MILNE Duncan   *MA 1951
sqn ldr: head ling. br HQ Air Force s Naples 1964–
66; pers serv sqn RAF Locking Weston-super-Mare
1966–68; syst analyst/progr RAF pers man. centre
Glos 1968–72; milit asst to comm NATO defence coll
Rome 1973–78; c o RAF High Wycombe from 1978

MILNE Elizabeth Honor   MB ChB 1943
g p Harrow from 1964

MILNE Elizabeth Jane   *MA 1927
retd 1968; resid Aber

MILNE or McCabe, Elizabeth Mary Isabella
                ***MB ChB 1944**
S Af; s m o Frere hosp East London 1973–78; s
m o dept of fam health H F Verwoerd hosp Pretoria
from 1978
husb *d* 24.5.72

MILNE Ella Jean   MA 1921
no longer on GC reg

MILNE or Mackay, Elspet Wilkie
                BSc 1927 DSc 1934
resid Edin

MILNE or Cameron, Elspeth Margaret   *MA 1929
resid Stirling

MILNE Eric   MB ChB 1939
MRACGP 1971 FRACGP 1975
regist surg Preston 1958–59; Mount Isa Aust: m o
1960–62, med pract from 1962
m Auckland NZ 15.12.78 Gladys L. Welbourne nurse
d of Ernest W.

MILNE or Marnoch, Euphemia Jane   MA 1945
teacher Tarves p s 1946–60, part time 1960–72, full
time from 1972

MILNE Evander Mackay McFarquhar   *MA 1948
lect univ coll Gold Coast till 1952; edit. Thomas
Nelson and Sons (Edin & Lond) from 1952

MILNE Frances Forbes   MB ChB 1949
DObstRCOG 1958 DPM 1964 MRCPsych 1973

C of S med missionary Rajputana India 1952–61; sen h o Goodmayes hosp Ilford 1961–62; regist Cell Barnes hosp St Albans 1962–64; regist/sen regist ch guid trg centre Hampstead Lond 1964–71; consult. psychiat ch guid clin Luton from 1971

MILNE Frank Marr   MB ChB 1946
g p Coupar Angus from 1952

MILNE Frederick Alexander   BSc(agr) 1934
farm./man. dir Montrose Auction Co from 1942; panel arbiter DAFS from 1947

MILNE Gavin   MA LLB 1950
asst gen secy NFU of Scot. Edin from 1956

MILNE George   MB ChB 1905 *MD 1908
g p Streatham 1974
d Streatham 1.2.75 *AUR* xlvi 234

MILNE George   MA 1911
d St Andrews 26.3.75 *AUR* xlvi 234

MILNE George   MB ChB 1927
d Pietermaritzburg Natal 21.9.69 *AUR* xliii 330

MILNE George Alexander   MA 1935
min Pacific City and Nestucca presb churches Cloverdale and Pacific City Oregon USA from 1971

MILNE George Graham   BSc(agr) 1952
prin teacher biol Belmont acad Ayr from 1974

MILNE George James   *MA 1905
d Aber 3.2.73 *AUR* xlv 223

MILNE George Panton   MB ChB 1934
clin reader obst/gyn Aberd 1972–76; retd member univ court Aberd from 1980
wife *d* 29.6.73
m(2) Melrose 3.11.75 Mary A. Watt teacher d of James W.

MILNE or Astle, Gladys   MA 1945

MILNE Harold Samuel   BSc(eng) 1928
retd 1964; resid Aber

MILNE Helen   MA 1924 *1926
d Daviot Inverurie 29.7.71 *AUR* xliv 320

MILNE Herbert John Mansfield   *MA 1909
d 11.2.65 *AUR* xli 54

MILNE Herbert Stewart   MB ChB 1909 DPH 1912
retd col; resid Lymington

MILNE Hugh Fraser   MA 1949
head: Dunecht p s 1961–70, Milltimber 1970–73, Scotstown Aber from 1973

MILNE Ian   BL 1949
sole ptnr Mayer & Fraser solic Keith 1955–76; retd
m 22.6.68 Jeannie C. W. Stevenson
d Keith 16.2.80

MILNE Irene   MB ChB 1948
DObstRCOG 1971
private g p Mt Isa Queensland Aust from 1963

MILNE or Ingram, Irene   MA 1950
resid Llandrindod Wells Powys

MILNE or Grant, Isabella   MA 1930

MILNE Isobel Goring   BL 1939
retd; resid Aber

MILNE James   *MA 1934
M o T (D o E): fin. div Blackpool/Lond 1940–52, Lond: bridges eng div/lect trg branch 1954–58, parl estimates clerk 1958–67, dep chief regist 1967–73; retd; resid Catford, Lond
m Inverurie 1.9.37 Adelaide Joss

MILNE James   *MA 1951
teacher classics Morgan acad Dun 1954–63; spec asst classics Kirkcaldy h s 1963–68; prin classics: Airdrie acad 1968–72, Albyn s for girls Aber from 1972

MILNE James Bate   MA 1930
head Braes p s Perthsh 1947–52, Longforgan from 1952
m 1938 Anna M. Henderson

MILNE James Pratt   BSc(eng) 1945

MILNE James Scott   MA 1940
no longer on GC reg

MILNE or MacKean, Janet Elizabeth   *MA 1939
resid Wallasey

MILNE or Edmond, Jeannie   MA 1949

MILNE Joan Margaret   MB ChB 1948
h s Aber 1949–52; regist Nuffield dept surg Oxford 1952–54; regist ch dept Newcastle 1954; resid Vict, Aust
m Braemar 1955 Joseph H. Scudamore MB ChB(Brist) obst/gyn s of William E. S. Usk Mon

MILNE John   MA 1919 BSc(agr) 1921

MILNE John   MA 1930
d Aber 30.3.74 *AUR* xlv 448

MILNE John   *MA 1934
teacher: prin mod lang Dollar acad from 1938, acting dep rector 1960–62; retd 1977

MILNE John Bruce   *BSc(eng) 1947

MILNE John Clark   *MA 1922
d Aber 3.12.62 *AUR* xl 86

MILNE John Coutts   MB ChB 1923 DPH 1925
m o h Farnborough, Fleet & Hartley Wintney 1959–68, part time m o Surrey c c from 1968

MILNE John George   MB ChB 1946
g p Yorks from 1955

MILNE John Irvine Wallace   *MA 1931
prin teacher classics Dunbar g s from 1946

MILNE John Maxwell   MA 1949
man. dir James G. Bisset univ bookseller Aber from 1953

MILNE John Nelson
BCom 1922 *MA 1946 LLB 1947 LLD 1960
retd 1970
Aberd: member univ court 1949–70; member bus. comm of Gen Council 1930–70, convener 1944–70

MILNE Joseph Peter   MB ChB 1934
g p Keith from 1935

MILNE or Dobbs, June Ishbel   MB ChB 1951
dir ch dev center ch hosp Milwaukee, Wisconsin USA/assoc prof paediat med coll of Wisconsin from 1965

MILNE Kenneth Grant Sim   MB ChB 1951
g p Edin from 1956

MILNE Kenneth Panton   MB ChB 1946
brig/advis ophth M o D Lond from 1973

MILNE Lawrence Walker   MA LLB 1950

MILNE Leonard McDonald Emslie   MB ChB 1937
g p; retd; resid Wales

MILNE Leslie   MA 1951
head Tullynessle p s from 1966
m Deskford 24.7.65 Isobel J. Currie bank clerkess d of William C. MBE Deskford

MILNE or Cant, Lizzie Fowlie Bruce   MA 1924
d Aber 23.12.69 *AUR* XLIII 445

MILNE Lorna Christian   MB ChB 1947
Dip Psychiat(McG) 1954 CRCP(C) 1968 FRCP(C) 1973
asst psychiat Montreal ch hosp 1954–55; USA: instr clin psychiat univ of Vermont coll of med Burlington 1961–67, psychiat/consult. ch health State of Vermont 1965–67; Kingston Ontario: ch psychiat reg ch centre from 1968, asst prof psychiat Queen's univ from 1972
m Kingston Ontario 1.7.50 Thomas J. Boag MB ChB(Liv) dean fac of med Queen's univ Kingston s of John H. B. Liv

MILNE or Jamieson, Mabel   MA 1924
resid Edin
husb d Edin 2.3.67

MILNE or Mitchell, Mabel Davidson   MA 1915
resid Sanderstead

MILNE Malcolm Ross   *MB ChB 1943
FFARCS 1960 FFARACS 1961
dist m o Broome W. Aust 1947–50; dep dir dept of anaest royal Perth hosp W. Aust from 1962

MILNE or Summers, Margaret   MA 1936
teacher Ruthrieston s s Aber from 1950

MILNE or Ribton-Turner, Margaret Mirren
MA 1934
resid Whetstone Lond

MILNE Marian Byrne   *MA 1929 MB ChB 1937
d Aber 15.4.72 *AUR* XLV 128

MILNE Marjorie Isabel   *MA 1932
AIL 1967
teacher Beechwood s Aber 1958–73; stud. Italian Aber coll of comm/univ centre of culture for foreigners Florence Dip(Adv) 1966

MILNE Marjorie Mary
MA 1916 *MB ChB 1920 DPH 1922
d Edin 30.11.75

MILNE Mary Ann   MA 1911
no longer on GC reg

MILNE Mary Ann Urquhart   MA 1917
d 9.7.63

MILNE Mary Cheyne   BSc 1927
no longer on GC reg

MILNE or Stephen, Mary Evelyn
BSc 1932 MA 1933
resid Groombridge

MILNE or Allman, Mary Gordon
MA 1917 MB ChB 1921

MILNE Mary Isabella   *MA 1924 BSc 1924
retd 1960; resid Bieldside Aber

MILNE or Barrie, Mary Stronach   MA 1937
resid Stonehaven

MILNE or Hampson, Marybell Grant   BSc 1949
Cert Dip Acct & Finance 1977
teacher sc N Manc g s for girls 1961–71; comp secy/dir Becketts bakery eng Heywood Lancs from 1971

MILNE Maurice   *BSc(eng) 1936
FIMunE 1953 FICE 1954 FIWE 1956 FIStruct 1968 FRTPI 1968 FIHE 1968
dep dir gen highways D o E Lond 1970–76; pres Permanent International Assoc of Road Congresses Paris from 1977

MILNE Moira Agnes   MA 1931
retd 1973; resid Stonehaven

MILNE Murdoch McIntyre
MB ChB 1928 ^cMD 1936
d Hawick 15.2.64 *AUR* XL 400

MILNE Norman   BSc(eng) 1951 *1952
elect. eng AEI 1952–63; lect eng Aberd from 1963

MILNE Peter   MB ChB 1941

MILNE Peter Weir   MA 1925 LLB 1929 BCom 1930
resid Peterhead
d 16.4.81

MILNE Robert Alfred Charles   MA 1949

MILNE Robert Blair   MA 1902
no longer on GC reg

MILNE Ronald Douglas   *BSc(eng) 1952
PhD(Lond) 1962 FIMA 1965 FRAeS 1970
MSc 1971
reader aeronaut. eng Lond (QMC) 1964–71; prof eng
maths Brist from 1971

MILNE Ronald George   MB ChB 1946
consult. anaest NE reg hosp board Aber from 1963

MILNE Rosalind Margaret Paul   MB ChB 1934
consult. anaest NE reg hosp area Aber from 1948

MILNE Royston John   *MA 1934 LLB 1937

MILNE or Cruickshank, Sheila Craig   *BSc 1942

MILNE Sheila Isabel Duguid   BL 1949
d Aber 25.3.68 *A UR* XLII 374

MILNE Stephen George   *BSc 1936

MILNE Thomas   *MA 1947

MILNE Thomas Beattie   BSc(eng) 1938
d Calgary Canada 12.3.75 *A UR* XLVI 240

MILNE Thomas Charles Craighead   *MA 1950

MILNE Valerie MacAra   MB ChB 1950
g p
resid Bridgend Glam

MILNE Victor Edmond   MB ChB 1921 DPH 1923
d Sutton Coldfield 9.9.71 *A UR* XLIV 319

MILNE William   MA 1903
d 5.10.63

MILNE William   MA 1951

MILNE William   BSc(eng) 1952

MILNE William Alexander   BCom 1929 *BSc 1931

MILNE William Francis Jamieson   BSc 1936 *1937

MILNE William Guthrie   MA 1935 LLB 1939
solic Milne & Reid advoc Aber from 1948

MILNE William James   BSc 1952 *1953

MILNE William Mitchell   BSc(agr) 1923
no longer on GC reg

MILNE William Proctor
                    MA 1903 DSc 1910 LLD 1946
d Glack 3.9.67 *A UR* XLII 178

MILNE William Shirreffs   MB ChB 1939
consult. ophth NE reg hosp board and asst in
ophth Aberd 1948–77; retd

MILNER George Algernon Webb   MB ChB 1949
FACS 1960
consult. surg univ hosp of W. Indies from 1959

MILNER Robert Webb   MB ChB 1949
DA(Dub) 1953 FFARCS(Lond) 1954
m o Kingston Jamaica 1949–53; spec in anaest:
Kingston Jamaica 1954–56, St Boniface hosp
Winnipeg 1956–68; chief of anaest Victoria gen hosp
Winnipeg from 1968

MILNER or Kidson, Ruth   MA 1937
resid Aberystwyth

MILNER Thomas Gordon   BSc(eng) 1947

MILTON Alexander Gordon   *MA 1924
retd 1970; resid Glasg
d 21.7.77

MILTON or Faulds, Andrena Dorothy Margaret
                                        MA 1932
d Aber 24.2.72 *A UR* XLIV 433

MILTON George John Geddes   *BSc 1934
rector Invergordon acad 1959–75; retd; resid
Portgordon
d England –.9.80 (on holiday) *A UR* XLIX 68

MILTON James Sutherland   MA 1915
d 26.10.64

MILTON John Alexander   BSc(agr) 1928
MA(Dub) 1965
private vet pract Rutland 1960–61; lect anim husb
vet s Trinity coll Dublin 1962–77; retd

MINDE Max   MB ChB 1921

MINTO Alfred   MB ChB 1951
DPM(Lond) 1960 MRCPsych 1972
FRCPsych 1975
Nott: sen hosp m o 1959–60, consult. psychiat from
1960

MINTO Charles Nicholson   MB ChB 1944 DPH 1949
MFCM 1972
county m o h and dist hosps off. for Caithness 1953–
74; dist m o Northern dist Highland health board
from 1974
m Horsham 6.2.68 Elizabeth Bremner

MINTO William Henry Peter
                    MB ChB 1941 DPH 1947 MD 1955
d 24.10.63 *A UR* XL 303

MINTY Agnes Mavor   MA 1930
teacher Northfield acad Aber from 1956

MINTY Eliza   MA 1915
d Newmachar 8.4.78

MINTY Gladys   *MA 1927
retd 1968; resid Fraserburgh

MINTY Herbert   MA 1931
i/c Af dept J. P. Coats Glasg 1960–71
d Glasg 15.1.74

MINTY Jessie   *MA 1930
teacher Fr Aber acad 1950–60, 1966–69; retd; resid
Fraserburgh

MINTY or Templeton, Mary Bisset   MA 1943
deceased

MINTY Schona Margaret   MA 1953

MIRRLEES Stewart Turnbull Alexander   *MA 1914
d Aber 27.1.70 *AUR* XLIII 441

MIRRLEES William Minto   MA 1920 BCom 1922
d Liverpool 1.5.63 *AUR* XL 202

MIRTLE William Pirrie   BSc(eng) 1952
CEng 1960
English Elect. co: div prod. man. MRI div Stafford
1958–61, asst gen man. Madras 1961–70; consult.
dept of employ. Glasg 1970–73; gen man. Control
panels Glasg from 1973, dir 1974

MITCHELL or Porter, Agnes Henderson   MA 1922

MITCHELL or Norwell, Ailsa Janette Isabel
resid Aber   **MA 1934**
husb *d* 1976

MITCHELL Alan Ogston   BSc(eng) 1954
MICE 1961
asst civ eng Halcrow Lond 1959–63; sen civ eng:
Balfour Beatty & Co water eng and power dev consult.
London/Sidcup 1963–73; man. eng Rendel, Palmer &
Tritton Lond from 1973
m Wimbledon 14.7.62 Caroline D. Waters secy d of
Frederick G. W. Eastbourne

MITCHELL Alastair James Lendrum   BSc(for) 1949

MITCHELL Alexander   MB ChB 1910 MD 1925
no longer on GC reg

MITCHELL Alexander Lessel Stephen   BL 1931
theatrical prod. Lond from 1937
wife *d* Lond 27.7.57

MITCHELL Alexander Mennie
MA 1895 MB ChB 1899
no longer on GC reg

MITCHELL Alfred William Coutts   *MA 1909
no longer on GC reg

MITCHELL Andrew Alexander Smith   MA 1930
retd 1972; resid Bonnyrigg

MITCHELL Andrew Henry   MB ChB 1916
retd 1966; resid Cardiff

m(2) Cardiff 6.5.69 Beatrice M. Clode d of Sidney
H. C. Cardiff

MITCHELL Ann Christine   MA 1955
teacher Ellon p s from 1961

MITCHELL or Reid, Anne Margaret   MB ChB 1954
g p Hinton Alberta from 1956

MITCHELL or Florence, Annie Gray Adams
resid Cults Aber   **MA 1931**
d 22.12.81

MITCHELL or Morgan, Betty   MB ChB 1924
retd 1966; resid Cothal Dyce

MITCHELL Brian Redman   *MA 1952
Cantab: res off. dept applied econ 1960–65; sen res
off. 1966–67; lect econ/fell. Trinity coll from 1967
marr diss
m(2) Lymington Hants 11.9.68 Ann L. Birney SRN
d of David L. B. BA(Cantab) Rusper

MITCHELL or Guy, Catherine Hutcheon
MB ChB 1945
FRCOG 1973 FAGO 1974 BA 1978
retd 1974; resid Canberra Aust

MITCHELL Charles Duncan   BSc 1942 *1948
Birm: prod. man. Polymers Dunlop chem div
1958–68, market res man. Dunlop chem. div
1968–72, quality control man. Dunlop Semtex 1972–
79, tech proj man. Dunlop Semtex from 1979

MITCHELL Charles Gordon   *MA 1911 *BSc 1913
d Inv 12.5.65 *AUR* XLI 149

MITCHELL Charlesina Jessie   MA 1947
asst head New Elgin p s 1972–77, head Greenwards
p s Elgin from 1977

MITCHELL or Gibb, Christian   MA 1925
d Ealing –.12.80

MITCHELL Colin George   MB ChB 1953
g p Aber from 1956

MITCHELL David   MA 1929
head St Mungo p s Lockerbie 1962–70; retd; resid
Langholm
m 14.7.33 Mary Douglas d of David D. Langholm

MITCHELL or Younie, Dorothy
MB ChB 1921 ᶜMD 1929
sen asst m o h Aber corp 1953–63; res fell. dept of
ment health Aberd 1968–72; retd; resid Dyce

MITCHELL or McIntosh, Dorothy Margaret
MA 1934
secy/int decorator; resid Hemel Hempstead

MITCHELL Edith Lawrence   *MA 1924
d Aber 3.7.66 *AUR* XLI 340

MITCHELL or Brebner, Eileen Jean   *MA 1954

MITCHELL or Duce, Eleanor Kerr *MA 1932
resid Norwich

MITCHELL or Bown, Elizabeth Milne BSc 1954

MITCHELL Elspeth Madge MA 1936
resid Aber

MITCHELL Ernest Renan *MA 1933
teacher Engl: Charters Towers East Grinstead 1936, Buckingham coll Harrow 1937, Internat s Yokohama 1937–39, Cath boys' s Shanghai 1940–43; interned by Japanese at Shanghai 1943–45; teacher Engl: Aberdeensh 1946, Whitwood tech coll Castleford 1946, Lamlash s 1946–48, Peterhead acad 1948–50, Dunfermline h s 1950–56, George Watson's coll Edin 1956–72, asst prin Engl 1972–74; retd

MITCHELL Ethel Margaret *MA 1926
teacher: prin mod lang Witney g s later Henry Box comp Oxford 1961–66, spec asst mod lang Aber h s for girls later Harlaw acad 1966–68; retd; resid Edin

MITCHELL Evelyn Jean MA 1952
BEd(Br. Col) 1958
Canada: teacher Fr Queen Elizabeth h s Surrey 1960–61, Engl/Fr Belmont h s 1961–63, substitute teacher Inuvik NWT 1966–67; part-time Parkland elem s Coquitlam 1972–75; learning assistance Langdale p s Gibsons BC from 1977
m Huntly 25.8.62 Robert J. Wetmore B Ed(Vict) teacher/prin s of James A. M. W. Vict BC

MITCHELL or Rose, Evelyn May MA 1921
head Brae p s Stonehaven 1931–62; retd; resid Aber
d Aber 31.7.80

MITCHELL Florence Mary MA 1929
retd 1969; resid Aber

MITCHELL or Stott, Frances Maureen MA 1954
resid Goring-on-Thames

MITCHELL George Archibald Grant
*MB ChB 1929 ᶜChM 1933 DSc 1950
FRCS 1968
prof anat Manc univ 1946–74; dean Manc univ med s 1955–60, pro vice-chancellor Manc univ 1959–63
author of many books and articles and contributor of sections or chapters to *Encyclopaedia Britannica* and other encyclopaedias and books

MITCHELL George Mutch MB ChB 1951
FPS 1942 off. brother O St J 1974
sen lect materia medica/pharmacology WNSM Cardiff from 1965; hon consult. clin pharmacology and toxicology from 1969

MITCHELL George Patrick MB ChB 1940
lect orthop surg Edin from 1957; nat delegate UK to SICOT from 1972; UK repres monospecialist sect. UEMS orthop surg from 1973

MITCHELL Gladys Muriel *MA 1919 ᵈLLB 1921
retd 1957; resid Aber

MITCHELL Hannah Isabel Elizabeth MA 1937

MITCHELL Hannah King *MA 1923
teacher Fordyce acad Banffsh 1924–64; retd; resid Cullen

MITCHELL or Smith, Helen Elizabeth MA 1936
d Aber 8.2.69 *AUR* XLIII 216

MITCHELL Helen Milne MA 1925
teacher Fordyce acad Banffsh 1926–63; retd; resid Cullen

MITCHELL or Thomson, Hilda MA 1935

MITCHELL Hunter Diack BSc(eng) 1951
resid St Albans

MITCHELL Ian Falconer BCom 1932
no longer on GC reg

MITCHELL Ian Harper *MA 1939

MITCHELL Ian James BSc(eng) 1945

MITCHELL Ian McRae MA LLB 1952
prin leg. asst corp of city of Aber 1969–75, sen solic to city of Aber from 1975

MITCHELL or Macdonald, Irene Elsie Helen
MA 1954
teacher: AGS 1960–61, Airyhall p s 1966–68

MITCHELL or Simmonds, Irene Margaret MA 1953
teacher Engl Aber: Ruthrieston s s 1964–67; part time coll of comm 1969–73, Harlaw acad 1973–78, Cults acad from 1978

MITCHELL James BSc(agr) 1923
d Edin 7.8.69 *AUR* XLIII 330

MITCHELL James *BSc 1955

MITCHELL James Durno BSc(eng) 1946

MITCHELL James Elmsly MB ChB 1907 *MD 1910
d Hartlepool 25.5.67 *AUR* XLII 347

MITCHELL James Frederick MB ChB 1931
g p Northampton from 1946

MITCHELL James Gault
*BSc 1952 Dip Ed 1955 PhD 1978
FRAS 1957 M Inst P 1958 MIElectronics 1972
teacher sc Aber acad 1953–56; res scient AEI Aldermaston 1956–62; res phys SRNE (instrumentation) Hayes 1962–67; lect med phys dept Aberd from 1967
m Aber 1.7.55 Jean C. Illingworth d of William I. Ballater

MITCHELL James Mitchell MB ChB 1915
d 3.8.61 *AUR* XXXIX 279

MITCHELL James Wilkie MB ChB 1927
d Luton 6.1.71 *AUR* XLIV 211

MITCHELL John   MA 1928 LLB 1930
d 2.12.72

MITCHELL John Alexander   MA 1952
head Marybank p s Urray Muir of Ord from 1962

MITCHELL John Charles   MB ChB 1948 ᶜMD 1956
sen consult. path. Rush Green hosp Romford from 1962

MITCHELL John Marsters   MB ChB 1911
d Edin –.1.75

MITCHELL John Phimister
**   MB ChB 1907 MD 1911**
d Cults Aber 1.4.62 *AUR* xxxix 375

MITCHELL John Souter   *MA 1921 BSc(agr) 1922
d Aber 8.6.69 *AUR* xliii 329

MITCHELL or Whyte, Maggie   MA 1911
d Stonehaven 27.10.68 *AUR* xliii 78

MITCHELL Malcolm James   MB ChB 1953
g p Crieff from 1956

MITCHELL Margaret   *MA 1948
head moderns dept Dr F. J. Donevan Collegiate Oshawa Canada 1958–59; teacher Fr Whitby Canada from 1974
m Toronto 11.10.58 Rex E. Hopkins acct s of William H. Bristol

MITCHELL or Williamson, Margaret Amy
**   MA 1952**

MITCHELL or Gordon, Margaret MacGregor
**   Gordon   MA 1930**
resid Inv

MITCHELL or Duncan, Margaret Reid   MA 1929
resid Aber

MITCHELL or Smith, Margaret Rowan   MA 1952
Aber: teacher Ferryhill s 1953–61, remed Tullos p s from 1975

MITCHELL or Macdonald, Mary   MA 1949
part time teacher: Engl Farr s Bettyhill 1964–65, remed 1969–73; resid Brora

MITCHELL Muriel Craig   *MA 1947
conference secy Royal Soc of med Lond

MITCHELL Nellie   MA 1932
m Crawford
d 1970

MITCHELL Norma Constance   MA 1943

MITCHELL or Mair, Patricia Mary Reid   MA 1927

MITCHELL Patrick   MA 1924 BSc 1926 *1927
d Aber 14.8.71 *AUR* xliv 320

MITCHELL Patrick Charles   MB ChB 1937
consult. dermat Cumberland and North Westmorland Carlisle from 1961
marr diss 1973
m(2) Carlisle 1.11.75 Alison E. S. Burnett farm. d of John G. B. of Powis MA(Oxon) Old Aber

MITCHELL Patrick Malcolm   MA LLB 1951
ptnr Craigens, Glennie & Whyte advoc Aber from 1958 (amalg John & W. G. Craigen and Glennie & Whyte)

MITCHELL Peter Edward Gordon
**   MB ChB 1953 MD 1960**
T.D. 1969 MRCPath 1964 FRCPath 1976
lect path. Aberd 1956–66; consult./hon sen lect Dund from 1966
m Aber 26.10.62 Bessie T. Fulton d of Robert M. F. Aber

MITCHELL Philip Rene   MB ChB 1936
d Galmpton 8.1.73 *AUR* xlv 227

MITCHELL Robert Alexander   MB ChB 1950
LMCC 1959 DABPsych & Neurol 1961
Clin MITAA 1972 Teaching MITAA 1973
USA: fell. commun psychiat Albany med coll NY 1960–61, private pract psychiat Shenectady NY from 1961; clin dir upstate NY transactional analysis seminar from 1972

MITCHELL Robert Hartley Ogilvie   *BSc(eng) 1950
MICE 1956
eng asst Motherwell 1950–55; 2nd lt RE (nat serv) Hants 1952–54; contractor's site eng Shetland Is/Lond/Glasgow area 1955–59; sen asst eng Argyll c c 1959–63; sen eng Stirling 1963–68; dep county surv Aber 1968–75; div road surv Grampian reg c from 1975
m Motherwell 6.4.56 Isabella M. Coutts teacher d of William A. C. Motherwell

MITCHELL Robert Lumsden
**   BSc 1930 *1931 PhD 1934**
d Aber 13.12.72 *AUR* xlv 227

MITCHELL Robert Lyell   PhD 1934
head dept spectrochem Macaulay inst for soil res Aber until 1968, dir until 1975

MITCHELL Robert Wilson Downie   BSc 1954
prin teacher maths/sc Stanley s Perthsh 1959–63; head Brechin h s annexe 1963–66; head Portmoak s Kinross 1966–70, Muthill Perthsh from 1971

MITCHELL or Ashby, Sheila Mary   MA 1944

MITCHELL Stanley Matthew   BSc(for) 1950
prin Kersewell coll Lanarksh 1961–69; head Bovington mod s Dorset from 1969

MITCHELL Thomas Chalmers   BSc(for) 1948

MITCHELL Walter Alexander   MA 1955 LLB 1957
ptnr A. C. Morrison & Richards advoc Aber from 1962

m Aber 17.9.64 Freda A. Butt millinery asst d of Frederick W. B. Aber

MITCHELL William   *MA 1902
no longer on GC reg

MITCHELL William   BCom 1922
no longer on GC reg

MITCHELL William   MA 1924
retd 1964; resid Foveran

MITCHELL William Anderson   *BSc 1947
d Aber 15.5.70 *AUR* XLIV 111

MITCHELL William Cameron   MB ChB 1926
g p N'cle-u-Tyne 1934–67; med referee DHSS 1947–74; retd; resid Canonbie, Dumfriessh
m(2) N'cle 18.2.67 Ida Scott acct d of William E. S. Manc
d 7.9.79

MITCHELL William George Drummond   MA 1930
d Aber 24.1.76

MITCHELL William Ian Cameron   BSc(agr) 1924
man. Sungei Arak estate Perak Malaya 1929–30; rep: Sun Life assur comp of Canada Aberdeensh, SAI 1931–36; acting man. rubber estates (Harrison & Crossfield) Malaya 1937–41; served with FMSVF, captivity in Singapore 1942–45; man. Cluny estate Perak Malaya 1947–49; in bus. Forres 1951–61; curator MacRobert Trusts Tarland from 1962
m Penang 11.5.39 Penelope Ogston d of Thomas O. Elgin
d Tarland 9.12.80

MITCHELL William Smith   PhD 1951
lib univ of N'cle 1963–73, lib fell. 1973–74; retd
wife d 1972
m(2) N'cle-u-Tyne 9.6.73 Christina B. Denniston or Crawford loc govt off. d of James D. Trinidad

MITCHELL William Thom   MA 1950
teacher Engl/dep head St Paul's s São Paulo Brazil from 1969

MITCHELL or Morfey, Winifred Isobel Leslie
                                            MA 1930
d 26.1.81

MOAR John William Hunter   *MA 1951
higher exec off. GCHQ Cheltenham from 1963

MOFFAT or Wallace, Elizabeth Jean   *MA 1930
Clarkston Glasg: part-time teacher Fr Radleigh private s 1956–62, teacher Fr/Ger Eastwood s 1962–65
d Glasg 27.2.78 *AUR* XLVII 359

MOFFAT or Kaye, Margaret   MA 1928
resid Tayinloan Tarbert Argyll

MOIR or Taylor, Agnes   MA 1937
prop. ironmongery shop Turriff from 1963

MOIR Beatrice Milne   MA 1928
head Tipperty s 1962–74; retd; resid Sauchen

MOIR or Hale, Catherine Watt Baird   MA 1946
teacher Port Vale j s Hertford 1960–63; resid Solihull

MOIR Donald Meldrum   MB ChB 1950
d –.8.67

MOIR Douglas Lennox   BSc(eng) 1948

MOIR Duncan Wilson   *MA 1954
sen lect Span S'ton from 1972
publ: *The Golden Age: Drama 1492–1700* Lond and New York and Spanish lang edit. 1971 and 1974 with prof E. M. Wilson; scholarly introductions to facsimile edit. of emblem books
m Monimail Fife 18.12.63 Adelyn L. Ross MA(St And) univ lect d of David R. MB ChB(Glas) Cupar

MOIR Eva   MA 1922
retd 1960; resid Kinellar

MOIR George Alexander   BSc(agr) 1932 PhD 1935
d 30.9.77

MOIR George Lumsden   BSc(eng) 1937

MOIR George Wellington   BCom 1931
no longer on GC reg

MOIR Harry   BSc 1949

MOIR Ian Alexander   *MA 1936 BD 1939
lect Christian origins (NT) Edin 1961–74, sen lect from 1974, acting head of NT dept 1974–75

MOIR or Birnie, Isabel   MA 1948
teacher: Melness Sutherland 1959–61, Aberchirder j s s 1963–66, Findochty j s s 1966–69; resid Annbank Ayr

MOIR James Glegg   MB ChB 1939
g p Ballater 1947–77; retd

MOIR John   MA 1912 MB ChB 1915
d 9.4.67 *AUR* XLII 350

MOIR John McInnes   MA 1952 BD 1955
teacher Aber 1958–61; C of S min Glenelg 1961–66; teacher: Kasama trg coll Zambia 1966–68, Aber from 1968

MOIR John Reid   MB ChB MA 1927
retd 1966; resid Grange-over Sands

MOIR Leonard James   MB ChB 1913

MOIR Leonard James   BSc(agr) 1946
estate man. Perak Malaysia 1947–62; self-employed oyster farm. from 1962; resid Lochgilphead

MOIR Lesley   MA 1942

MOIR Maureen Agnes   MA 1954
Sydney Aust: teacher Engl 1968–73, head Engl/ humanities NSW dept tech and f e from 1973
m Sydney 15.6.68 Winston A. Kraal

MOIR Murdo Logan   *BSc 1939
d 8.11.65

MOIR or Cormie, Stella Anne   MA 1955
DipEd(Dund) 1971
teacher: Cummings Park p s Aber 1956–61, adjust-
ment ch guid centre Perth 1968–70, remed reading
from 1970

MOIR Sylvia Margaret   MA 1954
m Jones

MOIR William Keith   BSc(agr) 1924 MA 1925
d Stracathro 23.10.67 AUR XLII 363

MOLLIÈRE Frédéric Herman   MB ChB 1921

MOLLISON George   BSc(eng) 1948
advis tech educ (Brit govt) Middle East countries
Beirut, Lebanon from 1965

MOLLISON James Bain   MA 1926
d 3.9.64

MOLLISON or Brind, Janet Elizabeth
                    BSc 1937 *1938 PhD 1941
resid Harpenden

MONCRIEFF or Watson, Winifred Mary
                    MB ChB 1947
med asst dermat Shrewsbury group hosps and
Staffs central inf from 1965
m Chelsea 1950

MONCRIEFF or Fitzgerald, Zina Eveline
                    MA 1934 MB ChB 1938
FRCP 1970
head dept paediat Royal free hosp Lond from 1971;
examiner in DCH Lond from 1973

MONCUR or Taylor, Helen Ramsay   MA 1934
teacher St Combs p s Fraserburgh 1956–72; head
Craigo p s Montrose 1973–76; retd; resid Montrose

MONIES Thomas Harold   BSc(for) 1922
d Leeds 3.8.71 AUR XLIV 320

MONRO Hector   MA 1915
d Aber 29.10.61 AUR XXXIX 279

MONRO James Scott Campbell
                    BSc 1937 MB ChB 1940
aural surg Darlington mem hosp from 1947

MONRO or Booth, Jeannie   MA 1912
no longer on GC reg

MONRO or Hamilton, Margaret Webster
                    *MA 1934
teacher Ger: Aber High s for girls 1963–70, Aber p
s 1970–78
husb d 10.6.74

MONRO May   MA 1941 MB ChB 1956 MD 1965

MONTEITH or Milne, Margaret Duncan   MA 1939
teacher: Skene s s 1957–69, Bankhead acad from
1969

MONTEITH Robert Dugald   MB ChB 1937
g p Chaddesley Corbett Kidderminster from 1966
d Luton 21.5.80

MONTGOMERY Donald   MA 1928
retd 1968; resid Aber

MONTGOMERY George Morison   MA 1928
d –.5.62

MONTGOMERY Ian Fife   MA 1925
retd 1970; resid Kyle of Lochalsh
d 6.11.81

MONTGOMERY John Aitken   BSc(eng) 1949
sect. head works lab Mullard Blackburn from 1969
d 15.4.80

MONTGOMERY Murdo   MA 1921 BSc 1923
d 20.8.69

MOODIE James Stanley Ross   BSc(agr) 1951
Balloan farm Lairg 1952–58; Rogart: Rovie farm
from 1956, dairying until 1974; acquired Auchnabuach
sheep farm 1967; beef and sheep from 1974

MOODIE or Shewan, Jean Isobel   MA 1922
d Aber 6.2.70 AUR XLIII 444

MOODY or Gill, Ivy Rae   MB ChB 1955
DPH(Tor) 1965 Dip Psychiat(Tor) 1970
Cert Psych 1971 Fell. Psych 1972
publ health off.: Kingston Jamaica 1962–64; Canada:
north York Toronto 1965–67, resid psychiat U M Tor
1967–70; psychiat: Lakeshore psychiat hosp 1970–72,
Scarborough gen hosp from 1974

MOODY Robert George Neasham   *BSc 1941
teacher biol Bishop Wordsworth s Salisbury 1967–
73; retd
d 1981

MOONIE or Ley, Alexandrina Jessie   MA 1953

MOORE Walter
                    BSc 1923 BSc(agr) 1924 *1925 DSc 1942
d Aber 15.4.69 AUR XLIII 212

MOORHOUSE or Geddes, Doris May   MB ChB 1955
formerly sen m o Essex; now g p Clacton-on-Sea
from 1976

MORDAUNT or Fraser, Frances Galloway
                    *MA 1919 *1920
d 1.2.74

MORE Charles George Robb
                    MB ChB 1943 DPH 1948
F Amer Publ Health Assoc 1964 FRSH 1965
MFCM 1973
m o h Red Deer Alberta from 1948

MORE David   MA 1908
d Lond 21.6.74 *AUR* XLVI 107

MORE Isabella Main   MA 1926
retd 1972; resid Aber

MORE or Weir, Katharine Ishbel Davidson   MA 1943
resid Harrow-on-the-Hill

MORE William   *MA 1925
d 17.1.72 *AUR* XLIV 430

MORETTI or Howitt, Lina Armida Cilinda
**   MA 1937**
resid Macduff

MORGAN Alan Douglas
**   MA 1931 MB ChB 1935 *MD 1955**
FRCPath 1964
prof path. Westminster hosp Lond from 1962

MORGAN Boyd Hepburn   MA 1927 BSc 1930
JP 1959
head Dunbarney j s s Perthsh 1960–71; retd; resid
Burghmuir Perth; chmn Scot. Caravan Club 1967–69,
pres 1975–77

MORGAN George Roderick   MB ChB 1924
d Aber 2.4.67 *AUR* XLII 363

MORGAN Henry Wright   BCom 1923
MBE 1943
sen asst Harrisons & Crosfield Kuala Lumpur 1924–
36; secy chamber of commerce: Kanpur UP India
1937–48, Chittagong E. Pakistan/Bangladesh 1949–
55, Forth Valley Falkirk 1956–58, Canadian London
England 1958–63; retd; resid Sutton
m Kanpur 24.1.48 Lorna D. Pryce d of Ernest J. P.,
Simla India
d 4.7.79

MORGAN James   BSc(eng) 1938

MORGAN Jessie Mackenzie   MA 1938
head Bramble Brae p s Aber from 1969

MORGAN John Smith   *MA 1929
retd 1971; resid Aber

MORGAN Lewis   MB ChB 1925
no longer on GC reg

MORGAN Mary   MA 1934
secy Ladysbridge hosp Banff 1934–37; asst publ
assistance off. New Pitsligo 1937–48; Scot. organis
Barnardo's helpers' league 1948–58; resid Cullen

MORGAN or Taylor, Muriel Reid   MA 1931
resid New Deer

MORGAN Robin Milne   *MA 1952
teacher hist George Watson's coll Edin 1960–70;
head Campbell coll Belf 1970–76; prin Daniel
Stewart's & Melville coll & The Mary Erskine School
for girls Edin from 1976

MORGAN Thomas Newall
**   *MB ChB 1931 *MD 1934**
FRCPE 1966
hon reader in med Aberd from 1959
d Aber 4.5.69 *AUR* XLIII 215 & 242

MORGAN William James   BSc(eng) 1955

MORISON or Watson, Edith Minnie   MA 1939
d New Pitsligo 10.4.69 *AUR* XLIII 216

MORISON Isabella   MA 1930
retd 1969; resid Fraserburgh

MORISON Robert Ainslie   MA 1913 LLB 1915
no longer on GC reg

MORREN William Leith   MA 1908
d 31.12.63 *AUR* XLI 54

MORRICE Alexander   MA 1926
retd 1968; resid Dollar

MORRICE Alexander Mackay   MB ChB 1924
no longer on GC reg

MORRICE Charles Smith
**   *MA 1954 ᵈBD 1957 PhD 1959**
C of S min Newarthill ch Motherwell 1959–71,
St Andrew's Scots Presb ch Buenos Aires 1971–76,
Mauchline from 1976

MORRICE or Davidson, Elizabeth Castle Burnett
**   MA 1927**

MORRICE George   MB ChB 1936
g p Salford; retd 1973

MORRICE Helen Imlach   BSc 1929 MA 1930
d Aber 18.8.75 *AUR* XLVI 323

MORRICE James Kenneth Watt
**   MB ChB 1946 MD 1954**
FRCPsych 1972
consult. Fort Logan Mental health center Denver
USA 1966–67; consult. psychiat Ross clin Aber/clin
sen lect Aberd from 1968

MORRICE James Wilson   BL 1947
farm. Torphins 1966–78; retd

MORRICE John   MB ChB 1930
retd 1973; resid Salford

MORRICE Maggie Jane   MA 1923
d 6.2.63

MORRICE or Carswell, Margaret Christian
**   MA 1924**
resid Edin
d Edin 17.9.77

MORRICE Margaret Christina   MA 1947
no longer on GC reg

MORRICE William   MA 1920 BD 1921
d Motherwell 13.1.71 *AUR* xliv 210

MORRICE William Gorman
　　　　　　***MA 1951 BD 1954 PhD 1957**
C of S min: Auchterarder 1957–65, Motherwell 1965–70; NT advis Brit and foreign Bible soc Lond from 1970; NT lect New coll Lond from 1972; NT tut. and lib. St Jns coll Durham from 1975

MORRIS Alexander George   BSc 1953
ptnr pharm Colchester 1963–69; pharm prop. Colchester and West Mersea from 1969
m 16.9.61 Moira T. Peacock pharm dispenser d of Andrew R. P. Farnborough

MORRIS Andrew Bernard   MB ChB 1903
no longer on GC reg

MORRIS Brian Taylor Jordan   BSc(eng) 1954
MIEE C Eng 1971 MIWES 1975
applications eng AEI Trafford Park Manc 1958–61; sen tendering eng (contr) dept Harland eng Alloa 1961–66; sen proj and contr eng James Howden & Co Glasg 1967–73; elect./mech eng Lanarksh water board Hamilton 1973–75; div mech/elect. eng Strathclyde reg c water dept lower Clyde div from 1975

MORRIS James Pressley   *MA 1954

MORRIS William Drummond   MA 1891
no longer on GC reg

MORRIS William James   MA 1923
FEIS 1960
retd 1965; resid Aber

MORRISON Adeline Isobel   BCom 1935
retd; resid Lond
d Stonehaven 30.9.77

MORRISON or Allan, Agnes Whitelaw
　　　　　　　　　　　　MB ChB 1942
resid Cheltenham

MORRISON Alexander   *MA 1899 *BSc 1899
no longer on GC reg

MORRISON Alexander   MA 1912
no longer on GC reg

MORRISON Alexander   BSc(for) 1951

MORRISON Alexander James   *MA 1909 DD 1955
d 29.1.64 *AUR* xl 396

MORRISON or Donald, Alice Barbara   MA 1927
retd 1970; resid Aber
d Aber 30.8.79

MORRISON or Law, Alice Jean   MA 1943
d Stevenston 5.1.76

MORRISON or Gibson, Ann   MA 1917
teacher maths Golspie s s 1951–63; retd
d Golspie 13.4.81

MORRISON or Currier, Ann   *BSc 1927
retd 1966; resid Inv

MORRISON or Morrison, Annie   MA 1945

MORRISON Archibald   MB ChB 1952
h o ARI 1952–53; nat serv RAMC 1953–55; regist: psychiat Oldham 1955–57, ARI 1957–58; sen regist psychiat de la Pole hosp Willerby, E Yorks 1958–62; consult. psychiat Fife from 1962
m Gatley 12.6.58 Ruth Goodier MB ChB(Manc) med pract/regist paediat d of James W. G. Cheadle

MORRISON Audrey Elizabeth   MA 1948
teacher Surrey: Engl commonwealth girls' s Purley 1963–66, prin Engl Court Lodge s s Horley 1966–73, Engl Sutton Common h s Sutton 1973–76, prin Engl Sutton Common h s from 1976

MORRISON Catherine
　　　　　　MA 1955 Dip Ed 1956 *MEd 1967
educ psych Aber 1967–71; lect educ psych Callendar Park coll of educ Falkirk 1972–76; part time lect psych univ Hong Kong from 1977
m Bearsden 22.6.74 William J. Greig BSc 1948 *qv*

MORRISON or Grant, Catherine Mary   MA 1933
teacher Fr Rubislaw acad/AGS from 1967
d Aber 21.11.80 *AUR* xlix 68

MORRISON Charles Albert   *MA 1950
MA(Oxon) 1965
asst lect laws S'ton 1953–54; asst lect/sen lect/sub-dean of fac of laws King's coll Lond 1954–68; dean of fac Inns of Court s of law Council of Leg. Educ Lond from 1968; QC 1977
m Calverton 19.12.59 Elizabeth A. Coales catering man. d of Reginald C. Timaru NZ

MORRISON Colin George   MA 1935
Dumfries h s: prin teacher maths 1964–72, asst head 1972–73, dep head from 1973

MORRISON Donald   MA 1916
retd 1964; resid Croy Invsh
d Croy 24.5.79

MORRISON Douglas   BSc(agr) 1944
head crop husb dept s of agr Aber/part time lect Aberd 1968–71; chmn crop prod. group s of agr Aber/part time sen lect Aberd from 1972

MORRISON Douglas Bannerman
　　　　　　　　BSc 1927 MA 1928
d Chapel-en-le-Frith Manc 10.5.73 *AUR* xlv 320

MORRISON Edith Jane Douglas   *MA 1909
d Bath 16.7.64 *AUR* xl 396

MORRISON or Little, Elizabeth Ann   MB ChB 1944
dept m o Redbridge Lond from 1965

MORRISON Eric Elmslie   *MA 1940
FIMA 1967
Aberd: sen lect maths from 1969; edit. *AUR* from 1969; member univ court 1968–79; convener bus. comm General Council from 1979

MORRISON Eric Keir   *MA 1936
FIL 1951
reg army off. 1940–60; prin lect Ger Bristol polytech 1960–78; retd

MORRISON or Davidson, Ethel   MA 1943
Aber: teacher Lat h s for girls 1965–73, prin classics St. Margaret's s for girls from 1973
m diss 1976

MORRISON Frank Tregear   BSc(for) 1948
d 17.6.67

MORRISON George Clark   MA 1930
retd HMIS 1972; reg commun dev off. Grampian reg Scot. council of soc serv Edin from 1973
wife *d* 17.6.81

MORRISON George Will   MB ChB 1945
MRCGP 1957
g p Inverbervie from 1951

MORRISON or Henderson, Helen Shepherd
                                                    MA 1929
resid Maryculter

MORRISON Henry Philip   MA 1912
FCBA 1914 FSA 1926
resid Illinois USA

MORRISON Ian Middleton   MB ChB 1944
consult. thoracic surg Liv from 1958

MORRISON or Finlayson, Isabella   MA 1934
teacher N Tolsta p s Is of Lewis 1958–72; retd; resid Stornoway

MORRISON Isobel Milne   MA 1925 *BSc 1925
retd 1967; resid Juniper Green Edin

MORRISON James   BSc(agr) 1924
OBE 1963
prof crop/anim husb Belf and dir agr res inst of N Ireland Hillsborough Co Down 1945–65; retd

MORRISON James Alexander   MA 1905
d Aber 20.4.63 *AUR* XL 198

MORRISON James Dey   MA 1939
TD 1966 JP Aber 1971
comm 51(H) div regt RCT(TA) h q Perth 1963–67; brevet col on relinquishing comm of reg 1967; head Walker Rd p s from 1967; dist comm Dee dist city of Aber scout assoc 1967–73; retd

MORRISON James Gilbert   MA 1937
chap. to the Forces 1942–70; min of the Community ch Nicosia Cyprus 1971–72; min of the Scots ch Rotterdam Neths from 1972

MORRISON James Macdonald   MB ChB 1917
d 5.9.68 *AUR* XLIII 79

MORRISON or Thomson, Jane Ann   MA 1935

MORRISON or Mackie, Jean Bruce   MA 1928
resid N. Berwick

MORRISON or Simmers, Jean Robertson   MA 1937
teacher Kintore 1962–77; retd

MORRISON or Brockie, Jeanette   *MA 1941
d Northland NZ 17.3.63
husb *d* Northland NZ 1.3.71

MORRISON Jeannie Marr   MA 1927
d Aberdeensh 27.11.68 *AUR* XLIII 84

MORRISON Jessie Ann   MA 1930
teacher: Engl/hist/geog Ordiquhill j s s Banff 1932–47, geog/woman advis Macduff h s 1947–69, geog house mistress Banff acad 1969–73; retd; resid Macduff

MORRISON or Macleod, Jessie Mary   MA 1911
d 25.12.70

MORRISON John
          MA 1915 MB ChB 1918 DPH 1921 MD 1932
d Shrewsbury 8.2.68 *AUR* XLII 354

MORRISON John   *MA 1936
teacher Aber Lond Glasg
killed in road accident 7.7.53

MORRISON John   MB ChB 1939
g p Portree from 1952; med supt Portree hosp from 1965

MORRISON John Alexander   *BSc(eng) 1940
civ eng contr ag Aber from 1940
m Glasg 11.4.62 Mary C. J. Graham MA(Glas) teacher d of Thomas L. G. Glasg

MORRISON John Edgar   BSc 1955
food tech Rothamsted res stat 1958–64; dir res and quality assur Quaker Aust from 1964

MORRISON John James Todd
                    MB ChB 1937 DPH 1939 MD 1947
d 15.8.73

MORRISON John Peter   *BSc 1948
FInstP 1966
div man. Aircraft Marine Prod. (GB) Parkstone Dorset 1960–68; man. dir Cochrane & Johnson Paisley 1968–72, consult. from 1972

MORRISON or Morrice, Katharine Jean   MA 1954
resid Mill Hill Lond

MORRISON or Kennedy, Kathleen Montgomery
                                                    MA 1955

MORRISON or Hadden, Kathleen Murray
                                        MB ChB 1945
g p Aber from 1957

MORRISON Kenneth James   BSc(eng) 1942
elect. supt BICC Wrexham N Wales from 1968

MORRISON or Jennings, Leona Adolphus   MA 1927
teacher: Coventry 1953–55, Aber 1955–57, asst

head Middlefield p s Aber 1957–59, Aber 1959–66, retd; resid Aber
d 23.10.81

MORRISON Lewis   BSc(agr) 1921
    d 25.3.68

MORRISON Margaret   MA 1937

MORRISON Margaret   MA 1942

MORRISON Margaret   MA 1953 LLB 1955
    leg. asst: Paull & Williamsons advoc Aber/Dundas & Wilson solic Edin 1958–65; resid Saxilby
m Aber 15.2.65 David M. Shewan BA(Cantab) med pract s of Henry A. S. MA 1928 *qv*

MORRISON or Innes, Margaret Barbara
                                          BSc(agr) 1943
    resid Aber

MORRISON or Thomson, Margaret Garden
                                          MB ChB 1944
    Founder Fell. Brit Soc Med & Dent Hypnosis FRSM
g p Cullen 1948–58, Southport Lancs 1963–64; locum cas off. Westmorland and N Lancs 1964–67; asst m o coll of educ Aber from 1967
m Southport 14.12.62 Thomas W. Quigley

MORRISON Margaret Hall   MA 1939
    teacher Newmachar p s from 1957

MORRISON or Simpson, Margaret Jane   MA 1953

MORRISON or MacKintosh, Margaret Jane Barclay
                                          MA 1934
    teacher: St Peter's epis s Fraserburgh 1959–61, Fraserburgh North s 1961–64; spec s Fraserburgh 1964–69, Denend p s Cardenden 1969–77; retd; resid Glenrothes

MORRISON Margaret Leith   MA 1953
    teacher geog/Engl Inverurie acad 1961–64; credit advis Hudson Bay Co, Victoria BC Canada 1964–66; writer of ch's books
m Victoria BC –.11.65 Robert J. Minter supervis of construct. for Greater Victoria s board s of Francis R. M. Victoria BC

MORRISON or Williams, Margaret McLean
                        Macfarlane   MB ChB 1933
    lect anat univ of Wales (Univ Coll Cardiff) 1963–76, sen lect from 1976

MORRISON Marion   MA 1925
    retd 1964; resid Bath

MORRISON or Watson, Marjorie Elizabeth
                                          BSc 1946
    resid Shrewsbury

MORRISON Marjory Watson   MA 1942

MORRISON or Brownlee, Mary Dempster   BSc 1953

MORRISON Mary Gordon   *MA 1935
    sen lect Fr univ Brist from 1963; retd 1977

MORRISON Mary Macleod   MA 1953
    teacher Stornoway from 1960
m Aber 31.3.62 David D. MacKenzie draper s of Donald G. MacK. Stornoway

MORRISON Murdo   MA 1901
    d Troon 11.4.75 *AUR* XLVI 320

MORRISON or Whitelaw, Nettie   MA 1951

MORRISON Norman   *MA 1923
    d Kirkcaldy 17.1.71 *AUR* XLIV 211

MORRISON Roy   BSc(agr) 1953
    Belf: sales man. BOCM 1965–70, man. dir Assoc Agr Merchants 1970–75; Cambridge: reg man. United Agr Merchants from 1975

MORRISON Sheila Catherine   MA 1953
    teacher: Walker Rd p s Aber from 1954

MORRISON Stephen Duncan   MA 1948
    dep head: Woodside p s Aber 1961–66, Springhill p s Aber from 1966

MORRISON Susan Hay   MA 1925
    prin teacher Engl/lady supt Bankhead acad 1961–68; retd; resid Turriff

MORRISON Thomas Affleck
                        MA BSc(agr) 1923 MB ChB 1931
    retd 1967; resid Brighton
wife *d* 17.10.67

MORRISON Thomas Ian   BSc 1950 *1951
    MSc(Glas) 1973 FRIC 1968 TD 1969
lect chem Jordanhill coll of educ Glasg 1963–70; asst rector Brechin h s 1971–74; advis sec educ Angus div Tayside reg from 1974
major 2 i/c 153(H) regt royal corps of transport, T and AVR, Dunfermline; rtd brevet lieut colonel 1971
pres Scot. Hockey Assoc 1974–76
m Stirling 16.4.73 Isabel C. Forgan MA(St And) lect Jordanhill coll of educ d of Robert F. Stirling

MORRISON or Reith, Violet Margaret   MA 1938

MORRISON William   MA 1939
    leading seaman RN 1939–46; teacher: Chiltern St Boys' s Hull 1946–52; Hornsea s Yorks: head Engl dept/housemaster 1952–58, sen housemaster 1969–75, head of middle s from 1975
m Hull 10.2.44 Phyllis M. Hutchinson SRN d of Frederick A. H. Hull

MORTIMER or Forbes, Dorothy Elizabeth
                                          MA 1953
    teacher: Brit army s Singapore 1959–60, Naracoorte S Aust 1962–66, Oak Farm p s Hillingdon Mddsx 1966–68; Melb Aust: emergency teacher/volunteer crippled ch kindergarten from 1973; resid Melb Aust

MORTIMER or McConnachie, Dorothy Isabel
MB ChB 1938
med asst psychiat Penyval hosp Monmouthsh from 1969

MORTIMER or Ironside, Dorothy Norris
MB ChB 1953 DPH 1956
MFCM 1973
h o RACH/Halifax hosp 1953–54; sen h o South-mead hosp Bristol 1954–56; j h m o Slade hosp for infect. diseases 1956–60; dep m o h Thanet 1960–64; sen clin m o and dep m o h Tunbridge Wells from 1964

MORTIMER Douglas MB ChB 1948

MORTIMER or Troup, Elizabeth Campbell
MA 1898
d Aber 28.12.73 *AUR* XLV 444

MORTIMER Gordon William James
MA 1948 *BSc 1951 BD 1960
C of S min Thurso W parish ch 1961–64; spec teacher relig educ Brechin h s from 1965
m Careston 6.10.73 Catherine M. Sefton BSc(St And) teacher d of George A. S. MA 1921 *qv*

MORTIMER Hector MB ChB 1914

MORTIMER John Burnett *MA 1950
d 18.6.62

MORTIMER Margaret Forbes MA 1912
retd; resid Peterhead

MORTIMER or Allan, Margaret McWilliam Milne
MA 1946

MORTIMER or Mackie, Mary Pirie MA 1924
retd 1964; resid Edin

MORTIMER or Brown, Muriel Margaret MA 1946
teacher: Aboyne till 1960, Turriff p s from 1972

MORTIMER William *MA 1941
chief acct Standard Life Assur Co Edin from 1970

MORTON or Demaine, Barbara Reid Alexander
MB ChB 1922
d Wigan 1.3.70 *AUR* XLIV 110

MORTON (formerly di Veri) Charles Bertie
***MA 1920**
retd 1971; resid Ladysmith, Natal

MORTON Richard Grenfell *MEd 1951
lect hist dept extra-mural stud. Queen's univ Belf from 1967

MOSS Francis John BSc 1953

MOUAT or Scott, Joanna Mary Isobel MA 1927
no longer on GC reg

MOUAT John Stephen Veitch MB ChB 1950
d 21.12.67

MOUAT Stephen James Veitch MB ChB 1926
d Dumfries 14.3.75 *AUR* XLVI 236

MOULI Kalluri Chandra BSc(agr) 1924

MOWAT Alexander Goodsir MB ChB 1924
retd 1965; resid Ashton-u-Hill, nr Evesham

MOWAT Brenda *MA 1947
teacher: prin mod lang Kirkwall g s from 1955

MOWAT Donald Arthur Edward MB ChB 1953
MRCGP 1970
g p: Newtyle 1963–65, Montrose from 1965

MOWAT or Ross, Esther Margaret MA 1928
Alloa: temp teaching posts various s then Lornshill acad Grange sect./Forebraes 1950–70; retd; resid Aber husb *d* 7.11.64

MOWAT or Leslie, Esther Mary MA 1946
teacher: Anstruther Wester s 1963–69, Cellardyke 1969–72; teacher Engl Waid acad from 1972

MOWAT George MB ChB 1898
d Bolton 22.1.61 *AUR* XXXIX 198

MOWAT George Nicol Garson MA 1928
retd 1968; resid Mansfield

MOWAT James Lawson *MA 1922 PhD 1927
chief admin div ILO Geneva 1960–64; retd; resid Geneva

MOWAT or Philip, Jane Fowler Sim MA 1950
teacher Kineff p s 1951–53, Portlethen p s 1953–54, Gatehouse p s Kirkcudbright 1954, Crossford p s Fife 1959–62, Edin 1962–64, Glasg 1964–68, Edin from 1968

MOWAT John *MB ChB 1942
d Dun 10.1.72 *AUR* XLIV 433

MOWAT John BSc 1952
d Aber 19.4.66 *AUR* XLII 90

MOWAT Lesley Anderson MA 1938 LLB 1941

MOWAT or Stirling, Marion Elizabeth MB ChB 1921
d Edin 27.10.73

MOWAT or Munro, Mora Jean MA 1950
teacher Kiltearn p s Evanton 1967–73

MOWAT Robert Philip MA 1934 BCom 1936
prin teacher econ/bus. stud. RGC Aber from 1944; retd 1978

MOWAT Ronald Rae MB ChB 1950 MD 1959
DPM(Lond) 1956
consult. psychiat Brighton & Hove SE metrop reg hosp board Royal Sussex County hosp Brighton/Lady Chichester hosp Hove and E. Sussex ch's dept from 1960
author *Morbid Jealousy and Murder* 1966

MOWAT William Paton   *BSc 1954

MOWATT Thomas Douglas   *MA 1927 *MEd 1929
teacher Engl/hist Glenluce s s 1952–65; retd; resid
Newton Stewart
d Dumfries –.9.80 *AUR* xlix 68

MUIR Agnes Gibson   MA 1954

MUIR or Maclean, Annie Elizabeth   MA 1930

MUIR Charles Mackenzie   BCom 1923

MUIR Colin   *BSc 1955 PhD 1959
lect nat hist dept St And

MUIR Duncan McNicol   MA 1948
Aber: dep head Kittybrewster p s 1962–67, head
Seaton p s from 1967
wife d Jan. 1970
m (2) Inverurie 6.8.71 Elizabeth M. Cook ward sister
d of Alexander C. Kemnay
d Aber 18.8.79 *AUR* xlviii 354

MUIRDEN John Robert   MA 1937
d Rosskeen Alness 21.8.68 *AUR* xliii 85

MULCAHY Maurice Joseph   BSc(for) 1949
scient off. Macaulay inst soil res Aber 1949–53;
Australia res scient CSIRO: Adelaide 1953–54, Perth
from 1954

MULHOLLAND William Hamilton   BSc(for) 1949

MULLER Ernst Robert   BSc(eng) 1940
MICE 1971 MIMH 1971 F Inst Pet 1972
prop. bakery eng firm from 1947; now gen eng and oil
field eng from 1972

MULLICK Dwijendra Nath   PhD 1939

MULLIGAN Hugh Waddell
                        MB ChB 1923 *MD 1930 DSc 1934
CMG 1954
dir Wellcome res lab Beckenham 1960–66; visiting
lect univ of Salford 1967–76

MULLIGAN James Anderson   MB ChB 1925
g p Inverbervie 1928–67; retd; resid Cadnam
Southampton

MULLIGAN John Henry   *MB ChB 1920
lect histology and neurology St And 1949–60; retd;
resid Edzell

MULLIGAN or McManus, Kathleen Marie
                                        MA 1955
resid Dun

MULLIGAN Malachi Finn-Barr
                        MA 1949 LLB 1952

MULLIGAN William Percival   *MB ChB 1913

MUNDAY Kenneth Albert   PhD 1949

MUNDIE John Harold   *BSc 1949

MUNDIE Sheila Margaret   *MA 1950

MUNN James Marshall   MB ChB 1954
g p Stirling from 1966
m Stepps 26.5.67 Fiona M. Anderson comm artist
d of John M. A. Stepps

MUNRO Alexander Fraser
                        BSc 1934 *1935 PhD 1941

MUNRO Alexander John   MA 1953
teacher: prin Engl Auchterarder 1966–68; head:
Stanley p s 1968–73, Robert Douglas mem s Scone
from 1973

MUNRO or Skarda, Annabelle Farquharson
                                        MA 1924
teacher: Edin 1949–56, York 1961–67, Aber 1968–
73; retd

MUNRO Anne Morrison   *MA 1921
retd 1961; resid Edin

MUNRO Annie Stark   MA 1930

MUNRO or Booth, Charlotte Annie   MA 1931
resid Dumfries

MUNRO Christine McCulloch   MA 1926

MUNRO Colin Ross   MA 1910
d Castlecary 28.3.61 *AUR* xxxix 201

MUNRO Donald   MA 1907
retd 1949; resid Lochmaben
d 9.1.78

MUNRO Donald   MA 1922 LLB 1924
retd 1968; resid Purley

MUNRO Donald George   BSc(agr) 1915
d Tain 13.5.74

MUNRO Donald Gunn   MA 1912 BSc 1913
d Brora –.3.71 *AUR* xliv 209

MUNRO Donald Sinclair   MB ChB 1947 ᶜMD 1957
FRCP(Lond)
univ of Sheffield: reader clin endocrinology 1963–67,
prof clin endocrinology 1967–73, Sir Arthur Hall prof
of med from 1973

MUNRO or Meston, Dorothea   *MA 1953
teacher mod lang Queen's Park s s Glasg 1959–60,
Powis acad Aber from 1976

MUNRO Dorothy Margaret   MA 1915
deceased

MUNRO or Mitchell, Elizabeth Gray   BL 1934
d Torquay 22.3.73 *AUR* xlv 227

MUNRO or Cowie, Eva Jean   MA 1951
teacher: Engl Powis j s s Aber 1951–58, Engl Kaimhill j s s Aber 1959–60, Fr Aber acad 1968–69, Rubislaw acad Aber from 1969
m 29.3.58 Gordon F. G. Cowie MA 1972 teacher s of James B. C. Aldershot

MUNRO or Mitchell, Evelyn Jane Morrison
MA 1928
resid Cults Aber

MUNRO George Francis   MA 1897
no longer on GC reg

MUNRO George Gauld   BSc(eng) 1945

MUNRO Harry William   MA 1926 BSc 1929
retd 1969; resid Kinghorn

MUNRO or MacLean, Hilda Margaret Lind
BSc 1929
resid Inv

MUNRO Hugh   MA 1924
resid supervis Craibstone coll Aber NOSCA 1960–67; retd; resid Montrose

MUNRO Hugh David Ross   MB ChB 1955
MRCOG 1972
g p Crosshills 1962–67, g p hosp practitioner (obst/gyn) conjoint appt Livingston New Town and Bangour gen hosp from 1967

MUNRO Ian Mackenzie   MB ChB 1929
resid Lond SW15

MUNRO Irene   MA 1954 Dip Ed 1955
teacher Engl: Perth h s 1955–60, Dunbarney j s s 1960–62, Kinross s s from 1969
m Aber 16.7.60 Iain A. Robertson MA(Dund) teacher f e s of George R. Perth

MUNRO James   MA 1948
teacher various schools Aber 1949–77; retd from prin maths Linksfield acad

MUNRO James John   MB ChB 1924
no longer on GC reg

MUNRO James Scott Gray   BL 1939
MBE 1964
ptnr Stephen & Smith advoc Aber from 1946; DL for County of City of Aber from 1964; DL for County of Aber from 1973

MUNRO Jessie Barbara   MA 1931

MUNRO Jessie May   MA 1930
inf mistress Elgin W End s 1959–72, asst head from 1972

MUNRO Joan   BSc(agr) 1950 PhD 1954
sen scient off. Hill Farming Organis 1959–61
m Inv 8.6.61 Michael T. Fotheringham farm. s of Alfred F. Laurencekirk

MUNRO John George   MB ChB 1938
FRCGP 1972
g p Beauly from 1946

MUNRO John George Clarke
*BSc 1947 MB ChB 1954
g p Nambour Queensland Aust 1963–76; sen lect commun pract univ Queensland med s from 1976

MUNRO or Cran, Margaret Campbell   MA 1947
resid Falkirk
husb d 27.1.71

MUNRO or Cox, Margaret Isabel   BSc 1951
exper off. MAFF 1951–59; physiol Epsom dist hosp Surrey from 1973

MUNRO or Wilson, Margaret Tennant   MA 1925
Canada: teacher Athlone boys' s Vancouver 1963–64, remed for London (Ont) board of educ 1964–70; retd
husb d 7.11.54

MUNRO or Keith, Mary Bella   MA 1929

MUNRO Murray   MA 1944

MUNRO Neil   BCom 1931
free-lance journalist *Daily Express/Evening Standard/Daily Mail* Lond 1958–65; tax. off. Inl Rev and free-lance journalist *Evening Standard* Shoreham-by-Sea from 1965; retd from civ serv 1977; secy/treas Royal Brit Legion Shoreham
m Lond 20.6.49 Andree G. J. Taylor d of Herbert T. major RASC

MUNRO Norman Morrison
MB ChB 1925 ᶜMD 1931
retd 1972; resid Luton
d Luton 27.12.77 *AUR* XLVII 356

MUNRO or McGregor, Rachel Catherine   MA 1916
d 16.4.69

MUNRO Robert   MB ChB 1915
no longer on GC reg

MUNRO or Ross, Robina   MA 1918
d 9.4.79

MUNRO Roderick Alexander   MA 1948 *MEd 1951
FEIS 1971
Aber: dep head Kirkhill p s 1960–65, head Victoria Rd p s from 1965

MUNRO Ronald   MA 1929
no longer on GC reg

MUNRO Stewart Sinclair Fowler   MB ChB 1945
consult. ophth surg to Herefordsh and Radnor group of hosps from 1960

MUNRO or Adan or Matheson, Winifred Davidson
MA 1926
d Aber 22.2.73

MUNRO-FERGUSON Arthur Brocklehurst Luttrell
                                      BSc(for) 1951
resid Evanton

MURCHISON or Blues, Catherine   MA 1924
teacher Inv 1925–28; resid Dalkeith

MURDOCH or Day, Elizabeth Helen McRobert
                                      MA 1944
resid Stockport

MURDOCH Eric   BSc(eng) 1954
MICE 1960
sen asst eng: Inv c c 1966–67, Aber c c 1967–71; chief
asst eng Aber c c 1971–75, chief asst eng Grampian
reg c from 1975
m Inv 29.9.61 Mary A. M. Gillies asst matron d of
Donald G. Portree

MURDOCH George Clark   *MA 1952
dist off. Tanganyika 1955–61; teacher: Dollar acad
1962–64, Daniel Stewart's coll Edin 1964–68; prin
mod lang Fraserburgh acad 1968–76; asst rector
Elgin acad from 1976

MURDOCH or Semmence, Henrietta Scorgie
                                      MA 1919
d Galashiels 7.2.77

MURDOCH Ian Martin Calder   BSc 1951
1978 Brit patent no 1507899
teacher maths/sc Methlick j s s 1961–64; retd

MURDOCH or Alderson, Jessie Elliott   MA 1904
d 1977 *AUR* XLVII 286

MURDOCH John Henry   MB ChB 1944
g p Vancouver from 1951

MURDOCH or Simpson, Lizzie Jane   MA 1919
d Colchester 10.6.68 *AUR* XLIII 80

MURDOCH or Henderson, Marguerita Bridgeford
                                      MA 1953
teacher: supply Kincardine 1967–74, Arduthie p s
Stonehaven from 1974

MURDOCH or Simmons, Marjorie Henry   MA 1946
inf teacher Lothian reg Edin from 1974

MURDOCH or Imlach, Moyra Isobel   MA 1947
sub-post mistress Lintmill Cullen 1964–65; teacher
Portsoy from 1965

MURDOCH Sophie Allardyce Farquharson
                                      MA 1907
d Banff 30.4.76 *AUR* XLVI 414

MURDOCH Thomas Henderson   MA 1930
spec in spoken Engl Roxburghsh s 1962–72; head
of div for English as an acquired lang Engl-speaking
board from 1972; resid Hants

MURISON Alfred Ross
                ***MA 1912 *1914 *1919 LLD 1951**
d Glasg 21.2.68 *AUR* XLII 351

MURISON Charles Alexander   *MA 1929
F Inst P 1944
sen lect med physics Edin 1968–72; retd
wife *d* 18.2.75

MURISON Charles Fraser   MB ChB 1939
d St Anne's on Sea 19.12.70 *AUR* XLIV 215

MURISON David Donald   *MA 1933
resid Fraserburgh

MURISON or Taylor, Dorothy   MA 1955
resid Peterhead

MURISON Helen Ross   MA 1943
teacher: p s Aberdeensh 1945–55, Roxburghsh
1955–57, Toronto 1958–61; study in France 1961–63;
teacher Fr: Lyng Hall Coventry 1963–65, Sutherland
House s Cromer Norfolk 1965–71; retd; secy

MURISON James Fraser   BSc(eng) 1945
sen stressman Hunting Aircraft (Airframes) 1960–
61; stress off. airborne radar div EMI Hayes from
1961

MURPHY Helen Burgess   MA 1933

MURPHY Peter Alexander   *MA 1955 MEd 1958
prin teacher Engl Summerhill acad Aber 1965–71;
head Logie s s Dun 1971–75; rector Whitfield h s Dun
from 1976
m Aber 7.8.61 Margaret J. Christie chem d of John C.
Keig

MURPHY Vincent John   MB ChB 1953

MURPHY William Turnbull   *BSc 1954

MURRAY or Ogilvie, Agnes Davidson   MA 1924
no longer on GC reg

MURRAY Alexander James   MA 1949
M of H 1949–59; dept chem Surr 1963–68; microbiol dept nutrit and food sc Westminster tech coll
from 1968; resid Sutton

MURRAY Alexander John Robertson
                           ***BSc 1943 PhD 1949**
ICI plastics div Thornton Lancs: plant man. 1961–
64, sect. man. 1964–69, asst works man. 1969–71; dep
gen man. plastics div ICI Europa Brussels 1971–77;
works oper man. ICI Holland BV from 1977

MURRAY Alexander McPherson
                           ***BSc 1953 PhD 1956**

MURRAY Alfred Edward   BSc(eng) 1933

MURRAY or Mackenzie, Alice Annand
                           ***MA 1905 *BSc 1906**
no longer on GC reg

MURRAY or Hugo, Alison Elisabeth   BSc 1946
teacher: Kitwe N Rhodesia later Zambia, 1950–68,
s s Aber from 1968

MURRAY Andrew John   MB ChB 1922
d Littlehampton 26.7.60 *A UR* xxxix 105

MURRAY Angus McKay   MA 1907
no longer on GC reg

MURRAY Angus Sutherland   MA 1948
d Aber 26.2.81

MURRAY Arthur Farquhar   MB ChB 1937
no longer on GC reg

MURRAY Campbell   MB ChB 1955
MRCPE 1965 MRCGP 1966
m o stud. health serv Aberd 1960–67, chief m o 1967–
74, reg m o SHHD from 1974

MURRAY Charles Mitchell Macquibban
MB ChB 1931
prof orthop surg Ahmadu Bello univ Kano Nigeria
1971–74; retd; resid Hayling Is, Hants

MURRAY Charles Peter   MB ChB 1924
d 14.4.67 *A UR* xlii 363

MURRAY or Duff, Chrissy Isobel   MA 1920
retd 1964; resid Torphins

MURRAY Donald Roderick   MB ChB 1950

MURRAY Douglas Dalgarno   BSc(eng) 1933

MURRAY Duncan   MB ChB 1954
LMCC 1970 Cert Coll Fam Pract 1971
g p Hinton Alberta from 1957

MURRAY Edward George Morrison   MA 1914
d 8.11.64 *A UR* xli 56

MURRAY Ellis Edward Paul
BSc 1934 *MB ChB 1937
consult: surg Portsmouth group hosps 1951–71;
retd; resid Eastbourne
d Eastbourne 7.4.81 *A UR* xlix 138

MURRAY Eric Taylor   MB ChB 1944
consult. gen surg Basildon and Orsett hosps from
1960; resid Brentwood

MURRAY Ethel Macgregor   *MA 1915
d 26.4.72

MURRAY Frank   MB ChB 1938

MURRAY George   *MA 1931
d Haddington 31.5.69 *A UR* xliii 215

MURRAY George   *MA 1936

MURRAY George Alexander   MA 1910
d Aber 14.4.61 *A UR* xxxix 201

MURRAY George Alexander   MA 1930
no longer on GC reg

MURRAY Gordon Souter   BSc(eng) 1945
MIME 1979
reg marine market. man. indust and marine div Rolls
Royce Coventry from 1970

MURRAY Helen Taylor Kippen   BSc 1926
retd 1970; resid Laurencekirk

MURRAY Hugh Alexander   *MA 1929
d Wellington NZ 17.10.73 *A UR* xlv 448

MURRAY or Reid, Irene Brown   MA 1944

MURRAY or Henderson, Isabel Bisset   *MA 1955
MA PhD(Cantab) 1963 FSA Scot
asst keeper nat lib of Scot. 1966–74, asst lib off. Camb
univ lib from 1975

MURRAY or Budge, Isabella Marion Hodgson
MB ChB 1921
resid Towcester

MURRAY Isobel Alice   *MA 1934
BA(Lond) 1967 Dip St Colm's Missionary Coll,
Edin
teacher Fr/Lat Lossiemouth 1935–36; sen classics
mistress Albyn s for girls Aber 1936–37; i/c s for C of S
Poona/Madras/Arkonam India 1938–44; sen classics
mistress Cranley s Edin 1945–47; tut. Paterson's
coll Edin 1947–49; sen classics mistress: Ackworth s
Yorks/Stratford s Lond/Skinners Company's s Lond
1949–67; teacher Fr/Russian Aber h s for girls 1967–
73; retd

MURRAY James   *MA 1926
C of S min St Brides Newtonmore 1962–75; retd;
resid Whiterashes

MURRAY James Durno   *MB ChB 1923
d Hamilton NZ 14.7.64 *A UR* xli 57

MURRAY James Greig   MB ChB 1942 ChM 1961
FRCS(Eng) 1966
prof surg Lond/hon consult. surg King's coll hosp
Lond from 1964; member Senate Univ of Lond;
member SE Thames reg health auth

MURRAY James John Christie
MA 1934 Dip Ed 1961
head: Woodlands p s Durris 1962–68, Midmar s
1968–73; retd; resid Banchory

MURRAY James Robbie Duncan
MA 1935 LLB 1938
secy White Fish Auth Edin from 1973
d Kinross 28.12.79 *A UR* xlviii 442

MURRAY James Robertson
MB ChB 1911 *MD 1914 DPH 1919
d Lond 19.6.72 *A UR* xlv 124

MURRAY James Stannard   BSc(for) 1949
FIF
Aberd: sen lect for. 1961–73, reader from 1973

MURRAY Jane Elizabeth   BSc 1926
teacher prin maths Lond 1926–28; temp head Glenfoudland p s Aberdeensh 1928–31; teacher maths/sc Montrose 1942–45, 1948–52, 1957–58; head: Clochcan p s Aberdeensh 1945–48, Inch p s/Cookney p s Kincardine 1952–57, Whittinghame E. Lothian 1958–64; retd; resid Haddington
m Huntly 21.6.31 John W. Mackie farm./estate off. s of Alexander M. Glenfoudland

MURRAY Jean   MA 1918
d Edin 1.11.73 *AUR* XLV 447

MURRAY Jessie   MA 1901
d 9.7.69

MURRAY John   *MA 1900 LLD 1930
d Lond 28.12.64 *AUR* XLI 53

MURRAY John   MB ChB 1907

MURRAY John   MA 1922
no longer on GC reg

MURRAY John   MA 1939

MURRAY John   MA 1951
Is of Lewis: dep head Bayble j s s 1960–71, head Tolsta p s from 1971

MURRAY John Kerr   *MA 1924
retd 1962; resid Nottingham

MURRAY John Paton   MA 1919
no longer on GC reg

MURRAY John William   *MA 1923
retd 1957
d Knaresborough 7.1.67 *AUR* XLII 360

MURRAY or Smith, Kathleen Marjory Fletcher MB ChB 1945
d 30.10.76 *AUR* XLVII 214

MURRAY Kathleen Taylor Finnie   *MA 1936

MURRAY Kenneth Alexander George *MA 1938 *MEd 1949
civ serv selection board: chief psych 1951–63, dir from 1963; resid Leatherhead
m Aber 4.4.42 Elizabeth W. Simpson soc worker d of Arthur S. Aber

MURRAY Malcolm Gordon   MB ChB 1931
g p unit Queen Elizabeth II hosp Welwyn Garden City

MURRAY Malcolm Murdo   MA 1929
retd 1971; resid Stornoway

MURRAY or Banka, Margaret Harvey   MA 1932
d Regina Canada 18.9.70 *AUR* XLIV 110

MURRAY or Fraser, Margaret Helen Sim   MA 1943
resid Aber

MURRAY Margaret Isabell   *MA 1918
resid Laggan Newtonmore

MURRAY or Horne, Margaret Jamieson   MA 1923
resid Blackpool
husb *d* –.9.65

MURRAY or Gardiner, Mary   *MA 1948

MURRAY Mary Adams Bisset   MB ChB 1955
regist anaest: Lambeth hosp Lond 1959–62, Aber 1962–67; med asst anaest Royal Alexandra Inf Paisley 1967–79; asst anaest Perth RI from 1979
m Aber 22.8.62 William B. R. Macmillan MA 1951 *qv*

MURRAY or MacIver, Mary Sutherland   MA 1923

MURRAY May Forbes   MA 1929
Aber: inf mistress St Margaret's epis p s 1953–59, Hanover St p s 1960–65, Walker Rd p s 1965–71; retd
d Aber 15.3.78

MURRAY Moira   MA 1948
teacher Tarves p s from 1949
m Aber 4.4.60 James Massie market gardener s of George M. Tarves

MURRAY Murdo   MA 1913
d Strathpeffer 30.5.64

MURRAY Nathaniel Munro   MA 1905
no longer on GC reg

MURRAY Norman   MB ChB 1949
g p Stornoway from 1959

MURRAY Robert Garden   MB ChB 1941 DPH 1947 MFCM 1972
m o h/prin s m o Rochdale from 1963

MURRAY Robert MacKay   *BSc 1950
teacher sc Portree h s 1955–76; retd

MURRAY Robert Walker   *MA 1948

MURRAY or MacDonald, Roberta Elspeth MA 1930
teacher Engl/hist Ardersier j s 1956–70; retd; resid Inv

MURRAY Sheila   *MA 1931
b 21.8.08
retd 1968; resid Fochabers
m Aber 15.7.69 William J. McGeorge retd

MURRAY Sheila   MA 1941
teacher Skene Square p s Aber 1946–79; retd

MURRAY or Fawcett, Sheila Jean   *MA 1951

MURRAY or Gray, Stella Watt   MA 1953
teacher maths Inverbervie 1954–58; resid Laurence-kirk

MURRAY Thomas Patrick Edward
                    MA 1921 LLB 1923
  DL county and city of Aber from 1964
ptnr Stewart & Murray advoc Aber from 1927; clerk/
treasurer Deeside dist c 1944–73

MURRAY William   MA 1891
  no longer on GC reg

MURRAY William George   MB ChB 1921
  d Aber 15.3.61 *AUR* xxxix 203

MURRAY William George Duncan
                    MB ChB 1947 MD 1958
FRSM 1958 DIH(RCS) 1961 FRIPHH 1968
occup health Lond 1958–71; asst secy Med Protect.
Soc Lond from 1972; resid West Malling

MURRAY William Nicoll   MA 1927 MB ChB 1932
  retd 1971; resid Fochabers

MURRAY William Robert   MA 1937
  Mackie acad Stonehaven: spec asst Engl 1967–72,
asst prin Engl 1972–76; retd

MURRAY or McAulay, Williamina Sinclair
                    MA 1943
  lived W Cameroon 1950–68; teacher: Benedict p s
Mitcham 1969–71, Canterbury Rd p s Morden from
1971
husb *d* 10.10.69

MURRISON or Milne, Annie Mary   MA 1928
  resid Aber

MURSELL or Sinclair, Margaret Fraser
                    BSc(agr) 1926
  no longer on GC reg

MUSTARD or Capper, Catherine Ella   MA 1942
  resid Huyton-with-Roby, nr Liverpool

MUSTARD Donald Kennedy   BSc 1952

MUSTARD or Graham, Elizabeth Grant
                    BSc(agr) 1945
  publ health apptment (milk and food hyg) Fife c c
1973–75, Dunfermline dist c from 1975

MUSTARD James   BSc 1948 *1956
  Aber: teacher sc Rosemount s s 1949–67, lect chem
coll of comm from 1967

MUTCH Alexander   *MA 1929
  no longer on GC reg

MUTCH Andrew Mollison   MA 1927 LLB 1928
  no longer on GC reg

MUTCH or Durnin, Elizabeth Anne   MA 1952
  teacher: Aber 1953–64, Galashiels 1964–65, Dumfries from 1965

MUTCH Forbes Robertson   MB ChB 1923
  d Nottingham 3.5.68 *AUR* xlii 361

MUTCH George   *MA 1927
  retd 1968; resid Helensburgh

MUTCH Harry   *MA 1951 PhD 1962
  lect nat phil Aberd 1962–68; head of maths s RGIT
Aber from 1968; member of BA comm (seismological
investigation) 1966
m Aber 15.5.59 Susan Edgar d of John A. E. Inv

MUTCH or Johnston, Isabel Margaret   *BSc 1946
  resigned Macaulay inst for soil res Aber 1960

MUTCH or Zamoyski, Isobel Margaret (Countess)
                    MA 1951

MUTCH or Bisset, Isobel Stephen   BSc 1944
  teacher: sc/maths Keith g s 1965–69, sc Mackie
acad Stonehaven from 1969

MUTCH John   MA 1913
  d Aber 9.11.66 *AUR* xlii 84

MUTCH John Bernard   MB ChB 1917
  no longer on GC reg

MUTCH John Simpson   MA 1913 BD 1915
  retd 1960
d Cleveleys 14.7.77 *AUR* xlviii 226

MUTCH or Milne, Leila Davidson   MA 1923
  resid Laurencekirk

MUTCH Robert James   BSc 1931
  head Mintlaw s s 1961–71; retd

MUTCH Sheena Doris   MA 1954

MUTCH or Pitty, Sophia Anderson   MA 1930
  d of William F. farm.; b Crimond 27.7.07
teacher: St Combs 1932–37, supply Hyde educ div
Cheshire 1950–57, girls' s s Hyde 1959–66; retd;
resid Bridlington
m Aber 20.7.37 Harold E. Pitty teacher/headmaster
s of Frank P. Manc

MUTCH William Alexander   MA 1911
  no longer on GC reg

MUTERER James George
                    MB ChB 1908 DPH 1912
  no longer on GC reg

MYERS Algernon Edgar Cyril   MB ChB 1907
  no longer on GC reg

MYERS John Wade   *MA 1954

MYLES Robert Boulton   MB ChB 1915
  d 12.8.72 *AUR* xlv 125

MYLROI Derek   *MA 1952
  DipEd(Durh) 1953
head hist dept Faraday Hall s Billingham 1961–65;
dep head St Francis RC g s Hartlepool 1965–69; head
St Bede's RC comp s Peterlee from 1969

MYRON or Ross, Agnes Warwick   MA 1949
resid Cults Aber

MYRON or van Niekerk, Margaret Sutherland
MA 1945
resid Mandini Natal

NAPIER George   *BSc 1920
no longer on GC reg

NAPIER George   *MA 1923

NAPIER or McAuslan, Mary Elizabeth   MA 1925
no longer on GC reg

NAPIER or Wilkie, Sheila Ruth   *MA 1948
Adult Educ Cert Russian Lang (Leeds) 1967
teacher Ger Lawnswood h s Leeds 1972–73; tut. Engl
for overseas stud. Swarthmore educ centre Leeds
1977

NAPIER William Ross   *MA 1952 Dip Ed 1955
prin teacher classics Tain royal acad 1968–72, asst
rector from 1972

NARAHARI Kosarazu   BSc(agr) 1923
no longer on GC reg

NASH Charles Anthony Mariott   BSc(for) 1949
d Honiara BSIP 25.8.71 *AUR* xlv 128

NASR Hamed Nasr Mohamed   PhD 1950

NAUGHTIE Alexander   MA 1930
d Aber 5.3.73 *AUR* xlv 227

NAUGHTON or Alexander, Margaret   MA 1948

NAUGHTY Alexander Wilson   *MA 1926

NAYLOR or Youngson (Brown), Elizabeth Gisborne
***MA 1948**
lib univ Edin 1970–74; resid Canberra, Aust

NAYLOR Roy Stewart   BSc(eng) 1950
no longer on GC reg

NEATE Harry Lingwood   *MA 1914
d 3.8.76

NEILL Freda Katherine   *MA 1942
teacher classics: head Lat dept Selkirk h s 1943–46,
Mary Erskine s for girls Edin 1946–49; educ edit.
Blackie & Son Glasg 1949–55; head Lat dept Baston
s for girls Bromley Kent 1959–64; edit. ch's books
Blackie Lond 1965–67; head classics dept Hill House
s for boys Doncaster from 1974
m Bridge of Allan 7.1.55 John Kemsley BSc(Lond)
C.Eng NCB Doncaster
d Italy 30.8.78 *AUR* xlviii 107

NEILL or Logie, Kathleen Margaret Cameron
BSc 1940
resid Aber
husb d 15.3.72

NEILL Robert Macfarlane   DSc 1941 LLD 1965
d 30.7.69

NEILSON Christina McLeod (Lynda)   MA 1941
teacher: Dunure s Ayrsh 1961–70, Russel St s Ayr
1970–71, Alloway s Ayr 1971–77; retd

NEILSON or Petters, Eleanor   *MA 1954

NEILSON Gladys Brock   MA 1938

NEILSON Matthew Welsh   PhD 1928
retd 1958; resid Ayr
d Ardrossan 12.5.81 *AUR* xlix 137

NEILSON or Burns, Winifred   MA 1930
resid Bieldside Aber

NEISH Ian Douglas   MB ChB 1954
MRCGP 1969
g p Stockton-on-Tees from 1958

NEISH Isobel Kennedy   MA 1955

NEISH William John Pirie   *BSc 1943

NELSON or McDonald, Elizabeth Margaret
MA 1926
resid Port Appin, Argyll

NELSON or Duthie, Marion Bell   *MA 1926
retd; resid Okehampton
husb d –.10.74
d 26.10.77

NELSON Mary Masson   MA 1939 BL 1948

NEMETH Alexander   *MA 1954
Cert City & Guilds RTEM Aber 1978; naturalized
Brit citizen 1978
photographer Aber from 1960
m Aber 15.4.63 Margaret M. Archibald nurse, photogr
asst d of William J. A. Aber

NESS Thomas Dick   MB ChB 1948
hon orthop surg Prince Henry hosp and Prince of
Wales hosp Sydney/clin teacher orthop dept univ of
NSW from 1961

NEUSTEIN Stephen Andreas   BSc(for) 1952
for. comm: silviculturist (North) Edin 1961–74, asst
conserv Chester from 1974

NEVILLE Hugh Henry   MA 1943 *BSc 1946
prin scient off. bldg res estab Watford from 1962

NEWLANDS Annie   MA 1938
teacher Culter 1953–76; resid Kintore
m Edin 7.8.76 Alexander Singer sqn ldr RAF (retd)
s of Alexander S. St Katherine's Aberdeensh

NEWLANDS Constance Jean   MA 1955

NEWLANDS Janet Roy   MA 1914
resid Aber

NEWLANDS or McVean, Mary Isabella   MA 1942
  teacher Rothes p s from 1946

NEWLANDS William   MB ChB 1937
  g p Aber; retd
d Majorca 12.6.74 *A UR* xlvi 110

NEWTON or Dowie, Frances Elena   MA 1914
d Putney 13.11.71 *A UR* xliv 317

NEWTON John Philip   BSc(for) 1950
  man. dir Fountain Forestry Wells later Cheddar
Somerset 1960–75; vice chmn Fountain Forestry from
1975 and dir Matthews Wrightson Land from 1971

NICHOL Edith Margaret   MA 1930
  teacher maths Findochty j s s till 1968; retd
d 12.7.74

NICHOLLS Thomas Burtonshaw   MB ChB 1908
  no longer on GC reg

NICHOLSON Andrew Broadfoot   BSc(agr) 1954
  member Stock Exchange Edin; ptnr Macgregor,
Walker & Co from 1962, merged to become Bell,
Lawrie Macgregor & Co from 1975
m Lond 11.4.73 Joanna M. Bechely-Crundall d of
Noel B.-C. Ramsbury

NICHOLSON or Milne, Annie   MA 1905
d Streatham Lond 19.1.72 *A UR* xliv 427

NICHOLSON or Fielding, Doreen   BSc(agr) 1948
  resid Forres

NICHOLSON or Nicol, Eva MacIntosh   MA 1923
d Forres 4.12.78

NICHOLSON George Duncan   BSc(eng) 1945
  dep resid eng Mangla dam proj Preece Cardew &
Rider W Pakistan 1963–70; proj man. Kehan and
Gokcekaya transmission proj Ankara and Istanbul
from 1970

NICHOLSON or Lyon, Helen   MA 1910
d 25.8.64

NICHOLSON John Archibald   MB ChB 1916
  no longer on GC reg

NICHOLSON William Dallas   MB ChB 1949
  g p Sale Cheshire from 1960

NICOL or Jackson, Agnes   MB ChB 1945
  MFCP 1972
dep m o h Ross & Cromarty (mainland) 1970–74; sen
m o Highland health board (Ross & Cromarty) from
1974

NICOL Aileen Annette   MB ChB 1926 DPH 1928
  retd 1963; resid Inverurie

NICOL Albert Reid   *MA 1924
d 2.1.67

NICOL Alexander   *MA 1915
d Lymington 19.10.62 *A UR* xl 84

NICOL Alexander   *MA 1927
  retd 1966; resid Nairn
d 8.12.81

NICOL Alexander   MB ChB 1949 ᶜMD 1962
  MRCPath(Lond) 1964 FRMS 1972
FRCPath(Lond) 1976
sen regist clin path RI Manc 1962–64, dir area lab
Glos royal hosp Gloucester from 1964

NICOL Alexander Adam McIntosh
                              MB ChB 1922 MD 1926
  member hosp man. comm/advis in med N'cle-u-
Tyne reg hosp board/assoc clin teacher med King's
coll N'cle 1948–65; retd; resid Whitburn Sunderland

NICOL Alexander Corskie   MB ChB 1926
d 25.11.70

NICOL Alice Ann   MA 1910
  sen mistress Stanley g s Co Durham till 1947; retd;
resid Insch

NICOL or Markwick, Amy Taylor   MA 1930
  fell./tut./lect classics Girton coll Cantab 1961–67;
retd; resid Lymington
husb d 1946

NICOL Bruce Milligan   MB ChB 1935
  Coronation Medal 1953
advis nutrit UNICEF for FAO New York 1960–62;
Rome: asst to dir for nutrit div FAO 1962–63, dep dir
nutrit div FAO 1963–73; consult. for FAO to govt of
Malaysia Kuala Lumpur 1974–75; consult. for FAO
to govt of Indonesia Djakarta 1974; retd from FAO
1973; still doing consult. work for overseas govts

NICOL Cameron Macdonald
                      MA 1911 MB ChB 1915 MD 1919
d Welwyn 19.2.65 *A UR* xli 31

NICOL or Walker, Charlotte Jane Donald   BSc 1942
  head Netherley p s Stonehaven from 1947

NICOL Duncan   MA 1933
  head Drumblade p s Huntly from 1957

NICOL or Bell, Elizabeth Andrew   MA 1918
d Glasg 9.1.77

NICOL Ethel Lumsden   MA 1931
  retd; resid Aber

NICOL Harvey   MB ChB 1951
  MRCGP 1974
g p Fraserburgh from 1956
wife d 3.12.76

NICOL or Brown, Helen Hendry   MA 1919
  husb d 1972
resid Portpatrick
d Stranraer 2.11.79

NICOL James Lendrum MB ChB 1928
MRCGP 1964 MNZCGP
retd 1974; resid Christchurch NZ

NICOL James Rae *MA 1937
d Lond 13.3.69 *AUR* XLIII 216

NICOL or Simpson, Janet Cruickshank
MA 1917 *MB ChB 1921
d Lymington 26.9.68 *AUR* XLIII 79

NICOL Margaret Melville MA 1904
d Aber 28.4.68 *AUR* XLII 345

NICOL or Robson, Marjory Helen *MA 1952

NICOL or Geater, Mona MA 1926
no longer on GC reg

NICOL Nancy Jane MA 1929
d 11.12.73

NICOL Norman Thomas MB ChB 1950
FFR(Lond) 1959 TD 1963
consult. radiotherap Leic RI 1960–64; consult. radioth
i/c radioth dept Leic RI/assoc consult. radioth centre
Sheffield from 1964

NICOL Patrick Blaikie MB ChB 1938 DPH 1953
MRCPath 1965
regular navy 1939–71; QHP 1969–71; sen m o Rolls-
Royce (1971) Derby

NICOL Peter Lyon MA 1935
head Port Elphinstone p s from 1950; town councillor Inverurie from 1970; chmn commun serv panel
Garioch from 1966; convener swim. pool Inverurie
from 1971; retd 1975; pres Inverurie Bowling Club
1978

NICOL Robert MA 1903
d Crieff 10.10.71 *AUR* XLII 316

NICOL Thomas James Trail MA 1938 DD 1968
dep asst chaplain-gen BAOR Germany 1963–67;
asst chaplain-gen Edin 1967–72; min Crathie church
1972–77; domestic chaplain to Queen in Scot. from
1972; resid St Fillans

NICOL William Bernard de Bear *MA 1938

NICOLL Alfred BSc(eng) 1945

NICOLL or Watson, Annie *MA 1934
d 12.1.75 *AUR* XLVI 239

NICOLL David Ross MA 1951

NICOLSON or MacIntyre, Helen MA 1923
head Corgarff p s 1957–63; retd; resid Elgin

NICOLSON Jessie Ann MA 1930
teacher p s Kinlochiel/Eigg/Barra 1932–35; head:
Southlaggan p s 1935–38, Tomachartich Fort William
1938–72; retd

NICOLSON Thomas Henry *BSc(agr) 1950
lect/sen lect bot Queen's coll Dund 1961–69; reader
biol sc Dund from 1969

NIDDRIE James MA 1954
p s teacher Aber: Stockethill 1959–61, Cornhill
1961, Fernielea 1961–67; lower s master AGS 1967–
70; dep head Westerton p s 1970–74; head Craighill
p s from 1974
m Aber 4.4.60 Hazel C. McIntosh teacher d of James
C. McI. Aber

NISBET Alexander *MA 1950 Dip Ed 1952
dist insp Dumfries and Galloway 1969–70; HMIS
(higher grade) 1970; dist insp Ayr Bute Dumfries and
Galloway 1972–77; Lothian reg from 1977

NISBET Alister MacGregor MB ChB 1954
DObstRCOG 1959
g p Bridlington from 1961

NISBET Frederick Cawthorne Hutchinson
***BSc(eng) 1955**
FICE FIStruct E
consult. civ eng/ptnr W. A. Fairhurst & Ptnrs Aber
from 1966

NISBET John Donald PhD 1952
prof educ Aberd from 1963

NISH or Chapman, Anna Aileen McInnes MA 1934

NIVEN Alan Fowler *MA 1951 LLB 1960
d Torphins 4.7.71 *AUR* XLIV 322

NIVEN Alexander Francis MB ChB 1940
g p Chatham from 1947

NIVEN Charles David *MA *BSc 1918

NIVEN or Graham, Jean Margaret *MA 1939
resid Glasg

NIVEN John Scott MA 1901
no longer on GC reg

NIVEN or Sorley, Marjorie Davidson
***MA 1913 *1914**
d Leura NSW 5.4.74 *AUR* XLV 447 & XLVI 107

NIVEN William MB ChB 1924
consult. radiol; chmn Huddersfield hosp comm
1964–68; retd
no longer on GC reg

NIVEN William Dickie *MA 1900 DD 1928
d Glasg 26.2.65 *AUR* XLI 145

NOBLE Alexander MB ChB 1906 DPH 1908
no longer on GC reg

NOBLE Andrew MB ChB 1940
g p Montrose from 1946

NOBLE Benjamin BSc 1946 DSc 1962

NOBLE or Griffith, Christina MA 1925
retd 1965; resid Kirby Underdale York

NOBLE Donald Haddow Macrae BSc(agr) 1954

NOBLE Douglas Oswald MA 1939
rector: St Michael and All Angels Helensburgh 1959–71, St Columba's Largs from 1971; canon of St Mary's cath Glasg from 1971

NOBLE Elizabeth Duthie MA 1929

NOBLE Isabel Mary MB ChB 1954

NOBLE John MA 1952
dep head Oakbank s Aber 1962–66; B.C. Canada: supt Brannan Lake s 1966–73, exec dir soc serv 1973–76, dep min. ministry of human resources from 1976

NOBLE or Porter, Lilian McLean MA 1952

NOBLE or Emslie, Margaret MA 1922
d Glasg 24.9.68 *AUR* XLIII 83

NOBLE or McGill, Mary MA 1929

NOBLE Mary Jane MA 1950
teacher Sandhaven till 1977; peripatetic remed teacher Grampian reg c from 1977
m Aber 31.3.67 Charles M. Watt eng s of Alexander D. W. Fraserburgh

NOBLE Mary Mearns MA 1949

NOBLE or Russell, Patricia MA 1945
teacher Crimond j s s 1961–74; head Crimond p s from 1974

NOBLE Peter Scott *MA 1921 LLD 1955
Kt 1966
vice-chancellor Lond univ 1961–64; retd; resid Edin

NOBLE Robert William Smith *MA 1938
head Newburgh Mathers p s nr Ellon 1964–78; retd; resid Aber

NOBLE Sheila Mary Grant MA 1942
Aber: teacher Fr/Engl Middle s, Frederick St s s 1970–75, Linksfield acad from 1975

NOBLE Thomas Alexander Fraser
**   *MA 1938 *1940 LLD 1968**
Kt 1971 LLD(Leic) 1976
Secy/treas Carnegie Trust 1957–62; vice-chancellor and principal: Leic 1962–76, Aberd 1976–81; retd; resid Nairn
chmn UK comm vice-chancellors and principals 1970–72

NOLTIE Henry Robert *MA 1925 BSc 1927 *1931
retd 1968; resid Broughty Ferry

NORBY Douglas Morton *MA 1952

NORQUAY or Laird, Margaret Helen
**   MB ChB 1951**
radiol Wellington publ hosp NZ from 1966
husb d 3.8.73

NORRIE George Beaton BSc(agr) 1945

NORRIE John BSc 1906
no longer on GC reg

NORRIE or Roberts, Mary Bedford MA 1928
teacher: Zambia/Swaziland/S. Africa; retd from Wesley s s Salt River Cape Town 1974
m Ndola Zambia 23.6.34 Horace E. Roberts asst postmaster-gen N. Rhod s of Sidney R. Evesham

NORRIE Mary Helen *MA 1914
resid Aber from 1944
d Aber 5.12.78

NORRIS Forbes James Anderson MB ChB 1935
no longer on GC reg

NORTH Alastair Macarthur
**   *BSc 1954 PhD 1957 DSc 1965**
FRSE 1971 FRIC 1971
Burmah prof physical chem Strath from 1967

NOTHOLT Arthur John George *BSc 1951
FGS 1954 MIMM 1963
employed mineral resources div overseas geol surv inst of geol sciences Lond from 1956

NOTTINGHAM Peter Maxwell PhD 1952

NOUR Ibrahim Mohamed MA 1954
MEd(Harv) 1960
prin tech inst Khartoum 1964–65, UNESCO expert: Riyad Saudi Arabia 1966–70, Baghdad Iraq 1970–73; dir higher educ Khartoum from 1973

NUTTEN Albert John *BSc 1948

NUTTEN Horace Edward MB ChB 1951 DPH 1955
MFCM 1971
m o h NW Derbyshire Buxton from 1965; m o stud. health serv: Buxton from 1968, Matlock from 1970; m o gen c of British Shipping 1974

NUTTEN Robert Edward Page MB ChB 1943
g p Aber from 1947

OAG John Alexander BSc(agr) 1922
no longer on GC reg

O'BRIEN Kevin MB ChB 1941
g p Birm; prin from 1954

O'BRIEN or Sim, Ruth *MA 1930
Fraserburgh acad: teacher Engl 1956–60, spec asst Fr/Ger 1960–72

O'CONNOR Christine Greig *MA 1915
d 5.10.65 *AUR* XLI 244

O'CONNOR William John   MB ChB 1922
d 8.2.76

OFFICER Alice Edith   MA 1927
no longer on GC reg

OFFICER Henry Sylvester   BSc(agr) 1947

OGG George
*MA 1912 BD 1919 *BSc 1919 DD 1951
d 18.1.73 *AUR* XLV 224

OGG Lindsay Robert Arbuthnott   MB ChB 1931
d 22.12.63

OGG William Gammie
MA 1912 BSc(agr) 1913 *BSc 1914 LLD 1951
retd; resid Edzell
d Edzell 25.9.79 *AUR* XLVIII 350

OGILVIE Alexander   MA 1902
d 15.12.66

OGILVIE Allan   MA 1913
d Laurencekirk 24.9.68 *AUR* XLII 352

OGILVIE Helen   MA 1916
d Aber 11.3.68 *AUR* XLII 355

OGILVIE Hugh Alexander   *MA 1937

OGILVIE James   MA 1933
teacher Banff acad 1969–73; retd; resid Macduff

OGILVIE Lawrence   MA *BSc 1921
retd 1964; resid Dundry Bristol
wife *d* 1965
d Bristol 16.4.80 *AUR* XLVIII 440

OGILVIE or Craig, Mary Cowie   MA 1947

OGILVIE Roberta   MA 1914
resid Edin

OGILVIE Walter Johnston
MA 1919 MB ChB 1923

OGSTON Alexander   MA 1912

OGSTON Derek
MA 1952 *MB ChB 1957 PhD 1962 *MD 1969
DSc 1975
MRCPE 1963 MRCP(Lond) 1967 FRCPE 1972
FRCP(Lond) 1977
lect med Aberd 1962–69, sen lect 1969, reader 1975,
regius prof physiol from 1977
m Aber 19.7.63 Cecilia M, Clark MB ChB 1962 *qv*

OGSTON or Nicol, Elizabeth Marion Ross
*MA 1937

OGSTON or Townroe or Bullimore, Helen Charlotte
Elizabeth Douglas   *BSc 1906
no longer on GC reg

OGSTON Henry   MA 1936 ᵈLLB 1938
ptnr Clark & Wallace advoc Aber from 1949
d Aber 7.1.80 *AUR* XLVIII 442

OGSTON Isabella Sophia   MA 1928
sen asst teacher Cornhill p s Aber 1951–69; retd

OGSTON John   BCom 1924
d Aber 10.4.70 *AUR* XLIII 445

OGSTON or Ingram, Lillias   MA 1947
resid Wishaw

OGSTON William Duncan   MB ChB 1955
sen lect dept mental health Aberd 1968–77; chief of
psychiat Martinez VA hosp and vice chmn univ of
Calif, Davis from 1977

OGSTON William Leslie   MA 1927

OLDMAN Ella Geddes   MA 1954

O'LEARY Anne Rose   *MA 1954
teacher Engl St Augustine's Priory Ealing 1958–62

OLIPHANT or Geddes, Elsie Mary   MA 1945
teacher: Turriff 1955–68, Peterculter from 1968

OLIVER Francis William Anderson
BSc(for) 1922 BSc 1923
H.M. for. comm: div off. Dumfries 1938–46; conserv
E Scot. Aber 1947–64; retd; resid Skene

OLIVER or Abrahamsson, June Marie
MB ChB 1951
Swedish med regist 1959
consult. anaest: (locum) Stockholm 1968, Ekmanska
hosp Gothenburg from 1969 (formerly Elmanska
hosp, later Östra hosp)

OLIVER or Robb, Wilma Margaret   MA 1949
Kelso h s: teacher part time 1960–70; maths asst
from 1970

OLSON James William   MA 1915
resid Clarkston, Glasg
d Glasg 12.3.78

OMINDE Simeon Hongo   *MA 1954

OMOND or Burn, Agnes   MA 1906
no longer on GC reg

O'NEIL or Sharp, Eleanor Mary   MA 1928
resid Whittlesford Cambridge
husb *d* 23.12.66

ORAM Alan Kenneth   BSc(for) 1952

ORCHARDSON Ian Quiller   BSc 1904
no longer on GC reg

ORD Arthur Frederic Trotter   MB ChB 1934
d 21.1.71

ORD or Mackie, Mary Bremner   MA 1910
d Aber 2.4.77

ORE or Beatty, Margaret Isobel   BSc(agr) 1949
resid Loanhead

ORKIN Philip Alexander   PhD 1951
sen lect zool Aberd 1963–79; retd

ORMISTON Margaret   MB ChB 1944 DPH 1948
MFCM 1973
Aber: asst m o h 1952–58, sen asst m o h 1958–63;
Leeds: sen m o 1963–69, prin m o (ch health) 1969–
74; spec in commun med (ch health) Leeds area health
auth (teaching) from 1974

ORR or Barton, Elizabeth Joan Boyd   MB ChB 1939
intermittent g p m o Stracathro hosp Angus 1956–73

OSBORNE James Bourke   BSc(agr) 1950
FRICS 1966
chartered land ag Taunton and Beds from 1960
m Great Horkesley nr Colchester 2.7.60 Susan K.
Skinner teacher d of Edgar L. S. BA(Oxon) Great
Horkesley

OTTY Eric Horsfield   *MA 1929 *MEd 1934
FEIS 1970
prin The David Dale coll Glasg from 1949; retd 1974

OTTY Helena Horsfield   *MA 1926
retd 1965; resid Gateshead

OTTY John Horsfield   MA 1925 MB ChB 1927
d Bradford 10.5.74 *AUR* xlvi 109

OUTRAM Marjorie Isabella
                              MB ChB 1923 DPH 1924
retd 1974; resid Tenterden

OVERELL Philip Alexander Wyrill   BSc(for) 1951
H.M. for. comm: conserv E Eng 1962–68, NW Eng
from 1968

OWEN Edwin Cecil   PhD 1940

OWLER or Watt, Heather McDonald Anderson
                                            MA 1936
resid Edin
d Edin 4.10.78

OWUSU-AFRIYIE Abraham Kwabena
                              BSc(for) 1953
MF (CSU Colo. USA) 1959
Ghana: asst conserv for. 1954–57, sen asst 1957–59,
conserv for. 1959–61; dep chief conserv for. 1961–62,
chief conserv for. 1962–70; dir Volta Lines (shipping
co) Accra from 1970
m Lond 16.11.63 Emma Oppong hotelier d of
Christian O. Dormaa-Ahenkro Ghana

PACE Eda Mary   MA 1954

PACKMAN or Honigmann, Elsie McConnachie
                              ***BSc 1951 PhD 1954**
OU tut. 1977

PACKMAN or Carter, Hazel   MA 1951

PAISLEY Duncan Herbert   MA 1955

PAISLEY William Duncan   BSc 1951

PAL Dewan Har Charan Das   BSc(agr) 1924

PALIT or Martin, Marion Nasmyth Clifton
                              MA 1953
teacher: Engl lycée Cayenne Fr Guyana 1968–70,
Nuffield spec Fr course Airyhall, Craighill and Hazlehead p s Aber from 1972
husb *d* 25.7.72

PALMER George   MA 1932
teacher phys Preston Lodge h s Prestonpans 1968–
76; retd

PALMER James Hugh   MB ChB 1953
d Cults, Aber 18.9.67 *AUR* xlii 186 & 375

PALMER Kenneth John Raymond   BSc 1948
man. dir Legal and General Volkskas Assur (S Af
comp) Johannesburg from 1980

PALMER Ronald Mills   BSc(for) 1942
chief conserv for. 1960–61; cler off. D o E Hastings
from 1961

PANTON John Stuart   MA 1931 *BSc(agr) 1933
d Aber 10.2.73 *AUR* xlv 227

PANTON Robert Watt   MA ChB 1939
g p Croxteth Liv from 1953

PAPLEY or Stevenson, Margaret   MA 1932
resid Stromness

PARDOE John George   MB CM 1892
no longer on GC reg

PARDY Alexander Angus   BSc 1924 BSc(for) 1926
asst bot dept Aberd 1957–72; retd

PARK Alastair Henry   MB ChB 1954
d Penarth 16.8.65 *AUR* xli 153, 252

PARK Alexander William Chrystal   MA 1919
no longer on GC reg

PARK Alexandra Jane   MA 1944

PARK Catherine Hazel   MB ChB 1954

PARK or Murray, Cecilia Mitchell   MB ChB 1942
clin m o Lond borough of Lewisham from 1966

PARK George Thomson Booth   BSc(eng) 1953
AM(SA)ICE 1954 MICE 1959 Pr. Eng 1965
civ eng: Natal roads dept Pietermaritzburg S Africa,
John Miles & Ptnrs Bulawayo S. Rhodesia 1957–60;
Johannesburg: O Grinaker (Pty) 1960–68, McAlpine
(Pty) 1968–70, Union Constr Co 1970–72, AECI
from 1972

PARK or Townshend, Gillian Mitchell   *MA 1950
resid Upper Langford

PARK or Milne, Helen Margaret   *MA 1922
resid Dun

PARK Herbert Foster   MB ChB 1933
g p Norham-on-Tweed from 1936
d 21.6.76

PARK Ian   *MA 1949 Dip Ed 1950

PARK James Robert   MA 1910 *LLB 1911
no longer on GC reg

PARK [James] Vincent   *MA 1949
d Binghampton New York 10.1.74 *AUR* xlv 450

PARK John Mitchell   MB ChB 1945
g p Hong Kong from 1948

PARK Leonora Willox   MA 1933

PARK Louisa Benton   *MB ChB 1923
g p Pendleton, Salford

PARK Mary Ella Gordon   MA 1936

PARK Wilson Henry Gordon
                     MA 1919 MB ChB 1923
d Aber 14.8.71 *AUR* xliv 317

PARKER Gilbert   MB ChB 1934
orthop surg Teesside from 1948

PARKINSON John Thompson Low   BSc(eng) 1954
MIME 1969 MIEE 1969 MIHVE 1970 MRSH 1970
Aber: eng J. T. L. Parkinson 1959–63, dir J. T. L.
Parkinson 1963–68, man. dir 1968–71; also man. dir
J. T. L. Parkinson-Twaddle Glasg 1969–71; dir Aber
Construction Group Aber/dir M & E div incorpor-
ating the two comps 1971–75; man. dir reconstructed
fam bus. group including Parkinson and Parkinson-
Twaddle from 1975; member Grampian reg c 1977
and 1978

PARTHASARATHY Dasika   PhD 1952

PATERSON or Wells, Agnes   MA 1912
no longer on GC reg

PATERSON Albert John Horne   MA 1950 LLB 1953

PATERSON Alexander   MB ChB 1926
d 7.1.66

PATERSON Alexander Cardno   MA 1911
d 19.1.73

PATERSON Alexander James   MA 1930 BL 1936
d Kyoto Japan 28.9.67 *AUR* xlii 186

PATERSON or McDonald, Anne Innes   MA 1926
resid Ballater

PATERSON or Mackenzie, Annie Christie Dickson
                     *MA 1940
asst prin teacher mod lang Golspie h s 1974–76;
retd

PATERSON Duncan   BSc 1926
retd 1965; resid Cults

PATERSON Duncan   BSc(agr) 1940

PATERSON Edward Alexander   MB ChB 1926
g p Hastings 1938–73; retd; resid St Leonards-on-
Sea

PATERSON or Beal, Elizabeth McPherson
                     MA 1929

PATERSON or Clunas, Emmaline Scott   MA 1940

PATERSON George Wood   MA 1937
Glasg: dir Thermotank 1963, fin. controller Hall-
Thermotank Internat 1967–75; internal audit. Strath-
clyde reg c Paisley from 1975

PATERSON Hamish Barron   MA 1954

PATERSON or Hardie, Helena Mackie   MA 1907
no longer on GC reg

PATERSON Henry Knox   MB ChB 1938

PATERSON or Weatherston, Isabella   MA 1924
teacher maths St Denis Edin 1955–68; retd

PATERSON James Alexander Rogerson
                     *MB ChB 1925
no longer on GC reg

PATERSON Jean   MA 1936

PATERSON Jean Forbes   MA 1949
teacher infants Peterhead 1958–61
m Aber 28.3.62 James P. Gray farm. s of James W. G.
Oldmeldrum

PATERSON Jeannie Hardy   MA 1930
retd 1968; resid Aber

PATERSON Joseph Middleton
                     MB ChB 1928 DPH 1931
m o Castleford and Normanton 1947–70
d 12.7.77

PATERSON or Holm, Leila Gordon   MA 1939
teacher: Engl/Lat Gordon s Huntly 1958–60, Engl/
geog Inv royal acad 1960–63, Engl/geog h s Inv
1963–70, Engl Dingwall acad 1970–71, Engl/geog
Fortrose acad from 1971, also prin guid from 1972

PATERSON Maggie Ann Lyall   MA 1927
retd 1965; resid Macduff

PATERSON or Hunter, Margaret Davidson
                     ᶜMB ChB 1948
part time g p Hawick from 1960

PATERSON or Lumsden, Mary Stuart   BSc 1924
prin sc Albyn s for girls Aber 1943–66 and second
mistress 1953–66; retd
m(2) Lond 15.4.70 Alexander L. Sandison progress
eng Monsanto (Chemicals) Internat s of Alexander
L. S. Inv

PATERSON Robert Edward Mitchell   MB ChB 1938
g p Burton-on-Trent from 1940; retd 1978

PATERSON or Wright, Sarah Rose   MA 1931

PATERSON Thomas Maver   *MA 1922
no longer on GC reg

PATEY Thomas Walton   MB ChB 1955
d Durness 25.5.70 *AUR* xliv 111

PATIENCE or Stalker, Annie Brodie   MA 1944
resid Toronto

PATIENCE Elizabeth   MA 1941
teacher Avoch p s Rosssh from 1962

PATIENCE James   *MA 1947

PATON Andrew Watts   BSc(eng) 1955

PATON Annie Findlay   MA 1948

PATON Cumming   BSc 1955 PhD 1959

PATON or Rae, Elsie Mary   MA 1920
teacher: sc Inverurie acad 1940–42, sc/maths
Kintore j s s 1959–63; retd; resid Rothienorman
m Aber 12.12.35 John N. Rae farm. s of David R.
Maud
d Banchory 22.12.77

PATON Ethel Anne Scott   BSc 1952
Assoc FIMA 1964 FBCS 1969
nat eng lab E. Kilbride: exper off. 1960–67, sen exper
off. 1967–72, sen scient off. from 1972

PATON John   MA 1948
teacher maths/sc Rubislaw acad from 1973

PATON John Alexander   *MA 1949
FIL 1964
head mod lang coll of comm Aber from 1964

PATON Robert Charles   MA 1953
d Cloppenburg Germany 14.7.77

PATRICK or Smith, Doris Neil   *MA 1949
d Manchester 4.1.80 *AUR* xlviii 443

PATTERSON or Baxter, Constance Rose   MA 1953
Aber: teacher Powis acad 1954–69, Cummings Park
p s from 1970

PATTERSON David McDonald   BSc(eng) 1952

PATTERSON Douglas Gordon   BL 1949
ptnr Watt & Cumine advoc Aber 1950–76,
Stronachs advoc from 1976

PATTERSON Iain Alexander Miller   BSc(agr) 1954

PATTERSON Janet Bothwell   MB ChB 1939
semi retd 1974; resid Middlesbrough

PATTERSON Kenneth Harper   *MA 1938
VRD 1960
teacher Edin till 1960; instr lt cdr RNVR/sen instr off.
Forth div RNVR till 1960; dir acad stud. metrop
police from 1960

PATTERSON or Massie, Lavina Cowie   BSc 1954
part-time asst exper off.: endocrinology Torry res
stat Aber 1965–66/marine lab DAFS Aber 1966–68,
prod. sect. marine lab DAFS Aber 1968–70, exper
off./higher scient off. from 1970

PATTERSON Robert Shanks   BSc(eng) 1931
d 22.11.65

PATTILLO Alan Hutchison   *MA 1951
employed film indust Lond from 1955

PATTILLO John Alexander   MB ChB 1953
g p Shrewton Salisbury from 1966

PATTISON David Dickie   MA 1907
d 1972

PATTISON Iain Henry   BSc(agr) 1937
FRCVS 1965
dep dir agr res council inst for res on anim diseases
Compton nr Newbury Berks 1967–76; retd

PATTULLO Jean   MB ChB 1944 DPH 1949

PATTULLO William Ogilvy   MA ^dLLB 1948
sen lect mercantile law Aberd 1959–61; prof commercial law Khartoum 1961; advoc Edin 1961–62;
sheriff Lanarksh 1962–74
d Thorntonhall 1.11.75 *AUR* xlvi 418

PAUL Douglas Lamont   BL 1949

PAUL Elizabeth Hay   *MA 1913
resid Dufftown
d Dufftown 20.6.78

PAUL or Annand, Elizabeth Helen   MA 1955
teacher p s St Margaret's s for girls Aber 1967–73

PAUL Ian Alexander   *MA 1953
civ serv M o D (navy) 1953–75
m W Calder 1960; marr diss 1977
resid Dufftown

PAUL John Milne   MA 1924
d Elgin 22.8.77

PAUL William   *MA 1946 PhD 1951
AM(hon)(Harv) 1960
Gordon McKay prof of applied phys Harvard USA
from 1963; prof associé faculté des sciences univ de
Paris 1966–67; fell Clare Hall Camb 1974–75; assoc
Clare Hall from 1975

PEACE Sydney   MB ChB 1951
DObstRCOG 1964
h o obst Raigmore hosp Inv 1963; g p Kirkwall/obst
and med apptments Balfour hosp from 1963

PEARCE or Latter or Shaw, Jessie (Janette)
MA 1947

PEARCE Peter Anthony   BSc(for) 1953

PEARCE Terrance Arthur Albert   MB ChB 1950
DPM(Lond) 1960 MRANZCP 1964 FACMA 1968
MRCPsych 1972
regist psychiat NW Glasg reg hosp board Woodilee
hosp Lenzie 1960–62; Victoria Aust: consult. psychiat
mental hyg dept Sunbury hosp 1962–63, consult.
psychiat 1960, dep psychiat supt mental hyg dept
Mont Park hosp 1963–66, psychiat supt 1966–76,
supt commun ment health centre Chatsworth House
clin Frankston from 1976

PEARSON Edgar Alan [Hamilton-]
see Hamilton-Pearson

PEARSON Gavin Duffus   *BSc 1937

PEARSON or Cruickshank, Margaret Duffus
*MA 1940
teacher Aber: sc/maths Middle j s s 1941–42, sc
Central s s 1942–51, High s for girls 1962–65, mus
Torry s s 1966–69, sc pre-nursing coll 1969–71, phys
St Margaret's s for girls from 1971

PEARSON or Arnett, Mary Helen   BSc 1929

PEARSON Robert Graham   MA 1951 LLB 1954

PEARSON William Ellis   MA 1924
retd 1955; resid Trimley

PEAT Alfred Augustus   MB ChB 1931
m o Research Unit Rockefeller Foundation
Trelawny Jamaica 1933–34, m o h St Catherine Ja
1935–42, ADMS Jamaica 1943–48, DMS Trinidad
1948–56, CMO Jamaica 1956–64, Ag MOH St
Thomas Ja 1966–77; retd

PEAT or Stewart, Catherine   MB ChB 1926
med pract Mulanje Malawi 1930–72; retd; resid
Edin
d Edin 18.4.81

PEAT Reginald Albert   MB ChB 1943
m o: publ gen hosp Kingston Jamaica 1945–46,
Port Royal 1946, Georgetown Cayman Is 1946–48,
Malvern and ag MOH St Elizabeth Jamaica 1948–55,
Highgate Jamaica 1955–58; med practice Highgate
from 1968

PEDDIE John Cameron   MA 1910
d 14.1.68 *AUR* XLII 349

PEDERSEN Christian Peter   BSc 1955
AMIMM 1960 AMAIMM 1973
dist geol Chartered Explor (AAC) Lusaka Zambia

1960–65; div geol (Charter Consolidated) Jos Nigeria/
Whitby Yorks/Akjoujt Mauretania 1965–69; Aust:
sen geol John Taylor & Sons NSW WA NT Papua
New Guinea 1969–71, sen geol Noranda Aust
Koongarra uranium proj NT 1972–75, man. South
Alligator Joint Venture 1975–77

PEEBLES or Lewis, Catherine Grimmond Robertson
MB ChB 1941
d Aldershot 12.5.77

PELLY Frank Le Quesne   MB ChB 1903
no longer on GC reg

PENNIE Donald Durance   MB ChB 1942
MRCGP 1958
g p Forfar from 1948

PENNIE or Taylor, Elisabeth Dewar   *MA 1954

PENNIE Gibb Niven   *MA 1930 ᵈBD 1944
rector St John's ch Greenock 1957–61, canon St
Mary's cath Glasg from 1961; retd 1977; hon canon
1977

PENNIE Helen Skene   MA 1929

PENNIE Ian Durance   MB ChB 1939 MSc 1967
g p Golspie 1952–66; ARO Nature Conserv
Sutherland 1967–68; g p W Lothian 1969–70,
Edrachillis Sutherland from 1970
wife *d* 1971
m(2) Dornoch 10.8.72 Edith M. Wilkinson
MB BS(Durh) anaest d of William W. N'cle-u-Tyne

PENNIE James Hamilton   MA 1935
d Elgin 28.2.75 *AUR* XLVI 239

PENNY Alan Bruce   MA 1953 Dip Ed 1954
teacher classics Montreal 1958–60; prin classics
Port Credit Ontario 1961–63; prin lang Glenrothes
1964–72; grocer Hatton from 1972
m Aber 2.8.60 Cecilia Rennie MA 1953 *qv*

PENNY Alexander   BSc(agr) 1949
Rothamsted exper stat Harpenden: exper off. 1958–
65, sen exper off. 1965–71, sen scient off. 1971–76, prin
scient off. from 1976
m Luton 24.9.60 Katherine C. Graham lab asst d of
James T. H. G. LRCPGlas Luton

PENNY Alfred Alexander   BSc 1933 *1934
d 23.8.71 *AUR* XLIV 321

PENNY Charles   MB ChB 1922
d Derby 21.9.66 *AUR* XLI 339

PENNY or Sabiston, Emma   BSc 1926
resid Longside

PENNY Ian Francis   *BSc 1953 PhD 1956
sen scient off. low temperature res stat Cambridge
1961–67; prin scient off. meat res inst Langford from
1967

PENNY James Chalmers   BSc(eng) 1953
d 22.12.61 *AUR* xxxix 284

PEREIRA Denis Joseph Viegas   MB ChB 1917
no longer on GC reg

PERTor Baxter, Wilma Watt   MA 1951
teacher Engl/Fr Montrose acad from 1972

PETER James Clark   BSc(agr) 1955

PETER Jean Elizabeth   MA 1952
teacher Southesk s Montrose till 1960
m Montrose 5.3.60 William Thomson farm. s of
William T. St Cyrus

PETERKIN Charles Duncan   MA 1908 LLB 1911
d Aber 8.5.62 *AUR* xxxix 377

PETERKIN Constance Elizabeth   MA 1907
d Lond 15.7.66 *AUR* xli 336

PETERKIN or Black, Elizabeth   *MA 1905
d Lond 12.6.65 *AUR* xli 145, 238

PETERKIN or MacIver, Ethel Marion   MA 1907

PETERKIN Frank Gellie Tennant   MB ChB 1903
no longer on GC reg

PETERKIN Gilbert Burgher   BSc(agr) 1929

PETERKIN Janet Smith   MA 1923
retd; resid Portsoy
d Portsoy 18.8.77

PETERKIN or Cowie, Millie   BSc 1933
resid Oldmeldrum

PETERKIN Reginald Carnie   BCom 1922
no longer on GC reg

PETERS or Robb, Anne Macdonald   *MA 1930
Aber acad: spec asst Engl 1958–60, woman advis
1960–79; retd; resid Braemar

PETERS David Cargill   *MA 1955

PETERS James Henderson   MB ChB 1923
d 12.7.63

PETERS Janet Hunter   *MA 1924
Aber acad: spec asst Fr 1956–65, prin asst Fr
1965–66; retd; resid Braemar
d Braemar 7.8.79

PETERS Martha McLaren   MA 1908
no longer on GC reg

PETERS William   *MA 1910 *1911
d Romsey 5.3.64 *AUR* xl 397

PETERS William   *MA 1951

PETERS Willy Ernst   MA 1907 *1908

PETERSON or Milne, Emily O'Hanlon   MA 1930
d 27.10.70

PETERSON George Peter Scott   MA 1955
Shetland: teacher Bridgend p s Burra Isle 1958–59,
Hamnavoe j s s Burra Isle 1959–61; teacher Engl Brae
j s s 1961–66, Engl/geog Aith j s s 1966–69, Engl/geog
Brae j h s from 1969, dep head from 1971
m Lerwick 9.8.65 Frances A. Doull knitter d of Adam
D. Brae

PETERSON James McInnes
                         BSc(agr) 1922 BSc 1925 DSc 1933
prof physiol univ of Wales 1947–66; chmn edit.
board *Journal of Physiology* 1947–66; retd; resid Edin

PETERSON James Magnus   BSc(eng) 1954
test eng Rolls-Royce Derby 1961–63; tech sales eng
Serck Radiators Birm 1963–65; S Aust: maintenance
eng Eng & Water Supply dept 1966–67, des eng
Woods & Forests dept 1967–68; maintenance eng
Railways dept NSW Aust 1968–72; proj eng Serck
Heat Transfer B'ham from 1972

PETERSON Magnus Fraser   BCom 1924
prod. eng *Manchester Guardian* 1928–37; prod. dev
eng Fairey Aviation Co. Stockport 1938–65; retd;
resid Christchurch
m Manc 1928 Evelyn S. Bakewell teacher d of William
B. Aber

PETERSON Peter Hewitt   MB ChB 1940
g p Bixter Zetland 1963–73; retd (except for s
dental anaest); resid Whiteness Zetland

PETERSON William Gordon   BCom 1927 MA 1930
retd 1963; resid Aber
d Aber 4.9.78

PETRIE Adeline Frances   MB ChB 1937

PETRIE Alexander   *MA 1903
retd; resid Pietermaritzburg
d Johannesburg 1.12.79 *AUR* xlviii 350

PETRIE Annie Jane   MA 1904
no longer on GC reg

PETRIE Beryl Gertrude   MB ChB 1937
m o Westminster c c from 1964

PETRIE Charles William   MB ChB 1939
d Wigan 8.2.70 *AUR* xliii 446

PETRIE David   MA 1900
d Sidmouth 7.8.61 *AUR* xxxix 268

PETRIE or Baird, Elizabeth Mary   MA 1936
exec off. MAFF 1949–76; retd; resid Lond
m(2) Lond 1.9.51 Telesfor M. Kuzminski (*d* 13.1.76)
s of Kazimierz K. Skolimow Poland

PETRIE Gordon   *MA 1952
lect geog Glas 1958–64, sen lect from 1964; Carnegie
res fell. internat trg centre for aerial surv Delft, Neths
1969–70, prof from 1977

PETRIE Ian Clark   MA 1948
teacher Manc 1949–51; Wigan: teacher 1951–55, graded post 1955–58, head Engl dept 1958–60, dep head from 1960
m Wigan 28.7.54 Eunice A. Ashurst beauty consult./ hosp receptionist d of John A. Wigan

PETRIE James Beattie
                    MA 1932 *MB ChB 1936 DPH 1939
d Lond 3.6.66 *A UR* xli 340

PETRIE James William Gorrod   BSc(eng) 1948
MICE 1951 FICE 1966
Port of Lond auth: asst eng 1951–62, div eng new works 1962–64, div eng (plans & proj man.) 1964–67, asst chief eng (proj) 1967–71, chief eng Upper Docks 1971–72, chief eng PLA from 1972

PETRIE Robert John   MA 1950

PETTIGREW or Brown, Ellen Elizabeth   MA 1950

PHEMISTER or Munro, Helen Reid   MB ChB 1949
Dip Med Radiother(Lond) 1973
regist radiotherap Sheff from 1974

PHILIP Alexander Gunn   BL 1951

PHILIP Alexander James   *BSc 1922
d Sherbrooke Quebec 20.2.67 *A UR* xlii 185

PHILIP or McGregor, Alice Mary   MA 1916
no longer on GC reg

PHILIP Alice Mary   MA 1921 BSc 1923
d Aber 18.4.75

PHILIP Andrew William   BSc(agr) 1949
lect NOSCA from 1960

PHILIP or Glass, Annie Jane Isabel   MA 1919
d Aber 25.7.63 *A UR* xl 302

PHILIP Audrey   MA 1954
teacher geog Airdrie from 1968
m Edin 24.3.59 Robert F. Shirra des draughtsman

PHILIP Catherine   MA 1935
Peterhead acad: woman advis 1969–75, asst head 1972–75; retd

PHILIP Cecil Sleigh   MB ChB 1928
retd 1966; resid Elgin

PHILIP Charles Robert   MB ChB 1921 ᶜMD 1929
d 17.9.69 *A UR* xliii 329

PHILIP Elizabeth   MA 1908
d Aber –.9.69 *A UR* xliii 327

PHILIP Flora   MA 1935

PHILIP George Mackenzie   MA 1951
C of S min: Sandyford-Henderson mem ch Glasg from 1956

m Glasg 26.4.61 Patricia J. Morrison MA(Edin) teacher d of Donald J. M. MB ChB(Edin) Edin

PHILIP Hardy   MA 1896 BL 1898
no longer on GC reg

PHILIP or Robertson, Helen Jane   MA 1937
resid Montrose
d 31.7.78

PHILIP Henry Leslie   *MA 1950
HMIS Edin/Renfrew 1962–69; head Liberton s s Edin from 1969

PHILIP Isabel Mary   *MA 1952

PHILIP James   MA 1942
C of S min: Holyrood Abbey Edin from 1958
m Aber 19.11.60 Mary F. Moffat MB ChB(Edin) h o d of Unwin J. M. BSc(agr)(Glas) Broken Hill Zambia

PHILIP James Fiddes   MB ChB 1933 *ChM 1937
clin prof oncology Aberd from 1975; clin dir Roxburghe House Tor-Na-Dee hosp Aber from 1977

PHILIP Jessie Stuart   *MA 1926
retd 1964; resid Aber

PHILIP John   MA 1930
warden Tertowie resid s 1960–70; retd; resid Kintore

PHILIP John George Walker
                    BL 1954 MA LLB 1956
ptnr Philip & Wadsworth advoc Aber from 1973

PHILIP Kathleen   *MEd 1950

PHILIP or Stokeld, Kathleen May Colvine   MA 1945
resid N. Berwick

PHILIP or Hendry, Margaret Isabella   MA 1932
teacher Kittybrewster p s Aber 1940–72; retd
husb d 15.8.73

PHILIP or Startup, Marjorie Ellson   MA 1926
no longer on GC reg

PHILIP Richard Lewis   BCom 1923

PHILIP Robert Alexander David   *BSc(eng) 1950

PHILIP or Campbell, Una Jessie   *BSc 1935
teacher maths: St Margaret's s for girls Aber 1936–39, Cambridge county h s for girls 1942–44, Mary Erskine s for girls Edin 1944–48; head Queen Margaret coll Wellington NZ 1949–52; lect maths Homerton coll Cambridge 1957–59; head The Royal Masonic s for girls Rickmansworth 1959–72; retd; resid Cambridge

PHILLIPS Calbert Inglis   MB ChB 1946 ᶜMD 1957
PhD(Brist) 1961 MSc(Manc) 1969 FRCSE 1972 Hon F BoA 1975
consult. ophth surg St George's hosp Lond 1963–65;

prof ophth Manc/hon consult. surg Manc royal eye hosp; prof ophth Edin/hon consult. ophth surg ERI from 1972
m Edin 29.12.62 Christina A. Fulton MB ChB(Edin) ophth d of Angus A. F. BSc(eng)(St And) Edin

PHILLIPS Ernest Johnston   BSc 1930
statist: col off. Lond 1960–62, central statist off. Lond 1962–71; retd; resid Ditchling

PHILLIPS James   MB ChB 1936
g p: Grange-over-Sands Lancs 1946–47, Sale Cheshire from 1948

PHILLIPS John Charles Lewis   BSc(for) 1951

PHILP Alexander George   BSc 1949 MB ChB 1954
MRCGP 1963
g p Brentford from 1956
m Lond 3.12.60 Margaret F. Hutchinson MA(Lond) teacher d of Humphrey H. OBE BSc(Durh) S. Hetton Co Durh

PHILP Ronald Richard   *MA 1950
teacher: Lossiemouth 1961, prin geog Forres acad 1961–72, asst rector from 1972

PHIMISTER George   BSc 1948
analyst Colombo Comm Co Ceylon 1948–70; teacher Aber from 1971

PHIMISTER Ronald McLean   MA 1947
head Dunecht p s from 1973

PICKFORD or Milne, Mabel Mary   MA 1948

PICKLES John William   MB ChB 1932 DPH 1940
Commander St John amb organis 1966
retd 1966; locum tenens apptments tuberculosis hosps/clin Cape Province S. Af 1966–76; emigrated to NSW Aust 1976; locum tenens apptments g p, immunological clin Mittagong shire c NSW

PICKUP Eric   PhD 1940

PIKSIS Velta   MA 1953
teacher Aberchirder j s s 1954–62
m Aber 11.7.61 Robert M. Forsyth BSc 1953 *qv*

PIMLEY Kenneth Gordon   MB ChB 1946

PIMLEY Terence Franklin Philip   MB ChB 1950
Kingseat hosp Newmachar: h o 1951–52, regist 1953–56, jun hosp m o 1956–65, asst in psychiat 1965–66; Bilbohall hosp Elgin: asst in psychiat 1966–74, consult. psychiat from 1974
m Aber 29.11.63 Sheila K. Chalmers MB ChB(St And) med asst in psychiat d of Malcolm C. MA(Glas) Broughty Ferry

PINNOCK Malcolm Raymond   MB ChB 1950
g p Feckenham and Astwood Bank from 1956

PIRIE Alexander Anderson   MA 1891
d Oldmeldrum 20.8.72 aged 104 *AUR* xlv 123

PIRIE Alexander Irvine
                    ***MA 1902 BD 1907 DD 1952**
d Edin 10.9.62 *AUR* xl 74

PIRIE Alexander James   *MA 1948
teacher prin hist: Blairgowrie h s 1961–65, Elgin acad 1965–69; head Craigshill h s Livingston W. Lothian from 1969

PIRIE Alexander Maxwell   MA 1948

PIRIE Alfred James   MB ChB 1907
no longer on GC reg

PIRIE or Adams, Annie Roger   MA 1941
resid Anguston Peterculter

PIRIE Bruce Geddes   MB ChB 1951
FFARCS(Lond) 1961
regist anaest Addenbrookes hosp Cambridge 1958–62; sen regist anaest Norfolk and Norwich hosp 1962–65; consult. anaest Queen Elizabeth II hosp Welwyn Garden City from 1965
m Pattishall 4.2.61 Diana J. Collins MA(Oxon) med pract

PIRIE Ella Elizabeth Philip   MA 1928
resid Edin

PIRIE or Douglas, Elma   MA 1947
teacher Fernielea p s Aber from 1964

PIRIE Frances   MA 1930

PIRIE George   MB ChB 1913
no longer on GC reg

PIRIE George Jamieson   MB ChB 1898 DPH 1905
d 27.12.64

PIRIE or Pirie, Helen Calder   MA 1949
teacher Engl: Middle s s Aber 1950–59, Old Aber s s 1968–75, Linksfield acad from 1975

PIRIE or Egerton, Isobel Jean   MA 1944
resid Milltimber Aber

PIRIE James Elphinstone   MA 1921 BD 1923
C of S min: chaplain RN Malta/UK 1932–53; Kinellar 1953–56, Heriot Midlothian 1956–59; retd; resid Edin
wife *d* Edin 9.11.72

PIRIE John Riddell Knight   BSc 1931 BL 1936
edit. NEL newsletter 1964–68; retd; pres Glasg branch of Aberd Alumnus Assoc 1967; founded E coast branch of Aberd Alum. Assoc, secy & treasurer 1968; resid Scone

PIRIE Margaret Christian   *MA 1944
prin teacher mod lang St Margaret's s for girls Aber from 1963

PIRIE Nora Mary   BSc 1922
d Huntly 19.6.77

PIRIE Norman James   *MA 1929
d 31.1.69

PIRIE Rhoda Ellen   MA 1950

PIRIE Richard Thomas   BSc(eng) 1949 *1950
Cia Shell de Venezuela: head of transportation Maracaibo 1959–61; Shell Int Petr: head of trans The Hague 1961–67; Shell BP Nigeria: supplies & services man. Port Harcourt 1967, man. mid west Warri 1967–69; Basrah Petr Coy gen man. Basrah Iraq 1970–72; Assoc Octel Coy: man. supply/plan. Lond 1972–73, man. pers/man. serv Ellesmere Port from 1973

PIRIE Robert William   MA 1947
Aber: prin teacher sc St Peter's RC s s 1962–66, prin sc/phys Summerhill acad from 1966, asst head from 1973

PIRIE or Graham, Vivien Winifred
**   *BSc 1950 PhD 1955**
resid Carluke

PIRIE William   MA 1953
head Tillydrone p s Aber from 1973

PIRRIE Margaret Jane   MA 1945
teacher Rothiemay p s from 1949

PITHIE or Askew, Alice   MA 1918
no longer on GC reg

PITHIE Mary   MA 1910
no longer on GC reg

PITTENDRIGH Agnes Margaret   BSc 1926
volunt soc worker Aber from 1946
d Aber 20.4.78 *AUR* XLVIII 357

PLANT Donald   BSc(for) 1953
Methwold h s: prin maths/sc 1957–77, sen tut. from 1978; retd 1.4.80

PLEASANCE or Ogilvy, Sybil Emily Knox
**   MA 1916**
no longer on GC reg

POLE or Yule, Constance Margaret   MB ChB 1949
g p Maryport Cumbria from 1966

POLE James Denham   MB ChB 1921
d Australia

POLE or Morrison, Kathleen St Clair Montford
**   MA 1954**
teacher: various p s 1955–62, 1967–73; head Port Erroll p s Aberdeensh from 1974

POLLOCK George Tullo   MB ChB 1953 DPH 1957
MFCM 1972
m o h/prin s m o Coventry 1972–74; area m o Coventry AHA from 1974

POLLOCK William Patrick   BSc(for) 1924
no longer on GC reg

POLLOCK William Stott   MB ChB 1932
retd 1973; resid Alford

POLYCARPOU Andrew   BSc(for) 1952
dir dept of for. Nicosia Cyprus 1960–66; progr co-ordination off. for. div FAO Rome 1966–68; dir dept of for. Nicosia 1968–70; gen man. Cyprus For. Indust Nicosia 1970–71; sen agr advis/FAO country rep Cairo 1972–73; chief for. conserv and wild life br for. dept FAO Rome 1974–76; asst to ADG for. dept FAO Rome from 1977

PONTING Frederick William   PhD 1953
FIMA 1964
sen lect maths Aberd 1961–70, reader from 1970

POPE James Albert   *MA 1948
FRSS 1949
head statist and computing team Marine Lab DAFS Torry Aber from 1950

POPPLEWELL Newman   MA 1908 BD 1911
d 1961 *AUR* XXXIX 273

PORTEOUS James Duncan   BSc(eng) 1945
CEng 1965
asst chief eng John Brown Land Boilers Clydebank 1965–66; Foster Wheeler John Brown Boilers: eng man. Whitecrook Clydebank 1966–67, proj man. Aberthaw Lond 1967–68; eng and contr man. Diamond Power Specialty Dumbarton from 1968

PORTEOUS or Melvin, Margaret   MB ChB 1919

PORTER Dorothy May   MB ChB 1955
h o obst Edgware gen hosp 1959; g p Newmarket 1960–69; sen m o health dept Bury St Edmunds 1969; g p: Cuminestown 1975–76, Leighton Buzzard from 1977
m Aber 28.12.64 Colin H. Walker MB BS(Lond) g p s of Wilfrid E. W. Chingford; marr diss 1974

PORTER or Bell, Edith Barnett   MA 1952
teacher: Lanarksh 1969–76, Dr Barnardo's Coltness 1976–77; lect Motherwell tech coll from 1977

PORTER Elma   BSc 1950
Glaxo labs: analytical chem Montrose 1952–59, tech 1959–70, head of correspondence sect. Greenford 1970–78, tech exec, tech dir Lond from 1978

PORTER Helene Sievewright   MA 1946
teacher p dept RGC Aber from 1958

PORTER or Morrison, Isabel Murray   BSc 1952
Cambridge: part time lect Cambridgeshire coll arts and tech from 1976

PORTER or Ellis, Jean Bruce Maitland
**   BSc 1940 MB ChB 1946**
member Gen Nursing Council Scot. from 1970, member Grampian health board from 1974, chmn Royal Cornhill and assoc hosp board of man. 1971–74

PORTER or Diack, Laura   MA 1943
resid Torphins

PORTER Richard Reginald Maitland
                              MA 1908 *MB ChB 1912
  Kt order of St John 1972
resid Aber
d Aber 24.7.79 *AUR* xlviii 350

POTTER or Alexander, Eva Augusta   MA 1930
  d Aber 12.12.75

POTTINGER or Sutherland, Jessie Maggie   MA 1911
  d 19.1.68

POZZI Joseph   MA 1893 MB ChB 1897
  d St Fillans 23.3.62 *AUR* xxxix 370

PRATT Audrey   MA 1955

PRATT Donald Reginald   MA 1949 MB ChB 1954
  DObstRCOG 1958
g p Bournemouth from 1958
m Lytchett Matravers 16.6.62 Pamela J. Sheppard
SRN d of Douglas H. S. Lytchett Matravers

PRATT James Barrie   BSc(agr) 1923 BSc 1926
  resid Nairn

PRATT James Davidson   *MA 1912 ^dBSc 1913
  joint edit. *Chemical Industry* series of monographs
for Pergamon Press 1965–72; retd; resid Ightham
d Ightham 26.7.78 *AUR* xlviii 102

PRATT or Williams, Lora Young
                              MA 1949 MB ChB 1954
  g p Leeds from 1975

PRATT Margaret Ann   MA 1936
  no longer on GC reg

PRATT or McCullough, Mary Christina
                              BSc(agr) 1922 MA 1923

PRATT or Palmer, Moira Kathleen Margaret
                              MB ChB 1951
  part time g p Caloundra Aust from 1960 and m o h
from 1976

PRATT or Pennycuick, Susanna Andrew Calder
                              *MA 1938

PRATT Sydney Alexander Milne   *MA 1951

PRATT William Reginald   MB ChB 1924
  d Bournemouth 28.12.61 *AUR* xxxix 382

PREDDY Adeline Jane   MA 1915
  d Aber 3.1.70 *AUR* xliii 442

PRESLY or Smith, Helen Mackenzie   MA 1945
  resid Keith

PRESSLY Isabella Pearson   MA 1902
  d 21.10.68

PRESTON Charles Desmond   MB ChB 1931
  d 7.1.75 *AUR* xlvi 238

PRICE John William   MB ChB 1949
  LDS RCS(Eng) 1960
sen hosp dent. off. Staffs 1961–65; g p Stoke-on-Trent
1965–66; sen dent. off. Staffs c c from 1966

PRICE or Pougiales, Mary Lomas   MB ChB 1947
  ophth Olmsted med group Rochester Minnesota
USA from 1955

PRICE or Yule, Mona Margaret   MA 1941 LLB 1947
  ptnr John S. Yule & Son solic Aber from 1966

PRIEST or Hewitt, Anna Ross   MA 1924
  retd 1965; resid Bedford

PRIEST Elizabeth Anne Forbes   MB ChB 1950
  med asst diabetic serv ARI from 1972
m Aber 21.11.62 James J. Dickie LLB(Dunedin)
barrister-at-law s of John Dickie MA 1895 *qv*(i, ii, iii)
husb *d* 13.3.67

PRIEST or Cox, May Wilson   MA 1924
  MBE 1945
teacher Hants 1948–51; retd; resid Farnborough
d 22.12.78

PRIEST or Turner, Mina Wilson   MA 1930
  retd 1968; resid Farnborough

PRIESTLEY or Reid, Phyllis Jane Holden
                              MB ChB 1938
  g p Auchterarder from 1939

PRINGLE Alexander Ferguson
                              MB ChB 1904 *MD 1916
  d Aber 10.9.62 *AUR* xl 91

PRINGLE Ivan Terence   MA 1909
  no longer on GC reg

PRINGLE or Hunter, Joyce
                              BSc(agr) 1949 PhD 1953
  lect soil phys dept soil sc N'cle from 1963

PRINGLE or Cooper, Norna
                              MB ChB 1948 DPH 1955
  departmental m o Aberdeensh 1963–70; clin m o
Cupar 1970–76; sen clin m o NE Fife from 1976

PRISE Edward   *BSc(eng) 1955
  W. A. Fairhurst & ptnrs Aber: eng 1957–72, assoc
1973–77, ptnr from 1977

PRITCHARD Donald Forsyth Buchanan   BSc 1927
  d 22.8.79

PRITCHARD or McDonald, Margaret   MA 1953
  teacher Swanland E Yorks from 1973

PROCTOR David Maxwell   MB ChB 1944
  OBE

PROCTOR George Rennet   *BSc 1952 PhD 1956
  visiting fell. univ of Zurich 1960; Royal Soc visiting
fell. Yale univ New Haven USA 1963; lect chem

Strath 1964–70, sen lect from 1970; visiting expert Nat Cancer Inst Bethesda Md USA

PROFEIT or Watson, Mary Helena   *MA 1909
no longer on GC reg

PROFEIT Robert Alexander   MA 1889
no longer on GC reg

PROSSER Dorothy Claire   MA 1920
no longer on GC reg

PROSSER Douglas   *MA 1947 Dip Ed 1948
dep rector Inverurie acad 1971–75; head Hazlehead acad Aber from 1975
wife d –.2.78

PROSSER Oswald George   MB ChB 1925
d Hull 20.12.67 *AUR* xlii 366

PRYOR Graeme Derek   MA 1955

PUCCI Peter Vincent   MB ChB 1940
g p Chesterfield 1950–69; Edzell: commun med 1969–80

PUDDY Claude Austin   PhD 1934

PURCHASE Arthur Richard   BSc 1953

PURDY Henry David   MA 1894
no longer on GC reg

PURVES John Elder Bootland   MA 1936 *BSc 1939

PYCROFT or Baillie, Norma Cotesworth   MA 1947

PYKA William Swienczyk   BL 1955
CA 1960 Assoc Member Institute of Taxation 1964 Polish Gold Cross of Merit 1967 Polish Home Army Cross 1970
ptnr Cooper & Hay advoc Aber 1961–68; lect RGIT Aber 1968–70, sen lect from 1970; private advoc & NP/CA from 1968

PYLE Douglas   MA 1930

PYPER or Stewart, Catherine Mary   MA 1925
no longer on GC reg

PYPER or Hillelson, Ida Burton   *MA 1909
d 26.8.63

PYPER Ida Malcolm Birnie   *MA 1932
retd 1968; resid Peterhead

PYPER or Thomson, Mary Milne
                              MA 1918 *MB ChB 1921
g p Kei Mouth S Af 1923–61; semi-retd; resid Kei Mouth Cape Province

PYPER William Esplin   MB ChB 1936
retd; resid Tamworth

QUINE John Waddington   *MA 1952
econ intell asst Pontypool 1954–58; econ Brit Nylon Spinners Lond 1958–65; econ ICI Fibres Harrogate from 1965

QUINLAN Audrey   MA 1953
Aber: teacher Inchgarth p s 1966–73, Craighill p s from 1973

RAE or Bain, Anne Bruce Lumsden   MA 1910
d Perth 11.5.72 *AUR* xlv 224

RAE Beatrix   MA 1916 BSc 1920
d 16.11.70

RAE Bennet Birnie   MA 1926 *BSc 1929 PhD 1938
FRSE 1961
Buckland prof (lect various fishing ports) 1958; sen prin scient off./asst dir Marine lab DAFS Aber 1959–71; retd

RAE Cornelius Thomson   MA 1910 BD 1913
d 12.12.74 *AUR* xlvi 235

RAE or White, Elizabeth   MA 1913
d 2.3.74

RAE or Thom, Elizabeth   MA 1926

RAE Francis William   MA 1931 BD 1934 DD 1965
C of S min: Cardonald par ch Glasg 1948–70, Dairsie and Kemback, Fife from 1970; convener home mission comm home board 1964–68, moderator Glasg presb 1968–69, convener joint home and deaconess board comm 1970–74; moderator Cupar presb 1973–75; retd; resid St Andrews

RAE Frederick Sutherland   MB ChB 1937
MRCGP 1956
g p Aber from 1947

RAE George Cornelius   MB ChB 1937
DPM 1940
h o Kettering hosp Northants 1938–39; asst m o Bexley mental hosp Kent 1939–41; war serv m o RAF 1941–46; asst m o Bexley mental hosp 1946–48; sen m o Banstead mental hosp Surrey 1948–56, St Andrew's mental hosp Norfolk 1956–69; retd; resid Norwich
m Norfolk 5.12.70 Barbara J. Eagling d of William A. E.

RAE Gordon   *MA 1934
FEIS 1976
prin lect geog Jordanhill coll of educ Glasg 1947–76

RAE or Chakko, Grace Jane Hurry   MA 1933

RAE or Hutcheson, Isabella Jessie   MA 1915
no longer on GC reg

RAE or Mathers, Isabelle Josephine   *MA 1934

RAE or Margetts, Isobel Watson   MB ChB 1944
g p: Beeston Notts 1950–70, Elgin from 1970; also part time m o Bilbohall hosp Elgin
husb d 29.2.68

RAE James   MA 1910 BD 1914 DD 1956
d Lond 4.5.60 *A UR* xxxviii 589

RAE James William   MB ChB 1939
d 25.12.66

RAE John James   BSc(agr) 1954

RAE or Clark, Mary Janetta   MA 1921
resid Aber

RAE Nancy Margaret   MA 1954
teacher remed reading Craigbank p s Sauchie Alloa
from 1975
m Aber 22.8.59 John A. R. Colman BSc(Glas) petr
geol s of Ernest C. Gatehouse-of-Fleet

RAE William   MA 1903 ᵈBL 1906
d Victoria BC 11.11.73 *A UR* xlv 444

RAE William   MA 1949
head St Boswells p s from 1958

RAE William   *MA 1951

RAE William Duff   BSc 1941 PhD 1946
AIRI 1967
group chief chem Silentbloc Holdings Surbiton from
1971

RAE William Jack Watson
                MB ChB 1950 DPH 1957 MD 1962
MFCM 1972
Aber: sen asst m o h 1959–63, jun dep m o h 1963–68,
asst sen m o NE reg hosp board 1968–71, prin asst sen
m o 1971–74; spec commun med Grampian health
board 1974–78; retd

RAE William James   *MA 1950

RAEBURN George Ferguson   LLB 1938
ptnr Raeburn, Christie, Buthlay & Rutherford
advoc Aber/solic Ellon from 1947; town clerk Ellon
till 1975

RAFFAN Alfred William   MB ChB 1938
anaest NE reg hosp board from 1948; member NE
reg hosp board Scot. from 1971; member bus. comm
General Council Aberd from 1971; retd hosp serv
1977
wife *d* Aber 1.9.75
m(2) 23.12.76 Hellen P. Ledingham or Gilchrist

RAFFAN Hamish McLennan
                MB ChB 1943 ᶜMD 1948
FRCP(C) 1972
internal med Guelph Ontario from 1953

RAFFAN Helen Mary   *MA 1917
retd; resid Edin
d Edin 27.4.80

RAFFAN Ian Duffus   BSc 1955
teacher sc: St Andrew's s s Lhanbryde 1958–61,
Rothes s s 1962–63, Lossiemouth h s 1963–65, spec

asst 1965–69; sp asst sc Milne's h s Fochabers 1969–
73, asst prin guid from 1973
m Elgin 8.7.64 Margaret A. McArthur cook d of
James H. McA. Garmouth

RAFFAN John Buie   MB ChB 1939
path. mid Glam AHA from 1949

RAFFAN Stanley James   MA 1947
C of S min: Martyr's and North ch Greenock
1956–62, Ellon par ch 1962–73, Ellon and Slains par
ch 1973–77; chaplain Crichton Royal & Nithbank
hosps Dumfries from 1977

RAINNIE George Fraser   *MA 1949
univ of Leeds: sen lect 1964–78, chmn of econ stud.
from 1978

RAIT Robert Bain   MB ChB 1935
h o Darlington 1935–36; g p Ilford 1936–41; RAMC
1941–44; g p Ilford 1944–72; retd; resid Ringwood

RAIT Williamina Alice   MA 1910
d –.12.72

RAITT John Stewart   BSc 1947 *1949 PhD 1953

RAITT or Fallowfield, Kathleen Mary   *BSc 1953
head sc dept St Bride's s Helensburgh from 1971

RAITT Norah Patricia   MB ChB 1951
part-time cytologist Raigmore hosp Inv
m Aber 26.8.61 John R. G. Watters MB ChB(Edin)
g p Ullapool

RAITT William John   MB ChB 1925
d Aber 3.7.61 *A UR* xxxix 205

RAITT William Lindsay   *BSc 1955

RALPH Ian Fraser   MB ChB 1953

RALPH or Neill, Maggie   *MA 1928
d Glasg 9.12.60 *A UR* xxxix 105

RAMKISSOON Ramdath   MB ChB 1954

RAMSAY Andrew Melvin
                MA 1923 MB ChB 1926 MD 1939
consult. phys infectious diseases unit Royal Free
hosp Hampstead from 1948

RAMSAY or Duncan, Charlotte Edna   MA 1944
teacher Drumgarth s Aber from 1961

RAMSAY Doris   MB ChB 1945
g p: Shapinsay Orkney 1963–72, Thurso from 1972

RAMSAY or Dalrymple, Isobel Stuart Wyness
                MB ChB 1931
d Aber 1.12.76

RAMSAY Mary Paton   MA 1908
d Edin 5.7.67 *A UR* xlii 179

RAMSAY Rowellyn   BCom 1923
minister emeritus presb ch of Aust 1966; hon chaplain presb homes for the blind Brisbane Queensland from 1967
d 1981

RAMSAY William Leslie   MB ChB 1926
retd 1970; resid Shorne Kent

RANKIN Alexander Douglas
                    MB ChB 1925 DPH 1927
no longer on GC reg

RANKIN Andrew   MA 1922
retd 1966; resid Inv
d Inv 21.9.80 *AUR* XLIX 67

RANKIN Andrew Logan   MA 1954

RANKIN or Chalmers, Anita Joyce Graham
                                    MA 1947
resid St Albans

RANKIN or Junor, Margaret Elizabeth
                    MA 1920 MB ChB 1923
resid Grahamstown S Africa

RANKIN Wilfred   PhD 1929

RANKIN William James   MA 1935
major TARO
retd
wife *d* 1966
d Aber 30.9.80 *AUR* XLIX 69

RANKINE Annie Anderson Primrose   BSc 1937 *1938
asst head Fraserburgh acad; retd 1976; resid Gullane

RANKINE Henry William   BSc 1938
MICE 1945 MIStructE 1945
county surv E Lothian c c Haddington 1962–75; consult. to Mason & ptnrs consult. eng Edin 1975–78; retd; resid Gullane

RANKINE or Binns, Janet   MA 1912
d Jedburgh 3.10.70 *AUR* XLIV 109

RANKINE Rachel Levie   MA 1910
resid Aber
d Aber 7.4.79 *AUR* XLVIII 226

RANNIE James   MB ChB 1921 MD 1924
d Beckenham 14.7.77

RANNIE Melville Elliot McAlpine   BL 1948
secy/treas: board of man. Aber spec hosps 1963–71, hon secy/treas assoc of Scot. hosp boards of man. 1965–69; secy/treas board of man. Foresterhill and assoc hosps Aber 1971–74; private leg. practice Crieff 1974–77

RAO Gargestwari Narayana Subba
see Subba Rao

RATTRAY Arthur Smith   BSc 1942
d Sutton Coldfield 12.9.74 *AUR* XLVI 110

RATTRAY William   MA 1899
d 2.1.71

RAWCLIFFE Gordon Hindle   DSc 1944
FIEE 1946 FIEEE 1970 FRS 1972
prof elect. eng Brist 1944–75; retd
d 3.9.79

RAY Santosh Chandrah   PhD 1938

RAYNER or Bain, Kathleen   *BSc 1951
teacher phys St David's s Ashford Middx from 1969

REAICH or Ewing, Maggie Jane Cowie   MA 1923
resid Cults Aber
d Aber 11.7.78

REAICH or Brooks, Williamina   MA 1925
teacher Abbotswell p s Aber 1953–66; retd

REAPER Alexander   MA 1909
d Aber 2.2.66 *AUR* XLII 82

REAY or Jason, Aileen Anne Elizabeth   *MA 1952
resid Cults Aber

REAY George Adam   MA 1921 *BSc 1923
d Aber 20.1.71 *AUR* XLIV 210

REAY John Sinclair Shewan   *BSc 1953
SAI Edin 1958–67; Warren Spring lab DTI Stevenage: head intelligence sect. 1968–71, head air pollution div 1972–77; DTI: head prospectives unit from 1977

REDDING or Munro, Mary Elizabeth   MA 1941
resid Edin

REDINGTON George   DSc 1929
no longer on GC reg

REEKIE Andrew George   MB ChB 1917
resid Edin

REES David Cooper   MA 1911
d 5.1.63

REES Lovat Victor Charles
                    ***BSc 1950 PhD 1953 DSc 1977**
sen lect chem Imperial coll Lond from 1970

REGAN Nils Albert   MB ChB 1949
Lond: prin g p from 1957; clin asst hosp pract grade venereology/fam plan. Westminster hosp from 1964, St Stephen's hosp from 1977

REID Alastair David   *MA 1950
teacher Engl/liberal stud. Aber coll of comm from 1960

REID Alexander   MA 1921
d Edin 28.8.65 *AUR* XLII 85

REID Alexander   BSc 1923
d Peterhead 29.6.62 *AUR* XL 88

REID Alexander MB ChB 1924
no longer on GC reg

REID Alexander MB ChB 1924
d Manc 2.5.72 *AUR* XLIV 430

REID Alexander MA 1925 BSc 1927
d Australia

REID Alexander *BSc 1949
d Inv 1.7.74 *AUR* XLVI 110

REID Alexander Edwin MB ChB 1921 DPH 1923
retd 1969, resid Towcester

REID Alexander Gordon MA 1954 LLB 1956

REID or Crossman, Alice MB ChB 1922
d Cheddar 17.12.69 *AUR* XLIII 445

REID Alister Ure BSc(eng) 1954
MICE 1960 MSc(Lond) 1965 DIC 1965
CEng: Lond c c 1960–65, GLC from 1965
m Dunfermline 14.10.61 Sheila C. M. Cumming d of
David O. C. Dunfermline

REID or Buchan, Ann Buchan MA 1914
d 2.5.50

REID Anne Isabella MA 1952
Dip Sec Stud.(Glasg) 1953
teacher comm subj Aber coll of comm 1970–72, sen
lect from 1972
m Inverurie –.4.60 Clayton B. W. Angus sen asst
registrar Aber s of John A. Aber
husb *d* 1977

REID Annie MA 1914
d Aber 22.3.65 *AUR* XLI 149

REID or Allan, Annie Elsie MA 1926
resid Alvah, Banff

REID or Allan, Annie Isabella MA 1942
d Aber 11.4.61

REID Archibald Charles MB ChB 1925
no longer on GC reg

REID Arthur George *MB ChB 1916 *MD 1919
d Aber 21.5.62 *AUR* XXXIX 381

REID Arthur George MB ChB 1938
FRCGP 1970 MBE 1977
g p Auchterarder from 1940; clin asst Scot, g p res
support unit (attached dept g p Dund) 1971–74

REID or Dixon, Beatrice Rae MA 1925
resid Grantown-on-Spey

REID Catherine Williamine MA 1928
teacher maths Inverurie acad 1935–67; retd

REID Charles MA 1909
d Lond 24.1.69 *AUR* XLIII 209

REID Charles
*MA 1914 *BSc 1916 *MB ChB 1917 *MD 1926
DSc 1927
d 24.10.61 *AUR* XXXIX 276

REID Charles MA 1914 MB ChB 1921
d Craigellachie 7.9.72 *AUR* XLV 124

REID or McMillan, Charlotte Helen Mary MA 1933
resid Elgin

REID Donald Darnley MB ChB 1937 ᶜMD 1946
FRCP(Lond) 1965
prof epidemiology/dir dept med statist and epidemiology London s of hyg & trop med from 1959
d Hampton Middx 26.3.77 *AUR* XLVII 214

REID Donald Eric MA 1907
no longer on GC reg

REID or Mutch, Edith Grace MA 1931
resid Mintlaw

REID Edmund Lewis MB ChB 1910
surg ENT Sellyoak hosp Birm 1938–39; ADMS
Orkney & Shetland Defences; consult. nat health
hosp serv ENT Liv 1948–54; retd; resid Bicester
m Newport Mon 12.3.22 Flora M. Green physioth
d of James G. Newport

REID Edward Alexander MA 1951 MEd 1958
ABPsS 1961
educ psych/advis Banffsh 1965–68; dep prin educ
psych Fife 1968–70; lect/sen lect educ psych Callendar
Park coll of educ Falkirk 1970–71, prin lect from 1972

REID Ella Taylor MA 1916
d 13.7.72

REID Eric *BSc 1943
Univ Sur: reader biochem from 1965; also dir of
Wolfson bioanalytical centre from 1969

REID George MA 1920
d Aber 9.4.77

REID George MA 1939 LLB 1942
ptnr Alexander & Gillan advoc Aber from 1963

REID George Alexander BSc(eng) 1947

REID George Arthur *MB ChB 1916 *MD 1919
d Aber 21.5.62 *AUR* XXXIX 381

REID George Merson MB ChB 1942 DPH 1947
g p Sydney Aust from 1951

REID or Green, Grace Hendry MA 1955
teacher: Alves 1959–60, Halifax Canada 1968–69;
secy Parry Sound Canada 1978–79

REID Harry Campbell MA 1937 LLB 1938
ptnr James Milne & Co CA Aber 1951–62; member
exam board inst of CA Scot, 1955–63; man. indust
work therap unit royal Cornhill hosp Aber 1964–68;

acct Mackenzie & Wilson advoc Aber 1968–77, ptnr from 1977

REID Helen Margaret   MA 1940
Aber: teacher Sunnybank p s 1945–65, Mile End p s 1965–66, dep head Tullos p s 1966–73; head Kirkhill p s from 1973

REID or Keir, Helen Winifred   MA 1949
teacher Skene p s 1966–68; asst head (qualif in early educ) Culter s from 1969

REID or Bennett, Hilda Jean   *MA 1944

REID Ian Wilson Carlyle   MB ChB 1954
Canada: dist med examiner Hinton Alberta from 1957, indust m o Cardinal River Coals Hinton from 1974

REID or Sharp, Isobel Ellen   *MA 1939
county pres Brit Red Cross Soc Scot. Branch Banff 1967–75, pres Moray branch incorporating Banffsh from 1975; resid Keith

REID James   MA 1934
TD 1961
br man. Standard Life Assur Co Manc 1964–72; retd; resid Balerno

REID James Leckie   MA 1901
d Dun 24.3.70 *AUR* XLIII 440

REID James Vessman   MA 1930
resid Aber

REID or Russell, Jean   MA 1940
resid Elgin

REID or Couper, Jean Alison   MA 1942
teacher: North s Kirkcaldy 1960–68, Kinloss s Moray 1969–75, Applegrove s Forres from 1975

REID or McGlashan, Jean Margaret   *MA 1917
resid Regina Canada
husb d 31.5.66

REID or Still, Jean Milne Brebner   MA 1950
teacher Aboyne acad 1952–59

REID Jessie   MA 1929
teacher Fraserburgh cent s 1939–69; retd

REID or Ewart, Jessie   MA 1945

REID Jessie Sandison   MA 1935

REID or Morton, Joan Ririe   MA 1929

REID John   MA 1936 BD 1938
C of S min Arbroath Knox's from 1950

REID John   *MA 1944
TD 1965
prin teacher mod lang RGC Aber from 1963; CO Aberd OTC 1957–65

REID John Cameron   MB ChB 1945
MRCGP 1953 FRCGP 1975 JP Abdnsh 1964
g p Strathdon from 1948

REID John Carlyle   MA 1927
no longer on GC reg

REID John Henderson   *BSc 1932
d 8.10.81

REID John Low Thomson   BSc(agr) 1952
farm. Ellon from 1952

REID John Madden   *MA 1951

REID John Mortimer   *BSc(eng) 1951
MIWES 1964 FICE 1970
resid eng Howard Humphreys & Sons Trinidad/Kenya/Libya 1955–64, prin eng Ethiopia, Seychelles, Ghana, Sierra Leone 1964–69; man. dir Pietrangeli & Humphreys SPA Rome 1969–73; assoc ptnr Howard Humphreys England 1974–78, Howard Humphreys Jordan (resid Amman) from 1978—all work associated with water supplies and irrigation

REID John Ure   BL 1949
retd police serv 1960; Wiggins Teape Basingstoke: group safety trg advis

REID Kathleen Murray   MA 1924
no longer on GC reg

REID Laurence Milne   BSc(eng) 1955
MIEE 1965
hydro-elec sect. AEI heavy plant div Rugby 1961–62; J. Sykes & Ptnrs consult. eng Sheffield 1962–64; AEI electronic apparatus div which became GEC/Elliot process automation: head of power, mining and GPO sales Leicester 1964–70; careers advis univ of Brist from 1970
m Wolvercote 27.8.66 Jennifer A. Wolfe BA(Cantab) teacher d of Robert W. Oxford

REID Lydia Chisholm   *MA 1950
d 9.5.81

REID Margaret Anne   MB ChB 1919
no longer on GC reg

REID Margaret Elspeth Jaffray   MA 1951

**REID or Stacey, Margaret Farquharson Garrow
       MB ChB 1928**
asst venereologist (locum) Sheff hosps 1960–63, g p Bakewell Derbysh 1963–65; retd; resid Sheffield

REID Margaret Jane Cornfute   *MA 1910 PhD 1937
no longer on GC reg

**REID or Clay, Margaret Pamela Birnie
       cMB ChB 1948**
JP Reigate 1968
part time asst m o SE Surrey from 1963
d Redhill 5.6.80 *AUR* XLIX 70

REID or McGregor, Margaret Sarah Milne
                MB ChB 1926 MD 1932 DPH 1932
retd 1969; resid Dyce

REID Marshall Findlay   BCom 1922
no longer on GC reg

REID Martha   MA 1946
teacher: Aberchirder j s s 1947, Newhall 1948–56,
Golborne 1956–58, Slough 1958–66, Inv 1966–72
m Nairn 9.12.72 John T. Graham comp dir s of
Thomas G. Chryston

REID or Williams, Mary Ann Margaret   MA 1934
teacher Fr/Engl Buckie h s 1968–73; retd; resid
Portsoy

REID or Kellas, Mary Buchan Ponting   MA 1947
teacher Arrochar p s Dunbartonsh from 1968

REID or MacArthur, Mary Helen   MB ChB 1939
d Edin 23.2.59 *AUR* XXXVIII 218

REID or Moxley, Mary Loughran   MA 1950

REID or Mair, Mary Morrison   MA 1941
resid Aboyne

REID or Cartledge, Mildred Jean   MA 1951
teacher: Birm 1955–61, Warks from 1961

REID Peter   MB ChB 1911 DPH 1927
d Buckie 3.1.69 *AUR* XLIII 209

REID Robert Barron   BSc(agr) 1938
dep dir agr Lusaka N Rhodesia 1959–65; retd; sen
agr econ NOSCA Inv from 1965

REID Robert Stephen   MA 1925
no longer on GC reg

REID Robert Watson   MB ChB 1901
no longer on GC reg

REID or Ezles, Robina   MA 1927
no longer on GC reg

REID or Gray, Sheena Edward   MA 1954
teacher Fr gr s for girls Guernsey from 1975

REID or Fawcett, Sheila Macdonald   MA 1939
W Aust: lib asst Scarborough publ lib 1960–62, br
lib Canning Bridge, Melville, lib geol surv mines dept
of W Aust, Perth 1966–78

REID or Simpson, Sheila Margaret
                MB ChB 1947 DPH 1952
resid Newbury

REID Stanley McRae   MA 1934 MB ChB 1938
d Banstead 26.1.80 *AUR* XLVIII 442

REID or Nutten, Thomasina   MA 1925
resid Inv

REID or Bowie, Victoria Henrietta   BSc 1921
asst dept bot and zool NOSCA 1921–27
resid Aber

REID William   MA 1912
TD
d 23.6.64 *AUR* XL 397

REID William Brebner   BSc 1949
rector Earlston h s from 1965

REID William Clark   BSc 1951
prin teacher maths Eyemouth from 1963

REID William Ewen   MB ChB 1905
no longer on GC reg

REID William Ferris   BSc(agr) 1935
farm./cattle breeding; retd dir RH & A soc; resid
Montrose

REID William Innes   MB ChB 1947
d Hopeman 27.2.75 *AUR* XLVI 240

REID William James
      MA 1906 BSc 1908 *MB ChB 1910 *MD 1914
no longer on GC reg

REID William John Walker   BSc(eng) 1944
MICE 1951 MIWPC 1955 FIPHE 1967
county drainage eng Aber c c 1968–75; retd; with
Hunter Construction (Aberdeen) from 1975

REITH or Oliphant, Adeline   *MA 1934
teacher Engl/hist Ruthrieston s Aber 1952–70; retd

REITH Arthur   MB ChB 1933
d Manc 22.9.69 *AUR* XLIII 331

REITH Douglas   MA 1938 LLB 1945
QC from 1957; NHS commissioner from 1960;
standing jun counsel in Scot. to customs and excise
1949–51; advoc-dep Crown Off. Scot. 1953–57; pres
Pensions Appeal Tribunal (Scot.) 1958–64; chmn
NHS tribunal (Scot.) 1963–65

REITH Hellen Lind   MB ChB 1938
FRCOG 1971
consult. obst/gyn Paisley; retd

REITH James William Strachan
                *BSc(agr) 1943 PhD 1950
FRIC 1967
sen prin scient off. Macaulay inst Aber from 1977

REITH Margaret   *MA 1931
retd 1970
m Inv 18.9.70 Donald Macpherson wholesale area
man. s of Donald M. Uplawmoor Renfrewsh

REITH Ronald John   BSc(agr) 1932
d Lond 14.2.67 *AUR* XLII 371

RENDALL James Alexander   MA 1935
d Aber 19.8.62 *AUR* XL 93

RENNET David Lindsay   MA 1929 LLB 1932
ptnr Butchart & Rennet advoc Aber 1935–75; retd;
resid Bristow Norfolk

RENNET or Proctor, Margaret Joyce   MB ChB 1923
retd 1966; resid Aber
d 24.11.81

RENNET or Stewart, Nita Isobel   BSc 1923
resid Abinger Common Surrey

RENNIE or Bain, Agnes Craigen   MA 1933

RENNIE Alexander James
                    ***BSc(mech eng) 1947 *BSc(civ eng) 1948**
FICE 1968
Merz & McLellan consult. eng N'cle-u-Tyne: chief civ
eng 1968, assoc 1969–74, ptnr from 1974

RENNIE Alexander Milne   *MB ChB 1933
consult. orthop surg to army in Scot. 1960–76; prof
clin orthop surg Aberd 1972–76; retd; resid Kinellar

RENNIE Cecilia   MA 1953
oral Fr superv in Oakville area Ontario 1961–63;
teacher remed: Methil 1968–72, Ellon area 1972–76,
spec unit for sec maladjusted ch in Fraserburgh
teachers' centre from 1976
m Aber 2.8.60 Alan B. Penny MA 1953 *qv*

RENNIE Duncan   BSc(eng) 1945

RENNIE or Smith, Ethel Margaret   MA 1928
teacher: Chapel of Garioch 1930–35, Canongate
nursery s Edin 1940–45, Trefoil s Gogar Edin 1956–
72; retd; resid Ellon

RENNIE George Nicholson   *MA 1934
JP FEIS
d Aber 12.3.74 *AUR* XLV 449

RENNIE Gordon Grant   MB ChB 1953
regist anaest: Edin 1960–63, Greenock 1963; locum
consult. anaest: Greenock 1963, Glasgow/Lanarksh
1964–69; Lanarksh: med asst anaest 1969–70, consult.
anaest from 1970
m Largs 2.4.67 Morag L. Davis MB ChB(Glas) d of
Thomas J. D. Largs

RENNIE James Benjamin   MA 1955
C of S min Blackford ch Auchterarder from 1967
m Inverurie 6.6.59 Margaret G. Pirie s secy d of
George P. Inverurie

RENNIE James Fyfe   *MA 1922 BD 1925
d Hamilton NZ 20.3.80 *AUR* XVLIII 441

RENNIE or Beddie, Jane Christie   MA 1927
teacher Peterhead cent s 1930–63; retd
husb *d* 1968

RENNIE or Gavin, Jeannie Stephen   MA 1919
resid Fraserburgh

RENNIE Joan Elise   MA 1929
d 29.11.78

RENNIE John   MB ChB 1908 *MD 1912
no longer on GC reg

RENNIE John Milne   BSc(agr) 1922

RENNIE Lottie   MA 1937
teacher Hilton acad Aber from 1942

RENNIE or Wilkinson, Margaret Louisa   *MA 1930
d 1952

RENNIE Peter   *MA 1951
diplomatic serv off. FCO Lond 1961–71; 2nd secy
Brit Emb Belgrade 1971–74; FCO Lond from 1974

RENNIE Stephen   BSc(agr) 1923
d York 12.3.69 *AUR* XLIII 213

RENNIE Thomas Fyfe   MB ChB 1953 DPH 1958
FACMA 1968 Dip Health Admin (NSW) 1972
NSW Aust: m o h Western health dist 1961–67, m o h
Parramatta 1967–72, dir commun health serv health
comm from 1973

RENNIE Violet Falconer   MA 1949 Dip Ed 1963
lect prin methods Aber coll of educ 1966–67;
head Auchentoshan s for handicapped Dalmuir
Dumbartonsh 1967–72, asst advis spec educ Glasg
1972–78; advis spec educ Renfrew div Strathclyde reg
c from 1978

RENNIE William John   BSc 1955

REPPER Edwin Norman Duncan
                    MB ChB 1921 MD 1929
no longer on GC reg

RETIEF François Petrus Steyn (Frank) MB ChB 1924

RETTIE Hugh Leith   MB ChB 1925
d 1962 *AUR* XXXIX 383

RETTIE Ian Hazelwood   *MA 1953
Assoc FRAeS 1967
chief aero dynamicist BAC Brist div 1966–73; chief
eng aerodyn staff Boeing comm aeroplane co Renton
Washington USA from 1973

REYNARD or Greenhorn, Catherine Grainger
resid Cupar Fife   **MA 1930**

REYNARD James Grainger   BSc(agr) 1924
no longer on GC reg

REYNARD Marion Grainger   *MA 1932
teacher Engl Bell-Baxter s Cupar Fife 1949–74;
retd

RHIND or Walker, Alison Thackrah   *MA 1936
Red Cross Badge of Honour 1978
teacher Fr h s for girls Wolverhampton 1960; o/c
BRCS Wolverhampton from 1967; Red Cross rep at
Consulate-gen in Lyon France to assist Brit casualties
1965; member commun health council Wolverhampton from 1976

RHIND Douglas Haig   MB ChB 1939
g p Derby from 1946

RHIND Edward Gregson Grant   *MB ChB 1935
FRCP 1964
consult. phys Sheffield gen hosp 1946–77; retd
wife *d* 1960
m(2) Aber 5.12.64 Kathleen McCombie MB ChB 1947
qv

RHIND Gordon   *MA 1925
no longer on GC reg

RHIND Mary Elder   BSc 1941
C of S deaconess Glasg 1960–65; w c c schol
William Temple coll Rugby 1965–66; commun liaison
off. Corby from 1966

RHIND Robert Gordon   *MA 1931
prin teacher maths Br of Don acad Aber 1962–74;
retd

RHIND William   *MA 1928 BSc 1930
retd 1970; resid Lerwick

RHYNAS Ethel Isobel   MA 1927
FSA(Scot) 1973
retd teaching 1962; hon curator Elgin museum
1967–71

RIACH or McMorland, Amy Forbes   MA 1952
teacher: Edzell p s 1960–65, temp in Angus s from
1965

RIACH David Alexander   MA 1953 *1955

RIACH William Alastair Drage   MA 1937
MA(Kansas) 1970 PhD(Edin) 1978
asst prof educ Mem univ Newfoundland 1962–70,
assoc prof from 1970

RIBTON-TURNER Humphrey   BSc(for) 1934
security investig off. M o D royal milit acad Woolwich from 1965

RICE Agnes Walker   MA 1932

RICE Denis James   *MA 1955
Post Grad Cert Ed(Lond) 1960
Dip Soc St(Edin) 1960
Member Br Assoc Soc Workers 1970
educ off. RAF 1956–60; fam case worker Aber assoc
of soc serv 1961–62; warden Vaughan coll univ Leic
from 1962, sen lect from 1974

RICE James Inglis   *MB ChB 1939
d Corgarff 3.9.72 *AUR* xlv 128

RICE Maureen Agnes   MA 1948
dep head Corpus Christi RC s s Nott 1958–67
m Montrose 29.8.66 Peter W. Baxter jeweller s of
George W. B. Nott

RICE Thomas Inglis   MA 1928
no longer on GC reg

RICHARDS or Tewnion, Agnes Doreen   BSc 1944
teacher chem Dollar acad from 1971

**RICHARDS or Watt, Elizabeth Ferguson Carmichael
MA 1941**
resid Cults Aber

RICHARDS Ernest Glenesk   BSc(for) 1938
FIFor(GB) 1958
dir for. comm h q Lond from 1974

**RICHARDS John Charles Shenstone
*BSc 1947 PhD 1953**
reader nat phil dept Aberd from 1965
m(2) Aber 12.4.73 Alexandra G. Murdoch mus

**RICHARDS or Mortimer, Louisa Ravenscroft
MA 1940**
resid Edin

**RICHARDS Marion Brock
*MA 1907 *BSc 1909 DSc 1916**
d 19.6.64 *AUR* xl 395

**RICHARDS Robert
MA 1907 *MB ChB 1910 *DPH 1913 ᶜMD 1917**
d Aber 18.11.65 *AUR* xli 239

**RICHARDS Robert Lawrence
*MB ChB 1939 MD 1944**
FRCPGlas 1964
consult. phys Glasg Western/Gartnavel hosps; also
clin lect Glas from 1963

RICHARDS Robert Lawson   MB ChB 1932
d Inv 2.3.74 *AUR* xlv 448

RICHARDS William Leslie   MA 1938 ᵈLLB 1940
retd 1970; resid Somerset

RICHARDS William Powell Earle   MB ChB 1925
d 27.9.61 *AUR* xxxix 282

**RICHARDSON or McKenzie, Edith Smith
MA 1923**
deceased

RICHARDSON George Barclay   BSc 1944
CBE 1978
fell. St John's coll Oxon from 1951; member mon-
opolies comm 1969–74; member royal comm environmental pollution 1973–74; secy to delegates and chief
exec OUP from 1974

**RICHARDSON or Mackintosh, Kathleen Campbell
MA 1945**

RICHARDSON Walter Dudley   *BSc 1951
MSc(Lond) 1966
lect bot Imp coll Trop Agr, Trinidad 1956–62; lect/sen
lect bot SW Essex tech coll 1963–66; Goldsmith's coll
Lond: sen lect bot 1966–73, head biol sc dept from
1973

RICHES John Haddon   PhD 1936
no longer on GC reg

RICHMOND Archibald Johnston Roddan   MA 1941

RICHMOND Hendry Gilmour
                              MB ChB 1948 *MD 1958
FRCPath 1970
consult. path. Highland health board Inv from 1960

RICHMOND Robert Hill   MA 1947
C of S min Stonehaven South ch Stonehaven from
1967

RICHMOND Robert Leo   BSc(eng) 1949

RICHMOND Roland Denis   MB ChB 1953
anesthesia: g p Jamaica

RIDDEL or Thomas, Barbara Elizabeth   MA 1938
Whitmore Park j s Coventry: teacher 1962, teacher-
tut. for probationary and stud. teachers 1972–77; retd

RIDDEL Donald Olson   MB ChB 1912
d Aber 7.5.63 *AUR* xl 201

RIDDEL George William   MB ChB 1914 DPH 1919
d Norwich 5.2.70 *AUR* xliii 442

RIDDEL or Forbes, Isabella Malcolm   MA 1902
no longer on GC reg

RIDDEL Margaret Gertrude Black   BSc 1927
no longer on GC reg

RIDDELL or Riddell, Alison Mary   MB ChB 1946
resid Papatoetoe RD Auckland NZ

RIDDELL Clarence Eric   MB ChB 1922
h o/locums/asst Wrexham, London, Bolton 1923–
30; g p Point Kingston Jamaica 1930–41; locum/asst
Lond 1941–72; retd
d 2.3.79

RIDDELL or McWilliam, Dorothy Christina Gordon
                              MA 1935
teacher Bishopmill p s Elgin 1959–77; retd

RIDDELL George Alexander   BCom 1929
Lond: secy/acct D. Napier & Son 1933–47; comptroller Engl Elect. Co 1947–62, man. dir 1962–69; dep
man. dir/exec dir GEC 1969–73; retd

RIDDELL George Steedman
                *MB ChB 1939 DPH 1947 MD 1949
commun med spec Fife health board

RIDDELL or Gettliffe, Gladys May   MB ChB 1953
W Va USA: internship 1972–73, resid paediat
1975–76; hon fell. oncology S Carolina 1976–77;
paediat: Ponape TTPI 1977–78, Guam from 1979

RIDDELL John Scott   MB ChB 1937
retd 1973; resid Auldearn
wife *d* 3.9.63
m(2) Stockton-on-Tees –.7.64 Winifred Hemsley asst
matron mat. hosp d of Thomas H. S Shields

RIDDELL Sylvia Aileen   *MA 1955
sen clin psych: Banstead hosp Surrey 1960–62,
Mental h c Burnaby BC Canada 1962–66, McGill ch
learning clin Montreal from 1966

RIDDELL William Shewan   *MA 1913
resid Norwich

RIDDLER Munro   BSc(eng) 1950
MICE 1960 FFB 1971
asst civ eng: Perthsh 1952–56, Inv 1956–60; sen civ
eng Dun 1960–62; comm man. Glasg 1962–70; assoc
consult. eng Glasg from 1970

RIDDOCH Anne Lillias   MA 1919
d Athens 1979

RIDDOCH or Sawyer, Emily Caroline   MA 1899
d 28.5.62 *AUR* xl 74

RIDDOCH or MacLeod, Helen Eliza   MA 1928
resid Stonehaven
husb *d* 22.7.64

RIDDOCH Jean Walker   MA 1933
retd 1966; resid Aber

RIDDOCH Mary   BSc 1924 MB ChB 1927 MD 1934
d 4.3.66 *AUR* xlii 363

RIDDOCH Wyness David   BCom 1924
d Rothiemay 16.1.69 *AUR* xliii 213

RIGG or Kerr, Caroline Wilson   MA 1926
JP Ayr 1965
resid Girvan

RIOCH Charles Turner   MA 1947
pers man. Dunfermline 1948–50; retail man.
Callander 1950–60; teacher Stranraer 1960–69; head
Hoy s Orkney from 1969

RIOCH Margaret   *MA 1923
d Stirling 12.5.69 *AUR* xliii 213

RITCHIE Adam Alexander   MA 1912
d 11.2.74 *AUR* xlv 447 & xlvi 107

RITCHIE or Mathieson, Agnes Duguid Ferrier
                              *MA 1935
d 5.12.64

RITCHIE or Cordiner, Agnes Walker   *MA 1924
resid Aber
d Aber 5.1.80

RITCHIE Agnes Walker   MA 1937
retd 1974; resid Aber

RITCHIE Alfred   BSc 1926 PhD 1936
prin scient off. Scot. home dept from 1950; resid
Aber
d Aber 24.8.79

RITCHIE or Dickie, Alma Christina
                              MB ChB 1942 DPH 1947
g p Crimond in ptnrship with husb from 1953

RITCHIE Annetta Duthie   MA 1935
teacher Fraserburgh cent s from 1957

RITCHIE or Meldrum, Annie Miller   MA 1931

RITCHIE Anthony Elliot   MA 1933 BSc 1936
FCSP 1970 DSc(St And) 1972
secy/treas Carnegie Trust for univs of Scot. from 1969

RITCHIE Catherine   MA 1940
teacher Buckie h s from 1946

RITCHIE or Barker, Charlotte Mitchell   MA 1915
no longer on GC reg

RITCHIE David Alfred Rattray   MB ChB 1946
consult. radiol Perth/Perthsh group of hosps from 1962

RITCHIE Duncan Ferries   MB ChB 1938
retd; resid Elgin

RITCHIE Elizabeth   MA 1913
retd; resid Port Elphinstone, Inverurie

RITCHIE or Rutherford, Elizabeth   MA 1913
no longer on GC reg

RITCHIE Elsie   BCom 1927
d Fraserburgh 6.5.65 A UR XLI 151

RITCHIE or Kellas, Eveline Margaret   *MA 1920
resid Edin
husb d 12.11.67

RITCHIE or Munro, Frances Isabel MacCallum
                              MA 1928

RITCHIE or Graham, Frances Selma
                      MA 1945 MB ChB 1950
asst reg dir blood transfusion serv Dun till 1959;
resid Broughty Ferry

RITCHIE Frederick   MB ChB 1913 DPH 1922
retd Oct 1959
d Nov 1959

RITCHIE George Lee   MB ChB 1914
d Aber 29.7.73

RITCHIE George Lee May
                      MB ChB 1937 DPH 1939

RITCHIE Gordon Law   MB ChB 1947
FRCSE 1958 DMRT(Edin) 1960 FFR(Lond) 1963
surg regist: Law hosp Carluke 1953–57, ARI 1957–
58; regist/sen regist radiotherap Edin RI 1958–64;
consult. radiotherap West Gen hosp Edin from 1964

RITCHIE Herbert   MB ChB 1921
d Cowes I o W 24.7.74 A UR XLVI 108

RITCHIE Ian   *BSc 1954
geol explor dept California Standard Edmonton
1958–61; geol in res proj Calif res corp La Habra
Calif 1961–62; teacher Bankhead acad Aber 1963–64:
geol in explor and prod. Chevron standard Calgary
1964–69, dist geol 1969–75, geophys 1975–76, staff
geophys 1976–78

RITCHIE or Kinnear, Irene Lang   MA 1950
resid Lower Fargo, Fife

RITCHIE Isabella   MA 1945
teacher: Strichen j s s 1958–67, Lossiemouth h s
1967–68, Fraserburgh N s 1968–76, New Pitsligo
1977–78

RITCHIE James   MA 1911
d Kirriemuir 26.5.74 A UR XLVI 107

RITCHIE James   MA 1926
head: W Kirkton p s Dun 1949–51, Wallacetown
p s 1951–62, Liff Road p s 1962–64, Fintry p s
1964–67; retd
m Dun 6.8.32 Elsie J. Gorrie

RITCHIE James Cunningham   *BSc 1951 DSc 1962
Canada: assoc prof Manit 1960–65, prof biol Trent
univ 1965–68, Dalhousie univ 1968–70, prof/chmn life
sc Scarborough coll Tor from 1970

RITCHIE James Hunter   BSc(for) 1932

RITCHIE James MacPherson   *MA 1951
sen lect/assoc prof N'cle univ NSW Aust 1961–65;
sen lect/warden of Grant Hall Hull univ 1965–69;
prof/head dept Germanic stud. Sheff from 1969; pro
vice chancellor
m Glasg 8.9.58 Sheena M. C. Watson MA(Glas) univ
lib/teacher d of William W. BSc(Glas), Strathaven
Lanarksh

RITCHIE James Simpson   MB ChB 1945
OBE 1968 surg capt 1967 FCM 1973
sen ENT spec RN hosp Chatham 1958–61; joint
services staff coll, Latimer Bucks 1961; sen m o HMS
Blake Medit/WI 1961–63; sen ENT spec/sen m o
(surg) RN hosp Plymouth 1963–72; sen m o HMS
Bulwark UK/Far East 1966–67; m o i/c RN hosp
Gibraltar 1972–77; retd from RN; m o DHSS
Gosforth N'cle-u-Tyne from 1977

RITCHIE Jeanie Helen   MB ChB 1923
resid Aberdeensh

RITCHIE or Coull, Jessie   MA 1929
resid Aber

RITCHIE Jessie Ann   MA 1931

RITCHIE John   MB ChB 1910 MD DPH 1913
d Aber 10.9.66 A UR XLI 337

RITCHIE John Edwin   *MA 1913 *BSc 1914
retd; resid Aber

RITCHIE John Hall   MA 1912 BSc(agr) 1913
d 1976

RITCHIE John Miller   MB ChB 1930
retd g p 1966; member/chmn m o p & i i boards Middlesbrough 1948–73

RITCHIE John Milne   MB ChB 1925
no longer on GC reg

RITCHIE John Murdoch   *MA 1925
d 3.8.70

RITCHIE Joseph   BSc 1933
chief chem Carnegie Chemicals 1947–58; res chem Riker 3M 1958–73; retd; resid Rosehearty

RITCHIE Joseph Murdoch   BSc 1944
DSc(Lond) 1960 MA(Yale) 1968 FRS 1976
USA: prof pharm Albert Einstein coll of med NY 1963–68; Eugene Higgins prof pharm Yale univ Conn from 1968

RITCHIE Lewis William   MB ChB 1940
d 22.11.70 *AUR* XLIV 215

RITCHIE Macdonald Frey   MA 1893 BL 1896
no longer on GC reg

RITCHIE or Waters, Margaret Buchan   BSc 1941

RITCHIE Margaret Doreen   MA 1933
teacher Engl subj Cullen/Portknockie 1969–71; retd; resid Buckie

RITCHIE or Annand, Margaret Duncan   MA 1936
resid Aber
husb *d* 24.6.71

RITCHIE Mary Jane   MA 1939
retd 1979; resid Rosehearty

RITCHIE May   MA 1914
d Lonmay 4.6.67 *AUR* XLII 184

RITCHIE Michael Balfour Hutchison   MB ChB 1904
d 11.2.69

RITCHIE Robert Stephen   MB ChB 1948

RITCHIE or Konstam, Sheila Thompson
**   MB ChB 1943**
sessions in clin path. Orkney hosps from 1963

RITCHIE or Johnston, Stella Bremner   MA 1945
teacher maths Our Lady's Convent Abingdon 1964–70, head of maths dept from 1970, first sen mistress from 1976

RITCHIE Thora Garden   MA 1937

RITCHIE William   MB ChB 1945
d 1.12.69

RITCHIE William Duncan   MB ChB 1899
d Bovey Tracy 19.1.61

RITCHIE William Forbes   *MA 1930
prin teacher classics Arbroath h s from 1950 and dep rector 1959–74; retd; memb Scottish Classics Group

RITCHIE William Geddes   MA 1938
FRMetS 1968

RITCHIE William Miller   MB ChB 1924
no longer on GC reg

RITCHIE William Murray   MB ChB 1937

RITSON Joyce Manson   MA 1944

RITSON Roy Barker   MA 1949
MIPM 1962
asst head indust relations Texas Oil Co Bogota, Columbia 1959–60; pers off. Imp. Smelting Co Brist 1960–63; pers/trg off. Bookers (Zambia) Ndola Zambia 1963–69, group pers off. from 1969

RIXON David Dobson   *MA 1951
pers off./staff pers man. Thames Board Mills Purfleet Essex from 1961

RIXON Peter Ernest   MB ChB 1949
MRCPsych 1971
consult. psychiat: St George's hosp Morpeth 1960–63, St Audrys hosp Melton Woodbridge from 1963
m(2) Woodbridge 16.8.79 Dawn M. Tredre med soc worker d of Jack Norman Newmarket

ROBB Alexander Lawrence   MB ChB 1913
d Aboyne 12.5.64 *AUR* XL 398

ROBB or Mair, Catherine   MA 1946
teacher: Monquhitter s 1960–62, West Barns s E Lothian 1963–64, Damacre s Brechin 1964–66, Cults acad 1967–73; asst head Cults p s 1973–77, head Crombie p s Westhill Aber from 1977

ROBB David Bannerman   MB ChB 1929
retd 1971; part time m o Dept of Health E Midlands div from 1971; resid Leicester

ROBB Douglas Alexander   BCom 1927
Scott Peden & Co CA Edin from 1960, ptnr 1969–72; retd

ROBB Douglas George   MA 1905
d Southsea 1.1.68

ROBB Edwin Douglas   MB ChB 1932
Nott: sen m o DHSS 1963–73 retd; part time med referee DHSS from 1973

ROBB Elizabeth Agnes   *MA 1918
no longer on GC reg

ROBB George Cameron   *MA 1953 MEd 1957

ROBB George Mitchell McLeod   MB ChB 1953
FRCS(Can) 1965 Cert Spec Gen Surg RCP&S(Can)
temp lect biol chem Aberd 1960–62; resid surg
Canada: resid surg Vancouver/gen surg Royal
Columbian hosp/St Mary's hosp New Westminster
Surrey mem hosp, Burnaby gen hosp BC from 1965

ROBB Harold Phillips   MB ChB 1951

ROBB or Peers, Helen Margaret Taylor   MA 1926
no longer on GC reg

ROBB or McCulloch, Isabella Esslemont   MA 1920
resid Aber
husb *d* 28.8.62
d Banchory 9.9.78

ROBB James BSc(agr) 1920
no longer on GC reg

ROBB James Christie   *BSc 1945 PhD 1948
prof phys chem Birm from 1957

ROBB James Philip   BSc 1927 *1928 MA 1927
retd 1968; resid Aber

ROBB Jane Winifred   MA 1904
retd; resid Banchory

ROBB or Elliot, Jean Anne   MA 1941
Renfrewsh: teacher maths Giffnock j s s 1957–62,
woman advis Woodfarm h s 1962–69, asst head from
1969

ROBB Jean Campbell   MA 1925
d Banchory 27.1.70 *AUR* XLIII 445

ROBB John Walker   *MA 1951

ROBB or Laidlaw, Mary Brebner   MB ChB 1942

ROBB Nora   MA 1946
teacher Turriff acad from 1953

ROBB Peter Yeats   BSc(eng) 1949

ROBB Sheila McDonald   BSc 1947 *1948
lect biol sciences Exe from 1968

ROBB William Brebner   BSc 1952

ROBBIE Douglas Stewart   ᶜMB ChB 1954
DA(Lond) 1958 FFARCS 1960
Lond: s r Westminster hosp group/Brompton hosp
1958–63, consult. anaest and i/c pain clin Royal
Marsden hosp from 1963, consult. anaest (pain) St
Christopher's hospice 1968–77

ROBBIE James Andrew   *BSc 1933
d Edin 19.5.77 *AUR* XLVII 213

ROBBIE or Thomson, Lizzie Helen   MA 1931
teacher Gartly 1932–39; head Cushnie p s 1939–42,
Oldhamstocks p s 1959–65; teacher Earlston 1965–68,
Kinnesswood 1968–72; retd; resid Kirkcaldy

husb *d* Alyth –.10.75
now Mrs. Weir

ROBBIE Thomas Alexander   BSc(for) 1935
retd 1973; resid Glasg

ROBERTS Alexander   MA 1931

ROBERTS or Lanning, Helen Elizabeth   MA 1948

ROBERTSON Adrian Alfred Gibb   *MA 1942
head mod lang Wyke manor s Bradford 1962–65;
head lower s Maltby g s nr Rotherham Yorks 1966–
72; sen master Maltby comp s from 1973; member
council Cyrenians from 1971

ROBERTSON Alan Ogilvie   MA 1949 BD 1952
JP Aber 1968
Aberd: warden Crombie Hall 1964–66, warden
Crombie/Johnston Halls 1966–68, sen warden and
warden Hillhead Halls from 1968

ROBERTSON Albert John   *MA 1951

ROBERTSON Alexander   MB ChB 1908
no longer on GC reg

ROBERTSON Alexander   MA 1919 LLD 1958
d Grantham 9.2.70 *AUR* XLIII 444

ROBERTSON Alexander   MA 1929 BSc 1930 LLD 1971
CBE 1963 Kt 1970 FRSE 1945 FRIC 1946
FRSH 1950 FRCVS 1970 DVSc(Melb) 1973
Edin: prof anim health 1964–70, dean fac vet med
1964–70, prof tropical anim health/dir centre tropical
vet med 1970–78

ROBERTSON Alexander Duffus   *MA 1912
retd 1954; resid Carluke
d Carluke 27.5.79

ROBERTSON Alexander Findlay   *MA 1936

ROBERTSON Alexander John   MA 1925
retd 1968; resid Montrose

ROBERTSON Alexander Kay   *MA 1947 Dip Ed 1953
FO, CO and dept tech co-operation 1953–64, Min
of overseas dev Lond from 1964
m Kirkliston W. Lothian 2.4.65 Pamela Miller civ
serv d of George S. M. Kirkliston

ROBERTSON Alexander McQueen   MB ChB 1947
DTM & H(Edin) 1956 DPH(Lond) 1960
DIH(Lond) 1965
m o Sudan 1952–56; prin health off. N. Nigeria
1956–65; sen lect Liv s of tropical med 1966–71; sen
m o Esso Libya 1971–73; m o NCB N'cle 1974–77;
dir occup health serv Grampian health board Aber
from 1978

ROBERTSON Alexander Rollo   MA 1935 LLB 1937
d Sheffield 2.11.79

ROBERTSON Alfred Malcolm   ***BSc 1953**

ROBERTSON Andrew Forbes   ***MA 1932**
head Newmachar p s 1962–70; retd; resid Alyth

ROBERTSON Andrew Slora   ***MA 1950 *MEd 1956**
Aber: teacher p s 1956–59, asst mod lang AGS
1959–62, RGC from 1962, careers master from 1967,
prin guid from 1972

ROBERTSON Angus Graham   ***BSc 1947**

ROBERTSON or Russell, Anna   **MA 1932**
resid Insch

ROBERTSON or Finlayson, Anna Isabella
                              MB ChB 1955 DPH 1972
sen m o commun med Grampian health board
resid Cults, Aber

ROBERTSON or McDonald, Annie   **MA 1921**
d 23.1.66

ROBERTSON Arthur Kay   **MA 1951**
teacher Anderson h s Lerwick from 1957, asst head
from 1974
m Lerwick 27.3.64 Catherine D. Kerr nurs sister d of
Duncan K. Kingennie by Dun

ROBERTSON or Troup, Bessie   **MA 1930**
d nr Greenloaning 19.4.68 A UR XLII 370

ROBERTSON Bruce   **BD 1951**
resid Dunbar

ROBERTSON Castella Margaret   **MA 1928**
retd 1968; resid Kintore

ROBERTSON Charles   **BCom 1928**
no longer on GC reg

ROBERTSON Charles William   **MB ChB 1930**
resid Lee Green Lond

ROBERTSON Charles Wilson   **MA 1934**
teacher sc: Eastriggs, Eaglesfield, Ecclefechan 1937–
39, Annan acad 1939–40, 1946–47; head: Dalton s
Lockerbie 1947–54, Balmedie s 1954–76; retd
wife d 1964

ROBERTSON Christina Speed   **BSc 1925**
no longer on GC reg

ROBERTSON David
                  BSc(agr) 1924 PhD 1927 DSc 1937
retd 1968; resid Bieldside Aber
d Bieldside 10.12.80 A UR XLIX 137

ROBERTSON David   **BSc(for) 1945**
Dip. Man. Stud.(Edin coll of comm) 1971
man. Alex Cowan & Sons papermakers Penicuik
1961–68; lect man. Edin coll of comm 1968–72; lect
man. stud. Queen Margaret coll Edin 1972–73, sen
lect from 1973

ROBERTSON David John Clark
                  *BSc(mech eng) 1932 (elect. eng) 1933
CEng FIMechE MIEE
admin staff Birm poly 1971–76; retd

ROBERTSON Dawson Cameron   **MB ChB 1909**
d Burgess Hill 14.1.63 A UR XL 199

ROBERTSON Donald Angus   **BL 1929**
d 17.1.64 A UR XL 400

ROBERTSON or Fraser, Doreen Grant   **MA 1953**
teacher: Hinton, Alberta 1969–70

ROBERTSON or Simpson, Dorothy Mary   **MA 1934**
retd 1973; resid Peterhead

ROBERTSON Duncan Carmichael   **BSc(eng) 1944**

ROBERTSON Edward Macallan   **MA 1949**

ROBERTSON Elbert Louis Stevenson   **MB ChB 1944**

ROBERTSON Elizabeth   ***MA 1948**
asst rector: Banff acad 1972–73, Kirkwall g s from
1973

ROBERTSON or Michie, Elizabeth Woodrow
                                      MB ChB 1955
resid Cottingham

ROBERTSON Ella Bruce   **MA 1928**
retd 1969
d Aber 17.5.75 A UR XLVI 323

ROBERTSON or Smith, Ellen Dorothy   **MA 1942**
resid Farnham

ROBERTSON or Farquharson, Elma Jessie
                                      *MA 1950
resid Blairgowrie

ROBERTSON Elsie   **MA 1930**
m Craig

ROBERTSON Eric Desmond
                          BSc(for) 1934 BSc 1936
OBE 1964
BBC Lond: asst controller/controller overseas serv
1964–73, controller Engl serv/dep man. dir external
broadcasting from 1973

ROBERTSON Ethel Elizabeth   **MA 1932**
FRCPsych 1971
retd 1971; resid Edin

ROBERTSON Forbes William   ***BSc 1941**
FIBiol 1969 FRSE 1972
sen prin scient off. ARC unit of anim genetics Edin
univ 1968–70, prof genetics Aberd from 1970
m Edin 5.6.48 Katherine L. H. Brown MA(Edin)
WRNS/secy d of Henry H. B. MB ChB(Edin) Edin

ROBERTSON Frederick   ***MA 1949**
visiting prof Penn state univ USA 1968–69; sen lect

classics R'dg from 1969 and warden Windsor Hall R'dg from 1974, head classics dept R'dg from 1975

ROBERTSON Frederick Albert   BSc 1944
Marconi, Chelmsford: man. tech lab 1966–70, joint progr man. Marconi radar syst 1970–72, comp quality man. from 1972

ROBERTSON Frederick John   BSc(agr) 1954
Dip Agr(Cantab) 1956 DTA(Trinidad, Cornell USA) DVMS and MRCVS(Edin) 1965
agr. off. Transvaal S. Af 1957–60; g p vet med Falmouth Cornwall 1965–67; vet investigation off. Aber from 1967
m Elgin 4.10.69 Valerie A. W. Alexander MA(Edin) res physiol d of Thomas G. A. Fochabers

ROBERTSON George Booth
                            MA 1951 BD 1954 PhD 1971

ROBERTSON George Taylor   MB ChB 1938
g p Alness from 1947
d Alness 29.8.78 *A UR* XLVIII 106

ROBERTSON George Webster   BSc(eng) 1949

ROBERTSON or Killah, Georgina Mary   MA 1948
JP 1968
Cairney s: teacher 1961–67, head from 1967

ROBERTSON or Downie, Gertrude Isabel Buchan
                                        MA 1915

ROBERTSON Gilbert William   BSc 1944
prin teacher phys Forfar acad from 1967

ROBERTSON Grace   MA 1946
teacher: Engl/Lat Hopeman s s 1961–64, Elgin acad 1964–68, Engl Buckie h s 1968–70, Engl/Lat Keith g s 1970–73, prin classics Buckie h s from 1973

ROBERTSON Grigor Charles Allan
                            BSc(agr) 1913 MA 1914
d 27.6.70

ROBERTSON Hamish   *MA 1952
MBE 1966
HM overseas civ serv Nyasaland/Malawi 1955–67; UK civ serv (Scot. off.) from 1967

ROBERTSON Harry   BSc 1928 MA 1929
retd 1966; resid Aber

ROBERTSON or Walker, Henrietta Lord   MA 1941
resid Nelson NZ

ROBERTSON Henry Downie   *MA 1952

ROBERTSON or Conn, Hilda Helen   MA 1934
resid Huntly
d Huntly 14.3.78

ROBERTSON Hugh   *MA 1950
Forres: prin teacher hist 1960–70, asst rector 1971–77, dep rector from 1977

ROBERTSON Hugh Sinclair   *MA 1906 BSc 1908
no longer on GC reg

ROBERTSON Ian Alexander Donald   *BSc 1952

ROBERTSON Ian (John) Barr   MA 1939 LLB 1949
ptnr Cunningham & Robertson solic Stonehaven from 1949, later prin; town clerk Stonehaven 1964–75; reg councillor Stonehaven/Kinneff from 1974

ROBERTSON Ian Graeme   BSc(eng) 1954

ROBERTSON Ian Stewart   *BSc 1955 PhD 1959
lect nat phil Aberd from 1969
wife d 6.1.78

ROBERTSON Ida   MA 1920
d Banchory 22.7.68 *A UR* XLIII 80

ROBERTSON Irene Eliza   MA 1949

ROBERTSON or Waite, Isabella   MA 1906
d Gartly 4.5.78

ROBERTSON Isabella Ledingham   *MA 1929
teacher Broughton s s Edin 1944–68; retd; Cavaliere dell' Ordine al Merito della Repubblica Italiana 1976

ROBERTSON Isabella Leslie   *MA 1918
no longer on GC reg

ROBERTSON or Gray, Isobel Agnes   MA 1941
teacher hist Shotton Hall s s Peterlee Co Durh from 1963

ROBERTSON James   MA 1903 MB ChB 1907
d 28.9.65

ROBERTSON James   MB ChB 1925

ROBERTSON James   *MA 1954 Dip Ed 1958

ROBERTSON James Dewar   MB ChB 1910
d Swansea 29.12.60 *A UR* XXXIX 102 & 201

ROBERTSON James Kennedy   *MA 1923
d Elgin 22.2.73 *A UR* XLV 225

ROBERTSON James Kinnaird   BSc(agr) 1927
asst insp DAFS from 1957

ROBERTSON James Matheson   BL 1952
law app/solic/advoc in Aber Burnett & Reid advoc Aber 1958–61; leg. asst Stronachs advoc Aber 1962–63, ptnr from 1963

ROBERTSON James Stuart
                MB ChB 1928 DPH 1931 ᶜMD 1935
retd 1968; resid Bournemouth

ROBERTSON or Pickford, Janet Mary (Sheena)
                                        MA 1945

ROBERTSON or Anderson, Janet Watson *MA 1910
resid Aber
husb *d* 1953

ROBERTSON or Bremner, Jean Hosie MA 1930
teacher Portsoy 1958–71; retd
d 25.9.81

ROBERTSON or Gibb, Jeanie MA 1901
d Salford 23.12.61 *AUR* xxxix 270

ROBERTSON John BSc(agr) 1936
teacher agr Elmwood coll Cupar 1958–75; retd;
resid St Andrews

ROBERTSON John Archibald MA 1949 BD 1952
C of S min: John Knox ch Mounthooly Aber
1962–67, Parkdale presb ch Toronto 1967–77, par of
Strath Is of Skye from 1977

ROBERTSON Lawrence Don MB ChB 1923
d 24.1.73 *AUR* xlv 225

ROBERTSON Lewis Stevens MB ChB 1919
m o S Af chamber of mines Johannesburg 1936–70;
pres: S Af Red Cross soc 1950–51, med assoc of S Af
1963–64 (gold medal), nat cancer assoc of S Af
1952–75 (Oettle gold medal); retd; resid Johannesburg

ROBERTSON or Willans, Lillie Don MA 1924
d 8.8.76

ROBERTSON or Smart, Margaret Alexandrina
MA 1908
d 31.3.72

ROBERTSON or Perry, Margaret Alice *MA 1943
resid Perth

ROBERTSON Margaret Helen MA 1912
no longer on GC reg

ROBERTSON or McDonald, Margaret Jessie
*BSc 1949
teacher maths Bankhead acad from 1976

ROBERTSON or Melvin, Margaret Leslie
*MA 1947
resid Aber

ROBERTSON or Horne, Margaret Marian
MB ChB 1937
resid Tain

ROBERTSON Margaret Mitchell *MA 1910
resid Banff

ROBERTSON Marian Downie MA 1926
teacher Westhill Aber 1962–64; retd; resid Clinterty

ROBERTSON Mark Macdonald
MA 1953 PhD 1959

ROBERTSON Martha Ethelwyn Young MA 1909
d Edin 9.2.67 *AUR* xlii 179

ROBERTSON Mary Constance MA 1932
med secy Aber gen hosps 1955–66; retd

ROBERTSON Mary Isabella MA 1944
teacher Cummings Park p s Aber from 1973

ROBERTSON or Simpson, Mary Williamina Urquhart
*MA 1911
d 29.5.70 *AUR* xliv 107

ROBERTSON Maurice Charles Gordon
MB ChB 1925
g p Leeds

ROBERTSON Nellie Ann MA 1925
teacher maths/geog Kintore j s s 1962–65; retd

ROBERTSON Norman BSc 1944 *MA 1950
sen tut. fac of urban and reg stud. univ R'dg from
1974

ROBERTSON Norman Dale BSc 1946 *MA 1952

ROBERTSON or Fyfe, Patricia Stewart MA 1951
teacher inf Calder St s s Glasg 1961–63, supply
Gilburn p s Dun 1964–66, home-teaching/part time
work/St Nicholas C of E p s Newbury from 1966
marr diss 1975

ROBERTSON Patrick Dugan MB ChB 1954

ROBERTSON or Reay, Rhoda Donald
BSc 1953 *1954
resid Welwyn

ROBERTSON Richard Ross MA 1922 BD 1925
d Aber 11.12.69 *AUR* xliii 445

ROBERTSON Robert *MA 1927
retd 1964; resid Bellshill

ROBERTSON Roderick George MA 1934
head: Tullos p s Aber 1959–66, Hazlehead p s Aber
from 1966; retd
m Aber 12.8.58 Alice Douglas d of John D. Aber

ROBERTSON or Brown, Roma Learmonth
MA 1946

ROBERTSON Ronald MA 1935 BD 1938
C of S min Old Parish ch Scone from 1949
chap. to Lord High Commissioner Lord Mansfield
1961, 1962

ROBERTSON Ronald Graham BSc(for) 1954
retd Ghana for. dept 1961; asst conserv for. N
Nigeria for. dept 1962–65; dept lands and for. Truro
Nova Scotia: for. 1966–69, man. silviculture dept
from 1969
m Keith 30.6.62 Isobel J. Riddoch

ROBERTSON or Thomson, Sheila Mairi Jean
MB ChB 1946
s m o Aber from 1966

ROBERTSON Sibylla Georgia MA 1955

ROBERTSON Stephen Andrew Cormack
                          MA 1954 LLB 1957
1960 various posts Lond; leg. asst Aber c c 1961–62;
admin asst NE reg hosp board 1962–63; solic: Burnett
& Reid advoc Aber 1963–64, Allan Buckley Allan &
Co advoc Aber 1964–66, ptnr 1966–73; amalgamated
with and ptnr of Wilsone & Duffus advoc Aber from
1974

ROBERTSON Thomas   *MA 1897
d Aber 3.3.63 *AUR* XL 197

ROBERTSON Thomas George   MA 1926
retd head St Margaret's s Aberlour 1967; resid
Tower Villa Aberlour Farms Bruntlands etc Knockando from 1967

ROBERTSON Walter   BSc 1931
teacher Forfar 1933–38, head Logie Pert s Angus
1938–47; war serv R Sigs 1941–46; head: Tannadice
1947–66, Newtyle 1966–72; retd; resid Whitehills
Forfar
m Tannadice 28.2.38 Constance B. Reid d of Alexander
R. Tannadice

ROBERTSON William   *MA 1941
prin teacher classics Portobello s s from 1961

ROBERTSON William Allan   *MA 1902
d 25.5.62 *AUR* XXXIX 373

ROBERTSON William George   *MA 1951
teacher Engl Aber acad/Hazlehead acad from 1960

ROBERTSON William Leslie   MA 1934
H.M. civ serv customs and excise dept from 1934;
retd; resid Montrose

ROBERTSON William Rae
                          BSc(agr) 1951 MSc 1969
Dip App Econ(univ coll of Rhodesia and Nyasaland)
1966 PhD(Lond) 1974 ARICS 1976
Salisbury Rhodesia: sen agronomist 1967–69, sen
farm man. spec dept of conserv and extension 1969–74,
chief of crop prod. dept conserv and extension 1974–
75; world bank secondment staff serving as head of
agr proj evaluation and plan. unit fed govt Nigeria
from 1975

ROBERTSON William Stuart Justice
                          BSc(eng) 1953
MEd(R'dg) 1972
lect f e eng subjs/maths/phys The College Swindon
from 1960

ROBERTSON Williamina Charlotte   MA 1910
d Inverurie 9.11.75

ROBINS Alfred Brian   PhD 1952

ROBINSON or Maxwell, Grace Margaret
                          MB ChB 1925 DPH 1927
resid Edin

ROBINSON Margaret Alice Jocelyn   *MA 1953

ROBISON Walter   *MA 1931
prin maths Turriff acad from 1947, dep rector from
1970

ROBLEY John Alfred Watson   BSc(for) 1954
asst conserv for. Bamenda, S Cameroons 1960–61;
for. util off. Blantyre, Nyasaland 1961–64; W Aust:
div for. off. 1964–70, insp for. Harvey 1970–72, state
bush fire control off. Perth from 1972
m Inv 27.5.58 Sheila M. Sweeney BSc 1954 *qv*

ROBSON Alexander   BSc(eng) 1938

ROBSON Arthur   MA 1927
retd from Windsor Place ch Portobello 1971
d 29.11.74

ROBSON or Laing, Evelyn Margaret   MA 1954
LTCL (teacher's dip in Engl as second lang) 1971

ROBSON James   MA 1946
C of S min St John's ch Camelon Falkirk from 1957

ROBSON John Douglas   MB ChB 1953
g p Potton from 1956
d 4.4.81 *AUR* XLIX 139

ROBSON or Robertson, Margaret   MB ChB 1950
part-time publ health and g p Perth Aust from 1971

ROBSON Mary Hastings Edwards   MA 1951
m Crawford

ROBSON Norman Keith   BSc(agr) 1922
d Aber 10.2.63 *AUR* XL 204

ROBSON Norman Keith Bonner   *BSc 1951
FLS 1958
Lond: sen scient off. extra-Europ flowering plants
dept of bot Brit Museum (nat hist) 1962–67, prin
scient off. from 1967
m Folkestone Kent 3.9.60 Eve B. Reynolds d of
Donald H. B. R. MA(Cantab) Folkestone

ROBSON Thomas Falconer   MA 1934
ptnr Williamson & Dunn CA Aber from 1946

ROCHE Susan Mary Blair (Sr Véronique)   MA 1949
France: religious work in serv of old ladies of every
station and creed, mostly of peasant origin Sens
Yonne 1951–59, Cahors Lot 1959–68, Vence Alpes
Maritimes 1968–70, Rodez Aveyron from 1970

RODE or Castledine, Margaret Joyce   *MA 1942
d Nott 30.11.67 *AUR* XLII 373

RODE Robert Moir   *MA 1945
d –.11.63

RODEN Keith Serjeant   MB ChB 1919
d 1972

RODGER Jessie Roy   MA 1935

RODGERS Albert Nathaniel Ewing   MB ChB 1906
no longer on GC reg

ROE Charles Francis   MB ChB 1955
MD(NY) 1964 FACS 1969
USA: res fell. surg Harvard univ Boston 1961–
63 (Harvey Cushing award 1963–69); instr surg
Columbia univ NY city (member NY acad of sc); asst
prof surg Yale univ/consult. veterans admin hosps
New Haven Conn 1969–73; chief surg Lawrence mem
hosp New Lond Conn from 1973 (member internat
soc surg)
m NY city 31.7.69 Anita M. Bruckner MA(Corn) d of
Paul B. PhD(Prague) Vienna

ROE Maurice Robert André   *MA 1949
PMD(Harvard bus. s Cambridge Mass USA) 1962
man. consult. GB and France, pres Integrated Business
Systems Issy-les-Moulineaux
m Neuilly-sur-Seine France 30.12.71 Monique A. M.
Roca d of Santiago R. Barcelona Spain

ROGER Barbara   MA 1905
d Peterhead 30.7.72 *A UR* xlv 123

ROGER Henry   MA 1913 MB ChB 1917
retd; resid Banff
d Memsie 24.9.76 *A UR* xlvii 102

ROGER John Grant   *BSc 1937

ROGERS or Stanislas, Adeline Mary Kate   MA 1910

ROGERS Eric   BSc(eng) 1950
sen eng/ag Brit contr 1958–62; dep chief resid eng
Binnie & Ptnrs Mangla dam proj W Pakistan 1962–
69; repres World Bank Boké proj Guinea W Af
1969–72; contr man. dir William Tawse Aber from
1973

ROGERS James William   BSc(eng) 1950
CEng MICE 1959
gen man. Sierra Leone dev co 1967–70; asst man. dir
Williams Mills Staffs 1970–73, man. dir from 1973

ROGERS Thomas   *BSc 1951
eng Barr & Stroud Glasg from 1956

ROGIE or Crawford, Mary   MA 1920
d Alford 6.2.71 *A UR* xliv 210

ROLL Richard Clipperton   MB ChB 1951
MRCGP 1962
g p Nelson Lancs from 1954

ROLLO Ian McIntosh   BSc 1945
PhD(Manit) 1968
Canada: prof dept pharm and therap fac of med univ
Manit, Winnipeg from 1961

ROLLO James Cowie   MA 1953
teacher: Engl/hist/geog Old Deer j s s 1955–61,
Mintlaw s 1961–65; head Fetterangus p s 1965–69,
New Machar p s from 1970

RONALD or Gray, Winifred Jean   *MA 1931
resid Victoria BC Canada

ROSE Alexander Macgregor
                              MB ChB 1899 DPH 1901
d Cults 2.12.62 *A UR* xl 74

ROSE Beatrice Mary   *MA 1912 LLD 1953
retd; resid Guildford

ROSE Harry Baxter   BL 1954
teacher Powis s s Aber 1956–60; lect Aber coll of
comm from 1960

ROSE James   MB ChB 1949
MRCGP 1971 FRCGP 1977
g p Dun from 1956

ROSE Jessie Ann   MA 1915
d 30.9.67

ROSE or Marshall, Jessie Fraser   MA 1919
resid Kilsyth

ROSE John   BSc(agr) 1911
d 4.7.71

ROSE John Alexander Gilbert Fiddes   MB ChB 1927
consult. radiol AEA Winforth Dorset from 1960;
retd consult. radiol W Dorset hosp group 1971, elected
hon consult.; resid Dorchester

ROSE John Ingram
                ***MA 1952 Dip Ed 1953 MEd 1966**
lect educ psych Aber coll of educ 1966–74, lect
remed and spec educ Aber coll of educ 1974–76, sen
lect from 1976
wife d 3.4.63
m(2) Aber 12.8.65 Marjory E. H. Esslemont MA 1959 *qv*

ROSE or Hunter, Lydia Jane   MB ChB 1953

ROSE Margaret Elizabeth   MA 1950

ROSE Nancy Masson   MA BSc 1921
retd 1964; resid Aber
d Banchory 28.10.79

ROSEDALE John Lewis   DSc 1923
d 12.11.68

ROSS or Willox, Adeline Elsie Philip   MA 1927
war serv C of S ladywarden: Sullom Voe Shetland
1943; hostel Tel Aviv Israel 1945–46; teacher: Lanark
c c 1947–54, Carstairs s 1954–66; part time tut. hosp
Carstairs 1966–71; retd; resid Helensburgh

ROSS Alexander   MA 1909 BD 1913
d 26.5.65

ROSS Alexander Brown   MA 1905
no longer on GC reg

ROSS Alexander Fraser
                        BSc(for) 1930 MB ChB 1942
retd 1970; resid Fairlie Ayrsh

ROSS Alexander James BSc 1949 *1950
Bahrain: group head-prod. quality investigations 1966–80; chief chem from 1980

ROSS Alexander Wilson MA 1910
d 25.9.65 *AUR* XLII 83

ROSS or Mazur, Anabella Mackenzie *MA 1942

ROSS Andrew Cormack MB ChB 1944 DPH 1949
m o h Blaby/Lutterworth and asst m o h Leic from 1955

ROSS or Main, Anna Leila MA 1953
resid Barnhill Dun

ROSS Angus Alexander MA 1912
no longer on GC reg

ROSS Anne MA 1955
teacher Fr Alexandra s Singapore 1961–62; hosp teacher Berlin 1975–76
m Aber 25.7.60 William G. Johnston MB ChB 1958 *qv*

ROSS Anne Christina MA 1928
retd 1970; resid Stornoway

ROSS Annie Cameron MA 1911
no longer on GC reg

ROSS or Hindle, Caroline Frances MA 1925
no longer on GC reg

ROSS Carson Abbot Ainscough MA 1921 BSc 1923
d 1963

ROSS or Griffiths, Catherine Eliza *MA 1952
teacher: ESN Red Lodge Southampton 1971–72, remed Danemark s Winchester 1973–74, mus at Glen Eyre s S'ton from 1975

ROSS Catherine Ishbel MacKenzie MB ChB 1949
m Lee

ROSS or Rzechorzek, Catherine Jane Helen Smith Wallace MA 1945
Mackie acad Stonehaven: teacher mod lang/Engl 1962–68, woman advis 1968–72, asst rector from 1972

ROSS or Davie, Cecilia Durward *MA 1934
secy prisoners of war assoc Aber 1942–45; resid Glassel

ROSS or Burnett, Charlotte Bell MA 1930
resid Elgin

ROSS Christina Shearer MA 1923

ROSS Cormac Craig MB ChB 1927
no longer on GC reg

ROSS David Forbes MB ChB 1940

ROSS David George MA 1908
d Dumfries 1.11.62 *AUR* XL 78

ROSS David Warnock *MA 1953

ROSS David William MA 1935 BD 1938
d Dun 24.12.74 *AUR* XLVI 239

ROSS or Kerr, Davina MA 1924
resid Haddington
husb *d* 25.1.72
d 6.7.79

ROSS Donald MB ChB 1950
DPM 1965 MRCPsych 1971
h o psychiat Inv 1957–64; Greenock: regist psychiat 1964–65, med asst psychiat 1965–68; sen regist ch psychiat Dumfries/Glasgow 1968–71; consult. ch psychiat Lancaster from 1971
m Prestwick 8.7.65 Esther S. Paton MB ChB(Glas) med pract d of James D. P. Prestwick

ROSS Donald Ian MB ChB 1955
sen h o anaest Glasg WI 1960–62; RAMC from 1962
m Edin 8.10.60 Jean C. McCulloch nurse/midwife d of Robert McC. Northolt

ROSS or Grant, Edith Mary MA 1925

ROSS Edward Sim MA 1923
d Aber 15.11.64 *AUR* XLI 58

ROSS or McNaughton, Elizabeth MA 1913

ROSS or Davis, Elizabeth Irene Murray MA 1947 Dip Ed 1952
no longer on GC reg

ROSS or Glennie, Elizabeth Mary Aird MB ChB 1942
s m o dept health NZ from 1954; resid Christchurch NZ

ROSS George BSc(agr) 1922
FEIS 1960 JP 1935–70
retd 1962; resid Aber

ROSS George MB ChB 1947
g p Ilkeston from 1951/anaest Ilkeston gen hosp

ROSS George Alexander MB ChB 1926
retd; resid Bridport

ROSS George Cruickshank BSc(eng) 1953

ROSS George Innes Macdonald MB ChB 1942
FRCPath 1966
consult. path. Ashford hosp Middx from 1957; resid Weybridge

ROSS George Wesley MA 1928
retd 1973; resid Aber

ROSS George William *BSc 1946 PhD 1950
ICI plastics div from 1956; resid Welwyn Garden City

ROSS Gray Ernest Donald BSc(eng) 1952

ROSS Gregor Mackay   MA 1935
retd 1973; resid Fearn

ROSS Harold James   MB ChB 1932

ROSS or Davies, Helen Mary   MA 1930

ROSS Henrietta Mary Isabella   MA 1925
retd Kaimhill s s Aber 1970; teacher Fr Northfield
acad 1971–72; divinity stud. Aberd from 1973

ROSS Ian   BSc(agr) 1951
teacher agr: Bell Baxter h s Cupar Fife 1957–62;
Barony farm s Dumfries 1962–65, prin Balmacara
farm s Kyle 1965–73; teacher biol Invergordon acad
from 1973

ROSS Ian   MB ChB 1955
sen h o orthop ARI 1960–61; g p Aber from 1961

ROSS or Reid, Irene Philip   *MA 1948
teacher maths Queen Anne's s Caversham from
1965

ROSS Isabel Georgina Temple   *MA 1931
retd 1969; resid Aber

ROSS or McPherson, Isabel Mhairi   MA 1937
resid Aber

ROSS or MacLean, Isabella   MA 1923
d Kiltarlity 24.2.72

ROSS or Garner, Isabella   *MA 1927
teacher Kent 1928–48; resid Folkestone

ROSS or MacRitchie, Isobel Margaret   MA 1928
resid Aber

ROSS James   BCom 1923
d 6.10.58

ROSS James   BSc(for) 1936

ROSS James Alexander   *MA 1907
no longer on GC reg

ROSS James Alexander   *BSc 1948
staff off. M o D 1961–63; lt-col head of s branch inst
of army educ 1963–66; retd army 1967; bldg/civ eng
group Edin: educ and trg off. 1967–69, group pers
man. from 1969

ROSS James Cameron   MA 1908
no longer on GC reg

ROSS James Harper   BSc 1928
d Inv 13.8.62 *AUR* XL 93

ROSS James Matthews   *MA 1947

ROSS James Rae   *MA 1931
d Guernsey 21.3.64 *AUR* XL 400

ROSS James Wiseman   BSc 1928
d Alloa 7.11.64 *AUR* XLI 59

ROSS or Douglas, Jean Mary   MA 1924
retd 1964; resid Elgin

ROSS or McLachlan, Jeannie   MA 1914 BSc 1917
d Aber 13.10.75

ROSS or Napier, Johan   *MA 1929
teacher Engl Dumfries h s 1961–67; retd

ROSS John   MB ChB 1911
d Sydney Aust –.1.61 *AUR* XXXIX 202

ROSS John   MA 1927
d 1972

ROSS John   *MA 1930
dep rector Invergordon acad 1962–72; retd; resid
Fearn

ROSS John   MB ChB 1937
g p Fraserburgh from 1946

ROSS John Hugh Gunn   *MA 1935 BD 1938
C of S min Dundurn parish ch St Fillans from 1973

ROSS John Maclennan   BSc(for) 1932

ROSS John Marshall   MB ChB 1930
d Beckenham 30.9.72 *AUR* XLV 128

ROSS John Munro   MB ChB 1953
FCCFP 1971
Newfoundland Canada: sen m o Bonne Bay 1958–60,
Placentia 1960–70, Channel 1970–71; assoc prof/chmn
g p mem univ St John's 1971–75, dir residency progr
in fam med 1971–78
m Deer Lake Newfoundland Doreen Janes nurse d of
Sydney J. Lond

ROSS John Wilfrid Gwinnett   BSc(for) 1933

ROSS Kenneth Aird   MB ChB 1942
sen cas off. Addington hosp S Af 1967–73; retd
Tunbridge Wells
wife *d* 29.7.73
d Tunbridge Wells 31.8.75

ROSS Lewis Davidson   MA 1929
d 27.11.72

ROSS Lizzie   MA 1921
retd 1961; resid Aber

ROSS Lydia   MA 1926
teacher Inv 1958–71; inf mistress Dalneigh p s
1971; retd; resid Inv

ROSS or Deans, Madeline   MB ChB 1951 DPH 1954

ROSS or Thomson, Margaret   *MA 1917
resid Lond
husb *d* 14.9.55

ROSS or Macmillan, Margaret   MA 1932
retd; resid Aber

ROSS Margaret Cumming   MA 1907
d 11.8.64 *AUR* XL 395

ROSS Margaret Helen   MA 1904
no longer on GC reg

ROSS or Knox, Margaret Hellen   MA 1938
d 13.12.65

ROSS or Wiseman, Margaret Stewart   MA 1905
no longer on GC reg

ROSS or Bain, Mary Ann   MA 1910
d Stonehaven 4.1.71 *AUR* XLIV 209

ROSS or MacKillop, Mary Ann   MA 1929
teacher Lat/Engl Sir E. Scott's j s s Harris 1960–68,
p dept 1969–73; retd

ROSS or Milne, Mary Eleanor   MA 1913
d Bloemfontein S Af 20.4.74 *AUR* XLVI 107

ROSS Mitchell Cumming   BSc 1925
d Aber 21.7.70 *AUR* XLIV 110

ROSS Murdo   BSc(eng) 1944

ROSS or McBain, Muriel Mary   MA 1932

ROSS Norman Alfred   MB ChB 1936 DPH 1939
d Ketton 2.5.78 *AUR* XLVIII 106

ROSS Norman Cruickshank
BSc 1955 *1957 PhD 1960

ROSS Patricia Anne   *MA 1951
civ serv dip. wireless serv Lond 1951–55; Royal
Dutch Shell translator/edit. The Hague/Amsterdam
1955–61; bldg res stat D o E Garston: higher scient
off./tech information off. from 1965; resid St Albans

ROSS Percival   MB ChB 1922
d Shrewsbury 5.9.65 *AUR* XLII 86

ROSS Robert Forsyth   BSc(for) 1940

ROSS Robert Henry   *MA 1950

ROSS Robert James Ferguson   *MA 1951

ROSS Robert Lewis   MA 1940 LLB 1949

ROSS Robert Matthew Bruce   MA 1932
prin teacher geog Bo'ness acad from 1951

ROSS Ronald Gavin   MB ChB 1949
FRSM
d Orpington 31.1.74 *AUR* XLV 450

ROSS Ronald McLeod Stewart   BSc(eng) 1948

ROSS Simon Douglas   BSc(agr) 1930
d Inverurie 16.5.65 *AUR* XLI 152

ROSS Stewart   BL 1950

ROSS Sydney Duthie   *BSc 1941
teacher: papermaking Glenrothes tech coll 1968–72,
chem Ballingry j h s Fife 1972–74; teacher/tech. sc
dept Kirkcaldy tech coll from 1974

ROSS William Alexander   *MA 1897
d Elgin 29.1.67 *AUR* XLII 79 & 345

ROSS William Andrew   MB ChB 1949
g p Laurencekirk 1959–77; m o DHSS from 1977

ROSS William Wilson Michie   *MA 1928 BL 1930
date of marriage: 4.3.36
retd 1969; resid Lochailort Invsh

ROSS Williamina Ann   MA 1921
d Inv 11.10.75

ROSS Winifred   MA 1937

ROSS-KEYT Frederic Dudley
see Keyt

ROSSOUW James Petronellus Johannes
*MB ChB 1921
no longer on GC reg

ROTH Paul Bernard   MB ChB 1905
d Richmond Surrey 29.12.62 *AUR* XL 76

ROTHNEY or Deming, Flora Elspeth   *MA 1918

ROTHNIE Douglas Auchterlonie   MA 1896 DD 1952
d Kingston Jamaica 22.11.62 *AUR* XL 73

ROTHNIE George   *MA 1931
d Edin 6.11.70 *AUR* XLIV 110

ROTHNIE James Henry   MA 1955
head: Bogmoor p s Moray 1960–63, Fornighty p s
Nairn 1963–67; teacher Tullos p s Aber 1967–71,
head St Cyrus p s from 1971

ROULSTON Thomas Love   MA 1951 MEd 1955
prin Belmont House spec s Londonderry from 1961

ROWE Joseph Bevil Wrathall   MB ChB 1928
chief m o Kodak Harrow from 1936
m Bromley 14.10.63 Agnes A. Boddie d of Ronald
C. B. CVO DSO, Bromley

ROWLAND Roy MacDonald   MB ChB 1954
surg lt RN hosp Chatham 1958–62; h s obst/gyn
Hillingdon hosp Middx 1962; ptnr g p Wolverhampton from 1962

ROY Alistair Anderson   MA 1948 BD 1952
C of S min Bridge St ch Wick from 1955
m Banff 10.9.68 Jean M. McIntosh teacher d of Fred
McI. Banff

ROY Arnold George Rennie   MA 1944 *1948
prin teacher classics Blairgowrie h s from 1956

ROY Eric James   BSc(eng) 1929
no longer on GC reg

ROY Ian Leslie   MB ChB 1942
g p Carlisle from 1953

ROY John James   *MA 1914
retd 1956; temp teaching Engl subj Elgin acad,
Lossiemouth h s, temp head Lhanbryde j s s 1956–73

ROY Peter Rennie   MA 1924
no longer on GC reg

ROY or Stuart, Rosella Gladys   MA 1926
resid Aber
husb *d* Oyne 8.5.68

ROYSTON Elsie Henriette   BSc 1931

RUDDIMAN David   MB ChB 1952

RULE Alexander   MA 1920 BSc(for) 1921
tech asst to dir gen for. and timber bureau Canberra,
Aust 1957–60; retd; compiled *Forests of Australia*
publ Angus & Robertson Sydney 1964–66

RUMBLES Eleanor Lorimer   MA 1924
retd 1964; resid Arbroath

RUMBLES Francis   MA 1914
d Eastriggs Annan –.9.62 *AUR* XL 83

RUNCIE George Deans   *MA 1937
BBC chief asst (tv Scot.); retd 1974; resid Gartmore
Stirling

RUNDLE Leslie John   BSc 1952 *1953
CChem MRIC 1973 FCS 1973
ICI: chem Grangemouth 1953–58, plant man. 1958–
63, proj sponsor Calcutta 1963–69, area man. Grangemouth from 1969

RUSACK Louis Seton   MB ChB 1942
g p Haddington from 1950

RUSHTON Henry Glen   *BSc 1953
Regd Prof Eng(Ont) 1958
Regd Prof Geol(Alta) 1968 FGAC 1965 MCIMM 1968
Canada: geol Frobisher Tor 1956–58, Ventures
Noranda Quebec 1958–63; sen geol nickel Falcon-
bridge Val d'Or Quebec/Sudbury Ont 1963–66; sen
geol/chief geol Calgary 1966–71; man. explor Fording
Coal 1971–77; man. dev and explor Fording Coal
from 1977

RUSSELL Alexander Wilson   BSc(agr) 1925
Ceylon: tea planter 1925–40, 1946–49; army 1940–
46; retd 1949–51; farm. Insch from 1951
m Insch 26.3.53 Winifred Reid

RUSSELL Aubrey Ronald Laselve   MB ChB 1952
Fell Rosae Cross(Rosicrucian Order)(Calif) 1970
Cert Fam Plan.(Fertility Control)(Johns Hopkins)
1973
Jamaica: g p: Malvern 1957–63, part-time Kingston

1963–73, m o part-time Kingston publ hosp 1963–
64, dep m o part-time gen penitentiary Kingston
1964–70, m o part-time Bellvue psychiat hosp from
1964, m o part-time fam plan. clin Kingston from 1964
marr diss March 1973
m(2) Kingston 17.8.73 Phyllis C. Macpherson
BA(Lond) lect/res fell. WI univ d of J. A. M. Kingston

RUSSELL or Walker, Audrey Mary Brodie
MA 1952

RUSSELL Bruce Arnold   MB ChB 1924
no longer on GC reg

RUSSELL or Bernard, Christina   MB ChB 1924
dep m o h Finchley 1948–61; retd; resid Insch

RUSSELL David Campbell   BSc(eng) 1934

RUSSELL or Stirling, Eileen Catherine Smart
MA 1951

RUSSELL Helen Mary Margaret   MA 1944
teacher Broomhill p s Aber from 1965

RUSSELL James Alexander   *BSc 1951

RUSSELL James Knox   MB ChB 1942 MD 1954
N'cle: post-grad dean med s from 1968, consult.
WHO human reprod from 1965, hon obst MRC unit
on reprod/growth from 1966

RUSSELL or Must, Katrine   MA 1929
teacher: St Matthew's s Westminster Lond 1946–48,
RAF school Amman Jordan 1951–52, Westlands p s
Nairobi 1952–54
m Lond 6.12.32 John S. Must BA(Cantab) clerk in
holy orders s of Rev Henry M. Barnsbury Lond

RUSSELL Mildred Margaret Gray   MB ChB 1922
retd 1948; resid Budleigh Salterton

RUSSELL Rognvald Gordon   MB ChB 1931
OBE 1969 FRCGP 1970
g p Wingate, Blackhall, Castle Eden Co Durham from
1931; chmn Durh exec council 1962–76; memb
Hartlepool hosp man. comm from 1949, chmn 1959–74

RUSSELL Stewart Innes   MA 1922
d 20.4.63

RUSSELL William Affleck   *MA 1897
d 10.11.66

RUSSELL William Frederick
MB ChB 1939 MD 1949
g p Chaddesden, Derby from 1948/asst skin dept
Derbysh RI from 1955

RUSSELL William Smith   MB ChB 1931
g p Leic from 1933

RUST Margaret Philip   MA 1933 LLB 1935
archivist Town Clerk's dept Aber 1955–72; retd;
resid Durris

RUST Robert Alexander   *BSc 1954
tech off. (chem) ICI (Dyestuffs) Huddersfield 1956–60, Fleetwood 1961–64, Teesside from 1964
m Huddersfield 17.6.61 Margaret E. Bolton

RUTHERFORD Hamish   MA 1926
tut. mod. stud. Stowe s 1945–66; retd; resid Wicken, Milton Keynes
d Wicken 28.4.80 *AUR* XLVIII 441

RUTHERFORD Hubert Watson
**   MB ChB 1942 DPH 1948**
consult. venereologist NE reg hosp board/clin sen lect venereal diseases Aberd from 1966

RUTHERFORD William Armstrong   *MA 1929
d Golspie 30.1.73 *AUR* XLV 226

RUTHERFORD William Hay   MA 1936 LLB 1938
hon sheriff Aber, Kincardine & Banff from 1974
ptnr: Christie, Buthlay & Rutherford advoc Aber 1962–78, Raeburn, Christie & Co advoc from 1978; pres Royal Northern Agr Soc 1980

RUXTON or Watson, Annie Ellen   MA 1913
d Warminster 27.2.76

RUXTON or Lee, Ethel Lewis   MA 1912
d St And 24.1.78 *AUR* XLVIII 102

RUXTON Herbert William Black
**   MB ChB 1904 DPH 1905**
d St And 12.3.64 *AUR* XL 394

RUXTON Irene Tomina Joan   MB ChB 1919
d Newport Gwent 9.5.78 *AUR* XLVIII 103

RUXTON or Auld, Mary Margaret   MA 1907
d Aber 17.6.76 *AUR* XLVII 101

RYAN Daniel James   *MA 1953 *MEd 1958
teacher Engl AGS 1962–66; sen lect educ Avery Hill coll Lond 1966–72, head of grad dept 1972
m Aber 2.4.63 Rosalie Macdonald nurse
d Eltham 14.9.72

RYDER or Spiller, Elma Pirie   MA 1930
resid Stirling
husb d 5.3.66

RYDER Mary Elizabeth   MA 1924
d 10.2.62 *AUR* XL 91

SABISTON Gordon Harvey   BSc 1953
petrographer Arvida Canada 1953–56; field geol Boké Guinea W Af 1956–57; group leader Arvida 1957–68, sect. head 1968–74; supt min res Mandeville Jamaica 1974–76, chief geol from 1976
m Aber 20.8.53 Alison W. Robb

SABISTON James   MA 1936
teacher Keith g s from 1955
d Keith 16.8.75

SABISTON Louis   *BSc 1948
d Stoke-on-Trent 11.8.79

SACKS Ephraim   MB ChB 1925

SACKS Israel   MB ChB 1922 MD 1941
d Bloemfontein 11.4.64

SACKS Neville Zigmund   MB ChB 1950
FRCPE 1973
Bloemfontein S Af: consult. phys Pelonomi hosp 1960–73, part-time lect in med from 1973
m Bloemfontein 15.6.58 Julie Abrahamson B Soc Sci (Cape Town) soc sc worker

SAINT Dorothy   MA 1951
teacher Woodside Aber 1952–59; later at Hazlehead acad
m(1) Aber 16.5.59 Roger Mullard RAF; husb d 2.3.60
(2) Aber 26.7.77 John Gilmour BSc 1948 *qv*

SALISBURY or Ellis, Elizabeth Anne   MA 1948

SALMOND Robert Williamson Asher
**   *MB ChB 1907 DPH 1908 ChM 1910 *MD 1911**
no longer on GC reg

SALT or Durkin, Sheila Margaret
**   MB ChB 1944 DPH 1948**
MFCM 1973 FRSH
m o Is of Man 1971–73, prin s m o 1973–75; m o/dir Sturgeon health unit Alberta Canada from 1975

SALTER or Baird, Isabella   MA 1939
Elgin: teacher pre-nursing coll, asst 1955–58, head 1958–71; stud. advis tech coll from 1971

SAMMON David Campbell   *BSc 1951 PhD 1954
on staff UKAEA Harwell from 1954

SAMMON Paul Matthew   MB ChB 1950 DPH 1953
MFCM 1972
asst, sen asst div m o Lancs 1953–66, div m o W Riding c c, m o h urban districts Colne Valley Yorks 1966–71; div m o Lancs c c and m o h districts c Accrington area 1971–74; dis commun phys Ormskirk dist Lancs health auth from 1974

SAMSON Harry Philip   MB ChB 1923
g p Eccles Manc from 1929

SAMSON James Beahan   MB ChB 1922 MD 1931
retd 1960; resid Eastbourne

SANDERSON or Cochrane, Janet Andrews
**   MA 1935**
civ serv/asst lib microbiol res estab Porton Wilts 1966–72; retd; resid Salisbury Wilts

SANDFORD Cyril James   MB ChB 1924
d –.3.70

SANDISON or Simpson, Charlotte   MA 1931
resid Banff
husb d 26.7.74

SANDISON Isobel Fleming   *MA 1943
teacher mod lang Buckie h s 1964–72, prin Fr from 1972

SANDISON John Forbes William   MB ChB 1914
d Bournemouth 4.4.69 *AUR* XLIII 210

SANDISON John Henry   *BSc 1952
agr div ICI Middlesbrough 1964–75; seconded to Price Comm Lond from 1975
m Stockton-on-Tees 5.9.59 Carol Howitt clerk d of Robert F. H. Doncaster

SANDISON or Smith, Mary Wilhelmina   MA 1936
Shetland: head Eshaness p s till closure 1968; occasional relief teacher from 1968

SANDISON or Lewis, Sheila   MA 1930
resid Aber

SANDLER Hyman   MB ChB 1926
no longer on GC reg

SANDS or Wilkie, Mary Gavin   MA 1918
no longer on GC reg

SANG Charles George   BSc(eng) 1936

SANG Elma Mair   MA 1935
dep head Torry acad Aber 1972–76; retd

SANG or Eddie, Isabel Margaret   MA 1930

SANG James Henderson   BSc 1934 *1936
FRSE 1959
asst dir poultry res centre Edin 1958–65; prof genetics Sus Brighton from 1965, dean of s of biol sc from 1972

SANGSTER or Buchanan, Alexandra Adam
                                    MA 1948
resid Aber

SANGSTER Charles Low   BSc(eng) 1933 *1934
FIEE 1959 FIMechE 1960 OBE 1963
Crown Agents Lond: asst chief insp eng 1966–67, chief insp eng 1967–69, chief elect. eng 1969–70, dir 1970–73; dir (non-exec) Tradewinds Airways 1970–73; retd

SANGSTER or Bolland, Edith Mary   MA 1943
resid Brussels

SANGSTER or Leslie, Elizabeth Anderson   MA 1942
teacher Hampstead Garden Suburb s Lond from 1967
husb *d* 8.6.67

SANGSTER or Macaulay, Ella Murray   MA 1953
resid Peterculter

SANGSTER Eric Garden   BL 1942
Lond: dep dir paintmakers assoc 1963–65, dir fed. of painting contr 1965–72, dir nat fed. paint/decorating contr from 1972

SANGSTER Ernest George   *MA 1954 BD 1957
chaplain St And 1961–65; C of S min: Beechgrove ch Aber 1965–76, Blackhall St Columba ch Edin from 1976
m St And 23.8.63 Alison M. Runcie MA(St And) d of Alexander M. R. MB ChB(Edin) Kirkcaldy

SANGSTER George   MB ChB 1937 ᶜMD 1949
FRCPE 1976
consult. phys city hosp Edin from 1961

SANGSTER George Brown Cameron
                          MA 1945 BD 1948
C of S min: Murrayfield par ch Edin from 1964

SANGSTER Harry   BSc(agr) 1950
farm. Ladybank Fife from 1954

SANGSTER James Hay   *MA 1930
FEIS 1970
retd 1972; resid Edin

SANGSTER John   MB ChB 1905
no longer on GC reg

SANGSTER John Ramage Marshall   MB ChB 1934
d Lond 1969

SANGSTER or Macleod, Margaret Ingram   MA 1909
d 9.12.70

SANGSTER Robert Gray   BSc(for) 1933
CBE 1966
secy Scot. Woodland Owners Assoc Edin 1966–78

SANGSTER Robert John   BSc(agr) 1949
on staff of DAFS Dun from 1950

SANGSTER or McPherson, Violet   MA 1954
teacher Hopeman p s from 1969

SANGUINETTI John Fitzalan Burgoyne
                                MB ChB 1936

SARGISON Charles William   MA 1927
retd 1960; resid Majorca

SARGISON Kenneth Duthie   MB ChB 1955
FRCSE 1963
regist surg ARI 1960–63; regist orthop Agnes Hunt and Robert Jones hosp Oswestry 1963–65; sen regist orthop WI Glasg 1965–67; consult. orthop surg RI Hull from 1967

SAUL Donald   MA 1951

SAUNDERS Campbell Milne   MA 1949 BD 1952
C of S min St Leonard's ch Ayr from 1962

SAUNDERS or Davis, Ellen Jeanie   MB ChB 1919
no longer on GC reg

SAUNDERS Harold Gordon   MB ChB 1950
consult. in admin charge dept anaest N & S Teesside hosp groups 1973–75, South Tees health dist from 1975

m Ferryhill Co Durh 23.6.61 Thelma Wright SRN
theatre sister d of Harry W. Ferryhill
d Martin-in-Cleveland 13.12.79 *AUR* XLVIII 443

SAUNDERS John Herbert   *BSc 1951

SAUNDERS Maxwell James
**   MB ChB 1934 DPH 1936**
   g p Bournemouth from 1946
d –.4.80

SAUNDERS William Munro Hutchison   PhD 1953
   leader soil fertility Ruakura agr res centre Hamilton
NZ from 1966

SAVEGE Arthur Charles Mears   MB ChB 1912
   d Arbroath 11.12.66 *AUR* XLII 351

SAVEGE James Maxwell   MA 1913 MB ChB 1917
   retd col RAMC 1958; resid Harrogate
d 6.4.74

SAVEGE Ronald Maclure   MB ChB 1921
   retd 1966; resid Richmond-on-Thames

SAVIDGE Cecil Arthur Grant   MA 1927
   MBE
dir Brit nat comm internat Chamber of Commerce
1954–73; retd; resid Gt Missenden
d 9.12.75

SAVILLE Alan   BSc 1944 *1946
   FRSE 1976
sen prin scient off. marine lab Aber from 1968

SAVY Jacques   MB ChB 1947
   g p Kingston-on-Thames from 1958

SAYLE Anthony Cashen   BSc(for) 1954
   for.: Br Col: inventory div BC for. serv 1957–63,
for. valuation Min of Fin. 1963–73, co-ordinator
timber appraisal BC assessment auth from 1973
m Victoria BC 22.10.60 Anna M. Schmidt teacher d of
John H. S. Middle Lake Sask

SCATTERTY or Beaton, Margaret Smith   MA 1931

SCENCZI (formerly Schmidt) Nicholas Joseph
**   *MA 1928**
   d Budapest 10.7.77 *AUR* XLVII 357

SCHARENGUIVEL James Arthur   MB ChB 1906
   no longer on GC reg

SCHNEE or Cohen, Isadore Murray   MB ChB 1934

SCHOFIELD or Kirby, Margaret Ellerker
**   MB ChB 1946**
   teaching fell. anaest Jefferson med coll Philadelphia
USA from 1960

SCOLLAY John Thomas Gilbert   BSc(agr) 1921
   organis f e Shetland 1951–53; stud. div Edin 1953–
55; C of S min: Lanarksh 1955–61, Greenock 1961–66,
Waterside Ayr 1966–71; retd; resid Edin

SCORGIE or Neilson, Catherine Mitchell Johnston
**   MA 1929**
   resid Montrose
d Montrose 15.11.80

SCORGIE Dorothy Margaret   MA 1941

SCORGIE or Mackenzie, Elsie Johnston
**   MB ChB 1921**
   d 4.6.75 *AUR* XLVI 322

SCORGIE Frank   *MA 1914 BSc 1921
   d Aber 7.11.61 *AUR* XXXIX 277

SCORGIE or Purdie, Jean Smart   MA 1932
   d Edin 5.6.66 *AUR* XLI 341

SCORGIE John   MA 1916
   d 7.4.74

SCORGIE John   MB ChB 1939
   d 20.6.60 *AUR* XXXVIII 598

SCORGIE or Carr, Margaret Olga   MA 1939
   secy: Engl Elect. Co Rugby 1958–59, Gussen &
Wolff Northampton 1959–63, various posts Aber
from 1963

SCORGIE Penelope Dey   MA 1938
   on staff M o T Aber from 1958
d Aber 14.11.79

SCOTCHER Lilian Mary   MB ChB 1951
   dept m o s health serv Kent c c Maidstone from
1967
m Southborough 1.10.64 Gerald W. T. Norton bus.
exec s of John H. C. C. Tunbridge Wells

SCOTT or Allan, Agnes Mary Walker   MA 1926
   teacher Engl/maths Rochester 1949–66, head dept
Engl from 1958

SCOTT Alexander   *BSc 1954 PhD 1958
   lect zool Belf 1960–68; lect biol Strath 1968–73, sen
lect from 1973

SCOTT Alexander Daniel Jamieson   *MA 1928
   TD 1946 OBE 1960
army off. (lt-col) SEAC/India 1939–46; educ off./sen
educ off. Sierra Leone 1947–56; perm secy min of
educ/soc welfare 1956–60; perm secy/chief of protocol
PM's off. 1961–62; teacher/master i/c jun s Boroughmuir s s Edin 1962–72
m Glasg 13.3.37 Helen P. Galbraith secy d of Robert
G. Dunfermline

SCOTT Alexander Mackie   *MA 1947
   Scot. Arts Council award 1968
Glas: sen lect Scot. lit. 1963–71, head dept from 1971,
reader from 1976

SCOTT Alexander Robb   *MA 1953 Dip Ed 1956
   sen Engl master the Publ s Hyderabad W. Pakistan
1962–65; teacher Engl overseas Patoomwan teacher
trg coll Bangkok Thailand 1965–68; asst dept Engl/
commun coll of comm Aber from 1968

SCOTT or Pearson, Alice May   MA 1925
deceased

SCOTT or Adam, Alice Moir   *MA 1948
teacher Fr: Aber acad 1961–70, prin asst Hazlehead acad from 1970

SCOTT or Dobb, Alison Jean Anderson   *MA 1951
resid Cambridge

SCOTT Allan Harper   *BSc(eng) 1952

SCOTT Andrew George   MB ChB 1942 DPH 1947
b 20.6.19
MFCM 1972
Dept of Health NZ from 1974

SCOTT Andrew Maxwell   BSc(eng) 1939
Assoc Fell. Can. Aero/Space Inst 1962
test supt Rolls Royce Glasg 1939–50; chief test eng/sales and serv man./chief eng Rolls Royce of Canada Montreal 1950–62; sales and serv man. Rolls Royce Glasg 1962–68; comm man. Rolls Royce (1971) Derby 1968–77, asst comm dir from 1978
m Glasg 1943 Helen McCallum secy d of John R. McC. Glasg

SCOTT or Ashmore, Anne Elizabeth   *MA 1938
part-time examining/teaching from 1944; resid Manc

SCOTT or Urquhart, Annie Bella   MA 1925
teacher Lat/Greek Nicolson inst Stornoway 1956–66; resid Stornoway

SCOTT Charles   BSc 1934
FEIS 1963
head: Pitmedden p s 1941–71, Mintlaw s from 1971
wife d 27.5.71
m(2) Aber 23.10.73 Lena M. Innes
d Aber 1.8.79

SCOTT Charles Alexander Nelson   *MA 1933
Forres acad: prin teacher mod lang 1938–73, dep rector from 1960; retd 1976

SCOTT Charles Cameron   MB ChB 1954
d Dun 2.7.73 AUR xlv 321

SCOTT Charles Doig   BSc(agr) 1950
farm. Newburgh Aberdeensh from 1950

SCOTT Christian Austine   MA 1930
retd 1969; resid Edin

SCOTT David   BSc 1950

SCOTT Desmond Rodway   BSc(eng) 1938

SCOTT Donald   *BSc 1949
sen lect zool univ of Otago NZ 1967–71, assoc prof from 1971

SCOTT Douglas Somerville   MB ChB 1916
d –.4.66

SCOTT Edith   MB ChB 1938
DPH(Edin) 1958
resid Goring-by-Sea
m Edin 20.5.58 Albert J. Phillips pharm s of William P.

SCOTT or Roy, Elsie Ann Margaret   *MA 1947
resid Blairgowrie

SCOTT or Alexander, Ethel Adamson   MA 1941
lived in Hong Kong 1957–67; teacher Aber/Aberdeensh 1968–76

SCOTT Euphemia Ashley   MA 1930
teacher Dyce p s 1962–74; retd; resid Aber

SCOTT Frederick James   *MA 1929
Edin: part-time univ lect Greek from 1954; teacher classics Royal h s 1947–60, prin classics 1960–71; retd

SCOTT Geoffrey Burnett   MB ChB 1955
MRCPath 1964 FRCPath 1976
sen lect path. Aberd from 1969; hon consult. path. NE Scot. reg hosp board from 1969

SCOTT George Alexander   *MA 1930
retd 1969; resid Banff

SCOTT George Brebner   MB ChB 1896 MD 1900
d Reigate 6.3.65 AUR xl 197

SCOTT George Smith   *MA 1951

SCOTT Gordon   MA 1938
CA

SCOTT Helen   MA 1907
no longer on GC reg

SCOTT or Roll, Helen Camilla de Clèry
                                        MB ChB 1950
g p Nelson Lancs from 1958

SCOTT Helen Gordon   MA 1929
retd 1967; resid Rosemarkie

SCOTT Henry Norman   *MA 1928
retd 1965; resid Sauchen

SCOTT Herbert James   BSc(agr) 1921
no longer on GC reg

SCOTT James   MB ChB 1941
g p Alyth from 1947

SCOTT James Alexander   MA 1899
d Cincinnati Ohio 16.10.63 AUR xl 299

SCOTT James Henry   MA 1929 MB ChB 1939
g p Blackpool from 1947

SCOTT James Reid   BSc(eng) 1933

SCOTT Jean Gordon   *MA 1916
d Elgin 30.5.71 AUR xliv 317

SCOTT or Bottomley, Jean Innes
                                      ***BSc 1950 PhD 1953**

SCOTT Jean Macdonald   *MA 1939
  m Scott

SCOTT John   MA 1907
  d Kilmarnock 13.11.60 *AUR* xxxix 100

SCOTT John   *MA 1936
  retd 1978; resid Buckie

SCOTT John Adam   MB ChB 1932
  g p Kingston-u-Thames from 1945
  m Wick 8.3.37 Sylvia D. Fitzlanders

SCOTT John Shields   BSc(for) 1954

SCOTT Joseph   *MA 1901 *BSc 1909
  no longer on GC reg

SCOTT Kerry Owen   BSc(eng) 1951
  MICE 1958 MNZIE 1963
  NZ: with hydro-elect. proj investigations and construct. from 1956

SCOTT Lorna Stephen   BSc 1951

SCOTT or Skinner, Mabel   MA 1925
  resid Aber

SCOTT or Henderson, Maggie   MA 1919 BSc 1922

SCOTT or Bright, Margaret   MA 1935
  resid Chippenham

SCOTT Margaret McKenzie   MA 1921
  d Port Edward S Af 12.6.77

SCOTT Marguerite McDonald
                                      MB ChB 1943 MD 1960
  h o Highgate hosp Lond 1943–44; bact: Manc
  1944–46, publ health lab Salisbury 1953–57; sen
  bact/consult. Virus Ref Lab Colindale Lond 1957–70;
  dir Virus Ref Lab from 1970; co-dir WHO Collab.
  centre ref and res on influenza from 1975
  m Lond 1946 Helio G. Pereira D Med(Rio de Janeiro)
  head div virology nat inst for med res Lond s of
  Raul P.

SCOTT Mary Anne   BSc 1909
  no longer on GC reg

SCOTT or Meek, Mary Elizabeth   MA 1905
  no longer on GC reg

SCOTT or Hendry, Mary Elizabeth   *MA 1943
  teacher mod lang: St Leonard's s St And 1956–57,
  Madras coll St And 1962–69

SCOTT May   MA 1946

SCOTT Neil   BSc(eng) 1949

SCOTT Robert Gordon   MA 1938

SCOTT Robert James   BSc 1926 BSc(agr) 1928
  OBE 1964
  retd 1971; resid Dumfries
  d 28.9.79

SCOTT Robert McDonald   MB ChB 1951
  g p Portsoy from 1953
  d Aber 18.2.78 *AUR* xlvii 360

SCOTT Robert Orr   PhD 1942
  ARCST(Glas) 1939 ARIC 1939 FRIC 1973
  Aber: res chem dept spectrochem Macaulay inst 1939–
  69, head of dept from 1969
  m Aber 14.6.44 Mary R. Davidson d of William D.

SCOTT or Wynne-Edwards, Stella Julia   MA 1955
  instr dept Fr Queen's univ Kingston Canada 1966–
  70, admin asst dept Engl from 1970
  m(2) Gartland

SCOTT or Gray, Susan   *MA 1939
  resid Lumsden 1976

SCOTT or Annand, Wilhelmina Elliot   MA 1932
  resid Perth

SCOTT William   *MA 1936
  dep head Keith g s from 1970

SCOTT William Alexander   MA 1921
  retd 1965; resid Aber
  d Aber 2.4.80 *AUR* xlviii 441

SCOTT William Antony McDonald   MB ChB 1937
  FRSM 1947
  S Af: sen visiting phys Addington hosp Durban from
  1967, spec phys Durban from 1967
  m(2) Durban 13.11.72 Rosemary A. Gardner SRN
  d of George C. G. Dorking

SCOTT William Dawson   MA 1903
  d Inverurie 17.6.62 *AUR* xxxix 373

SCOTT William McQueen   MA 1950
  JP 1970
  prin teacher Engl Kinross s s 1959–69; dep head
  Kinross p s 1969–73, head from 1973

SCOTT William Russell   MB ChB 1931
  MRCGP
  d Weymouth 10.10.74 *AUR* xlvi 239

SCOTT or Coutts, Winifred Katherine   MA 1955
  MA(Edin) 1969
  resid Edin

SCRIMGEOUR Annie Somerville   BSc 1943
  exper off. Nat Eng Lab East Kilbride 1954–63; prin
  teacher maths Kilgraston s Bridge of Earn from 1964

SCRIMGEOUR Arthur Martin   MA 1930
  d Kent 29.4.74 *AUR* xlvi 109

SCROGGIE or Carnie, Anne Johnstone Stewart
                                              MA 1935
teacher Aber 1956–75
resid Banchory

SCROGGIE or Tait, Dorothy Findlay   MA 1945
asst teacher Quarryhill p s Aber from 1964

SCROGGIE George   MA 1952

SCROGGIE or Rice, Jane Meauras Findlay   MA 1936
husb d 3.9.72

SCROGGIE or Hay, Margaret Ruth   MA 1936
resid Wallasey

SCROGGIE or West, Mary Chalmers   MA 1933
retd 1970; resid Fochabers

SCROGIE Ishbel Margaret   MA 1911
resid Peterhead

SEAL David Trevor   BSc(for) 1950

SEATH James William   MA 1920
d 11.4.69

SECTOR Mary Margaret   MA 1931
teacher: St Paul St s Aber 1937–60, Springhill p s
Aber 1960–70; retd

SEED John   MB ChB 1930
consult. geriat med E Riding Yorks/Scarborough
HMCs 1963–72; retd; resid Bridlington

SEFTON Alexander Monro   *MA 1911
d 13.2.67

SEFTON George Arthur   MA 1921 BD 1924
C of S min: Fern and Careston 1937–66; clerk
presb of Brechin and Fordoun 1945–60; retd; resid
Brechin

SEGGIE or Jenner, Griselda Margaret
                                        MB ChB 1945
Dun: clin asst cytology unit Maryfield hosp 1963–
78, fam plan. clin doctor 1968–78; g p Brechin from
1969

SEGGIE or Allison, Rosalind Mary   MA 1948
resid Pitfodels Aber

SEIVEWRIGHT Robert Taylor   MA 1909
retd 1972; resid Melton Mowbray

SEIVWRIGHT Elizabeth Ross   *MA 1922
d Ellon 28.10.61 *A UR* xxxix 281

SELBIE Gordon Stewart   MB ChB 1949
g p Huddersfield from 1953

SELBIE Hector   MA 1932

SELBIE James Chalmers   BSc 1928 *1929
d Upminster 9.5.74 *A UR* xlvi 109

SELBIE John Stewart   BSc 1926
retd 1968; resid Gourdon

SELBIE William   MB ChB 1937
g p Moldgreen Huddersfield from 1939; retd

SELBIE William Philip   *MA 1910
d Bath 7.4.67 *A UR* xlii 349

SELKIRK Robert Andrew   BSc(for) 1934
d Perth 25.10.68 *A UR* xliii 85

SELLAR Beatrice Mary   MB ChB 1922
retd 1961; resid Aberlour

SELLAR Forbes Keith   BL 1953

SELLAR James   MA 1894 ᵈBL 1897
no longer on GC reg

SELLAR James Alexander   MB ChB 1915 DPH 1921
d Perth 25.12.71 *A UR* xliv 429

SELLAR James Alexander   BSc 1937 *BSc(eng) 1938

SELLAR Jean Henderson Graham   MA 1955

SELLAR Patrick James   BSc(eng) 1950
MIEE CEng
elect. eng British Gas (SE reg) Croydon from 1969

SELLAR Ronald Marischal   *MA 1952
retail sales man. Lond 1962–64; sales trg man.
Slough 1964–66, marketing man. 1966–68; reg man.
Manc 1968–74, nat sales man. Slough from 1974

SEMMENCE Adrian George   MA 1922
d 3.1.62 *A UR* xxxix 281

SEMMENCE Adrian Murdoch
                            MB ChB 1953 MD 1957
MSc 1972 FRCGP 1972 DIH(England) 1972
p m o civ serv dept from 1976

SEMMENCE Henry Rattray   BSc(eng) 1947

SEMPLE Agnes Loudon   *MB ChB 1918 DPH 1921
d Alexandria Dunbartonsh 22.2.63 *A UR* xl 202

SEMPLE John Ferguson
                BSc(mech eng) 1944 BSc(civ eng) 1948
man. consult. Aberdour Fife 1960–62; man. dir
Kinord Associates Aber from 1962

SEMPLE Mary Clark   *MA 1913
d Helensburgh 28.4.69 *A UR* xliii 210

SEMPLE Robert   *MB ChB 1910 MD 1915
d Aber 1.1.70 *A UR* xliii 441

SEMPLE Robert   *MB ChB 1939 ᶜMD 1952
FRCP(Lond) 1964
lect clin med Queen's coll Dund 1954–64; consult.
phys Ninewells and assoc hosps Dun from 1974 and
sen lect clin med Dund

SEMPLE Roderick Ferguson   BSc(eng) 1941
  MBE 1961
Brit army staff Washington USA 1961–64; c o 131
parachute eng regt TA Lond 1964–66; army instr
RAF staff coll Bracknell 1966–68; comm Spec Air
Service group Lond 1969–72; retd; dir gen defence
admin Muscat Sultanate of Oman from 1973

SENGUPTA Samaras Ranjan   PhD 1949

SERAPHIM George Michael   BSc(for) 1953
  asst dir Cyprus for. dept 1961–71, dir from 1971

SHAHID Ismail Ahmad   BSc 1949

SHAHWAN Aziz Áli Ismail   PhD 1953
  FASCE(USA) 1967
asst prof Baghdad univ Iraq 1958–59; dept tech advis
major proj admin Damascus Syria 1959–61; prof of
hydraulics Cairo univ from 1965; consult. eng Bank
du Cairo from 1968

SHAND Bessie Lindsay   MA 1910
  d 23.4.70

SHAND or Taylor, Dorothy   MA 1923
  no longer on GC reg

SHAND Frederick John Michael   *BSc 1953

SHAND George   BSc 1937 BSc(eng) 1939
  Manc: chief eng rly signals AEI 1964–67, chief eng
Manc group AEI gen signals 1967–69; tech author
Technivision serv 1970–78; retd

SHAND George Ernest   MB ChB 1909 *MD 1914
  no longer on GC reg

SHAND or Macdonald, Grace Ann   MA 1942

SHAND Harry Edward   MA 1913 BSc(agr) 1914
  no longer on GC reg

SHAND James Allan   MA 1936
  FEIS 1971
head Aberchirder s s 1962–76; retd

SHAND or Fleming, Jeannie   MA 1920
  no longer on GC reg

SHAND John   MA 1927

SHAND or Davidson, Margaret Milne   MA 1933
  teacher maths Morgan acad Dun 1959–73; retd;
resid Broughty Ferry

SHAND or Harrower, Mary Geddes   MA 1953
  teacher Dunfermline from 1954

SHAND or Durno, Matilda Jean   MA 1913
  d 1.7.67

SHAND William   MA 1897
  d Dun 1.3.62 *AUR* xxxix 376

SHAND William John   MA 1934
  d Australia 5.10.80

SHANKS John Alexander   MB ChB 1948
  MRCOG 1962 FRCS(C) 1964 FACOG 1972
FRCOG 1974
lect Aberd: dept path. 1960–62, dept obst/gyn 1962–
64; consult. obst/gyn private pract Brockville Ontario
from 1965

SHANKS Peter Lindsay   BSc(agr) 1927

SHAPIRO Charles   MB ChB 1921
  d Israel 13.8.74

SHARKEY John Austin   MB ChB 1927
  retd 1969; resid Shipton Green Itchenor W Sussex
m(2) Kingston Surrey 11.9.63 Margaret E. Baker d of
Henry B. Folkestone

SHARP Christabel Noel   MA 1905
  d Aber 24.2.66 *AUR* xlii 82

SHARP David   *MA 1932
  d 18.4.66

SHARP David Easton   BSc 1911
  d 1.6.75

SHARP George Alexander   MB ChB 1930
  retd g p 1972; sen ship surg P & O Brit India educ
cruise div 1972–76; retd

SHARP James Garden   MA *BSc 1930 PhD 1935
  d Cambridge 23.12.66 *AUR* xlii 88

SHARP or Mackie, Lindsay Lyall   MA 1946
  husb made life peer 1974—Lord Mackie of Benshie
in the County of Angus
resid Kirriemuir

SHARP or Dickinson, Margaret Isabel Anne
                                        ***MA 1931**
  resid Malta
m(2) Baron van Weesel

SHARP Michael Storie   MA 1947 LLB 1949
  ptnr Davidson & Garden advoc Aber from 1955

SHARP Neil Carter   MB ChB 1940
  MBE 1975
member Grampian health board from 1977

SHARP Peter Ogston   MA 1946 MB ChB 1951
  g p Banff from 1954

SHARP Richard Lyall   *MA 1937
  CB
i d c (served on staff Imp Def Coll)
prin Home Civ Serv 1946; Imp Def Coll 1961; under-
secy: Prices and Incomes 1966–68, HM Treasury
1968–76; ceremonial off. civ serv dept from 1977

SHAW Alastair   MA 1949
  teacher: St Peter's RC s Aber 1958–60, Aber coll of
comm from 1960

SHAW Ian Kirk   *MA 1952
Leeds: reg secy RIBA Yorks reg 1968–72, Yorks/NW/Northern reg from 1972

SHAW or McLean, Jessie Cormack   MA 1917
resid Longniddry

SHAW or Crombie, Jessie Tyson   *MA 1931
resid Dingwall

SHAW John   MB ChB 1912
no longer on GC reg

SHAW or Naughton, Mary Ann   MA 1950

SHAW Thomas   BSc(for) 1955

SHEACH Jean Mackenzie   MB ChB 1937 MD 1952
consult. Exeter clin area Devon from 1958

SHEACH or Dubreuil, Margaret Helen   *MA 1940
MA(Vermont) 1970
Canada: asst prof Engl Macdonald coll 1961–70, assoc prof Engl McG univ 1970–77
m(2) Montreal 12.5.72 Rodney Bruce BSc(Queen's univ Kingston Ontario) engineer

SHEACH Mary Ann   MA 1918
prin teacher Engl/Fr Kinross 1924–60; retd 1960; resid Aber
d Aber 15.2.76

SHEARER or Falconer, Evelyn Murray   MA 1923
loc exec secy Brit assoc: Aber 1962–63, Southampton 1963–64, Leeds 1966–67, Dun 1967–68, Exeter 1968–69; head secy duties dept Queensway secy coll Nairobi 1970–74; prin Pioneer comm coll Mombasa 1975–77; retd

SHEARER Janet   *MA 1947

SHEARER John Alexander   MB ChB 1934
FRCGP 1971
g p Bucksburn 1938–74; retd; resid Tarves

SHEARER John Craigen   BSc(eng) 1950

SHEARER Lewis George   MB ChB 1930

SHEARER Margaret Ferguson Plowman   MA 1917
d 1942

SHEARER William   *BSc 1953

SHEARER William Fraser   MB ChB 1922
no longer on GC reg

SHECHNER Isadore   MB ChB 1934

SHEED or Riddell, Annie Rennie   MA 1928
resid Aber

SHEED Jessie Smith   MA 1926
d 21.11.65

SHENNAN David John George   *BSc(eng) 1929
FICE 1959 FI Arb 1974
Sir Wm Arrol, J. Mowlem & E. Nuttall: eng/ag 1930–42, contr co-ordinator 1956–74; R E 1943–46; consult. and arbitrator from 1974

SHENNAN Edward Theodore
            MB ChB 1939 DPH 1947
DIH 1970 MFCM 1972
Jamaica WI: m o h parish of St Mary 1964–67, sen m o h min of health Kingston from 1967

SHEPHERD Anna   MA 1915 LLD 1964
edit. *AUR* 1957–64; author *The Living Mountain* publ 1977
d Aber 27.2.81 *AUR* XLIX 136

SHEPHERD Arnold Frederick   *BSc 1946

SHEPHERD David Ramsay   BSc 1952

SHEPHERD or Reaper, Elizabeth Nicol   MA 1917
no longer on GC reg

SHEPHERD Ella Christine   MA 1943

SHEPHERD Francis George Graham
            ᶜ**MB ChB 1948**
MRCGP 1967
g p Aber from 1952

SHEPHERD George Alexander   *MB ChB 1919
retd 1961; resid Estepona, Malaga, Spain

SHEPHERD Helen   *MA 1939
JP 1969
teacher: prin mod lang/housemistress Huyton coll 1953–59, prin mod lang Congleton g s 1959–61; head: March h s Cambs 1961–69, Hereward comp s March Cambs 1969–73; sen advis teacher mod lang Cambs 1973–76; retd

SHEPHERD Ian Leslie   MB ChB 1944
g p: Nott 1954–66, Burlington Ontario from 1966

SHEPHERD James Alexander   MA 1904
no longer on GC reg

SHEPHERD James Forrest   MB ChB 1922
d Farnham Surrey 21.10.72 *AUR* XLV 126

SHEPHERD James William Thomson
            MB ChB 1950

SHEPHERD Kathleen Mary   *MA 1947
prin teacher mod lang: Banchory acad 1966–70, Nairn acad 1970–71; prin Ger Inv royal acad from 1971

SHEPHERD Norman   BSc 1954 *1956

SHEPHERD Norman Alexander
            MA 1949 ᵈLLB 1952
QC 1978
Canada: br leg. off. indust dev bank London Ontario

1961–63, reg leg. off. indust dev bank Toronto 1963–65; ptnr Crawford, Shepherd & Hill Wingham 1965–69, sen ptnr Shepherd & Laschuk Kincardine from 1969; pres Bruce Law Assoc from 1976

SHEPHERD Norman James Brander
                              MA 1937 LLB 1941
  MBE
d Aber 1.7.71 *AUR* XLIV 321

SHEPHERD Robert Robertson   BSc(agr) 1952

SHEPHERD William Gray Aitken   *MA 1948
  PhD(Edin) 1962
prin teacher lang Leith acad Edin 1961–65; head Broughton s s later h s Edin from 1965

SHEPPARD Herbert Playford   MB ChB 1900
  no longer on GC reg

SHERRIFFS or Burn, Helen   MA 1914
  d Methlick 12.12.72 *AUR* XLV 224

SHERRIFFS or Gordon, Mary Ironside   MA 1911
  resid Bendigo Vict Aust
d Bendigo Australia 10.5.79

SHERRIFFS William Rae
                    MA 1903 BSc 1911 DSc 1919
  d Surrey 7.10.64 *AUR* XLI 53

SHEWAN or Robertson, Agnes   BSc 1953
  teacher sc Fyvie s s 1967–73; asst head Fyvie s from 1974

SHEWAN Alexander   BSc(agr) 1922
  no longer on GC reg

SHEWAN Frederick George Davidson
                              MA 1925 ᵈLLB 1927
  retd 1975; resid Aber
wife *d* 18.8.76

SHEWAN Frederick Robert   MA 1952 Dip Ed 1955
  teacher Ruthrieston s s Aber 1961–62; head Tough p s 1962–67, Cove p s 1967–71, Kinnoull p s 1971–77, North Muirton p s Perth from 1977

SHEWAN Henry Alexander   *MA 1928 ᵈLLB 1932
  OBE(mil) 1946 CB 1974
dep commissioner nat insur Edin 1955–66, commissioner from 1966
wife *d* 7.8.77

SHEWAN James Mackay
                    BSc 1931 *1932 PhD 1935 DSc 1969
  FRSE 1960 FIBiol 1960 FIFST 1965
retd 1975; resid Aber

SHEWAN or Milne, Jane Will   *MA 1917
  resid Pitmedden
husb *d* 3.12.62

SHEWAN John   MA 1920
  d Aber 25.4.68 *AUR* XLII 358

SHIACH or McIver, Doris Lorimer   *MA 1941
  resid Westhill Skene

SHIACH George Alexander   MA 1932

SHIACH George Alexander Morrison   *MA 1936
  Castle Douglas h s: teacher classics 1962–73, asst prin guid from 1973; retd 1978
wife *d* 1963
m(2) Bearsden 24.12.66 Margaret M. R. Davidson Dip Mus teacher d of Joseph J. D. Bearsden

SHIACH or Cowie, Helen Emily   MA 1954
  teacher: Toronto 1958–64, York county s Ontario 1964–75; vice-prin York county s from 1975

SHIACH Hendry   MA 1933
  head St Peter's s Galashiels 1951–72; retd

SHIACH or Diack, Irene McLeod   MA 1953
  resid Germany

SHIACH James George   BSc(eng) 1945 BSc(agr) 1950
  F Inst Agr E JP 1969
part-time sen lect agr Aberd from 1969; chmn eng/farm bldgs group Aber s of Agr from 1969

SHIACH William Geddes   MB ChB 1943
  Cook hosp Gisborne NZ: surg supt from 1958, visiting surg from 1963

SHIACH William Lorimer   MA 1911
  d Aber 12.4.61 *AUR* XXXIX 202

SHIACH Wilma Janet   MA 1944
  teacher Tillydrone p s Aber from 1954

SHIELDS Michael Anthony   MB ChB 1954
  g p: Inverurie 1958–60, Bucksburn 1960–61, Wrexham Denbighsh from 1961
m Aber 9.9.60 Valerie E. R. Birkbeck MA 1956 *qv*

SHILLAND John Kirkcaldy Murray   BSc(agr) 1952
  farm. nr Dun from 1954

SHILLINGFORD Dorian Cleophas   MB ChB 1954

SHINNIE Andrew James   MB ChB 1908 ᶜMD 1912
  d Twickenham –.5.63 *AUR* XL 199

SHINNIE or Shaw, Ann   MA 1909
  d Minehead 9.1.62 *AUR* XXXIX 377

SHIRRAS Joan   MA 1918
  resid Sevenoaks
d 1981

SHIRRAS or Philip, Kathleen Janet   MA 1943
  resid Eaglesham Glasg

SHIRRAS or Gray, Ruth Georgina Patricia   MA 1942
  resid Glasg

SHIRREFFS Helen Catherine   MA 1955 LLB 1957
  leg asst Guild & Guild WS Edin 1966–68; part time

man. Chamber of Commerce Dorval Quebec 1972–75
m Aber 29.7.60 Robert Bain BSc 1956 *qv*

SHIRREFFS James Gordon   MB ChB 1945
  g p Barrow-on-Soar nr Loughborough from 1948

SHIRREFFS or Campbell, Mary Annella
                              MB ChB 1947
  gp/anaest Loughborough from 1952

SHIRREFFS Percy Charles Brand   MB ChB 1931
  comp dir from 1945; resid Lodsworth nr Petworth

SHIVAS Alice   MA 1927
  retd 1968; resid Aber

SHIVAS Andrew Armitage
              MB ChB 1944 DPH 1947 *MD 1955
  TD 1965 FRCSE 1970 FRCPath 1971
sen lect Edin from 1959

SHIVAS Isobel Blanche Armitage   MB ChB 1951
  regist anaest Edin 1962–63 REHSC 1963–67; part-
time anaest Scot. borders hosps Melrose from 1967
m Aber 20.4.63 Stuart C. L. Barber BSc(for)(Edin) for.
consult. s of Arthur L. B. Heckmondwike Yorks

SHIVAS or Walker, Mary Grant   BSc 1949 *1950
  resid Benton N'cle-u-Tyne

SHORTT Henry Edward
            MB ChB 1910 ᶜMD 1936 DSc 1937 LLD 1952

SHRIMPTON Derek Howard   PhD 1954

SHU Hou Jen (Suvoong Cornelius Agnew)
            MA 1900 MB ChB 1903 DPH 1904 MD 1908
  d –.10.51

SIBBALD James Gray   MA 1950 LLB 1953
  prin solic Livingston dev corp from 1966

SILBERGH Alexander Edward
                              MA 1949 MB ChB 1956
  g p Buckie from 1961
m Aber 17.8.62 Anne B. Hutchison midwife d of
Gordon Hutchison MB ChB 1927 *qv*

SILBERGH Michael   BSc(eng) 1944 *1947

SILLARS Alexander   MB ChB 1950
  sen ptnr Sillars Crane & Brummitt Malmesbury
from 1972

SILVER Cyril John   MB ChB 1935 DPH 1939
  deceased

SILVER Douglas   *MA 1933
  teacher: prin mod lang Aboyne acad 1968–74; retd
councillor Mid Deeside Commun Council 1977, chmn
1978

SILVER Gerald Bain   MA 1929

SILVER or Shivas, Isabel Margaret   MA 1953

SILVER Kathleen Mary   MA 1946
  deceased

SILVER Rona McLaren   MA 1954
  teacher Edin

SIM Alfred Gall   MA 1910
  no longer on GC reg

SIM Arthur Henri   BSc(agr) 1923 BSc 1925
  no longer on GC reg

SIM or Penwarden, Dora Penny   MA 1946

SIM Douglas   BSc(for) 1945 Dip Ed 1964
  retd Ghana 1962; for. off. UN FAO advis on for.
educ Nyabyeya, Uganda 1964–72; proj man. UN Dev
Progr for. coll proj Malaysia, Kepong, Selangor 1972–
76; consult. for. educ Orgut-Swed Forest Consortium
Ethiopia from 1976

SIM Elizabeth Shand   MA 1908
  no longer on GC reg

SIM George   BSc(mech eng) 1944; BSc(civ eng) 1948
  MICE 1970
various apptmts UK/abroad with eng consult.
sen resid eng on construct. of new chem plant in Libya
from 1977
m Villablino León Spain 11.10.61 Aurora R. Alonso
MIL(Lond) lang teacher

SIM George   BSc 1952 *1953
  teacher sc/spec asst chem Fraserburgh acad 1957–
72; prin chem Lochaber h s Fort William from 1973
m Aber 4.4.61 Margaret M. Pennie radiogr d of Alfred
G. P. Aber

SIM John Wood   *MA 1947
  prin teacher Engl Fraserburgh acad from 1964

SIM John Wyness   *MA 1932
  MSc(Lond) 1967
C.O. RAF s of educ Uxbridge 1960–63; chief instr
basic stud. RAF tech coll Henlow 1963–64
m Mary J. Disbrey; wife *d* 19.1.79

SIM or Waugh, Marjorie Elizabeth   MA 1937

SIM or Fraser, Mary Badenoch   MA 1936
  resid Glasg
husb *d* 23.8.67
m(2) Paisley 24.8.76 William D. Buchanan comp dir
s of John S. B. Mauchline

SIM or Edwards, Mary Jane Forbes   BSc 1944
  resid Brechin

SIM or Littlejohn, Phyllis Margaret   MA 1949
  resid Ealing Lond

SIM Robert Stephen   *MA 1953
  prin teacher hist: Thurso h s 1961–66, Inverurie
acad 1966–74; advis hist Aber city 1974–75, Grampian
reg from 1975

SIM Stuart Anderson   MA 1919 BSc 1921
retd 1962; resid Wolverhampton
d 26.3.74

SIMMERS Forbes   MB ChB 1916
d 11.11.62

SIMMERS John Sandison   MB ChB 1935
g p Keith 1946–76; retd

SIMMERS or Bulkley, Williamina Isabella   BSc 1933
d Douglas I of M 27.12.75 *AUR* XLVI 417

SIMMINS or Slater, Mary Chalmers   MA 1938
lib s of nurs Royal Masonic hosp Lond 1966–75;
visitor Anchor Housing Assoc from 1975

SIMMONDS Trevor Henry   MA 1949
LTCL(TEFL) 1971
lect TEFL coll of comm Aber from 1963

SIMON John Hood   MA 1952 LLB 1956
nat serv Lond 1956–58; solic: Aber 1958–61, Inv
1961–67; asst secy (leg.) Aberd from 1967
m St And 23.6.67 Vida A. Skinner MB ChB(St And)
med pract d of David S. Wormit-on-Tay

SIMPSON Agnes Teresa   MA 1913
no longer on GC reg

SIMPSON Alan Walter   MB ChB 1953
FRCP(C) 1973
Canada: h o anaest gen hosp St John's Newfoundland
1958–59, McG univ hosps Montreal 1959–61; staff
anaest Kitchener-Waterloo St Mary's hosps Kitchener
Ontario from 1961 and chief of anaest St Mary's hosp
Kitchener 1972–76
m Montreal 20.5.60 Elizabeth S. Stewart RGN d of
John S. Law Lanarksh

SIMPSON Albert Allan   MB ChB 1925
Canada: g p Midland Ont 1961–64, Lower Sackville
Nova Scotia 1964–72
d Digley Nova Scotia 20.9.75 *AUR* XLVI 323

SIMPSON Alexander   BSc(agr) 1923

SIMPSON Alexander Bruce   MA 1954 *BSc 1957
PhD
Johannesburg: mine geol 1959–61, temp lect geol univ
Witwatersrand 1961, res worker econ geol res unit
1962–65, min nat inst metallurgy 1965–70 (study tour
univs etc Aust/USA/Europe 1966–67), chief min Brick
corp of S. Af. 1970–72; Cape Town: meteorite res
off./PhD stud. univ of Cape Town from 1972

SIMPSON Alexander George   BCom 1923
d Aber 3.11.66 *AUR* XLII 86

SIMPSON, Alexander Malcolm   MA 1929
retd 1973; resid Selkirk
wife *d* 7.7.73

SIMPSON or Houghton, Anne
                              MB ChB 1918 DPH 1920
d Banchory 5.1.64 *AUR* XL 399

SIMPSON or Payne, Annie   *MA 1913
d Fochabers 12.9.77

SIMPSON Beatrice Weir   MA 1913 *BSc 1917
resid Aber
d 14.2.81 *AUR* XLIX 135

SIMPSON Brian   BSc 1955
prin teacher maths: Kaimhill s s Aber 1966–71,
Kincorth acad 1971–74; asst head Northfield acad
Aber 1974–79, dep rector Westhill acad Skene from
1979
m Bieldside 28.12.68 Alice S. T. Watson law off.
cashier d of Thomas W. Aber

SIMPSON Charles Gregor   MA 1929 LLB 1931
NCB: dir gen staff 1957–67, pers consult. 1967–71;
retd; member nat staff comm of NHS 1967–70;
member chmn's panel civ serv selection board 1970–
77; resid Moreton-in-Marsh

SIMPSON Charles Harvey   *MA 1914
retd 1956; resid Edin 1956–74, Cheltenham from
1974
wife *d* 18.3.74
d Cheltenham 14.12.79

SIMPSON Colin Finlayson   MA 1906 *MB ChB 1910
d Aber 2.6.64 *AUR* XL 394, XLI 145

SIMPSON David   MA 1910 BSc(agr) 1912
d Jersey 19.1.76 *AUR* XLVI 414

SIMPSON Douglas Alexander Dunningham
                                         MA 1930
d 18.1.73

SIMPSON Elizabeth Margaret Murray
                                     MB ChB 1937
retd 1973; resid Carlisle

SIMPSON or McKenzie, Elma Moira   MB ChB 1948
med asst Craig Phadrig hosp for m/ph patients Inv
from 1969

SIMPSON Eric John   *MA 1952 Dip Ed 1953
prin teacher hist Hawick h s 1962–66; lect hist
Moray House coll of educ Edin from 1966

SIMPSON Ernest   BSc(eng) 1939
d 1960

SIMPSON Frank Douglas   MA 1890
d 24.5.62 *AUR* XL 73

SIMPSON George   MA 1949
branch man. Aber savings bank from 1972

SIMPSON George Donald   BSc(agr) 1938
MBE 1970
DAFS from 1939; resid Keith

SIMPSON Graham Robertson   *MA 1955

SIMPSON or Mullan, Helen Macdonald   *MA 1941

SIMPSON Henry Stewart   MA 1927
d Garmouth 3.5.67 *A UR* XLII 367

SIMPSON Ian Catto   MB ChB 1936

SIMPSON Ian James
     *MA 1920 MEd 1922 PhD 1942
retd 1962; resid Edin
wife *d* 3.5.68
d Edin 11.1.81

SIMPSON Ian Laing   MA 1954
prin sc teacher Kinross h s from 1964

SIMPSON James Morrison   MA 1927
 OBE 1960
solic Stewart & Watson Banff from 1965
d Banff 26.7.74 *A UR* XLVI 109

SIMPSON Jeffrey Randal   PhD 1955

SIMPSON or Brittain, Jenny Hay Anderson
       MB ChB 1921
 d Oldmeldrum 7.2.64 *A UR* XL 399

SIMPSON Jessie Mary   *MA 1911
d Edin 10.12.67 *A UR* XLII 350

SIMPSON John   BSc(eng) 1945
teacher sc/maths Gordon s Huntly 1962–65; prin sc
Lossiemouth h s 1965–73, dep rector from 1973
d Lossiemouth 21.2.76

SIMPSON John Alexander   *MA 1913
retd; resid Edin
d 1978

SIMPSON Joseph William   MA 1947 Dip Ed 1948
head: Stonehaven p s 1968–71, Arduthie p s Stonehaven from 1971

SIMPSON or Kiddie, Lilias Innes Anderson
      MA 1916 BSc 1920
 resid Dun

SIMPSON Lizzie Helen Barbara   MA 1907
d Aber 30.5.65 *A UR* XLI 146

SIMPSON or Simpson, Muriel Dohm   *MA 1920
d Oxford 3.5.68 *A UR* XLII 359

SIMPSON Norman Charles
      MB ChB 1921 *MD 1927
d Edin 12.12.67 *A UR* XLII 359

SIMPSON Peter McGregor   *MA 1935
head Torphins p s 1967–76; retd; resid Old Meldrum

SIMPSON Robert Hamilton McColm   BSc(eng) 1947

SIMPSON Ronald George   MB ChB 1943 *MD 1949
 FRCPE 1969 FRCP(Lond) 1975
lect geriatric med Dund from 1954

SIMPSON Ronald Ian   *MA 1948

SIMPSON Sheila May   MA 1955
teacher Skene Sq p s Aber 1963–74, asst head
Ashley Road p s Aber from 1974

SIMPSON or Low, Vera Catherine   MA 1949
teacher Engl: Queen Anne's s Dunfermline 1950–51,
Larkhall acad 1951–52; Griffith NSW Aust: teacher
Fr/head of lang dept cath h s 1965–75, i/c teaching
Engl as second lang to migrant ch cath h s 1976; retd

SIMPSON Walter Murray   *BSc(eng) 1953
oper eng commissioning dept EE Co Hinkley Point
'A' power stat 1961–64; dep chief comm eng comm
dept NDC Sizewell power stat 1964–67; chief comm
eng: BNDC Wylfa power stat 1967–73, chief comm
eng NPC Hartlepool AGR power stat from 1973

SIMPSON William Douglas
     *MA 1919 DLitt 1924 LLD 1960
 d Aber 9.10.68 *A UR* XLIII 24, 27

SIMPSON William John   BSc 1952

SIMPSON William Nightingale   MB ChB 1924
retd 1964; resid Melrose

SINCLAIR Alexander   *MA 1933
prin teacher classics Milne's h s Fochabers 1936–74,
dep rector from 1961; retd 1974

SINCLAIR Alistair   MB ChB 1955
DIH(Soc of Apoth) 1962
m o United Steel Co., Sheffield 1960–66; sen m o Brit
Steel Corp Ebbwvale 1967–73, group sen m o BSC
Scunthorpe from 1974

SINCLAIR Andrew David   MB ChB 1926
d 1974

SINCLAIR or Noble, Barbara Anne Mabel (Lady)
       MA 1937
 resid Nairn

SINCLAIR or Low, Catherine   MA 1925
no longer on GC reg

SINCLAIR David   BSc(agr) 1926
JP 1942
farm. Nigg Aber from 1967; retd; resid Aber

SINCLAIR or Mitchell, Ellen Carey   MA 1913
no longer on GC reg

SINCLAIR Frances Mary Grace   MB ChB 1921
d Walsall 29.5.66 *A UR* XLI 339

SINCLAIR George Alexander   *MA 1949 *MEd 1952
 FEIS 1975
prin teacher Engl/hist/geog Powis acad Aber 1961–65;
dep head Northfield acad Aber 1965–67; head Powis
acad from 1967

SINCLAIR George Murdoch   MB ChB 1942
part-time consult. radiol Tunbridge Wells hosp
man. comm from 1953

SINCLAIR or Robertson, Helen Slater   **MA 1951**

SINCLAIR Henry Macgregor   **MB ChB 1930**
retd 1969

SINCLAIR Ian Hunter   **BSc 1954**
teacher maths Aber coll of comm from 1962
m Aber 8.8.62 Violet M. Stockan teacher d of John
W. S. Aber

SINCLAIR Ian Wayman   **MB ChB 1947**
MFCM 1972
sen m o East Riding Yorks and Humberside from
1969

SINCLAIR or Goodlad, Isabel   **MA 1928**
d –.8.64

SINCLAIR Isobel Russell   **MA 1927**
retd 1968; resid Elgin

SINCLAIR or Lowe, Jean   **MA 1930**
d –.5.40

SINCLAIR or Robertson, Jean Boyes Wilson
            *MA 1931
retd 1969; resid Limuru Kenya
husb d 1974

SINCLAIR or McConnachie, Jessie   **MA 1930**

SINCLAIR Joan May   ***MA 1951**
teacher geog Peterhead acad from 1960

SINCLAIR John Henry   **MA 1955 Dip Ed 1956**
teacher Laurencekirk s s from 1959

SINCLAIR Magnus   ***BSc 1954**
teacher Hawick h s from 1967

SINCLAIR Margaret Macpherson
            MA 1917 BSc 1925
d Aber 30.9.61 *AUR* xxxix 280

SINCLAIR or Noble, Mary Bella   **MA 1937**

SINCLAIR Mary Elizabeth   **BSc 1921**
Dingwall acad: prin teacher biol 1962–63, woman
advis 1955–63; retd
d Inv 16.5.78 *AUR* xlvii 356

SINCLAIR or Babcock, Nita (Yuanita) Mary
            *MA 1928
retd 1971; resid NY

SINCLAIR or Wilson, Norah Boyes   ***MA 1933**
resid South Ascot

SINCLAIR Robert David   **PhD 1932**
no longer on GC reg

SINCLAIR Ronald McKerron   **MB ChB 1949**

SINCLAIR Wilfred George   **MA 1935**
d Aber 20.8.77

SINCLAIR William Dawson
            MB ChB 1943 DPH 1953
sen m o health dept Nott 1965–70; med asst
Glenfrith hosp Leic from 1970
m Ashford Kent 17.11.56 Lucy J. Moryson MEd
(Loughborough) lect d of Richard M. Wesel Germany

SINCLAIR William James   **BSc(agr) 1921**
no longer on GC reg

SINCLAIR William Roy   ***MA 1934**

SINGER Dennis Lewis   **BSc 1947 *1948**
teacher: asst head Lochaber h s Fort William from
1972

SINGER Roland Charles   ***MA 1932**
Dunoon g s: respons asst mod lang/i/c Ger dept
from 1958, dep rector from 1963
d Dunoon 13.7.75

SINGH-SONDHI Gurcharan   **BSc(for) 1927**
no longer on GC reg

SINGLETON Alfred Cahoon Bruce   **MB ChB 1939**
d Vancouver 30.12.75

SINGLETON or Basil, Neith Lucy Bruce
            MB ChB 1941
m(2) Coats

SINTON Eric John   **MB ChB 1951**
FRCS(C) 1972
Alberta Canada: ophth surg Red Deer/active staff
Red Deer reg hosp centre, chief of staff Red Deer reg
hosp centre; pres Ophthalmological Society of Alberta

SIVELL or Stowell, Elspeth Dolores   ***MA 1948**

SIVEWRIGHT Mary   **MA 1914**
d Aber 27.7.62 *AUR* xl 83

SIVEWRIGHT Robert Troup   **MA 1902**
no longer on GC reg

SKAKLE George Scott   **MA 1942**
C of S min Powis parish ch Aber from 1947
m Aber 15.4.67 Kathleen Duncan med secy d of
George D. Aber

SKEA Andrew James   **BSc(agr) 1932**

SKEA Edith Margaret   **MB ChB 1948**
resid m o House of Daviot Inverurie from 1950
m Aber 26.4.68 James D. Conway marine eng/SRN
s of James B. C. Coatbridge

SKELTON or Tosh, Eileen Joan   **BSc 1949**

SKENE or Grant or Williams, Annie Pirie   **MA 1935**

SKENE George   **BSc(eng) 1948**
CEng FIMechE
chief proj eng Foster Wheeler Reading from 1955

SKENE Macgregor   *BSc 1909 DSc 1914
  d 8.8.73 *AUR* xlv 316

SKENE Norman Hay   BL 1951

SKENE Ronald Fraser   MA 1930
  JP(Aber) 1961
permanent EEC exec delegate for Federation of British
Port Wholesale Fish Merchants' Associations
d Aber 26.3.74 *AUR* xlv 448

SKENE William John   BSc(eng) 1949

SKINNER Adam Gordon   MA 1924 BCom 1925
  OBE 1965
retd HMIS 1946; cler educ advis off. Edin 1967–70;
retd; resid Aber

SKINNER Alexander Hugh
                 MA 1903 *MB ChB 1907 *MD 1909
  d Auckland NZ 21.10.62 *AUR* xl 75

SKINNER Alfred   BSc 1952
  sen lect maths Aber tech coll 1965–69, head of
maths dept from 1969
m(2) Aber 23.6.72 Diane A. D. Wilmot lect gen stud.
dept Aber tech coll d of Thomas E. W. BSc(Glas)
Strathaven

SKINNER Anne   MA 1926
  retd 1971; resid Fordyce

SKINNER David   MB ChB 1924
  d Burnley 22.8.67 *AUR* xlii 185 & 364

SKINNER Henry Gray   MB ChB 1938
  DIH 1963 O(brother) St J 1969
DADAH hq Rhine dist Germany 1954–56; dem army
health RAM coll 1957; DADAH hq BFAP Aden
1957–58; DADAH War Office Lond 1958–61; asst
prof army health RAM coll 1961–63; consult. army
health 1964; ADAH Malaya 1964–66; prof army
health RAM coll 1966–70; DDAH Army Strategic
Comm 1970–72; retd rank of col; resid Conon Bridge

SKINNER James Beattie   *MA 1934
  OBE 1960 FEIS 1966
head Dalkeith h s 1961–74

SKINNER James Mackintosh   *MA 1955
  PhD(Kent) 1972
asst prof Brandon univ Canada 1965–73, asst prof
from 1973
m Aber 5.7.61 Hazel D. E. Barclay BSc 1960 *qv*

SKINNER James Sutherland   *MA 1936

SKINNER Jean   MA 1916
  d 18.11.72

SKINNER John   MA 1914 MB ChB 1919 DPH 1920
  d Jarrow 2.12.61 *AUR* xxxix 278

SKINNER Julia   MA 1909
  no longer on GC reg

SKINNER Leslie Clark   MB ChB 1950

SKINNER or Elliot, Margaret   MA 1928
  d 27.11.60

SKINNER Mary Louisa   MA 1925
  d 4.7.66

SKINNER Rowland Gordon Chalmers
                                   BSc(eng) 1942

SKINNER Silvester   MA 1938
  C of S min: Gardenstown 1961–72, Lumphanan
from 1972; retd; resid Banchory

SKROCZYNSKI or Szamocki, Jamna Zofia Maria
                                   MB ChB 1950

SLATER Alice Lawtie   MA 1923
  retd 1964; resid Portknockie

SLATER or Merson, Ann Cowie   MA 1953
  teacher Christian Brothers' coll Springs S Af 1966–
67; resid Buckie

SLATER August Henry Klie   *MA 1939
  on staff DTI Lond from 1964; Egypt explor soc:
hon treas from 1962, governor GB/E Europe centre
1968–78

SLATER David   *BSc 1955
  PhD(Leeds) 1965
res schol inst of Af geol Leeds 1961–65; geol Hunting
Geol/Geophysics Elstree 1965–66; sen scient off. inst
of geol sciences Lond 1966–69, prin scient off. 1969–75,
sen prin scient off. from 1975
m Manc 9.3.63 Margaret Morrell teacher d of Harold
M. Manc

SLATER Fife   MB ChB 1904
  d Germiston Transvaal 16.7.65 *AUR* xli 237

SLATER George Phimister   *BSc 1954
  PhD(Belf) 1961
Saskatoon Canada: post-doct fell. chem dept univ
Sask 1961–62, res off. Prairie reg lab, nat res council
from 1962

SLATER Helen Pirie   MA 1948
  teacher geog Buckie h s from 1962

SLATER Ira George   BSc(eng) 1945

SLATER Jeannie   MA 1936
  d Buckie 7.6.68 *AUR* xliii 85

SLATER or Mearns, Jessie   MA 1925
  d 26.5.77

SLATER John   MB ChB 1941
  g p Middlesbrough from 1946
d Yarm Cleveland 15.4.79 *AUR* xlviii 353

SLATER John   BSc 1954 *MA 1956
  marketing res Vancouver 1963–74; Policy Legis-

lation and Plan. Branch Min of Consumer and Corporate Affairs Victoria BC from 1975

SLATER John Cormack   *MA 1912 *BSc 1913
no longer on GC reg

SLATER Margaret   *MA 1953
secy/res asst to Sir Harold Mitchell Bt Geneva 1960–62
m Aber 30.4.62 Matthias H. Luchsinger textile eng s of Hermann L. Zürich

SLATER William   *MA 1936
d 13.3.73

SLATER William   MB ChB 1940
g p Nott from 1967

SLEIGH or Gillies, Agnes Mary   MB ChB 1945
d 1973

SLEIGH Frederick Roberts   MB ChB 1923
retd 1960; resid Biggar
d Biggar 5.7.79 *AUR* xlviii 351

SLEIGH Gordon Fraser   MA 1947

SLEIGH James Charles   MB ChB 1918 DPH 1931
d Harpenden 17.6.65 *AUR* xli 149

SLEIGH John   MB ChB 1940
m o h S Herefordsh from 1968; resid Ross-on-Wye

SLEIGH or Miller, Lesley Margaret   BSc 1955 *1956
resid Banchory

SLEIGH Rona   MA 1947

SLESSOR Donald Munro   MB ChB 1950
g p Aber from 1956

SLESSOR or Nutten, Dorothy   MA 1944
resid Aber

SLESSOR Isabel Mary   *MA 1929
retd 1971; resid Bridge of Allan
d Milnathort 25.1.81

SLESSOR James George   MA 1899
d 25.7.66 *AUR* xli 335

SLESSOR Robert Stewart   MB ChB 1935

SLORACH Albert Robert   MA 1938
MBE 1976
head Kinloss p s from 1946; retd 1978
wife *d* 26.8.76

SLORACH or McLachlan, Elizabeth   MA 1923
retd 1967; resid Helensburgh

SLORACH John   BSc 1929 MB ChB 1937
consult. psychiat Carlton Hayes hosp Leic 1951–72; member mental health review tribunal 1960–72; consult. psychiat emeritus Leic from 1972

SMAILES or Alp, Grace Elizabeth   *MA 1940
head lang Wanganui girls' coll NZ from 1965

SMALL or McCrea, Catherine Isabella   *MA 1918
deceased

SMART Alexander   MA 1918 PhD 1938 DD 1954
d Prestwick 8.7.65 *AUR* xli 150

SMART Annie Margaret   MA 1930
head Engl dept Hammersmith polytech Wilts 1939–45; res for M of Educ Wilts 1945–47; sen mistress Bath coll of tech 1947–54; head Peckham s Lond 1954–68; retd; resid Dulwich

SMART Christina Mary   MA 1930

SMART David Gordon   BL 1903

SMART Evelyn   *MA 1924
retd 1961; resid Langholm

SMART James Duncan   BCom 1924
d 18.10.70 *AUR* xliv 211

SMART or Clay, Margaret Caldwell Cathro   MA 1953
teacher: Northside inf s Canberra 1966–72, mistress i/c Canberra gr inf s from 1973

SMART Mary Edith   MA 1955
teacher: Blairgowrie 1956–59, Nairn 1959–60, Bankfoot 1960–61, Toronto from 1970
m Nairn 4.7.60 Ivan Haggart pres construct. comp s of James C. H. Stanley Perthsh

SMART Robert Arthur   MB ChB 1936
MRCP(Lond) 1965 FRCP 1977
dep chief m o Supreme HQ Allied Powers Europe 1960–62; dep dir army health BAOR 1962–64; dir army health M o D 1964–68; dir med serv: Far East Land Forces 1968–70, BAOR 1970–71; retd maj gen 1972; Esso Petr Co: sen m o 1972–75, chief m o from 1975; retd 1979
m Lond 6.12.47

SMART Robert Milne   MA 1914 BSc 1921
no longer on GC reg

SMART William Gerald   MB ChB 1942
Tanganyika: malaria lab Amani 1951–52; dist m o Shinyanga Tabora Mbulu 1952–61, sen m o W Lake Province 1961–63; Perth W Aust: Commonwealth dept health 1963–68, sen m o dept health 1968–72; sen m o dept soc secur from 1972; med counsellor dept health 1978
m Tranent 18.3.43 Alice M. Bannerman

SMIT Henry   MB ChB 1906
no longer on GC reg

SMITH Agnes Macdonald   BSc 1924 *BSc 1925
d West Wickham 28.1.66 *AUR* xli 245

SMITH Agnes Mary   MA 1908
d Turriff 30.8.73 *AUR* xlv 316

SMITH Alan   BL 1931
d Aber 13.2.65 *AUR* xli 152

SMITH Alasdair McIntyre   MB ChB 1920
(foundation) MRCGP
retd 1973; resid Camborne Cornwall
d Camborne 5.11.79 *AUR* xlviii 351

SMITH Alex John   *MA 1952
sec British Ports Assoc Lond from 1969

SMITH Alexander   MA 1902
no longer on GC reg

SMITH Alexander   MB ChB 1911

SMITH Alexander   MA 1929
retd 1968; resid Aber

SMITH Alexander Edmond   *MA 1926
d Dunoon 8.2.73 *AUR* xlv 226

SMITH Alexander James   MA 1936
SSC Edin 1961; ptnr Lindsay Duncan & Black WS
Edin from 1961
d Edin 18.10.78

SMITH Alexander James   MB ChB 1953
g p Brighton from 1958

SMITH Alexander John   MA 1943

SMITH Alexander John Vincent   MA 1905
d 16.1.70 *AUR* xliii 440

SMITH Alexander Johnstone Cameron   MA 1929
acct Aber 1929–40, Lond 1940–74; retd 1974; resid
Cobham

SMITH Alexander Mair   MA 1944 *1948 PhD 1952
KB 1975
Rolls Royce Derby: head adv res 1959–67, dir/chief
scient 1967–69; dir Manc polytech from 1969

SMITH Alexander Souter   BL 1946

SMITH Alexander Will Hampton   MA 1954

SMITH Alexandra Gordon   MB ChB 1954

SMITH Alfred James   *MA 1905 DLitt 1919
d Aber 15.2.62 *AUR* xxxix 374

SMITH Alfred Nicoll   *MA 1938
d 28.10.75

SMITH Alick Drummond Buchanan
see Buchanan-Smith

SMITH Alison Elizabeth   MA 1951

SMITH Allan Keppie   BSc(eng) 1953
CEng 1963 FIMechE 1975 FIWeldE 1975
Dip Man. St(Strath) 1966
Babcock & Wilcox Renfrew: facilities eng 1963–66,
indust eng man. 1966–74; prod. dir 1974–77, man. dir
from 1977
m Paisley 2.9.65 Mary B. Love typist d of James L.
Paisley

SMITH Andrew Ross   BSc(eng) 1952
gen man. A. Hall & Son (concrete) Aber 1965–67;
man. dir A. Hall & Son/George W. Bruce Aber 1967–
69; man. dir Aber Concrete Co from 1969
wife d –.10.72

SMITH or Frain, Annabella   *MA 1932

SMITH Anne-Leslie Armstrong Leonard
see Leonard-Smith

SMITH or Allan, Anne Mary   MB ChB 1930

SMITH Archibald   MA 1955
dep head Ashley Road s Aber from 1972
m Aber 24.12.59 Sheila Benzies nurs nurse d of Harry
B. Aber

SMITH Archibald James   *BSc(eng) 1943

SMITH Arthur Forbes   MA 1919
d 21.9.66 *AUR* xli 338

SMITH Audrey Fraser   BSc 1955 *1956
teacher sc Aber h s for girls/Harlaw acad from 1958

SMITH Benjamin Butler   *MA 1936
dir of educ Kincardinesh 1961–75; retd; teaching
Engl in Italy 1975–78

SMITH Bernard Hooper   *MB ChB 1940 *MD 1956
FRCP(Lond) 1965 FRCP(C) 1972 FRCPsych 1973
prof neurol State univ of NY at Buffalo s of med NY
from 1953

SMITH Bryan Taylor   MA 1939
head Airyhall p s Aber 1964–80; retd

SMITH Charles   *BSc(agr) 1955
DSc(Edin) 1976
anim breeding res organis(ARC) Edin 1958–68 and
from 1974; dept human genetics Edin 1968–74

SMITH Christina   MA 1929
spec asst maths Nicolson inst Stornoway 1942–68;
retd

SMITH or Lister, Christina Wilson   MA 1927
no longer on GC reg

SMITH Cyril Moore   *MB ChB 1904
no longer on GC reg

SMITH David   BSc(agr) 1952
farm. Arbroath from 1956

SMITH David Drummond   MA 1904
no longer on GC reg

SMITH David Flett   MB ChB 1935
FRCOG 1961
assoc lect obst/gyn N'cle from 1971

SMITH David Taiwan   MA 1900
d 23.10.62

SMITH or Arnaud, Dena Isabella
                        MA 1943 *MEd 1951
teacher Perth, Alyth 1952–54; asst educ psych
Banffsh from 1972

SMITH Donald   MA 1942

SMITH Donald   MA 1949
head Airidhantuim s Shader Is of Lewis from 1965

SMITH Donald Sinclair   MB ChB 1929 MD 1957
no longer on GC reg

SMITH or Reid, Dorothea Thomson   MA 1929
farm. Peterhead from 1947
husb *d* 29.6.62

SMITH Dorothy Aiken   MA 1926
no longer on GC reg

SMITH or Watson, Dorothy Jane Moir   MA 1929
teacher: Engl/maths/hist Mzuza s s Nyasaland
1960–62, Engl Blantyre comm coll 1962–64; Engl/
maths/hist/relig educ Aberfoyle s s 1965–70; resid
Salisbury Rhod

SMITH or Farquharson, Dorothy Margaret   MA 1926
d 7.4.75

SMITH Douglas Edward   *MA 1927 *MEd 1950
dep dir of educ Banffsh 1965–71; retd; resid Keith

SMITH Douglas William Cumming   MB ChB 1947
OBE 1972 TD 1966
g p Grays Essex from 1950; lt col City of Lond field
ambul 1964–67

SMITH Duncan Kenneth   *BSc 1952
asst dir Ont res foundation Mississauga Ontario
from 1976

SMITH or Galloway, Edith Annie   MA 1904
d Vancouver Is BC 6.3.53 *AUR* xxxix 100

SMITH Edna May   MA 1940
Aber: dep head Summerhill acad 1970–73, dep
head Harlaw acad 1973; head Hilton acad 1974–80;
retd

SMITH Edward Alexander   *MA 1924
BA(Lond) 1940
teacher classics: Bellshill acad 1925–28, Hamilton
acad 1928–38, AGS 1938–41; prin classics Dumfries
acad 1941–56; edit: printing firm Alva 1959–62, Oliver
& Boyd Edin 1962–70; retd

m Cults 2.8.44 Isabella L. Innes comm artist d of
John I. Aberlour

SMITH Elizabeth Helen   MA 1932

SMITH or Joss, Elizabeth Lillie Lindsay
                                MB ChB 1923
retd 1960; resid Edwalton

SMITH or Henderson, Elizabeth Margaret   *MA 1953
teacher Engl Dunfermline h s 1968–72; asst prin
Engl from 1972

SMITH or Law, Elizabeth Mary   MA 1930
retd 1967; resid Barnsley

SMITH Elizabeth Mary Geddes   MB ChB 1944
Canada: Indian health serv Edmonton 1955–59;
assoc path. Edmonton gen hosp 1963–71; private
med lab pract Edmonton from 1971

SMITH or Emslie, Elizabeth Pollock   MA 1912
d 4.10.72

SMITH or Brown, Elsie Coral   *MA 1940
teacher Elgin from 1950

SMITH or Duthie, Emily Rose Sinclair   MA 1929
teacher: Skene j s s 1953–55, part-time on relief
work 1955–69; retd; resid Aber
husb *d* 4.3.72

SMITH Emily Stevenson   MB ChB 1942

SMITH Eric Burnett   MB ChB 1942

SMITH Ethel Violet Guinevere   MB ChB 1921
d 29.1.71

SMITH or Elliott, Florence   MA 1914
resid Manitoba
d circa 1979

SMITH Frances Mildred Dorothy   *MA 1927
teacher: Kinellar 1945–54, Culter s 1954–65; retd;
resid Aber

SMITH or McLean, Frances Moira   MA 1945
teacher: Meiklerigg Crescent p s Glasg 1951–55,
Bromley Kent 1964–65; nursery teacher Edin 1966–
68; free-lance writer from 1965; council member The
Natl Children's Bureau from 1975

SMITH Francis Godfrey   BSc(for) 1949 DSc 1956
col serv/HM Overseas civ serv agr/for. dept Tabora/
Arusha Tanganyika 1949–62; W Aust dept agr i/c
apiculture and veg mapping Perth Aust 1962–74; dir
Nat Parks W Aust from 1974

SMITH Francis Taylor   MA 1955
C of S min: St Paul's ch Dunfermline from 1964;
moderator presb Dunfermline and Kinross 1973–74

SMITH George   MA 1893
no longer on GC reg

SMITH George   *MA 1929
retd; resid Methil

SMITH George   MA 1950
teacher Littleport Cambs 1961–66; head dept Hemel Hempstead 1966–69, dep head 1969–72; head Radlett 1972–78; head Garston from 1978
m Portgordon Banffsh 27.12.58 Patricia Innes

SMITH George Cameron   MA 1925
no longer on GC reg

SMITH George Carnegie
see Carnegie-Smith

SMITH George Murray Cowie   MB ChB 1939
m Bradford 20.6.40 Anne M. S. MacRae MB ChB 1939 *qv*

SMITH Gertrude Anne   *MA 1920
retd 1961; resid Turriff

SMITH Harold   *MA 1951

SMITH Helen   MA 1929

SMITH or Murison, Helen   MA 1930
d Edin 18.2.75

SMITH or Adam, Helen Ann   MB ChB 1939
g p Sheffield from 1963

SMITH or Wood, Helen Maggie   MA 1940
Banff acad: teacher Engl 1961–69 housemistress/asst prin guid/teacher Engl 1969–74, prin guid/Engl from 1974

SMITH or Mackechnie, Helen May   MA 1940

SMITH or Matheson, Helen Wilson   MA 1927
teacher inf: Annan acad 1929–32, Aber 1932–35, Glasg 1948–55; inf mistress Glasg 1955–70; retd

SMITH Helena   BSc 1926
retd 1968; resid Fraserburgh

SMITH Henry   *BSc(agr) 1952 PhD 1956
Cyanamid of G.B. Gosport: sen scient advis anim prod. 1956–69, tech man. agr prod. from 1969
m Kemnay 11.7.59 Elizabeth M. Downie teacher d of James D. Kemnay

SMITH Herbert Irving Gordon   BSc(eng) 1928
CEng MIMechE 1970
lect Glasg coll of tech 1969–75; retd

SMITH Hugh Gordon Tennant   MB ChB 1923
hon sheriff from 1964; retd 1966; resid Banff
d 15.10.80 *AUR* XLIX 67 & 136

SMITH Iain   *MA 1949
FRLS 1974   8 Arts Council awards
Oban: asst prin teacher Engl 1955–77, full time writer under name Iain Crichton Smith from 1977

m Perth 16.7.77 Donalda Logan school nurse d of Peter L. Oban

SMITH Ian Alexander   BSc 1949
teacher maths/sc: Daliburgh S Uist 1960–63, Dundee s s 1963–65, E Kilbride s s 1965–69; head dept maths/sc/phys Brisbane Aust from 1969

SMITH Ian Fyvie   BSc 1942 *1943

SMITH Ian Lewis   BSc(eng) 1935
MInstR 1960
chmn/man. dir Spark's of Aber from 1955

SMITH Ian Mackenzie   *MA 1955
housemaster Forest Hill s Lond 1964–68; dir of stud. Sir Henry Cooper h s Hull 1968–77; vice prin SE Essex Sixth Form Coll Benfleet from 1977

SMITH Ian MacLean   MA 1931
JP(Aberdeensh)
retd 1974; resid Aber

SMITH Ian Macrae   *MA 1953
head geog dept Dartford h s for boys from 1962

SMITH or Campbell, Irene   MA 1947

SMITH or Johnson, Isabel Copland   MB ChB 1903
no longer on GC reg

SMITH Isabella   MA 1926
retd 1965; resid Banff

SMITH or Bisson, Isabella Jane   MA 1917
no longer on GC reg

SMITH Isobel Marjorie   *MA 1945

SMITH Ivor Mitchell   MA 1950

SMITH James   *MA 1913 *BD 1916
d Elgin 16.7.70 *AUR* XLIV 109

SMITH James   MA 1923
d Portessie 10.4.67 *AUR* XLII 361

SMITH James Alexander   MB ChB 1929
g p Bolton from 1935

SMITH James David Maxwell   MA 1920
d Edin 5.3.69 *AUR* XLIII 211

SMITH James Donald   *MA 1939 BD 1957 DD 1978
C of S min: Cults East ch 1966–73, Auchtergaven Perthsh from 1973
Author *And All the Trumpets* 1954

SMITH James Douglas   BSc(for) 1953
Glasg: apptd to exec comm Home Timber Merch Assoc Scot. 1967, dir Robinson Dunn & Co from 1968, dir Temple Builders Market from 1972

SMITH James Edward   BSc 1926 PhD 1933
retd 1963; resid Sutton

SMITH James Gauld   MA 1946 *MEd 1949
Management Selection: dir Glasg from 1965; man. dir Lond from 1967; chmn MSL advertising serv Lond from 1970

SMITH James Grieve Murray   BSc 1949
Torry res stat Aber: higher scient off. civ serv 1958–72, sen scient off. from 1972

SMITH James Ian   MB ChB 1926
g p S Shields from 1926; resid E Bordon Co Durh

SMITH James Ross   *MA 1920
retd 1965; resid Airdrie

SMITH James William   BSc(agr) 1929
retd 1964; resid Glenrothes

SMITH Jane Cruickshank   *MA 1914
d Turriff 30.12.74 *AUR* XLVI 235

SMITH Janet Leslie   MA 1915
no longer on GC reg

SMITH or Downie, Jean Murray   BSc 1951
LTCL 1952
Aber: teacher sc Middle s 1958–63, prin sc Convent of the Sacred Heart 1963–71; Rubislaw acad: teacher phys 1971–73, asst head AGS from 1973

SMITH or Presly, Jeannie Grassie   MA 1927

SMITH Jessie Ann   MA 1926
retd 1966; resid Stonehaven

SMITH or Wattie, Jessie Beattie   MA 1942
teacher Engl Forrester s s Edin from 1963

SMITH or Cormack, Jessie Gordon   MA 1930
retd 1969; resid Newmachar

SMITH or Marsh, Joan Elizabeth   MB ChB 1949
LMCC 1955 Dip Psy(McG) 1968 CRCP(psy) 1968 FRCP(Can) 1972
Canada: fl/lt RCAF Aylmer 1952–55, h o psychiat Lond 1955–57, McG Montreal 1964–68, consult. psychiat veterans' affairs dept of nat defence RCMP Winnipeg from 1969
m Lond, Ont 24.7.54 Bernard C. Marsh commercial pilot

SMITH John   MA 1895
d 29.2.64

SMITH John   MB ChB 1915 DPH 1919 *MD 1922 DSc 1927 LLD 1965
d Aber 19.6.76

SMITH John   MA 1920

SMITH John   *MA 1930

SMITH John Anthony McCredie
                          MB ChB 1943 ᶜMD 1950
FRCOG 1960

consult. Burnley hosps from 1959
d 11.9.79 *AUR* XLVIII 353

SMITH John Charles   MA 1905
no longer on GC reg

SMITH John Couper   MB ChB 1928

SMITH John Geddes   MA 1916 *MB ChB 1918
d Aber 24.7.62 *AUR* XL 85

SMITH John Lansley   *MA 1927 BSc(eng) 1929
d Aber 9.4.65 *AUR* XLI 151

SMITH John Leslie Sidney   MA 1926
d Greenock 31.8.74 *AUR* XLVI 109

SMITH John Robertson   *MA 1952
prin mod lang/dep rector Grantown-on-Spey g s from 1965

SMITH Joseph Meston   BCom 1922
d 21.12.77

SMITH or Macpherson, Joyce Isabella   MA 1951
Canada: teacher Fr/Engl St John New Brunswick 1966–69, head mod lang dept Millidgeville N h s St John 1969–71, oral Fr dept Thunder Bay Ontario from 1971

SMITH or Blackie, Katharine Ironside   MA 1915
no longer on GC reg

SMITH or Tocher, Kathleen Mann   MA 1953
teacher Dalkeith h s 1959–63; resid Aber

SMITH or Hamilton, Kathleen Norah Ross   MA 1948
resid Wellington NZ

SMITH Kenneth   MA 1928
retd 1968; resid Back Is of Lewis

SMITH Kenneth   MB ChB 1939

SMITH Kenneth Donald   MA 1951
prod./organis Gaelic s broadcast unit Highland area (in assoc with BBC) Stornoway
m Inv 4.8.59 Rosemary Cowan hotel man. d of Douglas S. C. Rugeley

SMITH Kenneth Prahm   BSc 1949

SMITH Leslie Barnet   BSc(eng) 1952
teacher Baltasound Shetland from 1956

SMITH Leslie Johnston   MA 1931 LLB 1933
ptnr Clark & Wallace advoc Aber 1945–71; retd 1976; resid Anglesey
d 9.12.80 *AUR* XLIX 138

SMITH or Drew, Lilian Mary Buchanan   MA 1916
d St. Louis USA 16.10.80 *AUR* XLIX 66

SMITH Lorna   MA 1955
teacher 1960–70
m Aber 2.10.70 Charles B. Riddoch bus driver/insp

SMITH Lyndesay Raymond Duncan   MB ChB 1925
no longer on GC reg

SMITH Malcolm John Rognvald   BSc(eng) 1955
on res eng staff Livishie Works Glenmoriston 1959–61; Taylor Woodrow Construction Lond: contr eng atomic power dept 1961–62, chief eng Euston stat reconstr 1962–65, sen contr eng atomic power dept 1965–71; Rendel Palmer & Tritton Lond chief plan. eng Thames barrier proj from 1971
m Derby 23.4.60 Elizabeth M. Wallace BA(Oxon) advert copywriter, publ edit. d of Andrew M. W. Derby

SMITH or Slorach, Mara Heraughty   MA 1936
d Forres 26.8.76

SMITH or Currie, Margaret   MA 1916 *BSc 1917
resid Canberra

SMITH or Mathieson, Margaret   MA 1941

SMITH or Angus, Margaret Ann   MA 1925
resid Fintray Aberdeensh
husb d Aber 2.11.76

SMITH or Johnston, Margaret Baron   MA 1933
Enzie p s: teacher till 1963, head 1963–65; teacher Portgordon p s 1965–71; retd; resid Enzie

SMITH Margaret Campbell Gordon   MA 1942
advis primary educ Aberdeensh 1967–75, Grampian reg c from 1975

SMITH Margaret Elizabeth   MA 1932

SMITH or Gauld, Margaret Elizabeth
                                    ***MA 1948 Dip Ed 1949**
JP
teacher Fintry p s Turriff Aberdeensh 1962–63, Turriff acad: Engl 1963–71, prin Engl from 1971

SMITH Margaret Flett   MA 1927
retd 1966; resid Lerwick

SMITH or Hogarth, Margaret Isobel   MA 1928
teacher Sanquhar acad 1956–69
d Sanquhar 9.2.77

SMITH or Greig, Margaret Isobel   MA 1944

SMITH Margaret Mary   BSc 1945 MEd 1972
lect sc coll of dom sc Aber 1963–68; lect phys RGIT Aber from 1968

SMITH or Terris, Margaret Rodger   MA 1955

SMITH or Smith, Marguerette Thomson   MA 1947

SMITH Marion Coghill   MA 1929

SMITH Marshall Alexander Hosie
                                    MA 1950 *MEd 1952
ABPsS 1961

sen educ psych Far East milit command Singapore/Hong Kong 1968–71; consult. psych United World coll S.E. Asia Singapore from 1971

SMITH or Langtry, Mary   MA 1913
d Canada 26.10.73 *A UR* XLVI 107

SMITH or Trann, Mary   *MA 1922

SMITH Mary Bella   *MA 1919
no longer on GC reg

SMITH Mary Helen   MA 1943
m Nicholls

SMITH or Robertson, Mary Jane   MA 1908
no longer on GC reg

SMITH Mary Janet   MA 1928
teacher Nicolson p s Stornoway 1961–67; retd

SMITH Mary Lucy   MA 1928
FSA Scot.
retd 1969; resid Dun

SMITH Mary Milne   MA 1924
teacher Maud j s s 1956–60, Culter j s s 1960–64; retd; resid Aber
m Aber 29.7.42 Alexander S. Mather farm. s of Alexander M. Stuartfield

SMITH or Balfour, Olive Elizabeth Duthie   MA 1929
retd 1968; resid Aber

SMITH or Eady, Peggy Mairi   MA 1942
lect Engl Leicester coll of comm 1958–62; resid Aber

SMITH Peter   MA 1953
teacher Gordon s Huntly from 1957

SMITH Richard Williams   MB ChB 1948

SMITH Robert Adam   MA 1923
d Kilmarnock 27.5.68 *A UR* XLII 361

SMITH Robert Anderson   MB ChB 1949
g p Burslem from 1941; Treasury m o Burslem/Admiralty surg Stoke-on-Trent from 1944
wife d –.4.69
m(2) Leek 30.3.72 June Proctor comp dir d of Frederick G. P. Tunstall

SMITH Robert John   MB ChB 1916
no longer on GC reg

SMITH Ronald Alexander William Cochrane
                                    MB ChB 1952

SMITH Ronald Gordon Christie   BSc(agr) 1946
chief off. (Scot.) meat and livestock commission Perth from 1970

SMITH or Macdonald, Sadie Mary   BSc(agr) 1940

SMITH Sheena   MA 1953
journalist *Evening Citizen* Glasg 1960–61; teacher
Engl Kirkintilloch h s from 1972
m Aber 23.9.61 John C. Gray acct s of John R. G.
Philadelphia USA

SMITH or Duncan, Sheila   MA 1954
d Thurso 14.11.67 *AUR* XLII 375

SMITH or Presly, Sophie Caroline   MA 1941
resid Methlick

SMITH Stanley George   *MA 1936 BD 1941
spec in r e Beath h s Cowdenbeath 1956–70, prin
r e h s Peebles from 1970
d Peebles 21.7.77

SMITH Stephen Reed Naisby   MB ChB 1934
d –.6.72

SMITH or Walker, Sydney Eleanor   MB ChB 1929
g p Manc 1932–67; retd
husb *d* 21.8.69

SMITH Sydney Robertson   BSc(eng) 1933

SMITH Thomas James   MA 1926
MBE 1974
head Peterhead cent. s; retd 1970; Peterhead: provost
from 1971, chmn harbour trustees/chmn feuars from
1971; resid Aber 1978

SMITH Trevor Alexander Howard   MB ChB 1919
d 27.10.62

SMITH Trevor George   MA 1948 Dip Ed 1949

SMITH or Roger, Violet Margery Gatford
                              *MB ChB 1919 DPH 1924**
d Banff 7.9.70 *AUR* XLIV 109

SMITH Violet Mary   *BSc 1930
retd 1966; resid Glassel

SMITH William   MA 1907 BSc(agr) 1914
no longer on GC reg

SMITH William   MB ChB 1910

SMITH William   *MA 1912
d Wick 6.12.65 *AUR* XLII 84

SMITH William   BSc 1934 MB ChB 1937
d –.3.77

SMITH William Alexander   BSc(eng) 1950

SMITH William Gordon   *MB ChB 1948 *MD 1957
d Perth Aust 29.10.69 *AUR* XLIII 331

SMITH William James   *MA 1952
asst prin mod lang Hampton g s Middx 1962–66;
lect i/c lang Merton tech coll Wimbledon 1967–75,
prin mod lang Alford acad from 1975

SMITH William Kenneth   BSc(agr) 1923
emeritus prof genetics agronomy univ Wisc
retd 1965; resid Madison Wisconsin USA

SMITH William Murison   MB ChB 1928
retd 1967; resid Harrogate
d 23.3.81 *AUR* XLIX 137

SMITH William Rennie   BSc(eng) 1951

SMITH Wilma West   *BSc 1954 PhD 1958
LTCL 1960
scient off./sen scient off. Macaulay inst for soil res
Aber 1954–64; part-time curator dept geol/mineralogy
Aberd from 1973
m Aber 30.9.61 Angus Aitken BSc 1950 *qv*

SMITH Wilson Hird   MA 1926 LLB 1929
retd 1969; resid Aber

SMYLIE Henry Gordon   MB ChB 1954 *MD 1960
MRCPath 1963
sen lect Aberd hon consult. bact to NERHB from
1964

SMYLIE William Cecil Beveridge   BSc(eng) 1947
Sir Robert McAlpine: eng to ag 1949–64; Geo
Wimpey & John Laing Constr: sen ag 1964–70;
Simon Eng(Simonbuild) contr man. Manc from 1970
m Newton Mearns Ernestine A. Gaminek ch's nurse,
phlebotomist d of Josef G. W Ger

SNOOK Laurence Cecil   DSc 1939
anim prod. advis FAO Burma/Costa Rica 1963–69;
consult. FAO Latin America/Asia 1970–75; farm.
Bramley W. Aust from 1976

SNOW Charles Edward Francis Owen
                                          MB ChB 1894
no longer on GC reg

SNOWIE Robert Simpson   MB ChB 1913
d Ilkley 19.9.71 *AUR* XLIV 316

SOMERS Ernest Archibald   *BSc 1953

SOMERVILLE David Keltie   PhD 1943
rector Bathgate acad from 1954
d Edin 1.11.80

SOPER Thomas Pitt   PhD 1954
MA(Oxon) 1961
dir of stud. overseas dev inst Lond 1964–70; advis
Barclays Bank Lond from 1970
m(2) Lond 13.4.64 June E. Brown d of J. B. B. Oxford

SORLEY Anne Christina Niven   MA 1948

SORLEY or Thom, Helen Allan   MA 1917
d Aust 5.8.65 *AUR* XLI 244

SORLEY Herbert Tower   *MA 1914 DLitt 1939
d Salisbury Rhodesia 7.8.68 *AUR* XLII 353, XLV 447,
XLVI 107

SORLEY John Tower   MA 1921 MB ChB 1925
d Aber 1.4.79 *AUR* XLVIII 228

SORLEY John Tower   MB ChB 1955
d Aber 6.5.65 *AUR* XLI 154

SORRIE Alexander James Strath
                              *BSc 1951 PhD 1954
sect man. ICI petrochem div Teesside
date of marr 9.8.58

SORRIE or Skinner, Mary Ann   MA 1906
d 1969

SOUTAR Alastair James   MB ChB 1944
g p Downton Wilts from 1951

SOUTAR Charles Lewis Colby   MA LLB 1950
solic in loc govt Ayr, Perth, Dun 1966–75; chief
solic (conveyancing) Tayside reg c Dun from 1975

SOUTAR or Andrew, Ella Ann   MA 1941

SOUTAR Patricia Frances   MA 1952
supply teacher royal nat orthop hosp s Stanmore
Middx 1968–72; private tut. to dyslexic pupils Northwood from 1975
m Dun 1.6.61 Douglas D. Scott sen exec eng PO
telecom s of Robert W. S. Dun

SOUTAR Thomas   MA 1948
head Strichen s from 1962

SOUTER Alexander Wilson   *MB ChB 1937
g p Kirkland Lake Ontario from 1947
wife d –.12.67
m(2) Matheson Ont 20.9.71 Marlene A. McCabe
nurse d of Gerald McC. Kirkland Lake

SOUTER or Ritchie, Caroline Margaret
                              BSc 1938 *1940
d Elgin 4.6.74 *AUR* XLVI 110

SOUTER Edward Simpson   MA 1931 BCom 1933
FEIS 1971
prin teacher comm subj Perth acad 1949–73; retd

SOUTER or Broadhead, Elcy Cruickshank   *BSc 1942
part-time dem zool univ Leeds from 1954

SOUTER Eliza Hay   MA 1911
no longer on GC reg

SOUTER or Morgan, Evelyn Ashley   MB ChB 1945
g p Perth W. Aust from 1950

SOUTER Isabella   MA 1913
teacher math Forres acad 1933–62; retd; resid
Alves

SOUTER James   MA 1898 MB ChB 1902
no longer on GC reg

SOUTER James Callaghan   MB ChB 1921
d 3.5.61 *AUR* XXXIX 203

SOUTER James Lownie   MA 1954

SOUTER or Robbie, Jane Margaret   MA 1917
resid Aber
d Aber 27.1.80

SOUTER or Davidson, Kathleen May   MA 1926
resid Matua Tauranga NZ

SOUTER Leslie Morrison   MA 1929
teacher g tech s for boys S. Shields 1963–72; retd;
resid Whitley Bay

SOUTER or Middleton, Marjorie Mary Meredith
                              Gordon   MA 1933
resid Sunderland

SOUTER or Grimwood, Tresta Stephen   *MA 1937
retd from teaching in Kent 1974; resid N'cle-u-Tyne
husb d 1973

SOUTHERAN Margaret   MA 1954
teacher: Overdale j s Leic 1961–66, part-time Devon
from 1966
m Chesterfield 27.12.63 Alan L. Bentley headmaster
s of Harry B. Leic

SOUTHGATE Bernard Alfred   PhD 1929 DSc 1936
d 3.9.75 *AUR* XLVI 324

SOUTTER or Evans, Helen Mary   MB ChB 1948
d 29.3.74

SOUTTER James Tindal   MA 1910
no longer on GC reg

SOUTTER or Wernham, Rosemary Margaret
                              MA 1943
teacher Aber 1949; volunteer/teacher Ottawa assoc
for ment retarded 1968–69

SOUTTER William   MB ChB 1951
g p Aber 1964–74; CMP(REME) M o D from 1974

SOUTTER William Roberts   MB ChB 1925
retd 1963; resid Dunfermline
wife d 15.6.72

SPALDING or Holms, Florence Graham   MA 1941
resid Glasg

SPARK or Reive, Barbara Wilhelmina   MB ChB 1925
resid Cheadle Cheshire

SPARK Cecil Vivian   MB ChB 1923
d Mancetter 8.4.69 *AUR* XLIII 213

SPARK or Standeven, Elizabeth Mabel
                              MB ChB 1948
d 3.10.77

SPARK Gladys Agnes   MB ChB 1924
no longer on GC reg

SPARK Ian Denis   MB ChB 1951

SPARK Ian Fowlie   MA 1949

SPARK Ian Robert   *MB ChB 1921
  d Nott 2.10.74 *AUR* xLvi 236

SPARK Isabella Margaret   MA 1938

SPARK Robert Arthur   MB ChB 1951

SPEARING Antony Gustavus Byron   MA 1950
  Cert Proficiency Radio-phys(Lond) 1942
Lond: asst edit. *Process Control and Automation*
Colliery Guardian 1961–67, *Sheet Metal Journal*
Industrial Newspapers 1967–68, asst to information
eng Electrical Dev Assoc 1967–71; freelance edit., edit.
Proceedings Institute of Mechanical Engineers 1971–
73, asst edit. II British Standards Inst 1973
m Morden 4.4.62 Maria A. R. da Costa ch nurse/
teacher's aide d of Ernesto R. da C. Lisbon Portugal

SPEED Isobel   MA 1950
  Cert Soc Stud.(Glas) 1952
Sec Teacher's Cert(Vict) 1970
asst ch's off.: Dunfermline 1954–58, ch's off. Perth
1958–63; sen asst/dep ch's off. Aber 1963–65; Aust:
soc worker Vict soc welfare dept Melbourne 1965–66,
res asst Monash univ 1966–68; teacher Frankston
tech s Vict 1969–73, SW educ dept from 1973
m Frankston Vict Aust 10.3.69 Kevin Connolly

SPEIGHT Harold Edwin Balme   MA 1908 *1909
  d Victoria BC 9.8.75 *AUR* xLvi 320

SPEIRS Alexander Logan   MB ChB 1943 ᶜMD 1954
  FRCP(Lond) 1971 FRCPGlas 1971
consult. paediat Stirling RI/Falkirk RI/RHSC Glasg
from 1954

SPEIRS John Hastie   *MA 1928
  reader Engl lit Exe 1966–71; author *Poetry Towards
Novel*; retd; resid Lond
d Lond 22.3.79 *AUR* xLviii 229

SPENCE Alexander James   MB ChB 1943
  FRCSE 1968
consult. orthop surg E/W Fife from 1962

SPENCE Alexander Stewart   MB ChB 1938
  m o Leanchoil hosp Forres from 1944

SPENCE Charles Clouston   BSc 1951

SPENCE Douglas Roy   BSc(eng) 1949
  d Birm 8.7.77 *AUR* xLvii 287

SPENCE or Leese, Eileen Margaret   MB ChB 1949
  sen med regist Royal Free hosp group Lond 1956–
62, clin asst from 1962

SPENCE or Christie, Elizabeth Sylvia   *MA 1954
  secy DSIR psych res unit Aber 1961–63

SPENCE or Gray, Ida Lillian   MA 1905
  d Aber 15.10.61 *AUR* xxxix 272

SPENCE James Alexander   MA 1950

SPENCE Johanna   MA 1906
  d Aber 3.8.68 *AUR* xLiii 78

**SPENCE or Caseley, Katherine Carruthers
                              MB ChB 1922 ᶜMD 1928**
  Singapore 1929; RAMC Malaya till 1942; retd;
resid Devon

SPENCE or King, Mary Laughton   MA 1933
  teacher Hope j s s St Margaret's Hope Orkney
1958–72; retd; resid Kirkwall

SPENCE William Stewart   BSc(eng) 1929

SPIBY Thomas Dickson   MA 1939
  head Cummings Park p s Aber from 1968

SPILLER Cecil Gordon   *MA 1927
  d Kilmarnock 5.11.62 *AUR* xL 93

SPILLER Gerald Bernard   *MA 1930 LLB 1933
  d Edin 5.3.66

SPILLER Thomas Reuben   MA 1912 *1913
  d Aber 1.3.65 *AUR* xLi 149

SPRING Douglas Martin   MB ChB 1909
  no longer on GC reg

STABLES Rosabel   *MA 1922
  no longer on GC reg

STABLES William James   MA 1954

STALKER Alexander   MB ChB 1924
  d Portugal 19.5.67 *AUR* xLii 186 & 365

**STALKER Alexander Logie
                              *MB ChB 1942 *MD 1961**
  FRCPath 1970 DL county of city of Aber from 1967
Aberd: reader path. 1965–69, prof path. 1969–72,
regius prof from 1972; hon surg to HM the Queen
1963–65

STALKER or Mitchell, Ella McGregor   *MA 1918
  from 1939: youth serv club man. YWCA Nuneaton
Warks, hostel man. Northumberland/E. Sussex; stud.
hostel warden Lond; retd; resid Aber

STALKER James Stephen   MA 1912
  d Perthsh 6.1.61 *AUR* xxxix 103

STALKER John Alexander   BSc(eng) 1945

STALKER Robert   MB ChB 1951
  DPH(Leeds) 1961 MFCM(Leeds) 1971
div m o W Riding Yorks 1967–74; spec commun med
(soc serv) Doncaster AHA from 1974

STARK Walter John Kirkpatrick   MA 1908
  d 6.9.70

**STARTUP Collingwood William
                              BSc 1927 PhD 1935**
  no longer on GC reg

STEADMAN John   MA 1950 Dip Ed 1951
dep head Langlaw p s Dalkeith 1960–66; head:
Temple p s Midlothian 1966–69, Cornbank St James
p s Penicuik from 1969

STEDMAN Oliver Hall   MA 1949

STEDMOND John Mitchell   PhD 1953
FRSC 1971
Queen's univ Kingston Ont: assoc prof 1960–63, prof
1963–68, head dept of Engl 1968–77
wife *d* 1969

STEEL David   MA 1932 BD 1935 DD 1964
C of S min St Michael's ch Linlithgow from 1959
mod Gen Assembly of Ch of Scot. 1974–75

STEEL Eric Wilson   BSc 1952
teacher maths Bankhead acad Aber 1963–74; asst
prin maths Torry acad Aber from 1974

STEELE Archibald   *MA 1950
prin teacher Engl Ruthrieston s s Aber 1965–71,
dep head 1971–73, asst head Harlaw acad Aber from
1973

STEELE or Pimm, Constance Sophia   MB ChB 1923
retd 1961; resid S. Oakleigh Vict Aust

STEEN James Cameron   MB ChB 1954
g p: Blackburn Lancs 1956–63, Murrayville Vict
Aust 1963–67, Birregurra Vict from 1967

STEEN Margaret Lawson   MA 1927
no longer on GC reg

STEIN (Walter) Peter Gonville   PhD 1955
FBA 1974
dean fac of law Aberd 1961–64; regius prof civil
law/fell. Queen's coll Cantab from 1968; member
UGC 1971–75

STEINBACH Gustav Maxim   MB ChB 1933

STENHOUSE Andrew Strachan
                    BSc 1925 BSc(agr) 1927
d 26.4.72

STEPHEN Alexander   MA 1918 MB ChB 1922
d Aber 15.2.73 *AUR* xlv 224

STEPHEN Alexander   MB ChB 1941
FPsych RCP & S Can 1972
dir ch psychiat province of Sask Canada from 1970
d Saskatoon 18.5.79

STEPHEN Alexander Charles   *BSc 1919 DSc 1934
d Edin 3.6.66 *AUR* xli 338

STEPHEN Alexander Hutchison   *MA 1939
retd 1972; resid Kirkwall

STEPHEN Alexander Kynoch   MB ChB 1951
g p Redcar Yorks from 1956

STEPHEN Andrew   MB ChB 1928
s of Alexander S. farm.
Knighted 1972
g p Sheffield from 1930; chmn FA England 1967–76
d Sheffield 25.2.80 *AUR* xlviii 442 & xlix 68

STEPHEN Andrew William Phillips
                    BSc(elect. eng) 1935 (mech eng) 1936

STEPHEN Anne Margaret   MA 1953
tech asst Scot. Gas from 1953; resid Bucksburn

STEPHEN or Robertson, Annie   MA 1907
d 22.7.66

STEPHEN or Tait, Annie   MA 1945
resid Inverallochy

STEPHEN Bruce Smith   MB ChB 1951

STEPHEN David Bishop   MB ChB 1937
d Enfield 16.6.67 *AUR* xlii 186 & 371

STEPHEN Doris Leonora   MB ChB 1949
m o blood transfusion centre N'cle-u-Tyne from
1959

STEPHEN Douglas Alan   BSc 1948 *1949

STEPHEN Eleanor Elizabeth Lauder   MA 1923
teacher Finnart p s Greenock 1925–41; resid Cornhill Banffsh

STEPHEN or Innes, Elizabeth
                    MA 1913 MB ChB 1915
d Aber 9.6.69 *AUR* xliii 210

STEPHEN or Hartopp, Elizabeth Annie   *MA 1927
d Alford 26.3.71 *AUR* xliv 211

STEPHEN or Raffan, Elizabeth Mary   MA 1944
resid Forgue

STEPHEN Ella Mary Salmond   MA 1923
teacher St Stephen's coll Folkestone and Broad-
stairs 1932–62; retd; resid Aber

STEPHEN Ernest John   BSc(eng) 1943

STEPHEN or Johnston, Esther   MB ChB 1915
d Glasg 27.11.75

STEPHEN Florence   MB ChB 1937
g p Aber 1938–78; retd

STEPHEN George Allardyce   MB ChB 1937
d Enfield –.2.63 *AUR* xl 207

STEPHEN or McLeod, Helen Marr   MA 1929
teacher Fraserburgh cent s 1956–69; retd

STEPHEN Ian Trail   *MA 1946
teacher maths/asst head AGS from 1974

STEPHEN James Leiper   *MA 1952

STEPHEN James Lindsay   MA 1931

STEPHEN James Souter
*MA 1934 PhD 1936 BD 1943
C of S min Banffsh: Mortlach 1942–62, Botriphnie from 1962 and Boharm from 1971

STEPHEN or Clark, Janet Ann   MA 1950
teacher: Leicester 1963–66, Banff 1966–72; asst head Banff from 1972

STEPHEN Jean Thomson   MA 1944
infants' mistress Ashley Rd p s Aber from 1968

STEPHEN or Youngson, Jessie Kerr   MA 1909
d Aber 14.10.71 AUR xliv 316

STEPHEN John   MA 1902
no longer on GC reg

STEPHEN John   BSc(agr) 1922
no longer on GC reg

STEPHEN John Hector   *BSc 1900 *MB ChB 1902
d 24.6.63

STEPHEN John Herbert   MB ChB 1905 DPH 1920
d Aber 15.5.62 AUR xxxix 373

STEPHEN (formerly Zamory) John Joachim
MA 1948 *MEd 1958
Rossshire: sole educ psych 1963–66, prin educ psych 1966–75; reg prin educ psych Highland reg from 1975

STEPHEN John Low
MA 1931 MB ChB 1935 ᶜChM 1945
FRCS(Eng) 1968 FRSoc Med (vice-pres surg sect. from 1971)
Lond: surg St Mary's hosp from 1958/teacher in surg St Mary's hosp med s from 1950

STEPHEN John Ronald   MA 1944
teacher Elgin East End s 1954–57; some relief teaching from 1957
m Urquhart 4.3.72 Alice Petrie clerkess/typist d of James C. P. Urquhart

STEPHEN John Traill   *MA 1912
d Buckie 15.7.67 AUR xlii 182

STEPHEN or Skinner, Margaret   MA 1932
d 18.5.77

STEPHEN Margaret Agnes   MA 1938
King's coll lib Aberd: res asst 1961–71, sen lib asst 1971–77/mss and archives sect. 1969–77; retd

STEPHEN or Pirrie, Margaret Eleanor   BSc 1945
resid Turriff

STEPHEN or Noble, Mary (Lady)   *MA 1921
resid Edin

STEPHEN Mary Janet   MA 1925
no longer on GC reg

STEPHEN Mary Jean   BSc 1953
teacher sc: Inverurie acad 1959–65, Aber h s for girls (Harlaw acad) from 1965, spec asst from 1969

STEPHEN Mildred Wilken   MA 1935
Lond: secy 1936–40
m Lond 1940 Ben Smith

STEPHEN Moira Anne   MA 1951
asst dist lib N Angus from 1975

STEPHEN Norah Turner   MA 1942
Dip R Ed(Lond) 1964
teacher Wolston Coventry 1960–65, Arbroath 1965; Aber: Summerhill acad 1965–70, Harlaw acad 1971, Old Aber/Frederick St/Middle s from 1971

STEPHEN or Bain, Olive Margaret   MA 1930
resid Cults Aber

STEPHEN Robert Alexander
MB ChB 1930 MD 1933 ChM 1960
FRCS 1947 QHS 1960–67
dir surg/consult. surg to army 1959–64; substant col 1957, brig 1958, maj gen 1961; dir surg/consult. surg M o D(army) 1964–67; consult. surg Royal hosp Chelsea 1960–67; off. St John 1964, CB 1965
wife d 1972
m(2) 1977

STEPHEN Robert Alexander Nicol   *BSc 1949
teacher: phys Albyn s for girls 1961–66, prin phys Aber h s for girls (later Harlaw acad) from 1966

STEPHEN Robert John   MB ChB 1924
d Bristol 30.9.69 AUR xliii 330

STEPHEN Ronald John   MA 1944
no longer on GC reg

STEPHEN Roy Cameron   *BSc 1950 PhD 1956

STEPHEN Sheila Tyas   *MA 1946 *1947
Board of Inl Rev: spec work Somerset House from 1959; sen insp of Taxes dist insp Tunbridge Wells from 1978
m Wimbledon 2.2.71 Harry H. Leedale CBE control. Surtax Board of Inl Rev s of John L. New Malden

STEPHEN Susan   MA 1931
retd 1972; resid Rothienorman
m Aber 26.6.74 George Simpson

STEPHEN Walter Glennie   MA 1936
head Kingswells p s from 1953; retd 1975
d Aber 31.8.78 AUR xlviii 106

STEPHEN William   MB ChB 1942
MRCPsych 1971
sen m o HM prison med serv 1965–70, prin m o from 1970; resid Birm
wife d –.3.75
m(2) –.5.78 Caroline V. Cambridge

STEPHEN William Galloway Donaldson
BSc(agr) 1950

STEPHEN William Hendry   MB ChB 1923
d 18.12.73

STEPHEN William Irvine   *BSc 1950 DSc 1970
FRIC 1964 CChem 1970
Birm: sen lect chem 1966–71, reader analytical chem from 1971

STEPHEN William McLauchlan
                          MA 1931 BSc 1934
JP 1969
farm. Duffus Moray from 1938

STEPHEN William Robert   MB ChB 1940
g p Fochabers from 1946

STEPHEN or Sole, Williamina   MB ChB 1925
locum work Chester 1957–63; retd; resid Bieldside

STEPHEN (formerly Zamory) Wolfgang
                          BSc(eng) 1946

STEPHENSON Ian   *BSc(eng) 1940
eng surv off. Aber c c from 1948

STERRY John Roland   BSc(agr) 1954

STEVEN Andrew Marshall Macdonald
                          MA 1954 LLB 1955
Dip Ed(Belf) 1974
Queen's univ Belf: sen asst secy 1968–71, sen asst secy (pers)/head of pers dept 1971–73; lect humanities dept Castlereagh coll f e Belfast from 1968; area organis adult literacy proj from 1965; voluntary youth and community work in Belfast

STEVEN John   BSc(agr) 1936
asst insp DAFS from 1955; resid Watten

STEVEN Ranald Fyfe Findlay   MB ChB 1949
g p Aber from 1952

STEVEN Robert Clement   *MA 1947 LLB 1950
WS 1953 TD 1962 F Corp Insur Brokers 1970
Lond: on staff of Price Forbes & Co 1963–69, dir 1970–72; asst man. dir Sedgwick Forbes UK 1973; dep chmn Claverhouse Invest Trust 1974–77, chmn from 1977
m Lond 30.1.65 Judith C. Locker teacher d of James W. D. L. Madras India

STEVENS David Alan John   *MA 1936

STEVENS Helen Mary   *MA 1931
retd 1969; resid Uppingham

STEVENS Philip Theodore   PhD 1939
lect classics Cape Town 1938–41; war serv S Af milit intelligence 1941–45; lect Lat Liv 1945–50; prof Greek Bedford coll Lond 1950–74; emeritus prof Greek Lond 1974

STEVENSON Alexander   *MA 1938
internat bank for reconstruction and dev Washington DC from 1947

STEVENSON Douglas Ogilvie   MB ChB 1935
retd 1978; emeritus consult. venereologist S Lincs
d Penwortham Preston 15.1.81

STEVENSON Elsie Mary   MA 1929
no longer on GC reg

STEVENSON or Volpich, Hilda   MA 1925
teacher p s Dumbarton 1942–66

STEVENSON John Meikle   BSc(agr) 1953
founder/man. dir food manuf comp Bo'ness from 1962

STEVENSON Raymond William Henry   PhD 1953
sen lect nat phil Aberd 1965–69; prof phys univ of Rhodesia Salisbury from 1969

STEVENSON Walter Freeman   BL 1949
hon sheriff 1971
solic Thornhill from 1954

STEWART or Kerr, Agnes Mary   MA 1936
resid Laurencekirk

STEWART Aileen Keith   MA 1947
head: Torridon p s 1964–66, Raemoir p s 1966–68, Maryculter E p s from 1968

STEWART Albert James   *MA 1930 BSc 1931
dep dir of educ Argyll 1961–73; retd; resid Dunoon
d 21.6.78

STEWART Alexander   MA 1913
d Aber 1.12.61 *AUR* xxxix 275

STEWART Alexander   MB ChB 1946
g p Chapel-en-le-Frith from 1954

STEWART Alexander Boyd
        MA 1925 BSc 1927 *1928 PhD 1932 LLD 1971
CBE 1962
retd 1968; resid Aber
d Aber 27.2.81 *AUR* xlix 137

STEWART Alexander Graham   *MB ChB 1907
no longer on GC reg

STEWART Alexander Morrice Leighton
                          BSc(eng) 1955
d Edin 9.12.71 *AUR* xliv 434

STEWART or Garrow, Alice Watson
                          BSc 1928 *1929
teacher chem Harlaw acad Aber 1964–74; retd
husb *d* 27.5.63

STEWART or Paton, Alison Georgina   *MA 1942
JP Gloucester 1971
resid Gloucester

STEWART or Armstrong, Annie Kemp   MA 1918
no longer on GC reg

STEWART Augustus George
                    MA 1905 MB ChB 1909 *MD 1912
d Durban S Af 15.5.68 *AUR* XLII 346 & XLIII 77

STEWART or Bentley, Cecily Jean Macrae
                                        MB ChB 1948
DPH(Glas) 1973 MFCM 1977
s m o Glasg 1972–74; c m s Forth Valley 1978

STEWART Charles Murray   MA 1951
C of S min Viewforth St Oswald's par ch Edin
1960–72; dir youth/commun serv Scot. nat council of
YMCA; nat gen secy Scot. Nat Council of YMCAs
1975; resid Edin

STEWART Charles Nelson   MA 1920
d Aber 7.11.71 *AUR* XLIV 319

STEWART or Fletcher, Charlotte Simpson   MA 1931
resid Lewes

STEWART Christina   MA 1919
d Dufftown 1.12.69 *AUR* XLIII 444

STEWART Clyne Garden   MA 1921

STEWART Clyne Robert Bruce   MB ChB 1947
g p Shifnal from 1955

STEWART Colina May   MA 1915
no longer on GC reg

STEWART or Coulson, Constance Philippa
                                        MA 1954
teacher: Burgh p s Galashiels 1957–60, Kelso p s
1960–62, Victoria p s Falkirk 1962–69, Bridge of Weir
p s from 1974

STEWART David   BSc(agr) 1928
FISP(Inc Soc Planters) 1952
AMN(Malaysian govt) 1958
PJK(Negri Sembilan govt) 1958
planting advis Seafield Amalgamated Rubber Co
1960–65; retd; resid Nairn

STEWART David Lamb   *MA 1930
d Laurencekirk 2.2.68 *AUR* XLII 370

STEWART Dolina   MA 1950
teacher: Lat/geog and supt boarding house Fort
Victoria s Rhodesia 1959–70, part-time Coventry
1970–74, full-time (jun s) from 1974
m Salisbury Rhodesia 31.8.60 Bernard W. Lawson
elect. eng s of William E. L. Catford Lond

STEWART Donald   MA 1916
no longer on GC reg

STEWART Donald   BSc 1953
MSc(Manc) 1965
metall BP chem Grangemouth 1965–68; indust liaison
off. Strath from 1968

STEWART Donald Mackenzie   BSc 1941 *1948

STEWART Donald MacRae
                    MA 1918 *MB ChB 1922
d Ayr 23.12.70 *AUR* XLIV 210

STEWART Donald Sinclair
                    MA 1921 *MB ChB 1925
MRCGP 1952
retd g p/indust m o 1966; part-time med referee Dept
of Health Surrey 1966–74; resid Abinger Common

STEWART or Prentice, Doris Harvey
                                BSc 1944 *1947
teacher maths Harlaw acad Aber 1966–74, Albyn s
Aber from 1974

STEWART or Macphail, Dorothy Jean   *MA 1926
resid Edin
d Edin 31.3.80 *AUR* XLVIII 442

STEWART or Thomson, Dorothy Margaret
                                        BCom 1940
resid Penarth

STEWART Douglas Lawrence
                            ***MA 1934 MB ChB 1939**
g p Insch 1946–78; retd

STEWART Edith Gordon   MB ChB 1951
g p central Ottawa from 1957

STEWART Elizabeth Helen   MA 1940
teacher Engl Malvern girls' coll Worcs 1967–76,
sen tut. from 1976

STEWART or Fyfe, Elizabeth Mary Arthur
                                        ***BSc 1940**
resid Halifax Nova Scotia

STEWART or Pirie, Ethel Mackenzie   MA 1922
d Edin 9.12.72

STEWART or Mirrlees, Evelyn Marian   MA 1917
d Aber 22.5.62 *AUR* XXXIX 381

STEWART or Cronin, Evelyn Mary   MA 1915
resid Carnegie, Aust

STEWART Flora   MA 1915
retd 1958; resid Kyle

STEWART Florence   MA 1930 MB ChB 1941
g p Aber from 1949

STEWART or Watt, Freda Florence   MA 1941
resid Bramhall

STEWART Frederick Henry   *BSc 1937 DSc 1975
FRS 1964 Kt 1974 DSc(Leic) 1977
prof geol Edin from 1957; chmn nat environment res
council Lond 1971–73, chmn advis board for res
councils Lond from 1973

STEWART George   MA 1929
sen asst dept soc stud. Kingsway tech coll Dun
1962–72; retd

STEWART George   MA 1947
d Lond –.3.64 *A UR* XL 401

STEWART George Alexander Murdoch
                                MA 1953 Dip Ed 1957
Aber: teacher sc Summerhill s s 1962–68, Tullos p s
1968–69, sc Ruthrieston s s/Harlaw acad 1969–74,
asst prin sc Torry acad 1974; teacher sc Dumfries h s
from 1975
m Aber 2.8.66 Wilma Lawson pharm d of William
A. L. Inverurie

STEWART George Macdonald   BSc 1938

STEWART Georgina   MA 1924

STEWART Gordon Gray   MA 1908
d Ottawa 18.5.66 *A UR* XLI 336

STEWART or Hardy, Grace Henderson   *BSc 1940
resid Dun
d Dun 19.5.80

STEWART Helen   MA 1939
retd 1971; resid Buckie
m Buckie 24.6.68 William J. Low motor eng s of
James A. L.

STEWART or Merchant, Helen   MA 1944
teacher Cornhill p s Aber from 1957

STEWART or Mitchell, Hester Elizabeth   MA 1936
resid Edin

STEWART Hubert James   BSc 1919 BSc(for) 1921
retd AEI Richmond 1960; resid Aber
d Aber 7.7.81

STEWART Ian Edward   *MA 1954
Brit Steel Corp: group sales man. Scunthorpe 1967–
70, div comm man. Teesside 1970–72, asst div export
man. Lond from 1972

STEWART Ian Jackson   BSc(for) 1937
temp asst dept for. Aberd 1937–38; dist off. for.
comm E and W conservancies Scot. 1938–70; retd;
resid Arbroath

STEWART Ian Martin Steel
                                MB ChB 1944 DPH 1953
Order St J. serv brother 1962, off. brother 1966,
comm brother 1972
Order St J. Knight of Grace 1978
m o workers' compensation board Alberta Edmonton
from 1958

STEWART or Kemp, Isabella   MA 1935

STEWART or Dring, Isabella Cameron   *MA 1947

STEWART Isobel   MA 1924
retd Elgin acad 1964

STEWART James   BSc(agr) 1922
no longer on GC reg

STEWART James   *MA 1932
FSAScot 1961
head: Old Aber s s 1960–65, Hilton acad 1965–74;
retd

STEWART James Alexander Elder   MB ChB 1942
d Coventry 29.10.69 *A UR* XLIII 446

STEWART James Charles   BL 1930

STEWART James Douglas   *MA 1931
prin teacher classics Aber acad, Hazlehead acad
1966–73; retd

STEWART James Gordon   MB ChB 1924
OBE 1967
retd; resid Royton

STEWART James Guthrie   BSc(agr) 1902 MA 1903
d 3.3.68

STEWART James Harvey   MB ChB 1938
g p Hatton 1946–78; retd

STEWART James Smith   MB ChB 1913
d Aber 14.7.66 *A UR* XLI 338

STEWART Jane   MA 1920
retd 1961; resid Aber
d Aber 26.12.79 *A UR* XLVIII 440

STEWART Jemima Ann   MA 1936
town chamberlain and burgh collector Buckie
1960–75; retd

STEWART Jemina   MA 1942
teacher Lochcarron p s from 1970

STEWART Jessie Rae   MA 1912

STEWART Jessie Robertson   MA 1905
d Aber 8.4.73 *A UR* XLV 223

STEWART John   MA 1901
no longer on GC reg

STEWART John   MA 1926
teacher Aber: Middle s 1927–42, dep head Seaton
p s 1942–47, dep head Skene Square p s 1947–70
d Aber 22.2.77 *A UR* XLVII 212

STEWART John Duff   *MA 1924 PhD 1948
dep dir and head school of maths RGIT 1964–68
m Milngavie 31.3.66 Elizabeth Summerville McBride
d Benidorm Spain 3.6.74 *A UR* XLVI 108

STEWART John Gordon   *MA 1946 ᶜMB ChB 1950
d Manc 22.3.77 *A UR* XLVII 214

STEWART John Russell   MA 1901
no longer on GC reg

STEWART, John Sidney   MA 1948 Dip Ed 1962
FIL(Lond) 1964
teacher: Fr/Ger Aber g s 1962–67; prin mod lang
Chilliwack BC Canada 1968–78; resid Chilliwack

STEWART Johnstone Macpherson　MA 1936

STEWART Joseph Robert　BSc 1944 *1949
teacher sc Kirkcaldy 1950–55; prin sc: Peebles 1955–59, Dun 1959–65; dir Scot. schools sc equipment res centre Edin from 1965
d 29.6.81

STEWART or Donald, Leonora Frances　MA 1927
resid St And
d Edin 29.6.76

STEWART Margaret Anne　MA 1951
teacher: Lossiemouth j s s 1952–53, Forres acad 1953–56, Heathcote j s s Essex 1956–58, Hope s s Hope BC Canada 1958–60; studio potter/sculptor from 1962
m Hope 1.9.60 George B. F. Gibson BA(BC) teacher

STEWART Margaret Fleming　MA 1910
for. travel NZ, Aust, Europe, Can, USA; resid Lond
d Derby 6.11.79

STEWART Margaret Jameson　MA 1938
teacher Symbister House j h s Whalsay Shetland 1967–75; retd

**STEWART or Gardner, Margaret Mary Hain
　　　　　　　　　　　　　　MA 1947**
resid Musselburgh
husb deceased

STEWART or Brown, Margaret Maud　MA 1954
resid Oban

STEWART or Fraser, Margaret Taylor　MA 1930
resid Inv
husb *d* 27.7.61

STEWART Marjorie Cameron　*MA 1933
d 19.8.69

STEWART Marjorie Mitchell　*MA 1920
resid Aber

STEWART Marjory Jane　MA 1931
teacher p s: Johnshaven/Inverbervie 1934–52, Montrose 1952–71; retd

STEWART or Buchan, Mary　MA 1930
resid Carnoustie

STEWART or Sangster, Mary Adamson　MA 1929
retd 1971; resid Edin

STEWART or Nicol, Mary Ann　MA 1914

STEWART or Naylor, Mary Ann Forbes　MA 1908
d Stracathro 15.6.71 *AUR* XLIV 316

**STEWART or Gurrey, Mary Dobie Gilmour
　　　　　　　　　　　　　　MA 1945**
teacher inf Tadcaster s Yorks 1960–69; resid Collingham nr Newark

**STEWART or Vick, Mary Macfarlane
　　　　　　　　　　BSc(agr) 1928 PhD 1931**
resid Welwyn Garden City

STEWART or Hercus, Mary Macpherson　MA 1929
teacher prin Fr Elphinstone s s BC Canada 1964–73; retd; resid Gibsons BC

STEWART Neil Findlay　MB ChB 1953
g p Burton-on-Trent from 1959

STEWART Norman Geddes　*MA 1937

STEWART Peter　BSc(eng) 1954

STEWART Robert　MA 1905
no longer on GC reg

**STEWART Robert Douglas
　　　　MB ChB 1927 DPH 1932 MD 1933 DSc 1943**
d Abdnsh 5.5.68 *AUR* XLII 367

STEWART Robert Weir Gilmour　MB ChB 1953
d Hamilton Ont 27.8.70 *AUR* XLIV 111

STEWART Ronald　*BSc 1951

STEWART Theodore　MA 1920
d Edin 21.3.64

STEWART Victor Innes　*BSc 1954 PhD 1958
sen lect i/c soil sc unit dept biochem/agr biochem univ Wales Aberystwyth from 1971
m Aber 6.1.62 Shirley M. Robertson occup therap d of James R. Aber

STEWART Walter　MB ChB 1934
off. St J 1963 MFCM 1973
asst dir gen army med serv (army med dept pers br) War Office Lond 1961–64; dep dir army health E. Command Hounslow 1964–67; retd col 1968; dep m o h Gt Yarmouth 1968–74; s m o Norfolk AHA 1974–78; retd
wife *d* –.3.65
m(2) Norwich 24.5.75 Elizabeth G. Ridgway Cordon Bleu d of Leopold P. R. Dublin

STEWART Walter Allan　MA BSc(agr) 1913
retd 1958; resid Little Brington Northants

STEWART William　MA 1913
resid Aber
d Aber 20.12.79 *AUR* XLVIII 440

STEWART William　MB ChB 1929 DPH 1931
retd 1971; resid Welwyn Garden City

STEWART William　MB ChB 1940

STEWART William　BSc(eng) 1950

STEWART William Alistair　MB ChB 1954
DPM(Dublin) 1963 MRCPsych 1972
psychiat and hon clin lect mental health Ross clin day hosp and Royal Cornhill hosp Aber from 1972

STEWART William James Morrison
                    MB ChB 1952 DPH 1955
g p Huntly from 1956

STEWART Williamina   MA 1917
d 3.2.69

STICKLER William Harvey   *BSc 1951
asst dir of res John G. Stein & Co Bonnybridge
1959–65; United Fireclay Products Armadale: tech
dir 1965–71, works dir 1971–75, man. dir 1975–79;
man. dir Darngavil Minerals Larkhall from 1979
m Bonnybridge 19.5.61 Muriel M. Napier lab analyst
d of George G. N. Gosforth

STILL Athole Tosh   MA 1954
freelance journalist/broadcaster and external opera
stud. Morley coll, Guildhall Lond 1964–69; prin
tenor Scot. Opera, Glyndebourne Opera etc. 1969–76;
study in Naples 1972–73; freelance broadcaster/
journalist, swimming correspondent *Sunday Times*/
ITV; ptnr: Athole Still Assoc from 1978, Rawstron-
Still (internat opera man.) from 1980
m Aber 12.4.63 Isobel J. Cordiner tv prod. asst d of
John C. Lond

STILL or Watson, Edith Mary Simpson   MA 1948
teacher: Sunnybank s Aber 1959–63, Keephatch s
Wokingham Berks 1964–65; dep head Whiteknights
c p s Berks 1965–67; head Loddon inf s Berks from
1968

STILL Katherine Littlejohn   MA 1913
no longer on GC reg

STILL or Fletcher, Olive Adamson   MA 1916
Rhodesia: teacher Chaplin h s Gwelo 1940–43,
Queen Elizabeth s Salisbury 1944–48, govt correspondence s 1952–68
husb *d* Salisbury Rhod –.11.71

STILL Robert   *MA 1931
prin maths/dep head Aboyne s s 1966–68; dep
rector/prin maths Aboyne acad 1968–73

STILL Robert   BSc(eng) 1944 *1948

STILL Sydney Cardno   MA 1915
resid Aber
d Balmedie 16.6.79

STILL William James Sangster
                    MB ChB 1951 ᶜMD 1960
FRCPath 1964
sen lect path. R Free hosp Lond 1962–65; prof path.
med coll of Virginia Richmond Va USA from 1965

STIRLING or Verschelde, Barbara McKenzie
                    MA 1927 BCom 1929
no longer on GC reg

STIRLING George Scott   MB ChB 1949
FRCPsych 1977
consult. psychiat Crichton r hosp Dumfries from 1960

STIRLING Henry William   BSc(agr) 1945
NE Farms Aber: tech advis 1967–72, sales dev
man. 1972–77, tech man. from 1977

STIRLING Kenneth William   *MA 1950
prin mod lang Beath h s Cowdenbeath 1962–72;
asst head Grove acad Dun from 1972
marr diss
m(2) Edin 10.7.73 June Noble teacher home econ

ST LEGER Robert Geoffrey Tunstall   *MA 1952
OBE 1965 FRES 1973
E. Nigeria: dist off. 1953–60, sen asst secy 1960–61,
prin asst secy 1961–68; retd admin off. class I; prin
asst secy Lesotho 1968–70; econ plan. Louis Berger
Inc Uganda/Nigeria from 1970
m Enugu Nigeria 5.9.63 Priscilla A. Egiga nurse/
midwife d of Jonah L. E. Ikom Nigeria

STOBIE or Lawson, Bertha Mary   MA 1928

STODDART or Fletcher, Elizabeth   MA 1939
d Lockerbie 29.4.66 *AUR* XLI 342

STODDART or Valentine, Winifred   MA 1931
resid Haddington

STONE Eric Vaughan   BSc(for) 1948

STORMONTH Georgina Walker   MA 1917
retd 1961; resid Aber

STOTT Alexander Norman Barron   MB ChB 1954
Fell. Fac Occup Med 1979
chief m o UKAEA Harwell from 1965

STOTT Marion Mary   MA 1946
teacher Aber: Tillydrone s 1950–53; Middlefield s
1954–55; Cummings Park s 1956–57; Quarryhill s
1957–60; Springhill s from 1961
m Aber 23.3.51 Gordon D. Cruickshank MA 1969 *qv*

STOTT or Espley, Marion Mayo Josephine
                    MA 1925
resid Bromley

STOUT or Russell, Mary Barbara   MA 1933
head remed dept Gosford Hill comp s Kidlington
Oxford 1965–76; retd

STOVE Magnus James   MA 1936
JP Zetland
head Mid Yell j s s from 1948

STOWELL John Hilton   *MA 1949
PhD(Florida)

STRACHAN Alexander Bremner   MB ChB 1942
g p Goole/Treasury m o from 1947

STRACHAN Alice Mary   *MA 1919
d 1972

STRACHAN Arthur Allister   MB ChB 1945

STRACHAN Charles   *MA 1928
retd 1966; resid Stirling

STRACHAN Charles   *MA 1929
Fell. Corpus Christi Coll Cambridge 1934–37
reader nat phil Aberd 1964–77; retd
wife *d* –.8.71
m(2) Aber 14.12.73 M. Agnes Cuthell or Mathieson
BA(Kingston Ont) d of John C. Vict BC

STRACHAN Charles Henry   MB ChB 1928
fell. BMA 1960
retd g p 1971; part-time referee DHSS Manc from
1965; resid Wilmslow

STRACHAN David Buchan   MB ChB 1948
g p Bradford from 1952

STRACHAN Douglas John   MB ChB 1929
d Milltimber Aber 17.7.73 *AUR* xlv 320

STRACHAN or Whiteford, Elizabeth   MA 1927
retd 1968; resid Inverurie

STRACHAN or Wilkinson, Emma Elizabeth
**   *BSc 1951 PhD 1954**

STRACHAN Eric James   MB ChB 1934
g p Gatley from 1948

STRACHAN Florence Agnes   *MA 1925

STRACHAN or Knox, Frances Mary   MA 1939
resid Inverurie
husb *d* 9.9.55

STRACHAN Freda   BSc 1949 *1950

STRACHAN Georgina Thornton   MA 1924
teacher: Keith g s 1926–51, Kilmichael s Glassary
Argyll 1952–54, Stranraer acad 1954–58, Rephad p s
Stranraer 1958–65; retd
m Inv 4.8.51 Norman C. Mackenzie

STRACHAN or Wright, Hazel Chisholm   *MA 1955
asst press lib Inst of Internat Affairs Lond 1959–61;
head of BBC pronunciation unit Lond 1971–78

STRACHAN Henry James   *MA 1928

STRACHAN Ian Morrison   MA 1955 BD 1958
missionary Ghana 1959–66; C of S min: St Paul's
ch Cambuslang 1966–71, St John's ch Gourock from
1971

STRACHAN Ian Reid   *BSc 1951
MBE 1963
various admin posts: Nyasaland govt (later Malawi)
until 1968, Lanark c c 1968–75, Perth & Kinross dist c
from 1975
m Blantyre Malawi 3.6.67 Judith Michael teacher d of
Ian L. M. Blantyre

STRACHAN Ian William James   MB ChB 1950
g p Aber from 1954

m Aber 30.9.61 Susan Grant exec civ serv d of James
R. G. Aber

STRACHAN or Hunter, Isabel Craib   MA 1946

STRACHAN or Anderson, Isobel Marjorie   MA 1948
teacher ph/mh ch Beechwood s Aber from 1968

STRACHAN James   *MA *BSc 1899
d Slough 20.4.62 *AUR* xxxix 371

STRACHAN James   MA BSc 1913
no longer on GC reg

STRACHAN James   MB ChB 1923
retd 1970; resid Leyland Lancs
d 3.3.74 *AUR* xlv 447

STRACHAN James   MB ChB 1950
g p Elland W Yorks from 1958

STRACHAN James Forbes   BSc(eng) 1940
d Wembley 10.2.68 *AUR* xlii 373

STRACHAN James Milne   MA 1900
d 28.8.61 *AUR* xxxix 270

STRACHAN John   BSc(eng) 1951

STRACHAN John   MA 1951 LLB 1954
ptnr Davidson & Garden advoc Aber from 1958

STRACHAN Malcolm Ian   *MA 1928
d Aber 17.2.75

STRACHAN or Sim, Margaret Buyers   MA 1903
no longer on GC reg

STRACHAN or Peters, Margaret Elizabeth Jane
**   (Lady)   MA 1915**

STRACHAN or Milne, Margaret Jane   MA 1928
resid Keith

STRACHAN or McDonald or Melville, Margaret
**   Vivien   MA 1937**

STRACHAN Maureen Clark   MA 1955 Dip Ed 1956
teacher Cornhill p s Aber till 1962
m Aber 1.12.62 Charles J. Marshall agr machinery
manuf s of Charles M. Aber

STRACHAN or Kemp, Meta   *MA 1929
husb *d* Edin 25.11.67

STRACHAN Robert   MA 1910
d –.7.63

STRACHAN Robert Donald   *MA 1923
retd 1967; resid Aber
d Aber 21.5.79 *AUR* xlviii 228

STRACHAN Robert Stewart   BSc(for) 1948
d –.9.63

STRACHAN Ronald West MB ChB 1953
MRCPE 1961 MRCPGlas 1962 MRCP(Lond) 1964
FICA 1965 FRCPE 1972 FRCPGlas 1978
sen regist med Aber teaching hosps/clin tut. med
Aberd 1961–70; res fell. cardiol Case-Western Reserve
univ Cleveland Ohio USA 1967–68; consult. phys
Dumfries and Galloway RI from 1970

STRACHAN or Burgess, Sheila Ruth MA 1953

STRACHAN Stanley George *MA 1950
Dip Ed(Dund) 1968
trg advis Distrib Indust Trg Board

STRACHAN Theodore Percy *MA 1933 BD 1936
min King St presb ch (latterly URC) Oldham
1964–74; clerk of Manc presb 1965–72; min Holderness Road and E Hull joint pastorate Hull(URC)
1974–78; retd

STRACHAN or Hearn, Violet *MA 1921
no longer on GC reg

STRACHAN William *MA 1935

STRACHAN William MB ChB 1955
g p Edin from 1960

STRACHAN William Ellis MB ChB 1954
FRCSE 1961
regist surg Glasg RI 1959–61; regist neuro-surg St
George's hosp Lond 1961–64; sen regist neuro-surg
nat hosp nerv diseases Lond; sen regist neuro-surg
Edin RI; consult. neuro-surg Plymouth from 1967
m Bucksburn 15.10.60 Lilias M. Cuthbertson MA
1953 *qv*

STRACHAN or Spooner, Winifred Mary MA 1948
resid Ruislip

STRAND or Allcroft, Ruth PhD 1934
DSc(Wellington NZ) 1964
retd 1968; resid Waikanae NZ

STRANG Alastair *BSc(eng) 1955
AMIMechE 1970 MIMechE CEng 1971
acetate and synthetic lab Coventry: sect. leader 1968–
70, dep head 1970–71, head eng dev dept from 1971;
dir Mornington eng subsidy of Courtauld's eng Bolton
from 1972

STRATH or Rebecca, Evelyn May MA 1932
teacher Holburn St, Sunnybank p s Aber from 1955

STRATHDEE Roy Brown
MA 1920 BSc 1922 *1923 LLD 1975
retd 1965
d Guernsey 19.6.76 *AUR* xlvii 103

STRATTON Dorothy Isabella Bryce MA 1943
Bankhead acad: spec asst 1965–72, prin guid/spec
asst hist from 1972
m Aber 7.7.75 Alfred Tosh warehouse superv s of
George T.

STREETEN (formerly Hornig) Paul Patrick
MA 1944 LLD 1980
Fell. Balliol Coll Oxford 1948–66
visiting prof/res fell. to USA 1962–63, to World Bank
in 1973; dep dir gen econ plan. Min Overseas Dev
Lond; prof Sus/fell. and acting dir inst of dev stud.
Sussex 1966–68, dir inst of commonwealth stud./
warden Queen Elizabeth House/fell. Balliol coll
Oxford 1968–78; spec advis to World Bank from 1976

STRONACH Alexander Ruddiman MA 1913
d 1962

STROUD Robert Erskine Wetherly BCom 1929
d Aber 30.10.61 *AUR* xxxix 283

STUART or Simmers, Agnes MA 1926
no longer on GC reg

STUART or MacIntosh, Aileen Grant *MA 1953
Falkirk: teacher Engl Camelon h s 1974–78, Woodlands h s from 1979

STUART Alexander *MA 1937 *MEd 1939
FRGS 1946
Canada: teacher Engl/Fr/soc stud. Hamilton Ontario
1953–54, prin classics Aylmer Ont 1954–55, teacher
classics Etobicoke Ont 1955–56; Ottawa teachers'
coll: master psych in educ 1956–62, chmn psych in
educ from 1962
m Cairo 27.4.45 Marie Deith d of Edward D. Lond

STUART Alexander BSc 1953

STUART Alexander Mitchell MA 1933 BD 1936
C of S min Banchory-Ternan West par ch Kincardinesh from 1966

STUART Allan Ramsay MA 1948
Zaire: hosp admin inst méd évangélique Kimpese
1954–62, mission treasurer Amer baptist mission
Kinshasa 1964–66, bus. man. inst Pédagogique
évangelique Kimpese from 1966
m Leopoldville (Kinshasa) 1.11.57 Carrie E. Sprague
MD(Phil) med pract d of Guy B. S. Corning NY USA

STUART or Middleton, Annie Winifred MA 1929
retd 1968; resid Aber

STUART Barbara Rebecca *MA 1912
d 26.12.71

STUART or Ross, Catherine MA 1923
resid Kincraig

STUART or Pape, Catherine MA 1925
retd 1958; resid Coniston Cumbria

STUART or Hargreaves, Christina
MB ChB 1922 DPH 1923
d 5.4.68 *AUR* xlii 360

STUART Douglas MB ChB 1954
g p Nott from 1960

STUART or Elton, Elizabeth Mary   MA 1952

STUART Forbes Jackson   MB ChB 1906
  d 6.12.65

STUART George
          MA 1908 *MB ChB 1912 *MD DPH 1929
  d Spey Bay 3.8.72 *AUR* XLV 124

STUART George Nicolson   MA 1908
  no longer on GC reg

STUART or Mitchell, Gertrude Helen   MA 1930
  JP Aber 1957
teacher Burnside Inf s Aber 1961–78; retd
husb *d* 14.8.71

STUART Gladys Lee   MA 1918 BSc 1920
  d Aber 23.7.69 *AUR* XLIII 329

STUART Gordon   *BSc(eng) 1945
  MBIM 1960 CEng FIEE 1968 CDip AF 1973
sen lect RGIT Aber 1963–66; with Merz & McLellan
consult. eng N'cle-u-Tyne from 1966, assoc 1973–76;
with Motor Columbus consult. eng Baden Switzerland
from 1976

STUART Gordon William   MB ChB 1944
  g p Ramsgate from 1949

STUART Helen   MA 1944
  exchange teacher Ottawa 1959–60; inf mistress
Scotstown p s Bridge of Don Aber 1969–73, asst head
from 1973

STUART Helena Mary   MA 1931
  resid Aber

STUART Ian   MB ChB 1955
  JP Angus 1968
g p Arbroath from 1959

STUART Isabella Cameron   MA 1933
  retd 1972; resid Fochabers

STUART or Gordon, Janet Jane Reid   MA 1934
  head Ballogie p s Aboyne 1965–72; teacher Dyce
p s 1972–73; retd; resid Oldmeldrum

STUART or Menzies, Jean Elspeth   MB ChB 1940
  d Aber 13.10.66 *AUR* XLII 90

STUART John Charles   MA 1893
  no longer on GC reg

STUART John Mitchell   MB ChB 1931
  sen m o Vickers 1955–71; retd; resid Lyme Regis

STUART or Hinds, Joyce Angus   MA 1952
  resid Welwyn Garden City

STUART Lawrence Murray   *BSc 1946
  res chem Bakelite Birm 1946–47; works chem
Expanded Rubber Co Dun 1947–62; teacher: chem
Dun h s, prin chem RGC Aber from 1972

STUART or Angus, Maggie Ann   MA 1927
  d 24.7.77

STUART or Campbell, Margaret Gray Hitchcock
                                              ***MA 1914**
  retd 1953; resid Moffat

STUART Mary Ann   MA 1918
  no longer on GC reg

STUART or McMain, Mary Emslie   MA 1941
  teacher: Cairncry p s Aber 1966–68, Macalpine p s
Dun 1969–75, Craigie h s Dun from 1975

STUART Patricia May   *MA 1939
  resid Rothes

STUART Robert Douglas
          MB ChB 1927 DPH 1932 ᶜMD 1933 DSc 1943
  d Oyne 5.5.68 *AUR* XLII 367

STUART Roderick Allen   BSc 1930 MA 1931
  d Aber 12.7.70 *AUR* XLIV 110

STUART Ronald Sangster   *BSc 1950 PhD 1954

STUART Sophia Keith Grant
                          MA 1915 MB ChB 1918

STUART William   MA 1935
  ptnr Bower & Smith CA Aber from 1954

STUART William Innes   BSc 1954

STURM Maxwell Gerard de L'Isle   MB ChB 1927
  d Trinidad 17.11.68 *AUR* XLIII 215

STURROCK Robert John   BSc 1930 MA 1931
  d Stonehaven 12.7.73 *AUR* XLV 320

STURTON James   BSc(eng) 1938

STYLES Edward Currie Castell   *BSc 1951

SUBBA RAO Gargestwari Narayana   PhD 1948
  MSc(Mysore)
India: fish. tech Bombay 1949–50, tech food res inst
Mysore 1950–53; fish. tech FAO Rome 1953–59; reg
fish. off. FAO Bangkok Thailand 1959–71; proj oper
off. fish. Rome from 1971
m Mysore 30.10.50 Leela Rao d of K. V. Srinivaso
Rao BE(Bangalore) Bangalore

SUMITRA Svasti   BSc 1926

SUMMERS or Buchan, Ella Smith   MA 1952

SUMMERS George Noble
                          MB ChB 1944 DPH 1949

SUMMERS Gordon Jamieson   MB ChB 1932

SUMMERS or Connal, Sophia Lucy Mackworth
                      MA 1907 BSc 1909 DSc 1929
  d 17.3.64 *AUR* XL 395

SUMMERS or Brown, Williamina   *MA 1923
no longer on GC reg

SUNDARA-VICHARANA Yen   BSc 1927
no longer on GC reg

SURTEES Anne Dey   MB ChB 1946
m Kendrick

SUTHERLAND or Dyke, Alexandrina Booth
*MA 1954 PhD 1957
resid Bath

SUTHERLAND Andrew Norman   BSc(agr) 1935
head Brae j h s Shetland 1950–74; retd

SUTHERLAND Annie   MA 1929

SUTHERLAND Arthur Robert   MA 1904
no longer on GC reg

SUTHERLAND Audrey
MB ChB 1948 DPH 1964 MD 1967
FFCM 1972
Myers res fell. Aberd 1964–67; res fell. SHHD Aberd
1967–70; prin sen m o (res) Durh c c health dept
1970–74; SCM/information serv and res N reg health
auth 1974; SCM/information and serv plan. Durham
AHA from 1975
d N'cle-u-Tyne 15.4.81 *AUR* xlix 139

SUTHERLAND Christina Hunter
MA 1916 BSc 1918
d Gardone Riviera Italy 9.7.72 *AUR* xlv 125

SUTHERLAND David   MA 1932
min St Nicholas cong ch (union Albion & St Paul's
and Belmont) Aber from 1966; pres cong union of
Scot. 1968–69; chmn Aber & Dist Council of ch
1973–76; retd 1978; resid Rosemarkie

SUTHERLAND David Thompson   MB ChB 1947
g p Salford from 1950

SUTHERLAND Donald John Waters
MB ChB 1952
g p Terrington St Clement nr King's Lynn Norfolk
1960–66; Tasmania: royal Derwent hosp New Norfolk
1966–67, repatriation gen hosp Hobart 1967–68, g p
Boronia Kingston Beach from 1968

SUTHERLAND Dorothy Anne   MB ChB 1950
med asst paediat Royal Alexandra hosp Rhyl

SUTHERLAND Enid May   MA 1925
d Aber 19.7.74 *AUR* xlvi 109

SUTHERLAND Finlay Fraser   *MA 1950

SUTHERLAND or Carle, Florence Mackenzie
MA 1929

SUTHERLAND Frank Lamond   MA 1922
head Springhill p s Aber 1956–66; retd

SUTHERLAND George Graham Mackay
*MA 1952
FEIS 1978
prin teacher bus. stud. and econ Morrison's acad
Crieff from 1954

SUTHERLAND George Kenneth
MA 1909 *BSc 1911 DSc 1916
no longer on GC reg

SUTHERLAND George Pottinger   MB ChB 1945
g p Maybole from 1958
m Elgin 9.8.58 Beryl D. Harper nurs sister d of Henry
S. H. Mosstodloch

SUTHERLAND Gilbert   MA 1929 BCom 1931
dep head coll Sydney NSW; retd 1970; resid Edin
d 4.11.75

SUTHERLAND Gordon Alexander   MA 1950
Aber: teacher Kaimhill s s 1960–64, dep head
Broomhill p s 1965–73, head Muirfield p s from 1973

SUTHERLAND Gordon Wymess   *MA 1951

SUTHERLAND or Garson, Helen May   MA 1952
b 7.8.31
resid Ottawa

SUTHERLAND Herbert   BSc 1926

SUTHERLAND Iain Johnstone Macbeth   MA 1948
CMG 1974
first secy/head chancery Brit emb Havana Cuba 1959–
62; first secy Brit emb Washington USA 1962–65;
asst Northern Dept FO Lond 1965–67; counsellor/
consul gen Brit emb Djakarta Indonesia 1967–69;
head S Asian dept FCO Lond 1969–73; fell. center for
internat affairs Harvard univ Cambridge Mass 1973–
74; min Brit emb Moscow 1974–78; asst under secy of
state for European affairs FCO Lond 1976–78; HM
ambassador Athens Greece from 1978

SUTHERLAND James Runcieman
*MA 1921 LLD 1955

SUTHERLAND James Wilson   *BSc 1953

SUTHERLAND Jane Humphrey   *MA 1955
Dip Ed(Glas) 1956
teacher Engl Perth acad 1956–65; resid Romsey Hants
m Aber 29.12.64 Norman D. Thomson MA(Cantab)
schoolmaster/computer progr instruct. s of Robert T.
Leven

SUTHERLAND John Gairn   MB ChB 1951

SUTHERLAND John Stuart   MB ChB 1954
regist anaest ARI 1959–62; g p Coventry from 1963

SUTHERLAND John Wallace Milne   MB ChB 1934

SUTHERLAND Kenneth Ian   MB ChB 1950
MRCGP 1964
g p Udny from 1960

SUTHERLAND Maggie Alice   MA 1926
no longer on GC reg

SUTHERLAND or Alexander, Margaret Adamson
                                                              ***MA 1917**
asst edit. *The British Weekly* Lond 1942–46
resid Canterbury Kent

SUTHERLAND or Walker, Margaret Jean
                                                                MA 1931
resid Haslingfield Cambridge

SUTHERLAND Marie Sherriffs
                                        MB ChB 1935 DPH 1939
asst m o h Aber from 1941; retd 1974

SUTHERLAND or Wilson, Mary   MA 1928
resid Ellon

SUTHERLAND or Ross, Mary Baillie   MA 1920
deceased

SUTHERLAND Mary Elizabeth   *MA 1917
d 19.10.72 *AUR* XLV 125

SUTHERLAND Mary Isabel   MA 1947

SUTHERLAND or Carter, Mary Simpson
                                              ***MB ChB 1924**
retd 1965; resid N'cle Staffs
husb *d* 1951

SUTHERLAND Robert   MA 1922
d Aber 7.2.71 *AUR* XLIV 210

SUTHERLAND Robert
                            MB ChB 1928 DPH 1931 ᶜMD 1933
FRSMed 1943 FRSH 1943
F Internat Epidemiological Assoc
sen lect prev med and p h Leeds univ 1951–64; dir Br
Emp cancer campaign (Yorks council) cancer surv
Leeds 1954–64; retd; resid Harrogate

SUTHERLAND Robert William   BCom 1923
no longer on GC reg

SUTHERLAND Ruth Gordon   MA 1926
d Aber 4.12.76 *AUR* XLVII 212

SUTHERLAND Sinclair Stewart   MB ChB 1955

SUTHERLAND Victor Lloyd   MB ChB 1944

SUTHERLAND William   ᵈBL 1935
ptnr Smith & Sutherland advoc Aber from 1946

SUTHERLAND William   MA 1937 LLB 1939

SUTHERLAND William Alexander   MA 1912
d Aber 8.8.73 *AUR* XLV 317

SUTTAR Thomas   BSc(eng) 1949
DIC 1969 FIE Aust 1973
post grad stud. Imp coll Lond 1962–63; proj des eng
hydro-elect. comm Tasmania 1963–73; eng for civil

investig hydro-elect. comm 1973–77, asst chief civ eng
from 1977

SWAINE Dalway John   PhD 1952
sen prin res scient/head geochem sect. CSIRO div
of mineralogy North Ryde NSW Aust from 1959

SWAINSON Douglas Willan   *BSc(eng) 1939

SWAINSON or Fulton, Grace Robertson   *MA 1943
resid Blairgowrie

SWAINSON Willan   MA 1945
          (conferred for long service of exceptional merit)
Aberd: founder of dept music, reader at time of
retirement; founder of Aberdeen Bach choir, Aberdeen
Orchestral Soc and Aberdeen Chamber Music Club
d Ballater 28.9.70 *AUR* XLIV 111

SWAN Ronald   BSc(eng) 1949
contr man. for J. McAdam & Sons c e contractors
Aber 1954–78, sen estimator W. Tawse c e contr Aber
from 1978

SWANNEY Reginald Thomas Rosson   MA 1947

SWANSON Ian Reid   MB ChB 1952
DObstRCOG 1959
g p: Moe Vict Aust 1960–72, Lesmurdie W Aust from
1973

SWANSON Margaret   BSc 1945
teacher: Burnham Somerset 1946, Warrington
Lancs 1947–48, dep head Accrington 1953–58;
Crawley Suss: teacher g s 1958–70, prin maths 1971–
72, comp s from 1973
m Brent Knoll Somerset 9.8.47 James H. Tucker civ
serv s of Edward T. Southall

SWANSTON Thomas
                            MA 1952 *MEd 1954 BD 1960
C of S min: asst N and E St Nicholas ch Aber
1960–61, Holytown par ch Motherwell 1962–71, West
par ch Inv 1971

SWAPP or Diack, Catherine   MA 1919
resid Edin
husb *d* 4.5.67

SWAPP Garden Hepburn   MA 1925 MB ChB 1928
d Stonehaven 28.1.67 *AUR* XLII 367

SWAPP Garden Hepburn   MB ChB 1953
DObstRCOG 1960 DCH 1960 MRCOG 1963
FRCOG 1976
g p trainee Pitlochry 1960–61; regist obst/gyn Aber
hosps 1961–63; Aberd: sen lect dept obst/gyn 1966–70,
consult. obst/gyn Grampian area health board/clin
sen lect dept obst/gyn from 1970

SWAPP George   MB ChB 1924 LLD 1961
d Aber 24.5.69 *AUR* XLIII 213

SWAPP George David   *MA 1953 Dip Ed 1954
RAF stat. and s selection off. Luga Malta 1961–63;

h q trg command Brampton 1964; stud. RAF staff coll 1965; dir staff RAF staff coll; wing comm sen educ and trg off. RAF Lyneham 1969–71, dir educ serv (RAF) M o D Lond from 1971

SWEENEY Sheila May   BSc(agr) 1954
Dip Agr(R'dg) 1955
jun lect W of Scot. agr coll Ayr 1956–58; teacher: zool for. s Sunyani Ghana 1959, gen sc/biol Sir Robert Armitage s s Limbe Malawi 1964
m Inv 27.5.58 John A. W. Robley BSc(for) 1954 *qv*

SWEENIE or Davidson, Dorothy Mary McIntosh
MB ChB 1951
resid Lénzie Glasg

SWINNEY George Ewen   *MA 1936 *MB ChB 1941
phys/supt Woodilee and Stoneyetts hosps Glasg from 1961

SWINNEY William Dixon   MB ChB 1941 DPH 1947
d Eye Suffolk 11.3.77 *AUR* XLVII 214

SYED Philip Antony Ross   MA 1949
antiquarian bookseller: Cornwall 1966–70, Tewkesbury from 1970

SYKES or Maxwell, Greta Louise   MA 1929
resid Cambridge

SYME Peter Salmon   BSc(agr) 1919
no longer on GC reg

SYMES Bertram William (Barry)   BSc 1950
teacher: Aber 1960–65, spec asst 1965–68, prin asst 1968–73, year master/prin guid Kincorth acad from 1973

SYMMERS Godfrey Roy
BSc(civ eng) 1929 BSc(elect. eng) 1930

SYMMONS Saida   PhD 1950
lect nat hist dept Aberd from 1951

SYMON Archibald   MB ChB 1932
d Elgin 11.12.70 *AUR* XLIV 212

SYMON Ian Urquhart   BS(agr) 1954
with SAI from 1954; resid Berwick-on-Tweed

SYMON James Alexander   MA BSc(agr) 1911
d Edin 8.10.74 *AUR* XLVI 235

SYMON Jean   *MA 1949
translator Council of Europe Strasbourg France from 1961

SYMON John Walker   MA 1919
no longer on GC reg

SYMON Lindsay   *MB ChB 1951
Rockefeller trav fell. Wayne univ Detroit USA 1962–63; sen neurosurg regist nat hosps/Middx hosp Lond 1963–65; consult. neurosurg: nat hosps Lond 1965–78, St Thomas hosp Lond 1969–78; prof neurol

surg univ Lond Inst of Neurol Lond from 1978; civ consult. neurosurg RN from 1978

SYMON Lindsay James   MB ChB 1944
g p Lossiemouth from 1945

SYMON or John, Margaret Anne Cargill
MB ChB 1924
h o Lond 1927, Manc 1928; m o Dar-es-Salaam Tanganyika 1939–49; m o fam plan. Manchester/ Preston 1953–65; resid Somerset

SYMON or Ritch, Mary Barbara   MB ChB 1954
resid Oldmeldrum

SYMON Mary Susan   MA 1911
d Brechin 11.3.67 *AUR* XLII 350

SYMON Patrick Anderson   MA 1952 LLB 1954
solic: ptnr John Laurie & Co Aber from 1957, ptnr in Kemp & Auchinachie (Keith, Aberlour, Dufftown) from 1955, ptnr in Alex. Elder Anton & Son Buckie from 1977; resid Aber
m Aber 22.7.59 Isobel G. Pearson MA 1958

SYMONDS James   MB ChB 1948
MRCGP 1962
g p Bonnyrigg from 1955

SYMONS or Kurland, Elizabeth Fleming   MA 1929

SYMONS or Balnaves, Marion McDonald
*MA 1923
d Aber 11.12.72 *AUR* XLV 225

TAGGART Annie Ross   *BSc 1948
sen lect nutrit and dietetics RGIT Aber from 1965

TAGGART or Townsend, Eleanor Elizabeth
*MA 1933

TAGGART George Joss   MA 1923
d Aber 31.3.77 *AUR* XLVII 212

TAGGART Isabella Munro   MA 1924
retd 1971; resid Brechin

TAGGART James Sinclair   *MA 1950

TAGGART June Margaret   MA 1948
pers secy Kingseat hosp Newmachar 1960–77, pers secy med comp centre ARI from 1977

TAGGART Norman   MB ChB 1924
resid Is of Wight

TAIT Alexander   *MA 1933
retd 1976; resid Edin

TAIT Dorothy Fraser   *MA 1908
d 10.4.71

TAIT Eric Alexander   *BSc 1950
Aberd: lect geol 1961–65, sen lect 1965–70, reader 1970–72, Kilgour prof from 1972

TAIT Henry Alexander Gardner   *MA 1951 BD 1964
b 27.4.29
teacher: Calabar Nigeria 1955–61, Kinross s s 1964–65; C of S min: asst Shettleston Old par ch Glasg 1965, Crieff South and Monzievaird ch Crieff from 1966

TAIT Irene Margaret Hunter   MA 1945

TAIT John Gavin   *MA 1918
no longer on GC reg

TAIT or Moir, Kirsteen Maie   *MA 1939
part time teaching and coaching Edin from 1962

TALLACK John Aidan   MB ChB 1949
med regist Addenbrooke's hosp Cambridge 1956–57; Oldchurch hosp Romford Essex: locum regist 1957–67, asst phys from 1967
m Brentwood Essex 25.4.63 Mary M. Murphy SRN d of Patrick M. farm. Cork Eire

TARREL William   MA 1913
no longer on GC reg

TATE Joyce Kathleen   MB ChB 1944
private pract Jamaica from 1955

TATTON Henry   MB ChB 1937
d 15.4.74 *A UR* xlv 449

TAVENDALE Alexander Blease   BSc(eng) 1942

TAWSE Alastair Harry   BSc(eng) 1951
MICE 1959
assoc dir Wm Tawse Aber 1963–66; Shellabear Price Walton-on-Thames Surrey: contr man. 1966–70, contr dir from 1970
m(2) Enfield Middx 12.12.69 Doreen Paterson d of William D. P. Aber

TAWSE John George   MA 1932
dep head Mile End p s Aber 1950–75; retd

TAWSE Malcolm Harold   *BSc(eng) 1948
d Nairobi 31.12.70 *A UR* xliv 216

TAYLOR Alan King   *BSc 1951

TAYLOR Alan Neil   BSc 1953

TAYLOR Alan Skinner   MB ChB 1947
d Preston Ont 29.3.68 *A UR* xlii 374

TAYLOR Alexander Abel   *BSc 1953
AIFST 1962 FIFST 1973
sen scient off. ARC low temp res stat Cambridge 1961–67; prin scient off. ARC meat res inst Bristol from 1967
m Aber 16.3.63 Isabel D. Hyland d of Benjamin J. H. Aber

TAYLOR Alexander James   MB ChB 1950
FRCGP
g p Fyvie from 1960; lect in g p Aberd

TAYLOR Alexander James Gourlay   BL 1937
d Aber 28.10.75 *A UR* xlvi 417

TAYLOR Alexander Pyper   MA 1907 *BSc 1909
d 12.8.65 *A UR* xli 240

TAYLOR Alexander Robertson
                                          MA 1937 *MB ChB 1941
PhD(Belf) 1972
consult. neurol surg NI hosp auth 1952–73; sen lect med sc inst Dund from 1974
correspondence member neuro-surg Spanish, Ger, Scandinavian societies
d Dun 9.7.78 *A UR* xlviii 106

TAYLOR or Mearns, Alice Margaret   MA 1928
teacher: inf Ashley Rd p s Aber 1961–63, Rosewood inf s Aber 1963–71; retd

TAYLOR Alistair James   MB ChB 1944 MD 1957
MRACP 1970 FRCP 1976
NZ: respir phys Otago hosp board 1960–64, sen lect med Otago univ from 1964

TAYLOR or Tennant, Anna   MA 1923
no longer on GC reg

TAYLOR or Clark-Hutchison, Annie Calder Robertson
                                                               MA 1930

TAYLOR Annie Stewart   MA 1926
retd 1966; resid Edin

TAYLOR Arthur Henry Roan   MA 1950
secy NFU Scot.: Caithness area Thurso 1961–64, Dumbarton area Cardross 1964–73; Inverclyde area Cardross from 1973
d Lond 17.7.79

TAYLOR Bruce Drummond   MB ChB 1936
g p Wembley; retd to Aber 1976

TAYLOR Charles   *MA 1939

TAYLOR Charles George Smith   *MA 1927
retd 1970; resid Strathpeffer

TAYLOR Charles Matheson   MB ChB 1945
g p Harlow Essex from 1949

TAYLOR Colin Fraser   MA 1932
d Aber 12.1.66 *A UR* xlii 88

TAYLOR Daniel   MA 1952
prin teacher Engl/hist/geog Lossiemouth h s 1963–69; head: Port Erroll p s Cruden Bay 1969–71, Ellon p s 1971–75, Cults p s from 1975

TAYLOR David Scott   *MA 1949
teacher Fr/Ger Mackie acad Stonehaven from 1953

TAYLOR Douglass William
                                          MB ChB 1946 *MD 1957
univ of Otago med s, Dunedin NZ: sen lect physiol 1962–64, assoc prof 1964–68, pers prof from 1968; asst Dean (part-time) from 1974

TAYLOR Edward Russell   *MA 1921
d 23.1.69

TAYLOR Edwin William   MA 1944
head Bucksburn s 1961–69; lect Aber coll of educ
from 1969

TAYLOR Elizabeth Ann   MA 1948
teacher King St s Aber 1955–62
m Aber 1.9.62 George A. Duthie joiner s of George D.
New Pitsligo

TAYLOR Elizabeth Colville Anderson   MA 1927
d Edin 7.9.75 *AUR* xlvi 323

TAYLOR Elsie Constance Coutts   MA 1929
teacher Engl: Inverurie acad 1943–63, Monifieth/
Carnoustie s s 1963–68; retd; resid Monifieth

TAYLOR Elspeth Stewart   MA 1936
teacher Springhill p s Aber 1959–75; retd

TAYLOR Eric Forbes   MA 1950
head Sandhaven s from 1965

TAYLOR or Cutting, Flora Mysie   MA 1943

TAYLOR or Lessells, Frances Mary   MA BSc 1941
resid Aber

TAYLOR Gavin Beddie   MB ChB 1954
MRCGP 1965
g p Peterhead from 1959
m Doncaster 26.6.61 Margaret L. Woodmansey d of
Alfred B. W.

TAYLOR Gavin Catto   *MB ChB 1924
d Peterhead 6.10.62 *AUR* xl 91

TAYLOR George Alexander
                    MA 1926 BSc(eng) 1928 *1929 PhD 1949
d Tor-Na-Dee Aber 17.12.64 *AUR* xli 58

TAYLOR George Angus   MB ChB 1932
d Oldham 1961 *AUR* xxxix 283

TAYLOR George Gordon Massie   BSc(for) 1952

TAYLOR George Henry Carr   MB ChB 1940

TAYLOR George James Gibson   *MA 1926
part-time lect Fr Wolverhampton tech coll 1965–66;
part-time teacher Fr/Ger Wolverhampton girls' h s
1966–72; Fr oral exam. Lond univ 1965–74, exam. Fr
Oxf & Camb joint board from 1966
m Wolverhampton 4.7.64 Elsa A. Walker BA(Lond)
teacher

TAYLOR Harriet Johnston Sutherland
                                        MB ChB 1921

TAYLOR or Aldwinckle, Helene Lovie   MA 1942

TAYLOR Henry   *MA 1953 Dip Ed 1954
MEd(Edin) 1972

prin teacher geog: Mortlach sen s s Dufftown 1956–60,
Peterhead acad 1960–63; dep head Royal Blind s
Edin 1963–65, head 1965–72; lect educ of visually
handicapped ch Moray House coll of educ Edin from
1973

TAYLOR Henry Alistair   MA 1950

TAYLOR Henry Mitchell   BSc(eng) 1937
FRSA 1966 FIMechE 1967 CEng 1967
head dept eng tech Luton coll of higher educ from
1957

TAYLOR Ian Bryson   BSc(eng) 1947
FICE 1968
Richard Costain: dep ag Barbados 1956–60, ag 1960–
61; area rep Kaduna Nigeria 1962–66, asst comm
man. Lond 1966–68; contr eng Lond 1969–78, sen
contr eng from 1978

TAYLOR Irene Barlow   MA 1945
ordained Lond as priest of Christian Commun
1960; working Lond from 1960
m Lond –.6.63 Ormond St J. Edwards BSc(Keele)
printer/priest s of Alfred E. Shrewsbury

TAYLOR or Davidson, Isabel Mary Jane   MA 1946
resid Ellon

TAYLOR Isabella Florence Sutherland   MA 1909
no longer on GC reg

TAYLOR James   *BSc 1952
MIMM 1959 CE 1965 assoc M Aust IMM 1967
geol surv of Gt Brit Lond 1952–66; Aust: explor man.
United Uranium NL Darwin 1966–73, chief geol JOC
min resources Sydney/Perth 1973–74; geol Internat
Atomic Energy Agency UN, Afghanistan 1974–75,
Uruguay 1975, Ethiopia 1976, Greece 1976–77,
Nicaragua 1978, Bolivia 1978

TAYLOR James Fraser   MB ChB 1954
DPH(Edin) 1965 DIH(Lond) 1965 MFOM 1978
m o Chloride Group Swinton Manc from 1965

TAYLOR James Garden   *MA 1919 DSc 1966
d Hemel Hempstead 10.9.73 *AUR* xlv 318

TAYLOR James Ingram   BSc(eng) 1930 *1931
MBE 1953 FIWE 1950 FICE 1955
asst city eng Durh 1930–31; dep eng Kent river board
Maidstone 1932–53; major Royal Marines Burma/
India etc 1941–45; chief eng Kent river board Maid-
stone 1953–74
m Marden Kent 11.7.36 Joyce M. Wheeler d of
Leonard W. Marden

TAYLOR James Lennel   MB ChB 1935
g p Keith from 1936; retd 1977

TAYLOR James Michael   MB ChB 1955
h o mat. hosp Aber 1959–60; g p Peterhead from
1960

TAYLOR James Thomson   *MA 1915
d 13.5.72

TAYLOR James William   MA 1929
head Stromness p s 1961–70; retd; resid Dormans-land Surrey

TAYLOR James Wilson   MB ChB 1940
MRCGP 1953
g p Dyce from 1947

TAYLOR Jane Stuart   MA 1935

TAYLOR Janet Isabel   MA 1913
d Halkirk 15.3.67 *AUR* XLII 182

TAYLOR or Nelson, Jean Clyne   MB ChB 1945
FRCPE 1971 FRCP(Can) 1973
Canada: m o loc board of health Edmonton 1958–67; m o inst for delinquent adolescent girls Edmonton 1960–67; member prov royal comm to investigate juvenile delinquency Alberta 1967–68; member McGrath penology consult. stud. group Alberta 1968–69; asst dir Well Child progr univ of Alberta 1964–68; commun paediat loc board of health Edmonton 1967–74; lect dept paediat univ of Alberta from 1955; vice-pres Vanier Inst of the Family Ottawa 1973–74; dep Min of Health province of Alberta from 1975
d Edmonton 15.1.79 *AUR* XLVIII 233

TAYLOR or Stewart, Jean Mary   MA 1933
teacher p s Inverurie acad 1960–72

TAYLOR John   BL 1940

TAYLOR John Cuthill   MB ChB 1939
g p Goudhurst Kent 1946–76, part time g p Hawkhurst from 1977
m Maidstone 3.10.67 Daphne D. Haynes riding instr d of Lewis P. H. Hawkhurst

TAYLOR John Erskine   MA 1946 LLB 1949
solic in civ serv Edin from 1956

TAYLOR John Hamilton   *MA 1949
teacher: Moray/Banff 1960–72, Glasg from 1972

TAYLOR John Ingram   MB ChB 1925
retd 1966; resid Sheffield

**TAYLOR John Maxwell
                *MA 1899 MB ChB 1905 DPH 1913**
d Dun 11.2.65 *AUR* XLI 52

TAYLOR John Mitchell   MA 1954
rector: St Ninian's ch Pollokshields 1964–73, St John's ch Dumfries from 1973

TAYLOR John Murray   *MA 1931
d Banchory 12.1.72 *AUR* XLIV 433

TAYLOR John Stewart   MB ChB 1951
g p Elgin from 1955

TAYLOR John William   MA 1916
m(3) Lond 4.11.61 Joan M. Hickman d of Bernard V. H. Wolverhampton
d Lond 25.5.74 *AUR* XLVI 108

TAYLOR Keith McLean   *MA 1948

TAYLOR or Turner, Louise Barbara   *MA 1929
secy joint comm of Greek and Roman societies 1949–75; resid Fortrose
edit. *Aberdeen Shore Work Accounts*

**TAYLOR or McKenzie, Mabel Catherine
                MA 1939 BSc 1940 *1941**
teacher maths: Fraserburgh acad 1960–64, spec asst 1964–71, Mackie acad Stonehaven 1971–77; retd; resid Stonehaven

TAYLOR or Heald, Margaret Bella   MA 1943
insp MOH (insur dept) Nott 1943–46; regist of appeals (fam allowances dept) N'cle 1946–48; reg welfare off. MOH/soc security Leeds 1948–50; part-time teacher Leeds 1958–72; resid Wetherby

TAYLOR Margaret Buchan   MA 1952

**TAYLOR Margaret Jane McKenzie
                MA 1947 *MEd 1961**
ch guid centre Aber: educ psych 1961–67, sen asst educ psych 1967–68, prin psych 1968–75, reg psych Grampian reg from 1975

TAYLOR or Innes, Margaret Reid   MA 1926

**TAYLOR or Mackenzie, Marjorie Kathleen
                MA 1942**
Aber: teacher (temp) 1959, Muirfield p s 1960, Quarryhill p s 1961–68, Kingswood p s 1968–75

TAYLOR or Robertson, Mary   MA 1904
d 1962

TAYLOR or Stephen, Mary Elizabeth   MA 1936
teacher Kingswells p s from 1962

TAYLOR or Gray, Moira Margaret   BSc 1950
teacher maths/sc: Burnley h s for girls 1962–66; Tasmania: Huonville h s 1967–69, Prospect h s Launceston 1969–70, Kings Meadows h s Launceston from 1971

TAYLOR Moore   MB ChB 1921 MD DPH 1928
resid Nedlands W Aust

TAYLOR Patrick Hamilton   BSc(eng) 1953
MICE 1961
Terresearch Middx: eng 1958–60, contr man./superv 1960–61; DAFS Edin: asst civ eng 1961–65, civ eng 1966–72; Scot. dev dept Edin: civ eng 1972–77, sen civ eng from 1977

TAYLOR Phyllis Agnes   BSc 1937

TAYLOR Robert   BSc(agr) 1928
no longer on GC reg

TAYLOR Robert   MB ChB 1944

TAYLOR Robert Innes   MA 1934
retd 1972; resid Hillside Montrose

TAYLOR Robin Burness   BSc(eng) 1947

TAYLOR Ronald Gordon   BSc(eng) 1944

TAYLOR Thomas Murray (Sir)
*MA 1919 LLB 1922
prin and vice-chancellor Aberd 1948–62
d Aber 19.7.62 *AUR* xxxix 291–306

TAYLOR Thornton Lewins   *MA 1928
HMIS retd 1968; dealer antiques/fine art Glasg
from 1968
d Glasg 10.1.79 *AUR* xlviii 231

TAYLOR William   *MA 1913 LLD 1962
m Aber 28.9.63 Mildred Hartley MA(Cantab)
d Oxford 12.2.77 *AUR* xlvii 211

TAYLOR William   *MA 1953 MEd 1958
prin teacher classics John Neilson h s Paisley from
1965

TAYLOR William Alexander   BSc(eng) 1947

TAYLOR William Anderson   MA 1942 LLB 1949
ptnr Mackenzie & Grant solic Forres from 1960

TAYLOR William Clyne   MB ChB 1945
Canada: prof paediat Edmonton from 1968; asst
dir R. S. McLaughlin exam. and res centre Edmonton
from 1973
m Winnipeg Manitoba 24.4.54 Susie S. Paxton nurse
d of Thomas P. Oak River Manitoba

TAYLOR William Ferguson   *MA 1949

TAYLOR William John   MA 1931
d Lond 2.5.63 *AUR* xl 206

TELFER or McCredie, Kathrine Carmichael
MA 1928

TEMPLE John Stoddart   BSc(agr) 1952
insp DAFS Edin from 1970

TEMPLETON or Dent, Mary Agnes   MB ChB 1945
occasional work locum g p/fam plan. clin from
1947; resid Norwich

TENNANT Edward Robert Hector   MB ChB 1951
HM overseas civil serv (med dept) N Borneo Sabah
1959–66; dep m o h, dep prin schools m o Inv
1967–70; g p Ullapool 1970–77; s m o Esso Standard
Libya Inc Marsa, El Brega 1977–79; m o Brit emb
Warsaw from 1979
m Inv 15.8.59 Morag J. MacLeod matron ch's home

TENNANT or Russell, Ethel Law   BCom 1930
d Pitmedden 21.9.76

TENNANT John   MA 1937 BD 1946
C of S min Cluny par ch 1957–70; mod. presb
Garioch Inverurie 1961–63, clerk presb of Garioch
1964–69; mod. synod of Aber 1968–69; retd 1970;

locum tenens: par of Ardgour with Strontian 1971–72,
Duneaton 1972
d Gartly Aberdeensh 16.6.76

TENNANT Vivian Lloyd   MB ChB 1937
sen m o h Ksac Jamaica 1960–64; private pract
1964–73; retd; resid Kingston Jamaica
d Jamaica W Indies 18.10.74

TENNANT William Robert (Sir)
*MA 1914 *1915 LLD 1953
d St And 4.5.69 *AUR* xliii 329

TEUNON or Shiach, Clara Macandrew   MA 1937
occasional relief teaching Selkirksh 1951–72; retd;
resid Galashiels

TEUNON George John MacAndrew   MB ChB 1924
sen hosp m o/consult. radiol Blackburn & dist
group of hosps from 1955; retd 1963; resid Banchory

TEUNON or Sharma, Hilda Margaret
MB ChB 1937
resid Nainital UP India

TEUNON John   MA 1941

TEUNON Lilian Margaret   MA 1947

THAIN or Tellwright, Annie   *MB ChB 1921
resid Market Drayton

THERON Pieter Hendrick
MB ChB 1941 *ChM 1947

THICKNESSE or Garrow, Katharine Joyce
MB ChB 1950
resid Pinner

THIRD James Ross Sinclair   MB ChB 1933
g p Aber from 1947

THIRD John   *MA 1914 ᵈBSc 1915
d 28.10.67

THIRD or Duffus, Marjorie Ann Sinclair   MA 1934

THIRD or Lewis, Sheila   MB ChB 1946
d Gloucester 31.10.69

THOIRS or Queen, Isobel Louise   MA 1943
resid Richmond Hill Ontario

THOLT Elizabeth   MA 1929

THOM Alexander Davidson   MB ChB 1947
gen surg regist King Edward VII hosp Windsor
1958–61; surg CMC hosp Pendiya Cyprus 1961–64;
g p Maitland NSW Aust from 1964, hon obst/assoc
surg Maitland hosp from 1966

THOM Charles Denis   MA 1949

THOM Charles John   MA 1909
d Glasg 2.9.67 *AUR* xlii 180

THOM Elizabeth Henderson   MB ChB 1948
DPH(Glas) 1954
m Ayr 14.6.51 David A. R. Lawrie stockbroker s of
David L. Bearsden

THOM Isabella Scott   MA 1925
no longer on GC reg

THOM James William   BSc 1926
no longer on GC reg

THOM Jane Ann   MA 1918
resid Oldmeldrum
d 27.6.81

THOM or Duncan, Margaret Jean   MA 1949

THOM Marjory Ferguson   MA 1938

THOM Robert Jamieson   *MA 1933

THOM William   BCom 1922
no longer on GC reg

THOM William Cumming
MA 1917 BD 1920 PhD 1924 DD 1948
retd from Sydney Aust 1968; resid Aber
wife *d* 5.9.65
d Aber 25.3.79 *AUR* xlviii 227

THOMAS David   BSc 1950
HM geol surv later inst of geol sc: geol Lond
1950–52, Manc 1952–60, Leeds 1960–71, sen scient
off. from 1971; member Br Caucasus exped to USSR
1958; Lond univ exped to Jan Mayen Is 1961, Imp
coll exped to Jan Mayen Is 1963
m Wrexham Ruth E. Young d of Edward Y. Wrexham

THOMAS Ena Ernestine   MB ChB 1954

THOMAS Isabella Elsbeth Mary Ferguson
MB ChB 1950
clin m o h Carmarthen from 1970
m Caio Carmarthensh 14.6.65 Eric M. Grey
BA(Lampeter) clerk in holy orders s of Thomas G.
Llandybie Carmarthensh

THOMAS William (Sir)   PhD 1923
CB
d 22.11.74 *AUR* xlvi 322

THOMPSON or Donald, Alice
*MA 1907 *BSc 1909
d 7.7.74

THOMPSON Alice May   MA 1916
d Aber 4.9.73 *AUR* xlv 318

THOMPSON Barbara Anne   MA 1952
teacher: s s Aber 1959–61, Ghana 1961–67, p s
Lond from 1967
m Lond 2.9.75 Justice A. Neizer BSc(eng) 1960 *qv*

THOMPSON Edward John   MA 1910
no longer on GC reg

THOMPSON George Alexander   BSc(eng) 1948
CEng MIEE 1969
sect. leader Laurence, Scott & Electromotors Norwich
from 1973

THOMPSON Hugh Percy   BSc(eng) 1947

THOMPSON James McAllan Cormack
MA 1934 *BSc 1935
FRIC
retd 1972; resid W Kilbride

THOMPSON Jane Maver   MA 1927
teacher Fraserburgh acad 1947–63
resid Paisley
m Aber 1964 John I. McBurnie MA(Edin) C of S min
s of Walter M. McB. Loanhead Midlothian

THOMPSON John Arthur   BSc(for) 1954

THOMPSON John Edward   MB ChB 1909
no longer on GC reg

THOMPSON or Malcolm, Laura Blackhall Cormack
MB ChB 1943
clin m o Grampian health board (N dist)

THOMPSON or Craig, Maggie Wilken   MA 1929

THOMPSON Michael Scott   BSc(agr) 1955
Buxted Chicken Co.: superv farms E Anglia 1961–
66; res asst NIAB Cambridge 1966–68; herbicide
advis CIBA-GEIGY (UK) based on Cambridge 1968–
73; comp tech advis Key & Pell E Anglia/E Midlands
1973–76; trg advis man. 1976–78; trg man. agr area
BASF(UK) from 1978

THOMPSON or Morrice, Norah   MA 1945
resid Aber

THOMPSON Robert McLean   MB ChB 1924
d Tamworth 5.2.65 *AUR* xli 58

THOMSON Adam Edward   MA 1923 ᵈMB ChB 1927
retd Dagenham 1963; resid Banchory

THOMSON or Lyall, Agnes Ann   MA 1930
retd 1972; resid Aber

THOMSON or Gibson, Agnes Jane   *MA 1920
resid Tain

THOMSON Alan Russell   *BSc 1952 PhD 1955
leader biochem group eng sc div AERE Harwell
from 1969; visiting reader Wolfson bioanalytical
centre Sur univ 1973–76; comm techniques group
biochemical soc from 1977

THOMSON Albert Gordon   MA 1931

THOMSON Alexander Baird   MA 1926
retd 1968; resid Pencaitland E Lothian

THOMSON Alexander Francis   *BSc 1943
Rowntree-Mackintosh York: chief analyst 1960–67,
prod. dev man. and export div dir from 1967

THOMSON Alexander Louis George
                                        *MB ChB 1921
g p Kei Mouth S Af 1960–73; semi-retd

THOMSON Alexander Wilson   MB ChB 1944
g p Cullen from 1947
marr diss
m(2) Tarves 23.1.63 Nora I. Henderson dietitian d of
William H. Tarves

THOMSON or Davidson, Alexandra Margaret
                                        BSc 1929 MA 1931
resid Fraserburgh

THOMSON or Hendry, Alice Cushny   MA 1913
d Aber 28.9.62 *A UR* XL 82

THOMSON or Martin, Alice Margaret
                                        MA 1922 BSc 1924
resid Aber
d Newmachar 20.3.81 *A UR* XLIX 136

THOMSON Allister McAllister   BSc(eng) 1944

THOMSON or Shewan, Ann (Annie) Fraser
                                        MA 1929
d Edin 7.8.77 *A UR* XLVIII 287

THOMSON or Shennan, Ann Lindsay
             *MB ChB 1930 *MD 1934 ᵈDPH 1939
MFCM 1972
sen m o Aber c c 1968–74; retd
husb d –.10.48
m(2) Aber 30.9.61 Alan R. Edwards OBE MA(St And)
instr/comm RN
d Aber 21.1.81 *A UR* XLIX 138

THOMSON Annie Sutherland   MA 1922

THOMSON Arthur Landsborough (Sir)
        MA 1911 *BSc 1914 DSc 1920 LLD 1956
Buchanan Medal of Royal Society 1962
chmn trustees Brit Museum Lond (nat hist) 1967–69
d 9.6.77 *A UR* XLVII 286

THOMSON Atholl   MB ChB 1919
d Aber 5.12.69 *A UR* XLIII 444

THOMSON Beryl   MA 1955
teacher: Sunnybank p s Aber 1956–66, Beaconhill
p s Beaconsfield Quebec 1966–73; resid Pierrefonds
Quebec
m Beaconsfield Quebec 16.6.72 Gordon R. Biggar
instrum mech Air Canada s of Louis B. Florida USA

THOMSON Charles   BL 1938
d Aber 7.2.79 *A UR* XLVIII 232

THOMSON Charles David   MA 1950 MB ChB 1955
d Auchterarder 5.10.64 *A UR* XLI 61

THOMSON or Steele, Christina Williamina
                                        MA 1917
d 5.3.80

THOMSON David Landsborough
             MA 1921 *BSc 1924 LLD 1952
LLD(Sask) 1961 LLD(Manit) 1961
d Province of Quebec 20.10.64 *A UR* XLI 56

THOMSON Derick Smith   *MA 1947
prof Celtic Glas from 1963; pres Scottish Gaelic
Texts Soc from 1964; chmn Gaelic Books Council
from 1968

THOMSON Donald   MA 1915
no longer on GC reg

THOMSON Donald   MA 1929
OBE 1970
dep rector Oban h s 1967–72; retd; provost Oban
1959–62, 1968–71; pres An Comunn Gaidhealach
1962–65; chmn McCaig's Trust from 1968; chief
Camanachd assoc of Scot. 1971–73; member Argyll
c c from 1973
d Oban 8.7.80 *A UR* XLIX 68

THOMSON Dorothy Adèle   BSc 1953
analyst chem dept Aberd 1955–63; teacher maths:
Aber 1972–73; Glasg from 1974
m Aber 2.4.62 John S. Edmond MA 1955 *qv*

THOMSON Dorothy Isobel Grant   MA 1915
resid Galashiels
d Galashiels 26.4.80

THOMSON Douglas Stephen   MA 1952 LLB 1955

THOMSON Edward   BSc(eng) 1948
head dept telecomm Aber tech coll 1963–75; retd

THOMSON Edward Riddell   *MA 1938
asst head (curriculum) Inverurie acad from 1974

THOMSON Edward Worley   BSc 1926
FEIS 1967
retd 1968; resid Dun
d 17.6.78

THOMSON Elizabeth Forbes   MA 1920
retd 1960; resid Aber

THOMSON Elizabeth Fraser   *MA 1945
lib London patent off. lib (later sc ref lib) Lond
from 1960

THOMSON or Liddell, Elsie Jean   MB ChB 1937
g p Cults Aber from 1946
husb d Cults 15.6.74

THOMSON or Duncan, Ethel Elspeth Fyfe
                                        MA 1939
teacher Walker Rd p s Aber till 1948; resid Aber

THOMSON or Greig, Frances Isobel   MA 1927
resid Guildford

THOMSON or Milne, Freda Margaret   BSc 1954
lab tech: path. dept Weston-super-Mare gen hosp
1967–68, girls' g s Gloucester 1969–73

THOMSON Frederick Alexander   *MA 1954
prin teacher hist: Forfar acad 1963–67, Aber acad (Hazlehead acad) 1967–73; asst head Hazlehead acad from 1973
m Paisley 28.7.62 Elizabeth M. Muir MA(Glas) teacher d of John K. M. Paisley

THOMSON George   MA 1948

THOMSON or Ross, Gladys   MA 1955
head Chapel of Garioch p s from 1976

THOMSON or Glass, Hilda Macdonald   MA 1933
b Kirkwall 14.7.13
teacher Kincardinesh 1934–45; women's educ Omdurman, Sudan 1946–48; teacher maths Grove acad Dun 1956–73; retd
m Khartoum 14.12.46 George A. Glass chief publ health insp Sudan

THOMSON Horace Norman Michaelson
MB ChB 1944 DPH 1965
asst m o Banff c c 1965–66; m o/prin lect health educ Aber coll of educ from 1966
chmn educ comm joint c c Moray & Nairn Elgin 1962–64

THOMSON Ian   BSc(agr) 1951

THOMSON Ian Angus   BSc(eng) 1945
MIMavE 1958 MIMechE 1970
lect mech eng Gateshead tech coll 1951–59, sen lect 1959–61; head mech eng Wearside coll of f e Sunderland Co Durh from 1961

THOMSON Ian Gordon   MB ChB 1943 MD 1959
OBE 1965
m o Ndian/Pamol/Douala, Cameroons W Af from 1967; later m o gen council of British Shipping; resid Lond

THOMSON Ian Stephen   BSc(eng) 1934

THOMSON Ian Stewart
MA 1913 MB ChB 1921 MD 1924
retd 1958; resid York

THOMSON Isobel Margaret   MA 1937
teacher Airyhall p s Aber 1968–77; retd

THOMSON or Fröhlich, Isobel Pirie   MA 1946

THOMSON James   MA 1909
d Aber 26.4.68 *AUR* xlii 348

THOMSON James   MA 1910

THOMSON James   BSc 1925
teacher sc RGC Aber from 1942; retd 1963; resid Aber

THOMSON James   BSc 1926
d Aber 16.7.73 *AUR* xlv 320

THOMSON James   MB ChB 1929
d 20.11.67

THOMSON James Greig   MB ChB 1927 °MD 1937
FRCPath 1963
retd 1970; emeritus prof univ of Cape Town

THOMSON James Ian Fraser   MA 1936 LLB 1938
ptnr Edmonds & Ledingham advoc Aber from 1948
m 27.9.41

THOMSON James John George
***MA 1924 BSc 1925**
retd 1966; resid Edin

THOMSON James Laing   *MA 1900 BD 1903
d Edin 10.7.64 *AUR* xl 394

THOMSON James Laing Spalding   MB ChB 1932
MRCGP 1966 FHS 1970 FRSM 1971
g p Lond from 1933

THOMSON James Macfarlane
MB ChB 1935 DPH 1939
m o h Angus c c 1944–68; retd; police surg Angus constab 1945–66; secy loc med comm Angus 1950–67; resid Aber

THOMSON James Milne   MB ChB 1936
d 31.12.64

THOMSON James Oliver   *MA 1911
d 31.4.71

THOMSON James Simpson   MA BSc 1920
d Aber 10.2.62 *AUR* xxxix 382

THOMSON or Smitton, Jane Elizabeth Johnston
MA 1920
d Wick 3.7.77

THOMSON Jane Scott   BCom 1932

THOMSON or Meldrum, Janet Craig   MA 1900
d Newtonmore 29.4.61 *AUR* xxxix 199

THOMSON Janet Gladys   MA 1930

THOMSON Janet McAllan   MA 1925
no longer on GC reg

THOMSON Jean Shepherd   MA 1916
retd 1960; resid Aber
d 20.6.81

THOMSON Jeannie Grant   *MA 1903
d Aber 10.4.61 *AUR* xxxix 199

THOMSON or Diack, Jeannie Isabella   MA 1943
teacher Kemnay 1956–78

THOMSON or Wiseman, Jessie   MA 1920
resid Aber

THOMSON John Adam (Sir)   MA 1947
CMG 1972 KCMG 1978
HM dipl serv: first secy Washington 1960–64; FO

1964–66; acting head plan. staff FO 1966–67, head plan. staff 1967–68; chief of assessment staff Cabinet off. 1968–72; min and dep perm rep UK deleg to NATO 1972–73; asst under-secy FCO 1973–76; Brit high comm New Delhi from 1977

THOMSON John Hendry   *MA 1951

THOMSON John McNaughton   MB ChB 1955
   RAMC 1956–59; col med serv Dar-es-Salaam/ Njombe, Tanganyika 1959–62; g p Leic 1962–69; g p/part-time m o Natal prov admin Eshowe, Zululand from 1969

THOMSON John Maitland   BSc(eng) 1945

THOMSON John Peters   MA 1908
   d Falkirk 15.3.69 *A UR* XLIII 208

THOMSON or Watt, Lily Norrie   MA 1946
   resid Memsie

THOMSON Maggie   MA 1931
   d 13.1.71

THOMSON Magnus Louttit
                  MA 1926 MB ChB 1930 MD 1936
   d Cheadle Hulme 7.6.63 *A UR* XL 205

THOMSON Margaret Dawson   MB ChB 1944
   m Harries

THOMSON or Brodie, Margaret Elizabeth
                                      MA 1943

THOMSON or Wilde, Margaret Helen
                                   MB ChB 1948
   resid Bridgend Glam

THOMSON or Dunnet, Margaret Henderson
                                      MA 1952
   teacher Engl Mintlaw s from 1971

THOMSON or Cheyne, Margaret Isabel   MA 1929
   d Aber 30.5.69 *A UR* XLIII 331

THOMSON or Craig, Margaret Isabella   MA 1929
   resid Dollar
husb *d* Kirkhill Invsh 4.8.54

THOMSON or Holiday, Margaret Ishbel Hemingway
                                      MA 1955
   retd; resid Rowlands Gill Tyne and Wear
d 27.1.79

THOMSON or Edwin, Maribel
                           MA 1916 *BSc 1919
   writer; resid Dorking

THOMSON or Huber, Mary Duffus   MA 1913
   resid Hamburg, Cologne and then Munich
d Munich W Ger 22.7.80

THOMSON Mary Elizabeth   *MA 1901
   d Daviot Abdnsh 27.8.73 *A UR* XLV 315

THOMSON or Macinnes, Mary Margaret Gray
                                      MA 1948
   resid Tunbridge Wells

THOMSON or Davidson, Mattie Paterson   BSc 1924
   d Banchory 6.10.67 *A UR* XLII 365

THOMSON Robert   MB ChB 1922
   retd 1969; resid Louth Lincs

THOMSON Ronald Cooper   *BSc 1946
   ICI: seconded as works man. to Duperial Argentina 1961–64; prod. man. petrochemicals div Teesside from 1969

THOMSON Ronald Ross   *BSc 1949

THOMSON Roy Hendry   *MA 1955
   Thomson of Cults: dir 1960–63, man. dir from 1963; elected off. O St J 1972

THOMSON Sheila   *MB ChB 1932 DPH 1935
   MM(Soc Apoth. Lond) 1937 MFCM 1971
retd 1972; resid Edin

THOMSON Spence Ford   BL 1952
   prin leg asst Corp Aber until 1971; retd
d Trowbridge 25.2.75 *A UR* XLVI 240

THOMSON Thomas Bentley Stewart
                  *MA 1911 BD 1914 DD 1946
   d 10.8.73 *A UR* XLV 316

THOMSON Violet May   MA 1949
   dep head Woodside p s Aber 1967–77, head The Hillocks p s Bucksburn Aber from 1977

THOMSON Wilfred Nicolson   BSc(agr) 1948

THOMSON or Sinclair, Wilhelmina Downie Flett
                                      MA 1947
   relief teacher Moray from 1963

THOMSON William   LLB 1934
   retd 1972; resid Edin
d Edin 4.10.78

THOMSON William Eddie Spalding   *MA 1936
   scient edit. Blackie & Son Glasg from 1946

THOMSON William George   MB ChB 1947
   DIH 1967 DMJ 1969 MFOM 1978
chief m o Smith's Indust Lond from 1959

THOMSON William Norman   MB ChB 1944
   consult. radiol Edin N hosp group from 1953

THOMSON Williamina Netta   MA 1916
   d Carluke 14.10.61 *A UR* XXXIX 279

THOMSON or Gordon, Winifred   MA 1946

THORN or Wilson, Annie Florence Elizabeth
                                      MA 1908
   d Torphins 19.9.70 *A UR* XLIV 107

THORN Harold Leslie   BSc(eng) 1950

THORNILEY Garven Nesbitt   BSc(agr) 1952
no longer on GC reg

THORNTON Ronald   *MA 1937

THOW Gordon   MB ChB 1925
s h m o surg Elgin 1948–67; retd g p Elgin 1970
m(2) Elgin 12.1.60 Christina Davidson

THOW Henry Abernethy   MA 1920
no longer on GC reg

TIBBLES Joseph Russell   MB ChB 1915
no longer on GC reg

TINDALL Daisy   *MA 1933
lib Reform Club Lond 1947–71; retd

TINGLE Alfred   BSc 1896
no longer on GC reg

TOCHER Alexander McKenzie Innes   MA 1931
head Methlick p s 1966–72; retd; resid Aber

TOCHER Forbes Scott   *MA 1906 DD 1934
d 15.8.73 *AUR* XLV 316

TOCHER Francis Edward   *BSc 1951 PhD 1959
sen lect dept geol/mineralogy Aberd from 1969;
asst dean (advis) fac of sc Aberd from 1973

TOCHER or Milne, Hazel Allan   MA 1944

TOCHER Helen Howitt   MA 1939
teacher Aber: St Clement St p s 1943–58, Springhill
p s 1959–72, Sunnybank p s from 1972

TOCHER James Ross   MB ChB 1938
g p Arbroath from 1945
d Arbroath 14.1.79 *AUR* XLVIII 232

TOCHER Wilfred Ian McKenzie   MA 1945

TODD Edward Finlay Ross   MB ChB 1944
d 25.4.61

TODD Ian Douglas Hutchison   MB ChB 1950
MRCP 1958 FFR 1962 FRCP 1975 FRCR 1975
consult. radiotherap Christie hosp Manc from 1963;
hon lect radiotherap Manc from 1967

TODD John David   BSc(for) 1949
conserv of for. Zambia from 1964

TODD John Munro   *MA 1932
d Kingussie 28.4.73 *AUR* XLV 227

TODD Martha Simpson   *MA 1914
d 25.4.74

TODD Peter George   MB ChB 1953

TODD William George   MB ChB 1943
g p Kemnay from 1967

TODD William Maxwell   *BSc 1936
prin teacher chem Morrison's acad Crieff from 1966

TOGHILL Edith Mary   MA 1952

**TOLMIE or Mitchell or Mason, Elizabeth Mary
                                    Falconer   MB ChB 1939**
staff m o Harrods Lond from 1960

TOLMIE or White, Isabella Margaret   MA 1913

TOLMIE James Boyd   MB ChB 1937

TOLMIE John William   BSc(eng) 1946
FIEE 1975 Dip Man. St(H–W) 1965
Dip Inst Marketing 1968 BA(OU) 1977
NSHEB: dist eng Dingwall 1950–55; sen asst eng
(head off.) Edin 1955–69, area eng Dingwall 1969–71,
area eng Dun 1971–75; asst chief pers off. (head office)
from 1975

**TOMORY or Werdmuller, Louise
                            MB ChB 1919 MD 1923**
d Cape Town 5.9.73 *AUR* XLV 318

TOPPING Jeanie Bayne   *MA 1911
d Aber 11.12.73 *AUR* XLV 446

**TOPPING or Carey, Margaret Rosamond
                            MB ChB 1946**
resid Keynsham Bristol

TOPPING or Youngson, Robina Gordon   MA 1927

TOPPING William Renton   MB ChB 1927 MD 1942
d Birm 30.12.77 *AUR* XLVII 357

TORRIE Alfred   MA 1919 MB ChB 1924
d Richmond Surrey 21.4.72 *AUR* XLIV 429

TORVANEY Alastair William Logie   *MA 1948

**TORVANEY or Hemans, Janet Helen Alison
                            MA 1944**
coach Engl lang Harpenden 1962–63; teacher Engl
lit/lang St Michael's convent Leigh-on-Sea 1964, part-
time Steeple Bumpstead jun s 1965–68; lect: lib stud./
Engl coll of tech Southend 1969, bus. Engl f e coll
1972–78, 1st yr Fr evening class Brentwood from 1974

TOSH Annie Clarke   MA 1916
resid Aber

TOSH or Kendrick, Constance Stevenson   *MA 1949

TOSH Gordon Cameron   *BSc(eng) 1953
sen dev eng in telecommunications Lond from 1954
m Lond 11.8.56 Iris Farrer secy d of Victor S. F.
Mottingham Lond

TOSH Jack Rae   *MA 1950

TOSH Sheena Mary   MB ChB 1939

TOTT or Bevan, Patricia Murray   MA 1948

TOUGH or Brown, Aileen Taylor   MA 1952
freelance journalist Aber 1960–69; teacher: Aber 1970–71, Anlaby Yorks 1972–75, Glasg from 1975

TOUGH Andrew Crawford   BL 1949
ptnr Aikins MacAulay & Thorvaldson barristers and solic Winnipeg Canada

TOUGH Arthur Farquharson   *MA 1953 LLB 1956
Keele univ: admin asst 1961–63, asst regist 1963–67, dep regist from 1967

TOUGH David   *MA 1946
sect. man. ICI Manchester: dyestuffs div 1948–71, organics div from 1971; resid Rochdale

TOUGH or Lennie, Elizabeth Mary   MA 1946
teacher maths: Powis acad Aber 1959–63, Linksfield acad Aber from 1967

TOUGH Eric Alexander   BSc(eng) 1943
dir Internat Oil and Gas div PA man. consult. Lond from 1973

TOUGH George   *BSc 1951

TOUGH or Shepherd, Helen Isabella   MA 1924
no longer on GC reg

TOUGH or Davidson, Isabella Jane Ritchie
**   MA 1932**
resid Aber

TOUGH James Cormack   BSc(eng) 1941
teacher phys Banff acad from 1969

TOUGH or Hart, Jeannie Ann Christina   MA 1930

TOUGH Mary Fraser Roberts   MA 1929
head p dept High s for girls Aber 1964–70; retd

TOUGH Peter Henderson   MA 1911
d Daviot Abdnsh 13.6.68 *AUR* XLIII 78

TOUGH Robert   BSc(agr) 1921
no longer on GC reg

TOWERS or Ashburn, Janetta   MA 1946

TOWNS or Heggie, Audrey Margaret Gourlay
**   MB ChB 1950**
Newton Stewart: fam plan. clin work from 1962 and part time g p from 1966

TOWNSEND Patrick William   BSc(eng) 1950

TOWNSHEND Gerald Kilvington   *BSc 1949
MInst Packaging 1964
Procter & Gamble: Geneva 1959–61, Cincinnati USA 1961–62, Brussels 1962–65, N'cle-u-Tyne 1965; Bowater Packaging Gillingham Kent: dir sales 1969–71, gen man. 1971–74; Mardon Packaging Internat: man. group dev from 1975

TRAIL Hugh   MB ChB 1923
consult. chest phys hosp man. comm mid Glam area from 1948; resid Radyr Cardiff

TRAIL John Downie   MB ChB 1931 DPH 1933
consult. chest phys N'cle-u-Tyne RHB 1963–70; retd; resid Washington Tyne & Wear

TRAIL or Fraser, Leslie Mitchell   MA 1911
resid Belf

TRAIL or Cumming, Mabel   MA 1933

TRAIL Mary   MA 1926
head Fraserburgh inf s 1964–69; retd

TRAIL or Thomson, Mary Moir (Lady)   MA 1912
d Lond 12.1.69 *AUR* XLIII 209

TRAIL Richard Robertson
**   *MA 1919 *MB ChB 1923 *MD 1925**
d Lond 15.6.71 *AUR* XLIV 317

TRAIL Stephen Galt   *MB ChB 1910
no longer on GC reg

TRAIL William   *MA 1928
d Edin 5.9.73 *AUR* XLV 320

TRANTOR Alexander William Grant
**   BSc(eng) 1934**
FIME 1943
dir/gen man. BP refinery (Kent) 1960–68; dir: Cammell Laird shipbuilders Birkenhead from 1971, Oil Refinery Serv Internat Lond from 1972, Gas & Oil Acreage Lond from 1973, oil consult. to Royal Bank of Scot. Edin from 1973

TREACHER William John Floyd
**   MA 1932 MB ChB 1937**
d Pinner Middx 26.2.74

TRETHOWAN Henry Markham   MB ChB 1929

TRIBE Derek Edward   PhD 1949
D Agr Sci(Melb) 1966 OBE 1977
univ Melb Aust: prof anim nutrit from 1966; member Aust comm on advanced educ 1970–77

TRINGHAM Robert   MB ChB 1944
g p Bedford from 1965
m(2) Bedford 21.2.70 Isabel J. H. Colegate d of Ralph C. Norwich

TROTTER Robert Maxwell   MB ChB 1894
no longer on GC reg

TROUP Arthur David   MA 1925 LLB 1927
d 17.8.73

TROUP or Russell, Doris Isa   MA 1930
JP Castle Eden and Peterlee Durh 1961
chmn juvenile court 1971–73, dep chmn of bench from 1971

TROUP or Patterson, Isobel Robertson Stewart
MB ChB 1949
m o Hants from 1966

TROUP James Bannerman   MB ChB 1951
Dipl. Amer Board Orthop Surg 1963
Fell. Amer Acad Orthop Surg 1964
consult. orthop surg Winchester mem hosp Virginia
USA from 1961

TROUP or Jockel, Jean Davidson   MB ChB 1949
g p Tawa NZ from 1965

TROUP Margaret MacDonald   BSc 1921
d St Abbs 12.11.73

TROUP Robert George   MB ChB 1949
MRCGP 1965 FRCGP 1975
g p Hornchurch Essex 1956–77; reg m o DHSS from
1977

TROUP Robert Jamieson   MA 1914
no longer on GC reg

TROUP or Connon, Sylvia Helen Rose
MA 1948 Dip Ed 1952
resid Cults Aber

TROUP William Alexander   MA 1919
d Glasg 18.3.77

TULLOCH Alexander Guthrie   MA 1916
no longer on GC reg

TULLOCH Alistair John   MB ChB 1950 MD 1976
FRCGP 1975
g p Bicester Oxon from 1963; part-time res asst unit
of clin epidemiology regius dept med univ of Oxford
from 1969
m Birm 26.11.66 Christine Goffe BA(Nott) med soc
worker d of Cyril G. Birm

TULLOCH Hector Munro   BSc(agr) 1942

TULLOCH Lawrence Gardner
MB ChB 1938 MD 1950
d Astley nr Manchester 4.1.65 *AUR* xli 60

TULLOCH or Dixon, Margaret Beatrice   *MA 1912*
d Lerwick 11.10.74

TULLOCH or Macleod, Mary Ann   MA 1923
teacher Lochmaddy p s N Uist 1957–62; retd; resid
Inv

TULLOCH Mary Elizabeth   MA 1945

TULLOCH Mary Gardner   *MA 1931*

TULLOCH or Mackay, Nina June   MA 1954
res asst dept psych Strath 1973–74; res asst dept
psych Aberd 1974–75; teacher adult ment h'capped
Aber from 1976

TULLOCH Robert Grant   BSc 1941 *1947*
d 9.12.72 *AUR* xlv 228

TULLOCH William   *BSc 1945*
on staff inst of geol sc Edin (formerly geol surv of Gt
Br) from 1945

TULLOCH William James   MA 1955 Dip Ed 1956
dep head p s Montrose acad 1962–70; head East p
s Montrose 1970–76, N Links p s 1976–77, Borrowfield
p s from 1977

TURNBULL Alexander Cuthbert
MB ChB 1947 *MD 1966*
FRCOG 1966 Thursfield award Aberd 1966
MA(Oxon) 1973
sen lect obst/gyn Aberd and consult. NE reg hosp
board 1961–66; prof obst/gyn Welsh nat s of med
Cardiff 1966–73; Nuffield prof obst/gyn Oxford from
1973; fell. Oriel coll Oxford from 1973

TURNBULL George Harley   *MA 1950 MEd 1958*
PhD(Strath) 1970
sen lect educ psych Aber coll of educ 1967–75; head
psych dept Craigie coll of educ Ayr from 1975

TURNBULL Graham Dudgeon   MA 1952

TURNBULL James   *MEd 1946*
d 6.5.67

TURNBULL or Forsyth, Prudence Isobel   MA 1943

TURNER Adam Annand   MB ChB 1913 MD 1926
d 7.1.64 *AUR* xl 398

TURNER Alexander   *MA 1955*
March Group (Spain) Lond: teaboy 1957–58,
cashier 1958–59, chief cashier 1959–61, comp secy
1961–64, dir from 1964
m New Barnet 17.8.63 Ann Wilkin mus

TURNER Alistair Glass   MB ChB 1951
d Lond 11.3.69 *AUR* xliii 218

TURNER Isabella Coutts   MA 1955

TURNER or Donald, Louise   *MA 1923 LLB 1972*
Arundel s Salisbury Rhodesia: dep head 1962–64,
head 1964–68; retd; edit. vol iv *Roll of Graduates* until
her death
d Montrose 21.12.80 *AUR* xlix 136

TURNER or Wright, Margaret Elizabeth   MA 1930
resid New Elgin
husb d 2.7.71

TURNER William Tracey   EdB 1947 MEd 1966
MBE 1970
teacher: maths/sc St Columba's h s Fife 1940–45,
handicapped ch Frederick St s Aber 1945–47; educ
psych Cumberland 1947–49; organis off. Lancs c c
1949–64; asst educ off. Lancs 1964–72; retd; resid
Clayton-le-Woods nr Chorley

TURPIE John Lawson   *MA 1951*

TWEDDELL William   MB ChB 1924
retd; resid Clent Worcs

TWEDDLE or Main, Margaret Fimister
                                    MB ChB 1949
JP 1976
part time m o h Nott from 1959

TWORT or Raffan, Jean Crampton   MB ChB 1939
part time med asst diabetic dept ARI from 1962
d Aber 1.9.75 *A UR* XLVI 325

TWORT Reginald Frank   MB ChB 1908
d 9.2.69 *A UR* XLIII 208

TWORT Reginald Joseph   MB ChB 1936 ᶜMD 1944
d Nott 16.6.71 *A UR* XLIV 321

TYTLER Peter   MB ChB 1940
d Lerwick 28.12.68 *A UR* XLIII 217

URE Allan McCulloch   PhD 1954
prin scient off. Macaulay inst Aber from 1961

URE James Smith   BSc(agr) 1950

URQUHART Angus Munro   *MA 1899
no longer on GC reg

URQUHART or Russell, Cecilia Valentine
                                    MB ChB 1942 ᶜMD 1946
part-time m o mat./ch welfare N'cle-u-Tyne 1958–72

URQUHART Helen Edith   MA 1925
nurs trg and apptments 1951–71; retd; resid Beauly

URQUHART Ian Alexander   MA 1925
teacher: 1st asst Victoria s Falkirk, head Buchlyvie s
1956–63; retd
d Falkirk 30.12.72

URQUHART John   MA 1951

URQUHART or Taylor, Joy Munro   *MA 1946
teacher various schools till 1964; Lady Spencer-
Churchill coll of educ Wheatley Oxford: lect 1964–71,
head of educ dept from 1971; visiting lect Central
Michigan univ USA summer 1975; dean fac educ
stud. Oxford polytech from 1978

URQUHART or Blackman, Margaret McRobb
                                    MB ChB 1946
s c m o Maidstone health dist. from 1972
marr diss 1968

URQUHART Margery   BSc(agr) 1935
OBE 1977
dir soc work Aberdeensh/Kincardine 1969–75; dep
dir soc work Grampian reg 1975–76, acting dir 1976–
77; retd

URQUHART Robert William (Sir)
                                    MA 1920 LLD 1954
CMG 1944 KBE 1950
consul FO Lond 1938–39; insp gen consular establish-
ments; prin off. min of home security Bristol 1940–42;
consul gen Tabriz Iran 1942–43, New Orleans USA
1943–44; insp gen worldwide 1945–47; minister pleni-

potentiary Washington USA 1947–48; consul gen
Shanghai China 1948–51; amb Caracas Venezuela
1951–55; retd; chmn Crofters' Commission Inv 1955–
63; resid Edin
wife *d* 25.1.75
m(2) Edin 15.10.77 Jane Gibson MA 1921 *qv*

URQUHART William Spence
                        ***MA 1897 DLitt 1921 DD 1930**
d Torphins 16.7.64 *A UR* XL 394

UYSAL Ahmet Edip   MA 1948
Ankara univ Turkey: assoc prof Engl 1957–65, prof
Engl 1965 and from 1968; visiting prof: Engl dept
univ of Cologne W Ger 1963–64, Engl dept Texas
tech univ Lubbock, Texas USA 1966–68; Carnegie
fell. School of Scottish Studies Edin univ 1977–78;
prof Engl dept Ankara univ from 1978
m Ankara 17.12.52 Melek Genç d of Nuri G.
Iskenderun Turkey

VALENTINE Alfred Buyers   *MA 1919
d Guildford 21.2.70 *A UR* XLIII 444

VALENTINE Edward Jordan   MB ChB 1941
Jamaica: sen m o King George V sanatorium 1960–
69, prin m o MoH 1969–73; retd; consult. phys
King George V sanatorium from 1973

VALENTINE Gilbert Enos   MA 1910 MB ChB 1914
private pract Kingston Jamaica 1931–78; retd

VALENTINE Henry William   *MA 1931
retd 1967; resid Haddington

VALENTINE Irene Mary Findlay   MA 1930
retd 1971; resid Aber

VALENTINE John Cheyne   BSc(agr) 1954

VALENTINE or Mackintosh, Kate Margaret
                                    MA 1910
no longer on GC reg

VALENTINE Leslie MacKenzie
                            ***BSc 1946 PhD 1949**
dir res Berger Jenson & Nicholson Lond from 1968
marr diss 1972
m(2) Lond 19.8.72 Nina Flatto BSc(Lond) civ serv

VALENTINE Margaret Hunter Strachan   MA 1918
d Lond 7.11.62 *A UR* XL 85

VALENTINE Max Gordon
                            MB ChB 1940 MD 1946
MRCPsych 1971 FRCPsych 1971
consult. psychiat Bristol from 1959

VALENTINE May Fleming   MA 1925
teacher: Portessie p s 1955–60, Buckie h p s 1960–
66; retd

VAN BLOMMESTEIN Jack Henry Greite
                                    MB ChB 1922
member   pneumonocosis   compensation   board

Johannesburg 1962–72; part-time med consult.
western platinum mines Marikana S Af from 1972
d Transvaal S Af 9.7.78

VAN DER MÉRWE or Westhuysen, Katherina Francisia Elizabeth MB ChB 1921

VARTY Isaac William BSc(for) 1950 PhD 1954

VASS John MA 1937 BD 1940
d Aber 21.10.74 *A UR* XLVI 240

VENTERS Robert Sharpe MB ChB 1928
d Carlisle –.6.73 *A UR* XLV 320

VERE Raymond Andrew BSc 1951
FInstPet 1973
Esso res centre Abingdon Oxon: scient 1964–67, prin
scient from 1967

VERGNANO or Gambi, Ornella PhD 1952
resid Firenze, Italy

VLASTO or Higham, Patience Jane Marietta *MA 1947*
resid York

WADDELL Annie Fleck *MA 1924*
d 9.2.75

WADDELL Robert Lindsay BSc(agr) 1950

WADDINGTON William George MA 1901
no longer on GC reg

WADE Alan Hugh MB ChB 1953

WAGREL Martin James *BSc(eng) 1953*
BP: proj eng Venice/Aden 1960–62; dev eng distrib
Lond 1962–66; dev eng marketing: Milan 1966–70,
Lond from 1970
m(1) Venice 1961 Patricia E. Morgan; marr diss 1967
(2) Lond 1967 April B. Coats

WAINWRIGHT Richard William MA 1947
d 16.12.63

WAITER or Tulloch, Margaret Mary MA 1955
teacher: St Cyrus p s 1956–60, North Links p s
Montrose 1960–64; part-time remed Montrose dist
from 1973

WALKER or Taylor, Agnes MA 1943

WALKER or Thomson, Agnes Anne MA 1926
teacher p s Mintlaw 1961–71; retd; resid Longside

WALKER Alaster Charles Andrew BSc(for) 1950
d Hobart Tasmania 19.4.77

WALKER Alexander MA 1940

WALKER Alexander Adam *MA 1925*
d Aber 3.11.65 *A UR* XLII 86

WALKER Alexander Camfield Slessor MA 1937
head Tyrie p s 1963–72; dep head Fraserburgh
cent s from 1972

WALKER Alexander Donald *BSc 1953*
prin scient off. pedology dept Macaulay Inst for soil
res Aber from 1958
m Aber 29.6.62 Eleanor W. Booth

WALKER Alexander Lumsden MA 1928 BD 1932
d 27.10.63

WALKER Alexander Mackenzie *MA 1930*

WALKER or Donald, Amy Stewart *MA 1921*
resid Aber
husb *d* 8.7.55

WALKER Andrew MA 1932 LLB 1934 MB ChB 1942
g p Aber; retd
m Woking 25.9.54 Anne C. Paget physioth d of
Lancelot P. Beattock

WALKER or Milne, Ann MA 1940
resid Whitehills

WALKER Charles Herbert MB ChB 1951 MD 1958
g p Liverpool from 1952

WALKER Charles William MA 1915 *MB ChB 1924 *MD 1926*
retd 1964; resid Hereford

WALKER Cyril George MB ChB 1927 MD 1933
g p Oxted 1933–64; retd; resid Bexhill
d 24.10.78 *A UR* XLVIII 229

WALKER Doris *MA 1918*
no longer on GC reg

WALKER Dorothy June MA 1952
teacher p s Culter from 1964; exchange BC Canada
1967–68

WALKER Douglas (Bremner) MA 1951

WALKER Douglas Ewen MB ChB 1943 DPH 1948
s m o reg med off. SHHD Edin from 1975

WALKER Douglas Stewart MA 1921 LLB 1923
d Hereford 18.6.63 *A UR* XL 203

WALKER or Wray, Edith MA 1925
resid Aber
d Aber 3.9.80

WALKER or Tawse, Edith Margaret Helen MA 1929

WALKER or Murphy, Elizabeth MA 1933
resid Durris

WALKER Elsie Findlay MA 1901
d 26.8.67 *A UR* XLII 178

WALKER Frances   BCom 1935
retd 1972; resid Finzean

WALKER George Forbes
                        *BSc 1938 PhD 1948 DSc 1960
d Melbourne 17.2.70 *AUR* XLIII 446

WALKER or Mennie, Gertrude Milne   MA 1942
d Aber 5.9.77

WALKER Hector MacDonald   MB ChB 1925
d Manchester 21.8.69 *AUR* XLIII 330

WALKER or Hayman, Helenor Rona   MA 1949

WALKER Horace   *MA 1932 BD 1935 DD 1967
OBE 1978
retd 1977; resid Edin

WALKER Isabella   MA 1922
retd 1966; resid Cults Aber

WALKER or Walker, Isobel Helen   MA 1925
resid Hereford

WALKER James   MB ChB 1938
DADMS
RAMC Middle East/Italy 1940–47; g p Manchester
from 1947
m Aber 4.6.41 Roberta G. Bain d of Alexander T. B.,
Aber

WALKER James   MA 1945
PhD(Lond) 1962
scient MRC Univ Coll Lond 1947–66; sen lect
epidemiology/preventive med Glas 1966–70; sen prin
psych civ serv Lond from 1970
m Lond 30.12.65 Nesta J. Majeran

WALKER James Adam   *MA 1950 *MEd 1955
Dollar acad: prin maths 1964–73, asst rector from
1973

WALKER James Frederick   *MA 1922
d Aber 19.1.77 *AUR* XLVII 212

WALKER James Strachan
                    MB ChB 1922 DPH 1933 MD 1937
d Aber 21.10.70 *AUR* XLIV 110

WALKER John Davidson   MA 1898
no longer on GC reg

WALKER John Leiper   *BSc 1952

WALKER or Simpson, Kathleen Hazel
                        *MA 1955 Dip Ed 1956
resid Dalgety Bay by Dunfermline

WALKER or Newlands, Margaret Jessie
                                MB ChB 1938

WALKER or Mortimer, Margaret June   BSc 1952

WALKER Mary Jean   *MA 1917
d Edin 15.9.76 *AUR* XLVII 103

WALKER Norman John Jamieson
                        MA 1905 *BL 1908 LLB 1910
d 14.3.67 *AUR* XLII 178

WALKER Patricia May   MA 1952
no longer on GC reg

WALKER Patrick   MA 1915
d Port Elphinstone Inverurie –.8.79 *AUR* XLVIII 350

WALKER Peter Gordon   PhD 1952
prof chem path. inst orthop Lond

WALKER Ralph Spence   *MA 1928
emeritus prof McG 1970; resid Haslingfield Camb

WALKER Richard Jones   MB ChB 1937
d Aber 5.1.72 *AUR* XLIV 433

WALKER Robert Jackson   *MA 1925
d 16.4.71

WALKER Ronald Powlett   *MA 1931 *MB ChB 1936
Brit Red Cross Badge of Honour
g p Tettenhall Wolverhampton from 1939; area m o
Brit Red Cross Soc

WALKER Sheila Mair   MA 1954
teacher Engl Torry acad Aber from 1960

WALKER Sidney James Macara   MB ChB 1942
clin div indust hyg Ont Canada from 1952

WALKER William Alexander   BCom 1923

WALKER William Alexander   MB ChB 1942
g p Nelson NZ 1958–78; sen m o Ngawhatu
psychiat hosp Nelson from 1978

WALKER William Lumsden
                MB ChB 1941 DPH 1947 MD 1963
FRCPsych 1972
consult. ch psychiat United Brist hosps/Avon AHA
(ch/fam guid serv) from 1966; also clin lect ment
health Brist from 1970; visiting consult. Kingswood
spec unit Bristol from 1964

WALKER William Wood   *MB ChB 1924
g p Lee 1928–72; Treasury m o Lond 1929–72; clin
asst Gyre-Miller gen hosp 1928–71; retd

WALLACE Annabella   *MA 1926
no longer on GC reg

WALLACE Arthur Edward   MA 1922
retd 1968; resid Largs
d 3.1.80

WALLACE or Andersz, Evaline Euphemia Baxter
                                    MA 1944
teacher Port Elphinstone Inverurie from 1952

WALLACE Gordon Profeit   MA 1934 MB ChB 1939
prin m o areas 3/5 Maidstone Kent 1953–74; retd;
part time clin m o Kent from 1974

WALLACE James Gilbert   MA 1924 LLB 1925
d Blairs Aber 26.12.72 *AUR* XLV 225

WALLACE James Lamb   BSc 1952
Aber: prin teacher maths/sc Middle s 1967–69, prin sc Frederick St s 1969–71; prin maths Old Aber s 1971–73, year master Linksfield acad 1973–75; asst head Linksfield acad from 1975

WALLACE or Murray, Janet Keith   *MA 1931
d Tranent 29.11.70 *AUR* XLIV 212

WALLACE Kenneth Macdonald   BSc(for) 1955

WALLACE or Cruickshank, Mary Elizabeth
MA 1954
teacher Hull from 1965
m Aber 3.8.57 Stanley Cruickshank MB ChB 1963 *qv*

WALLACE Patrick Crawford   MB ChB 1933
g p Middleton-on-Sea Sussex from 1948

WALLACE Robert Strachan   *MA 1904 LLD 1928
d Canberra 5.9.61 *AUR* XXXIX 271

WALLACE William   MA 1931
d –.6.63

WALLER Patricia May   MA 1952
asst edit. Thos Nelson & Sons publ (overseas dept) Edin 1959–62
m Edin 23.9.61 Alexander Heward arch. s of Frederick W. H. Milngavie

WALTERS Louis George   MB ChB 1927 MD 1936
d Natal 12.4.75 *AUR* XLVI 323

WALTON Kenneth   PhD 1951
d Aber 2.1.79 *AUR* XLVIII 122

WANNOP Arthur Robson   BSc(agr) 1922
d Edin 11.9.72 *AUR* XLV 126

WARDLE Philip Arthur   *BSc(for) 1955
HM for, comm: Forest of Dean 1958–61, Alice Holt Lodge Farnham 1961–71; FAO UN Yugoslavia/ Surinam/Rome from 1971

WARE James McWilliam   BSc(agr) 1932

WARES Alastair Heddle   *BSc 1949

WARES or Wilson, Barbara Calder Sutherland
MA 1940

WARING Horace   DSc 1939
Clarke medallist Royal Soc of NSW 1952; hon DSc univ of W Aust; Britannica gold medal for sc 1970 vice-pres Aust acad of sc 1958–59; retd 1975; emeritus prof univ W Aust
d W Aust 9.8.80

WARK or Reid, Dorothy Elizabeth   *MA 1921
d 1.2.71

WARK James Miller   BSc(agr) 1950

WARNER Adrian Charles Irving   PhD 1955

WARRACK George Clark   BSc(for) 1940
MF(Michigan) 1960 FIFor(GB)
BC for. serv Victoria BC Canada: res progr superv 1960–71, dir res div from 1971

WARRACK John   MB ChB 1932 DPH 1939
retd 1971; resid Ashley Heath Shropsh

WARRACK John Hyslop   MB ChB 1947
g p Derby from 1953

WARREN or Beattie, Lucy   MA 1941
occasional teaching posts Elgin acad 1942–45, St John the Evangelist s Manchester 1970–73

WARREN Ronald Wilfred   BSc(agr) 1949

WARREN Thomas   *EdB 1951
d 19.10.71

WARREN Winifred Joyce   MA 1923 BSc 1925
chief chem Unigate Creamery Hemyock Devon 1930–65; retd; resid Church Stretton Salop

WATERS Margaret Fraser   MA 1941
resid Aber

WATERS or Waters, Mina Hunter   MA 1910
d Edin 11.2.67 *AUR* XLII 180

WATERS Russell McFarlane   BSc(for) 1951
d 8.12.69

WATKINS David Fraser   MA 1938
Aber: head Seaton p s 1965–67, Cornhill p s from 1967; retd 1980

WATKINS Richard Dawson   PhD 1954
MIEA 1956
sen lect civ eng Sydney univ Aust from 1956

WATKINS Sidney Maurice Kynoch   MB ChB 1937
RAMC 1940–45; house surg Royal hosp Chesterfield 1949; g p Dronfield 1950–73; retd; resid Bournemouth
m Dronfield 24.5.40 Isbel R. Fowler SRCN d of George H. F. BAOR Cologne

WATLER Donald Crosbie   MB ChB 1949
MRCPath 1964 FRCPath 1969 MMASC 1970 FRCPE 1972
Jamaica govt med serv Kingston: consult. path. 1960–64, dir laboratory serv from 1964

WATSON Adam   *BSc 1952 PhD 1956 DSc 1967
FRSE 1971
sen scient off. Aberd 1960–71, sen prin scient off. (spec merit in res) ITE Banchory from 1971

WATSON Alexander Hepburn   MA 1949
BA(Lond) 1970
Inverurie acad: spec asst 1959–73, asst prin Engl from 1973

WATSON Alexander James
                    ***MB ChB 1947 °MD 1960**
FRCPath 1973
lect path. Glas 1954–61; sen lect path N'cle 1961–70, reader from 1970

WATSON Alexander Lindsay   BSc(eng) 1948
CEng MIEE 1971 Cert Ed 1974
GEC Coventry: proj leader on Admiralty receiving equipment 1955–64; proj leader mobile radio receiving eqpment 1964–68; group leader: VHF mobile radio/ UHF mobile radio 1968–71; lect telecommun sect Coventry tech coll from 1971
m Coventry 29.5.66 Doreen A. Berry teacher d of Robert B. Worsley Manc

WATSON Alexander McKay Young   MA 1928
d Huntly 15.4.72 *A UR* XLIV 432

WATSON Alexander William   MA 1951
teacher maths Montrose acad 1961–72; prin guid Keith g s from 1972

WATSON or Husband, Alice Raeburn   BSc 1929
teacher: Invsh 1930–32, sc Castlebay Is of Barra 1932–34, S Harris/S Uist 1934–35; sc tech h s Inv 1940–43, biol Durh/N'cle-u-Tyne 1943–51; educ off. Ibadan/Zaria Nigeria 1951 –59; lect St Matthias coll of educ Brist 1960–72; retd; resid Bristol
m Inv 20.8.35 William A. Husband BCom(Durh) confid clerk/univ regist s of George H. N'cle-u-Tyne

WATSON Andrew Forbes   *MA 1953
asst solic: Eastbourne corp 1959–61, Ipswich corp 1961–63; sen asst solic Ilford corp 1963–65; asst town clerk Kingston-u-Thames 1965–67; dep town clerk Grimsby 1967–70, Plymouth 1970–74, chief exec/town clerk from 1974
m Northwood Middx 13.4.63 Penelope J. Archer housemother maladjusted ch d of Herbert W. A. OBE Northwood

WATSON Angelica   MA 1942
sen lect soc work Stir from 1972

WATSON or Gray, Annabella   MA 1915

WATSON Arthur Forbes   MB ChB 1942
g p Sinoia Rhodesia from 1960

WATSON Bessie Urquhart   MA 1935
retd 1973; resid Aber

WATSON or Orchiston, Charlotte Barbour   MA 1917
d NZ 1969

WATSON Christina Cruickshank   MA 1933
d Campbeltown 28.11.78

WATSON Constance Mary Anne   *MA 1924
d 7.12.81

WATSON Daniel Stewart   BSc(eng) 1932 *1933
CB 1961
Admiralty: chief scient off. 1961–68; head royal naval scient serv M o D 1968–72; retd; resid Churt Farnham

WATSON David Brown   MA 1928 MB ChB 1932
d 22.2.66 *A UR* XLI 248

WATSON David John   BSc 1951
teacher: sc Kelso h s 1961–70, prin biol from 1970

WATSON or Whalen, Elizabeth Law   MB ChB 1947
resid Shrewsbury New Jersey USA

WATSON or Adam, Elizabeth Margaret   MA 1915

WATSON George Alexander   BSc 1932
retd 1974; resid Luthermuir Laurencekirk

WATSON Gladys Nellie   *MB ChB 1922 DPH 1924
MRCGP 1953
g p Warley from 1947

WATSON Henry   MA 1948

WATSON Henry Gavin   BSc(agr) 1953

WATSON Herbert Louis   BSc 1911
no longer on GC reg

WATSON Hugh Glass   MB ChB 1923
d Bakewell 9.2.71 *A UR* XLIV 211 & 320

WATSON James   MA 1891
d Cults Aber 16.1.63 *A UR* XL 73

WATSON James   BSc 1932 MA 1933
retd 1970; resid Kirriemuir

WATSON James   BSc 1944 *1949
phys Alex Pirie & Sons Stoneywood 1953–58; self-employed Northampton 1958–69; phys Alex Cowan & Sons Penicuik 1969–73; teacher Stevenson coll of f e Edin 1973–74; lect Telford coll f e Edin from 1974

WATSON James Alexander   *MA 1912
d 21.6.75 *A UR* XLVI 320

WATSON James Henderson   BSc(eng) 1945
FIEE 1970
St Helens Lancs: works man. Fibreglass 1961–64, works man. Pilkington Bros 1964–71, chief eng from 1973

WATSON James Innes   MA 1912 MB ChB 1917
d Kelso 22.9.70 *A UR* XLIV 109

WATSON or Robson, Jane (Jean) Frances   MA 1919
d Aber 15.3.45

WATSON or Pickup, Jean Patricia   MB ChB 1951
cytologist Royal North Shore hosp Sydney Aust from 1964

WATSON John   MB ChB 1938
g p Perth W Aust from 1950

WATSON John   *BSc 1952
assoc prof maths Rensselaer polytech inst USA 1965–66; lect maths univ of E Anglia from 1966

WATSON John   MA 1953
no longer on GC reg

WATSON John Alexander   *MA 1938 LLB 1947
resid Ardrishaig

WATSON John Scott   MB ChB 1936
d Aber 28.9.65

WATSON or Stewart, Kathleen Elizabeth   *MA 1944

WATSON Kenneth Charles
MB ChB 1947 ᶜMD 1955
FRCPath 1968 MRCPE 1972
assoc prof microbiol univ of Natal S Af 1964–68, prof
1968–69; consult. microbiol Western gen hosp Edin
from 1969
m Canterbury Kent 8.5.59 Alys M. Gardener physioth
d of Edward G. A. G. MA(Cantab) Reculver

WATSON Louisa Margaret   *MA 1922
no longer on GC reg

WATSON Luke Methuen   MB ChB 1929

WATSON or Whiteley, Margaret Elsie   MA 1941
resid Otley

WATSON or Carmichael, Margaret Stewart
MB ChB 1936
resid Derby

WATSON Mearns Bruce   *BSc 1933 PhD 1936
FSAScot 1972
dep dir RGIT Aber 1968–71; retd

WATSON Murray James Alexander   MB ChB 1950
d Maidenhead 14.1.77 *AUR* XLVII 287

WATSON or Rae, Norma Reid   MA 1950
resid Aber

WATSON Pauline Bertha   MA 1919
no longer on GC reg

WATSON Stanley Wilson   MB ChB 1941
d 24.12.72

WATSON Thomas Yirrell   BSc(agr) 1929

WATSON Vincent Murray McAdam   MB ChB 1921
d Aber 6.12.62 *AUR* XL 85

WATSON or Wilson or Axford, Violet Irene
MB ChB 1945

WATSON William Ferguson
***BSc 1944 PhD 1947 DSc 1952**
CBE 1978
dir rubber and plastic res assoc Shrewsbury 1959–76;
dir Allied Polymer Group 1976–78; dir Portex Hythe
Kent

WATSON William Hay   *MA 1929 DD 1964
secy/educ secy Christian council (Nyasaland)
Malawi 1962–64; C of S min: asst St Machar's cath

Old Aber 1964–65, St Bride's ch Callander 1965–70;
team min City presb ch Salisbury Rhodesia from 1970

WATSON William Hugh   BSc(agr) 1954

WATSON William Mair   MA 1934

WATSON William Norman   BCom 1931

WATT Adam Niddrie Shirreffs   MB ChB 1925
d 18.5.66

WATT Adrian Gray   MA 1935
C of S min: Baillieston Old ch 1941–48, St Michael's
par ch Edin 1948–80; part-time chap. HM prison
Edin from 1973
wife *d* 4.10.78

WATT Aileen   *MA 1955 Dip Ed 1956
farm. Aberlour 1961–65; also teacher spec asst Engl
Nairn acad 1965–69; ptnr farm. Aberlour from 1969
m Aberlour 5.7.69 James Garrow farm. s of George
W. G. Aberlour

WATT Alan Crombie Robertson
***MA 1946 LLB 1949**
ptnr Gray & Kellas advoc Aber 1951–72; town
clerk Ballater 1952–71; a chmn indust tribunals
(Scot.) from 1972

WATT Alexander
MB ChB 1902 DPH 1904 MA 1904
no longer on GC reg

WATT Alexander   MB ChB 1935
DPM 1953 MRCPsych 1973
psychiat Worthing from 1960

WATT Alexander James Morrison   *MA 1932
teacher maths/phys Gordon s Huntly 1937–52;
spec asst maths Waid acad Anstruther 1952–72; retd;
resid Huntly
m Huntly 17.7.39 Jean Robertson nurse d of John
W. R. Huntly

WATT Alexander John   Dip Agr 1915 BSc(agr) 1919
d Aber 6.10.66 *AUR* XLII 85

WATT Alexander Stuart   MA 1913 BSc(agr) 1913
M Brit Soc Soil Sc 1948 M Bot Soc Brit Isles 1952
FRS 1957 Hon M Brit Ecol Soc 1961 Hon F For.
Soc(GB) 1965 Gold Medal Linnean Soc 1975
lect for. bot Cantab 1934–59; visiting lect Melb Aust
1950–51; visiting lect Colorado USA 1963; visiting
prof Khartoum Sudan 1965–66

WATT Alexander William Owen   BSc(agr) 1951
MBE
prin insp dept of agr for Scot. NE area from 1979

WATT Alice (Alison) Jean   MA 1941
admin off. secretariat ITA/IBA Lond from 1963

WATT Alice Mabel   MB ChB 1922 DPH 1923
retd 1961; resid Boston Lincs

WATT Andrew Philip   BSc(agr) 1955
farm. Maud from 1958

WATT Annetta Mary   MA 1951

WATT or Godsman, Annie Isabella   *MA 1922
head Fisherie p s Aberdeensh 1940–60; retd; resid
Aber
husb *d* Aber 1973
d Aber 9.1.79

WATT Archibald   MA 1923 DD 1959
moderator Gen Assembly of C of S 1965–66; retd
1969; resid Aber
d Aber 1.1.81 *AUR* XLIX 137

WATT Archibald   *MA 1936 MEd 1938
JP 1970 FSAScot 1970 FEIS 1976
prin Engl/dep rector Mackie acad Stonehaven 1962–
72, dep rector 1972–77; retd
m Edzell 21.12.64 Elizabeth P. White teacher d of
Arthur J. W. BA(Lond) Thame Oxon

WATT Arthur Stewart   MA 1910 LLB 1911
no longer on GC reg

WATT Catherine Ann   MA 1937
teacher: Causewayend p s Aber 1940–50, Powis s s
Aber 1951–76; retd
m Aber 24.7.43 Eric C. Wilson driver s of Alexander
W. Aber

WATT Colin John George   BSc(eng) 1953

WATT David Brand   MB ChB 1947
no longer on GC reg

WATT David Scott   MA 1939 *BSc 1947
Royal Dutch Shell Group: gen man. Shell BP &
Todd oil serv Wellington NZ 1960–66, staff assign-
ment Shell Lond 1967–68, exploration & prod. dir
A/S Norske Shell Stavanger Norway 1968–74; retd;
resid Pennan

WATT Donald Elmslie Robertson   *MA 1950
FRHistS 1960
sen lect mediaeval hist St And 1965–77, prof from
1977, visiting prof mediaeval hist Columbia univ
NY USA 1966–67

WATT or Saunders, Dorothy Margaret   MA 1950
teacher Minishant Ayrsh 1963–73; head Girvan
nursery s from 1974

WATT or Blackhall, Edith   MA 1916
HM off. of works/WRAF; demob 1919
resid Lordswood S'ton

WATT Edward William Murray   *MA 1935
secy/treas Inv hosp board of man. 1951–74; dist
gen admin Highland health board 1974–78; retd
d Inv 20.11.80 *AUR* XLIX 69

WATT or Thomson, Elizabeth Garrow   MA 1946
teacher maths Buckie h s from 1967

WATT or Klose, Elizabeth Mary   MA 1948

WATT or McNab, Elizabeth Mowat   *MA 1901
no longer on GC reg

WATT Francis   BSc 1933
dep head Tayport s s 1955–67; retd; resid Newport-
on-Tay

WATT George Andrew   BSc(eng) 1948

WATT George Beattie   MA 1912
d Johannesburg 19.3.69 *AUR* XLIII 210

WATT George Dewar   BSc(eng) 1955
MICE 1963 MIWE 1964 FIWES 1977
asst eng Blyth & Blyth consult. eng Inv 1961–62; sen
eng Aber c c water dept Aber 1962–68; group leader
new works NE Scot. water board Aber 1968–75; asst
dir resource plan. dept of water services Grampian reg
c 1975–76, dep dir 1976–78, sen dep dir from 1978

WATT George Esson   *MA 1951
teacher Engl Wemyss s s 1960–63; dep head
Mountfleurie p s Leven 1964–67; head Arncroach p s
by Pittenweem from 1968

WATT George Fordyce   *MA 1924 BSc 1924
no longer on GC reg

WATT or Morrison, Gladys Petrie   MA 1922
d Brighton 17.10.67

WATT Gordon   BSc(agr) 1930
d 31.5.74

WATT Gordon Imray   BSc(eng) 1951

WATT Gordon Lorimer   MB ChB 1949
g p Alford from 1961

WATT Harold Murray Robertson   *MA 1942
JP
man. dir Aber univ press from 1958; Aberd: member
univ court from 1970, vice-convener bus. comm of
General Council from 1971

WATT or Inkster, Helen Milne   *MA 1945
resid Gosforth N'cle-u-Tyne
d N'cle-u-Tyne 20.7.81

WATT Ian Allan   *MA 1950

WATT Ian Gordon   *BSc 1953

WATT Ian Mackenzie   BSc(eng) 1945

WATT Ian Stuart   BSc(for) 1948
for. comm: dist off. Perth 1955–70, Llandovery
S Wales from 1970

WATT or Greig, Irene Alice Ogilvie   MA 1924
d Aber 2.3.69 *AUR* XLIII 214

WATT or Ogston, Iris Campbell   MA 1941
resid Aber

WATT James   MB ChB 1945 *MD 1956
MRCPath 1965 FRCPath 1977
sen lect dept path. Liv from 1965

WATT James   BSc(eng) 1948 *1949

WATT James Alexander   MA 1936
sen tut. and dept head London comp schools 1960–77; retd

WATT James Mackenzie   MA 1929
head Old Deer p s 1961–71; retd; resid Old Deer
d Fraserburgh 7.10.78 *AUR* xlviii 104

WATT or Gauld, Jane   MA 1927
no longer on GC reg

WATT or Taylor, Jane Runciman   MA 1929
resid Aston Sheffield

WATT Jeannie Isobel   MA 1926
no longer on GC reg

WATT or Gatt, Jeannie Slessor   MA 1954

WATT John George Moncur   MA 1942
secy Scot. Marriage Guid Council from 1964

WATT John Taylor   MB ChB 1913
served in Merchant Navy during 1939–45 war
d Banchory 1.6.66 *AUR* xli 338

WATT John Valentine   MB ChB 1953
g p Erith Kent from 1958

WATT or Guthrie, Kathleen Milne   MB ChB 1949
d Dun 21.6.74 *AUR* xlvi 111

WATT Leslie   MB ChB 1940 ᶜMD 1947
phys i/c St Luke's clin and ven dis dept united Manc hosps/reg advis VD Manc RHB/lect in ven dis Manc univ from 1966

WATT or Davey, Lily Margaret   MB ChB 1923
no longer on GC reg

WATT Margaret   *MA 1910
d Banchory 9.1.80 *AUR* xlviii 440

WATT or Wesley, Margaret Crichton   BSc 1945
teacher: sc Aber tech coll 1961–68, maths Currie h s from 1971

WATT or Rhodes, Margaret Downie   BSc 1945
resid Shipley

WATT or McBeath, Margaret Jessie   MA 1939
teacher Banffsh 1940, Aberdeensh 1944, Aberdeensh 1963–68, Angus 1972; resid Letham

WATT Marjory Isabella Katherine   MB ChB 1951
regist obst/gyn Craigtoun hosp St. And 1958–60; m o Aber publ health dept/Grampian health board from 1970; s c m o commun med dept S Grampian dist

m Kincardinesh 26.5.60 Ian B. Hamilton off. RAF/CA s of Thomas H.

WATT Mary   MA 1925
no longer on GC reg

WATT or Cormack, Mary   MA 1930
retd 1967; resid Findochty

WATT Mary Florence   MA 1928
retd 1962; resid Aber
d Aber 19.12.78

WATT or Duncan, Mary Jessie   MA 1952

WATT or Roelich, Mary Webster   MA 1930
Dip Soc Sc(Lond) 1953
secy Red Cross depot Solihull Warks 1939–43; welf off. WLA Winchester 1943–45; teacher Ashford Middx 1959–75; retd
d 28.8.80

WATT Matilda   MA 1920
no longer on GC reg

WATT or Loots, Moyra Helen   MA 1952
teacher Harrytown h s Romiley 1969, remed Stockport 1970–71, St Paul's p s Hyde from 1972

WATT or Mutch, Myra   MA 1914
d Aber 19.5.74

WATT Raymond Ian Gordon   *MA 1939
lect: hist Kingsway coll for f e Lond 1948–66, hist/soc stud. Brixton coll for f e Lond 1966–67, hist/econ Princeton coll Lond from 1967; councillor Borough of Hornsey 1951–65
m Lond 22.3.63 Patricia A. Charlton med secy/lect comm subj d of Leonard F. C. Mevagissey

WATT Robert John McPherson   BL 1952
teacher: Springhill p s Aber 1963–65, Flotta publ s 1965–74, Cornhill p s Aber 1974–80; retd

WATT Robert Strachan   *MA 1955

WATT or Masson, Sandra Ryrie   MA 1949
teacher: Invergowrie p s Angus 1964–66, Callander p s 1967–68, Doune p s Perthsh from 1968

WATT William   *MA 1918
d Ellon 24.6.70 *AUR* xliv 109

WATT William   MB ChB 1942 DPH 1948
Canada: dir loc health serv Manitoba 1956–67, Alberta 1967–76; retd
wife *d* 1969

WATT William Alexander   MB ChB 1946
g p Cheltenham from 1951

WATT William Andrew Fraser   BSc 1951
FRSS 1970 MBCS 1973
head dept maths/sc coll of comm Aber from 1961

WATT William Gordon   MB ChB 1908 DPH 1909
d Aber 12.5.76

WATT or Marshall, Williamina Margaret   MA 1944
resid Newton Stewart

WATTIE Annie Kinnear
        MA 1919 *MB ChB 1922 DPH 1928
d Tynemouth 31.8.77

WATTIE James Alexander   MA 1907
no longer on GC reg

WATTIE John Nicholson   MB ChB 1947
g p Romsey Hants

WATTIE or Morgan or Cope, Katharine Betty
        McPherson   *MA 1917
examiner Engl civ serv commissioners 1934–47;
reviser Engl SED 1922–57; resid Lond

WATTIE Nora Isabel   MB ChB 1921
OBE 1964
retd 1964; resid Glasg

WATTY Edward Irving   MB ChB 1950
OBE 1973 DTM & H FRCP(C) F Coll Amer Path.
Dominica WI: dist m o 1951–63, govt path. from 1967
m Lond 26.12.55 Winifred P. Paul cyto tech d of
Ninas P. USA

WAYMOUTH Charity   PhD 1944
FAAAS 1966
USA: sen staff scient The Jackson Lab, Bar Harbor
Maine from 1963, asst dir (trg) 1969–72; asst dir (res)
1976–77; assoc dir (scient affairs) from 1977; hon lect
univ of Maine from 1964; Rose Morgan visiting prof
univ Kansas 1971; pres Tissue Culture Assoc 1960–
62; edit.-in-chief Tissue Culture Assoc 1968–75;
member exec council Episc ch 1967–70; vice-chmn
clergy deployment board Episc ch from 1970; chmn
Episc ch comm on state of the church from 1976;
member Faith & Order comm Nat Council of
Churches USA 1970–73

WEBSTER Alexander   BSc 1917
d Aber 21.11.68 AUR XLIII 80

WEBSTER Alexander   MA 1947 LLB 1953
d Tornaveen Torphins 24.7.64 AUR XL 401

WEBSTER Alexander Urquhart
        MA 1906 MB ChB 1909
d 23.10.75 AUR XLVI 414

WEBSTER Annie Strachan   *MA 1898
no longer on GC reg

WEBSTER Charles Urquhart   *MB ChB 1950
MA(Oxon) 1970
surg tut. univ of Oxford from 1960; consult. surg
United Oxford hosps from 1963

WEBSTER or Alexander, Dolores Frances
        MB ChB 1950
g p Smethwick W Midlands from 1958

WEBSTER Douglas James   MA 1955
teacher Middle s Aber 1956
d Cults Aber 12.4.77

WEBSTER Douglas William Lawrence   MA 1947

WEBSTER or Fleming, Frances Irene   MA 1950
farm. from 1969; resid Bieldside Aber
husb d Aber 1969

WEBSTER Francis Lindsay   MB ChB 1923
no longer on GC reg

WEBSTER Frances Milne   MA 1952
teacher Ballater p s from 1962

WEBSTER Fred   *MA 1938

WEBSTER George Waddell   MB ChB 1953
g p Margate from 1958

WEBSTER Grace Alexandra Mary   MB ChB 1947
DObstRCOG 1951 DPH(Lond) 1960 MFCM 1973
spec commun med (child health) Ealing, Hammersmith and Hounslow AHA from 1976

WEBSTER or Mackenzie, Helen Urquhart   MA 1914
d East Grinstead 20.5.71 AUR XLIV 317

WEBSTER James   MB ChB 1931 DPH 1933
retd 1968; resid N Berwick

WEBSTER or Robertson, Jessie Donald   MA 1955

WEBSTER John William England   MB ChB 1930
g p Malvern 1946–71; retd; resid Malvern

WEBSTER Maurice Holland
        MB ChB 1936 DPH 1938
FRSH 1971 MFCM(RCP) 1973 BL(Rhodesia) 1975
FFCM 1977
secy for health, dir gen med serv Rhodesia 1963–74;
retd; lect law univ of Rhodesia from 1976

WEBSTER Michael Charles   MA 1947

WEBSTER Peter   MA 1906
d Cambusbarron Stirling –.5.61 AUR XXXIX 200

WEBSTER Robert   MA 1903
no longer on GC reg

WEBSTER Ronald George   *MA 1953

WEDDERBURN or Hughes,Christobel Mary
        MA 1943
resid Bangor

WEE Hiap Tock   MB ChB 1920

WEINER Aaron Harry   MB ChB 1934

WEIR Charles Wilson   MB ChB 1912
d Leeds 11.6.62 AUR XXXIX 379

WEIR or MacQuoid, (Margaret) Florence Smith
MA 1916
resid Turriff
d Portsoy 21.4.81

WEIR George   LLB 1953

WEIR James Martin   *MA 1953
prin teacher Russian Aber acad (Hazlehead acad)
from 1965

WEIR John   MA 1909
retd; resid Hamilton

WEIR John   BSc(agr) 1950
teacher sc: Glenrothes 1961–66, Gordon s Huntly
from 1966

WEIR John Gordon
*MA 1945 MB ChB 1952 MD 1964
DPM 1960 MRCPsych 1971 FRCPsych 1976
Lond: sen regist St Mary's hosp 1960–63; consult.
psychotherap St Bernard's hosp Southall 1963; con-
sult. psychiat: Mildmay mission hosp from 1963, St
Mary's hosp from 1968, Royal Masonic hosp from
1970, St Dunstan's from 1973

WEIR John Park   MB ChB 1929
re-employed (war off.) FEMO combined serv re-
cruiting centre Bristol 1959–70
d 17.5.79

WEIR Kathleen England   MA 1946

WEIR Mackenzie Craigmile   MA 1932
organis p educ Kirkcaldy 1968–74; retd; resid
Selkirk

WEIR Robert   *MA 1912
d Dun 5.2.62 *A UR* xxxix 380

WEIR Roy Deans
MB ChB 1950 DPH 1954 MD 1962
MRCPE 1970 FFCM(Lond) 1973
sen lect soc med Aberd 1965–69; prof soc med Aberd
from 1969

WEIR William   MA 1911 BSc(agr) 1913
d Aber 7.11.65 *A UR* xlii 83

WELSH Frederick Hamilton   MB ChB 1905
d 20.4.64

WELSH Richard William Hepburn
MB ChB 1925 MD 1939
d Guildford 13.12.75 *A UR* xlvi 417

WELSH Robert Hepburn   MB ChB 1891
d S Af –.12.57

WERE Guy Laurenny   MB ChB 1940

WERNHAM Archibald Garden   *MA 1938
prof moral phil Aberd from 1960

WERNHAM or Wilson, Bertha   MA 1944
judge of Court of Appeal Ontario from 1976

WERNHAM James Chrystall Stephen   *MA 1943
prof phil Carleton univ Ottawa from 1954; chmn of
dept phil 1955–70; author *Two Russian Thinkers* 1968

WESLEY Andrew Marshall   BSc(eng) 1945
MIEE 1955
sen asst eng NSHEB Edin from 1968

WEST Alexander Wood   MB ChB 1927 DPH 1929
d 12.1.68

WEST or Duffin, Anne Thomson   MB ChB 1921
resid Greenford

WEST David   *MB ChB 1924

WEST David Alexander   *MA 1948
prof Lat N'cle-u-Tyne from 1969; pro vice
chancellor 1976–77 and 1978–81

WEST Emily   MA 1952

WEST Evelyn May   MA 1949
teaching for C of S mission pre marriage, and for
Government post marriage, in N Rhodesia/Zambia
1958–68; part time teacher Fr/Engl and latterly EFL
at coll of f e Welwyn Garden City 1968–78
m Lubwa mission 22.7.61 Peter D. Snelson
MA(Cantab) dir educ and trg progr Commonwealth
secretariat Lond s of Briscoe G. A. S. Cambridge

WEST George   *MA 1924
no longer on GC reg

WEST or Aitken, Gladys Mary
MB ChB 1922 DPH 1924
m o h Llantrisant and Llantwit Fardre rural dist
council Glam 1932–36; g p 1926–62
resid Creigiau nr Cardiff

WEST or Birkett, Margaret Adamson   MA 1926
resid Burton by Lincoln
husb *d* 1969

WEST Stephen   MA 1930
JP 1959
retd 1971; resid Fochabers

WEST Thomas Summers   *BSc 1949
DSc(Birm) 1962 Chem Soc Medallist in chem
analysis and instrumentation 1976
Imperial Coll Lond: reader chem 1963–65, prof
analytical chem 1965–75; dir Macaulay inst for soil
res Aber from 1975

WEST William Wiseman   MA 1905
d Aber 6.5.70 *A UR* xliii 440

WESTERMAN Arthur   MB ChB 1900 *MD 1904
d 8.1.63 *A UR* xl 198

WESTERN Robert Henry   *MA 1934
head Warddykes p s Arbroath from 1969; retd 1975

WESTIE Kathleen   MA 1952
  Rhodesia: teacher Engl Gatooma 1958–59, Roosevelt h s (girls) Salisbury 1959–60, i/c hist Girl's h s Salisbury 1960–74; hist at Mount Pleasant (co-ed) s Salisbury from 1974
  m(1) Salisbury Rhod 23.1.60 Geoffrey T. Eason prop. man. s of Tom E. Berks; husb *d* Salisbury –.6.69
  (2) Salisbury 20.12.78 Donald L. Forbes

WESTMORELAND Winnie   MA 1938

WESTOLL Thomas Stanley   DSc 1941 LLD 1979
  FRSE 1943 FRS 1952 Murchison medal geol soc Lond 1967 Clough medal geol soc Edin 1977 Linnean gold medal zool 1978
  Alexander Agassiz visiting prof Harvard 1952–53; prof geol N'cle (Durh from 1948) 1963–77; emeritus prof 1977; Leverhulme emeritus fell. 1977–79 member of council: Royal Soc Edin 1958–60, Royal Soc 1966–68; presid geol soc of Lond 1966–68, 1972–74; presid sect. C Brit assoc for advancement of sc Durh 1970; chmn convocation N'cle from 1979

WETHERLY James Marshall Rennie   MB ChB 1951
  MCSP 1936
  g p Aber from 1953; med asst dept phys med/ rheumatology ARI from 1959; retd 1978

WETHERLY Robert Erskine   BSc 1938 MB ChB 1951
  d Sunderland 16.1.63 *AUR* XL 207

WHAMOND William Duke   MB ChB 1916
  d 5.11.65

WHEELAN Lorna   MB ChB 1948 MD 1954
  AMInst Psychoanalysts 1959 FRCPsych 1971 consult. ch psychiat King's coll hosp Lond from 1954 m Lond 1962 Sir John D. N. Hill MB BS(Lond) prof psychiat s of Jack H. Orleton nr Ludlow

WHEELER Philip Theodore   MA 1953

WHELAN Lawrence Andrew   PhD 1936
  no longer on GC reg

WHIGHAM Jack Williamson   *BSc 1951
  phys with Admiralty Surface Weapons Estab from 1959
  m Fareham 26.4.80 Patricia T. Bergin

WHIMSTER John Rust   BL 1934
  admitted fac of advoc 1950; leg. asst 1960–71; leg. off. to foreign compensation comm Lond 1971–78

WHITE Adam Duncan Ferguson   MB ChB 1925
  deceased

WHITE Albert Arnold   MB ChB 1935 MD 1951
  chief m o BM corp Birm 1964–70; retd; resid Bigton Shetland
  d Shetland 10.12.76 *AUR* XLVII 214

**WHITE or Smith, Dorothy Mary Agnes
                                   MB ChB 1942**
  clin m o Hereford county hosp; resid Ledbury

WHITE or Waugh, Elizabeth Ann   MB ChB 1938
  g p E Kilbride from 1960

WHITE Eric Alfred Dutton   PhD 1951 DSc 1967
  Lond: dir crystal growth lab Imp Coll 1965–69, reader crystal growth from 1969

WHITE James George Charles   *MA 1942
  ptnr Baillie Gifford & Co from 1955, sen ptnr from 1975; dir: Claverhouse Invest. Trust from 1963, Winterbottom Trust from 1963, Scot. Equit Life Assur Soc from 1971, Scottish Mortgage & Trust Co from 1978

WHITE Leslie Scott   BSc 1955
  d Elgin 10.6.63 *AUR* XL 207

WHITE or Drosso, Lily   MB ChB 1941
  d 23.8.75

WHITE Michael David Ewing   *MA 1939
  BSc(Carleton) 1964
  analyst Canada Cement Lafarge Ottawa from 1964

WHITE or Anderson, Rosemary Helen   MA 1934
  d of John G. W. MA 1890 *qv*(I, II, III)
  teacher Fr Manc 1966–71; resid Bolton-le-Sands, Lancs

WHITE or Moss, Sheena Margaret Jean   MA 1952

WHITEFORD Allan Dinnell   *MA 1954
  teacher Engl Inv royal acad 1960–62; prin Engl: Portree h s 1962–67, Nicolson inst Stornoway 1967–72, dep rector from 1972
  m Aber 4.4.60 Christina M. Mackay MA 1953 *qv*

**WHITELEY Archibald White Maconochie
                                   MA 1928 Dip Ed 1929**
  MBE FSA Scot
  head Kemnay s s 1967–72; retd; resid Monymusk

WHITELEY Dorothy Mary   MA 1922
  retd 1965; resid Aber

WHITLAM John Campbell   MB ChB 1946

WHITSON Gordon Stuart   *MA 1934
  d 21.6.79

WHITSON William Harry Michael   BSc(agr) 1950

WHITTAM Thomas Vincent   PhD 1952

WHITTER Agnes Elizabeth   MB ChB 1951
  part time: asst m o h Aber 1960–61, med asst malignant diseases unit ARI from 1969; part time g p and sessional m o Marks and Spencer Aber
  m Aber 8.9.60 Alistair W. Forrest MB ChB 1927 *qv*

WHITTER Austin Fullarton   MB ChB 1951
  g p Perth W Aust from 1957

WHITTON or Oglethorpe, Anne Smith   MA 1913
  resid Hove Sussex
  d Hove 24.1.81

WHYTE or Macdonald, Agnes Elizabeth   MA 1955

WHYTE Alexander   *MA 1945 LLB 1949

WHYTE Alistair Gordon Donald
                            MA 1927 MB ChB 1931
FRSM 1948 FAS 1958 FSA Scot 1972
lect anat Aberd 1959–77

WHYTE Allan Taylor   MA 1946
C of S min: Kirkmichael and Tomintoul ch 1960–69, Ordiquhill, Cornhill and Ord ch from 1969

WHYTE Betty Hendry   *MA 1940
lib Publ Health lab serv Lond from 1948

WHYTE Catherine Isobel   MA 1920
no longer on GC reg

WHYTE David Fairweather   MB ChB 1938
g p Torridon 1966–74; retd; resid Kenilworth Warks

WHYTE Edward George   MA 1952
head Longside p s from 1973

WHYTE Elisabeth   *MA 1909
resid Lond

WHYTE Emily Park   MA 1909
no longer on GC reg

WHYTE or Campbell Allen, Ethel   *MA 1910
d Harrow-on-the-Hill 22.7.75 *AUR* XLVI 320

WHYTE or Tennant, Gertrude   MA 1936
resid Craigellachie

WHYTE James Alexander   MB ChB 1924
no longer on GC reg

WHYTE James Douglas   MB ChB 1932
retd g p 1972; Northumberland: med asst psychiat St George's hosp Morpeth/Collingwood day clin Gosforth/Tynemouth Victoria Jubilee hosp from 1972, clin asst Tynemouth Vict Jub Day Psychiat hosp N Shields
m Gateshead-u-Tyne 27.6.34 Elsie Davison health visitor d of Peter D. Hetton le Hole Co Durh

WHYTE James Harvey Strachan
                            MB ChB 1941 MD 1954
d 5.1.75 *AUR* XLVI 240

WHYTE James Smith   *MA 1933
MInstP 1970
prin tech coll Aber 1968–74; retd

WHYTE John Cowie   MB ChB 1947
g p Sydney NSW Aust from 1964

WHYTE or Miller, Maggie Bella   MA 1942

WHYTE or Ingram, Margaret Ritchie   MA 1941

WHYTE Margarita Russell   MA 1915
no longer on GC reg

WHYTE or Burbidge, Muriel Louvain   *MA 1941
lect Engl Camb coll of arts/tech Cambridge from 1965

WHYTE Robert Bruce   *BSc 1945 PhD 1948

WHYTE Sydney   MA 1949
Lib asst Sutherland county lib 1961–63; teacher Lhanbryde p s 1964–70; head Echt p s from 1970
m Methlick 19.7.73 Yvonne C. Yule teacher d of Alexander G. Y. Maud

WHYTE William John   *BSc 1937

WHYTE William John Arnold   *MA 1912
no longer on GC reg

WIGGINS Albert Leslie   BSc(agr) 1952
MSc(Glas)

WIGHT or Miller, Elizabeth Campbell Hendry
                            ***MA 1915**
teacher Engl: Gateside j s s 1954–61, Bellahouston and Shawlands acad Glasg 1962–66; retd; resid Aber

WIGHT Robert Muir   BL 1937
univ of Leic: sen lect educ 1961–62, dir p e from 1962

WILDGOOSE John Middleton   MA 1931
head Kittybrewster p s Aber from 1965
d road accident Berwickshire 1.5.79 *AUR* XLVIII 232

WILKIE Alfred   MB ChB 1928
d 14.11.67 *AUR* XLII 368

WILKIE Beryl Alice Gordon   MA 1955
teacher St Thomas's s Keith from 1956

WILKIE James   BSc(agr) 1929

WILKIE James   MB ChB 1948
prin g p Fraserburgh from 1960; m o Consolidated Pneumatic Tool Co from 1963; hon m o RNLI 1964–73

WILKIE John Ritchie   *MA 1943
MA(Cantab) 1972
univ of Leeds: sen lect Ger 1961–72, prof/head of dept 1972–77; prof Ger Aberd from 1978

WILKIE William Roy   *MA 1954
F Inst Scient Bus. 1973
Strath: res organisation theory 1962–63, lect 1963–65, sen lect 1965–66; dir J & J Denholm (MGT) 1966–67; reader/head dept of admin Strath 1967–72; personal professorship 1974

WILKINS Alan Harley   BSc(eng) 1951
FEDI 1967 MITE 1970 FICE 1971 FCIT 1972
Hong Kong: chief eng 1964–69, govt eng 1969–72, dir mass transit stud. from 1972

WILKINS Arthur James Walker
                    MB ChB 1926 DPH 1928

WILKINSON or Mitchell, Agnes Simpson   BSc 1935

WILKINSON James Anderson   *MA 1899
   no longer on GC reg

WILL Alan Addison   MB ChB 1949
   g p/m o to RNAD Coulport Kilcreggan from 1967

WILL or Lamont, Alexa Lee   MA 1922
   resid Aber

WILL or Park, Annie Bain   MA 1936
   teacher: SE Glamorgan 1966–68, Aber from 1968
husb *d* 16.8.65

WILL Charles John   BL 1940

WILL or Campbell, Enid Margaret Ogilvie
                              MB ChB 1925
   d 20.12.69

WILL Hunter McLeod   *MA 1928
   head Ruthrieston s s from 1961
d Aber 16.2.66 *A UR* XLI 249

WILL Ian   BSc(agr) 1950
   prin scient off. Ghana 1960–63; farm man. anim
breeding res organis Roslin from 1963

WILL Ida Mitchell   MA 1933 MB ChB 1938
   g p Arnold Notts from 1941

WILL or Bottomley, Isabella Margaret
                          BSc 1934 MB ChB 1937
   d Carluke 23.10.77

WILL or Walker, Jean Mitchell   MA 1947
   teacher: Brooklands tech coll Weybridge 1958–59,
St Mark's s Mbabane Swaziland S Af 1960–61, New
Town h s Hobart Tasmania 1961–65, Taroona h s
Tasmania from 1967
husb *d* Hobart Tasmania 19.4.77

WILL John   MA 1903 BD 1909
   d Edin 30.10.65 *A UR* XLII 81

WILL Margaret Oliver   MB ChB 1941
   Birm: j h m o St Margaret's hosp Great Barr
1958–62, All Saints hosp 1962–65; asst psychiat St
Margaret's hosp Great Barr from 1965

WILL or Brown, Mary Ann   MA 1932

WILL or Lyons, Mary Shewan   MA 1918
   no longer on GC reg

WILL William Miller   MB ChB 1911
   d Tunbridge Wells 6.1.63 *A UR* XL 201

WILLER Joseph   *MA 1929

WILLIAMS or MacGillivray, Alice Maude   MA 1941
   resid Aber

WILLIAMS Anthony Herbert Michael   *MA 1950
   d Salisbury Wilts 17.10.64 *A UR* XLI 61

WILLIAMS David Albert   MA 1936 BD 1940
   C of S min: Orphir and Stenness from 1964; county
councillor Firth and Stenness 1970–73; member
Orkney educ comm 1973–75

WILLIAMS Edward   BSc(agr) 1931
   retd HM overseas civ serv 1963; sen admin off.
commonwealth econ comm/chief res off. commonwealth secretariat Lond 1963–70; retd; resid Haywards Heath

WILLIAMS Elisabeth Myra   MB ChB 1938
   DA(RCS) 1967
various anaest apptments: Johannesburg/Cape Town
1941–51, Cheltenham/Gloucester from 1965
m(1) Aber 1941 Stanley W. Watson MB ChB 1941 *qv*
   (2) Lond 1951 Gordon S. Haggie rope maker

WILLIAMS or Brooke, Florence Margaret
                                      ***MA 1940**
   resid Keele

WILLIAMS Jean Helen   MA 1939
   teacher Seafield p s Elgin from 1960; retd 1976

WILLIAMS Marjorie Humphry   BSc 1916
   no longer on GC reg

WILLIAMS Michael James
                    MB ChB 1954 ᶜMD 1965
   sen regist ARI 1960–61; lect mat. medica/therap
Aberd 1961–68; consult. phys NE reg hosp board
from 1968
m Glasg 21.1.72 Mary P. McEwan MB ChB(Glas)
haemat d of Patrick McE. MA(Glas) Glasg

WILLIAMS Patrick Bertram Rotheroe
                              MB ChB 1939
   TD
TA and AER 1947–65, lt col; m o Worcs c c Worcester
from 1959
d Droitwich 19.3.79 *A UR* XLVIII 232

WILLIAMS Robin Vawer   MB ChB 1951
   d Malta 21.1.70 *A UR* XLIII 446

WILLIAMS William George   *BSc 1952 Dip Ed 1955
   prin teacher biol AGS from 1961

WILLIAMS William Holmes   MA 1929 BSc 1930

WILLIAMSON or Verel, Agnes Cobden Miller
                              MB ChB 1947
   Sheffield: part-time g p 1959–68, sessional m o
blood transfus serv 1969–72; comp m o from 1974

WILLIAMSON Alfred John
              MA 1905 MB ChB 1909 MD 1911
   d –.12.73 *A UR* XLV 446

WILLIAMSON Andrew Ritchie   BSc(eng) 1951

WILLIAMSON or Kirk, Annie Catherine   MA 1939
resid Taunton

WILLIAMSON Charles   MA 1889
d –.5.60

WILLIAMSON Douglas Harris
                                    BSc 1950 PhD 1952
MCIMM 1953 FGS(Lond) 1953 MAAAS 1964
MGeolAss(Can) 1968
Canada: Sir James Dunn prof geol Sackville NB
1954–66; prof geol/dept head Laurentian univ Sud-
bury Ont 1966–71, also dean of sc from 1969

WILLIAMSON Douglas Macgregor   MB ChB 1941

WILLIAMSON or Sutherland, Eliza Irvine   MA 1925
resid Aber

WILLIAMSON Eric Arthur   MA 1955
d Brunei 21.8.76

WILLIAMSON Freda   MA 1933
teacher King St p s, Ruthrieston s s Aber from 1936

WILLIAMSON George   BSc(agr) 1954

WILLIAMSON George Alexander (Sir)   BL 1926
d Adelaide 23.6.75 *AUR* XLVI 323

WILLIAMSON James   *BSc 1941

WILLIAMSON James Henderson
                                    MA 1946 MB ChB 1953
resid Roos N Humberside

WILLIAMSON Jessie Dalziel   MA 1932

WILLIAMSON Jessie Tulloch   MA 1905
retd 1946; resid Aber

WILLIAMSON John Bremner   BSc(eng) 1948
RE Germany 1948–50; Geo Wimpey & Co UK
1950–73; jun eng, serv ag GB & NI 1973; chief tech
off. Coleraine borough c from 1973
m N'cle-u-Tyne 23.2.57 Patricia Green

WILLIAMSON John Taylor   MA 1936 LLB 1941

WILLIAMSON Laurence Pierre de Loriol
                                    BCom 1926
d Ashford Middx 25.12.64 *AUR* XLI 58

WILLIAMSON Maurice Robert   BSc(eng) 1954
sen dev eng Solarton Farnborough, Hants 1961–63:
lect M o D: s of elect. eng REME Arborfield Berks
1963–67, s for signals Blandford camp Dorset from
1967

WILLIAMSON Robert Bertram
                                    MA 1922 LLB 1924
conducted law classes in POW camp—several
students while in captivity were able to pass univ
degree examinations; chmn Richards of Aberdeen
from 1960; dir, then chmn Lawson Turnbull & Co

Aber 1956–73; dir, then chmn Cruden Bay Brick and
Tile Co from 1937; dir Scot. Salmon and White Fish
Co from 1965; retd as sen ptnr Paull and Williamsons
advoc Aber 1971
d Aber 20.7.76 *AUR* XLVII 105

WILLIAMSON Thomas   MB ChB 1932
MC

WILLIAMSON William Turner Horace   BSc 1910
d Aber 26.4.68 *AUR* XLII 349

WILLIAMSON Williamina Catherine   MA 1911
retd 1955; resid Aber
d Aber 28.8.78 *AUR* XLVIII 102

WILLOCK Ian Douglas   MA 1951 LLB 1954
PhD(Glas) 1963
prof juris St And (now Dund) from 1965

WILLOX Alexander   MA 1930
d 9.10.81

WILLOX Alexander George   *MA 1910
d Kent 8.5.68 *AUR* XLII 350

WILLOX or Brown, Alice   MA 1928

WILLOX Charles Finnie   *MA 1922
FEIS
retd; resid Stonehaven

WILLOX Frank Gerrie   *BSc 1952
FRAeS 1968 MSc(Cranfield) 1972
chief proj eng BAe Preston Lancs 1961–66; proj man.
1966, exec dir from 1976

WILLOX Henry Norman   MA 1928 BD 1931
MBE 1971
C of S min Carnwath par ch/chaplain state hosp
Carstairs: clerk synod Clydesdale from 1967: war
serv: milit hosp Carstairs 1939–48, seconded Shetland
1943, Middle East 1945; retd; resid Helensburgh

WILLOX Marjory Matthew   MA 1954
teacher: Peebles h s 1959–62, King Richard's s
Dhekelia Cyprus 1962–63, Bourne s Singapore 1963–
67, McLaren h s Callander from 1967

WILLOX Norma Philip   MA 1953
tut./lib coll of dom sc Aber 1963–71; lib RGIT Aber
from 1971

WILSON or Panton, Agnes   MA 1913

WILSON Alexander   MB ChB 1909 *MD 1914
d Wimbledon 8.6.62 *AUR* XXXIX 377

WILSON Alexander   *MA 1925
retd 1962; resid Aber
wife *d* 3.12.73

WILSON Alexander Dey   MA 1936
dir soc educ Elgin acad 1967–72, asst rector (guid)
1972–75; retd

WILSON Alexander Hogarth   MB ChB 1925
MRCPsych 1971
med supt/consult. psychiat Leeds 1939–62; lect psychiat univ Leeds 1942–62; retd; resid Walton-on-Thames
m Southend-on-Sea 20.11.29 Jean M. Robertson MB ChB(Glas) m o mat. and ch welfare off. wife *d* 29.11.62

WILSON Alexander Roger   BSc(eng) 1933
retd 1973; resid Ellon

WILSON Andrew   BSc(eng) 1936

WILSON Andrew Strang   MA 1934 LLB 1936
ptnr Stuart & Wilson solic Huntly from 1946

WILSON or Thomson, Anne Edith Duncan
BSc(agr) 1945
dir farm. comp Nether Balgillo Forfar from 1966

WILSON or Hunter, Annie Fraser   *MA 1913
resid Stonehaven

WILSON Archibald Dey   MA 1915
d Chester 30.5.77

WILSON Catherine Johina Jane   MB ChB 1947
no longer on GC reg

WILSON Charles Stephen   BSc 1930 *1932
d –.4.69

WILSON or Bridges, Charlotte Mary
MA 1920 MB ChB 1925
d Lincoln 24.12.76

WILSON Christina Oliphant Binning   MA 1922
MA(Queensland) 1930
Aust: teacher Somerville Ho Brisbane h s for girls 1924–66; retd; part time Somerville Ho 1967–68; retd

WILSON or Simons, Claudine Isabel   *MA 1916
resid Muswell Hill Lond

WILSON or Austin, Cristina   MB ChB 1905
d Lond 17.6.60 *A UR* xxxviii 587

WILSON David Monro   BSc(eng) 1939

WILSON Douglas   MB ChB 1925
no longer on GC reg

WILSON Douglas   MB ChB 1934
DA(Lond) 1944 FRSM 1946
retd 1969; resid Dunstable

WILSON Edith   MA 1922
head Lakes s s (girls) Dukinfield 1945–61; retd
d Buckie 17.3.76 *A UR* xlvi 416

WILSON Edith Barton   MA 1924
d Nairn 27.4.70 *A UR* xliii 445

WILSON Edith Bruce   MB ChB 1925
retd 1967; resid Lond

WILSON Edward Bruce   MB ChB 1898
d –.11.63

WILSON or Drummond, Elizabeth Joyce   BL 1955

WILSON Elizabeth Margaret Davidson   *MA 1933

WILSON Eric Blackett   BSc(agr) 1925 BSc 1925
no longer on GC reg

WILSON Ernest   BL 1937
asst trustee man. Royal Bank of Scot. (merged with Nat Comm Bank) 1969–71; retd; resid Devon

WILSON Florence Eva   BSc 1927 MA 1930

WILSON or Inkson, Frances   MA 1928
teacher maths Dingwall acad 1954–67; retd

WILSON Francis Charles McKay   BCom 1927
no longer on GC reg

WILSON Frank Stanley   BSc(for) 1951
for. off. Attadale W Ross 1964–66; for./conservation off. Dun from 1966

WILSON George   MA 1913
d Nairn 10.1.70 *A UR* xliii 441

WILSON George Alexander   MB ChB 1928
d 9.7.62

WILSON George Alexander   MB ChB 1942
anaest The Rand Mutual hosp (formerly WNLA hosp) Johannesburg from 1980

WILSON George Paterson   MA 1954 BSc 1957
asst biol master Perth acad 1959–66; prin teacher biol Morrison's acad for boys Crieff from 1966

WILSON or Lawrence, Gladys Mary   BSc 1932 *1933
resid Harpenden

WILSON Gwendolene Jean Emslie
MA 1911 MB ChB 1918
no longer on GC reg

WILSON Helen Milne   MA 1924
retd 1961; resid Dingwall
d Dingwall 10.12.79 *A UR* xlviii 441

WILSON Herbert George Macdonald   MA 1907
d 1.9.67 *A UR* xlii 347

WILSON Hilda Eleanor   MA BSc 1922
d Banff 21.11.68 *A UR* xliii 84

WILSON Hugh   *MA 1946
dep rector Nairn acad from 1970

WILSON Hugh Norman Blackett   MA 1926
no longer on GC reg

WILSON Ian Edward   BSc 1949
sen tech off. nat inst of agr bot Cambridge from 1960

WILSON Ian Turner   BSc(for) 1939
d Cornwall 20.8.71 *AUR* XLIV 321

WILSON or Thomas, Irene Catherine   MA 1942

WILSON Isabella   MA 1917
resid Aber
d Aber 24.3.81 *AUR* XLIX 136

WILSON or Wheatley, Isabella Anne   MA 1935

WILSON or Ledingham, Isabella Elder   MA 1925
resid Aber
d Cults Aber 16.10.78

WILSON Isobel Mary   MA 1950

WILSON James Ingram Pirie
MB ChB 1907 MD 1910
resid Southgate Lond
deceased

WILSON Janet Duff   *MA 1910
no longer on GC reg

WILSON John   MA 1942 BD 1945
exec dir Consumers' Assoc of Canada (Ont) from 1975

WILSON John Alexander George   MB ChB 1923
retd; resid Sheffield

WILSON John Cameron   MB ChB 1933

WILSON John McIntosh   MA 1905 MB ChB 1907
d Aberdare 18.4.67 *AUR* XLII 346

WILSON John McIntyre   BL 1947
leg. asst Milne & Reid Aber 1948–60, corp of city of Aber 1960–69; second town clerk dep 1969–71, sen town clerk dep to corp of city of Aber 1972–75, dep town clerk and chief exec 1975–77, town clerk and chief exec from 1977

WILSON John McLaren   MA 1910
retd 1972; resid Fyvie
d Turriff 17.9.75

WILSON John McQueen   BSc(agr) 1944

WILSON John Sutherland Macintosh   MB ChB 1934
g p Aberdare Mid Glam from 1936

WILSON John Warwick   BSc(eng) 1953

WILSON Katharine Margaret   *MA 1917
author: *The Nightingale and the Hawk* (Allen & Unwin) 1964; *Shakespeare's Sugared Sonnets* (Allen & Unwin) 1974
resid Eltham Lond

WILSON or Moir, Kathleen Isabella   MA 1923
teacher Aber: Powis s s 1949–50; remed: Old Aber s s, Ashley Rd p s, Broomhill p s, Frederick St s s, St Peter's s s 1950–63; retd
d Newmachar 7.4.79

WILSON Laura Marie   *MA 1927
d Durris 28.3.72 *AUR* XLIV 431

WILSON Leslie Andrew
MA 1937 MB ChB 1941 MD 1954
FRCP(Lond) 1970 FRCPE 1971
consult. phys Aber gen hosps from 1955

WILSON or Gentles, Lisette Anne Macdonald
MB ChB 1905
no longer on GC reg

WILSON Louisa Mary   MA 1911
d Aber 7.12.74 *AUR* XLVI 235

WILSON or Taylor, Mabel
MB ChB 1923 DPH 1925
no longer on GC reg

WILSON Margaret Anderson   *MA 1921
retd 1961; resid Bieldside Aber

WILSON or Miller, Margaret Barbara   *MA 1930
d Daviot Aberdeensh 26.4.76

WILSON Margaret Doverty   MA 1930
teacher Engl/geog/hist Whitehills j s s 1948–69; retd; resid Macduff

WILSON or Scott, Margaret Elisabeth Mathewson
MA 1946
resid Newburgh Aberdeensh

WILSON or Bevan, Margaret Elspet   MA 1945

WILSON Mary   MA 1939
Edin: asst head: Moredun p s 1958–62; Peffermill p s 1962–78

WILSON Mary Annie Susana   MA 1925
retd 1965; resid Aber

WILSON Mary Helena Taylor   *MA 1939

WILSON Moira Mathewson   MB ChB 1955
regist obst/gyn South Lond hosp 1960–62

WILSON Muriel Isobel May   BSc 1922
no longer on GC reg

WILSON Norman James   MA 1921 *LLB 1923
no longer on GC reg

WILSON Robert   MA 1919 BD 1921
d Aber 20.9.67 *AUR* XLII 184

WILSON Robert   *MA 1926
retd 1972; resid Aber
d 1.11.81

WILSON Robert Angus   *MA 1924
teacher: Cottesmore s mod s 1951–58, Southend s m s Herts 1958–63; lect: Southend coll of tech 1963–67; retd; resid St Albans

WILSON Robert Cummins   *MA 1906
no longer on GC reg

WILSON or Brooks, Sarah Jane   MA 1926
teacher: Macduff h s 1951–69, Banff acad 1969–70; retd; resid Macduff

WILSON Stewart   *MA 1955
head arts dept Rushcliffe g s Notts 1961–63; dep head Moorside comp s Staffs 1963–66; head: Eston Grange s Yorks 1966–71, Stapylton s Teesside 1971–73, Sutton comp s/commun centre Notts from 1973

WILSON Thomas MacSkimming   MB ChB 1944
g p Stoke-on-Trent 1947–64; hotelier Aber 1964–66; g p: Audley Staffs 1966–68, Bucksburn/Dyce from 1968

WILSON Warren Woodrow   MB ChB 1949
FICS 1972
g p St Anns Bay Jamaica from 1952

WILSON William   MA 1909
no longer on GC reg

WILSON William Donald
                    MB ChB 1930 DPH 1938 MD 1948
d Aber 31.8.74 *A UR* xLvi 109

WILSON William Douglas   ᶜMB ChB 1953
MANZCP 1963
consult. psychiat s Canterbury hosp Timaru NZ from 1963; also private psychiat pract

WILSON William Glennie   MB ChB 1939
Treasury m o 1946–68; g p/police surg Salford 1958–68; g p Leuchars 1968–74; retd; resid Mintlaw
d 8.12.81

WILSON William Harvey   BSc(eng) 1955

WILSON William Milne   MB ChB 1927
g p Salisbury Rhodesia 1958–77; m o Rhodesian Iron & Steel Co (RISCO) Redcliff from 1977
d Rhodesia 15.12.78 *A UR* xLviii 229

WILSON William Murray   BSc(for) 1950
d Eassie, Forfar 12.10.77

WILSON William Trail   MA 1926
Dun: teacher Ancrum Rd p s 1927–35, first asst Morgan acad p s 1935–41, dep head Butterburn p s 1941–43, dep head St Michael's p s 1943–47, head Grove acad p s 1947–50, head Eastern p s 1950–71; retd; resid Broughty Ferry

WILSON William Wallace   MB ChB 1923
d 1.8.63

WINROW Stanley Richard   BSc(for) 1952
prin teacher biol Crawshaw s Pudsey from 1960

WINTERFLOOD Eric Gordon   BSc(for) 1950
for. comm: dist for. off. New Forest 1951–60, utilisation off. Chester 1960–67, dist for. off. New Forest 1967–72, asst conserv for. man. Cambridge from 1972
m Hove 22.7.50 Edna S. Burch nurse d of Sidney T. G. Brighton

WINTON or Jamieson, Helen Leslie   *MA 1945
resid Galashiels

WINTON or White, Margaret   MA 1929

WINTON Margaret Jane   MA 1938
first asst/asst head Hill p s Blairgowrie from 1969

WINTON Robert Mitchell   *MA 1941

WINTON William Cruickshank   MA 1919
no longer on GC reg

WISELY Jane (Jeannie) Troup   *MA 1927
prin lect Engl/head Engl dept City of Portsmouth coll of educ 1961–70; retd; resid Aber

WISEMAN Alfred James Thomas   BSc(agr) 1923
d Rhynie 5.1.63 *A UR* xL 204

WISEMAN David Flett   BSc(agr) 1925 MB ChB 1937
d Wanstead 28.6.70 *A UR* xLiv 110

WISEMAN Evelyn Mary   MA 1908
no longer on GC reg

WISEMAN Herbert Horace Eugene   MA 1907
d Edin 2.2.66 *A UR* xLi 241

WISEMAN James Charles   *MA 1930 PhD 1934
rector Forres acad 1961–68; retd; resid Aber

WISEMAN or Steele, Jane Mackie   MB ChB 1953
DOH(Syd) 1975
g p Sydney Aust from 1961

WISEMAN John   BSc(eng) 1951
FICE 1969 FIHE 1972 M Cons E 1977
resid eng: Sir Owen Williams & Ptnrs 1963–64, city eng dept Liv 1964–66; ptnr Wallace Evans & Ptnrs, W I from 1967, assoc ptnr UK 1972 and ptnr from 1975; resid Penarth Glam

WISEMAN John Thomson   *BSc 1948

WISEMAN Laermont Douglas   *MA 1937
dep rector Bo'ness acad 1962–64, rector 1964–74; retd

WISEMAN Robert Lindsay   MA 1928 *BSc 1931
retd 1972
d Greenford Middx 10.10.77 *A UR* xLvii 287

WISHART Agnes Gertrude (Nan)   *MA 1927

WISHART Emmie Orr   *MA 1936
retd 1968; resid Aber

WISHART John Christie   MB ChB 1929
g p Bromley from 1935
d Bromley 23.9.77 *A UR* xlvii 358

WISHART John Strath   *BSc(eng) 1938

WISHART William Philip   *MA 1909 BD 1917
d Edin 2.3.62 *A UR* xxxix 377

WITHERIDGE Edmund Alick   MB ChB 1944
d Stoney Stratford Bucks 29.12.73 *A UR* xlv 449

WITHERIDGE Neil Russell   MA 1948 Dip Ed 1949
teacher Engl spec asst Harlaw acad Aber from 1970

WITT Alexis John   MB ChB 1941
no longer on GC reg

WITTE William   PhD 1935
DLit(Lond) 1966
prof Ger Aberd 1951–77; retd

WITTET or Stewart, Veronica Mary   MA 1923
resid Edin
husb *d* 26.12.55

WOOD or Wilson, Agnes McRobie   MA 1910
no longer on GC reg

WOOD Alexander   MB ChB 1926
d Bournemouth 30.7.70 *A UR* xliv 110

WOOD Alexander Lawson   MA 1931
serv with Moral Re-Armament Europe/Af/Asia/
Amer from 1946; resid Lond

WOOD Alexander (Alistair) Ross   MB ChB 1921
MRCGP 1952
g p Preston till 1967; hon m o Preston North End
AFC 1946–66; dir Preston NE 1954–66; retd

WOOD or Topping, Alfreda Margaret   MA 1914
d Keynsham Somerset 27.11.72 *A UR* xlvi 321

WOOD Annabel   MA 1915
d 17.6.76

WOOD Bryan Ellis   *BSc 1951
FRGS 1959
dep dir of educ Sutherland 1961–75; div educ off.
Sutherland from 1975

WOOD Catherine Smith   MA 1950
teacher p s Findochty j s s 1961–65; supply teaching
Macduff/Whitehills/Bracoden 1972–76, Portnockie p
s 1976–77, Findochty p s from 1977
m Aber 29.3.61 William G. Ross MN capt/harbour
master s of Alexander R. Findochty

WOOD Charles Coutts   MB ChB 1908
no longer on GC reg

WOOD Charles Hutchieson   BCom 1922
no longer on GC reg

WOOD David   BSc(eng) 1954

WOOD Donald Alexander James   BSc(for) 1947

WOOD or Westoll or Will, Dorothy Cecil Isobel
BSc 1939

WOOD Douglas Moir   MA 1927 ᵈLLB 1929
retd 1972
d Dun 22.7.75 *A UR* xlvi 323

WOOD Edith   MA 1908
no longer on GC reg

WOOD Edward James   *MA 1925
retd prof Lat Leeds 1967; part time lect Greek
Leeds 1967–73

WOOD or Sked, Elsie Mackie   MA 1930
resid Glenrothes

WOOD Emily Margaret Leiper   MA 1950
teacher Skene Sq p s Aber from 1954

WOOD George   *BSc 1955 PhD 1959

WOOD George Alexander   MB ChB 1949
Edmonton Alberta from 1970

WOOD George Anderson   MB ChB 1951
g p Taranaki NZ from 1957

WOOD Harry Roy   MA 1951

WOOD Helen Ramsay   MA 1910
deceased

WOOD Helena   MA 1947
teacher Engl/hist: Brechin h s 1961–74, Kincardine
1974, Arbroath acad from 1974
m Aber 14.7.60 James R. Forbes H M off customs &
excise s of James F. MRCVS(Edin) Truro Cornwall

WOOD Henry   MA 1920 PhD 1933
d Aber 15.2.69 *A UR* xliii 211

WOOD or Jefferson, Ida Elizabeth
MA 1908 BSc 1911 MB ChB 1920
d 30.3.74 *A UR* xlv 446

WOOD Isabella Joss   MA 1948
m Smith

WOOD Isobel Milne   MA 1948 MB ChB 1953
various posts ENT dept ARI and RACH, part-time
1965–68; med asst ENT RACH from 1968
m Aber 15.3.65 John T. C. Gillan MA 1950

WOOD James Caie   MB ChB 1932
d 21.4.81 *A UR* xlix 138

WOOD James Challoner   MB ChB 1944
g p Hull from 1948

WOOD James Douglas   *BSc 1951 PhD 1954
head: physiol chem defence res med lab Toronto 1961–68, prof and head dept biochem univ of Saskatchewan Saskatoon from 1968

WOOD James Stewart   *MA 1929 DD 1971
C of S min: South ch Aber 1953–73; advis stud. (lay missionaries) Aber 1962–68; asst pract theol dept Christ's coll Aber 1971–77; relig advis Grampian TV from 1973; lib Christ's coll from 1976

WOOD James Walker   MB ChB 1914
d S Af 4.4.68 *AUR* XLIII 79

WOOD or Cruickshank, Jean Smith   MB ChB 1948
resid Blairgowrie

WOOD Jeannie Margaret Stewart   MA 1922
teacher: Engl/hist Stromness acad 1923–51, prim. subjs 1951–60; retd

WOOD John   MA 1920
d 6.10.63

WOOD John Armour   MB ChB 1955
MRCOG 1963 CRCS(C) 1966 FRCS(C) 1973
spec obst/gyn Nanaimo BC Canada
m Aber 21.7.60 Eleanor M. Allan d of James D. A. Aber

WOOD John Hay   MB ChB 1942 DPH 1947
MRCGP
g p Stoke on Trent from 1949

WOOD John Ramsay   MB ChB 1953
Dip Soc Med 1968
retd RAF 1969; dep med supt Edin R I from 1970; resigned 1977

WOOD Joseph   *MA 1946

WOOD Kathleen   MA 1928

WOOD Kathleen   MA 1946
teacher Aber

WOOD Kenneth Alexander   MA 1943 *1948

WOOD or Getty, Margaret   *MA 1923
d Aber 16.12.70 *AUR* XLIV 211

WOOD or Shearer, Margaret   MA 1914
no longer on GC reg

WOOD or Black, Margaret Caie   MB ChB 1947
MFCM 1973
sen clin m o ch health Wirral from 1973

WOOD or Bain, Mary   MA 1934
teacher Portsoy 1940–46; in bus. Cullen 1946–58; teacher Portessie/Findochty/Portsoy/Banff acad 1958–74; retd
d Portsoy 24.2.78

WOOD Mary Isobel   *MA 1922
retd 1963; resid Cupar

WOOD or McArthur, Millicent Mary Magdalene MA 1935
part-time prin psych civ serv dept Lond from 1962; resid Bowdon Cheshire
husb *d* –.8.58
m(2) Lond 13.10.62 Henry D. Whitehouse restaurant prop. s of Henry J. W. Disley Cheshire

WOOD or MacLennan, Patricia Miles   MA 1950
teacher: Inv 1965–70, Alness 1970–73, Invergordon 1973–78, Fortrose from 1978

WOOD Peter Murray   *MA 1953
d Glasg 20.1.69 *AUR* XLIII 218

WOOD or Wood, Rachael Anne Milne   MA 1946
teacher; girls' coll Aden 1960–62, boys' coll Aden 1964–65; Hatfield Travis s W Riding Yorks 1965–67, Sciennes s Edin 1967–78; retd

WOOD Ronald   MA 1931
MBE 1971 FEIS
retd Valley p s Kirkcaldy 1972; part time asst Abbotshall teachers' centre Kirkcaldy 1972–74

WOOD Stanley Whyte   BSc(eng) 1933

WOOD Thomas William Walter   BSc(for) 1952
asst conserv for. Sarawak 1953–67; FAO UN: for. off. Apia, W Samoa 1967–70, proj man. Paramaribo Surinam S Amer from 1971

WOOD William   MB ChB 1904 MD 1911
OBE 1966
wife *d* 1961
d Sydney Aust 22.12.74 *AUR* XLVI 234

WOOD William   *MA 1930
retd 1970
d Aber 21.1.75 *AUR* XLVI 238

WOOD Williamina   MA 1945
d –.1.67

WOODCOCK Henrietta   MA 1908
d 16.7.73

WOODCOCK or Brander, Margaret   MA 1910
resid Beaconsfield Bucks
d 20.11.81

WOOLCOTT John Foster   MB ChB 1941
m o publ health dept W Aust from 1951

WOOLLEY James Bernard   MB ChB 1940
d Chichester 17.12.65 *AUR* XLI 251

WORGAN Mary Eunice   *MA 1934
d Aber 21.10.71 *AUR* XLIV 321

WORK or Cromarty, Isabella Budge   MA 1903
d 5.11.62

WORK or Struthers, Margaret Garrioch   MA 1906
teacher Castle Douglas acad 1906–10; resid Edin

**WORLING or Grant or Sehrson, Euphemia Betty
MA 1944**

WRIGHT Alfred   *MA 1897
d 25.9.62

WRIGHT Daniel Overbeck   BSc 1926 BSc(agr) 1928
Malaysia: asst/man. KMS rubber plant, Kedah
1928–41, plant advis Guthrie & Co Lond/Kuala
Lumpur 1946–51; farm. Lanarksh/Surrey 1951–71;
retd
m Penang 27.9.39 Hannah Appleby

WRIGHT David Livingston   MA 1954 BD 1957
organist/choirmaster W St Clement's ch Aber 1946–
55; Chalmers mem ch Port Seton 1957–63; C of S
min: Lowson mem ch Forfar 1964–70, Old par ch
Hawick from 1971, linked with Teviothead from 1972
m Cockenzie 4.8.61 Margaret Brown bank teller d of
Thomas S. B. Port Seton

WRIGHT or McBain, Dorothy Evelyn   MA 1950
resid Maryculter

WRIGHT or Cowan Glegg, Effie Graham   MA 1912
Engl mistress Hermitage s Bath 1941–45; resid
Tunbridge Wells
d 23.7.76

WRIGHT Ella   MA 1920
no longer on GC reg

WRIGHT George Tod   MA 1913 BD 1915
retd 1955; resid Castle Douglas
d Dumfries 29.12.78

WRIGHT or Smith, Gladys May   MA 1921
d Aber 6.1.75

WRIGHT Herbert John   BSc(eng) 1944

WRIGHT Herbert MacPherson   MB ChB 1924
g p Birm from 1958

WRIGHT Ian McKenzie   BSc(eng) 1951

WRIGHT Iris Martin   MA 1949
teacher: Aber: St Margaret's epis p s 1950–59,
Causewayend p s 1960–68; dep head King St p s
1968–73, asst head Broomhill p s 1973–77; head King
St p s from 1977

WRIGHT Jack Clifford   *MA 1955
FRAS MPhilological Soc
prof Sanskrit univ of Lond from 1964 and also head
dept languages and cultures of India, Pakistan and
Ceylon at SOAS univ Lond from 1969

WRIGHT James   MB ChB 1925
d 16.10.75 *AUR* xlvi 417

WRIGHT John Milne   MA 1929
head Sunnybank p s Aber 1965–71; retd

WRIGHT John Norman   MA 1951
teacher Aber 1952–53; army educ off. capt Edin
1953–56, Kenya 1956–61; major housemaster QVS
Dunblane 1961–66; sen educ off. Bridge of Don
barracks Aber 1966–69; asst controller service
children's educ M o D Lond 1969–73; group educ off.
Plymouth 1973–76; group educ off. (Scot.) from 1976
m Blackpool 26.10.47 Hilda Chadwick

WRIGHT or Birnie, Joyce   MA 1951

WRIGHT Margaret Johanna   *MA 1937
Dornoch acad: woman advis from 1957, prin
teacher Engl from 1973, dep head from 1975

WRIGHT Maurice Richards   BL 1950 PhD 1956

WRIGHT or Seller, Muriel Christine   MA 1943
teacher: classics Wakefield girls' h s 1945–48, p s
AGS 1949–51; head of lower s Albyn s for girls Aber
from 1964

WRIGHT Ninian Blundell   MA 1926 BD 1929
retd 1973; resid Comrie

WRIGHT Nora Alexandra   MA 1954

WRIGHT Robert Daniel Barron   MB ChB 1931
Hull: g p from 1936; final examining m o RN/med
referee M o H from 1969

WRIGHT Robert Ian   BSc(eng) 1952
MIMunE 1958
sen eng: Midlothian c c 1965–68; field man. CITB
Scot. from 1968

WRIGHT Stanley Cooper   BSc 1932 MB ChB 1937
d Kendoon Kirkcudbrightsh 19.8.76 *AUR* xlvii 106

WRIGHT Thomas William   BSc(for) 1950 PhD 1953

WRIGHT Victor Oswald   MB ChB 1893
no longer on GC reg

WRIGHT William   PhD 1952
ScD(Dub) 1961 FICE 1964 CEng 1964 FRSE 1965
FInst Prod.E 1966 FIEI 1969
dean of fac math eng sc Dublin univ from 1969
m(2) Manc 14.7.61 Barbara Robinson BA(Dub)
Chevalier de l'ordre du merit prof Fr univ Dub d of
Edward Robinson Dublin

WRIGHT William Christie   BL 1939
resid Dornoch

WRIGHT William Neil   MA 1924
CA
no longer on GC reg

WYLIE James   MB ChB 1938
g p Sheerness Kent from 1946; m o HM prison
Standford Hill Eastchurch Sheerness from 1950

WYLIE Norman Richard   MA 1935 LLB 1939
admitted to fac of advoc Edin 1958

resid magistrate Kampala Uganda 1955–60; magistrate/dist court judge Hong Kong 1961–68; leg. asst Scot. off. 1969–74; retd
m Aber 24.1.61 Isabella R. Donaldson

WYLLIE James McLeod   *MA 1928
d Cumbria 8.4.71 *A UR* xliv 212

WYLLIE John Hamilton
                    BSc 1954 *MB ChB 1957 *MD 1961
FRCS 1964 FRCSE 1964 MS(Wash) 1966
surg trg posts/lect surg Aberd 1960–65; Harkness fell. commonwealth fund NY Seattle USA 1965–66; lect inst basic med sc Lond 1966–68; personal chair in surg stud. dept surg UCHMS Lond from 1976
m Aber 16.3.68 Kathleen R. Mackay MA(Edin) teacher

WYLLIE Violet McAndrew   MB ChB 1955
Dip Ophth(Lond) 1968
trainee g p Edin 1958–59; civ med pract BAOR W Ger 1960–63; g p Sutton Surrey 1964–67; ophth med pract Sutton hosp/s eye serv Sutton from 1968
m Kensington Lond 4.10.58 Emanuel G. Lucas MB ChB(Edin) consult. psychiat s of Max L. MB ChB(Edin) Bedford

WYND Alexander   BSc(agr) 1950
MSc(Edin) 1962 BD(Lond) 1973
agr advis Fife from 1958

WYNESS James Alexander Davidson   MB ChB 1928
resid Bramhall Cheshire

WYNESS William John Robertson   MB ChB 1935
MCRA 1952 FRACR 1972
Adelaide S. Aust: visiting spec radiol Royal Adelaide hosp 1960–68, repatriation gen hosp 1960–78, Aust army consult. radiol (lt-col RAAMC) 1962–73, private radiol pract from 1960
wife d 30.5.76
m(2) Mitcham S Aust 14.5.77 Mary L. Pitcher or Cleland d of C. K. P. Kingswood S Aust

WYNNE-EDWARDS Hugh Robert   *BSc 1955
FRS(C) 1968 Regd Prof Eng Ont 1968, Br Col 1972 DSc(hon) Memorial univ St John's Nfld 1975 Spendiarov Prize internat geol congress 1972
Canada: prof Queen's univ Kingston 1959–68, prof and head 1968–72; Cominco prof and head univ of Br Col 1972–77; asst secy (univs) min of state for sc and tech Ottawa 1977–79; vice pres and chief scient off. Alcan Internat Montreal from 1979

WYNNE-EDWARDS or Sorbie, Janet
                    MB ChB 1955 MD 1975
MSc(Queen's univ Kingston) 1969
Queen's univ Kingston Ont Canada: res asst in med 1966–75, lect fam med 1973–74, lect med 1974–75, asst prof fam med from 1977

YATES Barbara Gertrude   PhD 1953
sen lect maths Royal Holloway coll Lond from 1964

YEATS Alfred   MA 1929
head: Skene Sq p s Aber 1963–66, Springhill p s Aber 1966–70; retd

YEATS James Alexander   MA 1937
head Invergowrie s from 1955

YEH Shao Ying   MA 1918 LLB 1919
no longer on GC reg

YELL William Lyall   MB ChB 1917 MD 1928
d Macduff 7.1.63 *A UR* xl 201

YEOMAN Joseph Alexander   BL 1941
ptnr Paull & Williamsons advoc Aber from 1955

YEUDALL or Forbes, Agnes Gertrude   MA 1927
resid Inv

YORK Roland   *BSc 1951 *MEd 1954
educ psych Lothian reg from 1975
m Edin 7.8.65 Gillian M. A. McMath d of John S. McM. Edin

YORKE James Burgoyne   MA 1947
d Ayr 30.4.76

YORSTON James Roderick   MA 1951
teacher geog Kinross h s from 1969

YORSTON John McLeod   MA 1950
dep head Scotstown s Br of Don Aber from 1967

YORSTON Malcolm Bruce   MB ChB 1953
FFARCS(Eng) 1961
consult. anaest Wessex reg hosp board Southampton from 1962

YOUNG Agnes   MA 1928
retd 1970; resid Turriff

YOUNG Archibald Grahame Brown   MB ChB 1937
g p Aber from 1939

YOUNG Charles Allan   BSc 1945 *1948
scient civ serv RRE Malvern 1948–61; Johns Hopkins univ USA: radar syst analyst applied phys lab Silver Spring Md 1962–70, William S. Parsons fell. dept of earth and planetary sc Baltimore Md 1971–72, sen staff scient applied phys lab Silver Spring, later moved to Laurel, from 1972

YOUNG or Macdonald, Charlotte Roberta Dallas
                    *MA 1916
d 3.2.78

YOUNG Douglas Alexander   *MA 1951
sen progr and logic des Elliot Automation Borehamwood 1960–63; sen scient off. GPO res stat Lond 1963–66; asst prof/dean of computer sc univ of Manitoba Winnipeg 1966–67, assoc prof from 1967; sen res fell. Europ. molecular biol organis Edin 1970–72
m Winnipeg –.6.75 Joan G. Clark or Orman

YOUNG Evelyn Crighton   MA 1945
teacher Ruthrieston s 1946–70, year mistress Torry acad from 1970

YOUNG George Douglas Paton   *MA 1950

YOUNG George Forbes   MA 1939 LLB 1947
ptnr Watt & Cumine advoc Aber from 1953

YOUNG Hilda Margaret   MA 1930
retd 1969, resid New Deer

YOUNG Hilda Sutherland   MB ChB 1920
d 26.1.76 *AUR* xlvi 415

YOUNG Ian Robert   BSc 1954 PhD 1958
MInstMC 1964 CEng FIEE 1969
consult. elect. eng Lond 1967–70; tech dir Evershed Power Optics Chertsey Process Peripherals Thatcham 1970–76; dept head EMI Central Research Labs Hayes from 1976

YOUNG James Findlay   *BSc(agr) 1950 PhD 1958
advis off. in grassland husb NOSCA from 1958

YOUNG or Harper, Jane Ann Gray   MA 1921
d Toronto 16.10.79

YOUNG Jessie Wilson   MA 1929

YOUNG John   MA 1909
no longer on GC reg

YOUNG John   *MA 1929
retd 1973; resid York

YOUNG John Irving   *BSc(eng) 1947

YOUNG or Cowie, Sheila Stewart   MA 1949

YOUNG or Dee, Winifred Morrison   MA 1922
no longer on GC reg

YOUNGSON (or Brown) Alexander John
**   *MA 1947 DLitt 1953**
prof pol econ Edin 1962–74; vice-prin Edin 1970–74; dir res s soc sc Canberra from 1974

YOUNGSON Alexander Patrick
**   MA 1925 MB ChB 1929**
retd 1973; resid Broughton nr Stockbridge Hants

YOUNGSON Catherine Park   MA 1951

YOUNGSON Douglas Alexander Ritchie   BL 1934
ptnr Hunter & Gordon and Alexander Stronach & Son now Stronachs advoc Aber from 1934
d Aber 26.10.79 *AUR* xlviii 353

YOUNGSON George William   *BSc 1941 PhD 1948
CChem FRCS
sen lect chem RGIT from 1953

YOUNGSON or McRobie, Isobel   MA 1945
teacher: Aber 1945–49, 1953–57, Aberdeensh 1961–63, Glasg 1967

YOUNGSON James   MA 1921
chap. gen hosp board Aber 1945–71; retd; resid Aber

YOUNGSON James Donaldson   MA 1925
retd 1964; resid Perth

YOUNGSON or Robiette, Kathleen Campbell
**   MA 1927**
resid Great Missenden

YOUNGSON Robert Murdoch   MB ChB 1951
DTM & H 1964 DO(RCS) 1965 OStJ 1969
ophth trainee Brit milit hosp Gibraltar 1960–64; regist ophthal ARI 1964–65; spec ophth Tidworth milit hosp 1965–66; sen spec ophth Brit milit hosp Singapore 1966–69; ophth surg St John ophth hosp Jerusalem 1969–70; sen spec ophth: Brit milit hosp Iserlohn Germany 1970–74; consult. ophth Cambridge milit hosp Aldershot 1974–77; consult. ophth Brit milit hosp Hong Kong from 1977

YOUNIE Elspet Margaret   *MEd 1955
psych audience res BBC Lond 1957–62
m Aber 20.10.62 Alasdair H. Norton BA(Oxon) merch banker/dir Comalco Melbourne s of James E. N. BA(Oxon) Farnham

YOUNIE George Grant   MB ChB 1948
TD 1964
g p Aber from 1952

YOUNIE John Milne   *MA 1909
d Kippen 4.1.61 *AUR* xxxix 102

YOUNIE or Wardill, Mary   BSc 1949 MB ChB 1954
part-time clin with prov chest disease serv Sudbury Ontario from 1966

YOUNIE or Hamilton, Thora Dewar
**   *MA 1951 Dip Ed 1952**
Edin: lect hist coll of comm 1969–72, Stevenson coll from 1972

YUILL or McLean, Helen Isabel   MA 1925
resid Gorebridge

YUILL Robert   *MA 1922
deceased

YUILL William Edward   *MA 1947
prof Ger Bedford coll Lond from 1975

YULE Adam Thomson   *BSc 1948
indust chem Procter & Gamble Europ tech center Belgium from 1948

YULE Joseph Lockhart Downes   MB ChB 1913
lt col
d 18.8.68

YULE Robert Farquhar Spence   *BSc 1951
scient off. Glaxo labs Montrose from 1954
m Montrose –.5.59 Moira E. Ogilvie teacher d of William O. Grandtully

YULE Robert Mortimer   MB ChB 1949
g p Silloth Cumbria from 1957

YULE William   MA 1937 BD 1939
C of S min Kemnay 1964–72; retd; resid Crieff
d Perth 15.5.78 *AUR* XLVII 359

YUNNIE Clara Henrietta   *MA 1926
no longer on GC reg

ZAMORY John Joachim
see Stephen

ZAMORY Wolfgang
see Stephen

ZIMMERMAN or Simms, Madeleine Berta
**   *MA 1952**
MSc 1976
Lond: edit. Fabian soc publications 1960–64; press
off./gen secy Abortion Law Reform Assoc 1964–70,
res fell. The Eugenics Society 1970–75; co-author
Abortion Law Reformed 1971; sen Leverhulme stud.
Bedford coll Lond 1975–77; sen res off. Inst for Social
Studies in Medical Care, Lond from 1977

MARRIED WOMEN GRADUATES PRE–1956 WITH HUSBANDS' NAMES IN ALPHABETICAL ORDER

An asterisk (*) indicates an Aberdeen University graduate.
The year of graduation follows the husband's name if he graduated after 1955 and his name therefore appears in Section I of this volume.

ADAMS John P	HARKINS Anne	CAIRNS	JACK Marjorie
AIRD Alexander H	DIACK Mary M	CAMERON Antony D	MARSHALL Doreen G
*AITKEN Angus	SMITH Wilma W	CAMPBELL George	CARNIE Mary H
ALLAN	HARRIS Barbara M	CAMPBELL James	McDONALD Mary G
ALLEN William S	McCALLUM Aenea J	CAMPBELL John M	COLT Joan M R
ANDERSON	ABERNETHY Hilda M	CARDONA Juan	CUMMING Joyce E
ANDERSON Alexander C	BURLEY Flora M	*CHIN Sherlock S L (1966)	DOUGLAS Vivienne M
ANDERSON George W	KEMP Moyra S M	*CHISHOLM Alexander G	JENKINS Margaret W
ANGUS Clayton B W	REID Anne I	CHOPIN	JOHNSON Joan M
ASTLE	MILNE Gladys	CLARK Gordon	COWIE Jessie G
ATKINS Leonard B W	BLACK Jessie M	COATS	SINGLETON Neith L B
AUSTIN Jack	HOYLE Nancy J C	COCKBURN John T	LAWRIE Una
		COLMAN John A R	RAE Nancy M
*BAIN Robert	SHIRREFFS Helen C	CONNOLLY Kevin	SPEED Isobel
BAKHTAR Farhang	EDWARDS Jane L	*CONOCHIE Douglas A F	McLEAN or PETRIE, Cairine R M
BARBER Stuart C L	SHIVAS Isobel B A	CONWAY James D	SKEA Edith M
BARRETT-AYRES Reginald	CRAIG Esther M	COOPER John A	MERCHANT Margaret E S
BAXTER Peter W	RICE Maureen A	CORDINER Alexander M	MATHIESON Constance M
BAXTER William P	JOHNSON Rosemary A	CORSE David R	BULLEN Jennie
BECHHOFER Frank	CONOCHIE Jean B	COWIE David K	MACAULAY Murdina
BENNETT Alan D	FRASER Helen M	COWLEY	HUNTER Eilean A
BENTLEY Alan L	SOUTHERAN Margaret	COX	FINDLAY Diana A
BENWELL Francis E	DAVIDSON Margaret E M	CRAIG	HUSBAND Valentine M
BIGGAR Gordon R	THOMSON Beryl	CRAIG	ROBERTSON Elsie
BJARNASON Bjarni B	MACDONALD Catherine	CRAWFORD	MITCHELL Nellie
BOAG Thomas J	MILNE Lorna C	CRICHTON Daniel S	McCALLUM Isabella
BODIE William G R	GARDEN Margaret H	CUMMINE James	BEANGE Margaret H
BOORER Harold J	JOHNSTON Mary R	CURRIE William M	LESLIE Margaret E
BRAS Jan F	DUGUID Annabelle M		
BRIANT Andrew K	DICKSON Kathleen	DARMON Paul E	BRAND Margaret M
BROATCH Hugh W	BAXTER Flora L	DAWSON	BAINES Doreen
BROWN	CROMBIE Katherine I	DESMOND Edward J	EDWARDS Jean M
BROWN John A B	CHRISTIE Mary B	DICKIE James J	PRIEST Elizabeth A F
*BROWN Karl (1956)	McROBB Moira H	DICKINSON Leslie	MACDONALD Norma
BRUCE Rodney	SHEACH Margaret H	*DINNES James A (1956)	DAVIDSON Nancy R C
BUCHAN Stanley J	MacLEOD Margaret M	DORRELL Peter G	CONCHIE Julia G W
BUCHANAN William D	SIM Mary B	DUCHOVNY	MILLER or BUCHAN, Margaret
BUCK Alfons	INGRAM Anne	DUGUID William J	FYFE Grace C
BURNS Alfred J	BARRON Catherine A	DURKACZ Kazimierz P	KOPERSKA Janina F M
BURNS Norman	HAY Janet G	*DURNIN Patrick J	MUTCH Elizabeth A
BYRN Richard F M	BREBNER Lilias W	DUTHIE George A	TAYLOR Elizabeth A

EDMOND
*EDMOND John S
EDWARDS Alan R
EDWARDS Ormond St J
EVANS Maurice

FLOWERS John E
FORBES Donald L
FORBES James R
*FORREST Alistair W
*FORSYTH Robert M
FOTHERINGHAM Michael T

GABRIEL Ronald M
GARROW James
GARTLAND
GIBSON George B F
GILBERT Ian G
GILL
*GILLAN John T C
GILMOUR John
GLASS James R
GLOVER Harold G
GRAHAM John J
*GRAHAM Thomas C
GRANT Daniel B
GRAY James P
GRAY John C
GREEFF Lawrence J
*GREIG William J
GREY Eric M

HAGGART Ivan
HAMILTON Ian B
HARBORD John J G H
HARPER Alexander
HARRIES
HATCH
HATVANY
HEMPSEED Allan
HENDERSON
HERNER Saul
HEWARD Alexander
HILL John D N
HOPKINS Rex E
HOWIE George F
HOWIESON
HUNTER Robert S
HURRY

INNES David J L

JACK Neil McL
JEZZARD Robert
JOBLING Geoffrey L
*JOHNSTON William G (1958)
JONES
JONES Lloyd H P

*KEIR Alexander
KEMSLEY John
KENDRICK
KENNEDY
KERMACK Stuart D
KING John E

MILNE Jeannie
THOMSON Dorothy A
THOMSON Ann L
TAYLOR Irene B
DONALD Margaret P

CAMPBELL Rosemary E
WESTIE Kathleen
WOOD Helena
WHITTER Agnes E
PIKSIS Velta
MUNRO Joan

McGLASHAN Agnes M
WATT Aileen
SCOTT Stella J
STEWART Margaret A
DONALD Heather M
MACKENZIE Myra Aileen
WOOD Isobel M
SAINT Dorothy
MACKAY Lena
BURNETT Muriel
REID Martha
CRAN Jean J
MACKENZIE Sandra I
PATERSON Jean F
SMITH Sheena
GOVE Daisy D
MORRISON Catherine
THOMAS Isabella E M F

SMART Mary E
WATT Marjory I K
STRUTHERS Frances C
Law Sheila
THOMSON Margaret D
LAWSON Janet M
ELRICK Doris M
AITKEN Dorothy R
ALLAN Margaret M O
ALEXANDER Mary
WALLER Patricia M
WHEELAN Lorna
MITCHELL Margaret
DUNCAN Elizabeth E
MacDONALD Betsy
HAYMAN Ann E
Cow Catherine M

DUNCAN Margaret G

CUMMING Patricia M
LEASK Mary I M
KINDNESS Jane
ROSS Anne
MOIR Sylvia M
MILNE Angela A

HALL Agnes T C
NEILL Freda K
SURTEES Anne D
MORRISON Kathleen M
MACKENZIE Barbara
COCHRANE Helen B T

KOLIZERAS
KRAAL Winston A
KUZMINSKI Telesfor M

LASZEWSKI
LAUGHTON Bruce
*LAW George R (1957)
LAWRIE David A R
LAWSON Bernard W
LEE
*LEE Richard M (1957)
LEEDALE Harry H
*LEES Gordon M (1961)
LOGAN Garth
Low William J
Low-MITCHELL Lachlan G
LUCAS Emanuel G
LUCHSINGER Matthias H
LYNCH Patrick
LYTHGOE James P

McBURNIE John I
McCORKINDALE
MacDONALD Christopher I
*MacDONALD Kenneth J
MacDONALD Patrick D C L
MACDONALD Peter
McGEORGE William J
McINTOSH Robert C
MacIVER
MACKAY
MacKAY Andrew
MACKAY Thomas I
MacKENZIE
MacKENZIE David D
MACKENZIE Finlay
McKENZIE James
MACKENZIE Kenneth G F
MACKENZIE Norman C
McKIE John S
MACKIE John W
MACKINNON Norman N
MACLEAN Norman
MACLEOD Angus
McMILLAN
*MACMILLAN William B R
MACPHERSON Donald
MacWILLIAM Daniel
MARR Alfred J
MARSHALL Charles J
MASSIE James
MATHER Alexander S
MATHIE
MEIKLE W James
*MELVILLE William S
*MILLER Gordon R (1957)
MILLER Thomas A
MILLS Joseph E
MILNE Thornton G
MINTER Robert J
MONKS Edward J
MULLARD Roger
MURRAY
MURRAY Robert I
*MURRAY Stewart

BEATTIE Katrina
MOIR Maureen A
PETRIE Elizabeth M

KINEL Zofia K W
AIKEN Doris M
ABERNETHY Elizabeth A
THOM Elizabeth H
STEWART Dolina
ROSS Catherine I M
BLACK Arthurina R M
STEPHEN Sheila T
MANSON Doris I
ANDERSON Irene R
STEWART HELEN
CHALMERS Audrey M
WYLLIE Violet M
SLATER Margaret
CAMPBELL Mary S
MELVIN Anne

THOMPSON Jane M
FALCONER Catherine J
GAVIN Evelyn E
COCKER Phyllis M
GRANT Donella
FRASER Helen C
MURRAY Sheila
Low Norma
PETERKIN Ethel M
CRUICKSHANK Annie
McGOWAN Christina J
MAITLAND Gladys L
MACDONALD Janet B W
MORRISON Mary M
MacDONALD Agnes
MACDONALD Catherine
GORDON Helen E
STRACHAN Georgina T
CAMPBELL Jean M
MURRAY Jane E
MANSON Margaret F
BARCLAY Mary D
MACARTHUR Effie K
CRAIG Elma G
MURRAY Mary A B
REITH Margaret
FRASER Christine G
McINTOSH Irene M
STRACHAN Maureen C
MURRAY Moira
SMITH Mary M
DAVIDSON Ethel M F
GRANT Muriel C
CRAIG Jean F
SLEIGH Lesley M
MENZIES Joan I
MILLS Margaret M
CATTANACH Sandra I D
MORRISON Margaret L
MACRAE Ishbel M
SAINT Dorothy
MACKENZIE Annie M
CRAIB Kathleen
KEAN Helen M

*Neizer Justice A (1960)
Nicholls
Nicoll Alexander J D
Niven George G
Norrie James P
Norton Alasdair H
Norton Gerald W T

O'Gorman James

Park George
Parker
Peacock Lawrence
Peel
Pennie James
*Penny Alan B
Pereira Helio G
Perrée Frank Le Riche
Petrie David S
Petrie Ian G M
Philip John C
Phillips Albert J
Preece
Pritchard John E

Quigley Thomas W

Rae Alistair S L
Rae Herbert
Rae John N
Ramsay William
Rawlins Raymond H
Rayne Robert
Reeves William J
Reid Charles J
Reid William A P
Reynaud Jacques
*Rhind Edward G G
Riddoch Charles B
Roberts Horace E
Robertson Iain A
*Robley John A W
Ross Charles W
Ross William G

Sanderson William G
Sandison Alexander L
Scarth George W
Scherz Franz
Scott
Scott Douglas D
Scudamore
Sehrson
*Shepherd Ronald (1956)
Sheran John H
Shewan David M
Shirra Robert F
Shirran Douglas

Thompson Barbara A
Smith Mary H
Keith Elizabeth M
Dempster Mary R
Forbes Eleanor M
Younie Elspet M
Scotcher Lilian M

Anderson Janet W

Anderson Margaret J
Leach Gweneth R
Dunn Eileen C K
Barker Noël C B
Leith Helen S
Rennie Cecilia
Scott Marguerite M
Greene Anne C
Bell Aluinn N
McIntosh Irene M
Cowie Isabella S
Scott Edith
Davidson Sylvia H M
Heddle Inga P

Morrison Margaret G

Duguid Helen L D
Barron Jeannie H M
Paton Elsie M
Barron Annie
Brown Mabel K
Dinnie Doreen A
Gordon Diana M
Cockburn Mary
Dickson Margaret L
Lascelles Gladys M
McCombie Kathleen
Smith Lorna
Norrie Mary B
Munro Irene
Sweeney Sheila M
Harvey Jeanie
Wood Catherine S

Macleod Anne S
Paterson Mary S
Anderson Mary A
Craggs Joyce
Scott Jean M
Soutar Patricia F
Milne Joan M
Worling Euphemia B
Main Elsie M
Donald Ella
Morrison Margaret
Philip Audrey
Beveridge Evelyn E

Simpson George
Singer Alexander
Smith
Smith
Smith Ben
*Smith George M C
Snelson Peter D
Stephen Daniel J
Stephen George
Sterland George M S
Stewart Douglas C W
Strachan John
*Strachan William E
Stuart
*Suttie James M (1956)
Synge Francis M

Tanner John
Taylor William A
Telfer John M
Thomas David E W
Thomson
Thomson Norman D
Thomson William
Tosh Alfred
Tracy Robert W
Traill
Tucker Arthur E
Tucker James H

*Urquhart Robert W

Van Zyl Chris P
Vernon Louis O

Wagner John
Walker Alexander
Walker Colin H
Wallace Norman S
Waller Dudley
*Walterson Laurence I (1957)
Watt Charles M
Watters John R G
Weesel Baron van
Weston Roy F
Wetmore Robert J
*Whiteford Allan D
Whitehouse Henry D
Wilkinson
Williams
Willox Alexander R
Wilson

Wilson Eric C
Wilson George C
Wilson Leslie
Winter
Woolfenden Thomas

Stephen Susan
Newlands Annie
Duncan Elizabeth D
Wood Isabella J
Stephen Mildred W
MacRae Anne M S
West Evelyn M
Michie Ethel L
Ferries Catherine A
Macleod Mairi E
Forbes Jane M M
Crabb Catherine A
Cuthbertson Lilias M
Johnston Margaret H
Andrews Elizabeth R
Lancaster Margaret S

Benzie Sheila A
Edwards Phyllis A
Forrest Elsie M
Middler Dorothy F
Lyon Alice A C
Sutherland Jane H
Peter Jean E
Stratton Dorothy I B
Bromberg Priscilla B
Duthie Margaret S
MacKenzie Maimie M
Swanson Margaret

Gibson Jane

Keay Margaret E
McKenzie Nellie B

Gauld Katharine W
McDonald Marie W
Porter Dorothy M
Farquhar Moira
Hill Amelia
Anderson Jean
Noble Mary J
Raitt Norah P
Sharp Margaret I A
Donaldson Sheina M
Mitchell Evelyn J
Mackay Christina M
Wood Millicent M M
Strachan Emma E
Skene Annie P
Henderson Moira E K
Fallowfield or Mackay,
  Patricia M
Watt Catherine A
Mackenzie Elizabeth M F
Greig Hazel W
Campbell Violet M
Croll Jean F

HONORARY GRADUATES 1926–1955

This list does not include the names of those honorary graduates of the 1926–1955 period whose deaths have already been recorded in the previous volume of the Roll of Graduates.

An asterisk (*) is prefixed to the names of those who hold, or have held, degrees of Aberdeen University other than honorary degrees. Their first Aberdeen degrees are shown here and this will enable them to be identified in the appropriate Section(s) of this volume and other volumes of the Roll of Graduates.

ABEL John Jacob   LL D 1932
  deceased

ABELL George Edmund Brackenbury (Sir)   LL D 1947

ABERDEEN and TEMAIR George Gordon, Marquess of   LL D 1954
  d Aber 6.1.65

ADAM Ronald Forbes (General Sir)   LL D 1945

ADAMS John Esslemont   DD 1928
  deceased

ALLEN Edgar Leonard   DD 1946

ANDERSON John (Rt Hon Sir)   LL D 1926
  d 4.1.58

APPLETON Edward Victor   LL D 1935
  d 21.4.65

AUCHINLECK Claude John Eyre (Field Marshal Sir)   LL D 1948
  d 23.3.81

BAILLIE James Black   LL D 1926
  d 9.6.40

BAIRD Andrew Cumming   LL D 1939
  d 21.1.40

BALDENSPERGER Philippe Fernard   LL D 1954

BARCLAY William   LL D 1941

BARRON Evan Macleod   LL D 1936
  d Nairn 24.4.65 *AUR* xl 152

BELL Richard   DD 1927
  deceased

BENNET George H. (Rt Rev)   LL D 1931
  d 25.12.46

BENTWICH Norman   LL D 1942
  d 8.4.71

BERKELBACH van der SPRENKEL Simon Frederick Hendrik Jan   DD 1951
  d 18.1.67

BEST Maud Storr   LL D 1945
  d 18.1.69

BICKERSTETH Geoffrey Langdale   LL D 1955
  d 29.3.74

BLACK John Bennett   LL D 1954
  d 25.11.64

BLISS Kathleen (Mrs)   DD 1949

BLOCH Olaf   LL D 1937
  d 19.10.44

BOHR Neils Henrik David   LL D 1952
  d 18.11.62

BROAD Charlie Dunbar   LL D 1947
  d 11.3.71

BROWN Ivor John Carnegie   LL D 1950
  d 22.4.74

BROWNE Buckston (Sir)   LL D 1932
  d 19.1.45

BUBER Martin   DD 1953
  d Jerusalem 13.6.65 *AUR* xli 153

BUCHAN John Norman Stuart The Rt Hon Baron Tweedsmuir of Elsfield   LL D 1949

BUCKLER William Hepburn   LL D 1935
  d 2.3.52

BURLEIGH John Henderson Seaforth   DD 1938

BURT Cyril Lodowic   LL D 1939
no longer on GC reg

*BUTCHART Henry Jackson (Lt Col)   LL D 1952
BL(Aberd) 1905
d Aber 30.8.71 *AUR* XLIV 231

BUTLER Edwin John   LL D 1938
d 4.4.43

BUTTERFIELD Herbert   LL D 1952
d 1979

CAITHNESS The Rt Hon The Earl of   LL D 1931
d 25.3.47

CALLANDER John Graham   LL D 1932
d 18.3.38

CAMERON John LL D 1950

*CAMERON Lewis Legertwood Legg   DD 1953
BSc(Aberd) 1920
d Edin 19.3.73 *AUR* XLV 225

CARGILL James Jamieson   LL D 1955
d 28.6.71

CARRITT Edgar Frederick   LL D 1950
d 19.6.64

CARTON DE WIART Adrian (Lt Gen Sir)   LL D 1947
d 5.6.63

CHIRGWIN Arthur Mitchell   DD 1943
d 29.6.66

CHURCHILL Winston Spencer   LL D 1946
d 24.1.65

CLARK George Norman   LL D 1936
d 6.2.79

CLARKE John   LL D 1927
d 28.9.39

CLARKE Mary Gavin   LL D 1943
d 12.2.76 *AUR* XLVII 106

CRUICKSHANK Alexander   DD 1932
no longer on GC reg

CRUICKSHANK John   LL D 1955
d Aber 10.10.66 *AUR* XLII 91

*CURRIE George Alexander (Sir)   LL D 1948
BSc(agr)Aberd 1923

DAHLBERG Gunnar   LL D 1938
no longer on G C reg

DAIN Harry Guy   LL D 1939
d 26.2.66

DAVIDSON Francis   DD 1931
deceased

DEAN Henry Roy   LL D 1950
d 13 2.61

DEANE Frederick Llewellyn (Rt Rev)   DD 1931
d 12.1.52

de ZULUETA Francis   LL D 1953
d 15.1.58

DODD Charles Harold   DD 1930
d 1.9.73

DRIVER Godfrey Rolles   DD 1946

*DRUMMOND James Gilmour   DD 1951
MA(Aberd) 1907
d Glasg 20.2.63 *AUR* XL 199

DUFF James Fitzjames   LL D 1942
d 24.4.70

*DUTHIE Charles Sim   DD 1952
MA(Aberd) 1932
d Edin 11.1.81

DYSON George (Sir)   LL D 1942
d 28.9.64

*ELDER John Rawson   LL D 1943
MA(Aberd) 1902
d Dunedin NZ 12.4.62 *AUR* XXXIX 373

ELLIOTT James Sands (Sir)   LL D 1939
d 26.10.59

ELMSLIE William Alexander Leslie   DD 1928
d 14.11.66 *AUR* XLI 312

ELPHINSTONE The Rt Hon Baron   LL D 1931
d 28.11.55

*ESSLEMONT Mary   LL D 1954
BSc(Aberd) 1914

*FINDLAY Adam Fyfe   LL D 1948
MA(Aberd) 1889
d Aber 19.1.62 *AUR* XXXIX 268

*FINDLAY Alexander   LL D 1944
MA(Aberd) 1895
d 14.9.66 *AUR* XLI 286

FLEW Robert Newton   DD 1942

FORSTER Edward Morgan   LL D 1931
d 7.6.70

FOSTER John   DD 1945
d 3.11.73

FRASER Duncan   LL D 1951
d Aber 18.2.66

*FRASER John Annand   DD 1951
MA(Aberd) 1919

FYFE William Hamilton (Sir)   LL D 1949
d 13.6.65

GARDINER James Bruce   DD 1938
no longer on GC reg

GARROD Alfred Guy Roland (Air Marshal)   LL D 1943
d 3.1.65

GARSTANG John   LL D 1931
d 12.9.56

GILSON Etienne Henry   LL D 1931
no longer on GC reg

GOLDSCHMIDT Victor Moritz   LL D 1944

GORDON Dudley (Lord)   LL D 1948
d –.4.72

GRAHAM John Anderson   DD 1931
d 15.5.42

GRANT Francis James   LL D 1931
d 17.2.53

GRAY Alexander (Sir)   LL D 1949
d 17.2.68

GRAY James   LL D 1939
d 14.12.75

HARDY William Bate (Sir)   LL D 1928
d 23.1.34

*HASTINGS Edward   DD 1950
MA(Aberd) 1913
d Aber 31.7.80 *AUR* XLIX 66

HAY Malcolm Vivian   LL D 1950
d Aber 27.12.60 *AUR* XL 94

HERBERT Arthur Gabriel   DD 1949
deceased

*HENDRY George Stuart   DD 1949
MA(Aberd) 1924

HILL H Erskine (The Very Rev)   DD 1931
d 22.4.39

HILL Leonard Erskine (Sir)   LL D 1931
d 30.3.52

HNIK Frank Martin   DD 1942

HØEG Carsten   LL D 1948

HROMADKA Josef L   DD 1949
d 26.12.69 *AUR* XLIII 446

HUNT John (Brigadier Sir)   LL D 1954

IRVINE James Colquhoun (Sir)   LL D 1931
d 12.6.52

*JAMESON William Wilson (Sir)   LL D 1940
MA(Aberd) 1905
d Lond 18.10.62 *AUR* XL 75

JENKINSON Hilary   LL D 1949
d 5.3.51

JOHNSTON Thomas (The Rt Hon)   LL D 1949
d 5.9.65

KAHLE Paul   DD 1940
d 24.9.64

*KELLAS John   DD 1950
MA(Aberd) 1920
d Edin 12.11.67 *AUR* XLII 358

*KENNEDY Archibald Robert Stirling   LL D 1933
MA(Aberd) 1880
d –.10.38

KNOX Edmund Arbuthnott (The Rt Rev)   DD 1932
d 16.1.37

KOO Vi Kyuin Wellington (His Excellency)   LL D 1943
deceased

LAING Alexander James Louttit   LL D 1944
d Ashurst 24.11.62 *AUR* XL 94

LAMB David C   LL D 1934
d 7.7.51

LAMB John (Sir)   LL D 1931
d 3.7.52

*LIANG Lone   LL D 1945
MA(Aberd) 1917
d Yonkers NY State 12.6.67 *AUR* XLII 335

LIGHTFOOT Robert Henry   DD 1936
d 24.11.53

*LILLIE William   DD 1948
MA(Aberd) 1921

LINDEMAN Frederick Alexander   LL D 1940

LINDSELL Wilfred Gordon   LL D 1946
d 2.5.73

*LINKLATER Eric Robert Russell   LL D 1946
MA(Aberd) 1925
d Aber 7.11.74 *AUR* XLVI 10

LÖFSTEDT Einar   LL D 1937
deceased

*LOTHIAN (William) Arthur Cunningham (Sir)
LL D 1950
MA(Aberd) 1908
d Lond 16.11.62 *AUR* XL 77

MACAULAY Thomas Bassett   LL D 1930
d Montreal 3.4.42 *AUR* XXIX 248

MacARTHY Desmond   LL D 1932
d 7.6.52

*MACDONALD Robert Gordon   DD 1954
MA(Aberd) 1907
d 17.12.70

*MACKAY John Alexander   DD 1939
MA(Aberd) 1912

*McKENZIE John Grant   DD 1939
MA(Aberd) 1910
d Edin 17.5.63 *AUR* XL 199

*MACKINTOSH Robert   DD 1950
MA(Aberd) 1910
d Edin 1.1.62 *AUR* XXXIX 273

McNEUR George Hunter (The Very Rev)   DD 1948

MANSON Thomas Mortimer Yule   LLD 1951

MARSHALL Charles Robertshaw   LL D 1931
d 2.4.52

MASSEY Vincent (The Hon)   LL D 1937
d 30.12.67

MAXWELL John Stirling (Sir)   LL D 1935
  d 30.5.56

MAYO William James   LL D 1933
  d 28.7.39

MEIJERS Edward Maurits   LL D 1949

MERTON Thomas Ralph (Sir)   LL D 1955
  d 10.10.69

MEULENGRACHT Jens Einar   LL D 1939
  no longer on GC reg

*MILNE William Proctor   LL D 1946
  MA(Aberd) 1903
  d Glack 3.9.67 *AUR* XLII 178

MILON Yves   LL D 1950

*MORRISON Alexander James   DD 1955
  MA(Aberd) 1909
  d 29.1.64 *AUR* XL 396

*MURISON Alfred Ross   LL D 1951
  MA(Aberd) 1912
  d Glasg 21.2.68 *AUR* XLII 351

MURISON William   LL D 1928
  d Culter 26.6.41 *AUR* XXIX 87

*MURRAY John   LL D 1930
  MA(Aberd) 1900
  d Lond 28.12.64 *AUR* XLI 53

NICHOLSON Patrick Joseph (The Rt Rev)   LL D 1953

NIELSEL Wilhelm   DD 1954

*NIVEN William Dickie   DD 1928
  MA(Aberd) 1900
  d Glasg 26.2.65 *AUR* XLI 145

*NOBLE Peter Scott (Sir)   LL D 1955
  MA(Aberd) 1921

NORDAL Sigurdur   LL D 1947

NORTH Christopher Richard   DD 1946
  d –.7.75

NYGREN Anders Theodor   DD 1950

*OGG George   DD 1951
  MA(Aberd) 1912
  d 18.1.73 *AUR* XLV 224

*OGG William Gammie (Sir)   LL D 1951
  MA(Aberd) 1912
  d Edzell 25.9.79 *AUR* XLVIII 350

OLIVER Francis Wall   LL D 1926
  d 14.9.51

O'RAHILLY Thomas Francis   LL D 1949

ORR John Boyd (Sir)   LL D 1948
  d 25.6.71

PHILIP James Randall (Sir)   DD 1955
  d 2.5.57

PIGOU Arthur Cecil   LL D 1937
  d 7.3.59

*PIRIE Alexander Irvine   DD 1952
  MA(Aberd) 1902
  d Edin 10.9.62 *AUR* XL 74

RAVEN Charles Earle   DD 1946
  d 8.7.64

REITH John Charles Walsham (Sir)   LL D 1933
  d 16.6.71

ROBINSON of Kielder Forest and of Adelaide
                    (The Rt Hon Baron)   LL D 1951
  d Ottawa 6.9.52 *AUR* XXXV 104

ROBINSON Theodore Henry   DD 1929
  d 26.6.64

*ROSE Beatrice Mary   LL D 1953
  MA(Aberd) 1912

ROSS John Alexander   LL D 1941
  d 16.9.67

*ROTHNIE Douglas Auchterlonie   DD 1952
  MA(Aberd) 1896
  d Kingston Jamaica 22.11.62 *AUR* XL 73

SELWYN Edward Gordon   DD 1927
  d 11.6.59

SHENNAN Theodore   LL D 1937
  d 21.10.48

SHEPHERD-BARRON Wilfred Philip   LL D 1954
  d 6.5.79

*SHORTT Henry Edward (Colonel)   LL D 1952
  MB ChB(Aberd) 1910

SIEGFRIED Andre   LL D 1950
  d 28.3.59

SINCLAIR John Dickson   LL D 1949
  d Winchester 1951 *AUR* XXXIV 190

*SMART Alexander   DD 1954
  MA(Aberd) 1918
  d Prestwick 8.7.65 *AUR* XLI 150

SMITH Arthur Francis (General Sir)   LL D 1948
  d 8.8.77

SMITH Frank Edward (Sir)   LL D 1931
  d 1.7.70

SMITH Sidney Earle   LL D 1953
  d 17.3.59

SMITH William Wright (Sir)   LL D 1944
  d 15.12.56

SPENCER Herbert Ritchie   LL D 1934
  d 28.8.41

STEWART Findlater (Sir)   LL D 1931
  d 11.4.60

STONEHAVEN, John Lawrence Baird, Baron
                                        LL D 1931
  d 20.8.41

STORRS Ronald (Sir) LL D 1938
 d 1.11.55

SUTHERLAND David McBeth LL D 1953
 d 20.9.73

*SUTHERLAND James Runcieman LL D 1955
 MA(Aberd) 1921

SUTHERLAND John Donald (Colonel) LL D 1927

TAYLOR Eva Germaine Rimington LL D 1949
 d 5.7.66

*TENNANT William Robert (Sir) LL D 1953
 MA(Aberd) 1914
 d St And 4.5.69 *AUR* XLIII 329

*THOM William Cumming DD 1948
 MA(Aberd) 1917
 d Aber 25.3.79 *AUR* XLVIII 227

*THOMSON David Landsborough LL D 1952
 MA(Aberd) 1921
 d Province of Quebec 20.10.64 *AUR* XLI 56

THOMSON George Paget (Sir) LL D 1948
 d 10.9.75

*THOMSON Thomas Bentley Stewart DD 1946
 MA(Aberd) 1911
 d 10.8.73 *AUR* XLV 316

THURNEYSEN Edward DD 1934
 d 21.8.74

*TOCHER Forbes Scott DD 1934
 MA(Aberd) 1906
 d 15.8.73 *AUR* XLV 316

UNDERHILL or Moore, Evelyn DD 1939
 d 15.6.41

UNWIN Stanley LL D 1945
 d 13.10.68

*URQUHART Robert William (Sir) LL D 1954
 MA(Aberd) 1920

*URQUHART William Spence DD 1930
 MA(Aberd) 1897
 d Torphins 16.7.64 *AUR* XL 394

VISSER t'HOOFT Willem Adolf DD 1939
 deceased

Von THADDEN-TRIEGLAFF Reinold DD 1953

WALEY Arthur David LL D 1938
 d 27.6.66

*WALLACE Robert Strachan LL D 1928
 MA(Aberd) 1904
 d Canberra 5.9.61 *AUR* XXXIX 271

WATSON David Meredith Seares LL D 1943
 d 23.7.73

WATSON William DD 1929
 d 24.4.72

WATT George Fiddes LL D 1955
 d Aber 22.11.60 *AUR* XXXIX 106

WATT James Cromar LL D 1931
 d 19.11.40

WILSON Horace John (Sir) LL D 1934
 d 19.5.72

WIMBERLEY Douglas Neil (Major General)
                                     LL D 1948

WOOD Thomas Barlow LL D 1926
 d 6.11.29

WYON Olive DD 1948
 d Edin 1966 *AUR* XLI 342

ZIMMERN Alfred (Sir) LL D 1941
 d 24.11.57

APPENDIX

DEGREES AND DIPLOMAS AWARDED
FOR YEARS 1956–1970

DEGREES AND DIPLOMAS AWARDED

		HONORARY DEGREES		HIGHER DEGREES										ORDINARY AND									
		DD	LLD	D Litt	M Litt	PhD	MSc	DSc	MD	ChM	EdB(M Ed)	MTh	MA	MA(Hons)	BSc	BSc(Hons)	BSc(agr)	BSc(agr)(Hons)	BSc(eng)	BSc(eng)(Hons)	BSc(for)	BSc(for)(Hons)
1956	M	4	9	—	—	24	—	1	5	1	9	—	35	33	16	31	13	3	12	7	11	1
	W	—	—	—	—	4	—	—	2	—	—	—	64	19	12	8	4	—	—	—	—	—
1957	M	3	7	—	—	24	—	3	11	—	6	—	38	34	14	33	9	3	18	7	13	2
	W	—	—	—	—	6	—	—	—	—	—	—	59	19	12	4	—	—	—	—	—	—
1958	M	4	6	—	—	25	—	—	6	2	8	—	48	57	16	32	7	—	14	7	15	5
	W	—	1	—	—	2	—	—	—	—	2	—	70	19	13	4	1	—	—	—	—	—
1959	M	3	7	—	—	36	—	1	6	—	1	—	48	43	23	37	7	—	18	5	14	4
	W	—	—	—	—	1	—	—	1	—	—	—	73	19	15	11	—	—	—	—	—	—
1960	M	4	10	—	—	24	5	2	8	1	2	—	44	35	26	42	7	—	22	7	13	2
	W	—	2	—	—	3	—	—	2	—	2	—	71	19	21	9	—	—	—	—	—	—
1961	M	2	6	1	—	21	11	1	4	1	—	—	49	33	23	46	9	1	20	9	11	6
	W	—	—	—	—	—	1	—	—	—	3	—	92	30	14	5	—	—	—	—	—	—
1962	M	3	4	—	—	33	16	2	5	—	5	—	55	62	15	45	6	1	14	11	8	3
	W	—	1	—	—	2	—	—	2	—	2	—	82	27	19	9	—	—	—	—	—	—
1963	M	2	8	—	—	27	22	1	6	—	7	—	66	62	15	47	5	8	19	13	6	5
	W	—	—	—	—	1	1	—	3	—	1	—	79	24	3	5	—	—	—	—	—	—
1964	M	4	6	—	—	33	23	—	4	—	3	—	39	60	28	53	5	3	23	14	7	4
	W	—	1	—	—	2	3	—	—	—	—	—	103	31	18	10	—	—	—	—	—	—
1965	M	2	9	—	—	35	17	2	6	2	6	—	67	68	23	45	4	3	13	15	7	3
	W	—	—	—	1	1	—	—	2	—	3	—	116	39	20	16	—	—	—	—	—	—
1966	M	4	12	—	—	35	19	2	2	1	5	—	88	97	36	64	4	5	20	16	8	3
	W	—	1	—	—	1	1	—	2	—	4	—	127	55	24	20	1	1	—	—	—	—
1967	M	4	7	—	4	46	34	3	8	—	6	—	91	109	41	69	10	11	24	24	6	4
	W	—	—	—	1	7	1	—	1	—	5	—	173	52	19	21	—	1	—	—	—	—
1968	M	3	7	—	2	54	31	2	3	—	9	1	93	108	50	81	11	6	20	21	15	3
	W	—	2	—	3	8	3	—	—	—	2	—	192	89	25	25	—	—	—	—	—	—
1969	M	3	8	—	3	51	20	2	5	—	8	3	102	132	62	101	12	9	21	35	8	3
	W	—	1	—	2	6	7	—	1	—	2	—	218	103	25	29	—	—	1	—	—	—
1970	M	1	5	—	3	35	37	1	4	2	10	—	90	152	71	129	11	12	28	39	7	2
	W	—	—	—	4	4	7	—	2	—	5	—	197	91	50	25	1	1	—	—	—	—

NOTES

The degree of BEd is conferred in terms of a University Court Ordinance of 1965. To avoid confusion the degree of EdB was renamed MEd.

The figures for MD, ChM, MB ChB and BMedBiol include those with honours, commendation and distinction.

In the faculty of Law the degree of BL is no longer awarded; the LLB degree no longer requires candidates to have a previous degree.

FOR YEARS 1956–1970

HONOURS DEGREES								TOTALS (EXCLUDING HONORARY)			DIPLOMAS							
BD	BD(Hons)	BL	LLB	LLB(Hons)	MBChB	BMedBiol	BEd	MEN	WOMEN	TOTAL	DipStat	Dip Medieval Studies	CASS	DipEd	DMRD	DPH	DipPsychother	LTh
1	—	3	8	—	48	—	—	262		394	—	—	—	—	—	—	—	—
—	—	—	2	—	17	—	—		132		—	—	—	—	—	—	—	—
5	—	6	13	—	43	—	—	282		400	—	—	—	—	—	—	—	—
—	—	1	1	—	16	—	—		118		—	—	—	3	—	—	—	—
2	—	3	8	—	49	—	—	304		434	—	—	—	12	—	5	—	—
—	—	—	1	—	18	—	—		130		—	—	—	14	—	1	—	—
3	—	3	4	—	44	—	—	297		441	3	—	—	8	—	1	—	—
1	—	—	1	—	22	—	—		144		1	—	—	7	—	—	—	—
5	—	1	12	—	51	—	—	309		452	—	—	—	8	—	—	—	—
—	—	—	—	—	16	—	—		143		—	—	—	7	—	—	—	—
3	—	3	14	—	43	—	—	309		473	1	—	—	16	—	2	—	—
—	—	—	—	—	19	—	—		164		—	—	—	4	—	1	—	—
—	—	1	12	—	37	—	—	331		494	2	—	—	14	—	—	—	—
—	—	—	1	—	21	—	—		163		—	—	—	9	—	—	—	—
3	—	—	8	—	34	—	—	354		485	4	—	—	16	—	—	—	—
—	—	—	3	—	11	—	—		131		—	—	—	12	—	2	—	—
3	—	—	14	2	58	—	—	376		553	—	—	—	10	—	—	—	—
—	—	—	1	—	9	—	—		177		—	—	—	10	—	1	—	—
—	1	1	15	2	43	—	—	378		608	—	—	—	20	—	1	—	2
—	—	—	2	—	30	—	—		230		1	—	—	13	—	2	—	—
1	—	—	25	4	54	—	—	489		740	—	—	—	22	—	2	3	—
—	—	—	4	1	10		—		251		1	—	—	18	—	2	1	—
3	—	—	23	3	55	—	—	574		883	—	—	—	26	—	—	—	5
—	—	—	6	—	21	1	—		309		—	2	—	28	—	—	—	—
2	—	—	29	7	57	6	—	611		999	—	4	1	27	—	—	3	2
—	—	—	5	—	33	—	3		388		—	2	—	32	—	—	—	—
4	1	—	38	6	57	5	18	706		1,160	—	2	1	41	2	3	2	7
—	—	—	5	1	18	4	32		454		—	1	8	41	—	—	—	—
4	1	—	39	4	39	7	17	744		1,196	—	—	—	30	2	—	2	3
—	—	—	10	1	27	1	26		452		—	1	6	37	—	—	—	—